Carolyn Schwartz

HANDBOOK OF SCHOOL COUNSELING

HANDBOOK OF SCHOOL COUNSELING

EDITED BY

Hardin L.K. Coleman
Christine Yeh

Taylor & Francis Group
New York   London

Lawrence Erlbaum Associates
Taylor & Francis Group
270 Madison Ave,
New York NY 10016

Lawrence Erlbaum Associates
Taylor & Francis Group
2 Park Square,
Milton Park, Abingdon,
Oxon, OX14 4RN

© 2008 by Taylor & Francis Group, LLC
Lawrence Erlbaum Associates is an imprint of Taylor & Francis Group, an Informa business

Transferred to Digital Printing 2010

International Standard Book Number-13: 978-0-8058-5623-1 (Softcover) 978-0-8058-5622-4 (Hardcover)

Except as permitted under U.S. Copyright Law, no part of this book may be reprinted, reproduced, transmitted, or utilized in any form by any electronic, mechanical, or other means, now known or hereafter invented, including photocopying, microfilming, and recording, or in any information storage or retrieval system, without written permission from the publishers.

Trademark Notice: Product or corporate names may be trademarks or registered trademarks, and are used only for identification and explanation without intent to infringe.

Visit the Taylor & Francis Web site at
http://www.taylorandfrancis.com

and the LEA and Routledge Web site at
http://www.routledge.com

CONTENTS

Contributors ix

School Counseling from a Multicultural and
an Ecological Perspective: An Introduction xxvii
HARDIN L. K. COLEMAN AND CHRISTINE J. YEH

1 Introduction to the Field of School Counseling

I   History of School Counseling 3
        JOHN J. SCHMIDT

II   A Concept of Best Practices in Training School Counselors 15
        ROBBIE J. STEWARD, DOUGLAS M. NEIL, AND MATTHEW A. DIEMER

III   School Counseling: Moving Toward Standards and Models 37
        CAROL A. DAHIR

IV   Student Accomplishment: Equity and the School Counselor's Role 49
        HARDIN L. K. COLEMAN

V   Understanding Yourself as a School Counselor 63
        CHRISTINE J. YEH AND STEPHANIE T. PITUC

2 Diversity and School Counseling

VI   The Acculturative Environment of Schools and the School Counselor:
        Goals and Roles That Create a Supportive Context for Immigrant Adolescents 79
        EDISON J. TRICKETT AND DIANA FORMOSO

VII	Immigrant Children and Youth in Schools	95
	SARAH J. LEE AND KAREN A. CORT	
VIII	Racial Harassment in American Schools	111
	ROBERT T. CARTER, TAMARA R. BUCKLEY, AND SCHEKEVA P. HALL	
IX	The Role of Ethnic Identity in the Practice of School Counseling	127
	SHANNON CASEY-CANNON	
X	Understanding and Implementing Gay, Lesbian, Bisexual, Transgender, Questioning Affirmative Practices as School Counselors	135
	SHELBY J. SEMINO	
XI	Social Class in School Counseling	145
	WILLIAM MING LIU, ALICE FRIDMAN, AND THOMASIN E. TRANEL HALL	
XII	Disability in the Schools	157
	TINA M. ANCTIL AND STEPHANIE SAN MIGUEL BAUMAN	
XIII	Race and Ethnicity in School Counseling	177
	MARIE L. MIVILLE	
XIV	African American Empowerment in Secondary School Counseling	195
	LEON D. CALDWELL, RICHARD OLDFIELD, BETTINA M. BEECH, AND VANN PRICE	

3 Student Development

XV	Facilitating Personal and Social Development	209
	NANCY BODENHORN	
XVI	Physical Health and Emotional Development: A Primer for School Counselors	219
	LAURA FILLINGAME KNUDTSON AND HARDIN L. K. COLEMAN	
XVII	Adolescent Sexual Health and Development	243
	LAURA FILLINGAME KNUDTSON AND HARDIN L. K. COLEMAN	
XVIII	School Counselor's Role in Promoting Literacy in Elementary School–Aged Children	259
	CARRIE J. LINSKENS AND HARDIN L. K. COLEMAN	
XIX	Designing Culturally Responsive School Counseling Career Development Programming for Youth	269
	KIMBERLY A. S. HOWARD, V. SCOTT H. SOLBERG, NEETA KANTAMENI, AND MELISSA KRAEMER SMOTHERS	

4 School Counselor Competence

XX	School Counselor Training: School and Societal Needs in the 21st Century	293
	JOHN L. ROMANO, KAY HERTING WAHL, AND JULIE M. KOCH	

XXI	Supervision of Professional School Counselors 309
	DIANA GRUMAN AND MARY LEE NELSON
XXII	Multicultural Competence of School Counselors 321
	DELILA OWENS AND MADONNA G. CONSTANTINE
XXIII	Consultation With Teachers, Administrators, and Counseling Agencies 329
	ROBERTO CLEMENTE
XXIV	The School Counselor's Role in Creating Caring School Communities 351
	JENNIFER J. LINDWALL AND HARDIN L. K. COLEMAN

5 School-Based Interventions

XXV	Youth Development and Prevention in the Schools 381
	SALLY M. HAGE, JONATHAN P. SCHWARTZ, AND SARA BARNETT
XXVI	Individual Counseling as Intervention in the Schools 397
	JERI L. LEE AND STACIE E. PUTMAN
XXVII	Focused, but Flexible: A Developmental Approach to Small Group Work in Schools 409
	JEAN SUNDE PETERSON AND HEATHER L. SERVATY-SEIB
XXVIII	Conducting Groups in Schools: Challenges and Rewards 431
	DENISE BEESLEY AND LISA L. FREY
XXIX	Families in Context: An Essential Component of School Counseling 449
	TERENCE PATTERSON
XXX	Crisis Management in the Schools 459
	MICHELLE L. MURPHY
XXXI	Consultation and Collaboration as Essential Services for School Counseling Programs 481
	MICHAEL B. SALZMAN
XXXII	Career Development Interventions in Schools 497
	WEI-CHENG J. MAU
XXXIII	Creative Arts Counseling in Schools: Toward a More Comprehensive Approach 517
	CAROLINE S. CLAUSS-EHLERS
XXXIV	Counseling the Gifted and Talented 531
	CORISSA C. LOTTA, BARBARA A. KERR, AND ERICA A. KRUGER
XXXV	Cultural Identity Enhancement Strategies for Culturally Diverse Youth 563
	HARDIN L. K. COLEMAN, SARA CHO KIM, AND A. YANG

6 Working With Socioemotional Challenges

XXXVI	Interpersonal Relationships	587
	STEPHANIE T. PITUC AND TRACY R. JULIAO	
XXXVII	Suicide Prevention, Intervention, and Postvention	613
	SHERI BAUMAN	
XXXVIII	Working With School Failure	635
	KAREN A. CORT	
XXXIX	Measuring and Evaluating Adolescent Connectedness	651
	MICHAEL J. KARCHER, MICHELLE R. HOLCOMB, AND ELIAS ZAMBRANO	
XL	Bullying and Peer Victimization	673
	SUSAN M. SWEARER, ERIC S. BUHS, AMANDA B. SIEBECKER, KELLY BREY LOVE, AND COURTNEY K. MILLER	
XLI	School Violence	693
	ANNE GREGORY AND ELISE CAPPELLA	
XLII	Substance Abuse	717
	CHRIS WOOD AND LISA HINKELMAN	

7 Accountability and Professional Issues in School Counseling

XLIII	Evaluating School Guidance and Counseling Programs: Past, Present, and Future	739
	NORMAN C. GYSBERS	
XLIV	Research in and on School Counseling	751
	BRYAN S. K. KIM AND SAUL G. ALAMILLA	
XLV	The Essential Role of School–Community Partnerships in School Counseling	765
	MARY E. WALSH AND JILLIAN DePAUL	
XLVI	Law and Ethics in School Counseling	785
	PATRICIA L. WOLLEAT	
XLVII	Professional Activities in Professional School Counseling	811
	KEITH M. DAVIS, LAURIE L. WILLIAMSON, AND BARBARA A. SCARBORO	
	Author Index	825
	Subject Index	865

CONTRIBUTORS
(in alphabetical order)

Saul G. Alamilla
University of California at Santa Barbara

Saul G. Alamilla, MS, MA, is a doctoral candidate in the Department of Counseling, Clinical, and School Psychology at the University of California at Santa Barbara. He received a BA degree in sociology in 2002 and an MS degree in counseling in 2004, both from the California State University at Fullerton. He earned an MA degree in counseling psychology from the University of California at Santa Barbara in 2006. His current research interests include Latino/a mental health, ethnic/racial psychology, and the measurement of cultural constructs.

Tina M. Anctil
Washington State University

Tina M. Anctil, PhD, is Assistant Professor of counseling psychology at Washington State University. She coordinates the EdM in School Counseling Program at WSU and is the administrator of the WSU School Counseling Professional Education Advisory Board. In addition to teaching in the School Counseling Program, she is a licensed professional counselor and a certified rehabilitation counselor. She has worked in school settings across the country, assisting children and adolescents with disabilities with their educational and career development pursuits. Her research agenda is varied but is fundamentally concerned with how schools can empower all students to achieve in spite of life's challenges including disabilities, mental health disorders, poverty, and other risk factors.

Sara Barnett
Teachers College, Columbia University

Sara Barnett, MA, MEd, currently teaches fifth grade in the South Bronx as member of the New York City Teaching Fellows Program. She holds a BA from Harvard University and an MA and EdM in counseling psychology from Teachers College, Columbia University. Her research interests include minority student achievement, majority privilege, and racial-cultural identity development, among others.

Sheri Bauman
University of Arizona

Sheri Bauman, PhD, is Associate Professor in the Department of Educational Psychology and is director of the MEd program in School Counseling and Guidance at the University of Arizona. Her research focuses on school bullying, with an emphasis on relational bullying and teacher responses to bullying. In addition, she conducts research on professional issues in school counseling and on aspects of group work. She is editor-elect of the *Journal for Specialists in Group Work* and will become editor in July 2007. She is a licensed psychologist with a small clinical practice in Las Cruces, New Mexico.

Stephanie San Miguel Bauman
Washington State University

Stephanie San Miguel Bauman, PhD, is Associate Professor of counseling psychology at Washington State University. She coordinates the EdM in Counseling Program at the WSU Tri-Cities campus and is a member of the WSU School Counseling Professional Education Advisory Board. She received her PhD from the University of California at Santa Barbara in 1995. Her research interests include risk and resiliency factors for children of color, children with chronic illnesses, and their families. She has published in the areas of social support for families of children with autism, learning disabilities and social skills, and multicultural counseling.

Bettina M. Beech
University of Memphis

Dr. Beech is Associate Professor in the Department of Psychology. She received her DrPH in community health sciences in the School of Public Health from the University of Texas Health Science Center at Houston and a master's degree in public health from Temple University. She has focused her research in the area of behavioral risk factors that contribute to chronic diseases, specifically among adolescents and ethnic minority populations. Dr. Beech has been the Principal Investigator of 14 grants from the National Institutes of Health, The Assisi Foundation, and Memphis Alliance for Public Health.

Denise Beesley
University of Oklahoma

Denise Beesley, PhD, is Associate Professor of educational psychology at the University of Oklahoma (OU). She currently serves as the Coordinator for the school counseling program and as Director of the OU Counseling Psychology Assessment Clinic. Her research interests include school counselor and teacher training, working with at-risk youth, diversity issues, relational and behavioral health, and psychological and psycho-educational assessment. She serves on the Editorial Board of the *Journal of School Counseling*.

Nancy Bodenhorn
Virginia Tech

Nancy Bodenhorn, PhD, was a school counselor for 20 years before earning her PhD in counselor education. Nancy's career has included counseling at all three academic levels, alternative schools, and gifted and talented magnet schools. She has worked in schools in four different states as well as in international schools in Kuwait, Bangkok, and Brussels. After that exciting career, Nancy is following a new direction, transferring her passion to the next generation of school counselors. She earned her PhD at Michigan State and has been teaching at Virginia Tech since 2001.

Tamara R. Buckley
Hunter College, City University of New York

Tamara R. Buckley, PhD, earned her doctorate in counseling psychology from Columbia University, Teachers College in 2001. She is currently Associate Professor at Hunter College, City University of New York in the Department of Educational Foundations and Counseling Program, and she is a New York State licensed psychologist. Dr. Buckley's research focuses on racial identity and health, educational, organizational outcomes.

Eric S. Buhs
University of Nebraska–Lincoln

Eric S. Buhs, PhD, is Assistant Professor of educational psychology at the University of Nebraska-Lincoln in the Cognition, Learning, and Development program. His research interests include examining children's peer relationships and school adjustment with a focus on the role of behavioral correlates of peer rejection and the examination of cultural and ethnic differences in aggression. He has been conducting and publishing research using longitudinal examinations of peer rejection effects on victimization, social exclusion, and classroom engagement and is currently examining potential effects of aggression and victimization on adjustment in Latino adolescent populations.

Leon D. Caldwell
University of Memphis

Leon D. Caldwell, PhD, is Visiting Associate Professor of counseling psychology in the Department of Counseling, Educational Psychology, and Research at the University of Memphis. Dr. Caldwell's research focuses on the cultural determinants to health behaviors, African American male mental health promotion, adolescent mental health promotion, youth development and violence prevention intervention, and academic performance of African American and other underrepresented students. Dr. Caldwell has served as a consultant on national projects involving issues such as gang prevention, health disparities elimination, cultural competence, and the academic achievement gap.

Elise Cappella
Institute for Juvenile Research, University of Illinois at Chicago

Dr. Cappella is Assistant Professor at the Institute for Juvenile Research, University of Illinois at Chicago. She received her PhD in clinical–community psychology from the University of California, Berkeley. Her rescarch integrates education and psychology with the goal to understand the social–emotional and academic development of children in schools. She currently is studying an intervention to promote learning and positive behavior among students in urban high poverty schools and has conducted research on children's peer relationships and achievement trajectories. Dr. Cappella began an appointment as Assistant Professor in the Department of Applied Psychology at New York University in 2007.

Robert T. Carter
Teachers College, Columbia University

Robert T. Carter, PhD, is Professor of Psychology and Education in the Counseling Psychology Program at Teachers College, Columbia University. Dr. Carter is known internationally for his work on Black and White racial identity. He has published in the areas of psychotherapy processes and outcome, career development, cultural values, racial identity issues, educational achievements, and equality in education through the lens of racial identity. He also provides consultation on organizational, legal, and educational issues associated with race and diversity.

Shannon Casey-Cannon
Alliant International University

Shannon Casey-Cannon, PhD, is Assistant Professor at the California School of Professional Psychology at Alliant International University. She is currently doing research related to ethnic identity, cognitions associated with shifting between diverse cultural environments, and minority student achievement. Dr. Casey-Cannon teaches Psychometrics, Statistics, and Research Design, as well as courses related to cognitive behavioral therapy.

Sara Cho Kim
University of Wisconsin–Madison

Sara Cho Kim, MS Ed, is a 5th-year doctoral student in counseling psychology at the University of Wisconsin–Madison. She has presented and published on topics related to cultural identity formation, psychosocial factors in student achievement, and stereotype threat. Her major research interests are in studying cultural and contextual factors influencing psychological processes and outcomes for Asian Americans. In addition, she has taught courses on multicultural counseling and career development as an adjunct professor at Shippensburg University. She received her master's degree from the University of Pennsylvania.

Caroline S. Clauss-Ehlers
Rutgers, the State University of New Jersey

Caroline S. Clauss-Ehlers, PhD, is Assistant Professor of counseling psychology at the Graduate School of Education, Rutgers, the State University of New Jersey. Her research interests include cross-cultural psychology with children and families, bilingualism in psychotherapy, resilience, and public education through the media. A key interest is to explore what fosters resilience in children and adolescents at home, in the community, and in schools. Her recent books include *Diversity Training for Classroom Teaching: A Manual for Students and Educators* (Springer, 2006), and she was coeditor of *Community Planning to Foster Resilience in Children* (Kluwer Academic Publishers, 2004).

Roberto Clemente
Roosevelt University, Chicago

Roberto Clemente holds a PhD in counselor education from Oregon State University, a master's in school guidance, and a bachelor's in science education from the University of Puerto Rico. He was an Associate Professor at the University of Northern Iowa and is currently at Roosevelt University in Chicago in the Counseling and Human Services Department. He has written two book chapters and several refereed articles, and has coauthored a book on ethnically diverse children and counseling interventions. In addition to providing sensitivity and multicultural training in schools and mental health agencies, he has conducted international consultation activities in St. Petersburg, Russia, Guatemala, Mexico, and Puerto Rico.

Hardin L. K. Coleman
University of Wisconsin–Madison

Hardin L. K. Coleman, PhD, is Professor of counseling psychology and Associate Dean in the School of Education at the University of Wisconsin–Madison. His primary teaching and training focus is on the development of school counselors and professional development training in multicultural competence for teachers. His clinical focus is with lower income African American families with a particular interest in adolescents. His current research focus is on the noncognitive factors that affect minority student achievement in K–12 educational settings and interventions that enhance cultural identity development. His other research interests include the development of cultural identity, strategies for effectively coping with cultural diversity, and bicultural competence.

Madonna G. Constantine
Teachers College, Columbia University

Madonna G. Constantine, PhD, is Professor of psychology and education in the Department of Counseling and Clinical Psychology at Teachers College, Columbia University. The scope of her work includes exploring the psychological, educational, and vocational issues of African Americans; developing models of cross-cultural competence in counseling, training, and supervision; and examining the intersections of variables such as race and ethnicity in relation to mental health and educational processes and outcomes. She is currently involved on several editorial boards in her field, and she serves in various leadership capacities in counseling and psychological associations across the country.

Karen A. Cort
Teachers College, Columbia University

Karen A. Cort is currently a doctoral candidate in counseling psychology at Teachers College, Columbia University. She received her MA and EdM in psychological counseling, and MPhil from Teachers College, Columbia University. She has worked with students for over 10 years in academia, serving as a high school counselor for 5 years and as an adjunct faculty member at LaGuardia Community College, John Jay College of Criminal Justice, and Dowling College. Her research interests include race, education, and adolescent development, specifically focusing on students of color.

Carol A. Dahir
New York Institute of Technology

Carol A. Dahir, EdD, is Associate Professor in counselor education at New York Institute of Technology. Dahir is the coauthor of *The National Standards for School Counseling Programs* (1997) and has also coauthored *The Transformed School Counselor* (2006) and *School Counselor Accountability: A Measure of Student Success 2e* (2007) with Carolyn Stone. She writes and presents extensively about transforming school counseling, school counseling program development, and accountability in textbooks, journals, publications, and professional development venues across the nation.

Keith M. Davis
Appalachian State University

Keith M. Davis, PhD, NCC, is a Licensed North Carolina School Counselor and Associate Professor in the Department of Human Development and Psychological Counseling at Appalachian State University, Boone, North Carolina. He has worked in public education as a high school teacher and high school and elementary school counselor.

Jillian DePaul
Boston College

Jillian DePaul, MA, MEd, is a doctoral student in counseling psychology at Boston College's Lynch School of Education. She received clinical training at a variety of settings, including Fenway Community Health Center, the Tufts University Counseling Center, and Chelmsford High School. Her research interests include systemic interventions in schools, gender identity and socialization, and issues of sexual orientation in schools. Prior to pursuing graduate studies in psychology, Jillian taught fifth grade for 2 years in Austin, TX, as a member of the Alliance for Catholic Education, a service program housed at the University of Notre Dame.

Matthew A. Diemer
Michigan State University

Matthew A. Diemer, PhD, is Assistant Professor in the Michigan State University MA Counseling Program. His teaching and training interests include preparing culturally competent counselors, social justice counseling perspectives, comprehensive guidance models, and integrating career development into the practice of (particularly school) counselors. His research interests include the cultural context of career development, facilitating sociopolitical development and critical consciousness among oppressed/marginalized individuals, and synthesizing these domains to explore sociopolitical development/critical consciousness as a predictor of career development and occupational attainment among economically disadvantaged youth of color.

Laura Fillingame Knudtson
University of Wisconsin–Madison

Laura Fillingame Knudtson, MA, is a doctoral candidate in counseling psychology at the University of Wisconsin–Madison. She earned her master's in educational psychology from the University of Minnesota. Laura's clinical work focuses on working with diverse adolescent populations as well as the clinical supervision of master's level counseling psychology trainees. She has conducted research in the areas of positive youth development, racial/ethnic identity development, minority student achievement, body image, and training medical professionals' skills in working with adolescent patients. Laura's current work focuses on adolescent sexual decision making and sexual health education.

Lisa L. Frey
University of Oklahoma

Lisa L. Frey, PhD, is Assistant Professor in the counseling psychology program of the Department of Educational Psychology at the University of Oklahoma. Her teaching and research has been greatly influenced by her previous clinical experience, which focused on work with youth who have experienced trauma and/or perpetrated violence, as well as individuals from diverse populations. Dr. Frey has consulted extensively in schools and community agencies. Her research interests are in the areas of at-risk youth, particularly youth who have been identified as delinquent and girls involved in the juvenile justice system; diversity; applications of the relational cultural model; and relational development.

Alice Fridman
University of Iowa

Alice Fridman is a doctoral student in her 3rd year of the counseling psychology program at the University of Iowa. She received her BA in psychology from Carleton College in 2003. Her research interests include social class and other multicultural issues, and her clinical interests include trauma recovery, diversity issues, gender issues, and play therapy.

Anne Gregory
Curry School of Education, University of Virginia

Anne Gregory is Assistant Professor in clinical and school psychology at the University of Virginia. She received her PhD from the University of California, Berkeley. Her research identifies contributors to the overrepresentation of African American students in the discipline system. Co-authored recent publications include, "The Discipline Gap and the Normalization of Failure," in P. Noguera and J. Wing (Eds.), *Unfinished Business: Closing the Racial Achievement Gap in Our Schools* (2006) and "School Climate and Implementation of a Preventive Intervention," *American Journal of Community Psychology* (in press).

Diana Gruman
Western Washington University

Diana Gruman, PhD, NCC, is Assistant Professor in the Department of Psychology at Western Washington University in Bellingham. Her primary area of teaching is in the CACREP-accredited school and mental health counseling programs. Dr. Gruman received her bachelor's degree in psychology from Whitman College, her master's degree in school counseling at Western Washington University, and her doctorate in educational psychology, with an emphasis on counselor education and supervision, at the University of Washington, Seattle. Her research interests include student mobility, effectiveness of school prevention/intervention efforts, and the professional development of school counselors.

Norman C. Gysbers
University of Missouri–Columbia

Norman C. Gysbers, PhD, is Professor with Distinction in the Department of Educational, School, and Counseling Psychology at the University of Missouri–Columbia. He is a licensed school counselor in Missouri. Gysbers' research and teaching interests are in career development, career counseling, and school guidance and counseling program development, management, and evaluation. He is the author of 79 articles in 17 different professional journals, 31 chapters in published books, 15 monographs, and 17 books. Since 1967, he has served as director of numerous national and state projects on career development and career counseling, and school guidance program development, implementation, and evaluation.

Sally M. Hage
Teachers College, Columbia University

Sally M. Hage, PhD, is Assistant Professor of psychology and education at Teachers College, Columbia University, Department of Counseling and Clinical Psychology. She is a licensed psychologist who earned her doctorate at the University of Minnesota and an MDiv from the University of Notre Dame. Her areas of special interest and research include prevention and training, spirituality and counseling, prevention of interpersonal violence, and multicultural psychology. She has written extensively in the area of prevention and psychology and she is the lead author of the "Best Practice Guidelines on Prevention Practice, Research, Training, and Social Advocacy for Psychologists," *The Counseling Psychologist,* 2007.

Schekeva P. Hall
Teachers College, Columbia University

Schekeva P. Hall, BA, is a doctoral student in counseling psychology in the Department of Counseling and Clinical Psychology at Teachers College, Columbia University. Her research interests include racial identity development, racial discrimination, and mental health with Black immigrant populations.

Thomasin E. Tranel Hall
University of Iowa

Thomasin E. Tranel Hall graduated with a BA from Gonzaga University in 2004 with majors in psychology and Spanish. She is currently working toward a PhD in counseling psychology at the University of Iowa. Her specific interests are in the areas of child developmental disabilities and behavior disorders, acculturation among Latino adolescents, and social justice issues in counseling psychology.

Lisa Hinkelman
The Ohio State University

Lisa Hinkelman, PhD, is Assistant Professor in the counselor education program at The Ohio State University. She is licensed as a school counselor in the state of Ohio and is licensed as a professional counselor. Her work includes serving as Project Evaluator for Project Success, an Elementary School Counseling Demonstration Act project in the Columbus Public Schools. She has published and presented on topics such as the development of leadership in school counseling students, girls' career development, body image and eating disorders, sexual assault prevention, and mental health issues in schools.

Michelle R. Holcomb
University of Texas at San Antonio

Michelle R. Holcomb, MA, is a Licensed Professional Counselor (LPC) in the state of Texas. She received her Bachelor of Science Degree in psychology from Angelo State University in San Angelo, Texas and her Master of Education in counseling psychology from the University of Houston. She is currently pursuing a doctorate in counselor education and supervision at the University of Texas at San Antonio. Michelle worked as a high school guidance counselor for 2 years in Houston and an LPC working with at-risk youth grades K–12 in San Antonio for 5 years.

Kimberly A. S. Howard
University of Wisconsin–Madison

Kimberly A. S. Howard, PhD, is Assistant Professor, the Coordinator of the School Counseling track, and the Chair of the Masters in Counseling program in the Department of Counseling Psychology at the University of Wisconsin–Madison. Dr. Howard's research interests include the examination of the career development process of diverse, low-income youth. She is interested in factors that promote vocational development and resilience, including supportive relationships and personal agency beliefs. Her early research explored the reasoning processes used by children and youth to understand career choice and career attainment. At present, she is engaged in an international study of protective factors that predict positive academic, career, and life outcomes.

Tracy R. Juliao
Genesys Regional Medical Center

Tracy R. Juliao, PhD, earned her baccalaureate degree in psychology from the University of Michigan. She pursued her graduate studies at Teachers College, Columbia University where she earned a Master of Arts in developmental psychology, a Master of Education in psychological counseling, and a PhD in counseling psychology. Tracy currently practices full time as a Health Psychology Fellow at Genesys Regional Medical Center in Grand Blanc, Michigan. Her primary research and clinical interests include multicultural issues in clinical practice, women's issues, effectiveness of family interventions, integrating health psychology within primary care, incorporating multiculturalism and behavioral medicine into medical education, and developing comprehensive pain management programs.

Neeta Kantamneni
University of Wisconsin–Milwaukee

Neeta Kantamneni, MS, is a doctoral student in the counseling psychology program at the University of Wisconsin–Milwaukee. She received her master's degree in counseling from the University of Wisconsin-Madison. Her research interests include contextual factors in vocational development and career interests, as well as multicultural counseling and competencies.

Michael J. Karcher
University of Texas at San Antonio

Michael J. Karcher, EdD, PhD, is Associate Professor of Education and Human Development and Coordinator of the School Counseling Program at the University of Texas at San Antonio. He has studied the phenomenon of connectedness in schools for 10 years. In 2002, he became the principal investigator for the Study of Mentoring in the Learning Environment (SMILE) funded by the William T. Grant Foundation. He is on the editorial boards of *Journal of Primary Prevention, Professional School Counseling, Journal of Youth and Adolescence,* and *Psychology in the Schools,* and is coeditor, with David L. DuBois, of the *Handbook of Youth Mentoring* published by Sage Publications in 2005.

Barbara A. Kerr
University of Kansas

Barbar A. Kerr, PhD, is Williamson Family Distinguished Professor of Counseling Psychology at the University of Kansas. Her interests include the psychology of optimal human development, including giftedness, creativity, and spirituality; counseling and psychotherapy; and gender issues. She is also a member of the National Association for Gifted Children.

Bryan S. K. Kim
University of Hawaii at Hilo

Bryan S. K. Kim, PhD is Associate Professor in the Department of Psychology at the University of Hawaii at Hilo. Previously, he was Associate Professor in the Department of Counseling, Clinical, and School Psychology at the University of California, Santa Barbara, and Assistant Professor in the Department of Psychology at the University of Maryland, College Park. Dr. Kim's research focuses on multicultural counseling process and outcome, the measurement of cultural constructs, and counselor education and supervision. Dr. Kim is an associate editor of *The Counseling Psychologist* and *Cultural Diversity and Ethnic Minority Psychology.* He also serves on the editorial boards of *Measurement and Evaluation in Counseling and Development; Journal of Counseling Psychology; Psychotherapy: Theory, Research, Practice, and Training;* and *Educational Review.*

Julie M. Koch McDonald
University of Minnesota–Twin Cities

Julie M. Koch, MEd, is a doctoral candidate in the counseling and student personnel psychology program in the Department of Educational Psychology, University of Minnesota–Twin Cities. She has worked as a school counselor at both elementary and high school levels and is a certified K–12 school counselor in the state of Texas. Her research interests include school counseling, multicultural counseling, international and immigrant populations, and counselor training and development. She is an active member of the American Psychological Association, American Counseling Association, and American School Counselor Association.

Erica A. Kruger
University of Wisconsin–Madison

Erica A. Kruger, M.S., is a licensed professional school counselor in Madison, WI. She earned her master's degree in counseling from the University of Wisconsin–Madison in 2004, with dual specializations in community mental health and K–12 school guidance. From 2001 to 2004, Erica also worked as a residential coordinator of summer enrichment programs for the Wisconsin Center for Academically Talented Youth. In addition to her experience in educational settings, Erica has also worked as an in-home family therapist at a local community mental health agency. Her interests include socioemotional concerns of gifted and talented youth, strengths-based practices for families, creating effective school-based intervention programs, and the personal and professional development of beginning school counselors.

Jeri L. Lee
Tennessee State University

Jeri L. Lee, EdD, is an Associate Professor and Coordinator of the Graduate Program in School Counseling in the Psychology Department at Tennessee State University. Dr. Lee is licensed as a professional school counselor, a teacher, and a counseling psychologist. Her research interests include legal and professional issues, program evaluation, and parenting strategies. Publications include a book, *The Two Yes Maxim: Maximizing Parenting Effectiveness*, and articles appearing in *Tennessee Psychologist* and *The Southern Speech Communication Journal*.

Sarah J. Lee
Teachers College, Columbia University

Sarah J. Lee received her MA and EdM in psychological counseling from Teachers College, Columbia University. She has worked with diverse populations in the City College of New York system as an instructor, counselor, and advisor providing students with personal and career counseling, academic advisement, educational planning, and mentorship. For the past 5 years, Lee has focused her research efforts in the areas of Asian Americans and mental health and addressing needs of immigrant youths in schools.

Jennifer J. Lindwall
University of Wisconsin–Madison

Jennifer J. Lindwall, MS, is a doctoral student at the University of Wisconsin–Madison in the Department of Counseling Psychology. Upon receiving her masters in counseling from University of Wisconsin–Madison, she became licensed as a school counselor and worked with elementary and middle school students. Additionally, Ms. Lindwall has worked as a teacher, mentor, and counselor for youth and their families in other settings, including precollege programs, an after-school program, a community counseling agency, and most recently primary care settings. She is primarily interested in school counseling, school psychology, prevention science, and developing effective interventions for culturally diverse youth.

Carrie Jo Linskens
Office of the Attorney General, Nevada Department of Justice

Carrie Jo Linskens received an MS in counseling from the University of Wisconsin–Madison, where she prepared for certification in both school and community counseling. She is currently working for the Office of the Attorney General in Nevada in the Medicaid Fraud Control Unit. Her responsibilities include investigating abuse and neglect of patients. The information in her chapter is based on her master's thesis completed in cooperation with the second author.

William Ming Liu
University of Iowa

William Ming Liu, PhD, is Training Director for the Counseling Psychology Program at the University of Iowa. He received his doctorate from the University of Maryland. His research and clinical interests are in social class and classism, poverty, and men and masculinity. He is on the editorial boards for *The Counseling Psychologist, Cultural Diversity and Ethnic Minority Psychology*, and *Psychology of Men and Masculinity*.

Corissa C. Lotta
University of Wisconsin–Madison

Corissa C. Lotta, PhD, is a faculty associate at University of Wisconsin–Madison, Department of Counseling Psychology. Her areas of primary interest include gifted and talented/creativity, clinical/communications training, at-risk youth, and diversity/women's issues. Within the Counseling Psychology Department, she teaches a variety of courses, supervises students' clinical work, and is the Masters and Doctoral Practicum Coordinator. In addition, she is developing counseling and support services for students in the School of Veterinary Medicine and clients in the Veterinary Medicine Teaching Hospital.

Kelly Brey Love
University of Nebraska–Lincoln

Kelly Brey Love, MA, is a doctoral candidate in school psychology at the University of Nebraska–Lincoln. She is currently completing her predoctoral internship in professional psychology at McLean Hospital/Harvard Medical School in Belmont, Massachusetts, and is working with the Klarman Eating Disorders Center and the Franciscan Children's Hospital in Boston, Massachusetts. Her research interests include analysis of aggressive, depressive, and anxious symptomatology in adolescents who witness bullying interactions.

Wei-Cheng J. Mau
Wichita State University

Wei-Cheng J. Mau, PhD, NCC, is a professor of counselor education at Wichita State University where he has been teaching career development and other school counseling courses since 1991. Dr. Mau has published over 40 journal articles, books, book chapters, reviews, and monographs. He has presented numerous papers at national and international conferences. His primary research areas include cultural differences in educational/vocational aspirations and career planning, academic achievement, help-seeking attitudes and behaviors, and computer-based career interventions. He has served on the editorial boards of *Journal of Vocational Behavior, Career Development Quarterly*, and *Measurement & Evaluation in Counseling and Development*.

Courtney K. Miller
Catholic Social Services, Lincoln, Nebraska

Courtney K. Miller, PhD, is currently completing a postdoctoral fellowship with Catholic Social Services in Lincoln, Nebraska, and is a provisionally licensed psychologist in the state of Nebraska. She received her doctorate of philosophy in the area of school psychology from the University of Nebraska–Lincoln. Dr. Miller's research interests include bullying and victimization among school-age youth; multisystemic interventions to support youth and families; and integration of spirituality within the therapeutic context.

Marie L. Miville
Teachers College, Columbia University

Marie L. Miville, PhD, is Associate Professor of psychology and education at Teachers College, Columbia University. She also is the Program Coordinator and Director of Training of Counseling Psychology programs at Teachers College. Professor Miville has conducted research and developed workshops on social attitudes and universal-diverse orientation, Latino mental health, and the interrelations of various aspects of identity, as based on race, culture, gender, sexual orientation, and ego identity among populations of color. Dr. Miville is the author of nearly 40 journal articles and book chapters dealing with multicultural issues in counseling and psychology. She is currently serving or has served on several editorial boards.

Michelle L. Murphy
University of North Florida

Michelle L. Murphy, PhD, LMHC, NCC is Visiting Assistant Professor in the Department of Leadership, Counseling, and Instructional Technology at the University of North Florida. Dr. Murphy has a dual specialization in mental health counseling and school counseling and guidance, and her current areas of emphasis include crisis intervention, suicide prevention, sexual assault, and relationship violence. She has worked as a high school counselor and a mental health consultant, collaborating with schools and community agencies to provide counseling services to at-risk youth. Dr. Murphy is an instructor and trainer for the North Florida Crisis Intervention Team and works with a local EAP providing crisis response services and critical incident stress debriefings.

Douglas M. Neil
Michigan State University

Douglas M. Neil, PhD, is Assistant Professor at Michigan State University's MA Counseling Program. Dr. Neil promotes the development of school counselors through highlighting the importance of attention to psycho-socioemotional development across the life span in his areas of expertise in teaching and research, which include multicultural counseling competence development, counseling supervision, and assessment. Dr. Neil also provides training in counseling supervision for post-master's level professionals in the community.

Mary Lee Nelson
University of Wisconsin–Madison

Mary "Lee" Nelson is Professor in the Department of Counseling Psychology at the University of Wisconsin–Madison. Dr. Nelson has recently coauthored a book titled *Critical Events in Psychotherapy Supervision: An Interpersonal Approach*. She has practiced school counseling and has trained school counselors for 13 years. Her research has focused on supervision processes, the relation of appearance talk to body dissatisfaction in adolescents, and the psychological experience of social class. She is currently on editorial boards of *Psychotherapy Research, Training and Education in Professional Psychology,* and *The Clinical Supervisor*.

Delila Owens
Wayne State University

Delila Owens, PhD, is Assistant Professor at Wayne State University. Owens has nearly 10 years of experience working with adolescents. Her areas of specialization include school counseling, adolescent counseling, career and counseling/development. She has taught courses such as Diverse Learners in a Multicultural Perspective, Child Development, Career Counseling, and School Counseling and Consultation. Her research interests are in the areas of adolescent counseling, urban school counseling, early parental attachment and later adult adjustment, and college student adjustment.

Terence Patterson
University of San Francisco

Terence Patterson is Professor at the University of San Francisco. He is a licensed psychologist and is board certified in family psychology with the American Board of Professional Psychology and a Fellow of the American Psychological Association. He is on the board of *The American Journal of Family Therapy*, a reviewer for *Professional Psychology: Research, & Practice*, and senior consulting editor for the APA bulletin *The Family Psychologist*. He is author of *The Couple & Family Clinical Documentation Sourcebook* and *The Comprehensive Handbook of Psychotherapy (2nd ed., Vol. 2—Cognitive-Behavioral)*. He is currently active in promoting diversity and competence in specialty areas in psychology.

Jean Sunde Peterson
Purdue University

Jean Sunde Peterson, PhD, is Associate Professor in the Department of Educational Studies at Purdue University and coordinates school-counselor preparation. Her research has focused on underidentified and understudied populations of gifted children and adolescents, with particular attention to underachievement, bullying and other trauma, homosexuality, and giftedness as a risk factor. She is currently the chair of the Counseling & Guidance Division of the National Association for Gifted Children. She has published 70 books, articles, and chapters, including 3 books on group work with teens.

Stephanie T. Pituc
University of San Francisco

Stephanie T. Pituc, MA, MEd, earned her baccalaureate degree in psychology from Northwestern University in Evanston, Illinois. She earned a Master of Arts and Master of Education in psychological counseling from Teachers College, Columbia University. She is currently affiliated with the University of San Francisco, School of Education's Department of Counseling Psychology. Stephanie's clinical work and teaching experience include high school, community college, and university populations in the New York City area. Her research interests include multicultural counseling, interpersonal dynamics, Asian immigrant populations, cultural adaptation and acculturation, and racial/ethnic identity.

Stacie E. Putman
Tennessee State University

Stacie E. Putman, EdD, is Assistant Professor in the Graduate Program in School Counseling in the Psychology Department at Tennessee State University. Her research interests include posttraumatic stress disorder among sexually victimized children, multicultural counseling issues, and issues related to juvenile sexual offenders. Dr. Putman is a licensed professional counselor/mental health service provider in the state of Tennessee. Her publications include articles appearing in *The Journal of Counseling & Development*.

John L. Romano
University of Minnesota–Twin Cities

John L. Romano is Professor of educational psychology in the Counseling and Student Personnel Psychology Program at the University of Minnesota–Twin Cities. He received his PhD from Arizona State University. He was a core faculty member on the evaluation team that assessed the outcome and impact of the national *Transforming School Counseling Initiative*, originally supported by the Wallace–Reader's Digest Fund in partnership with the Education Trust. He has also conducted workshops and research with preK–12 school personnel on models to enhance student well-being. His current research interests include applying principles and concepts of prevention to counseling and applied psychology and international psychology.

Michael B. Salzman
University of Hawaii at Manoa

Michael B. Salzman, PhD, is Associate Professor in the Department of Counselor Education at the University of Hawaii at Manoa. He has worked with diverse populations as a teacher in an inner-city public school district in Brooklyn, a school counselor in the Navajo Nation, with Alaska Natives in a model rural mental health program, with the Native Hawaiian Leadership Project in Hawaii, and as a psychologist at a community mental health center in South Tucson, Arizona. Dr. Salzman has developed interests in the psychological functions of culture, cultural trauma, consultation, indigenous psychologies, movements of cultural recovery, ethno-cultural conflict, and the processes of psychological decolonization.

Barbara A. Scarboro
Appalachian State University

Barbara A. Scarboro, PhD, is Assistant Professor in the Human Development & Psychological Counseling Department at Appalachian State University. Previously, she worked in the public schools of North Carolina as a substance abuse prevention coordinator, student assistance program counselor, and professional school counselor. Her current research interests include mental health reform, professional school counseling, professional development; counseling students with emotional and behavioral challenges; substance abuse prevention, intervention, treatment and dual diagnosis; group counseling; and multiculturalism and diversity issues. She is a National Certified Counselor, Licensed Professional Counselor, Licensed School Counselor, Licensed Clinical Addictions Specialist, and Case Presentation Method Evaluator for the North Carolina Substance Abuse Professional Practice Board.

John J. Schmidt
East Carolina University, Greenville

John J. (Jack) Schmidt, PhD, is Executive Director of the International Alliance for Invitational Education and professor emeritus of counselor education at East Carolina University, Greenville, North Carolina. This year, Jack is a visiting professor at Wake Forest University. In addition to service as a university professor, Jack has been a social studies teacher; an elementary, middle, and high school counselor; a school system director of counseling and testing; and the state coordinator of school counseling with the North Carolina Department of Public Instruction from 1985 until 1989. Author of over 50 articles, professional manuals, book chapters, and book reviews, Jack has published more than a dozen books.

Jonathan P. Schwartz
University of Houston

Jonathan P. Schwartz, PhD, is a licensed psychologist and Assistant Professor in the Counseling Psychology Program at the University of Houston, Department of Educational Psychology. His research interests include prevention, intimate violence, and gender roles. He is the current Communication Officer for the American Psychological Association Division 17 Prevention Section and is the editor for the Section's publication, "Prevention in Counseling Psychology: Theory, Research, Practice and Training."

Shelby J. Semino
Fordham University

Shelby J. Semino, MEd, is a doctoral candidate in counseling psychology at Fordham University in New York City. She received her Bachelor of Science degree in human service studies from Cornell University and obtained her Masters of Education degree in psychological counseling from Teachers College, Columbia University. At this time, Semino is completing her psychology internship training at the Child and Family Institute of St. Luke's-Roosevelt Hospital Center. Simultaneously, she is working on her dissertation, which focuses on the psychological impact of racial and sexual identity development processes among nonheterosexual Black women.

Heather L. Servaty-Seib
Purdue University

Heather L. Servaty-Seib, PhD, a counseling psychologist, is Assistant Professor in the Department of Educational Studies at Purdue University and teaches graduate-level courses on counseling theories, group counseling, and children and death. Her research interests include a broad range of areas within the field of thanatology, with particular emphasis on adolescent grief and social support offered to the bereaved. She maintains a small private practice, counseling children, adolescents, and adults who are struggling with loss issues. Dr. Servaty-Seib has held a number of leadership positions, including Second Vice President, in the Association for Death Education and Counseling.

Amanda B. Siebecker
University of Nebraska–Lincoln

Amanda B. Siebecker, MA, is a fifth-year doctoral student in the School Psychology program at the University of Nebraska–Lincoln. She is the President-Elect of Student Affiliates in School Psychology (SASP). In addition, Amanda is a student-editor for *School Psychology Quarterly*. Her research interests include issues related to the measurement of bullying, the role of special education verification in bullying and victimization, and the identification of effective prevention and intervention programs for schools and communities.

Melissa Kraemer Smothers
University of Wisconsin–Milwaukee

Melissa Kraemer Smothers, MA, is a doctoral candidate in the counseling psychology program at the University of Wisconsin–Milwaukee. She graduated from Boston College with a master's degree in counseling psychology. Her research interests include supervision and psychotherapy process and multicultural counseling. She currently teaches in the areas of counseling theory and group counseling, as well as supervising master's level students in practicum.

V. Scott H. Solberg
University of Wisconsin–Madison

V. Scott H. Solberg, PhD, is Director of Wisconsin Careers in the Center on Education and Work at the University of Wisconsin–Madison where he is also a member of the faculty of the Department of Counseling Psychology. From 1995 to 2006, Dr. Solberg served as Associate Professor of educational psychology at the University of Wisconsin–Milwaukee. His primary work has focused on improving school classroom settings through intervention programming designed to promote a number of resilience characteristics including academic self-efficacy, motivation, positive relationships, stress management, and health. His intervention work has been published recently to be available to schools as *Success Highways* by ScholarCentric publishing.

Robbie J. Steward
Michigan State University

Robbie J. Steward, PhD, is Professor and Director of the Michigan State University Master's Counseling Program, whose training and teaching foci include the development of trainees' basic individual and group counseling skills and self-efficacy, appropriate selection and implementation of counseling strategies and consultation skills, and research competence. Her research specialty areas are multicultural counseling development, counseling supervision, the identification of trainees' cognitive and academic background and personal characteristics that influence optimal training outcomes in terms of counselor competence and self-efficacy, and the identification of variables that influence academic persistence in both K–12 and university settings.

Susan M. Swearer
University of Nebraska–Lincoln

Susan M. Swearer, PhD, is Associate Professor of school psychology in the Department of Educational Psychology at the University of Nebraska–Lincoln. She is the codirector of the Nebraska Internship Consortium in Professional Psychology and is a licensed psychologist in the state of Nebraska. Her research interests are in the areas of bullying prevention and intervention, comorbidity of internalizing and externalizing disorders, and cognitive-behavioral interventions for youth and their families. Dr. Swearer is Associate Editor for *School Psychology Review* and is on the editorial boards of *School Psychology Quarterly* and *Journal of Anxiety Disorders*.

Edison J. Trickett
University of Illinois at Chicago

Edison J. Trickett, PhD, is currently Professor of psychology and Chair of the Community and Prevention Research Division in the Psychology Department at the University of Illinois. Throughout his career, his research has focused on the development of an ecological perspective for conducting community research and intervention. His empirical work has focused on how to assess the social environments of public schools and their effects on adolescent development. In the past 15 years, the emphasis has been on the role of the schools in the acculturation and adaptation of immigrant and refugee adolescents and families. His current work focuses on school contributors to burnout among ESL and bilingual high school teachers.

Kay Herting Wahl
University of Minnesota–Twin Cities

Kay Herting Wahl, PhD, has been involved in school counseling training programs in several university programs, including in South Dakota, Iowa, Nevada, and Minnesota. She is a former school counselor, working at all three levels of education: elementary, middle, and secondary. She is currently involved in a federal grant that has hired school counselors in elementary schools in the inner city and a suburban school district to complete a comparison on the effectiveness of comprehensive programming by the school counselor.

Mary E. Walsh
Boston College

Mary E. Walsh, PhD, the Daniel E. Kearns Professor of Urban Education and Innovative Leadership in the Department of Counseling, Developmental and Educational Psychology at the Lynch School of Education at Boston College, directs the Boston College Center for Child, Family, and Community Partnerships. For the past several years, Dr. Walsh has been a lead partner in a school–community–university partnership among Boston College, the Boston Public Schools, and community agencies. This partnership, known as Boston Connects, addresses barriers to learning and promotes academic achievement by enhancing the school climate and the student support process for the school community and improving health and mental health resources for student and their families.

Laurie L. Williamson
Appalachian State University

Laurie L. Williamson, PhD, is a counselor educator and Professor in the Department of Human Development and Psychological Counseling and the Coordinator of the Professional School Counseling Program at Appalachian State University. Her clinical background is in medical social work, residential treatment, and mental health services. She has worked as a professional school counselor for 10 years, including in two international settings. As a counselor educator, her interests include school counseling, diversity, supervision, and career counseling.

Patricia L. Wolleat
University of Wisconsin–Madison

Pat Wolleat is a professor emerita from the Department of Counseling Psychology at the University of Wisconsin–Madison. She received her PhD from the University of Minnesota in 1971 and a law degree from the University of Wisconsin in 1987. She began her professional career as a seventh-grade English/social studies teacher. At the University of Wisconsin, she pursued research and teaching interests in law and ethics, clinical supervision, and career development of girls and women. She has supervised many school counseling practicum students and interns and published several articles in *The School Counselor* and *Elementary School Counseling and Guidance* journals.

Chris Wood
The Ohio State University

Chris Wood, PhD, NCSC is currently in the Counselor Education Program at The Ohio State University. He taught previously at the University of Arizona and has been on the editorial review board of *Professional School Counseling* for many years. He has authored numerous articles and book chapters advancing the field of school counseling. A nationally certified school counselor (NCSC), he has experience as a counselor educator, a high school counselor, and a counselor/group leader at a residential youth facility for troubled teens.

A. Yang
University of Minnesota–Twin Cities

A. Yang is a doctoral student at the University of Minnesota–Twin Cities. She received her Masters of Science from the University of Wisconsin–Madison. Her research interests can be encompassed under multicultural counseling, as it relates to promoting healthy psychological adjustment among culturally diverse groups through theory, research, and practice. For example, previous research topics of interest included studying racial/ethnic collective self-esteem; ethnic support network, and its influence on interracial dating and marrying; and cultural identity as a resiliency factor. Currently, she is investigating characteristics of counselors and therapists who encompass more ethno-relative worldviews and thus a greater capacity toward intercultural sensitivity competence.

Christine J. Yeh
University of San Francisco

Christine J. Yeh, PhD, is Associate Professor of counseling psychology and Coordinator, Educational Counseling/PPS Credential Program at the University of San Francisco. From 1998 to 2006, she was a Professor and Coordinator of the School Counseling Specialization at Teachers College, Columbia University. Her interests include developing school-based intervention programs for culturally diverse and immigrant children and youth and facilitating school counselor collaborations with teachers, staff, and outside agencies and organizations. She is currently Principal Investigator of a 5-year NIMH grant examining the cultural adjustment, academic achievement, and mental health of recent immigrant students. She is on the editorial boards of *Journal of Counseling Psychology* and *Training and Education in Professional Psychology*.

Elias Zambrano
University of Texas at San Antonio

Elias Zambrano, MA, is a doctoral student at the University of Texas at San Antonio, Counselor Education and Supervision. He is a retired certified school counselor, having worked as a professional school counselor for 28 years. During that time, he also served as the Safe and Drug Free Schools and Communities Program Coordinator and then Director of Guidance Services for Northside Independent School District in San Antonio.

SCHOOL COUNSELING FROM A MULTICULTURAL AND AN ECOLOGICAL PERSPECTIVE: An Introduction

HARDIN L. K. COLEMAN
University of Wisconsin–Madison

CHRISTINE J. YEH
University of San Francisco

As counseling psychologists, we (the editors) are committed to positive youth development, educational equity, and social justice. We seek to prepare school counselors who will help students become effective citizens in a democratic and pluralistic society through integrating theory, science, and practice in school counseling. We wanted to create a handbook for professional school counselors and counselor educators that reflects these commitments while contributing to the growing field of school counseling. This was an incredibly challenging and ambitious task that, due to the high quality of chapters created by our contributors, has been accomplished.

In planning the *Handbook of School Counseling*, we realized that today's schools are under pressure to meet the needs of an increasingly diverse student body. For example, in large cities such as New York City, only 15.3% of public school students are racially identified as White (Young, 2002). Across suburban, rural, and urban public schools in the United States, more than one third of students are from racial minority groups and this number continues to grow (Hoffman, 2000).

Due to the increasing diversity of school-aged children and youth, schools offer a unique and critical context for understanding multiple aspects of student development including race, disability, sexual orientation, social class, and linguistic differences. Specifically, in the past few decades, immigrants are the fastest growing and most culturally diverse group of school-aged children and youth in the United States (Zhou, 1997). In terms of linguistic diversity, 31% of all American Indian/Alaska Native, Asian/Pacific Islander, and Latino/a students enrolled in U.S. public schools speak English as a second language (U.S. Department of Education, 1996). Moreover, the percent of students at the poverty level continues to remain high (Fix & Capps, 2002; National Center for Children in Poverty, 2002). Due to the high costs of individual counseling, cultural stigmas, and other cultural barriers to mental health services, school counselors are an optimal choice for addressing socioemotional issues and fostering positive student development. Similarly, school counselors' daily contact with youth affords them opportunities to address many everyday issues facing students including academics, career development, literacy, interpersonal relationships, and sexual and physical health.

Understanding and incorporating multiculturalism in school counseling requires an appreciation of the range of values, customs, behaviors, and lifestyles represented within a school context (Kim & Yeh, 2002) and in the surrounding communities. Culturally diverse children and youth must learn to negotiate multiple sets of norms and identities across numerous social systems. Students experience challenges when they are expected to function and achieve according to the norms and goals of the "dominant culture" (Yeh, 2004). Helms (1990) defined the dominant culture as White European American with power and wealth. Because racialized interactions occur at multiple levels across various systems (Helms, 2003), school counselors with White privilege must explore and understand the influence of this power in the school setting and in their direct and indirect interactions with students (see Yeh & Pituc, this volume).

Children and youth are developing in a society that is undergoing a significant change because of the industrial revolution when schools transitioned from single-room houses in agrarian communities to comprehensive high schools in urban areas, followed by the consolidation movement across the United States in the 1960s and 1970s. Such shifts, in an increasingly multicultural society, mandate changes in the how we envision the role of the professional school counselor—a role that has evolved in the past three decades and will continue progress in the immediate future. There are also dramatic changes in technological advances that introduce a host of new challenges as well as resources for students and school counselors that are unprecedented. In this *Handbook*, we try to address the most current and pressing societal concerns and offer numerous current resources.

We hope that this *Handbook* can serve as a support system for school counselors as they move from the end of their preservice training and through the first 5 years of their professional career. We also hope that students, school counselors, school staff, counselor educators, and counseling psychologists will use the *Handbook* in their training and research as well as in program development and evaluation. Educational and psychology-based researchers may also use this *Handbook* as a guide for conducting research in school settings. In addition, many social systems that collaborate and interact with schools and students (e.g., families, community agencies, psychologists) may use this *Handbook* as a valuable resource for various student issues.

Most textbooks that specifically address the needs of school counselors tend to focus on understanding the history of the profession and the roles that school counselors take within the schools. Many textbooks provide specific techniques without providing the relevant conceptual, cultural, and scientific context. Certainly, our chapters provide specific skills, techniques, and discussions of roles. However, we also wanted to integrate critical issues related to child and adolescent development, positive youth development, diversity (in terms of ethnic, racial, cultural, geographic, gender, grade level, sexual orientation, ability, etc.), urbanization and immigration, social justice, and school-based interventions all within an ecological systems perspective (for an overview, see Bronfenbrenner, 1989, 1994).

The Organization and Overview of the Handbook

The Handbook consists of 48 chapters and it is divided into seven sections: Introduction to the Field of School Counseling, Diversity and School Counseling, Student Development, School Counselor Competence, School-Based Interventions, Working with Socioemotional Challenges, and Accountability and Professional Issues in School Counseling. We asked each contributor to include the most relevant current and past theory, research, and practice and to provide multicultural and contextual perspectives that include diversity in terms of ethnicity, race, sexual orientation, disability, social class, geographic location (e.g., rural, suburban, and urban) and grade level (e.g., elementary, middle school, and high school). We also asked contributors to highlight the connection between research and practice in relation to their topics. Because so many of our contributors have extensive experience in school settings (school counselors, school psychologists, program developers/evaluators, etc.), they were able to integrate their practical expertise in the chapters through case studies, examples of interventions, and student quotes. Many chapters also include discussion questions; suggestions for readings, videos, Web sites; and other resources for further development.

The first section includes five chapters and is an introduction to and overview of the field of school counseling. This section addresses the history of school counseling (Schmidt), the concept of "best practices" in school counseling (Steward, Neil, & Diemer) and a discussion of the development and implementation of National Standards in School Counseling (Dahir). In addition, our commitment to multiculturalism and context is underscored in chapters on student accomplishment and equity (Coleman) and in a chapter exploring school counselor worldview and cultural background as critical factors in training, practice, and research (Yeh & Pituc). This section lays the groundwork for more in-depth discussion of the role of diversity in the school setting.

The second section, Diversity and School Counseling, consists of nine chapters all dedicated to examining the important role of multiculturalism in our schools. The notion of multiculturalism is broadly defined and includes issues related to immigration, acculturation, racism, racial identity, ethnic identity, sexual orientation, social class, disability, and empowerment. These critical aspects of diversity are considered intersecting, dynamic, multidimensional, and contextually situated. For example, Edison Trickett and Diana Formoso's chapter, "The Acculturative Environment of Schools and the School Counselor: Goals and Roles That Create a Supportive Context for Immigrant Adolescents" provides an ecological perspective on immigrant youth development and interactions in schools. They discuss the reciprocal and complex nature of students' social systems (e.g., peers, family) as significant acculturative contexts. The chapter "Racial Harassment in American Schools" by Robert Carter, Tamara Buckley, and Schekeva Hall explores social, political, and institutional practices and policies that function as a basis of racial assumptions and beliefs. Issues of White privilege are examined at multiple levels (e.g., individual, school) across various structures (e.g., educational and political practices) to provide a context for understanding the systemic underpinnings of the racial harassment of students of color. Similarly, other chapters in this section are dedicated to helping school counselors address oppressive practices in schools and build a climate prioritizing equitable conditions and interactions.

The third section, Student Development, includes five chapters that incorporate major issues facing school-aged children and youth as they navigate through childhood and adolescence. There is a strong focus on the ways in which school counselors can promote positive youth development and health. The authors advocate for collaborative school counselor relationships with teachers, school staff, families, and communities to foster student development in areas such as literacy, career, and physical health. Further, as indicated in the chapter "Designing Culturally Responsive School Counseling Career Development Programming for Youth" (Howard, Solberg, Kantameni, & Smothers), positive development must be considered within its relevant cultural and social context.

The fourth section, School Counselor Competence, consists of five chapters that focus on the training, development, supervision, and practice of competent school counseling. Using a contextual and multicultural perspective, the authors view competence as not just an individual construct, but an integral aspect of counseling that involves teachers, administrators, counseling agencies, training programs, and supervisors. For example, as Jennifer Lindwall and Hardin Coleman discussed in their chapter, "The School Counselor's Role in Creating Caring Communities," competence entails the creation and development of caring school communities, not just individual counselors.

The *Handbook's* strong systemic approach is further underscored by the fifth section, School-Based Interventions. This section includes 11 chapters that range from examples of preventative intervention ("Youth Development and Prevention in the Schools," Hage, Schwartz, & Barnett) to "Crisis Management in the Schools" (Murphy). Multiple ecological levels are addressed including individuals, groups, and families. Given the high student-to-school counselor ratio, it is essential that we consider alternatives to the one-on-one counseling model. Given our strong multicultural focus, we also include chapters that provide various models of interacting with students (e.g., "Creative Arts Counseling in Schools: Toward a More Comprehensive Approach," Clauss-Ehlers) as well as different issues that can be addressed programmatically, such as the enhancement of cultural identity (Coleman, Cho Kim, & Yang).

The sixth section, Working With Socioemotional Challenges, includes seven chapters that highlight some of the most current challenges facing our schools and ways that school counselors can address these issues. Many of these issues create barriers to positive youth development and must be confronted systemically. For example, Susan Swearer, Eric Buhs, Amanda Siebecker, Kelly Brey Love, and Courtney Miller provided the most current research, theory, and practical offerings on the growing problem of bullying and peer victimization in our schools. Anne Gregory and Elise Capella discussed school violence from an ecological systems perspective examining the continuous and reciprocal interactions between individuals and contexts (e.g., the role of neighborhoods, families, and school policies). Karen Cort's chapter, "Working With School Failure," describes the racial and cultural contexts that are associated with school failure from an ecological perspective and challenges the discrete, unitary diagnostic category of an individual as being solely responsible for "failure."

The final section, Accountability and Professional Issues in School Counseling, includes five chapters focused on some of the most pressing professional issues that school counselors face and various laws and ethical issues that influence the role of the school counselor (see Wolleat, Chapter 46). This section examines issues of accountability by discussing how we evaluate school counseling programs (e.g., see Gysbers, Chapter 43) and the role of research in and on school counseling (see Kim & Alamilla, Chapter 44). Our commitment to integrating the science and theory of school counseling with practice is further highlighted in the chapter, "Professional Activities in School Counseling" by Keith Davis, Laurie Williamson, and Barbara Scarboro.

Hopes for the Handbook of School Counseling

We have several additional hopes for this *Handbook*. Our first hope is that, along with the journal, *Professional School Counseling*, the American School Counselor Association (ASCA), the efforts of the Educational Trust and the Transforming School Counseling Initiatives, and the work of counselor educators and school counselors across the country, this *Handbook* serves to highlight the importance and value of school counselors within the schools and in the field of counseling psychology. There are many challenges in modern education from school violence to the student achievement gap among many ethnic minority groups. School counselors must work collaboratively and systemically to prepare students to take on positive roles as citizens in a global economy. They must provide leadership in a culturally relevant comprehensive guidance and counseling program in order to foster positive youth development. Presently, the relationship between school counseling and counseling psychology has failed to live up to its full potential for collaboration (Romano & Kachgal, 2004).

Our second hope is that the material in this *Handbook* will help stimulate the integration of science into the practice of school counseling. To date, research and practice in school counseling have often occurred in two separate and distinct conversations. Part of this disconnect is shaped by the structure of training programs (Coleman, 2004) and the difference between the focus on research in doctoral level training in counseling psychology versus the focus on practice in master's degree level training in school counseling (Yeh, 2004). In addition, the scholarship and research associated with key topics in school counseling is spread across multiple disciplines (e.g., emotional intelligence, social competence, vocational psychology; Coleman, 2004).

Although there are numerous opportunities for multicultural research and practice in schools (Romano & Kachgal, 2004), the current research in counseling psychology does not adequately reflect school age populations (Yeh 2004). Romano and Kachgal asserted that school counseling has the potential to contribute unique research opportunities in terms of its emphasis on action research, qualitative methods, and developmental-contextualism. However, because doctoral students and their mentors in Counseling psychology programs tend not to specialize in School counseling research, few dissertations and later research activities address school counseling issues (Yeh, 2004). In this *Handbook*, school-based research, which incorporates an ecological systems perspective (Bronfenbrenner, 1989, 1994; Trickett & Schmid, 1993), is embedded throughout various chapters.

Our third hope is that this *Handbook* will provide guidance for greater collaboration between school counselors, other student pupil services professionals, teachers, and community members. According to the ASCA Delegate Assembly (2003),

> School counselors work with all students, including those who are considered at-risk and those with special needs. They are specialists in human behavior and relationships who provide assistance to students through four primary interventions: counseling (individual and group), large group guidance, consultation, and coordination. (¶ 1)

In order to serve as advocates for students, school counselors must work to ensure equal access to desired and necessary services. Hence, school counselors must collaborate to offer groups, outreach services, and programs in school and community settings.

Consistent with the ecological systems perspective (Bronfenbrenner, 1989, 1994; Trickett & Schmid, 1993), school counseling can greatly benefit not only from research that incorporates a systemic approach but also from practice applications as well. Specifically, ecological systems theory fosters our understanding of influences on children's and adolescents' psychological and emotional functioning across multiple contexts and helps shape relevant counseling approaches. Ecological settings are a group of reciprocal and interacting systems (Bronfenbrenner, 1994) that must be incorporated into current school counseling practices. Because many school-aged youth utilize differing coping strategies depending on their situation and environment (Coleman, Casali, & Wampold, 2001), school counseling practice must also involve important relationships for children and youth.

Colbert and Magouirk Colbert (2003) discussed the change from the individual focus in school counseling to the larger educational system as part of a necessary "culture-centered education reform" (p. 3). This framework is useful because it conceptualizes the role of the school counselor as a student advocate, organizational change facilitator, and consultant (Colbert & Magouirk Colbert) and removes the naïve perception that the individual student is accountable for the problems in a school setting. Along these same lines, we assert that school counselors must consider their role in the larger context of social justice and see their roles in fostering social, cultural, and institutional change. The chapters in the *Handbook* strive to meet this vision of the role of the school counselor.

Our fourth hope of the *Handbook* is that it will encourage school counselors and mental health practitioners in schools to use the principles of social science to guide and evaluate their practice. Moreover, we hope the *Handbook* will enhance and validate their identities as scientist-practitioners. Our contributors help us realize this goal by including recent research findings, critical theoretical perspectives, and the most pertinent clinical applications. Moreover, these chapters discuss the *links* that connect research, theory, and practice so that practicing school counselors may better understand the role of research in their everyday work. Similarly, training programs may better explain and validate this important connection through education and scientific inquiry.

The *Handbook* fulfills the vision of the editors and the numerous contributors and provides a clear agenda for research, practice, training, and practice in the growing, yet evolving field of school counseling.

References

American School Counselor Association Delegate Assembly. (2003). The role of the professional school counselor. Retrieved June 29, 2007, from http://www.schoolcounselor.org/content.cfm?L1=1000&L2=69

Bronfenbrenner, U. (1989). Ecological systems theory. *Annals of Child Development, 6*, 187–249.

Bronfenbrenner, U. (1994). *The ecology of human development.* Cambridge, MA: Harvard University Press.

Colbert, R. D., & Magouirk Colbert, M. (2003). School counselor involvement in culture-centered education reform. In P. B. Pederson & J. C. Carey (Eds.), *Multicultural counseling in schools: A practical handbook* (2nd ed., pp. 3–20). Boston: Allyn & Bacon.

Coleman, H. L. K. (2004). Toward a well-utilized partnership. *The Counseling Psychologist, 32*, 216–224.

Coleman, H. L. K., Casali, S. B., Wampold, B. E. (2001). Adolescent strategies for coping with cultural diversity. *Journal of Counseling and Development*, 356–365.

Fix, M. E., & Capps, R. (2002, August 31). Immigrant well-being in New York and Los Angeles. Retrieved October 24, 2003, from http://www.urban.org/urlprint.cfm?ID=7889

Helms, J. E. (Ed.). (1990). *Black and White racial identity: Theory, research, and practice*. New York: Greenwood.

Helms, J. E. (2003). Racial identity in the social environment. In P. B. Pederson & J. C. Carey (Eds.), *Multicultural counseling in schools: A practical handbook* (2nd ed., pp. 44–53). Boston: Allyn & Bacon.

Hoffman, L. (2000). *Overview of public elementary and secondary schools and districts: School year 1998–99*. Retrieved October 24, 2003, from the U.S. Department of Education, National Center for Educational Statistics Web site: http://nces.ed.gov/pubs2000/quarterly/summer/2feat/q2-5.html

Kim, A., & Yeh, C. J. (2002). Stereotypes of Asian American children and youth in schools. *ERIC Digest, 172*, EDO-UD-02-1.

National Center for Children in Poverty. (2002, September). Children of immigrants: A statistical profile. Retrieved October 24, 2003, from http://www.nccp.org/

Romano, J. L., & Kachgal, M. M. (2004). Counseling psychology and school counseling: An underutilized partnership. *The Counseling Psychologist, 32*, 184–215.

Trickett, E. J., & Schmid, K. D. (1993). The school as a social context. In P. H. Tolan & B. J. Cohler (Eds.), *Handbook of clinical research and practice with adolescents* (pp. 173–202). New York: Wiley.

Yeh, C. J. (2004). Multicultural and contextual research and practice in school counseling. *The Counseling Psychologist, 32*, 278–285.

Young, B. A. (2002). Characteristic of the 100 largest school districts in the United States: School year 2000–01. Retrieved October 24, 2003, from the U.S. Department of Education, National Center for Educational Statistics Web site: http://nces.ed.gov/pubs2002/100_largest/table_09_1.asp

1

Introduction to the Field of School Counseling

HISTORY OF SCHOOL COUNSELING

JOHN J. SCHMIDT, EdD
East Carolina University

School counselors are members of an expanded profession of practitioners who work in a variety of settings, including mental-health centers, family clinics, military services, hospitals, businesses, schools, and colleges among others (Gladding, 2000; Nugent, 2000; Schmidt, 2008; Vacc & Loesch, 2000). Within this burgeoning field of professional counseling, school counseling is a specialty field that has its roots in the vocational guidance movement of the Industrial Revolution during the late 19th and early 20th centuries (Gysbers & Henderson, 2000; Schmidt; Studer, 2005).

This first chapter of the *Handbook of School Counseling* provides an overview of the historical development of the school counseling profession, highlights the role that counselors have played in student development, and offers a brief synopsis of professional issues and trends that have had an impact on the practice of counseling in schools. By understanding historical influences and the emerging role of school counselors in American education over the past hundred years, a future school counselor or administrator can attain greater appreciation for the vital role that counselors will have in our 21st century schools.

In previous books and articles, Schmidt (2004, 2008) argued that, although school counselors serve students, parents, and teachers with seemingly dissimilar missions than their colleagues who practice in mental health, family clinics, or other arenas, all counselors are united professionally by criteria of preparation and standards of practice. These criteria and standards include a basic understanding and command of helping skills and techniques; a broad knowledge of psychological, sociological, and human development theories; an appropriate level of training in assessment, diagnosis, and intervention; and an appreciation of common goals and objectives that bring together counselors from a variety of specialty work settings as colleagues in the broader counseling profession. Before exploring the history of school counseling as a professional specialty, it is appropriate that we first take a brief glance at the counseling profession.

The Counseling Profession

The exact beginning of the counseling profession is unknown, but its roots may be found in a range of helping relationships that have spanned cultures and societies throughout the ages. In most instances, helping relationships that existed within early cultures and societies encouraged the development of young people and their acquisition of personal traits, social acceptance, and survival skills (Schmidt, 2008).

Numerous historical events, such as the U.S. Industrial Revolution, led to the emergence of professions to help people with social, personal, and vocational concerns. These professions include the fields of social work, psychology, psychotherapy, and counseling among others, and the theories of practice adopted and developed by the counseling profession have roots in the scholarly research and practical guidelines established during the 19th and 20th centuries.

> As a result, the counseling profession relies on a broad knowledge of human development, psychology, sociology, and education. At the same time, it incorporates effective communication and leadership skills with the essential human qualities of caring, genuineness, regard, and respect for others. (Schmidt, 2008, p. 5)

The counseling profession evolved from traditions and practices to help people formally assess their needs, design interventions, and provide services to assist people in identifying issues, developing self-awareness, making life-altering decisions, solving problems, and establishing healthy personal and social relationships. As such, professional counselors in a variety of work settings provide a range of services to help clients maximize their development and human potential, examine ways to prevent barriers or obstacles to their development, and alter behaviors or life situations that cause problems. In summary, professional counselors form different types of helping relationships and provide other services to assist clients in *preventing* future difficulties, *developing* optimal human potential, and *solving* problem situations.

The counseling profession is primarily represented and promoted by the American Counseling Association (ACA) and its many divisions, including the American School Counselor Association (ASCA). These organizations have guided the development of the counseling profession, established standards of preparation, set criteria for certification and licensure, and developed ethical guidelines and standards of professional practice for counselors. At the same time, other helping professions also use counseling processes in their roles. Social workers, psychologists, and psychiatric nurses are among those who apply processes similar to those used by counselors in mental-health centers, family clinics, prisons, hospitals, and schools.

The growth of all of these helping professions in the United States is largely due to social and economic changes during the 18th and 19th centuries that raised concern about personal, social, career, and educational development among young people. In another book, Schmidt (2008) commented,

> Because the U.S. prides itself on democratic principles, equal opportunity, and human service, it is understandable how so many related helping professions could emerge. In particular, it is especially clear why counselors have played such an important role in our schools, which themselves incorporate principles of democracy, equity, and opportunity for all students. (p. 6)

Within this framework of helping students develop their potential by accessing opportunities for personal, social, and education development, we introduce the school counseling profession and its attention to student development.

School Counseling and Student Development

School counselors work in elementary, middle, or high schools across the United States, and today the profession is expanding to many other countries throughout the globe.

These counselors matriculate in counselor education programs that stress human development, helping skills, and professional practice in school environments. As noted earlier, this educational focus is what links school counselors and other counselors as colleagues in an expanded counseling profession.

Before the 20th century in American schools, classroom teachers provided guidance to students for their social, personal, vocational, and in many cases, spiritual development. Most historical summaries point to the U.S. Industrial Revolution as the significant event or period during which the school counseling profession emerged as the guidance movement at the beginning of the 20th century (Schmidt, 2008; Sciarra, 2004). Some unfortunate consequences of the industrial growth of this era were urban blight, challenges of city life, and creation of ethnic ghettos. At the same time, industrial growth contributed to a factory mentality that frequently neglected or overlooked individual rights, freedom, and human value. In response to these conditions, some educators and social activists proposed programs and services to help students with their development, in particular with vocational aspirations and choices brought about by the change from an agrarian to an industrial society (Schmidt, 2008).

Emphasis on vocational guidance was an important part of this early response to industrialization. As one example, George Merrill began experimental efforts in vocational guidance at the California School of Mechanical Arts in San Francisco in 1895 (Miller, 1968). He proposed vocational experiences for students to explore occupational trades taught at the school and, in addition, offered counseling and job placement services to complement vocational experiences. In addition to vocational exploration, the guidance movement of the early 20th century helped students with their moral development, social skills, and interpersonal relationships. Leaders of this early guidance movement included Jesse B. Davis in Michigan, Frank Goodwin in Ohio, Anna Reed in Washington, Frank Parsons in Massachusetts, and Eli Weaver in New York.

Although his work did not focus directly on students in schools, Frank Parsons, also known as the "Father of Guidance," is considered to have started the guidance movement in the United States (D. Brown & Trusty, 2005; Gladding, 2000; Schmidt, 2008). In 1908, he established the Boston Vocational Bureau to assist young men in choosing their careers. Through his work with the bureau, Parsons focused on vocational development by helping young men make the career transition from high school to the world of work. Parsons (as cited in Schmidt) wrote a book, *Choosing a Vocation,* published after his death, in which he presented three essential factors for selecting a vocation: (a) clear self-understanding of one's aptitudes, abilities, interests, resources, and limitations; (b) knowledge of the requirements, advantages, disadvantages, and compensation for different types of employment; and (c) an understanding of the relationship between these two groups of facts.

As previously noted, this early guidance movement spread to many other states and cities across the United States including New York City, Grand Rapids, Seattle, and Cincinnati. Within a few short years, city school systems across the country had developed guidance programs. As an example, in 1889, before Frank Parsons created the Vocation Bureau, Jesse B. Davis established a guidance program in the curriculum of the public schools of Michigan (Gladding, 2000; Schmidt, 2008; Wittmer, 2000). From 1898 to 1907, Davis was a class counselor at Central High School in Detroit, Michigan, and was responsible for educational and vocational counseling with 11th-grade boys and girls. Named as principal of a high school in Grand Rapids, Michigan, in 1907, he soon established a schoolwide guidance program by having English teachers integrate into their classes guidance lessons for helping students acquire positive traits, choose appropriate behaviors, and address their vocational interests (Schmidt). Davis's work preceded other guidance programs established across the country. Anna Reed led the development of systematic vocational guidance in Seattle, Washington. Similarly, in 1908, Eli Weaver achieved national notoriety for his efforts at the Boys High School of Brooklyn to establish the first guidance services in New York City, and in 1911, Frank Goodwin organized a system-wide guidance program for the Cincinnati, Ohio, schools (Gibson & Mitchell, 1999; Miller, 1968; Schmidt). The focus of these guidance programs on student development formed the early years of what we know today as the school counseling profession. It is noteworthy that the school counseling profession throughout the years has continually addressed aspects of student development. The next several sections of this chapter chronicle that movement and emphasis.

Vocational Development

The early guidance movement of the 19th and 20th centuries gained strength from the founding of the National Vocational Guidance Association (NVGA) in 1913. One of the most significant activities of this organization was to publish the *National Vocational Guidance Bulletin*, which spread news and trends about the vocational guidance arena. Eventually, this publication would become the *Career Development Quarterly*, today published by the National Career Development Association (NCDA).

The early NVGA focused on vocational choice and career development, but its enduring legacy is the unification of counselors across a wide spectrum and the eventual identification of what today has become the counseling profession. During the next 3 decades and into the 1950s, many national and world events would give direction and momentum to the emerging counseling profession, particularly for counseling in schools. Related to this emphasis on vocational development was the country's growing interest in measurement and assessment of human traits and aptitudes. This interest increased dramatically during World War I, when the military began using assessments to screen and classify recruits and draftees.

Assessment and Vocational Development

Intelligence testing, first developed in the beginning of the 20th century, sparked interest in measuring human potential and other traits, and using results to place people in vocational tracks. The U.S. army adapted the work of French psychologist, Alfred Binet, later expanded by Arthur Otis and Lewis Terman, to create assessment procedures. A group intelligence test, developed by Arthur Otis (Miller, 1968), led to the military's *Army Alpha Examination* and the *Army Beta Examination* (Baker & Gerler, 2004). What followed was a proliferation of tests developed and marketed over the next decade, but many of these instruments were flawed due to inadequate design and inappropriate standardization processes (Schmidt, 2008):

> Nevertheless, the military's interest in using group measurement techniques was embraced by schools and the education profession when the war ended. The potential for applying testing and other measurement techniques to pupil assessment helped catapult the development and expansion of standardized testing in U.S. schools. (p. 9)

The testing movement contributed to the development of approaches to guidance and counseling that focused on measurement of students' traits and characteristics in the process of selecting vocational goals and planning career directions. As one example, E. G. Williamson, a professor at the University of Minnesota, promoted the perspective of a *directive* or *counselor-centered* approach to school counseling. In 1939, Williamson wrote that a school counselor should state his or her "point of view with definiteness, attempting through exposition to enlighten the student" (p. 136). Although he softened this view somewhat in later years (Schmidt, 2008), Williamson's direct approach continued through the 1950s to caution counselors about giving students too much latitude in making decisions for themselves. During this time, Trait-Factor Theory, as his approach became known, grew in popularity. Williamson (as cited in Schmidt) maintained, "[T]he development of individuality on the part of students must be balanced with concern for self-destructive and antisocial behaviors," and "people achieve individual freedom through effective group membership, interdependence, and adherence to high social ideals" (p. 9).

The Trait-Factor approach to counseling presented six steps in the process (Williamson, 1950). These steps included (a) *analysis*, which was the collection information and data about students and their environments; (b) *synthesis* of pertinent data to better identify and understand students; (c) *diagnosis* or rationale for intervention; (d) *prognosis* or the prediction of results that most likely will occur as a consequence of students' behaviors; (e) *treatment*, which outlined different strategies and techniques counselors might use in assisting students; and (f) *follow-up* or the evaluation of the outcomes of students' plans of action. The structure that Williamson (1950) and his colleagues gave to the counseling process helped give some sense of identity to the profession. However, not all counselors or counselor educators believed that the attention placed on students' traits and characteristics, or the limited focus of vocational development and career choice, adequately defined the role of counselors in schools. To some, vocational development and career decision making were only part of the developmental spectrum challenging students in schools. The voices of these professionals gained an audience and, consequently, the emphasis on counseling students in schools began to acquire a wider lens for the profession.

Personal and Social Development

During the early 1900s and through the 1930s, the country witnessed a seesaw of attitudes and beliefs about education and about the role of guidance and counseling in schools. For example, as the work of early guidance pioneers, such as educators Jesse Davis, Anna Reed, Eli Weaver, and Frank Goodwin, began to bear fruit from their efforts, American education entered the *progressive era*. Proposed by educational philosophers, such as John Dewey and others, *progressive education* advocated the personal, social, and moral development of students and handed schools the responsibility for addressing these issues. This progressive movement was relatively short-lived. Criticism from teachers, parents, and other groups who believed progressive education was too permissive and lacked a sound educational basis resulted in lost momentum after a few years. Also weakened by the decline in funding for public education, exacerbated by the Great Depression, progressive education disappeared as a popular movement, and coincidentally, support for guidance activities and counseling services in the schools was seriously weakened during this time (Nugent, 2000).

Nevertheless, many authorities in the school counseling profession continued to question the narrow focus on vocational development. Some encouraged a broader focus to include issues related self-concept development and other equally important aspects of student development. This broader view laid the groundwork for many of the counseling theories and approaches created in the years to come.

The years leading up to America's involvement in World War II witnessed significant change in U.S. education and influences on the practice of guidance and counseling in schools. Among the influences on the school counseling profession and the preparation of school counselors was the notable work of Carl Rogers (1942, 1951). The direction Rogers gave to the counseling profession as a whole, and the recognition his work gave to the importance of personal development in people's lives was significant for counselors in all mental-health arenas including the schools. Rogers' work helped to move the counseling profession away from counselor-centered models toward more developmentally oriented helping relationships. For school counselors, Rogers' emphasis helped move the profession from strict informational-gathering, decision-making, and problem-solving approaches to services intended to meet broader developmental needs of an expanded student population.

During the next five decades, Rogers' contributions would continue to identify and define an emerging counseling profession. Not all voices, however, praised how his work influenced the practice of counseling in schools. For example, Wittmer (2000) argued that inordinate attention to the person "somehow took us off-track in school counselor preparation and may have contributed to the inappropriate training of many school counselors" (p. 3). Wittmer particularly noted that the extraordinary attention placed on individuals seemed to lead the school counseling profession to place undue emphasis on one-on-one and remedial services while neglecting preventive and developmental approaches that are so vital in school curricula.

Gysbers and Henderson (2000) also criticized the overemphasis placed on the counseling function. They noted that the strong emphasis on counseling services maintained the historical roots of pupil personnel services and corresponding organizational models that had emerged from the pre-WWI era and continued through the 1960s. These models, such as the clinical-services model, promoted great interest in students' personal development with the focus being on the counseling function and the school counselor rather than on guidance curricula and guidance programs (Gysbers & Henderson).

During the 1940s, the nation became embroiled in World War II and, with its allies, fought against Germany, Italy, and Japan around the globe. United States entry into this conflict once again raised the military's interest and use of assessment and selection processes to identify personnel for specialist training and placement. After the war, this interest expanded from military use to educational testing and personnel screening in the business sector. As a result, the country saw an expanded use of assessment processes, which contributed to the growth of human services professions including counseling, psychology, and human resource development in business and industry (Gladding, 2000). This influence also affected the direction of school counseling services at this time and, furthermore, the attention that the federal government gave to this relatively new profession (Schmidt, 2008).

In 1946, the U.S. Congress passed the *George–Barden Act,* which allocated financial support for guidance and counseling services in schools. This legislation initiated the availability of funds and resources for state education supervisors, local school systems, and practicing school counselors. As Schmidt (2008) noted in another book, the available funds and resources from the *George–Barden Act* "fueled the start of a period of rapid growth for guidance and counseling services in schools" (p. 11). Simultaneously, rapid growth of the school counseling profession was complemented by various changes in government organization and oversight. Different federal and state offices under which school guidance and counseling was located and governed frequently changed names and organizational structure until the mid-1950s, when the Guidance and Personnel Services Section of the U.S. Office of Education was established. The direction provided by this office through the 1960s continued to emphasize areas of student development beyond the single focus on vocational development.

The next major world event to influence American education and the school counseling profession was the launching of the first unmanned satellite, Sputnik I, by the Soviet Union in 1957. This successful entry into the space age by an arch nemesis of the United States sounded a loud awakening in American politics and, simultaneously, rigorous debate about the ability of our educational system to prepare future scientists to compete in the race to space. The eventual fall out from the publicity, debate, and fear following the launch of Sputnik I was swift. Congressional action brought about significant change in educational direction and funding, both of which had tremendous impact on the emerging school counseling profession and greater emphasis on and attention to students' academic development.

Academic Development

Public fear, political criticism, and educational debate culminated in the passage of Public Law 85-864, called the *National Defense Education Act* of 1958 (NDEA). In sum, this bill provided direction and funding to improve assessment of student abilities, create systems for identifying students' potential (particularly in math, science, and foreign language) early in their school years, and encourage scholarships and other financial incentives to enable motivated and talented high school graduates to attend college. These directives aimed at the academic development of students to ensure the national safety and competitive place of the United States among the world's scientific achievements, exploration of space, military powers, and economic leaders.

Title V of the NDEA specifically addressed the need for more school counselors and, indirectly, the role of counselors in assisting students by assessing their educational potential and guiding them in their academic development. Essentially, this part of the bill noted that schools needed more counselors who were prepared to encourage students to complete high school, select academic courses that would ready them for college, and enter college upon graduation from high school.

Support from NDEA to improve guidance and counseling services in secondary schools came in the form of federal funds to the states for the purpose of establishing and maintaining assessment, counseling, and other guidance related services. NDEA also authorized the creation of institutes and graduate programs at colleges and universities to increase the number of counselors and strengthen the training for current and future counselors working in schools. During the summer of 1959, guidance and counseling institutes at 50 colleges and universities prepared over 2,200 counselors to meet the expectations put forth by NDEA. In addition, NDEA provided $15 million a year to assist local school systems and about $7 million a year to universities and colleges for the purpose of establishing and improving school counseling services, with particular emphasis on students' academic development (Miller, 1968; Shertzer & Stone, 1966).

The result of the NDEA, Title V, on the school counseling profession was remarkable. In his summary, Miller (1968) noted that, in a 5-year period, the number of school counselors increased from 12,000 to over 27,000 across the country, dropping the ratio of counselors to students from 1:960 to 1:530 during that period. In the process, the number of state consultants for school guidance and counseling increased two and one half times to over 250 consultants, and the federal government funded more than 400 institutes to prepare more than 13,000 counselors. Expenditures for the delivery of guidance and counseling services in local schools rose tremendously from 1958 until the mid-1960s, beginning in the $5.5 million range to over $127 million.

The federal government expanded NDEA in 1964 to include elementary school counseling as well as counseling in junior colleges and technical schools (Gibson, Mitchell, & Basile, 1993). As a result, NDEA training institutes added content about counseling young students in elementary schools. Despite this added emphasis, school systems were reluctant to employ elementary counselors. This hesitancy may have been due to schools' uncertainty about the role of counselor's in elementary education and the public's lack of general acceptance to the idea (Schmidt, 2008).

In 1965, the federal government once again intervened in public education due to continuing concerns about students' academic development. Despite the focus of NDEA, many students, particularly those from impoverished and lower income families, were not progressing educationally. Congress passed the *Elementary and Secondary Education Act* of 1965 (ESEA; Public Law 89-10) to provide states with funds and support for special instructional programs and counseling services to improve the educational opportunities of students from lower income families. This bill had an impact on the development of counseling services in elementary schools. Before 1965, only progressive school districts with strong financial bases were able to support school counseling services below the secondary level. ESEA allowed flexibility for states and local districts to identify federal funds for this purpose.

The overall effects of NDEA and ESEA on the focus of school counseling and guidance services through the 1960s and into the 1970s placed greater emphasis on helping students with their academic development. Nevertheless, development of new counseling theories and models of school counseling programs emerged at this time lending a more holistic perspective to the mission of the profession. In some measure, we can attribute this broader focus to the belief that school counselors and the programs they design to serve students should not compartmentalize human developmental needs and aspirations. By holding to a single perspective on academic growth and success, school programs risk neglecting important personal, social, and career issues that might influence students' intellectual and educational development. Contrarily, by emphasizing personal/social development while ignoring educational development, school counselors neglect a vital purpose for working in schools—students' academic success. Therefore, what we note in the emerging school counseling profession of this period is a range of newly proposed theories of counseling and models of service delivery that attempted to address interconnected and inter-related developmental aspects of students. From the 1960s and into the 21st century, these theoretical approaches and programmatic models helped give direction to the school counseling profession by attending to academic, career, and personal/social aspects of student development.

Academic, Career, and Personal/Social Development

The work of Carl Rogers in the 1950s fueled the development of new theories of counseling and approaches to professional helping. Many of the more popular approaches appeared in the 1960s and 1970s. These emerging theories included behavioral approaches, cognitive theories, ego-psychology, self-concept theory, and others. Models and approaches to group work also appeared during this period. Over the years, popular approaches to counseling that seemed compatible with the school setting and student development included Adlerian Counseling, Reality Therapy, Rational-Emotive-Behavioral Therapy, Person-Centered Counseling, and Multimodal Therapy, among others.

Various counseling approaches developed during the 1960s and 1970s encouraged counselors to consider broader student development issues. With this change in direction, the school counseling profession brought together three main developmental aspects that separately had defined the role of counselors in schools up to this point in time. Now the profession advocated for programs of services to address the academic, career, and personal/social development of students. In addition, this new direction encouraged the expansion of services to include all students in the schools, perhaps influenced by the Civil Rights movement of the time and subsequent integration of the public schools.

This broader mission for school counseling was complemented by greater emphasis on programmatic planning and delivery of services. The thrust behind this broader emphasis was the notion that counselors needed to work more closely with teachers in identifying school issues affecting student development, and by planning programs of services to address these obstacles to learning.

Since the 1970s, the school counseling profession has placed greater emphasis on well-designed programs of services to meet the developmental needs of a larger student population. Norman Gysbers (1978; Gysbers & Henderson, 2000; Gysbers & Moore, 1981), a counselor educator from the University of Missouri–Columbia, deserves much credit for initiating this professional direction by developing a comprehensive program model and researching its effectiveness. With his colleague, Patricia Henderson, a director of guidance in San Antonio, Texas, Gysbers provided a structure for school counseling program development, and equally important, set the stage for significant reform in the profession. Robert Myrick (1997) is another counselor educator who influenced the programmatic philosophy of school counseling through his developmental approach to program planning and service delivery.

Counselor educators and researchers, such as Gysbers and Myrick, helped guide legislative and educational action in many states during the 1970s and 1980s. States such as California, Missouri, North Carolina, Oklahoma, and Texas created guidelines for establishing comprehensive school counseling programs. For example, in the 1970s the North Carolina legislature endorsed the *North Carolina Master Plan for Guidance,* a plan that continued through the mid-1980s. North Carolina has revised its suggested plan using the *ASCA National Model* (American School Counselor Association [ASCA], 2003) as its template.

D. Brown and Trusty (2005) noted that several models for comprehensive school counseling programs exist in the literature. Although philosophical differences exist among these models, most suggest structures and strategies to design comprehensive programs of services, such as assessing and determining students' needs, setting goals and objectives, aligning services within the curriculum, coordinating and delivering appropriate services, and evaluating results. At the same time, many authorities view comprehensive school counseling programs of services as essential to the school curriculum (Schmidt, 2008). This belief maintains that school counseling services are no longer ancillary or simply supportive of the school mission. Rather, the indirect and direct services of a comprehensive counseling program are *essential* to helping each school reach its goals. To make this belief a reality, school counselors actively collaborate with classroom teachers, school administrators, and other school and community personnel integrating guidance activities and counseling services into the daily function of the school.

This section has explored the historical development of the school counseling profession by using aspects of student development as its framework. In addition, it has offered a brief summary about the introduction and development of comprehensive program models to further define the school counseling profession. We will return to comprehensive models later in this chapter when we review the *ASCA National Model* (ASCA, 2003) and other models, but before doing that, the next section gives a brief summary of the expansion of school counseling into elementary education.

Counseling in Elementary Schools

Elementary guidance and counseling had its birth as early as 1910 in the Boston schools where teachers were appointed counselors (Gysbers & Henderson, 2000). For several years, however, the elementary movement remained undeveloped until William Burnham began focusing on counseling in elementary schools during the 1920s and 1930s (Faust, 1968; Studer, 2005). Burnham emphasized the total well being of young students and the essential role classroom teachers played in working with the school counselor to focus on the mental health of children. Because few school systems employed counselors for elementary counseling programs (Gibson et al., 1993), a scarcity of information and knowledge about establishing programs for elementary schools existed. Consequently, in its infancy, elementary counseling adapted perspectives and approaches from secondary guidance programs of services (Schmidt, 2008).

During the early 1960s, schools witnessed an increase in the number of counselors employed for elementary school programs (Faust, 1968). National surveys and other studies of this period found that these early elementary counselors performed functions remarkably similar to the services provided in today's contemporary programs, including

- providing individual counseling with students;
- conferring with teachers and parents about children's needs, developmental characteristics, and school progress; and
- referring students and their families to community agencies (Foster, 1967; Greene, 1967; McKellar, 1964; Schmidt, 2008).

Greene's (1967) survey of more than 1,100 counselors nationwide examined over 100 possible functions and found that the services and activities performed at the upper elementary grade levels contrasted with those in the primary grades. "Counselors at the intermediate grades seemed to have more direct contact with children, whereas primary counselors spent more time consulting with parents and teachers. The most common services in both intermediate and primary grades were referral services" (Schmidt, 2008, p. 17). At about the same time, Foster (1967) used a survey consisting of 84 functions and reported that counselors, counselor educators, teachers, and administrators perceived counseling as the most important function of the elementary school counselor.

Faust (1968) chronicled the development of elementary counseling across three periods. The *traditional* phase from the early 1900s through World War II observed the adoption of secondary school beliefs and methods, as I noted earlier. The second phase, which he called the *neotraditional* period, saw less of a secondary school influence and more attention to using group process and emphasizing student learning. Faust termed the third phase, beginning in the 1960s, as the *developmental* period, which elevated student development over crisis intervention as a major program goal.

A 1966 report by the Joint Committee on the Elementary School Counselor (Association for Counselor Education and Supervision [ACES]–ASCA) helped to support this notion of focusing on student development while lending clarity to the role of the emerging role of elementary school counselors. This report delineated the major functions of elementary school counselors as counseling, consulting, and coordinating. At the same time, the report surmised, "Effective learning climates were to be central to the work of school counselors" (Gysbers & Henderson, 2000, p. 17).

As additional surveys and reports appeared in the professional literature, elementary school counseling gained visibility and acceptance across the country. From the late 1960s and through the 1970s, additional counselors were employed in elementary schools. This growth was accompanied by the publication of the *Elementary School Guidance and Counseling* journal of the ASCA beginning in 1968.

The growth in elementary school counseling was also an outcome of national legislation and government reports that helped give definition to and broaden the scope of the school counseling profession from the 1960s until today. For example, the 1975 *Education Act for All Handicapped Children,* commonly referred to as Public Law 94-142, influenced the consulting role of counselors in working with parents and teachers (Schmidt, 2008). Changes to that initial law continue to have an impact on how school counselors function with regard to exceptional students, even though counselors were not specifically mentioned in the original bill.

According to Gysbers and Henderson (2000), the *Elementary School Guidance and Counseling Incentive Act* of 1979, introduced in the U.S. House of Representatives, proposed funds to establish comprehensive counseling programs in elementary schools. Although not passed by Congress, the bill is significant because of its emphasis on elementary counseling and the importance of comprehensive programs. Congress passed and President Clinton signed the *Elementary School Counseling Demonstration Act* 20 years later, providing $20 million for schools to employ elementary school counselors (Sciarra, 2004).

Publication of the *A Nation at Risk* in 1983 by the National Commission of Excellence in Education focused attention on the declining achievement of U.S. students. The report alarmed the country, and combined with subsequent books and reports about the state of American education, launched the beginning of the educational reform movement we currently experience in schools today (D. Brown & Trusty, 2005). Not all authorities, however, accepted the findings of *A Nation at Risk*. Berliner and Biddle (1995) were two researchers who claimed the report contained more myth than fact about American students' academic performances (D. Brown & Trusty). Nevertheless, *A Nation at Risk* propelled the United States into an accountability mode known as the *effective schools* movement, which has guided how schools function, teacher preparation programs, and other aspects of American education including the school counseling profession (Schmidt, 2008).

The events and legislation mentioned here are but a few examples of the initiatives that have influenced the growth and direction of school counseling. All of them helped to focus on the need for counseling services in schools, the importance of organizing such services into comprehensive programs, and the demand for accountability in determining the outcomes and effectiveness of such programs. In the next section of this chapter, we revisit the emphasis on comprehensive models of school counseling programs.

Comprehensive School Counseling Programs

During the 1970s, several authorities emphasized the need for school counselors to plan comprehensive programs of services and some suggested specific models for program design and development (Gysbers & Henderson, 2000). Many of these models focused on program goals, objectives, and activities for career development and vocational guidance (e.g., Herr & Cramer, 1979; Hilton, 1979), while others advocated for programs with broader intent (e.g., Ballast & Shoemaker, 1978; J. A. Brown, 1977; Mitchell & Gysbers, 1978). Despite many attempts to describe a comprehensive role for these counselors in schools, school systems and state education departments faced the challenge of creating consistent descriptions and guidelines for the school counselor's role within a comprehensive program of services.

As noted earlier, Gysbers and Henderson (2000) pointed to the clinical-services model that emerged during the 1960s as focusing too heavily on the position, role, and function of the counselor, rather than on program development to meet developmental needs of students. D. Brown and Trusty (2005) discussed this history as well, but they referred to the clinical-services approach as the "essential services model" (p. 80), and credited Schmidt (2003) for promoting this model in recent years. Contrary to D. Brown and Trusty's interpretation, Schmidt did not use the exact term, "essential services model." Rather, he listed various essential services of a comprehensive program as being more than simply support or ancillary services. "A key element in describing a comprehensive counseling program is the notion that these services are *essential* to the school" (Schmidt, p. 62). The decision about which services are essential for a particular school, according to Schmidt, rests with the stakeholders in that school—counselors, teachers, administrators, parents, and students.

Schmidt (2003) did not present a specific model for a comprehensive school counseling program, but encouraged counselors and schools to adopt a philosophy of program planning, organization, implementation, and evaluation. Within such a framework, "[S]ome common processes and services are used by school counselors [and] these processes and services help define and describe the nature and scope of a comprehensive school counseling program" (p. 67).

D. Brown and Trusty (2005) distinguished types of comprehensive programs as either *prescriptive* or *nonprescriptive*. They suggested that the essential services model is nonprescriptive because it does not prescribe specific components or mission of a comprehensive program. Consequently, the "nature of the essential services model may increase the likelihood that school counselors will be assigned nonprofessional responsibilities" (p. 82). In contrast, they presented Gysbers and Henderson's (2000) Comprehensive Guidance Program Model (CGPM) and *The ASCA National Model: A Framework for Comprehensive School Counseling Programs* (ASCA, 2003) as two examples of prescriptive models that advocate "against the inclusion of nonprofessional activities as part of the school counseling program" (D. Brown & Trusty p. 83). D. Brown and Trusty compared and contrasted these two models, and although they concluded that both models "represent significant advances in conceptualizing the organizational structure of school counseling programs," both were lacking some aspects "deemed essential to strategic models" (p. 89). They recommended a Strategic Comprehensive Model (SCM), which seems to include some concepts, processes, and terminology proposed by Schmidt (2003), while at the same time adopting elements of the CGPM and ASCA National Model. Interestingly, D. Brown and Trusty claimed, "There are no prescribed roles or activities for school counselors in the SCM" (p. 90), which further contrasts their model with the prescriptive philosophies of the CGPM and ASCA National Model.

Some authorities in school counseling have promoted a general philosophy of program planning, development, and evaluation without identifying or naming specific models (Baker & Gerler, 2004; Schmidt, 2008). As one example, Baker and Gerler encouraged a balanced approach to school counseling programs. They defined *balance* as program goals that place equal importance on *prevention* and *intervention* strategies. To achieve such balance, they suggested two program goals: (a) managing intervention demands and (b) programming for prevention. In theory and practice, a comprehensive program is designed and developed around these two broad goals.

Based on the development and promotion of comprehensive school counseling programs as a means of better serving students, parents, and teachers in schools, it appears that the profession is making strides to identify itself. Through the long journey that began in the late 19th century and now in the 21st century, the quest of establishing a clear mission for counseling in schools as well as a consistent professional identity for school counselors continues.

The School Counselor's Professional Identity

In this first chapter, you learned that the earliest signs of an emerging school counseling profession began as a reaction to vocational, cultural, and social events during the U.S. Industrial Revolution. With that beginning, the profession continued to grow by responding to national and world events over the next hundred years and more. Although this reactive posture helped to describe the role of school counselors, this description has not been consistently recognized in developing a clear identity for the profession. Many authors have stressed the importance of school counselors' creating a professional identity to ascribe consistent purpose for their roles in schools (e.g., Baker & Gerler, 2004; Gladding, 2000; Myrick, 1997; Schmidt, 2008), but despite such encouragement, uncertainty about the school counselor's role continues in most states across the country.

Some authors have pointed to the use of inconsistent and confusing terms to describe the profession and its services as *guidance counselors*, *guidance services*, and *guidance programs*, in contrast to *school counselors*, and *school counseling programs* (e.g., Baker & Gerler, 2004; D. Brown & Trusty, 2005; Schmidt, 2004, 2008). This is not a new discourse for the profession. For over 50 years, the term *guidance* has been cited as vague and confusing for both the people who work and learn in the schools, including counselors, and the audiences served by the profession—students, parents, and teachers, and the public at large (Shertzer & Stone, 1966). Today, debate and confusion continue in part because traditions are sometimes difficult to change and one of the most popular authors and researchers in the field uses the terms *guidance program* and *guidance activities* (Gysbers & Henderson, 2000, p. 78). In contrast, the *ASCA National Model* (ASCA, 2003) uses the term *comprehensive school counseling program*, and D. Brown and Trusty commented that, although the differences remain an issue for the profession, "the scales seem to be tipping toward the ASCA terminology" (p. 6). Perhaps what is most important to the profession is that although some language remains problematic, common concepts and goals for developing comprehensive programs, expressed by many authors, might move school counseling in a clear direction (ASCA, 2003; Baker & Gerler, 2004; D. Brown & Trusty; Gysbers & Henderson; Schmidt; Studer, 2005).

In addition to the professional textbooks and other literature published about school counseling programs and practices, the future direction taken by the ASCA will have an impact. The ASCA has one of the largest memberships of the divisions of the ACA (Schmidt, 2008). The *ASCA National Model* (ASCA, 2003), in addition to other comprehensive models of program planning and service delivery, will help distinguish counselors who practice in educational settings from counselors who work in clinical environments. That distinction will not be based on a counselor's level of preparation or knowledge of clinical skills, but rather on the focus given to comprehensive programs of services to meet the developmental needs of an expanded audience.

The *ASCA National Model* (ASCA, 2003) and other examples of comprehensive program planning and service delivery provide the school counseling profession with an organizational framework and philosophical position with which to create, deliver, and evaluate services that help students with academic, personal/social, and career development. As such, these efforts have proposed national standards to help students be successful across a full range of developmental tasks. In chapter 2 of this *Handbook*, you will explore these standards more fully. The next historic step for the profession in the process of developing an identity for school counseling will be to create national standards of professional preparation and practices for counselor education programs and school counselors to follow (Schmidt & Ciechalski, 2001).

This *Handbook* introduces you to a number of professional issues about counseling standards, supervision, and competence when working with diverse populations. This *Handbook* also offers suggestions for specific interventions with particular students and school populations. In addition, you will learn about measures of program accountability, legal guidelines, and ethical standards to increase your knowledge in becoming an effective school counselor. This chapter has provided the historical foundation upon which you can learn this knowledge and skill and subsequently build a successful career as a professional school counselor.

References

Association for Counselor Education and Supervision (ACES)–American School Counselor Association (ASCA) Joint Committee on the Elementary School Counselor. (1966). The elementary school counselor: Preliminary statement. *Personnel and Guidance Journal, 44,* 658–661.

American School Counselor Association. (2003). *The ASCA national model: A framework for school counseling programs.* Alexandria, VA: Author.

Baker, S. B., & Gerler, E. R. (2004). *School counseling for the twenty-first century* (4th ed.). Upper Saddle River, NJ: Merrill/Prentice Hall.

Ballast, D. L., & Shoemaker, R. L. (1978). *Guidance program development.* Springfield, IL: Charles C. Thomas.

Berliner, D. C., & Biddle, B. J. (1995). *The manufactured crisis: Myths, fraud, and the attack on America's public schools.* Reading, MA: Addison-Wesley.

Brown, D., & Trusty, J. (2005). *Designing and leading comprehensive school counseling programs: Promoting student competence and meeting student needs.* Belmont, CA: Thomson Brooks/Cole.

Brown, J. A. (1977). *Organizing and evaluating elementary school guidance services: Why, what, and how.* Monterey, CA: Brooks/Cole.

Faust, V. (1968). *History of elementary school counseling: Overview and critique.* Boston: Houghton Mifflin.

Foster, C. M. (1967). The elementary school counselor: How perceived? *Counselor Education and Supervision, 6,* 102–107.

Gibson, R. L., & Mitchell, M. H. (1999). *Introduction to counseling and guidance* (4th ed.). Upper Saddle River, NJ: Prentice Hall.

Gibson, R. L., Mitchell, M. H., & Basile, S. K. (1993). *Counseling in the elementary school: A comprehensive approach.* Boston: Allyn and Bacon.

Gladding, S. T. (2000). *Counseling: A comprehensive profession* (4th ed.). Upper Saddle River, NJ: Prentice Hall.

Greene, K. (1967). Functions performed and preferred by elementary school counselors in the United States. *Dissertation Abstracts International, 28.* (UMI No. 67-14 780)

Gysbers, N. C. (1978). Comprehensive career guidance programs. In R. E. Campbell, H. D. Rodebaugh, & P. E. Shaltry (Eds.), *Building comprehensive career guidance programs for secondary schools* (pp. 3–24). Columbus, OH: National Center for Research in Vocational Education.

Gysbers, N. C., & Henderson, P. (2000). *Developing and managing your school guidance program* (3rd ed.). Alexandria, VA: American Counseling Association.

Gysbers, N. C., & Moore, E. J. (1981). *Improving guidance programs.* Englewood Cliffs, NJ: Prentice-Hall.

Herr, E. L., & Cramer, S. H. (1979). *Career guidance through the life span.* Boston: Little, Brown.

Hilton, T. L. (1979). *Confronting the future: A conceptual framework for secondary school career guidance.* New York: College Entrance Examination Board.

McKellar, R. (1964). A study of concepts, functions, and organizational characteristics of guidance in the elementary school as reported by selected elementary school guidance personnel. *Dissertation Abstracts International, 24,* 4477. (UMI No. 643601)

Miller, F. W. (1968). *Guidance: Principles and services.* Columbus, OH: Merrill.

Mitchell, A. M., & Gysbers, N. C. (1978). Comprehensive school guidance programs. In American Personnel and Guidance Association, *The status of guidance and counseling in the nation's schools* (pp. 23–39). Washington, DC.

Myrick, R. D. (1997). *Developmental guidance and counseling: A practical approach* (3rd ed.). Minneapolis, MN: Educational Media.

Nugent, F. A. (2000). *Introduction to the profession of counseling* (3rd ed.). Columbus, OH: Merrill.

Rogers, C. R. (1942). *Counseling and psychotherapy: New concepts in practice.* Boston: Houghton Mifflin.

Rogers, C. R. (1951). *Client-centered therapy: Its current practice, implications, and theory.* Boston: Houghton Mifflin.

Schmidt, J. J. (2003). *Counseling in schools: Essential services and comprehensive programs* (4th ed.). Boston: Allyn & Bacon.

Schmidt, J. J. (2004). *A survival guide for the elementary/middle school counselor* (2nd ed.). San Francisco: Jossey-Bass.

Schmidt, J. J., & Ciechalski, J. C. (2001). School counseling standards: A summary and comparison with other student services' standards. *Professional School Counseling, 4*, 328–333.

Schmidt, J. J. (2008). *Counseling in schools: Comprehensive programs of responsive services for all students* (5th ed.). Boston: Allyn & Bacon.

Sciarra, D. T. (2004). *School counseling: Foundations and contemporary issues*. Belmont, CA: Thomson Brooks/Cole.

Shertzer, B., & Stone, S. C. (1966). *Fundamentals of guidance*. Boston: Houghton Mifflin.

Studer, J. R. (2005). *The professional school counselor: An advocate for students*. Belmont, CA: Thomson Brooks/Cole.

Vacc, N. A., & Loesch, L. C. (2000). *Counseling as a profession* (3rd ed.). Muncie, IN: Accelerated Development.

Williamson, E. G. (1939). *How to counsel students*. New York: McGraw-Hill.

Williamson, E. G. (1950). *Counseling adolescents*. New York: McGraw-Hill.

Wittmer, J. (2007). Developmental school guidance and counseling: Its history and reconceptualization. In J. Wittmer & M. A. Clark (Ed.), *Managing your school counseling program: K–12 developmental strategies* (3rd ed., pp. 2–15). Minneapolis, MN: Educational Media.

II
A CONCEPT OF BEST PRACTICES IN TRAINING SCHOOL COUNSELORS

ROBBIE J. STEWARD, DOUGLAS M. NEIL, AND MATTHEW A. DIEMER
Michigan State University

The primary objective of this chapter is o provide a critical analysis of the literature addressing the best practices in training school counselors in attending to the most critical issues in K–12 school settings. The first section presents extensive training content and guidelines that extend beyond the minimal standards purported by the Council of Accredited Counseling and Related Educational Programs (CACREP), the American Counseling Association (ACA), and the Missouri Comprehensive Guidance Model (MCGM), which has been revised and adapted to fit the needs of individual states. The second section provides an overview of the literature describing the process uniquely associated with graduate education and the relevance to enhancing current professional guidelines in the training of school counselors. The third section describes a master's level, school counselor training model used at Michigan State University, which also includes additive training practices and that more comprehensively attend to the needs of both community counselor trainees and schools. The suggestions for consideration are based on the most recent literature and research findings, as well as on the authors' extensive professional experiences within the school setting as consultants, building coordinator in a professional development school, school counseling supervisors, service providers, and researchers. This latter information regarding the experiences of the authors is important given the trend found that most citations in the literature consist of university faculty who have had very limited, if any, direct professional experience within the K–12 school setting (N. S. Carlson, 2001).

Training and the Council for the Accreditation of Counseling and Related Educational Programs

Since 1981, the CACREP (2001), a national accrediting agency, has assumed the very important charge of establishing minimum standard training curriculum and practices for school counselors. Its incorporation as an independent body resulted from a culmination of years of work by the ACA toward defining the sets of knowledge and skills required for admission into the profession and to advocate that these requirements be adopted by the preparation programs offering counseling and student development practice degrees (Bobby & Kandor, 1995). Periodically contacting counselor educators and practitioners within the school setting to receive feedback and recommendations for guideline revisions (Schmidt, 1999), the CACREP consistently provides the essential training guidelines that are most meaningful to the current needs of K–12 students. (The information collection process through e-mail survey with this objective has already begun toward the development of the 2008 minimum standards.) Evidence of a commitment to maintain the critical link between training and service delivery is evident in the clearly established relationship between the eight core knowledge areas for all counselors (i.e., Professional Identity, Social and Cultural Diversity, Human Growth and Development, Career Development, Helping Relationships, Group Work, Assessment, and Research and Program Evaluation) and the K–12 school counseling program models that have been adopted by a number of schools across the nation to provide a balance between intervention responses and proactive prevention programming (Holcomb-McCoy, 2005): the national model for school counseling programs (American School Counselor Association [ASCA], 2003; Akos, Goodnough, & Milsom, 2004; Dahir, 2001; Perusse, Goodnough, & Noel, 2001), Missouri Comprehensive Guidance program model (Gysbers & Henderson, 2001), Myrick's (1993) Invitational Theory of Practice model (Stanley, Juhnke, & Purkey, 2004), and the Transformative Individual School Counseling model (Eschenauer, 2005). Although varying in degrees to which percentages of counselors' time is allocated toward each CACREP domain activity, each of these leading models is developmental in nature, has a guidance/career component, highlights attention to individual differences within student populations (i.e., race/ethnicity, culture, socioeconomic status), and acknowledges the importance of individual and group counseling competence, consultation, and program development and evaluation. Empirical research that has examined the effect of this linkage has found statistically significant results in pre- and post-implementation of CACREP guidelines in the relationship between training program status and on-site supervisors' perceptions of training (LaFountain & Baer, 2001). Accreditation status has also been significantly linked with higher entrance standards and academic potential of master of arts counseling students (Pate, 1990), graduates' increased multicultural counseling competence (Dinsmore & England, 1996), heightened attention to ethical issues in training, a willingness to follow through in addressing legal/ethical violations among trainees (Gaubatz & Vera, 2002), and faculty and students' perceptions of program improvement (Schmidt, 1999). Given the longevity of this major contribution to the profession of counseling, the level of respect among professionals within higher education and within K–12, and the long-standing vigilance of this agency to comprehensively evaluate graduate level programs' effectiveness in preparing individuals to most effectively assume the role of counselors, counselor educators' strict adherence to these currently existing minimum practice guidelines as the core foundation to any training environment is certainly warranted.

However, it remains imperative that counselor educators and school counselors remain committed to review the literature and to constantly assess and reflect on the strengths and limitations of training in preparation for standard practice and service delivery to student populations and school setting staff both locally and nationally. In a review of the literature, a number of studies have highlighted a wide range of responses from the professional arena to the existing CACREP guidelines related to school counselors, some including recommendations for additions and stronger statements about specific topic areas. In spite of the prevailing status of CACREP as the premier accrediting agency for master's level programs within this country, the benefits of the core curriculum standards have been found to be received with varying levels of acceptance within and between professional groups surveyed (i.e., American Mental Health Counselors Association, American School Counselors Association [ASCA], and Association for Counselor Education and Supervision) (McGlothlin & Thomas, 2004).

On one hand, those who most strongly support and embrace the existing guidelines have created opportunities to educate school districts concerning the importance of CACREP in training and service delivery within the school setting (LaFountain & Baer, 2001). Other strong CACREP proponents have developed a listing of Internet Web sites that align with the CACREP eight common core knowledge areas to assist training programs in more comprehensively and intentionally attending to each of the core guidelines (Keller & Goodman, 2003). The wide-range acceptance of the CACREP as an accrediting agency is also reflected in the fact that, as of May 2005, 159 master's level school-counseling programs have applied for and received accreditation by this agency. An average of 12 to 13 new applications are anticipated annually. The perception of legitimacy of CACREP as an accrediting agency within school counseling is well validated.

However, some within the profession raise questions about the limitations that are inherent within the CACREP guidelines. In other words, among these individuals, the guidelines for the most part are deemed acceptable but perceived as limited in scope. Some believe that these limitations impede optimal training outcomes in preparation for service delivery to the schools. To provide a brief overview, the authors have categorized the areas of concern purported in the literature into the following themes: (a) enhancement of currently required curriculum, (b) critical school setting issues, and (c) counselor-trainees' psycho-socioemotional development.

Enhancement of Currently Required Curriculum

In an online search of articles in ERIC and ACA journals, the most cited theme that emerged was the recommendation of the enhancement of currently required curriculum to specifically address deficits identified within the school setting. The following sections represent the content areas that had been highlighted within the literature in which authors suggested a need for greater attention and reflection given the changing K–12 student population.

Issues of diversity. The most predominant area of focus that surfaced highlighted the need for increased attention to some point of racial/ethnic diversity or individual difference such as gender (R. M. Hoffman & Myers, 1996), multicultural counseling competency development (Hays, 2002; Holcomb-McCoy, 1999; Margolis & Rungta, 1986), urban school counseling competence (Butler, 2003; Green, 2005; Lee, 2005; Schultheiss, Palma, & Manzi, 2005), spirituality and religion (Matthews, 1998; Young, Cashwell, Wiggins-Frame, & Belaire, 2002), and sexual orientation (R. M. Hoffman, 2004). Although each of these areas of experience and competence are considered critical for attention and inclusion in minimal standard training curriculum, authors also are well aware of the impossibility of faculty members' extensive attention to all areas given the CACREP required 48-credit-hour structure of most master's level counseling programs. This is particularly noteworthy for instructors of multicultural counseling courses who are sometimes expected to attend extensively, within a 16-week semester, to every possible point of diversity that is associated with culture and special populations that may exist within the school setting.

Assessment and diagnosis. These authors (Elmore, 2001; Hansen, 2003; R. M. Hoffman, 2001; Impara, 1995; Reeves, Wheeler, & Bowl, 2004; Schafer, 1995) have purported the necessity for counselor educators to more specifically attend to trainees' familiarity with the use and interpretation of measures toward diagnosis using the DSM-IV-R. Given the increasing prevalence of students' psychosocioemotional problems within the K–12 school setting, proponents purport that counseling programs must now better familiarize trainees with standard assessment measures used with the K–12 population, and develop competence in how to use the literature to interpret the results and develop recommendations for intervention (Giordano, Schwiebert, & Brotherton, 1997). These competences have typically been associated with nonschool counselors, but given the changing student population, these authors suggest the necessity for counselor educators' increased and concerted efforts toward remediation of this knowledge and skill limitation.

Legal/ethical practice in service delivery. This is another area that is based on a shifting of prevalence within the school setting (Jordan & Stevens, 2001; Lambie, 2005; Lawrence & Kurpius, 2000). With increased violence within school settings and within families and with the increased representation of those being harmed by others and students who may do harm to self and/or others, professionals within the school must understand the importance of assuming the responsibility of assessing when to report, identifying to whom a report is required, and actually reporting to authorities. Issues such as students' experiences with bullying (Embry & Luzzo, 1996; Lambie; Urofsky & Sowa, 2004) and nonconsensual sexual activity among students (K. A. King, Tribble, & Price, 1999) are only a few of those that counselors must address. Due to limitations of confidentiality, the definition of due process, and duty to warn, school counselors, like their nonschool counselor peers, should now adhere to specifying guidelines regarding parents' and students' informed consent rights. Given that informed consent forms are not standard practice within school settings, there is typically no systematic reminder of the importance of attending to legal and ethical issues in school counseling activity, which includes privileged communication with minors (i.e., Ahia & Martin, 1993). Consequently, it becomes even more critical for counselor educators to train school counselors, who are not only knowledgeable of the professional legal/ethical code (ASCA, 2004) but also aware of their responsibilities to assess when to report and to inform students and parents of the parameters of their counseling relationship and of what will happen if a specific kind of information is shared.

The authors have identified two patterns that may emerge within school settings that are in direct violation of school counselors' legal and ethic responsibilities to report. For example, in suburban, higher income communities, school counselors may tend not to report that which they should in order to protect family image and the reputation of the school. Whereas, in urban, lower income communities, school counselors may tend not to report that which they should because of the prevalence of perceived violations and past negative experiences with reporting. In both cases, increased harm for the students and potential professional harm to counselors and trainees due to possible litigation can be outcomes. Regardless of the community setting, school counselor-trainees must leave training understanding the anxiety that might surface as they assume this professional responsibility and with the willingness to do so in spite of nonsupport which can occur from those more senior within the profession, from teachers, from parents, and from administrators within practicum, internship, and eventually permanent work settings if the identification of common practices within the setting are not clear before placement.

The other side of the legal/ethical issue that seldom and hesitantly is addressed in master's programs is the responsibility for counselor educators to serve as gatekeepers to the profession by monitoring students' progress in terms of counseling competence (Gaubatz & Vera, 2002; Vacha-Haase, Davenport, & Kerewsky, 2004). Given that most school districts require all applicants to complete a felony report form and give permission for a background check by authorities, we propose that it would be equally as important for counselor educators to include within their program handbooks and application materials some statement of the necessity for all interested in the pursuit of certification as school counselors to consider this requirement prior to application. Of course, the same is true for all students who eventually wish to apply for the status of licensed professional counselors, in which the same kind of information is requested. Although CACREP does not address this issue directly, we believe that it is imperative to inform all applicants and remind current students of the influence of engagement in and potential convictions for illegal activity can have on practicum/internship placement and professional futures. Counselor educators need to be gatekeepers not only in terms of counselor competence but also in terms of character. This recommendation was even more salient due to the results of one state audit, which found that the Michigan Department of Education had failed to adequately track teachers convicted of sexual assault and other crimes. Several teachers convicted of crimes against minors never had their certifications revoked, and the Department to Education reported that it had never heard of the convictions from local prosecutors. This case of a communication glitch in a government system verifies the necessity for training programs to develop some guidelines for selecting students for admissions and for including this kind of information in the process of supporting endorsement of current students in the program. Although this presents somewhat of a sensitive legal issue in terms of faculty decision making, we strongly support that the minimum training policy should include at least a statement to inform applicants and current students of the short- and long-term implications for the engagement in criminal activity. In these cases, program faculties need to have access to professional legal assistance (Lawrence & Kurpius, 2000).

The third and final aspect of the legal ethical responsibility, which is frequently cited in the literature but not addressed specifically within the accreditation standards, is the role of school counselors as advocates for the academic success of every student (ASCA, 2003). According to the *National Model* (ASCA), school counselors' advocacy efforts involve leadership, collaboration, and systemic change. These efforts, which evolve out of an advocacy disposition, knowledge of resources, and effective communication skills with both children and adults, should have the following objectives: eliminating barriers to students' development, creating opportunities to learn for all students, ensuring access to a quality school curriculum, collaborating with others within and outside of the school to help students meet their needs, and promoting positive, systemic change in schools (Trusty, 2005). This means that school counselors are not only practitioners competent to work with K–12 student populations, but also social change agents who can effectively communicate and negotiate with adults in order to work toward equity and social justice within the school setting (Bemak, 2005; Dahir, 2004).

In light of the prior sections, both being multiculturally competent (Sue, Arrendondo, & McDavis, 1992) and addressing discrimination (Ponterotto, 1991; Trusty, 2002) are indicators of advocacy. However, in anticipation of the next section's addressing the role of school counselors as researcher–practitioner, Eriksen's (1997) definition of advocacy includes generating research on the efficacy of counseling. Myers, Sweeney, and White (2002) noted that any form of promoting counselors' credibility in the public's eye is a salient advocacy task and a noteworthy point that should be addressed in training.

Counselors as researcher–practitioners and scholars. In the face of the increasing necessity of establishing professional accountability of all professionals within the schools (Whiston, 2002), particularly given the most recent U.S. Department of Education (2001) legislation, No Child Left Behind, which mandates all federally funded programs be accountable for and directly connected to student learning and improvement (Hatch & Bowers, 2002), it becomes imperative for counselor educators to prepare students who not only are practitioners, but also have knowledge of how to use the literature to support the rationale for a study; understand the importance of human subjects approval and informed consent for participation in research; are able to collect, analyze, and interpret data; and can sustain a commitment to influence the profession and assist others with the community by committing to scholarship and professional presentations (ASCA, 2003; N. S. Carlson, 2001; Gordon, McClure, & Petrowski, 1994; Larson & Besett-Alesch, 2000). Trainees must have the experience with systematically implementing a research program for understanding students' development within the setting and evaluating the efficacy of the school counseling program's contribution to students' development and achievement (ASCA, 2003).

The authors identified five specific themes associated with recommendations for school counselors' research activities that might frame practitioner–researcher activities: (a) studies that identify school counselors' attitudes and practices (e.g., Astramovich, 2002; Scarborough, 2005), (b) studies that compare individual and group counseling processes with certain populations and client issues (e.g., Granello & Granello, 1998; Lin, Kelly, & Nelson, 1996), (c) studies that evaluate the impact of school-counselor-led interventions on student academic achievement and school success behavior (e.g., Brigman, 2003; Bruce, 1997), (d) studies that examine the relationship between school counselors' training and person variables on self-efficacy and students' evaluation of service delivery (e.g., Peterson, Goodman, Keller, & McCauley, 2004; Ray, Armstrong, Warren, & Balkin, 2005; S. L. Smith, Crutchfield, & Culbreth, 2001), and (e) studies that examine the relationship between students' personal variables and academic achievement and school success behavior (e.g., Trusty & Niles, 2004). Attention to each of these domains would increase accountability and be additive to both the local and broader professional community. Nevertheless, research and scholarship have traditionally been associated only with the doctoral educational process (LaPidus, 1998). Consequently, including this component within the training of master's level school counselors would be a major deviation from standard practice in training.

Nevertheless, this recommendation will be most challenging to attend to in training and in practice for two main reasons that extent beyond curriculum. Due to larger student cohort sizes and advisee loads and to a service delivery focus that extends beyond content presentation and integration, master's level faculty members' research activities and scholarship productivities have been consistently found to be more limited in number than doctoral level faculty. Consequently, the traditional thesis/dissertation model of working individually with novice researchers in the development of publishable manuscripts based on research activity will pose an additional challenge in the faculty members' professional development toward promotion and tenure at major research institutions. A parallel problem is that school counselor to student ratios strain their time for providing direct service to students. The ASCA (1999) suggested that the ideal ratio is 1 counselor per 250 students; however, Marino, Sams, and Guerra (1999) reported that the nationwide ratio is 1 counselor per 513 students. With these kinds of faculty load assignments and school counselors' service delivery loads, little or no time would be available to commit to research activities without support from administration and a systematic research activity imbedded within the structure of the school counseling program. Though seemingly important to both parties, the time for engagement in the standard practices within training programs and school settings is limited if not nonexistent.

School counselors as supervisors and career development. The significance of supervision in counseling is quite apparent in state licensing laws and professional accreditation standards that require students to have supervision during practicum, internship, and post-master's degree in order to secure licensure (Akos, Konold, & Niles, 2004; Crespi, 2003; Fischetti & Lines, 2003; Kahn, 1999; Remley, & Huey, 2002; Schultheiss et al., 2005; Studer, 2005). Consequently, it has become imperative that current practitioners, whose training did not include supervisory skills development, now pursue opportunities for training given the ACA Code of Ethics. In response, a number of doctoral level professionals in Counseling and Counseling Psychology are developing and providing 1 to 2 day ACA-criteria-based workshop opportunities to train currently practicing school counselors, school counselors are contacting universities for graduate level counseling supervision course work that has typically been reserved for doctoral students, and a few training programs are now considering how to infuse such training prior to degree completion. At this point, no evidence in the literature identifies a strategy for doing so that extends beyond the traditional addition of course work, which will certainly tax faculty in terms of time commitment during a period of sensitivity about budget cuts in higher education, and will also present additional financial overloads for students who seek master's level training without guaranteed funding and with limited income. Once again, the necessity for attending to this training issue is not to be argued, given the importance of providing only a service in which one has been trained, but strategies for infusing this experience within training have not been identified at this time.

Counselor-Trainees' Psycho-Socioemotional Development

The third theme addressed within the context of this chapter moves beyond recommendations associated with curriculum and instruction toward a more focused strategic framing, development, and integration of training experiences that provide in-depth attention to counselor-trainees' personal development as counseling competence and professional development evolves (Barbee, Scherer, & Combs, 2003; Downs, 2000; Tang et al., 2004). The almost nonexistent attention of the CACREP core components to the counselor-trainees' healthy psycho-socioemotional development is perceived by some as overlooking the well-established, tightly integrated, empirical link between counselors' personal variables and counseling competence (Haverkamp, 1994; Stein & Lambert, 1995; Stevens, Dinoff, & Donnenworth, 1998).

There is much support for those who recommend strong language and attention to trainees' personal development. Borders, Fong, and Neimeyer (1986) found that students at higher levels of ego development had a greater awareness of clients' needs than did those students at lower levels of ego development, while Carlozzi, Gaa, and Liberman (1983) found that students at lower levels of ego development were less empathic than those at higher levels were. Borders et al. (1986) found that most of the counseling graduate students were functioning at or above the conscientious level of ego development wherein individuals possess self-evaluated goals, differentiated self-criticism, and senses of responsibility on which genuine feelings and abilities to attend to the needs of others are based. Watt, Robinson, and Lupton-Smith (2002) found that the very process of training has a statistically significant effect on trainees' ego development, earlier studies have found the same to be true for students' cognitive development (Etringer, Hillerbrand, & Claiborn, 1995; Leach, Stoltenberg, McNeil, & Eichenfield,

1997) and interpersonal and intrapersonal skills even outside of the counselor–client relationship (Furr & Carroll, 2003).

Developing training experiences that strategically attend to personal development would seem even more imperative given the expectation that many trainees arrive with psychological wounds, eventually to become "wounded healers," and the implications for this population within the training cohort (Mander, 2004). Though these personal histories that remain in need of resolution can be instrumental in establishing effective working alliances with clients, such histories not addressed during training can have negative outcomes during practicum. One example of this phenomenon is the result of a study in which trainees' lower avoidance and higher anxiety, indicators of attachment, were found to be associated with highest levels of empathy, and higher avoidance and lower anxiety were associated with the lowest levels of empathy (Trusty, Ng, & Watts, 2005). In a review of literature addressing countertransference (CT), counselors' conscious and unconscious reactions toward clients based on counselor's unresolved conflicts (Gelso & Carter, 1985), Rosenberger and Hayes (2002) reflected that CT, strongly associated with state anxiety, can assume several forms of exhibition within the counseling relationship: cognitive responses (e.g., distorted perceptions of clients, inaccurate recall of client material, reactive, defensive mental activity, blocked understanding, uncertainty, changes in treatment planning); affective responses (e.g., anger, sadness, boredom, nurturing feelings); and behavioral responses (e.g., avoidance or withdrawal). It would seem safe to conclude that trainees' awareness and resolution of personal issues are required in order for trainees to draw from their own experience in working with clients (J. A. Hayes, 2002).

Inadvertently, some students will arrive seeking to correct and resolve difficulties from early childhood and sometimes even more recent life experiences; others will arrive to the training environment psychologically intact only to experience "wounding" by the new experience and psychological challenges and stress and strain involved in training and overexposure to problems within humanity (Miller, Wagner, Britton, & Gridley, 1998). Regardless of students' initial psychological status, the literature overall tends to support the premise that the nature of training and the role of counselors require the most effective training models to have a clearly defined objective to address heightened distress related to trainees' histories and affective and behavioral responses to training. Osborn (2004) recommended the inclusion of content that specifically attends to the development of the stamina, the endurance, and the strength to withstand, resist, or hold up under pressure of difficulty (Thomas, 1982). The objective of doing so would be twofold: (a) to facilitate optimal levels of skill development and (b) to teach trainees to practice effective preventative self-care (Cushway, 1996; Ungar, Mackey, Guest, & Bernard, 2000; Wolgien & Coady, 1997).

Researchers have found that counseling skill attainment during training, particularly after exposure to the Skilled Counselor Training Model (SCTM; Smaby, Maddux, Torres-Rivera, & Zimmick, 1999), does affect trainees' personality (Crews et al., 2005). The SCTM is the result of the fusion of two models: (a) Carkhuff's (1987) Human Resource Training/Human Resource Development Model (HRT/HRD), based on Toukmanian and Rennie's (1975) core conditions of counseling, and (b) the Microcounseling Skills Training Model (Ivey, Normington, Miller, Morrill, & Hause, 1968). Smaby & D'Andrea (1995) suggested that counselor skill training could, in fact, result in changes in trainees' interpersonal styles and ways of self-monitoring and, therefore, be therapeutic for both the clients to whom they are exposed and to the trainees themselves in their personal development.

Nevertheless, counselor educators must be cautioned not to assume full responsibility for trainees' psychological well-being and development. The severity and depth of some more debilitating personal issues exhibited in the training environment may not be attended to by the very nature of the training environment, and may in fact be exacerbated by training. Downs (2000) found trainees' experiences as clients to have a significant effect on both counseling self-efficacy and competence. Considering counseling as a viable option would therefore seem meaningful to the process of developing counseling competence and moving toward the required professional stamina as previously defined.

Critical School Setting Issues

The fourth and final theme addresses a collection of issues that are the most recent, critical areas of concern for K–12 school settings and believed to require special awareness, knowledge, and skills that extend beyond CACREP curricular guidelines: pharmacology (Bauer, Ingersoll, & Burns, 2004; J. H. King & Anderson, 2004), addictions (Morgan, Toloczko, & Comly, 1997), sexual abuse (Kitzrow, 2002), HIV-AIDS education (Hunt, 1996), school–family partnerships (Bryant, 2005), violence in the schools (Aspy et al., 2004; D'Andrea, 2004; Newman-Carlson & Horne, 2004; D. C. Smith & Sandhu, 2004), and grief and dying (Hodges, 2005). These were not the only school issues that were identified as important, and for the purpose of space, the list is not exhaustive and is intentionally limited. Most of these topics will require a need for attention in supervision and training during practicum and internship; however, some may not. Consequently, the existence of an unlimited list further supports the necessity of all trainees to understand the limitations of master's level training specifically attending to all potential issues with which they might be confronted in service delivery. Trainees must be initially informed during orientation of the limitations and prepare themselves to assume responsibility for continued education to remain informed and abreast of critical issues in the school setting. In addition, students may also choose electives during training that will highlight a specialty area noting one of the missing pieces in their training experience, which can make them more knowledge about a particularly content area and, therefore, more competitive within the world of work.

On the other hand, counseling programs can also attend to the content deficiencies in a number of ways: periodically providing in-service workshops based on the results of surveys of the needs of practitioners within surrounding community schools; current students, who have developed a specialty area in terms of knowledge of the literature and course work, may work with faculty to develop and lead a workshop for current practitioners; local practitioners, having expertise in specific areas, might be invited to attend brown bag faculty–student meetings; and faculty may develop a file accessible to students of all local speakers conferences and workshops addressing critical issues in counseling. These are only a few suggestions regarding the how-to of strategically addressing critical issues that cannot be more comprehensively covered within the parameters of the program curriculum.

The essential, strategic, and periodic compilation and processing of continually evolving perceived training programs could eventually lead to a body of knowledge and recommendations for training that will eventually result in the equivalent of a doctoral degree. However, there are a number of training models wherein counselor educators have made some concerted effort to extend training curriculum and practices beyond the minimum CACREP standards in order to attend to the many recommendations in the literature toward training enhancement. In the next section, master's level education will be briefly discussed and suggestions identified in the literature for the improvement of the training of school counselors.

Master's Level Training in School Counseling: Strategies for Extending Beyond Minimum Training Guidelines

In making any attempt to attend to the seemingly ever increasing list of recommendations from counselor educators, counselor-trainees, and the K–12 school setting, a brief review of the literature specifically addressing standard practices within master's level training programs is essential. This is particularly important as we are confronted with a trend for some programs and state regulations are choosing to increase the required number of credit hours from 48 (CACREP minimal requirement) to 60 credits, which is more associated with specialist degrees. Before describing master's level training models, this section describes the distinct process of master's training, presents strategies in the literature that purport to enhance standard information dissemination and increased preparation for master's entry level positions, and notes recommendations for future research.

The Process of Master's Level Counselor Education

Gordon (1990) described the role of graduate education as exploring, advancing, and determining the parameters of knowledge in a particular field. As indicated in the prior section, Hirt and Muffo (1998) added that graduate level professional programs are more often than not guided by professional disciplines such as the state and national accrediting agencies (e.g., CACREP) than by institutional standards. Master's degree curricula have typically been designed to train counseling students for entry level positions in schools (CACREP, 2001; Zimpfer, Cox, West, Bubenzer, & Brooks, 1997), they tend to emphasize skills and training over theory and scholarship (Nelson & Jackson, 2000), and they prepare students for careers to meet the needs of the marketplace (Association of American Universities, 1998; Syverson, 1996). However, very little empirical research has specifically examined the process through which these outcomes are pursued.

In a review of the literature, Nelson and Jackson (2000) found few descriptive studies that concerned the academic environments of either doctoral or master's levels counselor education programs (Boes, Ullery, Milner, & Cobia, 1999; Schmidt, 1999; Zimpfer et al., 1997). Given the professional trend toward increased expectations of school counselors in terms of both knowledge and competence as they begin entry-level positions, it would seem imperative that we as counselor educators are clearer about the distinctive parameters and nature of master's and doctoral level training experiences. Identifying the differences will provide some guide toward increasing our awareness of the direction for shifts in future instructional and training practice.

Master's and doctoral level training experiences. In a qualitative study of counselor educators who had extensive experience (10 or more years) with both master's and doctoral level CACREP-accredited counselor education programs, Nelson and Jackson (2000) compared the training process issues uniquely associated with master's and doctoral level programs. Findings indicated that faculty associated with doctoral programs prepared students for advanced professional leadership in teaching, clinical practice, supervision, and scholarship/research (e.g., CACREP, 2001; Zimpfer et al., 1997); had greater contact with trainees in the roles of mentor and collaborator in their professional development (CACREP; Hirt & Muffo, 1998); provided opportunities for engagement in numerous experiential learning activities; provided a learning environment based on a cohort model, which facilitated group cohesiveness and a sense of family (Boes et al., 1999; Hirt & Muffo); and in course instruction, expected students to focus on process, engage in higher order thinking, consider multiple perspectives of materials presented, and question their own and others' beliefs and knowledge. In contrast, faculty associated with master's programs highlighted beginning counseling skill acquisition; provided fewer opportunities for students to select electives; taught courses which were didactic, content driven, and survey in nature, involving the transmission of knowledge from the professor to the student; perceived students as consumers; reported less time with students; and had clearer boundaries between their role in the advisor–advisee relationship.

Given these stark differences, in order to meet the challenges in attempts to attend to the numerous recommendations in the literature discussed in the first section of the chapter, counselor educators must begin to creatively interject as best we can doctoral level training philosophy into training master's level school counselors. Although not explicitly stated in terms of transforming master's level training through infusing the doctoral level training process, a number of authors have recommended and used strategies that attend to the need for this transformation. The following section lists a few of such strategies that serve as a bridge toward new guidelines for training experiences in master's level counseling programs.

Strategies for Infusing Doctoral Level Training Process Into Master's Level Programs

More in-depth interaction with and mentoring from faculty. Faculty must provide counselor-trainees with significant time for ongoing and regular feedback and discussion so that students can work on areas in need of growth and development (Stoltenberg, McNeil, & Delworth, 1998; Vespia, Heckman-Stone, & Delworth, 2002). Jordan (2002) supported this strategy to assess students' readiness for training, to assure the quality of students' work, to encourage students' professional development, to more accurately evaluate students' professional competence, and to supply early identification and intervention with identity impaired student counselors. This ongoing and more extensive feedback from faculty will provide trainees with the kinds of information and learning that will facilitate growth in terms of counseling skills, enhance progress in professional identity, and assist in their ability to compare and contrast their thinking and responses with those of the more experienced senior members of the profession that they wish to enter (Deal, 2003).

Movement toward the inclusion of both didactic and experiential learning modes of instruction. Faculty must provide counselor-trainees with multiple opportunities for experiential learning that will allow time for personal introspection and reflection on how their person variables influence interactions and affective/behavioral responses to others within the cohort, to feedback regarding progress in counseling skill development, and to client issues discussed (Akos, 2004; Kim & Lyons, 2003; Parker, Freytes, Kaufman, Woodruff, & Hord, 2004) and that will allow them to integrate prepracticum curriculum and learning activities in a manner that approximates their roles as practitioners (Prieto & Scheel, 2002). The body of literature that emphasizes experiential learning in counselor education primarily attends to this as a strategy to enhance multicultural awareness about issues of diversity in the terms of structured exercises and games designed for this specific purpose, whereas the other body of literature identifies experiential learning as a means to facilitate the development of skills directly related to service delivery such as competence in case conceptualization and group counseling. At this time, recommendations for the use of the infusion of learning through experience appears to be limited, fragmented, and focused on individual areas of competence. Nevertheless, the merit of recommendations for training to move in this direction appears worthy of attention as we rethink the process of master's level counselor education given the positive correlation found between experience in an activity and counselor self-efficacy and the negative relationship with trainees' anxiety (Barbee et al., 2003; Tang et al., 2004).

Use of technology in replacement of more traditional modes of information dissemination. As in all arenas of personal and professional lives of many individuals in the United States, the use of technology in the field of counseling has emerged and continued to evolve (Baggerly, 2002; Baltimore, 2002; Quinn, Hohenshil, & Fortune, 2002). The existence of an online journal, the *Journal of Technology in Counseling*, which began in October of 1999 and was designed to specifically focus on this topic, is evidence of the emerging importance of technology within this discipline. Recommendations for the use of technology in counseling can be divided into two different foci: (a) use in service delivery and (b) use in counselor education and skills development. Literature supporting the link of technology with service delivery within the schools highlights the following areas: a means of advocacy (Stone & Turba, 1999), career counseling service delivery (Kuo & Srebalus,

2003; Pelling, 2002), assisting collaborative efforts between school counselors and special educators (Crutchfield, Baltimore, Felfeli, & Worth, 2000), and scheduling (e.g., aSc TimeTables, SchoolWorks, Daymark Software Systems, and Management Information Group–SIRS 3).

Recommendations for use in counselor education and skill development are to be more expansive and include teaching group counseling competence (Krieger & Stockton, 2004); connecting theory and practice through exposure to model videotapes (J. Carlson & Kjos, 1998); multimedia instruction in training counselors (B. G. Hayes, 1999); facilitating counseling skill development (Casey, 1999); counseling assessment (Lundberg & Cobitz, 1999); transcultural counseling education (McFadden & Jencius, 2000); instruction of counseling techniques (Jones & Karper, 2000); instruction teaming of school counseling, special education, and social work trainees (Stone & Seabrooks, 2000); supervision training (Barnes, Clark, & Thull, 2003; Getz & Schnurman-Crook, 2001; Pelling & Renard, 1999); distance learning in counseling education (Woodford, Rokutani, Gressard, & Berg, 2001); promoting active learning in training programs (Baggerly, 2002); and presenting online assignments (Clark & Stone, 2002). In addition, faculty are also beginning to more frequently use technology as a component in the process of data collection in both qualitative and quantitative research designs (McGlothlin, 2003).

There are a number of implications for the increasingly more common use of technology within the field of counseling. First, it presents one more component that counselor educators must use in training in order to best prepare students for the world of work. Graduates must at least know of programs with some degree of awareness of the role of technology within counseling. In addition, the relatively new role of technology in training will require some faculty to become more familiar with the strategic use of technology in order to be more effective and efficient in curriculum development, in classroom instruction, and in supervision. Technology can be one of the keys to freeing faculty classroom time, which has previously been reserved for lecture or examination, to engage in more meaningful discussions facilitating critical thinking skills among students about the content within the context of their roles as school counselors.

The integration of a developmental, across the life span, emphasis. Ivey and Goncalves (1987) suggested that counselors maintain the distinctiveness of being a specialized profession separate from psychology and continue to integrate developmental theory systematically into the curriculum and into the practice of counseling. Paisley and Benshoff (1996) and Akos and Galassi (2004) purported that school counselor education program faculty must use contemporary developmental research to train counseling students to serve as developmental advocates, whose primary role is to promote positive student developmental outcomes, and the research identified types of environments that nurture those outcomes. In addition, the emphasis on human development has extended to the critical training issue of professional development, more specifically, counseling supervision (Murray, Portman, & Maki, 2003; Nye, 2002; Vespia et al., 2002). No longer is it assumed that good counselors will make good supervisors; however, the link between the two professional activities, which highlight human development, has been respected and maintained (Bradley & Ladany, 2001; Milne, Pilkington, Gracie, & James, 2003). Human development remains a mainstay of distinction within the profession and this prominence is reflected in that it is a course requirement included in the 2001 CACREP guidelines as well as in the list of required course work for many state boards of counseling.

Although the concept of human development is firmly implanted as a point of attention in service delivery and training, there are a number of traditional curriculum, practices, and policy guidelines that result in limitations to the relevant knowledge in this content area. First, usually, attention to development in curriculum is too often relocated to the primary focus of one course and tangentially addressed within syllabi across core curricula. Theory and knowledge are seldom presented together in such a manner to assist in training's being able to effectively move from knowledge to application. Second, when students are exposed to developmental course work, trainees are seldom prepared for the role of supervisee and, eventually, supervisor (Vespia et al., 2002). Human development, in general, is addressed, but not associated with the experience in training. Without exposure to this body of knowledge, increased anxiety and misuse of the supervisory relationship may ensue (Bradley & Ladany, 2001). Third, some trainees arrive wishing to major in only one development stage. For example, some school counselor-trainees purport to feel comfortable with only a specific age group and choose to enroll in courses that attend to that stage. In addition, we have found that some students who choose school counseling as a career goal wish not to develop any competencies in work with adults. This decision is too often supported by program policies that support trainees in their decision to do so by maintaining complete separation between school counseling practicum sections and nonschool practicum sections. Such students are not challenged to attend to personal issues that they have with older or younger adult populations, and through choice, they are not exposed to training experiences wherein they are able to observe and develop the adult-to-adult or adult-to-child competencies. Such an outcome can impede the development of interpersonal competencies that are associated with assuming the role of effective student advocate with teachers, administrators, parents, or guardians. Not attending to human development in the most comprehensive manner could certainly be considered a debilitating influence in training programs that intend to prepare the most competent practitioners in the school setting.

The literature seemingly presents with clarity the necessary training content and process toward the development of the best prepared and most effective school counselors. However, there is also somewhat of a mixed message in that there is not currently a well-defined strategy for attending to the recommendations. For example, the national models developed by the profession were not intended to present an ideal program that could be used as a standard throughout the nation, but to provide school counselors with a document that would institutionalize the framework of a comprehensive school counseling program (Hatch & Bowers, 2002). With this in mind, it is no surprise that survey results indicate a great deal of variability in how and to what degree counselor educators implement the standards and literature in curriculum development, program practices, and policies (Perusse et al., 2001). Consequently, at this time, each individual program faculty body has the responsibility to attend to the challenge of developing, based on local demographic needs and political conditions, personalized programs that infuse recommendations from the literature and professional associations into students' training experiences (Hatch & Bowers). Although there may be as many different training models as there are training programs that purport to attend to both process and content recommendations within the confines of the structure of master's level training (e.g., Adelman & Taylor, 2001; Clarini & Greenwald, 2004; R. M. Hoffman, 2001; Johnson & Johnson, 2002), at this time, very limited literature identifies and specifically describes the content and process of training programs that do so in a comprehensive manner. The following section presents a case description of one school counseling training model that purports to do just that by attending to and extending beyond the current minimal standards as identified by the CACREP.

The Michigan State University School Counseling Training Model (MSU-SCTM): Extending Beyond the Minimum Standards

Graduate programs in school counseling are being reconstructed to facilitate the development of counselors-in-training who have the necessary information and skills to address the needs of a rapidly changing society. This section presents one CACREP-based, school counselor education program's curricular organization and structure designed to emphasize the integration of theory and practice in the process of simultaneously attending to the previously discussed, cutting-edge recommendations in the literature and guidelines established by professional organizations. The intent of the curriculum organization is to provide students with experience in assuming basic professional tasks associated with service delivery in school settings prior to real contact with K–12 student populations.

The Program Description

This two-year, cohort-model, CACREP-based, 48-credit-hour school counseling program is located in a large Midwestern state institution of higher education. Each year, 18 to 25 trainees are selected from a pool of 50 to 100 highly academically competitive applicants from around the world. Admission occurs only once each year during the fall semester. The program has consistently high graduation rates, has successful professional placement of graduates, and has a longstanding, successful admission of graduates to accredited doctoral programs (e.g., counseling psychology, counselor education, psychology, organizational psychology, and educational policy).

There are three program faculty, and all have doctoral degrees in counseling psychology; are members of ACA, the state Counseling Association, and the American Psychological Association (APA); have some experience of service delivery and research in the school setting; have research, scholarship, and service delivery experience associated with issues of diversity; and have developed program policies and practices that attend to the minimum standards of training exhibited in CACREP, the components of the Missouri Comprehensive Guidance Model, and the ASCA Counseling Program Guidelines.

The following sections provide an overview of the most defining characteristics of the program's pedagogy, curriculum integration, unique training components, and potential limitations of the program practices.

Pedagogy and counselor education. *Pedagogy,* the work of the teacher, is the systematized and strategic instruction of principles that promote students' learning. *Content pedagogy* refers to the teaching skills used to impart the specialized knowledge/content of the subject areas. Effective teachers display a wide range of skills and abilities that lead to creating an effective learning environment. Delineating effective practice and recognizing those who achieve it are important first steps in shaping the kind of teaching professional that America needs. This is the core challenge embraced by the National Board for Professional Teaching Standards (NBPTS; 1998), which recognizes that teaching is at the heart of education and the single most important action the nation can take to improve schools is to strengthen teaching. We believe that this is the core challenge that should also have some utility for counselor educators.

This language is borrowed from teacher education and is seldom addressed in the development of school counseling curriculum or recommendations for training, which tend to overlook the how-to and highlight the inclusion of content. Nevertheless, school counselor educators must address pedagogical and programmatic concerns if effective training process and outcomes are to result (R. M. Hoffman, 2001). We believe that for the best training outcomes to ensue, a clearly defined teaching philosophy to which all program faculty members must adhere is mandatory.

Teaching philosophy statement. In the introduction to the 30th anniversary edition of Brazilian educator Paulo Freire's *Pedagogy of the Oppressed*, Richard Shaull (1970) suggested that education has the capacity to facilitate students' abilities to accurately interpret and transform reality toward becoming effective social change agents. The central factors are the ability to challenge internalized images of established ways of life and the understanding of how to critically develop creative solutions to ill-formed problems. Attending to students' baseline competencies and knowledge and providing adequate support and challenge, teachers must provide conditions that allow counselor-trainees to develop knowledge, skills, and cognitive capacities necessary for dealing with complex social issues in the school setting (Kohlberg, 1975).

Although Freire's (1970) pedagogy provides an overarching frame for this program's model of training, faculty members have more specifically integrated components of a number of theories and models to facilitate the development of objective and effective social change agents. Developmental theory is perceived as critical to training in that faculty recognize and facilitate trainees' progress toward counseling competence (Stoltenberg & Delworth, 1988) through integrated curriculum, extensive and ongoing evaluations of counseling competence, and movement from self- to other evaluation of counseling competence. Phenomenological philosophy serves as the underpinning of the requirement that both faculty and students review and critique their videotaped counseling sessions and typewritten transcripts by using Kagan and Kagan's (1990) Interpersonal Process Recall. The Discrimination Model (Bernard, 1979; Luke & Bernard, 2006) is reflected in trainees' being provided with a map to critique the efficacy of their work with clients (e.g., process skills, conceptualization skills, and personalization skills). Finally, there is in-depth attention to the personal growth approach (Griffith & Frieden, 2000), which is person-centered and emphasizes heightening trainees' self-awareness, insight, and control of their own feelings and behaviors through requiring psycho-socioemotional self-assessment and development of a personal treatment plan.

Faculty members in this program have adopted a teaching style to inspire personal introspection and consciousness raising and to facilitate heightened understanding of personal values and the well-being of others. Students are challenged through use of what Freire (1970) called a "problem-posing" approach in which learning evolves from experiences that arouse interest, enjoyment, and challenge in the immediate experience of the student. Change in how a student knows is perceived as originating from movement from experience to thought and back again to construct and organized experience—what Schon (1987) referred to as "knowing in action." In this regard, teaching and learning are considered forms of research and experimentation and of questioning what is known in relationship to the problem-posing situation.

All core program faculty members have adopted this teaching philosophy in the development of course syllabi and classroom structure. The training environment and in-class experiences reflect each of Freire's (1970) philosophical main points: active, interactional, and participant learning opportunities; emphasis on acknowledgement of diverse perspectives; opportunities to learn how to effectively think critically about issues discussed; opportunities to become adaptive toward greater cognitive and behavioral flexibility; and extensive opportunities for self-assessment and heightened self-awareness. Students are reinforced to see themselves as agents of systemic change who are committed to improving themselves, their student cohort and training environment, the profession of counseling in terms of service delivery and research, their families, and the communities in which they live.

Core curriculum is based on national standards and the CACREP minimum standards guidelines; individual core course structures and required activities allow students opportunities to actually experience professional tasks associated with service delivery and practice within the school setting. For example, in the instruction of the course addressing individual counseling skills, students not only are exposed to the literature (knowledge) associated with skill acquisition, but are also allowed multiple opportunities for practice, which includes faculty, self-, and other evaluation of competence. Students have the opportunity to interface with program alumni and practicing school counselors during the first year of enrollment before the practicum experience. Both students and faculty are continuously informed of the needs within the current K–12 population. Technology is used in the dissemination of information and reading, and didactic and experiential learning are both used as modes of instruction and training.

Standard-based integrated curriculum. Often the applicability of effective educational models is identified and developed by faculty for primary implementation in the K–12 setting (Beane, 1993). Curriculum integration, one such model, has long been proposed as a way of organizing the common learnings or professional life skills considered essential to effective functioning in a life setting (Beane, 1997; McAuliffe & Eriksen, 2000). The primary objective is to assist students in making sense out of their experiences and learning how to participate in a democracy (Beane, 1997). Although the utility of such a model based on the professional standards of school counselors and counselor education programs would have the same benefits and positive outcomes in graduate education programs, few counselor education programs have attempted to strategically develop integrated curriculum in the training of school counselors (Hoachlander, 1999). The implementation of professional, standards-based integrated curriculum in K–12 instruction, having the goal of attending to student achievement in learning environments, has been significantly linked with increased mastery of much higher levels of knowledge and skill and with applying it in a coherently defined domain of the world of work (Gardner, 1993). The faculty members in this program have assumed that similar outcomes will occur in professional, standards-based integrated curriculum in counselor education graduate programs. Curriculum integration occurs at a number of levels within the MSU-SCTM. The following sections describe the levels of integration of training experiences that not only attend to professional standards, but also address the issues raised in the literature.

Integration of standards within course content. Increasing students' self- and other awareness and attitudes about individual differences is a critical recommended component of all counselor education training environments. In each of the required core courses related to service delivery, trainees experience the role of counselor and of faculty-constructed client in mock, videotaped counseling sessions in which evaluation and feedback based on professional standards and effective skill implementation are critical components of the training exercises. For example, in the diversity course among the first-year cohort, in their work with one another, students are requested to assume the roles of critical issues with which they will be confronted in the school setting (e.g., ADHD, substance abuse, parental physical abuse and neglect, anxiety, career counseling, academic underachievement) and special populations (e.g., racial-ethnic minority populations, GLBT students, gender issues, religious and spiritual issues) and to utilize effective multicultural counseling skills in work with their clients. Students develop knowledge and competencies in addressing legal/ethical issues with clients, effectively develop rapport, collect relevant information, write comprehensive progress notes, experience consultation, and develop a critical evaluation of counseling competence. This kind of activity allows students to experience a faculty guided, practicum-like, small group supervision experience prior to contact with actual clients.

Integration of curriculum/training across core courses. During the first semester, students enroll in three required core courses: (a) Individual and Group Counseling, (b) Multicultural Counseling, and (c) Counseling Theories and Ethics. The mock counseling sessions described in the previous section provide the crux of the training experience. Students are required to implement microcounseling skills learned and modeled in training videotapes in a culturally sensitivity manner in their work with their clients in the school setting. In addition, trainees are required to attend to legal/ethical issues that arise in their cases, presenting standard- and/or ethical-guideline-based rationales for their decision making and to conceptualize their clients presenting problems from multiple theoretical perspectives. The instructors of courses addressing each domain review the materials, but assume responsibility for evaluating and grading the final products based on the degree to which students attend to the standards presented in their perspective courses.

During the second semester of enrollment, trainees enroll in a career counseling course and are required to develop a school program module for implementation and evaluation during practicum the following fall semester of their second year of enrollment. Also during the second semester of enrollment, trainees enroll in two courses: (a) Counseling Assessment and Diagnosis and (b) Counseling Strategies. Training videotapes exhibiting model counseling strategies and clients with specific diagnoses are used to enhance trainees' understanding strategy implementation and clients' presentations of self within the counseling relationships. In work with videotaped mock counseling sessions, students collect relevant information and are required to select assessments, interpret results, develop DSM diagnoses, and identify the appropriate comprehensive treatment plans and literature-based strategies for intervention. Ongoing small group supervision sessions provide a forum for case presentations, consultations with colleagues and faculty, evaluation, and feedback. Trainees' products include a comprehensive formal write-up of all course requirements.

Integration of curriculum/training across first- and second-year student cohorts. During enrollment in practicum, trainees receive selected reading addressing counseling supervision and serve as secondary supervisors to first-semester students as they develop multicultural counseling competencies through the use of microcounseling skills in mock counseling sessions with one another. All training experiences are videotaped, which result in typewritten transcripts having both counselors' and clients' responses. Although faculty members in Individual and Group Counseling and Multicultural Counseling provide written feedback, practicum-level secondary supervisors review videotapes and transcripts and meet with trainees to assist them in preparation for improvement in their work during the final taped session of the semester.

During enrollment in internship, trainees serve as role-playing clients to the students who are enrolled in Counseling Assessment and Diagnosis, and Counseling Strategies as just described. Interns select cases and assume the role of clients with whom they have worked during practicum or with whom they are currently working. Multiple sessions begin with an intake interview and end with a final session that concludes with a supervisory session in which the intern discusses the counseling process and outcome, which includes a sharing of perspectives of strengths and limitations of the trainees' competence. The client also provides a formal evaluation of the counseling relationship and counselor effectiveness.

Finally, at the end of the semester of practicum, students participate in a panel discussion with the intent of preparing and guiding first-year students through the process of identifying a practicum site and the experience of practicum. In response, first-year students, who have almost completed their first semester of enrollment, develop and present papers describing their experiences in attending required professional development activities to the entire student body.

Integration of curriculum/training with community counseling curriculum. All students share core coursework that addresses both school and community literature, but the students are required to develop products that are associated with the setting in which they plan to work after graduation. For example, school counseling students will have clients and client cases associated with the school setting; those in community mental health will have client cases associated with community mental health. In order for trainees to have some understanding of service delivery and practices that extend across settings and developmental stages in work with children, adolescents, and adults, small group mock supervision activities are integrated, as are practicum and internship sections. Differences between the two programs are indicated in course products, practicum and internship placement site selection, and the selection of electives.

Unique model components that extend beyond the professional guidelines. The following provides a list of the components of the training model that further distinguish it from the common practices of most training programs: all core course work addresses issues related to development across the life span in addition to the CACREP required developmental course recommended; all core course work addresses issues of diversity in addition to the CACREP required diversity course recommended; a Program Diversity Model is designed to provide guidelines for sensitively attending to "cross-cultural collisions" (Steward, Gimenez, & Jackson, 1995) that occur during training; the program uses ongoing jury evaluation of trainees' counseling competencies; the program provides opportunity for research team participation and professional presentation/publication; the program provides a structured longitudinal programmatic research program for evaluation of training and faculty–student scholarship, wherein admission packet information and student course products during training are considered data for analysis; students engage in numerous opportunities to develop competence in self- and other evaluations of competence in professional activities; and the program provides extensive and ongoing supervision of trainees' counseling competence development throughout enrollment in the program. One of the most recent additions to the curriculum in the Counseling Strategies and Assessment courses is students being required to complete psychological measures that they would require of future clients, write an interpretation of the results and how the results will influence their experiences within the training environment and with future clients, and develop personal treatment plans that describe strategies they would use to self-monitor the issues that are revealed. This activity was designed to heighten students' senses of awareness and personal and interpersonal understanding and to increase their senses of responsibility to self-monitor personal issues that may negatively influence relationships within training and professional environments. Students' understanding of the intricacies and sensitivities of the assessment and interpretation process increased, and the outcome positively influenced small group discussions of mock counseling sessions.

Future planning toward a more comprehensive model of integration. Because this is a training model in progress, faculty members' continue to plan for continued enhancement of program curriculum and training practices through extension of the description of training during practicum and internship. First, extending practicum/internship sites to include the formal development of a trainee-instructed, faculty-supervised course that addresses students' academic achievements and skills for student success will allow students the direct instructional experience with the K–12 student population that is typically missing within training programs. Second, the inclusion of an on-site research experience and resulting publishable paper during internship would most directly address the researcher–practitioner model discussed in the literature. Third, in light of state legislation that removed teacher certification as a requirement for endorsement as a school counselor, faculty are currently also discussing the merit of requiring school counseling students to apply and serve as substitute teachers prior to program completion. Fourth, offering on-site practicum and internship supervisors opportunities for training in counseling supervision will provide a service to the community, establish a stronger and better integrated faculty–practitioner and university–community bond, and enhance the training experience of current and future students. Fifth, conversations are currently beginning to develop integrated training experiences across faculty related to other disciplines within the school setting (e.g., school psychology, teacher education, social work) in order to develop awareness of the parameters of knowledge of competence and increase awareness of the process of consultation toward effective treatment plans and subsequent positive student academic outcomes. Use of the findings from the longitudinal research program self-study will provide the basis for continued program enhancement and student training outcomes.

Limitations of the Training Model

Composition of student cohort. Although most student cohorts admitted have a critical representation of diversity in terms of race and ethnicity, the structure of the program tends to attract students whose lifestyles are more amenable to full-time enrollment given the nature of the integrated curriculum. Trainees tend to be female and between 22 and 32 years of age with limited professional experience after completing their undergraduate degrees. Therefore, the model does not accommodate other applicant populations, who may seek degree completion on a part-time, more long-term basis. The generalizability of this model to other student populations may not be feasible.

The challenge of the integration of curriculum and training model pedagogy. To be effective, an integration activity must accomplish an important, well-defined educational objective, emphasize connections and context, demand extensive faculty time commitment (Hoachlander, 1999) and must be dependent on the close, ongoing collaboration and consultation among program faculty in the development of syllabi, instructional styles, and standards for evaluations. Faculty must not only be aware of all professional standards but also, to some degree, be like-minded in terms of criterion used in evaluation of students' competencies, which can be a somewhat subjective process. This is particularly the case wherein multicultural counseling competence is evaluated and faculty members' personal biases and attitudes may be in direct opposition to those of other faculty members. In spite of the positive outcomes associated with integrated curriculum, these may be substantial obstacles to making it a more common practice in training programs, especially without a formal commitment to adhere to a diversity model designed to specifically address point of differences.

Professional identity of faculty. Despite an increasing concentration of counseling psychology programs within schools of education (80% today, as opposed to 50% in the mid-1980s; M. A. Hoffman & Carter, 2004), Pope (2004) noted that counseling psychology has shifted from a connection to master's level practice and the field of counseling to an emphasis upon doctoral-level practice and an emphasis upon the field of psychology. As this shift occurred, counseling psychology and counselor education competed for scarce resources within universities and developed distinct accreditation standards, award systems, ethical codes, and licenses for practice, creating some tension between these two fields. Counseling psychology also began to move away from its historical role in schools (Neimeyer, Bowman, & Stewart, 2001) and became more isolated from counselor education in order to meet the distinct demands of APA accreditation (Galassi & Akos, 2004). However, recent special issues of *The Counseling Psychologist* (cf. Romano & Kachgal, 2004; Walsh & Galassi, 2002) have revisited the role of counseling psychologists in our schools and, considering the natural fit between these two fields, have suggested that counseling psychologists may play an important role in the training of school counselors.

This historical divergence between counselor education and counseling psychology is reflected in the scholarship of these fields. Pope (2004) noted that although counseling psychologists routinely publish in counselor education journals, counselor educators do not encounter a "two-way" street in publishing within counseling psychology journals. Relatedly, Whiston (2002) noted that only 2 of the 25 editorial board members of *Professional School Counseling* are from counseling psychology programs.

Coleman (2004) noted that many counseling psychology training programs have made it difficult for graduates to become involved in schools and in the training of school counselors. For example, he noted the lack of child/adolescent-friendly counseling psychology doctoral programs, the lack of sequential school counseling course work for counseling psychology graduate students, and the lack of counseling psychology role models who were involved in the schools or in school counseling that leave few counseling psychology graduates prepared to direct a school counseling program.

Despite this trend, several counseling psychologists have taken active roles within schools and in the training of school counselors. For example, the "Achieving Success Identity Pathways" and "Tools for Tomorrow" career development interventions have had a significant impact upon the educational and vocational development of students in urban schools (Solberg, Howard, Blustein, & Close, 2002), in addition to providing counseling psychology graduate students with valuable experiences within our schools. Relatedly, Kenny, Waldo, Warter, and Barton (2002) and Walsh and Galassi (2002) both articulated and demonstrated the roles counseling psychologists may play within schools, such as in coordinating educational and social services or delivering mental health services within underserved schools.

The active roles these counseling psychologists have taken within schools reflect Romano and Kachgal's (2004) argument that "the influence of the two specialties [counseling psychology and school counseling] will be eminently stronger if they can form a strong partnership based on their overlapping philosophical foundations, scientific investigations, and psychological practices" (p. 184). They suggested that the theoretical and conceptual training of counseling psychology and school counseling is similar and that the theoretical foundations of counseling psychology can be helpful in training of school counselors. For example, the emphasis upon development, career development, and contextual bases of behavior and prevention (among other domains) within counseling psychology are well suited to the training and professional practices of school counselors.

Counseling psychology's emphases upon multiculturalism and research are also well suited to address school counselors' needs in our current context of accountability within schools. In particular, the Education Trust and the ASCA's (2003) model emphasizes school counselors' addressing the need of traditionally underserved students, such as racial/ethnic minorities, and closing the gap in academic achievement between White students and students of color. Counseling psychologists would be well suited to address issues of cultural identity and its relationship to academic performance among students of color and could train school counselors to understand these relationships, models of racial/ethnic identity development, and facilitate the cultural competence of counselor-trainees (Coleman, 2004). Relatedly, the research skills of counseling psychologists could be applied in training school counselors to utilize data and evaluation to drive decision making and advocate for the impact of school counselor within school systems (Whiston, 2002). For example, counseling psychologists could train school counselors to use research design skills to evaluate the impact of guidance programs upon the academic achievement of students of color and in closing the gap in academic achievement. In sum, considering the external threats faced by both counseling psychology (the closing of prominent doctoral programs) and school counseling (the recent trend of losing guidance counselors and programs), we suggest that the mutual benefits to these parties, in addition to the benefits students would receive, far outweigh historical tensions between these two fields.

Summary

To ensure the best outcomes in the training of school counselors, counselor educators must accept that it is an ever-evolving process that requires periodic review of the critical issues within the schools; ongoing contact with practitioners within the school settings; systematic, well-constructed, empirical research examining both process and outcome; and careful attention to the needs and issues that trainees bring to training. An updated literature review addressing professional standards in both practice and service delivery is incomplete without some attention to the parameters of restrictions associated with the master's degree. To prepare trainees who will be able to best meet the needs of children, teachers, and staff in the 21st century, there must be some understanding of how we must move to more effectively and efficiently incorporate what we must and can into the structure of training programs. This review and model of training, though quite comprehensive, is only a beginning to our fully understanding the process through which the necessary content and professional experiences can be infused into master's level training programs.

References

Adelman, H., & Taylor, L. (2001). *Framing new directions for school counselors, psychologists, and social workers.* Los Angeles: University of California (ERIC Document Reproduction Service No. ED450 299).

Ahia, C. E., & Martin, D. (1993). *The danger-to-self-or-others exception to confidentiality. ACA legal series* (Vol. 8). Alexandria, VA: American Counseling Association. (ERIC Document Reproduction Service No. ED403508).

Akos, P. (2004). Investing in experiential training appropriate for pre-service school counselors. *Journal for Specialists in Group Work, 29*(4), 327.

Akos, P., & Galassi, J. P. (2004). Training school counselors as developmental advocates. *Counselor Education & Supervision, 43*(3), 192–206.

Akos, P., Goodnough, G. E., & Milsom, A. S. (2004). Preparing school counselors for group work. *Journal of Specialists in Group Work, 29*(1), 127–136.

Akos, P., Konold, T., & Niles, S. G. (2004). A career readiness typology and typal membership in middle school. *The Career Development Quarterly, 53*(1), 53–67.

American School Counselor Association. (1999). *American School Counselor Association 1999–membership directory and resource guide.* Gainesville, FL: Naylor.

American School Counselor Association. (2003). ASCA national model: A framework for school counseling programs. Executive summary. *Professional School Counselor, 6,* 165–168.

American School Counselor Association. (2004). *Ethical standards for school counselors.* Alexandria, VA: Author.

Aspy, C. B., Oman, R. F., Vesely, S. K., McLeroy, K., Rodin, C., & Marhsall, L. (2004). Adolescent violence: The protective effects of youth assets. *Journal of Counseling & Development, 82,* 268–276.

Association of American Universities. (1998). *The AAU graduate education report and recommendations.* Washington, DC: Author.

Astramovich, R. L. & Holden, J. M. (2002). Attitudes of American School Counselor Association members toward utilizing paraprofessionals in school counseling—Statistical data included. *Professional School Counselor, 5*(1), 203–210.

Baggerly, J. (2002). Clicking with students: Using online assignments in counselor education courses. *Journal of Technology in Counseling, 2*(2). Retrieved October 3, 2007, from http://jtc.colstate.edu/issues.htm

Baltimore, M. (2002). Recent trends in advancing technology use in counselor education. *Journal of Technology in Counseling, 2*(2). Retrieved October 3, 2007, from http://jtc.colstate.edu/issues.htm

Barbee, P. W., Scherer, D., & Combs, D. C. (2003). Prepracticum service-learning: Examining the relationship with counselor self-efficacy and anxiety. *Counselor Education & Supervision, 43*(2), 108–119.

Barnes, P. Clark, P., & Thull, B. (2003). Web-based digital portfolios and counselor supervision. *Journal of Technology in Counseling, 3*(1). Retrieved October 3, 2007, from http://jtc.colstate.edu/issues.htm

Bauer, A. L., Ingersoll, E., & Burns, L. (2004). School counselors and psychotropic medication: Assessing training, experience, and school policy issues. *Professional School Counselor, 7*(3), 202–209.

Beane, J. A. (1993). *A middle school curriculum: From rhetoric to reality* (2nd ed.). Columbus, OH: National Middle School Association.

Beane, J. A. (1997). *Curriculum integration: Designing the core of democratic education.* New York: Teachers College Press.

Bemak, F., & Chung, R. C. (2005). Advocacy as a critical role for urban school counselors: Working toward equity and social justice. *Professional School Counseling, 9*(4), 327–331.

Bernard, J. M. (1979). The discriminative model of counseling supervision. *Counselor Education & Supervision, 19*(1), 60–68.

Bobby, C. L., & Kandor, J. R. (1995) CACREP accreditation: Assessment and evaluation in the standards and process. *ERIC Digests.* Greensboro, NC: ERIC Clearinghouse on Counseling and Student Services (ERIC Document Reproduction Service No. ED388884).

Boes, S., Ullery, B., Milner, V. S., & Cobia, D. (1999). Meeting the challenges of completing a counseling doctoral program. *Journal of Humanistic Education and Development, 37,* 130–144.

Borders, L. D., Fong, M. L., & Neimeyer, G. J. (1986). Counseling students' level of ego development and perceptions of clients. *Counselor Education and Supervision, 26,* 36–49.

Bradley, L. J., & Ladany, N. (2001). *Counseling supervision: Principles, process, & practice* (3rd ed.). San Francisco: Jossey-Bass.

Brigman, G., & Campbell, C. (2003). Helping students improve academic achievement and school success behavior. *Professional School Counselor, 7*(2), 91–98.

Bruce, M. A. (1997). Brief counseling versus traditional counseling: A comparison of effectiveness. *School Counselor, 44*(3), 171–184.

Bryan, J. (2005). Fostering educational resilience and achievement in urban schools through school-family-community partnerships. *Professional School Counselor, 8*(3), 219–227.

Butler, S. K. (2003). Multicultural sensitivity and competence in the clinical supervision of school counselors and school psychologists: A context for providing competent services in a multicultural society. *Clinical Supervisor, 22*(1), 125–141.

Carkhuff, R. R. (1987). *The art of healing.* Amherst, MA: Human Resource Development Press.

Carlozzi, A. F., Gaa, J. P., & Liberman, D. B. (1983). Empathy and ego development. *Journal of Counseling Psychology, 30,* 113–116.

Carlson, J., & Kjos, D. (1998, December 29–31). *Relating in a global community.* Proceedings of the Seventh International Conference on Counseling in the 21st Century, Sydney, Australia (ERIC Document Reproduction Service No. ED439359).

Carlson, N. S. (2001). Competent counselors as authors. *California Association for Counseling and Development, 21,* 55–56.

Casey, J. A. (1999). Computer assisted simulation for counselor training of basic skills, *Journal of Technology in Counseling, 1*(1). Retrieved October 3, 2007, from http://jtc.colstate.edu/issues.htm

Clarini, J., & Greenwald, M. (2004). Process and product in designing a new curriculum: The training of special care counselors at Vaier College. *Child & Youth Care Forum, 33*(4), 247–256.

Clark, M. A., & Stone, C. B. (2002). Clicking with students: Using online assignments in counselor education courses. *Journal of Technology in Counseling, 2*(2). Retrieved October 3, 2007, from http://jtc.colstate.edu/issues.htm

Coleman, H. L. K. (2004). Towards a well utilized partnership. *The Counseling Psychologist, 32*(2), 216–224.

Council for Accreditation of Counseling and Related Educational Programs. (2001). *The 2001 standards*. Retrieved October 3, 2007, from http://www.counseling.org/cacrep/2001standards700.htm

Crespi, T. D. (2003). Special section—Clinical supervision in the schools: Challenges, opportunities, and lost horizons. *Clinical Supervisor, 22*(1), 59–73.

Crews, J., Smith, M. R., Smaby, M. H., Maddux, C. D., Torres-Rivera, E., Cassey, J. A., et al. (2005). Self-monitoring and counseling skills: Skills-based versus interpersonal process recall training. *Journal of Counseling & Development, 83*, 78–86.

Crutchfield, L. B., Baltimore, M. L., Felfeli, M., & Worth, S. (2000). Empathic responding skills across counselor education training tracks: A comparative study. *Journal of Humanistic Counseling, Education & Development, 38*(3), 162–169.

Cushway, D. (1996). Tolerance begins at home: Implications for counselor training. *International Journal for the Advancement of Counseling, 18*(3), 189–197.

Dahir, C. A. (2001). The national standards for school counseling programs: Development and implementation. *Professional School Counseling, 4*(5), 320–327.

Dahir, C. A. (2004). Supporting a nation of learners: The role of school counseling in educational reform. *Journal of Counseling & Development, 82*, 344–353.

D'Andrea, M. (2004). Comprehensive school-based violence prevention training: A developmental-ecological training model. *Journal of Counseling & Development, 82*, 277–286.

Deal, K. H. (2003). The relationship between critical thinking and interpersonal skills: Guidelines for clinical supervision. *Clinical Supervisor, 22*(2), 3–19.

Dinsmore, J. A., & England, J. T. (1996). A study of MCT at CACREP-accredited counseling education programs. *Counseling Education and Supervision, 36*(1), 58–76.

Downs, L. (2000). *A study of the outcomes of required counseling during training at a CACREP accredited university* (Report No. CG030227). Greensboro NC: University of North Carolina at Greensboro. (ERIC Document Reproduction Service No. EDE444078).

Education Trust (2003). School counselors working for social justice. Retrieved October 4, 2007, from http://www2.edtrust.org/EdTrust/Transforming+School+Counseling/Social+Justice.htm

Elmore, P. (2001). Competencies in assessment and evaluation for school counselors. In G. R. Walz & J. C. Bleuer (Eds.), *Assessment: Issues and challenges for the millennium* (pp. 95–100). Greensboro, NC: ERIC Clearinghouse on Counseling and Student Services (ERIC Document Reproduction Service No. ED457432).

Embry, S. L., & Luzzo, D. A. (1996). The relationship between name-calling and peer beliefs among elementary school children: Implications for school counselors. *Elementary School Guidance & Counseling, 31*(2), 122–130.

Eriksen, K. (1997). *Making an impact: A handbook on counselor advocacy*. Washington, DC: Taylor & Francis.

Eschenauer, R., & Chen-Hayes, S. F. (2005). The transformative individual school counseling model: An accountability model for urban school counselors. *Professional School Counselor, 8*(2), 241–246.

Etringer, B. D., Hillerbrand, E., & Claiborn, C. D. (1995). The transition from novice to expert counselor. *Counselor Education and Supervision, 35*, 4–17.

Fischetti, B. A., & Lines, C. L. (2003). Views from the field: Models for school-based clinical supervision. *Clinical Supervisor, 22*(1), 75–86.

Freire, P. (1970). *Pedagogy of the oppressed*. New York: Continuum Publishing Company.

Furr, S. R., & Carroll, J. J. (2003). Critical incidents in student counselor development. *Journal of Counseling & Development, 81*(4), 483–489.

Galassi, J. P., & Akos, P. (2004). Déjà vu and moving the conversation: Reactions to an underutilized partnership. *The Counseling Psychologist, 32*(2), 235–244.

Gardner, H. (1993). Educating for understanding. *American School Board Journal, 180*(7), 20–24.

Gaubatz, M. D., & Vera, E. M. (2002). Do formalized gatekeeping procedures increase programs follow-up with deficient trainees? *Counselor Education and Supervision, 41*, 294–305.

Gelso, C. J., & Carter, J. A. (1985). The relationship in counseling and psychotherapy: Components, consequences, and theoretical antecedents. *The Counseling Psychologist, 13*, 155–243.

Getz, H. G., & Schnurman-Crook, A. (2001). Utilization of online training for on-site clinical supervisors: One university's approach. *Journal of Technology in Counseling, 2*(1). Retrieved October 3, 2007, from http://jtc.colstate.edu/issues.htm

Giordano, F. G., Schwiebert, V. L., & Brotherton, W. D. (1997). School counselors' perceptions of the usefulness of standardized tests, frequency of their use, and assessment training needs. *School Counselor, 44*(3), 198–205.

Gordon, E. W. (1990). Coping with communicentric bias in knowledge production in the social sciences. *Educational Researcher, 19*(3), 14–19.

Gordon, R. A., McClure, B. A., & Petrowski, E. L. (1994). *Research productivity in CACREP accredited programs*. Greensboro, NC: University of North Carolina at Greensboro (ERIC Document Reproduction Service No. ED412490).

Granello, P. F., & Granello, D. H. (1998). Training counseling students to the use outcome research. *Counselor Education and Supervision, 37*(4), 224–237.

Green, A. G., Conley, J. A., & Barnett, K. (2005). Urban school counseling: Implications for practice and training. *Professional School Counselor, 8*(2), 260–265.

Griffith, B. A., & Frieden, G. (2000). Facilitating reflective thinking in counselor education. *Counselor Education & Supervision, 40*(2), 82–93.

Gysbers, N. C., & Henderson, P. (2001). Comprehensive guidance and counseling program: A rich history and a bright future. *Professional School Counseling, 4*(4), 246–256.

Hansen, J. T. (2003). Including diagnostic training in counseling curricula: Implications for professional identity development. *Counselor Education & Supervision, 43*(2), 96–107.

Hatch, T., & Bowers, J. (2002). The block to build on. *School Counselor, 39*(5), 12–17. Retrieved May–June, 2002, from www.schoolcounselor.org

Haverkamp, B. E. (1994). Using assessment in counseling supervision: Individual differences in self-monitoring. *Measurement and Evaluation in Counseling and Development, 27,* 316–324.

Hayes, B. G. (1999). Where's the data: Is multimedia instruction effective in training counselors? *Journal of Technology in Counseling, 1*(1). Retrieved October 3, 2007, from http://jtc.colstate.edu/issues.htm

Hayes, J. A. (2002). Playing with fire: Countertransference and clinical epistemology. *Journal of Contemporary Psychotherapy, 32*(1), 93–100.

Hays, D. G. (2002). *Infusing multicultural counseling competencies into counselor training curriculum.* Greensboro, NC: University of North Carolina at Greensboro (ERIC Document Reproduction Service No. ED465137)

Hirt, J. B., & Muffo, J. A. (1998). Graduate students: Institutional climates and discipline cultures. *New Directions for Institutional Research, 25*(2), 17–33.

Hoachlander, G. (1999). Integrating academic and vocational curriculum—Why is theory so hard to practice? *National Center for Research in Vocational Education, 7,* 2–12.

Hodges, S. (2005). [Review of the book *In the presence of grief: Helping family members resolve death, dying, and bereavement issues*]. *Journal of Counseling & Development, 83,* 120–104.

Hoffman, M. A., & Carter, R. T. (2004). Counseling psychology and school counseling: A call to collaboration. *The Counseling Psychologist, 32*(2), 181–183.

Hoffman, R. M. (2001). *Theory to practice: A model for school counselor education.* Based on a paper presented at the Triennial Conference of the Association for Counselor Education and Supervision, New Orleans, LA, October 2731. 1999. Greensboro NC: University of North Carolina at Greensboro. (ERIC Document Reproduction Service No. ED452448).

Hoffman, R. M. (2004). Conceptualizing heterosexual identity development: Issues and challenges. *Journal of Counseling & Development, 82*(3), 375–380.

Hoffman, R. M., & Myers, J. E. (1996). *Gender issues in counselor education: Are the CACREP standards sufficient?* (ERIC Document Reproduction Service No. ED400481.)

Holcomb-McCoy, C. (2005). A descriptive study of urban school counseling programs. *Professional School Counselor, 8*(2), 247–252.

Holcomb-McCoy, C. C. (1999). Multicultural counseling training: A preliminary study. *Journal of Counseling & Development, 77*(3), 294–302. (ERIC Document Reproduction Service No. ED428301).

Hunt, B. (1996). HIV/AIDS training in CACREP-approved counselor education programs. *Journal of Counseling and Development, 47*(3), 295–299.

Impara, J. C. (1995). Assessment skills of counselors, principals, and teachers. *ERIC Digests.* Washington, DC: ERIC Clearinghouse on Assessment and Evaluation (ERIC Document Reproduction Service No. ED387708).

Ivey, A. E., & Goncalves, O. F. (1987). Toward a developmental counseling curriculum. *Counselor Education & Supervision, 26*(4), 270–278.

Johnson, C. D., & Johnson, S. K. (2002). Building stronger school counseling programs: Bringing futuristic approaches into the present. Washington, DC: Office of Educational Research and Improvement (ERIC Document Reproduction Service No. ED 464268).

Jones, K. D., & Karper, C. (2000). How to develop an online course in counseling techniques. *Journal of Technology in Counseling, 1*(2). Retrieved October 3, 2007, from http://jtc.colstate.edu/issues.htm

Jordan, K. (2002). Clinical training of graduate students: The need for faculty to balance responsibility and vulnerability. *Clinical Supervisor, 21*(1), 29–38.

Jordan, K., & Stevens, P. (2001). Teaching ethics to graduate students: A course model. *Family Journal: Counseling & Therapy for Couples & Families, 9*(2), 178–184.

Kagan, N. I., & Kagan, H. (1990). IPR: A validated model for the 1990s and beyond. *Counseling Psychologist, 18*(3), 436–440.

Kahn, B. B. (1999). Priorities and practices in field supervision of school counseling students. *Professional School Counselor, 3*(2), 128–136.

Keller, T. J., & Goodman, R. W. (2003). *Supporting CACREP programs and curriculum with World Wide Web resources.* Greensboro, NC: ERIC Clearinghouse on Counseling and Student Services (ERIC Document Reproduction Service No. ED481135).

Kenny, M. E., Waldo, M., Warter, E. H., & Barton, C. (2002). Theory, science, and practice for enhancing the lives of children and youth. *The Counseling Psychologist, 30,* 726–248.

Kim, B. S. K., & Lyons, H. Z. (2003). Experiential activities and multicultural counseling competence training. *Journal of Counseling & Development, 81*, 400–408.

King, J. H., & Anderson, S. M. (2004). Therapeutic implications of pharmacotherapy: Current trends and ethical Issues. *Journal of Counseling & Development, 82*, 329–336.

King, K. A., Tribble, J. L., & Price, J. H. (1999). School counselors' perceptions of nonconsensual sexual activity among high school students. *Professional School Counselor, 2*(4), 286–290.

Kitzrow, M. A. (2002). Survey of CACREP-accredited programs: Training counselors to provide treatment for sexual abuse. *Counselor Education & Supervision, 42*(2), 107–111.

Kohlberg, L. (1975). The cognitive-developmental approach to moral education. *Phi Delta Kappan, 56*(10), 670–677.

Krieger, K., & Stockton, R. (2004). Technology and group leadership training: Teaching group counseling in an online environment. *Journal for Specialists in Group Work, 29*(4), 343.

Kuo, Y., & Srebalus, D. J. (2003). The development of a Web-based career counseling course. *Journal of Technology in Counseling, 3*(1). Retrieved October 3, 2007, from http://jtc.colstate.edu/issues.htm

LaFountain, R. M., & Baer, E. C. (2001). Increasing CACREP's name recognition: The effect of written communication on site supervisors' awareness level. *Journal of Counseling & Development, 79*(2), 194–199.

Lambie, G. W. (2005). Child abuse and neglect: a practical guide for professional school counselors. *Professional School Counselor, 8*, 253–259.

LaPidus, J. B. (1998). If we want things to stay as they are, things will have to change. *New Directions for Humanistic Education, 26*(1), 95–102.

Larson, L. M., & Besett-Alesch, T. M. (2000). Bolstering the scientist component in the training of scientist-practitioners: One program's curriculum modifications. *Counseling Psychologist, 28*(6), 873–896.

Lawrence, G., & Kurpius, S. E. (2000). Legal and ethical issues involved when counseling minors in non-school settings. *Journal of Counseling & Development, 78*(2), 130–136.

Leach, M. M., Stoltenberg, C. D., McNeill, B. W., & Eichenfield, G. (1997). Self-efficacy and counselor development: Testing the Integrated Developmental Model. *Counselor Education and Supervision, 37*, 115–124.

Lee, C. C. (2005). Urban school counseling context, characteristics, and competencies. *Professional School Counselor, 8*(2), 272–277.

Lin, M., Kelly, K. R., & Nelson, R. C. (1996). A comparative analysis of the interpersonal process in school-based counseling and consultation. *Journal of Counseling Psychology, 43*(4), 389–393.

Luke, M., & Bernard, J. M. (2006). The school counseling supervision model: An extension of the discrimination model. *Counselor Education & Supervision, 45*, 282–295.

Lundberg, D. J., & Cobitz, C. (1999). Use of technology in counseling assessment: A survey of practices, views, and outlook. *Journal of Technology in Counseling, 1*(2). Retrieved October 3, 2007, from http://jtc.colstate.edu/issues.htm

Mander, G. (2004). The selection of candidates for training in psychotherapy and counseling. *Psychodynamic Practice: Individuals, Groups & Organizations, 10*(2), 161–172.

Margolis, R. L., & Rungta, S. A., (1986). Training counselors for work with special populations: A second look. *Journal of Counseling and Development, 64*(10), 642–644.

Marino, T., Sams, W., & Guerra, P. (1999). *ACA wins introduction of 100,000 new counselors and other counselor-friendly legislation in U.S. Senate.* Alexandria, VA: American Counseling Association. Retrieved March 10, 2001, from http://www.counseling.org/enews/volume_2/0210.htm

Matthews, C. O. (1998). Integrating the spiritual dimension into traditional counselor education programs. *Counseling & Values, 43*(1), 3–18.

McAuliffe, G., & Eriksen, K. (2000). *Preparing counselors and therapists: Creating constructivist and developmental programs.* Alexandria, VA: ACES (ERIC Document Reproduction Service No. ED467417).

McFadden, J., & Jencius, M. (2000). Using cyberspace to enhance counselor's cultural transcendence. In J. W. Bloom & G. R. Walz (Eds.), *Cybercounseling and cyberlearning: Strategies and resources for the millennium* (pp. 67–83). Alexandria, VA: American Counseling Association.

McGlothlin, J. M. (2003). The infusion of internet-based surveys and postal mail surveys. *Journal of Technology in Counseling, 3*(1). Retrieved October 3, 2007, from http://jtc.colstate.edu/issues.htm

McGlothlin, J. M., & Thomas, D. E. (2004). Perceived benefit of CACREP (2001) core curriculum standards. *Counselor Education & Supervision, 43*(4), 274–285.

Miller, G. A., Wagner, A., Britton, T. P., & Gridley, B. E. (1998). A framework for understanding the wounding of healers. *Counseling and Values, 42*(2), 124–132.

Milne, D. L., Pilkington, J., Gracie, J., & James, I. (2003). Transferring skills from supervision to therapy: A qualitative and quantitative N=1 analysis. *Behavioural & Cognitive Psychotherapy, 31*(2), 193–202.

Morgan, O. J., Toloczko, A. M., & Comly, E. (1997). Graduate training of counselors in the addictions: A study of CACREP-approved programs. *Journal of Addictions and Offender Counseling, 17*, 66–76.

Murray, G. C., Portman, T. A., & Maki, D. R. (2003). Clinical supervision: Developmental difference during preservice training. *Rehabilitation Education, 17*(1), 19–32.

Myers, J. E., Sweeney, T. J., & White, V. E. (2002). Advocacy for counseling and counselors: A professional imperative. *Journal of Counseling and Development, 80*, 394–402.

Myrick, R. D. (1993). *Developmental guidance and counseling: A practical approach* (2nd ed.). Minneapolis, MN: Educational Media Corporation.

National Board for Professional Teaching Standards. (1998). *A nation prepared: Teachers for the 21st century*. Washington, DC: Author. Retrieved October 3, 2007, from http://www.nbpts.org/

Neimeyer, G. J., Bowman, J., & Stewart, A. E. (2001). Internship and initial job placements in counseling psychology: A 26-year retrospective. *The Counseling Psychologist, 29*, 763–780.

Nelson, K. W., & Jackson, S. A. (2000). *Factors affecting the learning environment of doctoral students in counselor education*. Project funded by a Texas A&M University-Corpus Christi College of Education Faculty Research Grant. Greensboro, NC: ERIC Clearinghouse on Counseling and Student Services (ERIC Document Reproduction Service No. ED451 440).

Newman-Carlson, D., & Horne, A. M. (2004). Bully busters: A psychoeducational intervention for reducing bullying behavior in middle school students. *Journal of Counseling & Development, 82*(3), 259–267.

Nye, C. H. (2002). Using developmental processes in supervision: A psychodynamic approach. *Clinical Supervisor, 21*(2), 39–53.

Osborn, C. J. (2004). Seven salutary suggestions for counselor stamina. *Journal of Counseling & Development, 82*, 319–328.

Paisley, P. O., & Benshoff, J. M. (1996). Applying developmental principles to practices: Training issues for the professional development of school counselors. *Elementary School Guidance & Counseling, 30*(3), 163–169.

Parker, W., Freytes, M., Kaufman, C., Woodruff, R., & Hord, R. (2004). The mentoring lab: A small group approach for managing emotions from multicultural counselor training. *Journal for Specialists in Group Work, 29*(4), 361.

Pate, R. H. (1990). The potential effect of accreditation standards on the type of students who will enter counselor education programs. *Counselor Education and Supervision, 29*(3), 179–187.

Pelling, N. (2002). The use of technology in career counseling. *Journal of Technology in Counseling, 2*(2). Retrieved October 3, 2007, from http://jtc.colstate.edu/issues.htm

Pelling, N., & Renard, D. (1999). The use of videotaping within developmentally-based supervision. *Journal of Technology in Counseling, 1*(1). Retrieved October 3, 2007, from http://jtc.colstate.edu/issues.htm

Perusse, R., Goodnough, G. E., & Noel, C. J. (2001). Use of the national standards for school counseling programs in preparing school counselors. *Professional School Counselor, 5*(1), 49–55.

Peterson, J. S., Goodman, R., Keller, T., & McCauley, A. (2004). Teachers and non-teachers as school counselors: Reflections on the internship experience. *Professional School Counseling, 7*(4), 246–255.

Ponterotto, J. G. (1991). The nature of prejudice revisited: Implications for counseling interventions. *Journal of Counseling and Development, 70*, 216–224.

Pope, M. (2004). Counseling psychology and professional school counseling: Barriers to a true collaboration. *The Counseling Psychologist, 32*(2), 253–262.

Prieto, L. R., & Scheel, K. R. (2002). Using case documentation to strengthen counselor trainees' case conceptualization skills. *Journal of Counseling & Development, 80*(1), 11–22.

Quinn, A. C., Hohenshil, T., & Fortune, J. (2002). Utilization of technology in CACREP approved counselor education programs. *Journal of Technology in Counseling, 2*(2). Retrieved October 3, 2007, from http://jtc.colstate.edu/issues.htm

Ray, D. C., Armstrong, S. A., Warren, E. S., & Balkin, R. S. (2005). Play therapy practices among elementary school counselors. *Professional School Counselor, 8*(4), 360–365.

Reeves, A., Wheller, S., & Bowl, E. (2004). Assessing risk: Confrontation or avoidance—What is taught in counsellor training courses. *British Journal of Guidance & Counselling, 32*(2), 235–247.

Remley, T. P., & Huey, W. C. (2002). An ethics quiz for school counselors: Legal and ethical issues in school counseling [Special issue]. *Professional School Counselor 6*(1), 3–12.

Romano, J. L., & Kachgal, M. M. (2004). Counseling psychology and school counseling: An underutilized partnership. *The Counseling Psychologist, 32*(2), 184–215.

Rosenberger, E. W., & Hayes, J. A. (2002). Therapist as subject: A review of the empirical countertransference literature. *Journal of Counseling & Development, 80*(3), 264–270.

Scarborough, J. L. (2005). The school counselor activity rating scale: An instrument for gathering process data. *Professional School Counselor 8*(2), 278–283.

Schafer, W. D. (1995). *Assessment skills for school counselors*. (ERIC Document Reproduction Service No. ED387709).

Schmidt, J. J. (1999). Two decades of CACREP and what do we know? *Counselor Education and Supervision, 39*(1), 12–24.

Schon, D. A. (1987). *Educating the reflective practitioner, toward a new design for teaching and learning in the professions*. San Francisco: Jossey-Bass.

Schultheiss, D. E., Palma, T. V., & Manzi, A. J. (2005). Career development in middle school: A qualitative inquiry. *The Career Development Quarterly, 53*(3), 246–265.

Shaull, R. (1970). Introduction. In P. Freire (Ed..), *Pedagogy of the oppressed* (pp. 1–10). New York: Continnum Publishing Company.

Smaby, M. H., & D'Andrea, L. M. (1995). 1994 CACREP standards: Will we make the grade? *Journal of Counseling & Development, 74*, 105–109.

Smaby, M. H., Maddux, C. D., Torres-Rivera, E., & Zimmick, R. (1999). A study of the effects of a skills-based versus a conventional group counseling training program. *Journal for Specialists in Group Work, 24*(2), 152–163.

Smith, D. C., & Sandhu, D. S. (2004). Toward a positive perspective on violence prevention in schools: Building connections. *Journal of Counseling & Development, 82,* 287–293.

Smith, S. L., Crutchfield, L. B., & Culbreth, J. R. (2001). Teaching experience for school counselors: Counselor educators' perceptions. *Professional School Counselor, 4*(3), 216–224.

Solberg, V. S., Howard, K., Blustein, D. L., & Close, W. (2002). Career development in the schools: Connecting school-to-work-to-life. *The Counseling Psychologist, 30,* 705–725.

Stanley, P. H., Juhnke, G. A., & Purkey, W. W. (2004). Using an invitational theory of practice to create safe and successful schools. *Journal of Counseling & Development, 82*(3), 302–209.

Stein, D. M., & Lambert, M. J. (1995). Graduate training in psychotherapy: Are therapy outcomes enhanced? *Journal of Counseling Psychology, 63,* 182–196.

Stevens, H. B., Dinoff, B. L., & Donnenworth, E. E. (1998). Psychotherapy training and theoretical orientation in clinical psychology programs: A national survey. *Journal of Clinical Psychology, 54,* 91–96.

Steward, R. J., Gimenez, M., & Jackson, J. D. (1995). A study of personal preferences of successful university students as related to race, ethnicity, and sex. *Journal of College Student Development, 36,* 123–131.

Stoltenberg, C. D., & Delworth, U. (1988). Developmental models of supervision: It is development—A response to Holloway. *Professional Psychology: Research and Practice, 19,* 134–137.

Stoltenberg, C. D., McNeil, B., & Delworth, U. (1998). *IDM supervision: An integrated developmental model for supervising counselors and therapists.* San Francisco: Jossey-Bass.

Stone, C. B., & Seabrooks, J. (2000). Virtual teaming among pre-service professionals in school counseling, special education and social work services. *Journal of Technology in Counseling, 1*(2). Retrieved October 3, 2007, from http://jtc.colstate.edu/issues.htm

Stone, C. B., & Turba, R. (1999). School counselors using technology for advocacy. *Journal of Technology in Counseling, 1*(1). Retrieved October 3, 2007, from http://jtc.colstate.edu/issues.htm

Studer, J. R. (2005). Supervising school counselor-in-training: A guide for field supervisors. *Professional School Counselor, 8*(4), 353–359.

Sue, D. W., Arredondo, P., & McDavis, R. J. (1992). Multicultural counseling competencies and standards: A call to the profession. *Journal of Counseling and Development, 70*(4), 477–486.

Syverson, P. D. (1996). Assessing demand for graduate and professional programs. *New Directions for Graduate and Institutional Research, 92,* 17–29.

Tang, M., Addison, K. D., LaSure-Bryant, D. Norman, R., O'Connell, W., & Stewart-Sicking, J. A. (2004). Factors that influence self-efficacy of counseling students: An exploratory study. *Counselor Education & Supervision, 44*(1), 70–80.

Thomas, N. (1982). Educational information centers: One answer for adults. *New Directions for Experiential Learning, (Building on Experiences in Adult Development),* pp. 75–85 (ERIC Document Reproduction Service No. EJ267277).

Toukmanian, S. G., & Rennie, D. L. (1975). Microcounseling versus human relations training: Relative effectiveness with undergraduate trainees. *Journal of Counseling Psychology, 22*(4), 345–351.

Trusty, J. (2002). African Americans' educational expectations: Longitudinal causal models for women and men, *Journal of Counseling & Development, 80,* 332–345.

Trusty, J. (2005). Advocacy competencies for professional school counselors. *Professional School Counselor 8*(2), 266–271.

Trusty, J., Ng, K., & Watts, R. E. (2005). Model of effects of adult attachment on emotional empathy of counseling students. *Journal of Counseling & Development, 83,* 66–77.

Trusty, J., & Niles, S. G. (2004). Realized potential or lost talent: High school variables and bachelor's degree completion. *The Career Development Quarterly, 53*(1), 2–15.

Ungar, R., Mackey, L., Guest, M., & Bernard, C. (2000). Logotherapeutic guidelines for therapists' self-care. *International Forum for Logotherapy, 23*(2), 89–94.

Urofsky, R., & Sowa, C. (2004). Ethics education in CACREP-accredited counselor education programs. *Counseling & Values, 49*(1), 37–47.

U.S. Department of Education (2001). No Child Left Behind Act of 2001, Pub. L. N. 107–110, 115, STAT. 1424–2094, January 8, 2002.

Vacha-Haase, T, Davenport, D. S., & Kerewsky, S. D. (2004). Problematic students: Gatekeeping practices of academic professional psychology programs. *Professional Psychology: Research and Practice, 35*(2), 115–122.

Vespia, K. M., Heckman-Stone, C., & Delworth, U. (2002). Describing and facilitating effective supervision behavior in counseling trainees. *Psychotherapy: Theory/Research/Practice/Training, 39*(1), 56–65.

Walsh, M. E., & Galassi, J. P. (2002). Counseling psychologists and schools. *The Counseling Psychologist, 30,* 675–681.

Watt, S. K., Robinson, T. L., & Lupton-Smith, H. (2002). Building ego and racial identity: Preliminary perspectives on counselor-in-training. *Journal of Counseling & Development, 80*(1), 94–100.

Whiston, S. C. (2002). Response to the past, present, and future of school counseling: Raising some issues. *Professional School Counseling, 5*(3), 148–155.

Wolgien, C. S., & Coady, N. F. (1997). Good therapists' beliefs about the development of their helping ability: The wounded healer paradigm revisited. *International Journal for the Advancement of Counselling, 18*(3), 189–197.

Woodford, M. S., Rokutani, L. Gressard, C., & Berg, B. (2001). Sharing the course: An experience with collaborative distance learning in counseling education. *Journal of Technology in Counseling, 2*(1). Retrieved October 3, 2007, from http://jtc.colstate.edu/issues.htm

Young, J. S., Cashwell, C., Wiggins-Frame, M., & Belaire, C. (2002). Spiritual and religious competencies: A national survey of CACREP-accredited programs. *Counseling & Values, 47*(1), 22–23.

Zimpfer, D. G., Cox, J. A., West, J. D., Bubenzer, D. L., & Brooks, D. K. (1997). An examination of counselor preparation doctoral program goals. *Counselor Education & Supervision, 36*(4), 318–331.

III
SCHOOL COUNSELING:
Moving Toward Standards and Models

CAROL A. DAHIR
New York Institute of Technology

Today, in most high schools, counselors are not only expected to advise students about college, they are also asked to police for drugs, keep records of dropouts, reduce teenage pregnancy, check traffic in the halls, smooth out the tempers of irate parents, and give aid and comfort to battered and neglected children. School counselors are expected to do what our communities, our homes, and our churches have not been able to accomplish, and if they cannot, we condemn them for failing to fulfill our high-minded expectations.

(Boyer, 1988, p. 3)

For too many years, and for as long as the school counseling profession has existed, the scope and sequence of services delivered have been defined and influenced by forces outside of the profession more than by the profession itself (Dahir, 2001, 2004). State departments of education, school district administrators, and educational organizations and foundations have clearly dictated the functions, activities, and programs that professional school counselors should deliver to students (Cunanan & Maddy-Bernstein, 1994). School counseling programs were perceived as a collection of well-intentioned responsive services based upon the professional orientation of the counselor, the priorities of an individual school building, and administrative needs (Campbell & Dahir, 1997). Confusion existed as to what actually constituted a school counseling program and what role the school counselor assumed in a school setting.

School counseling has been on a continuous journey of change since the inception of the profession in the 1890s. One hundred years later, a concerted effort initiated by the American School Counselor Association (ASCA; 1994) and the Education Trust (1997, 1999) focused attention on the essential dimensions for effective school counselors and counseling programs in schools as represented in Table 3.1.

Today's 21st-century, professional school counselor is a systemic change agent, who uses leadership, advocacy, collaboration and teaming, and data-driven decision making skills to "become the academic conscience of the school, insuring that the school remains focused on student achievement and accepts responsibility for student outcomes" (Hart & Jacobi, 1992, p. 49). As student advocates, school counselors support equity in educational opportunities for all students and nurture dreams and aspirations. School counselors embrace the ethical and moral obligation to reduce and eliminate the institutional and/or social barriers that may stand in the way of every student's academic, career, or personal/social development (Lee & Walz, 1998; Stone, 2005). The profession of school counseling has embraced changing times. It displays a willingness to analyze, monitor, and adapt the school counseling program to the changing educational landscape and the goals of school improvement. School counselors recognize and embrace the critical part they play on the educational team. They also accept the challenge to share in the responsibility to prepare students to meet the expectations of higher academic standards and help them become productive and contributing members of society.

It is not to say that school counselors did not previously embrace this way of work; ASCA and the Education Trust's efforts at the national level promoted the transformation of the profession in ways that complemented the national agenda to improve schools and equitably address every student's educational needs. Twenty-first century school counseling programs are in a proactive and pivotal position to effectively demonstrate how the complement of academic rigor and affective development is the formula to student success (Stone & Dahir, 2007).

Table 3.1 Traditional vs. Transformed School Counseling

The Practice of the Traditional School Counselor	The Practice of the Transformed School Counselor
Counseling	Counseling
Consultation	Coordination of Services
Coordination	Consultation
	Leadership
	Advocacy
	Collaboration and Teaming
	Managing Resources
	Use of Data
	Technology
Service-driven model	Systemic and programmatic model

Note: Adapted from *Working definition of school counseling.* Education Trust. Washington, DC: Author, 1997.

National Standards: What Students Need to Know and Be Able to Do

At the heart of the national debate about education is simply what's working and what's not working in public schools. Since the publication of *A Nation at Risk* (National Commission on Excellence in Education, 1983), the education and business communities, and the public and private sector regularly deliberate the expectations of American public education. The school improvement agenda of the No Child Left Behind Act (U.S. Department of Education, 2001) evolved from the decades-old educational reform movement which is rooted in A Nation at Risk. America 2000 (USDE, 1990), and its reauthorization as *Goals 2000* (USDE, 1994) was the impetus for the development of national standards across all academic disciplines. Phrases such as "higher academic achievement," "increasing student potential," and "rigorous academic preparation," as well as the word *accountability*, have become commonplace in every community across the nation.

As the academic disciplines moved forward to develop statements of what "students should know and be able to do" (National Education Goals Panel, 1992, p. x). The development of the *National Standards* (Dahir, Sheldon, & Valiga, 1998) encouraged the school counseling community to look within itself to clarify its purpose and establish higher expectations for both students and the programs delivered. ASCA determined that the school counseling standards, like the academic subject standards, would define what K–12 students should know and be able to do as a result of participating in a school counseling program (Campbell & Dahir, 1997). ASCA believed that national standards would

- Promote equitable access to school counseling programs and services for all students,
- Identify and prioritize the key content components for school counseling programs, and
- Ensure that school counseling programs are comprehensive in design and delivered in a systematic fashion for all students (Campbell & Dahir).

A major research study was undertaken by ASCA in 1995 to analyze relevant school counseling and educational reform literature and to review existing school counseling program models developed at the state level. The findings confirmed the continued importance of the three widely accepted and interrelated areas of student development: (a) academic, (b) career, and (c) personal/social development (Campbell & Dahir, 1997). As a result of this work, the nine national standards (represented in Table 3.2) ensued. These standards offer school counselors, administrators, teachers, and counselor educators a common language to promote student success through school counseling programs, which also is readily understood by colleagues who are involved in the implementation of standards across other disciplines.

The National Standards for School Counseling Programs (ASCA, 1997) tied the work of school counseling programs to the mission of schools and encouraged school counselors to assume a leadership role in school reform (Bowers, Hatch, & Schwallie-Giddis, 2001). National standards-based school counseling programs are intended to help students develop attitudes, knowledge, and skills in academic, career, and personal/social development that are needed in today's and tomorrow's world. Higher expectations would also necessitate the development of new and different measures of school counseling accountability to evidence that the student competencies—and ultimately, the standards—are achieved. Measurable success resulting from this effort can be documented by an increased number of students completing school with the academic preparation, the career awareness, and the personal/social growth essential to choose from a wide range of substantial postsecondary options, including college (Education Trust, 1997).

Student Competencies

Expectations of student accomplishments or outcomes as a result of participating in a standards-based school counseling program are written in terms of student competencies. Student competencies support the goals of the *National Standards*, guide the development of strategies and

Table 3.2 *National Standards for School Counseling* Programs (ASCA, 1997)

Domain		Standard
Academic	A	Students will acquire the attitudes, knowledge, and skills contributing to effective learning in school and across the lifespan.
	B	Students will complete school with the academic preparation essential to choose from a wide range of substantial post-secondary options, including college.
	C	Students will understand the relationship of academics to the world of work and to life at home and in the community.
Career	A	Students will acquire the skills to investigate the world of work in relation to knowledge of self and to make informed career decisions.
	B	Students will employ strategies to achieve future career goals with success and satisfaction.
	C	Students will understand the relationship between personal qualities, education, training and the world of work.
Personal/ Social	A	Students will acquire the knowledge, attitudes and interpersonal skills to help them understand and respect self and others.
	B	Students will make decisions, set goals, and take necessary action to achieve goals.
	C	Students will understand safety and survival skills.

Note: From *Sharing the Vision: The National Standards for School Counseling*, Alexandria, VA: ASCA, 1997.

activities, and are the basis for assessing student growth and development. Competencies represent the specific knowledge, attitudes, and skills that students can acquire to support their academic, career, and personal/social success. The 122 ASCA student competencies are arranged in the three domain areas and provide the pathways to each, achieving the nine standards.

In addition to the concept of age appropriate and developmental needs, many sources influence the selection and formation of student competencies. State, district-level, and building-site comprehensive school counseling programs often include specific competencies or outcomes that are aligned with the school's or system's mission statement and the academic or curriculum standards, and are categorized according to elementary, middle, or secondary levels. Competencies that are identified through needs assessments and data analyses are pathways to documenting and demonstrating student growth and progress development to the achievement of the nine standards. School plans may identify the competency expectations by grade levels consistent with developmental expectations and local needs and priorities. The competencies are incorporated into a comprehensive, developmental school counseling program that emphasizes early intervention and prevention as well as responsive counseling services. Thus, they are delivered in the multitude of ways that school counselors provide services to students.

The ASCA National Standards and the student competencies provide a context for every student to acquire attitudes, knowledge, and skills. School counseling programs based on this framework advocate for a consistency in expectations for all students across all levels of education—elementary, middle, and high schools—and seek to close performance gaps among students from different economic classes, genders, races, or ethnic groups. Comprehensive national-standards-based school counseling programs seek to ensure that all students are served equitably and provide readily available data for assessing program equity and efficacy.

The Next Step: *The ASCA National Model*

With the continued progression of school improvement and standards-based education, the next logical progression was the development of the *ASCA National Model* (ASCA, 2003) to assist the field in delivering comprehensive school counseling programs. The concept of comprehensive programs was not new; first developed by Gysbers and Moore (1981), it has been continuously refined over the past 20 years (Gysbers & Henderson, 2000, 2001, 2002). The *ASCA National Model* (ASCA, 2003) integrated the work of Gysbers and Henderson (2000, 2001, 2002), C. D. Johnson & Johnson (2001), S. K. Johnson & Johnson (2005), and Myrick (2003), and added the content of the *National Standards* (ASCA, 1997) and the process of the *Transforming School Counseling Initiative* (Education Trust, 1999). The *ASCA National Model* has contemporized school counseling foundation and philosophy, management and delivery systems, and accountability, and has aligned the program with the expectations of 21st-century schools (Myrick, 2003).

An organizational structure emerged for the model that consisted of four quadrants: (a) Foundation and Philosophy, (b) Management, (c) Delivery, and (d) Accountability. The inside of the graphic shown in Figure 3.1 depicts the four interrelated quadrants that are the essential components of successful and effective comprehensive school counseling programs (ASCA, 2003). The *ASCA National Model* also facilitates the *new vision* of the transformed school counselor (House & Hayes, 2002; House, Martin, & Ward, 2002). The outside frame of Figure 3.1 represents the skills of leadership, advocacy, collaboration, and systemic change (Education Trust, 1997) needed to help every student succeed academically.

A brief summary of each quadrant follows.

1. The *Foundation* of the program describes the *what* of the program and discusses what every student should know and be able to do (ASCA, 2003, p. 22). The foundation of the program, based on the *National Standards*, highlights the importance of a mission statement and developing a proactive belief system to ensure that every student will benefit from the school counseling program.
2. *Delivery* monitors *how* the program will be implemented and defines the components of the comprehensive program—that is, guidance curriculum, individual planning with students, responsive services, and system support. The *ASCA National Model* details each of the components and offers examples and tools for implementation.
3. *Management* addresses the *when*, the *why*, and on what authority the program is delivered (ASCA, 2003, p. 22). This section also presents the organizational processes and tools needed to deliver a comprehensive school counseling program. The model presents sample agreements of responsibility, data application, and action plans. Time and task analysis tools are also presented.
4. *Accountability* answers the question: "How are students different as a result of the school counseling program?" The *ASCA National Model* encourages school counselors to demonstrate accountability by presenting the effectiveness of their work in measurable terms such as impact over time, performance evaluation, and undertaking a program audit.

Exploring Each Quadrant

The Foundation

The foundation of the program calls for school counselors to develop a proactive belief system that ensures that every student will benefit from the school counseling program. The vision and mission statements guide the development of an effective comprehensive school

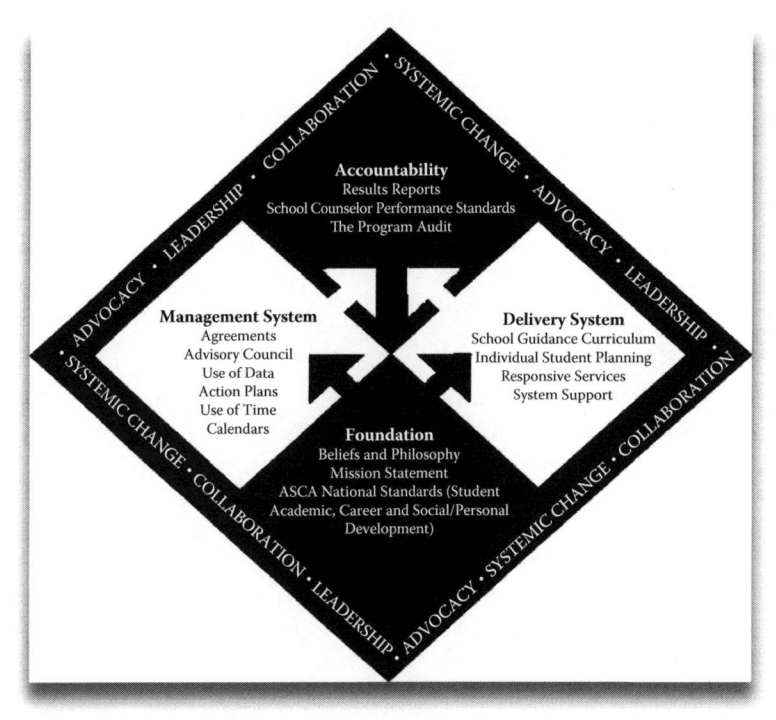

Figure 3.1 The ASCA National model.

counseling program while the *National Standards* and student competencies guide and support student development in academic, career, and personal/social domains. The foundation provides the basis for every student to benefit from a comprehensive school counseling program and serves as the solid ground upon which the rest of the program is built. Beliefs and philosophy are inextricably related to behaviors. What school counselors believe about students, families, colleagues, and community can strongly influence their approach to their work. The foundation addresses the *what* of the program, the content and beliefs about what every student should know and be able to do (ASCA, 2003, p. 22).

The Mission Statement The mission describes the purpose for the school counseling program, is aligned with the school's mission, and publicly commits the counselor's intent to provide every student with the skills needed to become lifelong learners and productive members of society. The mission statement promotes collaboration with colleagues to ensure that every student fully benefits from the educational opportunities offered in each school system. School counselors are reminded to align their work with their school's mission statement, which is a public proclamation about student success.

The ASCA National Standards: A Key Component of the Foundation The *ASCA National Standards* and competencies are an integral component of the *ASCA National Model*. The student competencies define the knowledge, attitudes, or skills students should obtain or demonstrate as a result of participating in a school counseling program. They clarify the relationship of school counseling to the educational system and they address the contributions of school counseling to student success. The foundation of the program, based on the *National Standards*, emphasizes the importance of having a mission, a vision, and a proactive belief system that ensures that every student will benefit from the school counseling program (ASCA, 2003).

The *National Standards* place student competencies first, move school counselors into the educational mainstream, and align school counseling programs with the academic disciplines (Dahir et al., 1998). The *National Standards* provide consistency in the description of school counseling programs and the services they provide. They are also a basis for assessing program quality. The information gained from the evaluation process tells what students have learned as a result of participating in a national-standards-based program. Measurable success demonstrates the effectiveness of a school counseling program. Collecting data, gathering information, and conducting research are critical to determine the success of a school counseling program. This empirical information provides the evidence to deliver a defined and accountable comprehensive program designed to help students be successful in school and in life.

The Delivery System

The delivery quadrant offers the methods for delivering an effective school counseling program. The scope of the program may differ across grade levels, thus the variation of delivery methodology is adjusted to meet developmental needs. For example, in elementary schools, the guidance curricula and group guidance activities are utilized more frequently than they are at the secondary level. Gysbers and Henderson (2000, 2002) offered a model for distributing the time allotment of each delivery component across grade levels. The challenge lies in the school counselor's ability to deliver a program that is balanced and blends the four delivery methods: (a) school counseling curriculum, (b) individual student planning, (c) responsive services, and (d) system support.

By carefully examining current practice and student needs revealed by school improvement data, school counselors can determine the amount of time they need to spend on each of the key areas:

1. school counseling curriculum (e.g., structured groups, classroom guidance, advisory programs);
2. individual planning with students (e.g., advising, assessment, placement, academic, career and personal/social goal setting, and follow up);
3. responsive services (e.g., individual and group counseling, consultation, and referral); and,
4. system support (e.g., program management, coordination of services, community outreach, and public relations).

Each of these delivery components has a significant purpose in the comprehensive school counseling program.

School Counseling Curriculum The school counseling curriculum is a sequential, standards-based instructional program designed to assist *all* students acquire, develop, and demonstrate competence in three content area domains: (a) academic, (b) career, and (c) personal/social development. The involvement of school faculty and administration is essential for effective and successful curriculum implementation. In most circumstances, the curriculum is intended to serve the largest number of students possible, and this is accomplished through large group meetings and classroom presentations. The curriculum gives attention to particular issues or areas of concern in the school building or district, such as eliminating bullying, resolving conflict, or raising aspirations.

Curriculum design requires building a scope and sequence, which helps to define and clarify the topics and competencies taught at each grade level and articulates what students should *know, understand,* and be able to *do* as a result of the curriculum. The curriculum can be delivered through classroom instruction in which *school counselors design, teach, and assess the impact of standards-based lessons and presentations* that meet the academic, career, and personal/social developmental needs of each student. It can also be delivered through *large group instructional activities and presentations* that convey information in a variety of ways by offering group activities, workshops, assemblies, and meetings to accommodate student needs and interests.

Individual Planning With Students Successful students learn to take ownership for their academic, career, and personal/social development. Individual student planning provides opportunities for students to plan, monitor, and evaluate their progress. Activities can include but are not limited to working with students to establish and monitor goals, develop a career plan, commit to behavioral goals, create an educational plan, and apply testing and assessment information to present and future plans. The planning process personalizes the educational experience and helps students develop a pathway to realize their dreams.

Individual student planning consists of ongoing, systematic activities that assist students with planning, managing, and monitoring their academic, personal/social, and career and employability goals. These activities are counselor directed and delivered on an individual or small-group basis. Each student is provided with the information, encouragement, and support needed to work toward his or her personal goals. Parents and/or guardians are frequently included in these activities.

Responsive Services When school counselors proactively address student-related concerns such as peer pressure, conflict resolution, family relationships, personal-identity issues, substance abuse, motivation, and achievement challenges, they deliver responsive services. Included in responsive services are interventions necessary to help students succeed, which include individual and group counseling, consultation, referrals to community agencies, crisis intervention and management, and prevention activities. The impetus for response and intervention can be dominated by crisis, school building and faculty concerns, parental trepidations, community concerns, and student requests. Responsive services can also proactively address concerns and prevent situations from occurring. Implementation strategies can include the following:

1. *Individual or small group counseling:* Counselors counsel students with identified needs/concerns or students who request counseling. This is an opportunity to discuss/clarify needs and guide therapeutic intervention. The school counselor must act ethically at all times in accordance with the ASCA Ethical Standards (ASCA, 2004) and with federal, state, and local laws and policies regarding confidentiality, suspected cases of abuse, and threats of harm or violence.
2. *Consultation:* Counselors work collaboratively with students, parents, teachers, and community members to develop a broad base of support and help for students.
3. *Referrals:* Counselors consult with and make referrals to community agencies to assist students facing personal crisis outside the scope of the school counseling program.
4. *Crisis counseling:* Counselors provide short-term prevention and intervention counseling and support to students and school staff dealing with crises.
5. *Crisis prevention* and *crisis management plans*: Specialized plans guide school prevention, intervention, and management of crisis response. Staff crisis training establishes readiness to meet student/school needs in emergency situations.
6. *Schoolwide prevention and intervention programs:* Counselors collaborate with all faculty, students, staff, and community-based organizations to expand responsive service outreach.
7. *Student support services team:* Counselors collaborate with school-based professionals such as the school psychologist or social worker to plan interventions for the academic, social, and emotional needs of students.

System Support School counselors, when engaged in system support, offer ongoing sustenance to the school environment by actively participating in school-based activities when delivering the comprehensive school counseling program. Involvement in system support sends a strong message to the faculty that the school counselors are committed to achieve the system's goals and mission. System support demonstrates the degree to which the school counseling program is aligned with the school district's priorities and with state and federal school improvement mandates.

System support usually consists of indirect services, which are not delivered directly to students. For example, chairing the school improvement team, coordinating student service volunteers, and facilitating the school peer mediation program are examples of proactive services that connect school counseling to the mission of the school. System support also provides school counselors with multiple opportunities to act as leaders and advocates by facilitating discussions around school improvement, examining data that may be impacting success of some groups of students, and assisting with professional development and in-service activities for the faculty. Indirect services including professional development to faculty, serving on school committees, coordinating safe school initiatives are essential to impact systemic change and support the "new vision" of transformed school counseling (Ripley, Erford, & Dahir, 2002).

The Management System

Effective programs require strong organization and effective management. The management component of the ASCA model addresses the *when* (action plan and calendar), the *why* (use of data), the *who* will implement (management agreement), and on what authority (management agreement and advisory council) the school counseling program is delivered. The *ASCA National Model* suggests the following key elements to manage the program.

Developing Management Agreements Management agreements are established annually between school counselors and the building administrator. The counselor(s) produce and present yearly a document that prioritizes school counseling, timelines, and the implementation plan. The principal then reviews the document and arrives at consensus with the school counselor as to how students, services, and activities are assigned. These decisions should be made based on site needs and data analysis. The agreement delineates counselor responsibilities, program implementation, and methods of accountability, and it offers a timeline for when these activities will occur.

When the principal and school counselors meet and agree on program priorities, implementation strategies, and the organization of the counseling department, the entire program runs more smoothly and is more likely to produce the desired results for students. Thus, the management agreement is a public statement to all stakeholders, and it demonstrates the commitment of school counselors and administrators to collaborate on an annual statement describing what the counselors hope to accomplish in the coming year.

Advisory Council An advisory council helps to solicit school and community support to inform the program's direction, to provide a sounding board for discussion about what is working and what needs to change, and to discuss the ways in which the comprehensive school counseling program can better support student success. An advisory council assists in the development of the school counseling program by annually reviewing program goals and results, and making recommendations for improvement. It provides a forum for open dialogue between schools and community and the perspective of community and parental expectations for the counseling program.

Council membership should reflect the community's diversity and can include school staff, parents, school board members, and student, business, and community representatives. Members selected must share an interest and enthusiasm for the school counseling program and representation could consider including the following stakeholders:

- Teachers
- Parents
- School counselors
- Administrators
- Community members (nonparent)
- Business/industry/labor leaders
- School board members
- Student(s)
- College (2- and 4-year) representatives
- Community-based organizations
- Counselor educators

Use of Data Monitoring student achievement data helps to ensure that all students have equity and access to a rigorous academic curriculum and identifies academic gaps. Counselors suggest systemic changes in policy and procedures to improve student performance. The use of data to effect change within the school system is integral to ensuring students' success. School counselors should be proficient in the collection, analysis, and interpretation of data, and they should monitor student progress through collection of three types of data:

1. Student achievement data, which can include standardized test scores, GPA, graduation rate, promotion/retention rates, and so forth;
2. School improvement data, which can include course enrollment patterns, discipline referrals, suspension rates, attendance rates, parent/guardian involvement, participation in extracurricular activities, and so forth; and
3. Student competency data, which can include percentage of students with a 4-year plan, percentage of students participating in job shadowing, and percentage of students achieving the competencies as determined by the faculty.

Action Plans Planning is necessary to detail annual program activities which show how the desired results will be achieved. Action plans usually contain

- Domain areas, national standards, and school improvement goals;
- Student competencies and descriptions of the activity;

- Curriculum/materials being used in the activity;
- Time lines;
- Methods of evaluation;
- Measurable outcomes;
- Person(s) responsible; and
- A description of the students involved.

Program Audit/Self-Study

An annual program audit or a self-study helps to determine the degree to which the school counseling program is being implemented and is in alignment with the ASCA model. Audit results provide information on the current state of the school counseling program, identify gaps and/or implementation challenges, and help the counselors plan for the following school year.

Use of Time Gysbers and Henderson (2000) offered specific recommendation for time distribution and suggested that school counselors spend 80% of their time in direct service to students and 20% of their time in indirect services and program management. While the amount of time counselors should spend delivering services in each component area may vary according to the individualized needs of each school, the ASCA has provided the recommendations shown in Table 3.3.

Calendars Calendars (district, departmental, and individual) are integral to maintaining a comprehensive counseling program because of the specificity in terms activities, actions, and events. An annual district calendar articulates the delivery of the various elements that comprise the program. Developed by the leaders of the district's school counseling program, the calendar allocates time for curriculum development, individual student planning, responsive and intervention services, and system support. When a calendar is developed and published, teachers, administrators, students, and families are aware of the scope and extensiveness of the activities of the school counseling program.

An annual school counseling department calendar follows the district calendar. The school counseling departments in each of the district's elementary, middle, and high schools construct calendars that align with the building calendar. This calendar is set up by month and by grade levels for the entire year for each school. Counselors list activities or themes to be delivered and specify how collaboration with school, district, family, and community stakeholders will occur. Yearly calendars also include quarterly grade reporting dates, state assessments, college entrance exams, orientation, graduation, as well as ongoing activities such as respect days, wellness days, career fairs, college expos, and other special events for students and their families.

Calendars ensure involvement. When stakeholders are aware of activities and services, the probability of becoming involved or participating increases. Calendars are also significant public relations tools and are public statements of the variety of services and activities offered both during the school day and in extended hours and/or weekends.

The management quadrant reminds us of the importance of organization and building a cadre of support for comprehensive school counseling. Although the program is coordinated by school counselors, many activities are shared by the entire staff and require a collaborative approach. These can include

- Planning and organizing tasks,
- Action plans around specific school issues,
- Organizing activities with teachers about program operation, and
- Publicizing activities and events.

The Accountability Quadrant

Accountability provides evidence of program accomplishments or student gains as a result of intentional efforts by the school counselors (Hart & Jacobi, 1992). School counselor accountability intentionally contributes to closing the achievement gap and meets the goals of school improvement.

Table 3.3 Sample Distribution of Total School Counselor Time Within the Delivery System Component*

Delivery System Component	Elementary School % of Time	Middle School % of Time	High School % of Time
Guidance Curriculum	35–45	25–35	15–25
Individual Student Planning	5–10	15–25	25–35
Responsive Services	30–40	30–40	25–35
System Support	10–15	10–15	15–20

* Adapted from Gysbers, N.C., & Henderson, P. (Eds.). (2000). *Developing and managing your school guidance program* (3rd ed.), Alexandria, VA: American Counseling Association.

School counselors are sometimes challenged to demonstrate the effectiveness of the school counseling program in measurable terms. The *ASCA National Model* (ASCA, 2003) encourages school counselors to collect and analyze data, use data-driven decision making, use evaluation methods that focus on student achievement, and contribute to the school and system improvement goals. By using their specialized training in group process, collaboration and teaming, and data analysis, school counselors demonstrate how the school counseling program moves school improvement data in a positive direction.

Using Data Data present the picture of the status of student needs and achievement issues and corroborate the development of practices that can lead students to higher levels of success. Data inform, confirm progress, and reveal shortcomings in student performance (Stone & Dahir, 2007). Annual school report cards publicize critical data elements such as attendance, demographics, graduation and postsecondary planning rates, and standardized testing results. These can be monitored and analyzed longitudinally and show how the work of school counselors impacts student achievement.

MEASURE-ing Success

MEASURE, a six-step accountability process, confirms the impact of the school counseling program on critical data, those elements of the school report card that are the backbone of the accountability movement. MEASURE supports the accountability component of the ASCA *National Model* (ASCA, 2003) and moves school counselors from a "counting tasks" system to aligning the school counseling program with standards-based reform (Stone & Dahir, 2007). MEASURE is a way of using information such as retention rates, test scores, and postsecondary going rates to develop specific strategies for connecting school counseling to the accountability agenda of today's schools. MEASURE is an acronym to help school counselors remember the following:

- *Mission:* Connect your program to the mission of your school and to the goals of your annual school improvement plan.
- *Elements:* Identify the critical data elements that are important to the internal and external stakeholders.
- *Analyze:* Carefully discuss which elements need to be aggregated or disaggregated and why.
- *Stakeholders-Unite:* Invite stakeholders to collaborate and address this school improvement issue and unite to develop strategies.
- *Results:* Reflect on your results; rethink and refine your strategies; refocus your efforts as needed.
- *Educate:* Show the positive impact the school counseling program has on student achievement and on the goals of your school's improvement plan.

MEASURE is a model of teaming and collaboration. It requires school counselors to work side by side with administrators, faculty, and stakeholders to identify and positively impact the critical data elements that are important barometers of student success (Dahir & Stone, 2003). MEASURE supports the accountability component of the ASCA *National Model* (ASCA, 2003) by helping school counselors move from a "counting tasks" system to aligning the school counseling program with standards-based reform. This process enables school counselors to demonstrate how they are accountable for results and contribute to student achievement.

Putting Theory Into Practice

During the 2004–2005 school year, a pilot project in New York City demonstrated that school counselors can use data to act on their belief system and assume a leadership role to identify and rectify issues that impact every student's ability to achieve at expected levels. The school counselors in three schools in Region 4 in Queens, New York, used MEASURE to initiate, develop, lead, and coordinate systems to improve the learning success for every student. The school counselors, working from an accountability perspective, contributed to key school improvement data and brought attention to student progress and results.

The school counselors identified a specific school improvement goal and analyzed the data that represented the issues surrounding that goal. As the school counselors aligned their services and activities to the issue, they shared accountability for student success with the administrators, faculty, staff, and students and contributed to the expectations of *No Child Left Behind* (USDE, 2001) and the accountability quadrant of the ASCA (2003) and New York State Models (New York State School Counselor Association, 2005). The baseline data was identified and disaggregated demographically. The results of three of the pilot school's projects are included in Table 3.4.

School counselors, working within an accountability framework, can challenge the pervasive belief that socioeconomic status and color determine a young person's ability to learn. Acting as agents of school and community change, school counselors can create a climate where access and support for quality and rigor is the norm (Lapan, 2005; Stone & Dahir, 2007). In doing so, underserved and underrepresented students now have a chance at acquiring the education skills necessary to fully participate in the 21st-century economy (S. Johnson, C. Johnson, & Downs, 2006; Stone & Martin, 2004). The *No Child Left Behind Act* (USDE, 2001) is a clear imperative for school counselors to accept the responsibility to support academic achievement, share the pressures of school accountability, and demonstrate advocacy for every student to experience success

Table 3.4 New York City School Counselor Accountability Project 2004–2005

School Site	Location	Student Population	School Improvement Data	Results
PS 229 Emanuel Kaplan Elementary School	Woodside	Caucasian/Non-Hispanic: 30.6% African American: 3.1% Hispanic: 38.7% Asian: 27.6% Free/Reduced lunch: 43.5% ESL: 19.0%	Increase the 4th grade English Language Arts test scores	Increased the number of students from level 2 (below standards) to level 3 (meets standards) by 8%
Long Island City High School 4100 students	Long Island City	Caucasian/Non-Hispanic: 15.9% African American: 15% Hispanic: 51.4% Asian: 17.7% Free/Reduced Lunch: 60.3% ESL: 15%	Improve the number of students achieving Regents diplomas	Increased the number of students achieving Regents diplomas by 5%
Newtown High School 4290 students	Elmhurst	Caucasian/Non-Hispanic: 8% African American: 6% Hispanic: 60% Asian: 26% Free/Reduced Lunch: 27% ESL: 40%	Improve attendance	Increase of 2% in average daily attendance

(Brigman & Campbell, 2003; Dahir & Stone, 2003; Gysbers, 2005; Stone & Dahir, 2006, 2007). With an accountable, data-driven school counseling program, school counselors are seen as powerful partners and collaborators in school improvement and most importantly, as proactively driving their own destiny (S. Johnson et al., 2006; Stone & Dahir, 2007).

Can school counseling continue to evolve with the times and openly examine paradigms and practices that forward the profession? The profession of school counseling has evolved in a very short period of time from a service driven approach to a systemic and programmatic model. *The National Standards* (ASCA, 1997), *Transforming School Counseling Initiative* (Education Trust, 1997), and the *ASCA National Model* (2005) have enabled school counselors to seize the present and forge a path to the future. School counselors now have a well designed approach to design, coordinate, implement, manage, deliver, and evaluate their programs. Leadership, advocacy, and systemic change are essential skills that ensure that school counselors can respond to the question, "How are students different as a result of what we do?"

No matter how comfortable the status quo or how difficult or uncomfortable change may be, every school counselor must work diligently to support every student's quest for success. The *ASCA National Model* (ASCA, 2003) has directed school counselors toward a unified, focused, and professional school counseling program with one vision and one voice.

REFERENCES

American School Counselor Association. (1994). *The school counselor's role in educational reform*. Alexandria, VA: Author.

American School Counselor Association. (1997). *Executive summary: The national standards for school counseling programs*. Alexandria, VA: Author.

American School Counselor Association. (2004). *Ethical standards for school counselors*. Retrieved September 8, 2005, from www.schoolcounselor.org

American School Counselor Association. (2005). *American school counselor association national model: A framework for school counseling programs* (2nd ed.). Alexandria, VA: Author.

Bowers, J., Hatch, T., & Schwallie-Giddis, P. (2001, September/October). The brain storm. *ASCA School Counselor, 42*, 17–18.

Boyer, E. L. (1988). Exploring the future: Seeking new challenges. *Journal of College Admissions, 118*, 2–8.

Brigman, G., & Campbell, C. (2003). Helping students improve academic achievement and school success behavior. *Professional School Counseling, 7*, 91–99.

Campbell, C., & Dahir, C. (1997). *Sharing the vision: The national standards for school counseling programs*. Alexandria, VA: American School Counselor Association.

Cunanan, E., & Maddy-Bernstein, C. (1994, August). *The role of the school counselor*. BRIEF v. 1, 1. Berkeley: National Center for Research in Vocational Education.

Dahir, C. (2001). The national standards for school counseling programs: Development and implementation. *Professional School Counseling, 4*(5), 320–327.

Dahir, C. (2004). Supporting a nation of learners: The development of the national standards for school counseling programs. *Journal of Counseling and Development, 82*(3), 344–353.

Dahir, C. A., Sheldon, C. B., & Valiga, M. J. (1998). *Vision into action: Implementing the national standards for school counseling programs.* Alexandria, VA: American School Counselor Association.

Dahir, C., & Stone, C. (2003). Accountability: A m.e.a.s.u.r.e. of the impact school counselors have on student achievement. *Professional School Counseling, 6*, 214–221.

Education Trust. (1997). *Working definition of school counseling.* Washington, DC: Author.

Education Trust. (1999). *Transforming school counseling.* Retrieved December 29, 2004, from http://www.edtrust.org/main/school_counseling.asp

Gysbers, N. C. (2005). Closing the implementation gap. *ASCA School Counselor, 42*, 37–41.

Gysbers, N. C., & Henderson, P. (2000). *Developing and managing your school guidance program* (3rd ed.). Alexandria, VA: American Counseling Association.

Gysbers, N. C., & Henderson, P. (2001). Comprehensive guidance and counseling programs: A rich history and a bright future. *Professional School Counseling, 4,* 246–256.

Gysbers, N. C., & Henderson, P. (2002). *Leading and managing comprehensive school guidance programs.* Greensboro, NC: ERIC/CASS Digest. (ERIC Document Reproduction Service No. ED462670)

Gysbers, N. C., & Moore, E. J. (1981). *Improving guidance programs.* Englewood Cliffs, NJ: Prentice-Hall.

Hart, P. & Jacobi, M. (1992). *Gatekeeper to advocate.* New York: College Board Press.

House, R. M., & Hayes, R. L. (2002). School counselors: Becoming key players in school reform. *Professional School Counseling, 5,* 249–256.

House, R. M., Martin, P. J., & Ward, C. C. (2002). Changing school counselor preparation: A critical need. In C. D. Johnson & S. K. Johnson (Eds.), *Building stronger school counseling programs: Bringing futuristic approaches into the present* (pp. 185–208). Austin, TX: Pro Ed.

Johnson, C. D., & Johnson, S. K. (2001). *Results-based student support programs: Leadership academy workbook.* San Juan Capistrano, CA: Professional Update.

Johnson, S., Johnson, C., & Downs, L. (2006). *Building a results-based student support program.* Boston, MA: Houghton Mifflin.

Johnson, S. K, & Johnson, C. D. (2003). Results-based guidance: A systems approach to student support programs. *Professional School Counseling, 6*, 180–184.

Lapan, R. (2005). Evaluating school counseling programs. In C. A. Sink (Ed.), *Contemporary school counseling: Theory, research, and practice* (pp. 257–293). Boston: Houghton Mifflin.

Lee, C. C., & Walz, G. R. (Eds.). (1998). *Social action: A mandate for counselors.* Alexandria, VA: American Counseling Association.

Myrick, R. D. (2003). *Developmental guidance and counseling: A practical handbook.* Minneapolis, MN: Educational Media Corporation.

National Commission on Excellence in Education. (1983). *A nation at risk: The imperative for educational reform.* Washington, DC: Author.

National Education Goals Panel. (1992). *Promises to keep.* Washington, DC: Author.

New York State School Counselor Association (2005). *The new york state model for comprehensive K-12 school counseling programs.* Albany, NY: Author.

Ripley, V., Erford, B., & Dahir, C. (2002) Planning and implementing a 21st century comprehensive, developmental professional school counseling program. In B. Erford (Ed.), *Transforming school counseling* (pp. 63–120). Columbus, OH: Merrill Prentice Hall.

Stone, C. (2005). *School counseling principles: Legal and ethical issues.* Alexandria, VA: American School Counselor Association.

Stone, C. & Dahir, C. (2006). *The transformed school counselor.* Boston, MA: Houghton Mifflin.

Stone, C., & Dahir, C. (2007). *School counselor accountability: A measure of student success* (2nd ed.). Upper Saddle River, NJ: Pearson Education.

Stone, C., & Martin, P. (2004). Data-driven decision makers. *ASCA School Counselor, 41*(3), 10–17.

U.S. Department of Education. (1990). *America 2000: An education strategy.* Washington, DC: Author.

U.S. Department of Education. (1994). *Goals 2000: The educate America act.* Washington, DC: Author.

U.S. Department of Education. (2001) *No child left behind act of 2001 (H.R.1).* Washington, DC: Author.

IV
STUDENT ACCOMPLISHMENT:
Equity and the School Counselor's Role

HARDIN L. K. COLEMAN
School of Education
University of Wisconsin–Madison

Introduction

Rarely does a child become accomplished on his or her own. For most of us, it takes a range of familial, school, and community support to be successful. Children from middle-class families are born with this support. Middle- and upper-class families are structured to prepare their children for school, to be available to the school for communication about the child, and to provide for the child those experiences (e.g., sports, music lessons, or sit down family dinners) that teach the social skills of school (e.g., delaying gratification, paying attention, deference to authority, and performance under pressure). The lower a family's economic status the more difficult it is to provide this support. As Wilson (1997) demonstrated, in low-income environments, particularly in urban areas where work is not available, children have fewer opportunities to see the behaviors that translate into school success. When adults are denied work opportunities, children are denied the opportunity to learn the social skills that lead to the work habits of a mainstream occupation.

It has always been the role of school to take children from their families to train them in the skills, knowledge, and attitudes that are necessary to be effective members of the community. In effect, schools have always been agents of enculturation. Within an increasingly diverse society, there are mounting challenges to this process of enculturation and challenges as to whether this should be the role of the school. Unfortunately, even as the role of the school to train children and parents in the social skills that lead to school success becomes more challenging, schools are cutting back on the staff members who are prepared to provide those trainings (e.g., school counselors and social workers) and emphasizing academic skill development in preparation for high-stakes tests. To succeed in this context, low-income and culturally diverse children need to develop personal skills and acquire social support systems that allow them to overcome the challenges to their success. In short, they need to be resilient. In our increasingly complex society, all children are coming to school with fewer social supports than they had a generation ago. With increased mobility, increased divorced rates, changing social roles, increasing disparities in wealth, and rapidly changing occupational choices, the demand for children to have the social competence to negotiate school has increased.

The central thesis of this chapter is that addressing this development of social competence should be the organizing principle for the school counselor who is committed to student accomplishment. As one reviews local, state, and competing national models of school counseling, it is apparent that a range of choices is provided for school counselors. Are they to focus on their role as consultant and systems change agent through a focus on data driven programming as promoted by the Transforming School Counseling Initiative (Education Trust, 1999)? Are they to focus on the tasks assigned by the principal as a function of the demands within the school or grade level? Are they to focus on developmental guidance, post-high-school planning, preventive services, parent involvement, truancy, bullying, or testing? These multiple responsibilities, obligations, and ranges of choices create tremendous variability in the manner in which school counseling programs are organized around the country and within districts. Some are organized around a model (e.g., the American School Counselor Association's [ASCA] model and the Transforming School Counseling Initiative [TSCI], as well as those of states or districts). Others are organized around certain types of programming, whether that is career focused or personal growth. Some are organized around the demands of a particular group (e.g., college applications in high-performance districts) or the demands of a context or principle (e.g., preparation for high-stakes testing). Still other programs are organized around the skills or predilections of the school counselor in the building. These confusions and variabilities challenge our ability to create a meaningful and accepted role for school counseling throughout PK–12 education. This challenge is part of what has driven the development of the *National Model* by ASCA and the TSCI by the Education Trust.

In this chapter, I will use what we know about minority student achievement to demonstrate the need to organize our thinking about school counseling around student outcomes. Minority students around the country are at risk for underperformance and failure in American public schools. It is my contention that many of the factors that put minority students' at risk are also factors that challenge the academic progress of all students. It is, therefore, important that the characteristics a student needs in order to overcome this risk status are—or should be—the focus of a systematic and developmental school counseling program. In this chapter, I will provide the justification for an outcome-oriented school counseling program around which the roles and tasks of a school counselor can be organized as appropriate to the particular needs of the context in which the program is being implemented.

To make this argument, I will present the various choices for organization that are available for school counselors. I will then present a process model for understanding student achievement that I will use to contextualize these choices. Using minority student achievement as the case example, I will propose a student outcome-oriented framework for implementing a systematic and developmental school counseling program. Prior to presenting this information, I want to define what I mean by the terms *accomplishment, achievement*, and *success*.

Although I will use these phrases interchangeably throughout the chapter, the important variable for me is accomplishment, which from my perspective includes achievement and is a predecessor of success. In the current conversations about schools, there is a huge focus on achievement, particularly as measured by academic performance. The minority student achievement gap is measured in the difference between groups on standardized academic tests such as the SAT or ACT. The effectiveness of a school and district is often measured by the percentage of children who go on to highly competitive colleges, which increasingly use grade point averages, challenging core academic courses, and standardized scores as their criteria for admissions. Obviously, academic proficiency is one measure of accomplishment; however, I think it is important that we consistently articulate that is it not the only useful measure.

Not every student is well served in a college preparatory curriculum. Not every student who participates in such a curriculum should be measured by his or her success in those subjects. The student who has significant accomplishments in the arts (instrumental, choral, or theatric) needs to be understood as having achieved success. The student who effectively organizes a service-learning experience, volunteers to work with the elderly, holds down a job, develops technical skills, comes to school every day, and makes it through classes in which he or she is not performing at a high level needs to be understood as accomplished and competent. When a school begins to focus on celebrating the many ways in which a student can be accomplished, they begin to create a culture in which many students can develop a sense of belonging and feel motivated to find a productive role as a citizen in a pluralistic society. From my perspective, this is the most important measure of success (see Lindwall & Coleman, chapter 24, this volume, for an in-depth discussion of the importance of creating a caring school community). As will be made clear in this chapter, I am advocating that school counselors take a leadership role in helping their students, colleagues, principals, parents, and communities to understand and act on the importance of focusing on what each child brings to the situation and what each child can gain from school, rather than applying an oppressive and outdated single model for success in school.

For me, therefore, accomplishment is developing the awareness, knowledge, and skills to become an effective citizen in a pluralistic society. What this accomplishment looks like will be incredibly diverse.

Organizational Choices

Since the history of school counseling and the development of the National Standards for School Counseling Programs are covered in other chapters, I will not repeat those discussions here. In this section, I will use this information to highlight the choices in models that school counselors have for developing a school counseling program. I will briefly outline the model promoted by the ASCA (2003), the *Transforming School Counseling Initiative* (Education Trust, 1999), and several other relevant models before proposing an integrative model.

The ASCA *National Model* is becoming the standard for organizing school counseling programs. The focus of this model is the acceptance of three standards for judging student outcomes from an effective school counseling program: (a) academic development (b) career development, and (c) personal/social development. The strength of this model is that it moves us away from the discussion about school counselors' skills to the outcomes we want for our students. The limitation of this model is its lack of specificity in either the behavioral representations of these outcomes, the school counselor's role in producing these outcomes, or how these outcomes will be assessed. Core to the standards movement in education (ASCA, 2003) is the proposition that the standards can be mastered and assessed. As the *National Standards* are more fully integrated into national practice, these limitations must be addressed in a systematic manner.

The TSCI, stimulated by the Education Trust (1999), is an alternate model upon which a school counseling program can be developed. In some ways, this model addresses one of the limitations of the ASCA model: A core principle of the TSCI is that programs should be data driven. One focus of this model is that a school counselor needs to be able to identify the data that supports his or her efforts in a particular area. The TSCI is deeply invested in the focus on helping students succeed in rigorous academic programs, with a particular interest in ensuring equitable access to these programs for culturally diverse students and changing the school systems to ensure the existence of a rigorous program and equity. The strengths of this model include the focus on equity, the use of data to inform practice, and the importance of system change. One central limitation to this model is that it accepts the notion—which does not have empirical support—that everyone can succeed in an academically focused program, and it seeks to judge the effectiveness of a school counseling program on this goal. As important as it is for school counselors to be sophisticated in their understanding of systems issues and participate in school reform, turning their focus away from a mental health and student-centered approach to an administrative-consultative focus may leave a broad group of students underserved.

One important issue to address here is the difference between academic achievement and accomplishment. The former assumes that the goal of school is to make sure that every student performs at a high level of achievement in his or her classes. This assumption facilitates the refocusing of a curriculum around the acquisition of content in core classes rather than the development of the whole person or addressing the needs of a diverse student population for which a college preparatory curriculum may not be universally appropriate. Such a school may not facilitate the type of connection and growth that will allow a student to explore her or his interpersonal self, artistic self, or mechanical self. A school that focuses on helping students to feel accomplished would be one that provides offerings to meet the diverse needs of students, including the academically talented, the artistically gifted, and the rest who are seeking to find a satisfying occupational role that may not be predicted by performance on an academically oriented test.

Process Model of Minority Student Achievement

Applying this conceptualization to minority student achievement means we need to focus on the conditions that contribute to minority student performance and the conditions of risk, and then identify situations when minority students overcome the high probability of failure. This process perspective views academic performance as an outcome. It is not random, and it is not purely a function of individual or group characteristics. Academic performance is predicted by a set of factors that, when manipulated, will produce different outcomes. The major reason to study this process model is to enhance our ability to effectively manipulate those factors in order to produce desirable outcomes. As Coleman (2007) has suggested, in this conceptualization (see Figure 4.1), three major categories of factors interact to predict minority student achievement: social stratification (e.g., class), contextual factors (e.g., parental involvement), and personal factors (e.g., social competence).

Social Stratification. The first category involves those factors that lead to social stratification within most societies, particularly those dominated by a capitalist economy (Bordieu, 1986). These factors are associated with the groups into which a person is born, which have, over time, regulated those group members to a particular status within a certain society that is reinforced by the values and practices of that society.

Social class. Within the United States, the reality of this process is readily apparent in educational outcomes. Performance, as measured by standardized tests, is predicted by a combination of social class status, with the poor underperforming the wealthy; racial/ethnic status, with those from historically disadvantaged groups—particularly students who have African, Latin, or Native American backgrounds—underperforming their European-descended peers; and gender, with girls historically underperforming boys, although this relationship is changing as a function of increased attention and change to policies and practices that have historically disadvantaged girls (Konstantinos & Wladina, 2003; Thernstrom & Thernstrom, 2003). Within the context of this paper, it is apparent that socioeconomic status can protect a child or put a child at risk. It is not poverty per se, however, that predicts academic performance, but the conditions of poverty that constrain the acquisition of the awareness, knowledge, and skills that lead to success in schools.

Gender. Gender is the next social stratification factor that has, historically, predicted academic performance. In many ways, this is an encouraging factor to acknowledge,

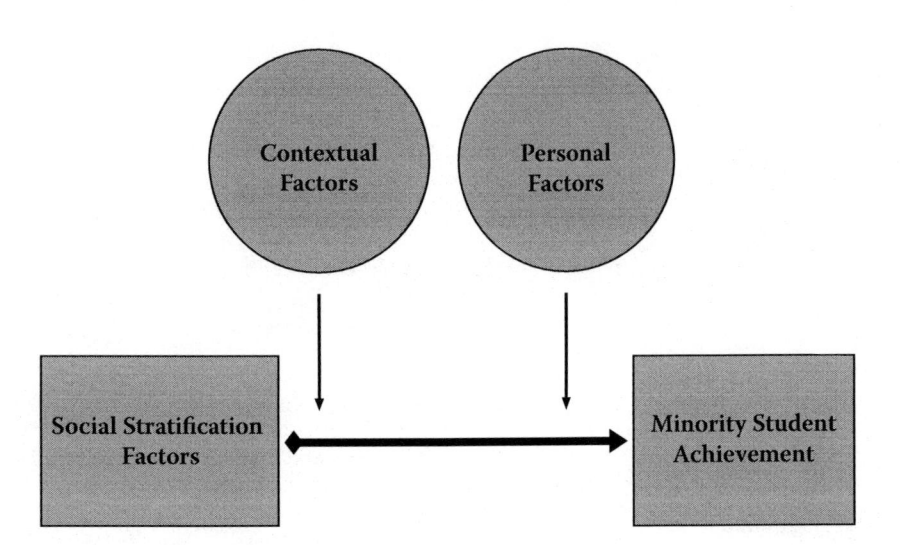

Figure 4.1 Process model of minority student achievement.

because with the changes in values, policies, and practices, the manner in which gender influences performance is changing. As Bleuer and Walz (2002) have found in an examination of national data, the gap between boys' and girls' academic performances is significantly reduced. This gives hope to the belief that the effects of these social stratification factors are malleable. In many ways, the manner in which gender influences academic performance is similar to the manner in which poverty has an impact, but it is also more complex.

Discrimination. Historical policies and practices of discrimination are the third social stratification factor that influences academic performance. How we, as a society, provide financial resources to schools is deeply reflective of our belief in replicating class structure. Allowing schools to be financed by the wealth of the community in which they reside also allows for this replication. A high-poverty area will not have the resources to meet its members' needs, while these resources may be available to a school in a wealthy community. Historical practices of racial discrimination in times of economic well-being (e.g., separate and unequal schools during the post-World-War-II boom) make it more difficult for members of those discriminated groups to take advantage of economic opportunities. They are more likely to be in poverty areas, which are more likely to have inadequate schools. Furthermore, those schools are less likely to send students to a quality postsecondary educational institution, which serves to keep the economic opportunities constrained. As such, a group stays within the lower reaches of the economic structure that reinforces an internal sense of possibility and the external ascriptions of competence. This process serves to maintain current forms of stratification. Changing this, therefore, requires extraordinary efforts at the individual, institutional, and societal levels.

Contextual Factors. Contextual factors interact with social stratification factors to influence minority student achievement. According to Brofenbrenner (1979), individuals develop within a complex weave of distal and proximal variables. He called those distal factors the "macrosystem," which involves a society's history, political, and economic structure (constitutions, federal government, religious traditions, or national media), and "exosystem," which includes the more immediate expressions of the macrosystem that have a direct impact on the functioning of a particular ecological niche (e.g., local government, school board, or employers). These elements influence the nature of the social stratification factors just described. More immediate to the development of a child is what Brofenbrenner called the "mesosystem," which encompasses the institutions and relationships that directly enculturated the child into the values and desired behaviors of their macrosystem. Four major elements historically make up a child's mesosystem: their (a) school, (b) family, (c) peers, and (d) institutions such as a church or similar community organization. These contextual factors influence minority student achievement. The stronger and more stable these factors are, the more likely it is that the student will overcome the social stratification factors that may predict his or her academic failure. Unfortunately, the higher the risk factors within the child's macrosystem, the more likely their mesosystem or context will negatively influence their school performance. Growing evidence suggests three contextual factors that have a direct influence on minority student achievement:

(a) parental involvement, (b) school and teacher quality, and (c) a caring and committed community, both within and outside of the school (Borman, Hewes, Overman, & Brown, 2003).

Parental involvement. There is evidence (Spera, 2005) that the more a parent attends to his or her child's academic progress, the better that child will do in school. This finding holds true across class, gender, and cultural lines (Bogenschneider, 1997; Jeynes, 2003). In order to be effectively involved in a child's schooling, the parent must (a) know where his or her child is on a regular basis, (b) provide the child with the space and materials he or she needs to do schoolwork, and (c) provide the structure and experiences that teachers expect a child to have prior to coming into the classroom. This often involves having the skills to effectively interact with school personnel to advocate for the needs of this child. As is readily apparent, having the resources to provide this attention will be a factor of the parent's class status. The more financial resources a parent has at his or her disposal, the better able the parent is to provide the stability and structure that correlates with good academic performance. The more a parent understands the culture of the school, the better able parent is to negotiate for the needs of their child. The less parents understand and know about the culture of the school, the more difficult it is to understand what the child needs or how to be his or her advocate. It, therefore, becomes more difficult to be involved. An important focus of an effective school counseling program with a focus on equity will be to develop strategies to increase parental involvement in the school and provide training in parenting techniques that facilitate student accomplishment.

School and teacher quality. Student performance is closely related to the quality of a school in terms of enriched curricular offerings, safety of the school, student/teacher ratio, and extracurricular activities (Borman et al., 2003; Borman & Rachuba, 2001; Griffith, 2003). Student performance is also closely related to the percentage of well-trained and experienced teachers on the staff of a school (Borman et al., 2003). In practice, well-trained and experienced teachers tend to gravitate to high quality schools in which they can spend more time engaged in the academic, rather than the social, development of students. Conversely, as a function of poverty and housing discrimination, minority students are more likely to be in schools that are overcrowded, have high mobility rates for both the students and teachers, and have teachers who are either inexperienced or underprepared to meet the diverse needs of an ethnically diverse school population with a high concentration of poverty. This interaction has a direct impact on constraining the academic performance of minority children.

Caring school and community. There is a growing body of evidence to show that schools that facilitate connections within classrooms (e.g., between faculty and students, and with the community at large) have better academic performance than schools that have not created this type of community (Karcher, 2005; Lindwall & Coleman, chapter 24, this volume). Schools possessing economic resources and cultural continuity between the school and the community in which it resides have an easier time creating an environment in which all children and parents believe they belong in the school and have shared expectations of performance. Unfortunately, too high a percentage of minority students do not attend this type of school, which serves to depress their academic performance in relationship to peers who attend schools with effective caring communities.

Personal Factors. Most sociological and education research has focused on the effect of social stratification and contextual factors on minority student achievement (e.g., Mehana & Reynolds, 2004). This evidence suggests, in a somewhat overwhelming manner, that these factors, external to the individual, are the primary predictors of performance, that to be poor, to be female, and to be an ethnic minority is to be at high risk for academic failure or underperformance. It is vitally important not to make the leap to suggest that this is an essentialist reality (Coleman, Norton, Miranda, & McCubbin, 2003). It is to suggest that the ecological contexts into which many ethnic minorities are socialized do not provide the awareness, knowledge, skills, and social resources necessary for them to be successful in American schools. It is also to suggest that ethnic minorities who are successful in schools have demonstrated resilience, as described earlier in this chapter. Given the probabilities, minorities who perform well in school have overcome significant risk factors and are, therefore, resilient. In order to increase the number of ethnic minorities who are resilient, we need to better understand the factors that contribute to this success.

To build resilience in minority students will require a multivariate approach, Figure 4.2. In order to truly change the process, economic and political strategies need to be employed to increase the economic opportunities of the poor and to eliminate the current effects of gender and racial discrimination. In addition, school reform efforts must successfully provide quality schools and teachers to all children across the country. In the meantime, we need to enhance the capability of individual minority students to overcome adversity in their lives. The first step in this process is to understand and address the personal factors that appear to help these students be resilient. Based on a review of the existing literature, those personal factors that are particularly relevant for minority students seem to

The Study of Resilience

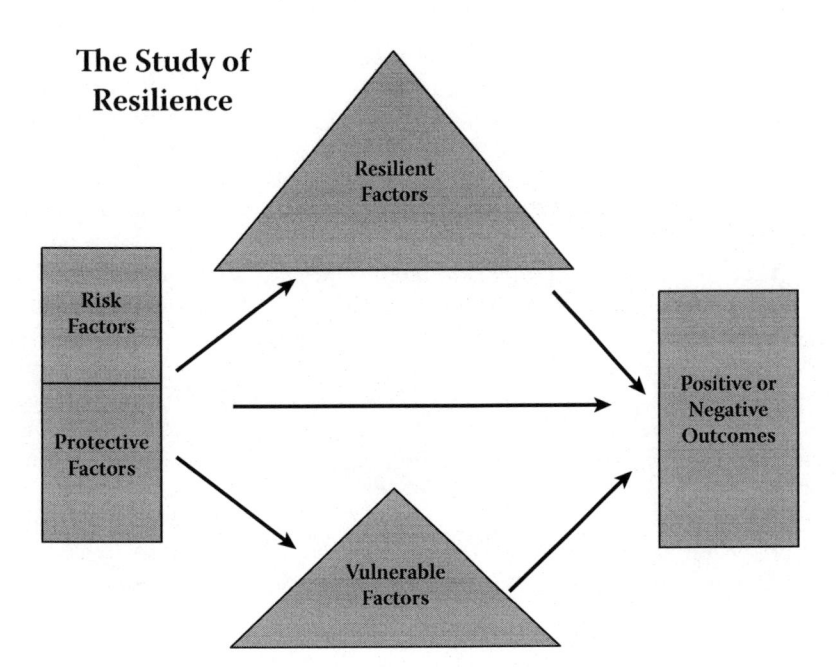

Figure 4.2 A resilience model of minority student achievement.

include intellective competence, social skills, cultural identity, and bicultural competence.

Intellective competence. The National Study Group for the Affirmative Development of Academic Ability (NSGADAA; 2004) has posited the concept of intellective competence rather than intelligence as a more useful way to think and talk about the skills an individual has that translate into academic success. They define intellective competence as

> systematic ways of reasoning, of inferring patterns from one's environment, and using them to maintain practices and to invent new ones; highly adaptive, rich habits of thinking; engagement in meaningful problem solving. Academic intellective competence is a highly specialized set of abilities that should be acquired as the result of particular kinds of experience over long periods of time in Western schooling. (p. 48)

The core thrust of this report is that the ability to perform well in an academic setting is not a function of biological endowment or other natural talent, but that this ability is something that can be acquired within the appropriate context. As stated above, being raised in a wealthy family and attending high-quality schools with high-quality teachers facilitate the acquisition of intellective competence, which leads to quality academic performance. The skills that are involved with intellective competence are presented in Table 4.1.

As the NSGADAA intended, this concept is appealing precisely because it identifies the range of skills, abilities, and dispositions that can be taught and that relate to academic performance. Although the report provides evidence of the validity of these dimensions and describes strategies that can be used in schools to develop these skills, abilities, and dispositions, it does not provide evidence that links the acquisition of these dimensions directly to academic performance. In this political period where the assessment of academic competence is becoming increasingly focused on the acquisition of content and performance on high stakes tests (U.S. Department of Education, 2001), this is a linkage that is important to demonstrate. Although the concept of intellective competence avoids the essentialist traps of intelligence testing as represented by Hernstein and Murray (1996), there is no evidence concerning the distribution of this competence across class, ethnic and racial, or gender groups. More research needs to be committed to this concept in order for us to understand its precise role in minority student achievement.

In theory, intellective competence could be a personal resilient factor. The more of this competence a poor minority student had in a low-quality school, the more likely he or she would be to outperform his or her peers. If this were the case, then strategies to enhance this competence would be a way to improve minority student achievement, which is the focus of the NSGADAA (2004) report. What is lacking is a reliable and valid measurement of this competence. McDermott (1999) has developed an approach to measuring intellective competence, but there are no stud-

Table 4.1 Skills, Abilities, and Dispositions of Intellective Competence (NSGADAA, 2004).

Skills	Abilities and Dispositions
Literacy and numeracy	Perceive critically
Mathematical and verbal reasoning	Explore widely
Creating, recognizing, and resolving relationships	Bring rational order to chaos
Problem solving from both abstract and concrete situations, as in deductive and inductive reasoning	Bring knowledge and techniques to bear on problem
	Test ideas against explicit and implicit assumptions
Sensitivity to multiple contexts and perspectives	Value and use empirical data
Skill in accessing and managing disparate bodies and chunks of information	Recognize and create relationships between concrete and abstract phenomena
Resource recognition and utilization	Channel ideas and energy into productive and pro-social activity
Self regulation	

ies to demonstrate its external validity. In lieu of such a measurement, attempts to measure the role of academic ability as a resilience factor need to be cautious about using measures that are culturally biased and dependent on the cultural competence of the assessor (Dana, 1996).

Social skills. In the literature related to resilience, there is an ongoing conversation about several elements in need of greater specification. In particular, literature that addresses risk and protective factors (e.g., Bogenschneider, 1996) or developmental assets (Search Institute, 2005) has a tendency to combine different levels of analysis. In terms of the framework in this chapter, they combine the social, contextual, and personal factors into the same level. In conversations about risk and protective factors or developmental assets, it is hypothesized that the sheer number of factors or assets predicts outcome without specifying which ones contribute more or in which way to outcome. One need in this area of research is to specify these relationships.

There are multiple ways in which scholars have discussed the manner in which social skills or social competence has a significant influence on the quality of outcomes in a child or adolescent's life. The core hypothesis in much of this literature is that the better a child's social skills, the more effectively he or she will be able to negotiate an ecological niche and reach developmental milestones. In many cases, social skills are seen as playing a central role in a child's emotional health and well-being, which also translates into positive academic performance (e.g., Parke & Welsh, 1998). The assumption in this chapter is that a social skill, applied in a situation of risk, is an individual resilience factor. One of the confusions in the resilience literature is the implication that these skills are somehow different than social skills are. An analysis of some of the theories concerning individual resilient and protective factors shows that social skills are protective factors that contribute to individual resilience.

This construction of resilience is powerful in its appeal about the character of children who are able to overcome conditions of risk. The conflation of attitudes and behaviors within each attribute makes it difficult to use it to guide scholarship in this area or to guide interventions (see Coleman et al., 2003, for an attempt to build such an intervention based on this model). Prior to using this model to guide a study of the relationship between personal factors of resilience and resilient outcomes, clarity needs to be drawn between which part of the relationship is a function of attitudes and which part is a function of skills or abilities. This important distinction should be consistently applied in the investigation of resilience.

Goleman (1995) has done an excellent job of describing the concept of emotional intelligence and how it can be considered a personal characteristic that, when used in situations of risk, could produce a resilient outcome. Table 4.2 is a summary of what he has identified as the characteristics of emotional intelligence: (a) emotional self-awareness, (b) managing emotions, (c) harnessing emotions productively, and (d) empathy, along with their behavioral correlates.

Goleman (1995) has suggested that the more emotional intelligence one has, the better able one is to accomplish developmentally appropriate tasks through the effective management of social relationships and of emotions.

Bogenschneider's (1996) work with risk and protective factors is typical of the field. As represented in Table 4.3, she has identified factors in the individual, peer group, family, school, and community that put an individual at risk for or protect an individual from negative personal outcomes. As mentioned earlier in this chapter, there is a continuum within a particular factor (e.g., family) from which behaviors indicate a condition of risk to which ones indicate a protective condition. This construction conflates the distinctions made here. For example, it describes that risk factors can be individual, family, or community without suggesting that a factor in one category may have more explanatory power than a factor in another. As presented earlier, social class status is a powerful explanatory factor in minority student achievement, certainly, in aggregate, more than an individual factor such as emotional intelligence. As we develop research and interventions on minority student achievement, addressing the differential impact of particular factors should be an important focus in the work. This paper advocates for a systematic analysis of the effect of each level on student performance.

Table 4.2 Characteristics of Emotional Intelligence (Goleman, 1995).

Characteristic	Descriptors
Emotional Self-Awareness	Improvement in recognizing and naming own emotions
	Better able to understand the causes of feelings
	Recognizing the difference between feelings and actions
Managing Emotions	Better frustration tolerance and anger management
	Fewer verbal put-downs, fights, classroom disruptions
	Better able to express anger appropriately, without fighting
	Fewer suspensions and expulsions
	Less aggressive or self-destructive behavior
	More positive feelings about self, school, and family
	Better at handling stress
Harnessing Emotions Productively	More responsible
	Better able to focus on the task at hand and pay attention
	Less impulsive, more self-control
	Improved scores on achievement tests
Empathy: Reading Emotions	Better able to take another person's perspective
	Improved empathy and sensitivity to others' feelings
	Better at listening to others
	Less loneliness and social anxiety

Cultural identity. Current research on minority student achievement indicates that an ethnic minority's sense of his or her cultural self may serve to facilitate his or her academic performance (Bass & Coleman, 1997; Chavous et al., 2003; Hrabowski, Maton, & Greif, 1998; Oyserman, Gant, & Ager, 1995). Within the resilience framework, the relevant hypothesis is that racial or ethnic identity is a personal factor that moderates between conditions of risk (social stratification and contextual factors) and desirable outcomes (e.g., high academic aspirations and efficacy; D. B. Miller, 1999). What limits investigation in this area are the challenges of defining the construct of racial or ethnic identity (Coleman et al., 2003) and of developing conceptually and psychometrically sound instruments to measure the construct.

When looking at individual factors that might explain the gap in minority student achievement, historically, it was presumed that differential academic orientation, ability, or motivation could explain underperformance in minority students. A bulk of recent research has refuted these claims, identifying that minority youth have similar or superior attitudes toward educational achievement, have attainment attitudes that in certain environments supersede peers in the majority group, believe that getting good grades is important, and work at the same level as peers (Arroyo & Zigler, 1995; Bok, 2003; Ferguson, 2002). In one of the largest studies of minority achievement, the Minority Student Achievement Network surveyed students in 15 school districts and found that the majority of students, regardless of ethnic membership, placed great value on academic success and reported essentially the same amount of homework time as students in the majority group, although rates of enrollment in higher level courses varied by ethnic group (Alson, 2003). These findings reveal that the gap for minority students cannot be explained by motivation or orientation hypotheses. In considering other factors, many authors have turned to internalized racism, stereotype threat, and ethnic identity as possible mechanisms that offer explanation for the minority achievement gap (Chavous et al., 2003; Oyserman et al., 1995; Steele & Aronson, 2000).

Bicultural competence. Gutter (2003), in an investigation of bicultural competence among successful African American women, provided an interesting finding concerning the relationship between cultural identity and behaviors that lead to success in a predominately White environment. The focus of Gutter's (2003) investigation was to test and extend LaFromboise, Coleman, and Gerton's (1993) theory of bicultural competence. This theory suggests that bicultural competence is a complex interaction between seven elements: (a) knowledge of both cultural groups, (b) positive attitudes toward both groups, (c) communication skills in both groups, (d) a role in both groups, (e) a support system in both groups, (f) bicultural efficacy, and (g) a sense of belonging in both groups. Fur-

Table 4.3 Risk and Protective Factors (Bogenschneider, 1996).

Primary Factor	Elements
Individual Risk Factors	Anti-social behavior
	Alienation or rebelliousness
	Favorable attitudes toward the problem behavior
Individual Protective Factors	Well-developed problem-solving skills and intellectual abilities
	Self-esteem, self-efficacy, personal responsibility
	Well-developed social and interpersonal skills
	Religious commitment
Family Risk Factors	Poor parental monitoring
	Distant, uninvolved, and inconsistent parenting
	Unclear family rules, expectations, and rewards
Family Protective Factors	A close relationship with at least one person
Peer Risk Factors	Association with peers engaged in similar behaviors
Peer Protective Factors	Truly intimate relationships
School Risk Factors	School transitions
	Academic failure
	Low commitment to school
School Protective Factors	Positive school experiences
Work Setting Risk Factors	Long work hours
	Stress of jobs
	Increased contact with older kids
	Increased financial autonomy
Work Setting Protective Factors	Required helpfulness
Community Risk Factors	Low socioeconomic status
	Complacent or permissive community laws and norms
	Low neighborhood attachment, community disorganization, and high mobility
	Media influences
Community Protective Factors	Belonging to a supportive community
	Bonding to family, school, and other social institutions

thermore, in a review of the literature on the psychological impact of being bicultural, these authors found that it had positive benefits and that a set of attitudes and skills makes up bicultural competence. They found that bicultural competence is the ability to effectively negotiate two cultures, either simultaneously or separately. They found that it has cognitive similarities to being bilingual, but that it was significantly more demanding at the affective level. What their review suggested, however, was that bicultural competence is a set of skills that may facilitate the ability for culturally diverse children to be successful in school. Furthermore, this suggests that being culturally competent in school is a factor in academic accomplishment, a construct relevant to all learners, regardless of race, class, or gender.

Gutter (2003) found that women who were successful in predominately White environments did demonstrate these dimensions of bicultural competence. Equally important is that the women in her study claimed that it was the strong sense of cultural identity—encouraged and developed by their families—that was the foundation upon which they based their efforts to become biculturally competent. Conversely, in an intervention to improve the academic performance of African American boys, Bass and Coleman (1997) found a different relationship. They created an intervention to enhance the cultural identity of these boys based on the Kwanza principles (see Coleman, Yang, & Kim, chapter 5, this volume, for more detail concerning this intervention). After 10 weeks, they found that the boys had an improved sense of cultural identity, but that their school performance had not improved. It was when the intervention focused on applying their positive sense of cultural self within a predominately White school, or on being bicultural, that their performance improved. Although the participants' positive sense of cultural identity improved during the first half of the intervention, once the intervention focused on how to apply that sense of self in school, their grades as well as teacher ratings on in-class behavior (e.g., being prepared to work and completing homework improved).

Based on these investigations, it can be hypothesized that bicultural competence is a resilient factor for ethnic minorities. The more competent they are in both cultures the better their personal (e.g., self-esteem) and social (e.g., academic performance) adjustment will be (Berry, 2003; Phinney, 2003). Specifying these effects is an important focus of future research.

Coleman's (2007) process model of minority student achievement, summarized in this chapter, suggests that intellective competence in one factor among many that leads to a positive outcome. There is substantive evidence that student accomplishment is as much a function of social stratification and contextual factors as it is a function of individual ability. Schools, as institutions, are structured to replicate existing social hierarchies that are becoming increasingly inequitable. Increasingly, a child's class and race are the characteristics that determine his or her academic and career opportunities. School counselors are in a unique position to implement practices that appear to build resilience in children and help them overcome barriers to success. These practices involve strategies to trigger institutional and individual change.

Implications for School Counseling

The balance of this chapter will focus on two areas. The first is to summarize the range of interventions that seem to work with minority students to help them overcome barriers to academic accomplishment. The second area will focus on the school counselor's role in implementing these practices for all students.

What works for minority students?

1. *Family/Parental involvement:* The more parents and family are involved in the life of a school, the better position they are in to help their child meet school expectations. Helping parents learn how to be involved in schools so that they can support their children is an important function of a school counseling program. Ideally, a strategy for facilitating school involvement by parents should be articulated throughout the K–12 classrooms in a district.
2. *Community involvement:* Effective schools have high levels of community involvement. In fact, schools become a focal point of a community. As Dryfoos (1994) has suggested, full-service schools that provide multiple services to the community enhance students' accomplishments. Communities that are involved in the needs of K–12 students also help with needed resources. As is noted in the literature on truancy, one of the effective strategies for reducing truancy is building a working relationship with the local community. For example, communities with after-school programs for youth or with structured alternative programs and a close relationship with truancy court have reduced truancy rates (U.S. Department of Education, 1996).
3. *Nonacademic opportunities for involvement and success:* The more students are availed the opportunity to have success within a school, the more they will value and participate within the core functions of a school. Not every student is motivated to focus on his or her academic responsibilities. When, however, they become involved in nonacademic opportunities within the school, from drama or music to sports or student council, students get to learn that school is a meaningful institution for them, which translates into academic performance.
4. *Quality teachers with a focus on accomplishment:* Ladson-Billings (1994) demonstrated that there is no such thing as a one-size-fits-all teacher. Her work shows that teachers who are deeply committed to the accomplishments of students are effective teachers with a diverse array of learners. It is the central assumption of this chapter and this *Handbook* that a quality school counselor is as important as a quality teacher in having an impact on minority students' achievements.
5. *Culturally competent teachers (counselors):* Ladson-Billings (1994) also demonstrated that being effective with one cultural group does not necessary mean one can be effective with all cultural groups. Being able to differentiate teaching or counseling services based on the context of a child's life allows teachers to effectively work with a culturally diverse array of students.
6. *Mastery learning:* Teachers who focus on the development of intellective competence and the mastery of context are more effective with a diverse array of students than teachers who teach to a theory of ability. Teachers, who focus on sharing content, rather than the mastery of that content, and who are therefore differentiating instruction, pace, and approach to help different learners master the content, facilitate student accomplishment.
7. *Respect:* Gregory (2006) has demonstrated that students are very responsive to levels of perceived respect. When students feel respected and cared for, they will actively engage in adult-mediated activities, such as school. If they feel judged and/or dismissed, they will actively disrupt the pro-

cess, even if such disruption leads to negative consequences.
8. *Being known:* Students who feel known by the adults in their environment are more likely to aspire to success in that context than students who have a sense of being anonymous. If students know that it means something to their teacher that they are there and engaged, it will mean something to the student to be there and be engaged. This can be accomplished by making sure there is an adult presence as spectators at events in which students get to demonstrate their competence from spoken word performance through school musicals and art exhibitions. Too often, the parents of the performers and the teacher who organizes the event are present, but other faculty and staff are not. It is also accomplished by knowing the names of students in the hall and talking with them, even if they are not in your class or on your roster. Being known can be accomplished by recognizing activities in which students are involved outside of school, or it can be as complex as expanding the recognition of student accomplishment outside of traditional areas such as academics or athletics.
9. *Facilitation of bicultural competence:* Negotiating multiple social contexts is difficult and taxing. Schools that help students learn and practice these skills are more effective than those that do not. Coleman, Yang, and Kim, chapter 35, in this *Handbook*, have addressed this process in more detail. The school counselor is in a unique position to help students think through how their membership in multiple cultural groups (e.g., culture of origin, culture of school, or culture of peers) affects their decision making concerning course selection, career goals, or even extracurricular activities. Gathering this information from individual students provides the school counselor an understanding of the manner in which a school may systematically disenfranchise—or include—students for involvement as a function of their cultural competence. For example, many schools that maintain an academic barrier to participation in school activities (e.g., drama or athletics) systematically exclude the students who may be in most need of being in an adult-mediated activity that will help them acquire the skills (e.g., self-regulation or communication) that are the foundation of academic accomplishment.

Many educators struggle with the paradox that programming for minority students may look very different from programming for majority students. They struggle with the concern that a different treatment may be an inequitable treatment. This struggle is embedded within the universalist conceit. This conceit starts with the premise that we are all the same or that the goal is to converge to some type of homogeneity. An alternate ideology draws evidence from the study of biology and economics, which demonstrate that difference adds value to a community. A differentiate economy and a diverse ecology are healthier are than those with high levels of homogeneity. For example, a cactus and Wandering Jew both need water, but it would be inequitable to give them the same amount of water. They would both fail to flourish if they were treated the same.

My core argument is that learning to effectively meet the needs of minority students within American public schools will lead the way to more effectively meeting the needs of all students in these schools. A tendency to value one type of student has led to increasing failure within the system. Learning to meet the needs of diverse students may lead to a flourishing system.

The school counselor can make a tremendous contribution to the development of a school that focuses on student accomplishment. It is important, however, that this contribution is guided not only by current practices, but also by a vision of how we can better serve students. Acceptance of the status quo, and our relatively low status within the current structure of schools, is to accept the many obstacles we face to providing quality counseling and guidance services to all students. To envision schools that allow us to prepare students to learn and facilitate their entry into their postsecondary lives is to find ways to truly transform our practice. Following are several dimensions of our role that are central to creating schools that focus on student accomplishment.

Caring communities. As Lindwall and Coleman (chapter 24, this volume) have suggested, school counselors have a vital role in creating the type of caring community in which all members feel they have a role and belong.

Focus on mastery of emotional intelligence. Being prepared to learn is a fundamental skill of accomplished students. Unfortunately, most developmental guidance lessons mirror traditional classrooms where the focus is on presenting the material at an appropriate developmental level and style, rather than mastery of the skill being taught (e.g., working in groups or managing conflict). School counselors can begin to model mastery learning with their teacher colleagues in three ways. The first is to implement curriculum that focuses on the master of emotional intelligence. The second is to collaborate with classroom teachers in the teaching and mastery of these skills. The third is to annually assess the level of emotional intelligence in the school and use this assessment data (analyzable by class, gender, and ethnicity) to acknowledge success and redesign curriculum to meet unmet needs.

Educator. School counselors regularly consult with their colleagues concerning student needs. It is important that school counselors are also involved in the training of their colleagues in their area of strengths.

Cultural competence. School counselor training programs across the country have integrated training in multicultural counseling into their curriculums. Teacher education programs have also addressed issues of multicultural education (Grant & Gillette, 2006; Ladson-Billings, 2005; Zeichner, 1992) within their curriculum. School counselors should have the skills to facilitate conversations about cultural diversity and equity within a school and train teachers in the skills to work effectively with diverse parents, children, and colleagues.

Interpersonal skills/negotiation. As Gregory (2006) has noted, effective teachers with diverse students may have effective interpersonal skills and the ability to negotiate conflict. School counselors have the skills to help train teachers in these skill areas. Microskills (Ivey & Ivey, 2003), motivational interviewing (W. R. Miller & Rollnick, 2002), and conflict resolution (Conflict Resolution Network, 2006) are all areas in which school counselors can lead professional development activities for their colleagues as a way of improving these colleagues' skills and establishing the school counselor as an effective consultant in these areas.

Interventions. Although school counselors have a primary commitment to positive youth development through effective developmental guidance programs, they also have the skills and responsibility to meet the needs of those who are not experiencing success within the school. This is particularly true when this progress is being impeded through institutional discrimination. School counselors, once they identify sources of inequity, can intervene at both the institutional and personal levels. It is important, for example, to have programs to facilitate cultural identity (e.g., positive images of self as a function of race or gender) for middle-school students, programs that help students who do not have access to precollege training or information, or programs that address the socioemotional aspects of truancy. School counselors need to be involved in the development, implementation, and evaluation of such programs. This is an excellent area in which they can collaborate with school counselor training programs to help develop and evaluate such programs and to provide practicum students to help with the running of such programs.

Data driven decision making. School counselors are facing a delicate balance between their commitment to direct service and the call for playing an administrative role within a school. Many calls for accountability within school counseling appear to ask the school counselor to become involved in the collection and analysis of student performance data. A different perspective is to suggest that school counselors become more proficient at applying social science principles to their work within schools. This does not mean becoming the administrator of the data process, but using social science skills to use the data to guide decisions within the school. This is most important when it comes to developing, implementing, and evaluating programming that addresses the inequitable effects of social stratification factors within modern American schools.

Conclusion

With an economy that has changed drastically in the past 50 years and a school system that looks and acts the same as it did in the 1950s, it is no wonder that there are areas of perceived failures in the school system. Over the next decade, schools will be radically reconfigured to meet the needs of a modern economy. This chapter highlights the importance of considering social stratification factors as we engage in this transformation and of encouraging school counselors to take a leadership role in ensuring that the central role that emotional intelligence plays in student accomplishment is recognized and integrated into the change. Specifically, school counselors are encouraged to use their social science and clinical training to develop, implement, and evaluate (a) training programs for their colleagues in cultural competence and interpersonal skills, and (b) training programs for their students in emotional intelligence, which has a demonstrable impact on student accomplishment.

Author's Note: This chapter integrates work and conversations that the author has had with Lali McCubbin, Romana Norton, Gina Miranda, Sara Karcher, Collette Bina, Shannon Casey-Cannon, Laura Fillingame, Amanda Sommerfeld, Jennifer Lindwall, William Hoyt, and multiple other students and colleagues with whom I have discussed these ideas in meetings, classrooms, and workshops.

References

Alson, A. (2003). The minority student achievement network. *Educational Leadership, 60,* 76–80.

American School Counselor Association. (2003). *American School Counselor Association National Model: A framework for school counseling programs.* Alexandria, VA: Author.

Arroyo, C. G., & Zigler, E. (1995). Racial identity, academic achievement, and the psychological well-being of economically disadvantaged adolescents. *Journal of Personality and Social Psychology, 69,* 903–914.

Bass, C., & Coleman, H. L. K. (1997). A culturally relevant group intervention with at-risk early adolescents. *Professional School Counselor, 1,* 48–51.

Berry, J. W. (2003). Conceptual approaches to acculturation. In K. M. Chun & P. O. Ball (Eds.), *Acculturation: Advances in theory, measurement, and applied research* (pp. 17–37). Washington, DC: American Psychological Association.

Bleuer, J. C., & Walz, G. R. (2002). *Are boys falling behind in academics? Part I. ERIC Digest.* Greensboro, NC: Clearinghouse on Counseling and Student Services.

Bogenschneider, K. (1996). An ecological risk/protective theory for building prevention programs, policies, and community capacity to support youth. *Family Relations, 45*(2), 127–138.

Bogenschneider, K. (1997). Parental involvement in adolescent schooling: A proximal process with transcontextual validity. *Journal of Marriage and the Family, 59*(3), 718–733.

Bok, D. (2003, October). Closing the nagging gap in minority achievement. *Chronicle of Higher Education,* 50.

Bordieu, P. (1986). The forms of capital. In J. Richardson (Ed.), *Handbook of theory and research for the sociology of education* (pp. 241–258). Westport, CT: Greenwood Press.

Borman, G. D., Hewes, G. M., Overman, L. T., & Brown, S. (2003). Comprehensive school reform and achievement: A meta-analysis. *Review of Educational Research, 73,* 125–203.

Borman, G. D., & Rachuba, L. T. (2001). *Academic success among poor and minority students: An analysis of competing models of school effects* (CRESPAR Report No. 52). Baltimore: John Hopkins University, Center for Research on the Education of Students at Risk.

Bronfenbrenner, U. (1979). *The ecology of human development.* Cambridge, MA: Harvard University Press.

Chavous, T. M., Bernat, D. H., Schmeelk-Cone, K., Caldwell, C. H., Kohn-Wood, L., & Zimmerman, M. A. (2003). Racial identity and academic attainment among African American adolescents. *Child Development, 74,* 1076–1090.

Coleman, H. L. K. (2007). Minority student achievement: A resilient outcome? In D. Zinga (Ed.), *Navigating multiculturalism: Negotiating change* (pp. 296–326). Newcastle, UK: Cambridge Scholars Press.

Coleman, H. L. K., Norton, R. A., Miranda, G. E., & McCubbin, L. D. (2003). Toward an ecological theory of cultural identity development. In D. B. Pope-Davis, H. L. K. Coleman, W. Liu, & R. Toperek (Eds.), *Handbook of multicultural competencies* (pp. 38–58). Thousand Oaks, CA: Sage.

Conflict Resolution Network. (2006). *HomePage.* Retrieved April 21, 2006, from http://www.crnhq.org/.

Dana, R. H. (1996). Culturally competent assessment practice in the United States. *Journal of Personality Assessment, 66*(3), 472–487.

Dryfoos, J. G. (1994). *Full-service schools: A revolution in health and social services for children, youth, and families.* San Francisco: Jossey-Bass.

Education Trust (1999). *Transforming school counseling.* Retrieved December 11, 2006, from http://www2.edtrust.org/EdTrust/Transforming+School+Counseling/main

Ferguson, M. P. (2002) Racial socialization of young Black children. In H. P. McAdoo (Ed.), *Black children: Social, educational, and parental environments* (2nd ed., pp. 57–72). Thousand Oaks, CA: Sage Publications, Inc, 2002.

Goleman, D. (1995). *Emotional intelligence.* New York: Bantam Books.

Grant, C. A., & Gillette, M. D. (2006). *Learning to teach everyone's children: Equity, empowerment, and education that is multicultural.* Belmont, CA: Thomson/Wadsworth.

Gregory, A. (2006). A window on the discipline gap: Defiance or cooperation in the high school classroom. *Dissertation Abstracts International Section A: Humanities and Social Sciences, 66*(8-A), 2831.

Griffith, J. (2003). A multilevel analysis of the relation of school learning and social environments to minority achievement in public elementary schools. *Elementary School Journal, 102,* 349–36.

Gutter, B. T. (2003). The construction and maintenance of bicultural competence: A phenomenological investigation and ecological perspective of african american women in the professions and executive management. *Dissertation Abstracts International: Section B: The Sciences and Engineering, 64*(5B), 2388.

Hernstein, R. J., & Murray, C. (1996). *The bell curve: Intelligence and class structure in American life.* New York: Simon & Schuster, 1996.

Hrabowski, F. A., Maton, K. I., & Greif, G. L. (1998). *Beating the odds: Raising academically successful African American males.* London: Oxford University Press.

Ivey, A. E., & Ivey, M. B. (2003). *Intentional interviewing and counseling with Infotrac: Facilitating client development in a multicultural society.* Belmont, CA: Thomson/Brooks/Cole.

Jeynes, W. H. (2003). A meta-analysis—The effects of parental involvement on minority children's academic achievement. *Education and Urban Society, 35*(2), 202–218.

Karcher, M. J. (2005). The effects of developmental mentoring and high school mentors' attendance on their younger mentees' self-esteem, social skills, and connectedness. *Psychology in the Schools, 42,* 65–77.

Konstantinos, A., & Wladina, A. (2003). The gender gap in science education. *Science Teacher, 70,* 30–33.

Ladson-Billings, G. (1994). *The dreamkeepers: Successful teachers of African American children.* San Francisco: Jossey-Bass Publishers.

LaFromboise, T. M., Coleman, H. L. K., & Gerton, J. (1993). Psychological impact of biculturalism: Evidence and theory. *Psychological Bulletin, 114*, 395–412.

Ladson-Billings, G. (2005). *Beyond the big house: African American educators on teacher education.* New York: Teacher College Press.

McDermott, P. A. (1999). National scales of differential learning behaviors among American children and adolescents. *School Psychology Review, 28*, 280–291.

Mehana M., & Reynolds A. J. (2004). School mobility and achievement: A meta-analysis. *Children and Youth Services Review, 26*(1), 93–119.

Miller, D. B. (1999). Racial socialization and racial identity: Can they promote resiliency for African American adolescents? *Adolescence, 34*, 493–501.

Miller, W. R., & Rollnick, S. (2002). *Motivational interviewing: Preparing people to change.* New York: Guilford Press.

National Study Group for the Affirmative Development of Academic Ability. (2004). *All students reaching the top: Strategies for closing academic achievement gaps.* Napierville, IL: Learning Point Associates.

Oyserman, D., Gant, L., & Ager, J. (1995). A socially contextualized model of African American identity: Possible selves and school persistence. *Journal of Personality & Social Psychology, 69*, 1216–1232.

Parke, R. D., & Welsh, M. P. (1998). Social relationships & academic success. *Trust for Educational Leadership, 28*(1), 32–34.

Phinney, J. S. (2003). Ethnic identity and acculturation. In K. M. Chun & P. Balls Organista (Eds.), *Acculturation: Advances in theory, measurement, and applied research* (pp. 63–81). Washington, DC: American Psychological Association.

Search Institute. (2005). *40 developmental assests.* Retrieved July 13, 2005, from http://www.search-institute.org/assets/forty.html.

Spencer, M. B., Noll, E., Stoltzfutz, J., & Halpalani, V. (2001). Identity and school adjustment: Revisiting the "acting White" assumption. *Educational Psychologist, 36*, 21–30.

Spera, C. (2005). A review of the relationship among parenting practices, parenting styles, and adolescent school achievement. *Educational Psychology Review, 17*(2), 120–146.

Steele, C. M., & Aronson, J. (2000). Stereotype threat and the intellectual test performance of African Americans, In C. Strangor (Ed.), *Stereotypes and prejudice: Essential readings (Key readings in social psychology)* (pp. 369–389). Philadelphia: Taylor and Francis.

Thernstrom, A, & Thernstrom, S. (2003). *No excuses: Closing the racial gap in learning.* New York: Simon & Schuster.

U.S. Department of Education (2001). *No child left behind act of 2001* (H.R.1). Washington, DC: Author.

U.S. Department of Education. (1996). *Manual to combat truancy.* Retrieved January 30, 2007, from http://www.ed.gov/pubs/Truancy/index.html

Wilson, W. J. (1997). *When work disappears: The world of the new urban poor.* New York: Vintage Books.

Zeichner, K. (1992). *Connecting genuine teacher development to the struggle for social justice.* East Lansing, MI: National Center for Research on Teacher Learning.

V
UNDERSTANDING YOURSELF AS A SCHOOL COUNSELOR

CHRISTINE J. YEH AND STEPHANIE T. PITUC
University of San Francisco

Most people would kill for the opportunity to seek a better life in America. My friends told me that Americans are so rich that money is strewn on the ground like garbage. A friend told me to stick gum on my shoe so I could pick up the money off the street without looking bad. Although I believed these myths, my life in a "good" American school was quite different. School was filled with racial problems. People of color did not understand each other and no one understood me. But everyone united in hating the Haitians. We were stereotyped as having bad hygiene, carriers of diseases, and people feared us because we practiced voodoo. People called me "HBO" for Haitian Body Odor. School was traumatic. I never had problems with who I was before because everyone in Haiti was the same as me. Now I had very negative feelings about who I was. I was constantly teased after school. I began to internalize the stereotypes and hate myself. The only way to survive was to speak and look like everyone else. I refused to talk or participate in class for fear someone would hear my accent. I had transformed from a very outgoing self-assured child in Haiti to a withdrawn depressed kid with a low self-esteem. I did not speak in public or admit I was Haiti until I went to college.

(quote from a Haitian immigrant student)

If you were a school counselor for this student, how would you address these problems? You might focus on the student's specific concerns, such as his "low self-esteem," "lack of confidence," or "depression." Many school-age immigrant youth, however, tend to keep their problems to themselves due to shame and embarrassment (e.g., Yeh et al., 2003; Yeh, Ma, et al., 2005). This student reported that he stayed quiet in class, tried hard to act and look like others, and did not even admit he is Haitian to himself anymore. In fact, due to cultural stigmas and racist encounters, a student may hide and internalize his feelings and experiences (D. W. Sue, 2001). As a school counselor, you might pathologize his experiences and attribute his withdrawn and quiet behavior in class to low academic performance, lack of interest in school, lack of effort and motivation, or depression, but there are multiple ways to understand the students we work with in schools. The purpose of this chapter is to recognize the important role that cultural values and worldview play when working with students. Specifically, as school counselors, we often fail to realize our own unconscious contributions to everyday interactions and to realize how our values and worldviews influence our interpretations of student experiences. In this chapter, we will pay particular attention to work with students of color and offer case examples to highlight our ideas. In addition, we will offer specific suggestions for how school counselors may explore their own biases, stereotypes, and assumptions.

In the past few decades, there have been, and will continue to be, dramatic changes in our society's demographics that will have a tremendous impact on the number of students of color and immigrants in our schools (Bemak & Chung, 2003). This increase in cultural and ethnic diversity has important implications for the field of school counseling (Sciarra, 2001). Counselors and educators need not only to be cognizant of the unique concerns of diverse students but also to recognize how their own cultural backgrounds and counselor–student interactions influence the school climate and students' psychological development. In fact, working with students of color must be viewed as a reciprocal process of growth and learning between counselor and student.

Worldview

Research and literature in the field of school counseling tends to focus on specific counseling and intervention techniques, skills, theoretical approaches, and strategies as well as particular student issues and concerns (e.g., eating disorders, violence, bullying), and with valid reason. School counselors must be informed and knowledgeable about the various problems facing our school-age children and youth. However, one of the most critical aspects to the process of counseling involves recognizing how our *own* cultural, personal, and educational background and experiences influences our interpretations, and subsequent understanding and management, of student development. For example, many years ago, when I (Christine) was one of a few students of color at a predominantly White K–12 school, I always thought that my own feelings of difference and isolation were my problem, not the students', teachers', or staffs' problems. Similar to the case of the Haitian student, I felt that if I just fit in and acted like everyone else, no one would notice how different I felt inside.

There is a quote by Anais Nin (as cited in Lewis, 2007) that states, "We don't see things as they are. We see them as we are." Specifically, our perception of reality is grounded in our own individual beliefs about the world and constructed by sociocultural interactions. *Worldview* refers to how a person sees the world (Ivey, Ivey, & Simek-Morgan, 1997), one's subjective reality (Ibrahim, 1985), or one's philosophy of life (D. Sue & Sue, 2003). According to Sodowsky and Johnson's (1994) review of culturally learned assumptions and values, worldview is associated with a person's relational, moral, spiritual, educational, economic, or political encounters. Worldview is also shaped by one's reference group, such racial or ethnic background, as well as one's geographic location and family system. Moreover, worldview has a strong grounding in cultural beliefs about knowledge, logic, and interpretation. Recent writings on worldview have expanded current definitions to include group identity, self-concept, language, and interpretations and perceptions of counseling (Dana, 1993).

Present understandings of worldview suggest that, for a given set of student behaviors, feelings, thoughts, and actions, there are many possible interpretations, many of which are culturally embedded. How a student describes his or her experiences in or outside of the classroom, and how a school counselor then makes meaning of these experiences, is largely based on the worldviews of both the school counselor and the student. Thus, when working with students of color, school counselors must learn to question their own assumptions, stereotypes, and biases. School counseling involves understanding not only students, but also yourself, your identity, where you come from, and how your education, family, social upbringing, class, and race and ethnicity—to name a few—shape who you are as a person.

In the case of the Haitian student, what are our assumptions when meeting someone from another country? How do media representations of and political relations with Haiti influence our impressions of this student? Although we may not be aware of it, any previous exposure to Haitian culture (especially negative stereotypes) may influence our assessment and evaluation of this student. Likewise, it was the student's belief that appearing different from others was a bad thing, perhaps because he came from a culture that emphasized homogeneity and collectivism (see Markus & Kitayama, 1991). Hence, according to the student's worldview, fitting in was a culturally and socially desirable way of coping with school racism.

A counselor's worldview is inextricably linked with his or her clinical intentions and actions (Ivey et al., 1997). However, many school counselors are not aware of their biases and assumptions, and their actions may contribute to an oppressive environment for students of color. Hence, increasing self-awareness of one's cultural values and worldview will allow school counselors to better understand their roles and participation in terms of individual, cultural, and institutional racism (for detailed definitions and discussion, see D. Sue & Sue, 2003).

Locus of Control and Locus of Responsibility

D. Sue and Sue (2003) described worldview as "how a person perceives his or her relationship to the world (nature, institutions, other people, etc.)" (p. 267). Further, "[N]ot only are worldviews composed of our attitudes, values, opinions, and concepts, but also they may affect how we think, define events, make decisions, and behave" (p. 268). If you have traveled, lived, and worked in a different culture or country, you know that members in various cultural settings perceive communication patterns, identity, relationships, and so forth, in a multitude of ways (Sodowsky & Johnson, 1994; D. Sue & Sue). As previously described, these cultural differences are referred to as cultural values or worldviews. Although the constructs of worldview and culture have been used interchangeably, *culture* refers to "the artifacts, achievements, and symbols of a people, and all of their actions and patterns of behavior" (Sodowsky & Johnson, 1994, p. 61). Thus, culture is observable and visible. In contrast, worldview is not directly communicated because it refers to an individual's relationship to the world (D. Sue & Sue) or one's assumptions and philosophy about how the world works (Ivey et al., 1997; Sire, 1976). An example of worldview that has been used to differentiate between White Americans and ethnic and racial minorities is *Locus of Control* (LOC) and *Locus of Responsibility* (LOR; D. Sue & Sue).

LOC refers to people's perception of how much they are able to control their situations and their surrounding context (Rotter, 1966, 1975; Sodowsky & Johnson, 1994). LOC is understood along a continuum with two dichotomous ends, external versus internal LOC. An *internal LOC* assumes that one believes one is in control of one's own experiences and environment. In contrast, *external LOC* entails perceiving control of one's life to be outside of oneself, such as due to religious/spiritual beliefs, nature, fate, chance, or contextual factors (e.g., geographical location, the school system, or society). As in the case of the Haitian student, his external LOC influenced his perception that his situation was shaped by his outside environment. Specifically, he felt that his behaviors, attitudes, and values were shaped by his geographic location and school setting. For example, he believed he was a different person when he was in the United States versus who he was in Haiti. In fact, research has shown that many ethnic minority groups, women, and people from lower socioeconomic statuses (for an excellent review, see D. Sue & Sue, 2003) tend to endorse an external versus internal LOC.

LOR refers to the amount of responsibility one attributes to successes and failures (Sodowsky & Johnson, 1994). LOR is also conceptualized along a continuum with two polar opposite ends. An *internal LOR* suggests that one attributes individual responsibility to achievements and weaknesses, and an *external LOR* is defined as perceiving responsibility to be within one's context, in others, or in the environment. In the case of the Haitian student, his external LOR attributed his poor performance in school to the school environment and context. In particular, he believed he was not doing well because of the racist climate in school.

It is fairly common in contemporary American society to value individual responsibility, accountability, and control. Idioms in the United States, such as "pull yourself up by your bootstraps" and "the squeaky wheel gets the grease," underscore the embedded assumption of autonomy and self-determination in our society and in our schools. These sayings refer to the importance of using individual efforts to improve your situation or to stand out in a crowd. If we apply these implicit cultural messages to the case of the Haitian student, a school counselor may interpret his withdrawn and quiet behavior through the lens of an internal LOR. According to this perspective, the student may be performing poorly due to lack of self-motivation, lack of initiative, and poor learning skills. All of these reasons hold the student *personally accountable* for his academic and social performance. Relatedly, an internal LOR in this case blames the student for his problems, and it assumes an internal LOC in which he is individually responsible for *changing* the situation.

There are numerous ways in which LOC and LOR impact our counseling across cultural groups (Roysicar-Sodowsky & Frey, 2003). Hence, it is imperative that we understand these tendencies in our worldview in order for us to bridge potential cultural gaps. For example, in our educational system, an overrepresentation of bilingual students is inappropriately referred to special education with "learning disabilities" (Ortiz & Maldonado-Colon, 1986). An internal LOR would attribute this overrepresentation in special education to the individual. Specifically, personal inadequacies, poor performance, low concentration, lack of motivation, and lack of effort would be used to explain why an individual is diagnosed as having a learning disability. One explanation may be that the individual is not applying himself or herself, not working hard enough, not born with the adequate tools to succeed, or not motivated by the course material. Hence, the blame or responsibility is placed on the individual, not on the system.

In contrast, using an external LOR, the overrepresentation of bilingual students who are referred to special education in the school system could be attributed to the context in which students of color must operate and learn (Locke & Parker, 1994). For example, rather than attribute blame to the individual, it would be important to consider aspects of the students' learning environment that contribute to a subsequent placement in special education (Ortiz & Maldonado-Colon, 1986). Alternative explanations include linguistic and cultural differences, experiences with racial discrimination, fewer educational opportunities, and biases in assessment procedures that place them at increased risk for diagnosis of a learning disability or behavioral disorder (Facundo, Nuttall, & Walton, 1994).

The answer may not be so clear-cut, and we need to consider that it may be a combination of both an internal and external LOC/LOR. For every student concern and issue that we encounter, there are multiple ways of approaching it based on differing worldviews. Part of being an effective multicultural school counselor is to understand our own tendencies in terms of LOC and LOR. Do we, as school counselors, have a tendency to look within the individual or to look at the system? Is our theoretical foundation and skills training based on an assumption of individualism? Research indicates that specific cultural groups may be oriented toward one approach over the other (see Locke & Parker, 1994). As discussed by Locke and Parker, a Native American student may have cultural values that dictate an external orientation. On the other hand, an overrepresentation of African Americans can live at or below the poverty level in the United States; their lower standard of living could be attributed to personal inadequacies *or* attributed to discrimination and lack of opportunities. Being aware of such biases and multiple interpretations will help us understand how our worldview may shape a student's experience in the school setting.

Even if we endorse an external LOR, a potential frustration is realizing how difficult it is to change our culturally diverse students' experiences with racism and discrimination. The reality is that we cannot change the system immediately. We can work toward that goal collaboratively, but most importantly, we can recognize the contexts in which our students function. The powerlessness we experience as school counselors in not being able to change the system is only a fraction of what our students must experience on a daily basis.

Assessment of Worldview

In multicultural counseling, assessment of your own and students' worldviews is a critical part of understanding the client's frame of reference (Carter, 1991; Ibrahim, Roysicar-Sodowsky, & Ohnishi, 2001). Some of the seminal conceptualizations of worldview by Ibrahim (1984) were influenced by the existential values model (C. K. Kluckhohn, 1951, 1956; F. R. Kluckhohn & Strodtbeck, 1961), and Ibrahim and Kahn (1987) created the Scale to Assess Worldview© (SAWV). According to research conducted by Sadlak and Ibrahim (1986, as cited in Ibrahim et al., 2001) and Cunningham-Warburton (1988, as cited in Ibrahim et al., 2001) using the SAWV, a shared frame of reference in worldview (e.g., common beliefs, values, and assumptions) contributed to successful engagement in counseling along with counselor effectiveness and self-efficacy. The SAWV has also been used to illustrate similarities and differences across various cultural groups (Ibrahim & Owen, 1994).

Cultural Values

Counselors who have not explored their worldviews and who continue to work with culturally diverse clients may be at risk for reinforcing cultural oppression (D. Sue & Sue, 2003). A critical aspect of understanding worldview relates to the value orientation model of worldviews (cultural values) by F. R. Kluckhohn and Strodtbeck (1961).

According to F. R. Kluckhohn and Strodtbeck (1961), basic values are core concepts that combine cognitive, conative, and affective elements. These elements are shaped by one's social and cultural setting and may be experienced and interpreted differentially across individuals. The notion of value orientations continues beyond basic values to include existential themes. Various cultural groups create cognitions, emotions, and tendencies from their beliefs about the world and life and form existential propositions (Carter & Helms, 1990; Yeh, Carter, & Pieterse, 2004). *Cultural value orientations* are thought to be culturally specific systems or perspectives for understanding the world. While there are inevitable within-group differences in cultural values, some homogeneity across cultural worldviews allows for direct empirical investigation and illustrates cultural values that are more general and that, to a certain degree, may be racially defined.

The F. R. Kluckhohn and Strodtbeck (1961) model of cultural value orientations may help school counselors to better understand their own, as well as their clients', worldviews and subsequent beliefs and interactions. Kluckhohn and Strodtbeck contended that individuals across races must address five common existential issues, each with three potential solutions or alternatives: (a) what is the character of human nature? (evil, mixed, or good); (b) what is the person–nature relationship? (subjugation, harmony, or mastery); (c) what is the proper temporal focus? (past, present, or future); (d) what is the proper manner of human activity? (being, being-in-becoming, or doing); and (e) what is the proper focus of social relations? (lineal, collateral, or individual). The answers to these questions determine and represent particular cultural value orientations.

Previous researchers have examined adaptations of the F. R. Kluckhohn and Strodtbeck (1961) model to explain how the value-orientation of a particular group may have unique patterns or value structures that may be understood independently of other racial groups (Carter & Helms, 1987; Carter & Parks, 1992). Moreover, D. Sue and Sue (2003) argued,

> Cultures differ also in their attitudes toward activity. In White culture, doing is valued over being, or even being-in-becoming. There is a strong belief that one's own worth is measured by task accomplishments. In White culture, statements such as "do something" indicate the positive value placed on action. Likewise, when someone is involved in being, it may be described as "hanging out" or "killing time." In most cases these represent pejorative statements. In counseling and therapy, the perceived "inaction" of a client who may adhere to a "being" orientation is usually associated with some form of personal inadequacy. (pp. 269–270)

The influence of cultural values cannot be separated from a school counselor's style of interaction and case conceptualizations. Several researchers and theorists have discussed at length how White cultural patterns of communication and conceptions of self are embedded in traditional counseling techniques (e.g., D. Sue & Sue; Yeh, Hunter, Madan-Bahel, Chiang, & Kwong, 2004; Yeh & Hwang, 1999). Specifically, many counseling techniques underscore the importance of direct, verbal, communication, and assertive problem solving as a means of coping and the importance of emotional catharsis as a means to alleviate psychological symptoms (Yeh, 2000). However, school counselors must be aware of indigenous and communal notions of health and healing (D. Sue & Sue, 2003; Yeh, Hunter, et al., 2004; Yeh & Hwang, 1999) and of how their own cultural and familial upbringing may shape their counseling interactions (D. Sue & Sue).

White Racial Identity

Racial identity theory is helpful in examining one's worldview and interactions with the others. Racial identity models describe patterns of thoughts, feelings, and behaviors associated with one's own race and that of the dominant White culture (Helms & Cook, 1999). In this chapter, we focus on White racial identity, as all too often, discussions about race focus on people of color, whereas White individuals may not consider themselves as racial beings and the implications of one's Whiteness (for a review of racial identity models for people of color, see Helms, 1995). In particular, if the school counselor is from the White, European-American majority culture, it would be necessary for him or her to understand his or her own White racial identity (see Helms & Cook). White racial identity development is the process of a White individual's understanding of him or herself as a racial being as well as his or her relationship with non-White individuals (Helms & Cook). Specifically, Helms asserted that most White individuals tend to believe that they are entitled to privileges, especially when they are socialized in an environment in which Whites are valued more in comparison with other racial groups. White individuals protect this privilege by rejecting their own racial status and denying attempts to threaten the racial status quo. As a result, developing a positive sense of self as a White person must entail realizing and abandoning the typical strategies Whites endorse in order to maintain their position in society (Helms & Cook).

White racial identity (Helms, 1995; Helms & Carter, 1990; Helms & Cook, 1999) involves the progression through a series of developmental statuses: contact (lack of consciousness of one's own race), disintegration (guilt and confusion regarding race), reintegration (White is considered to be superior), pseudoindependence (thinks about other groups racial problems and tries to help them acculturate, integrate, and fit in), immersion/emmersion (seeks to reeducate Whites about racism), and autonomy (able to identify White as not necessarily associated with being a racist).

In the case of the Haitian student, one might suggest that other students in the school context are in the contact status of White racial identity since they seem to lack an awareness of their own White status and seem to devalue that which is not White (in this case, being from Haiti). It would be particularly important in this situation for White counselors and teachers of the Haitian student to be aware of how the White students' racism, as well as their own racism, impacts their interactions with the Haitian student. Counselors who are at a higher level of White racial identity (e.g., immersion/emmersion and autonomy) might in fact seek to educate others about their own racist attitudes and behaviors toward the student and could incorporate counseling techniques and pedagogical practices that would exhibit antiracist beliefs and value cultural diversity. Depending upon the racial identity of the school counselor and that of the student, there may be predicted qualities of the counseling relationship and therapeutic process (see Carter, 1995; see Helms & Cook, 1999, regarding Helm's interactional model of racial identity in counseling dyads).

White Privilege

Related to White racial identity is the notion of White privilege (for in-depth discussion, see Neville, Worthington, & Spanierman, 2001), which refers to having unearned access to institutions (e.g., health care, housing, business, hospitals, schools), various settings (e.g., restaurants, neighborhoods, school districts, employment, credit, and tax benefits. It means that you are not discriminated against, and others assume you are intelligent, hardworking, and competent (Lazos Vargas, 1999) because you have White skin. McIntosh (1988) described White privilege as an "invisible package of unearned assets, which I can count on cashing in each day, but about which I was 'meant to remain oblivious'" (p. 10). McIntosh discussed these privileges as providing her with a sense of normality, of fitting in, and of being average. These assets also provided her with the necessary criteria to "[e]scape penalties or dangers which others suffer" (p. 11).

White privilege creates a system of race-based social benefits, rights, and opportunities that leads to a sense of entitlement as well as social and material advantages of White people (Neville et al., 2001). Neville and colleagues described White privilege as multidimensional and constructed on micro- and macrolevels. Microlevels focus on advantages that are observed at the individual and group level (e.g., a sense of entitlement to resources; p. 262). Whereas, macrolevel privileges are structural in nature and relate to having unearned entry, benefits, and immunities within various institutions (see the previously mentioned list). Neville and colleagues provided a list of such advantages including graduation from 4-year colleges, homeownership, health care, computer technology in schools, small class size, higher salaries, and so forth (p. 263; National Center for Education Statistics, 1997).

It seems that an essential aspect of working with students of color is being able to understand the role of White privilege in the school setting (as well as in other social systems in the student's life) and one's own White racial identity. On a related note, school counseling training programs should incorporate consideration of one's own experiences and participation with individual, institutional, and cultural racism. For example, how might the institutional racist structures of school (hierarchy of racial power, pedagogical decisions based on race, school activities, etc.) create and reinforce feelings of invisibility among students of color (Franklin, 1999; Yeh, 1999)?

It is critical for school counselors to be aware of their White privilege (if they are White) and/or aware of the dynamics associated with Whiteness at their school settings. White privilege cannot be separated from issues related to power. Moreover, White privilege provides a racial hierarchy in the school setting which normalizes and favors Whiteness, "[T]he sociocultural norms, values, modes of communication, and standard procedures that govern everyday life. . . . As a result, White privilege is institutionalized, based in White ethnocentric definitions of self and other, good and evil, right and wrong, and normal and abnormal" (Neville et al., 2001, p. 264).

Exploration of Whiteness is an often painful, emotional process that results in numerous types of emotional reactions. For example, some counselors (or counselor-trainees) may express feelings of guilt and shame (Neville et al., 2001; D. W. Sue, 2003; Thompson & Neville, 1999) as they discover their own privilege. Some counselors may feel angry that they are "made to feel bad about something they cannot control." They may wonder why people of color cannot "move on" from talking about race and just try to all get along. Oftentimes, this reaction is related to a misinterpretation of racism as a specific act (e.g., hate crime) versus a culturally embedded system of structures and norms. Other counselors may deny their own privilege as a way to consciously or unconsciously protect and maintain their benefits. And many counselors will experience all of the reactions listed previously. The exploration of Whiteness is a long process and cannot be oversimplified as an academic task. This deeply personal journey of discovery requires a constant evaluation of one's environment, relationships, interactions, behaviors, beliefs, values, and so forth.

Acculturation and Identity

When exploring White privilege and cultural norms, it is also important to recognize culturally informed ways of being that differ and conflict with the White majority. In addition to knowing about one's self (cultural self-awareness), school counselors must also be familiar with the cultural backgrounds and values of their students and how these backgrounds shape students' learning environment, relationships, communication patterns, and experiences. Oftentimes, students from varying cultural backgrounds must negotiate conflicting values from their culture of origin and values from the dominant culture (Roysicar-Sodowsky & Frey, 2003; Yeh, et al., 2003; Yeh, Ma, et al., 2005). Such cultural conflicts are most apparent as students of color try to negotiate contrasting learning styles and expectations (Yeh, Kim, Pituc, & Lee, 2005). School counselors must strive to be knowledgeable of such cultural differences and work with students to manage conflicting value systems.

To quote a ninth grade, Puerto Rican student,

> When I first came to America everything seemed so strange, the people, the clothes, the smells, the food, the music. My whole world was really messed up and confusing and I didn't know how to make sense of anything. Everything that I loved and everything that was familiar to me was now gone.

Students of color are a heteroegeneous group representing many different ethnic backgrounds, cultural histories, and varied levels of assimilation to American culture. Important aspects of understanding the experiences of students of color involve understanding their racial and ethnic identity development as well as their levels of acculturation. Knowledge about students' identities and acculturation informs counselor–student interactions and communication styles in the counseling relationship.

The construct of *acculturation* has been defined in numerous ways in the past several decades (Berry, 1980; Cuellar, Arnold, & Maldonado, 1995; Kim & Abreu, 2001). According to Berry (1989), acculturation is the process that individuals experience in response to shifting cultural settings. Acculturation strategies are techniques and skills individuals utilize in relating to a dominant society. Berry (1989) contended that there are four main acculturation strategies: (a) assimilation, (b) separation, (c) integration, and (d) marginalization.

Specifically, *assimilation* refers to when an acculturating student does not wish to keep his or her cultural identity and seeks regular interaction with the dominant culture. A student endorsing this strategy may deny his or her cultural background, may interact with only White students, and may idealize White culture and values. *Separation* refers to when a student chooses to hold onto his or her culture of origin, rather than participating actively in the dominant society. There is a desire to avoid interaction with others in the mainstream culture. Students utilizing this strategy may tend to keep to themselves and be quiet in classes. They may be reluctant to participate in group activities and discussions. They may also be reluctant to learn English and embrace styles of interaction that are more "American" (Berry, 1980, 1989).

Integration refers to an individual's interest in maintaining both his or her culture of origin and American culture. In this situation, some degree of cultural identity is maintained while actively participating and interacting in the larger dominant social network. Students who engage in this strategy may have friendships and interactional styles that reflect both the dominant culture as well as their cultures of origin.

Marginalization is a strategy that entails little or no interest in maintaining one's cultural identity and minimal interest in having relationships with others from the dominant culture (primarily rooted in experiences with discrimination). Students who use this strategy in many ways float from cultural contexts (i.e., American and their cultures of origin), and yet they do not feel as if they fit in with either. These students may feel alienated and alone and are often quiet and withdrawn in class. Although they may experience a tremendous amount of psychological conflict, they rarely express these feelings openly (Berry, 1980, 1989).

In the case of the Haitian student, his acculturation strategy was a combination of assimilation and marginalization. Due to numerous racist encounters, he denied his own cultural background and tried to look, speak, and act White as a means of survival. He believed that being and acting White was somehow better than acting and behaving Haitian; thus, he internalized the racist messages he was receiving. Although he attempted to assimilate, many people in the dominant culture continued to reject him based on his skin color, accent, and interactional styles. Rejected by White culture, and no longer fitting in with Haitian culture, the student was marginalized.

Such experiences with marginalization are not uncommon. In my experience at various school settings, one of the most frequent concerns that I encountered as a counselor with students of color was their perceptions that they did not fit in. Like the Haitian student, they were rejected by White students, as well as students from their own cultural backgrounds. In fact, being in a White-dominated school (or even a school with White norms and/or a primarily White staff and teachers) often alienates students of color from their own cultural community. Because of such marginalization, students of color may become depressed, alienated, and withdrawn.

When considering acculturation strategies, it is especially important to consider how the various strategies may impact student learning, behavior, presenting concerns, and interaction styles. In addition, it is also important to understand how, as a school counselor, you may misinterpret such strategies as deficiencies in academic abilities. For example, if a student is marginalized, he or she may feel inadequate, may sit apart from other students, and may not engage in class discussions. The student may also miss class due to depression or somatic complaints. The teachers and counselor of this student need to be careful not to misinterpret these reactions and behaviors as being academically grounded. The withdrawn behavior should not be seen as the student's inability to understand the material, and the lack of involvement and initiative in class discussions should not be viewed as representative of a learning disability.

Numerous factors can impact a student's level of acculturation or assimilation (Berry, 1980, 1989). In particular, level of schooling, employment, urbanization, popular culture, political participation, religion, language, daily customs, and social relations all need to be considered as essential contributing influences to how a student interacts with dominant society. Specifically, students are exposed to many of these factors in classrooms, curriculum, and peer relations in school. For the Haitian student, interpersonal interactions and classroom culture seemed to mandate that he assimilate in order to survive the largely White environment.

Acculturation and cultural adjustment can also be very emotionally and socially difficult and scary for students, and counselors need to be aware of possible negative reactions to being in a new cultural environment (Yeh et al., 2003; Yeh, Ma, et al., 2005). Two possible negative responses to acculturation are acculturative stress (Berry 1989; Bemak & Chung, 2003; Yeh, 2003) and culture shock (Lynch, 1992).

Acculturative stress refers to the stressors and stress behaviors that stem from the acculturation experience. Examples include mental health symptoms such as anxiety and depression, marginalization and alienation, psychosomatic symptoms, and identity conflict (Sodowsky & Lai, 1997; Yeh, 2003). *Culture shock* refers to a number of disorienting experiences that occur when an individual's basic values, beliefs, and patterns of behavior are challenged by culturally contrasting values, beliefs, and behaviors (Lynch, 1992). According to Lynch, negative responses to the acculturation process occur when (a) the typical strategies that the student uses to deal with problems, make decisions, and socially interact are no longer effective; (b) the student experiences an overpowering sense of uneasiness and discomfort with his or her new cultural setting; and (c) acculturative distress may be exhibited emotionally or physically with anger, depression, anxiety, or illness. When a student is experiencing such reactions, it is hard to engage in positive constructive strategies (p. 24).

Students who experience such negative reactions may withdraw from their peers and class or take numerous sick days from school. These reactions are important to consider when evaluating counselor–student and student–student interactions. Too frequently, poor academic performance and extended school absences are attributed to low student intelligence or achievement. Many school counselors have reported that they are referred students of color for "academic" counseling, only to discover that their situation was grounded in their negative experiences with acculturation and culture shock.

Understanding the process of acculturation is especially relevant when considering a student's sense of self. A particularly challenging aspect of acculturation is coming to terms with multiple cultural value systems (Yeh et al., 2003; Yeh, Ma, et al., 2005). Although students of color must negotiate various aspects of identity and self, an implicit expectation in their development is to express themselves in terms of coherent and stable identities (Yeh & Hwang, 2000). As we learned from the Haitian student, he did not feel comfortable identifying as both Haitian and American. He felt as if he needed to choose one identity in order to fit in.

The Multidimensionality of Ethnic Identity

To quote a 10th grade, Chinese-American girl,

> I do not know who I am. Am I the good Chinese daughter? Am I an American teenager? I always feel I am letting my parents down when I am with my friends because I act so American, but I also feel I will never really be American with my White friends. I never feel really comfortable with myself anymore because I have to act so many different ways all the time.

With students of color, ethnic identity or self should be understood as multidimensional (Phinney, 1996; Yeh & Huang, 1996) and dynamic (Yeh & Hwang, 2000). A student's ethnic identity is an evolving process that refers to individual shifts over time in identification, attitudes, values, and behavior through exposure to different cultures (Berry, Trimble, & Olmedo, 1986). Yeh and Huang asserted that ethnic identity may also be influenced by differing social, cultural, and educational contexts; family and peer relationships; and geography. In this chapter, we will only briefly touch upon the literature on ethnic identity and self as it relates to understanding worldviews and assumptions. For more detailed discussions of these issues, refer to the chapters in this *Handbook* by Casey-Cannon (chapter 9, this volume) and Coleman, Yang, and Cho Kim (chapter 35, this volume).

Yeh and Huang (1996) examined Asian American youth and discovered that ethnic identity development is strongly shaped by one's social setting and environment, such as geographic location, educational context, relationships, stereotypes, and racism. Yeh and Huang further contended that ethnic identity development theories should consider the situational specificity of self in collectivistic cultures. Current models of identity development assume that self is formed and influenced by internal processes rather than external factors. Cultural context is especially relevant for students of color who must constantly negotiate selves across various ethnic, racial, and cultural values, beliefs, and behaviors.

To fully comprehend the complexity and malleability of a student's ethnic identity, it is critical that counselors recognize how relational and cultural contexts contribute to one's sense of self. The literature on cultural notions of self describes how a culture's inclination toward independence or interdependence may shape identity. The independent self, which is representative of many Western cultures, may be described in part as a coherent, separate, and decontextualized entity containing specific dispositional attributes. According to Markus and Kitayama (1991),

> [A]chieving the cultural goal of independence requires construing oneself as an individual whose behavior is organized and made meaningful primarily by reference to one's own internal thoughts, feelings and actions, rather than by reference to the thoughts feelings and actions of others. (p. 226)

If we consider the quote at the beginning of this section from the Chinese-American girl, it seems apparent that it is not desirable in U.S. society to have more than one identity. She seems conflicted about who she is and how she should behave. Her confusion, however, may be rooted in an American emphasis on having a stable and coherent sense of self. A singular self is impossible to achieve for most culturally diverse youth because they must operate in many differing cultural systems.

As a counselor, do you value students who present strong, consistent voices and identities? What does this look like? For example, do you ask your clients "what are your preferences," "what do you want in life," or "how can you pursue what matters to you"? Do your counseling practices seem to emphasize forming and developing an independent and singular sense of self (e.g., "Do you feel more American or Chinese?")? Do you encourage multiple ways of being and interacting (e.g., "How can you nurture the various cultures you experience?")? See Yeh and Hwang (1999) for more detailed discussion and case analysis of working with clients with multiple and shifting cultural selves.

In the case of the Chinese-American girl, although she seemed confused about her different identities, she was, in fact, exhibiting the ability to negotiate differing self-systems and cultural values. Contrary to values emphasizing rigid individualism, such behavior is quite adaptive for students of color. Another way to consider how interdependent selves are manifested across cultural contexts is through the concept of bicultural competence (LaFramboise, Coleman, & Gerton, 1993). *Bicultural competence* is the integration of two cultures without feeling the tension between the two (Domanico, Crawford, & Wolfe, 1994). According to the alternation model of bicultural competence (LaFromboise et al.) an individual can adapt his or her behavior to a given social or cultural context without having to commit to a specific cultural identity. The ability to adjust across situational domains may include using different languages, as well as different problem-solving, coping, interpersonal, communication, and motivational styles of interaction (LaFromboise et al.). It would be important for a counselor to encourage her bicultural competence as a necessary aspect of being from a collectivistic culture.

Because most students of color do not fit into the dichotomous categories of interdependent or independent, cultural labels should not be conceptualized in stereotypical, polar terms. It is essential for counselors to be able to adapt and adjust to various aspects of students' multidimensional and shifting selves. As a school counselor, try to avoid pressuring students to pinpoint their beliefs, values, or styles of interactions. Instead, help them explore and recognize how varying cultural contexts influenced and shaped their ways of being a person. If appropriate, try also to encourage students to appreciate these dynamic aspects of their selves and not to feel pressure to choose only one cultural identity.

As in the case of the Haitian student, if he had encountered counselors and teachers who had created multicultural inclusive settings that encouraged Haitian as well as American aspects of his self, perhaps his experiences in school would have been more enriching. If his teachers and counselors had been more open to his culturally embedded styles of interaction and belief system, he may not have felt the pressure to deny his own cultural heritage. If his teachers and counselors were aware of their own assumptions and biases in working with students, perhaps he would not have internalized all of the discrimination he felt. Unfortunately, the case of the Haitian student is not unique, but increasingly more common.

Case Study: Amy

Amy is a 32-year-old, White, European-American (she states that her ethnic background is a "mix of British, Danish, Polish, and Russian") female, working as a school counselor at an urban high school. Amy grew up just outside of the city in a middle-class home, and Amy and her two siblings were raised by her mother (a teacher) and father (an accountant). Currently, she lives in the city with her husband and young daughter. Prior to her current job as a school counselor, Amy worked in both the for-profit sector in human resources and later in the administration of the school district where she currently works. Having found these previous work experiences personally unfulfilling, Amy decided to attend graduate school in order to become a school counselor.

Amy has been a school counselor at this high school for the past 2 years. The racially and ethnically diverse school's students primarily come from low-income, immigrant families, and 70% are placed in ESL classes their first years. The administration, teachers, and staff at the school, are predominantly White; there are only one Spanish-speaking counselor and a few Spanish-speaking teachers. In terms of performance, the school is currently on probation for not meeting the state's standards in math, science, and English/language arts. Historically, the school has also had a low-retention rate for African American males and growing truancy among Latino and Asian students.

Oftentimes, counselor education programs and the professional development literature focus on the characteristics of student populations, rather than examine the role of *counselors'* cultural values and worldview. The perceptions of and interactions between Amy and students may vary widely, dependent upon differences in cultural factors and life experiences. In this section, we explore aspects of school counselors' identities and worldviews in a case example and ask a number of questions that may be helpful in reflecting on how these might impact school counseling interactions.

To what extent has Amy examined her White identity and its effects on work with students? How aware is she of White privilege? Amy may be unaware of the powerful influence of Whiteness in her interactions with students. As race is socially constructed and largely based on phenotype (Carter, 1995), Amy's physical appearance (e.g., skin color, hair color and texture, and facial features) may represent various personal, societal, and historical symbols and evoke a wide range of emotions (Kiselica, 1999). For example, to a Black student whose own racial identity development exhibits rejection of White culture and a hypervigilance around issues of race (Helms, 1995), Amy may represent the oppressive White establishment. This student may react to her in a hostile or avoidant manner. Another Black student seeking to assimilate into and to be accepted by White culture may admire and look up to Amy; it is likely that their working alliance would look quite different from that of the previous student.

Amy's White privilege and her middle-class, American background also influence the development of her worldview and cultural values. As a White woman, Amy may assume a colorblind attitude, believing that all students face the same developmental and academic issues and can overcome any challenges through sheer self-determination. She may overlook the privileges afforded to her in her own experiences. For example, Amy's pursuit of a career in school counseling because of finding her previous work unfulfilling represents a set of privileges she possesses because of her socioeconomic status, education, and White racial status. Though well meaning and optimistic, such a worldview invalidates the very real effects of racism and discrimination for students of color.

More generally, how does Amy attribute student experiences with respect to LOC and LOR? The American value of individualism and the belief that anyone can overcome obstacles if one puts in enough effort represent internal attributions of LOC and LOR, which may obscure systemic, contextual forces at play in student adjustment and academic performance. The systems in which students exist profoundly influence their experiences and academic outcomes; school counselors must consider the students' family systems, the school environments, and the communities as possible factors in addition to internal attributions.

For example, Amy's perceptions of family and concomitant roles and obligations may be in direct conflict with the reality of students who come from more collectivistic cultures (Markus & Kitayama, 1991) and nontraditional families. In Latino families, for instance, relationships with extended family play a major role in one's life; a school counselor from a different culture may overlook the significance of these relationships. Similarly, low-income, immigrant families may expect their children to contribute to the families' incomes by working or acting as caretakers for younger siblings. A student in this situation may exhibit lack of focus in class or increased truancy. Perhaps due to her family's stable, middle-class status, Amy never had to work and her siblings were able to attend daycare while both of her parents worked. Because her worldview does not incorporate the same familial obligations as those of some of her students, Amy may advise these students to abandon those obligations and "stand up to their parents." Alternatively, she may overlook these contextual factors and assume that an individual's performance is due to a lack of motivation or aptitude. Both of these situations assume an internal LOC and LOR. The counselor must balance his or her expectations with the students' cultural norms and realities.

Another systemic factor school counselors should consider is the school environment. What kinds of resources are available? How culturally appropriate are the instructional methods and standards? Do the testing standards represent biased pedagogy or assessment methodology? Applying a strictly individualistic orientation to student issues would place the blame on the student and might overlook a number of barriers that exist in the school setting.

Student experiences should also be considered in light of the community and society. For example, is Amy attuned to the racial dynamics within the school and community? What are the community resources that might be of value to students such as community centers, churches, synagogues, or youth groups catering to different religious or cultural groups? What societal stereotypes, biases, or assumptions does she endorse? With the growing diversity in the United States, increasingly, more students' native languages are not English, and more students live in multilingual homes. How appropriate is a school's system for tracking ESL students? Some school counselors may assume that complete assimilation to English-speaking, American culture should be the goal of immigrants; however, it is imperative to validate students' cultures and provide opportunities for them to explore and take pride in their native cultures.

Amy should also be aware of her endorsement of stereotypes based on gender, race, ethnicity, disability, sexual orientation, and religion/spirituality. For example, Amy may not realize the homogeneity of Asian Americans, often confusing her Asian students with one another and saying, "They all look so similar!" This attitude may hinder authentic relationships with students and a lack of understanding of the variety of issues that face different Asian ethnic groups (e.g., those immigrants that are more recent, that are undocumented, or that have refugee status). She may also endorse the "model minority" stereotype, assuming that all Asians are intelligent, academically successful, and well adjusted. These types of assumptions are just as harmful as negative stereotypes about other racial and ethnic groups, as signs of distress may be overlooked if they are inconsistent with one's assumptions. School counselors may also underestimate students' abilities and resilience if they hold certain negative stereotypes (Coleman, 2007).

While Amy may have a certain degree of awareness about her personal beliefs and expectations of various reference groups, she must also consider what her worldview posits about basic existential issues. What are her expectations about the purpose of life? Amy's definitions of happiness and success in life will likely differ from some of her students' definitions due to their differences in cultural values and worldviews. White, American culture tends to value activity and productivity, while other cultures may emphasize the quality of life in terms of relationships with others, relationships with nature, or spirituality (F. R. Kluckhohn & Strodtbeck, 1961). How does Amy's view of social relations inform her work? What is her temporal orientation, and how does this influence her work with students? For example, the stereotypical American orientation to the future (F. R. Kluckhohn & Strodtbeck) may influence a school counselor to focus his or her work with students on long-term academic and career goals. However, this may be inappropriate for cultures more oriented toward the present; these students may seek more immediate coping strategies and solutions. Exploration of these larger questions about life and orientation to the world will help the school counselor recognize his or her tendencies and, consequently, recognize and adapt to the preferences of his or her students.

Implications for School Counselor Training

In order to effectively work with students of color, school counselors must understand their own worldviews, cultural values, identities, and White privilege. In particular, one's worldview or LOC and LOR may contribute to one's own interpretation of student concerns and issues. School counselor knowledge and self-awareness is especially influenced by one's understanding of issues concerning acculturation, identity development, and self-making.

The issues raised in this chapter lend themselves to many important implications for school counselor education and training. Specifically, counselor education programs need to address the importance of self-awareness, emotional growth, and introspective development. Because interpretations and interactions associated with school counseling techniques are constructed individually, socially, and culturally, the subjectivity of school counselors' worldviews plays a critical role in school environments. School counselor training should also include critical discussions of individual, institutional, and cultural racism and how counselors' racial identity statuses may contribute to racist counseling interventions.

Pedersen (1994) suggested that (a) cultural knowledge may be gained from an understanding of the institutional barriers in the educational system and in other sociopolitical systems that impact students of color; (b) counselors should have and pursue specific knowledge and information (e.g., history, lifestyles, role of education, socioeconomic background, preferred values, typical behaviors, inherited customs, slang, learning styles, and ways of thinking) about particular cultural groups and teach and share this knowledge with others; and (c) counselors should have information about teaching/learning resources about other cultures and be able to access those resources.

Clearly, it is unrealistic for a school counselor to obtain knowledge about every single student's cultural background. However, school counselors should make every effort not only to learn specific knowledge about students' cultural backgrounds but also to be able to integrate this knowledge into the counseling interactions. For example, it would be important for counselors to ask themselves, "Whose values are reflected in my assumptions about human development and in my counseling techniques?" In terms of knowledge, counselors also need to be cognizant of vast within-group cultural differences and avoid perpetuating stereotypes about groups. Knowledge also extends far beyond historical facts and customs and must include worldviews, perspectives of self, and histories of oppression.

Next Steps for School Counselor Development

As you read the other chapters in this book, which address a wide variety of topics, consider the cultural framework and worldview from which you understand these issues. Furthermore, we cannot emphasize enough that this type of self-exploration and acquisition of knowledge about alternative worldviews is an ongoing process. The following is a list of resources and readings to further enhance school counselor exploration; these should serve as just the starting point for a lifelong journey of reflection and growth.

Further Reading

Carter, R. T. (1995). *The influence of race and racial identity in psychotherapy: Toward a racially-inclusive model.* Westport, CT: John Wiley & Sons.

Helms, J. E. (1992). *A race is a nice thing to have: A guide to being a White person or understanding the White persons in your life.* Topeka, KS: Content Communications.

Helms, J. E., & Cook, D. A. (1999). *Using race and culture in counseling and psychotherapy: Theory and process.* Boston: Allyn & Bacon.

Kiselica, M. S. (1999). Confronting my own ethnocentricism and racism: A process of pain and growth. *Journal of Counseling & Development, 77*(1), 14–17.

Pedersen, P. B., & Carey, J. C. (Eds.). *Multicultural counseling in schools.* Boston: Allyn & Bacon.

Ponterotto, J. G., Casas, J. M., Suzuki, L. A., & Alexander, C. M. (2001). *Handbook of multicultural counseling* (2nd ed.). Thousand Oaks, CA: Sage.

Raheim, S., White, C., Denborough, D., Waldegrave C., Tamasese, K., Tuhaka, F., et al. (n.d.) *An invitation to narrative practitioners to address privilege and dominance.* Retrieved Octobere 5, 2007, from http://www.dulwichcentre.com.au/privilege.hm

Stewart, E. C., & Bennett, M. J. (1991). *American cultural patterns: A cross-cultural perspective* (Rev. ed.). Yarmouth, ME: Intercultural Press.

Sue, D., & Sue, D. W. (2003). *Counseling the culturally diverse: Theory and practice* (5th ed.). New York: Wiley.

References

Bemak, F., & Chung, R. C.-Y. (2003). Multicultural counseling with immigrant students in schools. In P. Pederson & J. Carey (Eds.), *Multicultural counseling in schools: A practical handbook* (2nd ed., pp. 61–83). Boston: Allyn & Bacon.

Berry, J., Trimble, J., & Olmedo, E. (1986). Assessment of acculturation. In W. Lonner & J. Berry (Eds.), *Field methods in cross-cultural research* (pp. 291–324). Newbury Park, CA: Sage.

Berry, J. W. (1980). Acculturation as varieties of adaptation. In A. M. Padilla (Ed.), *Acculturation: Theory, models, and some new findings* (pp. 9–25). Boulder, CO: Westview.

Berry, J. W. (1989). Psychology of acculturation. *Nebraska Symposium Motivation, 37,* 201–234.

Carter, R. T. (1991). Cultural values: A review of empirical research and implications for counseling. *Journal of Counseling and Development, 70,* 361–369.

Carter, R. T. (1995). *The influence of race and racial identity in psychotherapy: Toward a racially inclusive model.* Westport, CT: John Wiley & Sons.

Carter, R. T., & Helms, J. E. (1987). The relationship of black value-orientations to racial identity attitudes. *Measurement and Evaluation in Counseling and Development, 19,* 185-195.

Carter, R. T., & Helms, J. E. (1990). White racial identity attitudes and cultural values. In J. E. Helms (Ed.), *Black and White racial identity attitudes: Theory, research and practice* (pp. 105–118). Westport, CT: Greenwood Press.

Carter, R. T., & Parks, E. E. (1992). White ethnic group membership and cultural value preferences. *Journal of College Student Development, 33,* 499–506.

Coleman, H. L. K. (2007). Minority student achievement: A resilient outcome? In D. Zinga (Ed.), *Navigating multiculturalism negotiating change.* Newcastle, UK: Cambridge Scholars Press.

Cuellar, I., Arnold, B., & Maldonado, R. (1995). Acculturation Rating Scale for Mexican-Americans-II: A revision of the original ARSMA scale. *Hispanic Journal of Behavioral Sciences, 17,* 275–304.

Dana, R. H. (1993). *Multicultural assessment perspectives for professional psychology.* Boston: Allyn & Bacon.

Domanico, Y. B., Crawford, I., & Wolfe, A. S. (1994). Ethnic identity and self-concept in Mexican-American adolescents: Is bicultural identity related to stress or better adjustment? *Child and Youth Care Forum, 23*(3), 197–207.

Facundo, A., Nuttall, E. V., & Walton, J. (1994). Culturally sensitive assessment in schools. In P. S. Pedersen & J. C. Carey (Eds.), *Multicultural counseling in schools* (pp. 207–224). Boston: Allyn & Bacon.

Franklin, A. J. (1999). Invisibility syndrome and racial identity development in psychotherapy and counseling African American men. *The Counseling Psychologist, 27*(6), 761–93.

Helms, J. E. (1992). *A race is a nice thing to have: A guide to being a White person or understanding the White persons in your life.* Topeka, KS: Content Communications.

Helms, J. E. (1995). An update of Helms's White and people of color racial identity models. In J. G. Ponterotto, J. M. Casas, L. A. Suzuki, & C. M. Alexander (Eds.), *Handbook of multicultural counseling* (pp. 181–191). Thousand Oaks, CA: Sage.

Helms, J. E., & Carter, R. T. (1990). Development of the White racial identity attitude inventory. In J. E. Helms (Ed.), *Black and White racial identity: Theory, research, and practice* (pp. 105–118). New York: Greenwood Press.

Helms, J. E., & Cook, D. A. (1999). *Using race and culture in counseling and psychotherapy: Theory and process.* Boston: Allyn & Bacon.

Ibrahim, F. A. (1984). Cross-cultural counseling and psychotherapy: An existential-psychological perspective. *International Journal for the Advancement of Counseling, 7,* 159–169.

Ibrahim, F. A. (1985). Effective cross-cultural counseling and psychotherapy: A framework. *The Counseling Psychologist, 13,* 625–638.

Ibrahim, F. A., & Kahn, H. (1987). Assessment of worldviews. *Psychological Reports, 60,* 163–176.

Ibrahim, F. A., & Owen, S. V. (1994). Factor analysis structure of the Scale to Assess Worldview©. *Current Psychology: Developmental, Learning, Personality, Social, 13,* 201–209.

Ibrahim, F. A., Roysicar-Sodowsky, G., & Ohnishi, H. (2001). Worldview: Developments and directions. In J. G. Ponterotto, J. M. Casas, L. A. Suzuki, & C. M. Alexander (Eds.), *Handbook of multicultural counseling* (2nd ed., pp. 425–456). Thousand Oaks, CA: Sage.

Ivey, A. E., Ivey, M. B., & Simek-Morgan, L. (1997). *Counseling and psychotherapy: Skills, theories, and practice.* Englewood Cliffs, NJ: Prentice-Hall.

Kim, B. S. K., & Abreu, J. M. (2001). Acculturation measurement. In J. G. Ponterotto, J. M. Casas, L. A. Suzuki, & C. M. Alexander (Eds.), *Handbook of multicultural counseling* (2nd ed., pp. 394–424). Thousand Oaks, CA: Sage.

Kiselica, M. S. (1999). Confronting my own ethnocentrism and racism: A process of pain and growth. *Journal of Counseling & Development, 77*(1), 14–17.

Kluckhohn, C. K. (1951). Values and value orientations in the theory of action. In T. Parsons & E. A. Shields (Eds.), *Toward a general theory of action* (pp. 388–433). Cambridge, MA: Harvard University Press.

Kluckhohn, C. K. (1956). Towards a comparison of value-emphasis in different cultures. In L. D. White (Ed.), *The state of social sciences* (pp. 116–132). Chicago: University of Chicago Press.

Kluckhohn, F. R., & Strodtbeck, F. L. (1961). *Variations in value-orientations*. Evanston, IL: Row, Peterson.

LaFramboise, T., Coleman, H. L. K., & Gerton, J. (1993). Psychological impact of biculturalism: Evidence and theory. *Psychological Bulletin, 114*(3), 395–412.

Lazos Vargas, S. L. (1998). Deconstructing homo(geneous) Americans: The White ethnic immigrant narrative and its exclusionary effect. *Tulane Law Review, 72*, 1493–1596.

Lewis, J. J. (2007). *"Anais Nin quotes." About women's history*. Retrieved January 3, 2007, from http://womenshistory.about.com/od/quotes/qu_anais_nin.htm

Locke, D. C., & Parker, L. D. (1994). Improving the multicultural competence of educators. In P. B. Pedersen & J. C. Carey (Eds.), *Multicultural counseling in schools*. Boston: Allyn & Bacon.

Lynch, E. W. (1992). From culture shock to cultural learning. In E. W. Lynch & M. J. Hanson (Eds.), *Developing cross-cultural competence: A guide for working with young children and their families*, (pp. 17–34). Baltimore, MD: Paul H. Brooke.

Markus, H. R, & Kitayama, S. (1991). Culture and self: Implications for cognition, emotion, and motivation *Psychological Review, 98*(2), 224–253.

McIntosh, P. (1989). "White privilege: Unpacking the invisible knapsack." *Peace and Freedom* (July/August): 10-12.

National Center for Education Statistics (1997, January). Integrated postsecondary education data system (IPEDS): Fall enrollment survey. Washington DC: Author.

Neville, H. A., Worthington, R. L., & Spanierman, L. B. (2001). Race, power, and multicultural counseling psychology: Understanding White privilege and color-blind racial attitudes. In J. G. Ponterotto, J. M. Casas, L. A. Suzuki, & C. M. Alexander (Eds.), *Handbook of multicultural counseling* (2nd ed., pp. 257–288). Thousand Oaks, CA: Sage.

Ortiz, A. A., & Maldonado-Colon, E. (1986). Recognizing learning disabilities in bilingual children: How to lessen inappropriate referrals of language minority students to special education. *Journal of Reading, Writing, and Learning Disabilities, 2*(1), 43–56.

Pedersen, P. B. (1994). Multicultural training in schools as an expansion of the counselor's role. In P. B. Pedersen & J. C. Carey (Eds.), *Multicultural counseling in schools*. Boston: Allyn & Bacon.

Phinney, J. S. (1996). When we talk about American ethnic groups, what do we mean? *American Psychologist, 51*(9), 918–927.

Rotter, J. B. (1966). Generalized expectancies for internal versus external control of reinforcement. *Psychological Monographs, 80*, 1–28.

Rotter, J. B. (1975). Some problems and misconceptions related to the construct of internal versus external control of reinforcement. *Journal of Consulting and Clinical Psychology, 43*, 56–67.

Roysicar-Sodowsky, G., & Frey, L. L. (2003). Children of immigrants: Their worldviews value conflicts. In P. B. Pederson & J. C. Carey (Eds.), *Multicultural counseling in schools* (2nd ed., pp. 61–83). Boston: Allyn & Bacon.

Sciarra, D. T. (2001). School counseling in a multicultural society. In J. G. Ponterotto, J. M. Casas, L. A. Suzuki, & C. M. Alexander (Eds.), *Handbook of multicultural counseling* (2nd ed., pp. 701–728). Thousand Oaks, CA: Sage.

Sire, J. W. (1976). *The universe next door*. Downers Grove, IL: Intervarsity Press.

Sodowsky, G. R., & Johnson, P. (1994). World views: Culturally learned assumptions and values. In P. B. Pedersen & J. C. Carey (Eds.), *Multicultural counseling in schools* (2nd ed., pp. 59–80). Boston: Allyn & Bacon.

Sodowsky, G. R., & Lai, E. W. M. (1997). Asian immigrant variables and structural models of cross-cultural distress. In A. Booth, A. C. Crouter, & N. Landale (Eds.), *Immigration and the family: Research and policy on U. S. immigrants* (pp. 211–237). Hillsdale, NJ: Lawrence Erlbaum Associates.

Sue, D., & Sue, D. W. (2003). *Counseling the culturally diverse: Theory and practice* (4th ed.). New York: Wiley.

Sue, D. & Sue, D. W. (2007). Counseling the culturally diverse: *Theory and practice* (5th ed.). NY: Wiley.

Sue, D. W. (2001). Surviving monoculturalism and racism: A personal and professional journey. In J. G. Ponterotto, J. M. Casas, L. A. Suzuki, & C. M. Alexander (Eds.), *Handbook of multicultural counseling* (2nd ed., pp. 45–54). Thousand Oaks, CA: Sage.

Sue, D. W. (2003). *Overcoming our racism: Journey to liberation*. New York: Wiley.

Thompson, C. E., & Neville, H. A. (1999). Racism, mental health, and mental health practice. *The Counseling Psychologist, 17*, 155–223.

Wah, L. M. (Director). (1994). *The Color of Fear* [Motion picture]. United States: StirFry Seminars.

Yeh, C. J. (1999). Invisibility and self-construal in African American men: Implications for training and practice, *The Counseling Psychologist, 27*, 810–819.

Yeh, C. J. (2000). Depathologizing Asian American perspectives of health and healing. *Asian American and Pacific Islander Journal of Health, 8*, 138–149.

Yeh, C. J. (2003). Age, acculturation, cultural adjustment, and mental health symptoms of Chinese, Korean, and Japanese immigrant youth. *Cultural Diversity and Ethnic Minority Psychology Journal, 9*, 34–48.

Yeh, C. J., Arora, A. K., Inose, M., Okubo, Y., Li, R. H., & Greene, P. (2003). The cultural adjustment and mental health of Japanese immigrant youth. *Adolescence, 38*(151), 481–500.

Yeh, C. J., Carter, R. T., & Pieterse, A. L. (2004). Cultural values and racial identity attitudes among Asian American students: An exploratory investigation. *Counseling and Values, 48*, 82–95.

Yeh, C. J., & Huang, K. (1996). The collectivistic nature of ethnic identity development among Asian American college students. *Adolescence, 31*(123), 645–661.

Yeh, C. J., Hunter, C. D., Madan-Bahel, A., Chiang, L., & Kwong, A. (2004). Indigenous and interdependent perspectives of healing: Implications for counseling and research. *Journal of Counseling and Development, 82*, 410–419.

Yeh, C. J., & Hwang, M. (1999). The sociocultural context of Asian Pacific American ethnic identity and self: Implications for counseling. In D. S. Sandhu (Ed.), *Asian and Pacific Islander Americans: Issues and concerns for counseling and psychotherapy* (pp. 127–138). New York: Nova Science Publishers.

Yeh, C. J., Kim, A. B., Pituc, S. T., & Lee, S. J. (2005, August). *Asian Americans: Advocacy, culturally competent services, and public policy.* Paper presented at the annual Asian American Psychological Association Convention, Washington, DC.

Yeh, C. J., Ma, P.-W., Madan, A., Hunter, C. D., Jung, S., Kim, A., et al. (2005). The cultural negotiations of Korean immigrant youth. *Journal of Counseling and Development, 83*, 172–181.

2

Diversity and School Counseling

VI
THE ACCULTURATIVE ENVIRONMENT OF SCHOOLS AND THE SCHOOL COUNSELOR:
Goals and Roles That Create a Supportive Context for Immigrant Adolescents

EDISON J. TRICKETT AND DIANA FORMOSO
University of Illinois at Chicago

The core relevant question at the beginning of the new millennium is how we can best incorporate into our society the large number of immigrants who now call the United States their home. Nowhere is the need to responsibly address these issues greater than when it comes to immigrant children. . . . Schooling is at the heart of all these questions.

(C. Suárez-Orozco & M. Suárez-Orozco, 2001, p. 155)

The changing demography of public schools in the United States, in recent years, has challenged the existing structure of educational institutions to meet the varying and diverse needs posed by immigrant and refugee students. These students arrive with varied educational histories, including gaps due to political turmoil or war, differing levels of knowledge of English, differing levels of literacy in their languages of origin, limited social capital in terms of parental education and U.S. cultural knowledge, and sometimes histories of traumatic experiences related to their flights from their native countries (Olsen, 1997). They arrive in communities with different kinds of resources to aid the transitions to a new country, and they are placed in schools with many degrees of prior experience and competence in dealing with the cultural and linguistic diversity brought by immigrant and refugee students. Further, new waves or groups are constantly arriving because of turmoil or inadequate economic conditions in the rest of the world.

The challenge to public schools in coping with this changing and diverse influx of newcomers is enormous and is further complicated by the diversity of the immigrant populations themselves. In some locations, specific cultural groups will accumulate in significant numbers to provide a bilingual and bicultural challenge for schools. Here, the primary school task involves how to develop bilingual and bicultural resources relevant to their missions such as bilingual educational offerings, bilingual staffs, and the recruitment of parents from immigrant communities to serve as school–community culture brokers. In other locations, however, multiple groups enter the schools in small numbers, such that a particular school may include children from many countries speaking many languages and bringing with them many cultural histories. Here, the school challenges are somewhat different, focusing on the complex task of developing the kinds of community networks, linguistic resources, and cultural knowledge to understand the lives of the children from multiple cultural contexts. These multiple and contrasting kinds of school contexts suggest that the roles and functions of school counselors will be different depending on their schools' experiences in receiving immigrant student populations.

This chapter focuses on some of the multiple implications of this changing demography for the roles and competencies of school counselors (Bemack & Chung, 2003; Eschenauer & Chen-Hayes, 2005). The notion of school as an acculturative environment is posited as one way of providing a road map for exploring where and how schools can and do affect the educational and psychosocial adaptation of immigrant students and their families. Viewing the school as an acculturative context can aid school counselors in using their skills and knowledge to affect the success of immigrant and refugee students. In adopting this approach, we suggest that the school counselor role can include not only explicit activities at the individual student level but also those geared toward developing the school as a resourceful and hospitable community for immigrant and refugee students. This perspective draws on emerging calls in the school counselor literature for school counselors to engaging in activities designed to affect school culture more generally (Dollarhide, 2003; Hernandez & Seem, 2004; Ito, 2004; Sink, 2002; Tatar & Bekerman, 2002).

The chapter is organized in the following way. First, we present some of the distinctive issues facing immigrant and refugee students and their parents and discuss why the public school is such a critical setting for them. Next, we provide an ecological perspective underlying the notion of acculturative press and outline some if its implications for schools counselors. Of particular concern here is the value of viewing adolescents, families, and schools as interdependent—that is, of developing an understanding of how students' family lives impact their school behavior and performance as well as how students' school experiences can impact their family lives. We then outline a view of the school as an acculturative environment, emphasizing three central aspects of the schooling experience for immigrant children and their families—the classroom, relationships within the school, and parent involvement. In each section, we address key issues identified by the literature as impacting immigrant children in American schools and some implications for the role of school counselor. The final sections of the paper are dedicated to (a) providing examples of how some schools receiving an influx of immigrant and refugee children have chosen to respond to their needs and (b) discussing possible ways that school counselors can use their existing roles and/or engage in role expansion to attend to the acculturative press in their own schools.

The Multiple Education-Relevant Roles of Public Schools and Immigrant Children and Families

It is customary to think of schools as agents of socialization as well as education; that is, they provide a context for socializing students as well as serving an explicitly educational function through the formal curriculum. Such socialization functions are manifested in the overall school climate, peer group norms, teacher attitudes, and the availability of extracurricular offerings. They are expressed in the creation of such settings as in-school health centers, prenatal programs for pregnant adolescent girls, in-class health modules on AIDS or drugs, and the recent concern with the development of parent involvement programs. There is an assumed and anticipated connection between the educational function of schools and these broader socialization opportunities. For example, proponents of including social/emotional learning in the curriculum do so with the belief that a connection exists between such an emphasis and academic outcomes (Greenberg et al., 2003). Learning about safe sex is seen as a preventive intervention that affects life chances through the demonstrated connection between teen pregnancy, school completion, and future occupational options and economic potential. In engaging in these activities, schools attempt to prepare their students for the world in which they are living, with all its uncertainties, risks, and needed skills.

The role of the school in the lives of immigrant and refugee children, however, extends far beyond these normative educational and socialization functions.

> American public schools since the last century have served as quintessential agencies of acculturation. It is in school settings that immigrant youth come most directly in contact with their native peers—whether as role models or close friends, as distant members of exclusionary cliques, and as sources of discrimination or of peer acceptance. (Portes & Rumbaut, 2001, p. 203)

Thus, for these students, school is the central entry point into the new culture. It represents a setting of both language learning and acculturation. Schools are where immigrant and refugee children learn about the United States and what it means to be an American. It is a site where they receive messages from school personnel—well intended or unintended—about what it means to be an immigrant and a native language speaker and whether they are welcomed here. It is where native-born peers provide information, feedback, and role models for how students in the United States behave toward each other and toward teachers; how friendships are defined and on what basis they are made; and what kinds of aspirations are available for educational attainment in and after high school. The bottom line is that, for this group of students, the school, of necessity, must serve an acculturative as well as an educational function.

Immigrant and refugee children and adolescents share with native-born students hopes for academic school success. Yet they face additional challenges that place them in a potentially precarious position. First, they often do not have the linguistic skills to take full advantage of the offerings of local schools, particularly advanced classes. This issue is particularly complicated for those immigrant students whose educations have been interrupted in their countries of origin because of war, political upheaval, or rural residence. Thus, the importance of providing intensive language instruction is clear and compelling. In addition, they often either lack or have erroneous knowledge about the culture into which they have entered and the ways that schools function in that culture. These issues range widely, from how to access public transportation and needed services in the community to how to learn what is required from the schools in terms of dress, supplies, schedules, and teacher conferences. While these aspects of daily school life are taken for granted by native-born children and their families, they represent new learning for many immigrants. Indeed, considerable research suggests that these students often do not understand how schools operate, ranging from such basic knowledge as how to use lockers to how to relate to teachers and American peers, and do not understand the role of guidance counselors, the idea of scholarships for post-high-school education, and for undocumented immigrants, legal rights and reporting responsibilities of school personnel (Lucas, 1997; Portes & Rumbaut, 2001; C. Suárez-Orozco & Suárez-Orozco, 2001).

The school can serve an equally important role for parents through its structure, policies, and activities. Although children need guidance in their adaptation to U.S. culture and schools, parents often are unable to provide such guidance based on their own recent arrivals and limited language skills. Parents also may have no one to turn to for advice on guiding this process if their support networks consist mainly of family members and friends who have recently immigrated and if they live and work within ethnic enclaves that give them little exposure to native-born parents or coethnic parents with longer tenure in the United States. If parents are to support the educational progress of their children, they need to learn about the culture of schools as well as the culture of their new country. For many immigrant and refugee parents, schools may be the only available resource in terms of getting the information and support they need to assist their children effectively. Thus, the school experience is critical not only for immigrant children but for their families as well. When schools do not provide a welcoming and supportive port of entry for immigrant parents as well as children, immigrant students' educational prospects and life chances are impacted. Thus, the school is both an educational and acculturative setting of great significance to immigrant families.

Ecology and the Acculturative Press

In elaborating the implication of the changing school demography for the role of school counselor, two primary points are central to the remainder of the chapter. The first is the importance of ecology, of understanding the changing social and cultural context of the school and the students and parents it serves. Elsewhere, Trickett (e.g., Birman, Trickett, & Buchanan, 2005; Trickett, 1991; Trickett & Birman, 1989; Trickett, Kelly, & Todd, 1972; Trickett & Schmid, 1993) has written about the implications of an ecological perspective for understanding the school context and interventions in it. An ecological perspective suggests that both schools and students will continue to struggle unless interventions are based on a rich and thorough understanding of the issues facing both schools and students. Both schools and families will benefit when institutional agents take charge of learning about these issues and translating that knowledge into ways of making the school context as welcoming a reception for immigrant students as possible. This mind-set frames the potential for the school counselor as such a resource.

The second point stems from this ecological perspective on the ever-changing school contexts of today. In these often fluid contexts, it is useful to view any specific intervention effort from a "learning how to learn" perspective. This is important because the landscape of immigration can change rapidly depending on events around the world, and the ecology of schools changes over time in both numbers and diversity of immigrant populations. In this ecological context, what is adaptive for school personnel is the ability and energy to invest in self-education about how lives of students and parents from multiple cultures and contexts may affect students' school adaptations and performances. A learning how to learn perspective is critical because every school is different and because the immigrant wave it receives this year may be very different from the immigrant wave that arrives next year. Some of the issues described in this chapter will be present in a particular school, whereas others will not, and some (when present) may already be effectively addressed. Many issues will impact immigrant students from some countries, but not others. Finally, there will undoubtedly be issues present in schools that are not yet addressed in the literature on immigrant families or the school counseling literature. The distinctive positioning of school counselors at the interface of students' academic and social needs, as well as their access to teachers, parents, and students, renders them potential boundary spanners who can both seek out and communicate to relevant others information about the issues facing immigrant and refugee children and families.

Thus, the ecological perspective provides contours for conceptualizing the school context, while learning how to learn provides a mind-set for constructive engagement with the process of facing diversity in the present and a changing future. Such a perspective is intended to bring into sharp relief the needs and issues of immigrant and refugee children and families and to place them in a central position with respect to the counselor role.

One Example of an Ecological Mind-Set: The Interdependence Between Adolescent School Experiences and Family Lives

An ecological perspective suggests that schools, families, and students operate interdependently, with each system impacting and being impacted by every other (Bronfenbrenner, 1977; Trickett, Kelly, & Todd, 1972). In efforts to make a positive difference in the school lives of immigrant and refugee children, it is useful to understand how the family lives of both parents and students can spill over into the school experience, as well as how students' school experiences can spill over into their well-being and family lives. Two implications of this interdependence are cited here: (a) the ecology of family lives and school behavior/performance and (b) culture brokering, the acculturation gap, and school behavior/performance.

Ecology of Immigrant Family Lives

At its most general level, an ecological perspective draws attention to the circumstances and challenges facing immigrant and refugee families in their transitions to new lives. C. Suárez-Orozco and Suárez-Orozco (2001) provided a useful overview of many relevant issues in this regard. First, they found that only 20% of Mexican immigrant children in their sample came to the United States as part of a family. Thus, when immigrant children who were separated from parents went to school every day, they brought with them their worries around separation, loss, and family reunification.

When intact families do arrive in the United States, however, parents are busy with the tasks of finding work, housing, and transportation and, indeed, of enrolling their children in school, often without the benefit of English-language proficiency or the knowledge of how one goes about school enrollment in the United States. Undocumented immigrant families face additional challenges as they try to fill these important needs while avoiding detection, and many refugee families must simultaneously deal with the emotional consequences of having experienced war-related violence or political persecution. If and when jobs are found, the nature of the work (e.g., long hours and evening shifts) presents additional challenges for immigrant parents. These challenges permeate every aspect of immigrant parents' and children's lives and are not easily set aside for the purposes of engaging in or interacting with the school. Thus, learning about the ecology of the lives of these families is critical in understanding the school-related challenges of their children.

Culture Brokering, the Acculturation Gap, and School Behavior/Performance

The research literature suggests that immigrant students often play a number of important roles in their families that affect both their school performance and family dynamics as well, such as working to alleviate economic hardship and caring for younger siblings (Orellana, 2003). Two specific issues, however, have received considerable attention. The first involves the culture broker role played at one time or another by almost all immigrant children (Portes & Rumbaut, 2001). Here, children mediate between their families and external institutions such as schools through serving as translators, attending doctors' appointments and parent–teacher conferences, or otherwise helping parents negotiate complicated U.S. systems (Orellana, Dorner, & Pulido, 2003; Portes & Rumbaut, 2001; Trickett & Jones, 2007). While this role may be viewed as an unfair burden on children or a valuable opportunity for them to learn through experience, entering into these necessary activities can limit students' time to complete homework or participate in school activities.

The acculturation gap (Birman, in press; Portes & Rumbaut, 2001) is seen as resulting from the differential rates of acculturation of parents and children to the new culture. School is the primary setting for this to occur, as parents see their children becoming more Americanized than they are in terms of language acquisition, cultural values, and behavior, including choices of clothing and music. The acculturation gap may also be influenced as children fail to retain aspects of the culture of origin that are important to parents. The often cited parental fear of "losing one's child to the new culture" reflects both of these concerns and may contribute to family disagreements about various school-related involvements for their children. Because of their salience in the lives of immigrant students and families, the culture broker role and acculturation gap represent salient issues that can affect the family/student/school interdependence.

Of particular import here is the acculturation gap with respect to acquisition of a new language and retention of the language of the culture of origin. In one of the most broad-based studies of immigrant adolescents and families, Portes and Rumbaut (2001) followed over 5,000 second-generation immigrant students from 77 countries for a 3-year period (14–17 years old). Their findings are too numerous to cite here, but several are central to the interdependence of families, students, and schools. For example, they found that over 98% of these adolescent immigrants report speaking English well or very well, and while 90% also report speaking another language, the fluency level is significantly less. In addition, their data suggest that the acquisition of English is accompanied by a loss of native language, which results in an acculturation gap between children and their parents, who are less likely to have acquired English. Furthermore, they stressed that because language fluency does not simply involve the acquisition of a new skill but implies a broader sense of identification with the new culture (and perhaps a reduced sense of identification with the culture of origin), this pattern reinforces parental concern over losing their children to the new culture.

There are multiple implications of these findings for the interdependence of school and family life. Portes and Rumbaut (2001) demonstrated a link between such dissonant parent–child linguistic acculturation (an acculturation gap) and increased parent–adolescent conflict and decreased family cohesion and parent–child communication. Moreover, dissonant acculturation is associated with several child outcomes, including lowered self-esteem, increased family conflict, and grades in school. The loss of students' native languages can also disconnect them from the potential protective influence provided by extended families and coethnic community members and peers (see also C. Suárez-Orozco & Suárez-Orozco, 2001).

Portes and Rumbaut (2001) argued that limited bilingualism and its negative outcomes for youth and their families are "partly traceable to the inability of public schools to support immigrants' efforts to preserve their language" (pp. 145–146). Their recommendation with respect to literacy is twofold: First, bilingual education should focus on both the teaching of English and the retention of native language, not simply the former. Here, the notion is that while teaching English to immigrant children and youth is clearly a first priority of schools, its success may inadvertently heighten distance between children and parents and have deleterious consequences for both family life and school performance. Second, they recommended that efforts be made to increase parental fluency in English. This effort may both support positive family relationships by reducing the acculturation gap and help parents negotiate the educational system and bolster their children's school performances.

A focus on the ecology of immigrant lives and such issues as the culture broker role and acculturation gap can provide not only an appreciation of the challenges facing these students and families but also ideas for intervention. Such an understanding can be a resource as the school counselor interacts with other school personnel who lack such specific knowledge.

In addition, as one of the first major contacts that newly arrived immigrant students and families encounter, counselors are well-positioned to assist them in their transitions to American public schools (Williams & Butler, 2003). At the student level, varied potential roles have been described, including developing a set of coordinated and comprehensive strategies that focus on orientation and facilitating the acculturative process for newcomer students (e.g., Shepherd-Johnson, 1995). Elsewhere, these efforts have included orientations to the school and U.S. culture, adult or peer mentoring, Newcomer Clubs, conflict resolution and peer mediation programs, small group counseling, classroom guidance (Shepherd-Johnson), or indeed, the creation of Newcomer Centers or Newcomer Schools (e.g., Olsen, 1997). At the family level, efforts to link immigrant families with community agencies or supports that can help them to negotiate the transition to the United States have also been described as potentially beneficial (Taylor & Adelman, 2000).

The Acculturative Environment of Schools: An Ecological Overview

The Acculturative Press

Sarason's (1982) classic treatise on the culture of the school and the problem of change underscores the perspective that school counselors operate within a school culture that affects not only the lives of immigrant students but also what counselors can themselves accomplish (see Tatar & Bekerman, 2002). To sharpen the focus on the school as an acculturative environment for immigrant students, we employ the notion of acculturative press. This concept draws on the more general notion of environmental press derived from the early work of Murray (1938) and flows from Lewin's (1951) suggestion that individual behavior is a function of person and environment. Murray described the environmental press in terms of its resources, norms, and constraints that formed the context within which individuals function. Individuals, on the other hand, could be described in terms of needs that may or may not mesh with the environmental press. Thus, just as individuals differ in terms of their preference for nurturance and order, so may environments differ in the degree to which they may be viewed as nurturing or orderly. The acculturative press adopts this notion of fit as it relates to the ways in which the social context of the school supports, ignores, or inhibits the academic, social, and acculturative demands facing immigrant and refugee children and their families.

The notion of acculturative press is foreshadowed by Gordon (1964) in his classic book *Assimilation in American Life*. He distinguished three main historical philosophies or goal-systems of assimilation evident over time: "Anglo-conformity," "the melting pot," and "cultural pluralism." Anglo-conformity requires renunciation of culture of origin in favor of values and behavior of Anglo-Saxon core group. The melting pot envisions a new integration, a sociobiological merger, and creation of a new indigenous American type. Cultural pluralism postulates preservation of communal life and significant aspects of the culture of origin within the context of American citizenship and social and political integration into American society. While not pure types, these broad characterizations suggest different potential structures and processes in schools which, taken together, suggest to immigrant students how the school views the goals of their acculturation in a new land.

Levels of the Ecological Context and the Acculturative Press

While Gordon's (1964) typology provides a useful orienting set of ideas, specifics of the acculturative press are found in multiple levels of the ecological environment of the school (Bronfenbrenner, 1979; Trickett et al., 1972; Trickett & Schmidt, 1993). For purposes of this chapter, we are selecting three different aspects of the school representative of the acculturative press and relevant to existing and potential roles of school counselors. They include (a) the classroom, (b) out-of-class relationships with peers and school adults, and (c) opportunities for parent–school interactions. Each of these domains is reviewed for its relevance to the acculturative press and its implications for the educational and acculturative development of immigrant adolescents.

The Classroom as an Acculturative Context. The way immigrant children experience schools, particularly at the elementary school level, is greatly influenced by their classroom experiences. Although school counselors are not classroom teachers, counselors could play an important role in shaping immigrant students' experience in schools by learning about classroom issues at their school, facilitating conversations with teachers, counseling colleagues in anticipation of the issues facing immigrant students, and serving in a professional development capacity for those serving immigrant students. This potential role is supported by calls in the school counselor literature for a more central place for counselors in the professional development of teachers (Esquivel & Keitel, 1990) and increased communication and support among counselors, classroom teachers, and ESL teachers (e.g., Clemente & Collison, 2000). This section outlines key themes identified by the research literature as relevant to immigrant students' classroom experiences that provide examples of the kinds of issues school counselors may potentially affect at the classroom level.

Teacher attitudes and behavior. While a warm, respectful teacher–student relationship is a powerful protective resource for all students, it is particularly so for immigrant students (e.g., Stanton-Salazar, 2001). A focus on the classroom as an acculturative context directs attention to specific aspects of the classroom that contribute to creating such a context. C. Suárez-Orozco and M. Suárez-Orozco (2001), for example, found that many teachers who worked closely with immigrant students regarded them highly, whereas others viewed them as lazy, less intelligent, prone to get into trouble, and unlikely to assimilate or succeed. Classroom climate for immigrant students also is impacted by the extent to which teachers are knowledgeable about and inclusive of students' native cultures and languages in ongoing classroom processes, assignments, and classroom displays. In some schools, teachers have tied the curriculum to immigrant students' real life experiences (e.g., using immigration rates in math examples) in order to make lessons meaningful and to communicate an ethic of inclusion (Lucas, 1997). Such signs are noticed by students, and their absence seen by them as sending messages about the relevance or value of their cultures of origin (Olsen, 1997).

Similarly, conversations around students' native language use in schools can convey messages of inclusion or exclusion. Teachers have been found to interpret immigrant students' native language usage in many diverse ways, including as an endorsement of ethnic pride, a refusal to assimilate, an opportunity to speak unfavorably about teachers, or a lack of motivation to learn English (see Birman, 1998). Children with a short tenure in the United States are sometimes simply expressing themselves in the only language they speak. Nonetheless, these interpretations will inevitably shape how teachers respond to native language use, and teacher responses will convey information to immigrant students about what it means to be an American and what it will take for the doors to American schools to be open to them.

Gordon's (1964) images of Anglo-conformity, the melting pot, and cultural pluralism as contrasting acculturative goals are evident in the classroom through teacher attitudes and behavior regarding the cultural background of the students. Counselor-led discussions and classroom consultation around multicultural issues such as those raised previously may encourage teachers to develop a curriculum that is inclusive and respectful of diverse cultures and languages, which can go far toward helping immigrant students feel valued and welcome. Durodoye (1998) and Shepherd-Johnson (1995) outlined school counseling models used to foster such multicultural awareness among teachers.

Academic press. Academic press refers to the extent to which teachers provide exposure to advanced course work and closely link student performance and grades. Boyd and Shouse (1997) argued that for low-SES schools, emotional climate and academic press go hand-in-hand to improve student outcomes. In their study, the least academically effective schools were those that combined a supportive emotional climate and weak academic press, leading the authors to caution against viewing "positive social relations and student self-esteem as reasonable substitutes for meaningful academic demand and student effort" (p. 148). Teachers serving immigrant students are often faced with striking a delicate balance between accommodating the barriers some immigrant students bring to the classroom and maintaining an ethic of high expectations for student effort and success. Critical to this tension is the domain of academic expectations (Weinstein, 2002) teachers hold for immigrant students, particularly those entering school later or arriving with disrupted educational backgrounds. In addition, the lack of readily available diagnostic tools to differentiate linguistic issues from cognitive impairment complicates the situation. In this context, school counselors may be in a useful position to work with teachers around expectation issues and encourage them to translate their concern for the well-being of immigrant students into additional supports for learning instead of lowered expectations. Although concern for immigrant students and respect for their cultures and languages are important, they are not reasonable substitutes for high expectations and academic support.

Course placement and bilingual education. While the previous discussion focused on students already placed in classes, a critical role played by counselors in many schools is in course placement. As such, counselors serve as gatekeepers for classes and post–high-school options (Lucas, 1997). These placement decisions are determining for many immigrant students, as they affect the kind of acculturative classroom climate they will experience, the degree to which the classes count toward graduation, and the degree to which they will be tracked. Course placement decisions are complicated by what immigrant students themselves bring to the school: What was their schooling experience in their home country? Did they experience interrupted education? What is their level of English proficiency? What are their academic competencies and could these be masked by interrupted education or a lack of English proficiency? Like native-born students, immigrant students bring great diversity in terms of history, talent, and work ethic. Although the diversity among immigrant students should be considered when making course placement decisions, individualized assessments can be difficult and time consuming, particularly for counselors responsible for hundreds of students. Furthermore, assessment tools (when they exist) may not be valid for English-language learners (ELL) or may not generalize across countries.

Under these circumstances, school counselors are themselves often placed in difficult situations with few clear available and positive options. When faced with a rapid influx of immigrant students, students who share a common heritage or language may be assigned to the same classes, irrespective of their individual abilities or school experiences. To illustrate, interviews with school counselors revealed that there was no systematic plan in many schools to identify gifted students in ESL groups using bilingual assessment methods (Clemente & Collison, 2000).

These decisions are further complicated by what the school has to offer in terms of courses for immigrant students: What are the options for students in terms of general education courses, vocational training, or college prep classes? Which teachers are known to be committed to the education of immigrant students? Can incoming immigrant students be grouped together in common classes? Should they be? Unfortunately, while immigrant students are working to learn English, they are often enrolled in classes with shallow course content that does not adequately prepare them for classes that are more academically demanding and in classes that can essentially exclude them from the college track (C. Suárez-Orozco & Suárez-Orozco, 2001). Indeed, many ELL are "mainstreamed" into vocational education, lower academic tracks, and remedial courses (see Harklau, 1994a, 1994b) based on their English proficiency rather than on their academic competencies. This creates a dilemma for counselors who want to see immigrant students do well academically, but at the same time feel constrained by students' educational and linguistic limitations. Similarly, concerned counselors and teachers may wonder if it is fair to expect immigrant students to effectively participate in a challenging curriculum while they are facing multiple transitions and struggling to learn English. Although one solution is to place students in less challenging courses, some argue that all immigrant students can be exposed to the same high expectations and challenging curriculum and instead have access to varying levels of academic support (see Lucas, 1997; Mehan, Villanueva, Hubbard, & Lintz, 1996; Olsen, 1997).

In sum, course placement decisions for immigrant youth can have widespread implications for their English-language learning, native language fluency, academic performance, peer networks, and future life options. These decisions should be taken particularly seriously when working with immigrant students because family members or immigrant peers often do not understand the school system well enough to offer helpful guidance (McCall-Perez, 2000). Here is an area in which the school counselor can exert considerable control as he or she thinks broadly about child outcomes when making decisions around course placement and English-language learning. Another vital role for school counselors is to look beyond their particular school's policies around course placement for approaches and programs that have demonstrated success elsewhere, evaluate their potential for success in their own particular school context, and advocate for use of alternative strategies and the recruitment of qualified bilingual staff, if necessary. In support of this latter role, McCall-Perez concluded, "[I]n periods of challenges to the educational rights of immigrant and language minority students, informed counselors can serve as their most effective advocates and protectors" (p. 19).

Out-of-Class Relationships With Peers and School Adults. In addition to the classroom as an acculturative context, the acculturative press is found outside of the classroom in the extent and nature of relationships of immigrant and refugee students with both peers and school adults. Both peer relationships and adult connections have been highlighted in the literature, with quite differing emphases, and both have implications for the educational and psychological adaptation of immigrant and refugee students and the potential role of the school counselor in that process.

Peers and the acculturative press. Many qualitative studies of the school lives of immigrant children and adolescents have documented the stressors, challenges, opportunities, and school outcomes related to out-of-class interactions with peers and school adults (Portes & Rumbaut, 2001; C. Suárez-Orozco & Suárez-Orozco, 2001; Stanton-Salazar, 2001). Central to all of these accounts are encounters with perceived discrimination from both peers and adults. Anecdotal accounts include overhearing anti-immigrant sentiments in the casual conversations of teachers (C. Suárez-Orozco & Suárez-Orozco), ethnic slurs directed at students by peers (Portes & Rumbaut, 2001), and being asked ignorant and sometimes insulting questions about one's country of origin by both peers and adults (Birman, Trickett, & Bacchus, 2002).

Such accounts are substantiated by quantitative data derived from large-scale studies where immigrant adolescents have been asked about the nature and frequency of discrimination experience in schools. For example, Zhou (2001), in a sample of Vietnamese adolescents in San Diego followed over a 3-year period, found that 65% at Time 1 and 72% at Time 2 reported being discriminated against in school. The most common source was native-born students, both Black and White (38% and 41% overall at the two time periods, 3 years apart), but school adults were also mentioned, particularly teachers (17.5% and 29% at the two time periods) and school counselors (6% and 14%).

As Portes and Rumbaut (2001) suggested, race may be a paramount factor in the social context of reception for immigrant students and account for perceived discrimination. However, the experience of discrimination is not reserved for immigrants of color. Birman, Trickett, and Buchanan (2005), for example, sampled two groups of immigrant adolescents from the former Soviet Union living in different community contexts, one ethnically dispersed and one of high ethnic concentration. Of the adolescents, 90% in the Concentrated Community and 73% in the Dispersed Community reported experiencing at least one incident of discrimination in the school context within the previous month. Again, the sources of these perceptions were both other students and teachers.

However, peers can also be a source of support and access to the dominant culture and can provide social norms supportive of academic achievement and social integration. Indeed, a potentially important point of intervention may be in facilitating supportive peer relationships among newcomers and between newcomers and immigrant youth with longer tenure in the United States or native-born peers. For example, Conchas (2001) described an in-school academy within a larger school where Latino students reported feeling close bonds with one another and formed relationships with both Latino and non-Latino youth. Peer relationships were sources of both academic and social support, and students noted that school personnel played a key role in encouraging a sense of community.

School adults and the acculturative press. School adults, while clearly seen as a source of discrimination and as part of the problem, are also a potentially large part of the solution. One potential source of social capital for immigrant and refugee students in the out-of-class context involves the extent and nature of the connections they make with adults in the school: teachers, guidance counselors, administrative staff, and coaches. If there is any unanimity in the recent scholarly books describing the lives of immigrant children and adolescents in the context of the school, it is this point. As M. Suárez-Orozco (2001) pointed out, many immigrant students live in neighborhoods with schools characterized by a culture of violence, little social capital, overcrowded classrooms, and outdated texts. School adults offer the potential to be personally supportive prosocial models and can serve as advocates for immigrant students when their parents are often not knowledgeable about how to perform such functions. Stanton-Salazar and Dornbusch (1995) suggested that such "supportive ties with institutional agents represent a necessary condition for engagement and advancement in the educational system and, ultimately, for success in the occupational structure" (p. 117). Such connections can link immigrant students to other resources that can increase their social capital: college or job connections, scholarship opportunities, or school organizations previously unaware of the skills and competencies of immigrant students.

While many scholars and immigrants themselves have commented on the importance of a particular adult or small number of adults as relating to their eventual school success, Stanton-Salazar's (2001) beautifully written book *Manufacturing Hope and Despair: The School and Kin Support Networks of U.S. Mexican Youth* articulates some of the dynamics and processes that make school adults so important. His focus is on the role of supportive networks and help-seeking experiences of lower income, Mexican American youth in school. In addition to focusing on structural aspects of the school experience that constrain the development of networks with school adults, Stanton-Salazar used the concept of network orientation to describe how Mexican youth decide to approach or not approach school adults for support, advice, or guidance. Confidence or trust that adults are indeed interested is central here. His book is a provocative and compelling look at the ecology of schooling for these immigrant youth and the potentially protective web that caring school adults can help immigrant youth establish. In Stanton-Salazar's work, teachers and guidance counselors surface as important parts of the social networks of these immigrant students and often serve as coparents, informal mentors, child advocates, and informal psychologists. He suggested that intervention efforts in the school need to be assessed in terms of how well they open up the kinds of relationships and access to institutional resources needed by these students.

There are many reasons, however, why such critical relationships are difficult to achieve. These reasons range from the structural (e.g., lack of teacher time to develop such relationships) to the normative (perceived discrimination or lack of interest on the part of school adults). Interviews with Latino youth reveal that the lack of bilingual counselors can not only prohibit outright counselor–student communication in the case of monolingual Spanish speakers, but also serve as a barrier for bilingual students who find it difficult to discuss stressful situations or strong emotions in English (Clemente & Collison, 2000). Regardless of the many very real constraints, school adults can provide a potential safe haven for immigrant students as well as a link to other school resources of relevance to their adaptation both educationally and acculturatively (Portes & Rumbaut, 2001; C. Suárez-Orozco & Suárez-Orozco, 2001).

In sum, the out-of-class relationships formed by immigrant and refugee students with peer and school adults represent a critical part of the acculturative press of schools that influence their immediate options and longer term life changes. The school counselor role is not only central to supporting immigrant students in dealing with the structural issues in schools that inhibit making adult connections or yield identity-disconfirming experiences. It can serve as a springboard for school culture and intergroup assessment and intervention.

Parent Involvement. The acculturative environment of schools also encompasses the ways in which immigrant parents are included in or marginalized by the school. Parent involvement in children's education is consistently identified as a critical protective resource for children's school success (Eccles & Harold, 1993; Epstein, 1991; Hess & Holloway, 1984; U.S. Department of Education, 1994) across family income, education, ethnicity, and immigrant status (e.g., Birman & Ryerson-Espino, in press; Delgado-Gaitan, 1991; Epstein & Becker, 1982; Hao & Bonstead-Bruns, 1998; Mau, 1997). When parents provide for children's basic needs, support their education at home, and maintain communication with the school, their involvement can offset the negative impact of poverty and prevent high school drop out (Chrispeels & Rivero, 2001). This section reviews the considerable constraints experienced by immigrant parents that unfortunately can impede meaningful parent involvement.

Sociocultural constraints on immigrant parents. There are multiple reasons for the relative lack of immigrant parent involvement in the ongoing, everyday education of their children. Lack of adequate knowledge of English and, sometimes, lack literacy skills in their native languages are oft-cited by immigrant parents as primary barriers to traditional forms of parent involvement, including helping with homework, reading with children, and participating in school activities (Collignon, Men, & Tan, 2001; Delgado-Gaitan, 1991). They can have devastating effects on immigrant parents' perceived competence to helping support their children's education and can lead to disengagement from parent involvement activities more generally (e.g., Delgado-Gaitan, 1992; Hoover-Dempsey & Sandler, 1997). Thus, counselor efforts to develop and adapt parent involvement strategies that do not require formal education or English-language literacy, but may nonetheless support children's educational goals (e.g., discussions about the importance of education) can serve to increase parent self-efficacy and bolster student engagement.

In addition, as previously described, the tasks of resettling in a new country are multiple and complex, and the process of immigration and the existence of competing demands for time and resources can impede immigrant parents' availability to be more involved in children's schooling (C. Suárez-Orozco & M. Suárez-Orozco, 2001). Moreover, many immigrant families come from countries where parents were not expected to be involved in their children's education (Birman & Ryerson-Espino, in press; C. Suárez-Orozco & M. Suárez-Orozco, 2001; Trueba & Delgado-Gaitan, 1988). These experiences continue to shape parents' understanding of their sense of place in their children's education in the United States (Chrispeels & Rivero, 2001; Hoover-Dempsey & Sandler, 1997).

School constraints. Parent involvement depends, in large part, on the extent to which the school can provide accessible opportunities for parents to learn about the nature of schooling and the roles they can play (Chrispeels & Rivero, 2001; Hoover-Dempsey & Sandler, 1997). Delgado-Gaitan (1991) found that many traditional avenues for involving parents in schools were closed to immigrant parents because school-generated processes for parent involvement relied on specific cultural knowledge in order to participate effectively. She argued,

> Schools facilitate the exclusion of students and parents by (consciously or unconsciously) establishing activities that require specific majority culturally based knowledge and behaviors about the school as an institution. Frequently, these ideas are assumed and are not made explicit. The absence of appropriate sociocultural knowledge precludes acceptable participation in formal school activities, resulting in isolation for many parents, especially those who have not been schooled in the United States or are limited in English proficiency. (p. 21)

To best support their children's education, immigrant parents need information about the local school system, grades and graduation requirements, the school's approach to bilingual education and how decisions about class placement are made, how difficulties in school adjustment and behavior problems are handled, and expectations for students and parents in terms of their interactions with the school. To the extent that school counselors make this information available to immigrant parents through individual contact, group meetings, or initiating workshops, it can reduce a primary barrier to parent involvement and immigrant students' academic success (e.g., Birman & Ryerson-Espino, in press).

In addition to information about school practices, policies, and procedures, the availability of school personnel who can communicate in parents' native language or serve as cultural brokers affects the degree of immigrant parent involvement, particularly for parents with limited English proficiency or cultural differences. Available bicultural and bilingual school personnel are a tremendous resource for schools whose immigrant student body shares a common heritage and language. For schools where immigrant students come from many countries speaking many different languages, one approach is to identify school personnel or community members who can serve as liaisons, translators, and cultural brokers for parents and the school. This networking strategy has been used with some success in a variety of parent involvement efforts (e.g., see Chrispeels & Rivero, 2001; Delgado-Gaitan, 1991; Epstein & Becker, 1982), although the level of success depends largely on the level of training and support for this role (e.g., Epstein & Becker). Additional efforts have included school counselors hiring and supervising bicultural and bilingual home–school liaisons to serve in various roles that normally were part of a counselor's job (Clemente & Collison, 2000) and to serve as cultural consultants (Esquivel & Keitel, 1990). Thus, bicultural, bilingual school personnel or parent liaisons may prove to be an invaluable resource to both parents and schools, and counselor efforts to recruit and train such personnel or advocate for creating such a position may bolster parent involvement and facilitate the work of school counselors. (While immigrant students are sometimes recruited for some of these translational roles, translating or transmitting complex information from schools can place them in a difficult and stressful position, particularly when they themselves misunderstand such information or they may be invested in portraying their school performance in a more favorable light.)

In addition, school personnel have been found to differ from immigrant parents in their understandings of the extent of parent involvement and why some immigrant parents are not more involved (Olsen, 1997). Because they may not see immigrant parents at school as often as their native-born counterparts, school personnel may perceive immigrant parents as disinterested and uninvolved in their children's education (Collignon et al., 2001; Moll, 1992). Similarly, teachers working in low-income, urban schools reported that most parents were not involved in their child's education, did not want to be more involved, and were not capable of high-quality involvement (Becker & Epstein, 1982; Epstein, 1991).

These perceptions are in stark contrast to those of immigrant parents, who cite better educational opportunities for their children in the United States as a primary factor motivating their migration (C. Suárez-Orozco & Suárez-Orozco, 2001). Indeed, parents in the same low-income, urban schools referred to earlier (Becker & Epstein, 1982; Epstein, 1991) reported that they supported their children's education at home, but needed better information from teachers about what types of educational support to provide. This reflects a broader concern reported in the literature that immigrant parents value education but are unsure about how to proceed (Delgado-Gaitan, 1992; C. Suárez-Orozco & Suárez-Orozco). These important differences in how teachers view parents and how parents view themselves create additional barriers to successful parent involvement and are likely an important discussion point among counselors, teachers, and parents.

Several excellent reviews offer recommendations for parent involvement strategies (Becker & Epstein, 1982; Chrispeels & Rivero, 2001; Delgado-Gaitan, 1991, 1992; Epstein, 1991; Lucas, 1997), but few were developed with specific immigrant parents in mind and none directed toward schools whose student population reflects multiple cultures and languages. Armed with rich understandings of barriers to parent involvement, counselors are better positioned to adapt strategies to the needs of the group, incorporate parents' strengths in meaningful ways, and render parental limitations less limiting. From a learning how to learn perspective, school counselors could fill a number of roles, including learning about the barriers and facilitators of parent involvement for immigrant families, developing and adapting parent involvement strategies tailored to the needs of immigrant parents and the teachers who serve them, and identifying areas of misunderstanding and facilitating conversations and professional education around the issues at hand. The school counselor literature discusses methods for strengthening family–teacher–counselor connections (e.g., Amatea, Daniels, Bringman, & Vandiver, 2004) and creating school–community links (Taylor & Adelman, 2000) to facilitate parent involvement and student success. In addition, strategies for networking with relevant external agencies can enhance the resource pool for immigrant parents and school alike (Lucas, 1997).

Attending to the Acculturative Press: Reports From the Field

In discussing the potential school counselor role, it is useful to provide select examples of how the acculturative press of schools has been attended to in terms of both empirical research reports and case studies describing schools or programs within schools which have this focus. With respect to empirical reports, for example, Rich, Ben Ari, Mar, and Eliassy (1996) provided data from Israel on schools dealing with significant numbers of immigrants from the former Soviet Union. Their focus is on how to characterize those schools doing an effective job of integrating immigrant children into the ongoing workings of the school. In addressing this issue, they made clear that, for immigrant students, the school task includes not only academic but also social goals, in this instance, social integration into the school.

Through a combination of student and teacher quantitative data and interviews with senior school officials, Rich et al. (1996) assessed varied aspects of the school climate and school structure. Using self-report data from immigrant students on perceived teacher support and native-born student acceptance and inclusion, they divided schools into effective and ineffective in their responses to immigrant students. Effective schools were more likely to have a specific adult in the school responsible for the welfare of immigrant students, were more likely to integrate newcomers into existing classes rather than using pullout programs extensively, provided additional tutorial opportunities and work for immigrant students beyond regular classroom programming, and were led by principals who viewed their job with immigrant children as more encompassing and personal rather than one focusing primarily on academic goals. In addition, elementary school (grades 1–6 or 1–8) were more effective in integrating immigrant students than junior high schools (grades 7–9), suggesting somewhat different issues related to school climate and structure at these different levels.

Additional on-the-ground data come from reports of programs within schools designed to improve the acculturation and adaptation of immigrant students. For example, Mehan et al. (1996) investigated features of a particular program, the Medical Academy, which made schoolwork for a mixed group that included Latino immigrants. The goal was to restructure the school environment to promote academic engagement in the context of a school culture that was stratified by race and differential opportunities. Here, the key was the social scaffolding of institutional support systems, "the practice of combining heterogeneous grouping with a uniform, academically rigorous curriculum enhanced with strong supports" (p. 78). Reflecting the importance for immigrant students of learning about the culture of the school, the program "explicitly teach[es] aspects of the implicit culture of the classroom and hidden curriculum of the school" (p. 81).

This report outlines a litany of issues facing immigrant students that contributed to or reflected their marginalization in the school (Mehan et al., 1996). These included the effects of tracking, socialization patterns at school, and sitting together at lunch and in classes; stigma associated with lower track classes; perceived ignoring by guidance counselors; little contact with institutional agents; and the perceived unavailability of caring teachers.

The Medical Academy program was self-consciously designed to reflect an alternative context to the marginalization just described (Mehan et al., 1996). The Medical Academy model included enhanced institutional supports for students, including an advanced, challenging curriculum, support for an academically oriented peer network, tutors, and workshop-based academic support. These specific efforts were largely lacking in the general education track at the school. In the smaller Medical Academy, every teacher knew each student by name, teachers met regularly as a group to discuss ways of doing better, and there was frequent contact between school and home. In addition, a student peer educator program linked program students with other students, community members, and parents, and career mentors were available. Taken together, these efforts are described as creating a strong sense of community and resultant commitment to school and learning.

This program demonstrated a 93% graduation rate, with 98% of graduates enrolling in college, supporting the notion that high academic press and school-level institutional supports can help at-risk students succeed (Mehan et al., 1996). In addition, the racial and ethnic diversity of the program in the context of a safe and supportive program environment encouraged intergroup contact, with friendships and dating occurring across cultural boundaries. Taken together, these findings suggest a potentially important role for school counselors in helping schools to examine their policies and practices with respect to the provision of academically challenging classes and appropriate placement of immigrant students in those classes as well as availability of academic supports for immigrant youth. They also suggest the importance of considering how course placement options facilitate or constrain opportunities for intergroup contact.

Immigrant students' first placements in their schools are typically not their last, and the difficult transition to mainstream classes from Newcomer Centers or ESL/bilingual programs represents another potential intervention point. Lucas (1997) recommended that one person be responsible for coordinating these transitions, and school counselors are well positioned to oversee this process. This role could entail (a) planning a gradual transition that slowly reduces the number of ESL/bilingual classes and adds mainstream courses; (b) arranging for additional, ongoing supports, such as tutoring, bicultural/bilingual instructional assistants, and mentoring; and (c) monitoring the transition process for each student.

In addition to programs within schools, Newcomer Schools (e.g., Olsen, 1997) provide another example of some of the ways in which school climate and structure can facilitate the adaptation of immigrant students. Lucas (1997) provided a description of the International High School in New York: a "four year comprehensive alternative high school . . . designed specifically for limited English proficient students who have been in the United States for fewer than four years" (p. 161). Because it is a school of newcomers, immigrant students are central rather than peripheral to all aspects of school life. Appreciation for diversity thus permeates the curriculum and teachers are divided into thematic clusters, "each linking four subjects around a theme and involving approximately 75 students and four to eight staff members" (p. 162). A student-centered approach, as described previously in the Medical Academy, is adopted, with extensive efforts made to create learning experiences in which students must collaborate with each other to accomplish tasks. Evaluation processes emphasize the achieving of student-defined goals and standards that demonstrate the learning they need to accomplish. Though most teachers speak English exclusively or primarily, students can take a course focusing on native language development.

There are also examples from the field of how school counselors have engaged in processes designed to learn how to learn about creating a positive acculturative press for immigrant children. McCall-Perez (2000), for example, described an action research model where school counselors gathered information about the course placement and academic outcomes for ELL through meetings with ESL teachers, observations of ESL classrooms, review of student work, and panel discussions with ELL students. As a result, some counselors learned they had seriously misjudged the English-language proficiency of their advisees. Others learned that their ELL advisees indeed held college aspirations, but had not been placed in college prep courses. This information was used to improve the school's assessment and placement of ELL students and revise the school's course schedule to devote more time to intensive English instruction and move courses requiring extensive English fluency to later in students' high school careers. In addition, the model created an electronic database of students' school experiences in their home countries and English-language proficiency that facilitated course placement decisions, despite very high student caseloads. ELL students in participating schools studied English more intensively, remained in school, and accrued more credits toward graduation and college. The use of panel discussions to gather information from key stakeholders such as ESL and general education teachers, immigrant students and their parents, and fellow counselors can go far toward giving the perspectives of immigrant students a voice and has the additional advantages of efficiency with respect to time and the use of translators.

These examples provide but a small glimpse of the possibilities for attending to the acculturative environment surrounding immigrant students in the school context. They reflect teacher–student in-class relationships, curriculum issues, structural issues around the organization of instruction, and the provision of school roles specifically dedicated to aiding immigrant student adaptation. The primary purpose for discussing them is to (a) draw attention to some of the many possible ways that the acculturative environment of schools can become a central concern and (b) provide ideas for school counselors about some of the different ways in which they, in collaboration with school colleagues, can influence this context. We close this chapter with a more focused set of comments on the implications of all of the previous discussions for the role of school counselor.

Conclusion

The preceding has outlined a general perspective on the school as an acculturative environment for immigrant students. The primary rationale for this approach was twofold: (a) to provide a perspective on how encompassing school influences are on immigrant and refugee students as they attempt to cope with adaptation to a new school in a new land and (b) to suggest, in concert with emerging literature in the counseling area (Dollarhide, 2003; Hernandez & Seem, 2004; Ito, 2004; Sink, 2002; Tatar & Bekerman, 2002), that school counselors can play critical roles for these students both by attending to their traditional roles and by adopting newer roles that focus on their abilities to affect the school as a community with respect to the needs of immigrant students. Throughout, specific ideas for potential school counselor roles have been mentioned. They fall generally into two broad categories: (a) operating within the existing normative roles of school counselors and (b) role stretching or drawing on the skills and expertise of school counselors to engage in new activities designed.

The former is more likely to consist of direct service to students and parents. Examples here may include developing processes to ensure that immigrant students and families have access to understandable information about both the specifics of how to "do school" and the broader knowledge of how schools function and how issues such as course placement affect life chances. Here, several authors (Lucas, 1997; Stanton-Salazar, 2001) have provided ideas about the specific kinds of information that will help immigrant make the most of the opportunities available and keep future options open. These include understanding the implications of such practices as tracking, how placement decisions are made, and how to make sure the requirements for entry into the honors program are fulfilled.

However, the school counselor role can also be stretched to include additional functions in the purview of the school counselor but requiring additional activities. Lucas' (1997) list includes orientation workshops for families, translation of written documents for parents and children (however, some may not be literate in their native languages), ongoing parent workshops, special orientation classes, creating the role of transition counselor, integration of orientation information in ESL classes or content classes, field trips, and pairing recent immigrants with other students.

Similar role stretching can be found in Bemack and Cornely's (2002) description of their School and Family Intervention Model (SAFI) for school counselors working specifically with immigrant students and their families. Here, the expanded counselor role would include both family-focused and school-focused interventions. The family focus is manifested in creating collaborative, power-sharing, mutually influencing relations between family and school, including creating welcoming settings and opportunities for parents to get to know both counselors and school personnel and for school personnel to learn about the lives of parents. The school focus involves counselors serving as a resource for other school personnel, providing in-service training for teachers or consultation to administrators working with parent-school relationships. Structurally, it may involve developing flexible scheduling of meetings in terms of time and place to facilitate family availability due to work constraints. Bemack and Cornely viewed most of these role-stretching possibilities as extensions of the kinds of interpersonal and group dynamic skills that are part of the counselor repertoire, fully consistent with ASCA standards calling for school counselors to attend to the overall learning environment as part of their role.

Tatar and Beckerman (2002), reinforcing Bemack and Cornely's (2002) perspective on the challenges of multiculturalism for the counselor role, emphasized that knowledge of the organizational culture of the school is critical to effective school counselor role stretching. They suggested that if counselors are to engage in efforts to change aspects of the school culture, they must study the ongoing social practices of their schools. They advocated the adoption of a sociohistorical and cultural lens on the meaning of the behavior of immigrant students, fellow school personnel, and indeed, counselors as well.

To conclude, in outlining a perspective on the acculturative environment of schools, our intent has been less to recommend specific actions on the part of school counselors and more to provide a world view that can be adapted to local context. The experience of immigrant students and families in schools, of course, is varied with respect to success, as is the ability of school counselors to respond to these children and families. However, there is sufficient data on the difficulties experienced by immigrant children and families in terms of adaptation to a new country and way of life so that explicit attention to the acculturative environment of school and the potential role of the school counselor in affecting that environment is clearly warranted. The emerging calls for an expanded role for school counselors is fully consistent with this hope on our part that school counselors can build on their current training to address the bedrock questions of how our schools can better provide for their multicultural students and how school counselors can be valued resources to the families who have given so much in hopes that their children will have a better life.

References

Amatea, E. S., Daniels, H., Bringman, N., & Vandiver, F. M. (2004). Strengthening counselor-teacher-family connections: The family-school collaborative consultation project. *Professional School Counseling, 8*(1), 1–15.

Becker, H. J., & Epstein, J. L. (1982). Parent involvement: A survey of teacher practices. *The Elementary School Journal, 83*(2), 83–113.

Bemak, F., & Chung, R. (2003). Multicultural counseling with immigrant students in schools. In P. Pederson & J. Carey (Eds.), *Multicultural counseling in schools: A practical handbook* (2nd ed., pp. 84–104). Needham Heights, MA:

Allyn & Bacon.

Bemack, F., & Cornely, L. (2002). The SAFI model as a critical link between marginalized families and schools: A literature review and strategies for school counselors. *Journal of Counseling & Development, 80,* 322–331.

Birman, D. (1998). The adjustment of Russian students at Pikesville High School, Pikesville, MD. Refugee Mental Health Program, Center for Mental Health Services, Substance Abuse and Mental Health Services Administration, Rockville, MD.

Birman, D. (in press). Measurement of the "acculturation gap" in immigrant families and implications for parent-child relationships. In M. Bornstein & L. Cotes (Eds.), *Acculturation and parent child relationships: Measurement and development. (Monographs in parenting).* Mahwah, NJ: Lawrence Erlbaum Associates.

Birman, D., & Ryeson-Espino, S. (in press). The relationship of parental practices, school knowledge, English competence, and school contact to immigrant adolescent school adaptation. *Canadian Journal of School Psychology.*

Birman, D., Trickett, E. J., & Bacchus, N. (2002). *Somali youth report.* Denver, CO: Spring Institute for Intercultural Learning.

Birman, D., Trickett, E., & Buchanan, R. (2005). A tale of two cities: Replication of a study on the acculturation and adaptation of immigrant adolescents from the former Soviet Union in a different community context. *American Journal of Community Psychology, 35*(1–2), 87–101.

Boyd, W. L., & Shouse, R. C. (1997). The problems and promise of urban schools. In H. J. Walberg, O. Reyes, & R. P. Weissberg (Eds.), *Children and youth: Interdisciplinary perspectives* (pp. 141–165). Thousand Oaks, CA: Sage.

Bronfenbrenner, U. (1979. Toward an experimental ecology of human development. *American Psychologist, 32*(7), 513–531.

Chrispeels, J. H., & Rivero, E. (2001). Engaging Latino families for student success: How parent education can reshape parents' sense of place in the education of their children. *Peabody Journal of Education, 76*(2), 119–169.

Clemente, R., & Collison, B. B. (2000). The relationships among counselors, ESL teachers, and students. *Professional School Counseling, 3*(5), 339–348.

Collignon, F., Men, M., & Tan, S. (2001). Community-based perspectives on Southeast Asian family involvement with schools in a New England state. *Journal of Education for Students Placed at Risk, 6*(1–2), 27–44.

Conchas, G. Q. (2001). Structuring failure and success: Understanding the variability in Latino school engagement. *Harvard Educational Review, 71*(3), 475–504.

Delgado-Gaitan, C. (1991). Involving parents in the schools: A process of empowerment. *American Journal of Education, 100*(1), 20–46.

Delgado-Gaitan, C. (1992). School matters in the Mexican American home: Socializing children to education. *American Educational Research Journal, 29*(3), 495–513.

Dollarhide, C. (2003). School counselors as program leaders: Applying leadership contexts to school counseling. *Professional School Counseling, 6*(5), 304–308.

Durodoye, B. A. (1998). Fostering multicultural awareness among teachers: A tripartite model. *Professional School Counseling, 1*(5), 1–10.

Eccles, J. S., & Harold, R. D. (1993). Parent-school involvement during the early adolescent years. *Teachers College Record, 94*(3), 568–587.

Epstein, J. L. (1991). Effects on student achievement of teachers' practices of parent involvement. *Advances in Reading and Language Research, 5,* 261–276.

Epstein, J. L., & Becker, H. J. (1982). Teachers' reported practices of parent involvement: Problems and possibilities. *Elementary School Journal, 83,* 103–113.

Eschenauer, R., & Chen-Hayes, S. (2005). The transformative individual school counseling model: An accountability model for urban school counselors. *Professional School Counseling, 8*(3), 244–248.

Esquivel, G. B., & Keitel, M. A. (1990). Counseling immigrant children in the schools. *Elementary School Guidance & Counseling, 24,* 213–221.

Gordon, M. (1964). *Assimilation in American life.* New York: Oxford University Press.

Greenberg, M., Weissberg, R., O'Brien, M., Zins, J., Fredericks, L., Resnik, H., et al. (2003). Enhancing school-based prevention and youth development through coordinated social, emotional, and academic learning. *American Psychologist, 58*(6–7), 466–474.

Hao, L., & Bonstead-Bruns, M. (1998). Parent-child differences in educational expectations and the academic achievement of immigrant and native students. *Sociology of Education, 7,* 175–198.

Harklau, L. (1994a). "Jumping tracks": How language minority students negotiate evaluations of ability. *Anthropology and Education Quarterly, 25,* 347–363.

Harklau, L. (1994b). Tracking and linguistic minority students: Consequences of ability grouping for second language learners. *Linguistics and Education, 6,* 217–244.

Hernandez, T., & Seem, S. (2004). A safe school climate: A systematic approach and the school counselor. *Professional School Counseling, 7*(4), 256–262.

Hess, R. D., & Holloway, S. D. (1984). Family and school as educational institutions. In R. D. Parke (Ed.), *Review of child development research: Volume 7: The family* (pp. 179–222). Chicago: University of Chicago Press.

Hoover-Dempsey, K. V., & Sandler, H. M. (1997). Why do parents become involved in their children's education? *Review of Educational Research, 67*(1), 3–42.

Ito, A. (2004). Current and future direction of school counseling and preventive interventions: Implications for comprehensive and preventive programs in Japanese schools. *Japanese Psychological Review, 47*(3), 348–361.

Lewin, K. (1951). *Field theory in social science.* New York: Harper and Row.

Lucas, T. (1997). *Into, through, and beyond secondary school: Critical transitions for immigrant youths.* McHenry, IL: Delta Systems.

Mau, W. (1997). Parental influences on the high school students' academic achievement: A comparison of Asian immigrants, Asian Americans, and White Americans. *Psychology in the Schools, 34*(3), 267–277.

McCall-Perez, Z. (2000). The counselor as advocate for English language learners: An action research approach. *Professional School Counseling, 4*(1), 13–22.

Mehan. H., Villanueva, I., Hubbard, L., & Lintz, A. (1996). *Constructing school success: The consequences of untracking for low-achieving students.* Cambridge, UK: Cambridge University Press.

Moll, L. C. (1992). Funds of knowledge for teaching: Using a qualitative approach to connect homes and classrooms. *Theory Into Practice, 31*(1), 132–141.

Murray, H. (1938). *Explorations in personality.* London: Oxford University Press.

Olsen. L. (1997). *Made in America: Immigrant students in our public schools.* New York: The New Press.

Orellana, M. F. (2003). Responsibilities of children in Latino immigrant households. *New Directions for Youth Development, 100,* 25–39.

Orellana, M. F., Dorner, L., & Pulido, L. (2003). Accessing assets: Immigrant youth's work as family translators or "para-phrasers." *Social Problems, 50,* 505–524.

Portes, A., & Rumbaut, R. G. (2001). *Legacies: The story of the immigrant second generation.* New York: Sage.

Rich, Y., Ben Ari, R., Mar, Y., & Eliassy, L. (1996). Effectiveness of schools with mixed student body of natives and immigrants. *International Journal of Intercultural Relations, 20*(3/4), 323–339.

Sarason, S. B. (1982). *The culture of the school and the problem of change* (2nd ed.). Boston: Allyn & Bacon.

Shepherd-Johnson, L. (1995). Enhancing multicultural relations: Intervention strategies for the school counselor. *The School Counselor, 43,* 103–113.

Sink, C. (2002). Comprehensive guidance and counseling programs and the multicultural student-citizen. *Professional School Counseling, 6*(2), 130–137.

Stanton-Salazar, R. D. (2001). *Manufacturing hope and despair: The school and kin support networks of U.S. Mexican youth.* New York: Teachers College Press.

Stanton-Salazar, R., & Dornbusch, S. (1995). Social capital and the social reproduction of inequality: The formation of informational networks among Mexican-origin high school students. *Sociology of Education, 68,* 116–135.

Suárez-Orozco, C., & Suárez-Orozco, M. (2001). *Children of immigration.* Cambridge, MA: Harvard University Press.

Suárez-Orozco, M. (2001). Globalization, immigration, and education: The research agenda. *Harvard Educational Review, 71*(3), 345–365.

Tatar, M., & Bekerman, Z. (2002). The concept of culture in the contexts and practices of professional counseling: A constructivist perspective. *Counseling Psychology Quarterly, 15*(4), 375–384.

Taylor, L., & Adelman, H. S. (2000). Connecting schools, families, and communities. *Professional School Counseling, 3*(5), 298–307.

Trickett, E. J. (1991). *Living an idea: Empowerment and the evolution of an alternative high school.* Brookline, MA: Brookline Books.

Trickett, E. J., & Birman, D. (1989). Taking ecology seriously. A community development approach to individually-based preventive interventions. In L. Bond & B. Compas (Eds.), *Primary prevention in the schools* (pp. 361–390). Hanover, NH: University Press of New England.

Trickett, E. J., & Jones, C. (2007). Adolescent culture brokering and family functioning: A study of families from Vietnam. *Cultural Diversity and Ethnic Minority Psychology, 13*(2), 143–150.

Trickett, E. J., Kelly, J. G., & Todd, D. M. (1972). The social environment of the high school: Guidelines for individual change and organizational development. In S. Golann & C. Eisendorfer (Eds.), *Handbook of community mental health* (pp. 331–406). New York: Appleton-Century Crofts.

Trickett, E. J., & Schmid, K. (1993). The social context of the school: An ecological perspective on school, adolescents in schools, and intervention in schools. In P. Tolan & B. Cohler (Eds.), *Handbook of clinical research and practice with adolescents* (pp. 173–202). New York: Wiley & Sons.

Trueba, H., & Delgado-Gaitan, C. (Eds.). (1988). *School and society: Learning content through culture.* New York: Praeger.

U.S. Department of Education. (1994). *Strong families, strong schools: Building community partnerships for learning.* Washington, DC: Author.

Weinstein, R. (2002). *Reaching higher: The power of expectations in schooling.* Cambridge, MA: Harvard University Press.

Williams, F. C., & Butler, S. K. (2003). Concerns of newly arrived immigrant students: Implications for school counselors. *Professional School Counseling, 7*(1), 9–14.

Zhou, M. (2001). Straddling different worlds: The acculturation of Vietnamese refugee children. In R. Rumbaut & A. Portes (Eds.), *Ethnicities: Children of immigrants in America.* Berkeley: University of California Press.

VII
IMMIGRANT CHILDREN AND YOUTH IN SCHOOLS

SARAH J. LEE AND KAREN A. CORT
Teachers College, Columbia University

Currently, the demographic shift in the United States stems from the rapid increase in the influx of immigrants from around the world (U.S. Bureau of the Census, 2001). In the year 2002, there were 32.5 million immigrants living in the United States. Of those, 52.5% were born in Latin America, 25.5% in Asia, and 14% in Europe and the remaining 8% were from other parts of the world. Due to recent immigration trends and differential birth rates, people of color compose over 30% of the U.S. population, approximately 45% of whom are attending public schools (Sue & Sue, 2003; U.S. Bureau of the Census, 2000). According to A. Portes and Rumbaut (1996), immigrant children from a minority background constitute more than one half of the entire children immigrant population in the United States. Of these immigrant students, those who are of Asian and Hispanic descent make up the largest immigrant groups in the elementary and secondary schools (U.S. Department of Education, 1997). Vernez and Abrahamse (1996) also found that although immigrant children and youth were just as likely as nonimmigrants to enroll in U.S. primary and middle schools, they were less likely to attend high school. Because of this demographic shift, immigrant children and youth in schools now represent a major constituency within the public schools, and due to the challenges they face in school, this is an important focus for school counselors (U.S. Department of Homeland Security, 2004).

Past literature suggests that many immigrant students struggle to adapt to a new environment and culture, and they experience pressure to assimilate into the American mainstream (Sue & Sue, 2003). In contrast to native-born individuals in the United States, many immigrants experience additional barriers such as language acquisition, social economic status, cultural value conflict, racism and discrimination, and intergenerational conflicts (Chiu & Ring, 1998). In addition, Sue (2001) reported that many of the values, beliefs, and practices of today's society are structured to serve only a select portion of the population, which includes mainly individuals and groups from the host culture. Sue & Sue highlighted the importance for counselors to be culturally aware of their own values and biases that may be imposed onto individuals. As such, school counselors and teachers must avoid imposing these beliefs onto minority clients, as it may invalidate their own cultural values and experiences. Additional barriers to an immigrant student's academic success may be inherent to the school culture and environment. For example, school counselors and teachers may be responsible for the inappropriate instructional placements for immigrant youth, teacher prejudice, poor facilities, racism and discrimination, unmotivated teachers, and academic curricula that have little relevance to immigrants.

Due to the large diversity of the immigrant population, this chapter can give only an overview of common challenges and issues that are experienced by immigrant children and adolescents from diverse populations. This chapter will also discuss some of the between-group and within-group differences that exist among immigrant students and some of the ways in which school counselors and educators can begin effectively working with these students to provide them with the best educational support. The authors will also discuss implications for school counselors so they can begin addressing the concerns of immigrant students who have their own unique individual needs in major public school systems throughout the United States.

Research

Acculturative Stress

Many immigrants share a common experience coming into the United States—the process of migration and acculturation. This cultural change has posed new challenges for many immigrants who experience various types of stressors due to cultural and social adjustment, which is often referred to as "acculturative stress" (Garcia Coll & Magnuson, 1997; C. L. Williams & Berry, 1991). Oftentimes, stress is due to the acculturation process when an individual experiences conflict between two distinct cultures (Nwadiora & McAdoo, 1996). In addition, a major consequence of the acculturation process is associated with acculturative stress, which accounts for the variable mental health outcomes that have been observed among immigrants and refugees arriving in a new country (C. L. Williams & Berry; Nwadiora & McAdoo; Kuo & Roysircar, 2004). Within this general acculturation perspective, this notion is also found to be highly associated with culture shock (Furnham & Bochner, 1986) due to the affects of stress, which may eventually expose migrants to the risk of illness (C. L. Williams & Berry).

Research has revealed that various acculturative stressors are experienced differently among immigrants from diverse migration and generational statuses, which accounts for one's level of acculturation (Berry, Kim, Minde, & Mok, 1987; C. L. Williams & Berry, 1991). From a theoretical perspective, Berry et al. (1987) proposed four different modes of acculturation by which individuals who feel marginalized, as well as those who choose to remain separate, are likely to be highly stressed. In contrast, individuals who seek integration may experience minimal levels of stress, while those who assimilate tend to feel intermediate levels of stress. Thus, we can assume that acculturation occurs in different types of situations and that individuals may participate in and experience these changes as they vary from person to person.

More importantly, Berry et al. (1987) noted that the consequences of acculturative stress may not be applicable across cultures, especially for immigrant and refugee groups. The outcome of acculturative stress may not always be negative; positive outcomes include enhanced opportunities and mental health (Nwadiora & McAdoo, 1996). For example, although immigrants and refugees may experience similar adjustment problems, they may eventually become socialized to the norms, behaviors, and lifestyle of the dominant culture and, in turn, focus on striving for success rather than relying on a simple stress reduction (Torres & Rollock, 2004).

Because research on acculturative stress has shown varied results, Berry and Kim (1998) have suggested that acculturating groups have their own degree to which they experience stress, which can also account for their own unique ways in which they cope and deal with their problems (C. L. Williams & Berry, 1991). Thus, Coleman (1997) suggested that there is a need to understand individuals' coping mechanisms and strategies as they relate to cultural adjustment. Further, there is a need for future research to examine alternative conceptualizations of cultural adjustment and adaptation in order to provide a better understanding of this phenomenon.

Migration Pattern

Current research areas must focus more on recognizing the different types of immigrants who come into the United States, as each group has its own distinct migration experiences and sociocultural histories that play a significant role in its process of acculturation and lifestyle (Talmadge, 2002). Because of these different patterns of migration, many ethnic/racial groups are unevenly distributed within the United States. Specifically, many immigrant children and youth seem to be increasingly concentrated in urban areas such as New York City, Chicago, Los Angeles, Philadelphia, and other major cities (U.S. Bureau of the Census, 2000). Though many of the 30 million immigrants who have come to the United States since 1990 are still dispersed throughout the suburb and rural areas, most will likely affect the school systems in the aforementioned cities (F. C. Williams & Butler, 2003). This means that a core issue in the emerging field of urban education will involve the needs of immigrant children and youth.

As immigrant children and youth arrive in the United States, researchers have studied a variety of factors that may have impacted their assimilation process, such as immigration status (e.g., legal, illegal, refugee; Sue & Sue, 2003; U.S. Department of Homeland Security, 2004). In addition, Ogbu (1983) distinguished between voluntary immigrants (e.g., European) and involuntary immigrants (e.g., Africans). Involuntary immigrants came to the United States by force and enslavement, which will impact the process of acculturation and assimilation differently from groups who came to the United States by their own choice. Dawkins (2000) reported that Haitian and Cuban refugees have been found to be treated differently with the former being sent back to their homeland due to the variation of U.S. immigration policy. Similarly, Chinese immigrants are often considered as voluntary immigrants because they migrated to the United States by choice, whereas most Vietnamese refugees fled from their homelands due to war and violence (Chiu & Ring, 1998). Thus, it can be assumed that some immigrants may have an advantage of having made prior arrangements before migrating to the United States, whereas refugees are often unprepared to start a new life in an unknown country.

Roysircar-Sodowsky and Maestas (2000) reported, however, that many refugee experiences have been focused on adults and that research on immigrant youth has been very limited. Regardless, we need to be aware of the cultural stressors that may leave emotional scars for many immigrant youths who come into a new environment and, in turn, make learning difficult in school (Atkinson & Juntunen, 1994).

The heterogeneity of immigration statuses are now emerging in research literature and may assist school counselors and teachers to understand the mobility patterns and impact of circular migration within the United States. For example, while many immigrant parents bring their children to the United States for permanent residency, others many send their children back to their native country (Harkins, 2001). For example, Harkins studied a group of Kaigaishijo students, a significant subset of the Japanese population, and reported that these students returned to Japan shortly after their parents' businesses and responsibilities were completed. In other serial migration patterns, Smith, LaLonde, and Johnson (2004) found that many Caribbean parents migrated to the new country first, with the children following later, which presents other stressors for the family (Gopaul-McNicol, 1998). Thus, having an accurate assessment of children's adaptation to the host country requires an understanding of the impact of migration among immigrant families across cultures (Suarez-Orozco & Suarez-Orozco, 2001).

Acculturation

Immigrant students cannot be understood without considering the range of migration experiences that characterize these children and their families. Thus, the process of acculturation is one of the most explored topics in understanding the migration experiences for immigrants across cultures, which is also a significant part of their developmental process (Berry, 1997; Mitchell, 2005). One definition of *acculturation* refers to changes in cultures, values, and behaviors that individuals make as they gradually conform to the dominant group or society (Mitchell). For many Hispanics, the process of acculturation has been assessed by identifying differences among their generational status due to migration streams from Mexico, Central America, and South America, including the Caribbean, which is sending a large number of Hispanics into the urban areas of the United States (Rogler, Cortes, & Malgady, 1991). Coupling the importance of generational status, it is also imperative for school counselors to be aware of the heterogeneity of immigrants that enter the United States and understand the differences in immigration status (Chiu & Ring, 1998).

Consistent with other studies, B. S. Kim, Brenner, Liang, and Asay (2003) reported that one's level of acculturation is linked to generation status. These generation trends include 1st-generation, 1.5-generation, and 2nd-generation immigration statuses (B. S. Kim et al., 2003). Many immigrant children may identify most with the 1.5 generation, meaning they were born in their native country and later moved to the United States, whereas 2nd-generation individuals were born in the United States. Immigrants who were born in their native country and arrived in the United States sometime during their adult years are referred to as "1st-generation immigrants." Many Asian Americans use the term *1.5-generation* to describe individuals who have immigrated to the United States during early childhood or adolescent years, so that most of their developmental years were spent and their identity established in the United States (B. S. Kim et al.). The differences in generation statuses may be critical in helping school counselors to understand the adaptation experiences of each immigrant group, especially immigrant students in comparison with the adult immigrant population. Thus, the impact of generation statuses as part of the acculturation process is most likely to be experienced by children in the school setting because much of their development and socialization occurs within this context (James, 1997a). Hence, it is important for school counselors to have the awareness, knowledge, and skills to assess students' migration experiences, potential traumas, and challenges in acculturation as they settle into a new country (Sue & Sue, 2003). School counselors have a significant role in establishing the social and educational setting into which a student immigrates, so it is important for them to understand the complex process of acculturation as it impacts immigrant students' academic performance (Harkins, 2001).

Although immigrant children and youth are one of the fastest growing groups in the educational school system, there is still a paucity of research and resources available to better address the salient needs of this population (Gibbs, Huang, & Associates, 1989). In order to better meet the needs of each student, counselors need to gather more information about specific immigrant children and youth populations. As previously mentioned, each child is unique and has special needs and concerns that may be different from the group with which he or she identifies. Because little has been written about counseling immigrant youth, this chapter addresses some generic concerns and needs that are of great urgency when working with immigrant students in schools. It also offers some possibilities for individual and institutional changes that will lead to more effective education for students across cultures. This field needs studies that account for the various settlement patterns, immigration statuses, generational statuses, and behaviors exhibited by different immigrants across cultures.

Culture Shock

The influx of newly arrived immigrants into the United States is most affected by culture shock, which is described as a series of disorienting encounters that occur when individuals are faced with challenging events and contacts with a new culture that are inconsistent with their basic values, beliefs, cultures, and lifestyles (Lynch, 1992; Yost & Lucas, 2002). More specifically, culture shock is a psychological reality for many immigrant children and youth who come to a host culture that is different from their native country, especially in a new school setting (Kaplan & Eckermann, 1996; Eckermann, 1994). In addition, Eckermann (1994) argued that immigrant children who are able to identify with the school environment in terms of language, values, and experiences were more likely to have better adjustment than those who could not make this identification. On the other hand, the immigrant students who felt disconnected from the school environment were found to experience acute culture shock, which, in turn, negatively impacted their social development and performance in learning. As such, understanding the adjustment process as it relates to culture shock is extremely important because the experience of culture shock is often so great that it impedes individuals from effectively solving problems, making decisions, and interacting positively when they feel overwhelmed and uncomfortable in the environment (Draine & Hall, 1986).

According to Bhattacharya (2000), many immigrant children find that cultural differences between their native homeland and the host country play a significant part in their academic achievement. For example, in a study of Aboriginal children, Kaplan and Eckermann (1996) found that culture shock was highly associated with stress and anxiety, which was one of the major factors negatively impacting the children's ability to achieve in school. Similarly, many Asian immigrant adolescents may be disappointed after arriving to the United States when they realize that their new life does not meet their expectations. As a result, their disappointment may lead to distress such as feelings of anger, resentment, and depression (Yeh, 2003).

Culture shock is a common problem shared by many immigrants; however, it may also be more salient in the lives of refugees (Drachman & Halberstadt, 1992). According to Drachman and Halberstadt, refugees suffered psychological and physical trauma before their immigration, due to traumatic events such as war and violence (Chiu & Ring, 1998), which include feelings of isolation, fear, anxiety, and resistance to change (Igoa, 1995). Thus, experiencing both culture shock and the psychological effects from their homeland may be more severe than in other immigrant populations (Yost & Lucas, 2002); however, the affects of culture shock are prevalent across all cultures and must be further examined, as it clearly impacts the academic achievement of immigrant children in school (Bhattacharya, 2000).

Language Barrier

Statistics revealed that immigrant children and youth constitute a large percentage of public school enrollment from K–12 (U.S. Department of Homeland Security, 2004). Acknowledging potential barriers regarding lack of language proficiency is an important area to be considered (Graham, 1995). Students who speak another language and have limited proficiency in English are found to be one of the fastest growing populations in public schools in the United States (Smith-Davis, 2004a). In fact, 350 different languages are spoken in school districts across the United States.

The new immigrant populations are a diverse group, as they vary on their level of prior education and literacy in the native language (Smith-Davis, 2004b). Thus, it is important for school counselors to be aware of the heterogeneity of language spoken by immigrant students in both school and home settings. The variation in the immigrants' academic competence in their culture of origin compounds the difficulties many immigrant populations experience as they struggle to acquire English as a second language (Sue & Sue, 2003). Thus, learning a new language may impede academic performance and, in turn, become a source of stress, especially for students who fear speaking in a classroom setting, which is a common practice for schools in the United States (Bhattacharya, 2000; James, 1997a). Simultaneously, it is most noteworthy to recognize that immigrant students enter school with varying degrees of preparation and educational competencies, which can impact their academic performance. While understanding the challenges of learning a second language, it is also important to recognize that learning a second language may not be the main problem but it is the fact that students may have been illiterate or preliterate in their own native language. Kang, Kuehn, and Herrell (1994) found that Hmong students in grades K–12 face a difficult challenge because the Hmong language was only recently written (about 30 years ago); therefore, most of the children may not have received adequate academic preparation for their grade level (Schwartz & Stiefel, 2004).

Many immigrant students face different barriers and limitations than those faced by native-born children, such as developing English language skills, learning basic academic concepts needed to function in U.S. schools, overcoming difficulties in communication, and gaining cultural knowledge. Even when a child has learned the basic conversational aspects of the second language, it may still take some time for a child to fully comprehend on a level of cognitive and academic functioning (Schwartz & Stiefel, 2004). Thus, there is a particular concern in the cases where various schools are not adequately equipped with the tools and resources to help maximize the potential of immigrant populations. Further, it is crucial that school counselors understand the effects of acculturative factors such as generational status, language barriers, linguistic differences, lack of understanding of prior education, and experiences of immigrant students, which pose new challenges on educational achievement in working effectively with this population (Yeh & Inose, 2002).

Social Economic Status

As noted above, difficulty with language may be one of several stressors experienced by immigrant children and youth who transition into a new culture (Bhattacharya, 2000). Another increasing area of concern is the academic school achievement of immigrant youth and the effects of social economic status and parental support that children receive at home, which have an impact of academic performance (Coleman, 1997). The U.S. Bureau of the Census (2000) reported that 11% of nonimmigrants have income below the poverty level while 17% of immigrant households were estimated at being below the poverty level. In general, immigrant children who are raised in families whose incomes is below the poverty level may be more likely to fail academically and eventually drop out of school than nonimmigrants (Taylor, 2004).

Research suggests that social economic status may be linked to academic performance for many immigrant adolescents (James, 1997a). Several authors suggested that many adolescents who come from low-income families might work long hours to help support the family and that may impact their ability to attend school and, in turn, affect their ability to learn in school (Mitchell, 2005; Zhou, 2003). For example, in a culture of migration, adolescents may have to take the responsibility of becoming a labor migrant as part of their transition from adolescent into adulthood. To support this notion, Mitchell reported that Caribbean Americans had a high labor force participation and median income. Statistics indicated, however, that this population may also work multiple jobs to maintain a steady income for their household. Similarly, many Asian American families are reported to have higher median income compared with the general population; however, statistics do not take into account the high percentage of Asian American families with multiple individual family members contributing to the family income (Sue & Sue, 2003).

Many immigrant populations may struggle with low social economic status as it relates to language barrier. For example, several authors found that one of the overarching themes among the immigrant population is their inability to effectively communicate due to language barrier and the subsequent negative impact on their employment opportunities (Chun, Eastman, Wang, & Sue, 1998; Sue & Sue, 2003). Sandhu (1997) reported that many Southeast Asians are three times more likely to be on welfare compared with the general population due to lack of job skills and English language barriers. As a result, young adolescents may experience frustration, helplessness, and low self-esteem, which may lead to academic failure and various psychological problems (Yeh & Inose, 2002).

Racism/Discrimination

There is substantive support to the argument that immigrants may experience additional sources of stress and problems such as immigrant status, poverty, racism, discrimination, and prejudices by society in comparison with persons from the host country (Yeh & Inose, 2002; Sue & Sue, 2003; Yost & Lucus, 2002). More specifically, the impact of racism and prejudice may be an important development task for immigrant children and adolescents to manage, particularly immigrants of color and, in turn, such a task may affect their academic achievement (Garcia Coll & Magnuson, 1997). The increasing reports of racism and prejudices encountered by immigrant children and youth, however, have become more complex and difficult to document. As a result, this area of concern has been subject to limited research; more investigation to understand the behavioral and psychological impact of immigrant population is warranted.

In an attempt to better understand the impact of racism and discrimination, it is crucial to understand that these experiences may be largely dependent upon multiple factors for each immigrant as an individual and as a group. Many Asian immigrant youth may face additional challenges such as racial discrimination and stereotypes than their White American counterparts (Chiu & Ring, 1998). For example, many Asian immigrant youth are often labeled with the notion of the "model minority myth," which suggests that Asians are academically successful and do not exhibit major problems (Chiu & Ring, 1998). In addition, school counselors may have higher expectations of Asian students academically due to their reputation as good students while other students may engender hostility toward these students for the same reason (Herring, 1997). This myth can serve to invalidate the experiences of Asian immigrant children and youth because it assumes that they do not have any adjustment issues or problems (Yeh & Inose, 2002). It is also important to note, however, that many European immigrants from Eastern and Southern Europe (i.e., non-English immigrants) may experience prejudice and discrimination from "native" Anglo Americans who viewed them as being culturally inferior due to their disadvantaged status and language barrier (Giordano & McGoldrick, 1996). Thus, it is critical for counselors to recognize the salience of racism experienced by immigrant children across all cultures, regardless of race and ethnicity.

As previously mentioned, while many immigrant adolescents already struggle with the hardship of learning the English language, they may face an additional stressor of feeling stigmatized when speaking in class and may find discrimination and stereotyping to be a confusing experience (Yeh & Inose, 2002). In addition, the educational school system may also contribute to their stress through implicit and explicit racist educational policies, intergroup conflict and tension, and teachers who do not have or demonstrate multicultural competence. Sue & Sue (2003) stated that it is vital for educators, counselors, and teachers who work with immigrant youth to understand how social and cultural forces have impacted and shaped the lifestyle of this type of population. Within this frame of mind, educational systems must engage in careful examination of the values being taught and how these values influence culturally diverse groups as well as members of the dominant culture. Thus, educators are responsible for being aware of and countering particular stereotypes, prejudices, and discrimination that immigrant students face within the school environment. Overall, school counselors should be aware of the fueling of public stereotypes and prejudices against immigrant groups, which may potentially affect immigrant students' school performance and achievement.

Intergenerational Conflict

Generational conflicts between parents and adolescents in the United States have been a continuous challenge, as this conflict is a core theme within the acculturation process (Herring, 1997). In particular, immigrant adolescents experience intergenerational clash with their parents because of differences in values, customs, and lifestyles—as adolescents become more assimilated into the "American" lifestyle—that are at odds with their parents' expectations (James, 1997b). As a result, immigrant parents often perceive their children's attempts to separate and individuate from their family roots as a rejection of the entire family, its values, and the culture it represents. Further, many parents may resist their children's acculturation, as it causes family conflict between what adolescents aspire for in life contrasted with what is expected of them by their parents (James, 1997b). Another source of intergenerational conflict has been the experiences of immigrant children who are often caught between double roles when they serve as a cultural bridge for their parents (Garcia Coll & Magnuson, 1997). According to Baptiste (1993), school-age children were found to acculturate faster by adapting to a new culture and learning a new language more rapidly than their parents through their exposure to the school environment. In a study conducted with Southeast Asian immigrant children, S. Kim, Coletti, Williams, and Hepler (1995) found that when immigrant parents have limited English acquisition, the children feel obligated to master the English language more quickly in order to help translate for their parents. The child assumes a new role in the family and serves as the cultural translator for his or her parents by completing job applications, shopping, using public transportation, being an interpreter during doctor visits, and engaging in particular situations in which they would not otherwise engage (Baptiste; S. Kim et al., 1995). Thus, the generational boundaries are crossed because the parent may rely heavily on the child to take certain responsibilities and make decisions that impact the entire family and, in turn, cause distress for the child. Further, parents may also feel distressed and frustrated by the role reversal of the child–parent relationship and come to resent their dependence on the child (Garcia Coll & Magnuson, 1997).

Psychological Effects

Immigrating to a new country involves different types of adjustments and transitions that may affect the emotional and psychological health of the family unit as well as the individual family members (Smith et al., 2004). As discussed throughout the chapter, we can assume that the aforementioned challenges and barriers (i.e., culture shock, acculturative stress) may become a clinical issue when they manifests into various elevated symptoms and mental disorders (Berry et al., 1987; Furnham & Bochner, 1986; Garcia Coll & Magnuson, 1997). For many immigrant children and youth, stress may be a significant factor in understanding mental health and development during adolescence (Chiu & Ring, 1998; Colten & Gore, 1991) due to the transition of leaving behind a familiar language, culture, community, and society (James, 1997a). According to Berry (1990), stress is often precursor for many immigrants leading to lowered mental health, feelings of marginality, isolation, and high levels of psychosomatic symptoms.

At the same time, Sluzki (1979) reported that many immigrants may not be aware of the emotional and psychological impact of their new environment and, in turn, may negate the stressful experience of their migration process. James (1997b) asserted that psychological suffering and trauma may be less visible and more difficult to measure, especially for illegal immigrants, who must cope with the problem of being discovered and deported back to their homeland. Several researchers found specific circumstances inherent to the migration process that may be stressful for young immigrants. For example, in a study involving Chinese immigrants (i.e., student visa holders) and American-born students, the former group reported loneliness, isolation, language and communication barriers, and being homesick, in contrast with their American counterparts (Igoa, 1995; C. L. Williams & Berry, 1991; Zheng & Berry, 1991). As a result of various stressors, Chinese immigrants reported more general anxiety symptoms (Chung, 1994), which were also found to be related to depression (Constantine, Okazaki, & Utsey, 2004).

Similarly, Draine and Hall (1986) found that discomfort in the environment may lead to a series of emotional and physical distress such as frustration, anger, depression, withdrawal, and various illnesses that may be difficult for the individual to handle. Although recent psychology literature reveals that many immigrant youth demonstrate psychological problems (Chiu & Ring, 1998), they are less likely to seek mental health care services than nonimmigrants are (Munroe-Blum, Boyle, Offord, & Kates, 1989; Sue & Sue, 2003). In general, it is important to consider that although immigrant families may experience stress, they may not seek treatment for their members due to a myriad of cultural reasons, which include differences in values, beliefs, background, and experiences (Sue & Sue, 2003).

Conclusion

The aim of this chapter was to provide a comprehensive overview of problems and issues that are commonly encountered by immigrant children and youth from across cultures, particularly in the context of education. More importantly, the authors' intentions were to help readers understand the complexity of an immigrant student's migration history, level of acculturation, language, and cultural factors, as well as their effect on academic achievement, as each individual has his or her own unique and individual experiences. In addition, one cannot assume that all immigrant children and youth have the same exact experiences, but rather, one must recognize the heterogeneity of each immigrant youth and, in turn, embrace the diversity that exists within all students. Because immigrants are a heterogeneous group, it is critical that counselors, practitioners, and researchers explore other patterns of underlying issues that have not surfaced into discussion. Further, the next section will provide specific ways in which theoretical models and practical guidelines can be applied in counseling practice, education, and research.

Conceptual Frameworks

Several theories have influenced school counselors when working with immigrant youth. The cultural deprivation and the cultural diversity models, however, illustrate the dynamic influence and relationship between the individual students and their culture, which accounts for the essence of the working relationship between school counselors and immigrant students (Coleman, 1995).

Cultural Deprivation Model

Although school counseling has existed since the 1920s, the profession became officially standardized and uniform several decades later. In the 1950s and '60s, as a result of the creation of the American Personnel and Guidance Association in 1952 (now the American Counseling Association [ACA]), the passage of the National Defense Education Act in 1958, and the increased school enrollments caused by the baby boomers, the training programs of school counselors increased in number and became standardized (Baker & Gerler, 2004).

During this time period, the term *cultural deprivation* was frequently used to describe underachieving students in the public school system and to indicate that many groups performed poorly on tests or exhibited negative characteristics because they were culturally impoverished and lacked many of the advantages of White middle-class culture (Sue & Sue, 2003). Given the fact that school counselor training programs were being established during this time, we can assume that the cultural deprivation ideology heavily influenced the curricula and techniques of school counselor trainees, as well as those of practicing school counselors. This ideology unfortunately places the blame of deficiency on the individual, perpetuating the myth of minority inferiority and superiority of White middle-class values. The core thesis of the cultural deprivation model is that the host society (i.e., American society) is what is perceived as normal and valued. If one does not have that culture, one is deprived. This suggests that immigrant does not have a culture of value, which they bring to the school.

School counselors were, therefore, being trained to assimilate students into White American cultural norms and values. Pathology was being equated with deviation from these norms, which is particularly detrimental and harmful when working with immigrant youth who are from diverse cultures, especially immigrant students of color. Their cultural background was often being invalidated and was cited as the source of their pathology and lack of success in the American educational system. Unfortunately, this ideology predominated American culture for decades.

Culturally Diverse Model

As the United States has become more racially and ethnically diverse, the school counseling profession has been challenged and is being held accountable for promoting academic achievement for *all* students, through efforts such as the National Model of Comprehensive School Counseling Programs (Baker & Gerler, 2004). Through such initiatives and over time, a shift in the predominant ideology of cultural deprivation to cultural diversity has occurred. School counselors are now being called upon to recognize the legitimacy of alternative lifestyles and the value of cultural differences. The "cultural diversity" ideology implies that all racial/ethnic groups are equally valued and that all cultural perspectives are important in understanding human development and behavior. Comparisons of different cultural groups should not be made, in particular against the White American cultural standard (Sue & Sue, 2003). School counselors have slowly begun to develop interventions and instructional guidelines that reflect the racial and cultural experiences of racial/ethnic groups of people (Carter, 1995). This shift in ideology serves to empower immigrant students (who are often from racial/ethnic minority groups), instead of forcing them to assimilate and ascribe to foreign (and often oppressive) norms and behaviors (Constantine & Gushue, 2003).

Throughout the history of the school counseling profession, these two drastically different ideologies have influenced the practice and training of school counselors. The cultural deprivation model served to allow school counselors to focus on the assimilation of racially and ethnically diverse students and immigrant youth into White cultural standards and behaviors through attempts to realize the myth of the "melting pot." Although this practice was somewhat successful in facilitating the academic accomplishment of European immigrants through the 1940s, it has not demonstrated its effectiveness with non-European immigrants. As the United States has become more racially and ethnically diverse, particularly with immigrants from non-European backgrounds, the cultural diversity model has encouraged school counselors to assess and understand the value of different cultures, and how these differences can both positively and negatively influence the immigrant students. This focus on integration may be more effective at promoting academic accomplishment among recent immigrants than the assimilationist approach of a previous generation.

With a greater understanding of the conceptual frameworks that influence school counselors' training and role, the next section will examine the ways in which school counselors have engaged in their work with immigrant students.

Practice

Historically, the U.S. educational system has been constructed and defined by the dominant culture (i.e., White Anglo-Saxon Protestant middle-class American). This system focuses mainly on U.S.-born students without taking into account the broad spectrum of students who migrate from diverse cultures around the world (Bemak & Chung, 2003). In reviewing the experiences of immigrant children and adolescents in the American educational system, it is critical for school counselors to become involved in making the changes that will lead to greater success for immigrant youth. A school counselor is the first person in school that immigrant students encounter, since, in most school settings, the school counselor is the person responsible for initial registration, as well as academic scheduling and course planning. In these initial introductions, as well as through access to records, counselors are often the first to learn and identify the daily struggles to survive and the more immediate social and economic stressors with which the immigrant student may be dealing (which can be a higher priority in the immediate, than are the benefits of a seemingly abstract and far-reaching goal of graduation; Bemak & Chung). Counselors are, therefore, well positioned to work with immigrant students and assist in their successful transition to the American school environment. School counselors may, however, be called upon to extend themselves beyond their traditional roles when working with immigrant students, and they may need to serve as leaders, advocates, and social change agents in the school and in the community at large.

The next section will be a brief review of recommendations and strategies for school counselors to utilize when working with immigrant students in school.

Multicultural Competence

Before any helping professional begins his or her work with any client, he or she must strive to achieve multicultural competence. In the broadest sense, multicultural competence is the ability to effectively provide services cross-culturally (Sue & Sue, 2003), and it should be achieved through both didactic training and ongoing self-exploration and experiential learning. For school counselors, multicultural competence may involve broadening the roles that counselors play and pushing them to expand their repertoire of appropriate helping skills (Sue & Sue), especially when working with immigrant youth, who are often from cultural backgrounds that are different from the counselor's background. Research has found that school counselors with previous multicultural training and higher tolerance to ethnic diversity have been found to better conceptualize the mental health issues of immigrant students and are better able to consider and integrate salient cultural information in the context of conceptualizing and addressing their presenting concerns (Constantine & Gushue, 2003). Multicultural competence generally focuses on three domains: (a) understanding attitudes/beliefs of one's own culture, (b) understanding the worldview of others, and (c) the ability to determine and use culturally appropriate intervention strategies with clients (Sue & Sue).

Understanding Ourselves

School counselors must begin with awareness of their own assumptions, values, and biases, which will impact their work with clients (Sue & Sue, 2003). Counselors need to become knowledgeable about how race, culture, and all of their reference group memberships affect their thoughts, behaviors, and interactions with others. How we view and understand the world is from our cultural lens, and often unconsciously, our thoughts, behaviors, and interactions reflect our own values and beliefs (Sue & Sue). Counselors cannot assume that their values and beliefs are shared by others, and if they are not aware of their own cultural beliefs (on both an intellectual *and* emotional level), they may impose their perspective onto others and ultimately invalidate and oppress them.

Understanding Others

Once school counselors gain an understanding of themselves, they must then try to understand the worldview and experiences of their students. School counselors need to gain knowledge about cultural nuances and different cultural experiences, values, and norms of the immigrant population, as well as how acculturation may be impacting them in various ways (F. C. Williams & Butler, 2003). Counselors should not strive to become cultural "experts," nor do they have to hold these worldviews themselves. Instead, school counselors need to accept the worldviews of others in a nonjudgmental manner, in order to be able to effectively counsel and assist immigrant students (Sue & Sue, 2003).

For example, during a meeting with an Asian immigrant student to conduct initial course scheduling/planning, the school counselor must first be aware of his or her own assumptions and beliefs about Asians, as he or she may hold inappropriate, stereotypical beliefs about this group. The counselor may assume that the student is either highly intelligent (due to the belief in the model minority myth), or conversely low functioning (because of the belief that the student is not capable due to an assumed level of English language ability). These stereotypical beliefs may influence the counselor and result in misplacement of and unsuitable course selection for the student, setting the student up for potential failure. The counselor needs to be cognizant not only of his or her personal biases regarding Asians, but of Asian cultural values as well. Awareness of cultural values may help counselors assist immigrant students with the most suitable course selections. For instance, the aforementioned school counselor working with the Asian immigrant student should have some knowledge of the Asian cultural value system of cooperation and collectivism (versus the American values of competition and individualism). As such, the Asian immigrant student first entering an American school system could benefit from classes or teachers that work more collaboratively or in groups, as opposed to courses that focus more on individualism (e.g., debate class). Moreover, in class, this student may tend to keep to himself and be quiet in class discussions, especially during heated debates, and he may hesitate to confront others in order to avoid interpersonal conflicts. Although their behavior is congruent with their cultural value system, once they are in America, many Asian immigrant youth encounter values and customs that are contradictory to those of their country of origin. What these youth understand as accepted norms and behavioral patterns in their country of origin may be ridiculed or misunderstood in America, which can create confusion and discomfort for them (Yeh & Inose, 2002). Counselors with an understanding of Asian cultural values may be able to educate and train teachers on how to work effectively with immigrant youth, as well as how to deal with cultural tensions in the classroom.

Moreover, for many immigrant youth of color, the experience of racism and racial labeling is a unique and often traumatizing experience for them in the United States. Many did not encounter this experience in their native lands. Many immigrant youth are moving from countries that are racially homogeneous (e.g., Asian countries), or from places where ethnic categories are more important. For example, in some Muslim countries, it is more important to be identified by sect—such as Shiite—than by skin color (F. C. Williams & Butler, 2003). These youth may find being stereotyped and discriminated against due to the color of their skin very confusing (Yeh & Inose, 2002), and they may have to assume a new racial identity. Moreover, many West Indian immigrant youth may be contending with similar levels of racism as native-born Black Americans, which again may serve to confuse and paralyze them, as they were not socialized with the history of racial oppression found in the United States and may not understand how to adapt and survive discrimination and prejudice of this type (Albertini, 2004).

Multiculturally competent school counselors need to be aware of and acknowledge the insidious nature of racism and racial oppression in the United States, especially within the school environment. They must be supportive of their immigrant students of color instead of invalidating their experiences. On an individual level, school counselors should make an effort to check in and meet with new immigrant students, providing them with an opportunity to discuss their adjustment experiences. Moreover, on a larger scale, counselors can conduct workshops to educate not only the immigrant youth, but also the school faculty and staff overall about prejudice and discrimination within contemporary society. All too often in today's society, it is assumed that prejudice and discrimination no longer exist, due to the effects of the Civil Rights Movement and other social justice efforts. Although these efforts have been successful in decreasing overt discrimination and creating more opportunities for racial/ethnic minority groups, prejudice and discrimination continue to rear their ugly head sand impact all our lives. Media is often helpful in addressing these sensitive topics, and counselors can utilize films such as, *A Class Divided* with Jane Elliott, or a more recent film *Crash*. Both vividly depict how prejudice develops, as well as the lethal effects of discrimination.

On their quest to acquire cultural knowledge and information of others, school counselors need to be wary and careful not to stereotype. Although people from certain groups may share common values and worldviews, it does not mean that all people from these groups are the same; we are all individuals and group members (Sue & Sue, 2003). For example, many Asian immigrant youth suffer from the model minority myth. Some school counselors overlook the psychological problems of Asian immigrant youth and consequently fail to provide effective interventions to them, for they assume that all Asian students are well adjusted because many are compliant and may be excelling academically (Yeh & Inose, 2002).

Culturally Appropriate Strategies

Different racial/ethnic groups respond best to culture-specific strategies of helping, and this is especially true for immigrant youth. Greater effectiveness is most likely achieved when the school counselor takes on different roles and utilizes different modalities that may be more consistent with the life experiences and cultural values of their students (Sue & Sue, 2003). Most theories of counseling that school counselors are exposed to in their training programs generally prescribe the types of actions and roles played by a counselor; however, these may prove minimally helpful to immigrant students, and as such, school counselors may need to expand their range of helping responses (Sue & Sue). For example, "talk therapy" may not be congruent with Asian cultural values. For many Asians, it is not culturally appropriate to discuss personal concerns with others, as it may cause shame for the whole family and may be deemed culturally stigmatizing (Yeh & Inose, 2002). Therefore, in working with Asian immigrant youth, school counselors may have to utilize more creative techniques in order to understand their concerns and help

attain psychological well-being, instead of meeting individually with students in their offices.

The following section is a list of recommendations and culturally appropriate strategies and interventions that may be helpful for practicing school counselors working with diverse immigrant youth.

Recommendations

Work With Students Individually and in Groups

School counselors are often the first line of defense to identify students with psychological—as well as survival—issues, and their traditional training offers a wide variety of ways in which school counselors can intervene with immigrant students individually. Primarily though, when working with immigrant students, counselors should try to build on students' strengths. Many immigrant students are resilient and have learned how to survive in highly complex and confusing worlds. School counselors should capitalize on these strengths to increase student adjustment and academic achievement, and to help foster an overall positive outlook for students (Bemak & Chung, 2003).

School counselors should also work to determine aspirations and future plans of immigrant students. All too often, many immigrant youth are not aware of employment opportunities and educational experiences available to them in the United States. Counselors should work to provide students with a complete set of options into potential future careers and educational opportunities (Mitchell, 2005). One groundbreaking program in the area of career development has been conducted by Shea, Yeh, Ma, Lee, and Pituc (2007). This program, known as CEDAR (career exploration development and resource group), involved low-income, urban, Chinese immigrant youth. They participated in an 8-week group within the school, which was intended to incorporate cultural and systemic factors, such as racism and cultural values, related to career development process. The program provided students with specific career information, social support, and role modeling, and was aimed at promoting their self-efficacy in making career choices. One key element of the program was that the leader conducted the group sessions in the students' native Chinese language, making the program culturally sensitive and available to greater numbers of students. Overall outcome analysis of the group thus far reveals that group participants have demonstrated increased career decision-making self-efficacy and increased clarification of career interests.

School counselors must also remember that immigrant youth are similar to their American counterparts and are confronting the challenges of the transition from childhood to adulthood. They, too, need support and help in dealing with and conquering the developmental milestones, such as identity development, especially among the middle- and high-school years (F. C. Williams & Butler, 2003).

While school counselors are in the best position and are primarily trained to provide individualized attention to students, it has been well established that group work is quite effective with immigrant youth, especially for those from more collectivistic cultures where social relationships and cooperation are highly valued (Bemak & Chung, 2003). Therefore, school counselors need to involve themselves with greater numbers of students, such as forming support groups, transition groups, or academic circles with the goal of assisting immigrant students in becoming adept at survival in their new scholastic environment (F. C. Williams & Butler, 2003). One simple initiative school counselors can take is the formation of a peer support/mentoring group. Since school counselors have contact with all new students during course planning, they can identify potential group members, as well as immigrant peers who are more established within the school community. These groups may address such topics as (a) negative experiences such as racism and discrimination, (b) frustration caused by limited English proficiency, (c) cultural conflicts, (d) peer pressure, and (e) parental conflict. The development of peer groups offers an opportunity for immigrant youth to build supportive alliances and relationships *at school*, gain knowledge and advice from others who may be going through similar experiences, and identify a caring adult role model. In addition, this is a no-cost intervention involving minimal time for counselors.

Utilize Peers

Positive relationships with peers are essential for adjustment to school, not only for immigrant youth, but also for all school children, particularly in the adolescent years. Many immigrant youth may not be accepted by their peers when they first enter the American school system. This lack of acceptance may occur often because of misunderstanding based on differences in language, dress, and patterns of speech (F. C. Williams & Butler, 2003). School counselors can lead efforts to promote healthy peer relationships by introducing cross-cultural sharing and learning relationships and establishing cooperative learning activities, both social and academic. Moreover, counselors can train peers to work collaboratively with them as "peer counselors" (F. C. Williams & Butler).

Empower Families of Immigrant Youth

School counselors have an obligation to support and inform immigrant families about the educational system and their role in it, as well as empower families to become involved in shaping their child's future. They should work to encourage parental involvement of immigrant students, which may be challenging, as there may be many barriers impeding their involvement. Some of these include (a) language differences, (b) cultural conflict, (c) lack of familial support, (d) isolation in a new and strange country, (e) intergenerational conflict with their children, (f) employment/financial concerns, and (g) a general lack of knowledge of American institutions and organization, especially the school system (Fuligni, 1997). This is particularly exemplified with Caribbean immigrant parents. Caribbean parents are often unaware of the need to closely monitor their child's experience in school because of their culturally different understanding of the educational system. Parents in the Caribbean place ultimate trust in teachers as professionals who will make the best decisions for the child's academic progress, so these parents are less involved (however, they are still invested). Therefore, when American school personnel misguide students and push them into vocational programs and other nonacademic classes, Caribbean parents often believe that teachers are making the best educational decisions for their child and do not advocate for changes in their child's prescribed academic course (Mitchell, 2005); however, school faculty may view them as being complacent and not caring. School counselors need to make a concerted effort to learn as much as possible about immigrant families and the values that underlie the family unit, roles, and structure. They should be careful not to prejudge family structure from their own ethnocentric perspective (Sue & Sue, 2003). Moreover, counselors need to inform and educate immigrant parents about the American school system through parent informational meetings scheduled at convenient times for working parents. Meetings and materials should be written and translated into different languages (Mitchell). Additionally, programs or meetings with parents do not always have to be on school premises, especially since the families of immigrant youth often cannot attend meetings at school due to scheduling conflicts. One idea to involve parents would be to conduct parent meetings at apartment complexes where a large number of students reside, at churches, or even at community centers, in order to increase possible attendance and/or alleviate transportation concerns. Additionally, parent meetings should involve incentives for attendance, such as providing meals, babysitting, training (e.g., free income tax assistance), or school benefits for their child (e.g., trips).

Teach School Survival Skills

Learning basic school survival skills is essential, as immigrant students need to learn how to negotiate American schools and, in general, need assistance in adjusting to the school culture, given their lack of experience with American institutions. Simple procedures and tasks that most American students take for granted—such as moving from one class to another, being taught by several different teachers each day, and the length of classes and the school day—may all be foreign experiences to immigrant students (F. C. Williams & Butler, 2003). Moreover, the lack of English competence for so many immigrant youth compounds the situation even more and poses yet another challenge for immigrant students attempting to survive in the American public school system (Yeh & Inose, 2002). English competence, at the very least, is required in order to know and understand what is going on in their classrooms, and it is necessary to allow them to excel academically and to perform just as well as they did when they attended school in their home countries and in their native languages (Bemak & Chung, 2003).

Teaching basic school survival skills is within the scope of training and skills of multiculturally competent school counselors. School counselors can serve as "cultural translators," interpreting American cultural patterns and norms for immigrant youth and explicitly offering didactic training in methods and techniques for surviving the daily challenges of school. School counselors can provide orientation programs, create handbooks and/or guides for immigrant students to refer to policies and procedures and can initiate clubs for immigrant students to create support systems and opportunities for students to learn and benefit from each other (Juntunen, Atkinson, & Tierney, 2003).

Become Open to and Try Alternative Methods of Helping

School counselors should be open to and appreciate alternative and indigenous cultural methods of helping of their immigrant students. Traditional "talk therapy" is not the only manner in which people can be helped, though it is superior to other types of healing (although they may not seem "scientific").

In addition, spirituality and religion are important and powerful aspects of the lives of many immigrant youth. School counselors should consider student's religious and/or spiritual values and should work to incorporate these values and beliefs into ways in which they support immigrant students. For example, many Korean immigrant youth tend to utilize religious practices, as church plays the role of extended family and they feel more comfortable sharing their problems with the religious community (Yeh & Inose, 2002; Suh & Satcher, 2005).

Become an Advocate for Immigrant Youth in the School

The relationship between students and all school faculty and staff is an important bridge to students' school experience, and this is especially true for immigrant students. As immigrant students settle in the United States and spend more time in a school cultural environment that opposes their heritage cultural norms, they begin to have negative experiences in schools and exhibit declining achievement patterns. School counselors need to begin to identify what specific negative factors exist in the school environment that, over time, dampen aspirations and academic functioning of immigrants (Mitchell, 2005). School counselors should advocate for the creation of a school environment that actively supports students' development and expression of their heritage culture within the school environment. It is important to try to cultivate a climate for respect for cultural diversity, for this type of environment will ultimately be beneficial in allowing all students to not experience the school environment as oppositional to their cultural heritage. This may be achieved through consultation with teachers, coordinating diversity appreciation days, and working with student council/parent–teacher associations and the community to generate schoolwide, community-linked activities that pay tribute to cultural traditions and practices (Bemak & Chung, 2003).

Moreover, school counselors can become advocates for immigrant students by educating other school personnel about the importance of maintaining a culturally supportive environment so that immigrant students can attain personal and academic success (Mitchell, 2005). Counselors can provide in-service training and workshops educating other school personnel (especially teachers) to the diversity of immigrant students, including the differences in their cultural values and beliefs, as well as the impact of acculturative stress on their lives of immigrant youth. Moreover, school counselors must educate American teachers about different styles of teaching and learning that may be more appropriate for immigrant students (Bemak & Chung, 2003). For example, in Haiti, students are taught by the rote method, where they are expected to write down the teacher's words verbatim. This is in contrast to the teaching style of most American schools, where taking notes in class may involve summarizing or simply writing down the basic gist of a teacher's instruction. In addition, many immigrant students have never been exposed to different types of evaluation, such as multiple-choice tests, which are not commonly used in parts of the world outside of the United States (F. C. Williams & Butler, 2003).

Build Collaborative Relationships With Communities and Outside Support Networks

The community provides critical information for school counselors, who are in an ideal position to be liaisons. Communities provide immigrant students with support, especially since most immigrant groups typically live in clusters, providing a base of social and cultural support (Bemak & Chung, 2003). In a study conducted by P. R. Portes (1999), the immigrant students who maintained optimal performance in American schools established inroads in the community, which provided social and cognitive supports to these students.

School counselors should access community support systems and centers to be able to develop a resource list of services that may aid and assist immigrant youth, who are often in need of support to deal with immigration issues, as well as housing, financial, and employment concerns. This will expand contacts and experiences and offer a set of resources available to the counselor for future consultation.

Provide Ongoing Assessment and Review

Many immigrant students are placed in remedial courses and less rigorous academic and/or vocational classes based on poor testing or language skills. School counselors should challenge these placements and advocate for immigrant students by alerting officials to cultural differences and learning styles, language barriers, and acculturation issues that may impact evaluations and assessments. In determining classroom assignments and educational placements, school counselors can recommend the use of nontraditional measures that may be more accurate in assessing the abilities of immigrant students, as well as document the efficiency of best practices for working with particular students. It is also critical that counselors continue to assess the academic tracking of immigrant students and reevaluate their classroom placements, since their initial placements usually become permanent (Bemak & Chung, 2003).

Become an Agent for Social Change

School counselors also need to be involved in systemic changes beyond the individual level of intervention. Many of the problems and concerns of immigrant students are related to systemic and external forces, such as racism, poverty, and issues surrounding acculturation, rather than internal psychological problems. School counselors might be most effective in assisting their students to deal with these social forces on a systemic level, rather than focusing on self-exploration and assimilation into American culture (Sue & Sue, 2003).

Summary

School counselors can play a critical role in addressing the needs of immigrant students, and generally, in aiding their successful transition to American culture. Several recommendations and strategies have been suggested, some encouraging school counselors to go beyond their traditional roles, which would require additional support and training. It is important to note, however, that the authors' recommendations are only a general overview and that counselors, teachers, and practitioners must be able to assess their students' issues and concerns and then provide appropriate interventions and techniques that address their specific needs. No matter what interventions are implemented, though, school counselors must remember to be culturally sensitive when addressing the needs of immigrant students.

Implications

School counselors must become leaders in the school community in serving the needs of the rising population of immigrant students. In order for school counselors to become prepared for the challenges of their expanded work and roles in the school, changes need to be implemented in counselor training programs. Counselor training programs should emphasize multicultural counseling competencies as an integral part of school counseling curricula, infusing diversity throughout the curriculum instead of in just a single course (Constantine & Gushue, 2003). In addition, course offerings might be expanded to include more intense study of cultural nuances, exposure to different types of immigrants and groups, and introduction to the history of countries from which immigrants (F. C. Williams & Butler, 2003). Counselor education programs also need to consider incorporating a variety of theoretical orientations and approaches in theories courses, beyond the traditional psychodynamic, cognitive–behavioral, and person-centered approaches generally presented. The goals and techniques recommended by these theories may not be appropriate or culturally sensitive to immigrant students (Sue & Sue, 2003).

Beyond training programs, school districts should develop and offer regular in-service professional development programs for practicing counselors to help keep them current in their knowledge and level of proficiency with immigrant students (F. C. Williams & Butler, 2003).

The immigrant population is large, diverse, and on the rise in the United States due to recent shifts in the demographics of our society. Although there is a great influx in this population, there is a paucity of research that focuses on and highlights the needs and interests of immigrant, especially among youth and youth of color. As such, greater attention needs to be focused on addressing their concerns. Future directions should focus on development of programs and intervention efforts to assist immigrant youth with acclimation and adjustment to the United States and the American public school system. Additionally, the structure of the school system must change to be more inclusive. Research efforts toward curricular reform, including infusing diversity and different cultural perspectives within the curriculum, as well as new teaching methods, should be considered.

References

Albertini, V. L. (2004). Racial mistrust among immigrant minority students. *Child and Adolescent Social Work Journal, 21*, 311–331.

Atkinson, D. R., & Juntunen, C. L. (1994). School counselors and school psychologist as school-home-community liaisons in ethnically diverse schools. In P. Pederson & J. C. Carey (Eds.), *Multicultural counseling in schools* (pp. 103–119). Needham Heights, MA: Paramount Publishing.

Baker, S. B., & Gerler, E. R. (2004). *School counseling for the twenty-first century* (4th ed.). Upper Saddle River, NJ: Prentice Hall.

Baptiste, D. A. (1993). Immigrant families, adolescents, and acculturation: Insights for therapists. *Marriage and Family Review, 19*, 341–363.

Bemak, F., & Chung, R. C. Y. (2003). Multicultural counseling with immigrant students in schools. In P. B. Pearson & J. C. Carey (Eds.), *Multicultural counseling in schools: A practical handbook* (2nd ed., pp. 84–104). Boston: Person Education.

Berry, J. W. (1990). Acculturation and adaptation: A general framework. In W. H. Holtzman & T. H. Borneman (Eds.), *The mental health of immigrants and refugees* (pp. 90–102). Austin, TX: Hogg Foundation for Mental Health, University of Texas.

Berry, J. W. (1997). Immigration, acculturation, and adaptation. *Applied Psychology: An International Review, 46*, 5–34.

Berry, J. W., & Kim, B., U. (1998). Acculturation and mental health. In P. Dasen, J. W. Berry, & N. Sartorius (Eds.), *Health and cross-cultural psychology: Towards application* (pp. 207–236). London: Sage.

Berry, J. W., Kim, U., Minde, T., & Mok, D. (1987). Comparative studies of acculturative stress. *International Migration Review, 21*, 491–511.

Bhattacharya, G. (2000). The school adjustment of South Asian immigrant children in the United States. *Adolescence, 35*, 77–85.

Carter, R. T. (1995). *The influence of race and racial identity in psychotherapy*. New York, NY: John Wiley & Sons, Inc.

Chiu, Y. W., & Ring, J. M. (1998). Chinese and Vietnamese immigrant adolescents under pressure: Identifying stressors and interventions. *Professional Psychology: Research and Practice, 29*, 444–449.

Chun, K. M., Eastman, K. L., Wang, G. C. S., & Sue, S. (1998). Psychopathology. In L. C. Lee & N. W. S. Zane (Eds.), *Handbook of Asian American psychology* (pp. 457–484). Thousand Oaks, CA: Sage.

Chung, C. L. E. (1994). An investigation of the psychological well-being of unaccompanied Taiwanese stressors and interventions. *Professional Psychology: Research and Practice, 29*, 444–449.

Coleman, H. L. K. (1995). Cultural factors and the counseling process: Implications for school counselors. *The School Counselor, 42*, 180–185.

Coleman, H. L. K. (1997). Conflict in multicultural counseling relationships: Source and resolution. *Journal of Multicultural Counseling and Development, 25*, 195–200.

Colten, M. E., & Gore, S. (1991). Introduction: Adolescent stress, social relationships, and mental health. In M. E. Colten & S. Gore (Eds.), *Adolescent stress* (pp. 1–14). New York: Walter de Gruyter.

Constantine, M. G., & Gushue, G. V. (2003). School counselors' ethnic tolerance attitudes and racism attitudes as predictors of their multicultural case conceptualization of an immigrant student. *Journal of Counseling & Development, 81*, 185–190.

Constantine, M. G., Okazaki, S., & Utsey, S. O. (2004). Self-concealment, social self-efficacy, acculturative stress, and depression in African, Asian, and Latin American international college students. *American Journal of Orthopsychiatry, 74*, 230–241.

Dawkins, M. P. (2000). Rethinking U.S. immigration policy. *Black Issues in Higher Education, 17*, 120.

Drachman, D., & Halberstadt, A. (1992). A stage of migration framework as applied to recent Soviet emigres. *Journal of Multicultural Social Work, 2*, 63–78.

Draine, C., & Hall, B. (1986). *Culture shock!* Singapore, Indonesia: Times Books International.

Eckermann, A. K. (1994). *One classroom, many cultures*. Sydney, Australia: Allen and Unwin.

Fuligni, A. J. (1997). The academic achievement of adolescents from immigrant families: The roles of family background, attitudes, and behavior. *Children Development, 68*, 351–363.

Furnham, A., & Bochner, S. (1986). *Culture shock: Psychological reactions to unfamiliar environments*. New York: Methuen.

Garcia Coll, C., & Magnuson, K. (1997). The psychological experience of immigration: A developmental perspective. In A. Booth, A. C. Crouter, & N. Landale (Eds.), *Immigration and the family* (pp. 91–131). Mahwah, NJ: Lawrence Erlbaum Associates.

Gibbs, J., Huang L., & Associates. (1989). *Children of Color: Psychological interventions with minority youth*. San Francisco: Jossey-Bass.

Giordano, J., & McGoldrick, M. (1996). European families: An overview. In M. McGoldrick, J. Giordano, & J. Pearce (Eds.), *Ethnicity & family therapy* (pp. 427–441). New York: Guilford Press.

Gopaul-McNicol, S. (1998). Caribbean families: Social and emotional problems. *Journal of Social Distress and the Homeless, 7*, 55–73.

Graham, P. A. (1995). Assimilation, adjustment and access: An antiquarian view of American education. In D. Ravitch & M. A. Vinovskis (Eds.), *Learning from the past* (pp. 3–24). Baltimore: The John Hopkins University Press.

Harkins, L. F. (2001). Understanding the acculturation process for Kaigaishijo. *The Educational Forum, 65*, 335–43.

Herring, R. D. (1997). *Counseling diverse ethnic youth: Synergetic strategies and interventions for school counselors*. Orlando, FL: Harcourt Brace & Company.

Igoa, C. (1995). *The inner world of the immigrant child*. Mahwah, NJ: Lawrence Erlbaum Associates.

James, D. C. S. (1997a). Coping with a new society: The unique psychosocial problems of immigrant youth. *The Journal of School Health, 67*, 98–102.

James, D. C. S. (1997b). Psychosocial risks of immigrant students. *The Education Digest, 63*, 51–53.

Juntunen, C. L., Atkinson, D. R., & Tierney, G. (2003). School counselors and school psychologists as school-home-community liaisons in ethnically diverse schools. In P. B. Pederson & J. C. Carey (Eds.), *Multicultural counseling in schools: A practical handbook* (2nd ed., pp. 149–170). Boston: Pearson Education.

Kang, H. W., Kuehn, P. A., & Herrell, A. (1994). The Hmong literacy project: A study of Hmong classroom behavior. *Bilingual Research Journal, 18*, 63–83.

Kaplan, G., & Eckermann, A. K. (1996). Identity and culture shock: Aboriginal children and schooling in Australia. *McGill Journal of Education, 31*, 7–24.

Kim, B. S., Brenner, B. R., Liang, C. T. H., & Asay, P. A. (2003). A qualitative study adaptation experiences of 1.5 generation Asian Americans. *Cultural Diversity and Ethnic Minority Psychology, 9*, 156–170.

Kim, S., Coletti, S. D., Williams, C., & Hepler, N. (1995). Substance abuse prevention involving Asian/Pacific Islander American communities. In G. J. Botvin, S. Schinke, & M. A. Orlandi (Eds.), *Drug abuse prevention with multiethnic youth* (pp. 295–312). Thousand Oaks, CA: Sage.

Kuo, B. C. H., & Roysircar, G. (2004). Predictors of acculturation for Chinese adolescents in Canada: Age of arrival, length of stay, social class and English reading ability. *Journal of Multicultural Counseling and Development, 32*, 143–154.

Lynch, E. W. (1992). From culture shock to cultural learning. In E. W. Lynch & M. J. Hanson (Eds.), *Developing cross-cultural competence, A guide for working with young children and their families* (pp. 19–34). Baltimore: Paul H. Brookes Publishing Co.

Mitchell, N. (2005). Academic achievement among Caribbean immigrant adolescents: The impact of generational status on academic self-concept. *Professional School Counseling, 8*, 209–218.

Munroe-Blum, H., Boyle, M. H., Offord, D. R., & Kates, N. (1989). Immigrant children: Psychiatric disorder, school performance, and service utilization. *American Journal of Orthopsychiatry, 59*(4), 510–519.

Nwadioria, E., & McAdoo, H. (1996). Accultuarative stress among Amerasian refugees: Gender and racial differences. *Adolescence, 31*, 477–488.

Ogbu, J. U. (1983). Minority status and schooling in plural societies. *Comparative Education Review, 27*, 168–190.

Portes, A., & Raumbaut, R. G. (1996). *Immigrant America: A portrait* (2nd ed.). Berkeley: University of California Press.

Portes, P. R. (1999). Social and psychological factors in the academic achievement of children of immigrants: A cultural history puzzle. *American Educational Research Journal, 36*, 489–507.

Rogler, L. H., Cortes, D. E., & Malgady, R. G. (1991). Acculturation and mental health status among Hispanics. *American Psychologist, 46*, 585–597.

Roysircar-Sodowsky, G., & Maestas, M. V. (2000). Acculturation, ethnic identity, and acculturative stress: Evidence and measurement. In R. H. Dana (Ed.), *Handbook of cross-cultural and multicultural personality assessment* (pp. 131–172). Mahwah, NJ: Lawrence Erlbaum Associates.

Sandhu, D. S. (1997). Psychocultural profiles of Asian and Pacific Islander Americans: Implication for counseling and psychotherapy. *Journal of Multicultural Counseling and Development, 25*, 7–22.

Schwartz, A. E., & Stiefel, L. (2004). Immigrants and the distribution of resources within an urban school district. *Educational Evaluation and Policy Analysis, 26*, 303–2004.

Shea, M., Yeh, C. J., Ma., P. W., Lee, S., & Pituc, S. (2007). Development of a career exploration group for low income Chinese immigrant youth. Manuscript in preparation

Sluzki, C. E. (1979). Migration and family conflict. *Family Process, 18*, 379–390.

Smith A., LaLonde R. N., & Johnson, S. (2004). Serial migration and its implications for the parent-child relationship: A retrospective analysis of the experiences of the children of Caribbean immigrants. *Cultural Diversity and Ethnic Minority Psychology, 10*, 107–122.

Smith-Davis, J. (2004a). The world of immigrant students. *Principal Leadership (High School Ed.), 4,* 44–49.

Smith-Davis, J. (2004b). The new immigrant students need more than ESL. *The Education Digest, 69,* 21–26.

Suarez-Orozco, C., & Suarez-Orozco, M. (2001). *Children of immigration.* Cambridge, MA: Harvard University Press.

Sue, D. W. (2001). Multidimensional facets of cultural competence. *The Counseling Psychologist, 29,* 790–821.

Sue, D. W., & Sue, D. (2003). *Counseling the culturally diverse, theory & practice* (4th ed.). New York: John Wiley & Sons, Inc.

Suh, S., & Satcher, J. (2005). Understanding at-risk Korean American youth. *Professional School Counseling, 8,* 428–435.

Talmadge, C. G. (2002). Black immigrants of the Caribbean: An invisible and forgotten community. *Adult Learning, 12,* 18–21.

Taylor, J. A. (2004). Teaching children who have immigrated: The new legislation, research, and trends in immigration which affect teachers of diverse student populations. *Multicultural Education, 11,* 43–44.

Torres, L., & Rollock, D. (2004). Acculturative distress among Hispanics: The role of acculturation, coping, and intercultural competence. *Journal of Multicultural Counseling and Development, 32,* 155–167.

U.S. Bureau of the Census. (2000). *Data highlights.* Retrieved June 12, 2005, from www.census.gov

U.S. Bureau of the Census. (2001). *Population profile of the United States.* Washington, DC: U.S. Government Printing Office.

U.S. Department of Education. (1997). *Digest of educational statistics.* Washington, DC: U.S. Government Printing Office.

U.S. Department of Homeland Security. (2004). *Yearbook of immigrant statistics, 2003.* Washington, DC: U.S. Government Printing Office.

Vernez, G., & Abrahamse, A. (1996). *How immigrants fare in U.S. education.* Santa Monica, CA: RAND.

Williams, C. L., & Berry, J. W. (1991). Primary prevention of acculturative stress among refugees application of psychological theory and practice. *American Psychologist, 46,* 632–641.

Williams, F. C., & Butler, S. K. (2003). Concerns of newly arrived immigrant students: Implications for school counselors. *Professional School Counseling, 7,* 9–14.

Yeh, C. J. (2003). Age, acculturation, cultural adjustment, and mental health symptoms of Chinese, Korean, and Japanese immigrant youths. *Cultural Diversity and Ethnic Minority Psychology, 9,* 34–48.

Yeh, C. J., & Inose, M. (2002). Difficulties and coping strategies of Chinese, Japanese, and Korean immigrant students. *Adolescence, 37,* 69–82.

Yost, A. D., & Lucas, M. S. (2002). Adjustment issues affecting employment for immigrants from the former Soviet Union. *Journal of Employment Counseling, 39,* 153–70.

Zheng, X., & Berry, J. W. (1991). Psychological adaptation of Chinese sojourners in Canada. *International Journal of Psychology, 26,* 451–471.

Zhou, M. (2003). Urban education: Challenges in educating culturally diverse children. *Teachers College Record, 105,* 208–225.

VIII
RACIAL HARASSMENT IN AMERICAN SCHOOLS

ROBERT T. CARTER
Teachers College, Columbia University

TAMARA R. BUCKLEY
Hunter College, City University of New York

SCHEKEVA P. HALL
Teachers College, Columbia University

The aim of this chapter is to provide information about racial harassment and discrimination in schools that can be valuable to school counselors, officials, parents/guardians, and other interested persons who work with school-aged people. We have chosen this emphasis on race and have chosen to address racial harassment because we believe that, in our society, social and political systems and institutional practices and policies operate based on racial assumptions and beliefs. Whites, as the dominant group, tend to benefit from educational, social, economic, and political rewards, and more often than not, people of color have less access to educational, social, economic, and political rewards (Bell & Nkomo, 2001; McGrath, Berdahl, & Arrow, 1999; Oliver & Shapiro, 1997, 2006; Sidanius & Pratto, 1999). Unequal treatment in educational systems can lead to tension and hostility related to race, which ultimately can result in race-based stress and perhaps trauma. In the public school system, children and adolescents mat be the victims of such stress from racial harassment.

In this chapter, we begin with a brief description of the roles and functions of public schools and school counselors. Next, we outline legal and psychological distinctions between racial harassment, racially hostile environments, and racial discrimination. We then describe the psychological impact of racial harassment and discrimination on school-aged people, outline factors that influence perceptions of racial incidents, and conclude with recommendations for school officials.

Public Schools

Public schools are charged with lofty goals. Public schools are the institutions intended to create a common preparation for citizens in an increasingly multiracial society (Frankenberg & Lee, 2002). Public schools are required to care for and educate the offspring of every segment of society, including children of every color, race, and culture in the world and every young person, regardless of sickness or well-being, family economic status, language, and religion and regardless of whether the children are able-bodied or have special needs (Texas Association of School Boards). The Texas Association of School Boards' statement prepared on behalf of the National School Boards Association stated,

> [P]ublic schools, as the backbone of our American way of life, foster our ideals of freedom, shared values, and the integration of peoples, and meet the changing needs of our evolving society through a commitment that every child can succeed and become a contributing member of it.
>
> Liberty, democracy, domestic tranquility, economic prosperity, and all the other benefits traditionally associated with American society require an educated people. Ensuring the development of that educated populace is the bedrock purpose of public education. (¶ 1–2)

As socializing institutions, schools help students to become citizens (Sheldon & Biddle, 1998). Effective schools shape students' development, values, and attitudes, and teach them the rules of living and relating to themselves, each other, their families, and society as a whole (Dollarhide & Saginak, 2003). In studies of effective public schools, researchers have consistently described two principles of primary importance: a caring environment and holistic development (School Mental Health Project/Center for Mental Health in Schools [SMHP], 1999, p. 5). Therefore, effective schools promote connections among staff, teachers, students, communities, and caregivers so that young people feel welcomed and respected and so that they make important connections with caring adults. Effective schools are also characterized by consistent, fair decision making and discipline, an environment that encourages academic and personal achievement, realistic but high expectations for all, and high accountability for learning (Travers, Elliott, & Kratochwill, 1993). Education professionals including school counselors, teachers, and administrators are critical for creating caring learning environments that are free from racial bias and harassment. Dollarhide and Saginak (2003) described 16 expectations for professionals in school settings, several of which include instilling core values that transcend cultures, such as justice, honesty, caring, respect, and responsibility; providing a safe bias-free, exciting, fun invigorating learning environment; interacting positively with the community; and instilling respect for traditions and symbols of the country, state, and community.

Although the specific role of public schools varies by state and locality, with the passage of the *No Child Left Behind* Act (U.S. Department of Education [USDE], 2001), all schools in the United States are moving toward greater accountability for educational outcomes. In a climate of accountability, educational professionals are required to account for the relationship of time on task and educational impact (Stone & Dahir, 2004). In this culture of accountability, it is essential for school counselors to remain focused on their primary roles as student advocates and leaders charged with creating safe learning environments that are free from discrimination. The American School Counselor Association (ASCA; 2004) outlines the role of school counselors as student advocates who are responsible for increasing student development in three primary areas: (a) academic, (b) career, and (c) personal and social interactions. Student development is wholly dependent on safe, bias-free learning environments for all students. With increasing numbers of racial/ethnic minority students in public schools, school counselors should become leaders in raising awareness about how to recognize racial harassment and discrimination and to create school-wide strategies that can ensure that all students have an equally likely chance of success.

Racial Composition of Public Schools in the United States

A frequently noted fact is that, with each generation, the United States' population is becoming increasingly multiracial and culturally diverse. This demographic shift has changed the racial–ethnic composition of the nation's elementary, middle, and secondary schools. The USDE racial disparity in number of students and teachers National Center for Educational Statistics (NCES; 2007) stated that, in 2005, 42% of schoolchildren from kindergarten through 12th grade were members of nondominant racial/ethnic groups. More importantly, children from nondominant racial/ethnic groups constitute 80% of total school enrollment in the country's largest school districts (NCES, 2007). In contrast, 86% of new teachers are White, and fewer than 3% of new teachers speak a second language (Darling-Hammond & Sclan, 1996). White/minority teacher ratio has altered little in the past few years as percent of full-time teachers who represent minority groups constituted only 17% of elementary and secondary schools for the 2003–2004 fiscal year indicating only a three percent incline from previous years (USDE, NCES, 2007). The ratio may be problematic because many teacher preparation programs do not adequately prepare student teachers to recognize their own beliefs regarding race, class, and culture and the impact of such beliefs when working with diverse populations (Cockrell, Placier, Cockrell, & Middleton, 1999). Moreover, research suggests that racial groups differ in their perceptions of racially based experiences and incidents (e.g., Kailin, 1999). Whites often view people of color as responsible for acts against them, whereas people of color tend to view the perpetrators as responsible (Kailin, 1999). Racial disparities between school personnel and students may make it more difficult for racial incidents to be recognized and adequately addressed.

Scholars, educators, school counselors, parents, and community representatives have called for changes in school policy and practice as it related to incidents of racial harassment and other forms of racial discrimination. They have challenged the adequacy of current policy and practices aimed at preventing and addressing incidents of racial harassment and teacher training, and they have questioned the racial–cultural composition of teachers and school administrators (Carter, 2000; Darling-Hammond, 2000). These challenges appear well justified, particularly since there are many lawsuits against schools due to how they have dealt with racial harassment (Darling-Hammond; Kozol, 1991).

Although many forms of racial discrimination and harassment have been outlawed as a result of the Civil Rights Movement, many minorities encounter racial discrimination and harassment daily (Feagan, 1991; Landrine & Klonoff, 1996). To understand how powerful these encounters of discrimination and harassment may be, we will provide several examples of racial discrimination and harassment in the nations' schools.

Incidence and Prevalence of Racial Harassment and Discrimination

Media and publication outlets and researchers report a high incidence of racial harassment and discrimination in the public schools across the United States. These acts impact students from a variety of racial and ethnic backgrounds. In April 2005, Kaufmann (2005), a staff writer from the Gazette, a news supplier in Bethesda, Maryland, reported that four teenage students in Maryland were charged with racial harassment and vandalism for drawing and posting swastikas around the school. In another recent case, the *Rocky Mountain News* (Lindsay, 2005) and *The Denver Post* (Rouse, 2005) reported an incident at a middle school in Denver, Colorado, where a 13-year-old White boy was charged with racially harassing a 12-year-old Black girl by shouting racial slurs, including "n-----," "monkey," and "Blackie Chan." The harasser reportedly was accompanied by two, 12-year-old White girls, who were not charged with "ethnic intimidation." The same victim and her cousins reported that these students also spat on their sandwiches. No charges have been filed because officials have not been able to determine who was involved in the incident. In February 2005, the *Los Angeles Times* (Covarrubiac, 2005) reported that White teens had bullied, harassed, and continually physically attacked African American teenagers at a public school, based on "the color of their skin." No intervention has been taken on behalf of this incident, and community members reported feeling concerned and threatened for their children.

Many additional accounts of racial discrimination and harassment in the national media raise questions about whether these acts have been adequately cited and addressed. For example, both the *Northwest Herald* (Turner, 2005) and the *Chicago Tribune* (Starks, 2005) reported that a much discussed Civil Rights lawsuit in Chicago, Illinois, wherein a child who had been consistently racially harassed began to have suicidal ideation, had been dropped because school officials said they could not prove that the incidents were racially motivated. A similar case appeared in Vermont (Lecuyer & Ceccarossi, 2005) where a teenage girl was suspended from school for fighting. The girl felt wrongly accused, claiming that the fights were racially motivated and that the school is "a hostile environment" (¶ 6). Her mother claims school officials failed to address the [racial] issues and labeled her daughter "aggressive and a danger to the school" (¶ 12). The school reportedly also did not respond to the mother's requests for diversity education in the school.

Fortunately, not all parents have to fight so hard for diversity programs to be implemented in the public schools. A group of school officials in Anne Arundel County, Maryland, has taken allegations of racial harassment very seriously. Throughout several counties in Maryland in 2004, there were a large number of racial incidents in both middle and high schools. *The Baltimore Sun* (Kay, 2005) reported 237 racially biased "acts" that ranged from racial slurs to physical attacks. The preponderance (123) of these acts took place in 16 middle schools, fewer (77) racial incidents happened in 12 high schools, and 37 occurred in 20 elementary schools. Because of the alarming incidence of racial harassment, Maryland implemented diversity programming and a tracking system for reporting incidents.

In 1999, the USDE reported that 25% of students at school had experienced some form of racial harassment such as violent acts, vandalism, or name-calling. The U.S. Department of Education's Annual Report to Congress of the Office for Civil Rights (2007) indicated that the number of specific race-related complaints documented in OCR's yearly reports from 2000 to 2006 fiscal years had declined from the 25% in 1999, and maintained a stable 18%–19% rate of all complaints (USDE, OCR 2007). However, USDE's OCR reported race-related complaints remains the second largest issue affecting American schools below disability complaints. Following this was "multiple" complaints which OCR reports could contain "for example, allegations of both sex and race discrimination (p. 19). Researchers described a similar pattern of harassment and discrimination. Fisher, Wallace, and Fenton (2000) found that, among a sample of 177 African American and Hispanic youth, many reported frequent instances of institutional racism. These instances included being hassled by store personnel and by police officers, presumably because of their race. Asian and White students reported that they were verbally assaulted and excluded from school activities based on their race. All students of color in this study reported that racial incidents were a persistent stressor that had a negative impact on their academic performance. The students of color, with the exception of Asians, perceived that their race contributed to their being wrongfully disciplined, being discouraged from taking advance level courses, and receiving lower grades. Rosenbloom and Way (2004) found that when Black and Latino students perceived teacher preference toward Asian students, they retaliated by harassing the Asian students. Acts of aggression are a common outcome of perceived acts of racial discrimination (Rosenbloom & Way). The negative impacts of racial discrimination and harassment are wide reaching and have been reported to include actions taken by adults and peers both in and outside the school premises. Fisher and colleagues (2000) found that students experienced harassment from teachers, store owners, and police. Harassment and discrimination from peers was reported both among members from the same racial groups and across racial groups. These selected cases represent a small sampling of a much larger problem that exists in schools across the nation and that affects students and school officials from all racial and ethnic groups. As Dollarhide and Saginak (2003) stated, because schools are systems, all actions within a system affect all members of that system. Young people can be profoundly affected by the values and attitudes that are taught directly or indirectly in that system.

In the following section we will clarify the legal and psychological distinctions between racial harassment and discrimination, followed by a description of the psychological impact of such racial incidents.

Legal Definitions of Racial Harassment and Discrimination

The USDE's (1994) Office of Civil Rights (OCR) wrote,

> Title VI of the Civil Rights Act of 1964 (42 U.C.S. 2000d et seq.) prohibits discrimination on the basis of race, color, or national origin in any program or activity in schools receiving federal financial assistance.
>
> The USDE interpreted title VI as prohibiting racial harassment (Federal Register Vol. 59, No. 47, 1994), which is defined as an incident or environment that denies students the right of an education devoid of discrimination. Specifically, any act that excludes, denies or treats students differently due to race, color or national origin within a federally supported institution or during activities managed by such an institution can be found to violate title VI. Moreover, title VI states that a racially hostile environment 'that is created, encouraged, accepted, tolerated or left uncorrected by a recipient, constitutes different treatment on the basis of race and is in violation of title VI. (¶ 5)

The legal definition of racial discrimination involves situations in which someone is treated differently based on race, such as if a student were denied access to a program or a school solely based on his or her race. Racial harassment is also considered a form of racial discrimination that arises from disparate treatment or impact (i.e., violations of the 1964 *Civil Rights Act*, Title VII).

To determine if an act violates the provisions of title VI, a different treatment standard is applied such that a person must show a legitimate, nondiscriminatory reason for the different treatment. Specifically, the analysis must consider (a) if a student was treated differently, (b) if the treatment occurred within the purview of the school's duties and activities, (c) if the treatment was based on race, and (d) if there was a legitimate, nondiscriminatory (i.e., not a reason given as pretext) basis for the different treatment. If the first three conditions are met and the last condition was not, the institution has violated title VI. The determination of different treatment is distinct from establishing the existence of a racially hostile environment. (A hostile environment may also have aspects of racial harassment, but with schools, specific behaviors and actions also constitute racial harassment, which can be distinct from a racially hostile environment.) A more complete description of specific criteria of racial harassment will be provided later.

To determine whether a hostile environment exists, the analysis must consider if the institution or school officials have engaged in harassing conduct or are responsible for allowing harassing conduct (e.g., physical, verbal, graphic, or written) to occur without intervention. The conduct must be severe, pervasive, or persistent such that it limits a student or adult from taking full advantage of the service or activity offered by the school *and* meets the standard for different treatment noted previously. One of the differences between hostile environments and racial discrimination as previously described is that the harasser does not need to be an agent or employee of the institution because the school or institution has a duty to provide a nondiscriminatory educational environment. To be deemed a racially hostile environment, an investigation must establish that (a) a hostile environment existed and (b) school officials were notified or had knowledge of the environment and failed to redress the situation. To assess for severity and persistence, one must consider the nature, scope, and frequency of the incidents as well as the characteristics of the persons involved, such as their age, grade, race, gender, and developmental level, and the relationship between the parties. These distinctions are important because younger children might be more adversely impacted by verbal or physical assaults than older, more mature students. These factors are also important because they provide information that must be evaluated and interpreted by school counselors and administrators. For example, it might be determined that, in spite of the perspective of the student who was the target, the racial incident did not meet standards for severity or pervasiveness or that it was not racially motivated; therefore, the racial incident may not create a racially hostile environment. The USDE's OCR (1999) issued guidelines for assisting schools in determining racial harassment, entitled "Protecting Students From Harassment and Hate Crimes: A Guide for Schools." The guidelines offer a definition of racial harassment in schools, directions on how to develop policy that responds to harassment, and steps for creating a safe school setting for students.

The OCR defined racial harassment as "harassment that is oral, written, graphic, or physical conduct relating to an individual's race, color or national origin" (USDE, OCR, 1999, p. 16). The acts may be persistent and severe such that they create a hostile environment, which can impede a person's ability to benefit from the school activity or program. The act can involve implied or overt threats of physical violence, physical aggression, assault, property damage, demeaning racial jokes (depending on the circumstances), taunting, racial slurs, use of demeaning nicknames, and other negative remarks. Graffiti and other physical displays that have racial meaning or intent are considered acts of racial harassment. It is the responsibility of the school officials to investigate and determine if particular incidents meet the criterion established for racial harassment. While these criteria and guidelines are helpful, many additional factors influence school officials' abilities to label racial harassment accurately, such as their racial awareness and understanding, proclivity to break the silence about race, and understanding of distinctions among discrimination and harassment. Therefore, adherence to strict legal definitions might possibly obscure such distinctions. Carter (2007) suggested that legal definitions are an important first step in delineating between racial harassment and discrimination, but these definitions provide limited information about perceptions of racial discrimination or harassment and the psychological impact of race-related incidents on the target. To understand the emotional and psychological effects, each act needs to be understood as distinct, rather than interchangeable. According to Carter, racial discrimination often takes the form of avoidance, wherein the target is denied access and opportunity. In schools, therefore, limited access to academic preparation and gifted programs is an example of avoidant racial discrimination. Racial harassment, on the other hand, is a form of hostility that communicates to the nondominant group individual that he or she is powerless and inferior. Although Carter's definitions are not included in legal descriptions, they might help scholars and school personnel understand the psychological effects and differences in race-related incidents.

Distinctions Between Racial Harassment and Discrimination

Both racial discrimination and harassment have negative effects on the target, but the acts are not interchangeable (Carter, 2007; Carter, Forsyth, Mazzula, & Williams, 2005). Distinguishing between these two types of racially based incidents may provide a better understanding of the psychological and emotional effects associated with each. According to Carter and Carter et al. (2005), racial discrimination is a type of avoidant racism. It can be illustrated through behaviors, actions, policies, and strategies that have either the intentional or the unintentional effect of maintaining separation and/or minimizing contact between dominant and nondominant racial groups. For example, in schools, some would argue that limited access to academic preparation and gifted programs serves as an example of avoidant racial discrimination. In contrast, racial harassment "encourages a hostile or dominative environment" (Carter et al., p. 449). Harassment involves "actions, strategies and policies intended to communicate to nondominant racial groups' their inferior status" (p. 449). It is usually overt hostility toward the target that may be communicated through physical and verbal assaults (e.g., slaps, spitting, kicks, racial slurs, jokes), symbolic messages (e.g., swastikas, racist cartoons), or racial profiling.

Both racial harassment (hostility) and racial discrimination (avoidance) can occur on three different levels: (a) individual, (b) cultural, and (c) institutional or systemic through school policy (Carter et al., 2005). The individual level is usually interpersonal. At an individual level, an example of discrimination might involve a person with formal authority excluding another person from an activity based on race and/or the perceived inferiority. A typical example of harassment at an individual level might involve an individual calling another person a derogatory name. Cultural level discrimination and harassment exclusion are societal influences that directly and negatively affect individuals or groups by imposing rules that have the effect of exclusion (e.g., requirements for gifted programs, culturally biased tests as selection criteria for special programs, and advanced placement classes that limit Blacks and Hispanics). Systemic discrimination or harassment relates to institutional practices that are imposed on individuals or groups. Institutional policies and practices would be those that possibly and unknowingly advantage one racial/cultural group over another.

Fisher et al. (2000) contended that institutional and interpersonal acts of racism via discrimination or harassment create psychological distress for students, which negatively impact their academic lives and their senses of self-worth. The harassing acts, which seem far more perverse, are more troubling because they can lead to psychological disengagement from academic achievement and success (Schmader, Major, & Gramzow, 2001). Both racial discrimination and racial harassment have serious psychological outcomes for youth being educated in America.

Psychological Effects of Racial Discrimination and Harassment

Despite the seriousness of racial harassment and discrimination, school counselors and other mental health professionals often do not consider how students might be affected by these acts. This is troubling considering that racial harassment has been demonstrated by scholars to be involved in many aspects of daily living and in social and economic opportunity and resources (Carter, 2007). Thus, racial harassment and racism are likely involved in the developmental process, life adjustment, and school experiences of all students—White students and students of color. In studies with school-aged children and adults that examined symptoms from racial harassment and other race-related incidents, researchers found that these incidents produced symptoms ranging from daily stress to post-traumatic stress disorder (PTSD; Butts, 2002; Carter, 2005; Johnson, 1993; Taylor & Turner, 2002). Researchers have also found that racial harassment and discrimination impact self-esteem and self-worth (Fisher et al., 2000; Ladd, 1990; Wentzel & Asher, 1995;), depression (Romero & Roberts, 2003; Taylor & Turner), and aggressive behavior (Caldwell, Kohn-Wood, Schmeelk-Cone, Chavous, & Zimmerman, 2004; Rosenbloom & Way, 2004).

Carter et al. (2005) conducted a study to examine the prevalence of racial discrimination and harassment among 262 people of color. Overall, participants from a variety of settings reported almost twice as many incidents of racial harassment (54%) as incidents of racial discrimination (23%). Of the racial incidents that occurred in school settings (primary, secondary, and postsecondary), participants reported a higher incidence of harassment (43%) than discrimination (34%). When examining the psychological impact of these incidents, 75% of the sample reported that these incidents had long-term psychological effects on them, ranging from mild to extreme distress and hypervigilance. The severity of the psychological effect was influenced by the type of event (i.e., harassment or discrimination). On average, 85% of participants who experienced racial harassment reported long-term psychological effects. Conversely, on average, 59% of participants who encountered racial discrimination reported lasting psychological effects. This finding suggests that both types of incidents impact mental health, but harassment seems to engender stronger emotional effects.

Researchers (e.g., Ladd, 1990; Wentzel & Asher, 1995) found that young children who are teased or picked on by their peers at school are more likely to do poorly in school, have low self-esteem, and feel lonely in comparison with children who are not victimized. Similarly, Fisher et al. (2000) reported that 50% of students of color reported that the stress from racial discrimination impacted their self-worth. In a study of White (434) and Black (463) students, Taylor and Turner (2002) found a strong relationship between discrimination and depression for African American students but not among White students. Similarly, in a study of Mexican-American youth (994, both English and Spanish speaking), Romero and Roberts (2003) found a positive relationship between racial distress and depression, with greater levels of racial distress associated with higher levels of depression.

Rosenbloom and Way (2004) found that, for Black and Latino youth, intergroup tension resulted from their perceptions of teacher preferences toward Asians. Latinos and African Americans resented the perceived preference given to Asians, and they harassed them as a result. They reported that the teachers were unaware of their own behavior and the intergroup tensions that it created. These findings may reveal how structural and institutional racism operates and how it may be reflected in interracial group tension. This study also suggests that the stress associated with discrimination can lead to acts of aggression and violence, a finding supported by Caldwell et al.'s (2004) research, which finds that racial discrimination is a strong predictor of violent behavior in young, Black adults.

School Officials' Perceptions of Racial Harassment and Discrimination

Despite the research on psychological impact of racial incidents, school counselors and other mental health professionals have often not received adequate training about how race and ethnicity impact student development and intergroup relations (e.g., Cockrell et al., 1999). Researchers who examined school officials' responses to racism in schools found several themes. First, school officials frequently inaccurately labeled racial incidents, giving more credence to physical acts over emotional and psychological acts; therefore, the psychological impact of racial incidents was rarely a consideration in terms of punishment. Second, school officials tended to focus on individual-level variables such as the perpetrator's personality and disposition, while ignoring the larger sociocultural environment, particularly as it relates to how the racial/cultural climate might influence the prevalence of racial incidents. Third, school officials used race-avoidance strategies to deny the impact of race and race-related issues, which may be related to findings that they often lacked knowledge about how the cultural norms and practices might impact their ability to recognize racially and culturally biased acts.

In a study that examined teachers' and counselors' abilities to distinguish between bullying and other forms of conflict, Hazler, Miller, Carney, and Green (2001) found that school officials inaccurately labeled such acts, often minimizing emotional and psychological harassment and highlighting physical acts. When teachers and counselors examined over 20 scenarios depicting a range of conflictual situations, physical threat or abuse was seen as more severe than verbal, social, or emotional abuse. Additionally school officials were more likely to label physical conflicts as bullying rather than as racial harassment; perceiving an incident as "bullying" leaves more room for interpretation and leniency for officials and perpetrators. Conversely, labeling an act as racial harassment may have more serious consequences for the parties involved and the school. Furthermore, the idea that social and emotional abuse was less in frequently considered harassment suggested that school officials may be unaware of more subtle forms of racial harassment. Therefore, despite prohibitions against racial harassment, schools officials may not recognize such acts. If school officials are unable to accurately label racial harassment and to model appropriate behavior, school-aged children may be unlikely to do the same.

A second theme that researchers (e.g., McClelland & Hunter, 1992) found was that school officials relied primarily on the perpetrator's report when making a determination about the seriousness of acts of racial harassment rather than considering the larger sociocultural environment. In a study at a small college campus, participants' perceptions of racial harassment were wholly dependent on the harassing behavior, in isolation, with little consideration of possible antecedents contributing to the incident nor of the psychological impact on the target. For instance, the type of harassment directed toward the victim from his or her harassers (e.g., hostile comments or actions) and apologetic actions, excuses, or justifications were important factors for how seriously the act was considered. The researchers found that when covert forms of harassment included an apology, school officials perceived the act as less serious. There was no consideration of psychological or emotional impact. There was also no consideration of how the larger racial/cultural climate might have influenced the acts.

Relying on the perpetrator's account of a racial incident can be problematic because an individual's level of development and biological age impact accurate recognition of such acts. In a study about Puerto Rican children's and adolescents' abilities to recognize discrimination, Szalacha et al., (2003) found that age was a significant variable in an individual's ability to recognize instances of racial discrimination. Adolescents who were between ages 13 and 14 were more likely to recognize racial discrimination than were younger children between ages 6 and 11. It is unclear how actions taken against children would be deemed discriminatory since children themselves might not recognize such acts, and authority figures often misperceive such actions. What is more problematic is that researchers have begun to document that newer forms of racial harassment and discrimination may be more difficult to recognize because of their covert nature (Gaertner & Dovidio, 1986; Sellers & Shelton, 2003) or because they may be imbedded in other types of harassment and or discrimination such as language bias (Goto, Gee, & Takeuchi, 2002) or sexual harassment (Shelton & Chavous, 1999). Racial harassment can also be masked and take the form of microaggressive assaults such as walking in one's path, interrupting a conversation, or using symbols or coded language (e.g., using a play on words to communicate a racial slur). These acts may be both intentional and unintentional (McClelland & Hunter, 1992); as a result, rectifying these behaviors and enforcing policies that protect individuals in schools may be more challenging (Goto et al., 2002).

Recognizing and reporting racial incidents is challenging. Fine (1991, 2000) asserted that discussions regarding race are silenced in the nation's schools. "Inside low-income public schools, there is a systematic commitment to not name those aspects of social life that activate social anxieties" (Fine, 1991, p. 33). In particular, Fine asserted that there is a social pressure to be silent about aspects of education related to race and racism. Thus, when Black, Latino, or Native American students raise issues about social inequities and practices associated with race and racism such as racial harassment, teachers typically shift the topic and silence discussion. School counselors, acting in accordance with their professional training, often employ a similar strategy by focusing on individuals' personal or dispositional characteristics, rather than considering sociocultural or environmental factors, when assessing student problems. Employing this strategy, school counselors do not consider the situational or external impacts of racial harassment incidents nor the stress such events may produce for it targets.

School Officials

Few studies have addressed how school officials' can be more effective in detecting racial harassment, so they can more effectively assist children, parents, and administrators in detecting the same. Rather, more attention has focused on sexual discrimination and harassment within schools (McClelland & Hunter, 1992). We believe that it is more accurate to assess the effects of racial harassment as a possible psychological and emotional injury, rather than primarily focusing on the problematic behavior or disposition of the harasser and victim. The idea here is that racial harassment is a sociocultural environmental event, not a personal limitation that can damage a person (Herman, 1992; Johnson, 1993; Wallace & Carter, 2003). *Merriam-Webster's Collegiate Dictionary* (2003) defined injury as "an act that damages or hurts and is a violation of another's rights for which the law allows an action to recover damages" (p. 1040). We argue that racial harassment disrupts normal functioning and can cause psychological and emotional harm. Therefore, such acts should be understood as situational rather than dispositional. But it is also important to take into account the factors that influence the perception of race-related events in schools.

To consider how the sociocultural environment might influence acts of racial harassment, school officials must have knowledge about issues related to race, racism, and power. But, many educators and school counselors either do not recognize or choose to de-emphasize the significance of race and racism in our nation's schools (e.g., Davidman & Davidman, 1988; Fine, 2000; Milk, 1994). This is disturbing, given that in some American cities the majority of teachers are White whereas students of color compose a larger segment of the student enrollment. Cockrell (1999) examined teacher preparation programs and found that many student teachers did not understand how their own beliefs about race, class, culture, and other demographic characteristics impacted their work with diverse populations.

In describing the racial climate in American culture, Verkuyten, Kinket, and Van Der Wielen (1997) stated that if school leaders and staff reflect traditional American racial beliefs and attitudes, especially the belief that racism is a thing of the past, then they will likely attribute racial acts to individual aberrations and minimize possible racial undertones in the larger environment. Sleeter (1989) observes that White teachers who are often the majority seldom see racial oppression. White educators may also have difficulty engaging in discourse about race because they generally do not see themselves as members of a racial group (McIntosh, 1988, 1998). To the extent that their own racial group membership is de-emphasized, their awareness regarding the impact of racism on their own and others psychological development is also de-emphasized. Consequently, they do not understand or appreciate the role and significance of race and racism, nor are they aware of how racial harassment and discrimination impact the lives of students of color (Sleeter, 1989). In fact, Kailin's (1999) study finds that many liberal White teachers blamed Black students for racism. It seems reasonable to conclude that it is difficult to be socialized in this society without internalizing positive beliefs about Whites and negative attitudes about people of color. To offset standard racial socialization practices, educational training programs need to equip school leaders with the knowledge, attitudes, and skills to recognize racial issues such as racial harassment (Carter, 2000).

In the following section, we will use racial identity theory, a race-based approach to education (Carter, 2000), as an approach for increasing knowledge and awareness about race and racial issues. Because racial identity is an inclusive paradigm that incorporates and values all racial–cultural perspectives, the theory provides a way for all Americans, including White Americans, to participate in the dialogue about race, racial harassment, and racism in the nation's schools. Racial identity theory proposes that an individual's ascribed racial group (e.g., White, Black, or Latino) does not tell us about the nature of his or her psychological orientation to race. Indeed, more important from a racial identity perspective is an individual's psychological perspectives or perceptions about race (i.e., a person's racial identity ego status). Each person's racial identity ego status will have consequences for the way he or she interacts with people from his or her own group and from other racial groups. An individual's racial identity ego status might also impact the manner in which institutional practices and policies are established and followed. For example, the school principal's level of racial identity might impact whether he or she believes it is important to hire teachers from visible racial/ethnic groups. Incorporating racial identity theory as a framework for defining, understanding, and addressing issues of racial harassment in school systems offers an important and complex mechanism with which to develop and advocate for prevention and intervention programs. In the next section, we will briefly describe two racial identity models.

Racial Identity Theory and Education

The term *racial identity* refers to one's psychological response to race; it reflects the extent to which one identifies with a particular racial and cultural group and how that identification influences perceptions, emotions, and behaviors toward people from other groups (Carter, 1995). There are several models of racial identity. In this chapter, we describe the White and people of color racial identity models, originated by Helms (1990) and Thompson and Carter (1997), respectively. Each model comprises several distinct racial identity ego statuses, which are theorized to be aspects of personality. Each racial identity ego status comprises a constellation of beliefs, thoughts, emotions, and behaviors based on an individual's membership in a socially ascribed racial group. Although each racial identity ego status is presented separately, at any one point, an individual may endorse attitudes from each status, with one predominant status that has the largest influence on an individual's worldview (Helms & Piper, 1994). Therefore, racial identity is not a stage model wherein an individual is located in one status, but rather individuals have components of each status in their personality structures. An individual can develop sequentially from less differentiated, externally derived, and less mature status influences to more internally based, complex, and differentiated mature status influences, and the influences of statuses may change over time.

The following paragraphs provide an overview of the two models of racial identity for people of color and Whites. Racial identity models for people of color are described together; subsequently, the White racial identity model is described. We encourage the reader to consult other works for more detail (Carter, 1995; Carter & Goodwin, 1994; Carter & Pieterse, 2005; Helms & Cook, 1999; Thompson & Carter, 1997).

People of Color Racial Identity Model

In the first status of the people of color model, Conformity, an individual's worldview is consistent with dominant European-American cultural beliefs, for example, idealizing American culture. Race has limited personal or social meaning, rather social status is presumed to be determined by personality and ability. Individuals characterized by this status view people of color from a stereotypic perspective that is consistent with the dominant societal view. This person is likely to attribute racial incidents solely to personality rather than to see possible interactions with race. The second people of color identity status, Dissonance, is characterized by emotional and psychological confusion, triggered by a series of emotional blows that begin to shift an individual's externally held beliefs regarding race. An individual in this status would probably be unsure whether an event could be attributed to racial harassment or to personal conflicts. In the third status, Immersion–Emersion, an individual attempts to discover his or her racial–cultural heritage and begins to idealize his or her own racial–cultural group, while denigrating White culture. This individual would attribute racial incidents to racism and racial harassment. The fourth people of color identity status, Internalization, is characterized by an inner pride regarding an individual's own racial–cultural heritage and an acceptance of other racial–cultural groups. The final status, Integrative Awareness, is characterized by an active and visible support of nonracist perspectives and often involves social and political activism. In the final statuses an individual would be able to discern racial harassment and understand the differences between personal conflicts and racially based incidents.

White Racial Identity Model

Helms' (2001) theory of White racial ego identity proposes six statuses (Contact, Disintegration, Reintegration, Pseudo-Independence, Immersion–Emersion, and Autonomy). The first three statuses (Contact, Disintegration, and Reintegration) represent the abandonment of racism, and the second three latter statuses (Pseudo-Independence, Immersion–Emersion, and Autonomy) represent the establishment of a nonracist White racial identity. In the first status, Contact, an individual views the world as colorblind; therefore, race has little or no personal meaning. This person might attribute school-based incidents to personal issues rather than to race. The second status, Disintegration, is initially characterized by limited consciousness of one's Whiteness, with a subsequent recognition of racial inequalities, racially based social rules, and pressure to adhere to the color line in social and institutional situations. To cope with this new awareness, which is often conflictual, individuals' become defensive, convincing themselves that racism is a remnant of the past. This person would likely be unsure whether an event could be attributed to racial harassment or to personal conflicts but would tend to not see the role of race. In the third status, Reintegration, individuals adopt a belief in White racial superiority and non-White inferiority. An individual in this status reinterprets information to fit stereotypes commonly held in American society. This individual would tend to attribute encounters with race to the person of color as being overly sensitive and would deny that any action was the result of racism or racial harassment. In the fourth status, Pseudo-Independence, an individual reexamines externally derived information and questions whether Blacks and other people of color are innately inferior to Whites. Individuals also begin to understand that Whites have responsibility for racism. In Immersion–Emersion, the fifth status, an individual begins the emotional process of self-exploration and discovery, and he or she seeks out other Whites for discussions about race. This process often leads to positive, nonracist feelings about being White. In the final status, Autonomy, an individual has developed a new meaning of Whiteness, no longer oppresses or idealizes people based on group memberships, and is primarily able to abandon cultural, institutional, and personal racism. People whose racial identity is influenced by the final three statuses would be able to discern racial harassment and understand the differences between personal conflicts and racial ones. But the distinctions become more clear as the Immersion–Emersion and Autonomy statuses have more influence over one's racial identity ego structure.

In summary, racial identity is a psychological resolution within each person's personality that serves as a lens and filter for racial and cultural knowledge, experience, behavior, and emotion. Racial identity ego status resolutions provide a complex approach for understanding individual development and intergroup interactions. Racial identity sheds light on one's self-understanding, affect, perceptions, ideas, and behaviors toward those who belong to the same or different racial groups. By using racial identity constructs, the meaning of race does not focus entirely on physical markers such as skin color and physical features. Group membership based on demographic markers, alone, is a misleading indicator of whether a person values his or her ascribed racial and cultural group.

Racial Identity and School Applications

We contend that the variation in response to one's racial group membership, namely one's racial identity, has implications for school counselors, educators, students, administrators, and policy makers who address complaints of racial harassment. As school counselors and educators attempt to bring attention to the psychological, educational, and cultural needs of the members of racial groups, they typically do so with little recognition that individuals may vary in response to their racial group membership. We believe, however, that understanding that individuals respond in a variety of ways to their race is crucial to helping school counselors and other staff in dealing with encounters with racial harassment in schools. For example, it is important to consider that people view incidents through their particular views of race and culture.

School counselors who use less mature racial identity statuses as a lens to filter racial cultural information believe that all students are the same and that racial and cultural differences do not impact school events and interactions. Rather, they view students and staff from a universal perspective. Therefore, if a child reports a racial incident, school counselors operating at a low level of racial identity development would tend to blame the victim by viewing the child as lacking appropriate parental guidance; having an impoverished home life, social background, or community; or being overly sensitive about race. School counselors in this group might also believe that they hold high standards for protecting students from harassment and that they work for the interest of all children, a belief that is contrary to empirical studies of teachers' racial perceptions (Darling-Hammond, 2000). Counselors who hold such racial identity attitudes will employ seemingly racially sensitive counseling strategies when issues of racial harassment occur, yet by treating each complaint as an isolated event, he or she is not recognizing the possible patterns. This approach limits one's ability to see any systemic patterns or to discern that the events may be related to racial animus or to prior or current circumstances. Although these counselors may attempt to understand people in terms of racial-cultural distinctions, their own limited racial learning and perspective may distort their understanding. For instance, a White person who holds less mature racial identity attitudes may not recognize how he or she using his or her own background and experiences as the standard for other racial groups (Pseudo-Independence). Likewise, a person of color who holds less mature racial identity attitudes may distort information in favor of his or her racial group and be incapable of being balanced in his or her understanding of complex racial-cultural relationships and incidents.

The more mature and internally defined racial identify statuses are Autonomy and Immersion–Emersion (White statuses) and Internalization and Integrative Awareness (people of color statuses). These statuses are characterized by an internalized positive view of self as a racial being with a deeper understanding of racial and social–political issues in society. School counselors who endorse these racial identity attitudes recognize the complexity of relationships between schools, society, students, and teachers. They also recognize how each student is shaped and influenced by society, school, and teachers. For school counselors endorsing more mature racial identity ego statuses, they can identify racial–cultural patterns in student experiences and uncover subtle aspects of the reported incidents. School counselors who express these racial identity statuses work actively to expand their own knowledge and understanding of race and culture and integrate new knowledge into their work in meaningful ways. The school climate created by school counselors characterized by the more internally based racial identity statuses is one of support and confirmation of varying racial and cultural groups. "They create a [school climate] that is collaborative, purposeful, and supportive" (Hollins, 1999, p. 192).

Students, like counselors, understand the world and interpret classroom and school events through their own level of racial identity development. Students learn about who they are as racial/cultural beings from primary socializing agents (e.g., family, schools, and community) and distal socializing agents (e.g., television and other media). Primary socializing agents are the most powerful forces early in children's lives for learning which groups are valued. These messages are often internalized by students and acted on by school officials. Fine (2000) observed,

[I]nside schools . . . students who carry their genders, their race/ethnic identities, and their social class biographies into school "become"—that is, are seen as and see themselves as—bright or not; talented or deficient, filled with potential or filled with needs. I seek to understand the social psychological processes by which institutional hierarchies, patterned by race and ethnicity, gender and class, come to be embodied by students so that faculty and students can be so sure about who is promising and who is not. (p. 35)

For example, students functioning from different statuses of racial identity may have different reactions to the same educational environment. White students in the Contact or Reintegration statuses may experience an educational environment that supports traditional American cultural values as affirming. Similarly, a Black or a Latino student in the Conformity status may initially feel comfortable with a counselor who believes that American culture should be the conduit through which all learning and experience should take place. In contrast, students of color and White students who possess more advanced racial identity ego statuses may view this attitude as diminishing their race and culture; thus, they may experience such an educational environment as hostile and unwelcoming.

Racial identity development can also influence interpersonal interactions, group dynamics, and organizational policies and practices. The role of racial identity statuses in relationships, systems, and groups is affected by power and authority. Individuals who have more power and authority will exert greater force in terms of relationships. Racial identity researchers and theorists have delineated four types of relationships that can be used to understand interpersonal connections, groups, and organizational dynamics (Carter 1995; Helms, 2001; Thompson & Carter, 1997). The relationship types are regressive, parallel, progressive, and crossed. In a parallel relationship, both participants are at the same level of racial identity development and express the same types of attitudes about their own race and others racial groups. Such a relationship would be self-validating and socially confirming in that the individuals hold the same view and process information in a similar manner (Carter & Helms, 1992). If the victim and school official had a similar racial identity level, even if they were from different racial groups, they would likely be in agreement about what happened and how the incident should be addressed.

In a regressive relationship, the person with less formal power and authority (e.g., the student) has a more mature and advanced racial identity than the person(s) with more power and authority (e.g., school counselor or principal). This type of relationship often produces anxiety, resistance, and anger in the person with less power, who may believe his or her perspective is being disregarded, devalued, and dismissed. In a crossed relationship, similar to a regressive relationship, the participants have opposite racial identity ego statuses, with the person in power having a more mature racial identity than the person with less power. The progressive relationship is the most productive. In this relationship, the power holder(s) has more advanced racial identity status development. By virtue of the more developed status the person in authority can help the less powerful participant(s) learn, grow, and understand issues about race and racial identity. Consider this example of a progressive relationship. Black students engage in verbal name-calling directed at an Asian student. The Asian student lodges a complaint to the school counselor, a White professional in the Autonomy status. The school counselor recognizes that the Black students, even though they may not hold institutional power, were harassing the Asian student. The counselor acquaints the harassers with the policy and the consequences of violations, warns them about violating such policies, and suspends them.

Extending the racial identity relationship dynamics to groups and organizations is extremely powerful and represents an important advance in our abilities to understand race related issues in organizations and groups. As Thompson and Carter (1997) pointed out,

[I]ndividuals who comprise groups and organizations influence others according to the racial identity schema and conversely, are influenced by the racial identity statuses of those who hold power within these setting. Importantly, the racial identity of those in positions of influence contribute to the racial climate of a particular group or organization. (p. 29)

The racial climate refers to how open the group or organization is to addressing and resolving intra- and interracial conflicts and whether group members are able to encourage and facilitate the development of positive race relations (Helms, 1990). The definitions and dynamics are relevant irrespective of the particular racial group's members who may be a part of the organization.

In groups and organizations, racial identity coalitions may be formed on the basis of racial norms and perceptions of power. Coalitions operate based on how comfortable people feel in part due to the proportion of White people to people of color in the group or organization. Whites are more conformable when they are in power and outnumber people of color, and Blacks and self-identified people of color's comfort derives from equal number of Whites and people of color in the organization or group.

Understanding how the racial identity model applies to educational organizations such as classroom, schools, and school districts is important, particularly since these settings often have racial issues, which may become more apparent as those in positions of power are predominantly White and increasingly larger segments of parents and students are people of color. Racial climate plays a powerful role in shaping individual behavior within groups. School counselors and administrators are guided by the racial norms and expectations of those who have authority for the individual school and the school district. For example, if the racial climate of a school or district is characterized by racial denial and stagnation, parents, teachers, and community members who attempt to promote change are likely to have limited success because they are attempting to change their organization's racial norms. If group or organizational leaders avoid and minimize racial-related issues and conflicts or if they confront and address racial issues openly, then their behavior sends signals to group and organizational members about the racial climate and about what behavior is acceptable.

Organizations are usually plagued by stagnation and ambivalence about addressing race (Carter, 2000). Many organizations and schools claim to be concerned with improving race-related problems and conflicts, such as racial incidents or harassment, high rates of suspensions of students of color, disproportionate number of students of color referred to special education, and so on. However, many school leaders will nevertheless establish polices and procedures that ignore or even promote these very problems. Fine (2000) pointed out that race is a critical element in institutional and organizational life in our schools. However, she argued that rather than focus on people of color that we shift our attention to how Whiteness is created and maintained as an unseen process.

> First . . . whiteness, like all "colors," is being manufactured, in part, through institutional arrangements. This is particularly the case in institutions designed "as if" hierarchy, stratification, and scarcity were inevitable. Schools and work, for example, do not merely manage race; they create and enforce racial meanings. Second, in such institutions, whiteness is actually co-produced with other colors, usually alongside blackness, for instance, in symbiotic relation. Where whiteness grows as a seemingly "natural" proxy for quality, merit, and advantage, color disintegrates to embody deficit. Third, whiteness and color are therefore not merely created in parallel, but are fundamentally relational and need to be studied as a system; they might, in statistical terms, be considered "nested" rather than coherent or independent variables. Fourth, the institutional design of whiteness, like the production of all colors, creates an organizational discourse of race and a personal embodiment of race, affecting perceptions of self and "others," producing individuals' sense of racial "identities" and collective experiences of racial "tensions," even coalitions. Once this process is sufficiently institutionalized and embodied, the observer, that is, the scholar, can easily miss the institutional choreography, which has produced a stratified rainbow of colors. What remains visible are the miraculous ways in which quality seems to rise to the glistening white top. (pp. 38–39)

As we can see from Fine's (2000) example, aspects of race and its systemic effects and processes may go unnoticed; our attention may need to be on who benefits in our educational system and how, not just on who is excluded and why. Nevertheless, the example illustrates the use of racial identity analysis in group and organizational contexts. Another example is offered for how racial identity might impact an organization. Since groups are composed of individuals, it is possible for the individual levels of racial identity to combine and reflect the views of the group. For example, in a given middle school, a group of teachers may possess a low status of racial identity (e.g., Contact, Pre-Encounter, Disintegration, and Encounter). It is likely that their individual attitudes will combine to form a coalition (see Helms, 1990) that will become the predominant perspective of the school.

In this example, racial conflict or acts of racial harassment directed at students of color may be understood in terms of individual student personality issues rather than as violations of the law and school policy. Counselors who do not belong to the prevailing racial identity coalition, particularly those who may function from more developed statuses (e.g., Autonomy and Internalization) may feel marginalized and helpless in their efforts to enlighten their colleagues. It is likely that the school environment will be stressful, students will feel the frustration of their teachers, and the school and educational climate will not be conducive to learning. This circumstance is an illustration of regressive racial identity coalitions, since the groups interacting in the school are functioning from very different statuses of racial identity and the group with the greatest influence is characterized by lower statuses.

Recommendations for School Counselors

The increasing number of children from diverse backgrounds in the United States suggests that school counselors and administrators should gain knowledge about how to best meet the needs of these children and their families (Holcomb, 2004). This is particularly important because racial minorities continue to be negatively impacted by race-based harassment (Carter et al., 2005; Carter & Helms, 2002; Juvonen, Nishina, & Graham, 2000). In the following sections, we offer several recommendations based on literature and models presented earlier. These recommendations consider the growing movement in school counseling toward developing a balanced program in prevention and intervention programming.

Intervention Strategies

First, school officials should gain knowledge about the legal statutes and codes for recognizing and addressing allegations of racial harassment and discrimination. In this way, they will be poised to adequately address allegations of racial harassment. As described previously, the OCR established procedures for investigating incidents of racial harassment. Although this office was established to maintain students', teachers', and administrators' civil liberties, school officials would benefit from establishing their own guidelines that are specific to racial harassment and discrimination rather than grouped with other types of discrimination and harassment (sexual harassment, typical bullying, etc.). In developing their own guidelines, schools might develop a detailed process for reporting and resolving incidents of racial harassment. First, schools might develop procedures to adhere to when recording a complaint (i.e., what to look and listen for in the complainant's reactions and how to determine if the victim needs additional services such as psychological counseling, mediation, or conflict resolution). Second, school officials should be aware of complainant's rights to confidentiality. Third, a formal investigation should be launched.

Prevention Strategies

Ideally, schools would develop preventive programming aimed at increasing knowledge and awareness about race, before problems ensue. For example, Vermont recently established a set of guidelines and procedures for addressing instances of racial harassment (USDE, OCR, 1999) that includes school- and community wide interventions aimed at improving the racial climate of their schools. As mentioned earlier, Anne Arundel County, Maryland, has implemented systematic reporting and diversity programs to deter racial incidents at their schools. While this strategy may be in reaction to earlier events, it may also prevent such acts.

The most effective method for combating racial harassment and discrimination, however, is to develop prevention programming that targets the entire school population and that is aimed at increasing awareness and knowledge about race. Before training students, school officials must increase their knowledge. Therefore, professional development for school counselors should include training about race, ethnicity, racial identity, and power. At a minimum, this would require that school counselors attend several conferences on race and seek continuing education training and in-service training on the topic. Training that increases self-awareness, including the complexity of racial identity, will likely lead to a deeper understanding of the nuances of race and racial identity and how they impact the self and others. These requirements will be most successful if all school officials engage in the training. A school counselor is likely to face resistance if other school officials in the system have not had similar training. To ensure that the information is translated into practice, a consultant would be engaged to provide consultant-centered advice related to curriculum development, clinical work, and advocacy. The consultant might also meet monthly with school officials to discuss ways that race and power have been implemented into each person's respective role and practices; regular meetings are essential for creating lasting change and for expanding the organizational culture to include discussions of race and power. Expanding the culture will also increase school officials' comfort in having race-related discussions with students. For school counselors, it is even more imperative to develop skill in discussing issues related to race. Without a level of cultural comfort, students from diverse backgrounds may be unlikely to report acts of racial harassment and discrimination. In writing about how to create identity safety for students of color, Markus, Steele, and Steele (2000), stated,

> [C]lassrooms should be a climate in which group differences—the difference in the local worlds experienced by minority and non-minority students in the setting—is commonly recognized by all and used in achieving a respectful understanding and valuing of all students. (p. 252)

A first and critical step in increasing students' awareness, knowledge, and comfort talking about race, racial harassment, and discrimination is for school officials to begin openly having conversations about these topics. Therefore, school officials might consider implementing a school wide assembly where an expert in the topic discusses these issues with students. Second, school counselors can provide in-class guidance curriculum related to race and power; counselors and teachers can use video and other media on this topic that can appeal to students with varying learning styles; and school counselors and teachers should integrate race and culture into the larger school wide curriculum.

We believe that if students and school officials gain knowledge and awareness about race and power, racial incidents will be more readily reported and claims of racial harassment and discrimination will be adequately addressed. In this way, the unfortunate sequelae of racial incidents such as diminished self-esteem, depression, and negative academic performance will be minimized.

References

American School Counselor Association. (1999). *The role of the professional school counselor.* Retrieved August 4, 2005, from www.schoolcounselor.org

Bell, E. L. J. E., & Nkomo, S. M. (2001). *Our separate ways: Black and White women and the struggle for professional identity.* Boston: Harvard Business School Press.

Butts, H. F. (2002). The black mask of humanity: Racial/ethnic discrimination and post-traumatic stress disorder. *Journal of the American Academy of Psychiatry & the Law, 30*(3), 336–339.

Caldwell, C. H., Kohn-Wood, L. P., Schmeelk-Cone, K. H., Chavous, T. M., & Zimmerman, M. A. (2004). Racial discrimination and racial identity as risk or protective factors for violent behaviors in African American young adults. *American Journal of Community Psychology, 33*(1–2), 91–105.

Carter, R. T. (1995). *The influence of race and racial identity in psychotherapy: Toward a racially inclusive model.* Oxford, UK: John Wiley & Sons.

Carter, R. T. (2000). Reimagining race in education: A new paradigm from psychology. *Teachers College Record, 102*(5), 864–897.

Carter, R. T. (2007) Racism and psychological and emotional injury: Recognizing and assessing race-based traumatic stress. *The Counseling Psychologist, 35*(1), 13–105.

Carter, R. T., Forsyth, J. M., Mazzula, S., & Williams, C. B. (2005). *Handbook of racial cultural psychology.* New York: Wiley.

Carter, R. T., & Goodwin, A. L. (1994). Racial identity and education. In L. Darling-Hammond (Ed.), *Review of research in education* (Vol. 20, pp. 291–336). Washington, DC: American Educational Research Association.

Carter, R. T., & Helms, J. E. (1992). The counseling process as defined by relationship types: A test of Helms's interactional model. *Journal of Multicultural Counseling & Development, 20*(4), 181–201.

Carter, R. T., & Helms, J. E. (2002). *Racial discrimination and harassment: A race based traumatic stress disorder.* Paper presented at American Colleges of forensic examiners Conference, Orlando, FL.

Carter, R. T., & Pieterse, A. L. (2005). Race: A social and psychological analysis of the term and its meaning. In R. T. Carter (Ed.), *Handbook of racial-cultural psychology and counseling: Theory and research* (Vol. 1, pp. 41–63). New York: Wiley.

Cockrell, K. S., Placier, P. L., Cockrell, D. H., & Middleton, J. N. (1999). Coming to terms with "diversity" and "multiculturalism" in teacher education: Learning about our students, changing our practice. *Teaching & Teacher Education, 15*(4), 351–366.

Covarrubias, A. (2005, February 17). Alleged racial incidents shatter security of Santa Clarita Valley; some parents who moved from Los Angeles for a better family environment say their children are now under threat or attack. *Los Angeles Times.* Retrieved August 4, 2005, from the Lexis Nexis database.

Darling-Hammond, L. (2000). School contexts and learning: Organizational influences on the achievement of students of color. In R. T. Carter (Ed.), *Addressing cultural issues in organizations: Beyond the corporate context* (pp. 69–88). Thousand Oaks, CA: Sage.

Darling-Hammond, L., & Sclan, E. M. (1996). Who teaches and why: Dilemmas of building a profession for twenty-first century schools. In J. Sikula (Ed.), *Handbook of research on teacher education* (2nd ed., pp. 67–101). New York: Macmillan.

Davidman, L., & Davidman, P. (1988). Multicultural teacher education in the state of California: The challenge of definition and implementation. *Teacher Education Quarterly, 15*(2), 50–67.

Dollarhide, C. T., & Saginak, K. A. (2003). *School counseling in the secondary school: A comprehensive process and program.* Boston: Pearson Education.

Feagan, J. R. (1991). The continuing significance of race: Anti-black discrimination in public places. *American Sociological Review, 56,* 101–116.

Fine, M. (1991). *Framing dropouts: Notes on the politics of an urban public school.* Albany: State University of New York Press.

Fine, M. (2000). "Whiting out" social justice. In R. T. Carter (Ed.), *Addressing cultural issues in organizations: Beyond the corporate context* (pp. 35–50). Thousand Oaks, CA: Sage.

Fisher, C. B., Wallace, S. A., & Fenton R. E. (2000). Discrimination distress during adolescence. *Journal of Youth and Adolescence, 29*(6), 679–695.

Frankenberg, E. & Lee, C. (2002) *Race in American public schools: Rapidly resegregating school districts.* Retrieved October 13, 2007, from http://www.civilrightsproject.ucla.edu/research/deseg/Race_in_American_Public_Schools1.pdf

Gaertner, S. L., & Dovidio, J. F. (1986). The aversive form of racism. In J. F. Dovidio & S. L. Gaertner (Eds.), *Prejudice, discrimination, and racism* (pp. 61–89). San Diego, CA: Academic Press.

Goto, S. G., Gee, G., C., & Takeuchi, D. T. (2002). Strangers still? The experience of discrimination among Chinese Americans. *Journal of Community Psychology, 30*(2), 211–224.

Hazler, R. J., Miller, D. L., Carney, J. V., & Green, S. (2001). Adult recognition of school bullying situations. *Educational Research, 43*(2), 133–146.

Helms, J. E. (1990). *Black and White racial identity: Theory, research, and practice.* New York: Greenwood Press.

Helms, J. E. (2001). An update of Helms' White and people of color racial identity development models. In J. P. Ponterotto, J. M. Casas, L. A. Suzuki, & C. M. Alexander (Eds.), *Handbook of multicultural counseling* (2nd ed., pp. 188–198). Thousand Oaks, CA: Sage.

Helms, J. E., & Cook, D. A. (1999). *Using race and culture in counseling and psychotherapy: Theory and process.* Needham Heights, MA: Allyn & Bacon.

Helms, J. E., & Piper, R. E. (1994, April). Implications of racial identity theory for vocational psychology. *Journal of Vocational Behavior, 44*(2), 124–138.

Herman, J. L. (1992). *Trauma and recovery: The aftermath of violence from domestic abuse to political terror.* New York: Basic Books.

Holcomb, M. C. (2004). Assessing the multicultural competence of school counselors: A checklist. *Professional School of Counseling, 7*(3), 178–186.

Hollins, E. R. (1995). Revealing the deep meaning of culture in school learning: Framing a new paradigm for teacher preparation. *Action in Teacher Education, 17*(1), 70–79.

Hollins, E. R. (1999). Relating ethnic and racial identity development to teaching. In R. H. Sheets & E. R. Hollins (Eds.), *Racial and ethnic identity in school practices: Aspects of human development* (pp. 183–194). Mahwah, NJ: Erlbaum.

Johnson, R. (1993). Clinical issues in the use of the DSM-III-R with African American children: A diagnostic paradigm. *Journal of Black Psychology 19*(4), 447–460.

Juvonen, J., Nishina, A., & Graham, S. (2000). Peer harassment, psychological adjustment, and school functioning in early adolescence. *Journal of Educational Psychology, 92*(2), 349–359.

Kailin, J. (1999). How White teachers perceive the problem of racism in their schools: A case study in "liberal" Lakeview. *Teachers College Record, 100*(4), 724–750.

Kaufmann, K. (2005, April 6). Charges filed in Swastika incidents. *The Gazette*. Retrieved April 22, 2005, from http://www.gazette.net

Kay, L. F. (2005, July 22). School plan aims to curb bias acts. *Baltimore Sun*. Retrieved August 2, 2005, from http://www.baltimoresun.com

Kozol, J. (1991). *Savage inequalities: Children in American schools*. New York: Crown Publishers.

Ladd, G. (1990). Having friends, keeping friends, making friends, and being liked by peers in the classroom: Predictors of children's early school adjustment? *Child Development, 61*, 1081–1100.

Landrine, H., & Klonoff, E. A. (1996). The schedule of racist events: A measure of racial discrimination and a study of its negative and mental health consequences. *Journal of Black Psychology, 22*, 144–168.

Lecuyer, C., & Ceccarossi, K. (2005, March 29). Student race was a factor in suspension. *Brattleboro Reformer (Vermont)*. Retrieved August 4, 2005, from the LexisNexis database.

Lindsay, S. (2005, March 31). Teen charged with harassment; Jeffco student accused of using racial slurs against a classmate. *Rocky Mountain News*. Retrieved August 8, 2005, from the LexisNexis database.

Markus, H. R., Steele, C. M., & Steele, D. M. (2000). Colorblindness as a barrier to inclusion: Assimilation and nonimmigrant minorities. *Daedalus: Journal of the American Academy of Arts and Sciences, 129*(4), 233–259.

McClelland, K., & Hunter, C. (1992, February). The perceived seriousness of racial harassment. *Social Problems, 39*(1), 92–107.

McGrath, J. E., Berdahl, J. L., & Arrow, H. (1999). Traits, expectations, culture and clout: The dynamics of diversity in work groups. In S. E. Jackson & M. N. Ruderman (Eds.), *Diversity in work teams: Research paradigms for a changing workplace* (pp. 17–45). Washington, DC: American Psychological Association.

McIntosh, P. (1995). White privilege and male privilege: A personal account of coming to see correspondences through work in women studies. In M. L. Andersen and P. H. Collins (Eds.), *Race, class, and gender: An anthology* (2nd ed., pp. 76–87). Belmont, CA: Wadsworth Publishing Co.

McIntosh, P. (1998). White privilege: Unpacking the invisible knapsack. In M. McGoldrick (Ed), *Re-visioning family therapy: Race, culture, and gender in clinical practice* (pp. 147–152). New York: Guilford Press.

Merriam-Webster's collegiate dictionary (11th ed.). (2003). Springfield, MA: Merriam-Webster.

Milk, R. (1994). *Responding successfully to cultural diversity in our schools: The teacher connection*. Albany: State University of New York Press.

Oliver, M. L., & Shapiro, T. M. (1997). *Black wealth/White wealth: A new perspective on racial inequality*. New York: Routledge.

Oliver, M. L., & Shapiro, T. M. (2006). *Black wealth/White wealth: A new perspective on racial inequality* (10th ed.). New York: Routledge.

Romero, A. J., & Roberts, R. E. (2003). The impact of multiple dimensions of ethnic identity on discrimination and adolescents' self-esteem. *Journal of Applied Social Psychology, 33*(11), 2288–2305.

Rosenbloom S. R., & Way, N. (2004). Experiences of discrimination among African American, Asian American and Latino adolescents in an urban high school. *Youth and Society, 35*(4), 420–451

Rouse, K. (2005, June 13). Harassment has outcome that's Unique after 12-year-old Unique Irvin was racially harassed at Ken Caryl Middle School, she and her mother met the problem with forgiveness and a community education project. *The Denver Post*. Retrieved August 8, 2005, from the LexisNexis database.

Schmader, T., Major, B., & Gramzow, R. H. (2001). Coping with ethnic stereotypes in the academic domain: Perceived injustice and psychological disengagement. *Journal of Social Issues, 57*(1), 93–111.

School Mental Health Project/Center for Mental Health in School (SMHP). (1999, Fall). Promoting youth development and addressing barriers. *Addressing Barriers to Learning*, 1–8.

Sellers, R. M., & Shelton, N. J. (2003). The role of racial identity in perceived racial discrimination. *Journal of Personality and Social Psychology, 84*, 1079–1092.

Sheldon, K. M., & Biddle, B. J. (1998). Standards, accountability, and school reform: Perils and pitfalls. *Teachers College Record, 100*, 164–180.

Shelton, J. N., & Chavous, T. M. (1999). Black and White college women's perceptions of sexual harassment. *Sex Role, 40*(7–8), 593–615.

Sidanius, J., & Pratto, F. (1999). *Social dominance: An intergroup theory of social hierarchy and oppression.* Cambridge, UK: Cambridge University Press.

Sleeter, C. E. (1989). Doing multicultural education across the grade levels and subject areas: A case study of Wisconsin. *Teaching & Teacher Education, 5*(3), 189–203.

Starks, C. (2005, July 9). Harvard school bias suit dropped. *Chicago Tribune.* Retrieved August 4, 2005, from the LexisNexis database.

Stone, C. B., & Dahir, C. A. (2004). *School counselor accountability: A measure of student success.* Upper Saddle River, NJ: Pearson Education, Inc.

Szalacha, L. A, Erkut, S., Coll, C. G., Alarcon, O., Fields, J. P., & Ceder, I. (2003). Discrimination and Puerto Rican children's and adolescents' mental health. *Cultural Diversity & Ethnic Minority Psychology, 9*(2), 141–155.

Taylor, J., & Turner, R. J. (2002). Perceived discrimination, social stress, and depression in the transition to adulthood. *Social Psychology Quarterly, 65*(3), 213–225.

Texas Association of School Boards. (2007). *Supporting schools. The fundamental role of public schools.* Retrieved August 11, 2005, from http://www.tasb.org/schools/role.aspx

Thompson, C. E., & Carter, R. T. (1997). *Racial identity theory: Applications to individual, group, and organizational interventions.* Mahwah, NJ: Lawrence Erlbaum Associates.

Travers, J. F., Elliott, S. N., & Kratochwill, T. R. (1993). *Educational psychology: Effective teaching, effective learning.* Madison, WI: Brown & Benchmark.

Turner, K. (2005, July 9). Suit alleging racism in D-50 dismissed. *Northwest Herald.* Retrieved August 2, 2005, from http://www.nwherald.com

U.S. Department of Education. (1994, March). *Racial incidents and harassment against students at educational institutions; investigative guidance* (Federal Register, 59, No. 47). Retrieved June 15, 2005, from http://www.ed.gov/about/offices/list/ocr/docs/race394.html

U.S. Department of Education. (2001). *No child left behind act.* Washington, DC: Author. (ERIC Document No. ED 447-608)

U.S. Department of Education. (2007). A*nnual report to Congress of the Office for Civil Rights: Fiscal year 2006.* Washington, DC: Author.

U.S. Department of Education, National Center for Education Statistics. (2007). *The condition of education 2007* (NCES 2007-064). Washington, DC: U.S. Government Printing Office.

U.S. Department of Education, Office for Civil Rights & National Association of Attorneys General, Bias Crimes Task Force. (1999). *Protecting students from harassment and hate crime: A guide for schools.* Retrieved on October 7, 2007, from http://www.ed.gov/offices/OCR/archives/Harassment/harassment.pdf

Verkuyten, M., Kinket, B., & Van Der Wielen, C. (1997). Preadolescents' understanding of ethnic discrimination. *Journal of Genetic Psychology, 158*(1), 97–112.

Wallace, B. C., & Carter, R. T. (Eds.). (2003). *Understanding and dealing with violence: A multicultural approach.* Thousand Oaks, CA: Sage

Wentzel, K., & Asher, S. R. (1995). The academic lives of neglected, rejected, popular, and controversial children. *Child Development, 66,* 754–763.

IX

THE ROLE OF ETHNIC IDENTITY IN THE PRACTICE OF SCHOOL COUNSELING

SHANNON CASEY-CANNON
California School of Professional Psychology
Alliant International University

Multicultural programming and culture-based initiatives have recently become central to many school counseling programs (Bass & Coleman, 1997). Educators and psychologists better understand how youth view their cultural selves, including the intrapersonal and interpersonal psychological processes related to exploring and committing to a cultural or ethnic identity (Phinney, 1992; Sellers, Rowley, Chavous, Shelton, & Smith, 1997; A. Thernstrom & S. Thernstrom, 2003; Yeh, 2004). Racial and ethnic identity has been defined as a "type of group identity that is central to the self-concept of members" of an ethnic group (Roberts et al., 1999, p. 303) and as the significance and meaning that individuals attribute to membership in a certain group (Sellers et al., 1997). Development of positive ethnic identity has been related to numerous developmental outcomes, including psychological well-being, self-esteem, career development, and most notably for schools, academic achievement in young people (Dubow, Pargament, Boxer, & Tarakeshwar, 2000; Rumbaut, 1994; Yasui, Dorham, & Dishion, 2004). Theories regarding youth ethnic identity development are supported by research that acknowledges and celebrates diversity in school settings.

Counselors are charged with helping students develop positive and "comprehensive" identities based upon the many cultures to which they belong. Operating within larger systems of neighborhoods, school districts, and society, counselors advocate for students both individually and collectively. Empowering minority students helps to foster dynamic and accepting schools and communities where all students have the opportunity to thrive (Fusick & Bordeau, 2004; Yeh, 2004). This chapter summarizes the literature on ethnic identity, provides a framework for ethnic identity development within broader sociocultural contexts, and discusses strategies and evidence-based interventions for "counselor-assisted ethnic identity development" (Fusick & Bordeau). A case example of school-based counseling with a high-school girl immigrating to the United States from Peru is presented as a highlight of the encouragement of ethnic identity development.

Schools have become reflections of growing diversity in the United States, with an increase in the number of children from diverse ethnicities, bicultural backgrounds, and immigrating families (U.S. Bureau of the Census, 2001). The changing ethnic makeup of tomorrow's generations is accompanied by shifts in cultural values, customs, behaviors, and lifestyles (Yeh, 2004). To meet the demands of growing, dynamic student populations, counselors tailor interventions and programs to promote emotional, social, and cognitive growth of a diverse range of students (Baker & Gerler, 2001). In their National Model of School Counseling, the American School Counseling Association (ASCA; 2003) mandated that schools ensure every student has equitable access to school counseling programs. That includes providing comprehensive services to help students acquire knowledge, attitudes, and interpersonal skills necessary for understanding and respecting oneself and others (ASCA). Specifically, the ASCA advocates for facilitating minority and nonminority exploration of ethnic identity through purposeful programs in schools.

> School counselors would do well to integrate knowledge, awareness, and skills related to adolescents' ethnic identity development, acculturation experiences, perceptions of mattering, and overall wellness into their comprehensive counseling programs in order to meet the diverse needs of both minority and nonminority students. (Rayle & Myers, 2004, p. 89)

That includes shifting traditionally Eurocentric views of educational standards to multiculturally informed views of education, perceiving individuals who differ from traditional Western norms as positively adapting within new contexts.

Counselor-Assisted Ethnic Identity Development

During preadolescence and adolescence, youth make social comparisons to explore their identity relative to others in their social world, including family, peers, and authority figures such as teachers (Steiner & Feldman, 1996). One way school-aged children categorize themselves and others is according to race and ethnicity. Students begin to encounter their racial or ethnic makeup and affiliation, a process referred to as "racial identity" or "ethnic identity development" (Phinney, 1992; Sellers et al., 1997). Typically, the term *race* or *racial identity* has been used to describe the genetic or biological markers that differentiate individuals, with an additional focus on sociopolitical implications related to marginalizing groups based on visible group membership (Betancourt & Lopez, 1993; Helms, 1994; Ponterotto & Pederson, 1993). The broader and more widely accepted term *ethnicity* or *ethnic identity* has identified groups of individuals united by shared values, worldviews, and behaviors, who may have a similar heritage (Betancourt & Lopez; Phinney, 1990).

Historically, research about ethnicity for children focused on stereotyping, racism, and discrimination; more recently, literature focuses on the psychological relationship of minority group members with their own group (Holcolmb-McCoy, 2005). Distinguishing ethnic identity from other constructs such as racial identity and acculturation has been complicated and difficult (Coleman, Norton, Miranda, & McCubbin, 2003). Many authors, however, have elected to use the terms interchangeably to symbolize an individual's understanding of his or her cultural self, including self-identity, perspectives on group membership, and perceptions on how his or her group is perceived by others (Phinney, 1990; Sellers et al., 1997). Educators and psychologists focus less on disputing the nuanced understanding of terms such as *race* and *ethnicity*, and instead concentrate on the dynamic and changing nature of cultural socialization, in particular, for minority populations (Yeh & Hwang, 2000).

Regarding the development of ethnic identity, ecological models suggest that self-understanding and behavior result from ongoing dynamic interactions between individuals and their environment (Bronfenbrenner, 1979). Thus, identity development does not occur in a vacuum; it is part of a much larger system that integrates diverse layers of influence, including societal, neighborhood, school, and family influences (Yeh, 2004; Zayas, 2001). Ethnic identity is mutually constructed, built upon contacts with one's own and other cultures across the lifespan (Aldarondo, 2001; Yeh & Hunter, 2004). The transmission of cultural values and culturally appropriate behaviors, thoughts, and emotions is critical to the identity development process (Yeh & Hunter).

The context is not seen as an external driving force, but rather, it gives meaning to one's behaviors (Bronfenbrenner, 1979). The meaning that youth attribute to membership in a specific group or groups helps to form self-perceptions (Sellers, Chavous, & Cooke, 1998). Distal and proximal systems, such as neighborhoods and families, differentially influence the meaning associated with being a member of a certain ethnic group. That process of coconstruction of meaning has important ramifications for the development of identity, as patterns of socialization likely vary by cultural context (Yeh & Hunter, 2004). A student's identity, thus, may shift based upon the surrounding cultural context and the meaning attributed to being part of a cultural group within that context. For example, a student recently immigrating to America from Vietnam and attending a predominantly European-American high school might encounter others' perceptions of what it means to be Vietnamese, as well as what it means to be an immigrant. The meaning attributed to being from a certain ethnic group, by oneself and by others, provides a context for identity development (Yeh & Hwang, 2000).

Based on ongoing interactions, ethnic identity development is a multidimensional and dynamic process that shifts across time and context (Markus & Kitayama, 1991; Yeh & Hunter, 2004; Yeh & Hwang, 2000). Selves are continually adapting and changing in ways that vary for each individual and are based on previous experience and support for exploration in their community (Yeh & Hunter). Bridging across diverse contexts can be difficult for students (Yeh & Drost, 2002)—in particular, when there are cultural conflicts between one's own culture and the majority or dominant culture, which is frequently privileged by race and economic status. Identifying and confirming possible selves is a difficult process that deserves acknowledgment from psychological support staff (Markus & Kitayama, 1991). Rather than being marginalized or degraded for different values, students deserve recognition for the complicated and "stressful" process of negotiating across diverse contexts (Coleman, Casey-Cannon, & Fillingame, 2004).

Many authors have found that ethnic identity development is strongly influenced by discrimination, classicism, and unequal access to opportunity (Fusick & Bordeau, 2004). If a child is seen by educators as a stereotype, rather than an individual, then racism takes its psychological toll (Zayas, 2001). Children might feel estranged from themselves when they are defined by external notions, rather than innate self-definition (Zayas). Aldarondo (2001) observed that "experiences with racism, especially if this is internalized, may prompt some confusion related to personal identity" (p. 246). Students may experience conflict between what they experience to be true about themselves (e.g., they enjoy and excel in math) and what society says about students from their cultural group (e.g., they lack mathematic ability). It is likely that racism and discrimination lead to a stress response and evoke attempts at coping with the discrimination (Zayas). Thus, youth use a range of strategies to cope with cultural conflicts; some are more adaptive than others and some may relate more strongly to achievement (Coleman et al., 2004; Coleman, Casali, & Wampold, 2001).

The process of developing ethnic identity may be more complex for biracial or multiethnic populations (Rayle & Myers, 2004). In addition to conforming to mainstream social norms, students from multiethnic backgrounds may believe that they must identify with one group or another in order to consolidate the persons they are becoming (Aldarondo, 2001). Multiethnic students may struggle with creating an integrated sense of cultural identity based on compatible—or sometimes conflicting—norms and values (LaFromboise, Coleman, & Gerton, 1993). Development of ethnic identity may also be more complicated for immigrant students, who might encounter discrimination on a systemic level or feel stigmatized or stereotyped by society (Yeh et al., 2005). As such, immigrant students might rely more heavily on social support networks as they work to balance multiple aspects of the self (Yeh et al.).

Ethnic identity searching has been related to psychological well-being (Phinney, 1990; Rayle & Myers, 2004), academic achievement (LaFromboise et al., 1993), school experiences (Thernstrom & Thernstrom, 2003), and self-esteem (Holcolmb-McCoy, 2005; Phinney, 1992) in minority and nonminority populations. Research suggests that ethnic minority youth are at higher levels of risk for mental health problems, school problems, and school dropout (Dubow et al., 2000; Yasui et al., 2004). Thus, developing a positive sense of one's cultural self is critical for youth. Self-awareness and understanding contributes to maximizing student potential and well-being. School counselors serve as agents of change when they help students explore ethnic identity (Holcolmb-McCoy), facilitate negotiation of diverse contexts, and provide choices for defining who one wants and chooses to be (Fusick & Bordeau, 2004). Students benefit from understanding ethnic affiliation, including knowledge of cultures they seek to integrate, developing positive attitudes toward multiple groups, and understanding core values related to the groups to which they belong (LaFromboise et al.; Yang, Coleman, & Cho Kim, 2003).

Theories of ethnic identity development suggest that students internalize cultural messages about their ethnic group; how those messages are interpreted directly relates to self-identity, psychological well-being, and school performance (Holcolmb-McCoy, 2005; Thernstrom & Thernstrom, 2003). When messages toward one's cultural group are perceived to be favorable, or when there is minimal conflict in identity development, minority students have more support to excel and build a positive sense of self (Aldarondo, 2001). Even in the presence of external barriers such as racism and discrimination, positive racial identity serves to assist minority adolescents in overcoming obstacles present in hostile environments, which contributes to improved educational involvement and achievement (Miller, 1999; Spencer, Noll, Stoltzfutz, & Halpalani, 2001). This research supports that ethnic awareness and group affiliation are protective by facilitating the development of positive self-beliefs and personal potential.

Other theorists hypothesize that when messages are perceived as less than favorable, students might underperform relative to peers from majority cultures in spite of equivalent levels of motivation and ability. Students may "disidentify" with school or undervalue education, choosing to redefine their identity around pursuits other than academics (Steele, 1997; Wilson, Cooke, & Arrington, 1997). Thus, social conditions degrade student's perceptions of the self and create barriers for active engagement. Research evidence for a direct relationship between racial and ethnic identity and academic achievement is mixed, although recent attempts to clarify how identity and achievement are related show much promise (Coleman et al., 2004).

The Role of the School Counselor

It is clear from the research that students benefit from assistance in developing a positive identity (Phinney, 1992). "Counselor-assisted ethnic identity development" (Fusick & Bordeau, 2004, p. 110) has been described as a process of promoting positive ethnic identity development, helping students to resolve identity conflicts, and providing environments that support growing diversity (Aldarondo, 2001; Fusick & Bordeau). Based in relationships built on trust and mutual respect, interactions with multiculturally competent counselors empower young minority students to better negotiate cultures and take positions of strength (Yang et al., 2003). Allowing for exploration of ethnic identity in a nonjudgmental environment, through groups, assignments, and programming is critical (Phinney, 1992).

Research has identified many ethnic minority students as reluctant to seek counselor assistance due to fear of being stigmatized or of linguistic barriers (Yeh & Inose, 2002). Other research suggests that minority students report receiving less support from teachers and educators than their European-American counterparts receive (Bass & Coleman, 1997). In addition, cultures vary in their views of counseling and self-disclosure, with some cultural values that discourage sharing personal difficulty outside of the family (Sue & Sue, 2002; Yeh & Hunter, 2004). As a result, students will be at different levels of exploring ethnic identity for diverse reasons (Holcomb-McCoy, 2005; Phinney, 1992). Thoughtful and culturally sensitive counseling and outreach with students is imperative.

The Case of Marta

To illuminate the process of supporting ethnic identity development in school counseling, this chapter reviews a case example of recently immigrated Marta, a 17-year-old junior-high-school student born in Peru who approached school counselors for support. Marta had moved to the United States to live with her aunt and uncle after the sudden death of her parents in Peru for political dissent. While taking multiple honors courses and working 18 hours per week at a restaurant, Marta was caring for younger cousins to alleviate family burden. Initially, Marta identified having had difficulty making friends in her new school. Though she had excellent English skills, she struggled to balance school, work, and family life with her desire to succeed. At a first meeting, it became clear Marta was having difficulty creating a new identity based on her emergence in the United States absent the support of her parents. She had conflicted feelings about returning to Peru and about what she perceived as abandoning her native country. Responding in culturally appropriate ways that honored the complexity and profundity of her experience was critical.

Individual and Group Counseling

Several authors provide practical strategies for assisting youth with developing positive identities, a process that begins with a self-assessment of the counselor's cultural group membership, values, and multicultural competence, which lies at the core of building good rapport with students (Sue & Sue, 2002). Active exploration of biases and assessment of abilities and limitations provide positive role modeling for students developing their ethnic identity (Fusick & Bordeau, 2004). "If educators understand how ethnic identity affects their interactions and behaviors with students, they will be more equipped to change negative, ineffective relationships (with students and parents) into more positive, supportive relationships" (Holcomb-McCoy, 2005, p. 126). In building a relationship with Marta, it was important that the counselor ask herself "What values do I hold that I might expect Marta to also hold or that I might impose on her?" and "How does my role as a White woman privileged by skin color, education, and U.S.-born status affect our interactions?" It was important that the counselor directly address these cultural differences, including acknowledgment and discussion of her inability to provide service in Marta's native language. English proficiency, as well as both how it influences working with the student in counseling and how it impacts interpersonal relationships and classroom experiences, should be considered. Conversations exploring transference related to therapist–student ethnic match or peer–student interethnic issues help students understand how ethnic identity emerges in interpersonal relationships (Zayas, 2001). Though counselor–student ethnic match is helpful for many students (Bass & Coleman, 1997), it is ultimately having achieved ethnic identity exploration that is most beneficial.

As all counselors are aware, relationship building, caring, and fairness are critical components of successful counseling relationships (Sue & Sue, 2002). Mistrust or skepticism from either the counselor or client meaningfully interferes with the process of identity exploration (Fusick & Bordeau, 2004). Providing open-ended and nonjudgmental questions is critical. It may be particularly important for counselors to have high expectations of all students (Fusick & Bordeau). This serves to counteract stereotypes of ability based on ethnic group membership and provides a platform of belief that all youth have the potential for achievement in areas that are important to them (Thernstrom & Thernstrom, 2003).

In both individual and group settings, students benefit from discussing issues about race and ethnicity (Benedetto & Olisky, 2001). Students should be assured that discussing ethnic and multiethnic identities is a positive and normal part of development. Counselors are encouraged to directly engage in discussions of values, communication, and culture with students, proactively rather than reactively (Caldwell, Oldfield, & Beech, chapter 14, this volume). Through individual and group counseling, counselors invite students to talk with school personnel and fellow students about belief systems in nonjudgmental ways that engender mutual respect for differences (Fusick & Bordeau, 2004; Rayle & Myers, 2004). Specifically, research advocates for helping students place worth in traditional values, as well as in American education, to optimize success (Yang et al., 2003). Counselors might ask, "What values are important to you?" or "If you were describing for someone who you are as a person, what would you say?" Other questions to help youth understand their multiple identities could include "Are there times that you feel pulled between many different ideas of who you are?" or "Some people say they have competing values, like wanting to be their own person and feeling strong commitments to their family. Are there times you feel unclear about what is most important to you? What is that like for you?" In individual meetings, Marta was invited to describe her life in Peru, how it compared with her life in the United States, and value conflicts that emerged when comparing the two cultures. The counselor refrained from defining Marta by literature on Peruvian culture and from conceptualizing Marta exclusively by South American culture; instead, the counselor gleaned Marta's worldview from questioning her. Though it was tempting to suggest that Marta consider quitting her job or spending less time watching her cousins, it was important the counselor not prioritize or condemn Marta's values, but instead explore how and why those values were lived out in her behaviors, experiences, and choices she made.

Being multiculturally competent includes an awareness of the needs of students from diverse communities, including the needs of multiethnic and immigrant students (Aldarondo, 2001; Yeh, 2003). Counselors do well to consider that youth are struggling with negotiating a large and complex cultural landscape that includes multiple players (teachers, peers, parents and extended family, societal values, and cultural messages). Counselors benefit from making ongoing assessment of the sociological context of the school, including the neighborhood, communities, families, and society to which the students belong (e.g., noting the presence of mentors of color in schools; Thernstrom & Thernstrom, 2003). The development of identity is not a linear or unidirectional process from students to the environment, but instead a bidirectional dynamic between students and the environment. Thus, individuals move in and out of stronger and weaker affiliation with their ethnic identity based upon the cultural context; a holistic perspective of students, including both intrapsychic and interpsychic variables, illuminates the complexity of the student–environment interaction (Yeh, 2004). That includes making assessments of how racial identity is viewed, supported, and cultivated at home and at school (Benedetto & Olisky, 2001). Direct discussions of acculturation experiences and questions about students' new roles can be particularly helpful for immigrating students. Counselors might ask, "How do the people around you think or feel about the culture to which you belong?" or "Are there ever times when you feel as though people around you really support things you value or don't support things you care about?" or "In what settings are you able to feel most comfortable or true to all of the different parts of who you are?" Through counseling, Marta recognized that becoming successful and having the freedom to pursue personal interests were critically important to avenging the cruel death of her parents, although they were not values necessarily shared by those in her school. Marta also explored the importance of giving back to family through childcare to repay the debt she felt toward her aunt and uncle. She was not eager to change her affiliation with either of those value structures, in spite of the dilemmas they presented on occasion.

School counselors help students acquire skills and knowledge to identify, negotiate, and resolve cultural conflicts; to develop as unique individuals; to build coping strategies; and to thrive in spite of external obstacles (Fusick & Bordeau, 2004; Yeh & Hwang, 2000). By encouraging pride in oneself and recognition of individual potential, counselors promote exploration of abilities, interests, strengths, and self-reliance in students (Rayle & Myers, 2004). For example, counselors can directly ask, "What is it important for you to be good at?" or "What is one thing about yourself that you see as an asset and you cherish the most?" or "What is something your family or culture really values about you?" or they can say, "Tell me a few things that you do really well." Reflecting on these questions, students learn skills for integrating disparate parts of their identity to form and reform a sense of themselves and their culture from positive viewpoints (Aldarondo, 2001).

In addition, counselors have an opportunity to help students understand and manage stresses associated with racism, discrimination, and educational barriers and to help students refrain from self-limiting thinking (Fusick & Bordeau, 2004; Thernstrom & Thernstrom, 2003; Zayas, 2001). Because students are not likely to approach counselors with racism or discrimination as a presenting problem, counselors are encouraged to listen for covert material related to ethnic and racial self-definition (Zayas). Students can be invited to reflect directly on how perceptions of race and class help or hinder academic achievement, interpersonal relationships, and academic success (Fusick & Bordeau). Initially, Marta approached the counselor for help building a larger social circle; later, it emerged that she was feeling overwhelmed by keeping up appearances of "doing it all" to counter fear that other students would look down on her. Marta expressed concerns that working to support her extended family and save money for college would interfere with academic achievement, a stressor not shared by many of her middle-class majority peers. While sadness emerged from these realizations, they were instrumental in helping her consider how to respond to these constraints toward building a successful future. While open discussions about culture and values are not simple, when conducted with sensitivity, honesty, and humility, they can be enlightening and inclusive for students who feel marginalized or stereotyped based on ethnic group membership.

Research suggests counselors should consider tailoring programs for bicultural and immigrant youth, who may experience identity differently from monoethnic individuals (LaFromboise et al., 1993; Wardle, 1992; Yeh & Hunter, 2004). Benedetto and Olisky (2001) suggest that work with biracial youth in a school setting should recognize multiple factors related to biracialism; counselors need to become familiar with myths and stereotypes that perpetuate about biracialism. In addition, Benedetto and Olisky advocate for appreciation of advantages and disadvantages associated with biracial identity status.

Specific techniques such as strengths-based assessments, values-related activities, or exercises that develop a future orientation can be helpful. For example, creating a family genogram helps students explore values held by families, communities, and cultures. Guided imagery exercises helped Marta envision her future. She vividly described two future scenarios, as a fashionably dressed urban working professional, and in a large country home with rooms for extended family and a porch for family meals. Those images reassured Marta of her potential, reminding her that achievement was important to her, and solidified that maintaining family connectedness while excelling at a job was possible. Ultimately, Marta made the decision to shift her restaurant work to a position at a local library where she could study during work time; she also joined a group of students committed to improving conversations of culture at the school. Those shifts in commitments allowed her to remain true to her values while pursuing her social and academic goals.

Developing a multiculturally sensitive program includes acknowledging the dearth of resources available for many students, counseling staff, and schools. Limitations placed on school counseling budgets are real. It is increasingly difficult to engage in programming without sufficient fiscal and human resources. In addition, counselors are frequently called upon to engage in other important activities, such as college preparation or course scheduling. Working in an underserved school may present particular difficulty finding resources and time to discuss identity with individuals and groups. In spite of this, many of the strategies mentioned above involve shifts in attitudes and approaches, rather than costly programs. One of the most powerful interventions can be creating positive environments where ethnic identity is welcomed and celebrated, rather than minimized or disregarded.

Group interventions may be more cost-effective and may be more culturally appropriate for persons of diverse ethnicities (Benedetto & Olisky, 2001; Yeh, 2004). Some authors have found that belonging to specific types of groups, such as peer support groups for Asian immigrant youth, reduces acculturative stress; others have found that belonging to counseling groups allows for open exploration of student feelings of belongingness, affirmation, and commitment as they discuss issues of race and ethnicity (Baca & Koss-Chioino, 1997). Groups can include problem-solving activities and role-playing activities (cf. Holcolmb-McCoy, 2005). In addition, students can be encouraged to work toward changing the environments that are not helping them meet their goals (Cook, Heppner, & O'Brien, 2002). Interventions that highlight positive ethnic orientation and encourage cultural assets, as well as help students cope with cultural conflict, are particularly helpful (Yang et al., 2003). For example the Calm Heart: Ua Siab Tus Yees program promotes healthy cultural identity development and assists students with psychological well-being and school success (Yang et al.). Finding the balance of individual and group interventions for your school and community is an individual process related to resources, community acceptance, and student needs.

Building a Multicultural School Environment

Regardless of the school's ethnic makeup, counselors serve advocacy roles for increasing cultural sensitivity within the larger community (Holcomb-McCoy, 2005; Rayle & Myers, 2004). This includes working with students from the dominant culture—typically, White culture—to engage in self-awareness activities that explore ethnic heritage. Increasing the amounts of cultural references and resources (e.g., books, videos, and posters) available to people in the school, advocating for student uniqueness, and developing opportunities to explore culture are all effective community-building activities (Holcomb-McCoy). In addition, counselors are situated to increase the number of staff training sessions and parent workshops that address culture, as well as to advocate for additional mentors of diverse ethnicities on campus (Thernstrom & Thernstrom, 2003; Wardle, 1992). Both school wide and district wide interventions can increase exposure to race and ethnicity; inviting local leaders from diverse ethnic groups to speak, celebrating diverse holidays, or inviting families to the school for cultural celebrations are all examples of meaningful and cost-effective initiatives (see Benedetto & Olisky, 2001 for a review of multiple initiatives). The bottom line is that counselors must rally all of the resources at their disposal to build developmental guidance programs that are aware of issues of race and ethnicity, that address the importance of diversity, and that encourage respect for diverse cultures in school halls and the larger community.

Summary

The importance of ethnic identity to developmental success of young people highlights the need for counselors to assist all students with developing positive ethnic identity. Because of the dynamic nature of identity, counselors need to visit and revisit these issues with students from all ethnic groups and from the larger community. Experiences of racism or critical events that influence students' feelings about themselves and each other provide unique opportunities for engaging students in this area. The field deserves additional support for ongoing exploration specific to diverse ethnicities and contexts for optimizing learning and development for all students. Proactive school programs improve the cultural context, perpetuate safety, engender respect, and embrace diversity, benefits that are beyond measure.

References

Aldarondo, F. (2001). Racial and ethnic identity models and their application: Counseling biracial individuals. *Journal of Mental Health Counseling, 23*, 238–255.

American School Counselor Association. (2003). *The ASCA national model: A framework for school counseling programs.* Alexandria, VA: Author.

Baca, L. M., & Koss-Chioino, J. D. (1997). Development of a culturally responsive group counseling model for Mexican American adolescents. *Journal of Multicultural Counseling and Development, 25*(2), 130–141.

Baker, S. B., & Gerler, E. R. (2001). Counseling in schools. In D. C. Locke, J. E. Myers, & E. L. Herr (Eds.), *The Handbook of Counseling* (pp. 289–318). Thousand Oaks, CA: Sage Publications.

Bass, C., & Coleman, H. L. K. (1997). Enhancing the cultural identity of early adolescent male African Americans. *Professional School Counselor, 1*, 48–51.

Benedetto, A. E., & Olisky, T. (2001). Biracial youth: The role of the school counselor in racial identity development. *Professional School Counseling, 5*, 66–69.

Betancourt, H., & Lopez, S. R. (1993). The study of culture, ethnicity, and race in American psychology. *American Psychologist, 48*, 629–637.

Bronfenbrenner, U. (1979). *The ecology of human development.* Cambridge, MA: Harvard University Press.

Coleman, H. L. K, Casali, S. B., & Wampold, B. E. (2001) Adolescent strategies for coping with cultural diversity. *Journal of Counseling and Development, 79*, 356–364.

Coleman, H. L. K., Casey-Cannon, S., Fillingame, L. K. (2004). *Cultural identity, bicultural competence, strategies for coping with cultural diversity.* Paper presented at the Multicultural Education Conference, Melbourne, Victoria, Australia.

Coleman, H. L. K., Norton, R. A., Miranda, G. E, & McCubbin, L. D. (2003). Toward an ecological theory of cultural identity development. In D. B. Pope-Davis, H. L. K. Coleman, W. Liu, & R. Toperek (Eds.), *Handbook of multicultural competencies* (pp. 38–58). Thousand Oaks, CA: Sage.

Cook, E. P., Heppner, M. J., & O'Brien, K. M. (2002). Career development of women of color and white women: Assumptions, conceptualization, and interventions from an ecological perspective. *Career Development Quarterly, 50*, 291–305.

Dubow, E. F., Pargament, K. I., Boxer, P., & Tarakeshwar, N. (2000). Initial investigation of Jewish early adolescents' ethnic identity, stress, and coping. *Journal of Early Adolescence, 20*, 418–441.

Fusick, L., & Bordeau, W. C. (2004). Counseling at-risk Afro-American youth: An examination of contemporary issues and effective school-based strategies. *Professional School Counseling, 8*, 109–115.

Helms, J. E. (1994). The conceptualization of racial identity and other "racial" constructs. In E. J. Trickett, R. Watts, & D. Birman (Eds.), *Human diversity* (pp. 285–311). San Francisco: Jossey-Bass.

Holcomb-McCoy, C. (2005). Ethnic identity development in early adolescence: Implications and recommendations for middle school counselors. *Professional School Counseling, 9*(2), 120–127.

LaFromboise, T., Coleman, H. L. K., & Gerton, J. (1993). Psychological impact of biculturalism: Evidence and theory. *Psychological Bulletin, 114*, 395–412.

Markus, H. R., & Kitayama, S. (1991). Culture and the self: Implications for cognition, emotion, and motivation. *Psychological Review, 98*, 224–253.

Miller, D. B. (1999). Racial socialization and racial identity: Can they promote resiliency for African American adolescents? *Adolescence, 34*, 493–501.

Phinney, J. S. (1990). Ethnic identity in adolescents and adults: Review of research. *Psychological Bulletin, 108*, 499–514.

Phinney, J. S. (1992). The Multigroup Ethnic Identity Measure: A new scale for use with adolescents and young adults from diverse groups. *Journal of Adolescent Research, 7*, 156–176.

Ponterotto, J., & Pedersen, P. (1993). *Preventing prejudice: A guide for counselors and educators. Multicultural aspects on counseling series 2.* Newbury Park, CA: Sage.

Rayle, A. D., & Myers, J. E. (2004). Counseling adolescents toward wellness: The roles of ethnic identity, acculturation, and mattering. *Professional School Counseling, 8*, 81–91.

Roberts, R., Phinney, J., Masse, L., Chen, Y., Roberts, C., & Romero, A. (1999). The structure of ethnic identity in young adolescents from diverse ethnocultural groups. *Journal of Early Adolescence, 19*, 301–322.

Rumbaut, R. G. (1994). The crucible within: Ethnic identity, self-esteem, and segmented assimilation among children of immigrants. *International Migration Review, 28*, 748–794.

Sellers, R. M., Chavous, T. M., & Cooke, D. Y. (1998). Racial ideology and racial centrality as predictors of African American college students' academic performance. *Journal of Black Psychology, 24*, 8–27.

Sellers, R. M., Rowley, S. A., Chavous, T. M., Shelton, J. N., & Smith, M. (1997). Multidimensional inventory of Black identity: Preliminary investigation of reliability and construct validity. *Journal of Personality and Social Psychology, 73*, 805–815.

Spencer, M. B., Noll, E., Stoltzfutz, J., & Halpalani, V. (2001). Identity and school adjustment: Revisiting the "acting White" assumption. *Educational Psychologist, 36*, 21–30.

Steele, C. M. (1997) Race and the schooling of Black Americans. In L. A. Peplau & S. E. Taylor (Eds.), *Sociocultural perspectives in social psychology: Current readings* (pp. 359–371). Upper Saddle River, NJ: Prentice-Hall.

Steiner, H., & Feldman, S. S. (1996). General principles and special problems. In H. Steiner & I. D. Yalom (Eds.), *Treating adolescents* (pp. 1–42). San Francisco: Jossey Bass.

Sue, D. W., & Sue, D. (2002). *Counseling the culturally diverse: Theory and practice* (4th ed.). New York: Wiley.

Thernstrom, A., & Thernstrom, S. (2003). *No excuses: Closing the racial learning gap*. New York: Simon & Schuster.

U.S. Bureau of the Census. (2001). *Profiles of general demographic characteristics 2000: 2000 census of population and housing: United States*. Washington, DC: U.S. Census Bureau.

Wardle, F. (1992). Supporting biracial children in the school setting. *Education and Treatment of Children, 15*(2), 163–172.

Wilson, M. N., Cooke, D. Y., & Arrington, E. G. (1997). African American adolescents and academic achievement: Family and peer influences. In R. D. Taylor & M. C. Wang (Eds.), *Social and emotional adjustment and family relations in ethnic minority families* (pp. 145–155). Mahwah, NJ: Lawrence Erlbaum Associates.

Yang, A., Coleman, H. L. K., Cho Kim, S. (2003). Hmong adolescent cultural identity and academic achievement. Unpublished manuscript.

Yasui, M., Dorham, C. L., & Dishion, T. J. (2004). Ethnic identity and psychological adjustment: A validity analysis for European American and African American adolescents. *Journal of Adolescence, 19*, 807–825.

Yeh, C. J. (2003). Age, acculturation, cultural adjustment, and mental health symptoms of Chinese, Korean, and Japanese immigrant youths. *Culturally Diverse Ethnic Minority Psychology, 9*(1), 34–48.

Yeh, C. J. (2004). Multicultural and contextual research and practice in school counseling. *Counseling Psychologist, 32*, 278–285.

Yeh, C. J., & Drost, C. (2002). *Bridging identities among ethnic minority youth in schools*. Retrieved August 2, 2006, from http://eric.ed.gov (ERIC Document Reproduction Service No. ED462511).

Yeh, C. J., & Hunter, C. D. (2004). The socialization of self: Understanding shifting and multiple selves across cultures. In R. T. Carter (Ed.), *Handbook on racial-cultural psychology and counseling* (pp. 78–93). Hoboken, NJ: Wiley.

Yeh, C. J., & Hwang, M. Y. (2000). Interdependence in ethnic identity and self: Implications for theory and practice. *Journal of Counseling & Development, 78*(4), 420–429.

Yeh, C. J., & Inose, M. (2002). Difficulties and coping strategies of Chinese, Japanese, and Korean immigrant students. *Adolescence, 37*(145), 69–82.

Yeh, C. J., Ma, P. W., Madan-Bahel, A., Hunter, C. D., Jung, S., Kim, A. B., et al. (2005). The cultural negotiations of Korean immigrant youth. *Journal of Counseling & Development, 83*(2), 172–182.

Zayas, L. H. (2001). Incorporating struggles with racism and ethnic identity in therapy with adolescents. *Clinical Social Work, 29*, 361–373.

X

UNDERSTANDING AND IMPLEMENTING GAY, LESBIAN, BISEXUAL, TRANSGENDER, QUESTIONING AFFIRMATIVE PRACTICES AS SCHOOL COUNSELORS

SHELBY J. SEMINO
Fordham University

Introduction

School counselors have the grave responsibility of creating and maintaining a safe educational community in which diversified groups of children can experience, learn, and develop their social and emotional selves. It is expected that within this academic environment, a culture is created in which our students can reach these developmental milestones without exposure to discrimination or harassment. Unfortunately, for some students, the opportunity to learn in the absence of these harmful conditions fails to present itself, despite the great need. This chapter will focus on the experiences of these students, whose sexual orientation or gender expression is not seen as "the norm," and who are consequently ignored, bullied, or disregarded. Specifically, it is the goal of this chapter to illuminate salient aspects of theory, research, and practice relevant to working with, and promoting acceptance of, sexual minorities within various educational settings.

Before progressing any further, it is important to identify key terms (i.e., sexual orientation, sexual minority, heterosexism, and homophobia) that will be used throughout this chapter. As defined by Sandfort (1997), *sexual orientation* is a multidimensional term that reflects an individual's physical and/or emotional attraction to someone of the same or different gender, one's sexual behavior, and one's identity (i.e., gay, straight, heterosexual, homosexual, bisexual, etc.). For purposes of this chapter, the term *sexual minority* refers to any individual who recognizes within him or sherself an emotional and/or sexual attraction to someone of the same gender (gay, lesbian, bisexual, or questioning [GLBQ]). Additionally, *sexual minority* is inclusive of persons who may be experiencing an incongruity between their external and internal gender identities (transgender [T]). The term *heterosexism* was developed in the early 1990s to encapsulate, at a systemic or institutional level, a constellation of beliefs, statements, and actions that either explicitly or implicitly deny and/or stigmatize any behaviors, feelings, identities, relationships, or communities that are nonheterosexual (Herek, 1990). An example of a heterosexist perspective that often exists in the school environment is the presumption that the parental unit of each of our students consists of a mother and/or a father, without the acknowledgement of a potential same-sex parental unit (i.e., two moms or two dads). Heterosexism is not to be confused with *homophobia*, which is defined as the active fear, ignorance, and hatred toward individuals or communities who identify as having same-sex attractions. A homophobic response to a child with lesbian parents might be, "I cannot believe that Isaac's dikey mothers showed up to the holiday concert. Don't they know that no one should have to be exposed to their queer ways?"

As school counselors who are charged with such great responsibility, we are seen as the "point person" for many members of the academic community. We not only serve the children and adolescents who make up the student body, but we also serve as consultants and educators to the administrative staff, the faculty, and the parents of each child seeking our guidance. Given the nature of this responsibility and the many varied individuals with whom we come into contact, we are expected to be competent enough to assess the needs of the community we serve. This means, that we are first obligated to identify, and subsequently understand, the factors most relevant in the lives of our GLBTQ students and their families. Once these two fundamental tasks are underway, we can begin to implement effective practices that are inclusive, thoughtful, and respectful. And although it is unrealistic for one to be omniscient of the unique needs of this population, it should be expected that all of us remain open to, and curious about, learning as much as we can.

Forming a Sexual Orientation Identity

To best serve this population of interest, it is of primary import that one is aware of the unique individual developmental tasks and family experiences of members of the GLBTQ community. Fisher and Akman (2002), Reynolds and Hanjorgiris (2000), and McCarn and Fassinger (1996) provided comprehensive reviews of the most widely cited and informed sexual identity development models from the past 25 years (e.g., Cass, 1979, 1984; Chapman & Brannock, 1987; Coleman, 1982; Minton & McDonald, 1984; Sophie, 1986; Troiden, 1989). Citing the major limitations of these former models as being unidirectional with a straightforward trajectory, McCarn and Fassinger developed a more fluid and flexible identity development model that is also inclusive of racial/ethnic minorities (Reynolds & Hanjorgiris). While the McCarn and Fassinger initially proposed their model for understanding the course of sexual identity development for nonheterosexual females, they later extrapolated the model for the use with gay men, and it has received good initial empirical validation (Mohr & Fassinger, 2000). McCarn and Fassinger's model stresses the importance of understanding the bidirectional movement that can occur as one begins negotiating the complex process of coming out and forming one's sexual orientation identity. Diamond (2006) supported the notion that individuals may cycle back through the identity development process as they continue to grow psychologically, emotionally, and sexually and begin to encounter different experiences across changing environments. Counselors working with individuals across different age groups must be particularly sensitive to this suggestion and proceed cautiously with their assumptions regarding normative and pathological development.

As evidence of the previously mentioned point, the McCarn and Fassinger (1996) model comprises two parallel contextual planes (*Individual Sexual Identity* and *Group Membership Identity*) and four developmental phases which include (a) awareness, (b) exploration, (c) deepening/commitment, and (d) internalization/synthesis. The authors wanted to develop a model that addressed the different experiences that can occur within these two contextual planes (*Individual* vs. *Group*). For example, a woman may be successful in traversing the internal processes involved in integrating lesbian feelings and desires, but because of oppressive environmental conditions, she may not be able to fully integrate a lesbian group membership identity (McCarn & Fassinger). An important component of one's ability to move through these phases, at two different levels, is the individual's attitudes. Thus, this model incorporated a concept often built into popular ethnic/racial identity models that acknowledge an individual's "attitudes towards self, other lesbians/gays, and non-gays" (McCarn & Fassinger, p. 522).

Movement through the four phases, on the two parallel planes can be considered "reciprocally catalytic but not [necessarily] simultaneous" (McCarn & Fassinger, 1996, p. 521). These phases take into consideration the fluidity and flexibility often required in the ongoing negotiation process of developing self and group identity memberships within two worlds (*Individual* vs. *Group*; McCarn & Fassinger). While McCarn and Fassinger suggested that the more one accepts/integrates ones same-sex attractions and labels ones sexual orientation identity, the less one will experience psychic conflict and distress, Diamond (2006) posited that labeling oneself is not entirely necessary for developing a healthy sense of self.

From a practical perspective, we should be sensitive to the importance and value the student places on constructing a labeled identity for him- or herself. We should not assume that because the student does not label him- or herself gay, lesbian, or bisexual, he or she is living in denial of who he or she is or how he or she feels. Rather, we should accept the student where he or she is developmentally and explore with the student the meaning he or she attributes to his or her same-sex or both-sex attraction. When working with a student who is evidently moving through these developmental phases at both a personal and group level, it is important to maintain a theoretical understanding of the developmental process but not necessarily label these phases for the student. What is important, however, is being able to validate and normalize the student's feelings, which may include confusion, anger, sadness, joy, excitement, and curiosity. It is important that we provide the student with GLB resources that address his or her individual experiences and talk with the student about ways in which he or she can explore GLB support groups or community activities. As school counselors, we want to be able to show these students that positive GLBT role models and community organizations do exist and are available for them to access, whenever they feel ready to do so.

Talking with students about concerns pertaining to their sexual identity development can be very challenging for counselors and educators who have very little experience working with GLBTQ issues. As with any other form of counseling, it is important to meet the student where he or she is and not to pressure him or her to discuss anything he or she may not feel comfortable discussing. It is important, however, not to confuse your discomfort with what the student is feeling. The following brief excerpt is from a session between a school counselor and a 9th grade male student who sought guidance because he was being teased by students for acting "too girly."

School Counselor: Hey John, thanks for coming to visit me today. What's up? What's been going on?
John: Nothin. It's just that school is so crappy right now.
SC: Oh yeah? What is making school feel so crappy right now?
John: I dunno. It's . . . the kids. They're always runnin' their mouths, saying stuff to me behind my back, and saying that I'm a fag.
SC: Wow, that must not feel good, knowing that there are kids saying stuff about you.
John: I know. It isn't a good thing. And I don't even know what to say back to them. I mean, I don't know why I act the way I do, it just happens. I know I like more girly things but it still doesn't give them the right to say stuff. And my teacher totally lets it go on.
SC: Huh. . . . So it sounds like there are a couple of upsetting things happening right now. First, the other kids are saying stuff to you that you don't like. And, second, the teacher hears what is going on, and he's not stopping it. That doesn't really sound like it is too comfortable to be in class. It must be hard to listen and pay attention to the lecture.
John: Totally. I mean, am I wrong for how I am acting? I just was never into like football and being rude to the other girls in the class, saying nasty things to them, like the other boys do.
SC: Listen John, the first thing I want you to know is that there isn't anything wrong with the way you act. You are you, in whatever way, shape, or form that may appear. I am glad that you treat your peers with respect, and am disappointed that the other kids don't seem to be doing the same.
John: It's like, even if I were gay, I would so not tell anyone here at this school. People can be so close-minded.
SC: That's true John, there are a lot of close-minded people in this world, which is a really unfortunate thing. But coming to terms with your sexuality can be really confusing, and you may need to talk to someone eventually about that kind of stuff, ya know? So, do you feel like, if sexuality was something you felt confused about, or needed to talk with someone about, you had at least one person to do that with?
John: Um . . . no, not really. I mean I have friends from summer camp I could talk about it with, and I have a little bit, but no, no one here at school.
SC: Ok. Well, I want to let you know that you can come here and talk with me about this stuff whenever you want. OK? Although you may feel nervous or scared to come here and chat about it, this office is a totally safe space and we can talk about whatever and no other student or teacher needs to know. Alright? I know it must have taken a lot of guts to come visit me today and let me know what's going on, so I appreciate that a lot.
John: Thanks.
SC: And because it is a really important issue, I wanted to know if I had your permission to speak with the faculty about their responsibility to clamp down on all the name-calling stuff that seems to be happening in the classrooms. You should know that you are not the first student to bring it to my attention, and I really want to make sure that the staff knows, this kind of language is so not okay here at school.
John: Well, as long as you don't say my name, I'm cool with it. And I'm really not the only kid who has said this to you?
SC: Nope. John, you aren't alone here. My door is always open to you. Okay?
John: Kay. Thanks. Can you write me a pass so I don't get detention?
SC: No problem.

Researching the Educational Environment

Having a greater sense of the developmental process that many GLBTQ individuals endure while forming their sexual identities, one is able to begin to think about the potential factors that could either thwart this developmental course or contribute to the construction of a healthy identity. In recent years, research has focused primarily on the sexual identity developmental tasks faced by those in their middle to late adolescent years, as well as adults. Very little, if any, has focused on early childhood development as it relates to sexual orientation issues. The research, which has not focused on clarifying the developmental tasks and processes of sexual minority youth, has given more attention to examining the environments in which these students learn and the effects of these educational climates on variables such as self-esteem, mental health, and substance use.

As one might imagine, limited empirical data and literature are available, despite the great need for this knowledge. One of the greatest barriers to obtaining data specific to this population in the educational context is the individual's fear of being "found out," as many GLBTQ students feel the need to hide their orientations and fit in with the general population so they do not become victims of harassment (Hunter & Mallon, 2000). Another limitation of doing research with this population is the researcher's struggle to obtain a diverse sample of research participants (Croom, 2000). Because GLBTQ persons are not easily identifiable physically, researchers must rely on individuals who are willing to identify themselves as GLBTQ persons. This results in a skewed representation of GLBTQ persons comfortable with having and expressing their sexual minority statuses. Naturally, it behooves the field to develop more secure and confidential means of obtaining such sensitive information, so that the field can continue to make progress in understanding, more deeply, the needs of different GLBTQ persons.

One avenue of research that has presented itself over the past several years, and one which can continue to grow and proliferate worthwhile information, is the examination of the attitudes that school counselors, administrators, faculty, and general student bodies possess with respect to GLBTQ persons. Because students spend much of their days in the presence of other students and in the care of school professionals, school counselors must begin to take inventory of how their academic communities fare with respect to homophobia, heterosexism, and genderphobia. Institutionalized homophobia is a very real concern in many school systems, but can often be overlooked, and consequently perpetuate the message that it is okay to ignore GLBTQ issues (Fontaine, 1998). The following is a summary of a national research effort spearheaded by the Gay, Lesbian and Straight Education Network (GLSEN) that examined current school cultures across the United States.

GLSEN is one of the most comprehensive resources that all school counselors across the United States should consult. This organization provides invaluable information to administrators, educators, counselors, students, and the public about current and historical research and action-oriented efforts that have helped create safe educational environments for sexual minorities. In 2006, GLSEN reported findings from their 2005 National School Climate Survey, which assessed the experiences of over 1,700 gay, lesbian, bisexual, and transgender youth between the ages of 13 and 20 years old. This seminal study sheds light on some of the hostile and unwelcoming environments in which many of our children obtain their education and develop their self-esteem and identities. Results from this national survey found that over 75% of students had heard homophobic or antigender expression language spoken during the school day (GLSEN). Of these students, it was reported that 89.2% of them heard such comments on an often/frequent basis (GLSEN). Even more disturbing, however, is the percentage of students (18.6%) who reported hearing homophobic remarks and comments being made by teachers or other school staff (GLSEN, 2006). Some homophobic or transphobic comments often heard in the hallways and classrooms of schools are the following: "fag," "no homo," "dyke," "lezzie," "queer," "that's so gay," "homo," "fairy," "butch," and so forth.

Apart from the experience of hearing homophobic or antigender expression language, 64.3% of students reported feeling unsafe in their schools because of their sexual orientation, while 40.7% reported feeling unsafe due to the expression of their gender (GLSEN). Furthermore, 37.8% of students had faced physical harassment due to their sexual orientation, while 26.1% of students endured the same harassment due to the way in which they expressed their gender identity (GLSEN). These findings suggest that the school environment, while intended to be a place for learning, discovery, and achievement can, in reality, be a place of torment for this population. This is of even more concern given that many students already face rejection from their families and are highly vulnerable to low self-esteem and negative mental health symptoms (D'Augelli, 2006).

Another important area of research that must continue to grow is the exploration of the relationship between students' exposure to harassment and the impact it has on their well-beings and developing senses of self, identity, and connection within the community. The effects of experiencing harassment at school are just as worrisome as the actual occurrence of it. Fisher and Akman (2002) asserted that sexual minority youth who are harassed due to their assumed sexual orientation are at greater risk for being threatened and/or assaulted, are more likely to fear for their own safety, may avoid school altogether, and may be at greater risk for engaging in self-harming behaviors such as abusing substances and contemplating suicide. It is obvious that these negative consequences of pervasive school ignorance and incidents of harassment do not contribute to feelings of support and emotional containment. And although incidents of harassment or anti-GLBTQ assaults may not be as prominent in your academic community, it is important to consider what, if any, subtle messages of homophobia, heterosexism, or gender-phobia are being generated by administrative staff and faculty.

An example of heterosexist language that is often observed in early education classes is the persistent assertion of a mother and father dyad in a child's family. Also, many of the early stories we read or tell to our younger students are about families with a mother and a father as the parents. Further along in the educational system, teachers and counselors begin to speak with students about marriage, having children, and so forth, processes that for most GLBTQ persons are either illegal or very difficult to navigate due to systemic and institutional biases and prejudices. As educators, we must continue to be mindful of the language we choose to use in addressing our students (i.e., instead of saying, "when you get married," consider saying, "when you find a partner with whom you want to settle down"). Small modifications to the statements we make today can leave an indelible mark on our students of the future.

Putting Awareness and Knowledge Into Action

Thus far, this chapter has identified the processes by which individuals begin to identify and form their sexual orientation identities, it has acknowledged the reality of how hostile and unwelcoming academic environments can be, and it has provided insight into the negative impact that such toxicity can have on students' emerging self-esteem and mental health. Hence, there should be no question as to why school counselors must bear the responsibility of guiding and directing administrative staff, faculty, students, and their families. School counselors are expected to consult with these parties to help them create educational communities that accept all students, regardless of sexual orientation or gender expression and to sustain climates that do not tolerate hate, hostility, or ignorance. However, although the reasons may be clear as to why we must take on this responsibility, we may not know how to put our knowledge into action. This section will provide insight into affirmative practices that can help guide our efforts.

As cited in the *American School Counselor Association Ethical Standards for School Counselors* (American School Counselor Association [ASCA], 2004), section "E.2. Diversity," a professional school counselor is not only expected to affirm diversity in the school community, but he or she is also expected to increase awareness of one's own cultural attitudes and biases toward culturally different individuals and to obtain training and greater knowledge in areas that are deficient with respect to multicultural competence. This indicates that if an individual has very little understanding, awareness, or experience in working with GLBTQ students and families, he or she is expected to obtain adequate knowledge and insight through supervision, consultation, and various training opportunities. We must be able to assess our biases, judgments, strengths, and limitations of competence when it comes to working with this particular population and be willing to challenge others and ourselves so that we may continue to move forward in our efforts.

As evidenced in one school's report about promotion of an affirmative GLBTQ school environment, commitment level is one of the most important and primary factors to be assessed (Bauman & Sachs-Kapp, 1998). Beyond the commitment needed from the administration and the staff, Bauman and Sachs-Kapp acknowledged the importance of enlisting student leaders to help generate greater commitment among the student body. The goal here is to help create a network of peer support and peer-influenced affirmation of the GLBTQ population. Once a greater commitment level is experienced at administrative, staff, and student levels, school counselors can begin to have more in-depth dialogues with each level and determine what efforts are needed to promote greater acceptance. An exemplary model of a high school demonstrating a strong commitment level may include the following in their academic communities: (a) a GLBTQ and Straight Alliance Group, (b) awareness and promotion of National Coming Out Day, (c) implementation of a Zero Tolerance Week against homophobia and heterosexism, and (d) GLBTQ History Month (showcasing the contributions of major political figures of this community).

McFarland and Dupois (2001) provided a comprehensive overview of the strategies used in various school systems across the United States to create a safe school environment for their GLBTQ students. McFarland and Dupois specifically highlighted the work of the Massachusetts Governor's Commission on Gay and Lesbian Youth (1993) that has been successful in providing and implementing a useful framework for educators to follow. The Governor's Commission report, as cited by McFarland and Dupois, suggested implementing change in the following five areas: (a) establishing clear school policies regarding harassment, (b) training all school staff and administration about appropriate ways to prevent and intervene in harassment and violence against GLBTQ students, (c) developing active school-based GLBTQ–Straight Support Groups and Alliances, (d) providing relevant and useful resources about the GLBTQ community in visible areas and in libraries, and (e) infusing GLBTQ-related information and subject materials into schools' curricula. Serving as a consultant to educators and administrators across different academic levels, we can help schools implement these suggestions in earnest and applicable ways. With attention given to the developmental and educational abilities of varying grade levels, support from the administration, and creativity, these strategies can prove to be incredibly useful.

An intervention suggested by Nichols (1999) is the creation of a Diversity Room located in a very visible and easily accessible space in any school (elementary, middle, or high school). Depending on the grade level, the content shared will need to be modified, but the mission of the Diversity Room should be consistent and universal—providing a safe space for all students with zero tolerance for violence and harassment. Nichols further suggested that each Diversity Room be run by a Diversity Room Specialist (DRS), a professional who is multiculturally competent, who consults with the school counselor, and whose primary responsibility is to appropriately work with students and educate staff about diversity issues related to the GLBTQ community. To assist in such an effort, Kimmel (2000) provided a very clear outline of important topics specific to the developmental years of infancy, early childhood, middle childhood, early adolescence, and adulthood.

An example of how to work with students at the middle or high school level could be that the DRS serves as a consultant to the school's Social Studies/History Department and suggests the exploration of significant moments in the history of the GLBTQ community (e.g., Stonewall; AIDS epidemic; Marriage Equality Rights, etc.). Another example could be that DRS works with the English/Language Arts Department and helps teachers incorporate writings from several prominent GLBTQ authors into the curriculum. At the elementary school level, the DRS could organize a unit on teaching tolerance about diverse family systems, which includes children of same-sex parents, or a unit on accepting gender nonconforming play and dress.

Along the same lines, the school counselor could develop a monthly program, in cooperation with the Health Education Department (at both middle and high school levels), that helps to educate parents and students, individually and collectively, about important mental health concerns, safer sex practices, dangers of drug and alcohol use, and so forth. These monthly meetings could also be used as a forum in which GLBTQ alumni return to their schools and serve as positive role models. Alumni could meet with students, parents, teachers, and administrators to discuss their experiences in middle and high school and to inform them of the ways in which they have successfully navigated their college and professional careers.

Once these systemic interventions are implemented and are proving to be effective at the institutional level, school counselors must continue to think about how best to meet the individual student and his or her needs. Aside from the need to receive weekly individual supportive counseling, many GLBTQ students report feeling alone and isolated, wanting to develop a network of peers who are negotiating similar struggles (Savin-Williams, 1994). To reduce this sense of loneliness, it has been suggested that group counseling be implemented and effectively carried out (Muller & Hartman, 1998). Muller and Hartman provided several relevant topics that could be useful to process at the group level, which include homophobia in the school, feelings of loneliness and isolation, identity issues, alienation from family, suicidal ideation, drug and alcohol use, and perceptions of self and others' perceptions of self. Specifically, in a group session that is focusing on homophobia in the school, students can be encouraged not only to process their feelings related to this abuse, but also to use the support of each other to strategize ways in which they can effectively handle such situations so that they can protect themselves and not compromise their self-esteem and dignity. Furthermore, counselors can help students develop effective ways to inform teachers, staff, and administration when these incidents are occurring. Another specific example of how counselors can utilize group counseling is helping students focus on exploring and coping with feelings of loneliness and isolation because of their minority statuses. Trusted counselors can encourage students to not only to process their emotional experiences, but also to develop strategies that can help reduce the students' urge to self-medicate through the use of alcohol, drugs, overeating, or other self-harming behaviors. Such discussions, which occur in a safe and trusting space, can help serve as a buffer against negative emotional and psychological outcomes. Due to the often intense nature of this kind of support/process group, it will be of vital importance that the professionals coleading the group obtain excellent supervision.

An additional component to providing direct counseling services to our GLBTQ students is carving out a safe space in which collateral or family work can be conducted. While not all GLBTQ students may be out to their parents or families, some definitely are. As the literature indicates, parents often have difficulty in accepting their children's identifications as GLBTQ persons and may react negatively to this news (Fisher & Akman, 2002). What is hopeful, however, is the notion that parental support, when it is bestowed upon children, can have very positive effects on children's mental health (Hershberger & D'Augelli, 1995). Thus, the goal in working with families is to help parents explore their concerns, fears, and other negative feelings, while working toward a level of acceptance and support that is beneficial to children.

A key component to conducting successful family counseling is developing a working alliance with parents. Despite one's personal feelings toward a parent who is unsupportive of his or her GLBTQ child, it is important to find the strengths that the parent endorses and to capitalize on these positive attributes. Without the commitment on the part of the parents, family work cannot successfully meet the necessary goals, and you put the children at greater risk. Once you are able to get the parent "hooked in," you can begin to work on providing important psycho-education about the coming-out process, the GLBTQ community, related mental health issues, and so forth. It will be important to dispel myths that parents may believe and to answer any questions (no matter how ignorant) they may have. Oftentimes, parents wonder "where they went wrong" in their parenting, or they want to place blame on early childhood experiences that students may have endured. It is critical that you normalize their children's identities so that parents do not pathologize their parenting skills or their children's behaviors and feelings. Parents may express feelings of anger, sadness, confusion, disappointment, and fear regarding their children's identities. Just as with any other controversial topic, it is necessary that you appropriately draw boundaries and set limits with respect to the language that can be used in a child's presence. Providing parents with helpful resources and outlets to explore and discuss their feelings about their children's sexual orientation or gender identities is of absolute importance. One very comprehensive source of support for helping parents navigate this difficult process is PFLAG (Parents, Families and Friends of Lesbians and Gays), an organization whose presence is well represented and accessible across the United States.

The practical suggestions just discussed are to be seen as helpful resources that we can begin to implement as we focus on creating an affirmative GLBTQ environment. These suggestions are by no means exhaustive, but they do provide a sampling of ways in which we can be effective in our roles as schools' point persons for handling the diverse needs and crises of our students and their families. The following case study can be used to generate a discussion about case conceptualization and practice–planning strategies. With the theory, research, and practical applications just discussed, you are encouraged to challenge yourself in anticipation of working with a student such as Mariana.

The Case of Mariana

Mariana is a 17-year-old, Mexican-American female who is currently enrolled in 11th grade at a public high school in New York City. She is a particularly bright young woman who has historically excelled academically and who is well liked by her peers. Mariana immigrated to this country with her mother, father, and two younger brothers 7 years ago. Mariana's family has struggled financially throughout the years, especially during their immigration to this country. Because of these struggles, Mariana has developed a close relationship with both of her parents. Her father, who adores "Marianita" is a contractor and carpenter and has been able to successfully build a small business that he hopes to leave to his son when he retires. Mariana's mother, a religious woman, attended university in Mexico and was a practicing schoolteacher until she gave birth to Mariana 17 years ago. Since then, she has dedicated herself to raising her family and supporting her husband. Both of Mariana's parents are supportive of her desire to attend college, but they also have many expectations about her getting married and having three children, just as they had done. While Mariana is career-focused, she feels a lot of pressure to make her parents proud and fulfill the dreams they have for her. She feels that because they worked so hard to move the family to the United States, she owes this to them. Recently, Mariana's older female cousin and Mariana's mother began planning Rosa's wedding. Since this planning began, Mariana's mother has been pressuring Mariana to spend "some time" with a young male family friend visiting from Mexico. Mariana is aware that her mother wants her to spend time with Julio because she never "hangs out with boys," but Mariana wants to stay focused on her academics. Furthermore, Mariana finds Julio to be "annoying and childish" and finds him not sophisticated enough for her interests. Simultaneously, Mariana has become preoccupied with having an emotional and sexual attraction to one of her closest female friends. Despite this attraction, Mariana has not labeled herself as lesbian or bisexual, and she thinks that this is just a "weird thing" she is going through. She knows that lesbians do exist in the world, but she is unaware of any Chicana in her world liking another Chicana. Therefore, she thinks "that kind of thing" just happens with "White chicks with weird hairdos and piercings."

Recently, Mariana was referred to you for counseling because of a sudden drop in her grades and teachers' observations of increased sleepiness in class and a withdrawn attitude. Teachers report that this change in behavior was quite noticeable because of Mariana's past academic involvement and leadership in the classroom. Mariana has informed teachers that she is "fine, just tired, and stressed," but she has not been able to expound upon this with any of her teachers.

Points/Questions to Consider in the Case of Mariana

1. As her school counselor it will be important for you to align yourself with Mariana in a nonthreatening, nonjudgmental manner.
2. It is important to assess your assumptions about Mariana being a Mexican-American female who has a history of attraction to a close female friend.
3. Assess your own level of comfort being a male or female, heterosexual or nonheterosexual, or ethnically similar or different counselor working with a Hispanic female who is struggling with her sexual orientation.
4. Are there questions you have that you need clarification on from your supervisor? Do you feel like you have the appropriate resources to consult in order to best work with this student?
5. Once a rapport is established, it will be important to explore how Mariana understands the changes in her grade point average, class participation, and sleep patterns.
6. If Mariana discloses to you her same-sex attraction and her confusion regarding this attraction and her Hispanic identity, are you prepared to direct her to resources that embrace both a Hispanic and a GLBTQ identity?

7. Are you aware of any support groups in the school setting that you could involve Mariana in so that she may begin to meet peers who are negotiating a similar identity process?
8. Explore with Mariana any potential conflicts she may be experiencing related to her need to satisfy her parents' dreams for her and her own desires for her future.
9. How might you be able to work with the family if Mariana does end up identifying herself as a member of the GLBTQ community?
10. How might you be able to work with the family if Mariana accepts her same-sex attraction but does not want to disclose this to her parents?
11. How can you work with Mariana to effectively cope with the underlying anxiety and conflict she is experiencing so that she may continue to excel at school and once again become an active member of her classroom discussions?
12. Are you aware of what it means culturally to be a Hispanic female from a Mexican family with same-sex attractions?
13. If Mariana were to begin to be more open about her sexuality and began to experience forms of harassment or taunting, how might you work with the school system to intervene effectively? How might you work with the school system to prevent the development of a culture in which harassment is acceptable?

It is important to begin to consider these previously mentioned questions and to think in a multidimensional manner about how to best address the complicated and competing factors Mariana is facing. As school counselors, our abilities to work creatively, comprehensively, and thoughtfully will be challenged each day, and it is important that we be as prepared as we can be. Exercises such as this can help us do just that.

Recommendations for Future Research

As issues pertaining to sexual orientation and the GLBTQ community become increasingly prominent in entertainment, media, and public/political debates, it is important that we, as members of the field of psychology, provide accurate and useful information that can help create a general atmosphere of acceptance and understanding. As school counselors, we have an obligation to all of our students to become more actively involved in the research that is currently under way. While we continue to explore the developmental processes of GLBTQ youth and the effects of harassment on students' mental health and self-esteem, we must extend this research to be more inclusive of racial and ethnic minorities. These groups are often underrepresented in the literature regarding GLBTQ youth, but their experiences are just as critical to understand. We need to extend research to include younger developmental age groups so that we may fully understand when and how the process of sexual orientation/gender identity formation begins. As we implement practical strategies to help guide others, we must assess the efficacy of our efforts. It will be important to keep an open dialogue about what attempts appear to be facilitating optimal development, and what seems to be failing. Additionally, we need to develop more creative ways of reaching out to and assessing youth who may be apprehensive about sharing their experiences and otherwise remain outside of our purview.

Recommendations for Practice

As school counselors move forward in their work toward developing, maintaining, and sustaining GLBTQ affirmative practices in the school environment, it is essential that we convey the importance of these efforts to our school administrators, faculty, students, and their families. We can lead this effort by setting expectations of ourselves that require us to continuously look inward, assess our own biases and prejudices, and address our limitations head-on. We must enlist the help of our colleagues and our counselors-in-training to set a standard of practice that not just tolerates, but accepts and affirms our GLBTQ clients. As school counselors, we must actively consume the literature that continues to emerge and effectively transform what we read into practice. These efforts are not just limited to our counseling practices, but are far-reaching and include program development, advocacy, and community service. We must take the information disseminated from organizations such as GLSEN, PFLAG, the Human Rights Campaign, and the Safe Schools Coalition and clearly present it to those we serve and those with whom we work. It is no longer acceptable to simply react to the harassment and assaults that our students face on a daily basis. It is time now to advocate for these students' rights, to affirm their existence, and to inform even the most ignorant of offenders.

References

American School Counselor Association. (2004). *Ethical standards for school counselors: Revised.* Retrieved October 8, 2006, from http:www.schoolcounselor.org

Bauman, S., & Sachs-Kapp, P. (1998). A school takes a stand: Promotion of sexual orientation workshops by counselors. *Professional School Counseling, 1,* 42–45.

Cass, V. C. (1979). Homosexual identity formation: A theoretical model. *Journal of Homosexuality, 4,* 219–235.

Cass, V. C. (1984). Homosexual identity: A concept in need of definition. *Journal of Sex Research, 20,* 143–167.

Chapman, B. E., & Brannock, J. C. (1987). A proposed model of lesbian identity development: An empirical investigation. *Journal of Homosexuality, 14,* 69–80.

Coleman, E. (1982). Developmental stages of the coming out process. *Journal of Homosexuality, 8,* 31–43.

Croom, G. L. (2000). Lesbian, gay, and bisexual people of color: A challenge to representative sampling in empirical research. In B. Greene & G. L. Croom (Eds.), *Education, research, and practice in lesbian, gay, bisexual, and transgendered psychology* (pp. 263–281). Thousand Oaks, CA: Sage Publications.

Cross, W. E. (1971). The Negro-to-Black conversion experience. *Black World, 20,* 13–27.

D'Augelli, A. R. (2006). Developmental and contextual factors and mental health among lesbian, gay, and bisexual youths. In A. M. Omoto & H. S. Kurtzman (Eds.), *Sexual orientation and mental health: Examining identity and development in lesbian, gay, and bisexual people* (pp. 37–54). Washington, DC: American Psychological Association.

Diamond, L. M. (2006). What we got wrong about sexual identity development: Unexpected findings from a longitudinal study of young women. In A. M. Omoto & H. S. Kurtzman (Eds.), *Sexual orientation and mental health: Examining identity and development in lesbian, gay, and bisexual people* (pp. 73–94). Washington, DC: American Psychological Association.

Fisher, B., & Akman, J. S. (2002). Normal development in sexual minority youth. In B. E. Jones & M. J. Hill (Eds.), *Mental health issues in lesbian, gay, bisexual, and transgender communities* (pp. 1–16). Arlington, VA: American Psychiatric Press.

Fontaine, J. H. (1998). Evidencing a need: School counselors' experiences with gay and lesbian students. *Professional School Counseling, 1,* 8–14.

Gay, Lesbian, & Straight Educational Network. (2006). *GLSEN's 2005 National school climate survey sheds new light on experiences of lesbian, gay, bisexual and transgender (LGBT) students.* Retrieved on October 7, 2006, from http:www.glsen.org

Herek, G. M. (1990). The context of anti-gay violence: Notes on cultural and psychological heterosexism. *Journal of Interpersonal Violence, 5,* 316–333.

Hershberger, S. L., & D'Augelli, A. R. (1995). The impact of victimization on the mental health and suicidality of lesbian, gay, and bisexual youths. *Developmental Psychology, 31,* 65–74.

Hunter, J., & Mallon, G. P. (2000). Lesbian, gay, and bisexual adolescent development: Dancing with your feet tied together. In B. Greene & G. L. Croom (Eds.), *Education, research, and practice in lesbian, gay, bisexual, and transgendered psychology* (pp. 226–243). Thousand Oaks, CA: Sage Publications.

Kimmel, D. C. (2000). Including sexual orientation in life span developmental psychology. In B. Greene & G. L. Croom (Eds.), *Education, research, and practice in lesbian, gay, bisexual, and transgendered psychology* (pp. 59–73). Thousand Oaks, CA: Sage Publications.

Massachusetts Governor's Commission on Gay and Lesbian Youth. (1993). *Making schools safe for gay and lesbian youth: Breaking the silence in schools and in families.* Boston: Author.

McCarn, S. R., & Fassinger, R. E. (1996). Revisioning sexual minority identity formation: A new model of lesbian identity and its implications for counseling and research. *The Counseling Psychologist, 32,* 629–637.

McFarland, W. P., & Dupois, M. (2001). The legal duty to protect gay and lesbian students from violence in school. *Professional School Counseling, 4,* 171–179.

Minton, H. L., & McDonald, G. J. (1984). Homosexual identity formation as a developmental process. *Journal of Homosexuality, 9,* 91–104.

Mohr, J., & Fassinger, R. (2000). Measuring dimensions of lesbian and gay male experience. *Measurement and Evaluation in Counseling and Development, 33,* 66–90.

Muller, L. E., & Hartman, J. (1998). Group counseling for sexual minority youth. *Professional School Counseling, 1,* 38–41.

Nichols, S. L. (1999). Gay, lesbian, and bisexual youth: Understanding diversity and promoting tolerance in schools. *The Elementary School Journal, 99,* 505–519.

Reynolds, A. L., & Hanjorgiris, W. F. (2000). Coming out: Lesbian, gay and bisexual identity development. In R. M. Perez, K. A. DeBord, & K. J. Bieschke (Eds.), *Handbook of counseling and psychotherapy with lesbian, gay and bisexual clients* (pp. 35–55). Washington, DC: American Psychological Association.

Sandfort, T. G. M. (1997). Sampling male homosexuality. In J. Bancroft (Ed.), *Researching sexual behavior: Methodological issues* (pp. 261–275). Bloomington: Indiana University Press.

Savin-Williams, R. C. (1994). Verbal and physical abuse as stressors in the lives of lesbian, gay male, and bisexual youths: Associations with school problems, running away, substance abuse, prostitution, and suicide. *Journal of Consulting and Clinical Psychology, 62,* 261–269.

Savin-Williams, R. C., & Cohen, K. M. (1996). *The lives of lesbians, gays, and bisexuals.* Orlando, FL: Harcourt Brace College Publishers.

Sophie, J. (1986). A critical examination of stage theories of lesbian identity development. *Journal of Homosexuality, 12,* 39–51.

Troiden, R. R. (1989). The formation of homosexual identities. *Journal of Homosexuality, 17,* 43–73.

# XI
SOCIAL CLASS IN SCHOOL COUNSELING

WILLIAM MING LIU, ALICE FRIDMAN
AND THOMASIN E. TRANEL HALL
University of Iowa

School counselors understand the importance of comprehending and integrating context into their work (e.g., Bronfenbrenner, 1986). School counselors working in various situations from kindergarten to 12th grade understand that social, political, and historical contingencies have leverage in their practice. In this chapter, context refers to social constructions of race, gender, and social class, and the sociopolitical (e.g., the unequal distribution of power), sociohistorical (e.g., biased and inaccurate histories of peoples), and sociostructural (e.g., legal, educational, and economic systems) forces that perpetuate inequality and marginalization (Liu & Ali, 2005). Of all the different contexts, social class is one of the least understood in counseling and psychology. Therefore, the focus of this chapter will be on understanding and integrating social class perspectives into school counseling. Specifically, the chapter will address social class issues related to children and adolescents from low-income, poor, and impoverished environments, as well as those from the middle and upper classes. In the research review, keep in mind that many lower-class K–12 students are typically African American or Latino American; as a result, race and social class are often confounded in the extant research. Although this makes it difficult to tease apart the precise effects of the two variables, this is a bigger problem for research than for practice. Ethnicity and social class are fundamental personal characteristics that necessarily interact in affecting any individual with whom a practitioner works; therefore, it is unnecessary, and possibly even harmful, for practitioners to treat ethnicity and social class as separate entities. Because this chapter is concerned mainly with the role of social class in the practice of school counseling rather than in research, it will not attempt to untangle the effects of race and social class, but instead will examine their interaction in affecting the children with whom school counselors work.

Much has been written about social class, children, and schools. This chapter synthesizes some of the literature and provides a subjective approach to integrating social class into school counseling. The authors use the term *social class* rather than *socioeconomic status* (SES) for two reasons. First, the terms *social class* and *SES* have no real theoretical difference (Liberatos, Link, & Kelsey, 1988; Oakes & Rossi, 2003), and therefore, one term does not convey any more significance than the other does. We select the term *social class* because of the connotation that people operate from a worldview that tends to distinguish different groups (i.e., social classes such as middle class and lower class). Second, social class is more easily tied to classism if one believes that people operate from different social class groupings (Liu, 2001; Liu, Ali, Soleck, Hopps, Dunston, & Prickett, 2004; Liu, Soleck, Hopps, Dunston, & Pickett, 2004). Finally, the term *social class* is more compatible with a subjective/phenomenological approach to social class issues. This approach argues that individuals' subjective perceptions of their social standing are more important than objective indices of social class, such as income and education, in determining people's experiences of social class and the resulting psychological outcomes.

In this chapter, the authors will first discuss why social class should be used to inform school counseling practice. Specifically, the authors will discuss how social class has been used in the counseling research and practice literature. Second, the authors will address the current limitations to understanding social class in school counseling. Third, the authors will focus on two aspects of school counseling practice: developmental guidance and vocational guidance. The authors will critique the current theory and practice and provide examples of informing both aspects of school counseling through social class. Finally, the authors will present some practice implications and advocate the use of a subjective/phenomenological approach to social class.

Social Class and Counseling

Social class is difficult not only to operationalize, but also to integrate into clinical practice (Frable, 1997; Liu, Ali, et al., 2004; Liu, Soleck, et al., 2004). What do counselors imply when they describe a parent or student coming from a "working-class" or a "middle-class" background? Although we intuitively believe that people have a common agreed understanding of "working class" or "middle class," the research does not support this conclusion (M. T. Brown, Fukunaga, Umemoto, & Wicker, 1996). Certain characteristics do exist that people often use to make informal distinctions among different social classes. The most basic include amount of income, type of occupation, level of education, and location of residence; other, less concrete characteristics include manners of speech and dress, leisure activities, spending behavior, cars, jewelry, and other visible possessions. Although it is important for school counselors and researchers to be aware of these informal indicators of social class, we caution against relying on this information to make inferences about students' social class standings. Such an approach could lead to making incorrect assumptions that could anger or alienate the students with whom counselors work. Instead, school counselors should focus on students' subjective views and experiences in assessing the impact of social class in their lives, as suggested in the subjective/phenomenological approach.

Although social class is important, school counseling literature has not addressed it. For example, Holcomb-McCoy (2004) addressed the growing need for multiculturally competent school counselors and has suggested nine overarching areas under which a checklist of 51 competencies fall: the areas comprise (a) multicultural counseling, (b) multicultural consultation, (c) understanding racism and student resistance, (d) multicultural assessment, (e) understanding racial identity development, (f) multicultural family counseling, (g) social advocacy, (h) development of school–family–community partnerships, and (i) understanding cross-cultural interpersonal interactions. The author fails to include social class as a multicultural variable, however, and thus neglects one extremely pertinent form of competence for the multiculturally competent school counselor and ignores the potential impact of the intersection of race, gender, and ethnicity on children's social, emotional, and academic adjustment during their elementary school years.

The research on social class, children, adolescents, and schools suggests that school counselors must understand social class in order to develop appropriate interventions, prevention programs, and sensitive consultation practices. The extant empirical research reveals a number of ways in which social class is linked to developmental outcomes. For instance, the research shows that child and adolescent development is negatively affected by socioeconomic disadvantage (Evans, 2004; McLoyd, 1998), that parenting practices vary by social class (Hoffman, 2003; Lareau, 2003), and that poverty is related to child conduct problems (Dodge, Pettit, & Bates, 1994.) Mothers' low educational level and teenage pregnancy are related to physical aggression among boys (Nagin & Tremblay, 2001). Poverty and low income lead to poor physical health in infants, which is associated with cognitive deficiencies, poor socioemotional adjustment, psychophysiological stress, and developmental delays (Duncan, Brooks-Gunn, & Klebanov, 1994; Evans & English, 2002; Pollitt, 1994). Poverty also negatively impacts the quality of the home environment (Garrett, Ng'andu, & Ferron, 1994) and increases children's exposure to community violence (Ackerman, Brown, & Izard, 2004; Rasmussen, Aber, & Bhana, 2004). Unemployment and work interruptions are related to maternal stress and depression, and consequently, cognitive distress, low self-esteem, and developmental problems among some adolescents (Conger, Ge, Elder, Lorenz, & Simons, 1994; McLoyd, Jayaratne, Ceballo, & Borquez, 1994). Finally, poverty is associated with poor social competence (Garner, Jones, & Miner, 1994) and, along with maternal depression, jeopardizes early child development (Petterson & Albers, 2001).

Social class also has some specific implications for schools and school counselors. For instance, poverty is related to restricted access to resources and poor teacher quality (Lee, 1999). White students are more likely to be of higher social class and apply to college at higher rates than African American or Latino students (Valadez, 1998), and students who are poor are treated unfairly in comparison are middle- and upper-class White children (Bemak, 2005). All these effects of social class, both at school and in the home, demonstrate the importance of social class to children's lives and the necessity of considering this variable in the practice of school counseling.

Day-Vines, Patton, and Baytops (2003) also explored the complex interactions among race, culture, and social class, and the impact of such interactions on African American adolescents. Using a case study of "Tiffany," an upper-middle-class, 10th-grade African American, the authors illustrate the ways in which culturally responsive counseling practices challenge traditional stereotypes and the tendency for counselors and educators to view social class and race as mutually exclusive elements of one's identity. Such a model encourages counselors to investigate the relative contributions of race, class, gender, religion, sexual orientation, and geography to marginalized children's identities and experience of the world. The case example demonstrates one possible interaction between race and class, wherein class serves as a buffer from certain risk factors (e.g., malnutrition, inferior education), but does not lessen the experience of racism and discrimination for the individual. In addition, the example illustrates specific ways in which school counselors can encourage students and families to utilize community resources to promote academic achievement. Day-Vines et al. (2003) caution against making inaccurate generalizations about race and social class that could lead to further misunderstanding and miscommunication among counselors, educators, and students. They also offer important insight into the potential risks of considering only the upper and lower ends of the social class spectrum, and they highlight concrete methods by which class can enter into multicultural dialogues.

The association between social class and physical, emotional, and mental health has become the focus of research attention among middle- and upper-class individuals, who, until only recently, were considered relatively impervious to the risks experienced by their lower class counterparts (Luthar & Latendresse, 2005a, 2005b). Luthar and Latendresse addressed the importance of considering the entire continuum of social class in both counseling and research, and they described the problems associated with affluence. Adjustment difficulties, for example, are seen among suburban youth who face unique barriers to well-being, such as isolation from adults and increased pressure to achieve. Children of affluent parents often experience anxiety and depression as a result of failing to meet parental expectations, and they report distress associated with parent–child interactions. In addition, elevated rates of substance abuse are also seen among children and adolescents of popular standing among their peers (Luthar & Latendresse, 2005a, 2005b). Researchers have also shown that upper-class adolescents report feeling greater discrepancies between their bodies and the norm, which is, in turn, related to increased symptoms of eating disorders (Sanderson, Darley, & Messinger, 2002). These findings highlight the importance of considering the effects of social class across all individuals.

Limitations to Our Understanding of Social Class

How can we know so little about social class if there is so much research on social class, children, adolescents, and schools? A brief review of the literature suggests that the difficulty lies in the ways in which social class is used in research. Although the literature critiquing current conceptualizations of social class in counseling is far too extensive for this chapter, some highlights will be presented to help orient the reader.

Generally, much of psychology uses a social class conceptualization based in sociology (Liu, Ali, et al., 2004). While sociology is interested in group-level characteristics and phenomena, psychologists and counselors are interested in the ways an individual thinks, behaves, and conceptualizes the world. Sociologists tend to used income, education, and occupation to classify individuals into various social class groups (e.g., middle-class; e.g., Entwisle & Astone, 1994; Hauser, 1994), and thereby assume that everyone within those specific groupings thinks and behaves similarly. Consequently, within-group variation is not explored fully. In contrast, Liu, Ali, et al. suggested that counselors consider using social class as a descriptor for a psychological framework. For instance, Liu (2001) used social class to describe a particular type of worldview for his Social Class Worldview Model (SCWM). This suggestion would be consonant with the subjective/phenomenological approach and with the way that psychologists view other cultural constructs. For example, counselors study racial identity and acculturation instead of race itself, and they examine gender role identity and conflict rather than gender. By doing so, it is possible to address and validate individuals' subjective experience of race, culture, and social class.

There are also other problems with the way social class is used in counseling. Social class can vary from time to time depending on income, occupation, and other family circumstances and, therefore may not always be a static characteristic (Duncan & Magnuson, 2003). Poverty and low social class are often treated similarly (Huston, McLoyd, & Coll, 1994), race and social class are frequently intertwined (Huston et al.), and the effects of transient and persistent poverty need to be teased apart (Huston et al.). There are also gender differences in educational attainment and occupation between men and women (Bornstein, Hahn, Suwalsky, & Haynes, 2003). As previously addressed, our current understanding of social class is limited to the extant research, which has largely ignored the problems faced by upper- and middle-class individuals. Finally, income is an inconsistent measure of social class due to short-term variations and unreliable reporting (Bronstein et al., 2003).

Another difficulty with using social class in school counseling is that variables such as income, occupation, and educational level are common indices of social class, but the relationship between the three indices is small, and there are no data to suggest how a social class group might be affected by any combination of the indices (M. T. Brown et al., 1996; Liberatos et al., 1988). An additional problem is that these indices are primarily "adult" symbols of social class, which implies that children and adolescents do not have a social class apart from their parents, and by extension, do not experience classism. Research shows, however, that children and adolescents are highly attuned to social class messages, and that they experience and participate in various forms of classism (Carter, 2003; Goldberg, Gorn, Peracchio, & Bamossy, 2003; Goodman et al., 2000; Roberts, Tanner, & Manolis, 2005; Wood, 1998). Tudor (1971) found that children as early as the first grade developed social class awareness. Tudor studied 216 first-, fourth-, and sixth-grade students in a public school system, with ages ranging from 6 to 13. They were presented with a task of grouping pictures of objects (e.g., houses and cars) into upper, middle, and lower classes. Results showed that first-grade children could classify groups accurately, and by the sixth grade, children were nearly perfect in their classifications.

Issues of social class and classism are also widely present in children's daily activities and interactions; the following case vignette illustrates how such issues are likely to play out in a typical situation, as well as the social and psychological effects that are likely to ensue.

> John is a White, 12-year-old seventh grader whose family recently moved from a large city to one of its suburbs so that he could attend a better public school. The community he lives in is predominantly White and upper-middle-class; most of his classmates' parents work in white-collar jobs and have above-average incomes. John's own parents are employed as a bank teller and a teacher, and the family lives in one of the few apartment complexes in the community, which is dominated by single-family homes. After moving, John met some new friends at his apartment complex and on the sports teams that he joined at school, and spent time socializing with both groups; however, he soon began to find it difficult to fit in equally well with both sets of friends. When he wore khakis and sweaters like his friends on the basketball team, the kids at the apartment complex cracked jokes about his "preppy" clothes, but if he came to practice wearing an old T-shirt and jeans, the other players said that he looked like a bum. When he hung out at the mall with his basketball friends, the kids in his building accused him of being snobby, but if his teammates walked by as he and his friends sat on the steps of their complex, they joked about how "ghetto" he looked. Soon, John found himself dreading the prospect of being around members of both social groups at the same time and began to avoid situations where this might happen. He felt exhausted by his efforts to juggle the two groups' demands for appropriate behavior and appearance, and was constantly stressed out by their continuous jeering at his failures to conform to group norms. Although he liked both sets of friends, over time, John began to decrease his contact with the kids in his building and to spend most of his time with his teammates in order to avoid the stress of trying to fit in with both groups. Eventually, his friendships with his neighbors faded completely, and the basketball team became his primary social network.

This vignette demonstrates that children and adolescents are not only aware of social class, but also use it to form judgments about others and to make decisions about their own behaviors and choices of friends. All of John's friends' taunts stemmed form their sensitivity to subtle indicators of his social class, such as his clothing and recreational activities; moreover, the upward and downward classism that John experienced caused him substantial distress, and eventually forced him to modify his behavior and even abandon some of his friendships. This example also suggests that school counselors should be aware of the indicators of social class that are relevant to the children in their schools and must keep in mind the powerful influence that social class issues can have on students' behaviors and psychological well being.

Because social class is important in the lives of children and adolescents, it is imperative for school counselors to better understand its role in their work. While school counselors are employed in a number of different settings with varying responsibilities, we will focus on two issues especially pertinent in school counseling practice: (a) developmental guidance and (b) vocational development.

Developmental Guidance

Of all the tasks school counselors tackle, one of the most important in relation to academic achievement is developmental guidance in the classroom (Lapan, Gysbers, & Sun, 1997; Whiston & Sexton, 1998). The use of a counseling paradigm and the application of teaching theories, human developmental theories, and counseling theories are important frameworks in implementing developmental guidance (Goodnough, Perusse, & Erford, 2003). The school counselor provides direct (e.g., counseling) and indirect (e.g., consultation) services to assist teachers with the delivery of lesson plans, the implementation of discipline, and the creation of a positive school climate (Sink, 2005). Thus, school counselors become increasingly important "teachers" within the classroom (Goodnough et al., 2003).

Developmental guidance, which uses traditional developmental theories to inform and guide school counseling practice, helps facilitate our understanding of how social class may impact a child's or an adolescent's development. The extant literature on developmental guidance, however, typically suggests targeted interventions for different grade levels (e.g., behavioral or cognitive goals), but does not reflect how social class operates at the societal, family, or interpersonal levels. That is, the interventions are given irrespective of the resources to which teachers have access, the social class variations in parent–teacher interactions, and the effects of poverty on the cognitive and intellectual development of children and adolescents. Thus, the literature on developmental guidance, especially developmental theory, has largely ignored the role social class plays in the trajectory of children's and adolescents' cognitive, social, and personal development.

The problem with a developmental approach that does not integrate social class into its interventions or program structure is that what is likely to blame the child or adolescent for failing to achieve or to actualize the programs available to him or her. For instance, imagine a developmental guidance approach that is not race-sensitive or attuned to how teachers, especially middle-class teachers, view African American students. Under such an approach, a program might be established to raise the intellectual performance of African American students in an elementary classroom, but may fail to achieve the desired goal. Without an understanding of the interaction between social class and race, one conclusion might be that the program did not work because the African American students are intellectually deficient.

Research overwhelmingly shows, however, that this conclusion would be wrong. To begin, unfavorable attitudes from White teachers toward African American students depress standardized test scores (Oates, 2003). McLoyd (1998) and Evans (2004) have also shown that child and adolescent achievement is influenced negatively by poverty and low social class. Beginning at the perinatal stage and onward, complications stemming from stress, violence, exposure to toxins such as lead, and a lack of home-based cognitive stimulation all contribute to limiting intellectual and socioemotional functioning (Costello, Compton, Keeler, & Angold, 2003). Job loss or unemployment, persistent poverty, and exposure to violence also impact the psychological well being of parents, which in turn influences the child's or adolescent's sense of self (Farmer et al., 2004; McLoyd et al., 1994; Nagin & Tremblay, 2001; Petterson & Albers, 2001). Furthermore, research shows that low teacher expectations, along with poor academic readiness, contribute to low school achievement. The cocurricular and home environments and resources contribute to the intellectual progress of students. Entwisle, Alexander, and Olson (1997) found that home resources, such as books and computers, contribute to children's intellectual gains, especially when school is not in session. Parental involvement in the school and consistent parental discipline are also related to fewer absences and higher grade point average (Gutman, Sameroff, & Eccles, 2002). However, not all families have access to these resources, or the ability to provide optimal levels of parental involvement and structure.

There are also differences within classrooms, depending on context. For instance, Greenwood, Delquadri, Stanley, Terry, and Hall (1986) found that inner-city teachers typically used more audio–visual materials and teacher–class discussions, whereas suburban teachers assigned more independent work and more sustained study time. Consequently, inner-city children tended to have lower levels of teacher–student interaction and to be more passive when compared with suburban children. Therefore, when providing developmental guidance, school counselors need to be sensitive to the possible social class issues among students and to the impact of social class on the particular school and community. These factors affect the way families interact with society, the way they deal with the conflict and crisis that result from poverty, the way children come to school, and the expectations that teachers and school counselors have for parents.

School counselors should also be aware of communication differences between students and parents from different social class groups. For instance, children in lower social classes report more negative interactions with parents than children in higher social classes (Chen, Matthews, & Boyce, 2002). Hence, some of the low social class children may be more sensitive to criticism from teachers and counselors than other children are. Additionally, low social class parents tend to focus on obedience, respect, neatness, cleanliness, and staying out of trouble, whereas high social class parents focus on happiness, independence, creativity, curiosity, ambition, and self-control (Maccoby, 1980). Lower social class parents are also more power-assertive, authoritarian, controlling, and willing to use physical punishment in comparison with higher social class parents who tend to be democratic and permissive or authoritative (Maccoby). Finally, in contrast with parents from low social classes, parents from high social classes may reason and use complex language with their children (Maccoby).

All of these social class differences have implications for school counselors. The lower class children and adolescents with whom counselors work may expect direct and autocratic communication from teachers and may need help in understanding democratic or permissive language. School counselors should also help to develop behavioral contingencies for difficult-to-control children who avoid power-assertive techniques and focus only on control and avoidance of trouble.

Vocational Guidance

Another important role a school counselor plays is in providing vocational guidance (Baker, 1996). Vocational guidance can happen as part of vocational development and school-to-work transitions. In this role, school counselors provide reliable information about jobs and careers, help make appropriate vocational choices, and provide opportunities to explore various occupations (Baker). D. Brown (2003) provided several examples of developmentally appropriate career goals for each school class level. At kindergarten, children may be expected to identify their parents' jobs and duties. At third grade, they should identify five workers employed by the state and know their major responsibilities. By middle school (eighth grade), students may identify three interesting jobs and determine the skills and education needed for those jobs. By high school, adolescents may want to make a preliminary career choice, identify alternative career choices, and construct a path to obtain each career. Although helpful in the ideal, these suggestions are premised on a middle-class context where children and adolescents have opportunities and options to investigate. The other assumption is that children and adolescents develop career interests and goals that are independent of their parents and community; however, as we will discuss later, Rasheed (2001) found that these career goals might not be accurate or helpful, especially among some lower class and rural youth.

The primary limitation of contemporary career theories and research is that they are based mostly on the experiences of White and middle-class populations (Chaves et al., 2004). Buboltz, Miller, and Williams (1999) found in a content analysis of the *Journal of Counseling Psychology* that many of the participants in the studies were college students, even though only 25% of the United States population has a college education (U.S. Census Bureau, 2001). Many other studies on which career theories are based also rely on samples that are not representative of all segments of the population in terms of race, gender, or social class. Given these limitations, current career theories, many of which are used by school counselors, may have limited applicability to poor and working-class groups.

Some research shows that current career theories may have to be adapted for non-middle-class students. For instance, some research suggests differences between senior high school students from low and high social class groups in terms of investigating and planning for college. Low-income, ethnic minority, high school students are similar to higher-income White students with respect to future income expectations, especially in their expectations of returns on higher education (Rouse, 2004). The problem is that lower income, ethnic minority students are less able to translate their future plans, such as college, into actual college attendance (Rouse). Thus, school counselors need to be aware that barriers limiting higher educational attainment may be more pronounced for those in lower social class groups. Focusing simultaneously on overcoming these barriers and developing higher achievement motivation is imperative.

Work may also be differentially meaningful depending on the social class group of the child or adolescent. School counselors should be aware that adolescents from lower social class groups may approach career and job attainment differently than adolescents of higher social class might. For example, in Chaves et al.'s (2004) study of poor and working-class urban adolescents, the authors found that vocational education and exposure was expected to come through traditional school-to-work programs embedded in academic work in school. The premise of career theories is that people will find work that is meaningful, relevant, and rewarding. Yet, some poor and working-class individuals may not find work intrinsically rewarding or interesting. Chaves et al. found that high school students who lived in urban settings and were predominantly poor tended to view work as a means to make money, establish financial security, and keep themselves occupied; work was perceived by different students as enjoyable, boring, positive, and negative. In contrast, students from high social class groups tended to view work as a source of personal satisfaction and reported greater access to parental support and resources as well as higher levels of career adaptability (Blustein et al., 2002).

These results suggest that school counselors need to develop career programs and services that acknowledge the practical rewards of vocational choices as well as the potential intrinsic rewards of careers. Focusing specifically on the abstract and ideal goal of vocational choice (i.e., finding a career that is intrinsically rewarding) may be a social class bias that needs to be addressed before providing services. Additionally, school counselors should recognize the important role parents might play in students' career choices. Focusing on the students' career choices as independent and autonomous, without regard for the parents' wishes or support, may decrease the credibility and trustworthiness of the counselor.

Practice Implications

In this chapter, we have reviewed literature and critiqued theories relevant to school counseling practice. In addition to these reviews, practical examples and implications are also important in illustrating how school counseling practice can be informed by social class. In these examples, we will use the phenomenological/subjective approach to understanding social class in students' lives. This approach maintains that while income, education, occupation, and other "adult" indices are typically used to classify individuals into social class groups such as the middle class, research shows that people's perceptions of their situation or condition are more important to their psychological well-being than the objective indicators (Liu, Ali, et al., 2004; Liu, Soleck, et al., 2004).

The framework used here is an abbreviated SCWM (Liu, 2002; Liu, Soleck, et al., 2004). The premise is that individuals live in economic cultures that socialize them into ways of living that sustain their social class standing. Materialism, lifestyle considerations, and social class behaviors such as accents and table manners, to name a few, are all symbols of a person's social class standing. People are motivated to maintain a homeostatic position in their social class group. As a result of this motivation for homeostasis, people also experience and enact various forms of classism. Upward classism, for instance, consists of prejudicial attitudes toward those perceived to be in a higher social class group than oneself; these individuals may be regarded as snobby, elitist, or stuck up. Downward classism is prejudice and discrimination directed toward those in lower social classes. Lateral classism is prejudice experienced as "keeping up with the Joneses"—people work to maintain their standing in relation to others in their social class group in order to avoid the negative judgments and prejudicial treatment they would receive if they fell behind. Finally, internalized classism is anxiety, depression, fear, and anger resulting from an inability or a failure to maintain one's social class standing.

Even though many examples could be derived from the SCWM, we will touch on only a few to illustrate the application of social class to informing the practice of school counseling. Several forms of classism are salient for students coming from impoverished, poor, low-income, and low social class situations. Career motivations to achieve, save money, or work in service occupations, such as fast food, are often sabotaged by poor peer interactions. For instance, Newman (1999) describes how poor and urban youth often feel shamed or demeaned by their peers for "just working." They experience upward classism when other poor adolescents perceive them as "snobs" and lateral classism when these peers pressure them to conform and not work. This situation often becomes the proverbial "crabs in a bucket," where any "crab" attempting to escape is pulled back down by the others and, as a result, no one can get out. In such cases, school counselors need to recognize the possible deleterious role that peer pressure may play in students' job attainment or career choices. Not all students are motivated toward job attainment, and not all students are interested in supporting their peers' success. Consequently, in counseling, it would be important to acknowledge the multiple tiers of pressure that students experience and the barriers that they face. A counselor who is aware of social class issues would attempt to understand the feelings of internalized classism as well as the pressures of upward, downward, and lateral classism in students' lives.

Students in all grades also experience materialistic pressures to conform to their peers. Dress codes and norms, often fluctuating and reflecting the mercurial aesthetics of the broader society, may be easier to subscribe to for those who have financial resources. For those lacking such resources, feelings of internalized classism such as depression, anger, and anxiety may arise. School counselors could work with administrators to examine the physical characteristics of the students' environment. They should be observant of dress norms, jewelry, cars, and other possessions that force stratification among different students in the school. Such stratifications may create tension, anxiety, and stress among some students, who may then express these feelings through withdrawal, anger, or frustration. In their work, school counselors should acknowledge how these material pressures affect the students. Furthermore, school counselors need to be constantly aware of the ways in which they might explicitly or implicitly reinforce social class stratification in their schools. Students of different social classes may have different normative experiences as well as differential access to academic activities and resources, such as field trips and extra books. Counselors should be sensitive to these differences and careful not to make assumptions about the resources that students can access or the experiences that they have had.

In general, school counselors should communicate to the students they work with that they empathize with them and share similar values and worldviews. Esters (2001) investigated students' preferences for counselor characteristics. A sample of 66 high-risk students from the southern United States completed the Preferences for School Counselor Characteristics Questionnaire, which requires a forced choice between two characteristics. The results suggest that students prefer to work with a counselor who possesses characteristics similar to their own. After rank ordering the characteristics chosen by the participants, Esters found that the two most desirable counselor characteristics were (a) same attitudes and values and (b) same background and socioeconomic status as the student. This finding indicates that students' preferences with regard to similarity are not based on overt, easily available physical characteristics. Rather, students prefer counselors with worldviews and past experiences that are similar to their own.

School counselors can also act as informed mediators among schools, families, and communities. Giles (2005) asserted that educators send messages to poor and working class parents that undermine the role of the parents in their children's education. Using a conceptual framework, Giles outlined the ways in which counselors and educators in urban schools perceive the quality and nature of their relationship with parents. Barriers in these relationships often form as a result of social class, race, and power differences between parents and educators, and the author suggests that these barriers can be overcome by transforming the school–family–community culture from bureaucratic to relational. Giles suggested that parents and educators should strive for mutual interactions and assume mutual responsibility for the education of children. Going further, Bryan (2005) also addressed the need for school–family–community partnerships in order to foster resilience, build social capital (i.e., relationships), and make a positive difference in school achievement among ethnic minority and low-income children. According to Bryan, parents of these children are often regarded by educators as adversaries rather than supporters of their children's educations. Bryan suggested that barriers to low achievement can be overcome by fostering dialogue among educators, parents, and community members. School counselors may act as facilitators, advocates, or collaborators to help develop these necessary dialogues.

Although much research demonstrates the deleterious effects of poverty on children and adolescents, there is also evidence for the existence of certain protective factors that shield children from these effects and that can be used in planning and implementing school counseling interventions. For example, Lee (1999) found that supportive adult relationships were instrumental in boosting economically disadvantaged students' confidence and expectations of themselves and, thus, helped them to achieve academic and career success. Lee studied mentoring and its relationships with self-efficacy, aspirations, and ideas of future selves in disadvantaged students of various ages. The author explored the length of time that was required for mentoring relationships to significantly benefit the mentees. One hundred and thirty elementary- and secondary-school students participated in a mentoring program. Participants were mostly African American and were reported by the school staff to be economically disadvantaged. One group consisted of students on the waitlist for mentoring, another group of students had been mentored for 6 months or less, a third had been mentored for 7 to 12 months, and a final group had been mentored for more than 1 year. Lee found that aspirations were higher in students who had been mentored for more than 1 year when compared with students on the waitlist.

The results suggest that long-term mentoring is associated with more ambitious plans for future education and occupation in disadvantaged students. School counselors can therefore improve students' chances of future success by making efforts to establish long-term, consistent relationships with students, or by collaborating with other important mentors in the students' lives, such as parents and teachers, in their efforts to promote academic success. Although it is not feasible for school counselors and teachers to provide all students with the support and guidance they need and deserve, these individuals provide an important link between students and other potentially helpful community-based programs. Research has documented the benefits of mentoring programs (e.g., Big Brothers/Big Sisters) in promoting positive attitudes and healthy behavior and in reducing self-destructive, risk-taking behavior (Rhodes, Grossman, & Resch, 2000). Research on the effectiveness of the Big Brothers/Big Sisters program has noted the following benefits among mentees: a lower likelihood of initiating drug or alcohol use, more self-confidence with regard to schoolwork, better attendance, improvements in perceived scholastic achievement, and better relationships with parents, families, and peers (DuBois, Neville, Parra, & Pugh-Lilly, 2002). Given the potential for such extrafamilial relationships to provide benefits for at-risk youth, it is important for school counselors to work with parents and teachers in providing suitable recommendations and referrals.

One specific intervention that school counselors might consider in working with lower class students is to provide etiquette classes that focus on dining and socializing. This intervention may be particularly useful for counselors working with high-school seniors in school-to-work transition programs. Many of these students may find themselves in job interviews or performance evaluations that require dining with current or prospective employers in formal or semiformal settings. The goals of the etiquette class would be to reduce the students' anxiety and increase feelings of competency and self-efficacy in such situations; this could be accomplished by teaching specific skills relevant to the situation, such as ordering, dining, and formal socializing.

A final suggestion for school counselors is to be aware of their own social class backgrounds, assumptions, and prejudices. It is particularly important to avoid upward mobility bias (Liu & Pope-Davis, 2003), which is the belief that everyone is motivated toward upward social mobility (e.g., to gain a higher education or get a better job). In her dissertation work among Appalachian high-school youth, Rasheed (2001) found that many in this poor, rural community decided not to go to college or seek other postsecondary training. Instead, they intended to work in occupations associated with coal mining or other community jobs. Rasheed reported that these students' primary value was to stay close to their families; they were not interested in upward mobility as defined by conventional society. For these students, coal mining and service work were not seen as mundane or uninteresting, but as honorable and honest forms of work. Cases such as this illustrate how important it is for counselors to avoid making assumptions about others' social class related values and aspirations based on their own views or experiences.

In the following case vignette, we will synthesize several of the issues pertinent to school counseling intervention.

Marilyn is a school counselor working in a rural Midwestern high school, where she has been employed for eight years. A new manufacturing company was recently established in the town, bringing with it several hundred new families, most of whom were Hispanic and poor. With the addition of new students, Marilyn faced new challenges as a middle-aged, middle-class Caucasian school counselor, who had, until recently, worked primarily with White, middle-class students. Namely, Marilyn noted an increased incidence of bullying among the female students: It appeared that a popular "clique" of Caucasian girls was singling out, teasing, and ostracizing several of the new Hispanic girls. As a result, the new girls were cutting classes or not coming to school at all, homework was late or not turned in, and many had been seen in the nurse's office with complaints of physical ailments. Marilyn spoke with the girls individually, in an attempt to gather information about their predicament, as well as to express her concern. She knew that to be successful in communicating with the girls, she would have to identify some way in which she could share their worldviews and experiences. Rather than speaking directly about race or class, Marilyn attempted to drawn common ground via her own experience as an adolescent girl. She shared her memories of high school, remembering that other girls had always seemed to have nicer clothes and books; their parents dropped them off in newer cars; and they seemed to speak properly and effortlessly with teachers and other students. Marilyn encouraged the girls to talk with their parents and to become involved in activities in the community that were not directly school-related, such as 4-H. In doing so, she hoped the girls could begin to establish other friendships and bolster their social support networks. Marilyn also suggested that the girls become mentees in the Big Brothers/Big Sisters program and described to them the potential benefits of having someone to talk to who was not a parent. Throughout her work with the new students, Marilyn knew to be aware of her own values and background, and the way in which these could influence counseling. In turn, Marilyn asked the girls to describe their own beliefs and values to her. Over the course of the year, Marilyn developed important relationships with the girls that provided both support and information about community resources.

The previous vignette demonstrates how a school counselor can provide important guidance and direction for youth in a sensitive and empathetic manner. In addition, the vignette demonstrates the importance of the role of the school counselor as a mediator among school, family, and community, and as a referral source for adolescents to other supportive adult relationships.

The Subjective/Phenomenological Approach to Social Class

Much of the research evidence we have reviewed in this chapter supports moving to a subjective/phenomenological approach to social class. The literature shows that the subjective experience of poverty mediates the effects of poverty on psychological outcomes (McLoyd et al., 1994). The way an individual sees his or her current situation and makes meaning of poverty affects that person's psychological outlook and well-being. For instance, one person with a 10th-grade education and an income of $25,000 may blame herself for underachieving and feel constantly stressed out, while another with the same education and income may be happy and consider himself lucky to be free of the burden of managing large amounts of money and possessions. While these two individuals' objective social class status is the same, their perceptions of their situations, and the resulting psychological outcomes, are very different. A phenomenological approach to social class captures important subjective differences such as these. It also allows researchers to investigate situational nuances that are not apparent from a classification scheme. For example, Carter's (2003) qualitative analysis of 44 low-income African American youth in an urban school revealed that they often struggled to balance two different forms of cultural capital in maintaining their social class status. Cultural capital is the standards of speech, dress, musical tastes, and ways of interacting that distinguish between one group and another. The African American students struggled between African American cultural capital and the dominant cultural capital (i.e., White and middle class), which was believed to lead to success. The study of this and other subjective social class phenomena is impossible if social class is measured solely by objective indices; however, a phenomenological approach allows us to examine the attitudes, conflicts, and other psychological processes involved.

Summary and Conclusions

The purpose of this chapter was to provide an overview of social class in school counseling. Although social class is an important contextual variable in students' lives that affects them in many ways, it is difficult to understand

and integrate into research and practice. Social class is also often confounded with ethnicity, although this presents more of a problem for research than practice, where it is more important to understand the interaction between the two variables than to tease them apart. The literature reviewed in this chapter shows that various measures of social class, such as income, education, and occupation, are related to numerous indicators of child development, intellectual performance, and socioemotional functioning. Typically, the lower the social class of the family, the poorer the outcomes for children and adolescents. The authors also examined the role of social class in two major services provided by school counselors: (a) developmental guidance and (b) vocational guidance. The available evidence highlights the importance of integrating social class considerations into both services; otherwise, school counselors may find their work catering only to White, middle-class students while ignoring everyone else. The chapter concludes with some practice implications that illustrate how social class can be used to inform the work of school counseling. We hope that this discussion will help school counselors become aware of their own biases and worldviews when working with students of low social class and aid them in developing better programming for these students.

References

Ackerman, B. P., Brown, E. D., & Izard, C. E. (2004). The relations between persistent poverty and contextual risk and children's behavior in elementary school. *Developmental Psychology, 40,* 367–377.

Baker, S. B. (1996). *School counseling for the twenty-first century* (2nd ed.). Upper Saddle River, NJ: Prentice Hall.

Bemak, F. (2005). Advocacy as a critical role for urban school counselors: Working toward equity and social justice. *Professional School Counseling, 8,* 196–203.

Blustein, D. L., Chaves, A. P., Diemer, M. A., Gallagher, L. A., Marshall, K. G., Sirin, S., et al. (2002). Voices of the forgotten half: The role of social class in the school-to-work transition. *Journal of Counseling Psychology, 49,* 311–323.

Bornstein, M. H., Hahn, C. S., Suwalsky, J. T. D., & Haynes, O. M. (2003). Socioeconomic status, parenting, and child development: The Hollingshead Four-Factor Index of Social Status and the Socioeconomic Index of Occupations. In M. H. Bornstein & R. H. Bradley (Eds.), *Socioeconomic status, parenting, and child development* (pp. 29–82). Mahwah, NJ: Lawrence Erlbaum Associates.

Bronfenbrenner, U. (1986). Ecology of the family as a context for human development: Research perspectives. *Developmental Psychology, 22,* 723–742.

Brown, D. (2003). *Career information, career counseling, and career development* (8th ed.). Boston: Allyn & Bacon.

Brown, M. T., Fukunaga, C., Umemoto, D., & Wicker, L. (1996). Annual review, 1990–1996: Social class, work, and retirement behavior. *Journal of Vocational Behavior, 49,* 159–189.

Bryan, J. (2005). Fostering educational resilience and achievement in urban schools through school-family-community partnerships. *Professional School Counseling, 8,* 219–228.

Buboltz, W. C., Jr., Miller, M., & Williams, D. J. (1999). Content analysis of research in the *Journal of Counseling Psychology* (1973–1998). *Journal of Counseling Psychology, 46,* 496–503.

Carter, P. L. (2003). "Black" cultural capital, status positioning, and schooling conflicts for low income African American youth. *Social Problems, 50,* 136–155.

Chaves, A. P., Diemer, M. A., Blustein, D. L., Gallagher, L. A., DeVoy, J. E., Casares, M. T., et al. (2004). Conceptions of work: The view from urban youth. *Journal of Counseling Psychology, 51,* 275–286.

Chen, E., Matthews, K. A., & Boyce, W. T. (2002). Socioeconomic differences in children's health: How and why do these relationships change with age? *Psychological Bulletin, 128,* 295–329.

Conger, R. D., Ge, X., Elder, G. H., Jr., Lorenz, F. O., & Simons, R. L. (1994). Economic stress, coercive family process, and developmental problems in adolescents. *Child Development, 65,* 541–561.

Costello, J. E., Compton, S. N., Keeler, G., & Angold, A. (2003). Relationships between poverty and psychopathology: A natural experiment. *Journal of the American Medical Association, 290,* 2023–2029.

Day-Vines, N. L., Patton, J. M., & Baytops, J. L. (2003). Counseling African American adolescents: The impact of race, culture, and middle class status. *Professional School Counseling, 7,* 40–52.

Dodge, K. A., Pettit, G. S., & Bates, J. E. (1994). Socialization mediators of the relation between socioeconomic status and child conduct problems. *Child Development, 65,* 649–665.

DuBois, D. L., Neville, H. A., Parra, G. R., & Pugh-Lilly, A. O. (2002). Testing a new model of mentoring. In J. E. Rhodes (Ed.), *New directions for youth development: A critical view of youth mentoring* (pp. 21–57). New York: Wiley Periodicals.

Duncan, G. J., Brooks-Gunn, J., & Klebanov, P. K. (1994). Economic deprivation and early childhood development. *Child Development, 65,* 296–318.

Duncan, G. J., & Magnuson, K. A. (2003). Off with Hollingshead: Socioeconomic resources, parenting, and child development. In M. H. Bornstein & R. H. Bradley (Eds.), *Socioeconomic status, parenting, and child development* (pp. 83–106). Mahwah, NJ: Lawrence Erlbaum Associates.

Entwisle, D. R., Alexander, K., & Olson, L. (1997). *Children, schools, and inequality.* Boulder, CO: Westview Press.

Entwisle, D. R., & Astone, N. M. (1994). Some practical guidelines for measuring youth's race/ethnicity and socioeconomic status. *Child Development, 65,* 1521–1540.

Esters, I. (2001). At-risk high school students' preferences for counseling characteristics. *Profession School Counseling, 4,* 165–171.

Evans, G. W. (2004). The environment of childhood poverty, *American Psychologist, 59,* 77–92.

Evans, G. W., & English, K. (2002). The environment of poverty: Multiple stressor exposure, psychophysiological stress, and socioemotional adjustment. *Child Development, 73,* 1238–1248.

Farmer, T. W., Price, L. N., O'Neal, K. K., Leung, M. C., Goforth, J. B., Cairns, B. D., et al. (2004). Exploring risk in early adolescent African American youth. *American Journal of Community Psychology, 33,* 51–59.

Frable, D. E. S. (1997). Gender, racial, ethnic, sexual, and class identities. *Annual Review Psychology, 48,* 139–162.

Garner, P. W., Jones, D. C., & Miner, J. L. (1994). Social competence among low-income preschoolers: Emotion socialization practices and social cognitive correlates. *Child Development, 65,* 622–637.

Garrett, P., Ng'andu, N., & Ferron, J. (1994). Poverty experiences of young children and the quality of their home environments. *Child Development, 65,* 331–345.

Giles, H. C. (2005). Three narratives of parent-educator relationships: Toward counselor repertoires for bridging the urban parent-school divide. *Professional School Counseling, 8,* 228–236.

Goldberg, M. E., Gorn, G. J., Peracchio, L. A., & Bamossy, G. (2003). Understanding materialism among youth. *Journal of Consumer Psychology, 13,* 278–288.

Goodman, E., Amick, B. C., Rezendes, M. O., Levine, S., Kagan, J., Rogers, W. H., et al. (2000). Adolescents' understanding of social class: A comparison of White upper middle class and working class youth. *Journal of Adolescent Health, 27,* 80–83.

Goodnough, G., Perusse, R., & Erford, B. T. (2003). Developmental classroom guidance. In B. T. Erford (Ed.), *Transforming the school counseling profession* (pp. 121–151). Upper Saddle River, NJ: Merrill Prentice Hall.

Greenwood, C. R., Delquadri, J., Stanley, S. O., Terry, B., & Hall, R. V. (1986). Performance-based assessment of depriving environments: Comparison of context/response interactions within inner-city and suburban school settings. In S. E. Newstead, S. H. Irvine, & P. L. Dann (Eds.), *Human assessment: Cognitition and motivation* (pp. 319–340). Dordrecht, the Netherlands: Martinus Nijhoff.

Gutman, L. M., Sameroff, A. J., & Eccles, J. S. (2002). The academic achievement of African American students during early adolescence: An examination of multiple risk, promotive, and protective factors. *American Journal of Community Psychology, 30,* 367–399.

Hauser, R. M. (1994). Measuring socioeconomic status in studies of child development. *Child Development, 65,* 1541–1545.

Hoffman, L. W. (2003). Methodological issues in studies of SES, parenting, and child development. In M. H. Bornstein & R. H. Bradley (Eds.), *Socioeconomic status, parenting, and child development* (pp. 125–143). Mahwah, NJ: Lawrence Erlbaum Associates.

Holcomb-McCoy, C. (2004). Assessing the multicultural competence of school counselors. *Professional School Counseling, 7,* 178–184.

Huston, A. C., McLoyd, V. C., & Coll, C. G. (1994). Children and poverty: Issues in contemporary research. *Child Development, 65,* 275–282.

Lapan, R. T., Gysbers, N. C., & Sun, Y. (1997). The impact of more fully implemented guidance programs on the school experiences of high school students: A statewide evaluation study. *Journal of Counseling and Development, 75,* 292–302.

Lareau, A. (2003). *Unequal childhoods: Class, race, and family life.* Berkeley: University of California Press.

Lee, J. (1999). The positive effects of mentoring economically disadvantaged students. *Professional School Counseling, 2,* 172–179.

Liberatos, P., Link, B. G., & Kelsey, J. L. (1988). The measurement of social class in epidemiology. *Epidemiologic Reviews, 10,* 87–121.

Liu, W. M. (2001). Expanding our understanding of multiculturalism: Developing a social class worldview model. In D. B. Pope-Davis & H. L. K. Coleman (Eds.), *The intersection of race, class, and gender in counseling psychology* (pp. 127–170). Thousand Oaks, CA: Sage Publications.

Liu, W. M. (2002). The social class-related experiences of men: Integrating theory and practice. *Professional Psychology: Research and Practice, 33,* 355–360.

Liu, W. M., & Ali, S. R. (2005). Addressing social class and classism in vocational theory and practice: Extending the emancipatory communitarian approach. *The Counseling Psychologist, 33,* 189–196.

Liu, W. M., Ali, S. R., Soleck, G., Hopps, J., Dunston, K., & Pickett, T., Jr. (2004). Using social class in counseling psychology research. *Journal of Counseling Psychology, 51,* 3–18.

Liu, W. M., & Pope-Davis, D. B. (2003). Understanding classism to effect personal change. In T. B. Smith (Ed.), *Practicing multiculturalism: Internalizing and affirming diversity in counseling and psychology* (pp. 294–310). New York: Allyn & Bacon.

Liu, W. M., Soleck, G., Hopps, J., Dunston, K., & Pickett, T. (2004). A new framework to understand social class in counseling: The social class worldview and modern classism theory. *Journal of Multicultural Counseling and Development, 32,* 95–122.

Luthar, S. S., & Latendresse, S. J. (2005a). Children of the affluent: Challenges to well-being. *Current Directions in Psychological Science, 14,* 49–53.

Luthar, S. S., & Latendresse, S. J. (2005b). Comparable "risks" at socioeconomic extremes: Preadolescents' perceptions of parenting. *Development and Psychopathology, 17*, 207–230.

Maccoby, E. E. (1980). *Social development: Psychological growth and the parent-child relationship*. New York: Harcourt Brace.

McLoyd, V. C. (1998). Socioeconomic disadvantage and child development. *American Psychologist, 53*, 185–204.

McLoyd, V. C., Jayaratne, E., Ceballo, R., & Borquez, J. (1994). Unemployment and work interruption among African American single mothers: Effects on parenting and adolescent socioemotional functioning. *Child Development, 65*, 562–589.

Nagin, D. S., & Tremblay, R. E. (2001). Parental and early childhood predictors of persistent physical aggression in boys from kindergarten to high school. *Archives of General Psychiatry, 58*, 389–394.

Newman, K. S. (1999). *No shame in my game: The working poor in the inner city*. New York: Vintage Books.

Oakes, J. M., & Rossi, P. H. (2003). The measurement of SES in health research: Current practice and steps toward a new approach. *Social Science and Medicine, 56*, 769–784.

Oates, G. L. S. C. (2003). Teacher-student racial congruence, teacher perceptions, and test performance. *Social Science Quarterly, 84*, 508–525.

Petterson, S. M., & Albers, A. B. (2001). Effects of poverty and maternal depression on early child development. *Child Development, 72*, 1794–1813.

Pollitt, E. (1994). Poverty and child development: Relevance of research in developing countries to the United States. *Child Development, 65*, 283–295.

Rasheed, S. (2001). *Prediction of post secondary plans for rural Appalachian youth* (Doctoral Dissertation, University of Oregon, 2001). UMI Dissertation Services, AAT, 3024527.

Rasmussen, A., Aber, M. S., & Bhana, A. (2004). Adolescent coping and neighborhood violence: Perceptions, exposure, and urban youths' efforts to deal with danger. *American Journal of Community Psychology, 33*, 61–75.

Rhodes, J. E., Grossman, J. B., & Resch, N. L. (2000). Agents of change: Pathways through which mentoring relationships influence adolescents' academic adjustment. *Annual Progress in Child Psychiatry and Child Development, 16*, 183–190.

Roberts, J. A., Tanner, J. F., Jr., & Manolis, C. (2005). Materialism and the family structure-stress relation. *Journal of Consumer Psychology, 15*, 183–190.

Rouse, C. E. (2004). Low-income students and college attendance: An exploration of income expectations. *Social Science Quarterly, 85*, 1299–1317.

Sanderson, C. A., Darley, J. M., & Messinger, C. S. (2002). "I'm not as thin as you think I am": The development and consequences of feeling discrepant from the thinness norm. *Personality and Social Psychology Bulletin, 28*, 172–183.

Sink, C. (2005). *Contemporary school counseling: Theory, research, and practice*. New York: Lahaska Press.

Tudor, J. F. (1971). The development of class awareness in children. *Social Forces, 49*, 470–476.

U.S. Census Bureau (2001). *Census 2000 supplementary survey profile for the United States*. Retrieved May 16, 2005, from www.census.gov

Valadez, J. R. (1998). Applying to college: Race, class, and gender differences. *Professional School Counseling, 1*, 14–21.

Whiston, S. C., & Sexton, T. L. (1998). A review of school counseling outcome research: Implications for practice. *Journal of Counseling and Development, 76*, 412–426.

Wood, M. (1998). Socio-economic status, delay of gratification, and impulse buying. *Journal of Economic Psychology, 19*, 295–320.

XII
DISABILITY IN THE SCHOOLS

TINA M. ANCTIL AND STEPHANIE SAN MIGUEL BAUMAN
Washington State University

Introduction

Special Education Services Today

Since the landmark passage of P.L. 94-142, the Education of All Handicapped Children Act (1975), which guaranteed all children with disabilities a free, appropriate public education (FAPE), children with disabilities have been attending public schools. Prior to this legislation, children with disabilities were largely uneducated, residing in institutions or with family members. Today, the inclusion of students with disabilities in the general education classroom signifies a true revolution has occurred within education over the past 30 years as 95% of students with disabilities are now served in general education classrooms (U.S. Department of Education [USDE], 2002).

In the 2001–2002 school year, over 5 million school-age children, or 9% of the U.S. resident population of school-aged children, had been identified as requiring special education services due to specific disabilities. The most common disabilities represented in U.S. schools are specific learning disabilities, speech or language impairments, mental retardation, and emotional disturbance. Of those students, White students made up 62.3% of the students served; 19.8% were African American; 14.5% were Hispanic; 1.9% were Asian/Pacific Islander; and 1.5% were American Indian/Alaska Native (see Table 12.1; USDE, 2002). There continues to be overrepresentation of disabilities in some racial/ethnic groups according to specific disability categories, as well as under representation of certain disabilities in some racial/ethnic groups, when compared with the special education student population as a whole.

Research on the educational outcomes of students with disabilities is disappointing, with 31% of adolescents with disabilities dropping out of high school; this rate is much higher than for nondisabled adolescents (Phelps & Hanley-Maxwell, 1997; USDE, 2000). Unemployment rates for young women with disabilities are over four times the rates for nondisabled young women, while unemployment rates for young adult males with disabilities are approximately three times the rate for their nondisabled peers. Additionally, youth with disabilities attend postsecondary education or training at much lower rates than do nondisabled young adults (USDE, 2000).

The Inclusion Movement

Today, P.L. 94-142 has been amended five times and has evolved into the Individuals with Disabilities Education Act (IDEA), with the most recent amendments passed in 2004 renaming the legislation the Individualized Disability Education Improvement Act (IDEA). The amendments of 1997 (P.L. 105-107) were particularly significant in creating a renewed focus requiring that children with disabilities be guaranteed the "least restrictive environment" for learning while also addressing the importance of a thorough evaluation for services (including diagnosis by qualified professionals), individualized education programs for each student, student and parent participation in decision making, and the procedural safeguards to ensure that the regulations and the rights of students with disabilities are being followed. Furthermore, the 2004 amendments align IDEA closely to the No Child Left Behind Act, helping to ensure equity, accountability, and excellence in education for children with disabilities.

Table 12.1 Percentage of Students Ages 6 through 21 Served Under IDEA During 2000–2001

Disability	American Indian/ Alaska Native	Asian/ Pacific Islander	Black (non-Hispanic)	Hispanic	White (non-Hispanic)	All Students Served
Specific learning disabilities	56.3	43.2	45.2	60.3	48.9	50.0
Speech or language impairments	17.1	25.2	15.1	17.3	20.8	18.9
Mental retardation	8.5	10.1	18.9	8.6	9.3	10.6
Emotional disturbance	7.5	5.3	10.7	4.5	8.0	8.2
Multiple disabilities	2.5	2.3	1.9	1.8	1.8	2.1
Hearing impairments	1.1	2.9	1.0	1.5	1.2	1.2
Orthopedic impairments	.08	2.0	0.9	1.4	1.1	1.3
Other health impairments	4.1	3.9	3.7	2.8	5.9	5.1
Visual impairments	0.4	0.8	0.4	0.5	0.5	0.4
Autism	0.6	3.4	1.2	0.9	1.4	1.4
Deaf-blindness	0.0	0.0	0.0	0.0	0.0	0.0
Traumatic brain injury	0.3	0.3	0.2	0.2	0.3	0.3
Developmental delay	0.7	0.6	0.7	0.2	0.6	0.5
All disabilities	100.00	100.00	100.00	100.00	100.00	100.00

Note: Does not include New York State; Source: U.S. Department of Education, Office of Special Education Programs, Data Analysis System (DANS).

Of increasing importance to school counselors is Section 504 of the Rehabilitation Act, originally passed in 1973 as the first Civil Rights law that prohibited discrimination on the basis of disability. Specifically, this law required that all federally funded entities (e.g., schools, libraries, universities, local and state government agencies) provide physical as well as programmatic accommodations for people of all ages with disabilities. Many students with health impairments that do not interfere with classroom learning, such as juvenile diabetes, receive 504 accommodations instead of IDEA related services.

Notably, IDEA and Section 504 differ in their focus, goals, and funding. IDEA emphasizes educational remediation and attempts to address gaps in skills and abilities by providing modified instruction and additional services for students in need of special education. Section 504 focuses on the prevention of discrimination. It attempts to level the playing field for students who can succeed academically if their disabilities do not limit their access to learning. IDEA is a funded law, while Section 504 is not (Lockhart, 2003).

The latest flagship regular education law, No Child Left Behind (NCLB), was authorized in 2002, replacing the Elementary and Secondary Education Act (ESEA) and bringing broad changes to U.S. educational systems. While not a special education law in particular, NCLB does have significant impact on students with disabilities, especially in the terms of assessment. Building on IDEA, NCLB requires schools to measure how well students with disabilities have learned reading and mathematics curricula. The law includes provisions for students with the most significant cognitive disabilities, allowing for designed alternate assessments when appropriate. Because the majority of students with disabilities are required to meet the academic achievement goals of their schools, they must also have access to the general education curriculum. Assisting and advocating for students with disabilities to have adequate access to the general education curriculum are crucial roles for school counselors and will be discussed in greater detail later in the chapter.

Another point of consideration for school counselors is the unique educational and environmental differences between rural, suburban, and urban settings for students with disabilities. Kinnison, Fuson, and Cates (2005) summarized the most common barriers to special education students in rural settings as access to qualified and skilled special education instruction and a lack of future employment opportunities. Similarly, students in some high-poverty urban areas may also lack adequate access to specialized instruction. As school counselors engage and collaborate with special educators, it is imperative that they inquire about issues that may be unique to the school setting or community, allowing the counselor to design interventions that supplement the work of the special educators (e.g., a community that lacks adequate child psychologists may benefit from a school counseling program that offers group counseling for students with specific issues).

School Counselors and Students With Disabilities

In summary, school counselors need to understand that these laws mandate the education of students in the most inclusive setting possible. Understanding how school counseling practices fit into the national legal mandates for students with disabilities provides a framework for implementing comprehensive counseling and guidance programs across grade levels.

School counselors play a unique and varied role in supporting the personal/social, academic, and career development needs of students with disabilities. Despite the importance of the school counselor to this population, there is a dearth of literature on school counseling and students with disabilities in the school counseling literature. This chapter will address how school counselors can support the individual needs of the student with a disability through individual counseling, interdisciplinary teamwork, and family-oriented counseling and services. Key theories that impact students with disabilities (i.e., adjustment to disability, self-determination theory, and Social Cognitive Career Theory [SCCT]) will be discussed, as well as pertinent research and example of practice for each. Ethical and legal issues that pertain to school counseling practice and students with disabilities will be covered. Finally, recommendations for training future school counselors to meet the needs of students with disabilities will be addressed.

Theory

Personal and Familial Adaptation to Disability

School counselors who are knowledgeable about the factors that influence students and their family's response to disability are better prepared to meet the educational needs of students with disabilities. Referring again to Table 12.1, the most common disabilities found in schools today are specific learning disabilities, speech or language impairments, mental retardation, emotional disturbance, and other health impairments. In addition to students with disabilities, school counselors may encounter students who have a parent or a sibling with a disability. Understanding the basic theoretical construct of adaptation to disability and psychosocial functioning as it relates to the disability and the family is foundational to providing counseling services to this population.

What is the psychosocial impact of having a disability? One way of answering this question is to evaluate the many factors that interact with the disability. Despite considerable agreement in the literature that the onset of a chronic illness or physical disability constitutes a "crisis-like" situation in the lives of affected individuals, there continues to be considerable disagreement regarding the nature, process, and outcomes of adaptation to chronic illness or disability (Livneh, 1986; Shontz, 1975; Siller, 1976; Wright, 1983). It is generally agreed that there are changes in *self-representation* (i.e., sense of self, self-identity, body image) following the onset of a disability or the diagnosis of a chronic or life-threatening medical condition. There is little agreement, however, regarding the psychosocial factors that contribute to changes in self-representation (Livneh & Antonak, 1997).

In a review of the literature of ecological models of psychosocial adaptation to disability, Livneh and Antonak (1997) identified four primary classes of variables important to understanding variations in the process of psychosocial adaptation. The first class of variables are those associated with the specific disability (e.g., cause of condition, type of disability, type of onset, extent of condition, degree of functional involvement, body areas affected, extent of brain and central nervous system involvement, age at diagnosis, age of symptom onset, chronicity, stability of condition, lethality, and visibility). For example, a second-grade student diagnosed with juvenile diabetes encounters a very different set of variables than another second grader who suffers a severe head injury. Both families will be deeply affected, but in different ways. The family of the student with a head injury likely dealt with a life-threatening accident and the ensuing days or weeks of inpatient treatment and rehabilitation. On the other hand, the family of the student with juvenile diabetes may be working extensively with a diabetes educator to learn to administer and manage insulin, adjust to a new diet, and facilitate their child's understanding of the illness. Both families will have long-term worries about their child's future health and will need accommodations from the school to meet the disability related needs of their child, but each has a unique set of needs that the school must address and negotiate.

The second class of variables important to understanding variations in the process of psychosocial adaptation is associated with sociodemographic and organismic characteristics of the individual, including (a) sex and sex role identification, (b) chronological age, (c) life or developmental stage, (d) ethnicity, (e) socioeconomic status, (f) state of general health, (g) level of education, (h) marital status, (i) occupational attainment and job history, and (j) existing vocational skills. While these variables apply primarily to adults, the school counselor should be aware of them in the event that a parent of a student has an existing disability or obtains a new disability. For example, when a parent is injured on the job, the family's socioeconomic status may decline, causing marital discord, which could then impact the student's ability to academically achieve and/or result in behavioral problems at school.

Next, variables associated with personality and behavioral attributes of the individual can impact the psychosocial functioning of the individual. The coping strategies and defense mechanisms employed can be either negative or positive. The individual's perception of control, whether internal or external, can be critical to developing internal motivation and self-determination. Other examples of personality and behavioral attributes include (a) the personal meaning of the condition; (b) attitudes toward health, sickness, and deviance; (c) personal values and beliefs; (d) self-concept and ego strength; (e) body image; (f) cognitive competence or intellectual ability; (g) acceptance of disability; (h) premorbid psychosocial adaptation (i.e., before the occurrence of the disability); and (i) previous experience with crises of a similar nature. Developmentally, certain variables such as self-concept may be experienced quite differently depending on the age and grade level of the student. An elementary school student may not internalize the label of "learning disabled" in the same way as a middle school student diagnosed with a learning disability.

Finally, variables associated with the physical environment should be considered. Examples of this include the individual's access to social support systems, economic and institutional support, physical settings, attitudinal barriers or supports, and encountered stress. For children and adolescents, the primary environment is the family, which ultimately can dictate how each of these variables will interact with each other. For these reasons, it is particularly important that the school counselor include the family in as many interventions as possible related to psychosocial adjustment to disability.

Self-Determination Theory

Beginning in the 1980s, research regarding the factors and supports that may contribute to adult success for students with disabilities became a priority for special education researchers and policy makers (Kohler, 1993). One of the most significant findings from outcomes research has been the link between high levels of self-determination and positive adult outcomes (Gerber, Ginsberg, & Reiff, 1992; Reiff, Gerber, & Ginsberg, 1997; Wehmeyer & Schwartz, 1997). Research on self-determination as a motivational construct has highlighted the importance of promoting educational practices that lead to enhanced internal motivation for students with disabilities, which is also of great interest to school counselors.

Given these findings, the U.S. Department of Education created a series of national model demonstration projects to promote self-determination for youth with disabilities. With ever-increasing evidence that self-determination is essential for successful adult outcomes for youth with disabilities today (Sowers & Powers, 1995; Wehmeyer & Lawrence, 1995), there is clearly an assumption that higher levels of self-determination will lead to a better quality of life in adulthood. While most, if not all, of these demonstration projects focused on special education services, school counselors can work to support and supplement the special education services that promote self-determination by incorporating practices that enhance self-determination into comprehensive counseling and guidance programs.

There are many definitions of self-determination, all similar in nature. Field and Hoffman (1994) defined self-determination as "the ability to identify and achieve goals based on a foundation of knowing and valuing oneself" (p. 164). Deci and Ryan (1985) described self-determination as "the capacity to choose and to have those choices be the determinants of one's actions" (p. 38). Ward (1988) identified five traits underlying self-determination: (a) self-actualization, (b) assertiveness, (c) creativity, (d) pride, and (e) self-advocacy. In addition, Wehmeyer (1996) defined self-determination as "acting as the primary causal agent in one's life and making choices and decisions regarding one's quality of life free from undue external influence or interference" (p. 24).

Wehmeyer (1995) identified the four essential characteristics of self-determined behavior as (a) behavioral autonomy, (b) self-regulated behavior, (c) psychological empowerment, and (d) self-realization. Wehmeyer (1993) studied the relationship between several of these elements and found that adolescents with learning disabilities and mental retardation had more barriers to effective career decision making (e.g., self-regulation) than their nondisabled peers had. Additionally, internal locus of control (i.e., psychological empowerment) was strongly related to positive career decision making for all students. Wehmeyer and Kelchner (1995) examined problem solving (i.e., self-regulation) in social contexts with youth with mental retardation and found that they created fewer and less complex solutions. Locus of control orientation, self-efficacy, general self-esteem, and problem solving and self-concept, which are both measures of self-realization, contributed significantly to the variance among total problem solving scores. These findings suggest that the four elements of self-determination may be related but are also distinct in their contribution to the construct of self-determination (Wehmeyer, Kelchner, & Richards, 1996).

Research clearly states that self-determination is a developmental process that must begin well before students leave high school (Sands & Doll, 1996; Whitney & Moloney, 2001). Teaching students with disabilities to become more self-determined to identify and reach goals, to evaluate personal preferences and decisions, to solve problems, to self-evaluate performance, and to assume greater control over their lives are key building blocks to becoming successful adults. In fact, these skills are important for all students; however, as illustrated by the drop-out rate and poor employment rates of young people with disabilities, learning these skills is imperative for students with disabilities.

Social Cognitive Career Theory

Social Cognitive Career Theory (SCCT) was designed to promote understanding of the career development of a wide variety of students and workers by considering factors such as age, gender, race/ethnicity, culture, socioeconomic status, and disability status (Lent, 2005). The primary foundation for SCCT is Bandura's (1986) general social cognitive theory. Thus, SCCT emphasizes the complex mutual influence of people, their behavior, and their environments. Acknowledging that people possess the capacity to direct their own vocational behavior, SCCT considers three "person variables": (a) self-efficacy beliefs about one's capabilities (i.e., "Can I do this?"); (b) outcome expectations about the imagined consequences of particular courses of action (i.e., "If I try doing this, what will happen?"); and (c) personal goals regarding engagement in a particular activity or the production of a particular outcome (i.e., "How much and how well do I want to do this?"). SCCT also proposes conceptually distinct yet interlocking models for the following processes: (a) the development of academic and career interests, (b) the formation of educational and vocational choices, and (c) the nature and results of academic and career performance. In other words, the basic theoretical person elements (i.e., self-efficacy, outcome expectations, and goals) will operate in concert with other important aspects of the person (e.g., gender, race/ethnicity, and disability status); their contexts; and their learning experiences in the interest model, the choice model, and the performance model. In the process, academic and career development is shaped (Lent).

In discussing the practice implications of Social Cognitive Career Theory (SCCT), Fabian and Liesener (2005) commented that formal or informal assessment of efficacy beliefs and outcome expectations may be warranted with due consideration given to how these beliefs and expectations may have compromised an individual's interests, goals, and future expectations. Direct interventions could include strategies to bolster self-efficacy; to expose students to multiple career options and successful peer role models; to anticipate, understand, and address contextual barriers; and to build support systems (Fabian and Liesener, 2005).

Research

Personal and Familial Adjustment to Disability

Key themes in the seminal works of Shontz (1975), Roessler and Bolton (1978), and Wright (1983) suggest that adaptation to chronic illness is a "dynamic, gradually unfolding, and progressive process through which the individual strives to reach an optimal state of person-environment congruence regarded as adjustment" (Livneh & Antonak, 1997, p. 8). A person who has successfully reached a state of adjustment demonstrates (a) psychosocial equilibrium or reintegration, (b) awareness of remaining assets and existing functional limitations, (c) positive self-esteem and self-concept, (d) a sense of personal mastery, (e) successful negotiation of the environment, and (f) active participation in social, vocational, and recreational activities.

Because not all persons with disabilities reach this optimum level of adaptation, researchers (Livneh, 1986; Wright, 1983) have suggested that the adaptation process may also be conceptualized as a one-dimensional continuum ranging from failed adaptation (i.e., maladaptive psychosocial functioning) to successful adaptation (i.e., adaptive psychosocial functioning). The maladaptive end of the pole is characterized by the early reactions to disability, described in stage theories as shock, anxiety, and denial, while the adaptive end of the pole is characterized with the later reactions of acknowledgement, acceptance, and adjustment.

Behavioral correlates in the research have found behaviors such as problem solving, information seeking, and social support seeking are helpful to individual coping and can be viewed as a general reflection of successful psychosocial adaptation. Meanwhile, behaviors such as self-blame, avoidance, or externalizing blame are indicative of failed psychosocial adaptation (Livneh & Antonak, 1997).

Self-Determination Theory

Because the research on self-determination has identified self-determination as a positive predictor of adult success, many studies have focused on the federally mandated practice of individualized transition planning (ITP), which is required for all special education students beginning at age 14. The special education teacher is the identified party responsible for completing the transition plan (as well as the individualized education plan, or IEP); however, the school counselor is often identified as a key team member for the implementation of the individual student's plan. For example, if a student has a goal related to career exploration, the school counselor may facilitate a series of job shadowing experiences with local businesses.

Transition planning has been discussed as a dynamic vehicle by which students with disabilities can become empowered to identify and reach short- and long-term goals based on individual strengths and weaknesses (Blalock & Patton, 1996). Furthermore, many believe that self-determination is a skill that must be taught, and if education and transition goals are to address self-determination, the goals should be specific, systematic, and sequential (i.e., they should include the many small steps required to reach the main goal) to allow the student to practice self-determination (Hughes et al., 1997; Stowitschek, Laitinen, & Prather, 1999; Wehmeyer & Kelchner, 1995).

For students with developmental disabilities, studies that imbed early self-determination opportunities (such as choice making) have shown promise for eventually generalizing the skills outside of the classroom and in unique situations (Stowitschek et al., 1999). A broader review of transition practices, which are empirically and socially validated (Hughes et al., 1997), identified strategies that support students in their preparation to leave high school. Overall, these strategies can be characterized into those that "emphasize building supportive environments, assessing and teaching choice and preference, and increasing self-management, independence, social interaction, and social acceptance" (p. 10).

In addition to imbedding self-determination into the transition planning process and the classroom, Agran (1997) described the importance of student-directed learning strategies in the classroom as a means of enhancing self-determination. He contended that student-directed learning strategies facilitate skills acquisition, save teachers time, promote generalization, and promote the cultural benefits of education. Wehmeyer, Agran, and Hughes (1998) added that there is no better setting for student-directed learning than the educational and transition planning processes in special education.

Whitney-Thomas and Moloney (2001) studied student self-definition as a component of self-determination in adolescents with and without disabilities. Using cognitive psychology as a basis for their study, they proposed that in order for adolescents to develop self-determination, they must first have a positive future orientation with the cognitive tools necessary to explore and form a healthy self-identity. They maintained that in order for adolescents to expand their identities, they must first be challenged by their environments (e.g., school) in a manner that does not "overwhelm the current capacities of the adolescent . . . resulting in high levels of distress and disorder" (p. 376). They theorized that in many adolescents with disabilities, the transition from high school becomes too overwhelming and therefore results in poor individual outcomes.

Whitney Thomas and Moloney's (2001) results indicate that "students' self-knowledge and visions for the future develop from introspection, learning from mistakes and choices made, and interactions with significant others across contexts such as family life and school" (p. 385). They found social support and opportunities for independence to be mediating factors in the development of self-definition, as well as in coping with stress. Students with disabilities were most likely to have low self-definition, to experience high rates of stress, and to struggle with development of their identity.

Social Cognitive Career Theory

In terms of research, self-efficacy has received the most attention among the variables in SCCT. Intervention, experimental, and path analytic studies support hypotheses regarding causal relations among measures of self-efficacy, performance, and interests (Lent, 2005). In the area of disability, researchers have used SCCT to examine career self-efficacy beliefs among students with disabilities compared with their nondisabled peers (Fabian & Liesener, 2005). For example, investigations of students with learning and emotional disabilities (e.g., Ochs & Roessler, 2001) have suggested that the participants with disabilities have lower efficacy beliefs than their peers without disabilities. Other studies suggest that self-efficacy beliefs play an important role in understanding students' career choice and interests (Fabian & Liesener, 2005). For example, Paganos and DuBois (1999) found that self-efficacy, rather than outcome expectancies, was the strongest contributor to career interests for high school students with learning disabilities.

In turn, Ochs and Roessler (2004), in an examination of 77 special education students diagnosed with learning disabilities and 99 general education students, revealed through a backward regression that both career decision self-efficacy and career outcome expectations were key predictors of career exploratory intentions in both groups. Fabian and Liesener (2005) also identified studies (e.g., Willis, 2002) that examined self-efficacy beliefs as significant predictors of postschool employment in students with serious emotional disturbance. A limited number of studies (e.g., Conyers & Symanski, 1998) have also looked at efficacy beliefs in the context of intervention studies and found positive results in regard to mitigating negative feedback of environmental constraints that have limited vocational development. These studies, however, looked at college students or adults rather than school-aged participants (Fabian & Liesener).

School Counselors and Students With Disabilities

School counselor preparation. Preparation of counselors to serve children and adolescents with disabilities requires the clarification of counselors' feelings and attitudes about working with students who have disabilities, as well as the acquisition of relevant knowledge and skills (Tarver-Behring & Spagna, 2004). Unfortunately, minimal guidelines for disability training are provided by the program standards of national accrediting agencies such as The Council for Accreditation of Counseling and Related Educational Programs and the National Council for Accreditation of Teacher Education (Milsom & Akos, 2003). In the absence of specific guidelines, a look at current school counselor preparation may be instructive. For example, in their survey of school counselor education programs, Milsom and Akos found that 43% of the 137 participating school counselor education program coordinators reported that disability courses were required by their program, while 29% of the coordinators reported that elective disability courses were recommended. Milsom and Akos also found that information about disabilities often was integrated into existing program courses such as the basic school counseling course (integrated in 72% of the programs), the multicultural course (integrated in 64% of the programs), and the human counseling development course (integrated in 58% of the programs).

In terms of practical experiences, Milsom and Akos (2003) found that 26% of the school counseling programs required activities such as participating in an IEP, 504, or multidisciplinary meeting; consulting with teachers of students with disabilities; and/or providing individual counseling to a student with a disability. Moreover, in programs that did not specifically require involvement with individuals with disabilities, 55% of the program coordinators indicated that their students still became involved in experiences with, or that were related to, individuals with disabilities.

Activities school counselors perform with students with disabilities. The American School Counselor Association (ASCA) has encouraged school counselor involvement with students with disabilities (Milsom & Akos, 2003) and has recommended a variety of school counselor roles to that end (ASCA, 2000, 2004). In addition to providing school counseling activities that serve all students as part of a comprehensive school program, counselors may engage in other roles on behalf of students with disabilities. These roles may include the following: (a) serving on a school's multidisciplinary team; (b) assisting with the establishment, implementation, and modification of plans for accommodations; (c) collaborating with other student support specialists in the delivery of services; (d) providing group and individual counseling; (e) advocating in the school and in the community for students with special needs; (f) assisting with transitions between different grades and between school and postschool activities; (g) consulting and collaborating with staff and parents; and (h) making referrals to the appropriate specialists in the community (ASCA, 2004). Notably, professional school counselor roles may vary from school system to school system and from state to state due to the policies and regulations that state and local school boards may have in response to federal laws addressing students with disabilities (Lockhart, 2003).

In a survey of 100 randomly selected school counselors in elementary (28% of respondents), middle/junior high (38% of respondents), and high school (34% of respondents) settings, Milsom (2002) found that at least 75% the respondents indicated that they performed activities with students with disabilities. These activities included providing individual and group counseling, being a member of or providing feedback to multidisciplinary teams, and helping with behavior modification plans for students with disabilities. In turn, Wood Dunn and Baker (2002) surveyed 168 elementary school counselors in North Carolina. When asked to circle descriptors that best described what they believed about their role in working with students with disabilities, the percentage of participants who circled the following descriptors were as follows: counselor (92.9%), advocate (90.5%), listener (82.7%), team member (79.8%), consultant (78.6%), communicator (61.9%), and problem solver (55.4%). Wood Dunn and Baker concluded that the results of their research

> seem to depict a situation in which many school counselors acquired some formal education with students with disabilities prior to entering the profession. Yet, many may have found that the demands for them to possess expertise in this domain while working in the schools exceeded their perceived level of knowledge. (p. 282)

Practice

Counseling Services to Students With Disabilities and Their Families

The Individuals with Disabilities Act mandates access to a wide range of educationally related services for students with disabilities, including counseling. For the school counselors to provide competent counseling interventions to students with disabilities, they must first develop an awareness for the cognitive, affective, and social problems of these students (Bowen & Glenn, 1998). Generally speaking, within the entire population of students with disabilities, school counselors will likely provide the majority of their services to students with mild disabilities. Typically, this includes students with learning disabilities, other health impairments (e.g., attention deficit disorder), mild mental retardation, and emotional and behavioral disorders.

As discussed earlier, school counselors often receive little training specifically related to counseling students with disabilities, and there are few resources discussing best practices for school counselors when working with students with disabilities; however, many counselors possess the skills needed to work with these students and their families. Communication skills, empathy, conflict skills, and facilitation skills are essential. As evidenced by the vast array of functional impairments included in the diagnostic definitions of the 13 categories of disabilities eligible for special education and related services (see Appendix A), students with disabilities do not represent a homogeneous group, and there is no "one size fits all" counseling approach or intervention. Counselors who are willing to explore work with students and/or family to examine the specific student's functional strengths and weaknesses, while putting aside feelings of low expectations, pity, and biases can be very effective with this population (Tarver-Behring & Spagna, 2004).

Referring again to the evidenced-based theories of psychosocial adaptation to disability, self-determination, and career self-efficacy, school counselors will find a multitude of possible "jumping off points" for individual and small group counseling. For instance, we know that self-definition and self-understanding are critical to incorporating the diagnostic label into the student's past experiences, current self-concept, and future goals. Milson and Hartley (2005) discussed the importance of the school counselor to college bound students with learning disabilities, including the provision of counseling related services designed to assist the student to "explore the relationship between their skills and abilities and potential future careers" (p. 438). Elementary school counselors are also critical to meeting the educational and personal/social needs of students with disabilities. Bergin and Bergin (2001) suggested that elementary school counselors should be keenly aware of how language-based problems can impede the counseling process for some students with learning disabilities. School counselors should be knowledgeable of the functional limitations of the student with a learning disability, prior to engaging in counseling interventions. For example, a student with an auditory processing disorder may not benefit from cognitive therapy as much as play therapy.

Finally, consider a sixth-grade girl who was recently evaluated for a specific learning disability and is subsequently found eligible for special education. This student may need assistance reflecting on her past academic performance, her current academic needs, and her future career goals. She may need to be gently guided to take responsibility for ensuring that her teachers provide the accommodations she needs without externalizing blame when a teacher's instructional style clashes with her learning style. She may feel stigmatized by the label of L.D. and may feel embarrassed to be receiving special education services. The school counselor is in an ideal position to assist this girl with understanding herself and her learning needs and, by doing so, is building a solid foundation for both self-determination and career self-efficacy in adolescence and adulthood.

Individual and Group Counseling for Specific Problems or Issues

Social skills training. Social skills are often pointed to by educators as a key deficit area for many children, especially children and adolescents with disabilities (Swanson & Malone, 1992). Social skills training (SST) programs are based on behavioral therapy and have gained prominence for their hope of remediating social competence deficits in students, especially for students with specific learning disabilities, mental retardation, emotional disturbance, or attention deficit/hyperactivity disorder (Gresham, Sugai, & Horner, 2001). Gresham (1998, as cited in Gresham et al., 2001) noted that "SST has four primary objectives: (a) promoting skill acquisition; (b) enhancing skill performance; (c) removing competing problem behaviors; and (d) facilitating generalization and maintenance" (p. 338).

While many SST packages and curricula are available for purchase (see also, Greenberg, Kusché, & Mihalic, 1998; Hoffman, 2003; Katz, McClellan, Fuller, & Walz, 1995), school counselors should be knowledgeable about the type of social skills deficit that requires remediation, as well as the research on SST outcomes. Many training curricula may not take into account what skills the student already possesses and in what settings the student may need more practice and support. For example, it is not appropriate to pull a student out of class to teach a skill he or she already knows, when what he or she really needs is practice "in the moment." The most positive results have been found in studies that match the social skills deficits with the SST intervention strategy (Gresham et al., 2001). School counselors must work closely with classroom teachers and special educators to first assess the exact nature of the social skill deficit and then design an intervention strategy, avoiding a "cookie cutter" approach at all times. For example, comic book conversations are a positive behavioral support strategy that has been used successfully with students with autism, mild/moderate learning disabilities, and cognitive and behavioral disabilities (Gray, 1994; Pierson & Glaeser, 2005).

The final issue school counselors must be aware of is the lack of broad generalization and maintenance of many SST programs. In other words, many students are not able to transfer the skills they learn in SST into the real world, suggesting that pullout small group settings may not be the most effective way to deliver SST. As much as possible, school counselors should consult with teachers and educational assistants to work within the regular classroom or other real-world settings to capitalize on "teachable moments" as this kind of contextual approach has the greatest efficacy (Gresham et al., 2001).

Self-determination guidance. There are two primary approaches to teaching self-determination to students with disabilities in schools today: (a) specific guidance curriculum and (b) whole school imbedded practices. Generally, the curricular approaches are led by special educators; however, special educators can benefit from the expertise of the school counselor, who can provide additional resources and insight to enhance the delivery of the curriculum.

The broader approach of incorporating activities that enhance self-determination into larger school practices (e.g., general education curriculum, special education curriculum, extracurricular activities, or community based activities) lends itself easily to current models of comprehensive school counseling programs, which also seek to imbed specific social and emotional development goals into a variety of school services. To date, self-determination has not been a purposeful component of developmental comprehensive counseling and guidance programs or the ASCA's National Model (2003). Because elements of self-determination encompass such constructs as decision making and self-efficacy, however, components exist that could be readily expanded.

Field and Hoffman (2002) have developed a list of nine quality indicators for promoting self-determination in educational settings (see Table 12.2), which are based on an extensive review of the existing self-determination literature, qualitative interviews, and expert review. Since the indicators were developed to enhance the self-determination of the entire school community (i.e., students, parents, faculty, leadership, and staff), they naturally lend themselves to a comprehensive counseling and guidance program. Examples of these practices in schools are (a) the systematic infusion of self-determination across the curriculum, (b) parent and student involvement in individualized educational planning meetings, (c) students selecting their own courses, (d) encouraging families to support new strategies at home to reinforce classroom learning, (e) team projects that bolster relationship building between students, (f) the use of assistive technology to provide for individual needs and supports, (g) the encouragement and support of divergent opinions within the school community, (h) clear behavioral management expectations for students, and (i) the active involvement of the entire school community in school evaluation and school improvement activities. By developing these quality indicators, school counselors can support school teams and programs in an effort to help students develop self-determination within school environments.

School counselors who develop a self-determination focus in their comprehensive counseling and guidance programs should also focus on assisting students with disabilities to develop a lasting relationship with an adult. Research has shown that students who have a confiding relationship with an adult have more opportunities for self-determination development (Benz, Lindstrom, & Yovanoff, 2000). While it is unrealistic to expect school counselors to have close relationships with all students with disabilities, it is feasible that the school counselor can coordinate mentoring programs in addition to maintaining individual relationships with students with disabilities.

Building on research documenting positive relationships between student-centered planning practices and student self-determination, Benz et al. (2000) discovered that "what adolescents with disabilities appear to want, *and what many adolescents desperately need*, is a personal relationship with a trusted adult who will be available to encourage their efforts, validate their fears, and celebrate their accomplishments" (p. 525). According to self-determination theory, in order to be truly self-determined, students must learn not only to make decisions, but also to self-evaluate decisions and experiences (Wehmeyer, Sands, Doll, & Palmer, 1997). Developmentally speaking, this is a difficult task for all children and adolescents and can be directly enhanced through didactic exchanges that occur in relationships built upon mutual trust and respect. It is critical to the long-term success of this population that adolescents with disabilities have access to a trusted adult after high school graduation. It is during these early adulthood years that real-world learning is occurring; this period of development offers many opportunities for hands-on learning about oneself, along with opportunities for failure, which can then lead to personal growth. Without the ability to converse and reflect with a trusted adult, many young people with disabilities do not experience an adequate quality of life in adulthood.

Table 12.2 Self-Determination in School Environments (Field & Hoffman, 2002, pp. 114–117).

Quality Indicators of School Environments That Promote the Acquisition of Knowledge, Skills, and Beliefs Related to Self-Determination

Quality Indicator 1: Knowledge, skills, and attitudes for self-determination are addressed in the curriculum, in family support programs, and in staff development.

Quality Indicator 2: Students, parents, and staff are involved participants in individualized educational decision making and planning.

Quality Indicator 3: Students, families, faculty, and staff are provided with opportunities for choice.

Quality Indicator 4: Students, families, faculty, and staff are encouraged to take appropriate tasks.

Quality Indicator 5: Supportive relationships are encouraged.

Quality Indicator 6: Accommodations and supports for individual needs are provided.

Quality Indicator 7: Students, families, and staff have the opportunity to express themselves and be understood.

Quality Indicator 8: Consequences for actions are predictable.

Quality Indicator 9: Self-determination is modeled throughout the school environment.

Self-esteem enhancement. When a student is diagnosed with a disability, he or she also becomes labeled and categorized, and many students report feeling stigmatized by their special education status (Smart, 2001). Depending on the disability and the perception by others about the disability, the student may encounter varying degrees of insult to his or her self-image and self-concept. For example, a student with a specific learning disability may be perceived as mentally retarded because he or she is a slow reader, while a student with schizophrenia may be perceived as potentially violent. We know that the most successful adults with disabilities are those who are self-determined and, therefore, possess a strong sense of self-awareness. Because of these factors, self-esteem is foundational to accepting one's self, including one's strengths and weaknesses; therefore, self-esteem enhancing services are an important aspect of the school counselor's role in working with students with disabilities.

Whiston and Sexton (1998) evaluated school counseling outcome research according to Gysbers and Hendersons (1994) comprehensive developmental guidance model as a theoretical framework. Many studies were included as examples of responsive services that had self-esteem as the measurable outcome, with a few of the studies including students with disabilities as the targeted population. Of these studies, group counseling was the most popular method of service delivery across all grade levels. Because of the varying nature of the interventions, an overall analysis of the effectiveness of the multiple types of self-esteem interventions was not provided; however, school counselors can evaluate the efficacy of their own interventions through the use of pre- and posttests or by utilizing an evidence-based curriculum readily available.

Brief Family Interventions

When counseling students with disabilities and their families, the most effective model is "a broad-based service model in which the counselor creates a collaborative community with all individuals and resources necessary for the child or adolescent to experience success in every area of life to the greatest extent possible" (Tarver-Behring & Spagna, 2004, p. 220). Collaborative relationships between families and professionals who work with students with disabilities are optimal given the familial investment in the outcome of children with disabilities, as well as the association between parent involvement in both student and school performance. Furthermore, parents' knowledge of their children and of their own expectations helps guide educators in the selection of appropriate interventions (Blackbourn, Patton, & Trainor, 2004).

Simeonsson and Bailey (1990) have developed a framework that represents the full spectrum of professional involvement in the area of early intervention and the services provided for young children with special needs. This useful organizing framework can be applied to services provided to the families of school-aged students with disabilities. Using a numbering system that reflects a successive increase in the active involvement of the practitioner, Simeonsson and Bailey proposed the following professional functions: (0) informing families about available services and offering such services, (I) tracking and advising families, (II) providing or brokering child-related services, (III) consulting or teaching families as part of information sharing, (IV) working on practical concerns in the role of family advocate and focusing on personal concerns through relationship building, (V) setting goals to develop practical strategies and coordinating resources to help the family manage their ongoing needs and demands, and (VI) providing help with psychological or existential issues through counseling or therapy.

School counselors who effectively work with families of children with disabilities remember that parents' roles vary with the professional's role due in part to parents' comfort with parent–professional interaction and involvement in counseling services. When the practitioner's function is to provide information or to track and advise families, family involvement is modest. At the middle of the spectrum, when professionals take on the role of consultant or provide other guidance for families, families actively seek both information and skills. For example, parent education requires a commitment of time and a willingness to learn of the part of the parent. At the highest levels of Simeonsson and Bailey's (1990) framework, parents pursue counseling and thus invest much of themselves in personal, behavioral and psychological terms.

Rather than recognize and respect variations in involvement, practitioners may criticize parents who refrain from participation. On one hand, nonuse of services and limited involvement may signal extreme sensitivity, apathy, or resistance on the part of parents. In these cases, school counselors can employ strategies such as setting a positive tone, using active listening skills, or using written or verbal contracts to clarify expectations (Campbell, 1993). On the other hand, low parent involvement may reflect other issues. Realistically, parents may feel distracted or overwhelmed by financial, health, or job-related issues. Perhaps they value their privacy and will not disclose family concerns until their counselor earns their trust (Campbell, 1993). In most cases, there is no one best way for parents to be involved at any point in time. Ideally, a full range of services should be available to meet parents' current and evolving needs and desires for involvement (Fine & Gardner, 1991; Weissberg, Caplan, & Harwood, 1991).

Harry (1997) has used the concepts of leaning forward and bending over backwards to suggest guidelines for working with families, especially when there are viewpoint differences between parents and professionals. She commented,

> If I feel like I'm bending over backwards in working with families, then I'm probably doing something wrong! Not only am I doing something unnatural, but, by bending backwards, I'm actually looking away from the person I'm trying to help. (p. 62)

In order to build bridges between the counselors' and parents' points of view through a posture of reciprocity, a school counselor can undertake the following specific actions: (a) identify issues that divide the professional and the family with whom the professional is working, (b) identify beliefs or values that underlie the professional's position, (c) inquire into the beliefs and values that underlie the family's position, (d) explicitly discuss the two different but equally valuable points of view, and (e) identify a point of similarity between the professional's and the family's views as a first step in the process of collaboration (Harry, 1997). Certainly, building bridges is well worth the effort if, as a result, counselors can more effectively collaborate with and enhance the well-being and development of young children with disabilities.

Consultation Services With Teachers and Multidisciplinary Teams

Whether at a meeting operating under IDEA or Section 504, the school counselor must be a supportive member of the multidisciplinary team that uses a group decision-making process and works toward the goal of enabling a student with a disability to learn and succeed (Lockhart, 2003). Lockhart listed possible professional school counselor functions on a multidisciplinary committee, including (a) serving as a member of a multidisciplinary meeting, (b) chairing a multidisciplinary meeting, (c) participating in the development of an individualized education plan, (d) participating in the development of a transitional plan, (e) participating in the development of an individual treatment plan, (e) participating in the development of a Section 504 plan, and (f) participating in the planning for related services. Notably, school counselors have much to offer multidisciplinary teams. The previous discussion of services for students of disabilities and their families identified some ways to integrate school counselors' knowledge of psychosocial adaptation to disability, self-determination, and career self-efficacy into their work with students with disabilities and their families and, in the process, into their consultation with teachers. Often, the counselor is very familiar with the parents, the child, and the child's needs. Moreover, the school counselor can readily make sense of the larger issues. The counselor also has the expertise to foster a sense of trust as well as open communication (Greer, Greer, & Woody, 1995). The specific nature of the consultation will vary with the needs of a students and the nature of the disability.

Ethical, Legal, and Professional Issues

When providing services to students with disabilities, school counselors must be cognizant of the multitude of ethical, legal, and professional issue surrounding their practice. In 1999, the ASCA adopted an official position statement regarding the role of the school counselor and students with disabilities (this position statement was subsequently revised in 2004). Specifically, ASCA (2004) stated that,

> Professional school counselors encourage and support all students' academic, personal/social and career development through comprehensive school counseling programs. Professional school counselors are committed to helping all students realize their potential and make adequate yearly progress despite challenges that may result from identified disabilities and other special needs. (¶ 1)

The ASCA has also stated that the school counselor's role in working with students with disabilities must be clearly defined and understood by all parties. It is not the sole responsibility of the school counselor to make special education or 504 plan eligibility decisions or to prepare the individual education plan or 504 plans. The school counselor is, however, in a unique role to support and advocate for services for students with disabilities. Common interventions for school counselors include, but are not limited to (a) participating in multidisciplinary teams; (b) collaborating with teachers and other education staff to support individualized instruction; (c) providing social skills training; (d) conducting self-esteem enhancing counseling and guidance activities; (e) assisting with the establishment, implementation, and maintenance of behavior management plans; (f) providing career development and guidance activities, especially related to the transition from high school to adult life; (g) counseling parents and families; and (h) making outside referrals to a variety of community providers and resources (ASCA, 2004). Others have written that school counselors have an obligation to (a) assist other educators to identify students who might have disabilities, (b) assist with appropriate evaluation and testing to determine if students do have disabilities (provided it is not beyond the scope of the school counselor's training or expertise), (c) assist in monitoring the student's educational progress, and (d) help families understand their children's disabilities (Remley, Hermann, & Huey, 2003).

Special education and 504 eligibility criteria. The legal issues surrounding eligibility for special education (IDEA, P.L. 105-107) and section 504 services (i.e., Rehabilitation Act of 1973) are beyond the scope of this chapter; however, a broad overview will be provided with the caveat that school counselors must pursue further research prior to implementing the laws in educational settings. Figure 12.1 provides a flow chart illustrating the decision-making points and criteria educators must consider when making eligibility decisions.

While the ASCA maintains that school counselors must not be the sole decision makers of special education or section 504 eligibility decisions, many school counselors today are "unofficially" reporting that they are responsible for determining eligibility as well as for establishing and then maintaining 504 plans. As referenced earlier, Section 504 of the Rehabilitation Act has been a federal law since 1973 (including the provision that students with disabilities receive a free and appropriate education [FAPE]); however within the last 15 years, the Office of Civil Rights has become proactive in advocating for the education of students with disabilities (Council of Administrators of Special Education [CASE], 1999). Also, the Americans with Disabilities Act is being interpreted by the Office of Civil Rights as incorporating all Section 504 protections (CASE).

Both IDEA and Section 504 protect the right of students with disabilities to FAPE; however, a student who is eligible for 504 services may be ineligible for IDEA special education services. Recall again that IDEA defines *eligible* as (a) only those students whose disability qualifies as one of the 13 specific diagnostic categories, and (b) those who are also in need of specialized instruction due to their impairment. Section 504 is far more inclusive in its definition, protecting all students with disabilities that substantially limit one or more life activities (including education). Once the school determines that a student, because of a disability, requires either special accommodations or related services to participate in his or her regular classroom, eligibility for Section 504 accommodations must occur (Heyward, 1992). Following the evaluation, if the student is found eligible, a 504 plan must be secured and implemented.

Examples of potential 504 disability conditions not typically covered under IDEA include, but are not limited to, (a) medical conditions such as asthma, allergies, diabetes, or cancer; (b) attention deficit disorder (ADD); (c) communicable diseases such as HIV; (d) temporary medical conditions; (e) drug/alcohol addiction, or (f) behavioral difficulties (CASE, 1999). A student with a health impairment that does not directly impact learning, but still needs accommodations or assistance during the school day, would require an evaluation for 504 services. For example, if a second-grade student with attention deficit disorder needs a regular break during the day to receive medication, but has no other educational needs related to the ADD diagnosis, the school may establish a 504 plan, rather than an individualized education plan (IEP), to assure that this student has the necessary accommodations.

Representation within special education. Disability can and should be understood within the context of multicultural counseling, as the dynamic of dominant culture (i.e., nondisabled) versus the nondominant culture (i.e., disabled) is similar in nature to other cultural phenomenon. As evidenced by the simple statistics of characteristics of special education students, the variables of ethnicity and gender appear to bias the identification of students with disabilities. The reauthorization of IDEA in 2004 specifically calls for schools to begin addressing these issues as well.

Wehmeyer and Schwartz (2001b) have provided a review of the literature regarding gender bias in referral and admission to special education services, noting that the issue has been a focus of research for the past two decades. The authors have also noted that federal reports have consistently found twice as many males as females within the special education ranks. Some studies have accounted for this through biology and behavior, but many more have found that male overrepresentation may be a function of bias. An additional problem that may be created by such bias is female underrepresentation in special education. Wehmeyer and Schwartz (2001a) hypothesized that girls who need some academic support but who do not display behavior problems are neither being referred nor receiving services. Wehmeyer and Schwartz (2001b) noted that "referral bias is the degree to which persons responsible for referring students for evaluation of eligibility in special education . . . make such referrals based upon personal or professional opinions rather than objective indicators" (p. 274). School counselors must be aware of this bias and self-monitor their own referral practices accordingly.

In another comprehensive review of the literature, Coutinho and Oswald (2000) evaluated the disproportionality of representation in special education services. Studies have consistently found African American students to be overrepresented in every disability category, especially in the mental retardation and emotional disturbance categories. Meanwhile, Hispanic students today (U.S. Department of Education, 2002) are overrepresented in the learning disability category and underrepresented in the categories of mental retardation, emotional disturbance, and other health impairments (see Table 12.1). The numbers of American Indian/Alaska Native students

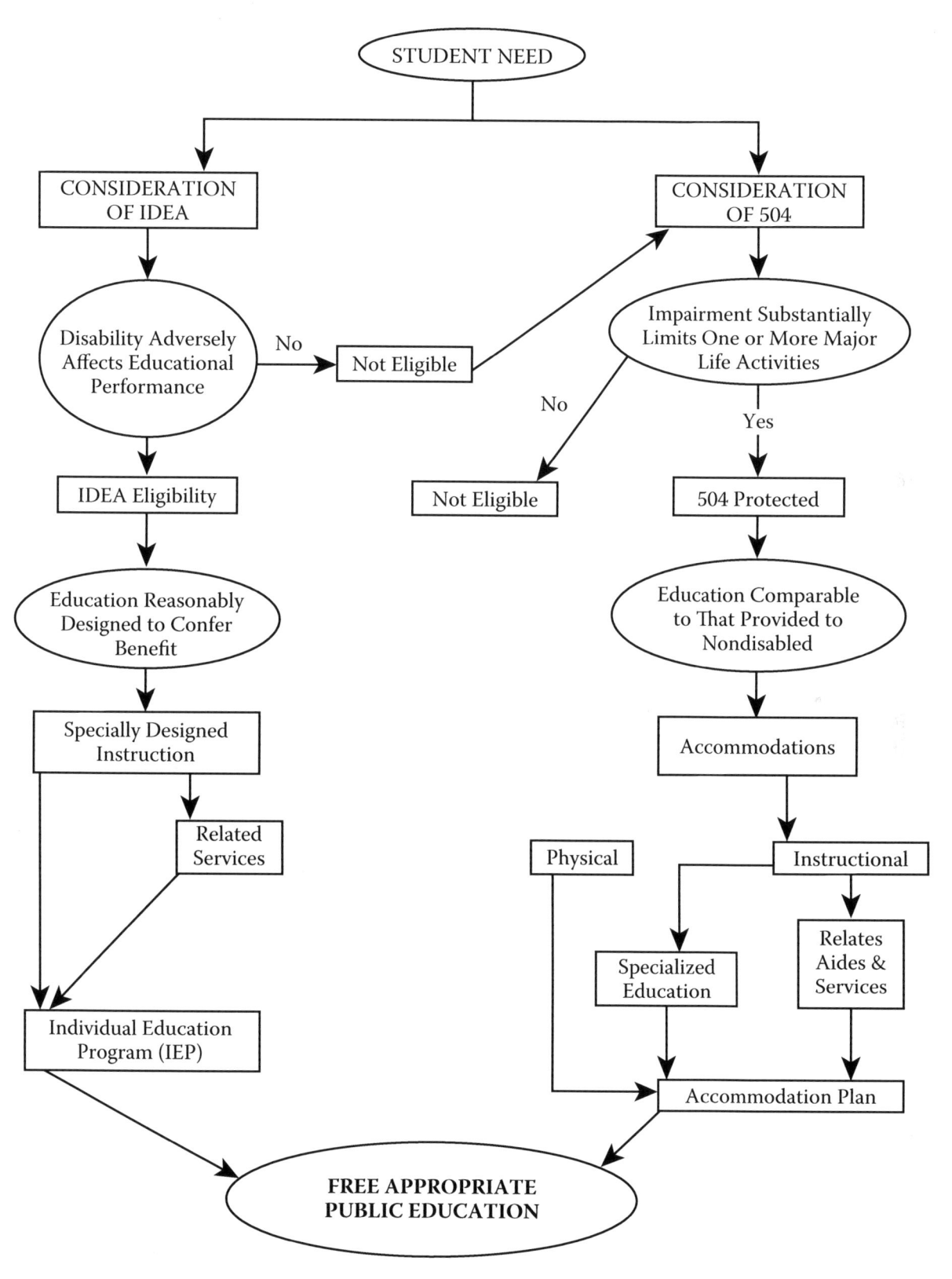

Figure 12.1 IDEA/504 Flow Chart. From *Section 504 and the ADA Promoting Student Access: A Resource Guide for Educators* by Council of administrators of Special Education, 1999, For Valley, GA: Author, p 5.

receiving services for specific learning disabilities were higher than that for all students with disabilities, and the percentage receiving services for mental retardation was lower. While there has been some variance in the past 25 years—the time when this issue began to gain prominence—these issues of disproportionality have remained largely unchanged. Concomitantly, underidentification of students from diverse backgrounds for gifted and talented programs is also an issue. There are few ethnic minority students in gifted and talented programs due to assessment instruments (e.g., those with a language bias), the reputation of sending schools that are not well regarded, and teacher training that does not emphasize the identification of student strengths (Boscardin, Brown-Chidsey, & Gonzalez-Martinez, 2003; Ford, 1998).

These statistics are important to school counselors because they describe the context of services to students with disabilities in schools today. If counselors are to become advocates for the needs of students with disabilities, they must first be aware of their own biases and the biases of other educators. How can this be accomplished by school counselors and other school personnel? Existing scientific evidence on stereotyping and cognitive automaticity indicates that biased perceptions often originate in processes that take place outside of conscious awareness (Abreu, 2001). Complicating the issue is the fact that stereotypes filter social reality. Citing Eagly and Kite (1987) Abreu explained, "in Western culture, male sex, White race, nondisabled physical status, heterosexual orientation, and young age are treated as cultural expectations, assumed to characterize a person if no dimension-relevant information is explicitly provided" (p. 495). With the objective of making covert attitudes and beliefs easier to acknowledge, Abreu provided a helpful review of theory and research on these perceptual processes and recommended sources of additional information on the topic for both multicultural counseling trainers and students on the topics.

Abreu (2001) discussed a variety of experiential educational experiences that are designed to promote self-awareness of prejudicial biases and stereotypes. These include the labeling exercise (Goldstein, 1997), which can be used with a group to illustrate the impact of stereotypes on perceivers, as well as the Implicit Association Test (Greenwald, Banaji, Noskek, & Baskhar, 1998; Greenwald, McGhee, & Schwartz, 1998), which can be accessed on the Internet and used by individuals to detect unconscious prejudice. In addition, counselors can promote equitable education for culturally diverse students with disabilities by becoming more knowledgeable about culturally and linguistically appropriate educational practices, facilitating culturally fair assessment, using culturally sensitive and inclusive school-based programs that support the academic and social success for all students, and quickly responding when academic risk factors first become evident (Tarver-Behring & Spagna, 2004).

While Abreu (2001) focused on racial biases, Rousso and Wehmeyer (2001) provided an extensive discussion of what educators should know about gender equitable education for male and female students who qualify for and would benefit from special education services. As previously mentioned, school counselors can help monitor that evaluative methods are free of gender bias and stereotyping. Additional guidelines of relevance to school counselors include creating a learning environment that encourages participation of all members, minimizes gender-segregated activities, uses diverse strategies given different learning strengths, encourages cooperation, and provides praise and recognition in an equitable manner. In sum, it is imperative that school counselors attend to racism, sexism, and other factors in the ecological context of a student's world and strive to address these critical elements within the role of a school counselor (Bemak & Chung, 2005).

Future Directions

Synthesis: Theories, Research, and Implications for School Counselors

As the field of school counseling has moved from a largely reactionary position to a proactive one of designing, implementing, and evaluating comprehensive school counseling programs, the school counselor's role with students with disabilities has been somewhat neglected. We know that school counselors often serve students with disabilities, especially students with learning disabilities and behavioral disorders. It appears that the role of the school counselor, in supporting students with disabilities, is probably as varied as the students with disabilities themselves. Allowing motivated school counselors a myriad of opportunities to tap into individual interests and strengths would improve their practice with students with disabilities; however, there does not appear to be any large-scale, focused movement within the field to advance theory, research, and practice with this population.

In this chapter, we have reviewed three important theories—(a) adjustment to disability, (b) self-determination, and (c) Social Cognitive Career Theory (SCCT)—all of which are excellent starting points for expanding one's knowledge about the experience of students with disabilities and their families. We have also reviewed examples of interpersonal counseling, group counseling, and classroom guidance activities that may be useful for enhancing the academic success of students with disabilities. In each of these areas, school counselors must learn to be advocates for students with disabilities and their families. The school counselor may be the one educational staff member who is knowledgeable about the psychosocial, as well as educational, aspects of the disability. Consequently, the school counselor may also be the only educational staff member who possesses the interpersonal counseling skills to assist all parties to negotiate a successful educational experience for the student.

Recommendations for Research

Counseling and consultation. As in all areas of school counseling practice, school counselors must collect evidence about the interventions they provide to evaluate their efficacy as well as promote their role within their schools. Since there is little research on school counseling practice and students with disabilities, recommendations for future research are very broad.

Based on the theories reviewed in this chapter, studies that address interventions that increase self-knowledge, self-esteem, self-efficacy, or self-determination in students with disabilities are critical. Special educators should not be expected to provide these interventions alone, and since we know that students with disabilities who possess self-knowledge, self-esteem, and self-determination have better adult outcomes, school counselors need to become active players in delivering these services and programs.

Furthermore, Benz et al. (2000) contended that while the standard-based school reform efforts of the past decade include many crucial benefits for special education students, "the achievement of academic skills alone is insufficient for improving post-school outcomes in continuing education, employment, and independent living" (p. 526). In addition to academic skills, students with disabilities must also have knowledge and skills in key transition content areas (e.g., independent living, careers, personal/social arenas), awareness of their own interests and abilities in order to match those to job opportunities, and the skills necessary to pursue vocational postsecondary educational and training goals.

Finally, given the current climate of educational reform and high-stakes assessment, the demand for school counselors to become experts at enhancing individual student's academic capabilities is ever increasing. Students with disabilities face especially difficult odds of passing classes—not to mention high-stakes exams—depending on the nature of their impairment. In the last 15 years, little has been written in the school counseling literature about the efficacy of study skills or specific academic interventions, making this an area appropriate for future research.

School counselor preparation. Whether addressed in stand-alone courses or integrated into core counseling courses, the following topics are important to cover in school counselor preparation: disability legislation, general characteristics, common cognitive issues, psychosocial issues, individualized education programs, effective counseling interventions, and transition planning (Milsom & Akos, 2003). One goal for school counseling educators would be to move beyond general knowledge of various disabilities and competence in dealing with students with disabilities and their parents and toward more familiarity with relevant legislation and the role of school counselors in implementing legislation (Wood Dunn & Baker, 2002). In addition, we concur with Milsom and Akos' observation that, "In a field that values practical experience, it seems that required, practical experiences with students with disabilities should merit more importance than school counselor education programs currently support" (p. 93). Both school counselors in training and professional school counselors can also obtain relevant knowledge through counseling workshops, consultation, supervision, current therapeutic literature, and community resources (Tarver-Behring & Spagna, 2004).

School counselor competencies. Just as other counseling specialties (e.g., counseling psychology and rehabilitation counseling) have developed essential components for multicultural counseling competence (e.g., Middleton et al., 2000; Sue, Arredondo, & McDavis, 1992), we propose that school counseling explore and develop the essential components of school counselor competence. We would expect that school counselor competencies would encapsulates the culturally relevant and effective intervention strategies for working with underrepresented student populations including students with disabilities.

Subsequent to the seminal work of the other counseling specialties, it would be essential for school counselors to consider the domains of beliefs and attitudes, knowledge, and skills. The following are examples of the types of considerations regarding students with disabilities that should be considered when developing the school counselor competencies. School counselors must assess their own beliefs and attitudes about the experience of disability, especially their "tendencies toward overidentification or paternalistic attitudes and the impact of these on" students with disabilities (Middleton et al., 2000, p. 226). In terms of knowledge, school counselors would need to be knowledgeable about not only diagnostic criteria, but also the psychosocial, and sociopolitical ramifications of the various types of disabilities. Furthermore, school counselors must be aware of how their own biases about specific disabilities may impact their practice (e.g., efforts to identify strengths, advocate for services, access to community resources). Lastly, we have identified a variety of specific counseling and advocacy related skills that effective school counselors should possess when working with students with disabilities. School counselors must continue to employ evidenced based interventions with all populations, especially those from underrepresented populations.

References

Abreu, J. M. (2001). Theory and research on stereotypes and perceptual bias: A didactic resource for multicultural counseling trainers. *The Counseling Psychologist, 29*, 487–512.

Agran, M. (1997). Teaching self-management. In M. Agran (Ed.), *Student directed learning: Teaching self-determination skills* (pp. xi–27). Pacific Grove, CA: Brooks/Cole.

American School Counselor Association. (2000). *The professional school counselor and attention deficit/hyperactivity disorder* (ADHD). Retrieved May 31, 2005, from http://www.schoolcounselor.org

American School Counseling Association. (2003). *The ASCA National Model: A Framework for School Counseling Programs*. Alexandria, VA: Author.

American School Counselor Association. (2004). *The professional school counselor and the special needs student*. Retrieved September 12, 2007, from http://www.schoolcounselor.org

Bandura, A. (1986). *Social foundations of thought and action: A socialc ognitive theory*. Englewood Cliffs, NJ: Prentice-Hall.

Bemak, F., & Chung, R. C. (2005). Advocacy as a critical role for urban school counselors: Working toward equity and social justice. *Professional School Counseling, 8*, 196–202.

Benz, M. R., Lindstrom, L., & Yovanoff, P. (2000). Improving graduation and employment outcomes of students with disabilities: Predictive factors and student perspectives. *Exceptional Children, 66*, 509–529.

Bergin, J. W., & Bergin J. J. (2001). Counseling children with learning disabilities. In D. Sandhu (Ed.), *Elementary school counseling in the new millennium* (pp. 183–191). Alexandria, VA: American Counseling Association.

Blackbourn, J. M., Patton, J. R., & Trainor, A. (2004). *Exceptional individuals in focus*. Upper Saddle River, NJ: Pearson Prentice Hall.

Blalock, G., & Patton, J. R. (1996). Transition and students with learning disabilities: Creating sound futures. *Journal of Learning Disabilities, 29*, 7–16.

Boscardin, M. L., Brown-Chidsey, R., & Gonzalez-Martinez, J. C. (2003). Counseling approaches to working with students with disabilities from diverse backgrounds. In P. B. Pedersen & J. C. Carey (Eds.), *Multicultural counseling in schools* (pp. 257–269). Boston: Allyn & Bacon.

Bowen, M. L., & Glenn, E. E. (1998). Counseling interventions for students who have mild disabilities. *Professional School Counseling, 2*(1), 16–25.

Campbell, C. (1993). Strategies for reducing parent resistance to consultation in the schools. *Elementary School Guidance and Counseling, 28*, 83–91.

CICHCY (National Dissemination Center for Children with Disabilities). (2002). General information about disabilities. Retrieved October 3, 2007, from http://www.nichcy.org/pubs/genresc/gr3.htm#categories

Conyers, L., & Szymanski, E. M. (1998). The effectiveness of an integrated career intervention on college students with and without disabilities. *Journal of Postsecondary Education and Disability, 13*, 23–34.

Council of Administrators of Special Education. (1999). *Section 504 and the ADA Promoting Student Access: A Resource Guide for Educators*. Fort Valley, GA: Author.

Coutinho, M. J., & Oswald, D. P. (2000). Disporportionate representation in special education: A synthesis and recommendations. *Journal of Child and Family Studies, 9*(2), 135–156.

Deci, E. L., & Ryan, R. M. (1985). *Intrinsic motivation and self-determination in human behavior*. New York: Plenum.

Eagly, A. H., & Kite, M. E. (1987). Are stereotypes of nationalities applied to both men and women? *Journal of Personality and Social Psychology, 53*, 451–462.

Education for All Handicapped Children Act of 1975, PL 94-142, 20 USC §§ 1401 et seq.

Fabian, S., & Liesener, J. J. (2005). Promoting the career potential of youth with disabilities. In S. D. Brown & R. W. Lent (Eds.), *Career development and counseling: Putting theory and research to work* (pp. 551–572). Hoboken, NJ: John Wiley & Sons.

Field, S., & Hoffman, A. (1994). Development of a model for self-determination. *Career Development for Exceptional Individuals, 17*, 159–169.

Field, S., & Hoffman, A. (2002). Quality indicators of school environments that promote the acquisition of knowledge, skills, and beliefs related to self-determination. *Journal of Disability Policy Studies, 13*, 113–118.

Fine, M. J., & Gardner, P. A. (1991). Counseling and education services for families: An empowerment perspective. *Elementary School Guidance & Counseling, 26*, 33–44.

Ford, D. Y. (1998). The underrepresentation of minority students in gifted education: Problems and promises in recruitment and retention. *The Journal of Special Education, 32*(1), 4–14.

Gerber, P. J., Ginsberg, R., & Reiff, H. B. (1992). Identifying alterable patterns in employment success for highly successful adults with learning disabilities. *Journal of Learning Disabilities, 25*, 475–487.

Goldstein, S. B. (1997). The power of stereotypes: A labeling exercise. *Teaching of Psychology, 24*, 256–258.

Gray, C. A. (1994). *Comic strip conversations: Illustrated interactions that teach conversation skills to students with autism and related disorders*. Arlington, TX: Future Horizons.

Greenberg, M. T., Kusché, C., & Mihalic, S. F. (1998). *Blueprints for violence prevention, book ten: Promoting alternative thinking strategies (PATHS)*. Boulder, CO: Center for the Study and Prevention of Violence.

Greenwald, A. G., Banaji, M., Nosek, B., & Bhaskar, R. (1998). *Implicit association test.* Retrieved October 10, 2005, from http://depts.washington.edu/iat/

Greenwald, A. G., McGhee, D. E., & Schwartz, L. K. (1998). Measuring individual differences in implicit cognition: The implicit association test. *Journal of Personality and Social Psychology, 74,* 1464–1480.

Greer, B. B., Greer, J. G., & Woody, D. E. (1995). The inclusion movement and its impact on counselors. *The School Counselor, 43,* 124–131.

Gresham, F. M., Sugai, G., & Horner, R. (2001). Interpreting outcomes of socials skills training for students with high-incidence disabilities. *Exceptional Children, 67*(3), 331–334.

Gysbers, N. C., & Henderson, P. (1994). Developing and managing your school guidance program (2nd ed.). Alexandria, VA: American Counseling Association.

Harry, B. (1997). Leaning forward or bending over backwards: Cultural reciprocity in working with families. *Journal of Early Intervention, 21,* 62–72.

Heyward, S. M. (1992). *Access to education for the disabled: A guide to compliance of Section 504 of the Rehabilitation Act of 1973.* Jefferson, NC: McFarland & Company.

Hoffman, A. (2003). *Teaching decision making to students with learning disabilities by promoting self-determination* (Report No. EDO-03-7). Arlington, VA: ERIC Clearinghouse on Disabilities and Gifted Education. (ERIC Document Reproduction Service No. ED481859).

Hughes, C., Bogseon, H., Kim, J., Killian, D. J., Harmer, M. L., & Alcantara, P. R. (1997). A preliminary validation of strategies that support the transition from school to adult life. *Career Development for Exceptional Individuals, 20,* 1–14.

Katz, L, McClellan, D. E., Fuller, J. O., & Walz, G. R. (1995). Building social competence in children: A practical handbook for counselors, psychologists and teachers. Austin, TX: *Pro-Ed,* Inc.

Kinnison, L. R., Fuson, S., & Cates, D. (2005). Rural transitions: What are the limitations? *Rural Special Education Quarterly, 24,* 30–34.

Kohler, P. D. (1993). Best practices in transition: Substantiated or implied? *Career Development for Exceptional Individuals, 16,* 107–121.

Lent, R. W. (2005). A social cognitive view of career development and counseling. In S. D. Brown & R. W. Lent (Eds.), *Career development and counseling: Putting theory and research to work* (pp. 101–127). Hoboken, NJ: John Wiley & Sons.

Livneh, H. (1986). A unified approach to existing models of adaptation to disability-II. *Journal of Applied Rehabilitation Counseling, 17*(2), 6–10.

Livneh, H., & Antonak, R. (1997). *Psychosocial adaptation to chronic illness and disability.* Gaithersburg, MD: Aspen.

Lockhart, E. J. (2003). Students with disabilities. In B. T. Erford (Ed.), *Transforming the school counseling profession* (pp. 357–409). Upper Saddle River, NJ: Pearson Education.

Middleton, R. A., Rollins, C. W., Sanderson, P. L., Leung, P., Harley, D., & Ebener, D., et al. (2000). Endorsement of professional multicultural rehabilitation competencies and standards: A call to action. *Rehabilitation Counseling Bulletin, 43,* 219–240.

Milsom, A. (2002). Students with disabilities: School counselor involvement and preparation. *Professional School Counseling, 5,* 331–338.

Milsom, A., & Akos, P. (2003). Preparing school counselors to work with students with disabilities. *Counselor Education & Supervision, 43,* 86–95.

Milson, A., & Hartley, M. T. (2005). Assisting students with learning disabilities transitioning to college: What school counselors should know. *Professional School Counseling, 8,* 436–441.

Ochs, L. A., & Roessler, R. T. (2001). Students with disabilities: How ready are they for the 21st century? *Rehabilitation Counseling Bulletin, 44,* 170–176.

Ochs, L. A., & Roessler, R. T. (2004). Predictors of career exploration intentions: A Social Cognitive Career Theory perspective, *Rehabilitation Counseling Bulletin, 47,* 224–233.

Paganos, R. J., & DuBois, D. C. (1999). Career self-efficacy development and students with learning disabilities. *Learning Disabilities Research and Practice, 4*(1), 25–34.

Phelps, L. A., & Hanley-Maxwell, C. (1997). School-to-work transitions for youth with disabilities: A review of outcomes and practices. *Review of Educational Research, 67,* 197–226.

Pierson, M. R., & Glaeser, B. C. (2005). Extension of research on social skills training using comic strip conversations to students without autism. *Education and Training in Developmental Disabilities, 40,* 279–284.

Reiff, H. B., Gerber, P. J., & Ginsberg, R. (1997). *Exceeding expectations: Successful adults with learning disabilities.* Austin, TX: PRO-ED, Inc.

Remley, T. P., Jr., Hermann, M. A., & Huey, W. C. (2003). *Ethical and legal issues in school counseling.* Alexandria, VA: American School Counseling Association.

Roessler, R. T., & Bolton, B. (1978). *Psychosocial adjustment to disability.* Baltimore: University Park Press.

Rousso, H., & Wehmeyer, M. L. (2001). *Double jeopardy: Addressing gender equity in special education services.* Albany, NY: State University of New York Press.

Sands, D. J., & Doll, B. (1996). Fostering self-determination is a developmental task. *Journal of Special Education, 30,* 58–76.

Shontz, F. C. (1975). *The psychological aspects of physical illness and disability.* New York: Macmillan.

Siller, J. (1976). Psychological aspects of physical disability. In J. Meislin (Ed.), *Rehabilitation medicine and psychiatry* (pp. 455–484). Springfield, IL: C C Thomas.

Simeonsson, R. J., & Bailey, D. B. (1990). Family dimensions in early intervention. In S. J. Meisels & J. B. Shonkoff (Eds.), *Handbook of early childhood intervention* (pp. 428–444). Cambridge: Cambridge University Press.

Smart, J. (2001). *Disability, society, and the individual*. Gaithersburg, MD: Aspen.

Sowers, J. A., & Powers, L. (1995). Enhancing the participation and independence of students with severe physical and multiple disabilities in performing community activities. *Mental Retardation, 33*, 209–220.

Stowitschek, J., Laitinen, R., & Prather, T. (1999). Embedding early self-determination opportunities in curriculum for youth with developmental disabilities using natural teaching incidents. *Journal of Vocational Special Needs Education, 21*(2), 15–26.

Sue, D. W., Arredondo, P., & McDavis, R. J. (1992). Multicultural counseling competencies and standards. A call to the profession. *Journal of Counseling and Development, 70*, 477–786.

Swanson, H. L., & Malone, S. (1992). Social skills and learning disabilities: A meta-analysis of the literature. *School Psychology Review*, 21, 427–442.

Tarver-Behring, S., & Spagna, M. E. (2004). Counseling with exception children. In A. Vernon (Ed.). *Counseling children and adolescents* (pp. 189–226). Denver, CO: Love Publishing.

U.S. Department of Education. (2000). *Twenty-second annual report to Congress on the implementation of the Individuals with Disabilities Education Act*. Washington, DC: Author.

U.S. Department of Education. (2002). *Twenty-fourth annual report to Congress on the implementation of the Individuals with Disabilities Education Act*. Washington, DC: Author.

Ward, M. J. (1988). The many facets of self-determination. *Transition Summary, 5*, 2–3.

Wehmeyer, M. L. (1993). Perceptual and psychological factors in career decision-making of adolescents with and without cognitive disabilities. *Career Development for Exceptional Individuals, 16*, 135–146.

Wehmeyer, M. L. (1996). Self-determination as an educational outcome: Why is it important to children, youth and adults with disabilities? In D.J.Sands & M. L. Wehmeyer (Eds.), *Self-determination across the lifespam: Independence and choice for people with disabilities* (pp. 17-36). Baltimore: Paul H. Brookes Publishing Co.

Wehmeyer, M. L., Agran, M., & Hughes, C. (1998). *Teaching self-determination to students with disabilities: Basic skills for successful transition*. Baltimore, MD: Paul H. Brookes.

Wehmeyer, M. L., & Kelchner, K. (1995). *Whose future is it anyway? A student-directed transition planning process*. Arlington, TX: The Arc of the United States.

Wehmeyer, M. L., Kelchner, K., & Richards, S. (1996). Essential characteristics of self-determined behavior of individuals with mental retardation. *American Journal on Mental Retardation, 100*(6), 632–642.

Wehmeyer, M. L., & Lawrence, M. (1995). Whose future is it anyway: Promoting student involvement in transition planning. *Career Development for Exceptional Individuals, 18*(2), 69–83.

Wehmeyer, M. L., Sands, D. J., Doll, B., & Palmer, S. (1997). The development of self-determination and implications for educational interventions with students with disabilities. *International Journal of Disability, Development and Education, 44*, 305–328.

Wehmeyer, M. L., & Schwartz, M. (1997). Self-determination and positive adult outcomes: A follow-up study of youth with mental retardation or learning disabilities. *Exceptional Children, 63*(2), 245–255.

Wehmeyer, M. L., & Schwartz, M. (2001a). Disproportionate representation of males in special education services: Biology, behavior, or bias? *Education and Treatment of Children, 24*, 28–45.

Wehmeyer, M. L., & Schwartz, M. (2001b). Research on gender bias in special education services. In H. Rousso & M. L. Wehmeyer (Eds.), *Double jeopardy: Addressing gender equity in special education* (pp. 271–287). Albany: State University of New York.

Weissberg, R. P., Caplan, M., & Harwood, R. L. (1991). Promoting competent young people in competence-enhancing environments. *Journal of Consulting and Clinical Psychology, 59*, 830–841.

Whiston, S. C., & Sexton, T. L. (1998). A review of school counseling outcome research: Implications for practice. *Journal of Counseling and Development, 76*, 412–426.

Whitney-Thomas, J., & Moloney, M. (2001). Who I am and what I want: Adolescents' self-definition and struggles. *Exceptional Children, 67*, 357–389.

Willis, S. (2002). *The relationship of social cognitive variables to outcomes among young adults with emotional disturbance*. Unpublished doctoral dissertation, University of Maryland, College Park.

Wood Dunn, N. A., & Baker, S. B. (2002). Readiness to serve students with disabilities: A survey of elementary school counselors. *Professional School Counseling, 5*, 277–284.

Wright, B. A. (1983). *Physical disability—A psychosocial approach* (2nd ed.). New York: Harper & Row.

Appendix A. Federal Definitions of Disabilities Qualifying for Special Education and Related Services (IDEA 1997, 20 U.S.C. 1401(3)(A) and (B); 1401(26)) (NICHC), 2002).

Federal Definitions of Disabilities Qualifying for Special Education and Related Services

Specific Learning Disability

- General. The term means a disorder in one or more of the basic psychological processes involved in understanding or in using language, spoken or written, that may manifest itself in an imperfect ability to listen, think, speak, read, write, spell, or to do mathematical calculations, including conditions such as perceptual disabilities, brain injury, minimal brain dysfunction, dyslexia, and developmental aphasia.
- Disorders not included. The term does not include learning problems that are primarily the result of visual, hearing, or motor disabilities, of mental retardation, of emotional disturbance, or of environmental, cultural, or economic disadvantage.

Speech or Language Impairment

- A communication disorder, such as stuttering, impaired articulation, a language impairment, or a voice impairment, that adversely affects a child's educational performance

Mental Retardation

- Significantly subaverage general intellectual functioning, existing concurrently with deficits in adaptive behavior and manifested during the developmental period, that adversely affects a child's educational performance.

Emotional Disturbance

- The term means a condition exhibiting one or more of the following characteristics over a long period of time and to a marked degree that adversely affects a child's educational performance:
  - an inability to learn that cannot be explained by intellectual, sensory, or health factors.
  - an inability to build or maintain satisfactory interpersonal relationships with peers and teachers.
  - inappropriate types of behavior or feelings under normal circumstances.
  - a general pervasive mood of unhappiness or depression.
  - a tendency to develop physical symptoms or fears associated with personal or school problems.
- The term includes schizophrenia. The term does not apply to children who are socially maladjusted, unless it is determined that they have an emotional disturbance.

Multiple Disabilities

- Concomitant impairments (such as mental retardation-blindness, mental retardation-orthopedic impairment, etc.), the combination of which causes such severe educational needs that they cannot be accommodated in special education programs solely for one of the impairments. The term does not include deaf-blindness.

Hearing Impairment

- An impairment in hearing, whether permanent or fluctuating, that adversely affects a child's educational performance but that is not included under the definition of deafness.

Deafness

- A hearing impairment that is so severe that the child is impaired in processing linguistic information through hearing, with or without amplification, that adversely affects a child's educational performance.

Orthopedic Impairment

- A severe orthopedic impairment that adversely affects a child's educational performance. The term includes impairments caused by congenital anomaly (e.g., clubfoot, absence of some member, etc.), impairments caused by disease (e.g., poliomyelitis, bone tuberculosis, etc.), and impairments from other causes (e.g., cerebral palsy, amputations, and fractures or burns that cause contractures).

Other Health Impairment

- Having limited strength, vitality or alertness, including a heightened alertness to environmental stimuli, that results in limited alertness with respect to the educational environment, that is:
  - due to chronic or acute health problems such as asthma, attention deficit disorder or attention deficit hyperactivity disorder, diabetes, epilepsy, a heart condition, hemophilia, lead poisoning, leukemia, nephritis, rheumatic fever, and sickle cell anemia; and
  - adversely affects a child's educational performance

Visual impairment

- Including blindness means an impairment in vision that, even with correction, adversely affects a child's educational performance. The term includes both partial sight and blindness.

Autism

- A developmental disability significantly affecting verbal and nonverbal communication and social interaction, generally evident before age 3, that adversely affects a child's educational performance. Other characteristics often associated with autism are engagement in repetitive activities and stereotyped movements, resistance to environmental change or change in daily routines, and unusual responses to sensory experiences. The term does not apply if a child's educational performance is adversely affected primarily because the child has an emotional disturbance.
- A child who manifests the characteristics of "autism" after age 3 could be diagnosed as having "autism" if the criteria in paragraph (c)(1)(i) of this section are satisfied.

Deaf–Blindness

- Concomitant hearing and visual impairments, the combination of which causes such severe communication and other developmental and educational needs that they cannot be accommodated in special education programs solely for children with deafness or children with blindness.

Traumatic Brain Injury

- An acquired injury to the brain caused by an external physical force, resulting in total or partial functional disability or psychosocial impairment, or both, that adversely affects a child's educational performance.
- The term applies to open or closed head injuries resulting in impairments in one or more areas, such as cognition; language; memory; attention; reasoning; abstract thinking; judgment; problem-solving; sensory, perceptual, and motor abilities; psychosocial behavior; physical functions; information processing; and speech.
- The term does not apply to brain injuries that are congenital or degenerative, or to brain injuries induced by birth trauma.

XIII
RACE AND ETHNICITY IN SCHOOL COUNSELING

MARIE L. MIVILLE
Teachers College, Columbia University

Let there be no misunderstanding about this, no easy going recognition. We are not going to share modern civilization just by deserving recognition. We are going to force ourselves in by organized far-seeing effort—by outthinking and outflanking the owners of the world today . . . if we think and learn and do.

(W. E. B. Dubois, 1930, cited in Butchart, 1988, p. 333)

Educators recently celebrated the 50th anniversary of the *Brown vs. Board of Education* decision mandating desegregation of public schools in the United States and opening access to educational resources for children and youth of color. Yet today, students of color, particularly those who are African American, Latina/o, and American Indian, continue to lag far behind White students on many educational milestones. For example, the overall graduation rate of all high school students in the United States is approximately 75%, but hovers around 50% for these three racial/ethnic groups (Orfield, Losen, Wald, & Swanson, 2004). Indeed, as one author noted, the graduation rates of many students of color have "the same odds as flipping a coin" (Swanson, 2004, p. 1). Moreover, recent statistics indicate that most students of color are attending schools that (a) are increasingly segregated, (b) are located in urban settings, (c) often lack basic materials, such as updated books and clean facilities, and (d) utilize rote forms of learning not found in other school settings (Kozol, 2005). In short, the United States is at risk of losing half of its minority youth from the educational pipeline.

Although highly challenging, the roles school counselors can play in helping to mitigate the crisis of educational equity are multilayered, long-term, and potentially effective. At a minimum, school counselors must recognize the impact that the societal forces of racism and ethnocentrism have on school systems serving children and adolescents of color. As D. W. Sue (2003) noted,

> It is probably fair to say that our school systems have done a poor job in educating our students to understand issues of diversity, cultural differences, bias, and prejudice because the curriculum and services are monocultural and ethnocentric in nature. (Pedersen & Carey, 2003, p. ix)

Thus, school counselors must be prepared for the urgent social realities present in their schools that will affect the efficacy of any interventions they may attempt with racially and ethnically diverse students.

In this chapter, I will provide a brief overview of some of the significant historical events and issues relevant to race and ethnicity in school settings, particularly for school counseling. I also will review theory, research, and practice initiatives centered on race and ethnicity issues for school counseling. Despite the dire state of education for many students of color, I will emphasize primarily successful approaches that school counselors might adopt, rather than ineffective ones (Garcia, 2001). Success stories about individuals, programs, and school settings will be described throughout the chapter in the hope of providing guidance as to how school counselors might be able to conceptualize, intervene, and evaluate the effectiveness of their work with students of color and others, such as families, teachers, and school administrators.

Although the terms *race* and *ethnicity* are often used interchangeably, they refer to distinct constructs. The term *race* refers to a social construct used to identify individuals based on their presumed biological makeup (e.g., Caucasian,

Asian; Helms, 1990). Visible physical characteristics commonly used to identify racial group membership include skin color, hair type and color, eye color, head shape and size, and facial features. Although the construct of race has been debunked regarding its genetic bases (Zuckerman, 1990), the term nevertheless refers to a form of demographic categorization that continues to profoundly affect many levels of society, including social policies, educational interventions, and psychological functioning, in powerful yet sometimes invisible ways. The term *ethnicity* has been defined very broadly to include physical characteristics: "groups defined by descent, real or mythical, and sharing a common history and experience" (Glazer, 1971, p. 447). In this chapter, however, I use a more narrow definition: "a group classification of individuals who share a unique social and cultural heritage (customs, language, religion, and so on) passed on from generation to generation" (Casas, 1984, as cited in Helms, 1990, p. 4). Examples of ethnic group membership include Mexican, Ethiopian, and French.

There are often strong interactions between race and ethnicity, such that the impact of oppression arising from racism and ethnocentrism may be commingled. My chapter will examine the unique impact of race and ethnicity as well as their nexus for students of color traditionally underrepresented in, or as some might argue "pushed out" of, school systems, including African Americans, Latinas/os, American Indians, and newly immigrated students (Swanson, 2004).

History of Race and Ethnicity Issues in Schools and School Counseling

As noted at the beginning of the chapter, the inclusion of students in school systems from diverse racial and ethnic backgrounds is relatively recent. Generations of legal and educational scholars fought for this right to educational access for people of color. Butchart (1988) described the importance of this process of inclusion:

> W. E. B. DuBois once argued that the proper education for oppressed groups such as African Americans had a special, critical purpose. He knew, as have all serious educators since Socrates accepted his cup, that education was always and everywhere political. For the oppressed, the political role of schooling had to be aimed precisely at finding the means to end the oppression. (p. 333)

Butchart further noted that the purpose of knowing history is to "provide a guide to action." Telling stories of what came before helps create a better understanding of the stories of today.

The end of the Civil War in the 1860s and the freedmen's educational movement led to free public schooling in the South, but at the same time, a focus on "industrial education" rather than progressive or liberal education for many Black school children (Butchart, 1988). Throughout the 19th century and well into the 20th century, state laws existed that systematically excluded or separated children and adolescents of African American, Latina/o (particularly Mexican), and American Indian heritage from mainstream schools. Not only were these students segregated, school systems who served these children often were hostile to their cultural values, customs, and native languages. Lomawaima (1994) poignantly described the experiences of American Indian children who attended an Oklahoma boarding school created to assimilate students into the mainstream. While the reported experiences of these youth were demoralizing and harmful, many students learned to bond together and develop an American Indian identity as well as reinforce their tribal affiliations. Del Castillo (cited in San Miguel, 1986) argued that the educational experiences of many Chicana/o students in the late 1800s and early 1900s were so negative that these students felt encouraged to leave school before completing their elementary education. This trend continues today. Latinas/os continue to have the highest dropout rates from high school of any racial–ethnic group in the United States (Pew Hispanic Center, 2004).

Sadly, the role that many school counselors played throughout this history is seemingly undocumented, and there are no publications regarding this topic. For example, a recent review of the history of school counseling (Gysbers, 2001) described the beginnings of the profession in the late 1800s as "a response to the economic, educational, and social problems of those times" (p. 97); however, social problems were described as referring more to child labor issues, rather than issues of racial and ethnic discrimination. Paisley and Borders (1995) implied the importance of race and ethnicity in their recent description of the evolution of school counseling as moving from "vocational and educational decision making, to personal growth, responsive services for special 'at-risk' populations, [and] to developmental programs" (p. 150), but they do not describe specific or unique historical issues related to this topic. In their review of recent trends in school counseling journals, Bauman et al. (2003) noted that articles with a multicultural focus went from 2% of all publications in the 1950s to 13% in the 2000s, indicating increased interest by the profession in race and ethnicity. Bauman et al. suggested that perhaps this increase was driven by recently revised Council for Accreditation of Counseling and Related Educational Programs (CACREP) standards that more directly incorporate these issues. Moreover, the American School Counselor Association (ASCA) developed a model training program that "focuses on equitable access of direct services to all students" (Fusick & Bordeau, 2004, p. 103). Paisley and McMahon (2001) identified increasingly diverse student populations as one of the major challenges currently facing school counseling. Green and Keys (2001), however, contended that although the profession of school counseling has no doubt evolved to be more in line with student needs, effective developmental strategies are still lacking, particularly for students of color.

One might infer from readings of educational histories, as well as from individual anecdotes, that despite the founding principles of the profession, many school counselors may have played a role, albeit unintentionally, of supporting the status quo of segregation and helping to deny students of color access to the educational pipeline. Like others in the school system, such as teachers and principals, some school counselors likely communicated their biases in a variety of ways, both overt and covert, for example, by having low expectations regarding the potential achievement of students of color. Over the past few generations, many students of color have shared the oft-told tale of segregation's more modern form, tracking, where disproportionately larger ratios of youth of color were placed into special education classes and other low-achieving or compensatory curricula (Herring, 1997). In support of this contention, Green and Keys (2001) recently critiqued traditional models of school counseling as providing insufficient focus on the social contexts in which development occurs, thereby neglecting to incorporate the many unique struggles that students of color must negotiate in their schools.

Theory

Although theories of counseling have existed since the beginning of the field, applications of these theories with racially and ethnically diverse students have been only recently introduced. A key issue of counseling theories as they relate to school counseling is how they help counselors conceptualize students regarding the nature of growth and development, maladaptive behaviors, and intervention techniques (Stone & Bradley, 1994). Although any theory potentially might be useful in conceptualizing and intervening with children and youth of color, a number of theoretical approaches have been found to be particularly effective in working with these populations. Some examples include racial and ethnic identity development models, cognitive–behavioral strategies, and ecological systems approaches for both families and schools. All of these approaches will be reviewed to highlight their emphases and potential for effective interventions.

Racial and Ethnic Identity Development Theory

For more than twenty years, counselors and psychologists have proposed that educational achievement is linked to how students see themselves as racial and ethnic beings. In a seminal paper, Fordham and Ogbu (1986) argued that due to the history of racial discrimination and segregation, many people of color, particularly African Americans, distrust school systems and are skeptical of these institutions' commitment and ability to educate them, resulting in conflict and ambivalence about seeking an education as well as poorer school performance. Part of this ambivalence comes from societal pressure that many students of color may feel to conform to White cultural norms in order to succeed in school ("acting White"). Social sanctions exist for those African American students who attempt to assimilate to White norms and behaviors (e.g., speaking Standard English) as a strategy for academic success. "Acting White" is viewed by many African American community members as a denial and potential loss of Black identity:

> When I encounter a group of Blacks on the street in my home community, I can't go up to them and say, "Good afternoon, gentlemen. How are you doing today?' (i.e., greet them in Standard English). They would laugh at me and then feel sorry for me. They'd think, "Poor Charles, when he left here for college, he was OK (That is, he talked appropriately like us and maintained his Black identity). But now look what they've done (i.e., White people or White educational institutions) to him!" (i.e., he has learned to "talk proper or "act White"). (Ogbu, 2004, p. 25)

It is important to understand, however, that it is not school success itself that garners criticism from others, but rather assimilation to White ways of thought, speech, and action (Ogbu & Simons, 1994). That is, many African Americans and other people of color do not view making good grades negatively, but instead are critical of speaking Standard English, acting smart during lessons, and having many White friends (Ogbu & Simons, 1998).

Fordham (1991) further asserted that in most school systems, both public and private, "a strong separation of 'I from us' and 'me from thee' is not only expected but deemed absolutely essential for academic success . . . [this represents] an inversion of fictive kinship in the Black community" (p. 473), which celebrates the group or collective rather than the individual: "A striking feature of the African American Self is members' unilateral focus on density in their interactions, [incorporating] a broad, detailed knowledge of community participants" (p. 472). Black youth are thus faced with a difficult—even impossible—choice between academic success and maintaining affinity with their communities. Indeed, Fordham reports that although many African American youth in private school settings may obtain excellent academic skills, the most important lesson learned may be "enduring the unendurable." One student described this process:

> Each of the two cultures considered me a foreigner, one who did not belong. Where my allegiance resided was their [both cultures'] question. Neither world [the housing project nor the prep school] fully understood me because these two cultures almost never meet. (Fordham, 1991, p. 478)

Distancing self from Black communities has been shown to be linked with depression (Arroyo & Zigler, 1995). Moreover, Ogbu (2004) described a number of strategies Black students may use to mediate these conflictual choices, such as (a) assimilation to White ways accompanied by a loss of Black identity and relationships, (b) adoption of White ways without giving up their Black identity or language, (c) opposition to engaging in any form of "acting White," and (d) encapsulation, or becoming raceless. Black students who choose the first two strategies—although high achieving—risk feelings of alienation, depression, and anxiety. Those students who engage in the latter strategies likely value other forms of education or learning than those found in traditional school settings, but may be at risk of poorer academic performance and dropping out.

Arroyo and Zigler (1995) found support for the negative psychological impact of adopting "raceless" strategies in their three-study project composed of mostly White and African American high school students. Interestingly, they found that components of racelessness, such as impression management, among both White and African American students. The authors speculated that high-achieving students of any race or ethnicity often feel pressured to choose academics over peer relationships. However, Arroyo and Zigler found that depression was clearly linked with racelessness for African Americans, but not for White students. Further, raceless attitudes were linked with negative collective self-esteem for African American students; these students felt their racial group was negatively viewed by others and were less identified with being Black.

Osbourne (1997) investigated a related phenomenon: disidentification, the lack of relationship between academic self-esteem and general self-esteem, which results from negative experiences with school, presumably due to reasons of racism and discrimination. Osbourne found that although White high school students' general self-esteem was stable through all years, African Americans' self-esteem increased from eighth to tenth grade, then decreased in the 12th grade, as did their grades and achievement scores (their self-esteem scores, however, were higher than Whites' scores). Hispanics' self-esteem increased over time, but their grades decreased, also showing a disidentification trend, though in a different way. Correlations between grades and self-esteem dropped over time for both Hispanics and African Americans, the most dramatic being for African American boys. Interestingly, the main exception to these latter findings was Hispanic girls, whose self-esteem and grades were increasingly linked over time.

School counselors can have potentially impactful roles in helping students negotiate these identity issues, for example, providing advocacy within the school system regarding norms and expectations about what are the factors that lead to academic success. Another avenue may be to provide a supportive and safe space for students to acknowledge and share with each other about these dilemmas, either through individual counseling or student support groups.

Helms (2003) proposed another way to conceptualize the importance of racial and ethnic identity to school success for students of color. The people of color identity development model proposes that individuals do not react identically to conditions of discrimination or privilege, but develop various schemas or strategies for interpreting these experiences (e.g., conformity, dissonance, immersion/emersion, and internalization). These strategies may be marked by naiveté and denial (conformity); ambivalence and conflict (dissonance); anger, curiosity, and growth (immersion/emersion); and awareness and acceptance (internalization). A key aspect of these identity models is that individuals experience conflict regarding their racial and ethnic identities that result in a variety of identity resolutions (Miville, Koonce, Darlington, & Whitlock, 2000). Helms has suggested that school counselors and other educators need to be aware of how students are dealing with experiences of racism and the cognitive and behavioral strategies they have adopted to cope with these experiences. For example, students experiencing dissonance or immersion may feel a great deal of anger and frustration regarding the racial status quo in the school system. Rather than responding with fear or minimization, counselors may develop interventions that help students to divert this emotional energy into positive outlets, such as a candlelight march to raise awareness.

Some scholars suggest that racial identity may be an important focus in helping students of color succeed in school (Ford, Harris, & Schuerger, 1993). For example, Parham (1989, as cited in Ford et al.) described two issues along racial identity lines with which gifted students of color may struggle: (a) "self-differentiation versus preoccupation with assimilation" (p. 411) and (b) "ego-transcendence versus self-absorption" (p. 411). The former refers to the importance of valuing self regardless of negative messages from Whites and others in the environment, whereas the latter describes the importance of developing a sense of security about self in order to develop ego strength. Another way of describing these identity struggles is finding congruence with self and being freed of racial stereotypes imposed by others. School counselors also can teach students of color how to deal with feeling different from or inferior to both school and community members. The acknowledgement of these struggles by counselors is critical to helping students begin to cope with these feelings.

Thomas, Townsend, and Belgrave (2003) further suggested that racial identity issues might be integrated with Afrocentric values for a more effective conceptualization of ethnic identity for African American students, particularly those in low-income or inner-city-school settings. Afrocentric values refer to enduring cultural beliefs and practices of African Americans, including "a spiritual orientation, a deep sense of kinship and identification with the greater collective . . . , extended family structure as a social support network, and a philosophy of unity" (p. 219). Thomas et al. found that both racial identity and Afrocentric values were predictive of child–school adjustment, as measured by behavior control, school interest, teaching ratings of child problems and strengths. Moreover, racial identity and self-esteem were important mediators of the relationship of Afrocentric values and child–school adjustment. Afrocentric values and racial identity have also been found to be significant predictors of drug attitudes and use among African American students (Belgrave et al., 1994; Townsend & Belgrave, 2000). Further, racial identity has been a positive predictor of academic self-efficacy among African American eighth graders (Oyserman, Harrison, & Bybee, 2001).

Oyserman and her colleagues (Oyserman, Bybee, Terry, & Hart-Johnson, 2004; Oyserman, Gant, & Ager, 1995; Oyserman & Markus, 1990; Oyserman, Terry, & Bybee, 2002) also have conceptualized identity issues for students of color utilizing the construct of "possible selves." Oyserman et al. (1995) proposed that identity negotiation among youth of color "involves the dual task of assembling a positive sense of self while discrediting negative identities attributed to African American males and females" (p. 1217). Part of this identity negotiation involves visualizing hypothetical or possible selves across a number of dimensions, including academic and occupational areas. Possible selves are future-oriented and involve aspects of the self-concept that put self into action and motivate goal-oriented behavior; balancing of positive and negative selves is posited to lead to perseverance in tasks. Oyserman et al. (1995) asserted that it is critical that racial–ethnic identity incorporate achievement "within the context of being African American" (p. 1220). By doing so, students of color will not experience the tension between achieving academic success and embracing Black identity. Indeed, research shows that it is *both* awareness of racism and achievement as salient identity components that may be linked with better performance in math tasks, rather than either individual component. The construct of possible selves also is potentially useful in other ways for students of color. For example, Oyserman et al. (2004) found that having a possible self as a self-regulator was linked with better academic performance, doing homework, and class participation. Oyserman et al. (2002) described interventions based on developing a balance of possible selves to enhance school performance.

Although much theory and research on racial and ethnic identity has focused on African Americans, some research indicates that identity issues also are important to other students of color. For example, Rolon-Dow (2004) explored the construction of ethnic identity among Puerto Rican middle-school girls in the Northeastern United States. Rolon-Dow utilized Black feminist critiques in understanding the multiple ways in which schools and teachers may impose images on Latina girls. She found that teachers often viewed these girls as overly sexualized with their language and dress and, as a result, not educable or potentially successful in school. In other words, "the image of the hypersexual girl was cast in opposition to the image of an educable girl interested in her schooling endeavors" (p. 17). The girls also cast themselves within these restricted, either–or roles, with many adopting the stereotyped image for Puerto Rican girls associated with low success in schools. Rolon-Dow urged school personnel to examine the images and stereotypes both teachers and students may adopt, often unconsciously, that may determine the educational outcomes of these youth.

Ecological and Family Systems Approaches

Another fruitful area has been the incorporation of theoretical approaches that contextualize individual students within their multiple systems, such as families and schools. As McKenna, Roberts, and Woodfin (2003) noted, children belong to two substantive systems: families and schools. Thus, forging links between these two systems in viable and consistent ways is essential to the future success of students, particularly students of color. Partnerships between schools and families are viewed as so important that the U.S. Department of Education has made these a codified requirement of the National Education Goals (McKenna et al.). Indeed, there is a wealth of research indicating that the single best predictor of student achievement is parental involvement (Henderson & Berla, 1994). Given the issues of racism and discrimination as well as cultural values emphasizing familism and collectivism for many racial–ethnic groups, parental involvement becomes even more important for school systems to cultivate in order to increase success for students of color.

Most family systems theories conceptualize children as being nestled within at least three to four generations. Problems that occur (e.g., a student who misses school) are conceptualized as not attributable to the individual, but as a "representative of a system that is faulty" (Goldenberg & Goldenberg, 2000, p. 10). Thus, it is relationships—for example, between parents and teachers—that become the target of intervention. A likely outcome of these interventions is to change the system(s), for example, by opening up new lines of communication or changing communication patterns, with the ultimate goal of further strengthening the systems.

Tucker (1999) and Yeh (2004) further suggested that the ecological model of Bronfenbrenner (1979) helps conceptualize the multiple systems present in most students' lives. These systems include (a) microsystems, such as the family, school, and neighborhood; (b) mesosystems, involving relationships among various microsystems; (c) exosystems, other systems that affect microsystems, such as parental employment, and (d) macrosystems, involving the values and norms of the larger society. As noted at the beginning of the chapter, most students will be negatively affected by the history of racism and discrimination at the macrosystemic level. Green and Keys (2001) further stated that it is critical students "be given opportunities to enhance their awareness of the multiple contexts that impact their lives" (p. 89). For example, they noted that students are best helped when both families and schools are consistent in their expectations and messages regarding appropriate behavior.

Juntunen, Atkinson, and Tierney (2003) described the role of school counselors as being potential liaisons at the mesosystemic level of schools, families, and community agencies. Within this framework, school counselors may be able to address some of the barriers that prevent school and families from working together. Such barriers include differences in language abilities, educational and literacy levels, communication styles, emphases regarding time and attendance, miseducation on the part of school officials regarding culturally different but effective parenting styles, and racial–ethnic tensions within the school setting. Juntunen et al. described a number of roles school counselors could play that could bring potentially disparate elements of school and family systems together, such as cultural interpreter or broker, referral base, advocate, program developer, social model for respect and acceptance, and mediator.

The ways in which counselors and teachers reach out to families is a critical first step toward building a bridge between families and school systems. Gaitan (2004) described a number of strategies that likely will be effective in reaching out to parents of color. These include

- building on cultural background, knowing important cultural values and including extended family, such as grandparents, aunts and uncles, and even older siblings;
- developing personal contact with parents, such as positive interactions, small talk, phone calls, and home visits;
- fostering communication by taking the initiative, making information accessible, and sharing experiences;
- creating a welcome environment that is warm, empathic, and engaging; and
- developing structural accommodations, such as parent centers, parent teams, and parent advisory committees.

It is also important to establish bidirectional relationships, particularly in inviting parents to discuss their expertise in disciplining or supporting their children. Evidence exists demonstrating how effective parents of color can be in shaping their children's academic success. For example, Romo and Falbo (1996) found that Latino/a parents whose children had graduated from high school had utilized the following strategies:

- Used two-way influence between parent and child
- Set limits
- Monitored the student
- Limited contact with peers about whom they had concerns
- Maintained a continuous message to their children to stay in school
- Were involved in school

As noted earlier, focusing on effective family-oriented strategies is key to the eventual success of many students at risk of low school performance. School counselors can liaison with families regarding their methods and create parenting groups to help identify such strategies.

Cognitive–Behavioral Approaches

Another theoretical approach that has been effective regarding the academic success of students of color is the cognitive-behavioral approach. This approach emphasize the link between thoughts and behaviors, and that the means by which to change behaviors is to the change the thoughts underlying them. As Pajares (2002) noted, "the beliefs [or cognitions] . . . that individuals create and develop and hold to be true about themselves form the very foundation of human agency and are vital forces in their success or failure in all endeavors (school)" (p. 1). Beginning with

Bandura (1986), cognitive–behaviorists have maintained that individuals are self-organized and self-regulating, and that central to this organization are beliefs they hold about their capabilities, also known as "self-efficacy." Self-efficacy refers to beliefs about self regarding the ability to "organize and execute the courses of action required to manage prospective situations" (Pajares, 2002, p. 8).

Self-efficacy influences behaviors in several ways, including choices of tasks, level of effort, perseverance, and resilience in the face of adversity. Sources of self-efficacy include mastery experiences (success with a task raises self-efficacy, whereas failure diminishes self-efficacy); vicarious experiences, particularly with a respected model; social persuasion (i.e., messages from others); and physiological states, such as anxiety, stress, and fatigue (Pajares, 1997). Considerable evidence exists showing the importance of positive self-efficacy in specific academic skills and tasks such as writing, mathematics, and motivation levels (Pajares, 2001, 2003). Current research, although sparse, indicates that many students of color, particularly African Americans and Latinas/os, may have lower academic self-efficacy, despite having positive self-concepts (evaluations about self as a whole). Given that self-efficacy perceptions influence such broadly important aspects of academic performance as choice of task, effort, perseverance, and anxiety level, assessing and intervening with self-efficacy beliefs may prove helpful to identify with "at-risk" youth (Pajares, 2003). Some recent research (De Los Santos & Miville, 2005) shows promise regarding academic self-efficacy beliefs as significant predictors of academic performance among Latinas/os. De Los Santos and Miville also found that biculturalism was a significant predictor of academic self-efficacy, indicating that involvement with both Latina/o and Anglo cultures was linked with positive beliefs about self in the academic environment.

Tucker (1999) also has developed academic interventions for students of color based on cognitive–behavioral approaches. Her research indicates that such interventions are effective if they are adapted for populations of color. For example, Tucker suggested that replacement of cognitions or self-efficacy beliefs needs to occur in a way that utilizes communication styles of the cultures of origin. She also strongly emphasized that cognitive–behavioral interventions should be contextualized within a self-empowerment paradigm which "focuses on facilitating self-motivation for academic achievement, self-control of academic progress (e.g., self-instruction-based learning), self-praise of academic progress and success, skills for academic success, and academic success behaviors" (p. 226). Tucker asserted that a focus on self-empowering strategies prepares students of color to perceive and facilitate their own academic success, regardless of their learning situation. She described a number of strategies that students, teachers, and counselors might use to help children and youth develop self-empowering strategies.

Research

Research regarding students of color, particularly in the realm of school counseling, has been sparse (Yeh, 2004). By far, the area of primary emphasis has been the alarming dropout rates of students of color discussed earlier in the chapter. Although clearly there are historical underpinnings for these rates, empirical research also has focused on identifying variables that may lead to the dropout rates, or conversely, help to retain students. Some of this research has already been described, particularly racial-ethnic identity variables that may play a role in student–feeling alienated from, or more hopefully, embedded within their school settings. Other variables that have been explored include (a) stereotype threat; (b) acculturation and acculturative stress; (c) language issues, particularly for newly immigrated students; and (d) resiliency. Although it is beyond the scope of this chapter to review all research findings relevant to each of these variables, I will highlight important findings and discuss future directions in research for school counselors working with students of color.

Stereotype Threat

Steele and Aronson (1995) coined the phrase *stereotype threat* to refer to "being at risk of confirming, as self-characteristic, a negative stereotype about one's group" (p. 797). As Steele (1997) further illuminated,

> it is a situational threat—a threat in the air—that, in general form, can affect the members of any group about whom a negative stereotype exists. . . . Where bad stereotypes about these groups apply, members of the groups can fear being reduced to that stereotype. And for those who identify with the domain to which the stereotype is relevant, this predicament can be self-threatening. (p. 614)

Stereotype threat has important implications for the academic performance of students of color for which stereotypes regarding their academic abilities abound in overt and covert ways. These stereotypes exist over and beyond the identity struggles already described of cultural values or roles that may discourage young students of color from becoming part of the academic world (Fordham & Ogbu, 1986). In addition, as Steele has argued, for those students of color wishing to be successful in academia who are already stigmatized regarding their potential abilities, stereotype threat can further push students from incorporating academic success into their identities. Stereotype threat can occur to any social group member, including Whites and middle-class people, and is situation-dependent, such during as a math test. Individuals do not have to believe in the threat themselves in order to be affected by it (e.g., their performance diminished as result). Moreover, stereotype threat has the greatest impact on more confident or academically identified students because they still see themselves as part of this domain. In contrast, low-performing students already may have disidentified as "good students" and not even attempt academic tasks. Evidence exists (Aronson, 2002; Steele, Spencer, & Aronson, 2002) indicating that stereotype threat is a factor in the lowered performance of many social group members, including African Americans and Latinas/os, for a number of academic tasks, such as reading and mathematics exams and standardized tests, including the Scholastic Achievement Test (SAT).

Two factors may be at play regarding potential areas of intervention for stereotype threat: (a) evaluative scrutiny, which may be associated with decreased enjoyment of learning, increased stress and anxiety, and lowered performance, and (b) group composition of those taking a test. In a series of interesting studies, Aronson and his colleagues (Aronson, Fried, & Good, 2002; Good, Aronson, & Inzlicht, 2003) examined how students' beliefs in the malleability of intelligence (vs. beliefs of the inherent nature of their limited abilities, as based on race and ethnicity) might affect performance. They arranged for college students to mentor seventh graders who were mostly students of color from low-income backgrounds. The college students highlighted the notions that intelligence was changeable and that the difficulties the younger students were having were due to being in a new school setting. The students in the experimental condition involving mentoring scored significantly higher on standardized reading tests than those in a control group. These findings indicate that it is possible to mitigate the effects of stereotype threat, for example, with messages to counter the immutability of academic potential due to presumed racial or ethnic heritage.

Acculturation and Acculturative Stress

Numerous definitions and models of acculturation exist, some of which are based on a particular racial–ethnic group, such as Mexican Americans or American Indians, and others that focus on a general approach presumably applicable to any racial–ethnic group. Most models and definitions of acculturation focus on an interactive learning process between an individual and a dominant host culture or society, such as Anglo society in the United States (Coleman, 1995; Gloria & Rodriguez, 2000; Stephenson, 2000). Models of acculturation generally are based on the presumption that the interactive learning process necessarily occurs in a sociopolitical context (Berry, 1993) and provide the basis for understanding how individuals may cope with and develop differently from one another within this context.

Many acculturation models distinguish between transmission of cultural information that emanates from politically dominant or host cultural groups (what some scholars refer to as "second culture acquisition"; LaFromboise, Coleman, & Gerton, 1993), and transmission of cultural information that emanates from one's racial–ethnic group. LaFromboise et al. distinguished six strategies in which second culture acquisition may occur. The first three represent traditionally linear approaches—(a) assimilation, (b) acculturation, and (c) separation—in which individuals may either attempt to join the second culture (acculturation or assimilation) or withdraw from or avoid the second culture (separation; Coleman, Casali, & Wampold, 2001). More recent conceptualizations of second culture acquisition reflect integrative processes, where involvement in both cultures is presumed. In other words, immersion into both dominant and ethnic cultures may be orthogonal, rather than polarized, processes (Oetting & Beauvais, 1991). These strategies include (a) alternation, involving changing from one set of cultural behaviors to another, based on the situation; (b) integration conceptualization, in which individuals interact with culturally different others, but maintain their own cultural identity; and (c) fusion conceptualization, involving the development of a new culture from the fusion of two or more cultures. Most assessment instruments of acculturation attempt to determine participant levels of acculturation, assimilation, separation, alternation, fusion, and/or integration (Coleman et al., 2001).

Coleman (1995) proposed a model for better understanding acculturation strategies that highlights goals individuals wish to achieve in particular settings, such that "the context in which an individual is coping with cultural difference and the goals that individual wants to achieve in that context [e.g., school] will influence the individual's choice of strategy" (Coleman et al., 2001, p. 357). Coleman et al. further asserted that choice of strategy occurs sequentially and arises from "a series of choices, consciously or unconsciously, about how he or she wants to associate with the new and old cultures" (p. 358). The first choice involves whether to associate with more than one cultural group, followed by deciding the extent of association with these groups. Thus, Coleman and his colleagues suggest that choices regarding second culture acquisition depend upon individuals' socialization, the context in which second culture contact occurs, and the goals individuals are attempting within that context.

Acculturation processes are believed to shape critical aspects of psychological functioning, including core beliefs, choice of language, attitudes, and expectations of behaviors. Indeed, inconsistencies and conflicts between cultures are often a source of stress for many people (Gloria & Rodriguez, 2000; Kim & Abreu, 2001), including students of color. Other scholars (Garza & Gallegos, 1995), however, have noted that interactions between cultures can also have positive outcomes, including increased academic performance, psychological adjustment, and the development of leadership skills.

Research on the link between acculturation and academic performance is sparse but suggests that acculturation processes and choices may affect academic performance. Coleman and his colleagues (Coleman, 1995; Coleman et al., 2001; Hamm & Coleman, 2001), for example, found that adolescents' choices regarding second culture acquisition were indeed context-dependent. Moreover, African American adolescents were more likely to use separation strategies than their White counterparts. Coleman et al. suggested that students might use one set of second culture acquisition strategies in one setting, such as assimilation or acculturation in the classroom, and another set of strategies in another setting, such as separation in a social situation.

Other research indicates that the link of acculturation with academic performance is complex and often produces mixed effects. For example, Lopez, Ehly, and Garcia-Vasquez (2002) found that high school "students identified as highly integrated and strongly Anglo-oriented bicultural tended to have higher academic achievement" (p. 245). Chea (2003), however, found that Cambodian adolescents between the ages of 12 and 17 who adhered to their culture of origin did well academically. Further, Tencer Garrity (2003) found that bicultural Latina/o students in Illinois (third and fourth graders) did not have high self-esteem and high academic performance. Adams (2000), using structural equation modeling, found that among 266 Mexican-American elementary schoolchildren, generation and socioeconomic status (SES) influenced acculturation which, in turn, influenced learning preferences (cooperative learning) which then affected academic performance for traditional Mexican-American students. Finally, research on Native youth in Alaska revealed that performance in mathematics and science was significantly improved for students participating in a three-year cultural program, as compared with students who did not participate in the program (Demmert, 2001).

It is clear that a great deal of further research is needed to explore how acculturation processes might be linked with academic performance. Theory- or model-driven research may help better illuminate these complex findings. Moreover, exploring how second culture acquisition differs among various racial–ethnic groups, such as Latinas/os and African Americans might further untangle this relationship. Finally, exploring context or school setting in which students are placed (e.g., White-dominated or ethnic-group-oriented) may be a critical moderating variable in the relations of acculturation and academic performance.

Immigration Status and Language Abilities

Intermingled with acculturation issues are the impact of immigration status and students' language abilities, particularly for limited-English-proficient students, on academic performance. For example, among Latinas/os, the largest immigrant group in the United States today, immigration status is the strongest predictor of the dropout rate (Garcia, 2001). Further, although the United States is now the fourth largest Spanish-speaking nation in the world, most school systems are based on English language proficiency.

Since the 1960s, U.S. school systems have been receiving a large number of newly immigrated students of color, mostly from Latin America, Asia, and the Caribbean (Roysircar-Sodowsky & Frey, 2003). Little information is available on the needs and stressors concerning these children and adolescents, although some research exists for late adolescents and college students. Important variables to consider are whether students themselves are newly immigrated, whether they immigrated as children or as adolescents, or are whether they are children of immigrants. Each of these statuses may influence, for example, the racial–ethnic identity these children and youth adopt and the level of stress they may experience in the school systems. Immigrant status has also been linked with a number of psychological issues that, in turn, may affect academic performance, including acculturation, changes in family relationships, self-esteem, anxiety, depression, and stress (Roysircar-Sodowsky & Frey).

Research on the impact of immigrant status on academic performance indicates a number of stressors might impede success in schools for many newly immigrated students. A major stressor appears to be adjusting to culture shock, as well as developing new skills and competencies that will facilitate success in school (Bemak & Chung, 2003). Without these new skills and competencies, evidence demonstrates that students may reject school-appropriate norms and behaviors in an effort to maintain their native cultural background (Gibson, 1997). Adjustment involves not only learning a new language and different ways of studying (e.g., individualistically oriented tasks), but also learning to deal with issues of racism, ethnocentrism, and discrimination as students of color that they may not be accustomed to or socialized to withstand. Moreover, antischool attitudes predominant in some urban settings will need to be addressed by these youth and their families, hopefully with the help of school counselors, to prevent disidentification with school and dropout (Bemak & Chung, 2003). Unfortunately, very little research exists demonstrating effective strategies for helping immigrant students of color to negotiate struggles arising from acculturation, language differences, and preexisting conditions that also might diminish academic performance. Future research might examine the impact of each of these variables—as well as their combination—on children of varying immigration status, age, and race–ethnicity.

Language abilities also affect many students of color, both newly immigrated students as well as those coming from racial–ethnic backgrounds that emphasize maintenance of native languages as part of their heritage and identity, such as Latinas/os. Historically, bilingual abilities have been viewed as a handicap, rather than an asset, to the learning environment (Pearson, 2001). Indeed, for much of the 20th century, many educators believed that being bilingual actually slowed learning and diminished intelligence, rather than increased performance and cognitive complexity. Unfortunately, most studies between the late 1800s until the 1960s yielded findings linking bilingualism with lower academic performance; however, recent reviews of this research have revealed many were flawed in their methodologies, including their definitions of intelligence and sampling techniques (August & Hakuta, 1997; Hakuta & Garcia, 1989).

Biases toward bilingualism also have been reflected in public policies affecting school systems that serve bilingual students. For example, a landmark and progressive 1976 law passed in California enabling education programs for limited-English-proficient students framed the issue as a "language problem" to be solved by transitioning students from their native language into English, with an unfortunate outcome of prejudicing these students against their own languages (Gándara, 2001). In short, the legislated goals of bilingual program were to dispense with native languages as quickly as possible, in order that English might be learned.

Although bilingual education continues in many public schools, legislation in more recent years has reflected increasingly hostile attitudes toward providing funding emphasizing learning in school using any other language than English. The ongoing debate regarding bilingualism in the United States may be summarized this way: "Is bilingualism strictly the knowledge and usage of two linguistic systems, or does it involve the social dimensions encompassed by the languages?" (Hakuta & Garcia, 1989, p. 374). Hakuta and Garcia illustrated the complexities of these issues for limited-English-proficient students in the following statement of a recently immigrated Mexican 9th grader:

There is so much discrimination and hate. Even from other kids from Mexico who have been here longer. They don't treat us like brothers. They hate even more. It makes them feel more like natives. They want to be American. They don't want to speak Spanish to us. . . . If they're with us, other people will treat them more like wetbacks, so they try to avoid us. (p. 374)

In the face of strong criticism regarding the need for more effective programs targeting limited-English-proficient students, scholars today emphasize the potential positive impact of dual language learning (Calderon & Carreon, 2001). Recent research indicates that learning in a second language may actually facilitate cognitive functioning, particularly cognitive flexibility and metalinguistic awareness (August & Hakuta, 1997). More sophisticated research has revealed that language learning, whether first- or second-language, uses the same basic cognitive processes, and that learning dual languages "share[s] and build[s] upon a common underlying base rather than compete[s] for limited [cognitive] resources" (Hakuta & Garcia, 1989, p. 375).

A related issue concerning bilingualism refers to children and youth serving as language brokers for their parents, other family members, and other adults, such as school administrators. Often, as families transition into a new cultural setting, children become the first members to learn English, resulting in their serving as translators and interpreters for others. These youth are often placed in complex, adultlike situations and are called upon to utilize more sophisticated skills in language and social interactions than other peers their age do. In a recent review of literature on language brokering, Morales and Hanson (2005) found that the majority of immigrant children, particularly females, served as language brokers, sometimes beginning as young as eight years of age, and translated and interpreted in a variety of settings, including school. Findings have been mixed regarding the psychological impact of language brokering, ranging from feelings of pride to frustration and embarrassment.

Language brokering may facilitate cognitive development, including a more sophisticated vocabulary, higher cognitive abilities and better problem-solving abilities, as well as being able to switch languages across settings and roles (Buriel, Perez, De Ment, Chavez, & Moran, 1998). Due to the cognitive complexity required of these tasks, some scholars have proposed that language brokering may facilitate school performance. For example, Buriel et al. found that for 122 Latina/o adolescents, language brokering was positively related with academic performance, and feelings about language brokering were positively linked with academic self-efficacy. Orellana and Bowman (2003) also found that language brokering was linked with increased performance on standardized reading and math tests. However, some scholars warn that pressures associated with the role of language broker in the family may be linked with early dropout or restricting of academic goals. Further, risks of children being placed in more adult roles and settings (e.g., explaining serious medical test results to parents) might lead to traumatizing outcomes for some of these youth, if limits are not placed on their brokering responsibilities. In sum, Morales and Hanson (2005) encourage further research in this area, particularly the impact of language brokering on the social and cognitive development and academic performance of students of color.

Resiliency

In addition to examining the impact of potential barriers on the academic achievement of students of color, some scholars have begun to explore potential protective factors to help mitigate the impact of these barriers. Resiliency refers to "the capacity of an individual to overcome difficult and challenging life circumstances and risk factors" (Bryan, 2005, p. 220). In short, resiliency is the ability to continue in the face of adversity, either by drawing strength from rising up to challenges or by not being detracted by such challenges. Resiliency is a capacity that can be fostered in a number of ways, such as interactions with skilled others, meaningful participation in schools and communities, reasonably high expectations regarding student performance, and a positive self-concept (Bryan, 2005; Gordon, 1996). In a review of resiliency studies, Rak and Patterson (1996) found several types of protective factors that increased the resiliency of potentially at-risk children, including personal characteristics, family conditions, environmental supports, and self-concept factors. Crosnoe and Elder (2004), for example, found that supportive relationships with parents were significantly important in helping to promote academic achievement in high school students of color. They further found positive relationships with teachers were linked with better academic performance.

Gordon (1996) explored important differences among Hispanic youth, using a sample of 36 participants, characterized as resilient (n = 9) and nonresilient, drawn from a pool of 123 Hispanic high school sophomores. Students identified as resilient came from low SES and stressful backgrounds and had a relatively high GPA (2.75 or better); nonresilient youth were from similar backgrounds, but were not achieving well academically. She found that resilient youth believed in their cognitive abilities, such as comprehension skills, and placed less importance on belongingness regarding their families and friends. Gordon interpreted the latter finding as a protective factor regarding the avoidance of negative peer pressure. Resilient youth also had stronger, more tenacious motivation regarding their cognitive abilities, and placed less emphasis on personal relationships, in contrast with nonresilient youth.

Using a similar method, Gordon (1995) also explored differences among 40 resilient and nonresilient African American high school students, drawn from a participant pool of 138 students. She found that, as with Hispanics, resilient African American youth had significantly different, more positive self-concepts, including beliefs about their cognitive abilities, environmental support, control over their cognitive goals, and recognition of the importance of these goals. These dimensions point to a stronger motivational pattern regarding academic performance. Resilient youth also placed greater emphasis on extracurricular activities and their relations to academic skills as well as on material gain; however, resilient and nonresilient youth differed minimally in terms of their social self. Gordon interpreted this finding as indicative of the dual cultures in which African Americans must operate, such that "being socially motivated may be vulnerability inducing for them . . . because their peers may see them as 'weird' or 'odd'" (p. 253).

Miller and MacIntosh (1999) examined how racial socialization and racial identity might serve as protective factors in promoting the resiliency of African American adolescents. Racial socialization refers to "the responsibility of raising physically and emotionally healthy children who are Black in a society in which being Black has negative connotations" (Peters, 1985, as cited in Miller & MacIntosh, p. 160). The authors describe racial socialization as providing a "suit of armor" against the hostilities of the environment. Participants included 131 African American adolescents in an urban school setting who completed measures of stress, racial socialization, racial identity, and collective self-esteem. Demographic information collected included GPA, school involvement, time spent on homework, and school attendance. Regression analyses indicated that positive racial identity and racelessness predicted higher GPA, although racial socialization and collective self-esteem did not.

Wayman (2002) hypothesized that educational resilience factors might play a role for students who return to obtain their high school degree after dropping out. He utilized longitudinal data gathered by the National Institute on Drug Abuse exploring substance abuse and other factors among 519 Mexican-American and non-Latino high school youth who had dropped out of school. Several types of resilience factors were included, as based on personal, family, peer, and school factors. Personal factors included personal self-esteem dimensions, including competence, self-confidence, and social acceptance, as well as attitudes toward high school completion; family factors were composed of family school support and family caring; peer factors included both alienation and support items; and school factors included extracurricular involvement, school liking, relationship with teachers, perception of school success, teacher caring, and supportive school environment. Logistic regression analyses indicated perception of school success, and peer educational support predicted degree attainment, and self-esteem; intent to graduate and identification as a student predicted type of degree (diploma or GED). Wayman noted that a primary benefit of exploring resilience factors among dropouts is that these factors "are typically more proximal to the student and thus make better use of the information that these students have to offer" (p. 176).

In sum, the research on resiliency among students of color provides a promising avenue for future research. Although some ambiguity exists regarding the definition of resiliency (Miller & MacIntosh, 1999), exploring the impact of protective factors that help youth recover or persist in the face of overwhelming odds is critical to identifying and developing effective interventions with these students. Future research needs to be conducted on a wider range of students from different grades, as well as, different racial–ethnic groups.

Practice

Thus far, I have reviewed theory and research most relevant to working with racially and ethnically diverse students. Many of these issues may be expressed as mental health concerns, such as identity development, self-esteem, culture shock and acculturative stress, depression and anxiety, and low motivation, each of which ultimately affect the retention and academic achievement of these students; as noted earlier, nearly half of all students of color are lost from the academic pipeline during the elementary and secondary school years. It is therefore critical for school counselors to develop and provide essential services and interventions that can help stem this tremendous loss for individuals, their families, and their communities, as well as the larger society.

Indeed, although the situation is dire, it is important to point out that there are schools whose personnel exhibit beliefs, attitudes, and behaviors that create a learning community that positively influences student achievement and personal functioning (Carey & Boscardin, 2003). Several educators have identified common factors of schools and school personnel that have been effective at retaining students of color (August & Hakuta, 1997; Darder, Torres, & Gutierrez, 1997; Gaitan, 2004; Romo & Falbo, 1996):

- put learning of students first (teachers, administrators, and counselors)
- clarify scholastic standards as skill-based, communicate high standards, and have accountability
- make participation rewarding
  - discourage skipping, encourage attendance
  - create strong peer groups
- emphasize hard work and persistence, not just abilities
- make schools accessible
  - involve parents in respectful and genuine ways (e.g., advocates, volunteers)
  - where appropriate, have bilingual personnel
  - share information in many ways (e.g., focus groups)
- create clear pathways to good outcomes
  - provide link to jobs, organizations, communities, higher education

Thus, there have been schools whose personnel were engaged such that their beliefs, attitudes, and behaviors created a learning community that positively influenced student achievement and personal functioning (Carey & Boscardin, 2003). Simply stated, it is people who matter most in promoting positive student outcomes. As Carey and Boscardin observed: "School counselors have the opportunity to play a crucial role in helping all constituencies [in a school system] collaborate in creative ways to produce positive outcomes that will benefit all those invested in creating a multiculturally effective school environment" (p. 278).

With the approval of the "Guidelines on Multicultural Education, Training, Research, Practice, and Organizational Change for Psychologists" by the American Psychological Association (APA; 2003), mental health professionals now have some general guidelines by which to develop and evaluate their interventions with diverse students. For example, Guideline 1 highlights that all mental health professionals are cultural beings who "may hold attitudes and beliefs that can detrimentally influence their perceptions of and interactions with individuals who are ethnically and racially different from themselves" (APA, p. 382). Thus, Guideline 1 states that multicultural competence begins for school counselors primarily by developing awareness regarding biases, stereotypes, misinformation, and the like regarding culturally different people. Guideline 1 strongly urges the avoidance of the "color-blind" approach (e.g., people are people), instead promoting the development of more complex social attitudes and worldviews that incorporate the multiple identities that people (including school counselors and their clients) may adopt.

In Guideline 2, mental health professionals "are encouraged to recognize the importance of multicultural sensitivity/responsiveness to, knowledge of, and understanding about ethnically and racially different individuals" (APA, 2003, p. 385). Thus, in addition to awareness of attitudes and biases, school counselors must develop an adequate racial–cultural knowledge base regarding their students, including historical influences, sociopolitical pressures and precedents, legal and policy issues, language concerns, values, customs, beliefs, acceptable behaviors (both verbal and nonverbal), social competencies, and important psychological processes, such as acculturation and racial and ethnic identity development.

Guideline 5 states that mental health professionals "are encouraged to apply culturally appropriate skills in clinical and other applied psychological practices" (APA, 2003, p. 390). This guideline applies to school counselors in at least two general ways. The first refers to learning to use general or microskills in culturally appropriate or sensitive ways (Ivey & Ivey, 2002). Thus, one focus of Guideline 5 is to promote the use of general counseling skills (e.g., attending, focusing, reframing) that invite dialogue among the various constituencies in school systems about issues of racism, oppression, discrimination, and so on. It is essential that persons in the more powerful or privileged positions (e.g., counselor, teacher, principal) initiate this dialogue given its sociopolitical and emotionally evocative nature (Ancis & Ladany, 2001). A second way to apply Guideline 5 to school counseling is in the provision of culturally appropriate techniques for specific racial and ethnic groups (e.g., NTU therapy) as well as indigenous healing methods (e.g., sweat lodge ceremonies). Culturally specific techniques are particularly important to utilize in school settings that primarily serve racially and culturally different students. Learning these techniques involves becoming familiar with indigenous forms of healing, as well as bridging with indigenous healers within the local community (Sue & Sue, 2003). Another way of approaching school counseling within Guideline 5 is to provide intervention strategies for specific topics (e.g., dealing with racism, identify conflicts, sexual education) that target racial and cultural groups.

A final guideline, Guideline 6, is particularly critical for school counselors to keep in mind, given the history of school systems' negative treatment of racially and ethnically diverse students, in which mental health professionals "are encouraged to use organizational change processes to support culturally informed organizational (policy) development and practices" (APA, 2003, p. 392). As already noted, school counseling does not occur in a vacuum. Indeed, school counseling that is provided with an eye to a larger context that emphasizes multicultural competence at *all* levels of students' experience with their school systems will be more effective than school counseling where this does not occur. One theoretical approach discussed earlier was ecological frameworks, which purport that school counseling necessarily occurs in a context, and that counselors' attitudes, knowledge, and behaviors are part of the context in which students learn, and hopefully survive and thrive.

Several scholars have identified ways in which these guidelines may be applied specifically to school counselors in their interventions with students of color and their families and communities. For example, utilizing ecological approaches, Juntunen et al. (2003) described the various roles that school counselors can play as liaisons among schools, families, and community agencies. These roles include being a cultural interpreter or broker, referral base, advocate, program developer, social model for respect and acceptance, and mediator. By adopting multiple roles, school counselors may be able to address some of the barriers that prevent students of color from being successful in today's school systems. Such barriers include differences in language abilities, educational and literacy levels, communication styles, emphases regarding time and attendance, as well as miseducation on the part of school officials regarding culturally different but effective parenting styles and racial-ethnic tensions within the school setting.

A major area in which school counselors may play a more effective role in combating institutionalized racism and ethnocentrism is by developing more effective or alternative assessment interventions that essentially "detrack" students of color. Hancock (1994, as cited in Tamminga, 2002) defined alternative assessment as "an ongoing process between the student and teacher [or counselor] in making judgments about the student's progress, using nonconventional strategies" (p. 1). Del Vecchio, Gustke, and Wilde (1998) provided the following "alternative assessment" approach as a more effective way to assess racially and ethnically diverse students. Assessment must incorporate the following:

- Clearly defined purpose
- Information gathered over time
- Assessing broad progress in multiple skills, such as conceptual understanding, problem solving, reflective thinking
- Focusing on process, not just drills
- Integrating diversity, such as language and learning styles (e.g., cooperative, rather than individualist/competitive)
- Active student and parent involvement
- Climate of trust
- Use of anecdotal records and observations, classroom products, checklists

By following these guidelines, school counselors can help ensure that students of color will be accurately assessed in terms of their strengths as well as the growth areas.

Involving students in community or bridge programs is another effective way of increasing motivation to achieve and complete school. Programs such as GEARUP and Upward Bound help provide targeted assistance to students that personalizes their unique goals and visions, increases academic self-efficacy, and connects them to more realistic and attainable goals (McLure & Child, 1998; O'Brien et al.,

2000). By personal visits to and from university officials, students also may receive greater recognition for their academic achievements. These programs help develop critical educational skills, such as verbal expression, writing, and learning how to negotiate larger educational systems such as admissions applications and financial aid. A major purpose of these programs is to bring closer the long-term goal of completing an education, a goal that often seems out of reach and impossible for many youth of color.

Other intervention ideas might involve parent/child programs, where students attend their parents' work settings for a day, career days, and university campus visits. Linking students to national networks and scholarship also is a vital intervention for many of these youth, given that financial woes often are the primary reason why students do not seek higher education. Herring (1997) described many other innovative practices that school counselors can use with racially and ethnically diverse students.

Ultimately, a primary goal for school counselors is to help engender a climate of trust and respect within the school system to which students belong. This may be achieved in a number of ways, in addition to those promoted through the Guidelines. Focusing on student strengths, rather than deficits, is generally viewed as a more effective approach (Bemak & Chung, 2003; Tucker, 1999). Consultation with other school personnel, families, and communities also is key to establishing a positive and engaged learning atmosphere. In particular, drawing in families, especially parents, has been viewed as essential to helping students stay in school and complete their education. Important questions school counselors might ask to begin their work include the following

- Who are the students being served?
  - examples include race, ethnicity, SES, generation, migration
- What are current educational challenges of these students?
  - helps to identify goals
- What are current educational successes of these students?
  - helps to identify strategies
- What are available resources?
  - helps to identity the means by which goals and strategies may be achieved (e.g., personnel, budget, space)

Future Directions

In this chapter, I have described theory, research, and practice issues of relevance to race and ethnicity in school counseling. Beginning with historical considerations, it is clear that the current difficulties facing many students of color and the school systems that serve them emanate from exclusionary laws and discriminatory policies of the past. These historical forces have helped to shape current theory and research, including the challenge for many students regarding the healthy development of their racial and ethnic identities; the inclusion of people and systems critical to these youth, particularly families; and the development of interventions that are effective and sensitive to these youth's cultural values and norms. Research on students of color has focused on such diverse topics as identity development and the impact of stereotype threat, acculturation and acculturative stress, immigration status and language abilities, and resiliency. Each of these areas provides promising directions for further research, particularly in identifying potential areas of strengths of students of color that can be incorporated into interventions (e.g., language differences as reflecting increased cognitive complexity). Unfortunately, research on students of color remains sparse and lacks programmatic emphases (Yeh, 2004); however, numerous grant projects and professional organizations today are targeting the needs of racially and ethnically diverse students. Although not a mandate, the recent approval of the Multicultural Guidelines (APA, 2003) as well as the model program approved by the ASCA, signifies the importance of considering race and ethnicity in the theory, research, and practice of school counseling. Several books, most notably by Herring (1997) and Pedersen and Carey (2003), are now available that focus specifically on school counseling issues for diverse student populations.

In considering future directions for theory, research, and practice regarding race and ethnicity in school counseling, it is critical to consider the continuing needs of students of color, particularly strategies and approaches that help motivate these youth to continue their education. Without a specific focus on race and ethnicity, it is likely that racially and ethnically diverse students will continue to be lost from the educational pipeline.

References

Adams, A. M. (2000). Learning preference and Mexican American students: Considering the significance of acculturation, socioeconomic status, and academic performance. *Dissertation Abstracts International, 61,* 491.

American Psychological Association. (2003). Guidelines on multicultural education, training, research, practice, and organizational change for psychologists. *American Psychologist, 58*(5), 377–402.

Ancis, J. R., & Ladany, N. (2001). A multicultural framework for counselor supervision. In L. J. Bradley & N. Ladany (Eds.), *Counselor supervision: Principles, process, and practice* (pp. 63–90). Philadelphia: Brunner-Routledge.

Aronson, J., Fried, C., & Good, C. (2002). Reducing the effects of stereotype threat on African American college students by shaping theories of intelligence. *Journal of Experimental Social Psychology, 38,* 113–125.

Aronson, J. M. (2002). *Improving academic achievement: Impact of psychological factors in education.* San Diego, CA: Academic Press.

Arroyo, C. G., & Zigler, E. (1995). Racial identity, academia achievement, and the psychological well-being of economically disadvantaged adolescents. *Journal of Personality and Social Psychology, 69,* 903–914.

August, D., & Hakuta, K. (Eds.). (1997). *Improving schooling for language-minority children: A research agenda.* Washington, DC: National Academy Press.

Bandura, A. (1986). *Social foundations of thought and action: A social cognitive theory.* Englewood Cliffs, NJ: Prentice Hall.

Bauman, S., Siegel, J., Falco, L., Szymanski, G., Davis, A., & Seabolt, K. (2003). Trends in school counseling: The first fifty years. *Professional School Counseling, 7,* 79–90.

Belgrave, F. Z., Cherry, V. R., Cunningham, D., Walwyn, S., Letlaka-Rennert, K., & Phillips, F. (1994). The influence of Africentric values, self-esteem, and Black identity on drug attitudes among African American fifth graders: A preliminary study. *Journal of Black Psychology, 20,* 143–156.

Bemak, F., & Chung, R. C. (2003). Multicultural counseling with immigrant students in schools. In P. B. Pedersen & J. C. Carey (Eds). *Multicultural counseling in schools: A practical handbook* (2nd ed., pp. 84–104). Boston: Allyn & Bacon.

Berry, J. W. (1993). Ethnic identity in plural societies. In M. E. Bernal & G. P. Knight (Eds.), *Ethnic identity: Formation and transmission among Hispanics and other minorities* (pp. 271–296). Albany: State University of New York.

Bronfenbrenner, U. (1979). *The ecology of human development: Experiments by nature and design.* Cambridge, MA: Harvard University Press.

Bryan, J. (2005). Fostering educational resilience and achievement in urban schools through school-family-community partnerships. *Professional School Counseling, 8,* 219–227.

Buriel, R., Perez, W., De Ment, T. L., Chavez, D., & Moran, V. R. (1998). The relationship of language brokering to academia performance, biculturalism, and self-efficacy among Latino adolescents. *Hispanic Journal of Behavioral Sciences, 20,* 283–297.

Butchart, R. E. (1988). "Outthinking and outflanking the owners of the world": A historiography of the African American struggle for education. *History of Education Quarterly, 28,* 333–366.

Calderon, M., & Carreon, A. (2001). A two-way bilingual program: Promise, practice, and precautions. In R. Slavin & M. Calderon (Eds.), *Effective programs for Latino students* (pp. 125–170). Mahwah, NJ: Lawrence Erlbaum.

Carey, J. C., & Boscardin, M. L. (2003). Improving the multicultural effectiveness of your school in the context of state standards, accountability measures, and high-stakes assessment. In P. B. Pedersen & J. C. Carey (Eds.), *Multicultural counseling in schools: A practical handbook* (2nd ed., pp. 270–289). Boston: Allyn & Bacon.

Chea, P. (2003). Effects of cultural and ethnic identity on academic performance and self-esteem of Cambodian adolescents. *Dissertation Abstracts International, 64,* 763.

Coleman, H. L. K. (1995). Strategies for coping with cultural diversity. *The Counseling Psychologist, 23,* 722–740.

Coleman, H. L. K, Casali, S. B, & Wampold, B. E. (2001). Adolescent strategies for coping with cultural diversity. *Journal of Counseling and Development, 79,* 356–364.

Crosnoe, R., & Elder, G. H. (2004). Family dynamics, supportive relationships, and educational resilience during adolescence. *Journal of Family Issues, 25,* 571–602.

Darder, A., Torres, R. D., & Gutierrez, H. (1997). *Latinos and education: A critical reader.* New York: Routledge.

De Los Santos, J., & Miville, M. L. (2005, August). *The relations of cultural influences and academia self-efficacy on Hispanic academia performance.* Poster session presented at the annual meeting of the American Psychological Association, Washington, DC.

Del Vecchio, A., Gustke, C., & Wilde, J. (1998). Alternative assessment for Latino students. In M. L. Gonzalez, A. Huerta-Macias, & J. V. Tinajero (Eds.), *Educating Latino students: A guide to successful practice* (pp. 329–356). Lancaster, PA: Technomic.

Demmert, W. G. (2001). *Improving academic performance among Native American students: A review of the research literature* (Report No. RC 023449). Washington, DC: Office of Educational Research and Improvement. (ERIC Document Reproduction Service No. ED463917).

Ford, D. Y., Harris, J. J., & Schuerger, J. M. (1993). Racial identity development among gifted Black students: Counseling issues and concerns. *Journal of Counseling and Development, 71,* 409–417.

Fordham, S. (1991). Racelessness in private schools: Should we deconstruct the racial and cultural identity of African American adolescents? *Teachers College Record, 92,* 470–484.

Fordham, S., & Ogbu, J. U. (1986). Black students' school success: Coping with the burden of 'acting White.' *Urban Review, 18,* 176–206.

Fusick, L., & Bordeau, W. C. (2004). Counseling at-risk Afro-American youth: An examination of contemporary issues and effective school-based strategies. *Professional School Counseling, 8,* 102–115.

Gaitan, C. D. (2004). *Involving Latino families in schools: Raising achievement through home-school partnerships.* Thousand Oaks, CA: Corwin.

Gándara, P. (2001). Learning in English in California: Guideposts for the nation. In M. M. Suarez-Orozco & M. M. Paez (Eds.), *Latinos: Remaking America* (pp. 306–320). Berkeley: University of California Press.

Garcia, E. E. (2001). *Hispanic education in the United States: Raices y alas.* Lanham: Rowman & Littlefield.

Garza, R. T., & Gallegos, P. I. (1995). Environmental influences and personal choice: A humanistic perspective on acculturation. In A. M. Padilla (Ed.), *Hispanic psychology: Critical issues in theory and practice* (pp. 3–14). Thousand Oaks, CA: Sage.

Gibson, M. A. (1997). Complicating the immigrant/involuntary minority typology. *Anthropology & Education Quarterly Review, 28*, 431–454.

Glazer, N. (1971). Blacks and ethnic groups: *The difference, and the political difference it makes. Social Problems, 18*, 444–461.

Gloria, A. M., & Rodriguez, E. R. (2000). Counseling Latino university students: Psychosociocultural issues for consideration. *Journal of Counseling and Development, 78*, 145–154.

Goldenberg, I., & Goldenberg, H. (2000). *Family therapy: An overview* (5th ed.). Belmont, CA: Wadsworth.

Good, C., Aronson, J., & Inzlicht, M. (2003). Improving adolescents' standardized test performance: An intervention to reduce the effects of stereotype threat. *Journal of Applied Developmental Psychology. 24*, 645–662.

Gordon, K. A. (1995). Self-concept and motivational patterns of resilient African American high school students. *Journal of Black Psychology, 21*, 239–255.

Gordon, K. A. (1996). Resilient Hispanic youths' self-concept and motivational patterns. *Hispanic Journal of Behavioral Sciences, 18*, 63–73.

Green, A., & Keys, S. (2001). Expanding the developmental school counseling paradigm: Meeting the needs of the 21st-century student. *Professional School Counseling, 5*, 84–95.

Gysbers, N. C. (2001). School guidance and counseling in the 21st century: Remember the past into the future. *Professional School Counseling, 5*, 96–105.

Hakuta, K., & Garcia, E. E. (1989). Bilingualism and education. *American Psychologist, 44*, 374–379.

Hamm, J. V., & Coleman, H. L. K. (2001). African American and White adolescents' strategies for managing cultural diversity in predominantly White high schools. *Journal of Youth and Adolescence, 30*, 281–303.

Helms, J. E. (1990). *Black and White racial identity: Theory, research and practice.* New York: Greenwood Press.

Helms, J. E. (2003). Racial identity in the social environment. In P. B. Pedersen & J. C. Carey (Eds). *Multicultural counseling in schools: A practical handbook* (2nd ed., pp. 44–58). Boston: Allyn & Bacon.

Henderson, A., & Berla, N. (1994). *A new generation of evidence: The family is critical to student achievement.* Washington, DC: National Committee for Citizens in Education.

Herring, R. D. (1997). *Counseling diverse ethnic youth: Synergetic strategies and interventions for school counselors.* Fort Worth, TX: Harcourt Brace.

Ivey, A. E., & Ivey, M. G. (2002). *Intentional interviewing and counseling with Infotrac: Facilitating client development in a multicultural society.* Pacific Grove, CA: Brooks-Cole.

Juntunen, C. L., Atkinson, D. R., & Tierney, G. (2003). School counselors and school psychologists as school-home-community liaisons in ethnically diverse schools. In P. B. Pedersen & J. C. Carey (Eds). *Multicultural counseling in schools: A practical handbook* (2nd ed., pp. 149–168). Boston: Allyn & Bacon.

Kim, B. S. K., & Abreu, J. M. (2001). Acculturation measurement: Theory, current instruments, and future directions. In J. G. Ponterotto, J. M. Casas, L. A. Suzuki, & C. M. Alexander (Eds.), *Handbook of multicultural counseling* (2nd ed., pp. 394–424). Thousand Oaks, CA: Sage.

Kozol, J. (2005). *The shame of the nation: The restoration of apartheid schooling in America.* New York: Crown.

LaFromboise, T., Coleman, H. L. K., & Gerton, J. (1993). Psychological impact of biculturalism: Evidence and theory. *Psychological Bulletin, 114*, 395–412.

Lomawaima, K. T. (1994). *They called it prairie light: The story of Chilocco Indian school.* Lincoln: University of Nebraska.

Lopez, E. J., Ehly, S., & Garcia-Vasquez, E. (2002). Acculturation, social support and academic achievement of Mexican and Mexican American high school students: An exploratory study. *Psychology in the Schools, 39*, 245–257.

McClure, G. T., & Child, R. L. (1998). Upward Bound students compared to other college-bound students: Profiles of nonacademic characteristics and academic achievement. *Journal of Negro Education, 67*, 346–363.

McKenna, N., Roberts, J., & Woodfin, L. (2003). Working cross-culturally in family-school partnerships. In P. B. Pedersen & J. C. Carey (Eds). *Multicultural counseling in schools: A practical handbook* (2nd ed., pp. 131–148). Boston: Allyn & Bacon.

Miller, D. B., & MacIntosh, R. (1999). Promoting resilience in urban African American adolescents: Racial socialization and identity as protective factors. *Social Work Research, 23*, 159–169.

Miville, M. L., Koonce, D., Darlington, P., & Whitlock, B. (2000). Exploring the relationships between racial/cultural identity and ego identity among African Americans and Mexican Americans. *Journal of Multicultural Counseling and Development, 28*, 208–224.

Morales, A., & Hanson, W. E. (2005). Language brokering: An integrative review of the literatura. *Hispanic Journal of the Behavioral Sciences, 27*, 471–503.

O'Brien, K. M., Bikos, L. H., Epstein, K. L., Flores, L. Y., Dukstein, R. D., & Kamatuka, N. A. (2000). Enhancing the career decision-making self-efficacy of Upward Bound students. *Journal of Career Development, 26*, 277–293.

Oetting, E. R., & Beauvais, F. (1991). Orthogonal cultural identification theory: The cultural identification of minority adolescents. *The International Journal of the Addictions, 25*, 655–685.

Ogbu, J. U. (2004). Collective identity and the burden of "acting White" in Black history, community, and education. *Urban Review, 36*, 1–35.

Ogbu, J. U., & Simons, H. (1994). Cultural models of school achievement: A quantitative test of Ogbu's theory. Berkeley, CA: National Center for the Study of Writing and Literacy.

Ogbu, J. U., & Simons, H. (1998). Voluntary and involuntary minorities: A cultural-ecological theory of school performance with some implications for education. *Anthropology and Education Quarterly, 29*, 155–188.

Orellana, M. F., & Bowman, P. (2003). Cultural diversity research on learning and development: Conceptual, methodological, and strategic considerations. *Educational Researcher, 32*, 26–32.

Orfield, G., Losen, D., Wald, J., & Swanson, C. (2004). *Losing our future: How minority youth are being left behind by the graduation rate crisis.* Cambridge, MA: The Civil Rights Project at Harvard University. Retrieved for Orfield, G., Losen, D., Wald, J., & Swanson, C. (2004). add: Retrieved September 1, 2007, from http://www.civilrightsproject.ucla.edu/research/dropouts/LosingOurFuture.pdf

Osbourne, J. W. (1997). Race and academic disidentification. *Journal of Educational Psychology, 89*, 728–735.

Oyserman, D., Bybee, D., Terry, K., & Hart-Johnson, T. (2004). Possible selves as roadmaps. *Journal of Research in Personality, 38*, 130–149.

Oyserman, D., Gant, L., & Ager, J. (1995). A socially contextualized model of African American identity: Possible selves and school persistence. *Journal of Personality and Social Psychology, 69*, 1216–1232.

Oyserman, D., Harrison, K., & Bybee, D. (2001). Can racial identity be promotive of academic efficacy? *International Journal of Behavioral Development, 25*, 379–385.

Oyserman, D., & Markus, H. R. (1990). Possible selves and delinquency. *Journal of Personality and Social Psychology, 59*, 112–125.

Oyserman, D., Terry, K., & Bybee, D. (2002). A possible selves intervention to enhance school involvement. *Journal of Adolescence, 25*, 313–326.

Paisley, P. O., & Borders, L. D. (1995). School counseling: An evolving specialty. *Journal of Counseling and Development, 74*, 150–153.

Paisley, P. O., & McMahon, G. (2001). School counseling for the 21st century: Challenges and opportunities. *Professional School Counseling, 5*, 106–115.

Pajares, F. (1997). Current directions in self-efficacy research. In M. Maehr & P. R. Pintrich (Eds.), *Advances in motivation and achievement* (Vol. 10, pp. 1–49). Greenwich, CT: JAI Press.

Pajares, F. (2001). Toward a positive psychology of academic motivation. *Journal of Educational Research, 95*, 27–35.

Pajares, F. (2002). Self-efficacy beliefs in academic contexts: An outline. Retrieved May 6, 2006, from http://des/emory.edu/mfp/efftalk.html

Pajares, F. (2003). Self-efficacy beliefs, motivation, and achievement in writing: A review of the literature. *Reading and Writing Quarterly, 19*, 139–158.

Pearson, B. Z. (2001). Bilingual infants: Mapping the research agenda. In M. M. Suarez-Orozco & M. M. Paez (Eds.), *Latinos: Remaking America* (pp. 306–320). Berkeley: University of California Press.

Pedersen, P. B., & Carey, J. C. (2003). *Multicultural counseling in schools: A practical handbook* (2nd ed.). Boston: Allyn & Bacon.

Pew Hispanic Center (2004). *Latino teens staying in high school: A challenge for all generations.* Retrieved September 1, 2007 from http://pewhispanic.org/files/factsheets/7.3.pdf

Rak, C. F., & Patterson, L. E. (1996). Promoting resilience in at-risk children. *Journal of Counseling and Development, 74*, 368–373.

Rolon-Dow, R. (2004). Seduced by images: Identity and schooling in the lives of Puerto Rican girls. *Anthropology and Education Quarterly, 35*, 8–29.

Romo, H. D., & Falbo, T. (1996). *Latino high school graduation: Defying the odds.* Austin, TX: University of Texas Press.

Roysircar-Sodowsky, G., & Frey, L. L. (2003). Children of immigrants: Their worldviews value conflicts. In P. B. Pedersen & J. C. Carey (Eds.) *Multicultural counseling in schools: A practical handbook* (2nd ed., pp. 61–83). Boston: Allyn & Bacon.

San Miguel, G. (1986). Status of the historiography of Chicano education: A preliminary analysis. *History of Education Quarterly, 26*, 523–536.

Steele, C. M. (1997). A threat in the air: How stereotypes shape intellectual identity and performance. *American Psychologist, 52*, 613–629.

Steele, C. M., & Aronson, J. (1995). Stereotype threat and the intellectual test performance of African Americans. *Journal of Personality and Social Psychology, 69*, 797–811.

Steele, C. M., Spencer, S., & Aronson, J. (2002). Contending with group image: The psychology of stereotype and social identity threat. In M. Zanna (Ed.), *Advances in experimental social psychology* (pp. 379–440). San Diego, CA: Academic Press.

Stephenson, M. (2000). Development and validation of the Stephenson Multigroup Acculturation Scale (SMAS). *Psychological Assessment, 12*, 77–88.

Stone, L. A., & Bradley, F. O. (1994). *Foundations of elementary and middle school counseling.* White Plains, NY: Longman.

Sue, D. W. (2003). Foreword. In P. B. Pedersen & J. C. Carey (Eds.), *Multicultural counseling in schools: A practical handbook* (2nd ed., pp. ix–x). Boston: Allyn & Bacon.

Sue, D. W., & Sue, D. (2003). *Counseling the culturally diverse: Theory and practice* (4th ed.). New York: Wiley.

Swanson, C. B. (2004). *Real kids, real numbers.* Washington, DC: The Urban Institute. Retrieved September 1, 2007, from http://www.urban.org/url.cfm?ID=311114

Tamminga, J. L. (2002). Alternative assessment in mathematics. Retrieved June 13, 2006, from http://ldn.tamu.edu/Archives/studprojs/MathAlternativeAssessment.ppt#1

Tencer Garrity, T. L. (2003). An investigation of the relationship between acculturation and academic performance, self-esteem, and ethnic identity with Mexican-American children. *Dissertation Abstracts International, 64,* 2943.

Thomas, D. E., Townsend, T. G., & Belgrave, F. Z. (2003). The influence of cultural and racial identification on the psychosocial adjustment of inner-city African American children in school. *American Journal of Community Psychology, 32,* 217–228.

Townsend, T. G., & Belgrave, F. Z. (2000). The impact of personal identity and racial identity on drug attitudes and use among African American children. *Journal of Black Psychology, 26,* 421–436.

Tucker, C. M. (1999). *African American children: A self-empowerment approach to modifying behavior problems and preventing academic failure.* Boston: Allyn & Bacon.

Wayman, J. C. (2002). The utility of educational resilience for studying degree attainment in school dropouts. *Journal of Educational Research, 95,* 167–178.

Yeh, C. J. (2004). Multicultural and contextual research and practice in school counseling. *The Counseling Psychologist, 32,* 278–285.

Zuckerman, M. (1990). Some dubious premises in research and theory on racial differences. *American Psychologist, 45,* 1297–1303.

XIV
AFRICAN AMERICAN EMPOWERMENT IN SECONDARY SCHOOL COUNSELING

LEON D. CALDWELL AND BETTINA M. BEECH
University of Nebraska, Lincoln

RICHARD OLDFIELD AND VANN PRICE
North Star High School, Lincoln, Nebraska

The psychological well-being of African American students deserves greater attention in the literature, given the amount of research describing the academic underperformance. This is especially true of African American boys, who are disproportionately represented in special education classes and have an alarming prevalence of adolescent psychopathology diagnosis (i.e., attention deficit disorder, attention deficit with hyperactivity disorder, conduct disorder, etc.), (Porter, 1997). While the analyses of African American academic underachievement are replete in the literature, studies investigating resilience and protective factors for African American boys are scant. Even more distressing is the dearth of school counseling literature disseminating prevention interventions that promote academic performance, reduce academic underperformance, and address psychological well-being. This chapter asserts that school counselors have a role in developing prevention intervention for underserved students. We then propose the Progressive School Counseling Advocacy Model; next, we discuss the African American males and educational interventions, and then we provide an example of a culturally consistent school-based intervention, the African American Empowerment Curriculum (AAEC). Finally, we discuss the implications of this approach for school counselors to develop culturally responsive interventions.

SCHOOL COUNSELING AND PREVENTION: A MATTER OF PUBLIC HEALTH

School counselors have a unique role within the education system. While their primary role is to support the educational mission of the school, they provide socioemotional support to students and families. School counselors are conduits and brokers between educational success and psychological well-being. Shrinking resources and expanding student problems, however, have varied the task of professional school counselors. Administrators, pressured to respond to national mandates, place greater resources in student achievement than in student health. Several researchers have demonstrated that academic performance and student health are associated (Arroyo & Ziegler, 1995; Davis, Ajzen, Suanders, & Williams, 2002; Kiesner, 2002). Particularly during adolescence, developmental changes and challenges may lead to mental health disorders (Lambert, McCreary, Joiner, Schmidt, & Ialongo, 2004) (e.g., conduct disorder, depression, anxiety disorder) and the adoption of risk behaviors (e.g., substance abuse, teen parenting, suicide) if protective factors are absent (Aro, 1994; Fuller, 1992; Keisner, 2002). Given this critical developmental period, secondary school counselors have access to adolescents at a point that could impact the national public health agenda.

Despite their importance, school counseling resources, like many other school resources, are shrinking. The suggested counselor-to-student ratio proposed by the American School Counselor Association (ASCA) serves only as a reminder of the U.S. educational systems' distance from the ideal. Creativity is required of successful school districts in the face of resource starvation. Considering the public health implications of educational failure, we call for proactive instead of reactive models of intervention by school counselors.

A comprehensive school guidance model (Gysbers, 1990) is one example of how to insert prevention intervention to meet the needs of high school students regardless of students' risk classification. Risk behavior prevention and health promotion in the form of curricular units satisfies the needs of administrators who are concerned with compliance to national mandates. In addition, curricular-based intervention models offer a cost-effective and efficient method of meeting students' social-emotional needs. The advantage of moving beyond remediation is that greater numbers of students benefit from primary prevention rather than secondary or tertiary interventions. Too often, the requirement for services is an at-risk label (Porter, 1997). Of course, the problem with the "at-risk criterion" is that not all students may demonstrate psychological need with misconduct (Spencer, Kim, & Marshall, 1987). In fact, depending on the student's characteristics, misconduct is rarely followed by a mental health screening. We argue that the common intervention approach—serve the high-risk first—may account for the increasing numbers of students in that high-risk category. This conclusion can be easily reached if you begin with an assumption that all students at this developmental stage are "at-risk" and, therefore, in need of interventions (Aro, 1994).

Erford, House, and Martin (2003) asserted that two essential ideological shifts are necessary as the school counseling profession prepares for the 21st century: (1) the need to understand and apply the language of educational reform to school counseling and (2) the need to advocate for all students, not just some students, on important educational issues and their continuous improvement. While these proposed shifts clearly allow for more inclusive school counseling practices, they narrowly render the role of school counseling as an agent of educational systems. The emerging role of school counselors as violence prevention interventionists, high-risk student service providers, and agents of diversity and multicultural sensitivity (Erford et al., 2003) has implications well beyond educational institutions. We assert that the emerging realities of school counselors require an additional ideological shift:

the need to place the roles and duties of school counselors within the continuum of public health.

This assertion is a matter of semantics, to a great extent. School counselors, by nature, have been local (i.e., school building or district) interventionists. This additional shift, however, places the school counselor as an important component of a national priority (i.e., public health) contrary to its current undesirable position in the achievement score chase. School counselors, depending on the resources, have engaged in group interventions for specific groups of students and have addressed school topics (e.g., suicide, eating disorders, etc.) as the need arises. By proclaiming a prevention and health promotion approach, however, school counselors begin to connect with a discourse that extends beyond school building parameters. Prevention and health promotion are a matter of public health for minority adolescents (see Wilson, Rodrigue, & Taylor, 1997). Prevalence trends in child and adolescent psychopathology suggest growth in numbers of school-aged children who require several layers of service. We purport that school counselors should enter the discourse on adolescent health from a public health perspective or it will be relegated to a reactionary position. In fact, school counselors should be on the vanguard of health interventions given the importance of school outcomes to quality of life.

Furthermore, we believe that given the nature of compulsory education, schools are important in dispensing various health interventions to underserved populations, especially ethnic/racial groups who have been historically marginalized and disenfranchised by status quo health enterprises. Native American, African American, Latino, Hispanic, and Asian American children and adolescents are likely to come from families who are described in health care and health status disparities (see LaVeist, 2005). The Surgeon General's (U.S. Department of Health and Human Services, 1999) mental health report and supplement outlining minority health disparities created national concern. School counselors could be extremely important in reducing health care disparities, as schools are often the first manifestation of health concerns. Thus, well-trained school counselors are also the first responders to health behaviors for children and adolescents. For this reason, we place great importance on the school counselor's role in service delivery to students from underserved populations. Schools offer excellent opportunities to disseminate a myriad of interventions that while not directly educational, have a grave impact on learning. For example, interventions that address depression, test anxiety, and suicide are extremely important to the learning process (Kaslow, Price, Wychoff, Grall, Sherry et al., 2004; Keisner, 2002; Sagrestano, Paikoff, Holmbeck, & Fendrich, 2003). This is especially important for those communities who have historically underutilized professional community-based services.

School Counselors and Health Disparities

Given the reported health disparities in the United States, schools can be a repository of interventions that impact health and learning for African American students and families (Bemak, Chung, & Murphy, 2003). We propose that school counselors can be instrumental in addressing public health initiatives aimed at reducing health disparities. Unfortunately, even despite several national headlines about school violence, some school administrators and board members need convincing that mental health is as important to the learning environment as sports teams are to school community building. Although some school administrators dismiss mental health as part of the mission of education, others recognize that healthy students are optimal learners (Keisner, 2002).

School counselors, like school psychologists, if properly trained, can provide screening, referral, and prevention interventions for children and adolescents who are uninsured or underinsured and thus least likely to receive professional psychological services (Doll, 1996). Thomas and Holzer (1999) reported that there is a dearth of appropriately trained clinicians and social workers to provide services to children and adolescents. In many cases, school counselors are the first responders to psychological issues. The Surgeon General's Mental Health Report (U.S. Department of Health and Human Services, 1999) suggests that this shortage places an additional burden on school counselors and other gatekeepers to identify children for screening and treatment decisions. Children and adolescents from historically underserved communities could benefit greatly from public health oriented school counseling programs.

The desperate educational status of African American students in general and young men in particular has received extensive national attention. Dubbed as the "achievement gap," several educators and politicians have allocated a plethora of resources to describe and understand the extent to which African American students score below their White classmates in standardized achievement tests and underperform in classroom indicators of educational attainment (e.g., Fordham & Ogbu, 1986). Yet, there has been far less analysis of how educational outcomes impact the future health of African American adolescents. Few are surprised that the nation's educational underperformers are the nation's most vulnerable to homicide and other crimes, according to statistics from the Office of Juvenile Justice and Delinquent Prevention and Center for Disease Control and Injury Prevention. Yet, there is a dearth of research investigating mental health and academic outcomes for African American males.

The obligation of providing primary education to the next generation has become burdensome by a national misappropriation of resources. There is no doubt that the "achievement gap," if made a priority, could be diminished in U.S. education. Required are bold educational leadership, progressive interventions (prevention), and more accurate indices of educational success, without political intrusion, yet with democratic accountability. Educational leadership requires innovation. Given over 20 years of researching the issue, an expectation of successful strategies is not far-fetched. We advocate that education in the United States is past analyses of the problems and should be focused on solutions to address educational inequities in this country (Perry, Steele, & Hilliard, 2003).

The following section describes a school-based, culturally relevant, academic performance intervention—the African American Empowerment Curriculum—that applies African centered psychology (see Hilliard, 1997, for more detail) and social learning theory (Bandura, 1986). As a follow-up to the introductory section, we discuss the roles of the school counselor for advocating prevention interventions in what we call the Progressive School Counseling Model. Then we discuss African American males and school-based interventions and their implications for public health. Next, we outline the African American Empowerment Curriculum and provide preliminary results from an evaluation of its effectiveness, and finally, we provide future directions for culturally responsive school-based prevention interventions. We offer this chapter as an exemplar of school counselors confronting the challenge of developing innovative interventions to promote student success and health.

THE PROGRESSIVE SCHOOL COUNSELING MODEL AND ADVOCACY

Authors have suggested a need for change and transformation of the professional school counselor (Capuzzi, 1998; Erford, 2003). Advocacy for educational achievement by school counselors is an important role in the mission of schools. Because school counselors are often repositories of emotional and behavioral issues influencing learning, we believe advocating for academic achievement without considering students' psycho-emotional needs is unproductive. Academic performance may be impacted when school counselors advocate for fairness and equity in the educational process by developing prevention interventions that meet the needs of all student groups (Baker, 1996; Caldwell & Siwatu, 2003).

The National Standards for School Counseling Programs proposed by the ASCA urges school counselors to be change agents and leaders in school reform (Campbell

& Dahir, 1997). ASCA recommends the following: (1) coordinate comprehensive developmental guidance programs for all students, (2) advocate all students navigate through the school systems for postsecondary school options, (3) call attention to systemic factors that enhance or hinder academic success for all students, (4) utilize achievement data to identify patterns and behaviors that facilitate academic success, and (5) to leadership roles to identify the issues that need to change in the school and help develop change strategies that benefit every student. This call to the profession sets the stage for innovative school interventions by school counselors.

Ethnically and culturally marginalized groups will require interventions unique to their challenges in educational settings. Whether they are socially alienated for being in advanced learning programs (i.e., gifted), are educationally alienated for being placed in special education, or bring an ethnic-based stigma and disposition to the learning environment, these students require psycho-emotional attention that could enhance the learning experience (Caldwell, 2000). As an extension of Gysbers' (1990) Comprehensive School Guidance Model, we offer the Progressive School Counseling Model as a health promotion and risk reduction strategy for school counselors. We acknowledge the many obstacles for schools to effectively meet the mental health needs of students, especially if conducted by nonschool personnel (Doll, 1996; Evans & Weist, 2004). Furthermore, schools with limited resources have fewer options for delivering services to identified students, nonetheless providing screening and prevention. A progressive extension of comprehensive school guidance models is to deliver health promotion and risk reduction interventions through the curriculum for groups of students who demonstrate the highest risk is critical to a adolescent's healthy promotion.

The Progressive School Counseling Model postulates the following:

1. All students are "at-risk"; therefore, prevention interventions are useful for all students.
2. Academic and emotion-focused interventions should be integrated.
3. Education has implications for public health.
4. Worldview commonalities and differences provide opportunities for culturally responsive interventions.
5. Prevention is ecological.
6. Interventions should be informed by culturally competent research.

A progressive school counseling program recognizes its limits in delivering effective services to its students and takes the role of advocate/broker for service providers.

AFRICAN AMERICAN MALES AND EDUCATIONAL INTERVENTIONS

Males of African descent have had a precarious history in the United States. Participation in several social and political institutions was forbidden, with potentially lethal consequences for violation. Space does not permit a detailed account of the historical legacy of "mis-education" (Woodson, 1933) of African Americans in the United States; however, we believe any serious discussion of interventions for African American males must have a historical perspective (Caldwell & White, 2003). We assume that the current status of African American boys in school is influenced by past institutional, family, and community beliefs, attitudes, actions, and reactions (Caldwell, 2000; Saunders, Davis, Williams, & William, 2004).

The statistics describing the current educational and health status of African American males are overwhelming (see the Web sites for the National Institute of Health, the Bureau of Justice, the Office of Juvenile Justice and Detention Programs, and the Centers for Disease Control and Injury Prevention, and the Department of Education). What is even more distressing is that a majority of the commentary generated about this national epidemic has been in the form of critiquing the legislation commonly referred to as the No Child Left Behind Act. Despite debatable gains in the educational status of African American male students following this legislation, there remains the need for a comprehensive school-based intervention strategies.

Some of the challenges to developing school-based interventions for African American males are (1) lack of strength-based and positive research on African American males; (2) overreliance on Eurocentric theory to explain African-centered behaviors, creating different equals deficient interpretations; (3) absence of preservice teaching models to confront racism and stereotypes (Milner, Calwell, & Murray, 2004); (4) reluctance to utilize African American and African educational pedagogy and praxis; (5) exclusion of African American community resources; (6) lack of recognition and healing the historically oppressive educational practices; (7) false accusation that African American communities devalue formal education; (8) reluctance of African American communities to democratically confront educational policies that are not in their best interest; and (9) a lack of knowledge and implementation of African American centered educational theory and research by school administrators. By not confronting these challenges, educational systems and the African American communities have contributed to the invisibility of African American males (Franklin, 2004; Osborne, 1999).

Responding to the call from ASCA, we suggest that school counselors take leadership roles in providing intervention models for African American males. There is little argument that educational outcomes have a strong influence on such life outcome indicators as income, health, mental health, suicide, homicide, substance and alcohol abuse, and risky sexual behavior (Anderson, 2002; Beymer, 1995). For this reason, we argue that culturally responsive, school-based prevention interventions are important to eliminating health disparities among African American males. Mahoney and Merritt (1993) found a higher percentage of African American male students more likely than White students to seek school counseling services to overcome academic weaknesses and for job and educational placement. Positive experiences with interventions disseminated by school counselors may increase the likelihood of African American males later accessing help or at least voluntarily participating in health-focused interventions. We urge that school counselors confront the aforementioned challenges and create culturally responsive interventions that meet the psychosocial, educational and health needs of African American male students.

Culture-centered school-based prevention interventions. Universally applied (etic), school-based intervention may be marginally successful, depending upon the target audience and the content of the intervention; however, school administrations often fear the political fallout of targeted interventions by those who qualify them as "set aside" programs. While gender-specific topics usually meet very little hesitation, ethnic/racial segregation is usually confronted with resistance. School counselors should advocate for opportunities for African American students to navigate through their unique challenges without emotional or social intrusion from those they perceive as antagonists. Empowered school counselors can advocate for interventions that are culturally consistent with a target population. Employing the communication style and pattern, cultural worldview, and method of information dissemination by a target group may render it culturally consistent.

Cicero and Barton (2003) advocated that professional school counselors find ways to collaborate with community service agencies to meet the needs of children and families. Oftentimes, culturally centered interventions are avoided because of limited culturally competent school personnel. In the case of the AAEC, the school counseling staff was proactive in partnering outside of the school district to find a culturally competent facilitator of the intervention. The shortage of African American males in leadership and instructional positions within school districts provide opportunities for creativity. We request that schools no longer hide behind "racial" politics as the excuse to underserve ethnic "minority" groups of students and thus exacerbate their invisibility. Under the leadership of professional counselors, a school can be challenged to find the appropriate resources to address educational and health issues.

African American EMPOWERMENT CURRICULUM

Responding to the districtwide academic underperformance of a majority of African American male students, the counseling staff at a midwestern high school sought an intervention to address the "achievement gap" in their school. Prompted by the shortage of solutions proposed by the school district to address standardized test score discrepancies, the counseling staff, which consisted of three females (an African American, a Latina, and a European-American) and one male (a European American) initiated an intervention that would target African American male students. The African American Empowerment Curriculum was developed as a prevention intervention to address academic motivation and underperformance, and to promote school participation among African American boys.

The school counseling department sought and received a grant from a local funding foundation to pilot the AAEC during the second semester (January to June) of the school year. The mission of the counseling center was to develop a culturally responsive intervention that would address the following issues from their experiences providing services to African American male students: (1) feelings of cultural alienation from the educational process; (2) beliefs that the educational process lacks cultural relevance; (3) "anti-intellectualism," including negative peer pressure for academic participation or commitment; (4) fear of competing in the academic arena as a result of being presented with race/ethnic based stereotypes suggesting the intellectual inferiority of African American males; (5) other forms real or perceived racism; (6) ethnic and cultural identity issues; and (7) victimization and coping issues related to school culture issues. Although several issues were relevant to other student groups (e.g., African American females), it was hypothesized that a culturally consistent intervention would yield the greatest impact.

African-centered educational psychology (see Hilliard 1997; Kunjufu 1995, 2000; Sanyika, 1999) and social cognitive theory (SCT; Bandura, 1986) provided a conceptual framework for this intervention. In particular, African-centered educational psychology posits that African American learning is optimized when the following exist: (1) there are culturally consistent teaching styles; (2) learning is expected to develop character; (3) there are high expectations for high performance and achievement; and (4) learning is holistic (Hale, 2004). In addition, the triadic model of social cognitive theory comprising person, behavior, and environment interaction complimented the African-centered educational psychology framework. For example, individual, person-level factors such as skills, outcome expectancies, and self-efficacy spurred by the African-centered teaching approaches may increase the likelihood of that individual executing a behavior; conversely, individual behaviors can shift group norms among others in a learning environment, which can potentially shift a student's personal motivation (i.e., self-efficacy) and future behavior. Environmental factors (e.g., seating configuration, caller-response teaching method) can either enhance or hinder individual motivation. Reciprocal determinism, the dynamic interaction of the personal factors, environmental factors, and behavior, is a useful conceptual tool for developing interpersonal interventions for African American adolescents (Resnicow, Braithwaite, & Kuo, 1997). However, SCT alone does not provide the cultural context necessary to account for the unique educational history of African American male students.

The Progressive School Counseling Model Applied: African American Empowerment Class. The following describes the AAEC. African American males were randomly selected from a midwest high school population to participate in the AAEC. The selection criteria established by the counseling center staff were (1) schedule clear during the time the class was offered (3rd period) and (2) volunteer to participate. We intentionally did not use grade point averages, attendance records, or records of behavioral history as selection criteria to increase the diversity in performance level, motivation, and disposition toward school. Of the 21 boys invited to participate in the class, 18 volunteered. The reasons of those declining participation are unknown, but of interest. The class met daily during the third period (47 minutes) of the second semester (January to June) every school day as a regular academic course. Because of scheduling conflicts, the principal investigator was absent for 5 of the 65 classes. In addition, the intervention was concluded prior to the summer break because of the first author's overseas teaching obligation that began before the end of the school district's academic year.

African American Empowerment Curriculum (The Intervention) Description

The AAEC was implemented as a culturally consistent intervention for African American males (Akbar, 1998; Caldwell & White, 2001). Students were greeted at the door with a handshake and the classes began with a discussion about expectations. The environment was manipulated by placing the desks in an oval shape, which was different from the line of four rows, so each member could view the others. Students had to address each other by first names and the instructors by their titles. Ground rules were established and are summarized as respecting self, each other, and the class space. In addition, collective accountability was discussed as an expectation to create a sense of group cohesiveness.

Employing the previously mentioned conceptual models and research literature, the AAEC consisted of four conceptual target attitudes and behaviors: (1) cultural consciousness, (2) academic competence, (3) life skills, and (4) social responsibility. The following are descriptions of the conceptual targets:

Cultural consciousness is one's ability to understand his or her ethnic history and how it influences his or her thoughts, actions, and future (Kambon, 1998). Ethnic identity has been demonstrated to influence the learning of African American students (Cunningham & Boykin, 2004). Lesson plans in this domain consisted of the discussion and exercises, which explored identity in ethnicity and masculinity. For example, students were asked to list their images of African American males, discuss where these images come from, and to think critically about the utility of these images on their academic self-concept. Not surprisingly, the students' original list of images could all be characterized as negative. The list included "hustler," "violent," "dumb," "lots of children," "womanizer," and "abusive." These images are consistent with media portrayals and mainstream sentiment. The point of this exercise and this phase of class was to introduce cognitive restructuring and critical thinking. The students were asked to discuss where these images may have come from. In addition, they were asked to write a short paper about how these images could be changed and to what would they be changed. A hip-hop analysis using the song "I know I can" by hip-hop artist Nas was conducted during this section. The class was given the charge of creating the image of the ideal African American male student and then challenged to live up to that image (Akbar, 1998).

Academic competence focused on the influence of the cultural unconsciousness on the development of learning strategies. The aforementioned images exercise led to a discussion about academic performance. The central question extracted from the previous phase was, "Is your academic performance a result of the images you have about African American men?"

Students were presented with academic achievement data for the district and were asked to interpret the data. This experience allowed the students to critically analyze how their self image influenced their academic behavior. The class role-played how to encourage an underperforming classmate who is presenting as low achieving. The class actively discussed such issues as peer underperformance, teacher–student conflicts, deep breathing, and test anxiety. There is scant published research that investigates preventative strategies with African American high school males.

The lyrics and songs from music CD "The Journey," by Dr. Cornel West, were used as stimulus to discuss the legacy of African American intellectualism. Students were then given an assignment to research, using the Internet, African American scholars and inventors.

Life skills were discussed in the context of navigating the school environment. We addressed such behaviors as language, self-presentation, and code-switching. Emotional clarity, management, and expression were stressed. The intent of this phase was to address behavioral and time management. Many of the conduct issues that arose in the school could be classified by teachers as anger management issues. We believed, however, that in some cases, students were provoked or misunderstood by teachers who were impacted by stereotypical images of African American males. Students in the class were prompted, employing rational emotive therapy techniques, to understand their own behavioral reaction to being "played" (disrespected) or embarrassed. For example, in one class, we role-played how to code-switch when an individual perceived that a teacher had "dissed" him. Students were taught that emotions are natural, but that they must be controlled in a manner that was consistent with their ideal image of African American masculinity. Each student was asked to identify how mismanaged emotions led to negative consequences. Code-switching was taught as a life skill, where students mastered their emotional response and then found the appropriate outlet to vent when they believe they had been "dissed." Active learning techniques were used to encourage code-switching. The goal of this section was to engage the students in critical thinking and introspection while introducing such life skills as thought stopping and code-switching to reduce the likelihood of misconduct when emotionally vulnerable.

In addition, career exploration activities were conducted. Guided imagery exercises that promoted dreaming and strategic planning were conducted in class. Students were given an assignment to write down their dreams and a plan to see them accomplished. This required the class members to participate in a realistic self-appraisal of skills, talents, and necessary resources to realize their dreams. Such life skills as time management, study skills, conflict resolution, decision making, and communication of intentions were taught.

Social responsibility is an outcome of an empowering educational process for African American high school students. The class discussed empowerment in the context of creating and managing the ideal African American male image. Being self-sufficient, collaborative, and able to garner resources to address issues that promoted success in their community were central to the class's definition of empowerment.

The students were given an assignment to identify problems in their community that they wanted to fix. The music of hip-hop artist Mos Def was used as a stimulus for addressing the issue of social responsibility. In addition, class participants were tasked with developing a youth focused intervention for African American middle school students. The assignment included completing a Google search with assigned search terms for community and school-based interventions. The objective was to develop an intervention and propose it to the leadership of a local community center historically associated with African American families.

Measuring Culturally Responsive Interventions: Outcome Research

While research is not a major focus of this manuscript, we thought it important to give some insight into how we measured the success of this intervention. Perry (1993) called for professional counselors to understand outcomes research. It is important that consumers of culturally responsive school-based interventions understand outcome research. We advocate that culturally responsive outcome measures be utilized to measure the effectiveness of ethnic specific interventions.

We advocate expanding intervention success indicators beyond behavior and class grade indicators to include attitudes toward learning promoting strategies, learning compromising strategies, and academic self-efficacy. Of particular interest was the concept of academic self-efficacy (e.g., students' self-belief in completing academic tasks) (Multon, Brown, & Lent, 1991). Generally, we hypothesized that students who felt confident in their academic abilities (i.e., high self-efficacy) would perform to their ability and demonstrate fewer learning compromising behaviors. A mixed-method evaluation procedure was implemented to monitor the impact and influence of the course on academic performance.

Because this chapter is not intended to be a research paper, we are providing limited information about the results. A selection of the measures included in the evaluation is provided as a point of reference for future school-based prevention intervention outcome research. Questionnaires were administered to the class participants on the first day of the class, at the midterm, and again at the end of the semester. Feedback from the participants at the 6-month follow-up indicated that the last data collection (June) was not a good time to collect data because of the students focus on the upcoming summer. In addition, three focus groups were conducted at the beginning of the semester (January), at midsemester (March), and at the conclusion of the semester (June). Below are the titles, brief descriptions, and reliability coefficients for this sample for each instrument:

Academic Self-Efficacy (PATTERNS OF ADAPTIVE LEARNING SCALES (PALS), 2000, p. 24)
Scale Description: This refers to students' perceptions of their competence to complete their class work.
Internal Consistency: .86

Self-Presentation of Low Achievement (PALS, 2000, p. 27)
Scale Description: This refers to students' preferences to keep peers from knowing how well they are achieving in school.
Internal Consistency: .85

Performance-Avoidance Goal Orientation Revised (PALS, 2000, p. 13)
Scale Description: When oriented to performance-avoid goals, students' purposes or goals in an achievement setting is to avoid the demonstration of incompetence. Attention is focused on the self. A performance-avoid goal orientation has been associated with maladaptive patterns of learning.
Internal Consistency: .70

Performance Approach Goal Orientation Scale Revised (PALS, 2000, p. 12)
Scale Description: When oriented to performance-approach goals, students' purposes or goals in an achievement setting is to demonstrate their competence. Attention is focused on the self. A performance-approach orientation has been associated with both adaptive and maladaptive patterns of learning.
Internal Consistency: .90

Mastery Goal Orientation Revised (PALS, 2000, p. 11)
Scale Description: This refers to students' reasons or purposes for engaging in academic behavior. Different goals foster different response patterns. These patterns include cognitive, affective, and behavioral components, which have been characterized as more or less adaptive.
Internal Consistency: .88

Academic Self-Handicapping Strategies (PALS, 2000, p. 22)
Scale Description: This refers to strategies that are used by students so that if subsequent performance is low, those circumstances, rather than lack of ability, will be seen as the cause.
Internal Consistency: .79

Racial Awareness of Achievement Scale (Caldwell, 2003)
Scale Description: This measures race-based attitudes toward academic achievement and tests assumption of race-based anti-intellectualism.
Internal Consistency: .81

Castenell Achievement Motivation Scale (Catenell, 1994)
Scale Description: This assesses how various areas, such as peers, home, and academic influence, affect motivation within the student.
Internal Consistency: .78

Presence of Caring Individual Protective Factors
Scale Description: This measures how much the person feels he has an important person who supports him.
Internal Consistency: .70

Preliminary qualitative results obtained from two focus groups provided statements that indicated positive attitudes and experiences towards the AAEC and a change in motivational attitudes. Preliminary quantitative results from a longitudinal descriptive analysis revealed positive trends in learning promoting behaviors, reduction in learning compromising behaviors, and acquisition of an affirming disposition toward education. Preliminary quantitative results from a descriptive analysis indicated positive trends in all measures. A partial order correlation analysis found significant relationships between *Mastery Goal Orientation* and *Academic Self-Efficacy*, and between *Presence of Caring Individual Protective Factors* and *Academic Self-Efficacy*. These two variables warrant further analysis, as they could be used in future interventions for this population.

Future Directions

The purpose of this chapter was to assert the importance of a public health perspective in the role of school counselors. Because school counselors have a relatively captive audience, they are positioned as conduits for prevention interventions and health promotion. Recognizing the realities of school districts across the country (i.e., shrinking financial resources, legislative pressure to increase standardized test scores, and personnel shortages), we advocate that school counselors create progressive school counseling models that extend comprehensive guidance models by targeting proven risk and protective factors through the curriculum. In addition, we wanted to call attention to the need for culturally consistent school-based interventions that address the needs of underserved students and families. Although the focus of this chapter was not empirical research, we provided an example of an evaluation method and preliminary results.

The African American Empowerment Class demonstrates the importance of a progressive school counseling model for the provision of culturally consistent school-based prevention interventions. School counselors are positioned to advocate for underserved and marginalized students. Despite the abundance of national attention given to the "achievement gap," the literature is scant regarding interventions. There is even a larger void in research that investigates the associations between academic performance and psychological variables (e.g., wellness, distress, anxiety). Culturally relevant strength-based research concerning African Americans adolescents is noticeably missing from the literature. We hope that this chapter can initiate more dialogue that includes school counselors who play a vital part in the health of school-aged students. By proactively addressing the needs of underserved students—for example, African American males—school counseling departments may be able to increase academic performance and promote healthy attitudes and lifestyles for high-risk students. Curriculum-based interventions models are effective ways for school counselors to engage in disseminating educational and health interventions (Borders & Drury, 1992; Gysbers & Henderson, 2000).

Furthermore, we call for more interventions and research that provide faculty and staff with the skills and tools necessary to increase the learning competencies, academic self-efficacy, and general wellness of African American male students. The current teacher training and counselor education models inadequately prepare school personnel to provide services to students and families who are socially marginalized or economically disadvantaged. We suggest school counseling professionals and training programs create a discourse and training models to address the needs of students whose families have been historically underserved.

The progressive school counseling model asserts that the integration of academic underperformance and socioemotional interventions in a culturally consistent method should be included in the range of intervention options. Progressive interactions are proactive, culturally consistent, and employ community resources (Caldwell, 2001). Professional school counselors who employ this model must be multiculturally competent and community savvy to be effective. We believe that this model can be applied to a variety of marginalized students and families.

In conclusion, we advocate for a modification in school counseling language. For example, we refer to both the student and family in our interventions. This ecological perspective provides us with multiple points of intervention and acknowledges the complexity of student services. Also, we choose the term *academic performance* as opposed to *academic achievement* in our intervention because we believe that school counselors can encourage resiliency, instill hope, and help students navigate educational institutions, thus affecting their performance. We make the distinction of achievement as being a function of scores on a test which has been politicized, is culturally encapsulating, and does not adequately differentiate between external and internal influences. Professional school counselors engaged in progressive school counseling models are integral to providing leadership for accurately representing the educational potential and, ultimately, the health of historically underserved ethnic students and families in their schools.

REFERENCES

Akbar, N. (1998). *Know thyself.* Tallahassee, FL: Mind Productions.

Anderman, E. M. (2002). School effects on psychological outcomes during adolescence. *Journal of Educational Psychology, 94,* 795–809.

Aro, H. M. (1994). Risk and protective factors in depression: A developmental perspective. *Acta Psychiatrica Scandinavica, 89,* 59–64.

Arroyo, C. G., & Zigler, E. (1995). Racial identity, academic achievement, and the psychological well-being of economically disadvantaged adolescents. *Journal of Personality and Social Psychology, 69,* 903–914.

Baker, S. (1996). *School counseling for the twenty-first century* (2nd ed.). Columbus, OH: Merrill.

Bandura, A. (1986). *The social foundations of thought and action: A social cognitive theory.* Englewood Cliffs, NJ: Prentice-Hall.

Beymer, L. (1995). *Meeting the guidance and counseling needs of boys.* Alexandria, VA: American Counseling Association.

Borders, L. D., & Drury, S. M. (1992). Comprehensive school counseling programs: A review for policymakers and practitioners. *Journal of Counseling and Development, 70,* 487–498.

Caldwell, L. D. (2000). The psychology of black men. In L. Jones (Ed.), *Brothers of the academy, 30 up and coming black males in higher education.* Sterling, VA: Stylus.

Caldwell, L. D. (2001). Education as talent development: Preparing African American students for a new millennium: The greenhouse or the flower shop. *Illinois Committee on Black Concerns in Higher Education Journal.* Carbondale, IL: Southern Illinois University Carbondale.

Caldwell, L. D., & Siwatu, K. (2003). Promoting academic persistence in African American and Latino high school students. *High School Journal, 87,* 30–38.

Caldwell, L. D., & White, J. L. (2001). African-centered therapeutic and counseling interventions for African American males. In G. Brooks & G. Good (Eds.), *A new handbook of counseling and psychotherapy approaches for men.* San Francisco: Jossey-Bass.

Campbell, C. A., & Dahir, C. A. (1997). *The national standards for school counseling programs.* Alexandria, VA: American School Counseling Association.

Cicero, G., & Barton, P. (2003). Parental involvement, outreach, and the emerging role of the professional school counselor. In B. T. Eford (Ed.), *Transforming the school counseling profession.* Upper Saddle River, NJ: Merrill Prentice Hall.

Cunningham, R. T., & Boykin, W. (2004). Enhancing cognitive performance in African American children: Infusing Afro-centric perspectives and research. In R. L. Jones (Ed.), *Black psychology.* Hampton, VA: Cobb & Henry.

Doll, B. (1996). Prevalence of psychiatric disorders in children and youth: An agenda for advocacy by school psychology. *School Psychology Quarterly, 11,* 20–47.

Erford, B. T., House, R., & Martin, P. (2003). Transforming the school counseling profession. In B. T. Eford (Ed.), *Transforming the school counseling profession.* Upper Saddle River, NJ: Merrill Prentice Hall.

Evans, S. W., & Weist, M. D. (2004). Implementing empirically supported treatments in the schools: What are we asking? *Clinical Child and Family Psychology Review, 7*(4), 263–267.

Fordham, S., & Ogbu, J. U. (1986). Black students' school success: "Coping with burden of 'acting white.'" *The Urban Review, 18,* 176–206.

Fuller, T. (1992). Masked depression in maladaptive Black adolescents. *The School Counselor, 40,* 24–31.

Gysber, N. (1990). *Comprehensive guidance programs that work.* Ann Arbor, MI: ERIC/CASS.

Gysbers, N., & Henderson, P. (2000). *Developing and managing your school guidance program.* Alexandria, VA: American Association for Counseling and Development.

Hilliard, A. G. (1997). *SBA: The reawakening of the African Mind.* Gainesville, FL: Makare.

Kambon, K. K. K. (1998). *African/Black psychology in the American context: An African-centered approach.* Tallahassee, FL: Nubian Nation.

Kaslow, N. J., Price, A. W., Wyckoff, S., Grall, M. B., Sherry, A., & Young, S. (2004). Person factors associated with suicidal behavior among African American women and men. *Cultural Diversity and Ethnic Minority Psychology, 10,* 5–22.

Keisner, J. (2002). Depressive symptoms in early adolescence: Their relations with classroom problem behavior and peer status. *Journal of Research on Adolescence, 12,* 463–478.

Kunjufu, J. (1995). *Countering the conspiracy to destroy Black boys.* Chicago: African American Images.

Kunjufu, K. (2000). *Developing positive self-images and discipline in Black children.* Chicago: African American Images.

Lambert, S. F., McCreary, B. T., Joiner, T. E., Schmidt, N. B., & Ialongo, N. S. (2004). Structure of anxiety and depression in urban youth: An examination of the tripartite model. *Journal of Consulting and Clinical Psychology, 72,* 904–908.

LaViest, T. A. (2005). *Minority populations and health: An introduction to health disparities in the United States.* San Francisco: Jossey-Bass.

Midgley, C. (2002). *Goals, goal structures, and patterns of adaptive learning.* Mahwah, NJ: Lawrence Erlbaum.

Milner, H. R., Caldwell, L., & Murray, I. (2004). When race shows up in the curriculum: Teacher (self) reflective responsibility in students' opportunities to learn. In E. W. Ross (Eds), *Defending public schools.* Westport, CT: Praeger.

Multon, K. D., Brown, S. D., & Lent, R. W. (1991). Relation of self-efficacy beliefs to academic outcomes: A meta-analytic investigation. *Journal of Counseling Psychology, 38,* 30–38.

Osborne, J. W. (1999). Unraveling underachievement among African American Boys from an identification with academics perspective. *Journal of Negro Education, 68*(4), 555–565.

Perry, T., Steele, C., & Hilliard, A. (2003). *Young gifted and black: Promoting high achievement among African American students.* Boston: Beacon Press.

Porter, M. (1997). *Kill them before they grow: Misdiagnosis of African American boys in American classrooms.* Chicago: African American Images.

Sagrestano, L. M., Paikoff, R. L., Holmbeck, G. N., & Fendrich, M. (2003). A longitudinal examination of the familial risk factors for depression among inner-city African American adolescents. *Journal of Family Psychology, 17,* 108–120.

Saunders, J., Davis, L., Williams, T., & William, J. H. (2004). Gender differences in self-perceptions and academic outcomes: A study of African American high school students. *Journal of Youth and Adolescence, 33*(1).

Spencer, M. B., Kim, S., & Marshall, S. (1987). Double stratification and psychological risk: Adaptational processes and school achievement of Black children. *Journal of Negro Education, 56,* 77–87.

Stevenson, H. W., Chen, C., Uttal, D. H. (1990). Beliefs and achievement: A study of Black, White, and Hispanic children. *Child Development, 61,* 508–523.

Thomas, C. R., & Holzer, C. E., III (1999). National distribution of child and adolescents psychiatrists. *Journal of the American Academy of Child and Adolescent Psychiatry, 38*, 9–15.

U.S. Department of Health and Human Services (1999). *Mental health: A Report of the Surgeon General.* Rockville, MD: U.S. Department of Health and Human Services, Substance Abuse and Mental Health Services Administration, Center for Mental Health Services, National Institutes of Health, National Institute of Mental Health.

Wilson, D. K., Rodrigue, J. R., & Taylor, W. C. (1997). *Health-promoting and health compromising behaviors among minority adolescents.* Washington, DC: American Psychological Association.

Woodson, C. G. (1933). *The mis-education of the Negro.* Trenton, NJ: The Associated Publishers.

3

Student Development

XV
FACILITATING PERSONAL AND SOCIAL DEVELOPMENT

NANCY BODENHORN
Virginia Tech

The *American School Counselor Association (ASCA) National Standards*, and most school counseling programs, indicate provision of student development in three areas: (a) personal/social, (b) career, and (c) academic. One of the suppositions of this chapter is that the differentiation between these areas of development is somewhat artificial. In other words, if an area of the school counseling program is ostensibly geared to personal/social development, this will also affect students' career and academic development. The Collaboration for Academic, Social, and Emotional Learning (CASEL; http://www.casel.org) provides updated research on the synergy between these areas of student development. For planning, programmatic, and accountability reasons, it can be helpful to differentiate these areas, but from a holistic point of view, student development in these areas is intertwined.

That being said, this chapter will focus on those programs that are primarily geared to personal/social development.

> Personal/social development includes the acquisition of skills, attitudes, and knowledge that help students understand and respect self and others, acquire effective interpersonal skills, understand safety and survival skills, and develop into contributing members of society. Personal/social development standards and competencies ensure that students have learned to negotiate their way successfully and safely in the increasingly complex and diverse world of the twenty-first century. (Baker & Gerler, 2004, p. 380)

More than any other area of the school counseling program, the responsibility for personal/social development is in the realm of the entire school staff. Indeed, some of the programs described later in the chapter indicate that the whole staff, including custodians, bus drivers, and cafeteria workers as well as teachers and administrators, need to be trained in order to fully support students. Needless to say, parents and families are essential in their students' personal/social development. School counselors frequently serve as consultants for parents and families who may struggle with facilitating development in this area.

The themes of the *ASCA National Model* (advocacy, leadership, collaboration, and systemic change) are productive lenses through which to view personal/social development in the schools. Collaboration is needed with all constituents of the school and community. Schools showing the most success in personal/social development have been those in which comprehensive guidance programs are more thoroughly implemented (Lapan, Gysbers, & Petroski, 2001), schools with integrated prevention programs across grade levels and courses, and schools that work systematically to establish a community where personal/social learning is integrated with academic learning (Elias, Hunter, & Kress, 2001). Advocacy, leadership, and commitment to systemic change to implement programs with children's holistic development at the core are needed to ensure that the personal/social realm is included in schoolwide efforts.

Personal/social development is supported in a variety of ways in the schools. The programmatic avenues that will be covered in this chapter include character education, moral development, emotional intelligence, self-efficacy, self-esteem and other-esteem, decision making, and assertiveness. Anger management, conflict resolution, and goal setting are not included here, though they are considered areas of personal/social development, because they are covered in other chapters.

Theory

Character Education

According to the ASCA (2005) position statement on character education,

> Inclusion of character education in the school curriculum helps students acquire the knowledge, skills and positive attitudes necessary for student achievement and success in life. The professional school counselor understands that the acquisition of positive character values promotes healthy student development. These universal values include such traits as honesty, integrity, trustworthiness, respect, responsibility, fairness, caring and citizenship, which all affirm basic human worth and dignity and support healthy communities. Character education emphasizes key social values and encourages students to become responsible, contributing members of society. (¶ 2)

Character education has sometimes come under criticism based on a misperception that schools are selecting and endorsing specific values that do not represent all populations, undermining or overstepping families as the primary purveyors of ethics and values. Some critics indicate that this is the purview of families and religious organizations, rather than of schools. The values espoused in character education programs, however, are basic to student development in a pluralistic classroom and society, and they are not contradictory to behavioral values espoused by parents or religions (Lickona, 1991).

Many states currently mandate that character education be included in the school curriculum. The coordination and selection of the program frequently falls within the school counseling program development. This responsibility is endorsed by ASCA.

Good character is conceptualized in three domains: (a) moral knowing, (b) moral feeling, and (c) moral action. The three domains interact and build on each other as we develop.

- Moral knowing incorporates moral awareness (recognizing that an issue may be considered right or wrong), knowing moral values (values to which one's society, family, and/or culture ascribe), perspective taking (ability to take another person's viewpoint), moral reasoning (understanding why being moral is important and understanding how to be moral), decision making (ability to think through a moral problem), and self-knowledge.
- Moral feeling incorporates conscience (knowing what is right and feeling an obligation to do what is right), self-esteem, empathy (emotional perspective taking, identifying with another person), loving the good (taking pleasure in doing good), self-control, and humility.
- Moral action incorporates competence (ability to turn moral judgment and feeling into effective action), will (acting on hard choices), and habit (developed through frequent practice). To create a school environment that encourages character development based on respect and responsibility, the school, parents, and community must develop a partnership of commitment; a positive moral climate must be created in the school; and caring must be expanded beyond the classroom (Lickona, 1991).

Moral Development

Moral development can overlap with character education, but there are specific theories of moral development that are important to understand and that inform the practices of school counseling. Kohlberg (1969) outlined six stages of moral judgment based on his research. His research has come under some criticism, partly because his subjects were exclusively male, and other researchers have added a responsiveness or care dimension to Kohlberg's stages as a "different voice" in moral development (Gilligan, 1982).

Kohlberg's (1969) stages of moral development include six stages in three levels. When people are in level 1, Preconventional, their moral values are externally based. Within this level, stage 1 is earmarked by recognizing whether a behavior is rewarded or punished and then acting out of personal concern to avoid punishment. During stage 2, people begin to recognize that others are affected, but the main rationale behind choosing an action is based on whether the action will benefit the self in some way. The hallmark for this stage is, "What is in it for me?" When people are in level 2, Conventional, they extend their understanding of reciprocal relationships. Within this level, people in stage 3 are motivated by desire for approval and acceptance, so they tend to conform to group norms. During stage 4, people begin to consider a broader scope of society, but rely on laws, rules, social order, and duty as their guidelines for behavior. When people are in level 3, Postconventional, they begin to utilize principles to determine their actions. During stage 5, societal and legal contracts are differentiated from legal absolutes, and judgments can be made based on the greatest good for the greatest number and the concept of cooperative collaboration.

Stage 6, apparently rarely reached, is earmarked by utilizing universal ethical principles that would be applicable for all people in all cultures at all times (Kohlberg; Newman & Newman, 1995; Paisley & Hubbard, 1994).

More recently, theorists have reconfigured moral development into three schemas (Rest, Narvaez, Bebeau, & Thoma, 1999; Rest, Narvaez, Thoma, & Bebeau, 2000). As opposed to stages, the schemas are conceptualized as changes in frequency of usage, understanding that development occurs at a variety of rates. Rest et al. (2000) also acknowledged that cross-cultural similarities and differences remain as and raise questions in morality, rather than presenting morality as a universal concept. The reconfiguration is named a neo-Kohlbergian approach, as the basis of Kohlberg's theory remains.

Rest et al. (1999, 2000) indicated that elementary children are in the Personal Interests Schema, which corresponds to Kohlberg's stages 2 and 3. Adolescents begin to recognize societal needs and they begin to think in terms of "macromorality." Macromorality, as opposed to earlier micromorality, situates moral resolutions in the context of what is good for the greater good beyond self, family, and friends, and it wrestles with the questions of how to organize a network of cooperation on a societywide basis and on issues of social justice. When these issues can be cognitively dealt with, people move into the Maintaining Norms Schema, which corresponds to Kohlberg's stage 4. According to this schema, law and order are critical to organizing societies, respect for the social system is demonstrated by obeying authority, and maintaining the social order defines morality. Entering into adulthood, people start to utilize a Postconventional Schema, corresponding to Kohlberg's stages 5 and 6. According to this schema, moral obligations are to be based on shared ideals, are fully reciprocal, and are open to scrutiny. Shared ideals are not mandated, but they need to be recognized, acknowledged, and justifiable. Laws, roles, codes, and contracts are recognized as social arrangements that can be successfully designed in a variety of ways, and thus, they can be changed.

Understanding students' developmental levels and ability to conceptualize society is important for school counselors. We work directly with students on moral development issues, both one-on-one, in small groups, and in classroom guidance lessons. We also consult with teachers and parents who interact with students as they develop their moral identities.

Emotional Intelligence

The most comprehensive definition of emotional intelligence (EI) is

> the ability to perceive accurately, appraise, and express emotion; the ability to access and/or generate feelings when they facilitate thought; the ability to understand emotion and emotional knowledge; and the ability to regulate emotions to promote emotional and intellectual growth. (Mayer & Salovey, 1997, p. 10)

Thus, EI relates to both our self-knowledge and knowledge of others' emotions and emotional expressions, as well as to the regulation of our own emotions.

EI is directly related to many of the prevention education programs targeting drugs, sex, anger, and relationships. These programs, in general, may include lessons on identifying feelings, reacting to and managing feelings, and making decisions based on a variety of factors, not solely on emotions (Ciarrochi, Forgas, & Mayer, 2001; Goleman, 1994). Rational Emotive Behavior Therapy (REBT) counseling, frequently used with adolescents, is also dependent on the skills of Emotional Intelligence.

Self-Efficacy, Self-Esteem, and Other-Esteem

Self-efficacy is one of the cornerstones of social cognitive theory. Self-efficacy is defined as "beliefs in one's capabilities to organize and execute the courses of action required to manage prospective situations. Efficacy beliefs influence how people think, feel, motivate themselves, and act" (Bandura, 1995, p. 2). Each of us has a sense of our efficacy in particular areas of our lives, so one may have a sense of high self-efficacy regarding math, but low self-efficacy regarding basketball.

Self-efficacy is differentiated from self-esteem in that self-efficacy is derived from accomplishments and is specific to areas of activity, whereas self-esteem is a global sense of self-worth derived from messages of love, support, admiration, and approval (Newman & Newman, 1995). School counseling programs and educators seem to be shifting their focus from developing student self-esteem to developing student self-efficacy as the standards-based movement takes hold. These concepts are certainly intertwined and can build upon each other, but people may have a high level of self-efficacy (especially when limited to one particular area of accomplishment) and not have a high level of self-esteem, and vice versa.

Other-esteem is not seen widely in the literature, but it is a reaction to previous focus on developing self-esteem. Other-esteem serves as a reminder that we need to balance self-worth with recognizing and respecting the worth of others as well. Multiculturalism, prejudice reduction, anti-bullying, conflict resolution, and peer helper programs are all based on the need for increased other-esteem.

Decision Making

Decision-making skills are a major part of the *ASCA National Standards* in all of the three components. Students make daily decisions regarding their academic and career choices, as well as their personal/social choices. Teaching a decision-making model of identifying options; listing potential positive and negative consequences; and choosing, acting, and evaluating the decision has probably been included in school counseling programs since their inception. Decision making is, similar to EI, commonly included in prevention education programs.

Assertiveness

Assertiveness incorporates self-advocacy and independent communication. Children and adolescents frequently need training and practice in how to ask for support in productive ways. Self-advocacy skills include being able to identify one's needs through self-knowledge and to recognize that one's personal needs also have an impact on others. Communication skills are then built upon recognizing others' needs as well as one's own and asking persistently for solutions to meet ones own needs without infringing on the needs of others. Counselors frequently provide role modeling, role-play practice, and support for students in developing these skills.

Research

The school counseling profession has historically been weak in producing outcome research, so research findings on programs that serve to develop personal/social competence stem from a variety of sources.

Character Education

Character education is an area that, while widely implemented in schools nationwide, has not been widely researched in comparative studies. Additionally, most character education programs are developed to be used by all school staff members, primarily delivered by classroom teachers, rather than necessarily using a school counselor. SUNY Cortland's Center for the Fourth and Fifth R's (n.d.) Web site listed 43 programs or organizations that deal with character education, and more are devoted specifically to bullying or violence prevention that overlap significantly with character education programs. These programs and organizations may change over time, so updated information is best found on the Internet. Research on particular programs can be difficult to evaluate for objectiveness. School systems that choose to purchase any given program are invested in obtaining positive results, as are the organizations that produce the programs.

Developing or utilizing a character education program comprehensively is undoubtedly better than either doing nothing or patching a program together nonsequentially and nontheoretically. At this point in time, however, research has not identified one program as the most superior when compared with others. One study based on longitudinal (three-year) data of five systems in one state that implemented different programs found a significant increase in indicators of school climate in all systems implementing a program. Recommendations are made to match the program characteristics to aspects of the community, but evaluators were not able to identify differences between the programs utilized (Skaggs & Bodenhorn, 2006). One very well-designed study utilized one group of schools that did not receive any character education program and another group of schools that implemented the Second Step program (Committee for Children, 2007) in second and third grades. Researchers, who relied on trained behavior coders who did not know which students had received the program and which had not, found significant differences in aggressive behaviors and prosocial skills that remained over a 6-month period after the program was initiated (Grossman et al., 1997). Similarly, *Character Counts!* (Josephson Institute of Ethics, n.d.) includes a variety of studies and anecdotal evaluations that include indications that the program increases academic achievement and lowers disruptive behaviors, including cheating, vandalism, absenteeism, racial incidents, fights, and discipline referrals. While these studies identify one particular program, the results indicate that the program is better than no program, not that it is better than another particular program.

Research on character education programs will, I hope, continue to grow. Some of the continual challenges to research in this area are measuring and attributing the outcomes. A variety of efforts are made throughout the community to develop children's character. The types of measurements that are currently used to assess character education are either behavioral (i.e., changes in discipline, aggression) or attitudinal in terms of safety and comfort in school (school climate). These are expected behaviors related to an increase in the values espoused in character education programs, but are really a by-product of character development.

Moral Development

Simplified categorizations of approaches to moral development are as "direct" and "indirect." Direct approaches rely on presenting role models, telling stories with heroes and heroines who exhibit moral characteristics, studying various virtues, and providing opportunities to reason through moral dilemmas. Indirect approaches rely on holding class meetings, presenting opportunities for perspective taking and role-taking, using literature to stimulate discussions, and exhibiting a commitment to increase the level of student autonomy. A more comprehensive way to understand approaches to moral education, and a reasonable way for school counselors to evaluate or design programs for moral development, is to understand the psychological, moral, and educational assumptions behind the approach and to identify the contingent factors involved or assumed (Sanger & Osguthorpe, 2005). Similar to a counselor's identifying a counseling theory that works best for that counselor and a particular setting, identifying an approach to moral education can be dependent on the belief systems and characteristics within the school.

Situations arise on a regular basis in schools that involve student moral development. All school staff intervene with children if they are behaving in ways that would be considered morally inappropriate (e.g., bullying, fighting, ridiculing, ostracizing). Ideally, programs are in place to prevent this type of inappropriate behavior.

Creating cognitive dissonance is necessary to provoke someone developmentally (Piaget, as cited in Paisley & Hubbard, 1994). Dissonance is achieved when thoughts, feelings, and behaviors are not balanced, and it is stimulated by interaction with the social environment, especially with peers, when conflicts arise. Many situations present opportunities to discuss moral decisions, including children's books related to moral issues; situations that have occurred and are presented in various disciplines, such as history, literature, or science; hypothetical but believable dilemmas; spontaneous experiences that occur in everyday life; and simulations such as a "blue-eyed/brown-eyed" oppression experience (Maslovaty, 2000). With any of these open-ended stimulants, a dilemma discussion can be developed for students to contemplate and convey their own reasoning about decision making in challenging situations.

Counselors are advised to recognize the various cognitive and moral developmental stages. Using plus-one reasoning, discussions should be geared to the current developmental level and one above. Students are able to understand their own level and those developmentally below them, but are only able to grapple with issues represented within one step above their level. Students are overwhelmed and frustrated with discussions that are too far above their developmental level (Paisley & Hubbard, 1994).

Emotional Intelligence

Emotional intelligence is conceptualized as three different skills: (a) recognizing our own emotions, (b) recognizing others' emotions, and (c) managing our emotions.

Recognizing our own emotions is a basis of person-centered therapy, wherein the counselor reflects emotions indicated either directly or indirectly. All counselors have developed the skills to be able to support children in identifying and recognizing their emotions.

Recognizing others' emotions is similar to the trait of empathy. Research on empathy development leads us to the ambiguous generalization that empathy can probably be learned within limitations of age, maturity, and experience (Duan, Rose, & Kraatz, 2002). The key ingredients to empathy development seem to be role- and perspective-taking (Duan et al., 2002). One activity that uses role-taking is theater. Kruger, Samuelson, Kapsch, Flanigan, and Harris (2003) presented results of a pre-post study with 111 middle school students experiencing an actor-in-residence over a 2-year period. The control group empathy scores decreased, while the intervention group's increased. For this group, the experience of exploring others' perspectives through the dramatic arts increased the component skills of empathy in a measurable way. Similarly, volunteer service is advocated for students at all levels, starting in preschool. Contributory service has resulted in increased empathy as well as valuing everyone's contributions (Elias et al., 2001).

Managing emotions is a basis of the various forms of cognitive–behavioral therapy, wherein the counselor helps students balance their feelings and behaviors in avenues that will avert problems.

Emotional intelligence correlates positively with life satisfaction, ability to maintain self-esteem and positive mood in a negative situation, ability to maximize the impact of positive mood, interpersonal relationship quality, academic success, occupational success, and leadership effectiveness (Ciarrochi et al., 2001). Additionally, EI moderates the effects of stress on mental health. In other words, those people with high emotional intelligence who experience stress experience fewer mental health problems than those with low emotional intelligence do under the same stress (Ciarrochi, Deane, & Anderson, 2002).

Self-Efficacy, Self-Esteem, and Other-Esteem

Self-efficacy contributes to resiliency, perseverance, positive risk-taking, and lower anxiety levels. Self-efficacy is learned through direct mastery experiences, through vicarious experiences of watching others (role models), and through persuasion or encouragement (Bandura, 1995). Fall and McLeod (2001) developed a self-efficacy scale for student learning. Identifying students with low self-efficacy can help counselors and teachers understand student behavior and provide appropriate interventions.

Self-esteem is also related to resiliency, positive risk-taking, optimism, and social relationships. Self-esteem is enhanced through a sense of belongingness, continuity of values and experiences, and relationships with at least one person who extends unconditional positive regard, as well as through reinforcement of skill areas (Newman & Newman, 1995). Outcome research on elementary school programs designed to enhance self-esteem has found no consistent results regarding self-esteem, but it did find an impact on achievement (Whiston & Sexton, 1998).

Research specific to other-esteem in the form of prejudice reduction is also scarce. One study reported positive findings for a program with fourth graders receiving a 1-week group guidance session. Students who received the program exhibited more cooperative social skills than those who did not receive the program (Omizo & D'Andrea, 1995). Similar to findings with character education and comprehensive guidance programs, the success of antibullying and respect programs seems to be reliant on the commitment of the entire school staff to interact with students exhibiting antisocial behavior.

Decision Making and Assertiveness

Little research has been conducted specific to these areas of practice. Social skills training in general, which can incorporate decision making and assertive communication, was an area that showed a trend of positive results, according to a review of school counseling outcome research (Whiston & Sexton, 1998).

Practice

This section is divided into two parts. The first part focuses on the different roles that school counselors perform at different academic levels in the realm of personal and social development. The second part focuses on some sample resources and programs that can be utilized to guide practice.

Elementary School

Elementary school counselors, according to comprehensive guidance program suggested guidelines, spend between 35 and 45% of their time delivering guidance lessons in a classroom setting. School counselors should advocate for a developmentally appropriate, theoretically sound, research-based program suitable to their school setting. Character education, moral education, and emotional intelligence programs frequently organized into 30 to 45 minute lesson plans are widely available, but can be expensive for cash-strapped school systems. Individually developed lessons can be effective and valuable, but not as effective as comprehensive programs that are integrated into the school culture.

Many elementary school counselors also offer small group sesssions for students with particular developmental needs (e.g., students whose parents are divorcing). These offer understanding, skill-building opportunities, and socialization for children who need particular support in areas either where their circumstances are special or where they may lag behind their peers. Group counseling was found to be especially effective for elementary students (Prout & Prout, 1998; Whiston & Sexton, 1998).

Individual counseling is an appropriate practice for processing situations that occur in schools. Some elementary school children need the focus and attention offered only in individual meetings. Counselors need to use good judgment to not spend too much time in individual sessions, to the detriment of all the other students in the school.

Consultation is critical to the development of a school counseling program in elementary schools. Elementary school counselors perceive their role in school–community partnerships as being more important to their school than secondary school counselors do (Bryan & Holcomb-McCoy, 2004). Elementary counselors have more contact with and provide more consultation for families and teachers than secondary counselors do (Isaacs & Stone, 1999). Keys, Bemak, Carpenter, and King-Sears (1998) advocated for a collaborative consultation model for counselors to work with families, teachers, and community providers. The collaborative consultation model is based on the parity of team members, mutual goals, interdependence of support, and shared responsibility, resources and accountability. This type of support, especially for at-risk children, could be instrumental in providing continuity and stability for children.

Middle School

Middle school counselors need to be masters of transition. Not only do they oversee the students' transition from elementary to middle and then on to high schools, but adolescence itself is a time of personal and physical transitions.

Many middle school counselors are instrumental in building communities that support the transitions their students' experience. A variety of programs that essentially establish smaller communities within the school have proven to be beneficial (Akos & Galassi, 2004; Lawson, McClain, Matlock-Hetzel, Duffy, & Urbanovski, 1997; Myrick, 1997). Overseeing these programs and/or providing activities or guidelines for the small community meetings to support emotional development are frequently the responsibility of the school counselor. These communities (perhaps established as teacher-advisory or school-within-school) can provide support similar to the elementary classroom guidance, utilizing many staff members as facilitators.

Consultation and training with staff is therefore critical in developing these programs.

Small group sessions are also frequently held in middle schools. Some counselors find groups especially beneficial for adolescents, who are frequently hyper-aware of peer reactions, status, and pressures. Through the group interaction process, they learn how to interact appropriately, if the group is well-constructed, with some role models and students at slightly different levels of development so that students are exposed to the plus-one reasoning described earlier (Brown & Trusty, 2005; Paisley & Hubbard, 1994).

High School

Some high school counselors indicate that because they are so involved in the academic and career aspects of student development, the personal/social aspects get less attention. It is important to remember the interaction of holistic development. College and career choices, as well as academic achievement, are intertwined with personal values, decision-making, self-efficacy, interpersonal relations, and goals. Students are best served by counselors who work from a holistic framework and support the student in balancing these various aspects of their development.

Coordinating small group meetings can be more difficult in high schools, where students are in different class sections and teachers may be very protective of their class time. More time is usually spent in individual planning sessions. Gysbers and Henderson (1994) have recommended that high school counselors spend between 25 and 35% of their time with this avenue of delivery.

Consultation with families of high school students is a complex practice. Families are still very important support systems for most students, but adolescents want, need, and deserve more autonomy and independence as they mature. The most common and most challenging ethical dilemmas reported by school counselors are situations involving confidentiality of student personal issues (Bodenhorn, 2006), which would most likely occur in counseling sessions involving personal and social issues. Consultation with parents of adolescents with whom the counselor holds personal confidences is challenging because the counselor needs to balance the team building process with family supporters and the confidentiality needs of the student.

Identifying Programs

School counselors should ideally be at the forefront of deciding what program will best fit in their particular school and community, as well as the implementation, follow-through, and evaluation of the program. As indicated from some of the research described above, the context of the community is important to implementation decisions. School counselors know their community, the values and norms of their community, and the developmental needs of the students in the community. School counselors may need to adapt a program to their particular community. For example, cultures vary in the value placed on assertiveness, expression of emotion, and independence. If a particular skill is not likely to be valued in the community, some of the lessons in these areas might best be downplayed.

Several agencies provide ratings and evaluations of programs designed to target personal/social development. The titles, descriptions, marketing, and evaluation of the programs included may be specific to one domain of personal/social development. Personal/social development can impact academic development; therefore, the various domains of personal/social development are not easily separated. Drug and violence prevention programs include many aspects of emotional intelligence, moral development, other-esteem, and decision making. Because of the overlap between personal/social development and drug and violence prevention, the agencies that evaluate programs specific to these prevention efforts are included. Due to the constant improvement and development of educational programs, school counselors are advised to check the following Web sites for updated information evaluating related programs when selecting programs to use in their schools. Based on the rigorous research requirements used by these agencies, comprehensive programs have an advantage in the evaluation process. While these programs are undoubtedly more effective, they are also significantly more expensive to implement. School counselors may advocate for the model programs endorsed by these agencies, but realistically need to be prepared to creatively develop and adapt programs and curricula for their schools.

1. www.casel.org. The Collaborative for Academic, Social, and Emotional Learning delineates five developmental areas: (a) self-awareness, (b) social awareness, (c) self-management, (d) relationship skills, and (e) responsible decision making. For each of these areas, the site offers an evaluation of each program covered (currently 80, with 22 indicated as "select"). This site also includes a general indication of the cost of the program and the level of support provided.
2. www.modelprograms.samhsa.gov. The Substance Abuse and Mental Health Services Administration provides a database of programs with information regarding target population, strategies, outcomes, and approximate costs. Currently, 67 programs are included in their model program selection.
3. http://www.nida.nih.gov/Prevention/Prevopen.html. The National Institute on Drug Abuse currently

includes information about 10 programs that address 14 principles of prevention. The principles identified are common to resiliency and personal/social development.
4. http://www.colorado.edu/cspv/blueprints/index.html. With support from the Office of Juvenile Justice and Delinquency Prevention, the Center for the Study and Prevention of Violence provides an evaluation of programs geared to preventing violence. This site currently designates 11 programs as "model," and an additional 16 as "promising."

The programs described in the next section are not meant to be an endorsement of these particular programs, but instead to serve as a guide to what implementing these and similar programs may involve for the school counselor. Each of the programs included is evaluated positively by at least one of the previously mentioned agencies.

I Can Problem Solve (ICPS)

ICPS (Shure, 2001) is a series of three books with lessons focused on resolving conflicts and preventing antisocial behavior for different elementary levels: (a) preschool, (b) primary, and (c) intermediate elementary. Each book contains a series of lessons designed to teach children how to think about problems. The lessons involve games, stories, puppets, and role play. Each lesson contains a script and reproducible materials. The author has also developed a parent involvement component: *Raising a Thinking Child Workbook*. Training and consultation are provided, but the books are sold independently and could be used by an elementary school counselor in classroom guidance lessons.

Promoting Alternative Thinking Strategies (PATHS)

PATHS (Kusche & Greenberg, 1994) is a curriculum for kindergarten through sixth grade geared to violence prevention. The areas of development targeted in this program include self-control, emotional awareness, self-esteem, and interpersonal problem solving. The curriculum is designed for classroom teacher delivery of 20-minute lessons three times per week, so school counselors can either be consultants for the teachers or participate in the delivery. Parent involvement, encouraged through letters, handouts, and activities, provides many avenues for school counselors to integrate the PATHS lessons into the school counseling program.

Training in program implementation is optional, but recommended. Training can be completed on-site, either with an entire staff or by a process of training trainers who then train the remaining staff. The school counselor would likely be one of the trainers, although there may be advantages to having others who are less familiar with the original concepts have the most direct training. The school counselor should monitor the integrity of the training delivered to other staff, even if not directly involved, and serve as a resource for any staff member who has difficulty implementing the expected communication skills or lesson material. If a school were to purchase the program but not the training, the school counselor would be the logical person to implement the program and train the teachers as necessary, based on the specialty education earned in school counselor master's programs.

Second Step

Second Step was developed by the Committee for Children (2007; http://www.cfchildren.org/programs/ssp/overview/). Although Second Step is identified as a violence and bullying prevention program for grades pre-K through 9, the focus of the program includes familiar personal/social skills of empathy, anger management, impulse control, and problem solving. Second Step, named to recognize that families are the first step in social skill building and schools are the second, provides parent workshops during which parents learn and practice the communication skills their children are learning, as well as how to reinforce the skills at home. Materials are provided for teachers of each grade and subject level to infuse the message of respect in all learning areas. Either training is offered for the on-site staff, or a few staff members are trained as trainers for the rest of the staff.

Tribes TLC®

Tribes TLC®, developed by CenterSource Systems (n.d.; www.tribes.com), is designed for grades K–12. The goal of the program is to increase respect for differences, self-efficacy, and belongingness through developing a positive classroom and school environment. Group work and collaborative learning are critical to developing this environment, which involves empathy, active listening, goal setting, and conflict resolution. Teachers learn about the stages of group development and select strategies appropriate to the developmental stage of long-term cooperative learning groups (called "tribes"). School counselors, with background and training in group dynamics, would be natural leaders and/or consultants in implementing this program.

Future Directions

School counselors, through their leadership and advocacy, need to keep personal/social developmental issues within the mission of their schools. Education has a history of following trends, and the current trend is for standards and high-stakes testing. It is easy for personal/social issues to be set aside in this climate. It is our responsibility to keep holistic development, meaning all three areas of the *ASCA National Standards*, central to the educational process.

Clearly, we also need to activate more research with school counselor involvement in all areas of development, especially personal/social. It is disturbing that none of the major studies describing character education and moral development within the schools referred to utilizing the skills of the school counselor. Of the three developmental areas, personal/social development may be the most difficult to assess because it is hard to quantify. Accountability is a major component of a school counseling program, according to the *ASCA National Model*. As a profession, we need to be able to indicate the impact that our programs have on student development. Sadly, school counselor positions are still in jeopardy in some school systems based on funding and budgets. Until we prove, through research, that our programs are essential to student development, we will continue to be in jeopardy, which means that the students we serve are in jeopardy of losing our skills of supporting personal/social development.

References

Akos, P., & Galassi, J. P. (2004). Middle and high school transitions as viewed by students, parents, and teachers. *Professional School Counseling, 7*(4), 212–221.

American School Counselor Association. (2005). Position statement: Character education. Retrieved August 30, 2007, from http://www.schoolcounselor.org/content.asp?contentid=193

Baker, S. B., & Gerler, E. R. (2004). *School counseling for the twenty-first century* (4th ed.). Upper Saddle River, NJ: Merrill Prentice Hall.

Bandura, A. (1995). Exercise of personal and collective efficacy in changing societies. In A. Bandura (Ed.), *Self-efficacy in changing societies* (pp. 1–45). Cambridge, UK: Cambridge University Press.

Bodenhorn, N. (2006). Exploratory study of common and challenging ethical dilemmas experienced by professional school counselors. *Professional School Counseling, 10,* 195-202.

Brown, D., & Trusty, J. (2005). *Designing and leading comprehensive school counseling programs.* Belmont, CA: Brooks/Cole.

Bryan, J., & Holcomb-McCoy, C. (2004). School counselors' perceptions of their involvement in school-family-community partnerships. *Professional School Counseling, 7*(3), 162–171.

CenterSource Systems. (n.d.). Tribes learning communities. Retrieved August 30, 2007, from http://www.tribestlc.com

Ciarrochi, J., Deane, F. P., & Anderson, S. (2002). Emotional intelligence moderates the relationships between stress and mental health. *Personality and Individual Differences, 32,* 197–209.

Ciarrochi, J., Forgas, J. P., & Mayer, J. D. (Eds.). (2001). *Emotional intelligence in everyday life: A scientific inquiry.* Philadelphia: Psychological Press.

Committee for Children. (2007). Second step. Lessons for school and life. Retrieved August 30, 2007, http://www.cfchildren.org/programs/ssp/overview.

Duan, C., Rose, T. B., & Kraatz, R. A. (2002). Empathy. In G. S. Tryon (Ed.), *Counseling based on process research: Applying what we know* (pp. 197–231). Boston: Allyn & Bacon.

Elias, M. J., Hunter, L, & Kress, J. S. (2001). Emotional intelligence and education. In J. Ciarrochi, J. P. Forgas, & J. D. Mayer (Eds), *Emotional intelligence in everyday life* (pp. 133–149). Philadelphia: Psychology Press.

Fall, M., & McLeod, E. H. (2001). Identifying and assisting children with low self-efficacy. *Professional School Counseling, 4,* 334–341.

Gilligan, C. (1982). *In a different voice.* Cambridge, MA: Harvard University Press.

Goleman, D. (1994). *Emotional intelligence.* New York: Bantam.

Grossman, D., Neckerman, H. J., Koepsell, T. D., Liu, J. Y., Asher, K. N., Beland, K., et al. (1997). The effectiveness of a violence prevention curriculum among children in elementary school. *Journal of the American Medical Association, 277,* 1605–1611.

Gysbers, N. C., & Henderson, P. (1994). *Developing and managing your school counseling guidance program* (2nd ed.). Alexandria, VA: American Counseling Association.

Isaacs, M. L., & Stone, C. (1999). School counselors and confidentiality: Factors affecting professional choices. *Professional School Counseling, 2,* 258–266.

Josephson Institute of Ethics. (n.d.) Character counts! The evidence. Retrieved May 30, 2003, from http://www.charactercounts.org/doing/survey-reports.htm

Keys, S. G., Bemak, F., Carpenter, S. L., & King-Sears, M. F. (1998). Collaborative consultants: A new role for counselors serving at-risk youth. *Journal of Counseling and Development, 76,* 123–133.

Kohlberg, L. (1969). Stage and sequence: The cognitive-developmental approach to socialization. In D. A. Goslin (Ed.), *Handbook of socialization theory and research* (pp. 347–480). Chicago: Rand McNally.

Kruger, A. C., Samuelson, P., Kapsch, L., Flanigan, G., & Harris, K. (2003, April). Experience in dramatic writing promotes empathy. Paper presented at the Meeting of the Society for Research in Child Development, Tampa, FL.

Kusche, C. A., & Greenberg, M. T. (1994). *The PATHS curriculum.* Seattle, WA: Developmental Research and Programs.

Lapan, R. T., Gysbers, N. C., & Petroski, G. (2001). Helping seventh graders be safe and successful: A statewide study of the impact of comprehensive guidance programs. *Journal of Counseling and Development, 79,* 320–330.

Lawson, D. M., McClain, A. L., Matlock-Hetzel, S., Duffy, M., & Urbanovski, R. (1997). School families: Implementation and evaluation of a middle school prevention program. *Journal of Counseling and Development, 76,* 82–89.

Lickona, T. (1991). *Educating for character: How schools can teach respect and responsibility.* New York: Bantam Books.

Maslovaty, N. (2000). Teachers' choice of teaching strategies for dealing with socio-moral dilemmas in the elementary school. *Journal of Moral Education, 29*(4), 429–444.

Mayer, J. D., & Salovey, P. (1997). What is emotional intelligence? In P. Salovey & D. Sluyter (Eds.), *Emotional development and emotional intelligence: Educational implications* (pp. 3–34). New York: Basic Books.

Myrick, R. D. (1997). *Developmental guidance and counseling: A practical approach* (3rd ed.). Minneapolis, MN: Educational Media Corporation.

Newman, B. M., & Newman, P. R. (1995). *Development through life: A psychosocial approach.* Pacific Grove, CA: Brooks/Cole.

Omizo, M. M., & D'Andrea, M. (1995). Multicultural classroom guidance. In C. C. Lee (Ed.), *Counseling for diversity: A guide for school counselor and related professionals* (pp. 143–158). Boston: Allyn & Bacon.

Paisley, P. O., & Hubbard, G. T. (1994). *Developmental school counseling programs: From theory to practice.* Alexandria, VA: American Counseling Association.

Prout, S. M., & Prout, H. T. (1998). A meta-analysis of school-based studies of counseling and psychotherapy: An update. *Journal of School Psychology, 36,* 121–136.

Rest, J., Narvaez, D., Bebeau, M., & Thoma, S. (1999). A neo-Kohlbergian approach: The DIT and schema theory. *Educational Psychology Review, 11*(4), 291–324.

Rest, J. R., Narvaez, D., Thoma, S. J., & Bebeau, M. J. (2000). A neo-Kohlbergian approach to morality research. *Journal of Moral Education, 29*(4), 381–395.

Sanger, M., & Osguthorpe, R. (2005). Making sense of approaches to moral education. *Journal of Moral Education, 34*(1), 57–71.

Shure, M. (2001). *I can problem solve: An interpersonal cognitive problem-solving program.* Champaign, IL: Research Press.

Skaggs, G., & Bodenhorn, N. (2006). Relationships between implementing character education, student behavior, and student achievement. *Journal of Advanced Academics, 18,* 82-115.

State University of New York College at Cortland, Center for the 4th and 5th Rs. (n.d.). Character education orgaizations and initiatives. Retrieved August 30, 2007, from www.cortland.edu/character/chared_orgs.html

Whiston, S. C., & Sexton, T. L. (1998). A review of school counseling outcome research: Implications for practice. *Journal of Counseling and Development, 76,* 412–426.

XVI
PHYSICAL HEALTH AND EMOTIONAL DEVELOPMENT:
A Primer for School Counselors

LAURA FILLINGAME KNUDTSON AND HARDIN L. K. COLEMAN
University of Wisconsin–Madison

Most of the time, when we imagine the typical child, we visualize a happy, energetic, giggly, innocent small person who craves new knowledge, who yearns for adult attention, and whose mind encompasses an imagination full of colorful, new ideas. We also envision the average child to be physically healthy. This assumption is not unwarranted due to the fact that the majority of children and adolescents are in good to excellent physical health (Centers for Disease Control and Prevention [CDC], 2004b). In addition, the majority of the physical conditions that impact children/adolescents during childhood are illnesses (or death) that could have been prevented (CDC, 2004b). Therefore, when discussing child and adolescent physical health, the prevention of childhood illnesses should be the primary focus. School counselors, as prevention specialists, have a unique opportunity to engage in this conversation. This chapter presents a brief overview of the physical health conditions that impact child/adolescent emotional development. This chapter is not intended to be a comprehensive literature review on any of the key areas, nor is it a medically based guide describing condition diagnosis. Instead, it is intended to serve as a primer (1) to help school counselors and other educators attain a basic understanding of how physical health issues affect students within a school context, (2) to present school counselors with knowledge that can inform community-based referrals for students, and (3) to provide a brief review of how school counselors and other educators can implement interventions in their schools to promote child/adolescent physical health.

The majority of American children live to see their 18th birthdays (CDC, 2004b); however, many children and adolescents encounter significant health conditions that occasionally result in death. According to the National Vital Statistics Report (CDC, 2004b) the top cause of mortality in children and adolescents ages 5 through 19 is accidents (e.g., automobile accident or drowning). Additionally, the next two causes of mortality in adolescents ages 15 through 19 are homicide and suicide (suicide is also the number 3 cause of death in children ages 10 through 14). For younger children (ages 5 through 14), malignant neoplasms (cancers) and congenital malformations, deformations, and chromosomal abnormalities are also significant causes of death. Based on these statistics, it is apparent that many deaths (those due to accidents, homicide, and suicide) are preventable.

When looking at the physical health of America's youth, there are many disparities between the health status of racial/ethnic minorities and European Americans, and between the health of the working class and the middle/upper class in this country. These disparities are reflected in the prevalence of diseases such as asthma and obesity and in other health disparities between wealthy European Americans and other Americans such as the adolescent pregnancy/birth rate. Additionally, there are large inequalities in health care access and quality that are tied to the higher prevalence of disorders in some racial/ethnic minority and working-class populations. It is particularly important for school counselors and educators to recognize the racial and class impacts upon child and adolescent physical health.

The Importance of Prevention in Child and Adolescent Physical Health

Due to the fact that the majority of children and adolescents are very healthy and the majority of physical conditions that affect children are preventable, the importance of preventive care for children and adolescents is obvious.

One of the most encouraged elements of preventive care for children are periodic "well child" visits to a physician. These visits may include elements such as immunizations, sports-participation physicals, and child/family counseling regarding child health issues such as nutrition, adolescent sexual health, and home gun safety. In the end, however, physicians have only limited time with children and families during these visits, and occasionally, critical issues are not covered. Therefore, other members of children's and adolescents' communities can be important contributors to child/adolescent preventive care. Schools provide an ideal context in which to be involved with child/adolescent preventive physical health care due to their frequent and continuous contact with children and their families. In a survey conducted with directors and adolescent health coordinators of the Maternal and Child Health Bureau, respondents identified four suggestions as to what could be done to improve youth health outcomes. Three of these suggestions mentioned the involvement of schools, including (1) integrating physical health, mental health, and school-based health services for youth; (2) strengthening community and school-based health services; and (3) strengthening schools overall (Blum, 1998). Schools are seen by the health community as integral to the promotion of healthy youth in this country, and they are ideal locations for child/adolescent health prevention efforts.

Why are schools important resources for impacting adolescent physical health and emotional development? First of all, schools have a continual and concentrated access to youth and are able to impart information upon children at developmentally appropriate times. Additionally, schools have the opportunity to implement school-wide health programs that become an integral part of children's and adolescents' time at school. Finally, the development of healthy children has long been a mission of American schools (National Association of State Boards of Education, 2002). School counselors are key players in the healthy physical, cognitive, social, and emotional development of youth. First, school counselors are trained to manage the emotional development of youth, and they are taught to assess how many elements of life (including childhood physical health) may effect a child's emotional development. Additionally, many school counselors have acquired some research and program evaluation training while in graduate school. This provides school counselors with the important opportunity to aid in conducting program evaluation to ensure that interventions are effective. Finally, many school counselors are trained in consultation skills, which provide them with the ability to coordinate with community resources to ensure that students are receiving the best possible physical health education and that school staff is being supported through trainings, help in curriculum development, and funding. In the end, schools become one of the most ideal locations to address child and adolescent physical health, with school counselors being one of the most appropriate school personnel to lead implementation of these programs.

Racial/Ethnic and Socioeconomic Disparities in Child and Adolescent Physical Health Care

National initiatives such as *Healthy People 2010* (Department of Health and Human Services [DHHS], 2005) have demonstrated our nations' commitment to addressing and eliminating health disparities based on gender, race/ethnicity, education, socioeconomic status, disability, geographic location, or sexual orientation; however, disparities in primary care access, quality, and satisfaction continue to prevail. Additionally, many children in the United States continue to be uninsured or underinsured in regards to private or public health insurance. Overall, the U.S. health care system persists in providing adequate health care for some—but not all—of the nation's children and adolescents.

In preface to the discussion of racial/ethnic disparities in health status among children/adolescents, it is necessary to discuss the issue of the relationship between race and socioeconomic status (SES) in the United States. Since high proportions of racial/ethnic minority children in the United States also are more likely than White families to be of lower income, it is difficult to attribute disparity findings to just race/ethnicity. Only recently have studies begun to control for SES and/or race/ethnicity in their research. Therefore, conclusions regarding this area of research need to take the relationship between race/ethnicity and SES into account when interpreting findings in this area.

The United States continues to be the *only* Western industrialized nation that does not guarantee primary care preventative medical services to its citizens through universal health care coverage (G. D. Stevens & Shi, 2003). According to the U.S. Census Bureau (Bhandari & Gifford, 2003), 12.1% of children age 18 and younger were uninsured in 2001. Racial/ethnic minorities continue to be the majority of uninsured children, with 24.9% of Hispanic children, 22.3% American Indian children, 14.3% African American, 12.1% Asian/Pacific Islander, 11.4% Whites, and 7.6% non-Hispanic Whites all uninsured (Bhandari & Gifford). Although government initiated programs such as Medicaid and state Child Health Insurance Program (CHIP) insured over 29 million children in 2003, 62% of the 10 million uninsured children who were eligible for the programs were not enrolled (Kaiser Commission on Medicaid and the Uninsured, 2005). Uninsured Medicaid-eligible children are twice as likely as those insured by Medicaid to have an unmet medical need, to not have seen a doctor, and to have large out-of-pocket family expenditures on medical care (Kaiser Commission on Medicaid and the Uninsured). Additionally, due to the current budget cuts in the United States, the national government has cut funding to Medicaid, and some state-based programs have frozen new CHIP enrollment, raised premiums, and made enrollment in health insurance programs more difficult for families (Kaiser Commission on Medicaid and the Uninsured). Although policy initiatives demonstrate a national recognition regarding the alarming health disparities in the United States, without proper funding, it is likely that this health care crisis will continue to challenge low-income families in accessing quality preventative health care for their children.

Healthy People 2000 developed a list of 18 Health Status Indicators (HSIs) for all people to determine the health of the nation in multiple key areas, as well as to examine differences and/or disparities between populations. Overall, the final profile of the 1990s showed many racial/ethnic health disparities between populations (children and adults). The HSIs that showed the greatest degree of racial/ethnic disparity were in tuberculosis case rates, syphilis case rates, homicide death rates, and live birth rates (Keppel, Pearcy, & Wagener, 2002). The populations that made the smallest improvements as compared with other racial/ethnic groups regarding these HSIs were the American Indian and Alaskan Native population (Keppel et al., 2002). Overall, there continue to be great differences between the overall health of racially/ethnically specific groups in the United States.

Although few studies have been conducted specifically on racial/ethnic disparities in primary medical care for children and adolescents (G. D. Stevens & Shi, 2003), research in the area of racial/ethnic child/adolescent populations continues to grow. One of the main areas that continue to be addressed both in the adult and child literature around racial/ethnic health disparities is *access* to health care. Shi and Stevens (2005) found that prior to and after controlling for poverty status and demographic variables, racial/ethnic minority children (Asian, Black, Hispanic) were less likely than White children to have a regular source of care (physician, clinic, etc.), to have had a health professional or doctor visit in the past year, and to have had a dental visit in the past year (except Asian/Pacific Islander). Additionally, in another study, Weinick and Krauss (2000) found that, after controlling for health insurance and SES, Black and Hispanic children were substantially less likely than White children to have a usual source of care. Interestingly, when language ability was controlled for, it completely eliminated the differences between Hispanic and White children. Therefore, Weinick and Krauss added that language difference puts Hispanic children at a great disadvantage in terms of access to care. In addition, low-income children with Medicaid coverage were found to be more likely to have a usual source of care and to receive care within an appropriate time interval as compared with low-income children without Medicaid (St. Peter, Newacheck, & Halfon, 1992). Finally, Newacheck, Hughes, and Stoddard (1996) found that poverty, minority status, and absence of insurance exerted independent effects on access to and use of primary care. They found that low-income, minority, and uninsured children were twice as likely as children in the reference group (children above the poverty line, children not belonging to a racial/ethnic minority group, and children with health insurance) to lack usual sources of care and used only about half as many physicians' services (after adjustment was made for health status). Overall, it appears that racial/ethnic minority children continue to have significant barriers in access to health care, along with low-income children, children (or caretakers) that do not speak English, and children who do not have health insurance.

Although access to care is a significant health disparities issue and some scholars believe that by increasing access to care many socioeconomic disparities in health status will lessen (Andrulis, 1998), even when access to care is granted, the disparities in quality of care provided to racial/ethnic minorities as well as lower income individuals continues to be an issue. When looking at quality of care, funding of care (facilities, availability of treatment, etc.) and provider characteristics (provider's cultural competence in caring for patients) become large issues. Additionally, *quality* continues to be a very value-laden and culturally determined construct which creates challenges in determining a definition. Therefore, quality of care is a difficult construct to measure and tends to be looked at through self-report satisfaction measures as well as frequency counts of particular events taking place within the visit. Shi and Stevens (2005) found in 1996 (but not in 2000) that Hispanics and African Americans were more likely to be dissatisfied with the quality of care provided (after controlling for sociodemographics and poverty status). Additionally, St. Peter et al. (1992) found that low-income children with Medicaid were less likely than children living above the poverty line to have continuity between usual sources of routine care and sick care as well as were less likely to receive routine care in physicians' offices.

One of the frequently cited issues regarding access and quality of health care is the high number of children and adolescents that use the emergency room as their primary source of care over a clinic or physician's office. Emergency rooms are not designed to serve as primary care settings, the consistent use of which creates a barrier to the delivery of quality care (Bliss, 1982). In looking at population-specific differences of those individuals who frequent emergency rooms, African Americans were noted in a 1996 study to use emergency departments as their regular source of care at twice the frequency of White children (Halfon, Newacheck, Wood, & St. Peter, 1996). Additionally, in a hospital in Honolulu, Hawaii, Yamamoto and colleagues (1995) found that Polynesian children (i.e., Hawaiian, Samoan, and other Pacific Islanders) were more likely to use emergency departments than European and African Americans. However, these frequent users of emergency rooms were not noted as being a function of not having insurance and/or a primary care physician. Mayberry, Mili, and Ofili (2000) concluded that the frequent use of emergency rooms or their use as a primary source of care may be explained by sociocultural factors more than socioeconomic issues (such as insurance). Therefore, it is still not completely understood why specific populations use emergency rooms for primary care purposes more frequently than others do. If, however, sociocultural factors are a significant factor in this aspect of health care, school counseling programs can address these concerns within their curriculum.

Many health professionals are seeing a great need in the field to educate doctors, nurses, and other health specialists in how to work with patients from a culture different from their own. Curricula for training physicians in culturally competent care, specifically for adolescents, are being developed (Sylvester et al., 2003); however, few practitioners have had training in cultural competence, particularly for working with children and/or youth. Even when culturally diverse youth do receive medical care, it is likely that it comes from a physician who does not take into account their cultural background, beliefs, or values. This ultimately affects the quality of care that the adolescent receives, as well as his or her satisfaction regarding that care.

Poor quality of care and limited access to care can impact on students and their learning. School counselors are likely to be confronted with multiple students who do not have access to health insurance and may not be receiving adequate care for illnesses. This requires school health staff (nurses, school counselors, school psychologists, etc.). to be able to attend to children with unmet health needs and to be knowledgeable regarding community-based health resources for students and families if there is a need for a referral.

Physical Health Disorders in Children and Adolescents

Chronic Illness in Children

Although the majority of children are healthy and do not have to manage living with chronic disease, illnesses such as AIDS, cystic fibrosis, sickle cell anemia, epilepsy, diabetes, and asthma are diagnosed in children and significantly impact their lives. Many children with chronic illness are able to effectively manage their disease while maintaining close relationships with their caregivers, building lasting friendships with peers, and earning good grades in school; however, these children tend to face additional challenges. School in particular can be a challenging environment for children whose peers and teachers may have incorrect assumptions regarding a child's disease or may not understand the impact that a particular disease has on that child. Although this section will not discuss the particulars of all chronic diseases that are diagnosed in childhood and adolescence, it will address how educators can establish an effective and supportive learning environment for students diagnosed with chronic disease in their schools.

What is chronic illness? The medical and educational communities continue to be challenged in how to define chronic illness for children. Different definitions of chronic illness are required in order to provide multiple types of services for children with chronic health conditions. For instance, medical model diagnoses (such as type 2 diabetes) are needed for medical professionals to classify and reach a common understanding of the etiology and treatment of a particular illness. Additionally, the federal government has created chronic illness definition policy (like the Individuals with Disabilities Act—IDEA) to determine who is eligible to receive particular services at schools. Typically, definitions of chronic illness differ between the medical and the educational community, which causes challenges for school districts in providing services to youth (Thies, 1999). In one attempt to create a more integrative definition of chronic illness, Stein, Bauman, Westbrook, Coupey, and Ireys (1993) created a multidimensional, noncategorical approach to defining chronic illness in children. A chronic condition is defined as one of biological origin that persists for at least 3 to 12 months and is supplemented with at least one of the following issues: (1) limitations in daily functioning; (2) reliance on things such as medications, special diets, or assistive devices; and (3) a need for services beyond routine medical care (Stein et al., 1993).

More than 200 chronic health conditions are diagnosed in children and adolescents aged 18 and younger (Thies, 1999). Dependent upon the definition of chronic illness, it has been estimated that between 6.5% and 31% of children at some time in their childhood could be diagnosed with a chronic illness (Thies). Many educators and school health professionals are challenged by understanding the breadth and depth of each of these illnesses and particularly how they individually affect each child. The following section briefly addresses some common characteristics of a few of the more prominent chronic illnesses in children and adolescents. Educators and school health professionals are encouraged to supplement their reading in this area with information about illnesses with which students in their schools are diagnosed.

Asthma. Asthma is the leading chronic illness among children (American Lung Association [ALA], 2005). About 12% of children in the United States have been diagnosed with asthma (CDC, 2004c), which translates to about 3 children in every classroom of 25 children (CDC, 2004a). Asthma prevalence rates in the United States do not appear to be leveling off or decreasing. The prevalence of asthma in children increased an average of 4.3% per year from 1980 to 1996 (CDC, 2005a). Children ages 5 through 17 missed 14.7 million school days due to asthma (CDC, 2002a). Educators are being confronted with increased responsibility in the prevention and management of childhood asthma in their schools.

Asthma is a chronic respiratory disease that is characterized by the inflammation and narrowing of the bronchial tubes which may be accompanied by respiratory attacks (CDC, 2002a) and is a response to various environmental triggers such as cockroaches, dust mites, furry pets, mold, tobacco smoke, certain chemicals (CDC, 2005a) and allergens, infections, exercise, or abrupt changes in weather (CDC, 2002a). The severity of asthma ranges from mild to life-threatening (CDC, 2002a). Asthma is the third leading cause of hospitalization for children under age 15 (Hall & DeFrances, 2001). Over a 17-year period (1979–1996), the number of childhood deaths attributed to asthma increased almost threefold from 93 in 1979 to 266 in 1996 (CDC, 2005a). From 1980 to 1998, adolescents had a higher death rate from asthma than younger children (almost twice as large) (Akinbami & Schoendorf, 2002). Overall, asthma continues to be a significant risk factor for children that can considerably affect quality of life.

There continue to be many racial and ethnic disparities regarding asthma prevalence and quality of care for children. Akinbami and Schoendorf (2002) used multiple data sources to assess trends in childhood asthma rates in the United States. They reported that the gap between Black and White children who were diagnosed with asthma widened from 15% higher rates for Black youth in 1980–1981 to 26% higher in 1995–1996. Additionally, Black children had an asthma attack prevalence rate 44% higher than that of White children in 2000. Hispanic children were reported to have an average annual prevalence rate higher than White children from 1995–1996 (76.1 per 1000, as compared with 65.3 per 1000), but then in 2000, had a lower rate of asthma attack (42.1 per 1000, as compared with 53.4). From 1998–1999, Black children were over 3 times as likely as White children to be hospitalized due to asthma, and in 1997–1998, Black children were 4 times as likely as White children to die from asthma. Finally, Hispanic children's death rates due to asthma were comparable with those of White children. Overall, Akinbami and Schoendorf (2002) demonstrated that there continue to be large disparities between Black and White/Hispanic populations with regard to asthma prevalence, hospitalization, and mortality.

Socioeconomic disparities have also been noted regarding prevalence rates of asthma. Children from lower income families have a higher asthma prevalence rate (16%) as compared with children from families that were not low-income (11%; CDC, 2004c). Halfon and Newacheck (1993) demonstrated that lower income children were more likely to have more than 7 bed days in the last year, to have 40% fewer doctor's visits, and 40% more hospitalizations in the previous year. Additionally, lower income children were found to be at higher risk for inadequate asthma therapy (taking maintenance medications such as inhaled corticosteroid, cromolyn, or theophylline; Halterman, Aligne, Auinger, McBride, & Szilagyi, 2000), which is intended to prevent asthma complications that may require hospitalization. This suggests that the disparity in asthma rates may be due to the negative interaction between environmental stressors and access to health care among lower income Americans. It also suggests that the inadequate management of the illness will have a direct impact on the child's learning as a result of repeated absences from school. At very least, facilitating the process of making up for lost learning is one in which the school counselor needs to be involved at both the individual and systemic level.

Since asthma continues to be a significant health issue that affects many children, schools continue to need resources to manage and prevent childhood asthma among students. The Centers for Disease Control (2005e) has developed strategies for schools to effectively address asthma within a school health program. These strategies include (1) establishing management and support systems for asthma-friendly schools; (2) providing appropriate school health and mental health services for students with asthma; (3) providing asthma education and awareness programs for students and school staff; (4) providing safe and healthy school environment to reduce asthma triggers; (5) providing safe, enjoyable physical education and activity opportunities for students with asthma; and (6) coordinating school, family, and community efforts to better manage asthma symptoms and reduce school absences among students with asthma (CDC, 2005e). Schools should contract with students, parents, and physicians in the form of an "asthma action plan" that provides students, parents, and educators with a detailed and personalized method to handle asthma emergencies at school (CDC, 2005e). Additionally, schoolwide case management of students with asthma needs to take place between counselors, school nurses, teachers, and administrators to effectively aid students with frequent school absences, emergency room visits, and/or hospitalizations due to asthma (CDC, 2005e). Overall, pre-planning and effective communication between school personnel can aid in helping students effectively manage their asthma.

Although asthma is a common disease in childhood, many schools do not have adequate school resources in place to effectively serve these students. A part-time or full-time nurse is on staff in 76.8% of schools, but only 52.9% of schools have the recommended nurse-to-student ratio (1:750) or better (CDC, 2000b). Only 44.6% of schools have Tobacco-Free Environment policies that prohibit cigarette, cigar, and pipe smoking use by students, faculty, staff, and visitors in school buildings, on school grounds, and at off-campus school sponsored events (CDC, 2000b). Students are allowed to self-administer an inhaler in 68% of schools (CDC, 2000b). Finally, the median percentage of schools that provided asthma education to school staff was 51.9% (CDC, 2000b). Many schools are not effectively managing asthma among their students. As part of the student personnel team, a school counselor needs to consistently raise the issue of physical health as a part of student achievement. A plan to ensure compliance with interventions and with quality prevention needs to be integrated into a comprehensive developmental guidance program.

Cancer in children and adolescents. Over the past 30 years, there have been numerous medical advances that have aided in the diagnosis and treatment of childhood cancer. Many more children are surviving cancer than had previously. Overall, the death rates of children from cancer are declining about 2% to 3.2% per year (Ries, 1999). Many children diagnosed with cancer during childhood are living into adulthood. Over the past 30 years, the survival rate for children diagnosed with cancer has increased from 30% to 80% (National Cancer Institute, 2005). Additionally, these children are more likely to have a better quality of life throughout childhood and into adulthood, and they are less likely to suffer from negative long-term effects following treatment (National Cancer Institute). Although medical researchers are making great progress regarding the treatment of childhood cancer, it is still a disease that affects a large number of children and adolescents. Cancer is the second leading cause of mortality in children ages 5 to 14 years old (CDC, 2004b). Cancer continues to be an extremely serious disease that immensely impacts the lives of many children in the United States.

The most common form of cancer in childhood is leukemia (National Cancer Institute, 2005). Leukemia is a cancer of the blood that develops in the bone marrow, which is the location in the body that creates blood cells (National Cancer Institute). The majority of childhood leukemia cases are diagnosed as acute lymphoblastic leukemia (ALL) type (Smith, Ries, Gurney, & Ross, 1999). Although little is known regarding the risk factors involved with ALL, potential causes include prenatal exposure to X-rays and genetic syndromes such as Down syndrome (Smith et al.). ALL is most likely to be diagnosed between ages 2 and 5; however, it can be diagnosed from infancy into adolescence (Smith et al.). There are 30% more males diagnosed with ALL than females (Smith et al.). Additionally, European-American children have a two-fold higher increase of being diagnosed with ALL than African American children (Smith et al.). Overall, approximately 80% of children diagnosed with ALL survive into adulthood, with children diagnosed older than 1 year of age having the most favorable survival rates (Smith et al.).

Children diagnosed with cancer can receive many different types of treatment. The most common treatments are chemotherapy and radiation. These treatments can cause multiple side effects and can cause challenges to individual student learning. Every child responds differently to cancer treatment; however, radiation has been shown to impact learning through impaired attention, short-term memory, visuomotor coordination, and information processing (Thies, 1999). Additionally, chemotherapy treatment can impact student learning through increased fatigue, greater risk for infection, and fears of going to school (due to physical appearance differences such as hair loss; Thies). Educators can help aid students with chronic illnesses by more specifically understanding the side effects of treatments and the implications for child learning in their classroom. They also need to recognize and respond to the social and learning challenges associated with absence from school due to treatment.

Diabetes. Diabetes is an illness in which the body does not produce or properly use insulin (American Diabetes Association [ADA], 2005). Insulin is a hormone in the body that is required for the conversion of food (such as sugar and starch) into energy (ADA, 2005). There are two main types of diabetes diagnosed in children and adolescents: Type 1 diabetes and type 2 diabetes. Type 1 diabetes (previously labeled "juvenile diabetes") is typically diagnosed in children and adolescents (ADA, 2005). People with type 1 diabetes do not produce insulin in their bodies. This makes it difficult for their bodies to use sugar and to create energy (ADA, 2005). Type 2 diabetes is typically diagnosed in adolescence or adulthood and is the most prevalent type of diabetes (ADA, 2005). Individuals with type 2 diabetes do not produce enough insulin or their cells ignore the insulin produced (ADA, 2005). There has been an increase in the number of children/adolescents diagnosed with type 2 diabetes over the past few decades (ADA, 2000; Fagot-Campagna et al., 2000).

Until recently, type 1 (or juvenile diabetes) was the only type of diabetes deemed appropriate to diagnose during childhood or adolescence (ADA, 2000); however, medical experts have made a shift in how they think about type 1 and type 2 diabetes. The American Diabetes Association (2005) has reported that about 2 million overweight American adolescents have prediabetes. They indicate that diagnoses of type 2 diabetes in children and adolescents continues to be rare, but provide the caveat that we have not developed a sophisticated tracking system of type 1 versus type 2 diabetes diagnoses in children. It continues to be unclear how the number of type 2 diabetes diagnoses in children has shifted in recent decades.

The majority of children with type 2 diabetes are obese at diagnosis (ADA, 2000). Type 2 diabetes is typically diagnosed in children when they are in middle to late puberty or over the age of 10 (ADA, 2000). It has been speculated, however, that as younger and younger children become more overweight, the incidence of type 2 diabetes in children may increase and may be found in younger children (ADA, 2000). Risk factors associated with a type 2 diabetes diagnosis include (1) having a family member with type 2 diabetes, (2) being an obese adolescent, (3) being female, and (4) being a member of a racial/ethnic minority group (including American Indian, African American, Hispanic-American, and Asian/South Pacific Islander populations; ADA, 2000).

Children and adolescents in racial/ethnic minority groups are more likely to be diagnosed with type 2 diabetes than are their European-American counterparts (ADA, 2000). In particular, the Pima Indians of Arizona have been shown to have one of the highest prevalence rates of type 2 diabetes in any racial/ethnic group. In a study from 1992 to 1996, the prevalence rate for type 2 diabetes in Pima Indians ages 15 to 19 was 50.9 per 1000, and for Pima Indian children ages 10 to 14 it was 22.3 per 1000 (Fagot-Campagna et al., 2000). Overall, there have not been substantial population-based studies on the prevalence of type 2 diabetes in other racial/ethnic minority populations, but it is believed that these rates are higher than in European-American populations.

In a study regarding school nurses' perceptions of how adolescents diagnosed with diabetes manage school, 98% of nurses surveyed agreed that adolescents with diabetes need more support at school (Nabors, Troillett, Nash, & Masiulis, 2005). First of all, the nurses indicated that school staff needs to be further educated regarding diabetes and how it affects students. Teachers and other school staff need to make accommodations for students with diabetes to provide them with access to food and water at all times and to allow them to carry their testing equipment with them through the school (which may violate backpack carrying rules). Next, communication between the student, parents, school nurse, and the student's doctor needs to take place to ensure that the student is receiving appropriate care in school. Teachers need to be involved in these discussions as well to ensure that the student's health needs are being met in the classroom. Additionally, the nurses discussed how parental involvement was extremely important. Without continuity between caretakers and the school's management of a child's diabetes, it can be challenging to support the student in the healthy management of the student's diabetes. Finally, school staff (in particular, school counselors) need to be aware of how diabetes affects student mental health and social involvement with peers. It can be very challenging for a child with diabetes to have to avoid hanging out with peers due to their food choices or to endure being rewarded for good behavior in class with foods that they cannot eat. Many students can feel left out, depressed, and angry when they are constantly put in situations where they cannot participate in social functions that involve eating. School staff need to find ways to best facilitate overall support of children with diabetes in school.

How can educators provide appropriate services for children with chronic illness? Schools are faced with multiple challenges in offering appropriate services to children with chronic illnesses. Providing services for children with chronic illnesses can be particularly challenging due to the fact that these children tend to frequently fluctuate between states of good and poor health (Thies, 1999). Unlike with disabilities such as mental retardation and emotional/behavioral disorders, school health professionals and educators are required to more frequently alter their approach for working with these students' absences from school and daily abilities to participate in classroom activities. Thies provided five guidelines for schools to address the educational implications for students with chronic health conditions:

1. Schools should recognize that many students do have chronic health conditions and that this population is not shrinking.
2. Schools may need to identify students with chronic illness without self-disclosure from students or their families.
3. Educators and school health professionals need to create a system for identifying and aiding students with chronic illness.
4. Schools need to address the difference between providing accommodations for chronic illness (such as giving more time to make up assignments) and education for students with chronic illness (providing students with lessons, etc.). Just allowing students time to make up missed work may not give

them the necessary instruction to understand and learn certain lessons.
5. Schools can begin to think creatively about students with chronic illnesses and not try to fit them into previously existing programs.

It becomes extremely important for schools to begin to treat students with chronic health conditions as a separate population that has specific needs and will benefit most significantly from policies and programs catered to these needs.

Children who reenter school following hospitalization or other treatment for chronic illnesses may face many challenges to learning at school. First of all, many children may experience lethargy, chronic nausea, fatigue, and overall weakness that may make it difficult for them to learn (Sexson & Madan-Swain, 1993). Additionally, many children may be experiencing a lot of pain, which can hinder concentration (Sexson & Madan-Swain). Various medications can cause sedation, increase irritability, and decrease attention span in some students (Sexson & Madan-Swain). Finally, certain medical treatments can decrease children's immunity to common illnesses such as colds, which can lead to more absences from school (Sexson & Madan-Swain). All of these physical symptoms can make it challenging for students to attend to academic learning.

Children with chronic illnesses are also likely to suffer from symptoms of mental disorders as well. In a study of depression in adolescents with asthma, sickle cell disease, cystic fibrosis, insulin-dependent diabetes, and spina bifida, Beck Depression Inventory (BDI) scores were compared between healthy controls and adolescents with one of these chronic illnesses. Key, Brown, Marsh, Spratt, and Recknor (2001) found that a higher percentage of adolescents with chronic illness had moderate or severe BDI scores than the control group. Additionally, adolescents with chronic illness who rated their disease as moderate to high in severity reported more symptoms of depression than those adolescents that reported their chronic disease as mild (Key et al.). It appears that adolescents suffering from moderate to severe mental illness are also likely to experience multiple symptoms of depression, which can create additional challenges for adolescent learning in school.

In addition to physical challenges, students with chronic illnesses face many social challenges at school as well. Students are faced with the reality that many of their teachers do not completely understand their illness and many are not trained to work with children with chronic illnesses. In a survey of Midwestern teachers, almost all the teachers in the sample reported working with children with chronic illness, yet 64% reported no on-site training for working with these students (Clay, Cortina, Harper, Cocco, & Drotar, 2004). This lack of training can result in teachers' inaccurate assessment of the child's physical symptoms, as well as their academic and social skills (Sexson & Madan-Swain, 1995). In addition to a lack of training, many teachers have lower expectations for children with chronic illness (Northham, 1997), which can place children at risk for academic failure (Clay et al.). Teachers have reported feeling frustrated, helpless, and apprehensive regarding working as both educators and health managers in the classroom (Clay et al.). Additionally, many teachers are not given the support within their schools to personally deal with the death of a student (Rowling, 1995). Schools need to address the training needs of educators around chronic illness in students to improve teacher efficacy in working with these students, to increase the teacher's fund of knowledge about chronic illness that can address the questions of students in the classroom, and to provide a higher standard of care to children diagnosed with chronic health conditions.

In a qualitative study looking at the inclusion of students with chronic illness in mainstream schooling, students communicated what support they needed from their school and from their teachers in particular. Students in this study felt the need for support in managing school absences, taking part in school activities, developing and maintaining peer relationships, aiding other students to understand their health condition, and having someone to talk to at school about their illness (Mukherjee, Lightfoot, & Sloper, 2000). Teachers and school counselors could help students with chronic illness in their school by asking them what sources of support they feel are needed for them to succeed at school and by facilitating the previously identified support systems in classrooms and the school as a whole.

School counselors and other school staff need to pay particular attention to how other students in the school environment think about a child's illness and how they treat this child. In a study on fourth-, fifth-, and sixth-grade students' perceptions of peers with chronic illness, Cole, Roberts, and McNeal (1996) found that fourth graders were more likely to indicate that children diagnosed with the diseases studied (diabetes, asthma, AIDS, and cystic fibrosis) were contagious and that they were the least accepting of their peers diagnosed with these illnesses. This finding confirmed other research that older children tend to be more accepting of children with chronic illness (Royal & Roberts, 1987). Additionally, Cole and colleagues (1996) found that the students studied considered children with AIDS to carry the most responsibility for their diagnosis as compared with children with other chronic illnesses. The authors remarked that this finding is consistent with other researchers and may be due to the fact that AIDS is a frequently discussed disease and that children are taught about AIDS prevention (which may inadvertently teach the presumption that individuals are responsible for their AIDS diagnosis). Overall, many children have biased and inaccurate perceptions regarding chronic illnesses. School counselors and other educators need to address disease contagion perceptions, children's responsibility for their disease, and acceptance of peers with chronic illness to provide students with accurate education about chronic disease and to provide students with chronic illnesses a supportive social space at school.

Other Childhood Medical Conditions

Weight-related disorders. One of the most prevalent and concerning current health conditions for people in the United States involves weight-related disorders (including obesity, eating disorders, and disordered eating behaviors). Not only are adults battling with being overweight or underweight, but an increasing number of children and adolescents are also being diagnosed with weight-related diseases (CDC, 2005d; Hoek & van Hoeken, 2003). These conditions are very prevalent in both staff and students at schools, with very few educators knowing how to best aid their students (or themselves) in developing and maintaining healthy body weight (Yager & O'Dea, 2005). Many schools are taking it upon themselves to provide preventive curricula for eating disorders and obesity. Many curricula, however, focus on only one end of the spectrum of weight-related disorders, which may end up unintentionally causing one disorder (e.g., anorexia nervosa) while teaching a curriculum to prevent another weight-related disorder (e.g., obesity; Neumark-Sztainer, 2003). Although anorexia nervosa is not necessarily the "opposite" of obesity, it can be helpful for educators to view weight-related disorders along the spectrum represented in Figure 16.1 in order to address both the extreme weight-related disorders, as well as more minor disordered eating behaviors. Some researchers in the field of weight-related disorders are encouraging prevention efforts to provide more of an integrated approach that focuses on many facets of disordered eating in an attempt to provide considerably clearer (nonconflicting) messages to children about weight, more cost-effective interventions (focusing on all weight-related disorders rather than one piece, e.g., eating disorders), and fewer time-intensive programs for students (and staff trainings; Neumark-Sztainer, 2003). The following overview of weight-related disorders focuses on defining the significance of weight-related conditions in the child/adolescent population, briefly defining the characteristics of these disorders, and finally, reviewing a few school-based interventions to prevent weight-related disorders in children and adolescents.

Overweight and Obesity The U.S. Surgeon General has named the obesity "epidemic" as one of the greatest health problems facing Americans today (DHHS, 2001). Over the past 20 years, individuals have made dramatic environmental, cultural, and vocational lifestyle changes that have ultimately contributed to the increased prevalence of overweight and obesity in the United States. Many factors have played a role in this epidemic, including (1) increased access and dependence on high-fat and high-caloric fast food, (2) increased consumption of sugary beverages (e.g., sodas, sports drinks, fruit juices with less than 100% fruit juice), (3) larger food portion sizes, (4) decreased vigorous physical activity, (5) increased sedentary leisure time (i.e., TV watching, Internet surfing, videogame playing), and (6) increased reliance on automobile and train transportation, to name a few. Additionally, research continues to uncover the genetic underpinnings of overweight and obesity diagnoses (CDC, 2002b). Alarmingly, not only are America's adults becoming fatter, but this epidemic has reached child and adolescent populations as well. Clearly, radical steps need to be taken to reverse the harmful effects of obesity and overweight in America's children.

In the medical community, overweight is typically defined as being children who are at or above the 95th percentile for Body Mass Index (BMI) for their particular age and sex (CDC, 2005b). Additionally, children who are classified as being "at risk" for overweight are those whose BMI scores fall ≥85 percentile and <95 percentile. BMI is the proportion of total body weight to skeletal height and is measured through national growth chart data collected since 1963 on population height and weight (CDC, 2000a). The national growth chart data are collected through a stratified, multistage probability sample of civilians, or noninstitutionalized people, living in the 48 contiguous United States (CDC, 2000a). In addition to BMI scores, many studies collect additional data on the triceps skinfold

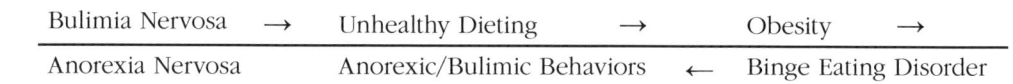

| Bulimia Nervosa | → | Unhealthy Dieting | → | Obesity | → |
| Anorexia Nervosa | | Anorexic/Bulimic Behaviors | ← | Binge Eating Disorder | |

Figure 16.1 The spectrum of weight-related disorders. (From Obesity and eating disorder prevention: An integrated approach?, D. Neumark-Sztainer, 2003, *Adolescent Medicine, 14*(1), 159–173).

thickness (TSF) test and the subscapular skinfold test (SSF), which measure skinfold thickness in participants. Finally, some studies estimate body fat mass through bioelectrical impedance analysis (BIA), which uses electrical signal to estimate body fat mass. Overall, BMI, TSF, SSF, and BIA tend to be moderately correlated in studies.

Overweight and obesity is greatly affecting the child and adolescent population. From 1999 to 2002, 16% of American children ages 6 to 19 were overweight (Hedley et al., 2004). Additionally, 31% of children and adolescents were at risk of becoming overweight (BMI ≥ 85 percentile and < 95 percentile). The current frequency of overweight in children has more than *doubled* and for adolescents has more than *tripled* since 1980 (Hedley et al.; Ogden, Flegal, Carroll, & Johnson, 2002). Additionally, it does not appear that these numbers have substantially improved in the years 2001–2003 (CDC, 2004d). Children and adolescents in the United States are much larger now than they have been in recent years, and it does not appear that these numbers will change any time in the near future.

Similar to other diseases, there continue to be large disparities between European-American populations and racial/ethnic minority populations regarding prevalence of overweight population. The National Health and Nutrition Examination Survey (NHANES) studied children and adolescents ages 6 to 19. The results from 1999 to 2002 demonstrated that non-Hispanic Black children and adolescents had a 20.5% obesity prevalence rate and a 35.4% prevalence rate for being at risk for overweight (Hedley et al., 2004). Mexican-American children and adolescents had a 22.2% prevalence for obesity and a 39.9% prevalence for being at risk for overweight (Hedley et al.). Additionally, in a smaller scale study in Washington, DC, El Salvadorian children had comparable numbers to Mexican-American children and adolescents of 38% overweight (BMI ≥ 95th percentile) and 22% at risk for overweight (BMI 85th–94th percentile; Mirza et al., 2004). These numbers are significantly different from the prevalence rates for non-Hispanic White populations at 13.6% and 28.2%, respectively (Hedley et al.). Because few large population-based studies have assessed the prevalence of obesity and overweight among Native American populations living on reservations (Story et al., 2003), the majority of our data regarding obesity and overweight in Native American populations turns to relatively small sample size studies. This makes it more challenging to establish prevalence rates for overweight and obesity in the Native American population. In general, these studies indicate that prevalence rates for obesity in Native American children/adolescents (BMI ≥ 95th percentile) range between 13.7% for both boys and girls (CDC, 2001) to 22% for girls and 18% for boys (Zephier, Himes, & Story, 1999). Additionally, prevalence rates for overweight in Native American children/adolescent populations (BMI 85th–94th percentile) ranged from 29.3% in both boys and girls (CDC, 2001) to 40% for girls and 35% for boys (Zephier et al.). Although it is still relatively unclear regarding specific prevalence rates, it appears that Native American populations are facing an obesity epidemic similar to other racial/ethnic minority populations. Overall, racial/ethnic minority populations have significantly higher rates of overweight than their European-American counterparts, which continues to speak to the marked rates of health disparities between groups.

In addition to racial/ethnic disparities in obesity rates, there are also disparities in obesity rates, based on socioeconomic status (SES), in children and adults. It appears that childhood obesity is more common in children of lower SES (Crawford, Drury, & Stern, 1999; Sobal & Stunkard, 1989). Additionally, it appears that childhood SES may have an impact on adult obesity status. In a cross-sectional study, Power, Manor, and Matthews (2003) found that social class from birth to 7 years of age predicted adult obesity for women and men. Although lower SES seems to be a risk factor for obesity, there tend to be differences among racial/ethnic groups. Zhang and Wang (2004) found that the degree of socioeconomic inequality varied considerably across ethnic group, gender, and age. Additionally, in a study of 9- and 10-year-old African American and Caucasian girls, Crawford et al. found that for the Caucasian girls, the prevalence of obesity dropped for girls with higher household income and higher parental education, but that for the African American girls, there was no significant correlation between household income, higher parental education, and prevalence of obesity. Overall, it appears that SES is a risk factor for childhood obesity, although this impact is dependent upon other variables such as gender, age, and race/ethnicity.

One hypothesis regarding the higher prevalence of obesity in lower SES groups is the lower prices of high-energy dense foods (e.g., butter, oil, margarine) as compared with lower energy dense foods (e.g., lean meats, vegetables, fruits). It has been shown that energy dense foods such as margarine, oil, and butter cost less than lower energy dense foods such as lettuce, other fresh vegetables, and frozen fish (Drewnowski & Specter, 2004). Additionally, the price of high-fat and high-sugar foods has become cheaper over the past few decades as compared with fresh fruit and vegetables (McCarthy, 2004). It is not surprising that it becomes more challenging for lower SES families to eat healthy foods such as lean meats, fresh vegetables, and fresh fruit.

Additionally, another factor that may be related to obesity in children of lower SES is the characteristics of their neighborhood. It has been shown that children of lower SES are more likely to live in urban neighborhoods and are more likely to encounter high crime rates in their neighborhoods. This makes it challenging for these children to play outside and to engage in physical activity outside of school time. In a study of children who live in urban neighborhoods, it was found that neighborhood safety and social disorder were significantly associated with less physical activity (Molnar, Gortmaker, Bull, & Buka, 2004). Additionally, a study on preschool children's neighborhood safety, outdoor playtime, and television time demonstrated that children whose mothers perceived that their neighborhood was unsafe watched significantly more television, but did not play outside less than children in perceived safe neighborhoods did (Burdette & Whitaker, 2005). Some communities are attempting to address neighborhood safety issues by creating safe spaces for children to exercise in their neighborhood and/or at schools and/or by creating programs that promote safe transportation to school through walking or biking.

Children and adolescents who are overweight are at risk for having additional damaging health conditions. Recently, typical weight-related conditions that were previously diagnosed only in adults are now plaguing children as well. For instance, type 2 diabetes, more commonly known as "adult onset" diabetes, is becoming more frequently diagnosed in overweight youth (ADA, 2000). Additionally, it is estimated that 61% of children/adolescents who are overweight also have at least one risk factor for heart disease, including high blood pressure and high cholesterol (Freedman, Dietz, Srinivasan, & Berenson, 1999). Obesity is also associated with higher rates of sleep apnea and gallbladder disease in children (Dietz, 2004). Being an overweight child carries with it great risks of other significant health conditions.

In addition to the health concerns associated with being overweight during childhood, it is apparent that being an overweight child also carries risks for being overweight in adulthood. Children who are overweight are more likely to remain or become overweight as adults (DHHS, 2001). Additionally, adults who were overweight as children are more likely to have more severe obesity than adults who were not overweight as children (Dietz, 1998; Freedman, Khan, Dietz, Srinivasan, & Berenson, 2001). Similar to children who are overweight, being an overweight adult carries with it many health risks, including higher risk for type 2 diabetes, multiple cancers, cardiovascular disease, stroke, osteoarthritis, and premature death (DHHS, 2001). Given the health disorders that are associated with weight problems, it is vitally important to prevent childhood obesity, not only to improve child/adolescent health and well-being, but also to improve future quality of life in adulthood. Learning the proper management of nutrition and exercise needs to be integrated into all aspects of a child's schooling. School counselors need to integrate these concerns into their guidance programs from issues related to self-regulation and emotional self-awareness to the role of physical status on social relationships.

Obesity and overweight are not only diseases that impact individuals' physical health, but also have large influences on childhood mental health. Americans have been socialized to discriminate against overweight people. Typical stereotypes carried regarding overweight people include that they are lazy or lack self-control. The American media teaches us that the ideal body is very thin and that beauty is a function of physical appearance. All of these factors contribute to body dissatisfaction and low self-esteem in many youth, particularly in those who can be considered overweight or obese. Schwimmer, Burwinkle, and Varni (2003) found that severely obese children and adolescents scored lower on a measure of health-related quality of life than children and adolescents who had been diagnosed with cancer. Other studies have shown decreases in physical and social functioning in obese children, but not significant decreases in emotional and school functioning for obese children as compared with children who were not overweight (Williams, Wake, Hesketh, Maher, & Waters, 2005). In a study of African American youth (ages 5 to 10), overweight was associated with low appearance self-esteem and body size dissatisfaction with low global self-worth (Young-Hyman, Schlundt, Herman-Wenderoth, & Bozylinski, 2003). Additionally, Young-Hyman and colleagues (2003) found that weight-related peer teasing was associated with low self-esteem in African American youth. It appears that the emotional influences of obesity and overweight are incredibly apparent in children and adolescents.

Eating Disorders In addition to weight-based illnesses such as obesity, eating disorders have also become alarmingly prevalent among children and adolescents. Among adolescent women (ages 15 to 19), eating disorders are considered to be the third most common chronic illness (M. Fisher et al., 1995). Females are much more likely than males to develop an eating disorder, with only 5% to 15% of the people diagnosed with anorexia and bulimia being male (Andersen, 1995). The estimated mortality rate for people diagnosed with anorexia is very high at 0.56% per year which is 12 times higher than the annual death rate for all other causes of death for females 15 to 24 years of age (Sullivan, 1995). In looking at adult populations, anorexia is considered to have the highest mortality rate of any psychiatric illness (Gardner, Vitousek, & Pike, 1997). Due to the high relapse and mortality rates from eating disorders (specifically anorexia nervosa; Sullivan, 1995), prevention efforts are extremely important. Schools become an excellent context for evidence-based prevention of eating disorders for children and adolescents, interventions that can be delivered through the coordination of the departments of guidance, home economics, and nursing.

Similar to other diseases, the etiology or causes of eating disorders are biological, developmental, sociocultural, and psychological (APA, 2000). Although it is not completely known to what extent, eating disorders tend to be inheritable (Strober, Freeman, Lampert, Diamond, & Kaye, 2000; Walters & Kendler, 1995). Current research is finding genetic underpinnings of eating disorders (Kaye et al., 2000). One main predictor of eating disorders is excessive dieting and exercise (Patton, Selzer, Coffey, Carlin & Wolfe, 1999). Other predictors of eating disorders are physical and sexual abuse (Logio, 2003), early puberty, body dissatisfaction, and negative emotionality (Leon, Fulkerson, Perry, & Cudeck, 1992). Additionally, researchers hypothesize the reason that eating disorders tend to emerge during adolescence may be due to the vast and rapid physical changes that occur in the body during this period of emotional and physical development (Smolak & Levine, 1996). Although the actual combination of factors that are the prescription for the development of eating disorders is unknown, current research in the field points to the predictors described above.

The *Diagnostic and Statistical Manual of Mental Disorders IV-TR* (*DSM-IV-TR*; APA, 2000) provided the prescribed method that physicians and mental health professionals use for eating disorder diagnosis. The three eating disorders as classified by the *DSM–IV–TR* include anorexia nervosa (AN), bulimia nervosa (BN), and binge eating disorder (APA, 2000). The diagnostic criteria for assessing and diagnosing eating disorders can be helpful with older adolescent and adult populations but provides many challenges for diagnosing children and younger adolescents (M. Fisher et al., 1995; Kreipe et al., 1995). Kreipe et al. remarked that diagnosis is difficult because (1) menses is unpredictable in early menarche (and absence of a menstrual period is one component of a diagnosis of AN), (2) normal adolescents have limited ability to engage in abstract thinking (which may affect motivation to lose weight and self-awareness), and (3) there is an overall large variability in the rate and timing of height and weight gain during puberty among adolescents. Therefore, the typical criteria for diagnosing eating disorders in children and adolescents may be difficult to assess and may also be inapplicable.

Although the assessment of children and adolescents for anorexia nervosa (AN) continues to be a challenge, the *DSM–IV–TR* provides a framework that clinicians use to diagnose AN (APA, 2000). The onset of AN occurs at a variety of times within the population (Hoek & van Hoeken, 2003), and the lifetime prevalence rate for AN in females is estimated at 0.5% to 3.7% (National Institute of Mental Health [NIMH], 2001a). Many experts in the field, however, see a large number of adolescents with the disease, hypothetically due to the rapid periods of physical and emotional maturation during this time period (Steiner & Lock, 1998). People with AN have a fear of gaining weight or becoming fat, even when they are at or below their expected body weight (APA, 2000). Although these individuals reach points of being well below ideal body weight, individuals with AN are unable to understand the severity of their condition and do not see themselves as malnourished (APA, 2000). For many people with AN, self-esteem is highly tied to their weight and how they see themselves (which, typically, is a body shape or size much larger than they appear to others). To continue to lose weight in an attempt to reach their ideal body size, people with AN will heavily restrict caloric intake or practice excessive exercise, and some will even practice binging (consuming a large amount of food in a short period of time) and purging. In the end, some individuals with AN may reach such a low body weight that they are not able to function and may need to be hospitalized. AN can cause multiple other developmental issues during the onset of adolescence, and some studies indicate that many health risks associated with eating disorders may be irreversible (Katzman, 2005). Children/adolescents can suffer from acute and severe malnutrition, damage to the brain, and damage to bone tissue (Rome et al., 2003). In the end, the most common causes of death from anorexia nervosa are cardiac arrest, electrolyte imbalance, and suicide (NIMH).

Bulimia nervosa (BN) is an eating disorder that is less frequent in childhood/adolescence than AN, and it seems to have an onset in later adolescence (Steiner & Lock, 1998). The typical onset of BN is between 14 and 25 years of age (Bogliatto, Delvenne, & Flament, 1996); however, clinician reports of BN have been seen in children as young as 10 (Bogliatto et al.). Similarly to AN, BN is more common in females than in males (Hoek & van Hoeken, 2003). The lifetime prevalence rate for females with BN is higher than that of AN, with 1.1% to 4.2% of females acquiring BN in their lifetime (NIMH, 2001b). BN is characterized by uncontrollable episodes of binge eating (APA, 2000). These episodes almost always occur in private, due to the recognition of individuals with BN that this behavior is not "right" and the significant feelings of guilt around engaging in binge eating behavior that individuals with BN have (APA, 2000). Following episodes of binge eating, individuals with BN engage in some form of purging, which may include self-induced vomiting, fasting, use of laxatives, use of diet pills, use of enemas, excessive exercise, or rigid dieting (APA, 2000). Typically, after engaging in this purging behavior, individuals report feeling "relieved" (NIMH, 2001a). Overall, individuals with BN tend to be of normal body weight as compared with individuals with AN (NIMH, 2001a). Similarly to AN, the self-esteem of individuals with BN is highly tied to their body weight and shape (APA, 2000). Many individuals with BN fear gaining weight, feel very unsatisfied with their body size and shape, and have a strong desire to lose weight (NIMH, 2001a). The process of binging and purging can cause significant health concerns for individuals with BN, including acute and severe malnutrition, brain damage, and bone tissue damage (Rome et al., 2003). Although the mortality rates for individuals with BN are not as high as they are for those with AN (Birmingham, Su, Hlynsky, Goldner, & Gao, 2005), the consequences of BN continue to carry great health risks for children and adolescents.

Binge Eating Disorder Binge eating disorder is one of the more recent eating disorders that has been added to the *DSM–IV–TR* as a "Criteria set and axes provided for further study" (APA, 2000). These disorders are included in the *DSM–IV–TR* because they are likely to have clinical validity but continue to have limited information to include as bona fide disorders (APA, 2000). The research criteria in the *DSM–IV–TR* indicates that individuals with binge eating disorder engage in frequent episodes of out-of-control eating (similar to bulimia nervosa) and have significant stress about the binges, but do not engage in compensatory behaviors such as purging and fasting (APA, 2000). These individuals are likely to present with varying degrees of obesity (APA). Additionally, it is proposed that, similarly to AN and BN, binge eating disorder tends to begin in adolescence or the early 20s (APA, 2000). Multiple population-based studies have confirmed the presence of binge eating disorder (Bruce & Agras, 1992; Spitzer et al., 1993); however, there continues to be questioning in the field regarding the presence of binge eating disorder (Fairburn, Welch, & Hay, 1993). Additionally, similar to other disorders, there is limited research in the area of binge eating disorder in adolescent populations and among racial/ethnic minority populations. As the creation of the *DSM V* is in progress, it is unclear whether binge eating disorder will be included in the next revision of the *DSM*.

A common misconception around eating disorders is that they are only prevalent in Caucasian, female, middle/upper-class populations. Although the majority of people that suffer from eating disorders are female, it is estimated that around 10% to 15% of people who are diagnosed with eating disorders are males (Carlat, Camargo, & Herzog, 1997). Overall, research has shown few differences between how eating disorders are manifested in female versus male populations, and there is a relative consensus that eating disorders are clinically similar in the male and female population (National Eating Disorder Association, 2002); however, a few differences have surfaced in research studies. First, as compared with females (mainly adults) with eating disorders, a higher percentage of males diagnosed with eating disorders identify as being homosexual (Bramon-Bosch, Troop, & Treasure, 2000; Carlat et al.). Only one of the studies that found the high association of homosexuality in the males diagnosed with eating disorders used a design that matched a female comparison group with each of the males studied. No population-based studies have been conducted that observe the incidence of homosexuality in the population and look at the incidence of males who identify as homosexual and are diagnosed with eating disorders within the overall population. Additionally, multiple studies have demonstrated a higher level of comorbidity of eating disorders and other psychiatric conditions (depression, anxiety disorders) in males as compared with females. Because the cultural standards of beauty for men and women are different, it is possible that additional differences regarding the etiology of eating disorders in men and women may surface in coming years.

Similarly to misconceptions around eating disorders and gender, information regarding eating disorders in ethnic minority populations continues to be limited. Since eating disorders tend to be highly tied to cultural ideals of beauty, it becomes increasingly important to study eating disorders within specific ethnic groups. It is possible that many within-group differences regarding eating disorders may be lost when the majority of studies on eating disorders in racial/ethnic populations pool multiple ethnicities under one racial group (e.g., Asian American, Latino/a; Pratt, Phillips, Greydanus, & Patel, 2003). In the end, we have a very limited understanding of how culture impacts the manifestation of eating disorders in racial/ethnic minority populations.

Although eating disorders can be viewed as a disease of affluence, there are considerable incidences of eating disorders in many populations of people worldwide (Pratt et al., 2003). Eating disorders tend to manifest themselves differently in racial/ethnic minority populations as compared with their European-American counterparts. It has been reported that racial/ethnic minority populations tend to have a lower level of "compensatory behaviors" such as dieting, purging, and excessive exercise, but are more likely to engage in binge eating and be diagnosed with partial eating syndromes (Pratt et al.). In a population-based study on dieting behaviors and body image perceptions of adolescents in Minnesota, population-specific differences were found among different racial/ethnic groups; SES was also found to be a factor. Story, French, Resnick, and Blum (1995) found that, in general, unhealthy weight control behaviors were not found just in White females of high SES. African American male and female adolescents were more likely to report being satisfied with their bodies, but also reported higher rates of vomiting as compared with their White counterparts. Asian females reported the highest frequency of binge eating and out-of-control eating, yet at the same time, Asian females were the least likely (along with African American females) to view themselves as overweight. As compared with White males, Asian males reported more binge eating, out-of-control eating, and dieting in the past year. Hispanic females reported the highest prevalence of frequent dieting and use of laxatives or other diuretics to lose weight. Additionally, when looking at SES, there were significant differences between females of low, middle, and high SES. Females of lower SES reported less frequent dieting and were less likely to view themselves as overweight, but reported more intentional vomiting and use of diuretics to lose weight as compared with females of middle SES. In addition, females of higher SES reported less binge eating or vomiting and were more likely to report feeling proud of their bodies. In the discussion section, Story et al. (1995) presented the caveat that the measures used in this study were validated on Caucasian populations and it is unknown if these unmodified measures were used appropriately within the other populations. It appears that we continue to have a vague understanding of how adolescents of racial/ethnic groups view and understand disordered eating as well as the manifestation of eating disorders in racial/ethnic minorities and individuals of lower SES as compared with their White, middle/upper-class adolescents.

Although school counselors and other educators are typically not immediately involved in all aspects of eating disorder treatment, they become extremely important in aiding prevention efforts and in facilitating appropriate school conditions for children/adolescents who are in treatment for eating disorders. First of all, school counselors and other educators have the tremendous asset of spending large amounts of time with youth. This places them in an ideal context to model healthy body image, eating, and exercise routines. Additionally, they are in an ideal situation to see early signs of the disorders as they develop. Early detection of eating disorders can make the recovery much more successful (Rome et al., 2003). If a counselor or school educator believes that a child may have an eating disorder, the following strategies can be used to facilitate the process of helping the child and his/her family receive treatment (Manley, Rickson, & Standeven, 2000):

- Express concern to the student and a willingness to help, while still respecting his or her need for autonomy and privacy
- Do not force the student to eat
- Observe, describe, and document behaviors of concern across times and settings
- Find out where to go for support and encourage the student to seek help
- Consult with parents and the child on an information-sharing basis
- Consult with the school-based team regarding referrals to other experienced professionals for a thorough assessment.

Treatment for eating disorders takes place in both inpatient and outpatient settings. Therefore, students may be away from school for a large part of their treatment, or they may be attending classes while part of an outpatient program. School counselors and other school staff need to create an individualized plan for students' diagnosed with eating disorders to meet their emotional, educational, physical, and social needs while in school. This may include creating an individualized education plan (IEP) for the student, which can aid him or her in catching up on missed classes and provide physical education that is appropriate for his or her current health (Manley et al., 2000). Additionally, it is extremely important for educators to establish a healthy social environment for students which encourages students to find a support network within the school and involves a no-tolerance policy on weight-based harassment (Manley et al.).

Although many schools have good intentions in attempting to create a school environment that fosters healthy physical and emotional development, for many students diagnosed with eating disorders, school contexts can be extremely toxic and harmful to their recovery (Rich & Evans, 2005). In a qualitative study on the challenges of British adolescents who had been diagnosed with eating disorders, Rich and Evans described the many struggles that these students met when returning to school. Many students discussed how their private struggles with an eating disorder became very public knowledge to teachers and students at the school. The comments that many well-meaning teachers made were hurtful to these students in the recovery process. One student discussed returning from an outpatient unit during the sixth grade and remarked that the first time a teacher saw her in the hallway, he shouted across the corridor, "Are you putting on weight?" Another student remarked that while she was in line at the cafeteria, a teacher remarked, "Well, Hayley, is this really you in a queue for food?" The identities of these students end up being tied up in the sheer fact that they have an eating disorder (Rich & Evans). The school environment can be an extremely difficult context for a student to establish a different identity than the "anorexic" and to manage a successful recovery.

School-Based Prevention Efforts in Obesity and Eating Disorders Because obesity and eating disorders are difficult to treat (Power, Lake, & Cole, 1997; Pratt et al., 2003), prevention efforts are extremely important, particularly for children and adolescents. Although researchers are developing more effective weight-loss treatments, overall, these treatments tend to be costly, can be dangerous, and may have limited time-based effects. Additionally, due to the high mortality rate of anorexia nervosa and the limited success in treatment, it becomes particularly beneficial to prevent eating disorders. It is extremely important, therefore, to raise children in a culture of physical health that includes frequent physical exercise, limited inactive leisure time, and healthy food intake, along with developmentally appropriate discussions of healthy weight levels and the impact of the media on our societal perpetuation of the thin ideal. By making healthy lifestyle choices routine and enjoyable for youth, it is presumed that they will continue to maintain these lifestyle choices into adulthood.

One of the challenges to effective weight-related health education is to teach extremely complicated lessons about weight-related health to children and adolescents, while also reaching them at a developmentally appropriate level. It can be difficult to work with younger students in particular, who may more easily create concrete associations of fat as being "bad" and thin as being "good." Therefore, educators need to be extremely savvy in their approach to working with younger children so as not to perpetuate cultural stereotypes about weight. Additionally, as children age and become more complex in their thinking, educators are given an opportunity to encourage children to think more abstractly about weight-related health, which will better help them to understand the complexities regarding these issues. It is hoped that if children are exposed to effective weight-related school-based interventions as they age, they will be more knowledgeable and prepared to understand the idiosyncrasies and current societal issues around weight and also to maintain a healthy weight into adulthood.

Since schools are one of the primary contexts in which most youth spend a large portion of their time, school communities are an ideal location to address healthy lifestyle choices that include obesity/eating-disorder prevention. Although many schools have high aspirations for adequately addressing the healthy physical development of their students, many fall short of creating an environment that facilitates healthy lifestyles. First, many educators report a lack of training in obesity/eating disorder prevention (Neumark-Sztainer, Story, & Harris, 1999). Although many teachers, counselors, coaches, and school nurses report an interest in acquiring more knowledge, few schools are providing these resources for their staff (Neumark-Sztainer et al.). Second, although attempts to establish effective school-based prevention efforts may be made in schools, occasionally, these uninformed attempts can be harmful to students. This may be due to curriculum choices (e.g., one that promotes an unhealthy body size and perpetuates the thin ideal). Curricula that promote these negative cultural images may sanction negative labeling of children who are overweight and lead students to make unhealthy drastic weight-loss choices such as enacting excessive food restrictions or vomiting (Yager & O'Dea, 2005). Additionally, individual educators can also be harmful to youth when they advertently (or inadvertently) promote drastic weight loss as the "ideal" picture of health or provide outdated weight loss prescriptions to overweight adolescents (those that focus only on decreasing caloric intake and increasing physical activity while ignoring genetic factors; Yager & O'Dea). It becomes extremely important for schools to correctly choose evidence-based programs that effectively teach students about healthy eating and exercise behaviors and also ensure that the educators who are delivering these materials correctly promote the curriculum through their teaching and role modeling.

The Centers for Disease Control (CDC) and other organizations have taken an active role in providing schools with assistance in developing their own prevention programs for obesity and eating disorders prevention. Many resources are now available for educators online, with assistance for implementing programs within schools and school districts. For instance, the CDC has published 10 guidelines that are most likely to promote lifetime healthy eating and physical activity in students (CDC, 1997; see also Wechsler, McKenna, Lee, & Dietz, 2004):

1. Address physical activity and nutrition through a Coordinated School Health Program (CSHP) approach
2. Designate a school health coordinator and maintain an active school health council
3. Assess the school's health policies and programs and develop a plan for improvement
4. Strengthen the school's nutrition and physical activity policies
5. Implement a high-quality health promotion program for school staff
6. Implement a high-quality course of study in health education
7. Implement a high-quality course for students in physical education
8. Increase opportunities for students to engage in physical activity
9. Implement a quality school meals program
10. Ensure that students have appealing, healthy choices in foods and beverages offered outside the school meals program.

The most effective curricula are "skill-based" programs that teach skills to adopt healthy behaviors, promote the practice and mastery of these skills, and aid students in overcoming barriers to achieving these skills (Wechsler et al., 2004). An important role for the school counselor in this process is in the evaluation of the effectiveness of existing programs. Often, the provider of the curriculum is focused on the transmission of content, so it is the school counselor who is in position to evaluate how well the curriculum translates into behavior. As changes in the school counseling program (see C. Dahir, chapter 3, this volume) call for school counselors to take an advocacy and leadership role, a focus on the acquisition of skills related to healthy behavior is certainly an important area of concern.

Many educators and schools are overwhelmed with education funding cuts and additional work responsibilities that have been added due to the demands of the "No Child Left Behind" legislation. It appears that schools are feeling pressure to cut program areas such as prevention programs and physical education in an effort to allocate more funding for required standardized testing and programs to improve student standardized test scores. These legitimate, pressing demands can be rationales for schools to reject plans of implementing school health programs and allocating additional resources to obesity and eating disorders prevention. It can be argued, however, that schools are required not only to educate and develop the minds of young learners, but also to teach youth skills in developing healthy bodies as well. Additionally, it has been shown that physically healthy (i.e., active and nutritionally fed) youth are more prepared and better equipped to learn than those who are not healthy (Chan, 2002; King et al., 2005). Therefore, it can be a tremendous asset for student learners when their schools provide them with adequate resources to reach optimum physical health. One way to address this challenge is to avoid the either/or thinking too common in schools. Rather than having to choose between socioemotional skill development and academics, addressing health issues such as nutrition can be integrated across the curriculum. For example, a seventh-grade curriculum might be an ideal time to address issues of assertion in guidance, nutrition in health class, exercise in physical education, gender images in social studies, self-image in English, and the underlying biology of nutrition in science class. Such an integrated curriculum would enhance the learning experience.

Additionally, many educators and school counselors feel overwhelmed regarding the prospect of treating children and adolescents with weight-related conditions. It is extremely important, however, to remind educators of their role in weight-related health condition prevention and treatment. Schools can be adequately trained to aid in the *prevention* of obesity and eating disorders, but not in the *treatment* of these diseases. It is not a school counselor's role to treat anorexia in a ninth grader or the physical education teacher's responsibility to prescribe a weight-loss treatment program for an overweight third grader. Instead, educators serve the role of teaching students about how to live healthy lives and teaching behavioral skills that students can use to achieve lifetime physical health. Additionally, educators play the important role of referring students who are struggling with weight-related conditions to the appropriate community resources for treatment (e.g., counselors, pediatricians, nutritionists) This role clarification allows educators to help struggling students within the scope of their training and expertise.

In addition to the CDC and other national organizations, many additional programs are being implemented in schools. The American Indian community has seen a high prevalence of overweight and obesity (Story et al., 2003). In an attempt to lower the percentage of body fat of American Indian children, a culturally grounded, large-scale, multi-site, school-based intervention entitled "Pathways" was implemented in 21 schools. The curriculum components included (1) a culturally based classroom curriculum designed to encourage healthy eating and increase physical activity, (2) a physical activity piece that emphasized maximum energy expenditure during physical education classes, (3) a food service component which intended to lower the amount of fat in school meals, and (4) a family program that contained take-home information for parents and encouraged them to prepare lower fat meals and promote exercise in their children (Steckler et al., 2003). School personnel (including food service staff) at the intervention schools were trained in the curriculum. In comparison with students at control schools (who were not involved in the Pathways intervention), the students exposed to the Pathways curriculum had an increase in healthy food intentions (intentions to choose more healthy foods over less healthy foods) and participation in physically active behaviors (J. Stevens et al.). Additionally, knowledge of messages about nutrition and physical activity increased in the intervention group (J. Stevens et al., 2003). The children involved in Pathways reported a significant decrease in the mean percentage of calories from total fat and saturated fat consumed in school lunches, and they reported a significant increase in the percentage of total calories from carbohydrates as compared with the control group (Himes et al., 2003). In looking at self-efficacy, girls were more efficacious to be physically active in the intervention group as compared with the control group, but this did not change for boys (J. Stevens et al.). Additionally, there were no differences between the intervention and control groups regarding student self-efficacy to make more healthy food choices (J. Stevens et al.). Finally, perception of healthy body size and weight-loss attempts did not demonstrate differences between intervention and control groups (J. Stevens et al.). Overall, it appears that the Pathways intervention was moderately successful in changing the eating behaviors and physical activity behaviors of American Indian students within a school context.

School-Based Health Centers

School-based health centers (SBHCs; also called coordinated school health programs) are clinics located in schools that provide students with comprehensive physical and mental health services. Students who receive parental consent are able to receive care for basic health needs such as annual physicals, immunizations, asthma care, sexually transmitted infection treatment, smoking cessation behavioral interventions, and preventative counseling for various health issues. SBHCs are staffed by qualified health professionals such as nurse practitioners, physicians, social workers, and counselors. In a 2002 survey, there were 1498 SBHCs in the United States (Center for Health and Health Care in Schools, 2002). Many experts agree that SBHCs are an effective means to increase health literacy in students, reach student populations that do not have a primary source of care, and provide effective preventative health services for children.

There are eight basic components of effective coordinated school health programs (CSHPs): (1) health services; (2) counseling, psychological, and social services; (3) health education; (4) health promotion for staff; (5) healthy school environment; (6) nutrition services; (7) physical education; and (8) family/community involvement (C. Fisher et al., 2004). Organization of these programs typically comes from a state and community level. Many CSHPs have advisory boards that include teachers, school nurses, school principals, coaches, parents, and students to ensure that the CSHP is meeting the needs of the community. Funding for these programs includes federal, state, and private grants. Additionally, some CSHPs are able to receive payment through managed care and Medicaid.

Parents, students, and schools benefit from establishing SBHCs in their schools. First, it has been hypothesized that healthy students are more effective in the classroom than unhealthy students are. By providing all students with access to quality health care, students are better able to maintain good to excellent physical and mental health, which can have an impact on their academic performance (Geierstanger, Amaral, Mansour, & Walters, 2004). Next, SBHCs provide a convenient place for students to receive access to health care. By providing quality health care in schools, parents are able to avoid taking time off from work to transport children to physician's appointments. Additionally, since transportation time is not an issue, students are able to miss less classroom instruction time. Finally, many SBHCs are located in urban areas with higher physician-to-child ratios (Center for Health and Health Care in Schools, 2002). By coordinating with the community to establish health care for students in schools, it is likely that more underserved students will have access to health care, particularly in these areas with few available pediatricians (Center for Health and Health Care in Schools).

Effectiveness of School-Based Health Centers

Many schools have found measurable benefits from implementing SBHCs in their schools. For instance, after implementing an SBHC in a middle school in Florida, the school reported that school attendance increased from 92.1% to 94.2%, the percentage of students scoring above a 3.0 on a Florida writing exam increased from 86% to 99%, the percentage of students scoring above the 50th percentile on a mathematics standardized test increased from 69% to 79%, and the number of disciplinary actions of students was reduced (Marx, 2003). Although SBHCs account for only a portion of the multiple interventions used to aid students in succeeding academically, they can provide a service that allows students to become healthier and thus improve the likelihood that they will succeed in school. A quote from Jackson, Davis, Abeel, & Bordonaro (2000), *Turning Points*, demonstates the focal idea, "Good health does not guarantee that students will be interested in learning and able to learn, but the absence of good health makes learning all the more difficult" (pp. 168–169). Therefore, in the advent of a time when schools are required to demonstrate the use and benefit of every dollar spent within school systems, researchers have begun to conduct studies that show the effectiveness of SBHCs.

Health related impacts of school-based health centers. It has been demonstrated that students who have access to SBHCs at the elementary school level are more likely to see a health professional and receive higher quality care. Kaplan et al. (1999) conducted a comparison study between students at a school that had an SBHC and a neighboring comparison school that did not. Both schools enrolled children who were from large households, had parents with lower education levels, and were receiving high levels of public assistance, and about half of the students did not have health insurance. They found that students who had access to the SBHCs had significantly less difficulty receiving physical health care, used emergency departments less frequently, were more likely to have seen a physician in the past year, and were more likely to have had an annual dental exam. SBHCs can be a very effective method to provide elementary students with access to quality physical health care.

Additionally, SBHCs have been shown to be very effective in working with children who have asthma. In a longitudinal study conducted from 1997 to 2003, researchers found that children with asthma who received care within the context of a SBHC were less likely to be hospitalized (due to asthma complications) and were less likely to make emergency room visits as compared with children in non-SBHC schools (Guo et al., 2005). Additionally, Guo et al. estimated that the potential cost-savings for hospitalization per child was $970. In a another study on the impact of SBHCs on children with asthma, researchers found that children with access to SBHCs in the Bronx, New York, had a reduction in hospitalizations and gained 3 school days in comparison with children who did not have an SBHC (Webber et al., 2003). Overall, it has been shown that SBHCs are able to provide both quality and cost-effective care for children with asthma.

Academic impacts of school-based health centers. The evaluation of the impacts of SBHCs continues to be a challenge for many school districts. Although many school districts intuitively believe that their programs are making an impact on students' academic performance, there continue to be insufficient well-conducted quantitative studies that demonstrate this relationship (Geierstanger et al., 2004). In a review of the literature on the relationship between SBHCs and academic performance, Geierstanger and colleagues found seven studies that met the methodological qualifications for studies that used an experimental or quasi-experimental design and were published in peer-reviewed journals. Of these seven studies, six found a statistically significant relationship between at least one academic indicator (i.e., absence/attendance, tardiness, promotion to the next grade, withdrawal/drop-out rates, graduation rates, disciplinary referrals, suspension rates, standardized test scores, GPA, educational motivation, receipt of failing grade, educational aspirations, or credit accumulation) and the presence or use of a SBHC. They concluded that although there continues to be insufficient evidence regarding the direct link between SBHC and positive academic performance outcomes, the intermediate outcomes of SBHCs along with other social or educational factors can influence academic performance indirectly (Geierstanger et al., 2004).

In a similar review of the same seven studies on the relationship between SBHCs and academic performance, the National Assembly on School-Based Health Care (Geierstanger & Amaral, 2005) also concluded that it is difficult to establish a direct link between SBHCs and academic performance. Additionally, some individuals on the committee argued that because SBHCs are not a direct educational intervention, they should not be held responsible for directly accounting for the educational performance of students. They wrote that due to the idea that SBHCs are primarily created to impact student health, any benefits to academic performance should be seen as secondary. The committee also acknowledged, however, that schools are being held to increasingly higher standards to demonstrate where their dollars are being spent, and that if SBHCs cannot demonstrate a direct link between their presence in schools and the effects of academic achievement, that it will be difficult to rationalize the funding of these programs. In the end, the committee also communicated a great need to improve the methodological design in studies used to demonstrate the relationship between SBHCs and academic outcomes (Geierstanger & Amaral). It is currently unclear if more rigorous studies of SBHCs will demonstrate significant, direct links between SBHCs and academic outcomes. More importantly, it may be more advantageous for SBHCs in the long run to argue for their inclusion in school programs as an indirect influence on academic performance and as being an integral component of the development of the whole student with both mind and body included.

Implementation of school-based health centers. School counselors can be instrumental in establishing SBHCs in their schools. By networking with other individuals in their community (including superintendents, principals, teachers, parents, students, community leaders, etc.), school counselors can create a unified group that can lobby state and local leaders for support. Although many communities fear that establishing SBHCs is too expensive, there are many grants available through organizations such as the Centers for Disease Control's Division of Adolescent and School Health (CDC, 2005c). As key players in establishing prevention efforts within schools, counselors are able to work with the community to recognize how creating SBHCs can be more cost-effective in the long run.

Additionally, the CDC has created a free publication entitled *Stories from the Field: Lessons Learned about Building Coordinated School Health Programs* (Marx, 2003), which aids educators in adopting, initiating, implementing, and institutionalizing SBHCs in their schools. In addition to a practical implementation guide, this publication tells the stories of nine school districts across the country who successfully implemented SBHCs in their communities. This publication can be an extremely helpful resource for communities looking to address physical and mental health issues in their schools.

Ultimately, the creation of SBHCs in schools is highly dependent on funding and those organizations that contribute to the payment for health based services. Because health care tends to be funded primarily through Health Management Organizations (HMOs), national programs (e.g., Medicaid), and personal contributions, if schools are to implement SBHCs, it would be necessary to encounter means to provide services that would be covered by various payment entities. This is a potential barrier to the establishment of SBHCs in some areas, which may need to be addressed at a state policy level. Regardless of the ultimate method of delivery, it is important for schools to find a means to coordinate how to effectively meet the physical and emotional health needs of students in schools.

Conclusions

School counselors and other educators are being required to have increased influence over the physical health of their students. This additional responsibility is a reality that requires that educators have access to appropriate training and funding for these school programs that address physical health issues. It is hoped that by increasing physical health based prevention programs in school, children will be less likely to suffer from preventable physical health conditions and that they will be better prepared to learn and succeed academically. School counselors can be excellent resources in schools to help address, advocate for, plan, implement, and evaluate school health initiatives. Through coordinated school health efforts, which may include school-based health centers (SBHCs), schools can be at least one environmental context that is concerned with not only the successful mental and social development of youth, but also their optimal physical development as well.

References

Akinbami, L. J., & Schoendorf, K. C. (2002). Trends in childhood asthma: Prevalence, health care utilization, and mortality. *Pediatrics, 110*(2), 315.

American Diabetes Association. (2000). Type 2 diabetes in children and adolescents. *Diabetes Care, 23*, 381–389.

American Diabetes Association. (2005). *All about diabetes.* Retrieved October 30, 2005, from http://www.diabetes.org/

American Lung Association. (2005). *Asthma and children fact sheet.* Retrieved July, 2005, from http://www.lungusa.org/

American Psychiatric Association. (2000). *Diagnostic and statistical manual of mental disorders: DSM–IV–TR* (4th ed.). Washington, DC: American Psychiatric Association.

Andersen, A. (1995). Eating disorders in males. In K. D. Brownnell & C. G. Fairburn (Eds.), *Eating disorders and obesity: A comprehensive handbook* (pp. 177–182). New York: Guilford Press.

Andrulis, D. P. (1998). Access to care is the centerpiece in the elimination of socioeconomic disparities in health. *Annals of Internal Medicine, 129*(5), 412.

Bhandari, S., & Gifford, E. (2003). *Children with health insurance: 2001.* Washington, DC: U.S. Census Bureau.

Birmingham, C. L., Su, J., Hlynsky, J. A., Goldner, E. M., & Gao, M. (2005). The mortality rate from anorexia nervosa. *International Journal of Eating Disorders, 38*(2), 143–146.

Bliss, H. A. (1982). Primary care in the emergency room: High in cost and low in quality. *New England Journal of Medicine, 306*(16), 998.

Blum, R. W. (1998). Improving the health of youth: A community health perspective. *Journal of Adolescent Health, 23*(5), 254–258.

Bogliatto, C., Delvenne, V., & Flament, M. (1996). *Early onset of bulimia.* Paper presented at Seventh New York International Conference on Eating Disorders, New York.

Bramon-Bosch, E., Troop, N. A., & Treasure, J. L. (2000). Eating disorders in males: A comparison with female patients. *European Eating Disorders Review, 8*(4), 321–328.

Bruce, B., & Agras, W. S. (1992). Binge eating in females: A population-based investigation. *International Journal of Eating Disorders, 12*(4), 365.

Burdette, H. L., & Whitaker, R. C. (2005). A national study of neighborhood safety, outdoor play, television viewing, and obesity in preschool children. *Pediatrics, 116*(3), 657–662.

Carlat, D. J., Camargo, C. A., Jr., & Herzog, D. B. (1997). Eating disorders in males: A report on 135 patients. *American Journal of Psychiatry, 154*(8), 1127–1132.

Centers for Disease Control and Prevention. (1997). Guidelines for school and community programs to promote lifelong physical activity among young people. *MMWR Weekly, 46*(RR-6), 1–36.

Centers for Disease Control and Prevention. (2000a). *Clinical growth charts.* Retrieved August 15, 2005, from http://www.cdc.gov/

Centers for Disease Control and Prevention. (2000b). *Fact sheet: Asthma.* Retrieved August 15, 2005, from http://www.cdc.gov/

Centers for Disease Control and Prevention. (2001). *1999 Pediatric surveillance system.* Atlanta, GA: U.S. Department of Health and Human Services.

Centers for Disease Control and Prevention. (2002a). *Asthma prevalence, health care use and mortality, 2002.* Retrieved August 15, 2005, from http://www.cdc.gov/

Centers for Disease Control and Prevention. (2002b). *Obesity and genetics: What we know and what we don't know.* Retrieved August 15, 2005, from http://www.cdc.gov/

Centers for Disease Control and Prevention. (2004a). *Addressing asthma in schools.* Retrieved August 15, 2005, from http://www.cdc.gov/

Centers for Disease Control and Prevention. (2004b). *Leading causes of death and numbers of deaths, according to age: United States.* Retrieved August 15, 2005, from http://www.cdc.gov/

Centers for Disease Control and Prevention. (2004c). *Summary health statistics for U.S. children: National health interview survey, 2002.* Retrieved August 15, 2005, from http://www.cdc.gov/

Centers for Disease Control and Prevention. (2004d). *Trends in the prevalence of overweight.* Retrieved August 15, 2005, from http://www.cdc.gov/

Centers for Disease Control and Prevention. (2005a). *Asthma's impact on children and adolescents.* Retrieved August, 2005, from http://www.cdc.gov/

Centers for Disease Control and Prevention. (2005b). *BMI—Body mass index: BMI for children and teens.* Retrieved August 15, 2005, from http://www.cdc.gov/

Centers for Disease Control and Prevention. (2005c). *Healthy youth!: Funded education agencies.* Retrieved August 15, 2005, from http://www.cdc.gov/

Centers for Disease Control and Prevention. (2005d). *Prevalence of overweight among children and adolescents: United States, 1999–2002.* Retrieved August 15, 2005, from http://www.cdc.gov/

Centers for Disease Control and Prevention. (2005e). *Strategies for addressing asthma within a coordinated school health program, with updated resources.* Retrieved August 29, 2005, from http://www.cdc.gov/

Centers for Health and Healthcare in Schools. (2002). *2002 State survey of school-based health center initiatives.* Retrieved August 15, 2005, from http://www.healthinschools.org/

Chan, W. (2002). *Preparing our children to learn: Report of the select committee on California children's school readiness and health.* Sacramento: California State Legislature.

Clay, D. L., Cortina, S., Harper, D. C., Cocco, K. M., & Drotar, D. (2004). Schoolteachers' experiences with childhood chronic illness. *Children's Health Care, 33*(3), 227–239.

Cole, K. L., Roberts, M. C., & McNeal, R. E. (1996). Children's perceptions of ill peers: Effects of disease, grade, and impact variables. *Children's Health Care, 25*(2), 107–115.

Crawford, P. B., Drury, A., & Stern, S. (1999). Childhood obesity and family SES racial differences. *Healthy Weight Journal, 13*(3), 42–43.

Department of Health and Human Services. (2001). *The Surgeon General's call to action to prevent and decrease overweight and obesity.* Retrieved August 15, 2005, from http://www.surgeongeneral.gov/

Department of Health and Human Services. (2005). *Healthy people 2010.* Retrieved August 15, 2005, from http://www.healthypeople.gov/

Dietz, W. H. (1998). Health consequences of obesity in youth: Predictors of adult disease. *Pediatrics, 101,* 518–525.

Dietz, W. H. (2004). Overweight in childhood and adolescence. *The New England Journal of Medicine, 350*(9), 855–858.

Drewnowski, A., & Specter, S. E. (2004). Poverty and obesity: The role of energy density and energy costs. *American Journal of Clinical Nutrition, 79*(1), 6–16.

Fagot-Campagna, A., Pettit, D. J., Engelgau, M. M., Burrows, N. R., Geiss, L. S., Valdez, R., et al. (2000). Type 2 diabetes among North American children and adolescents: An epidemiological review and a public health perspective. *The Journal of Pediatrics, 136*(5), 664–672.

Fairburn, C. G., Welch, S. L., & Hay, P. J. (1993). The classification of recurrent overeating: The "binge eating disorder" proposal. *International Journal of Eating Disorders, 13,* 155–159.

Fisher, M., Golden, N. H., Katzman, D. K., Kreipe, R. E., Rees, J., Schebendach, J., et al. (1995). Eating disorders in adolescents: A background paper. *Journal of Adolescent Health, 16,* 420–437.

Fisher, C., Hunt, P., Kann, L., Kolbe, L. J., Patterson, B., & Wechsler, H. (2004). *Building a healthier future through school health programs.* Retrieved October 15, 2005, from http://www.cdc.gov/

Freedman, D. S., Dietz, W. H., Srinivasan, S., & Berenson, G. S. (1999). The relation of overweight to cardiovascular risk factors among children and adolescents: The Bogalusa heart study. *Pediatrics, 103*(6), 1175–1183.

Freedman, D. S., Khan, L. K., Dietz, W. H., Srinivasan, S. R., & Berenson, G. S. (2001). Relationship of childhood obesity to coronary heart disease risk factors in adulthood: The Bogalusa heart study. *Pediatrics, 108*(3), 712–719.

Gardner, D. M., Vitousek, K. M., & Pike, K. M. (1997). Cognitive-behavioral therapy for anorexia. In D. M. Garner & P. E. Garfinkel (Eds.), *Handbook of treatment for eating disorders* (2nd ed., pp. 94–144). New York: Guilford.

Geierstanger, S. P., & Amaral, G. (2005). *School-based health centers and academic performance: What is the intersection?* Washington, DC: National Assembly on School-Based Health Care.

Geierstanger, S. P., Amaral, G., Mansour, M., & Walters, S. R. (2004). School-based health centers and academic performance: Research, challenges, and recommendations. *Journal of School Health, 74*(9), 347–352.

Guo, J. J., Jang, R., Keller, K. N., McCracken, A. L., Pan, W., & Cluxton, R. J. (2005). Impact of school-based health centers on children with asthma. *Journal of Adolescent Health, 37*(4), 266–274.

Halfon, N., & Newacheck, P. W. (1993). Childhood asthma and poverty: Differential impacts and utilization of health services. *Pediatrics, 91*(1), 56.

Halfon, N., Newacheck, P. W., Wood, D. L., & St. Peter, R. F. (1996). Routine emergency department use for sick care by children in the United States. *Pediatrics, 98*(1), 28.

Hall, M. J. & DeFrances, C. J. (2003). 2001 National Hospital Discharge Survey. *Advance Data from Vital & Health Statistics, 332,* 1–18.

Halterman, J. S., Aligne, C. A., Auinger, P., McBride, J. T., & Szilagyi, P. G. (2000). Inadequate therapy for asthma among children in the United States. *Pediatrics, 105*(1), 272.

Hedley, A. A., Ogden, C. L., Johnson, C. L., Carroll, M. D., Curtin, L. R., & Flegal, K. M. (2004). Prevalence of overweight and obesity among US children, adolescents, and adults, 1999–2002. *JAMA: Journal of the American Medical Association, 291*(23), 2847–2850.

Himes, J. H., Ring, K., Gittelsohn, J., Cunningham-Sabo, L., Weber, J., Thompson, J., et al. (2003). Impact of the Pathways intervention on dietary intakes of American Indian schoolchildren. *Preventive Medicine, 37,* S55–S61.

Hoek, H. W., & van Hoeken, D. (2003). Review of the prevalence and incidence of eating disorders. *International Journal of Eating Disorders, 34*(4), 383–396.

Jackson, A., Davis, G. A., Abeel, M., & Bordonaro, A. (2000). *Turning points 2000: Educating adolescents in the 21st century.* New York: Teachers College Press.

Kaiser Commission on Medicaid and the Uninsured (2005). *Enrolling uninsured low-income children in Medicaid and SCHIP.* Washington, DC: Henry J. Kaiser Family Foundation.

Kaplan, D. W., Brindis, C. D., Phibbs, S. L., Melinkovich, P., Naylor, K., & Ahlstrand, K. (1999). A comparison study of an elementary school-based health center. *Archives of Pediatrics and Adolescent Medicine, 153,* 235–243.

Katzman, D. K. (2005). Medical complications in adolescents with anorexia nervosa: A review of the literature. *International Journal of Eating Disorders, 37,* S52–S59.

Kaye, W. H., Lilenfeld, L. R., Berrettini, W. H., Strober, M., Devlin, B., Klump, K. L., et al. (2000). A search for susceptibility loci for anorexia nervosa: Methods and sample description. *Biological Psychiatry, 47*(9), 794–803.

Keppel, K. G., Pearcy, J. N., & Wagener, D. K. (2002). Trends in racial and ethnic-specific rates for the health status indicators: United States, 1990–98. *Healthy People 2000 Statistical Notes/National Center for Health Statistics, 23,* 1–16.

Key, J. D., Brown, R. T., Marsh, L. D., Spratt, E. G., & Recknor, J. C. (2001). Depressive symptoms in adolescents with a chronic illness. *Children's Health Care, 30*(4), 283–292.

King, G., McDougall, J., DeWit, D., Hong, S., Miller, L., Offord, D., et al. (2005, December). Pathways to children's academic performance and prosocial behaviour: Roles of physical health status, environmental, family, and child factors. *International Journal of Disability, Development & Education, 52*(4), 313–344.

Kreipe, R. E., Golden, N. H., Katzman, D. K., Fisher, M., Rees, J., & Tonkin, R. S. (1995). Eating disorders in adolescents: A position paper of the Society for Adolescent Medicine. *Journal of Adolescent Health, 16,* 476–489.

Leon, G. R., Fulkerson, J. A., Perry, C. L., & Cudeck, R. (1992). Personality and behavioral vulnerabilities associated with risk status for eating disorders in adolescent girls. *Journal of Abnormal Psychology, 102,* 438–444.

Logio, K. A. (2003). Gender, race, childhood abuse, and body image among adolescents. *Violence Against Women, 9*(8), 931–954.

Manley, R. S., Rickson, H., & Standeven, B. (2000). Children and adolescents with eating disorders: Strategies for teachers and school counselors. *Intervention in School and Clinic, 35*(4), 228.

Marx, E. (2003). *Stories from the field: Lessons learned about building coordinated school health programs.* Washington, DC: CDC.

Mayberry, R. M., Mili, F., & Ofili, E. (2000). Racial and ethnic differences in access to medical care. *Medical Care Research & Review, 57*(3), 108.

McCarthy, M. (2004). The economics of obesity. *The Lancet, 364*(9452), 2169–2170.

Mirza, N. M., Kadow, K., Palmer, M., Solano, H., Rosche, C., & Yanovski, J. A. (2004). Prevalence of overweight among inner city Hispanic-American children and adolescents. *Obesity Research, 12*(8), 1298–1310.

Molnar, B. E., Gortmaker, S. L., Bull, F. C., & Buka, S. L. (2004). Unsafe to play? Neighborhood disorder and lack of safety predict reduced physical activity among urban children and adolescents. *American Journal of Health Promotion, 18*(5), 378–386.

Mukherjee, S., Lightfoot, J., & Sloper, P. (2000). The inclusion of pupils with a chronic health condition in mainstream school: What does it mean for teachers? *Educational Research, 42*(1), 59–72.

Nabors, L., Troillett, A., Nash, T., & Masiulis, B. (2005). School nurse perceptions of barriers and supports for children with diabetes. *Journal of School Health, 75*(4), 119–125.

National Association of State Boards of Education. (2002). *Fit, healthy, and ready to learn: A school health policy guide.* Alexandria, VA: Author.

National Cancer Institute. (2005). *Young people with cancer: A handbook for parents.* Retrieved October 15, 2005, from http://www.nci.nih.gov/

National Eating Disorders Association. (2002). *Males and eating disorders: Research.* Retrieved August 15, 2005, from http://www.nationaleatingdisorders.org/

National Institute of Mental Health. (2001a). *Eating disorders: Facts about eating disorders and the search for solutions.* Bethesda, MD: National Institute of Health.

National Institute of Mental Health. (2001b). *The numbers count: Mental disorders in America.* Retrieved September 1, 2005, from http://www.nimh.nih.gov/

Neumark-Sztainer, D. (2003). Obesity and eating disorder prevention: An integrated approach? *Adolescent Medicine, 14*(1), 159–173.

Neumark-Sztainer, D., Story, M., & Harris, T. (1999). Beliefs and attitudes about obesity among teachers and school health care providers working with adolescents. *Journal of Nutrition Education, 31*(1), 3–9.

Newacheck, P. W., Hughes, D. C., & Stoddard, J. J. (1996). Children's access to primary care: Differences by race, income, and insurance status. *Pediatrics, 97,* 26–32.

Northham, E. A. (1997). Psychosocial impact of chronic illness in children. *Journal of Paediatric Child Health, 33,* 369–372.

Ogden, C. L., Flegal, K. M., Carroll, M. D., & Johnson, C. L. (2002). Prevalence and trends in overweight among US children and adolescents, 1999–2000. *Journal of the American Medical Association (JAMA), 288,* 1728–1732.

Patton, G. C., Selzer, R., Coffey, C., Carlin, J. B., & Wolfe, R. (1999). Onset of adolescent eating disorders: Population based cohort study over 3 years. *BMJ: British Medical Journal, 318*(7186), 765–786.

Power C., Lake J. K. J., & Cole, T. J. (1997). Measurement and long-term health risks of child and adolescent fatness. *International Journal of Obesity Related Metabolic Disorders, 21*, 507–526.

Power, C., Manor, O., & Matthews, S. (2003). Child to adult socioeconomic conditions and obesity in a national cohort. *International Journal of Obesity, 27*(9), 1081–1086.

Pratt, H. D., Phillips, E. L., Greydanus, D. E., & Patel, D. R. (2003). Eating disorders in the adolescent population: Future directions. *Journal of Adolescent Research, 18*(3), 297.

Rich, E., & Evans, J. (2005). Making sense of eating disorders in schools. *Discourse: Studies in the cultural politics of education, 26*(2), 247–262.

Ries, L. A. G. (1999). *Childhood cancer mortality.* Retrieved October 15, 2005, from http://seer.cancer.gov/

Rome, E. S., Ammerman, S., Rosen, D. S., Keller, R. J., Lock, J., Mammel, K. A., et al. (2003). Children and adolescents with eating disorders: The state of the art. *Pediatrics, 111*(1), 98–108.

Rowling, L. (1995). The disenfranchised grief of teachers. *Omega: Journal of Death and Dying, 31*(4), 317–329.

Royal, G. P., & Roberts, M. C. (1987). Students' perceptions of and attitudes toward disabilities: A comparison of twenty conditions. *Journal of Clinical Child Psychology, 16*, 122–132.

Schwimmer, J., Burwinkle, T., & Varni, J. (2003). Quality of life in obese children. *Nutrition Research Newsletter, 22*(5), 6–8.

Sexson, S. B., & Madan-Swain, A. (1993). School reentry for the child with chronic illness. *Journal of Learning Disabilities, 26*(2).

Sexson, S. B., & Madan-Swain, A. (1995). The chronically ill child in the school. *School Psychology Quarterly, 10*, 359–368.

Shi, L., & Stevens, G. D. (2005). Disparities in access to care and satisfaction among U.S. children: The roles of race/ethnicity and poverty status. *Public Health Reports, 120*(4), 431–442.

Smith, M. A., Ries, L. A. G., Gurney, J. G., & Ross, J. A. (1999). *Leukemia.* Retrieved August 15, 2005, from http://seer.cancer.gov/

Smolak, L., & Levine, M. P. (Eds.). (1996). *Adolescent transitions and the development of eating problems.* Hillsdale, NJ: Lawrence Erlbaum Associates.

Sobal, J., & Stunkard, A. J. (1989). Socioeconomic status and obesity: A review of the literature. *Psychological Bulletin, 105*(2), 260–275.

Spitzer, R. L., Yanovski, S., Wadden, T., Wing, R., Marcus, M. D., Stunkard, A., et al. (1993). Binge eating disorder: Its further validation in a multisite study. *International Journal of Eating Disorders, 13*(2), 137.

St. Peter, R. F., Newacheck, P. W., & Halfon, N. (1992). Access to care for poor children: Separate and unequal? *Journal of the American Medical Association, 267*, 2760–2764.

Steckler, A., Ethelbah, B., Martin, C. J., Stewart, D., Pardilla, M., Gittelsohn, J., et al. (2003). Pathways process evaluation results: A school-based prevention trial to promote healthful diet and physical activity in American Indian third, fourth, and fifth grade students. *Preventive Medicine, 37*, S80–S90.

Stein, R. E., Bauman, L. J., Westbrook, L. E., Coupey, S. M., & Ireys, H. T. (1993). Framework for identifying children who have chronic conditions: The case for a new definition. *Journal of Pediatrics, 122*(3), 342–347.

Steiner, H., & Lock, J. (1998). Anorexia nervosa and bulimia nervosa in children and adolescents: A review of the past 10 years. *Journal of the American Academy of Child & Adolescent Psychiatry, 37*(4), 352–359.

Stevens, G. D., & Shi, L. (2003). Racial and ethnic disparities in the primary care experiences of children: A review of the literature. *Medical Care Research & Review, 60*(1), 3–30.

Stevens, J., Story, M., Ring, K., Murray, D. M., Cornell, C. E., Juhaeri, et al. (2003). The impact of the Pathways intervention on psychosocial variables related to diet and physical activity in American Indian schoolchildren. *Preventive Medicine: An International Journal Devoted to Practice and Theory, 37*(Supp. 1), S70–S79.

Story, M., French, S. A., Resnick, M. D., & Blum, R. W. (1995). Ethnic/racial and socioeconomic differences in dieting behaviors and body image perceptions in adolescents. *International Journal of Eating Disorders, 18*(2), 173–179.

Story, M., Stevens, J., Himes, J., Stone, E., Holy Rock, B., Ethelbah, B., et al. (2003). Obesity in American-Indian children: Prevalence, consequences, and prevention. *Preventive Medicine, 37*, S3–S12.

Strober, M., Freeman, R., Lampert, C., Diamond, J., & Kaye, W. (2000). Controlled family study of anorexia nervosa and bulimia nervosa: Evidence of shared liability and transmission of partial syndromes. *American Journal of Psychiatry, 157*(3), 393–401.

Sullivan, P. F. (1995). Mortality in anorexia nervosa. *American Journal of Psychiatry, 152*, 1073–1074.

Sylvester, M. S., Aughey, D., Sieving, R. E., McNeely, C. A., Singh, N., Oliphant, J., et al. (2003). *Preventive care for adolescents: A training plan for primary care providers.* Minneapolis, MN: Division of General Pediatrics & Adolescent Health, University of Minnesota.

Thies, K. M. (1999). Identifying the educational implications of chronic illness in school children. *Journal of School Health, 69*(10), 392.

Walters, E. E. & Kendler, K. S. (1995). Anorexia nervosa and anorexic-like syndromes in a population-based female twin sample. *American Journal of Psychiatry, 152*(1), p. 64–71.

Webber, M. P., Carpiniello, K. E., Oruwariye, T., Lo, Y., Burton, W. B., & Appel, D. K. (2003). Burden of asthma in inner-city elementary schoolchildren: Do school-based health centers make a difference? *Archives of Pediatrics and Adolescent Medicine, 157*, 125–129.

Wechsler, H., McKenna, M. L., Lee, S. M., & Dietz, W. H. (2004). The role of schools in preventing childhood obesity. *The State Education Standard*, 4–12.

Weinick, R. M., & Krauss, N. A. (2000). Racial/ethnic differences in children's access to care. *American Journal of Public Health, 90*(11), 1771.

Williams, J., Wake, M., Hesketh, K., Maher, E., & Waters, E. (2005). Health-related quality of life of overweight and obese children. *JAMA: Journal of the American Medical Association, 293*(1), 1–5.

Yager, Z., & O'Dea, J. A. (2005). The role of teachers and other educators in the prevention of eating disorders and child obesity: What are the issues? *Eating Disorders: The Journal of Treatment & Prevention, 13*(3), 261–278.

Yamamoto, L. G., Zimmerman, K. R., Butts, R. J., Anaya, C., Lee, P., Miller, N. C., et al. (1995). Characteristics of frequent pediatric emergency department users. *Pediatric Emergency Care, 11*(6), 340–346.

Young-Hyman, D., Schlundt, D. G., Herman-Wenderoth, L., & Bozylinski, K. (2003). Obesity, appearance, and psychosocial adaptation in young African American children. *Journal of Pediatric Psychology, 28*(7), 463–472.

Zephier, E., Himes, J. H., & Story, M. (1999). Prevalence of overweight and obesity in American Indian school children and adolescents in the Aberdeen area: A population study. *International Journal of Obesity Related Metabolic Disorders, 24*(2), S28–S30.

Zhang, Q., & Wang, Y. (2004). Socioeconomic inequality of obesity in the United States: Do gender, age, and ethnicity matter? *Social Science & Medicine, 58*(6), 1171–1180.

XVII
ADOLESCENT SEXUAL HEALTH AND DEVELOPMENT

LAURA FILLINGAME KNUDTSON AND HARDIN L. K. COLEMAN
University of Wisconsin–Madison

Currently, one of the most controversial topics regarding adolescent physical health is sexuality. Parents, educators, counselors, physicians, and youth leaders continue to struggle with issues around adolescent sexuality including but not limited to abstinence-only versus comprehensive sex education, the role of schools versus parents in sexual health education, minors' rights in consenting to receive sexual health services and/or birth control, the role of religion/spirituality in sexual health, communicating with adolescents about sexuality, and our nation's overwhelming discomfort in talking about sex. The politically charged nature of the topic of adolescent sexual health can be particularly challenging for school counselors and other school personnel who readily observe the developmental changes of middle and high school students and become closely integrated into adolescents' negotiation of this challenging developmental milestone, but are increasingly meeting roadblocks in how they are allowed to be involved in the life transition of sexual development in their students. Although, states differ in their legal requirements around sexual health education, this chapter can aid school personnel in understanding the issues around adolescent sexual health and then applying the information to their current state's legal statutes about counselors' and educators' roles in sexual health education and counseling. (The Alan Guttmacher Institute has excellent fact sheets on state specific policies on sex education and minor access to contraception, STI treatment, abortion, etc., available at http://www.guttmacher.org/statecenter/spibs/index.html.) Additionally, this chapter will provide information about coordinated school-based health centers as a beneficial addition to school programs that address issues of adolescent physical and sexual health.

Current State of Adolescent Sexual Behaviors

The state of adolescent sexual behaviors has changed over the past 12 years in the United States. The number of teens who have *never* had sexual intercourse is declining (from 54.1%, CI [confidence interval]: ±3.5%, in 1991 to 46.7%, CI: ±2.6%, in 2003) and continues to be a significant issue for almost half of all adolescents (Centers for Disease Control and Prevention [CDC], 2005b). See Table 17.1 for racial-/ethnic-specific rates for adolescents who have reported having sexual intercourse. Every year about 1 million teens become pregnant (which is about 10% of all women aged 15 to 19; Alan Guttmacher Institute, 1999). The teen pregnancy rate in the United States has declined (Singh & Darroch, 2000). However, the United States continues to lag behind other developed nations regarding adolescent pregnancy, abortion, and birth rates. See Table 17.2 for pregnancy, abortion, and birth rates as reported per 1,000 adolescents aged 15 to 19. See Table 17.3 for race/ethnic pregnancy and birth rates in the Unites States and Table 17.4 for information on pregnancies and out-of-wedlock births for adolescents under age 20. It is estimated that 78% of teen pregnancies are unplanned (Alan Guttmacher Institute, 1999). This is a major health issue, as adolescent pregnancy carries with it many risks. One third of pregnant teen mothers receive inadequate prenatal care. Babies born to adolescent mothers are more likely to be of low birth weight, to have childhood health problems, and to be hospitalized than are babies born to older mothers. Additionally, adolescent mothers are less likely than nonparenting teens to go on to college (Alan Guttmacher Institute). As compared

Table 17.1 Race-/Ethnic- and Gender-Specific Percentages of Teens That Report Ever Having Sexual Intercourse

Race	Percentage of Teens (15–19) Who Report Ever Having Sexual Intercourse	
	Female	Male
African American	60% (1995)	80% (1995)
Asian/Pacific Islander	27.9% (aggregate)[a]	28.5% (aggregate)[a]
Caucasian	50% (1995)	50% (1995)
Latino	56% (1995)	61% (1995)
Native American	52.3% (2001)[b]	65.5% (2001)[b]
Total—All Youth	51% (1995)	55% (1995)

[a] Combined data from the 1991, 1993, 1995, 1997 Youth Risk Behavior Surveys—due to small sample size of Asian/Pacific Islander students. [b]Survey conducted by the Bureau of Indian Affairs in 2001. National percentages were reported as 42.9% for females and 48.5% for male adolescents in 2001. From National Campaign to Prevent Teen Pregnancy, 2004a, 2004b, 2004c, 2005b.

Table 17.2 Developed Nations' Adolescent Pregnancy, Abortion, and Birth Rates (per 1000 adolescents aged 15–19 years)

Nation	Pregnancy Rate	Abortion Rate	Birth Rate
Australia (Singh & Darroch, 2000)	43.7	19.8	23.8
Canada (WHO, 2004)	45.4	21.2	24.2
Denmark (WHO, 2004)	Not reported	14.4	8.3
Finland (WHO, 2004)	Not reported	10.7	9.8
United Kingdom (WHO, 2004)	46.9	18.6	28.4
United States (Singh & Darroch, 2000)	83.6	29.2	54.4

Note: From World Health Organization. (2004). *Adolescent pregnancy: Issues in adolescent health and development.* Geneva, Switzerland: Author.

Table 17.3 Race-/Ethnic-Specific Pregnancy and Birth Rates in the United States (per 1000 youth surveyed)

Race	Pregnancy Rate (2000)[a]	Birth Rate (2002)
African American	153.3	66.6
Asian/Pacific Islander	Not available[b]	18.3
Caucasian	54.7	28.5
Latino	137.9	83.4
Native American	Not available[b]	53.8
Total—All Youth	83.6	43.0

Notes: [a] 2000—latest year available for pregnancy rates. [b] Not available due to lack of information on number of abortions. From National Campaign to Prevent Teen Pregnancy, 2004a, 2004b, 2004c, 2005b.

with adolescents of similar socioeconomic status, adolescent mothers are more likely than their nonparenting counterparts to end up on welfare (52% of women on welfare were teen mothers; National Campaign to Prevent Teen Pregnancy, 2002). The reality is that adolescents in the United States *are* engaging in sexual behaviors and although pregnancy rates are dropping, they continue to be much higher than other developed countries. We need to continue to promote greater adolescent sexual health awareness and effective interventions to align pregnancy, abortion, and birth rates more equally with other developed nations as well as to curb some of the inherent risks of adolescent pregnancy for youth.

Table 17.4 Race-/Ethnic-Specific Percentages of Teens Who Become Pregnant at Least Once by Age 20, and Percent of Teens Who Gave Birth out of Wedlock

Race	Percent that Become Pregnant at least Once by age 20	Percent of Teens that Give Birth Out of Wedlock (2001)
African American	57%	95.7%
Asian/Pacific Islander	Not available	71.5%
Caucasian	25%	75.4%
Latino	51%	73.9%
Native American	Not available	86.6%
Total—All Youth	35%	80%

Note: From National Campaign to Prevent Teen Pregnancy, 2004a, 2004b, 2004c, 2005b.

In addition to the number of adolescent births and abortions, adolescent sexual behaviors carry an increasing risk of acquiring sexually transmitted infections (STIs). Adolescents and young adults are at a higher risk for acquiring STIs than other adults are (CDC, 2003b). Every year, about 3 million (or 1 in 4) sexually experienced teens will acquire an STI (Alan Guttmacher Institute, 1999). In 2003 (and similarly in previous years), adolescent women aged 15 to 19 years had the highest gonorrhea rates at 634.7 cases per 100,000 females (CDC, 2003b). In adolescent males, aged 15 to 19 years, this rate was 262.4 per 100,000 males for gonorrhea in 2003 (CDC, 2003b). The *National Job Training Program* tracks chlamydia rates for young people entering their program (typically a diverse group of working class young people). In women entering the program in 2003, the median state-specific rate for chlamydia infection was 9.9% and for men was 7.8% (CDC, 2003b). Some studies report as many as 15% of sexually active teenage women have been infected with the human papillomavirus, which has been linked with cervical cancer (Alan Guttmacher Institute). In 2003, there were an estimated 7,081 adolescents and young adults aged 15 to 24 living with AIDS in the United States, which was a 37% increase in AIDS cases from 1999 (CDC, 2005a). Although it is unknown exactly how these youth acquired HIV/AIDS (e.g., unprotected sex, sharing needles, blood transfusion, perinatal transmission), it is likely that many of these youth acquired the AIDS virus through unprotected sexual behavior. African Americans are the largest group of young people affected with HIV, with 56% of all new HIV infections (CDC, 2004). Additionally, young men who have sex with men (particularly of minority racial/ethnic groups) are at a high risk of HIV infection (CDC, 2001). The inherent risks associated with adolescent sexual behavior continue to raise our concerns and additional interventions are needed to encourage safe sexual experiences for all adolescents.

Why Have Pregnancy Rates Dropped in the United States?

It is unknown exactly why national teen pregnancy rates have dropped. Overall, it appears that teens can take a large amount of credit for this decrease in adolescent pregnancy rates because they are making more educated and responsible decisions regarding their sexual health (Kirby, 2001). In addition to teens' making better choices, many programs have been established to encourage teens to practice abstinence or to use contraception if they have sex (Kirby). Although it is currently unclear exactly what has led to the drop in teen pregnancy rates, some researchers credit the greater use of contraception (e.g., condoms and birth control), while others credit delayed sexual behavior initiation for this decrease in births. In the end, it is probably a combination of these two concepts that have contributed to the decrease in adolescent pregnancies.

Racial/Ethnic Differences in Contraceptive Use

In 1991, the percentage of youth that reported using condoms at last intercourse was 46.2% (CI: ±3.3%) and, in 2003, it was 63% (CI: ±2.5%; CDC, 2005b). See Table 17.5 for information pertaining to adolescents' use of contraception at first and most recent intercourse and Table 17.6 for information pertaining to male adolescents' report of consistent use of condoms. Similarly, 17% (CI: ±2.3%) of adolescents reported using birth control pills in 2003 (CDC, 2005b). In an attempt to explain the current decline in teen pregnancy rates during the 1990s, Santelli et al. (2004) used data on estimated youth sexual activity and contraceptive use from the *National Youth Risk Behavior*

Table 17.5 Percent of Female Teens Who Used Contraception at First Intercourse and Most Recent Intercourse

Race	Percent of Female Teens Who Reported Using Contraception at First Intercourse (1995)	Percent of Females Who Reported Using Contraception at Last Intercourse (1995)
African American	68%	70%
Asian/Pacific Islander	Not available	49.9%
Caucasian	81%	71%
Latino	53%	52%
Native American	Not available	Not available
Total—All Youth	75%	68%

Note: National Campaign to Prevent Teen Pregnancy, 2004a, 2004b, 2004c, 2005b.

Survey along with method-specific contraceptive failure rates to estimate the degree to which delayed initiation and improved contraceptive practice contributed to the decline in teen pregnancy rates. Although Santelli et al. reported an almost equal contribution between delayed initiation and improved contraceptive practice, they also reported extremely large confidence intervals (CI: ±25%), which virtually rendered their results inconclusive as to the contribution of either factor (Constantine, 2004). However, when these data are examined looking at group specific outcomes over and above the pooled data, Santelli et al. found very different population specific data. They reported change rates in initiation as being a 16% decline for the combined group, 14% in the White group, 28% in the Black group, and no change in the Hispanic group (Santelli et al.). Additionally, the reported change rates in contraceptive method risk were 15% for the combined group, 9% among White teens, 20% among Black teens, and 24% among Hispanic teens (Santelli et al.). Apparently, it appears that larger change rates are taking place in specific ethnic groups (e.g., Black adolescents). It will be important for researchers to determine why specific ethnic groups are making greater changes over others and using this information, they may be able to determine how to target more focused interventions to specific populations. Additionally, school counselors will need to be knowledgeable about the ethnic characteristics of their students in order to adequately address the sexual health needs of their students.

Issues in Adolescent Sexual Health

What Is Considered "Sex" to Current Teens?

Although there is a broad scope of behaviors involved in the act of sex, many teens feel that sexual intercourse (vaginal/penile sex) is the only type of "real" sex. As Remez (2000) suggested, it appears that current youth and adults tend to equate sex with vaginal/penile sexual intercourse. In a study with Midwestern university students, 59% believed that oral sex was not "sex," and 19% believed that anal sex was not "sex" (Sanders & Reinisch, 1999). Therefore, engaging in oral and/or anal sex appears to be an option that youth believe will not get them pregnant, will not expose them to STIs, and will allow them to maintain "virgin" status.

However, many of these beliefs are myths that can have harmful consequences. There continue to be many inherent risks (e.g., STI and HIV/AIDS infection) that are involved in other noncoital sexual acts, including oral and anal sex. First, noncoital behaviors are seen as a gateway to further sexual experimentation (Smith & Udry, 1985). Although oral and anal sex may not be immediately involved in causing pregnancy, youth may be more likely to experiment with further sexual behaviors such as sexual intercourse. Furthermore, many STIs including gonorrhea, syphilis, chlamydia, human papillomavirus, herpes simplex virus, and hepatitis B can be transmitted through

Table 17.6 Percent of Male Adolescents Who Reported Consistent Use of Condoms (100% of the time)

Race	Percent of Male Teens Who Reported Using Condoms 100% of the Time (1995)
African American	47%
Asian/Pacific Islander	Not available
Caucasian	46%
Latino	29%
Native American	Not available
Total—All Youth	44%

Note: National Campaign to Prevent Teen Pregnancy, 2004a, 2004b, 2004c, 2005b.

oral and anal sex (CDC, 1999, 2000). It is rare to transmit HIV through oral sex (CDC, 2000), but relatively easy to transmit the HIV virus through anal sex (CDC, 2003a). Additionally, it is perceived that few if any teens or adults use dental dams or condoms when practicing noncoital sex. Boekeloo and Howard (2002) found that very few adolescents reported using barrier protection during oral sex. Finally, many sexual health curricula, sexual health educators, parents, and clergy have failed to define exactly what "sex" is for our youth. This may be out of fear that, if we define what sexual behavior is, we will be telling our youth how to engage in sex, and therefore, they will engage in sexual activity. However, without proper definitions of what "sex" is, it becomes difficult for youth to abstain from sex. Therefore, America's youth are creating their own definitions of what constitutes "sex," which is currently placing them at risk.

It is not only America's youth who struggle with defining sex and abstinence from sex. The definitions for what constitutes sex and abstaining from sex are largely dependent on the type of sexual health information taught (abstinence-only, comprehensive, religious-based, parental-only education) and an individual's critical analysis of personal beliefs. Even adults including sexual health educators struggle in determining a definition for abstinence from sex. In a 1999 survey, 30% of health educators believed that oral sex was abstinent behavior and 71% believed that mutual masturbation was abstinent behavior (Mercer, 1999, as cited in Remez, 2000). It appears that to work effectively with youth around issues of sexual health development, one of our goals, as school counselors and educators, is to define for ourselves what constitutes abstinence from sex and also encourage our schools and districts to reach a solid definition of abstinence that allows us to communicate with youth, other educators, and parents without confusion.

Oral Sex Prevalence in the Teen Population

It is presumed that teens are engaging in unprotected oral and anal sex. However, due to the controversial nature of asking teens about these sexual behaviors, there is little research available on the prevalence of oral and no specific research on anal sex in the teen population (Remez, 2000). In a recent study of ethnically diverse 9th graders, more participants reported ever having oral sex (19.6%) than vaginal sex (13.5%) and more participants reported intending to have oral sex (31.5%) than vaginal sex (26.3%) in the next 6 months (Halpern-Felsher, Cornell, Kropp, & Tschann, 2005). Additionally, these participants found oral sex to be significantly less risky, to be more acceptable than vaginal sex among their peers, and to be less of a threat to their values/beliefs (Halpern-Felsher et al.). In a retrospective study on college students, over 50% of participants reported engaging in fellatio or cunnilingus prior to their first experience with vaginal intercourse (Schwartz, 1999). Finally, there tends to be a difference in the engagement of Black and White adolescents in noncoital sexual behaviors (e.g., oral sex). Smith and Udry (1985) found that Whites were more likely than Blacks to engage in a predictable series of noncoital behaviors before their first vaginal intercourse. Although no recent studies have been conducted in this area, there may be differences in the amount that certain racial groups engage in noncoital behaviors prior to first sexual intercourse. Overall, it appears that adolescents are engaging in noncoital behaviors prior to first intercourse, but little is known regarding the specifics of these behaviors.

Anal Sex

Overall, there is very limited data on the prevalence and characteristics of anal sex in adolescents. There are many reasons regarding this limited research body. First, anal sex tends to be considered very taboo in our society (Remez, 2000). Adults are very uncomfortable talking about anal sex and adolescents tend to avoid discussing anal sex as well. Second, anal sex tends to be attributed to a sexual behavior that takes place only between men who have sex with men in our society. Therefore, many individuals assume that only gay men have anal sex, even though anal sex is a sexual behavior that is not solely attributed to a particular sexual identification. Men who have sex with men (but may not identify as gay) have anal sex as well as men who have sex with women, and so forth. For people who are uncomfortable or unfamiliar with same-sex sexual behaviors, there can be a tendency to consider anal sex wrong because they associate it with homosexuality. Finally, since anal sex continues to be such a difficult topic to discuss in our society, many human subject review panels, parents, and schools are reluctant to allow researchers to ask adolescents questions about anal sex. Therefore, the majority of our research on anal sex revolves around adult men who have sex with men and HIV/AIDS prevention research.

In a study on anal sex in heterosexual college students, Baldwin and Baldwin (2000) found that 22.9% of nonvirgins indicated that they had engaged in anal intercourse. These students reported using condoms during anal intercourse 20.9% of the time as compared with 42.9% of the time with vaginal intercourse. Finally, individuals in the study who had engaged in anal intercourse were more likely to report having had at least one STI and having had been tested for HIV as compared with those that did not report having anal intercourse. Although many individuals feel that anal intercourse is prevalent only in gay communities, it is apparent that both heterosexual and gay/

lesbian/bisexual students need to be educated regarding the risks of anal intercourse.

When Does Sexual Initiation Occur for Teens?

Although the majority of school-based sexual health programs begin to teach students about abstinence, teen pregnancy, contraception, and STIs in the ninth-grade year, many teens report having initiated sexual behaviors prior to their ninth-grade year. One in five teens reported having had sex before age 15 (National Campaign to Prevent Teen Pregnancy, 2003d). Additionally, the percentage of adolescents in the United States who reported having engaged in sexual intercourse before the age of 13 was 7.4% (CI: ±1.2%) in 2003 (Grunbaum et al., 2002). Although the majority of adults (and teens) do not believe that young adolescents are prepared to be sexually active (Moore & Stief, 1991; National Campaign to Prevent Teen Pregnancy, 2004d, 2005a), many are engaging in sexual behaviors at very early ages.

Since around half of all teens will have sex prior to graduating from high school, where are they having sex? It appears that the majority of 16- to 18-year-olds who reported having sex for the first time in 2000 are having sex in their family's home, in their partner's family home, or in a friend's home (National Campaign to Prevent Teen Pregnancy, 2003e). Additionally, much smaller numbers reported having sex in their own home/partner's home (e.g., apartment, dorm room), in a car or truck, in a hotel or motel, in a park or outdoors, or somewhere else. Most teens (70%) report that their first sex occurred in the evening or nighttime. However, African American teens were more likely to have sex during the late afternoon hours than other racial/ethnic groups were. There do not seem to be any significant seasonal differences in when teens first initiate sex (National Campaign to Prevent Teen Pregnancy, 2003e). Overall, it appears that most teens are engaging in sex in their family's home (or partner or friend's home) and that first sex appears to be taking place in the evening hours (possibly when parents are present). It has been shown that first sexual experience increases with the number of hours teens spend unsupervised (Cohen, Farley, Taylor, Martin, & Schuster, 2002). Therefore, prevention efforts may be directed at structuring more afternoon and evening times when teens are involved in adult-mediated activities.

What are the first sexual partners of adolescents typically like? Many teens report that their first sexual partners was a friend first (National Campaign to Prevent Teen Pregnancy, 2003c). Additionally, teens report having met their first sexual partners at school or a place of worship. Few teens report that their first sexual partners were strangers. Most teens report having participated in "couple-like" behavior (e.g., going out together in a group, going out together alone, meeting their partners' parents, thinking of themselves as a couple, telling others that they were a couple, exchanging presents, and exchanging the words "I love you") prior to their first sexual experience. This percentage is higher for non-Hispanic White and Hispanic teens than African American teens. Additionally, most adolescents reported having engaged in intimate behavior with their partners (i.e., kissing, holding hands, and touching each other under clothes or with no clothes on) prior to their first sex. The majority of teens (69%) reported having touched their partners' genitals before having sex for the first time. In looking at contraception, 40% of adolescents surveyed never discussed contraception with their partners before having sex for the first time. Adolescents who reported engaging in more couple-like behaviors were more likely to discuss contraception prior to sex as compared with those that did not. Finally, teens who had sex at or before 14 years of age reported less couple-like activity and were less likely to discuss contraception with their partners (National Campaign to Prevent Teen Pregnancy, 2003c). Overall, it appears that teens who engage in couple-like behaviors with their partners appear to have better communication skills with their partners and may feel more comfortable talking with their partners about contraception.

Early sexual initiation in adolescents is correlated with some other health risk behaviors. For teens who were sexually active before the age of 13 in 1991, fighting, carrying a weapon to school, and early experimentation with cigarettes and alcohol were associated with early sexual activity (Coker et al., 1994). Additionally, Coker et al. found that those teens who initiated sex early had a greater number of sexual partners, were 50% less likely to use condoms, and were more likely to have been pregnant or have caused a pregnancy, and females who initiated sex early were more likely to have had an STI. For those teens who are initiating sex prior to age 13, it is apparent that they are likely to be engaging in other health risk-taking behaviors and that they are less likely to have received formal education about health behaviors. It seems that, to reach this population of adolescents, sexual health education needs to take place prior to age 13.

Alcohol and Teen Pregnancy

When looking at risk factors for sexual risk taking and teen pregnancy, many studies have pointed to the possible risk of using alcohol prior to sex as decreasing the likelihood that adolescents will act responsibly (i.e., use protection) during intercourse (Biglan, Metzler, Wirt, & Ary, 1990; Gold & Skinner, 1992; Hingson, Strunin, Berlin, & Heeren, 1990; McEwan, McCallum, Bhopal, & Madhok, 1992; Mott & Haurin, 1988; Robertson & Plant, 1988; Rotheram-Borus et al., 1994). This is based upon the hypothesis that adolescents who are drinking will be unable to behave responsibly while affected by alcohol and also that adolescents who engage in underage drinking are more likely to be risk takers overall and, thus, are more likely to take risks in sexual behavior as well. Additionally, other researchers have pointed to the probability that adolescents will be more likely to be victimized sexually when alcohol has been used by the perpetrator or the victim. Champion et al. (2004) found that both binge drinking in the past 2 weeks and age of first drink were associated with sexual victimization (among females). However, other studies have found no association between alcohol use and sexual risk taking (Fergusson & Lynskey, 1996; Fortenberry & Orr, 1997; Halpern-Felsher, Millstein, & Ellen, 1996; Lowry et al., 1994; Santelli, Robin, Brener, & Lowry, 2001). In a study on adolescents with a high level of sexual risk taking, rates of condom use did not differ significantly between sexual events that were preceded by drinking (use in 54% of events) versus those that did not (use in 52% of events; Morrison et al., 2003). It appears that few conclusive findings have demonstrated that adolescent alcohol use conclusively diminishes the likelihood that adolescents will engage in protected sexual encounters. Additionally, the data on middle school and high school students suggest that sexual activity occurs within ongoing intimate relationships (National Campaign to Prevent Teen Pregnancy, 2003c). Although, researchers and youth workers should continue to be concerned about ensuring that adolescents have the knowledge and skills necessary to decrease involuntary sexual experiences, educational efforts also should focus around the likely perception that intercourse is more likely to be a natural progression within a relationship.

Sexual Identity Development of Gay, Lesbian, and Bisexual Teens

The majority of research on adolescent sexual health tends to be on adolescents who identify as heterosexual or the researchers make assumptions that all adolescents in the sample identify as heterosexual. However, a small population of teens identifies as gay or bisexual and/or have sex with same-sex partners. This population tends to be overlooked in research even though many adolescents and adults who have sex with same-sex partners engage in sexual risk-taking behaviors (CDC, 2001). Particularly, in an adolescent population where sexual identity development is an evolving process, many adolescents may choose to have sex with same-sex partners and not identify as gay/lesbian/bisexual, while other adolescents who will later identify as gay/lesbian/bisexual will choose to have sex with the opposite sex. Sexual identification does not necessarily predict behavior in adults and is particularly inaccurate among adolescents. Given the nature of the evolving process of sexual identity development in adolescence, school counselors and other educators need to be aware of the fluid process of sexual identity to work with this population of youth appropriately.

How Are Religious Teens Different From Teens Who Are Not Religiously Identified in Terms of Sexual Behavior?

Since sexual behavior tends to be largely tied to values and morals in the United States, many researchers have turned to the role of religion in sexual behavior to understand why some adolescents tend to delay sexual intercourse and others do not. Multiple studies have found that adolescents that identify as being religious and attend religious services frequently are at a reduced likelihood of engaging in sexual intercourse (Billy, Brewster, & Grady, 1994; Brewster, Cooksey, Guilkey, & Rindfuss, 1998; Resnick et al., 1997; Thornton & Camburn, 1989). Additionally, Brewster (1994) found that women without a preidentified religious affiliation are at a greater risk of engaging in sexual intercourse than are mainline Protestants.

Although it appears that there is a connection between religiousness in adolescents and delayed first intercourse, not all studies have found this conclusion. Meier (2003) found that there was only an effect of religiosity on first sex for females and that over and above religiosity, personal and relational attitudes about sex (cost/benefits of sex) were more influential for both males and females. Miller and Gur (2002) found that the personal devotion (i.e., an adolescent's sense of personal connection to God) was positively associated with decreased risk of sexual activity outside of a romantic relationship. Personal devotion and attendance at religious events were found to be associated with sexual responsibility. Additionally, they found that personal devotion, institutional conservatism, and participation in religious events were associated with decreased number of sexual partners in the last year. However, they found that no dimension of religiousness (e.g., personal devotion, institutional conservatism, personal conservatism, and participation in religious events) was associated with a decreased likelihood of sexual intercourse. Additionally, they found a marginally significant trend that personal conservatism (i.e., a close or rigid adherence to religious creed) actually posed a risk for sexual risk taking behavior such as unprotected sex. It seems that, overall, religious participation continues to be a protective factor in terms of adolescent sexual activity but that it may not protect adolescents from intercourse to the degree previously hypothesized (especially when adolescents follow personal strict guidelines around sexual behavior). It might be that religious activities tend to be adult mediated and occur during the times in which youth, not similarly occupied, may be initiating sexual activity.

Another reason religiosity and spirituality may delay sexual activity is not due inherently to a belief in God and adherence to a specific religious denomination, but due to a connection with a group of people involved in spirituality. Holder et al. (2000) found that "spiritual interconnectedness" (supportive components of an individual's ties to friends and associates within a body of faith) was the only spirituality variable negatively associated with a history of sexual activity. Additionally, the booming adolescent pledge movement (where adolescents publicly pledge to abstain from sex until marriage) also indicates ties to the importance of building a pledge identity within a moral community (Bearman & Bruckner, 2001). Adolescent pledgers are found to be significantly less likely to have intercourse than adolescents who do not pledge. However, this significance is heavily contingent upon the number of pledgers in the community (where too few or too many pledgers are not effective) and on the age of the pledger (the effectiveness of pledging tends to be less effective for older adolescents; Bearman & Bruckner, 2001). Overall, it appears that adolescents who have built connected relationships with other adolescents around religious/spiritual issues are more likely than other adolescents are to delay sexual intercourse. This delay in sexual intercourse appears to have more to do with these spiritually connected relationships with the people involved in the faith community than with their religiosity or spirituality.

Although it appears that pledging significantly delays sexual initiation, it may not completely protect adolescents from getting STIs. Based on data from the *National Longitudinal Study of Adolescent Health,* the rate of STI for pledgers was not significantly different than it was for nonpledgers (Bruckner & Bearman, 2005). The authors proposed that this may be due to the finding that pledgers are less likely than nonpledgers are to use condoms at their sexual debut and that they are less likely to be tested and therefore diagnosed with STIs (Bruckner & Bearman, 2005). From this study, it appears that the pledge movement has not been effective in decreasing STI acquisition in adolescents.

Debate Around Sexual Health Education

The extremely political debate over how to educate our students on sexual health issues centers the decision to teach our youth through abstinence-only curriculum or through comprehensive sexual health education. Abstinence-only programs focus on values, character building, and occasionally sex-refusal skills. These programs promote abstinence from sex, refrain from presenting information on contraception and abortion, and give information about STIs and HIV/AIDS as reasons to abstain from sex (Collins, Alagiri, & Summers, 2002). Comprehensive sex education programs or "abstinence-plus" curricula explore and discuss sex through the promotion of abstinence and the dissemination of information about contraception, STIs, HIV/AIDS, and abortion (Collins et al.). The type of sex education that a student receives in school is largely dependent on state statutes, parental wishes, public/private education, and federal funding.

Since 1981, the federal government has played a large role in the funding and promotion of abstinence-only education programs. Most recently, in 1996, Congress added a provision to welfare legislation indicating that any program that wishes to receive funding must teach that "sexual activity outside of marriage is likely to have harmful psychological and physical effects" (Starkman & Rajani, 2002, p. 316). To receive this money, states were required to match federal dollars with state dollars, a challenge that most states have met. Overall, from 1996 to 2002, funding for abstinence-only education has increased by 3,000% (Starkman & Rajani, 2002). The federal government has taken large measures (through funding allocation) to determine the type of sex education students receive in the United States. Although individual states (and many times local governments) have the right to determine the type of sex education provided to youth in schools, through the restriction of funding, the federal government is making a tremendous impact on how today's youth are being educated around sexual health issues.

What Does the Evidence Say?

In the end, there is no confirmatory evidence regarding which types of programs work better to delay adolescent sexual initiation, prevent teen pregnancy, and decrease STIs in adolescents (Kirby, 2001). In an attempt to compile and make conclusions upon the large amount of quality research on sexual health programs, Kirby and the

National Campaign to Prevent Teen Pregnancy compiled a report to develop some conclusions based on the programs that have been effective. In the end, Kirby came to a few basic conclusions. First, he found that there were few rigorous studies conducted on abstinence-only programs and only three programs ended up meeting the research criteria for inclusion within the report. Of the three programs included, none of them demonstrated an overall positive effect on the sexual behavior of participants (Kirby). Kirby commented that we cannot make a definitive conclusion regarding the effectiveness of abstinence-only programs at this time due to the diversity of abstinence-only programs and the scarcity of programs that have been subjected to rigorous research. Next, he concluded that programs that discuss sex and HIV education do not increase adolescent sexual activity. Although many parents, educators, politicians, and so forth believe that, by talking with children about contraception and sex, they will initiate sexual behaviors, the review of these rigorous studies has shown that is not the case. Finally, Kirby found that many of the sex and HIV education programs evaluated were effective in delaying adolescent sex, increasing condom or contraceptive use, and decreasing unprotected sex. These effective sex and HIV programs all shared the following necessary characteristics. These programs

1. focused on reducing one or more sexual behaviors that lead to unintended pregnancy or HIV/STD infection;
2. were based on theoretical approaches that have been demonstrated to influence other health-related behavior and identify specific important sexual antecedents to be targeted;
3. delivered and consistently reinforced a clear message about abstaining from sexual activity and/or using condoms or other forms of contraception (this appears to be one of the most important characteristics that distinguishes effective from ineffective programs);
4. provided basic, accurate information about the risks of teen sexual activity and about ways to avoid intercourse or use methods of protection against pregnancy and STDs;
5. included activities that addressed social pressures that influence sexual behavior;
6. provided examples of and practice with communication, negotiation, and refusal skills;
7. employed teaching methods designed to involve participants and have them personalize the information;
8. incorporated behavioral goals, teaching methods, and materials that were appropriate to the age, sexual experience, and culture of the students;
9. lasted a sufficient length of time (i.e., more than a few hours); and
10. selected teachers or peer leaders who believed in the program and then provided them with adequate training (Kirby, 2001).

Our current knowledge regarding effective programs to delay sexual behaviors, prevent teen pregnancy, and decrease unprotected sex among adolescents has shown that there are many components of effective programs and in particular those programs that stress both abstinence and contraception are the most effective.

What Does the American Public Want?

Although the United States government has painted a picture that the majority of American adults and teens want abstinence-only education provided to youth, this is not the case. In a national 2003 survey to adults and teens, the National Campaign to Prevent Teen Pregnancy (2003b) found that 75% of adults and 60% of teens wish that adolescents were getting more information about abstinence *and* contraception. Additionally, 67% of adults and 66% of teens surveyed reported that they would urge policy makers in Washington to place greater emphasis on abstinence *and* contraception in their legislation and funding allocation. Given this wish to have access to comprehensive sex education for teens, nearly all teens and adults surveyed (92% and 94%, respectively) believe that teens should be given a strong message from society that they should not have sex until they are at least out of high school. Additionally, most teens and adults (77% and 68%) feel that offering comprehensive sex education to teens does not offer a confusing or mixed message about teenage sexual activity (National Campaign to Prevent Teen Pregnancy, 2003b). Overall, it appears that the American public supports providing comprehensive sex education to adolescents that stresses abstinence.

Many national organizations have publicly announced their support of comprehensive sex education for all adolescents in an effort to encourage school districts to provide this for their students and in hopes that our national government will begin to change its funding policy of supporting exclusively abstinence-only sexual health programs. The American Medical Association, the American Academy of Pediatrics, the American College of Obstetricians and Gynecologists, the American Nurses Association, and the American Public Health Association, to name a few, have all endorsed comprehensive sex education for adolescents (Starkman & Rajani, 2002). Overall, it appears that both the American public and prominent medical associations within the United States are in support of comprehensive sex education.

Sexual Health Education for Gay, Lesbian, and Bisexual Youth

In order to provide comprehensive sexual health education for all adolescents, it is very important that any education or interventions include information and conversation about same-sex partners among youth. Although many school districts and states do not allow for the discussion of homosexuality within the context of adolescent sexual health, students have questions and need correct answers to provide them with education to avoid risks and to promote healthy adolescent sexual identity development. School counselors and sexual health educators are likely to face barriers to the education and discussion of homosexuality in schools. However, in order to provide sexual health education for all students, this is a necessary component of all sexual health curricula.

In a 1995 study of school health teachers, Telljohann, Price, Poureslami, and Easton found that only 46% of teachers surveyed formally taught about homosexuality in their health classes. Additionally, only 1 in 4 teachers felt that they were very competent to teach about homosexuality in their health classes. Finally, teachers were asked to identify where they received their information regarding homosexuality, and the four leading sources of information were the mass media (66%), textbooks (50%), college classes (44%), and professional journals (44%). Overall, it appears that even when teachers are attempting to talk about issues related to homosexuality in health classes, many do not feel completely competent and may not be teaching correct information to their students.

When access to information about sexual health is not available or incomplete, many students choose to gain their sexual health education through other sources such as the Internet. Students who are engaged in the process of sexual identity formation may find some of these sites particularly appealing when they are not educated about gay, lesbian, and bisexual sexual health issues elsewhere. However, even when searching the Internet, it appears that many students are not given correct and adequate information regarding gay, lesbian, and bisexual sexual health. In a study of online sexuality education sites, Bay-Cheng (2001) found that only 9 of the 52 sites evaluated communicated an expanded definition of sex that extended beyond just vaginal–penile intercourse. Many sites failed to address the reality of same-sex sexual behaviors. Students who are engaging in same-sex relationships are rarely given spaces where they can ask questions about these sexual relationships and/or learn the risks inherent in same-sex sexual relationships.

Many teachers and school counselors desire to incorporate effective teaching about homosexuality in sexual health curriculum and overall school climate. The "Advocates for Youth" (2005) Web site provides multiple guidelines that educators can use to attempt to create inclusive programs in their schools. In particular, they suggested that educators (a) assess their own values and beliefs regarding sexual orientation and gender identity, (b) make it clear that homophobic sentiments and actions have no place in your class or school, (c) consider posting a "Safe Zone" sticker, (d) use inclusive language such as talking about "partners" or using ambiguous names such as Leslie or Chris when talking about relationships, (e) schedule training sessions (for both staff and students) to debunk myths and stereotypes, (f) provide peer support, (g) ask GLBTQ youth and adults to participate in panel discussions or as speakers, and (h) consider working with students to begin gay/straight alliances. By providing a safe space to ask questions about homosexuality, sexual health teachers and counselors can begin to address many of the incorrect assumptions children/adolescents have about gay/lesbian/bisexual youth and also to allow for supported sexual identity development of all youth.

How Can We Talk About Sexual Development Using a Positive Youth Development Approach?

At this point in their sexual development, adolescents are looking to adults in their lives to fulfill their curiosity about sex. However, for many, it appears that adults are unwilling to discuss or, more likely, uncomfortable in discussing sex with youth, which can lead teens to learning information about sex from their friends or to making assumptions on their own (which can come from erroneous details learned through the media, online searches, friends, uninformed adults, etc.).

One of the challenges for sex educators, school nurses, school counselors, youth mentors, and parents is learning to communicate the inherent risks of sex with youth while also emphasizing the positive aspects of sex. Although sexual education heavily emphasizes the biology of sexual development, the psychological impact of sexual development can be far more relevant for students who are looking for answers. This psychological piece of teen sexuality is a critical component of most sexual development curricula (more than the biological) because it draws youth in by addressing the values and morals inherent in sexual behavior. This component tends to attract teens because it is here that they can begin to answer the burning questions, including the following: When will I be ready for sex? How will I know if I love someone? What if I am attracted to someone of the same sex? How can I say "no" to having sex? What will people think of me if I decide not to have sex? And, what will they think of me if I do? However, when particular sets of values and morals are integrated into sexual health curriculums, these questions tend to be stifled. It is much easier for educators to deliver messages of complete abstinence until marriage and fear-based messages around STIs and HIV/AIDS than it is to really talk to America's youth about the emotional and behavioral components of sex. Obviously, no sex educator can tell any teen when he or she is ready for sex. However, a positive youth development framework would ask educators and counselors not to frighten our youth about sex. Instead, teens want us to provide them with valid and comprehensive information, real-life discussions about feelings and desires during adolescence, lessons in negotiating relationships, and ultimately, a little faith that they are going to be able to make healthy choices about their sexual health as most teens do. Although sexual behavior carries with it many risks for youth, we are doing our youth a disservice by instilling guilt, secrecy, discomfort, fear, and alienation around sexuality.

What would a positive youth development approach to adolescent sexual health education look like? Just as the more academic subjects taught in schools, sexual health programs need to promote critical thinking skills in their students. In addition to factual information about the physical aspects of sexual development, adolescent pregnancy, birth control, and STIs, a comprehensive sexual health program would include discussions around sex and the media; America's discomfort in talking about sex; positive aspects of sexuality; how to negotiate teen relationships; feelings around sex including pleasure, desire, guilt, anxiety, and so forth; and ways to assert oneself in sexual encounters (when and how to say "no" or "yes" to sex; how to ensure that a partner uses protection; how to get oneself out of an uncomfortable sexual situation, e.g., you can say "no" at anytime). Adolescents want honest and real-world answers about how to manage their sexual development. If this information is not provided in discussions with knowledgeable adults they will find it elsewhere (which may not be adequate or healthy information). Although challenging, adults need to trust that if they provide our youth with comprehensive, factual, relevant, and real-life information, they will be able to make positive and responsible choices in their own lives.

Another means by which schools can integrate information about sexual health in the school community is by forming school-based health centers (SBHCs). SBHCs are clinics located in schools that provide students with basic health care including annual physicals, immunizations, asthma care, STI treatment, smoking cessation behavioral interventions, and preventive counseling for various health issues (for further information on SBHCs, see "Physical Health and Emotional Development," Knudtson & Coleman, chapter 16, this volume). It is important to note that SBHCs do not just offer services pertaining to adolescent sexual health (and some SBHCs do not even offer sexual health services for their students). SBHCs are mentioned because school-based clinics are an important means by which schools can create safe spaces for students to gain knowledge and receive services pertaining to adolescent sexual health. Providing students with sexual health resources at school can alert students that their school is concerned with helping them negotiate romantic relationships and is investing in their students' abstention from sex as well as helping students to prevent unplanned pregnancies and STIs.

How Can School Counselors and Educators Be Involved in the Sexual Health Education of Their Students?

The educational attainment of students is greatly affected by teenage pregnancy. Only 41% of teens who begin families prior to age 18 complete high school (National Campaign to Prevent Teen Pregnancy, 2001). Additionally, only 1.5% of teenage mothers earn a college degree by the time they are 30 years old (Maynard, 1996). The children of teen parents are also likely to struggle in school. It is reported that the children of teen parents are 50% more likely to repeat a grade in school (National Campaign to Prevent Teen Pregnancy, 2001). Educational failure and teen pregnancy seem to have a reciprocal relationship. Manlove (1998) found that 28.2% of teen parents had dropped out of school prior to becoming pregnant and 30.3% dropped out after they had become pregnant. Additionally, educational failure has been found to be a key predictor of adolescent pregnancy (Robbins, Kaplan, & Martin, 1985). Overall, teen pregnancy is a barrier to educational attainment of high school students, and it is more likely that adolescents will become pregnant if they are not in school or are performing poorly while in school.

School counselors and educators can help to curb the likelihood that adolescents will engage in sexual activity or become pregnant by creating a safe school environment where students feel connected to their school (for information concerning creating a caring school community, see Lindwall & Coleman, chapter 24, this volume). Blum (2005) found that students who feel a strong connection to their school and have a higher GPA were more likely to postpone sexual activity. Additionally, female athletes have been found to postpone sex until later in life, to have sex less often, to have fewer partners, to be less likely to get pregnant, and to be more likely to use contraception (National Campaign to Prevent Teen Pregnancy, 2003a). Adolescents have identified counselors and teachers as the second most reliable source of sexual health information they receive (parents were first; Ehrlich & Vega-Matos, 1998). Overall, adolescents are better able to negotiate their sexual health development successfully when they feel connected to their schools and are able to communicate openly and honestly with their counselors and teachers about their sexual health.

School counselors can be important team members in the construction and delivery of sexual health education curriculum. In particular, the major factors that facilitate and constrain sexual activity are the core components of a developmental guidance curriculum. For example, in the state of Wisconsin, students are to acquire 10 skills as an outcome of a development guidance program. These skills include the abilities to (a) understand the connections among family, school, and work; (b) solve problems; (c) make decisions; (d) set and achieve goals; (e) harness emotions productively; and (f) be empathic. As has been consistently presented in this chapter, these are the skills adolescents need to effectively negotiate the risks and opportunities of sexual development. With these skills, an adolescent is better prepared to use the content provided in sex education. We advocate for the integration of sex education with social skill development as a potentially more effective educational model. However, there are no examples of such integration in the literature. Ultimately, school counselors can contribute significant information and skills to their schools' discussions on how to educate their students around issues pertaining to sexuality and sexual health.

School counselors can be instrumental in facilitating individual student growth around sexual health issues. The following includes two case study examples of how a school counselor may address sexual health issues with a student.

Mariah

Mariah is an 11-year-old, Latina sixth grader at an urban middle school. In the past 10 years, her community has experienced an increase in violence, including two public sexual assaults that occurred in her neighborhood. Mariah became sexually active at age 10 and has been involved the previous year with four male partners. After discovering that Mariah was sexually active, her mother contacted the school counselor, Delia, to attempt to support Mariah in stopping her risky sexual behavior. After speaking with Mariah, Delia discovered that Mariah had made the decision that she no longer wanted to have sex (at this stage of her life), but that she was struggling in creating a new identity for herself as a girl who is not "easy." Mariah was struggling in school because she was experiencing teasing from her peers around her past sexual involvement. Additionally, she struggled with developing healthy relationships with her male peers that were not grounded in having sex. Delia determined that Mariah would benefit from the development of positive social skills as well as psycho-education around healthy relationships. Mariah joined a healthy relationships girls' group at the school to allow her to connect with other female students and learn skills in developing healthy friendships and romantic relationships. Additionally, she worked individually with Delia to address how Mariah could learn to connect with others in romantic relationships without the need to use sexual activity as a means to build connections.

Abdulle

Abdulle is a 16-year-old, Somali 10th-grade student at a suburban high school. He has been coming to see the school counselor, James, for one year due to academic struggles and depression. During his most recent meeting, Abdulle discloses to James that he has been involved sexually with other males in the community. Abdulle adamantly states that he does not consider himself gay and that he has not told his friends or family about his relationships with other men. James asks Abdulle if he has been using condoms when he has sex with other men. Abdulle states that he does not need to use condoms because he is not gay and he storms out of the office.

The next week, Abdulle returns to see James for their regular weekly meeting. James tells Abdulle that he did not make the assumption that Abdulle was gay and that he was sorry that he had given Abdulle that impression. Abdulle states that it is not okay for people to be gay in his community and that he does not want to be associated with this label or for others to know that he has been having sex with men. James stresses confidentiality with Abdulle and states that he will not share Abdulle's disclosure with anyone in Abdulle's community unless it appears that he is harming himself or someone else. James also tells Abdulle that he encourages all students to use condoms when having sex regardless of sexual orientation and regardless of whether they are having sex with same-sex or opposite-sex partners. James indicates that he is concerned about the potential of Abdulle acquiring an STI like HIV if he continues to have unprotected sex. Additionally, he encourages him to be tested for STIs at the confidential teen clinic in town. Abdulle continues to state that he does not believe that he needs to protect himself because he is not gay.

Over the next 6 months, James continues to work with Abdulle on understanding his evolving sexual identity as well as coming to terms with the need to protect himself from STIs even when he does not identify as gay. James continues to encourage Abdulle to engage in healthy relationship-building activities (e.g., discussing past sexual history with sexual partners, encouraging sexual partners to wear a condom, and practicing open communication with sexual partners). Additionally, he works with Abdulle at understanding his community's prejudice around gay people and how this impacts how Abdulle feels about himself and his current sexual experimentation with men.

Conclusions

In our roles as educators, parents, siblings, grandparents, caretakers, and adults, we are consistently reminded of the saying "children grow up too fast." As we watch children grow up, we are amazed at how fast they learn to crawl and walk on their own, begin their first days of kindergarten, read their first books aloud, attend their first sleepovers away from home, dance at their first boy/girl parties at school, and kiss their first boyfriends/girlfriends. These huge milestones tend to come very quickly for most adults, and it can be hard to comprehend that once young children will soon be adults. Therefore, many adults struggle with realizing that children need information regarding romantic relationships and sexual health at a younger age than many adults feel is appropriate. It is important for us to remember that as children age, they *will* find answers to their curious questions about relationships and sexual health. Therefore, to prevent them from learning at times inappropriate and incorrect information about relationships and sex through the media, the Internet, and their peers, we must provide them with timely and accurate information about their developing sexuality. SBHCs are an excellent addition to any sexual health education program that can provide students not only with information about their sexuality but also with the sexual health services that are needed as adolescents begin to learn about themselves as a sexual beings. Schools are perfectly situated not only to provide students with academic knowledge and skills, but also to assist them in learning how to successfully manage romantic relationships with others as well as begin to understand their developing sexuality.

References

Advocates for Youth. (2005). *Advocates for youth*. Retrieved August 15, 2005, from http://www.advocatesforyouth.org

Alan Guttmacher Institute. (1999). *Teen sex and pregnancy: Facts in brief*. Retrieved August 15, 2005, from http://www.guttmacher.org/

Baldwin, J. I., & Baldwin, J. D. (2000). Heterosexual anal intercourse: An understudied, high-risk sexual behavior. *Archives of Sexual Behavior, 29*(4), 357–373.

Bay-Cheng, L. Y. (2001). SexEd.com: Values and norms in Web-based sexuality education. *The Journal of Sex Research, 38*(3), 241–251.

Bearman, P. S., & Bruckner, H. (2001). Promising the future: Virginity pledges and first intercourse. *American Journal of Sociology, 106*(4), 859–912.

Biglan, A., Metzler, C. W., Wirt, R., & Ary, D. V. (1990). Social and behavioral factors associated with high-risk sexual behavior among adolescents. *Journal of Behavioral Medicine, 13*(3), 245–261.

Billy, J. O. G., Brewster, K. L., & Grady, W. R. (1994). Contextual effects of the sexual behavior of adolescent women. *Journal of Marriage & the Family, 56*(2), 387–404.

Blum, R. W. (2005). A case for school connectedness. *Educational Leadership, 62*(7), 16.

Boekeloo, B., & Howard, D. E. (2002). Oral sexual experience among young adolescents receiving general health examinations. *American Journal of Health Behavior, 26*(4), 306–314.

Brewster, K. L. (1994). Race differences in sexual activity among adolescent women: The role of neighborhood characteristics. *American Sociological Review, 59*(3), 408–424.

Brewster, K. L., Cooksey, E. C., Guilkey, D. K., & Rindfuss, R. R. (1998). The changing impact of religion on the sexual and contraceptive behavior of adolescent women in the United States. *Journal of Marriage & the Family, 60*(2), 493–504.

Bruckner, H., & Bearman, P. (2005). After the promise: The STD consequences of adolescent virginity pledges. *Journal of Adolescent Health, 36*, 271–278.

Centers for Disease Control and Prevention. (1999). Increases in unsafe sex and rectal gonorrhea among men who have sex with men—San Francisco, California—1991–1997. *Morbidity and Mortality Weekly Report, 48*(3), 1–4.

Centers for Disease Control and Prevention. (2000). Preventing the sexual transmission of HIV, the virus that causes AIDS: What you should know about oral sex. Retrieved August 15, 2005, from http://www.cdc.gov/hiv/pubs/Facts/oralsex.pdf

Centers for Disease Control and Prevention. (2001). HIV incidence among young men who have sex with men: Seven U.S. cities, 1994–2000. *MMWR Weekly, 50*(21), 440–444.

Centers for Disease Control and Prevention. (2003a). *Can I get HIV from anal sex?* Retrieved August 15, 2005, from http://www.cdc.gov/

Centers for Disease Control and Prevention. (2003b). *STDs in adolescents and young adults.* Retrieved March 18, 2005, from http://www.cdc.gov/

Centers for Disease Control and Prevention. (2004). *HIV prevention in the third decade.* Retrieved July 1, 2005, from http://www.cdc.gov/

Centers for Disease Control and Prevention. (2005a). *HIV/AIDS among youth.* Retrieved July 1, 2005, from http://www.cdc.gov

Centers for Disease Control and Prevention. (2005b). *Trends in the prevalence of sexual behaviors: National youth risk behavior survey: 1991–2003.* Retrieved August 15, 2005, from http://www.cdc.gov/HealthyYouth/yrbs/pdfs/trends-sex.pdf

Champion, H. L., Foley, K. L., DuRant, R. H., Hensberry, R., Altman, D., & Wolfson, M. (2004). Adolescent sexual victimization, use of alcohol and other substances, and other health risk behaviors. *Journal of Adolescent Health, 35*(4), 321–328.

Cohen, D. A., Farley, T. A., Taylor, S. N., Martin, D. H., & Schuster, M. A. (2002). When and where do youths have sex? The potential role of adult supervision. *Pediatrics, 110*(6).

Coker, A. L., Richter, D. L., Valois, R. F., McKeown, R. E., Garrison, C. Z., & Vincent, M. L. (1994). Correlates and consequences of early initiation of sexual intercourse. *Journal of School Health, 64*(9), 372–377.

Collins, C., Alagiri, P., Summers, T., & Morin, S. F. (2002). *Abstinence only vs. comprehensive sex education: What are the arguments? What is the evidence?* Retrieved August 30, 2007, from http://www.ari.ucsf.edu/science/reports/abstinence.pdf

Constantine, N. A. (2004). Changes in sexual behaviors among high school students. *Journal of Adolescent Health, 35*(6), 430–431.

Ehrlich, G., & Vega-Matos, C. A. (1998). *Policy update: The role of education in teen pregnancy prevention.* Alexandria, VA: Policy Information Clearinghouse.

Fergusson, D. M., & Lynskey, M. T. (1996). Alcohol misuse and adolescent sexual behaviors and risk taking. *Pediatrics, 98*(1), 91.

Fortenberry, J. D., & Orr, D. P. (1997). Sex under the influence. *Sexually Transmitted Diseases, 24*(6), 313.

Gold, R. S., & Skinner, M. J. (1992). Situational factors and thought processes associated with unprotected intercourse in young gay men. *AIDS, 6*(9), 1021–1030.

Grunbaum, J. A., Kann, L., Kinchen, S.A., Williams, B., Ross, J.G., Lowry, R., et al. (2002). Youth risk behavior surveillance—United States, 2001. *Morbidity and Mortality Weekly Report, 51*(SS04), 1–64.

Halpern-Felsher, B., Cornell, J. L., Kropp, R. Y., & Tschann, J. M. (2005). Oral versus vaginal sex among adolescents: Perceptions, attitudes, and behavior. *Pediatrics, 115*(4), 845–851.

Halpern-Felsher, B., Millstein, S. G., & Ellen, J. M. (1996). Relationship of alcohol use and risky sexual behavior: a review and analysis of findings. *Journal of Adolescent Health, 19*(5), 331–336.

Hingson, R. W., Strunin, L., Berlin, B. M., & Heeren, T. (1990). Beliefs about AIDS, use of alcohol and drugs, and unprotected sex among Massachusetts adolescents. *American Journal of Public Health, 80*(3), 295–299.

Holder, D. W., Durant, R. H., Harris, T. L., Daniel, J. H., Obeidallah, D., & Goodman, E. (2000). The association between adolescent spirituality and voluntary sexual activity. *Journal of Adolescent Health, 26*(4), 295–302.

Kirby, D. (2001). *Emerging answers: Research findings on programs to reduce teen pregnancy.* Washington, DC: National Campaign to Prevent Teen Pregnancy.

Lowry, R., Holtzman, D., Truman, B. I., Kann, L., Collins, J. L., & Kolbe, L. J. (1994). Substance use and HIV-related sexual behaviors among US high school students: Are they related? *American Journal of Public Health, 84*(7), 1116.

Manlove, J. (1998). The influence of high school dropout and school disengagement on the risk of school-age pregnancy. *Journal of Research on Adolescence, 8*(2), 187–220.

Maynard, R. A. (Ed.). (1996). *Kids having kids: A Robin Hood Foundation special report on the costs of adolescent childbearing.* New York: The Robin Hood Foundation.

McEwan, R. T., McCallum, A., Bhopal, R. S., & Madhok, R. (1992). Sex and the risk of HIV infection: The role of alcohol. *British Journal of Addiction, 87*(4), 577–584.

Meier, A. M. (2003). Adolescents' transition to first intercourse, religiosity, and attitudes about sex. *Social Forces, 81*(3), 1031–1052.

Miller, L., & Gur, M. (2002). Religiousness and sexual responsibility in adolescent girls. *Journal of Adolescent Health, 31*(5), 401–406.

Moore, K. A., & Stief, T. M. (1991). Changes in marriage and fertility behavior: Behavior versus attitudes of young adults. *Youth and Society, 22*(3), 362–386.

Morrison, D. M., Gillmore, M. R., Hoppe, M. J., Gaylord, J., Leigh, B. C., & Rainey, D. (2003). Adolescent drinking and sex: Findings from a daily diary study. *Perspectives on Sexual and Reproductive Health, 35*(4), 162–168.

Mott, R. L., & Haurin, R. J. (1988). Linkages between sexual activity and alcohol and drug use among American adolescents. *Family Planning Perspectives, 20*(3), 128–136.

National Campaign to Prevent Teen Pregnancy. (2001). *Halfway there: A prescription for continued progress in preventing teen pregnancy.* Washington, DC: Author.

National Campaign to Prevent Teen Pregnancy. (2002). *Teen pregnancy: Not just another single issue.* Retrieved July 8, 2005, from http://www.teenpregnancy.org/

National Campaign to Prevent Teen Pregnancy. (2003a). *Fact sheet: Not just another single issue: Teen pregnancy and athletic involvement*. Retrieved August 15, 2005, from http://www.teenpregnancy.org/

National Campaign to Prevent Teen Pregnancy. (2003b). *Science says: American opinion on teen pregnancy and related issues 2003*. Retrieved July 1, 2005, from http://www.teenpregnancy.org

National Campaign to Prevent Teen Pregnancy. (2003c). *Science says: Characteristics of teens' first sexual partner*. Retrieved July 1, 2005, from http://www.teenpregnancy.org

National Campaign to Prevent Teen Pregnancy. (2003d). *Science says: The sexual behavior of young adolescents*. Retrieved July 1, 2005, from http://www.teenpregnancy.org/

National Campaign to Prevent Teen Pregnancy. (2003e). *Science says: Where and when teens first have sex*. Retrieved July 1, 2005, from http://www.teenpregnancy.org

National Campaign to Prevent Teen Pregnancy. (2004a). *Teen sexual activity, pregnancy and childbearing among Asians and Pacific Islanders in the United States*. Retrieved August 15, 2005, from http://www.teenpregnancy.org

National Campaign to Prevent Teen Pregnancy. (2004b). *Teen sexual activity, pregnancy and childbearing among Black teens*. Retrieved August 15, 2005, from http://www.teenpregnancy.org

National Campaign to Prevent Teen Pregnancy. (2004c). *Teen sexual activity, pregnancy and childbearing among Latinos in the United States*. Retrieved August 15, 2005, from http://www.teenpregnancy.org

National Campaign to Prevent Teen Pregnancy. (2004d). *With one voice 2004: America's adults and teens sound off about teen pregnancy*. Retrieved August 15, 2005, from http://www.teenpregnancy.org/

National Campaign to Prevent Teen Pregnancy. (2005a). *Science says: Teens' attitudes toward sexual activity, 2002*. Retrieved July 1, 2005, from http://www.teenpregnancy.org

National Campaign to Prevent Teen Pregnancy. (2005b). *Teen sexual activity, pregnancy, and childbearing among Native Americans*. Retrieved November 30, 2005, from http://www.teenpregnancy.org/

Remez, L. (2000). Oral sex among adolescents: Is it sex or is it abstinence? *Family Planning Perspectives, 32*(6), 298–304.

Resnick, M. D., Bearman, P. S., Blum, R. W., Bauman, K. E., Harris, K. M., Jones, J., et al. (1997). Protecting adolescents from harm: Findings from the national longitudinal study on adolescent health. *JAMA: Journal of the American Medical Association, 278*(10), 823–832.

Robbins, C., Kaplan, H. B., & Martin, S. S. (1985). Antecedents of pregnancy among unmarried adolescents. *Journal of Marriage and the Family, 47*, 567–583.

Robertson, J. A., & Plant, M. A. (1988). Alcohol, sex and risks of HIV infection. *Drug & Alcohol Dependence, 22*(1), 75–78.

Rotherham-Borus, M. J., Rosario, M., Meyer-Bahlburg, H. F. L., Koopman, C., Dopkins, S. C., & Davies, M. (1994). Sexual and substance use acts of gay and bisexual male adolescents in New York City. *Journal of Sex Research, 31*(1), 47.

Sanders, S. A., & Reinisch, J. M. (1999). Would you say you "had sex" if? *JAMA: Journal of the American Medical Association, 281*(3), 275–277.

Santelli, J. S., Abma, J., Ventura, S., Lindberg, L., Morrow, B., Anderson, J. E., et al. (2004). Can changes in sexual behaviors among high school students explain the decline in teen pregnancy rates in the 1990s? *Journal of Adolescent Health, 35*(2), 80–90.

Santelli, J. S., Robin, L., Brener, N. D., & Lowry, R. (2001). Timing of alcohol and other drug use and sexual risk behaviors among unmarried adolescents and young adults. *Family Planning Perspectives, 33*(5), 200.

Schwartz, I. M. (1999). Sexual activity prior to coital interaction: A comparison between males and females. *Archives of Sexual Behavior, 28*(1), 63–69.

Singh, S., & Darroch, J. (2000). Adolescent pregnancy and childbearing: Levels and trends in developed countries. *Family Planning Perspectives, 32*, 14–23.

Smith, E. A., & Udry, J. R. (1985). Coital and non-coital sexual behaviors of White and Black adolescents. *American Journal of Public Health, 75*(10), 1200–1203.

Starkman, N., & Rajani, N. (2002). The case for comprehensive sex education. *AIDS Patient Care & STDs, 16*(7), 313–318.

Telljohann, S. K., Price, J. H., Poureslami, M., & Easton, A. (1995). Teaching about sexual orientation by secondary health teachers. *Journal of School Health, 65*(1), 18–22.

Thornton, A., & Camburn, D. (1989). Religious participation and adolescent sexual behavior and attitudes. *Journal of Marriage & the Family, 51*(3), 641–653.

World Health Organization. (2004). *Adolescent pregnancy: Issues in adolescent health and development*. Geneva, Switzerland: Author.

XVIII
SCHOOL COUNSELORS' ROLE IN PROMOTING LITERACY IN ELEMENTARY SCHOOL-AGED CHILDREN

CARRIE J. LINSKENS
Office of the Attorney General, Nevada Department of Justice

HARDIN L. K. COLEMAN
University of Wisconsin–Madison

Introduction

According to Bloome (2001), literacy is not an abstract and independent concept, but one that depends on the context for its meaning. How individuals, especially students, identify, use, and interpret reading and writing and how written texts are constructed depends on and differs across communities. Every personal encounter and situation entails a construction of a new style of communication. Thus, even though a community often creates the definition and patterns of literacy, it is significant to note that our understanding of literacy is a continuously evolving process that is often specific to a community. In this chapter, we want to accomplish two goals. The first is to help school counselors understand and have the language to describe how important literacy is to academic accomplishment. The second is to share a model, derived from interviews with school counselors, of how literacy skills can be developed through participation is a school counseling program.

Why Literacy Is Important in Childhood

According to Serpell (2002), three themes capture the importance of literacy and children being literate: (a) entertainment, (b) skills, and (c) everyday life. First, literacy can be a form of entertainment to children because they can read books they enjoy, write stories, and assist in finding new interests that can steer them out of troublesome activities. Second, literacy is also important because it can assist children in acquiring certain skills. For example, literacy activities can encourage children to recite the alphabet, to recognize letters, and to learn letter sound correspondences and can even aid children in practicing reading words from cards or lists. These literacy skills can be important early in a child's life and can promote future reading achievement or language development in later school years (L. Baker, Scher, & Mackler, 1997). The third and final theme emphasizing the importance of literacy identified by Serpell is everyday life. In this form of literacy, children who read find it is useful and beneficial in everyday activities, such as going to the grocery store or reading traffic signs. It is also important for children to become literate in order to function in society, for instance by reading the bus schedule, paying bills, or looking up phone numbers.

Other authors have written about additional ways in which literacy during childhood leads to positive outcomes. For example, literacy development is linked to early interest in reading and achievement (L. Baker et al., 1997). Furthermore, interactions about literacy may foster social connections, promote interests in reading and writing, and motivate activity by engaging the children in reading and writing with adults or other peers in order to achieve goals (Morrow, 1997). Finally, literacy fosters family interactions and communication (L. Baker et al.). In sum, literacy development is viewed as a crucial component in a child's life. Becoming literate appears to be important in order for children to succeed in school and to become successful citizens in society.

Current Perspectives on Literacy Definitions and Acquisition

To understand the topic of literacy, it is necessary to analyze current definitions of literacy and different perspectives regarding the process of becoming literate. A study by Evans, Shaw, and Bell (2000) describes young children's early literacy and oral language skills as letter name knowledge, letter sound knowledge, phonological sensitivity, and receptive vocabulary. This study examined what types of activities are done with children (e.g., being read to regularly), which do or do not enhance literacy skill development. Their findings support the role of parental involvement in enhancing children's reading achievement—both before and during early formal reading instruction at school. In contrast, Duffy (2003) defined literacy mostly in terms of reading behavior and contended that one should not only teach reading but should also explain and model the process of reading. He discussed four critical aspects of reading: (a) concepts about reading, (b) vocabulary, (c) skills that readers learn automatically, and (d) strategies that readers employ thoughtfully and adaptively. Duffy illustrated that the most effective way to explain the concepts of reading to children is via scaffolding. Scaffolding uses cues that focus students on key elements and then gradually reduces the amount of assistance when the students show evidence of achieving the objectives. As students make sense of the material, they observe each student's responses closely in order to determine how the student is making sense of the cues provided. All of this is done in order to be able to change or modify a cue in response to the child's level of understanding.

According to Pressley (2002), there has been too much controversy about literacy instruction between the skills instruction approach and the whole language approach. Pressley believed that literacy is better taught by maintaining a balance of skills instruction and holistic reading and writing experiences by both methods. Pressley claimed that literacy development strongly depends on the type of instruction and that it is important to have a balance in order to meet all different reading and learning styles in the classroom.

In addition to focusing on how literacy is acquired in particular domains (e.g., at school or at home), Morrow (1997) suggested that literacy can be acquired by different processes and methods. Morrow asserted that the following four processes assist learners in acquiring literacy abilities and skills: (a) observation, (b) collaboration, (c) practice, and (d) performance. First, children may often observe different literacy behaviors in others. For example, children may watch other children being read to or may see other children reading and writing. This may introduce the child to the idea of reading and writing and may begin to formulate ideas in the child's head regarding literacy activities. One hopes that the child will see a positive interaction between an adult and a child reading a book, for instance, and become more interested in pursuing a book him- or herself. Second, children may experience collaboration with classmates and peers regarding literacy activities. For instance, a child may have a social interaction with a learner or with other children who may provide encouragement, help, or motivation about reading and writing skills. Third, after a child observes and possibly receives some positive feedback and collaboration from other children about literacy activities, the child may practice literacy activities on his or her own. For example, a child may actually try out what was learned by reading and writing with the other children or by him- or herself. Fourth, a child may actually perform the literacy activity and share what he or she accomplished. The child may then seek approval or guidance from others about what he or she read or wrote. Overall, there are many different processes involved in literacy besides the actual performance portion of reading and writing.

Overall, there is a wide range of literacy-based activities that promote literacy in children (Serpell, 2002). Joint storybook reading with parents or with peers and teachers, language games, visits to the library, observation of pictures and written texts, and even dinnertime conversations can all be forms of literacy in children. Even activities such as reading picture books, magazines, newspapers, comic books, word puzzle activity books, or any other kind of book can promote reading skills in young children. Not only do reading activities promote literacy in children, but writing activities do as well. For instance, drawing; coloring; writing letters, stories, and poems; playing games involving words and writing; and even writing in journals and diaries promote writing skills in children, which may also enhance literacy development.

While many view literacy as a set of cognitive–linguistic skills that are acquired by an individual, literacy can also be viewed as a set of social and cultural practices that are enacted by a group (Bloome, 2000). This point of view examines the interactions among individuals in social and cultural activities that usually involve written language. It also examines how certain literacy abilities may affect the individual's social and cultural identities as well. This view of literacy examines the variations in literacy practices that may reflect individual's cultural differences, socioeconomic differences, gender relationship differences, or even different orientations in political activities.

Literacy has also been conceptualized by Gee (1989) in terms of the use of discourses. He described discourses as a way of being in the world and as a form of life that integrates words, values, beliefs, acts, attitudes, and social identities, not excluding body positions, clothes, gestures, and glances. However, he defined literacy as "the mastery of or fluent control over a secondary discourse" (p. 8). Primary discourses usually involving home life, and peers are the way we make sense of the world and others. On the other hand, secondary discourses include interactions with various non-home-based social institutions in the public sphere that is beyond the family and peer group (e.g., schools, local stores, churches, community groups, and local, state, and national businesses, agencies, and organizations). Secondary discourses entail being able to "use" the discourses and function in the discourse. For instance, literacy involving school discourse may mean reading and writing. However, to be literate in this discourse is to be able to function in school and to be able to read and write in order to complete tasks.

Gee (1989) argued that literacy is not taught; rather, it is acquired. For example, teachers do not teach literacy in school. Rather, teachers provide the opportunity for children to acquire literacy through experiences at school. In addition, the school gives children opportunities to practice what they are acquiring. Gee also stated that learning cannot take place unless literacy skills are acquired both in school and through experiences at home. Thus, school does not directly enable children to become literate; it does equip children with metalevel cognitive and linguistic skills that they can use to critique discourses in their lives. This may pose a problem to children who are not receiving school congruent literacies at home or the opportunity to acquire these literacy abilities in a school setting. Disadvantaged children may have few opportunities for the acquisition of these secondary discourses within the home setting; thus, they cannot use the learning and teaching to develop the metalevel cognitive skills within the school setting. Another problem that may occur is that nonmainstream children's discourses may be very different from the mainstream discourses provided and taught, which may cause a conflict with the child's family values and beliefs. Although Gee's construction of the literacy process may reinforce a deficit model for those whose secondary discourse is different from the discourse of schools, it is important to acknowledge that this difference creates learning challenges for the child who has to learn these different discourses in order to be effective in either context.

There are many secondary discourses; thus, there are many forms of literacy (Gee, 1989). We have all acquired some forms of literacy and have failed to have others. Today's modern society and its secondary discourses usually involve print. However, literacy can take on many forms, including interactions and conversations, for example. Thus, it is important to understand that when one is using a mainstream definition or understanding of literacy and what constitutes literacy, it may be different from what constitutes a child's culture, family, discourses, and access to literacy activities.

A recent article by Daggett (2003) examines three separate definitions of literacy that were taken from the National Adult Literacy Survey (NALS) and the International Adult Literacy Survey (IALS). Daggett highlighted three definitions of literacy, and he reported that school counselors must play an integral role in redefining education to coincide with essential 21st century employability skills and technology competencies. Daggett also noted the importance of the need to redefine literacy and the ambiguity that comes along with it. The three definitions are as follows: First, prose literacy is described as the knowledge and skills needed to identify, understand, and use information from continuous text sources (e.g., newspaper editorials, magazine articles, reference sources, and fiction). Second, document literacy is defined as the knowledge and skills required to locate and use information contained in functional materials (e.g., job applications, payroll forms, transportation schedules, online consumer surveys, maps, graphs). Third, quantitative literacy is defined as the knowledge and skills required to apply arithmetic operations, either singly or sequentially, using numerals and quantitative data embedded in printed materials (e.g., balancing a checkbook, figuring out a tip, completing an order form). These three definitions are often helpful to contexutalize literacy and how it may be defined differently in many domains and to different researchers.

In this chapter, we will focus primarily on Gee's (1989) concept of secondary discourses. From this perspective, literacy is the ability to manipulate symbols and to communicate and express one's understanding of self and of the world and to understand how others express these experiences. This includes the understanding that the dominant form of literacy is through print, but that other forms of communication (e.g., music, film, or drawing), are legitimate methods for expressing and understanding ways of sharing views of the self and the world. Being literate, therefore, means being competent to express and understand the process of communication. We believe that effective communication is one outcome of a school counseling program. For this reason, we think an understanding of literacy and how school counselors are involved in its development is an important professional competency.

The School Counselor and Literacy

What is the school counselor's role in the process of developing literacy in school-aged children? The American School Counselor Association's (ASCA; 2003) *National Model* summarizes what is evolving as a set of expectations for the school counselor's role. The ASCA model of school counseling has four main systems (i.e., accountability, delivery, foundation, and management). The ASCA model also incorporates four themes to guide the school counselor's role: leadership, advocacy, collaboration, and systemic change as part of the framework. The four themes represent the importance of the school counselors' work within these areas. School counselors play an important role in improving student achievement and are unique in that they are advocates for students and systems.

Hardesty and Dillard (1994) examined the role of the elementary school counselor in comparison with middle and secondary school counselors and found three major differences in the ranking of school counselor activities by elementary school counselors. First, elementary school counselors were found to perform more coordination activities and consultative activities (e.g., consulting with faculty and parents, and coordinating programs). Elementary school counselors were also found to perform fewer administrative activities, such as paperwork and scheduling, than middle school counselors were. Finally, even though both elementary and middle school counselors were found to work with student concerns on an individual basis, elementary school counselors tended to work systemically (e.g., with families, community agencies, and teachers). In addition, the least likely activity performed by elementary school counselors involved vocational and post-high-school educational activities. However, the larger emphasis on coordination activities is consistent with ASCA's suggestion that classroom guidance and curriculum is an important component of elementary school counseling.

One of the shortcomings in the current understanding of the school counselor's role is that none of the existing models address how the school counselor's responsibilities apply to core areas of academic competence such as literacy. Specifically, research is vague or nonexistent on the school counselor's role in literacy. This leads to questions about whether school counselors even have a role in promoting literacy in school-aged children and, if so, why. These common questions are not answered in the current literature.

According to Delpit (1995), "[S]tudents must be taught the codes needed to participate fully in the mainstream American life, not by being forced to attend to hollow, inane, de-conceptualized sub-skills, but rather within the context of meaningful communicative endeavors" (p. 45). Delpit highlighted the multiple flaws that take place in our educational system, especially when it comes to children of color and even more so when it comes to the development of literacy. She emphasized the difficulty that children of color have in academia because they are being taught in a White American frame of reference, by White teachers, and like White children. She pointed out that children of color do not learn well this way and, therefore, they often lag behind their White peers and fall behind in school. Referring back to Gee's (1989) perspective, the cultural difference in primary discourses increases the difficulty of effectively acquiring secondary discourses such as literacy. Delpit's quote illustrates the importance for all cultures to be brought into the classroom and for having literacy interactions and different methods of literacy to which students of color can relate and from which they can learn. Teachers are not capable of achieving this ideal goal alone; hence, other school personnel have an important role regarding literacy development. Delpit suggested that school counselors are in a unique position to use developmental guidance and counseling as an aid for teachers and other school staff in the promotion of literacy and "meaningful communicative endeavors." From this perspective, literacy is not only a teacher's job but also an important focus of schoolwide activity. School counselors can collaborate with parents, students, teachers, and other school personnel and can join and take part in the literacy movement that needs to occur in order to make classroom instruction more effective across various cultural groups.

The perspective that school counselors should be involved in literacy development in school-aged children was also shared by Daggett (2003). He suggested that school counselors who take leadership roles in schools need to question current definitions about literacy and learning and expectations about student achievement and success. School counselors need to track changes happening in the world that require new ways of thinking in order to assist students in gaining those resources to adapt to the changes. School counselors are also equipped to integrate relevant activities into classrooms, especially using technological information. If school counselors can become educated in the manner in which computer and Web industries are redefining literacy, they will be able to assist students in becoming computer literate in order to keep up with the current job market and computer industry. Daggett asserted that school counselors can be student literacy advocates by alerting parents, decision makers, and students that the reading tasks required by adult roles now involve higher readability levels than ever before. The current gaps between graduates and employer needs are continually increasing; school counselors can help bridge the gap. Daggett emphasized, "With the influence school counselors hold in student curriculum decisions, their leadership in promoting greater attention to literacy cannot be understated" (p. 240). Daggett suggested that school counselors need to expand their influence, assume a role in mentoring teachers about the changing workplace, convince administrators to provide only rigorous and relevant learning options, and alert parents and students of the increasing literacy expectations in society. He also argued that if school counselors do not assume some leadership roles in academics and greater levels of achievement, their roles in modern schools will soon become irrelevant. It is important that school counselors become involved in any type of movement that will prepare students with the literacy skills they will need to succeed.

Another perspective suggests that some students struggling in literacy may not need expert instruction at all times (Allington, 2001). Some instruction sessions could be taught by other school personnel (e.g., the school counselor) who would allow the teacher more time to assist students who are having difficulty. It would also give the school counselors a chance to get involved in literacy development. Allington believed school counselors should support teachers in their efforts to become more expert and reorganize all of the aspects of the educational system so that they can teach as expertly as they know how. School counselors can be supportive in literacy development in many ways. For example, they can support the children and help with one-on-one assistance or instruction of literacy, and they can also support the teachers in learning more about literacy instruction and what works best for the students.

D'Andrea (1995) gave a final example of the school counselor's role in literacy development in school-aged children. He emphasized the importance of multicultural literacy, which is defined as a state of being knowledgeable and respectful of the history, traditions, and values of persons from diverse backgrounds. With the increase in cultural diversity in the United States, the need to increase multicultural literacy among students is crucial. D'Andrea proposed that elementary school counselors, teachers, and administrators will soon be pressed to implement educational strategies that help children develop skills necessary to manage the technological demands and the interpersonal challenges related to living in a highly diverse society. He suggested that elementary school counselors, who continue to increase their own level of knowledge and skills in the areas of multiculturalism, in turn, can consult with teachers and administrators about ways to bring multicultural and computer literacy into the curriculum.

Although the research on the role of school counselors in the development of literacy in school-aged children is still in its infancy and most of it is theoretical, it is clear that scholars in this area are advocating for a more explicit focus on literacy as a pathway to student achievement and an appropriate focus for school counselors. The existing literature suggests several ways in which school counselors can integrate a focus on literacy within their current role. The first is as a change agent within a school. In this role, the school counselor would focus on ways in which teachers can be provided more resources to address literacy development (e.g., culturally relevant curriculum or support within the classroom to focus on students with higher needs). The second is as a coordinator of services. In this role, the school counselor would work with parents, teachers, students, and others to increase the focus on the literacy needs of particular children or the whole school. The final approach is that of a direct stimulant to literacy. Hence, the school counselor would be explicit about the developmental guidance program used to promote literacy. Each of these approaches has conceptual merit, yet each is not based on empirical support.

In the research on literacy development, many limitations and strengths are important to note. Some of the weaknesses in the existing research are that many of the articles and books continually focus on what is wrong within school systems, with certain models, or in what is currently being done in literacy that is not working well. Rarely do studies actually test methods to determine the changes needed to improve the literacy of children. Generalizability is difficult because situations and problems related to literacy development are often context specific. Another common limitation of the literature is the lack of recognition of the many duties that the school counselors already have. School counselors are having trouble finding time to do direct services as it is, much less finding time to work on literacy activities. Finally, the articles do not talk about training for literacy educators. It is difficult for school counselors to become more involved in literacy development, for example, when their training programs have not adequately prepared them.

There are also many strengths of the literature examined. Almost all give a definition of literacy. This literature comprises books, national guidelines, instructional guides, articles, and qualitative and quantitative studies, providing many different views on the topic. Some of the books presented provide examples of programs and interventions for literacy improvement, which serve as a groundwork for future programs. A final strength of the literature is that it examines cultural factors by recognizing that mainstream culture sometimes tries to teach literacy only in one "mainstream" form. However, programs and research are being implemented to consider children of color and the influence of sociocultural factors on their literacy development.

Even though there are strengths and limitations in the domain of literacy development, there are still some gaps in the literature that need to be filled. More needs to be known about literacy development, especially in relation to school counselors' roles. Rowell and Hong (2002) suggested that new standards for education would enhance counselor involvement in students' academic development; would help strengthen the bond among school counselors, teachers, administrators, students, and parents; and would help demonstrate the importance of school counselor involvement in the educational system. They suggested school counselor training should involve more academic support of students.

More research needs to examine what school counselors actually do, what their stated job responsibilities are, and what roles can be altered to best improve the student and the educational system as a whole. Therefore, given Bloome's (2001) earlier definition of literacy and how it depends on a child's culture and interactions, it seems important to understand how practicing school counselors perceive their role in literacy. In this chapter, we share a phenomenological understanding of how professional school counselors perceive their involvement in the development of literacy in school-aged children.

A Beginning Phenomenological Understanding of the School Counselor's Role in Promoting Literacy

Given the lack of research examining the role of the school counselor in promoting literacy in school-aged children, there is a need for creating a baseline understanding of the school counselor's role in the development of literacy. To achieve this understanding, we asked eight practicing school counselors to share with us the activities they use to promote literacy in their developmental guidance and counseling programs. To focus the interviews we defined literacy as the ability for children to understand and manipulate a written word. What we found reinforces the hypothesis that school counselors can be actively engaged in helping all students develop and practice literacy skills. Using a thematic analysis, we found four core themes (represented in Table 18.1) around which a school counselor may organize his or her involvement in the process of literacy development.

Table 18.1 Four Core Themes

1. The school counselor has multiple roles.
2. Contextual considerations are crucial.
3. School counselors are promoters of literacy, not instructors.
4. Ambivalence leads to enlightenment.

Theme 1: The School Counselor Has Multiple Roles

Across all of the interviews, it was evident that school counselors in every school and in every district have multiple roles and duties. The primary duties that were consistent for all of the participants were to (a) produce desired outcomes in students, (b) adopt a team approach with other school staff, (c) facilitate socioemotional development as primary, and (d) promote literacy as a secondary outcome to their work. For instance,

> My role is to support the child in academics, not to teach the child in academics. My role is to make sure that the child is healthy enough so that he or she can be learning in the way that he or she needs to. I see it certainly as part of what I'm helping the child do by means of helping with the things that are impeding his or her academics, so that I can remove those impediments then indirectly I'm helping with literacy.

Theme 2: Contextual Considerations Are Crucial

Many of the interviewees found contextual factors to be crucial considerations in their jobs, suggesting that certain structural school considerations, such as contextual factors (e.g., family) or the difference in school counselor training program, may hinder what work is done with the children. The school counselors stated that the work that they do with students largely depends on the contextual considerations. For instance, if a school has very involved parents, the school counselor may not need to be as involved in the promotion of literacy in the students. Another example could be, "I have 800 to 900 children that I am responsible for as a school counselor," or on a positive note in relation to literacy, "In our district, anyway, there are really a lot of people dedicated to specific literacy issues that are helpful to the teachers." Thus, contextual considerations, whether positive or negative, were consistent across all eight interviewees and in their duties as school counselors.

Theme 3: School Counselors Are Promoters, Not Instructors, of Literacy

The third core theme was that the school counselors were promoters or enhancers of literacy development in children, but not instructors. These school counselors felt that they were not trained to instruct literacy-related lessons and that it was more of a teacher's job for the phonetics and instruction of literacy. However, they stated that they do play a strong role in enhancing literacy activities in children, even if they did not realize it before sharing their stories in these interviews. The school counselors in the study promoted literacy through the techniques and interventions that they employed in developmental guidance and counseling situations (e.g., focus on communication of ideas or reading about situations of relevance to the students) by facilitating socioemotional development and developmental guidance instruction. One school counselor stated,

> Sometimes we'll play a game where they have to read the cards or read the problem-solving cards. That is not my specific goal; I think it happens as a side sometimes. I don't set up the literacy components, I get them ready to be able to be receptive to them.

This is an example of the manner in which school counseling programs support literacy development. Many of the school counselors described the multiple literacy-related techniques that they do with children, however, they did not think of them as explicitly related to literacy promotion because often times it was not their intention. With reflection, they were able to see how much of their work did provide the underpinning for literacy.

Theme 4: Ambivalence Leads to Enlightenment

The final core theme was that the interviewees began the interviews by saying that they did not promote literacy and that teachers primarily fulfilled that role. However, during the hour interview, almost all participants had an increased awareness of "enlightenment," meaning that after they told of the activities that they did with children, they realized that many of them were involved in literacy promotion. For example, one interviewee stated at the end of the interview,

> If you would have asked me that first I think my answer might have been different. Now we've been talking as long as we have and I've made some realizations on what I've been doing, I feel I'm doing a pretty good job in promoting literacy in the time frame that I have. I'm incorporating it into my developmental guidance lessons, I'm trying to use it on a whole school basis with the assemblies. I feel overall that I'm doing a good job with it and just having a positive attitude with literacy in general and promoting reading. I'm actually realizing now that I do quite a bit with it. At first I would have been like I don't know. . . . I could do more. I think that every one of my guidance lessons has something to do with literacy.

Another example was a comment that, "I'm seeing that it is important and there are things that I do and there are more things that I could do to promote literacy in the classroom." Once again, the theme emerged that once discussing the topic of the promotion of literacy, school counselors realized that they actually did more than they thought. Furthermore, they also considered the notion that they could possibly do more in this area of academic development. Along with the enlightenment phase of this theme, there was also some ambivalence about saying that they do promote literacy. For example, the same counselor who was just quoted said,

> I'm not instructing literacy, am I promoting it? I mean I guess I am! Do I see that as part of my job though? I see that as something that I do, but I don't know if as a counselor I see this as part of my job expectation.

Overall, this last core theme represents the increased awareness of what school counselors actually do, including the promotion of literacy development as a large part of their job description once they look at it from that perspective. In this manner, school counselors are providing opportunities for students to develop their skills in the secondary discourse of literacy that Gee (1989) suggested is fundamental to the learning process.

Implications from the Phenomenological Exploration of Elementary School Counselors and Promotion of Literacy

The purpose of this chapter is to heighten the fields' understanding of the importance of literacy in the academic progress of students and to show that school counselors are actively involved in the process of literacy development. Using Gee's (1989) conception of secondary discourses (which suggests that literacy is the ability to manipulate symbols and communication to express one's understanding of self and of the world and to understand how these experiences can be expressed by others), we wanted to show how school counselors perceive their role in this process. What we have found is that the dominant relationship school counselors have with literacy development is one of ambivalence. School counselors assert that they are not reading specialists, that they are not teachers, and therefore, that they do not organize their daily activities around literacy development. Upon reflection, however, school counselors came to understand that their work is focused on helping children develop a deep and emotional understanding of the secondary discourses, which creates their sense of the world. In turn, this understanding is a fundamental stepping-stone in becoming literate. We found that this insight could move school counselors from

Figure 18.1 School counselor's role in Literacy Development.

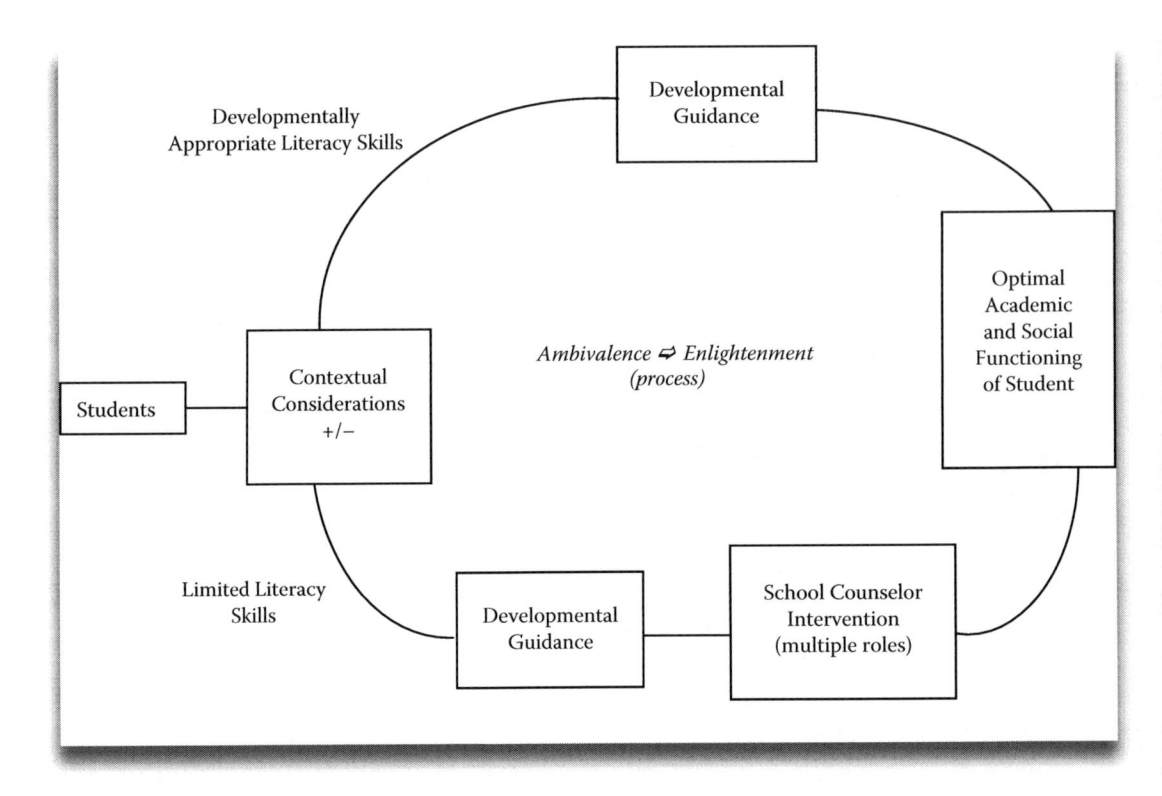

ambivalence concerning their role in literacy development to one of enlightenment as to how much of their work created the context in which students developed literacy.

As represented in Figure 18.1, there are four core themes that represent this perspective on the school counselors' role in literacy development. The first is that they are charged with understanding and working with the contextual factors that affect a student's preparation to become literate. Contextual factors include family conditions, teacher competence, quality of instruction, and other factors around the child, which influence or facilitate his or her preparation for becoming literate. If these contextual factors facilitate literacy, then the school counselor can focus on a developmental guidance program, which supports, enhances, and practices the literacy skills and perspectives a child gains from his or her parents, peers, and teachers. If they do not, then the school counselor uses developmental guidance to stimulate the student's interest in acquiring an understanding of secondary discourses through reading about emotional and behavioral issues as a way to motivate the student to develop school-oriented literacy. If developmental guidance activities are insufficient to the task, the school counselor uses a variety of roles (individual or group counseling, consultation, or teaching) to stimulate the child to acquire literacy.

The middle of the model has a bubble that represents the movement from ambivalence to enlightenment. This area is the process that occurred throughout these interviews. This model was formulated after the school counselors realized how much literacy promotion they actually did with their students and how different it was with each student at each school. This core theme happened with many of the different school counselors at many different times throughout the interviews. Some participants experienced ambivalence to enlightenment while in the midst of the interview, and some realized it at the end. We are not suggesting that this model is applicable to each child, let alone each school counseling program. We are suggesting that there may be a pattern to the paths that students take to develop their literacy skills through a school counseling program.

Erford (2003) supported our notion that school counselors can support the facilitation of literacy acquisition. He described 10 roles of a school counselor, over half of which can impact literacy development. First, Erford suggested that developmental guidance could be a means of achieving academic achievement in children. We found that most of the literacy-based activities these school counselors do with children are done during either individual counseling or developmental guidance periods. Second, Erford stated that school counselors should be collaboration specialists between community and school members. We also found that school counselors act as collaborators by teaching parents how to enhance literacy skills in the home setting. Third, Erford stated that a school counselor's role is as a career and educational planning specialist. The school counselors we interviewed also said they perform literacy enhancing tasks with children involving career and computer activities and in academic areas in which the child may be struggling within the classroom. Fourth, the school counselor performs individual and group counseling as a role, which can be utilized as a way to incorporate literacy activities in counseling interventions. For instance, a group on self-esteem issues might give the children an opportunity to read a book on positive self-affirmations or allow them to engage in a writing activity in which they write down positive things about themselves in a journal. Fifth, Erford suggested that a school counselor's role is an advocate for social justice. This role involves school counselors working toward removing the barriers that students may experience in an effort to educate students and promote social and emotional development. This is reflected in the experiences that were shared by the participants in the study via the literacy-based activities that they had implemented. Finally, Erford suggested that school counselors are agents of diversity and multicultural sensitivity. The school counselors that we interviewed fulfilled this role by creating diversity groups or making signs of diversity and putting them around the school. D'Andrea (1995) also suggested that it is important for school counselors to help with the promotion of multicultural literacy. In the study that we presented, we found that many of the school counselors had discussions on multicultural and diversity topics in the developmental guidance periods or during individual or group counseling.

Delpit (1995) suggested that school counselors can help teachers minimize cultural barriers and can act as an additional supportive person who can provide literacy to children, which would maximize the effectiveness with the child. We found that other barriers, which are a focus of school counseling programs, also impede student academic achievement. Furthermore, many of the school counselors knew that a proper diet and clothing, social skills, love, support outside of the school, and positive peer interactions were crucial before a child could learn academically. As school counseling programs focus on the socioemotional development of children, they are serving to promote literacy.

Finally, these findings are consistent with Allington's (2001) thesis that school counselors should help struggling readers and be supportive of teachers in literacy development. Although many of the interviewees did not feel they were instructing literacy, they did see that they were promoting and enhancing literacy in their office by reading and writing with children and doing other literacy-based activities besides instruction. Many of the school counselors interviewed stated that before delivering developmental guidance lessons, they would talk with the teachers about current issues in the classroom at the time and then could address the issues (e.g., bullying) via literacy activities or other means in their lessons—thus supporting the teachers.

We suggest that there are some important conclusions regarding the school counselor's role in literacy development that warrant further consideration. First, it is clear that there is a paucity of research in this area, resulting in little empirical evidence to guide research or practice. When the school counselors were initially asked about their roles in literacy, they were often confused as to why the question was even being asked. This speaks to a gap in their training as school-based professionals. Literacy is often viewed as a teacher's role and the school counselor deals only with socioemotional issues. However, after the interviews it was clear that school counselors do have a large role in the promotion of literacy in elementary school students—they just did not realize it. It was well stated by the participants that their ultimate goal when working with children was fostering their socioemotional development and that involvement in literacy-oriented experiences was just a means of achieving this goal. However, after discussion, it became apparent that there is a direct link between socioemotional development and literacy—they go hand in hand. It was very rare to talk about socioemotional development without literacy being a part of the discussion or to discuss literacy without issues of socioemotional development being raised.

While school counselors do have a role in promoting literacy in elementary school students, it is significant to note that often their role in literacy is indirect. Teachers are viewed as having the direct role of promoting literacy because they instruct literacy; however, school counselors promote literacy indirectly because they are using it as a means to achieve an alternative goal—socioemotional development.

A final conclusion is that even though school counselors are promoting literacy, not instructing it, they are not trained or told to do so; they just pick up that responsibility based on the school needs. Some schools may need the school counselors to take on an extra role in literacy development and some may not, depending on contextual considerations. It is also significant to note that the personal view that the school counselor has may also impact his or her role in literacy development. If a school counselor firmly believes that it is not his or her role and was not instructed to do so, he or she is oftentimes hesitant to take on that role of literacy promotion much less admit that it is a role of the school counselor. On the other hand, some school counselors who take on the "team approach" to helping students see literacy promotion as everyone's role and are more likely to be actively involved and admit it is also their responsibility.

We also found that awareness was a key issue, which was explained in the ambivalence-to-enlightenment section. The interviewees who realized how much literacy promotion they do became excited to do more, to recognize what they were already doing as positive, and to be a member of the "literacy bandwagon." Many of the participants did not realize how they specifically promoted literacy, which includes more than simply reading a book with a child.

We suggest that training guidelines for school counselors be altered in order to articulate literacy promotion as a role of the school counselor. It is clear that this assistance and help from the school counselors in relation to literacy is greatly needed; thus, school counselors need to be trained to develop this competence. For school counselors practicing right now, it is important to review current research on this topic and to provide proper training on how to promote and assist in literacy development. It is also important to be aware of the amount of literacy promotion they do and what more they could do to benefit the child, e.g., finding alternative literacy techniques that could facilitate their goals in working with children.

Conclusion

Socioemotional development is a foundation of academic achievement and is the primary goal of school counselors. This chapter indicates that school counselors reinforce socioemotional development in children by using literacy-related techniques. How is a child going to be able to learn academically if he or she has barriers preventing the academic achievement? It is true that a teacher or a reading specialist may instruct literacy and may be the first person called to help a struggling reader; however, who follows through and makes sure that the child is emotionally stable in order to fulfill this academic instruction? Who is the one who connects the socioemotional development with literacy development? That individual is a school counselor. School counselors, both directly and indirectly, reinforce literacy and academic instruction through counseling techniques and developmental guidance. School counselors remove barriers in children's lives and prepare children to succeed academically. School counselors have a critical and valuable impact on the development of literacy and the socioemotional wellbeing in children's lives.

References

Allington, R. L. (2001). *What really matters for struggling readers: Designing research-based programs.* New York: Addison-Wesley Educational Publishers.

American School Counselor Association. (2003). *The ASCA national model: A framework for school counseling programs.* Alexandria, VA: Author.

Baker, L., Scher, D., Mackler, K. (1997). Home and family influences on motivations for reading. *Educational Psychologist, 32*(2), 69–82.

Bloome, D. (2000). Interpellations of family/community and classroom literacy practices. *Journal of Educational Research, 93*(3), 155–164.

Bloome, D. (2001). Building literacy and the classroom community. *Theory Into Practice, 25*(2), 71–76.

D'Andrea, M. (1995). Using computer technology to promote multicultural awareness among elementary school-age students. *Elementary School Guidance & Counseling, 30*(1), 45–55.

Daggett, W. R. (2003). School counselors and information literacy from the perspective of Willard Daggett. *Professional School Counseling, 6*(4), 238–243.

Delpit, L. (1995). *Other people's children: Cultural conflict in the classroom.* New York: The New Press.

Duffy, G. (2003). *Explaining reading: A resource for teaching concepts, skills, and strategies.* New York: The Guilford Press.

Erford, B. T. (2003). *Transforming the school counseling profession.* Upper Saddle River, NJ: Prentice Hall.

Evans, M. A., Shaw, D., & Bell, M. (2000). Home literacy activities and their influence on early literacy skills. *Canadian Journal of Experimental Psychology, 54*(2), 65–75.

Gee, J. P. (1989). Literacy, discourse, and linguistics: Introduction and what is literacy? *Journal of Education, 171*(1), 5–25.

Hardesty, P. H., & Dillard, J. M. (1994) The role of elementary school counselors compared with their middle and secondary school counterparts. *Elementary School Guidance & Counseling, 29*(2), 83–92.

Morrow, L. M. (1997). A family literacy program connecting school and home: Effects on attitude, motivation, and literacy achievement. *Journal of Educational Psychology, 89*(4), 736–742.

Pressley, M. (2002). *Reading instruction that works* (2nd ed.). New York: The Guilford Press.

Rowell, L. L., & Hong, E. (2002). The role of school counselors in homework intervention. *Professional School Counseling, 5*(4), 285–292.

Serpell, R. (2002). Intimate culture of families in the early socialization of literacy. *Journal of Family Psychology, 16*(4), 391–405.

XIX
DESIGNING CULTURALLY RESPONSIVE SCHOOL COUNSELING CAREER DEVELOPMENT PROGRAMMING FOR YOUTH

KIMBERLY A. S. HOWARD
University of Wisconsin–Madison

V. SCOTT H. SOLBERG, NEETA KANTAMENI, AND MELISSA KRAEMER SMOTHERS
University of Wisconsin–Milwaukee

The focus and scope of school counseling has expanded in recent years from a primary focus on work transition to include a comprehensive range of developmental services that address academic, interpersonal, and vocational readiness. Currently, the design of most school counseling programs is on the provision of "comprehensive" services that include a developmental guidance curriculum; individual services to children, youth, and their families; and responsive services (American School Counselor Association [ASCA], 2003; Gysbers, 2001). Recent large-scale evaluations indicate that programs offering comprehensive services result in positive outcomes for youth (Lapan, Gysbers, & Petroski, 2003; Lapan, Gysbers, & Sun, 1997; Sink & Stroh, 2003). Youth attending schools that implement a comprehensive school counseling model reported higher grades and higher achievement test scores; they believed that more career information was available to them, could see the relevance of their current school work to their future endeavors, and perceived a more positive school environment, in terms of feeling safe in school and feeling connected to their teachers (Lapan et al., 1997, 2003; Sink & Stroh). One such study also examined student outcomes by various types of student characteristics, including race/ethnicity and socioeconomic indicators (Lapan et al., 1997). The researchers discovered that, overall, students of color reported lower grades on average than White students did. While comprehensive guidance programs were found to positively influence grades for all students, these programs did not reduce the achievement gap between youth from racially and ethnically diverse backgrounds and White youth or between youth from lower income and higher income backgrounds.

This achievement gap is troubling and deserves immediate attention for we know that youth from low-income and diverse backgrounds are three times more likely to leave high school prior to gaining a degree and that growing up in poverty is the strongest predictor of future unemployment (National Research Council, 1993). Reducing the achievement gap refers not only to increasing high school graduation rates, but also to providing youth from racially and ethnically diverse backgrounds and youth from lower income backgrounds with the skills needed to successfully enter and graduate from 2- and 4-year colleges. Adults with a 4-year college degree earn a median income of $41,800 while those who do not graduate from high school earn a median income of $18,300—a difference of $23,500 per year (U.S. Census Bureau, 2005). When considered over a 45-year work life, this totals more than $1 million. Figure 19.1 breaks down the economic implications of a college degree by racial and ethnic background. While individuals from African American and Latino backgrounds continue to earn less than individuals from White and Asian American backgrounds, the relative income differences that result from having a college degree across all groups is quite staggering.

At the same time, however, we must also keep in mind that economic success is not solely reflected by one's annual income, but also entails avoiding periods of unemployment and poverty. As we would expect, unemployment and poverty rates are closely tied to level of education. In 2003 (U.S. Census Bureau, 2005), 12.5% of Americans lived in poverty. When considering just those individuals who did not complete high school, we see a jump in poverty

[Figure 19.1: Bar chart showing income levels by ethnicity (White, Black, Asian, Latino) comparing High School and Bachelor's Degree]

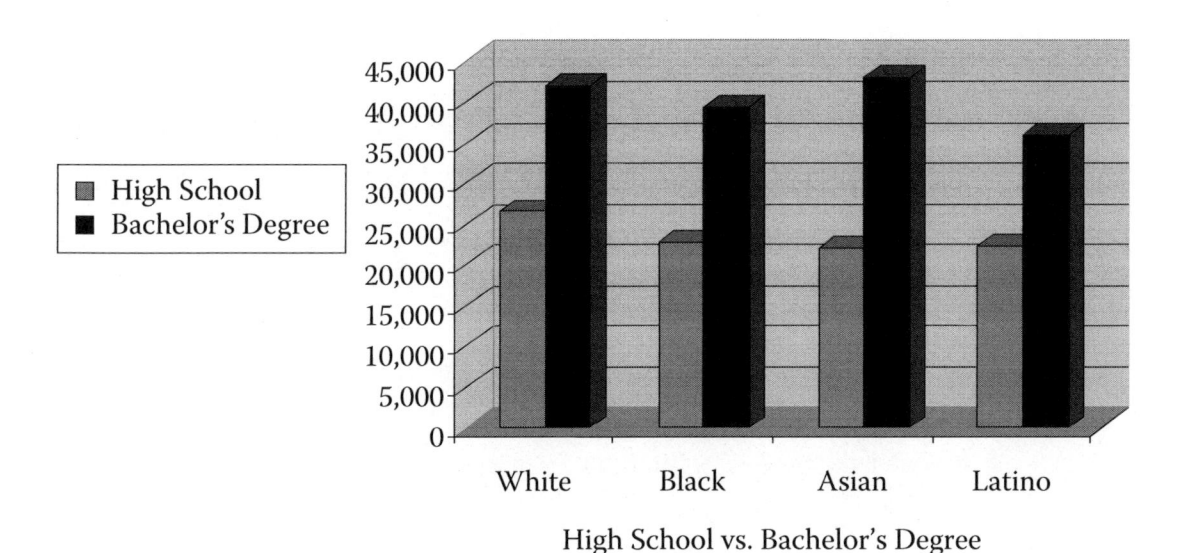

Figure 19.1 Income levels by ethnicity and degree.

rates to 21.3%. This rate steadily declines with additional education; high school degree or GED: 11.3%; some college: 8.5%; and a 4-year degree or more: 4.2%. So, too, does the unemployment rate. Individuals 25 years and older who did not have a high school diploma were almost twice as likely as high school graduates and over three times more likely than those with a 4-year college degree to be unemployed (U.S. Bureau of Labor Statistics, 2005). Figure 19.2 examines poverty rates by academic degree status and by racial/ethnic group. Even among individuals possessing no high school diploma we see differences in poverty rates for African-Americans and Latinos versus their White and Asian-American counterparts.

In short, unless the achievement gap is addressed, serious economic inequities are likely to continue in the United States. One of the most serious signs of the severe inequities occurring in the United States is that the median net worth for individuals from White backgrounds has been estimated at $120,000 compared with $17,000 for individuals from non-White backgrounds (Aizcorbe, Kennickell, & Moore, 2003). By establishing culturally responsive comprehensive school counseling programs that narrow the achievement gap, school counselors are promoting a more socially just society. While some critics of the multicultural movement believe that good practice should work equally

[Figure 19.2: Bar chart showing poverty rates by ethnicity comparing No High School vs Bachelor's Degree. White: 18, 3.7; Black: 33.7, 5.5; Asian: 20.4, 8; Latino: 26, 8]

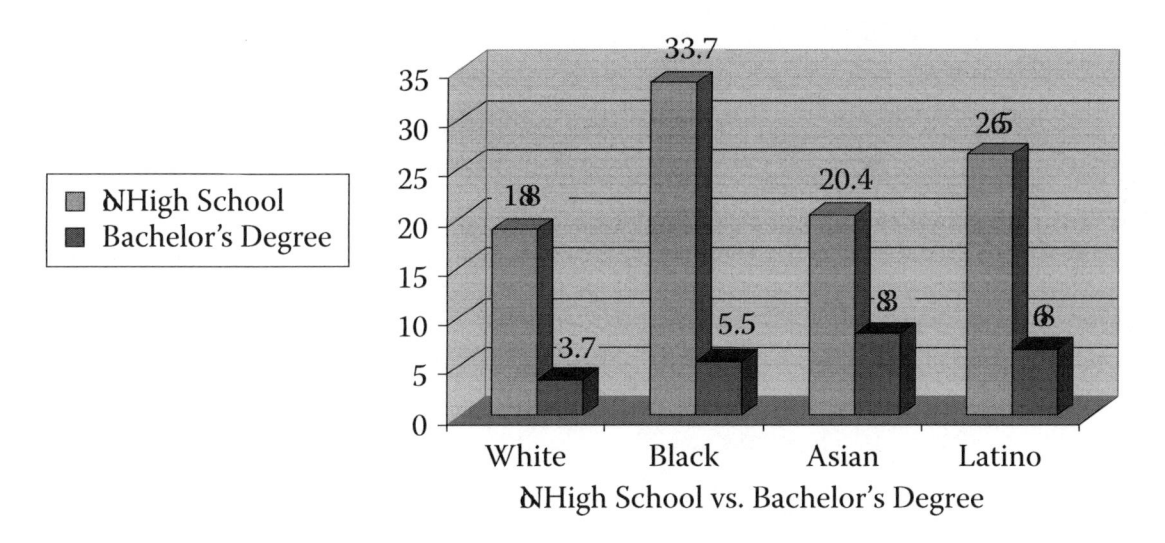

Figure 19.2 Poverty by education level.

for everyone (an assertion with which we disagree), the Lapan et al. (1997) investigation suggested that "working equally well" with all groups, in fact, serves to maintain the status quo of unequal outcomes for culturally diverse and low-income youth. Instead of focusing on strategies that work equally well across groups, we must, instead, turn our attention to strategies that provide opportunities for youth to experience *equal levels of success,* both in school and in their postsecondary plans.

Where, then, do we begin when aiming to provide culturally responsive programs of career development for children and youth? One logical place to start is consulting the *ASCA National Model* of comprehensive school counseling (ASCA, 2003). This model includes four main components: (a) the theoretical foundation underlying the profession, (b) a management system for the school counseling program, (c) a services delivery system, and (d) accountability methods (ASCA). It was designed to support school counselors' efforts to develop and implement a comprehensive, developmentally appropriate program of school counseling. The *ASCA National Model* clearly describes the importance of disaggregating outcome data in order to evaluate whether services are effectively impacting all youth. It does not, however, provide adequate discussion with regard to "how" to design such services in a manner that makes these services responsive to youth from culturally diverse or low-income backgrounds. We agree with the many advocates who have argued that a culturally appropriate school-counseling program begins with both preservice training and professional development opportunities in multiculturally competent counseling (Coleman & Baskin, 2003; Constantine & Yeh, 2001; Hobson & Kanitz, 1996; Schwallie-Giddis, Anstrom, Sánchez, Sardi, & Granato, 2004).

In the remainder of this chapter, we will discuss the topic of culturally appropriate, school-based career interventions for youth. We concur with scholars and practitioners in the field that the application of counseling knowledge and skills to the career domain, as in the academic and personal/social domains, requires an integration of multicultural competence (Arbona, 2000; Hargrove, Creagh, & Kelly, 2003) and a social justice perspective (Vera & Speight, 2003). It requires knowledge of major career theories and contemporary developmental perspectives that are relevant to school-age children and youth. It requires familiarity with the current state of research knowledge in career interventions with youth in school settings, as well as with exemplars of well-developed and effective school-based career intervention programs. Thus, after reviewing the literature on multiculturally competent career counseling and interventions, we will describe a social justice perspective to school counseling and then review relevant theory, summarize the current state of research in school-based career interventions, and describe two examples of career interventions designed for culturally diverse youth. Let us now turn our attention to the role of multicultural counseling competence in school counseling.

Multicultural Competence

Each year the United States' population becomes more and more diverse. It is projected that by the year 2050 people of color will compose roughly 50% of the national population (U.S. Census Bureau, 2005). With the growing diversity in our nation's population comes an increased recognition regarding the importance of working in ways that are knowledgeable, respectful, and affirming of other cultures' ways of being (Carey & Reinat, 1990; Hobson & Kanitz, 1996). D. W. Sue and D. Sue (2003) explained that multicultural counseling competence has historically been conceived of as including three core dimensions: (a) an awareness of one's own cultural self; (b) knowledge of the history, values, and worldviews of various racial, ethnic, and cultural groups; and (c) skills to create and implement culturally responsive interventions. Holcomb-McCoy (2003) explained that for school counselors, practicing in a culturally competent manner demands a "paradigm shift" in how one conceptualizes students and student issues. This shift requires one to understand the influence of a number of factors on students' academic and social functioning at school. These factors include students' racial and/or ethnic identity, language status, and country of origin; their socioeconomic status, social resources, and family status; and their cultural expectations of school counseling. Further, practicing in a multiculturally competent way requires that school counselors appreciate the ways that a student's home, community, and cultural contexts shape how they perceive schooling and their roles as students. Indeed, for Coleman and Baskin (2003), it is the ability to naturally incorporate an understanding of these contexts into the therapeutic process and method of service delivery that captures the "essence" of being a multiculturally competent school counselor.

Previous research found that practicing school counselors recognized the need to become more skilled at working with culturally diverse students (Carey & Reinat, 1990). Specifically, school counselors reported a need for becoming more aware of their own cultural background, more effective in interacting and working with culturally diverse youth, and more aware of how their actions were being perceived by students (Carey & Reinat). More recent research has found that for school counselors, multicultural counseling knowledge and awareness is related to the number of multicultural courses taken previously, a commitment to interacting with culturally diverse individuals, and an appreciation for and a valuing of the ways that we are all similar as well as different (Constantine et al., 2001). Thus, establishing multicultural competence as a school counselor includes maintaining an appreciation for the diverse ways of being and thinking found across racial and ethnic groups and actively seeking out cultural experiences and new learning opportunities.

Scholars within the field of career development, too, have called for multiculturally competent approaches to the generation and application of career theory, research, and practice (e.g., Betz, 1993; Swanson & Fouad, 1999). Hargrove and colleagues (2003) explained that three foci have emerged in the area of studying multiculturally competent career counseling. These foci include (a) attempts to articulate racial/ethnic group-specific career-counseling guidelines, (b) the identification of culturally appropriate principles of career counseling that may be used with all clients, and (c) the creation of multicultural career-counseling competencies. Seeing the need for a model of multiculturally competent career counseling to guide the work of practitioners and scholars, Hargrove et al. proposed a three-part framework based, to some extent, on the multicultural counseling competencies of the American Counseling Association (ACA). Consistent with D. W. Sue and D. Sue (2003), this framework includes the importance of career counselor self-awareness, awareness of the client's worldview, and the development and use of culturally appropriate interventions and strategies.

It is hard not to recognize that becoming multiculturally competent is critical for success as a school counselor. At the same time, however, we argue that multicultural competence is a necessary, but not a sufficient condition for working in optimal ways with culturally diverse and low-income youth. The disparities apparent in high school graduation rates, college attendance, incomes, poverty rates, and unemployment rates make it clear that a more proactive stance is needed to address the differential life outcomes experienced by our young people. We concur with Vera and Speight (2003) who argued that multiculturally competent practice will be limited in its impact without a focus on promoting a more socially just world. It is our contention that in order to be well prepared to provide appropriate and culturally relevant career development services, one must adopt a social justice perspective.

Social Justice Perspective

While the multicultural competencies (American Psychological Association, 2003) describe the characteristics and qualities necessary for working with individuals from diverse cultural backgrounds, a social justice perspective expands the role of school counselors to include efforts to change the school context in ways that promote academic, interpersonal, and vocational success for youth. From a school-based social justice perspective, the primary goal is for youth to experience power and the ability to influence their academic and life outcomes in self-determined ways (Howard & Solberg, 2006). According to Prilleltensky (1997), traditional service delivery methods focus on working with individual clients in ways that encourage them to take ownership of the problem and establish a plan for ameliorating it. Traditional methods assume that problems lie within the individual and that the individual possesses the ability to address the problems that he or she may have in a relatively independent manner. Cognitive therapeutic methods, for example, focus on the beliefs of the individual as the source of the problem; treatment consists of helping the individual learn to become aware of the problematic thoughts and to actively challenge and replace them with more effective thoughts.

Prilleltensky (1997) articulated an Emancipatory Communitarian (EC) framework that is notably different from traditional service delivery methods. The EC framework identifies problems as being relational, such that both the individual and the context in which one finds one's self share responsibility for the development of the problem as well as its solutions. In school settings, the EC framework seems particularly applicable because school counselors can work with youth and the school context. For example, one of the authors helped a school decrease its truancy rate by working with the administration to establish a new late-arrival policy. Rather than having tardy youth wait in an atrium outside of school until they were processed one at a time, a new procedure was enacted whereby all youth who were late to school entered the cafeteria. Two things occurred when they entered: First, opera music playing, creating a situation that these youth found to be "unpleasant." Second, the students completed a short survey about the reasons for their tardiness. A paradox was created by the school whereby youth avoided being late so they did not have to listen to the opera music. As a result, the number of students late for school dropped substantially within 2 months time from approximately 100 per day to fewer than 25.

At the same time, an examination of youths' written statements regarding their tardiness revealed that many of them had legitimate reasons for being late. The administrators realized that it was not uncommon for these students to be responsible for dropping off siblings at elementary school in the morning making them late as a result. Now the administrators knew that many of these students wanted to arrive on time, but had family responsibilities that prevented them from doing so. Armed with this knowledge, they began to work with these students differently to address their tardiness. Such an intervention is consistent with an EC framework because the context that contributed to the problem was being addressed in ways that prevented the problem of late arrival from occurring while simultaneously empowering youth to influence the perceptions of administrators by writing down their reasons for being late.

A social justice perspective in school settings defines the problematic behavior of a student as an interpersonal problem between the individual and the context within which the problem occurs. As such, solutions to problem behaviors must involve changing both the individual and the context. From this perspective, youth are perceived as having potential, while the context is perceived as either facilitating the development of or subverting this potential. Rogers (1961) argued that at the root of one's problems are interpersonal relations that provide conditional regard. Within such contexts, one is challenged to actualize one's true potential. These types of contexts are deemed "oppressive" in nature. Currently, large populations of youth from diverse cultural and economic backgrounds are not achieving to their true potential, as indicated by persistent achievement gaps in standardized and college entrance examinations, differential dropout rates, and lower college participation rates (National Center for Education Statistics, 2001). This suggests that, at best, many schools are failing to facilitate equal levels of achievement across students and, at worst, they are contributing to oppressive conditions experienced by youth. Oppression occurs through policies and procedures that result in differential educational and economic outcomes for specific groups of individuals in our society. In the truancy example just discussed, administrators initially felt at some level that students were late for school because they did not value the importance of being on time and were not interested in learning. Waiting outside in the building atrium on a cold morning communicated to the students that the school did not care about their well-being. The school policy that required youth to wait outside and enter one at a time only contributed to the problem because any student anger was interpreted by school administrators as further evidence that they were not interested in school. Reorganizing the rules for being late facilitated more positive patterns of behavior in three ways: First, moving the youth inside to the cafeteria was appreciated by the students. Second, the opera music that was played created a different motivation for arriving on time. And, finally, students' written explanations for their chronic tardiness challenged the administrators' assumptions as to why students were late for school.

While changing the rules and resources that contribute to maintaining oppression is certainly important, according to Freire (1970), oppression operates most significantly at the psychological level. He argued that individuals in the oppressed category and individuals in positions of power share common beliefs that maintain the status quo. From this perspective, battling oppression is accomplished when both individuals—the oppressed and oppressor—become aware of their own unconscious beliefs and how the rules and resources within the context contribute to the problem. Friere's position allows schools to move away from attributing blame to focus instead on becoming aware of the shared responsibility that the school context has in maintaining differences in academic achievement. There is no doubt that youth from culturally diverse and lower economic backgrounds enter school with different levels of readiness. And there is no doubt that many families from lower income communities are working in jobs that do not allow them to participate as fully in their child's education as they would like. School counselors engage in EC when they work with their school to identify ways to address these challenges so that all youth achieve their highest potential.

In multicultural counseling, research has identified a number of models for understanding how unconscious belief patterns—worldviews—impact behavior. Four lines of research drawn from the multicultural literature are described here, including false versus critical consciousness, racial identity development models, White racial identity development models, and collectivism versus individualism. Each of these models offers school counselors useful tools for assessing how both students and educators approach their racial identity and their understanding of racial issues. Thus, an understanding of these models is important for the provision of culturally responsive career programs in schools.

False Versus Critical Consciousness

Recently, Quintana and Segura-Herrera (2003) catalogued the unconscious beliefs that influence one's racial identity into two categories. They described false consciousness as being marked by an internalized inferiority and mental colonization—a situation in which the oppressed have been convinced of the legitimacy of their oppression. Alternatively, critical consciousness is described as "contesting the legitimacy of the oppression . . . without reifying negative in-group stereotypes" (p. 275). Quintana and Segura-Herrera also described the conditions necessary for the development of critical consciousness. They explained that engaging in a critical examination of oppression and of the claims of "truth" used to justify it requires a certain level of sophistication of social cognitive abilities. They explained, "Being able to formulate a generalized group perspective for other racial groups provides an important development in the ability to contest the legitimacy of oppression as well as the truth claims attempting to justify the oppression" (p. 279).

Racial Identity Development Models

Other models of identity development attend to the degree to which individuals from diverse racial and ethnic backgrounds share in majority culture perspectives and practices, react against the majority culture, or have established integrated perspectives that allow them to participate in society in a self-determined manner (Ponterotto & Pederson, 1993). Although several models have dominated multicultural literature over the past several decades, the Minority Identity Model developed by Atkinson, Morten, and Sue (1998) includes many of the characteristics of these models. One shared feature is that these models consist of different worldview orientations (initially referred to as developmental stages). The first worldview orientation of the Atkinson et al., model is related to conformity to the majority culture. This worldview is characterized by the individual from a culturally diverse background maintaining a clear preference for the majority cultural values over their own cultural values. The second worldview orientation is labeled Dissonance and Appreciation. This worldview is characterized by the individual questioning and challenging of one's own beliefs and values, specifically those related to the assumptions regarding majority culture values. The third worldview orientation is entitled Resistance and Immersion. Individuals within this orientation actively challenge their beliefs and tend toward endorsing views and beliefs from their culture of origin while rejecting the majority culture values and beliefs. The fourth worldview orientation is Introspection. Individuals within this orientation begin to evaluate the efficacy of values and beliefs from both their culture of origin and the majority culture. Finally, the Integrative Awareness worldview orientation occurs when individuals develop an inner sense of security and an appreciation of one's cultural values and beliefs as well as the dominant culture's values and beliefs (Atkinson et al.).

White Racial Identity Development Models

A social justice perspective involves consciousness raising on the part of the individuals within the oppressed position *as well as* individuals within positions of power. The White Racial Identity Development model was established for individuals from White cultural backgrounds to evaluate the degree of conscious awareness they have developed regarding race and factors that maintain oppression (Helms, 1984, 1995). Helms (1995) described the worldview orientations as ego statuses and elaborated on the dynamic process involved in racial identity. According to Helms, the first ego status is called Contact Status. A person who possesses a Contact Status worldview orientation is one who lacks complete awareness of racism and factors within his or her community that contribute to racial differences. The Disintegration worldview orientation is characterized as an existential conflict the individual experiences whereby he or she begins to understand that differences do exist in how people from different racial/ethnic groups are treated, but simultaneously want to believe that his or her values and beliefs do not contribute to these differences. The Reintegration worldview orientation often evolves from the Disintegration orientation whereby the individual regresses to a pro-White values orientation and perception of inferiority as the main cause for perceived racial differences. The Pseudoindependence worldview orientation often occurs when a person is finally faced with an experience of injustice that cannot be accounted for by inferiority attributions. Such an orientation may involve renewed efforts at helping individuals from culturally diverse backgrounds to understand the White values and beliefs in order to avoid future injustice. The Immersion/Emersion worldview orientation involves becoming aware of White privilege and the ways that one contributes to racism. As a result, the individual is likely to become involved in efforts to educate other individuals from White backgrounds about privilege and work to actively intervene against racism. The Autonomy worldview orientation involves the strengthening of one's own understanding of one's White privilege and increasing understanding of the role one plays in supporting the continuation of racism.

Collectivism Versus Individualism

Another identity model evaluates whether the society in which a person lives operates according to an individualist or collectivist worldview orientation (Triandis, 1995). Individualist societies are those that value autonomy and perceive normal human development in terms of separating from the family through the articulation of unique and personal goals and attributes. Societies that value individualism are characterized as highly competitive and support meritocracy based on individuals' competing for status, recognition, and achievement.

Other societies rely on a collectivist orientation that values family over individual goals and cooperative versus competitive work environments. Collectivist cultures often have an interdependent nature, placing the needs and interests of the larger group over the desires of individuals (Triandis, 1995). This is clearly displayed within the family, when individuals in the family are expected to work together to fulfill needs and goals. Individuals with a collectivistic orientation often consider the benefits for everyone in the group not just individual needs. Thus, when they compete, they work to gain status, recognition, and achievement for their group as a whole. This orientation is sometimes hard for individuals in the mainstream U.S. culture to understand and is often overlooked when work-

Sample Characteristics of a Social Justice Perspective

- School counseling must contribute to achieving social equality and economic inequity by establishing culturally relevant strategies for narrowing the achievement gap.
- The achievement gap results from oppression operating in school settings and communities that contribute to youth from culturally diverse and low incomes from performing below their true potential.
- Intervention strategies battle against oppression when they help educators challenge prevailing worldviews that contribute to educational inequity.
- Intervention strategies battle against oppression when they establish intervention strategies that help youth experience power to influence their academic, interpersonal, and vocational outcomes.
- Problems youth experience are perceived as emerging from interpersonal problems between the individual and the context.

Figure 19.3 Social justice perspective.

ing with clients. Many times over, certain clients have been described as "dependent" without a thorough examination of their cultural background (Sue & Sue, 2003). From this perspective, oppression can also occur when someone whose culture of origin is collectivist is living within a society that values individualism. Oppression occurs when the individual in the oppressed position values a collectivist worldview while the person in the position of power values and judges others from an individualist worldview.

Social Justice and School Counseling

In order for school counselors to effectively address the academic, interpersonal, and vocational development needs of youth from diverse cultural and low-income backgrounds, they must maintain a social justice perspective that incorporates multicultural competence and an understanding of the complex individual and context interactions that maintain differential rates in achievement and life success (Figure 19.3). As such, school counselors must perceive their role as intervening both with youth and with the school context in order to eradicate the achievement gap, lower dropout rates, and increase the number of youth from diverse and low-income backgrounds participating in postsecondary education. At the core of these interventions are unconscious beliefs that are held by both youth and educators. Many of these beliefs consist of patterns, or worldview orientations, that can be understood in terms of the degree to which they possess a critical consciousness of their racial and ethnic background, their level of identity development, and/or the collectivist versus individualist perspective they hold (Figure 19.4).

In sum, the unequal academic, career, and economic outcomes of diverse and low-income youth require that school counselors develop and provide culturally responsive programs of career development. Such an undertaking necessitates the development of multicultural competencies and an adoption of a social justice perspective on the part of school counselors. It also requires school counsel-

Worldview Conceptualizations

False versus Critical Consciousness (Quintana and Segura-Herrera, 2003)

For individuals from culturally diverse backgrounds, false consciousness is characterized by internalized inferiority beliefs that result from sensing legitimacy of prevailing oppressive forces existing in one's community. Critical consciousness is achieved by challenging sources of oppression and claims of "truth."

Racial Identity Models (Ponterotto & Pederson, 1993)

For individuals from culturally diverse backgrounds, these models describe a number of worldview orientations associated with the degree of conformity to majority culture values and beliefs versus movement toward appreciation and value for one's own culture of origin.

White Racial Identity Models (Helms, 1995)

For individuals from White ethnic backgrounds, this model describes worldview orientations associated with becoming aware of racism and oppression. Worldviews range from a complete lack of awareness of racism to possessing an understanding of how one's personal privilege status contributes to racism.

Individualism versus Collectivism (Triandis, 1995)

Describes how cultures vary according to worldview orientations associated with individual, personal goals versus family, collective goals. Collectivist worldview orientations are associated with valuing cooperation versus competition, down playing personal achievements for the collective efforts, and maintaining group harmony versus striving for individual goals.

Figure 19.4 Worldview conceptualizations.

ors to be knowledgeable of both common and contemporary theoretical approaches to understanding the career development of youth. The next section of this chapter will briefly summarize relevant career theories and models of development.

Vocational and Career Development: Past and Present

Vocational guidance traces it roots to the beginning of the 20th century. During this time, the United States was experiencing frequent waves of immigration, an increasing industrialization of the work world, and a growing number of individuals and families moving from rural to urban areas. It was in this time that Frank Parsons (1909) established the Vocations Bureau in Boston, Massachusetts. The purpose of this bureau was to help youth and adults assess their interests and skills, learn about the world of work, and identify work opportunities that would allow them to utilize their skills while providing enjoyable work activities. Parsons argued that choosing a vocation involves the following three conditions:

> First, a clear understanding of yourself, aptitudes, abilities, interests, resources, limitations, and other qualities. Second, a knowledge of the requirements and conditions of success, advantages and disadvantages, compensation, opportunities and prospects in different lines of work. Third, true reasoning on the relations of these two groups of facts. (p. 5)

Parsons' early vocational work laid the foundation for the later person–environment fit models of vocational development (Baker & Gerler, 2004; Schmidt, 1999).

At the same time that Parsons was establishing the Vocations Bureau, early pioneers in this field were establishing vocational guidance programs in schools (Baker & Gerler, 2004; Schmidt, 1999). Individuals such as Anna Reed, Jesse Davis, and Eli Weaver (Gibson & Mitchell, 2003) were designing and implementing programs to assist youth in transitioning into the world of work. In 1910 Boston Public Schools became the first school district in the United States to begin assigning vocational counselors to elementary and secondary schools (Gysbers, 1997).

Beginning in the 1920s, Western countries saw the rise of the psychometric movement—a movement that was fueled by the development of intelligence testing by Binet in France. During World War I, the American military developed and began using the Army Alpha Test—an assessment designed to quickly determine the best placement for recruits. Soon, vocational guidance counselors began using testing techniques to determine the interests, personality characteristics, and relative strengths and weaknesses of their clients and, in school settings, youth (Baker & Gerler, 2004; Gibson & Mitchell, 2003; Schmidt, 1999). The decades of the 1950s and 1960s were intense periods of theory development in vocational psychology. During this period, theorists such as Ginzburg, Holland, Roe, Super, and Tiedeman provided professionals of career development with conceptual frameworks in which to ground their work (Schmidt).

Alarmed by the Soviet Union's successful launch of the Sputnik I satellite in 1957, the U.S. Congress passed the National Defense Education Act of 1958 (Public Law 85-846, U.S. Congress, 1958). Among other things, this act provided funding to high schools to identify and guide talented students into careers deemed as critical to the national good. It also improved and expanded school counselor preparation programs to meet the guidance needs created by the new NDEA funding. As a result, within the next 10 years the number of counselors in schools increased fourfold (Baker & Gerler, 2004; Schmidt 1999; U.S. Congress, 1958). Whereas traditional vocational guidance focused on helping youth transition into the world of work, the NDEA shifted the focus of the field to include the identification of individuals with math and science aptitude. These youth were often tracked into special course offerings to further develop their math and science skills.

Recent changes in the world of work and the advent of standards-based education (e.g., No Child Left Behind) have changed the role of vocational guidance, and with that has come a change in title from vocational guidance to school counselor. Current conceptualizations of the role of school counselors organize the foci of their work into three developmental domains: (a) academic, (b) interpersonal, and (c) vocational (ASCA, 2003). It is not uncommon for today's school counselors to feel pulled in multiple directions. Schools need school counselors to support their school improvement efforts to meet grade-level expectations as mandated under new federal legislation. Yet, youth will not be prepared to enter the world of work without requisite readiness skills. The Secretary's Commission for Achieving Necessary Skills (Resnick & Wirt, 1996; SCANS, 1992) provides a template of academic, social, technology, and related readiness skills that youth will need to be competitive in today's world of work. While it appears that school counselors are being faced with a multitude of responsibilities, the methods needed for being effective in each task are not mutually exclusive. For school counselors working with youth from culturally diverse and low-income backgrounds, their support of efforts to increase youth literacy and numeracy test scores, for example, can also result in improvements in academic achievement as well as better postsecondary readiness skills. Both of these outcomes position youth better for their post-high-school plans. In other words, school success is the foundation for career development.

Traditional Career Development Perspectives

Presently, vocational psychology and career development theory can be divided into three categories: (a) person–environment fit theories, (b) developmental theories, and (c) social cognitive theories.

Person-Environment Fit Theories

The rise of survey assessment methods in the early and mid-1900s brought about an emphasis in personality measurement. Assuming that personality consists of stable "traits," it was possible to identify the traits a person possessed and then match the individual to the types of work environments that effectively used those traits (Chartrand, Strong, & Weitzman, 1995). Holland's (1996) theory of vocational types and work environments is one of the best known person–environment fit theories. His Self-Directed Search (SDS) instrument allows youth to select from a variety of interests, skills, and occupations in order to generate scores that vary along six personality types: (a) realistic, (b) investigative, (c) artistic, (d) social, (e) enterprising, and (f) conventional. According to Holland, the six personality types emerge as dispositions within complex family contexts. While genetics plays a role in the formation of these types, interactions within the family and community shape their development. From a social justice perspective, the issue is whether youth from culturally diverse or low-income backgrounds receive the same range of opportunities for developing their personality type. While a family from a low-income background may expose their child to realistic-type experiences, corresponding assessment evaluations may confirm a realistic personality type, but one must wonder if there is a range of other dispositions that could emerge if the learning contexts offered other experiences. With art, music, and theater programs being cut from many schools in lower income areas, it is possible that youth may have a disposition for artistic-related career interests but may not be provided the opportunity to develop this part of their personality.

Holland (1996) recognized that personality does not consist of hard-wired traits. As dispositions, these types can be modified and will change through interactions with the environment. As a consequence, school counselors should consider waiting to use interest assessments until after they have provided youth with opportunities to explore different interests. The caution against interest assessment is advised especially for youth who have experienced lower academic achievement. Interest assessments designed to help these youth explore how their personality types may fit within the world of work and postsecondary opportunities should occur after they have experienced school success and have developed the confidence that they can succeed in school. Otherwise, their results will be more indicative of their low academic self-efficacy than their true interests or potential.

Developmental Theories

Developmental theories of vocational psychology focus on helping youth develop a healthy self-concept. Super's Life-Span, Life Space theory is the best known of these theories (Super, 1953, 1990; Super, Savickas, & Super, 1996). Similar to person–environment fit models, this theory views career choice as an extension of one's selfhood processes. Super posited that each individual carries with him or her a unique set of interests, abilities, goals, and values. Work settings, too, have unique combinations of values, abilities required, etc. Individuals, by virtue of their constellation of interests, values, and abilities, can "fit" well within various types of work settings (Super, 1953, 1990; Super et al., 1996).

According to Super (1953, 1990), individuals construct self-concepts (e.g., of self as worker) through feedback from themselves and important others. Self-concepts develop throughout childhood and adolescence and become relatively stable as an individual matures. Super et al. (1996) defined self-concept as "a product of the interaction of inherited aptitudes, physical makeup, opportunity to observe and play various roles, and evaluations of the extent to which the results of role-playing meet with the approval of supervisors and peers" (p. 125). Occupational choice is one instance of the implementation of self-concepts. Thus, this theory posits that career choices are influenced by one's natural abilities and acquired skills, one's occupationally related experiences, vicarious learning, and feedback from significant others such as parents, authority figures, siblings, and peers. School counselors can support the development of a healthy self-concept by providing elementary and middle school youth with world-of-work experiences. By visiting various work environments and meeting individuals from similar cultural or socioeconomic backgrounds, youth have the opportunity to meet important role models. During adolescence and into young adulthood, school counselors should offer experiences that help youth explore career options, learn how to secure selected career options, and develop a plan of action with regard to how they will begin realizing these career options (Super, 1953, 1990; Super et al.).

Social Cognitive Theories

Social cognitive theories of career development make up the third general category of career theories. Emerging from the application of Bandura's (1986) social cognitive theory to vocational development (Betz & Hackett, 1981), social cognitive career theory (SCCT) is a model of vocational development that focuses on how one's occupational self-efficacy beliefs determine the direction of one's career interests (Lent, Brown, & Hackett, 1994). According to Bandura, self-efficacy is defined as the confidence one feels in one's ability to successfully perform a specific task. Occupational self-efficacy refers to one's confidence in his or her ability to perform tasks associated with specific occupations. Betz and Hackett's seminal application of Bandura's work found that women who were confident in their ability to complete math and science related tasks expressed stronger career interests in those fields. In the context of 1981, women were facing a number of challenges with regard to entering what at that time were termed "nontraditional" careers.

Bandura (1986) has empirically validated four ways in which the learning context could be designed to promote self-efficacy. An individual's confidence beliefs associated with a given occupation increase when he or she is provided with learning opportunities that offer mastery experiences, modeling (vicarious) experiences, verbal persuasion, and anxiety management (Bandura). Mastery experiences involve the successful performance of the targeted skill, while modeling refers to watching someone successfully perform the skill. Verbal persuasion involves someone such as a school counselor or teacher expressing a belief in the person's ability to successfully perform the task by pointing out other related skills the person possesses. The final source refers to developing the skills needed to manage the anxiety often associated with learning new tasks. Breathing and relaxation exercises are two avenues for helping in this regard.

Fouad and Smith (1996) tested the social cognitive career theory with a diverse population of predominately Latino and African American, urban middle school youth. Consistent with social cognitive career theory, results indicated that self-efficacy expectations related to math/science, decision-making, and outcome expectations were associated with career interests in math and science. Also, interest in math/science careers was related to intentions to complete math and science courses and, unexpectedly, self-efficacy was also directly related to these intentions. Fouad and Smith also found a strong relationship between self-efficacy and outcome expectations; that is, youth who felt able to successfully perform math and science tasks also believed that math and science pursuits would help them achieve desirable outcomes.

Bandura's social cognitive theory has also been applied to "career search self-efficacy" (V. S. Solberg, 1998) and academic self-efficacy (Multon, Brown, & Lent, 1991). Career search self-efficacy refers to an individual's confidence in his or her ability to successfully perform career search tasks such as exploring career values and interests, conducting job interviews, seeking out information about possible careers, and networking with peers and others who may offer job leads. Career search self-efficacy has been found to be linked to a number of interpersonal and vocational outcomes. Individuals with high career search self-efficacy have indicated higher assertiveness and more career readiness, and they have engaged in more career exploration (V. S. Solberg, 1998). Academic self-efficacy refers to one's confidence for performing specific classroom learning tasks such as reading textbooks, asking questions, and relating to peers. This type of self-efficacy has been found to be an important determinant of school success. In a meta-analysis of the literature, Multon et al. found that academic self-efficacy yielded a medium effect size with regard to school outcomes. This means that academic self-efficacy should be considered a central contributing factor in school performance. Youth with higher academic self-efficacy expectations are more likely to perform better, persist longer when performing challenging tasks, and approach challenging tasks rather than avoid them.

The SCCT model has also been extended to the study of school engagement. Recently, Wettersten et al. (2005) successfully created and tested such a model with rural high school youth. Specifically, they found that students' academic self-efficacy and outcome expectations, career outcome expectations, perceived level of social support, and parents' involvement in their education accounted for 40% of the variance in their school engagement attitudes. While not as strong, results also indicated that this model successfully predicted a significant amount of the variance in school engagement behaviors, such as time spent on various academic courses. In sum, the SCCT model is a useful tool for school counselors wishing to create programs that support youths' school engagement as well as their academic and career development.

Social Justice and Traditional Career Theory

Person-environment fit approaches were initially used with adult populations in order to help match personality traits to occupations that were deemed to support those traits. As mentioned earlier, we caution the use of interest assessments with youth for a number of reasons. First, with regard to youth development, personality is in formation during childhood and adolescence, and there are differences of opinion with regard to whether personality consists of traits or modifiable dispositions (Lerner, 2002). Consistent with life-span, life-space theory, it is essential that all youth receive a full range of opportunities to explore the world of work and become aware of the relevance and value of education to one's developing identity. Moreover, school counselors should focus their efforts on collaborating with educators in schools to establish the conditions for optimal growth and development. Social cognitive applications to career development describe four sources of self-efficacy beliefs that can be used to design such experiences. In addition, a number of contemporary developmental perspectives are described here that offer additional ideas in regard to designing school experiences in ways that maximize youth development (Figure 19.5).

Contemporary Developmental Perspectives

Developmental Contextualism

Developmental contextualism (DC; Lerner, 1995) is a metatheory that describes how academic, interpersonal, and career development emerge from complex interactions between youth and the various systems in which youth are embedded. Drawing from Bronfenbrenner (1979), three interrelated systems include (a) microsystems, (b) exosystems, and (c) macrosystems. Microsystems involve direct interactions youth encounter in school, home, and community. Exosystemic factors indirectly impact youth development through their influence on microsystems.

Traditional Career Development and Contemporary Developmental Theory

Person–Environment Fit (Chartrand, Strong, & Weitzman, 1995)

Successful transitions into work are expected when individuals make career decisions that represent a fit between personality traits and skills, and occupations that need those traits and skills. Assessment tools are often used to evaluate personality traits, interests, and skills and then offer individuals a fit index with regard to a range of occupational possibilities.

Life-Span, Life Space (Super, Savickas, & Super, 1996)

Evaluates the role of work as one role within the person's self-concept. Developmental in nature, this theory encourages exposure to various occupational settings in order to help individuals develop an understanding of different opportunities.

Social Cognitive Theory (Bandura, 1986)

From social cognitive theory, the concept of self-efficacy has been applied to career development through the Social Cognitive Career Theory (Lent, Brown, & Hackett, 1994), academic self-efficacy (Multon, Brown, & Lent, 1991), and career search self-efficacy (V.S. Solberg, 1998). This theory provides four developmental sources of self-efficacy which has been defined as one's confidence to successfully perform a targeted task.

Developmental Contextualism (Lerner, 2002)

A meta-theory that conceptualizes development in terms of human potential being realized only through supportive contexts that effectively promote growth. As such, the context – such as the school or classroom – becomes the focus of interventions rather than the individual.

Developmental Assets (Search Institute, 2002)

The Search Institute has identified 40 individual and contextual factors that promote optimal development. Divided into 20 external (i.e., contextual) and 20 individual characteristics, youth possessing more assets and who are embedded in environments that offer more assets demonstrate better academic outcomes.

Selection, Optimization, and Compensation Model (SOC) (Baltes, 1997)

Research indicates that helping individuals make better life transitions occurs when they learn how to select a few goals, optimize their chances of achieving a goal by taking advantage of opportunities to develop the skills, and are able to compensate by selecting back-up goals when challenges are too great.

Self-Determination Theory (Deci & Ryan, 1985)

Individuals who are learning in environments in which they feel connected to adults in authority and peers will perform the activities because they are enjoyable and meaningful. In school settings, youth will become motivated to engage in school when interventions focus on building stronger relational connections between youth and their teachers and peers.

Figure 19.5 Traditional career development and contemporary developmental theory.

For example, the quality of work available to a parent or guardian impacts youth through the amount of financial resources available to the home and the energy and enthusiasm the parent or guardian may have when at home. Differential school resources impact youth in relation to quality of textbooks, access to technology, and the quality of the school environment. McLoyd (1998) described in detail how living in lower income communities severely impacts one's ability to actualize his or her true potential. Macrosystems involve the cultural context and history of the community and society. One primary assertion in DC is that the various systems in which youth interact are interconnected such that change in one area can impact other areas. While it is clearly understood that what happens in students' home lives can seriously impact their school performance, from a DC perspective, the school counselor can still promote development even though he or she may not be able to intervene directly in the family system. Instead, school counselors can provide opportunities for youth to learn how to cope with these home pressures, and thus indirectly support the well-being and continued academic success of their students. In severe situations, school counselors can mobilize social service providers in the community to provide support and intervention. As the home becomes more stable, youth will be better able to focus on learning. As such, positive development and change that occur in school impact home and vice versa. DC also emphasizes that the impact of school-based interventions that help at-risk youth generate conceptions of self as a "competent learner" can extend beyond the school walls. This new conception of self can serve to encourage youth to seek out experiences both at home and in the community that support and reinforce the belief that one is a skilled and curious seeker of knowledge (Ford & Lerner, 1992). With regard to school counseling, DC conceptualizes education as a powerful learning context that can positively shape youth development, regardless of income levels and home situations. Consistent with the *ASCA National Model* (ASCA, 2003), DC challenges school counselors to examine the types and quality of the learning experiences they offer to youth and to design such experiences so as to facilitate youths' realization of their true potential with regard to academic, interpersonal, and vocational development.

Developmental Assets

The Search Institute in Minnesota has been studying the individual and contextual variables—called developmental assets—that support positive youth development. They have identified 40 developmental assets that include 20 external and 20 internal assets. The 20 external assets are organized into four categories that include (a) support, (b) empowerment, (c) boundaries and expectations, and (d) constructive use of time. Similarly, the 20 internal assets are also grouped into four categories: (a) commitment to learning, (b) positive values, (c) social competencies, and (d) positive identity. Research indicates that youth who reported possessing more assets are found to experience better life and academic outcomes (Figure 19.6). In a longitudinal study conducted by Scales and Roehlkepartain (2003), it was found that the level of developmental assets present in youths' lives during the ninth grade was significantly correlated with their ninth-grade GPA. This relationship continues to exist even after controlling for gender, family composition, socioeconomic status, and race/ethnicity (Scales & Roehlkepartain; Sesma & Roehlkepartain, 2003).

Selection, Optimization, and Compensation Model

The selection, optimization, and compensation (SOC) model developed by Paul Baltes and colleagues (Baltes, 1997; Freund & Baltes, 1998) contends that there are three sets of strategies that individuals use in their strivings to be successful. Individuals are more likely to achieve their desired goals when they (1) selectively choose future goals, (2) develop methods to optimize their chances for success, and (3) utilize compensatory strategies when faced with barriers or losses. Thus far, this model has effectively predicted positive health outcomes among aging (Freund & Baltes) and adult populations (Wiese, Freund, & Baltes, 2000). Application of the SOC model to youth populations seems especially relevant to youth career interventions because it focuses not just on selecting an occupational choice, but also on how youth maximize the skills and opportunities available to them in order to achieve the occupational choice, as well as how they manage when the path to that occupational choice is particularly challenging or potentially blocked.

Self-Determination Theory

Self-determination theory describes a model of motivation that focuses on four reasons youth will perform a task, such as attending school. Whereas social cognitive theory focuses on youth's belief in their ability to perform a task, self-determination theory (Deci & Ryan, 1985) is concerned with *why* youth are motivated to perform the task. While social cognitive theory is concerned with whether "I think I can" perform the task, self-determination theory is concerned with "why do I want to" perform the task. According to self-determination theory, there are four types of motivation involved in performing a task—two external

External Assets

Support
Family support, positive family communication, other adult relationships, caring neighborhood, caring school climate, and parent involvement in schooling

Empowerment
Community values youth, youth as resources, service to others, safety

Boundaries and Expectations
Family boundaries, school boundaries, neighborhood boundaries, adult role models, positive peer influence, and high expectations

Constructive Use of Time
Creative activities, youth programs, religious community, and time at home

Internal Assets

Commitment to Learning
Achievement motivation, school engagement, homework, bonding to school, and reading for pleasure

Positive Values
Caring, equality and social justice, integrity, honesty, responsibility, and restraint

Social Competencies
Planning and decision-making, interpersonal competence, cultural competence, resistance skills, and peaceful conflict resolution

Positive Identity
Personal power, self-esteem, sense of purpose, and positive view of personal future

Figure 19.6 Search Institute's developmental assets. (Reprinted with permission from *The Asset Approach: 40 Elements of Healthy Development.* Copyright © 2002 by Search Institute[SM], Minneapolis, MN.)

and two internal. The two external reasons include performing the task so that others will not be let down or feeling forced to perform the task. The two internal reasons include performing the task because it is enjoyable or because it is perceived as meaningful. Self-determination theory also prescribes the conditions within which youth will be more likely to perform the tasks because it is enjoyable or meaningful. These include learning contexts in which youth feel strong connections to their teachers and peers.

A study by Close (2002) integrated social cognitive and self-determination theories in a study of predominately Latino urban high school youth. She found that students reporting stronger connections with teachers and peers were more likely to report that they attended school because it was meaningful and enjoyable (internal motivation). She also found that students who were confident in their ability to perform the academic tasks (academic self-efficacy) and were attending school because it was enjoyable and meaningful recorded higher attendance and grades. The implication of this research is that the sources of self-efficacy and internal motivation can be found in the classroom context. Armed with an understanding of how to promote the development of academic self-efficacy and internal motivation, school counselors can work with teachers in classroom settings to create optimal learning contexts (V. S. Solberg, Howard, Blustein, & Close, 2002).

Career Interventions Research

Career development research with youth has not enjoyed the same level of interest as research on career development of adults, especially college-aged adults (Whiston, Sexton, & Lasoff, 1998). Similarly, research assessing the impact of career *interventions* is not conducted as readily as research that examines aspects of career development more generally. Nevertheless, there is much to be learned from a review of the small body of available career intervention research with youth. This research has covered such diverse topics as personal definitions of occupational success and career decision-making self-efficacy and has focused primarily on interventions with middle school and high school youth.

Sample research

As explained earlier, one important area of focus in the field of vocational development is the confidence that individuals feel for performing various career-related tasks. Several researchers have explored the ability of various interventions to improve youths' career self-efficacy. Through a series of activities, discussions, and observations of role models, O'Brien and her colleagues were able to raise middle school youths' beliefs that they had the skills necessary to engage in career planning and exploration activities and that they had the academic skills necessary to pursue career paths of interest to them (O'Brien, Dukstein, Jackson, Tomlinson, & Kamatuka, 1999). Turner and Lapan (2005) were also able to successfully improve these same areas of career self-efficacy by utilizing a computer-based program that includes two exploration and career development activities as well as an interpretation and discussion session with a counselor. Kraus and Hughey (1999) targeted career decision-making self-efficacy specifically and found that their eight-session course assisted female students to become more confident.

Along with feeling confident in one's ability to engage in career development tasks, one must also be able to use a range of career exploration activities so as to capitalize upon the exploration opportunities that are presented. Jones, Sheffield, & Joyner (2000) found that, while there is some variation from instrument to instrument, interest inventories can encourage youth to use various approaches to career exploration. Engagement in career planning and exploration activities, active decision making, and pursuing and using occupational information can be successfully fostered by parent–student activities (Palmer & Cochran, 1988). Further, engagement in exploration behaviors is also impacted by the importance one assigns to making a career choice (Jones et al., 2000). Thus, timing of interventions designed to teach exploration behaviors may be important to consider. During times when youth are being asked to make decisions for their future plans (e.g., 8th graders choosing high school courses; high school students planning for post–high school), they may be particularly ready to learn career exploration strategies.

Just as important as the confidence one has for engaging in the process and tasks of career development and the actual career exploration behaviors one uses is the number of occupations one considers. As Gottfredson (1981) asserted, youth narrow the range of occupations that they believe are appropriate for them by a number of variables including gender typing. Thus, for many interventionists and practitioners, the focus of their work is to stall and, it is hoped, reverse this trend of circumscription. Programs of career development (e.g., O'Brien et al., 1999) and even career interest inventories (Jones, 2000) can help youth to increase the number of occupations they consider as possibilities for themselves, as well as the congruence between their personal characteristics (e.g., skills, interests, and abilities) and occupations considered (O'Brien et al.). Further, programs that actively engage youth in identifying and challenging traditional notions of career gender typing encourage both males and females to consider a broader range of nontraditional careers (Turner & Lapan, 2005). Similarly, a four-session curriculum designed to help youth explore and reflect on what they value in life and translate those values into a thoughtful definition of life success assisted youth to define success in broader, more holistic terms that de-emphasized material goods and emphasized enjoyment, satisfaction, and overall quality of life (Mosconi & Emmett, 2003).

Lapan and colleagues (Lapan, Tucker, Kim, & Kosciulek, 2003) investigated the impact that school-to-work partnership programs have on the career development of rural youth. Results indicated that the career guidance curricula used in the school-to-work programs and the level of teacher and counselor support perceived by youth positively impacted youth outcomes such as career-related self-efficacy, engagement in career exploration activities, and work-readiness skills. Youth who experienced improvements in their level of career development were more likely to aspire to continue their education and/or training after high school and were more likely to feel satisfied with the preparation they had received. Perceived support and the guidance curricula also had small, but important effects on both post-high-school plans and satisfaction with preparation (Lapan, Tucker, et al., 2003).

Further, both Schlossberg, Morris, & Lieberman (2001) and Lapan, Gysbers, Hughey, and Arni (1993) explored the impact of classroom-based career interventions on various career development competencies. Specifically, it was found that such programs improved students' knowledge of careers, their abilities to explore and plan for careers, and to make decisions about post-high plans, and to understand how gender relates to jobs and careers (Lapan et al., 1993). Students reported high levels of satisfaction with the intervention. Youth who made progress on the competencies also demonstrated higher postintervention vocational identity scores (Lapan et al., 1993).

Meta-Analyses Related to Career Interventions

Also important to our summary of relevant school-based career intervention research is a review of several important meta-analyses (Brown & Ryan Krane, 2000; Whiston, Sexton, & Lasoff, 1998) of career intervention efficacy conducted over the past 10 years. Both the Whiston, Sexton, and Lasoff and the Brown and Ryan Krane meta-analyses were undertaken to update and expand upon previously published meta-analyses (i.e., Oliver & Spokane, 1988; Spokane & Oliver, 1983). Whiston et al. found an average effect size of .45, indicating that career interventions, in general, demonstrated a moderate level of effectiveness. Stated another way, career interventions produced meaningful and moderately strong improvements in career development. School-based career interventions, too, were found to be effective, especially those at the middle school level. In fact, of all age groups included in this study, middle school students appeared to benefit the most from career interventions. Intuitively it makes sense that middle school students are a particularly impressionable group. For many youth, middle school (and 8th grade in particular) is the first time that they are asked to make decisions based upon their career interests. They are confronted with the task of needing to choose courses for high school and, thus, to consider what types of courses would best prepare them for potential career paths.

Both meta-analyses also examined the impact of various types of career interventions. While results varied some between the two analyses, they both consistently found that individual and group career counseling activities as well as classroom-based interventions were more powerful than self-directed and counselor-free activities (Brown & Ryan Krane, 2000; Whiston et al.). However, when examined by level of impact of the intervention by cost per individual, classroom-based and computer-based interventions surpassed individual and group counseling activities in their usefulness and their efficiency (Whiston et al., 1998).

The impact of an intervention also varied by the number of sessions included. Specifically, it was found that effect sizes rose steadily across sessions until reaching the 4 to 6 sessions mark (Brown & Ryan Krane, 2000; Whiston et al.), and again at 9 to 10 sessions (Whiston et al.). This is important information for school counselors to have as they are planning their career development curriculum.

Finally, Brown and Ryan Krane (2000) also coded studies not just by intervention type and number, but also by components of interventions. They found that out of 18 possible treatment components, five components were most influential. These included written exercises, individualized interpretations and feedback, world of work information, modeling opportunities, and attention to building support for choices within one's social network. Studies that included one component had average effect sizes of .45 (moderate effect); those with two components had effect sizes of .61; and those with three components had large effect sizes of .99. No studies were found that included 4 or 5 of these components. This information is particularly useful to school counselors and other interventionists as it provides clear guidance as to the types of activities and program elements that should be included in career development curricula.

Practice

Having reviewed traditional theories of career development and contemporary developmental models as well as research on career interventions, it is now time to focus our attention on the practice of culturally responsive career programming for youth. The literature previously reviewed provides guidance as to key aspects of such work. In the remainder of this chapter, we will offer practice recommendations for school counselors and describe two examples of career development programs for youth that were designed to be culturally responsive in nature.

First, the growing diversity in our nation's population makes it clear that multicultural competence is necessary for effective, respectful school counseling practice. Research by Lapan and colleagues (1997) demonstrated that even very effective school counseling programs may not provide opportunities for low-income and diverse youth to experience the same levels of success as their White, middle-class peers. Efforts to create career development programming for culturally diverse and low-income youth must be based upon a solid knowledge of diverse cultural practices and beliefs, models of acculturation and racial identity development, and worldview orientations.

A multicultural perspective is not, however, sufficient on its own. Vera and Speight (2003) have articulated well the need to expand our professional work to include a commitment to promoting a more socially just world. School counselors cannot ignore the serious economic consequences of the achievement gap that impact the life outcomes of this nation's culturally diverse and low-income youth. Embracing a social justice perspective expands the role of school counselor from solely engaging in one-on-one treatment strategies to focusing on creating a school context that promotes youth development academically, interpersonally, and vocationally. Thus, by incorporating a social justice perspective into one's work, school counselors commit themselves to intervening at the system's level within (and perhaps outside of) the school to shape policies and create programs that are designed to support optimal development for all youth.

Furthermore, youth will benefit both immediately and in the long term from opportunities to develop the competence and skills necessary to enter *and succeed in* postsecondary settings, such as 2-year and 4-year colleges. Career interventions should be designed with this purpose in mind. The Secretary's Commission for Achieving Necessary Skills (Resnick & Wirt, 1996; SCANS, 1992) describes the range of skills and dispositions necessary to be effective in transitioning into the world of work. The SCANS report is consistent with the *ASCA National Model* (ASCA, 2003), which identifies the role of school counselors as promoting development in three domains: (a) academic, (b) interpersonal, and (c) career. SCANS clearly articulates that one's ability to transition into the world of work is predicated upon an integration of all three of these areas. According to this report, in order for youth to make effective work transitions, they must possess basic literacy and numeracy skills, be able to think critically, and possess personal qualities such as honesty and integrity. In addition to the basic skills, a number of competencies were also outlined in the SCANS report. These competencies include managing time effectively, interpersonal skills, the ability to gather and use information, understanding the relatedness of various systems, and use of technology (Figure 19.7). It is recommended that educators and interventionists who work with youth from culturally diverse and lower income backgrounds should create career interventions that integrate the academic and interpersonal domains. The focus of intervention efforts should be on helping develop competent learners who understand how to navigate the world of work and possess the skills needed to make effective school-to-work-to-life transitions (V. S. Solberg, Howard, et al., 2002).

Next, academic, career, and life success is supported by a number of internal and external protective factors described in the resilience and developmental assets literature. Professionals can create interventions that help youth develop internal and interpersonal assets, such as academic self-efficacy, internalized motivation, stress and health management skills, and relational connections with family members, teachers, and peers. Further, they can work at the school level to create programs and policies that offer opportunities for youth empowerment, provide supportive relationships, and allow youth a range of creative, enriching extracurricular options.

Finally, research indicates that the effectiveness of career interventions will be stronger when they are conducted in classroom or group settings (Whiston et al., 1998). Brown and Ryan Krane (2000) further espoused that career interventions will be more effective when the classroom or group methods incorporate a number of key ingredients, which include the following: written exercises, individualized interpretations and feedback, world-of-work information, modeling opportunities, and attention to building support for choices within one's social network. Theory and research also suggest additional ingredients that should be considered. From social cognitive theory (Bandura, 1986), adding mastery, vicarious, and anxiety management experiences will increase youth's confidence for performing the tasks outlined in the intervention. From self-determination theory (Deci & Ryan, 1985), interventions that incorporate activities designed to establish stronger relational connections between youth and their teachers and peers will result in youth engaging in the career activities because they find them enjoyable and meaningful (Figure 19.8).

Sample Programs

We will now turn our attention to two examples of culturally responsive career intervention programs that were derived from research and theory: the Career Horizons (O'Brien et al., 1999) and the Achieving Success Identity Pathways (V. S. Solberg, Close, & Metz, 2002; V. A. Solberg et al., 1998) programs.

Necessary Skills and Competencies (based on SCANS, 1992)

Basic Skills
Reading, writing, arithmetic, listening, and speaking

Thinking Skills
Creative thinking, decision-making, problem-solving, visualization, knowing how to learn, and reasoning

Personal Qualities
Responsibility, self-esteem, sociability, self-management, integrity/honesty

Competency Areas
Resources
Time management, money management, material and facilities, able to evaluate others

Interpersonal
Participates as member of a team, teaches skills to others, serves customer, exercises leadership, negotiates, and works well with diverse populations

Information
Acquires, evaluates, organizes, interprets information

Systems
Understands systems, monitors and corrects performance, improves based on feedback

Technology
Selects technology, applies technology to tasks, can problem-solve technology related issues

Figure 19.7 Secretary's Commission for Achieving Necessary Skills.

Effective Career Curriculum Ingredients

Written exercises[1]
Individualized interpretations and feedback[1]
World-of-work information[1]
Modeling/vicarious opportunities[1,2]
Building support networks[1]
Mastery experiences[2]
Verbal persuasion[2]
Anxiety management[2]
Building social connections between youth, adults and peers[3]

Figure 19.8 Effective career curriculum ingredients. [1]Brown & Ryan Krane, 2000; [2]Bandura, 1996; [3]Deci & Ryan, 1986.

Career Horizons

The Career Horizons program was designed to increase career readiness skills among middle school youth from culturally diverse and lower income backgrounds (O'Brien et al., 1999). This summer transition program targeted youth who were deemed by their sixth-grade teachers as at risk for academic difficulties. Career Horizons was designed to increase student's confidence to explore and plan for careers, increase self-knowledge, improve student's perceived relevance with regard to the importance of math and science, and increase the range of career interests. A series of 20 classroom-based sessions were provided to youth (details of the curriculum may be obtained by contacting Karen O'Brien). Throughout the intervention, the curricula incorporated exploration activities designed to increase youths' self-efficacy for performing the specific tasks. For example, in a class devoted to increasing math and science interests, role models not only discussed the range of career options related to their area of math and science and the importance of math and science in relation to many career options, but also supervised an activity in which youth performed hands-on experiments. O'Brien et al. used measures drawn from the Missouri Comprehensive Guidance Evaluation Survey (Gysbers, Lapan, Multon, & Lukin, 1992) to evaluate whether exposure to the program was associated with increased career search self-efficacy. They reported significant differences between pre- and posttest scores such that students exposed to Career Horizons reported more confidence in being able to engage in career planning and career exploration, more awareness regarding the relevance of math and science to academic and career interests, and an increased number of career options.

Career Horizons attempts to increase youth's career readiness competence as a method for helping at-risk youth from culturally diverse and low-income backgrounds make more effective transitions into middle school. This program clearly incorporates a number of the practice strategies related to social justice. As part of its design, Career Horizons includes at least 11 of the developmental assets identified by the Search Institute as being related to competence. With regard to external assets, the program offers adult role models, promotes positive peer influences, maintains high expectations, and offers creative activities. With regard to internal assets, the program helps youth engage in planning and decision making; fosters school engagement, achievement motivation, and bonding to school; and encourages the development of a sense of personal power and purpose as well as a positive view of one's future. With regard to the design of the curriculum, Career Horizons incorporated a number of processes identified by Brown and Ryan Krane (2000) as well as related research and theory as being influential in promoting youth competence. Specifically, the program offers mastery and vicarious experiences whereby youth are able to learn by doing and watching others perform various tasks. Youth received knowledge about the world of work, engaged in written exercises, and received individualized assessment information. Youth were also engaged in social support activities.

Achieving Success Identity Pathways

The Achieving Success Identity Pathways (ASIP; formally titled the Academic Success Identity Plan) is a curriculum school counselors can use to challenge all students to improve academically (V. A. Solberg et al.; V. S. Solberg, Close, & Metz, 2002, 1998). The goal of the program is to help youth build "success identities" and the skills needed to make effective school to work-to-life transitions. The curriculum is implemented in classroom settings and consists of the ASIP Navigator, Hear My Story, and Action Theater. The ASIP Navigator provides youth with individualized feedback about how they perceive their academic self-efficacy, motivation, health, stress, and social support. Through classroom conversations about these topics, youth are provided the opportunity to share their life experiences, discuss career goals, and listen as the school counselor, teachers, and peers discuss their experiences as well. Youth complete a workbook that helps them articulate their challenges and develop self-determined plans of action. Hear My Story encourages youth, the school counselor, and their teacher to write about their lives according to any number of strategies including poetry and autobiographical short stories and then share their writings with the class. Action Theater uses sculpting exercises, short plays, and live improvisational techniques to help youth learn the nature of how problem and success behaviors evolve during their daily experiences, Close, & Metz.

The ASIP program was derived from theory and research (Solber, Closer, & Metz, 2002) in academic self-efficacy (e.g., Zimmerman, 1995; Zimmerman, Bandura, &

Martinez-Ponz, 1992), vocational self-efficacy (e.g., Betz & Hackett, 1981; Lent, Brown, & Hackett, 1994), motivation (e.g., Deci & Ryan, 1985), and social support (e.g., Wentzel, 1998; Wickrama, Lorenz, & Conger, 1997), as well as best practices in vocational education (e.g., Brown & Ryan Krane, 2000) and group theory (e.g., Yalom, 1995). ASIP was piloted in an urban high school that serves lower income youth of predominately Latino background. The student population consisted of about 65% Latino youth and about half of these youth were classified as English language learners. African American youth compose the second largest ethnic group (20%) and 90% of the youth receive free or reduced lunch. Due to the large number of Spanish-speaking youth and low entering-reading levels, the curriculum has been translated into Spanish and is written in both English and Spanish for a fourth-grade reading level. Evaluations of the program's effectiveness indicate that youth who were exposed to three or more classroom experiences using the ASIP curricula recorded better grades, more credits earned, and higher end-of-semester attendance (V. S. Solberg, 2001, 2005). Grade improvements were found to continue 2 years following intervention (V. S. Solberg, Carlstrom, & Kowalchuk, 2001). More importantly, the program has been credited with helping to transform a low-performing school by helping students establish stronger relationships with teachers and peers and helping teachers establish a clearer understanding of the challenges facing their lower income students.

ASIP attempts to increase youth's competence to make effective transitions into high school. The program incorporates a number of the practice strategies related to social justice. Throughout the curriculum, students are encouraged to define for themselves the challenges they experience and to express their personal stories in their own terms through conversation, written exercises, and theater. ASIP incorporates at least 21 of the developmental assets identified by the Search Institute as being related to competence. With regard to external assets, the program encourages family support, positive family communication, relationships with adults, a caring school climate, and a community that values youth; it views youth as a resource, addresses safety in school and the community, reinforces school boundaries and clear consequences, provides adult role models, encourages positive peer influences, holds high expectations, and offers creative activities. With regard to internal assets, the program encourages planning and decision making, school engagement, achievement motivation, bonding to school, equality and social justice, interpersonal competence, cultural competence, personal power, sense of purpose, and positive view of one's future. With regard to the design of the curriculum, ASIP also incorporates a number of key ingredients identified by Brown and Ryan Krane (2000) as well as related research and theory as being influential in promoting youth competence. Specifically, the program offers mastery and vicarious experiences whereby youth are able to learn by doing and watching others perform various tasks. Youth receive knowledge about the world of work, engage in written exercises, and receive individualized assessment information. Youth also receive opportunities for establishing stronger connections with teachers and peers.

Conclusion

As our nation's population continues to grow more diverse, school counselors will increasingly be challenged to create and provide culturally responsive comprehensive school counseling programs. By focusing on the provision of services that offer opportunities for all youth to realize their academic, career, and personal potential, school counselors are promoting a more socially just society for the youth with whom they work. Culturally responsive career development programming will rest on a base of cultural knowledge and competence, will incorporate a commitment to social justice, and will provide opportunities for youth to develop the academic and transitioning skills needed to pursue and excel in their postsecondary plans. Further, it will promote the development of the resilience characteristics and internal assets that support positive outcomes for youth and will incorporate a range of external assets and protective factors as well. Finally, culturally appropriate career programming will be informed by research and theory of "best practices," and will include aspects of interventions that have been found to contribute to positive career development outcomes.

References

Aizcorbe, A. M., Kennickell, A. B., & Moore, K. B. (2003, January). Recent changes in U.S. family finances: Evidence from the 1998 and 2001 survey of consumer finances. *Federal Reserve Bulletin, Board of Governors of the Federal Reserve System (U.S.)*, 1–32.

American Psychological Association. (2003). Guidelines on multicultural education, training, research, practice, and organizational change for psychologists. *American Psychologist, 58,* 377–402.

American School Counselor Association. (2003). *The ASCA national model: A framework for school counseling programs.* Alexandria, VA: Author.

Arbona, C. (2000). The development of academic achievement in school aged children: Precursors to career development. In S. D. Brown & R. W. Lent (Eds.), *Handbook of counseling psychology* (3rd ed., pp. 270–309). New York, NY: John Wiley & Sons, Inc.

Atkinson, D. R., Morten, G., & Sue, D. W. (1998). *Counseling American minorities* (5th ed.). Boston: McGraw-Hill.

Baker, S. B., & Gerler, E. R., Jr. (2004). *School counseling for the twenty-first century* (4th ed.). Columbus, OH: Pearson.

Baltes, P. B. (1997). On the incomplete architecture of human ontogeny: Selection, optimization, and compensation as foundation of developmental theory. *American Psychologist, 52,* 366–380.

Bandura, A. (1986). Self-efficacy. In A. Bandura (Ed.), *Social foundations of thought and action: A social cognitive theory* (pp. 390–453). Englewood Cliffs, NJ: Prentice Hall.

Betz, N. E. (1993). Toward the integration of multicultural and career psychology. *CareerDevelopment Quarterly, 42,* 53–55.

Betz, N. E., & Hackett, G. (1981) A self-efficacy approach to the career development of women. *Journal of Vocational Behavior, 18,* 326–339.

Bronfenbrenner, U. (1979). *The ecology of human development.* Cambridge, MA: Harvard University Press.

Brown, S. D., & Ryan Krane, N. (2000). Four (or five) sessions and a cloud of dust: Old assumptions and new observations about career counseling. In S. D. Brown & R. W. Lent (Eds.), *Handbook of counseling psychology* (3rd ed., pp. 740–766). New York: Wiley.

Carey, J. C., & Reinat, M. (1990). School counselors' perceptions of training needs in multicultural counseling. *Counselor Education & Supervision, 29*(3), 155–168.

Chartrand, J. M., Strong, S. R., & Weitzman, L. M. (1995). The interactional perspective in vocational psychology: Paradigms, theories, and research practices. In B. W. Walsh & S. H. Osipow (Eds.), *Handbook of vocational psychology: Theory, research, and practice* (2nd ed., pp. 35–65). Mahwah, NJ, England: Lawrence Erlbaum Associates.

Close, W. M. (2002). Integrating self-determination theory and social cognitive theory to predict urban high school students' distress, achievement, and retention. *Dissertation Abstracts International, 62,* 3688A.

Coleman, H. L. K., & Baskin, T. (2003). Multiculturally competent school counseling. In D. B. Pope-Davis, H. L. K. Coleman, W. M. Ling, & R. L Torporek (Eds.), *Handbook of multicultural competencies in counseling and psychology* (pp. 103–113). Thousand Oaks, CA: Sage.

Constantine, M. G., Arorash, T. J., Barakett, M. D., Blackman, S. M., Donnelly, P. C., & Edles, P. A. (2001). School counselors' universal-diverse orientation and aspects of their multicultural counseling competence. *Professional School Counseling, 5*(1), 13–18.

Constantine, M. G., & Yeh, C. (2001). Multicultural training, self-construals, and multicultural competence of school counselors. *Professional School Counseling, 4*(3), 202–207.

Deci, E. L., & Ryan, R. M. (1985). *Intrinsic motivation and self-determination in human development.* New York: Plenum.

Ford, D. H., & Lerner, R. M. (1992). *Developmental systems theory: An integrative approach.* Newbury Park, CA: Sage.

Fouad, N. A., & Smith, P. L. (1996). A test of a social cognitive model for middle school students: Math and science. *Journal of Counseling Psychology, 43,* 338–346.

Freire, P. (1970). *Pedagogy of the oppressed.* New York: Herder & Herder.

Freund, A. M., & Baltes, P. B. (1998). Selection, optimization, and compensation as strategies of life management: Correlations with subjective indicators of successful aging. *Psychology and Aging, 13,* 531–543.

Gibson, R. L., & Mitchell, M. H. (2003). *Introduction to counseling and guidance* (6th ed.). Columbus, OH: Merrill Prentice Hall.

Gottfredson, L. S. (1981). Circumscription and compromise: A developmental theory of occupational aspirations (Monograph). *Journal of Counseling Psychology, 28,* 545–579.

Gysbers, N. C. (1997). Involving counseling psychology in the school-to-work movement: An idea whose time has come. *Counseling Psychologist, 25,* 413–427.

Gysbers, N. C. (2001). School guidance and counseling in the 21st century: Remember the past into the future. *Professional School Counseling, 5,* 96–105.

Gysbers, N. C., Lapan, R. T., Multon, K. D., & Lukin, L. E. (1992). *Missouri comprehensive guidance evaluation survey: Grades 6–9.* Jefferson City, MO: Missouri Department of Elementary and Secondary Education.

Hargrove, B. K., Creagh, M. G., & Kelly, D. B. (2003). Multicultural competencies in career counseling. In D. B. Pope-Davis, H. L. K. Coleman, W. M. Ling, & R. L Torporek (Eds.), *Handbook of multicultural competencies in counseling and psychology* (pp. 392–405). Thousand Oaks, CA: Sage.

Helms, J. E. (1984). Toward a theoretical explanation of the effects of race on counseling: A Black and White model. *Counseling Psychologist, 12*(3), 153–165.

Helms, J. E. (1995). An update of Helm's White and people of color racial identity models. In J.G. Ponterotto, J.M. Casas, L.A. Suzuki, & C. M. Alexander (Eds.), *Handbook of multicultural counseling* (pp. 181–198). Thousand Oaks, CA: Sage.

Hobson, S. M., & Kanitz, H. M. (1996). Multicultural counseling: An ethical issue for school counselors. *The School Counselor, 43,* 245–255.

Holcomb-McCoy, C. C. (2003). Multicultural competence in school settings. In D. B. Pope-Davis, H. L. K. Coleman, W. M. Ling, & R. L Torporek (Eds.), *Handbook of multicultural competencies in counseling and psychology* (pp. 406–419). Thousand Oaks, CA: Sage.

Holland, J. (1996). Exploring careers with a typology: What we have learned and some new directions. *American Psychologist, 51,* 397–406.

Howard, K. A. S., & Solberg, V. S. H. (2006). School-based social justice: The Achieving Success Identity Pathways Program. *Professional School Counseling, 9*(4), 278–287.

Jones, L. K., Sheffield, D., & Joyner, B. (2000). Comparing the effects of the Career Key with Self-Directed Search and Job-OE among eighth-grade students. *Professional School Counseling, 3*(4), 238–247.

Kraus, L. J., & Hughey, K. F. (1999). The impact of an intervention on career decision-making self-efficacy and career indecision. *Professional School Counseling, 2,* 384–390.

Lapan, R. T., Gysbers, N. C., Hughey, K., & Arni, T. J. (1993). Evaluating a guidance and language arts unit for high school juniors. *Journal of Counseling and Development, 71,* 444–451.

Lapan, R. T., Gysbers, N. C., & Petroski, G. F. (2003). Helping seventh graders be safe and successful: A statewide study of the impact of comprehensive guidance and counseling programs. *Professional School Counseling, 6*(3), 186–197.

Lapan, R. T., Gysbers, N. C., & Sun, Y. (1997). The impact of more fully implemented guidance programs on the school experiences of high school students: A statewide evaluation study. *Journal of Counseling & Development, 75,* 292–302.

Lapan, R. T., Tucker, B., Kim, S., & Kosciulek, J. F. (2003). Preparing rural adolescents for post-high school transitions. *Journal of Counseling and Development, 81,* 329–342.

Lent, R. W., Brown, S. D., & Hackett, G. (1994). Toward a unifying social cognitive theory of career and academic interest, choice, and performance. *Journal of Vocational Behavior, 45,* 79–122.

Lerner, R. M. (1995). *America's youth in crisis: Challenges and options for programs and policies.* Thousand Oaks, CA: Sage.

Lerner, R. M. (2002). *Concepts and theories of human development.* Mahwah, NJ: Lawrence Erlbaum Associates.

McLoyd, V. C. (1998). Socioeconomic disadvantage and child development. *American Psychologist, 53,* 185–204.

Mosconi, J., & Emmett, J. (2003). Effects of a values clarification curriculum on high school students' definitions of success. *Professional School Counseling, 7,* 68–78.

Multon, K. D., Brown, S. D., & Lent, R. W. (1991). Relation of self-efficacy beliefs to academic outcomes: A meta-analytic investigation. *Journal of Counseling Psychology, 38,* 30–38.

National Center for Education Statistics. (2001). *NAEP summary data tables* [Electronic version]. Washington, DC: U.S. Department of Education.

National Research Council. (1993). *Losing generations: Adolescents in high-risk settings.* Washington, DC: National Academy Press.

O'Brien, K. M., Dukstein, R. D., Jackson, S. L., Tomlinson, M. J., & Kamatuka, N. A. (1999). Broadening career horizons for students in at-risk environments. *Career Development Quarterly, 47,* 215–229.

Oliver, L. W., & Spokane, A. R. (1988). Career intervention outcome: What contributes to client gain? *Journal of Counseling Psychology, 35,* 447–462.

Palmer, S., & Cochran, L. (1988). Parents as agents of career development. *Journal of Counseling Psychology, 35,* 71–76.

Parsons, F. (1909). *Choosing a vocation.* Boston: Houghton Mifflin Co.

Ponterotto, J., & Pederson, P. B. (1993). *Preventing prejudice: A guide for counselors and educators.* Thousand Oaks, CA: Sage.

Prilleltensky, I. (1997). Values, assumptions, and practices: Assessing the moral implications of psychological discourse and action. *American Psychologist, 52*(5), 517–535.

Quintana, S. M., & Segura-Herrera, T. A. (2003). Developmental transformations of self and identity in the context of oppression. *Self and Identity, 2,* 269–285.

Resnick, L. B., & Wirt, J. B. (1996). *Linking school and work: Roles for standards and assessments.* San Francisco: Jossey-Bass.

Rogers, C. R. (1961). *On becoming a person: A therapist's view of psychotherapy.* Boston: Houghton Mifflin.

Scales, P. C., & Roehlkepartain, E. C. (2003). Boosting student achievement: New research on the power of developmental assets. *Search Institute Insights & Evidence, 1*(1), 1–10.

Schlossberg, S., Morris, J., & Lieberman, M. (2001). The effects of a counselor-led guidance intervention on students' behaviors and attitudes. *Professional School Counseling, 4*(3), 156–164.

Schmidt, J. J. (1999). *Counseling in schools: Essential services and comprehensive programs* (4th ed.). New York: Allyn & Bacon.

Schwallie-Giddis, P., Anstrom, K., Sánchez, P., Sardi, V. A., & Granato, L. (2004). Counseling the linguistically and culturally diverse student: Meeting school counselors' professional development needs. *Professional School Counseling, 8*(1), 15–23.

Secretary's Commission on Achieving Necessary Skills. (1992). *Learning a living: A blueprint for high performance.* Washington, DC: U.S. Department of Labor.

Search Institute. (2002). *The asset approach: 40 Elements of healthy development.* Minneapolis, MN: Author.

Sesma, A., & Roehlkepartain, E. C. (2003). Unique strengths, shared strengths: Developmental assets among youth of color. *Search Institute Insights & Evidence, 1*(2), 1–13.

Sink, C. A., & Stroh, H. R. (2003). Raising achievement test scores of early elementary school students through comprehensive school counseling programs. *Professional School Counseling, 6*(5), 350–364.

Solberg, V. A., Gusavac, N., Hamann, T., Felch, J., Johnson, J., Lamborn, S., et al. (1998). The Adaptive Success Identity Plan (ASIP): A career intervention for college students. *Career Development Quarterly, 47,* 48–95.

Solberg, V. S. (1998). Assessing career search self-efficacy: Construct evidence and developmental antecedents. *Journal of Career Assessment, 6,* 181–193.

Solberg, V. S. (2001). *ASIP evaluation report.* Milwaukee, WI: Author.

Solberg V. S. (2005). *ASIP evaluation report.* Milwaukee, WI: Author.

Solberg, V. S., Carlstrom, A. H., & Kowalchuk, R. K. (2001, August). *Longitudinal evaluation: School success intervention with low-income diverse youth.* Paper presented at the 109th annual convention of the American Psychological Association, San Francisco.

Solberg, V. S., Close, W., & Metz, A. J. (2002). Promoting success pathways for middle and high school students: Introducing the adaptive success identity plan for school counselors. In C. L. Juntunen & D. R. Atkinson's (Eds.), *Counseling across the lifespan: Prevention and treatment* (pp. 135–157). Thousand Oaks, CA: Sage Publications.

Solberg, V. S., Howard, K. A., Blustein, D. L., & Close, W. (2002). Career development in the schools: Connecting school-to-work-to-life. *The Counseling Psychologist, 30,* 705–725.

Spokane, A. R., & Oliver, L. W. (1983). The outcomes of vocational intervention. In W. B. Walsh & S. H. Osipow (Eds.), *Handbook of vocational psychology* (pp. 99–116). Hillsdale, NJ: Erlbaum.

Sue, D. W., & Sue, D. (2003) *Counseling the culturally diverse: Theory and practice* (4th ed.). New York: John Wiley & Sons.

Super, D. E. (1953). A theory of vocational development. *American Psychologist, 8,* 185–190.

Super, D. E. (1990). A life-span, life-space to approach to career development. In D. Brown & L. Brooke (Eds.), *Career choice and development: Applying contemporary theories to practice* (2nd ed., pp. 197–261). San Francisco: Jossey-Bass.

Super, D. E., Savickas, M. L, & Super, C. M. (1996). The life-span, life-space approach to careers. In D. Brown & L. Brooks (Eds.), *Career choice and development* (3rd ed., pp. 121–178). San Francisco: Jossey-Bass.

Swanson, J. L., & Fouad, N. A. (1999). *Career theory and practice: Learning through case studies.* Thousand Oaks, CA: SAGE Publications, Inc.

Triandis, H. C. (1995). *Individualism and collectivism.* New York: Simon & Schuster.

Turner, S. L., & Lapan, R. T. (2005). Evaluation of an intervention to increase non-traditional career interests and career-related self-efficacy among middle-school adolescents. *Journal of Vocational Behavior, 66,* 516–531.

U.S. Bureau of Labor Statistics. (2005). *Labor force statistics from the current population survey.* Retrieved November 7, 2005, from http://data.bls.gov/cgi-bin/surveymost

U.S. Census Bureau. (2005). *Detailed poverty tables: 2003.* Washington, DC: Author.

U.S. Congress. (1958). *National Defense Education Act of 1958* (Public Law 85-846). Washington, DC: Author.

Vera, E. M., & Speight, S. L. (2003). Multicultural competence, social justice, and counseling psychology: Expanding our roles. *The Counseling Psychologist, 31*(3), 253–272.

Wentzel, K. R. (1998). Social relationships and motivation in middle school: The role of parents, teachers, and peers. *Journal of Educational Psychology, 90,* 202–209.

Wettersten, K. B., Guilmino, A., Herrick, C. G., Hunter, P. J., Kim, G. Y., Jagow, D., et al. (2005). Predicting educational and vocational attitudes among rural high school students. *Journal of Counseling Psychology, 52*(4), 658–663.

Whiston, S. C., Sexton, T. L., & Lasoff, D. L. (1998). Career-intervention outcome: A replication and extension of Oliver and Spokane. *Journal of Counseling Psychology, 45,* 150–165.

Wickrama, K. A. S., Lorenz, F. O., & Conger, R. D. (1997). Parental support and adolescent physical health status: A latent growth-curve analysis. *Journal of Health and Social Behavior, 38*(2), 149–163.

Wiese, B. S., Freund, A. M., & Baltes, P. B. (2000). Selection, optimization, and compensation: An action-related approach to work and partnership. *Journal of Vocational Behavior, 57,* 273–300.

Yalom, I. D. (1995). *The theory and practice of group psychotherapy* (4th ed.). New York: Basic Books, Inc.

Zimmerman, B. J. (1995). Self-efficacy and educational development. In A. Bandura (Ed.), *Self-efficacy in changing societies* (pp. 202–231). Cambridge, UK: Cambridge University Press.

Zimmerman, B. J., Bandura, A., & Martinez-Ponz, M. (1992). Self-motivation for academic achievement: The role of self-efficacy beliefs and personal goal setting. *American Educational Research Journal, 29,* 663–676.

4

School Counselor Competence

XX

SCHOOL COUNSELOR TRAINING: School and Societal Needs in the 21st Century

JOHN L. ROMANO, KAY HERTING WAHL, AND JULIE M. KOCH
University of Minnesota–Twin Cities

Introduction

The evolution of the education and training of school counselors has progressed as the role of the school counselor, the profession of school counseling, and the educational enterprise have changed over the years. This chapter will give a brief historical review of school counselor training and practice during the past 100 years, commenting on the development of the profession and highlighting the major training developments during this period. The major objective of the chapter is to examine the theoretical and curricular frameworks of more recent school counselor training initiatives, including empirical evidence related to the impact of the educational programs that train school counselors. In conclusion, the chapter will suggest recommendations for the training of school counselors to maximize the effectiveness and impact of school counselors in the 21st century.

The history of school counseling can be traced back to the early part of the 20th century as the United States was experiencing major societal changes as a result of the influx of new immigrants to the country and urbanization (Baker & Gerler, 2004). School counseling, which generally focused on vocational guidance activities, was undertaken by personnel in the schools with no formal training in counseling. In succeeding years, school counseling was influenced by different societal and professional developments, including the standardized testing movement of World Wars I and II, protection of children through child labor laws, the vocational guidance centers of Frank Parsons, and the mental health movement. In addition, theoretical concepts of Carl Rogers and his nondirective theory of counseling greatly influenced the profession. In the 1950s, school counseling reached a level of professional recognition through the formation of the American School Counseling Association (ASCA) and the National Defense Education Act (NDEA), which provided federal funding to staff schools with counselors and to train school counselors at universities throughout the country. During this period, the training of school counselors and their roles in schools were not clearly defined (Baker & Gerler, 2004). Training programs, as well as school counselor positions, were usually open only to those with a classroom teacher's license or certificate, and the training programs tended to be offered during the summer months and part-time during the academic year, to accommodate licensed teachers.

During the decades of the later 20th century, the training of school counselors became more defined. Different training models were initiated, including the Comprehensive School Guidance Model (Gysbers & Henderson, 1988) and the Developmental Model as proposed by Myrick (1987). The models emphasized a comprehensive K–12 approach to school guidance and counseling, and recommended that school counselors focus on the career, educational, personal, and social development of students. These models made major contributions to the training and practice of school counselors compared with earlier years. In recent years, however, educational leaders both within and outside of the field of school counseling were concerned about the lack of influence and impact of school counselors (Stone & Dahir, 2006). In addition, concerns about the adequacy of the training of school counselors have been raised (Schmidt, 2003). Among the concerns are the lack of understanding of new school counselor professionals about the changing dynamics of schools and the students they serve (Sears & Granello, 2002). As a result, two initiatives were developed. One, called the *Transforming School Counseling Initiative* (TSCI), focused on the graduate-level training of school counselors, and the other, the *ASCA National Model*, focused on the practice of school counselors in the field. These models of training and practice will be described more fully below.

While the school counseling profession continues to develop the best possible training models and delivery of services in the schools, the academic and mental health needs of children and adolescents are issues of concern to school stakeholders. These stakeholders include educational policy makers, teachers and administrators, parents, community leaders, and students. The No Child Left Behind federal legislation focused on student academic achievement and high-stakes testing programs throughout the country. Academic disparities across the educational landscape showed large achievement differences between students from lower socioeconomic communities and students from some ethnic communities compared with Caucasian students and those from more affluent communities. Sometimes referred to as the "achievement gap," data show that while some progress has been made in reducing the achievement gap, there are still systemic differences between students from different socioeconomic and ethnic groups (Perie, Grigg, & Donohue, 2005).

In addition to academic achievement indicators, children and adolescents have needs for mental health services, and schools provide a large proportion of these services (Rones & Hoagwood, 2000). A recent study by the U.S. Department of Health and Human Services addressed the country's school mental health services (Foster et al., 2005). One of the major findings of the study was that 20% of students received some type of school-supported mental health service. The most frequent mental health concerns for males and females were social, interpersonal, and family problems. The second and third most cited concerns for female students were anxiety and adjustment problems, while aggression and behavioral problems were most frequent for males. School districts reported that while the need for student mental health services has increased since 2000, funding for such services has decreased. School counselors were the most frequently identified mental health professional in the school. Given the high demand for services, many districts were attempting to meet the student mental health needs through community-based providers. Among the recommendations of the study was the need for additional school-based research that specifically examines the type and number of student problems presented, and the most effective combination of services, given the skills and training of school personnel who are assigned to deliver them and the availability of community resources for referral. The study did not collect data about the training and professional development needs of school personnel to adequately meet student mental health needs, nor did the study examine job responsibilities and school administrative structures that may reduce the effectiveness of school personnel (e.g., high school counselor-to-student ratios and administrative duties).

The profession is at a critical time in the training of school counselors for several reasons. Despite a recent history that includes well-articulated statements about purpose and roles of professionals in the field, the school counselor role continues to be met with ambiguity within many school systems. In some school districts and universities, there is a major discrepancy between the role of the school counselor and the preservice school counselor training that counselors receive. Too many school counselors are spending too much of their time on quasi-administrative tasks and too little time directly serving students in ways that are compatible with their training (Baker & Gerler, 2004; Burnham & Jackson, 2000; Partin, 1993). The ASCA model hopes to correct this, by recommending that school counselors spend 80% of their time in direct service to students (ASCA, 2003). School counselors may believe that they are adequately trained to deliver direct service given their graduate level curriculum; however, traditional training programs may not prepare students in areas necessary to be effective in new roles required of school counselors, such as providing schoolwide leadership to facilitate systemic school change. This latter criticism of school counselor preservice training was the impetus for the *Transforming School Counseling Initiative*. For change to occur in both school counselor preservice training and school counseling practice, major coordination between universities that train school counselors and school districts that hire counselors is needed. However, other aspects of school counselor preservice training are important, and this chapter will examine the training of school counselors and recommend ways to strengthen the training.

Theoretical Bases and Models of Training

School counselor training programs have undergone a metamorphosis in theoretical bases from the inception of school counseling to the present. The earliest training program models were created with the idea of training school counselors to help students prepare for successful vocations after high school. This model of training included preparing high school students for a future career and successful adjustment into adult society (Thompson, 2002).

These training programs primarily focused on vocational development theory.

Compulsory education laws in the 1920s, along with industrialization, urbanization, and immigration, placed new demands on schools for providing more than academic instruction. A sharp increase in numbers of students unsure about school attendance as well as their futures (Baker, 2000) created a need for changes in education to help bridge the gap between school and the adult world and the transition from school to work. School counselors began to answer those needs as school counselor training models focused on psychological adjustment as well as vocational guidance (Erford, 2003). School counselors needed to be trained to assist high school students with social skills for successful and independent living after high school (Baker & Gerler, 2004). In addition, psychometrics became a component of school counselor training after World War I (Sciarra, 2004). Schools were the ideal setting to utilize a variety of psychological measures to help students with vocational and life planning, as well as adjustment issues (Erford).

Gradually, more sophisticated models to train school counselors evolved; however, many training programs developed from the theoretical bases of counselor educators, who were not necessarily focused or experienced in public schools and the practice of school counseling, leaving the profession without a unified direction or theory of training.

In 1958, the U.S. government, through the NDEA, provided funding for school counselors to help high school students choose courses that would promote knowledge and interest in science and math as well as careers in these fields (Baker, 2000). As a result, school counselor training programs were quickly developed, with little theoretical direction other than the dictated purpose of the NDEA. Training programs were inconsistent in their theoretical models related to training curricula, skills, and requirements.

The mental health components of school counselor training programs evolved with the popularity of psychological counseling theorists such as Carl Rogers and his Person-Centered Theory. Humanistic theories influenced the training and practice of school counselors in the 1950s and remained a strong influence in the following decades (Baker & Gerler, 2004). The mental health theoretical approach to school counselor training seemed to be the answer to criticisms that the mental health needs of children and adolescents should be met in their natural environments, including the schools (Erford, 2003). Generic counselor training programs educated school counselors in foundational counseling theory and techniques, and required other courses specific to school counseling. This practice of course integration across the curriculum continues in the majority of school counselor training programs today. The unfortunate circumstance of this practice is that there is little or no connection between information imparted in the counseling foundation courses and those more specific to the role of school counselors (Martin, 2002).

ASCA, founded in 1958 as a division of the American Personnel and Guidance Association (now called the American Counseling Association, began to bring unification and standards to the field of school counseling (Cobia & Henderson, 2003). A major revolution in school counselor training models came with the advent of the comprehensive guidance model developed by Dr. Norman Gysbers at the University of Missouri and later refined by Gybers and Henderson (2000), which has become the basis for almost all current school counselor training models. This model focused on preparing school counselors to serve all K–12 students in the schools and was comprehensive in terms of addressing the career, academic, and social development needs of students (Sink, 2005).

Training programs across the country began to adopt the comprehensive model for training school counselors, but these programs also adapted the model to meet the needs of schools in their own states (Sink, 2005). The comprehensive model called for school counselors to develop prevention and intervention programs at all levels in the schools and to work with students individually, in groups, and in classrooms. The comprehensive model organized programs into three major areas called domains—personal/social, academic, and career development—assuming that these areas encompassed the needs of all students. The comprehensive model detailed activities and duties into components assigned to each domain. The components consisted of individual planning, system support, classroom guidance, and responsive services. Gysbers and Henderson (2000) specified amounts of time that counselors should spend in these components at the different levels of education, realizing that student needs at elementary schools were different from those in middle and high schools. The comprehensive model also called for K–12 programming on all topics. For example, the model asserted that career education must start at the kindergarten level and continue in each grade level until graduation. The comprehensive model provided well-defined structure, procedures, and system for school counselors to organize their programs and time. The comprehensive guidance model was considered a template from which other models of training and practice could be formed to meet local needs (Thompson, 2002).

In 1987, Myrick proposed the Developmental Theory for school counselors in his publication, *Developmental Guidance and Counseling: A Practical Approach*. Myrick's theory added the aspect of awareness and developmental stages to Gysbers and Henderson's (2000) comprehensive model. According to Myrick, the development of children throughout their growth stages must be an integral part of the planning of all work with children. The physical, emotional, cognitive, and psychological development of children must be recognized as school counselors work to help all students be successful throughout childhood and adolescence. Developmental guidance stressed cooperation between school counselors and school staff, particularly teachers. It stated that setting goals and determining curriculum and programs must be established with developmental stages in mind.

In practice, the comprehensive and developmental models were often combined in school counselor training programs and in school counseling literature. While school counselors continued to be trained in generic counseling programs, comprehensive and developmental guidance perspectives became the unifying theme of school counselor training curricula within counselor training programs in the 1980s and 1990s (Thompson, 2002).

In the 1980s, federal funding and a new emphasis on the future of high school students advanced a practical concept called "school-to-work" (Erford, 2003; Worthington & Juntunen, 1997). This renewed emphasis on vocational guidance, or "career development" as it is now called, was added to school counselor comprehensive training programs (Baker & Gerler, 2004). In the same decade, the mental health movement in U.S. society in general, and more specifically, in the school counseling field, added a renewed emphasis on the mental health of school children (Schmidt, 2003). As theories of psychotherapy gained greater emphasis in society at large, they also emerged as counseling models for school counselors, such as Solution Focused Brief Theory (Rye & Sparks, 1999), Rational Emotive Behavior Therapy (REBT; Ellis, 1994), and Choice Theory (Glasser, 1998). Counseling theories were usually taught as part of counselor training programs, and the application of the theories to school counseling was expected to be taught in the school counseling specialty courses within the training program. School counselor specialty courses were now focusing on counseling skills to serve all students, prevention and intervention programs for all students, and the need to address mental health as well as career issues for all students. School counselor training also included the expanded role and function of the school counselor as defined by comprehensive and developmental guidance programs, including the 3 C's: counseling, coordinating, and consulting (Erford, 2003).

Although the comprehensive and developmental guidance and school counseling training models have been the cornerstone in school counseling programs throughout the 1990s, many individualized and unique models have developed in recent years. The common thread among new training initiatives remains the comprehensive and developmental approach to school counseling. A few of the newer models are summarized in the following paragraphs.

The Support System Approach was proposed by Rye and Sparks (1999). This is a consumer-centered program, with a community-based decision-making foundation. This approach has a new focus on consumer participation, but is also meant to be delivered in a comprehensive and developmental school counselor model, thereby allowing training programs to maintain their adherence to the comprehensive developmental model while adding a consumer or community-based aspect. The Support System Approach to training includes the school counselor, the entire school staff, and the community. In this approach, values and beliefs known and understood by the community and the school are developed into goals for the school and for the school counseling program. The uniqueness of the model lies in preparing graduates to work with a school staff, including teachers and administrators, and with the community. School counselors are trained to develop and share a vision and a mission with constituents from all areas. A major goal of the program is to strengthen the bond among the school, the school counseling program, and the community through collaboration.

The School-Community Collaboration Model (Adelman & Taylor, 2002) is a similar approach to the Support System Approach. The School-Community Collaboration Model includes the creation and maintenance of collaborative connections with public and private agencies, higher education, business and professional organizations, churches, and volunteer organizations. School counselors are trained to begin with local and neighborhood levels of collaboration and eventually expand to broader based connections.

In the 1990s, the *Transforming School Counseling Initiative* (TSCI), supported by the Wallace Reader's Digest Fund and managed by the Educational Trust National Center for Transforming School Counseling, developed a model to transform the training of school counselors. Advocates believed that the training of school counselors had to change to strengthen their impact in the schools. A major goal of TSCI is to train school counselors to have a significant impact on students by helping to close the achievement gap between different groups of student (Seashore, Jones, & Seppanen, 2001). To accomplish this goal, according to TSCI, school counselors must be trained to reduce barriers to academic achievement and become advocates for equity in all aspects of education. School counselor training includes learning about schools and their cultures, advocacy skills to promote important school changes, skills to increase collaborative activities with other school personnel and the community, and the use of data and technology for informed decision making. Other goals of TSCI are the inclusion of the school counselor as a member of the school leadership team, the focus on systemic change for the betterment of all students, and partnerships with community agencies. An extremely important practice within the goals of the TSCI is the linkage of the school counselor training program to indicators of student success, such as improved attendance, behavior, test scores, and graduation rates. The linkage to student academic success lends itself to further research on the relationship between student mental health and academic success. Therefore, future research will help to inform training programs about the importance of the inclusion of mental health training in all school counselor programs.

The TSCI model supported the call for school counselors to take a more active leadership role in schools (Erford, House, & Martin, 2003). Educators at all levels seemed to agree that school counselors could effect change for all students, especially in closing the achievement gap and increasing the academic success of all students. This goal seemed to alter somewhat the comprehensive and developmental training models of some programs, but the goal did not eliminate the earlier conceptual training models from school counselor training. Since the TSCI model is relatively new, research on its implementation and effectiveness is limited; however, the model is given further attention in the research section of this chapter.

The *ASCA National Model: A Framework for School Counseling Programs* incorporates the ASCA National Standards for School Counseling Programs (Baker & Gerler, 2004) and has been adopted by ASCA as the national model for school counselor practice (ASCA, 2003). A major goal of the ASCA model is to develop comprehensive school counseling practice models that are integral to high student academic achievement across the school population. In this regard, the National ASCA model complements the transformation of school counselor training supported by TSCI.

The ASCA Model highlights the National Standards for School Counselors and reflects current educational trends, including the No Child Left Behind legislation. Therefore, school counseling programs must meet the needs of all students and include components such as a districtwide delivery system that includes a guidance curriculum, individual student planning, responsive services, and system support. In addition, the model requires a management system that is based on student needs, is data-driven, offers services for academically underperforming students, and infuses strategies for systemic change, leadership development, and advocacy throughout all components of the program.

Gysbers and Henderson (2002) reported that the *ASCA National Model* consists of three elements: (a) content, (b) organizational framework, and (c) resources. *Content* is defined as the curriculum through which K–12 students achieve developmental competencies. The organizational framework consists of delivery modes and the K–12 scope of guidance activities. Delivery modes include classroom guidance, schoolwide counseling activities, and individual student planning. Student planning requires that the counselor be competent in student appraisal techniques, student advising, and career and personal/social counseling skills. The ASCA model also stresses the importance of regular program evaluation, planning, and management; continuing professional development for counselors; maintaining communication and relationships with important stakeholders (e.g., parents, community leaders, school administrators, and teachers); school counselor service on advisory boards; and community outreach. School counselors are encouraged to advocate for students and schools in the political process through their state legislators and local school boards. Again, these are goals that are addressed in the TSCI training model.

The ASCA model incorporates the comprehensive development model of training, as well as the more recent models. The newer training models require that prospective school counselors be trained in leadership and counseling skills. This is a paradigm shift from the focus on individual and group counseling and comprehensive programming to the facilitation of school-based systemic change. It must be noted that the ASCA model does not deemphasize the comprehensive and mental health models of school counseling practices. Instead, the ASCA model incorporates previous models into a more integrated model. To summarize, in the ASCA model, the counselor's role is as an advocate for all students, supporting and strengthening their academic, career, and emotional and social needs, while delivering a comprehensive program with a focus on systemic change.

The ASCA and TSCI models create a new vision for the school counselor role. Traditional practices must be enhanced to include, emphasize, and utilize the collaboration and leadership skills of school counselors. A major function of the new school counselor role is to be an agent of systemic change, with the academic success of all students as a major goal. To reach this goal, school counselors need training in accountability and evaluation strategies, public relations and marketing skills, and presentation skills. With little training or perceived need for accountability and evaluation skills in the past, school counselors are now being called on to discuss the efficacy of their programs to school boards and community groups and to deliver the presentations using PowerPoint and other technology-enhanced strategies. These types of activities are necessary to help stakeholders understand the role of the school counselor; to communicate the impact of school counseling on the academic, career, personal, and social development of students; and to support the need for school counseling funding for prevention and intervention programs. School counselor training programs must ensure that students graduate with evaluation and presentation skills.

The change in school counselor practices also requires a change in training. Currently, the majority of school counselor training programs, whether they are accredited by the Council for Accreditation of Counseling and Related Educational Programs (CACREP) or by regional or state agencies, require a master's degree in counseling. A typical program usually includes training in individual and group counseling theory, application, and skills; career development and multicultural counseling; and foundational courses in psychology, statistics, and research methods. School counseling specialty courses also usually include development and planning of comprehensive school counseling programs, prevention and intervention program development, and crisis intervention and consulting skills (Thompson, 2002). In order for school counseling students to attain the skills needed in newer school counseling delivery models, training curricula must include skills in leadership, creative planning, public relations and marketing, program accountability, public speaking, and community relations. Current trends in public schools and school counselor training models require that the practicing school counselor be trained and skilled in much more than traditional individual and group counseling—sometimes referred to as a "mental health focus" or "therapy focus"—if the position of the school counselor is to remain a vital and integral part of education.

A major dilemma facing the school counseling profession is that students usually choose the profession because they wish to engage in personal counseling with children and adolescents to help them solve problems. Historically, school counselors desired to be change agents for students, but not necessarily for schools or school districts. Taking on a leadership role may not be the career they intended nor the career for which they feel best suited. School counselors already in the field may be satisfied with the comfortable status quo, while new school counselors in training may be resistant to the leadership aspect of their school counseling roles. Therefore, school counselor training programs, through marketing and recruitment of new students, must articulate newer models of training and roles so that appropriate students are attracted and admitted to the training program.

Another dilemma for training programs is that additional theoretical and skills courses will be needed to complement existing training programs, and current faculty may not have the interest or qualifications to teach the courses. Further, most training programs may find it difficult to add new courses and content areas to an already full, two-year master's degree counseling program. Therefore, training programs will need to find innovative ways to give students the necessary training and skills, perhaps through focused assignments in existing classes and through small group course modules for school counseling students.

Another training area that needs attention is the need to infuse information about the role of the school counselor in the education of school administrators (Martin, 2002). Without school administrators' cooperation and awareness of the new trends in school counselor training and practice, the new school counseling initiatives may well be met with resistance in the schools. Change has generally been constant but slow in education; thus, the changes suggested for school counselors in the new models will require cooperation and coordination among school and community stakeholders, and especially among school administrators.

Field Experiences

At present, the only current, standardized guidelines for school counseling fieldwork training experiences are those accredited by CACREP. While state departments of education may require field experiences, they are not standardized. The 2001 CACREP standards give guidelines for instructor, student, and site supervisor qualifications. In addition, the standards state that the "clinical instruction environment . . . is conducive to modeling, demonstration, and training and . . . ensures adequate and appropriate access by the faculty and students" (2001, Section III.D., p. 11). The CACREP standards offer explicit requirements regarding physical necessities of the learning environment, such as access to technology. In addition, CACREP requires that students complete a 100-hour supervised practicum experience and a 600-hour supervised internship, both of which require a specific number of direct service hours, individual supervision, group supervision, and evaluation of the graduate student. In addition, the CACREP standards state that clinical experiences should provide the opportunity for students to gain experience interacting as counselors with students who represent "the ethnic and demographic diversity of their community" (Section III.K. p. 13). The CACREP standards emphasize that "practicum and internship requirements are considered to be the most critical experience elements in the program" (Section III, p. 11).

There are a few concerns, however, regarding the CACREP standards. First, currently, 188 counselor training programs are CACREP accredited, but there are also training programs that are not CACREP accredited. Research does not indicate how many of the nonaccredited programs follow the CACREP standards. Some professionals have criticized CACREP for not providing enough structure. One concern, for example, is that the fieldwork experience and site supervision is an individual training program decision (Bradley & Fiorini, 1999). On the other hand, others fear that CACREP is overly rigid and restrictive, allowing for no flexibility in its requirements. A recent major concern expressed by some is CACREP's insufficient attention to multicultural and social justice issues (M. D'Andrea, personal communication, 2005). This concern is particularly worrisome due to the importance of school counselors' being trained and experienced in working with multicultural populations in schools. Therefore, while CACREP is the only national body to accredit school counseling programs, some institutions may choose not to seek accreditation, but, as an alternative, to ensure that their programs meet state license guidelines.

Perusse, Goodnough, and Noel (2001) surveyed school counselor training programs to assess the consistency of training program requirements. Among their findings was that the fieldwork component was "one of the greatest areas of difference among programs" (p. 257). They found that over half of the training programs provided some sort of prepracticum field experience in a school setting, such as classroom observation, shadowing, and interviews. While almost all (96%) programs required a practicum experience, they ranged widely from a total requirement of 20 to 700 hours, and only 68% required these experiences to be in school settings. Most (86%) programs also required an internship, and again, they ranged from a total requirement of 100 to 1,500 hours. Some programs based the hour requirement on the students' prior teaching experience.

Perusse et al.'s (2001) findings confirmed Stickel's (1995) results from a similar survey. Stickel found that while counselor educators viewed the field placement experience as "very positive" (p. 9), expectations for activities that students engage in during their practicum or internship were inconsistent. For example, school counselor trainees may find that their duties include "activities considered noncounseling such as discipline, general staff duties, and clerical duties" (p. 9). One respondent wrote, "Many counselors are locked in to doing administrative, noncounseling work. Tradition is strong; change is slow" (p. 9). Stickel also found that programs emphasized individual counseling more than group work and consultation, which are considered important components of school counseling programs.

Bradley and Fiorini (1999) surveyed CACREP accredited programs' fieldwork requirements. They first looked at prerequisite coursework and training for enrollment in the practicum course, and they found that over half of the surveyed programs required theory, professional orientation, and human development courses. The least common courses required prior to practicum were appraisal, career, multicultural, and research. Bradley and Fiorini looked at how students were evaluated, and they found that most (63%) programs used letter grades rather than a credit/no credit grade (30%). They found that most programs relied heavily on self-report measures such as student case presentations (83%), but also considered site supervisor feedback (96%) for student evaluation. Regarding counselor competencies, they found that most programs felt that attending skills and self-awareness were important. The researchers were surprised at some of their findings, including that while most programs said that they incorporated multicultural counseling into practicum course content, only 33% of the programs required a multicultural course prior to practicum. Bradley and Fiorini were also surprised that only 60% of the programs stated they expected students to be able to facilitate a counseling group and that it is not adequate to rely on microcounseling skills as the only measure of counseling competency.

In terms of field placements, the TSCI model includes some components to strengthen the fieldwork experience. First, all practicum and internship experiences are required to be in school settings, and fieldwork experiences are developed in collaboration with the university training program, the local school district, and local community agencies. Beginning in the first semester, students are expected to have some field experience in the schools. These experiences can be in the form of shadowing school counselors, observing their work, or participating in different school activities (e.g., after-school tutoring programs). During practicum and internship, students are expected to engage in individual and group counseling, classroom guidance activities, outreach to community groups, and opportunities to participate in evaluation and research studies and to be a member of the school team that includes administrators, teachers, parents, and community members. The TSCI model emphasizes the importance of qualified supervisors who are knowledgeable and support the TSCI goals. One way that the TSCI model achieves this is by recruiting TSCI alumni to serve as site supervisors. However, if TSCI alumni are not available, site supervisors "for whom TSCI goals resonate and who have strong school counseling programs" are recruited as practicum and internship supervisors (Michlin & Meath, 2005, p. 23). Incentives for the site supervisors might include monetary remuneration or the opportunity for continuing education training at the university. Since the quality of site supervision is emphasized in TSCI, supervisors may receive supervision training and continuing education credits. A supervisor's manual is often provided for supervisors with targeted skills, steps toward skill acquisition, and methods of student evaluation. A developmental model of supervision that matches field experiences to the needs of the graduate student is used. University program faculty are actively involved in the field experience and supervision, thereby avoiding the need to rely exclusively on student self-report and supervisor feedback. The field experience is periodically evaluated and reviewed (Michlin & Meath, 2005).

Improved collaboration among school districts, communities, and university training programs is likely to increase the quality of field placements throughout the students' training and strengthen the role of site supervisors. Students are likely to be assigned more meaningful experiences in their field placements, and are likely to participate in activities that are reflective of the new school counseling models. Site supervisors will have a closer affiliation with the training program, and communication between the school and university will be improved.

Research

Unfortunately, there is little to report in the area of research related to the impact on students and schools of different school counseling training models or programs. In looking for research in this area, a number of search engines were used, such as PsycInfo and ERIC. Any articles that hinted at being related to research in this area were perused, as were their references. Faculty who appeared to do research of this nature were contacted. Finally, specific Web sites such as those of the Center for Applied Research and Educational Improvement (University of Minnesota–Twin Cities), TSCI, universities that participated in TSCI, and the Center for School Counseling Outcome Research (University of Massachusetts–Amherst), were investigated. There is a wide range of highly specialized, unreplicated research in areas such as the effect of training school counselors in a unique play therapy technique (Kagan, 2003); the training of school counselors in working with exceptional children (McEachern, 2003); and the training of school counselors to conduct family therapy (Hinkle, 1997). Most of this research is based on in-service training of practicing school counselors rather than preservice school counselor students. The only large-scale research project that has been completed on the training of school counselors has been conducted as an evaluation of the TSCI project (Seashore et al., 2001). Although there might be some concerns with the ability to generalize from this research project because the TSCI emphasized urban, highly diverse populations, nevertheless, it was hoped that the TSCI evaluation would produce empirical evidence that TSCI training is more beneficial than other training models are on school achievement and the lives of students. The TSCI evaluation research did not, however, specifically investigate school counselor trainee outcomes, K–12 student outcomes, or the impact of TSCI-trained school counselors on schools. The 2000 TSCI *Executive Summary* (CAREI, 2000) focuses mainly on the challenges in implementation of the TSCI training model. The final TSCI report (Michlin & Meath, 2005) emphasizes the actual implementation of the training programs and does not address the impact of the training on students or schools. Therefore, the profession is left with unanswered questions about the best school counselor training model to improve student academic achievement and overall student well-being, and about which components of any given training model will best meet the needs of school aged youth in the 21st century.

Future Directions

Future directions for the training of school counselors will require comprehensive planning and the involvement of school stakeholders, including school-based educators, policy makers, counselor educators, students, and parents. Several recommendations are offered in developing a process for the implementation of school counselor training in the future.

Practicing school counselors should be involved in the development and implementation of school counselor training programs. Involvement of in-service master school counselors is important in the development and delivery of school counselor preparation programs. Practicing school counselors have firsthand knowledge of the skills and duties that are necessary to be an effective school counselor. As stated by Sisson and Bullis (1992),

> We hope that practicing school counselors will be afforded the opportunity to and will begin to take a proactive role in the design of these curricula. It will be through such ongoing scrutiny of educational needs that the field of school counseling can become consistent with the needs of the students who are served. (p. 114)

School district personnel should be better educated regarding the role of school counselors. School counseling training programs, in collaboration with departments of educational policy, administration, and curriculum and instruction, should work to ensure that future teachers and administrators understand appropriate tasks and duties of school counselors. It is possible for counseling faculty to work with faculty within these areas of university schools and colleges of education. Counseling faculty may act as guest lecturers or may coordinate a collaborative effort among school administration trainees, teacher trainees, and counselor trainees in order to help students understand how they will work together in the future. These students could be assigned group projects or presentations for credit within their respective courses. In addition, school counseling training programs can reach out to school administrators currently employed by school districts and coordinate training activities such as staff development workshops to promote understanding of the role and potential of the school counselor in their schools and districts.

Faculty who teach required school counseling courses should have some knowledge of school counseling and should understand how to incorporate school counseling content into their courses. For faculty members who are not familiar with school counseling, professional development training could be offered within their programs or funds could be allocated for professional development outside the program. Faculty can visit and observe school counselors in action. It may be possible for faculty who are unfamiliar with school settings to work with their local school districts in various ways in order to become better acquainted with the culture of schools. It may also be possible for faculty members to work with other faculty in related university departments (e.g., curriculum and instruction) who are familiar with schools in order to incorporate school-related issues into counseling curricula and courses. Collaborative opportunities may exist through joint research activities, guest lectures, and consultation with schools. University programs that offer doctoral programs in counseling and counseling psychology may also offer training opportunities for doctoral students to prepare a new generation of counseling faculty who have some school-based experience. The training may include practicum and internship placements in the schools, supervision of master's students in on-campus practicum courses, and participation in school-based research and evaluation projects.

Some training components, but not all, should be specifically focused for school counselor trainees. School counselors have specific training needs in areas of counseling that their peers in other counseling specialties may not. For example, the importance of training in advocacy, public speaking, data-driven decision making, and collaboration should be emphasized in school counselor training. In addition, school counselor trainees need to be informed about the culture of schools, and the roles of different professionals in the schools (e.g., school psychologist, special education teacher, school social worker). Students will also need training in brief counseling, group work, and child and adolescent counseling (Jackson et al., 2002). School counselor trainees should be well instructed on school-based prevention and intervention theories and applications (Keys, Bemak, & Lockhart; Romano & Kachgal, 2004, 1998). Since school counselors are increasingly called on to be activists and leaders in schools to promote practices and policies that encourage student development (Stone & Dahir, 2006), they must learn these skills, along with training in collaboration and partnership formation. Finally, school counselor trainees must develop skills in program evaluation, research methods (qualitative and quantitative), and how to effectively present their findings to professional and lay constituent groups. Some courses will also cut across the different counseling specialties, such as counseling theory, career development, multicultural counseling, and ethics. Even within these courses, however, it is useful to structure assignments and content that addresses their applications in school settings.

The school counselor training curriculum should be standardized. Stickel (1995) found that there was wide variability in training programs in areas such as the number of credit hours required, accreditation of training programs, practicum/internship experiences, and methods of student evaluation. In another study, Bradley and Fiorini (1999) found that there was no uniform requirement of a multicultural counseling course. Because school counselors are credentialed by state departments of education, there will be variability across the country in order to meet state license or certification requirements; however, as a profession, it behooves school counselors and counselor educators to come to an agreement, without imposing rigidity, about the most effective curriculum and training components of training. Although CACREP offers standards, and ASCA and TSCI have offered practice and training models, there is not always agreement about the curriculum for school counselor trainees. Programs should be allowed the flexibility to tailor their programs to their students' needs and the local context. The question that should be asked when designing school counseling curricula, therefore, should not be, "Does this conform to CACREP (ASCA, TSCI) models?" but rather, "Does this program fully consider our students' needs in order to prepare them for the changing world of school counseling and the districts where they will seek employment?"

Effort must be made to recruit school counselor students who represent a wide variety of cultural backgrounds. Diversity is a reality in U. S. schools, with dramatic increases projected in the years ahead. The changing demographics will affect schools, and school counselors must be prepared to respond in a prosocial manner. School counselor training programs should exert effort to recruit potential school counselors who are members of traditionally underrepresented populations into the field of school counseling. Once accepted into school counselor training programs, students will need a safe place to gather and share experiences. A mentor program may be beneficial, so that students of color feel welcomed and supported in their programs. The TSCI institutions have made concerted efforts to recruit students from communities of color through recruitment in school districts, community media outlets, and mentoring of undergraduate students.

Multicultural counseling competencies must be a goal of all school counselor training programs. School counselor trainees must be given knowledge and skills related to addressing student diversity in school communities. Diversity includes not only U.S. ethnic and gender diversity, but also diversity of sexual orientation, disabilities, and international populations. The learning of multicultural counseling competencies should include a field component in which students are actually interacting with diverse populations, rather than just learning about diverse populations in textbooks or classroom activities. Additionally, school counselors must be trained regarding how to help their school community learn about the importance of understanding cultural differences.

Field experiences should be integrated into the student's program of study from the very beginning of the training program. Students should be provided with opportunities to experience the culture of schools in fieldwork prior to their practicum placements. These experiences may include a variety of school-based experiences. For example, in a career counseling course, school counseling students could observe a career counseling session at a high school, while the counselor uses an online career counseling resource. Someone interested in the career development of elementary school children could assist a school counselor in preparing and delivering an in-class group lesson in which students play a game that encourages them to explore future career possibilities. In addition, the initial field experiences can be integrated as assignments in regular courses. As another example, a program can require school counseling students to engage in three days of shadowing an elementary school counselor, a middle school counselor, and a high school counselor, to help students decide at what level they would like to focus as school counselors. Finally, mentoring programs, in which school counseling students are assigned to a practicing professional school counselor over a given period of time, have also been found to be successful as an induction into the school counseling profession (Jackson et al., 2002).

Field experiences should include a wide range of activities. In order for school counselor trainees to be prepared for a career in school counseling, they should have the opportunity to experience and be supervised in a wide range of duties and responsibilities that are necessary in the new models of school counseling practice. These include activities such as advocacy, use of technology, and program evaluation. Stickel (1995), however, found that some trainees were involved in activities that were non-counseling related such as student discipline, and general staff and clerical duties. Stickel also found that trainees spent less time than was desirable in individual and group counseling and consultation. While most school counselor supervisors provide adequate administrative and programmatic supervision to students, more supervision of counseling skills are needed (Roberts & Borders, 1994). Sisson and Bullis (1992) found that at the elementary level, counselors wanted more training in their graduate programs in consulting skills with teachers, and at the middle and high school level, counselors wanted more training in consulting skills with health service professionals and community leaders. Freeman and McHenry (1996) support the need for counseling and consulting skills, and they support Lanning's (1986) emphasis on training in professional issues and ethics. In their integrated approach for supervision of school counselor interns, Nelson and Johnson (1999) stress the importance of counselor trainees learning self-supervision skills. They wrote, "Considering that the internship typically marks the end of graduate training and possibly the last time that school counselors will receive any formal supervision, it seems prudent to culminate the evaluation process with a focus on self-supervision skills" (pp. 97–98). Students should also be informed of the importance of continuing their education and supervision, and should be introduced to sources of continuing professional development and potential supervision (Nelson & Johnson). Students also must have opportunities to utilize leadership skills under supervision such as serving on important school committees. Finally, school counselor trainees can assist with program evaluation projects, such as being involved in project planning, data collection, and presentation of results to stakeholder groups.

Applied experiences must be managed skillfully within an overall training model. Good communication must exist between the trainee, the on-site supervisor (an experienced school counselor), the on-site administrator (usually the school principal), and the professor in charge of the practicum or internship experience (Jackson et al., 2002). The site supervisor and university professor should have face-to-face or telephone contact in addition to periodic written evaluations of the trainee. The on-site administrator should be provided information about the internship or practicum and should receive contact information for the university professor as well. A handbook that includes expectations of the site supervisor, guidelines for the student, evaluation forms, and contact information will facilitate communication. Collaboration with a school district is essential in order for the two entities to be familiar with and support each other's goals and training objectives (Blackman, Hayes, Reeves, & Paisley, 2002). Stickel (1995) found that trainees wanted better and more established practicum and internship sites and more quality control of sites, which could be remedied with strong university–school partnerships. In order for the site supervisor to create an environment and relationship with the trainee that allows for two-way feedback and open communication in a safe environment (Bernard & Goodyear, 2004), expectations of the site and site supervisor should be clearly articulated by the training program and agreed upon by the supervisor and training program. These expectations may include (a) supervisor qualifications and credentials, (b) a certain number of required hours of supervision per week, (c) student learning expectations (e.g. learning contract), (d) expectations about introducing the student to the site, (e) supervisor evaluations of trainee, and (f) expectations regarding communication with the university.

It is also important to explicitly state student expectations. These may include (a) required coursework concurrent with the practicum or internship, (b) required hours in direct contact with students, (c) required individual and group supervision, (d) required assignments, including written self and site evaluations, (e) appropriate use of supervision, and (f) consultation about ethical dilemmas. It is important that the practicum or internship agreement between the site, student, and university be signed by the relevant parties.

School counselor supervisors should be trained in supervision theory and skills. Most practicing school counselors, while familiar with the typical duties and expectations of school counselors, have not received training in supervision (Henderson & Lampe, 1992; Jackson et al., 2002). Peace and Sprinthall (1998) stated that it is important to train school counselors in supervision methods to strengthen their supervision of school counselor trainees. They have indicated that training programs should consider trainees' needs. Therefore, the supervision model used by school counselor supervisors should be flexible and should consider trainee professional development stage and supervisor roles (Nelson & Johnson, 1999; Sisson & Bullis, 1992). Nelson and Johnson developed a model of counselor supervision that integrated the models proposed by Littrell, Lee-Borden, and Lorenz (1979) and Bernard (1979, 1997). The Nelson and Johnson model is flexible because it incorporates stages of the supervision process with supervisor roles and the skills and needs of trainees.

More outcome research must be conducted in the area of school counselor training. As reviewed earlier, there has not been enough research in the area of school counselor training to determine which models are most effective. Of course, one's perception of effectiveness or whether a school counselor is adequately trained depends on one's definition of the role of the school counselor. The efficacy of a counselor's training on any given school or district is strongly impacted by the support of administrators for counselors to engage in appropriate activities. A number of questions must be answered before it is asserted that any given training program is more or less successful compared with others at preparing school counselors. Research questions that must be answered include, "What are the differential outcomes for school counselors trained under different training models and structures? For example, are school counselors who are trained under the TSCI model more successful than those trained at a non-TSCI training program?" "Do new counselors feel prepared for their work in the schools, and how are they received by administrators, teachers, parents and other stakeholders?" "Are trainees developing the needed skills as they move through their graduate program, and does their self-efficacy increase?" and "What are the long-term effects of school counselors' work on the academic and personal development of students?" Other research questions include, "How do students respond to counselors trained under different models?" "Does the training of school counselors impact student attendance, disciplinary referrals, postsecondary plans, and academic achievement test results?" "What are students' and parents' perceptions of being welcomed by the school, and how accessible are the school counselors?" and "Are school counselors skilled to address the needs of multicultural student populations, and are they skilled in advocacy and community outreach?"

We recognize that complete answers to questions such as those posed above are difficult to answer, and the school counseling profession is not the only profession that needs to conduct research on effective training models. Public education is continually debated, however, at local and national levels, regarding its effectiveness and appropriate allocation of public resources. School counseling is often a part of this debate, as stakeholders assess how best to utilize limited educational resources, during a period of intense pressure on public schools to meet the myriad needs of students and communities. Universities that train school counselors must produce graduates who will make a major impact in the schools, and programs must engage in regular evaluation of their training models to help assure that their graduates are meeting the needs of students and their schools. The newer training and practice models of school counseling offer an opportunity for university programs, school districts, and the school counseling profession to come together to evaluate the efficacy of these models.

Summary

In many respects, the profession of school counseling is at an important crossroads. As the educational enterprise in the U.S. and abroad receives increased scrutiny, and as key education stakeholders demand greater accountability of schools and student learning, it is imperative that universities evaluate their school counselor training programs to assure that they are graduating school counselors who are exceptionally well prepared to contribute to the needs of students and schools. School counselor training programs must assure that they recruit students with a vision of school counseling that reflects the newer training and delivery models of school counseling practice. School counselor training programs must adjust their programs to graduate students who are not only knowledgeable about traditional counseling and psychological theories and skilled in counseling techniques, but also are informed about contemporary schools and skilled in the delivery of the most current models of school counseling practice. Student field experiences must be carefully selected to give students important learning activities under the supervision of a master school counselor. School counselors must receive training through which they develop competencies in multiculturalism, advocacy, and educational accountability, and they must be encouraged to become leaders in their schools and communities and to become advocates for needed school reforms. Further, not only must school counselors be skilled in crisis intervention and remedial counseling, but they must also know about prevention science and must be skilled in the development of prevention interventions that will reach large numbers of students. Given budget constraints, it is unlikely that a counselor's large student caseload will be reduced in the near future, and therefore, school counselors must be innovative in effectively serving the total student population. Finally, school administrators must be adequately educated to help them understand the appropriate roles of school counselors so that the considerable knowledge and skills of school counselors are not wasted on clerical and administrative tasks that erode the school counselor's effectiveness.

School Counselor-Centered Training: The Ideal Program

While our ideal program incorporates some of the traditional elements of school counselor training models, the biggest difference is that our training program is school counselor–centered. The needs of school counselor trainees, students, parents, and communities are of paramount importance. This training program should be completed in two academic years, culminating with a master's degree and a school counseling license or certification. While we prefer the cohort model, flexibility should be allowed for nontraditional students (such as those with families or those who must work full-time) to complete the program in three years. While we estimate that the program will require 54 semester credit hours to complete, variations may depend on university and license requirements.

It is understood that the reality of school counselor training programs usually will not allow for completely separate sections or courses for school counselor trainees, and classes may be completed in other university departments (e.g., human development, social work, or psychology). However, these courses can be supplemented, however, by small group sessions that apply the course content to school counseling practice. These sections can be taught by instructors knowledgeable about the practice of school counseling (e.g., master school counselors from the community). The sessions could be integrated with student field experiences. In any given course, instructors could separate students according to interest (e.g., school counseling, community mental health). Different readings and assignments could be required depending on area of interest. For example, in a career counseling course, school counselors may focus on career exploration and college major selection, and appropriate career development models of middle school students. In an ethics course, students can be given ethical dilemmas commonly faced by school counselors. We also recommend that school counseling students be placed in practicum courses and on-campus supervision groups with other school counseling practicum students, rather than in heterogeneous groups of students who are completing their practicum in different types of settings (e.g., community mental health).

The following is an example of one possible program of study.

Semester One

Field Placement: First Encounter With School Counseling Students are assigned to a school and school counselor supervisor for one semester or the entire school year. CACREP calls this a "practicum," and 100 hours is required. Some programs may be able to arrange for their students to participate in field placements at the elementary, middle school, and high school levels across one academic year. This is especially important for school counseling students who have not previously worked in a school environment. School counseling practicum students will begin by observing professional school counselors and participating in nondirect service roles, such as staff development, navigation of career exploration software, and organization of school mentoring programs and the guidance curriculum. They can gradually be allowed to provide some direct services, such as participating in classroom guidance activities, individual academic advising, and individual or group career counseling services, perhaps in a co-counselor role. A total of 40 direct contact hours (i.e., time spent with students, teachers, and parents) should be completed by the end of the practicum placement. The main point of this initial experience is for students to become familiar with a school environment and school counselor responsibilities and activities.

Counseling Theory In this course, students learn about counseling theories and the history of counseling, including school counseling. Students learn about counseling theories that are typically applied in schools and how they might be useful. These theories will include person-centered, brief counseling models, and cognitive–behavioral counseling. Other approaches that are sometimes used in school, for example, the use of play, art, and narrative approaches, can also be included.

Multicultural Counseling This course may be best taught in the first year to help students fully realize the importance of the cultural context in which students live. Issues related to cultural bias, stereotyping, and prejudice must be covered. Course activities should provide opportunities for students to examine their personal histories and increase their own self-awareness related to issues such as race, ethnicity, gender, and socioeconomic status. Students should also be taught models of advocacy and leadership to promote tolerance and reduce discriminatory practices. The course should include both didactic and experiential learning.

Helping Relationships The instructor of this course should be cognizant of the fact that school counseling students will have specific, unique needs and, therefore, will allow for flexibility in assignments and classwork. When requiring students to write an informed consent statement, for example, the instructor will allow students to write a "Welcome to Central City Guidance Department" statement which, while informing students and parents of their rights, is written in a more family-friendly or child-friendly manner. Students should also learn counseling skills appropriate with children and their parents.

Introduction to School Counseling School counseling students "rule" here! Uniquely designed for only school counseling students, this course intends to prepare school counselors for their unique roles in schools. Students are taught consultation, how to interact professionally with parents, how to not "side" with a high school student when the student complains about a teacher, and how to communicate effectively with principals. Students learn how to work within the broader community and collaborate with cultural leaders. The course should be flexible according to the needs of the community and the students, and it should address common school counselor activities at the different educational levels. Finally, the course should inform students about the use of technology in decision making, and it should require technology-enhanced presentations for student presentation assignments.

Semester Two

Field Placement Continues It may be preferable for students to change school settings the second semester to have a broader experience as well as the opportunity to interact with another school counselor supervisor.

Group Counseling It is important for school counselors to be competent in leading a range of groups in schools (i.e., support groups, psycho-educational groups, and task groups). Students should develop skills leading informational groups for parents and community leaders, and leading task groups of stakeholders. Graduate students should be given the opportunity to observe or co-facilitate a group in a school setting. Students should become familiar with the Association of Specialists in Group Work Best Practice guidelines.

Ethics It is important for the instructor of this course to be familiar with the unique ethical dilemmas faced by school counselors. For example, is it appropriate for a school counselor to be the head coach of the girls' basketball team? Is it appropriate for the school counselor to date a teacher or a child's parent? How do school counselors keep case notes, if any? How do school counselors protect their students while respecting parents' rights? Who is the "client" of the school counselor: parent, student, teacher, or administrator? In addition to professional ethical codes (i.e., American Counseling Association) and ASCA Best Practices Guidelines, the course must familiarize trainees with state (and perhaps school district) rules and regulations concerning issues such as confidentiality, informed consent, duty to warn, and reporting possible abuse.

Career Counseling Developmental models of career counseling are preferred for school counseling students, recognizing that career counseling used with high school students is not appropriate for elementary children. Post-high-school planning is appropriate for high school students, but acquainting children about careers and decision-making are more appropriate for elementary school students. School counselor trainees should become familiar with relevant assessment instruments, such as aptitude, achievement, and interest tests, and with career exploration computer software.

Contemporary Student Issues In this course, students become familiar with topics that are most pressing for children, adolescents, and their families. Important topics for school counselor trainees to learn about include crisis intervention, school violence, suicide, sexuality and sexual harassment, drug and alcohol use and abuse, teen pregnancy, dropout prevention, gangs, divorce and custody laws, child abuse (including specific information about how to report and handle the aftermath), and bullying. Special populations within the schools, such as gay and lesbian students, immigrant and refugee students, students who receive assistance through special education, gifted and talented students, and unmotivated students, can also be addressed in this class. Graduate students should also learn about broader issues related to schools and how they affect students (e.g., state and national achievement tests and legislative and political forces that impact school funding).

Semester Three

Practicum or Internship This is a more intense field experience that builds upon previous field placements. CACREP calls this an "internship," and 600 hours is required. Because graduate students have had school-based field experience, they are able to begin providing direct service early in their practicum setting. Counseling students should have the opportunity to work with students individually and in large and small groups and also to interact with teachers, administrators, and parents. Specific activities include individual student planning, crisis intervention, delivering guidance lessons, and consulting with teachers, administrators, and parents about student and school systemic needs. School counselor supervisors should be provided with training in supervision by the training program faculty, and students should be supervised on-campus through their graduate program by supervisors knowledgeable about school counseling. This supervision can be conducted in small groups of student peers. Depending on the number of school counseling practicum students, it may be preferable to form supervision groups based on the educational level of the practicum placement (i.e., elementary, middle, or high school). Some jurisdictions may require students to complete a practicum across three different levels of schools (i.e., elementary, middle, and senior high schools). While such a requirement may provide students with familiarity to determine which school counselor license they would like to pursue, it may not actually allow them enough time to determine which environment is best for them. In addition, this requirement seems unnecessary for those who know they would like to work at a specific level. Some states may license counselors across K–12 grades and may allow students to complete a practicum at the elementary school level, but accept a job later at the high school level. This allows flexibility for the school counselor trainee, but may not allow for full familiarization with different needs at the various levels.

Statistics and Measurement School counseling students must be conversant in basic statistical and measurement techniques to understand the professional literature and to develop strategies to evaluate their programs. These classes ideally focus on applied statistics and measurement, with students using examples of concepts and data from school situations. Students should learn about statistical computer software and ways to present statistical information to be meaningful to education stakeholders. Students should also learn concepts from measurement theory to adequately evaluate and use psychological tests with their students.

Child/Adolescent Development School counseling students must be knowledgeable about child and adolescent development across the domains of social, cognitive, and emotional development. With this background, school counselors learn what is developmentally appropriate for students in order to assist teachers, administrators, and parents in understanding students. An understanding of child and adolescent development also helps school counselors promote the most effective and developmentally appropriate interventions for students.

Semester Four

Practicum or Internship The practicum/internship assignment continues as summarized above; however, the trainee should have responsibility for increasingly demanding school counseling activities under supervision. Trainees should also be encouraged to engage in self-supervision and reflection and to articulate ways that they manage stress and care for themselves.

Research Methods and Evaluation Students learn how to develop surveys and questionnaires in order to evaluate their programs. They learn and practice the fundamentals of research methods, including qualitative research methods. At least some research examples should be relevant to the role of the school counselor. Experiential components are extremely important. Students should be asked to complete a research project that is relevant to a school context. Students should also be required to present their research project in some local forum (e.g., department poster session or local school district presentation). As presentation aids, students should be encouraged to use computer technology to enhance their presentation (e.g., PowerPoint). It is also important for school counseling students to be encouraged to submit their projects to professional conferences and journals, perhaps with faculty as coauthors.

Assessment School counseling students must learn about psychological and educational assessments typically used in schools (e.g., intelligence, achievement, aptitude tests, and career interest inventories). It is also important for students to become familiar with assessments such as the clinical interview and measures of personality. Even if school counselors do not administer psychological and educational instruments, they will receive assessment reports and will be expected to understand the results and convey them to relevant parties (e.g. students, parents, teachers). For example, if parents receive a written assessment report from the school psychologist, the parent may ask the school counselor to interpret the report. Therefore, the school counselor must be able to read a psychological assessment report and translate it in a meaningful way to parents and other stakeholders. Other examples include interpreting the meaning of intelligence test results, of tests that assess learning difficulties, of SAT or ACT measures, and of state and national achievement tests. School counseling students should have direct experience administering, scoring, and interpreting some of the more common measures that they will use. They can also self-administer some others to better understand the tests. Finally, the course should give students skills to help them understand the quality of the technical information about any given test (e.g., reliability, validity, norms).

References

Adelman, H. S., & Taylor, L. (2002). School counselors and school reform: New directions. *Professional School Counseling, 5,* 235–248.

American School Counselor Association. (2003). *The ASCA national model: A framework for school counseling programs.* Alexandria, VA: Author.

Baker, S. B. (2000). *School counseling for the twenty first century* (3rd ed.). Upper Saddle River, NJ: Pearson Education.

Baker, S. B., & Gerler, E. R. (2004). *School counseling for the twenty first century* (4th ed.). Upper Saddle River, NJ: Pearson Merrill Prentice Hall.

Bernard, J. M. (1979). Supervisor training: A discrimination model. *Counselor Education and Supervision, 19,* 60–68.

Bernard, J. M. (1997). The discrimination model. In C. E. Watkins, Jr. (Ed.), *Handbook of psychotherapy supervision* (pp. 310–327). New York: Wiley.

Bernard, J. M., & Goodyear, R. K. (2004). *Fundamentals of clinical supervision* (3rd ed.). Boston: Pearson Education Inc.

Blackman, L., Hayes, R. L., Reeves, P. M., & Paisley, P. O. (2002). Building a bridge: Counselor educator-school counselor collaboration. *Counselor Education and Supervision, 41,* 243–255.

Bradley, C., & Fiorini, J. (1999). Evaluation of counseling practicum: National study of programs accredited by CACREP. *Counselor Education and Supervision, 39,* 110–120.

Burnham, J. J., & Jackson, C. M. (2000). School counselor roles: Discrepancies between actual practice and existing models. *Professional School Counseling, 4,* 41–49.

CAREI (Center for Applied Research and Educational Improvement), University of Minnesota College of Education and Human Development. (2000, October). *Evaluation of the transforming school counseling initiative. A report on first year experiences: Executive summary—October 2000.* Retrieved October 25, 2007, from http://cehd.umn.edu/CAREI/Reports/DeWitt/year-1.html

Cobia, D. C., & Henderson, D. A. (2003). *Handbook of school counseling.* Upper Saddle River, NJ: Pearson Education.

Council for Accreditation of Counseling and Related Educational Programs (CACREP). (2001). *The 2001 standards.* Retrieved April 24, 2005, from http://www.counseling.org/cacrep/2001standards700.htm

Ellis, A. (1994). *Reason and emotion in psychotherapy revised.* New York: Kensington.

Erford, B. T. (Ed.). (2003). *Transforming the school counseling profession.* Columbus, OH: Merrill Prentice Hall.

Erford, B. T., House, R., & Martin, P. (2003). Transforming the school counseling profession. In B. T. Erford (Ed.), *Transforming the school counseling profession* (pp. 1–20). Columbus, OH: Merrill Prentice Hall.

Foster, S., Rollefson, M., Doksum, T., Noonan, D., Robinson, G., & Teich, J. (2005). *School mental health services in the United States, 2002–2003* (DHHS Publication No. SMA054068). Rockville, MD: Center for Mental Health Services, Substance Abuse and Mental Health Services Administration.

Freeman, B., & McHenry, S. (1996). Clinical supervision of counselors-in-training: A nationwide survey of ideal delivery, goals, and theoretical influences. *Counselor Education and Supervision, 36,* 144–158.

Glasser, W. (1998). *Choice theory.* New York: Harper Collins.

Gysbers, N. C., & Henderson, P. (1988). *Developing and managing your school guidance program* (2nd ed.) Alexandria, VA: American Association for Counseling and Development.

Gysbers, N. C., & Henderson, P. (2000). *Developing and managing your school guidance program* (3rd ed.). Alexandria, VA: American Counseling Association.

Gysbers, N. C., & Henderson, P. (2002). *Implementing comprehensive school guidance programs: Critical leadership issues and successful responses*. Washington, DC: Office of Education Research and Improvement.

Henderson, P., & Lampe, R. E. (1992). Clinical supervision of school counselors. *The School Counselor, 39*, 151–157.

Hinkle, J. S. (1997). Training school counselors to do family counseling. In W. Walsh & G. R. Williams (Eds.), *Schools and family therapy: Using systems theory and family therapy in the resolution of school problems* (pp. 201–207). Springfield, IL: Charles C. Thomas.

Jackson, C. M., Snow, B. M., Boes, S. R., Phillips, P. L., Stanard, R. P., Painter, L. C., et al. (2002). Inducting the transformed school counselor into the profession. *Theory Into Practice, 41*, 177–185.

Kagan, S. (2003). Short-term child-centered play therapy training with school counselors and teachers in Israel. *Dissertation Abstracts International, 64* (6-A), 1985.

Keys, S. G., Bemak, F., & Lockhart, E. J. (1998). Transforming school counseling to serve the mental health needs of at-risk youth. *Journal of Counseling and Development, 76*, 381–388.

Lanning, W. (1986). Development of the supervisor emphasis rating form. *Counselor Education and Supervision, 27*, 331–342.

Littrell, J. M., Lee-Borden, N., & Lorenz, J. A. (1979). A developmental framework for counseling supervision. *Counselor Education and Supervision, 19*, 119–136.

Louis, K. S., & Gordon, M. F. (2006). *Aligning student support with achievement goals*. Thousand Oaks, CA: Corwin Press.

Martin, P. J. (2002). Transforming school counseling: A national perspective. *Theory Into Practice, 41*(3), 148–153.

McEachern, A. G. (2003). School counselor preparation to meet the guidance needs of exceptional students: A national study. *Counselor Education and Supervision, 42*, 314–325.

Michlin, M., & Meath, J. (2005). *Effective training for school counselors, advocates of academic achievement for all*. Minneapolis: Center for Applied Research and Educational Improvement, University of Minnesota.

Myrick, R. D. (1987). *Developmental guidance and counseling: A practical approach*. Minneapolis, MN: Education Media.

Nelson, M. D., & Johnson, P. (1999). School counselors as supervisors: An integrated approach for supervising school counseling interns. *Counselor Education and Supervision, 39*, 89–100.

Partin, R. L. (1993). School counselors' time: Where does it go? *The School Counselor, 40*, 274–281.

Peace, S. D., & Sprinthall, N. A. (1998). Training school counselors to supervise beginning counselors: Theory, research and practice. *Professional School Counseling, 1*, 2–8.

Perie, M., Grigg, W., & Donahue, P. (2005). *The nation's report card: Mathematics 2005* (NCES 2006-453). Washington, DC: U.S. Government Printing Office.

Perie, M., Grigg, W., & Donahue, P. (2005). *The nation's report card: Reading 2005* (NCES 2006-451). Washington, DC: U.S. Government Printing Office.

Perusse, R., Goodnough, G. E., & Noel, C. J. (2001). A national survey of school counselor preparation programs: Screening methods, faculty experiences, curriculum content, and fieldwork requirements. *Counselor Education and Supervision, 40*, 252–262.

Roberts, E. B., & Borders, L. D. (1994). Supervision of school counselors Administrative, program, and counseling. *The School Counselor, 41*, 149–157.

Romano, J. L., & Kachgal, M. (2004). Counseling psychology and school counseling: An underutilized partnership. *The Counseling Psychologist, 32*, 184–215.

Rones, M., & Hoagwood, K. (2000). School-based mental health services: A research review. *Clinical Child and Family Psychology Review, 3*, 223–241.

Rye, D. R., & Sparks, R. (1999). *Strengthening K-12 school counseling programs*. (2nd ed.). Ann Arbor, MI: Taylor & Francis.

Schmidt, J. J. (2003). *Counseling in schools: Essential services and comprehensive programs* (4th ed.). Upper Saddle River, NJ: Pearson Education.

Sciarra, P. T. (2004). *School counseling: Foundations and contemporary issues*. Pacific Grove, CA: Brooks/Cole Thomson Learning.

Sears, S. J., & Granello, D. H. (2002). School counseling now and in the future: A reaction. *Professional School Counseling, 5*, 164–171.

Seashore, K. R., Jones, L. M., & Seppanen, P. (2001). *Transforming school counseling: A report on early evaluation findings*. Minneapolis: Center for Applied Research and Educational Improvement, University of Minnesota.

Sink, C. A. (2005). *Contemporary school counseling: Theory, research and practice*. Boston: Houghton Mifflin Company.

Sisson, C. F., & Bullis, M. (1992). Survey of school counselors' perceptions of graduate training priorities. *School Counselor, 40*, 109–117.

Stickel, S. A. (1995, March). *The internship in school counseling: A national survey of school counselor training programs*. Paper presented at the annual meeting of the Eastern Educational Research Association, Hilton Head, SC.

Stone, C., & Dahir, C. A. (2006). *The transformed school counselor*. Boston: Houghton Mifflin.

Thompson, R. A. (2002). *School counseling: Best practices for working in the schools*. (2nd ed.). New York: Brunner-Routledge.

Worthington, R. L., & Juntunen, C. L. (1997). The vocational development of non-college bound youth: Counseling psychology and the school-to-work transition movement. *The Counseling Psychologist, 25*, 323–363.

XXI
SUPERVISION OF PROFESSIONAL SCHOOL COUNSELORS

DIANA GRUMAN
Western Washington University

MARY LEE NELSON
University of Wisconsin–Madison

INTRODUCTION

It is rare to find a professional who emerges from a graduate training program and feels entirely prepared for the work that lies ahead. Inevitable gaps exist between the graduate school–based training and internship practice, and the personal and professional demands of the "real world." Time and experience may be needed to integrate and apply prior training experiences to professional practice. For example, research within the teacher education field suggests that it is not until a teacher's third year of teaching that he or she is prepared to implement many of the methods introduced during the teacher training programs because he or she is too busy simply "surviving."

Similarly, when a student leaves a counselor training program to embark on a career in the schools, he or she is only partially trained to provide competent, comprehensive services (Matthes, 1992; Page, Pietrzak, & Sutton, 2001). In part, the road through the induction period will become less rocky through time on the job. Time is needed, for instance, to understand the unique needs of the school and community in which one works. Time is also required to establish trust with colleagues both inside and outside the school. In addition, time is needed to learn how to navigate the politics of the building and district including styles of leadership and competing agendas as one tries to find one's place in a team of educators.

In addition to the initial tasks that will be mastered through time on the job, other tasks facing school counselors will require considerable effort. In fact, numerous authors have stressed that these efforts should span a practitioner's entire professional career (Brott & Myers, 1999; Skovholt & Rønnestad, 1992). For example, counseling skills introduced during the graduate training program may need constant refinement. Knowledge obtained during graduate school can quickly become outdated. No matter how many years of experience, counselors may also encounter new types of cases or crisis situations that are baffling, ethically challenging, and stress provoking.

In addition to these individual challenges, school counselors who are proceeding down the path toward professional competency face a unique set of contextual challenges. First, pressing social problems intensify and fade in a very short period, requiring school counselors to stay abreast of current issues impacting their students. For example, while gang involvement may provoke a high level of panic in one year, the impact of proliferating meth labs in a community may eclipse the problems that gangs pose in the following year. Second, methods of treating people with problems are in a constant state of evolution. Counselors must seek out continual skill development regarding such things as medications for children's psychiatric disorders and best practices in reducing violence in the schools.

A final challenge is that school counselors work in the ever-changing political and social context of schools. Politically, national and local reform efforts to improve the system of education inevitably shape and reshape the priorities of all those personnel working within the walls of the school. Effective school counselors must understand and attempt to stay aligned with the new priorities and directions of their buildings and districts. Socially, the population of citizens in the United States is becoming increasingly more diverse, with projections estimating a shift for European Americans from majority to minority status over the next 50 years (Sue & Sue, 2003). School counselors who have not already examined their prejudices, biases, and culturally embedded identities must make cultural awareness and action a priority in order to effectively meet the needs of students and their families (Paisley & McMahon, 2002).

A final concern about professional development for school counselors is that skill delivery in the training program is learned rather quickly, but timing and judgment in the use of skills takes much longer to acquire (Holloway & Neufeldt, 1995). Meyer (1978) found that, without supervision, skill levels decrease after training. Crutchfield & Borders (2002) were concerned with discover that practicing counselors scored in the subtractive range on a test of empathetic responding—a basic skill we might assume they had acquired at a certain level of mastery. Likewise, Granello (1997) found that, compared with their counterparts in mental health, community, and marriage and family counseling, who increased cognitive development with training, school counselors demonstrated a trend toward regressive cognitive development as they progressed in training.

Of most concern is a 10-year follow-up survey of school counselors who were rated by supervisors and teachers as low, average, and high in effectiveness (Wiggins, 1993). Contrary to the notion that school counselors, in general, will naturally develop greater competence with years of experience, results indicate that only 12 of the 193 evaluated counselors received a higher rating after 10 years on the job. In the sample, 33 counselors received lower ratings and 148 received the same effectiveness rating. Without a concerted effort to address these individual and contextual challenges, numerous authors have warned that practicing school counselors face a number of professional risks, including a regression in skills, stagnation, and burnout (Crutchfield & Borders, 1997; Herlihy, Gray, & McCollum, 2002; Meyer, 1978; Wiggins, Wilkerson, & Bellini, 2006).

Given the many challenges, it seems clear that, as they continue to work toward proficiency across their professional lives, professional school counselors will need to access many sources of development and support. Pioneering researchers Skovolt and Rønnestad (1992) proposed that counselor development is a multiyear process involving many different influences, wherein counselors greatly benefit from supervision, particularly early on. The process of moving from novice to skilled requires feedback from clients, peers, and more experienced professionals. Skovolt and Rønnestad suggested that with careful attention to training and supervision, proficiency may take a minimum of ten years. How do school counselors best tackle the wide-reaching need for ongoing training, supervision, and support throughout their careers?

The purpose of this chapter is to review what is known about supervising the journey of school counselors as they move from novice counselors fresh from training programs to more experienced professionals. We will examine the theoretical base and research findings surrounding on-the-job professional development and school counselor supervision. We will also examine the research on potentially supportive practices that may help counselors move smoothly toward competence and effectiveness. Finally, we will review the latest innovations regarding professional development and future directions.

THEORY

The Role of Supervision in Counselor Development

The development of counseling expertise is a fuzzy process. It is not linear or straightforward, and in the case of school counseling, it usually feels like "learning on the fly." So many circumstances arise daily in the life of a school counselor that it would be impossible to write a textbook or a series of textbooks that could address every potential challenge. Supervisors can play a vital role in assisting new professionals to manage the uncertainty inherent in the school counselor role. In fact, research on stages of counselor development tells us that supervisors exert a strong influence on new professionals' conceptualizations about their work, decisions about how to practice, and development of a professional identity (Skovholt & Rønnestad, 1992). Counseling students and early professionals relies on supervisor expertise—either *in vivo* or in memory—well into their first few years of practice.

Because learning to be an expert demands an understanding of how to manage ambiguity and complexity, developing professionals are thought to pass through a predictable set of stages. In counseling, this progression has been described as the integrated developmental model, or the IDM (Stoltenberg, McNeill, & Delworth, 1998). According to the IDM, Level One supervisees have limited training, or at least limited experience, in the specific domain in which they are being supervised. Both motivation and anxiety are high. Supervisees are focused on acquiring skills; they want to know "the correct" or "best" approach with their students and other clientele. At Level One, supervisees are dependent on their supervisors. They are highly self-focused, but with limited self-awareness, and they are apprehensive about evaluation. Thus, they need structured education, positive feedback, and little direct confrontation.

At Level Two, supervisees are transitioning from being structure-dependent to being structure-independent. They experience fluctuating confidence. Although functioning more independently, they may experience conflict between autonomy and dependency, much as one does in adolescence. This conflict can manifest as pronounced resistance to supervisors and superiors. With regard to awareness, supervisees at Level Two have a greater ability to focus on and empathize with their students; however, "balance" is still an issue. In younger supervisees, the problem may become manifest in role confusion and enmeshment with their students and students' families. Supervision can be somewhat turbulent in this stage. Supervision of the Level Two counselor may require supervisors to recognize the resistance and/or enmeshment as developmental in nature and to work to facilitate the supervisee in his or her growth toward autonomy.

The Level Three supervisee has achieved a degree of autonomy and tends to focus more on a personalized approach to practice, as well as on the use and understanding of "self" in counseling. Motivation is consistent; occasional doubts about effectiveness will occur, but will not be immobilizing. A solid belief in one's own professional judgment has developed as the supervisee moves into independent practice. Supervision tends to be more collegial, as differences between supervisor and supervisee expertise diminish.

Level Three supervisees return to being self-aware, but with a very different quality than at Level One. Supervisees at this level are able to remain focused on the students while also stepping back to attend to their own personal reactions to the students and using this awareness in decision making about students.

Stoltenberg et al. (1998) proposed a second phase to Level Three development: Level Three, Integrated (Level 3i). At the integrated phase of Level Three, the supervisee is able to apply developing knowledge and awareness across domains of work. Thus, a school counselor at this level would feel confident across tasks such as developing guidance curricula; interacting with parents; interacting with administrators, teachers, and other school personnel; and mastering the technicalities of scheduling and advising practices. Though not completely seasoned, the supervisee at this phase also feels confident in assessing student needs and developing collaborative interventions to address them. Supervisees at this level are able to identify their strengths and weaknesses and can make good use of supervisors who assist them in this process and help them to identify sources of continuing education.

Continuous Professional Reflection: The Key to Developmental Progress

Though counselor development may seem to progress along a linear pathway, counseling professionals occasionally encounter situations that challenge their current procedural models of how to handle situations and result in crisis-like experiences. A good example of such a situation is feeling confident about knowing how and when to make a report to child protective services regarding the abuse of a child. You have had several experiences of doing so and you have even developed a relationship with someone in the agency upon whom you can rely. A situation arises with a student who confides in you that her father has beaten her on several occasions and threatened to kill her and her siblings if she tells. She has no observable symptoms of abuse, and other school personnel have told you that protective services have investigated the home previously but could not get clear evidence from any of the children that abuse was occurring. You fear that reporting the student's allegations to protective services might result in further harm to the student.

This concern disrupts your procedural knowledge about how to address allegations of child abuse, and you experience the crisis of having encountered an unfamiliar "shade of gray" with respect to child abuse reporting. At times like this, supervisors can be extremely helpful. They can provide needed "inside information" about how these squeaky situations are handled in the school or in the district, they can help the counselor with cognitive dissonance and fears about negative outcomes for the student, and they can provide needed support throughout the process.

With new knowledge and experience with managing a complex, challenging situation, the developing counselor can again relax and feel confident because he or she has developed another level of informational and procedural understanding. Unfortunately, however, calm is only temporary in the life of a school counselor. The complexity of the job ensures that new crises will erupt and that wise supervisors will be necessary to provide brainstorming, information, and support.

It takes complex skills to think through complex problems. Optimal development of expertise relies on an attitude of openness and willingness to reflect on one's learning process (Neufeldt, 1999; Neufeldt, Karno, & Nelson, 1996). This process of *continuous professional reflection* (Skovholt & Rønnestad, 1992) involves observing one's work, as well as one's thoughts and feelings about decisions that go into the work. Given the contextual challenges facing school counselors, such as the diversification of the population, reflectivity must be practiced continuously to provide responsive and ethical services.

Reflectivity is a process one may undertake after completing a task (much like debriefing after a practice counseling session or viewing and discussing a taped session with a supervisor). Schön (1983) referred to this process as "reflection on action." Reflectivity can also take place while one is in the process of doing a task—a kind of "thinking on one's feet." Schön referred to the latter as "reflection in action." When professionals have developed reflective skills, they are armed with the capacity to process problem situations more quickly and seek productive courses of action. Professionals who learn reflectivity skills are less prone to "premature foreclosure" of development (Skovholt & Rønnestad, 1992); that is, they are less likely to get stuck in brittle, rigid ways of thinking and working that can ultimately lead to dissatisfaction and burnout. Through careful feedback and questioning, supervisors can be helpful in assisting counselors to develop reflective skills that will last a lifetime.

Reflectivity is both a skill and a propensity. The word connotes a capacity to identify areas of one's work that need to be examined, to engage in thorough processing of these situations, and to identify courses of action based upon engagement with them. Reflectivity also implies capacity for self-examination, including consideration of the impact of one's behavior on others and identification of more productive ways of relating. A good supervisor does more than simply share information or provide skills training. He or she provides a sounding board for the developing counselor, offering encouragement for the counselor to wrestle with problems. A good supervisor provides an opportunity for the developing counselor to engage in self-examination in a safe and supportive relationship.

The Supervision Needs of School Counselors

Skovholt and Rønnestad's (1992) work illustrated how professional counselors continue to draw on supervision experiences well into their careers; however, those authors did not specifically investigate the experiences of school counselors, who may or may not benefit from standard forms of clinical supervision. The use of *clinical supervision* has been the most widely discussed method of facilitating professional development for school counselors. Supervision, in general, has been defined as an intensive, interpersonally focused, one-to-one relationship in which one person is designated to oversee the work of others with the express purpose of improving performance and enhancing professional development (Feldstein, 2000; Henderson & Lampe, 1992; Loganbill, Hardy, & Delworth, 1982).

Clinical supervision, specifically, often refers to a relationship focused on direct service delivery or enhancing the clinical knowledge and skills for working with individual students, groups, or in consultation with parents or teachers (Roberts & Borders, 1994). The focus on clinical supervision for school counselors most likely stems from the profession's roots in therapy and clinical practice. As Holloway and Neufeldt (1995) remarked, "supervision is embedded in our beliefs about what constitutes training in psychotherapy" (p. 212).

While supervision may be an essential element in ensuring that counselors become competent and developed professionals, a number of persistent barriers to providing quality clinical supervision in the schools have been identified, including a lack of funding and a lack of time to conduct supervision (Crutchfield, McGarty, Pennington, Richardson, & Tsolis, 1997). An additional barrier, pointed out by Sutton and Page (1994), is that counselors themselves may not seek out clinical supervision because they lack awareness of why supervision may be helpful and are not sure how to obtain it. Moreover, school counselors may anticipate that traditional clinical supervision may not provide them with the skills and knowledge they need to operate within a school setting; thus, they may feel stymied about how to acquire the help they truly need.

These findings raise the question: Given observed barriers to the provision of clinical supervision for school counselors, are there are other avenues for development and support that may meet school counselors' professional needs? Further, given the demands of school reform efforts such as No Child Left Behind, are school counselors facing professional development demands that reach beyond the common scope of clinical supervision? In the following sections, we will take a comprehensive look at the research on the many avenues of supervision and professional development available to school counselors.

RESEARCH

The need for supervision within the counseling field has been widely recognized for decades (Bernard & Goodyear, 2004). Yet the dialogue regarding appropriate supervision and professional development practices for *school counselors* was not initiated in journals until the mid 1970s. Referring to the lack of adequate supervision provided to most school counselors, Boyd and Walter (1975) likened the school counselor to a cactus plant, suggesting that "both survive on a minimum of nutrients" (p. 103), and they called for increased attention to school counselor professional development.

Since the early writing on the topic, numerous authors have stated concerns regarding inadequate practices and limited research (Barret & Schmidt, 1986; Brott & Meyers, 1999; Crespi, 1998). Professional organizations have also weighed in on the issue. In 1989, the AACD (now ACA) School Counseling Task Force declared a need for counseling supervision of practicing school counselors, concluding that, "proper supervision of school counselors is lacking at best, nonexistent at its worst" (p. 20). Recognizing the lack of research, they also recommended that counselor educators at the university level take a lead in initiating new research studies. In the years since the AACD report, many articles have been published, but the empirical evidence regarding effective means of supervision is very limited (Agnew, Vaught, Getz, & Fortune, 2000; Crespi, 1998).

What can we draw from the existing literature? First, a number of researchers have attempted to draw a link between supervision and job performance. Wiggins and Weslander (1986) found that counselors rated as most effective by their building administrators had higher ratings of job satisfaction, self-esteem, and tolerance for ambiguity than did their less-effective counterparts. Moreover, a recent study by Halverson (2000) demonstrated that school counselors willing to pursue ongoing training and supervision demonstrated higher levels of moral development than their counterparts, and that those with higher levels of conceptual development demonstrated greater levels of job satisfaction. Given that we do know that supervision—compared with no supervision—promotes counselor development (Wiley & Ray, 1986), we might be able to hypothesize that adequate supervision may contribute to counselor conceptual development, which, in turn, may promote job satisfaction and greater competence.

A number of surveys have made it clear that counselors themselves recognize a need for significant professional support. In a qualitative study of Australian school counselors, participants cited concerns regarding "blind spots," unchecked prejudices, and being "trapped into . . . using a narrow range of skills" due to professional isolation and lack of supervised practice (McMahon & Patton, 2000). Several surveys also have shed light on how practicing school counselors view their supervision needs. Participants in the Roberts and Borders (1994) survey of school counselors in North Carolina indicated that they wanted counseling supervision to enhance professional growth, provide professional support, and avoid burnout. In a national survey of American school counselors (Page et al., 2001) and a smaller Maine survey (Sutton & Page, 1994), participants' top two supervision goals included (a) taking appropriate action with clients and (b) developing skills and techniques.

Research also has revealed that many school counselors *wish* they had exposure to clinical supervision, but they do not *receive* it (Page et al., 2001; Roberts & Borders, 1994; Sutton & Page, 1994). For example, in a national survey, Page et al. found that 67% said they desired some type of clinical supervision, but only 24% were receiving it. This finding also implies that 33% of school counselors feel they have no need for clinical supervision.

As corroborating evidence, in their survey of National Certified Counselors (NCCs), Borders and Usher (1992) found that a large number of school counselors reported that they had no need for clinical supervision. They also found that school counselors (39% of the 357 NCCs in the sample) were different from other counselors in terms of their existing practices and reported need for supervision. Specifically, counselors in the schools received significantly fewer hours of postdegree supervision than community or private practice counselors. They also were more likely to be receiving no supervision and reported wanting supervision less frequently than their peers in other settings did. Finally, the authors reported that, "school-based counselors' most frequent reason for receiving supervision was that it was a requirement of the work setting" (p. 596) rather than a desire for professional development.

How might we explain why some school counselors feel they do not need clinical supervision and others feel they need more of it? It is possible that school counselors, such as those in the Borders and Usher (1992) study, who say they do not need clinical supervision think of it as supervision for traditional psychotherapists rather than as supervision for counselors in schools. Indeed, many traditional clinical supervisors who have not worked in schools may not understand the needs of or complex roles assumed by school counselors. Additionally, school counselors are commonly supervised by administrators or school principals who have little or no counseling experience (Borders & Usher; Mathes, 1992; Roberts & Borders, 1994). Perhaps as a result of negative experiences, the school counselors who lack interest do not think supervision is a worthwhile endeavor. The underlying problem is that the dearth of supervisors with adequate expertise leaves school counselors vulnerable to a lack of potentially valuable support and professional training.

On the face of it, reports of limited interest in and poor provision of clinical supervision raise ethical concerns. The ethical code of the American Psychological Association (APA; 2002) states, "Psychologists provide services, teach, or conduct research in new areas or involving new techniques only after undertaking appropriate study, training, supervision, and/or consultation from persons who are competent in these areas or techniques" (p. 4). This mandate suggests that professionals need consultation and supervision when they confront client difficulties that are outside the range of their experience. Second, the ethical code developed by the American Counseling Association (ACA; 1995) strongly suggests that professional counselors participate in ongoing and regular clinical supervision. In contrast to the specific guidelines regarding supervision in the ACA codes, the American School Counseling Association (ASCA) offers a much broader recommendation. ASCA focuses on professional development rather than taking a specific stand on clinical supervision. Specifically, within the professional responsibilities section of the ASCA *Ethical Standards for School Counselors* (2004) is the following statement: "The professional school counselor strives through personal initiative to maintain professional competence and to keep abreast of professional information" (ASCA, 2004, p. 125). The ASCA *Ethical Standards* also state, "Professional and personal growth are ongoing throughout a counselor's career" (p. 125). In contrast to the APA and ACA codes of ethics, the ASCA code seems to reflect the reality of counseling in school settings: Because of funding priorities in schools, professional supervision is largely unavailable to school counselors. All ethical codes, however, imply that a counselor is responsible for obtaining ongoing professional consultation.

If, as the aforementioned research suggests, few school counselors actually receive clinical supervision as a means of professional development, how do they comply with the ethical standards of their organization? Numerous articles shed light on how school counselors find ways to "maintain professional competence" and grow on an ongoing basis. First, informal networks of counselors in a region, as well as more formalized meetings of district teams, may be vital ways to combat isolation and stress (McMahon & Patton, 2000). These informal and formal networks may be the best way for geographically isolated counselors in rural areas to consult on critical supervision issues. Second, professional development activities provided through workshops and professional affiliations with state or national organizations may be critical components in terms of skills acquisition and program development (Fairchild & Zins, 1986). Counselors such as those working in elementary settings with no direct colleagues may breathe new life into their programs by attending workshops with peers who understand the challenges they face. Finally, a compelling argument was made by Barret and Schmidt (1986) that clinical supervision might be successfully augmented by other types of supervision, including administrative and program supervision

PROFESSIONAL DEVELOPMENT PRACTICES

Prevailing Trends and Recent Innovations

In this section, we review current trends and recent innovations in professional development practices. First, we address the contributions to school counselor development that can be made by administrative and program supervision. Second, we address peer group supervision practices and describe some proposed models for conducting peer supervision groups. Finally, we describe university–school counseling collaboratives and professional development schools as broader collaborative efforts to provide supervision and development opportunities for school counselors.

Administrative Supervision

Administrative supervision has been described as supervision focused on employee job performance and effectiveness, staff relations, and outreach to parents and other constituents (Henderson, 1994; Roberts & Borders, 1994). Administrative supervision appears to be the most common form received by counselors, given that school principals and district-level administrators often take a primary role in overseeing the work of school counselors (Schmidt & Barret, 1983; Sutton & Page, 1994). While concerns are frequently cited, several authors have provided a vision of how administrative supervision can be beneficial.

One school district in Virginia developed a professional growth program whereby counselors, with the support of administrators, created an individual action plan to target areas for professional development (Kaplan, Geoffroy, Pare, & Wolf, 1992). Progress was documented through written evaluations, observations, self-reports, video tapes, and teacher surveys. Preliminary evaluations indicated that the plans encouraged constructive dialogue between administrators and counselors and helped the counselors identify their strengths and weaknesses. The authors also speculated that, "administrator participation in the process encourages their continued support for [counseling] activities" (p. 168).

In Mississippi, mandated job assessments were required starting in 1982 and the Mississippi Counseling Association took a lead role in developing a set of counselor competencies to comply with the new law. Housely, McDaniel, and Underwood (1990) initiated a survey to investigate the impact of the new assessments. They reported that almost half of the counselors reported an increase in clarity of purpose as a counselor, feelings of competence, and feelings of self as a professional. The only significant change ($p < .05$), however, was in increased organizational skills. They also found that inexperienced counselors reported greater benefits from the assessment process than did experienced counselors.

Program Supervision

Program supervision is defined as supervision focused on program development, implementation, coordination, and evaluation. Given that school counselors working within the comprehensive contexts of the *ASCA National Model* (2003) and Developmental School Counseling and Guidance programs (Gysbers & Henderson, 2000, 2001) are called upon to develop large-scale preventative education programs, the elements addressed by a program supervisor, such as a lead counselor or district coordinator, may be critical to the success of a school counseling program. Again, rather than dismissing it as "beneath" the professional school counselor's standards, program supervision may be vital for success, given the programmatic demands on today's school counselor.

As an example, in a national survey of practicing school counselors, Fairchild and Zins (1986) found that over half of the respondents were collecting program accountability data to enhance their professional development. The researchers reported that counselors used the data in a number of ways including "demonstrating one's effectiveness to others (75.6%) and improving the quality of services (71%)" (p. 198). Of those counselors not collecting accountability data, the greatest percentage (52%) said they were not familiar with the methods for obtaining it. The authors emphasized that counselor training programs "need to play a more instrumental role in ensuring that counselors in training acquire self-evaluation and program evaluation skills" (p. 198). We would also suggest that program administrators take a lead role in guiding counselors through the process of data collection and evaluation.

A final example that combines administration and program supervision involves the use of performance evaluations in the restructuring of the Austin (Texas) School District guidance and counseling program (Synatschk, 2002). The 5-year restructuring process began when a team established a well-defined and accepted job description for counselors and created a yearly appraisal system. The appraisal process involved each counselor's completing a "campus priority plan" based on student needs assessments, reviewing the plan with the school administrator, collecting evidence of work in all areas of the comprehensive guidance model, and participating in a year-end evaluation conference. Though Synatschk did not collect data following the implementation process, she did report anecdotally that administrators gained a great appreciation for the benefits of a comprehensive counseling model.

Peer Group Supervision

In addition to the one-to-one relationships in clinical supervision models, several authors have nominated peer group supervision as an alternative, cost-effective means of providing supervision to school counselors (Agnew et al., 2000; Benshoff, 1993; Benshoff & Paisley, 1996; Crutchfield & Borders, 1997; Spice & Spice, 1976). Moreover, peer supervision may be experienced by members as more collegial and supportive, as well as less threatening, than clinical supervision based upon the hierarchical structure of the "expert" and "learner" configuration typically found at clinical training sites (Borders, 1991; Crutchfield & Borders, 1997).

Though professional ethical codes suggest that supervision should be provided by senior members of the same profession—a mandate that might seem to conflict with the practice of peer supervision—supervision is not a formalized professional activity in most school settings; hence, all school counselors are technically peers—both novice and seasoned counselors alike. The second author of this chapter has conducted numerous professional development groups for school counselors in which some members were much more senior than others. Moreover, a less experienced school counselor may have expertise in a particular area that more senior counselors do not. For instance, a novice school counselor with experience in the paraprofessional role of psychiatric technician may know more about psychotropic medications than other school personnel and thus be able to advise more senior counselors about a student's medication side effects. One way to ensure the quality of peer supervision is to have counselors with expertise in particular areas take the lead when a consultation is requested within their area of expertise. If no expertise pertaining to a particular problem exists in a consult group, a professional with experience in that area can be brought in as a guest consultant.

Peer group supervision can be organized in a number of ways. C. G. Spice and W. H. Spice (1976) described a triadic peer supervision model wherein counselors met on a weekly or biweekly basis to provide support and consultation to each other. As group members, the counselors served alternately in roles of supervisee, facilitator, and commentator, much in the same fashion as counseling students work in class as they are learning basic skills. These groups decide on their own membership, structure, and meeting times, based on supervision needs and interests such as particular theoretical orientations, grade levels served, and interpersonal attributes.

Borders (1991) proposed a structured group supervision format that offered multiple suggestions for participant roles, as well as group activities, including case presentation and recommendations, role playing, providing constructive feedback, and viewing case presentations from different theoretical orientations. Though the Borders model was generic and not limited to school counseling peer supervision groups, it provided detailed rationales and strategies for organizing and participating in peer group supervision and is a "must read" for any professional counselor group wishing to pursue collaborative peer supervision.

More recently, Benshoff and Paisley (1996) provided a format for nine-week structured dyadic peer supervision meetings. In their model, structured activities included examination of appropriateness of roles and expectations for counselors in participants' individual schools, discussions of needed changes in school counseling services at each participant's school, and ongoing review of counseling audio or videotapes. Early participants in the Benshoff and Paisley model indicated strong satisfaction with their experiences. Though the model was time-limited and designed for peer supervision dyads, recommended activities could easily be adopted and adapted as needed by collaborative peer supervision groups.

Crutchfield and Borders (1997) compared the relative effectiveness of the Borders (1991) and Benshoff and Paisley (1996) models and found that, regardless of format, participants expressed satisfaction and increased counseling self-efficacy as a result of their participation. Additionally, a qualitative examination of the effectiveness of the Borders model also yielded promising results (Crutchfield et al., 1997). Though more research is needed on the effectiveness of peer supervision, we strongly recommend that practicing school counselors make a serious effort to either join or initiate regular peer supervision meetings, whether in dyadic or group format.

University–School Counseling Collaboratives & Professional Development Schools

Collaborative professional development efforts between counselor education departments and school districts seem to provide support, renewal, and ongoing learning to professional school counselors, as well as counselor educators (Blackman, Hayes, Reeves, & Paisley, 2002; Hayes, Paisley, Phelps, Pearson, & Salter, 1997; Thomas, 2005). A collaborative between the University of Georgia School Counseling faculty and the Clarke County School District has been ongoing since 1992. School counselors and counselor educators meet for 3 hours monthly at the university campus to discuss mutual concerns, share information, and participate in professional trainings. A qualitative program evaluation of this effort revealed that participants found the collaborative to be a source of personal and professional renewal and support, professional development, and sense of community (Blackman et al., 2002). School counselors revealed that this type of participation shattered their sense of isolation and contributed greatly to a sense of validation that they were doing a good job.

Similar opportunities for ongoing support and training may be available through professional development schools, wherein a college or school of education partners with a school to provide collaborative education and training to school personnel, faculty, and education students (Clark & Horton-Parker, 2002). Splete and Grisdale (1992) described a professional development academy for school counselors in 28 districts in Oakland County, Michigan. Academy participants attended a full day of training per month for 12 months. Those who wished to receive continuing education credit for participation were able to do so. Needs assessments at the beginning of each academy year identified training content that would be specific to practicing counselors' current needs. Evaluations of the Oakland Academy were uniformly positive, with participants indicating that academy participation increased their motivation, perceived counseling efficacy, and professional sophistication (Waidley & Pappas, 1992). Subsequently, academies for school counselors based upon the Oakland Academy model have been established in several Michigan counties. Though research has not yet established the relationship between self-efficacy and professional competency, one can hypothesize that the combination of experienced self-efficacy and motivation would enhance outcomes in school counseling.

FUTURE DIRECTIONS

Clearly, there is a voiced need for increased supervision for school counselors. Evidence also points toward the benefits of ongoing professional development for school counselors in terms of sense of community, enhanced self-efficacy, experiences of professional support, validation for good work, and burnout prevention. Moreover, ethical codes of both ACA and ASCA emphasize the importance of regular supervision or pursuit of professional development opportunities. Our ongoing challenge as a profession continues to be how to provide these opportunities and to evaluate the outcome of our ongoing efforts. In this section, we summarize the critical issues we have addressed with regard to both practice and research on supervision of practicing school counselors and make recommendations for how professionals at all levels can contribute to counselors' ongoing development and provision of optimal services to students.

Implications for Practice

In their survey, Borders and Usher (1992) found that a majority of practicing counselors would like to have some form of supervision, and most would like supervision to be provided at their place of employment. Borders and Usher called for the training of more supervisors to meet the professional training needs of all postdegree counselors, including school counselors. Goodyear and Bernard (1998) contended that, ideally, supervisors of any profession should be senior members of the same profession who are actively pursuing their own professional development and who are trained supervisors. Likewise, Page et al. (2001) found that school counselors wished to be supervised by senior school counselors who were also trained supervisors. Given current funding limitations in American schools, it is highly unlikely that many districts will be able to provide such experts to supervise their counselors on a regular basis. Only the fortunate few will be able to avail themselves of such services. In addition, we recognize that many schools do offer school counselors excellent opportunities to consult with colleagues and other school personnel such as psychologists, nurses, occupational therapists, and speech therapists through participation in student intervention team meetings.

It is possible, however, for institutions such as school districts and universities to provide professional development for credit, as the Oakland County, Michigan, and neighboring districts have demonstrated. The creation of professional development schools has demonstrated how schools and universities can partner together to address common critical concerns.

Though research has shown that peer supervision groups and professional development efforts are effective in the sense that they can enhance motivation and self-efficacy, the field has yet to demonstrate what kinds of professional development and supervision opportunities are more efficacious than others or that represent "best practices." That is a goal for ongoing research efforts. Based upon the findings of the studies we have reviewed in this chapter, however, we would like to make the following recommendations:

- Counselor education programs should become familiar with outreach and continuing education units on their campuses for the purpose of offering for-credit, continuing professional education courses for school counselors. Continuing professional education courses might involve ongoing supervision in group format or systematic training in peer supervision formats.
- Counselor education programs should offer coursework in supervision to students in their programs, to postdegree school counselors, or to both. Ideally, this coursework should be provided by professional school counseling supervisors and should involve training on mentoring counselors within school settings.
- The professional training of school counselors should emphasize the importance of obtaining ongoing supervision during professional employment and practicing counselors' responsibility for getting that supervision. Such an emphasis should be a part of the ethical training of all school counselors.
- School counseling professionals should take it upon themselves, as an ethical obligation, to pursue ongoing supervision and professional development in the form of coursework, professional supervision, and peer supervision throughout their careers.

Implications for Research

Numerous authors have pointed out the dearth of research on school counseling supervision (Agnew et al., 2000; Bernard & Goodyear, 2004; Crespi, 1998). Moreover, Bernard and Goodyear addressed the need for more research on the effectiveness of supervision, especially for school counselors.

Research on school counselors is difficult to conduct because of the bureaucracy one must negotiate to get adequate sample sizes. Any given school often has so few counselors that many schools must participate in a large-scale data collection effort. This is one reason that survey research on school counselors is common. Qualitative methods also lend themselves to small samples, and numerous widely cited studies on counselor development and supervision process exist.

More work is needed, however, to document the types of supervision that contribute to ongoing professional school counselors' development and the efficacy of their work. We have identified the types of supervision that may be available to school counselors: (a) administrative supervision, (b) program supervision, and (c) clinical supervision. We have also recommended that professional school counselors participate in some form of peer supervision on a regular basis. An appropriate agenda for research on postdegree supervision would compare the relative contributions that each of these types of supervision makes to school counselor development and efficacious work. Both quantitative and qualitative methods would be useful in this effort.

CONCLUSION

Existing knowledge on the work lives of practicing school counselors suggests that there is an overall need for more supervision and professional development opportunities. Counselors who do not receive adequate postgraduate developmental supervision evidence greater burnout and stagnation. Moreover, without ongoing professional input, counselors—particularly those who work in isolation in one or more schools—can be at risk for unknowingly violating ethical principles. Peer group supervision and participation in professional development workshops can enhance school counselors' self-efficacy, motivation, and sense of community.

Though research has yet to document which professional development opportunities for school counselors are most efficacious, we believe that practicing school counselors are ethically obliged to pursue supervision and development activities throughout their careers. Further, counselor education programs in the United States should take a stronger role in supporting the work of school counselors by providing ongoing professional development opportunities.

References

AACD School Counseling Task Force. (1989). *School counseling: A profession at risk [Final Report]*. Alexandria, VA: American Association for Counseling and Development.

Agnew, T., Vaught, C. C., Getz, H. G., & Fortune, J. (2000). Peer group clinical supervision fosters confidence and professionalism. *Professional School Counseling, 4*(1), 6–12.

American Counseling Association. (1995). *Code of ethics and standards of practice*. Alexandria, VA: Author.

American Psychological Association. (2002). Ethical principles of psychologists and code of conduct. *American Psychologist, 57*, 1060–1073.

American School Counseling Association. (2003). *The ASCA national model: A framework for school counseling programs*. Alexandria, VA: Author.

American School Counselor Association. (2004). *Ethical standards for school counselors*. Alexandra, VA: Author.

Barret, R. L., & Schmidt, J. J. (1986). School counselor certification and supervision: Overlooked professional issues. *Counselor Education & Supervision, 26*(1), 50–55.

Benshoff, J. M. (1993). Peer supervision in counselor education. *Clinical Supervisor, 11*, 89–102.

Benshoff, J. M., & Paisley, P. O. (1996). The structured peer consultation model for school counselors. *Journal of Counseling & Development, 74*(3), 314–318.

Bernard, J. M., & Goodyear, R. K. (2004). *Fundamentals of clinical supervision* (3rd ed.). Needham Heights, MA: Allyn & Bacon.

Blackman, L., Hayes, R. L., Reeves, P. M., & Paisley, P. O. (2002). Building a bridge: Counselor educator-school counselor collaborative. *Counselor Education and Supervision, 41*(3), 243–255.

Borders, L. D. (1991). A systematic approach to peer group supervision. *Journal of Counseling and Development, 69*, 248–252.

Boyd, J.D., & Walter, D.B. (1975). The school counselor, the cactus, and supervision. *The School Counselor, 23*, 103-107.

Borders, L. D., & Usher, C. H. (1992). Post-degree supervision: Existing and preferred practices. *Journal of Counseling and Development, 70*, 594–599.

Brott, P. E., & Myers, J. E. (1999). Development of professional school counselor identity: A grounded theory. *Professional School Counseling, 2*(5), 339–348.

Clark, M. A., & Horton-Parker, R. (2002). Professional development schools: New opportunities for training school counselors. *Counselor Education and Supervision, 42*, 58–75.

Crespi, T. D. (1998). School counselors and clinical supervision: Perspectives to facilitate counseling services in the schools. *Special Services in the Schools, 13*(1/2), 107–114.

Crutchfield, L. B., & Borders, D. (1997). Impact of two clinical peer supervision models on practicing school counselors. *Journal of Counseling & Development, 75*(3), 219–230.

Crutchfield, L. B., McGarty, D., Pennington, D., Richardson, J., & Tsolis, A. (1997). Challenge and support: Group supervision for school counselors. *Professional School Counseling, 1*(1), 43–46.

Fairchild, T. N., & Zins, J. E. (1986). Accountability practices of school counselors: A national survey. *Journal of Counseling and Development, 65*, 196–199.

Feldstein, S. B. (2000). The relationship between supervision and burnout in school counselors. *Dissertation Abstracts International, 61*(2-A), 507. (UMI No. AAI9959913)

Goodyear, R. K., & Bernard, J. M. (1998). Clinical supervision: Lessons from the literature. *Counselor Education and Supervision, 38*(1), 6–22.

Granello, D. H. (2002). Assessing the cognitive development of counseling students: Changes in epistemological assumptions. *Counselor Education and Supervision, 41*, 279–293.

Gysbers, N. C., & Henderson, P. (2000). *Developing and managing your school guidance program* (3rd ed.). Alexandria, VA: American Counseling Association.

Gysbers, N. C., & Henderson, P. (2001). Comprehensive guidance and counseling programs: A rich history and a bright future. *Professional School Counseling, 4*, 246–256.

Halverson, S.E. (2000). Relationships between experience, credentials, moral development, conceptual level, and self-efficacy of school counselors. *Dissertation Abstracts International, Section A: Humanities and Social Sciences, 60* (8A), 2813. (Dissertation No. AA19942552)

Hayes, R. L., Paisley, P. O., Phelps, R. E., Pearson, G., & Salter, R. (1997). Integrating theory and practice: Counselor educator-school counselor collaborative. *Professional School Counseling Special Partners in Research: School Counselors and Counselor Educators Working Together, 1*(1), 9–12.

Henderson, P. (1994). *Supervision of school counselors* (Report No. ED 372353 1994-04-00). Greensboro, NC: ERIC Clearinghouse on Counseling and Student Services. (ERIC Document Reproduction Service No. EDOCG9421)

Henderson, P., & Lampe, R. L. (1992). Clinical supervision of school counselors. *The School Counselor, 39*, 151–157.

Herlihy, B., Gray, N., & McCollum, V. (2002). Legal and ethical issues in school counselor supervision. *Professional School Counseling, 6*(1), 55–60.

Holloway, E. L., & Neufeldt, S. A. (1995). Supervision: Its contributions to treatment efficacy. *Journal of Consulting and Clinical Psychology, 63*(2), 207–213.

Housely, W. F., McDaniel, L. C., & Underwood, J. R. (1990). Mandated assessment of counselors in Mississippi. *The School Counselor, 37*(4), 294–302.

Kaplan, L. S., Geoffroy, K. E., Pare, P., & Wolf, L. (1992). Using an individualized action plan to enhance the professional development of elementary school counselors. *The School Counselor, 39*, 164–170.

Loganbill, C., Hardy, E., & Delworth, U. (1982). Supervision: A conceptual model. *The Counseling Psychologist, 10*(1), 3–42.

Matthes, W. A. (1992). Induction of counselors into the profession. *The School Counselor, 39*, 245–250.

McMahon, M., & Patton, W. (2000). Conversations on clinical supervision: Benefits perceived by school counselors. *British Journal of Guidance & Counseling, 28*(3), 339–351.

Meyer, R.J., Jr. (1978). Using self-supervision to maintain counseling skills: A review. *The Personnel and Guidance Journal, 57*, 95–98.

Neufeldt, S. A. (1999). *Supervision strategies for the first practicum* (2nd ed.). Alexandria, VA: American Counseling Association.

Neufeldt, S. A., Karno, M. P., & Nelson, M. L. (1996). A qualitative study of experts' conceptualizations of supervisee reflectivity. *Journal of Counseling Psychology, 43*, 3–9.

Page, B. J., Pietrzak, D. R., & Sutton, J. M. J. (2001). National survey of school counselor supervision. *Counselor Education & Supervision, 41*(2), 142–150.

Paisley, P. O., & McMahon, H. G. (2001). School counseling for the 21st century: Challenges and opportunities. *Professional School Counselor, 5*, 106–115.

Roberts, E. B., & Borders, L. D. (1994). Supervision of school counselors: Administrative, program, and counseling. *School Counselor, 41*(3), 149–157.

Schmidt, J. L., & Barret, R. L. (1983). Who's in charge? Counseling supervision in North Carolina. *Counselor Education and Supervision, 23*, 109–116.

Schön, D. A. (1983). *The reflective practitioner: How professionals think in action.* New York: Basic Books.

Skovholt, T., & Rønnestad, H. (1992). *The evolving professional self: Stages and themes in therapist and counselor development.* New York: John Wiley and Sons.

Spice, C. G., Jr., & Spice, W. H. (1976). A triadic method of supervision in the training of counselors and counseling supervisors. *Counselor Education and Supervision, 15*, 251–280.

Splete, H. H., & Grisdale, G. A. (1992). The Oakland Counselor Academy: A professional development program for school counselors. *The School Counselor, 39*, 176–182.

Stoltenberg, C. D., McNeill, B. W., & Delworth, U. (1998). *IDM supervision: An integrated developmental model for supervising counselors and therapists.* San Francisco: Jossey-Bass Publishers.

Sue, D. W., & Sue, D. (2003). *Counseling the culturally diverse: Theory and practice.* New York: John Wiley & Sons.

Sutton, J. M., & Page, B. J. (1994). Post-degree clinical supervision of school counselors. *School Counselor, 42*(1), 32–39.

Synatschk, K. O. (2002). *Ensuring professionally relevant supervision and professional development: A district-level experience.* Austin, TX: ERIC Database. (Eric Document Reproduction No. ED461796)

Thomas, S. R. (2005). The school counselor alumni peer consultation group. *Counselor Education and Supervision, 45*, 16–29.

Waidley, J. W., & Pappas, J. G. (1992). An evaluation of the Oakland Academy Model: Do counselor academies really work? *The School Counselor, 39*, 183–188.

Wiggins, J. D. (1993). A 10-year follow-up of counselors rated high, average, or low in effectiveness. *The School Counselor, 40*, 380–383.

Wiggins, J. D., & Weslander, D. L. (1986). Effectiveness related to personality and demographic characteristics of secondary school counselors. *Counselor Education and Supervision, 26*, 26–35.

Wiley, M. O., & Ray, P. B. (1986). Counseling supervision by developmental level. *Journal of Counseling Psychology, 33*, 439–445.

Wilkerson, K., & Bellini, J. (2006). Intrapersonal and organizational factors associated with burnout among school counselors. *Journal of Counseling and Development, 84*, 440–450.

XXII
MULTICULTURAL COMPETENCE OF SCHOOL COUNSELORS

DELILA OWENS
Wayne State University

MADONNA G. CONSTANTINE
Teachers College, Columbia University

Multicultural Competence of School Counselors

According to recent estimates (U.S. Department of Education, 2003), students of color in elementary and secondary schools constitute nearly 40% of the nation's school-aged population. In states such as Alabama, California, Georgia, Hawaii, Illinois, Louisiana, Maryland, Mississippi, New Jersey, New York, and Texas, students of color represent over 70% of the school-aged population in many large and mid-sized cities. The multicultural competence of school counselors has received increasing attention in the literature over the past decade (e.g., Carey, Reinat, & Fontes, 1990; Holcomb-McCoy & Day-Vines, 2004; Lewis & Hayes, 1991; Reynolds, 1999). School counselors are challenged but uniquely poised to promote the academic, career, and psychosocial development of their students in light of the complex constellations of racial, ethnic, and socioeconomic backgrounds of their clients (Lee, 2005). As such, this chapter (a) discusses academic, career, and cultural considerations for school counselors in relation to working with students of color, and (b) delineates competencies needed by school counselors in their provision of culturally competent services to students of color.

Academic Considerations

Multiculturally competent school counselors recognize that family background and family expectations can shape the academic and educational aspirations of many students of color directly and through these students' educational experiences (Kao & Tienda, 1998). However, to address the needs and experiences of students of color, it is important that school counselors be wary of academic aspiration and achievement differences relevant to culturally diverse students. Kao and Tienda found that students of Asian descent tended to have higher academic aspirations than their Latino, Black, and White counterparts; notably, African American males were found to experience a decrease in their educational aspirations from 8th to 10th grade. However, their study also reported that although adolescents of color evidence high academic aspirations at any point in time, the maintenance of their high aspirations, however, is tentative.

Some students of Asian descent may be expected to perform well academically by their teachers as a function of the model minority stereotype (i.e., the belief that students of Asian descent tend to perform well academically, particularly in math and science courses and that their strong performance is indicative of positive psychological well-being). Additionally, students of East Asian descent may be influenced by familial and cultural values of filial piety, wherein their primary duty is to honor parents and elders (Shon & Ja, 1982), along with high educational achievement. In contrast, African American and Latino students, as compared with White students and students of Asian descent, may experience negative peer sanctions for excelling academically (Suarez-Orozco, 1991), which might partially explain differences in academic achievement and aspirations. Moreover, some students of color, particularly African American students, may have internalized Eurocentric standards that may denigrate their academic potential and performance and may contribute to their struggle in building a strong sense of academic self-efficacy and performance (Constantine & Blackmon, 2002; Spencer, Noll, Stoltzfus, & Harpalani, 2001). On the other hand, some students of color who have developed a positive, authentic, and proactive internalized racial identity may possess coping strategies that thwart negative expectations of academic performance and, consequently, may exhibit higher levels of academic self-efficacy and achievement (Constantine & Blackmon, 2002; McMahon & Watts, 2002; Spencer et al., 2001). Hence, school counselors may promote the maintenance of academic aspirations among students of color by providing opportunities for these students to develop affirming cultural identity attitudes.

Some students of color may experience incongruities between worldviews informed by their racial–cultural backgrounds and the values and norms of the school and dominant society, which may factor into their academic disengagement at times (Schwallie-Giddis, Anstrom, Sanchez, Sardi, & Granato, 2004). These students may experience "cultural contradictions" (Allen-Meares, 1999), wherein they feel they are unable to relate their cultural heritage to that which is represented in the classroom. For example, some Latino students may struggle to identify with academic materials and educational content if they feel that their heritage and customs are not represented therein. Additionally, independent and competitive forms of learning in the classroom may conflict with cooperative and collaborative learning styles that are encouraged by collectivistic cultural value orientations (Butler, 2003).

Socioeconomic issues also have been hypothesized to contribute to racial disparities in educational aspirations to the degree that access to material resources enhances or detracts from some youths' dispositions to achieve (Kao & Tienda, 1998). For example, more than 35% of African American youth under age 18 live in poverty and are exposed to various negative environmental factors (e.g., unemployment, exposure to crime and violence, and financial struggles within the home) that can interfere with academic pursuits (Butler, 2003). Urban African American youth are often labeled "at risk" by researchers and educators and may be placed on vocational or trade-specific tracks geared toward low-wage jobs because they are not expected to succeed academically (Constantine, Erickson, Banks, & Timberlake, 1998). The overrepresentation of students of color in the lower socioeconomic strata has numerous implications for interventions that multiculturally competent school counselors may apply to encourage academic achievement among this population, including advocating for parity in the assessment of "at-risk" students.

Another hypothesis concerning racial differences in educational outcomes focuses on structural and social barriers that preclude access to educational and/or occupational success. According to this hypothesis, in response to classification in minority status, some people of color may overcompensate and achieve highly; others may internalize social meanings of minority status and negative stereotypes about their racial/ethnic group and become dubious about education as a means toward social mobility (Kao & Tienda, 1998). It is possible that this internalized racism can influence not only psychological well-being, but also career aspirations and development (Ladany, Melincoff, Constantine, & Love, 1997).

Cultural Considerations

The promotion of academic retention and achievement and positive psychosocial adjustment may not be mutually exclusive roles for school counselors, particularly with respect to complex needs of students of color and immigrant students (Kopala, Esquivel, & Baptiste, 1994; Sciarra, 2001). Over and above normative developmental concerns, students of color and immigrant students may experience multiple psychological and psychosocial concerns such as culture shock, racism, learning multiple cultural identities, school disengagement, depression, and intergenerational conflict (Constantine & Gushue, 2003; Yeh, 2003). However, these students may resist seeking help for these concerns from school counselors as a function of unfamiliarity with counseling, cultural mistrust attitudes, differences in expectations of service providers, somatic expressions of distress, or culturally appropriate values of forbearance (Constantine, Okazaki, & Utsey, 2004; Holcomb-McCoy). Despite differences in help-seeking behaviors between people of color and members of the dominant White culture, the majority of youth of color continue to receive counseling services from school counselors (Holcomb-McCoy, 2003). Moreover, in light of increasing rates of mental health concerns among school-aged children (e.g., depression, suicide, and attention deficit/hyperactivity disorder), decreased availability of community mental health programs (Lockhart & Keys, 1998), and increased attention to the psychological welfare of young people following the Columbine school shooting, school counselors are placed in critical roles to provide free personal mental health services to young people. Thus, it is critical for school counselors to be aware of and attentive to the psychological needs of students of color.

Upon meeting with students of color, culturally competent school counselors need to be cognizant of differences in affective expression across racial–cultural groups. For example, there may be cultural differences in the ways in which students of diverse racial and ethnic backgrounds express emotions as a function of values that encourage emotional restraint (Constantine & Gainor, 2001). School counselors need to be cognizant of how emotional states are expressed differently across cultures, for they risk misinterpreting, pathologizing, and inappropriately treating students of color if they are not attuned to potential cultural differences in affective presentation. Similarly, it is valuable for school counselors to apply their knowledge and awareness of cultural differences in expressing empathy so as to attend effectively to diverse students (Constantine & Gainor).

Multiculturally competent school counselors also need to be aware of the diverse and complex concerns of newly arrived immigrant students. For example, students and families who are Jamaican immigrants may contend with racism, socioeconomic disparities, and job difficulties, whereas students from Iraq or Kosovo may contend with war-related trauma concerns (Williams & Butler, 2003). Despite differences in concerns among immigrant student populations, Williams and Butler outlined several primary issues faced by immigrant students, including English language acquisition, posttraumatic stress disorder, lack of social support networks, racial labeling and categorization, adjustment to different learning styles and expectations, acquisition of new cultural scripts (i.e., behaviors, ideas, thoughts, and role expectations that are specific to a given culture), and struggles to gain social acceptance. The degree to which school counselors interact with recent immigrant students and their families may be a function of how these psychosocial stressors impact their subjective (e.g., personal distress and dysphoria) and objective (e.g., academic difficulties or acting out) experiences; that said, it is possible that immigrant students who tend to maintain academic performance and avoid teachers' attention may not present their needs readily to school counselors, and thus may "slip between the cracks." Hence, culturally competent school counselors can address the potential needs of newly immigrant students through reaching out toward the immigrant student body by engaging with student groups and collaborating with immigrant community groups outside of school (Williams & Butler).

Linguistically and culturally diverse students may experience challenges to their racial and ethnic identity development within their families and in the larger society. Students may experience intergenerational cultural conflicts, wherein the students acculturate to the dominant society more quickly than their parents or guardians. Students may feel conflicted between how their values, influenced by both their parents' cultures and the dominant society's cultures, contrast with those of their family and community; similarly, parents and guardians may feel betrayed by their children's willingness to contest their ways of being and their cultural identity. Thus, concomitant with normative struggles of separation and individuation that can result in family conflicts, students of color may present with interacting challenges of intergenerational conflict.

Racial and ethnic identity development may present psychosocial concerns for students of color as well (Reynolds, 1999). As students' cognitive scopes broaden from egocentric to peer-centered, they may become more cognizant of how their race and ethnicity have subjective and social valence (Constantine & Blackmon, 2002). Moreover, students of color may encounter educational challenges to conform to the dominant society in order to succeed and thwart negative stereotyped expectations while maintaining allegiances to their racial–cultural reference groups (e.g., family, racially similar peers, and community members). It is possible that students of color switch codes between the differing racial–cultural contexts of family, peers, and school and begin to question the degree to which they are compromising their racial and ethnic identity. School counselors are in a critical position to validate these experiences of students of color, particularly before they enter postsecondary institutions, and encourage adaptive biculturalism (LaFromboise, Coleman, & Gerton, 1993). Through individual, group, family, and schoolwide interventions, multiculturally competent school counselors can provide a space for students of color to feel empowered about the strengths regarding their families' racial–cultural experiences and values, as well as their agentic decisions to navigate in the dominant culture without compromising their cultural sense of self.

Although many school counselors have been trained in traditional counseling paradigms to identify intrapsychic sources of presenting problem etiology, multiculturally competent school counselors are encouraged to consider external, systemic influences of their students' presentations, including racial discrimination, access to resources, socioeconomic difficulties, and social concerns related to poverty (Atkinson, Thompson, & Grant, 1993). For example, a 14-year-old African American female who lives with her maternal grandmother presented to an African American female school counselor through a teacher's referral for classroom behavioral problems including frequent outbursts and disinterest.* A school psychologist administered a series of achievement tests, including the Wide Range Achievement Test–3, wherein the student struggled to read words longer than four letters and perform mathematical operations entailing long division and converting fractions to decimals. When presented with this information, the school counselor hypothesized that the student may be illiterate and had been tacitly promoted through ninth grade without adequate attention to her academic needs. Initially, the school counselor conceptualized the student' difficulties as stemming from a learning disability, attention deficit/hyperactivity disorder, and other intrapsychic concerns that resulted in both classroom misbehavior and

---

* Example was adapted from a colleague's recent experience.

shame regarding her literacy struggles. Upon later reflection, the school counselor acknowledged that stereotyped assumptions of unruly classroom behavior and poor academic performance, inadequate access to early psychological assessment, and limited school and familial resources to supplemental services may be external forces that influenced how the student's needs were not identified. Furthermore, the school counselor reflected on her biases based on her social-class identity, in which she assumed that all students have access to equitable attention regarding their academic challenges and that this young woman's struggles were a function of her and her family's difficulties. In processing her reflections in peer supervision, she realized that her biases might compromise her conceptualization of her client's concerns and treatment options that would be commensurate to more inclusive conceptualizations.

Career Considerations

Multiculturally competent school counselors employ lenses that acknowledge the conjoined influences of intrapsychic and external forces on career development in various student populations. In recognizing the concomitant forces of cultural values, racism and discrimination, and inequitable access to resources alongside positive factors, such as coping self-efficacy, racial socialization, and resilience, school counselors can play a vital role in promoting higher academic achievement among all students and foster opportunities for greater representation of people of color in the workforce (Constantine & Blackmon, 2002; Constantine, Wallace, & Kindaichi, 2005; Sciarra, 2001). Although all students may experience career exploration and other career development issues at different paces, some students of color may perceive additional career and educational barriers that might inhibit their career exploration (Ladany et al., 1997). For example, Constantine et al. (2005) found that perceptions of occupational barriers were positively predictive of career indecision among African American adolescents. Conversely, however, Evans and Herr (1994) found that perceptions of neither racial nor gender discrimination were significantly related to the career aspirations of Black college students. Additionally, Rollins (2001) found that African American adolescents who perceived greater racial discrimination toward themselves reported greater career decision-making self-efficacy. It appears that although some adolescents of color may internalize perceptions of educational and vocational barriers, others still possess high career goals and confidence in their abilities to pursue their goals successfully (Constantine et al., 2005).

Constantine et al. (1998) encouraged school and career counselors who work with urban youth of color to address the potential conflict that may arise between wanting to succeed academically and vocationally and feelings of loyalty to their families and communities. It is critical for multiculturally competent school counselors to be cognizant of the multiple forces that can influence the career development of students of color and to differentiate between normative career development experiences and those that are of more critical psychological concern.

Multicultural Competencies for School Counselors

Although the literature on multicultural counseling competence has offered several training "best practices," it has been suggested that the field lacks a consistent and "comprehensive taxonomy of training objectives that describe cross-cultural competence" (Carey et al., 1990, p. 156). In summarizing recent literature that articulates specific competencies for multiculturally competent school counselors, it is possible that a sense of consistency and specificity can emerge among school-counseling training programs.

Newer models of cultural competence for school counselors draw from the tripartite model of multicultural counseling (Sue, Arredondo, & McDavis, 1992), while providing specific suggestions regarding school characteristics and areas of intervention (e.g., personal, career, or academic). For example, Lee (2005) articulated six competencies specific to school counselors who work in urban environments: (a) cultural competence (i.e., possessing awareness, knowledge, and skills appropriate to intervene responsibly with culturally diverse students and families); (b) skills for promoting empowerment (i.e., engaging youth to become empowered to address challenges implicit in urban contexts that can hamper their academic and vocational achievement); (c) taking a systemic perspective to counseling (i.e., acknowledging and integrating the multiple personal, familial, social, and societal influences on urban adolescent development in multifaceted interventions); (d) advocacy (i.e., implementing change on systemic levels to address inequitable barriers to student development); (e) collaboration (i.e., forming alliances with familial and community stakeholders in urban student education to promote educational development initiatives); and (f) leadership (i.e., active participation in school, district, and political initiatives that attend to the needs of urban students). Although these competencies were written specifically for counselors working in urban school environments, tenets such as employing a systemic perspective, collaborating with important others in the students' environments, and promoting empowerment and advocacy are applicable to school counselors who work with racially and ethnically diverse students across environments.

Specific competencies for multicultural career counseling also have been presented in the literature. Constantine et al. (1998) encouraged counselors to be aware of how cultural (e.g., acculturation, ethnic and racial identity, and cultural values), familial (e.g., parental education attainment), and environmental (exposure to poverty, violence, and crime) factors may contribute to urban youths' perception of attainable careers. Using this awareness, counselors may identify and employ interventions designed to foster the pursuit of career-related information and increase students' knowledge of the qualifications needed to succeed in their career choices. Additionally, counselors can assist students of color to identify occupational role models from their racial and ethnic group and/or in their communities and encourage adolescents of color to address potential barriers (e.g., financial, sociocultural, and systemic) to their career aspirations (Constantine et al., 2005). Moreover, counselors should be skilled in determining the degree to which the career development struggles of adolescents of color are developmentally appropriate, related to their perceptions of career barriers or having limited career-related information, or a combination of multiple psychological, environmental, and structural factors (Ladany et al., 1997). Counselors could collaborate with teachers and school administrators to foster coping and resilience strategies to help adolescents of color address discrimination, racism, and prejudice as they pursue their career goals and to encourage the integration of vocational information and themes within school curricula. For example, school counselors could offer teachers workshops that address such issues as working with culturally diverse student populations, addressing diverse learning styles, understanding cultural influences on learning, and addressing racism. Additionally, counselors could liaise with local business leaders to provide work apprenticeships and/or meaningful part-time jobs that may influence the career development of adolescents of color. Moreover, counselors might want to engage the support of community and political organizations that address the myriad societal barriers that may impact the career development of youth of color.

In the aforementioned competencies for multicultural school counseling and career counseling, the theme of advocacy is brought into relief. According to the American School Counselor Association (ASCA; 2003) *National Model*, school counselors' advocacy efforts are designed to help counselors eliminate barriers to students' development; foster opportunities for all students to learn; ensure equitable access to quality education; collaborate with important others outside of the school body to help meet students' needs; and promote systemic change. School counselors may advocate for students and families and particular groups of students within the school body; additionally, school counselors may advocate for better school counseling programs and resources and for the visibility of the school counseling profession on local, state, regional, and national levels (Kiselica & Robinson, 2001). Trusty and Brown (2005) presented three general advocacy competencies for school counselors: *dispositions*, which include advocacy (i.e., autonomous and altruistic motivation to take risks in helping students meet their needs), family support/empowerment (i.e., recognizing that parents and guardians are often the primary advocates for students), social advocacy (i.e., addressing inequities and barriers affecting all people), and ethical (i.e., valuing professional codes of ethics); *knowledge*, which includes knowledge of resources, parameters (e.g., school regulations, rights of families and individuals, and scope of their practice), dispute resolution mechanisms (e.g., mediation), advocacy models, and systems change; and *skills*, which include those regarding communication (e.g., listening and empathy), collaboration (e.g., joining families and administration in advocacy efforts), problem assessment and problem solving, organization, and self care.

Advocacy competencies are intrinsic to school counselors' multicultural counseling competence and to changing roles of school counselors given the changing needs of the diverse school population. For example, school counselors working with students of color need to enact their knowledge and awareness of diverse familial and cultural values to join and collaborate effectively in advocacy efforts. Moreover, school counselors' mediation between parental bodies and school administration might entail employing awareness of how the role of school as a socialization agent in students' lives may differ by culture. Further, efforts to assess and address problems may entail culturally relevant intervention mechanisms, including involving external, family/community-based important others as mediators or group cofacilitators. Lee (2001) noted that school counselors should advocate and become voices for students who have been disenfranchised historically by the educational system, especially students of color and students from low socioeconomic backgrounds.

Multiculturally competent school counselors also could advocate for the needs of their profession regarding increased multicultural training. For example, advocacy efforts may be directed toward encouraging ASCA to state explicitly its intention with regard to servicing the needs of linguistically and culturally diverse students (Williams & Butler, 2003). Furthermore, school counselors and professionals devoted to the needs of school counselors and students of color may encourage the Council for Accreditation of Counseling and Related Educational Programs (CACREP) to institute explicit guidelines that encourage training programs to infuse multicultural training beyond the one-course method (First, 1988). Doing so may promote the multicultural competence of future school counselors and address the needs of the increasingly diverse student population in a much more effective manner.

Best Practices in School Counseling: Promoting Multicultural Issues in Schools

Culturally diverse school-aged children whose emotional, social, and behavioral concerns are not addressed sufficiently may experience diminished opportunities to learn and grow in school environments (Rones & Hoagwood, 2000). School counselors are in vital positions to help eliminate or reduce the impact of barriers that keep children of color from achieving academically in school systems (Butler, 2003). The needs of children of color must be addressed in ways that consider the complex milieus in which they live. For example, it is important to note that some school-aged children may come from home settings in which poverty, interpersonal violence, or even substance abuse may be prevalent. These types of circumstances may make it challenging at best for some children to attend sufficiently to academic endeavors. Differences between the home and school environments of children of color, particularly in urban settings, must be considered in the context of identifying culturally appropriate interventions for these students (Patton & Day-Vines, 2004). Moreover, school counselors' identification and implementation of enrichment initiatives geared toward promoting the academic achievement of student populations affected by achievement gaps would be helpful (Yowell & Gordon, 1996).

Many school counselors may over rely on individual counseling interventions in working with children of color. Such interventions not only lack research data and accountability with regard to outcomes in school settings (Eschenauer & Chen-Hayes, 2005; Whiston, 2003), but also may not consider how the cultural values of these students might not be congruent with the use of such interventions. Because accountability and cultural sensitivity are particularly important issues in many school districts, the use of individual counseling interventions, absent data regarding their efficacy and cultural appropriateness in school settings, may be both ineffective and inappropriate (Burnham & Johnson, 2000).

It also is crucial that school counselors identify an array of interventions with students of color that focus not only on responding to existing problems or issues, but also on the prevention of mental health issues or concerns that could arise in school environments (Holcomb-McCoy & Mitchell, 2005). Programming and small-group discussions on topics such as body image, self-esteem, peer pressure, and social skills could be instituted prior to an age in which school-aged children of color begin to be concerned more specifically about these issues. In addition, vocational guidance and career interventions, beginning as early as elementary school, would seem important in underscoring the salience of career exploration and development at a relatively young age.

School systems and districts also should consider ways to promote the recruitment, hiring, and retention of qualified counselors that, to some degree, reflect aspects of the student populations with which they work. For instance, it may be difficult for some students of color to consider seeing a White school counselor to address deeply personal issues. Because some students of color experience cultural mistrust attitudes toward Whites generally, such attitudes may play a role in their willingness to seek help from a counselor who is racially or ethnically different. The opportunities for students of color to seek school counseling services from a culturally similar counselor might help these students to seek such services more deliberately.

School counselors increasingly are being challenged to become social justice advocates in school systems, particularly with regard to ensuring that all students, regardless of cultural background or socioeconomic status, have the chance to achieve to their greatest potential (Lee, 2005). Thus, school counselors should be leaders in the context of their school environments in terms of ensuring a milieu that actively promotes multiculturalism and antidiscrimination so that students of color do not have to be exposed to attitudes and behaviors that might circumvent their opportunities for academic, personal, and social successes. Setting up a multicultural task force comprising students, teachers, administrators, parents, and other community members might be effective in ensuring relatively system-wide support for multicultural initiatives. In addition, programs that address the strengths and assets of an inclusive and multicultural environment might be helpful in educating both students and teachers about the importance and necessity of cultural diversity. School counselors also are in a unique position to support a diverse student body by (a) examining school policies and practices as well as student activities to ensure equity and access among the student body, (b) encouraging teachers to explore issues of diversity in the context of the courses that are offered, (c) acting as an advocate for students who possess limited English proficiency, and (d) advocating for equal access in educational attainment and course-taking opportunities for all students (Stone & Dahir, 2006).

References

Allen-Meares, P. (1999). African American males: Their status, educational plight, and the possibilities for their future. In I. E. Davis (Ed.), *Working with African American males: A guide to practice* (pp. 117–128). Thousand Oaks, CA: Sage.

American School Counselor Association (ASCA). (2003). *The ASCA national model: A framework for school counseling programs.* Alexandria, VA: Author.

Atkinson, D. R., Thompson, C. E., & Grant, S. K. (1993). A three-dimensional model for counseling racial/ethnic minorities. *The Counseling Psychologist, 21,* 257–277.

Burnham, J. J., & Johnson, C. M. (2000). School counselor roles: Discrepancies between actual practice and existing models. *Professional School Counseling, 4,* 41–49.

Butler, S. K. (2003). Helping urban African American high school students to excel academically: The role of school counselors. *High School Journal, 87,* 51–57.

Carey, J. C., Reinat, M., & Fontes, L. (1990). School counselors' perceptions of training needs in multicultural counseling. *Counselor Education and Supervision, 29,* 155–169.

Constantine, M. G., & Blackmon, S. M. (2002). Black adolescents' racial socialization experiences: Their relations to home, school, and peer self-esteem. *Journal of Black Studies, 32,* 322–335.

Constantine, M. G., Erickson, C. D., Banks, R. W., & Timberlake, T. L. (1998). Challenges to the career development of urban racial and ethnic minority youth: Implications of vocational intervention. *Journal of Multicultural Counseling and Development, 26,* 83–95.

Constantine, M. G., & Gainor, K. A. (2001). Emotional intelligence and empathy: Their relation to multicultural counseling knowledge and awareness. *Professional School Counseling, 5,* 131–137.

Constantine, M. G., & Gushue, G. V. (2003). School counselors' ethnic tolerance attitudes and racism attitudes as predictors of their multicultural case conceptualization of an immigrant student. *Journal of Counseling and Development, 81,* 185–190.

Constantine, M. G., Okazaki, S., & Utsey, S. O. (2004). Self-concealment, social self-efficacy, acculturative stress, and depression in African, Asian, and Latino international college students. *American Journal of Orthopsychiatry, 74,* 230–241.

Constantine, M. G., Wallace, B. C., & Kindaichi, M. M. (2005). Examining contextual factors in the career decision status of African American adolescents. *Journal of Career Assessment, 13,* 307–319.

Eschenauer, R., & Chen-Hayes, S. F. (2005). The transformative individual school counseling model: An accountability model for urban school counselors. *Professional School Counseling, 8*(3), 244–248.

Evans, K. M., & Herr, E. L. (1994). The influence of racial identity and the perceptions of discrimination on the career aspirations of African American men and women. *Journal of Vocational Behavior, 44,* 173–184.

First, J. M. (1988). Immigrant students in the U.S. public schools: Challenges with solutions. *Phi Delta Kappan, 70,* 205–210.

Holcomb-McCoy, C. C. (2003). Multicultural competence in school settings. In D. B. Pope-Davis, H. L. K. Coleman, W. M. Liu, & R. L. Toporek (Eds.), *Handbook of multicultural competencies in counseling and psychology* (pp. 406–419). Thousand Oaks, CA: Sage.

Holcomb-McCoy, C. C., & Day-Vines, N. (2004). Exploring school counselor multicultural competence: A multidimensional concept. *Measurement and Evaluation in Counseling and Development, 37,* 154–162.

Holcomb-McCoy, C., & Mitchell, N. (2005). A descriptive study of urban school counseling programs. *Professional School Counseling, 8,* 203–208.

Kao, G., & Tienda, M. (1998). Educational aspirations of minority youth. *American Journal of Education, 106,* 349–384.

Kiselica, M. S., & Robinson, M. (2001). Bringing advocacy counseling to life: The history, issues, and human dramas of social justice work in counseling. *Journal of Counseling and Development, 79,* 387–397.

Kopala, M., Esquivel, G., & Baptiste, L. (1994). Counseling approaches for immigrant children: Facilitating the acculturative process. *School Counselor, 41,* 352–359.

Ladany, N., Melincoff, D. S., Constantine, M. G., & Love, R. (1997). At-risk urban high school students' commitment to career choices. *Journal of Counseling and Development, 76,* 45–52.

LaFromboise, T. A., Coleman, H. L. K., & Gerton, J. (1993). Psychological impact of biculturalism: Evidence and theory. *Psychological Bulletin, 114,* 395–412.

Lee, C. C. (2001). Culturally responsive school counselors and programs: Addressing the needs of all students. *Professional School Counseling, 4,* 163–171.

Lee, C. C. (2005). Urban school counseling: Context, characteristics, and competencies. *Professional School Counseling, 8,* 184–188.

Lewis, A. C., & Hayes, S. (1991). Multiculturalism and the school counseling curriculum. *Journal of Counseling and Development, 70,* 119–125.

Lockhart, E. J., & Keys, S. G. (1998). The mental health counseling role of school counselors. *Professional School Counseling, 1,* 3–6.

McMahon, S. D., & Watts, R. J. (2002). Ethnic identity in urban African American youth: Exploring links with self-worth, aggression, and other psychosocial variables. *Journal of Community Psychology, 30,* 411–431.

Patton, J. M., & Day-Vines, N. L. (2004). *A curriculum and pedagogy for cultural competence: Strategies to guide the training of special and general education teachers.* Richmond, VA: Virginia Department of Education.

Reynolds, A. L. (1999). Working with children and adolescents in the schools: Multicultural counseling implications. In R. H. Sheets & E. R. Hollins (Eds.), *Racial and ethnic identity in school practices: Aspects of human development* (pp. 213–229). Mahwah, NJ: Erlbaum.

Rollins, V. B. (2001). Perceived racism and career self-efficacy in African American adolescents. *Dissertation Abstracts International, 61*(9-B), 5059.

Rones, M., & Hoagwood, K. (2000). School-based mental health services: A research review. *Clinical Child and Family Psychology Review, 3,* 223–241.

Schwallie-Giddis, P., Anstrom, K., Sanchez, P., Sardi, V. A., & Granato, L. (2004). Counseling the linguistically and culturally diverse student: Meeting school counselors' professional development needs. *Professional School Counseling, 8*, 15–23.

Sciarra, D. T. (2001). School counseling in a multicultural society. In J. G. Ponterotto, J. M. Casas, L. A. Suzuki, & C. M. Alexander (Eds.), *Handbook of multicultural counseling* (2nd ed., pp. 701–728). Thousand Oaks, CA: Sage.

Shon, S. P., & Ja, D. Y. (1982). Asian families. In M. McGoldrick, J. K. Pearce, & J. Giordano (Eds.), *Ethnicity and family therapy* (pp. 208–228). New York: Guilford.

Spencer, M. B., Noll, E., Stoltzfus, J., & Harpalani, V. (2001). Identity and school adjustment: Revisiting the "acting White" assumption. *Educational Psychologist, 36*, 21–30.

Stone, C., & Dahir, C. (2006). *The transformed school counselor.* Boston: Houghton Mifflin/Lahaska Press.

Suarez-Orozco, M. (1991). Immigrant adaptation to schooling: A Hispanic case. In M. A. Gibson & J. U. Ogbu (Eds.), *Minority status and schooling: A comparative study of immigrant and involuntary minorities* (pp. 37–61). New York: Garland.

Sue, D. W., Arredondo, P., & McDavis, R. J. (1992). Multicultural counseling competencies and standards: A call to the profession. *Journal of Multicultural Counseling and Development, 20*, 64–88.

Trusty, J., & Brown, D. (2005). Advocacy competencies for professional school counselors. *Professional School Counseling, 8*, 259–265.

U.S. Department of Education. (2003). *Overview of public elementary and secondary schools and districts: School year 2001-02: Statistical analysis report* (NCES 2003-411). Retrieved on May 3, 2005, from http://nces.ed.gov/pubs2003/2003411.pdf

Whiston, S. C. (2003) Outcomes research on school counseling services. In B. T. Erford (Ed.), *Transforming the school counseling profession* (pp. 435–447). Upper Saddle River, NJ: Merrill Prentice Hall.

Williams, F. C., & Butler, S. K. (2003). Concerns of newly arrived immigrant students: Implications for school counselors. *Professional School Counseling, 7*, 9–14.

Yeh, C. J. (2003). Age, acculturation, cultural adjustment, and mental health symptoms of Chinese, Korean, and Japanese immigrant youths. *Cultural Diversity and Ethnic Minority Psychology, 9*, 34–48.

Yowell, C. M., & Gordon, E. W. (1996). Youth empowerment and human service institutions. *Journal of Negro Education, 65*, 19–29.

XXIII
CONSULTATION WITH TEACHERS, ADMINISTRATORS, AND COUNSELING AGENCIES

ROBERTO CLEMENTE
Roosevelt University, Chicago

Introduction

The daily routines of school counselors reflect the complexities of an ever evolving and multifaceted society. The stereotypical perception of a school counselor sitting passively behind a desk, providing career advice or counseling students one-on-one, is a mirage of the past. It is no secret that our society is experiencing drastic changes and is facing a severe crisis in most sectors; this is supported by both anecdotal and empirical evidence (Lockhart & Keys, 1998; Luongo, 2000). Our students cannot be isolated from the severe stress found in our society and cannot function in a vacuum. National data on poverty, joblessness, divorce rates, substance abuse, violence, sexual abuse and homelessness are all evidence of a convoluted society in search of answers. As an illustration, there are more than 5 million children with special educational needs receiving some type of services in our schools (Albert, Brown, & Flanigan, 2003) approximately one third of the student population is taking some type of psychotropic medication for attention deficit disorders, anxiety, depression, or other types of mental health conditions (Nastasi, Bernstein-Moore, & Varjas, 2004), the suicide rate among school-aged children has risen substantially, and the unintended pregnancy rate among adolescents remains a challenge although some steady progress has been achieved in this area.

To make matters more complicated, who can forget the horrific images displayed on television during the Columbine High School shootings or more recently, the events in which a teen gunman carried out a deadly killing spree at Red Lake High School in Minnesota? The level of violence in our schools has increased to the point that we are facing one of the most severe challenges in the history of our educational system. School shootings perpetrated by disgruntled and disenfranchised students living on the outskirts of the school cultures are a unique American phenomenon that has education experts scrambling for answers. On top of all the new challenges encountered by school counselors and students, the nature of the concerns and challenges brought by the students is testing the professional flexibility and adaptability of today's counselors.

Another example of the increased challenges to school counselors is responding to behavior that was once socially acceptable, but may now be the precursor of severe negative behaviors accompanied by potential lawsuits against the school or district, as in the case of bullying. Today's school counselors have to be well versed in areas such as law, educational policies, state mandates, and health policies in addition to the expected traditional areas (e.g., career, individual and group counseling, classroom guidance) as addressed in their training programs. This list of challenges also includes increased focus on the use of the school counselor to facilitate academic achievement among all students with a movement to increase the academic rigor of each student's program of study.

Each student who is on a school counselor's caseload presents challenges that are complex and can be a challenge to develop an effective plan of action. Consider Case Vignette 23.1. This vignette exemplifies a challenging situation that is becoming more the norm than the exception and forces school counselors to draw on their knowledge and experience as well as increase their need to seek and

CASE VIGNETTE 23.1: HECTOR—LACK OF MOTIVATION IN CLASS

The homeroom teacher has referred Hector, a 10th-grade Latino student, to the school counselor because he seems to be unmotivated, does not participate in class, and most of his homework in other classes is either incomplete or not completed at all. Occasionally, he falls asleep and lacks physical energy. The teachers suspect that Hector may be experimenting with drugs or alcohol. After a thorough interview with Hector and his mother, the counselor realizes that Hector has been working two part-time jobs to help supplement the family income. Since he is the oldest child and has four siblings, it is expected that he must contribute. The family's sole other income is his mother's. His father is a chronic alcoholic who abuses the children and his wife constantly. His mother is encouraging Hector to leave school and work full-time.

Questions for Analysis:

1. As a counselor, what issues would take precedence and why?
2. How would you "calm down" the teachers without violating confidentiality?
3. What are the cultural issues?
4. How can you reconcile the consultation and counselors' roles?
5. How important are the cultural variables?
6. If you are not proficient in the Latino culture, how can you demonstrate sensitivity and implement a plan of action that addresses Hector's needs?

provide consultation. In this case, the poor academic performance is only a symptom of the real problem.

This chapter provides an operational definition of the consultation concept as it represents a shift in paradigm for counselors as well as several modes of consultation. It also provides a series of theoretical approaches and practical approaches to the process of consultation. Furthermore, it presents a generic consultation model along with challenging areas accompanied by basic communication strategies to ameliorate those difficulties. Finally, the differences between client- and group-focused consultation are discussed along with suggested areas of research and future directions.

Consultation as Part of a Developmental–Comprehensive School Counseling Program

In a developmental–comprehensive school counseling (DCSC) perspective, consultation becomes one of the program components. The traditional approach of working with students was based on providing services for those who requested them or those who were referred by teachers, school principals, or parents. In contrast, the DCSC program is based on a proactive platform for delivering sequential programming to all students (Ripley, Erford, Dahir, & Eschback, 2003). According to the American School Counselor Association's (ASCA) model, a DCSC has three interrelated components that are the foundation. These components are the delivery system, the management system, and accountability.

Within these three integral components, the following areas are targeted: systemic change, leadership, advocacy, collaboration, and leadership. All of the aforementioned are based on three key domains: academic, career, and personal/social development. Also, the Transforming School Counseling Initiative (TSCI) emphasizes the areas of equity, justice, and consultation as part of a strong DCSC program (Carey, 2003). In essence, consultation is not an optional skill or intervention but an instrumental strategic aspect of implementing and targeting some of the areas of a DCSC program.

Consultation: A Practical Definition

The term *consultation* is informally used among friends, coworkers, and even family members. In essence, *consultation* implies sharing advice or information when there is a lack of knowledge or uncertainty about making a decision. The professional literature provides multiple definitions that have common traits that will vary slightly depending on the focus given (Brown, Pryzwansky, & Schulte, 2001; Friend & Cook, 1992; Gallessich, 1982; Gutkin, 1999; Parsons, 1996; Parsons & Kahn, 2005). For example, when a student is trying to choose between several postcollege opportunities and seeks perspective from peers, family members, or the school counselor, the student is seeking consultation. If the same student is struggling with his or her anxiety about the situation or understanding the pressure he or she is getting from parents to make a particular decision, the student is seeking counseling.

Fundamentally, consultation is a voluntary relationship of a triadic nature (Gutkin, 1999) and involves a consultant or provider of help (e.g., a school counselor; Friend & Cook, 1992), who will work with a person/group or help seeker (consultee) in order to benefit a client (e.g., student). School-based consultation is unique because of the context in which it occurs. Several variables will determine the outcome and direction of the consultation process, for instance, the intensity of the problem or issue, the competence and qualifications of the consultee to solve the situation, and who initiates the consultation process. It is common for the consultee to initiate the consultation process; however, it is not unlikely for the consultant to initiate it by being proactive instead of reactive, particularly within a school setting where the consultant may have responsibilities concerning the consultee's choices (Parsons & Kahn, 2005).

Problem–Solution Orientation

An effective way in which to sustain the boundaries of the triadic nature of consultation is for the school counselor (consultant) to keep a problem-solution orientation toward the resolution of the client's situation as opposed to focusing on the consultee's needs. Consider Case Vignette 23.2, which provides an illustration in which the boundaries of the consultant and consultee can be easily transgressed due to role confusion. That is, the consultee expects that the consultant will serve as a personal counselor to deal with her emotional issues.

Although it may seem simple, maintaining the role of a consultant and focusing on the original tasks that often start the conversation, can be somewhat difficult. It is not atypical for consultees to explore the possibility of getting counseling by the consultant. This can be dealt with by keeping in mind the original purpose of the triadic relationship and the problem-solution orientation that will ultimately benefit the client(s). However, if the consultant believes that the consultee could benefit from personal counseling, then the consultee may be referred to another mental health professional who can assist her in dealing with those personal issues. As a word of clarification, this particular problem-solution orientation is based on a triadic relationship, and then the previous example emphasizes the client as a beneficiary via the assistance of the consultee. Therefore, this does not imply that at some point and by utilizing other types of services the school counselor cannot provide direct services. Thus, these are not rigid processes, modes, orientations, or models that cannot change as the interactive dynamics evolve. The best strategy to deal with the uncertainty of whether the consultant is providing consulting services or counseling services to the consultee is by having a pictorial characterization of both processes as illustrated in Figure 23.1 and Figure 23.2.

Modes of Consultation

Since consultation is practiced in different contexts and areas of the counseling profession (e.g., community, agencies, industry, and schools) and is an essential part of

---

CASE VIGNETTE 23.2: BETTY'S ROLE CONFUSION

Betty is a third-grade teacher and is extremely angry and disturbed after seeing sexual abuse signs displayed by Katisha who is in her class. She contacted the father and after a short dialogue "concluded" that he was the perpetrator. As a result, she engaged Katisha's dad in a very nasty argument. After she calmed down and the parent left the classroom, she consulted with the school counselor and concluded that she might have overreacted. By Betsy's own admission, she was sexually molested by her uncle when she was young and was carrying a lot of anger and probably misplaced it against Katisha's dad without having proof that he was the perpetrator. Betsy is asking for professional help by the counselor in order to deal with her own issues.

Questions for Analysis:

1. What would be your first reaction when dealing with Betty's outbursts of misplaced anger?
2. How would you balance the delicate role of consultant/counselor?
3. What are the possible ethical and legal issues involved?
4. How would you report the sexual abuse case to the proper authorities and agencies?

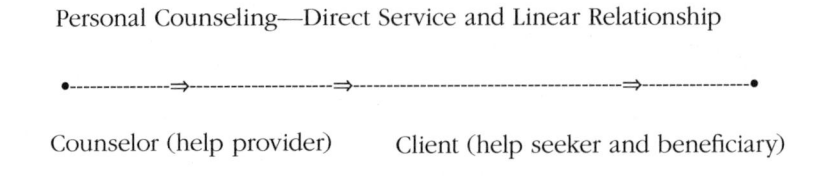

Figure 23.1 These diagrams serve as a pictorial depiction of the differences between the processes and not the exclusion of direct services over consultation (Parsons, 1996).

Personal Counseling—Direct Service and Linear Relationship

●--------------⇒--------------------⇒--------------------------------------⇒----------------●

Counselor (help provider)　　　Client (help seeker and beneficiary)

other disciplines (e.g., engineering, marketing/finances, and medicine), there are many different forms that consultation can take. Most importantly, like any of the other modalities (e.g., individual, group, and family counseling), consultation is guided by a theoretical conceptualization. Furthermore, consultants will operate based on their views, concerns, problems, or issues; how these must be resolved; what the expected outcomes are; and how soon results must be obtained. This section provides a short overview of some modes of consultation based on assumptions of the complexity of the problem, its focus, and styles of implementation.

Behavioral Consultation

The pillar of behavioral consultation is the social learning theory that stresses observable behaviors displayed by the consultee and the client (Bergan & Kratochwill, 1990; Martens, 1993). It stresses that the environment influences the individual's learning process and the way he or she functions on a daily basis. Strategies such as modeling, self-management, monitoring, reshaping, and social modeling are typical interventions drawn from both behavioral and social learning theories. Like a behavioral counselor, behavioral consultants adopt a directive, generally authoritative position when monitoring and assisting their consultees. They are actively involved in the data-gathering process or can use the consultee as a source to collect the necessary information for evaluation and intervention planning.

Client-Focused Consultation

The client-focused consultation approach is perhaps the most popular and common type of consultative interventions. It is typically used with teachers, administrators, parents, and individuals from the community when they need advice and guidance on how to help their students. The ultimate goal of the client-focused consultation is to look for a change in the behavior of an individual client. The typical methods utilized to promote these changes are field observations, individual interviews, and paper-and-pencil instruments of evaluation or testing. The main focus of the process is the client and not the consultee or group of the client.

Crisis-Oriented Consultation

When school counselors are consulted by an individual or group to provide advice or shed light on an issue, it is very likely that at that point a high degree of dysfunctionality is present and very likely that discomfort and hurt are felt. Using the metaphor of a mental health condition and the severity of its symptoms, the consultant has to determine the swiftness of the consultation process to quickly bring back the original degree of stability to the system (Sheridan, Bergan, & Kratochwill, 1996). For example, Mrs. Hanson is extremely frustrated with Eddie's behavioral outbursts in the classroom; likewise the school principal has tried several methods of disciplinary actions without success. Because there is no school counselor appointed in

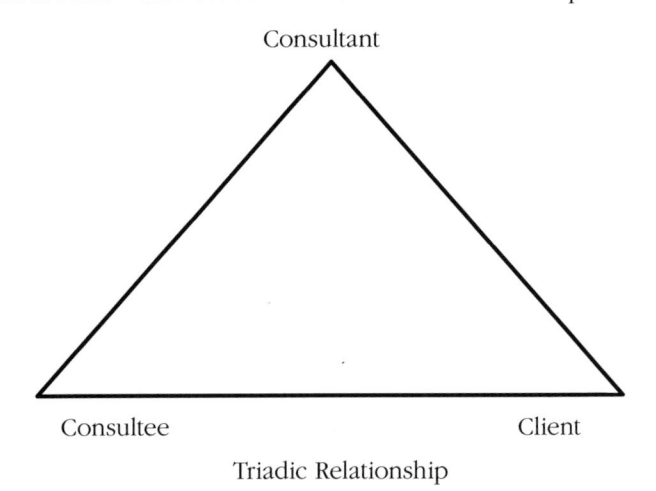

Consultation Process—Indirect Service and Triadic Relationship

Consultant

Consultee　　　　　　　　　　　　　　Client

Triadic Relationship

Figure 23.2 A triadic relationship places the emphasis on the client as the ultimate beneficiary of the consultation process (Parsons, 1996).

the school, they have brought in a part-time school counselor as a consultant to deal with cases such as Eddie's. Obviously, the main goal of the consultant is to improve Eddie's interpersonal skills, self-monitoring skills, and social behavior. The main point is to restore the quality of the teaching environment in the school, increase Eddie's school performance, decrease Mrs. Hanson's stress and the school principal's preoccupation about an unstable school atmosphere. Due to the triadic nature of this situation, the consultant will be targeting the teacher, school principal and student. All of them need to change in order to reestablish the precrisis level of the school environment. In essence, the consultant will touch upon the three points of the consultation triangle.

Consultee-Focused Consultation

This consultation approach focuses on assisting the consultee by providing the necessary skills or tools that will eventually help him or her provide better services to the client. To be exact, the consultee is the provider of the services and is being instructed or coached on areas that need improvement. In spite of the fact that the focus of this approach is the consultee, the client will reap benefits as a result of the consultative interventions (Brigman, Mullis, Webb, & White, 2004). By obtaining some additional training, the provider (consultee) is better equipped to assist the client. Again, the consultant is investing his time and energy on the consultee with the expectation that the consultee will provide better services to the client. For example, Jamie, a 5th-grade teacher, lacks a knowledge base of attention deficit disorders and its implications; she would like to "reach" Kennie, who has been diagnosed with ADD. The consultant can provide Jamie with information and specific classroom intervention strategies to assist her in being more effective in teaching Kennie. For instance, the consultant (counselor) can obtain Jamie's evaluation records and establish recommendations on: (a) follow up of psychotropic medication monitoring in conjunction with the parents and school nurse, (b) eating habits, (c) distraction elements, (d) breaks or relaxation periods between activities, (e) seating arrangements in the classroom, and (f) exploiting strengths to compensate for deficiencies.

Mental Health–Focused Consultation

In many ways the mental health–focused consultation is a more elaborated and extensive version of the client-focused approach. The consultant is seen as a teacher who delivers information but does so in a collaborative fashion with strong democratic principles. G. Caplan and R. Caplan (1993) saw this approach as a coordinated effort between the consultant and the consultee. G. Caplan and R. Caplan considered the relationship as an egalitarian negotiation in which the consultant does not claim to be an expert who imposes his or her views about how a problem must be approached and solved, but rather an individual who offers a different point of view and coordinates the resolution efforts. As a way of illustration, a mental health agency is struggling with a new influx of Bosnian immigrants who have received refugee status and are being integrated in the community. Many of them are facing issues related to postwar trauma and posttraumatic stress disorders. They are puzzled by their symptoms but unsure how to contextualize their realities in the U.S. context. A mental health consultant with expertise in refugees is hired not only to provide information to the staff, but to explore issues related to cross-cultural concerns that are having a negative impact on developing effective programs.

Developmental-Focused Consultation

In contrast to other types of consultation such as crisis-focused consultation, developmental-focused consultation is initiated by the consultant (counselor) and not the consultee. Instead of looking at what currently is not working, consultants will offer their services even when there are no difficulties in the areas of delivery services, clientele, or staff. This approach adopts a preventative perspective angle that looks at maintaining and improving current services. For instance, James, an experienced school counselor, learns that in the next two years the main factory in town will start downsizing to reduce the cost of operation. He knows that it will mean changes in the family structure of many of the students at the school, and therefore, the teachers must be prepared to deal with issues related to unemployment such as divorce, substance abuse, and domestic violence. James has offered a series of workshops to help teachers deal with this upcoming reality. The emphasis is on prevention as opposed to remediation.

Collaborative-Focused Consultation

Collaboration implies sharing, that is, allocating the resources to solve a situation. In this model, the consultant and consultee are actively giving out the best of their knowledge in a partnership in order to resolve a challenge. They not only share and combine resources, but also are responsible for the outcome. Therefore, the consultant and the consultee work as partners (Kurpius & Faqua, 1993). By using this approach, the probability of success increases substantially. For instance, let's use the previous case in which James, the school counselor, is expecting serious changes in the school environment as a result of the factory's closing. Despite the fact that he is an

CASE VIGNETTE 23.3: MR. PETERSEN AND PAPO

Reason for Referral

Papo was referred to you by Mr. Petersen, a seventh-grade teacher. According to Mr. Petersen, Papo has serious disciplinary problems in his class. He describes Papo as extremely disruptive, anxious, attention seeking, loud, and cocky. Mr. Petersen indicates that he is always late and comes with "lame" excuses to justify his tardiness. He describes Papo as the class clown but also believes that he seems to be involved in some type of gang activities because he is always hanging out with older kids who wear distinctive colors and make certain hand signs at school.

Mr. Petersen—The Consultee

Mr. Petersen accepted a teaching appointment at a middle school in the South Bronx last year as a result of a giveback-to-America program designed to appoint teachers to inner-city schools with a forgivable student loan program as an incentive. This is Mr. Petersen's first teaching appointment since his graduation last year from a university in Iowa. Mr. Petersen comes from a traditional farm town in Iowa with a population of 1,500 people, mostly of Swedish descent. He had never visited New York or the East coast prior to this teaching appointment. He thought that teaching a couple of years in a different part of the country would give him the opportunity to see other places in addition to the financial benefit of not having to pay back his student loans. At this point, he feels frustrated by Papo's situation because he was taught that a good teacher does not need a school counselor or social worker to deal with classroom disciplinary problems.

Papo—The Client

Papo is a fourth-generation Puerto Rican–American from the South Bronx, New York. He is currently living with his paternal grandparents. Prior to this, he lived with his uncle, mother, and maternal grandparents. He is the youngest of three siblings; one of them is living with another relative and the older one was sent to Puerto Rico. His dad is currently serving time in the state penitentiary for armed robbery, and his mother lost custody of the children due to physical abuse. In spite of the difficult family picture, Papo keeps a 2.80 G.P.A. and has not had serious disciplinary difficulties in the past.

The Context—School

The middle school (seventh to ninth grades), located in the South Bronx, has a population of 1,500 students, 60 classroom teachers, four school counselors, one school psychologist, one school administrator, and three assistant administrators. Ninety-five percent of the student body is eligible for either free or reduced lunch. The majority of the students are African American, Puerto Rican, and Dominican. Only one percent of the students are European American. According to the school district, the school has achieved some progress during the last academic year; however, the school remains under academic probation due to its low scores on the state tests. This came as a result of the No Child Left Behind mandate and its achievement standards. There is a high level of tension among the staff and a certain degree of discontent due to the lack of funding provided by the federal government to achieve these goals.

CASE VIGNETTE 23.3: MR. PETERSEN AND PAPO (continued)

Questions for Analysis and Application:

1. Conceptualize this case based on the following consultation modes:
   a. Behavioral Consultation:
   b. Client-Focused Consultation:
   c. Crisis-Oriented Consultation:
   d. Consultee-Focused Consultation:
   e. Mental Health Consultation:
   f. Developmental-Focused Consultation:
   g. Collaborative-Focused Consultation:
   h. System-Focused Consultation:
2. According to the case and based on your conceptualization, which consultation mode is most effective? Elaborate.
3. What are the major issues to be considered as a consultant?

---

experienced school counselor, he lacks knowledge about the aftermath of downsizing a company and its effects in an area's schools. He decides to seek consultation from Jackie, an experienced school counselor from a neighboring town that experienced the same situation eight years ago. James and Jackie shared experiences and put them together to create a plan of action. In reality, both were equally involved in the process and shared the workload in order to devise a proactive intervention.

System-Focused Consultation

This mode of consultation attempts to target various components or subsystems of an organization to bring collective awareness of how to resolve a conflict or a problem. The consultant works directly with those involved in the system to assist them in identifying the areas that are creating the current conditions (McDaniel, Campbell, Wynne, & Weber, 1986). The consultant will assist those involved in the system to conceptualize the current situation from a different angle and see how all participants can work together to achieve a "new system." From an organizational standpoint, many times the members of a system reflect the structural dynamics of the organization itself; that is, if the organization is extremely rigid, bureaucratic, and hierarchical, the members will feel alienated from those in power. Typically, a sense of detachment and a lack of collective responsibility surface, which creates oppositional behaviors among employees. By nature, systems try to maintain their homeostasis (balance) and will inevitably resist change. If a consultant is conducting an evaluation of the system, this may be seen as a threat to the current balance of the organization. As a result, it is not atypical for consultants to deal with high levels of resistance (Kuh, 1993). Consider the previous case in which James, the school counselor, is trying to be proactive by utilizing a systemic mode of consultation.

James is aware that many of the faculty and administrators will be resistant to change in their current daily routines unless they are involved in the process. In order to ameliorate their opposition and gain their support, he creates a consultation committee in which members of the faculty, administration, and parents work in conjunction with him and outside consultants. The strategy is to validate the concerns of all the subsystems in the school and obtain their support once proactive measures are recommended and implemented. The chance of successful consultation process will increase by considering all the elements of the system.

Phases in the Consultation Process

Regardless of the mode of consultation, there appear to be phases in each consultation. Depending on the consultative style, theoretical orientation of the consultant, and nature of the consultation, there will be variations in the sequencing and pacing of the phases in each consultation and some phases may not be present at all. Occasionally, the consultant will invest a lot of time on one phase and barely any on another. However, the following overview of the consultation phases serves as a guiding map that provides direction, structure, and order of action for any school consultant.

Consultation mimics the counseling process in many ways but most specifically mirrors the uncertainty of the outcome and the fluidity of the action process. It is important to clarify that despite the fact that the phases of consultation are presented in a linear fashion, they are not always experienced in this way, and at times some of these phases seem to be more ambiguous and unpredictable than others.

Preentry

This phase of consultation is critical because it sets the stage for all the participants. Similar to group counseling, the preentry phase serves for the consultant to explore the existing norms of the institution. It is vital for the school counselor (consultant) to explore the views or opinions that the administrators and teachers hold toward the school counselor with regard to referral procedures, expectations, and outcomes. As an illustration, Mr. Parker refers "trouble students" to Mrs. Atkinson (the school counselor) and expects her to be able to evaluate and "fix" them in a couple of days. This is the traditional way of interaction with school counselors as consultants; teachers or administrators refer students and then remove themselves from the remaining process expecting the school counselor to resolve the situation or give them quick advice.

To avoid this antiquated dynamic, the school counselor must redesign the traditions and norms of the school with regard to the consultation process. That is, teachers and administrators must take an active role during the consultation process and remain active throughout its resolution by providing feedback to the consultant, keeping the communication channels open, and incorporating the input of the consultant. The best way to change the perception and expectations of the school staff with regard to the duties of the school counselor as a consultant is to demystify those ingrained beliefs. This can be achieved by using a predetermined period of time during in-service activities at school to explain the process of consultation and counseling to the staff and by clarifying that this is not an individual process but a concerted effort from all the staff. These concepts can be introduced by making available a conceptualization diagram of a DCSC and all its respective components. Familiarizing the school staff with these concepts will facilitate their involvement in the consultation process.

Entry

Similar to individual counseling, the first meeting will set the stage for success or failure in the consultation process. The focal point of the very first meeting will be based upon the crisis level brought by the consultee or the intensity of the situation. For example, Katherine, a 28-year-old parent, has been struggling with her daughter's apathy toward school and has resorted to contacting the counselor for assistance after trying ideas of her own. It is obvious that Katherine is frustrated, angry, and discouraged at the point of contact with the counselor. As a result, Katherine may be looking for a quick fix and not necessarily for active collaboration with the counselor. It may be necessary for the school counselor to take remedial direct action for a short period of time until some degree of stability is brought to the situation.

When a consultee is in a state of crisis, collaborative partnership will not be a priority, but rather the expectation will be for the consultant to devise a "magic" plan for prompt resolution with minimal assistance from the consultee. It is indispensable, especially during the first session, to demonstrate empathy through the power of listening. The following are some key points for the consultation process during the entry phase:

1. Use basic listening skills; let the consultee finish the whole story.
2. Be empathic.
3. After dealing with the emotive part of the process, establish the logistics of the process, such as where to meet, what is needed for the next meeting, expectations, and collaborative goals.
4. As in individual counseling, the professional code of ethics must be applied, especially the issue of confidentiality and its exception (i.e., duty to warn). That is, if the consultee or client are in danger or will harm him- or herself, the consultant is obligated to report it to the respective authorities.
5. Create a written contract if necessary. Sometimes a written document provides some degree of accountability.

Exploration

Whether the consultation is formal or informal, this is the phase in which the school consultant collects data in the form of verbal reports and observations or documents and paper-and-pencil instruments. The school consultant must adopt the attitude of a field researcher in which all possible sources of information are investigated. As in counseling, at first the school consultant has to rely on the version and perspective of the consultee. At this point, the school consultant may be considering whether the description of past events is accurate or if the perception of the consultee needs to be corroborated due to a lack of consistency. Consequently, trust is an important element at this phase. The following points must be considered during this phase:

1. Explore what efforts and strategies have been tried to resolve the problem in the past. Which did not work and which were partially successful?
2. In a nonjudgmental way, explore the "filter" of the consultee, moreover, whether traumatic experiences, current mental health conditions, or severe biases are altering the perception of a situation.
3. Gather information about the client via documents, observations, or instruments to help answer the following questions: "What is occurring at this moment? Previously? Or, if the situation is not corrected, what will happen in the near future? What could be the potential consequences if the pattern is not altered?
4. Explore if there are systemic variables influencing the current or past situations of the client.
5. Rank, in order of importance, the series of problems (challenges) that may be causing the client(s) to behave in a particular way.

Setting Concrete Goals, Objectives, and Carrying Them Out

Once the school consultant has gathered a series of preliminary explanations of the origin of the problem, then he or she is ready to answer the following question: "How can I help the client change, alleviate the consultee's current situation, and help the system evolve?" Most of the time, the primary goal is to find a way to help the client change to ameliorate the situation. However, occasionally, one has to refocus the consultation process toward altering the consultee or even the organizational structure of the system in order to provoke change in the client. Independent of the focus of the consultation, the ultimate goal is to provoke some type of change to create homeostasis (balance in the system).

Case Vignette 23.4 is an illustration of how concrete goals can be set.

CASE VIGNETTE 23.4: MRS. BOWER'S CONCERNS—SETTING CONCRETE GOALS

Mrs. Bowers—The Consultee

Mrs. Bowers, a twelfth-grade English teacher has been very concerned about the rumors in school regarding her intolerance toward African Americans students. According to her, everything started when Tyrone, an African American male, complained about the absence of notable African American authors in the class's reading list. She explained that the selection of books was predetermined by the school district and that she had very limited flexibility on the selection of new titles for the course. She consulted with the school counselor on how to find a solution for the situation.

Tyrone and parents—The Clients

Tyrone and several parents indicated that Mrs. Bowers is somewhat racist because she gives preference to all the European novels and 19th-century American classics without taking into account authors of color. Tyrone and a group of African American parents presented their complaints to the school principal and school counselor.

The School Counselor as Consultant—Setting Concrete Goals

The immediate goal of the consultee is "I want the rumors about my supposed racial intolerance to stop." In order to achieve this basic goal, the consultant (school counselor) explored alternative options regarding her curricular flexibility prior to setting up a meeting with the parents of the concerned students. The consultant came up with several alternatives that could provide curricular flexibility to the teacher without compromising the original academic guidelines. He recommended the utilization of more special reports, alternate projects, and films and videos in class addressing African American icons such as Dr. Martin Luther King, Rosa Parks, and Malcom X. These options were approved by the school principal and board and immediately a special meeting with the African American parents was scheduled to inform them of the curricular changes.

CASE VIGNETTE 23.4: MRS. BOWER'S CONCERNS— SETTING CONCRETE GOALS (CONTINUED)

Questions for Reflection and Analysis:

1. How can Mrs. Bowers keep in touch with the African American parents and get feedback before similar issues get out of hand?
2. What other long-term goals should Mrs. Bowers be advised to keep in mind?
3. How can the consultant evaluate the effectiveness of the interventions?

Regardless of the angle or focus of the consultation, a set of manageable and realistic goals will lead the way to achieve concrete objectives. Occasionally, goals are mistaken for objectives but they are not the same. A goal is a general, positive statement intended to achieve an outcome (Midgley, 2002). These general goals take the form of broad declarations such as

1. I would like my son to be more responsible with his homework.
2. I wish that Casey could be on time for his biology class after the lunch break.
3. I would like Mr. Ramsunsen to be more organized as a teacher.
4. We (i.e., teachers, administrators, and school staff) would like the students and parents to embrace the idea implementing a uniform for all the students beginning the next academic year.

As evidenced by the aforementioned declarations, vagueness tends to be the central issue among all of them. At times goals acquire the form of wishful thinking but lack a directional force that would propel the consultee to execute them. Goals are stated in a positive fashion and not with a negative connotation (Midgley, 2002). On the other hand, objectives are a refined version of goals because they are the tangible proof that the goals have been achieved. The objectives will serve as a measure of accountability to determine the direction of the process (Matsumura, 2005). The key difference between goals and objectives is that the objectives operationalize the goals and make them concrete and achievable. Goals are not always achieved because they fall within the realm of wishful thinking, but objectives provide direction. For instance, the aforementioned goals can be converted into achievable objectives in the following manner:

1. To promote school responsibility and the completion of my son's homework, I will create a more enticing and quiet environment at home conducive to academic work. I will set up a desk, reading lamp, and quiet place for him to study at the same time every day. The TV, stereo, video games and other distractions will be turned off during the two hours of daily study. And, I will provide a series of rewards by stages (i.e., weekly, monthly, quarterly, midterm, semester) as incentives.
   a. Different from the initial *goal* (i.e., I would like…), these *objectives* have a measurable outcome in which the progress is monitored and can be evaluated or rectified if not effective.
2. I will provide positive encouragement to Casey every time he is on time for biology class. At first, the hall monitor will remind Casey to go for a drink of water and use the restroom five minutes before the bell rings. I will find strong motivators and encouragement factors and utilize them to help Casey with his tardiness.
   a. Unlike the initial goal of "I wish that…" these objectives concretize a vague idea into action.
3. I will send Mr. Ramsunsen to some time-management and organizational workshops provided by the school district. I will pair up Mr. Ramsunsen with Mrs. Jones as a mentor.
   a. Instead of desiring to have a more organized teacher in Mr. Ramsunsen, providing the training and educational tools will increase the chances that he will be more apt to change. Criticizing or providing vague feedback will not necessarily invoke change.
4. We will send monthly letters and provide a series of workshops informing parents of the benefits of implementing a school uniform. Students will be exposed to similar information through classroom guidance activities throughout the semester. Also, creating an environment of inclusiveness and cooperation, parents and students will have the opportunity to select the school logo and colors of the uniform.
   a. Instead of wishing that the parents and students could embrace the idea of a school uni-

form, the goals allow the conversion of a wish into the operationalization of an idea.

The process of operationalizing the goals will follow after these are clearly depicted. Implementation of action strategies needs to be a communal effort on the part of the consultant and consultee. After the interventions are implemented, the consultant and consultee must look at the objectives carefully to see whether or not the intervention strategies are on the right track. In sum, the objectives are not affirmative statements but ways on how to transform a vague idea into a manageable purpose.

Evaluation

Evaluation serves as a way to monitor the accomplishment of the initial goals and objectives. Monitoring change in the client serves as a function to determine if there is a need to alter the initial goals or objectives or if the interventions have to be modified. How does the school consultant know if the consultation process was successful? The following points serve as a measuring device:

1. The implementation strategies were achievable and manageable.
2. The "true" problem or the source of concern was effectively targeted.
3. The concrete goals for the system, consultee, and/or client were attainable.
4. All causes of resistance were identified during the consultation process and were dealt with effectively.

Termination

Ideally, the termination process must be mutual although this may not necessarily happen. Termination is not only a matter of reviewing the attainment of goals and objectives but also a way to provide the necessary tools of awareness and knowledge for the consultant to maintain the current conditions. In other words, to conclude the consult, the consultee should be able to

1. Keep the actions used during the consult to sustain progress;
2. Monitor change in the future; and
3. Find sources of support in the absence of the consultant.

In sum, the process of consultation is not a linear one in which all the phases are achieved and every part of the process can be clearly identified. On the other hand, knowledge of the phases of consultation is critical as it serves as a roadmap that provides direction and understanding of the whole process.

Research on Consultation

Effectiveness of Consultation

As in any other branch of the human services, measuring change and success as a result of consultative interventions is not an easy task. However, it is not only an option to know whether the interventions provoked some positive change but an ethical mandate established by the Code of Ethics and Standards of Practice (American Counseling Association, 1995, C.2.d). When compared with group, individual, and family counseling, the modality of consultation lacks solid research in the areas of efficacy (Parsons & Kahn, 2005). In order to increase the quality of consultative services rendered, it is necessary to increase the body of research and information (ACA, 1995, C.2.f).

One of the main concerns about consultative interventions is whether school consultants are using interventions that have some validity and can be empirically supported (Erchul, 1992). As previously mentioned, school districts operate under the assumption that empirical studies with strong statistical support are more valid than anecdotal experiences. Therefore, these are some recommendations when conducting a consultation project:

1. Write a strong rationale that supports the study.
2. Translate the problem or situation into a hypothesis.
3. Use a large pool of participants (when appropriate). If not available, compile the results of several individual case studies.
4. Extrapolate results with school documents and national statistics.
5. If being hired by another school district, collaborate with other school counselors who can serve as action researchers.
6. Do not discard any form of data (e.g., number of phone calls, e-mails, interviews) that can be later used as research.
7. Follow the district guidelines for publication and dissemination of research (e.g., human subjects' standards).
8. Present results at local, regional, and national school counseling conferences.

Consultation and research in the multicultural arena
Multiculturalism has produced substantial changes in the areas of counseling and psychology (i.e., direct services) and it is slowly bringing about modifications to the modality of consultation (Jackson & Hayes, 1993). Because cultures do not remain stagnant, the consultant's skills should evolve and develop accordingly. Understanding the culture and values of a system is a prerequisite of any successful

consultation and a sign of a consultant with updated skills (Hansen, Himes, & Meier, 1990).

According to Parsons (1996), it is the consultant's responsibility to increase his or her own cultural knowledge and develop skills that are consistent with the diverse cultural populations. Also, a more effective consultant should accomplish the following: (a) awareness of one's own culture and its influence, (b) awareness of the narrowness of a single mainstream perspective, (c) understanding and valuing an alternative worldview, and (d) employing culturally sensitive approaches to diagnosis and intervention (p. 233).

The consultation modality will remain productive and vibrant by embracing and infusing multiculturalism. Acknowledging the demographic changes of the nation is paramount in developing services that are consistent with the belief systems and cultures represented by those who will benefit in a consultation process (Worzbyt, O'Rourke, & Dandeneau, 2003).

Areas deserving research interest in the future As a result of sudden cultural and social changes experienced in our society, school counselors as consultants will have to keep abreast by reaching out and tapping into other resources in order to remain effective. The following are some areas that deserve more research:

1. *Gang-intervention programs.* Although there are myriad gang-intervention programs with an emphasis on intervention and prevention, there is limited research on the consultation process that goes along with such programs (Tabish & Orell, 1996). School counselors can serve an instrumental role as consultants when prevention programs sponsored by community agencies cannot fully reach into the school. Utilizing the knowledge, educational background, and insights of the school's culture may possibly increase the chances of success of these programs.
2. *Formal consultation with mental health and community agencies.* It is best practices for community counselors to have staff meetings in which clients' issues are discussed as a way to obtain input and feedback from the rest of the colleagues. Rarely are school counselors considered in such processes, and they are routinely seen as ancillary providers of basic information as opposed to equals and participants in a coordinated event (Caplan & Caplan, 1993; Parsons, 1996). Research is needed to see how the outcome of the consultation process would change if school counselors are seen as equal collaborators and invested participants.
3. *Internet, school counselors, and their consultation role.* School counselors are in the initial stages of realizing the potential of the Internet as a tool to facilitate consultation (see www.scan21st.com).
4. *The* No Child Left Behind *initiative.* Currently, there are no provisions in the original document regarding school counseling. This should be a red flag for counselor/educators and school counselors in the field as it reflects various trends: (a) a lack of knowledge of services rendered by school counselors by those who developed the document, (b) an invalidation of these services as secondary to the traditional disciplines, and (c) a lack of leadership and political involvement in developing educational policies that benefit the school-counseling profession. All of these deserve the attention of researchers. Long-term and data-driven studies in conjunction with qualitative investigations should help advance the school-counseling profession and make it more relevant to our current reality.

Practice

Communication Strategies

Regardless of the intuitive abilities of a consultant, communicating effectively remains at the core of any consult. Damage to a professional relationship is not atypical if the communication between the parties has not been clear, purposeful, and honest (Brown, Pryzwansky, & Schulte, 2001). The following is a short synopsis of some communication strategies that the consultant must be aware of when interacting with the consultee and the client.

Rapport is established when the consultant displays careful and reflective listening and is empathic toward the consultee (Brammer, 1994; Ivey, 1994). Rapport is established when there is a sense of mutual trust and comfort in the communication process as illustrated in the example below.

Consultee (Parent)—Mrs. Ali
Consultant (School Counselor)—Mrs. Pitch

Dialogue:

Mrs. Ali: Hello, Mrs. Pitch. I am here because some students are harassing my son Abdul for his beliefs, looks, etc. I am very concerned, upset, and scared at the same time for his safety.

Mrs. Pitch: You must be going through a difficult time as I can tell that you are a responsible and loving parent who is concerned about Abdul's well-being. I cannot fully understand what you are going through because I am not Muslim, but I am a mother like you.

Mrs. Ali: Yes, you know how hard it is to hear other kids say that my son is a terrorist? It hurts a lot because we are a good Muslim family and we do not believe in violence. That's not the way Abdul has been raised. This situation is very difficult. I think that most kids and even some teachers do not know what the true Islam is.

Mrs. Pitch: First, I want to know how Abdul is coping with the situation and what kind of help he has. Second, I also want to know what kind of support your family is getting. Abdul is our responsibility and our school wants to foment a sensitive and embracing environment. You seem very hurt about this problem and I am concerned about you and your family.

Mrs. Ali: Thank you so much for being a good listener, you are the first person that I have talked to about this situation outside the family. You seem to understand what we are going through.

Mrs. Pitch: You are very welcome. I have some ideas on how to promote a more tolerant environment. I believe that some kids and parents are reacting like that because they lack information. I can certainly mediate some type of classroom guidance activities in which perhaps members of your mosque who do out-reach activities can visit us and provide information to the students and staff of the school. Then, I can do some follow up activities with regard to diversity and tolerance. What do you think?

Before engaging in a full process of consultation, Mrs. Pitch addressed the emotional needs of Mrs. Ali by validating her feelings of pain and insecurity. As in a counseling session, connecting with the client is the precursor of a successful outcome, thereby building rapport.

Persuasion is not the equivalent of manipulation. It can be defined as a motivational strategy based on positive encouragement, especially when the consultee is frustrated and unmotivated (Brigman, Mullis, Webb, & White, 2004). The following example illustrates a series of skills such as validation, persuasion, and advice giving.

Consultant (School Counselor)—Mrs. Robinson
Consultee (Teacher)—Mr. Byrd

Dialogue:

Mr. Byrd: I don't think that I was born to be a teacher. I don't have what it takes to do it. I feel that I am putting out fires all the time. I feel disorganized and never relaxed. It is taking a toll and even affecting my lectures, which are my only strength. I am going to quit... .

Mrs. Robinson: Based on your tone of voice and your whole demeanor I can tell that you are very affected by your situation. However, I commend you for coming to my office and seeking help. How long have you been teaching?

Mr. Byrd: This is my first year. It has been really rough.

Mrs. Robinson: I hear your struggle and I don't want to invalidate or minimize your experience but that's exactly how I felt during my first year as a teacher. I started as an English teacher and after seven years made the transition to school counseling. I was so close to throw my teaching degree out of the window and start a new career... .

Mr. Byrd: Really? You look so organized and comfortable with what you do that I would have never imagined that. I don't know if I can make it though.

Mrs. Robinson: If you allow me, this is what I see. I see a very talented and energetic teacher who cares about his students. And, I see a person that can make a difference, somebody who is invested and willing to work hard.

Mr. Byrd: Thanks, I appreciate it. I have not had feedback in a long time because Mrs. Carter (school principal) is too busy these days... .

Mrs. Robinson: Do you still want to give it a try if I give you some assistance?

Mr. Byrd: Sure.

Mrs. Robinson: It seems to me that organization and time distribution are the issues here and not a lack of talent. That's easy to correct. We just have to work on an organizational system.

Persuasion can be combined with advice giving and positive encouragement. Once the consultee is encouraged to alter a behavior or pursue a goal, then that can be followed with advice giving and more concrete instructions.

Informing. Because the consultation is a psychodidactic process, being a good listener is not enough. At some point, it is expected that the school consultant will provide information and deliver concrete details and ways of implementing ideas. The school consultant will play the role of a teacher during some stages of the consultation process (Schmidt, 2003).

Consultant (School Counselor)—Mrs. Ramírez
Consultee (Teacher)—Mr. Castro

Dialogue:

Mr. Smith: I am having a hard time motivating some Latinos in my senior class to follow through the necessary steps to complete college applications, ACT/SAT forms, and college visits. They do not seem to be motivated at all.

Mrs. Ramírez: You seem pretty frustrated about it. What have you tried up to this point?

Mr. Smith: I have talked about the importance of a college degree in life, brought the brochures, and offered help to fill them out, etc.... .

Mrs. Ramírez: I see. All of those are good strategies and perhaps we could enhance those to build up the motivation by using reverse psychology.

Mr. Smith: Uhm. Good idea. But how exactly can I do it?

Mrs. Ramírez: I can assist you with locating speakers from the community who are ex-convicts and ex-gang members, who have had a really rough time in life, and are giving back to the community by demystifying the idea that you can have it easy in our society without a college degree. These are very powerful guys who speak their language and are reliable. Once they start realizing that it is not that easy, we will come up with other strategies of positive encouragement to apply for college. Step by step.

Mr. Smith: Excellent. When do we start?

Utilizing a basic pedagogic technique of delivery and application of information, the consultant provided the idea (reverse psychology or prescribing the symptom) and later explained how to apply it (bringing speakers). This will have a follow up of more specific interventions.

Reinforcing. The reinforcement strategy is based upon the constant reaffirmation that the consultation process is being implemented (Brigman, Mullis, Webb, & White, 2004). More importantly, it consolidates the commitment toward positive change.

Consultant (School Counselor)—Mrs. Stuart
Consultee (Parent)—Mr. Blagovejic

Dialogue:

Mrs. Stuart: Okay, let's see if things have changed with Tommy at home. Are you following the instructions that I gave you last week?

Mr. Blagovejic: More or less.

Mrs. Stuart: Remember that it is critical to keep a stable routine with regard to behavior and be persistent. ADHD is a condition that aside the medication can be controlled with a solid routine at home. Let's go over some of the basic instructions again, okay?

Mr. Blagovejic: Okay, that sounds good.

In a way, reinforcing is based on repetition. The school counselor could provide the same information from a different angle or simply remind about aspects of the consultation. The idea is to refresh the initial interventions with positive encouragement.

Paraphrasing. The basic message delivered by the consultee is reflected back by the consultant. The idea is to keep the content intact as a reflective strategy (Thompson, 2002). Paraphrases tend to be shorter than the initial statement and should not be convoluted in nature.

Consultant (School Counselor)—Mrs. Uribe
Consultee (Teacher)—Mr. Ramazzoti

Dialogue:

Mr. Ramazotti: I am so upset right now...I don't believe it. How did that parent dare to say that I am not a good teacher? I bet that she is upset because her daughter got a C on the last test. Well, I am sorry but that's the grade that she earned, plain and simple. She insulted me on the phone and is demanding a parent–teacher conference this afternoon! I have another commitment. God, I am so upset! I feel like...

Mrs. Uribe: You are upset and feel invalidated as a professional because that parent does not appreciate your hard work. And, you feel that you are losing control and about to do something that you may regret.

Mr. Ramazotti: Yes, that's how I feel, exactly.

Mrs. Uribe: Let's talk a little bit more about how you feel and later on I have a couple of strategies that will definitively help you in dealing with these kinds of challenges. Usually, these situations can be diffused with the appropriate interventions. So you will apply them and keep me posted. Okay?

In essence, the consultant is utilizing some of the same words that the consultee is using and emphasizing their importance. This is a basic counseling strategy that is transferable into the consultation arena. After the emotions are under control, the school counselor (consultant) can provide the consultee with strategies on how to deal with difficult parents and keep the potential crisis under control, but it was important to let him know that she was listening by paraphrasing the content of the conversation.

Listening. Listening is more than hearing. It implies an active process in which the nonverbal and verbal messages are carefully considered. Listening implies action; it is not a passive process (Marks, 1995). More importantly, listening must be empathic and not judgmental.

Consultant (School Counselor)—Mrs. Crede
Consultee (Student)—Jani

Dialogue:
Jani: I have tried to be nice to the art teacher; I have tried everything, believe me. I mean, I raise my hand, bring my materials, and do my homework but she always finds an excuse to pick on somebody. I am really tired of her. What's wrong with her? I am not an artist like most of my friends but at least I am trying. She thinks that she is Picasso, perfect, you know. I am sick of her and the class.
Mrs. Crede: Uhm, you are really upset. I can see it in your eyes. Tell me more about how you feel.
Jani: I am tired, period. I want to confront her personally. You will see…
Mrs. Crede: You did the right thing by coming here. This is a safe place to talk and I will help you. Please, what do you have in mind? After we talk about your feelings of discontent and distrust I can give you some techniques that you can use to handle your own feelings and how to deal with your art teacher. You can implement them and you will come back to me. Then, if those don't work, we can certainly look for other alternatives. I realize that your teacher is a very demanding teacher and has her own way of teaching the class.

The consultant (school counselor) is promoting full disclosure without invalidating the story and without being judgmental. After listening carefully, the consultant is ready to provide specific information on how to deal with the art teacher and other difficult people.

Exploring Resistance

Using the analogy of individual counseling, at times the consultant will encounter resistance from the consultee even if his or her intentions are noble. At times, the consultee may behave in a defensive manner and adopt an adversarial position (Cowan, 2005; Shelton & James, 2004). This should not take the consultant by surprise; levels of resistance are to be expected at some point.

Consultant (School Counselor)—Mr. Ferro
Consultee (Group of Parents)—Parents

Dialogue:
Parents: We cannot believe the attitude of the school principal. We are ready to send a letter to the superintendent and go to the press if necessary!
Mr. Ferro: This is our third meeting. Let's review our plan of action as delineated two weeks ago…
Parents: We don't think that the plan is working very well and we want to take action right away.
Mr. Ferro: Can you be more specific and let me know what is not working? As I recall, we all came up with the plan as a group.
Parents: Well, it is too slow…and…
Mr. Ferro: I believe that we had talked about getting a consensus from all the parents by collecting some surveys and running some focus groups in order to come up with a more comprehensive plan to change the situation in the school. I believe that we mentioned that it was not the school principal's fault but that it was a more systemic situation.

As in counseling, sometimes the consultee believes that the consultation process will provoke changes overnight and without the investment of energy. Reinforcement of the process is necessary and a challenge of preconceived ideas.

Exploring the Source of Resistance. There are many possible sources that can be attributed to the resistance displayed by the consultee. Among them are the nature or personality of the consultant, the lack of structure of the consultative process, the degree of dysfunctionality of the system, and the individual traits of the consultee. Resistance is defined as any intentional or unintentional behavior designed to obstruct a positive outcome (Cowan, 2005).

Understanding and Managing Resistance. Resistance is an indirect way of communicating that there is something making the consultee uncomfortable. Ideally, the consultant would like to know what is impeding the progress of the consult, but as in any other type of human interaction, communication is not always direct. Resistance can create frustration and discouragement, and it can slow down or block the consultation process if it is not managed appropriately. If the consult involves drastic implementation changes on the part of the consultee, resistance may be an appropriate reaction. If Mr. Ramos, a ninth-grade teacher, is instructed to assertively communicate with the school principal, Mrs. Richardson, he may present some degree of resistance out of natural fear of the potential consequences, because he does not hold a permanent position at the school. It is very likely that Mr. Ramos will not follow the recommendations of the consultant; his reaction is somewhat rational. In a case like this, the consultant and the consultee may have divergent outlooks about the consult (Randolph & Graun, 1988). Mr. Ramos may think that he is losing total control of the process and is feeling helpless— control tends to be a critical point that is at times conspicuously disregarded in consultation (Block, 1981).

Similarly, if Mr. Ramos discloses that he is not the most assertive person and he tends to be respectful and a passive follower, that could bring up feelings of inadequacy. When consultees feel vulnerable and inadequate, they may be worried that they are responsible for the problem (Alderman & Gimpel, 1996).

Consultant's Cultural Insensitivity. Mr. Tupec, a ninth-grade teacher, is a first generation Guatemalan-American of Native Indian heritage who left his country when he was an adolescent. He still speaks his native Indian language and Spanish. Respect and deference to people who hold positions of authority are highly regarded values held by Mr. Tupec. He has experienced difficulties with the school principal, Mrs. Richardson, who has put an immense degree of pressure on him in spite of the fact that he is a first-year teacher and has just completed his bachelor's degree in education a couple of months previously.

The school (counselor) consultant is a little exasperated with Mr. Tupec because he is not following the advice given. He is reluctant to "stand up" to Mrs. Richardson, and he seems to take it all without responding assertively. It is clear that there is a cultural gap between the consultant and Mr. Tupec. The consultant is unable to see that the cultural values held by Mr. Tupec are the reason behind his behavior and not a stubborn attitude.

As indicated by Sue, Arredondo, and McDavis (1992), consultants must be open to alternative worldviews and should employ techniques that respect and honor other cultures. In order to respect other cultures and worldviews, the counselor (consultant) must be aware of his or her own culture and biases (Vernon & Clemente, 2005). As the consultant engages in a journey of self-exploration, several issues such as applying culturally sensitive interventions, exploring other cultural views, the concept of time, personal versus collective responsibility, internal versus external locus of control, learning styles, and challenging European-driven interventions as the only alternatives should be carefully explored.

Individual-Focused Consultation

As indicated in previous sections of the chapter, the school consultant will work with different types of consultees at different levels: individual, group, and system. This section points out the unique characteristics of individuals that can require the services of a school consultant and how these individuals' needs in the school context may require completely different consultative approaches.

The Student

As in any interpersonal relationship there are issues of power, status, and control, and school consultation is not an exception. It is vital to acknowledge that in the school system students find themselves on the lowest rung of the ladder when issues of power are considered. More than the teacher and the administrator, students are vulnerable. Students will approach school counselors for consultation when they have tried other resources such as friends, family members, or even teachers. They recognize that the school counselor is a source of information but he or she is not always the first selection of choice. As a result, the school counselor must be aware that when a student knocks on the door out of his or her own volition, a sense of discouragement or vulnerability may be present.

For instance, Christie, a high school junior, is extremely anxious about her academic performance in her chemistry course. She had been thinking about a career in medicine but during the last two years her performance in science has not been the best. Due to her low grade in chemistry she is having self-doubts about her future. She stopped by the office of the school counselor to seek information about other careers that may not be science oriented. As indicated previously, the school counselor must let Christie finish her story and realize the magnitude of her situation and the impact it is having in her life. There are two different issues: (1) self-efficacy and personal doubts and (2) information about other careers. One falls within the consultative role (information) and the other one (self-efficacy) falls within the counseling role. The consultative role (information) can be easily addressed by presenting options and directing Christie to additional sources that she can access.

Either the consultative or the counseling roles are led by the theoretical orientation of the school counselor. For instance, an Adlerian consultant would teach Christie specific psychoeducational ways to deal with the situation (e.g., realigning goals, study habits, life style; Dreikurs, 2004), and a constructivist school consultant might deal with the language used and how it creates a reality that is socially constructed (Gutterman, 1994). For example, a situation becomes a problem if it is seen as a problem, otherwise it is not.

The following points should be considered when working with a student regardless of the theoretical orientation:

1. Identify the problem, acknowledge the breadth of its impact, and decide if remedial action is to be taken. Convey a sense of hope and resolution.
2. Prioritize the goals and objectives.
3. Respecting confidentiality, carefully present the idea of collaboration with other professionals (e.g.,

social worker, school psychologist, tutor, administrator, special education teacher) as a way to enhance the consultation process.
4. Monitor the process by reviewing the objectives and communicating what is being achieved with the student.

The Teacher and the Administrator

The professional dynamics between the teacher or administrator and the school consultant are considerably different from those with the students. The school consultant operates in a more collegial fashion with the teacher than with the administrator, who is seen as a superior and an evaluator. The power differential dynamics can exert some influence when the school consultant is facing a possible ethical dilemma. For example, the school consultant knows that Mrs. Richardson (school administrator) has been unfair with Mr. Ramos (ninth-grade teacher). The consultant must deal with the intransigent and rigid behavior of Mrs. Richardson, who is the consultant's supervisor as well. If her approach is too abrupt, she fears that Mrs. Richardson could retaliate in the evaluations. On the other hand, Mr. Ramos needs assistance. Thus, an ethical dilemma is created.

Unless the consult came as a result of a very specific interactional dynamic, most interventions that require skill training or development for teachers and administrators work better in a psychoeducational format rather than in individual one (Caplan & Caplan, 1993; Parsons & Kahn, 2005). Consultations in schools, therefore, can take the form of workshop training for teachers and administrators, as well as with parents. When developing a series of workshop training sessions, the following should be considered:

1. Pick an in-service training day as opposed to an optional training day. This way you will be able to target a broader audience.
2. Send various announcements and reminders via e-mail or school letters about the content of the workshop.
3. Compile some input from teachers and administrators about other areas that should be addressed.
4. As you deliver the workshop, do not mention the names of specific teachers or supervisors. This could either embarrass them or create the illusion that the sole purpose of the workshop is to correct the deficiencies of certain colleagues.
5. Develop clear goals and objectives.
6. Create learning activities devised to target specific subgroups.
7. Do not exclude the school administrators. Select a day in which all the administrators can be present and actively participate.

Consultant (School Counselor)—Mrs. Burton
Consultee (School Principal)—Mr. Brown

Dialogue:
Mr. Brown: I have noticed that there is a high degree tension among teachers, and I've seen a lot of overly stressed teachers. In fact, I know that the degree of absenteeism among teachers is high because of the stress levels. I am very concerned about five or six teachers specifically. Do you have any ideas on how to address this issue?
Mrs. Burton: I have seen the same thing because some students have complained to me about how grouchy some teachers are lately. I am glad that you came to me because I have a couple of ideas.
Mr. Brown: Excellent. Tell me more about it.
Mrs. Burton: I believe that I can send a short survey to explore the current climate of the school and add a section about areas of personal growth. Based on the feedback, I can arrange a series of workshops of one hour every two weeks during our early-release day or a morning session during our next in-service meeting. I can do some of the workshops and I can invite one or two colleagues who are very good at stress management techniques for teachers. What do you think?
Mr. Brown: I really like that idea, let's work on our calendars.

In the example above, the school counselor (consultant) included the school principal (consultee) in the process and in a way demanded his commitment to the consultation process and its implementation. Also, the input of the teachers is respected by asking them what their needs are via a survey. Another aspect of it could be that the survey may bring information about the school principal, which is another dimension of the consultation process. In other words, the survey may reflect that the school principal (Mr. Brown) is being too demanding and intolerant by not listening to the teachers' demands and needs. That would help the consultant to have a frank conversation with the consultee and explore other options.

The Mental Health or Community Counselor

Although one may have the impression that school counselors are isolated, they do not operate in a vacuum. They are constantly relying on feedback from teachers, students, administrators, parents, and professionals in the community. As an illustration, Mr. Carsinni consulted with the school counselor about Irina (tenth-grade student) regarding her lack of emotional affect in the class and her pattern of withdrawn behavior. He is very concerned about her. By interviewing Irina, the school counselor found out that she is facing a severe depression and is at a high risk for committing suicide if the pattern continues. Due to lack of training in using the *DSM-IV-TR* (American Psychiatric Association, 2000) and diagnosing mood disorders, it was imperative that the school counselor consult a mental health counselor.

Depending on the school district's resources, there are specific contracts between schools and mental health agencies via area education agencies. The mental health counselor should be seen as a close ally who can provide a rich source of information and immediate help to the students (Caplan & Caplan, 1993). The following criteria must be considered in determining if there is a need to consult a mental health counselor:

1. The school counselor does not possess the knowledge base to help a student.
2. Issues of mental health take precedence over academic areas.
3. There is a clear pattern of poor mental health conditions among the student's relatives.
4. The student's emotional issues put his or her life at risk as well as those of his or her classmates.
5. Skill development or career interventions are ineffective as a result of the hindrance created by the mental health condition.
6. The emotional spiral of a student is disrupting the normal course of school activities.
7. Access is available to mental health treatment.

Once the first contact has been established with the mental health counselor, the school counselor should not "release" the student without any follow ups. On the contrary, the school counselor should keep in close communication with the mental health counselor and monitor the student's progress and try to get a release of information from the student or parents so as to be able to keep abreast of the treatment and progress. School interventions should be consistent with the treatment provided by the mental health counselor and should not create antagonism.

Group-Focused Consultation in Schools

A school is more than a physical building containing teachers and students. As a complex system, a school is situated in a community, but at the same time, a school is part of a school district. The school district is ruled by the State Department of Education, which is influenced to a certain extent by the federal government and by the taxpayers, parents, and corporate businesses. Just as individuals have needs, schools have deficiencies and strengths. According to Parsons and Kahn (2005) schools are affected due by changes in demographics, industries, and the economy. In order to explore the needs of a school, consultants can develop formal *needs assessments to explore the current state, identify the gap*, and *formulate what is sought* or the *desired state*. Most school districts prefer to work with data-driven results as opposed to speculative experiential reports. To justify funding for new programs or new teaching positions, school districts rely on quantitative results with projective numbers. Serving as a consultant in a school is a major task because of the complexity of the interactive subsystem. For instance, Mrs. Carter, a school counselor in district B, was hired to conduct a consultation project in a school located in district A. The school principal is noticing that as a result of the configuration of the school boundaries more African American students are entering the school.

The number of European-American students has been declining drastically, various European-American teachers have resigned or requested transfers to other districts, and the real estate market has suffered. The school principal sees a trend that he is already labeling "White flight," and he is afraid of a decline in funding and an eventual erosion of the quality of education. Mrs. Carter has been hired to explore the reasons why more students are leaving (aside of the obvious racism) and to come up with a set of recommendations to ameliorate the situation.

A system analysis implies that Mrs. Carter will have to survey and interview teachers, students, parents, administrators, leaders of the community, and business individuals in order to formulate a systemic explanation of the problem. She may have to triangulate her results with existing documents or similar studies conducted in other districts that mimic district A. There are several aspects that must be considering when assessing a school:

1. Explore all the elements, forces, and variables affecting the school, that is, internal and external forces (Gallessich, 1974).
2. Explore the supportive and negative elements; do not concentrate on only the negatives.
3. Evaluate the unique culture of the school as well as the institutional history, physical surroundings, traditions, and collective patterns.
4. What are the symbols that characterize the school (e.g., logos, symbols, rites)?
5. Assess the common assumptions about the school (e.g., reputation of being good at sports, or a tough place).

6. In addition to the surveys, analysis of existing documents, and interviews, the school consultant must be a naturalistic observer. Without intruding on the system and prior to getting any form of documentation, observe the general dynamics of the school; for instance, the quality of interactions among teachers, students, administrators, and individuals from the community.

In sum, the consultant must have the mind of an investigator by being open to all kinds of explanations and by exploring areas that may have been ignored or taken for granted. Because the school is a complex system that does not operate in a vacuum, all possible subsystems must be considered as interrelated elements. Trying to find one cause or precipitant of a problem is not the best approach, but observing all the elements as each influencing the other facilitates the consultation process.

Future Directions in Consultation

National Cultural and Ethnic Changes: Creating a Multicultural Environment

Our society is faced with some of the biggest challenges ever; globalization, the Internet, and the disappearance of national and economic boundaries are just a few. As a result, the United States is facing rapid ethnic changes and, as a consequence, a shift in cultural standards. The shift in cultural standards implies that the way education has been delivered will change because a more diverse majority of non-European descent will dictate the standards.

Members of underrepresented ethnic groups are expected to constitute 50 percent or more of the U.S. population by the year 2050 (U.S. Bureau of the Census, 2000). These statistics are being used to highlight the importance of more inclusive and culturally responsive interventions for a growing number of young diverse ethnic clients (Atkinson, Morton, & Sue, 1998). According to the U.S. Bureau of the Census (2000), Latinos (Hispanics) have reached demographic parity with African Americans and would perhaps surpass them if undocumented individuals are taken into account. By the year 2020, an estimated 57 million Latinos will be residing in the United States, according to the current demographic growth (Dana, 1993; Marin & Marin, 1991).

In order to be abreast with the multicultural changes of our society, the school consultant, regardless of his or her ethnic background, has to promote a local environment that invites and welcomes consultees and clients from different ethnic backgrounds. This promotion of an inviting multiethnic environment starts with the office.

According to Clemente (2004), the following are considerations on how to create an inviting environment

1. Decoration, furnishings, and equipment—Although the presence of diplomas and certificates enhances the professional image of the counselor, a delicate balance should exist between friendly artwork and professional emblems. Art that represents nature, space, freedom, hope, and relaxation may enhance the counseling process. Natural elements such as wooden ornaments, plants, and a small fish tank are appropriate. Wooden furniture, as opposed to metal, as well as a sofa, promotes relaxation.
2. Aroma—The human brain is highly influenced by the presence of certain fragrances, and certain behavioral experiences are connected to the sense of smell (Vroon, 1997). Taking this into account, soft herbal, citrus, or vanilla scents create a comfortable environment.
3. Space—Provide space for children to play, paint, lie on the floor, and get "dirty" without being concerned about cleaning the area. And remember that the way furniture is arranged can communicate status, quality of relationships, and frivolity or warmth (Whiton & Abercrombie, 2002). Also, take into account the concept of personal space. Depending on the gender, age, and level of acculturation of the client, the physical distance between the counselor and the client may vary.
4. Sound, color, and light—Very loud sounds provoke anxiety and discomfort, whereas musical elements and natural sounds contribute to a peaceful and healing atmosphere (Wigram, Pedersen, & Bonde, 2002). For this reason, it maybe helpful to incorporate a small water fountain that mimics the soft sound of a stream. Like the power of sound, light and color stimulate the visual modality; a room that is too bright with artificial fluorescent lights is not as conducive to self-discovery as is the use of pastel colors and ambient lighting.

Ethical Considerations

School counselors who perform consultation duties are ruled by the same code of ethics that regulates the counseling profession (ACA, 1995; ASCA, 1998). Consultants must be familiar with the basic expectations of the code of ethics. The code of ethics does not always provide clear guidelines on how to make ethical decisions; ultimately, the consultant has to rely on his or her values and judgment. The most important aspect to maintaining ethical behavior is to keep oneself in check by conducting self-reflection exercises on a daily basis. Consultation is not a value-free process because we are not value free (Newman, 1993). Parsons and Kahn (2005) indicate devised an exercise that assesses the consultant's values and provides perspective. These are some of the key areas of the exercise; for each one of the following one is to identify one's belief, attitude, or value about the issue presented.

- Equality of genders
- Need and value of unions
- Use of recreational drugs
- Alternative lifestyles
- Absolute right of privacy
- Value of competition versus cooperation (p. 313)

A basic tenet that governs the consultation profession is confidentiality. The consultant–consultee relationship is based on trust and honesty. Because the consultee is expected to disclose personal information, the consultant must be able to protect the identity of the consultee and the content of conversations. Also, it is critical for the consultant not to use power to take personal advantage of those interpersonal dynamics. The idea is to always maintain a collaborative relationship as opposed to an unbalanced one. As a reminder, the consultee has the right to terminate the relationship at any time.

Conclusion

As a result of the drastic changes in our society and in the educational system, school counselors are called upon to respond to the challenge of consultation. School counselors are coordinators, mediators, teachers, administrators, community liaisons, team builders, and human service experts. Consultation is an exciting challenge that requires serious preparation and analysis in order to deliver responsible services.

Coordinating and integrating all the services that school counselors provide are critical when responsibly attending to the needs of consultees and clients. Consultation should not be seen as another "task" on the list but as a critical element that enhances their already diverse repertoire. Consultation will become more important as the boundaries of the community, school, and businesses become more fluid than ever.

WEB SITES

American Counseling Association—http://www.counseling.org

American School Counselor Association—http://www.schoolcounselor.org

School Counseling Resources—http://www.libraries.wright.edu/libnet/subj/cou/cpmeta/sc.html

Tools for Professionals—http://www.brightfutures.org/metalhealth/pdf/professionals/schoolcnsltn.pdf

References

Albert, B., Brown, S., & Flanigan, C. M. (2003). *14 and younger: The sexual behavior of young adolescents.* Washington, D.C.: National Campaign to Prevent Teen Pregnancy.

Alderman, G. L., & Gimpel, G. A. (1996). The interaction between type of behavior problem and type of consultant: Teacher's preferences for professional assistance. *Journal of Education and Psychological Consultation, 7,* 305–313.

American Counseling Association (ACA). (1995). *Code of ethics and standards of practice.* Alexandria, VA: Author.

American Psychiatric Association (2000). *Diagnostic and statistical manual of mental disorders,* (4th ed., text revision). Washington, DC: Author.

American School Counselor Association (ACA). (1998). *Ethical standards for school counselors.* Alexandria, VA: Author.

Atkinson, D. R., Morton, G., & Sue, D. W. (1998). *Counseling American minorities* (5th ed.). Boston: McGraw-Hill.

Bergan, J. R., & Kratochwill, T. R. (1990). *Behavioral consultation and therapy.* New York: Plenum Press.

Block, P. (1981). *Flawless consulting.* San Diego, CA: Pfeiffer & Comp.

Brammer, L. M. (1994). *The helping relationship: A process of skills* (5th ed.). Englewood Cliffs, NJ: Prentice Hall.

Brigman, G., Mullis, F., Webb, L., & White, J. F. (2004). *School counselor consultation: Skills for working effectively with parents, teachers, and other school personnel.* Hoboken, NJ: J. Wiley & Sons.

Brown, D., Pryzwansky, W. B., & Schlte, A. C. (2001). *Psychological consultation.* Needham Heights, MA: Allyn & Bacon.

Caplan, G., & Caplan, R. (1993). *Mental health consultation and collaboration.* Prospect Heights, IL: Waveland.

Carey, K. (2003). *The funding gap: Low-income and minority students still receive fewer dollars in many states.* Washington, DC: The Education Trust.

Clemente, R. (2004). Counseling culturally and ethnically diverse youth. In A. Vernon (Ed.), *Counseling Children and Adolescents* (pp. 227–253) (3rd ed). Denver, CO: Love.

Cowan, E. W. (2005) *Ariadne's thread: Case studies in the therapeutic relationship.* Boston: Lahaska Press.

Dana, R. H. (1993). *Multicultural assessment perspectives for professional psychology.* Boston: Allyn & Bacon.

Dreikurs, R. (2004). *Discipline without tears: How to reduce conflict and establish cooperation in the classroom.* Mississauga, ON, Canada: J. Wiley & Sons.

Erchul, W. P. (1992). On dominance, cooperation, teamwork, and collaboration in school-based consultation. *Journal of Educational and Psychological Consultation, 3*(4), 363–366.

Friend, M., & Cook, L. (1992). *Interactions: Collaboration skills for school professionals.* New York: Longman.

Gallessich, J. (1974). Training the school psychologist for consultation. *Journal of School Psychology, 12,* 138–149.

Gallessich, J. (1982). *The profession and practice of consultation.* San Francisco: Jossey-Bass.

Gutterman, J. T. (1994). A social constructionist position for mental health counseling. *Journal of Mental Health Counseling, 16,* 226–244.

Gutkin, T. B. (1999). Collaborative versus directive/prescriptive/expert school-based consultation: Reviewing and resolving a false dichotomy. *Journal of School Psychology, 27*(2), 161–190.

Hansen, J. C., Himes, B. S., & Meier, S. (1990). *Consultation concepts and practices.* Englewood Cliffs, NJ: Prentice Hall.

Ivey, A. E. (1994). *Intentional interviewing and counseling.* Pacific Grove, CA: Brooks/Cole.

Jackson, D. N., & Hayes, D. H. (1993). Multicultural issues in consultation. *Journal of Counseling and Development, 72*(2), 144–147.

Kuh, G. D. (1993). Appraising the character of a college. *Journal of Counseling and Development, 71,* 661–667.

Kurpius, D. J., & Fuqua, D. R. (1993). Introduction to speed issues. *Journal of Counseling and Development, 71,* 596–697.

Lockhart, E. J. & Keys, S. G. (1998). The mental health counseling role of school counselors. *Professional School Counseling, 1,* 3–6.

Luongo, P. F. (2000). Partnering child welfare, juvenile justice and behavioral healthy with schools. *Professional School Counseling, 3,* 308–314.

Marín, G., & Marín, B. V. (1991). *Research with Hispanic populations.* Newbury Park, CA: Sage.

Marks, E. S. (1995). *Entry strategies for school consultation.* New York: Guilford Press.

Martens, B. K. (1993). A behavioral approach to consultation. In J. E. Zins, T. R. Kratrochwill, & S. E. Elliot (Eds.), *Handbook of consultation services for children* (pp. 65–86). San Francisco: Jossey-Bass.

Matsumura, L. C. (2005). *Creating high-quality classroom assignments.* Lanham, MD: Scarecrow Education.

McDaniel, S., Campbell, T., Wynne, L., & Weber, T. (1988). *Family Systems Medicine, 6,* 391–403.

Midgley, C. (2002). *Goals, goal structures, and patterns of adaptive learning.* Mahwah, NJ: L. Erlbaum Associates.

Nastasi, B. K., Bernstein-Moore, R., & Varjas, K. M. (2004). *School-based mental health services: Creating comprehensive and culturally specific programs.* Washington, D.C.: American Psychological Association.

Newman, J. L. (1993). Ethical issues in consultation. *Journal of Counseling and Development, 7*(2), 148–156.

Parsons, R. D. (1996). *The skilled consultant: A systematic approach to the theory and practice of consultation.* Needham Heights, MA: Allyn & Bacon.

Parsons, R. D., & Kahn, W. J. (2005). *The school counselor as a consultant: An integrated model for school-based consultation.* Belmont, CA: Thomson/Brooks/Cole.

Randolph, D. L., & Graun, K. (1988). Resistance to consultation: A synthesis for counselor–consultants. *Journal of Counseling and Development, 67,* 182–184.

Ripley, V., Erford, B. T., Dahir, C., & Eschaback, L. (2003). Planning and implementing a 21st-century comprehensive developmental counseling program. In B. T. Erford (Ed.), *Transforming the school counseling profession* (pp. 63–120). Upper Saddle River, NJ: Pearson Education.

Schmidt, J. J. (2003). *Counseling in schools* (4th ed.). Boston: Allyn & Bacon.

Shelton, C. F., & James, E. L. (2004). *Best practices for effective secondary school counselors.* Thousand Oaks, CA: Corwin Press.

Sheridan, S. M., Bergan, J. R., & Kratochwill, T. R. (1996). *Conjoint behavioral consultation.* New York: Plenum Press.

Sue, D. W., Arredondo, P., & McDavis, R. (1992). Multicultural counseling competencies and standards: A call to the profession. *Journal of Counseling and Development, 70,* 477–486.

Tabish, K. R., & Orell, L. H. (1996). RESPECT: Gang mediation at Albuquerque, New Mexico's Washington Middle School. *School Counselor, 44,* 65–70.

Thompson, R. A. (2002). *School counseling: Best practices for working in the schools.* (2nd ed). New York: Brunner Routledge.

U.S. Census of Bureau (2000). 2000 Census of Population. General Population Characteristics. Washington, D.C.: U.S. Government Printing Office.

Vernon, A., & Clemente, R. (2005). *Assessment and intervention with children and adolescents: Developmental and multicultural approaches* (2nd ed.). Alexandria, VA: American Counseling Association.

Vroon, P. (1997). *Smell: The secret seducer.* New York: Farrar, Strauss and Giroux.

Whiton, S., & Abercrombie, S. (2002). *Interior design and decoration.* Upper Saddle River, NJ: Prentice Hall.

Wigram, T., Pedersen, I. N., & Bonde, L. O. (2002). *A comprehensive guide to music therapy: Theory, clinical practice, research, and training*. Philadelphia, PA: Jessica Kingsley Publ.

Worzbyt, J. C., O'Rourke, K., & Dandeneau, C. (2003). *Elementary school counseling: A commitment to caring and community building*. (2nd ed). New York: Brunner Routledge.

XXIV
THE SCHOOL COUNSELOR'S ROLE IN CREATING CARING SCHOOL COMMUNITIES

JENNIFER J. LINDWALL AND HARDIN L. K. COLEMAN
University of Wisconsin–Madison

A community orientation based in caring and support allows children to appraise school as a meaningful social context in which to function. The ensuing sense of belonging and psychological safety, combined with significant academic work that promotes engagement in the community, enables children to achieve to their potential.

(Baker, Terry, Bridger, & Winsor, 1997, p. 586)

This quote by Baker et al. (1997) sends a powerful message concerning the impact of the school context, the environment in which youth spend a great deal of time as they develop into young adults. Although the focus of school is often placed on gaining knowledge and increasing cognitive skills (Scott, 1974), much more takes place throughout one's experience within the educational context. School becomes the primary environment in which children are socialized, develop their identities, and become equipped with the skills and the knowledge that are prerequisites for a healthy development. However, youth also face a multitude of challenges within the educational context and the broader society that may prevent them from having positive experiences in school. Therefore, it is critical that school be thought of as not only a physical place, but also a *community* where students feel valued by and connected to the peers and adults with whom they interact every day. School should be established and promoted as an environment that strives to meet the needs of *all* students and that promotes their positive development.

Focusing on the school environment and on how it can best meet the needs of youth is a shift away from a "fix the child" perspective that places the responsibility for change within the student when he or she exhibits difficulties during the educational process. Instead, a focus on the school context involves thinking about how the structure of the school needs to change in order to become a supportive environment that promotes the healthy development of all children. A way in which to establish a positive school environment for youth is by fostering a *caring school community*, a context that provides the foundation for promoting the positive well-being of youth. In establishing

a stronger, more caring community, it more effectively meets the basic needs of students—their needs for physical and psychological safety; for a sense of belonging and connection to others; for a sense that one is a competent, worthy person; and for a sense of autonomy. (Schaps, 2002, p. 3)

This chapter will discuss the importance of creating a caring community within a school, highlighting the research and conceptual frameworks that illustrate the necessity of making each individual feel as if he or she belongs within the school environment. In the literature, it is well documented that belongingness leads to a myriad of positive outcomes within the educational setting, including the development of basic psychological processes that facilitate success in school, attitudes and motivation toward school, social and personal attitudes, one's degree of engagement and participation, and academic success (Osterman, 2000). It is clear that each individual within the school, including the students and adults, impacts the school climate and the degree to which all individuals feel cared for by others and engaged in the process of learning.

One member of the school community who possesses the knowledge and the skills to foster a caring environment is the school counselor. Worzbyt, O'Rourke, and Dandeneau (2003) advocated that caring and community building should be at the heart of the elementary school counselor's role. In this chapter, however, the authors believe that school counselors at all grade levels play a critical role in fostering caring school communities. The school counselor has a unique "whole-school, cross-grade level perspective" (Beale & McCay, 2001, p. 258) that enables him or her to implement strategies for building a caring learning environment within the school on multiple levels. School counselors should consider community building as a priority within their comprehensive developmental guidance program, attempting to make each individual feel positive about being a member of his or her school environment. The school counselor plays a pivotal role in addressing the school context and coordinating activities that allow each individual within the school, children and adults alike, an opportunity for "identification and commitment" (Battistich, Solomon, Watson, & Schaps, 1997, p. 138) within the school community. It is this creation of a caring school community, influenced a great deal by the efforts of the school counselor, which will be suggested as a way to promote the positive development of all students.

The first part of this discussion will explore the human desire for a sense of community and, more specifically, what constitutes a school community. Second, six theoretical frameworks that advocate for the creation of school communities will be presented in an effort to conceptualize the ways in which a sense of community is established within schools. Third, the discussion will shift to an analysis of the unique role of the school counselor, articulating why he or she is an appropriate leader in facilitating the development of a school community within a Positive Youth Development perspective. Specific strategies that can be utilized by the school counselor on multiple levels will be presented. Next, the chapter will discuss the implementation process of creating and maintaining a caring school community by presenting a model to guide practice, thoughts about evaluation strategies, and a case example that illustrates how a counselor might implement strategies on multiple levels in order to foster a sense of community for a child in need of support. Finally, challenges to implementing caring community-building strategies will be considered along with suggestions for future directions regarding this critical area of school counseling.

What Is a Community?

In an effort to fully understand what constitutes a community, it is useful to begin thinking about why individuals feel compelled to be part of a community along with the multiple characteristics that are present in effective communities. These ideas will be presented first, followed by a more specific definition of a *school community*. Finally, the benefits of a caring school community will be reviewed in order to gain an understanding of the positive impacts that are felt by the establishment of this kind of positive environment.

The Need for Community

All human beings have the innate desire to establish caring, meaningful relationships with other individuals and feel as if they belong (Baumeister & Leary, 1995; Noddings, 1992; Sergiovanni, 1994). This need to feel connected to others begins in adolescence and continues throughout adulthood (R. M. Lee & Robbins, 1995). A sense of belongingness occurs when individuals engage in positive interpersonal experiences on a regular basis within an environment that includes concern for the well-being of others (Baumeister & Leary, 1995). The community context is defined not only as a physical entity that can be delineated by geographical boundaries but as one that includes a psychological component as well. This latter element is a critical piece that is present in effective communities and includes a feeling of solidarity and support that is experienced by the members (Magrab, 1999). Therefore, the process of creating communities appears to be an appropriate way to satisfy the natural drive to belong, promote one's psychological well-being, and allow an individual to engage and identify with a collective group.

School as a Caring Community

Just over 10 years ago, the idea of structuring schools as communities was discussed by Sergiovanni (1994). He explained that we must shift our conceptualization of schools as organizations to schools as communities in order to make them successful, positive environments for students and adults alike. He stated,

> Community building must become the heart of any school improvement effort. Whatever else is involved—improving teaching, developing sensible curriculum, creating new forms of governance, providing more authentic assessment, empowering teachers and parents, increasing professionalism—it must rest on a foundation of community building. (p. xi)

This shift in thinking involves understanding that youth want to feel included in their school community and experience it as a context that facilitates their positive growth and development (Kuranz, 2002). Furthermore, youth perceive school as a critical context of safety (Cookson, 2004). When one feels as if one belongs to this safe school context, it means one is feeling "needed, as well as needful, and believing that you have something vital to contribute" (Charney, 1992, p. 14). Therefore, conceptualizing schools as communities and fostering a sense of belonging and security for youth appears to be a critical focus that warrants the attention of educators and educational researchers alike.

A critical piece of understanding schools as caring communities is the realization that *community* is used in a broad, inclusive sense of the word. The process of establishing a sense of community within schools involves *every* individual, ensuring that he or she feels a part of the school community. Furthermore, a sense of community is not only fostered between students, but among *all* individuals within the school. This includes fostering a sense of community among students, between staff and students, among staff, and with those beyond the school. When one examines schools by looking at the whole "school context" in this way, one is utilizing a relational approach to school improvement. This type of approach facilitates caring relationships among all individuals within the school while creating a sense of meaning from academic work as well (Baker et al., 1997).

For students, a sense of community must be fostered with other students as well as with adults in the school. Feeling connected to peers impacts the degree to which students feel comfortable participating in their learning process. For example, one place to build positive connections among students is within the classroom. If these connections are established, the classroom becomes a supportive context for learning, and it can be compared with that of a supportive "family" (Lewis, Schaps, & Watson, 1996). When this type of environment is created, "the caring classroom provides a sense of belonging that allows lively, critical discussions and risk-taking" (Lewis et al., 1996, p. 21) to occur. Students also need to develop positive connections with adults in the school. *All* school staff, such as teachers, administrators, counselors, custodians, and assistants, should make an effort to establish caring relationships with students in an effort to facilitate the success of every student (Kuranz, 2002).

A sense of community is also critical among the adult staff. For example, the school staff members need adequate time to share ideas, collaborate, and communicate with one another in order to help them feel supported by their colleagues. Furthermore, a positive collegial community is also beneficial to the students. For example, when staff members have the time and skills to effectively communicate with one another, they are more likely to work together to create an inclusive environment for the students; particularly for those with special needs who are oftentimes feeling left out of the educational experience (Carpenter, King-Sears, & Keys, 1998). Also, creating a "community of colleagues" to help new teachers feel supported will help them to meet their needs within the school; in turn, they are more likely to better serve the students in their classrooms (Lundeen, 2004).

In addition to fostering positive relationships among all members within a school, it is imperative to include those who extend *beyond* the school. Building caring school communities also involves active collaboration with families and partnerships within the greater community in which the school is located. It has been suggested that families and the larger community have a significant impact on the educational and developmental success of students. Therefore, a combination of educational and social supports will help not only students, but also their families to feel supported (Azcoitia, 2002; Brandt, 1991). It has also been suggested that specific efforts, such as addressing school violence, need to involve multiple contexts in order to be most successful (Collins, 2003). School–family–community collaborative efforts may also help to foster important protective factors in at-risk youth (Bryan, 2005). In the words of Stanley, Juhnke, and Purkey (2004), it is critical to remember that "[e]verybody and everything in and around the school adds to, or subtracts from a safe and successful school" (p. 307). When one individual or a group of individuals, whether they are students, staff, parents, or community members, experiences something positive or negative, the entire school community feels the effects of that experience.

Furthermore, the increasing diversity within American schools calls for not only the establishment of caring communities, but also *multiculturally* competent educational environments. One component of developing these types of schools is creating a sense of community with culturally diverse members by shifting toward a "salad bowl" concept of diversity rather than the "melting pot" metaphor (C. C. Lee, 2001). School staff should recognize that creating caring school communities helps youth become competent and able to succeed in an increasingly diverse world (Pohan, 2003). Therefore, the establishment of a school community that truly cares for each individual should be promoted. Cultural diversity should be recognized and celebrated among the school community rather than used as a means for further isolating and segregating students based on race/ethnicity, gender, sexual orientation, socioeconomic status, immigration status, religion, ability, and so forth.

Critical Elements of Successful School Communities

In an effort to improve the educational experience for youth, particularly those considered at-risk, a study was conducted for the Office of Educational Research and Improvement, U.S. Department of Education (Rossi &

Stringfield, 1996). The sites for individual case studies were 18 schools that had been recognized as effective in working with at-risk youth. One major implication that was reported from this effort was the fact that establishing and maintaining a strong sense of community within the school was critical for meeting the needs of students. In their review, Rossi and Stringfield identified a number of key elements that are present within those schools that function as true communities. These components, several of which are closely related, include a shared vision, shared purpose, and shared values; incorporation of diversity; communication and participation; caring, trust, and teamwork; and respect and recognition. The first set of elements, *shared vision, shared purpose, and shared values* involves having well-established educational goals and efforts to provide supportive relationships to reach those goals. The second key element, *incorporation of diversity*, includes promoting the strengths of students, embracing diversity, celebrating culture, and involving family and community. Next, *communication and participation* refer to opportunities for ongoing dialogue among adults and youth in an effort to allow all individuals to have a voice in the educational experience. *Caring, trust, and teamwork* consist of conscious behaviors that allow both students and adults to feel cared for and valued by their school community (e.g., giving handshakes, assigning mentors to students, acknowledging one another by name), and they are oftentimes present because of having effective communication and active participation among everyone in the school. Finally, *respect and recognition* include positive affirmation and acknowledgement of each individual and his or her contributions to the school community. According to Rossi and Stringfield, these elements create the foundation for facilitating positive relationships among students, among staff, and among staff and students in fostering a successful educational context.

The creation of a caring school community clearly involves *all* of its members, both children and adults, as well as individuals and agencies in the larger community, including family and community partnerships. Once a school understands this concept, they must also realize that the decision to foster a caring environment involves much more than simply identifying it as such.

> It requires us to think community, believe in community, and practice community—to change the basic metaphor for the school itself to community. We are into authentic community when community becomes embodied in the school's policy structure itself, when community values are at the center of our thinking. (Sergiovanni, 1994, p. xiii)

In sum, creating and maintaining a caring school environment needs to be integrated into every aspect of daily life within the school and requires a commitment on behalf of all of its members to contribute positively to that community. The critical elements that have been identified by Rossi and Stringfield (1996; a shared vision, shared purpose, and shared values; incorporation of diversity; communication and participation; caring, trust, and teamwork; and respect and recognition) are useful in understanding what constitutes a successful school community.

Schools as Caring Communities: Positive Benefits for Youth

Establishing schools as caring communities strives to fulfill the basic need of belongingness among youth, allowing students to feel as if they are cared for and valued by peers and adults alike. In a review of the literature, Osterman (2000) reported that a feeling of belongingness is related to five significant outcomes within a school setting: development of basic psychological processes that facilitate success in school, attitudes and motivation toward school, social and personal attitudes, one's degree of engagement and participation, and academic success. These five outcomes provide a useful way in which to understand how helping to facilitate a sense of belongingness within the school environment, through the creation of a caring school community, impacts youth in multiple positive ways.

Development of Basic Psychological Processes

Researchers have suggested that through the process of engaging in a caring school community, youth are likely to have their basic psychological needs met (e.g., belonging, autonomy, and competence). In other words, a higher involvement in the school community will lead to a more complete fulfillment of one's basic needs. Taking part in a caring school community will also facilitate one's intellectual, social, and moral development (e.g., acquiring knowledge of academic material, thinking/problem-solving skills, empathy, social skills, and understanding of others and of the community's values). The development of these factors also leads to the fulfillment of one's basic psychological needs, especially a sense of self-efficacy (Schaps, Battistich, & Solomon, 2004). Worzbyt et al. (2003) write, "As children learn how to build caring connections, through their smiles, positive feedback, self-affirmations, and planned acts of kindness, they begin to experience total well-being" (p. 10). Furthermore, when youth feel as if their developmental needs are met and feel supported by and cared for within their school environment, they are more likely to embrace the shared values of the school community (Solomon, Watson, Battistich, Schaps, & Delucchi, 1996).

Attitudes and Motivation Toward School

Establishing a caring community can potentially help improve students' attitudes and motivation toward school by helping students to feel more valued and included in the educational process. A positive educational environment that fosters belongingness, such as a caring school community, is more conducive to learning and increases students' sense of connection to school and sense of safety. When a caring community of learners is present within a school, its members feel valued by and connected to others and therefore more committed to and motivated in the learning process (Lewis et al., 1996). As a result, students who are more connected to school may have a more overall positive attitude about school and may feel more motivated to take part in school-related activities. For example, Karcher and Lindwall (2003) described those high school students who volunteered to serve as mentors for elementary school students as being more connected to school than those in the comparison group. Therefore, youth who feel more connected to, or a part of, their school community may be motivated to become even more involved by taking part in activities that are offered within the school context.

Social and Personal Attitudes

Fostering a caring school community has the potential to help students develop positive social and personal attitudes about one another and the school. For example, middle school students reported that they value caring relationships with their teachers and perceive their teachers as helpful when they display caring words and behaviors. These students also felt a greater sense of control and safety within their classroom when caring was present (Alder, 2002). This study suggested that when adults model a caring environment, the students will adopt and internalize these values and come to appreciate this type of context. Another study conducted by Perry (2002) examined an elementary school that utilized a "Community of Caring" program that aimed to facilitate healthy youth development and positive decision-making skills. Several values including respect, trust, caring, responsibility, and family were emphasized within the school and modeled by the adults. In general, the majority of the students within the school reported a high sense of belonging and felt that they were respected by all of the individuals within the school. Both the staff and the students attributed their school's sense of community to the "Community of Caring" program. Solomon, Battistich, Watson, Schaps, and Lewis (2000) reported findings from schools that implemented the Child Development Project (CDP), which included a community-building component. In this study, five CDP schools that "progressed in implementation," compared with non-CDP schools, showed positive benefits in personal, social, and ethical attitudes, values, and motives within students. Caring relationships with adults have also been suggested to be a protective factor for at-risk youth. When youth were asked about their descriptions of caring adults, they identified seven characteristics: trust, attention, empathy, availability, affirmation, respect, and virtue. These characteristics helped foster trust within the youth, allowing them to establish a positive connection with an adult (Laursen & Birmingham, 2003).

Engagement and Participation

The first theme that emerges within "engagement and participation" is the notion that facilitating a caring school community can help *increase* the positive engagement and participation of youth in school and related activities. For example, youth who attended a school that specifically focused on building a caring community as part of the CDP were more involved in school, showed a greater commitment to school, and were more prosocial (Battistich, Schaps, & Wilson, 2004). In another CDP study, elementary schools where classroom teachers exhibited practices that focused on fostering a school community were associated with more positive outcomes, including engagement in school and positive behaviors, than the comparison schools. Community building within classrooms included teacher practices that emphasized prosocial values, facilitation of youth's thinking and sharing of ideas, cooperation, warmth, and supportiveness. In addition, low use of extrinsic control was associated with positive classroom behaviors among the students. Furthermore, the positive outcomes were related to the students' sense of school community (Solomon, Battistich, Kim, & Watson, 1997). In another longitudinal study, Epstein and Sheldon (2002) reported that family–school–community partnership strategies were effective in increasing student attendance. These authors suggested that elementary schools might be able to increase student attendance by using strategies that involve community and family collaborative relationships.

The second theme suggests that fostering a caring school community can help *decrease* negative school and other youth behaviors. For example, schools where students felt a stronger sense of school community have been linked to lower average drug involvement and delinquency rates (Battistich & Hom, 1997). Also, students who attended a CDP school engaged in fewer problem behaviors than youth who belonged to schools that did not have a specific caring community-building program in place (Battistich et al., 2004). Teachers at schools who actively included community building within their classrooms reported that youth exhibited fewer discipline problems, and as a result, fewer referrals were made (Chesswas, Davis, & Hanson,

2003). Schools with higher levels of sense-of-community scores had lower average drug involvement and delinquency among students. This may suggest that the environment of the school moderates relationships among risk factors, protective factors, and developmental outcomes. Therefore, when students perceive school to be a community, this experience may foster increased resiliency (Battistich & Hom, 1997). Finally, collaborative relationships between families, schools, and communities have been shown to decrease chronic absenteeism in students (Epstein & Sheldon, 2002).

Academic Success

Finally, school community building efforts have also been shown to have an impact on the academic accomplishments of students. For example, youth who attended well-run CDP schools during elementary school were more academically successful and associated more with prosocial and less with antisocial classmates than the matched comparison students (Battistich et al., 2004). Community building, in combination with high expectations and challenging, engaging opportunities to learn, has also been shown to promote academic achievement particularly for low-income students (Schaps et al., 2004). Finally, in a review of literature on the impact of parental involvement on academic performance, Spera (2005) reported that parental involvement in school and monitoring of after-school activities promotes the academic success of youth.

Consideration of Cultural Diversity

Although the authors of this chapter advocate that fostering a caring school community includes helping all youth to feel a sense of belongingness and connection to school and emphasizes that the process of doing so has benefits for all youth, it is important to consider how those from diverse backgrounds might particularly benefit from such an effort. For example, those youth who differ in some way from mainstream culture—whether by race, ethnicity, sexual orientation, and so forth—might be at an increased risk for feeling disconnected from school and lack a sense of belongingness since it, too, is modeled after mainstream culture and may not be culturally sensitive to the diverse needs of its students.

In the literature, several examples emerge that highlight the notion that youth from diverse backgrounds will particularly benefit from the establishment of a caring school community. One group that is at risk of being disconnected from school is racial/ethnic minority youth, who overall are not performing as well academically as their European American peers. McMillian (2004) suggests that in order to truly address this achievement gap, it is the responsibility of educators to help minority youth feel as if they are valued by society and within their schools. Therefore, creating a sense of school community can be a step in this direction. Youth from economically disadvantaged families may also be at risk for feeling disconnected from school. Battistich et al. (1997) reported that the potential for improving a sense of school community appears to be greatest within those schools with significant populations of low-income students. Perhaps for this group of youth, a caring school community has the potential to provide a sense of safety and security despite the economic hardships within their families. Finally, young women in schools may be vulnerable for feeling disconnected from the school community if issues of gender are not taken into consideration when addressing their needs. Cook, Heppner, and O'Brien (2002) discussed the importance of using an ecological perspective in providing vocational guidance with women of color and White women, which can also be applied to school counselors who work with young women. These examples highlight how a caring community environment within a school can be specifically responsive to and respectful of the cultural diversity among youth. The report discussed earlier by Rossi and Stringfield (1996) did, after all, examine schools that were particularly effective at addressing the needs of at-risk youth, and one of the primary ways in which those schools were effective was the way in which they fostered a sense of community.

Clearly, the establishment of a school as a caring community positively impacts youth in numerous ways. Battistich et al. (1997) summed up the importance of creating a caring school community by describing that it

> provides the individual with a focus for identification and commitment, rather than simply offering personal support. Students' needs for competence, autonomy and belonging are thus met when they are able to participate actively in a cohesive, caring group with a shared purpose; that is, a community. (p. 138)

With this idea in mind, the discussion will now turn to a consideration of multiple perspectives that offer suggestions about how community building in schools actually looks.

Six Perspectives: A Foundation for Understanding School as a Caring Community

Within the literature, a number of different theoretical frameworks emphasize the importance of addressing the context of the school and, particularly, advocate for building a sense of community. As we know from the literature on effective counseling (Wampold, 2001), having a theory to guide practice translates into improved effectiveness. Wampold also pointed out that there are many theories that lead to effective practice. These findings suggest that a school counselor is well served if he or she uses theory to guide practice but that the theory needs to be compatible with the school counselor's worldview. In order to represent the range of options, we will review the following theoretical frameworks for creating a caring community: *Tribes* (Gibbs, 2001); Frank's (2004) "The Caring Classroom"; Kohn's (1996) "The Classroom as Community"; the Search Institute's (2003, 2004) "40 Developmental Assets"; the Child Development Project (Battistich et al., 2004; Battistich et al., 1997; Developmental Studies Center, 2005; Schaps et al., 2004); and the Invitational Theory of Practice (Purkey & Aspy, 2003; Purkey & Schmidt, 1996; Stanley et al., 2004). It is important to note that these frameworks differ somewhat in their approaches. For example, some, such as *Tribes*, describe the creation of a caring school community as the main goal, while the Search Institute, for example, describes it as one of the key components involved in comprehensively addressing the needs of youth. Some theories, such as the one proposed by Frank, focus on classroom contexts, while others, including the Invitational Theory of Practice, target the larger school environment. However, each offers valuable insight into how community building takes place within a school. Therefore, each will be briefly reviewed followed by a discussion about its applicability for school counselors and the ways in which they all illustrate the characteristics of effective communities.

Tribes

Jeanne Gibbs (2001) outlines the Tribes TLC (Tribes Learning Community) philosophy, calling for a pattern of interaction that involves educators, parents, and students working together toward common goals on behalf of youth. The overall goal of Tribes is "to engage all teachers, administrators, students, and families in working together as a learning community that is dedicated to caring and support, active participation, and positive expectations for all students" (p. 22). A critical element of this framework is the promotion of inclusion by encouraging each individual to reflect on and share his or her own personal thoughts and experiences. Students and adults are encouraged to utilize a democratic group process that allows them to collaborate on the creation of a positive, supportive environment that facilitates growth, development, and learning.

The Tribes framework calls for the redefinition of the role of teachers in particular and the way in which they structure their classrooms. First, teachers are to work together in groups, rather than in isolation, in order to build critical connections and support networks among the school staff. Second, classrooms are to be arranged so that students sit and work collaboratively in small groups, or "tribes." This creates a student-centered classroom where youth have ownership and participation in classroom functioning. By belonging to a group, each individual feels included and valued in the learning process. This is in contrast to the traditional classroom setting where students most often work independently in a teacher-centered classroom; this type of classroom, however, does not give students much voice in their classroom community. Third, teachers are called upon to use culturally appropriate teaching strategies and promote the development of critical thinking and collaboration skills. Caring, sharing, active participation, and positive expectations are integrated throughout the Tribes process. Because of the practices just mentioned, the Tribes classroom is democratic in nature, promotes inclusion, and fosters a sense of connection and belonging among students. This is largely the result of frequent opportunities for students to collaborate and contribute to their classroom (Gibbs, 2001).

A key component of Tribes includes building a strong community. This process emphasizes four "agreements" which help to foster a positive, collaborative environment. These agreements include attentive listening, giving "appreciations" (e.g., positive statements directed toward others) rather than "put-downs" (e.g., negative statements directed toward others), having the "right to pass," and showing mutual respect for all members of the community. Throughout the process of Tribes, community members are taught collaborative skills and taught how to reflect on the learning that takes place within the school. Through these interactions, a learning environment is created that promotes cooperative learning and positive interaction while establishing continuity for the community of individuals. Tribes recognizes that students' learning and development is greatly influenced by multiple people and contexts, including family, friends, school, and community. Furthermore, it actively seeks to address the multiple environmental factors that impact a student's well-being (Gibbs, 2001).

In recent years, the Tribes process has been evaluated using repeated measures and quasi-experimental design, producing promising results. After 2 years of an ongoing evaluation study (Chesswas, Davis & Hanson, 2003), 13 schools from the original 84 schools that had been implementing Tribes for at least 1 year in grades 2 through 5 participated by completing surveys and engaging in interviews. Several of the authors' overall conclusions supported positive effects related to the creation and maintenance of a caring school community. First, the authors reported increased student inclusion, respect for diversity, sense of value, collaboration, safe and supportive learning environments, and the development of increased resiliency in adults and youth. Second, results suggested that student engagement and participation in the educational process significantly increased in Tribes schools. Third, both adults and students classified their schools as safe and supportive environments. The majority of students in Tribes schools (82% to 89%) felt that the adults at their schools cared for them, while most of the adults who were interviewed described Tribes as "building community." Fourth, youth were more likely to collaborate with their classmates. Finally, student achievement was also shown to increase in some academic areas in Tribes schools significantly more than in comparison schools: fifth-grade reading and second-grade mathematics (Chesswas et al., 2003). In the subsequent year, similar results were reported when a second evaluation was conducted with fourth- through sixth-grade students (Chesswas & Davis Sosenko, 2004). In addition, findings indicated that there was evidence of mutual respect, improved student-centered work, increased problem-solving skills, improved classroom management, and improved teacher collaboration. Furthermore, a lower incidence of student referrals and suspensions was reported by adults (Chesswas & Davis Sosenko).

Although this research offers support for the effectiveness of Tribes for creating caring school communities, there are limitations and areas in need of further examination. First, there are some discrepancies between what is reported by adults and what is reported by students. For example, 87% of teachers reported giving students opportunities to be "leaders" or "helpers," while only 64% of students reported being given these roles. In addition, 87% of teachers stated that they actively involved students in determining classroom rules while a mere 28% of students endorsed being given this opportunity (Chesswas et al., 2003). Discrepancies were again found in the results presented one year later (Chesswas & Davis Sosenko, 2004). Future research is needed to understand these discrepancies and to determine how the program components are received by both adults and youth. One challenge that was endorsed by nearly all adult participants was lack of time to fully implement the Tribes strategies (Chesswas & Davis Sosenko, 2004). Further research that addresses this issue and efforts to provide support to educators through this process will be important to prevent burnout and/or lack of comprehensive implementation. Finally, the characteristics of the populations used in the studies (e.g., cultural background, geographic location) are unclear, making it difficult to interpret the findings and understand how they apply to diverse populations of youth.

Laurie Frank's "The Caring Classroom"

Frank (2004) described a process for creating caring environments within classrooms by combining theories that promote community building with those that emphasize experiential/adventure-based education. Her framework emphasizes collaboration, and she states, "Once a class of individuals comes together to work toward common goals, with everyone valued and respected, the business of learning can take place fully, without reservation" (p. 17).

Frank (2004) described her "community-building sequence" as a way in which to work toward creating a caring community within a classroom. The first stage in her model is cooperation, which involves working together to create a safe, inclusive environment. Frank indicated that the teacher should encourage the use of "put-ups" (e.g., positive statements about others) rather than "put-downs" (e.g., negative comments directed toward others). In this stage, cooperation is emphasized and students receive consistent encouragement. In addition, active listening and perspective-taking skills are emphasized by the teacher in an effort to allow the students to get to know and work with one another. Trust, the hallmark of stage two, develops when students feel included in the classroom activities and are able to positively work with one another. The students learn that their classroom is a safe environment in which to make mistakes and take positive risks. Empathy is also taught and modeled by the teacher, and there is an understanding that everyone's physical and emotional well-being is protected within the classroom. Cooperation and trust create the foundation for stage three, problem solving. Students feel confident and comfortable taking on group challenges and being able to work through conflict by engaging in effective communication. Finally, challenge is the fourth step that encourages students to set and work toward individual goals. Youth are taught that their community is supportive through both success and failure (Frank).

Frank (2004) described three "community-building tools" that help in the creation of safe, positive classroom communities. First, a "full-value contract" is decided upon by the group. This contract acts as a starting point and establishes the agreements for the functioning of the classroom. It ensures the safety of the classroom environment and each individual's responsibility to contribute to that safety. This tool is applicable to the group's needs and establishes group norms. The second tool is "challenge by choice," which pertains to the individual needs of the students in the classroom. An emphasis is placed on each individual's control over his or her choices, including the choice about the degree to which he or she will participate in different classroom activities. The third tool, "goal setting," includes both group and individual goals. It creates a framework from which to work through conflicts and make decisions.

Although Frank (2004) provided a well-developed model of community building within schools, there has not been a great deal of research to date that directly evaluates her model. Fortunately, research is currently underway to investigate her model of "The Caring Classroom," which will begin to shed light on the effectiveness of her techniques. Furthermore, Frank asserted that some literature in the areas of brain research and social/emotional learning indirectly support her ideas (L. Frank, personal communication, September 2, 2005). Nevertheless, she does provide important strategies related to community building that warrant consideration and would benefit from future empirical research.

Alfie Kohn's "The Classroom as Community"

Kohn (1996) suggested that in a classroom established as a community environment, the students and adults care for one another and continually receive messages that reflect this sense of caring. Each individual feels valued and thinks "in the plural" by referring to "us," which illustrates the importance of considering the needs of each person within the community. The classroom is established as a physically and emotionally safe context where students feel a sense of connection to one another.

An emphasis of Kohn's (1996) philosophy is the creation of a supportive educational context. He asserted that students' well-being, choices, thoughts, and behaviors are all impacted not only by what they learn, but also by the context of their school classroom. In his words, "A community not only preserves and nourishes the individuals who compose it but also underscores the relationships among these individuals" (p. 107). Therefore, a feeling of community supports the individual members and fosters the development of critical positive relationships among them. Kohn believes that it is necessary to establish a caring environment along with a meaningful, engaging curriculum and regular opportunities for students to participate in the educational experience. If these characteristics are present in the classroom, students will be able to make meaningful choices about their learning process.

The process of building a community within the classroom revolves around creating a sense of safety on four levels. First, it is critical to foster relationships between the students and adults. Children are more likely to care about others if they themselves feel as if they are cared for by others. Second, children need to experience positive relationships with their peers. An important way to facilitate these relationships is by providing cooperative learning experiences for students throughout the school day. Third, classroom and schoolwide activities should be employed as a means through which students and adults are allowed to reflect upon their experience at the school and share those reflections with one another. Finally, academic instruction should be used as a way to incorporate community building activities and cooperative learning throughout the children's educational experience (Kohn, 1996).

In order to employ the strategies just mentioned, Kohn (1996) described three important prerequisites for building a community. He pointed out that a community is built over *time*, with an *appropriate size* of individuals (i.e., within a school that is not overcrowded), and includes staff who feel connected to one another as an *adult community*. Furthermore, two important ideas of Kohn's community-building philosophy are related to competition and discipline. He asserted that competition within schools acts to break down a community, and therefore, it should not be integrated into the students' daily activities. Kohn believes that we also need to move beyond traditional definitions of discipline and instead focus on community building.

Kohn's (1996) ideas, although valuable for understanding how to build community within schools, have not been systematically evaluated. This is somewhat due to the fact that his concepts are not intended to comprise a particular programmatic framework that can be subjected to evaluation. However, Kohn (personal communication, August 8, 2005) has informally received many narrative reports that support the utilization of his ideas and suggest positive benefits within schools that employ his strategies. Therefore, Kohn's work serves as a heuristic for understanding important aspects of community building within schools and can help guide the implementation of these strategies.

The Search Institute's 40 Developmental Assets

The Search Institute (2004) developed a list of 40 developmental assets which are defined as "positive factors in young people, families, communities, schools, and other settings that have been found to be important in promoting young people's healthy development" (p. 2). The assets are grouped into two major types: external and internal. The four categories of external assets include support, empowerment, boundaries and expectations, and constructive use of time. The four groupings of internal assets encompass commitment to learning, positive values, social competencies, and positive identity. When youth possess these assets, they are less likely to engage in alcohol, tobacco, and other drug (ATOD) use regardless of their socioeconomic, family, or racial/ethnic characteristics. The more assets that are present in a particular child, the less likely he or she is to engage in any ATOD use. Furthermore, developmental assets are beneficial to the healthy development of youth whether a risk is present in their environment (Search Institute, 2004).

It is important to note that some of the Search Institute's (2003, 2004) 40 developmental assets are particularly related to school. For example, a "caring school climate" is one example of an external asset that provides support for youth. "School boundaries" and "adult role models" are other external assets that can be fostered within the school context. Furthermore, "school engagement" and "school bonding" are listed as internal assets as well as "caring." These characteristics can be fostered within the school environment to promote the well-being of students.

It is recommended that strategies and programs should be designed to specifically foster the developmental assets within all youth in order to contribute to their healthy growth and development. In addition to lowering the chance that youth will engage in ATOD use, the Search Institute reports that the developmental assets have shown positive benefits for youth in other ways. For example, they report that those youth who possess more developmental assets show a decrease in problematic behaviors in school, violence, antisocial behavior, gambling, eating disorders, and depression (Search Institute, 2004).

Along with the promotion of developmental assets, the Search Institute (2004) calls for building community collaborations in order to facilitate the positive, healthy development of youth and prevention efforts aimed at ATOD use. A model for community capacity building is presented that includes first fostering community dedication and efforts focused on building a community. This involves deciding on a "shared vision" as well as a "common purpose and commitment." Next is the establishment of an organizing community structure that will support positive asset building. Finally, the community engages in capacity-building strategies that give both adults and youth opportunities to be actively involved (Search Institute, 2004).

Multiple investigations conducted by the Search Institute (2003, 2004) have shown strong positive relationships between the levels of developmental assets of youth and their school attendance and grades. Recent research has provided stronger evidence because it examines the relationships between developmental assets and actual student grade reports as opposed to relying on self-reports. For example, a longitudinal study was conducted that examined youth from grades six to eight and again from grades ten to twelve. The most prominent finding indicated that the more assets youth possessed, the higher their overall GPA. This finding held true even three years later (Search Institute, 2003). Furthermore, research has also looked at the link between developmental assets and ATOD behaviors. After examining a large dataset of youth in grades 6 through 12, the results are summed up as follows. First, the more assets youth possess, the less likely they are to engage in ATOD use. Second, possessing developmental assets decreases the likelihood of engaging in all types of ATOD use. Third, developmental assets are beneficial across diverse youth. Fourth, youth who have more developmental assets show a delayed ATOD onset. Sixth, developmental assets are more closely linked to ATOD use than demographic factors. Seventh, assets are involved in other positive outcomes for youth, such as academic success and maintenance of good health. Finally, possessing certain assets, including boundaries and expectations, are particularly related to ATOD prevention (Search Institute, 2004).

The findings that support the importance of possessing developmental assets in youth clearly have been linked to positive outcomes. Because several of the assets are directly related to a sense of caring school community, this area of research justifies attention from educators. However, there are some limitations to keep in mind when interpreting these results. The primary issue is the lack of diverse samples of youth that have been used in these studies. The Search Institute (2003) reports that sample sizes for racial and ethnic minority youth are too small in their longitudinal samples to make strong conclusions. In conducting future research, it will be critical to examine larger numbers of students of color and determine how developmental assets impact their well-being.

Child Development Project

The Child Development Project (CDP) began approximately 25 years ago, and it is described as a comprehensive improvement program designed primarily for elementary schools. It attempts to increase academic, ethical, emotional, and social learning and includes community building as a key component. By building a community, the groundwork is laid for implementing strategies that help students becoming caring, prosocial individuals (Schaps et al., 2004).

The CDP attempts to create

> caring communities of learners—environments that are characterized by caring and supportive relationships, and collaboration among students, staff, and parents; a sense of common purpose and a clear commitment to salient norms and values of caring, justice, responsibility, and learning; responsiveness to students' developmental and sociocultural needs; an accessible, meaningful and engaging curriculum; and opportunities for students to meaningfully participate in decision-making and otherwise be actively involved in the intellectual and social life of the classroom and school. (Battistich et al., 2004, p. 244)

The creation of this type of school community is greatly influenced by certain strategies utilized by teachers, including warmth and supportiveness; a promotion of cooperation; elicitation of student thinking and discussion; emphasis on prosocial values; and low use of extrinsic control. Students should also be given regular opportunities to work collaboratively with their peers toward shared goals; assist others in a meaningful way when needed and vice versa; participate in discussions that help them to develop empathy; reflect on how one's behavioral choices contribute to the development of "prosocial values"; learn and implement behaviors and words that demonstrate appropriate social skills; and demonstrate an appropriate level of independence within the classroom while actively taking part in decision making and establishing the classroom context (Battistich et al., 1997).

In contrast to some types of programs that are implemented within schools, the CDP places an emphasis on the "promotion" of healthy growth and development of *all* children rather than the "prevention" of problems in only those children who are identified as at risk (Battistich et al., 2004). These authors, along with others, believe that a sense of school as community serves as a critical lens through which the context of education can be examined. By using this lens, educators will be able to better understand and to more fully meet the needs of all individuals within the school. Furthermore, they propose that students' needs are most likely to be met when they feel connected to their environment and identify with the values of school (Battistich et al., 1997). Since the CDP was originally developed and introduced in 1980, the community-building element has been developed into its own program called "Caring School Community" or CSC. The CSC program focuses on facilitating an environment of caring by fostering positive relationships between youth, adults, and families (Developmental Studies Center, 2005).

The Child Development Project is based on a great deal of research that has been done over the past 15 years with a diverse sample of youth in various elementary schools in the United States (Battistich et al., 1997). Multiple schools have implemented the CDP, and numerous studies have been conducted to determine the effectiveness of the program as well as to search for areas of improvement. The findings have suggested positive results in youth where the CDP was implemented. For example, Battistich, Schaps, Watson, and Solomon (1996) examined the impact of the CDP that was implemented in elementary schools from six school districts around the United States. Over the course of a three-year period, the authors reported that those students in the CDP program showed significant decreases in drug use and delinquency compared with their peers in non-CDP schools. In another study, Battistich et al. (1997) reported that elementary students who participated in a CDP school had a greater sense of community than students in comparison schools. In addition, the authors suggested that the positive benefits of improving school community may be greatest for economically disadvantaged students. In an examination of third- through sixth-grade students in CDP schools, Solomon et al. (2000) found that the youth exhibited gains in personal, social, and ethical attitudes, values, and motives. Furthermore, the authors noted that a sense of school community was found to be a significant mediating variable for nearly all of the dependent variables, illustrating that the CDP resulted in positive effects only to the extent that it was able to establish a caring community within the school. Battistich et al. (2004) conducted a follow-up to an earlier study with middle school students who were first exposed to the CDP in elementary school. Overall, the authors reported that CDP students were more involved in and had greater dedication to school, were more "prosocial," and were involved in fewer problem behaviors than comparison youth.

Schaps et al. (2004) summed up the findings from research on CDP schools over the years by noting that the children who participated in CDP schools exhibited an increased sense of community at school, which enhanced their academic motivation and goals, fostered the development of positive character traits, facilitated social and emotional learning, and decreased the number of behavior problems. Furthermore, many of these benefits lasted through middle school and produced positive effects on academic success (although they did not consistently produce academic gains in elementary school). The positive results of the CDP have led it to be recognized as a model program by which to pattern effective youth programs. For example, the Substance Abuse and Mental Health Services Administration (SAMHSA) has named the CDP a "Model Program" for reducing high-risk behaviors (U.S. Department of Health and Human Services, SAMHSA, Center for Substance Abuse Prevention, 2005). The Promising Practices Network (2005) on Children, Families, and Communities named the CDP as one of several "Programs that Work" for promoting positive youth outcomes. Finally, the Caring School Community Program (the community-building element of the CDP) was listed as a "Promising Program" by the U.S. Department of Education's (2001) Safe, Disciplined, and Drug-Free Schools Expert Panel.

The amount of research that has gone into the creation and refinement of the CDP is quite impressive and has produced many positive results. However, one limitation is the fact that the CDP does little to address a sense of community among adults, which is an important issue to address in future research (Battistich et al., 1997). Furthermore, future research that looks specifically at the CSC program, the community-building program of the CDP, would add further knowledge about the direct impact of the curriculum upon youth.

Invitational Theory of Practice

The previous frameworks provide valuable insight into how one can begin to conceptualize a "caring school community" and what kinds of strategies are implemented to foster this environment. However, at this point, it is also important to ask the question: Where do *school counselors* fit into the caring community-building process? These frameworks do not include an explicit discussion as to how school counselors are involved in the process of community building. Instead, the roles of other educators, such as teachers and principals, are often emphasized. Although these are equally important discussions, this area of work would be strengthened by additional conversations about the school counselor's role in creating a caring school community, particularly in light of the changing role that the school counselor has faced over the years. While it is important to note that the previous philosophies *do* mention the importance of including the entire school staff within the community-building process, which includes the school counselor, it still remains difficult to ascertain his or her specific role within this process. To being the conversation concerning the school counselor's role in creating a caring community, we will now examine a sixth framework, the Invitational Theory of Practice (ITOP), which provides more explicit guidance on how a school counselor can be involved in the creation and maintenance of a caring school community.

The ITOP is a framework that has self-concept as its foundation and integrates other relevant theories and strategies to create a model for human development. ITOP reflects four primary assumptions that can be utilized within a counseling relationship. First, individuals are able-bodied, valuable, and self-directed beings and should be treated accordingly. Second, the nature of the helping process is a cooperative, collaborative alliance. Third, each individual has an "untapped potential" that exists across each stage of development. Fourth, in order to realize this potential, there need to be individuals and conditions that facilitate its development. School counselors who utilize this approach use optimism, respect, trust, and intentionality in the helping process. Furthermore, there is an acknowledgement that each individual's functioning occurs on one of four levels: intentionally disinviting, unintentionally disinviting, unintentionally inviting, and intentionally inviting (Purkey & Schmidt, 1996).

Stanley et al. (2004) extended the ITOP framework to the establishment of a safe school environment where youth could experience academic success. It took on a holistic, schoolwide perspective, emphasizing the importance of considering the entire school context. The authors wrote, "The four elements of ITOP—respect, trust, optimism, and intentionality—provide a constant 'stance' or conceptual framework from which school counselors and others can effectively create and maintain a truly safe and welcoming academic environment" (p. 304). These elements of ITOP serve as a conceptual framework that strives to address the overall atmosphere of the school, attempting to make it a positive and rewarding environment for students, school staff, family, and community members. The authors noted that the ITOP philosophy could be used as a guiding force by which to meet the established goals of the school. It emphasizes the school counselor working in multiple collaborative relationships with students, staff, and family (Stanley et al.).

ITOP posits that each individual operates at one of four different patterns of communication (i.e., intentionally disinviting, unintentionally disinviting, unintentionally inviting, and intentionally inviting) at any given point in time (Purkey & Schmidt, 1996). School counselors can help individuals understand these different communication processes and educate them about what kinds of communication strategies are most effective. Furthermore, ITOP includes the "Five Ps" (i.e., people, places, policies, programs, and processes) that provide the means by which school counselors can implement ITOP. For example, counselors can address *people* by facilitating after-school training sessions for staff to promote positive listening skills, handling challenging situations, building intentional communication skills, and role-playing situations that arise in working with students. School counselors can address *places* by giving attention to the physical environment and to how to make it as attractive and welcoming as possible. The school counselor can be involved in school *policies* by ensuring that they reflect the values that are promoted by the school. School counselors can influence *programs* by ensuring that they are truly beneficial for students. For example, those that attach labels to students and are not inclusive can have many negative effects. Therefore, school counselors can advocate for programs that promote student strengths and allow them opportunities to participate in the larger school community. Finally, the school counselor can recognize how he or she is part of educational processes through his or her interactions with each person and each thing within the school, and the degree to which these interactions contribute to the establishment of an overall positive atmosphere. Together these strategies help the school counselor "to transform the total school culture by applying steady and continuous pressure from numerous sources over time, much like the starfish conquers oysters" (Stanley et al., 2004, p. 305).

The ITOP framework is helpful to the field of school counseling because it includes the role of the school counselor in the discussion of creating caring school communities. Suggestions are made about how the counselor can begin to foster a sense of community within his or her school. Purkey and Aspy (2003) described how ITOP was implemented in the nine lowest performing schools within a large, inner-city district. After physical renovations were made and new staff was hired at the schools, the starfish analogy of this framework was presented to the staff at these schools. Specific strategies were implemented at the five levels that are critical to this approach (i.e., people, places, policies, programs, and processes). At the end of the school year, preliminary findings suggested that all schools showed improvement in test scores. Furthermore, three of the nine schools were categorized as "exemplary" because district reading and math scores were met or exceeded. These findings provided positive support for the ITOP process, and in the words of the authors, invitational education can "effectively create and maintain healthy school environments" (Purkey & Aspy, 2003, p. 154). However, this area needs further empirical investigation and exploration into how other areas of concern (e.g., emotional, social, and behavioral well-being) are impacted because of utilizing the ITOP model.

Although most of the frameworks reviewed here do not explicitly include a discussion about the school counselor's role in facilitating caring school communities, they are valuable conceptualizations that shed light on what community building actually looks like within a school. Together, the strategies that are illustrated within these philosophies can be extended to the school counselor, which will be addressed in more detail later in this discussion. It is hoped that gaining an understanding of all six of these approaches will help to illustrate more fully that community building occurs in multiple ways using different strategies. Even though differences exist among these philosophies, each works toward a similar outcome: a caring school community. Furthermore, each will help to more fully understand how and in what ways the school counselor's role can be conceptualized to include community building.

Commonalities Among the Frameworks

After reviewing the six selected theoretical frameworks, it is helpful to analyze the components of these various frameworks and reflect upon the commonalities and differences that emerge. The elements of a successful school community that are described by Rossi and Stringfield (1996), reviewed earlier, provide a meaningful structure by which to compare the tenets of these various frameworks (see Table 24.1).

As evidenced by the table, each of these philosophies fosters the critical components of a successful school community as proposed by the Rossi and Stringfield (1996). A primary commonality between all of these frameworks is the focus on the school *environment* as a way in which to create a more positive learning experience for youth. This focus is highlighted in the shared vision, purpose, and values that are key to each perspective. All six also address multiple aspects of diversity and culture, including the celebration of culture and the consideration of cultural factors on the educational experience of youth. Each perspective calls for the effective participation and communication among multiple individuals (e.g., students, school staff, families, and community) when engaging in efforts of community building. Caring, trust, and teamwork are clearly included in each perspective either directly or indirectly in program implementation. Finally, each of the six theoretical frameworks emphasizes the need to respect and recognize the uniqueness of each individual.

Although all six perspectives foster the critical elements of successful communities, they do also differ. One major difference is the level of program implementation. For example, some programs focus more specifically on building community within the classroom (e.g., Frank's, Kohn's, CDP) while others take a more school-wide approach (e.g., Tribes, ITOP, Search Institute). A second difference is the amount of empirical support that is available in the literature. For example, of the six perspectives discussed here, the CDP enjoys the most empirical support and has been nationally recognized as a model program. The Search Institute has also made quite an effort to evaluate their model of developmental assets within schools and is attempting to conduct future research with more diverse samples of youth. Their work, however, is not focused on evaluating specific programs or interventions. The well-defined Tribes program has been implemented in many schools around the country, and support for the program is promising (Chesswas et al., 2003; Chesswas & Davis Sosenko, 2004). The ITOP will benefit from future research that supports the utilization of this model and how it is appropriate to guide school counseling practices. Frank's and Kohn's theoretical frameworks lack empirical support at this time, but nevertheless, they do contribute valuable ideas to the topic of school community building.

The School Counselor's Role in Building Caring School Communities

These six frameworks provide a foundation for understanding multiple approaches aimed at building caring communities in schools. They also provide guidance for how the school counselor can play a role in this process. The next

Table 24.1 Rossi and Stringfield's (1996) Elements of Successful School Communities (1996)

	Shared Vision, Shared Purpose, and Shared Values	Incorporation of Diversity	Communication and Participation	Caring, Trust, and Teamwork	Respect and Recognition
Tribes (Gibbs, 2001)	–Goal: "[T]o engage all teachers, administrators, students, and families in working together as a learning community that is dedicated to caring and support, active participation, and positive expectations for all students" (Gibbs, 2001, p. 22). –Four agreements: Attentive Listening, Appreciations/No Put Downs, Right to Pass, Mutual Respect	–Culturally appropriate strategies –Organized into diverse Tribes –Values uniqueness of each individual –Considers impact of cultural factors on student's well-being (e.g., family, community, friends)	–Reflect on and share own experiences, creating inclusion –Involve family, schools, and community using a democratic process –Student-centered classroom allows students to have active participatory role	–Teachers work collaboratively in groups –Educators, parents, and students work together –Caring and support is critical –Promote collaboration –Foster connection and belonging	–Respect diversity –Inclusion so that each member feels valued
Laurie Frank's (2004) "The Caring Classroom"	–"Full-value contract" describes group agreements –Each individual has a responsibility to contribute to the safety of the environment –"Goal-Setting" helps establish & understand group and individual goals	–Inclusion allows diverse individuals to be valued within the community	–Participation is valued: It is "OK" to make mistakes and take risks –Problem solving takes place at Stage 3 –Effective communication –"Challenge by Choice" gives individuals ownership about their individual participation	–Collaboration and cooperation are emphasized –Cooperative learning takes place at Step 1 –Establishes safety –Active listening and perspective-taking –Trust is created at Step 2 –Empathy –Community support	–Value and respect for each individual –"Put-ups" rather than "Put-downs" –Consistent encouragement –Challenge takes place at Step 4 (recognize individual goals)
Alfie Kohn's (1996) "The Classroom as Community"	–Take steps to establish the classroom as a physically and emotionally safe context for all individuals –Moving beyond discipline and competition to focus on community-building	–Focus on context and the factors that contribute to a safe, successful school environment	–Frequent opportunities for participation and engagement –Open dialogues about experiences within the school	–Continuously show caring for one another –Foster sense of connection among individuals –Supportive context –Build positive relationships –Caring environment –Community-building activities within the classroom	–Demonstrate supportive and caring attitudes toward youth and adults

Search Institute (2004)	–Strategies and programs should be designed to specifically foster developmental assets within all youth –Establish a "shared vision" along with a "common purpose and commitment"	–Consideration of multiple contextual/cultural factors that impact the development of youth –Focus on "assets," or strengths of each individual –Community capacity building	–School engagement –Building community collaborations –Active involvement of school, family, and community –Involve both adults and youth	–Establishment of a caring school climate –Caring	–Recognize that each individual has a unique set of developmental assets
CDP (Battistich et al., 1997; Battistich et al., 2004; Developmental Studies Center, 2005; Schaps et al., 2004)	–Create a "caring community of learners" –Community-building is key –Shared sense of purpose and common norms and values of caring, justice, responsibility, and learning	–Responsiveness to youth's diverse developmental and sociocultural needs –Promote development of all students rather than prevent problems in those identified as "at risk"	–Accessible, meaningful, engaging curriculum –Opportunities to participate meaningfully –Active role in decision-making process	–Facilitate development of caring, prosocial individuals –Caring and supportive relationships –Collaboration –Shared decision-making process –Teacher warmth and supportiveness	–Low use of extrinsic control –Recognize when help is needed and assist others –Empathy
ITOP (Parkey & Schmidt, 1996)	–Four primary assumptions: Individuals are able-bodied and valuable; helping process is collaborative alliance; each individual has "untapped potential"; strategies are implemented to promote one's "untapped potential"	–Address multiple contextual factors of the school in order to make it positive for students, adults, parents, and community	–Various levels of communication are utilized by individuals –Collaboration among school staff, students, parents, and community	–Trust and intentionality –Safe and welcoming environment	–Respect and optimism

part of the chapter will begin by considering the role of the school counselor in general, followed by a reflection on how the Positive Youth Development (PYD) perspective is a suitable framework from which to approach community building. Next, specific strategies that the counselor can utilize in the community-building process will be presented.

The Redefined Role of the School Counselor

In recent years, the American School Counselor Association (ASCA) has attempted to clarify the school counselor's role and emphasize his or her importance as an integral member of the school. The *ASCA National Model* (ASCA, 2003) is an attempt to describe how youth are positively affected by the school counselor and the multiple roles that the school counselor plays in an attempt to facilitate healthy youth development. The model defines the school counseling program as an essential component that contributes to the successful functioning of the school. It also emphasizes that *each* student is given equal access to the services provided by the school counselor, and the guidance curriculum in turn is designed to teach *all* students the appropriate knowledge and skills that they need in order to be successful individuals. Therefore, the school counseling program is defined as "comprehensive" in the sense that it is designed to reach all students in order to promote their academic, career, and personal/social development (ASCA). This perspective is in contrast to previous definitions of the school counselor, which described the counselor as working primarily with a subset of students, such as those identified as "talented and gifted," "at risk," or "with special needs." Within the literature on school counseling, it is clear that many authors embrace the redefinition of school counselors and call for their active facilitation of collaborative relationships and fostering a sense of community within the school as an integral part of this redefined role (e.g., Beale & McCay, 2001; Hernandez & Seem, 2004; Holcomb-McCoy, 2004; Keys & Lockhart, 1999).

This redefinition of school counseling that includes a shift from working with only a portion of the school population to providing services to all students is one that fits in well with the idea of creating a caring school community. Both call for the school counselor to address *all* students and provide *each* student with the knowledge and skills that needed to experience a healthy developmental process. Furthermore, both the ASCA definition of the school counselor and the process of building caring communities require the counselor to be *fully integrated* into the educational environment rather than functioning as an ancillary set of services.

Using a Positive Youth Development Perspective

In the past, programs for youth in our society were developed to address the negative behaviors that were exhibited by children who were labeled "at risk." This deficit approach targeted at-risk youth and attempted to "fix" them by decreasing these negative behaviors. However, beginning in the 1980s, research began to show that this strategy was not effective because it narrowly focused on specific problems (e.g., drug abuse, violence, or teen pregnancy) and failed to address the important elements of *healthy youth development*. In response to these findings, the focus of youth programs shifted to a resiliency approach that addressed what *all* children need to be successful and experience a healthy developmental process (Community Network for Youth Development, 2001). This shift is reflected in Damon's (2004) description of PYD: "The positive youth development approach aims at understanding, educating, and engaging children in productive activities rather than correcting, curing, or treating them for maladaptive tendencies or so-called disabilities" (p. 15). Furthermore, the importance of considering the impact of environmental factors (e.g., family, school) on the development of youth became apparent (Catalano, Berglund, Ryan, Lonczak, & Hawkins, 2002).

This change in thinking resulted in the emergence of PYD, which was a shift away from the intervention perspective that had formerly been promoted. Advocates of a PYD approach over an intervention focus argued that efforts aimed at youth cannot simply intervene with existing problem behaviors, but must also facilitate the development of positive characteristics as well (Catalano et al., 2002). An ecological perspective that considers contextual factors (e.g., Bronfenbrenner, 1979) was also included within the PYD approach as well as developmental components which highlighted the fact that certain competencies must be gained at particular stages of life (Catalano et al.).

Catalano et al. (2002), in an attempt to create a better definition of PYD, reviewed the PYD literature and identified 10 common goals that PYD programs have in common: facilitate bonding; increase resiliency; foster social, emotional, cognitive, behavioral, and moral development; build self-determination; foster spirituality; build self-efficacy; promote positive identity; promote positive belief in the future; recognize positive behavior and activities that allow for prosocial development; and build prosocial norms. Different programs included a different combination of the ten objectives; however, all programs tried to improve social, emotional, cognitive, and/or behavioral competencies; self-efficacy; and prosocial norms/family and community standards for healthy social and personal behavior. The authors also showed that PYD programs targeted one or more of three critical contexts: school, family, and community. Of the programs reviewed, 88% included a school component. Those programs that were most effective used a manual or curriculum to deliver the program and were in place for a period of at least nine months. The authors report that each program reviewed reported significant changes in youth's positive or problematic behaviors. These are preliminary findings on programs that utilize the PYD framework and warrant future research that evaluates program outcomes.

Utilizing a PYD perspective is appropriate for school counselors, given their redefined role to become more integral in supporting the well-being of students. When considering the PYD approach within the broader discussion of developmental guidance and, more specifically, in the creation of a caring school community, there are several parallels that are important to highlight in an attempt to understand the commonalities among the three. First, each is directed toward *all* students and promotes their positive well-being. Second, each considers the multiple contextual factors that impact youth and addresses the critical contexts of school, family, and community. Finally, all recognize the importance of using a developmental perspective in order to promote the acquisition of skills and knowledge at the appropriate stages in the developmental process. Although the ASCA calls for a developmental program that is "proactive and preventive in focus" (Campbell & Dahir, 1997, p. 9), it seems more appropriate to approach the process of creating a caring school community from a PYD perspective. The preceding commonalities that are evident among a PYD perspective and a developmental guidance program in general and, more specifically, creating a caring school community in particular, seem to make it a likely perspective from which a school counselor can guide his or her work within a school.

The school counselor has an exciting and critical role within the school. Using a PYD perspective, he or she is in the position to equip youth with the awareness, knowledge, and skills that will help them to become healthy and successful individuals. Unlike other school staff members, the school counselor is in a position that allows him or her to reach out to and establish him or herself as a positive source of support for all students within the school. Using the PYD perspective, the school counselor is fortunate to operate from a perspective that allows him or her to work not only with students but also with school staff, families, and community members in creating supportive relationships that promote the positive development of youth. The school counselor is truly an individual who can take initiative in creating a sense of community and establish him or herself at the "hub" of this process.

Building Caring School Communities on Five Levels

So far in this chapter we have laid a foundation that clarifies the nature of caring school communities and describes a select group of theories that show how to facilitate community building. Furthermore, a rationale as to why the counselor is well suited to play a key role in fostering caring communities within a PYD perspective has been articulated. This discussion will now turn to the more explicit ways in which the counselor can implement strategies on five levels within the school using individual and group counseling, classroom guidance lessons, staff consultation and collaboration, schoolwide initiatives, and community outreach and partnerships. Many of the strategies suggested by the six philosophies presented earlier in this discussion will be integrated into approaches described here that are specific to the school counselor's role in creating a caring community.

Individual and group counseling. School counselors can utilize their counseling relationships with students as opportunities to foster a sense of connection to the greater school community. For example, counselors can facilitate discussions about topics such as school success, anger management, relationship difficulties, dealing with bullying behavior, and coping skills as suggested by the ITOP framework (Stanley et al., 2004). Students who are in counseling because they are struggling with one of these critical areas of development will be able to discuss their feelings and experiences within the safe context of the counseling sessions. These opportunities can serve as crucial moments by which to facilitate the healthy growth and development of students who need support dealing with specific issues. In addition, counselors can use individual and group counseling sessions as opportunities to reflect on and share their experiences within the school environment, as suggested by Tribes (Gibbs, 2001), to address issues of diversity and other aspects related to the well-being of students.

Individual and group counseling sessions can also be utilized as opportunities to create more of a sense of inclusion among students. For example, individual and group counseling sessions can be a safe context in which to discuss diversity issues (Bradley & Jarchow, 1998). Students who are struggling with feeling a part of the community due to racial/ethnic, socioeconomic, religious, sexual orientation, or other cultural differences can benefit from discussions with the school counselor about this experience and ways in which to cope. On the other hand, students who seem to have a difficult time embracing diversity might benefit from discussions led by the counselor that help them understand the importance of respecting cultures that are different from their own. Small groups might also be used to discuss career development issues for ethnic minority youth, including conflicts, questions, and challenges that they might be facing as they consider their future educational and career choices (Constantine, Erickson, Banks, & Timberlake, 1998). Addressing these concerns for racial and ethnic minority youth might help them to feel as if their needs are being more fully addressed within the school environment. Other youth who might initially feel disconnected from the school community are new students. One way to create a sense of connection to the school is by creating a "new student group," headed by the school counselor, as a way to help these students feel welcomed into the school (Bradley & Jarchow, 1998). The counselor can help familiarize the students with the school community, help them discuss their experiences in the new school environment, and ensure that their needs are being met.

Counselors can also serve as liaisons to connect youth to supportive programs and resources. For example, after-school academic support programs and peer mentoring programs are two helpful environments that can meet the needs of students and help them to feel more connected to school (Stanley et al., 2004). Through individual and group counseling sessions, counselors will be able to identify those students who would benefit from programs such as these and help them to become involved. Furthermore, counselors should have books and other resources available to students on issues such as diversity (Bradley & Jarchow, 1998) and other important topics related to youth development that will help students to feel better about themselves and their membership in the larger school environment.

Classroom guidance. In order to establish a sense of a caring community during classroom guidance lessons, school counselors can employ the many techniques that are suggested by previously reviewed theories. For example, school counselors can follow the Tribes approach of structuring the classroom, ensuring that the lessons are organized in such a way that promotes a student-centered environment (Gibbs, 2001) where there is ample opportunity for students to work in groups (Battistich et al., 1997; Frank, 2004; Gibbs). Constantine et al. (1998) also promoted student collaboration in the use of career development activities in the classroom, which have the potential to increase self-esteem, academic achievement, and retention of at-risk youth. As suggested by both Gibbs and Frank, the counselor could model and encourage the use of "appreciations" or "put-ups" while discouraging "put-downs." He or she could make a conscious effort to design curriculum that is truly engaging and meaningful, as emphasized by the CDP (Battistich et al., 2004) and Kohn

(1996). Finally, school counselors could be cognizant of displaying warmth and supportiveness, using techniques to elicit thinking and discussion, emphasizing prosocial values, and using a low level of extrinsic control, which is related to the students' feelings of a sense of community within the classroom (Battistich et al., 1997; Solomon et al., 1997). Instead of attempting to exert control over students, the counselor should focus on how he or she could help to empower students so that they would be able to develop and exhibit self-control (Sautner, 2001).

One important topic for school counselors to address in classroom guidance lessons is diversity. Lessons can be designed to specifically create a space for students to discuss this topic, and counselors can target ways in which to reduce prejudice and stereotyping within the classroom. These lessons will allow students to learn to understand and respect the worldviews of others (Bradley & Jarchow, 1998). Also, counselors could be conscious about using culturally appropriate teaching methods within the classroom, as proposed in the Tribes philosophy (Gibbs, 2001). By demonstrating and teaching respect for diversity, it is hoped that students of diverse backgrounds will feel appreciated and supported within the school environment. Furthermore, adults should serve as role models for youth by embracing and celebrating diversity.

Staff consultation and collaboration. A major role that school counselors have when working with staff is the role of consultant. Because of his or her training, skills, and knowledge, the school counselor is in a desirable position to facilitate after-school or in-service training sessions for staff. Through these activities, counselors can educate their colleagues on topics such as positive listening skills, handling challenging situations, and building intentional communication skills. Furthermore, they can engage staff in role-playing situations that may come up with their students (Stanley et al., 2004). These opportunities not only help teach school staff the strategies that create a sense of community within their classrooms, but are also skills that can be used when interacting with other staff members, parents, and community members in effective ways.

Strategies that the counselor uses within the classroom to establish community can also be taught to teachers. These strategies include establishing the physical environment to promote collaborative learning (Gibbs, 2001); promoting collaborative learning experiences (Battistich et al., 1997; Frank, 2004; Gibbs); using "appreciations" or "put-ups" and discouraging "put-downs" (Frank; Gibbs); designing meaningful, engaging curriculum (Battistich et al., 2004; Kohn, 1996); using culturally appropriate teaching strategies (Gibbs); and helping teachers learn how to show warmth and supportiveness, techniques that elicit student thinking and discussion, prosocial values, and a low level of extrinsic control (Battistich et al., 1997). Counselors can educate staff about the Search Institute's (2004) developmental assets and help them understand how they can promote these assets within students.

In accordance with Kohn's (1996) philosophy, counselors can help other staff move away from promoting competition among students and using discipline strategies and, instead, toward the celebration of participation and community building. He or she can utilize Kohn's steps in creating a safe environment within classrooms as a way for educators to conceptualize how this process looks, which involves thinking in the plural as "us" rather than individualistically.

Counselors can also help facilitate a discussion with school administrators, teachers, and other school staff to reflect upon the shared values of the school (Stanley et al., 2004). Because the shared values of a community are so core to its success, it is important to ensure that this set of values is appropriate, agreed upon by the members of the school, inclusive, and promoted within the school. In order for these values to be shared by the students, the adults must appropriately model these values and continually reinforce them throughout the school year. Likewise, school counselors can also facilitate an examination of the various programs that are offered by the school. Those that attach labels to students and are not inclusive can have many negative effects on the school as a community (Stanley et al.).

Due to the increasing diversity in our country, the schools in the United States are becoming much more diverse and we are more in touch with global events which affect our everyday lives. As a result, both school staff and students need to gain the knowledge and the skills to successfully navigate within a diverse world. Counselors can collaborate with teachers to promote not only a classroom that is global, but also one that celebrates diversity. Staff trainings or workshops can be organized and facilitated by the counselor in an effort to teach staff about diversity and facilitate an open dialogue so that staff members can openly discuss this issue (Bradley & Jarchow, 1998). It is critical that these discussions embrace a broad definition of diversity that includes not only race and ethnicity, but all aspects of culture such as gender, socioeconomic status, sexual orientation, religion, immigration status, ability, and language.

Finally, school counselors can develop programs that foster a sense of community among staff and between staff and students. For example, he or she can coordinate a staff wellness program or implement a mentoring program that connects staff with students in need of positive role modesl (Stanley et al., 2004). These types of efforts highlight the importance of including the adult staff in the community-building process.

Schoolwide initiatives. School counselors can begin to address the school community on a whole-school level by giving attention to its physical environment and ensure that it is as attractive and welcoming as possible to all individuals within the school (Stanley et al., 2004). This might include paying particular attention to posters, banners, and pictures that are visible within the school context and making certain that they are truly characteristics of an environment that promote a sense of community.

It is clear that any successful community needs a shared set of values. School counselors can play a key role in helping to identify that set of values and connect it to the mission of the school. For example, the four "agreements" that are core to the Tribes (Gibbs, 2001) philosophy serve as a unifying set of values that all members are continually encouraged to uphold. School counselors can then help to articulate and promote these values, such as caring, respect, and responsibility, in a proactive manner through character education programs, for example (Britzman, 2005). The counselor can also collaborate with staff members to promote the shared values in a coherent, schoolwide manner. For example, the school could promote a particular value or idea related to a value promoted within the school on a monthly basis so that students consistently receive messages about these values.

A school counselor can also help facilitate a caring school community by consciously establishing him or herself as what C. C. Lee (2001) defined as a "culturally responsive counselor" who is a "facilitator of student development" (p. 258). By being culturally responsive, the counselor recognizes that each student has the desire and the ability to learn and acknowledges that cultural differences do exist. C. C. Lee described the importance of understanding the "cultural realities" of youth and how they affect their development on academic, personal/social, and career levels. By doing so, C. C. Lee explained that the counselor has five responsibilities for each student: facilitate positive self-identity, promote positive relationships between students of diverse backgrounds, promote academic achievement of students, promote attitudes and skills for success in school, and help youth explore career options and promote career development by considering the multiple factors that influence career development of racial/ethnic minority students. When counselors are culturally competent in these ways, they demonstrate an appreciation for diversity and an understanding of the multiple factors that influence the development of racial/ethnic minority children.

Another way in which to promote a sense of community at this level is by coordinating schoolwide connectedness-building activities in collaboration with other staff members (Holcomb-McCoy, 2004), such as schoolwide assemblies (Stanley et al., 2004). These activities will give the school a chance to celebrate its school community as a whole and emphasize those components that are most important to the school environment, such as the shared value system.

School counselors can also serve as leaders in school reform efforts that are related to caring-community building. For example, he or she might ensure that educational goals are met and that the whole school is, in fact, promoting a safe environment (Bemak, 2000). Counselors can help, for example, review school policies with other staff members to make certain that the policies do support and reflect the values of a caring school (Stanley et al., 2004). Another way to assess the ways in which the school community as a whole is perceived by both staff and students is to administer a climate survey. The school counselor can take a leadership role in the administration and interpretation of the survey (Hernandez & Seem, 2004). By gaining a sense of the school climate and what specific areas need to be addressed, the counselor can gain insight into the sense of school community that exists and what kinds of efforts can be introduced to improve that sense of community.

One way in which the school counselor can collaborate with others to create a caring community is by providing opportunities for students to participate in caring behaviors. In order for this to take place, all staff must first make a commitment to serve as role models for positive, caring behaviors. Next, school counselors can collaborate with staff to provide students with opportunities for students to practice behaviors in an effort to create a positive school climate (Noddings, 1992). Providing opportunities for students to engage in these caring behaviors is critical for establishing a caring context that feels like a true community (Ferreira & Bosworth, 2001). This might take form in service-learning activities, a "Random Act of Kindness" week, or pairing up students with other students in mentoring or "buddy" relationships.

In thinking about the school counselor as a leader in addressing the school climate, Hernandez and Seem (2004) wrote,

> While changing a school climate is everyone's responsibility, school counselors can play a leadership role in this effort because of their specialized knowledge and training. As catalysts for a safe school, school counselors can oversee and coordinate the school community's efforts at programming, provide leadership in the assessment of such efforts, and play a key role in communicating with students, teachers, staff, administration, parents, and the community at large. While being an advocate for a safe school climate may appear overwhelming, serving as a catalyst in a school will help foster programs and policies that create a climate that reflects a community that cares about all youth. Ultimately, the school counselor's leadership role in the creation of a safe school climate will result in the academic and personal success of all students and help schools achieve their educational missions. (p. 261)

These authors' ideas highlight the importance that counselors can indeed play a leadership role in promoting and evaluating a caring school climate, but also the necessity of collaborating with other staff members in order to create change.

Community outreach and partnerships. In a study conducted by Bryan and Holcomb-McCoy (2004), school counselors across grade levels reported that their participation in school–family–community partnerships was an important part of their role as school counselors. After reviewing the literature, these authors reported that nine partnership programs were oftentimes implemented in schools: mentoring programs, parent centers, family and community members as teachers' aides, parent and community volunteer programs, home visit programs, parent education programs, school-business partnerships, parents and community members in site-based management, and tutoring programs. These types of programs facilitate the development of critical positive relationships among the school, families, and community. The school counselor can be instrumental in building these relationships that connect schools, families, students, and the larger community. Bryan (2005) discussed the three roles that school counselors could undertake in order to build collaborative relationships: team facilitator, advocate, and collaborator.

An important way to foster a sense of connection with parents to the larger school community is by making parent contacts. For example, Kohn (1996) suggested that it is important to take the time to write positive notes to parents or make phone calls that inform them not only what their child needs to improve upon but more importantly what their child is doing *well*. When possible, holding parent–counselor meetings or even making home visits allows parents to know that they are truly valued. It is also critical for the school counselor to allow parents opportunities to express their ideas and experiences so that he or she can think from the parents' point of view. Furthermore, C. C. Lee (2001, 2005) suggested that the counselor should attempt to be flexible with his or her schedule, when possible, in order to accommodate different cultural backgrounds and different family circumstances. For example, the counselor might consider periodically having evening appointments available for parents who cannot make it to school during the regular school hours. Being flexible with one's schedule and ways of interacting with parents is likely to give the impression that the counselor is willing to meet the parents "where they are" and is striving to make them feel welcomed and a part of the school community.

In working with families, community members, and organizations, the school counselor is in an ideal role to take leadership of these collaborative efforts. He or she might consider building partnerships with mental health and related agencies, for example, to establish a positive working relationship (Bemak, 2000). As a result, a school counselor is in a position to consult with mental health providers who are working with students at his or her school (provided consent is obtained) and to collaborate on interventions for students. Furthermore, counselors will develop an understanding of the services that are provided in the area and will be able to make referrals to students and their families when necessary. As a result, school counselors can work with community agencies to develop programs and services for children and families (Bemak).

When developing school–family–community partnerships, eight communication processes are included in the process: trust, flexibility, help exchange, responsive listening, individuation, group functioning, nurturance, and problem solving (Swick, 2003). Because of the experience and skills that school counselors possess in the area of communication, they serve as valuable resources for teaching the individuals involved in these partnerships about these processes of communication. Counselors can also lead educational and experiential discussions about diversity and multicultural issues with parent and community groups in order to create a safe environment in which these conversations can take place (Bradley & Jarchow, 1998).

In attempting to create community partnerships, it is helpful to have a framework from which to begin this process. The community capacity-building model provided by the Search Institute (2004) provides one set of steps from which to understand this process. The school counselor can take an initiative to educate all parties involved about how to identify and promote the strengths of the community, as well as promote a democratic decision-making process.

Implementation

To help school counselors consider the implementation process of caring-community building the next section of the chapter will address three key issues. First, a model for implementation will be articulated that will help school counselors understand how they play a central role in this continuous, interrelated process. Second, a consideration of evaluation efforts will be important to reflect upon in order to assess the impact of community-building strategies. Finally, a case example will be presented as a practical illustration that applies the ideas presented throughout this discussion to one school counselor's efforts at community building.

A Model for Implementing Strategies for Fostering a Caring School Community

One helpful way to conceptualize how a school counselor builds caring school communities is to visualize the process on a wheel. The school counselor is centered at the hub of the wheel, serving as a key individual who can facilitate and maintain caring community building on the five levels described in this discussion. Each of these levels—individual and small group counseling, classroom guidance, staff consultation and collaboration, schoolwide initiatives, and community outreach and partnerships—is contained on one of the spokes of the wheel, directly connected to the school counselor who continuously implements strategies throughout the school year to address each of these levels. Between each spoke is one of the key elements of successful school communities identified by the OERI (1996): shared vision, shared purpose, and shared values; incorporation of diversity; communication and participation; caring, trust, and teamwork; and respect and recognition. The school counselor is mindful of incorporating these elements into the caring school community–building process. As a result, when each of the five levels of implementation is addressed and each of the five elements of successful school communities is fostered, a caring school community will be created as the overarching outcome of the school counselor's efforts (in collaboration with the students, staff, families, and community). The sense of caring school community is represented as the rim on the wheel diagram that is the goal of the efforts of the school counselor, at the center of the wheel (see Figure 24.1).

The representation of community building as a wheel also represents the fact that it is a circular, continuous process. There is not necessarily a clearly outlined, step-by-step process leading to the establishment of a caring school community; rather, it is the result of a continuous process of implementing strategies among the five levels and fostering the five key areas of successful school communities in order for the caring school community to persist. It is critical to point out that the school counselor does not act alone in fostering and maintaining a caring school community; rather, he or she serves as an appropriate individual who can facilitate the active efforts of each individual who is a part of the school community. Furthermore, it is important to remember that each of the components on the wheel is interrelated. For example, a school counselor's efforts to collaborate and consult with staff can also be interpreted as a schoolwide initiative that assists educators in working effectively with students. The school counselor's efforts during individual and group counseling sessions will also impact his or her work in classroom guidance lessons as those students in counseling will be encouraged to use what they learn in counseling within

Figure 24.1
Model for fostering a caring school community.

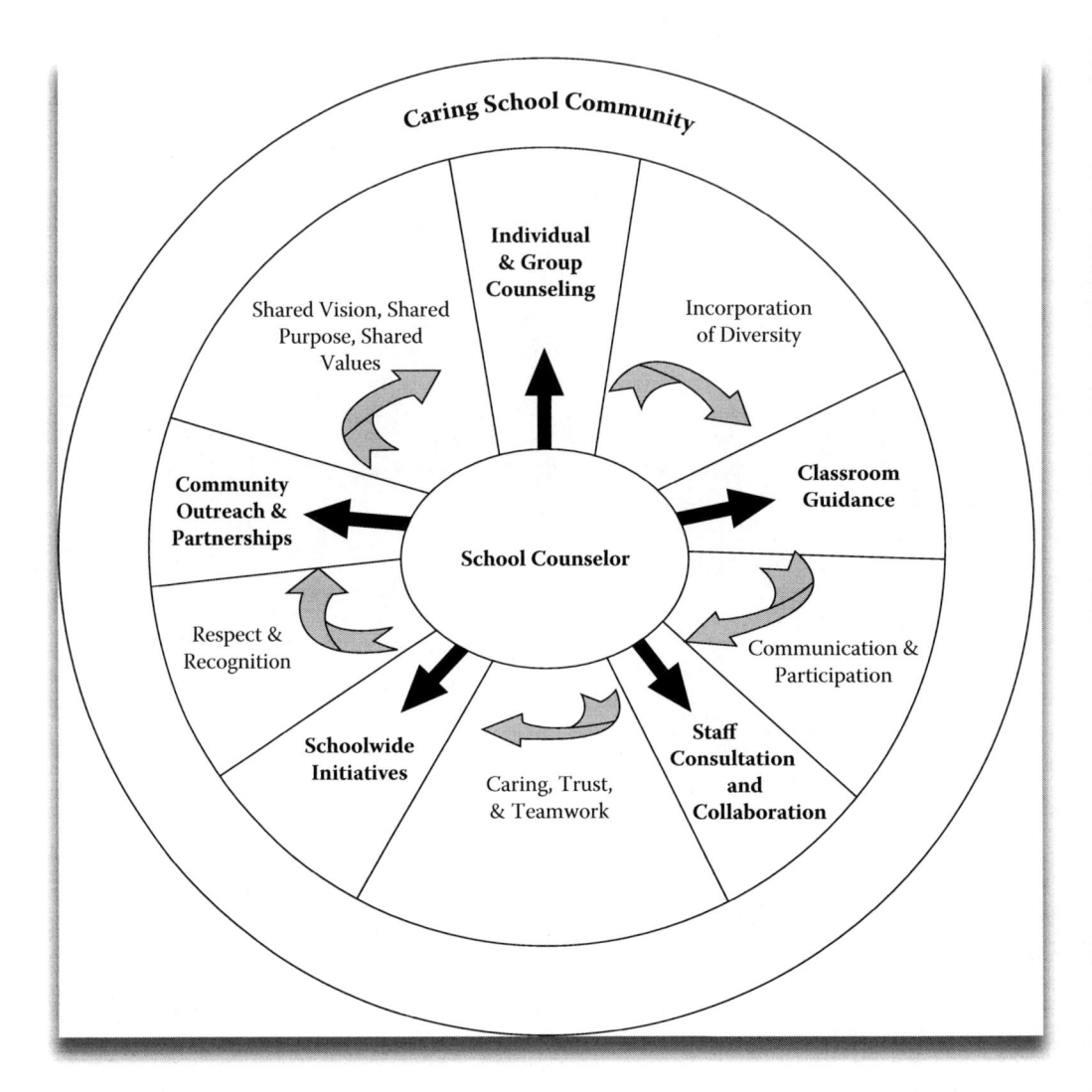

the classroom. Finally, it will be essential for the school counselor to consider the unique cultural context of his or her school, including the critical issues, concerns, and needs of his or her school, in order to develop a more specific plan that illustrates how caring community building will take place on the wheel.

Evaluation

Evaluation in the field of education can be an overwhelming concept. With an increasing focus on accountability, evaluation can even feel like a threat. With increasing emphasis on administrative roles for school counselors, evaluation can be perceived as a burden. With challenges to the mental health role of the school counselor, being involved in evaluation can lead to a sense of role conflict. We want to suggest that evaluation, too often the last element to be considered when implementing new programs, can be perceived as the source of useful feedback and an important aspect of continual improvement. We also want to suggest that program evaluation need not be an onerous project.

As part of the implementation plan for creating a caring community, we advocate that the implementation team, which should include the school counselor, identify the behaviors and attitudes that they associate with a caring community. Each plan should articulate its goals in terms of attendance, academic performance, participation rates, and even discipline referrals. Much of this information is already collected as part of the data that schools are required to report to the district. At the start of the program, the team should identify the current state of affairs.

We recommend that the team, in the first few years of implementation, collect the data on a monthly basis to identify the trends. As we all know, there are seasonal trends to behaviors that get lost in yearly reports. We also advocate that this process of evaluation not be confused with research. The goal is not to develop an experimental test of the theories guiding the plan, but to see how, in a particular school, behaviors change over time.

With this data, the team can see where and in which ways the plan is working. If there is a change in the participation rates or the attendance rates, then the team can see which part of the plan may be affecting that change. If there is not a change in a targeted behavior, such as discipline referrals, then the team can make targeted changes in the plan rather than feel they have to change everything.

Most importantly, this data can help the team and the school to celebrate change. As stated earlier in the chapter, one of the characteristics of a caring school community is taking the time to reflect on what they do. The data that is collected as part of that evaluation is a wonderful way to trigger that self-reflection.

Case Example

This case of Sam provides an example of how one school counselor served as a key individual in helping the student to become integrated into the school community. Sam was a third-grade student who felt very disconnected from the school. He and his family had recently moved to the community and were one of a few racial/ethnic minority families in the small, rural town. The transition to his new school was challenging, and he did not feel like he belonged among his classmates. From the beginning of the school year, Sam appeared to be isolated from his peers, teachers, and other school staff. Sam preferred working alone on all tasks, even when the students were placed into small groups or were encouraged to choose a partner. Sam lacked appropriate social skills that oftentimes made his peers hesitant to interact with him and made his teachers uncertain of how to best meet Sam's needs. During lunch and recess, Sam chose to distance himself from others, finding a far-off corner where he could eat or play by himself. If a teacher or other adult in the school encouraged him to work with the group, Sam displayed a great deal of anxiety, frustration, and anger that was often interpreted by both children and staff as inappropriate hostility. There was a growing concern about Sam that was expressed by his teachers, his school counselor, his parents, and other members of the school who observed Sam become more and more withdrawn. It was evident that Sam was lacking a connection to his school community, and the school community evidently had to shift in order to help Sam feel cared for and connected to his peers, teachers, and other school staff.

In order to evaluate Sam's needs, the school counselor initiated a meeting among multiple individuals within Sam's life, including his classroom teacher, the school psychologist, a special education teacher, and Sam's parents.

These individuals met and shared their perspectives in order to understand how each one of them could help Sam to become more a part of the community. It was particularly important for Sam's parents to be able to express their thoughts and gain a more complete picture of Sam's well-being both at school and outside of school. Collaboratively, these individuals worked toward a *shared vision* and were united by a common purpose: to help Sam feel as though he was cared for and accepted into the school community. After a great deal of thinking, sharing, and planning, several interventions were put into place in order to meet the goal of welcoming Sam into the community. The school counselor took on the responsibility of coordinating regular communication among these individuals in order to assess Sam's progress across the interventions. Furthermore, she would ensure that meetings would be held periodically in order to continue sharing ideas, reflections, and questions related to Sam's well-being. Through this process, effective *communication* and active *participation* was established among all of the individuals involved in Sam's well-being.

On an *individual level*, Sam worked with the school counselor to develop more appropriate social skills. The school counselor met weekly with Sam and engaged him in role-plays where they practiced appropriate ways of asking for help, saying thank you, and answering someone appropriately when he or she asks a question. Additionally, the school counselor would take responsibility for informing the other individuals, such as the special education teacher, who were working with Sam about the importance of emphasizing these skills. Through this process, Sam began to develop *trust* in his teachers and classmates and felt as if they truly did *care* for him. After Sam was able to learn basic social and communication skills and felt comfortable in role-plays with the school counselor, he began engaging in a social skills class that was facilitated by the special education teacher. Along with a small group of his peers, Sam learned how to make eye contact when speaking, to speak slowly and clearly, and to appropriately express his feelings to others in a nonthreatening manner. Within their small group, they engaged in role-plays and approached others in appropriate ways with the support of one another and the special education teacher. These skills were encouraged and reinforced by Sam's school counselor, his teacher, and his parents, who were all aware of what he was being taught in his social skills classes. Although this was challenging for Sam, he worked hard at refining his social skills and was beginning to understand how to positively interact with others in his school environment. Throughout this process, the special education teacher consulted with the school counselor about what kinds of skills Sam most needed to develop and what kinds of activities would best facilitate Sam's acquisition of these skills.

In the *classroom*, Sam's homeroom teacher also worked with him to express appropriate social behaviors with his classmates. She maintained regular contact with the school counselor, who kept her informed about Sam's development of social skills. The homeroom teacher and the school counselor also brainstormed strategies that she could use within the classroom in order to help Sam feel more welcomed by the school community. For example, Sam's teacher wrote daily notes to Sam's parents in order to inform them of their son's progress. She emphasized the strides that Sam was making and gave him personal notes of encouragement. She also gently suggested that Sam work with other students in the class, who were also in need of a friend. These students began to build friendships and began to sit next to one another in the lunchroom and play together at recess. For the first time during the school year, Sam was not always alone on the playground and was choosing to be with someone that he considered a friend. Sam was beginning to be *respected* and *recognized* as part of his classroom community.

Sam also engaged in *small group counseling* by participating in a friendship group that was facilitated by the school counselor. In the friendship group, Sam and the other children discussed and learned about what it means to be a friend and how to make friends and shared stories with one another related to friendship. Being part of this group helped Sam express himself in a way that had rarely been seen by others in the past—through drawing and writing stories. He laughed, smiled, and engaged with his peers in a creative manner that had not been seen previously by his teachers. The school counselor realized that drawing and writing might be something that could help Sam to socially engage with his peers during recess. Therefore, when the weather was suitable, the school counselor would encourage Sam to take paper, crayons, markers, and other art supplies out to the picnic tables on the playground and invite some of his peers to draw and tell stories together.

The school counselor also collaborated with Sam's *after-school program* to help reinforce the skills he was building into other contexts outside of school. The school counselor consulted with the teachers at the program and suggested that they incorporate specific lessons about the importance of belonging, showing respect for others, and giving appreciations. Sam had been especially uncomfortable around his peers in this program and would remove himself from social activities that were planned for all of the students. The school counselor suggested that the teachers at the after-school program have the students write and illustrate a story together as a group, which is something that would be a strength for Sam. With some encouragement, Sam agreed to join his peers, and over time, he felt welcomed into the group. The school counselor also suggested that the program teachers ask students to share "appreciations," or positive statements, about one another, and for the first time, Sam was able to make positive statements about others. In turn, his peers were expressing their appreciation for him being part of the group. This also became a way for the teachers to facilitate other important discussions, such as the importance of working with others and respecting multiple perspectives that are held by others. During these times, it was evident that Sam was beginning to be acknowledged by his peers as a valuable community member. The students were becoming more aware and accepting of diversity in the sense that each classmate was unique in terms of race, ethnicity, gender, and learning ability, but equally deserving of respect.

Throughout this process, the school counselor facilitated regular contact with Sam's *parents*. The school counselor met with Sam's parents and made them aware of the skills that Sam was building in school. She encouraged them to practice these same skills with him in the home and gave Sam's parents opportunities to express their ideas, questions, and frustrations. Sam's parents understood that it was very important for them to ensure that the skills Sam learned in school were also being used outside of school. They were grateful for the support that they had gained for their child and for themselves. Through this process, Sam's entire family felt cared for and involved in the school community.

The experience of being part of a caring school community was a new one for Sam. It took the collaborative efforts of multiple individuals to help address his needs. The school counselor played a key role in working with the teachers, parents, and after-school program to ensure that the environment that was once unwelcoming and uncomfortable to Sam became one that felt safe and inviting. Over time, and with a great deal of effort on the part of Sam and all of those who cared for him, Sam began to feel as if he was a true member of his community. In turn, the community was now more complete because Sam was a part of it.

This case example highlights the efforts to integrate one student into his school community and help him feel cared for by peers and adults. Sam's story illustrates how the school counselor played a central role in insuring that each of the five levels of intervention was addressed. Furthermore, throughout the process it is evident that the key elements of successful communities emerged. The school counselor employed a PYD approach that focused on the skills that Sam needed to acquire in order to experience a more positive development in school. Additionally, these efforts also addressed the other students and the larger school context by helping all individuals to develop greater respect and acceptance of Sam, a student that initially appeared to be an outcast within the school community.

Challenges and Future Directions

Although this chapter advocates that school counselors be central figures in fostering and maintaining caring school communities, the challenges inherent in doing so need to be considered. For example, school counselors continue to face misunderstanding and or conflicting ideas about their roles and responsibilities within the school (Paisley & McMahon, 2001). It is possible that taking on an active role in promoting a sense of community will not be embraced by all. In addition, school counselors, along with all educators, face countless responsibilities and need to have the time available to devote to community–building efforts. It is evident that fostering a caring school community takes a great deal of time, energy, and commitment. From a research perspective, this area of school counseling deserves more attention. Well-designed studies, both qualitative and quantitative in nature, are needed to provide a better understanding of the role of school counselors in creating caring school communities. It is important to consider conducting this research across K–12 settings. As described previously, much of the research to date has focused on implementing caring community-building programs with elementary and middle school youth. Unfortunately, a lack of attention has been given to fostering caring communities in high schools. Clearly, it is important for youth to feel a sense of belonging and connection to school throughout their educational careers. Therefore, future work will be needed to extend research and practices more fully into high schools as well.

In looking toward the future of school counseling, it is helpful to reflect back upon the quote by Baker et al. (1997) from the beginning of this discussion. In a time when youth face a multitude of challenges throughout their development, it is critical for educators to create positive, supportive learning environments that allow students to tap into their full potentials. The case example describing Sam's initial disconnect from the school community is not an uncommon story. Not only was he suffering because of his lack of connection to the school community, but the entire school context was less of a community because he was not initially part of it. The multiple strategies employed by the school counselor highlight the way in which she was able to operate from a PYD perspective to facilitate a variety of community-building strategies through collaborative efforts with students and staff. Furthermore, the case example also illustrates that school counselors need to take what Sautner (2001) calls "the challenge for educators, which is to view troubled students in terms of their strengths and potentials rather than their problems or disabilities" (p. 195). School counselors can step up to this challenge by actively engaging in efforts to create a context that allows youth to feel valued and connected to their educational process. That context is a caring school community.

References

Alder, N. (2002). Interpretations of the meaning of care: Creating caring relationships in urban middle school classrooms. *Urban Education, 37*(2), 241–266.

American School Counselor Association. (2003). *The ASCA national model: A framework for counseling programs.* Alexandria, VA: Author.

Azcoitia, C. M. (2002). Comprehensive community schools . . . Chicago style. *The School Community Journal, 12*(1), 137–141.

Baker, J. A., Terry, T., Bridger, R., & Winsor, A. (1997). Schools as caring communities: A relational approach to school reform. *School Psychology Review, 26*(4), 586–602.

Battistich, V., & Hom, A. (1997). The relationship between students' sense of their involvement in a community and their involvement in problem behaviors. *American Journal of Public Health, 87*(2), 1997–2001.

Battistich, V., Schaps, E., Watson, M., & Solomon, D. (1996). Prevention effects of the child development project: Early findings from an ongoing multisite demonstration trial. *Journal of Adolescent Research, 11*(1), 12–35.

Battistich, V., Schaps, E., & Wilson, N. (2004). Effects of an elementary school intervention on students' "connectedness" to school and social adjustment during middle school. *The Journal of Primary Prevention, 24*(3), 243–262.

Battistich, V., Solomon, D., Watson, M., & Schaps, E. (1997). Caring school communities. *Educational Psychologist, 32*(3), 137–151.

Baumeister, R., & Leary, M. (1995). The need to belong: Desire for interpersonal attachments as a fundamental human motivation. *Psychological Bulletin, 117*(3), 497–529.

Beale, A., & McCay, E. (2001). Selecting school counselors: What administrators should look for in prospective counselors. *The Clearing House, 74*(5), 257–260.

Bemak, F. (2000). Transforming the role of the counselor to provide leadership in educational reform through collaboration. *Professional School Counseling, 3*(5), 323–331.

Bradley, L. J., & Jarchow, E. (1998). The school counsellor's role in globalizing the classroom. *International Journal for the Advancement of Counseling, 20*, 243–251.

Brandt, R. (1991). America's challenge. *Educational Leadership, 49*(1), 3.

Britzman, M. J. (2005). Improving our moral landscape via character education: An opportunity for school counselor leadership. *Professional School Counseling, 8*(3), 293–295.

Bronfenbrenner, U. (1979). *The ecology of human development: Experiments by nature and design.* Cambridge, MA: Harvard University Press.

Bryan, J. (2005). Fostering educational resilience and achievement in urban schools through school-family-community partnerships. *Professional School Counseling, 8*(3), 219–227.

Bryan, J., & Holcomb-McCoy, C. (2004). School counselors' perceptions of their involvement in school-family-community partnerships. *Professional School Counseling, 7*(3), 162–171.

Campbell, C., & Dahir, C. (1997). *Sharing the vision: The national standards for school counseling programs.* Alexandria, VA: American School Counselor Association.

Carpenter, S. L., King-Sears, M. E., & Keys, S. G. (1998). Counselors + educators + families as a transdisciplinary team = more effective inclusion for students with disabilities. *Professional School Counseling, 2*(1), 1–9.

Catalano, R. F., Berglund, M. L., Ryan, J. A. M., Lonczak, H. S., & Hawkins, J. D. (2002). Positive youth development in the United States: Research findings on evaluations of positive youth development programs. *Prevention and Treatment, 5*(1).

Charney, R. S. (1992). *Teaching children to care: Management in the responsive classroom.* Greenfield, MA: Northeast Foundation for Children.

Chesswas, R. J. D., Davis, L. J., & Hanson, T. (2003). Evaluation of the implementation and impact of tribes TLC. Preliminary evaluation report. San Francisco: WestEd Regional Educational Laboratory.

Chesswas, R. J. D., & Davis Sosenko, L. J. (2004). Evaluation of the implementation of tribes TLC: Second year study. Final evaluation report. San Francisco: WestEd Regional Educational Laboratory.

Collins, L. (2003). Building caring communities through conflict resolution: The new challenge for principals. *Delta Kappa Gamma Bulletin, 69*(2), 17–19.

Community Network for Youth Development. (2001). *Youth development guide: Engaging young people in after-school programming.* Retrieved December 3, 2005, from http://www.cnyd.org/trainingtools/CNYD_YD_Guide.pdf

Constantine, M. G., Erickson, C. D., Banks, R. W., & Timberlake, T. L. (1998). Challenges to the career development of urban racial and ethnic minority youth: Implications for vocational intervention. *Journal of Multicultural Counseling and Development, 26*(2), 83–95.

Cook, E. P., Heppner, M. J., & O'Brien, K. M. (2002). Career development of women of color and White women: Assumptions, conceptualization, and intervention from an ecological perspective. *The Career Development Quarterly, 50*(4), 291–305.

Cookson, P. W. (2004). Building a community. *Teaching pre K–8, 35*(1), 10.

Damon, W. (2004). What is positive youth development? *Annals of the American Academy of Political and Social Science, 591,* 13–24.

Developmental Studies Center. (2005). Community building: Caring school community. Retrieved December 3, 2005, from http://www.devstu.org/csc

Epstein, J. L., & Sheldon, S. B. (2002). Present and accounted for: Improving student attendance through family and community involvement. *The Journal of Educational Research, 95*(5), 308–318.

Ferreira, M. M., & Bosworth, K. (2001). Defining caring teachers: Adolescents' perspectives. *Journal of Classroom Interaction, 36*(1), 24–30.

Frank, L. S. (2004). *Journey toward the caring classroom: Using adventure to create community and beyond.* Oklahoma City, OK: Wood 'N' Barnes Publishing and Distribution.

Gibbs, J. (2001). *TRIBES: A new way of learning and being together.* Sausalito, CA: CenterSource Systems, LLC.

Hernandez, T. J., & Seem, S. R. (2004). A safe school climate: A systematic approach and the school counselor. *Professional School Counseling 7*(4), 256–262.

Holcomb-McCoy, C. (2004). Assessing multicultural competence of school counselors: A checklist. *Professional School Counseling, 7*(3), 178–183.

Karcher, M. J., & Lindwall, J. (2003). Social interest, connectedness, and challenging experiences: What makes high school mentors persist? *Journal of Individual Psychology, 59*(3), 293–315.

Keys, S. G., & Lockhart, E. J. (1999). The school counselor's role in facilitating multisystemic change. *Professional School Counseling, 3*(2), 101–107.

Kohn, A. (1996). *Beyond discipline: From compliance to community.* Alexandria, VA: Association for Supervision and Curriculum Development.

Kuranz, M. (2002). Cultivating student potential. *Professional School Counseling, 5*(3), 172–179.

Laursen, E. K., & Birmingham, S. M. (2003). Caring relationships as a protective factor for at-risk youth: An ethnographic study. *Families in Society: The Journal of Contemporary Human Services, 84*(2), 240–246.

Lee, C. C. (2001). Culturally responsive school counselors: Addressing the needs of all students. *Professional School Counseling, 4*(4), 257-261.

Lee, C. C. (2005). Urban school counseling: Context, characteristics, and competencies. *Professional School Counseling, 8*(3), 184–188.

Lee, R. M., & Robbins, S. B. (1995). Measuring belongingness: The social connectedness and the social assurance scales. *Journal of Counseling Psychology, 42*(2), 232–241.

Lewis, C. C., Schaps, E., & Watson, M. S. (1996). The caring classroom's academic edge. *Educational Leadership, 54,* 16–21.

Lundeen, C. A. (2004). Teacher development: The struggle of beginning teachers in creating moral (caring) classroom environments. *Early Child Development and Care, 174*(6), 549–564.

Magrab, P. R. (1999). The meaning of community. In R. N. Roberts & P. R. Magrab (Eds.), *Where children live: Solutions for serving young children and their families* (pp. 3–29). Westport, CT: Alex Publishing Co.

McMillian, M. (2004). Is no child left behind "wise schooling" for African American male students? *High School Journal, 87*(2), 25–33.

Noddings, N. (1992). *The challenge to care in schools: An alternative approach to education.* New York: Teachers College Press.

Osterman, K. F. (2000). Students' need for belonging in the school community. *Review of Educational Research, 70*(3), 323–367.

Paisley, P. O., & McMahon, G. (2001). School counseling for the 21st century: Challenges and opportunities. *Professional School Counseling, 5*(2), 106–115.

Perry, C. M. (2002). Snapshot of a community of caring elementary school. *School Community Journal, 12*(2), 79–101.

Pohan, C. A. (2003). Creating caring and democratic communities in our classrooms and schools. *Childhood Education, 79*(6), 369–373.

Promising Practices Network. (2005). Programs that work: Child development project. Retrieved December 3, 2005, from http://www.promisingpractices.net/program.asp?programid=138

Purkey, W. W., & Aspy, D. (2003). Overcoming tough challenges: An instrumentional theory of practice for humanistic psychology. *Journal of Humanistic Psychology, 43*(3), 146–155.

Purkey, W. W., & Schmidt, J. J. (1996). *Invitational counseling: A self-concept approach to professional practice.* Belmont, CA: Brooks/Cole Publishing Co.

Rossi, R. J., & Stringfield, S. C. (1996). *Education reforms and students at risk: Findings and recommendations* (Vol. 1). Retrieved September 17, 2005, from http://www.ed.gov/PDFDocs/At_Risk1.PDF

Sautner, B. (2001). Safe and caring schools and communities. *Reclaiming Children and Youth, 9*(4), 194–195.

Schaps, E. (2002, June). *Community in school: Central to character formation and more.* Paper presented at White House Conference on Character and Community, Washington, DC.

Schaps, E., Battistich, V., & Solomon, D. (2004). Community in school as key to student growth: Findings from the child development project. In J. E. Zins, R. P. Weissberg, M. C. Wang, & H. J. Walberg (Eds.), *Building academic success on social and emotional learning: What does the research say?* (pp. 189–205). New York: Teachers College Press.

Scott, L. (1974). The caring school. *Delta, 15,* 10–17.

Search Institute. (2003). Boosting student achievement: New research on the power of developmental assets [Electronic version]. *Search Institute, Insights & Evidence, 1*(1), 1–10.

Search Institute. (2004). Tapping the power of community: Building assets to strengthen substance abuse prevention [Electronic version]. *Search Institute, Insights & Evidence, 2*(1), 1–14.

Sergiovanni, T. J. (1994). *Building community in schools.* San Francisco: Jossey-Bass.

Solomon, D., Battistich, V., Kim, D., & Watson, M. (1997). Teacher practices associated with students' sense of the classroom as a community. *Social Psychology of Education, 1*(3), 235–267.

Solomon, D., Battistich, V., Watson, M., Schaps, E., & Lewis, C. (2000). A six-district study of educational change: Direct and mediated effects of the child development project. *Social Psychology of Education, 4*(1), 3–51.

Solomon, D., Watson, M., Battistich, V., Schaps, E., & Delucchi, K. (1996). Creating classrooms that students experience as communities. *American Journal of Community Psychology, 24*(6), 719–748.

Spera, C. (2005). A review of the relationship among parenting practices, parenting styles, and adolescent school achievement. *Educational Psychology Review, 17*(2), 125–146.

Stanley, P. H., Juhnke, G. A., & Purkey, W. W. (2004). Using an invitational theory of practice to create safe and successful schools. *Journal of Counseling and Development, 82,* 302–309.

Swick, K. (2003). Communication concepts for strengthening family-school-community partnerships. *Early Childhood Education Journal, 30*(4), 275–280.

U.S. Department of Education. (2001). Safe, disciplined, and drug-free schools expert panel: Exemplary and promising safe, disciplined, and drug-free schools programs. Retrieved December 3, 2005, from http://www.ed.gov/admins/lead/safety/exemplary01/exemplary01.pdf

U.S. Department of Health and Human Services, Substance Abuse and Mental Health Services Administration, Center for Substance Abuse Prevention. (2005). SAMHSA model programs: Child development project. Retrieved December 3, 2005, from http://modelprograms.samhsa.gov/template_cf.cfm?page=model&pkProgramID=3

Wampold, B. E. (2001). Contextualizing psychotherapy as a healing practice: Culture, history, and methods. *Applied and Preventive Psychology, 10*(2), 69–86.

Worzbyt, J. C., O'Rourke, K., & Dandeneau, C. J. (2003). *Elementary school counseling: A commitment to caring and community building.* New York: Brunner-Routledge.

5

School-Based Interventions

XXV
YOUTH DEVELOPMENT AND PREVENTION IN THE SCHOOLS

SALLY M. HAGE AND SARA BARNETT
Teachers College, Columbia University

JONATHAN P. SCHWARTZ
University of Houston

Recent examinations of the status of children and families in the United States concluded that our nation is in the midst of a "health crisis" (Satcher, 2000). Social indicators point to the fact that youth are at significant risk with regard to such areas as substance abuse, violence, and school dropout rates, and that access to quality services is limited (Weissberg, Walberg, O'Brien, & Kuster, 2003). For instance, 30% of 14- to 17-year-olds report involvement in multiple high-risk behaviors that jeopardize their potential for successful development (Dryfoos, 1997). In addition, about 20% of youth experience mental health problems annually, yet 75% to 80% of those do not receive appropriate interventions (Ringel & Sturm, 2001; U.S. Department of Health and Human Services, 1999). This gap in services is even larger among youth of color, who may view mental health treatment as stigmatizing (U.S. Surgeon General, 2001).

At the same time, growing evidence points to the effectiveness of preventive interventions in enhancing the development of children and youth and in averting maladjustment for individuals at risk of mental disorders or other negative outcomes (Catalano, Berglund, Ryan, Lonczak, & Hawkins, 2002). The cost burden of not addressing children's and families' mental health is enormous. Early and focused interventions have been shown to limit both the chronicity and severity of symptoms and functioning limits (Cicchetti & Toth, 1992). Therefore, expanding prevention efforts significantly reduces the costs of later mental health and other care (Cohen, 1998; Conduct Problems Prevention Research Group, 1999; Tolan & Dodge, 2005). Tolan and Dodge argued that accumulating evidence of the value of early intervention and prevention points to the need for preventive interventions to become "regular, integrated, and substantial components" (p. 603) of our nation's school and communities. This vision is consistent with the recommendation of the President's New Freedom Commission on Mental Health (2003), which has called for an expansion of early intervention services and supports that emphasize prevention, early identification, and intervention in order to maximize positive outcomes.

In this chapter, a definition of prevention is provided. A rationale for expanding the role of prevention in the schools is also clarified, and considerations for fostering prevention research and practice in school settings are presented. Finally, the chapter concludes with an appeal for school counseling training programs to assist school professionals in developing their competence in integrating prevention in their work.

What Is Prevention?

When referring to *prevention* in this chapter, the authors' definition includes one or more of the following: (a) stopping a problem behavior from ever occurring; (b) delaying the onset of a problem behavior; (c) reducing the impact of a problem behavior; (d) strengthening knowledge, attitudes, and behaviors that promote emotional and physical well-being; and (e) promoting institutional, community, and government policies that further physical, social, and emotional well-being (Romano & Hage, 2000).

This definition builds upon the most frequently cited definition of *prevention* by G. Caplan (1964), which includes three dimensions of prevention activities: primary (i.e., stopping the problem before it occurs), secondary (i.e., delaying the onset of a problem), and tertiary (i.e., reducing the impact of a problem). The authors of this chapter extend G. Caplan's definition to include efforts to enhance personal and collective well-being as well as initiatives that create social and political change aimed at improving environments where people live, learn, and work (Romano & Hage, 2000). The most successful school-based prevention programs maintain the flexibility to administer prevention at all five levels.

Historical Context of Prevention in Schools

Earlier in this book, you learned that school counseling maintains a century-long history of providing diverse kinds of services to students. Notably, prevention efforts lie at the heart of many of these services, as is illustrated by a brief overview of the history of prevention in the schools.

In response to unfortunate circumstances that resulted from America's Industrial Revolution at the start of the 20th century, vocational guidance in schools was essentially established to help *prevent* students from succumbing to a life of working long hours, making low wages, and subsisting in poverty. In the 1950s, American public schools administered air raid drills in order to prepare students for nuclear attacks, and in this way, *prevent* their physical harm. In the early 1980s, reported decline in the academic achievement of American students led school counselors to focus on students' time-management and study skills, essentially in an attempt to *prevent* continued academic underachievement (Schmidt, 2003). Thus, prevention has long been recognized as an important aspect of the work of school counselors. Yet, while school-based prevention efforts have been ever-evolving, these efforts are only now assuming a central focus in the identity of the school counselor, despite the fact that a focus on prevention is deeply rooted in the history of school counseling.

Models of Prevention

Theoretical Models of Prevention in the Schools

Prevention practice in the schools should be informed by theory as well as by research. Having a foundation in theory is 1 of the 13 principles of effective prevention programs identified by Nation et al. (2003). School-based prevention programs that are grounded in theory are considered more likely than atheoretical approaches to address the complex interactions of risk and protective factors that operate across multiple contexts (Black & Krishnakumar, 1998; Durlak, 2003; Maggs & Schulenberg, 2001; Nation et al.).

The focus of this section will be an overview and critique of the most significant theories for prevention work in schools. A number of differing theoretical models for prevention in schools have emerged in the literature, each giving varying attention to individual, contextual, and systemic factors; exhibiting a diversity of delivery mechanisms; and including divergent measures of success (Albee, 1996; Cowen, 1983; Durlak & Wells, 1997; Lorion, Price, & Eaton, 1989; Mrazek & Haggerty, 1994; Romano & Hage, 2000).

Disorder reduction or at-risk model. One of the most influential models in the field of prevention is the Disorder Reduction Model (DR; Coie et al., 1993) or At-Risk Model (AR; McWhirter, McWhirter, McWhirter & McWhirter, 1995). The DR model is defined by a biological, intrapsychic, and developmental understanding of the individual, targeting identifiable deficit through a focus on negative symptomology or empirically derived risk factors (Mrazek & Haggerty, 1994). The AR component to this model is grounded in the theoretical assumption that *all individuals* are at risk for disordered behavior, thought, or affect. One's vulnerability to dysfunction exists along a continuum, and once hallmarks of "gateway behaviors" are identified, preventive intervention may be applied to reduce one's risk of negative outcomes (McWhirter et al., 1995). Preventive efforts are directed toward the reduction of clinically defined symptoms of disorders or risk factors, as generally outlined by the *Diagnostic and Statistical Manual of Mental Disorders IV-TR* (American Psychiatric Association, 2000). A strength of this model is its flexibility, making it possible to target individuals at a variety of prevention sites—schools, families, communities, or organizations—and to employ a number of different prevention methods (e.g., school support, psycho-educational groups, mentoring).

However, the limitations of the DR model for work in the schools are significant. Under this model, prevention efforts are confined to the reduction of identified symptomology or risk factors that reside within individual students. Risk assessment, intervention strategies, and programmatic success are all conceptualized at an individual level. Broader ecological or systemic changes that could potentially disrupt factors that engender dysfunction are not a major focus of the model. Further, sustainable, self-perpetuating mechanisms of change are not a significant consideration in prevention efforts in this model. As a result, prevention professionals must repeatedly intervene when identified "gateway behaviors" emerge, rather than more profitably addressing those societal or contextual factors that foster such trajectories (Caplan & Caplan, 2000; Conyne, 1994, 2004; Vera, 2000).

Hence, not enough attention is given to addressing the broader social context for the display of negative symptoms. The result is that the model risks pathologizing the worldview and lifestyle of marginalized populations, including ethnic minorities, women, and low-income students, by not acknowledging the systemically based and socially orchestrated origins of stressors and risk factors common to many of these populations (American Psychological Association, 2003; Brooks-Gunn & Duncan, 1997; Rogler, 1999: Vera, 2000). Mock (2001) suggested that systems-based prevention efforts offer a more effective model for work with ethnic minorities than solely addressing individual needs, facilitating greater sensitivity to the focus on the collective "we" within these communities, as opposed to the "I" value that is stressed in Western cultures.

Health promotion model. A second prevention model found in the literature is the Health Promotion (HP) model (Cowen, 1994, 1996). The HP model aims to strengthen and enhance individual well-being by fostering social and emotional competencies and developing an individual's resilience. This model "assumes that as individuals become more capable and competent, their psychological well-being improves and thus they are better able to withstand or deal with the factors or influences that lead to maladjustment" (Durlak & Wells, 1997, p. 117).

A major strength of the HP model for school settings is the focus on encouraging healthy behavior and in developing protective factors, or those attributes that have been shown to lead toward stronger well-being. Such a focus supports school counselors' work in providing strength-based counseling services, while identifying risk and protective factors and creating school prevention programs designed to increase youths' resiliency to combat targeted behaviors (E. J. Smith, 2006; Wolin & Wolin, 1993). At the same time, the HP model, similar to the DR model, is limited by its individual focus and failure to address systemic, community, and institutional barriers that impede the academic progress of low-achieving students. Thus, individual gains may be difficult to sustain in systems, communities, and institutions that remain static.

Wellness model. In the Wellness model, prevention efforts aim to be proactive and to nurture five dimensions of mental health: (a) healthy caregiver–child relationships, (b) developmentally appropriate competencies for children, (c) healthy environments for human relationships, (d) effective management of stress, and (e) empowerment of people in their lives (Cowen, 1991, 1994, 2000). Hence, a major strength of this model is its focus on primary prevention and early intervention, as Cowen (1994, 2000) believed that everyone would benefit from preventive measures. In addition, this model supports a broad focus on systemic change. School professionals' work, using this model, would promote programs to strengthen healthy relationships as well as social and academic competencies and coping strategies for managing psychological stress (Cowen, 1991). Success in this model is measured not merely through individual gains, but through environmental and systemic gains.

The Wellness model overcomes many of the limitations of the DR, AR, and HP models because of its early, universal, and multidimensional approach to prevention work. Cowen's model encourages prevention professionals to address universal factors that protect against dysfunction—parent–child relationships and competencies that buffer against pervasive risk—while addressing systemic factors that may lead to dysfunction, such as powerlessness, oppression, and the caustic environments created by racism, sexism, homophobia, ableism, and other forms of oppression (Conyne, 2004; Prilleltensky & Prilleltensky, 2003; Romano & Hage, 2000).

Ecological model. A fifth model of prevention that emerges from the literature is the Ecological model (Bronfenbrenner, 1979). The grounding principle of the Ecological model is the theory that behavior occurs in a context and that to understand and prevent disordered behavior, thought, or affect, prevention professionals must consider the context in which dysfunction emerges. Furthermore, one cannot successfully prevent dysfunction without in some way addressing the contextual factors that contribute to such behavior (Bronfenbrenner; Conyne & Cook, 2004; Lewin, 1951).

A major strength of the Ecological model is that school professionals who work under this model aim to address *both* individual *and* systemic well-being (Chronister, McWhirter, & Kerewsky, 2004; Conyne, 2004; Sheras, Cornell, & Bostain, 1996). As mentioned, evidence suggested that prevention efforts that address both individual and contextual factors are more effective than prevention efforts aimed at individual factors alone (August, Lee, Bloomquist, Realmuto, & Hecter, 2003; De La Rosa, Recio Adrados, Kennedy, & Milburn, 1993; Johnson et al., 1990; Stevenson, McMillan, Mitchell, & Blanco, 1998). Thus, like the Wellness model, the Ecological model addresses systemic forces that lead to dysfunction—such as racism, violence, poverty, and oppression. However, the Ecological model is not without its limitations. Unlike the Wellness model, the Ecological model does not explicitly advocate for early, universal prevention efforts. Also, the Ecological model is limited by its tendency to engage individuals or systems only after problem behaviors or pathologies are manifested (Conyne, 2004).

Social justice model. The Social Justice (SJ) model of prevention is theoretically grounded in the notion that pervasive sociopolitical inequity is the greatest contributor to psychological distress and dysfunction. Advocates of the SJ approach have argued that "prevention needs to be directed at the basic social, economic and political conditions that serve to maintain economic disparity" (Conyne, 2004, p. 19).

Unlike the individual focus of the DR, HP, and AR models, the SJ model is largely focused on challenging the political and socioeconomic structures of power, privilege, and poverty. For example, school professionals, in addressing issues such as male abuse of girls and women, would need to challenge "patriarchal power and the influence of male-dominated religion, corporate structure, media violence and sexuality" (Albee, 2000a, p. 850). In sum, advocates of this approach suggest that prevention professionals must address entrenched cultural values and social forces that perpetuate dysfunction in societies (Albee, 2000a, 2000b). Hence, successful prevention efforts in the SJ model not only ameliorate injustice, but also create sustainable, self-perpetuating systems that maintain a just society (Albee, 1996; Albee & Canetto, 1996; Albee & Perry, 1998; Mirowsky & Ross, 1989; Perry, 1996; Stevenson et al., 1998). A strength of the SJ model for schools is that, at its core, the SJ model is distinguished by a metaperspective of prevention and a focus on broader, socially just goals that are grounded in cultural competency and attention to inequities. Hence, unlike the five previous models, the goal of the SJ model is to dismantle all forms of oppression, rather than simply attend to the individual, family, or context.

A School-Based Prevention Model

While each of the prevention models previously outlined has unique strengths and limitations, together they highlight the fact that there is no single theoretical perspective specified for prevention practice and research in schools. However, several theoretical assumptions from these theories can be found in the renewal document provided by the American School Counselor Association (ASCA) *National Model* (2003). These assumptions may, in turn, be further integrated into the design of preventive programs and interventions that will simultaneously prevent negative outcomes and enhance positive development (Bogenschneider, 1996; Lerner, 2001; Weissberg, Kumpfer, & Seligman, 2003). The *ASCA National Model* recommends that school counselors adopt a preventive and developmental orientation, suggesting that students needing more intensive and long-term counseling should be referred to community agencies. The model advocates that school counselors provide leadership for systemic school change, particularly in the areas of academic achievement and career decision making.

This approach emphasizes a developmental, preventive, contextual, strength-based, and multicultural approach to the specialty of school counseling. School counseling programs need to apply the theoretical and research perspectives of developmental, counseling, and multicultural psychology, in partnership with school personnel, to strengthen student academic achievement, career development, and successful school transitions, especially of students from low-income or marginalized communities. In support of quality and equitable education, school counselors must advocate for all students to achieve successful educational outcomes.

Hence, in addition to providing direct services to students, school counselors need to address systemic community and institutional barriers that impede the academic progress of low-achieving students. For example, school counselors ought to work to ensure that all students receive quality academic and career information and counseling so that they are fully prepared to meet the challenges of postsecondary education and future employment opportunities. As agents of systemic change, for example, school counselors could be involved on school curriculum committees to advocate for changes that address the educational needs of students, such as selecting culturally relevant educational materials. A strong focus in the area of multicultural competency offers the means through which the professions can contribute to the academic success of students from culturally and racially diverse backgrounds, as well as to broader educational reforms that promote equity and social justice (Romano & Kachgal, 2004).

In addition, school counselors need to focus on providing strength-based counseling services, while identifying risk and protective factors and designing school prevention programs designed to increase youths' resiliency to combat targeted behaviors (E. J. Smith, 2006; Wolin & Wolin, 1993). The school counselor assists students with building strengths that include a commitment to learning, positive values that guide their choices, social competences that help them build positive relationships and succeed in life, and positive identities to promote a sense of their own power and self-worth (Benson, 1997). In sum, counselors need to adopt a multisystems approach that involves the peer group, school, and community in addition to the family as a way to fully understand students' behaviors in the contexts of their lives (Keys & Lockhart, 1999). A final component of effective school counseling emphasizes the importance of conducting needs assessments and program evaluations to strengthen school programs that deserve continuation and discontinue those that do not. This goal seems especially important in the current climate of high-stakes testing and school accountability (Osborne & House, 1995).

In sum, the ASCA (2003) model represents an exciting renewal in the training and practice of school counselors. This renewal supports a broader role for the school counselor in attending to the academic, career, and personal/social development of students. School counselors are encouraged not only to address major student issues that affect learning, but also to develop school–community partnerships, to implement comprehensive and developmental school-counseling programs, and to address issues across multiple delivery systems from remediation to prevention for *all* students (ASCA, 2003).

Prevention Practice in Schools

Recognizing that school is often the place where students' activities, experiences, and behaviors can be most closely monitored (E. P. Smith, Boutte, Zigler, & Finn-Stevenson, 2004), school counselors are perhaps in the best position to offer prevention programming to children and adolescents. Increased funding by the federal government for school-based prevention programs provides support for these efforts (Shepard & Carlson, 2003). Still, school counselors must be proactive about garnering the funds they need to effectively run a school-based prevention program. The inclusion of teachers, parents, and administrators is often integral to a school counselor's ability to successfully administer prevention programs to students. Stressing the need for such programs, highlighting risk factors within specific school communities, and reviewing research on the positive affects of prevention programming through presentations, writing letters and conducting both formal and informal meetings are just a few of the ways that school counselors can generate support for prevention.

A tailored, integrative and collaborative school-based prevention program caters to the needs of a specific school population and infuses prevention curriculum into all aspects of student life. With regard to these program goals, a systemic approach is best used to assess and intervene for the sake of preventing risky behavior and promoting positive performance in students. School counselors must consider not just what students are exposed to when they are in school, but so too what they face outside of school. This consideration helps enable school counselors to tailor prevention programming to the needs of specific student populations. Furthermore, because prevention programming that targets only the child, and in turn neglects the needs of home, school, and community environments is less effective than the more holistic approach (E. P. Smith et al., 2004), it is necessary for school counselors to serve as change agents both within and beyond the school grounds.

School-based prevention scholars have generally supported a tri-partite model to delineate the importance of contextual development considerations when it comes to designing and implementing a school-based prevention program (Miller, Brehm, & Whitehouse, 1998; Shepard & Carlson, 2003). School-based prevention programs are divided into three groups: (a) classroom approaches, (b) schoolwide approaches, and (c) multisetting approaches. A brief explanation of each approach will follow. Each part of this model stresses the need for school-based prevention programs to be tailored, integrative, and collaborative.

Classroom Approaches

One downside to the federal government's recent plan for improving public school education is that social and emotional student development efforts have taken a backseat to test-taking preparation in the classroom. In schools that embrace integrative prevention programs, however, classroom offerings are not limited to test-taking tips and training. Instead, teachers recognize the way "communication skills naturally fit into the language arts curriculum, problem solving into science and math, social skills into social studies, and mental health concepts into health and science" (Borders & Drury, 1992, p. 488).

For example, in a school where bullying hinders students' ability to concentrate in class or feel at ease on the playground, group activities in which students must work together, discussions about ethical decision making, and demonstrations of the importance of health and safety send meaningful messages and teach valuable life skills that benefit students both during and after their mastery of the content of a certain grade level. With this example in mind, school counselors should encourage teachers to integrate exercises that promote the general well-being and moral character of students into their daily classroom activities, as well as increase students' awareness of the dangers of involvement in risky behavior (Walsh, Galassi, Murphy, & Park-Taylor, 2002).

Schoolwide Approaches

In contrast to classroom-based approaches to prevention programming, schoolwide approaches deal less with direct interactions between school personnel and students, and more with the overall structure of the school schedule and school environment. Once again, as is the case with all types of effective prevention programming, "knowledge of risk and protective factors will inform the identification of target groups and program goals" (Kenny, Waldo, Warter, & Barton, 2002, p. 729). For example, a school from which the majority of students are not supervised by adults when they return home from school may offer affordable after-school care to families with parents who work in the late afternoon and early evenings. Similarly tailored to a specific student population, in a school where students feel a great deal of pressure to succeed academically, instruction on relaxation techniques and reasonable goal setting and stress management may be incorporated into the daily schedule. At first glance, decisions regarding after-school programs and lesson planning appear to fall under the jurisdiction of school boards and school administrators. Yet, it is often the school counselor—the faculty member with a background in child and adolescent psychology and an awareness of the multitude of factors affecting students' development—who knows how to best structure a school schedule and school environment most likely to turn out well-adjusted students.

Multisetting Approaches

One major limitation to restructuring school schedules and school environments is the lack of funding that exists within so many schools. In light of this, it is important to note that an alternative—yet equally, if not more, important—way to extend prevention efforts beyond the traditional classroom is for school counselors to work with parents as part of a multisetting approach to prevention programming. For decades, schools have provided parents with psycho-educational information via home mailings and yearly meetings. However, research shows that more involved "home-school collaboration" (Shepard & Carlson, 2003, p. 642) is required in order to help parents provide the most developmentally beneficial home environment for their children. Parent-information sessions need to be complemented with parent-training sessions. The most effective of these training sessions imbue parents with specific skills, such as how to create and manage a system of rewards for household chores and how to monitor a child's academic progress by way of homework checks and test record keeping (Shepard & Carlson). Individualized consultation for parents whose children struggle in a particular area—be it socially, academically, or otherwise—is also integral to an effective home–school collaboration, as is the option of family therapy. Benefits of parental involvement in their child's school include "higher academic performance, positive student attitudes and behavior, better attendance, increased student time spent with parents, and higher graduation rates" (Shepard & Carlson, p. 643). It seems that for the sake of students' positive experience in the home—the environment said to influence students the most—school counselors must partner with families, essentially serving as a constant and reliable source of guidance and support.

Making the Tri-Partite Approach Work

Certainly, when it comes to a tailed, integrative, and collaborative school-based prevention programs, it is not enough to say that school counselors should advocate, inform, and train all those who might possibly be able to help prevent students' involvement in risky behavior. True partnerships must exist between school counselors, school administrators, teachers, and parents. To best serve students, these relationships should be distinguished by "mutual respect, collaboration and cooperation" (Borders & Drury, 1992, p. 494). School counselors must recognize the demands that weigh on school administrators, teachers, and parents, as it is neither respectful nor beneficial to criticize an administrator's policies, a teacher's approach in the classroom, or a parent's parenting skills without harboring a measure of understanding and acting with genuine diplomacy, for most school administrators, teachers, and parents operate the best way they know how with the resources they are given.

That said, school administrators who suffer under tremendous pressure with regard to the academic achievement of their respective schools may make decisions that conflict with the best interests of students' overall development. Teachers who are overwhelmed by overcrowded classrooms may be able to best serve only the minority of these students. Single parents who work two jobs and care for three children may resolve to focus on putting food on the table rather than drawing up chore charts. For these and other reasons, school counselors must recognize and acknowledge the respective efforts of school administrators, teachers, and parents, ultimately offering constructive consultation and plans for improved action, rather than harsh condemnation and unsympathetic censure. A collaborative school-based prevention program that works must be characterized by partnerships and shared goals, rather than by turf wars and animosity. In this way, the maintaining of an effective school-based prevention program makes for a challenging balancing act.

Effective Implementation

Once various key players commit to taking part in the "balancing act" that makes for a tailored, integrative, and collaborative school-based prevention program, careful consideration of how information is best received by students is necessary for ensuring a program's effective implementation. For decades, "[S]chools have been inundated with well-intentioned prevention and promotion programs that address such diverse issues as HIV/AIDS, alcohol, careers, character, civics, conflict resolution, delinquency, dropout, family life, health, morals, multiculturalism, preg-

Table 25.1 School-Based Prevention Implementation for the Tri-Partite Model

Needs Assessment	Timing	Climate	Curriculum	Presentation	Cultural Adaptation	Evaluation
Stopping a problem behavior from ever occurring						
Delaying the onset of a problem behavior						
Reducing the impact of a problem behavior						
Strengthening knowledge, attitudes, and behaviors that promote emotional and physical well-being						
Promoting institutional, community, and government policies that further physical, social, and emotional well-being						

nancy, service learning, truancy and violence" (Greenberg et al., 2003, p. 467). However, these programs are at times unsuccessful due to a lack of congruency between the ways in which students are most powerfully influenced and the ways in which said programs are implemented. This lack of congruence underscores the utility and necessity of a comprehensive needs assessment to design and evaluate the multifaceted aspects of prevention programming. Sensitive to this, the following section will focus on basic aspects of a school-based prevention program, which will be informed by a comprehensive needs assessment (see Table 25.1 for an outline of each aspect)—namely, timing, climate, curriculum, presentation, cultural adaptation, and evaluation—all of which combine to largely determine a program's level of effective implementation.

Timing. Researchers have found that children and adolescents are most likely to adopt positive behaviors if prevention education is delivered before they become exposed to risky situations (Yoshikawa, 1994). It is important to note that "children's capacity to learn depends on a number of attributes (e.g., curiosity, motivation, and ability to seek help from adults) that develop during infancy and the preschool years" (E. P. Smith et al., 2004, p. 222). This means that students can benefit from exposure to prevention programming from start to finish of their academic careers, from the time they learn to finger paint to the time they learn to read Shakespeare.

Recognizing this, creators of the 21st Century Program, developed at Brown University and included as part of President Bush's *No Child Left Behind* mission, focused their efforts on preparing children for entrance into preschool. Implemented in more than 600 schools in 17 states, the 21st Century Program provides families—that are able to pay a small fee—with high-quality childcare from 6 A.M. to 6 P.M. every weekday, easy access to health care, home visits from experienced social workers, and weekly parenting workshops (E. P. Smith et al., 2004). With a goal for cultivating prosocial habits in young children, programs such as the 21st Century Program help lay a foundation of resiliency upon which students can build as they progress through childhood and adolescence.

Climate. In addition to targeting students before risk factors transform into risky behavior, effective implementation of a school-based prevention program depends largely on a school climate that is characterized by positive psychology. Positive psychology is defined as "positive subjective experience, positive individual traits, and programs that assist in improving an individual's quality of life while simultaneously preventing, or at least reducing, the incidence of psychopathology" (Akin-Little, Little, & Delligatti, 2004, p. 157). To be sure, "positive environments that evoke and reinforce positive behaviors are necessary in order to shape and maintain the optimal human experience" (Akin-Little et al., p. 160), so it is no surprise that school counselors need to secure a positive school climate—a climate of hope, trust, support, contentment, satisfaction, and understanding—in order to implement an effective school-based prevention program. Research has shown that teachers who subscribed to the practice of positive psychology "created more productive learning environments, were more complimentary of students, were more positive in their interactions with students, had more positive views of themselves as teachers, and reported greater job satisfaction" (Borders, & Drury, 1992, p. 493); all of which works to create a more promising school climate, ultimately supporting the notion that positive psychology is best adopted by all school personnel.

Curriculum. The curriculum offered in an effective school-based prevention program must be topical by not only addressing issues that affect specific school populations, but also adapting to the changing nature of today's world. In turn, effective implementation of a school-based prevention program requires that traditional curriculum, such as antidrug, antialcohol, and antiviolence initiatives, be complimented with curriculum aimed at assailing more modern risk factors as well. Since most American families have at least one computer in the home, effective implementation of a school-based prevention program now entails stressing the dangers of communicating with strangers on the Internet along with the dangers of becoming involved with drugs or alcohol. Likewise, due to the increasingly sexual nature of mainstream television and the Internet, lessons on how to detect and dissuade sexual advances from classmates and others makes for relevant and necessary preteen and teenage prevention education.

That said, it is important for school counselors to recognize the way media images that center on superficial beauty bombard anyone who merely walks down the street. K–12 students are particularly susceptible to this type of bombardment—messages sent via billboards, magazine articles, movies, and commercials suggesting that in order to be successful and accepted, girls must be feminine, skinny, and the center of the partying scene, while boys must be masculine, buff, and the center of the sports scene. As students maneuver their way through the awkward stages of childhood and adolescence, pressure to conform to these implausible standards can negatively affect students' self-esteem, potentially leading to destructive behavior, such as disordered eating and steroid use, possibly resulting in lifelong emotional scarring. Devoted to reducing the occurrence of these results, the Victorian Center for Excellence in Eating Disorders (VCEED) published *An Eating Disorder Resource for Schools*, a model program guide for preventing, detecting, and intervening in cases of eating disorders in students (VCEED, 2004).

Presentation. As a rule, school-based presentations should be nonbiased, age appropriate, structured, and time-limited with the majority resulting in either one-on-one activity or small-group work. Peer counseling and peer-mediation programs have also proven beneficial to school-based prevention efforts. Technological advancement can also factor into an effective school-based prevention presentation if it is used to enhance the program's appeal, for lessons that combine audio, video, and computing tend to resonate with the always plugged-in E-generation ("E" standing for electronic; Borders & Drury, 1992). As part of the Midwestern Prevention Project, for example, high school students view video of real-life drunk driving accidents, which essentially make palpable the dire consequences of drug and alcohol abuse (Shepard & Carlson, 2003).

To be sure, an effective school-based prevention program does not amount to students simply watching a video. Instead, interactive activities that present with problem-solving tasks must complement high-tech presentations. Whereas spectatorship alone fails to procure the type of critical thinking that prompts students to take stock of their own goals and actions, "group games, cooperative learning, discussion, role plays, and other forms of behavior rehearsal" (Clayton, Ballif-Spanvill, & Hunsaker, 2001) challenge students to put what they learn into practice and to critique one another's skills (e.g., refusing alcohol at a party, backing down from a fight, or telling the truth).

Cultural adaptation. The cultures of students who are impacted by a preventive program can vary enormously. However, many school-based prevention programs emphasize Western values and were developed and validated in middle-class communities (Kumpfer, Alvarado, Smith, & Bellamy, 2002; Vera & Reese, 2000). Prevention scholars emphasize the importance of tailoring interventions to the specific context in which they will be implemented (Durlak, 2003; Kumpfer & Alvarado, 2003; Lerner, 1995; Nation et al., 2003; Vera & Reese, 2000; Weissberg, Walberg, et al., 2003). Recommendations suggest that school interventions should be carefully designed to meet the cultural, community, and developmental characteristics of the child, school, and community (Castro, Barrera, & Martinez, 2004; Durlak, 2003; Gottfredson, Fink, Skroban, & Gottfredson,

1997; Nation et al., 2003; Weissberg, Walberg, et al., 2003). Existing research suggests that preventive interventions that are culturally adapted to fit the specific context of the student participants are more successful in recruiting and retaining participants (Kumpfer et al., 2002).

Several cultural factors are important to consider in designing prevention programs; these include students' level of acculturation, acculturative stress, migration and relocation history, language preferences, socioeconomic status, geographic location, education, religion and spirituality, extended family support, racial and ethnic identity, relationship to nature, time orientation, and culturally specific risks and coping strategies (Kumpfer et al., 2002). In addressing these factors, cultural adaptations should go beyond superficial changes, from including ethnic minorities in written materials to addressing important cultural values and practices (Kumpfer et al.). In determining adaptations, however, efforts to preserve the integrity of core program elements should be made, and as much as feasible, program strength and dosage should be sustained (Castro et al., 2004; Greenberg et al., 2003; Kumpfer et al.). Such efforts support the design and implementation of culturally relevant and effective preventive interventions. Finally, school professionals who adapt and deliver programs with cultural sensitivity and awareness of cultural nuances need to be provided with a high level of cultural competence (Castro et al.).

Evaluation. Feedback from students, teachers, and parents is critical to a school counselor's ability to make necessary adjustments to a school-based prevention program, ultimately contributing to a constant refinement process. Historically, program evaluation has consisted of descriptive reports on kinds of services offered, amount of time spent on each activity, and number of students served. Increasingly, program evaluation focuses on program results, rather than on program services, in order to truly gauge a program's effectiveness. Specifically, scholars suggest that school counselors specify learning domains (e.g., attitudes, behavior, and academic achievement) with which to structure a program's evaluation. Then, through observation, case study, participant/nonparticipant comparison, and interviews, school counselors can assess the specific areas in which students have either made improvement or remained largely unaffected by program efforts. This data helps school counselors to reevaluate and restructure future programs, as well as identify students who are in need of additional guidance and support. Additionally, included in any valid and reliable program evaluation is assessment made by program participants. In turn, it seems student assessment of school-based prevention programming is necessary for ensuring its continued success.

Prevention Research in Schools

Research knowledge supporting the efficacy of prevention in school and community settings has accumulated substantively in recent years (Catalano et al., 2002; Durlak, 2003; Greenberg, Domitrovich, & Bumbarger, 1999; Greenberg et al., 2003; Nation et al., 2003; Vera & Reese, 2000; Weissberg, Walberg, et al., 2003). The benefits of prevention are further supported by research indicating that it is more effective and less costly to promote positive development in the absence of a crisis than to intervene after a problem has developed (Albee & Ryan-Finn, 1993; Catalano et al.; Durlak; Elias, 1997; Luthar & Cicchetti, 2000). In the next section, a brief overview of the literature informing prevention practice in schools will be presented.

One of the most significant reviews of prevention research was carried out by The APA Task Force on Prevention, Promotion, and Intervention Alternatives in Psychology, which contacted 900 experts on prevention to identify 14 model prevention programs (Price, Cowen, Lorion, & Ramos-McKay, 1988). A similar effort by the second APA task force on prevention, named Prevention: Promoting Strength, Resilience, and Health in Young People, resulted in the synthesis of a larger body of research into a special issue of the *American Psychologist* in June/July 2003, which identified key findings and standards for evidence-based prevention practice for children and youth (Weissberg, Kumpfer, & Seligman, 2003). An additional function of the APA task force was to identify effective practice in the prevention of youth behavior problems by reviewing two federal studies sponsored by the National Institute of Justice's Office of Juvenile Justice and Delinquency Prevention and the Center for Substance Abuse Prevention (Kumpfer & Alvarado, 2003). Based upon their analysis of these prior studies, Kumpfer and Alvarado identified 13 principles of effective family-focused intervention. These strategies included tailoring for age, developmental level, and cultural traditions, as well as providing sufficient treatment dosage and intensity to address risks.

In addition, another comprehensive review of positive youth development programs was conducted by Catalano et al. (2002), who examined 161 programs that focused on developing youth competencies, such as positive relationships with adults, peers, school, community, or culture; social, emotional, cognitive, behavioral and moral competence; prosocial norms; identity development; self-efficacy; adaptive coping; spirituality; and belief in the future. Of those 161 programs, 77 had methodologically sound evaluations and had enough detail of the intervention, participants, and evaluation measures to warrant further consideration. Among the 77 programs, 25 were found to be effective in promoting varied positive outcomes, as well as reducing problem behaviors.

The 25 programs that were most effective had been carried out over a longer period of time (9 months or more) and used structured materials to facilitate consistency in delivery. The review also provided support for extending interventions across multiple contexts, including school, family, and community settings. Seventeen of the 25 effective programs were implemented in either two (usually school and family) or three contexts (community, school, and family). All of the effective programs were directed toward strengthening social, emotional, cognitive, or behavioral competencies and standards for healthy social behavior within the family and community. The majority of the effective programs also strove to build healthy relationships between youth and adults and provide recognition for prosocial involvement.

Catalano et al. (2002) suggested that more evaluation research is needed to demonstrate the effects of model prevention programs in new settings. This recommendation is consistent with ASCA's (2003) suggestion that school counselors conduct needs assessments and program evaluations to strengthen school programs that deserve continuation and discontinue those that do not.

Furthermore, Nation et al. (2003) conducted a "review-of-reviews," surveying 35 comprehensive reviews of prevention research published between 1990 and 1999 that focused on five problem areas: (a) substance abuse, (b) risky sexual behavior, (c) violence, (d) delinquency, and (e) school failure, and/or dropout. From these reviews, Nation et al. identified 252 characteristics of effective prevention programs. The authors further analyzed these characteristics to determine practices that were generalizable across the five problem areas. Through this process, Nation et al. identified nine characteristics of effective prevention programs. Overall, effective programs (a) were comprehensive, (b) used varied instructional methods, (c) were of sufficient dosage or intensity to affect change, (d) were based upon theory, (e) promoted positive interpersonal relationships, (f) were appropriate for participants in terms of developmental level and culture, (g) provided sound training for staff, and (h) included meaningful program evaluation. Nation et al.'s work builds upon Durlak and Wells' (1997) meta-analysis of research on 177 primary prevention programs for children and adolescents, 18 years of age or younger, that were delivered across school, home, clinic, and other settings and evaluated in comparison with a control condition. The meta-analysis revealed that both competence-building and problem-reduction programs were largely effective (59% to 82% of participants in the primary prevention programs were doing better on the target criteria in comparison with the control groups), although nine of the programs had some negative impact.

Finally, Greenberg et al.'s (2003) synthesis of the research literature on school-based prevention and youth development programs identified a number of effective strategies (e.g., designing comprehensive, multiyear programs that foster respectful relationships) that are also consistent with Nation et al.'s (2003) recommendations (Weissberg, Walberg, et al., 2003). Taken together, these reviews provide a substantial body of research evidence to inform the work of prevention practitioners in school settings.

At the same time, while an expanding body of prevention research has clarified practices that contribute to program effectiveness, many prevention efforts have not demonstrated efficacy. It is not clear whether some programs are not effective or just not appropriately evaluated. Catalano et al.'s (2002) suggestion that more evaluation research is needed to demonstrate the effects of model prevention programs in new settings is consistent with the ASCA (2003) recommendations that school counselors conduct needs assessments and program evaluations to strengthen school programs that deserve continuation and discontinue those that do not.

Youth Development Programs in School Settings

The next section of this chapter will present several model school-based prevention programs that have been developed for different grade levels. These examples illustrate the type of prevention program that may be collaboratively developed by prevention-oriented professionals in school settings.

High/Scope Perry preschool project. This longitudinal project (Schweinhart & Weikart, 1988), beginning in 1962, followed 123 African American children from low-income families living in Michigan. Fifty-eight children were randomly assigned at ages 3 and 4 to a high-quality preschool program offering parent information and support while 65 children did not participate in a preschool program. An evaluation completed when participants were 25 years of age (Barnett, 1993) revealed that participants who attended the aforementioned preschool program had higher levels of academic achievement, college attendance, employment, and earnings, and lower levels of special education, antisocial behavior, incarceration, and teenage pregnancy in comparison with those not attending the preschool program. Estimated taxpayer savings were $30,000 to $90,000 per participant. Furthermore, continued benefits of the program have been documented through interviews with 97% of the study participants at age 40 (Schweinhart et al., 2005). In comparison with those who did not attend the program, preschool participants continued to demonstrate higher earnings, higher rates of home ownership and savings, and fewer arrests, with a societal return of $17 for every tax dollar invested in the program.

Although the findings of Schweinhart et al.'s (2005) study cannot be generalized to early intervention programs that do not offer similar program components (e.g., highly trained teachers, home visits by teachers at least every 2 weeks, and low teacher–student ratios), the findings do suggest that high-quality early intervention can support adult success. The study is notable for the random assignment of children to program and no-program groups and for the long-term follow up on multiple indicators with low rates of participant dropout.

Assertiveness Training Intervention. An example of a primary prevention program for elementary students with no identified interpersonal problems is the Assertiveness Training Intervention (Rotheram-Borus & Weinkart, 1988). This intervention is based on evidence suggesting that assertion is linked to positive self-esteem and adjustment in elementary school. An assertiveness training program was conducted for 2 hours per week for 12 weeks in elementary school classes. The assertiveness training intervention was based on social learning theory (Bandura, 1977) and followed a manualized treatment of didactic presentation and behavioral practice with feedback. A sample group of 343 fourth to sixth graders at a predominately White middle-class school were assigned to three conditions: (a) assertiveness training, (b) a no-treatment control, and (c) an alternative treatment (self-confidence-training simulation game).

An evaluation of the Assertiveness Training Intervention (Rotheram-Borus & Weinkart, 1988) found that participants in the assertiveness training program demonstrated more assertive responses to problem solving, initiated more contacts with teachers, showed less problem behavior in the classroom, and had higher academic achievement at 1-year follow up when compared with the control and alternative treatment groups. A limitation of the study was the lack of diversity in the sample, while a strength of the study was the utilization of control and comparison groups as well as assessment at 1-year follow up.

Strengthening Families Program (SFP). The SFP was first administered in 1982 as a 14-session program with parent and youth skills training components for children ages 6 to 12 and parents who abused drugs or alcohol (Kumpfer et al., 2002). Five culturally modified interventions were developed and evaluated in 27 separate studies with rural and urban African Americans in Alabama and Detroit, Asian/Pacific Islanders in Hawaii, Spanish-speaking Hispanic families recruited from schools and community housing, and Ojibwa tribe Native Americans in Iowa. When the results of the culturally adapted interventions were compared with studies assessing the effects of the generic version of SFP, findings revealed levels of participation and retention were 41% higher for the culturally modified interventions, with only slight improvements in outcome.

The Midwest Prevention Project. The Midwest Prevention Project (Pentz, 1998) was an example of a community-based substance-abuse prevention program, which demonstrated efficacy in preventing adolescent substance abuse by addressing casual factors across individual and contextual domains. The components of the project included a parent communication-skills program, a social skills training program for youth, a mass-media campaign, and school and community policy modifications regarding the availability of alcohol and tobacco (Wandersman & Florin, 2003). School programming began in grade six as students entered middle school and continued over 5 years, with the school program being delivered in the first and second years, community interventions and changes in tobacco and alcohol policy being instituted in the third through fifth years, and mass-media coverage taking place across all years.

Eight of the 50 schools in the Midwest Prevention Project were randomly assigned to either the full prevention program or a delayed intervention control condition. The other schools were assigned to prevention and control conditions based upon school scheduling and demographic matching. Longitudinal research with 8,500 students (70% White, 23% African American, and 7% other) in 50 schools indicated that the combination of school and community programming contributed to larger and more enduring effects in preventing serious levels of drug use throughout the high school years than did a program of school-based intervention alone. Although the findings suggested the superiority of interventions that extend across multiple contexts, further research is needed to understand the impact of each program component and to determine an optimal and most cost-effective combination of program components, frequencies, and duration in preventing substance use and abuse and in promoting positive educational outcomes.

The Teen Outreach Program. The Teen Outreach Program (Allen, Philliber, Herrling, & Kuperminc, 1997) was developed as a collaborative program between the Association of Junior Leagues International, local Junior League chapters, and school districts across the United States. The program was designed to prevent teenage pregnancy and school failure, as well as to foster prosocial norms, positive identity, self-determination, and belief in the future by involving high school students in volunteer service in their communities, coupled with school-based activities focusing on self-management and life skills, decision making, and adaptive coping. This was an experimental design in which 695 high school students from 25 schools nationwide were randomly assigned to either Teen Outreach or a control condition to assess program effectiveness.

Adolescents who participated in Teen Outreach evidenced lower rates of pregnancy, school failure, and academic suspension in comparison with teens assigned to a control condition. These findings provide support for the effectiveness of the Teen Outreach Program specifically, as well as for the benefits of volunteer service in promoting positive development as an alternative to problem-focused intervention. Long-term follow-up data is needed to determine whether program effects last over time and whether similar effects may be found for males in promoting academic achievement and engagement.

Future Directions for School-Based Prevention

As the school counseling field continues to redefine the roles and identity of its members, we urge school leaders to take necessary steps to overcome any existing barriers that may .hinder the development of a prevention focus and to move toward a deeper commitment to a prevention agenda, as articulated in this chapter. Given that traditional mental health services systems have failed to significantly reduce the effects of debilitating social and emotional distress in the vast majority of the people in the United States, a movement toward a primary prevention focus in the schools offers much hope for improving the health and well-being of our nation's children and families (U.S. Department of Health and Human Services, 2000).

Without a doubt, the movement toward a prevention focus in school settings has important implications for the training and preparation of school counselors and other school professionals. In order to ensure a high level of professional competency among school counselors in the area of prevention, it is essential that students receive specialized training and supervised practice in the development, implementation, and evaluation of prevention programs. While we recognize the difficulty in adding additional course work to already overburdened school-counseling training programs, content related to prevention needs to be incorporated into existing counseling program course work, such as theoretical foundations, evaluation, group, consultation, practica, and internships. In addition, incentives need to be created to encourage midcareer school professionals to further incorporate prevention approaches into their work with children and families (Mrazek, 2002; Tolan & Dodge, 2005). Finally, efforts to build stronger collaboration between school and community professionals need to be put into place.

In closing, strengthening a prevention orientation in the school counseling field would orient school-based professionals to a *broader application* of their work, with the goal of more effectively and sensitively responding to the tremendous social needs that exist in our communities. The result of this shift would be to change the lens and context for their efforts from an individually focused, adaptation approach to one that includes before-the-fact intervention involving groups, communities, and social systems and is ultimately aimed at social change. As noted by Greenberg et al. (2003), "The choice is clear. We have the science to foster children's social, emotional, and academic learning" (p. 473). The future beckons school-counseling professionals to work together with researchers, educators, and policy makers to design, coordinate, implement, manage, and evaluate youth-development programs for every student's success. Through these collaborative efforts, school counselors can make sure that no child is left behind and that all children and adolescents have the opportunity to realize their potentials.

References

Akin-Little, K. A., Little, S. G., & Deligatti, N. (2004). A preventative model of school consultation: Incorporating perspectives from positive psychology. *Psychology in the Schools, 41*, 155–162.

Albee, G. W. (1996). Social Darwinism and political models of mental/emotional problems. *Special Issue of Journal of Primary Prevention, 17*, 3–16.

Albee, G. W. (2000a). Commentary on prevention and counseling psychology. *The Counseling Psychologist, 28*, 845–853.

Albee, G. W. (2000b). The future of primary prevention. *Journal of Primary Prevention, 21*, 7–9.

Albee, G. W., & Canetto, S. S. (1996). A family focused model of prevention. In C. A. Heflinger & C. T. Nixon (Eds.), *Families and the mental health system for children and adolescents: Policy, services, and research* (Vol. 2, pp. 41–62). Thousand Oaks, CA: Sage.

Albee, G. W., & Perry, M. (1998). Economic and social causes of sexism and of the exploitation of women. *Journal of Community and Applied Social Psychology, 8*, 145–160.

Albee, G. W., & Ryan-Finn, K. D. (1993). An overview of primary prevention. *Journal of Counseling and Development, 72*, 115–123.

Allen, J. P., Philliber, S., Herrling, S., & Kuperminc, G. P. (1997). Preventing teen pregnancy and academic failure: Experimental evaluation of a developmentally based approach. *Child Development, 68*, 729–742.

American Psychiatric Association. (2000). *Diagnostic and statistical manual of mental disorders* (4th ed., text revision). Washington, DC: Author.

American Psychological Association. (2003). Guidelines on multicultural education, training, research, practice, and organizational change for psychologists. *American Psychologist, 58*, 377–402.

American School Counselor Association. (2003). *The ASCA National Model: A framework for school counseling programs.* Alexandria, VA: Author.

August, G. J., Lee, S. S., Bloomquist, M. L., Realmuto, G. M., & Hecter, J. M. (2003). Dissemination of an evidence-based prevention innovation for aggressive children living in culturally diverse, urban neighborhoods: The *Early Risers* effectiveness study. *Prevention Science, 4*, 271–286.

Bandura, A. (1977). *Social learning theory.* New York: General Learning Press.

Barnett, W. S. (1993). Benefit-cost analysis of preschool education: Findings from a 25-year follow-up. *American Journal of Orthopsychiatry, 63*, 500–508.

Benson, P. L. (1997). *All kids are our kids: What communities must do to raise caring and responsible children and adolescents.* San Francisco: Jossey-Bass.

Black, M., & Krishnakumar, A. (1998). Children in low-income urban settings: Interventions to promote mental health and well-being. *American Psychologist, 53*, 635–646.

Bogenschneider, K. (1996). Family related prevention programs: An ecological risk/protective theory for building prevention programs, policies, and community capacity to support youth. *Family Relations, 45*, 127–138.

Borders, L., & Drury, S. (1992). Comprehensive school counseling programs: A review for policymakers and practitioners. *Journal of Counseling & Development, 70*, 487–498.

Bronfenbrenner, U. (1979). *The ecology of human development.* Cambridge, MA: Harvard University Press.

Brooks-Gunn, J., & Duncan, G. J. (1997). The effects of poverty on children: The future of children. *Future of Children, 7*, 55–71.

Caplan, G. (1964). *Principles of preventive psychiatry.* New York: Basic Books

Caplan, G., & Caplan, R. B. (2000). The future of primary prevention. *The Journal of Primary Prevention, 21*, 131–136.

Castro, F. G., Barrera, M., Jr., & Martinez, C. R., Jr. (2004). The cultural adaptation of prevention interventions: Resolving tensions between fidelity and fit. *Prevention Science, 5*, 41–45.

Catalano, R. F., Berglund, M. L., Ryan, J. A. M., Lonczak, H. S., & Hawkins, J. D. (2002). Positive youth development in the United States: Research findings on evaluations of positive youth development programs. *Prevention & Treatment, 5*(15). Retrieved August, 1, 2002, from http://journals.apa.org.osiyou.cc.columbia.edu:2048/prevention/volume5/pre0050015a.html

Chronister, K. M., McWhirter, B. T., & Kerewsky, S. D. (2004). Prevention from an ecological framework. In R. K. Conyne & E. P. Cook (Eds.), *Ecological counseling: An innovative approach to conceptualizing person-environment interaction* (pp. 109–142). Alexandria, VA: American Counseling Association Press.

Cichetti, D., & Toth, S. L. (1992). The role of developmental theory in prevention and intervention. *Development & Psychopathology: Special Developmental Approaches to Prevention and Intervention, 4*, 489–493.

Clayton, C., Ballif-Spanvill, B., & Hunsaker, M. D. (2001). Preventing violence and teaching peace: A review of promising and effective antiviolence, conflict-resolution, and peace programs for elementary school children. *Applied & Preventative Psychology, 10*, 1–10.

Cohen, M. A. (1998). The monetary value of saving a high-risk youth. *Journal of Quantitative Criminology, 14*, 5–33.

Coie, J. D., Watt, N. F., West, S. G., Hawkins, J. D., Asarnow, J. R., Markman, H. J., et al. (1993). The science of prevention: A conceptual framework and some directions for a national research program. *American Psychologist, 48*, 1013–1022.

Conduct Problems Prevention Research Group. (1999). Initial impact of the Fast Track prevention trial for conduct problems: I. The high risk sample. *Journal of Consulting and Clinical Psychology, 67*, 631–647.

Conyne, R. K. (1994). Preventive counseling. *Counseling and Human Development, 27*, 1–10.

Conyne, R. K. (2004). *Preventive counseling: Helping people to become empowered in systems and settings.* New York: Brunner-Routledge.

Conyne, R. K., & Cook, E. P. (2004). Understanding persons within environments: An introduction to ecological counseling. In R. K. Conyne & E. P. Cook (Eds.), *Ecological counseling: An innovative approach to conceptualizing person-environment interaction* (pp. 3–35). Alexandria, VA: American Counseling Association.

Cowen, E. L. (1991). In pursuit of wellness. *American Psychologist, 46*, 404–408.

Cowen, E. L. (1994). The enhancement of psychological wellness: Challenges and opportunities. *American Journal of Community Psychology, 22*, 149–179.

Cowen, E. L. (1996). The ontogenesis of primary prevention: Lengthy strides and stubbed toes. *American Journal of Community Psychology, 24*, 235–249.

Cowen, E. (2000). Community psychology and routes to psychological wellness. In J. Rappaport & E. Seidman (Eds), *Handbook of community psychology* (pp. 79–99). New York: Kluwer.

Cowen, R. L. (1983). Primary prevention in mental health: Past, present and future. In R. Felnes, I. Jason, J. Moritsuqu, & S. Farber (Eds.), *Preventive psychology: Theory, research, and practice* (pp. 11–25). New York: Pergamon.

De La Rosa, M. R., Recio Adrados, J. L., Kennedy, N. J., & Milburn, N. (1993). Current gaps and new directions for studying drug use and abuse behavior in minority youth. In M. R. De La Rosa & J. L. Recio Adrados (Eds.), *Drug use among minority youth: Advances in research and methodology* (pp. 321–341). Rockville, MD: NIDA Research Monograph 130, NIDA.

Dryfoos, J. G. (1997). The prevalence of problem behaviors: Implications for programs. In R. P. Weissberg, T. P. Gullotta, R. L. Hampton, B. A. Ryan, & G. R. Adams (Eds.), *Healthy children 2010: Enhancing children's wellness* (pp. 17–46). Thousand Oaks, CA: Sage.

Durlak, J. (2003). Effective prevention and health promotion programming. In T. P. Gullotta & M. Bloom (Eds.), *Encyclopedia of primary prevention and health promotion* (pp. 61–69). New York: Kluwer.

Durlak, J. A., & Wells, A. M. (1997). Primary prevention mental health programs for children and adolescents: A meta-analytic review. *American Journal of Community Psychology, 25,* 115–152.

Elias, M. J. (1997). Reinterpreting dissemination of prevention programs as widespread implementation with effectiveness and fidelity. In R. P. Weissberg, T. P. Gullotta, R. L. Hampton, B. A. Ryan, & G. R. Adams (Eds.), *Establishing preventive services* (pp. 253–289). Thousand Oaks, CA: Sage.

Gottfredson, D. C., Fink, C. M., Skroban, S., & Gottfredson, G. D. (1997). Making prevention work. In R. P. Weissberg, T. P. Gullotta, R. L. Hampton, B. A. Ryan, & G. R. Adams (Vol. Eds.), *Issues in children's and families' lives: Vol. 9: Healthy children 2010: Establishing preventive services* (pp. 219–252). Thousand Oaks, CA: Sage.

Greenberg, M. T., Domitrovich, C., & Bumbarger, B. (1999). *Preventing mental disorders in school-age children: A review of the effectiveness of prevention programs.* Washington, DC: Center for Mental Health Services, Substance Abuse Mental Health Services Administration, U.S. Department of Health and Human Services.

Greenberg, M., Weissberg, R., O'Brien, M., Zins, J., Fredericks, L., Resnik, H., et al. (2003). Enhancing school-based prevention and youth development through coordinated social, emotional and academic learning. *American Psychologist, 58,* 466–474.

Johnson, C. A., Pentz, M. A., Weber, M. D., Dwyer, J. H., Baer, N., MacKinnon, D. P., et al. (1990). Relative effectiveness of comprehensive community programming for drug abuse prevention with high-risk and low-risk adolescents. *Journal of Consulting and Clinical Psychology, 58,* 447–456.

Kenny, M., Waldo, M., Warter, E., & Barton, C. (2002). School-linked prevention: Theory, science, and practice for enhancing the lives of children and youth. *The Counseling Psychologist, 30,* 726–747.

Keys, S. G., & Lockhart, E. J. (1999). The school counselor's role in facilitating multisystemic change. *Professional School Counseling, 3,* 101–107.

Kumpfer, K. L., & Alvarado, R. (2003). Family-strengthening approaches for the prevention of youth problem behaviors. *American Psychologist, 58,* 457–465.

Kumpfer, K. L., Alvarado, R., Smith, P., & Bellamy, N. (2002). Cultural sensitivity and adaptation in family-based prevention interventions. *Prevention Science, 3,* 241–246.

Lerner, R. M. (1995). *America's youth in crisis: Challenges and choices for programs and policies.* Thousand Oaks, CA: Sage.

Lerner, R. M. (2001). Promoting promotion in the development of prevention science. *Applied Developmental Science, 5,* 254–257.

Lewin, K. (1951). *Field theory in social science.* New York: Harper.

Lorion, R. P., Price, R. H., & Eaton, W. (1989). The prevention of child and adolescent disorders: From theory to research. In D. Shaffer, I. Philips, & N. B. Enzer (Eds.), *Prevention of mental disorders, alcohol and drug use in children and adolescents* (pp. 55–96). Rockville, MD: DHHS (DHHS Pub. No. ADM 89-1646)

Luthar, S., & Cicchetti, D. (2000). The construct of resilience: Implications for interventions and social policies. *Development and Psychopathology, 12,* 857–885.

Maggs, J. L., & Schulenberg, J. (2001). Editors' introduction: Prevention as altering the course of development and the complementary purposes of developmental and prevention sciences. *Applied Developmental Science, 5,* 196–200.

McWhirter, J., McWhirter, B., McWhirter, A., & McWhirter, E. H. (1995). Youth at risk: Another point of view. *Journal of Counseling & Development, 73,* 567–569.

Miller, G. E., Brehm, K., & Whitehouse, S. (1998). Reconceptualizing school-based prevention for antisocial behavior within a resiliency framework. *School Psychology Review, 27,* 364.

Mirowski, J., & Ross, C. E. (1989). *Social causes of psychological stress.* Hawthorn, NY: Aldine de Gruyter.

Mock, M. (2001). Working with Asian American families. In interventions with multi-cultural families (Part 2). *The Family Psychologist, 17,* 5–7.

Mrazek, P. J. (2002). *Enhancing the well-being of America's children through the strengthening of natural and community supports: Opportunities for prevention and early mental health intervention.* Paper prepared for the Subcommittee on Children and Families, President's New Freedom Commission on Mental Health.

Mrazek, P., & Haggerty, R. (1994). *Reducing risks for mental disorders: Frontiers for preventive intervention research.* Washington, DC: National Academy Press.

Nation, M., Crusto, C., Wandersman, A., Kumpfer, K., Seybolt, D., Morrissey-Kane, E., et al. (2003). What works in prevention: Principles and effective prevention programs. *American Psychologist, 58,* 449–456.

Osborne, J. L., & House, R. M. (1995). Evaluation of counselor education program: A proposed plan. *Counselor Education and Supervision, 24*, 253–268.

Pentz, M. A. (1998). Preventing drug abuse through the community: Multicomponent programs that make a difference. In A. Sloboda & W. B. Hansen (Eds.), *Putting research to work for the community* (pp. 73–86). Rockville, MD: National Institute on Drug Abuse. (NIDA Publication No. 98-4293)

Perry, M. J. (1996). The relationship between social class and mental disorder. *Journal of Primary Prevention, 17*, 17–30.

President's New Freedom Commission on Mental Health. (2003). *Achieving the promise: Transforming mental health care in America. Final report* (U.S. DHHS Publication No. SMA-03-3832). Rockville, MD: U.S. Department of Health and Human Services.

Price, R. H., Cowen, E. L., Lorion, R. P., & Ramos-McKay, J. (1988). *Fourteen ounces of prevention: A casebook for practitioners*. Washington, DC: American Psychological Association.

Prilleltensky, I., & Prilleltensky, O. (2003). Synergies for wellness and liberation in counseling psychology. *The Counseling Psychologist. 20*, 1–9.

Ringel, J., & Sturm, R. (2001). National estimates of mental health utilization and expenditure for children in 1998. *Journal of Behavioral Health Services & Research, 28*, 319–332.

Rogler, L. H. (1999). Methodological sources of cultural insensitivity in mental health research. *American Psychologist, 54*, 424–433.

Romano, J. L., & Hage, S. M. (2000). Prevention and counseling psychology: Revitalizing commitments for the 21st century. *The Counseling Psychologist, 28*, 733–763.

Romano, J. L., & Kachgal, M. M. (2004). Counseling psychology and school counseling: An underutilized partnership. *The Counseling Psychologist, 32*, 184–215.

Rotheram-Borus, M. J. (1988). Assertiveness training with children. In R. H. Price, E. L. Cowen, R. P. Lorion, & J. Ramos-McKay (Eds.), *Fourteen ounces of prevention* (pp. 83-97). Washington, DC: American Psychological Association.

Satchere, D. (2000). Foreword. In U.S. Public Health Service. *Report of the Surgeon General's Conference on Children's Mental Health: A National Action Agenda*. Washington, DC: Department of Health and Human Services, 2000. Retrieved March 2, 2006, from http://www.hhs.gov/surgeongeneral/topics/cmh/childreport.htm#ack

Schmidt, J. (2003). *Counseling in schools*. New York: Pearson Education.

Schweinhart, L. J., Montie, J., Xiang, Z., Barnett, W. S., Belfield, C. R., & Nores, M. (2005). *Lifetime effects: The High/Scope Perry preschool study through age 40*. (Monographs of the High/Scope Educational Research Foundation, 14). Ypsilanti, MI: High/Scope Press.

Schweinhart, L. J., & Weikart, D. P. (1988). The High/Scope Perry Preschool Study though age twenty-seven. In R. H. Price, E. L. Cowen, R. P. Lorion, & J. Ramos-McKay (Eds.), *Fourteen ounces of prevention: A casebook for practitioners* (pp. 53–65). Washington, DC: American Psychological Association.

Shepard, J., & Carlson, J. (2003). An empirical evaluation of school-based prevention programs that involve parents. *Psychology in the Schools, 40*, 641–656.

Sheras, P., Cornell, D., & Bostain, D. (1996). The Virginia youth violence project:Transmitting psychological knowledge on youth violence to schools and communities. *Professional Psychology: Research and Practice, 27*, 401–406.

Smith, E. J. (2006). The strength-base counseling model. *The Counseling Psychologist, 34*, 13–79.

Smith, E. P., Boutte, G., Zigler, E., & Finn-Stevenson, M. (2004). Opportunities for schools to promote resilience in children and youth: A strengths perspective. In K. Maton, C. Schellenbach, & B. Leadbetter (Eds.), *Investing in children families, schools and communities: Resilience and strengths-based research and policy* (pp. 213–231). Washington, DC: American Psychological Association.

Stevenson, J. F., McMillan, B., Mitchell, R. E., & Blanco, M. (1998). Project HOPE: Altering risk and protective factors among high risk Hispanic youth and their families. *The Journal of Primary Prevention, 18*, 287–317.

Tolan, P. H., & Dodge, K. A. (2005). Children's mental health as a primary care and concern: A system for comprehensive support and service. *American Psychologist, 60*, 601–614.

U.S. Department of Health and Human Services. (1999). *Mental health: A report of the Surgeon General—Older adults and mental health*. Rockville, MD: U.S. Department of Health and Human Services, Substance Abuse and Mental Health Services Administration, Center for Mental Health Services, National Institutes of Health, National Institute of Mental Health.

U.S. Department of Health and Human Services (2000). Healthy people 2010 (Conference 1 & 2). Washington, DC: Author.

U.S. Surgeon General. (2001). *Mental health: Culture, race, and ethnicity*. Washington, DC: U.S. Department of Health and Human Services.

The Victorian Centre of Excellence in Eating Disorders and the Eating Disorders Foundation of Victoria. (2002). *An eating disorder resource for schools*. Retrieved September 17, 2007, from http://www.mercyministries.com.au/resource/CEED_Eating_Disorder_Resource.pdf

Vera, E. M. (2000). A recommitment to prevention work in counseling psychology. *The Counseling Psychologist, 28*, 829–837.

Vera, E. M., & Reese. L. E. (2000). Preventive interventions with school-age youth. In S. D. Brown & R. W. Lent (Eds.), *Handbook of counseling psychology* (pp. 411–434). New York: Wiley.

Walsh, M., Galassi, J., Murphy, J., & Park-Taylor, J. (2002). A conceptual framework for counseling psychologists in schools. *The Counseling Psychologist, 30*, 682–703.

Wandersman, A., & Florin, P. (2003). Community interventions and effective prevention. *American Psychologist, 58*, 441–448.

Weissberg, R. P., Kumpfer, K. L., & Seligman, M. E. P. (2003). Prevention that works for children and youth: An introduction. *American Psychologist, 58*, 425–432.

Weissberg, R. P., Walberg, H. J., O'Brien, M. U., & Kuster, C. B. (2003). *Long-term trends in the well-being of children and youth*. Washington, DC: Child Welfare League of America Press.

Wolin, S. J., & Wolin, S. (1993). *The resilient self: How survivors of troubled families rise above adversity*. New York: Villard Books.

Yoshikawa, H. (1994). Prevention as cumulative protection: Effects of early famous support and education and chronic delinquency and its risks. *Psychological Bulletin, 115*, 28–54.

XXVI
INDIVIDUAL COUNSELING AS INTERVENTION IN THE SCHOOLS

JERI L. LEE AND STACIE E. PUTMAN
Tennessee State University

Intervention in the schools takes the form of individual counseling when immediacy, brevity, and specialized solution focus are required to assist in solving problems, reducing stress, or enhancing a student's academic and social success. To understand the role and applications of individual counseling in the schools, it is necessary for professional school counselors (PSCs) to consider the following:

- Definitions/model for individual counseling in the schools
- Mandates for scope of practice for individual counseling in the schools
- Basic competencies required for individual counseling in the schools
- Appropriate theoretical orientations for individual counseling in the schools

Kutash and Duchnowki (2004) described the importance of individual counseling in the schools during their examination of urban children with emotional disturbances: "The most common service currently being supplied by school personnel was individual counseling and this was provided for 63% of the students while child-serving agency personnel were providing individual counseling for 17% of the youth" (p. 235).

Definitions/Model for Individual Counseling in the Schools

Defining Individual Counseling in the Schools

Gibson and Mitchell (2003) stated that individual counseling is "a one-to-one relationship involving a trained counselor and focuses on some aspect of a client's adjustment, developmental, or decision-making needs" (p. 76). More specifically, individual counseling in the schools takes two forms: traditional and focused. Traditional individual counseling in the schools is offered to all students. By contrast, focused counseling is reserved for those experiencing significant personal problems. In other words, the traditional type depicts the relationship between a PSC and all students in his or her caseload; the focused type depicts the relationship between a PSC and students identified as at risk.

Traditional individual counseling in the schools. Baker and Gerler's (2004) description of individual counseling, applied here as a definition for traditional individual counseling in the schools, is "part of an individual planning process for which the goals are to help students monitor their career, academic and personal development" (p. 118).

Focused individual counseling in the schools. Focused individual counseling in the schools refers to a confidential relationship between a student and a PSC counselor focused on enhancing the student's academic and/or social success at school by identifying a problem, establishing and implementing a solution involving both internal and external resources, and then monitoring the results to determine effectiveness. Focused individual counseling is geared toward at-risk students.

The concept of at-risk students can be difficult to operationalize. Baker and Gerler (2004) listed eight critical personal problems identified in the schools as

- Acting-out behaviors
- Underachievement
- Disabilities
- Grief
- Suicide ideation and depression

- Substance abuse
- Social isolation
- Floundering career planning

For each of these personal problems, the PSC assists students by clarifying their problems, identifying internal and external resources, and referring out when a diagnosable condition is suspected and further treatment is warranted.

A Model for Individual Counseling in the Schools

Orton's (1997) counseling model, consistent with the previous definitions, suggested four stages:

- Build a counseling relationship
- Assess specific counseling needs
- Design and implement interventions
- Conduct evaluation and closure

These four stages apply whether you are offering traditional or focused individual counseling. A relationship must be formed before any student will open up to you. Assessing needs or identifying problems is a critical role in both prevention and intervention. Interventions that draw upon a student's internal and external resources become the solutions to identified problems. Follow-through in the form of ongoing evaluation and, ultimately, closure completes the relationship.

Mandates for Scope of Practice for Individual Counseling in the Schools

Determining when to provide individual counseling in the schools requires a clear grasp of the PSC's scope of practice regarding individual counseling. Three initiatives establish individual counseling as a critical function of PSCs: The American School Counselor Association's (ASCA) National Model for Comprehensive School Counseling Programs (1998), The National School Counselor Training Initiative (Guerra, 1998), and The School–Community Collaboration Model (Campbell & Dahir, 1997).

Evidence-Based Treatment

Even though PSCs possess a rich tradition as the designated providers of individual counseling in the schools, the methods used for individual counseling should be evidence based, relying on research to establish the effectiveness of different approaches in the context of each presenting problem. In other words, while individual counseling is the intervention, evidence-based treatment (EBT) is the standard of care.

EBT is said to be taking place in a school's guidance office when the effectiveness of interventions can be justified according to research. Historically, PSCs were not enthusiastically involved in research. Cramer, Herr, Morris, and Frantz (1970) noted, "Too much effort is spent by counselors in evading the issue of validated knowledge, or in scoffing at research because the counselor is too incompetent to use the results" (p. viii).

More recently, Allen (1992) found that 84% of the PSCs in his study agreed that conducting research is valuable, and Bauman (2004) discovered that 69.5% of the PSCs in her study reported researching evidence of effectiveness before implementing a program. Finally, Cunningham and Henggeler (2001) pointed out, "If school-based services are to have a significant impact on targeted problems, logic dictates that evidence-based interventions hold the most promise" (p. 222).

Scope of Practice

Determining when to provide individual counseling requires a clear grasp of scope of practice issues. Otherwise, it would be impossible to justify spending several hours with one at-risk student while spending considerably less time with other students. Individual counseling in the schools is predicated on federal legislation, professional standards, ethical standards, state statutes, and case law. School policy, job description, principal's expectations, and school-specific characteristics give specific guidance (and protection) as well.

Scope of practice defined. Scope of practice refers to the boundaries establishing which duties fall to a specific group of licensed professionals and which fall outside their purview. Traditionally, licensed professionals acting outside of their mandated scope of practice face liability; hence, PSCs do not perform (among other things) hypnosis, appendectomies, or even assessments of intellectual functioning.

Much of the academic training for PSCs is geared also to mental health professionals seeking licensure as psychologists, clinical social workers, or professional counselors. Consequently, it is not surprising that some PSCs emerge from their academic training overwhelmed by the far-reaching breadth of a field that appears at times to promise healing of all school-age maladies. Scope of practice serves as a reminder of reasonable boundaries.

Federal Mandates

A good start to determining when and with whom individual counseling is appropriate is to examine federal laws establishing appropriations for school counselors to perform specific duties and to review PSCs' professional and ethical standards. See chapter 46 of this text for a discussion of relevant federal laws and professional and ethical standards.

State Mandates

PSCs must be aware of the types of counseling they are specifically mandated by state law to provide, for such is the framework for grasping scope of practice of individual counseling. Many states refer to counseling that offers assistance with academic and career decisions and with social and personal problems. Posting your state's description of the PSC position serves to remind you and others daily of the state-mandated reasons for your presence in the schools.

State education laws and, to a lesser degree, state mental health laws, establish the PSC's scope of practice. From the section of the state code that establishes the school counselor position to the detailed school employee guidelines to the mental health professional dictates of confidentiality and a higher duty to report and to protect, state legislation is full of applicable references to the duties of PSCs. State code also offers scope of practice delineation among related professions that is significant to avoid overstepping of boundaries that draw the lines between PSCs and school administrators, teachers, and other mental health specialists, making the PSC's job more manageable, the caseload for individual counseling more reasonable, and the liability less tenuous.

When principals call on PSCs to administer corporal punishment or refill snack machines, a good grasp of scope of practice comes in handy. For example, one portion of the *Tennessee Education Laws Annotated's* outline of the duties of the school guidance counselor clearly establishes that they are "not responsible for general school administration or reports, except such as may be connected with the school's guidance program" (LexisNexis, 2003, p. 250). If your state doesn't have such a law to limit scope of practice, then legislative advocacy may be in order.

Likewise, when a student presents with significant mental health issues requiring long-term, intensive treatment, a firm grasp of scope of practice lead PSCs to refer the student to an appropriate mental health professional rather than attempting to operate outside of their training. Treating a student in need of professional mental health intervention is outside the PSC's scope of practice and as such opens the PSC up for liability as well as an unreasonable individual counseling caseload.

Look at the middle school basketball coach, for example. She may become concerned with one of her star player's golf swing or algebra difficulties or recent ankle sprain, yet realizing these fall out of her area of expertise, she would refer each of these problems to the applicable expert. Her job then becomes simply monitoring the progress by asking questions and being interested and concerned. Likewise, the PSC sometimes identifies serious problems getting in the way of school success. Realizing which of these problems to refer is as important as handling the problems that fall clearly within the scope of practice.

No profession can define a scope of practice (and give meaningful legislative input) without having a firm grasp of related professionals' scopes of practice. This is a challenging task, yet has the potential of reducing inappropriate demands and bad feelings in general. It is critical to know where our own boundaries end and another professional's take over, as it can become frustrating when another professional repeatedly does not understand your priorities, your limitations, your legal and ethical guidelines, or your scope of practice in general. It is your duty to communicate it professionally (citing sources) and repeatedly (if necessary), particularly when called upon to offer individual counseling that you have deemed inappropriate.

Besides the statutory mandates establishing scope of practice for PSCs, there are also significant statutory mandates establishing scope of practice for the professionals with whom the PSC most frequently comes in contact—teachers, principals, school psychologists, school social workers, school nurses, and the agencies that serve as in-school providers or outside referral sources, including mental health agencies, juvenile courts, and the state's children's services departments.

Teachers. Teachers are often the major source for identifying students who need individual counseling services because teachers spend so much time with students yet are unable to get off task long enough to offer specialized assistance. Mental health consultations, timely classroom intervention, classroom guidance instruction, feedback on standardized testing, and supportive listening are some of the ways to support teachers. Most of the teachers' legal mandates established by state law apply to PSCs as well, so there is a clear scope of practice overlap. Teachers need to be apprised on a need-to-know basis regarding students they refer to the guidance office, providing only the information obtained during individual counseling that is necessary to assist the student's success in that class.

Principals. The PSC shares many of the principal's foci regarding individual counseling, such as maintaining student record confidentiality, parents' rights, identifying at-risk students, enforcing zero-tolerance breaches, protecting civil rights, and adhering to all relevant state and federal laws. Therefore, communication with the principal regarding individual counseling with students is a necessary duty within the PSC's scope of practice. Such communication, however, never discharges the PSC's professional obligations, such as duty to protect, as PSCs are professionals within their own right. Still, principals, as the administrative supervisors of PSCs, deserve to be kept abreast of all matters that fall under their purview, including but not limited to, notification when communicating with the following:

- School's attorney
- Department of children's services
- Police
- Courts
- High-risk students
- Anyone complaining about the guidance office services

Related professionals. Regarding school psychologists, school social workers, school nurses, and workers in mental health agencies, juvenile courts, and state children services departments, it would behoove the PSC to become as familiar as possible with the mandated roles of each of these in order to facilitate appropriate interactions.

Case Law

Case law (court decisions) constantly interprets scope of practice accountability. Criminal and civil cases at the state, regional, and federal level regarding PSCs specifically and education and mental health employees in general impact PSCs. Although many aspects of education law and mental health law fall outside of their purview, PSCs still benefit from studying court cases involving professional educators and mental health counseling professionals as well as those naming guidance counselors specifically.

Job Description, School Policy, School Characteristics, Principal's Expectations

Although it may seem self-evident, a clear understanding of and adherence to the duties described in the PSC's job description provide focus, decrease risk of liability, and justify the use of time. Likewise, school policy provides guidance and protection and should be carefully followed and regularly cited.

Hopefully, from the first interview as a prospective hire, the PSC has a firm grasp of the principal's expectations, from theoretical approach to school management to specific view of the priorities of a guidance office and where individual counseling falls in the organizational structure. School characteristics such as attrition, crime, pregnancy rate, and achievement scores likely impact the principal's emphasis (or de-emphasis) on individual counseling activities.

Facilitation of School Operations

Enhanced school functioning is the focus of all PSC's counseling services. Even if that is the clear aim, and it is determined that it cannot be accomplished in limited visits, a referral might prove more appropriate. The line between providing an open door and receptive manner and fostering dependence is one easily blurred, so the PSC needs to refocus students to the task of getting successfully through the school day when personal issues arise and empowering them to handle future problems with minimal intervention.

Since anarchy is the enemy of the school system, PSCs justify their individual counseling duties (and their very existence, for that matter) based also on their role in facilitating the smooth operation of the school. In their pursuit of efficiently running schools, principals and teachers often call on PSCs to act immediately to refocus students who have had their school day interrupted or who are interfering with the learning of others. The PSC who remains flexible can be a critical ally in the school's overall academic mission.

For example, a child may begin to cry in class due to grief issues or a teenager may become anxious and overly distracted due to an unplanned pregnancy scare. In both cases, the PSC must be able to accept a referral on short notice, complete an intake, and determine the necessary intervention to get the student refocused and back on task in the classroom. A short-term, solution-focused approach serves the needs of the school best. When a higher level intervention is needed, the PSC refers the student to the appropriate resource and targets the student as at risk, providing case management oversight.

Schools represent all of society's problems, and PSCs are called upon to intervene when children and adolescents behave as a manifestation of these problems. In order for teachers to focus on academics, PSCs intervene with students who are experiencing personal and social distractions from academic pursuits with the goal of restoring the student's academic present mindedness. The ethical standards of ASCA (1992) address personal needs of the student as the PSC's domain, making it appropriate for school personnel to rely on the PSC to intervene.

Safe Place

The guidance office should be viewed as a safe place for students who may have difficulty fitting in at times, such as those who are gay or lesbian, foreign born, homeless, of a minority culture, mentally ill, handicapped, or intellectually impaired, and even those who are intellectually or artistically gifted. Individual counseling with these students can offer acceptance and belonging.

After identifying the types of students for whom your student population seems an unlikely match, your efforts can ensure that they feel accepted and welcome in your office and in seeking your services. You cannot offer individual counseling if they never come into your office, so try to attract these students by making a point to target each identified population in ways such as the following:

- Acknowledge holidays and news events celebrating them.
- Highlight teachers and other school employees (as well as celebrities) with whom they identify.
- Provide information regarding laws and court decisions that dissuade prejudicial treatment of their population.
- Use and encourage embracing language which avoids heterosexism, sexism, eurocentricity, religiosity, and so forth.

Efforts such as these will not go unnoticed by the other school staff and should provide an opportunity for the guidance office to foster acceptance, embrace differences, and model the school official's role in supporting students.

Screening

Whether the students drop by just to talk or are referred due to behavior problems, use the opportunities to screen them. File student interests (both in your mind and in their file) such as "interested in debate" or "needs assistance with standardized test anxiety," so you can contact them personally when resources or opportunities arise. Try to remember that just because the squeaky wheel usually gets the grease does not mean the easygoing student should not rate your attention as well.

Every time you meet with a student, be mindful of ruling out the existence of any of the following:

- Danger of harm to self or others
- Duty to report or warn
- Zero-tolerance issues
- Medical problems
- Handicapping condition
- Need for an immediate response to facilitate school's functioning
- Good fit with any existing counseling groups
- Possible *Diagnostic and Statistical Manual* (*DSM-IV-TR;* American Psychiatric Association, 2000) diagnosis

DSM-IV-TR. School counselors must be aware of critical mental health problems common among children and adolescents, such as those listed in the *DSM-IV-TR,* just as they should be familiar with developmental milestones. Identifying and referring, rather than treating, becomes the focus when significant mental illness is suspected.

Regarding individual counseling, a good rule of thumb for referral versus in-school treatment is the inclusion of a preponderance of the students' presenting problems in the *DSM-IV-TR*. Problems that clearly fall short of a *DSM-IV-TR* diagnosis yet directly interfere with a student's ability to achieve academic goals during the school day are the purview of PSCs.

Just as some parts of society in general (Berk, 2003) and some early psychologists specifically (Buckley, 1989) treated children as little adults, "[h]istorically our understanding and classification of child psychopathology has been based on knowledge obtained from adult disorders" (Last, 1993, p. 29). The *DSM-IV-TR*, however, has a separate section devoted to disorders first evidenced in infancy, childhood, or adolescence, including

- Adjustment disorders;
- Attention deficit/hyperactivity disorder;
- Disruptive behavior disorders;
- Anxiety disorders;
- Mood and depressive disorders; and
- Substance and related disorders (American Psychiatric Association, 2003).

The *DSM-IV-TR* serves as a helpful tool during screening intakes to determine if the symptoms of a diagnosable mental problem are potentially present. If enough of the criteria is met to warrant concern, a referral to a licensed mental health professional to rule out or to confirm the diagnostic impression is in order. Although PSCs are not trained mental health diagnosticians, it is reasonable to expect they possess sufficient skills to make a diagnostic impression in the context of referring and assisting with educational plans.

Basic Competencies for Individual Counseling in the Schools

As stated earlier, PSCs should be competent to give help to those students who are in need of individual counseling. Egan (2004) offered as the operational definition of counseling, "An interpersonal relationship between someone actively seeking help and someone willing to give help who is capable of, or trained to help in a setting that permits help to be given and received" (p. 31).

Counseling is a skill and a process that is distinguished from advising, listening, and directing. It involves being tuned in to the student client both in thought and in feeling (Sciarra, 2004). While the student must assume some responsibility to participate fully, cooperatively, and willingly in the counseling process, counselor competence is also an important factor, making positive outcomes possible.

So what makes a counselor competent to provide individual counseling in the schools? This is the question that many school counselor training programs seek to answer through their programs of study. Often, these training competencies are determined by outside credentialing bodies such as The National Council for Accreditation of Teacher Education or The Council for Accreditation of Counseling and Related Educational Programs. Accreditation by such entities is designed to protect the public against those who would masquerade as possessing certain skills and training. Credentialing provides, at the very least, minimally acceptable training and experience requirements and seeks to offer a common core of learning to all PSCs who graduate from accredited degree programs (Gibson & Mitchell, 2003; Sciarra, 2004). State licensure requirements may enhance competency further by requiring the demonstration of competency in additional, specialized areas.

The National Standards for School Counseling Programs and Suggested Student Competencies

Campbell and Dahir (1997) identified nine standards, three in each of the three areas: academic development, career development, and personal and social development. Attached to each standard is a list of competencies or desired learning outcomes of students served by school counseling programs. In order for school counselors to help students achieve these learning outcomes, they must be skilled in implementing interventions and programs that are designed to illicit results in these three areas of development. Keeping the national standards in mind when counseling students and competently implementing programs that address these areas helps maximize student learning and overall social and personal development.

Competencies in each of the following areas should be demonstrated when conducting individual counseling with students:

- multicultural issues;
- personal limitations;
- an understanding of how personal values and beliefs impact work with students, families, teachers, communities, and so forth;
- a repertoire of interventions and strategies that are developmentally appropriate;
- a familiarity with theories and theoretical techniques that are most effective with certain populations, issues, cultures, and so forth;
- access to appropriate referral sources;
- a knowledge of community resources, climates, and so forth that impact student performance; and
- discernment regarding legal and ethical issues, including case law that impacts school counselors' roles and functions.

While this list is not exhaustive, it gives PSCs an idea of the critical areas of professional development and training required to remain competent, skilled, and knowledgeable.

Appropriate Theoretical Orientations for Individual Counseling in the Schools

Once PSCs determine that a student is right for individual counseling, they must decide on which theoretical approach will best fit that student's unique set of circumstances. Theories provide guidelines that have been tested by experienced counselors and proven reliable through validated research. Theories help explain human behaviors and predict behavioral outcomes in certain circumstances. Theories also can help school counselors make sense of the human data they are given by students, parents, teachers, and administrators and then apply it in a coherent, meaningful framework that will assist the school counselor in developing strategies appropriate for each student's situation (Sciarra, 2004), such as their cultural identity. School counselors need to consider the larger contextual framework, plus the perspective of the student when choosing theoretical interventions. For example, failure to recognize, plan, and adapt to cultural considerations when working with students is unethical behavior and could harm the student.

Given the vast array of theories and theoretical techniques from which to choose, combined with the unique set of student circumstances, the PSC can be left feeling overwhelmed and unsure. This section will address those theories that have been proven most useful in dealing with student populations when conducting individual counseling.

Person-Centered Therapy

Developed by Carl Rogers, the person-centered theory stresses students' capability and responsibility to identify new and better ways to cope with their own lives. Students are experts on themselves and their lives, and they grow through self-exploration. Rogers (1951) emphasized the importance of the counselor who is warm, genuine, empathic, and caring. Counseling, according to Rogers, is a collaborative effort between the counselor and the client/student.

In order for the counselor to facilitate change in the client, three conditions must be present in the counselor:

1. Congruence/genuineness: Counselors are truly themselves when relating to students.
2. Unconditional positive regard: Counselors should have a deep and genuine caring for the student. According to Sciarra (2004), "in order to create an environment in which the child feels secure, school counselors cannot be judgmental, and they cannot personalize the child's successes or failures" (p. 23). Condemn the behavior, not the child.
3. Empathic understanding of the child's frame of reference: The school counselor must convey this understanding in a way that the child can feel. School counselors must see the child's world through their "glasses" while still retaining their own separateness.

Greenwood (2002) described the role of person-centered intervention with students who have survived trauma:

> Some children have such traumatic experiences that they need to defend vigorously against any thoughts or feelings which threaten to bring the painful memories back into consciousness. Repeated hurtful and traumatic experiences can affect the deeper structures of the brain, causing behaviour and learning difficulties, which are difficult to reverse. These defensive behaviours can be very hard for teachers to appreciate and cope with. Sometimes, when the threatened and feared feelings are triggered, a child's reaction can be beyond conscious control and reason, until they have calmed down. Very damaged children need emotional "holding," as well as a facilitating environment, to be able to learn and function acceptably in school. (p. 295)

Although the person-centered approach is an overriding philosophy in the schools (Colvin, 1999) and has been shown effective in several applications such as high school delinquency and crime prevention (Cassel, 2001) and self-acceptance promotion for children with disabilities (Williams & Lair, 1991), in its actual practice it is often superceded by time constraints and the immaturity of some at-risk students, resulting in a more directive, advice-giving approach (Colvin). While Roger's (1951) theory advocates for the counselor to assume a nondirective role that may prove to be ineffective in today's fast-paced world of academics, his underlying counselor characteristics are critically important, especially when building therapeutic relationships with children and adolescents in individual counseling and in other venues.

Reality Therapy

Developed by William Glasser (2000), reality therapy focuses on the here and now or the student's present behavior, and it does not emphasize the student's past. The past is only explored in order to understand the student's present behaviors. The goal of reality therapy is to help students take more effective control of their lives.

Glasser (2000) focused on the idea that all behavior is goal directed, that is, that people do not engage in behaviors from which they do not get something. All behavior is goal directed and designed to meet both psychological and physiological needs within the individual. It is the school counselor's role to determine what need(s) students are attempting to meet by the behaviors in which they engage and then to work with students in developing more appropriate coping plans for meeting those needs. This is often done through individual counseling with students. Through individual counseling, school counselors can explore, in more depth, the needs that drive student behavior and choice making. Students who learn to meet their needs in a positive and realistic manner develop a success identity (Glasser). Those students who meet their needs in irresponsible ways assume a failure identity. It is not the needs themselves that cause a student's problems, but rather the way he or she goes about meeting those needs. Reality therapy focuses on helping individuals develop personal responsibility for their own happiness and well-being.

Reality-therapy techniques have been shown effective with emotionally disturbed middle school students (Passaro, Moon, Wiest, & Wong, 2004). Also, Kyung-hee Kim (2002) incorporated reality therapy and choice therapy with play in developing the Responsibility Behavior Choice Program, increasing internal control and responsibility in Korean fifth graders.

When used in the school setting, and specifically within the context of individual counseling, reality therapy can provide the PSC with insight into what motivates student behavior. It can further help students see both short- and long-term consequences of their choices and behaviors, and help them learn to make better and more successful choices. The blending of reality therapy and choice therapy helps students understand that they can control their behavior and choose to behave appropriately (Grossman, 1990).

Adlerian Therapy/Individual Psychology

Much like reality therapy, Adlerian therapy views the total individual and sees all behavior as goal directed. Adlerian therapy has had a tremendous impact on today's school systems because of its utility of *social interest* or a sense of belonging to something outside of ourselves (Pryor &

Tollerud, 1999). Adler (1930, 1958) believed that developing social interest was most realized in the school setting and therefore, should be primarily addressed there.

According to Adler (1930, 1958) all behavior is purposeful and is designed to overcome perceived inferiorities and to develop self-actualization. Given a positive environment, human growth will take place. Much as in reality therapy, it is the counselor's role to determine what perceived inferiority is driving student behavior and interfering with a sense of belonging. Adler encouraged teachers and counselors to investigate the purpose of the negative behavior of students instead of simply reacting to that child's behaviors. An example of this principle in action follows.

A student was repeatedly sent to the counselor's office for attempting to "boss" his peers and his teacher. Whenever the teacher gave instructions to the class, the student would openly correct the teacher, reiterate the instructions, and point out peers who weren't following those instructions. His behaviors became frustrating for his teacher who felt he was attempting to usurp her authority in the classroom. Furthermore, his behaviors were isolating him from his peers because they saw him as a bully and a tattle-tale. The student, himself, was angry and frustrated at both his teacher and his peers, so the counselor decided to work with him in individual counseling twice a week for 30 minutes.

The counselor attempted to understand the purpose of the student's behaviors in the classroom by exploring how he felt before, during, and after his behaviors. She also explored his family situation, discovering that the student's family was homeless, often sleeping in several different places throughout the week, leaving the child feeling powerless and frustrated over his lack of control in his family life. The PSC then explored the student's feelings when he was bossing his teacher and peers, discovering that the student felt powerful and in control while acting out. The student was attempting to gain power and control in the only area of his life where he could: at school.

Once she discovered the purpose of the behavior, she was able to redirect his power seeking behavior to help him find ways to have healthy power, such as appointing him hall monitor at least once a week, allowing him an opportunity to exhibit healthy power. An immediate reduction in his bossing behaviors at school was observed, and rather than feeling isolated from his peers, he began to develop more of a sense of belonging.

Using the Adlerian approach in schools helps teachers, counselors, and administrators look beyond their emotional reactions to student misbehavior and deal more democratically with those behaviors. By seeking to understand the purpose of behavior rather than condemning/blaming the child, teachers and counselors maintain academic and therapeutic alliances with their students, increasing the overall likelihood of student success.

Although the Adlerian approach traditionally incorporates teachers and families when working with students who disrupt (Dinkmeyer, Pew, & Dinkmeyer, 1979), individual counseling has to suffice when families are unable or unwilling to participate (Sonstegard & Dreikurs, 1973).

Conflict resolution is one way, according to Clark (1994), to apply Adlerian principles to individual counseling in the schools. Focusing on cooperation, social equality, and mutual respect, the four steps in resolving conflicts, according to Clark, include

- Establish respect;
- Pinpoint the issue;
- Explore alternatives; and
- Share decision-making responsibility.

The Adlerian lifestyle construct is often a good fit with Latino Americans, as they interact individually within their Latin culture and with the majority culture (Frevert & Miranda, 1998). Therefore, counselors must gain competence in understanding and respecting the influences of their lifestyle, such as their history, cultural subgroups, effects of discrimination, family and social networks, possible language barriers, and the tendency to somaticize.

As with Latino Americans, Asian Americans tend to somaticize when feeling psychologically stressed, likely contributing to their reluctance to seek counseling and their preference for medical or spiritual intervention (Carlson & Carlson, 2000). In addition to reluctance to seek treatment, their reputation as a "model minority" due to their educational and economic successes (Sandhu, 1997) may be the reason Asian Americans are underrepresented in the cultural diversity literature. Still, J. M. Carlson and J. D. Carlson identified four specific aspects of the Adlerian model that are conducive to working with the Asian American population: "the focus on the client's social and cultural context, the emphasis on collaborative goal setting, the importance placed on the family environment, and social interest" (p. 214).

Watts (2003) summed up the appeal of an Adlerian approach to populations struggling to assimilate:

> Consistent with important multicultural emphases, Adlerian therapy is a *positive psychology* and approach to therapy that emphasizes prevention, optimism and hope, resilience and growth, competence, creativity and resourcefulness, social consciousness, and finding meaning and a sense of community in relationships. (p. 144)

Behavioral Theory

There are some situations where students, due to either developmental age, cognitive deficits, or other disorders, are unable to grasp the abstract nature of some theoretical interventions. In these cases, often a straight behavioral approach can prove successful. Developed by B. F. Skinner (1953), behavioral theory views all behavior as a set of learned responses to events, experiences, or stimuli in a person's life. The behaviorist believes that behavior can be modified by providing appropriate learning conditions and experiences. By setting up specific experiences and conditions, the counselor can help students "relearn" more acceptable ways of behaving. The goal is for counselors to "recondition" students by focusing on specific behavioral goals, emphasizing precise and repeatable methods (James & Gilliand, 2003). Feelings are secondary to behaviors when using behavioral theory and the counselor takes on a more directive role. Behavioral counselors attempt to uncover the antecedents, circumstances, and consequences of human behavior, and to thereby probe into the ABCs of human behavior. Once these are uncovered, the school counselor can then develop interventions or behavioral plans that will recondition student behavior.

Many school counselors utilize this approach with younger or developmentally delayed students because it is simplistic and straightforward. The key to utilizing any type of behavioral therapy/plan is consistency in its implementation. School counselors must have the buy-in of teachers and others who interact with the student in order for behavioral plans to be effective across milieus.

School-based behavioral consultation and collaboration with mental health professionals is becoming more common (MacKenzie & Rogers, 1997; Reeder et al., 1997). Hussey and Guo (2003) measured behavior changes resulting when mental health professionals offered school-based behavioral intervention aimed at enhancing social competence and reducing negative emotions and behaviors in an urban elementary school with a population of severely disturbed students, made up predominately of African American males. They found decreased conduct disordered behavior, depressive symptomatology, and attention/deficit hyperactivity. Another study by Sapp and Farrell (1995) found a relationship between cognitive-behavioral therapy and academic achievement among African American middle school students. Additionally, cognitive-behavioral interventions stressing individualistic and self-deterministic qualities of feeling in control despite the environment are recommended for bicultural Hispanic Americans (Valdez, 2000).

Furthermore, prevention of antisocial behavior is potentially associated with positive behavioral intervention (McCurdy, Mannella, & Eldridge, 2003). Another study conducted by Miranda and Presentacion (2000) suggested cognitive-behavioral intervention, combined with anger management training is also efficacious in treating children with attention deficit hyperactivity disorder. Childhood anxiety disorders, when treated by cognitive–behavioral therapy, show long-term treatment gains, lasting 5 to 7 years (Barrett, Duffy, Dadds, & Rapee, 2001). Even preschool-aged children at risk for anxiety disorders can potentially benefit (Hirshfeld-Becker & Biederman, 2002). Cognitive–behavioral intervention may also be effective in dealing with childhood traumatic grief (Brown, Pearlman, & Goodman, 2004).

Solution-Oriented Therapy

Solution-oriented, or solution-focused, therapy was first established by Milton Erickson (1954). Due to the simplistic nature and unique approach of solution-oriented therapy (de Shazer, 1991), it has become a prime choice of school counselors when counseling students individually (Sciarra, 2004). The key to solution-oriented therapy lies in uncovering and utilizing exceptions to problem behaviors/issues in children.

When utilizing solution-oriented therapy, PSCs will first attempt to elicit from the students an example of a time when their problem was not present, that is, an exception. Once the exception has been identified, PSCs can then begin to look for the source of the exception. Was the teacher the source? The student? The environment? Under what conditions did the exception occur? By probing the exception instead of the problem, the counselor and the child are forced to look at preventative/corrective measures that they might have overlooked. Once it has been determined what source or sources are responsible for the exception, the PSC can then work with the student, teachers, parents, and administrators to expand the exception to other situations within which the child may be struggling.

As the counselor, students, and others work to expand the exception to other areas of the child's life, it is important to evaluate the process and to set goals for the student. Goals set for students should be specific, manageable, and meaningful to the student (de Shazer, 1991; Sciarra, 2004). They must also be measurable to the student and others who are invested in the student's progress.

The last step of solution-focused therapy is maintaining change over time. The idea here is to "teach the student to fish." One of the primary roles of a PSC, and any other counselor, is to empower clients to help themselves in the future. By helping students utilize the same process to solve other potential problems, PSCs are empowering their young charges to be self-actualized and to focus on solutions in their lives, rather than problems.

School counselors' use of interventions focusing on student outcomes has been shown to improve students' academic, social, and self-management behaviors (Webb,

Brigman, & Campbell, 2005). These interventions may also be in order during work with Asian Americans who often appreciate the prescriptive, brief approach the school day demands. Not only does the school environment often force the faster, more directive approach, but Asian American students themselves may press for a quick solution from the "expert" counselor (Corey, 1991).

Hope theory offers a goal-directed cognitive approach for PSCs. Research suggests students' level of hope plays a positive role in predicting well-being, academic success, and even athletic success (Snyder, Feldman, Shorey, & Rand, 2002). Another approach to solution-oriented therapy focuses on the stories adolescent students tell themselves and others. This involves the counselor's talking with students until stories emerge, and then facilitating the conversation until more useful stories develop. Biever and McKenzie (1995) accomplished this by

1. Maintaining a "not knowing" stance, by not being an expert about what is best for the student;
2. Being open to and helping to generate alternatives;
3. Thinking in terms of both/and, not either/or;
4. Assuming the student has both strengths and resources;
5. Being aware of own personal values and beliefs;
6. Working with the students, not their labels;
7. Including necessary others in the counseling process; and
8. Working toward understanding the students' situation and point of view.

Solution-oriented counseling in the schools can provide maximum benefit to students and counselors without lengthy, numerous individual counseling sessions, making it an excellent choice for today's overburdened school counselors.

Play Therapy

While play therapy will be discussed more in-depth in a future chapter, it bears mentioning here that PSCs need to play when conducting individual counseling with young children and even some adolescents. Young children (and those who have difficulty expressing themselves verbally) often will communicate through play. The Montessori school system was developed on the idea that play is the work of children (Sciarra, 2004). School counselors should be prepared to allow children the opportunity to draw, play, act out, and use drama and fantasy in their individual sessions with children. Often this is as simple as having a child color a picture and then tell the counselor about the picture. Play therapy can be as involved as having a child act out a family drama, or it can fall somewhere in the middle with the counselor and child shooting hoops in the gym while talking.

Fall (1999) found a connection between increased self-efficacy and a half-hour of play therapy each week for 6 weeks. Specifically, developmental play therapy is often utilized with prekindergarten children, aged 3 and 4, to help them with communication, interpersonal skills, self-esteem, and feelings of competency (Hoffman, 1991). Jungian play therapy may be effective in treating separation and enmeshment issues of elementary students (Allan & Brown, 1993). For the mentally deficient and the mentally retarded, even with accompanying emotional problems, play therapy may improve how they cope (Bernhardt & Mackler, 1975).

Individual cognitive–behavioral play therapy may be effective in treating encopresis (Knell & Moore, 1990) and other serious conditions. Adlerian play therapy is used for helping children build relationships, explore lifestyles, gain significance in school and in their families, and understand their behavior in the context of the school setting (Kottman & Johnson, 1993). Also, play therapy is recommended for disaster prevention and intervention in the elementary school (Yih-Jiun & Sink, 2002).

Hall, Kaduson, and Schaefer (2002) detailed 15 specific play therapy techniques to assist with understanding and expressing feelings, worries, and fears, and increasing self-control, impulse control, awareness of mind-body connections, self-esteem, problem-solving skills, relationship skills, and decreasing depression. One play therapy technique they suggested for students 4 to 8 years old is the use of puppets. It is less threatening to create a symbolic client (Kaduson & Schaefer, 1997) by allowing the child to talk through a puppet rather than directly about self.

Regardless of the age or presenting problems of the child, play therapy can provide the PSC with another avenue with which to explore meaning and discourse in the child's world. Utilizing play therapy can also help demystify the counseling experience for some children and make the school counselor's office a place to go for refuge and solace, as well as a place to discuss other, more serious issues. Despite these applications of play therapy, a survey of 381 elementary school counselors found that although most believed in its effectiveness, lack of specialized training and available time were barriers to its use (Ray, Armstrong, Warren, & Balkin, 2005).

While PSCs have their own theoretical orientations, they are often called upon to utilize a variety of techniques and interventions. Theories of counseling are the means to approaching a specific student with a specific problem because each student presents to counseling differently and must be treated as a unique individual.

References

Adler, A. (1930). *The education of children*. South Bend, IN: Gateway.

Adler, A. (1958). *What life should mean to you*. New York: Perigee Books.

Allan, J., & Brown, K. (1993). Jungian play therapy in elementary schools. *Elementary School Guidance and Counseling, 28*, 30–41.

Allen, J. (1992). *Action-oriented research: Promoting school counselor advocacy and accountability*. (ERIC Digest ED347477). Retrieved May 25, 2005, from http://www.ed.gov/databases/ERIC_Digest/ed347477.htm/

American Psychiatric Association. (2000). *Diagnostic and statistical manual* (4th ed., Text rev.). Washington, DC: Author.

American School Counselor Association. (1992). Ethical standards for school counselors. *School Counselor, 40*, 84–88.

American School Counselor Association. (1998). *The national standards for school counseling programs*. Alexandria, VA: Author.

Baker, S. B., & Gerler, E. R. (2004). *School counseling for the twenty-first century* (4th ed.). Upper Saddle River, NJ: Pearson Prentice Hall.

Barrett, P., Duffy, A., Dadds, M., & Rapee, R. (2001). Cognitive-behavioral treatment of anxiety disorders in children: Long-term (6-year) follow-up. *Journal of Consulting and Clinical Psychology, 69*, 135–141.

Bauman, S. (2004). School counselors and research revisited. *Professional School Counseling, 7*, 141–151.

Berk, L. (2003). *Child development* (6th ed.). Boston: Allyn and Bacon.

Bernhardt, M., & Mackler, B. (1975). The use of play therapy with the mentally retarded. *The Journal of Special Education, 9*(4), 409–414.

Biever, J., & McKenzie, K. (1995). Stories and solutions in psychotherapy with adults. *Adolescence, 30*(118), 491–499.

Brown, E., Pearlman, M., & Goodman, R. (2004). Facing fears and sadness: Cognitive-behavioral therapy for childhood traumatic grief. *Harvard Review of Psychiatry, 12*(4), 187–198.

Buckley, K. W. (1989). *Mechanical man: John Broadus Watson and the beginnings of behaviorism*. New York: Guilford Press.

Campbell, C. A., & Dahir, C. A. (1997). *Sharing the vision: The national standards for school counseling programs*. Alexandria, VA: American School Counselor Association.

Carlson, J. M., & Carlson, J. D. (2000). The application of Adlerian psychotherapy with Asian American clients. *The Journal of Individual Psychology, 56*, 214–225.

Cassel, R. (2001). A person-centered high school delinquency prevention program based on eight "hallmarks" for success in a democracy. *Education, 121*(3), 431–435.

Clark, A. (1994). Conflict resolution and individual psychology in the schools. *Individual Psychology, 50*(3), 331–340.

Colvin, G. (1999). Person-centered counseling after fifty years: How is it fairing in school-land? *American Secondary Education, 28*, 19–26.

Corey, G. (1991). *Theory and practice of counseling and psychotherapy*. Pacific Grove, CA: Brooks/Cole.

Cramer, S. H., Herr, E. L., Morris, C. N., & Frantz, T. T. (1970). *Research and the school counselor*. Boston: Houghton Mifflin.

Cunningham, P., & Henggeler, S. (2001). Implementation of an empirically based drug and violence prevention and intervention program in public school settings. *Journal of Clinical Child Psychology, 30*(2), 221–232.

de Shazer, S. (1991). *Putting differences to work*. New York: Norton.

Dinkmeyer, D. C., Pew, W. L., & Dinkmeyer, D. C., Jr. (1979). *Adlerian counseling and psychotherapy*. Monterey, CA: Brooks/Cole.

Egan, G. (2004). *The skilled helper: A problem management and opportunity-development to helping*. Pacific Grove, CA: Brooks/Cole.

Erickson, M. (1954). Special techniques of brief hypnotherapy. *Journal of Clinical and Experimental Hypnosis, 2*, 109–129.

Fall, M. (1999). A play therapy intervention and its relationship to self-efficacy and learning behaviors. *Professional School Counseling, 2*(3), 194–209.

Frevert, V., & Miranda, A. (1998). A conceptual formulation of the Latin culture and the treatment of Latinos from an Adlerian psychology perspective. *The Journal of Individual Psychology, 54*(3), 291–309.

Gibson, R. L., & Mitchell, M. H. (2003). *Introduction to counseling and guidance* (6th ed.). Upper Saddle River, NJ: Merrill Prentice Hall.

Glasser, W. (2000). *Reality therapy in action*. New York: HarperCollins.

Greenwood, A. (2002). The child who cannot bear to feel. *Psychodynamic Practice, 8*(3), 295–310.

Grossman, H. (1990). *Trouble free teaching solutions to behavior problems in the classroom*. Mount View, CA: Mayfield Publishing Company.

Guerra, P. (1998). Revamping school counselor education: The DeWitt Wallace Reader's Digest Fund. *Counseling Today, 40*(8), 19–36.

Hall, T. M., Kaduson, H. G., & Schaefer, C. (2002). Fifteen effective play therapy techniques. *Professional Psychology: Research and Practice, 33*(6), 515–522.

Hirshfeld-Becker, D., & Biederman, J. (2002). Rationale and principles for early intervention with young children at risk for anxiety disorders. *Clinical Child and Family Psychology Review, 5*(3), 161–172.

Hoffman, L. (1991). Developmental counseling for prekindergarten children: A preventive approach. *Elementary School Guidance and Counseling, 26*, 56–66.

Hussey, D., & Guo, S. (2003). Measuring behavior change in young children receiving intensive school-based mental health services. *Journal of Community Psychology, 31*(6), 629–639.

James, R. K., & Gilliand, B. E. (2003). *Theories and strategies in counseling and psychotherapy* (5th ed.). Needham Heights, MA: Allyn and Bacon.

Kaduson, H. G., & Schaefer, C. E. (Eds.). (1997). *101 favorite play treatment techniques*. Northvale, NJ: Jason Aronson.

Kim, K. (2002). The effect of a reality therapy program on the responsibility for elementary school children in Korea. *International Journal of Reality Therapy, 22,* 30–33.

Knell, S., & Moore, D. (1990). Cognitive-behavioral play therapy in the treatment of encopresis. *Journal of Clinical Child Psychology, 19,* 55–60.

Kottman, T., & Johnson, V. (1993). Adlerian play therapy: A tool for school counselors. *Elementary School Guidance and Counseling, 28,* 42–51.

Kutash, K., & Duchnowski, A. (2004). The mental health needs of youth with emotional and behavioral disabilities placed in special education programs in urban schools. *Journal of Child and Family Studies, 13*(2), 235–248.

Last, C. G. (Ed.). (1993). *Anxiety across the lifespan: A developmental perspective*. New York: Springer.

LexisNexis. (2003). *Tennessee education laws annotated: 2003 edition*. Charlottesville, VA: Matthew Bender & Company, Inc.

MacKenzie, D., & Rogers, V. (1997). The full service school: A management and organizational structure for 21st century schools. *Community Education Journal, 25*(3–4), 9–11.

McCurdy, B., Mannella, M., & Eldridge, N. (2003). Positive behavior support in urban schools: Can we prevent the escalation of antisocial behavior? *Journal of Positive Behavior Interventions, 5*(3), 158–170.

Miranda, A., & Presentacion, M. (2000). Efficacy of cognitive-behavioral therapy in the treatment of children with ADHD, with and without aggressiveness. *Psychology in the Schools, 37*(2), 169–182.

Orton, G. L. (1997). *Strategies for counseling with children and their parents*. Pacific Grove, CA: Brooks/Cole.

Passaro, P., Moon, M., Wiest, D., & Wong, E. (2004). A model for school psychology practice: Addressing the needs of students with emotional and behavioral challenges through the use of an in-school support room and reality therapy. *Adolescence, 39*(155), 503–517.

Pryor, D. B., & Tollerud, T. R. (1999). Applications of Adlerian principles in school settings. *Professional School Counseling, 2,* 299–304.

Ray, D., Armstrong, S., Warren, E., & Balkin, R. (2005). Play therapy practices among elementary school counselors. *Professional School Counseling, 8*(4), 360–365.

Reeder, G., Maccow, G., Shaw, S., Swerdlik, M., Horton, C., & Foster, P. (1997). School psychologist and full-service schools: Partnerships with medical, mental health, and social services. *School Psychology Review, 26*(4), 603–621.

Rogers, C. R. (1951). *Client-centered therapy: Its current practice, implications, and theory*. Boston: Houghton Mifflin.

Sandhu, D. (1997). Psychocutural profile of Asian and Pacific Islander Americans: Implications for counseling and psychotherapy. *Journal of Multicultural Counseling and Development, 25,* 7–23.

Sapp, M., & Farrell, W. (1995). Cognitive-behavioral therapy: Applications for African American middle school at-risk students. *Journal of Instructional Psychology, 22*(2), 168–178.

Sciarra, D. (2004). *School counseling: Foundations and contemporary issues*. Belmont, CA: Brooks/Cole.

Skinner, B. F. (1953). *Science and human behaviors*. New York: McMillan.

Snyder, C., Feldman, D., Shorey, H., & Rand, K. (2002). Hopeful choices: A school counselor's guide to hope theory. *Professional School Counseling, 5*(5), 298–108.

Sonstegard, M. A., & Dreikurs, R. (1973). The Adlerian approach to group counseling of children. In M. M. Ohlsend (Ed.), *Counseling children in groups: A forum* (pp. 47–77). New York: Holt, Rinehart, & Winston.

Valdez, J. (2000). Psychotherapy with bicultural Hispanic clients. *Psychotherapy, 37*(3), 240–246.

Watts, R. (2003). Adlerian therapy as a relational constructivist approach. *The Family Journal: Counseling and Therapy for Couples and Families, 11,* 139–147.

Webb, L., Brigman, G., & Campbell, C. (2005). Linking school counselors and student success: A replication of the student success skills approach targeting the academic social competence of students. *Professional School Counseling, 8*(5), 407–413.

Williams, W., & Lair, G. (1991). Using a person-centered approach with children who have a disability. *Elementary School Guidance & Counseling, 25*(3), 194–204.

Yih-Jiun, S., & Sink, C. (2002). Helping elementary-age children cope with disasters. *Professional School Counseling, 5*(5), 322–330.

XXVII
FOCUSED, BUT FLEXIBLE:
A Developmental Approach to Small Group Work in Schools

JEAN SUNDE PETERSON AND HEATHER L. SERVATY-SEIB
Purdue University

Introduction

The Call to Be Proactive

In recent years, school counselors have been admonished to devote a significant portion of their time to proactive, prevention-oriented activities. Such curricula are intended to develop skills, attitudes, and knowledge that will support students throughout life (Campbell & Dahir, 1997). By intervening before problems begin or by addressing existing problems before they become crises, counselors can help students navigate complex developmental challenges, develop important interpersonal skills, gain support and skills for problem solving, and connect with peers in ways that contribute to being comfortable in the school environment. Prevention programs can be geared to optimizing wellness and school adaptation from the very beginning of the school years (Cowen, 1997).

Both large- and small-group work can be geared to prevention. Psycho-educational large-group work in the form of sequential classroom lessons or presentations to larger groups can target entire populations, such as age or grade groups (Kulic, Dagley, & Horne, 2001). Large-group work can serve as *primary prevention* (i.e., preventing academic, social, and emotional problems, offering support for meeting developmental challenges, and fostering resilience). Small-group work in schools also usually focuses on prevention, but is more likely to represent two levels of prevention work: (a) primary prevention and (b) secondary prevention (i.e., focusing proactively on populations targeted because of particular risk factors or problems). Small groups can also focus on *remediation* (i.e., working with populations already experiencing significant problems) for "a small but hardcore segment of the school population" (Baker & Gerler, 2004, pp. 4–7). According to Kulic et al., prevention should be recognized as a long-term goal, with effects of preventive group work often unclear until much later. They also distinguished prevention from intervention in regard to strategies and noted that "prevention efforts should not become interventive" (p. 214).

Overview

This chapter presents small-group work as a component of proactive, preventive school counseling programs. These groups are intended to help students learn and succeed in life. The main focus of our chapter is on the *practice* of group work, including what distinguishes group work in schools from group work in other venues, as well as how they are similar, the latter discussed in regard to theories. The practice-oriented research section emphasizes how practitioners can access pertinent literature, rather than summarizing empirical studies of outcomes. Finally, after discussing group work practices in general, we present a specific model for small-group work in schools: a focused, flexible, development-oriented approach, appropriate and potentially effective for both prevention and remediation.

Theory

How School Groups Are Similar to Other Groups

Therapeutic factors. Small-group work in schools is similar to group work in agencies, youth centers, and treatment facilities in many ways. First, school groups can be as rich, complex, dynamic, and life altering as groups elsewhere, and Yalom's (1985) therapeutic factors apply to groups regardless of venue:

- interpersonal learning (learning about others' views of self and gaining skills related to interaction with others);
- self-understanding (learning about self);
- catharsis (experiencing and expressing, not holding in, negative and positive feelings);
- cohesiveness (having a sense of belonging);
- altruism (being helpful to others);
- universality (discovering common concerns, thoughts, feelings);
- installation of hope (seeing that others have solved problems similar to one's own);
- existential factors (facing issues related to life, death, pain, responsibility for actions);
- family reenactment (gaining understanding of self and family from family-like group);
- guidance (receiving advice, suggestions, information from group members); and
- identification (identifying with and imitating leader's and group members' behaviors).

Shechtman, Bar-El, and Hadar (1997) found that participants in psycho-educational and counseling groups for adolescents did not differ in attributing therapeutic factors to the group process. The language of comprehensive, developmental guidance (Gysbers & Henderson, 2001) includes learning about self and others as a key goal, and the Yalom (1985) factors of interpersonal learning, catharsis, self-understanding, family reenactment, universality, and identification are all related to that goal. Cohesiveness is related to the need to belong, commonly cited in literature as salient during the school years (Nelson, Rubin, & Fox, 2005; Risi, Gerhardstein, & Kistner, 2003). Installation of hope is certainly a desirable objective when working in the modes of secondary prevention and remediation. Existential factors apply to all modes of group work in schools, most notably in regard to children and adolescents coping with troubling life events and situations and accepting responsibility for behavior. Though it is possible that the last three therapeutic factors listed above would also be least noted by school-aged group members, they nevertheless apply here. School groups are not likely to focus much on family dynamics, per se, but insightful students capable of abstract thinking might indeed become aware of their own family's dynamics through interaction with others.

Well-trained facilitators avoid giving advice, but the factor of psycho-educational information might be part of a small-group curriculum in a school. Facilitators might judiciously provide information (e.g., about substances, disorders, careers, and development), and group members might offer suggestions for coping with problems. An intimate group setting provides opportunities for students to become well acquainted with each other, allowing for various positive behaviors that might not be visible elsewhere in school. Affirming and validating positive member and facilitator behaviors provides additional "information."

Group stages and dynamics. Second, group dynamics are likely to be similar. When school groups are closed and meet regularly over several weeks, they are likely to experience the stages of group development often noted in group counseling textbooks: Initial, Transition, Working, and Final (Corey & Corey, 2006) and Dependency and Inclusion, Counterdependency and Fight, Trust and Structure, and Work and Termination (Wheelan, 2005). When written and physical activities are frequently used, school-aged group members can challenge and resist the facilitator, group rules, and the curriculum in general. Unexpected movement into new levels of intimacy and investment can also occur, even when meetings are semistructured. Students and facilitators are both likely to notice when group dynamics shift. Facilitators cannot "make" a group cohesive, but by thoughtfully reflecting on group dynamics before and after meetings, they can develop strategies to enhance communication. For example, if a homogeneous group of high-control, verbally dominant high-achievers still seems to be collectively skittish about discussing social and emotional issues after five meetings, processing that perception is in order. If male and female eighth graders seem inhibited and distracted by each other, that perception can also be addressed, perhaps resulting in important forthright discussion about distractions, social development, gender identity and roles, and sexuality.

Norming. Third, the process of norming is as important and inevitable in school groups as it is in other venues, and it may occur through overt facilitator direction, or it may happen spontaneously over the first few sessions. We differ in our approaches to establishing guidelines in this regard, and therefore, we argue that the role of the facilitator in this process should vary according to style of facilitation, group composition, and size of group.

Termination. Fourth, school groups need as much careful attention to termination as do groups elsewhere. Regardless of age, members may have bonded with each other and the facilitator, and they may depend on the group for support and stability. Therefore, preparation for termination needs to occur in advance of the final session, and associated feelings need to be explored. Some sort of closing ritual, meant to affirm each group member and the group as a whole, is often the focus of the last meeting.

We typically advise our students not to change the basic format for the final group meeting (e.g., activity–discussion) because a changed format often significantly changes group dynamics. Some students might be uncomfortable in a more social context than previously, for instance, and no further meetings will provide opportunities to regain ease. Sometimes facilitators are also uncomfortable with the change, even though it is the group members who are the primary concern here.

Strengths-focus. Fifth, counselors of all varieties are trained to pay attention to client strengths. Effective school counselors, moving students toward self-awareness and successful coping, are alert for opportunities to stroke students' strengths credibly, with "accumulated evidence." In fact, group work is ideal for discovering and affirming strengths, including resilience, because facilitators can observe complex interpersonal processes, which provide rich information for generating feedback.

When group facilitators learn that struggling students have factors of resilience in their lives, they can note that these offer hope for breaking destructive and challenging cross-generational patterns. According to several noted figures in the resilience (e.g., Benard, 2004; Rak & Patterson, 1996; Werner, 1986) and hardiness literatures (Kobasa, 1979; Maddi, 2002), the following are factors that characterize individuals who thrive in spite of adverse conditions:

- problem-solving skills;
- ability to engage others;
- ability to be alert, spontaneous;
- desire for novel experiences;
- sustained primary caretaker early in life;
- role models outside of the home;
- various caretakers, a confidant;
- structure at home;
- proactive perspective;
- optimistic view of circumstances;
- positive vision of a meaningful life;
- self-understanding;
- not feeling responsible for family difficulties; and
- intelligence.

The first four might actually characterize students with attention-deficit problems, who may be quite successful as adults if they can find a good fit in employment and spouse/partner. These factors might also be found in students who simply know how to ask for help or build a relationship with a helpful adult. The next four may provide solid footing in the present. The next three represent potential movement. Proactive instincts help students to *do* something about difficulties. Being able to self-validate and look ahead, instead of becoming mired in the present, may propel young students forward positively. Self-knowledge, including understanding what is and is not one's responsibility, can help someone to stay above the fray. Last, intelligence is typically on lists of resilience factors and has been found to help generate options, among several benefits.

Facilitators can note strengths and factors of resilience even in students for whom school is uncomfortable (e.g., persistence in coming to school), in those who lack social skills (e.g., energy, ability to get attention), and in underachievers (e.g., courage not to do what everyone wants them to). Group members can also be encouraged to be alert to others' strengths and resilience and offer support and validation.

Specific theoretical approaches. Just as Yalom's (1985) therapeutic factors are applicable to group work in the schools, many other theoretical approaches to group counseling have been adapted for use in K–12 settings. More specifically, the scholarly literature includes formats/investigations associated with orientations such as Adlerian (Campbell, 2003; Clark, 1995), solution-focused (LaFountain, Garner, & Boldosser, 1995; LaFountain, Garner, & Eliason, 1996), reality therapy (Comiskey, 1993; Kim & Hwang, 1996), multimodal (Gerler, Drew, & Mohr, 1990; Stickel, 1990), cognitive-behavioral, and humanistic (Bauer, Sapp, & Johnson, 2000; Schechtman & Pastor, 2005). Adlerian and multimodal groups likely work well in school settings because they tend to be flexible, eclectic, and holistic and have an educational emphasis focused more on health than on sickness (Gladding, 2003; Lazarus, 2005; Mosak, 2005). The use of reality-therapy groups in schools is not surprising. This approach is straightforward, offers definable procedures for group facilitation, and stresses the importance of responsibility and accountability (Glasser, 1986; Wubbolding, 2001).

Many features of cognitive–behavioral groups make them a good fit for intervening with children and adolescents. They emphasize learning and the process of defining and evaluating specific goals, and they are focused on teaching specific skills, such as social skills (Gazda, Ginter, & Horne, 2001; Gladding, 2003). Humanistic approaches are attractive for group work with children and adolescents because they generally emphasize assets as well as deficits, unconditional positive regard, and the improvement of social skills (Raskin & Rogers, 2005). Also focused on strengths, solution-focused groups with children and adolescents allow for grouping children with diverse issues together and emphasize creating solutions rather than discussing problems (LaFountain et al., 1995, 1996).

Research

Although conducting literature reviews and building knowledge of research methodology and statistics may not be central foci within most school counseling training programs, it is crucial that practicing school counselors remain abreast of the existing empirical and nonempirical literature and be knowledgeable and comfortable with the process of program evaluation. Familiarity with the steps involved in gathering and evaluating literature and applying basic research skills can help school counselors to plan groups, argue the need for and value of groups, and meet the challenges related to accountability. Rather than summarizing the data from outcome evaluations (see excellent reviews of the research in Riva & Haub, 2004; Claiborn, Kerr, & Strong, 1990), we offer practical tips for how school counselors can enhance their group work by using their research skills.

Planning for a group with a specific focus, whether related to presenting issue, member composition, or theory, can be facilitated by a review of the literature. Searches performed through databases such as PsycINFO and ERIC (often available in schools or in local community or university libraries) or through the Internet require the use of key words. These words are terms related to the purpose of the search. For example, for a group for children who have experienced divorce, a school counselor can examine previous empirical and nonempirical literature using key words such as *divorce, children, counseling*, and *group*. The database or Internet search engine then locates articles, chapters, books, or Web sites that contain these words. We recommend that these words be put in separately, adding an *and* between each key word while searching in PsycINFO and ERIC (including the word *and* between key words is not required for searching on the Internet). It is important to note that the search process frequently involves taking the attitude of a detective, since multiple attempts, using a variety of key words, usually produces the most appropriate references. For example, the word *counseling* could be replaced with *therapy*, the word *counseling* could be dropped to widen the search, or *school* could be added to include only citations specifically mentioning the school setting. Although school counselors may initially see them as tedious, these searches can result in valuable information that can be incorporated into their work with groups. Examples of the resources available include material on the effects of certain life events on the functioning of children/adolescents, suggestions for working in a group setting with specific populations, and various group formats previously developed and used by others.

A solid literature search of how children/adolescents are affected by specific life events can reveal important emphases and/or approaches that can be incorporated into the design of a group. For example, a review of literature on teenage mothers indicates that they have fewer interpersonal relationships than nonpregnant teens and less frequent and less positive interactions with peers and family members (Bogat, Caldwell, Guzman, Galasso, & Davidson, 1998; Passino et al., 1993). Outcome investigations also suggest that pregnant teens benefit from educational material on child development, parenting skills, and life-skills training (Griffin, 1998; Kiselica, Gorczynski, & Capps, 1998). Discovering and incorporating such information during the group-planning phase likely enhances the ultimate outcome of the intervention.

Issues that may be unique to certain populations often become relevant when facilitating groups, and the scholarly literature provides interesting insights into working in the schools with children/adolescents from various populations, for example, Korean American elementary school children (Smith, 1997), African American/Black high school students (Goldberg & Tidwell, 1990; Muller, 2000), and Native American youth (Appleton & Dykeman, 1996; Herring, 1996). In addition, Bilides (1990) offered guidelines for confronting issues of race, color, ethnicity, and class as they arise in the school-based group setting. Beyond issues of race/ethnicity, Muller and Hartman (1998) wrote about working in a group setting with sexual minority youth, and Peterson (1990) and Humes and Clark (1989) offered strategies for providing group counseling to gifted high school students.

The literature on counseling groups implemented in the schools contains a number of potential models and formats for groups focused on specific presenting issues. For example, models can be found for working in a group setting with children/adolescents who have experienced a variety of life events such as divorce (DeLucia-Waack & Gerrity, 2001; Pedro-Carroll, 1997), death loss (Finn, 2003), adoption (Kizner & Kizner, 1999), and parental military deployment (Mitchum, 1991). Formats can be found for school-based groups focused on students with diagnosed conditions such as ADHD (Webb & Myrick, 2003), mild handicaps (Hess, Rosenberg, & Levy, 1990), and learning disabilities (Flitton & Buckroyd, 2002). Innovative approaches to group work in schools have also been described. For example, group formats have been used to debrief middle school students after the sexual assault of a peer (Fenlon & Mufson, 1994), in rural settings to help parents guide high school students' career decision making (Jeffery, Hache, & Lehr, 1995), and in a collaboration between university and public school personnel, with graduate students providing group interpretations of career-related assessments to ninth-grade students (Usher et al., 1994). At a more macrolevel, group interventions have been integral to school-based physical and mental health clinics in urban settings (Chatterji, Caffray, Crowe, Freeman, & Jensen, 2004; Dryfoos, 1994).

PsycINFO and/or ERIC searches can illuminate empirical research that can help school counselors argue the value of group work to administers, teachers, and parents, including the effectiveness of various formats and approaches. Both databases have a "limit search" option that allows for searching only empirical articles that contain the key words entered. School counselors should have at their disposal copies of meta-analyses done on school counseling outcomes (Prout & DeMartino, 1986; Prout & Prout, 1998) and group counseling outcomes for children and adolescents in a variety of settings (Hoag & Burlingame, 1997). These studies clearly show that group counseling is an effective intervention in schools.

Specifically, outcome studies support the use of school-based groups to improve social skills and interactions, as well as to enhance friendships (Salzman & D'Andrea, 2001; Schechtman, 1994; Schechtman & Bar-El, 1994; Schechtman, Vurembrand, & Hertz-Lazarowitz, 1994), raise academic performance (Brigman & Campbell, 2003; Slate & Jones, 2003; Webb, Brigman, & Campbell, 2005), decrease test anxiety (Wei, 2000), and reduce acting out and aggressive behaviors (Brantley, Brantley, & Baer-Barkley, 1996; Schechtman, 2001). Investigations of groups designed to address the difficulties faced by students at risk for poor outcomes and students who have experienced parental divorce found improvements in social, emotional, behavioral, and academic domains (Bauer et al., 2000; Hett & Rose, 1991; Kostoulas, Berkovitz, & Arima, 1991; Larkin & Thyer, 1999; Page & Chandler, 1994; Pedro-Carroll, Sutton, & Wyman, 1999; Sanders & Riester, 1996; Schechtman, 1993; Stolberg & Mahler, 1994; Zinck & Littrell, 2000).

Knowledge of the process of program evaluation can help school counselors to respond to recent and growing calls for accountability (Isaacs, 2003; Webb et al., 2005). Although empirical research on school-based group counseling does exist, more studies need to evaluate the effectiveness of such interventions (Riva & Haub, 2004; Whiston, 2002). Developing and implementing a plan for assessing the outcome of a group intervention can add depth and power to a group proposal, assist school counselors in more effectively and efficiently managing time, offer information on improving the delivery of the group, and provide valuable information to other colleagues within the field.

School counselors may find the prospect of engaging in research to be daunting, but it does not need to be an anxiety-provoking process (Corey & Corey, 2006). It is important to approach the process with an open mind. The ultimate goal of research does not need to be publication in an academic or other professional journal. Research can make a difference in the daily activities of school counselors and the students with whom they work—in program evaluation, for example. Program evaluation is a systematic approach to determining if a program "works"—that is, if a program has merit, value, and worth. Although a detailed description of the process is beyond the scope of this chapter, excellent and easily accessible resources are available for self-directed learning about program evaluation. For example, we recommend texts such as *Evaluation: A Systematic Approach* by Rossi, Freeman, and Lipsey, *Educational Evaluation:* by Popham, and *Utilization-Focused Evaluation* by Patton. A cost-effective place to begin is with online resources like those provided by the National Science Foundation, such as *The User-Friendly Handbook for Project Evaluation,* currently available at http://www.nsf.gov/pubs/2002/nsf02057/start.htm.

Practice

Explaining the Lack of Group Work

School counselors at all levels report that they value group work and that group work is possible at their schools (Dansby, 1996). Small-group work allows counselors to provide meaningful and high-impact services to several students at one time, including in several groups conducted concurrently. Therefore, counselors whose programs include substantial group work may not understand why others do not incorporate this efficient, effective delivery of services into their programs. After all, the American School Counselor Association (ASCA) advocates group work (Campbell & Dahir, 1997), and the Council for the Accreditation of Counseling and Related Education Programs (CACREP; 2001) requires preparation programs to train for it. However, regardless of how much can be accomplished by groups and regardless of research evidence about the effectiveness of group work in schools (Akos, Goodnough, & Milsom, 2004), group work may not be a significant part of school counseling programs. It is important to understand why groups may not be employed regularly or at all. Rare empirical studies of barriers to group work in schools have noted that nonguidance duties (Burnham & Jackson, 2000) and lack of time and access to students (Dansby) are obstacles; however, there may be other factors.

How Group Work in Schools Differs

Basic differences between group work in schools and group work in other venues may partially explain a frequent absence of group work in schools. In fact, awareness of these differences can help school counselors promote group work to school staff and other counselors—by highlighting what it is and what it is not. What follows here is a discussion of some significant differences.

Purpose. First, the purpose of school groups is usually different from the purpose of group work elsewhere. For instance, preventive group work occurs only rarely outside of the school setting, largely because hospitals and agencies are not expected to focus on primary prevention (Kulic et al., 2001). School groups are seen as school-guidance curriculum, which both proactively and reactively supports academic, social, and emotional development. In addition, expectations regarding academic achievement often distinguish the school context. Implicit in the guidelines about development are the beliefs that counselors' work is fundamentally to help children learn and succeed in school and that learning is affected by personal, social, and emotional development. Understandably, given their pressures to raise test scores, teachers and administrators may perceive that the sole purpose of groups should be to help students achieve better academically. School counselors may also appropriately justify program components as ultimately "helping students learn." Group work focusing on social and emotional concerns might help students concentrate better, for example.

Second, school groups are generally not seen as part of a treatment plan. Though these groups potentially have an important therapeutic function, they are not intended to be therapy in the way that scholars and the public usually consider "therapy." For example, according to standard group work texts, group psychotherapy is focused on the remediation of difficulties in individuals with severe psychological disturbance (Corey & Corey, 2006; Gladding, 2003). Whether the purpose is prevention or intervention, school groups intentionally bring students together for focused discussion. Instead of being treatment-oriented, the groups are meant to enhance functioning in the school context.

Justification. School groups usually have a curriculum, which must be approved by administrators. It is difficult to justify taking time from academic work or other activities for group work if personnel perceive it to be only "hanging out" with the counselor. Group curriculum may indeed focus on particular behavior problems (e.g., anger management issues, Schechtman, 2001; poor social skills, Shechtman & Bar-El, 1994), life transitions (e.g., bereavement, Finn, 2003; parental divorce, Hett & Rose, 1991), or proactively on development (e.g., Peterson, 2007; Vernon, 1998a, 1998b, 1998c).

Session Structure. Because there should be defensible curriculum, some structure is warranted. A series of coordinated, sequential topics may guide discussion, for example; however, film clips, brief written activities, and kinesthetic activities can also provide structure and variety, help students to engage with each other, and move the group beyond superficial communication. Everyone is then likely to participate, even after being given permission to "pass." Shy, reticent, perfectionistic, or environmentally hypersensitive members may appreciate being able to share what they have written on a brief questionnaire.

They have time to consider their thoughts, and sentence stems and other prompts provide expressive vocabulary, which then becomes familiar and accessible later. In addition, dramatic, crisis-prone members are less likely to dominate when all become used to the rhythm of taking turns sharing what they have written or created, at least during "go-arounds." Furthermore, inappropriate directions and disruptive behavior can be reined in by guiding the group back to the topic for the day. However, the structure referred to here is really semistructured, because discussion may move spontaneously in important, interesting, pertinent, and unexpected directions.

Having paper for "doodling" may help to diminish the emotional intensity associated with some topics for troubled students (Peterson, in press). Unsettling emotions are difficult for some children and adolescents to tolerate and express, and some structure and activities may help everyone be involved comfortably. Having quiet "toys" to manipulate may also help both young and older members to cope with emotions—for example, pipe cleaners, bendable sticks, or squeezable balls. If disrespect and disruption are issues, having speakers take turns holding a ball while the rest of the group listens might improve group behavior.

Recruitment. Recruitment is another challenge because group membership is typically voluntary, instead of being a required part of treatment. If group work is not familiar to a school population, recruitment may not be easy. Children and adolescents alike usually wonder who will be in the group being described to them. They may also be unconvinced that recess, being able to eat lunch with their friends, an interesting classroom activity, or time to prepare for an upcoming test is worth sacrificing for a group meeting, especially when they have no conception of what being in a group entails. Adventurous, social students might find the idea of a group appealing; others might view a first group experience as an uncomfortable unknown. Many facilitators prefer to screen students via individual meetings, not revealing names of other potential group members. The interviewer might say, "It's usually an advantage for a group to be organized without kids knowing who will be in it. Whether friends end up in the group or not, the experience will be a chance to know a *variety* of peers better."

The inherent social microcosm in each small group means that group work lends itself to important cross-cultural dialogue. Not only can communication among children and adolescents from various cultural and ethnic groups be facilitated, but discovery of developmental commonalities can also break down cultural barriers; however, organizers may have to be strategic during recruitment to accomplish this. Twice, we have seen how intentional mixing of cultures and ethnicities in small groups can have positive outcomes. As a pilot project in one large middle school, school counselors invited approximately 60 students living in high-risk circumstances to participate in weekly, prevention-oriented groups for a semester. Intentionally, half of those invited were children of color. Of the 45 who returned signed parent-permission forms, half again were from minority groups. Each small group was culturally mixed, and the minority-culture students appeared to feel comfortable in group interaction. Until the final meeting, there was no mention of culture, per se; however, several indicated, when asked then, that they had indeed noticed the cultural mix and had appreciated the opportunity to become acquainted with each other. A follow-up, locally funded grant currently supports a larger group program called ON TRACK. Inviting almost all students of color in the participating middle schools (where they are approximately 20% of the school population), with less than half returning the permission forms, and inviting a much smaller percentage of the schools' Anglo students has resulted in evenly balanced mixed-culture groups and similar productive and barrier-breaking dialogue. We have concluded that students' being able to anticipate and experience cultural support in small groups is important. Once group work is successful, word spreads and recruitment becomes easier.

Marketing. In agencies and treatment centers, group work is likely to be unquestioned as an intervention; in schools, group work must *become* part of the school or guidance curriculum. In a sense, group work must be marketed—not just to students, but also to parents, whose permission is needed for students' participation; to teachers, whose cooperation will be essential; to administrators, who can help to generate support and who must provide space; and possibly also to the school board, who may need to be convinced that group work is an appropriate component of a school counseling program. These adult players in the school context, given current demands for accountability, may all perceive that affective development has little or no bearing on academic achievement and that group time could be better spent in the classroom or in tutoring. There may also be a collective uneasiness about group work, based on past experiences or misperceptions about group work. In regard to generating teacher support, one study found positive process evaluations when involving teachers collaboratively in referral and group-formation processes (Sullivan & Wright, 2002).

Some proactive marketing is therefore part of one course in the school counseling program at our university. Principals-in-training are required by their program to take Introduction to School Counseling. Their presence in the course generates important real-world dialogue, they gain perspective on appropriate roles for school counselors, and invariably they are awed by the complexity of school counseling and the rigor of the training. Among a multitude of course components, in order to create some understanding of counseling in general and school counseling in particular, this course includes an introduction to active listening through brief skill-building exercises, simulations of semistructured small-group work, and a demonstration of brief counseling.

The principals-in-training are typically skeptical about group work, including their concerns about parent complaints. Initially, they are noticeably uneasy during group activities, often joking that the class has now become "touchy-feely" and sometimes referring to well-known media figures who engage in confrontational problem solving. After a few instructor-facilitated demonstrations, they are required to engage the class in ten minutes of a semistructured small group activity, based on *Essential Guide* materials (Peterson, 2007). They gain an appreciation for the challenges of generating interaction, and they consider a wide variety of developmentally oriented topics in the process of choosing their focus. Ultimately, they recognize that small-group work is not what they had assumed, and that, even in brief experiences, some degree of depth in communication is possible. They quickly find commonalities, become better acquainted, and have some understanding of the possibilities and parameters of small-group work in schools.

Wise school counselors make no assumptions about receptivity among parents, administrators, teachers, or students to group work. Accordingly, counselors might devise a formal or informal marketing plan, potentially including newsletter items, informational letters sent home with students, and oral explanations at faculty meetings prior to and continuing after implementation. Through a newsletter, parents might be given a timeline, organizational structure (e.g., length of group series, number of groups facilitated concurrently, and an explanation of how missed classroom time will be accommodated), sample discussion topics, clarification of the "prevention" concept and the purpose of small groups, a description of the function of a facilitator, and a permission form. The last item may be included in a packet of forms at the outset of the school year for field trips and other activities where parent permission is needed. In addition, superintendents and school board ideally receive a rationale and explanatory material before an extensive group program is implemented, with the promise of an evaluation of the program after one year and perhaps again after a second or third year (since outcomes are not likely to be apparent quickly). Newsletters are useful for cultivating the soil for group work and can continue to provide updates regarding developmental foci.

To students, small groups can be advertised as "clubs," as the elementary-level exemplar in Littrell and Peterson's (2005) ethnographic study did, or as "discussion groups," as Peterson (1990) did at the high school level. The former believed that kids like the idea of being in a club. The stigma potentially associated with "counseling" argues for creativity and sensitivity in marketing small groups to students. Counselors in one large midwestern middle school, whose groups generally targeted children with identified risk factors, called all groups "concerns" groups, appropriate for the secondary prevention function of the groups. Choice of term should depend on whether the groups are intended to serve as primary or secondary prevention or remediation. As we will note later in this chapter, however, primary prevention language can be used regardless of purpose.

Facilitation. Group facilitation also differs in schools. Effective early-elementary groups should have an appropriate format, enough hands-on activities to engage members, activities that match their range of small-motor development, and a meeting length appropriate for short attention spans. In fact, developmental differences in school-age children across a wide continuum require that group structure, group size, screening, facilitator language, expectations about what constitutes "discussion," and meeting focus differ from age level to age level. Facilitation must be creative, skilled, flexible, poised, and tuned in to developmental levels. A discussion of several aspects of facilitation of school groups follows here.

The relationship. Because children and adolescents may understandably mistrust counselors, wise counselors take steps to build a comfortable relationship with them. An appropriate physical environment, clarity about what will be experienced, and language are all important (Thompson & Henderson, 2007). In addition, group facilitators should be comfortable with the populations they work with; genuine in communication; congruent in demeanor, language, and attitude; able to harness emotional reactivity; able to corral "teacher" instincts; and interested in working with groups of school-aged youth. The facilitator must be a person—with a personality, yes, but not someone who needs affirmation from the group, who self-discloses in self-serving ways, and who voyeuristically *needs* to know about the private lives and concerns of group members (Peterson, 2007).

Skills. Active listening skills are as important in group work as in individual counseling. When facilitators remember that the groups are about the group members, not about the facilitators, they are likely to employ appropriate reflection, validation of feelings, checking for accuracy, paraphrasing, and summarizing and to avoid self-disclosure, except, perhaps, in the form of immediacy (e.g., "I'm sensing some discomfort in the group. I'm seeing that in your faces."). Instead, they focus, with a one-down posture (i.e., group member as authority), on entering the world of the students, being taught by them, and facilitating interaction. They resist the urge to "fix" group members.

Facilitation of school groups typically does not employ hard-edged confrontation or intentionally create discomfort for therapeutic purposes. Group membership is voluntary. Any actions that appear to have the goal of discomfort are likely to turn away students with already tenuous commitment. Instead, the focus is another basic counseling tenet, an emphasis on personal strengths (Gelso & Fretz, 2001), helping students discover and affirm them in the interest of coping effectively with developmental and other challenges (e.g., "You'll use your intelligence to figure this out and get what you need." "You're a survivor." "It took courage to speak up for yourself.").

Nonjudgment. A nonjudgmental facilitator posture is crucial to building trust, particularly important when working with students who find it difficult to trust adults. All group members, regardless of age and circumstances, observe verbal and nonverbal nuances in facilitator responses. In groups in any venue, however, students who do not trust easily may immediately test the facilitator with rough language, comments meant to shock, and other disruptive actions. In fact, all or most members of a group might do this collectively, depending on group composition. Such behavior poses particular concerns in schools.

Rules. For defensible reasons, many group facilitators in schools set firm rules about behavior at the outset, adhering to school policy about language and behavior, thereby making a roller-coaster ride of "testing" less likely (but not impossible). Usually, some reference to basic courtesies is enough:

- respect for everyone and, therefore, no put-downs;
- eye contact, if that is comfortable, and respect for whoever is speaking;
- no talking when someone else is talking; and
- no talking about someone who is not present.

Asking young children to set rules for their group may certainly be appropriate; however, since many—if not most—school-aged group members have had no previous small-group experience, they sometimes appear to be uncomfortable when asked what rules should be set. They probably have no sense of what their "group" experience will be. Therefore, we recommend that the initial meeting involve an engaging, noninvasive, semistructured activity and discussion. At the end, the facilitator can say, "This is what we're going to be doing in our group—talking and doing things together." Because membership is likely voluntary, a positive first experience is essential. If rules appear to be needed, they can be established at the second meeting. In fact, at the end of the first meeting, members might be asked to think about what rules would be helpful, to be discussed at the next meeting. Whatever guidelines are set, facilitators need to be consistent in encouraging and enforcing them, orchestrating with arms and hands if necessary (e.g., extending the arm in the direction of inappropriate behavior and saying, with palm facing away, "Hey—now wait a minute. Remember the rule about respect."). Such an action often suffices when needing to curb inappropriate behavior. Among several responsibilities, the facilitator is expected to lead and "manage."

Disruptive behavior. Some groups pose considerable challenges collectively. We argue that if facilitators can remain poised and nonreactive during disruptions, foul language, or disrespect of peers, while not allowing the behavior to escalate out of control, they are likely to gain the trust of the group. Then, language seems invariably to improve over time, as members relax and connect with each other in new ways, even though old language habits for expressing strong feelings may reappear now and then. It should be noted that, a week after a "breakthrough" discussion in which students leave bravado and façade behind, it is not unusual for a group with trust issues to slide back into testing the facilitator at the next meeting. Intimacy and expression of feelings may have been quite unsettling. Wise facilitators process the past week's session and present sessions, and then normalize the upheaval. It does indeed "make sense."

Modeling respect and poise. Facilitators also have the opportunity to model for group members. When they are unconditionally respectful of behaviors that might seem strange to others (e.g., a group member who cannot make eye contact and who may doodle microscopically throughout each meeting, one who cries easily, one with poor hygiene, one unconnected to peers in school), they model respect, affirmation, and nonjudgment. When facilitators do not challenge a "pass," saying instead, "I respect your choice" or "I'm glad you can set a boundary like that," they affirm a member's autonomy. When they do their job as a facilitator of discussion among student peers, without drawing attention to themselves with self-disclosure, they model objectivity and unconditional, focused attention, which can be amazing to students from emotionally enmeshed families. When facilitators reframe ineffective behaviors or revelations concerning "bad" behaviors, they model respect for and understanding of the function of behavior. When they stay poised in response to shocking disclosures, they demonstrate that *anything* can be discussed, no matter how painful and uncomfortable. When they respond to an inappropriate question about themselves, they can deflect it:

> It makes sense that you're curious, but the group is for you, not for me. My job is to help you communicate with each other as peers, and I'm not your peer, so I have to keep myself out. That's what I'm trained to do.

Access. Group facilitators in schools can have daily access to students between meetings, including being able to observe them in classrooms and lunchroom and to check in, informally. Such a vantage point may be especially important when bullying has been revealed or when symptoms of depression, suicidal ideation or attempts, an eating disorder, or substance use have been evident or hinted at in group meetings. For weeks and months after school or personal tragedies, facilitators can also monitor students beyond group meetings. In our experience, even students without personal connections to victims can continue to be highly troubled by deaths and other tragedies—sometimes because "the world went on" too quickly.

Logistics. Group work in schools is fraught with logistical challenges. These can be daunting to school counselors, who may decide that the payoff is not worth the energy required to make groups happen. Logistical concerns include finding space for meetings, not easy in buildings with 95% to 100% room utilization; scheduling meetings at times which interfere least with classes; developing a method for reminding students of meetings; and securing parent permission, since even supportive parents may forget to respond. When group work is embraced by parents and school personnel, logistical hurdles are easier to overcome, of course.

Space. Group privacy is essential, but not always easy to secure in schools. Any quiet room, preferably smaller than a classroom and with a door that closes, can suffice for group work. In the authors' experience, interns, required by standards of CACREP (2001) to conduct groups, have creatively used concession areas, media rooms, and corners of cafeterias for group meetings when conference or counseling rooms have not been available. Veteran counselors, wisely using needs assessments, evaluations, and formal and informal communication with teachers and administrators, can sometimes secure other areas as well for groups.

Scheduling. Scheduling group meetings can also be a challenge. Some principals discourage counselors from taking students out of classes such as physical education, art, and music, since the teachers in those areas typically do not see the students every day and often have skills, performances, or projects for which regular attendance is critical. Other principals deny pullout for classes in the core curriculum. Still others recognize that meeting social and emotional needs is crucial to the success of the school and overtly support group work, including leaving any classroom. School counselors must, therefore, build credibility and market program components carefully, and they must be skilled in negotiation. They may be able to vary meeting times so that students do not miss the same class more than once during a 6-week period, for instance.

Certainly, school counselors must be sensitive to teachers, pressured as the latter are to increasing student achievement. Some teachers are likely to be unwilling to allow students to leave for groups under any circumstances. It might take a few years to build a relationship with those teachers sufficient to gain access to their students. Until then, groups scheduled during breakfast, lunch, or after school might be the only options for those students.

In terms of length and frequency, we believe that it is better to meet regularly—weekly—for even a relatively short series of meetings than to meet infrequently over a longer period of time. Teachers are likely to prefer a weekly rhythm, which helps them to know when to expect absences. Students then are also more likely to remember to come to group meetings; however, students usually need reminders, regardless of their ability, commitment, or school level. Basic to successful facilitation of school groups is determining the most efficient way to notify teachers and students. Especially for middle school and high school students, it is important to emphasize to both teachers and group members that missed work should be completed, students should remind their teachers before class that they will be leaving or will be absent, and they should get the assignment for the day.

Group Size and Composition. Group size needs to vary according to age and ability level, and this consideration makes school groups, certainly in elementary and middle schools, somewhat different from groups in other venues. A general guideline might be to match the number of members with age, conservatively, with perhaps 3 at grades two and three, 4 at grade four, and 6 to 7 in middle school (Peterson, 2007). The higher the verbal ability, level of social skills, and level of behavior, the larger groups can be. We do not recommend more than 8 or 9 at any level, however, even with gifted high school students. It is important that everyone be heard adequately at each meeting, including when structured activities require everyone in a circle to speak. A small group size means that members have an opportunity to become well acquainted beyond a superficial level. Small numbers, therefore, also contribute potentially to a sense of comfort and safety, less peer evaluation, and less perceived competitiveness.

With students at risk for poor outcomes, at any age or grade level, limiting group size is important because they especially need opportunities to be heard and to make significant social and emotional connections. Although it is possible that meetings can be as long as a class period, it is not unusual that school groups must fit into a 20- or 30-minute time period. In those situations, a small group size helps everyone to be heard.

Principals and teachers may request that the counselor "do something about" students with diagnosed ADHD, behavior problems, or suspected drug use. Counselors who are site supervisors often feel unable to address such needs because of time constraints. They may therefore recommend that an intern create a homogeneous group according to a particular behavior or disorder for their first group experience; however, a group of hyperactive students, for instance, is not conducive to focus. In general, we do not recommend that interns (or school counselors in general) facilitate groups made up entirely of students with significant behavior problems or with another kind of severe problem as the common denominator. Having group members who can model appropriate behavior and effective coping is important. In this regard, Kulic et al. (2001) recommended in-group heterogeneity, but "not so much that the group members have nothing in common on which to work" (p. 213). However, support groups for bereavement, divorce, or pregnancy are examples of groups justifiably homogeneous according to a common concern.

We believe that groups should be homogeneous according to age, when possible (Peterson, 2007). One or two years of age difference can mean a great deal of difference in social and emotional maturity. Even cognitively precocious gifted students may not be socially or emotionally advanced, even if they connect easily with adults. In this regard, grade-accelerated children may be mismatched with grade peers in an affectively oriented discussion group. Regardless of ability, it is more likely that 5 fourth graders will have similar concerns related to social and emotional development than 3 fourth graders and 2 sixth graders in a similar group. We hasten to add, however, that we prefer to group gifted children homogeneously by age and by ability because their sense of differentness means that they often do not trust that others can relate to their concerns. It may be difficult for them to be vulnerable and reveal limitations and concerns in mixed-ability groups. The literature suggests that though they experience the same developmental milestones as others, their developmental experiences are qualitatively different (Mendaglio, 2003).

Groups can help the genders—at any age—learn to comfortably communicate with each other. In that regard, it has been recommended that genders be mixed in groups (Thompson & Henderson, 2007). We recognize, however, that boys and girls often communicate differently and may share more when the other gender is not present. Therefore, we often form same-gender groups when they are geared to primary prevention, especially prior to high school. When the goal is secondary prevention (e.g., coping with divorce or bereavement), we typically form mixed groups. We do recognize that there is controversy related to mixing genders in groups (Gazda, 1989).

Attendance. Attendance is another factor to consider in schools. A group comprised of seven students with poor school attendance may actually have only two or three attending on a given day. While the smaller number can be conducive to intimacy and depth of discussion, attendance patterns should be taken into consideration when ascertaining group size. In addition, though closed groups are preferable to open groups (Jacobs, Masson, & Harvill, 2002), erratic attendance can contribute to closed groups resembling open groups. Group dynamics then differ from meeting to meeting, with consequent loss of trust likely. In general, we recommend that group composition not change after the group is underway, no matter how much a new student might seem to fit a particular ongoing group.

Needs Assessment. In addition, some sort of needs assessment, formal or informal, should be conducted—not only to justify the groups to parents, teachers, and administrators, but also perhaps to market the groups to prospective members. Understaffed and with full, highly fragmented days, school counselors often find it difficult to step back far enough to assess needs formally, but such assessments can help to generate support for group work.

Confidentiality. Because more than one client is involved, confidentiality cannot be guaranteed in group work (American Counseling Association, 1995). In addition, regardless of how much facilitators emphasize it, several factors somewhat specific to schools may challenge a facilitator's ability to maintain it. Ethical standards related to parent rights, potential harm, and informing administrators are only general guidelines, and pertinent dilemmas are common.

In addition, significant differences in members' abilities and social and emotional development, even when homogeneous according to grade level, may mean that facilitators must take seriously the guidelines in pertinent ethical codes (American Counseling Association, 1995; ASCA, 1998) about protecting members—from each other and from themselves. The latter is especially important for school-aged children. In our experience, children and adolescents are usually discreet when choosing personal information to share. Nevertheless, we encourage counseling students to employ "orchestration" immediately when a group member says, soberly, "I'm going to tell you guys something I've never told anyone before." We advocate holding up a flat hand at arm's length, with fingers tipped up, and saying something like this:

> Hang on for just a minute. I want to say something to the rest of you. He is probably going to tell us something serious and important, and I want to remind you of our agreement about confidentiality. Are you trustworthy? He's respecting you here when he shares this. Now [looking at the talker], are you sure you want to share what you were going to say?

Facilitators should be *prepared for* indiscreet comments or dramatic revelations, including date rape, eating disorders, domestic violence, and substance abuse. In our experience, however, such disclosures are more likely to occur during one-on-one sessions outside of the group because facilitators are trusted.

"Jan," a first-year counselor in a middle school, experienced a complex ethical dilemma when her principal dramatically challenged her about confidentiality. She had established a group component in her program, facilitating several groups each week. Eventually, an eighth grader revealed to his group that he had committed minor vandalism to a teacher's home the previous year. A fellow group member told this to his parents, who were teachers in the system, and they in turn told the principal. No name was revealed. The principal, who did not support group work, pressured Jan to reveal the name of the vandal, saying that she would be fired if she did not comply with his request. After consulting with her former supervisor and considering pertinent ethical codes, principles of ethical decision making (Kitchener 1984), legal obligations, and the always tenuous trust factor in schools, she decided to hold her ground. She wrote a letter to her superintendent, focusing on ethical standards and her process of deciding, and fortunately, he supported her, although she decided before the end of the school year to accept a counseling position in another district.

Parents may also pressure group facilitators to reveal particulars—because they are afraid of what their children may disclose or because they are simply curious. It is important for facilitators to explain, perhaps in the permission letter, the parameters surrounding communication with parents, not unlike what might be explained about individual counseling. We also recommend, however, that group work be presented to parents as a "curriculum," which serves as a framework for discussion of development-related topics. Counselors should not expect laypersons to understand ethical guidelines, of course, and therefore, should be ready to articulate pertinent standards if asked.

Subgrouping. Subgrouping, which involves members splitting off into smaller groups in or outside of group meetings, is usually seen as potentially destructive to groups; however, contact among school group members is usually unavoidable between meetings, and it is possible that good friends find themselves in the same group. Friendships may also develop in the group, and in fact, that may be a goal of some groups. Nevertheless, group facilitators need to address, in meetings, any subgrouping that appears to be detrimental to group functioning.

Effect on Context. Effective small-group work, particularly when extensive and coupled with regular and coordinated large-group work, has the potential to improve the general school culture and climate over time. When bullying is pervasive, when teachers are hostile to each other and impatient with students, when "discipline" is usually punitive and harsh, when cultural and ethnic groups are at odds, and when parents believe that teachers are not sensitive to their children's needs, the very presence of group work in the system sends an important message: students have social and emotional concerns. That message, in turn, can generate sensitivity, compassion, and mutuality among school personnel. In addition, as students make connections and break through stereotypes, a ripple effect may occur — behavior and attendance improve, teachers relax and are able to focus on teaching, principals face fewer student attitude and behavior problems, and parents notice positive differences at home. More positive feelings about school, and about cross-cultural interactions, contribute to school pride and commitment to learning.

Peterson and Ray (2006) found that victims of bullying believed that their not being known by classmates made them vulnerable (e.g., when they were new to a school or when beginning middle school). Quality and quantity of friends are related to whether students are victimized (Hodges & Perry, 1999). Groups can serve an important school-climate function by helping students to make connections, be known, gain confidence, and find peers with common interests.

Littrell and Peterson's (2005) *Portrait and Model of a School Counselor* detailed a comprehensive program comprising almost exclusively small- and large-group work. Counselor Claudia Vangstad involved over half of the students in her school in her clubs simultaneously, while also regularly doing planned and ad hoc classroom lessons. Eventually, after her troubled K–5 school had been transformed into harmony and cooperation, she found that individual counseling was needed only rarely.

As another example, the first author, responsible for a special population, facilitated ten groups for gifted students per week for several years in a high school of 1500 students and perceived a significant, positive shift in teacher and administrator attitudes about social and emotional concerns of that population (Peterson, 1990). Arrogance became less of a problem in classrooms and elsewhere, and teachers regularly referred students to the groups when concerned about them. Group members found mind-mates, shy students had social contact, and group members greeted each other in the halls. At year's end, some students indicated that their group had helped them through difficult family or personal transitions. Some self-referred for individual counseling as a result of their group experiences.

Because group work in schools can be extensive, depending on investment and support, and because the student population is fairly stable over time, group work has the potential to effect significant change in an entire school. When groups help students find commonalities, lessen socioeconomic and cultural divisions, and become involved and comfortable at school, students can then turn at least some of their focus from social competition, bullying, and fighting to academics and school-based activities.

Development—Group Raison d'etre

The Common Concern. For primary and secondary prevention, there is often no one common concern that brings students together, unlike group work which is part of treatment (e.g., substance use, bereavement, anger management, eating disorders, problems with authority, criminal activity, or sexual molestation). In that sense, school groups are unlike community support groups or therapy groups in treatment centers. Developmental challenges can be viewed as the common denominator for school groups, regardless of whether groups are formed to address problematic behavior, career development, socialization, family transitions, peer relationships, or prevention of problems. Before we present our model for group work in schools, we will focus briefly on development, as related to school groups.

Developmental Goals. Counselors often work with people facing challenges related to life transitions, including normal developmental transitions (Corey & Corey, 1998). Indeed, a key tenet of school counseling, which is especially emphasized in comprehensive developmental guidance programs (Gysbers & Henderson, 2000), is that it is based on developmental principles and intentionally structured to support and enhance development, with curriculum selected according to students' developmental levels. Indeed, school counselors are to attend to students' academic, career, and personal/social development (Campbell & Dahir, 1997). School counselors are resident developmental specialists in their schools, and ideally, their programs support development in *all* students, not just in those with obvious problems or those at risk for serious problems or those who are motivated and ready to learn. Group work is well suited to meeting broad developmental goals.

Formidable Challenges. All school-aged children are developing, of course, and they will continue to do so throughout their lifespan. All face, and will continue to face, general developmental tasks, with timing of task accomplishment varying along a wide continuum. For some students, these challenges are formidable. Traumatic life events, disabling conditions, family characteristics, environmental contexts, biochemical and neurological predispositions, and significant peers and adults all potentially affect developmental progress, no less so during the school years than earlier or later in life. Developmental "stuckness" can occur at any stage. School-aged children and adolescents, normally experiencing rapid change, however, are probably particularly affected by life circumstances largely beyond their control. It is important that educators, including school counselors, continue to learn about child and adolescent development and continue to use it as one template when assessing and providing educational and supportive services (Gazda et al., 2001).

A Template for Prevention and Remediation. A developmental emphasis in group work is appropriate for both types of prevention, regardless of where group members are on a continuum of development and regardless of their behavior or current emotional state. Facilitators can focus on pertinent developmental tasks (e.g., establishing a sense of competence, developing social skills, forging identity, finding career direction, differentiating from family, or developing mature relationships). This emphasis can help students of any age normalize developmental challenges, move over developmental hurdles, increase self-awareness, enhance sense of personal agency, anticipate developmental transitions (e.g., entering puberty, moving to a new school level, establishing romantic relationships, or leaving home after high school), and move confidently into the next stage of development. Students can share insights about cognitive, physical, social, and emotional development and can dissect the stress that often accompanies developmental challenges. Unfortunately, talking about development *as* development probably happens only rarely—even with peers. An actively listening, poised, developmentally savvy adult, with competence as a facilitator, may also be an unusual experience.

All students can benefit from small-group work. Those who appear to be functioning optimally, including gifted students (Peterson, 1990, 1998, 2000, 2002), might actually not be doing well behind a façade of confidence. They can benefit from group discussion on any number of developmental topics, feel heard, find support, connect to peers in a safe context, and feel more confident when facing future challenges. Students already having concerns in academic, social, and emotional areas can discover commonalities, feel heard and understood, and be supported by fellow group members during difficult times. Students who are in need of responsive services because of problems related to anger management, loss and grief, family illness, traumatic life events, problems with authority, or social alienation, for example, can benefit from straightforward discussion related to specific problems in support-type groups (Rainey, Hensley, & Crutchfield, 1997), but they can also benefit from interaction limited generally to developmental concerns (Peterson, 1990, 2007). The latter inevitably connects them to other group members, and that connection may be crucial to their moving forward positively. Similarly, students returning from treatment for addictions, eating disorders, or mental health crises may attend not only to issues related to their treatment, but also to related developmental challenges.

A Model for Small Group Work in Schools

The model we advocate for small group work in schools is versatile and defensible. Groups are supportive, facilitators are nonevaluative, and sessions are focused, but flexible. The group curriculum is intended to enhance functioning in the present and in the future, but not to "solve problems." When focusing on fostering students' social and emotional growth, facilitators are alert to personal strengths.

Versatile and Flexible, yet Focused. One distinguishing feature of the model we advocate for small-group work in schools is that it is appropriate for a wide variety of groups, regardless of whether there are presenting issues or risk factors. It is flexible in that facilitators are encouraged to be nimble, following strands that emerge in the interaction; however, there is also a clear, defined, defensible, and developmentally appropriate focus for each meeting. This approach can potentially enhance present and future functioning through increasing self-awareness and awareness of others and providing a rare opportunity to learn important, new communication skills. Achieving these objectives can lessen the severity of presenting issues and also help well-functioning students avoid problems. Fundamentally, developmental challenges, not presenting issues, are the focus of group discussions, even in groups geared to remediation. Regardless of group purpose, each topic is presented to group members as being important to "growing up." Each topic is presented as a "normal" challenge.

With this model, groups do not focus on symptoms of pathology or on "bad behavior," per se. Regardless of presence or absence of significant issues, and regardless of age, gender, culture, socioeconomic circumstances, comfort level in school or at home, or personal problems, we have found that children and adolescents appreciate an opportunity to focus on general developmental concerns in a small group with their peers and a stable, attentive, nonjudgmental adult. School-age children are more than their labels or problems, of course, and small-group work can function as crucial support during years of rapid and complex development. Furthermore, adults, including educators, do not know much about the inner world of youth. It is dangerous to assume anything about the internal experiences of students in schools—whether faces and behavior reflect distrust and animosity or competence and social ease.

Justifiable. As discussed earlier, any group curriculum must be justified to administrators. They need to be generally aware of what groups are discussing so that they can be prepared to respond to parents who suspect that group discussions air "family laundry" and teachers who wonder if groups criticize teachers or wonder if missed classroom time is justified. Facilitators, too, should be able to articulate the curriculum. Being able to say, "We've been dealing with stress for the past four weeks," "We're focusing on self-awareness and identity development this semester," or, more specifically, "We've been talking about bullying" helps to lessen anxiety and suspicion and also underscores that the groups deal with significant issues and are worth the effort required to surmount logistical challenges. Topics can be defended as developmentally appropriate and developmentally informative.

Generated by Assumptions. Several assumptions helped to generate our model and apply to groups regardless of age and developmental level:

- All students need to be heard and taken seriously.
- Shy students also want to be recognized and known.
- All students need support, no matter how strong and successful they seem and no matter how rough their exterior or how great their bravado.
- All students feel stressed at times.
- All students are sensitive to family tension.
- All students feel angry at times.
- All students feel socially inept and uncomfortable at times.
- All students worry about the future at times.
- All students, no matter how smooth and self-confident they may appear, need practice talking about social and emotional concerns.
- All students wear a façade at times.

Therefore, all students deserve and can benefit from development-focused discussion in small groups. Groups can provide a safe environment for addressing whatever students bring to meetings—stress, anger, social discomfort, anxiety, guilt, rebelliousness, and doubts, for instance. Group meetings can also help peers and facilitator "stand beside" members who are experiencing crises. In addition, students with problems related to classroom behavior, substance abuse, eating disorders, depression, obsessive-compulsive disorder, or conduct disorder, for instance, can make positive connections with peers and with a caring, nonjudgmental adult. Referrals to community resources are appropriate for severe disorders, given school counselors' time constraints and probable lack of specific expertise, but concurrent with receiving therapy elsewhere, students can participate in the group curriculum at school. The message to group members is that everyone is developing and facing basic, universal developmental challenges, even though circumstances make each individual's experience qualitatively unique.

Supportive, Nonevaluative. Ideally, small-group work in schools moves students momentarily out of a potentially competitive, evaluative environment into a context where no one dominates, no grades are given, and no one judges. The model presented here holds assiduously to the idea of nonjudgment, which is particularly important in the U.S. education system, which typically reflects the dominant culture value-orientation of individual, competitive, conspicuous achievement (Spindler & Spindler, 1990).

Unconditional affirmation may be absent elsewhere in students' lives—in homes with nonsupportive or inattentive parents, in homes where parents control with constant criticism and negativity, and even in situations where parents are highly invested in the school and social successes of their children. Potentially, all students appreciate a nonevaluative group facilitator who does not evaluate performance, and who can accept them without a "Yes, but . . . ."

Fundamentally, the groups we advocate put development at the center, rather than instructing, advising, or problem solving, which often characterize remedial groups. Development is the vehicle for establishing connections with others and fostering awareness and affirmation of self, regardless of whether group purpose is prevention or remediation. Members learn to adopt the nonjudgmental, developmentally oriented posture of the facilitators. Peers understand that it takes great energy to manage difficult situations. Academic work may not be a priority for some students, and casual conversations elsewhere may be difficult because life does not *feel* casual. Regardless of school performance, group members support each other and explore coping strategies, while keeping the focus on development. Facilitators can affirm students where they are, not be preoccupied with where they ought to be.

Not Problem Solving. The model we present here also includes conscientiously maintaining a one-down posture, which puts group members into the "teacher" position. We have concluded that inviting students to talk about their own development-related experiences generates rich and edifying content; decreases alienation and loneliness; normalizes thoughts, feelings, and behaviors; and offers hope for success in the ongoing journey of development. Goals are not explicitly to eradicate problems or problematic behaviors or even to instruct, but instead to provide support for development. Developmental assistance potentially helps students to cope with difficult circumstances, assuage doubts and discomforts, and feel more connected to peers.

Personal and behavior problems might be resolved gradually as a result of the emphasis on development. Depending on etiology, such issues as underachievement, outbursts of temper, or substance abuse may gradually diminish. Study skills might be enhanced through having members talk about what strategies work and do not work for them, rather than approaching the topic didactically. Whole-classroom lessons are more appropriate for addressing study-skills training, but small groups can explore social, emotional, and environmental issues related to studying. Learning to study can be framed as a developmental challenge, one to be figured out. Obviously, if a problem is presented, or if a destructive group dynamic needs attention, the situation should be processed in the group. A brief, solution-focused approach (Littrell, 1998) can also be employed ad hoc, but specific problem solving is generally not the focus otherwise. A common stereotype of counselors is that they "solve problems." Therefore, providing students with an experience different from what was expected helps them to broaden their understanding of counseling and diminish negative stigma associated with it. They might readily seek it out in the future when needed—and before situations escalate into crises.

Developmental Objectives. The focus is on development—helping students understand it, normalize it, and manage it. Expectations are geared to the age and developmental level of the group. Developmental objectives such as the following, however, usually are appropriate for any age and level:

- increase self-awareness and affirm personal strengths
- gain understanding of developmental tasks
- gain insights about human nature
- gain skills related to expressing and articulating feelings
- develop social skills
- learn to give and receive feedback and compliments
- discover shared developmental concerns
- break down stereotypes
- develop trust
- develop effective coping strategies
- learn how to deal with stress, anger, fear, anxiety, and worry
- understand and find support for dealing with life transitions, including change/loss
- learn how to ask for and accept help when needed
- consider ways to relate with teachers and people in authority effectively
- learn how to deal effectively with "the system"
- develop skills related to self-advocacy

For all ages, probably most crucially for adolescents, the skills learned through small-group discussion will also help them in dating, marriage/partnership, employment, and parenting relationships. All of these areas represent ongoing development. New skills can help to break negative, nonnurturing patterns.

Focused. In general, the focus for group meetings is normally not a particular issue, behavior, need, or goal, even for remedial groups. Rather, the focus, not announced to members ahead of time, might be a concept or construct (e.g., multiple intelligences, success/failure, maturity, or depression), a theme (e.g., courage, transitions, personal strengths and limitations, loss, stress, coping, having fun, or making mistakes), a developmental task (e.g., forging an identity, developing relationships, or finding career direction), an issue (e.g., bullying, gossip, social exclusion, loneliness, expressing anger without hurting self and others, or unmet needs), a skill (e.g., giving and receiving compliments, or active listening), or an idea (e.g., that people allow tests and evaluations to "define" them, or that adolescents have more challenges now than in the past). A short series of meetings might be organized around one of these—stress, for example. Generally, we encourage facilitators to have some degree of closure on the topic at the end of each meeting—with reflection and summation. Closure gives facilitators an opportunity to commend group members for their seriousness, cooperation, and contribution. Even noting their progress in "becoming a group" is important affirmation.

Why have a topic to explore—an "umbrella idea"? Not all adolescents are as flexible as they might appear. On the other hand, some are quite flexible and, especially if they are verbal and spontaneous, may prefer a loose format. They might say, "Just let us come in here and talk about whatever we want to." The flexible structure that we recommend is appropriate for a wide continuum of needs and personalities—from those who resist structure to those who are uncomfortable without it. By not announcing topics in advance of a meeting, facilitators avoid having students prematurely deem them "not interesting." If students ask, facilitators can say, "It will be a good one. Trust me." Facilitators probably should come to a meeting with two related topics in mind, however, in case one topic fails to generate discussion—perhaps because it was not developmentally salient.

Students who like order and structure and are uncomfortable without a "map" usually want group time to be worthwhile in specific terms. They might choose not to attend when something else seems preferable. They might also object to the fact that assertive or dramatic members set the pace and direction each time. They might conclude that the groups "don't really do anything." Discussion groups should not be just for students who talk easily—or for those who talk because they want to have control. In our experience, students appreciate the universality of developmentally oriented topics. They also are often surprised when they discover commonalities with peers in the group. Otherwise, socioeconomic status, culture/ethnicity, ability level, and course selection, for instance, may preclude communication with each other. Having structure, including a focus, "levels the playing field." Everyone is developing. No one can claim that growing up is not a challenge. Everyone needs skills—and practice.

Even with structure, group discussions need not be rigidly programmed. Direction can be changed nimbly. An altered group dynamic might need to be processed, or a school crisis or death of a peer might completely replace the planned topic for the day. A group member's potentially dangerous misinformation (e.g., about various drugs, sexually transmitted diseases, or depression) might prompt a facilitator to offer to bring pertinent information to the next session. In short, a good facilitator can accommodate various strands that emerge, yet gently steer the group to closure, overtly acknowledging that the focus inspired unexpected directions. Especially when topics appear to be intimidating and difficult, the focus is an excuse to persist with tough questions and deal with developmental challenges, not just gripes and frustrations. In that sense, the topic has an important function.

When facilitators are nonjudgmental and nonevaluative, maintain a one-down posture, and keep the focus on development, students who may be secretly distressed are likely to seek them out for consultation. Facilitators who have earned the trust of their groups can provide a critical and potentially life-saving function by generating a request for help.

Avoiding Jargon. We believe that focusing on self-esteem, motivation, or friendship, per se, is generally not productive. That is not to say that enhancing these is not a worthy goal. Rather, by facilitating meaningful and pertinent discussion about developmental challenges, helping students make solid connections with each other, enhancing social skills through activities and discussion, and generating rich information about development, groups potentially enhance how members feel about and view themselves and how much they care about schoolwork. Whether they are all pregnant teens, unwed fathers, substance abusers, underachievers, extreme introverts, or high achievers, or whether they fit more than one of these categories, focused, flexible, topic-organized discussion can indeed help all to survive and find support, enhance well being, and feel better about present and future. Self-esteem and motivation are probably both related to developmental challenges, and friendship skills can be enhanced through making connections about development. Therefore, focusing on developmental topics makes sense.

Sample Sessions

Primary prevention. An example of a primary prevention session format and focus, using a paper-and-pencil activity, is entitled "Family Roles" (Peterson, 2007) and can be used at late-elementary through high school grade levels. In this session, students check which of approximately 30 family roles (e.g., peacemaker, gets the most attention, gets the least attention, easy to raise, easily upset, sensitive, responsible, hot-tempered, or leader) are theirs at home. After they read their list of roles, other members can ask for elaboration on various roles. The facilitator keeps track of the roles mentioned, and the group guesses, at the end, which roles were listed most often. Members then mark roles they enjoy or are uncomfortable with and articulate associated feelings. The facilitator introduces the idea that a family member may do a role so well that no one else has to do it. Discussion follows. Students speculate about whether they think they will assume similar roles at work or at home in the future. This session's focus is on development as related to relationships—in this case, with siblings, parents, and family.

Secondary prevention, focusing on teens beginning to be involved in cross-cultural harassment. This session, without a hands-on activity, is entitled "Does the Stereotype Fit?" (Peterson, 2007) and is related to identity development. The group may purposely include students from two or more cultural groups. After being asked to define *stereotype*, students share how they themselves might be stereotyped in school. Then the facilitator asks how they do and/or do not fit the stereotypes mentioned. The discussion then shifts to what members wish classmates, teachers, and parents understood about them.

Even early adolescents and late-elementary children generally engage readily around this topic. The word *stereotype* might be new to them, but they certainly know about critical judgment of and by peers who do not know them. Usually, having group members first speak about how they think others view them, instead of vice versa, safely opens up the dialogue to direct references to positive and negative assumptions. The dialogue isn't *about* people from another culture; it is *with* them. As after any discussion, it is important to process it: "What was it like to talk about stereotypes with a group that has kids from many cultures in it?" It is not unusual to hear comments that begin with "I never thought about that before . . ." or "I think it's not very nice to look at someone you don't know and judge them" or "We are a lot alike" or "I think it's nice how they care about their cousins and relatives so much."

Remediation, focusing on students expelled for fighting. A session entitled "In Control, out of Control," again involving just discussion, encourages students to reflect on the idea of control. The facilitator invites them first to describe situations and locations where they feel in control (e.g., manipulating, intimidating, having a temper outburst, being with a best friend, or working at a job) and then what they associate with feeling "out of control" (e.g., intense emotions, violence, social situations, drug use, fears and anxiety, developmental transitions, walking in crowded school hallways, or sexual feelings). Discussion then focuses on the extent members feel in control, their feelings about people who seem to be in control, normalizing out-of-control feelings, and how adults in their lives reflect "control." Though the facilitator maintains a nondidactic, non-problem-solving posture, discussion may move toward strategies for achieving a sense of control. This strand can be framed (and summarized to members later) as related to social, emotional, career, and academic development; skill-building; and support for moving to the next stage of "growing up."

Enhancing Lives in the Present and in the Future. Not only can school groups enhance mental health and help students survive difficult situations, but they also might help to decrease domestic and community violence in the future. Improved communication skills and the discovery that others are also struggling with developmental concerns are likely to help future partner and parent–child communication, not to mention work relationships. Behavior in those contexts will likely be affected by the interpersonal skills, attitudes toward others, and self-concepts that develop during the school years.

Groups provide both well-functioning and poorly functioning students an opportunity to develop skills related to expressing "emotional language." For example, they can learn that fear, worry, anxiety, frustration, irritation, sadness, disappointment, and anger can be talked about with others, as can joy, satisfaction, delight, and intense interest. Adolescent difficulties related to identity are normalized when group members share their confusion and concerns. Discovering that peers share many of their concerns helps adolescents to feel less lonely, less awkward, and less concerned about a critical "imaginary audience" (Elkind, 1984). If students feel connected to others, they are less likely to feel disenfranchised, perhaps resulting in less aggressive behavior and externalizing difficulties (Hymel, Rubin, Rowden, & LeMare, 1990), improved classroom adjustment (Mannarino, Christy, Durlak, & Magnussen, 1982), and even decreased criminal activity in the community (Schaeffer, Petras, Ialongo, Poduska, & Kellam, 2003).

Discussion can also explore real and potential relationships—with siblings, teachers, peers, persons in authority, and romantic interests. Perfectionism, substance abuse, eating disorders, depression, and sexual orientation are potential foci as well. Groups can also talk about "the system" and consider ways to self-advocate effectively in it. They can learn how to ask for help when needed and can be encouraged to be appropriately "selfish" in terms becoming educated—for present and future benefit. They can also learn how to give and receive compliments and other kinds of feedback.

Future Directions

Recommendations for Preparation and Practice

Because group work is integral to a well-planned, well-articulated school counseling curriculum, counselor educators need to maximize the impact of the typical group-training course on future school counselors by integrating content related to group work in schools and also by attending to group principles elsewhere in the preparatory curriculum, especially during field experiences (Akos et al., 2004). In terms of later professional development, workshops need to address real needs of school counselors in regard to group work. Wiggins and Carroll's (1993) subjects, for instance, had many concerns related to group leadership, group process, organizational issues, techniques, rules, and goals. Systematic national advocacy of small-group work in schools, with easily accessed workshops for training and retraining, can help veterans and novices alike to incorporate small groups regularly into their programs.

Recommendations for Research

Process and outcome research have been neglected. Kulic et al. (2001) examined a large body of research literature related to prevention-oriented group work for youth and made recommendations for ensuring quality and replicability: (a) careful documentation (e.g., member characteristics, prevention goals, techniques, theoretical orientation, duration); (b) true experiments; (c) follow-up assessments, including parents and teachers; and (d) facilitator training, especially for unstructured group processes. Experimental process and outcome studies comparing groups employing the practice-based model presented here with control groups would illuminate the impact of a strictly developmental focus. Follow-up studies could examine developmental gains and hardiness, with implications for "teaching resilience."

In addition, more studies of the long-term effects of large-scale, systemic group programs on school climate, school metrics, family, and community are needed. Cross-cultural groups, in contrast to culturally homogeneous groups (Bilides, 1990), offer opportunities for examination of the effects of developmentally focused group work on cross-cultural communication, school violence, attendance, and academic achievement, for example.

Conclusion

A small-group component in school counseling programs allows counselors to provide an important, multifaceted service to many students concurrently. Groups can be directed toward primary or secondary prevention or remediation. Regardless of purpose, however, development is at the heart of group work in schools, with the focus on helping students successfully meet developmental challenges. School groups are usually similar to groups elsewhere in terms of therapeutic factors, group dynamics, norming, termination, and strength-focus. However, group work in schools often differs significantly from group work elsewhere in regard to purpose, content, structure, recruitment, marketing, facilitation, logistics, group size and composition, attendance, needs assessment, confidentiality, subgrouping, and effect on context, as well as the reality that development is the common concern and can be addressed, per se. Several of these differences might explain the lack of group components in many school counseling programs. The model for group work presented here incorporates all of these similarities and differences, but sustains focus on development regardless of presenting issues and regardless of group purpose.

References

Akos, P., Goodnough, G. E., & Milsom, A. S. (2004). Preparing school counselors for group work. *Journal for Specialists in Group Work, 29,* 127–136.

American Counseling Association. (1995). *American Counseling Association code of ethics and standards of practice.* Alexandria, VA: Author.

American School Counselor Association. (1998). *Ethical standards for school counselors.* Alexandria, VA: Author.

Appleton, V. E., & Dykeman, C. (1996). Using art in group counseling with Native American youth. *Journal for Specialists in Group Work, 21*(4), 224–231.

Baker, S. B., & Gerler, E. R., Jr. (2004). *School counseling in the twenty-first century.* Upper Saddle River, NJ: Pearson Education.

Bauer, S. R., Sapp, M, & Johnson, D. (2000). Group counseling strategies for rural at-risk high school students. *High School Journal, 83*(2), 41–50.

Benard, B. (2004). *Resiliency: What we have learned.* San Francisco, CA: WestEd.

Bilides, D. G. (1990). Race, color, ethnicity, and class: Issues of biculturalism in school-based adolescent counseling groups. *Social Work with Groups, 13*(4), 43–58.

Bogat, G. A., Caldwell, R. A., Guzman, B., Galasso, L., & Davidson, W. S., II (1998). Structure and stability of maternal support among pregnant and parenting adolescents. *Journal of Community Psychology, 26,* 549–568.

Brantley, L. S., Brantley, P. S., & Baer-Barkley, K. (1996). Transforming acting-out behavior: A group counseling program for inner-city elementary school pupils. *Elementary School Guidance & Counseling, 31*(2), 96–105.

Brigman, G., & Campbell, C. (2003). Helping students improve academic achievement and school success behavior. *Professional School Counseling, 7*(2), 91–98.

Burnham, J. J., & Jackson, C. M. (2000). School counselor roles: Discrepancies between actual practice and existing models. *Professional School Counseling, 4,* 4–9.

Campbell, C. A., & Dahir, C. A. (1997). *The National Standards for School Counseling Programs.* Alexandria, VA: American School Counselor Association.

Campbell, C. (2003). Student success skills training: An Adlerian approach to peer counseling. *Journal of Individual Psychology, 59*(3), 327–333.

Chatterji, P., Caffray, C. M., Crowe, M., Freeman, L., & Jensen, P. (2004). Cost assessment of a school-based mental health screening and treatment program in New York City. *Mental Health Services Research, 6*(3), 155–166.

Claiborn, C. D., Kerr, B. A., & Strong, S. R. (1990). Group interventions in the schools. In T. B. Gutkin, & C. R. Reynolds (Eds.), *The handbook of school psychology* (2nd ed.), (pp. 703–732). Oxford, England: John Wiley & Sons.

Clark, A. J. (1995). The organization and implementation of a social interest program in the schools. *Individual Psychology: Journal of Adlerian Theory, Research & Practice, 51*(4), 317–331.

Comiskey, P. E. (1993). Using reality therapy group training with at-risk high school freshmen. *Journal of Reality Therapy, 12*(2), 59–64.

Corey, M. S., & Corey, G. (1998). *Becoming a helper* (3rd ed.). Pacific Grove, CA: Brooks/Cole.

Corey, M. S., & Corey, G. (2006). *Process and practice groups.* Belmont, CA: Thomson Brooks/Cole.

Council for Accreditation of Counseling and Related Educational Programs. (2001). *CACREP accreditation manual.* Alexandria, VA: Author.

Cowen, E. L. (1997). Schools and the enhancement of children's wellness: Some opportunities and some limiting factors. In R. P. Weissberg & T. P. Gulotta (Eds.), *Healthy children 2010: Establishing preventive services: Issues in children's and families' lives* (Vol. 9, pp. 97–123). Thousand Oaks, CA: Sage.

Dansby, V. S. (1996). Group work with the school system: Survey of implementation and leadership role issues. *Journal for Specialists in Group Work, 21,* 232–242.

DeLucia-Waack, J. L., & Gerrity, D. (2001). Effective group work for elementary school-age children whose parents are divorcing. *Family Journal: Counseling & Therapy for Couples & Families, 9*(3), 273–284.

Dryfoos, J. G. (1994). Medical clinics in junior high school: Changing the model to meet demands. *Journal of Adolescent Health, 15*(7), 549–557.

Elkind, D. (1984). *All grown up and no place to go.* Reading, MA: Addison-Wesley.

Fenlon, M. J., & Mufson, S. A. (1994). Psychological first aid for children exposed to sexual violence. *School Counselor, 42*(1), 48–58.

Finn, C. A. (2003). Helping students cope with loss: Incorporating art into group counseling. *Journal for Specialists in Group Work, 28*(2), 155–165.

Flitton, B., & Buckroyd, J. (2002). Exploring the effects of a 14 week person-centered counseling intervention with learning disabled children. *Emotional & Behavioural Difficulties, 7*(3), 164–177.

Gazda, G. M. (1989). *Group counseling: A developmental approach* (4th ed.). Boston: Allyn & Bacon.

Gazda, G. M., Ginter, E. J., & Horne, A. M. (2001). *Group counseling and group psychotherapy: Theory and application.* Boston: Allyn & Bacon.

Gelso, C., & Fretz, B. (2001). *Counseling psychology* (2nd ed.). Belmont, CA: Thomson.

Gerler, E. R., Drew, N. S., & Mohr, P. (1990). Succeeding in middle school: A multimodal approach. *Elementary School Guidance & Counseling, 24*(4), 263–271.

Gladding, S. T. (2003). *Group work: A counseling specialty.* Upper Saddle River, NJ: Merrill/Prentice-Hall.

Glasser, W. (1986). *The control therapy-reality therapy workbook.* Canoga Park, CA: Institute for Reality Therapy.

Goldberg, B., & Tidwell, R. (1990). Ethnicity and gender similarity: The effectiveness of counseling for adolescents. *Journal of Youth & Adolescence, 19*(6), 589–603.

Griffin, N. C. (1998). Cultivating self-efficacy in adolescent mothers: A collaborative approach. *Professional School Counseling, 1,* 53–58.

Gysbers, N. C., & Henderson, P. (2000). Comprehensive guidance and counseling programs: A rich history and a bright future. *Professional School Counseling, 4,* 246–256.

Herring, R. D. (1996). Synergetic counseling and Native American Indian students. *Journal of Counseling & Development, 74*(6), 542–547.

Hess, A. M., Rosenberg, M. S., & Levy, G. K. (1990). Reducing truancy in student with mild handicaps. *RASE: Remedial & Special Education, 11*(4), 14–19, 28.

Hett, G. G., & Rose, C. D. (1991). Counselling children of divorce: A divorce lifeline program. *Canadian Journal of Counselling, 25*(1), 38–49.

Higgins, G. O. (1994). *Resilient adults: Overcoming a cruel past.* San Francisco: Jossey-Bass.

Hoag, M. J., & Burlingame, G. M. (1997). Evaluating the effectiveness of child and adolescent group treatment: A meta-analytic review. *Journal of Clinical Child Psychology, 26*(3), 234–246.

Hodges, E. V. E., & Perry, D. G. (1999). Personal and interpersonal consequences of victimization by peers. *Journal of Personality and Social Psychology, 76,* 677–685.

Humes, C. W., & Clark, J. N. (1989). Group counseling and consultation with gifted high school students. *Journal for Specialists in Group Work, 14*(4), 219–225.

Hymel, S., Rubin, K. H., Rowden, L., & LeMare, L. (1990). Children's peer relationships: Longitudinal prediction of internalizing and externalizing problems from middle to late childhood. *Child Development, 61*(6), 2004–2021.

Isaacs, M. (2003). Data-driven decision making: The engine of accountability. *Professional School Counseling, 6,* 288–295.

Jacobs, E. E., Masson, R. L., & Harvill, R. L. (2002). *Group counseling: Strategies and skills* (4th ed.). Pacific Grove, CA: Brooks/Cole.

Jeffery, G., Hache, G., & Lehr, R. (1995). A group-based Delphi application: Defining rural career counseling needs. *Measurement & Evaluation in Counseling & Development, 28*(1), 45–60.

Kim, R., & Hwang, M. (1996). Making the world I want: Based on reality therapy. *Journal of Reality Therapy, 16*(1), 26–35.

Kiselica, M. S., Gorczynski, J., & Capps, S. (1998). Teen mothers and fathers: School counselor perceptions of service needs. *Professional School Counseling, 2*, 146–152.

Kitchener, K. S. (1984). Intuition, critical evaluation and ethical principles: The foundation for ethical decisions in counseling psychology. *The Counseling Psychologist, 12*, 43–55.

Kizner, L. R., & Kizner, S. R. (1999). Small group counseling with adopted children. *Professional School Counseling, 2*(3), 226–229.

Kobasa, S. C. (1979). Stressful life events, personality and health: An inquiry into hardiness. *Journal of Personality and Social Psychology, 42*, 707–717.

Kostoulas, K. K., Berkovitz, I. H., & Arima, H. (1991). School counseling groups and children of divorce: Loosening attachment to mother in adolescent girls. *Journal of Child & Adolescent Group Therapy, 1*(3), 177–192.

Kulic, K. R., Dagley, J. C., & Horne, A. M. (2001). Prevention groups with children and adolescents. *Journal for Specialists in Group Work, 26*, 211–218.

LaFountain, R., Garner, N., & Boldosser, S. (1995). Solution-focused counseling groups for children and adolescents. *Journal of Systemic Therapies, 14*(4), 39–51.

LaFountain, R. M., Garner, N. E., & Eliason, G. T (1996). Solution-focused counseling groups: A key for school counselors. *School Counselor, 43*(4), 256–267.

Larkin, R., & Thyer, B. A. (1999). Evaluating cognitive-behavioral group counseling to improve elementary school students' self-esteem, self-control and classroom behavior. *Behavioral Interventions, 14*(3), 147–161.

Lazarus, A. A. (2005). Multimodal therapy. In R. J. Corsini & D. Wedding (Eds.), *Current psychotherapies* (7th ed., pp. 337–371). Belmont, CA: Brooks/Cole.

Littrell, J. M. (1998). *Brief counseling in action.* New York: Norton.

Littrell, J. M., & Peterson, J. S. (2005). *Portrait and model of a school counselor.* Boston: Lahaska Press/Houghton Mifflin.

Maddi, S. R. (2002). The story of hardiness: Twenty years of theorizing, research, and practice. *Consulting Psychology Journal: Practice and Research, 54*, 175–185.

Mannarino, A. P., Christy, M., Durlak, J. A., & Magnussen, M. G. (1982). Evaluation of social competence training in the schools. *Journal of School Psychology, 20*(1), 11–19.

Mendaglio, S. (2003). Heightened multifaceted sensitivity of gifted students: Implications for counseling. *The Journal of Secondary Gifted Education, 14*, 72–92.

Mitchum, N. T. (1991). Group counseling for Navy children. *School Counselor, 38*(5), 372–377.

Mosak, H. H. (2005). Adlerian psychotherapy. In R. J. Corsini & D. Wedding (Eds.), *Current psychotherapies* (7th ed., pp. 52–95). Belmont, CA: Brooks/Cole.

Muller, L. E. (2000). A 12-session, European-American-led counseling group for African American females. *Professional School Counseling, 3*(4), 264–269.

Muller, L. E., & Hartman, J. (1998). Group counseling for sexual minority youth. *Professional School Counseling, 1*(3), 38–41.

Nelson, L. J., Rubin, K. H., & Fox, N. A. (2005). Social withdrawal observed peer acceptance, and the development of self-perceptions in children ages 4 to 7 years. *Early Childhood Research Quarterly, 20*(2), 185–200.

Ohlsen, M. M. (1977). *Group counseling* (2nd ed.) New York: Holt, Rinehart & Winston.

Page, R. C., & Chandler, J. (1994). Effects of group counseling on ninth-grade at-risk students. *Journal of Mental Health Counseling, 16*(3), 340–351.

Passino, A. W., Whitman, T. L., Borkowski, J. G., Schellenbach, C. J., Maxwell, S. E., Koegh, D., et al. (1993). Personal adjustment during pregnancy and adolescent parenting. *Adolescence, 28*, 97–122.

Pedro-Carroll, J. (1997). The children of divorce intervention program: Fostering resilient outcomes for school-aged children. In G. W. Albee & T. P. Gullotta (Eds.), *Primary prevention works* (pp. 213–238). Thousand Oaks, CA: Sage Publications, Inc.

Pedro-Carroll, J. L., Sutton, S. E., & Wyman, P. E. (1999). A two-year follow-up evaluation of a preventive intervention for young children of divorce. *School Psychology Review, 28*, 467–476.

Peterson, J. S. (1990). Noon-hour discussion groups: Dealing with the burdens of capability. *Gifted Child Today, 13*(4), 17–22.

Peterson, J. S. (1998). Six exceptional young women at risk. *Reclaiming Children and Youth, 6*, 233–238.

Peterson, J. S. (2000). A follow-up study of one group of achievers and underachievers four years after high school graduation. *Roeper Review, 22*, 217–224.

Peterson, J. S. (2002). A longitudinal study of post-high-school development in gifted individuals at risk for poor educational outcomes. *Journal for Secondary Gifted Education, 14*, 6–18.

Peterson, J. S. (2007). *The essential guide to talking with teens: Ready-to-use discussions for school and youth groups.* Minneapolis, MN: Free Spirit.

Peterson, J. S. (in press), Individual counseling practice. In A. Vernon (Ed.), *Counseling children and adolescents* (4th ed.). Denver, CO: Love.

Peterson, J. S., & Ray, K. E. (2006). Bullying among the gifted: The subjective experience. *Gifted Child Quarterly, 50*, 252–269.

Prout, H. T, & DeMartino, R. A. (1986). A meta-analysis of school-based studies of psychotherapy. *Journal of School Psychology, 24*, 285–292.

Prout, S. M., & Prout, H. T. (1998). A meta-analysis of school-based studies of counseling and psychotherapy: An update. *Journal of School Psychology, 36*, 121–136.

Rainey, L. M., Hensley, F. A., & Crutchfield, L. B. (1997). Implementation of support groups in elementary and middle school assistance programs. *Professional School Counseling, 1*, 36–40.

Rak, C., & Patterson, L. E. (1996). Promoting resilience in at-risk children. *Journal of Counseling & Development, 74,* 368–373.

Raskin, N. J., & Rogers, C. R. (2005). Person-centered therapy. In R. J. Corsini & D. Wedding (Eds.), *Current psychotherapies* (7th ed., pp. 130–165). Belmont, CA: Brooks/Cole.

Risi, S., Gerhardstein, R., & Kistner, J. (2003). Children's classroom peer relationships and subsequent educational outcomes. *Journal of Clinical Child & Adolescent Psychology, 32*(3), 351–361.

Riva, M. T., & Haub, A. L. (2004). Group counseling in the schools. In J. L. DeLucia-Waack, D. A. Gerrity, C. R. Kalodner, & M. T. Riva (Eds.), *Handbook of group counseling and psychotherapy* (pp. 309–321). Thousand Oaks, CA: Sage.

Salzman, M, & D'Andrea, M. (2001). Assessing the impact of a prejudice prevention project. *Journal of Counseling & Development, 79*(3), 341–346.

Sanders, D. R., & Riester, A. E. (1996). School-based counseling groups for children of divorce: Effects on the self-concepts of 5th grade children. *Journal of Child & Adolescent Group Therapy, 6*(1), 27–43.

Schaeffer, C. M., Petras, H., Ialongo, N., Poduska, J., & Kellam, S. (2003). Modeling growth in boys' aggressive behavior across elementary school: Links to later criminal involvement, conduct disorder, and antisocial personality disorder. *Developmental Psychology, 39*(6), 1020–1035.

Shechtman, Z. (1993). Group psychotherapy for the enhancement of intimate friendship and self-esteem among troubled elementary-school children. *Journal of Social & Personal Relationships, 10*(4), 483–494.

Shechtman, Z. (1994). Group counseling/psychotherapy as a school intervention to enhance close friendships in preadolescence. *International Journal of Group Psychotherapy, 44*(3), 377–391.

Shechtman, Z. (2001). Prevention groups for angry and aggressive children. *Journal for Specialists in Group Work, 26*(3), 228–236.

Shechtman, Z., & Bar-El, O. (1994). Group guidance and group counseling to foster social acceptability and self-esteem in adolescence. *Journal for Specialists in Group Work, 19*(4), 188–196.

Shechtman, Z., Bar-El, O., & Hadar, E. (1997). Therapeutic factors in counseling and psychoeducational groups for adolescents: A comparison. *Journal for Specialists in Group Work, 22,* 203–213.

Shechtman, Z., & Pastor, R. (2005). Cognitive-behavioral and humanistic group treatment for children with learning disabilities: A comparison of outcomes and process. *Journal of Counseling Psychology, 52*(3), 322–336.

Shechtman, Z., Vurembrand, N., & Hertz-Lazarowitz, R. (1994). A dyadic and gender-specific analysis of close friendships of preadolescents receiving group psychotherapy. *Journal of Social & Personal Relationships, 11*(3), 443–448.

Slate, J. R., & Jones, C. H. (2003). Helping behaviorally at-risk middle school students with the no bad actions program: Winning with the N.B.A. *Journal of Education for Students Placed at Risk, 8*(3), 351–362.

Smith, S. E. (1997). Willingness of Korean-American elementary school children to participate with counselors in a developmental guidance program. *International Journal of Adolescence & Youth, 6*(4), 329–341.

Spindler, G., & Spindler, L. (1990). *The American cultural dialogue and its transmission.* London: Falmer Press.

Stickel, S. A. (1990). Using multimodal social-skills groups with kindergarten children. *Elementary School Guidance & Counseling, 24*(4), 281–288.

Stolberg, A. L., & Mahler, J. (1994). Enhancing treatment gains in a school-based intervention for children of divorce through skill training, parental involvement, and transfer procedures. *Journal of Consulting Psychology, 62,* 147–156.

Sullivan, J. R., & Wright, N. (2002). The collaborative group counseling referral process: Description and teacher evaluation. *Professional School Counseling, 5,* 366–368.

Thompson, C. L., & Henderson, D. A. (2007). *Counseling children* (6th ed.). Pacific Grove, CA: Brooks/Cole.

Usher, C. H., Carns, A. W., Carns, M. R., Jones, L., Wright, J., Garcia, J. L., et al. (1994). Highlights of a career assessment project with ninth grade students: A collaborative effort between university and public school personnel. *TCA Journal, 22*(1), 29–34.

Vernon, A. (1998a). The passport program. *A journey through emotional, social, cognitive, and self-development, grades 1–5.* Champaign, IL: Research Press.

Vernon, A. (1998b). *The passport program. A journey through emotional, social, cognitive, and self-development, grades 6–8.* Champaign, IL: Research Press.

Vernon, A. (1998c). *The passport program. A journey through emotional, social, cognitive, and self-development, grades 9–12.* Champaign, IL: Research Press.

Webb, L. D., & Myrick, R. D. (2003). A group counseling intervention for children with attention deficit hyperactivity disorder. *Professional School Counseling, 7*(2), 108–115.

Webb, L. D., Brigman, G. A., & Campbell, C. (2005). Linking school counselors and student success: A replication of the student success skills approach targeting the academic and social competence of students. *Professional School Counseling, 8*(5), 407–413.

Wei, X. (2000). Application of group psychotherapy in exam anxiety in high school students. *Chinese Mental Health Journal, 14*(3), 191–192.

Werner, E. E. (1986). Resilient children. *Young Children, 40,* 68–72.

Wheelan, S. A. (2005). *Group processes: A developmental perspective.* Boston: Allyn & Bacon.

Whiston, S. C. (2002). Response to the past, present, and future of school counseling: Raising some issues. *Professional School Counseling, 5,* 148–155.

Wiggins, J. D., & Carroll, M. R. (1993). Back to the basics: Perceived and actual needs of group leaders. *Journal for Specialists in Group Work, 18,* 24–28.

Wubbolding, R. E. (2001). *Reality therapy for the 21st century.* New York: Brunner/Mazel.

Yalom, I. D. (1985). *The theory and practice of group psychotherapy* (3rd ed.). New York: Basic Books.

Zinck, K., & Littrell, J. M. (2000). Action research shows group counseling effective with at-risk adolescent girls. *Professional School Counseling, 4*(1), 50–59.

XXVIII
CONDUCTING GROUPS IN SCHOOLS:
Challenges and Rewards

DENISE BEESLEY AND LISA L. FREY
University of Oklahoma

Introduction

Groups are integral to human development. We enter the world as part of a family group; we work, learn, and often play in groups. For these reasons, in schools, group counseling is a crucial component of every comprehensive developmental guidance program. Fortunately, the school setting actively lends itself to the constructive use of group counseling as a vehicle for addressing the respective developmental needs of elementary, middle school/junior high, and secondary students. In addition, group counseling has other important advantages, including the following: (a) It is a time- and cost-effective modality for helping students achieve academic, personal/social, and career success, consistent with the National Standards for School Counseling Programs; (b) it allows counselors to serve larger numbers of students with a greater variety of problems; (c) it provides real world experiences, including a sense of belonging, connection with others, and opportunities to learn from others; and (d) it allows students to help each other with problem solving, modeling, and practicing skills (Baker & Gerler, 2004; Campbell & Dahir, 1997; Davis, 2005; Gladding, 2003; Schmidt, 1999; Sciarra, 2004; Studer, 2005). Groups are also recognized as the preferred mode for delivering a range of counseling and psychoeducational services in educational settings by the American School Counselor Association (ASCA; 2003).

In this chapter, we present an overview of the unique issues involved in conducting groups in schools. These include definitions of terms and purposes and discussion of challenges and considerations; extant theories, research, and practice; accountability; and future trends and innovative practices. We also examine the contributions and limitations of various theories and the impact of contextual variables on the academic, social, and emotional functioning of children and adolescents in school settings. In the discussion of future trends and innovative practices, we propose consideration of the relational–cultural theory (Jordan, Kaplan, Miller, Stiver, & Surrey, 1991; Miller, 1984) as a vehicle for maximizing the potential of group work in promoting social and emotional competence among students, counselors, teachers, parents, and administrators. In order to infuse the material presented with a more practical, user-friendly format, we intersperse facets of a group counseling scenario throughout various sections. We hope that the mix of pertinent background information interwoven with aspects of a group in action will be a useful resource for school counselors and will encourage and support them in their continued good work with students.

Definitions, Purpose, and Rationale

Schmidt (1999) defined group counseling as "a confidential helping relationship in which the counselor encourages members to focus on developmental, preventive, or remedial issues with which they are concerned" (p. 161). The purpose of group counseling, according to Schmidt, is "for members to explore issues affecting their development and to form intimate relationships in which they accept and support one another in the process of resolving and coping with their concerns" (p. 163). Obviously, group work in schools may be conducted using small groups or larger group classroom guidance formats. While the two are similar in some respects, they do differ in several key areas including size, purpose, scope, functioning, interaction processes, and group dynamics. For example, guidance lessons are generally preventative and psycho-educational in nature and are conducted with all students in a particular grade within the confines of the classroom. Small groups, on the other hand, focus more on counseling-related issues such as personal growth and interpersonal relationships. For the purposes of this chapter, we focus on small group counseling work in schools.

Children and adolescents come to school with an array of needs and problems. With the realities of war, school and community violence, and domestic abuse graphically displayed in the media and, sometimes, in students' daily lives, it is no wonder that students are often apprehensive and anxious about their feelings, experiences, and relationships. Because groups mirror real-world relationships and schools, in many respects, are microcosms of the larger society, educational settings provide an ideal environment for individuals to safely explore relationships and personal beliefs, values, and feelings. For example, group processes foster the development of deeper intrapersonal and interpersonal insight, empathy, perspective-taking skills, and social and emotional competencies that are imperative for building and nurturing healthy relationships with others. They allow members the opportunity for self-examination, to learn and practice new coping and relationship skills, to problem solve, and to share their experiences in a caring, supportive environment (Davis, 2005; Schmidt, 1999; Sciarra, 2004).

Historical Perspectives on Group Work

The history of group counseling in America can be traced back to hospitals and schools at the beginning of the 20th century. The first psychotherapeutic group was conducted in 1905 in a Boston hospital setting with tuberculosis patients. At about this same time, classroom guidance work was being implemented by such pioneers as Eli Weaver, Jesse B. Davis, and Frank Parsons. Their seminal work in guidance and counseling continues to proliferate in schools across the nation today. Group work continued to evolve during and after the mental health movement of the 1920s. During this period, group counseling was prominent in child guidance centers using a model developed by Alfred Adler. Group counseling entered a new phase after World War II, when large numbers of returning veterans and a shortage of therapists led Dr. Carl Rogers and several of his colleagues to develop a model based on his Person-Centered Counseling Theory to train counselors to work with individuals in a group format. This eventually led other theorists such as Albert Ellis (Rational Emotive Behavior Therapy), William Glasser (Reality Therapy), and Fritz Perls (Gestalt Therapy) to adapt their techniques to group work as well. Shortly thereafter, these theories, among others, were adapted for use with groups in school settings. Other types of group modalities emerged during the 1960s and the 1970s; some are more accepted than others.

As a result of ethical concerns related to certain types of group practices during this period, the Association for Specialists in Group Work (ASGW) was established in 1973. This professional organization went to work quickly to establish practice guidelines and standards for the field and promote research and best practices in order to better regulate the specialty profession of group work. Since then, other counseling organizations have added divisions to represent counselors who do group work (e.g., American Psychological Association [APA], Division 49, Group Psychology and Group Psychotherapy). Today, group work is conducted in a variety of settings, including schools, universities, hospitals, community mental health clinics, private practice offices, businesses, and so forth.

Theories of Group Counseling in Schools

Developmental Theory

As mentioned previously, several theories for counseling individuals have been modified for work with small groups. However, because any counseling intervention in an educational setting must be appropriately adapted to students' current levels of functioning, developmental theories are used to undergird other counseling interventions. Utilizing developmental theory in working with children and adolescents is especially important in view of its emphasis on physiological, psychological, and social processes from birth as well as the interactions among individuals and their environments. The developmental needs and processes of children and adolescents have been explored and examined in the works of Gesell and Ilg (1946), Gesell and Ames (1956), Havighurst (1953), Kagan (1962), Bloom (1964), Erikson (1963), Piaget (1970), Kohlberg (1969), Gilligan (1982), and Super (1990), to name a few. Developmental theories, especially those that consider the impact of contextual issues on student functioning and identity development (e.g., Gilligan), are an excellent fit for group work in schools because they provide a structure for gauging development in children and adolescents and for developing age-appropriate activities and competencies to promote optimal skill development for all students.

Counseling Theories

In conjunction with these developmental perspectives, a variety of counseling theories have been developed and utilized in school settings to conceptualize and illuminate individual and group functioning. Some of the most frequently applied models include (a) Person-Centered Therapy (Rogers, 1951), with its emphasis on the therapeutic conditions of genuineness, empathy, and unconditional positive regard to promote interpersonal awareness, insight, and positive change; (b) Rational Emotive Behavior Therapy (REBT; Ellis, 1962), which focuses on challenging irrational thinking; (c) Reality Therapy (RT; Glasser, 1965), which emphasizes the development of the "identity" and taking responsibility for one's behavior; (d) Adlerian Therapy (Adler, 1998), with its emphasis on examining the purpose and goals of behavior to gain insight and develop prosocial behavioral alternatives; (e) Cognitive, Behavioral, and Social Learning Theories (Bandura, 1969; Beck, 1976; Krumboltz & Thoresen, 1969, 1976), which advocate assessing the problem, developing goals for behavior change, and utilizing techniques such as cognitive restructuring, self-monitoring, reinforcement, modeling, and behavioral rehearsal to ameliorate the problem; and (f) Solution-Focused Therapy (deShazer, 1985; O'Hanlan & Weiner-Davis, 1989; Walter & Peller, 1992), with its focus on looking for "exceptions" in order to turn them into solutions.

According to more recent research, the majority of counseling groups in schools use a combined cognitive and behavioral approach (Barlow, Burlingame, & Fuhriman, 2000; Kulic, Hore, & Dagley, 2000). However, Shechtman (2002) suggested that to assume that cognitive–behavioral therapy is more effective than other approaches for working with groups in school settings is presumptuous to say the least. This may be the case simply because other approaches have not been the focus of frequent study.

Process and Outcome Research on Group Work in Schools

Of the dearth of literature on counseling groups in general, there is even less information available on group work in schools, which, of course, has led to the continued call from various entities for more research on the effectiveness of group counseling in schools (e. g., Jacobs, Masson, & Harvill, 2002). Among the studies that have been done, Burnham and Jackson (2000) found that 90% of school counselors conduct small groups in their school setting. This research and the few other studies available suggest that small group interventions in schools can be effective with a range of student issues. Among the issues where group work has demonstrated effectiveness are the areas of (a) interpersonal skills (Amerikaner & Summerlin, 2001; Ciechalski & Schmidt, 1995; Rosenthal, 1993; Shechtman, 1994); (b) family issues (Arman, 2000; Kizner, 1999; Omizo & Omizo 1987b; Tedder, Scherman, & Wantz, 1987); (c) aggression and other behavioral problems (Brake & Gerler, 1994; Omizo, Hershberger, & Omizo, 1988; Shechtman, 2000; Shechtman & Ben-David, 1999; Shechtman & Nach- shol, 1996; Taylor, Liang, Tracy, Williams, & Seigle, 2002; Utay & Lampe, 1995; Verdyn, Lord, & Forrest, 1990); (d) academic achievement (Rowell & Hong, 2002; Shechtman, Gilat, Fos, & Flasher, 1996); (e) stress management (Brooks, 2004); (f) study/organizational skills (Cook & Kaffenberger, 2003); (g) self-esteem (DeLuca, Hazen, & Cutler, 1993; Hlongwane & Bason, 1990; Omizo et al., 1988; Riddle, Bergin, & Douzenis, 1997); (h) at-risk students (Blum & Jones, 1993; Ripley & Goodnough, 2001; Zinck & Littrell, 2000); (i) diversity issues (Bemak, Chi-Ying, & Siroskey-Sabdo, 2005; Bradley, 2001; Muller, 2000; Muller & Hartman, 1998; Reeder, Douzenis, & Bergin, 1997); (j) learning disabilities, ADHD, and gifted (Ciechalski & Schmidt; Omizo & Omizo, 1987a; Webb & Myrick, 2003); (k) improved attitudes (Myrick & Dixon, 1985); and (l) career (Barkhaus, Adair, Hoover, & Bolyard, 1985; Glaize & Myrick, 1984).

Limitations in the Research

Despite the previously cited research, one of the consistent criticisms of the literature in the field of group counseling in schools is the limited information on group counseling outcomes. Potential explanations for this phenomenon include the inherent difficulty in effectively measuring the complex dynamics of the group process. Another consideration is that much of the group work that is conducted occurs in school settings by school counselors, who do not have the time, the necessary training, or the inclination to conduct research on the groups they administer. Also, despite a general consensus in the existing literature that group counseling in schools is effective for children and adolescents (Hoag & Burlingame, 1997; Kulic et al., 2000; Shechtman, 2002; Whiston & Sexton, 1998) and as effective as individual counseling (Hoag & Burlingame; Shectman & Ben-David, 1999), narrative reviews point to a lack of sophistication and rigor in methodology (Hoag & Burlingame). It seems that there is a consensus that groups are effective, but specifics on what makes them so and evidence of overall impact are lacking in the literature (Shechtman, 2002). Shechtman further added that process research is particularly important for the continued development of theory in the area of group work with children and adolescents and is crucial to informing counselors about evidence-based practice.

Of the limited number of studies that have been conducted examining process variables in group work with youth, there is some indication that the process of group development departs to some extent from what research has shown with adults. For example, research with children has shown that the "working" stage of group development occurs very quickly, which is congruent with observations of children's openness and willingness to self-disclose (Shechtman, 2002). As for therapeutic factors identified in the adult literature, only two of those factors were consistently found in work with adolescent groups—namely, catharsis and interpersonal learning (Shechtman, 2002). A third influential factor, which has rarely been found in research with adult groups, was social skill learning (Shechtman, 2002). This research provides further evidence that developmental factors play an important role in group work with youth and echoes a cautionary note about assuming that adult theories and models can be applied across the board with children and adolescents.

Additional Perspectives on Extant Research and Theory

While it is clear that a range of techniques from various theories has been applied in working with small groups in school settings, there is some concern, given the technological, demographic, and sociopolitical changes in society, that existing theories may fall short of being sufficient for working with students in the 21st century. This lack of preparedness to effectively deal with schools' changing demographics across the country leads to many students feeling isolated and alienated. This isolation, in turn, often leads to problems with truancy, classroom behavior, academic failure, and increased drop out rates. Shechtman (2002) suggested that what is needed is a theoretical model that accounts for children's and adolescents' needs for emotional expression, social connectedness, and practical support with problem issues.

While various developmental theories and traditional therapies such as Client-Centered Therapy, REBT, RT, Adlerian Therapy, and Cognitive and Behavioral Therapies have served as a foundation for working with children, adolescents, and adults throughout the 20th and into the 21st century, it is important to recognize that these perspectives may be limited in their abilities to adequately address the needs of a changing society. Some of these limitations have been discussed in the literature and include the observations that, for the most part, existing traditional theories (a) were based on societal and family dynamics from the previous century, (b) were developed for use in clinical settings, (c) reflect deep-seated Eurocentric perspectives, and (d) lack sensitivity to gender differences and diversity issues (Gilligan, 1982; Jordan et al., 1991; Stiver, 1991). Thus, new theories and models are desperately needed to address these concerns adequately. It is also important to remember that theories, while they are necessary supports to counseling, are a bit like cars—in need of constant care, maintenance, overhaul, and eventual trade-in. Because school counselors are dealing with issues and concerns unique to special populations, it is crucial to find, develop, and utilize theories conducive for working in school settings that are flexible and that provide for the consideration and appreciation of a range of contextual factors.

Diversity Competence: A Call for Contextual Models

Relational-cultural model. *Diversity* has been defined as "differences between people and the way we deal with those differences" (Jordan & Dooley, 2001, p. 23). These differences include, for example, age, gender, race, ethnicity, language, culture, class, exceptionalities, sexual orientation, gender identity, and geography and highlight perhaps the most important role of school counselors in the 21st century, that of advocate. While aspects of existing traditional theories may be adapted for use in working with groups on diversity issues, they do not provide a comprehensive base for addressing many students' special needs. A more recent theory that holds potential for working with these particular issues is the Relational–Cultural Model (Jordan et al., 1991; Miller, 1984). This model is based on the premise that human development and self-identity occur within a sociocultural context and that individuals "grow through action in relationship with others" (Walker, 2004, p. 4). According to the Relational–Cultural Model, authentic and mutual relational connections are necessary for optimal development, a premise that stands in contrast to more traditional models, which emphasize the importance of separation and individuation (Miller & Stiver, 1997). The Relational–Cultural Model's emphasis on mutuality and relatedness seems ideal for group counseling in schools in its ability to capitalize on the potential for building growth-fostering relationships in groups. As pointed out by Fedele (2004), "The ongoing process of connection, disconnection, and reconnection with the aim of enlarging relational possibilities is the very essence of group work" (p. 194). In this environment, members work and learn together about themselves and others in a climate of openness, mutual respect, appreciation, and support, thereby promoting opportunities for individual and collective empowerment.

One such group counseling program utilizing the Relational–Cultural Model, the Open Circle Competency Program (Wellesley Centers for Women, 2005), was developed for use with K–5 students, teachers, parents, and administrators. The program, based on social and emotional learning principles, reflects the Relational–Cultural Model's emphasis on the importance of relationships in fostering the academic, personal/social, and career success of children. It integrates the latest research on child development with evidence-based teaching practices and emphasizes concepts designed to build upon and reinforce each other as students move from grade to grade. The yearlong curriculum is presented in 15- to 30-minute sessions twice a week and covers the areas of active listening; self-calming;

assertiveness; coping with teasing, harassment, discrimination; and anger management. The training includes providing teachers, parents, and administrators with social competency and facilitation skills so that they can model and implement the strategies throughout the school setting and at home. To date, the Open Circle Competency Program has trained more than 5,600 teachers and counselors and has been implemented in public, private, parochial, urban, suburban, and rural school settings across New York, New Jersey, and New England (Wellesley Centers for Women).

Research thus far on the Open Circle curriculum has pointed to its usefulness in teaching relational and communication skills, addressing interpersonal issues, and assisting children and adolescents in feeling like part of the larger community. Studies by Black (1995) and Taylor et al. (2002) have revealed that students participating in this curriculum report improved self-worth; increased empathy, collaboration, mutuality, responsibility, and participation; and increased feelings of empowerment. Also, results showed some gender effects, with teachers reporting higher adjustment and assertiveness in girls, boys reporting improved self-control and fewer problems with fighting, and girls reporting improved adjustment (Taylor et al., 2002).

Applying the relational–cultural model. The following middle school case scenario is included in order to illustrate the application of the Relational–Cultural Model to group work in schools and to serve as a backdrop for the various "Group in Action" sequences that thread throughout the rest of the chapter.

Myer Middle School, consisting of grades 6 through 8, was constructed 20 years ago in a small bedroom community with a population of 6,000. Since that time, the community has tripled in size. Myer's enrollment has increased substantially, too, reflecting the growing diversity in the community. Currently, 64% of Myer's middle school students are identified as Caucasian, and 36% of the students are identified as one of several racial and ethnic minority groups. Given the rapidly changing demographic climate, Ms. Evans, the new school counselor, conducted a needs assessment among the students, teachers, parents, and administrators to identify salient issues for group counseling and classroom guidance. The feedback suggested a pressing need for working with students, teachers, parents, and administrators on diversity-related issues. As a result, Ms. Evans and the school's guidance advisory committee have worked to incorporate material on appreciating and respecting differences into the core guidance curriculum. Within this curriculum, a pilot, nine-session small group plan based on relational–cultural theory was developed for use with students in conjunction with an in-service workshop for school personnel and a PTA presentation for parents.

Flyers advertising the group were placed in various locations around the school campus. Several boys and girls were selected for prescreening interviews based on self, teacher, and/or parent referral, suggesting that these students seemed isolated and lacking in peer support. Interviews focused on explaining the purpose of the group, group goals, and group norms. A brief discussion covered issues of informed consent, privacy, and the importance of confidentiality and respect for other members. Potential participants were asked to sign a contract stating they would abide by the expectations for confidentiality. Parental permission forms were also distributed. Of the 10 students interviewed, 8 returned signed permission forms to participate in the group. Of the 8 participants, 4 were female and 4 were male; 5 were 7th graders and 3 were 8th graders. For 4 of the students, this was their 1st year at Myer. Of the students, 2 were African American, 2 were Asian American, 1 was biracial, 1 was Native American, and 2 were Hispanic/Latino. Arrangements were made with all teachers for the group to meet during alternate elective periods.

Multicultural responsiveness. With the increasingly diverse climate in society and public school systems, it is imperative that counselors attend to racial and ethnic diversity issues in their respective settings. Despite an increased call for multicultural competencies in education, there is much room for improvement in several important areas. For example, it is predicted that by the year 2020, ethnic minority students will make up 50% of the student body in public schools (Holcomb-McCoy, 2003). This stands in contrast to the fact that the majority of counselors in school settings are White females (Erford, House, & Martin, 2003). This underscores the responsibility of school counselors to be culturally responsive and competent (C. C. Lee, 2001; Locke, 2003). In this regard, Arredondo (1996) stated, "multicultural competencies were developed and defined to systematically address the centrality of culture, ethnicity, and race to counselor education, research, and practice" (p. 3). Research by Sodowsky, Taffe, Gutkin, and Wise (1994) revealed four multicultural competency areas for counselors: (a) multicultural counseling skills, (b) awareness (of life and professional experience levels), (c) counseling relationship (e.g., comfort with differences, sensitive to trust issues), and (d) counseling knowledge (e.g., see Roysircar, Arredondo, Fuertes, Ponterotto, & Toporek, 2003, for a more detailed discussion of multicultural counseling competencies). Thus, school counselors must begin with self-examination of personal biases and work toward recognizing the effects of oppression on students from minority populations, the privileges that the majority culture offers, and the existence and impact of overt and covert racism and discrimination. Utilizing input from minority students, teachers, administrators, and families in developing the guidance curriculum and in making decisions that affect students is imperative for ensuring that counseling services provided in the school setting are responsive to individual students' needs.

Specific to the school setting, Locke (2003) suggested the following strategies are necessary for improving multicultural competence among educators:

- being open and honest in relationships with culturally diverse students, including talking positively with students about their traits, attributes, and cultural characteristics
- seeking out and possessing knowledge about one's own culture and background and how that impacts one's value and belief system
- recognizing and valuing different cultures and providing opportunities for students of various cultural groups to interact in a way to help them differentiate feelings of superiority from feelings of pride and self-worth
- utilizing opportunities to get involved in cultural groups in the community and finding ways to involve various cultural groups/organizations and leaders in the community in working to improve intergroup relationships
- working to balance views of students as members of a cultural group but also as unique human beings with individual differences
- challenging and eliminating personal biases and prejudices and doing the same with students, teachers, parents, and administrators
- working with school personnel to ensure that the school climate acknowledges the contributions of all racial and ethnic groups through mutually agreed upon solutions reflecting respect for differences
- maintaining consistent expectations for all students and providing opportunities for students to develop and value their self-identity
- recognizing the importance of students' cultural heritage by seeking out information on cultural diversity and sharing the information with students, teachers, parents, and administrators
- developing and implementing programs that foster cultural appreciation and being attuned to and eliminating practices that employ grouping procedures of racial and ethnically diverse groups

In applying these competencies to group counseling, counselors must have knowledge and awareness of both the impact of diversity-related factors on group work and how these factors may affect group participation and process. For instance, relevant diversity-related factors include (a) racial identity development (e.g., see Sue & Sue, 2003, for a more comprehensive discussion of racial identity development), (b) cultural influences on gender role expectations, (c) disclosure and privacy issues related to cultural norms (e.g., loss of face), (d) family or group (i.e., collectivistic) versus individualistic worldview orientation, and (e) acculturation conflicts, including ambivalence regarding balancing traditional and mainstream cultural values.

GROUP IN ACTION—MULTICULTURAL

Group goals and rules are briefly reviewed. Members introduce themselves using a "making connections" activity, which allows them to identify strengths and assets in themselves as well as in other members of the group. Members reflect on the concept of unity and the strength associated with being part of something bigger than themselves and how the group will become what each member is willing to bring to it. At this point, members suggest possible names for the group. A consensus is reached and the group is officially christened the X-Squad. Members like the idea that, much like in the X-Men comics, they all bring unique individual talents and strengths to the group. Next Ms. Evans, the school counselor, tosses a loose ball of yarn into the center of the group circle and asks each member to identify of what the pile of yarn looks like. After summarizing the different views, a discussion follows with several group members talking about advantages in "seeing things differently." Ms. Evans takes this opportunity to encourage Christina, an Asian American student, to join the discussion. She haltingly begins to talk about how she struggles with conflicts between her parents' expectations and the expectations of her teachers and some of her peers. Her parents push her to excel in school and to observe traditional customs, while her teachers and some of her friends encourage her not to push herself so hard academically and, instead, to be more socially active. She explains that it is hard for her to talk about these conflicts because her parents expect such issues to be dealt with privately. She adds that she feels "different" and confused a lot of the time and just wants to be able to be more like the other students at Myer so she can fit in. It is obvious from the reaction that some of the other group members share Christina's struggle, and Ms. Evans makes a mental note to follow up in the next group session with an activity to stimulate more discussion related to issues of acculturation and racial identity development.

Other Diversity Issues

Sexual harassment. Ample opportunities also exist in schools for group work with other areas of diversity. For example, the authors' experience, which is supported in the literature, is that group work in schools related to sexual harassment is almost nonexistent. Despite the fact that sexual harassment issues in schools have received some media attention since the 1990s, it continues to be a serious problem in educational settings as evidenced by research that suggests that 90% of all sexual harassment incidents in schools go unreported (American Association of University Women [AAUW] Educational Foundation, 2001).

The U.S. Department of Education, Office of Civil Rights (1997) has defined sexual harassment as "sufficiently severe, persistent, or pervasive (behavior) that adversely affects a student's education or creates a hostile or abusive educational environment and the conduct must be sexual in nature" (p. 12036). According to Stone (2004), sexual harassment may also be recognized by examining whether

> the behavior is unwanted or unwelcome, the behavior is sexual or related to the gender of the person, and the behavior occurs in the context of a relationship where one person has more power, such as the informal power one student can have over another. (p. 354)

The AAUW defined sexual harassment as "unwanted and unwelcome sexual attention that interferes with your life" (AAUW Educational Foundation, 2001, p. 2) in their study, *Hostile Hallways*. This study revealed that 83% of girls and 79% of boys have been sexually harassed in a school setting. Although victims of harassment were both male and female, girls were represented in greater numbers and suffered from more negative consequences (AAUW Educational Foundation; Fineran & Bennett, 1999; Hand & Sanchez, 2000; V. E. Lee, Croninger, Linn, & Chen, 1996; Timmerman, 2003). More recently, the Supreme Court has weighed in on the issue of sexual harassment in schools via *Davis v. Monroe County Board of Education* (1999). The ruling in this case stated, "public schools can be forced to pay damages for failing to stop student-on-student sexual harassment" (Stone, 2004, p. 355), providing a wake-up call to schools as to the extent of their responsibility in implementing a zero tolerance policy related to incidents of sexual harassment.

GROUP IN ACTION—SEXUAL HARASSMENT

The group begins with Ms. Evans asking the members to define *sexual harassment*. Once the group has reached an agreement on a working definition, members are asked to pair up to review several scenarios describing potential sexual harassment of males and females. Next, the group members are asked to move to the floor in a tight circle. Ms. Evans places a plastic bucket in the center of the circle within everyone's reach. She hands out a cup full of water to each member. Then she begins to read several statements related to harassment. For example, "Have you been teased or called names" and "Have you ever been embarrassed by suggestive comments?" She asks the members to pour out some of their water into the center bucket every time they have had a similar experience. At the end, each member is asked to look at his or her "self-worth" cup and to reflect on how harassment affects his or her self-esteem.

Sexual orientation and gender identity. Information about group counseling interventions focused on exploring sexual orientation (i.e., "an enduring emotional, romantic, sexual, or affectional attraction toward others," [APA, 2004, ¶. 1]), gender identity (i.e., "the psychological sense of being male or female," ¶ 1), and social gender role (i.e., "adherence to cultural norms for feminine and masculine behavior," ¶. 1) issues are even more underrepresented in the school counseling literature, no doubt because these subjects have long been considered taboo in school settings. Ignorance, fear, and denial around these issues makes work with gay, lesbian, bisexual, transgendered, and questioning (GLBTQ) students especially challenging. For the most part, the needs of GLBTQ students have been neglected by school systems. Students from these groups have been at best ignored and at worst teased, harassed, and physically assaulted. A survey conducted by the Gay, Lesbian, and Straight Education Network (1999) revealed that 59% of GLBTQ youth were verbally harassed or physically attacked; 50% reported being harassed daily. In addition to harassment from their peers, many of these young people experience ridicule and/or abuse from family members. Although some schools would like to believe that students from these groups are not represented in their settings, the reality is that every school likely has at least one and probably more GLBTQ students. Many students do not reveal their orientation or questions for fear of rejection or physical assault. The other harsh reality is that because of their plight, these students often cope by socially isolating, abusing alcohol and drugs, engaging in risky and/or indiscriminant sex, and acting on suicidal impulses (Ryan & Futterman, 1998).

GROUP IN ACTION—SEXUAL ORIENTATION, GENDER IDENTITY, GENDER ROLES

The group begins with a review of the previous session, which focused on an activity designed to spur a discussion of the "realities" of being heterosexual versus homosexual and male versus female in today's society and, more specifically, in Myer Middle School. Next, Ms. Evans asks the members to move to a large table with various materials for making paper masks. She asks the members to make two masks, one for the way they think others see them and one for how they see themselves.

When everyone is finished, members discuss feelings and experiences related to having others "fail to see" them and whether "wearing a mask" is good or bad. One group member, Susan, brings up the example of people who act tough in order to protect themselves from getting hurt and how this can backfire and keep people from wanting to connect with them.

Making it Happen—Practical Considerations in Group Work

First Steps

As has been demonstrated by the limited research, small group counseling in schools represents a viable conduit through which to address a range of issues and concerns for students, teachers, administrators, and parents. To facilitate effective groups, however, school counselors must have an understanding of theory, diversity issues, and training in leadership skills, including not only group leadership skills but also skills for marketing group interventions. This would include, more specifically, background and training in how developmental theory works in conjunction with counseling theory to promote personal growth across different age and grade levels. Counselors must be knowledgeable in a variety of content areas and have training in and an understanding of the purposes of groups and processes related to optimal group functioning in order to be able to effectively utilize these skills to improve student performance. Finally, they must possess self-awareness and knowledge of how contextual factors influence student functioning and skills grounded in theory and research that accurately reflect the many nuances of diversity.

Building support and assessing need. Educating stakeholders such as teachers, administrators, and parents on how groups can effectively support and enhance students' academic, personal/social, and career achievement and promote the mission of the school is an important first step. This may be accomplished in various ways. For example, orientation programs presented at staff development workshops, parent support organizations, and regular faculty meetings can be used to inform and solicit program support from internal and external entities. Creating guidance curriculum advisory committees comprising teachers, administrators, parents, students, and community/business leaders to work together to develop and plan comprehensive guidance curricula is another excellent way to get much needed support for guidance and group counseling. Once support for group services is procured, the next step is conducting a needs assessment (Davis, 2005; Jacobs & Schimmel, 2005; Studer, 2005). Needs assessments can be administered formally by sending out short surveys or checklists to students, teachers, administrators, and parents, asking them for feedback on the kinds of groups they think would be helpful and informally by observing changes in the school climate and by talking with students, parents, and teachers about recurring problems. Once this information is collected, it is shared with members of the guidance advisory committee. Then the committee can use the data to prioritize needs and plan what types of groups should be offered to students in that setting.

Utilizing a knowledge base. Group dynamics are complex, and knowledge of group stages, group processes, and facilitative skills are crucial to the effective functioning of the group (Schmidt, 1999; Sciarra, 2004; Studer, 2005). Most of the literature on group processes pertains to adults, but a few studies have looked at group counseling with children and adolescents (e.g., Shechtman, 2002). While some differences in processes and group stages have been found with younger group members, in general, the dynamics tend to be quite similar.

The four stages of group involvement identified by Myrick (2003) are (a) involvement, (b) transition, (c) working, and (d) ending. The involvement stage is characterized by group members getting to know one another, establishing appropriate rules for the group, discussing the importance of confidentiality, and laying the necessary groundwork for building trust within a safe, supportive environment. The following brief excerpt illustrates the involvement stage:

> "Hello and welcome to the group. We hope that this group will allow you to talk about your experiences at Myer. We are going to be together for the next 9 weeks to help you get to know and respect yourselves and others better and to learn about connecting in relationships and about how to handle conflict (disconnection) in relationships. To do this, everyone must try to support and encourage each other and be open to new and different ways of thinking, feeling, and looking at the world. As we talked about earlier, what we discuss in the group is confidential and should not be shared with anyone outside the group. Does anyone have any questions?"

In the transition stage, members are learning to trust and work together. It is generally characterized by the beginnings of self-awareness and insight into behaviors evidenced by tentative self-disclosure and feedback from members. During this stage, group members begin to connect around their similarities and to recognize and talk about their differences (Fedele, 2004), similar to the following scenario:

> "Last week, toward the end of the group session, Lena was talking about how hard it is to be a new student at Myer this year. John and Keisha added that, although they've been at Myer since 6th grade, they still don't feel "accepted" by the other students. Others of you also expressed similar feelings. Let's begin today by talking more about how the lack of connections with others affects each of you and see whether your experiences with this are similar or different." As the group members begin to describe their feelings of disconnection and isolation in more detail, Lena comments that, for her, the worst part is the "loneliness." Several other members agree that they, too, feel lonely, and the group begins to join around the shared experiences of several of the members.

The working stage occurs once members develop trust and are comfortable enough to self-disclose and provide constructive feedback to other group members. This stage is characterized by deeper investment in the group and the confidence to try out new skills and behaviors. An important aspect is the emerging of conflict and disconnection and the willingness to work through it, for example, to "make and hold connections between apparent opposites" (Fedele, 2004, p. 205). An example of group dynamics during this stage is illustrated by the following:

> "The last time we met, several of you talked about your feelings of disconnection and loneliness. In doing that, some of you were able to connect around others' shared feelings and experiences. I noticed, however, that a couple of you were silent about your own experiences and instead focused on advising other group members what they should do to 'get through the day.' I sensed some tension in this process, and I would like to start by talking about what might be going on here."

Finally, the ending stage is focused on how to apply what has been learned in the group to other settings. New emotions and concerns may surface around "losing" access to the relational process and authentic connections formed in the group at this point. It is important in this stage for school counselors to acknowledge these concerns and allow members to vent their feelings so that they can be processed effectively. Emphasis on summarizing progress in the group and focusing on where members are headed can often allay many of these fears. The final stage of the group process might look something like the following:

> "We've been preparing for this day for a couple of weeks now. I'd like to begin by having everyone share a little about what the group experience has been like for them, what you've learned about yourself and others, and how you can use what you've learned about relationships to help you in the future." During this process, Christina says that being in the group has helped her to feel better about "things," but she is worried that once she is away from the group, everything will just go back to the way it was. Other members are able to point out to her that even though the group won't be meeting together, they will still have some classes together and see each other at lunch and sometimes after school. They remind Christina that she has started to make a couple of new friends outside of the group as a result of what she learned about connecting with other group members and that she can use what she's learned about herself and others to build new relationships and to work through problems and conflict in current relationships.

Who Is Your Audience? Issues Related to Development and Geographical Locale

Groups for elementary students. One strength of small group counseling is that the format can be used with students of all ages from elementary school to high school and in rural, urban, and suburban locales. Elementary schools are especially conducive to group work because the classes tend to be self-contained, providing easier access to students and the opportunity to get to know students and their particular needs. Also, elementary counselors tend not to be responsible for time-consuming duties such as scheduling, record keeping, and preparation for high school and college. The early years of elementary school are also a crucial developmental period for children. Their identities, values, attitudes, and beliefs are just beginning to form. They are starting to acquire social skills, and they are eager and enthusiastic about learning and pleasing those around them. Even during these early years, however, children are susceptible to peer influence and can often learn better by watching others (Davis, 2005). Groups allow this observational learning and help young children to understand their feelings and emotions, which can sometimes be confusing, frustrating, frightening, and overwhelming. Counseling in groups provides young children with modeling, skill building opportunities, and support in a safe, nonjudgmental environment. Topical groups that are appropriate for young children include building authentic and mutual connections with others, communicating, dealing with ADHD symptoms, anger management, study skills, coping with loss, parental divorce, behavior problems, and achievement issues.

Groups for middle school/junior high. The middle school/junior high years are challenging. Adolescents in this period are struggling with asserting their autonomy, while still wrestling with their needs to be dependent. Puberty, with its hormonal changes, can be a confusing, frightening, and frustrating time for some youth. Moods may fluctuate, and because their bodies are growing and changing so rapidly, adolescents may feel awkward, gawky, and clumsy, which may have a negative impact on their sense of self-worth. On a developmental note, groups with adolescents tend to be more complex as students become better at communicating, expressing emotions, and abstract thinking. Counseling at this age can provide opportunities for increasing problem-solving and decision-making skills; promoting awareness, appreciation, and acceptance of difference; improving communication and self-worth; learning to hold on to connection while working through conflict (Fedele, 2004); and experiencing mutual empathy and "power with" (Surrey, 1991, p. 165) another. Groups also capitalize on the influence of peers and pressures to conform in constructive ways. In groups, adolescents can help each other learn and practice new skills and behaviors, deal with peer pressure, work through identity issues, and manage stress.

Groups for high school. High school students are also prone to experiencing multiple stressors. Pressures from peers and parents as well as expectations for college and career may weigh heavily on older adolescents. At this age, students are still learning about interdependence and testing the limits of their independence. They are faced with having to make many important decisions and are learning to use their relational networks in new ways as they practice solving their problems. Groups at the high school level tend to focus on issues such as romantic relationships, substance use, sexuality, body image, teen parenting, stress management, family issues, peer influence, diversity and identity issues, and college and/or career planning.

Groups and geographical considerations. According to the U.S. Department of Education's Office of the Deputy Secretary (2003), approximately 43% of all schools are classified as rural, and rural schools educate nearly one third of all students in the United States. Preconceived notions about the differences in rural, urban, and suburban schools are common. For example, while rural schools may be viewed as being located in poor, backward, agricultural communities, they may also be viewed as safer and less prone to crime and violence. In contrast, it may be assumed that urban schools are fraught with issues related to poverty and lack of resources, such as lower academic achievement, truancy, higher dropout rates, increased behavioral problems, and student violence. Somewhere in the middle, of course, are the suburban school settings, which, to some, may appear idyllic in their perceived insulation from crime and poverty and in their access to supportive community resources. Obviously, the reality is that schools, whether rural, urban, or suburban, struggle with many of the same problems, and all have their own particular strengths and weaknesses.

It is true, however, that group work in more isolated rural educational settings can be hindered by a variety of factors, including limitations in the facility (e.g., older, cramped buildings) and lack of tax-based funding and supplemental community resources (Hines, 2002). At a minimum, counselors must possess both awareness and knowledge of the local culture in order to help facilitate effective groups. Furthermore, although rural students may have a strong sense of community and connection and an accessible support system, they may experience considerable social, cultural, and academic isolation and may be quite anxious about making academic, career, and life decisions (Gibbs, 2000). Thus, counselors doing group work in rural settings must capitalize on community-based strengths by cultivating ongoing partnerships with business, industry, and professional organizations. Partnerships such as these can provide a foundation for exploring additional resources and opportunities for students and promote a collaborative vision of the school as an extension of the community and the larger society. This reality echoes, once again, the importance of developing and utilizing brief surveys to elicit feedback on the needs of rural, suburban, and urban schools in order for group work to be a viable guidance program adjunct in addressing the unique issues in each setting.

Decisions to Make

What type of group to offer. Groups conducted in schools tend to fall into two categories—namely, psycho-educational or counseling. Within these categories, the format for groups may be open, allowing members to enter and leave the group at any time, or closed, requiring all the members to begin and end the group process together. Many school groups tend to be closed because having students enter and leave the group at different points can interfere with natural group processes such as building trust, connecting, and disclosing. Some groups, however, might be conducive to an open format. For example, an ongoing group to orient new students to the school could run year round, with new students entering the group until they have the lay of the land and leaving once they feel that they can function on their own.

Groups may also be homogenous or heterogeneous. Homogenous groups are composed of members who share very similar characteristics, such as age, grade, SES, race, ethnicity, gender, and/or sexual orientation. Heterogeneous groups are composed of members with widely varying characteristics. The purpose of the group is a key factor in, for example, deciding the question of group composition. For instance, if the group is designed to be more supportive in nature and to foster healing and growth through universality, then homogenous membership may work better. Having other students with the same characteristics and similar experiences and concerns creates a sense of understanding and acceptance. If the purpose of the group is to challenge perspectives and to promote learning through relational modeling and peer influence, then heterogeneous groups are a better fit. In groups with a remedial focus, heterogeneity among the members provides positive modeling; challenges existing perspectives; and offers opportunities for mutual feedback, peer influence, and relational learning. Ritchie and Huss (2000) suggested that heterogeneous groups are superior because they include a mix of students with and without specific problems and they can be designed to be supportive, preventative, or remedial in their focus. Perhaps this is because of the differences and, sometimes, the conflict that occurs in a heterogeneous group. From the perspective of the Relational–Cultural Model, conflict offers a relational opportunity: "In the larger picture, building bridges means confronting prejudices rather than ignoring them to create an illusion of solidarity" (Fedele, 2004, p. 205).

Size, frequency, duration, and location. The size of the group depends on various conditions (e.g., age, purpose). Most experts agree that 5 to 8 members, with smaller numbers for groups with very young children and larger numbers for adolescents (e.g., Myrick, 2003), are ideal. Corey (2000) suggested the rule of thumb should be, "the group should have enough people to afford ample interaction so that it doesn't drag and yet be small enough to give everyone a chance to participate frequently without, however, losing the sense of the 'group'" (p. 90). Groups usually meet once a week for 6 to 12 weeks. The length of the group time differs with developmental considerations. Younger children have shorter attention spans, so 20- to 30-minute sessions are generally recommended. Because the group sessions are shorter, some groups for younger children may meet twice a week. For adolescent groups, sessions usually correspond to one class period (approximately an hour in most cases).

Finding an appropriate place to meet in order to ensure confidentiality and privacy can often be a challenge because many schools lack a surplus of space. When to schedule group meetings, however, is probably the biggest challenge. Teacher and administrator opposition to group counseling often hinges around the issue of students missing class and instructional time to participate in the group. Another concern that may arise with group work has to do with students returning to class upset over something that transpired in the group. Nevertheless, there are creative ways around these sticky issues. For instance, groups can be organized around a rotating schedule so that students do not miss the same class every week. In some school settings, group meetings can be held during homeroom, study hall, or lunchtime. Also, counselors should be prepared for the need to help individual group members decompress after highly charged group work.

Who's right for the group? Members can be recruited through self-, teacher, or parent referral. Once potential members are identified, it is vitally important to have a screening procedure in place to determine if the student is appropriate for the proposed group. Unfortunately, as important as groups are to a comprehensive developmental guidance program, they are not suited to working with students with severe problems. In this case, referrals to outside agencies or private practitioners who specialize in working with children and adolescents with serious behavioral disorders should be made.

Other purposes of the screening process are to give potential members information about the group goals and the expectations for participation and to get a sense of how each student may function in the group. Although the screening process requires another time commitment for the school counselor, it will save time in the end by allowing an opportunity to assess whether a student will be able to work effectively in or be a hindrance to the group process.

Once the members for the group have been selected, a letter with information about the group purpose and goals and seeking signed permission for student participation should be sent to parents. Another way to handle getting parental permission is to present a counseling program orientation for parents at a beginning of the year. Here, you can provide parents with information and materials on different groups that will be offered. Counselors may want to include a brief form for parents to sign if they do not want their son or daughter to participate in any type of group work in the school setting.

It Finally Begins: Leading the Group

In order to facilitate group work in school settings, school counselors must be trained in developing leadership skills.

These skills are crucial to guiding the group process and include basic skills such as communicating effectively, active listening, observing, modeling, questioning, challenging, problem solving, interpreting, supporting, linking, and summarizing. In addition, the school counselor must pay special attention to several key aspects of group leadership: (a) creating a safe and consistent relational place, (b) being present, (c) pushing the envelope, and (d) promoting altruism.

Creating a safe and consistent relational place. It is important for school counselors to clarify expectations and boundaries related to the group process (Fedele, 2004). In contrast to traditional models, however, boundaries are not understood as rigid lines of demarcation, but emphasize mutuality, genuineness, and respect and exist within a context defined by the members (Jordan, 2000). This emphasis is consistent with the Relational–Cultural Model and the group goal of "enlarging relational possibilities" (Fedele, 2004, p. 194). This focus on flexibility in allowing group members to express what they need in order to make the group work helps to provide a safe environment in which to meet and interact. It also helps reduce the negative effects of power differentials resulting from social hierarchies among students, with its emphasis on "power with" versus "power over" (Surrey, 1991).

Assertively communicating information about the roles in group work and what is expected helps to set the stage for more proactive participation among members. Likewise, dealing with behavior problems and enforcing mutually agreed upon group rules in a consistent, forthright manner communicates the importance of group work conveys a respect for group members' abilities to accept responsibility, and it assists the leader in helping members connect more effectively and authentically with each other.

Creating a safe and consistent relational space (Fedele, 2004) in the group also includes confidentiality. While counselors are ethically bound to protect the confidentiality of every person in the group (American Counseling Association, 1995; ASCA, 1998), there is no guarantee that members of the group will take this commitment as seriously. With this caveat in mind, the counselor must do his or her best to emphasize the importance of maintaining confidentiality during the screening process, in the first session as group rules are being developed, and thereafter as necessary. In addition, counselors may want to provide potential members with a written statement outlining the parameters of confidentiality before allowing individuals to participate in the group.

Ms. Evans, the counselor, welcomes everyone to the group and begins by reviewing the purpose and rules of the group and their commitment to confidentiality. Members then begin a "getting to know" you activity. Here members are provided one large and several smaller strips of construction paper to create a "unity chain." First, the students sign their names on a large strip. Then, each student is instructed to write the names of people in their lives that they feel connected to on each of the smaller strips, using as many as they need. The small strips are stapled together to form links in a chain for each student. Finally, all the "connection" chains are attached to the larger circle containing the names of everyone in the group. The completed "unity chain" is fastened to the wall of the group meeting room as a reminder of the members commitment to each other and the group.

Being present. Observation and active listening are key to keeping the group on task and moving the members in the appropriate direction toward a specified goal. Collectively, these skills also help to capitalize on positive aspects of peer influence and promote mutuality through openness to change and connection with others. They allow the group leader to take note of important comments, recognize patterns of connection and disconnection, model moving through conflict and disconnection back into reconnection, and model good listening skills to group members. This modeling is an important leadership skill in that it allows group members to see the leader and other members demonstrate appropriate behavior.

Over the last two weeks, Ms. Evans has observed several of the group members moving toward connection. As might be expected, some members have been more open in their disclosure in the group, while others still seem suspicious and tentative in their interactions. In order to create a climate for more open discussion, the counselor provides each member with a large piece of butcher paper and instructs all to create a map of their lives, including drawing in places and people that have special meaning for them. Once the maps are complete, Ms. Evans demonstrates how members will use their personal maps to give the others a "tour" of their world.

Pushing the envelope. From the perspective of the Relational–Cultural Model, an important relational goal is to teach youth to "value conflict as an opportunity for greater connection" (Dooley & Fedele, 2004, p. 243). Thus, exploration of conflict and challenging students to understand others' perspectives can be used to take the group process to a new level, increase ownership of feelings and vulnerabilities, and assist members in the development of empathy toward feelings and vulnerabilities in others. Challenging can be used to encourage exploration of inconsistencies in group members' comments and behaviors, and discrepancies among what they are thinking, feeling, and doing. In addition, questioning and probing can be used effectively to clarify comments and solicit more information from members. This, in turn, can stimulate discussion that is more productive and allow for more breadth and depth in exploring problems and concerns. Last, interpretation helps group members better understand the potential causes for their problems and can stimulate self-awareness and insight. On a cautionary note, interpretations are really just educated guesses and, as such, should be done tentatively and respectfully and in a way that enhances mutual communication, allowing the group member to process and respond as to whether the speculation is indeed a good fit. In addition, it is essential that interpretations be congruent with the developmental level of the child or adolescent.

The group has been making good progress, but the last session was characterized by some silence and tension. Ms. Evans asks the group to sit in a tight circle on the floor. She places a large plastic ring with different-colored crepe paper streamers tied to it to represent the united group. Next she assigns each member a color. She explains that she is going to read several statements about different experiences and situations and asks the members to pull off a streamer in their color when the statement applies to them. For example, "When I speak up in group I feel like some people are judging me"; "Sometimes when people share advice, it reminds me of my mom, dad, or my teachers"; and "I'm not sure if I can really trust everyone in the group." At the end of the activity, students are asked to check how many of their streamers are still connected to the center ring. The counselor then asks the group to talk about what has happened. Students are encouraged to discuss their feelings of connection and disconnection.

Promoting altruism. Linking is a technique that allows the group leader, through active listening, to tie together what has been said by different members. It can be used to make important thematic connections within the group process, promote increased self-clarity and clarity about others, and create a sense of community by highlighting similarities in thinking, feeling, and experiencing. In addition, these connections free up members to help one another. Problem solving is useful for encouraging individual members to think about their own or other group members' situations or concerns in different ways, generating options, and encouraging other members to weigh in on how they would handle or have handled similar problems. Fostering this type of mutual empathy is important to the group process. Providing and capitalizing on opportunities for students to encourage and support each other and problem solve is crucial for establishing cohesiveness and trust, the glue of the group process.

"Last week, Susan talked about how her mom is "breathing down her neck" all of the time wanting information about where she is going and who she is hanging out with. The constant questions make Susan feel like her mom doesn't trust her. Can any of you relate to her experience at home? If so, how have you tried to handle the situation?" Several group members take turns speaking up about their own situations at home and about how they deal with rules. Tony and Keisha, in particular, suggest potential ways for Susan to negotiate on issues and ideas she might try to gradually earn more parental trust. Jonah, who tends to be very quiet, begins talking about how his mother works two jobs and is so tired when she gets home that she doesn't even seem to care what he's been doing or who he's been hanging out with. Group members, again, respond with concern and support and begin to help Jonah problem solve ways that he can connect with and communicate feelings to his mother.

Evaluation of Group Work and Commitment to Accountability

Merely conducting group activities in school settings does not ensure that they will be effective. Group practices should be rigorously tested and processes should be explored to demonstrate their effectiveness in accordance with evidence-based practices (APA, 2005). In light of the most recent educational reforms such as the *No Child Left Behind Act* (U.S. Department of Education, 2002), school counselors, along with their teaching colleagues, must be able to demonstrate accountability. They must commit to demonstrating that the services they provide have a positive impact on the students they serve. This may prove to be a difficult challenge for several reasons: (a) lack of training in research and evaluation; (b) lack of available time for school counselors to conduct research, given that studies have shown counselors often spend time performing duties that are inappropriate (i.e., record keeping, clerical work, substitute teaching, etc.; e.g., Ober & Beesley, 2004); and (c) reluctance on the part of school counselors to conduct research due to a lack of self-efficacy in this area. For these reasons and others, school counselor training programs must provide opportunities for counselors in training to develop and conduct needs assessments and to collect outcome data on the groups they facilitate in order to evaluate their effectiveness in working with students.

One possible way to stimulate this kind of accountability would be to require regular reports on group program status using readily available data (e.g., attendance, grades, achievement testing, number of discipline referrals) to demonstrate the positive impact of group counseling on the achievement and functioning of all students. These reports could be disseminated in school newsletters, on school Web sites, and in packet form for presentations at school board, parent organizational, and faculty meetings. Demonstrating that groups work with children and adolescents in school settings will do much to encourage support from teachers, administrators, and parents. In addition, helping counselors recognize that they already use data (e.g., attendance, grades, test scores) to advocate for students may help allay some of the anxiety about evaluation and accountability issues. Finally, the survival of the profession may depend on counselors' being able to consistently demonstrate that what they do makes a positive difference in the lives of all of their students.

Final Thoughts and Future Directions

Although research suggests that group work in school settings with children and adolescents is effective, the studies are limited in number and often not reflective of rigorous research methods. Also, concerns exist about the ability of traditional theoretical models to conceptualize issues related to our rapidly changing society. This has resulted in a call both for using theoretical perspectives that more accurately capture and reflect the complexities of contextual influences and for the development of new theories of group counseling. One such model that shows promise for use in school settings is the Relational–Cultural Model (Wellesley Centers for Women, 2005).

Group work in school settings serves as a centerpiece for a comprehensive developmental guidance program. It is not, however, without considerable challenges. To facilitate groups in schools successfully, counselors must have appropriate training in leadership skills, group process skills, research, evaluation, and diversity competence. It is not enough for school counselors to conduct groups for the benefit of all of the students they serve; they must also be committed to evaluating group outcomes to demonstrate the effectiveness of their work with children and adolescents.

References

Adler, A. (1998). *Understanding human nature*. Center City, MN: Hazelden Foundation.

American Association of University Women Educational Foundation. (2001). *Hostile hallways: Bullying, teasing, and sexual harassment in school*. Retrieved September 18, 2005, from http://www.aauw.org

American Counseling Association. (1995). *Code of ethics and standards of practice*. Alexandria, VA: Author.

American Psychological Association. (2004). *Sexual orientation and homosexuality*. Retrieved September 15, 2005, from http://apahelpcenter.org

American Psychological Association. (2005, August). *Policy statement on evidence-based practice in psychology*. Retrieved September 21, 2005, from www.apa.org/practice/ebpstatement.pdf

American School Counselor Association. (1998). *Ethical standards for school counselors*. Alexandria, VA: Author.

American School Counselor Association. (2003). *The ASCA national model: A framework for school counseling programs*. Alexandria, VA: Author.

Amerikaner, M., & Summerlin, M. L. (2001). Group counseling with learning disabled children: Effects of social skills and relaxation training on self-concept and classroom behavior. *Journal of Learning Disabilities, 15*, 340–343.

Arman, J. F. (2000). A small group model for working with elementary school children of alcoholics. *Professional School Counseling, 3*, 290–293.

Arredondo, P. (1996). Evolution of the multicultural counseling competencies: Background and context. In G. Roysircar, P. Arredondo, J. N. Fuertes, J. G. Ponterotto, & R. L. Toporek (Eds.), *Multicultural counseling competencies 2003: Association for Multicultural Counseling and Development* (pp. 1–16). Alexandria, VA: American Counseling Association.

Baker, S. B., & Gerler, E. R. (2004). *School counseling for the 21st century* (4th ed.). Upper Saddle River, NJ: Merrill Prentice Hall.

Bandura, A. (1969). *Principles of behavior modification*. New York: Holt, Rinehart, & Winston.

Barkhaus, R. S., Adair, M. K., Hoover, A. B., & Bolyard, C. W. (1985). *Threads* (3rd ed.). Dubuque, IA: Kendall/Hunt.

Barlow, S. H., Burlingame, G. M., & Fuhriman, A. (2000). Therapeutic application of groups: From Pratt's "thought control classes" to modern group psychotherapy. *Group Dynamics, 4*, 115–134.

Beck, A. T. (1976). *Cognitive therapy and the emotional disorders*. New York: Penguin Group.

Bemak, F., Chi-Ying, R., & Siroskey-Sabdo, L. A. (2005). Empowerment groups for academic success: An innovative approach to prevent high school failure for at-risk, urban African American girls. *Professional School Counseling, 8*, 377–389.

Black, B. (1995). *Reach out to schools: Social competency program*. Wellesley, MA: Stone Center, Wellesley College.

Bloom, B. S. (1964). *Stability and change in human characteristics*. New York: John Wiley.

Blum, D. J., & Jones, L. A. (1993). Academic growth group and mentoring program for potential dropouts. *School Counselor, 40,* 207–217.

Bradley, C. (2001). A counseling group for African American adolescent males. *Professional School Counseling, 4,* 370–373.

Brake, K. J., & Gerler, E. R. (1994). Discovery: A program for fourth and fifth graders identified as discipline problems. *Elementary School Guidance and Counseling, 28,* 170–181.

Brooks, V. (2004). Stress management: The school counselor's role. In R. Perusse & G. E. Goodnough (Eds.), *Leadership, advocacy, and direct service strategies for professional school counselors* (pp. 328–352). Belmont, CA: Brooks/Cole.

Burnham, J. J., & Jackson, C. M. (2000). School counselor roles: Discrepancies between actual practice and existing models. *Professional School Counseling, 4,* 41–49.

Campbell, C. A., & Dahir, C. A. (1997). *Sharing the vision: The national standards for school counseling programs.* Alexandria, VA: American School Counselor Association.

Ciechalski, J. C., & Schmidt, M. W. (1995). The effects of social skills training on students with exceptionalities. *Elementary School Guidance and Counseling, 29,* 217–222.

Cook, J. B., & Kaffenberger, C. J. (2003). Solution shop: A solution-focused counseling and study skills program for middle school. *Professional School Counseling, 7,* 116–123.

Corey, G. (2000). *Theory and practice of group counseling* (5th ed.). Pacific Grove, CA: Brooks/Cole.

Davis, T. (2005). *Exploring school counseling: Professional practices and perspectives.* Boston: Houghton Mifflin Company.

Davis v. Monroe County Board of Education et al. 120F.3d 1390. (Supreme Court, May 24, 1999).

DeLuca, R. V., Hazen, A., & Cutler, J. (1993). Evaluation of a group counseling program for preadolescent female victims of incest. *Elementary School Guidance and Counseling, 28,* 104–114.

deShazer, S. (1985). *Keys to solution in brief therapy.* New York: Norton.

Dooley, C., & Fedele, N. M. (2004). Mothers and sons: Raising relational boys. In J. V. Jordan, M. Walker, & L. M. Hartling (Eds.), *The complexity of connection: Writings from the Stone Center's Jean Baker Miller Training Institute* (pp. 220–249). New York: Guilford.

Ellis, A. (1962). *Reason and emotion in psychotherapy.* Secaucus, NJ: Citadel.

Erford, B. T., House, R., & Martin, P. (2003). Transforming the school counseling profession. In B. T. Erford (Ed.), *Transforming the school counseling profession* (pp. 1–20). Upper Saddle River, NJ: Merrill Prentice Hall.

Erikson, E. H. (1963). *Childhood and society.* New York: W. W. Norton.

Fedele, N. M. (2004). Relationships in groups: Connection, resonance, and paradox. In J. V. Jordan, M. Walker, & L. M. Hartling (Eds.), *The complexity of connection: Writings from the Stone Center's Jean Baker Miller Training Institute* (pp. 194–219). New York: Guilford.

Fineran, S., & Bennett, L. (1999). Gender and power issues of peer sexual harassment among teenagers. *Journal of Interpersonal Violence, 12,* 626–641.

Gay, Lesbian, and Straight Education Network. (1999). *National school climate survey.* New York: Author.

Gesell, R., & Ames, L. (1956). *Youth: The years from ten to sixteen.* New York: Harper & Row.

Gesell, R., & Ilg, F. (1946). *The child from five to ten.* New York: Harper & Row.

Gibbs, R. (2000). The challenge ahead for rural schools. *Forum for Applied Research and Public Policy, 15,* 82–87.

Gilligan, C. (1982). *In a different view: Psychological theory and women's development.* Cambridge, MA: Harvard University Press.

Gladding, S. T. (2003). *Group work: A counseling specialty* (4th ed.). New York: Merrill.

Glaize, D. L., & Myrick, R. D. (1984). Interpersonal groups or computers? A study of career maturity and career decidedness. *Vocational Guidance Quarterly, 32,* 68–176.

Glasser, W. (1965). *Reality therapy.* New York: Harper & Row.

Hand, J. Z., & Sanchez, L. (2000). Badgering or bantering? Gender differences in experience of, and reactions to, sexual harassment among U.S. high school students. *Gender & Society, 12,* 718–746.

Havighurst, R. J. (1953). *Human development and education.* New York: Longmans.

Hines, P. L. (2002). Transforming the rural school counselor. *Professional School Counseling, 41,* 192–201.

Hlongwane, M. M., & Bason, C. J. (1990). Self-concept enhancement of Black adolescents using transactional analysis in a group content. *School Psychology International, 11,* 99–108.

Hoag, M. J., & Burlingame, G. M. (1997). Evaluating the effectiveness of child and adolescent group treatment: A meta-analytic review. *Journal of Clinical Child Psychology, 26,* 234–246.

Holcomb-McCoy, C. (2003). Multicultural competence. In B. T. Erford (Ed.), *Transforming the school counseling profession* (pp. 317–330). Upper Saddle River, NJ: Merrill Prentice Hall.

Jacobs, E., Masson, R., & Harvill, R. (2002). *Group counseling: Strategies and skills* (4th ed.). Pacific Grove, CA: Brooks/Cole.

Jacobs, E., & Schimmel, C. (2005). Small group counseling. In C. A. Sink (Ed.), *Contemporary school counseling: Theory, research, and practice* (pp. 82–115) Boston: Houghton Mifflin Company.

Jordan, J. V. (2000). The role of mutual empathy in relational-cultural therapy. *Journal of Clinical Psychology/In Session: Psychotherapy in Practice, 56,* 1005–1016.

Jordan, J. V., & Dooley, C. (2001). *Relational practice in action: A group manual.* Wellesley, MA: Stone Center Publications.

Jordan, J. V., Kaplan, A. G., Miller, J. B., Stiver, I. P., & Surrey, J. L. (1991). *Women's growth in connection: Writings from the Stone Center.* New York: Guilford.

Kagan, J., & Moss, H. A. (1962). *Birth to maturity.* New York: Wiley.

Kizner, L. R. (1999). Small group counseling with adopted children. *Professional School Counseling, 2,* 226–230.

Kohlberg, L. (1969). Stage and sequence: The cognitive developmental approach to socialization. In D. Goslin (Ed.), *Handbook of socialization theory and research* (pp. 347–480). Chicago: Rand-McNally.

Krumboltz, J. D., & Thoresen, C. E. (1969). *Behavioral counseling.* New York: Holt, Rinehart, & Winston.

Krumboltz, J. D., & Thoresen, C. E. (1976). *Counseling methods.* New York: Holt, Rinehart, & Winston.

Kulic, K. R., Hore, A. H., & Dagley, J. C. (2000). *A comprehensive review of prevention groups for children and adolescents.* Paper presented at the annual meeting of the American Psychological Association, Washington, DC.

Lee, C. C. (2001). Culturally responsive school counselors and programs: Addressing the needs of all students. *Professional School Counseling, 4,* 257–261.

Lee, V. E., Croninger, R. G., Linn, E., & Chen, X. (1996). The culture of sexual harassment in secondary schools. *American Educational Research Journal, 33,* 383–417.

Locke, D. C. (2003). Improving the multicultural competence of educators. In P. B. Pedersen, & J. C. Carey (Eds.), *Multicultural counseling in schools: A practical handbook* (2nd ed., pp. 171–189). Boston: Allyn & Bacon.

Miller, J. B. (1984). *The development of women's sense of self* (Work in Progress No. 12). Wellesley, MA: Stone Center.

Miller, J. B., & Stiver, I. P. (1997). *The healing connection: How women form relationships in therapy and in life.* Boston: Beacon Press.

Muller, L. E. (2000). A 12-session, European-American-led counseling group for African American females. *Professional School Counseling, 3,* 264–269.

Muller, L. E., & Hartman, J. (1998). Group counseling for sexual minority youth. *Professional School Counseling, 1,* 38–41.

Myrick, R. D. (2003). *Developmental guidance in the schools: A practical approach* (4th ed.). Minneapolis, MN: Educational Media Corporation.

Myrick, R. D., & Dixon, R. W. (1985). Changing student attitudes and behavior through group counseling. *The School Counselor, 32,* 325–330.

Ober, K., & Beesley, D. (2004). A survey of school counselors regarding job role and job satisfaction. *Journal for the Professional Counselor, 19,* 43–58.

O'Hanlon, W. H., & Weiner-Davis, M. (1989). *In search of solutions: A new direction in psychotherapy.* New York: Guilford.

Omizo, M. M., & Omizo, S. A. (1987a). The effects of eliminating self-defeating behavior of learning-disabled children through group counseling. *The School Counselor, 34,* 282–288.

Omizo, M. M., & Omizo, S. A. (1987b). Group counseling with children of divorce: New findings. *Elementary School Guidance and Counseling, 22,* 46–52.

Omizo, M. M., Hershberger, J. M., & Omizo, S. A. (1988). Teaching children to cope with anger. *Elementary School Guidance and Counseling, 22,* 241–245.

Piaget, J. (1970). *Science of education and the psychology of the child.* New York: Onion Press.

Reeder, J., Douzenis, C., & Bergin, J. J. (1997). The effects of small group counseling on the racial attitudes of second grade students. *Professional School Counseling, 1,* 15–18.

Riddle, J., Bergin, J. J., & Douzenis, C. (1997). Effects of groups counseling on the self-concept of children of alcoholics. *Elementary Guidance and Counseling, 31,* 192–203.

Ripley, V. V., & Goodnough, G. E. (2001). Planning and implementing group counseling in a high school. *Professional School Counseling, 5,* 62–65.

Ritchie, M. H., & Huss, S. N. (2000). Recruitment and screening of minors for group counseling. *The Journal for Specialists in Group Work, 35,* 146–156.

Rogers, C. R. (1951). *Client-centered therapy.* Boston: Houghton Mifflin.

Rosenthal, H. (1993). Friendship groups: An approach to helping friendless children. *Educational Psychology in Practice, 9,* 112–120.

Rowell, L. L., & Hong, E. (2002). The role of school counselors in homework intervention. *Professional School Counseling, 5,* 285–291.

Roysircar, G., Arredondo, P., Fuertes, J. N., Ponterotto, J. G., & Toporek, R. L. (2003). *Multicultural counseling competencies 2003: Association for Multicultural Counseling and Development.* Alexandria, VA: American Counseling Association.

Ryan, C., & Futterman, D. (1998). *Lesbian and gay youth: Care and counseling.* New York: Columbia University Press.

Schmidt, J. J. (1999). *Counseling in schools: Essential services and comprehensive programs* (3rd ed.). Needham Heights, MA: Allyn & Bacon.

Sciarra, D. T. (2004). *School counseling: Foundations and contemporary issues.* Belmont, CA: Brooks/Cole.

Shechtman, Z. (1994). The effect of group psychotherapy on close same-sex friendships among preadolescent boys and girls. *Sex-Roles: A Research Journal, 30,* 829–834.

Shechtman, Z. (2000). Short-term treatment of childhood aggression: Outcomes and process. *Psychology in the Schools, 37,* 157–167.

Shechtman, Z. (2002). Child group psychotherapy in the school at the threshold of a new millennium. *Journal of Counseling and Development, 80,* 293–299.

Shechtman, Z., & Ben-David, M. (1999). Group and individual treatment of childhood aggression: A comparison of outcomes and process. *Group Dynamics, 3,* 1–12.

Shechtman, Z., Gilat, I., Fos, L., & Flasher, A. (1996). Brief group therapy with low-achieving elementary school children. *Journal of Counseling Psychology, 43,* 376–382.

Shechtman, Z., & Nachshol, R. (1996). A school-based intervention to reduce aggressive behavior in maladjusted adolescents. *Journal of Applied Developmental Psychology, 17,* 535–553.

Sodowsky, G. R., Taffe, R. C., Gutkin, T. B., & Wise, S. L. (1994). Development of the Multicultural Counseling Inventory: A self-report measure of multicultural competencies. *Journal of Counseling Psychology, 41,* 137–148.

Stiver, I. P. (1991). The meaning of care: Reframing treatment models. In J. V. Jordan, A. G. Kaplan, J. B. Miller, I. P. Stiver, & J. L. Surrey (Eds.), *Women's growth in connection: Writings from the Stone Center* (pp. 250–267). New York: Guilford Press.

Stone, C. B. (2004). School counselors as leaders and advocates in addressing sexual harassment. In R. Perusse & G. E. Goodnough (Eds.), *Leadership, advocacy, and direct service strategies for professional school counselors* (pp. 353–377). Belmont, CA: Brooks/Cole.

Studer, J. R. (2005). *The professional school counselor: An advocate for students.* Belmont, CA: Brooks/Cole.

Sue, D. W., & Sue, D. (2003). Racial/cultural minority identity development: Therapeutic implications. In D. W. Sue & D. Sue (Eds.), *Counseling the culturally diverse: Theory and practice* (4th ed., pp. 205–234). New York: John Wiley & Sons, Inc.

Super, D. E. (1990). A life-span, life-space approach to career development. In D. Brown, L. Brooks, & Associates (Eds.), *Career choice and development: Applying contemporary theories to practice* (2nd ed., pp. 197–261). San Francisco: Jossey-Bass.

Surrey, J. L. (1991). Relationship and empowerment. In J. V. Jordan, A. G. Kaplan, & J. B. Miller, I. P. Stiver, & J. L. Surrey (Eds.), *Women's growth in connection: Writings from the Stone Center* (pp. 162–180). New York: Guilford.

Taylor, C. A., Liang, B., Tracy, A. J., Williams, L. M., & Seigle, P. (2002). Gender differences in middle school adjustment, physical fighting, and social skills: Evaluation of a social competency program. *The Journal of Primary Prevention, 23,* 259–272.

Tedder, S. L., Scherman, A., & Wantz, R. A. (1987). Effectiveness of a support group for children of divorce. *Elementary School Guidance and Counseling, 22,* 102–109.

Timmerman, G. (2003). Sexual harassment of adolescents perpetrated by teachers and by peers: An exploration of the dynamics of power, culture, and gender in secondary schools. *Sex Roles, 48,* 231–244.

U.S. Department of Education. (2002). *No child left behind: A desk reference.* Washington, DC: Office of Elementary and Secondary Education.

U.S. Department of Education, Office of Civil Rights. (1997). *Sexual harassment policy guidance: Harassment of student by school employees, other students, or third parties.* 62 Fed. Reg. 12034–12051.

U.S. Department of Education, Office of the Deputy Secretary. (2003). *Rural education.* Retrieved September 25, 2005, from http://www.ed.gov/about/offices/list/ods/ruraled/index.html

Utay, J. M., & Lampe, R. E. (1995). Use of a group counseling game to enhance social skills of children with learning disabilities. *Journal for Specialists in Group Work, 20,* 114–120.

Verdyn, C. M., Lord, W., & Forrest, G. C. (1990). Social skills training in schools: An evaluation study. *Journal of Adolescence, 13,* 3–16.

Walker, M. (2004). How relationships heal. In M. Walker & W. B. Rosen (Eds.), *How connections heal* (pp. 3–21). New York: Guilford Press.

Walter, J. L., & Peller, J. E. (1992). *Becoming solution-focused in brief therapy.* New York: Brunner/Maxel.

Webb, L. D., & Myrick, R. D. (2003). A group counseling intervention for children with attention-deficit/hyperactivity disorder. *Professional School Counseling, 7,* 108–115.

Wellesley Centers for Women. (2005). *What is Open Circle?* Retrieved September 15, 2005, from http://www.open-circle.org

Whiston, S. C., & Sexton, T. L. (1998). A review of school counseling outcome research: Implications for practice. *Journal of Counseling and Development, 76,* 412–426.

Zinck, K., & Littrell, J. M. (2000). Action research shows group counseling effective with at-risk adolescent girls. *Professional School Counseling, 4,* 50–59.

XXIX
FAMILIES IN CONTEXT: An Essential Component of School Counseling

TERENCE PATTERSON
University of San Francisco

Introduction

Before delving into the realities faced by school counselors in the complex environment of today's schools, let us establish a framework for viewing the role of families: historically, conceptually, professionally, and practically.

On a practical level, the profession of social work recognized the centrality of families with the establishment of settlement houses such as Jane Adam's Hull House in Chicago in 1889 (Lissak, 1989). Serving many functions in the lives of immigrants and low-income city residents, the settlement house provided a refuge and a resource for those in need, and designed programs to involve parents in their children's activities, to keep families active and intact, and to assist those in need. As families moved out to more remote areas of cities and suburbs, those efforts evolved into the Family Service Association (FSA) of America, which provided services both centrally and in the home itself in order to accommodate changing living and family patterns. In the center and in the home, social workers engaged in social casework (Robinson, 1962), which involved connecting individuals and families with concrete services and also providing counseling, which might be seen as an early form of family therapy, and later became known as "clinical social work."

Thus the first family counselors (*therapist* and *counselor* will be used interchangeably) were social workers, and other mental health professionals did not recognize the essential role of families in intervention until the late 1940s and 50s. First a form of "family group therapy" (Bell, 1963), then "family network therapy" (Attneave, 1974), and "child guidance" (Levy, 1968) were identified, until "conjoint family therapy" (Satir, 1983) became the norm. The last became the standard for family therapists of all disciplines, including psychology, psychiatry, social work, nursing, counseling, and the profession of family therapy itself, and involves a counselor treating the entire family as a unit. Recent models, acknowledging the realities of modern life, include counseling family members both together and separately within a systemic context.

School professionals have long known that in every dimension, it is wise and necessary to involve parents and families in the life of the school. Thus, physical and mental health clinics were established in schools in the 1980s, providing both convenience and outreach for students and their families. Health providers and counselors not only began to come to the schools, but the schools were inviting the community, primarily families, into the school as part of a system of comprehensive, integrative services.

Theory

We now turn to the question, "What theories and developmental perspectives can serve as a foundation for comprehensive school counseling today?" The first element is General Systems Theory (GST; von Bertalanffy, 1968), which, in essence, views biological and social units as interacting elements that mutually influence each other. Major premises of GST are that systems have their own structure and processes; that a ripple in one part of a system can become a wave in the others, and each component has the potential of changing the entire system; and that systems cannot remain static, but must change or dissolve. GST was derived from the biological and physical sciences, was later applied to social science, and has become integrated into family psychology and therapy and, to a lesser extent, into organizational development.

For schools, the major elements are students, teachers, administrators and policymakers, staff, families, and the community. A school is a system in itself, but has subsystems within it and is itself a subsystem of a school district and the larger community, nation, and world. Thus, federal and state education policies affect local schools and communities, and developments in schools such as violence and test results affect state and local policies and funding.

GST also refers to closed systems and open systems that are regulated by feedback (i.e., communication), and indicates that an open system has boundaries that are somewhat permeable and allow for the exchange of information with the outside so that the system can remain viable. Closed systems, on the contrary, have rigid boundaries and poor communication, and they lead to chaos and disorganization. In schools, this points to the need for clear structures and a free flow of communication, both internally with teachers, counselors, administrators, and students, and externally with the larger community, so that mutual understanding and decision making can occur within the school and among the home, school, and community.

A related, still-relevant concept began in the early 1960s when President Kennedy initiated the community mental health movement, in which not only were facilities in each local area designed to provide emergency and rehabilitative psychological programs, but *community education and prevention services* were included to coordinate networks of services in order to prevent social and mental health problems from occurring (Caplan, 1964; Cutler & Huffine, 2004). Although never fully funded, some model centers developed school–family–business–nonprofit partnerships involving parents and residents in decision making and in assisting children, parents, and educators to focus on the central mission of educating and socializing children in a stable environment.

Also in the mental health field, the family therapy movement took root in the '50s and '60s, first with the concept of *family group therapy* (Bell, 1963), in which families with similar needs were brought together in a large group to share experiences and solve problems. A related process, *family network therapy* (Attneave, 1974), was based in Native American communities and incorporated the tradition of bringing together significant community members, including elders, to deal with family issues. Most recently, the concept of *ecosystemic therapy* (e.g., McDaniel, Lusterman, & Philpot, 2001) recognizes the interrelatedness of religious, educational, recreational, health, law enforcement, and other key institutions in providing comprehensive, integrated, stable environments for families.

Most mental health therapists and counselors who practice from a systems or family perspective recognize the need for significant others in a child or adolescent's life to be involved when problems arise, if not for intervention, at least for assessment. Thus, the *conjoint therapy* model, in which as many family or other individuals as possible are involved in treatment, is most desirable. Similarly, school personnel who refer to counselors understand the vital role that family members, relatives, and others in the community play in students' lives, but time often interferes with taking an approach that involves families and community members, and thus, solutions often become partial and inadequate. In this brief review of the foundations of family involvement, it is hoped that counselors and others will recognize the essential importance of including families in all aspects of working with students, and internalize the concept that it truly "takes a village" to raise and nurture children in a complex, changing environment.

Over the last two decades in particular, concepts and practices involving *multicultural competence* and diversity have informed practitioners of the advisability and necessity of taking culture, values, and traditions into account in engaging, assessing, and intervening with individuals and families. Most school counselors understand the critical importance of not only understanding the entire context of students' lives in assisting them appropriately, but of taking into account the individuality of each student and family, perhaps an even more difficult task. Concepts involving respect for elders, extended families, and alternative family forms, rituals, *personalismo,* and *familismo* (Falicov, 1998) have become integrated in counseling practice and have provided valuable lessons for all who work with families. The vital role of diversity will be examined in detail in the case example later in this chapter and in recommendations for the future.

Research

Many counselors' eyes instantly gloss over when scholarly research is mentioned. Let us briefly examine the reasons for this and present some practical examples of research that are directly useful in practice today. Psychoanalytic theories dominated the mental health field for the first half of the century and were largely theoretical and based on major disorders; that is, they were often derived from observations and clinical treatment of severely disturbed individuals in large treatment facilities. In addition, samples were usually small or uncontrolled for sources of variance. Following the 1950s, newer approaches began to appeal to the growing numbers of counselors who did not find traditional psychoanalytic models relevant to their practices. By the 1980s, many of the popular models of counseling were based on the writing and demonstrations of charismatic and leading-edge thinkers and clinicians, and research rarely involved systematic procedures or large samples from actual practice. Humanistic approaches to counseling and psychotherapy, including those of Carl

Rogers, Rollo May, and Abraham Maslow, attracted many. Behavioral techniques, although not popular in concept often because of inadequate explanation or misrepresentation, were often integrated into community counseling programs and agencies along with humanistic concepts, and they resulted in more practical approaches to counseling in neighborhood agencies and schools.

During the 1970s, psychotherapy and counseling practices came into vogue that involved two new, fundamental elements. First, clients were often seen before audiences of trainees or on videotape, and some systematic methods were used. This is particularly critical, as it pertains to the treatment of children, couples, and families, and because assessment instruments, ethical standards, and advanced technologies were developed to respond to this *glasnost*, or opening of the consulting room door. Second, controlled investigations using the scientific method of generating hypotheses, gathering data, and ruling out sources of variance in order to test the true effects of an intervention took place, primarily within behavior modification and therapy models. This is not surprising because systematic, scientific procedures are inherent in behavioral assessment and treatment, and modifications are continually made that are based on new findings. The following section will discuss one of the earliest and most rigorous series of research studies pertaining to adolescent conduct disorders and families, and it has direct relevance to school counseling.

In 1975, Dr. Gerald Patterson founded the Oregon Social Learning Center (OSLC) and published *A Social Learning Approach: Families with Aggressive Children* (Patterson, Reid, Jones, & Conger, 1975). Since that time, dozens of rigorous studies have been done focusing on the general topics of children and adolescents in schools, conduct orders and delinquency, and the relationship among schools, families, and the community. The following is an example of a research project by the OSLC that is highly relevant for school counselors.

Linking the Interests of Families and Teachers (LIFT) is a research intervention program designed to prevent the development of aggressive and antisocial behavior. Classes from 12 schools (first and fifth grades) located in neighborhoods with a high rate of juvenile crime have been included. All families in the selected grade level were asked to participate. The enrichment school participants participated in the assessment-only phase of the program. The assessment included observations on the playground, peer ratings, teacher ratings, family interviews, parent and child questionnaires, family interaction tasks, and school and court records queries. In addition to the assessment described, the prevention school participants received an intervention designed to prevent problem behaviors from developing or progressing by simultaneously influencing parents, teachers, and children to (1) enhance family interactions, (2) increase prosocial and reduce negative peer interactions, and (3) improve the coordination between home and school. The effectiveness of the intervention is being evaluated through a research design that includes preintervention, postintervention, and yearly follow-up assessments of all participants. In addition, these assessments provide an opportunity to comprehensively examine the factors that support or impede the success of important transitions children and families make as the child begins elementary school and moves into middle school, high school, and young adulthood (Eddy, Mayne, & Reid, 2000).

In reviewing the dimensions of this study, it is hard to imagine a project that would be more comprehensive or useful to anyone involved with schools. Over the 30-year history of the OSLC, studies have demonstrated the positive results that occur through providing prevention and education programs and fostering close collaboration between families and schools. School counselors often serve as a bridge between students, teachers, administrators, and parents, and provide the expertise to foster communication and provide valuable information.

The Oregon studies and others also highlight a key function, and in the author's view, the most critical one a school counselor can play in the family–school interface: a *consultant* and *facilitator* role. More than counselor/therapist or educator, the school counselor is in a unique position to provide a framework and perspective for teachers, parents, and administrators to both prevent and solve problems faced by students. In this role, the key tool for the counselor with a scientific or empirical approach is to assess needs and problems carefully, to generate options, rule out irrelevant variables, and collaborate with others in implementing the most efficient and effective solution. Thus, a student who is referred to a counselor for disruption in the classroom may not benefit from ongoing one-to-one counseling so much as having the various circumstances (times, locations, persons, significant changes, etc.) explored carefully with the teacher, student, and family, so that appropriate interventions can be made. The successful approach may be as simple as recommending that the teacher ignore disruptive comments and reward constructive ones, or moving the student to another section. The OSLC has also conducted investigations into delinquency, substance, abuse, and violence. Brigman, Mullis, Webb, and White (2005) emphasized that the role of consultant for school counselors is the most effective one they can serve and pointed out that it reaches the greatest number of students and creates a more responsive school environment.

Another significant area that closely links theory, research, and practice is the *scholarship of engagement*, a concept that incorporates collaboration between academic and community professionals and consumers of services. The process of top-down, ivory-tower-generated research becomes reversed, and issues to be addressed originate in the real needs of those who are to be studied.

One example is a study in Australia (Dancer & Fiebig, 2001).

> Using a sample of several hundred students enrolled in the Faculty of Economics at the University of Sydney, we modeled progression in the first-year econometrics course. Our primary interest was the identification of "students at risk." This interest highlighted the need to distinguish between students who dropped the course and those who completed, but ultimately failed, the course. The models allowed identification and quantification of the factors that were most important in determining student progression and thus made them a potentially useful aid in educational decision making. There was some evidence that students who discontinued and those who failed have different characteristics; however, there was very clear evidence that these two groups do have different characteristics from the group of students who passed the course. It is vital to identify those "students at risk" early in the semester, and these results help this process. (p. 21)

The key element in this practical research study was to involve the community in determining the problem to be studied, generating hypotheses, gathering data, analyzing results, and developing solutions—a fundamental "bottom-up" approach.

Another multisite research project, funded by the federal government, found substantial benefits from family involvement in adolescent substance abuse treatment (Liddle, 1991). Other widely implemented projects with extensive research foundations have demonstrated the benefits of prevention and intervention programs for at-risk children, including a large program implemented in Australia by Mark Dadds (2002) and another used throughout the United States for adolescents and their families by Thomas Sexton and James Alexander (2002). Others of interest to school counselors include studies on the relationship of family environment and marital quality to child adjustment (Jouriles & Farris, 1992; Miller, 2002), parent management training (Kazdin, 1997), and the *Steps to Respect* Program, a large-scale study in elementary schools in the Pacific Northwest designed to teach respect and avoid bullying (Frey, 2005).

Pragmatic research findings such as those mentioned can often demonstrate cause-and-effect relationships in common situations and provide a framework for counselors to explore the specifics of a given context. Thus, school counselors are encouraged to become conversant with relevant research and intervention programs that have been proven effective and to serve in a consultative role, providing prevention and education programs; counseling students; serving as a bridge between students, administrators, and parents; and making informed referrals to external services.

Practice

Let us now clearly define what we mean by involving families in schools and closely examine what is done now. The key concept is for parents and other family members, including anyone with significant responsibility for caretaking or providing important services to students, to be in a *partnership* with teachers, administrators, and counselors so that there will be a seamless integration with the school, home, and community. This may seem like an unattainable ideal, but it is the ultimate objective for school personnel who attempt to solve common problems and to serve students' needs. Participating in parent–teacher organizations, volunteering, fund-raising, serving on school and community boards, chaperoning, and coaching have all provided opportunities for parents and other community members to be actively involved in the life of the school. In addition to these types of traditional parent involvement activities, school counselors can provide information to parents and the community on the services they provide, such as academic, career, and personal counseling and education and support on peer relationships, coping strategies, social skills, communication, problem solving, conflict resolution, substance abuse, and diversity issues (American School Counselor Association [ASCA], 1999). It is essential for counselors to establish clear lines of communication with parents and be an effective liaison with officials and specialists in the community to obtain input and support on these and other important activities.

Counselors who will readily agree with this concept may point out the difficulty of involving family and community members due to scheduling, distance, disinterest, lack of staff, and disorganization. While these are realistic concerns and not all students will have family members who participate, an *ethic of partnership* that pervades a school from top to bottom can elicit involvement and create an atmosphere that is contagious and draws people to take part in vital activities.

In fact, the opposite of partnership often occurs regarding family involvement. Aside from traditional "back-to-school night," occasional newsletters, and crisis situations, the school counselor can be alone when it comes to involving parents in the school lives of their children.

When policies do not require parent participation and resources are not allocated, counselors are frequently left carrying the ball when a student is identified with a problem. Difficult behaviors such as disruption, withdrawal, lateness or truancy, and poor academic performance that are left solely on the counselor's plate can exacerbate and become intractable if parents do not feel part of the program, and administrators and teachers do not "own" a share of the problem and collaborate on developing solutions.

School counselors cannot do it alone. School boards, parent organizations, and principals who develop expectations and meaningful activities for families to share in the life of the school as a condition of admission and retention can facilitate regular contact between teachers, counselors, and other staff. Whether written, verbal, or electronic, information provided on a regular basis to parents keeps them "in the loop" and diminishes anxiety when student problems arise. As innovative programs or partnerships with nonprofit or business organizations are publicized, a sense of pride develops that strengthens parents' sense of partnership with the school. The underlying concept is one of positively reinforcing parents and increasing awareness of student and school achievements, rather than waiting for problems to arise. Although they may be well beyond their school years, parents, too, feel a tinge of apprehension when teachers, principals, or counselors call if contacts occur only around problems, and an avoidance response can inadvertently develop and further separate families from their children's lives in school.

Dos and Do Nots of Effective and Efficient Family Involvement

School boards, administrators, and teachers are urged to

- develop policies that provide encouragement and procedures for community partnerships between schools and businesses, social agencies, health facilities, law enforcement, and other community groups;
- provide incentives for parents to become involved on an ongoing basis from the time a student is admitted to school through graduation; and
- frequently publicize successful collaboration, especially examples of preventing potential problems and of social and academic success.

The concept of partnership, based on positive reinforcement and awareness, leads to some clear practices for counselors, supported by their schools, to facilitate parent involvement. In the earlier section on the genesis of the family therapy movement, a rationale was provided for involving *entire* families, or as many critical members as possible, in education, prevention, and counseling. Thus, school counselors are in a unique role to advocate for school–community partnerships, develop them, and take advantage of opportunities to draw parents into their children's activities: *as many as possible and as often as possible*. Specifically, in order to facilitate and strengthen parent involvement, school counselors can

- advocate and develop procedures and activities to involve families;
- provide useful, relevant information to parents on a regular basis through newsletters, workshops, Web sites, and e-mail;
- give parents periodic updates on social, emotional, vocational, and other relevant progress of their children;
- when critical situations arise, give background and other relevant information and arrange for key family members and other caregivers and professionals to meet together as appropriate, scheduling meetings—whenever possible—near worksites and at home; and
- assess problem situations systematically and provide options in order to reach collaborative, comprehensive solutions.

Administrators, board members, teachers, and parents are urged *not* to

- contact parents and invite their involvement only when funds are needed or problems arise;
- refer to counselors and utilize their services only when problems arise with students, and fail to collaborate in the assessment and treatment of problems; and
- expect school counselors to deal with complex family, social, and psychological issues that require specialized or ongoing treatment and referral.

School counselors are strongly encouraged *not* to

- operate as though they were in private practice, seeing students in ongoing, individual sessions without involving, families, teachers, administrators, and the community, as appropriate, and
- ignore the boundaries of their competence, and fail to refer to specialists as needed.

Counselors are required to serve many masters: teachers, administrators, parents, students, and the community. Therefore, they need to define their roles clearly and uphold the ethical standards of their profession. For a discussion of the ethics of school counseling, please refer to "Ethical School Counseling: Managing a Balancing Act" (T. E. Patterson, 1998).

Case Example and Implications for Multicultural Counseling

A highly visible public relations campaign says it best: *Si usted puede llegar aqui, se puede visitar la escuela de sus niños: participe, collabore!* (If you can arrive here, you can visit your children's school: participate, collaborate!) In that spirit, and to illustrate the concept of partnership, please consider the following example.

Armando and Estella Rivas are parents in their late 30s and have two boys, Esteban, age 10, and Hector, age 9, and one girl, Leida, age 7, in Buena Vista Elementary School in a major city. Both parents work in demanding jobs (Armando works 6 P.M. to 2 A.M. and Estella works 8 A.M. to 4 P.M.) and have been in the United States (they are from Nicaragua) for 12 years. Estella's mother and younger sister live with them and assist with child care and provide small incomes, although finances are still tight. Esteban is a high achiever and Leida is quiet, yet she has some friends and does well academically. Hector has a learning disorder (dyslexia) and a short attention span, and he has had to repeat his current grade (grade three) due to academic and behavioral difficulties. The parents have been interested in his progress and have responded to phone calls and attended teacher conferences, yet Hector's problems have been ongoing.

In October of Hector's second year in the third grade, Mr. Yi, his teacher, asked the school counselor, Ms. Jackson, to see Hector due to his difficulties with paying attention and completing his assignments, saying that his behavior was distracting to other students in class. Ms. Jackson scheduled a conference with Mr. Yi and obtained detailed information about Hector's past and present classroom activities (Mr. Yi was his teacher the previous year also), and requested an opportunity to observe Hector in class. She also obtained Hector's cumulative school folder and included significant academic and behavioral information in the file she had started on Hector. Ms. Jackson then contacted Mr. and Mrs. Rivas and, learning of their work schedules, arranged to meet them in their home between their respective shifts (at 4:30 P.M.) to discuss Hector's situation. She discovered that the parents experienced some of the same difficulties with Hector at home and in outside social situations, but they did not consider him to be *malcriado* (bad intentioned), but rather *dificil* (difficult). Their pediatrician had suggested that Hector was hyperactive at age 4, but they did not want him to be on medication.

Ms. Jackson wondered whether his attention span and task completion varied according to where he was, the task itself, or whom he was with. She noted in his school folder that similar problems had been observed since kindergarten, although when he was with one other person or was working on an art project (drawing or painting), he could sit for 30 minutes or more, was not disruptive, and could finish his project with some prompting. Rather than seeing Hector in individual counseling, she asked the parents if they could arrange a frequent time and place for Hector to draw in a quiet location with a sibling or friend. She suggested to Mr. Yi that he allow Hector to work with a classmate of his own choosing in a corner of his large classroom once each morning and afternoon, beginning with drawing and then shifting to the class assignment. Fortunately, Mr. Yi had a teaching assistant and agreed to try this approach, and after one week, he reported that Hector's behavior and attention were fine during the special periods and somewhat improved at other times also.

Ms. Jackson then contacted the school psychologist and requested that Hector be tested and that an individualized education plan (IEP) be developed. The testing confirmed the dyslexia as moderate, and the attention deficit appeared to depend upon the specific task and context. Weekly sessions with an educational specialist for Hector's dyslexia were arranged at a community center near his home, and Ms. Jackson found that a group had been formed there to assist adults and English as a Second Language (ESL) children who also had reading difficulties. Unfortunately, this group met only in the evenings, and Ms. Jackson successfully petitioned for a group to be formed to meet at the Buena Vista School on alternate Saturday afternoons. Hector attended the group there with children with other learning problems and was given special attention, and the parents were provided with information and the support of other parents. As a result, Armando and Estella also made it a point to arrange time off from work to attend parent teacher activities and other activities at the school because they saw the direct benefits of being actively involved in order to improve Hector's behavior and education.

It is notable that instead of automatically seeing Hector in individual counseling for the referred problem, Ms. Jackson took a broader approach and explored the history and current context of his situation. She did not view his inattention or disruptive behavior as an indication of either an emotional or a family problem, but rather as a specific deficit that could be addressed with environmental changes in the classroom, with specialized services, and with family and community support. She also went beyond the context of the school itself in arranging home visits and engaging the parents and community, which undoubtedly resulted in some lasting changes that benefited other parents and students. She embodied the concept of partnership, and she used a basic systems approach in creating a comprehensive solution to the referred problem. Ms. Jackson was also attuned to the cultural and specific context of this family, and she successfully discovered and expanded available resources. School counselors are urged to consider this model, which initially requires a period of assessment and outreach and ultimately necessitates less individual effort and responsibility and results in longer term solutions.

Although this case involved a Latin American family, its applications are widespread. If we consider the terms *culture* and *diversity* to encompass every type of difference, such as personality style, gender, sexual orientation, race, ethnicity, religion, socioeconomic status, geography, occupation, immigration, and disability, the first thing that becomes obvious is that just as group membership may be crucial to one's identity, such affiliation does not solely define an individual. Nor is it the purpose of this chapter to specify cultural differences, as illustrated by many excellent texts such as one by D. W. Sue and D. Sue (1999). It is also incorrect to assume that "minorities" are different from the norm, as the very definition of a "dominant culture" is constantly shifting, in both metropolitan and rural areas. Examples of differences that can intersect all groups are emphasis on individual versus community goals, loyalty to family, adherence to rituals, organized religion, career and education, and other dimensions. Thus, we may find a Native American who was raised in urban North Dakota by college-educated parents to have more in common with an Irish American from Chicago than with a Native American raised on a reservation in South Florida, though the Native Americans might adhere to the tradition of revering one's ancestors to a similar degree. This value might be shared by an African American from Louisiana who was raised in a Creole folklore tradition. The element essential for counselors to be *culturally competent* is to become knowledgeable about diversity as much as possible, while assessing the aspects of each individual that make her or him think, feel, and act in unique ways. Thus, awareness and skill in dealing with diversity is critical, and it is equally important to avoid stereotyping on the basis of group identification.

Future Directions

This chapter has reviewed the foundations and the impact of family involvement in schools and the importance of bringing community resources to bear in devising solutions. It has also outlined the models and practices in the mental health field to address family participation in assessment and intervention, particularly from a systems perspective. Practical, relevant research supports the roles of parents, nuclear and extended family, and other community individuals and groups in school activities. Numerous examples exist of successful collaboration, or partnership, which prevents and resolves problems, and enhances the quality of students' lives in schools, but much remains to be done.

The *scholarship of engagement* concept offers some of the brightest promise for school counselors to engage in partnerships with others in a relevant context to improve services to students while contributing scholarly information to the field. Projects can range from engaging students interested in careers in environmental management by studying pollution levels in disadvantaged communities to soliciting feedback from parents about their expectations of how they might be assisted most effectively when their children experience behavior problems. Teachers might be involved in exploring and testing alternative methods for counselors to observe and obtain systematic feedback on classroom and other school behaviors, and administrators can be surveyed and interviewed regarding their perceptions of the effectiveness of referrals made to school counselors and how to generate community resources in solving school-based problems. Alternatively, the experiences of students could be used as a basis for applying existing research to address bullying in middle schools. In similar fashion, the ideas of secretaries, custodians, teacher aides, and parent volunteers might be solicited for their observations and suggestions regarding student interactions in hallways, playgrounds, and in the cafeteria as part of developing a comprehensive model of assessment and intervention (for further information on this concept, see Boyer, 1996, and http://www.scholarshipofengagement.org).

In practice, counselors are encouraged to consider the example described above of Ms. Jackson, the school counselor who did not view Hector's difficulties in terms of an individual conduct disorder or family dysfunction, but rather as an issue to be systematically evaluated by engaging key individuals and groups in order to devise a comprehensive solution. Perhaps counselors who immediately take it upon themselves to address referrals from teachers and administrators only through private, individual sessions either do not feel that others are willing to be involved or are trained in a model of counseling that views problems only as pathologically based, or residing within the person.

Without debating the merits of different theories, it is apparent to nearly everyone that too many issues arise and not enough time or counselors exist to address problems solely in private sessions and that greater, more enduring outcomes can be achieved with a collaborative approach. We are not, however, encouraging counselors to be social workers, and we urge what one author has stated: "Solve school problems at school and home problems at home" (Palmatier, 1998, p. 442). Achieving the proper balance requires counselors to have a clear definition of their roles, and to serve as bridges between the school and the home and community. Thus, counselors are encouraged to (1) collaborate with teachers and administrators in developing effective referral, assessment, and intervention policies and procedures to address student issues; (2) assess presenting issues systematically and thoroughly when they are referred; (3) obtain as many records and reports relating to the problem as possible; (4) involve relevant specialists in obtaining a detailed assessment; and (5) involve key individuals within the school and in the community in generating alternative solutions and involve them in the implementation and evaluation of the plan.

The role of trainers and educators of school counselors emerges directly from the systemic model, the concept of partnership, the scholarship of engagement, and the examples described above. Instead of teaching only theory (especially an individual, problem-based one), training should involve a comprehensive model, include opportunities in the curriculum for students to explore real problems faced in the schools, and provide an empirical, student–family–community based perspective. Besides taking on cases referred by counselor–mentors, counseling trainees can then evaluate the dimensions of referred problems, talk with those involved, and produce a practical term paper to be shared with personnel in the school. Trainees should be expected to meet with families in their homes and become knowledgeable about community resources. Collaboration with training faculty can generate grants to fund such projects, based on the scholarship of engagement and coordinated with programs such as *Teach for America*. With this model, counselors can be initiated into a partnership that actively engages them in academic and practical approaches and prepares them for effective careers that will immediately benefit schools, students, families, and communities.

The significant understanding that has emerged from the study and experiences with diversity needs to be expanded in working with students, families, and communities. There may be no better context for examining cultural values and developing new approaches than in the complex environments of today's schools. The diversity present in our schools presents opportunities for counselors to collaborate and consult not only on promoting equality, but also in teaching invaluable lessons for students to use throughout their lives.

In summary, what should be the role and objectives of school counseling? Certainly, all of the goals and tasks detailed in ASCA (1999) guidelines should be included. While individual counseling is one appropriate role for counselors, state guidelines defining the scope of practice of school counseling clearly do not specify that role to be *psychotherapy* or any type of in-depth, long-term private sessions. Experienced school counselors, teachers, and administrators will readily acknowledge that this is not possible or expected in most situations, nor do students or parents understand or give informed consent to such a process. They do expect needs and problems to be anticipated, prevented, and addressed directly in the most efficient and effective manner. The school counselor is therefore in a central position to be an *evaluator* and *facilitator*, rather than the sole agent to address students' individual problems. Counselors' expertise is based on their ability to understand, from a systems perspective, the complex ways in which situations impacting students develop and on their skill in collaborating with others to craft efficient, effective solutions. While individual, family, or group counseling may be one element in that process, other methods such as careful assessment, outreach, and collaboration can be more comprehensive and enduring. This model is offered as a universal one for school counseling professionals to consider, recognizing the vast experience, accumulated wisdom, and continuing crucial role that school counselors play in the lives of students.

References

American School Counselor Association. (1999). *The ASCA National Model: A framework for school counseling programs*. Alexandria, VA: Author.

Attneave, C. (1974). *Family networks*. New York: Vintage Books.

Bell, J. E. (1963). A theoretical position for family group therapy. *Family Process, 2*(1), 1–12.

Boyer, E. (1996). The scholarship of engagement. *Journal of Public Outreach, 1*(1), 11–20.

Brigman, G., Mullis, F., Webb, L., & White, J. F. (2005). *School counselor consultation: Skills for working effectively with parents, teachers, and other school personnel*. New York: John Wiley & Sons, Inc.

Caplan, G. (1964) *Principles of preventative therapy*. New York: Basic Books.

Cutler, D. L., & Huffine, C. (2004). Heroes in community psychiatry: Professor Gerald Caplan: Community mental health around the world. *Community Mental Health Journal, 40*(3), 193–197.

Dadds, M. R. (2002). An early intervention approach to children and families at risk for psychopathology. In F. W. Kaslow & T. E. Patterson (Eds.), *Comprehensive handbook of psychotherapy: Vol. 2: Cognitive behavioral approaches* (pp. 51–72). New York: John Wiley & Sons.

Dancer, D., & Feibig, D. (2001). *The Vice-Chancellor's showcase of scholarly inquiry in teaching and learning—Program & abstracts*. Sydney, New South Wales, Australia: Institute for Teaching and Learning.

Eddy, J. M., Reid, J. B., & Fetrow, R. A. (2000). An elementary school–based prevention program targeting modifiable antecedents of youth delinquency and violence: Linking the interests of families and teachers (LIFT). *Journal of Emotional and Behavioral Disorders 8*(3), 165–176.

Eddy, M., Mayne, T., & Reid, J. (2005). *Linking the interests of families and teachers*. Eugene: Oregon Social Learning Center.

Falicov, C. J. (1998). *Latino families in therapy*. New York: Guilford.

Frey, K. S. (2005). Reducing playground bullying and supporting beliefs: An experimental trial of the "Steps to Respect Program." *Developmental Psychology, 41,* 3.

Jouriles, E. N., & Farris, A. M. (1992). Effects of marital conflict on subsequent parent-son interactions. *Behavior Therapy, 23,* 355–374.

Kazdin, A. E. (1997). Practitioner review: Psychosocial treatments for conduct disorder in children. *Journal of Child Psychology & Psychiatry & Allied Disciplines, 38*(2), 161–178.

Levy, D. M. (1968). Beginnings of the child guidance movement. *American Journal of Orthopsychiatry, 38*(5), 799–804.

Liddle, H. A. (1991). A multidimensional model for treating the adolescent drug abuser. In W. Snyder & T. Ooms (Eds.), *Empowerment families: Family centered treatment of adolescents with mental health and substance abuse problems* (pp. 91–100). Rockville, MD: U.S. Department of Health & Human Services.

Lissak, R. S. (1989). *Pluralism and progressives: Hull House and the new immigrants, 1890–1919*. Chicago: University of Chicago Press.

McDaniel, S. H., Lusterman, D.-D., & Philpot, C. L. (2001). *Casebook for integrating family therapy: An ecosystemic approach*. Washington, DC: APA Press.

Miller, T. (2002). Associations between marital quality and parenting: Does marital quality affect the degree to which parents encourage autonomy in their children? *Berkeley McNair Research Journal, 10,* 153–171.

Palmatier, L. L. (1998). Parental involvement with certain school problems. In L. L. Palmatier (Ed.), *Crisis counseling for a quality school community: Applying Wm. Glasser's choice theory* (pp. 439–464). Washington, DC: Accelerated Development, Taylor & Francis.

Patterson, G. R., Reid, J. B., Jones, R. R., & Conger, R. E. (1975). *A social learning approach to family intervention: Vol. 1: Families with aggressive children*. Eugene, OR: Castalia Publishing Company.

Patterson, T. E. (1998). Ethical school counseling: Managing a balancing act. In Palmatier, L. L. (Ed.), *Crisis counseling for a quality school community: Applying William Glasser's choice theory* (pp. 77–90). Washington, DC: Accelerated Development, Taylor & Francis Group.

Robinson, V. P. (1962). *Jessie Taft: Therapist and social work educator*. Philadelphia: University of Pennsylvania Press.

Satir, V. (1983). *Conjoint family therapy*. Palo Alto, CA: Science & Behavior Books.

Sexton, T. L., & Alexander, J. A. (2002). Functional family therapy for at risk adolescents and their families. In F. W. Kaslow & T. Patterson (Ed.), *Comprehensive handbook of psychotherapy: Vol. 2: Cognitive-behavioral approaches* (pp. 117–140). New York: John Wiley & Sons.

Sue, D. W., & Sue, D. (1999). *Counseling the culturally different: Theory and practice*. New York: Wiley.

von Bertalanffy, L. (1968). *General systems theory: Foundations, theory, applications*. New York: Braziller.

XXX
CRISIS MANAGEMENT IN THE SCHOOLS

MICHELLE L. MURPHY
University of North Florida

Introduction

As an organized body of knowledge, skills, and practice, the field of crisis intervention is relatively young. However, it has experienced heightened momentum in the last decade because of the widespread media coverage of growing numbers of school tragedies and the resulting ripple effect felt in school communities throughout the country. Nationwide, there is increased awareness of the need for effective crisis prevention and intervention in schools (Allen, Jerome, et al., 2002; Brock, 1998; Dwyer, Osher, & Hoffman, 2000; Klicker, 2000; Malley, Kush, & Bogo, 1994; Poland & McCormick, 2000; Wittmer, 2000). Crises of varying types and degrees can and do happen in all types of school communities every day, and school personnel and students are exposed to an increasing number of personal crises and traumatic events. According to Stephens (1994), schools face two types of crises: those they are currently dealing with and those about to happen. Thus, even with the most diligent prevention efforts, it is highly likely that a school counselor, at some point, will be called upon to provide crisis intervention services and/or be involved in larger scale crisis management efforts.

Crisis intervention is typically defined as a short-term, goal-directed helping process focused on resolution of an immediate problem and stabilization of resulting emotional conflicts. Prompt intervention should be geared toward reestablishing emotional and behavioral stability, providing support, and facilitating the needs of those most closely impacted by the crisis (Klicker, 2000). School counselors have the opportunity to become the response initiator, trainer, service provider, and advisor for crisis situations in the schools. However, their current roles must be expanded to include developing, training, and implementing strategies and support services designed to address crises that impact the school community.

Although school counselors have knowledge of a broad range of adolescent developmental issues, they need to acquire specific skills in developing and implementing prevention programs as well as the competence to intervene and respond to various crisis scenarios. Comprehensive crisis management involves efforts to prevent crises, such as school violence and suicide, as well as postvention efforts designed to minimize the impact of traumatic events, such as homicide, student deaths, and natural disasters, on the school community. However, effective prevention and intervention become unrealistic expectations when school counselors are not competent, capable, or adequately prepared to understand and handle a wide array of crisis situations. Given the increasing number and variety of crises impacting schools, a thorough understanding of the crisis intervention process and training in crisis intervention skills, with a specific emphasis on suicide intervention, are essential for school counselors.

This chapter establishes the scope and significance of crises in the schools and provides a rationale for the importance of school-based intervention in crisis situations, including a discussion of prevention efforts, crisis training activities, and crisis response procedures. I present an overview of the nature of crises, crisis theory, and the field of crisis intervention, with particular emphasis on crisis intervention in the schools. A review of the current literature in the field and a framework to guide school counselors toward effective prevention, preparation, intervention, and postvention efforts is provided. The benefits of developing a crisis intervention team, obstacles that can impede the development and implementation of the crisis intervention plan, and strategies for minimizing identified obstacles are also discussed.

Scope of the Problem

Every day in America, on average, 15 children are killed by firearms, 13 are victims of homicide, and 6 commit suicide. According to the *Indicators of School Crime and Safety 2000*, during the 1997–1998 school year, there were 60 violent deaths at school, including 47 homicides, 12 suicides, and 1 student killed by a police officer in the line of duty (National School Safety Center, 2001). However, widely publicized, school-based crises are still relatively rare compared with the rising incidences of depression, suicide, and physical, sexual, and psychological abuse/neglect, which are frequent causes of crises among children and adolescents. Schools are also faced with deaths in the school community, accidents, natural disasters, and terrorism concerns, all of which require crisis intervention in the schools on a much more frequent basis. According to Pitcher and Poland (1992), these types of traumatic stress, which result from unpredictable and uncontrollable losses, are the most common crises experienced in schools. These crisis situations expose students to "threat, loss, and traumatic stimulus" and undermine their "security and sense of power" (Johnson, 2000, p. 3).

Suicide is the second leading cause of death for adolescents and, thus, an integral part of any discussion of school crises (Hayden & Lauer, 2000; King, Price, Telljohann, & Wahl, 1999, 2000; Poland & McCormick, 1999; Popenhagen & Qualley, 1998). Gallup polls have indicated that 60% of teens reported personally knowing someone who had attempted and 15% knew someone who had actually completed suicide (Cohen & Fish, 1993). Students' lives are often grievously impacted by those who attempt or complete suicide, and adjustment after a completed suicide often impacts the entire school community because of the atypical nature of the death and the social stigma involved (Clark, 2002).

Issues related to overall school climate, such as bullying, alienation, and harassment, can influence the likelihood of school crises. For instance, Petersen and Straub (1992) cited the following environmental factors in schools that increase the risk of suicide or violence: transitions and restrictions imposed by "the system," lack of specialized programs and services, a social climate with strong cliques and factions, and the alienation and rejection of certain types and/or groups of students. Bullying, the most common form of violence occurring in schools, is continuing to increase. Nearly 30% of U.S. students report being involved in bullying as either a target or a perpetrator, and more than one in three students said they did not feel safe at school (National School Safety Center, 2001). Tolerance of bullying behaviors creates a hostile school climate that increases the likelihood of crisis (Olweus, Limber, & Mihalic, 1999). According to Hazler and Carney (2000), violence can be viewed along a continuum, with peer-on-peer types of abuse, such as teasing, harassment, and bullying, at the lower end and school assaults, murders, and suicides at the higher end. In fact, a history of bullying, persecution, and threats has been associated with 66% of the school shooting incidents (Vossekuil, Reddy, & Fein, 2000). These data also indicate that children who are bullied report more loneliness and social isolation, while those who are doing the bullying were more likely to perform poorly academically and engage in substance abuse. All of these behaviors and characteristics are considered risk factors that would place both targets and perpetrators at greater risk for crisis.

Furthermore, the impact of more "typical" developmental crises is multiplied and magnified by the increasingly complex issues facing today's school-aged youth and by declining family and community support systems. The influence of societal problems on adolescents is reflected in dramatic increases in substance abuse, suicide, child abuse, teen pregnancy, truancy, school dropout, and random acts of violence (Pitcher & Poland, 1992; Wittmer, 2000). According to Caplan (1964), crises challenge coping resources, jeopardize an individual's sense of emotional balance and stability, create psychological distress, and cause individuals to feel trapped (i.e., unable to escape or effectively deal with the problem at hand). Given the inevitability of crisis and its damaging impact, it is clear that crisis intervention in schools is a necessary mechanism for helping students deal with these increasingly common threats to their growth and well-being.

The Nature of Crisis

The Chinese symbol for crisis is a combination of two characters that represent both danger and opportunity. The *Encarta World English Dictionary* (2002) defined *crisis* as

> A time when something very important for the future happens or is decided [and] a situation or period in which things are very uncertain, difficult, or painful, especially a time when action must be taken to avoid complete disaster or breakdown.

A crisis entails the unexpected and usually involves change and loss (Erickson, 1963; Hendricks & Thomas, 2002; Lindemann, 1944). A typical crisis consists of the following five components: a hazardous event, a vulnerable state, a precipitating factor, an active response state, and the resolution (Roberts, 1990).

Crisis situations occur periodically throughout the life span, and they may be triggered by either a single catastrophic event or the cumulative effect of successive stressors. Although once viewed as pathological, crisis reactions are now recognized as normal responses to abnormal situations. The following characteristics of crisis situations have been identified: (1) the presence of both danger and opportunity, (2) complicated symptomatology and ineffability, (3) seeds of growth and change, (4) the absence of panaceas or quick fixes, (5) necessity of choice and action, (6) time-limited acuteness, (7) universality and idiosyncrasy, and (8) an obstruction of goals and loss of control (Gilliland & James, 1997; Romano, 1990, as cited in Hendricks & Thomas, 2002).

The emotional intensity of a crisis reaction may range from severe pain to numbness but is typically characterized by some degree of confusion, discomfort, anxiety, vulnerability, disorganization, helplessness, and/or disequilibrium. The crisis state produces distress that is primarily associated with an overwhelming precipitating event and an inability to cope with or adapt to the resulting circumstances. Personality characteristics of individuals in crisis include a lowered span of attention, an inability to discriminate between stimuli, introspection, uncontrolled emotional responses, impulsivity, limited perspective, and subtle and/or overt help-seeking behaviors (Hendricks & Thomas, 2002).

Crisis is a subjective reaction to a stressful life experience; it is an individual's perception of and reaction to an event that shapes a crisis, not the situation itself (Roberts, 1990). In other words, a person's feelings of shock and distress *concerning* the disruption will determine the crisis reaction, not the disruption itself. Therefore, an individual's perceptions, skills, experiences, and abilities cannot be viewed in isolation (Palmatier, 1998). Crisis is essentially a relational phenomenon and cannot be understood, prevented, or resolved without attending to the contexts and structures surrounding a distressed individual. According to Hendricks and Thomas (2002), "[T]he *interpersonal* experience of the individual in response to the *event* that in some way involves others in the *interpersonal* environment is the foundation for understanding the dynamics of crisis formation" (p. 7).

Expectations and assumptions for handling traumatic situations are shaped by an individual's worldview. For example, values associated with culture, gender, religion, and social roles influence the interpretation of and reaction to crises and may have implications for coping strategies, communication styles, emotional expression, and help-seeking behaviors. Counselors must be aware of how their own values and assumptions about crisis situations influence their work. For instance, cultural norms prescribing emotional restraint for Asians or expression of grief for African Americans may be viewed as maladaptive when viewed through a Eurocentric lens. It is important to remember that crisis is a normal reaction to an abnormal event; each individual's unique, personal experience of the crisis should be validated and accepted without imposing one's own values on how the crisis response should be manifested or effectively resolved.

Crisis is an intrinsic part of life, and despite efforts aimed at prevention, crises will continue to occur. Timely, efficient intervention frequently leads to the positive resolution of a crisis and minimizes the likelihood of future physical or emotional deterioration. According to Terr (1992), "[I]f a traumatic response does not have the chance to become entrenched, it will become only a small scar on a very large life" (p. 77). Increased awareness and understanding of the nature and impact of crisis as well as comprehensive intervention strategies increase the likelihood that individuals will emerge through a crisis stronger and more enriched, as opposed to hopeless and defeated. Well-resolved crises provide the opportunity for the development of improved coping strategies and increase an individual's resistance to the impact of future stressors. Thus, within each crisis lies the opportunity for growth.

School Crises

Schools are one of the major socializing institutions affecting children's lives and are therefore the context within which they experience frequent crises of varying degrees and impact. Within this context, counselors and educators have the opportunity and responsibility to teach students how to effectively resolve crises, cope with the associated and causal factors, and develop an increased sense of resiliency. A school crisis may be defined as an incident occurring either at school or in the community that negatively impacts students, staff, and/or other members of the school community (Trump, 2000).

The simplest criterion for an incident to be considered a crisis is an implied threat to the health, safety, or welfare of students. According to Johnson (2000), a school crisis "brings chaos" that "undermines the safety and stability of the entire school" (p. 18). Similarly, situations that create, or have the potential to create, a disruption of the educational process or normal school operations may be considered crises. Implications for school crisis intervention are particularly significant because of the intensity and frequency of both developmental and situational crises experienced by school-aged children and the unique social dynamics, capable of either alleviating or exacerbating a crisis, of school communities.

Situational school crises typically fall into one of the following three categories: (1) purposeful, human-caused disasters, such as violent crimes, shootings, bombings, hostage taking, teacher victimization, assault, suicide, or murder; (2) accidental disasters, such as transportation accidents, gas leaks, chemical spills, fires, or faulty equipment; and (3) natural disasters, such as hurricanes, tornadoes, floods, or earthquakes (Hill & Hill, 1994). However, given that crises are shaped by individual perceptions, it is important to realize that developmental crises, such as social isolation or interpersonal conflict (although less consensually traumatic) can evoke feelings that create a crisis state solely for the individual experiencing them.

Developmental crisis refers to the stress and anxiety associated with transitioning from one developmental stage to another and often relates to meeting the demands and resolving the tensions of the new stage. For example, the transition from middle to high school comes at a time when many students are worrying about their values and personal identities. This transition period frequently leads to crises when personal decisions cause conflict between family and/or cultural values and the values of their peers or social groups. The frequency, intensity, and duration of developmental crises vary depending on the individual's combination of personal, social, and environmental resources.

According to Johnson, Casey, Ertl, Everly, and Mitchell (1999), crises that are ignored or resolved ineffectively create posttraumatic stress responses that compromise the achievement of the goals of education in the following ways: (1) creating adverse reactions that affect learning, (2) reducing the ability to concentrate, (3) disrupting attention, (4) interfering with socialization, (5) causing difficulties in memory retention and retrieval, (6) becoming preoccupied with the traumatic experience, (7) regressing to earlier levels of coping, and (8) heightening physiological arousal and startle reflexes. Johnson et al. suggested that school personnel often misinterpret many of these problems and associated crisis-related behaviors as discipline issues, and thus, students are frequently punished as opposed to receiving appropriate intervention services.

The experience and resolution of crises in the schools is influenced by the unique dynamic of each school community. Factors, such as preexisting school climate, administrative support (or lack thereof), geographic location, facilities, and surrounding community resources, combine to enhance or inhibit crisis management. The location of a school in a particular urban, suburban, or rural area has implications for access to multiple resources during a crisis as well as for the amount of ripple effect that is felt throughout the surrounding community. For instance, a completed suicide in a small, rural town with strong religious ties may impact the community differently than if the same event were to occur in a large urban school, where violence is a more frequent occurrence. Similarly, for schools in areas where services are limited, proactive planning efforts should establish links with neighboring communities and develop networks for obtaining necessary support and resources, as needed. School counselors must know their schools and communities in order to effectively tailor their intervention efforts to respond to the specific needs.

Crisis in the context of schools is complex because of the unique features of a school's social structure and the shared sense of community. An efficiently managed crisis can provide valuable opportunities to model care and concern and can be used to unite students and staff, forming a sense of understanding, trust, and cohesiveness. Minimizing or denying the effects of crisis sends the message that an individual's distress is insignificant and may suggest that the crisis was so overwhelming that school staff was not able to deal with it directly. According to Hendricks and Thomas (2002), "[A] common crisis-producing event is the feeling that 'I have failed to cope adequately'" (p. 5). In the midst of a crisis, feelings of failure, isolation, and guilt increase the likelihood that another crisis will occur. Schools should be prepared to provide students with a sense of hope, stability, security, and optimism. The sense of community that comes from sharing an emotionally charged experience will not be realized if schools choose to maintain a "business as usual" approach to crisis situations or personal tragedies.

Suicide and aggression. Furlong, Morrison, and Pavelski (2000) suggested more implications for prevention and intervention become apparent when the definition of school crisis is broadened to include a continuum of harmful behaviors encompassing social and psychological harm. Furthermore, the scope of prevention and intervention activities should be expanded to include a focus on both outwardly directed acts and inwardly directed acts of aggression. There is support for the idea that maladaptive behaviors often occur in crisis situations in which isolated teens see no other option (Beautrais, Joyce, & Mulder, 1999; Bolton, 1993; Hazler & Carney, 2000; Kalafat, 1993). That is, adolescents often perceive that there are no solutions to their problems, and they turn to suicide or violence as the means to reduce their pain and torment or to cope with their out-of-control emotions. Violence toward oneself or others is frequently used by youth to release pent up feelings of anger or frustration. Statistics on adolescent suicide alone "require the school practitioner to develop skills to intervene with suicidal students and to develop primary prevention strategies for the school" (Davis, Sandoval, & Wilson, 1993, p. 265).

Suicide and aggression are inherent risks associated with crisis because of the hopelessness and despair that often accompany the crisis response. As problem-solving skills and coping abilities become overwhelmed, a crisis gains momentum, personality fragmentation occurs, and the crisis victim/survivor moves toward specific patterns of maladaptive behavior (Hendricks & Thomas, 2002). Researchers have suggested that poor impulse control may be the common link that influences the co-occurrence of these maladaptive behaviors (Simon & Crosby, 2000).

Specifically, a link has been found among the subjective experience of problem irresolvability, the sense of loss of control, and suicidal behavior (Jacobs, as cited in Orbach, Mikulincer, Blumenson, Mester, & Stein, 1999), all of which are essential issues to be addressed in any comprehensive crisis intervention program. An accumulation of negative life events and experiences in conjunction with inadequate problem-solving skills has a major impact on the frequency and intensity of anger experienced at school (Fryxell & Smith, 2000) and contributes to feelings of hopelessness and suicidal ideation (Ayyash-Abdo, 2002; Bolton, 1993; Simonds, McMahon, & Armstrong, 1991). Both suicide and aggressive behavior represent ineffective means of coping or resolving crises.

According to Studer (2000), "[B]ecause individuals experiencing a crisis are often difficult to be around (Aguilera, 1998), the real or imagined distance created between the suicidal individual and significant others may result in greater isolation, loneliness, and loss of a support system" (p. 270). Jobes (2000) asserted, "Suicidality is essentially a relational phenomenon. Specifically, the presence and/or absence of certain key relationships can paradoxically be both suicide causing and suicide preventive" (p. 8). For example, repeated disruptions of family life, such as parental discord, separation, caretaker changes, and physical or sexual abuse, have been linked to suicidal behavior, and 52% of adolescent suicide attempters revealed having problems with their parents (Studer). Thus, the school counselor's overall knowledge regarding adolescent suicide may directly determine the likelihood that at-risk students will successfully be identified and given the proper help (King et al., 2000). These findings have implications for the importance of school counselors' being able to identify, build rapport with, and convey empathy to students in crisis quickly and efficiently.

Risk factors. Using the categories developed by Hazler and Carney (2000), factors which would make a student more likely to experience a crisis and/or contribute to difficulties in the resolution of crises can be classified as follows:

- *Biological risk factors:* developmental transition issues, rapid physical and psychological changes, and dramatic hormonal fluctuations
- *Psychological risk factors:* depression, helplessness, hopelessness, low self-esteem, loss of motivation, anxiety, irritability, feelings of personal futility concerning the future, and hostility
- *Environmental risk factors:* lacking social competence, peer acceptance, family support, and meaningful relationships with others; academic or legal difficulties; high levels of chronic stress; and physical, emotional, or sexual abuse
- *Cognitive risk factors:* negative self-attribution, idealistic thinking, increased egocentrism, rigid or inflexible thinking, poor problem-solving skills, a negative or hopeless outlook, and an inability to foresee future consequences

All of the factors just mentioned are considered risk factors for youth suicide and violence. However, the strongest risk factors for suicide in youth are depression, alcohol or other drug use disorder, and aggressive or disruptive behaviors. It should be noted that any factors that increase the likelihood of rejection or peer alienation would also place students at higher risk for maladaptive coping. For instance, gay, lesbian, bisexual, and questioning youth face considerable obstacles both at home and school, and they often experience bullying, social isolation, and the loss of family support. Counselors should take steps to identify students who are more vulnerable to risk factors and attend closely to warning signs of potential crises so that interventions targeting these students will be timely and effective.

Females are 3 times more likely than males to attempt suicide, males are 5 times more likely than females to complete suicide, and gays/lesbians are 3 times more likely than heterosexual youth to engage in suicidal behavior (King et al., 2000). Caucasian adolescent males complete suicide at much higher rates than any other ethnic group, so extra efforts should be made to identify vulnerable students and involve them in early intervention efforts. Similarly, because Native Americans and Alaskan Natives have the highest adolescent suicide rates rate of any ethnic group, school personnel and parents should be aware of early warning signs and take efforts to prevent the development of at-risk behaviors (Capuzzi & Gross, 2004). According to Metha, Weber, and Webb (1998, as cited in Capuzzi & Gross, 2004), suicide rates for both Hispanic-American and Asian American adolescents continue to be lower than those for Native-American and African American youth, even though the period between 1980 and 1994 indicated higher rates than previously recorded. Similarly, despite significant increases in African American suicide rates during the same time, overall patterns in the data indicate that the suicide rate for African American adolescents remains lower than that of Caucasian adolescents. Some models indicate that cultural pressures associated with oppression may help to create protective factors that lower the risk of suicide.

Theory

The Origins of Crisis Intervention

Crisis intervention is a process by which trained crisis workers identify, assess, and intervene with distressed individuals to restore balance and reduce the negative effects of crisis in their lives. It involves an immediate response to and resolution of an urgent problem, focusing particularly on stabilizing emotional functioning and minimizing the long-term ramifications of the crisis (Hoff & Adamowski, 1998). Intervention becomes necessary when individuals have exhausted their skills for coping and feel hopeless and overwhelmed by their current situation. In 1906, the establishment of the nation's first suicide prevention center, in New York City, confirmed that effectively resolving a crisis frequently requires the provision of support and resources external to the individual experiencing the crisis (Brown, 2002; Roberts, 1990). According to Hoff and Adamowski, "A truism about the human condition is the community's recognition that most individual members cannot manage stressful or traumatic life events alone if they are to avoid potential pathologies or fatal outcomes" (p. 5).

According to Hendricks and Thomas (2002), early research, conducted without the benefit of the umbrella term "crisis intervention," focused on diverse and seemingly unrelated areas, such as "mental conflict," "hysteria," "time-limited mental health care," "short-term psychotherapy," and "acute grief." These early studies laid the foundation and provided support for many important crisis intervention concepts, including objective mediation, prioritizing patient treatment over problem diagnosis, directly addressing an individual's crisis, and the use of advanced empathy. It is generally recognized that the current field of crisis intervention, theory, and practice began with the groundbreaking efforts of Eric Lindemann (1944) and gained momentum through the work of Erickson (1963), Caplan (1964), and Quierdo (1968). Their numerous studies examined the effects of accidents and disasters on human functioning and shed new light on trauma response, crisis theory, and intervention practices. However, since the original work of these early pioneers, very few new theoretical approaches have been proposed to advance the crisis field (Hoff & Adamowski, 1998). Implications from their theories and practice are so fundamental that virtually all scholars and practitioners in the crisis field rely on their major concepts as a foundation (Hoff, 1995).

Grief postponement. In the early 1940s, 493 people were killed in the Boston Coconut Grove fire. Lindemann (1944) provided psychological assistance to individuals in various states of crisis, and his well-known study of the acute grief caused by this crisis provided the foundation on which the current understanding of crisis reactions is built. Lindemann identified five main characteristics of grief, including somatic distress, preoccupation with grim images, guilt, hostility, and loss of patterns of conduct. He discovered that acute crisis situations trigger similar patterns of grief and that individuals who were supported in expressing their grief experienced rapid stress relief.

Lindemann (1944) highlighted the seriousness of grief postponement, which is a type of crisis that occurs when a person displays little or no reaction to a tragedy, and noted the common experience of seeking to avoid the intense pain and distress associated with grief and loss. He concluded that, without intervention, denial and grief postponement were likely to lead to the development of personality disturbances, morbid reactions, and maladaptive behaviors. Lindemann's studies established a sequence of probable reactions and predicted how individuals might proceed through a crisis, depending on their reactions to grief. Later studies examined the effects of crisis-related stress on the human body and revealed that crises are detrimental to a person's physical health as well as his or her mental well-being. Current application of Lindemann's theories on acute grief, psychosomatic illness, and the crisis response emphasize the importance of immediate intervention, debriefing, and postvention efforts in order to lessen the long-term impact of crises.

Typologies of crisis. Erickson's (1963) work concentrated on the typologies of crisis. In particular, Erickson extended early definitions of crisis to include changes that occur naturally throughout the human growth and aging cycle and arise from situational, developmental, or sociocultural sources. According to Erickson, there are two categories of crisis: (1) maturational developmental crises, which involve physical, social, and emotional changes that occur because of the natural aging process and (2) accidental situational crises, which involve trauma and/or unexpected loss triggered by an unpredictable situation that taxes an individual's normal coping mechanisms. These categories of crisis also have been referred to as "internal" or "external" crises.

Situational crises are triggered either by a single, specific occurrence or by a compounded series of events, and typically, these occurrences are universally recognized as crises. These potentially traumatic crisis events can be classified in one of the following six categories (Brock, Sandoval, & Lewis, 2001; Slaikeu, 1990): (1) severe illness or injury; (2) violent and/or unexpected death; (3) threatened death and/or injury; (4) acts of war; (5) natural disasters; and (6) man-made/industrial disasters. Although Erickson's categories are still the primary classifications used today, Burgess and Baldwin outlined an expanded taxonomy that also includes crises associated with disposition, anticipated life transitions, psychopathology, and psychiatric emergencies (as cited in Hendricks & Thomas, 2002; Pitcher & Poland, 1992).

Mental health consultation. In 1946, Caplan joined with Lindemann to establish one of the first community mental health programs (Brock et al., 2001). Basing his theory on

Erickson's (1963) theories of life span development, Caplan (1964) believed that crises are often triggered by predictable developmental "tasks" that occur at various stages of life. Caplan suggested that failure to negotiate transitions from one developmental stage to another plays a role in the development of psychopathology and that personal and social resources are the key to determining how an individual resolves both developmental and situational crises. The concept of preventative mental health stemmed from the notion that because developmental crises could be anticipated, they also could be prevented (Pitcher & Poland, 1992).

Caplan (1964) also was one of the first theorists to address the concept of homeostasis, suggesting that people constantly employ coping strategies to maintain emotional equilibrium. Thus, he viewed crisis "as an upset of and an inability to maintain a steady emotional state" (Caplan, as cited in Brock et al., 2001, p. 12). Caplan suggested that crisis overwhelms an individual's normal problem-solving strategies and creates a state of disequilibrium associated with the inability to maintain emotional control.

Psychological first aid. Quierdo (1968) conducted studies during the 1930s in postwar Amsterdam, and his research determined that the effectiveness of crisis intervention is directly related to the intervention's proximity in both time and place to the crisis event. Quierdo's method, referred to as emergency first aid, was used extensively by the military during the Vietnam War, Korean War, and World War II. According to Hendricks and Thomas (2002), "[S]oldiers suffering from combat fatigue were sent to the rear of the combat zone to receive support. Research indicates that these soldiers were successful in regaining equilibrium within their immediate, albeit threatening, environment" (p. 12). Today, Quierdo's method is referred to as psychological first aid and is considered synonymous with crisis intervention.

Review of the Literature

Evaluation of Crisis Intervention Efforts

Crisis intervention is a relatively new responsibility for school systems in the United States. Prior to 1990, responsibility for school crisis intervention was not clearly defined; community mental health professionals, in fact, provided the bulk of mental health care for students impacted by crises (Johnson, 2000). However, schools are now increasingly relying on professionals within school systems for crisis intervention services (Brock et al., 2001; Johnson; Poland, 1994). Although there is heightened emphasis on crisis response in the schools, the field of school crisis intervention is still in its infancy. As a result, research, education, and training have not kept pace with the mounting need for the application of crisis intervention skills in the schools, and many school professionals feel they have inadequate training for the crisis intervener role (Allen, Jerome et al., 2002; Brock et al., 2001; King et al., 2000). This growing need for crisis preparedness and trauma response has highlighted the need for school counselors to develop specialized crisis intervention skills.

Although empirical support for the long-term effects of crisis intervention programs is unavailable, numerous qualitative accounts of school personnel who have "weathered" actual school crises attest to the value of having well-trained crisis teams and structured response efforts in place (Brock et al., 2001; Decker, 1997; Pitcher & Poland, 1992; Poland & McCormick, 1999; Trump, 1998; Wanko, 2001). Subsequent reviews of trauma response in the schools demonstrate that children who are able to verbalize their feelings and reactions in a timely manner recover most quickly and are better able to deal with the crisis in the long term.

A summary of crisis intervention and critical incident stress management research (Mitchell, 2003) yields the following conclusions in support of early intervention and debriefing efforts: multifaceted approaches to intervention are most effective; training, skill, and leadership style can impair or enhance the success of a debriefing; appropriate training determines the effectiveness of interventions; and when implemented effectively, debriefing reduces the signs and symptoms of distress associated with acute psychological crisis.

Furthermore, research indicates that the absence of effective intervention causes the crisis victim/survivor to reach a physical and psychological breaking point and increases the likelihood of permanent or long-term damage (Hendricks & Thomas, 2002; Palmatier, 1998; Poland & McCormick, 2000; Terr, 1983, 1992; Weinberg, 1993). The "Chowchilla bus incident" provided groundbreaking support for the importance of postvention services for victims of trauma. In Chowchilla, California, in the early 1970s, a busload of schoolchildren was kidnapped and buried underground for 27 hours. After their escape, no mental health care or counseling support was provided to the victims. As a result, follow-up and review of the incident indicated that, 5 years later, 100% of the children had clinical symptoms of depression, fear, and anxiety (Terr, 1983).

Additional research supports the improbability of adolescents being able to integrate traumatic experiences adequately, including suicide attempts or completions, without appropriate intervention and postvention efforts (Gilliland & James, 1997; Palmatier, 1998; Poland, 1994; Poland & McCormick, 2000; Terr, 1983; Weinberg, 1993). Moreover, if appropriate intervention and postvention activities are not carried out, Gilliland and James suggested, "[A]lthough the original crisis event may be submerged below awareness and the individual may believe the problem has been resolved, appearance of new stressors may bring the individual to the crisis state again" (p. 6).

Since few intervention and prevention programs have been evaluated rigorously enough to conclusively determine the most effective approach, the Centers for Disease Control (CDC) and Prevention (as cited in Brener, Krug, & Simon, 2000) recommended that programs not rely on any single strategy. Pitcher and Poland (1992) recommended that prevention efforts begin with programs that address the major causes of death for children: accidents, homicides, and suicides. The most effective programs will involve multiple stakeholders and utilize multifaceted approaches that target specific at-risk behaviors in addition to addressing attitudes and skills that can serve as protective factors. Integrated prevention models and universal interventions, applied to everyone in the same manner and degree, maximize the cost-effective use of school resources and

> provide an ideal means for school settings to develop, implement, and monitor a comprehensive management system that addresses the needs of all students . . . it is a fair system in that normally developing students are not penalized by being denied access to potentially beneficial interventions. (Sprague & Walker, 2000, p. 376)

Suicide prevention programs. Suicidal thoughts and behaviors are so closely linked to the crisis experience (e.g., suicide can lead to a school crisis and a school crisis can lead to suicide) that suicide prevention efforts are integral to comprehensive crisis management. Suicide is widespread among school-aged children. Prevention programs increase the likelihood that students at risk for suicide will be more readily identified and assessed, in order to receive the services they need. School-based programs can be effective in increasing knowledge of suicide, dispelling myths related to youth suicide, reducing suicidal ideation and behavior, and promoting expectancies for engaging in help-seeking behaviors (Thompson, Eggert, & Herting, 2000).

In response to the lack of current prevention and intervention programs, the *Youth Suicide Prevention Plan for Washington State* recommended comprehensive education and prevention programs for youth, screening students for suicide ideation, training teachers as gatekeepers, and helping high-risk youth with support groups, drug programs, and life-skills training (Hayden & Lauer, 2000). Indeed, comprehensive, systematic, and multifaceted approaches to prevention and early intervention, involving both students and staff and including curriculum-based and staff in-service programs, have been consistently recommended in the literature (Dwyer, Osher, & Hoffman, 2000; Garland, Shaffer, & Whittle, 1993; Hayden & Lauer; Miller, Eckert, DuPaul, & White, 1999; Mitchell, 2003).

However, many suicide prevention programs are out of date with current scientific knowledge and, thus, are patterned after universal stress models, which maintain that suicide is simply a response to an extremely stressful situation (Popenhagen & Qualley, 1998). Therefore, Garland et al. (1993) recommended program components that sensitize and train school staff to have better understanding of the factors that increase the likelihood of crisis and the risk of suicide and that teach participants to more reliably identify and provide resources for high-risk youth. The most commonly included topics in existing prevention programs include suicide facts and warning signs, death/dying education, signs of emotional disturbance, psychological development in adolescents, accessing community resources, confidentiality issues, stress reduction/coping strategies, and interviews with suicide survivors and attempters.

Barriers to Crisis Intervention Efforts

Despite evidence to the contrary, many school personnel erroneously believe that a crisis cannot happen in their school and unconsciously detach themselves from crisis training and planning activities. These schools function in a reactive mode, minimizing the importance of preparation efforts and postponing prevention activities. Their behavior is guided by a false sense of security, and as a result, the school community is left vulnerable. It is important to understand that crises can and do happen in all types of school communities. After a well-publicized crisis or tragedy occurs, parents, community leaders, and school officials all over the nation begin to cry out for increased efforts at school security and crisis response. However, once the fear begins to subside and the immediate threat begins to fade, they often lack the sustained motivation to follow through with thorough planning, training, and preparation activities.

Many schools are ill prepared to prevent, intervene with, and follow up with students in crisis. For example, in a survey of 163 school districts in Washington State, Hayden and Lauer (2000) found that the majority of districts did not have suicide programs, policies, or procedures, and they were not actively involved in prevention or intervention efforts. Their research indicates that the largest perceived roadblock to implementing suicide programs is insufficient staff and the greatest perceived need is additional information and training. Although research has shown that school counselors are knowledgeable about risk factors, they still do not feel confident in their abilities to recognize at-risk students and have indicated a need for more effective preparation in suicide and crisis intervention (Coder, Nelson, & Aylward, 1991; Fitch, Newby, Ballestero, & Marshall, 2001; King, Price, Telljohann, & Wahl, 1999, 2000).

A U.S. national survey conducted by Berman revealed that few professional schools, including programs for health and other human service professionals, incorporated formal coursework on crisis theory and practice (as cited in Hoff & Adamowski, 1998). Hoff and Adamowski believed every person working in human services, including school counselors, should understand the basic concepts and practices of the crisis model. Although feedback from school counselors suggests that recent graduates are receiving more preparation for crisis intervention than in the past, almost one third of school counselors continue to enter the profession with no formal course work or supervised experiences (Allen, Burt, et al., 2002).

The most common reaction to a crisis is to ignore it due to lack of training and awareness or fear that a response will worsen the situation and result in criticism (Klicker, 2000; Poland, 1994). Crisis intervention activities are often neglected due to lack of knowledge, overreaction, denial, or paralysis by analysis (overthinking to the point of inaction). Misconceptions of the problem and ineffective strategies inhibit crisis prevention and intervention efforts (Trump, 1998). Furthermore, reluctance to commit to comprehensive crisis intervention efforts is frequently linked to costs, to the stigma involved, to the logistics of putting on a program, and to a lack of understanding of the associated mental health issues (Tierney, Ramsey, Tanney, & Lang, 1990).

The Evolving Role of the School Counselor

It is apparent that increasing numbers of students are experiencing extreme mental and emotional pain that is influencing how they relate to themselves and others (Fryxell & Smith, 2000; Hazler & Carney, 2000; Minden, Henry, Tolan, & Gorman-Smith, 2000; Sandhu, 2000). Counselors must strive to formulate and adhere to visions that foster the intellectual, physical, emotional, and psychological well-being of the entire school community. As the role of the school counselor changes, counselors must adapt to support the new vision of school counseling. According to the American School Counselor Association (ASCA; 1997a), responding to and advocating for the emotional needs of all individuals impacted by crisis is part of the professional school counselor's role. School counselor involvement in crisis management efforts demonstrates a proactive commitment to ensuring that every student acquires the safety and survival skills necessary to emerge from a crisis stronger, more resilient, and better prepared to cope with difficulties in the future (ASCA, 1997b).

According to Sears and Granello (2002), "the preparation of counselors with individual and group counseling and guidance skills for academic, career, and personal/social counseling continues to be necessary, but is no longer sufficient" (p. 170). In light of the current emphasis on crisis response in the schools, Sears and Granello encouraged school counselors to develop the leadership skills necessary to impact systemic change and to transform school counseling to better meet the increasingly complex needs of today's school communities. As expectations for school crisis response and preparedness continue to increase, "educators must further their ability to consciously reflect on the provision of these services. Soon it will no longer be acceptable to respond in a reflexive fashion to crisis events . . . school crisis preparedness will be expected" (Brock et al., 2001, p. 7).

Professional literature is consistent in stating that school counselors should play a vital role in preventing and minimizing the impact of crises by advocating and providing leadership for crisis intervention and suicide prevention efforts (King et al., 2000; Remley & Sparkman, 1993). School counselors are the "experts" regarding student mental health issues and should be responsible for educating school personnel and helping them effectively deal with these concerns (King et al., 1999). Most school counselors feel that it is their role to identify and intervene with students at suicidal risk and that doing so would reduce the chances that the student would commit suicide (King et al., 1999). Thus, school counselors have an ethical, and, in many cases legal, responsibility for taking appropriate steps to effectively identify at-risk students, recognize potential lethality, and intervene with students in crisis.

According to Hoff and Adamowski (1998), "Excellence in crisis care requires appropriate education and training, access to consultation, and smooth interagency coordination" (p. xiii). Crisis intervention requires the acquisition and application of specific knowledge, attitudes, and skills in order to intervene effectively. Appropriate crisis management training should include the following: (1) knowledge of the nature of crisis and crisis responses, assumptions, and logic necessary for dealing with a crisis; (2) a general model and practical guidelines to prepare schools for crisis situations; (3) information on implementing a crisis plan; and (4) preparation activities, including role-plays and crisis drills. Furthermore, school counselors should be knowledgeable about the nature and extent of adolescent suicide; the warning signs and risk factors for adolescent suicide; student at-risk profiles; appropriate prevention, intervention, and postvention techniques; and the available mental health resources in the community (King et al., 2000; Popenhagen & Qualley, 1998; Remley & Sparkman, 1993).

Ethical and Legal Considerations

According to Decker (1997), schools have both a moral obligation and a legal responsibility to provide for the protection of the life, health, and property of students, faculty, and staff in emergencies. The *No Child Left Behind Act of 2001* (U.S. Department of Education [USDE], 2001) requires schools to anticipate acts of violence, be prepared to work through and manage crises, and ensure safety and order by implementing programs that protect students and teachers, encourage discipline and personal responsibility, and combat illegal drugs. To that end, districts must use federal school-safety funding to establish plans that include appropriate and effective discipline policies, security procedures, prevention activities, student codes of conduct, and a crisis management plan for responding to violent or traumatic incidents on school grounds (USDE).

School counselors should document and keep accurate records regarding consultation, notification, and intervention efforts with at-risk students. When there is a reasonable expectation that a student intends to do harm to self or others, counselors must disclose this information. According to Stone and Dahir (2006), "the school counselor's legal liability ends when school authorities or parents have been notified that a student is at risk and appropriate actions have been recommended" (p. 313). Though confidentiality is clearly paramount to the school counselor's role, a student's right to privacy becomes secondary to the duty to protect students from harm. Therefore, ASCA's (1997a) *Ethical Standards for School Counselors* includes the following guidelines with regard to situations which pose a danger to self or others: (1) After careful deliberation and consultation, when possible, inform parents/guardians or appropriate authorities when the student's condition indicates a clear and imminent danger to the student or others; and (2) attempt to minimize threat to a student by informing the student of actions to be taken, involving the student in a three-way communication with parents/guardians when breaching confidentiality, or allowing the student to have input as to how and to whom the breach will be made.

Because standards within each state are not consistent, it is imperative that counselors familiarize themselves with their state guidelines as well as specific school and district policies. Hermann and Remley (2000, as cited in Capuzzi & Gross, 2004) noted that, even though school personnel are expected to take reasonable precautions to prevent harm to students, courts have been reluctant to assign liability for injuries related to self-harm or violence. These claims typically fail because much of today's school violence, including suicide, can be considered spontaneous acts of violence. However, schools should not allow this fact to create a false sense of security, as "a growing number of legal opinions have indicated that an unanticipated act of violence can be predictable and, thus, actionable under state law" (Capuzzi & Gross, p. 290). Thus, schools can best protect themselves by taking a proactive stance toward crisis management and establishing comprehensive prevention, intervention, and postvention efforts as well as policies and procedures that mandate staff development and training.

Practice

Caplan (1964) proposed a model of mental health consultation that has become the foundation of school crisis intervention programs and crisis response (Pitcher & Poland, 1992). His model involves a three-part approach to crisis that includes primary, secondary, and tertiary intervention efforts. Primary care, or prevention, focuses on reducing the incidence of crises. Secondary care, or intervention, involves the immediate provision of assistance to individuals experiencing a crisis. Tertiary care, or postvention, reduces the long-term effects experienced by those directly or indirectly impacted by the crisis. Furthermore, Caplan emphasized community responsibility in facilitating the recovery of those in crisis and he called

> for the community and its agencies to work together to assist individuals in need . . . advocates trained in crisis intervention do this by training and networking community programs and by promoting general community welfare through preventative programs and response efforts. (Hendricks & Thomas, 2002, p. 11)

Crisis Prevention

Primary prevention, in the form of education, training, consultation, and crisis intervention, is designed to reduce the occurrence of mental distress, reduce exposure to hazardous situations, and reduce vulnerability to crises by increasing coping ability (Hoff, 1995). The goal is to promote growth, development, and crisis resistance in both individuals and the community. Therefore, prevention refers to proactive attempts by school leaders to teach students new and/or improved coping skills before difficult or traumatic events occur or immediately after a crisis in order to minimize long-term effects. The ideal objective for educators, counselors, and human service workers should be to establish prevention programs so effective that crisis intervention will seldom be needed.

The intent of expanding the notion of what constitutes a complete, thorough education is not only to help students learn but also to help them function as productive members of both the school community and the larger society. Character education programs are a key component of the implementation of the *No Child Left Behind Act* (USDE, 2001) and an integral part of the solution for improving school climate and creating a safe environment in which students can learn and achieve (Stone & Dahir, 2006). Classroom guidance activities as well as individual and group counseling efforts aimed at character education and focusing on the identified traits of students at risk for poor coping should begin in elementary school. Early prevention efforts aimed at increasing the resiliency of all students are more effective than waiting for suicidal ideation or specific warning signs to emerge.

In addition, counselors should take leadership roles in developing and providing workshops, staff development materials, in-services, and training opportunities to all stakeholders. Parent education programs designed to promote awareness of high-risk behaviors, such as suicide and violence, as well as strategies for increasing protective factors and accessing additional resources and support are an integral component of a comprehensive crisis management program. Similar programs should be offered to teachers, in order to prepare them to serve as gatekeepers. Clearly, age-appropriate guidance lessons and small and large group counseling units should be provided for all students, in addition to providing specific interventions for those identified as high risk.

Developmental approaches. Much time, effort, and money can be exhausted in the process of identifying at-risk target students with whom to intervene. In the meantime, comprehensive, school–wide preventative measures would ensure that all students are taught the skills necessary to deal with a wide range of social, emotional, and behavioral difficulties, before they escalate into serious crises. Hazler and Carney (2000) described a humanistic and developmental approach to intervention and prevention as one that targets general characteristics as they appear in anyone, as opposed to focusing on only those who demonstrate the most clear danger to society. It may be more effective to concentrate efforts on promoting healthy behaviors as opposed to targeting the elimination of specific, negative behaviors. Therefore, schools will need to move increasingly away from a focus on individual pathology to one that integrates human development theories and the risk and resilience literature.

Hawkins et al. (2000) suggested a prevention model based on a social development perspective and employing multiple strategies across multiple systems (e.g., family, peers, school, and community). An effective program seeks not only to reduce or eliminate risk factors but also to build and maintain protective factors that buffer against risk. Thus, the following competencies should be included in a comprehensive curriculum: interpersonal communication skills, assertiveness, goal setting, negotiation, managing multiple projects, group communication, multicultural sensitivity, and knowledge of sound nutrition and health practices (Likona, 2004; Palmatier, 1998). Also important would be topics related to general coping skills, including stress and anxiety management, problem solving, conflict resolution, and anger management. Guidance lessons that specifically explore perceptions of crisis and the crisis experience can be very effective and may include discussion of the following: What is a crisis? How does crisis occur? How do you feel during a crisis? Where do you go for support? What behaviors from others are helpful or not helpful when you are in crisis?

Bullying prevention. The bullying prevention program targets bullying behaviors at the school, individual, and classroom levels. Program components include assessing the nature, severity, and prevalence of bullying with anonymous surveys; targeting school areas requiring additional supervision; providing classroom lessons and rules designed to discourage bullying and intimidation; providing individual and group counseling to both perpetrators and victims of bullying; and inviting parents of students receiving counseling to participate in family counseling. Outcomes of the program have shown statistically significant reductions in the number of reported victimizations as well as fewer discipline problems, improved attitudes toward academics, and improvements in peer social relationships (Olweus et al., 1999).

Crisis Preparation

The creation and maintenance of safe, orderly, growth-oriented climates, in which students can thrive, requires commitment, collaboration, vision, ownership, and comprehensive preparation. In the midst of turmoil, a comprehensive, easily implemented plan helps crisis workers respond, in a timely manner, with confidence, and enables them to give their full attention to those in need of their assistance instead of wasting valuable time planning and making decisions. During a crisis it is difficult to think clearly, even for those in charge; people need direction, structure, and support. Cornell and Sheras (1998) highlighted the importance of leaders taking charge by assessing the situation, making decisions, giving directions to others, and supervising activities. Without proper preparation, including in-services, familiarization of school crisis plans, and crisis drills, the school crisis literature suggests that people become more afraid and disoriented and, as a result, less likely to do what needs to be done in a moment of crisis. School crisis plans establish interventionist roles and detail specific steps for reestablishing stability, providing support, and facilitating the needs of the school community (Klicker, 2000). According to Poland and McCormick (2000), advance crisis planning, at both school and district levels, minimizes chaos, conflict, and misunderstanding surrounding what should be done and who can do it when a crisis occurs.

Crisis intervention team. Bennis and Nanus (as cited in Hill & Hill, 1994) described effective leaders as "capable of achieving attention through vision, meaning through communication, trust through positioning, and [possessing] a willingness to self-deploy and empower others" (p. 28). The burden of crisis intervention activities will not fall solely on the counselors' shoulders if they take a leadership roles in developing comprehensive crisis intervention programs and promoting the visions of awareness and prevention in their schools. Collaboration, consultation, and the provision of in-service programs can help counselors generate gatekeepers among the entire school community. Counselors have a responsibility to teach parents, school personnel, and peers to recognize at-risk students and identify situations that may precipitate or exacerbate crises.

The key to managing crises is a crisis intervention team that is competent, capable, and adequately prepared to handle an emergency situation and a crisis management plan that clearly specifies the team's goals and responsibilities. Crisis intervention teams typically consist of some combination of teachers, parents, counselors, social workers, school psychologists, school nurses, and school administrators. Team members should be taught how to facilitate prevention efforts as well as how to respond to individuals experiencing a crisis or in need of postvention efforts (Capuzzi & Gross, 2004). School administrators must encourage familiarization of the staff with the plan, and team members must share a common vision, have well-defined roles, and be willing to work together in a coordinated manner.

Essential content for training crisis team members includes crisis definition and theory, types of school crises, childhood reactions to crisis and grief, direct intervention skills, and factors that affect both the severity of the crisis experience and the resolution of crisis responses. According to Gilliland and James (1997), effective crisis workers are energetic, sensitive to issues of diversity, organized, and systemically oriented; above all, they are optimistic in their outlook and philosophy of helping others. Crisis team members should also be flexible, adaptable, intuitive, multitasked, and able to think/react under pressure. Team responsibilities include developing an intervention plan, coordinating with community services, educating and training staff, monitoring plans, and conducting postvention activities. In addition, periodic in-service training, crisis drills, and role-plays and frequent utilization of the crisis response team will help to ensure the performance of the team and the continued effectiveness of the plan.

Training activities. According to Hoff and Adamowski (1998), there is a differentiation between training and teaching, and "the design of crisis training programs is a highly specialized area of practice, involving small group skills, effective communication style, and other strategies that are not easily mastered in didactic (classroom-based) instruction" (p. 99). Education and training in crisis intervention are best accomplished through the use of a variety of modalities of instruction: lecture, readings, role-plays, modeled role-plays, small group exercises, audiovisual resources, Internet sites, survivor stories, simulated interviews with suicidal students, and observations of experienced trainees by their less experienced colleagues (Hoff & Adamowski; Weinberg, 1993).

Lecture is typically viewed as the method of last resort because trainees can absorb essential written content through training manuals, handouts, and recommended readings or Web sites. In a study by Murphy (2004), students who had combined (didactic/experiential) crisis intervention training indicated higher levels of comfort, preparation, and confidence than those who had didactic training alone. This is consistent with recommendations in the literature that have suggested that limited training time is spent more efficiently on experiential/role-play activities (Gilliland & James, 1997; Hoff & Adamowski, 1998; King et al., 2000).

Role-playing crisis intervention scenarios is an essential component of a thorough training program and is emphasized as a central aspect of training by every certified crisis or distress center (Gilliland & James, 1997; Hoff & Adamowski, 1998; King et al., 2000). Role-play provides valuable opportunities to develop familiarity with various situations, practice crisis intervention skills, learn creative ways to deal with unexpected contingencies, and evaluate the efficiency of the response. Honest, constructive feedback is crucial to the process because it provides the opportunity to examine blocks to rapport, identify overlooked elements to the interaction (e.g., missed suicidal clues), and allows for objective interpretation of skills. According to Gilliland and James, a critical component of training is not just talking about problems but practicing the direct application of specific intervention skills. Simulating authentic situations enables team members to find out what works and does not work for them in the safety of a training situation and to receive constructive feedback concerning the effectiveness of their skills.

Murphy (2004) examined the impact of a 2-hour crisis intervention training module on school counselor education students' knowledge of crisis intervention and suicide prevention theories and concepts and their skills for responding to individuals in a variety of crisis scenarios. Because of participation in the training, participants' knowledge of crisis intervention theories and concepts improved significantly. However, there was no concomitant improvement in skills. This finding is consistent with other findings in the literature that suggested knowledge of crisis intervention does not necessarily translate into intervention skill (Coder et al., 1991; King et al., 1999, 2000). Although more than half of the participants reported feeling more confident in their ability to *recognize* an individual at risk for suicide, more than half also indicated that they did not feel adequately prepared to *intervene* with individuals in crisis, further demonstrating the discrepancy between "knowing" and "doing," and lending support for the need for more skill-based training. Furthermore, although self-perceptions of confidence and preparation increased, skill measures indicated that students' abilities to produce the most facilitative responses to individuals in crisis did not change significantly. Thus, increases in knowledge and self-efficacy were not translated into significant skill improvement.

According to King et al. (2000), additional time should be spent on helping counselors develop the practical skills needed to identify and assess at-risk students. Similarly, Hoff and Adamowski (1998) highlighted the importance of helping trainees understand the structure and value of the role-play process, including the use of appropriate content and the responsibility of fellow trainees for providing useful feedback. The authors also suggested that trainers model a brief role-play, containing both strengths and weaknesses, in order to illustrate the format and provide helpful feedback for the group. In particular, Hoff and Adamowski advocated modeling a role-play requiring a lethality assessment because "trainees with little or no experience in addressing the issue of suicide find it helpful to hear an experienced person ask directly about the client's self-destructive thoughts and behaviors or emotional pain from abuse" (p. 111). King et al. recommended that school counselor preparation programs increase the coverage of practical information pertaining to adolescent suicide and utilize role-play scenarios to provide valuable skill-building experiences.

Training Content

The six core competencies necessary for effective Critical Incident Stress Management (CISM) are closely aligned with the roles of a professional school counselor (ASCA, 1997b) and are key components of crisis management in the schools. These competencies include (1) assessment skills, (2) strategic planning skills, (3) skills to aid individuals in need of assistance, (4) large group intervention skills, (5) small group intervention skills, and (6) follow-up and referral skills (Mitchell, 2003).

Core crisis content falls into three categories that lay the foundation for objectives that demonstrate acceptable knowledge, attitudinal, and skill outcomes (Hoff & Adamowski, 1998). These categories parallel the established domains of multicultural competence (Sue & Sue, 1999). Although crisis is a universal phenomenon, its manifestation and resolution is influenced by the values, biases, and assumptions of both the individual experiencing the crisis and the crisis worker. School counselors should be aware of their ethical responsibility for providing culturally appropriate crisis intervention services and demonstrating multicultural competence concerning awareness of their own values and biases, awareness of the worldviews of diverse clients, and the provision of culturally appropriate intervention strategies (Sue & Sue). Culturally appropriate intervention requires school counselors to be sensitive to issues of diversity, which may influence communication styles, emotional expressiveness, coping strategies, help-seeking behaviors, and social support. Thus, mastery of knowledge, attitudes, and skills requires school counselors to consider each domain within the framework of multicultural competence.

Hoff and Adamowski (1998) provided the following example: A trainee should be able to "*identify* the steps of the crisis management process (knowledge), *demonstrate* a nonjudgmental attitude in role play, and *apply* the techniques of assessing suicide risk or victimization trauma in a real or simulated case situation (skill)" (p. 77). The elements of core content for crisis training curriculum were derived from the collective experience and knowledge of nationally and internationally recognized crisis specialists, suicidologists, and crisis organizations, including the National Institute of Mental Health (NIMH), the National Organization for Victim Assistance (NOVA), the American Association of Suicidology (AAS), and the Life Crisis Institute (LCI).

Knowledge. The knowledge component of core crisis content is the easiest to master because there are extensive resources available for self-learning, including books, audiovisual materials, and Internet resources. Essential concepts that should be mastered by crisis workers include the following list adapted from Hoff and Adamowski (1998): (1) crisis theory and principles of crisis management; (2) suicidology; (3) victimology; (4) death, dying, and grief work; (5) principles of communication; (6) identification and use of community resources; (7) ethical and legal issues regarding suicide, crime, and victimization; and (8) team relationships and self-care in crisis work.

Familiarization with definitions, types, and characteristics of crisis should be at the core of effective crisis training strategies. Essential content that counselors should be trained on include crisis definition and theory, types of school crises, developmental reactions to crisis and grief, warning signs and characteristics of suicide, assessment of danger to self or others, crisis intervention/grief counseling strategies, and factors that affect both the severity of the crisis experience and the resolution of crisis responses (Breland, Brody, Hunter-Ebeling, O'Shea, & Ronk, 1993; Cohen & Fish, 1993; Davis et al., 1993; Weinberg, 1993).

According to Cohen and Fish (1993), specific areas of knowledge related to suicide include prevention and postvention activities, warning signs, coping techniques, crisis intervention, handling the returning suicidal student, dealing with the friends of suicide attempters or completers, the contagion hypothesis, and managing the aftermath of a teacher, famous pop-culture idol, or parent/family member suicide attempt or completion. Breland et al. (1993) believed that issues of denial and preventability, the emotional impact of suicide, steps to take when facing a suicidal student, how to identify and talk to a depressed or suicidal person, and postvention plans for responding to the aftermath of a suicide are also key elements. According to Davis et al. (1993), "learning how to talk to students about suicide may reduce adult fears about such discussions, while training in listening skills and available school and community resources may allow staff to fulfill their roles more effectively" (p. 265).

Attitudes. Core crisis content includes the following attitudinal outcomes for training, adapted from Hoff and Adamowski (1998): (1) acceptance of and nonjudgmental response to persons different from oneself and toward controversial, emotional, and/or value-laden issues; (2) a balanced, realistic attitude toward oneself in the provider role; (3) a realistic and humane approach to death, dying, self-destructive behavior, victimization, and other human issues; (4) coming to terms with one's own feelings about death, dying, and the potential for violence, insofar as these feelings might deter one from helping others; and (5) activating with conviction one's advocacy role in client empowerment.

Helping people in distress is not a value-free endeavor, and counselors must be aware of personal attitudes and beliefs that may present barriers to impartial and compassionate crisis response. According to Hoff and Adamowski (1998), "it is important to note that rejection of problematic or challenging clients or value-laden responses to them may arise from insufficient knowledge of the dynamics and ramifications of some psychosocial and crisis situations" (p. 83). The authors recognized that some practitioner attitudes may remain fixed but suggested that new knowledge often leads to the kind of empathy and flexibility necessary to intervene with distressed persons.

Skills. Knowledge of crisis concepts and nonjudgmental attitudes are insufficient, without the ability to intervene with distressed individuals systematically and effectively. According to Hoff and Adamowski (1998), skilled intervention involves guiding each person toward "problem solving, empowerment, and crisis resolution consistent with the individual's values and meaning system . . . [and helping] distressed people avoid negative crisis outcomes such as violence, alcohol and other drug abuse, or chronic emotional or mental disability" (p. 84). School counselors must be able to apply the techniques for comprehensive crisis management, which include assessment, planning, implementation, and evaluation.

The skills necessary to work effectively with people in crisis include the following list adapted from Hoff and Adamowski (1998): (1) communicating well, listening actively, questioning discretely, responding empathically, and giving appropriate information and direction; (2) prioritizing to ensure an organized, systematic intervention process; (3) mobilizing community resources efficiently and effectively; (4) implementing agency policy and keeping records accurately and efficiently; (5) using consultative and referral processes appropriately; and (6) carrying out crisis management steps while withholding judgment on controversial behaviors and not imposing values on the distressed individuals.

A knowledgeable, well-trained counselor should be able to assess the level of risk, build rapport, and actively intervene with the immediate emotional crisis. In addition, counselors should be able establish procedures for receiving referrals from staff and contacting parents, as appropriate. The ability to provide additional resources and referrals to community-based services and to follow up on any actions taken is also important.

Crisis Intervention

Crisis intervention is an organized approach to helping distressed people; it is a specific helping activity, with its own unique set of theories, skills, attitudes, and knowledge. Crisis intervention is related to but differs from psychotherapy in that psychotherapy tends to be longer term and directed toward changing a person's maladaptive patterns of thinking, feeling, and behaving. Typically, the goal of psychotherapy is personal growth, and the therapeutic relationship is not characterized by the same sense of urgency and immediacy necessary for effective crisis intervention (Pitcher & Poland, 1992). Due to its emphasis on short-term stabilization, crisis intervention has been referred to as "emotional first aid" or "psychological triage" (Brock et al., 2001; Myer, 2001).

Crisis assessment. Crisis assessment involves determining a person's vulnerability to and resources for managing traumatic life situations, including the recognized standard of explicitly ascertaining current and past victimization trauma and risk of suicide (Hoff & Adamowski, 1998). Hoff (1995) proposed a model of assessment that involves two levels: (1) safety, which would include an exploration of the presence of imminent threat or harm as well as suicidal or homicidal intent, and (2) the ability to function, which involves consideration of an individual's personal and social characteristics and resources. Hoff's model has been described as a "vulnerability model" because crisis workers are able to assess an individual's overall vulnerability to a maladaptive crisis response by considering the nature of the hazardous event (an event that, in terms of timing and/or severity, stretches a person's ability to cope and increases susceptibility to a full-blown crisis response), the precipitating factor, and the person's reactions to the event (Myer, 2001).

Preliminary assessment and intervention should focus on a hierarchy of needs (e.g., survival, safety, food, shelter) before attempts are made to process the associated psychological distress. This is particularly relevant concerning intervention efforts in response to natural disasters, as restoring equilibrium requires first attending to an individual's basic survival needs. Clearly, physical healing must take precedence to emotional healing.

According to Hoff (1995), assessing a person's reactions to crisis includes examining the following distress signals: difficulty managing feelings, suicidal and/or homicidal behaviors, alcohol or substance abuse, trouble with the law, and an inability to utilize available assistance. Gathering information on a person's assets and liabilities with respect to family and social resources is essential in terms both of understanding family and social factors that may be exacerbating a crisis and of identifying possible resources and support that can be mobilized to help with the crisis.

Debriefing. Once an individual is determined to be in a state of crisis, there is agreement among crisis intervention scholars and practitioners that sound crisis intervention requires effective interpersonal communication, an ability to focus the client on the experience of the crisis, and skill in guiding an individual through the process of recovery (Hendricks & Thomas, 2002). The process includes but is not limited to debriefing, which is often referred to as Critical Incident Stress Debriefing (CISD). The common goal of debriefing models is to allow a semistructured format for traumatized individuals to discuss the details of the traumatic event they have experienced. This detailed processing of a crisis event is most frequently conducted in small groups, and since most of the principles are the same, the process can be viewed as "group crisis intervention." Debriefing should be initiated as soon as possible after a critical event occurs and typically involves listening, emotional support and catharsis, psycho-education about "normal" crisis response, and referral for follow-up counseling, as needed (Hoff & Adamowski, 1998). Crisis counselors should be able to anticipate and explain common crisis reactions as well as empathize with and validate the wide range of emotions experienced.

MEETU: A model for crisis response. The mnemonic "MEETU" (i.e., "I'm going to 'meet you' to provide assistance") is a helpful device for remembering the steps involved in psychological first aid (Brock et al., 2001):

Make psychological contact
Explore dimensions of the problem
Examine possible solutions
Assist in **T**aking concrete action
Follow-**U**p

Slaikeu (1990) characterized the just described mnemonic crisis intervention process as involving the following steps: (1) making psychological contact through empathy, warmth, and respect; (2) exploring dimensions of the problem, including direct inquiries about the immediate past (crisis precursors), the present (the crisis story), and the immediate future (crisis-related problems); (3) examining possible solutions by asking about the coping strategies already used, facilitating an exploration of additional coping techniques, and proposing other problem-solving options; (4) taking concrete action by facilitating implementation of solutions to crisis problems (if lethality is high, crisis intervener should assume greater responsibility for assuring that direct action is taken); and (5) establishing a plan to follow-up with the crisis victim.

School counselors need to listen actively, openly name and discuss taboo subjects (e.g., suicide, rape, or divorce) as soon as they become apparent, demonstrate empathy, and remain nonjudgmental. A skilled interventionist uses these behaviors to build rapport and lessen an individual's anxiety, thus allowing for the expression of vulnerabilities in a climate of safety, understanding, and acceptance. In addition, counselors should be prepared to provide individuals impacted by a crisis with specific information concerning the affective, cognitive, behavioral, physiological, interpersonal (Gilliland & James, 1997), and psychological responses to traumatic events, in order to help them predict and prepare for the various stages of the trauma response.

Although the characteristics of crisis are fairly universal, the manifestation of symptoms and the ability to intellectually and emotionally process the crisis experience will vary according to a student's developmental stage. Although a thorough discussion of age-related symptomology is beyond the scope of this chapter, school counselors should be mindful of providing developmentally appropriate prevention and intervention efforts for various grade levels. Crisis management activities should be reflective of the types of services counselors are already providing. For instance, adolescents are more capable of "talk techniques," while younger children may benefit from artistic outlets or play counseling activities designed to more effectively facilitate their understanding of the thoughts, behaviors, and emotions associated with their crisis response. There are a multitude of structured games and activities to help younger children process difficult events. One example is the Crisis Intervention Game (ages 6 to 12), which helps professionals counsel children who are coping with the devastating effects and emotions caused by a trauma or crisis in their lives. The game is designed to help children explore their feelings, make positive self-statements, and understand normal reactions to crisis situations.

Suicide deaths. According to Bolton (1993), not all counselors are willing to state categorically that addressing the issue of suicide will not trigger suicidal behavior. However, suicide literature clearly stresses the therapeutic importance of being able to discuss suicidal thoughts and behaviors openly, in terms of understanding both the person's own suicidality and that of others. The issue then appears to be not whether suicide should be discussed, but rather how it should be addressed. Intervention after a completed suicide should reestablish immediate coping with survivors in a way that minimizes identification with and glorification of the victim (Brock et al., 2001). It is a mistake to mystify the suicide or categorize it as unexplainable. For example, instead of saying, "It doesn't make any sense, she had everything going for her," say, "There were obviously serious things troubling her that we may never know about" (Rouf & Harris, 1988, as cited in Brock et al., 2001).

Youth Suicide Prevention Services at Albert Einstein Medical Center in Philadelphia offers school-based post-suicide crisis intervention services. They recommend a proactive approach wherein crisis workers act quickly to assess students' needs and provide immediate support to alleviate the shock and fear experienced by survivors of completed suicide. Discussing themes of permanent and reversible loss, death, hopelessness, and problem solving can be integral to the process of dispelling myths related to suicide and addressing the inevitable confusion experienced by survivors. Following a suicide death, it is also important to plan for and establish short-term support systems, utilize support groups, and provide access to more in-depth evaluation or therapy (Carter & Brooks, 1990).

Common intervention errors. In order to determine the common limitations of helping professionals in responding to distressed and self-injurious clients, Neimeyer and Pfeiffer (1994) analyzed participants' responses to the items on the Suicide Intervention Response Inventory (SIRI). According to Neimeyer and Pfeiffer, 10% to 40% of the interventionists in their study committed significant errors in the treatment of potentially self-destructive clients. The goal of their study was to identify common themes underlying various frequently occurring errors and less than desirable responses, in the hopes that identification of such common themes might be used to focus professional education in a way to redresses these weaknesses.

Thus, categories of suboptimal responses were identified in relation to the following themes: (1) superficial reassurance, (2) avoidance of strong feelings, (3) professionalism, (4) inadequate assessment of suicidal intent, (5) failure to identify the precipitating event, (6) passivity, (7) insufficient directiveness, (8) advice giving, (9) stereotypic responses, and (10) defensiveness. Neimeyer and Pfeiffer stated, "the frequency with which these errors occurred in our sample is as much an indictment of professional education . . . as it is a statement about the skill deficits of these generally well-intentioned helpers" (p. 218). It is believed that thorough discussion and role play of these common errors (including examples of both desirable and undesirable responses) will provide valuable opportunities to correct deficiencies in these previously identified areas of weakness.

Sample statements from the SIRI, which could be used to develop brief role-play scenarios, include the following: "I decided to talk to you because I really feel like I might do something to myself . . . I've been thinking about suicide"; "I've tried going to a therapist once before, but it didn't help . . . Nothing I do now will change anything"; and "I'm so lonely, so tired [crying]. There just isn't anywhere left to turn." It is important to remember that significant errors in responding to these types of statements, which are commonly associated with the crisis response, were highlighted in the research. Therefore, school counselors are encouraged to familiarize themselves with the analysis of these common intervention errors and to utilize the questions and responses on the SIRI as valuable training and practice materials.

Postvention

Postvention, or tertiary prevention, involves the provision of services (e.g., debriefing activities) designed to reduce the long-term effects experienced by those directly and indirectly impacted by crises. According to Weinberg (1993), postvention is considered a form of prevention, as it is designed to block the occurrence of new tragedies in response to the triggering event and associated symptoms. The recovery process includes not only restabilization but also learning new ways of coping with stress through positive crisis resolution (Hoff, 1995). An effective crisis resolution helps individuals compensate for past vulnerabilities and bolsters the individual with an expanded repertoire of coping skills that will serve as a buffer against future distress (Roberts, 1990). Therefore, crisis resolution involves cognitive mastery of the situation, the restoration of equilibrium, and the development of new coping strategies.

Students are more likely to be responsive to additional evaluation, treatment, and postvention efforts when the counselor has established sufficient rapport and trust by demonstrating empathy and utilizing timely, effective crisis intervention skills. School and community officials should be sensitive to the fact that the most painful and stressful aspects of crisis management frequently continue well after the initial incident has passed (Trump, 2000). In fact, postcrisis experiences can often be much worse than the original crisis event in terms of length, intensity, and strain. What occurs during the immediate aftermath of the crisis event determines whether the person is able to assimilate the experience effectively and, thus, prevent the occurrence of chronic, long-term symptoms.

Postvention activities should focus on helping students achieve a reality-based understanding of the trauma, including common themes and experiences as well as common psychological and behavioral symptoms. It is also important to reinforce and praise students for their courage in the face of trauma and to help them regain a sense of control and confidence in their ability to deal with crises in the future. Students need to understand that, although their memory of a crisis may remain, with time, the pain lessens and symptoms disappear. After the immediate crisis subsides, school personnel should follow up with the individual, make appropriate referrals, and connect him or her with additional resources in order to provide ongoing support and reinforce positive changes.

In practical terms, it can be helpful for counselors to identify individuals who seem to have had a particularly difficult time dealing with the crisis, and make reminder appointments on a calendar for checking in with these students at specified dates in the future. For instance, 2 weeks after an incident, when the immediacy of the crisis has died down, students may often feel isolated, as though everyone has moved on. Follow-up activities can be a valuable opportunity to communicate care and concern when a counselor "spontaneously" reaches out to see how the student is handling the recovery process.

Suicide contagion. The contagion issue causes many schools to be hesitant about engaging in appropriate postvention activities because the conditions under which students will imitate suicidal behavior are not clearly understood. Although contagion in the form of distress may occur among survivors and increase the risk of suicidal behavior, postvention activities can be a counteracting process (Carter & Brooks, 1990). Davis et al. (1993) wrote, "Research suggests that contagion is more likely when suicidal behavior is modeled without discussion. Discussion may reduce the contagion effect" (p. 267). Counselors must address issues and concerns related to contagion and dispel myths that talking about suicide will glorify the behavior and cause it to happen.

Postvention-as-prevention is successful when survivors are encouraged to express their personal reactions to and struggles dealing with a suicide death. Thus, potentially self-destructive feelings can be expressed, tolerated, and diminished in a safe, open environment. Honest discussions that address students' confusion and concerns and dispel myths associated with suicide reduce the likelihood of their becoming suicidal (Bolton, 1993; Leenaars & Wenckstern, 1998; Poland & McCormick, 2000).

Research on the contagion hypothesis suggests that teens closest to a suicide victim may be at increased suicidal risk for suicide attempts (Brent et al., 1989; Carter & Brooks, 1990). Some researchers advocate screening exposed students, particularly those who were friends of the victim, for suicide risk, and it is recommended that counselors pursue the survivors as opposed to waiting for them to seek help (Brent et al.; Carter & Brooks). Small group counseling, large group assemblies, dispelling rumors, and comprehensive debriefings are recommended following a student death (Cohen & Fish, 1993). Debriefings after a completed suicide should address the following: guilt and anger, the nature of grief, validation of common reactions, the individuality of experienced grief and the recovery process, opportunities for the expression of thoughts and feelings, and provision of additional resources and support services (Bolton, 1993).

Debriefing for crisis workers. Postvention tasks should include thorough debriefing for those directly impacted by the crisis as well as the crisis workers. Working with people in crisis is draining physically and emotionally, and those involved in the intervention must make sure that their own needs are being attended. Due to the severity of many crisis-producing experiences and the intensity of the crisis response, working with individuals who have been traumatized makes counselors vulnerable to secondary traumatization. Furthermore, as members of the community, school counselors are frequently personally impacted by the same crisis for which they are assisting others.

The risk of burnout is very high, and team members must work together to provide support, encouragement, and guidance not only to the victims of crisis but also to one another. Counselors must be willing to attend to their own issues of self-care, so it is helpful to have procedures built into the crisis response plan that allow for rotation and replacement of "frontline" interveners and the integration of additional resources and/or outside assistance, as necessary. In addition, crisis workers need to be given the opportunity to share their personal feelings of both the actual crisis and the intervention process with other members of the response team. As is common practice for many emergency response professionals, all crisis workers should be encouraged to participate in debriefing efforts, regardless of whether they are exhibiting signs of compassion fatigue, burnout, or secondary traumatization.

In order to use each crisis situation as a learning experience, team members and relevant stakeholders should also meet to debrief the practical elements of the crisis management process. This meeting should occur in a timely enough manner for participants to remember specific details and clear impressions of the process but not so soon that their own crisis resolution is not complete. Feedback should be provided about logistical concerns, plan effectiveness, and the team's strengths and weaknesses. It is important to provide constructive feedback and suggestions for improvement, including areas where additional training is needed. Examining the effectiveness of comprehensive crisis management efforts provides a valuable opportunity to evaluate, revise, and improve current procedures.

Future Directions

Research assessing future school administrators' perceptions of the school counselor's role indicated that responding to crisis and working with teachers in crisis situations were of primary importance (Fitch et al., 2001). Furthermore, a survey of school staff perceptions of student support services rated crisis intervention roles, including serving on a crisis team and providing direct intervention services during crises, as very important (Watkins, Crosby, & Pearson, 2001). Counselor educators can use this information in preparing school counselors to better fulfill the expectations of their positions. Since school administrators and personnel view crisis management as an essential task for counselors, school counselors should make training in crisis management a priority and be proactive in educating the school community about the importance of developing and implementing comprehensive crisis management efforts.

According to Hoff and Adamowski (1998), "the growth of professionalism emphasizes the training of various experts across settings and provider disciplines. A major outgrowth of this trend is the development of the crisis model as a distinct body of knowledge and practice" (p. 7). An increased understanding of crisis theory and training in crisis intervention skills can increase the efficiency with which crises are both recognized and handled. Early recognition of potential crises encourages timely, proactive responses that may prevent or minimize the impact of crises. Crisis training thus will help to increase knowledge, skills, and confidence levels and maximize opportunities for efficient intervention (Poland & McCormick, 2000; Weinberg, 1993).

According to Cornell and Sheras (1998), weaknesses in leadership, problems in teamwork, and failings in responsibility often precipitate or exacerbate crisis situations in schools. School leadership contributes to the morale of students and faculty and influences the nature of the school climate. If counselors intend to be proactive advocates for their students, they must be instilled with a vision for leadership that allows them to campaign for the prioritization of crisis intervention activities in their school communities.

References

Allen, M., Burt, K., Bryan, E., Carter, D., Orsi, R., & Durkan, L. (2002). School counselors' preparation for and participation in crisis intervention. *Professional School Counseling, 6*(2), 96–102.

Allen, M., Jerome, A., White, A., Marston, S., Lamb, S., Pope, D., et al. (2002). The preparation of school psychologists for crisis intervention. *Psychology in the Schools, 39*(4), 427–439.

American School Counselor Association. (1997a). *Ethical standards for school counselors*. Retrieved March 26, 2004, from http://www.schoolcounselor.org

American School Counselor Association. (1997b). *Executive summary: The national standards for school counseling programs*. Retrieved March 26, 2004, from http://www.schoolcounselor.org

Ayyash-Abdo, H. (2002). Adolescent suicide: An ecological approach. *Psychology in the Schools, 39*(4), 459–476.

Beautrais, A. L., Joyce, P. R., & Mulder, R. T. (1999). Personality traits and cognitive styles as risk factors for serious suicide attempts among young people. *Suicide and Life-Threatening Behavior, 29*(1), 37–47.

Bolton, I. M. (1993). Responding to suicide. In J. J. Cohen & M. C. Fish (Eds.), *Handbook of school-based interventions: Resolving student problems and promoting healthy educational environments* (pp. 274–275). San Francisco: Jossey-Bass.

Breland, M. E., Brody, P., Hunter-Ebeling, J., O'Shea, J. A., & Ronk, P. (1993). A suicide prevention program manual. In J. J. Cohen & M. C. Fish (Eds.), *Handbook of school-based interventions: Resolving student problems and promoting healthy educational environments* (pp. 277–279). San Francisco: Jossey-Bass.

Brener, N. D., Krug, E. G., & Simon, T. R. (2000). Trends in suicide ideation and suicidal behavior among high school students in the United States, 1991–1997. *Suicide and Life-Threatening Behavior, 30*(4), 304–312.

Brent, D. A., Kerr, M. M., Goldstein, C., Bozigar, J., Wartella, M., & Allan, M. J. (1989). An outbreak of suicide and suicidal behavior in a high school. *Journal of the American Academy of Child and Adolescent Psychiatry, 28*, 918–924.

Brock, S. E. (1998). Helping classrooms cope with traumatic events. *Professional School Counselor, 2*(2), 110–116.

Brock, S. E., Sandoval, J., & Lewis, S. (2001). *Preparing for crises in the schools: A manual for building school crisis response teams* (2nd ed.). New York: Wiley.

Brown, M. P. (2002). Ethics in crisis intervention practice. In J. E. Hendricks & B. D. Byers (Eds.), *Crisis intervention in criminal justice/social service* (3rd ed., pp. 32–76). Springfield, IL: Charles C. Thomas.

Caplan, G. (1964). *Principles of preventive psychiatry*. New York: Basic Books.

Capuzzi, D., & Gross, D. R. (2004). *Youth at risk: A prevention resource for counselors, teachers, and parents* (4th ed.). Alexandria, VA: American Counseling Association.

Carter, B. F., & Brooks, A. (1990). Suicide prevention: Crisis or opportunity? *The School Counselor, 37*, 378–390.

Clark, R. D. (2002). Suicide. In J. E. Hendricks & B. D. Byers (Eds.), *Crisis intervention in criminal justice/social service* (3rd ed., pp. 293–325). Springfield, IL: Charles C. Thomas.

Coder, T. L., Nelson, R. E., & Aylward, L. K. (1991). Suicide among secondary students. *School Counselor, 38*, 358–361.

Cohen, J. J., & Fish, M. C. (1993). *Handbook of school-based interventions: Resolving student problems and promoting healthy educational environments*. San Francisco: Jossey-Bass.

Cornell, D. G., & Sheras, P. L. (1998). Common errors in school crisis response: Learning from our mistakes. *Psychology in the Schools, 35*(3), 297–307.

Davis, J. M., Sandoval, J., & Wilson, M. P. (1993). Primary prevention of adolescent suicide. In J. J. Cohen & M. C. Fish (Eds.), *Handbook of school-based interventions: Resolving student problems and promoting healthy educational environments* (pp. 265–267). San Francisco: Jossey-Bass.

Decker, R. H. (1997). *When a crisis hits: Will your school be ready?* Thousand Oaks, CA: Corwin Press.

Dwyer, K. P., Osher, D., & Hoffman, C. C. (2000). Creating responsive schools: Contextualizing early warning, timely responses. *Exceptional Children, 66*(3), 347–365.

Encarta World English Dictionary. (2002). *Crisis*. Retrieved March 26, 2002, from http://www.dictionary.msn.com

Erickson, E. H. (1963). *Childhood and society* (2nd ed.). New York: W.W. Norton.

Fitch, T., Newby, E., Ballestero, V., & Marshall, J. L. (2001). Future school administrators' perceptions of the school counselor's role. *Counselor Education and Supervision, 41*(2), 89–99.

Fryxell, D., & Smith, D. C. (2000). Personal, social, and family characteristics of angry students. *Professional School Counseling, 4*(2), 86–94.

Furlong, M., Morrison, G., & Pavelski, R. (2000). Trends in school psychology for the 21st century: Influences of school violence on professional change. *Psychology in the Schools, 37*(1), 81–89.

Garland, S., Shaffer, D., & Whittle, B. (1993). Are suicide prevention programs effective? In J. J. Cohen & M. C. Fish (Eds.), *Handbook of school-based interventions: Resolving student problems and promoting healthy educational environments* (pp. 272–273). San Francisco: Jossey-Bass.

Gilliland, B. E., & James, R. K. (1997). *Crisis intervention strategies* (3rd ed.). Pacific Grove, CA: Brooks/Cole.

Hawkins, J. D., Herrenkohl, T. L., Farrington, D. P., Brewer, D., Catalano, R. F., Harachi, T. W., et al. (2000). *Predictors of Youth Violence*. Rockville, MD: Office of Juvenile Justice and Delinquency Prevention.

Hayden, D. C., & Lauer, P. (2000). Prevalence of suicide programs in schools and roadblocks to implementation. *Suicide and Life-Threatening Behavior, 30*(3), 239–251.

Hazler, R. J., & Carney, J. V. (2000). When victims turn aggressors: Factors in the development of deadly school violence. *Professional School Counseling, 4*(2), 105–112.

Hendricks, J. E., & Thomas, M. W. (2002). Historical and theoretical overview. In J. E. Hendricks & B. D. Byers (Eds.), *Crisis intervention in criminal justice/social service* (3rd ed., pp. 3–31). Springfield, IL: Charles C. Thomas.

Hill, M. S., & Hill, F. W. (1994). *Creating safe schools: What principals can do*. Thousand Oaks, CA: Corwin Press.

Hoff, L. A. (1995). *People in crisis: Understanding and helping* (4th ed.). San Francisco: Jossey-Bass.

Hoff, L. A., & Adamowski, K. (1998). *Creating excellence in crisis care: A guide to effective training and program designs*. San Francisco: Jossey-Bass.

Jobes, D. A. (2000). Collaborating to prevent suicide: A clinical-research perspective. *Suicide and Life-Threatening Behavior, 30*(1), 8–17.

Johnson, K. (2000). *School crisis management: A hands-on guide to training crisis response teams* (2nd ed.). Alameda, CA: Hunter House.

Johnson, K., Casey, D., Ertl, B., Everly, G. S., Jr., & Mitchell, J. T. (1999). *School crisis response: A CISM perspective*. Ellicott City, MD: The International Critical Incident Stress Foundation.

Kalafat, J. (1993). The school's response to adolescent suicide. In J. J. Cohen & M. C. Fish (Eds.), *Handbook of school-based interventions: Resolving student problems and promoting healthy educational environments* (pp. 268–270). San Francisco: Jossey-Bass.

King, K. A., Price, J. H., Telljohann, S. K., & Wahl, J. (1999). How confident do high school counselors feel in recognizing students at risk for suicide? *American Journal of Health Behavior, 23*(6), 457–467.

King, K. A., Price, J. H., Telljohann, S. K., & Wahl, J. (2000). Preventing adolescent suicide: Do high school counselors know the risk factors? *Professional School Counseling, 3*(4), 255–263.

Klicker, R. L. (2000). *A student dies, a school mourns: Dealing with death and loss in the school community.* Philadelphia: Taylor & Francis.

Leenaars, A. A., & Wenckstern, S. (1998). Principles of postvention: Applications to suicide and trauma in schools. *Death Studies, 22*(4), 357–391.

Likona, T. (2004). *Character matters.* Carmichael, CA: Touchstone Press.

Lindemann, E. (1944). Symptomatology and management of acute grief. *American Journal of Psychiatry, 101,* 141–148.

Malley, P. B., Kush, F., & Bogo, R. J. (1994). School-based adolescent suicide prevention and intervention programs: A survey. *School Counselor, 42,* 130–136.

Miller, D. N., Eckert, T. L., DuPaul, G. J., & White, G. P. (1999). Adolescent suicide prevention: Acceptability of school-based programs among secondary school principals. *Suicide and Life-Threatening Behavior, 29*(1), 72–85.

Minden, J., Henry, D. B., Tolan, P. H., & Gorman-Smith, D. (2000). Urban boys' social networks and school violence. *Professional School Counseling, 4*(2), 95–104.

Mitchell, J. T. (2003). *Crisis intervention and CISM: A research summary.* Ellicott City, MD: International Critical Incident Stress Foundation.

Murphy, M. L. (2004). Crisis intervention training for students in school counselor preparation programs. *Dissertation Abstracts International, 65*(08), 2909A. (UMI No. 3145954)

Myer, R. A. (2001). *Assessment for crisis intervention: A triage assessment model.* New York: Brooks/Cole.

National School Safety Center. (2001). *NSSC review of school safety research.* Retrieved April 16, 2001, from http://www.nssc1.org

Neimeyer, R. A., & Pfeiffer, A. M. (1994). The ten most common errors of suicide interventionists. In A. A. Leenaars, J. T. Maltsberger, & R. A. Neimeyer (Eds.), *Treatment of suicidal people* (pp. 207–225). Washington, DC: Taylor & Francis.

Olweus, D., Limber, S., & Mihalic, S. F. (1999). Blueprints for violence prevention: Book 9. *Bullying prevention program.* Boulder, CO: Center for the Study and Prevention of Violence.

Orbach, I., Mikulincer, M., Blumenson, R., Mester, R., & Stein, D. (1999). The subjective experience of problem irresolvability and suicidal behavior: Dynamics and measurement. *Suicide and Life-Threatening Behavior, 29*(2), 150–164.

Palmatier, L. L. (1998). *Crisis counseling for a quality school community: Applying William Glasser's choice theory.* Washington, DC: Taylor & Francis.

Petersen, S., & Straub, R. L. (1992). *School crisis survival guide: Management techniques for counselors and administrators.* West Nyack, NY: The Center for Applied Research in Education.

Pitcher, G. D., & Poland, S. (1992). *Crisis intervention in the schools.* New York: Guilford Press.

Poland, S. (1994). The role of school crisis intervention teams to prevent and reduce school violence and trauma. *School Psychology Review, 23*(2), 175–189.

Poland, S., & McCormick, J. S. (1999). *Coping with crisis: Lessons learned.* Longmont, CO: Sopris West.

Poland, S., & McCormick, J. S. (2000). *Coping with crisis: A quick reference.* Longmont, CO: Sopris West.

Popenhagen, M. P., & Qualley, R. M. (1998). Adolescent suicide: Detection, intervention, and prevention. *Professional School Counseling, 1*(4), 30–35.

Quierdo, A. (1968). The shaping of community mental health care. *The British Journal of Psychiatry, 114*(4), 293–302.

Remley, T. P., Jr., & Sparkman, L. B. (1993). Student suicides: The counselor's limited legal liability. *School Counselor, 40,* 164–169.

Roberts, A. R. (1990). Crisis intervention handbook: Assessment, treatment, and research. Belmont, CA: Wadsworth.

Sandhu, D. S. (2000). Alienated students: Counseling strategies to curb school violence. *Professional School Counseling, 4*(2), 81–85.

Sears, S. J., & Granello, D. H. (2002). School counseling now and in the future: A reaction. *Professional School Counseling, 5*(3), 164–171.

Simon, T. R., & Crosby, A. E. (2000). Suicide planning among high school students who report attempting suicide. *Suicide and Life-Threatening Behavior, 30*(3), 213–221.

Simonds, J. F., McMahon, T., & Armstrong, D. (1991). Young suicide attempters compared with a control group: Psychological, affective, and attitudinal variables. *Suicide and Life-Threatening Behavior, 21*(2), 135–150.

Slaikeu, K. A. (1990). *Crisis intervention: A handbook for practice and research* (2nd ed.). Needham Heights, MA: Allyn & Bacon.

Sprague, J., & Walker, H. (2000). Early identification and intervention for youth with antisocial and violent behavior. *Exceptional Children, 66*(3), 367–379.

Stephens, R. D. (1994). *Coping with school violence: How to turn schools into safe havens for children.* Westlake, CA: National School Safety Center.

Stone, C. B., & Dahir, C. A. (2006). *The transformed school counselor.* Boston: Houghton Mifflin.

Studer, J. R. (2000). Adolescent suicide: Aggression turned inward. In D. S. Sandhu & C. B. Aspy (Eds.), *Violence in American schools: A practical guide for counselors* (pp. 269–284). Alexandria, VA: American Counseling Association.

Sue, D. W., & Sue, D. (1999). *Counseling the culturally different: Theory and practice* (3rd ed.). New York: John Wiley & Sons.

Terr, L. C. (1983). Chowchilla revisited: The effects of a psychic trauma four years after a school bus kidnapping. *The American Journal of Psychiatry, 140,* 1543–1555.

Terr, L. C. (1992). Mini-marathon groups: Psychological "first aid" following disasters. *Bulletin of the Menninger Clinic, 56,* 76–86.

Thompson, E. A., Eggert, L. L., & Herting, J. R. (2000). Mediating effects of an indicated prevention program for reducing youth depression and suicide risk behaviors. *Suicide and Life-Threatening Behavior, 30*(3), 252–271.

Tierney, R., Ramsey, R., Tanney, B., & Lang, W. (1990). Comprehensive school suicide prevention programs. *Death Studies, 14,* 347–370.

Trump, K. S. (1998). *Practical school security: Basic guidelines for safe and secure schools.* Thousand Oaks, CA: Corwin Press.

Trump, K. S. (2000). *Classroom killers? Hallway hostages? How schools can prevent and manage school crises.* Thousand Oaks, CA: Corwin Press.

U.S. Department of Education. (2001). *The No Child Left Behind Act.* Washington, DC: Author.

Vossekuil, B., Reddy, M., Fein, R., Borum, R., & Modzeleski, W. (2000). *U.S.S.S. Safe school initiative: An interim report on the prevention of targeted violence in schools.* Washington, DC: U.S. Secret Service, National Threat Assessment.

Wanko, M. A. (2001). *Safe schools: Crisis prevention and response.* Lanham, MD: Scarecrow Press.

Watkins, M. W., Crosby, E. G., & Pearson, J. L. (2001). Role of the school psychologist: Perceptions of school staff. *School Psychology International, 22*(1), 64–73.

Weinberg, R. B. (1993). A student death response plan. In J. J. Cohen & M. C. Fish (Eds.), *Handbook of school-based interventions: Resolving student problems and promoting healthy educational environments* (pp. 275–277). San Francisco: Jossey-Bass.

Wittmer, J. (2000). *Managing your school counseling program: K–12 developmental strategies* (2nd ed.). Minneapolis, MN: Educational Media Corporation.

XXXI
CONSULTATION AND COLLABORATION AS ESSENTIAL SERVICES FOR SCHOOL COUNSELING PROGRAMS

MICHAEL B. SALZMAN
University of Hawaii at Manoa

The intention of this chapter is to examine the nature and variations of *consultation* and *collaboration* in school settings. The chapter will focus on relevant research, the major models of consultation and collaboration, and the importance of multicultural and historical contexts in relation to the processes of consultation and collaboration.

Consultation and collaboration are essential functions of school counseling programs and essential skills for school counselors. This has been true historically and is true today as school counselors seek to develop comprehensive counseling programs that are integral to the mission of the schools and communities they serve. Three important initiatives have been articulated that conceptualize a vision of school counseling where all students are served programmatically. The *National Model for Comprehensive School Counseling Programs* is sponsored by the American School Counselor Association (ASCA), the *National School Counselor Training Initiative,* and the *School–Community Collaboration Model* all stress the need for collaboration within and outside the schools and for the provision of consultation services (Baker & Gerler, 2004).

Consultation (along with counseling, coordinating, and appraising) has been considered one of the essential services performed by school counselors, and *collaboration* has been described as an important aspect of all relationships (e.g., with parents, teachers, and community agencies formed by school counselors; Schmidt, 1999). Although there is a great need for further research on all aspects of the consultation process in schools, there is a mounting body of empirical evidence demonstrating the efficacy of consultative services (e.g., Sheridan, Welch, & Orme, 1996). The Council for Accreditation of Counseling and Related Educational Programs (CACREP) has recognized the importance of consultation.

Collaboration in problem solving is well supported in the school psychology literature as a model for service delivery and is consistent with directions in federal law and educational initiatives designed to improve student outcomes (Allen & Graden, 2002). Collaboration is a necessary part of a school counselor's job (Porter, Epp, & Byrant, 2000). Groups and individuals working collaboratively can achieve goals and overcome challenges that would be difficult for an individual to accomplish and generally have more power to change systems (DeVoss & Andrews, 2006). The Education Trust (2002) emphasized the need for school counselors to be team builders and collaborators by working with teachers, administrators, staff, students, family members, and the community in service of the school's mission. Indeed, the need for professionals to work collaboratively has increased in recent years because of ever more complex sources of psychological, economic, social, and physical stress that impact people's lives (Nugent & Jones, 2005). School counselors are well prepared for this role by virtue of their training in group processes and dynamics as well as basic communication skills.

Definition of Terms

The terms *consultation* and *collaboration* have suffered from some definitional imprecision in the counseling literature

(Kampwirth, 2006). For the purpose of clarity, it is useful to consider, first, bedrock dictionary definitions of the terms. The *Oxford Encyclopedic English Dictionary* defines consult as "to seek information or advice" and defines consulting as "to give professional advice to others" (Pearsall & Trumble, p. 309). The consultant, then, is a person who gives advice. The consultant, then, is a person who gives advice. *Collaboration* is defined as working with others cooperatively.

Efforts have been made to both differentiate and synthesize these terms as they relate to school-based practices. For example, Erchul and Martens (2002) described school-based consultation as "a process for providing psychological and educational services in which a specialist (consultant) works cooperatively with a staff member (consultee) to improve the learning and adjustment of a student (client) or group of students" (pp. 13–14). The process, according to this definition, helps the consultee through systematic problem solving, social influence, and professional support. The consultee, then, assists the client by selecting and implementing the interventions generated in the consultation process. This essential triadic relationship characteristic of school-based consultation is supported by other scholars (e.g., Brown, Pryzwansky, & Schulte, 2006; Friend & Cook, 2003). They understand the process as a voluntary one in which one professional helps another address a problem concerning a third party by helping the consultee develop attitudes and skills that will promote more effective consultee functioning with an individual, group, or organization for which the consultee has responsibility.

Gelso and Fretz (2001) considered consultation to be a professional service that uses knowledge of human behavior, interpersonal relationships, and group and organizational processes to help others become more effective in their roles. They have suggested that, regardless of work settings, the consultation process involves a client, a consultee, and a consultant. The consultation relationship and process is voluntary, nonjudgmental, and nonrestrictive in that the consultee is free to accept or reject any suggestions or recommendations made by the consultant. The focus of the process and relationship is on the client's problems. Nugent and Jones (2005) described various types of consultation: (a) consultation with other counselors and mental health professionals; (b) consultation with faculty, administrators, parents, or families in educational settings; and (c) consultation with staff members of community organizations serving mental health needs.

Hackney and Cormier (2005) found a wide divergence of views on consultation. They did find general agreement that consultation is a process whereby one professional assists a consultee with a work-related problem with a client or client system. The lack of definitional clarity of consultation has been noted for at least 20 years (Brown et al., 2006). This definitional imprecision may be due to the varying theoretical models of consultation used by consultants working in different fields and settings. Confusion may have been further exacerbated or perhaps clarified by the introduction of the term *collaborative consultation* (Idol, Paolucci-Whitcomb, & Nevin, 1986; Reyes & Jason, 1993). Consultation is an essential function of school counselors. In the service of clarity, it may be defined in simple terms as a process whereby the first party (consultant) assists the second party (consultee) in finding a solution to a problem that concerns the third party (client) (Nugent & Jones, 2005).

The term *collaboration* has been used to describe "those instances in which two or more people agree to take somewhat equal responsibility for the implementation of the interventions" (Kampwirth, 2006, p. 3), generated by an interaction between coequal parties who voluntarily share decision making in working toward a common goal. This view is consistent with Sheridan, Napolitano, and Swearer's (2002) description of collaboration as being characterized by a "diversity of individuals and vantage points working together as coequal parties, sharing in the identification of goals and solution of problems, and forging trusting relationships wherein resources, power, and responsibilities are shared" (p. 322).

In an effort to clarify the definitional imprecision, other scholars (e.g., Schulte & Osborne, 2003) differentiated the two services in terms of direct and indirect services. They described consultation as an indirect service where the consultant does not work directly with the client, whereas collaboration is a direct service where the collaborators share responsibility for the implementation of the intervention. Gladding (2006) compiled *The Counseling Dictionary* of "concise definitions of frequently used terms in counseling." In this compilation, *consultation* was defined as follows:

> A voluntary *relationship* between a professional helper and an individual or group that needs help. In such a relationship, the *consultant* provides assistance by *helping* to define and resolve a *problem* or potential problem of the *client*. Consultant relationships are defined as triadic (i.e., client, consultant, problem) and are *content* based, goal directed, and *process* oriented. (p. 35, italics added)

Interestingly, Gladding's *Counseling Dictionary* does not define *collaboration*.

Collaboration and consultation are similar in that they both involve professionals engaged in a problem-solving process that requires a relationship based on mutual respect, cooperation, and shared goals. Collaboration and consultation, however, differ in that they are separate processes distinguished by who delivers the intervention. G. Caplan and R. B. Caplan (1999) and Pryswansky (1977) attempted to differentiate the two processes by stating that in consultation, the consultee delivers the intervention developed in the consultation process, whereas in collaboration, the responsibility for the implementation of the intervention is shared.

Consultation and Collaboration as Efficient Interventions

Although there continues to be a great need for further research on all aspects of consultation and collaboration, the practice of school-based consultation and collaboration is supported in the literature and by a mounting body of empirical evidence demonstrating the efficacy of consultative services and collaboration with school stakeholders (e.g., Brown et al., 2006; Elizalde-Utnick, 2002; Gutkin & Curtis, 1999; Porter et al., 2000; Wilkinson, 2003). A central goal of the consultation process is to enhance and empower the consultee systems and thereby enhance the students' well-being and performance. By enhancing and empowering the consultee, the consultation process serves both a remedial and a prevention function. That is, the severity of current client problems may be reduced, and similar problems in others may be prevented due to an increase in the awareness, knowledge, and skills of the consultee so that the environmental factors that elicit and maintain problematic behaviors may be altered or eliminated (Zins & Erchul, 2002). This preventative focus inevitably shifts the target of consultation away from individual students to entire systems such as classrooms, schools, and larger communities. This shift requires an analysis that attends to organizational variables such as decision-making processes, opportunities to feel a sense of belonging, and the availability of avenues through which young people can achieve a positive sense of significance as human beings that have value.

Collaboration within the school, school system, and community helps counselors identify and address the needs of students by accessing appropriate services to meet the identified needs. By collaborating with relevant agencies, counselors facilitate access to needed services for students and families. This is most important in rural areas where schools and communities often do not have the resources and funds to address essential needs (Schmidt, 1999). School counselors have a primary responsibility for developing comprehensive programs in order to address the needs of all students. Given the scope of this function, it is necessary to gain the cooperative support of other professionals and persons within the school system and community. Collaborative relationships should certainly be developed with parents, teachers, students, and other counselors in order for them to cooperate in the solution of problems and in meeting real needs. Counselors may also develop fruitful collaborations with nurses, psychologists, social workers, and community social service and health agencies. Consultation and collaboration may effectively and efficiently extend the reach of counselors to effect positive change and serve the best interests of the school and its students.

In the section that follows, a generic model, as well as theory-based models, of consultation will be reviewed. These theory-informed models are mental health (four types), behavioral, Adlerian, and organizational consultation. Table 31.1 provides an abbreviated summary of the theoretical foundations, target of consultation ("Who is the client?"), type of consultation/collaboration, relevant data, and other major ideas and issues related to these models of consultation.

Overview of Pertinent Theoretical Models and Perspectives

Commonalities: A Generic Model

In general, all models of consultation share certain functions and stages. Although definitional precision remains elusive, the most frequently employed approaches all stress the use of problem solving as the mechanism through which interventions are generated, the focus on work-related problems, and the view of participation in the consultation process as voluntary (Zins & Erchul, 2002). Kratochwill, Elliot, and Callan-Stoiber (2002) noted that the major models of consultation all emphasize enhancing the problem-solving expertise of the consultee within the triadic relationship of consultant–consultee–client. The counseling intern and practicum student may benefit by conceptualizing the process of consultation along the generic dimensions shared by most models. While some variations exist across different models of consultation due to their theoretical and historical antecedents, each phase of the process presents shared challenges. These dimensions or stages may be broadly categorized as *entry, assessment, intervention, evaluation,* and *follow-up.*

The *entry* phase presents challenges. The consultant must enter the consultee–client system. The entry phase must address the ethical mandate of *informed consent,* whereby the consultee is given all necessary information about the process in order to make an informed decision about whether to engage in consultation. Entry requires the consultant to fully explain the process of consultation and to define what confidentiality is and what it is not. Potential consultees need to be assured that the relationship is voluntary, nonhierarchical, and confidential. It is important that consultees be aware that consultation is an indirect service and that the consultant will not be working directly with the client, whereas in collaboration, responsibility for the implementation of the selected intervention

Table 31.1 Summary of Consultation Models

	Theoretical Foundations	Who is Client?	Type of Consult/Collaboration	Relevant Data	Other Major Ideas/Issues
Generic	Eclectic	Individuals, families, organizations	Problem solving All models stress problem solving	Problem definition, relevant data depends on guiding theories	Mutual respect, informed consent, shared expertise Cultural context Historical context
Mental Health	Psychodynamic theory	1. Individual client 2. Primary focus on consultee working on case 3. A program or organization 4. Effectiveness of consultee with organizations, programs	1. Client-centered case consultation *2. Consultee-centered case consultation 3. Program-centered administrative 4. Consultee-centered administrative consult problem solving	Assess level of knowledge, skill, confidence, objectivity regarding client, situation, issue	Consultee intrapsychic factors (e.g., theme interference, biases, feelings, attitudes, and beliefs) Cultural context Historical context
Behavioral	Classical, Operant, and Social Learning	Individuals, families, organizations	Consultee directed Problem solving	Contingencies of reinforcement, role models	Cultural context Historical context
Organizational	Systems theory Field theory	Organizations	Systemic approaches to organizational change. Organization as client Problem solving	Communication & decision making processes, organization norms & values	Subsystems, feedback loops, reciprocal causality Cultural context Historical context
Adlerian	Adlerian theory	Individuals, families, organizations	Collaborative, psycho-educational Problem solving	Purpose of behavior, "pathways to significance"	Social interest, mutual respect Cultural context Historical context

*Type most closely identified with Caplan (1970; Caplan & Caplan, 1999) and is synonymous with "mental health consultation."

is shared. The power of consultation lies in its indirect nature, in which the consultee emerges from the process with greater expertise and skills. In addition, the consultee is empowered with increased effectiveness in addressing a particular issue, such as classroom management, that may impact many students. The consultee must be informed that the consultation relationship may be terminated at any time by the consultee and that the consultee is free to reject any suggestions made by the consultant. In this phase and throughout the process, *mutual respect* is a necessary condition for a successful consultation. If the entry phase is not successfully negotiated, the consultation process is unlikely to be successful.

All models of consultation require that both consultant and consultee *assess* the nature of the concern in order to achieve a common understanding of the problem or challenge under consideration. The specific data collected and considered is largely a function of the theoretical foundation of the model used and of the identified client. Behavioral consultation, for example, informed by behaviorism and social learning theory, focuses attention on the contingencies of reinforcement and the available models that may serve to stimulate observational learning. Mental health consultation models, informed by psychodynamic theory, may focus on data relating to factors and tendencies within the consultee, such as expectations, themes, biases, and degree of consultee knowledge and confidence. Decisions about what data is relevant, what sources of data may be accessed, and the collection of relevant data lead to a clear *problem definition*. A clear problem definition focuses the attention and efforts of all parties in the process.

The *intervention* phase requires the generation of possible intervention strategies that may ameliorate, solve, or better manage the defined problem. The degree of collaboration in this phase may vary across models. In some models, the consultant may assume a more directive role in suggesting intervention, while in other models, the generation of the interventions may proceed through a cooperative brainstorming process that produces a large number of possible strategies to be evaluated and ultimately selected by the consultee. When the intervention is agreed on and selected, the consultee, with the support of the consultant, implements the intervention.

Evaluation of the intervention is the next challenge of the consultation process. The data required for a competent evaluation must necessarily be related to the defined problem or opportunity. At this point, new data may be generated by even an unsuccessful intervention leading to a reconceptualization and definition of the problem or opportunity that was the initial focus of the consultation. In such cases, the consultant and consultee may "loop back" to the assessment stage to reexamine the concern in the light of new data (e.g., family stress). If the evaluation indicates a substantial improvement in the consultee's abilities and the client's situation, then a *follow-up* process begins to support a gradual withdrawal of the consultant from the system.

This generic model is useful to understand the process of consultation. Variations are largely dictated by the theoretical assumptions informing different forms of consultation and by who the consultee and client are in the consultation process. These variations influence the type of data collected, the nature of the interventions generated, and the criteria used to evaluate the effectiveness of the consultation. Students in counselor education programs would be well advised to become well grounded in the predominant counseling and psychological theories that inform the consultation models as well as counseling practice. A student well grounded in theory will have the intellectual flexibility to apply illuminating and coherent systems of data gathering, assessment, intervention generation, and evaluation to their observations. The importance and utility of theory in school-based consultation was emphasized by Brigman, Mullis, Webb, and White (2005): "To be successful in the consultant role, school counselors must have a theoretical base and models from which to operate. Theory provides a basis for understanding what helps people change their attitudes, skills, behaviors and expectations" (p. 9). They note that all models of consultation, regardless of their theoretical basis, are similar in that they utilize a problem solving approach to help consultees with school-related problems. Four theory-informed models of consultation will be briefly considered and described now.

Mental Health Consultation

G. Caplan (1970, 2004), a leader in the development of community psychiatry, has been enormously influential in the field of psychological consultation. He viewed consultation as an effective means for the prevention of mental disorders. A fundamental assumption of his model is that that both intrapsychic and environmental factors are important in explaining and changing behavior. More than any other model of consultation, mental health consultation focuses on the importance of intrapsychic factors such as consultee feelings, attitudes, and beliefs (Brown et al., 2006). In their book *Mental Health Consultation and Collaboration*, G. Caplan and R. B. Caplan (1999) placed collaboration alongside consultation as a major tool for mental health professionals to infuse psychological and preventive principles into varied work settings They suggest that when mental health professionals are internal to an organization (e.g., school counselors), collaboration may represent a better fit with the circumstances than consultation. As noted, within the collaborative model, the collaborators assume joint responsibility for aspects of the process including the implementation of the selected intervention (Brown et al.).

Caplan (1990) thought that consultation with caregivers such as teachers, parents, and mental health professionals would reduce the need for more intensive mental health services. Caplan's influence on consultation has been significant. He conceptualized consultation as a nonhierarchical, cooperative relationship between professionals where each possesses his or her own expertise that may serve to inform effective interventions. In this conceptualization, the consultee is free to accept or reject any suggestions offered by the consultant and bears sole responsibility for carrying out any interventions.

Caplan (2004) distinguished between four types of consultation along two major dimensions (Brown et al., 2006): (a) whether the content focus of the consultation is a difficulty with a particular client or an administrative difficulty, or (b) whether the focus of the consultation is on providing information in the consultant's area of expertise or an improvement of the consulteee's problem-solving capacity.

In the case of *client-centered case consultation*, the process is essentially prescriptive in that the consultant assesses the client and provides information and expertise in order to assist the consultee in working more effectively with the client. In *consultee-centered case consultation*, the primary goal is to increase the skills and effectiveness of the consultee in working with the client and other clients with similar issues. In *program-centered administrative consultation*, the focus is on the development of a new program or the improvement of an existing one. In this case, an administrative/program counterpart of client-centered case consultation, the program or organization is the client and those responsible for it are the consultees. The consultant makes recommendations for program improvement and organizational development. Last, *consultee-centered administrative consultation*, analogous to consultee-centered case consultation, focuses on increasing consultee effectiveness and professional functioning regarding specific organizations, programs, or policies for which they bear responsibility.

Brown et al. (2006) suggested that of the four types Caplan (1970) delineated, consultee-centered case consultation is the type of consultation most closely identified with him and is synonymous with the term *mental health consultation.* The primary goal in this type of consultation is the remediation of deficiencies in the consultee's professional functioning that are responsible for difficulties with a particular case. Caplan suggested four major categories that necessitate different actions on the part of the consultant: (a) lack of knowledge, (b) lack of skill, (c) lack of confidence, and (d) lack of objectivity.

Interventions are generated depending on an assessment of the source of consultee difficulties. If *lack of knowledge* is a significant source of consultee difficulties due to, for example, a lack of knowledge of psychological, social, or developmental factors, then an intervention designed to increase relevant consultee knowledge of these factors would likely enhance consultee functioning. This may be accomplished by supplying information to the consultee. If the consultant assesses that this need is pervasive in an organization, then the problem may be systemic, suggesting the need for a system level intervention such as providing professional development opportunities. If the consultee possesses the relevant knowledge but has difficulty in applying that knowledge, then the difficulties might be attributed to a *lack of skill* in applying that knowledge. In this case, the consultant may work with the consultee in identifying appropriate sources for skill development within or external to the organization. If a *lack of confidence* is assessed as a significant source of consultee difficulties, the consultant may work to encourage and support the consultee and to find sources of support and encouragement within the organization and profession of the consultee.

In Caplan's (2004) view, when supervisory and administrative subsystems are working well in an organization, the majority of consultee-centered consultation cases will be the result of a consultee's *lack of objectivity* (Brown et al., 2006). Caplan identified five intrapsychic contributors to this problem. A *direct personal involvement* of the consultee with the client may occur, for example, when a professional relationship crosses a boundary to a personal relationship that may confound professional objectivity and functioning. *Simple identification* may be another contributor to a lack of objectivity. This may occur when the consultee identifies with the perceived situation of the client and superimposes his or her own experiences and struggles onto the case of the client, thereby losing professional objectivity. Similarly, in the case of *transference* (a psychodynamic concept), the consultee imposes her or his past experiences and expectations onto the client, thereby missing the real nature of the client's difficulties. In such cases, the consultee engaging in transference may well be an important source of the client's difficulties. A fourth category contributing to a consultee's lack of objectivity, *characterological distortion,* is perhaps the most extreme example. In this case, there is an enduring aspect of the consultee's personality that interferes with professional functioning. A perfectionist consultee, for example, with a deep need to perceive himself or herself as completely competent, may react negatively to a client who is not doing well, thereby contributing to client discouragement and difficulties.

A fifth, related source of consultee's lack of objectivity is given central importance in Caplan's (1970) thinking. *Theme interference* represents an unsolved problem or perceived defeat that was experienced by the consultee. The consultee makes a syllogistic link between a perceived situation and an undesirable outcome that is seen as inevitable. Linking a "broken home" to inevitable behavioral difficulties may create expectations in the consultee that make behavioral difficulties more probable in a kind of self-fulfilling prophecy. The consultee may in fact be manipulating the situation to conform to his or her preconceived expectations. Theme interference is more likely to occur when a particular situation makes a theme resident in the consultee more salient, reflecting the assumption that behavior is a function of a person–environment interaction. In this case, the consultant may work with the consultee to demonstrate that given a particular circumstance (e.g., a "broken home"), an expected outcome is not inevitable. In cross-cultural and multicultural consultation, particular themes regarding "how *they* are" are potent sources of a lack of objectivity. Biases and stereotypes may be particularly destructive themes resident in consultees, as they may assign clients to stereotypical categories rather than perceiving them as unique human beings.

Caplan's (2004) contributions have had enormous impact. His work focused attention on the relevance of variables resident in the consultee (e.g., perceptions, feelings, and attitudes) that may impact his or her interactions with clients. His emphasis on the importance of consultee involvement in the problem-solving process supports the effectiveness of consultation in cross-cultural and multicultural consultation contexts.

Research has found that mental health consultation has produced positive outcomes (Medway & Updyke, 1985; Sheridan et al., 1996); however, Brown et al. (2006) noted that a continuing problem in consultation research is a lack of data documenting how consultation has been implemented.

Behavioral Consultation and Collaboration

Behavioral consultation (BC) is informed by the principles of behaviorism and the learning theories and empirical evidence upon which it is constructed (Conoley & Conoley, 1992). After reviewing the consultation outcome research from 1985 to 1995, Sheridan et al. (1996) found that there was a well-established empirical basis for behavioral consultation. They found that more research was conducted with BC than with other models, that BC studies used the most rigorous experimental designs, and that BC tended to yield very favorable results (95% of the BC studies reported at least some positive results). The earliest models relied on the operant learning theory as a conceptual basis for consultation in schools. Since the 1980s, behavioral models of consultation have taken a more eclectic approach with the inclusion of classical and social learning theories into its conceptual framework. Behaviorists see behaviors as a function of the contingencies that support them (Kampwirth, 2006). A primary focus of data collection and analysis are the antecedent events and situations that occur prior to the behavior of concern (e.g., tantrum) and the environmental consequences of that behavior. Some children find unstructured activities such as recess to be anxiety producing. In order to avoid this anxiety-producing situation, the child may purposefully not complete the required work prior to recess. If the teacher then keeps the child in during recess (environmental consequences), the behavior is reinforced and will likely continue. Behaviorists assert that a behavior that is not being reinforced by the environment (including teachers, peers, and parents) will not continue. There is research that supports this approach. Wilkinson (2003), for example, found that behavioral consultation was effective in reducing "challenging behaviors" in the classroom.

So, as theory indicates which data are important, behaviorists collect and seek to understand how the environment may trigger and support behaviors of concern. While traditional behaviorism (Skinner, 1969) was not concerned with internal cognitive events, the importance cognitive mediation such as self-talk is now widely recognized (e.g., Meichenbaum, 1977; Schloss & Smith, 1998). Bandura (1977) and his development of social learning theory provided an additional emphasis on the role of observational learning and modeling in the acquisition of learning and behaviors. In Bandura's framework, cognitive constructs are important. Self-efficacy (the confidence that one can perform a task) and appraisal (the importance one attaches to a goal or task) are important influences on human behavior. It is important to recognize that, across cultures, behavioral reinforcements, as well as how people tend to learn, may vary. In Hawaiian culture, for example, the mode of observational learning is particularly stressed (Dela Cruz, Salzman, Brislin, & Losch, 2006).

Bergan (1977) and Bergan and Kratochwill (1990) developed a comprehensive model of behavioral consultation. Consistent with the generic approach to consultation previously outlined, the major steps in their model are (a) problem identification, (b) problem analysis, (c) plan implementation, and (d) problem evaluation. These scholars emphasize that, in all cases, the consultant should have expert knowledge in learning principles and should use social learning theory and the principles of behaviorism to analyze problems and to design, implement, and evaluate interventions (Harrison, 2004). Brown et al. (2006) refer to a *behavioral eclectic* model of behavioral consultation and collaboration that is informed by operant, classical, and social learning theories. The behavioral orientation emphasizes that behavior is contextual and cannot be understood when decontextualized. Relevant context(s) may not be immediately observable, but they can be accessed by a multiculturally competent consultant or collaborator. History is context. Culture is context. The historical and cultural contexts of behavior offer powerful antecedents and consequences that may escape the ethnocentric or uninformed consultant. Such attitudes or lack of knowledge do not enhance the likelihood of effective problem analysis or intervention in multicultural consultation (Salzman, 2005). An American Indian child may not want to behave in a manner that would diminish the status of others in his peer group in accordance with cultural norms. To assess this behavior as a "problem" would indeed be problematic.

An aspect of behavioral consultation that has produced some controversy is the degree to which the consultant directs the process, as well as consultee compliance with consultant recommendations. Bergan (1977) and Bergan and Kratochwill (1990) emphasized the importance of consultant control over the consultation process, rather than the more collaborative approach previously described, where consultant and consultee each enter the process with his or her own expertise relevant to the case or problem under consideration. In cross-cultural and diversity contexts, this emphasis could prove problematic. When the consultant is unfamiliar with the cultural or class context of the consultee and client, the accuracy of assessment and the effectiveness of interventions may be compromised. A consultant from an urban community may not comprehend the power of an impoverished rural context on behavior and perception. A due respect for the relevant expertise of all parties would reduce the probability of this type of error. A due respect for the limits of one's knowledge is a foundation of competence and wisdom.

Adlerian Consultation and Collaboration

Adlerian theory and its applications (see Ansbacher & Ansbacher, 1956; Dreikurs, Grunwald, & Pepper, 1998) inform another theory-based model of consultation. Brigman et al. (2005) have found that Adlerian theory offers a sound educational premise for use with both students and adults in school systems because "it is future oriented, collaborative, and realistic. It emphasizes social interest and the importance of contributing to society" (p. 10). Bedrock Adlerian principles include the following:

- "Reality" is subjective
- Equality between the consultant and consultee

- Encouragement: Courage is an essential quality
- Mutual respect and social equality
- Humans are social beings, and human behavior has social meaning
- Behavior is purposeful, guided by a "private logic," and goal directed
- Useful and "mistaken" goals of behavior
- Logical and natural consequences

Teachers informed by Adlerian principles strive to create democratic classrooms where students participate in developing the structure of the learning environment and the reasonable rules and consequences that guide responsible behavior. This may be accomplished by the consultant working with the consultee (teacher) in developing democratic practices in the classroom. Such practices may include establishing weekly class meetings that address problems and classroom goals. Rules and consequences for violating them could be determined by students under the leadership— but not domination—of the teacher. Since Adlerian theory posits that humans struggle to compensate for feelings of inferiority, a high value is assigned to developing relationships based on *mutual respect* and *social equality*.

Adlerian theory informs teachers that all young people seek a sense of significance. Positive (e.g., contribution to school community and real achievement) and negative paths (e.g., attention seeking and bullying) may be taken to achieve the goal of feeling that one matters and is a person who is indeed "somebody." Consultants can work with teachers (consultees) to develop opportunities for children to experience a sense of belonging to the class through contribution, service, and participation. Adler emphasized the central importance of courage and encouragement as an antidote to discouragement, which is the basic orientation from which mistaken, antisocial, and self-defeating goals of behavior (e.g., attention, power, revenge, and withdrawal) are pursued. Adlerians think that courage is required to seek challenging positive *pathways to significance* and that discouragement produces a tendency to seek "mistaken" goals in the striving for significance.

Teachers informed by Adlerian theory seek data that may help them understand the purpose of behaviors and learn to reorient clients away from *mistaken goals* to useful, meaningful, and responsible behaviors that help achieve goals that are healthy for the client, the community, and the planet. A well-constructed classroom environment offers multiple positive pathways to significance, thus addressing a core human need ("self-esteem") in ways that are not self-defeating for the client and not destructive to the larger community. Adler thought that children who receive encouragement, feel a real sense of connection and belonging, and are given the opportunity to develop their strengths would turn to the useful side of life. Such children develop *social interest*, courage, and the ability to make responsible decisions. Social interest is seen as that quality which motivates one to contribute to the greater good, the group or community (Ansbacher & Ansbacher, 1956). Interventions guided by Adlerian theory might focus on classroom and school organization where efforts are made to ensure that each child has meaningful responsibilities to help the class achieve its educational goals in a supportive, encouraging, and respectful environment.

Brown et al. (2006) acknowledged that "empirical support for the Adlerian approach to consultation is sparse" (p. 93). They did, however, find some support for parent–teacher consultation. They cited Palmo and Kuzniar (1972, as cited in Brown et al., 2006), who compared the effectiveness of Adlerian teacher-parent plus Adlerian group counseling with parent–teacher consultation alone, with Adlerian group counseling, and with a no-treatment control group on classroom behaior. They found that all treatment groups produced significant results based on teacher ratings. They also found, however, that only the parent–teacher consultation treatment significantly decreased troublesome classroom behavior based on classroom behavior observations.

Schmidt (1999) found that Adlerian and behavioral approaches to consultation are common in school settings where teachers or parents may be consultees. Gianotti and Doyle (1982), for example, used Parent Effectiveness Training (PET) with parents of children who were diagnosed as have "learning disabilities." They investigated parental attitudes, children's perceptions of parent behavior, children's self-concepts, and children's behavior in school using a pretest–posttest control group design. The study found significant differences on all four variables. Children of parents in the PET group scored higher on self-concept measures than the control group. Students whose parents were in PET were seen as less anxious about school achievement, and they had more self-reliance and sought more positive relationships with their teachers. Parents who participated in PET reported more confidence in their parenting skills, a greater awareness of the effect of their behavior on their children, a better understanding of their own needs, and that they were more willing to trust their children than parents who did not participate in PET. Two studies of Systematic Training for Effective Parenting (STEP), an Adlerian-based program, demonstrated some support for this type of consultation. Williams, Omizo, and Abrams (1984) showed significant positive changes in parents' attitudes after participating in a STEP program. The study, utilizing a pretest–posttest experimental design, produced results indicating that the STEP parents were more accepting and trusting after participation in the program, and they perceived their own behavior as more of a contributing factor in their children's behavior.

One of the primary goals of consultation is the prevention of mental health and behavioral problems (Brown et al., 2006). A strength of Adlerian consultation is its emphasis on prevention. By addressing core human needs, human problems may be prevented. What do young people really need? Adlerian theory addresses the core needs of feeling valued, significant, and respected, as well as a sense of belonging and usefulness. Problems may be fruitfully analyzed and interventions may be generated with such needs in mind. Counselors as consultants would be well advised to see the entire school as their client. The Adlerian approach offers a useful lens to analyze the school organization itself for its ability to address the basic human needs of its constituents by focusing on such variables as the availability of "positive pathways to significance" for all, opportunities for students to exercise meaningful responsibilities in their school community, democratic versus autocratic practices in the classroom and school, sources of encouragement and discouragement, and the degree to which *social interest* is nourished. By seeing the *school as client*, the consultant is engaged in *organizational consultation*.

Organizational Consultation

When the counselor sees the entire school community as the client, she or he is functioning as an organizational or process consultant. A consultation or collaboration problem-solving process may be approached by examining such internal systemic variables as (a) communications patterns, (b) clarity of roles and functions, (c) processes and procedures for group problem solving and decision making, (d) group norms, (e) leadership and authority, (f) intergroup (subsystems) cooperation and competition, (g) formal and informal power structures, (h) clarity and prioritization of organizational goals, (i) incentive and reward systems, and (j) organizational climate and health factors. External variables may exert a powerful influence on organizational change efforts, whether attempted through consultation or collaborative interventions. External variables affecting a school organization include (a) accrediting bodies, (b) union agreements, (c) legislation (e.g., "No Child Left Behind"), (c) community pressure groups, (d) community political organizations, (e) tenure laws, (f) environmental factors such as socioeconomic status of the surrounding community, and (g) cultural factors such as community values, beliefs, assumptions, and norms. The quality of school climate varies tremendously across the United States (Kozol, 1992), especially in environmental contexts (i.e., rural, urban, and suburban) that exert powerful influences on organizations that are embedded in them.

As in the cases of the previously discussed consultation models, the focus of the consultation or collaboration and the theoretical basis of the models used dictate the variables of interest and the relevant data needed to inform all phases of the process of consultation or collaboration (e.g., entry into the system and relationship development, problem analysis and definition, intervention generation and selection, and evaluation strategies).

The "client" in organizational or process consultation and collaboration is the system (organization or family) itself, where the consultant/collaborator contributes expertise to facilitate positive systemic change (Erford, 2003). Organizational consultation may be well informed by the previously—but briefly—outlined theoretical models. Organizational consultation is also a triadic model (consultant–consultee–client) that is informed by Lewin's (1951) *field theory* and by *systems theory* (e.g., Bertalanffy, 1962; Katz & Kahn, 1978). Brown et al. (2006) noted a review of the professional literature from a wide variety of applied fields within the social sciences that reveals a remarkable theoretical convergence in *systems theory* and its applications to understanding organizations, family therapy, education, and community functioning. These theoretical foundations emphasize that individuals and their behaviors are functionally interrelated with the groups, organizations, communities, cultures, and socioeconomic systems to which they belong. Lewin (1951) offered a simple formulation that human behavior is a function of a person/environment interaction $B = f(P \times E)$. *Systems theory* indicates that in a system where all elements are interrelated, causality cannot be seen in linear terms (where A causes B), but instead is complex and reciprocal, where all elements in a system influence all other elements as well as the system itself.

Bronfenbrenner (1979) emphasized the importance of context. Developmental–ecological models of human development rest on the principle that human development and its behavioral expressions are strongly influenced by context and that an analysis of an event or behavior cannot be conducted independently of the ecological–cultural–systemic and social context(s). The ecological model posits four levels for classifying context (Bronfenbrenner). This classification begins with those ecologies the child directly interacts with (microsystems), such as the family and school. It proceeds to social, cultural, and historical forces that, while operating at higher levels of abstraction (e.g., mesosystems, exosystems, and macrosystems), may powerfully impact human development and experience. The macrosystem represents the broadest level of systemic influence. This contextual force includes ideological and institutional patterns and events that define social reality and influence psychological experience and its behavioral manifestations. The macrosystem represents an overarching context that includes historical events such as colonization, decolonization, community, and cultural trauma (Salzman, 2001). The relevance to multicultural consultation is clear—a people's and a person's history and culture are influential contexts that cannot be ignored without risking serious and perhaps harmful error at all stages of the consultation process.

Welch (1999, as cited in Kampwirth, 2006), offers a set of general guidelines that may assist organizational consultants and collaborators to solve systemic problems that may improve the ability of the school organization to achieve its mission to provide a quality education to all of its students. The acronym DECIDE outlines this generic process:

D. Define and clarify the situation. What is currently happening? What is not happening that needs to happen? Describe in behavioral terms what the problem/issue/challenge is and who is involved and impacted by it.
E. Examine the environment and the systemic variables (i.e., reward and incentive system) that could be contributing to the problem.
C. Create a goal statement that includes
   1. Behaviors: Describe actions and events that are concrete, observable, and measurable.
   2. Conditions: Where and under what circumstances will the change occur?
   3. Criterion: Set a standard that must be achieved.
   4. Duration: For how long should the change be carried out?
I. Invent an intervention plan: The plan should address what will be done to accomplish the goal statement. This process may include stakeholders brainstorming ideas in a free and nonjudgmental atmosphere, evaluating the brainstormed interventions through a cost–benefit analysis, and selecting interventions that would address needs and identified goals. In order to develop an intervention plan that has a high probability of success, it is important to evaluate the availability and accessibility of the resources needed to undertake the intervention.
D. Deliver the action plan: Implement the plan that was designed to achieve the goals that, if achieved, would improve organizational functioning.
E. Evaluate the intervention action plan: This should include both formative and summative evaluations.

"School climate" is an excellent focus for organizational consultation or collaboration. It has been described (Lehr & Christenson, 2002) as a relatively enduring quality of the entire school that is experienced by members. It is the atmosphere for learning and includes the feelings people have about the school and whether it is a place where learning can occur. A positive school climate makes a school a place where both staff and students want to be. School climate has been recognized as an important component of effective schools. Lehr and Christenson cited numerous studies that have documented the association of school climate with improved student outcomes (e.g., Hoy & Hannum, 1997; Kuperminc, Leadbeater, Emmons, & Blatt, 1997; Rumsberger, 1995). Varying descriptions of the components of this complex construct converge on the construction of a sense or order and discipline, parental involvement, staff dedication to student learning, high expectations for academic performance and behavior, caring relationships, and respectful interactions among all stakeholders (students, parents, teachers, etc.) in the system.

Reality demands that schools be places where people feel safe and where learning takes place that prepares students to function competently in the world. How these demands of reality are achieved may vary according to contexts (e.g., cultural, historical, and rural–urban–suburban) but may share certain characteristics that are based on meeting fundamental human needs. Can we construct school environments where all feel valued, respected, connected, responsible, challenged, supported, and recognized for positive effort and accomplishment? How would such a school look? What would be happening that is not happening now? What would not be happening that is currently happening? If we want to raise responsible, self-respecting young people, should we not develop mechanisms for their meaningful participation in the decisions that affect them, rather than being the objects of the plans and actions of others? Is it not possible to construct a better world beginning with the schools we depend on to educate and nourish our children and young people?

Levels, Targets, and Contexts for Consultation and Collaboration

The targets of intervention identified by Brown et al. (2006) include individuals, groups, organizations, and communities. Another important issue is the level and purpose of the intervention. Primary prevention is true prevention. It aims at enhancing the positive development and mental health of a general population assumed to be "normal." It is designed to prevent problems before they may occur, for example, by enhancing life and coping skills needed to address the problems and challenges that life inevitably presents. Primary prevention may focus on individuals (enhancing skills), groups (improving communication patterns), organizations (improving decision making), and communities (community development). Secondary prevention addresses the early treatment of problems before they become serious and have significantly negative consequences for the individual, group, organization, or community. Such secondary-level interventions may include a mentoring system for students facing stressful transitions, job enrichment programs, and professional development opportunities for school personnel, as well as community development efforts designed to improve community environments. Tertiary preventions are remedial in nature. They address serious problems and dysfunctions in persons, groups, organizations, and communities. Tertiary prevention is perhaps better described as treatment. Consultation with a parent of a self-destructive child would be an example of a tertiary-level intervention. Organizational consultation or collaborative efforts to reduce dangerous gang violence would be an example of tertiary prevention at the group and organizational levels. Consultation and collaboration can be effective interventions in these cases. It is, of course, preferable to prevent problems before they occur. We can do this by proactively and intentionally acknowledging and addressing real human needs.

The Cultural Context of Consultation and Collaboration

Various theory-based models of consultation have been presented, and we must consider when Western-based theories are applicable in working with culturally diverse populations. Are the theoretical foundations of the models discussed in this chapter irrelevant to non-Western clients, consultees, and collaborators due to a Eurocentric bias in the foundational assumptions upon which these theories are constructed? Can they be effectively adapted in the service of multicultural consultation and collaboration?

The American Psychological Association (2003) published a set of six guidelines on multicultural education, training, research, practice, and organizational change for psychologists. These guidelines may assist consultants in considering how to think about cultural variation in the practice of consultation. The guidelines encourage us to recognize that we, as cultural beings, may hold attitudes and beliefs that can detrimentally influence perceptions and interactions with individuals who are racially, ethnically, and/or culturally different from ourselves. Stereotypical and prejudicial beliefs resident in a consultant, consultee, or client may confound the consultation process as indicated previously in the case of theme interference in mental health consultation. The guidelines also encourage us to recognize the importance of acquiring specific knowledge, skills, and understanding about culturally, ethnically, and racially different individuals in order to inform our practice.

Brown et al. (2006), for example, considered the cultural limitations of Adlerian theory and its approach to consultation with Native American, Asian, and Hispanic people due to different orientations to time, hierarchy, independence, and other variables that tend to vary across cultures. While cross-cultural differences exist and are important, in order to avoid the error of stereotyping we must acknowledge that within-group differences along these dimensions also exist. Perhaps culture, as well as other diversity variables, is best considered as a hypothesis to be tested. The power of a consultee to accept or reject consultant recommendations reduces the probability of error in these cases. The client in the triadic relationship is usually not afforded the same prerogative. Consultant and consultee can work to empower the client to have a voice in the process to the maximum extent possible when cultural differences exist between the consultee and client.

The theory-based models presented in this chapter may, however, be adapted in the service of effective multicultural consultation and collaboration. Salzman (2002) described a successful consultation at a Bureau of Indian Affairs Boarding School in a traditional area of the Navajo Nation in Arizona. The consultant emphasized one aspect of Navajo culture in order to address the defined problem. Traditionally, Navajos give great responsibilities to their children. Children make important contributions to the family by grazing sheep (family wealth), finding missing horses, or cutting wood for elders so they would be warm. When problems arise in the family, a family meeting is called where all members are expected to offer their views and contribute to a solution. This egalitarian, democratic, social, and social-interest orientation is resonant with aspects of Adlerian theory.

The problem as presented was the relationships among staff (Navajo) and students (Navajo) in the school's dormitory. There was conflict between the staff and the students, as well as conflict among the students. The Bureau of Indian Affairs system was a top-down command structure. Incident reports piled up, and people were miserable. The consultant met with dormitory staff and students to assess the problem. He called a mass meeting in the dormitory and offered the residents the option to take responsibility for running the dormitory consistent with two principles dictated by the demands of reality, which were nonnegotiable. These "nonnegotiables," which no one would really argue against, were that the dormitory must be safe for all and that it must be a place where studying and learning could take place. Students were asked to elect a representative council (also consistent with Navajo culture) and to determine what was needed to improve the situation. Navajo dormitory staff then assumed supportive roles in assisting the students in their task and efforts. The students determined what rules should exist to support the "nonnegotiable" requirements of safety and study, as well as the consequences that should be delivered by staff when the rules were violated. The staff quickly moved from the BIA "command" system to a role more consistent with Navajo culture. After four visits where the consultant worked with the consultees (staff), the democratic structure developed by the students was worked on and refined to the point where the consultant was informed that the students were essentially "running the dorm themselves." Incident reports dropped dramatically, the students found ways to involve their parents, a newsletter was developed, and recreational and cultural events nourished the system. This scenario, abbreviated in its description, is an example of adapting a "Eurocentric" theory to a non-Western people by finding and utilizing compatibilities between the cultural and theoretical systems in all phases of the process.

As previously indicated, other theoretical systems may be adapted or modified in cross-cultural and multicultural contexts. Consequences that may be considered reinforcing in one culture may be aversive in another. Being singled out for praise or being elevated above the group by a teacher may bring negative consequences from the group in collectivist-oriented cultures (e.g., Navajo or Hawaiian). This same situation may be highly reinforcing to someone from an individualistically oriented culture.

Consultants working across cultures must access the historical and cultural contexts of their observations. Ridley, Li, and Hill (1998) remind us of two types of error that counselors need to consider when working across cultures. Type I errors may occur when a symptom or behavior is decontextualized from the client or consultee's culture thereby labeling a culturally appropriate response as pathological where no pathology exists. In this case, the cultural worldview and values of the consultant are imposed thereby interpreting the "symptom" or behavior according to the cultural worldview of the consultant or counselor. This "pathologizing" error may have serious consequences as the label, erroneously applied, may be internalized by the person being labeled. A Type II error may occur when pathology is not identified when it exists because the behavior or manifestation is considered "cultural" and therefore "normal." Both types of error may have serious consequences. Ridley et al. offered a comprehensive system of multicultural assessment that might serve to minimize the likelihood of Type I and Type errors.

Consultants working across cultures must access the cultural context of the client and the consultee. This may be accomplished by seeking cultural consultants, reading, and inquiry. Consultants working across cultures may access traditional healers and resources within the culture of the client as a source of information that may serve to illuminate the analysis and definition of "the problem" and provide intervention possibilities in both consultation and collaboration processes. Culturally competent consultants and collaborators are aware of their own cultural socialization and that of the consultee, client, or collaborators.

Consultants working across cultures must access the historical context of the client and the consultee. Salzman (2005) looked at the symptom of "anger" among many Hawaiian people in the context of a history of colonization and the processes of decolonization and recovery. The symptom of anger may be viewed very differently when the historical context of anger is acknowledged or ignored. The approach to "anger management" would be quite different if one sees anger as a necessary force for psychological liberation from internalized oppression and for political emancipation. Another example would be the author's experience as a fourth grade teacher in a poor, tense, and stressed African American community in Brooklyn during the tumultuous year of 1968. Fortunately for the author, the politically aroused community gave an in-service to new teachers (mostly Euro Americans) about how parents tended to perceive teacher behaviors. These perceptions and attributions where highly influenced by a history of oppression and disrespect. The author remembers being told that parents tended to experience the phrase "these children" negatively. It was as if their children were considered inferior subspecies of children. This in-service given by the community allowed new teachers access to the cultural, historical, and political realities that contextualized behaviors and attributions.

Behring, Cabello, Kushida, and Murguia (2000) examined the use of current consultation approaches and modifications used by European-American, African American, Asian American, and Latino consultants and students. They found that consultants from all cultural backgrounds reported using modifications with teachers and parents for all cultural groups of students except the Euro American group. Interestingly, they found that non-European-American consultants reported using more and different modifications when working with culturally similar parents as compared with Euro American consultants. The results of this study strongly suggest that modifications to current consultation approaches must be used when working with non-European-American students and families. The modification most reported with teachers of non-European-American students was helping the teacher to develop an awareness of the students' cultural differences in the class. Other modifications included

> the consultant helping the teacher to develop an openness to discussing culture with students, the consultant helping the teacher to develop culturally sensitive skills with students, the consultant helping the teacher to allow more time for relationship building with the student and the consultant offering teacher support to cope with cultural differences of students. (Behring et al., 2000, p. 360)

A culturally competent consultant or collaborator seeks interventions that are appropriate and is respectful of the cultural orientation of those with whom they work.

Extant Research and Future Directions

Schmidt (1999) noted that while research on consultation is plentiful, methodological problems make it difficult to draw concise and accurate conclusions. Medway and Updyke (1985) averaged effect sizes over 24 studies examining the effectiveness of mental health, behavioral, and organizational consultation in a meta analysis. They concluded that all three models of consultation were effective across consultants, consultees, and clients. Brown et al. (2006) concurred, noting that methodological problems, fragmented studies, and definitional problems often characterize consultation research with the most frequent problem being the lack of control or comparison groups. In order to address the difficulty of finding appropriate control groups, because it is problematic to withhold a service that can be of immediate assistance to a consultee, these scholars recommended the use of time series research designs. They also stressed the need for outcome research "that measures multiple outcomes and is based on actual consultation efforts" (p. 326). In addition, in view of the continuing problem of definitional imprecision of consultation noted earlier, the theoretical propositions of the model should be elucidated to avoid atheoretical and therefore unreplicatible studies. Finally, Brown et al. suggested that consultation research mirror the complexity of the process using multiple measures of process and outcome dimensions of consultation involving consultee and client variable in order to establish interactions among independent and dependent variables. They further asserted that research cannot yet answer the question of which model of consultation is most effective for a particular problem. They suggested that the selection of a model of consultation should take into consideration the theoretical orientation and personal biases of the consultant as well as the nature of the presenting problem, the characteristics of the consultee, and the resources and constraints embedded in the setting.

Conclusion

School counselors are increasingly pressed to serve the needs of all students through comprehensive programming in the domains of career, academic, personal, and social development. At the same time the ratio of students to counselors is usually far beyond the capabilities of counselors to directly serve all students. Consultation and collaboration skills and services offer the possibility of reaching far greater numbers of students than individual counseling can achieve. This chapter has outlined generic and theory-based models of consultation and collaboration that will hopefully stimulate both beginning and seasoned counselors in their efforts to develop comprehensive school counseling programs that serve all students by helping them develop essential life skills that will empower them to meet life's challenges and the inevitable problems life presents. Consultation is effective because it can empower and improve the functioning of those whose actions affect many students (i.e., teachers, parents, and principals). Collaboration with other professionals, parents, community, and social service agencies combines the skills and expertise from diverse sources to address problems and needs. Both services may serve both the prevention and remediation of problems. Both services can positively impact individuals, groups, school organizations, and communities. Consultation and collaboration are essential and powerful services and competencies for school counselors to offer and cultivate in our efforts to construct a better world beginning with the schools that serve our children and young people.

References

Allen, S. J., & Graden, J. L. (2002). Best practices in collaborative problem solving for intervention design. In A. Thomas & J. Grimes (Eds.), *Best practices in school psychology* (Vol. 1, pp. 565–582). Bethesda, MD: National Association of School Psychologists.

American Psychological Association. (2003). Guidelines on multicultural education, training, research, practice, and organizational change for psychologists. *American Psychologist, 58*(5), 377–402.

Ansbacher, H. L., & Ansbacher, R. R. (Eds.). (1956). *The individual psychology of Alfred Adler.* New York: Basic Books.

Baker, S. B., & Gerler, E. R., Jr. (2004). *School counseling for the twenty-first century* (4th ed.). Upper Saddle River, NJ: Pearson.

Bandura, A. (1977). *Social learning theory.* Upper Saddle River, NJ: Prentice Hall.

Behring, S. T., Cabello, B., Kushida, D., & Murguia, A. (2000). Cultural modifications to current school-based consultation approaches reported by culturally diverse beginning consultants. *School Psychology Review, 29*(3), 354–367.

Bergan, J. R. (1977). *Behavioral consultation.* Columbus, OH: Charles E. Merrill.

Bergan, J. R., & Kratochwill, T. R. (1990). *Behavioral consultation and therapy.* New York: Plenum.

Bertalanffy, L. V. (1962). General systems theory: A review. *General Systems, 7*, 1–20.

Brigman, G., Mullis, F., Webb, L., & White, J. (2005). *School counselor consultation: Skills for working effectively with parents, teachers, and other school personnel.* Hoboken, NJ: John Wiley and Sons.

Bronfenbrenner, U. (1979). *The ecology of human development.* Cambridge, MA: Harvard University Press.

Brown, D., Pryzwansky, W. B., & Schulte, A. C. (2006). *Psychological consultation and collaboration* (6th ed.). Boston: Pearson.

Caplan, G. (1970). *The theory and practice of mental health consultation.* New York: Basic Books.

Caplan, G. (2004). Recent advances in mental health consultation and collaboration. In N. M. Lambert, I. Hylander, & J. H. Sandoval (Eds.), *Consultee-centered consultation: Improving the quality of professional services in schools and community organizations* (pp. 21–36). Mahwah, NJ: Erlbaum.

Caplan, G., & Caplan, R. B. (1999). *Mental health consultation and collaboration* (Rev. ed.). Prospect Heights, IL: Waveland.

Conoley, J. C., & Conoley, C. W. (1992). *School consultation: A guide to practice and training* (2nd ed.). Upper Saddle River, NJ: Merrill: Prentice Hall.

DeLa Cruz, K., Salzman, M., Brislin, R., & Losch, N. (2006). Hawaiian attributional perspectives on intercultural interactions in institutions of higher education: Development of an intercultural sensitizer. *International Journal of Intercultural Relations, 30*(1), 119–140.

DeVoss, J. A., & Andrews, M. F. (2006). *School counselors as educational leaders.* Boston: Houghton Mifflin.

Dreikurs, R., Grunwald, B. B., & Pepper, F. C. (1998). *Maintaining sanity in the classroom* (3rd ed.). Washington, DC: Accelerated Development.

Education Trust. (2002). *National school counselor training initiative.* Jacksonville, FL: Author.

Elizalde-Utnick, G. (2002). Best practices in building partnerships with families. In A. Thomas & J. Grimes (Eds.), *Best practices in school psychology* (Vol. 1, pp. 413–429). Bethesda, MD: National Association of School Psychologists.

Erchul, W. P., & Martens, B. (2002). *School consultation: Conceptual and empirical bases of practice* (2nd ed.). New York: Kluwer Academic Plenum.

Erford, B. T. (2003). *Transforming the school counseling profession.* Upper Saddle River, NJ: Pearson.

Friend, M., & Cook, L. (2003). *Interactions: Collaboration skills for school professionals* (4th ed.). Boston: Allyn and Bacon.

Gelso, C. J., & Fretz, B. R. (2001). *Counseling psychology* (2nd ed.). Fort Worth, TX: Harcourt Brace.

Giannoti, T. J., & Doyle, R. E. (1982). The effectiveness of parental training on learning disabled children and their parents. *Elementary School Guidance and Counseling, 17*, 131–136.

Gladding, S. T. (2006). *The counseling dictionary: Concise definitions of frequently used terms.* Upper Saddle River, NJ: Pearson.

Gutkin, T.B., & Curtis, M.J. (1999). School-based consultation theory and practice: The art and science of indirect service delivery. In C. R. Reynolds & T. B. Gutkin (Eds.), *The handbook of school psychology* (3rd ed., pp. 598–637). New York: Wiley.

Hackney, H., & Cormier, S. (2005). *The professional counselor: A process guide to helping.* Boston: Pearson.

Harrison, T. C. (2004). *Consultation for contemporary helping professionals.* Boston: Pearson.

Hoy, W.K., & Hannnum, J.W. (1997). Middle school climate: An empirical assessment of organizational health and student achievement. *Educational Administrative Quarterly, 33*, 290–311.

Idol, L., Paolucci-Whitcomb, P., & Nevin, A. (1986). *Collaborative consultation.* Rockville, MD: Aspen.

Kampwirth, T. J. (2006). *Collaborative consultation in the schools: Effective practices for students with learning and behavior problems.* Upper Saddle River, NJ: Pearson.

Katz, D., & Kahn, R. L. (1978). *The social psychology of organizations.* New York: Wiley.

Kozol, J. (1992). *Savage inequalities: Children in America's schools.* NY: HarperCollins.

Kratochwill, T. R., Elliot, S. N., & Callan-Stoiber, K. (2002). Best practices in school-based problem solving consultation. In A. Thomas & J. Grimes (Eds.), *Best practices in school psychology* (Vol. 1, pp. 583–608). Bethesda, MD: National Association of School Psychologists.

Kuperminc, G. P., Leadbeater, B. S., Emmons, C., & Blatt, S. J. (1997). Perceived school climate and difficulties in social adjustment of middle school students. *Applied Developmental Science, 1*(2), 76–88.

Lehr, C. A., & Christenson, S. L. (2002). Best practices in promoting a positive school climate. In A. Thomas & J. Grimes (Eds.), *Best practices in school psychology* (Vol. 1, pp. 929–947). Bethesda, MD: National Association of School Psychologists.

Lewin, K. (1951). *Field theory in the social sciences.* New York: Harper and Row.

Medway, F. H., & Updyke, J. F. (1985). Meta-analysis of consultation outcome studies. *American Journal of Community Psychology, 13*, 489–505.

Meichenbaum, R. (1977). *Cognitive behavior modification.* New York: Plenum.

Nugent, F. A., & Jones, K. D. (2005). *Introduction to the profession of school counseling* (4th ed.). Upper Saddle River, NJ: Pearson.

Pearsall, J., & Trumble, B. (Eds.). (1995). *The Oxford encyclopedic English dictionary* (2nd ed.). New York: Oxford University Press.

Porter, G., Epp, L., & Bryant, S. (2000). Collaboration among school mental health professionals: A necessity, not a luxury. *Professional School Counseling, 3,* 315–322.

Pryswansky, W. P. (1977). Collaboration or consultation: Is there a difference? *Journal of Special Education, 11,* 179–182.

Reyes, O., & Jason, L. A. (1993). Collaborating with the community. In J. E. Zins, T. R. Kratochwill, & S. E. Elliot (Eds.), *Handbook of consultation services for children* (pp. 224–242). San Francisco: Jossey-Bass.

Ridley, C. R., Li, L. C., & Hill, C. L. (1998). Multicultural assessment: Reexamination, reconceptualization, and practical application. *The Counseling Psychologist, 26*(6), 827–910.

Rumsberger, R. W. (1995) Dropping out of middle school: A multilevel analysis of students and schools. *American Educational Research Journal, 107,* 1–35.

Salzman, M. (2001). Cultural trauma and recovery: Perspectives from terror management theory. *Trauma, Violence & Abuse: A Review Journal, 2*(2), 172–191.

Salzman, M. (2002). A culturally congruent consultation at a Bureau of Indian Affairs boarding school. *Journal of Individual Psychology 58*(2), 132–147.

Salzman, M. (2005). Contextualizing the symptom in multicultural consulation: Anger in the family a cultural-historical context. *Journal of Educational and Psychological Consultation, 16*(3), 223–237.

Schloss, P., & Smith, M. (1998). *Applied behavioral analysis.* Boston: Allyn & Bacon.

Schmidt, J. J. (1999). *Counseling in the schools: Essential services and comprehensive programs* (3rd ed.). Needham Heights, MA: Allyn & Bacon.

Schulte, A. C., & Osborne, S. (2003). Why assumptive worlds collide: A review of definitions of collaboration and consultation. *Journal of Educational and Psychological Consultation, 14*(2), 109–138.

Sheridan, S. M., Napolitano, S. A., & Swearer, S. M. (2002). Best practices in school-community partnerships. In A. Thomas & J. Grimes (Eds.), *Best practices in school psychology* (Vol. 1, pp. 321–336). Bethesda, MD: National Association of School Psychologists.

Sheridan, S. M., Welch, M., & Orme, S. F. (1996) Is consultation effective? A review of outcome research. *Remedial and Special Education, 17,* 341–354.

Skinner, B. F. (1969). *Contingencies of reinforcement.* Upper Saddle River, NJ: Prentice Hall.

Wilkinson, L. (2003). Using behavioral consultation to reduce challenging behavior in the classroom. *Preventing school failure, 47*(3), 100–105.

Williams, R. E., Omizo, M. M., & Abrams, B. C. (1984). Effects of STEP on parental attitudes and locus of control of their learning disabled children. *School Counselor, 31,* 126–133.

Zins, J. E., & Erchul, W. P. (2002). Best practices in school consultation. In A. Thomas & J. Grimes (Eds.), *Best practices in school psychology* (Vol. 1, pp. 625–643). Bethesda, MD: National Association of School Psychologists.

XXXII
CAREER DEVELOPMENT INTERVENTIONS IN SCHOOLS

WEI-CHENG J. MAU
Wichita State University

Introduction

Historical Perspectives of Career Development in School Settings

Systematic vocational guidance in America can be traced back to the late 19th and early 20th centuries when social reformers saw the need of helping dislocated workers who flocked into urban cities because of the Industrial Revolution. Frank Parsons was one of the many persons who were striving to make the world a better place in which to live. His book, *Choosing a Vocation* (Parsons, 1909), and his tripartite model of vocational guidance have significantly impacted the theories and practice of vocational guidance for centuries. In his view, vocational guidance consisted of three steps: (a) develop a clear understanding of self, (b) develop knowledge of the requirements and conditions of work, and (c) use *true reasoning* relating these two groups of knowledge.

During the early 20th century, several forerunners had advocated the involvement of career guidance in school settings. Jessie D. Davis (1914), for example, was able to implement the tripartite steps — self-study, occupational study, and examination of self — in relation to students' chosen occupations throughout the 7th through 12th grades, while he was the principal of Central High School in Detroit. Anna Reed (1871–1946) established guidance services in the Seattle school system, and by 1910, 35 cities had plans to establish vocational guidance in their schools (Aubrey, 1977).

During the last 30 years, career education has been influential in the evolution of career services (Herr & Cramer, 1996). It was introduced as a federal priority by the U.S. Commissioner of Education, Sidney Marland, on January 23, 1971.

Career education is the systematic attempt to influence the career development of students and adults through various types of educational strategies, which include providing occupation information, infusing career related concepts into the academic curriculum, promoting various worksite-based experiences, and offering career planning courses (Isaacson & Brown, 2000). Since its introduction, there have been numerous attempts to translate the ideas into action, with funding from private and public sectors. Meta-analyses on the effects of career education intervention have suggested that career education has moderate effects (Baker & Taylor, 1998). Although the term *career education* is being used less frequently, the concepts it connotes continue to be viable and supported by a variety of federal and state programs (Hoyt & Shylo, 1989). Given the continuing need to help children and adolescents prepare for the transition from school to work, the career education goal that was first presented about three decades ago still seems to be salient.

By the late 1960s and early 1970s, the term *career guidance* began to appear in the literature as interchangeable with vocational guidance. The redefinitions and paradigm shifts associated with the emerging term *career guidance* were creating new metaphors. Career guidance was being termed a lifestyle concept that embodied the need to combine work and leisure counseling (McDaniels, 1978). Super's theory (1957) led to a paradigm shift within the career development field. In contrast to the Trait-and-Factor approach, which focuses on matching individuals with comparable occupations at a single point in time, Super's career development approach emphasized a lifelong development of interests, abilities, values, work, and leisure activities. Super's career development concept is especially helpful for school-aged students in understanding the stage-specific needs of these students and predicting their future behaviors. As definitions of career and career development have evolved and become broader and more encompassing, particularly during the past 20 years, there has been a corresponding broadening and expansion of career guidance programs and services to children and young people in our schools.

Recent Development

Moving into the 21st century, we are faced with many different career developmental concerns in the school setting: increases in school population, increases in diversity of student population, and increases in emphasis on school to work (V. S. Solberg, Howard, Blustein, & Close, 2002). In responding to this demand, it is important that counselors have a clear understanding of the career development needs diverse student populations have and effective career interventions that are developmentally appropriate.

Career development is a lifelong process that starts the minute a child is born (Super, 1990). Perhaps the most critical point in a child's career development is when he or she is still in school, is active in learning, and is in a learning environment that provides a preventive/developmental approach. Research has shown that students are more likely to stay in school and engaged in learning when they see the relevance of their course work to career work (Lapan, Gysbers, & Petroski, 2001). For children and adolescents, their school and leisure activities represent their work. These activities provide essential learning experiences that shape self-perception and understanding of the world of work (Niles & Harris-Bowlsbey, 2005). Career counseling and education are critical components in a comprehensive counseling program in school settings. School counselors play a key role in facilitating the career development of students. Herr (1992) asserted that schooling, human development, and economic development are now linked in this nation in an irreversible fashion. Thus, connecting students' learning in school with the world of work is more important than ever. Students must demonstrate not only basic skills in reading, writing, and performing arithmetic and mathematical operations, but also demonstrate higher order thinking skills in making decisions and solving problems, as well as effectively applying personal qualities in self-management (U.S. Department of Labor, 1991). If our schools fail to graduate students with these skills, graduates will not be able to compete in the global marketplace.

School Counseling Standards

Increasingly, counseling practitioners are required to be accountable for the effectiveness of the services they provide. It is critical that school counselors be knowledgeable about the types of career interventions that have been proven effective. Another trend in school counseling is the utilization of standards-based, developmentally appropriate counseling approaches. The American School Counselor Association (ASCA) has established standards for career development of school-aged students. The standards related to career development are as follows:

- Standard A. Students will acquire the skills to investigate the world of work in relation to knowledge of self and to make informed career decisions.
- Standard B. Students will employ strategies to achieve future career success and satisfaction.
- Standard C. Students will understand the relationship among personal qualities, education and training, and the world of work.

The National Career Development Guidelines (National Occupational Information Coordination Committee [NOICC], 1992) described the personal competencies individuals should have in order to successfully manage their careers throughout their lives. The Guidelines, released in 1989, represented consensus among the government and leading career counseling organizations as to what is necessary to foster excellence in career development. The framework outlined the organizational and personnel requirements necessary for effective comprehensive career development, as well as the specific competencies that career development programs should be instilling. The Department of Education has recently revised the National Career Development Guidelines in order to bring them into alignment with the goals of the *No Child Left Behind* legislation.

National Career Development Guidelines

The newly revised guidelines consist of three domains: (a) Personal Social Development (PS), (b) Educational Achievement and Lifelong Learning (ED), and (c) Career Management (CM). The three domains organize content that is further described by 11 goals. The goals define broad areas of career development competency as shown here.

Personal Social Development Domain

- GOAL PS1 Develop understanding of self to build and maintain a positive self-concept.
- GOAL PS2 Develop positive interpersonal skills including respect for diversity.
- GOAL PS3 Integrate growth and change into career development.
- GOAL PS4 Balance personal, leisure, community, learner, family, and work roles.

Educational Achievement and Lifelong Learning Domain

- GOAL ED1 Attain educational achievement and performance levels needed to reach personal and career goals.
- GOAL ED2 Participate in ongoing, lifelong learning experiences to enhance ability to function effectively in a diverse and changing economy.

Career Management Domain

- GOAL CM1 Create and manage a career plan that meets your career goals.
- GOAL CM2 Use a process of decision making as one component of career development.
- GOAL CM3 Use accurate, current, and unbiased career information during career planning and management.
- GOAL CM4 Master academic, occupational, and general employability skills in order to obtain, create, maintain, and/or advance employment.
- GOAL CM5 Integrate changing employment trends, societal needs, and economic conditions into career plans.

In the standards-focused climate of today's schools, school counselors take a leadership role when they help administrators, teachers, parents, and others recognize the link between career development, academic development, and personal/social development of students. Professional school counselors play a critical role in the career development of school-aged students. Although some schools use professionals such as social workers to perform counseling interventions, professional school counselors are often the only professionals with specific training in career development (Niles & Akos, 2003). Professional school counselors possess knowledge of career development theory and skills of program development and implementation, which allows them to take a leadership role in the standards-focused climate in today's schools.

Collaboration with other school professionals is critical in implementing a career intervention program. Although ASCA has suggested an ideal counselor–student ratio as 1:250, many counselors work with a larger counselor–student ratio. One counselor cannot accomplish all the goals and objectives necessary for a successful career intervention program. Therefore, incorporating teachers, students, parents, and community participants becomes inevitable.

The Career Development Research Team of the National Research Center for Career and Technical Education established a comprehensive list of career intervention programs that occur in secondary schools and created a taxonomy of the identified interventions (Dykeman et al., 2001). The creation of the taxonomy (see Table 32.1) helps to standardize the career guidance in terms of both content and structure; it provides school counselors with a parsimonious framework to judge where their school's career guidance efforts are underdeveloped. The career intervention taxonomy as described by Dykeman et al. can be classified into four major taxons:

Taxon 1: Work-Based Interventions
Work-based interventions are those activities that promote career development through providing students with meaningful interactions at a job site(s).

Taxon 2: Advising Interventions
Career advising interventions are designed to provide direction and help students plan for both the present and the future. The majority of advising takes place in late middle school through high school. It is usually done on a more individual basis, tailored fit to the specific student's strengths.

Taxon 3: Introductory Interventions
Introductory interventions have the purpose of awakening a student's interests for both personal and professional growth. This intervention is generally short in duration and is a "snapshot" of experiences and/or information. These usually prepare students for a follow-up of information that has more depth. Introductory interventions are tied closely with curriculum-based interventions, with the main differences being in the amount of time and detail.

Taxon 4: Curriculum-Based Interventions
Curriculum interventions are designed to aid students in learning academic knowledge and career skills that are relevant to the work world. They are generally longer in duration and encompass a large variety of presentation avenues. This taxon can be transferred through a variety of people; for example, school counselors, classroom teachers, presenters, and community members.

The following sections review research related to career development of school-aged populations and career interventions. The career developmental needs, counselor's role, and effective career intervention are each described at elementary, middle, high school, and college levels.

Table 32.1 A Taxonomy of Career Development Interventions

Work-Based Interventions

Cooperative Education
Internship
Job Shadowing
Job Coaching
Job Placement Mentorship Programs
Service Learning/Volunteer Programs
Work-Based Learning Project
Work Study
Youth Apprenticeships

Advising Interventions

Academic Planning Counseling
Career Focused Parent/Student Conference
Career Peer Advising/Tutoring
Career Map
Career Maturity Assessment Career Counseling
Career Interests Assessment
Career Library/Career Resource Center
Career Cluster/Pathway/Major
Career Passport/Skill Certificate
College Admissions Testing
Computer-Assisted Career Guidance
Cooperative/Dual Enrollment
Information Interviewing
Job-Hunting Preparation
Personal/Social Counseling
Portfolio/Individual Career Plan
Recruiting
Referral to External Training Programs
Referral to External Counseling/Assessment

Introductory Interventions

Career Day/Career Fair
Career Field Trip
Career Aptitude Assessment
Community Members Speak in Classroom
Guidance Lessons on Personal/Social Development
Guidance Lessons on Career Development
Guidance Lessons on Academic Planning

Continued

Table 32.1 (Continued)

Curriculum-Based Interventions

Career Information Infused into Curriculum
Career/Technical Education Course
Career Skills Infused into Curriculum
Career Academy/Career Magnet
School School-Based Enterprise
Student Clubs/Activities
Tech Prep/2+2 Curriculum

Source: The National Research Center for Career and Technical Education (Dykeman et al., 2001).

Career Development in School Settings

Elementary School

The specific career development competencies identified as appropriate for elementary school children are

- Self-knowledge
  - Describe positive characteristics about self
  - Demonstrate skill in resolving conflicts
  - Identify ways to express and deal with feelings
- Educational and occupational exploration
  - Awareness of the benefits of educational achievement
  - Awareness of the relationship between work and learning
  - Skills to understand and use career information
  - Awareness of the importance of personal responsibility and good work habits
  - Awareness of how work relates to the needs and functions of society
- Career planning
  - Understanding how to make decisions
  - Awareness of interrelationship of life roles
  - Awareness of different occupations and changing male/female roles
  - Awareness of the career planning process

Characteristics and Developmental Needs. According to Super (1990), elementary school children are typically at the *growth* stage of their career development, which is characterized by fantasy, formation of career interests, and capacity. Gottfredson (1981) described this stage as one in which children begin to develop a sense of sex role (ages 6–8) and become aware of social class in the work world (ages 9–13). Children of elementary school age are perhaps the most moldable because they are generalists in the sense that they are typically open to a broad range of stimuli and learning modes (Herr, Cramer, & Niles, 2004). Yet, they are also vulnerable to any inaccurate, stereotyped, and distorted information to which they are exposed. The sexual stereotyping of occupations begins at a young age. For example, Pierce (1993) investigated fiction in teen magazines and concluded that girls are portrayed as dependent rather than independent and that occupations are typically segregated by gender. Using qualitative research methods to study elementary school children, Adler, Kless, and Adler (1992) concluded that boys achieve popularity based on their toughness and athletic abilities, whereas girls achieved high status based on their physical appearance, social skills, and academic success.

Gender and Racial/Ethnic Differences. Gender differences in perception of occupations are well documented. Many studies concern children's gender-stereotyped beliefs and knowledge about occupations, often reporting a high degree of sex-typing along traditional occupational gender lines (McMahon & Patton, 1997; Trice, 2000). Children develop a belief that certain occupations are not appropriate for them because of their gender. Boys generally perceive more opportunities in the world of work than girls do. At the same time, boys tend to have more rigid sex-based preferences than girls do (Awender & Wearne, 1990).

Racial stereotyping could also play a profound role in children's career development. Restricted choice is a phenomenon seen in the career choices of minority students. For example, it is well known that African Americans are underrepresented in enterprising and investigative types of occupations and overrepresented in realistic and social types of occupations as measured by Holland's (1997) RIASEC typology. Asian Americans, on the other hand, are constricted to science and engineering types of occupational choice. In a study conducted by Leong and Hayes (1990), for example, male Asian Americans were seen as successful engineers, computer scientists, and mathematicians, but not as successful insurance salespersons.

Students in this stage could easily and prematurely constrict their career choices based on perceived prestige or sex-type factors. Research has indicated a widening gap in occupational aspirations across race, sex, and socioeconomic status with advancing age, suggesting that as children age, they become more aware of career barriers in relation to their sex, race, and socioeconomic status (Hartung, Porfeli, & Vondracek, 2005).

Elementary school years set the tone for developing the skills, knowledge, and attitudes necessary for our children to become successful and productive adults. It is critical that children at this stage be exposed to a wider variety and range of options in activities, hobbies, interests, roles, and behaviors. They need to experience sex-fair education, counseling, and curriculum at school (Sundal-Hansen, 1984).

Counselors' Roles. Counselors play a critical role in young pupils' lives. Historically, elementary school counselors have been defined by the three C's: Counseling, Coordinating, and Consulting. How much each of these is used depends on the needs and resources that characterize a local setting. The American School Counselor Association described the role of elementary school counselor as one who will

- Implement effective classroom guidance focusing on understanding of self and others; coping strategies, peer relationships, and effective social skills; communication, problem solving, decision making, conflict resolution, and study skills; career awareness and the world of work; substance education and multicultural awareness.
- Provide individual and small group counseling dealing with self-image, self-esteem, personal adjustment, family issues, interpersonal concerns, academic development, and behavior modification.
- Provide assessment by helping students identify their skills, abilities, achievements, and interests through counseling guidance activities and interpretation of standardized tests.
- Develop students' career awareness as a lifelong process of forming basic values, attitudes, and interests regarding their future world of work.
- Coordinate school, community, and business resources, schoolwide guidance-related activities, and extracurricular programs that promote students' personal growth and skill development. (Campbell & Dahir, 1997, p. 69)

Classroom guidance activities. Classroom guidance activities are very common counseling activities in the elementary school setting. School counselors use classroom guidance activities to facilitate career development of young children. For example, Beale (2003) described an innovative classroom guidance activity through which he helped third and fourth graders learn about the importance of teamwork and conflict resolution in a workplace. Herr and colleagues (2004) suggested several classroom guidance activities that may be useful for elementary school students:

- Select a career cluster requiring competence in a particular subject matter, such as math, science, or language and identify occupations related to it.
- Do oral reports on different occupations with the student pretending to be a worker in the report.

- Use ingredients of emotional intelligence as the focus of discussion with students.
- Have students prepare autobiographies and address at least three ways in which their lives are influenced by family, school, and peers.
- Build interest centers around different career clusters or ways to assess self-characteristics.
- Provide listening centers that include individual earphones, recording devices, CD-DVD, tapes, and cassettes dealing with worker interviews, study skills, and topics related to self-understanding.
- Provide reference books or biographies that portray personal decision making.
- Show guidance films on selected topics. (pp. 357–358)

Group activities. Other common counseling activities that are appropriate for elementary school children could be delivered through group activities. Herr and colleagues (2004) provided examples of group activities. Several are highlighted here:

- Using a supply of magazines, have students locate pictures that break down traditional male–female occupational role stereotyping (e.g., male nurse, female physician, male secretary, female truck driver). Discuss.
- Have students keep a log of all examples of occupational stereotyping that they discover while watching TV.
- In a role playing situation, have students break into pairs and role-play an employer who is interviewing an applicant for a job. The interviewer wants to know why the person wants the job—besides the money.
- Invite resource persons to discuss how personal characteristics contribute to daily functioning or ask them to discuss their vocational history in relation to what they now do.
- Develop and organize lists of resource speakers and field trips to observe the workers' roles in various occupations.
- Have students design games to play about different approaches to decision making, career options, or other life situations.
- Have students design creative drama skits that deal with self-concept, values, making choices, and other pertinent topics.
- Using pictures of people at work, have students distinguish between those involving the production of goods and those in the performance of services.
- Have students match pictures of tools and what they are used for. Discuss the use of tools for different purposes in school and in work. (pp. 358–360)

Research. Empirical studies on children's career development are sparse. Although counselors seek to advance students' career development across all grade levels, relatively few career development activities are offered in elementary school settings. Researchers pay less attention to the career development of young children, even though research suggests that tentative career aspiration and college plans begin emerging in elementary school (Trice & King, 1991). Infusion of career development into curriculum has been proven effective in the elementary school setting. For example, in an empirical study, McMahon, Gillies, and Carroll (2000) investigated the effect of career education on elementary students' perceptions of the relationship between school and occupations. Findings clearly suggested that students were able to link school-based learning with jobs that they were interested in pursuing.

Middle School

Characteristics and Developmental Needs. According to Super (1990), middle school students are in the beginning stages of *exploration*. While some preteens begin to form tentative career choices, typical students are not ready to commit to career choices. This age period is also described by Gottfredson (1981) as a period of orientation to the internal, unique self and specification of career aspirations. Developmentally, middle school students begin cognitive and moral processing, and many school activities play a role in shaping their identity development. For example, ability becomes an important determination of group membership, and career aspirations are tested in novel experiences such as extracurricular activities and part-time jobs (Herr et al., 2004). These identity formation processes in middle school ideally include increased exploration in relation to career development (Akos, Konold, & Niles, 2004). The needs of middle school students are well defined by NOICC:

- Self-knowledge
  - Knowledge of influence of a positive self-concept
  - Skills to interact with others
  - Knowledge of the importance of growth and change
- Educational and occupational exploration
  - Knowledge of benefits of educational achievement to career opportunities
  - Understanding of the relationship between work and learning
  - Skills to locate, understand, and use career information
  - Knowledge of skills necessary to seek and obtain jobs

- Understanding of how work relates to the needs and functions of the economy and society
- Career planning
  - Skills to make decisions
  - Knowledge of interrelationships of life roles
  - Knowledge of different occupations and changing male/female roles
  - Understanding of the process of career planning

The primary focus of career development during middle school is on exploration. Students need to explore by learning more about self—their interests, skills, and values. Career development tasks for students in middle school should also continue the task of developing students' self-awareness, which began in elementary school.

Guidance activities directed at junior high school students had the largest effect sizes, indicating that guidance efforts may be most effective with preteen aged (rather than high school or college) students (Oliver & Spokane, 1988). Career interventions that assist students with the assessment of their personal aptitudes, abilities, and interests are especially helpful.

Middle school students also need to explore the world of work. Hartung et al. (2005) reviewed literature on child vocational development and concluded that preteens explore the world of work much earlier than theorists and researchers have typically assumed. Teaching students how to locate educational and career information and how to interpret and use it could pave the way for the development of subsequent career tasks.

Counselor's Roles and Career Interventions. To help guide students in their exploration, counselors can administer career assessments. Career decision making is a complex process by which the decision makers are required to process information about themselves and information about the world of work (Jepsen, 1984). Information about self including interests, skills, and values is particularly useful for career exploration purposes and can be assessed formally and informally. Counselors can use individual counseling, group activities, or classroom guidance activities to help students better understand themselves. For example, the counselor could help students identify "transferable skills" in a group activity. Students could complete a worksheet containing a list of transferable skills. They then could identify situations in which skills are used in school and also situations when skills could be used in a career.

Counselors could also conduct a formal assessment using interest inventories. For example, the Career Decision-Making System developed by Harrington and O'Shea (1992) has color-coded interest clusters that are especially user-friendly for middle school students.

Another effective approach could be to use career portfolios as a counseling intervention for the middle school students. Portfolios are a way of assessing the skills students have mastered and the progress students have made toward educational and vocational planning. Counselors could then review a portfolio with students to help them evaluate where they were, where they are now, and where they want to be. An example of a portfolio is shown in Figure 32.1.

Research. Research has suggested that middle school students, in general, are lacking understanding of how school relates to the real world (Schultheiss, Palma, & Manzi, 2005). They are also lacking awareness of the knowledge and skills needed for success in the work world (Akos et al., 2004; Johnson, 2000). Many young adolescents have sex-stereotyped views of occupations and often have already limited their aspirations (McDonald & Jessell, 1992). They have difficulty seeing a connection between what they learn in school and future careers, and they often lack guidance in selecting courses that lay the groundwork for their high school and post–high school plans.

Connecting students' learning in school with the world of work is important especially for middle school students. Career counseling and education are critical components in a comprehensive counseling program in school settings. Research has shown students are more likely to stay in school and engaged in learning when they see the relevance of their course work (Lapan et al., 2001). This research examined the relationships between statewide implementation of comprehensive guidance programs and indicators of safety and success for seventh graders. After accounting for differences between schools due to socioeconomic status and enrollment size, students attending middle schools with more fully implemented comprehensive programs reported believing that their education was more relevant and important for their futures.

Using a nationally representative sample, Mau (2003) investigated persistence of career aspirations in science and engineering professional careers (SE) as a function of race and gender. A nationally representative sample of eighth graders who initially aspired to science and engineering careers and persisted for six years in the same career aspirations were identified. Results showed that males are more likely than females to persist in SE career aspirations. Academic proficiency and math self-efficacy were among the strongest predictors of persistence in SE careers. Seymour (1995) argued that females may be concerned that by being accepted by their male peers, they may lose their "femininity." They may also have to deal with discrimination and hostility from some faculty and male students (Stafford, 1991). For adolescent women, the

My Career Portfolio
(Grades 7–9)

NAME _____ TELEPHONE NUMBER _____

ADDRESS _____ SOCIAL SECURITY NUMBER _____

_____ BIRTHDATE _____

CONTENTS
Include the following kinds of documents in this folder:

- ☐ SAMPLE RESUME
- ☐ TRANSCRIPT OF GRADES
- ☐ LIST OF REFERENCES
- ☐ COPP MATERIALS
- ☐ MY CAREER PLANNER
- ☐ CAREER INTEREST SEARCHES
- ☐ CAREER INFORMATION MATERIAL

CONTENTS
Include the following kinds of documents in this folder:

- ☐ STANDARDIZED TEST SCORES
- ☐ EMPLOYMENT CREDENTIALS
- ☐ SKILL COMPETENCIES EARNED IN VOCATIONAL CLASSES
- ☐ LETTERS OF RECOMMENDATION
- ☐ COPIES OF COMPETENCY EXAM RESULTS
- ☐ SOCIAL AWARDS
- ☐ OTHER _____

9th GRADE

Interests/Activities → Strengths/Abilities → Awards/Certifications → Volunteer/Community Service

What do I need to reach this goal?

Short-term plan _____

Long-term plan _____

← Goals ← Career Options ← Work Experiences

pressures of trying to balance current and future gender relations in an environment that challenges conventional norms for women creates additional tensions and contradictions (McKinnon & Ahola-Sidaway, 1995). Other factors, such as lower teacher expectations (Anderson, 1992) and lack of role models (Dryler, 1998; Nauta & Kokaly, 2001) may also explain the loss of women in the pipeline. Career interventions that expose students to female role models in engineering and science may inspire students to pursue SE careers. It would appear that programs designed to encourage adolescent women to enroll in SE-related courses need to be sensitive to the intimidation and subtle pressures they may face. Bright young women and underrepresented minorities simply cannot be recruited into the SE pipeline without continued support and encouragement. Informal support groups may be helpful in addressing problems that young women and ethnic minority students enrolled in nontraditional programs or course work may face. Efforts to strengthen support systems and lessen barriers may better enable students to persist toward their career goals (R. W. Lent & Brown, 1996).

Given the importance of self-efficacy, interventions developed to build confidence and increase self-understanding of minority and female students are crucial. Betz (1992) suggested the following interventions to increase efficacy expectations: structuring performance accomplishments, observational learning, anxiety management, and verbal persuasion and encouragement. Given the unique contribution of gender and race factors in predicting SE persistence, counselors need to take a proactive approach in tailoring developmentally appropriate and culturally sensitive career interventions for individuals from diverse cultural backgrounds (Mau, 2003).

These findings suggest that middle school students need to learn to think about the future; recognize their responsibility for educational planning; broaden their aspirations beyond the stereotypes of gender, ethnicity, and socioeconomic level; develop and maintain self-esteem; develop cognitive complexity (essential for the knowledge work of the future); have parental support for career choices; understand how school relates to future life roles; and recognize the broad scope of work in the 21st century.

High School

Characteristics and Needs. As students transition to high school, they focus more directly on the task of identifying occupational preferences and clarifying career choices. High school students are developmentally characterized by Super (1990) as being in the exploration stage of their career development. The tasks of crystallizing, specifying, and implementing tentative career choices occur during this stage. Many individuals during this stage crystallize their daydreams into a publicly recognized vocational identity. Through more focused effort, they eventually complete the task of specifying an occupational choice by translating privately experienced occupational self-concept into educational/vocational choices (Super, Savickas, & Super, 1996). The needs of high school students are well defined by NOICC (1992):

- Self-knowledge
  - Understanding of the influence of positive self-concept
  - Skills to interact positively with others
  - Understanding of the impact of growth and development
- Educational and occupational exploration
  - Understanding of the relationship between educational achievement and career planning
  - Understanding of the need for positive attitudes toward work and learning
  - Skills to locate, evaluate, and interpret career information
  - Skills to prepare to seek, obtain, maintain, and change jobs
  - Understanding of how societal needs and functions influence the nature and structure of work
- Career planning
  - Skills to make decisions
  - Understanding of the interrelationship of life roles
  - Understanding of the continuous changes in male and female roles
  - Skills in career planning

Counselors' Roles and Career Interventions. The immediate concern of high school students upon graduation is whether to participate in the work force or go to college. They must decide earlier in school whether to take a vocational track, a college preparatory track, or pursue other options such as an apprenticeship training program. Students need to be aware of the array of postsecondary school options—college, other postsecondary education, work, nonwork, military, or government service. Counselors could help students examine the advantages and disadvantages of each option, including those occupations that do not require a college degree. Many good jobs do not require a college degree. However, the labor market continues to drastically increase its skill demands, especially in the technology domain, and college graduates also generally have earning advantages (Niles & Harris-Bowlsbey, 2005). Thus, helping students developing a long-term goal to achieve some form of college degree becomes essential.

A recent National Center for Educational Statistics (NCES) report (Parsad, Alexander, Farris, & Hudson, 2003) on high school guidance counseling indicated that when asked about the activities that take up more than 20% of guidance staff's time, the most often cited activity was assisting students in their choices and scheduling of high school courses. The second most commonly cited activity was postsecondary admissions and selections, and one third of the schools said that dealing with student attendance and discipline took up more than 20% of their guidance staff's time. While it appears that high school counselors are not spending much time directly engaged in assisting students with career planning, the NCES survey shows that guidance programs are generally equipped with tools students can use on their own. The vast majority of schools stock computerized and noncomputerized career information sources and college catalogues, as well as conduct testing for career planning.

Tracey, Robins, and Hofsess (2005) suggested that high school years are a time of focus for career interventions because students' career interests begin to stabilize. This study suggested that career development systematically increases with age during the high school years. The major component of career development involves discussing jobs with parents, talking with workers in certain jobs, attending job fairs, and taking tours of local businesses. The major career development emphasis in high school needs to be on the specific and comprehensive planning of immediate, intermediate, and future educational and vocational choices after high school (Herr et al., 2004). The examples of comprehensive sequential career intervention activities at the high school level differ from those at the elementary or middle school level. In many parts of the United States, large school districts have created a sequential program of career intervention that blends career guidance and career education. For example, South High School in USD 259 Wichita Public Schools, Kansas, created a career development program that is committed to allowing opportunities for self and career exploration, as well as the development of communication and workplace skills that will help students become productive and responsible citizens. The comprehensive program, aligned with National Career Development Guidelines and reviewed with National Standards for School Counseling Programs (American School Counselor Association, 2003), consists of (a) career portfolio (b) special career planning activities, (c) a career resource center, and (d) grade-level activities. Examples of grade level activities are

1. Freshmen—English 1
   - Goal Setting
     – Portfolio Insert Card
     – Writing Activity
   - Job Seeking and Keeping
     – Teamwork Activity
2. Sophomores—English 2
   - Goal Setting
   - Portfolio Insert Card
   - Interest Inventory—Harrington O'Shea CDM
   - Interests, Values, Perceived Strengths
   - Career Research Assignment
   - Internet Search
   - Use of Printed Resources
   - Sophomore Research Project
   - PowerPoint Presentation
3. Juniors—English 3 / U.S. History 2
   - Personality and Careers
     – Myers-Briggs Based Assessment
   - College/Scholarship Search
     – PowerPoint Presentation
   - Goal Setting
     – SMART Formula and Career Timeline
   - Problem-solving in the Workplace
     – Six-step Process
     – Teamwork Activity
4. Seniors—English
   - Goal Setting
     – Portfolio Insert Cards
   - Resumes and Interviewing
     – Use of Career Resource Center
     – Provide CD-Roms

Research. One major role of high school counselors is to advise students in class scheduling, college preparation, and post–high school selection of work or school. Advising can take many forms and functions and is often delivered in the form of individual or group guidance. Some forms of advising interventions include academic planning, career maps, interest assessments, interviewing information, career libraries or resource centers, college admissions testing, and job hunting guidance (Dykeman et al., 2001). Dykeman and his colleagues (2003) found through a student opinion poll that students who were advised and given directions for planning had increased motivation in mathematics. Peterson, Long, and Billops (1999) found that eighth graders who received assistance with course planning were more able to understand the importance of their class choices. Helping students set goals for the future may increase academic efforts and performance because students have more direction and motivation for their academic work.

Studies (e.g., Mau, Hitchcock, & Calvert, 1998) have shown that counselors are the last people from whom students seek help. They tend to seek help from their peers, parents, or teachers first. Counselors, therefore, could act as consultants, trainers, or program coordinators to involve parents, teachers, students, and community experts in career intervention programs. Formal programs can be developed to assist parents of minority students in communicating to teachers and counselors their academic expectations for their sons and daughters (Atkinson, Morten, & Sue, 1993). These programs also can be utilized by counselors to encourage parents to view educational choices in a realistic fashion, to help parents communicate these views to their children, and to help parents understand the curricular options and consequences of various academic choices (Commission on Precollege Guidance and Counseling, 1986).

Minority students are underrepresented in higher education. A national survey has indicated that Hispanic and African American high school students have lower college aspirations than White or Asian American high school students (Mau & Bikos, 2000). Programs that target minority students in exploring higher education options are especially appropriate. Findings based on a nationally representative high school student sample indicated that counseling services are not equally available to public school students (Lee & Ekstrom, 1987). Similarly, the final report of the Commission on Precollege Guidance and Counseling (1986) also indicated that many students have either little or no access to counselors at this critical time. As suggested by Lee and Ekstrom, counselors may be so busy with paperwork or other responsibilities that individual counseling and advising situations are rare. High student-to-counselor ratios also may limit the availability of counseling or advising services (Boyer, 1983). Students of minority background are less likely to access guidance counseling for making important educational and vocational decisions. Nevertheless, counselors need to be aware of cultural barriers that may inhibit minority students from seeking counseling help, such as feelings of shame (Mau & Jepsen, 1988), biased nature of the services (Sue & Sue, 2003) differences in coping strategies (Mau & Jepsen, 1990; Yeh & Inose, 2002), and differences in counseling expectancies (Altmaier & Rapaport, 1984). Considering, the high student-to-counselor ratios, computer-assisted career intervention systems may be implemented to ease the heavy workload of counselors. However, computer-based intervention shouldn't replace the counselor's work. Computer interventions with the counselor's follow up produce the most effective outcomes. Counselors need to be aware of the effective use of computer-assisted guidance systems (Sampson, 1994). Because students prefer to seek help from their peers, counselors may need to use approaches that are less threatening to students (Mau, 1995). Programs such as "Natural Helpers" (Comprehensive Health Education Foundation, 1997), which utilize informal or natural support systems, may be implemented.

Enhancing career self-efficacy of students is an important component of career interventions for high school students. A number of studies have investigated the effects of various interventions on career self-efficacy. O'Brien and her colleagues (2000) conducted a small-group career exploration and planning for Upward Bound students. Results indicated that students who received the career intervention exhibited significantly higher levels of career decision-making self-efficacy than did the students in the control group. McWhirter, Rasheed, and Crothers (2000) investigated the impact of a 9-week career education class on the career decision-making self-efficacy, vocational skill efficacy, and perceived educational barriers, outcome expectations, and educational plans among a sample of 166 high school students. Results suggested that students in the course as compared with students in the control group, showed increases in career decision-making self-efficacy and in vocational skill self-efficacy, and a short-term gain in outcome expectations.

College

Characteristics and Needs. Late adolescents and young adults are involved in multiple developmental challenges and transitions (Schultheiss, 2000). One of the most important career developmental tasks for young adults attending college is making a successful transition from school to work. For many college students, acquiring a satisfying career is the main reason for pursuing a college degree. National statistics have indicated that more than half of high school graduates attend some form of college and about 50% of students who enter colleges and universities graduate within six years (Gray & Herr, 2000). A Gallup survey sponsored by the National Career Development Association (NCDA) showed that 60% of college graduates would try to get more information about job and career options if they were starting over (NCDA, 1999). The survey also indicated that more ethnic minorities than Whites and more traditional (aged 18–25) than nontraditional students (aged 26 and over) reported a greater need for career assistance.

Herr and colleagues (2004) have identified segments of the college population that require special counseling support. Among these subpopulations, visible minorities include students such as physically challenged persons and ethnic minorities. Examples of less visible minority groups are students with gay, lesbian, and bisexual orientations. The needs of these subpopulations extend beyond "normal" boundaries because they may encounter internal barriers (e.g., low self-efficacy, financial difficulties) and external barriers such as prejudice and discrimination. Herr et al. also pointed out that international, adult/nontraditional, gifted, and liberal arts students also have unique concerns that require special attention.

This increased diversity suggests that career development interventions in colleges and universities must be comprehensive and planned systematically to meet the diverse needs of students today. The effectiveness of career counseling practices depends largely on the manner in which the unique needs of diverse populations are recognized and addressed. As with K–12, the National Career Development Guidelines (NOICC, 1992) also identified adult-level competencies:

- Self-knowledge
  - The skills to maintain a positive self-concept
  - The skills to maintain effective behaviors
  - Understanding of developmental changes and transitions
- Educational and occupational exploration
  - The skills to enter and participate in educational training
  - The skills to participate in work and lifelong learning
  - The skills to locate, evaluate, and interpret career information
  - The skills to prepare to seek, obtain, maintain, and change jobs
  - An understanding of how the needs and functions of society influence the nature and structure of work
- Career planning
  - The skills to make decisions
  - Understanding of the impact of work on individual and family life
  - Understanding of the continuing changes in male/female roles
  - The skills required to make career transitions

Counseling Intervention. The actual competency to be developed, the process, and the specific activities to be used will vary based on the nature and philosophy of the institution. There are several career intervention models for college students that can be used to address the competencies identified by NOICC. For example, Reardon (1996) described a comprehensive career intervention model used at Florida State University. The model is a curricular-based career information service model that consists of five modules. The focuses of this career service model are on providing students with an introduction to the service, helping students engage in self-assessment and locate career information, and helping students match majors and jobs. Isaacson and Brown (2000) suggested the following approach:

1. Outreach
   a. Career seminars in housing units
   b. Informal rap sessions in housing units to establish contact
   c. Activities designed for special groups (e.g., international students) delivered at their meeting
   d. Mentoring program using alumni or upper classmen
   e. Parental involvement such as career development seminars
2. Classroom instruction
   a. Required classes for credit
   b. Optional classes for credit
   c. Noncredit, short-term classes
   d. Employability skills training classes
   e. Unit in regular classes dealing with careers
3. Counseling
   a. Individual career counseling
   b. Group career counseling
   c. Employability groups
   d. Special programs for alumni such as group counseling activities
   e. Support groups for job hunters
4. Assessment
   a. Screening examinations given at entry to focus on career/decision making
   b. Ongoing assessment offered to students in counseling/career planning and placement center
   c. Assessment used as part of career counseling
   d. Computer-assisted services
   e. Self-direct assessment (e.g., self-directed search)
   f. Needs assessment
5. Information
   a. Orientation session/information
   b. Catalogs
   c. Advising information/careers
   d. Career information center
   e. Articles in student newspapers
   f. Computer-assisted systems
   g. Handouts that relate educational programs to career opportunities
   h. Alumni newsletters
6. Placement
   a. Regular job placement
   b. Job fairs to link employers and workers
7. Work experience
   a. Internship program
   b. Placement for part-time work
   c. Cooperative educational/work programs
   d. Work–study programs
8. Consultation
   a. With faculty advisors to make them aware of education–career connection; needs of certain students
   b. With residence hall assistants and directors to provide assistance

c. With instructors who wish to infuse more career information
   d. With club/social activities advisors to suggest career related activities
9. Referral
   a. To workers in the community for career information
   b. To mental health professionals to get assistance with personal problems blocking career related decisions.

Herr et al. (2004) suggested that career interventions should proceed in an orderly, systematic fashion to meet the unique needs of students at different points during college life. For example, during the freshman year, information concerning curriculum and career implications in different majors is especially helpful. For sophomores, assistance in exploration of an academic major is very much needed. For juniors, engagement in internships, cooperative education, or job search skill training is especially appropriate. During the senior year, assistance with access to world of work, resume writing, and mock interviewing to facilitate school-to-work transitions are critical.

Course-based career interventions. A career planning course is one of the most common programs offered in college and university settings. Folsom and Reardon (2003) documented the efficacy of course-based career interventions and reported the results of their examination of 46 studies of course-related outcomes published from 1976 to 2001. Their report indicated that a majority of these course-based interventions produced positive outcomes such as career decision-making skills, career decidedness, career maturity, persistence, retention, and satisfaction.

Savickas (1990) also designed and tested a career exploration course consisting of the following components: (a) become involved now, (b) explore your future, (c) choose based on how things look to you, (d) control your future, (e) work, a problem or opportunity, (f) view work positively, (g) conceptualize career choices, (h) clear up career choice misconceptions, (i) base your choice on yourself, and (j) four aspects of self as choice bases. He found students enrolled in this course were more oriented to a future time perspective. S. Solberg et al. (1998) used a curriculum-based college-age intervention called the Adaptive Success Identity Plan (ASIP). It measured the construct of success identity as the core guiding factor in college success. The study showed that students who received the ASIP curriculum were more likely to define their role in college around the success identity construct. Students were given a list of questions that were coded into four units of thought. After the ASIP interventions, students were more likely to broaden their "success vocabulary" from self-determination to words such as *self-efficacy, social integration, faculty integration,* and *outcome expectations.* This led to the conclusion that ASIP curriculum caused changes in student perceptions, and these results might generalize to other settings.

Robbins and Smith (1993) evaluated the effectiveness of an enhancement program for students entering college. The program is designed to help college students just entering school adjust quickly and smoothly. This class consisted of 10 weeks of curriculum including study skills, campus resources, visiting the career planning office, and instruction on how to have positive relationships with professors. After 10 weeks, results of the class were assessed. Robbins and Smith found that the class did broaden and quicken the students' knowledge base about college. Students felt more satisfied with their college experience after participating in the class. One negative knowledge point they found was a drop in student knowledge about a specific acquired field. This might mean the students had a lack of focused interest during their first college semester.

Computer-assisted career guidance system (CACGS). Most of the CACG systems are designed to assist individuals in learning about themselves (i.e., career assessment approach), or learning about the world of work, (i.e., career exploration approach). CACGS are often coupled with counseling interventions and various print and media-based support resources and are used within an organization to assist individuals in making current career decisions as well as to improve their capacity to make effective career decisions in the future. About 10.6% of college students reported that they had used one of the CACGS (Hoyt & Lester, 1995). College counselors and professional academic advisors have large client loads and heavy demands on their time. Therefore, students' requests for more personal assistance with academic planning may not be met by individual or group counseling, simply because the professionals do not have enough time or there are other students or other problems considered more pressing. CACG systems come in many forms. Studies in general have shown the CACGS to have a positive impact on career development of college students. For example, the CACGS has increased students' career self-efficacy and career decidedness (Fukuyama, Probert, Nevill, & Metzler, 1988), career decision commitment (Pinder & Fizgerald, 1984), and vocational identity and exploratory behavior (Mau, 1999).

Career fairs and internships. Career centers help college students better connect school to the community. Programs such as "Way with Words" help increase civic responsibility in students (Flores et al., 2002). The more college students connect with the community, the more efficient and prepared they will be to enter the workforce.

Deciding on a major field of study is one of the most important tasks for college students. Elliot (1988) described a program that helps students with choosing a college major. Undecided students along with faculty representatives of various academic programs were invited to attend an evening program in which students and faculty could interact about major areas of study. The program was well received by the participants.

Research. The perception of career related barriers and decision-making difficulties plays a significant role in the career development of women and ethnic minorities (W. L. Lent, Brown, & Hackett, 1994). Studies have shown that women and ethnic minorities perceived more career related barriers than did White Americans (Luzzo & McWhirter, 2001). In a cross-national study, Mau (2001) found that Taiwanese college students perceived more career decision-making difficulties than American college students. He also found that the clusters of difficulty had a different impact on career indecision depending on students' nationalities. Parallel to this study, Mau (2004) also compared the racial differences in career decision-making difficulties among college students. Results showed that Asian American students perceived significantly more difficulties in career decision making than other groups, whereas White American students perceived the fewest difficulties compared with other groups.

While minority students are more likely to experience decision-making difficulties, they do not always seek professional counseling help. A national survey on career services in postsecondary education has indicated that about 1 out of every 2 students has never used career counseling services (Mau & Fernandes, 2001), with Hispanic students the least likely to utilize career counseling services. Aggressive outreach efforts that target this group and that are tailored to increase utilization of services should be created. Counseling professionals need to take a proactive role in reaching this population. For example, Flores and Spanierman (1998) suggested that flyers be posted in the community at establishments that serve these targeted students. Providing information and/or making a presentation at a Hispanic American Student Association meeting may be more appropriate than waiting for students to seek counseling help at the center.

Consideration should be given to taking programs and services to locations where various subpopulations of students naturally congregate (Bishop, 1990). The ability to reach out effectively to minority students will be increasingly important, and service delivery systems must be adapted in order to accommodate such populations. Counseling professionals need to be more sensitive to potential barriers that may inhibit those who underutilize these services in seeking professional help. Needs assessments can be conducted to examine the unique concerns of this diverse population (Davidson, Heppner, & Johnston, 2001). The type of services provided through the career center should be appropriate to the needs of all students including the culturally diverse. When professionals acknowledge the unique factors of these students and their cultural beliefs, attitudes and types of career concerns, the students may be more likely to return for continued services.

Future Directions

Career interventions have generally been shown to have positive effects. Baker and Popowicz (1983) reported an overall effect size of .50 for career education studies, and Spokane and Oliver (1983) obtained an average effect size of .85 over all types of career interventions. Oliver and Spokane (1988) extended their meta-analyses and reported a similar overall effect size. They also reported effect size by age group with the middle school age having the biggest effect size (1.28), then, high school age (1.02), and college age having the smallest effect size (.85). In their meta-analyses, only one study involved the elementary school age population, which had an effect size of −.001. It is therefore not meaningful to evaluate the effectiveness of career intervention for this population based on one single study.

It is quite disturbing to find the lack of empirical studies investigating the effectiveness of career interventions with elementary school and middle school students. Whiston, Brecheisen, and Stephens (2003) documented that almost 50% of the studies conducted in the last 50 years involved college populations. There was only one experimental study on elementary-aged children conducted between 1983 and 1995 (Whiston, Sexton, & Lasoff, 1998).

Despite the importance of career developmental tasks as described by Super (1990), little systematic investigation has been conducted to confirm theoretical assumptions evident in children's models of life span career development. Research focusing on contributing conceptual knowledge of childhood career development is urgently needed to inform early career interventions and help children develop a meaningful understanding of the relevance of school-based learning to their future careers (Johnson, 2000).

Whereas college students received the most research attention, the effect size generated from those outcome studies appears to be smaller than other age groups. It is unclear if this is because college students face different types of career problems or they are less amenable than younger age groups. Further research may be able to clarify this issue.

Meta-analysis studies over the last 2 decades (e.g., Brown & Ryan Krane, 2000; Brown et al., 2003; Oliver & Spokane, 1988; Spokane & Oliver, 1983; Whiston et al., 1998) have continued to indicate that career interventions in general are effective. However, career interventions are not a homogeneous group producing a homogeneous effect. Previous meta-analyses have begun to analyze the effectiveness by treatment types, outcome measures, and participant's characteristics. Nevertheless, none of the meta-analysis studies have examined the treatment impact on racial/ethnic groups.

Unfortunately, most school-based studies do not have rigorous experimental control. It is extremely difficult to conduct experimental studies involving a control group in the school setting. However, school outcome researchers should consider the use of wait-list control groups that are commonly used in general counseling outcome research (Whiston et al., 1998). Research also needs to examine longitudinal effects of career interventions. Most of the studies are based on one-shot, short-term interventions. Results generated from these studies tend to be artificial and tentative. One pathway for future research involves responding to recent calls for research on life-span vocational development that uses truly longitudinal designs (Savickas, 2002). National databases sponsored by the Department of Education, such as the Early Childhood Longitudinal Study and the National Educational Longitudinal Study provide researchers with ample research topics examining the educational/vocational behaviors of school-aged students.

More recent meta-analyses (i.e., Brown & Ryan Krane, 2000; Brown et al., 2003) of career choice intervention literature have identified five critical ingredients involving any effective career intervention. The five critical ingredients are (a) workbooks and written exercises that require participants to write their goals and future plans; (b) individualized interpretations and feedback that provide participants individualized feedback regarding test results, goals, and future plans; (c) in-session occupational information explorations that provide opportunities to gather information on the world of work or specific career options; (d) modeling through counselor self-disclosure, guest speakers, and interaction with appropriate models; and (e) support-building that facilitates participants to gain support from their social network. Based on these findings, Brown et al. have made specific suggestions and hypotheses on how to improve career interventions.

Career counseling must take into consideration students' racial/ethnic backgrounds. A recent meta-analysis of race/ethnicity differences in career development suggested that significant differences exist among racial/ethnic groups in regard to the perception of career related opportunities and barriers (Fouad & Byars-Winston, 2005). It is important that a discussion of opportunities and barriers be incorporated into career interventions with minority students. Much of the existing research has been conducted with middle-class suburban youth, limiting the knowledge of more diverse groups in terms of socioeconomic status (Schultheiss et al., 2005).

It is predicted that by 2020, the majority of school-aged children in the United States will be from racial/ethnic minority groups, and persons of color will constitute a numerical majority sometime between 2030 and 2050 (Sue & Sue, 2003). Career counseling in the 21st century is called to shift paradigms when responding to the changing population and the standards-focused climate in our schools today. Traditional approaches to counseling that emphasize an individual-focused, client-centered, self-actualization approach may be insufficient or counter-productive in working with racial/ethnic minority students. Pedersen (2000) noted that society and culture in the United States is based on the concept of individualism and that competition for status, recognition, and achievement form the basis for Western tradition. Basic to this individualistic assumption is that the individual has the primary responsibility for his or her own actions. Independence and autonomy are highly valued, and one should be internally directed and controlled (Sue & Sue, 2003). However, from a cross-cultural perspective, the validity of these assumptions has yet to be verified. For example, the meaning of "self" varies across cultures. Individuals from a collective-oriented culture may conceive of self as interdependent, whereas persons from individualistic cultures may view the self as independent. For the latter, career decision making may be an individual matter, while for the former, career decision making may be a familial matter based on group interests, values, and needs. Leong and Brown (1995) strongly suggested that we need to continue to study the cultural validity of Western-based models of career intervention and development with diverse populations.

D. W. Sue and D. Sue (2003) have challenged the notion that "cultural-bounded" values may in fact be barriers to effective multicultural counseling. They suggested that the traditional one-on-one, in-the-office delivery of services must be supplemented by those that are more action oriented and involve roles and activities in natural settings (community, neighborhood, churches, etc.). Counselors need to address the problems that are related to systemic and external forces (e.g., poverty, discrimination, and prejudice) in addition to internal psychological problems. Counselors also should expand their roles to include advocacy of social justice and to be the change agent for student clients when necessary.

In recent years, more and more scholars have begun to reformulate existing counseling theories and approaches, with much attention to issues of cultural context in career development and counseling. For example, Super and colleagues (1996) described how the constructs of roles and values make career theories more relevant to women and minorities. Hartung et al. (1998) adapted Super's Career-Development Assessment and Counseling model (C-DAC) for use in career counseling with racial and ethnic minorities. Their extended model includes cultural identity as a core C-DAC element, and culturally sensitive assessments and counseling interventions as part of the assessment and counseling process. Criticizing past research that overly focused on universal dimensions of personality, Leong (1996) proposed an integrative model that proposes the notion that individual clients must exist at three levels—the universal, the group, and the individual. Career counselors using this model recognize that work is universal but its meaning is embedded in a cultural context that shapes and colors its nature and experience. These models have made advances in their effort to improve the process and outcome of career interventions for clients of diverse racial and ethnic minority backgrounds in the school setting (Leong & Tan, 2003).

Career counseling in the school setting has a relatively long history. Substantial research related to career development has been documented. However, there is still not substantial evidence about what works best with clients under what conditions. To achieve this goal, more systematic research that focuses on process and outcome of career counseling is needed (Whiston, 2003).

References

Adler, P. A., Kless, S. J., & Adler, P. (1992). Socialization to gender roles: Popularity among elementary school boys and girls. *Sociology of Education, 65,* 169–187.

Akos, P., Konold, T., & Niles, S. G. (2004). A career readiness typology and typal membership in middle school. *Career Development Quarterly, 53,* 53–66.

Altmaier, E. M., & Rapaport, R. J. (1984). An examination of student use of a counseling service. *Journal of College Student Personnel, 25,* 453–458.

American School Counselor Association. (2003). *ASCA national model: A framework for school counseling programs.* Alexandria, VA: Author.

Anderson, B. T. (1992). Minority females in the science pipeline: Activities to enhance readiness, recruitment, and retention. *Initiatives, 55*(2), 31–38.

Atkinson, D. R., Morten, G., & Sue, D. W. (1993). *Counseling American minorities: A cross-cultural perspective* (4th ed.). Dubuque, IA: W. C. Brown.

Aubrey, R. F. (1977). Historical development of guidance and counseling and implications for the future. *Personnel and Guidance Journal, 55,* 288–295.

Awender, M. A., & Wearne, T. D. (1990). *Occupational choices of elementary school children: Traditional or non-traditional?* Paper presented at the 16th annual National Consultation on Vocational Counseling, Ottawa, Ontario, Canada.

Baker, S. B., & Popowicz, C. L. (1983). Meta-analysis as a strategy for evaluating effects of career education interventions. *Vocational Guidance Quarterly, 31,* 178–186.

Baker, S. B., & Taylor, J. G. (1998). Effects of career interventions: A meta-analysis. *Career Development Quarterly, 46,* 376–385.

Beale, A. V. (2003). It takes a team to run a restaurant: Introducing elementary students to the interrelatedness of occupation. *Journal of Career Development, 29,* 211–220.

Betz, N. E. (1992). Counseling uses of career self-efficacy theory. *Career Development Quarterly, 41,* 22–26.

Bishop, J. B. (1990). The university counseling center: An agenda for the 1990's. *Journal of Counseling and Development, 68,* 408–413.

Boyer, E. L. (1983). *High school: A report on secondary education in America.* New York: Harper & Row.

Brown, S. D., & Ryan Krane, N. E. (2000). Four (or five) sessions and a cloud of dust: Old assumptions and new observations about career counseling. In S. D. Brown & R. W. Lent (Eds.), *Handbook of counseling psychology* (3rd ed., pp. 740–766). New York: Wiley.

Brown, S. D., Ryan Krane, N. E., Brecheisen, J., Castelino, P., Budisin, I., Miller, M., et al. (2003). Critical ingredients of career choice interventions: More analyses and new hypotheses. *Journal of Vocational Behavior, 62,* 411–428.

Campbell, C. A., & Dahir, C. A. (1997). *The national standards for school counseling program.* Alexandra, VA: American School Counselor Association.

Commission on Precollege Guidance and Counseling. (1986). *Keeping the options open: Recommendations.* New York: College Entrance Examination Board.

Comprehensive Health Education Foundation. (1997). *Natural helpers: A peer-helping program* (3rd ed.). Seattle, WA: Altschul Group Corporation.

Davidson, M. M., Heppner, M. J., & Johnston, J. A. (2001). Transforming career centers for the new millennium. *Journal of Career Development, 27,* 149–151.

Davis, J. B. (1914). *Moral and vocational guidance.* Boston: Ginn & Co.

Dryler, H. (1998). Parental role models, gender and choice. *British Journal of Sociology, 49,* 195–209.

Dykeman, C., Ingram, M., Wood, C., Charles, S., Chen, M., & Herr, E. (2001). *The taxonomy of career development interventions that occur in America's secondary schools.* A research report funded by the National Research Center for Career and Technical Education, University of Minnesota.

Dykeman, C., Wood, C., Ingram, M., Gitelman, A., Mandsager, N., Chen, M., et al. (2003). *Career development interventions and academic self-efficacy and motivation: A pilot study.* Columbus, OH: National Dissemination for Career and Technical Education. (ERIC Document Reproduction Service No. ED458408)

Elliot, E. S. (1988). Major fairs and undergraduate student exploration. *Journal of College Student Development, 29,* 278–280.

Flores, L., Scott, A., Wang, Y., McCloskey, C., Spencer, K., & Logan, S. (2002). Practice research in career development and counseling and development—2002. *Career Development Quarterly, 52,* 98–131.

Flores, L. Y., & Spanierman, L. B. (1998). An examination of a culturally sensitive university career center: Outreach, services, and evaluation. *Journal of Career Development, 25,* 111–122.

Folsom, B., & Reardon, R. (2003). College courses: Design and accountability. *Journal of Career Assessment, 11,* 421–450.

Fouad, N. A., & Byars-Winston, A. M. (2005). Cultural context of career choice: Meta-analysis of race/ethnicity differences. *The Career Development Quarterly, 53,* 223–233.

Fukuyama, M. A., Probert, G. J., Nevill, D., & Metzler, A. E. (1988). Effects of DISCOVER on career self-efficacy and decision-making of undergraduates. *The Career Development Quarterly, 37,* 56–62.

Gottfredson, L. S. (1981). Circumscription and compromise: A developmental theory of occupational aspirations. *Journal of Counseling Psychology, 28,* 545–579.

Gray, K. C., & Herr, E. L. (2000). *Other way to win. Creating alternatives for high school graduates.* (2nd ed.). Thousand Oaks, CA: Corwin Press.

Harrington, T. F., & O'Shea, A. J. (1992). *Career decision-making system revised.* Circle Pines, MN: American Guidance Service.

Hartung, P. L., Porfeli, E. J., & Vondracek, F. W. (2005). Child vocational development: A review and reconsideration. *Journal of Vocational Behavior, 66,* 385–419.

Hartung, P. J., Vandiver, B. J., Leong, F. T. L., Pope, M., Niles, S. G., & Farrow, B. (1998). Appraising cultural identity in career-development assessment and counseling. *Career Development Quarterly, 46,* 276–293.

Herr, E. L. (Ed.). (1992). *The school counselor and comprehensive programs for work-bound youth.* Alexandria, VA: American Counseling Association/National Occupational Information Coordinating Committee.

Herr, E. L., & Cramer, S. H. (1996). *Career guidance and counseling through the lifespan. Systematic approaches* (5th ed.). New York: Harper Collins.

Herr, E. L., Cramer, S. H., & Niles, S. G. (2004). *Career guidance and counseling through the lifespan. Systematic approaches* (6th ed.). Boston: Allyn and Bacon.

Holland, J. L. (1997). *Making vocational choices* (3rd ed.). Englewood Cliffs, NJ: Prentice-Hall.

Hoyt, K. B., & Lester, J. N. (1995). *Learning to work. The NCDA Gallup survey.* Alexandria, VA: National Career Development Association.

Hoyt, K. B., & Shylo, K. R. (1989). *Career education in transition: Trends and implications for future.* Columbus, OH: The National Center for Research in Vocational Education.

Isaacson, L. E., & Brown, D. (2000). *Career information, career counseling, and career development* (7th ed.). Boston: Allyn and Bacon.

Jepsen, D. A. (1984). The developmental perspective on vocational behavior: A review of theory and research. In S. D. Brown & R. W. Lent (Eds.), *Handbook of counseling psychology* (pp. 178–215) New York: Wiley.

Johnson, L. S. (2000). The relevance of school to career: A study in student awareness. *Journal of Career Development, 26,* 263–276.

Lapan, T. T., Gysbers, N. C., & Petroski, G. F. (2001). Helping seventh graders to be safe and successful: A statewide study of the impact of comprehensive guidance and counseling programs. *Journal of Counseling & Development, 79,* 320–330.

Lee, V., & Ekstrom, R. (1987). Student access to guidance counseling in high school. *American Educational Research Journal, 24,* 287–310.

Lent, R. W., & Brown, S. D. (1996). Social cognitive approach to career development: An overview. *The Career Development Quarterly, 44,* 310–321

Lent, W. L., Brown, S. D., & Hackett, G. (1994). Toward a unifying social cognitive theory of career and academic interest, choice, and performance. *Journal of Vocational Behavior, 45,* 79–122.

Leong, F. T. L. (1996). Toward an integrative model for cross-cultural counseling and psychotherapy. *Applied & Preventive Psychology, 5,* 189–209.

Leong, F. T. L., & Brown, M. T. (1995). Theoretical issues in cross-cultural career development: Cultural validity and cultural specificity. In W. B. Walsh & S. H. Osipow (Eds.), *Handbook of vocational psychology: Theory, research, and practice* (2nd ed., pp. 143–180). Mahwah, NJ: Lawrence Erlbaum Associates.

Leong, F. T. L., & Hayes, T. J. (1990). Occupational stereotyping of Asian Americans. *Career Development Quarterly, 39,* 143–154.

Leong, F. T. L., & Tan, V. L. M. (2003). Cross-cultural career counseling in schools. In P. B. Pederson & J. C. Carey (Eds.), *Multicultural counseling in schools: A practical handbook* (2nd ed., pp. 234–253). Boston: Allyn and Bacon.

Luzzo, D. A., & McWhirter, E. H. (2001). Sex and ethnicity differences in the perception of educational and career-related barriers and level of coping efficacy. *Journal of Counseling and Development, 79,* 61–67.

Mau, W. C. (1995). Educational planning and academic achievement of middle school students: A racial/cultural comparisons. *Journal of Counseling and Development, 73,* 518–526.

Mau, W. C. (1999). Effects of computer-assisted career decision making on vocational identity and career exploratory behavior. *Journal of Career Development, 25*, 261–274.

Mau, W. C. (2001). Assessing career decision-making difficulties: A cross-cultural study. *Journal of Career Assessment, 9*, 353–364.

Mau, W. C. (2003). Factor influencing persistence in science and engineering career aspirations. *Career Development Quarterly, 51*, 234–243.

Mau, W. C. (2004). Cultural dimensions of career decision-making difficulties. *Career Development Quarterly, 53*, 67–77.

Mau, W. C., & Bikos, L. H. (2000). Educational and vocational aspirations of minority and female students: A longitudinal study. *Journal of Counseling and Development, 78*, 186–194.

Mau, W. C., & Fernandes, A. (2001). Characteristics and satisfaction of students who utilized career counseling services. *Journal of College Student Development, 42*, 581–588.

Mau, W. C., Hitchcock, R., & Calvert, C. (1998). Career plans and perceived counselors' and other influential persons' expectations of high school students. *Professional School Counseling, 2*, 161–166.

Mau, W. C., & Jepsen, D. A. (1988). Attitudes toward counselor and counseling processes: A comparison of Chinese and American graduate students. *Journal of Counseling and Development, 63*, 189–192.

Mau, W. C., & Jepsen, D. A. (1990). Help-seeking perceptions and behaviors: A comparison of Chinese and American graduate students. *Journal of Multicultural Counseling and Development, 18*, 94–104.

McDaniels, C. (1978). The practice of career guidance and counseling. *INFORM, 7*, 1–2, 7–8.

McDonald, J. L., & Jessell, J. C. (1992). Influence of selected variables on occupational attitudes and perceived occupational abilities of young adolescents. *Journal of Career Development, 18*, 239–250.

McKinnon, M., & Ahola-Sidaway, J. (1995). Working with the boys: A north American's perspective on non-traditional work initiatives for adolescent females in secondary schools. *Gender and Education, 7*, 327–339.

McMahon, M., Gillies, R. M., & Carroll, J. (2000). Links between school and occupations: The perceptions of children. *Guidance and Counseling, 16*, 12–17.

McMahon, M., & Patton, W. (1997). Gender differences in children and adolescents' perceptions of influences on their career development. *School Counselor, 44*, 368–376.

McWhirter, E. H., Rasheed, S., & Crothers, M. (2000). The effects of high school career education on social-cognitive variables. *Journal of Counseling Psychology, 47*, 330–341.

National Career Development Association. (1999). *Career connection in a changing context: A summary of the key findings of the 1999 national survey of working America.* Tulsa, OK: Author.

National Occupational Information Coordinating Committee. (1992). *The National Career Development Guideline, local handbook.* Washington, DC: Author.

Nauta, M. M., & Kokaly, M. L. (2001). Assessing role model influences on students' academic and vocational decisions. *Journal of Career Assessment, 9*, 81–99.

Niles, S. G., & Akos, P. (2003). Fostering educational and career planning in students. In B. T. Erford (Eds.), *Transforming the school counseling* (pp. 153–170). Upper Saddle River, NJ: Merrill Prentice Hall.

Niles, S. G., & Harris-Bowlsbey, J. (2005). *Career development interventions in the 21st century.* Upper Saddle River, NJ: Pearson Prentice Hall.

O'Brien, K. M., Bikos, L. H., Epstein, K. L., Flores, L. Y., Dukstein, R. D., & Kamatuks, N. A. (2000). Enhancing the career decision-making self-efficacy of Upward Bound students. *Journal of Career Development, 26*, 277–293.

Oliver, L. W., & Spokane, A. R. (1988). Career-intervention outcome: What contributes to client gain? *Journal of Counseling Psychology, 35*, 447–462.

Parsad, B., Alexander, D., Farris, E., & Hudson, L. (2003). *High school guidance counseling* (NCES 2003-015). Washington, DC: U.S. Department of Education, National Center for Education Statistics.

Parsons, F. (1909). *Choosing a vocation.* Boston: Houghton Mifflin.

Pederson, P. B. (2000). *A handbook for developing multicultural awareness.* Alexandria, VA: American Counseling Association.

Peterson, G. W., Long, K. L., & Billops, A. (1999). The effects of three career interventions on educational choices of eighth grade students. *Professional School Counseling, 3*, 34–42.

Pierce, K. (1993). Socialization of teenage girls through teen-magazine fiction: The making of new women or old lady? *Sex Roles, 29*, 59–68.

Pinder, F. A., & Fitzgerald, P. W. (1984). The effectiveness of a computer guidance system in promoting career decision making. *Journal of Vocational Behavior, 24*, 123–131.

Reardon, J. R. (1996). A program and cost analysis of a self-directed career decision-making program in a university career center. *Journal of counseling and Development, 74*, 280–285.

Robbins, S., & Smith, L. (1993). Enhancement programs for entering university majority and minority students. *Journal of Counseling and Development, 71*, 510–514

Sampson, J. P., Jr. (1994). Factors influencing the effective use of computer-assisted career guidance: The North American experience. *British Journal of Guidance and Counseling, 22*, 91–106.

Savickas, M. L. (1990). The career decision making course. Description and field test. *Journal of College Student Development, 38*, 275–284.

Savickas, M. L. (2002). Reinvigorating the study of careers. *Journal of Vocational Behavior, 61,* 381–385.

Schultheiss, D. E. P. (2000). Emotional-social issues in the provision of career counseling. In D. Luzzo (Ed.), *Career counseling of college students. An empirical guide to strategies that work* (pp. 43–62). Washington, DC: American Psychological Association.

Schultheiss, D. E. P., Palma, T. V., & Manzi, A. (2005). Career development in middle childhood: A qualitative inquiry. *The Career Development Quarterly, 53,* 246–262.

Seymour, E. (1995). The loss of women from science, mathematics, and engineering undergraduate majors: An explanatory account. *Science Education, 79,* 437–473.

Solberg, S., Gusavac, N., Hamann, T., Felch, J., Johnson, J., Lamborn, S., et al. (1998). The adaptive success identity plan (ASIP): A career intervention for college students. *The Career Development Quarterly, 47,* 48–91.

Solberg, V. S., Howard, K., Blustein, D. L., & Close, W. (2002). Career development in the schools: Connecting school-to-work-to-life. *The Counseling Psychologist, 30,* 705–725.

Spokane, A. R., & Oliver, L. W. (1983). Outcome of vocational intervention. In S. Osipow & W. B. Walsh (Eds.), *Handbook of vocational psychology* (pp. 99–136). Hillsdale, NJ: Erlbaum.

Stafford, A. (1991). *Trying work, gender, youth, and work experience.* Edinburgh, UK: Edinburgh University Press.

Sue, D. W., & Sue, D. (2003). *Counseling the culturally diverse: Theory and practice.* (4th ed.). New York: Wiley.

Sundal-Hansen, L. S. (1984). Interrelationship of gender and career. In N. C. Gysbers (Ed.), *Designing careers: Counseling to enhance education, work, and leisure* (pp. 24–41). San Francisco: Jossey-Bass.

Super, D. E. (1957). *The psychology of career.* New York: Harper & Row.

Super, D. E. (1990). A life-span, life-space approach to career development. In D. Brown & L. Brook (Eds.), *Career choices and development: Applying contemporary theories to practice* (pp. 197–261). San Francisco: Jossey-Bass.

Super, D. E., Savickas, M. L., & Super, C. M. (1996). A life-span, life-space approach to career development. In D. Brown & L. Brook (Eds.), *Career choices and development: Applying contemporary theories to practice* (3rd ed., pp. 121–178). San Francisco: Jossey-Bass.

Tracey, T. J. G., Robins, S. B., & Hofsess, C. D. (2005). Stability and change in interests: A longitudinal study of adolescents from grades 8 through 12. *Journal of Vocational Behavior, 66,* 1–25.

Trice, A., & King, R. (1991). Stability of kindergarten children's career aspirations. *Psychological Reports, 68,* 1378.

Trice, A. D. (2000). Italian, Bulgarian, and U.S. children's perception of gender-appropriateness of occupations. *Journal of Social Psychology, 140,* 661–663.

U.S. Department of Labor. (1991). *What work requires of schools: A SCANS report for America 2000.* Washington, DC: U.S. Government Printing Office.

Whiston, S. C. (2003). Career counseling: 90 years old yet still healthy and vital. *The Career Development Quarterly, 52,* 35–42.

Whiston, S. C., Brecheisen, B. K., & Stephens, J. (2003). Does treatment modality affect career counseling effectiveness? *Journal of Vocational Behavior, 62,* 390–410.

Whiston, S. C., Sexton, T. L., & Lasoff, D. L. (1998). Career-intervention outcome: A replication and extension of Oliver and Spokane. *Journal of Counseling Psychology, 45,* 150–165.

Yeh, C. J., & Inose, M. (2002). Difficulties and coping strategies of Chinese, Japanese, and Korean immigrant students. *Adolescence, 37,* 69–82.

XXXIII
CREATIVE ARTS COUNSELING IN SCHOOLS:
Toward a More Comprehensive Approach

CAROLINE S. CLAUSS-EHLERS
Rutgers, The State University of New Jersey

Creative Arts Counseling in Schools: A Sound Approach With Significant Barriers

Research indicates that creative arts counseling is a highly effective intervention in preschool, elementary, middle school, and high school settings. Fall, Balvanz, Johnson, and Nelson (1999) found that children who received play therapy from school counselors experienced a significant increase in self-efficacy in comparison with the control group of children who did not receive play therapy. Johnson, McLeod, and Fall (1997) examined the efficacy of play therapy in school settings and found the intervention had a significant positive impact. Ray, Armstrong, Warren, and Balkin (2005) investigated elementary school counselor beliefs about creative arts counseling in the schools and learned that they strongly believed in its utility.

Creative arts counseling in schools is a developmentally appropriate intervention that helps children and adolescents cope with challenging situations (Cobia & Henderson, 2003). The provision of creative arts counseling within school systems makes intervention more accessible as youth receive treatment in their natural settings rather than having to be transported to a clinic or private office (Clauss-Ehlers & Weist, 2002). Creative arts counseling also addresses issues associated with stigma. Students may not feel that they are in counseling per se, but rather are engaged in a creative art form that fosters their self-expression, coping skills, and overall well-being.

Despite empirical evidence and a host of substantial benefits, however, very little literature exists about the ways in which creative arts counseling can be implemented more comprehensively in schools (Wengrower, 2001). Lack of knowledge about the counselor's role is one impediment to greater implementation. Within the school setting, the role of the creative arts counselor is often confused with that of the art teacher. The counseling profession itself does not necessarily understand the theoretical concepts, interventions, and unique contributions made by the creative arts approach. To this end, the current author introduces the term *creative arts school counselor* to further identify the role of the counselor who uses creative arts techniques in counseling. It is hoped that this new definition will differentiate the function of the creative arts school counselor from that of art educator, drama teacher, and others. The term *creative arts school counselor* will be used throughout the chapter, including when works by other authors are discussed.

A discussion of creative arts counseling techniques and relevant strategies must first consider the very real barriers associated with implementing creative arts counseling in schools. The culture of creative arts counseling and the culture of school-based education have differences that make it challenging for the two to work together (Wengrower, 2001). The therapy culture, for instance, focuses on the individual or group in contrast to an educational culture that focuses on the class or school. Creative arts counseling emphasizes each child's uniqueness while educational systems focus on common aspects of age level and shared grade, and assume similar learning styles and speed.

The culture of creative arts counseling deals with uncertainty, process, and introspection. In contrast, the educational culture focuses on knowledge of clear concepts, learning rather than doubt or uncertainty, lesson plans, measurable results that are evaluated, and a practical, action-oriented approach to learning. The creative arts school counselor views the therapeutic relationship as a tool to be used in counseling with the child. This differs from the relationship between educator and student that occurs amidst a classroom full of students (Wengrower, 2001).

Wengrower (2001) mentioned other factors that deepen the divide between therapeutic and educational cultures. The concept of parataxic distortion is applicable to those teachers who develop strong relationships with students and subsequently doubt that the creative arts school counselor can do the same (Sullivan, 1954). As a result, the possibility for a collaborative team effort between counselor and teacher becomes difficult, if not impossible, to achieve. The teacher may also be jealous of the creative arts school counselor's work role. The teacher who is in the classroom with students all day, for instance, may feel that the creative arts school counselor does not work as much since she only meets with students on a session-by-session basis (Wengrower).

For creative arts school counselors, an additional barrier is the challenge to maintain a clinical setting (Carroll, 2000). For those schools that have not yet fully integrated creative arts counseling interventions, the creative arts school counselor may find it difficult to acquire consistent office space that ensures ongoing sessions and confidentiality. Educators and administrators may also be concerned about a child being pulled out of class to attend creative arts counseling sessions. If a child leaves the same class once a week for sessions, the result is a 20% absentee rate for a class offered five days a week. After-school sessions may not be an option if the child depends on school transportation to return home. Lack of counseling support from the educational community may mean that the child does not get any counseling or does not attend on a regular basis (e.g., has sessions on a biweekly or monthly basis).

The school calendar itself can act as an impediment to ongoing creative arts counseling (Carroll, 2000). Winter holidays are significant times of stress for many families, yet children are on break during this time and do not have access to counseling within a school setting. Summer breaks last an average of 2 months during which time children do not benefit from school services offered during the academic year. This is unfortunate given that major developmental changes occur during the summer as children prepare for another grade. The lengthy break also interrupts treatment gains for those who have been in counseling, making it difficult to begin where client and creative arts school counselor left off when classes resume.

Another barrier concerns the provision of creative arts counseling to culturally diverse youth in schools. Culturally diverse youth are the fastest growing group in the United States (Porter, 2000). In the year 2000, culturally diverse youth made up almost 30% of the population. An estimated 3,000 immigrants arrive in the United States each day (Martin & Midgeley, 1994).

An evident trend is the young age composition of culturally diverse groups: 35% of Latinos, 33.9% of American Indian/Alaska Natives, 31.9% of Native Hawaiian/Pacific Islanders, 31.4% of Blacks/African Americans, and 24.1% of Asian/Asian Americans are under the age of 18. In comparison, Whites constitute the oldest group with only 22.6% of the total population under 18 years of age (U.S. Bureau of Census, 1996). These findings highlight the reality that we live in a young, diverse society (Clauss-Ehlers, 2003).

Within this cultural context, it is crucial that the creative arts school counselor consider how creative arts counseling can be effective in work with culturally diverse students. Very little attention has been devoted to how creative arts counseling applies to culturally diverse youth in school settings. The importance of cultural factors in the delivery of creative arts counseling needs to be addressed more fully so that the needs of all students are better met.

Despite these barriers, educational settings provide an excellent environment for creative arts counseling. What follows is a discussion about how future research, training, and practice can provide school-based creative arts counseling in a more comprehensive, systemic, developmentally appropriate, and culturally diverse manner. The chapter elaborates on the role of the creative arts school counselor with a focus on strategies associated with a more comprehensive, schoolwide approach. The chapter defines play and reviews creative arts counseling theory, discusses the state of research in creative arts counseling, looks at educational and training requirements for practice, and reviews the key creative arts counseling techniques of play therapy, art therapy, drama therapy, poetry therapy, and sandplay therapy. The review of each technique focuses on relevant definitions, processes, age appropriateness, and application to counseling culturally diverse youth. The conclusion presents an overall theory of creative arts counseling in schools and how communities can work toward a more comprehensive provision of such services.

Theoretical Basis for Creative Arts Counseling in Schools

Theories of play. The debate over how to define and conceptualize play has spanned the course of two centuries (Stagnitti, 2004). Theories of play are generally divided into classical theories and modern theories (Mellou, 1994). Classical theories of play began in the 1800s and examined the purpose of play. The surplus energy theory of play developed by Spencer (1878), for instance, concluded that play did not add anything to a child's development. In Spencer's conception, play simply occurred because children had extra energy. Other tenets of the classical framework believed play gave children a way to relax and was thus part of an evolutionary biological process that weakened primitive instincts (Lazarus, 1883; Hall, 1920).

Modern theories believe that play influences child development (Berlyne, 1960; Erikson, 1985). Play is thought to facilitate exploration and reduce arousal when new scenarios are encountered (Hutt, 1985). Psychodynamic theories of play focus on the emotional component that play brings to the lives of children. These theories state that children can play out their feelings and in so doing, master trauma (Erikson, 1985; Freud, 1961). Sociocultural theories of play examine the socialization process that play provides and how it helps children develop necessary skills for the adult world (Bateson, 1955; Mead, 1934).

The major change seen in the shift from classical to modern theories of play is the importance placed upon the role of play in childhood development. While classical theories saw play as something more functional in the life of a child (i.e., something children engage in to use extra energy), modern theorists take the stance that play has both a functional and therapeutic value as it facilitates the child's emotional, cognitive, and social development (Erikson, 1985; Freud, 1961; Mead, 1934).

Out of these contrasting and evolving theories, contemporary theorists have begun to piece together a definition or, more accurately, to put together characteristics that embody the concept of play. Play is currently described as something that is exploratory; an intrinsically motivated transaction between the individual and the environment; something that is internally motivated, reflects and transcends reality, is controlled by the player, is spontaneous, safe, fun, and concerned with process not product (Stagnitti, 2004).

Similar to modern theories of play, much of the theoretical linkage to creative arts counseling can be traced to both developmental (Piaget, 1962) and psychoanalytic theory (Naumburg, 1950). Piaget had a keen understanding of the different ways in which children and adults understand information. According to Piaget, children between 2 and 7 years of age are at the preoperational stage where they learn language skills and experience both rigid and magical thinking (e.g., the child creates an improbable explanation for something he or she does not understand).

The child experiences the concrete operational stage of development between the ages of 8 and 11 (Piaget, 1962). Here the child is able to organize material and develops the ability to reason logically. The focus of the child's thinking at this time, however, is on physical objects rather than on abstract thoughts or feelings. Creative arts counseling can help children bridge the gap between concrete and abstract thought, provide an opportunity to organize abstract thoughts, and enhance a sense of control and an ability to cope (Ray et al., 2005).

Creative arts therapies are also based on the psychoanalytic tradition in that they involve the expression and interpretation of unconscious material. In art therapy, for instance, children draw pictures and are asked to free associate their meanings. The creative arts school counselor offers interpretations and facilitates goals aimed to "support the ego, foster the development of identity, and promote maturation" (Kahn, 1999, p. 292).

Change in psychoanalytic approaches to creative arts counseling occurs within the context of a dynamic therapeutic relationship between counselor and child. Expression, self-exploration, and understanding are promoted through creativity and play, which is the child's natural way to communicate. Interpretations of play are used to help the child gain awareness of unconscious conflicts.

State of Research in Creative Arts Counseling

Research is an important aspect of a comprehensive approach to school-based creative arts counseling as empirical evidence can support the efficacy and expansion of interventions. Process and outcome research and narrative case study are three current research trends used with children (Carroll, 2000). *Process research* refers to studies that examine factors that emerge during the course of treatment that help children. *Outcome research* examines the child's level of functioning at the end of therapy. *Narrative case study* refers to a narrative written about a particular clinical case that documents the course of treatment and highlights specific aspects of treatment.

Process research. A strength associated with process research is that it explores what fosters a positive counseling process for children. Through empirical examination of those aspects of counseling that most benefit children, counselors have greater awareness of what to replicate and incorporate in their work. Weaknesses associated with process research include extenuating factors such as maturation and the environment that are beyond the researcher's control. As a result, it is difficult to state for certain that specific aspects of the counseling process influenced a positive counseling experience in isolation from extenuating factors.

Outcome research. A key strength associated with outcome research is its more recent focus on methodological issues (Carroll, 2000). Landreth, Homeyer, Glover, and Sweeney (1996), for instance, analyze play therapy studies and provide a comprehensive empirical review of positive counseling outcomes. In their meta-analysis of clinical intervention research with children, Weisz and Weiss (1993) found overwhelmingly positive outcomes.

Weaknesses associated with outcome research often center on problems with design. Outcome research often determines a baseline of functioning among children before the intervention is delivered (Carroll, 2000). Children are then randomly placed in different research groups and their functioning is remeasured at the end of the study. Problematic with this design strategy is that it measures behavioral symptoms only and does not consider other factors that contribute to changes in functioning.

Measuring outcomes among children also implies that they improve and respond to interventions at the same pace. Some children may respond quickly to an intervention while others may need more time to react (Carroll, 2000). Because the post measures are administered at the same time, diversity of the pace in which each child makes progress is not considered.

Narrative case studies. A key strength of the narrative case study is the ability to pay attention to details that would get lost in a larger study. As a result, this research can demonstrate effective, innovative interventions through documentation of what occurs in treatment. Written accounts that comprise the narrative case study rarely interfere with counseling; thus, the child's therapeutic process is largely uninterrupted (Robson, 1993). The narrative case study approach is also useful for practitioners engaged in research as material is presented in the consulting room rather than an outside environment (Carroll, 2000).

A major weakness associated with narrative case study is the large variability in how different issues are addressed. Some researchers base their narrative on session details while others focus their writing on the therapeutic process in general. This variability makes it difficult to assess the overall contribution and efficacy of narrative case study findings. The uniqueness of each case makes questions of validity, reliability, and generalizability difficult to answer.

Education and Training: The Association for Play Therapy and the American Art Therapy Association

The Association for Play Therapy (APT) and the American Art Therapy Association (AATA) are two professional organizations that provide formal training guidelines for creative arts counseling. Each organization provides a list of approved graduate-level academic training programs (for a comprehensive listing, see Webb, 1999). At the time of this writing, the American Psychological Association (APA) did not offer specific guidelines regarding the practice of creative arts counseling.

The APT provides various types of training for professionals specifically interested in the practice of play therapy. The APT issues credentials for being a Registered Play Therapist (RPT) and Registered Play Therapy-Supervisor (RPT-S) for those who meet their professional standards. Additional training and professional development is provided through the Annual APT International Conference as well as through distance-learning courses in play therapy.

A key organizational activity of the AATA is to examine the quality of training provided by graduate degree programs. The AATA has developed educational standards for master's level graduate programs. Art therapy education courses cover topics such as psychopathology, diagnostic categories, group work, human development, multiculturalism, ethics, research, and assessment. Educational programs will often have additional requirements in counseling theory and practice as many art therapists become licensed as professional counselors. After completion of required master's level course work in art therapy, the student must complete a supervised postgraduate internship. Upon completion of the postgraduate internship, the student is eligible to apply to become an Art Therapist Registered (ATR).

The art therapy education literature acknowledges that its objectives resemble those of the counseling profession, it states that art therapy education is different in three key ways. These differences apply to various types of creative arts counseling (e.g., drama therapy, sandplay therapy). First, materials used in the creative arts counseling process are usually not used in counseling. For instance, a client may use clay, sand, or draw during a creative arts counseling session, mediums that are not traditionally used in counseling.

Art expression is the second major difference and refers to the understanding among art therapists about the significance and meaning of the artwork created by their clients. Part of the creative arts school counselor's task is to be familiar with "normal developmental levels of artistic expression" as well as those that might suggest neurological problems, trauma, or mental illness. Thus, the creative arts counselor must be able to assess the client's artwork from a developmental perspective to make these determinations.

The third major difference involves the nature of the counseling relationship. For the creative arts school counselor, the counseling relationship incorporates both creative art materials and the creative process as part of the therapy process. This differs from a traditional counseling approach that largely focuses on the client's verbalizations as the primary aspect of the therapeutic relationship.

While these guidelines and differences pertain to student members of the APT and AATA, students enrolled in other graduate programs (e.g., counseling psychology programs) do not necessarily receive training in creative arts counseling. A study of elementary school counselors and their use of play therapy in the schools, for instance, found that 67% of participants had not taken a university-level play therapy course, 21% had taken one university-level play therapy course, and only 12% had taken two or more courses (Ray et al., 2005). Participants indicated that their lack of training was a key barrier to providing play therapy in the elementary schools where they worked. The researchers concluded that less training resulted in less play therapy for school-based clients.

Creative Arts Counseling Techniques: Definition, Process, Age Appropriateness, and Use With Diverse Populations

This section focuses on actual techniques the creative arts school counselor uses with children and adolescents in schools. Discussion of each technique addresses three areas: (a) definition and description of the processes and strategies associated with the technique; (b) the appropriate age for the technique; and (c) use of the technique with culturally diverse youth. The creative arts counseling techniques discussed in this framework are play therapy, art therapy, drama therapy, poetry therapy, and sandplay therapy. The purpose of this section is to familiarize practitioners and interested students with the various ways in which creative arts counseling is practiced in schools and among developmentally and culturally diverse youth.

Play Therapy

Play therapy definition and process. Axline (1947) described play therapy as "an opportunity which is given to the child to 'play out' his feelings and problems just as, in certain types of adult therapy, an individual 'talks out' his difficulties" (p. 9). Schaefer (1993) defined play therapy as "an interpersonal process wherein a trained therapist systematically applies the curative powers of play to help clients resolve their psychological difficulties" (p. 3). What happens in play therapy depends largely upon the approach taken in the session. Different theoretical approaches to play therapy incorporate different techniques and strategies. The commonality across approaches is that the creative arts school counselor always uses play to develop rapport and communicate with the child. Three prominent types of play therapy are (a) behavioral play therapy, (b) child-centered play therapy, and (c) structured play therapy (Cochran, 1996).

In behavioral play therapy, the creative arts school counselor uses play to help the child relax and role play alternative, more adaptive behaviors (Cochran, 1996). Play therapy largely relies on helping the child be an active participant in behavioral change and management. The bridge technique is an example of one strategy. The creative arts school counselor encourages the client to draw a bridge that extends from current behavior to the way he or she would like to be. The client then spells out the sequential steps that must be taken to achieve this new vision of self.

Child-centered play therapy focuses on the use of play to help children self-actualize through self-expression (Cochran, 1996). The child-centered philosophy of play therapy believes that play is the natural, developmentally appropriate way that children communicate, that children will naturally grow and mature, and that children can act responsibly and move in positive life directions (Landreth, 2002). Having children draw a picture that illustrates how they view themselves is an example of a child-centered technique.

Like the child-centered approach, the goal of structured play therapy is the child's self-expression and self-actualization. The difference between the two, however, is that the structured play therapist identifies barriers that interfere with the child's healthy development. Upon identifying the problem, the creative arts school counselor directs the child to develop skills aimed to overcome it. One example is the creative arts school counselor who discovers using play that the child experiences significant peer conflicts at school. The counselor then shares this observation with the child and engages in directed play therapy experiences aimed to enhance peer relationships.

Play therapy age appropriateness. Play therapy is appropriate for preschools and elementary schools with young children aged 10 and under who lack abstract verbal reasoning skills. The language of children is that of play; hence, understanding and communication is enhanced through play rather than verbal communication. This is in direct contrast with traditional talk therapies (Clauss, 1998).

Play therapy with culturally diverse youth. Play therapy is an effective tool in work with culturally diverse students in school settings (Cochran, 1996; Kalish-Weiss, 1989; Shen & Herr, 2003). Because the language of play therapy is play, cultural differences such as language that may otherwise interfere with the counseling process are not an issue. Many diverse cultures are context-dependent, meaning they rely more on context and nonverbal communication than the spoken word. Traditional counseling, however, is often focused on the client's direct verbalizations. Play therapy is culturally syntonic in that it naturally promotes the creative arts school counselor's focus on context, meaning how and with what the child plays. Additionally, a common practice is for play therapists to name the emotions the child indicates through play. For the student for whom English is a second language, the counselor's naming of feelings not only allows for greater insight and identification, but also expands the student's vocabulary for emotions (Cochran).

Cochran (1996) examined how play therapy helps culturally diverse students overcome educational barriers such as difficulty learning cognitive material, social problems, and assimilation stress. Children's diverse cultural values may interfere with their ability to perform in a classroom with different cultural norms (Clauss-Ehlers & Lopez Levi, 2002). For instance, if a child's culture is group oriented, he or she may have difficulty performing in a competitive, individualistic classroom setting where class participation and individual decision making are required. Play therapy enhances these academic skills as the creativity of play provides decision-making opportunities such as with what and with whom to play during a session.

Social problems can be another impediment to school success. Culturally diverse students may feel they do not fit in with their majority classmates and teachers. They may feel misunderstood or rejected, which can lead to poor attendance and missed academic material. Friend-making groups can be organized in diverse school settings where children develop a common interest, activity, and connection through play (Cochran, 1996).

Assimilation stress refers to the stress that individuals experience when they move from their culture of origin to a new host country. Stress occurs as individuals try to adapt to the new country's values, language, and work force; cope with their immigration experience; drop to a lower social class status that results in less economic mobility; and confront feelings of isolation and loneliness (Clauss-Ehlers, 2006). For the immigrant child in the U.S. school system, assimilation stress develops as he or she tries to master a new language, learn course content in the new language, adjust to the culture of the U.S. educational system, and establish peer relationships.

Due to a drop in social class standing, both of the child's parents may now have to work, leaving less time for parent–child contact and support. The immigrant child may also be mourning the loss of loved ones in the country of origin, particularly if the child's parents came to the United States first and he or she was being raised by grandparents who acted as surrogate parents. Given the loss of family in the country of origin, play therapy is culturally appropriate in that it has been shown to reduce separation anxiety (Milos & Reiss, 1982). Because play allows children to express themselves, they can play out feelings of separation, stress, loss, sadness, anger, fear, and anxiety.

Shen and Herr (2003) examined the status of play therapy in Taiwanese elementary schools to determine its compatibility with Chinese culture and possible expansion in Taiwan. These investigators wanted to determine how counselor educators and elementary school counselors perceived play therapy, how they perceived play therapy in school counseling, and how they perceived the adoption of Western play therapy in Taiwanese society. They found that play therapy in Taiwanese society had "developmental potential" but also faced a "disadvantaged environment."

With regard to developmental potential, Shen and Herr (2003) found that research participants were positive about the expansion of play therapy in Taiwan, agreeing with the benefits play can have for children. Focusing on how play helps children communicate, one participant said that play therapy is more beneficial for Chinese children than American children because "[American] kids are more verbally expressive than ours are" (p. 32). Certainly, this view corresponds with culturally diverse youth from less traditionally expressive cultures who have recently immigrated to the United States.

Disadvantaged environment refers to cultural and societal barriers associated with the expansion of school-based play therapy in Taiwan. One participant wrote, "[The problem] is that most parents ... think that play is a waste of time . . .. Many elementary school teachers even think the same way" (Shen & Herr, p. 33). Because environmental foundations for play therapy support are not always present in Taiwan, public education and outreach are increasingly important. Interestingly, this finding is not so different from the clash between therapeutic and educational cultures discussed earlier. Clearly, greater professional training and public awareness about the benefits of play are needed to provide a more comprehensive approach to creative arts counseling in school systems at home and abroad.

Art Therapy

Art therapy definition and process. Shostak (1985) defined art therapy as a "psychotherapeutic intervention that focuses upon art media as primary expressive and communicative channels" (p. 19). Art therapy provides both visual and verbal ways in which children can express themselves. Children tend to be open to the art-making process as it is less threatening than engaging in verbal expression about difficult issues.

Like play therapy, what occurs in an art therapy session depends upon the art therapist's theoretical approach. Strategies can vary from having a child create a collage that illustrates how he views his family to having a child draw a series of objects that illustrate her home life. In the more structured approach, the art therapist either selects the media to be used in session or presents a limited choice of materials. In the less structured framework, the client chooses from a range of materials. Like play therapy, theoretical orientations to art therapy include behavioral, child-centered, and structured art therapy.

Objectification is one process that occurs in art therapy. *Objectification* refers to the "process through which the [child or] adolescent externalizes threatening feelings and ideas onto a neutral art form" (Kahn, 1999, p. 293). Having projected these feelings outwardly, youth talk about them from a distance and slowly incorporate them into a sense of self. Objectification addresses resistance as the feelings reflected in the art objects remain an ongoing symbol of what the child experiences. While the child may subsequently deny these feelings or experiences, the art therapist can refer back to the artwork and inquire about its significance over the course of counseling.

Despite the benefits associated with art therapy, it is used less often in school settings. Kahn (1999) attributed less use to a lack of training, the misconception among counselors that they themselves must be artistically inclined, and the inability to match art directives with counseling goals. She recommended that the schools invested in art therapy start by setting up an art station. The next step is to normalize the use of art in counseling by sharing its purpose with students, parents, and colleagues. Trust can be further developed by talking about confidentiality during the initial session and explaining that artwork will not be shown to others without the student's permission.

Kahn (1999) provided a model of integrating art with counseling in school settings. The key is to recognize relevant objectives at each stage of counseling and choose art directives that reflect those goals (Kahn, 1999). As counseling directives change throughout the process, so must the art directives given to the client. The three stages in Kahn's model are (a) entry, (b) exploration, and (c) action-taking.

The *entry stage* refers to the initial phase of counseling where trust is a major goal. Because therapeutic rapport is critical at this juncture, Kahn (1999) recommended art productions that foster communication. Art directives are open ended and allow students to share who they are with the art therapist. Two examples are "Tell your story," and "Make a collage about who you are" (Riley, 1994).

Exploration is the second stage and reflects the part of the process where the client increasingly explores his or her problems. Art directives at this point are concerned with the actual problem areas presented by the client. Directives during the exploration stage tend to be more structured. Two examples are "Create a collage that depicts your understanding of why you are coming to counseling" and "Choose a picture that represents your involvement in your academic work" (Kahn, 1999).

During the *action-taking stage* the client examines solutions to problem areas. Here relevant art directives focus on setting action-oriented goals that promote change. Specific goals and potential barriers are also discussed. Kahn (1999) provided examples of art directives that reflect this stage of counseling that include "Draw one time when the change that you want to occur did happen, even if just a little" and "Draw yourself in a scene 15 years from now. What goals will you need to reach during this time?"

Art therapy age appropriateness. Art therapy is appropriate for use in preschools, elementary schools, middle schools, and high schools. Like play therapy, art therapy with young children provides a nonverbal means of self-expression. For older children, adolescent developmental needs of separation and individuation are met in that adolescent clients have control over the process, are provided with a creative outlet, and have the opportunity to use media that illustrate group symbols (Riley, 1994). The ability to externalize feelings onto artwork can help adolescents be less defensive during initial phases of counseling. Less defensiveness sets the tone for an atmosphere where the adolescent client feels accepted by the adult counselor. This can be a unique experience for adolescents who struggle with authority and feel adults in general do not support their experience.

Art therapy with culturally diverse youth. Little research and writing exists about conducting art therapy with culturally diverse youth. Campanelli (1991) stated that art therapists who work with diverse populations must be trained in how "symbols and images in art may have different meanings depending on the client's ethno-cultural background: preferences regarding the use of line, color, and form may vary because every culture has a unique approach to art" (p. 34). It is the art therapist's responsibility to be aware of these different forms of art expression so that artwork in counseling is not misread. For instance, a Mexican American student may draw figures with heavy outlines, because this type of drawing is part of Mexican tradition and has nothing to do with wanting stronger boundaries in interpersonal relationships (Campanelli).

Kalish-Weiss (1989) described work with the Los Angeles Unified School District and the Los Angeles County Department of Mental Health to address some of the problems faced by culturally diverse families. The focus of the treatment plan was to offer play and art therapies for students. The treatment team included experts in art therapy who reviewed the various cases and determined what type of art and play therapy would most benefit the student. The success of the program included fewer symptoms among students (i.e., depression, attention problems, and academic difficulties), continued referrals from parents and the school system, and providing children with a way to discuss their problems (Kalish-Weiss).

Omizo and Omizo (1989) found that the Hawaiian children in their study had low self-esteem primarily due to growing up in a different culture and attending a Westernized school system. They developed an art therapy program to address the experience of Hawaiian students in Western-oriented schools who suffered from low self-esteem. Art therapy was provided through art activities conducted in small groups that fostered self-expression. The result of the program was that native Hawaiian youth experienced significantly greater self-esteem in social and academic arenas.

Drama Therapy

Drama therapy definition and process. The word *drama* comes from the Greek word *drao*, which means to struggle. The word *theatre* comes from the Greek word *theatron*, which means to show (Casson, n.d.). Drama therapy uses drama as the therapeutic method (Casson). The client shows the counselor her struggles through dramatization. The drama therapist works to provide a safe environment and engages clients with activities that include music, images, drawing, and movement. Participants take on characters and roles to act out conflicts through the drama presented. Drama therapy is a group technique that aims to increase self-awareness and expression.

Two approaches to drama therapy are psychoeducational drama and psychodrama. Psychoeducational drama utilizes dramatic productions to further self-awareness. Characters act out real-life problems over a brief period of time (one to five minutes). The goal of the staged dramatic presentation is to create a "believable and familiar situation of psychological and/or social significance with which the audience can identify" (Urtz & Kahn, 1982, p. 327). The three units of structure in psychoeducational drama are (a) exposition of the scene, (b) complication or development of the characters and scene, and (c) the scene where the drama is heightened.

Unique to psychoeducational drama is that the dramas end with the problem unresolved. The purpose of an unresolved ending is to encourage discussion among audience members who are now identified with the drama. This group discussion is facilitated by trained group leaders. Urtz and Kahn (1982) wrote,

> [T]he psychoeducational drama leaders evoke an emotional experience in their audience and explore the psychological, social, and educational issues involved by discussing the reactions of the viewers and helping the audience to relate the dramatized experience to their own lives. (p. 327)

Psychodrama is similar to psychoeducational drama in that it occurs in a group modality and characters must confront authentic issues. Psychodrama is not as brief as the psychoeducational approach, however, and does not necessarily end with issues unresolved. The structure of psychodrama also differs and includes the three phases of warm-up, enactment, and sharing (Casson, n.d.).

In the first phase, warm-up, creative activities help participants be spontaneous and get ready to share. A group member is selected to express his or her experience through dramatic reenactment. In phase two, enactment, the group acts out scenes that represent the selected group member's life. A therapist facilitates this phase and works to foster catharsis, insight, and change. Sharing is the final phase of the psychodrama. Here group members explore the similarity and difference of experience between their lives and that of the protagonist. The goal of such sharing is greater awareness, the realization that one is not alone, and enhanced confidence and empowerment.

Drama therapy age appropriateness. Like art therapy, the use of drama therapy cuts across age groups and can be used in preschools, elementary schools, middle schools, and high schools. As with the other creative art therapies, drama therapy with young children provides a nonverbal means of self-expression. Young children may act out a character, for instance, through movement and interaction with other characters in a dramatic reenactment.

For elementary and middle school children, the drama therapy process can involve the telling of stories to one another about real-life situations. Storytelling is age appropriate and fits with the reading of stories that occurs at home and in the classroom. Theatrical experiences such as the use of make-up and costumes may further allow this age group to identify with the characters and stories they aim to portray. Even the creation of scenery can foster creativity, a sense of excitement about the process, and build confidence and resulting social skills in the process.

Drama therapy's peer-oriented nature makes it a developmentally appropriate intervention for adolescents. Dramatic enactment and the ensuing discussion with the audience directly correspond with the peer interaction that is so valued during this time. Adolescence is also a time of identity development and independence. Both are fostered through drama therapy in that adolescents get to bring their particular viewpoints to the characters that they embody. In addition, feedback, while facilitated by a group leader, is very much focused on input from peers. Given that some adolescents may rebel or feel distrusting toward adults at this point in their lives, the combination of facilitator and peer commentary is developmentally sound.

Drama therapy with culturally diverse youth. Almost no literature exists that explores the use of drama therapy with culturally diverse youth. Therapeutic Noh Theater is one approach that reflects an ancient Japanese dramatic art form (Green & Reinhard, 1995). Dating back to 14th-century sacred temple rituals, Noh therapy uses mime, music, and dance to convey a story. Protagonists use character masks to confront themselves in front of a mirror and engage in *kihon-no-kata*, a meditative approach to dealing with problems. The use of Noh therapy may be particularly appropriate with Japanese youth who have recently immigrated to the United States or who are familiar with the Noh tradition.

Drama therapy is also effective in helping culturally diverse youth work through complex sociocultural issues such as racism, discrimination, and grief related to the immigration process. Youth of all ages may have difficulty discussing such experiences and drama therapy can help them identify complex emotions. In addition, the creative arts school counselor may have limited personal experience with racism and immigration. Drama therapy helps the creative arts school counselor who is unfamiliar with these issues in that the sharing of their complexity stems from the youth's dramatic enactment. Thus, the culturally skilled creative arts school counselor who uses drama therapy must listen, empathize, and follow up on the cues communicated by clients.

Drama therapy is linguistically relevant for youth where English is a second language. Youth may have difficulty communicating in English. They may also be unable to access the emotions tied to a situation unless communication occurs in their language of origin (Clauss, 1998). Drama therapy provides a wonderful solution to this problem as youth can act out characters in their native tongue. The audience can consist of youth who speak the same language and thus provide further support and empowerment around the issue. For the facilitator who does not speak the same language, one strategy is to have the protagonist translate the main themes expressed during the drama. In this way, the facilitator understands what has been said and the youth is able to access the emotionality of experience through the language of origin (Clauss).

Poetry Therapy

Poetry therapy definition and process. Poetry is often considered a classroom tool and overlooked as a creative arts counseling technique. *Poetry therapy* refers to

> the use of poetry in a therapeutic experience that may involve a one-to-one relationship, a group process, or both. Such poetry is an ancillary tool that can be employed by any school of psychotherapy. The emphasis in poetry therapy is upon the person, while the accent in a typical poetry workshop is on the poem. The basic thrust of poetry in therapy is the use of metaphor and simile. (Lerner & Bettinger, 1991, p. 213)

Poetry therapy involves the reading and writing of poetry. It provides a healing experience in that individuals can share much of who they are through identification with a poem they have read or written themselves. The reading and writing of poems in creative arts counseling functions as a projective instrument through which emotions are expressed. Poetry therapy promotes greater self-expression, understanding of feelings, and self-esteem in a safe environment.

Gustavson (1999) presented several techniques that apply to the use of poetry therapy in school counseling situations. The *conversation poem* is a poem that tells a story through conversation. In using this technique, the creative arts school counselor provides an example of a conversation poem to the client who is then asked to write his or her own version. The creative arts school counselor can have the client write about a particular theme or the client can select a topic of choice.

I used to be . . . but now I am is another technique used in poetry therapy. Here clients are asked to write a poem about who they used to be and how they have changed to become their current selves. The *I used to be…but now I am* technique fosters insight about change over the course of time. Reflection about important life changes also provides the impetus for thinking about changes in the future and how counseling can facilitate the transformation process.

The *prose poem* is another technique. Creative arts school counselors introduce the prose poem format to their clients. Like the conversation poem, clients are asked to write about a particular theme or select their own topics. *Advice-giving poems* are poems selected by the creative arts school counselor that present advice about a given situation. Clients share their reaction to the advice given by the poet and subsequently write their own advice-giving poem.

In the *who I am* technique, the creative arts school counselor selects a poem that reflects a theme that is presented by the client in counseling. Gustavson (1999) used the example of the poem "I'm the Single Most Wonderful Person I Know" (Prelutsky, 1987) for clients who have conflicts with their peers. The main character brags about his personal qualities and then wonders why no one likes him. The poem concludes as follows: "[T]here's only one thing that I can't understand—why nobody likes me . . . not ever!" (p. 137). Upon reading the poem, the client is asked to discuss the difference between self-esteem and arrogance (Gustavson). The client then writes his own *who I am* poem that incorporates both personal strengths and weaknesses.

With the *suggest the line* technique, the creative arts school counselor reads a poem out loud that reflects critical themes in the client's life. The creative arts school counselor then presents an alternative line to the poem that the client is encouraged to finish. Gustavson (1999) used President Jimmy Carter's (1995) poem entitled "With Words We Learn to Hate" as an example of this technique. The creative arts school counselor reads the poem and discusses themes of hatred and intolerance with the client. The counselor then presents another line (e.g., "with words we learn to celebrate"; Gustavson, 1999) that the client must subsequently finish.

Poetry therapy age appropriateness. Poetry therapy can be used with children from preschool through high school depending on the specific technique employed. For pre-readers and writers, the creative arts school counselor can read the poem and encourage young children to share their reactions. Older children and adolescents who read and write can engage in all the aforementioned poetry therapy techniques.

Poetry therapy with culturally diverse youth. Poetry therapy provides an excellent way to capture the experience of culturally diverse youth. Critical to a culturally diverse approach is that diverse authors and themes are selected throughout the process. A culturally diverse application of the *conversation poem* technique, for instance, is Ntosake Shange's (1987) poem "Ancestral Messengers" (Gustavson, 1999). This poem depicts an authority figure who tells Señora Rodriguez why she cannot take her goat up to the 13th floor of a project building. The poem's theme centers on the clash between rural and urban cultures. After the poem is presented, the creative arts school counselor can have clients/students write poems about cultural differences (Gustavson, 1999).

Similarly, the *prose poem* techniques *I used to be . . . but now I am*, and *who-I-am* can focus on how clients view themselves in terms of their racial, ethnic, and cultural backgrounds. These mechanisms help clients focus on issues of identity, difference, and change. With the *prose poem* technique, for instance, Gustavson (1999) suggested the poem "Lil" (Gustavson, 1995)—a poem about an old woman who smells and is avoided by children and adults. After reading the poem, clients write a prose poem about someone who is misunderstood because they are of a different culture or race (Gustavson, 1999).

Sandplay Therapy

Sandplay therapy definition and process. Sandplay therapy uses sand as part of the healing process. Clients select and organize figures in a tray of sand that is usually 29" x 19" and 3" deep. The purpose of sandplay therapy is to

> 1) create in the sandtray a symbolic arena where conscious and unconscious dynamics can be presented and contained, and 2) allow for the rearranging and/or transforming of the objects in this symbolic arena in ways that foster and promote therapeutically positive changes in an individual's life. (Tennessen & Strand, 1998, p. 109)

Sandplay therapy incorporates Jungian theory as the use of sand is thought to encourage the unconscious mind to move toward its innate drive for healing (Weinrib, 1983).

Two approaches to sandplay therapy are the traditional approach and the directed approach. In traditional sandplay therapy, the sandtray is full of toys. The client works with miniatures (objects in the sandtray) as he or she chooses with no interference from the creative arts school counselor. The client is subsequently asked about what he or she created but no directives are given. Before the sandtray is disassembled, the creative arts school counselor photographs the client's work. Photographs are shown later when an interpretation is provided.

Directed sandplay therapy provides clients with guidance and direction. The directive approach believes that more involvement from the creative arts school counselor leads to greater change. Specific techniques are used to promote change more quickly. Directives include questions that ask clients to think about whether they want to change anything in the sandtray, requests to make specific changes, asking clients to depict particular scenarios, and questions about how miniatures are used in the sandtray (e.g., what a miniature wants to say and whether new miniatures should be introduced; Tennessen & Strand, 1998). Such directives are in direct contrast to the traditional approach that believes change will occur with nonverbal types of free play (Tennessen & Strand, 1998).

Sandplay therapy age appropriateness. Similar to art and drama therapy, sandplay therapy can be used in preschools, elementary schools, middle schools, and high schools. The traditional sandplay therapy approach is more relevant for younger, preverbal children as it allows the young child to move toward healing at a slower, less intrusive pace. Middle school and high school children are better candidates for directed sandplay therapy as they have the ability to use language. Youth in the formal operations stage of development can grasp the meaning of directives, understand their symbolism, and work with miniatures in new ways.

Sandplay therapy with culturally diverse youth. Cultures throughout time have viewed sand and circles of Earth as having magical, healing powers (Tennessen & Strand, 1998). Sand paintings, for instance, were often used in traditional Navajo healing ceremonies. Sandplay therapy is culturally appropriate for cultural groups that are less comfortable expressing their emotions. For instance, Asian groups that may talk about educational problems rather than emotional distress and Latino groups that may somaticize may be more likely to be receptive to this less intrusive approach (Javier & Camacho-Gingerich, 2004).

Sandplay therapy is also culturally appropriate for non-Western groups that are context dependent and thus view the individual in context. Sandplay therapy, for instance, encourages the expression of the individual in context, allows for verbal and nonverbal communication, and provides a whole-body activity that fosters greater emotional expression than the mere focus on abstract words (Enns & Kasai, 2003). This is in contrast to Western psychotherapies that tend to focus on the individual in isolation, verbal communication, direct expression of emotion, a cause-and-effect model of problems, and the separation of physical and mental states (Sue & Sue, 1999).

Enns and Kasai (2003) discussed how sandplay therapy integrates Eastern and Western values and thus is culturally appropriate for Asian/Asian American youth. They presented four commonalities between sandplay therapy's Jungian roots and Asian traditions that include

> (a) a belief in a fundamental internal drive for wholeness and healing, and a human capacity to transcend current circumstances; (b) an appreciation of symbols, metaphors, and mythology as important forms of communication; (c) an emphasis on mind-body and person-environment connections; and (d) the importance of balancing apparently opposing psychic forces such as rationality and irrationality. (Enns & Kasai, p. 96)

Hakoniwa is a Japanese version of sandplay therapy that incorporates these dual traditions and is used with children and adults in Japan. *Hakoniwa* means miniature garden and the organization of the sandtray is considered a garden that reflects the client's experience. This orientation builds upon the concept of the Japanese garden that depicts artistic and spiritual values, also known as the *karesansui* or Zen dry landscape (Enns & Kasai, 2003). Hakoniwa and sandplay therapy are appropriate for those cultural groups that express feelings through nonverbal symbols, have a time orientation focused on the here-and-now and unity between mind and body, and use discipline and relaxation techniques to regain a sense of tranquility (Enns & Kasai).

Future Directions: A New Theory of Creative Arts Counseling in Schools

The national movement toward school-based mental health provides a timely opportunity to reconceptualize the role of creative arts counseling in schools. Empirical evidence underscores the positive benefits of creative arts counseling in schools. School-based creative arts counseling increases self-efficacy, self-esteem, insight, and sense of empowerment among students. Creative arts therapy programs have been empirically proven to decrease clinical symptoms such as depression and anxiety and enhance academic performance.

The foundational techniques of creative arts therapy such as play therapy, art therapy, drama therapy, poetry therapy, and sandplay therapy are developmentally appropriate for children from preschool to high school. Creative arts counseling is naturally conducive to a school environment in that it occurs where children live and does not necessitate that they travel to an outside office. Stigma is decreased by the very nature of creative therapies; teachers can be informed of therapeutic progress when given the appropriate parental consent, and the school benefits from greater harmony among its youngest participants.

The current author has introduced the term *creative arts school counselor* to further delineate the role of the creative arts counselor who works in the schools. It is hoped that the naming of such a term decreases the confusion between the creative counselor's role and that of the art or drama teacher, among others. Creative arts school counselors can be viewed as having a specialized area that combines the creative arts with counseling in the context of school life.

Despite what creative arts school counselors provide, multiple barriers exist in the provision of comprehensive creative arts counseling in schools that include (a) differences between the culture of creative arts counseling and the culture of school-based education; (b) difficulties creating a collaborative schoolwide team effort; (c) lack of support for clinical space and process; (d) problems with allocation of classroom time for creative arts counseling sessions; (e) interruptions by the academic school calendar; (f) need for cultural competence; (g) developing/improving credentialing for creative arts school counselors; (h) development of APA guidelines regarding the practice of creative arts counseling; (i) developing/improving curriculum course offerings, programs, and requirements for creative arts school counselors; (j) additional courses in creative arts counseling in graduate-level counseling psychology programs; (k) additional training in research methods to provide a more comprehensive research approach for children's mental health; (l) eliminating the view that mental health services are not relevant to the school community; (m) helping the creative arts school counselor develop a clear role; (n) enhanced monetary support for creative arts counseling programs; and (o) educating the general public about the benefits of creative arts counseling.

A comprehensive approach to creative arts counseling in schools must largely focus on knowledge and communication. Given research that supports the efficacy of creative arts counseling in schools along with findings that indicate these techniques are underused, it is imperative that school administrators gain additional knowledge about creative arts counseling as an effective intervention. In addition, counselors themselves need additional training with regard to the theory and practice of creative arts counseling. This reality is particularly evident in research that indicates school counselors recognize the benefit of creative arts counseling but cite their lack of training as a key barrier to greater implementation (Ray et al., 2005).

Creative arts counseling research can take a more comprehensive approach by exploring broader trends that suggest what is effective with youth in schools. Truax and Mitchell (1971), for instance, examined process and outcome variables across several studies and found that empathy, non-possessive warmth, and a genuine response to children and families in distress promote helpful outcomes. Additional studies and measurement techniques are needed that move beyond process and outcome research and narrative case studies. Future research needs to better isolate those factors that promote a positive counseling experience for children in educational settings. In this way, creative arts counseling research will have greater validity, reliability, and generalizabilty.

With regard to training and standards, a lack of training among counselors is a major barrier in and of itself. In the Ray et al. (2005) study, counselors identified lack of training as the second highest barrier to using play therapy. To further promote the effectiveness of creative arts counseling in schools, research needs to investigate types of creative arts counseling training available in school counselor programs and identify areas where training is not available (Ray et al.). From this research, graduate-level programs can begin to consider the ways in which they want to expand their course offerings so that creative arts counseling is part of the future school counselor's clinical repertoire. School districts that use creative arts counseling can also work to decrease barriers that interfere with the implementation of creative arts counseling by offering training and training materials to their school counselors.

The move toward a comprehensive approach to creative arts counseling in the schools requires that these barriers are addressed by all who are involved with creative arts counseling. A comprehensive effort means that educators, administrators, parents, graduate program administrators and educators, public policy makers, creative arts school counselors, and community advocates create partnerships that make the delivery of creative arts therapies available in schools. These efforts will provide alternative ways to meet the academic and emotional needs of schoolchildren who are developmentally and culturally diverse.

References

Axline, V. (1947). *Play therapy*. Cambridge, MA: Riverside.

Bateson, G. (1955). A theory of play and fantasy. *Psychiatric Research Reports, 2*, 39–51.

Berlyne, D. E. (1960). *Conflict, arousal and curiosity*. New York: McGraw-Hill.

Campanelli, M. (1991). Art therapy and ethno-cultural issues. *American Journal of Art Therapy, 30*(2), 34–35.

Carroll, J. (2000). Evaluation of therapeutic play: A challenge for research. *Child and Family Social Work, 5*, 11–22.

Carter, J. (1995). *Always a reckoning*. New York: Times Books.

Casson, J. (n.d.). *Dramatherapy and psychodrama*. Retrieved August 19, 2005, from http://www.123webpages.co.uk/user/index.php?user=Casson&pn=104

Clauss, C. S. (1998). Language: The unspoken variable in psychotherapy practice. *Journal of Psychotherapy, 35*(2), 188–196.

Clauss-Ehlers, C. S. (2003). Promoting ecological health resilience for minority youth: Enhancing health care access through the school health center. *Psychology in the Schools, 40*(3), 265–278.

Clauss-Ehlers, C. S. (2006). *Diversity training for classroom teaching: A manual for students and educators*. New York: Springer.

Clauss-Ehlers, C. S., & Lopez Levi, L. (2002). Working to promote resilience with Latino youth in schools: Perspectives from the U.S. and Mexico. *International Journal of Mental Health Promotion, 4*(4), 14–20.

Clauss-Ehlers, C. S., & Weist, M. (2002). Children are news worthy: Working effectively with the media to improve systems of child and adolescent mental health. In H. Ghuman, M. D. Weist, & R. Sarles (Eds.), *Providing mental health services to youth where they are: School and community-based approaches* (pp. 225–239). New York: Brunner-Routledge.

Cobia, D., & Henderson, D. (2003). *Handbook of school counseling*. Upper Saddle River, NJ: Merrill Prentice Hall.

Cochran, J. L. (1996). Using play and art therapy to help culturally diverse students overcome barriers to school success. *School Counselor, 43*(4), 287–298.

Enns, C. Z., & Kasai, M. (2003). Hakoniwa: Japanese sandplay therapy. *The Counseling Psychologist, 31*(1), 93–112.

Erikson, E. H. (1985). Play and actuality. In J. S. Bruner, A. Jolly, & K. Sylva (Eds.), *Play: Its role in development and evolution* (pp. 688–704). New York: Penguin Books.

Fall, M., Balvanz, J., Johnson, L., & Nelson, L. (1999). A play therapy intervention and its relationship to self-efficacy and learning behaviors. *Professional School Counseling, 2*, 194–204.

Freud, S. (1961). *Beyond the pleasure principle.* New York: Norton.

Green, M. Y., & Reinhard, R. (1995). When art imitates life: A look at art and drama therapy. *Public Welfare, 53*(2), 34–43.

Gustavson, C. B. (1995). *In-versing your life: A poetry workbook for self-discovery and healing.* Milwaukee, WI: Families International, Inc.

Gustavson, C. B. (1999). The use of poetry in exploring the concepts of difference and diversity for gifted/talented students. *Journal of Poetry Therapy, 12*(3), 155–160.

Hall, G. S. (1920). *Youth.* New York: A. Appleton.

Hutt, C. (1985). Exploration and play in children. In J. S. Bruner, A. Jolly, & K. Sylva (Eds.), *Play: Its role in development and evolution* (pp. 202–215). New York: Penguin Books.

Javier, R. A., & Camacho-Gingerich, A. (2004). Risk and resilience in Latino youth. In C. S. Clauss-Ehlers & M. D. Weist (Eds.), *Community planning to foster resilience in children* (pp. 65–81). New York: Kluwer Academic Publishers.

Johnson, L., McLeod, E., & Fall, M. (1997). Play therapy with labeled children in the schools. *Professional School Counseling, 1*, 31–34.

Kahn, B. B. (1999). Art therapy with adolescents: Making it work for school counselors. *Professional School Counseling, 2*(4), 291–298.

Kalish-Weiss, B. (1989). *Creative arts therapies in an inner city school.* Los Angeles: Los Angeles Unified School District and Los Angeles County Department of Mental Health. (ERIC Document Reproduction Service No. ED 341 911)

Landreth, G. (2002). *Play therapy: The art of the relationship* (2nd ed.). New York: Brunner-Routledge.

Landreth, G. L., Homeyer, L. E., Glover, G., & Sweeney, D. S. (1996). *Play therapy interventions with children's problems: Case studies with DSM-IV diagnoses.* Northvale, NJ: Aronson Press.

Lazarus, M. (1883). *Die reize des spiels* [The stimuli of play]. Berlin: Fred dummlers-Verlagsbuch-handlung.

Lerner, A., & Bettinger, S. (1991). Some semantic considerations in poetry therapy. *A Review of General Semantics, 48*(2), 213–219.

Martin, P., & Midgeley, E. (1994). Immigrants to the United States: Journey to an uncertain destination. *Population Bulletin, 49*(2), 1–47.

Mead, G. H. (1934). *Mind, self, and society.* Chicago: University of Chicago Press.

Mellou, E. (1994). Play theories: A contemporary review. *Early Childhood Development and Care, 102*, 91–100.

Milos, M. E., & Reiss, S. (1982). Effects of three play conditions on separation anxiety in young children. *Journal of Consultation and Clinical Psychology, 50*, 389–395.

Naumburg, M. (1950). *An introduction to art therapy: Studies of the "free" art expression of behavior problems of children and adolescents as a means of diagnosis and therapy.* New York: Teachers College Press.

Omizo, M. M., & Omizo, S. A. (1989). Art activities to improve self-esteem among native Hawaiian children. *Journal of Humanistic Education and Development, 27*, 167–176.

Piaget, J. (1962). *Play, dreams, and imitation in childhood.* New York: Routledge.

Porter, R. Y. (2000). Understanding and treating ethnic minority youth. In J. Aponte & J. Wohl (Eds.), *Psychological intervention and cultural diversity* (pp. 167–182). Boston: Allyn and Bacon.

Prelutsky, J. (1987). *The new kid on the block.* New York: Scholastic, Inc.

Ray, D. C., Armstrong, S. A., Warren, E. S., & Balkin, R. S. (2005). Play therapy practices among elementary school counselors. *Professional School Counseling, 8*(4), 360–365.

Riley, S. (1994). Rethinking adolescent art therapy treatment. *Journal of Child and Adolescent Group Therapy, 4*, 81–97.

Robson, C. (1993). *Real world research: A resource for social scientists and practitioner-researchers.* Oxford, UK: Blackwell.

Schaefer, C. E. (1993). *The therapeutic powers of play.* Northvale, NJ: Aronson.

Shange, N. (1987). *Ridin' the moon in Texas.* New York: St. Martin's Press.

Shen, Y., & Herr, E. L. (2003). Perceptions of play therapy in Taiwan: The voices of school counselors and counselor educators. *International Journal for the Advancement of Counselling, 25*(1), 27–41.

Shostak, B. (1985). Art therapy in schools: A position paper of the American Art Therapy Association. *Art Therapy, 14*, 19–21.

Spencer, H. (Ed.). (1878). *The principles of psychology* (Vol. 2). New York: A. Appleton.

Stagnitti, K. (2004). Understanding play: The implications for play assessment. *Australian Occupational Therapy Journal, 51*, 3–12.

Sue, D. W., & Sue, W. (1999). *Counseling the culturally different: Theory and practice* (3rd ed.). New York: John Wiley & Sons.

Sullivan, H. S. (1954). *The psychiatric interview.* New York: W.W. Norton.

Tennessen, J., & Strand, D. (1998). A comparative analysis of directed sandplay therapy and principles of Ericksonian psychology. *The Arts in Psychotherapy, 25*(2), 109–114.

Truax, C. B., & Mitchell, K. M. (1971). Research on certain therapist interpersonal skills in relation to process and outcome. In A. E. Bergin & S. L. Garfield (Eds.), *Handbook of psychotherapy and behavior change* (pp. 229–344). New York: John Wiley & Sons.

Urtz, F. P., & Kahn, K. B. (1982). Using drama as an outreach and consultation tool. *The Personnel and Guidance Journal,* 326–328.

U.S. Bureau of Census. (1996). *Current population reports: Population projections of the United States by age, race, and Hispanic origin, 1995–2050.* Washington, DC: U.S. Government Printing Office.

Webb, N. B. (1999). *Play therapy with children in crisis.* New York: Guilford.

Weinrib, E. (1983). *Images of the self: The sandplay therapy process.* Boston: Sigo Press.

Weisz, J. R., & Weiss, B. (1993). *Effects of psychotherapy with children and adolescents.* Newbury Park, CA: Sage.

Wengrower, H. (2001). Arts therapies in educational settings: An intercultural encounter. *The Arts in Psychotherapy, 28,* 109–115.

XXXIV
COUNSELING THE GIFTED AND TALENTED

CORISSA C. LOTTA AND ERICA A. KRUGER
University of Wisconsin-Madison

BARBARA A. KERR
University of Kansas

Introduction

Gifted and talented students are some of the most rewarding and challenging students for the school counselor. It is surprising, then, that these students are so seldom discussed in counseling training programs, despite evidence that these students are at risk for negative academic and social–emotional outcomes, including underachievement, dropout, stress, and depression (Colangelo & Davis, 1997; Kerr, 1991; Lovecky, 1993; Moon, Kelly, & Feldhusen, 1997; Silverman, 1993). While there is a great deal of literature and research on gifted students, very few school counselors have been required to demonstrate proficiency in these topics in the course of their education and training. Of course, this does not mean that they will not encounter these students in their school counseling work—gifted students are in every school at every grade level. It does, however, mean that school counselors may not have the knowledge required to identify and support this population, nor the ability to recognize the importance of providing services that address their specific needs (Adams-Byars, Whitsell, & Moon, 2004; VanTassel-Baska & Baska, 2004).

The Unique Academic and Social/Emotional Needs of Gifted Students

The importance of being knowledgeable about these students is illustrated by the following vignettes. Although identifying information has been changed, each of these scenarios is based on actual individuals with whom the authors have worked in a counseling setting.

Matt, a third-grade Caucasian student at a small suburban elementary school, has a history of excellent school performance. He is well liked by all of his teachers, involved in extracurricular activities, and appears to have friends. A recent phone call from Matt's mother, however, indicates that Matt has been increasingly withdrawn and has been having difficulty sleeping.

Anita is a fifth-grade Latina student at a medium-sized urban elementary school who has been referred to the school counselor due to frequent absences and issues with homework completion. Teacher reports about Anita's performance are inconsistent. Most teachers report that Anita is struggling, but her math teacher notes that Anita's work is often excellent, although at times it is often incomplete or not turned in at all. Anita comes from a home in which Spanish is spoken as the primary language, and receives extra support, at school, because of her English language learner (ELL) status.

Jackie, a seventh-grade African American student at a large urban middle school, has been referred to the Student Services Team by her teacher because she has become increasingly disruptive in the classroom. In particular, her teacher is frustrated with Jackie's "attitude problem," including complaining about certain assignments, talking out of turn, and her tendency to negatively influence other students. Jackie's grades are average.

Before you read further, take a moment to consider the following questions: What are your initial impressions about these students and the issues that they are facing? What do you think your role as a school counselor would be in each of these situations? What interventions do you think would be needed in order to best meet the academic and social/emotional needs of these individuals?

Now, think about how your responses to these questions might change if you also had the following additional information.

Matt was identified as gifted in first grade and has been excelling in the school's gifted programs. His teachers have described him as well behaved and creative, although he occasionally seems to be preoccupied and "in his own head." Matt's mother states that he has a vivid imagination and has always been highly sensitive. Although Matt has always had friends, he currently spends most of his time alone or with one particular friend, often playing elaborate fantasy games. Matt's parents went through a difficult divorce 2 years ago, and Matt now lives with his mother, seeing his father every other weekend. School has always been enjoyable for Matt, although lately he seems less enthusiastic.

Anita and her family moved from Mexico when Anita was in the first grade. Spanish is the primary language spoken at home. Because her parents both work several jobs to support them and their extended family, Anita is responsible for caring for her younger siblings and often does not get to her homework until late at night. Her math teacher states that Anita is a quick learner and often provides tutoring and support for other students in the class. When asked, Anita states that she loves school, especially math.

A review of Jackie's cumulative file indicates above average scores on standardized tests and strong academic performance throughout grade school. Previous teachers have described her as "well-liked, assertive, and determined." Jackie is very involved at the community center near her home and is widely considered a leader. She expresses a passion for acting and singing, and participates in her church choir and a local children's theater group. Jackie reports that she doesn't like school very much anymore because "it's boring."

Even though each of these stories is very different, there *is* a common thread that ties these students' experiences together—giftedness. These vignettes illustrate that gifted students are diverse, both in terms of demographics and in how their giftedness is expressed. In addition, these vignettes help us to understand why accurate identification and knowledge of the specific academic, social, and emotional concerns of gifted students are so essential. Without appropriate support, Matt could become depressed and begin to underachieve; Anita may never be identified as having high ability and receive the guidance she needs to reach her potential; and Jackie may become increasingly bored and frustrated and eventually drop out of school. It is easy to see how, if one is not familiar with the characteristics and issues common to gifted children and adolescents, the specific needs of these students may go unmet. Although the school counselor may recognize that there are problems or concerns, and even make efforts to intervene, without a comprehensive understanding of the role that giftedness plays in the student's experience, these intervention attempts may not be the most effective or efficient.

Mixed Messages

It is difficult to understand why school counselors are often not provided with the knowledge, training, and resources to effectively meet the needs of their gifted and talented students. In large part, however, it may be due to society's mixed messages regarding its hopes for the youth within our educational systems. On the one hand, there are proclamations that our nation must support our youth in reaching their potential in order to be innovative and competitive in a global economy. At the same time, however, society sends messages that suggest that nurturing the potential of those youth with outstanding talent is elitist (Colangelo & Davis, 2002; Galbraith & Delisle, 1996; Silverman, 1993; Winebrenner, 2001). The U.S. Department of Education's (USDE) report (1993) *National Excellence: The Case for Developing America's Talent* stated, "The belief espoused in school reform that children from all economic and cultural backgrounds must reach their full potential has not been extended to America's most talented students." This report went on to assert that within our schools, bright students are underchallenged and underachieving, and that the students who are most neglected are those who are economically disadvantaged or from racial/ethnic minority groups.

Given the complexity and confusion regarding how our society views and values the gifted, it is not surprising that education systems have been inconsistent in both the nurturing of these students and in the training of those who provide services to them. This inconsistency means that school counselors are often lacking information and training regarding gifted children, leaving them unprepared to recognize or meet the academic or social/emotional needs of these students (VanTassel-Baska & Baska, 1993).

Myths About Giftedness

Further complicating matters are a number of common misconceptions that hinder the provision of services for gifted children. You might encounter these in teachers, school staff, and individuals outside of the school. You might even struggle with them yourself. The following are three myths that you may frequently encounter within the school setting regarding gifted children and their needs:

Myth 1: Gifted kids are easily identified—"You'll know one when you see one."

Myth 2: Gifted kids don't need academic or vocational guidance—"What do they need help with? They can *do* anything and *be* anything they want!"

Myth 3: Gifted kids don't have any social or emotional problems—"They've got it all (and if they don't, they are smart enough to figure it out themselves)."

As we will examine in this chapter, these myths not only are inaccurate, but can also be dangerous to the academic and social/emotional well-being of gifted students. Unless school counselors are prepared to challenge these myths, there can be serious impact on the development of gifted students—gifted students will not be accurately identified, nor will they receive appropriate services. The academic repercussions of this include underidentification, boredom, frustration, underachievement, behavioral issues, and dropping out. Social/emotional repercussions include stress, anxiety, isolation, depression, and struggles with interpersonal relationships.

Providing appropriate services for gifted students requires a solid understanding of how giftedness shapes the way a child experiences his or her world. As described in the American School Counselor Association's (ASCA; 2005) position statement on gifted student programs, professional school counselors play a critical role in supporting their gifted students through counseling, consultation, and advocacy. School counselors need to be aware of and sensitive to the numerous challenges faced by gifted students—from an educational system that is often not designed to develop their academic potential to a social and emotional landscape fraught with internal and external challenges (Colangelo & Davis, 2002; Silverman, 1993). Without the understanding and support of a well-informed school counselor, these children may be left to navigate this difficult terrain alone, with little guidance into their futures. Furthermore, they may even be met with hostility or ambivalence—from peers, teachers, counselors, administrators—and an overall political climate that does not support intellectualism (Colangelo & Davis, 2002; Gallagher, 1991; Marland, 1972; Sherman, 1997; Silverman, 1993; Webb & Kleine, 1993).

Naturally, school counselors want to meet the needs of and support *all* students. As school counselors strive to be culturally competent, it is important to remember that sensitivity to diversity includes recognizing gifted students. Although there is not one specific comprehensive model of school counseling for gifted children within the literature, this chapter seeks to present information and research on some of the most salient issues and concerns faced by gifted students so that school counselors can be better prepared to understand and meet the needs of this population.

We recognize the challenges that limited budgets, lack of resources, and increasing student needs place on the school counselor. Erford (2003) noted that "over the past several decades, many professional school counselors and counselor educators have come to realize that the job descriptions and role responsibilities, coupled with the work and caseload realities, are overwhelming for all but the superhuman" (p. 12). Our hope is that by providing this information, it will help the school counselor to be more *effective* and *efficient* in recognizing and supporting gifted students. Furthermore, we hope that this chapter will not only inform the school counselor's own practice, but also increase his or her capacity to be an advocate and resource for parents and other school staff. Lastly, and most importantly, we hope to provide sufficient guidance to support school counselors in nurturing the potential of students like Matt, Anita, and Jackie.

Chapter Goals

Within this chapter, we will

- present useful models for understanding the academic and social/emotional issues of gifted students;
- present salient and culturally relevant research that will further a school counselor's understanding of the primary academic and social/emotional issues of gifted students;
- provide frameworks to help school counselors understand the multiple roles that they play in effectively serving the gifted population;
- illustrate how the literature is applied to practice and provide suggestions for interventions to aid in meeting the academic and social/emotional needs of gifted students; and
- explore recommendations for future research and practice with the gifted population.

Dispelling the Myths

Gifted children have many of the same needs as other children—they experience the same physical maturation process, they go through the same developmental stages (although often at an earlier age), and they may face similar family issues such as poverty, divorce, or alcoholism

(Webb & Klein, 1993). In addition, it has been well documented within the literature that gifted children also have academic and social/emotional needs specifically related to their giftedness, yet these needs frequently go unmet (Colangelo, 1991; Davis & Rimm, 1989; Kerr, 1991, 1994; Moon et al., 1997; Silverman, 1993). The myths presented in the introduction have a profound impact on how these students are perceived, and they contribute to a lack of understanding, support, and guidance for gifted students in the school setting. In the following section, we will take a closer look at these myths and the research that dispels them. In addition, we will familiarize the school counselor with important information about gifted issues and practices that he or she will encounter, including identification, curriculum guidance, career guidance, and social/emotional concerns.

Myth 1: Gifted kids are easily identified—"You'll know one when you see one."

There is a misperception that all gifted kids are alike—that they do well on achievement tests, have As in all subjects, are mature, well behaved, and enjoy school. In reality, however, there is tremendous diversity among gifted students, differences in what they look like and in how they think, feel, and act (Fiedler, 1993; Sanborn, 1979). Unfortunately, the methods of identification that are commonly used by school systems do not produce gifted and talented student populations that reflect this diversity. Historically, school-based identification and assessment practices have resulted in a disproportionate representation of certain types of students in gifted and talented programs, namely students who are White or Asian American, academically successful, English speaking, middle to upper class, and well behaved (Galbraith & Delisle, 1996; Hunsaker, 1995; Sherman, 1997). These are the kids who rise to the surface in the traditional classroom as "teacher pleasers" and are most likely to be recognized by teachers and school staff (Davis & Rimm, 1989). Because they match the assumptions of what gifted kids are like, they are typically the ones identified as gifted.

Students like Anita and Jackie who are also gifted but are not recognized by the traditional methods of identification are in those same classrooms. According to the U.S. Department of Education's (1993) report *National Excellence: A Case for Developing America's Talent* there are several groups of children who are often neglected in gifted programs. These are the gifted students who are non-White, are from a lower socioeconomic background, have a disability, are female (who are underserved in mathematics and science programs), are underachieving in school, are from rural communities, or are those whose talents are primarily in the arts (Colangelo & Davis, 2002; Davis & Rimm, 1989; Galbraith & Delisle, 1996; Silverman, 1993). They also include students who have behavioral problems, are LL, and come from families who are less familiar with how to successfully navigate through the school system.

The assumption that gifted kids are easy to identify reflects a misunderstanding of what it means to be gifted. Who, exactly, fits under the category of "gifted"?

Definition and identification of gifted. There have been numerous definitions of gifted and talented over the years. The federal definition of gifted and talented has changed several times since it was originally developed for the 1972 *Marland Report to Congress*. According to the National Association for Gifted Children (NAGC) Web site (2005), the current definition is

> The term gifted and talented student means children and youths who give evidence of higher performance capability in such areas as intellectual, creative, artistic, or leadership capacity, or in specific academic fields, and who require services or activities not ordinarily provided by the schools in order to develop such capabilities fully.

While the federal definition is comprehensive and inclusive, states and districts are not required to use the federal definition (NAGC, 2005). Furthermore, what is defined is not always what happens in practice. In practice, there is wide variability in the identification process, with some processes being more broadly defined (e.g., utilizing multiple criterion in multiple areas) and some being more narrowly defined (e.g., a single standardized assessment). One procedure for identification that is commonly used in schools is teacher referral (Naglieri & Ford, 2003). This method has received criticism because researchers have found that teachers often underrefer certain groups of students for gifted education screening and programs (Ford, 1998; Naglieri & Ford). Furthermore, the No Child Left Behind Act, the continued opposition to intelligence testing, and the severe underfunding of schools have created a situation in which most schools have had to cut back on the identification of gifted students or end the procedure entirely (Davidson, Davidson, & Vanderkam, 2004).

Many gifted students are overlooked because they are not academically successful across all subjects; that is, they are not straight-A students at the top of the class in all subject areas (Winebrenner, 2001). These same students may not do well on all portions of standardized assessments—such as an IQ test—therefore, their cumulative IQ may not meet certain cutoff criteria set by the school district. Many students are high ability in certain areas and below average in others (Galbraith & Delisle, 1996; Gardner, 1983). It is also possible that some children might be challenged by a behavior or learning disability that "masks" their giftedness and impacts their performance in certain areas (Colangelo & Davis, 2002; Galbraith & Delisle, 1996; Silverman, 1993). Others may be bored by certain subjects; they may be excelling in one class where they feel sufficiently challenged, but failing another where they are uninterested or unmotivated (Galbraith & Delisle, 1996; Webb, 1994). Another group of gifted students who may have varied academic performance are those who are creative. These students tend to be less visible within traditional course work and less likely to be identified as gifted (Davis & Rimm, 1989; Renzulli & Reiss, 1986).

Additional factors, such as peer pressure, may also cause certain groups of gifted students to self-mask their own giftedness. This is especially true for adolescent girls. Although gifted girls in elementary school often surpass their male counterparts in academic performance, a significant shift can occur in the middle school years (Kerr & Nicpon, 2003). During adolescence, gifted girls begin to self-select out of higher level academic classes, particularly in the areas of math, science, and technology and may deliberately downplay their giftedness in order to conform to the expectations of their peer group (Callahan, Cunningham, & Plucker, 1994; Colangelo & Peterson, 1993; Frey, 1998; Kerr, 1994; Orenstein, 1994).

Current practices in identification are missing a large number of other students as well. There continues to be an underrepresentation of racial/ethnic minority and economically disadvantaged populations in gifted programming despite the fact that many researchers have called attention to this problem (Maker, 1996; Piirto, 1999; Silverman, 1993). Although evidence of intelligence is found in all children regardless of race, ethnicity, socioeconomic status, or geographic location, investigation into gifted programming has found that some minority groups are more likely to be served than others are (Colangelo, Assouline, & Gross, 2004; Schwartz, 1997). In her examination of national demographics of gifted programming, Ford (1996) reported the trend that Black, Hispanic, and Native American students have consistently been underrepresented in gifted education. The National Education Longitudinal Study of 1988 (NELS 88) found that about 8.8% of all 8th-grade public school students participated in gifted and talented programs (National Center for Education Statistics, 2000). Racial and ethnic groups were represented as follows: 17.6% of Asian students; 9.0% of White (non-Hispanic) students; 7.9% of African American students; 6.7% of Hispanic students; and 2.1% of American Indian students. The study also reported that states that use IQ-score cutoffs to identify gifted and talented students are more likely to have larger disparities among racial and ethnic groups. A growing body of literature has highlighted the fact that African American students are overrepresented in special education programs and underrepresented in gifted and talented programs (Ford, 1995; Ford, Harris, Tyson, & Trotman, 2002; Harmon, 2001; Morris, 2002; Patton, 1998). This literature suggests that the lack of identification of minority gifted students is due to a combination of factors, including cultural biases in assessment procedures, a lack of multicultural awareness on the part of referring teachers and school staff, and the existence of both covert and overt institutional racism. Negative stereotypes and inaccurate perceptions of the abilities of children from minority groups contribute to underrepresentation of racial/ethnic minority students (Ford, 1998; McCarty, Lynch, Wallace, & Benally, 1991; Patton, 1998).

As with adolescent females, the identification of gifted students of color may also be impacted by the influence that peer pressure has on these students' willingness to openly display their giftedness. Research suggests that this is especially true for academically successful African American students, who may receive negative feedback from both White and African American peers (Ford, 1994; Kitano, 1998; Kruger, 2004; Tatum, 1997). Concerns about social acceptance may further hinder accurate identification for this population.

According to the NELS 88 data, another group of significantly underserved gifted students were those who were economically disadvantaged (National Center for Education Statistics, 2000). Only 9% of students in gifted and talented education programs were in the bottom quartile of family income, while 47% of program participants were from the top quartile of family income.

Many believe that current definitions of giftedness do not adequately address culture, ethnic, economic, ability, and linguistic differences (Ford, 2001; Maker, 1996; McCarty et al., 1991; USDE, 1993). According to McKenzie (1986), identification procedures that use standardized achievement tests and intelligence scales reinforce social inequalities and miss some of the most promising students. Since the passing of the Jacob K. Javits Gifted and Talented Students Act of 1988, there has been a movement toward seeking alternative ways of identifying gifted children to better represent historically underidentified populations (Hertzog, 2003). Clearly, the identification and assessment of gifted and talented students is complex. A single test for all students is not an adequate approach to identify diverse students and talents (USDE, 1998). Many researchers and practitioners, as well as the NAGC (2005), recommend multiple assessment approaches to give students several opportunities to demonstrate their skills and performance potential (Maker; USDE). The ASCA (2005) advocates identifying gifted and talented students through the use of multiple criterion systems, which may include intellectual ability, academic performance, visual and performing arts ability, practical arts ability, creative thinking ability, leadership potential, parent/teacher/peer nomination, and expert evaluation.

Using multiple intelligences can help to recognize students who would traditionally be left unidentified, particularly those from diverse cultures. Most well known is the work of Gardner (1983), who proposed the Multiple Intelligences Theory, which states that there exist not one intelligence but many, including linguistic, mathematical–logical, spatial–visual, musical, interpersonal, intrapersonal, and kinesthetic. The intelligences can function independently or be combined in any number of ways. Multiple Intelligences Theory has gained increasing interest, yet has not consistently found its way into schools (Galbraith & Delisle, 1996). Within most classrooms, the intelligences that are recognized and supported are those related to language and math. Students demonstrating the other intelligences are not as likely to have their gifts valued and nurtured. While Gardner's Multiple Intelligences Theory has not been empirically validated through research (Pfeiffer, 2003), it can serve as a useful way to identify more diverse students and guide counselors in supporting individual students' needs.

In addition to recommendations for multiple criterion and assessment approaches in identifying gifted students from organizations such as NAGC and ASCA, researchers also note the importance of considering the values and beliefs of the particular culture when choosing the procedures for identifying gifted and talented students (Maker, 1996; Tonemah, 1987; USDE, 1993). By utilizing both qualitative and quantitative data, the assessment of gifted students can be more comprehensive and inclusive.

Myth 2: Gifted kids don't need academic or vocational guidance—"What do they need help with? They can *do* anything and *be* anything they want!"

Those who are identified as gifted are often perceived as on the fast track to a lifetime of accomplishments and success, requiring little support or guidance (Galbraith & Delisle, 1996; Winebrenner, 2001). It is assumed that a gifted student will thrive throughout his or her school years and into any number of career areas. Little consideration is given to the multitude of barriers—academic, social, and emotional—that can interfere with the academic and vocational development of gifted children. It is surprising to many that students like Matt, who are identified as gifted and talented as early as elementary school, are at high risk for underachievement and dropping out of school. In addition, there is little understanding or sensitivity to the struggle the decision-making process can present to a gifted student who is multipotential, placing these students at further risk of not achieving their dreams and goals (Kerr, 1991).

Underachievement and dropping out. An area that has gained increasing attention among researchers is the underachievement of gifted students (Reis, Colbert, & Hebert, 2005; Seeley, 1993). According to Seeley, an underachiever is a student "who do[es] not achieve in the academic areas at a level consistent with his or her capability" (p. 263). According to the National Commission on Excellence in Education's (1983) report *A Nation at Risk,* over one half of gifted students do not achieve in school at the level predicted by their tested ability. Those who are gifted may also be at risk for dropping out of school (Renzulli & Park, 2000). There have been reports that up to 18% of all high school dropouts are gifted students (Solorzano, 1983). A study by Renzulli and Park further pointed out that many gifted dropouts are racial minorities from low socioeconomic backgrounds.

There are a variety of potential reasons that gifted students may perform below their potential, including disabilities (Mendaglio, 1993; Seeley, 1993), behavioral issues (Seeley), and boredom due to a curriculum that does not challenge them or meet their needs (Reis et al., 2005; USDE, 1993). As previously discussed, the pressures of peer acceptance can also have a direct impact on gifted students' attitudes toward academic achievement. As early as elementary school, some students (especially girls) report deliberate underachieving, or "dumbing down," so that they would be more accepted by peers (Colangelo et al., 2004; Colangelo & Peterson, 1993; Kerr, 1994). Another explanation for underachievement among the gifted is that schools are not appropriately serving this population. Seeley stated, "When schools do not actively identify giftedness among young children, culturally different children, gifted girls, or special populations, they 'underserve' these students who consequently underachieve in relation to their potential" (p. 264).

Pressures from nongifted peers not to perform well in school (Olszewski-Kubilius & Scott, 1992) may also contribute to dropout rates for gifted minority students. A number of researchers have reported concern about gifted racial/ethnic minority students who are underachieving because of their concern with being accused of "acting White" if they achieve academically (Ford, 1995; Kitano, 1998; Tatum, 1997; USDE, 1993). In a survey administered to 144 ethnically and economically diverse gifted students in grades 6 through 8, the most significant reason that respondents gave for lowered academic performance was their fear of losing friends (Reis, Callahan, & Goldsmith, 1996). Bell's (1989) ethnographic study of ethnically diverse preteens found that participants frequently avoided, or downplayed, success because they viewed their success as others' failure and were concerned that openly acknowledging their achievements would make others "feel bad" (p. 122). Bell has suggested that the conflict that this creates can become internalized as "ambivalence about success" and lead to a hesitancy to value one's own accomplishments, decreased academic risk taking, and underachievement (p. 123). Friendships with other achieving students have been found to be a protective factor against underachievement among economically disadvantaged, ethnically diverse high school students (Reis et al., 2005).

Some suggest that a prevalence of White teachers and lack of culturally relevant curriculum in gifted education programs can also make it challenging for gifted minority students to feel inspired to achieve to their potential, thereby leading to underachievement (Day-Vines, Patton, & Baytops, 2003; Tatum, 1997). Ford (2001) discussed the importance of students being able to "see themselves reflected (and affirmed) in the curriculum" (p. 142), through multicultural books, materials, lesson plans, discussions, and culturally diverse role models.

In a study of economically disadvantaged, ethnically diverse high school students, Reis and colleagues (2005) reported that negative interactions with teachers and "questionable counseling experiences" were also associated with underachievement (p. 116). In working with gifted underachievers, these authors proposed that school counselors focus on resilience for gifted students. This study found that protective factors for underachieving youth included involvement with supportive adults (including caring teachers and counselors), friendships with other gifted students, challenging course work, participation in multiple extracurricular activities, and the development of a strong belief in self. In addition, these students benefited from strategies for coping with negative aspects of their school, an urban environment, and for some, their families.

Poverty has a major impact on school success (Seeley, 1993). Seeley emphasized that the "underachievement and higher drop out rates for minority students is a function of *poverty*, not race or ethnicity" (p. 265). Living in poverty is strongly related to low educational achievement and low self-efficacy (Schunk, 1991; Yee et al., 1995), even for those who are considered gifted (Moon et al., 1997). Some reported that children from poor families are three times more likely to drop out of school than economically advantaged families (Horowitz & O'Brien, 1989), and others reported that they may be up to eight times more likely to drop out (National Center for Education Statistics, 1997). Poverty not only limits opportunities in education and careers, but also contributes to increased rates of substance abuse and depression (Yee et al., 1995). VanTassel-Baska, Patton, and Prillman (1989) conducted a national study of culturally diverse, low-income gifted students. These authors concluded that these students were especially at risk and would benefit from additional opportunities beyond those provided to more advantaged gifted students, such as tutoring, mentoring, and counseling. Kitano (2003) also advocated for qualitatively different services designed to meet the unique needs of economically disadvantaged students. Increasing involvement of parents and families, particularly of those at risk because of poverty, can also be a critical factor in improving academic success. For those gifted children who are immigrants, school counselors may need to help them and their families obtain special services to address linguistic and cultural differences, economic and health factors, and stress from culture shock (Harris, 1991).

An often overlooked group of gifted students are those from rural communities. There are unique barriers often faced by gifted students in rural communities, including small numbers of students, limited resources, and low socioeconomic status (Lewis, 2000; Milligan, 2004). These challenges contribute to gifted students' being underidentified and underserved in rural schools, leaving them at increased risk for underachievement (Benbow, Argo, & Glass, 1992; Luhman & Fundis, 1989). The school counselor must be sensitive to the ways in which geographic location can affect gifted students' access to resources. Key intervention strategies for this population of gifted students include helping them develop relationships with other academically engaged peers and assisting them in accessing enrichment opportunities, such as online classes and summer programs.

In a nationwide study, McCoach and Siegle (2003) found that gifted achievers and gifted underachievers differed in their attitudes toward school, attitudes toward teachers, motivation/self-regulation, and goal valuation. To provide interventions for these youth, these authors suggested that school counselors should assess whether underachieving gifted students value the goals of the school and whether they are motivated to reach these goals, stating, "If they value neither the task nor the outcome, they will not possess the motivation to give the task their best effort" (p. 144). Goal-setting and future-planning activities can help students find both intrinsic and extrinsic benefits to school.

Academic guidance. The academic needs of gifted children frequently go unmet, making academic guidance for gifted students a critical component of their education throughout their years in school (VanTassel-Baska, 1993a). School counselors are often in the position to provide consultation in helping parents understand the options and make decisions about education planning for their children. Over the years, there have been a number of strategies and recommendations for meeting the academic needs of gifted students, often creating controversy and confusion. Gifted education as a profession was so shaken by accusations in the 1980s of "tracking" and elitism from the federal level to the local level that gifted education offerings in many school systems underwent profound changes (Kerr, 1991). Programs that featured ability grouping were often watered down or eliminated; programs that emphasized acceleration were often replaced with enrichment programs that promised to be less elitist by focusing on more defensible characteristics than intellectual ability, such as task commitment. An even stronger push in the 1990s for "inclusion" (Salend, 2004) sent gifted children back to the regular classroom entirely, where teachers were expected to provide differentiated education for gifted children as well as children of various abilities and disabilities. The irony of the move away from grouping and acceleration is that virtually all the research on education of gifted students shows these two practices to not only be best for bright students, but also not harmful to nongifted students. Two groundbreaking meta-analyses of research on educational approaches for gifted students found clear evidence that ability grouping for gifted students was associated with higher academic achievement for gifted students and positive social and emotional outcomes (Kulik & Kulik, 1992; Rogers, 1998). In addition, grouping gifted students together has had little negative effect or no effects on nongifted students.

School counselors need to be aware of the various approaches, including benefits and drawbacks, in order to provide useful consultation to parents and to best facilitate a match between needs of the student and education options. The array of curricular alternatives for gifted students is far too broad to review thoroughly in this chapter. Three models have been chosen here for purposes of illustrating the major models in use in schools: acceleration, enrichment, and differentiation. School counselors who desire to investigate curricular options more fully should refer to some of the excellent books available on the topic, such as VanTassel-Baska and Reis' (2003) *Curriculum for Gifted and Talented Students*. In reviewing these three models, the counselor should keep in mind that most schools do not employ a single model or program to meet the needs of all gifted students. Unfortunately, many of these practices are fragmented and discontinuous in scope and unsatisfactory in meeting the full-time needs of gifted students. Counselors who wish to serve as academic advocates for gifted students need to understand that most gifted students in this country are *not* receiving an appropriate or challenging education, and that many of the problems that gifted children face are linked to the lack of services or programming that truly suit their needs.

Acceleration. Acceleration is an approach that involves "moving students through an educational program at rates faster, or at a younger ages, than typical" (Colangelo et al., 2004, p. xi). It has been demonstrated that acceleration is effective, is economical, and can benefit students from poor schools as well as those from wealthier schools. Further, it has been suggested that acceleration may be the only alternative for meeting the curricular needs of gifted students growing up in most rural settings where resources, both personnel and economic, are limited (Benbow et al., 1992; Milligan, 2004).

Early admission. Early admission is thought to be the easiest form of acceleration, but the policies and politics of school districts and state education agencies may make it difficult indeed (Colangelo et al., 2004; Kerr, 1991). In a school district where little else can be done for gifted students, such as in many rural settings, early admission to kindergarten is a sensible choice for any child who has good social skills and emotional development for his or her age (Kerr, 1991). The school counselor who wishes to be an advocate for gifted children should be knowledgeable about the literature that shows clear benefits of early admission for gifted children and be ready to defend those parents who are struggling with rigid policies that keep gifted children from receiving this easy and economical method of acceleration (Colangelo et al.).

Grade skipping. Grade skipping was once a common practice, but is now seldom heard of. Like early admission to kindergarten, critics assailed this practice because of their desire to keep all children of the same age together (Kerr, 1991). Nevertheless, skipping 1 or 2 years has been found to be an effective practice, particularly for the highly gifted and when the extent of acceleration matches the student's abilities (Swiatek & Lupkowski-Shoplik, 2003). Grade skipping can be an especially challenging situation when a gifted child has academic skills far beyond his or her age mates, but social and physical skills at or below that of his or her age mates (Roedell, 1990). This asynchronous development can be confusing for parents and teachers. It can also be confusing and frustrating for the elementary child. When they already have the academic curriculum mastered, do not fit in intellectually with their age mates, and are not supported in their intellectual interests by their teachers, these gifted students can become increasingly frustrated, losing their natural enthusiasm for learning. Further, some may cope with their frustration by developing behavioral problems, while others may begin to deny or hide their abilities in order to fit in with their classmates. Skipped students seem to experience few negative effects of being smaller or less mature than other students and tend to feel more comfortable and be more socially adjusted with their intellectual peers than their age peers

(Swiatek & Lupkowski-Shoplik, 2003). Also, any gaps in curriculum seem to fade in just a few weeks, as bright students rapidly catch up to their classmates' level. The earlier that grades are skipped, the better for bright students; that way they have most of their education at the proper level and are able to stay with their new friends longer (Colangelo et al., 2004). An excellent way to provide grade skipping is whole grade acceleration when a group or entire class of children is "skipped" together. With this method, gifted children not only receive appropriately challenging education, but also have a peer group of bright students with whom to relate.

Talent search. The talent search approach is another form of acceleration. The goal of this program, begun at Johns Hopkins University and now expanded to all regions of the United States, is to identify young students of extraordinary mathematical reasoning ability and to help them find appropriate curricular alternatives to develop their abilities (Colangelo et al., 2004; Kerr, 1991). In order to identify these highly able students, the concept of an annual talent search was initiated in 1972. The talent search model first used out-of-level testing to identify middle school students capable of college work. By the year 2000, talent searches had become one of the most rigorously studied forms of gifted education, and hundreds of thousands of students had participated in some aspect of the search. Although each of these talent searches keeps to the same basic program of using "out-of-level testing" as a means of identifying highly gifted students, precise identification criteria and educational options made available to identified students vary from location to location.

Most talent searches are open to students in the seventh or eighth grades who achieve high test scores on standardized achievement tests designed for their grade level (identification cutoffs range from the 95th to the 97th percentile on these tests). Students who meet these cut-offs and learn of the talent search through a counselor or school publications sign up independently to take one of the standardized aptitude tests offered on a national basis several times each year. Students request that these test scores be reported directly to a talent search institution. Students who achieve a test score that meets the criteria of that particular talent search are then invited to participate in several advanced educational opportunities.

Evolving from the talent search models are several promising practices that the school counselor can use (Stanley & Benbow, 1982). These practices include the Diagnostic Testing followed by Prescriptive Instruction (DT-PI) model. Using this model, high-ability students are given a standardized test, which is then analyzed to identify specific content areas of lower competence that require instruction. Students are then assigned to a teaching strategy that specifically addresses the area in which work is needed.

Advanced placement. Advanced placement (AP) courses, developed by the College Board, have been one of the most successful means of accelerating high school students into rigorous, college-level study (Colangelo et al., 2004). One million high school students a year participate in these programs in a wide array of courses. The 34 subject areas include physical and natural sciences, mathematics, literature, languages, music, art, and social sciences. Students who are successful on the AP tests given after the courses are completed may be able to skip college courses, allowing them to take more advanced courses in college and even finish college early. Participation in AP courses has been found to increase the chances that students will graduate from college and go on to advanced education. School counselors should encourage all bright students to take as many of these courses as will fit into their schedule, as well as encourage teachers to take the special training that will allow them to teach these courses. School counselors may have to advocate in order to get some students into AP classes if these students do not fit the stereotype of a gifted student held by teachers or administrators. Counselors may also need to provide extra support and encouragement to students who—due to the negative messages that they have previously received from peers and/or school staff—do not see themselves as capable of advanced placement work.

There are potential issues related to acceleration that school counselors need to be aware of and anticipate (Kerr, 1991). The acceleration model is likely to produce students in high school who have advanced far ahead of their peers in at least one area. These students may already have exhausted all the resources available to them in their area of talent in their high school. For instance, the student who has been radically accelerated in math may already have completed calculus after a few summers at summer institutes at university programs such as Johns Hopkins or Duke. This leaves the counselor with the job of determining (a) how to factor these courses into a student's graduation requirements and (b) how to provide this student with additional appropriate academic opportunities in either mathematics or related disciplines. Another related difficulty may be that the student who has experienced highly accelerated, intellectually stimulating classes during the summer may return during the regular school year only to feel bored and frustrated with the slow pace of high school classes. Counselors may need to help students deal with these frustrations by assisting them in discovering other sources of intellectual stimulation as well as in helping them find ways of making the materials that they are studying more interesting to them.

One other outcome of accelerated programs is that students, for the first time, may have spent long periods with their intellectual peers (Colangelo et al., 2004). As a result, they have often made close friendships and have discovered a social group that has more importance for them than any they have previously experienced. Consequently, the return from a summer program or the return to a regular program from a highly accelerated program of any kind may be associated with feelings of loneliness and alienation. As with their academic transition, the school counselor can play an important role in helping gifted students successfully transition socially and emotionally back into their regular school environment.

The Enrichment Triad/Revolving Door Identification Model. Enrichment is another common method of curriculum modification and involves supplementing a student's regular curriculum with increased breadth and depth of material (Swiatek & Lupkowski-Shoplik, 2003). The Enrichment Triad/Revolving Door Identification Model (Renzulli, Reis, & Smith, 1981) is the system of identification and curriculum modification that is most widely used in schools in the United States today. The Enrichment Triad Model includes three types of student enrichment activities that progress in sequential, but qualitatively different, steps. These steps include Type I, *general exploratory activities,* in which students are exposed to a wide variety of content areas and topic experiences designed to help learners to understand their areas of personal interests; Type II, *group training activities,* which consist of materials, methods, and instructional techniques that enhance high-level thinking skills, facilitate feeling processes, may include creative problem-solving training, reflective thinking, training in inquiry, and other creative or productive thinking activities; and Type III *enrichment activities,* which provide students with opportunities to investigate a real problem by using appropriate inquiry methods, requiring students to have strong interests and task commitment. Type I and Type II are considered appropriate and valuable for all students, while Type III activities are thought to "require the special creativity, ability, and energy of truly gifted students" (Davis & Rimm, 1989, p. 162).

The Revolving Door Identification Model (RDIM) (Renzulli et al., 1981) is paired with the Enrichment Triad Model. The RDIM is the process by which a pool of approximately 15% to 20% of the student population is selected. Generally, these are students with above-average intelligence, as measured by a variety of intelligence instruments, who have also shown evidence of ability to commit themselves to tasks, and who have above-average creativity. These students are exposed to Type I activities and receive Type II process training usually on a weekly basis. During the time, the students are exposed to Type I enrichment activities and Type II training, and it is assumed that they will become interested in the more challenging Type III activities. Students "revolve into" these options as they show an interest and a desire to pursue advanced work.

Generally, an Enrichment Triad/RDIM gifted program is implemented through a pullout process. That is, students are pulled out of the regular classroom for a period of 1 to 3 hours a week in which they engage in special activities. Usually, these activities take place in a resource room with a resource teacher specially trained in facilitating student exploration in the three types of activities.

The advantages of the Enrichment Triad/RDIM are fourfold: (1) these programs do allow at least some interaction with intellectual peers, (2) only a small number of teachers are needed, (3) the teacher can concentrate on thinking and research skills because he or she does not have responsibility for basic skill development, and (4) the absence of the gifted child from the regular classroom allows other children to rise to the attention of the teacher.

According to Belcastro (1987), however, there are clear disadvantages for at least some gifted students, because pullout programs that are tied to the regular curriculum are quite rare. Instead, he said, many such programs are a smorgasbord of offerings that have no common thread and are disconnected from the regular curriculum. Too often, this becomes a collection of games and activities that do not actually constitute a qualitatively different curriculum for the gifted child. For example, the problem-solving strategies that are taught may not be associated with such content areas as biology or mathematics but instead with puzzles or mysteries. Creativity is used in future problem solving rather than applied to mathematics or social studies. In addition, the inclusion of so many non-gifted students with very gifted students often results in a dilution of the program so that it is not truly a differentiated program. In addition, a program that meets for only a few hours a week has a minimal impact on the academic experience of the gifted student (Belcastro). Time out for the gifted program is often time misused. Moreover, students who miss regular classes in order to go to the resource room are often made to finish the work they missed at other times, thus putting more pressure on them. Because of the short amount of time, students gain few opportunities to interact with their intellectual peers. Faster pacing is seldom used, although the model allows for it, and even though a wide variety of strategies is encouraged, in practice this often does not occur.

Perhaps Belcastro's (1987) criticism of the politics of pullout programs is most apt. He said that although the Enrichment Triad Model is simple and expedient, it creates the impression that something substantial is being done for the intellectually gifted. The pullout program, he said, both delays *and* impedes progress toward sounder programs because it allows administrators and teachers to be comfortable with the status quo. Regular teachers often resent the program because gifted students find the classes more exciting or stimulating than their own, and project planning is difficult due to the timing of programming. In practice, programs tended to be isolated, fragmented, time limited, and lacking in continuity with other school programs. Furthermore, negative attitudes toward gifted students in the regular classroom can be instilled when the pullout program causes an interruption of regular school programs.

The Renzulli Enrichment Triad/RDIM may lead to problems when highly gifted students are not admitted to the gifted education program. Because Renzulli's identification procedures involve selecting students of above-average intelligence who are task committed and who demonstrate creativity, it is often possible that a very high-IQ student will not be admitted. Most frequently, the very high-IQ student who is not admitted to an enrichment program is an underachiever whom teachers have a difficult time motivating. Occasionally, however, teachers or program directors have vented their resentment or hostility toward very bright students by denying them access to the program based on a subjective judgment that the student is "test-bright, but not creative" (Kerr, 1991). The unhappy scenario that often unfolds in this case is one in which the student and parent appeal their case to an administrator or board. The gifted student then is admitted to the gifted program only to learn that there is little there to meet his or her needs. Extremely bright students may feel that enrichment programs are too insubstantial and slow paced for their intellectual needs. Students in these situations may seek the counselor's aid in finding more challenging activities or even in making the enrichment program more rigorous.

Differentiation. As statewide, high-stakes testing has gained impetus throughout the United States, school administrators and teachers find themselves in the position of having to be constantly concerned about maintaining high overall scores for their school in order to receive an adequate "report card" from the state (Winebrenner, 2001). Most schools have chosen to raise their school scores by putting tremendous emphasis on raising the achievement of the lowest-scoring students. As a result, gifted students, who are already facing decreased programming as a result of budget cuts, are truly left behind.

However, grouping gifted students together in their own classroom for either acceleration or enrichment has been vigorously and persistently attacked by critics of gifted education who believe that any grouping is elitist and detrimental to disadvantaged or less academically able students (Colangelo et al., 2004; Richert, 2003). As Richert pointed out, identification practices that led to school segregation by class and ethnicity and unfair differences in the quality of the content and the instruction between gifted and regular classes have sometimes left gifted education vulnerable to these criticisms. Although efforts are being made to improve identification practices, the reality is that, with the increasing frequency of severe cuts to education budgets, gifted education classes are at continued risk for termination.

Therefore, it is likely that in the near future, most gifted students will spend most of their time in the regular classroom, with a regular classroom teacher, rather than in a resource room or self-contained classroom with a trained educator of gifted students. Of course, for most of the history of American education, this has been the way gifted students were educated. However, in the one-room schoolhouse, gifted students were allowed to work independently at their own pace and in larger schools, gifted students were skipped a grade or more or graduated early. In the present day, especially in more complexly organized schools, with less curriculum flexibility, it has been difficult for teachers of gifted students to implement even these simple options (VanTassel-Baska, 2003).

A number of scholars have developed creative responses to this situation. Richert (2003) developed innovative strategies for identifying giftedness that she claimed were ethical, equitable, and defensible in Project Apogee. In an attempt to overcome the tendency of gifted programs to serve mainly White, middle-class populations, Richert used local norms and a strategy for selecting the top 25% of every identifiable demographic group for differentiated education. The Maximizing Potential Model (Richert & Wilson, 1994) provided instruction to teachers in differentiating subject areas for individual interests, learning styles, and achievement levels. This model identified the strengths of all students through needs assessment, and then provided a wide variety of teaching strategies to maximize student strengths. Although in Project Apogee not all differentiation was within the heterogeneous classroom, the large numbers of children identified as having potential resulted in improved practices in regular classrooms. The use of Richert's identification procedures and Maximizing Potential model have led to substantial changes in numbers of students identified as well as improvements in school achievement on high-stakes state performance assessments in Connecticut, Louisiana, and New Jersey. Richert said, "Overall these results demonstrate that with intensive staff development and on site follow up, these strategies maximize students' cognitive, affective, and ethical potential" (p. 155).

Finally, VanTassel-Baska (2003) has developed detailed guides for curriculum differentiation for gifted students in the regular classroom. The Integrated Curriculum Model (ICM) takes into account the paradigm shift in educational reform focusing on learning communities and maximum competency standards. In addition, she has adapted the national and state standards to the needs of gifted students by emphasizing higher level thought processes in differentiation techniques for the regular classroom. The curricula developed by VanTassel-Baska and her colleagues include the possibilities of acceleration, increased task complexity, increased depth, increased challenge, and application of creativity to the work of the gifted student. Assessment of students is realistically based on available sources of information. Interventions are keyed to learner outcomes in a carefully planned design. Materials are provided to teachers so that each teacher need not reinvent curriculum for gifted students. Finally, a strong focus on evaluation keyed to learner outcomes ensures accountability. Evaluations of the implementation of the language arts curriculum (VanTassel-Baska, Bass, Ries, Poland, & Avery, 1998), the science curriculum (VanTassel-Baska & Baska, 2004), and the use of the ICM as a whole (VanTassel-Baska, Zuo, Avery, & Little, 2002) have shown that teachers can effectively implement differentiation of the curriculum for gifted students and can attain desired learner outcomes. Curriculum differentiation for gifted students in the regular classroom can be enhanced by the assessment techniques, the intervention strategies, and the teacher training components of many existing models of gifted education.

Some of the same criticisms that are leveled at enrichment hold true for differentiation in the regular classroom. When gifted children receive only a small portion of a teacher's attention, their education becomes fragmented (Colangelo et al., 2004). Teachers may become overwhelmed by the need to individualize education for each student, and end up resenting the amount of time and energy required by gifted children who use up educational resources rapidly. It takes a great deal of training and professional development to meet the needs of gifted children in the regular classroom in a skillful manner. Because differentiation models are fairly new, few teachers have been exposed to them in the course of their education.

Problems that can occur with differentiation models include isolation, distraction, and the pressure to help other children (Kerr & Kurpius, 2005). When there are only one or two gifted children in a classroom, bright children have little opportunity to interact with gifted peers. The gifted child can feel lonely and odd, and begin to camouflage his or her giftedness as a coping strategy (Buescher, 1986). Feelings of isolation may be further exacerbated for the gifted child of color if he or she is placed in a predominantly White classroom or for any child for whom the cultural characteristics of his or her classmates are very different from his or her own (Grantham & Ford, 1998). It is important for the school counselor to be aware of, and watch for, signs of boredom and/or withdrawal within the classroom. Research suggests that girls are more likely to withdraw as demonstrated by an unwillingness to go to school, poor class participation, daydreaming, and sadness, whereas boys are more likely to act out behaviorally (Kerr, 1994).

Distraction is a problem observed when gifted children in a differentiated classroom are given workbooks or computer-based instruction as tasks while the other children are being taught a regular curriculum. Gifted children may rapidly work through the advanced problems they are given and then spend the rest of their time doodling or reading "fun" material. On the computer, the gifted students may stray from the online curriculum to engage in instant messaging and playing games without the teacher's noticing that they have become distracted.

Finally, one of the most difficult situations for gifted children is pressure to tutor and help other students. Although they may at first enjoy their status as a peer tutor, gifted children may become tired and frustrated and begin having conflicts with their peers as a way of escaping their burdensome role. School counselors may hear parents of gifted children in the regular classroom complain that differentiated education for the gifted amounts to their children being used as tutors for children who are learning less rapidly.

When providing academic guidance, school counselors may find themselves in the position of consultant—providing parents with information about various educational approaches and assisting them in advocating for the needs of their student. Counselors may also need to work closely with teachers in developing curriculum to facilitate the development of gifted programs that are developmentally appropriate, carefully differentiated, and proactive.

Career guidance. Even Terman's (1925) highly gifted subjects from his historical study were often found to have had great difficulty translating their extraordinary intellectual ability into meaningful, productive work. Over half of the gifted women became homemakers despite earlier career aspirations; and even those who eventually achieved satisfaction and success had difficulty deciding among many career options (Terman & Oden, 1935, 1947). More recent clinical case studies and research on the gifted show that the path from youthful talent to adult accomplishment is not always straight and smooth. National Merit Scholars (Watley, 1969), Presidential Scholars (Kaufmann, 1981), and graduates of major learning programs (Kerr, 1985) all have been found to experience problems in career decision making or life planning.

One missing ingredient in the development of most gifted individuals is career guidance (Kerr, 1991). Although special education programs exist for about one third of the gifted in the nation's schools, few include a guidance career component. In a study surveying the parents, school personnel, and related professionals, Moon and colleagues (1997) found that there were strong perceptions of need for career guidance and planning of postsecondary education for gifted children and their families. Career guidance may be particularly powerful for gifted students from lower socioeconomic status or from rural settings. Students from disadvantaged backgrounds often do not have enough contact with those who could provide academic and vocational information and feel less informed about how to make career choices (Olszewski-Kubilius & Scott, 1992). These students may have limited knowledge of the world of work and a restricted sense of occupational options. Parents of these students, especially those who do not have personal experience with postsecondary education options, will also need resource information about how to support their gifted children in making appropriate academic and vocational choices.

While gifted girls and boys can both benefit from career interventions, girls seem to be at greater risk for not achieving their career goals (Kerr, 1994; Kerr & Fischer, 1997). Adolescence may be particularly difficult for gifted and talented girls, who often struggle with the conflict between achievement and affiliation needs (Clasen & Clasen, 1995; Kerr & Fischer; Moon et al., 1997) as well as with declining self-esteem (Greenberg Lake Analysis & American Association for University Women, 1991). It is also during this time that gifted girls' confidence and career aspirations begin to decline, initiating the gap between boys' and girls' career achievements that continues to widen throughout their lifetimes (Kerr, 1994).

One of the most important decisions that the school counselor will assist the gifted student in making is the choice of a college (Kerr, 1991). Gifted students are often unsure of their own characteristics and the ways in which their needs might be met by various kinds of higher education institutions. Bright students and their parents often have strong, and sometimes conflicting, opinions about college choices. Students, parents, and counselors are all often hampered by misconceptions of generalizations about what kind of college is best for gifted students. Some of the confusion about college choice is related to a lack of clarity about career choice.

There are several reasons why career interventions need to begin very early—as early as elementary school—for gifted and talented students and continue throughout schooling (Kerr, 1991). Many of the careers that gifted children find interesting require many years of advance planning. This does not mean that bright students should be pressured into making early career choices. Instead, career education and career guidance strategies should be infused into the curriculum to help gifted students progress through the stages of fantasy, exploration, crystallization, and commitment to a career.

Early emergence theory. This characteristic in the career development of some gifted students is usually not a concern for individual students, but is often the source of misunderstanding and concern for parents, counselors, and society. "Early emergers" (Marshall, 1981) are children who have an extremely focused career interest from a very early age. These children may become completely absorbed by their interests early in life and commit themselves to a career without exploring or considering other options (VanTassel-Baska, 1993a). This may be problematic for some, if this foreclosure creates a situation where a student feels locked into an early career decision and loses his or her love of learning. However, for others, this early vision of their career path means following their sincere passion and is more like a "calling."

Kerr's (1991) theory of career development for early emergence is based on the need to "scout" out specific, extraordinary talent, support early emerging interests, and provide adequate mentoring in the domain of talent. Neglecting early emergence means not noticing the talent or interest at all or failing to provide education and resources. Counselors and teachers need to be alert to the appearance of unusual talent and interests not only in traditional academic areas, but also in such areas as inventiveness and leadership. They should also be aware that a child's passion and brilliance at such recreational activities as video games, "Dungeons and Dragons," or skateboarding may be a sign of early emerging spatial–visual genius, verbal creativity, or athletic excellence, respectively. Ignoring these abilities because they emerge in play may be costly to the student's career development.

Despite the strength of the early emerger's passion, it is possible for it to be destroyed by others' belittling the talent or interest ("Who cares about someone who doodles and draws all the time instead of listening?"; "So what makes you think you will ever be able to get a job as an anthropologist?"; Kerr, 1991). It can also be done by insisting on "well-roundedness." Although the concept of the well-rounded person is deeply embedded in American educational tradition, research does not support the notion that eminent adults are knowledgeable in all fields or competent in all skills. Too often teachers and parents mistake a specialized interest as evidence of imbalance or poor adjustment when there is no basis for this evaluation. Sometimes parents or schools actively disallow needed training (e.g., refusing to allow a mathematically precocious child to accelerate in math), causing a talent to wither. Finally, overly enthusiastic encouragement and pressure may also remove the intrinsic pleasure the child feels in the interest talent area. When a child's first, tentative explorations of piano playing show precocious ability, too intense a practice schedule and concentrated parental focus may kill the child's natural desire to play well.

Career guidance must begin early for early emergers so that their precocious interests do not fade away for lack of affirmation from adults (Kerr, 1991). Early emergers will need encouragement for their profound passions, and the counselor's role will most frequently center around protecting the student from well-meaning teachers who want to focus on making these children well rounded. Counselors can help early emergers find the mentors they need in their chosen domain and impress upon parents the importance of respecting the child's desires to pursue his or her unique interests even outside of school.

Career education and guidance for gifted students needs to take into account not only their special career development needs, but also their preferences for intellectually challenging materials and methods. Career materials are often boring to bright students, and well-written biographies of diverse eminent people may be much more appropriate than the generic career guidance booklets found in most career centers. Web sites for the various professions, and organizations specially geared to children with specialized interests can be valuable to bright children who want to get a taste of what it is like to be a physician, engineer, poet, entrepreneur, or politician. Finally, career education and guidance need to be based on the discovery of a vocation or purpose rather than on the search for a job. Teaching students how to "package" themselves via resumes and interviewing skills should be deemphasized in favor of teaching students the importance of career development as a search for *meaning*.

Multipotentiality. Multipotentiality is the cause of most gifted students' difficulties in career development (Kerr, 1981b). *Multipotentiality* is defined as the ability to select and develop any number of competencies at a high level (Frederickson & Rothney, 1972). Gifted students and those who are concerned with their guidance have long recognized that having multiple potentials can be a mixed blessing. Without appropriate career guidance, multipotentiality may become a curse.

Gifted students are often multipotential because they possess a high level of general ability, which makes them able to perform capably in almost any intellectual endeavor (Kerr, 1991). Unlike students of average ability, who must make academic and career choices based on their areas of greatest strengths, many gifted students must make their choices based on some other criterion than ability. Unfortunately, vocational interests, when measured at grade level by current standardized measures, are also of limited usefulness for career decision making. The evidence that multipotentiality poses a significant barrier to effective decision making is available from decades of research, primarily from case studies and longitudinal studies. Hollingworth (1926) found that the many subjects from the large pool of gifted students she interviewed had experienced considerable difficulty both in choosing from among their many interests and in confining themselves to a reasonable number of enterprises. From 1957 until 1984 at the Wisconsin Research and Guidance Laboratory for Superior Students (where the term *multipotentiality* was coined), researchers consistently found that the gifted students attending the laboratory had excellent grades across the board in their course work, high scores across achievement tests, and multiple expressed interests on vocational instruments (Frederickson & Rothney, 1972; Perrone, Karshner, & Male, 1979; Sanborn, 1979). In the Study for Mathematically Precocious Youth at Johns Hopkins University, Fox (1978) found that junior-high-age gifted students identified by the talent search were higher on most basic interest scales than nongifted students and tended to have patterns of interest that were not clearly differentiated. Finally, studies of high school juniors and seniors scoring in the 95th percentile on the ACT showed elevated interests across five of the six occupational theme groups, all except business operations (Kerr & Colangelo, 1988).

A multipotential student may take a vocational test only to learn that he or she is "similar" in interests and abilities to biologists, librarians, musicians, reporters, English teachers, and ministers. Attaining straight As and uniformly high achievement-test scores means that the student cannot make decisions based on what he or she "does best" (Kerr, 1991). After graduation from high school, the multipotential student may vacillate between career choices, delaying career decisions until financial need and the end of a nonfocused education drive the student to take a job by default. As an adult, the multipotential gifted individual may dabble in a series of jobs, finding success but little satisfaction in any. Parents, teachers, and counselors are puzzled throughout the disappointing and spotty career of the multipotential individual. They continue to insist, "But you could be anything you want to be!" not understanding that this is precisely the problem. Thus, for many gifted students, career decision making can be an existential dilemma (VanTassel-Baska, 1993a). Having many viable vocational options and choosing only one of your dreams means that there is the loss of another. There can also be the pressure to make the "right" choice and the fear of making the wrong choice.

Too often, multipotential students make misinformed or misguided career choices. Today's gifted students make career choices based on conformity with peers, money-making potential, and pragmatism, like the rest of their generation (Astin, Green, & Korn, 1988). Unfortunately, the decisions they make are often not related to interests, needs, strongly held values, or even finely developed talent. The study of college major and career choices of the upper 10th, 5th, and 1st percentile scorers on ACT composites (Kerr & Colangelo, 1988) and the study of the choices of those students who scored perfectly on at least one scale of the ACT (English, math, social studies, natural science; Colangelo & Kerr, 1990), showed that the majority of the gifted had narrowed their career interests to business, engineering, premed, prelaw, and communications. Recent surveys of college freshman have shown similar patterns, but with stronger interest of gifted students in computer technology and biomedicine (Astin et al.). Although perfect scorers had extraordinary abilities in English, math, science, and social studies, only a small fraction were interested in majors in those areas. It is difficult to achieve a perfect score on any of these scales without unusual amounts of extracurricular reading and home study. Yet, these young people, who may value the study of the liberal arts and sciences above all other activities, seem to be discouraged about actually pursuing careers in these areas.

When providing vocational guidance for gifted students, school counselors need to be aware of the struggles faced by gifted students in their decision-making process. Silverman (1993) stated,

> Career counseling for the gifted needs to be sensitive to their multiple interests, the existential dilemmas they face in making choices, their fear of making the error, their fear of being less than their ideal or not living up to their potential, the depth of their sadness over the road not taken, and their fear that if they try to nurture all of their potential, they will end up second-rate at everything. (p. 220)

Multipotential students from elementary school throughout high school will need assistance learning to focus on one task at a time; they will need help prioritizing among their many interests; and even more important, they must learn to understand how their developing sense of identity and values relate to their interests (Kerr, 1991). They cannot be allowed to become exhausted achievers who try to excel in everything, being "all things to all people." Throughout school, counselors need to help multipotential students to understand that a true passion for one or two activities and academic areas is preferable to a competitive urge to be the best at everything they try.

Olszewski-Kublius and Scott (1992) stated that economically disadvantaged, minority gifted students are especially in need of early encouragement, exposure, and access to information, yet are less likely to receive it. Some literature suggests that even a brief career counseling intervention can have a positive impact on career development with minority students, but it is essential to respect the worldview and values of the participants (Darou, 1987; Herring, 1990; LaFromboise, Trimble, & Mohatt, 1993; Lotta & Benally, 2005). For example, it is important for school counselors to understand that academic and career decision making may be more complicated for gifted students from some collectivist cultures, because they are taking more into consideration than just themselves and their nuclear family—they are also considering the needs of their extended family and community. For many gifted students, there is recognition that the life decisions they make affect more than just themselves—they also affect the family, extended family, and community, or "home" (Lotta & Benally). Consider the following scenario:

> Beverly is a 10th-grade Native American student at a small rural high school who is participating in a career intervention program. Beverly reports that her career goal is to become a dentist. While she is a multipotential student with high grades in all subjects, her vocational assessments and interest inventories are not at all consistent with those in the field of dentistry; rather, her profiles are much more consistent with creative writing or journalistic careers. When the school counselor explores this with her, Beverly acknowledges that she enjoys writing "more than anything else," but remains adamant that she will become a dentist, adding, "It's what my people need."

Although Beverly has the potential to pursue numerous career paths, her career goals are heavily influenced by what she perceives as being needed in her community. Part of attaining her career goal involves being able to "give back" in a way that benefits her family and community, as well as herself. Community responsibility is a crucial value in her culture that may even supersede her own personal goals or decisions. Being respectful of Beverly's worldview may change the way a school counselor approaches career guidance. For example, rather than having Beverly focus on making the "appropriate career choice" based on her abilities or profiles (a more traditional approach), it may be more culturally sensitive and appropriate to help her find a "fit" between her career interests, needs, and values. Beverly has expressed her value of community by her firm commitment to provide much-needed services. The school counselor can respect Beverly's worldview by supporting her vocational decision while also helping her to find ways to also honor her other dreams; perhaps Beverly can find ways to become the dentist her community needs, and also balance her life by following her passion of writing in her avocational pursuits.

Myth 3: Gifted kids don't have any social or emotional problems—"They've got it all (and if they don't, they are smart enough to figure it out themselves)."

There is a misconception that gifted students do not have social and emotional needs. This assumption is dangerous because it means that these students do not receive the understanding and support to cope with their social/emotional struggles (Galbraith & Delisle, 1996; Kerr, 1991, Lovecky, 1993). Because gifted students may present as advanced in their cognitive abilities, it is often assumed that their emotional maturity matches their intellectual maturity. Even when it is recognized that gifted children may have social, interpersonal, or intrapersonal concerns, it may be assumed that they have intellectual abilities that provide certain coping advantages. This is the sentiment that gifted students should be able to "figure out" and manage any personal or emotional challenges that they may encounter on their own. Yet, gifted students do not always have the emotional development, life experiences, and skills to effectively cope.

While some have proposed that, overall, gifted children are better adjusted and have stronger self-concepts than regular students (Coleman & Fults, 1982; Davis & Rimm, 1989; Terman & Oden, 1951) and are socially and emotionally more mature than same-age peers (Colangelo et al., 2004), the literature and research on gifted children clearly show that gifted students *do* have social/emotional concerns. They may struggle with typical childhood and adolescent struggles, as well as additional social/emotional issues specifically related to their giftedness, including relationship issues, stress, perfectionism, and depression.

Before exploring some of the common social/emotional concerns of these students in more detail, we provide a theory of emotional development that may help the reader to understand the inner experience of gifted children.

Dabrowski's Theory of Emotional Development. One of the few psychological theories specifically focusing on giftedness and creativity is Dabrowski's Theory of Emotional Development, based on the work of Kasmirez Dabrowski. This theory emphasizes emotional and affective development in addition to cognitive development (Piirto, 1999). Dabrowski explored the notion of overexcitabilities (OEs), proposing that gifted children have greater capacities to respond to various stimuli (Piechowski, 1991), and that they may respond to even small stimuli more strongly and longer than would generally be considered normal (Tolan, 1999). These extreme intensities are thought to be innate and present from infancy, resulting from highly sensitive nervous systems (Blackburn & Erickson, 1986; Dabrowski, 1938, cited in Silverman, 1993; Tolan). The OEs are an abundance of energy and may be experienced in various areas, including sensual, imaginational, psychomotor, intellectual, and emotional. Highly gifted people tend to evidence all five of the OEs, but may "lead" with different ones (Tolan). Dabrowski's (1972) study of a group of gifted youth in Warsaw found considerable manifestations of OEs. Several studies of gifted youth have found significantly higher levels of OEs than those of nongifted students (Ackerman & Paulus, 1997; Dabrowski).

Sensual overexcitability. From a very early age, those with sensual OE experience a heightened sensory awareness. They derive great pleasure from experiencing the world through their senses, yet may also feel bombarded and easily overwhelmed by such stimulation (Silverman, 1993; Tolan, 1999). These children may be completely awed by the beauty of nature or have a powerful negative reaction to foul odors or bright lights.

Imaginational overexcitability. Imaginational OE is related to creativity and may be demonstrated through elaborate fantasies and daydreams, use of images and metaphors in thinking and communicating, and detailed visual recall (Silverman, 1993; Tolan, 1999). These students are inventive and may also have a tendency to blend truth with fiction and often possess a flair for the dramatic. As young children, they may have had an imaginary friend, and as adolescents they may be drawn to science fiction or fantasy. Because they tend to think in vivid images, it may be challenging and even frustrating for these students to communicate their thoughts and feelings verbally. Investigations have found that imaginational OEs tend to be present in artists and creative children (Piechowski, Silverman, & Falk, 1985) and are higher in gifted adolescents than in nongifted peers (Piechowski & Colangelo, 1984; Schiever, 1985).

Psychomotor overexcitability. Those with psychomotor OEs tend to be highly active, talkative, impulsive, competitive, and enthusiastic (Piechowski, 1991). As infants, they may have required less sleep. In case studies of young gifted students ages 4 though 6, psychomotor OE was noted in their high levels of enthusiasm, rapid speech, impulsive actions, and surplus of energy. These children may be misdiagnosed with Attention Deficit/Hyperactivity Disorder

(Schetky, 1981; Silverman, 1993). A notable difference is that children with psychomotor OE are able to sustain focused attention and concentration when they are sufficiently interested. Problems tend to arise when they are bored or feel that the activity or topic is not meaningful. It is important to note that psychomotor OE needs to be accompanied with other OEs in order to be considered significant and differentiate a gifted student from an average student (Piechowski & Cunningham, 1985; Silverman, 1993).

Intellectual overexcitability. The OE that is predominantly correlated with high intelligence is intellectual OE (Silverman, 1993; Tolan, 1999). This OE involves fervent curiosity, persistent intellectual effort and concentration, introspection, and analytical thinking. These youth develop the ability for abstract thinking early on and are often asking probing questions. It is also typical that they will have complex and highly developed moral reasoning and interest in theory. It must be noted that intellectual OE is not the same as intelligence (Piechowski, 1979). It is possible that someone who has a high IQ may not necessarily have an abundance of energy and intensity regarding learning, theorizing, and problem solving. Those who score high in intellectual OE are not always intellectually gifted. In a study by Piechowski and Cunningham (1985), artistically gifted adults scored just as high on intellectual OE as intellectually gifted.

Emotional overexcitability. Of all of the OEs, emotional OEs are central to the energies of the others (Tolan, 1999). Individuals with emotional OEs have intense feelings that are often evidenced from a very young age (Silverman, 1993). They are highly aware of their moods and emotional highs and lows, which may include intense feelings of joy, pain, guilt, self-criticism, and anxiety (Galbraith & Delisle, 1996; Silverman; Tolan). There is a depth and complexity to their own emotions as well as a heightened sensitivity to the emotional experience of others. In addition, there is a need for meaningful connections to other people or animals. These youth may have a profound concern with existential issues such as death and may also experience their emotions somatically such as a sense of having tension in their heart or stomach. There can be a tendency to become totally absorbed in thoughts, emotions, activities, or issues that matter to them. It is believed that the level of intensity and sensitivity of emotional response increases with the degree of giftedness (Piechowski, 1997). Higher levels of emotional OE have been found in gifted children, adolescents, and adults (Piechowski & Colangelo, 1984; Schiever, 1985; Silverman, 1983; Silverman & Ellsworth, 1980).

Children with sensual, imaginational, psychomotor, intellectual, and emotional OEs feel differently, experience the world differently, express themselves differently, and learn differently. They also have unique social and emotional needs related to their extraordinary sensitivities (Silverman, 1993). Experiencing the world with greater intensity than others can feel overwhelming, scary, and isolating. These youth are often on the receiving end of overt and covert messages from peers, adults, and society that they are overreacting or melodramatic. School counselors can be instrumental in helping these students understand, manage, and even celebrate their sensitivities and passions.

Common Social/Emotional Concerns for Gifted Students. An exhaustive description of possible social/emotional concerns experienced by gifted youth is beyond the scope of this chapter. However, we provide information from the literature about some common issues school counselors may encounter in their work with gifted students.

Relationship issues. Dating back to the work of Leta Hollingworth (1926), studies have found that the great differences in intellect between gifted and average peers often creates difficulty in establishing relationships. Webb, Meckstroth, and Tolan (1982) reviewed the major problems gifted and talented students have in peer relationships. Many difficulties gifted students have in peer relationships relate to their uneven, or asynchronous, development. Often, from the very beginning of elementary school, gifted young people's intellectual development outstrips that of their same-age peers to the point where they become "group deviants": they are simply too different intellectually to be accepted by their age-mates (Webb et al., 1982) and are often on the receiving end of negative nicknames such as "nerd," "dweeb," or "egghead" (USDE, 1993). These students tend to enjoy playing with older children, with whom they relate on a cognitive and humor level (Silverman, 1993; Webb, 1994). Webb et al. suggested that gifted children need several different peer groups that fit their different physical, intellectual, and social levels of development. They also pointed out that what adults consider to be satisfactory peer relationships may be very different from what the gifted child considers to be satisfactory. Pressuring gifted children to "fit in" makes them feel as if they must hide their gifts and their true selves. Too often, adults assume that a gifted child lacks social skills when the actual case is that the child has social skills, but chooses not to use them. Lovecky (1993) described gifted children as being particularly at risk for social ostracism, stating, "Many are more interested in following their own inner vision than in conforming in ways that will bring acceptance from peers. However, they are not always happy about the results" (p. 34). School counselors can help these students explore the process of their own decision making about social relationships. These students can benefit from support for their decisions, while also being encouraged to examine the consequences of their choices.

Relationships and "fitting in" often become increasingly important to gifted girls as they enter adolescence (Fielder, 2005). Whereas their focus in lower elementary school may have been on academic achievement, the bright girl approaching middle school may quickly shift her focus to friendships, romantic interests, and acceptance by peers. It is at this point that self-esteem declines and the gifted female may begin to hide her giftedness, intentionally underachieve, and begin to engage in risky behaviors (Kerr, Foley-Nicpon, & Zapata, 2005). Bright girls, in particular, need consistent encouragement and support in resisting the intense pressures to fit in or evaluate themselves primarily in terms of their attractiveness or their relationships (Kerr, 1994).

Culturally diverse gifted students may have additional struggles with peer relationships and acceptance (Grantham & Ford, 1998). Research has suggested that racial/ethnic minority students in gifted programs often find that access does not always result in acceptance. Because of their underrepresentation in gifted education programs, minority students (especially those in predominantly White schools) are often in predominantly White gifted classes and struggle with feelings of social isolation and exclusion, which may have a negative impact on their cultural identity. Students in these environments report having to adopt new behaviors and styles of speaking in order to try and fit in with White peers. Even with these alterations, gifted minority students are often the targets of covert and overt acts of racism on the part of their White classmates.

Peer issues do not occur solely in relationships with White peers. Often, gifted racial/ethnic minority students also experience peer rejection within their own racial/ethnic social groups. Similar to the way in which gifted adolescent females are ostracized for "acting smart" (Kerr, 1994), gifted minority students that achieve academically are often accused by their peers of rejecting their own culture and "acting White" (Ford, 1995; Kitano, 1998; Kruger, 2004; Tatum, 1997; USDE, 1992). In a survey of 31 gifted Black females in a predominantly Black, low-income community, Ford found that 54% of participants had experienced being teased by peers for academic achievements. Moreover, nearly one third of the participants had been accused of "acting White," and approximately 28% stated that they did not think that people would be friends with kids who were smart. In her interviews with gifted African American women, Kitano noted similar results. Six out of the 15 women interviewed reported that, during the school years, doing well academically frequently led to peer conflict.

Stress. Gifted students often feel a great deal of pressure to achieve from parents, teachers, peers, administrators, and their community (Grantham & Ford, 1998; Kerr, 1991). For some gifted children, meeting others' expectations has become a way of life (Kerr, 1981a). Jim Delisle (1984), in his book, *Gifted Children Speak Out*, gave many examples of students' beliefs that others hold expectations of them that are too high. Many gifted students describe a cycle in which achievement is followed by expectation of higher achievement, which is then followed by higher achievement in a never-ending spiral, so that the student believes that no matter how much he or she may try, no attainment will ever be enough. Pressure can also be experienced from within when gifted students set their own internal standards too high (Kerr, 1991). Many gifted students seem to "raise the stakes" on their own, even when parents, teachers, and counselors assure them that their performance is excellent. In their attempts to meet the expectations of themselves and others, gifted students may face antagonism from peers for their achievement focus, thus adding to the potential for stress (Clinkenbeard, 1991; Grantham & Ford).

Another common source of stress in the lives of gifted students is overcommitment to school activities, which often begins in elementary school. Multipotential students, with multiple interests and skills, often seem to find themselves involved in nearly every extracurricular activity available (Kerr, 1981a). It can be difficult for these students to prioritize in order to make their lives more balanced. Decision making can be particularly challenging for the gifted student (Kerr, 1991; Webb, 1994). Often adults expect that gifted children can make difficult decisions simply because of their excellent reasoning abilities, not recognizing that they may have limited skills and life experience from which to make these decisions. If students are given choices beyond their capacity for decision making, they may react with avoidance, confusion, and anxiety.

Poverty is a contributing factor to stress for some gifted students and is often related to rates of substance abuse (Beauvais, Oetting, Wolf, & Edwards, 1989; Husted, Johnson, & Redwing, 1995; Yee et al., 1995) and depression (Husted et al.). Those students who are racial/ethnic minorities may have the added stress of minority status (Smith, 1985). This stress can place these students further at risk as they attempt to cope with potential racial discrimination, alienation, and social isolation, in addition to the internal and external pressures they feel related to their giftedness.

Prolonged stress can have an impact of physical, mental, and emotional well-being (Greenberg, 2004). Strategies for preventing stress and coping with stress can be crucial skills for gifted students to develop (Galbraith & Delisle, 1996). School counselors can help gifted students prevent stress through strategies such as encouraging creative play and teaching students time-management and prioritization skills (Kerr, 1991). Discussion of both maladaptive coping strategies (e.g., withdrawal or alcohol/drug use) and adaptive coping strategies (e.g., relaxation training or changing cognitions) can empower gifted students to better manage stress within their lives. Gifted students can benefit from the guidance and support of school counselors as they develop healthy coping strategies and seek balance and meaning.

Perfectionism. Within the literature, perfectionism is a commonly described problem of gifted individuals from very young ages. (Kerr, 1991; Gallagher, 1990; Robinson & Nobel, 1991; Roedell, 1984). Webb (1994) stated that, in high-ability children, up to 15% to 20% may be significantly impacted by perfectionism. Kerr (1991) described perfectionism as a complex of characteristics and behaviors including compulsiveness with regard to work habits, overconcern for details, unrealistically high standards for self and others, indiscriminate acquiescence to external evaluation, and rigid routines. In comparison with their same-aged peers, gifted children often have the ability to perfectly carry out many tasks, especially cognitive tasks, expected of their age level. In this way, perfectionism becomes entrenched and part of the child's identity early on (Kerr, 1991, 1994).

Another potential contributing factor to perfectionism is extrinsic motivation (Kerr, 1991; Winebrenner, 2001). Gifted children whose abilities have been shaped by ever-increasing contingencies and who have been pressured into performing for points, grades, and awards soon lose a sense of ownership of their talents. An overemphasis on rewards can lead to less creative, more automatic behavior. A gifted child can develop perfectionistic behavior when he or she responds to all situations as an opportunity to gain "points." Gifted perfectionists tend to generalize their perfectionism to other areas of their lives, such as relationships and hobbies.

Gifted kids need help in overcoming the "fear of failure" (Kerr, 1994; Galbraith & Delisle, 1996), as well as the "fear of success." As early as elementary school, these students need encouragement to take risks and appreciate that true learning is an often frustrating struggle that takes effort (Winebrenner, 2001). Learning how to make mistakes can be one of the most critical skills a talented student can learn (Galbraith & Delisle). When gifted kids have opportunities to fail within a supportive environment, they can develop the skills necessary to "fail gracefully," make sense of the experience, learn from their mistakes, and persist in the task.

Related to the benefits of gifted students' learning how to make mistakes is learning how to tolerate frustration. Perfectionism can be related to asynchronous development, or uneven development in the rates of cognitive, emotional, and physical abilities (Silverman, 1993). One common example of this is the young elementary gifted students who become extremely frustrated when their limited physical coordination in writing with a pencil does not allow them to express their thoughts as neatly or quickly as their mind is working. They demand perfection, yet are not able to produce it in a way that meets their expectations. The school counselor can provide the necessary adult guidance in helping the gifted students in setting realistic goals and developing strategies for coping and problem solving, without compromising their ideals and goals (Roedell, 1990).

Some have asserted that perfectionism may also have positive aspects (Dabrowski, 1972; Robinson & Noble, 1991), stating that it can provide the driving energy toward achievement (Roedell, 1984). When understood and channeled appropriately, perfectionism can be used productively as a positive way to achieve excellence (Silverman, 1993). School counselors can help gifted students turn perfectionism from something that hinders their achievement and satisfaction into something that brings them success and pleasure.

Depression. Depression among gifted students is increasingly becoming a concern of parents and educators (Kerr, 1991). Many of the same situations that lead to stress for the bright child can also become precursors of depression. Kaiser and Berndt (1985) reported pervasive feelings of depression, anger, and loneliness in one eighth of the 175 gifted junior and senior high students in their study. Under conditions of prolonged stress, a student may gradually lose motivation, energy, and the will to go on. While the research is unclear whether gifted students are statistically at greater risk than average students for suicide, there is evidence that a high proportion of students who commit suicide are at least above-average students (Delisle, 1996; Kerr, 1991; Silverman, 1993). Some speculate that their heightened sensitivity and tendency toward perfectionism may place gifted youth at higher risk for suicide (Delisle, 1996).

One type of depression that seems to be unique to gifted students is a kind of premature existential depression (Webb et al., 1982). Existential depression occurs in gifted children and adolescents when their capacity for absorbing information about disturbing events is greater than their capacity to process and understand it. Second graders who are capable of reading news magazine accounts of war and pollution may understand the information but not be able to deal with their helplessness to do anything about it. As Hollingworth (1926) pointed out long ago, many gifted children feel trapped in a world created by adults that is somehow out of control. Some gifted students seem to experience existential depression as a result of having wrestled with concepts with which even the wisest of adults have struggled, such as the meaning of life, the inevitability of death, and the beginning and end of the universe. Asynchronistic development, or the incongruence between the child's developmental stage and intellectual abilities, may play a part in existential depression (Silverman, 1993; Webb et al., 1982). A young person whose cognitive development is still "dualistic," that is, still perceiving the world in terms of absolutes such as right and wrong or good and bad, may be disturbed by reading and thinking about questions for which there simply are no right or wrong answers. Unable to resolve the ambiguity, the student lapses into anger and despair.

While it is clear from the literature and research that gifted students have a number of social and emotional concerns related to their giftedness, there can be a danger in attributing all of their struggles to giftedness. Many people hold a stereotype that because of their advanced abilities, all gifted individuals are so "different" that they are unable to relate to or connect with others and that they are difficult to deal with (Galbraith & Delisle, 1996). This may be the gifted child who seems to be in his or her own world, withdrawn and isolating. It may be the gifted student who is pegged as the "know it all"—constantly answering questions in class, easily frustrated with peers who don't "get it" (particularly in group activities), unreceptive to feedback, and even correcting the teacher. Or it may be the student who persistently asks the difficult questions that challenge the adult's expertise or authority. These students are often seen as contributing to their own social rejection, garnering very little sympathy from others. Perhaps the most dangerous concern about this misconception is that it can perpetuate the idea that gifted students' issues are solely a result of their intelligence, and therefore they cannot be understood or helped.

Recommendations for Practice

The preceding sections of this chapter have been designed to (a) increase your understanding of some of the most salient academic and social/emotional concerns of gifted and talented youth, and (b) familiarize you with some important research and strategies that can help guide the design and delivery of school-based interventions with this population. In the following section, we will focus in more depth on practical application of this knowledge, paying specific attention to suggested intervention strategies that address three key areas of concern for gifted and talented youth: (a) academics, (b) career planning, and (c) social/emotional needs.

Within each area of concern, we will concentrate on three primary roles that the school counselor can play, namely, (a) counselor, (b) consultant, and (c) advocate. Examples of each of these roles are provided in Table 34.1. It is important to note that these roles are consistent with those recommended by the ASCA in their position statement of gifted student programs (See Appendix A).

Addressing Academic Needs and Concerns

As we have discussed previously in this chapter, providing academic support and guidance is one of the most critical roles that the professional school counselor can play for the gifted and talented population because their academic needs are often not met within the context of the regular school program (Kerr, 1991; VanTassel-Baska, 1993b). Gifted students and their families need assistance in developing a course of study that will best meet their academic needs. In addition, they may be unfamiliar with available enrichment opportunities outside of the school setting that could supplement their school-based experiences. This may be especially true for those in rural settings. Four key ways in which the school counselor can provide academic support are (a) being knowledgeable about identification practices, (b) advocating for curricular interventions, (c) consulting with students and parents about academic planning, and (d) serving as a resource for enrichment options. Each of these will be briefly discussed. In addition, a summary of recommendations for addressing academic needs and concerns is provided in Table 34.2.

Understanding identification. As illustrated earlier, the process of identifying and assessing gifted and talented students is complex. Identification methods and qualifying

Table 34.1 Roles of the School Counselor Working with Gifted and Talented Youth

	Counselor	Consultant	Advocate
EXAMPLES OF INTERVENTIONS	• Providing individual and group counseling to address social/emotional needs • Facilitating developmental guidance programming focused on career exploration	• Providing resource information to parents and teachers regarding specific academic and social/emotional needs • Serving as a resource regarding weekend and summer enrichment opportunities in the community	• Promoting use of appropriate criteria for assessment and identification • Encouraging continued support for programs that address the specific needs of gifted and talented youth.

Table 34.2 Recommendations for Addressing Academic Needs and Concerns by Grade Level

	Elementary School	Middle School	High School
Be knowledgeable about identification criteria and processes for your school district and be prepared to advocate for students who may not "fit" the stated criteria.	*	*	*
Assist parents and families in understanding and negotiating the education system.	*	*	*
Assist gifted students (and their families) in developing academic decision-making skills.	*	*	*
Consult with parents and help advocate for challenging curriculum and academic interventions (e.g., acceleration, enrichment, differentiation) when appropriate.	*	*	*
Advocate for the use of culturally relevant curriculum in gifted programming.	*	*	*
Be able to recognize underachievement and intervene appropriately.	*	*	*
Serve as a resource for out-of-school Saturday programs and summer opportunities for gifted children.	*	*	*
Assist parents and school staff in determining appropriateness of early admission to kindergarten.	*		
Encourage gifted students to participate in Talent Search process and take necessary tests (e.g., SAT, ACT) to qualify them for Talent Search program participation.		*	
Help students begin a college planning time line and explore opportunities for preparing for admission (e.g., enrolling in high school–level classes, volunteer work)		*	*
Provide developmental guidance experiences, with topics such as time management, study skills, and course selection.		*	*
Assist in finding appropriate online courses.		*	*
Encourage AP classes; provide advocacy for admission into AP classes when necessary.		*	*
Encourage continued college preparation activities such as practicing the PSAT (10th grade), taking the PSAT (11th grade), college visitations, and review of college reference books.			*
Assist gifted students in exploring, applying for, and deciding about college options.			*

criteria are variable and often fail to create gifted and talented populations that are diverse and representative of the school as a whole. Consequently, in order to best meet the needs of *all* gifted students within the school, it is critical that the school counselor (a) have a solid understanding of how giftedness is defined within his or her school district and (b) advocate for assessment practices that are inclusive of cultural diversity, such as a multiple criterion system (ASCA, 2005).

It is also important that the school counselor be familiar with the ways in which students from different cultural backgrounds may manifest their giftedness, as well as the impact that other issues, such as learning disabilities, language barriers, or family circumstances, might have on how a student's giftedness is expressed. For Anita, it was critical for her school counselor to understand that her English language proficiency and significant family responsibilities were contributing to her uneven academic performance and even masking her mathematical giftedness. By being sensitive to the characteristics of diverse gifted populations, the school counselor can help to ensure that *all* gifted students have the opportunity to access the specialized services that they need (Evans, 1997; Mendaglio, 1993).

Curricular approaches. Some of the most important tools that a school counselor can utilize to promote the positive academic experience of gifted students are curricular interventions, such as acceleration, enrichment, and differentiation. The appropriate use of curricular modifications plays a critical role in ensuring that gifted and talented students stay engaged in their academic experience. The school counselor must be informed about intervention options in order to effectively support gifted students, their parents, and their teachers in the design of appropriate academic programs.

Academic planning. Supporting gifted students with academic planning is vital to ensuring that they have access to the most appropriate and engaging programs available (VanTassel-Baska, 1993b). As you have learned in this chapter, underachievement and dropout are salient issues for the gifted and talented student population. Effective academic planning serves an important preventative function in addressing this issue. Academic planning can occur in individual settings (e.g., meeting with students to discuss their course schedules) or group settings (e.g., talking with an eighth-grade accelerated math class about high school course selection options). Three key questions for the school counselor to keep in mind when planning with a gifted student are

1. What classes will allow this student to feel engaged and challenged, academically?
2. What classes are essential for allowing this student to keep many doors open regarding higher education options and career interests?
3. What classes might be needed to help this student develop in important interest and skills areas in which he or she is less proficient?

Many gifted students are multipotential and have the ability to be successful in multiple areas. Consequently, they may have difficulty with deciding how to pursue diverse interests and make choices about academic courses (Silverman, 2000; Kerr, 1991). The school counselor can address this issue by helping gifted students develop academic decision-making skills. This could involve helping the student clarify values, set goals, and establish priorities. In addition, the school counselor could assist the student in finding ways to pursue some of his or her interests outside the school setting through extracurricular involvement and summer programs.

In contrast, some gifted and talented students may underestimate their ability in certain areas and intentionally choose less rigorous classes, such as girls not pursuing or persevering in math- and science-related curriculum (Kerr, 1994). Peer pressure and concerns about social acceptance can also cause gifted students to make inappropriate course choices. In both of these situations, the school counselor can provide support in working through these concerns and encourage the student to make decisions that will prevent them from foreclosing on future opportunities.

Enrichment resource. As previously mentioned, it may not be possible to meet all of a gifted student's academic interests within the school setting. In these instances, the school counselor can act as a valuable resource for enrichment opportunities, such as summer programs, weekend workshops, and online courses that are available outside of school. These extracurricular options serve an important function in allowing gifted students to have experiences (e.g., interest exploration, skill development) that their school environment does not provide, and may be particularly valuable for gifted students from low-income (Yee et al., 1995) and rural schools (Benbow et al., 1992; Luhman & Fundis, 1989).

School counselors can also facilitate another kind of enrichment opportunity—mentorships. A mentorship allows the gifted student the opportunity to work one on one with an individual, providing exposure to and information about a certain area of interest (Silverman, 1993). The mentorship relationship can support the gifted student in identifying, understanding, and taking pride in his or her greatest strengths and passions (Kerr, 1994; Schatz, 1999). In addition, mentorships have the potential to enhance self-esteem, career development, and social/emotional growth. Establishing a mentor relationship can be especially valuable for gifted students who feel disenfranchised by school, permitting them a chance to see others who have succeeded despite the obstacles (Van-Tassel-Baska, 2003).

Addressing Career Planning Needs and Concerns

The provision of career exploration and planning support is another important service that school counselors can offer their gifted and talented students. Two key ways in which the school counselor can address the career concerns of gifted and talented students are: (1) providing early access to career planning services, and (2) incorporating personality needs and values to the career decision making process. Both of these will be briefly discussed below. In addition, a summary of recommendations for addressing career planning needs and concerns is provided in Table 34.3.

Early access to career planning. As we reviewed previously, career counseling is a critical service for gifted students and often needs to happen at an earlier stage. Because of their developmental advancement, gifted children begin to be concerned about vocational choice much earlier than their peers. School counselors can encourage discussion and exploration of various careers, even with elementary school students. It can also be useful to involve parents in the discussion about the student's dreams and goals.

Incorporating personality needs and values. Multipotentiality, as we have explored, has a profound impact on career planning for gifted students. These students have interest and ability in many career fields, thus making the decision to pursue a specific career complicated. As Silverman (2000) noted, "When one is capable in many areas, aptitude is an insufficient criterion for selecting a career" (p. 215). Career guidance can be more effective in meeting the special needs of gifted students by looking beyond abilities and vocational interests alone, and incorporating personality needs and deeply held values (including cultural values). This model, called Values-Based Career Counseling (Kerr & Erb, 1991; Kerr & Kurpius, 2005) can help gifted students navigate the often confusing and complex

Table 34.3 Recommendations for Addressing Career Planning Needs and Concerns by Grade Level

	Elementary School	Middle School	High School
Provide realistic exposure to the world of work. Encourage parents to share information about their work and expose gifted students to diverse career options.	*		
Encourage career fantasies through dress-up and play.	*		
Encourage focus on activities that require goal setting and follow-through (class projects, achievement clubs, etc.).	*		
Use biographies of eminent people as primary career education material. Facilitate book discussion groups centered around the lives of eminent people in science, the arts, education, government, and entertainment.	*		
Help teachers and parents evaluate skills, talents, and interests carefully in order to help gifted students understand possible areas of greatest interest.	*		
Help gifted students discuss the meaning and value of work.		*	
Discuss family, cultural, and community values pertaining to work.		*	
Assist students in accessing career exploration opportunities such as volunteer work, job shadowing, and informational interviews.		*	
Help gifted students set priorities and make choices about extracurricular interests to prevent over-involvement.		*	
Help student plan a solid curriculum of course work in order to ensure against inadequate preparation for a later career choice.		*	*
Provide appropriate vocational testing for interests, personality characteristics, aptitudes, and values.			*
Encourage more extensive career exploration through volunteer and paid work experiences, internships with professionals, and visits to college classes in subjects of interest.			*
Provide values-based guidance emphasizing choosing a career that fulfills deeply held values. Understand the role that culture might play in shaping values.			*
Encourage nonconformist, nonstereotyped career choices.			*

process of making vocational decisions and help them to find career paths that have personal meaning for them. A values-based career intervention helped Beverly find ways to balance her dreams and pursue her passion, while also honoring her career goal and cultural values.

Addressing Social/Emotional Needs and Concerns

Throughout this chapter, we have provided literature and research that bring to light the importance of providing support to address social/emotional needs of gifted and talented students. School counselors will encounter gifted students who are struggling with concerns such as interpersonal issues with peers, as well as intrapersonal challenges such as stress, perfectionism, and depression. Gifted students need appropriate support in these areas. In her edited text *Counseling the Gifted and Talented*, Silverman (1993) provided a developmental model for counseling the gifted. This model, grounded in the unique shared traits of gifted and talented individuals, is designed to help the counseling professional in creating appropriate interventions for this population. Silverman described these interventions as "life preservers," necessary for "preventing alienation, depression, underachievement, and damage to their self-esteem" (p. 51). She suggested that, ultimately, counselors can help gifted students strive to live lives deeply imbued with immutable values, have the wisdom to choose the path of integrity, have the compassion to choose the path of service, and have the courage to become their best selves in the face of a world that often settles for less.

School counselors may believe that they have little time for social and emotional counseling for gifted students. However, a little attention to these special needs can go a long way toward keeping gifted students balanced and focused in their lives. Four key ways in which the school counselor can provide social/emotional support are (1) consulting with parents and teachers about how to best meet the social/emotional needs of their gifted and talented students, (2) providing individual counseling services, (3) providing group counseling services, and (4) serving as a resource for social enrichment opportunities.

Table 34.4 Recommendations for Addressing Social/Emotional Needs and Concerns by Grade Level

	Elementary School	Middle School	High School
Help parents and teachers understand asynchronous development and other social and emotional needs.	*	*	*
Act as a resource; make appropriate referrals when family or mental health counseling outside of school is needed.	*	*	*
Help students develop and maintain good peer relationships.	*	*	*
Encourage emotional expression through writing, art, and music.	*	*	*
Provide individual and group counseling to address social and emotional concerns.	*	*	*
Create prevention strategies—in-services for teachers, support groups for students—to support populations at risk of underachievement (such as adolescent girls, and African American adolescents) in maintaining their involvement in academically rigorous classes.	*	*	*
Encourage "failing gracefully" and finding meaning in making mistakes.	*	*	*
Teach stress-management strategies.	*	*	*
Use bibliotherapy; develop library of books with gifted individuals as protagonists.	*	*	*
Honor and encourage their dreams and goals.		*	*
Help students negotiate concerns with teachers and parents.		*	*
Facilitate the promotion of self-esteem and self-efficacy.		*	*
Facilitate the development of cultural identity.		*	*
Foster resiliency (e.g., through relationships with supportive adults, friendships with other gifted students, and participation in extracurricular activities).		*	*
Support students in individuation process.			*
Facilitate mentorship relationships.			*

Each of these will be briefly discussed. In addition, a summary of intervention strategies for addressing social/emotional needs and concerns is provided in Table 34.4.

Consulting with parents and teachers. The school counselor may be the first person parents approach with questions or concerns about their gifted child. Teachers may also seek consultation with the school counselor regarding social/emotional issues that they observe within the classroom setting or find are having an impact on academic performance. Both parents and teachers may need information about how to recognize and understand various social/emotional issues from the asynchronous development of the gifted kindergartner to the existential depression of the high school sophomore. School counselors may also need to provide referral information for outside support if additional resources, mental health support, or family counseling is needed.

Individual counseling. Gifted students may seek support from the school counselor for a variety of reasons, but it is unlikely that they will explicitly state that they need help "dealing with their giftedness." This makes it all the more important for the school counselor to be aware of the various ways giftedness may be a contributing factor when conceptualizing student concerns and considering possible interventions. Within the individual counseling context, there are opportunities for the student to explore *what it means to them* to be gifted. This may involve helping the student understand common experiences and struggles of gifted students or exploring how giftedness is incorporated into their overall identity. These general conversations can begin as early as elementary school. There are also opportunities to provide interventions for more specific issues they may be facing, such as concerns over peer relationship, stress, or depression. In individual counseling, Matt benefited from learning about and discussing how his emotional OEs impacted how he experienced his world, thereby helping him to gain self-understanding and self-acceptance.

Group counseling. It does not typically occur in a school day that gifted students are able to group together and talk about nonacademic concerns (Colangelo & Peterson, 1993). Providing gifted students with the opportunity to meet in a group setting gives them a chance to share their thoughts, feelings, and concerns with peers who may be more understanding and accepting. When facilitated by a school counselor who is sensitive to their social/emotional concerns, it creates a safe space for these students to share their fears, struggles, and dreams and to seek support from others who identify with what they are experiencing. Group counseling may also be more culturally appropriate for those gifted students who come from a cultural background that is more collectivist. Because some cultures tend to value collaboration over an individual focus, it has been proposed that interventions in a group setting may be particularly effective with these adolescents in order to promote confidence, self-esteem, and identity (Aponte, Young Rivers, & Wohl, 1995). Within a group setting, Jackie demonstrated her leadership skills and was able to discuss her frustrations with class curriculum that was not challenging or meaningful. She was also able to share her concerns about being accused of "acting White" for academic achievement with other gifted minority girls who had faced similar situations and in so doing found the support and encouragement she needed to overcome these pressures.

Potential topics for counseling groups are endless and can be adapted for different developmental levels: gifted elementary students may benefit from discussions about peer relationships; middle school students may explore underachievement; gifted high school students may share career hopes and dreams as part of college planning. One group counseling approach that has been shown to be especially effective in working with this population is bibliotherapy (Silverman, 1993). In her book *Counseling the Gifted and Talented*, Silverman recommended a list of books dealing with gifted students as protagonists that can be used as a springboard for discussing challenges that students experience.

Social Enrichment Opportunities. Group experiences do not have to be limited to the school setting. Many students note the important role that outside activities for the gifted and talented can play in their social and emotional well-being. Even programs with an academic focus can provide gifted students the chance to engage in social relationships with their intellectual peers. School counselors play an important role in providing gifted students and their parents with information about such opportunities as weekend or summer enrichment programs, Midwest Talent Search, or mentorship programs.

Future Directions

Throughout this chapter, we have shared information and research about a frequently misunderstood and often underserved population within our schools. The numbers of counselors who are interested and trained in the needs of gifted and talented are growing. The Guidance and Counseling Division of the National Association for Gifted Children (NAGC) has seen extraordinary growth in its membership, and more teachers are reaching out to counselors for advice and support for their gifted students (Mahoney, 2005). It is likely that as counselors learn more about this population, they will increase their involvement in this professional area. Counselors should consider becoming involved in this division, as well as seeking opportunities at the American Counseling Association to gather with other counselors to discuss the needs of gifted students. The NAGC Web site (www.nagc.org) provides a wealth of additional information and resources that are valuable to the school counselor.

In addition, the growth of guidance laboratories at the university level has increased the knowledge and practice with gifted and talented. Guidance laboratories now operating at major universities include the Nebraska Guidance Laboratory for Gifted at University of Nebraska–Lincoln, the Iowa Counseling Laboratory for Gifted at the Belin Blank National Center for Gifted and Talented at the University of Iowa, and the Positive Psychology Laboratory at the Center for Psychoeducational Services at the University of Kansas. Special guidance laboratories for girls and for boys have been developed at Arizona State University with the sponsorship of the National Science Foundation. It is likely that university-based counseling programs for gifted will continue to be developed, and counselors should check with their local school of education or college counseling center for special programs for gifted and talented students.

As research continues on the special needs of gifted and talented, it is likely that more attention will be paid to such topics as dual exceptionalities, including gifted attention deficit disorder, gifted bipolar, gifted Aspergers/autism, and gifted personality disorders (Webb et al., 2005). In addition, it is likely that issues of gifted and gay (Cohn, 2003) and giftedness and gender will rise in importance (Kerr & Cohn, 2001). A new generation of bright students who have been raised in times of national crisis and war is coming of age, and the impact of these events on this sensitive and complex population is unknown.

Pfeiffer (2003) surveyed authorities in the field of gifted, asking their perspectives on current trends, concerns, and future directions. The experts in the study most frequently reported the continuing need to reach a consensus on how to define and identify giftedness, concern about how to increase the identification of gifted minority students, and the importance of translating the research on meeting the needs of the gifted and talented into practice. Furthermore, these veterans of the field expressed a need to "build a more compelling case for the value of supporting one of America's most precious resources—its gifted children" (p. 161).

Appendix A

American School Counselor Association (ASCA) Position Statement: Gifted Student Programs

The Professional School Counselor and Gifted and Talented Student Programs. (Adopted 1988; revised 1993, 1999, 2001)

ASCA Position

The professional school counselor assists in providing technical assistance and an organized support system within the developmental comprehensive school counseling program for gifted and talented students to meet their extensive and diverse needs as well as the needs of all students.

The Rationale

An organized support system throughout the formative years is imperative for such students to be able to realize their potential. A part of this support system is participation in a school counseling program that meets the extensive and diverse needs of the gifted and talented students.

The Professional School Counselor's Role

The role of the professional school counselor in gifted and talented programs may be as follows:

1. Assisting in the identification of gifted and talented students through the use of a multiple criterion system utilized in their school district, which may include
   - Intellectual ability
   - Academic performance
   - Visual and performing arts ability
   - Practical arts ability
   - Creative thinking ability
   - Leadership potential
   - Parent, teacher, peer nomination
   - Expert evaluation
2. Advocating for the inclusion of activities that effectively address the personal/social and career development needs, in addition to the academic needs of identified gifted and talented students
3. Assisting in promoting understanding and awareness of the special issues that may affect gifted and talented students including
   - Underachievement
   - Perfectionism
   - Depression
   - Dropping out
   - Delinquency
   - Difficulty in peer relationships
   - Career development
   - Meeting expectations
   - Goal setting
   - Questioning others' values
4. Providing individual and group counseling for gifted and talented students, as warranted
5. Recommending material and resources for gifted and talented programs and for teachers and parents of gifted and talented students
6. Engaging in professional development activities through which knowledge and skills in the area of programming for the needs of the gifted and talented are regularly upgraded

Summary

Gifted and talented students come from many backgrounds, and their special abilities cover a wide spectrum of human potential. Specifically planned educational experiences can greatly enhance the continued development of gifted and talented persons. Professional school counselors work in a collaboration with other school personnel to maximize opportunities for these students. The professional school counselor is an integral part of the educational team that delivers a comprehensive school counseling program to meet the needs of all students (ASCA, 2005).

References

Ackerman, C., & Paulus, L. E. (1997). Identifying gifted adolescents using personality characteristics: Dabrowski's overexcitabilities. *Roeper Review, 19*(4), 229–236.

Adams-Byars, J., Whitsell, S. S., & Moon, S. M. (2004). Gifted students' perceptions of the academic and social/emotional effects of homogeneous and heterogeneous grouping. *Gifted Child Quarterly, 48*(1), 7–20.

American School Counselor Association. (2005). *Position statement: Gifted student programs.* Retrieved August 30, 2005, from http://www.schoolcounselor.org/content.asp?contentid=209

Aponte, J. F., Young Rivers, R., & Wohl, J. (1995). *Psychological interventions and cultural diversity.* Needham Heights, MA: Allyn and Bacon.

Astin, A., Green, K. C., & Korn, W. S. (1988). *The American freshman: Twenty year trends.* Los Angeles: Higher Education Research Institute.

Beauvais, F., Oetting, E. R., Wolf, W., & Edwards, R. W. (1989). American Indian youth and drugs, 1976–87: A continuing problem. *American Journal of Public Health, 79*(5), 634–636.

Belcastro, F. (1987). Elementary pull-out program—boon or bane? *Roeper Review, 9*(4), 208–212.

Bell, L. A. (1989) Something's wrong here and it's not me: Challenging the dilemmas that block girls' success. *Journal for the Education of the Gifted, 12*(2), 118–130.

Benbow, C., Argo, T., & Glass, L. (1992). Meeting the needs of the gifted in rural areas through acceleration. *Gifted Child Today, 18*(2), 1–5.

Blackburn, A. C., & Erickson, D. B. (1986). Predictable crises of the gifted student. *Journal of Counseling and Development, 9*, 552–555.

Buescher, T. M. (1986, March). *Adolescents' responses to their own recognized talent: Issues affecting counseling and adjustment.* Paper presented at the 63rd annual meeting of the American Orthopsychiatric Association, Chicago.

Callahan, C. M., Cunningham, C. M., & Plucker, J. M. (1994). Foundations for the future: The socio-emotional development of gifted, adolescent women. *Roeper Review, 17*(2), 99–104.

Clasen, R. D., & Clasen, R. E. (1995). Underachievement of highly able students and the peer society. *Gifted and Talented International, 10*, 67–76.

Clinkenbeard, P. R. (1991). Unfair expectations: A pilot study of middle school students' comparisons of gifted and regular classes. *Journal for the Education of the Gifted, 15*, 56–63.

Cohn, S. J. (2003). The gay gifted learners: Facing the challenge of homophobia and antihomosexual bias in schools. In J. A. Castellano (Ed.), *Special populations in gifted education.* Boston: Allyn and Bacon.

Colangelo, N. (1991). Counseling gifted students. In N. Colangelo & G. A. Davis (Eds.), *Handbook of gifted education* (pp. 273–284). Needham Heights, MA: Allyn and Bacon.

Colangelo, N., Assouline, S. G., & Gross, M. U. M. (2004). *A nation deceived: How schools hold back America's brightest students.* Iowa City: University of Iowa, The Connie Belin & Jacqueline N. Blank International Center for Gifted Education and Talent Development.

Colangelo, N., & Davis, G. A. (Eds.). (1997). *Handbook of gifted education.* Boston: Allyn and Bacon.

Colangelo, N., & Davis, G. A. (Eds.). (2002). *Handbook of gifted education* (3rd ed.). Boston: Allyn and Bacon.

Colangelo, N., & Kerr, B. A. (1990). Extreme academic talent: Profiles of perfect scorers. *Journal of Educational Psychology, 8*, 404–409.

Colangelo, N., & Peterson, J. S. (1993). Group counseling with gifted students. In L. K. Silverman (Ed.), *Counseling the gifted and talented* (pp. 3–28). Denver, CO: Love Publishing Company.

Coleman, J. M., & Fults, B. A. (1982). Self-concept and the gifted classroom: The role of social comparisons. *Gifted Child Quarterly, 26*, 116–120.

Dabrowski, K. (1972). *Psychoneurosis is not an illness.* London: Gryf.

Darou, W. G. (1987). Counseling the northern native. *Canadian Journal of Counseling, 21*(1), 33–41.

Davidson, J., Davidson, B., & Vanderkam, L. (2004). *Genius denied: How to stop wasting our brightest young minds.* New York: Simon and Schuster.

Davis, G. A., & Rimm, S. B. (Eds.). (1989). *Education of the gifted and talented* (2nd ed.). Needham Heights, MA: Allyn and Bacon.

Day-Vines, N., Patton, J., & Baytops, J. (2003). Counseling African American adolescents: The impact of race and middle class status. *Professional School Counseling, 7*, 40–51.

Delisle, J. R. (1984). *Gifted children speak out.* New York: Walker.

Delisle, J. R. (1996). Death with honors. *Journal of Counseling and Development, 64*, 558–560.

Erford, B. T. (Ed.). (2003). *Transforming the school counseling profession.* Upper Saddle River, NJ: Merrill Prentice Hall.

Evans, K. M. (1997). Multicultural training needs for counselors of gifted African American children. *Multicultural Education, 5*, 16–19.

Fiedler, E. D. (1993). Square pegs in round holes: Gifted kids who don't fit in. *Understanding Our Gifted, 5*(5A), 1, 11–14.

Fielder, K. V. (2005). Understanding teenage girls: Career and development perspectives. In S. Kurpius, B. A. Kerr, & A. Harkins (Eds.), *Handbook for counseling girls and women* (Vol. 1, pp. 19–31). Mesa, AZ: Nueva Science Press.

Ford, D. Y. (1994). Underachievement among gifted and nongifted black females: A study of perceptions. *The Journal of Secondary Gifted Education, 6*, 165–175.

Ford, D. Y. (1995). *Counseling gifted African American students: Promoting achievement, identity, and social and emotional well-being.* Storrs: The University of Connecticut, National Research Center for the Gifted and Talented.

Ford, D. Y. (1996). *Reversing underachievement among gifted Black students: Promising practices and programs.* New York: Teachers College Press.

Ford, D. Y. (1998). *Factors affecting the career decision making of minority teachers in gifted education.* Storrs: The University of Connecticut, National Research Center on the Gifted and Talented.

Ford, D. Y. (2001). *Infusing multicultural content into the curriculum for gifted students.* ERIC Digest. (Report No. E601). Arlington, VA: ERIC Clearinghouse on Disabilities and Gifted Education, Council for Exceptional Children. (ERIC Document Reproduction Services No. E0449635)

Ford, D. Y., Harris, J. J., III, Tyson, C. A., & Trotman, M. F. (2002). Beyond deficit thinking: Providing access for gifted African American students. *Roeper Review, 24*(2), 52–59.

Fox, L. H. (1978). Interest correlates to differential achievement of gifted students in mathematics. *Journal for the Education of the Gifted, 1*, 24–36.

Frederickson, R. H., & Rothney, J. W. M. (1972). *Recognizing and assisting multipotential youth*. Columbus, OH: Merrill.

Frey, C. P. (1998). Struggling with identity: Working with seventh and eighth grade gifted girls to air issues of concern. *Journal for the Education of the Gifted, 21*(4), 437–451.

Galbraith, J., & Delisle, J. (1996). *The gifted kids' survival guide: A teen handbook*. Minneapolis, MN: Free Spirit Publishing.

Gallagher, J. J. (1990). The public and professional perceptions of the emotional status of gifted children [Editorial]. *Journal for the Education of the Gifted, 13*(3), 202–211.

Gallagher, J. J. (1991). Educational reform, values, and gifted students. *Gifted Child Quarterly, 35*, 12–18.

Gardner, H. (1983). *Frames of mind: The theory of multiple intelligences*. New York: Basic Books.

Grantham, T. C., & Ford, D. Y. (1998). A case study of the social needs of Danisha: An underachieving gifted African American female. *Roeper Review, 21*(2), 96–102.

Greenberg, J. S. (2004). *Comprehensive stress management*. New York: McGraw-Hill.

Greenberg Lake Analysis Group & American Association for University Women. (1991). *Shortchanging girls, short changing America*. Washington, DC: AAUW.

Harmon, D. (2001). They won't teach me: The voices of gifted African American inner-city students. *Roeper Review, 24*(2), 68–75.

Harris, C. R. (1991). Evaluation of programs for disadvantaged gifted students. *Journal for the Education of the Gifted, 17*, 441–466.

Herring, R. D., (1990). Attacking career myths among Native Americans: Implications for counseling. *The School Counselor, 38*, 13–19.

Hertzog, N. B. (2003). Impact of gifted programs from the student's perspectives. *Gifted Child Quarterly, 47*(2), 131–143.

Hollingworth, L. S. (1926). *Gifted children: Their nature and nurture*. New York: Macmillan.

Horowitz, F. D., & O'Brien, M. (1989). In the interest of the nation. *American Psychologist, 4*, 441–445.

Hunsaker, S. (1995). The gifted metaphor from the perspective of traditional civilizations. *Journal for Education of the Gifted, 18*(3), 255–268.

Husted, J., Johnson, T., & Redwing, L. (1995). Multi-dimensional adolescent treatment with American Indians. *American Indian and Alaska Native Mental Health Research, 6*(3), 23–30.

Kaiser, C. F., & Berndt, D. J. (1985). Predictors of loneliness in the gifted adolescent. *Gifted Child Quarterly, 29*, 74–77.

Kaufmann, F. (1981). The 1964–1968 presidential scholars: A follow-up study. *Exceptional Children, 48*, 2.

Kerr, B. A. (1981a). *Career education for the gifted and talented*. Columbus, OH: ERIC Clearinghouse on Adult Career and Vocational Education. (ERIC reproduction Service No. 205778)

Kerr, B. A. (1981b). *Career education strategies for gifted and talented*. Columbus, OH: Education Resources Information Center Clearinghouse on Adult, Career, and Vocation Education.

Kerr, B. A. (1985). Smart girls, gifted women: Special guidance concerns. *Roeper Review, 8*(1), 30–33.

Kerr, B. A. (1991). *A handbook for counseling the gifted and talented*. Alexandria, VA: American Counseling Association.

Kerr, B. A. (1994). *Smart girls—A new psychology of girls, women, and giftedness* (Rev. ed.). Scottsdale, AZ: Gifted Psychology Press.

Kerr, B. A., & Cohn, S. J. (2001). *Smart boys: Talent, manhood, & the search for meaning*. Scottsdale, AZ: Great Potential Press.

Kerr, B. A., & Colangelo, N. (1988). The college plans of academically talented students. *Journal of Counseling and Development, 67*(1), 42–49.

Kerr, B. A., & Erb, C. (1991). Careers counseling with academically talented students: Effects of a value-based intervention. *Journal of Counseling Psychology, 38*(3), 309–314.

Kerr, B. A., & Fischer, T. (1997). Career assessment with gifted and talented students. *Journal of Career Assessment, 5*(2), 239–251.

Kerr, B. A., Foley-Nicpon, M., & Zapata, A. L. (2005). The development of talent in girls and young women. In S. Kurpius, B. A. Kerr, & A. Harkins (Eds.), *Handbook for counseling girls and women* (Vol. 2, pp. 15–39). Mesa, AZ: Nueva Science Press.

Kerr, B. A., & Kurpius, S. R. (Eds.). (2005). *Counseling girls and women: Ten years of NSF gender equity studies: Vol. 2 Talent development*. Arlington, VA: National Science Foundation.

Kerr, B. A., & Nicpon, M. F. (2003). Gender and giftedness. In N. Colangelo & G. A. Davis (Eds.), *Handbook of gifted education* (3rd. ed., pp. 493–505). Boston: Allyn and Bacon.

Kitano, M. K. (1998). Gifted African American women. *Journal for the Education of the Gifted, 21*(3), 254–287.

Kitano, M. K. (2003). Gifted potential and poverty: A call for extraordinary action. *Journal for the Education of the Gifted, 26*(4), 292–303.

Kruger, E. A. (2004). *"I haven't really met many girls like me": A qualitative exploration of barriers and facilitative conditions for the academic achievement and socio-emotional well-being of gifted African American adolescent females.* Unpublished Master's thesis, University of Wisconsin-Madison.

Kulik, J. A., & Kulik, C. C. (1992). Meta-analytic findings on grouping programs. *Gifted Child Quarterly, 36,* 73–77.

LaFromboise, T. D., Trimble, J. E., & Mohatt, G. V. (1993). Counseling intervention and American Indian tradition: An integrative approach. In D. R. Atkinson, G. Morten, & D. W. Sue (Eds.), *Counseling American minorities* (pp. 145–170). Dubuque, IA: William C. Brown Communications.

Lewis, J. (2000). *Rural gifted education: Enhancing service delivery.* Alexandria, VA: Capitalizing on Leadership in Rural Special Education, Making a Difference for Children and Families. (ERIC Document Reproduction Service No. ED 439 874)

Lotta, C. C., & Benally, N. (2005). Counseling talented, at-risk Native American girls. In S. R. Robinson-Kurpius, B. A. Kerr, & A. Harkins (Eds.), *Handbook for counseling girls and women* (Vol. 1, pp. 67–89). Mesa, AZ: Nueva Science Press.

Lovecky, D. V. (1993). The quest for meaning: Counseling issues with gifted children and adolescents. In L. K. Silverman (Ed.), *Counseling the gifted and talented* (pp. 29–50). Denver, CO: Love Publishing Company.

Luhman, A., & Fundis, R. (1989). *Building academically strong gifted programs.* Washington, DC: National Association for Gifted Children. (ERIC Document Reproduction Service No. ED 308-060)

Mahoney, A. S. (2005). *The gifted identity formation model.* Retrieved November 9, 2005, from http://www.counselingthegifted.com/articles/insearchofID.html#sub

Maker, C. J. (1996). Identification of gifted minority students: A national problem, needed changes and a promising solution. *Gifted Child Quarterly, 40*(1), 41–50.

Marland, S., Jr. (1972, March). *Education of the gifted and talented. Report to the Congress of the United States by the U.S. Commissioner of Education.* Washington, DC: U.S. Government Printing Office.

Marshall, B. C. (1981). Career decision-making patterns of gifted and talented adolescents. *Journal of Career Education, 7,* 305–310.

McCarty, T. L., Lynch, R. H., Wallace, S., & Benally, A. (1991). Classroom inquiry and Navajo learning styles: A call for reassessment. *Anthropology and Education Quarterly, 22,* 42–59.

McCoach, D. B., & Siegle, D. (2003). Factors that differentiate underachieving gifted students from high achieving gifted students. *Gifted Child Quarterly, 47*(2), 144–154.

McKenzie, J. A. (1986). The influence of identification practices, race, and SES on the identification of gifted students. *Gifted Child Quarterly, 30,* 93–95.

Mendaglio, S. (1993). Counseling gifted learning disabled: Individual and group counseling techniques. In L. K. Silverman (Ed.), *Counseling the gifted and talented* (pp. 3–28). Denver, CO: Love Publishing Company.

Milligan, J. (2004, Winter). Leadership skills of gifted students in a rural setting: Promising programs for leadership development. *Rural Special Education Quarterly,* 1–17.

Moon, S. M., Kelly, K. R., & Feldhusen, J. F. (1997). Specialized counseling services for gifted youth and their families: A needs assessment. *Gifted Child Quarterly, 41*(1), 16–25.

Morris, J. E. (2002). African American students and gifted education: The politics of race and culture. *Roeper Review, 24*(2), 59–62.

Naglieri, J. A., & Ford, D. Y. (2003). Addressing underrepresentation of gifted minority children using the Naglieri Nonverbal Ability Test (NNAT). *Gifted Child Quarterly, 47*(2), 155–160.

National Association for Gifted Children. (2005). *What is gifted?* Retrieved September 20, 2005, from http://www.nagc.org/index.aspx?id=574&ir

National Center for Education Statistics. (1997). *Dropout rates in the United States: 1996* (NCES 98-250). Washington, DC: U.S. Government Printing Office.

National Center for Education Statistics. (2000). *National education longitudinal study: 1988–2000.* (Data files and electronic codebook). Washington, DC: U.S. Department of Education.

National Commission on Excellence in Education. (1983). *A nation at risk.* Washington, DC: U.S. Government Printing Office.

Olszewski-Kubilius, P. M., & Scott, J. M. (1992). An investigation of the college and career counseling needs of economically disadvantaged, minority gifted students. *Roeper Review, 14,* 141–148.

Orenstein, P. (1994). *SchoolGirls: Young women, self-esteem, and the confidence gap.* New York: Anchor Books, Doubleday.

Patton, J. M. (1998). The disproportionate representation of African Americans in special education: Looking behind the curtain for understanding and solutions. *The Journal of Special Education, 32*(1), 25–31.

Perrone, P. A., Karshner, W. W., & Male, R. A. (1979). Identification of talented students. In N. Colangelo & R. T. Zaffrann (Eds.), *New voices in counseling the gifted* (pp. 251–263). Dubuque, IA: Kendall/Hunt.

Pfeiffer, S. I. (2003). Challenges and opportunities for students who are gifted: What the experts say. *Gifted Child Quarterly, 47*(2), 161–169.

Piechowski, M. M. (1979). Developmental potential. In N. Colangelo & R. T. Zaffrann (Eds.), *New voices in counseling the gifted* (pp. 25–57). Dubuque, IA: Kendall/Hunt.

Piechowski, M. M. (1991). Emotional development and emotional giftedness. In N. Colangelo & G. Davis (Eds.), *Handbook of gifted education* (pp. 285–306). Needham Heights, MA: Allyn and Bacon.

Piechowski, M. M. (1997). Emotional giftedness: The measure of intrapersonal intelligence. In N. Colangelo & G. A. Davis (Eds.), *Handbook of gifted education* (2nd ed., pp. 366–381). Boston: Allyn and Bacon.

Piechowski, M. M., & Colangelo, N. (1984). Developmental potential of the gifted. *Gifted Child Quarterly, 28,* 80–88.

Piechowski, M. M., & Cunningham, K. (1985). Patterns of overexcitability in a group of artists. *Journal of Creative Behavior, 19*(3), 153–174.

Piechowski, M. M., Silverman, L., & Falk, R. F. (1985). Comparison of intellectually and artistically gifted on five dimensions of mental functioning. *Perceptual and Motor Skills, 60,* 539–549.

Piirto, J. (1999). *Talented children and adults: Their development and education* (2nd ed.). Upper Saddle River, NJ: Prentice-Hall.

Reis, S. M., Callahan, C. M., & Goldsmith, D. (1996). Attitudes of gifted adolescents toward their achievement, education, and future. In K. D. Arnold, K. D. Noble, & R. E. Subotnik (Eds.), *Remarkable women: Perspectives on female talent development* (pp. 209–224). Cresskill, NJ: Hampton Press, Inc.

Reis, S. M., Colbert, R. D., & Hebert, T. P. (2005). Understanding resilience in diverse, talented students in an urban high school. *Roeper Review, 27*(2), 110–119.

Renzulli, J. S., & Park, S. (2000). Gifted dropouts: The who and the why. *Gifted Child Quarterly, 44*(4), 261–271.

Renzulli, J. S., & Reis, S. M. (1986). The enrichment triad/revolving door model: A schoolwide plan for the development of creative productivity. In. J. S. Renzulli (Ed.), *Systems and models for developing programs for the gifted and talented* (pp. 217–268). Mansfield Center, CT: Creative Learning Press.

Renzulli, J. S., Reis, S. M., & Smith, L. H. (1981). *The revolving door identification model.* Mansfield Center, CT: Creative Learning Press.

Richert, E. S. (2003). Excellence with justice in programming for gifted children. In N. Colangelo & G. Davis (Eds.), *Handbook of gifted education* (pp. 146–158). Boston: Allyn and Bacon.

Richert, E. S., & Wilson, R. (1994). Maximizing urban student and teacher potentials: Preliminary research results. In G. Ohwheri (Ed.), *Developing strategies for excellence in urban education* (pp. 189–218). New York: Nova.

Robinson, N. M., & Nobel, K. D. (1991). Social-emotional development and adjustment of gifted children, In M.C. Wang, M. C. Reynolds, & H. J. Walberg (Eds.), *Handbook of special education: Research and practice* (Vol. 2, pp. 56–76). New York: Pergamon Press.

Roedell, W. C. (1984). Vulnerabilities of highly gifted children. *Roeper Review, 6,* 127–130.

Roedell, W. C. (1990). *Nurturing giftedness in young children.* Washington, DC: National Association for Gifted Children. (ERIC Digest No. EC E487)

Rogers, K. B. (1998). Using current research to make good decisions about grouping. *National Association of Secondary School Principals Bulletin, 82*(595), 38–46.

Salend, S. (2004). *Creating inclusive classrooms: Effective and reflective practices for all students.* New York: Pearson.

Sanborn, M. P. (1979). Differential counseling needs of the gifted and talented. In N. Colangelo & R. T. Zaffrann (Eds.), *New voices in counseling the gifted* (pp. 154–164). Dubuque, IA: Kendall-Hunt.

Schatz, E. (1999). Mentors: Matchmaking for young people. *The Journal of Secondary Gifted Education, 11*(2), 67–87.

Schetky, D. H. (1981). A psychiatrist looks at giftedness: The emotional and social development of the gifted child. *Gifted Child Today, 18,* 2–4.

Schiever, S. W. (1985). Creative personality characteristics and dimensions of mental functioning in gifted adolescence. *Roeper Review, 7,* 223–226.

Schunk, D. H. (1991). Self-efficacy and achievement motivation. *Educational Psychologist, 26,* 207–231.

Schwartz, W. (1997). *Strategies for identifying the talents of diverse students.* New York: Eric Clearinghouse on Urban Education. (ERIC Document Reproduction Service No. ED 410323)

Seeley, K. (1993). Gifted students at risk. In L. K. Silverman (Ed.), *Counseling the gifted and talented* (pp. 263–276). Denver, CO: Love Publishing Company.

Sherman, L. (1997). Research review. *Northwest Education.* Retrieved September 1, 2005, from http://www.nwrel.org/nwedu/fall_97/article6.html

Silverman, L. K. (1983). Personality development: The pursuit of excellence. *Journal for the Education of the Gifted, 6*(1), 5–19.

Silverman, L. K. (1993). *Counseling the gifted and talented.* Denver, CO: Love Publishing Company.

Silverman, L. K. (2000). *Identifying visual spatial and auditory sequential learners.* Proceedings of the Henry and Jocelyn Wallace Symposium, Iowa City, IA.

Silverman, L. K., & Ellsworth, B. (1980). The theory of positive disintegration and its implications for giftedness. In N. Duda (Ed.), *Theory of positive disintegration: Proceedings of the third international conference* (pp. 179–194). Miami, FL: University of Miami School of Medicine.

Smith, E. M. (1985). Ethnic minorities: Life stress, social support, and mental health issues. *The Counseling Psychologist, 13*(4), 537–579.

Solorzano, L. (1983, August 8). Now, gifted children get some breaks. *U.S. News & World Report, 8,* 32.

Stanley, J. C., & Benbow, C. P. (1982). Educating mathematically precocious youth: Twelve policy recommendations. *Educational Researcher, 11*(5), 4–9.

Swiatek, M. A., & Lupkowski-Shoplik, A. (2003). Elementary and middle school student participation in gifted programs: Are gifted students underserved? *Gifted Child Quarterly, 47*(2), 118–130.

Tatum, B. V. (1997). *Why are all the black kids sitting together in the cafeteria?: And other conversations about race.* New York: Basic Books.

Terman, L. (1925). *Genetic studies of genius: Vol. 1. Mental and physical traits of a thousand gifted children.* Stanford, CA: Stanford University Press.

Terman, L. M., & Oden, M. H. (1935). *Genetic studies of genius: Vol. 3. The promise of youth.* Stanford, CA: Stanford University Press.

Terman, L. M., & Oden, M. H. (1947). *Genetic studies of genius: Vol. 4. The gifted child grows UP.* Stanford, CA: Stanford University Press.

Terman, L., & Oden, M. (1951). The Stanford studies of the gifted. In P. Witty (Ed.), *The gifted child.* Lexington, MA: Health.

Tolan, S. (1999). Dabrowski's overexcitabilities—A layman's explanation. *Metro EGT Newsletter, 2.*

Tonemah, S. A. (1987). Assessing American Indian gifted and talented student abilities. *Journal for the Education of the Gifted, 10,* 181–194.

U.S. Department of Education. (1993). *National excellence: A case for developing America's talent.* Washington, DC: U.S. Government Printing Office.

VanTassel-Baska, J. (1993a). Academic counseling for the gifted. In L. K. Silverman (Ed.), *Counseling the gifted and talented* (pp. 201–214). Denver, CO: Love Publishing Company.

VanTassel-Baska, J. (1993b) *Comprehensive curriculum for gifted learners.* Boston: Allyn & Bacon.

VanTassel-Baska, J. (2003). *Curriculum planning and instructional design for gifted learners.* Denver, CO: Love.

VanTassel-Baska, J., & Baska, L. (1993). The roles of educational personnel in counseling the gifted. In L. K. Silverman (Ed.), *Counseling the gifted and talented* (pp. 181–200). Denver, CO: Love Publishing Company.

VanTassel-Baska, J., & Baska, A. (2004). Working with gifted students with special needs: A curriculum and program challenge. *Gifted Education Communicator, 35*(2), 4–27.

VanTassel-Baska, J., & Reis, S. M. (2003). *Curriculum for gifted and talented students.* Thousand Oaks, CA: Corwin Press.

VanTassel-Baska, J., Bass, G. M., Ries, R. R.., Poland, D. L., & Avery, L. D. (1998). A national pilot study of science curriculum effectiveness for high ability students. *Gifted Child Quarterly, 42,* 200–211.

VanTassel-Baska, J., Patton, J., & Prillman, D. (1989). Disadvantaged gifted learners at risk for educational attention. *Focus on Exceptional Children, 22*(3), 1–15.

VanTassel-Baska, J., Zuo, L., Avery, L., & Little, C. (2002). A curriculum study of gifted-student learning in the language arts. *Gifted Child Quarterly, 46*(1), 30–43.

Watley, D. J. (1969). *Stability of career choices of talented youth.* Evanston, IL: National Merit Scholar Corporation.

Webb, J. (1994). *Nurturing social-emotional development of gifted children.* Arlington, VA: ERIC Clearinghouse on Disabilities and Gifted Education. (ERIC Document Reproduction Service No. E527)

Webb, J. T., & Kleine, P. A. (1993). Assessing gifted and talented children. In J. Culbertson & D. Willis (Eds.), *Testing young children* (pp. 383–407). Austin, TX: Pro-Ed.

Webb, J. T., Amend, E. R., Webb, N. E., Goerss, J., Beljan, P., & Olenchak, F. R. (2005). *Misdiagnosis and dual diagnoses of gifted children and adults: ADHD, bipolar, OCD, Asperger's, depression, and other disorders.* Scottsdale, AZ: Great Potential Press.

Webb, J. T., Meckstroth, E. A., & Tolan, S. S. (1982). *Guiding the gifted child: A practical source for parents and teachers.* Columbus, OH: Psychology.

Winebrenner, S. (2001). *Teaching gifted kids in the regular classroom.* Minneapolis, MN: Free Spirit Press.

Yee, B., Castro, F. G., Hammond, W. R., John, R., Wyatt, G. E., & Yung, B. R. (1995). Panel IV: Risk-taking and abusive behaviors among ethnic minorities. *Health Psychology, 14*(7), 622–631.

XXXV
CULTURAL IDENTITY ENHANCEMENT STRATEGIES FOR CULTURALLY DIVERSE YOUTH

HARDIN L. K. COLEMAN AND SARA CHO KIM
University of Wisconsin–Madison

A. YANG
University of Minnesota–Twin Cities

Introduction

Over the past decade, culminating with passage of the *No Child Left Behind* (NCLB) legislation, the focus of the educational establishment has been on academic achievement as measured by performance on high-stakes examination. The American School Counselor Association (ASCA) has aligned with this focus through the development of national standards designed to facilitate the academic accomplishment of students. As Coleman (Chapter 4, this volume) has suggested, student academic accomplishment is not achieved through a singular focus on the acquisition and mastery of academic content. Despite the fact that not all students go on to attend 2- or 4-year institutions of higher education, there is substantive evidence that student academic accomplishment is facilitated by a host of nonacademic factors (Coleman, in press). As has been suggested elsewhere in the handbook (e.g., see Hage, Schwartz, & Barnett, Chapter 25, this volume), the singular focus on academic content reduces a focus on the emotional development of children, which is a key factor in performance. The central focus of this chapter is both on the role that cultural identity plays in facilitating academic accomplishment and to provide school counselors with an approach to enhancing cultural identity, which they can integrate into their developmental guidance program.

A review of the literature suggests that a positive view of one's culture and ethnicity and developing a healthy cultural identity is important to academic success and is predictive of psychological adjustment (Bernal, Saenz, & Knight, 1991; Coleman, Norton, Miranda, & McCubbin, 2003; LaFromboise, Coleman, & Gerton, 1993; Phinney, 1991, 1992; Phinney & Kohatsu, 1997; Roberts & Romero, 1999; Taylor, Casten, Flickinger, Roberts, & Fulmore, 1994). A significant task of early and middle adolescence developmental growth focuses on forming cultural identities (Manning, 1999/2000). Oftentimes, culturally diverse adolescents find themselves living in two very different cultures and struggle with developing an integrated sense of cultural identity (Coleman et al., 2003).

Studies on the general development of adolescents help us understand the biological and innate processes that are unique to each individual; however, less research has been devoted to understanding the impact of environmental and psychosocial factors on the identity development of culturally diverse adolescents. Culturally diverse adolescents, who face difficulties with adjustments to the school environment, are too often referred to as "at risk" by teachers and school counselors. Issues that many do not take into account are the multiple factors with which many of these adolescents have to contend with, such as cultural identity development, navigating multiple contexts, language, and various familial and social expectations that are too often different from the expectations of school. We suggest that addressing these concerns is a developmentally appropriate focus for a middle school counseling program. Integrating these conversations into classroom guidance, small group interventions, and support to the curriculum development in academic courses is an important role that a school counselor can play. This chapter will provide explicit examples of what such a curriculum can look like for African, Latin, and Hmong descended students.

Thernstrom and Thernstrom (2003) and others (Bok, 2003; Ferguson, 2004) have noted that the achievement gap between African Americans, Latinos, and Asians is unacceptably large and continues to grow. It can be argued that in the middle school years the structure of the curriculum begins to separate children based on perceptions of their aptitude and motivation to do higher level math, leading to disparities in academic achievement. This process creates an implicit (and sometimes explicit) tracking system. As Thernstrom and Thernstrom have identified, this tracking system leads to systematic segregation within these classes by race and, historically, by gender (Denbo, 2002; Oyserman, Gant, & Ager, 1995). As this segregation increases with tracking, there is a greater chance of ethnic minority adolescents losing interest and potentially dropping out of school (Choi, Harachi, Gilmore, & Catalano, 2005). As Coleman (2006) has suggested, it is vital that we identify those resilience factors that help culturally diverse youth overcome the obstacles to their academic accomplishment and implement processes to facilitate the acquisition of these resilience factors among these youth. The purpose of this chapter will be to show how cultural identity may be one of those factors and give examples of how to facilitate its acquisition among particular populations. This chapter contributes to our understanding that a key role of a school counseling program for middle school adolescents is helping them understand their cultural identity as they prepare to find their place in society. In this chapter, we will focus on ethnic identity, but believe that similar activities to enhance gender or class identity are equally important. Grounded in theory, this chapter discusses the relationship among cultural identity, psychological adjustment and development implications, and culture specific interventions for cultural identity enhancement. Cultural identity and ethnic identity will be used interchangeably in this article. The rationale is that minority individuals in the United States may develop an ethnic identity but because of the influence of American society the term cultural identity is more appropriate.

In an attempt to address the multiple factors influencing culturally diverse adolescents, an integration of literature from counseling and developmental psychology, positive psychology, and cultural identity theories is provided for insight in constructing culturally sensitive strategies for optimal development in culturally diverse adolescents. In an effort to decrease the achievement gap along racial lines and to promote healthy cultural identity development, intervention programs tailored to specific cultural groups are discussed, with an in-depth look at one specific school-based intervention created by the authors. As noted by Harvey and Hill (2004), the model for the program, which can be tailored to specific cultural groups, focuses on the strengths and assets of adolescents to build on cultural values and self-awareness. Suggestions for further research on cultural identity enhancement are offered.

Cultural Identity Research

Research on cultural identity development has proliferated over the past three decades. In the past 20 to 30 years, there has been tremendous growth in the number of theoretical and empirical studies examining the process of cultural identity development (Parham & Helms, 1985; Phinney, 1990; Cross, 1991). Terms such as *ethnic identity development, racial identity*, and *multiculturalism* are included in this rapidly growing movement to understand the meaning and influence of culture in the lives and well-being of individuals. A number of studies have examined specific ethnic and racial groups based on the development of major racial categories of African Americans, Asian Americans, and Latinos. Upon closer examination, much of this research has focused on young adult or college-aged populations (Cross; Parham & Helms). There has been less focus on younger cohorts of children and adolescents (Phinney, 1990; Quintana, 1998).

A focus on the middle school years, adolescents between the ages of 11 and 14, is crucial. During this significant stage in their lives, culturally diverse adolescents are up against challenges that other adolescents from the dominant culture are less likely to face. Research has suggested that this is a time when adolescents are starting to develop a coherent sense of their cultural self. Historically, a monocultural perspective has dominated that study of human development where the focus has been on one's sense of self-identity (Erickson, 1968). More recent perspectives believe that one's sense of self is deeply integrated into one's contextual relationships (Bronfenbrenner, 1979). It is, at this time, important that systematic interventions need to be implemented to facilitate the development of one's sense of cultural self.

Positive Psychology

The field of positive psychology informs us of the various approaches offered through the examination of optimal functioning: character development, strength-based intervention programs, asset building, and core values development. In recent years, the concept of focusing on the strength-based model, as opposed to a deficit-based model was reinvigorated by Seligman and associates (Seligman, 1999; Seligman & Csikszentmihalyi, 2000). Seligman suggested that the field of psychology must shift the focus of the field to promoting a stronger "I–We balance" in which the family and the community are also included. Too often, the value of individualism in the dominant culture makes it easy to ignore the other important variables of connecting with family and community in creating conditions for optimum functioning (Seligman).

An extension of the field of positive psychology has focused on developing interventions for adolescents based on the premise of strengths and assets. Recent scholars have attempted to create a strength-based intervention model to be used with adolescents (Smith, 2006). Smith emphasized the importance of integrating cultural values in developing strength-based interventions for at-risk adolescents. By connecting adolescents to their culture, they are in effect extending the bond with family and community. As noted earlier, by creating a balance of the collective or "I–We balance," culturally diverse adolescents can strengthen their ties to their native culture and ultimately feel a stronger sense of self grounded in their bicultural identity (Seligman, 1999).

Cultural Identity Development

In the field, a widely accepted definition of *cultural identity* has been provided by Jean Phinney (2003). She used the term *ethnic identity* whereas we will use *cultural* and *ethnic identity* interchangeably in this chapter. Phinney stated that cultural identity development is a dynamic, fluid understanding of self and ethnicity. The development of cultural identity involves a process whereby an individual develops a sense of self based on at least race, ethnicity, culture, religion, language, or kinship. It is important to note the multiple factors that influence identity and the dynamic nature of identity formation.

Adolescents from ethnic minority groups find themselves living in two very different cultures and struggle to develop an integrated sense of cultural identity (Coleman et al., 2003). Many children want to belong with their ethnic community and at the same time they want to become mainstream Americans. They experience much confusion and ambivalence from feeling stereotyped by mainstream Americans in their community and schools and feeling culturally isolated from their original culture. At home they cannot talk about school and social activities because parents may not understand them, and at school they cannot talk about their cultural traditions to Americans who would not understand them (Trueba, Jacobs, & Kiron, 1990). They might even possibly risk being ridiculed for certain traditional practices.

Phinney (1991) suggested that identification with both one's own group and the mainstream culture is predictive of psychological adjustment. Bernal and colleagues (1991) went on to further suggest that positive ethnic identity with one's culture may promote academic achievement by acting as a cushion for the psychological stresses experienced by minority adolescents in school. Other researchers have consistently shown the positive relationship of ethnic identity to self-esteem (Phinney, 1992; Phinney & Kohatsu, 1997; Roberts & Romero, 1999) and school involvement (Taylor et al., 1994).

When considering the identity development of culturally diverse adolescents, an examination of the dominant culture and the ethnic culture is necessary. LaFromboise et al. (1993) noted that students have to learn to cope in two different cultures to succeed academically. They identified seven elements of bicultural competence: (1) knowledge of both cultures, (2) positive attitudes toward both groups, (3) communication competency, (4) role repertoire, (5) social support systems in both cultures, (6) bicultural efficacy, and (7) groundedness. These competencies are more descriptive of adults navigating in two (or more) cultures; two of the competencies are developmentally appropriate for adolescents, that is, knowledge of both cultures and positive attitudes toward both groups. Coleman (1995) also suggested learning about positive qualities that are core to the culture, an emphasis on group solidarity, and learning to negotiate dominate culture from a position of strengths as foci for cultural specific interventions.

Programs for Enhancing Cultural Identity Among Culturally Diverse Adolescents

Based on LaFromboise et al.'s (1993) assertion that bicultural competence facilitates successful adaptation to the risks ethnic minorities face living in a European American dominated society, Bass and Coleman (1997) developed an effective program for enhancing cultural identity within African American adolescents. Since that time, Coleman, Yang, and Cho Kim (2004) and de la Luz and Coleman (2003) have developed similar program for Hmong and Hispanic adolescents, respectively.

Bass and Coleman (1997) hypothesized that one source of academic underachievement in African American adolescents was that they were not grounded in their culture of origin but were acculturating to dominate society where their culture of origin was devalued, leaving them to feel like second-class citizens. In other words, they were not learning the positive values of their own culture as they were asked to perform within a second culture. To test the hypothesis, they developed a 20-week school-based intervention called the *Kwanzaa* program (see Appendix A), which was designed to initially ground the participants in Afrocentric ideology and then work with them to apply that perspective within a predominately White institution. They found significant improvement in the participants' GPAs and social performances as measured by frequency of detention and teacher evaluation of in-class behavioral performance. The findings in this intervention reinforced three assumptions: (1) that cultural identity is an important factor in adolescent development, (2) that middle school is a critical time to address these developmental issues, and (3) that using a group to address these issues has developmental and practical value.

Yang, Cho Kim, and Coleman (2004, see Appendix B) and de la Luz and Coleman (2003, see Appendix C) have developed similar programs for Hmong and Hispanic adolescents, respectively. Manuals were developed using LaFramboise et al.'s (1993) model of bicultural competence as the basis for cultural identity enhancement and the common elements that promote positive cultural identity. The interventions are based on the notion that culturally diverse adolescents gain knowledge of American culture and history from school and their daily interactions with the dominant society (directly or through the media) but often lack knowledge of their own culture and history of origin. The best strategy for understanding how their culture of origin functions is to identify the core values and traditional practices of that culture. Culturally diverse adolescents will need to know the positive aspects of these core values and be able to relate these concepts into their daily lives so that they can negotiate the dominate culture from a position of strength, while group solidarity of members in the programs acts as a support network.

The manuals were developed with the assumption that each culture has a set of core values that separate it from others. It is not that these values are not present in other cultures; it is that there is a set of values that members of the culture identify as representing their culture. The first step for each program was to identify those core values. For each program, those values were identified differently. For the African American program, the decision was made to use the *Kwanzaa* principles developed by Karenga (1980). For the Hmong program, *Calm Heart: Ua Siab Tus Yees*, given the lack of written history, the authors interviewed Hmong elders in the Midwest to gain a sense of what these elders understood to be the Hmong core values (Coleman et al., 2004). For the Hispanic program, *Fortaleciendo Nuestras Raíces: Strengthening Our Roots*, the author completed an extensive review of the counseling and values literature concerning Latino values (de la Luz, 2003; de la Luz & Coleman, 2003). Once the values were identified, a manual for each group was developed to share these values with adolescents from that particular culture.

The *Kwanzaa* program was the beta model. It was created and tested first. The subsequent programs based their structure on the success of the *Kwanzaa* program. Each session was designed to teach about a particular value, give the participants an opportunity to discuss how that value was, or was not, operational within his or her life, and how knowing about this value might affect his or her decision making. Working within the group format helped to create safety and build group cohesion; however, these factors alone did not change behavior. Bass and Coleman (1997) determined that it is necessary to directly discuss ways in which one can express his or her cultural values within the dominate society in order to facilitate change. The results support LaFromboise et al.'s (1993) supposition that bicultural efficacy, the confidence to act in a bicultural manner, is an essential element in bicultural competence. The final and most significant factor in the development of the manuals involved creating activities within the group that would allow the participants to practice a culturally specific action that integrated the value under consideration.

Traditional models of identity development (e.g., Erickson, 1968) suggested that the task of middle adolescence is to develop an autonomous and integrated sense of self. We would suggest that this is the appropriate task within a homogenous setting where one's cultural framework dominates the values and behaviors within the significant institutions (e.g., schools) with which the adolescent interacts. If the school curriculum in which one is being enculturated represents your values and your history, provides models of how people like you have been successful, and uses the language of your home to facilitate your learning, then accomplishing the task of demonstrating how you will represent this culture as an individual becomes the appropriate task. If you come from a cultural group that is not central to the values and behavior of a particular institution such as school, then the adolescent identity development task becomes more complex. We suggest that the task for minority students (and others who are not reflected in the core curriculum such as gay individuals) changes from how to develop an autonomous and integrated sense of self and personal agency to how to develop a positive, connected, and integrated sense of cultural self within a heterogeneous setting. We are advocating that middle school counselors learn to explicitly address this developmental task within their counseling programs through the use of small culturally specific groups that focus on cultural identity development.

To give an example of how this process can work, we will describe the program for Hmong adolescents in more detail.

Calm Heart: Ua Siab Tus Yees

Interviews were conducted with Hmong elders and compared with existing literature to determine core Hmong values. Five general core values were identified: (1) respect, (2) care, (3) hard work, (4) ethics, and (5) wisdom. As an example, *wisdom* is defined as choosing and acting in culturally appropriate ways to accomplish tasks and responsibilities in the best interests of your life, family, and future; and wisdom is a life-long process that includes but is not exclusive to learning in school; from family, friends, and work; and through society's examples. Based on these core values, the *Calm Heart: Ua Siab Tus Yees* program is created to teach Hmong youth about these values in a culturally relevant manner (Coleman et al., 2004; Yang, Cho Kim, & Coleman, 2005).

This program incorporates various domains of an adolescent's life—peer group, community, and family members—to facilitate an understanding of their cultural identity. The goals of the program encourage the development and utilization of a positive ethnic orientation as a coping strategy for managing in a pluralistic society (Coleman, 1995; Tajfel & Turner, 1979) and to increase developmental assets (Hutchinson, 1997; Koltyk, 1997) within ethnic minority adolescents. Evidence from previous studies shows that a positive cultural identity may promote academic achievement by acting as a cushion for the psychological stresses experienced by minority adolescents in school (Bernal et al., 1991). As suggested by Coleman, this is achieved through teaching and facilitating the learning of positive qualities that are core to the culture (in this case, the five core Hmong values), an emphasis on group solidarity, and strategies for negotiating the dominant culture from a position of strength. The desired outcomes are to strengthen adolescents to become more engaged in school, home, and their community.

The program was developed with the assumption that Hmong culture has a set of core values separating this culture from others. Values guide how a person makes decisions and lives life. Hmong American adolescents live in two cultures with different values and need assistance in finding the strengths in both of these cultures. The Hmong core values are present in the lives of adolescents but may not be apparent in behaviors that represent adaptation to the American context (e.g., by not adhering to traditional courting methods). Parents think that their children have lost all values, and adolescents may feel isolated from their parents and the Hmong community as a whole; the adolescents may come to believe that their values are in opposition to traditional Hmong values. However, if we dig deeper at the meaning of the adolescents' activities and thoughts, we will see that some of these core Hmong values are very much in practice.

Based on the values assumption, the *Calm Heart: Ua Siab Tus Yees* program is structured to teach and stimulate discussions about Hmong history and values with a particular focus on how the pragmatic aspects of these values are apparent in the adolescents' everyday lives as Hmong Americans. The manual consists of 11 sessions; the first session is an introduction to the group, and the last session is dedicated to group termination and a celebration. One session focuses on Hmong history, five sessions are dedicated to each of the five core values (e.g., respect, ethics), and the remaining sessions are syntheses of two values (e.g., caring and hard-working in our lives) or an in-depth focus on a core value in everyday life (e.g., wisdom in our lives). The program defines the values in terms of how they might manifest in Hmong American adolescents and their experience living within a Hmong and American community. Within each session, group members have the opportunity to share any recent news or events in the community, home, or school, and to participate in structured exercises and open discussions related to the session topic.

Historically, Hmong culture was transmitted using oral and pictorial traditions. The Hmong would embroider family and historical events onto their clothing as a form of communication, called *pa ndau*. As a closing ritual, each session ends with group members making a modified version of *pa ndau* that reflects his or her reaction to or understanding of the value address within that session. As an opening ritual, group members will finish their *pa ndau* from the previous session. The closing and opening rituals serve as a bridge between sessions. At the end of the program, individual *pa ndau* squares from all group members are collected and sewn to make a quilt, creating a pictorial story. It is suggested that the quilt be donated to the setting where the group is initiated (e.g., school), further solidifying group members' experiences.

To date, the authors' have only anecdotal reactions and responses to the Hispanic and Hmong programs. Based on program evaluations, de la Luz and Coleman (2003) reported that the students enjoyed and were engaged in the program. A common response was that it was helpful to experience their culture of origin within the school to give their cultural being a sense of being valued. In both the African and Hispanic program, the groups were run by a member of the group's cultural group. In the Hmong program, teachers were trained to run the groups. We trained 16 counselors and teachers (all European American) to run the groups with Hmong adolescents. The groups were run in a school located in a rural area of a mid-Western state where there has been a significant growth in the Hmong population. Although data concerning the adolescents was not collected in this round, the feedback from facilitators suggested an increase in awareness of culture and the roles that they can play in working with students from diverse cultures. The teachers reported that they enjoyed learning about Hmong culture and were emotionally moved by the stories their students' shared about their experiences of negotiating two cultures. This served to make the teachers more sensitive to the Hmong experience and more aware of the unique concerns of their Hmong students. The teachers also reported that parents contacted them concerning the group and were interested in attending a few of the sessions. The teachers also reported that the students enjoyed teaching the teachers about their culture and the opportunity to discuss the tension of living within two cultural frames of reference. These responses suggest that more systematic investigation of the process may yield useful information concerning ways to increase the multicultural competence of teachers.

Role in a School Counseling Program

The authors of this chapter consider group and classroom guidance a vital and central aspect of every school counseling program. We advocate that an important element of guidance in the middle school years should include an active discussion of the effect of cultural factors on an adolescent's sense of self. We believe that issues of class, gender, race, and other elements of culture should be a part of the regular conversation in schools. We believe, therefore, that an important aspect of classroom guidance should include these conversations. At the same time, there is a place for targeted conversations about these cultural factors among these adolescents, particularly influenced by factors such as gender or race. We advocate for the use of the type of programs presented in this chapter to be a central part of a middle school guidance curriculum. Whether these programs should be led by members of the cultural group reflected in the manual is an open question. We have utilized ethnic matching of leader and participant, for example, in the *Kwanzaa* program. In another program the *Calm Heart: Ua Siab Tus Yees* program, we have not used ethnic matching. Both approaches have been found to be valuable and effective. We do advocate, however, that pre- and postmeasures of academic performance and/or motivation be used in the evaluation of the groups.

Future work in the area should include empirical data to support the effectiveness of these interventions for their specific targeted groups; the use of comparison groups will further provide information on their effectiveness. Bass and Coleman (1997) found that the *Kwanzaa* program reinforced three assumptions: (1) cultural identity is an important factor in adolescent development, (2) middle school is a critical time to address these developmental issues, and (3) using a group to address these issues has developmental and practical value. Considering that ethnic/cultural identity development is not a static phase, future research should be extended to include postsecondary ethnic minority students and how they might benefit from such programs.

School counselors can play an important role in the proliferation of these types of programs. By introducing them into their counseling programs and evaluating their effectiveness, school counselors can develop models that other counselors in their district and state can emulate. As school counselors supervise the training of preservice school counselors, they can teach these models, which the school counselor in training can take to other schools. As to be expected, development, implementation, and evaluation of programs is a time-consuming activity. This activity, however, is a perfect way to collaborate or partner with university programs that train school counselors. The university partner is well situated to help with the development, evaluation, and dissemination of such a program, while the school counselor is well situated to implement and train staff to use such a program. We advocate for the school counselor to work with teachers to implement such programs as a way to enhance the multicultural competence of the teacher and his or her connections with the culturally diverse communities within the school.

Conclusion

We argue that middle school is an important time to help adolescents develop a positive image of cultural self and to become articulate about the challenges they face as members of their particular cultural groups. Cultural identity enhancement groups perform this very valuable function. This chapter has tried to convey that there is a way to help culturally diverse students enhance their sense of cultural identity. We believe that one's sense of self is deeply integrated into one's contextual relationships as articulated by Bronfenbrenner (1979). It is at this time, therefore, that systematic interventions need to be utilized to facilitate the development of one's sense of cultural self. The effectiveness of these programs suggests that at the minimum an equally important focus should be on how we see ourselves as members of a cultural group and what that means within the social contexts in which we live and work. By focusing more energy on formulating effective programs based on culturally relevant research, school counselors will be able to better address the issues related to the challenges culturally diverse adolescents are facing in achieving their best academically and to foster psychological adjustment. The work of Bass and Coleman (1997) suggests that this can have a positive impact on the academic and social performance of culturally diverse adolescents. Furthermore, this chapter suggests that the more we engage teachers in the process, the more teachers will be committed to this important aspect of student development.

Implicit within this chapter is the belief that school counselors are the pupil services professionals within schools and have a primary responsibility for the positive emotional development of children. School counselors are best suited to facilitate the process of positive emotional development that will lead to academic accomplishment. In the middle school years, we can think of no developmental task that is more central than the acquisition of a positive and integrated identity. For culturally diverse students, this must include an articulate sense of cultural self in a pluralistic society. We believe that the programs presented in this chapter provide models for developing this positive sense of cultural identity and that this should be a focus of the school counselor's role within the middle school years.

References

Bass, C., & Coleman, H. L. K. (1997). Enhancing the cultural identity of early adolescent male African Americans. *Professional School Counselor, 1,* 48–51.

Bernal, M. E., Saenz, D. S., & Knight, G. P. (1991). Ethnic identity and adaptation of Mexican American youths in school settings. *Hispanic Journal of Behavioral Sciences, 13,* 35–154.

Bok, D. (2003). *Universities in the marketplace: The commercialization of higher education.* Princeton, NJ: Princeton University Press.

Bronfenbrenner, U. (1979). *The ecology of human development: Experiments by nature and design.* Cambridge, MA: Harvard University Press.

Choi, Y., Harachi, T., Gilmore, M., & Catalano, R. (2005). Applicability of the social development model to urban ethnic minority youth: Examining the relationship between external constraints, family socialization, and problem behaviors. *Journal of Research on Adolescents, 15,* 505–534.

Coleman, H. L. K. (1995). Strategies for coping with cultural diversity. *The Counseling Psychologist, 23,* 722–740.

Coleman, H. L. K. (2006). Minority student achievement: A resilient outcome? In D. Zinga (Ed.), *Navigating multiculturalism: Negotiating change* (pp. 296–326). New Castle, UK: Cambridge Scholars Press.

Coleman, H. L. K., Norton, R. A., Miranda, G. E, & McCubbin, L. D. (2003). Toward an ecological theory of cultural identity development. In D. B. Pope-Davis, H. L. K. Coleman, W. Liu, & R. Toperek (Eds.), *Handbook of multicultural competencies* (pp. 38–58). Thousand Oaks, CA: Sage.

Coleman, H. L. K., Yang, A., & Cho Kim, S. (2004). *Minority student achievement: The role of cultural identity.* Paper presented at the Diversity Challenge Conference, Institute for the Study and Promotion of Race and Culture, Boston College.

Cross, W. E. (1991). *Shades of black: Diversity in African-American identity.* Philadelphia: Temple University Press.

de la Luz, M. (2003). *Fortaleciendo nuestras raíces: Strengthening our roots.* Unpublished master's thesis, University of Wisconsin, Madison.

de la Luz, M., & Coleman, H. L. K. (2003). *Fortaleciendo nuestras raíces: Strengthening our roots.* Unpublished manuscript, University of Wisconsin, Madison.

Denbo, S. J. (2002). Why can't we close the achievement gap? In S. J. Denbo & L. Moore Beaulieu (Eds.), *Improving schools for African American students: A reader for educational leaders* (pp. 13–16). Springfield, IL: Charles C Thomas.

Erickson, E. (1968). *Identity and crisis.* New York: Horton.

Ferguson, R. F. (2004). An unfinished journey: The legacy of brown and narrowing the achievement gap. *Phi Delta Kappan, 85,* 656–669.

Harvey, A., & Hill, R. (2004). Afrocentric youth and family rites of passage program: Promoting resilience among at-risk African American youths. *Social Work, 49,* 65–74.

Hutchinson, R. (1997). *The educational performance of Hmong students in Wisconsin.* Thiensville: Wisconsin Policy Research Institute.

Karenga, M. (1980). *Kawaida theory: Kwanzaa, origin, concepts, and practice.* Inglewood, CA: Kawaida Publications.

Koltyk, J. (1997). *New pioneers in the heartland: Hmong life in Wisconsin.* Boston: Allyn and Bacon.

LaFromboise, T., Coleman, H. L. K., & Gerton, J. (1993). Psychological impact of biculturalism: Evidence and theory. *Psychological Bulletin, 114,* 395–412.

Manning, M. L. (2000). Developing responsive multicultural education for young adolescents. *Childhood Education, 76,* 82–87. (Original work published 1999)

Oyserman, D., Gant, L., & Ager, J. (1995). A socially contextualized model of African American identity: Possible selves and school persistence. *Journal of Personality and Social Psychology, 69*(6), 1216–1232.

Parham, T., & Helms, J. (1985). Attitudes of racial identity and self-esteem of black students: An exploratory investigation. *Journal of College Student Personnel, 26,* 143–147.

Phinney, J. S. (1990). Ethnic identity in adolescents and adults: A review of research. *Psychological Bulletin, 108,* 499–514.

Phinney, J. S. (1991). Ethnic identity and self-esteem: A review and integration. *Hispanic Journal of Behavioral Sciences, 13,* 193–208.

Phinney, J. S. (1992). The multigroup ethnic identity measure: A new scale for use with diverse groups. *Journal of Adolescence Res., 7,* 156–176.

Phinney, J. S. (2003). Ethnic identity and acculturation. In K. Chun, P. B. Organista, & G. Marin (Eds.), *Acculturation: Advances in theory, measurement, and applied research* (pp. 63– 81). Washington, DC: American Psychological Association.

Phinney, J. S., & Kohatsu, E. (1997). Ethnic and racial identity development and mental health. In J. Schulenber, J. Maggs, & K. Hurrelman (Eds.), *Health risks and developmental transitions in adolescence* (pp. 420–443). New York: Cambridge University Press.

Quintana, S. M. (1998). Children's developmental understanding of ethnicity and race. *Applied and Preventative Psychology, 7,* 27–45.

Roberts, C., & Romero, A. (1999). The structure of ethnic identity in young adolescents From diverse ethnocultural groups. *Journal of Early Adolescence, 19,* 301–322.

Seligman, M. E. P. (1999). The president's address. *American Psychologist, 54,* 559–562.

Seligman, M. E. P., & Csikszentmihalyi, M. (2000). Positive psychology: An introduction. *American Psychologist, 55,* 5–14.

Smith, E. J. (2006). The strength based counseling model. *The Counseling Psychologist, 34,* 13–79.

Tajfel, H., & Turner, J. C. (1979). An integrative theory of intergroup conflict. In W. C.Austin & S. Worchel (Eds.), *The social psychology of intergroup relations* (pp. 33–47). Monterey, CA: Brooks/Cole.

Taylor, R., Casten, R., Flickinger, S., Roberts, D., & Fulmore, C. (1994). Explaining The school performance of African American adolescents. *Journal of Adolescence Res., 4,* 21–44.

Thernstrom, A., & Thernstrom, S. (2003). *No excuses: Closing the racial gap in learning.* New York: Simon & Schuster.

Trueba, H. T., Jacobs, L., & Kiron, E. (1990). *Cultural conflict and adaptation.* Bristol, PA: The Falmer Press.

Yang, A., Cho Kim, S., & Coleman, H. L. K (2004). *Calm heart: Ua siab tus yees.* Unpublished manuscript, University of Wisconsin, Madison.

Yang, A., Cho Kim, S., & Coleman, H. L. K. (2005). Hmong youth intervention program: The role of cultural identity. In L. M. Edwards (Chair.), *Navigating cultural contexts: Theory, research, and practice on bicultural and intercultural competence.* Symposium presented at the annual American Psychological Association Conference, Washington, DC.

Appendix A

Please note: The first three sessions are included. The complete manual can be found at http://www.education.wisc.edu/cp/faculty/hcoleman/

Kwanzaa/Sphinx Program: A Program for Academic Motivation Enhancement in African American Male Middle School Students

Christopher K. Bass, MS and Hardin L. K. Coleman, PhD

University of Wisconsin–Madison

Session 1 Overview
Concept: Umoja (Unity)

The principle Umoja will be presented to the boys and discussed. The key concept is the placing of high value upon relationships. The activity will involve having each boy self-disclose personal information about himself. This is a powerful exercise because it enables the boys to learn more about the other members of the group.

Session Objectives

- By the process of bonding/joining, participants will be able to let their defenses down and participate.
- Each participant will learn why he is in the group.
- Participants will learn about the rules and benefits of group membership.

Session Format

1. Opening exercise
2. African/African American history
3. Discussion on Kwanzaa Symbols
4. Member responsibilities
5. Group discussion of week activities ("Open Forum")
6. Introduction of concept
   a. What does this mean to you?
   b. Group discussion
7. Closure of session

Lesson 1 Plan
Opening Exercise (approximate time: 15 minutes)

Introduction Exercise

Introduce yourself to the group members. Ask each person to talk briefly about where he is from, how he came to be in the group, what he hopes to accomplish in the group, and what are his dreams.

Ground Rules

Briefly outline the following group parameters. These should be shared in a positive manner as the parameters are meant to facilitate group cooperation and cohesiveness. Group members are also encouraged to add to this list of ground rules.

- What goes on in group, stays in group.
- Attendance at each session is very important. Ask members to plan to attend all sessions.
- Knowledge of the motto and pledge of the group is important.
- Support of others is welcome. Constructive criticism used to facilitate work is acceptable. However, negative criticism and rudeness are not accepted and are discouraged.
- Each member is responsible for his own behavior.
- Members are responsible for the wearing and keeping of group symbols.

At the end of the discussion concerning ground rules, give members a chance to ask questions.

African/African American History (approximate time: 15 minutes)

This section is created to expose the African American young men to African world views and to enhance self-esteem/self-perception by including African/African American history in the formal learning environment. Facilitators of this group must be knowledgeable of some African/African American history. Information for different subjects may be gained through reading any African/African American history literature.

Open Forum (approximate time: 20 minutes)

This section of the program is created to give the participants an opportunity to discuss what has happened in their week. Whether they have good information to share or bad information to share, this section is designed for students to speak on what events have occurred during the week. Many times, participants may speak on events occurring at home (encourage this) or at school. Remember this is their time to speak. This is their space. Try to limit discussion time to 15 minutes. However, if a subject is too intense to disrupt, allow ample time for wrap up (use your own judgment).

Introduction of Concept
(approximate time: 15 minutes)

The Kwanzaa group, which is Afrocentric in nature, will incorporate into it the concepts of Kwanzaa. This part of the Kwanzaa group is powerful in the fact that it not only teaches the young men important aspects of their culture but links them to positive qualities of a past history that they might not have gotten an opportunity to experience. Giving the boys a past history (besides slavery) gives them something to draw upon when confronted by the ugliness of racism in this society.

The principles are based on *Kawaida Theory* (Karenga, 1980). The principles are used to expose and connect the boys to positive images in the African American culture. The seven principles are (1) *Umoja* (unity), (2) *Kujichagulia* (self-determination), (3) *Ujima* (collective work and responsibility), (4) *Ujamma* (cooperative economics), (5) *Nia* (purpose), (6) *Kuumba* (creativity), and (7) *Imani* (faith).

Principle one, which is Umoja, should be discussed in the first session. Participants should know how to pronounce the word and tell what it means to them. Each student should speak on unity. A group discussion on unity should ensue after each has described the concept in his own words.

Materials Needed

- Copy of the Kwanzaa Group Pledge
- Copy of the Kwanzaa Group Shield
- Afrocentric symbols (Ankh) for each member

Lecture Format

The following sample lecture is provided for you. Its content covers the major points just outlined. You may use the lecture verbatim or you can use your own words to convey the information. If you choose to use your own words, be careful to cover the major content and themes that are contained in the sample lecture.

Sample Lecture

Greetings, my name is .... Congratulations on being accepted into the Kwanzaa Group. I am the leader of the group but this group belongs to you. This is **your** group. Can anyone tell me what he thinks this group is all about? In a minute I would like for us to go around and tell who we are, why we are here in the group, and what you hope to learn from the group. You already know my name, but a little background information on me is .... This group is called the Kwanzaa Group. It will meet for 16 sessions. In these sessions we will discuss a lot of different things. We will talk about school, home, and how we feel. I want to start this session off by explaining the pledge of the group. The pledge goes, **"Through knowledge perseverance and self-respect, I shall uplift myself and my race."** Each of you will receive a copy of the pledge. All of you should know it by the next session. We say this pledge at the beginning and end of each meeting. Also, in time you will be expected to learn about the shield of the group. Like all groups, we have a shield that represents us. In the shield there are many different symbols and hidden meanings. The main symbol on the shield is the Sphinx. The Sphinx is a mystical figure originating in the African country of Egypt. Although we will discuss the origins of the Sphinx and many other symbols, for the shield, the Sphinx means pharaohs (who were Egyptian kings). The next symbol is the torch, on the shield the torch means knowledge. The next symbol is the Ankh; this symbol looks like a cross with a hole in the top; this means life. The next symbol is the pyramid, which means strength. As with all great clubs, all of these symbols are secret. Do not discuss these outside of the group.

Each of you will receive an Ankh to wear. These Ankhs are very special. You are responsible for them. Each member must wear his Ankh to each meeting. This is one of the ground rules. Other rules include (refer to rules section). Each week we will talk about things that are happening with you; whether it's school related or home related. It's up to you, we can talk about whatever you need to talk about.

Each week we will talk about a lot of different things. Can anyone tell me the name of this group? [The Kwanzaa group is the name]. Does anyone know about Kwanzaa? Can anybody tell me a Kwanzaa principle? This week we will talk about *Umoja*, which is Kiswahilii for unity. Let's talk about what it means to have unity. **Have each student discuss unity.** [It is important to talk to the young men in terms they can understand. Make it fun for them]. By this time, the hour should almost be completed, and participants should be encouraged to ask questions. It is important to also discuss with them the different types of paper work for which they will be responsible. The paperwork includes *Weekly behavior charts* (to be given to their teacher and returned to you at the end of each week) and *Academic goal planner/and chart miscellaneous homework projects.*

Closure of Session (approximate time: 5 minutes)

1. Summary of major points covered in session
2. Reminder of next scheduled meeting
3. Questions
4. The pledge
5. Goodbye

Session 2 Overview

Concept: Kujichagulia (Self-Determination)

This session will be presented in the form of a walk back through history. We will dissect some of the terms of African American culture and challenge the boys to enlighten their minds by asking questions relating to topics such as ancient African civilizations, kings, slavery, crime, and drugs in the community. Because of the lack of culturally relevant topics presented to the boys in the public school system, we believe that this exercise is more of an educational tool that will help the boys understand what they were and what they are as a people. The first phase of the rites of passage will be completed.

Session Objectives

- To explore myths and falsehoods about the African American culture
- To give participants an opportunity to discuss issues regarding their neighborhoods
- To expose participants to African history
- To complete the first phase of the rites of passage experience

Session Format

1. Opening exercise
2. Review of Session 1
3. African/African American History (Ceremony 1: Presenting of Ankhs)
4. Open forum
5. Introduction of new concept
   a. What does it mean to you?
   b. Group discussion
6. Closing exercise
7. Session closure

Lesson 2 Plan

Opening Exercise (approximate time: 7 minutes)

1. Kwanzaa pledge
2. Go over the symbols of the Kwanzaa shield and their meanings.
3. Collect teacher response sheets.

Review of Session 1 (approximate time: 15 minutes)

1. Go over group rules.
2. Briefly revisit past concept (Umoja).

African/African American History (approximate time: 20 minutes)

This week you should talk about Africa. Mention facts such as Africa is the second-largest continent in the world with an area of 12 million square miles. Find a current map of Africa and explain how most maps show the United States and Africa as equal in size, but Africa is almost 3 times as large. Understand that the only information about Africa that these children have is what has been presented to them by the media and the current educational system. These two realms of education often depict Africa in a negative light. It is up to you to add new insight to this great land. More information that you should mention includes Africa is not one country, but 54 different countries; the longest river in the world, the Nile, is located there (the Nile will be explored further in the Sphinx Club). Talk about the great empires and statues of Egypt, specifically the reigns of Ramses, Akenaten, and Tutankhamen, the Pyramids (Giza) and, the Sphinx (mention Chephren). After the history session, participants should be lined up according to height (shortest to tallest) and presented with their first Ankhs.

Bibliography

Diop, C.A. (1974). *The African origin of civilization.* New York: Lawrence Hill.

Kunjufu, J. (1987). Lessons from history: A celebration in Blackness Jr.–Sr. high edition. *African American Images,* Chicago, IL, 1–11.

Open Forum (approximate time: 15 minutes)

This section of the program is created to give the participants an opportunity to discuss what has happened in their week. Whether they have good information to share or bad information to share, this section is designed for students to speak on what events have occurred during the week. Many times participants may speak on events occurring at home (encourage this) or at school. Remember that this is their time to speak. This is their space. Try to limit discussion time to 15 minutes. However, if a subject is too intense to disrupt, allow ample time for wrap up. (Use your own judgment.)

Introduction of Concept (approximate time: 15 minutes)

The new concept this week is Kujichagulia, which means self-determination. Participants should be taught how to spell and pronounce the word and should tell what it means to them. Each student should speak on self-determination. A group discussion on self-determination should ensue after each has described it in his own words.

Materials Needed

- Copy of the Kwanzaa Group Pledge
- Copy of the Kwanzaa Group Shield
- Afrocentric Symbols (ANKH) for each member
- Map of Africa
- World map

Lecture

Closure of Session (approximate time: 5 minutes)

1. Summary of major points covered in session
2. Reminder of next scheduled meeting
3. Questions
4. The pledge
5. Goodbye

Session 3 Overview

Concept: Ujima *(Collective Work and Responsibility)*

The principle of Ujima will be presented to the boys in the form of an activity that will involve going to a neighborhood grocery store and picking out the groceries needed to create a meal. Each participant will be responsible for making one dish. After all dishes are completed, each will present the dish to the group. This activity was chosen for many reasons: (1) the boys will depend on each other for help in preparing their dish; (2) they will have the responsibility of creating a piece of the meal; and (3) the skills for grocery shopping and preparation of food are skills that young men should experience and have knowledge of (having the capabilities to take care of oneself).

Session Objectives

- To expose participants to the concept of *Ujima*
- To allow participants to be responsible for preparing a part of a collective project
- To give participants a life skill (grocery shopping and food preparation)
- To further the bonding process among participants

Session Format

1. Opening exercise
2. Review of Session 2
3. African/African American history
4. Open forum
5. Introduction of new concept
    a. What does it mean to you?
    b. Group discussion
6. Closing exercise
7. Session closure

Lesson 3 Plan

Opening Exercise (approximate time: 5 minutes)

1. Kwanzaa Pledge
2. Have participants go over the symbols of the Kwanzaa shield and their meanings.
3. Collect teacher response sheets.

Review of Session 2

1. Ask questions such as, What is the longest river in the world? What is a pyramid? Who was King Tut?

2. Briefly revisit past concept (*Kujichagulia*).

African/African American History

Because grocery shopping and cooking times may get extensive, this week's discussion should be centered on the topics discussed last week (i.e., the pyramids, pharaohs, Egypt, etc.). The discussion may take place in the car, grocery store, or even during cooking.

Open Forum

This entire session is basically an open forum. However, if participants want to speak about events in their community, home, or school, specifically encourage this.

Introduction of Concept

The new concept this week is Ujima, which means collective work and responsibility. Participants should be taught how to spell and pronounce the word and should tell what it means to them. Each student should speak on collective work and responsibility. A group discussion on collective work and responsibility should ensue after each has described the concept in his own words. Point out that this week's events have been an example of *Ujima*.

Materials Needed

- Copy of the Kwanzaa Group Shield
- Transportation to and from grocery store
- Approximately $25 for groceries
- A cooking facility

Lecture

Closure of Session

1. Clean up
2. Reminder of next scheduled meeting
3. Questions
4. The pledge
5. Goodbye

Appendix B

Please note: The first three sessions are included. The complete manual can be found at http://www.education.wisc.edu/cp/faculty/hcoleman/

Ua Siab Tus Yees: Calm Heart Manual

A Yang, MS
University of Minnesota–Twin Cities

**Sara Cho Kim, MS Ed
and Hardin Coleman, PhD**
University of Wisconsin–Madison

Session 1 Overview

Introduction

Session Format

1. Opening introductions
2. Cultural identity exercise
3. Introduction of Hmong values
4. Closure of session

Materials Needed

- Cloth squares
- Fine point permanent markers (variety of colors)
- Copies of the cultural values exercise

Session 1 Introduction

Opening Introductions

1. Member introduction
2. Facilitator introduction
   - My name is _____. Congratulations on being accepted into the Calm Heart: Ua Siab Tus Yees group. We are the leaders of the group but this group belongs to you. This is your group.
3. Ask members what their purpose is in joining the group and what they hope to learn from the group.
4. Inform members of the general purpose and structure of group:
   - I want to tell you about the Calm Heart: Ua Siab Tus Yees group. It will meet 11 times. We will start each session with a ritual and end with a ritual. Each one of you will have the chance to do many individual drawings, similar to a *pa ndau*.[1] We will work on this in the beginning and end of each session. At the end of our time together, the individual drawings will be sewn together into a quilt and perhaps we can donate it to the school. In the group we will discuss a lot of different things. We will talk about school, home, what we think, how we feel, and being Hmong American.
5. Discussion of what it means to be a member of a group:
   - Developing ground rules (from the group or by facilitator), for example, confidentiality, attendance, support of other, negative criticism and rudeness are not accepted. "These rules will be announced each week by a different member to remind us of where we are and what other members would like and need from us."

Cultural Identity Exercise

My two worlds exercise from *Who Am I?*[2] can lead to discussion of cultural identity and biculturalism.
Start the group on the *pa ndau*, or cloth drawing,[3] for example, a drawing of things they like in Hmong culture and American culture.

Introduction of Hmong Values

1. Introduce concept of Calm Heart: Ua Siab Tus Yees:[4]
   - What does Calm Heart: Ua Siab Tus Yees mean?
   - Open discussion and interpretation.
2. Hmong values
   - What are some values that your parents have?
   - Introduce Core Values as focus of sessions.[5]

---

[1] *Pa ndau* are stitched needlework that was originally used to adorn Hmong clothing and also became used as a way to record Hmong history and culture. The embroidery on the *pa ndau* tells a story that depicts aspects of the Hmong experience (e.g., war and death; village life).
[2] *Who Am I?* is an activity book designed to help Latina girls develop positive self-esteem (efforts of the U.S. Department of Health and Human Services). For more information see www.soyunica.gov. The activity worksheet has been adapted for the purposes of this manual.
[3] Each group member will complete one square cloth drawing reflecting how each of the five values may manifest in their lives today as a Hmong-American youth (for a total of five squares per group member). Fine point permanent markers should be used. The individual squares will be sewn together to create a quilt. It is suggested that the quilt be donated to the setting where the group is initiated (e.g., school).
[4] *Calm Heart: Ua Siab Tus Yees* is an ideal principle that encompasses the core Hmong values which guide how to live life as a good Hmong person. For more detail, see the introduction to the manual.
[5] See introduction to the manual for description of the five core values.

Closure of Session

1. Summary of major points covered in session
2. Reminder of next scheduled meeting
3. Questions

My Values

It is very important to know your values. What are values? They are guides to show you how to live and act. Therefore, they have great meaning in your life; they show that you are part of your family and culture.

These are basic elements for your identification as a person and to learn about your cultural heritage. That way, you will feel proud of it.

These values are a part of your identity, and they influence the decisions you make and your conduct, habits, ideals, rules, and goals.

You live in a Hmong culture and a North American culture. It is also important to your identity to know what aspects of each culture that you like.

My Two Worlds

Aspects of Hmong culture that I like: (Example: the food)	Aspects of American culture that I like: (Example: the music)
_____	_____
_____	_____
_____	_____
_____	_____
_____	_____
_____	_____
_____	_____
_____	_____

Session 2 Overview Hmong History

Session Format

1. Have member read ground rules.
2. Opening ritual
3. Open forum
4. Purpose
5. Hmong history
6. Exercise
7. Open discussion
8. Closure of session
9. Closing ritual

Materials Needed

- Cloth squares
- Fine point permanent markers (variety of colors)
- Paper, pens, and pencils
- Maps of Southeast Asia

Session 2 Hmong History

Ground Rules

Have a group member read the list of group rules generated in Session 1.

Opening Ritual

Cloth drawing (Finish picture from last session.)

Open Forum

To share any recent news or events in the community, home, or school. (Facilitators should use their best judgment on sensitive or negative topics.)

Purpose

To provide the group with a background of Hmong history. This will give group members a base from which the Hmong values stem. Participants will have the opportunity to compare and contrast Hmong history with the present conditions of Hmong life.

Hmong History

The main focuses of Hmong history:[6] (1) origins, (2) life in Laos, (3) role and outcome in the Vietnam War, (4) political asylum/immigration, and (5) life in the United States.

Exercise and Open Discussion

Have members write what they know about Hmong history related to the five main points just listed. Ask for two volunteers to share what they have written. This will be an open discussion; other members are welcome to expand or add anything else that they know. Facilitators should be prepared with information to fill in what members have not brought up.

Break main group into five smaller groups; each group will be assigned one of the five main foci of Hmong history and collaboratively write

---

[6] For more information, facilitators should read about Hmong history, for example, Fadiman, A. (1997). *The spirit catches you and you fall down.* New York: Noonday Press.

what was just discussed and information that was given. The written material will be put together into a book and each member will receive a copy along with a map of Southeast Asia.

Closure of Session

1. Summary of major points covered in session
2. Reminder of next scheduled meeting
3. Questions

Closing Ritual

Cloth drawing (Draw new one on history.)

Session 3 Overview Hard Working

Session Format

1. Have member read ground rules
2. Opening ritual
3. Open forum
4. Purpose
5. Introduce value of hard work
6. Exercise
7. Open discussion
8. Closure of session
9. Closing ritual

Materials Needed

- Cloth squares
- Fine point permanent markers (various colors)
- Copies of the folk story

Session 3 Hard Working

Ground Rules

Have a group member read the list of group rules generated in Session 1.

Opening Ritual

Cloth drawing (Finish picture from last session.)

Open Forum

To share any recent news or events in the community, home, or school. (Facilitators should use their best judgment on sensitive or negative topics.)

Purpose

To provide a group experience that will allow participants to gain insight into the value of hard work in traditional Hmong culture. To revisit the history of Hmong people, particularly related to the value of hard work. To give participants the opportunity to compare and contrast their personal view of hard work with that of their elders.

Value: Hard work

Saving for the future, laborious work, thrift, do well in school, housework (cook, clean), not complaining, not sitting around and doing nothing but instead being productive, and delayed gratification of work.

Exercise

Read a folk story that reflects the meaning of hard work just described. The group may alternate reading each sentence or paragraph if agreed upon.

Folk Story: Raising Rice[7]

Before we plant the rice, we must clear the fields. We use an ax or knife to cut the trees. We use a shovel to clear the land and make it smooth. We let the trees dry in the sun for several months. Then we burn the trees that we have cut. After we plant the rice seeds, we check on the rice every day. There is an insect called the *kooj*, or grasshopper, that eats the rice. We have to catch the grasshopper. We catch the grasshoppers at night with a light and put them in a bamboo basket with a top. We also spray the fields. When the rice is tall, the birds eat it, so the men use a *hneev*, or crossbow, to kill the birds that eat the rice. When the top of the rice plant curves down, the rice is ready to cut. We cut the tops off the plants. The men and women shake a flat bamboo basket. The leaves fall on the ground, and the rice stays on the flat basket. The rice is stored in a big bamboo storage bin. When the family needs rice to cook for food, it gets rice from the bamboo bin. The women put the rice seeds into a big round wooden barrel. The barrel has a long pole on one side. The women step on one end and make it move like a hammer. The hammer hits the rice seed and knocks the rice off the shell, and then it is ready to cook.

Open Discussion

- In Laos: What sort of work did Hmong families (for example, each family member) have to do?

---

[7] Folk story was taken from Cha, D. & Livo, N.J. (2000). *Teaching with folk stories of the Hmong: An activity book*. Westport, CT: Libraries Unlimited.

- In the United States: What sort of work do Hmong families do in the United States? What are the similarities and differences?
- How do you think these changes are affecting the Hmong parents, children, grandparents, and so on?
- What does hard work mean to you? How are you a hard worker? What does hard work look like?

Closure of Session

1. Summary of major points covered in session
2. Reminder of next scheduled meeting
3. Questions

Closing Ritual

Cloth drawing (Draw new one on hard work.)

Appendix C

Please note: The first three sessions are included. The complete manual can be found at http://www.education.wisc.edu/cp/faculty/hcoleman/

Fortaleciendo Nuestras Raíces (FNR): Strengthening Our Roots Manual

Maria de la Luz Perez de Olmos, MS and Hardin Coleman, PhD

University of Wisconsin–Madison, Department of Counseling Psychology

FIRST STAGE

Session 1

Value: Personalismo

Objectives

Students will know the rules and goals in general of this group and will learn the first value, Personalismo.

Getting Started

Optional: Before the group starts, take a picture of everybody and put the pictures with their names on a poster with a cornstalk drawing, so everybody will see it during each session. The corn plant will be a central element in our group process. You also can have Latin music while waiting for everybody to get ready to start. (You can ask the students to bring Latin music that they like to listen to before starting the session.)

You can write the proverb in a corner of the board before the group starts. Do it every time in the same place so the participants become familiar with it.

Dicho/Proverb: "No dejes para mañana lo que puedas hacer hoy." Don't leave for tomorrow what you can do today.

Activities (approximate time: 35 minutes)

1. (5 minutes) Introduce yourself to the group members. Congratulate them for being part of the Fortaleciendo Nuestras Raíces group. Tell them that the group belongs to them. Ask what they think this group is about. Ask each person to talk briefly about where he or she is from, what he or she likes to do in his free time, and what he or she hopes to accomplish in the group. Tell them a little bit about your background and your expectations in general.

2. (5 minutes) Tell participants about the ground rules and ask them if there are more rules they would like to include.

Ground Rules

- **Respect.** Constructive criticism is acceptable, but negative criticism or rudeness is not.
- **Responsibility.** Attendance at each session is very important. Each member is responsible for his or her own behavior.
- **Confidentiality.** What goes on in group, stays in group.
- **Membership.** Members are responsible for wearing and keeping of group symbols.

3. (5 minutes) Latino culture and history. You can start by asking where students come from, where their families come from, what countries Latinos come from, and where most of the Latinos are in the United States. Ask if they have relatives in the United States and where they live. You can bring a map to facilitate the discussion. You can give a brief narration of the Latino history in the United States. Tell participants briefly about the Latino history since the Spaniards colonized the Latin American countries. Tell them about the race mixture that is among Latinos (Spaniards, Indians, and African descendents). Ask if they know about their own race background. You can get Latino history in the books or any other resource accessible to you.

4. (10 minutes) Introduce the idea of the corn plant. Tell students about the importance of corn among Latinos. Ask who eats tortillas or other corn products. Tell them how the corn was first harvested by the Aztecs. Make the analogy of this group and the corn plant: At the end of the group we are going to harvest corn (goals), but first we need to strengthen the roots of this corn plant and then get ready to produce our fruit, the corn.

Tell them what every part of the corn stalk means in relation to the process of the group. "We are going to develop our corn plant. First, we will have to strengthen the roots of it, so our plant can be strong and can absorb the soil nutrients. The roots of our plant will be our values. Our values as Latinos are Personlismo, Respeto, Simpatía, Dignidad, Confianza, Familismo, and Fe/Espiritualidad. Once we learn and strengthen our values (root), we are going to develop our corn stalk. This means that we will learn more about ourselves. Later we will develop the leaves, which means that we are going to get ready to put forth the product, the corn. In this part we are going to learn skills that will help us to be able to produce. Finally, we are going to produce our last product, the corn (changes and actions)."

Symbols

El maiz
Raices (Roots) = Latino values
Caña (Stalk) = knowing my self
Hojas (Leaves) = learning, getting ready to produce
Maiz (Corn) = service, change, action

5. (5 minutes) Necklace Initiation Ceremony

Explain that the first 8 weeks will be dedicated to strengthening our values. Therefore, participants will be using a necklace with an image of roots. Then in the second part we will develop everything else in our corn plant (stalk and leaves) to leave it ready to harvest. In this part, participants will be using another necklace with an image of corn stalk on it that will represent what they are getting ready to produce.

The participants will receive their first symbol for the first 8 weeks. When the students receive the necklace, they say the pledge aloud. Once everybody has his necklace, all say the pledge again. Tell students that the pledge will be used always at the beginning and end of each session. You can ask the students what the pledge means.

Pledge

Através de nuestras raíces culturales fortaleceremos nuestro ser y nuestro espíritu. (Through our cultural roots we strengthen our self and spirit.)

For the first session you can make copies of the pledge for each one. Participants should memorize it for the next sessions.

6. (5 minutes) Introduce the first value: Personalismo. *Personalismo* is a very important value for Latinos. It emphasizes personal interactions. For us, Latinos, our relationships are very important. For example, our relationships with our family, friends, neighbors, and classmates are very important. For us, the interdependency and cooperation are important as part of Personalismo. Who can tell me what you know about interdependency? Interdependency is the belief that we are social beings, and we depend on others as others depend on us. For example, the teachers need us and we need them as well. Another example is a soccer team. Everybody needs everybody else to win. What does cooperation mean? Why do you think this is important for Latinos to be cooperative?

Group Discussion (approximate time: 10 minutes)

During this time, participants can talk about their experiences during the week. They can share good or bad news. Students can talk about what happens at school or at home. Emphasize that this is a time to speak. Be aware of the time and be sure to wrap up the conversation before moving to the closure.

Closure (approximate time: 5 minutes)

- Summary of major points covered in session
- Reminder of next scheduled meeting. Ask the participant to think of a person that they *respect* in their family and in their communities and think about why
- Questions
- The pledge

Material

- Latin music
- Boom box
- Big corn drawing
- Camera
- Corn drawing on which to put students' pictures
- Stickers on which to put names
- Symbols
- Copies of the FNR pledge
- Necklaces for first period

Session 2

Value: Respeto (Respect)

Objectives

Students will learn and talk about respect. Students will learn about Latino history.

Dicho: "El respeto al derecho ajeno es la paz" (Peace will come if we respect what is not ours.) Being honest is a very important virtue.

Latin Music

Activities (approximate time: 35 minutes)

1. (2 minutes) In group, say the FNR pledge.

2. (3 minutes) Review last session. Remember the ground rules. Revisit the last value (Personalismo).

3. (10 minutes) The value that we will talk about today is Respecto. *Respect* has two elements. One is the attitude of not being rude or damaging oneself or others. The other is related to the admiration of authority figures.

You can ask the students these questions to enrich the discussion:

- Who are authority figures for you?
- What do you do to respect them?
- What do people do when they do not respect others?
- What do you do when others do not respect you?

4. (10 minutes) Individual activity. Ask the students to do the exercise in Appendix 2. Explain that they have to write what they have done to respect themselves and what they have done to not respect themselves. Then ask them to write what they have done to respect others and what they have done to not respect others. Finally, they have to write what they could do differently to respect themselves and others. Once everybody has finished, ask volunteers to share some of their responses.

5. (10 minutes) Latino history. "Respect has existed since the ancient cultures in America. Old people were considered wise. They had a high status in society."

Ask students the following question to enrich the discussion:

- What cultures have you heard about? (Mayas, Aztecs, Incas, etc.) If you can, bring pictures of the Indians who inhabited Latino America.
- What do you know about those cultures?
- Where do Latinos come from?
- What are Latino America countries?
- Where are they located on a map?
- What traditions do those countries have?
- What do you know about these countries?

Group Discussion (approximate time: 10 minutes)

During this time, participants can talk about their experiences during the week. They can share good or bad news. Students can talk about what happened at school or at home. Emphasize that this is a time to speak. Be aware of the time and be sure to wrap up the conversation before moving to the closure.

Closure (approximate time: 5 minutes)

- Summary of major points covered in session
- Reminder of next scheduled meeting
- Questions
- The FNR pledge

Material

- Boom box
- Latin music
- Copies of *respecto* activity
- Copies of pledge

Session 3

Value: Simpatia

Objective

Students will learn more about the Latino history and about the Simpatia value.

Dicho: "Aquellos son ricos, que tienen amigos." (Those who have friends are rich.)

Activities (approximate time: 35 minutes)

1. (2 minutes) In group say the FNR pledge.

2. (3 minutes) Briefly review last session value, *Respecto*.

3. (10 minutes) Explain today's value. "The value to talk about today is *Simpatia*. Latinos like to be perceived as likeable, attractive, fun to be with, and easygoing. In general this emphasizes the promotion and maintenance of harmony with people around us, such as friends, family, neighbors, and classmates."

4. (20 minutes) Tell students that they will do a collage about what friendship and harmony mean to them. Invite them to think about their friends, why they are their friends, and what they like about their friendship. Later you will ask the students to share their collage with everyone else and talk about what friendship means to them.

Alternative Activity: Instead of doing the collage, you can ask the students to select a rock, which they will paint and give to a member in the group as a symbol of friendship. When they give the rock to somebody else, they have to say what friendship means to them and what they like about this person. To be sure that all students receive a rock from somebody else, you can do a lottery with participants' names so everybody will pick a different group member.

Group Discussion (approximate time: 10 minutes)

During this time, participants can talk about their experiences during the week. They can share good or bad news. Students can talk about what happened at school or at home. Emphasize that this is a time to speak. Be aware of the time and be sure to wrap up the conversation before moving to the closure. Ask the students to share experiences with friends.

Closure (approximate time: 5 minutes)

- Summary of major points covered in session
- Reminder of next scheduled meeting
- Questions
- The pledge

Material

- Boom box
- Latin music
- Video
- Magazines with Latino people and others
- Papers
- Scissors
- Glue

If you do the friendship rocks activity, you will need the following:

- Rocks
- Paint and brushes
- Water
- Towel
- Bowl of water
- A basket

6

Working with Socio-Emotional Challenges

XXXVI
INTERPERSONAL RELATIONSHIPS

STEPHANIE T. PITUC
University of San Francisco

TRACY R. JULIAO
Genesys Regional Medical Center, Grand Blanc, Michigan

Students' experiences in school are hardly limited to individualized academic endeavors. Academic achievement and personal development occur within the context of a number of interpersonal relationships among peers. Interactions with classmates, friends, foes, cliques, and romantic interests color the everyday experience for students, and the literature on childhood and adolescence recognizes the important role that peer interaction plays in the socialization process and academic adjustment (Parker & Asher, 1987). School counselors play a critical role in facilitating students' positive interpersonal relations and managing the challenges involved at the dyadic, group, and schoolwide level. Possessing the requisite knowledge and skills to attend to facilitating positive peer relations, school counselors can bridge the gap between students' needs with respect to academic success and positive psychosocial functioning.

Currently, a number of academic fields (e.g., School Counseling/Counseling Psychology, Educational Psychology, School Psychology) examine various interpersonal issues in isolation or address personal/social development at the individual level (see Bodenhorn, chapter 15, this volume). This chapter synthesizes the research and theory on the major socioemotional issues in student interpersonal relationship development within a peer-centered, relational framework. We also acknowledge the complex factors and forces which impact these connections, taking into account not only individual characteristics but also more systemic influences such as school and community contexts. We provide a general review of the literature in these areas as a backdrop for thinking about how school counselors can facilitate positive interpersonal relationships through individual, group, and systemic interventions. The first half of the chapter will provide an overview of theory and research in the areas of (a) friendship; (b) social networks; (c) rejection, withdrawal, and isolation; and (d) romantic relationships. The second half of the chapter will discuss school counseling intervention strategies emphasizing the facilitation and promotion of positive interpersonal relationships. We provide a general review of the literature in these areas as a backdrop for thinking about how school counselors can facilitate positive interpersonal relationships through individual, group, and systemic interventions.

Friendship

Once children begin school, their social world expands beyond the family, and their roles shift from child to student/peer. As students spend a greater proportion of time with their peers, peer relations become increasingly important and mere propinquity fosters the formation of close friendships. These relationships are usually unlike more involuntary relationships formed prior to coming to school, such as those associated with family. Bukowski, Newcomb, and Hartup (1996) described friendships as a unique kind of interpersonal relationship with respect to three conditions: (a) *reciprocities* (i.e., benefits that come about from mutual social exchange), (b) *liking* (i.e., preferring to spend time with one over others), and (c) *emotions* (e.g., affection and having fun).

Functions Served by Friendship

Developmental needs alter the way the conditions of friendship are sought and fulfilled (Brown, 1989; Gifford-Smith & Brownell, 2003). During the early school years, friendships are formed primarily around play and small classroom activities. In middle childhood, the child begins to seek acceptance from peers (Brown & Klute, 2003). In preadolescence and adolescence, there is an emerging need for intimacy and a desire for friends who are sensitive to one's needs and can supply mutual satisfaction (Berndt, 2002; Sullivan, 1953). Friendships also act as social support and facilitate school adjustment in the transitions between grades and schools (Berndt & Keefe, 1995; Ladd & Kochenderfer, 1996; Wentzel, Barry, & Caldwell, 2004).

During the middle and high school years, close interpersonal relationships may facilitate the critical task of identity formation (Erikson, 1968). The friendship patterns along race and ethnicity suggest that this may be an especially critical period for racial and ethnic identity development. Racial/ethnic minority students tend to choose culturally similar friends (Way & Chen, 2000) despite differences in academic orientations and deviant behaviors and attitudes (Hamm, 2000; Tolson & Urberg, 1993). For example, African American students, more than Asian American and European American students, showed less similarity than their friends in terms of academic variables such as GPA and goals but were more similar on ethnic identity and substance use (Hamm). Racial/ethnic minority adolescents who demonstrate strong in-group preferences also choose racially/ethnically similar friends (Hamm, Brown, & Heck, 2005), which may be a function of the relative importance of social group membership to their self-definition above other factors (Fordham & Ogbu, 1986). Grounded in these similarities, friendships provide the context for exploring a range of attitudes and behaviors (Hamm).

Types of Friendships and Associated Outcomes

Research regarding childhood friendship has unequivocally reported that having friends is associated with more positive outcomes than not having friends (Bukowski et al., 1996). Having friends has been correlated with positive outcomes for self-esteem, adjustment to school, family relationships, preventing delinquency, buffering of relational aggression from other peers, promotion of prosocial skills, cognitive development, and the development of morality (Bagwell, Newcomb, & Bukowski, 1998; Berndt & Keefe, 1995; Bukowski & Sippola, 1996; Hartup, 1996; Hodges, Boivin, Vitaro, & Bukowski, 1999). Benefits such as successful social coping and greater psychological well-being extend into adulthood and old age as well (Hartup & Stevens, 1997).

In response to criticism regarding assumptions found in the literature that all friendships are the same (Bukowski et al., 1996), recent research on friendship has extended beyond a focus of merely having friends to characteristics of friendships and their possible consequences (Hartup & Stevens, 1997). There has been a recent push to distinguish between types of friendships, such as close and general friendships (Harter, 1990; Way, 1996), and positive and negative qualities of friendships. For example, exploratory research on the close and general friendships of racial/ethnic minority adolescents from low-income families showed that the correlates of friendship quality (e.g., family support, school climate, and psychological well-being) differed across friendship type (Way & Chen, 2000).

Friendships can also be supportive and mutually satisfying or imbalanced and conflict-ridden though they often encompass both positive and negative traits. Research has found that both characteristics in friendships impact multiple areas of an individual's adjustment and well-being. For example, Berndt and Keefe (1995) found that students who reported more negative friendship characteristics (i.e., conflicts and rivalry) demonstrated greater disruptive behavior. This outcome was magnified when the friendship was also seen as highly supportive, thus reinforcing negative social interaction styles with other peers and teachers. Higher quality friendships (as measured by companionship, affection, disclosure, nurturance, instrumental aid, approval, support, reliable alliance, and satisfaction; Furman & Buhrmester, 1985) also appeared to protect against social anxiety. On the other hand, adolescents with lower quality best friendships (as measured by reported conflict, criticism, exclusion, dominance, and pressure; Furman & Buhrmester) reported more symptoms of social anxiety and depression (La Greca & Harrison, 2005). In one of the few studies on cross-race friendships, Aboud, Mendelson, and Purdy (2003) found that having a high-quality friend of a different race was associated with attitudes of less racial bias.

While some researchers posit that high-quality friendships increase self-esteem, a review of work in this area reveals inconsistent findings (Berndt, 2002). A limitation for much of the research regarding friendship outcomes is that studies are primarily correlational in nature, and thus do not provide insight into the processes mediated by high- or low-quality friendships. Further, the direction of the relationship between the correlated variables is unclear (Berndt; Bukowski & Sippola, 1996; Hartup, 1999).

Conflict in Friendships

In the research on the interpersonal dynamics of friendship, conflict often serves as a marker for low-quality friendships, in addition to other negative behaviors and attitudes such as dominance, criticism, exclusion, and pressure (e.g., Furman & Buhrmester, 1985). Yet friends experience conflict through fighting and arguing just as much as nonfriends do (Berndt & Perry, 1986). As children become older, they come to understand that the mere presence of conflict or disagreement does not threaten relationships but that the quality of the friendship is a function of how conflicts are handled (Laursen, 1996). Ways of coping with interpersonal conflict vary widely, perhaps as a function of gender and cultural socialization. For example, some research suggests that females are more sensitive to the costs of conflict and tend to emphasize compromise and negotiation (Collins & Laursen, 1992); concomitantly, females tend to negotiate conflict by withdrawing less and utilizing higher communication skills and support-validation (Black, 2000).

Variables such as cultural values, immigration status, and acculturation may particularly play a role in interactions for culturally diverse youth. Language barriers, the school climate, and school practices such as tracking may obscure opportunities for cross-cultural interaction (Hamm et al., 2005) and add another layer of complexity to friendships. Further, school counselors should reflect on these variables, as well as their own worldview and cultural values (see Yeh & Pituc, Chapter 5, this volume), when mediating peer conflicts.

Social Networks

The social ecology of students extends beyond individual relationships with peers into larger social networks. Brown (1989) classified these systems of peer interaction into three categories: dyads, cliques, and crowds. One-on-one dyadic relationships (e.g., friendships and romantic relationships) are the smallest units of the complex social network. The other two dimensions, *cliques* and *crowds,* become a discernable part of the social landscape beginning in late elementary school and into adolescence, facilitating students' navigation toward status and identity in an increasingly larger pool of formerly unfamiliar peers (Brown). Taken together, this tripartite model of social interaction creates a powerful dialectical source of influence in which social networks and individuals continually impact each other. Friendships and romantic relationships are addressed elsewhere in this chapter. Thus, this section of the chapter will discuss the influence of crowds and cliques as parts of students' social ecology on their interpersonal relationship development.

Crowds

Crowds are large, *reputation-based* groups, made up of individuals who are similarly stereotyped regarding attitudes and behaviors. The concept of crowds emerges into consciousness in preadolescence, likely due to the higher cognitive functioning necessary to create these heuristics (Brown & Klute, 2003). Examples of crowd labels include jocks, brains, druggies, normals, music kids, loners, and other categories or hybrids. The types of crowds in a school vary depending on the social context and community. For instance, multiethnic communities may utilize ethnic labels (e.g., Puerto Ricans or Polish), while British schools might lack a "jock" crowd (Thurlow, 2001). Crowds serve as reference groups for adolescents and may even channel friendships with in-group members (Urberg, Degirmencioglu, Tolson, & Halliday-Scher, 2000), although individuals belonging to the same crowd may not necessarily have close friendships exclusively within that crowd.

Outcomes associated with crowd affiliation. Crowd affiliation appears to impact students' well-being and adjustment, thereby warranting attention by clinicians. Psychosocial adjustment has been linked with crowd status, with high status affiliations related to higher levels of self-esteem (Brown & Lohr, 1987) and lower levels of social anxiety and depression (La Greca & Harrison, 2005). On the other hand, dysphoric characteristics were demonstrated in students who were rated negatively by peers and who held negative self-perceptions of their own status (Kistner, Balthazor, Risi, & David, 2001). However, there is some evidence that suggests belonging to a crowd, no matter the status, may have protective effects (La Greca & Harrison).

What about students who do not seem to fit into any category? Not belonging to a group may have consequences as well because crowd affiliations presume characteristics of one's identity. Fortunately, the individual's perspective on personal status can mitigate possible negative effects to the self-concept. Students who were outsiders, yet did not care about their status, demonstrated more positive psychological well-being than their fellow low-status peers who assigned importance to being part of a crowd (Brown & Lohr, 1987). The interpersonal associations a student is presumed to have and his or her perception of this status should be considered in counseling interventions.

Crowds and stereotypes. The projected images of various crowds naturally give rise to positive and negative stereotypes, which may be internalized by the individual and/or impact the way in which peers interact with each other. The assignment of certain labels may cause distress for some students. Unfortunately, mobility between crowds proves difficult, as membership is not voluntary, but rather assigned. Mobility not only relies upon individuals changing their own attitudes and behaviors but also necessitates change in the perceptions of their peers (Brown, 1989). For example, a student who is known as an antisocial "druggie" may participate in an intervention and/or decide to change his or her behavior, yet may find it difficult to socialize with peers who insist on treating him or her as a deviant. Alternatively, a male "jock" who is gay or questioning his sexual orientation may feel heightened pressure to conform to traditionally male gender expectations and heterosexist norms.

Such prejudices may also have implications for a student's perceived self-efficacy, leading to underestimation of his/her potentials across multiple competencies (Aronson & Inzlicht, 2004; Bandura, 1977). While some studies have suggested that the importance of crowd affiliation tends to diminish toward the end of adolescence (Brown, Eicher, & Petrie, 1986; Brown & Klute, 2003), the long-lasting effects of labels may persist as students encounter future social situations. Consequentially, it is imperative for school counselors and educators to attend to the attitudes and behaviors reinforced by the peer network. More systemic group and schoolwide interventions aimed at psychosocial issues such as identity formation, stereotyping, conflict, teamwork, and respect may be more appropriate in addressing the powerful influence of peer crowds and cliques. The second half of this chapter describes examples of these interventions and highlights some programs with evidence of positive outcomes.

Cliques

Clique formation and stability. Cliques are uniquely *interaction-based* groups, composed of anywhere from 3 to 10 members who consider the clique to be their primary source of interaction among peers. Unlike crowds, cliques form based upon voluntary interaction patterns between students. Cliques tend to be homophilous in demographics such as age, gender, and race/ethnicity, although they gradually move from same-sex groups to mixed-sex groups as they grow older (Connolly, Craig, Goldberg, & Pepler, 2004; Dunphy, 1963). Research in multiethnic schools has shown that tighter-knit cliques were less likely to be ethnically heterogeneous (Zisman & Wilson, 1992) and that students of color were more socially isolated than White students were (Zirkel, 2004). School counselors looking to facilitate positive peer relationships among diverse populations must take into account the existence and implications of the school's racial–cultural dynamics, as well as their assumptions and biases. Clique dynamics and racial–cultural dynamics are likely to be intertwined.

Similar to peer crowds, cliques become prominent in later years of development, although as early as preadolescence (Adler & Adler, 1995). In earlier school years, children tend to associate with fewer peers, based on proximity. As they get older, children and adolescents encounter a wider variety of peers as they transition into middle and high school, as well as through extracurricular activities. These changes in social context can result in shifts in individual identity, friendships, and group memberships.

Although the cliques themselves tend to be stable over time, membership and social positioning within cliques frequently changes (Adler & Adler, 1995; Eder, 1985; Ennett & Bauman, 1996; Shrum & Cheek, 1987). Social network analysis research has found that there tend to be three roles within a clique structure: (1) *member* (i.e., associates with primarily one friendship group), (2) *liaison* (i.e., has links with a member of more than one clique or other liaisons, but is not a clique member), and (3) *isolate* (i.e., has few or no links to peers in cliques (Ennett & Bauman). Over time in late adolescence, it appears that cliques become looser in membership, incorporating greater numbers of individuals with few or no links to cliques (i.e., isolates) and those with multiple affiliations (i.e., liaisons) in addition to core members (Ennett & Bauman; Shrum & Cheek). Dunphy's (1963) seminal ethnographic study on Australian peer networks demonstrated how cliques also change in their gender composition, from same-sex groups to mixed-sex groups, as clique members begin to date each other and their groups merge. The sometimes transient nature of clique membership feeds clique dynamics which have implications for the relationships between students and the psychological adjustment of the individual.

Clique stratification and dynamics. Qualitative study of cliques provides a vivid glimpse into the developmental changes of intricate clique dynamics and stratification—both within and between cliques (Brown & Klute, 2003). P. A. Adler and P. Adler's (1998) six-year study of fourth, fifth, and sixth graders demonstrated how early adolescent peer cliques are stratified by status and prestige. Four main strata were found (in descending order of status): the *popular clique* (the most exclusive and highest in status), the *wannabes* (who hung around the popular clique in hopes of inclusion), the *middle group* (smaller, independent friendship circles), and *social isolates* (who tend to spend most of their time independently (Adler & Adler, 1998).

The popular clique's status in the hierarchy often dictated ways in which students related to each other. Those lower in status often were subject to antagonism by popular peers, yet the wannabes tolerated these imbalanced relationships and often went to great lengths (e.g., carrying out favors, belittling other students lower in status) to fit in with and be accepted by the popular clique (Adler & Adler, 1998). Middle groups of students, however, were more accepting of their peers and tended to be better adjusted (e.g., had better self-concepts) than the wannabes and social isolates who were preoccupied with moving up in status. Social isolates endured the most teasing and rejection from all levels of peers; they were often forced to play alone or eventually allied with other stigmatized peers.

Early adolescent peer cliques are also characterized by dynamics of power maintenance and domination motivated by popularity. Leaders of popular cliques often vacillated between derision and temporary acceptance of followers and peripheral members seeking acceptance (Adler & Adler, 1995), seeking to keep their own elevated status. Those ranked lower in status within the popular clique as well as wannabes ingratiated themselves to the leaders in hopes of upward mobility. When working with students in early adolescence, school counselors should investigate the student's clique experiences. The desire to be a part of a certain clique and/or the threat over being displaced from one's current clique may create a great deal of stress to the individual. Additionally, he or she may experience negative relational patterns such as coercion and aggression as a function their place in the social hierarchy.

In middle and late adolescence, clique experiences become less antagonistic and focused on popularity and power. Although some cliques are more popular than others are and there may still be leaders/followers within the clique, the culture of rigid control by leaders and derision seems to be less prominent in middle and high school (Brown & Klute, 2003; Eder, 1985). Peer cliques in late adolescence particularly serve as a sort of home base, providing social support to their members and little concern with "who's in" and "who's out" (Brown & Klute). Interventions will likely focus on the dyadic level, rather than examining clique systems.

The Influence of Social Networks

Social networks have the potential to influence students strongly through norms. However, it is noteworthy to distinguish between the formation and maintenance of norms within peer crowds and cliques. Crowd norms are imposed from outside the group based upon perceived stereotyped attitudes and behaviors. Conversely, clique norms are formed within the group. Further, clique membership hinges upon one's ability to conform to the group norms (Brown, 1989). Concerns about fitting in and acceptance, highly salient in childhood and early adolescence, create conditions under which students are likely to be influenced by their peers.

Peer influence and antisocial behaviors. Another area of concern and interest is the influence of peer groups on antisocial behaviors, such as smoking or sexual activity. Prior research has shown that greater individual substance use is associated with greater use within the peer social network (Bauman & Ennett, 1996; Downs & Rose, 1991). Some studies are aimed at differentiating the influences of the various peer contexts (i.e., friendships, cliques, or crowds). One study (Hussong, 2002) found that adolescent substance use was most strongly predicted by a best friend's use (e.g., a student was more likely to smoke if he or she had a friend who did). Usage in the student's clique moderated the effects of best friend's usage as well—if the clique used more than a best friend, there was exacerbated risk, and if the clique used less than a best friend, there were protective effects (Hussong). It appears that one's peer affiliations have the power to influence behaviors both positively and negatively.

We must also note that several studies suggest that research and conventional folk wisdom runs the risk of overemphasizing the influence of peers on substance abuse and overlooking individual factors. The most cited alternative explanation is the adolescent's selection of friends and membership into cliques who exhibit certain behaviors (e.g., students who smoke tend to pursue friendships with other smokers). Research showing that cliques play a greater influence in the maintenance, rather than the onset, of antisocial behaviors corroborates the selection hypothesis (Ennett, Bauman, & Koch, 1994). Additionally, when asked to report the behaviors and attitudes of friends, students tend to project their own traits onto their friends (Bauman & Ennett, 1996).

Peer pressure. Conformity and resilience against peer pressure seem to mediate the effects of peer pressures. A study regarding high school drinking and its consequences (Arata, Stafford, & Tims, 2003) found that individual susceptibility to peer pressure was highly correlated with binge drinking (Urberg, 1992). Cultural factors also seem to mediate students' susceptibility to peer pressure. For instance, Black youth have shown lower levels of peer pressure and a need for peer approval when compared with White youth (Giordano, Cernkovich, & DeMaris, 1993). Adolescents of Mexican origin, whose families had most recently immigrated to the United States, demonstrated more resistance to peer pressure, perhaps influenced by Mexican cultural values related to a stronger identification with family as opposed to friends (Umaña-Taylor & Bámaca-Gómez, 2003). Therefore, interpersonal interventions should examine the interplay between individual characteristics (e.g., values, background, and attitudes) and the norms of the peer group.

Little has been studied in terms of the emotional response to peer pressure (Lashbrook, 2000). Qualitative study regarding the experience of peer pressure may provide insight into the psychological costs of conformity for students. For example, in Lashbrook's study regarding conformity to alcohol use, themes regarding fear of isolation, ridicule, and inadequacy emerged. Although the sample was composed of all White, college-aged students in a rural area, the implication that there is an affective consequence to peer pressure suggested that cognitive and behavioral interventions and programs (e.g., "Just Say No") may prove inadequate (Lashbrook).

Social Rejection, Withdrawal, and Isolation

At a time when peer acceptance is so important, the interpersonal experience of the socially rejected child or adolescent can be difficult and unsatisfying. What does it mean for a student to be "rejected?" Sociometric research utilizes peer nominations and ratings to categorize individuals within a context into one of five categories: popular, rejected, neglected, controversial, or average. Students who receive the highest number of negative nominations and ratings are categorized as "rejected." Researchers have naturally taken interest in the possible consequences of this status. Conventionally, the outcomes associated with a lack in peer acceptance have been thought to manifest in mid- to late childhood (Boivin, Hymel, & Bukowski, 1995; Ladd & Burgess, 1999). However, at least one study suggested that as early as kindergarten, rejection was linked to subsequent low self-confidence in the first grade (Phillipson, Bridges, McLemore, & Saponaro, 1999).

In studies focusing on mid- to late childhood, students with low peer-rated status have been found to be more aggressive and withdrawn and less sociable and cognitively skilled (Newcomb, Bukowski, & Pattee, 1993). Students who are rejected also experienced more academic, externalized (e.g., "acting out," dropping out of school, criminality), and internalized (e.g., self-esteem, anxiety, depression) problems (Bagwell et al., 1998; Coie, Terry, & Hyman, 1992; Coie, Terry, Lenox, Lochman, & Hyman, 1995; DeRosier, Kupersmidt, & Patterson, 1994; Panak & Garber, 1992; Parker & Asher, 1987). While these general tendencies are common to most rejected students, not all rejected students respond to being rejected in the same way. Many studies point toward two different subtypes: *aggressive-rejected* and *withdrawn-rejected* (McDougall, Hymel, Vaillancourt, & Mercer, 2001).

Aggressive-Rejected Students

Some studies indicate that aggression, in combination with rejection, predicts greater academic difficulties (Kupersmidt & Coie, 1990; Wentzel & Asher, 1995), higher levels of inattention and hyperactivity, and lower levels of prosocial skills (Bierman, Smoot, & Aumiller, 1993). In the extant literature, aggressive-rejected students were uniquely characterized by their difficulties with externalized outcomes. Aggression plus rejection correlated with later delinquency, more serious offenses, dropout, and physical acting out (Coie et al., 1992; Coie et al., 1995; French & Conrad, 2001; Kupersmidt & Coie, 1990; Miller-Johnson, Coie, Maumary-Gremaud, Lochman, & Terry, 1999). However, each of these consequences appears to be more severe for boys than for girls (Coie et al., 1995; McDougall et al., 2001). Rejection alone appears to be a stronger predictor of delinquency for girls (Miller-Johnson et al., 1999). These gender differences may be due to the operationalization of aggression in studies that are stereotypic for males. Females, on the other hand, tend to engage in *relational aggression* (see Chapter 40, this volume), which involves causing harm by intentionally hurting feelings, tainting reputations, and damaging relationships (e.g., teasing, spreading rumors, and exclusion).

Withdrawn-Rejected Students

While students who are thought of as aggressive-rejected do not demonstrate internalized maladjustment (McDougall et al., 2001), the reverse is true for withdrawn-rejected students. There appear to be few to no externalized difficulties for withdrawn-rejected students. Rather than characterized by peers and teachers as aggressive, these students are seen as shy and passive (Bierman et al., 1993). Withdrawn behavior in students has uniquely been found to be associated with greater depression, feelings of loneliness, and anxiety (Hymel, Rubin, Rowden, & LeMare, 1990; Newcomb et al., 1993; Rubin, Chen, & Hymel, 1993; Rubin & Mills, 1988), particularly in withdrawn-rejected girls (Bell-Dolan, Foster, & Christopher, 1995). Interestingly, some studies suggest that students' feelings about being categorized into this status mediated the link between status and internalized outcomes (Valas & Sletta, 1996, as cited in McDougall et al., 2001; Panak & Garber, 1992). In other words, those who were rejected *and* felt bad about it tended to feel greater anxiety, loneliness, and depression than those who were rejected but did not care.

Peer Relationships of Rejected Students

By virtue of a students' peer-assigned rejected status, the nature of their relationships with their peers warrants close attention. In Leary, Kowalski, Smith, and Phillips' (2003) examination of 15 events of school violence from 1995–2001, interpersonal rejection was involved in most cases. Of the cases, 12 involved a pattern of ongoing teasing, bullying, or ostracism. The U.S. Secret Service and Safe School Initiative data show that over two thirds of the recent school shootings have been associated with bullying, ostracism, and social rejection (Vossekuil, Reddy, Fein, Borum, & Modelski, 2000). Rejection from peers in adolescence tends to take on these chronic forms of victimization (Leary et al., 2003).

While rejection of peers can begin in early childhood, this kind of victimization does not seem to become salient until mid to late childhood (Boivin et al., 1995). Not every case of peer victimization toward rejection results in violence, but the possible volatile consequences behooves clinicians and researchers to pay attention to the way in which rejected students are treated by their peers (for a more comprehensive discussion of peer victimization and bullying, see Swearer, Buhs, Siebecker, Love, & Miller, Chapter 40, this volume).

Interpersonal relationship development, particularly in close interpersonal relationships, is another potentially troubling area for socially rejected children. There is contradictory evidence regarding the friendships of rejected students. Some studies indicate that rejected students have just as many friends as average children (Bagwell et al., 1998; Ladd & Burgess, 1999), while others indicate they have fewer close friendships (Brendgen, Little, & Krappmann, 2000; Kupersmidt, DeRosier, & Patterson, 1995). Researchers indicate that, despite the numbers of friendships that rejected students have, these friendships tend to be lower in quality with respect to mutual caring, conflict management, and intimate exchange (Parker & Asher, 1993). Conflict appears to occur at higher levels for students categorized as aggressive-rejected as opposed to simply rejected (Patterson, Kupersmidt, & Greisler, 1990). Interestingly, nominated friends viewed the relationship as lower in quality than the rejected students themselves did (Brendgen et al., 2000). Preserving these interpersonal relations with rejected students should be of import to school counselors, given the protective functions of friendship with respect to victimization (Hodges et al., 1999) and aggressive behavior (Ladd & Burgess, 1999, 2001).

In addition to tenuous friendships, rejected students tend to be peripheral members (i.e., less central and influential) of smaller cliques with other low-status peers (Bagwell, Coie, Terry, & Lochman, 2000). Bagwell and colleagues suggested that less central clique members may engender greater conformity to antisocial behaviors in hopes of greater acceptance or to achieve higher status within the clique. As aforementioned, the influence may very well be bidirectional: Students may self-select to be part of deviant peer cliques *and* the clique's norms may influence the student. In either situation, researchers have pointed out that deviant cliques membership may reinforce maladaptive, antisocial behaviors while precluding development and rehearsal of prosocial behaviors (Bagwell et al., 2000; Patterson, Capaldi, & Bank, 1991).

Contributing Factors to Rejected Status

One possible attribution of the rejected status may be due to perceived poor social skills (Newcomb et al., 1993). Aggressive-rejected children exhibit antisocial behaviors such as responding to ambiguous social situations with aggression and hostility (Dodge & Coie, 1987; Wood & Gross, 2002), while nonaggressive-rejected students may be seen by peers as socially awkward, incompetent, or strange (Bierman et al., 1993). Rejected students have also been found to have trouble monitoring their own strong emotions, as well as those of peers (Miller-Johnson et al., 1999). It seems that rejected students may not have developed the acumen for reading interpersonal cues, such as being able to recognize that they are upsetting their peers by being too bossy or persistent. Zakriski and Coie (1996) also found that while aggressive-rejected children were able to identify negative feedback directed at someone else, they tended to overlook negative feedback directed at themselves.

Theories describing rejection as incidental to individual characteristics, taken together with models theorizing sources of causality (McDougall et al., 2001), may be useful for clinicians to consider when choosing interventions or targeting student populations. For example, Parker, Rubin, Price, and DeRosier (1995) proposed a *transactional* model, which integrates predisposing factors, negative social behaviors, negative beliefs about the self and others, and peer relationships. It would be useful to consider all of these factors to come up with possible areas of intervention. For instance, Sandstrom and Coie (1999) found that fourth and fifth graders who were previously rejected tended to improve in status when they became more involved with extracurricular activities, when they developed better ideas of locus of control, and when their parents monitored the social activity of their peers.

When considering the way in which peers view or treat other students, various cultural factors inevitably come into play as well. For example, students may be viewed negatively because they are more reticent than other students are. Yet, their cultural values may prescribe silence as a form of respect; they may have learned that one should talk only when necessary. Difficulties in communication due to limited English proficiency may be misinterpreted as antisocial behavior. More generally, students who are "different" from the majority are susceptible to rejection by peers or differential treatment teachers and other school personnel. For example, a study of kindergarteners found that in the transition to first grade, Black children were more likely to experience chronic peer rejection and less likely to receive social support from their teachers and friends than were their White peers (Ladd & Burgess, 2001). It may be that the communication styles and ways of relating for Black children are viewed as "antisocial" or "inappropriate" (Sue & Sue, 2003) to their culturally different teachers or peers. Children with disabilities are particularly at risk for rejection, especially given that establishing and maintaining close friendships can be difficult (Brinton & Fujiki, 2002; Fukiji, Brinton, Hart, & Fitzgerald, 1999). Discrimination based on differences from the majority culture can have unfortunate outcomes for students, and counselors and educators have a responsibility not only to facilitate positive peer relations and a climate of respect for all students but also to be an advocate for those historically oppressed (Sue & Sue, 2003).

Dating and Romantic Relationships

The prominence of dating and romantic relationships in childhood and adolescent life are very important as evidenced by their depictions in popular culture through music, movies, and television. Mass consumption of popular culture depicting adolescent dating and romance speaks to how these issues resonate with the highs and lows of these experiences in adolescent life. Yet, the corpus of research into these issues is new (Furman, Brown, & Feiring, 1999). Researchers have only recently stressed that these interpersonal relationships are more than trivial matters in adolescence (Collins, 2003).

Characteristics of Dating and Romantic Relationships

In this section, we discuss the unique dynamics and consequences of dating and romantic relationships on interpersonal relationship development. A romantic relationship, defined as "an ongoing pattern of association and interaction between two individuals who acknowledge some connection with each other" (Brown, Feiring, & Furman, 1999, p. 3), is different from all other close relationships in its voluntary nature and element of attraction (Brown et al., 1999). There are usually intense and passionate, although sometimes fleeting, feelings which may include sexual attraction (Brown et al.; Larson, Clore, & Wood, 1999). Attraction usually extends beyond mere sexual chemistry, however, and encompasses companionship, intimacy, and caring in a way different from friendship.

It should be noted that certain hallmarks of dating (e.g., autonomy in choosing whom to date, public displays of romantic affiliation, and sexual behavior) reflect Western norms. One's personal, religious, or cultural background may preclude many of these experiences or cause distress for the student and his or her partner. For example, romantic relationships are thought to help establish autonomy and individuation from parents (Gray & Steinberg, 1999), which may lead to intergenerational conflict between parents and children. Similarly, partners from different cultural backgrounds may have contrasting relationship expectations and consequently experience distress.

Conventionally, adolescent relationships have been thought of as transient and frivolous (Collins, 2003); however, current research shows that may not be the case. About 20% of adolescents 14 years old or younger, 35% of 15- to 16-year-olds, and almost 60% of 17- and 18-year-olds reported romantic relationships lasting 11 months or more (Carver, Joyner, & Udry, 2004). There is great variation between age groups regarding what constitutes feelings such as "being in love" (Bouchey & Furman, 2003). Research regarding externalized behavior, internalized outcomes, and academic achievement (Brendgen, Vitaro, Doyle, Markiewitcz, & Bukowski, 2002; Neemann, Hubbard, & Masten, 1995) correlated these negative outcomes with early adolescent relationships. These findings suggest that late adolescent students may be more developmentally equipped for romance and dating, regardless of their subjective experience of romantic feelings.

Counseling interventions may be aimed at developing the interpersonal and cognitive skills relevant to successful romantic relationships. Healthy romantic relations rely on secure relationship style (Furman & Simon, 1999), capacity to give and receive intimacy (Collins & Sroufe, 1999), and adequate management of emotions (Larson et al., 1999). Formal operations cognitive skills such as perspective taking and negotiating hypothetical situations also become increasingly important. Working on these prerequisites to healthy romantic relationships will likely prove valuable in enhancing the student's other interpersonal relationships as well.

In addition to the euphoric feelings of being involved with another person, dating and romantic relationships provide the context for many other benefits. These relationships provide an opportunity for experimentation of roles and ways of behaving (Furman & Simon, 1999) and can serve as precursors to adult relationships (Sullivan, 1953). Dating may also be a way of gaining social leverage, increased popularity, or affirmation from peers (Brown, 1999).

The adage "you can't have love without pain" seems to ring true in the preadolescent and adolescent years, even in the shortest of relationships. Studies have demonstrated that students who had broken up with a partner in the last 6 months reported more externalizing symptoms (Kuttler, La Greca, & Prinstein, 1999), and the stresses of managing a romantic relationships can lead to greater depressive affect (Davila, Steinberg, Kachadourian, Cobb, & Fincham, 2004; La Greca & Harrison, 2005). Further, being in a relationship can consume great time and energy, possibly sacrificing academic performance (Brendgen et al., 2002) or the quality of friendships and relationships with others (Connolly & Goldberg, 1999).

Students who identify as gay, lesbian, or bisexual or those are still exploring their sexual orientation face additional stressors (Diamond & Savin-Williams, 2003; Diamond, Savin-Williams, & Dubé, 1999). Internal struggles over their identities may be exacerbated by the unique interpersonal challenges of being in the sexual minority. For example, identifying potential partners can be difficult and even dangerous in a homophobic community. Those currently in gay or lesbian relationships may also lack the social support of friends and family members. Moreover, the student may be distressed about how his or her sexual orientation will be accepted by the community at large. Counselors should keep in mind these unique factors when developing interpersonal interventions with gay, lesbian, and bisexual youth.

Dating and Romantic Relationship Expectations and Influences

Popular culture reflects the value of dating and romance as part of the normative adolescent experience. As a result, those who are not involved in a romantic relationship may experience anxiety and dysphoria (La Greca & Harrison, 2005). Adolescents currently dating or in a romantic relationship may also experience incongruities with their expectations (Connolly & Goldberg, 1999; Furman & Simon, 1999), often idealized in the media (Connolly & Goldberg). Counselors working with students on romantic relationships should differentiate exploring what they expect from actual/potential partners from the relationship itself.

The role of parents and peers in romantic relationships should be considered, as they are strong socializing forces for adolescents. Parents often directly influence certain relationship decisions, including who is acceptable to date, especially in non-Western traditional cultures and religions (Bouchey & Furman, 2003). Parents also indirectly affect the construction of representations of close relationships through their style of caregiving (Furman & Simon, 1999) and modeling of important interpersonal competencies (e.g., communication skills, conflict resolution, and displays of affection; Gray & Steinberg, 1999).

Romantic relationships also form under the strong influence of one's peer social context (see Brown, 1999; Connolly & Goldberg, 1999). Norms of peer groups at the clique or crowd level possess the power to shape individuals' dating decisions, such as who is "unacceptable" or "desirable" to date given one's prescribed social status or image. At the dyadic level, friends serve as social supports through various roles. For example, a friend can buffer potential rejection by acting as a messenger between the two parties, facilitate communication in the nascent stages of a romantic relationship, or act as an arbiter of wrongdoing in order to comfort a jilted friend (Brown). The interpersonal relationships at play within dating and romantic relationships, therefore, extend beyond the couple in question. This intricate interplay deserves attention in both research and intervention.

Romantic Rejection

Rejection in dating and romantic relationships can also cause distress for adolescents individually or between the couples involved in romantic relationships. In Leary and colleagues' (2003) examination of 15 cases of school violence, at least 6 of the perpetrators experienced recent romantic rejection (i.e., breakups or being rebuffed). As aforementioned, individuals vary in their abilities to manage emotions (Larson et al., 1999), and this may have serious implications given the strong emotions elicited by romantic rejection. Downey, Bonica, and Rincón (1999) proposed a model of *rejection-sensitivity*, which is the tendency to develop anxious or angry expectations of rejection based on interactions with parents and peers. Heightened sensitivity to rejection is later transposed onto romantic relationships. Individuals who are highly sensitive to rejection may react to ambiguous cues with hostility, despondence, withdrawal, or other efforts at gaining acceptance, which may escalate into either initiating or tolerating a unhealthy relationship.

Downey et al. (1999) postulated that rejection-sensitivity places individuals at risk for utilizing violence or coercion (e.g., angry reactions) or enabling these destructive relationship patterns (e.g., anxious reactions). In fact, more than 25% of adolescents (Wolfe & Feiring, 2000), and anywhere from 9% to 45% of middle school children studied (Downey et al.) experienced dating violence or aggression. Dating violence is generally thought to encompass "any attempt to control or dominate another person physically, sexually, or psychologically, resulting in harm" (Wolfe & Feiring, p. 360). Such a broad definition lends itself to subjective interpretation especially in nebulous situations, and sometimes the two parties involved experience a situation differently. Techniques for handling these sensitive interventions follow in the second half of this chapter.

Peer Sexual Harassment

Interpersonal antagonisms centered around sexual themes in schools additionally take the form of peer sexual harassment. The American Association of University Women (AAUW; 2001) conducted a nationwide study of sexual harassment in schools and found that 8 of 10 students experience some form of unwelcome and unwanted behavior. The most prevalent types included sexual comments, jokes, gestures, or looks; being touched, grabbed, or pinched in a sexual way; and spreading sexually related rumors (e.g., calling someone "gay" or claiming so-and-so had sex; AAUW). Over one third of students reported their first experience of unwanted behavior in sixth grade or earlier, and the most common places reported were in halls, classrooms or the gym area, or outside on school grounds (AAUW). Many students reported emotional consequences (e.g., feeling upset, angry, and embarrassed) and behavioral responses (e.g., avoidance of the perpetrator, becoming more withdrawn, and not wanting to come to school) to these experiences. Of those students affected, 20% said that they would tell no one, and only 20% said that they would tell a teacher or school employee (AAUW). Given the reality of peer sexual harassment in schools, the active promotion of positive peer relations should supplement school policies on harassment and remedial intervention.

Summary of Interpersonal Relationship Development

The previous discussion broadly addressed major issues related to interpersonal relationships among peers in schools including friendship; social networks; social rejection, withdrawal, and isolation; and romantic relationships. One limitation of the research on the development of interpersonal relationships among children and adolescents is the primary focus on school-related relationships. For example, students of color in lower socioeconomic statuses tend to be significantly influenced by nonschool networks (Dolcini, Harper, Watson, Catania, & Ellen, 2005). This finding, along with the acknowledgement of cultural and familial influences, may have implications for greater efficacy in more broad-based interventions (Dolcini et al.).

In addition, the ubiquity of technology and the Internet today provides the landscape for new dimensions to interpersonal relationships among youth. With about 87% of teenagers ages 12 through 17 using the Internet (Lenhart, Madden, & Hitlin, 2005), youth today connect with their peers, family, and the outside world in ways unimaginable even 5 to 10 years ago. Youth frequently interact with others online through instant messaging, e-mail, discussion boards, social networking sites (e.g., MySpace, Facebook, Friendster), and Web journals (also known as "blogs"). While the literature on the nature and implications of these "virtually" contextualized relations is still nascent and the virtual landscape is constantly changing, some existing research looks at online analogs to traditional peer relations phenomena such as bullying and relational aggression. Ybarra and Mitchell (2004) found that 19% of young regular Internet users were involved in online harassment as an aggressor, victim, or both. Online harassment takes on diverse forms ranging from directly communicating physical threats and rude comments between people to indirectly defaming others via online postings. Initial research into online aggression finds that there are similarities in the profiles of conventional and online aggressors/targets (i.e., individuals who are engaged both as a bully and as a target), specifically marked by psychosocial challenge.

There is also suggestion that, like victims of conventional harassment, online harassment targets experience distress because of these incidents (Finkelhor, Mitchell, & Wolak, 2000). It appears then that current knowledge on conventional peer relations can inform work with youth regarding online interactions. At the same time, researchers and practitioners should also investigate the unique nature and consequences of this ever-changing Internet peer culture.

Interpersonal Intervention Strategies

The remainder of this chapter will focus on intervention strategies within schools that will address the aforementioned areas of interpersonal relationship development, some in more detail than others. Some of the interpersonal interventions discussed in this section are more general in nature although some general interventions can be tailored toward more nuanced concerns regarding interpersonal relations. In particular, the intervention strategies that follow will emphasize enhancing students' interpersonal relationships with one another, school personnel, and their families. In an article summarizing intervention history within schools, Sandoval (1993) aptly defined the term *intervention* as "imposing a change or something new (an activity, strategy, or approach) in an already ongoing relationship between an adult (teacher, parent, administrator, and so on) and a child (or sometimes another adult) with the goal of improving it" (p. 195). He further indicated that interventions may also be directed at the internal state of the child, as well as toward observable behavior. Additionally, he noted that the purpose of an intervention is to bring about positive outcomes, particularly when negative ones might occur in the absence of an intervention. We would like to expand his definition to include targeting change in an ongoing relationship between two or more students as well. In other words, many times interventions aimed at improving interpersonal relationships will be directed at members of the student peer group.

Factors to Incorporate in Intervention Strategies

There are several factors to consider when planning and implementing interpersonal interventions within the school setting, including, but not limited to, culture, language, nonverbal communication, power, and developmental level of the student. Additionally, there is a wide range of interventions to choose from, growing out of various theoretical orientations and treatment approaches. This large repertoire demands that school counselors be well versed in all theoretical orientations and approaches offered within the field of psychology (Sandoval, 1993). For instance, many intervention strategies grow out of the following schools of thought: developmental psychology, social psychology, learning, psycho-educational, humanistic, cognitive–behavioral, psychodynamic, neuropsychological, and ecological perspectives. Further, even when interpersonal issues are of primary concern, the focus of the actual interventions can vary as well, including emphasis on prevention, social behavioral problems, academic problems, family/parental issues, friendships, peer rejection and isolation, and romantic relationships/dating (Kratochwill & Stoiber, 2000). Additionally, in order to intervene effectively, school counselors must assess relevant influences within students' social world including peer group memberships and defining characteristics of various peer relationships. Further, school counselors must enlist the assistance of other adults to teach and reinforce effective interactions within students' various social contexts (Sheridan, Buhs, & Warnes, 2003). Finally, in order to determine if the intervention strategies are effective, school counselors must evaluate the interventions they choose to implement. It is imperative that school counselors, taking all of these issues into consideration, remain flexible and thoughtful rather than mechanistic or formulaic in seeking intervention strategies (Villa, Udis, & Thousand, 1994).

Culture

Regardless of the interpersonal issue or treatment approach, culture is an ever-present factor (Lee, 1995; Rogers & Lopez, 2002). School, family, and community environments are driven by their unique cultures, which children must learn to respond to appropriately and sometimes very distinctly (Bronfenbrenner, 1979a, 1979b). The importance of familiarity with multicultural counseling theory and research becomes clear when school counselors acknowledge the culturally embedded nature of children's behaviors, as well as the interventions developed to modify many of those behaviors (Kratochwill & Stoiber, 2000). In an effort to be multiculturally competent, school counselors must work toward increasing awareness of culturally diverse individuals and groups within the school system, as well as increasing the sensitivity of students, parents, and school personnel to cultural diversity (American School Counselor Association [ASCA], 2004; Crockett, 2003; Kwon, 2001).

Language and Nonverbal Communication

Like culture, language and communication are important variables to consider when implementing interpersonal interventions in schools. Communication involves sending and receiving messages, understanding, and being understood (Pedersen & Carey, 2003). Effective communication is impeded not only when native languages differ but also when the meaning of words and/or the way in which information is communicated varies according to cultural norms. Communication occurs not only through spoken word but nonverbally as well. Similar to spoken word, nonverbal cues may hold different meaning for individuals dependent upon cultural background and worldview (Sue & Sue, 2003). It is thus important for school counselors to be aware of various communication modalities and worldviews in order to effectively intervene when interpersonal difficulties arise.

Social Power

Social power is another important factor to consider when developing and implementing interpersonal interventions. Kehe and Smith (2004) defined *social power* as the "ability to expand or diminish opportunities for oneself and/or others" (p. 335). Smith, Richards, Granley, and Obiakor, (2004) described the invisible nature of power by noting that those who have the power often take it for granted without acknowledging its presence, while those who are denied access to power notice its absence. Power is present at multiple levels in all interpersonal interaction, and as a result, it is necessary for school counselors to recognize it, consider it, and address it in the development and implementation of all interpersonal interventions.

Developmental Level of Students

Finally, school counselors must also be aware of the developmental level of the student(s) with whom they are intervening. As described earlier in the chapter, the nature and quality of interpersonal relationships grow and change as children mature. Thus, interpersonal interventions that are appropriate for one age group are likely not appropriate for other age groups. With all these factors in mind, let us turn our attention to specific interventions that target interpersonal relationship difficulties within the school.

Individual Interventions

School counselors may consider intervening with individual students. While individual counseling relationships may be developmentally based (i.e., assisting students to achieve their interpersonal potentials), most individual interventions will be reactive or remedial in nature (Schmidt, 2003). For instance, while individual interventions aimed at self-discovery and understanding oneself through one's own worldview might be of great benefit for healthy interpersonal development (Hoare, 1991; L. J. Myers et al., 1991), such interventions are not realistic in schools where counselors have student caseloads in the hundreds (Pedersen & Carey, 2003; Schmidt, 2003). Instead, individual interventions that are more plausible may include cognitive–behavioral-oriented approaches, which are remedial, developmentally appropriate, short-term, and solution-focused (J. E. Myers, Shoffner, & Briggs, 2002; Prout & Prout, 1998). Regardless of the nature of individual counseling relationships, key to the success of such interventions is that counselors model positive interpersonal interaction patterns with their students. This modeling can occur with children of all ages, from elementary to high school, although it is likely to occur in differing fashions for the various age levels.

Since individual interventions rely primarily upon verbal exchange, individual counseling typically occurs with older students. In fact, Thompson and Rudolph (2000) argued that verbal skills are not the only key component to effective individual counseling relationships, but behavioral maturity and cognitive development are needed as well. Behavioral maturity enables students to sustain attention and focus on a single issue, while sufficient cognitive development ensures that students are able to understand the relationship between their behaviors and associated outcomes. Examples of individual interpersonal interventions with middle school and high school age children might include those aimed at reducing antisocial behavior patterns, typically focusing on the behavior and skills of the student in question (Farmer & Cadwallader, 2000). However, given the powerful impact of peer relationships as previously discussed, such interventions may not succeed without supplemental interventions emphasizing changing the social context within which the behaviors typically occur inclusive of peer affiliations, classroom social structures, and social role supports within the school (Farmer & Cadwallader, 2000; vanManen, Prins, & Emmelkamp, 2004). Such interventions will be described in more detail in the following section.

Sexual harassment issues many times require individual intervention. When addressing concerns regarding sexual harassment, it is important that counselors foster an atmosphere/environment of mutual respect. This issue may lend itself well to the principles and approaches of Gender Aware Therapy, which focuses on social customs and expectations that influence one's development as a member of a particular gender (Gilbert & Scher, 1999; Good, Gilbert, & Scher, 1990). Gilbert and Scher recommended specific responsive intervention techniques when counseling individuals who have experienced sexual harassment. Their recommendations include (a) validation of feelings (feelings are appropriate, not an overreaction); (b) validation of harassment (sexual harassment is a form of sexual discrimination; one's rights have been violated); (c) framing the experience (sexual harassment arises from abuse of power, not physical attraction; it is not self-induced); and (d) developing effective strategies (determining healthy ways to process the emotional experience and manage any remaining interactions as a result of legal actions, if any). Clearly, these interventions are most likely to occur with high school students.

Individual counseling can be effective with elementary children when it emphasizes counselors modeling effective interpersonal interactions, as well as nonverbal interactions. Play therapy and art therapy are techniques that might be useful for school counselors working with elementary children. Through these nonverbal modes of communication, the counselor may be able to gain information that may be useful in informing alternative intervention strategies for these youngsters. Additionally, particularly for children experiencing interpersonal difficulties in other relationships in their lives, many times, they are able to benefit from the individual counseling relationship by developing a trusting relationship where they can communicate in an effective and nonthreatening manner (Nemiroff & Annunziata, 1990; Peterson & Hardin, 1997; Webb, 1991).

Interventions with elementary students may be delivered by noncounseling personnel as well. For instance, in an effort to mediate the effects of peer rejection, Buhs and Ladd (2001) recommended intervention early in the elementary school experience. In particular, they suggested that teachers encourage active classroom participation of all young children, as active engagement in classroom activities is related to better academic and emotional adjustment for students who are rejected by their peers.

Group Interventions

Although individual interventions can be effective with students, counselors are more likely to choose group counseling interventions to address students' interpersonal difficulties. Group counseling is an efficient way to address interpersonal concerns, as groups facilitate relationship development and positive interpersonal interactions (ASCA, 1999; Prout & Prout, 1998). Like individual interventions, group interventions can also be preventive, developmental, or remedial in nature. Again, like individual counseling, group counseling interventions are largely remedial in nature. For example, interpersonal group interventions can take on many shapes, such as focusing on activities (e.g., to build self-esteem), being problem focused (e.g., divorce), emphasizing social skills training (i.e., developing skills in specific areas of deficit, which can be generalized to behavior and interactions outside of therapy), as well as being structured as self-help groups (e.g., Alateen or Weight Watchers) or support groups (e.g., grief/loss;

Greenberg, 2003; Hansen, Nangle, & Meyer, 1998; Pedersen & Carey, 2003; Yalom, 1995).

Group counseling interventions typically brings together 6 to 10 students with similar concerns, focuses on a specific concern/issue, and has one or more counselors facilitating the group discussion, sometimes using curriculum and planned activities. Within each group, the counselor(s) establish a supportive and trusting environment among group members, direct the helping process, and facilitate the development of a group culture where students assist one another, both actively and passively. The development of the group culture is likely the factor that makes group counseling the most attractive way to intervene with students' interpersonal difficulties. As students engage in the group process, they become aware that others experience similar difficulties and that they are not alone in their struggles. Furthermore, with the assistance of the counselor(s) leading the group, the students are able to develop more effective ways of interacting with their peers, providing them with in vivo experience (usually success) of improving their interpersonal skills (Pedersen & Carey, 2003; Thompson, 2002). Examples of interpersonal group counseling interventions may include multiple sessions within a friendship skills group, where the focus of one session is on identifying attitudes and behaviors that generally result in making and keeping friendships. Such a session would be followed by another where the focus becomes addressing the kinds of attitudes and behavior that prevent the development of friendships. A later session might then bring the two previous sessions together and begin to personalize what the students have learned (e.g., "In what way am I impeding the development of friendships and in what way am I facilitating it?"; Greenberg, 2003).

There are few evidence-based group counseling interventions that have been implemented in school settings, and those that have tend to be limited in scope. Many group interventions have been developed in order to address interpersonal difficulties youngsters encounter, yet many of these interventions have not been located within school settings, but rather within community and clinical settings. Romasz, Kantor, and Elias (2004) argued that it is not only important to locate such programs within the school, but also ideal, as schools provide students with opportunities to both learn and practice social skills in an environment where academic instruction and personal life experience are intertwined. In other words, due to the interpersonally interactive nature of the school setting, by default students are given the opportunity to interact interpersonally with their peers both within and outside the structured group setting. Fisher, Masia-Warner, and Klein (2004) noted additional benefits of providing group interventions in the school setting including (a) making treatment more acceptable to children and families due to the context (no need for outside referral), (b) reducing common barriers for treatment including cost and transportation, and (c) increasing the likelihood of learned behaviors generalizing to the "natural" environment, as school is the environment where youngsters spend the majority of their time. Fisher and colleagues noted that it is very apparent that a gap exists between evidence-based interventions and services typically provided in schools. Further, they indicated of import at this point is determining which evidence-based programs can be effectively transported into school settings. Since there are limited examples of evidence-based school group interventions for counselors to draw upon, counselors are encouraged to look to community and clinical settings for evidence-based group interventions that can be transported into the school setting.

A few examples of group interventions that have demonstrated success within school settings do exist, but as previously mentioned, they tend to be limited in scope. Brief descriptions of these interventions follow. One example targeted toward the treatment of social phobia is Cognitive–Behavioral Group Therapy for Adolescents (CBGT-A), which focuses on psycho-education, cognitive restructuring, problem solving, social skills, and behavioral exposure and consists of sixteen 90-minute sessions (Hayward et al., 2000). Another example, also targeting the treatment of social phobia, is Social Skills Training (SST), which focuses on social skills training, exposures, problem solving, cognitive restructuring, and relaxation techniques and consists of 12 one-hour group sessions, each followed by a 30-minute practice of learned skills in a simulated environment (Spence, Donovan, & Brechman-Toussaint, 2000). A third example of a group intervention targeting the treatment of social phobia is Social Effectiveness Therapy for Children (SET-C), which focuses on behavioral exposure and social skills training and consists of 24 sessions delivered over a 2-week period (Beidel, Turner, & Morris, 2000) Two sessions are conducted weekly—one is an individual exposure and social skill training session, while the other is a group social activity. Fisher and colleagues (2004) modified the SET-C model for delivery to high school students, creating the Skills for Academic and Social Success program (SASS), which focuses on psycho-education, realistic thinking, social skills training, exposure, and relapse prevention and consists of 12 weekly group meetings, two group booster sessions, two brief individual meetings, and four weekend social events. Finally, a group intervention targeting at-risk children entitled Teaching Empowerment through Active Means (TEAM) focuses on teaching skills such as conflict resolution, anger management, responsible decision making, healthy interpersonal boundaries, managing unfairness, positive communication and listening skills, and respect (Redivo & Buckman, 2004). TEAM meetings typically consist of 90-minute sessions including an initial "huddle up," a stretching/yoga routine, an activity requiring the group to work together, and a closing "huddle up." Of note, the TEAM approach has demonstrated effectiveness in encouraging cross-clique interactions, with lasting impact of at least two years following participation in the intervention.

It is important to note that while group counseling interventions are attractive strategies to utilize, there are difficulties inherent with their use (Schmidt, 2003). Counselors many times encounter scheduling obstacles, particularly when a group is being formed by students who have differing class schedules. Additionally, sometimes conflicts with teachers arise because of the disruption of classroom instruction that occurs by pulling students out of class to participate in a group. Although counselors strive to develop and implement interventions that are the least disruptive to the learning environment for students, it is inevitable that some disruption will occur. It is the counselor's job to minimize the disruption (Greenberg, 2003; Schmidt, 2003).

A nontraditional group counseling intervention that is more commonly found in school settings is structured programs that are integrated into classroom curriculum (Adalbjarnardottir, 1993; Fraser et al., 2005; Johnson, Johnson, Dudley, & Magnuson, 1995). For example, a group intervention aimed at improving children's social–cognitive competence and skills was introduced in elementary school classrooms (Adalbjarnardottir, 1993). Teachers were trained to deliver curriculum that emphasized social problem-solving skills such as generating alternative strategies, anticipating consequences, and selecting a "best" strategy. In addition to the formal curriculum, as social conflict occurs throughout the week, the teacher has the opportunity to work with the students to address the conflict in a constructive manner. Another classroom intervention is Making Choices: Social Problem Solving Skills for Children (MC; Fraser et al., 2005). MC was developed to promote social competence and reduce aggression. MC's instructional program focuses on teaching children how to encode and interpret social and environmental information, identify and manage feelings, and generate appropriate goals and responses in play and classroom interactions.

Finally, peer mediation training has been introduced at the classroom level, teaching children how to negotiate agreements and mediate fellow classmates' conflicts (Johnson et al., 1995). Students who successfully learn these strategies demonstrate advantages over others, such as being empowered to regulate their own behaviors, increasing their abilities to cope with stress and adversity, and developing and maintaining high quality interpersonal relationships with peers (Johnson et al.).

Another group counseling intervention that may be utilized to address interpersonal difficulties is family therapy. This is the least utilized strategy by most school counselors, due to time constraints, as well as difficulties in coordinating the schedules of counselors, students, and family members. Despite these difficulties, Sandoval (1993) asserted that family therapy is an intervention that targets an important system within which the child must function. Further, school counselors report family problems as the most frequent type of problem encountered in counseling relationships (H. T. Prout, Alexander, Fletcher, Memis, & Miller, 1993). As stated previously, there are times when the family's mode of operation and expectations are in direct conflict with that of the school. In these instances, the counselor's role is to mediate between the school and the family in order to increase the likelihood of reducing the interpersonal conflict and acting out behavior demonstrated by the student (Harrison et al., 2003). As modeling of appropriate interpersonal interaction styles is a key component to a youngster's learning regarding developing and maintaining positive and healthy interpersonal relationships, interventions with parents and family members can prove beneficial when the interventions serve to improve the social modeling that occurs within the family. As such, family therapy is not always necessary, nor the only way to intervene within families. Parent conferences with school counselors and/or teachers that address interpersonal issues such bullying or harassment may also be effective means of impacting the social modeling that occurs within the home environment. Additionally, offering educational programs to parents regarding common interpersonal difficulties encountered by students may not only serve to strengthen the relationship between the school and parents, but can also provide parents with much needed information allowing them to initiate informed discussions with their children regarding interpersonal relationship issues. Finally, a more structured approach to parent education might include models such as the Parent-Management Training (PMT) model described by Carolyn Webster-Stratton (1997). This model focuses on direct intervention with parents aimed at improving parenting skills, which in turn has demonstrated a reduction in student conduct problems, improved student social competence, and overall improvement in student functioning.

Schoolwide Interventions

In contrast to individual and group counseling interventions, schoolwide interventions are typically preventative in nature and offer an alternative strategy to school counselors, assisting them in promoting and facilitating positive interpersonal relationships to a wider audience (Romasz et al., 2004; Schmidt, 2003). For instance, educational assemblies on special topics (e.g., violence; peer pressure;

gender roles, expectations, and relationships; friendships; aggression and bullying; and sexual harassment) are useful means of providing information to a large group of students. Many times, this format can be very effective, particularly when the programs are interactive and multimodal in nature, involving the students in the audience (e.g., performance, role-playing, interactive games, and art-related projects; Close, 2005). Further, when ongoing classroom curriculum is developed to coincide with schoolwide programs, the structure, stability, and skill building focus in the classroom improves the effectiveness of the educational assemblies and schoolwide programming (Romasz et al., 2004). Braswell and colleagues (1995) asserted that schools are the ideal site for preventative interventions because of opportunities that naturally present themselves in the school setting enabling students, parents, and school personnel to interact collaboratively to achieve positive outcomes.

There is an increasing trend for the development and maintenance of social competency programs as schoolwide preventative intervention programs (Frey, Hirschstein, & Guzzo, 2000; Leadbeater, Hoglund, & Woods, 2003; Taylor, Liang, Tracy, Williams, & Seigle, 2002). Such programs grow out of social and emotional learning theories and are designed to create a safe and cooperative learning environment that promotes the intellectual, social, and emotional development of children (Taylor et al.). One such program, Reach out to Schools: Social Competency Program (SCP), is an elementary primary prevention program that consists of curriculum delivered to students in grades K–5 by the teachers in their classrooms (Taylor et al.). The yearly curriculum consists of 42 regular lessons and 32 supplemental lessons, implemented twice per week for approximately 15 to 30 minutes. Communication, self-control, and social problem solving are the three areas of focus within the curriculum, with the structure allowing students to address current classroom issues as well. Taylor and colleagues reviewed literature that provided support for this model by demonstrating beneficial effects of the program including improved social skills, a greater sense of self-worth and empowerment, increased classroom participation, more time spent on academics, and reduced problem behaviors.

Another schoolwide social competency program is Second Step, which consists of a violence-prevention curriculum that is delivered by teachers and school counselors from preschool through middle school (Frey et al., 2000). Second Step emphasizes teaching children perspective taking, problem solving, and anger management strategies, enabling students to decide "what to do"; as well as behavioral skills training, enabling students to rehearse specific steps for "how" to do it. Second Step also includes parent training in the form of six video-based instruction modules. Similar to Second Step, Steps to Respect: A Bullying Prevention Program (Frey et al., 2005) consists of school policy development and staff training to address adult and systemic factors, along with classroom curriculum promoting prosocial beliefs and social–emotional learning. This program is associated with decreases in bullying behaviors for students who engaged in bullying behaviors prior to intervention. Of note, 77% of children were observed either engaging in or encouraging bullying behavior at one point or another. Thus, successful intervention not only reduced active engagement in bullying behavior, but also the encouragement of bullying behavior as well (Frey et al.).

Finally, another example of a schoolwide social competency program is the Walk away, Ignore, Talk, and Seek help program (WITS; Leadbeater et al., 2003). WITS was developed collaboratively by elementary school teachers, community-based police officers, and a university-based psychologist with the goal of reducing school and classroom levels of victimization. Since its development, WITS has been widely implemented by various school personnel, community organizations, parents, and older students. WITS is an acronym that has been easily utilized to consistently convey to young children workable, developmentally appropriate strategies for managing conflict within peer relationships. Leadbeater and colleagues reported that utilization of WITS has been related to decreases in levels of relational and physical victimization, as well as increased levels of classroom social competence. Researchers argue that prevention programs such as those just described demonstrate the best results when a commitment to the underlying beliefs and practices of the program is adopted and enacted schoolwide (Frey et al., 2000) and if possible, within families and the community at large (Leadbeater et al.). In other words, social competency curriculum delivered in the classroom is most beneficial for students who consistently witness modeling and reinforcement of constructive problem solving by all school personnel, by their family members, and within the community.

Specific issues that may be prime for schoolwide interventions programs are interpersonal difficulties that arise within the peer social network. Similar to the larger sociocultural, community-at-large, school, and family contexts, peer social networks serve as one of the systems in which youth operate. As such, school counselors and researchers should develop and implement interventions pertaining to cliques and peer networks on a systemic level. These can take the form of schoolwide programs to facilitate teamwork, understanding, and respect among students of all different backgrounds and social circles. School counselors can implement groups or peer mentoring programs to address the issues of identity formation and peer pressure. Administrators, educators, and counselors can work together to develop a service-learning component to existing curricula, which would encourage students to get out into the community and gain experience beyond their insulated social networks. The dearth of systemic, evidence-based interventions addressing the structure and dynamics of peer social networks behooves school counselors to implement and evaluate these types of programs.

Other Interventions and Various School Counselor Roles

Finally, counselors are likely to find themselves negotiating between various constituents in their students' lives to facilitate interpersonal relationship success. For instance, counselors take on roles in the school as liaisons, mediators, network therapists, and parent/family educators (Pedersen & Carey, 2003; Thompson, 2002). Additionally, counselors sometimes train students to provide peer mediation interventions with their fellow classmates. Further, counselors also provide training to teachers, school administrators, and other counselors.

Counselor as Liaison

As liaisons, counselors interface between the student and his or her family, the school, and the community in order to gain a better understanding of the student and to assist in improving a student's interpersonal interaction success with individuals at school, as well as outside of the school environment (Hiatt-Michael, 2001; Pedersen & Carey, 2003). In the role of liaison, counselors may become "cultural brokers" who attempt to educate various parties (e.g., parents, teachers) regarding alternative perspectives/worldviews and assist them in identifying and working toward mutually acceptable goals for the students (Gentemann & Whitehead, 1983; Sheridan et al., 2004). For instance, for children whose parents speak limited English or no English at all, communication between the school and home environment is at best difficult, if not impossible. Additionally, children in such situations many times not only serve as the interpreter between the family and school, but also find themselves caught between conflicting familial and school expectations or cultural norms. School counselors who take on the liaison role might locate a trained interpreter to assist with effectively communicating with such families. Then, once the student has been removed from serving as the interpreter, the counselor can effectively assess familial cultural norms and begin to educate parents regarding school cultural norms as well. As the counselor gains a better understanding of familial cultural norms, these norms can be communicated to the student's teacher(s), particularly when familial norms may be in conflict with school norms and/or expectations. As a relationship with the family is developed, the counselor can facilitate enlisting familial support for school goals, while acknowledging the importance of incorporating and/or accommodating for conflicting familial goals. Beyond serving as a liaison between the school and home environments, counselors as liaisons also develop networks and negotiate with organizations outside the school system. The development of these relationships many times increases students' access to and utilization of much needed community resources and services that cannot be provided by the school (Crockett, 2003).

Counselor as Mediator

When interpersonal relationship difficulties are at their worst, counselors are likely to take on the role of mediator between various parties. Many counselors are trained in conflict resolution strategies, which involve intervening with at least two individuals (perhaps more) who are experiencing conflict. Conflict resolution and mediation includes monitoring problematic interaction patterns and modeling effective interaction patterns, as well as direct intervention within social relationships and encounters. For instance, counselors may mediate conflict between students and teachers, teachers and parents, parents and students, parents and school administrators, and so forth. As a mediator, counselors attempt to reduce the participants involved in mediation to the bare minimum to increase the likelihood of conflict reduction, mutual understanding, and eventual conflict resolution (Pedersen & Carey, 2003). For example, in the role of mediator, the school counselor may be asked to settle a dispute between a student and teacher, where the student perceives his/her grade to be negatively impacted by factors other than academic performance. In the mediator role, the counselor would encourage both parties to communicate directly with one another and attempt to resolve their differences with minimal direct intervention from the counselor. The counselor's main role as mediator is to facilitate calm interaction between the parties and encourage utilization of positive problem-solving skills.

Counselor as Network Therapist

Another strategy that might be utilized by counselors in an effort to improve interpersonal relationships with a variety of parties in students' lives is Network Therapy. Network Therapy grows out of ecological models and emphasizes the importance of including the various contexts of students' lives when attempting to implement change (T. B. Smith, 2004). Such an intervention might include simultaneous intervention with students, family members, friends, teachers, and so forth. Intervening in this manner not only acknowledges the importance of the multiple contexts that students operate within (Bronfenbrenner, 1979b), but actually harnesses the power and influence of each of the contexts at the same time. For instance, some students may receive consistent feedback from friends, family members, teachers, and so forth regarding behaviors that elicit unwanted responses. While the student struggles to take in this feedback received during various individual encounters, which makes it difficult for the student to take ownership of his/her behavior and make efforts toward change, the message becomes more powerful when delivered by multiple important others all at the same time. The counselor who utilizes Network Therapy as an intervention strategy would invite the student and multiple members of the student's interpersonal relationship network (e.g., family, friends, and teachers) to meet together at one place and begin to discuss as a group common behavioral difficulties demonstrated by the student. It is highly likely that during the meeting time, the student will engage in the problematic behavior. When that occurs, it provides an in-the-moment example that can be discussed and explored by all members, with the guidance of the counselor.

Counselor as Parent/Family Educator

Another role common to school counselors is that of parent/family educator (DiCamillo, 2001). In this role, counselors intervene with the goal of improving parental participation in the academic and social lives of their children, as well as providing parents with the skills to effect behavioral changes in their children (ASCA, 2003). An example of such an intervention includes counselors conducting parent education classes and collaboratively developing strategies with parents to increase their involvement in the academic and extracurricular lives of their children. One such program might be an after-school tutoring program that includes the involvement of students, parents, and other school personnel. Such a program would not only address the academic needs of the students involved, but would assist the parents in becoming more familiar with school personnel, as well as the academic demands faced by their children, while at the same time providing students with the support, guidance, and expertise of the various school personnel involved in the program. In most cases, parent/family education occurs in a group setting and is tailored toward the parenting needs of the school in question. Thus, programming around specific issues (e.g., talking to your teen about sex, managing your child's anger) might be developed, announced, and delivered at parent–teacher organization meetings.

Peer Mediation

More and more frequently, counselors will train students in strategies that allow students to intervene with their fellow classmates (ASCA, 2000b). Peer mediation is a popular method of intervening with students experiencing interpersonal difficulties. Through peer mediation, trained students counsel and help facilitate the growth and development of other students through the use of their leadership skills (Buck, 1977), as well as through modeling behaviors within the interpersonal relationship that is developed between the peer counselor and student (ASCA, 2002b). A distinct advantage of the peer counseling relationship is that it provides students with positive interpersonal relationship experiences with peers at or near the same age (Salmivalli, 1999; Salovey, 1996). A variety of interventions can be offered through peer mediation, including one-to-one relationships with peers assisting with personal and academic difficulties; group interactions as group leaders, group counseling assistants, and trainers of peer-mediators-in-training; tutoring and educational consultant/assistant relationships; welcoming and orienting new students and parents to the school; and finally, serving in an outreach capacity to increase the awareness and understanding of the role of counseling and its services within the school (ASCA, 2002b).

Researchers agree that peer mediation is widely utilized within schools, despite limited research demonstrated its efficacy. Bickmore (2002) summarized recent research findings indicating that peer mediation programs are associated with a reduction in physical aggression and disciplinary actions. While acknowledging the dearth of available data, S. W. Smith, Daunic, Miller, and Robinson (2002) noted research findings indicate that, when peer mediation was utilized, (a) 85–95% of mediated conflicts resulted in lasting agreements and (b) referrals to school administrative personnel for inappropriate student behaviors decreased. Bickmore also reported that peer mediation programs are associated with improved problem solving, decision making, communication skills, critical thinking, conflict resolution, and self-discipline skills for those trained as peer mediators. Finally, the strength, sustainability, and effectiveness of peer mediation programs are improved when mediation teams are more diverse (i.e., academically, socially, culturally, and with regard to gender; Bickmore). Cunningham and colleagues (1998) argued that there are many potential benefits to implementing peer mediation programs including (a) students may be able to identify conflict and relational aggression more easily than adults; (b) since peer mediation programs span primary, middle, and secondary school years, they may be an important component of managing difficulties that arise at various developmental levels; and (c) given the relatively low cost, mediation programs are affordable even when resources are limited. While there are many variations of peer mediation programs in existence, programs commonly include curriculum for defining the problem, exploring feelings, and negotiating solutions (Bell, Coleman, Anderson, Whelan, & Wilder, 2000).

Training of Professional Staff

In addition to training students, counselors may also conduct training sessions for teachers, administrators, and other counselors (Kirschenbaum, 2001). These sessions emphasize interpersonal skills that can be incorporated into classroom curriculum and schoolwide programming. Such topics might include emotional education and/or competence (Buckley, Storino, & Saarni, 2003; Goleman, 1995), character education (ASCA, 1998), and moral education (Elias & Clabby, 1992). Essentially, each of these topics targets teaching children how to get along with each other (Pedersen & Carey, 2003). The social–emotional learning and social competency program models that were just described in detail are examples of programs that grew out of teacher training. Once teacher training is complete, the curriculum can be introduced into the classroom as an intervention strategy.

Indirect Interventions

Finally, interpersonal interventions may be indirect in nature, in other words, not an actual intervention strategy, but rather an active creation of an environment that facilitates positive interpersonal relationships (ASCA, 2002a). For instance, obstacles to gender equality and the underlying attitudes and associated behaviors can be addressed through the use and modeling of acceptable language, organizational structure, leader selection, expectations of students, and the development and implementation of school programming. Counselor awareness, as well as the counselor's role in actively creating an inclusive and accepting environment, is particularly important when considering students' sexual orientations (D'Augelli & Pilkington, 2002). Sexual minority youth are more likely to encounter difficulties with the development of self-acceptance and healthy self-esteem, particularly when exclusive language, misinformation, stereotypes, and myths are allowed to be perpetuated (ASCA, 2000a). Thus, in instances such as these, school counselors should intervene proactively and in broad environmentally structuring ways, rather than with targeted, specific interventions, to assist with the healthy interpersonal development of all students. For example, when discussing intimate relationships, counselors and other school personnel who are actively creating an environment of inclusion would inquire about a student's "partner" or "significant other," rather than "girlfriend" or "boyfriend."

Interventions Summary

As has been demonstrated throughout the intervention section of this chapter, social modeling is the key to success when intervening with regard to any issue or utilizing any strategy or technique. Additionally, it has been highlighted that school counselors take on many roles and interact with many constituents in order to facilitate healthy interpersonal development for students. Counselors must respond not only to the needs of the school and its personnel but also to the larger environmental contexts within which students operate. As such, Galassi and Akos (2004) summarized the role of school counselors and the importance of their interventions well:

> The school counselor is a leader within the educational community who works with students, teachers, administrators, parents, and other members of the community to build a supportive learning environment that nurtures the development of academic, career, and personal/social competence among students and fosters an appreciation of diversity and a commitment to social justice. (p. 155)

Interpersonal relationships in the lives of students are complex and impact many aspects of their lives, including academic performance and overall mental health. Utilizing developmentally and culturally appropriate means, school counselors proactively and reactively intervene with students in efforts to facilitate optimal interpersonal development.

Evaluation of Programs and Interventions

Today's culture of accountability in our nation's schools mandates that school counseling follow suit in providing evidence for the field's effectiveness. However, school counselors have traditionally been absent in this trend (Green & Keys, 2001). It has been suggested that school counseling has lagged in evaluating its effectiveness for a number of reasons: inadequate knowledge of and training in assessment practices, ethical issues around confidentiality, time and funding restraints, and an overall lack of self-efficacy on the part of school counselors to conduct evaluations (Foster, Watson, Meeks, & Young, 2005). Further, even when evaluation is effective and demonstrates benefits, sometimes the data is not sufficient motivation for those implementing the programs. For example, many intervention programs target decreasing undesirable behaviors, which may not be readily apparent for teachers, in the midst of day-to-day experiences with students. As a result,

Frey and colleagues (2000) noted that the benefits of many primary intervention programs are not always apparent to those implementing the programs despite objective data indicating success. In the absence of subjectively observable benefits, teachers may lose the motivation to continue expending the time and energy necessary for successful implementation.

Evaluation practices will vary according to the type of intervention implemented. Foster and colleagues (2005) highlighted the applicability of a *single-subject research design*, which looks at repeated measurements of target behavior for an individual student or single group. By comparing baseline and treatment levels of target behaviors, the counselor/evaluator gathers data to determine the effectiveness of an intervention. While Foster and colleagues' suggested research designs call for the measurement of behaviors, it may be more salient in the area of interpersonal relationships to more broadly assess for both attitudes and behaviors which serve as markers for psychosocial functioning (e.g., depressive symptomology, quality of relationships, or experiences with conflict).

In light of the pressures to be accountable, formal evaluation theory cautions against taking a purely outcomes-driven approach, especially with respect to systemic programs and interventions. The result can be a "black box evaluation" in which there is a lack of an articulated program theory to explain what might be contributing to the outcomes and why (Rossi, Lipsey, & Freeman, 2004). Prior to implementation and evaluation of a program, evaluators should explicitly articulate its assumptions and expectations, service implementation plans, inputs or resources, and other factors which may be at play in the school and community contexts. Identifying these factors can help the counselor/evaluator to understand the results of an evaluation more fully. In fact, Romasz and colleagues (2004) argued for the importance of an action-research model, which "involves the testing of theories and models by putting them into practice, evaluating their impact, and using the results to refine future theory, method, and practice" (p. 94).

When conducting evaluations on systemic interventions, evaluators should also aim to look beyond traditional experimental field-methods for isolating a program's effect. One research design that provides a comprehensive alternative is the Extended-Term Mixed-Method (ETMM) (Chatterji, 2004). It is theoretically grounded and defined by five characteristics: (a) use of a developmental, long-term research plan, tracking the course of a program over the course of its life, beginning with formative needs assessments through to summative outcome evaluations; (b) use of systemic, contextually grounded methods in earlier studies followed by more analytical, quasi-experimental designs in later phases; (c) deliberate consideration of environmental variables as part of the research; (d) use of multiple research methods (e.g., quantitative and qualitative) to understand relationships and causality; and (e) explanation of causality based on empirical data and substantive knowledge gained on the program and its setting (Chatterji, 2004, p. 7). The ETMM method provides a systematic approach to conducting evaluations and allows evaluations to be grounded in the complex realities of school-based programs.

School counselors must begin incorporating the role of "evaluator" as an integral part of their functioning (Green & Keys, 2001). This entails including training and practice of assessment and evaluation in school counselors' ongoing professional development. One way that school counselors can bridge this current gap in knowledge and expertise is to build coalitions with other agents in the school system, including administrators, educators, school psychologists, school social workers, parents, and community leaders. This synergy of energy, knowledge, and expertise can better serve the field of school counseling and unite the shared goals of these stakeholders in ensuring the positive psychosocial functioning of today's students.

Conclusion

Given the profound effects of interpersonal relations on student achievement and development, school counselors should take measures to be acquainted with the vicissitudes of students' interpersonal relationships. This chapter has highlighted some prevalent issues relevant to the school-age years. Facilitating positive peer relations around these issues necessitates a wide repertoire of skills and knowledge for school counselors. School counselors must see beyond an individualistic, dyadic model and address both contextual and systemic factors, while bringing together research and practice. As school counselors, we must be proactive in promoting positive peer relations, for these are life-long developmental concerns.

References

Aboud, F. E., Mendelson, M. J., & Purdy, K. T. (2003). Cross-race peer relations and friendship quality. *International Journal of Behavioral Development, 27*(2), 165–173.

Adalbjarnardottir, S. (1993). Promoting children's social growth in the schools: An intervention study. *Journal of Applied Developmental Psychology, 14*, 461–484.

Adler, P. A., & Adler, P. (1995). Dynamics of inclusion and exclusion in preadolescent cliques. *Social Psychology Quarterly, 58*(3), 145–162.

Adler, P. A., & Adler, P. (1998). *Peer power: Preadolescent culture and identity.* New Brunswick, NJ: Rutgers University Press.

American Association of University Women. (2001). *Hostile hallways: Bullying, teasing, and sexual harassment.* Washington, DC: Author.

American School Counselor Association. (1998). *Position statement: Character education.* Retrieved May 1, 2005, from http://www.schoolcounselor.org/

American School Counselor Association. (1999). *Position statement: Group counseling.* Retrieved May 1, 2005, from http://www.schoolcounselor.org/

American School Counselor Association. (2000a). *Position statement: Sexual orientation of youth.* Retrieved May 1, 2005, from http:www.schoolcounselor.org/

American School Counselor Association. (2000b). *Position statement: Use of non-credentialed personnel.* Retrieved May 1, 2005, from http://schoolcounselor.org/

American School Counselor Association. (2002a). *Position statement: Gender equity.* Retrieved May 1, 2005, from http://www.schoolcounselor.org/

American School Counselor Association. (2002b). *Position statement: Peer helping.* Retrieved May 1, 2005, from http://www.schoolcounselor.org/

American School Counselor Association. (2003). *Position statement: Family/parenting education.* Retrieved May 1, 2005, from http://www.schoolcounselor.org/

American School Counselor Association. (2004). *Position statement: Cultural diversity.* Retrieved May 1, 2005, from http://www.schoolcounselor.org/

Arata, C. M., Stafford, J., & Tims, M. S. (2003). High school drinking and its consequences. *Adolescence, 38*(151), 567–579.

Aronson, J., & Inzlicht, M. (2004). The ups and downs of attributional ambiguity: Stereotype vulnerability and the academic self-knowledge of African American college students. *Psychological Science, 15*(12), 829–836.

Bagwell, C. L., Coie, J. D., Terry, R. A., & Lochman, J. E. (2000). Peer clique participation and social status in preadolescence. *Merrill-Palmer Quarterly, 46,* 280–305.

Bagwell, C. L., Newcomb, A. F., & Bukowski, W. M. (1998). Preadolescent friendship and peer rejection as predictors of adult adjustment. *Child Development, 69*(1), 140–153.

Bandura, A. (1977). Self-efficacy: Toward a unifying theory of behavioral change. *Psychological Review, 84,* 191–215.

Bauman, K. E., & Ennett, S. T. (1996). On the importance of peer influence for adolescent drug use: Commonly neglected considerations. *Addiction, 91*(2), 185–198.

Beidel, D. C., Turner, S. M., & Morris, T. L. (2000). Behavior treatment of childhood social phobia. *Journal of Consulting and Clinical Psychology, 68,* 1072–1080.

Bell, S. K., Coleman, J. K., Anderson, A., Whelan, J., P., & Wilder. C. (2000). The effectiveness of peer mediation in a low-SES rural elementary school. *Psychology in the Schools, 37,* 505-516.

Bell-Dolan, D. J., Foster, S. L., & Christopher, J. S. (1995). Girls' peer relations and internalizing problems: Are socially neglected, rejected, and withdrawn girls at risk? *Journal of Clinical Child Psychology, 24*(4), 463–473.

Berndt, T. J. (2002). Friendship quality and social development. *Current Directions in Psychological Science, 11,* 7–10.

Berndt, T. J., & Keefe, K. (1995). Friends' influence on adolescents' adjustment to school. *Child Development, 66*(5), 1312–1329.

Berndt, T. J., & Perry, T. B. (1986). Children's perceptions of friendships as supportive relationships. *Developmental Psychology, 22,* 640–648.

Bickmore, K. (2002). Peer mediation training and program implementation in elementary schools: Research results. *Conflict Resolution Quarterly, 20*(2), 137–160.

Bierman, K. L., Smoot, D. L., & Aumiller, K. (1993). Characteristics of aggressive-rejected, aggressive (nonrejected), and rejected (nonaggressive) boys. *Child Development, 64,* 139–151.

Black, K. A. (2000). Gender differences in adolescents' behavior during conflict resolution tasks with best friends. *Adolescence, 35*(139), 499–512.

Boivin, M., Hymel, S., & Bukowski, W. M. (1995). The roles of social withdrawal, peer rejection, and victimization by peers in predicting loneliness and depressed mood in childhood. *Development and Psychopathology, 7,* 765–785.

Bouchey, H. A., & Furman, W. (2003). Dating and romantic experiences in adolescence. In G. A. Adams & M. D. Berzonsky (Eds.), *Blackwell handbook of adolescence* (pp. 313–329). Oxford, UK: Blackwell Publishing.

Braswell, L., August, G. J., Bloomquist, M. L., Realmuto, G. M., Skare, S. S., & Crosby, R. D. (1995). School-based secondary prevention for children with disruptive behavior: Initial outcomes. *Journal of Abnormal Child Psychology, 25*(3), 197–208.

Brendgen, M., Little, T. D., & Krappmann, L. (2000). Rejected children and their friendships: A shared evaluation of friendship quality. *Merrill-Palmer Quarterly, 46*(1), 45–70.

Brendgen, M., Vitaro, F., Doyle, A. B., Markiewitcz, D., & Bukowski, W. M. (2002). Same-sex peer relations and romantic relationships during early adolescence: Interactive links to emotional, behavioral, and academic adjustment. *Merrill-Palmer Quarterly, 48*(1), 77–103.

Brinton, B., & Fujiki, M. (2002). Social development in children with specific language impairment. In P. K. Smith & C. H. Hart (Eds.), *Blackwell handbook of childhood social development* (pp. 588–603). Malden, MA: Blackwell Publishers.

Bronfenbrenner, U. (1979a). Contexts of child rearing: Problems and prospects. *American Psychologist, 34*(10), 844–850.

Bronfenbrenner, U. (1979b). *The ecology of human development.* Cambridge, MA: Harvard University Press.

Brown, B. B. (1989). The role of peer groups in adolescents' adjustment to secondary school. In T. J. Berndt & G. W.

Ladd (Eds.), *Peer relationships in child development* (pp. 188–215). New York: John Wiley & Sons.

Brown, B. B. (1999). You're going out with who? Peer group influences on adolescent romantic relationships. In W. Furman, B. B. Brown, & C. Feiring (Eds.), *The development of romantic relationships in adolescence* (pp. 291–329). New York: Cambridge University Press.

Brown, B. B., Eicher, S. A., & Petrie, S. (1986). The importance of peer group ("crowd") affiliation in adolescence. *Journal of Adolescence, 9*(1), 73–96.

Brown, B. B., Feiring, C., & Furman, W. (1999). Missing the love boat. In W. Furman, B. B. Brown, & C. Feiring (Eds.), *The development of romantic relationships in adolescence* (pp. 1–16). New York: Cambridge University Press.

Brown, B. B., & Klute, C. (2003). Friendships, cliques, and crowds. In G. A. Adams & M. D. Berzonsky (Eds.), *Blackwell handbook of adolescence* (pp. 330–348). Oxford, U.K.: Blackwell Publishing.

Brown, B. B., & Lohr, M. J. (1987). Peer-group affiliation and adolescent self-esteem: An integration of ego-identity and symbolic-interaction theories. *Journal of Personality & Social Psychology, 52*(1), 47–55.

Buck, M. R. (1977). Peer counseling in an urban high school setting. *Journal of School Psychology, 15*(4), 362–366.

Buckley, M., Storino, M., & Saarni, C. (2003). Promoting emotional competence in children and adolescents: Implications for school psychologists. *School Psychology Quarterly, 18*(2), 177–191.

Buhs, E. S., & Ladd, G. W. (2001). Peer rejection as an antecedent of young children's school adjustment: An examination of mediating processes. *Developmental Psychology, 37*(4), 550–560.

Bukowski, W. M., Newcomb, A. F., & Hartup, W. W. (1996). *The company they keep: Friendship in childhood and adolescence*. New York: Cambridge University Press.

Bukowski, W. M., & Sippola, L. K. (1996). Friendship and morality: (How) are they related? In W. M. Bukowski, A. F. Newcomb, & W. W. Hartup (Eds.), *The company they keep: Friendship in childhood and adolescence* (pp. 238–261). New York: Cambridge University Press.

Carver, K., Joyner, K., & Udry, J. R. (2004). National estimates of adolescent romantic relationships. In P. Florsheim (Ed.), *Adolescent romantic relations and sexual behavior: Theory, research, and practical implications* (pp. 23–56). Mahwah, NJ: Erlbaum.

Chatterji, M. (2004). Evidence on "What works:" An argument for extended-term mixed-methods (ETMM) evaluation designs. *Educational Researcher, 33*(9), 3–13.

Close, S. M. (2005). Dating violence prevention in middle school and high school youth. *Journal of Child and Adolescent Psychiatric Nursing, 18*(1), 2–9.

Coie, J. D., Terry, R. A., & Hyman, C. (1992). Predicting early adolescent disorder from childhood aggression and peer rejection. *Journal of Consulting and Clinical Psychology, 60*, 783–792.

Coie, J. D., Terry, R. A., Lenox, K., Lochman, J. E., & Hyman, C. (1995). Childhood peer rejection and aggression as predictors of stable patterns of adolescent disorder. *Development and Psychopathology, 7*, 697–713.

Collins, W. A. (2003). More than myth: The developmental significance of romantic relationships during adolescence. *Journal of Research on Adolescence, 13*, 1–24.

Collins, W. A., & Laursen, B. (1992). Conflict and relationships during adolescence. In C. U. Shantz & W. W. Hartup (Eds.), *Conflict in child and adolescent development*. New York: Cambridge University Press.

Collins, W. A., & Sroufe, L. A. (1999). Capacity for intimate relationships. In W. Furman, B. B. Brown, & C. Feiring (Eds.), *The development of romantic relationships in adolescence* (pp. 216–241). New York: Cambridge University Press.

Connolly, J. A., Craig, W., Goldberg, A., & Pepler, D. (2004). Mixed-gender groups, dating, and romantic relationships in early adolescence. *Journal of Research on Adolescence, 14*(2), 185–207.

Connolly, J. A., & Goldberg, A. (1999). Romantic relationships in adolescence: The role of friends and peers in their emergence and development. In W. Furman, B. B. Brown, & C. Feiring (Eds.), *The development of romantic relationships in adolescence* (pp. 266–290). New York: Cambridge University Press.

Crockett, D. (2003). Critical issues children face in the 2000s. *School Psychology Quarterly, 18*(4), 446–453.

Cunningham, C. E., Cunningham, L. J., Martorelli, V., Tran, A., Young, J., & Zacharias, R. (1998). The effect of primary division, student-mediated conflict resolution programs on playground aggression. *Journal of Child Psychology and Psychiatry, 39*(5), 653–662.

D'Augelli, A. R., & Pilkington, N. W. (2002). Incidence and mental health impact of sexual orientation victimization of lesbian, gay, and bisexual youths in high school. *School Psychology Quarterly, 17*(2), 148–167.

Davila, J., Steinberg, S. J., Kachadourian, L., Cobb, R., & Fincham, F. (2004). Romantic involvement and depressive symptoms in early and late adolescence: The role of a preoccupied relational style. *Journal of Personal Relationships, 11*(2), 161–178.

DeRosier, M. E., Kupersmidt, J. B., & Patterson, C. J. (1994). Children's academic and behavioral adjustment as a function of chronicity and proximity of peer rejection. *Child Development, 65*(6), 1799–1813.

Diamond, L. M., & Savin-Williams, R. C. (2003). The intimate relationships of sexual-minority youths. In G. A. Adams & M. D. Berzonsky (Eds.), *Blackwell handbook of adolescence* (pp. 393–412). Oxford, U.K.: Blackwell Publishing.

Diamond, L. M., Savin-Williams, R. C., & Dubé, E. M. (1999). Sex, dating, passionate friendships, and romance. In W. Furman, B. B. Brown, & C. Feiring (Eds.), *The development of romantic relationships in adolescence* (pp. 175–210). New York: Cambridge University Press.

DiCamillo, M. P. (2001). Parent education as an essential component of family involvement programs. In D. B. Hiatt-Michael (Ed.), *Promising practices for family involvement in schools* (pp. 153–184). Greenwich, CT: Information Age Publishing.

Dodge, K. A., & Coie, J. D. (1987). Social-information processing factors in reactive and proactive aggression in children's peer groups. *Journal of Personality & Social Psychology, 53*, 1146–1158.

Dolcini, M. M., Harper, G. W., Watson, S. E., Catania, J. A., & Ellen, J. M. (2005). Friends in the 'hood: Should peer-based health promotion programs target nonschool friendship networks? *Journal of Adolescent Health, 36*(3), 267.e6–267.e215.

Downey, G., Bonica, C., & Rincón, C. (1999). Rejection sensitivity and adolescent romantic relationships. In W. Furman, B. B. Brown, & C. Feiring (Eds.), *The development of romantic relationships in adolescence* (pp. 148–174). New York: Cambridge University Press.

Downs, W. R., & Rose, S. R. (1991). The relationship of adolescent peer groups to the incidence of psychosocial problems. *Adolescence, 26*(102), 473–492.

Dunphy, D. (1963). The social structure of urban adolescent peer groups. *Sociometry, 26*(2), 230–246.

Eder, D. (1985). The cycle of popularity: Interpersonal relations among female adolescents. *Sociology of Education, 58*, 154–165.

Elias, M., & Clabby, J. F. (1992). *Building social problem skills: Guidelines from a school-based program.* San Francisco: Jossey-Bass.

Ennett, S. T., & Bauman, K. E. (1996). Adolescent social networks: School, demographic, and peer group homogeneity. *Journal of Adolescent Research, 11*, 194–215.

Ennett, S. T., Bauman, K. E., & Koch, G. G. (1994). Variability in cigarette smoking within and between adolescent friendship cliques. *Addictive Behaviors, 19*(3), 295–305.

Erikson, E. (1968). *Identity, youth, and crisis.* New York: Norton.

Farmer, T. W., & Cadwallader, T. W. (2000). Social interactions and peer support for problem behavior. *Preventing School Failure, 44*(3), 105–109.

Finkelhor, D., Mitchell, K., & Wolak, J. (2000). *Online victimization: A report on the nation's youth.* Alexandria, VA: National Center for Missing & Exploited Children.

Fisher, P. H., Masia-Warner, C., & Klein, R. G. (2004). Skills for social and academic success: A school-based intervention for social anxiety disorder in adolescents. *Clinical Child and Family Psychology Review, 7*(4), 241–249.

Fordham, S., & Ogbu, J. U. (1986). Black students' school success: Coping with the "burden of 'acting White." *Urban Review, 18*, 176–206.

Foster, L. H., Watson, T. S., Meeks, C., & Young, J. S. (2005). Single-subject research design for school counselors: Becoming an applied research. *Professional School Counseling, 6*(2), 146–155.

Fraser, M. W., Galinsky, M. J., Smokowski, P. R., Day, S. H., Terzian, M. A., Rose, R. A., et al. (2005). Social information-processing skills training to promote social competence and prevent aggressive behavior in third grade. *Journal of Consulting and Clinical Psychology, 73*(6), 1045–1055.

French, D. C., & Conrad, J. (2001). School dropout as predicted by peer rejection and antisocial behavior. *Journal of Research on Adolescence, 11*(3), 225–244.

Frey, K. S., Hirschstein, M. K., & Guzzo, B. A. (2000). Second step: Preventing aggression by promoting social competence. *Journal of Emotional and Behavioral Disorders, 8*(2), 102–112.

Frey, K. S., Hirschstein, M. K., Snell, J. L., Van Schoiack Edstrom, L., MacKenzie, E. P. et al., (2005). Reducing playground bullying and supporting beliefs: An experimental trial of the Steps to Respect program. *Developmental Psychology, 41*(3), 479–491.

Fukiji, M., Brinton, B., Hart, C. H., & Fitzgerald, A. (1999). Withdrawn and sociable behavior of children with specific language impairment. *Topics in Language Disorders, 19*, 34–48.

Furman, W., Brown, B. B., & Feiring, C. (Eds.). (1999). *The development of romantic relationships in adolescence.* New York: Cambridge University Press.

Furman, W., & Buhrmester, D. (1985). Children's perceptions of the personal relationships in their social networks. *Developmental Psychology, 21*, 1016–1024.

Furman, W., & Simon, V. A. (1999). Cognitive representations of adolescent romantic relationships. In W. Furman, B. B. Brown, & C. Feiring (Eds.), *The development of romantic relationships in adolescence* (pp. 75–98). New York: Cambridge University Press.

Galassi, J. P., & Akos, P. (2004). Developmental advocacy: Twenty-first century school counseling. *Journal of Counseling and Development, 82*(2), 146–157.

Gentemann, K. M., & Whitehead, T. L. (1983). The cultural broker concept in bicultural education. *Journal of Negro Education, 52*, 118–129.

Gifford-Smith, M. E., & Brownell, C. A. (2003). Childhood peer relationships: Social acceptance, friendships, and peer networks. *Journal of School Psychology, 41*, 235–284.

Gilbert, L. A., & Scher, M. (1999). *Gender and sex in counseling and therapy.* Boston: Allyn and Bacon.

Giordano, P. C., Cernkovich, S. A., & DeMaris, A. (1993). The family and peer relations of Black adolescents. *Journal of Marriage and the Family, 55*(2), 277–287.

Goleman, D. (1995). *Emotional intelligence.* New York: Bantam Books.

Good, G. E., Gilbert, L. A., & Scher, M. (1990). Gender aware therapy: A synthesis of feminist therapy and knowledge about gender. *Journal of Counseling and Development, 68*(4), 376–380.

Gray, M. R., & Steinberg, L. (1999). Adolescent romance and the parent-child relationships: A contextual perspective. In W. Furman, B. B. Brown, & C. Feiring (Eds.), *The development of romantic relationships in adolescence* (pp. 235–265). New York: Cambridge University Press.

Green, A., & Keys, S. (2001). Expanding the developmental school counseling paradigm: Meeting the needs of the 21st century student. *Professional School Counseling, 5*(2), 84–95.

Greenberg, K. R. (2003). *Group counseling in K-12 schools: A handbook for school counselors.* Boston: Allyn and Bacon.

Hamm, J. V. (2000). Do birds of a feather flock together? Individual, relationship, and contextual bases for African American, Asian American, and White adolescents' selection of similar friends. *Developmental Psychology, 36*(2), 209–219.

Hamm, J. V., Brown, B. B., & Heck, D. J. (2005). Bridging the ethnic divide: Student and school characteristics in African American, Asian-descent, Latino, and White adolescents' cross-ethnic friend nominations. *Journal of Research on Adolescence, 15*(1), 21–46.

Hansen, D. J., Nangle, D. W., & Meyer, K. A. (1998). Enhancing the effectiveness of social skills interventions with adolescents. *Education and Treatment of Children, 21*(4), 489–513.

Harrison, P. L., Cummings, J. A., Dawson, M., Short, R. J., Gorin, S., & Palomares, R. (2003). Responding to the needs of children, families, and schools: The 2002 multisite conference on the future of school psychology. *School Psychology Quarterly, 18*(4), 358–388.

Harter, S. (1990). Self and identity development. In S. S. Feldman & G. R. Elliot (Eds.), *At the threshold: The developing adolescent.* (pp. 352–387). Cambridge, MA: Harvard University Press.

Hartup, W. W. (1996). Cooperation, close relationships, and cognitive development. In W. M. Bukowski, A. F. Newcomb, & W. W. Hartup (Eds.), *The friends they keep: Friendship in childhood and adolescence* (pp. 213–237). New York: Cambridge University Press.

Hartup, W. W. (1999). Constraints on peer socialization: Let me count the ways. *Merrill-Palmer Quarterly, 45*(1), 172–183.

Hartup, W. W., & Stevens, N. (1997). Friendships and adaptation in the life course. *Psychological Bulletin, 121*(3), 355–370.

Hayward, C., Varady, S., Albano, A. M., Thienemann, M., Henderson, L., & Schatzberg, A. F. (2000). Cognitive-behavioral group therapy for social phobia in female adolescents: Results from a pilot study. *Journal of the American Academy of Child and Adolescent Psychiatry, 39*, 721–726.

Hiatt-Michael, D. B. (2001). Home-school communication. In D. B. Hiatt-Michael (Ed.), *Promising practices for family involvement in schools* (pp. 39–57). Greenwich: Information Age Publishing.

Hoare, C. H. (1991). Psychosocial identity development and cultural others. *Journal of Counseling and Development, 70*(1), 45–53.

Hodges, E., Boivin, M., Vitaro, F., & Bukowski, W. M. (1999). The power of friendship: Protection against and escalating cycle of peer victimization. *Developmental Psychology, 35*, 91–101.

Hussong, A. M. (2002). Differentiating peer contexts and risk for adolescent substance use. *Journal of Youth and Adolescence, 31*(3), 207–219.

Hymel, S., Rubin, K. H., Rowden, L., B., & LeMare, L. (1990). Children's peer relationships: Longitudinal predictions of internalizing and externalizing problems from middle to late childhood. *Child Development, 61*, 2004–2021.

Johnson, D. W., Johnson, R., Dudley, B., & Magnuson, D. (1995). Training of elementary school students to manage conflict. *Journal of Social Psychology, 135*(6), 673–686.

Kehe, J. V. & Smith, T. B. (2004). Glossary. In T. B. Smith (Ed.), *Practicing multiculturalism: Affirming diversity in counseling and psychology* (pp. 325-337). Boston: Pearson: Allyn & Bacon.

Kirschenbaum, H. (2001). Educating professionals for school, family, and community partnerships. In D. B. Hiatt-Michael (Ed.), *Promising practices for family involvement in schools* (pp. 185–208). Greenwich, CT: Information Age Publishing.

Kistner, J., Balthazor, M., Risi, S., & David, C. (2001). Adolescents' perceptions of peer acceptance: Is dysphoria associated with greater realism? *Journal of Social and Clinical Psychology, 20*(1), 66–81.

Kratochwill, T. R., & Stoiber, K. C. (2000). Diversifying theory and science: Expanding the boundaries of empirically supported interventions in school psychology. *Journal of School Psychology, 38*(4), 349–358.

Kupersmidt, J. B., & Coie, J. D. (1990). Preadolescent peer status, aggression, and school adjustment as predictors of externalizing problems in adolescence. *Child Development, 61*, 1350–1362.

Kupersmidt, J. B., DeRosier, M. E., & Patterson, C. P. (1995). Similarity as the basis for children's friendships: The roles of sociometric status, aggressive and withdrawn behavior, and academic achievement and demographic characteristics. *Journal of Social and Personal Relationships, 12*(3), 439–452.

Kuttler, A. F., La Greca, A. M., & Prinstein, M. J. (1999). Friendship qualities and social-emotional functioning of adolescents with close, cross-sex friendships. *Journal of Research on Adolescence, 9*(3), 339–366.

Kwon, K.-L. K. (2001). Models of racial and ethnic identity development: delineation of practice implications. *Journal of Mental Health Counseling, 23*(3), 269–277.

Ladd, G. W., & Burgess, K. B. (1999). Charting the relationship trajectories or aggressive, withdrawn, and aggressive/withdrawn children during early grade school. *Child Development, 70*(4), 910–929.

Ladd, G. W., & Burgess, K. B. (2001). Do relational risks and protective factors moderate the linkages between childhood aggression and early psychological and school adjustment? *Child Development, 72*(5), 1579–1601.

Ladd, G. W., & Kochenderfer, B. J. (1996). Linkages between friendship and adjustment during early school transitions. In W. M. Bukowski, A. F. Newcomb, & W. W. Hartup (Eds.), *The company they keep: Friendship in childhood and adolescence* (pp. 322–345). New York: Cambridge University Press.

La Greca, A. M., & Harrison, H. M. (2005). Adolescent peer relations, friendships, and romantic relationships: Do they predict social anxiety and depression? *Journal of Clinical Child and Adolescent Psychology, 24*(1), 49–61.

Larson, R. W., Clore, G. L., & Wood, G. A. (1999). The emotions of romantic relationships: Do they wreak havoc on adolescents? In W. Furman, B. B. Brown, & C. Feiring (Eds.), *The development of romantic relationships in adolescence* (pp. 19–49). New York: Cambridge University Press.

Lashbrook, J. T. (2000). Fitting in: Exploring the emotional dimension of adolescent peer pressure. *Adolescence, 35*(140), 747–757.

Laursen, B. (1996). Closeness and conflict in adolescent peer relationships: Interdependence with friends and romantic partners. In W. M. Bukowski, A. F. Newcomb, & W. W. Hartup (Eds.), *The company they keep: Friendships in childhood and adolescence* (pp. 186–210). New York: Cambridge University Press.

Leadbeater, B., Hoglund, W., & Woods, T. (2003). Changing contexts? The effects of a primary prevention program on classroom levels of peer relational and physical victimization. *Journal of Community Psychology, 31*(4), 397–418.

Leary, M. R., Kowalski, R. M., Smith, L., & Philips, S. (2003). Teasing, rejection, and violence: Case studies of the school shootings. *Aggressive Behavior, 29*, 202–214.

Lee, C. C. (1995). School counseling and cultural diversity: A framework for effective practice. In C. C. Lee (Ed.), *Counseling for diversity: A guide for school counselors and related professionals* (pp. 3–17). Boston: Allyn and Bacon.

Lenhart, A., Madden, M., & Hitlin, P. (2005). *Teens and technology: Youth are leading the transition to a fully wired and mobile nation.* Washington, DC: Pew Internet & American Life Project.

McDougall, P., Hymel, S., Vaillancourt, T., & Mercer, L. (2001). The consequences of childhood peer rejection. In M. R. Leary (Ed.), *Interpersonal rejection* (pp. 213–247). New York: Oxford University Press.

Miller-Johnson, S., Coie, J. D., Maumary-Gremaud, A., Lochman, J. E., & Terry, R. A. (1999). Relationship between childhood peer rejection and aggression and adolescent delinquency severity and type among African American youth. *Journal of Emotional and Behavioral Disorders, 7*(3), 137–146.

Myers, J. E., Shoffner, M. F., & Briggs, M. K. (2002). Developmental counseling and therapy: An effective approach to understanding and counseling children. *Professional School Counseling, 5*(3), 194–202.

Myers, L. J., Speight, S. L., Highlen, P. S., Cox, C. I., Reynolds, A. L., Adams, E. M., et al. (1991). Identity development and worldview: Toward an optimal conceptualization. *Journal of Counseling and Development, 70*(1), 54–63.

Neemann, J., Hubbard, J., & Masten, A. S. (1995). The changing importance of romantic relationship involvement to competence from late childhood to late adolescence. *Development and Psychopathology, 7*, 727–750.

Nemiroff, M. A., & Annunziata, J. (1990). *A child's first book about play therapy.* Washington, DC: American Psychological Association.

Newcomb, A. F., Bukowski, W. M., & Pattee, L. (1993). Children's peer relations: A meta-analytic review of popular, rejected, neglected, controversial, and average sociometric status. *Psychological Review, 113*(1), 99–128.

Panak, W. F., & Garber, J. (1992). Role of aggression, rejection, and attributions in the prediction of depression in children. *Development and Psychopathology, 7*, 145–165.

Parker, J. G., & Asher, S. R. (1987). Peer relations and later personal adjustment: Are low-accepted children at risk? *Psychological Bulletin, 102*(3), 357–389.

Parker, J. G., & Asher, S. R. (1993). Friendship and friendship quality in middle childhood: Links with peer group acceptance and feelings of loneliness and social dissatisfaction. *Developmental Psychology, 29*(4), 611–621.

Parker, J. G., Rubin, K. H., Price, J. M., & DeRosier, M. E. (1995). Peer relationships, child development, and adjustment: A developmental psychopathology perspective. In D. Cicchetti & D. Cohen (Eds.), *Developmental psychopathology: Vol. 2: Risk, disorder, and adaptation* (pp. 96–161). New York: John Wiley & Sons.

Patterson, G. J., Capaldi, D., & Bank, L. (1991). An early starter model for predicting delinquency. In D. J. Pepler & K. H. Rubin (Eds.), *The development and treatment of childhood aggression* (pp. 139–168). Hillsdale, NJ: Elrbaum.

Patterson, G. J., Kupersmidt, J. B., & Greisler, P. C. (1990). Children's perceptions of self and of relationships with others as a function of sociometric status. *Child Development, 61*, 1335–1349.

Pedersen, P. B., & Carey, J. C. (2003). *Multicultural counseling in schools: A practical handbook* (2nd ed.). Boston: Allyn and Bacon.

Peterson, L. W., & Hardin, M. E. (1997). *Children in distress: A guide for screening children's art*. New York: W. W. Norton & Company.

Phillipson, L. C., Bridges, S. K., McLemore, T. G., & Saponaro, L. A. (1999). Perceptions of social behavior and peer acceptance in kindergarten. *Journal of Research in Childhood Education, 14*(1), 68–77.

Prout, H. T., Alexander, S. P., Fletcher, C. E. M., Memis, J. P., & Miller, D. W. (1993). Counseling and psychotherapy services provided by school psychologists: An analysis of patterns of practice. *Journal of School Psychology, 31*, 309–316.

Prout, S. M., & Prout, H. T. (1998). A meta-analysis of school-based studies of counseling and psychotherapy: An update. *Journal of School Psychology, 36*(2), 121–136.

Redivo, M., & Buckman, R. (2004). TEAM: Teaching empowerment through active means. *Journal of Systemic Therapies, 23*(4), 52–66.

Rogers, M. R., & Lopez, E. C. (2002). Identifying critical cross-cultural school psychology competencies. *Journal of School Psychology, 40*(2), 115–141.

Romasz, T. E., Kantor, J. H., & Elias, M. J. (2004). Implementation and evaluation of urban school-wide social-emotional learning programs. *Evaluation and Program Planning, 27*, 89–103.

Rossi, P. H., Lipsey, M. W., & Freeman, H. E. (2004). *Evaluation: A systematic approach*. Thousand Oaks, CA: Sage Publications.

Rubin, K. H., Chen, X., & Hymel, S. (1993). Socioemotional characteristics of withdrawn and aggressive children. *Merrill-Palmer Quarterly, 39*, 518–534.

Rubin, K. H., & Mills, R. S. L. (1988). The many faces of social isolation in childhood. *Journal of Consulting and Clinical Psychology, 65*(6), 916–924.

Salmivalli, C. (1999). Participant role approach to school bullying: Implications for interventions. *Journal of Adolescence, 22*, 453–459.

Salovey, P. (1996). What is peer counseling? In V. J. D'Andrea & P. Salovey (Eds.), *Peer counseling: Skills, ethics, and perspectives* (2nd ed., pp. 3–18). Palo Alto, CA: Science and Behavior Books, Inc.

Sandoval, J. (1993). The history of interventions in school psychology. *Journal of School Psychology, 31*, 195–217.

Sandstrom, M. J., & Coie, J. D. (1999). A developmental perspective on peer rejection: Mechanisms of stability and change. *Child Development, 70*(4), 955–966.

Schmidt, J. J. (2003). *Counseling in schools: Essential services and comprehensive programs* (4th ed.). Boston: Allyn and Bacon.

Sheridan, S. M., Buhs, E. S., & Warnes, E. D. (2003). Childhood peer relationships in context. *Journal of School Psychology, 41*, 285–292.

Sheridan, S. M., Erchul, W. P., Brown, M. S., Dowd, S. E., Warnes, E. D., Marti, D. C., et al. (2004). Perceptions of helpfulness in conjoint behavioral consultation: Congruence and agreement between teachers and parents. *School Psychology Quarterly, 19*(2), 121–140.

Shrum, W., & Cheek, N. H. (1987). Social structure during the school years: Onset of the degrouping process. *American Sociological Review, 52*(2), 218–223.

Smith, S. W., Daunic, A. P., Miller, D. W., & Robinson, T. R. (2002). Conflict resolution and peer mediation in middle schools: Extending the process and outcome knowledge base. *The Journal of Social Psychology, 145*(5), 567–586.

Smith, T. B., Richards, P. S., Granley, H. M., & Obiakor, F. (2004). Practicing multiculturism: An introduction. In T. B. Smith (Ed.), *Practicing multiculturalism: Affirming diversity in counseling and psychology* (pp. 3-16). Boston: Pearson: Allyn & Bacon.

Spence, S. H., Donovan, C., & Brechman-Toussaint, M. (2000). The treatment of childhood social phobia: The effectiveness of a social skills training-based, cognitive-behavioral intervention, with and without parental involvement. *Journal of Child Psychology and Psychiatry, 41*, 713–726.

Sue, D. W., & Sue, D. (2003). *Counseling the culturally diverse: Theory and practice* (4th ed.). New York: John Wiley & Sons.

Sullivan, H. S. (1953). *The interpersonal theory of psychiatry*. New York: W. W. Norton & Company.

Taylor C.A., Liang B., Tracy A.J., Williams L.M., Seigle P. (2002). Gender differences in middle school adjustment, physical fighting, and social skills: Evaluation of a social competency program. *Journal of Primary Prevention, 23*(2), 259-272.

Thompson, R. A. (2002). *School counseling: Best practices for working in the schools* (2nd ed.). New York: Brunner-Routledge.

Thompson, R. A., & Rudolph. (2000). *Counseling children* (5th ed.). Belmont, CA: Brooks/Cole.

Thurlow, C. (2001). The usual suspects? A comparative investigation of crowds and social-type labeling among young British teenagers. *Journal of Youth Studies, 4*(3), 319–334.

Tolson, J. M., & Urberg, K. A. (1993). Similarity between adolescent best friends. *Journal of Adolescent Research, 8*, 274–288.

Umaña-Taylor, A. J., & Bámaca-Gómez, M. Y. (2003). Generational differences in resistance to peer pressure among Mexican-origin adolescents. *Youth & Society, 35*(2), 183–203.

Urberg, K. A. (1992). Locus of peer influence: Social crowd and best friend. *Journal of Youth and Adolescence, 21*(4), 439–450.

Urberg, K. A., Degirmencioglu, S. M., Tolson, J. M., & Halliday-Scher, K. (2000). Adolescent social crowds: Measurement and relationship to friendships. *Journal of Adolescent Research, 15*(4), 427–445.

vanManen, T. M. A., Prins, P. J. M., & Emmelkamp, P. M. G. (2004). Reducing aggressive behavior in boys with social cognitive group treatment: Results of a randomized, control trial. *Child and Adolescent Psychiatry, 43*(12), 1478–1487.

Villa, R. A., Udis, J., & Thousand, J. S. (1994). Responses for children experiencing behavioral and emotional challenges. In J. S. Thousand, R. A. Villa, & A. I. Nevin (Eds.), *Creativity and collaborative learning: A practical guide to empowering students and teachers* (pp. 369–390). Baltimore: Paul H. Brookes Publishing.

Vossekuil, B., Reddy, M., Fein, R., Borum, R., & Modelski, W. (2000). *U.S.S.S. Safe School Initiative: An interim report on the prevention of targeted violence in the schools.* Washington, DC: U.S. Secret Service, National Threat Assessment Center.

Way, N. (1996). Between experiences of betrayal and desire: Close friendships among urban adolescents. In B. Leadbeater & N. Way (Eds.), *Urban girls: Resisting stereotypes, creating identities* (pp. 173–193). New York: New York University Press.

Way, N., & Chen, L. (2000). Close and general friendships among African American, Latino, and Asian American adolescents from low-income families. *Journal of Adolescent Research, 15*(2), 274–301.

Webb, N. B. (1991). Play therapy crisis intervention with children. In N. B. Webb (Ed.), *Play therapy with children in crisis: A casebook for practitioners* (pp. 26–42). New York: Guilford Press.

Webster-Stratton, C. (1997). From parent training to community building. *Families in Society, 78*(2), 156–171.

Wentzel, K. R., & Asher, S. R. (1995). The academic lives of neglected, rejected, popular, and controversial children. *Child Development, 66*(3), 754–763.

Wentzel, K. R., Barry, C. M., & Caldwell, K. A. (2004). Friendships in middle school: Influences on motivation and school adjustment. *Journal of Educational Psychology, 96*(2), 195–203.

Wolfe, D. A., & Feiring, C. (2000). Dating violence through the lens of adolescent romantic relationships. *Child Maltreatment, 5*(1), 360–363.

Wood, C. N., & Gross, A. M. (2002). Behavioral response generation and selection of rejected-reactive aggressive, rejected-nonaggressive and average status children. *Child and Family Behavior Therapy, 24*(3), 1–19.

Yalom, I. D. (1995). *The theory and practice of group psychotherapy* (4th ed.). New York: Basic Books.

Ybarra, M. L., & Mitchell, K. J. (2004). Online aggressor/targets, aggressors, and targets: A comparison of associated youth characteristics. *Journal of Child Psychology and Psychiatry, 45*(7), 1308–1316.

Zakriski, A. L., & Coie, J. D. (1996). A comparison of aggressive-rejected children's interpretations of self-directed and other-directed rejection. *Child Development, 67*, 1048–1070.

Zirkel, S. (2004). What will you think of me? Racial integration, peer relationships, and achievement among White students and students of color. *Journal of Social Issues, 60*(1), 57–74.

Zisman, P., & Wilson, V. (1992). Table hopping in the cafeteria: An exploration of "racial" integration in early adolescent social groups. *Anthropology and Education Quarterly, 23*, 199–220.

XXXVII
SUICIDE PREVENTION, INTERVENTION, AND POSTVENTION

SHERI BAUMAN
University of Arizona

Introduction

Suicide-related crises (dealing with a suicide gesture or suicidal ideation) were two of the top four types of crisis situations encountered by a sample of school counselors (Mathai, 2002). They are also one of the most challenging and disturbing situations a school counselor ever faces, regardless of how much experience and training the counselor has. School counselors may be involved in all aspects of suicide, from prevention programs and activities to intervention with suicidal students, and unfortunately, with response services to students following a completed suicide. School counselors are important resources for students, educators, administrators, and family members who seek advice and expertise. "Counselors are on the front line for identification, prevention, intervention, and postvention of suicidal behavior. As oppressive as that may feel to counselors, it is nonetheless a fact" (Stefanowski-Harding, 1990, p. 334). The purpose of this chapter is to provide useful and current information for school counselors and counselor educators so that they might be better informed and prepared to address youth suicide.

Definition of Terms

Definitions of *suicide* convey the harsh reality of this behavior: self-murder, self-inflicted death, deliberate self-annihilation, self-destructive act with intent to die—these are among the definitions found in the literature (Stauffer, 2004; Stillion & McDowell, 1996). Suicide is usually a conscious, planned, and premeditated act, but it can also be impulsive and unplanned (particularly in adolescents), a desperate attempt to end unbearable pain. A suicidal event (gesture, attempt, or threat) may be what brings a student to the attention of the school counselor, but it is often the case that the reason for seeking help is something other than suicidal thinking. School counselors may also work with survivors of suicide (friends and loved ones of someone who completes an act of suicide), and when a student commits suicide, the school counselor must cope with his or her own personal loss while providing support to others.

The term *completed suicide* is used to accurately describe a death by suicide. The phrase *successful suicide* implies that this act can be an effective solution to a problem, and it should be avoided. *Suicidal ideation* refers to thoughts of suicide that are nonspecific as to plan or timing (e.g., "Sometimes I think I'd be better off dead"). The term *suicide gesture* describes an act that implies suicidal behavior but which is of very low lethality (e.g., making a very superficial cut on the wrist, taking five aspirin) and is intended to be a cry for help or a way to express the depth of pain an individual is experiencing. A *suicide attempt* is more lethal (e.g., taking a bottle of sleeping pills) and implies that the person believed their action would result in death (even if that belief was based on inaccurate information) and, if the individual survives an attempt, it is because someone intervened or interrupted the act. The *lethality* of a suicide attempt describes the likelihood that the action will result in death. Both thoughts and actions related to suicide are collectively referred to as *suicidal behaviors*.

Prevalence

In 2004 (the most recent year for which data were available) suicide was the third leading cause of death among youth aged 10 to 19 years old. Although suicide rates in this age group declined from the mid-1990s until 2003, the rates increased dramatically in 2004 for 10- to 14-year-old females (an increase of 76% from 2003–2004), and in 15- to 19-year-olds of both genders, with the rate for females increasing by 32% and male by 9% in one year (Center for Disease Control, 2007). In 2004, 8.2 persons per 100,000 in the population aged 15 to 19 committed suicide (12.65 for males and 3.52 for females). There were 283 confirmed suicides among 10- to 14-year olds in that year (American Association of Suicidology [AAS], 2006). It is estimated that 170 children younger than age 10 commit suicide each year (Zametkin, Alter, & Yemini, 2001). Most experts agree that these figures are an underestimate, as some deaths recorded as accidental may actually be suicides.

Despite the recent overall decline in suicide rates among youth in general, the rate for males aged 10 to 14 actually increased from 1981 to 2001, with the largest overall increase found for Black males aged 10 to 14. The rate for this group increased 233% from 1980 to 1995 (AAS, 2006). Male youth commit suicide at a rate five times that of females (National Institute of Mental Health [NIMH], 2005), although females make more attempts and have more suicidal ideation than males. In 2003, 21% of female students reported seriously considering suicide, compared with 13% of males (National Adolescent Health Information Center [NAHIC], 2006). Data from a national sample of high school students in grades 9 through 12 (National Center for Health Statistics [NCHS], 2004) reveal interesting trends over the last decade or so. The percent of students who seriously considered suicide declined from a high of 29.0 in 1991 to 16.9 in 2003 for males, and from 37.2 to 21.3 for females. Similar reductions are evident for all grades and ethnic groups. For students who acknowledged having made a suicide attempt, however, an increase was found. In 2001, the percentages were 3.9% for males, and 10.7% for females; in 2003, those percentages were 5.4% and 11.5%, respectively. An increase is also detected in the percentage of students who made a suicide attempt requiring medical attention; males increased from 1% in 1991 to 2.4% in 2003; females increased from 2.5% to 3.2% in the same time period. Thus, although rates of completed suicide have declined, these data suggest there is no reason to be complacent.

Combining data from the U.S. Census Bureau and the NCHS, the following profile emerges. The overall U.S. population increased approximately 27% in the years from 1980 to 2002. In that same period, the number of deaths of children aged 5 to 14 years declined by 33%, suggesting considerable progress given the population increase. Declines are found in the number of accidental injuries, as well as deaths from cancer. In contrast, during this same period, the number of suicide deaths in that age group increased by 86%. For the 15- to 24-year-old age group, death from all causes declined by 33%, and the rate of suicide also decreased by 23%. It seems that there is a greater reduction in suicide among older teens and young adults than in younger children and early teens. Although the rate has declined among older teens, it lags behind the improvement seen for other causes of death.

Role of Schools

Schools are a logical context in which to address the issue of child and adolescent suicide. Most children attend school 5 days a week for 36 weeks a year, where they are in contact with trained professionals who are in a position to provide information, observe behavior, recognize an increase in stress, and build trusting relationships. Key among those professionals is the school counselor, whose specialized training and skills argue for a central role in the school's efforts to reduce suicidal behaviors among youth.

Prevention. The concepts of primary, secondary, and tertiary prevention are useful frames for the schools' role in suicide reduction (Poland, 1989). Primary prevention efforts target the general population (all students) and have as a goal increasing awareness and knowledge of suicide along with enhancing resilience in students in order to prevent suicidal ideation from emerging. Primary prevention programs are usually components of the curriculum (e.g., health) delivered by teachers or school counselors in a classroom setting. Some programs include a screening component, by which students at risk for developing suicidal behaviors are identified, either by staff or by students themselves. These students are encouraged to seek assistance in order to prevent the emergence of suicidal behaviors. One of the resources for help for students at risk is the school counselor.

Secondary prevention efforts target those who are known or believed to be at risk for developing suicidal behaviors. These students may be identified by screening procedures, referred by self or others (parents, teachers, administrators), or referred by contact from outside agencies (police, health providers). Services to these students may take the form of support groups, other counseling groups (e.g., self-esteem building), monitoring, and programs designed to address other risk factors (e.g., substance abuse) and thus may indirectly impact the risk for suicide. Even programs (such as buddy systems) for new students can be considered secondary prevention of suicide, as transitions are known stressors that increase risk for suicide in vulnerable students. These prevention efforts are often provided, initiated, and monitored by the school counselor.

Tertiary prevention involves actions directed at those who have already been affected by a suicide, including students who have made an attempt and then return to school and students who have been exposed to the suicide of a friend or family member. The goal of tertiary prevention is to reduce the level of distress and assist students in returning to their former level of functioning. This includes monitoring for signs of increased suicidal ideation, as loss is frequently a precipitant of suicidal behavior. Again, it is the school counselor who is largely responsible for providing these services.

Intervention. The role of the school becomes one of intervention when a student has been identified as suicidal. The student is provided with support, while the counselor assesses the lethality of the student's suicidal behaviors. The specifics of this task will be discussed in greater detail in the Practice section below. At this point, it is important to note that the counselor has a responsibility to notify the parents or guardians and assist them in obtaining appropriate psychological services for the student, from outpatient counseling to hospitalization. The school counselor must also notify the school administration according to established procedures.

Postvention. One of the most difficult aspects of dealing with suicide in the school is responding to the suicide of a student. Again, details of postvention strategies will be discussed below, but it is important to recognize that there is a fine line to walk between ignoring and glamorizing a suicide while providing support to those students who are most affected. In addition, a topic that receives too little attention is that of the impact of a student suicide on the counselor who may be providing support for students, family, and teachers and whose own needs are often ignored.

Court rulings. School counselors' concerns about liability increase their stress when dealing with a possibly suicidal student. The school counselor must weigh the potential impact on the counseling relationship if confidentiality is breached against the responsibility for protecting students and taking all possible steps to prevent a suicide. Despite the prevailing view that "It is not easy for bereaved parents to hold a school board liable for their child's suicide" (Cafaro, 2000, p. 25), and the collateral belief that courts are reluctant to hold school counselors or other school personnel liable for injuries, the courts have increasingly ruled that certain acts of violence (to self or others) can be predicted, which means that school counselors could be sued on that basis (Capuzzi, 2002). Some of the influential court cases will be summarized below.

A case that signaled a willingness of courts to hear cases in which a school's liability for a student suicide is the basis of the suit was that of *Kelson v. City of Springfield, Oregon* (1985; Mathai, 2002). Although the case was settled out of court, it was the first case in which a lawsuit was allowed when the school did not intentionally harm the child. The basis of the suit was the inadequate training of district employees to respond to this situation. In this case, a 14-year-old boy killed himself with a gun he had brought to school. Administrators had seen the gun, read a suicide note written by the student, denied his request to see the school counselor, and permitted the student to go to the restroom alone, where he shot himself.

Another relevant case, particularly for school counselors, is that of *Eisel v. Board of Education of Montgomery County, Maryland* (1991; Pate, 1992). This case was significant in that the highest state court overturned the rulings of lower courts, which had held that school counselors were immune from liability for the suicide of a student. Earlier rulings had released school counselors from liability unless the counselor had "physical responsibility for the client" (p. 16). In this case, the friends of a 13-year-old student told their school counselor that a friend of theirs told them she intended to commit suicide. The friends' counselor told the student's counselor, who discussed it with the student. The student denied that she had made the reported statements. The counselor took no further action, and the student later died in a murder–suicide pact with another girl. The victim's father sued, saying that the counselor should have notified him in order to prevent the suicide. The case was returned to lower courts to determine whether the counselors in the case had information and whether the suicide was related to their failure to contact her parent, but the appeals court was clear that school counselors have a duty to prevent the suicide of a student when they are aware of the danger. The ruling, which stated that "school counselors have a duty to use reasonable means to prevent a suicide when they are on notice of a child or adolescent student's suicidal threat" (*Eisel v. Board of Education of Montgomery County, 1991*, as cited in Milsom, 2002, p. 456), should be the basis of school counselors' decision making in these situations. Note that notifying a parent is often the "reasonable means."

These cases stress that school counselors should take any threat of suicide seriously, and that they are expected to respond in a way that demonstrates they are exercising the same degree of care as would other school counselors of similar education and experience (Hermann, 2002).

Training of School Counselors for the Role in School Suicide Prevention, Intervention, and Postvention

Specific training for the school counselors' role in dealing with suicide is lacking in most graduate training programs (Foster & McAdams, 1999). Council for Accreditation of Counseling and Related Educational Programs (CACREP) guidelines do not require training for suicide response, and most programs, even those not accredited by that organization, follow CACREP guidelines in designing their curricula. If an elective course in crisis intervention or suicide is available, not all students will have that training. Thus, most school counselors rely on general counseling skills and techniques, and professional training workshops and other sources, for their skill development.

A national survey of 186 high school counselors revealed that only 57% had received information about suicide from college classes. Professional workshops and conferences on suicide were the source of information for 84% of respondents, with on-the-job training (66%) and in-service programs (40%) also utilized (King, Price, Telljohann, & Wahl, 2000). Mathai (2002) found that only 68% of her sample of 517 school counselors believed they were adequately prepared to respond to a crisis involving suicide; 93% and 81% reported feeling prepared to deal with suicidal ideation and suicidal gestures, respectively. She observed that more school counselors in the sample said they were prepared than said they had had training in responding to a crisis involving suicide, and concluded that experience must be an important factor in school counselors' self-efficacy in responding to a suicidal crisis.

Several studies investigated the knowledge and confidence of high school counselors regarding working with suicidal students. King et al. (2000) found that the majority of counselors were knowledgeable about the risk factors for adolescent suicide, and most knew the appropriate steps to take if a student was suicidal. Most also knew what should be done in the event of a suicide (postvention strategies). Results also indicated, however, that only 38% of their sample of high school counselors believed they could recognize a student at risk for suicide. This finding is a concern, as knowing what to do if a student threatens suicide is useful, but if the counselor is unable to identify students at risk, he or she may not have the opportunity to intervene. It is important to note that this study utilized a questionnaire, and one cannot predict actual behavior from the responses.

By comparison, King and Smith (2000) reported that of the school counselors in Dallas, Texas, who participated in the SOAR (Suicide Options, Awareness, and Relief) training provided by the district, 56% indicated they believed they could identify a student at risk for suicide. This finding suggests that training is helpful in increasing counselors' confidence and self-efficacy regarding suicide intervention. Counselor educators must recognize the frequency with which school counselors deal with all aspects of suicide, and they must ensure that their graduate programs prepare them for this role. Commenting on the lack of suicide training in graduate psychology programs, Dexter-Mazza (2004) noted, "Overall, graduate programs need to do a better job of providing formal training to students in working with suicidal clients. Students should be provided with opportunities to receive formal training through special topic courses, lectures, workshops, and practicum experiences" (¶ 7). This recommendation seems appropriate for graduate programs in school counseling as well.

Theory

There is no single widely accepted theory of suicidal behavior. In fact, theory development has been overlooked in the field of suicidology (Laux, 2002; Rogers, 2001; Westefeld et al., 2000). Several theories have been proposed and will briefly be described below (see Laux; Westefeld et al., 2000).

The Overlap Model developed by Blumenthal and Kupfer (1986) proposed five areas or domains that influence suicidal behaviors. These domains are (1) the psychosocial milieu (which includes social support), (2) biological vulnerability (including early development), (3) psychiatric disorders, (4) personality factors (including aggression and impulsivity), and (5) family history and genetics. Each domain is conceived of as a circle, with portions of the circles overlapping. The greater the area of overlap of the five circles, the higher the risk for suicide.

Jacobs, Brewer, and Klein-Benham (1999) suggested a three-element model, which includes (1) predisposing factors, (2) potentiating factors, and (3) a suicide threshold. In this model, predisposing factors are mental disorders, substance abuse, and schizophrenia. Potentiating factors are family history, the social context, personality disorders, stressors, and access to firearms or other lethal means. The combination of these factors impels a person toward the suicidal threshold and suicidal behavior.

The Suicide Trajectory model was proposed by Stillion, McDowell, and May (1989, as cited in Stillion & McDowell, 1996) and is based on the premise that a combination of biological, cognitive, psychological, and environmental risk factors interact to bring the individual to consider suicide (suicidal ideation). Suicidal ideation begins when the combined pressure from the four risk factors overtaxes the individual's coping skills. Once suicidal ideation has occurred, if a triggering event ("last straw") is added to the mix, the individual engages in suicidal behavior.

The Cubic model (Shneidman, 1987) is composed of 125 cubelets which together form a cube with three planes: (1) press, (2) pain, and (3) perturbation. *Press* involves things that happen to a person, both positive and negative, with more negative presses (e.g., humiliation, failure, and rejection) moving the person closer to suicide. In the model, the opposite sides of the plane are positive and negative. It is not the events that create the press, but the individual's interpretation of those events that is critical. *Pain* results from unmet psychological needs. Those needs include autonomy, achievement, recognition, nurture, and avoidance of shame and humiliation. The third plane, *perturbation*, refers to the condition of being upset, which can lead to black and white thinking and tunnel vision (constriction). This plane ranges from low to high. The three planes can be rated from 1 to 5, with 5 being the greatest intensity. With three ratings of 5, an individual is at maximum risk for suicide because the individual is experiencing maximum pain, press, and perturbation. Shneidman expressed the belief that intolerable pain is the central feature of suicide and that all other risk factors are only important in the ways they cause current pain. He also suggested that the model provides keys to treatment: "(a) reduce the hurt, (b) lift the blinders, (c) pull back from action, and (d) lighten the pressure, even just a little bit" (p. 177).

A comprehensive theory of suicide developed by Rogers (2001) was based on both existential principles and constructivist theory. He proposed that humans attach meaning to the world and the people who populate it. The meaning is created in a social context and is in some ways constrained by the environment. In this theory, environmental challenges (triggering events) cause the individual to consider response options, which, according to Rogers, consist of altering constructions (*accommodation*), keeping constructions (*assimilation*), or suicide. The school counselor might find this theory useful when there is an identifiable precipitating event. For example, if the triggering event is a loss of a relationship, the underlying construction might be "Important relationships must last forever," or "If he or she stops loving me, I am not worthy of being loved" (p. 23). The counselor might then assist the student in revising the underlying constructions, helping them be less rigid (modifying "must," "always," and "never" ideas) or reframing the event, so the loss is viewed as an opportunity for learning. Rogers considered these interventions to be short-term crisis response strategies, which is the kind of intervention the school counselor might make. The student would be referred to outside resources, who would help the student examine the various influences that contributed to the maladaptive constructions, with a potential outcome of revising the constructions so that they are more flexible.

Although none of these theories is widely accepted, each has something to contribute, and the school counselor's thinking about suicide might be clarified using a theoretical model. Research related to suicide is the topic of the next section.

Research

Much of the research in suicide has been devoted to identifying risk and protective factors for suicidal behaviors. A knowledge of risk factors allows the school counselor to be more vigilant with vulnerable youth. In this section, we will briefly review research on risk and protective factors, and then summarize the research related to depression in children and adolescents, which has been strongly linked to suicidal behavior. Then we will examine the available research on the efficacy of suicide prevention programs in schools. We will consider the impact of this information on the counselor's ability to predict suicidal behavior. Finally, we will discuss the methodological concerns with research in this field. First, however, we will review aspects of development that help explain suicidal behavior in children and adolescents, as these factors (which can be both risk and protective factors) are necessary to understand this population.

In addition to the known risk factors, what do we know about children that might explain suicidal behavior in youth? In younger children, a lack of cognitive maturity may allow them to maintain a belief that death is temporary or that death is a pleasant state (Pfeffer, 1997). They may believe that their death will reunite divorced parents, or that they will be the constant preoccupation in the thoughts of others once they are dead. Other misunderstandings, such as the belief that they will have a reunion with dead family members or the fantasy that they will watch others grieve over their death, may impel some children to this extreme behavior (Stefanowski-Harding, 1990). Some may have a heightened experience of hopelessness under stress because of their cognitive immaturity and inability to think abstractly and hypothetically.

Prepubertal children think concretely, often in black and white dichotomies, which make it difficult for them to generate multiple solutions to a problem. Young children are not able to estimate the lethality of a method or to envision the outcomes of their behavior (Pfeffer, 1997). The good news is that their ability to plan and carry out a suicidal plan is also limited by their immaturity (Goldman & Beardslee, 1999).

Some risk factors, such as depression, are difficult to detect in children, as symptoms manifest differently in children than in adults. (Bauman, 2004). This is also true for adolescents, who may mask depression with a variety of behaviors such as promiscuous sexual activity, acting out or delinquency, substance abuse, eating disorders, and even physical symptoms. Some have theorized that adolescent substance abuse often begins as an attempt to ameliorate depressive symptoms (Allberg & Chu, 1990). Other characteristics of adolescent thinking, originally described by Elkind (1967), are the imaginary audience or adolescent egocentrism, and the personal fable of invincibility. Adolescent egocentrism influences suicidal thinking in several ways: Adolescents have a sense that others are watching them closely and notice any deviation from perfection, which magnifies any perceived flaw or mistake, thereby increasing the level of distress. In addition, they may also believe that their death will have a momentous impact on others, that those who have wronged them will be overwhelmed with guilt and shock, and that their death will show the world how badly they have been treated. Although most adolescents have the cognitive understanding of the finality of death, they may "forget" this in their preoccupation with romanticized notions of the impact of their death on others. Their need to communicate or make a statement to the world predominates, and the finality of death is relegated to a minor role in their thinking (Allberg & Chu, 1990).

Many adolescents who engage in suicidal behavior have experienced a significant loss and may come from families in which mental illness, addictions, and other unhealthy environmental elements are common. These children and adolescents lack models for effective coping skills and are unequipped to deal with stresses in their own lives. Further, they may not be able to communicate their pain to adults in the family and by generalization to any adult, and so they experience acute isolation and a sense of helplessness and hopelessness. Such conditions are the breeding grounds for suicidal thinking. Even in families with a more positive environment, adolescents are in the process of separating from parents and establishing their own identities, which may deprive them of parental support at a time when it would be most needed. They are more likely to confide in peers than in adults, and adolescents may not have the skills to respond to a suicidal friend.

Any discussion of risk and protective factors for youth suicide must begin with a caveat. The presence of a single risk factor is not evidence of suicidal tendencies, with one exception: A previous attempt is a major risk factor (Zametkin et al., 2005). In fact, many individuals, both youth and adult, possess multiple risk factors and never contemplate suicide. Haley (2004) categorized risk factors into two categories: (1) *predisposing factors*, which are those underlying, more chronic and enduring factors, and (2) *potentiating factors*, which are the immediate situational influences on a suicidal event. Moscicki (1995, as cited in McKeown et al., 1998) used the terms *distal factors* (mental disorders, genetics, and family factors) and *proximal* (situational factors and stressors) to distinguish the two categories. It is widely accepted that predisposing distal factors combine with proximal factors in a social context to increase the risk for suicidal behavior (McKeown et al., 1998). Here we focus mainly on proximal factors.

Proximal Factors

McKeown and his colleagues (1998) have cautioned that focusing on stressors may cause one to overlook the important influences of mental disorders and family factors in suicidal behavior in adolescents. That is, while stressors might be the immediate factor, they are unlikely to impel a youth to suicide without the presence of the other underlying factors.

Stressful life events contribute to the risk for suicide in youth. In younger children and adolescents, conflict with parents is associated with increased risk for suicidal behavior, while for older adolescents, romantic problems and breakups are seen more often. The loss of an important relationship is a factor in up to 70% of suicide attempts or completions (Jacobs, 1999). It is likely that in children and adolescents whose suicidal behavior is precipitated by an actual or perceived loss, there were other risk factors present prior to the stressor. Children may not have the cognitive maturity to generate alternative solutions to problems, and if they also lack coping skills and the support of a caring adult, suicide may appear to be the only choice.

Kirk (1993) grouped adolescent stressors into two different groups: (1) those that are *expected and normative* (such as puberty, physical changes, school changes, and/or cognitive changes) and (2) those that are *unexpected* or *extreme* stressors (such as physical illnesses; developmental delays; parental separation, divorce, or death; death of a friend; abuse; legal difficulties, and/or sexual problems). A nationwide Gallup Organization (1994) survey was conducted in 1991 and was then repeated three years later. Of those participants who came close to or actually made an attempt, the most often cited stressor preceding an attempt was family problems, followed by depression, low self-esteem, peer problems, life in general, and school problems.

Kalafat (1990) distinguished between *causes* (risk factors) and *precipitants*, events that occur in an at-risk student's life that may push that student to make an attempt. He observed that it is not simply being in trouble (with school or police) that is the precipitant, but uncertainty and intense fear of what might happen increase the danger. Disappointment and rejection (however minor they may seem to someone else) may also be the impetus. I recall a suicide that shocked a community because the high school senior seemed to "have it all." He was a top student, an athlete, from an affluent family, and so forth. Although he had received several attractive offers from colleges, when he was rejected by the prestigious institution that was his first choice, he shot himself. Anxiety over impending change (again, however small to an outsider) can become so intense that the youth becomes desperate. A change in schools, or even in classes, as well as major changes in family constellations, can trigger some youth to suicide. If a vulnerable youth has experienced the death of someone important, the anniversary of that loss might revive the sadness and impel the youth to make an attempt.

In addition to evidence for risk factors, several protective factors have been identified. Using data from a sample of 13,110 students in grades 7 through 12, Borowsky, Ireland, and Resnick (2001) found that for all subjects, perceived strong relationships with parents and family reduced the risk for suicide. For females, an additional protective factor was emotional well-being, while for boys, grade point average served as a protective factor. Data indicated that for some males, high parental expectations for school achievement, more people residing in the household, and religiosity were protective; while for girls, counseling services at school and parental presence at home at important times in the day were protective. Interestingly, these findings for girls or boys did not apply to the opposite gender. Further analysis showed that for females with all identified risk factors, including a previous attempt and few protective factors, the probability of a suicide attempt in the time period between two interviews (interval averaged 11 months) was 36%. For African Americans with no risk factors and high levels of protective factors, the probability was 0.2%. Most important, for all racial/ethnic groups and both genders, the presence of three of the protective factors reduced the probability of an attempt by 70% to 85%. Family closeness and religiosity were also found to be protective in Latino adolescents (O'Donnell, Stueve, Wardlaw, & O'Donnell, 2003). Social support is a protective factor, in contrast to social isolation, which elevates risk for suicide (Rutter, 2004).

Prevention Programs

The absence of solid research evaluating the effectiveness of suicide prevention programs has been noted by researchers (e.g., Aseltine & DeMartino, 2004; Breton, Tousignant, Bergeron, & Berthiaume, 2002; Eggert, Thompson, Randell, & Pike, 2002). Although many schools have formal suicide prevention programs, less than 40% of a sample of high school counselors agreed that their school or district had a written policy specifying how a prevention and intervention program is evaluated (Malley, Kush, & Bogo, 1996). A review of school-based suicide prevention programs with suicide or suicide attempts as outcome measures was conducted in 2001 by the Harborview Injury Prevention and Research Center (HIPRC) at the University of Washington. Based on six studies published between 1997 and 2000, the reviewers concluded that there was only weak evidence for the effectiveness of such programs, but there was also no evidence that the programs resulted in an increase of attempts or suicide associated with the programs.

A more recent review (Doan, Roggenbaum, & Lazear, 2003) examined several school-based programs, including evaluation information. Most of these evaluations used outcome measures other than suicide attempts or suicide. HIPRC (n.d.) noted that there is insufficient empirical evidence that other outcome measures other than attempts or suicides correlate with suicide risk. Nevertheless, a brief overview of 10 of these programs will be included here, based on the Doan et al. review, unless other sources are cited.

BRIDGES is a program designed to increase skills of school personnel, including school counselors. Participants learn assessment and intervention skills to use with students, families, and peers and are assisted in developing school policies and procedures for dealing with all aspects of suicide. Evaluation information was not available at the time this chapter was written.

Project C-CARE is an individualized assessment interview, using a computer-assisted program (Measure of Adolescent Potential for Suicide) followed by a brief counseling session and contact with the parents. Extensive evaluation studies have been conducted on this approach.

Project CAST is often used with the C-CARE program when the student is found to be at risk for suicidal behavior. The program begins 4 weeks after the C-CARE component, and utilizes a 12-session structured group program at the student's school over a 6-week period. Research using randomized experimental design compared effects of C-CARE, C-CARE plus CAST, and treatment "as usual" with 341 potential school dropouts who were identified as at risk for suicidal behaviors (Eggert et al., 2002; Randell, Eggert, & Pike, 2001). As expected, participants in all three conditions demonstrated reductions in suicidal behaviors, depression, and drug involvement, but the reduction in depression was greater for the two experimental conditions than for the usual care group. In addition, the CAST program participants evidenced greater reductions in problem alcohol and drug involvement compared with the other two conditions. C-CARE plus CAST students demonstrated increases in other factors considered to have an impact on suicidal behaviors: personal control, problem solving, coping skills, and perceived family support. Both C-CARE and C-CARE plus CAST students showed decreased depression and enhanced self-esteem, and met family goals. Note that in all cases, the effects were measured at the end of the CAST program for all three groups; follow-up data were not reported. The same research team, however, also examined the program's effects on 460 at-risk youth and included a 9-month follow-up assessment. Results showed a faster rate of decline in attitude toward suicide and suicidal ideation in the two treatment groups compared with the control group, and the reductions in suicidal behaviors were maintained at a 9-month follow-up. The two treatment conditions also showed long-term decreases in depression and hopelessness, and CAST showed increases in personal control and problem-solving abilities (Thompson, Eggert, Randell, & Pike, 2001). Overall, research has provided promising empirical evidence of the possible effectiveness of the program.

Signs of Suicide (SOS) resulted in an increase in the number of youth seeking counseling for themselves or friends following the program (Aseltine & DeMartino, 2004). This program has been selected by the Substance Abuse and Mental Health Services Administration (SAMHSA; 2007) as a Promising Program, which means it has been deemed to have demonstrated positive outcomes, but has not yet provided evidence of consistent positive outcomes in carefully controlled research designs. The program utilizes a video and discussion guide that are covered in one to three class periods, as well as a depression screening instrument (the Columbia Depression Scale). The students are taught the elements of the acronym ACT: *acknowledge* the signs of suicide in peers, let the person know you *care* about them, and *tell* a responsible adult. An experimental design using random assignment to treatment and control conditions was used to evaluate the program by posttest only. Students in the treatment group self-reported significantly 40% fewer suicide attempts than the control group. The impact of the program on student help-seeking, however, was not significant nor was level of suicidal ideation. Despite some limitations, this research was important in that it evaluated a school-based program using a randomized experimental design (Aseltine & DeMartino).

Miami-Dade County Department of Crisis Management Prevention Program was established in 1987 to assist staff in schools (and community agencies) in identifying, assisting, and referring at-risk students by training "crisis care core teams" in each school. The program includes a hotline to provide assistance to staff, and a curriculum component for K–12; the topic of suicide is not directly addressed until the 10th grade component. Data indicate that the program did not decrease reported suicidal ideation, but did decrease suicide attempts and completions. Note that there was no comparison group reported, and participants were not randomly assigned to treatment.

Services for Teens at Risk (STAR) offers three programs directed at school personnel. In the first program, teachers and other school staff are taught to recognize risk factors and make appropriate referrals. The next level provides training in evaluation of risk and working with families and providers of mental health services as well as students. The third level trains school personnel to deliver the first level training in their setting. No evaluation data were available.

The Columbia TeenScreen Program conducts screening and assessment for depression and other disorders that put a youth at risk for suicide. The program makes available a computerized interview to those who are identified in a paper-and-pencil screen as in need of the more in-depth interview. An evaluation conducted in 1996 found that the process identified many teens at risk for suicide whose risk was not known prior to the screening. Their Web site (http://www.teenscreen.org/) indicates the program is used in 40 states. Although program implementation may vary among sites, precluding overall evaluation, research was conducted to determine whether asking about suicide (as in a screening or follow-up interview) caused distress or increased suicidal behavior (Gould et al., 2005). The randomized controlled study with 2,342 high school students found no evidence that the suicide screening increased either distress or suicidal behaviors.

Dallas school counselors were involved in a program to train all counselors in the district on interviewing and assessment techniques for use with students who threaten suicide. An evaluation of Project SOAR (Suicide, Options, Awareness, and Relief) observed that efficacy for suicide intervention was higher in the school counselor group receiving the SOAR training than in those who did not. The overall rate of those who strongly believed they could identify a potentially suicidal student, however, was only 56% (King & Smith, 2000). This speaks to the importance of school counselors' need for information, training, and supervision in working with suicide prevention, intervention, and postvention.

A curriculum program was developed and delivered to Zuni (American Indian) adolescents attending their local high school. Researchers developed a life skills program (treatment condition) that was delivered by two nonnative teachers paired with two Zuni cultural resource persons; one nonnative teacher provided the usual curriculum, which was the no-intervention condition. A life skills curriculum was chosen because it was thought to be effective in reducing cognitive and behavioral risk factors for suicide and to be culturally appropriate for the population. Three methods were used in an attempt to measure the effectiveness of the program, and results were equivocal. The researchers concluded, however, that there were statistically significant positive effects from the program (LaFromboise & Howard-Pitney, 1995).

A multilevel program that includes a program for educators, parents, and students is ASAP (Adolescent Suicide Awareness Program; Kalafat & Ryerson, 1999). Program developers were concerned that programs were not maintained after initial implementation efforts, and they surveyed schools in which the program had been implemented to assess how well the program had been institutionalized. Over time, many schools dropped the ongoing educator and parent training, but most retained the student training, although for less time that the original 6-hour format. As 33 of 46 public high schools in the county had received the training, suicide rates for 15 to 24 year olds were examined for three 5-year periods (preimplementation, implementation, and postimplementation). While rates for that county were lower than those of the state and nation at all three time periods, the drop postimplementation was quite large. The authors acknowledged that this decline cannot be attributed to the program, but also noted that the decline in a county so heavily saturated with suicide prevention programming gives support to the notion that talking about suicide does not increase suicide rates. They do not provide data regarding attempts or ideation for comparison.

For school counselors interested in implementing a suicide prevention and intervention program, there are clearly a number of models from which to choose. They vary in the degree of empirical support for effectiveness, and also in target populations (staff, parents, students, community resources) and in other components, so that counselors can determine the best fit for their environments—and they do not have to reinvent the wheel!

Prediction of Suicide

Unfortunately, the accuracy with which counselors and mental health professionals are able to predict suicide on an individual basis is quite poor (Goldney, 2000; Overholser & Spirito, 2003). Because suicide has a low base rate (is fairly rare), and because the risk factors are not specific (i.e., many with the risk factors do not commit suicide), prediction on an individual basis is an educated guess. Pokorny (1983) concluded that it was not feasible to identify specific individuals who will commit suicide. Goldney (1990) conducted a follow-up to the Pokorny study (1983) and reported similar findings, saying that our ability to "predict suicide is very limited" (p. 50). Muzina (2004) observed that despite all that is known about risk factors for suicide, "it is very difficult to predict whether an individual patient will attempt it" (p. 244). This suggests that school counselors, as others who encounter suicidal individuals, are far from infallible and, thus, need to accept their limitations. Despite all the best efforts of the most skilled and concerned school counselor, it is possible that some students will commit suicide. How such events affect the counselor is the subject of the next section.

Effect on the Counselor of a Completed Suicide

Much of the literature related to the impact of client suicide has been done with psychiatrists or interns in clinical settings. No study of the impact on school counselors was located. Many of the dynamics, however, are comparable, and the lessons from the research have important implications.

Ruben (1990) identified two types of reactions in clinicians who had experienced the suicide of a client. The first is the grief response, which was similar to that of anyone experiencing the loss of an important person. Those reactions include guilt, anger, denial, and repression. In addition, there are clinician-specific reactions, such as self-blame, a sense of inadequacy, and responsibility for the death. The clinician's grief response is complicated by the need to respond to family members, colleagues, supervisors, and others. In the case of the school counselor, this includes having to be of assistance to students. At times, the family may seek to assuage their own guilt by blaming others, which intensifies any guilt the counselor may already feel.

Gorkin (1985) proposed two factors that affect the clinician's ability to deal with a suicide. First, the greater the level of omnipotence (the belief that the clinician should be able to do everything for a client or student) the more difficult the impact of the loss might be. The second factor is the nature of the relationship to the deceased client. If the relationship included hostility (expressed or unexpressed), the grief process will be more difficult. Gorkin's signs of "pathological mourning" include the following: excessive feelings of guilt, expectations of harsh judgment from colleagues and supervisors, obsessing about one's ability to continue to do the job, and doubts about the value of counseling or therapy. When these factors are present, it is difficult for school counselors to be effective in their work, as they may avoid the mention of suicide or working with student at risk for suicide, or they may become overly careful and reactive when the subject comes up.

Other researchers cited by Ruben (1990) found young or less experienced therapists felt desolated by the lack of support from peers. He recommended that when a counselor learns of a suicide of a client, the counselor should gather as much unbiased, accurate information as possible before talking with others. Counselors should seek trusted colleagues and supervisor for support and should recognize that some symptoms, such as nightmares, are common. Depending on how severe the symptoms are, Ruben has advised counselors to seek professional help. This advice certainly applies to school counselors.

Several other studies could be reported here, but results are similar to those already discussed. It is important to consider the case of a school counselor who experiences the loss of a student. I have unfortunately had that experience and can attest to the accuracy of the research findings. An added difficulty for a school counselor, as opposed to a counselor in another setting, is the isolation from colleagues who can provide support (and hopefully, relieve the grieving counselor of some duties in the immediate aftermath). Some high schools have large counseling departments, but small or rural schools may not. In addition, principals and other administrators may not be prepared to deal with suicide and may in their own shock and grief be unable or unwilling to provide needed support. The presence of district crisis response teams can be a lifeline for the counselor in this situation. In my case, they were available, responsive, supportive, and helpful. Had they not been, it is likely that the experience would have been far more devastating. Speaking to school counselors who were actively involved in postvention after the suicide of a student, Stefanowski-Harding (1990) said, "If you do not talk to a crisis team, talk to someone—other staff people, other counselors, friends, or mental health professionals. Be sure to nurture yourself the way you nurture your clients" (p. 335).

Practice

In this section, we will discuss the elements of good prevention programs, review available assessment instruments that are appropriate for children and adolescents, discuss intervention and referral practices, and review important components of an effective postvention response. Then we will examine the needs of elementary and secondary school counselors, and reflect on pertinent ethical issues. We will end this section with a discussion of issues related to diversity.

Prevention Programs

Because specific prevention programs were reviewed early in this chapter, the focus here will be to identify elements that have been found to be important for implementation in schools; however, experts do not agree on which components of a suicide prevention program are necessary or helpful. For example, while most experts support training of staff, suicide awareness in the student curriculum is still quite controversial. In their training materials, the Center for Mental Health in the Schools (CMHS; 2002) urged caution in using an education component with students. They have based their concern on the scant research findings which indicate that while students do gain some *knowledge* about suicide, they do not change *attitudes* towards suicide or help-seeking *behaviors* after such education. Further, they point out that at least one study found harmful effects on students who had made a prior suicide attempt.

Garland and Zigler (1993) are concerned that some curricula, in an effort to destigmatize suicide, avoid mentioning the link to mental illness. The intent is to make help-seeking for suicidal thinking or behaviors more acceptable to youth who may have a negative perception of mental illness. Doing so, however, may indirectly suggest that suicide is a normal (if extreme) response to stress, a view that can easily be misinterpreted by vulnerable youth. Some programs may utilize popular media, which tend to glamorize suicide and send the wrong message to those at risk. Kalafat (1990) has also advised against using media that depict a suicide. Another concern is that because many students at risk are not actually attending school (runaways, dropouts, incarcerated youth, and truants), the message may not reach the target population (Garland & Zigler).

Others (Kalafat, 1990; Poland, 1989) believe that students already know about suicide and that accurate information is important. They encourage educators to incorporate suicide awareness into the curriculum, but advise careful planning and scrutiny of that curriculum. One recent approach that merits such scrutiny is outlined by J. S. Wodarski, L. A. Wodarski, and Dulmus (2003) in their book, which serves as a manual for the educator. The curriculum is a student team–based approach because the authors believe that students increase self-esteem and develop positive peer relationships in such a format. There are both adolescent and parent components: Adolescents focus on education, skill development, and problem solving, while parents receive the same information that the students do, along with communication techniques designed to strengthen the parent–child relationship. The student curriculum is a 6-week course, using 50 minutes per day. The parent program is delivered to parent groups in six 2-hour weekly sessions. No evaluation of the program is provided.

School counselors who are considering how best to prevent suicide in their schools might ponder this statement from the Center for Disease Control: "Many suicide researchers believe that broad-based primary prevention programs focusing on health enhancement may be of greater value than programs that address only suicide" (MHS, 2002, p. 24). Note that in the description of prevention programs earlier in this chapter, several programs do take the broader approach to educating students. Dyck (1991) reviewed the obstacles to implementing suicide prevention in schools, and the eager school counselor might refer to his chapter before moving forward.

Kalafat (1990) and Poland (1989) stress the importance of effective and frequent training for all staff. As cafeteria workers, custodians, bus drivers, and so forth all interact with children and may have different perspectives for observing them, they should all be included in the training. A single training, delivered in one or two hours, can provide adequate background for staff. In addition to providing information and statistics about youth suicide, staff should receive information on specific procedures for identifying and referring potentially suicidal students. Garland and Zigler (1993) contend that educating school counselors, teachers, and other staff does not involve the danger that curriculum-based programs have for imitation effects on adolescents. Parent training is also recommended by many experts, and several developed programs have a parent component as part of the package.

Screening and Assessment

Whether large-scale screening should be conducted in schools is also open to debate. There is no doubt, however, that school counselors are the school professionals who will have responsibility to assess risk for suicide (Davis & Sandoval, 1991; Poland, 1989; Stefanowski-Harding, 1990). In this section, we will discuss some principles related to suicide assessment, review available assessment tools the school counselor may wish to use, and also provide some informal, widely used assessment techniques.

Before discussing the specifics of assessment, we should point out the importance of basic clinical communication skills. Talking about suicide is not everyday conversation, and approaching an adolescent on this topic requires sensitivity and empathy. Further, the counselor needs to be firm in conveying that suicide is not an acceptable option. The school counselor should appear comfortable discussing death and suicide, genuinely concerned about the student, and competent to make appropriate decisions and take necessary action. Some counselors choose to tell students that they have helped many suicidal students and that they will help the present student as well.

The school counselor must also wrestle with the issue of trust and confidentiality. In the current climate, it is wise to notify parents when there are any concerns about suicide, but counselors may fear that they will lose the student's trust by doing so. First, school counselors should always make sure all students are informed about the limits of confidentiality by explaining those limits clearly and often. Many school counselors have posters in their offices with that information. Second, if the counselor explains to the student why the contact must be made, students are less likely to feel betrayed. In many cases, the counselor may offer to have the student and counselor tell the parents together. This is where sensitivity and clear communication are essential.

In addition to suicide risk factors we have discussed, there are also danger signals that should alert school counselors that a complete assessment should be conducted. Kirk (1993) pointed out that students may not communicate suicidal thinking or behaviors directly, but reading between the lines can help the skilled counselor identify clues. Seemingly, vague statements such as, "I'm sick of everything" or "I wish I had never been born" should be considered as communication of possible suicidal thinking and should be explored with the student. Some students will reveal their feelings or fantasies about death in poems, writing, and art, which also need to be taken as signals worthy of attention. The giving away of possessions is a very clear and loud signal that suicide is a real possibility, and the counselor must intervene if that information is known. The same is true for funeral arrangements (or invitations) that are sometimes discounted. These signals are messages that must not be ignored. This is a time for more in-depth assessment of suicide risk

I will describe in some detail several widely used assessment approaches. Each uses an acronym to help the clinician remember to inquire about all pertinent issues.

The SLAP method is used when the counselor learns of a client's suicidal ideation:

S = How SPECIFIC is the plan? Has the client thought about details? Does the client have a time frame? Has the client made special arrangements to make sure the plan will work? A client whose plan is more specific is at higher risk. For example, a client who says, "I'm going to take some pills" is at lower risk than one who says, "I'm going to pick up a refill on my prescription for Valium and take them all with a stiff Bloody Mary."

L = How LETHAL is the plan? Firearms are the most lethal, along with jumping from high places or jumping in front of moving cars. Hanging, overdose, and cutting can also be lethal, but can more easily be reversed if the person has second thoughts, and they are also more easily interrupted by others. The more lethal the plan, the higher the risk.

A = How AVAILABLE is the method? If the client intends to shoot himself in the head, does he have a gun, or does he plan to go to a store and buy one? Does the client who intends to overdose on barbiturates already have them, or will she have to make an appointment and request a prescription? Does the client who intends to use a knife have a knife selected? The more available the means, the higher the risk.

P = Are others in close PROXIMITY? Are there significant others who could interrupt or interfere with the plan? Are there others whose help can be enlisted (e.g., to remove firearms from the home, flush medication, remain with the client)? The greater the distance and isolation of the client, the higher the risk.

One potent risk factor for suicide is a previous attempt. When the clinician learns that there has been such an attempt, the DIRT method is a useful tool to assess the seriousness of that attempt:

D = How DANGEROUS was the attempt, or how lethal was the method used?

I = What was the client's IMPRESSION of the lethality? In this case, the clinician wants to know how lethal the client believed the method to be. For example, taking ten Tylenol may not be highly lethal from a medical perspective, but if the client *believed* he would die, that is more important in assessing the seriousness of the attempt.

R = What was the probability of RESCUE? Did the client take pills when others were at home? Did the client expect a friend to arrive? Did client announce his plan to others? Did she or he choose a public place (e.g., a school restroom) where she was likely to be observed and stopped?

T = What was the TIME frame of the most recent suicide attempt? The more recent the attempt, the higher the current risk.

Poland (1989) mentioned a system known as SAL for determining the lethality of a student with a plan to commit suicide. This is a mnemonic for gathering information about the *specificity* of the plan, the *availability* of the method, and the *lethality* of the method.

Another scale that utilizes an acronym as a mnemonic device for clinicians is the SAD PERSONS scale (Patterson, Dohn, Bird, & Patterson, 1983). This scale has been adapted for use with children and adolescents (Juhnke, 1996); its modified version is called the Adapted Sad Persons Scale (A-SPS). Goldston (2003) noted that there is no research providing data on reliability of validity of this measure, but there are few measures with such data. Reliability and validity of suicide assessments are problematic for ethical reasons. No researcher would choose not to intervene in the case of a client assessed at high risk for suicide in order to test the validity of the scale.

This scale is more formal in that there are guidelines for interpretation. The scale has demonstrated usefulness in accurately evaluating suicide risk. This method is easily learned and used, and is a systematic approach that the school counselor can use in a crisis situation. The scale and interpretation for the child/adolescent version is described in the box below. Note that for sex, score 10 for males and 0 for females.

Scoring is 0 (absence of risk factor) to 10 (significant manifestation of risk)

S = Sex	Score if the person is male
A = Age	Score if the person is over 15
D = Depression	Score if there are signs of depression
P = Previous attempt	Score if there was a previous suicide attempt
E = Ethanol (Alcohol)	Score if there are symptoms of substance abuse
R = Rational thinking loss	Score if person is psychotic, disoriented, has bizarre thoughts, is confused, is irrational, etc.
S = Social support loss	Score if person has no close friends
O = Organized plan	Score if the person has a fairly detailed plan that is lethal
N = Negligent parenting	Score if person has had negligent parents, family stressors, or suicidal modeling by parents or siblings
S = School problems	Score if there are aggressive behaviors at school or deterioration in academic performance, or if there is an embarrassing or humiliating experience

Recommended intervention:

0–29	Encourage counseling services; counselor should follow-up; provide emergency 24-hour numbers (e.g., hotline).
30–49	Strongly recommend counseling and follow-up services, contact parent or guardian, get "no suicide" contract
50–69	Have formal evaluation for hospitalization unless follow-up arrangements and counseling plan are highly reliable
70 +	Arrange for immediate hospitalization

Juhnke (1996) provided some very useful additional information. He recommended that all students, even those in the lowest risk category, receive a card so that if there is a change in suicidal status, they have phone numbers at hand. He suggests putting emergency contact information on a business card and taping a quarter to it so the student can make a phone call. In the current era of cell phones, the quarter may not be necessary. It might be helpful to have emergency information printed on the reverse side of the school counselor's business card. There might also be a place to indicate a follow-up appointment. Juhnke also recommended that a student's parents be contacted if the score is above 30, but it is advisable to do so in almost all cases. If an outside evaluation is needed, and parents refuse, Juhnke has advised that the counselor contact the local child protective service agency.

Another useful tool is the Suicidal Tendencies Scale (Crocitto, 1990) a quick initial assessment tool easily used in the school setting. No psychometric data are presented, but is easy for the school counselor to learn and apply.

Many formal assessments are available to the counselor (see Goldston, 2003, for a thorough review of every instrument available for children and adolescents as of the publication date). The most widely used assessments in schools for screening purposes are the Suicide Ideation Questionnaire (SIQ; Reynolds, 1987) and the Suicide Probability Scale (SPS; Cull & Gill, 1988). The SIQ has forms for both high school and grades 7–9. It is available only in English, and it does not ask about suicide attempts. Given that previous attempts are a high risk factor, that information is essential in identifying high-risk students. That information may not always be forthcoming from students or parents, so obtaining that information is essential to good assessment (Kirk, 1993). The SPS was designed for use with adolescents over age 13 and contains 36 statements to which students indicate how much the statement fits them on a 4-point scale. The title on the instrument does not mention suicide. Goldston noted that the cutoff score was not very useful in identifying youth who eventually made suicide attempts. Unlike the SIQ, there is not strong empirical evidence of its usefulness.

A newer set of assessments that I have found very helpful is the Beck Youth Inventories of Emotional and Social Impairment (Beck, Beck, & Jolly, 2005). The set includes five inventories that can be used separately or together with children from 7 to 14 years of age: (1) Beck Depression Inventory for Youth, (2) Beck Anxiety Inventory for Youth, (3) Beck Anger Inventory for Youth, (4) Beck Disruptive Behavior Inventory for Youth, and (5) Beck Self-Concept Inventory for Youth. Each inventory contains 20 items written at second-grade level; the profile is very useful in looking for risk factors. The revised Beck Depression Inventory can be used with students age 13 and older, but the Beck Hopelessness Scale is normed on those age 17 and older. All of these assessments are easy to score and interpret, and have excellent psychometric properties.

Intervention

Crisis response. During a crisis, suicide or other, school counselors must deal with increased demands in a context of heightened tension and anxiety. Nevertheless, the counselor needs to remain calm and supportive. If the student senses panic on the part of the counselor, she or he is unlikely to self-disclose and may even feel guilty for creating distress on the part of the counselor. It is crucial that the counselor not minimize the concerns that have brought the student to this juncture but demonstrate sincere concern and empathy for the student's pain. Despite any personal beliefs that suicide is wrong, immoral, or stupid, the counselor must be nonjudgmental so that the student is not fearful of censure or scolding as he or she talks about suicidal feelings or behaviors. The counselor must do a thorough assessment—ideally, with the assistance of a colleague. The student can be told honestly that the counselor is very concerned and wants to enlist the additional help of Colleague X, who has been helpful in the past in such situations. Then both counselors can consult as to the best strategy for managing the crisis, including notifying parents, contacting outside agencies, and so forth. In many schools, when there has been a concern about suicide, students are required to have an outside evaluation by a qualified professional before returning to school (Capuzzi, 2002).

Many schools and school districts have created crisis response teams so that there are established policies and procedures in place before the crisis emerges, and one does not have to make decisions without guidelines. Crisis teams have organized plans and procedures and have delegated tasks to individuals with specific responsibilities and training. The school counselor should always implement the established crisis response procedure, and enlist the aid and support of team members.

Kirk (1993, pp. 97–99) outlined the steps for a school counselor to take if a suicide attempt is in progress: (1) Ensure the attempter's survival, using appropriate methods (contacting emergency services, administering first aid, etc.). (2) Assess method, gathering as much specific information as possible (type and quantity of drug ingested, location of wounds, etc). This is useful in communicating with emergency personnel. (3) Notify parents or legal guardians. If they are unwilling to respond, contact the appropriate child protective services agency. (4) Activate the school crisis team. (5) Document and report the crisis. (6) Follow-up with emergency personnel in order to be able to provide accurate information to those involved and, later, to serve as liaison with outside agencies to assist the student in reentry to school.

Kirk (1993) also provided useful guidelines when an attempt has not been made but the school counselor has reason to suspect a student is imminently suicidal: (1) Make and maintain contact with the student, making sure the student knows the counselor is listening and concerned. (2) Assess for the existence of a plan and the lethality of the method. (3) Consult with another professional. If possible, the counselor should enlist the aid of a trained colleague. (A strategy for accomplishing this without leaving the student alone will be discussed below.) (4) Notify parents and assist them in making arrangements for immediate appointment with a professional. (5) Initiate a suicide watch. It is essential that the student not be alone at all, so it may be necessary to involve others while arrangements are being made for parents to arrive. (6) Document the event. (7) Follow up as above.

When a student is at imminent risk for suicide, it is critical not to leave the student alone. It is also important to begin the process of notifying parents and consulting colleagues. It would seem that those two priorities cannot be accomplished at the same time. The use of an established procedure in such events, however, is efficient and effective. For example, in one setting in which I worked, the plan was as follows. If the counselor had a student in the office in a crisis situation, the counselor would tell the student that the counselor just needed a moment to phone to cancel a doctor's appointment. The counselor would then phone (or contact on the intercom) the secretary, telling her to please cancel my appointment with Dr. Codename. The secretary's job was then to alert others to the situation, and send someone to the counselor's office immediately. A similar code can be created to alert teachers of a high risk situation in the school, initiating a prescribed procedure to assure everyone's safety. Depending on the situation, the secretary would alert all members of the building's crisis response team to the situation, so that they are on hand to do whatever tasks are necessary. All procedures need to be clear, in writing, and reviewed on a regular basis; crisis teams should receive ongoing training and support.

No suicide contracts. This is another issue on which there are differing opinions and little empirical data to support either position. There is consensus, however, that a "no suicide" contract should never be the only intervention strategy; rather it should be one of the tools used. Weiss (2001) expressed the preference for less legalistic terminology, such as "no suicide" *pact, agreement,* or *understanding.* Poland (1989) favored the use of "no suicide" contract and recommended a written document on official school stationary. Both counselor and student sign the contract, and both receive copies. The content should include the name of the student and words to clearly state an agreement that if the student is having suicidal thoughts, he or she will contact the counselor (contact info provided), a 24-hour crisis line (number provided), or the nearest adult for help. Range et al. (2002) recommended a specific period (until the next appointment, over the weekend, etc.) because time-limited agreements are easier to keep. These experts also suggest including as one of the options going to the hospital emergency room. They also begin each contract with a statement such as "I want to live long and be happy" (p. 72). This article is an excellent source of sample contracts for children and adolescents.

Additional components of a contract might include agreements to self-care, such as getting adequate sleep and food, how unscheduled time will be structured (e.g., weekends, after school), and most important, an agreement to remove any potentially lethal means from the home, such as guns, other weapons, and medication (Capuzzi & Gross, 2004). Motto (1999) made the point that a "no suicide" contract is only appropriate in the context of a mutually trusting relationship. For the school counselor, this means that a contract is appropriate in the case of a student with whom the counselor has established a solid relationship and who has been open with the counselor about the suicide issue. A student who is referred by someone else and denies any suicidal thoughts is not one for whom such a strategy is appropriate. The student may well sign the contract in order to end the discussion, but is unlikely to have much commitment to upholding the agreement. Miller (1999) referred to a strategy of not asking the client to agree not to commit suicide, but to focus on not taking any action until the client has taken all the steps in the contract (contacting the counselor, going to the emergency room, etc.). The point of this approach is to emphasize to the client that suicide is a permanent solution, and so the counselor wants the client to try everything else before taking such a terminal step. This strategy might have some use in acknowledging the client's pain, but school counselors should be very cautious that this not be interpreted as an endorsement of suicide.

Brent and Kolko (1990) have recommended that the family also sign the contract, which is consistent with the schools' obligation to notify parents when suicide is an issue. They stress that a contract should be considered only when certain elevated risk conditions are not present: current substance abuse, psychosis, or bipolar disorder. The school counselor should follow-up the contract with questions such as, "What would you do if [the precipitant of the episode] happened again?" If the student does not refer to the agreement, there would be a concern about the value of the contract. With children, it is advisable to test their understanding of the contract by having the child repeat or explain the agreement. Kirk (1993) has also supported the use of "no suicide" contracts, which he has stated are useful because they provide structure and time while other interventions are explored and arranged (professional counseling, hospitalization). He added that proposing the contract is a useful way to assess the effectiveness of intervention so far. If the student refuses to make an agreement, that is a signal of the need for a more restrictive intervention (e.g., hospitalization). On the other hand, Weiss (2001) pointed out that a refusal to sign a contract may also signal that the relationship between the counselor and the client is fragile. Both Poland (1989) and Kirk (1993) also provided examples of written "no suicide" contracts.

Advantages of "no suicide" contracts are that they clearly specify contingency behaviors the student can use other than suicide. Students may perceive the request for the contract as evidence of the counselor's concern, which would strengthen the relationship. These contracts can reduce both the student and the counselor's anxiety in outlining such a specific protocol. In addition, the request for a contract can be used as an adjunct to more formal evaluation of risk by noting the degree of the student's willingness to agree to the contract. The contract also provides partial documentation of the counselor's effort to prevent the suicide (Range et al., 2002).

The disadvantages of the contract include the possibility that older students may see it as an attempt by the counselor to protect against lawsuits, rather than as a measure of concern for the student. It also may be perceived as coercive. There is the danger that the counselor will overly rely on such contracts, which is ill-advised, as the contract should be a component, not the sole measure, of intervention with a suicidal student (Kelly & Knudson, 2000). The counselor may also mistakenly believe that he or she is immune from liability when a contract has been signed, which is not the case (Range et al., 2002). The counselor must also remember that the contract does not eliminate the suicide risk.

What are some best practices to follow if and when a contract will be used? One is not to use a preprinted form, but to design the specifics of the individual contract collaboratively with the student. Students may provide the names and phone numbers of people to contact, and some specific strategies to manage unstructured times; this process gives them more ownership of the agreement. Also helpful is the use of positive wording wherever possible, (e.g., "I agree to keep myself safe"). Best practice includes outlining a specific time period, providing copies to appropriate persons (including parents), and employing a follow-up mechanism (Range et al., 2002).

Postvention

Following the suicide of a student (or staff member), a plan for postvention should be implemented. Ideally, members of the building crisis response team, the school district crisis response team, and community resources will work together to plan the response. Tasks that must be accomplished are (1) providing accurate information to all constituents, including students; (2) assessing survivors who might be at risk for suicide themselves; (3) providing support to grieving students and staff; and (4) dealing with media.

Postvention efforts should begin as soon as possible after the suicide (Leenaars & Wenckstern, 1991). In many cases, if the event becomes known or occurs after school hours, a phone tree can be activated to notify staff and plan a meeting before students come to school. The exact wording on any announcement to students should be agreed upon (and checked by police or other sources for accuracy). It is strongly recommended that such announcements be delivered in classroom groups by regular teachers whenever possible, and at an agreed upon time, so that all students get the same information at the same time.

When students learn of the suicide, there are a variety of possible responses. Many students who knew or were close to the deceased will be visibly upset, and they should be allowed to leave the classroom setting to see the counselor. Group support sessions can be conducted with the assistance of district and community team members. Other students who did not know the student involved may also exhibit grief responses related to other losses they have experienced. If any students had argued with the deceased student, or is being blamed by others for the death, they need to be quickly identified and provided with considerable support. In one case I recall, a popular and talented student committed suicide after being told by his girlfriend that she thought they were getting too serious and that she wanted to spend less time together. Out of their own anger at the loss, many students blamed the girl, saying if she had not broken his heart, he would be alive. The rejection she experienced and the guilt she felt became so intense that she had to change schools in addition to receiving outside counseling.

Parents of students who knew the deceased should be contacted, provided with the same information the students received, and urged to be alert to signs of complicated grief. Any student who might have had negative feelings or interactions toward the student who died may feel increased anger and/or guilt, and should be reassured that it is not one event that causes suicide. The school counselor is often the person who will contact the family of the student who died and offer condolences, especially if there was a prior relationship with the family. The counselor must also be alert to teachers who are particularly impacted by the death and encourage them to gain support.

Dealing with the larger system should be left to other members of the crisis team. The district office must be notified, and team members of that level will deal with media and will also notify crisis teams of other schools who should be notified immediately (e.g., feeder schools, schools attended by siblings of the deceased student). School counselors will undoubtedly be involved in discussions of funeral attendance (will students be excused if the funeral occurs during the school day, will staff be free to go, should there be any memorial at school, etc.) and should be best informed about recommended practices. Memorials are widely discouraged, but each individual case should be considered carefully.

In addition to the immediate tasks of postvention, follow-up will also be in the school counselor's arena. If at-risk students are referred for outside counseling, the school counselor should follow up and ensure that the counseling is occurring. At-risk and grieving students should be monitored so that signs of lingering problems can be observed and appropriate action taken.

Elementary Versus Secondary Counselors

While the roles in prevention, intervention, and postvention are similar at elementary and secondary levels, there are some important differences. Curriculum approaches to suicide awareness are not recommended for elementary students, but classroom guidance lessons that address many of the risk factors for suicide are typically conducted by the counselor. At these times, the counselor needs to be alert to students whose reactions suggest that they need further assessment. Although rare, suicides do occur in elementary students, and any mention of suicidal thoughts or behaviors should be taken seriously, regardless of the age of the child. Elementary counselors usually provide group counseling and guidance to students, and grief groups are not uncommon. Parental contact tends to be more frequent at the elementary level, so counselors may have more information about family climate and changes in the family than do secondary counselors. Secondary school counselors with large caseloads may not have the opportunity to get to know each student well and, thus, may not have had the opportunity to build a trusting relationship with the student who is referred for suicidal concerns. Despite these differences, the roles of school counselors at all levels are much more similar than different.

Ethical Issues

There are a number of ethical standards that apply to the school counselor dealing with suicidal students. The first relates to a student who is a danger to her or himself. The American School Counselor Association's (ASCA) Ethical Standards includes this principle:

A.7. Danger to Self or Others

The professional school counselor:

a. Informs parents/guardians or appropriate authorities when the student's condition indicates a clear and imminent danger to the student or others. This is to be done after careful deliberation and, where possible, after consultation with other counseling professionals.
b. Will attempt to minimize threat to a student and may choose to 1) inform the student of actions to be taken, 2) involve the student in a three-way communication with parents/guardians when breaching confidentiality or 3) allow the student to have input as to how and to whom the breach will be made. (ASCA, 2004, p. 2)

This ethical principle makes it quite clear that the counselor is obligated to break confidentiality when the student is a "clear and imminent" danger. Unfortunately, those terms are not defined, and the school counselor is left to consider whether lesser degrees of suicidal behavior (e.g., ideation, vague comments) qualify. It is best to err on the side of caution given the cost of an error in the wrong direction and the inability of professionals to accurately predict suicide.

The other area of ethics that is involved in working with suicide in the schools is professional competence. From the standards:

E.1. Professional Competence

The professional school counselor:

a. Functions within the boundaries of individual professional competence and accepts responsibility for the consequences of his/her actions.
b. Monitors personal well-being and effectiveness and does not participate in any activity that may lead to inadequate professional services or harm to a student.
c. Strives through personal initiative to maintain professional competence including technological literacy and to keep abreast of professional information. Professional and personal growth are ongoing. (ASCA, 2004, p. 4)

Given that school counselors are unlikely to have had sufficient training in their graduate programs, it behooves them to seek opportunities to develop competence in working with all areas of suicide. Professional development opportunities such as in-service trainings and crisis response team trainings can be helpful. Professional conferences and workshops on the topic are another avenue to increasing knowledge and skills. Reading professional literature and staying current are additional measures to ensure that all school counselors are competent to assume their responsibilities on the "front line" of suicide prevention, intervention, and postvention.

Issues of Diversity

Although the majority of completed suicides in adolescents are in Caucasian youth, rates of other groups have been increasing dramatically. Rutter (2004) is concerned that because racial and ethnic minority students may express suicide risk differently, they can be overlooked, and assessments may be inaccurate. With the increasingly diverse population in America's schools, it is essential the school counselors be aware of racial/ethnic differences that might affect how students respond to suicide prevention, intervention, or postvention efforts. Although minority youth are vulnerable to the same risk factors as other youth, they may also be subject to unique risk factors based on their status that elevate risk for suicide. As a result, efforts to reduce suicidality in these youth must acknowledge and respond to these risk factors.

In their study of ethnic differences in patterns of suicide over the lifespan, Garlow, Purselle, and Heninger (2005) examined records of suicides in Fulton County, Georgia, from 1994 through 2002, and found that rates and patterns mirrored those reported in national samples. As in other studies, African Americans commit suicide at lower rates than Whites, and females had the lowest rates of all groups. Among victims younger than age 20, significantly fewer Black youths tested positive for substances at time of death than did Whites in the same age group. In attempting to account for their findings, these researchers noted that although the rates of psychiatric disorders (including depression) have been found to be similar in both groups, the availability of mental health treatment for African Americans is limited and is of lesser quality. Perhaps as a consequence, young African Americans may be reluctant to seek treatment. On the other hand, African American culture may mitigate against suicide. The protective factors of family support and religiosity are suggested to explain the overall low rates of suicide in this group, and the widely held attitude among African Americans that suicide is not acceptable also may serve as a protection. School counselors need to access the community support, and in an intervention it would be advisable to consider including extended family members as well as clergy. Based on this study, the best prevention strategies would be those that serve to strengthen the protective factors (e.g., educating parents and involving them in school programs) and those that include screening for depression.

Although Latino youth in the United States commit suicide at lower rates than other ethnic groups do, they are much more likely (particularly females) to make suicide attempts (Canino & Roberts, 2001). The Latino or Hispanic group is not homogeneous, and although the following discussion will generalize some concepts, there are intragroup differences depending on country of origin. Suicide ideation and attempts of Latino-American youth (Mexican American, Cuban American, and Dominican American) are higher than rates among comparable youth in their country of origin. This fact may indicate that acculturative stress is responsible for the increased ideation and attempts. A detailed discussion of that concept is beyond the scope of this chapter, but acculturative stress refers to a group of stressors such as conflicts in values between cultures, perceived discrimination, language difficulties, and perceived poor opportunities. Family support and positive expectations about the future appeared to protect against acculturative stress and, thus, protect against suicidal behaviors. Canino and Roberts also cautioned that as most studies of rates of suicide among adolescents are conducted in school settings, the many Latino youth who drop out of school (approximately 30%) and are probably at higher risk for suicide are often excluded from the data, presenting a false picture of the resilience of this group. No suggestions are offered for school counselors, but it would be wise to consider acculturative factors in planning suicidal prevention, intervention, and postvention. The protective factor of family support is important, but many school counselors face a language barrier when communicating with Spanish-dominant or monolingual Spanish-speaking parents about their students. Parent training and education programs are usually presented in English, excluding those parents who are not fluent in the language. In addition to recruiting more bilingual counselors, current school counselors need to make special efforts to collaborate with parents of those students so that the school and home can work together to prevent suicide.

American Indian youth have the highest rate of suicide among all groups. These youth experience many of the risk factors of other groups, but also have added risk factors unique to this group: social disintegration and cultural conflict (Metha & Webb, 1996). While some tribes have maintained their separate cultural identities, others have integrated with the majority culture. For many American Indian youth, adopting the majority cultural values means a loss of pride in their culture and decreased self-esteem. High rates of alcoholism and suicide may be the effect of "social alienation, social confusion, and self-hate" (p. 25).

Gary, Baker, and Grandbois (2005) have stated that suicide among American Indian youth is a fatalistic suicide, a reaction to the historical regulation by the dominant culture, including loss of their land, exploitation of natural resources, forced relocation, and forced assimilation. These experiences have led to pessimism about the future, and suicide may be the result. Living conditions on many reservations are substandard, with high unemployment and inadequate health and education facilities and services. In addition to the high rates of suicide, these authors point out that American Indian youth die at high rates from preventable injuries, some of which may actually be suicides. Previous research found that for a large sample of Navajo adolescents in grades 6 through 12, risk factors for suicidal behavior included feelings of alienation from family and community, having a friend who made a suicide attempt, and use of alcohol on a regular basis. Family history of suicide, a history of physical abuse and violence in the family, and sexual abuse were additional risk factors. Protective factors were also detected. Girls were protected by attention in the family, positive feelings about school, and caring by family and other adults. For boys, positive experiences at school, participating in traditional activities, good academic performance, and caring by family and other adults were the most prominent protective factors. For both boys and girls, support and caring by tribal leaders was a protective factor. Another previous study on Northern Plains reservations found that commitment to cultural spirituality was associated with reduced suicidal behaviors. In addition to common risk factors, an additional risk is the presence of guns in the homes. As many American Indians hunt for food, guns are among the basic tools found in the homes of many families.

Metha and Webb (1996) cited LaFramboise and Bigfoot (1998), who observed that the governmental pressures to assimilate (via boarding schools and prohibition of native language use in government schools for many years) may have created only one road to freedom: suicide. Further, some cultural attitudes may make suicide a more viable option to at-risk youth. The self-control that is admired in the culture may cause some youth who are experiencing psychological problems to internalize those problem. In some tribes, death is not as feared as it might be in other cultures, and the belief in ongoing contact between the human and spirit world may diminish the fear as well. In some tribes, large ceremonies (sometimes involving giveaways) that occur after a death, including a suicide, may be attractive to vulnerable youth.

Implications for schools counselors include the high need for suicide awareness programs for American Indian youth (Metha & Webb, 1996). Parent education is also crucial and often difficult to implement. Outreach to parents should be ongoing and should use personal visits and tribal liaison personnel to encourage involvement in school programs and activities. To increase attendance at programs for suicide awareness, school counselors can encourage the use of raffles and food as an incentive for attendance and can also support the use of tribal members as speakers. Finally, staff training in suicide awareness for professionals working with American Indian youth should be mandatory and should include follow-up sessions on a regular basis, to increase vigilance about adults who have many opportunities to observe and interact with the youth.

In addition, intervention strategies should employ traditional native practices (such as the healing circle and the medicine wheel), and the role of the school counselor might be to refer to tribal sources for these practices. When the only mental health providers are non-Indians, the use of traditional healers is especially important to avoid conflicts with cultural beliefs. In addition to involving parents when a student is at imminent risk, bringing members of the extended family into the consultation may increase the effectiveness of the intervention. As involvement in traditional cultural practices is a protective factor, encouraging and supporting that involvement is a useful preventive effort (Gary et al., 2005).

Although no literature on suicide in Asian American/Pacific Islander children and adolescents was located, suicide is the third leading cause of death in youth from 10 to 24; this group should not be ignored in efforts to reduce suicide among students. Chung (2002) noted that Asian American youth are considered to be prone to depression. She cited racism, the absence of Asian teachers and professionals in the school system, conflict with parents (students are likely to be more acculturated than parents are), and parental emotional unavailability as unique risk factors for this group.

Non-heterosexual youth are also at higher risk for suicide than their heterosexual peers (Russell, 2003). For this group, an additional risk factor is the possibility of abuse from relatives and family members who reject the child's sexual orientation. These students are often victims of violence and bullying at school as well. The adolescent task of identity formation may be difficult for sexual minority youth because of societal attitudes (Kirk, 1993). Social support from other LGB peers, family support, and self-acceptance of the sexual minority identity are protective factors. School counselors must be available to these students and must advocate for measures to protect them in the school environment. Further, with student consent, school counselors can provide parents with information about community resources that might be helpful as they adjust to their child's sexual orientation.

Overall, members of these diverse groups experience additional risk factors not present in Caucasian students. School counselors must be sensitive to these differences and must work to provide programming that is responsive to the needs of all students. Ideally, we would have a more diverse population of school counselors; presently, school counselors would do well to create collaborative relationships with diverse professionals who work in other settings whom they can call upon when needed.

Future Directions

There appear to be two needs in which future work in this area should focus: (1) research and (2) training. For school counselors, accountability has become a watchword, and in an area as important as suicide, they should be able to examine the evaluation of prevention programs to make evidence-based decisions for their schools. To date, such research has not provided the counselor with solid evidence of the effectiveness of any program, although some are better evaluated than others and seem promising. The availability of federal dollars to assist in establishing programs is good news, but unless schools incorporate stringent evaluation designs, those dollars may not be well spent.

School counselors are the logical choice of professionals to take leadership in suicide prevention/intervention/postvention efforts in their schools. To do so requires that they receive the best current information and training available. When this training is not provided in schools, counselors should be strong advocates for change. Further, school counselors must keep informed of opportunities for training outside of their local school or district and seek support for attendance at such conferences. Belonging to professional organizations is one way to keep up to date with new research and practices. The task of dealing with suicide is a daunting one, and school counselors need to be armed with the best information and training possible.

Shneidman (1987) said that "the most dramatic and tragic of all suicides (as a group) . . . is suicide among the young" (p. 178). School counselors have a unique role in schools, and they have the opportunity and the duty to reduce these tragic deaths. In this difficult work, it is easy to focus on the few tragic losses. Counselors must also focus on the many students whose path toward suicide was diverted by a competent and compassionate school counselor.

References

Allberg, W. R., & Chu, L. (1990). Understanding adolescent suicide: Correlates in a developmental perspective. *School Counselor, 37*, 343–350.

American Association of Suicidology. (2006). *Youth suicide fact sheet*. Retrieved September 20, 2007, from http://www.suicidology.org/associations/1045/files/Youth2004.pdf

American School Counselor Association. (2004). *Ethical standards for school counselors*. Alexandria, VA: Author.

Aseltine, R. H., & DeMartino, R. (2004). An outcome evaluation of the SOS suicide prevention program. *American Journal of Public Health, 94*, 446–451.

Bauman, S. (2004). *Recognizing depression*. Retrieved September 20, 2007, from http://www.guidancechannel.com/default.aspx?index =1520&cat=19

Beck, J., Beck, A., & Jolly, J. B. (2005). *Beck Youth Inventories* (2nd ed.) San Antonio, TX: Harcourt Assessment.

Blumenthal, S. J., & Kupfer, D. J. (1986). Generalizable treatment strategies for suicidal behavior. *Annals of the New York Academy of Sciences, 487*, 327–340.

Borowsky, I. W., Ireland, M., & Resnick, M. D. (2001). Adolescent suicide attempts: Risks and protectors. *Pediatrics, 107*, 485–493.

Brent, D. A., & Kolko, D. J. (1990). The assessment and treatment of children and adolescents at risk for suicide. In S. J. Blumenthal & D. J. Kupfer (Eds.), *Suicide over the life cycle: Risk factors, assessment, and treatment of suicidal patients* (pp. 253–302). Washington, DC: American Psychiatric Press.

Breton, J., Tousignant, M., Bergeron, L., & Berthiaume, C. (2002). Informant-specific correlates of suicidal behavior in a community survey of 12- to 14-year-olds. *Journal of the American Academy of Child & Adolescent Psychiatry, 41*, 723–730.

Cafaro, C. S. (2000). Student suicides and school system liability. *School Law Bulletin, 2*(3), 17–25.

Canino, G., & Roberts, R. E. (2001). Suicidal behavior among Latino youth. *Suicide and Life Threatening Behavior, 31*, 122–131.

Capuzzi, D. (2002). Legal and ethical challenges in counseling suicidal students. *Professional School Counseling, 6*, 36–45.

Capuzzi, D., & Gross, D. R. (2004). Counseling suicidal adolescents. In D. Capuzzi (Ed.), *Suicide across the lifespan: Implications for counselor* (pp. 235–270). Alexandria, VA: American Counseling Association.

Center for Disease Control. (2007, September 6). *Press release: DCD report shows largest one-year increase in youth suicide rate in 15 years*. Retrieved September 20, 2007 from http://cdc.gov/od/media/pressrel/2007/r070906.htm

Center for Mental Health in Schools. (2002). *A Center quick training aid . . . Suicide prevention*. Los Angeles: Author. Retrieved September 20, 2001, from http://smhp.psych.ucla.edu/pdfdocs/quicktraining/suicideprevention.pdf

Chung, I. (2002, May). *The prevalence of mental health problems among Asian-American adolescents and children: Symptoms and treatment issues*. Paper presented at the eleventh annual International Conference on Health Problems Related to the Chinese in North America, Chinese American Medical Society, New York City.

Crocitto, J. A. (1990). Message from the guest editor: Suicide and the school counselor. *The School Counselor, 37*, 324–327.

Cull, J. G., & Gill, W. S. (1988). *Manual: Suicide probability scale*. Los Angeles, CA: Western Psychological Services.

Davis, J. M., & Sandoval, J. (1991). *Suicidal youth: School-based intervention and Prevention*. San Francisco: Jossey-Bass.

Dexter-Mazza, E. (2004). The lack of graduate school training in suicide assessment and management. *Behavior Emergencies Update, 1*(1). Retrieved September 6, 2004, from http://www.apa.org/divisions/div12/sections/section7/news/sp04/lack.html

Doan, J., Roggenbaum, S., & Lazear, K. (2003). *Youth suicide prevention school-based guide (c/p/r/s) – P: School-based prevention programs* (FMHI Series Publication #219-P). Tampa: Louis de la Parte Florida Mental Health Institute, University of South Florida.

Dyck, R. J. (1991). System-entry issues in school suicide prevention education programs. In A. A. Leenaars & S. Wenckstern (Eds.), *Suicide prevention in the schools* (pp. 41–49). New York: Hemisphere Publishing.

Eggert, L. L., Thompson, E. A., Randell, B. P., & Pike, K. C. (2002). Preliminary effects of brief school-based prevention approaches for reducing youth suicide—risk behaviors, depression, and drug involvement. *Journal of Child and Adolescent Psychiatric Nursing, 15*(2), 48–64.

Eisel v. Board of Education of Montgomery County. 324 Md. 376, 597 A. 2d 447 (Md Ct. App. 1991).

Elkind, D. (1967). Egocentrism in adolescence. *Child Development, 38*, 1025–1034.

Foster, V., & McAdams, C. R., III (1999). The impact of client suicide in counselor training: Implications for counselor education and supervision. *Counselor Education & Supervision, 39*(1), 22–34.

Gallup Organization. (1994). *Teen suicide: A report on the 1991 Gallup survey among teens and the 1994 Gallup update survey*. Princeton, NJ: The George H. Gallup International Institute.

Garland, A. F., & Zigler, E. (1993). Adolescent suicide prevention: Current research and social and policy implications. *American Psychologist, 48*, 169–182.

Garlow, S. J., Purselle, D., & Heninger. M. (2005). Ethnic differences in patterns of suicide across the lifecycle. *American Journal of Psychiatry, 162*, 319–323.

Gary, F., Baker, M., & Grandbois, D. (2005). Perspectives on suicide prevention among American Indian and Alaska native children and adolescents: A call for help. *Online Journal of Issues in Nursing, 10*(2). Retrieved September 20, 2007, from http://nursingworld.org/ojin/hirsh/topic4/tpc4_3.htm

Goldman, S., & Beardslee, W. R. (1999). Suicide in children and adolescents. In D. G. Jacobs (Ed.), *The Harvard Medical School guide to suicide assessment and intervention* (pp. 417–442). San Francisco: Jossey-Bass.

Goldney, R. (1990, July 25). *The prediction of suicide*. Paper presented at the conference of the Australian Institute of Criminology, Canberra, Australia. Retrieved October 31, 2007, from http://www.aic.gov.au/publications/proceedings/13/goldney.html

Goldney, R. D. (2000). Prediction of suicide and attempted suicide. In K. Hawton & K. van Heeringen (Eds.), *The international handbook of suicide and attempted suicide* (pp. 585–595). West Sussex, UK: John Wiley & Sons.

Goldston, D. B. (2003). *Measuring suicidal behavior and risk in children and adolescents*. Washington, DC: American Psychological Association.

Gorkin, M. (1985). On the suicide of one's patient. *Bulletin of the Menninger Clinic, 49*, 1–9.

Gould, M. S., Marrocco, F. A., Kleinman, M., Thomas, J. G., Mostkoff, K., Cote, J., et al. (2005). Evaluating iatrogenic risk of youth suicide screening programs: A randomized controlled trial. *Journal of the American Mediccal Association, 293*, 1635–1643.

Haley, M. (2004). Risk and protective factors. In D. Capuzzi (Ed.), *Suicide across the lifespan: Implications for counselor* (pp. 95–138). Alexandria, VA: American Counseling Association.

Harborview Injury Prevention and Research Center. (n.d.). *Best practices: Suicide*. Retrieved online 20, 2007, from http://depts.washington.edu/hiprc/practices/topic/suicide/index.html

Hermann, M. A. (2002). An ethical and legal perspective on the role of school counselors in preventing violence in schools. *Professional School Counseling, 6*, 46–55.

Jacobs, D. G. (Ed.). (1999). *The Harvard Medical School guide to suicide assessment and intervention*. San Francisco: Jossey-Bass.

Jacobs, D. G., Brewer, M., & Klein-Benham, M. (1999). Suicide assessment: An overview and recommended protocol. In D. G. Jacobs (Ed.), *The Harvard Medical School guide to assessment and intervention* (pp. 3–39). San Francisco: Jossey-Bass.

Juhnke, G. A. (1996). The Adapted-SAD PERSONS: A suicide assessment scale designed for use with children. *Elementary School Guidance and Counseling, 30*(4), 252–258.

Kalafat, J. (1990). Adolescent suicide and the implications for school response programs. *The School Counselor, 37*, 359–369.

Kalafat, J., & Ryerson, D. M. (1999). The implementation and institutionalization of a school-based youth suicide prevention program. *The Journal of Primary Prevention, 19*, 157–175.

Kelly, K. T., & Knudson, M. P. (2000). Are no suicide contracts effective in preventing suicide in suicidal patients seen by primary care physicians. *Archives of Family Medicine, 9*, 1119–1121.

Kelson v City of Springfield, Oregon. 767 F.2d 651 (9th Cir. 1985).

King, K. A., & Smith, J. (2000). Project SOAR: A training program to increase school counselors' knowledge and confidence regarding suicide prevention and intervention. *Journal of School Health, 70,* 402–407.

King, K. A., Price, J. H., Telljohann, S., & Wahl, J. (2000). Preventing adolescent suicide: Do high school counselors know the risk factors? *Professional School Counseling, 3,* 255–263.

Kirk, W. G. (1993). *Adolescent suicide: A school-based approach to assessment and intervention.* Champaign, IL: Research Press.

LaFromboise, T., & Howard-Pitney, B. (1995). The Zuni life skills development curriculum: Description and evaluation of a suicide prevention program. *Journal of Counseling Psychology, 42,* 479–486.

Laux, J. M. (2002). A primer on suicidology: Implications for counselors. *Journal of Counseling and Development, 80,* 380–384.

Leenaars, A. A., & Wenckstern, S. (1991). *Suicide prevention in schools.* New York: Hemisphere.

Malley, P. B., Kush, F., & Bogo, R. (1996). School-based suicide prevention and intervention programs. *The Prevention Researcher, 3*(3), 9–11.

Mathai, C. M. (2002). *Surveying school counselors via the internet regarding their experiences and training needs in crisis intervention.* Unpublished doctoral dissertation, Virginia Polytechnic Institute and State University, Blacksburg.

McKeown, R. E., Garrison, C. Z., Cuffe, S. P., Waller, J. L., Jackson, A. B., & Addy, C. L. (1998). Incidence and predictors of suicidal behaviors in a longitudinal sample of young adolescents. *Journal of the American Academy of Child and Adolescent Psychiatry, 37,* 612–619.

Metha, A., & Webb, L. D. (1996). Suicide among American Indian youth: The role of the schools in prevention. *Journal of American Indian Education, 36*(1), 22–32.

Miller, C. M. (1999). Suicide prevention contracts: Advantages, disadvantages, and an alternative approach. In D. G. Jacobs (Ed.), *The Harvard Medical School guide to suicide assessment and intervention* (pp. 463–481). San Francisco: Jossey-Bass.

Milsom, A. (2002). Suicide prevention in schools: Court cases and implications for principals. *NASSP Bulletin.* Retrieved May 22, 2005, from http://www.findarticles.com/p/articles/mi_qa3696/is_200203/ai_n9080589

Motto, J. A. (1999). Critical points in the assessment and management of suicide. In D. G. Jacobs (Ed.), *The Harvard Medical School guide to suicide assessment and intervention* (pp. 224–238). San Francisco: Jossey-Bass.

Muzina, D. J. (2004). What physicians can do to prevent suicide. *Cleveland Clinic Journal of Medicine, 71,* 242–250.

National Center for Health Statistics. (2004). *Health, United States, 2004 with chartbook on trends in the health of Americans.* Hyattsville, MD: Author.

National Health Information Center. (2006). 2006 *Fact sheet on suicide: Adolescents and young adults.* Retrieved Setpember 20, 2007, from http://nahic.ucsf.edu//downloads/Suicide.pdf

National Institute of Mental Health. (2005). *Antidepressant medications for children and adolescents: Information for parents and caregivers.* Retrieved June 2, 2005, from http://www.nimh.nih.gov/healthinformation/antidepressant_child.cfm

O'Donnell, L., Stueve, A., Wardlaw, D., & O'Donnell, C. (2003). Adolescent suicidality and adult support: The reach for health study of urban youth. *American Journal of Health Behaviors, 27,* 633–644.

Overholser, J., & Spirito, A. (2003). Integrating clinical practice and current research. In A. Spirito & J. Overholser (Eds.), *Evaluating and treatment adolescent suicide attempters* (pp. 323–328). San Diego, CA: Elsevier.

Pate, R. H., Jr. (1992). Student suicide: Are you liable? *American Counselor, 1*(3), 14–19.

Patterson, W. M., Dohn, H. H., Bird, J., & Patterson, G. A. (1983). Evaluation of suicidal patients: The SAD PERSONS scale. *Psychosomatics, 24,* 343–349.

Pfeffer, C. R. (1997). Childhood suicidal behavior: A developmental perspective. *Pediatric Clinics of North American, 20,* 551–562.

Pokorny, A. D. (1983). Prediction of suicide in psychiatric patients. Report of a prospective study. *Archives of General Psychiatry, 40,* 249–257.

Poland, S. (1989). *Suicide intervention in the schools.* New York: Guilford.

Randell, B. P., Eggert, L. L., & Pike, K. C. (2001). Immediate post intervention effects of two brief youth suicide prevention interventions. *Suicide and Life Threatening Behavior, 31*(1), 41–61.

Range, L. M., Campbell, C., Kovac, S. H., Marion-Jones, M., Aldridge, H., Kogos, S., et al. (2002). No suicide contracts: An overview and recommendations. *Death Studies, 25,* 51–74.

Reynolds, W. M. (1987). *Suicidal ideation questionnaire.* Odessa, FL: Psychological Assessment Resources.

Rogers, J. R. (2001). Theoretical grounding: The "missing link" in suicide research. *Journal of Counseling and Development, 79,* 16–25.

Ruben, H. L. (1990). Surviving a suicide in your practice. In S. J. Blumenthal & D. J. Kupfer (Eds.), *Suicide over the life cycle* (pp. 619–636). Washington, DC: American Psychiatric Press.

Russell, S. T. (2003). Sexual minority youth and suicide risk. *American Behavioral Scientist, 46,* 1241–1257.

Rutter, P. A. (2004). Adolescent suicide risk: Four psychosocial factors. *Adolescence, 39,* 295–302.

Shneidman, E. S. (1987). A psychological approach to suicide. In G. R. Vandenbos & B. K. Bryant (Eds.), *Cataclysms, crises, and catastrophes: Psychology in action* (pp. 151–183). Washington, DC: American Psychological Association.

Stefanowski-Harding, S. (1990). Child suicide: A review of the literature and implications for school counselors. *School Counselor, 37,* 328–336.

Stillion, J. M., & McDowell, E. E. (1996). *Suicide across the lifespan: Premature exits* (2nd ed.). Washington, DC: Taylor & Francis.

Substance Abuse and Mental Health Services Administration. (2007). *Intervention summary: SOS Signs of Suicide.* Retrieved October 28, 2007, from http://www.nrepp.samhsa.gov/programfulldetails.asp?PROGRAM_ID=66

Thompson, E. A., Eggert, L. L., Randell, B. P., & Pike, K. C. (2001). Evaluation of indicated suicide risk prevention programs for potential high school dropouts. *American Journal of Public Health, 91,* 742–752.

Weiss, A. (2001). The no-suicide contract: Possibilities and pitfalls. *American Journal of Psychotherapy, 55,* 414–419.

Westefeld, J. S., Range, L. M., Rogers, J. R., Maples, M. R., Bromley, J. L., & Alcorn, J. (2000). Suicide: An overview. *The Counseling Psychologist, 28,* 445–510.

Wodarski, J. S., Wodarski, L. A., & Dulmus, C. N. (2003). *Adolescent depression and suicide: A comprehensive empirical intervention for prevention and treatment.* Springfield, IL: Charles C. Thomas.

Zametkin, A. J., Alter, M. R., & Yemini, T. (2001). Suicide in teenagers: Assessment, management, and prevention. *Journal of the American Medical Association, 286,* 3120–3125.

XXXVIII
WORKING WITH SCHOOL FAILURE

KAREN A. CORT
Teachers College, Columbia University

Introduction

In the United States, the educational system has become a significant medium for the preparation of children's transition into adulthood. Contemporary school systems are responsible for imparting basic academic knowledge and skills and didactic job-skills training, as well as assuming many of the socialization functions that earlier had been the sole responsibility of the family (J. J. McWhirter, 1998). Also consider that the school is the location in which children spend 30% to 40% of their waking hours, has mandatory attendance from about age 5 to at least 16 years, and is a primary source of constant evaluation of their performance (which oftentimes determines the child's level of aptitude for his or her lifetime; Harvey, 1984). As such, the effect of the schooling process probably has a more meaningful impact on the development of the individual than any other social institution. Therefore, outcomes of school must play an important role in the outlook and future livelihood of students. Unfortunately, though, the outcome for too many students in school is that they have not been able to satisfactorily fulfill the expectations placed upon them, and thousands of students "fail" the school system.

When students fail to achieve, there are numerous implications and consequences that may occur above and beyond their overall individual achievement level. Students with failing grades are at risk to fall down a spiral that can derail their educational and occupational trajectories well into adulthood (Needham, Crosnoe, & Muller, 2004). Academic struggles predict short-term problem behaviors and may eventually lead to dropout, creating disorder and undermining the general mission of schools. Moreover, as the United States faces global economic competition, children at risk for school failure represent a subgroup of the population whose fate will help shape the future of this country. High levels of school dropouts will cause the country to squander money, as society pays six times more to maintain an uneducated adult than it pays to keep a student in school through graduation. These trends will lead to billions of dollars in lost earnings, further expansion of welfare, and criminal justice expenses for this country, and will ultimately make the United States less economically competitive in the world (Becker & Luthar, 2002). Thus, what appears to be merely an aspect of the adolescent experience actually has far-reaching consequences across a variety of social phenomena. Children and adolescents who fail become "a problem" not only to the school system that was created to serve them, but also to society in general.

School failure is often viewed as a negative consequence to an individual student's actions and/or behavior. The burden of school failure is often placed upon the individual student particularly because in the U.S. educational system, student advancement is predicated on individual effort and graded performance in a series of classes. When students don't pass, it becomes their fault—often because they are "lazy" or "not trying hard enough." While some students do not live up to their potential, lack of effort alone cannot explain school failure, especially when one examines the discouraging statistics demonstrated in the disproportionate numbers of adolescents of color who "fail" and completely drop out of the educational system (approximately 50% of Black and Latino students combined in the year 2001; U.S. Department of Education [USDE], National Center for Educational Statistics [NCES], 2005; also see Coleman, Chapter X, this volume).

Placing the sole responsibility for the problem of school failure upon the student is narrow and skewed. This individualistic perspective does not acknowledge the fact that people's functioning is dependent upon their unique strengths and deficits, who or what they interact with on a daily basis, as well as those systems that structure the individuals' day-to-day realities. Ecological systems theory provides a conceptual foundation for emphasizing individual development within the immediate social environment and the impact of the larger social context on this environment (Neville & Mobley, 2001). Utilizing an ecological model provides a systematic and comprehensive approach to understanding the "bigger picture," identifying those personal, as well as environmental, factors contributing to a student's performance. Examining school failure from a broader ecological perspective places one in a stronger position to both better understand the source or sources of the student's difficulties and identify a range of possible responses and interventions (Abrams, Theberge, & Karan, 2005). Instead of focusing primarily on the student, an ecological approach would simultaneously recognize and, at times, carefully modify the balance between the person and the systems that interact both directly and indirectly with that person to organize his or her behavior. Working from an individualistic perspective—focusing on only the person or the system by itself—will not likely demonstrate sustained improvement and may simply contribute to the dilemma of "failing students." This may explain why our nation is becoming less competitive with other countries, as well as our consistent 11% dropout rate (for the past 15 years) and increasing numbers of students of color dropping out of the system, despite all of the research efforts to date, high-stakes testing, and dollars spent in educational reform. Think about it: How effective can individual change be if the individual has to return to a "sick" system?

In this chapter, school failure is examined from an ecological perspective, not as a discrete, unitary diagnostic category of an individual. More specifically, *school failure* is defined as a set of presumed cause-and-effect relationships among individual and environmental dynamics that place a child or adolescent in danger of negative future events in school (J. J. McWhirter, 1998). The purpose of this chapter is to explore school failure along a continuum, examining four different degrees of "failure"—academic failure, truancy, grade retention, and dropout. Each degree of school failure will be examined in terms of the varying ecological trends and contributing factors that define the problem. The chapter will conclude with practical strategies and suggestions, from an ecological perspective, that school counselors can utilize to address the needs of students who "fail."

Academic Failure

Academic achievement is generally known as student performance in school as measured by grades. Academic failure is, therefore, defined as the failing performance of a student because he or she receives extremely low grades (e.g., "F") in a class(es) (Dimmitt, 2003). Academic failure generally is thought of as the first step in the continuum of school failure (Kaplan, Peck, & Kaplan, 1997). The variable most directly related to academic failure is poor academic performance in the classroom. However, a student's academic performance can vary considerably between content areas (e.g., science, mathematics) and over time. Poor performance in one content area does not necessarily generalize to other areas. For example, according to the National Assessment of Education Progress (NAEP), fourth graders' average reading scale score has not been significantly different in the past 10 years (approximately 40% of students consistently perform below the basic level nationwide), while fourth graders' average mathematics scale scores have changed significantly in the same time period, with student performance steadily improving (50% of students below basic level in 1992 decreased to 35% in 2003; USDE, NCES, 2005).

Failing to achieve passing grades often disables students in a number of ways. When a student fails, he or she is often restricted from entering more rigorous curricula and may be subjected to repetitious, remedial course work. Moreover, "no pass, no play" policies in many school districts prevent students who have failed courses from participating in extracurricular activities (many of which have positive influences on child and adolescent development; Needham et al., 2004). Low-performing students are less likely to graduate from high school and less likely to go on to college, directly affecting their future adult financial livelihood, as most high school dropouts and people who don't attend college earn substantially lower wages than those who do (Kaplan et al., 1997). This has been found especially among rural youth. Only 54% of rural students apply to college, compared with 62% of their suburban peers (Hines, 2002).

Furthermore, calls for educational accountability over the past 2 decades have resulted in a move toward enhanced graduation requirements and mandated proficiency tests. Implementation of high-stakes testing and school accountability policies has escalated, broadening the consequences of academic failure. Academic achievement and failure has advanced beyond school grades and has become equated with student-outcome scores on standardized tests. Proficiency tests alone are often being used as a blanket measure of school success, making it possible for those outside of the school system to selectively apply test results to bring sanctions against teachers and schools that are floundering (McEvoy & Welker, 2000). This is reflected in the current federal policy incorporated within the No Child Left Behind Act, which identifies schools as needing improvement if their overall performance does not improve from year to year, or if subgroups do not make adequate yearly progress (Christenson & Thurlow, 2004). These new actions on the surface seem to be attempting to address the need for school reform and appear to be raising the standards of education in the U.S. school system. Unfortunately, however, these same actions are also placing unnecessary pressure on students creating another area in which they can possibly fail, as well as increasing the numbers of students who are becoming academic failures. For example, urban students are less likely to meet the minimum standards on national tests and less likely to complete high school in 4 years (Lee, 2005). Moreover, rural and urban students consistently scored at about the same level in math, reading, and writing, but significantly lower than their suburban cohorts in the same areas (Hines, 2002).

In addition, some teachers' attitudes are changing toward students due to these systemic pressures. Many teachers, in particular in urban areas, whose professional success tends to be measured by the percentages of their students who pass standardized tests, are beginning to adopt a militant "sink or swim" attitude toward students. Some have developed a tendency to pressure students to perform and may also concentrate their efforts only on those students who are perceived as being able to "swim" (McEvoy & Welker, 2000).

Factors Contributing to Academic Failure

Individual Factors

Academic failure has been linked to several factors intrinsic to students. These include cognitive deficits, attention problems, mental health challenges, and behavioral difficulties (McEvoy & Welker, 2000). Moreover, student motivation is another significant factor that may influence academic failure. Often, student's beliefs about and perceptions of the futility of school, as well as the value of specific subjects may often detract from their level of motivation and effort toward their academic progress (Dimmitt, 2003). In addition, students who lack the social skills to develop friendships, as well as those who perceive rejection by students and teachers, are at high risk for academic difficulties (Kaplan et al., 1997). Students who do not have social skills and/or positive relationships at school often lack the daily social support that enhances and contributes to positive academic performance. Lastly, lack of homework completion has also been found to be a significant individual factor contributing to academic failure. Homework is often used as a tool for reinforcement of class work and new material, as well as an opportunity to practice and improve skills. When homework is not completed, a student becomes at risk for academic failure. Material presented in class often builds upon previous material. If the student did not comprehend or become proficient with this material, the student begins to have gaps in his or her learning that often make subsequent learning difficult, and eventually impossible in some cases. This was supported in a study conducted by Dimmit, in which students, parents, and teachers were asked why they thought students were failing specific classes. All three groups identified not doing homework as the most significant factor (70% of teachers, 73% of parents, and 61% students).

Family Factors

Families have a tremendous impact on what happens to students in schools. The most significant family factors that are related to school achievement are the amount of family involvement with the school and family attitudes and beliefs about schooling. Parent–teacher communication and parental expectations of academic success also affect student achievement. When a student and/or the school are aware that family members are monitoring their child's progress, a greater interest arises. These external supports help students feel more motivated and supported for their efforts. Moreover, within the school, the student begins to receive greater attention, as faculty and staff recognize that this child's family supports his or her efforts and are willing collaborators. This makes their job easier and more effective.

There are also family factors that are not directly related to school–family relationships that have an impact on student success. These include family cohesion (e.g., divorce or death of a parent), lack of structure and instability, ineffective and inconsistent discipline practices, lack of parental supervision and monitoring, and little parental education (Dimmitt, 2003). These factors may cause family stress. Often stressors detract from family attention and school involvement, leaving no structure to guide the student and little support for the student to depend on. Another consequence of family instability and stress may oftentimes lead a child to change schools frequently. Changing schools impacts the coherence of students' academic experience and can result in knowledge gaps, lack of school connections, and the absence of appropriate educational service (Dimmitt).

School Factors

In the broadest sense, the general school climate has a tremendous impact on how all the people in the building—students, teachers, and administrators—feel about being in that environment. Students are more likely to do well when there is a school culture that has an academic emphasis, and when there are adequate educational resources to provide support for student learning within the school (Dimmitt, 2003). In addition, school practices, such as ability grouping or tracking, dramatically affect student conceptions of ability and sense of futility. For academically failing students, placing them in low-achieving "ability groups" or tracks with low expectations for academic success is especially detrimental to their subsequent school performance and to their nonacademic behavior. Tracking also heightens tensions and promotes segregation between groups ("failures" and "achievers"; McEvoy & Welker, 2000).

Teacher expectations and judgments of student's academic ability are also strong contributors of academic failure. Student perceptions of their academic ability and a sense of academic futility are greatly influenced by their teachers, as they are often the dominant daily reinforcement in a student's world. Students who are involved with teachers who do not hold a widely shared belief that *all* of their students will master grade-level objectives, irrespective of their background and life circumstances, have less support within school and are at greater risk for failure (McEvoy & Welker, 2000).

Community/Societal Factors

The complex interaction of culture and race must be taken into consideration when considering school failure. Many schools in this country continue to have students of color primarily being taught by White teachers. As such, curriculum, materials and/or didactic methodologies often reflect White American middle-class culture and not the range of learning styles and cultural experiences of all students in the classroom. This may result in students of color being at risk in school because their experiences and different learning styles are discounted, misunderstood, and not appreciated but instead viewed as pathological (Dimmitt, 2003).

Academic failure is the first step along the continuum of school failure. Historically, academic failure was measured only in terms of grades and G.P.A. However, in recent years, with the implementation of educational reforms, such as the No Child Left Behind Act, academic failure has included such measures as standardized testing. These efforts not only have caused stress and pressure among students and school faculty, but have also increased the number of academic "failures."

From an ecological perspective, a number of factors have been explored that contribute to academic failure. These include individual factors, such as cognitive deficits, lack of motivation, and lack of homework completion. Several family factors were also discussed, including the amount of family involvement and family attitude toward school, as well as family stress. School culture and teacher expectations have also been found to contribute to academic failure. Lastly, the influence of the broader context of dominant White Eurocentric American culture was examined to demonstrate its possible impact on academic failure.

Although academic failure is detrimental by itself, there are other levels of school failure. Often as a consequence of academic failure, the next more destructive level of school failure—truancy—occurs.

Truancy

Truancy is defined as a student's repeated unlawful and willful absence from school without knowledge and consent from parents (Kearney, 2003). In broad terms, truancy includes several school refusal behaviors, such as repeated tardiness in the morning, repeated absences and/or difficulty remaining in classes for an entire day, complete absenteeism for a certain period of the school year, to the extreme case of complete absenteeism for an extended period of time (Kearney).

Truancy is often used as a coping mechanism due to negative feelings toward school and/or can be utilized by some as attention-seeking behavior. It can begin as a result of academic failure, but may be due to other reasons. Regardless of the initial motivation, truancy can interrupt social development and has been identified as a precursor to undesirable outcomes and negative consequences in childhood, adolescence, and adulthood (McCluskey, Bynum, & Patchin, 2004). Short-term consequences include declining grades, legal difficulties, social alienation, family conflict, and distress (Kearney, 2003). Long-term consequences of truancy include academic failure, juvenile delinquency, school dropout, and occupational and social problems in adulthood (e.g., lower status occupations, less stable career patterns, and higher rates of unemployment; Kearney).

The inclination to miss school increases significantly by grade level. Skipping school accounted for 9% of all days eighth graders missed in 2000, compared with 16% for tenth graders, and 26% for twelfth graders (USDE, NCES, 2005). School systems do recognize the damaging effects of high levels of absenteeism and appoint truancy officers to search for missing students, particularly those in secondary schools (McCluskey et al., 2004). However, the issue of truancy has largely been ignored on the elementary school level.

Factors Contributing to Truancy

Individual Factors

A variety of factors is associated with truancy at the individual level. Poor social and cognitive skills, health problems, learning disabilities, and emotional disorders have all been found to influence the school experience generally and ultimately affect school attendance (McCluskey et al., 2004). Among elementary school students in particular, cognitive skills can affect coping and self-perception. Often if a student has low comprehension of class material or is not as competitive academically in comparison with his or her peers, he or she experiences negative feelings, such as frustration, anger, and sadness. As a coping mechanism to avoid these feelings and their negative perceptions of themselves, students begin to avoid school attendance. In addition, social skills can influence the ability of children to develop relationships with teachers and other students. Those with awkward or immature social skills may have a more difficult time acclimating to school and making new friends year to year. This may contribute to a consistently unpleasant experience day to day, year to year, increasing the likelihood of absenteeism and potential truancy (Barth, 1994).

Parent and Family Factors

Parent and family factors have been linked with school absenteeism. These include chaotic family structure, alienated families, poor parenting skills, and child abuse/neglect. Children and adolescents who are members of chaotic families often lack structure, support, and resources—all of which are necessary to maintain school progress. It is more difficult to attend to a child or even notice his or her infrequent pattern of attendance when there are too many distractions and other potential stressors (McCluskey et al., 2004).

School Factors

School characteristics that have been linked with school attendance broadly include teachers and the larger school environment. Teachers who are supportive of students and those with high expectations for student achievement are likely to encourage attendance and are also more likely to have higher attendance rates (McCluskey et al., 2004). In addition, schools that have consistent and stricter enforcement of attendance policies are more likely to have fewer problems with truancy (Kearney, 2003). For example, McCluskey and his colleagues conducted a study with chronic absentee elementary school students. A significant increase in attendance was found when the school enforced stricter attendance policies, such as sending a letter home to parents informing them of their child's attendance problem, along with a visit by the school attendance officer.

Student absenteeism also has been significantly associated with school climate. When morale is higher and when students and teachers feel physically and emotionally safe in the building, students are more inclined to attend school. However, in schools characterized by teacher reports regarding students with weapons and increased physical conflicts among students, higher rates of truancy, tardiness, and absenteeism can be found, as students have no desire to attend and be part of such an environment (Lee, 2005).

Community/Societal Factors

Among the larger community characteristics, the presence of delinquent peers and street gangs also contributes to truancy. As children age, the importance of school and community (peers in particular) emerges and negative influences in the surrounding community may serve to detract and coerce students from attending school (Garry, 1996).

Truancy is another level of school failure and is defined as a student's repeated willful absence from school without parental knowledge and consent. The reason for truancy may vary. However, it is often used as coping mechanism to deal with negative experiences in school and can have many short-term and long-term consequences. Among the individual factors that contribute to truancy, poor social and cognitive skills rank highest. Chaotic family structure has also been linked to chronic absenteeism and truancy. Finally, the surrounding communal environment has also been shown to contribute to distracting and coercing children and adolescents away from school, leading eventually to truancy for some.

Truancy is another degree of school failure, but unfortunately there are more severe levels along the negative continuum. Along that continuum, the next level is grade retention.

Grade Retention

Grade retention is the practice of not promoting students to the next grade level (Randolph, Fraser, & Orthner, 2004). The rationale behind this method of intervention is that by repeating the previous year's instruction, children will "catch up" with their new grade cohorts (McCoy & Reynolds, 1999). Back in the 1960s, social promotion (movement from one grade to the next based on age rather than achievement) was employed to reduce the stigma associated with not achieving and progressing academically. However, concern about social promotion grew in response to numerous reports on the deterioration of the American educational system. Some educators fought for the return to academic standards as the basis for promotion. Consequently, many school districts today around the country have established minimum promotion and graduation standards. Grade retention has returned as a popular method of remediating poor academic performance, where an estimated 1 in 5 children has been retained at least one time by the time he or ahe has reach third grade (Alexander, Entwistle, & Dauber, 1994), especially because teachers and principals are often being held more accountable for student performance.

Although grade retention is used as a strategy to strengthen academic performance, research has consistently demonstrated that the benefits don't outweigh the costs. Results of longitudinal retention research consistently demonstrates that grade retention fails to provide greater benefits to students with academic or adjustment difficulties than does promotion to the next grade (Jimerson, Anderson, & Whipple, 2002). By sixth grade, the emotional well-being of retained students was significantly lower than that of their same age, nonretained peers. Also, by the time they reached high school, the academic adjustment of retained students was significantly lower than that of their never retained peers (McCoy & Reynolds, 1999). Moreover, when students were compared with their "low-achieving but promoted" peers in high school, retained students were more likely either to have enrolled in alternative educational programs or to have dropped out of school (Jimerson & Schuder, 1996). In general, grade retention increased the risk of school dropout from 30% to 50%, regardless of socioeconomic level (Jimerson, 1999; Grissom & Shepard, 1989). The major indication is that grade retention does not appear to benefit many of the children it is designed to help. For all achievement comparisons, the research has shown that retained children consistently and usually significantly underperformed compared with their promoted peers (Randolph et al., 2004; Rumberger, 1995).

Factors Contributing to Grade Retention

Individual Factors

Several factors have been found to contribute to grade retention. Children who are retained tend to have lower cognitive skills and abilities, especially in reading and mathematics test scores and standardized achievement tests (prior to retention). In addition, retained students often demonstrate poor classroom conduct, poor social skills and peer relationships, and low self-esteem (Blair, 2001; McCoy & Reynolds, 1999).

Parent and Family Factors

A number of significant family factors contribute to retention. These include low parent educational attainment (e.g., high school dropout), socioeconomic disadvantage, frequent school changes or residential instability, and lack of parental involvement (Blair, 2001; McCoy & Reynolds, 1999). Children are also more likely to be retained when their parents view them as being less capable. When children are viewed as less capable by their parents, there are fewer expectations of their success. Consequently, teachers' recommendations for retention often go unchallenged by these parents and alternatives to retention are not pursued (McCoy & Reynolds).

School Factors

Teacher expectations are an important factor contributing to grade retention in particular because they are a source of daily reinforcement. When teachers have low expectations and perceptions of a student's academic competence, at times a self-fulfilling prophecy ensues (Blair, 2001). There are fewer expectations for success placed upon the student, and instead the child is viewed negatively. Since no one expects the child to do well, he or she lives up to these limited expectations. Self-fulfilling prophecies do occur, in particular with students from marginalized groups (Jussim & Harber, 2005).

Community and Societal Factors

Unfortunately retained children are more likely to be from racial/ethnic minority groups (Meisels & Liaw, 1993). This in part may be due to racism, which is an entrenched part of the normative American culture and, as a consequence, is transmitted and perpetuated through the various social institutions, including schools (Harvey, 1984). At times, racial/ethnic minorities face a cultural discontinuity between the day-to-day experiences that they encounter in their homes and neighborhoods and the philosophical ideals presented as fact in their school curriculum (Allen & Boykin, 1992). These stark differences at times cause confusion for children of color, who are ultimately forced to either conform to ideals they may not understand nor believe in or else be retained in the system until they learn and espouse values and ideals that ultimately may not benefit their well-being.

Grade retention occurs when a student is not promoted to the next level. In the past, social promotion (movement from one grade to the next based on age rather than achievement) was frequently practiced, and often students were not retained. However, social promotion was abandoned by most school districts due to the belief that this practice weakened the American educational system. Although grade retention is a common practice in contemporary society, research continually demonstrates the harmful effects of this practice on overall student performance and progress.

As with other levels of school failure, individual, family, and societal factors were examined. Individual factors contributing to grade retention were similar to other levels of school failure and included poor cognitive and social skills and abilities. Parental and teacher expectations and perceptions were found to greatly contribute to those students who were retained. On a broader, societal level, the impact of racism and cultural discontinuity among children of color was discussed as a major influence among those students who are retained.

Thus far, three destructive levels of school failure have been examined: academic failure, truancy, and grade retention. The final and most detrimental level that defines the continuum of school failure is often a result, consequence, or culmination of the other three levels. This level is known as dropout.

Dropout

A *dropout* is defined as a pupil who leaves school before his or her program of study is completed, before graduation without transferring to another school (M. J. McWhirter, 1998). Thousands of American youth are school dropouts, with an estimated 1 in 8 children never graduating from high school (Christenson & Thurlow, 2004). In fact, approximately 11% of the 35.2 million 16- to 24-year-olds in the United States in 2001 were not enrolled in a high school program and had not completed high school, and this estimate has not changed significantly since 1990 (USDE, NCES, 2005). Dropout rates are highest among the most vulnerable student populations including students with emotional and behavioral disabilities (half of whom dropped out of school in 1998–1999), students who are from low-income backgrounds, and those who attend rural and urban schools (approximately 12% dropout rate in these settings; Christenson & Thurlow, 2004; Hines, 2002). Moreover, dropout rates are disproportionately high for Black (11%) and Latino (27%) students, and this statistic has also remained fairly constant since 1990 (USDE, NCES, 2005).

These dropout statistics are particularly alarming because jobs that pay decent wages and benefits have virtually disappeared for youth without high school diplomas. High school dropouts may find themselves without the skills or qualifications to acquire secure, well-paying jobs with potential for advancement (McCluskey et al., 2004). The economic impact of school dropout is reflected in both short- and long-term loss of career options and earning potential. On the average, high school graduates earn $6,415 more per year than high school dropouts. Over their lifetime, high school dropouts can expect to earn $200,000 less than the students who graduated from high school. Not only are dropouts being paid less, they also are at increased risk for unemployment. The unemployment rate is approximately 4 times greater for high school dropouts than for graduates (Lever et al., 2004). As a result, high school dropouts have higher rates of unemployment, are more likely to receive public assistance, and earn less money when employed than do high school graduates (M. J. McWhirter, 1998). Moreover, for society, the costs of dropping out are staggering, estimated in billions of dollars in lost revenues, welfare programs, unemployment programs, underemployment, and crime prevention and prosecution (Becker & Luthar, 2002).

Factors Contributing to Dropout

Individual Factors

The decision to leave school without graduating is not an instantaneous one, but rather a process that occurs over many years. Research shows that leaving school early is the outcome of a long process of disengagement from school (M. J. McWhirter, 1998). Dropout is preceded by indicators of withdrawal (e.g., poor attendance and/or truancy) or unsuccessful school experiences (e.g., academic failure and grade retention) that often begin in elementary school (Christenson & Thurlow, 2004). Other factors shown to be associated with dropout include low self-esteem, frequent confrontation and lack of acceptance by teachers and peers, low involvement in extracurricular activities, and a general dislike for school (Lever et al., 2004).

Parent and Family Factors

The major family factor associated with dropout is lack of parental support and supervision. In a study conducted by Rumberger (1995), students who reported less parental supervision had 34% higher odds of dropping out than other students did. Moreover, students from homes with parents who have lower expectations regarding school performance, as well as a low regard and attitude toward education in general tended to leave school before graduating (M. J. McWhirter, 1998). In addition, lack of educational resources and support in the home (e.g., study aids, books, computers) contributed significantly as a factor to increase dropout (M. J. McWhirter, 1998).

School/Community/Societal Factors

Dropouts rarely mention a lack of desire to learn as a reason for their decision to leave school. A lack of relevance between the school's curriculum and the circumstances of student's lives as well as a lack of belongingness are often major reasons. This is especially significant for racial/ethnic minorities in the U.S. educational system. Many of the students who do not graduate are the victims (at least partially) of school systems that failed to understand and respond to their legitimate educational and cultural differences and needs. Schools cannot effectively educate children without giving consideration to the economic, cultural, and familial contexts from which they come (M. J. McWhirter, 1998). We all don't come from White middle-class families with two heterosexual parents and lots of resources and support.

Dropout is considered when a student "officially" or "unofficially" leaves school before his or her program of study is complete, without transfer. This is the most extreme and detrimental level of school failure. Dropout rates have been found to be steady and are consistently found among the most vulnerable student populations. Dropping out of school has been found to have lifelong economic and financial negative consequences, not only for the individual but also for society in general.

It is important to recognize that dropout is rarely a quick decision and is often a long process of slow disengagement from school. The typical dropout has already experienced many of the other levels of school failure, including academic failure, truancy, and grade retention. Dropouts also don't receive much social support from their families, school environments, and society in general.

Summary

Four levels of school failure have been discussed: academic failure, truancy, grade retention, and dropout. Each level has unique defining characteristics, but unsurprisingly all of the levels have similarities. Each level involves students who are struggling with their social and cognitive development, have limited or no social support from family and the school environment, and often find themselves culturally disconnected from values and ideals of the system that they are mandated to attend. Consequently, these students fail the school system, impacting their personal and professional livelihood forever.

Identifying the "problem" is not enough. It is important to make efforts toward change and decrease all levels of school failure. School counselors need to be involved in these intervention and/or prevention programs and efforts throughout school systems nationwide because they occupy a key position within the school environment. The next section will discuss the role of school counselors in working with school failure, discussing various interventions and/or preventive efforts they can employ in an effort to abolish school failure.

Practice—The Role of the School Counselor

School counselors are an essential factor in working with students who fail in school. It is their goal, according to the national standards for school counseling, as school counselors to facilitate, promote, and enhance academic, career, and personal/social development for the total student population in school (Baker, 2000). However, the wide-ranging demands of helping to improve the academic achievement of students who have not previously received full benefits from the educational system (and have consequently "failed") are challenging, especially as counselors continue to have large student-to-counselor ratios and deal with increasingly difficult, diverse student problems and parental issues. In addition, school counselors often are also required to spend a great deal of time on administrative tasks and other duties unrelated to their position and/or training, sometimes reaching up to 40% of their time (Gysbers, 2004). Moreover, as a result of federal interventions as No Child Left Behind Act, school counselors are facing increasing pressure to demonstrate how the work they do with students contributes to avoiding school failure and increasing student academic achievement (Baker).

School counselors can become more effective in their roles if they become more flexible, adopting an ecological approach to their work. From an ecological perspective, counselors should consider and incorporate factors inherent within the student, as well as factors within the student's environment (i.e., school, family, and community; Abrams et al., 2005) An ecological framework recognizes that each individual's life is affected by the attitudes and ideologies of his or her environments and considers interventions that address some of the pressures and stressors on students' lives stemming from these influences. Interventions may focus not only on addressing the individual student (e.g., direct individual counseling services), but also on more broad systemic levels of intervention, such as the student's family, school, community, and/or others having either direct or indirect influence on that student. The following are recommendations for school counselors from an ecological framework, to effectively work with students who are failing within the school system.

Individual Level

The Counselor

Before any steps are taken toward any level of intervention, school counselors must first "look in the mirror," and begin with their own personal development. School counselors must develop multicultural awareness and competence in order to provide effective and relevant educational experiences for all students. The first stage of multicultural competence is self-awareness. Awareness of self includes introspection of one's own thoughts and feelings regarding culture (Fusick & Charkow Bordeau, 2004). Self-introspection involves gaining an awareness and understanding of the values, behaviors, and beliefs of one's various reference group memberships (e.g., race, ethnicity, gender, social class, sexual orientation), and how these affect one's interactions in the world. This is a vital process before one begins to try to understand others. Without awareness of self, counselors may unknowingly discount or dismiss cultural influences and differences among the students they serve, and subconsciously believe they understand the culturally different when, in fact, they view others from their own cultural lens, which may cause certain things to be taken for granted (Locke, 2003). Counselors need to remember that they bring their own cultural worldview to their interactions with students, and their perspectives and experiences are not mutually exclusive to everyone else.

Counselors need to explore other cultures and the worldviews of others as well. School counselors need to understand and accept the worldviews of others in a nonjudgmental manner in order to work effectively with all students. This is particularly important in urban settings where there is increasing cultural diversity, and counseling interventions are continuously impacted by language issues and cultural differences (Lee, 2005). School counselors need to acquire practical knowledge about a student's cultural background and daily living experiences (Sue & Sue, 2003). However, one must be careful not to overgeneralize things learned about other cultures as applicable to all members of that population. Cultural group membership does not mean that people are not individuals with uniqueness or differences. All students must be seen as both individuals *and* members of their particular cultural groups (Locke, 2003).

Counseling Services—Individual

With a greater understanding of one's own cultural awareness and of others, school counselors can provide effective individual counseling services to students. The school counselor is often the first line of defense to identify critical issues occurring with the student, as well as to intervene in crisis situations. School counselors can provide short-term counseling as well as referral to community mental health resources. This is particularly important for children and families who do not have the financial resources or insurance benefits to support mental health services outside of schools (Romano & Kachgal, 2004).

Counseling Services—Group

While there are clear benefits to offering individual counseling, it is not always financially feasible, practical, or even culturally appropriate for many students (Yeh, 2004). Therefore, school counselors may need to reduce the amount of time in individual counseling with students and work toward serving larger groups of students. Working with students in groups may provide opportunities for doing outreach, developing and implementing programs that effectively deliver preventive interventions to larger numbers of students, and encouraging students to learn from each other (Yeh). For example, elementary and/or middle school counselors can offer direct instruction in social skills to groups of students in the classroom as an intervention, especially when social isolation and feelings of rejection have been found to contribute to a student's performance. This is most appropriate for students at these earlier stages of development. In addition, there may be more classroom time available for counselors to run psycho-educational groups, as there are fewer requirements for graduation for students at these levels.

Parent/Family Level

Difficulties that begin in the home often manifest themselves within the school setting (Abrams et al., 2005), and counselors need to be at the forefront for identifying those students with familial stressors. This may involve counselors stepping outside of their office from their traditional role and becoming advocates and liaisons for students (J. J. McWhirter, 1998). School counselors can explore the chaos, pressure, and stress that may result from multiple activities and demands on the lives of parents and/or caretakers that may be contributing to the students' school performance. As an advocate, the school counselor identifies a need that is not being met or a past injustice that has not being corrected by the school and speaks for or in support of the student and/or family in requesting a needed service (Juntunen, Atkinson, & Tierney, 2003).

As a liaison, school counselors can advocate for appropriate social services for students and their parents. This is especially pertinent for students living in poverty, usually in urban and rural areas (approximately 22% to 24% of urban and rural children live in poverty; Hines, 2002). Concentrated poverty heightens the probability that school children will lack access to regular medical care, have a parent who never finished high school, become pregnant, or drop out (Lee, 2005). Medical and mental health services are limited and community services are usually fragmented in high poverty areas, and the school counselor can facilitate access to information for students and parents and serve as a liaison or mediator among student, parents, the school, and other agencies (Locke, 2003).

It is clearly important for school counselors to have good working relationships with the families of their students. In general, it is essential to make every effort to involve parents and other caregivers in the academic lives of youth. Adults were found to exert a large influence on the behaviors that bolster mental health among marginalized youth. Although peers are increasingly more important during adolescence, all children and adolescents remain attached to parents even as they expand their networks of associations (Estell, Farmer, Cairns, & Cairns, 2002). School counselors can help parents structure their worlds and offer a support network so that the school tasks students need to accomplish are achievable (Ungar, 2004). As an intervention, counselors can suggest to parents to make time to talk and listen to their children. This simple intervention requires no additional financial resources or funds and can increase quality time spent between children and their parents, increase parental awareness of their child's behaviors and opinions, and improve their relationships (Abrams et al., 2005).

School Level

Schoolwide Prevention/Intervention Program Development

In general, successful intervention and/or prevention programs to address school failure need to be comprehensive, interfacing family, school, and community efforts rather than offering a single, narrow intervention in one environment (McCluskey et al., 2004). Programs should be implemented over time and have a longitudinal focus, rather than focusing on a single period in time. Change to reverse school failure should be considered in terms of years rather than weeks, especially since most types of failure among children and adolescents are the result of a long process of disengagement (McEvoy & Welker, 2000).

School counselors may also need to be creative with their interventions and not stress the school faculty and its resources. In school settings, such as urban and rural schools, there are often fewer resources and less money to spend per student, as well as less access to educational technology, and greater teacher and administrator shortages (Hines, 2002; Lee, 2005). Counselors may need to stretch funding and find alternative ways to pay for programs.

Interventions should be tailored to fit individual students' needs, rather than adopting a programmatic "one-size-fits-all" orientation. All attempts should be made to personalize education for students. Counselors should strive to understand the nature of academic, social, and personal problems affecting students and tailor services to address students' individualized concerns (Christenson & Thurlow, 2004).

Programs should also do more than focus on increasing student productivity. They should help students and families who feel marginalized in their relations with teachers and peers feel connected to school and with learning.

Student engagement across the school years depends on the degree to which there is a match between the student's characteristics and the school environment, so that the student is able to handle the academic and behavioral demands of school. Effective programs should focus on building and fostering positive relationships between students and those who will be supportive to them (e.g., teachers, parents, and peers), as well working on developing students' academic skills (Christenson & Thurlow, 2004).

Additional Points to Consider

Identify risk factors early. Identifying factors that interfere with academic success is a crucial first step in the process of choosing interventions to address this issue, and the best way to gain an accurate picture of interfering factors is the use of data. Concrete information about which students are failing (e.g., failing specific classes, increased absenteeism rates, etc.) can give counselors valuable knowledge to advocate for programs and polices that will be effective (Dimmitt, 2003). School counselors can build a database that provides them with information about the most salient factors for their population and continue to collect data consistently to identify problems within their system (Dimmitt).

For example, school districts could examine patterns of absenteeism within their school to identify youths at risk for dropout and to design subsequent preventive programs. Factors to consider may be number, frequency, and types of absences. Child reports are particularly important to understanding concerns in specific classes. Also as part of the data collection, consideration must be given to whether a child's absenteeism is primarily related to parental factors, such as illness, pregnancy, homelessness, or maltreatment. All of this data and information can be obtained from a combination of child, parent, teacher, and school attendance reports (Kearney, 2003).

School counselors can build collaborations and research partnerships between school counseling programs and counselor education programs at the university and graduate levels to assist them with data collection and research efforts within their school. These collaborations can provide needed resources and information for all involved. For the counselor already working in schools, partnerships with graduate students can provide assistance with research information and data analysis. In exchange, school counselors can provide useful educational experiences for graduate students who will learn more about the interplay of theory and practice in school counseling (Dimmitt, 2003).

Try to get all school faculty and staff involved. Within school, children and adolescents interact with and are impacted by a variety of school personnel, and as such, everyone within the school has a considerable impact on the students' educational success. It is important to try to gain an atmosphere of collegiality and collaboration so all within the school who are expected to implement new systems of change feel as though they have been given a voice in their design and can begin to "buy in" or gain a vested interest in the effort to ensure its success. Because time is a scarce resource, potentially successful interventions will receive little support if school personnel consider them to be too labor intensive. Often, intervention efforts fail because they are imposed from the top down as an additional responsibility. School counselors can use their group dynamic skills and training to bring together a team of individuals who are willing to work together, and then be leaders of the group to facilitate the intervention process (Abrams et al., 2005).

Moreover, school counselors can offer workshops to educate and inform other school personnel about the needs of the student population. If programs will be developed to "add on" responsibilities for teachers and other staff, there is a need for proper training and staff development opportunities. For example, counselors can act as consultants creating workshops to discuss curricular changes to make content more relevant to students' needs. Moreover, counselors can have discussions with teachers about multiple learning styles, the use of multimodal teaching methods, and/or multiple types of assessment to share information about differing student learning styles based on cultural background and differences (J. J. McWhirter., 1998).

Establish a coherent and clear framework for programs. In the absence of a clear rationale, many school-based programs for students who fail may be constructed in a seemingly random and inconsistent manner (McEvoy & Welker, 2000). Schools with mission statements, comprehensive curriculum plans, schoolwide assessments, and coordinated intervention programs are more likely to have greater success (Dimmitt, 2003).

Emphasize students' strengths instead of deficits. All school personnel must emphasize the development of students' competencies rather than dwelling on their deficits (Christenson & Thurlow, 2004). School counselors' and teachers' beliefs and attitudes about students have considerable impact on the educational process. When significant adults believe that their students are competent and capable, those students are more likely to be successful (Dimmitt, 2003).

Continue to have ongoing assessments of programs. Ongoing assessments of implemented programs are necessary to evaluate their effectiveness within the school and with its students. As the school's climate changes and programs are implemented, there may be a need to add or delete aspects of the program. This requires the school to have in place a system for monitoring students' changes and goals, which can be led by school counselors (McEvoy & Welker, 2000).

Case Examples

Brooks-McNamara and Pederson (2006) illustrated an excellent real-life example of a systemic intervention program initiated by a school counselor, created from an ecological theoretical conceptualization. An elementary school counselor observed that a high percentage of third-grade students were failing state standardized tests. This spurned a further, more detailed investigation of this third-grade "low-scoring" cohort. An examination of several factors, including student family background profiles, revealed that most of the students in this cohort came from single-parent, low-income families in the same apartment complex. This was the beginning of the development of a powerful intervention program at this school. Strategic planning teams were developed that resulted in the following intervention. In school, strategies for supplemental help in reading, writing, and math were created. In addition, middle and high school students were recruited from the district as peer tutors. (These students also lived near if not within the same apartment complex as most of the third-grade students.) The counselor was able to recruit educators to conduct parent workshops for encouraging and supporting academic achievement at home, using the resources available to them. After the initial development of the program, a 2-year post follow-up review was conducted. One new strategy was developed. Some of the parents developed an agreement for release of information between the school and the "Homework Club" personnel. (These were the peer tutors and teachers who were involved in tutoring the students.) Once this agreement was signed, the school was able to discuss and assist with monitoring student progress without having to first consult with the parent. This was an effective new strategy as many parents were not able, due to conflicting work schedules, to be as directly involved in the program. However, their children were not sacrificed, rather communal efforts helped to maintain their academic progress. The school counselor continued to track the overall achievement of the cohort of students. Results indicated that the intervention was a success; 88% of the third-grade students passed the reading exam, and 86% passed the math!

Another fascinating, effective example of an intervention program for school failure utilizing a group approach is EGAS (empowerment groups for academic success; Bemak,

Chi-Ying Chung, & Siroskey-Sabdo, 2005). This program was developed by the principal author, who worked closely with a school counselor in an urban Midwestern school identified as having students at the highest level of risk for school failure. This school experienced high rates of expulsion and suspension, academic failure, absenteeism, and school dropout. The goal of the program was to assist in resolving the difficult personal and interpersonal issues faced by high-risk students, as a means of improving academic performance and attendance. The program took a group approach, and its members were composed of 7 African American girls in the 10th grade, all of whom were identified by counselors, teachers, and administrators, as being at the highest level of risk, and who had been involved in previous failed school interventions. The key element to the EGAS approach is that it emphasizes empowerment through group process, moving away from the traditional structured group format. Group members controlled the group so that true empowerment resulted as members had an actual say in how the group was run, instead of a "facilitator" determining what was important and relevant to discuss. The group decided on a weekly agenda, meeting once a week for 45 minutes during school hours. Topics of discussion included family and peer relationships, death of friends and loved ones, pregnancy and single parenting, experiences with first sexual encounters, smoking, confrontations and poor relationships with teachers, and general school and academic concerns. Interestingly, the group felt that it was able to reenact a "family" through its members, providing support, which is an important and necessary aspect of healing, as well as a crucial factor to promote future school success. Moreover, through the exploration of real-life issues and struggles the group members faced, for the first time group members were able to examine the relevance and the relationship between these factors and their school performance. As a result of their participation in this group, marked academic improvements were evident in the group members.

On a more individualistic perspective, TeamMates is another example of an intervention program working with school failure. Dappen and Isernhagen (2006) studied this Midwestern, statewide, school-based, one-to-one mentoring program. TeamMates was initiated formally in 1991 by a football coach at a state university. He asked his players to volunteer to mentor local youth. During the first year, 25 student athletes volunteered to mentor seventh- and eighth-grade students in an urban school district. The program slowly grew, and by 2000, there were 1,490 students and mentors in the program. The TeamMates structure includes a state advisory board, executive director, and four regional coordinators who work with different districts. The state offices provide technical assistance for operation of the mentorship program. The mentors meet once a week with students during school time. The primary task of the mentor is to establish a positive, personal relationship with the student and assist him or her in any way possible. The program works with students beginning in early middle school through high school, with the goal of post secondary education. Although this particular program was not initiated by a school counselor, school counselors can follow this successful model and work to incorporate similar programs within their school districts.

Community/Societal Level

One must acknowledge that schools were created and designed to meet the needs of the dominant group (i.e., White American middle class); however, with the changing demographics of America's school children (currently almost 40% of the total public school population is students of color; U.S. Department of Health & Human Services, 2001), changes need to be made to the structure of the school system (J. J. McWhirter, 1998). Societal injustices, such as racism, are all aspects of a culture that must be understood and examined as a part of one's personal belief system, as well as a part of the larger culture in which one functions (Sue & Sue, 2003). Social injustices can be seen in the attitudes and beliefs of the school system in which the counselor works, and the counselor may be supporting these attitudes solely on the basis of participation in his or her school (Locke, 2003). For example, in the past 10 years, the majority of states have adopted statewide student assessment systems (usually in the form of testing), based upon standard state curricula. State policy makers believe that setting high standards will improve the state of education in the United States and decrease school failure. Because the tests are intended to communicate high expectations, all students in the state are required to pass the same test. However, according to the NAEP in 2003, White students outperformed racial/ethnic minorities in almost all subjects (USDE, NCES, 2005), and dropout rates are disproportionately high for students of color (approximately 50%). Are these high-stakes testing reforms serving to improve the educational achievement of everyone or is this another method to marginalize groups that are already culturally, racially, and linguistically disadvantaged?

As agents of systemic change, school counselors can be involved in educational reform efforts. First and foremost, though, school counselors must understand the system and learn how the system works. The chances for success increase if one consults first, rather than intruding and demanding change (Baker, 2000). Moreover, the school counselor who works as an agent for social change must be realistic when supporting the causes of inequity, injustice, and unfair practices within a school and advocating for promoting educational equity for all students. It is essential for school counselors to have the skills and support to balance the institutional realities of working within systems where they may have minimal power (Bemak et al., 2005). They can begin by soliciting community support. Most communities have a wide range of resources including medical professionals, social workers, or spiritual leaders, who together can exert power and pressure to effect change once they are informed of the issue via the school counselor. In particular, within communities of color and in rural communities, school counselors can tap into the inherent support and power within the community to help elicit change (Hines, 2002).

On an individual level, school counselors may serve on school curriculum committees to advocate for changes that address the educational needs of students, such as selecting culturally relevant educational materials (Romano & Kachgal, 2004).

It is important to note that school counselors who accept the challenge to be social change agents should be realistic with their efforts and not try to be martyrs. Counselors need to be careful and protect themselves from burnout; otherwise they will be used up by the same systems they are trying to help their students understand and manage (Baker, 2000).

Summary and Implications

School failure is a pervasive problem that continues to persist in our society in multiple forms. This chapter sought to examine the multiple degrees of school failure beginning with academic failure, which is generally the precursor to more serious levels of school failure, to truancy, grade retention, and most severe, dropout. In general, most understand the problem of school failure as an individual consequence to negative behaviors, and as such, plan interventions based on this individualistic perspective. However, from an ecological perspective, school failure can be understood as a cumulative result of multiple layers of influence on a child's performance, including their family, school, and communal environments. From this broader perspective, one can better identify the stressors (beyond the individual) that impact the student and identify multiple possibilities and ways to respond, intervene, and affect lasting change. The school counselor plays a critical role in helping students and schools address major issues that affect learning and academic achievement. School counselors should expand their role beyond "counselor," to act as consultants, advocates, and social change agents to attend to the full development of students, offering a range of services that include individual and small-group counseling, psycho-educational classroom activities, and consultation with teachers, parents, and community agencies. An ecological approach offers school counselors a useful framework for identifying appropriate interventions in their work with students whose behaviors fit along the school failure continuum.

American society is plagued with rampant social issues that affect students attending school and result in school failure for some. School counselors are in a position in which they cannot ignore these issues and are called upon to intervene with students in ways that may be intimidating, overwhelming, and unfamiliar. Although the training and practice of school counselors has experienced renewed attention in recent years, all training programs need to expand their programs and develop trainees to take on broader roles in their professional identity as school counselors. Training programs need to expose their students to a variety of roles outside the traditional counselor role, such as advocate, consultant, and social-change agent, and help trainees to understand how they can incorporate these identities into the political–social system of the school. Moreover, training programs need to infuse their curriculum with diversity and train students to be more multiculturally competent, especially since our school-aged population is becoming increasingly more racially and ethnically diverse, and these students have been found to be the most vulnerable to school failure.

References

Abrams, K., Theberge, S. K., & Karan, O. C. (2005). Children and adolescents who are depressed: An ecological approach. *Professional School Counseling, 8*, 284–292.

Alexander, K., Entwistle, D., & Dauber, S. (1994). *On the success of failure: A reassessment of the effects of retention in the primary grades.* New York: Cambridge University Press.

Allen, B. A., & Boykin, A. W. (1992). African-American children and the educational process: Alleviating cultural discontinuity through prescriptive pedagogy. *School Psychology Review, 21*, 586–596.

Baker, S. B. (2000). *School counseling for the twenty-first century* (3rd ed.). Upper Saddle River, NJ: Prentice Hall.

Barth, R. P. (1994). Reducing nonattendance in elementary schools. *Social Work in Education, 6*, 151–166.

Becker, B. E., & Luthar, S. S. (2002). Social-emotional factors affecting achievement outcomes among disadvantaged students: Closing the achievement gap. *Educational Psychologist, 37*, 197–214.

Bemak, F., Chi-Ying Chung, R., & Siroskey-Sabdo, L. A. (2005). Empowerment groups for academic success: An innovative approach to prevent high school failure for at-risk, urban African Americans. *Professional School Counseling, 8,* 377–389.

Blair, C. (2001). The early identification of risk for grade retention among African American children at risk for school difficulty. *Applied Developmental Science, 5,* 37–50.

Brooks-McNamara, V., & Pederson, L. (2006). Practitioner inquiry: A method to advocate for systemic change. *Professional School Counseling, 9,* 257–260.

Christenson, S. L., & Thurlow, M. L. (2004). School dropouts: Prevention considerations, interventions, and challenges. *Current Directions in Psychological Science, 13,* 36–39.

Dappen, L., & Isernhagen, J. C. (2006). Urban and nonurban schools: Examination of a statewide student mentoring program. *Urban Education, 41,* 151–168.

Dimmit, C. (2003). Transforming school counseling practice through collaboration and the use of data: A study of academic failure in high school. *Professional School Counseling, 6,* 340–349.

Estell, D. B., Farmer, T. W., Cairns, R. B., & Cairns, B. D. (2002). Social relations and academic achievement in inner-city early elementary classrooms. *International Journal of Behavioral Development, 26,* 518–528.

Fusick, L., & Charkow Bordeau, W. (2004). Counseling at-risk Afro-American youth: An examination of contemporary issues and effective school-based strategies. *Professional School Counseling, 8,* 102–115.

Garry, E. M. (1996). *Truancy: First steps to a lifetime of problems.* Washington, DC: U.S. Department of Justice, Office of Juvenile Justice and Delinquency Prevention.

Grissom, J., & Shepard, L. (1989). Repeating and dropping out of school. In L. A. Shepard & M. L. Smith (Eds.), *Flunking grades: Research and policies on retention* (pp. 16–33). London: The Falmer Press.

Gysbers, N. C. (2004). Counseling psychologist and school counseling partnerships: Overlooked? Underutilized? But needed! *The Counseling Psychologist, 32,* 245–257.

Harvey, W. B. (1984). The educational system and black mental health. *Journal of Negro Education, 53,* 444–454.

Hines, P. L. (2002). Transforming the rural school counselor. *Theory into Practice, 41,* 192–201.

Jimerson, S. R. (1999). On the failure of failure: Examining the association between early grade retention and education and employment outcomes during adolescence. *Journal of School Psychology,* 243–272.

Jimerson, S. R., Anderson, G. E., & Whipple, A. D. (2002). Winning the battle and losing the war: Examining the relation between grade retention and dropping out of high school. *Psychology in the Schools, 39,* 441–457.

Jimerson, S. R., & Schuder, M. R. (1996, June). *Is grade retention an appropriate academic intervention? Longitudinal data provide further insights.* Paper presented at Head Start's Third National Research Conference, Washington, DC.

Juntunen, C. L., Atkinson, D. R., & Tierney, G. (2003). School counselors and school psychologists as school-home-community liaisons in ethnically diverse schools. In P. B. Pederson, & J. C. Carey (Eds.), *Multicultural counseling in schools: A practical handbook* (2nd ed., pp. 149–170). Boston: Pearson Education, Inc.

Jussim, L., & Harber, K. D. (2005). Teacher expectations and self-fulfilling prophecies: Knowns and unknowns, resolved and unresolved controversies. *Personality & Social Psychology Review, 9,* 131–155.

Kaplan, D. S., Peck, B. M., & Kaplan, H. B. (1997). Decomposing the academic failure-dropout relationship: A longitudinal analysis. *The Journal of Educational Research, 90,* 331–343.

Kearney, C. A. (2003). Bridging the gap among professionals who address youths with school absenteeism: Overview and suggestions for consensus. *Professional Psychology: Research and Practice, 1,* 57–65.

Lee, C. C. (2005). Urban school counseling: Context, characteristics, and competencies. *Professional School Counselor, 8,* 184–188.

Lever, N., Sander, M. A., Lombardo, S., Randall, C., Axelrod, J., Rubenstein, M., et al. (2004). A drop-out prevention program for high-risk inner-city youth. *Behavior Modification,* 513–527.

Locke, D. C. (2003). Improving the multicultural competence of educators. In P. B. Pederson & J. C. Carey (Eds.), *Multicultural counseling in schools: A practical handbook* (2nd ed., pp. 171–189). Boston: Pearson Education, Inc.

McCluskey, C. P., Bynum, T. S., & Patchin, J. W. (2004). Reducing chronic absenteeism: An assessment of an early truancy initiative. *Crime & Delinquency, 50,* 214–234.

McCoy, A. R., & Reynolds, A. J. (1999). Grade retention and school performance: An extended investigation. *Journal of School Psychology, 37,* 273–298.

McEvoy, A., & Welker, R. (2000). Antisocial behavior, academic failure, and school climate: A critical review. *Journal of Emotional and Behavioral Disorders, 8,* 130–141.

McWhirter, J. J. (1998). An introduction to at-risk issues: The tree. In J. J. McWhirter, B. T. McWhirter, A. M. McWhirter, & E. H. McWhirter (Eds.), *At risk youth: A comprehensive response for counselors, teachers, psychologists, and human service professionals* (2nd ed., pp. 3–19). Pacific Grove, CA: Brooks/Cole Publishing Company.

McWhirter, M. J. (1998). School dropouts. In J. J. McWhirter, B. T. McWhirter, A. M. McWhirter, & E. H. McWhirter (Eds.), *At risk youth: A comprehensive response for counselors, teachers, psychologists, and human service professionals* (2nd ed., pp. 95–113). Pacific Grove, CA: Brooks/Cole Publishing Company.

Meisels, S. J., & Liaw, F. R. (1993). Failure in grade: Do retained students catch up? *Journal of Educational Research, 87,* 69–77.

Needham, B. L., Crosnoe, R., & Muller, C. (2004). Academic failure in secondary school: The inter-related role of health problems and educational context. *Social Problems, 51,* 569–586.

Neville, H. A., & Mobley, M. (2001). Social identities in contexts: An ecological model of multicultural counseling processes. *Counseling Psychologist, 29,* 471–486.

Randolph, K. A., Fraser, M. W., & Orthner, D. K. (2004). Educational resilience among youth at risk. *Substance Use & Misuse, 39,* 747–767.

Romano, J. L., & Kachgal, M. M. (2004). Counseling psychology and school counseling: An underutilized partnership, *The Counseling Psychologist, 32,* 184–215.

Rumberger, R. W. (1995). Dropping out of middle school: A multilevel analysis of students and schools. *American Educational Research Journal, 32,* 583–625.

Sue, D. W., & Sue, D. (2003). *Counseling the culturally diverse, theory & practice* (4th ed.). New York: John Wiley & Sons, Inc.

Ungar, M. (2004). The importance of parents and other caregivers to the resilience of high-risk adolescents. *Family Process, 43,* 23–41.

U.S. Department of Education, National Center for Education Statistics. (2005). Retrieved May 19, 2005, from http://nces.ed.gov//programs/coe/2004/section2/indicator11.asp

U.S. Department of Health and Human Services. (2001). *Mental health: Culture, race and ethnicity—A supplement to Mental Health: A Report of the Surgeon General.* Rockville, MD: U.S. Department of Health and Human Services, U.S. Public Health Service.

Yeh, C. J. (2004). Multicultural and contextual research and practice in school counseling. *The Counseling Psychologist, 32,* 278–285.

XXXIX
MEASURING AND EVALUATING ADOLESCENT CONNECTEDNESS

MICHAEL J. KARCHER, MICHELLE R. HOLCOMB, AND ELIAS ZAMBRANO
University of Texas at San Antonio

Introduction

School counselors who can demonstrate that their guidance and counseling programs result in improvements in their students' connectedness to school, teachers, and peers are less likely to be pulled in 100 different directions by administrators, teachers, and parents. Based on our experiences, we argue that this is because such counselors are viewed as providing unique and highly valued services. However, school counselors who utilize a comprehensive and organized approach to deliver guidance presentations, individual student planning, system support, and responsive services (American School Counselor Association [ASCA], 2003), and who can demonstrate that this coordinated set of services results in improved connectedness among their students are less likely to be asked (or expected) to engage in nonguidance activities, such as supervising testing, scheduling classes, or supervising lunch. Or, if asked, these counselors can point to their impressive body of evaluative evidence. They can use it to define the borders of their professional duties and, thereby, educate parents and colleagues alike about the unique and valuable role that professional counselors play in schools.

It is, therefore, incumbent upon school counselors to create and organize a quality program that is amenable to evaluation in order to demonstrate accountability. The planning of such thoughtful, focused, and intentional services takes time, but also requires forethought in order to anticipate desired outcomes that, from the outset, are measurable. Compounding these time constraints on program planning, many school counselors may believe they have limited training or insufficient tools at hand to link their program component's activities to program outcomes.

This chapter provides a guide to help school counselors to both systematically assess and strengthen the impact of their school counseling programs by focusing on promoting changes in students' connectedness. The theory of adolescent *connectedness* (Karcher, 2001) presented in this chapter defines connectedness as movement toward others through positive affect and activity. Connectedness is reflected in a student's response to feelings of relatedness and belonging. This definition provides the first key to intervention: To promote connectedness, school counselors must create school contexts where youth feel a sense of belongingness at school and relatedness to teachers and peers. When youth feel a sense of relatedness and belonging, they typically value those relationships and social institutions in which they experience the belongingness and relatedness. But school counselors then must help students pursue related activities and relationships which cement their connections through behavioral and affective commitment. Finally, connectedness can be captured in adolescents' own perceptions of their own involvement in and affection for others, activities, and organizations. Given this, connectedness is measurable and can be used as an indicator of program outcomes.

Of course, connectedness is but one outcome or construct a school counselor might wish to measure as evidence of outcomes. Other important constructs include social skills, self-esteem, peer attachment, cultural competence, and other behavioral and attitudinal indices of social competence and a positive orientation to school. For the purposes of this chapter, connectedness is solely emphasized in order to provide a comprehensive overview of one measure, its uses and evaluative procedures, which we believe will allow the reader to make generalizations and comparisons with other measures.

The Problem—Capturing the Effects of School Counseling Programs

The notion of connectedness has become increasingly popular in the media as well as in academic and educational settings (Lezin, Rolleri, Bean, & Taylor, 2004; Resnick, Harris, & Blum, 1993). The construct of connectedness is viewed by many as increasingly important in a mobilized, postindustrialized, multicultural, and technologically alienating society, such as is found in the United States. Children and adolescents need healthy connectedness to family, siblings, friends, and eventually romantic partners in order to weave themselves tightly into a supportive social network. Connectedness to school, teachers, and peers during the middle and high school years is a particularly strong predictor of academic and future success, but it also helps to prevent alienation, which can lead to violence such as that of the Columbine massacre; the Washington, DC, shootings; or the countless other acts of desperation performed by students in recent years (Henrich, Brookmeyer, & Shahar, 2005; Karcher, 2002). Adolescents also need to learn to effectively connect with culturally different peers, the world of reading, a source of spirituality (regardless of persuasion, denomination, or creed), and their neighborhoods. Because parents and researchers alike recognize the ubiquitous necessity of connectedness, it is important for school counselors to know how they can promote and measure connectedness.

Using Connectedness to Capture, Profile, and Predict Developmental Assets

The *Measure of Adolescent Connectedness* described in this chapter had direct parallels to the Developmental Assets presented by the SEARCH Institute. The 40 Assets listed in the SEARCH framework focus the attention of school counselors, teachers, parents, and youth on the positive relationships, opportunities, skills, and values that can support the healthy growth and development of youth (Scales & Leffert, 1999). The model asserts that the more young people experience these 40 Developmental Assets, the more likely they are to engage in prosocial behaviors and conversely, the less likely they are to participate in harmful behaviors (Benson, Galbraith, & Espeland, 1995). Using data collected with the SEARCH Developmental Assets survey, we refer to key assets in later sections to illustrate ways in which the measure of adolescent connectedness can serve as a proxy measure of assets and can thereby be used to facilitate and extend the use of the Developmental Assets framework.

The SEARCH Institute's Developmental Assets constructs have become a central organizational framework for many school districts, helping school counselors organize efforts to promote external and internal assets among students (Scales, 2005). Numerous school districts have used the SEARCH Institute's Developmental Assets framework to make fundamental changes in the structure of their schools and to improve students' relationships with teachers and peers. In addition, statewide initiatives, such as California's Proposition 49, actually require that school connectedness be assessed, in addition to other constructs currently informing guidance programming in schools. The *Measure of Adolescent Connectedness* can be used to supplement and extend the Developmental Assets framework by linking guidance program content with measurable outcomes. We argue that using the connectedness construct and measure described in this chapter may make the asset-promoting activities they propose even more useful in guidance programming.

Finally, our approach is based on the authors' combined experiences of conducting research on connectedness and our firsthand experience as school counselors and the director of school guidance programming for a large urban school district that used the SEARCH Developmental Assets framework as its organizing framework. Based on these experiences, we focus on illustrating ways to track changes in connectedness that result from guidance programming within the schools. In order to help the reader better understand how to assess connectedness among middle and high school–aged students, we present a theory of adolescent connectedness, describe *The Hemingway: Measure of Adolescent Connectedness*, provide normative data for one district and new research on connectedness, and finally bring this theory and research to practice by describing several strategies for developing a program of services that carefully links evaluation with efforts to promote assets and connectedness as part of a comprehensive guidance program.

Theory

Connectedness has been described as one of the five "Cs" that Lerner, Fisher, and Weinberg (2000) suggested youth development programs must target. This is due, in part, to its usefulness as a predictor of a number of developmental competencies as well as risk behaviors. However, while to date no theoretically derived measure of adolescent connectedness has been empirically tested for use in schools, adolescent connectedness has landed squarely in the middle of the emerging field of applied youth development (Roth & Brooks-Gunn, 2003). For example, in their review, Roth and Brooks-Gunn found that all of the youth development programs they reviewed attempted to promote one or more forms of connectedness. Of these programs, 73% explicitly "sought to improve adolescents' connections; connections with their families (40%) and peers (42%) were the most common connection goals for the programs" (p. 207). Yet, only half of those programs designed to promote connectedness actually used a measure of connectedness to evaluate program success. "More programs held goals of promoting . . . connections than actually measured these characteristics in the evaluations. Of 35 programs promoting connectedness only 19 (54%) reported measures of connectedness" (p. 215).

The absence of a measure of adolescent connectedness and definitional framework presents a huge barrier to fully exploiting the usefulness of the connectedness construct as a target of school counseling programs. Adolescent connectedness must be clearly defined and reliably measurable before research can have a positive influence on the field of school counseling and the applied developmental sciences. Measures used in most studies have been ad hoc, and when described within each study, the term *connectedness* often has been used interchangeably with other words such as *bonding*, *attachment*, *belongingness*, and *relatedness*. Not until a clear nomenclature for connectedness is established and measures of connectedness receive sufficient validity evidence will this, the third of the five Cs of applied youth development programs, be a useful and meaningful target for programmatic influences of school counseling on youths' developmental competencies.

The Ecology of Adolescent Connectedness

The model of connectedness presented in this chapter is derived from ecological and developmental theory. From these perspectives each world of the adolescent's social ecology—school, friends, family, and neighborhood—can be viewed as a world of connectedness. Used in this way, the term *world* refers to common and important contexts, relationships, and activities of engagement in the lives of adolescents (Nakkula & Selman, 1991).

The concept of *connectedness* has sometimes been restricted to participation or involvement in interpersonal relationships (Gilligan, 1991; Jordan, Kaplan, Miller, Stiver, & Surrey, 1991), but this definition is needlessly restrictive and inconsistent with the public's broader use of the term, which is more ecological in nature. Broadly defined, connectedness includes the acts of giving back to, being involved with, and investing oneself in an affective manner in places and activities as well as in relationships with other people. "Connectedness occurs when a person is actively involved with another person, object, group or environment, and that involvement promotes a sense of comfort, well-being, and anxiety-reduction" (Hagerty, Lynch-Sauer, Patusky, & Bouwsema, 1993, p. 293). Connectedness is not restricted to relationships. For example, youth can be connected to school and to reading just as they may care for, enjoy, and be actively involved with a teacher, peer, friend, or parent.

We suggest that there is a connectedness to self, which emerges during adolescence as a sense of self that is influenced by unique relationships with family memberships, teachers, and friends (Erikson, 1950; DuBois, Felner, Brand, & Phillips, 1996). Adolescents' self-esteem in these contexts informs a connectedness to self that is primarily present oriented. In addition, the ability to think abstractly results in the differentiation of a *present self* and from a *future self* (Harter, 1999). Because youth can have feelings about and engage in activities directed toward each of these selves, we include them as well.

The ecology of adolescent connectedness includes all of the significant ecological systems (e.g., micro-, macro-, and meso-) that adolescents experience in their day-to-day lives (Bronfenbrenner, 1979). Microsystems include youths' important relationships at home with parents and siblings, in school with teachers and peers, and in youths' neighborhoods with friends. Macrosystems of connectedness are the larger institutions in youths' lives in which these microsystemic relationships and activities occur and include one's neighborhood, family, school, religion, and cultural group. The mesosystems are those processes of connection that link micro- and macrosystems. For example, reading is one main mesosystem that links the home and school by orienting interpersonal connections. Reading is an activity that links the youth to school, teachers, and friends. Adolescent connectedness generalizes beyond immediate dyadic relationships (or microsystems) toward activities associated with these contexts, such as reading. In principle, using this same logic, one could suggest that smoking, drinking, and fighting (as something youth may participate in with friends) are mesosystems as well, but we restrict the term connectedness to types of affective and behavioral engagements that are (at least potentially) catalysts for positive youth development. And although connectedness to one's friends and neighborhood can contribute to risk-taking behaviors, a sufficient degree of connectedness to friends and one's neighborhood environment is essential to positive youth development. By comparison, because smoking and drinking do not provide a similar protective function for youth, they are not forms of connectedness included in our conceptualization.

The Continuum From Conventional to Unconventional Connectedness

Each of these worlds of connectedness can be characterized as falling somewhere along a continuum of conventionality. This concept of *conventionality* was initially proposed and described by R. Jessor and S. L. Jessor (1977), and it is used here as it is defined in *The Oxford Compact English Dictionary*: *Convention* refers to the "way in which something is usually done" and "socially acceptable behaviors" (Soanes, 2003, p. 234). *Conventional* means "following social convention; not individual or adventurous" (p. 234), where the conventions are those behavioral prescriptions set by adult society. Connectedness, then, can be characterized as either conventional (adult sanctioned) or unconventional (youth sanctioned).

Highly conventional worlds include those contexts, relationships, and activities that are structured, sanctioned, and supervised by adults. These conventional worlds of connectedness are antithetical to problem behaviors and risk taking (Donovan, Jessor, & Costa, 1988). Conventional connectedness typically includes the social worlds of school, teachers, reading, religion, and family—all of which are structured by adults and directed toward the future. Positive orientations toward and active involvement in all of these worlds serve to buffer against violence (Honora & Rolle, 2002; O'Donnell, Hawkins, & Abbott, 1995).

Conversely, connectedness to peers, friends, and the neighborhood may be conventional if the nature of these relationships and activities reflects attitudes and conventions prescribed by adults. However, this tends not to be the case for many youth (Karcher, 2001). Due to its customarily unsupervised nature, connectedness to neighborhoods and time spent with peers, friends, romantic partners, and (for some) siblings is primarily unconventional. Being antithetical to adult conventions, unconventional connectedness often elicits activities that may lead to problem behaviors. The *un*conventional worlds of connectedness are those social ecologies in which youth themselves typically dictate the norms, activities, and structures that govern or dictate appropriate interaction. Youths' neighborhoods (for early adolescents), friendships, and romantic relationships (for older adolescents) are the most common examples of contexts/relationships in which unconventional connectedness develops and directs behaviors.

All adolescents need to achieve a minimum amount of connectedness across their social ecology and in both conventional and unconventional worlds. Problems typically emerge for those youth who are not able to establish sufficient connectedness within the family, school, and other conventional contexts, relationships, and activities (e.g., reading). Youth at risk for academic underachievement often establish an imbalance, engaging in more unconventional than conventional connectedness.

Promoting connectedness in the school setting can serve to counterbalance the increasing importance of connectedness to peers, friends, and romantic partners during adolescence by providing an opportunity for conventionally disconnected youth to form connections with more conventional peers and adults at school. Youth whose primary affections and engagement are with peers and friends engage in more unconventional, illicit behaviors and are more likely to denounce school and other conventional contexts and relationships. In contrast, youth who are actively involved in, enjoy, and feel positive about school are less likely to engage in violent behavior, substance use, and other related problems that interfere with academic success (Cernkovich & Giordana, 1992; Farrington, 1991; O'Donnell et al., 1995; Olin, 2001). For this reason, promoting active engagement in school and positive feelings about school (viz., connectedness to school) should be at least one of the primary targets of school-based violence prevention programs. Promoting connectedness to friends who engage more in conventional, prosocial behaviors, such as by encouraging students to participate in extracurricular activities, clubs, and organizations where friendships grow in the context of conventional activities should be another target of programs.

The Developmental Origins of Adolescent Connectedness

Connectedness has several likely precursors, including attachment to caregivers, relatedness to others, and feelings of belongingness within social groups. Karcher (2004) proposed that connectedness develops in reaction to (a) attachment, (b) interpersonal social support, and (c) group-level experiences of belonging (see Figure 39.1). We define *connectedness* as youth's active involvement and caring for other people, places, and activities. Connectedness is the reciprocation of the support and positive affect that other people have provided youth in specific places. This reciprocal process reveals an opportunity for structuring programs and experiences in schools that aim to promote connectedness.

Connectedness is not a feeling of belonging or relatedness; rather connectedness reflects an extension and reciprocation of basic attachment and bonding processes into the adolescents' widening social ecology. As with indicators of attachment, connectedness reflects proximity seeking (i.e., movement toward) and positive affect for people, places, and activities in the adolescent's life. This is an important definitional distinction. Connectedness is not a bond that is felt, but a volitional, active "bonding" with other people, places, and activities. In this way, promoting connectedness in schools means not *only* "helping students feel supported" but *also* creating supportive conditions, such as through group work, activities, and collaborative learning, which act to foster connections in the form of action-based, attitude-driven involvement in school.

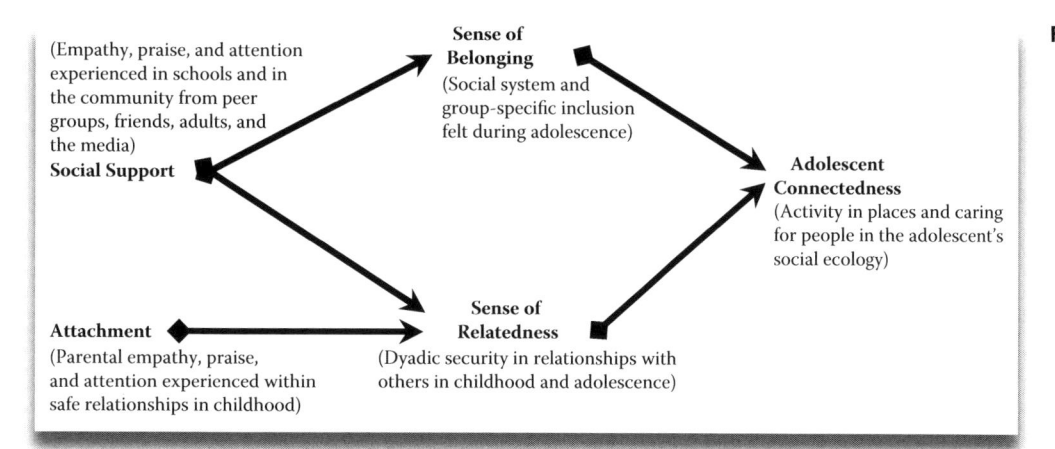

Figure 39.1 A hypothesized model of how attachment, social support, relatedness, and belonging contribute to adolescent connectedness.

Connectedness: The Reciprocation of Belonging, Relatedness, and Attachment

Connectedness has, as its source, positive relationships and experiences with others, and more specifically, relationships and experiences from which youth garner esteem and competence. Ideally, early in life, primary experiences of relatedness with caregivers result in positive attachments with caregivers and provide children with their initial sources of support, esteem, and praise (Ainsworth, 1989; Kohut, 1977). Later, other forms of social support build upon these early experiences, and provide interpersonal relatedness outside the family (e.g., teachers, peers, and friends) and experiences of group belonging beyond the family (see Figure 39.1). These socially supportive interactions usually result in positive feelings of relatedness and belonging. Youth reciprocate these feelings and "connect" with others by assigning them positive affect and seeking continued interaction with them (Baumeister & Leary, 1995). This reciprocation is similar to that of plugging in a power cord whereby one actively seeks out the source of connectedness (relatedness and belonging). Connectedness is not synonymous with relatedness and belonging; connectedness is a behavioral and attitudinal response to those feelings.

Attachment. Connectedness is present early in life in the caregiver–child bond. Attachment reflects the behavioral reciprocation of affective experiences by the child to the caregiver through proximity seeking and positive affect (Chodorow, 1978; Stern, 1985). Like the toddler, the adolescent becomes connected to those social worlds that provide the adolescent the basic interpersonal ingredients of development—empathy, praise, and attention within relationships in which they receive clear, consistent structure (Ainsworth, 1989; Kohut, 1977; Kohut & Elson, 1987). Likewise, adolescents report positive affect and demonstrate proximity seeking most strongly toward those people—parents, siblings, peers, friends, or teachers—who have provided them with empathy, praise, and attention in a clear and consistent manner.

This is key to intervention and may explain why these qualities have been found in the most effective prevention programs (Catalano, Berglund, Ryan, Lonczak, & Hawkins, 2002; Schorr, 1988). Arguably, no amount of skills training or heightened knowledge will effectively curb risk taking among youth if such interventions are devoid of positive interpersonal relationships in which youth can feel competent, understood, and important.

Social support. Past and present levels of social support will affect youths' receptivity to interpersonal interventions. There is evidence that early attachment experiences predict individuals' openness to receiving help and willingness to accept social support during adolescence. For example, Mallinckrodt (1991) found that the quality of late adolescents' relationships with their families and with important nonfamily members was a significant predictor of the quality of their therapeutic working alliance. The author argued, "[T]he ability to meaningfully connect with others is presumed to be a good indicator of their capacity to form productive working alliances" (p. 402). Therefore, adolescents' ability to benefit from social support will be constrained by the quality of their experiences with other people (Lee & Davis, 2000), such that those who have received the least social support in the past may be the hardest to reach by school counselors. Indeed, others have found that aggressive youth who overestimate their social relatedness (and report excessively high self-esteem) can be the most difficult to reach through interventions (Prasad-Gaur, Hughes, & Cavell, 2001). Relatedness and belonging are two indicators of how open youth may be to receiving social support from others.

Relatedness. Relatedness is the felt sense of closeness and of being valued by another individual. Relatedness is determined, in part, by the security youth experienced in early caregiver–child relationships, and relatedness predicts the degree to which youth will seek interpersonal connection in later relationships with peers, friends, and teachers (Kuperminc, Blatt, & Leadbeater, 1997). Hagerty et al. (1993) suggested that relatedness is a "functional, behavioral system rooted in early attachment behaviors and patterns," such that "affiliation or exploration are activated only after the attachment behavioral system" (p. 292). Breaks in relatedness, such as through forced separations, undermine connectedness by lessening youths' willingness to invest time and energy in relationships with others (Kuperminc et al., 1997; Richters & Martinez, 1993). For example, Midgley, Feldlauffer, and Eccles (1989) reported that students who moved from elementary classrooms where they experienced high teacher support to middle school classrooms where they perceived less teacher support showed decreases in their interest in learning. In short, undermined relatedness creates a lapse in connectedness. When teachers do not provide consistent sources of empathy, praise, and attention, as well as a clear, consistent structure, youth will become less involved in school and will become less inclined to establish conventional school-based relationships (van Aken & Asendorpf, 1997).

Belonging. When relatedness occurs in groups of people or in defined contexts, the result is the experience of belonging. Belonging is of paramount importance to adolescents. *The need to belong* is defined, not as the need to be the passive recipient of supportive relationships, but as the need for "frequent [positive and pleasing] interaction plus persistent caring" (Baumeister & Leary, 1995). Hagerty et al. (1993) described connectedness to others, as well as to organizations and their activities, as a reciprocation of experienced belonging and relatedness that has, directly or indirectly, primary attachment relationships at its source. How accepted and valued a youth feels by a particular group shapes how connected, involved, and concerned that youth will be with people and activities in that organization. This is because youth confirm and acknowledge their experience of belonging by becoming connected through increased interaction and caring for other people and places (see Figure 39.1).

Defined from an ecological point of view, then, adolescent connectedness reflects a youth's volitional involvement in relationships, contexts, and activities that he or she deems positive, worthwhile, and important. As a reciprocation of one's positive experiences of relatedness and belonging with others in particular places, connectedness is a function of the social support presented to individuals, his or her openness to receiving that social support, and security in those relationships and contexts. School staff and peers can vary the social support they provide to students; however, they cannot as easily change students' openness to receiving that social support. Receptivity to social support is partly driven by prior experiences with others, including early interactions with caregivers. In addition, openness to social support is influenced by recent and current experiences both of inclusion with or exclusion from groups and teams as well as experiences of failure in relationships and academics, all of which suggest to a given youth whether others view him or her as positive, worthwhile, and important.

Three Additional Dimensions Key to Understanding Connectedness in Schools

Many school counselors work with a student body that reflects a great deal of ethnic, racial, and socioeconomic diversity. Increased immigration from countries whose cultural beliefs differ from middle-class American and White Protestant values encourages school counselors to think more broadly about how adolescents experience connectedness as a function of their cultural backgrounds. Three key dimensions that need to be considered are time orientation, collectivism versus individualism, and familism, all of which will influence how the school counselor's efforts to promote assets and connectedness are understood and received by students.

The temporal nature of connectedness: Present and future-oriented connectedness. Distinctions between conventional and unconventional connectedness parallel, but are distinct from, future- versus present-oriented connectedness. Just as connectedness may have both protective and risk-promoting properties, depending on those to whom or to what place the connectedness refers, most places and relationships can be considered to be future or present oriented. Time with friends and family tends to be present oriented as it focuses on the here and now; whereas time spent in school, with teachers, and to some degree even in religious practice, is more oriented to the future. Future-oriented connectedness tends to serve as a protective factor in adolescent development by buffering difficult circumstances and inhibiting impulsive, risky behavior that could pose negative consequences on future opportunities.

Collectivistic versus individualistic connectedness. Some manifestations of connectedness reflect a relational emphasis, while others reflect a primarily self-oriented, individualistic emphasis (Cooper, 1999). For example, connectedness to schools is largely a reflection of attitudes toward individual achievement. Students feel positive, worthwhile, and important in large part as a function of the assessment process conducted by schools and teachers. By contrast, in families, friendships, neighborhoods, and romantic relationships, interdependent efforts and attention to relationships are deemed more positive, worthwhile, and important.

Familial versus nonfamilial connectedness. Some cultural groups make primary distinctions between family and nonfamily worlds, instead of between youth worlds and adult worlds (as is typical in the United States). For example, in Taiwan, confirmatory factor analyses of the connectedness scales indicate that family/nonfamily is a better way to characterize the nature of adolescent connectedness than is youth/adult-focused (Karcher & Lee, 2002).

The Shape of Adolescent Connectedness

By plotting an individual's or group of students' scale mean scores on a two-dimensional diagram that reflects each of the connectedness dimensions described previously, the shape of a youth's or group's overall connectedness can be represented graphically. The diagram in Figure 39.2 arranges each of the connectedness scales according to these dimensions. In the center of the diagram is *one* (on a one to five metric scale) referring to the lowest possible score. Each scale has a corresponding line that goes outward from the center to a maximum of five. Placing a dot where each group or individual's mean for each scale falls, and then connecting the dots around the center, allows one to see the "shape" of adolescent connectedness.

A triangle can be used to capture this shape by connecting with straight lines just the Family, School, and Friends mean scores for an individual or group. The different shapes of the connectedness triangle convey different emphases. For example, in Figure 39.3, each of three dif-

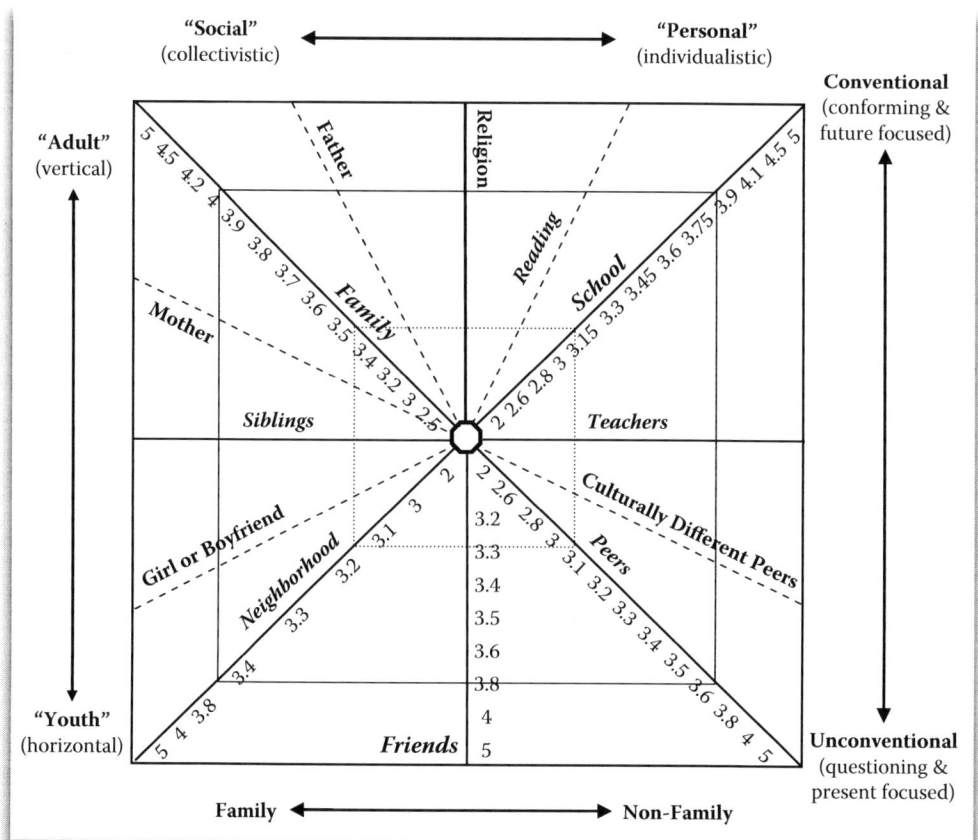

Figure 39.2 A means of plotting the ecology of adolescent connectedness by its dimensions. Copyright© 2007 by Michael J. Karcher.

Shape A:
Unconventional
Connectedness

Subscale Means
School = 2.5
Family = 2.7
Friends = 4.7

Shape B:
Conventional
Connectedness

Subscale Means
School = 3.9
Family = 4.6
Friends = 3.3

Shape C:
Collectivistic
Connectedness

Subscale Means
School = 2.7
Family = 4.6
Friends = 4.9

Figure 39.3 The "shape" of adolescent connectedness: Three types. Copyright© 2007 by Michael J. Karcher.

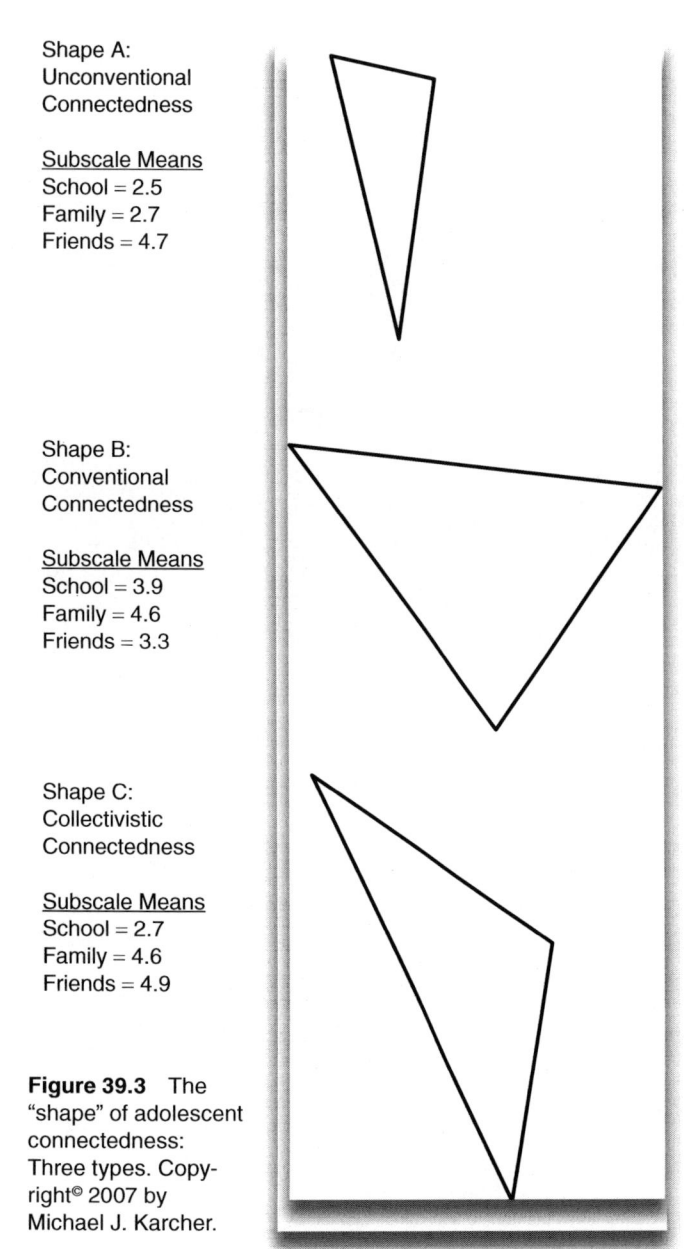

ferent triangles reflects the plotting of the Friends, Family, and School scales for a different pattern of connection.

Shape A in Figure 39.3 reveals that this particular youth prioritizes unconventional connectedness, because the youth rated his or her connectedness to friends as 4.7 out of a 5-point scale, while both conventional worlds of parent and school connectedness were rated below 3 ($M = 2.6$). Such a youth is likely quite vulnerable to peer pressure and, vis-à-vis, to risk-taking behavior and underachievement (especially when the youth's friends are also highly unconventional in their connectedness). This youth needs help increasing connections with adults and, therefore, may be a good candidate for having a mentor. Receiving extra attention from teachers and being given additional opportunities to interact in adult-oriented contexts also may provide positive experiences that make the youth feel important, valued, and seen as worthwhile by adults.

In contrast, Shape B highlights the importance this youth places on school and family connections (which share conventionality—viz., adult-oriented connections) over unconventional connectedness to friends, neighborhood, and peers. Some counselors might not view this child as having a problem. Certainly, this is not the type of youth typically described by parents, counselors, or teachers for presenting as disconnected, disobedient, or disengaged. However, the virtual absence of any connection with peers does not work to facilitate social skills and peer-based self-esteem. More than likely, this youth demonstrates lower than average social skills or high peer stigmatization that may in fact render the youth at risk for extreme, isolation-related, aggressive outbursts or at least for an unsatisfactory developmental experience with peers.

Shape C conveys a more collectivistic (friend and family) oriented connectedness because individualistic connections (school) were rated lowest. Children whose parents have little experience with postsecondary education, and by extension, many ethnic minority youth, may more often report this pattern of connectedness if their families are not able to model and strongly encourage individualistic achievement at school. Such youth may be more vulnerable to the long-term consequences of de-emphasizing the type of school-based, conventional connections that would help them secure future opportunities for employment or academic achievement. In regards to the particular student in Shape C, there may not be an immediate problem. However, the absence of future-oriented and individualistic connectedness presents warning signs. Such youth should be encouraged to participate in school programs (e.g., sports, extramural, or after-school academic enrichment) in order to help them feel positive, worthwhile, and important at school. These activities can provide opportunities to experience relatedness and belonging to which students can *reciprocate* through increased connection to school.

A Summary of the Theory of Adolescent Connectedness

Drawing on theories of problem behavior, belonging and attachment, and ecological development, we describe adolescent connectedness as an ecologically specific form of engagement with others and the environment. It occurs in response to feelings of belonging and relatedness, which can be fostered by increasing the social support a youth encounters in specific contexts and relationships. Building on the phenomenon of connectedness as a reciprocation of social support, the school counselor's main leverage gained by using this construct may come through applying the principle of connectedness compensation. In doing so, the counselor may encourage youth high in unconventional connectedness (Shape A) to participate in activities that boost conventional connectedness, but also encourage youth overly high in conventional connectedness and low in unconventional connectedness (Shape B) to engage in social activities with a broader range of peers. The starting place for such work, however, is for the school counselor to understand the behavioral consequences of disconnection in each world and to have tools that can be used to assess students' connectedness. One such tool is the connectedness diagram just described, which provides a way for students to see the shape of their connectedness in terms of the following dimensions: (a) conventional (adult sanctioned) and unconventional (youth sanctioned) connectedness, (b) present-focused and future-oriented connectedness, (c) collectivistic and individualistic connections, and (d) family and nonfamily connections. By considering the interplay of these connectedness dimensions, and creating opportunities for youth to better understand the "shape" of their own ecology of connectedness, school counselors may be better able to target meaningful interventions for youth and measure important postintervention changes in the adolescents' connectedness. Being successful at both, however, assumes the school counselor has a grasp of the research on connectedness and a valid assessment tool handy.

Research

Establishing and maintaining connectedness to others, to society, and to oneself is a pervasive human concern (Baumeister & Leary, 1995; Gilligan, 1982; Hagerty et al., 1993; Kohut, 1977; Nakkula & Selman, 1991). Baumeister and Leary proposed, 25 years after Maslow (1968) described belongingness as the third most fundamental need of the self, that belongingness is perhaps the most important psychological resource for overall human well-being.

Adolescents Need a Balance of Connectedness Across Their Social Ecology

Connectedness is a function of the need to belong, such that when an individual in one social ecology does not experience belonging and relatedness, he or she will become more connected to other social ecologies as a compensatory act (Baumeister & Leary, 1995). For example, research confirms that when disconnection occurs with family members, connectedness with friends may increase; when adolescents become disconnected from school, they often seek connectedness outside of school in their neighborhood (see Hirschi, 1969; Joo & Han, 2000). Other research suggests that adolescents' sense of self is born out of these sometimes divergent connections to family, teachers, friends, and peers (Buhrmester, 1990; DuBois et al., 1996) which facilitate the development of a sense of oneself in the present as well as oneself in the future.

An Emphasis on Unconventional Over Conventional Connectedness Promotes Risk Taking

Because connectedness reflects the presence (often in the form of expectations) of such profoundly important experiences as relatedness and belonging, connectedness has been linked to physical health, clinical disorders, and risk-taking behaviors (Bonny, Britto, Klostermann, Hornung, & Slap, 2000; Hendry & Reid, 2000; Lee & Robbins, 1998; Resnick et al., 1993). A long line of research on delinquency and violent behavior among youth shows that connectedness and alienation are intimately linked with problem behaviors (Hawkins, Catalano, & Miller, 1992; Hirschi, 1969; Jessor & Jessor, 1977) and, therefore provide important targets for effective prevention programs in schools (Allen, Kuperminc, Philliber, & Herre, 1994; Hawkins, Von Cleve, & Catalano, 1991; Jason & Kobayashi, 1995; Jessor, 1992).

Not all forms of connectedness decrease risky behavior, however, because the protective functions of connectedness vary across the relationships and contexts of adolescents' lives. Depending on the individual youth and his or her specific set of peers, connectedness to peers can reflect the conventions of either the adult world or the unsupervised activities and norms of the adolescent world. As one good example, it is commonly believed that peer relationships facilitate misbehavior through processes of negative peer pressure, yet research shows that associating with conventional peers is one of the best protective factors against violent behavior (Hawkins, Farrington, & Catalano, 1998; Hawkins et al., 1991; Olin, 2001).

Connectedness to friends, however, is usually positively correlated with risk taking (Karcher, 2002; Karcher & Finn, 2005). Although connectedness to friends could be called conventional because most parents/adult caretakers want their children to have friends, connectedness to friends serves a different function than connectedness to school or family does.

> Adolescents who describe positive relationships with parents and teachers show greater adaptation to school in terms of their academic coping, engagement, self-regulation, and perceived control. Relationships with friends are generally unrelated

to these outcomes, suggesting the different functional significance of students' relationships during early adolescence. In addition, adolescents who strongly identify with parents and teachers show more positive school adjustment and motivation, whereas emulation of friends is negatively related to these variables. (Lynch & Cicchetti, 1997, pp. 83–84)

Therefore connectedness to friends has *both* positive and negative effects on adolescent development and behavior. On one hand, any connectedness to friends is better than no connectedness at all in terms of promoting social development, avoiding experiences of alienation, and preventing aggression (Collins, 2002; Nakkula & Selman, 1991). On the other hand, when connectedness to friends is high, but connectedness to school or family low, this imbalance increases youths' risk for engaging in risk taking and misbehavior (Jessor, 1993).

More recently, Dishion, R. Jessor, and others (i.e., Dishion, McCord, & Poulin, 1999; Jessor, 1992; Patterson, Dishion, & Yoerger, 2000) have found that spending unsupervised time in one's neighborhood, with friends, or in other youth-governed contexts increases the risk that a youth will engage in unconventional behaviors. Taken to the extreme, unconventional connectedness can lead to activities that are unlawful and potentially damaging to self and others (Jessor & Jessor, 1977). Behaviors, such as stealing, drinking, delinquency, and violence, are most common when strong connectedness to friends is not balanced by equally strong connectedness to school or to family (Hirschi, 1969; Olin, 2001). In this way, conventional connectedness serves as a control against nonnormative, antisocial, illicit, and aggressive behaviors (Hirschi).

School Counselors Should Avoid Grouping Highly Unconventional Youth

The conventionality phenomenon presents an important consideration for school counselors when choosing members for group counseling. Although formally screening youth in order to identify appropriate candidates for school counseling groups or other interventions has not been a standard practice in school counseling (Ripley & Goodnough, 2001; Sullivan & Wright, 2002), there is persuasive research suggesting that it should be. For example, Dishion et al. (1999) presented surprising findings from a 30-year study of comprehensive services provided to youth at risk for delinquency. Analyses revealed that the long-term impact of aggregating at-risk youth within groups (e.g., in a counseling group) was to *increase* delinquency, regardless of the efforts of the counselors. Given this, it is wise to selectively include within group counseling both those youth at risk for specific problems and those not at risk. In terms of the connectedness framework, this means school counselors should include youth with high and youth with low levels of unconventional connectedness as opposed to targeting and aggregating only unconventionally connected youth within the group counseling setting.

The Promise and Perils of Connectedness Compensation

There appears to be an interaction between forms of conventional and unconventional connectedness, such that when connectedness is not achieved in one context it is overemphasized in others (Ainsworth, 1989). Baumeister and Leary (1995) argued that because the need to belong is so pervasive, there is a compensatory function which allows the absence of belonging in one ecology (e.g., family) to be countered by belonging in another (e.g., friends). They stated,

> Relationships should substitute for each other, to some extent, as would be indicated by effective replacement of lost relationships partners and by a capacity for social relatedness in one sphere to overcome potential ill effects of social deprivation in another. (p. 500)

Although the absence of conventional connectedness with one parent can be compensated by connectedness with the other, unconventional connectedness cannot take the place of absent parental connectedness (van Aken & Asendorpf, 1997). The intervention opportunity presented by this compensatory function is the possibility for conventional experiences and relationships, such as in after-school programs or through natural mentoring by teachers (DuBois & Silverthorn, 2005), to compensate for prior deprivations of conventional connectedness that resulted from poor parental bonding, peer rejection, or school failure and underachievement.

The Ecology of Connectedness Widens and Becomes More Unconventional During Adolescence

R. Jessor and S. L. Jessor (1977) found that, as the adolescent's ecology widens, so too do the opportunities to engage both in unconventional behaviors that are encouraged by peers (e.g., risk-taking behaviors) and in contexts not governed by parents (e.g., the neighborhood). This is partly because of normative declines in conventional behaviors (e.g., reading, working at school, and spending

Table 39.1 Connectedness Report: District Profile of Average Level of Connectedness by Sex, Grade, & Related Developmental Asset.

Connectedness Domain	Related Developmental Asset	Conn. for kids with/out asset – Does not have	Conn. for kids with/out asset – Does have asset	Average Level by Sex – Girls	Average Level by Sex – Boys	6th	7th	8th	9th	10th	11th	12th	α (#)
School Connectedness: Future-oriented, Conventional	Asset Number												
School: Involvement in and positive feelings toward school	24. Bonding to School (5)	3.2	3.7 (72%)	3.5	3.2	3.8	3.5	3.5	3.5	3.3	3.4	3.3	.84 (6)
Teachers: Caring for; wanting respect; working to gain trust	14. Adult Role Models	3.5	3.7 (83%)	3.7	3.5	3.8	3.6	3.6	3.5	3.5	3.5	3.6	.83 (5)
Reading: Reading regularly, independently, and for fun	25. Reading for Pleasure	2.5	3.4 (88%)	2.8	2.5	3.3	2.9	3.0	2.8	2.8	2.9	3.0	.92 (4)
Peers: Can work cooperatively with and likes one's own peers	15. Positive Peer Influence	3.0	3.4 (68%)	3.3	3.1	3.1	3.2	3.3	3.2	3.2	3.2	3.3	.74 (6)
Culturally different peers: Interest in being around them	34. Cultural Competence	3.2	4.3 (85%)	3.9	3.6	4.0	3.6	3.6	3.6	3.9	3.7	3.9	.91 (3)
Self-Perception: Temporal	Asset number	Don't have	Does have	Girls	Boys	6th	7th	8th	9th	10th	11th	12th	α (#)
Self-in-the Future: Actively working toward hopeful future	37. Personal Power (& 40)	3.6	4.2 (62%)	3.9	3.8	4.0	4.0	3.8	3.7	3.7	3.7	4.0	.79 (5)
Self-in-the-present: Feels esteemed, unique, likeable	38. Self-Esteem (17)	3.2	3.7 (71%)	3.4	3.4	3.5	3.5	3.5	3.3	3.3	3.3	3.4	.78 (5)
Social Connectedness: Present Oriented, Unconventional	Asset number	Don't have	Does have	Girls	Boys	6th	7th	8th	9th	10th	11th	12th	α (#)
Friends: Trusts, spends time with, & talks openly w/ friends	33. "Social" Competence	3.4	3.7 (72%)	3.7	3.4	3.7	3.7	3.7	3.3	3.4	3.5	3.6	.85 (6)
Neighborhood: Activity in and sense of safety & belonging	20. (−) Time at Home (10 Safe)	3.5	3.2 (−63%)	3.3	3.4	3.7	3.4	3.3	3.2	3.2	3.1	3.2	.80 (6)
Romantic partner: Has, relies on, values boyfriend/girlfriend	31. Restraint	3.5	2.7 (67%)	3.3	2.9	3.2	3.2	3.0	2.8	2.9	3.3	3.2	.95 (4)

(Continued)

Table 39.1 Continued

Connectedness Domain	Developmental Asset	Conn. for kids with/out asset Don't have	Does have	Average Level by Sex Girls	Boys	Mean Level of Connectedness in Each Grade 6th	7th	8th	9th	10th	11th	12th	α (#)
Family Connectedness: Present-oriented, Conventional	Asset number												
Parents: Spends time with, wants trust, cares for	1. Family Support	3.3	4.0 (77%)	3.7	3.6	3.9	3.6	3.7	3.7	3.4	3.6	3.6	.83 (6)
Mother: Feels close to, cares for, & communicates well with	2. Positive Family Communication	3.6	4.2 (77%)	3.9	3.8	4.3	4.0	3.7	3.8	3.9	3.7	3.8	.83 (4)
Father: Feels close to, cares for, & communicates well with	2. Positive Family Communicatioin	3.3	4.1 (76%)	3.9	3.8	3.9	4.0	3.8	3.5	3.5	3.4	3.7	.86 (4)
Siblings: Frequent, enjoyable contact with siblings	1. Family Support	2.8	3.3 (70%)	3.5	3.0	3.2	3.0	3.0	3.2	3.0	2.9	2.9	.89 (5)

Notes: α = scale reliability (<.70 fair; .70 –.79 good; >.80 very good)
Scale Anchors: 1 = Not at all true; No 2 = Not really true; 3 = Sort of true; 4 = True; 5 = Very true
Low connectedness includes anchors 1–3 (Mean < 3.5) and High connectedness includes anchors 4–5 (Mean > 3.5)
Copyright© 2007 by Michael J. Karcher.

---

time with family) relative to the increased opportunities to spend time with friends.

In several studies, both with adolescent samples from the United States and Asia, it appears that conventional connectedness declines during adolescence while unconventional connectedness increases (Karcher, 2001; Karcher & Lee, 2002). These differences in mean levels of connectedness across the adolescent social ecology over time are illustrated in Table 39.1. This table is based on data from 342 students from a Midwestern town who completed both the Hemingway measure and the SEARCH Developmental Assets survey. Students in grades 6 through 12 were equally represented. The majority were Caucasian (*n* = 265) and 185 were female. For the present purpose, notice mean changes among students in connectedness to school between 6th, 9th, and 12th grades, which go from 3.8 to 3.5 to 3.3 during that time period (with 5 being very connected and 1 being very disconnected). Similarly, changes in connectedness to parents are 3.9 to 3.7 to 3.6 during this time. This is expectable as increased freedom and mobility invite increased time spent with friends, peers, and romantic partners during adolescence. It also suggests that an *imbalance* between conventional and unconventional connectedness is *normal* in adolescence.

Girls Usually Report Higher Levels of Connectedness Than Boys Do

Gender differences have received perhaps the most attention within the research on connectedness even though many of the studies of connectedness actually measured belonging. Statistical tests of the hypothesis that girls report greater relatedness and belonging than boys has been the focus of much research (e.g., Lang-Takac & Osterweil, 1992), but empirical studies "connectedness" that used measures of belonging and relatedness (rather than connectedness) have failed to consistently reveal clear gender differences (Hagerty et al., 1993; Harter, Waters, Pettit, Kofkin, & Jordan, 1997; Jacobson & Rowe, 1999; Lee, Keough, & Seagal, 1999; Lee & Robbins, 1995). In most studies using the connectedness measure described in the following section, girls scored higher on all of the scales of connectedness except on the Connectedness to Neighborhood and Self-in-the-Present scales (Karcher, 2001, 2001a; Karcher & Finn, 2005; Karcher & Lee, 2002;). Consistent with these findings, Table 39.1 reveals the girls, in this Midwestern sample of 342 middle and high school students, reported greater connectedness than boys did. This may be interpreted to mean that while experiences of belonging and relatedness may not differ between adolescent boys and girls, the response to these feelings—that is, their efforts to connect with others—appears to be stronger for girls than boys. These differences, however, may be detected only with a measure of adolescents' *engagement* (i.e., of connectedness) rather than of belongingness or relatedness.

A Description of *The Hemingway: Measure of Adolescent Connectedness*

The Hemingway: Measure of Adolescent Connectedness is a self-report instrument that includes scales that assess engagement through caring for and involvement in close relationships and important contexts. The Hemingway consists of 78 items that are averaged to create scales for 15 ecological worlds and 4 composite scales. The 15 scales fall into 3 dimensions of connectedness: self, others, and society. *Connectedness to self* includes 2 scales: (1) positive feelings about the self in the present (e.g., self-esteem; DuBois et al., 1996; Harter, 1999) and (2) sense of one's self in the future (Nakkula & Selman, 1991). *Connectedness to others* includes 5 scales: connectedness to (3) parents, (4) friends, (5) teachers, (6) siblings, and (7) peers. Because the scales measuring connectedness to religion, race, and romance are sometimes problematic for school administrators, both short and long versions were created. Connectedness to others scales which are included only in the longer version are connectedness to one's (8) mother, (9) father, (10) a romantic partner, and (11) culturally different peers. *Connectedness to society* includes scales measuring connectedness to (12) school, (13) neighborhood, and (14) reading. Included in only the longer version is the (15) connectedness to religion scale. The 4 composite scales reflect the mean of all scale items in each of 4 domains: family (parents and sibling items), friends (friends and neighborhood items), school (school and teacher items), and self (present and future self items).

The psychometric properties of the scales across several samples as well as findings from multiple validity studies can be found in the manual and validity study (Karcher, 2001, 2003), which is available upon request from Karcher (first author). In addition, in the last column in Table 39.1, reliability estimates for the sample used for the analyses discussed previously are reported.

Scoring. Responses to each of the items are made using a 5-point, Likert-type response scale which includes (1) not true at all, (2) not really true, (3) sort of true, (4) true, and (5) very true. There is at least one reverse-scored item in each scale (identified in bold in Table 39.2). The items within each of the 15 scales are averaged (once the reverse worded items are reverse-scored) to get separate scale score means.

Table 39.2 Items for Several Scales of the Hemingway Measure of Adolescent Connectedness

Scale Items—Reverse score items 2, 7, 13, 18, 26, 30, 34, 45, 51, 55, 64, 70, 71

Neighborhood (6 items)
(1) I like hanging out around where I live (like my neighborhood).
(11) I spend a lot of time with kids around where I live.
(21) I get along with the kids in my neighborhood.
(31) I often spend time playing or doing things in my neighborhood.
(41) I hang out a lot with kids in my neighborhood.
(51) **My neighborhood is boring.**

Friends (6 items)
(2) **Spending time with friends is not so important to me.**
(12) I have friends I'm really close to and trust completely.
(22) Spending time with my friends is a big part of my life.
(32) My friends and I talk openly with each other about personal things.
(42) I spend as much time as I can with my friends.
(52) My friends and I spend a lot of time talking about things.

Self-in-the-present (6 items)
(3) I can name 5 things that others like about me.
(13) **There is not much that is unique or special about me.**
(23) I can name 3 things that other kids like about me.
(33) I really like who I am.
(43) I have special hobbies, skills, or talents.
(53) I have unique interests or skills that make me interesting.

Parents (6 items)
(4) My family has fun together.
(14) It is important that my parents trust me.
(24) I enjoy spending time with my parents.
(34) **My parents and I disagree about many things.**
(44) My parents and I get along well.
(54) I care about my parents very much.

Siblings (5 items)
(5) I have a lot of fun with my brother(s) or sister(s).
(15) I feel close to my brother(s) or sister(s).
(25) I enjoy spending time with my brothers/sisters.
(35) I try to spend time with my brothers/sisters when I can.
(45) **I try to avoid being around my brother/sister(s).**

School (6 items)
(6) I work hard at school.
(16) I enjoy being at school.
(26) **I get bored in school a lot.**
(36) I do well in school.
(46) I feel good about myself when I am at school.
(56) Doing well in school is important to me.

(Continued)

Table 39.2 Continued

Peers (6 items)
(7) **My classmates often bother me.**
(17) I like pretty much all of the other kids in my grade.
(27) I like working with my classmates.
(37) I get along well with the other students in my classes.
(47) I am liked by my classmates.
(57) I rarely fight or argue with the other kids at school.

Teachers (6 items)
(8) I care what my teachers think of me.
(18) **I do not get along with some of my teachers.**
(28) I want to be respected by my teachers.
(38) I try to get along with my teachers.
(48) I always try hard to earn my teachers' trust.
(50) I usually like my teachers.

Self-in-the-Future (5 items)
(9) I will have a good future.
(19) Doing well in school will help me in the future.
(29) I do things outside of school to prepare for my future.
(39) I do lots of things to prepare for my future.
(49) I think about my future often.

Reading (4 items)
(10) I enjoy spending time by myself reading.
(20) I like to read.
(30) **I never read books in my free time.**
(40) I often read when I have free time.

Kids from other cultures (3 items)
(60) I like getting to know kids from other cultural or racial groups.
(65) I would like to know more people from different cultural groups.
(69) I like getting to know people who are culturally different from me.

Copyright© 2007 by Nichael J. Karcher.

The Hemingway is one of few self-report measures of adolescent connectedness that has undergone considerable empirical scrutiny and generated considerable validity evidence (Karcher, 2001). The measure was developed through a series of exploratory and confirmatory factor analyses, which revealed the same family, friend, and school higher order factors (underlying scale groupings) across several U.S. samples. These three factors, which were used to create Figure 39.2, may be described as the Social Connectedness (i.e., to friends), Academic Connectedness, and Family Connectedness composite scales. These composite scales reflect the three corners of the Y-framed triangle in the Connectedness Diagram (Figure 39.2). The *unconventional connectedness* factor includes connectedness to friends, the neighborhood, a self-in-the-present, and romantic partner scales. The *academic connectedness* factor includes connectedness to school, teachers, peers, culturally different peers, reading, and self-in-the-future scales. The *family connectedness* factor includes the connectedness to parents, siblings, mother, father, and religion scales.

The scales in each of these three factors also can be characterized in terms of the dimensions or continuum described earlier: *temporality, conventionality,* and *relational orientation* (collectivist/individualist; family/nonfamily). The items in each of the scales reflect the two primary means of connection—through activity or involvement and through caring (e.g., "I work hard at school" and "I enjoy being at school"). These scales also reflect a time orientation. The family and social composite connectedness scales are generally present oriented, and the academic connectedness scale is typically future oriented. Scales measure either conventional, adult-mediated behaviors and attitudes that are vertical (adult-driven) and future-oriented or unconventional behaviors and attitudes that are horizontal (peer-driven) and questioning and which reflect youth-directed behaviors and youth-specific attitudes in the present. Finally, the collectivistic and family-oriented scales emphasize larger groups and social hierarchy, and conversely, the individualistic, nonfamily, and future-oriented scales reflect individual (self-directed) connections and achievement. These continua are presented as two-way arrows in Figure 39.2.

The Value of Connectedness in Predicting Assets

We believe the Hemingway connectedness measure can facilitate the use of the Developmental Assets framework and survey by providing an interim or proxy measure of assets. Here we provide just three examples of this. First, in Figure 39.2, the two concentric squares (dotted and thin lines) reflect the mean scale scores for two groups of youth from a Midwestern sample of 224 middle and high school aged youth. A sample of youth who completed both the SEARCH Institutes *A/B Assets Survey* and *The Hemingway: Measure of Adolescent Connectedness* sample was divided into three groups: low, medium, and high internal assets. The inside line reflects the mean for youth reporting low (fewest) internal assets, and the second line reflects the mean scale score for those youth reporting many high (the most) developmental assets. These lines provide one gauge of whether a given youth or group's scale score should be considered low or high (keeping in mind that girls tend to report .15 to .30 higher mean scores than boys on most scales; see Table 39.1).

Second, we can compare scores on specific connectedness scales with the presence/absence of related developmental assets. One important asset is the "Adult Role Models" asset. Using data from the same Midwestern sample described earlier, we could reliably predict (with 83% accuracy using logistic regression) the presence or absence of this asset from the youth's mean scale score on the connectedness to teachers scale (see second row in Table 39.1). Table 39.1 illustrates the prediction accuracy of several key Developmental Assets from related connectedness scales. The first two columns of numbers indicate the mean on each connectedness scale for youth who *did* or who *did not* have the related asset. In parentheses is the degree of predictive accuracy. For example, connectedness to reading scores predicted the presence or absence of the asset "Reading for Pleasure" with 88% accuracy. The connectedness to religion scale (not shown) predicted having the Religious Community asset with 84% accuracy. In short, several of the connectedness scales can serve as reliable proxy measures of specific assets.

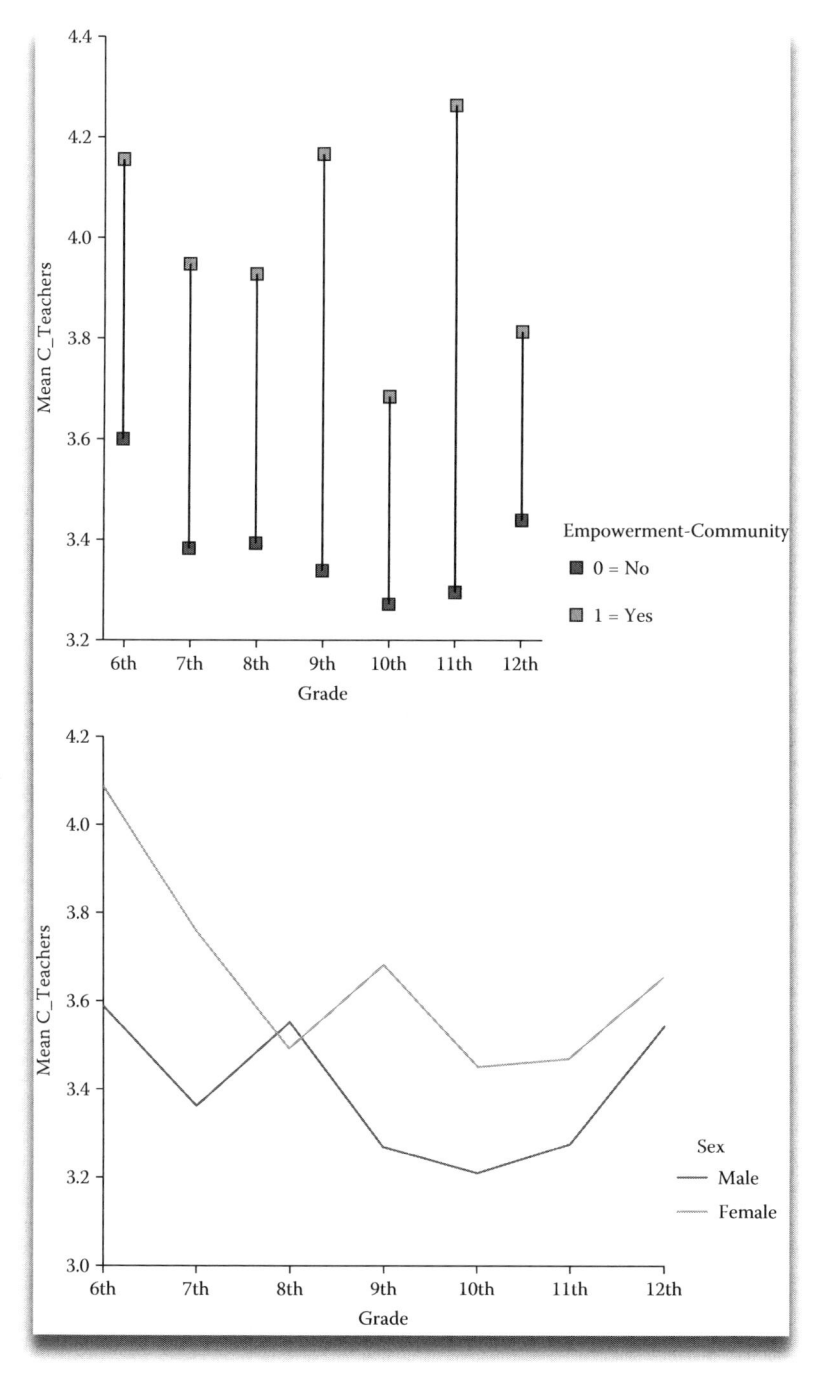

Figure 39.4 Two charts of connectedness to teachers across adolescence by assets and sex. Copyright© 2007 by Michael J. Karcher.

For a given school district, the relationship between Developmental Assets and connectedness may be linked in order to identify targets for interventions or guidance program goals. For example, in Figure 39.4, the means for connectedness to teachers at each grade were plotted for those who did and did not report having the asset "Community Values Youth," which assesses whether students perceive that adults in their community value youth. Across all grades, youth whose means on the connectedness to teachers scale was low (e.g., between 3.4 and 3.5) did not feel their community valued youth. How much improvement in connectedness to teachers would indicate that students in general did feel youth were valued by adults in the community? Well, this depends on the grade, because the mean level of connectedness to teachers among youth who had the "Community Values Youth" asset ranged from 3.7 in 10th grade to 4.3 in 11th grade. However, a good range to set as a goal to measure the success of an intervention to increase this asset among students might be to have the majority of youth score between 3.8 and 4.2, depending on the grade. A school district could begin a campaign to promote feeling valued by starting with teacher relationships in the school but extending efforts beyond the school as well, and measure changes in connectedness to teachers every semester until that goal is achieved.

Charting Developmental Trends for Boys and Girls Across Grades to Identify Program Goals

Another way to use research to link the Developmental Assets and connectedness scales in a manner that can help school counselors plan guidance activities and program objectives is to plot connectedness scales for boys and girls across grades. In the second chart in Figure 39.4, we see that girls report greater connectedness to teachers, but similar to boys, the girls show declines in connectedness to teachers from middle school to high school. By 11th grade, both boys and girls (those who have not dropped out, of course) are beginning to report more connectedness to teachers. The gap between the sexes is largest in 6th and 9th grades in this school district, which is a time of transition from one school level to another. Boys, it appears, are in particular need of connectedness to teachers at these times. For both sexes, the key times to target teacher connectedness (e.g., as a way to increase the "Community Values Youth" asset) appear to be during the 7th, 8th, and 9th grades. Such efforts could ward off declines in the assets as well.

Practice

A comprehensive school guidance and counseling program provides an organizational framework with a specific configuration of planned, sequenced, and coordinated guidance and counseling activities and services based on student, school, and community needs and resources (Gysbers & Henderson, 2006). As previously stated, many school counselors are stretched for time and must serve the needs of parents, teachers, administrators, and students. However, through involving teachers, parents, and administrators as well as the students in a comprehensive guidance and counseling program, greater clarity about the guidance program goals and the role of the counselor can be achieved. Our experience suggests that school counselors are less likely to be pulled in 100 different directions when they (a) base goals and related services on assessed needs of students and other stakeholders, (b) make the content and focus of their guidance program known to teachers, parents, and administration, (c) make clear to students and stakeholders how the four key components of their guidance programs (system support, guidance curriculum, individual student planning, and responsive services) are linked, and (d) demonstrate the effectiveness of these programmatic efforts.

The Developmental Assets framework (presented by the SEARCH Institute) is one approach chosen by many school districts with which to organize their comprehensive guidance model. The Northside Independent School District in San Antonio is an example of a large school district (the sixth largest in Texas) that has oriented its programming around the Developmental Assets framework. This district was the testing ground for Gysbers and Henderson's (2006) developmental guidance model (which informed and mirrored the ASCA, 2003, model). We also know this district well. It is where two of the authors worked, one as a licensed professional counselor and the other as the director of guidance, and from this district, the third author received his high school diploma. Northside, already a nationally recognized program, enhanced its model by using the Developmental Assets framework and by developing materials and guidance activities based on this approach. The Developmental Assets framework has been used district-wide to facilitate guidance program staff development efforts with counselors, teachers, administrators, and staff. The model informs such activities as campus mentoring, parent programs, policies, the content of the guidance program curriculum, intervention services, and the district's federal Safe and Drug Free Schools programming.

The Assets framework has provided a useful model for many of Northside's programs but has not provided an accessible tool for assessing the needs that individual students bring to the classroom. Formal and informal asset surveys have been used to assess the presence of assets among the student body at Northside at the district level. The results have provided a collective profile of students but no data representing the individual student's assets.

This is because the Developmental Assets survey cannot be conducted frequently enough to gauge change resulting from guidance, individual planning, and responsive services for subgroups of students over a short period, and it is not currently used for individuals, only for groups (e.g., districts).

For these reasons, *The Hemingway: Measure of Adolescent Connectedness* (Karcher, 2001) can be utilized as a complementary tool in order to also assess individual student needs regarding their connectedness to friends, school, and family, and by extension provide a proxy measure of Developmental Assets for individual students. This allows counselors and others to better plan and provide needed services for individual students. Combining the specificity of information provided by the connectedness measure with the collaborative and positive effects on school climate that a program oriented around the 40 Developmental Assets framework can engender, school counselors can be better poised to enhance student success across the four delivery components of a comprehensive guidance program with this integrated approach. In the sections that follow, we provide examples of how the connectedness measure and its accompanying constructs can be used to facilitate an asset-promoting comprehensive program of school guidance in a school district.

System Support: Teaching Teachers About Connectedness and Developmental Assets

The work that school counselors do with teachers can indirectly help students form connections to the school and foster developmental assets. By providing in-service training to staff, in accordance with the systems support component of the comprehensive guidance program model (ASCA, 2003), counselors can provide leadership and advocacy in promoting systemic change on behalf of students. Providing in-service training using the Developmental Assets framework to teachers and other staff members is a useful way of helping them promote students' healthy development and protect youth from negative and harmful behaviors (Benson et al., 1995). The 40 Assets also reveal types of youth-oriented attitudes and activities that promote or discourage students' conventional connectedness to the school.

As one example of promoting students' connectedness to school, counselors can work with teachers through staff development sessions to teach them how to utilize the connectedness constructs and assessment. Some teachers might want to use the connectedness measure to identify needs among their students. Either during staff development or with smaller groups of interested teachers, school counselors can illustrate for teachers the uses and interpretation of the measure. These teachers can be taught how to use the data to address and promote those assets that are absent in the students' lives. For example, if a student's connectedness profile suggests a marked degree of unconventional connections to peers, teachers and others can collaborate to build more conventional connections to peers through individual peer mentoring or collaborative learning projects. Teachers might also encourage youth who are disconnected from school to participate in school organizations related to the students' expressed interests.

Through such system support activities, school counselors also can indirectly help facilitate experiences of belonging and relatedness in classrooms, hallways, and other areas of the school that may result in increased student connectedness. Through small and large group staff development presentations on the Developmental Assets and the connectedness research mentioned previously, school counselors may promote a fuller utilization of comprehensive guidance activities by teachers and students.

School Guidance Curriculum: "The Connections I Make"

Classroom guidance provides counselors an opportunity to become familiar with the student climate as well as to screen students for appropriateness for other services (e.g., individual and group counseling, mentoring, tutoring, or after-school programs). School counselors may find the connectedness scales particularly useful in guidance lessons because they provide a framework for introducing students to the four domains of adolescent connectedness (viz., friends, school, family, and self).

Cobia and Henderson (2003) advised that all well-designed guidance lessons have a clear purpose, age-appropriate activities, coordinated and sequential lessons, and a summary or evaluative wrap-up. Each guidance lesson is designed to reach all students by delivering concepts that build on those learned in previous guidance lessons. Even though introducing the four domains of adolescent connectedness to students through classroom guidance must be delivered in an age-appropriate manner, it also can be done in ways that are fun, interactive, and memorable.

One example of a guidance lesson that can create an interactive and playful way to introduce the connectedness domains is entitled "The Connections I Make." This lesson asks students to place themselves on one or the other end of connectedness continua depicted in Figure 39.2. The goal of this guidance lesson is for students to better understand how much importance they place in different forms of connectedness by weighing the pros and cons of conventional and unconventional connectedness. This is achieved through two different activities. The first activity is interactive and interpersonal, and the second is reflective and more personal. Before beginning the activity, students are asked to complete the connectedness measure. Students should be told their answers will be kept confidential but that the counselor might talk with students afterwards about their own responses. To foster buy-in, the students should clearly understand that this measure provides the basis for the content conveyed in that day's and perhaps in subsequent guidance lessons.

After the students complete the connectedness measure, it is set aside, unscored, and students are asked to participate in the first activity. This activity requires them to identify their connectedness statuses by indicating which of two ends of each connectedness continuum shown in Figure 39.2 they more commonly engage in. To indicate their preference, students are asked to move from one side of the room to the other, providing a visual representation of each end of the continuum. The goal is for each student to identify the types of connections he or she is most inclined toward for each of the dimensions listed in Figure 39.2.

In the second part of the lesson, the school counselor guides the students through a student-centered discussion by encouraging the class to discuss the pros and cons of each type of connectedness. These dimensions should be discussed in an age-appropriate manner, such that discussing the terms conventional and unconventional connectedness may only be appropriate with older youth. Instead, the basic terms—youth versus adult focused—can be defined and written on either an overhead screen or chalkboard. Once defined, the counselor sets the stage for discussion by providing some of the research findings presented in the research section of this chapter. For example, if the youth are familiar with the Developmental Assets framework, this language can be incorporated into the discussion by linking assets to types of connectedness. The pros and cons of high connectedness in each world should be presented by the counselor for middle school students, while for high school students, these can be solicited from the students themselves. During the summary portion of the guidance lesson, the counselor asks students for feedback regarding lessons they learned in order to make sure their understanding is accurate and so that no one feels criticized or labeled. The goals of this activity are to help students identify variations in their connectedness and to more fully understand the benefits and risks posed by each kind of connection as well as to help school counselors identify the needed direction of future guidance lessons or individual planning sessions. Similarly, the counselor's next step toward integrating connectedness-promoting activities into the guidance program can be to take the students' connectedness measures, score them, and use the data to identify individuals who could be appropriate for individual planning meetings or specific responsive services.

Individual Planning: Assisting Present-Oriented Students

Having completed this guidance activity, the school counselor now has accessed valuable data through the collection and scoring of the completed connectedness measures and through information gathered from the guidance activity discussions. The individual student-planning component of the comprehensive guidance program provides the counselor with a vehicle for assisting all students in developing, monitoring, and assessing educational, occupational, and personal goals (ASCA, 2003). However, the connectedness data gleaned from the classroom guidance activity can be used to identify and assist students whose connectedness profile suggests a high degree of unconventional connectedness or a greater orientation to the present than to the future. Using this information, the school counselor might invite such students to participate in individual planning meetings. In doing so, the school counselor could then work with targeted students individually or in groups in order to establish future-oriented goals related to specific careers. A sample activity may include an individual planning session where the student and counselor investigate the student's areas of interest and strengths with the assistance of a computer-based interest inventory. This can help the student begin to connect present performance in the classroom and potential participation in related clubs and community activities to future interests and aspirations.

Responsive Services: Incorporating Unconventionally Oriented Youth More Fully Into School

Finally, working in the component of responsive services, school counselors can use the measure of adolescent connectedness as a tool for screening students for appropriate counseling groups. Keeping in mind that there are two main types of connectedness—conventional and unconventional—the counselor's goal in group selection should be to identify youth whose interpersonal needs, problems, and skills could complement those of other students in the group. Doing so can help to avoid the problem described by Dishion et al. (1999), wherein well meaning interventions actually become contexts for deviancy training.

Once the students have been identified for a group, connectedness may be used to provide the underlying theme for the group's work or to help link the youths' connectedness to specific developmental assets. For example, the school counselor might encourage discussions centered on the importance of establishing a balance between conventional and unconventional connectedness. The connectedness terms also may provide a shared language for the group, allowing a variety of individual problems (e.g., dealing with divorce, problems with peers, risk-taking behaviors) to be discussed indirectly and more inclusively by referring to the role of connectedness within each of these individual issues.

Another way to introduce the issue of connectedness would be for the school counselor to start the group by asking group members to determine with which one of the three shapes in Figure 39.3 they most identify. The school counselor can then facilitate a discussion regarding the group members' experiences of connection and disconnection and regarding how these experiences have led the students to take on the "shape" they identified. One goal the counselor may pursue is helping the group members encourage one another to seek out connectedness where it may previously have been lacking in the youth's life. The counselor might encourage group members both to create an action-oriented connectedness plan that facilitates their own connectedness and to support fellow group members' creation and the achievement of their own plans.

Counselors also should move beyond promoting feelings of belongingness and relatedness in the counseling group to helping students find ways to establish desired connections outside the group. For example, a group member may lack connectedness to school and decide he or she would like to become more involved at school. This group member's action-oriented connectedness plan may include joining a school club, sport, or after-school program. The school counselor could assist this student by helping the student identify *and achieve* concrete steps toward becoming more connected to school. For example, the counselor may assist the student by setting up the initial appointment for the student to meet with the club sponsor or coach.

Afterword: The Naming of "The Hemingway"

In 1994, Brad Powell and Father Patrick Gahan, at Saint Stephen's Episcopal School in Austin, Texas, asked the measure's creator, Michael Karcher, to develop an instrument that could help them assess student changes resulting from their cross-age peer mentoring program. The main concept of connectedness was derived from a paper by Michael Nakkula and Robert Selman (1991), both of whom were Karcher's academic mentors at Harvard. Nakkula's notion of youth development suggests that programs should serve to promote youth's "interpretation of his or her connectedness to the world over time" (p. 186). This suggestion served as the basis of *The Hemingway* and guided the development of adolescent connectedness theory (Karcher, 2001).

The name, Hemingway, also has its origin in the biography of Michael Nakkula. The first son of a blue-collar family in the Upper Peninsula of Michigan, Michael Nakkula was the first individual in his family to attend college. Nakkula's subsequent attainment of a professorship at Harvard led Karcher to ask him how he understood his extraordinary academic achievements. Nakkula explained his connectedness to academe through a story involving one of his high school teachers, who, after reading a paper Nakkula wrote for a class assignment, told Nakkula that he wrote like Hemingway. The interpretation Nakkula made about his connectedness to school and the future (that he had special writing gifts) helped him achieve his potential in the world of postsecondary education and ultimately as a published author. In honor of that high school teacher's impact, this measure of adolescent connectedness was named *The Hemingway*.

Acknowledgments

We would like to thank Gwen Louden-Gerber for her feedback on an early draft of this chapter. This chapter incorporates and further elaborates text, figures, and concepts from an earlier work on connectedness in schools by M. J. Karcher (2004) entitled, *Connectedness and School Violence: A Framework for Developmental Interventions*, which was printed in E. Gerler (Ed.), *Handbook of School Violence* (pp. 7–42), Binghamton, NY: Haworth Press. Permission to reproduce text and Figure 39.1 has been provided by the Haworth Press and Ed Gerler. Copies of the measure (both short and long forms in English and Spanish), scale norms, and related research can be found at www.adolescentconnectedness.com.

References

Ainsworth, M. S. (1989). Attachments beyond infancy. *American Psychologist, 44*(4), 709–716.

Allen, J. P., Kuperminc, G., Philliber, S., & Herre, K. (1994). Programmatic prevention of adolescent problem behaviors: The role of autonomy, relatedness, and volunteer service in the teen outreach program. *American Journal of Community Psychology, 22*(5), 617–637.

American School Counselor Association. (2003). *The ASCA national model: A framework for school counseling programs*. Alexandria, VA: Author.

Baumeister, R. F., & Leary, M. R. (1995). The need to belong: Desire for interpersonal attachments as a fundamental human motivation. *Psychological Bulletin, 117*(3), 497–529.

Benson, P. L., Galbraith, J., & Espeland, P. (1995). *What kids need to succeed: Proven practical ways to raise good kids*. Minneapolis, MN: Free Spirit Publishing.

Bonny, A. E., Britto, M. T., Klostermann, B. K., Hornung, R. W., & Slap, G. B. (2000). School disconnectedness: Identifying adolescents at risk. *Pediatrics, 106*(5), 1017–1021.

Bronfenbrenner, U. (1979). *The ecology of human development: Experiments by nature and design.* Cambridge, MA: Harvard University Press.

Buhrmester, D. (1990). Intimacy of friendship, interpersonal competence, and adjustment during preadolescence and adolescence. *Child Development, 61,* 1101–1111.

Catalano, R. F., Berglund, M. L., Ryan, J. A. M., Lonczak, H. S., & Hawkins, J. D. (2002). Positive youth development in the United States: Research findings on evaluations of positive youth development programs. [Electronic Version] *Prevention & Treatment, 5.*

Cernkovich, S. A., & Giordana, P. C. (1992). School bonding, race, and delinquency. *Criminology, 31,* 261–291.

Chodorow, N. (1978). *The reproduction of mothering: Psychoanalysis and the reproduction of mothering.* Berkeley: The University of California Press.

Cobia, D., & Henderson, D. (2003). *Handbook of school counseling.* Columbus, OH: Merril Prentice Hall.

Collins, W. A. (2002, April 13). *The development of physical aggression from early childhood to adolescence.* Paper presented at the Society for Research on Adolescence; ninth biennial meeting, New Orleans, LA.

Cooper, C. R. (1999). Multiple selves, multiple worlds: Cultural perspectives on individuality and connectedness in adolescent development. In A. S. Masten (Ed.), *Cultural processes in child development: The Minnesota symposia on child psychology* (Vol. 29, pp. 25–57). Mahwah, NJ: Lawrence Erlbaum.

Dishion, T. J., McCord, J., & Poulin, F. (1999). When interventions harm: Peer groups and problem behavior. *American Psychologist, 54,* 755–764.

Donovan, J. E., Jessor, R., & Costa, F. M. (1988). Syndrome of problem behavior in adolescence: A replication. *Journal of Consulting and Clinical Psychology, 56,* 762–765.

DuBois, D. L., Felner, R. D., Brand, S., & Phillips, R. S. C. (1996). Early adolescent self-esteem: A developmental-ecological framework and assessment strategy. *Journal of Research on Adolescence, 6,* 543–579.

DuBois, D. L., & Silverthorn, N. (2005). Characteristics of natural mentoring relationships and adolescent adjustment: Evidence from a national study. *Journal of Primary Prevention, 26,* 69–92.

Erikson, E. H. (1950). *Childhood and society.* New York: W. W. Norton.

Farrington, D. (1991). Childhood aggression and adult violence: Early precursors and later life outcomes. In D. Pepper & K. Rubin (Eds.), *The development and treatment of childhood aggression* (pp. 5–29). Hillsdale, NJ: Erlbaum.

Gilligan, C. (1982). *In a different voice: Psychological theory and women's development.* Cambridge, MA: Harvard University Press.

Gilligan, C. (1991). Women's psychological development: Implications for psychotherapy. Women, girls, and psychotherapy: Reframing resistance [Special issue]. *Women & Therapy, 11*(3–4), 5–31.

Gysbers, N. C., & Henderson, P. (2006). *Developing and managing your school guidance and counseling program.* Alexandria, VA: American Counseling Association.

Hagerty, B. M., Lynch-Sauer, J., Patusky, K. L., & Bouwsema, M. (1993). An emerging theory of human relatedness. *Journal of Nursing Scholarship, 25*(4), 291–296.

Harter, S. (1999). *The construction of the self: A developmental perspective.* New York: Guilford.

Harter, S., Waters, P. L., Pettitt, N. W., Kofkin, J., & Jordan, J. (1997). Autonomy and connectedness dimensions of relationship styles in men and women. *Journal of Social and Personal Relationships, 14*(2), 147–164.

Hawkins, J. D., Catalano, R. F., & Miller, J. Y. (1992). Risk and protective factors for alcohol and other drug problems in adolescence and early adulthood: Implications for substance abuse prevention. *Psychological Bulletin, 112*(1), 64–105.

Hawkins, J. D., Farrington, D., & Catalano, R. F. (1998). Reducing violence through the schools. In D. S. Elliott, B. A. Hamburg, & K. R. Williams (Eds.), *Violence in American schools* (pp. 188–216). Cambridge, UK: Cambridge University Press.

Hawkins, J. D., Von Cleve, E., & Catalano, R. F. (1991). Reducing early childhood aggression: Results of a primary prevention program. *Journal of American Academy of Child Adolescent Psychiatry, 30*(2), 208–217.

Hendry, L. B., & Reid, M. (2000). Social relationships and health: The meaning of social "connectedness" and how it related to health concerns for rural Scottish adolescents. *Journal of Adolescence, 23*(6), 705–719.

Henrich, C. C., Brookmeyer, K. A., & Shahar, G. (2005). Weapon violence in adolescence: Parent and school connectedness as protective factors. *Journal of Adolescent Health, 37,* 306–312.

Hirschi, T. (1969). *Causes of delinquency.* Berkeley: University of California Press.

Honora, D., & Rolle, A. (2002). A discussion of the incongruence between optimism and academic performance and its influence on school violence. *Journal of School Violence, 1*(1), 67–82.

Jacobson, K. C., & Rowe, D. C. (1999). Genetic and environmental influences on the relationships between family connectedness, school connectedness, and adolescent depressed mood: Sex differences. *Developmental Psychology, 35*(4), 926–939.

Jason, L. A., & Kobayashi, R. B. (1995). Community building: Our next frontier. *Journal of Primary Prevention, 15*(3), 195–208.

Jessor, R. (1992). Risk behavior in adolescence: A psychosocial framework for understanding and action. *Developmental Review, 12*, 374–390.

Jessor, R. (1993). Successful adolescent development among youth in high-risk settings. *American Psychologist, 48*, 117–126.

Jessor, R., & Jessor, S. L. (1977). *Problem behavior and psychological development: A longitudinal study of youth.* New York: Academic Press.

Joo, E., & Han, B. (2000). An investigation of the characteristics of "classroom alienated" middle school students in Korea. *Asia Pacific Education Review, 1*(1), 123–128.

Jordan, J. V., Kaplan, A. G., Miller, J. B., Stiver, I., & Surrey, J. (1991). *Women's growth in connection: Writings from the stone center.* New York: Guilford Press.

Karcher, M. J. (2001, August 24). *Measuring adolescent connectedness: Four validation studies.* Poster presented at the 109th Annual Convention of the American Psychological Association, San Francisco. (ERIC/CASS No. CG032433)

Karcher, M. J. (2002). The cycle of violence and disconnection among rural middle school students: Teacher disconnection as a consequence of violence. *The Journal of School Violence, 1*(1), 35–51.

Karcher, M. J. (2003). *The Hemingway: Measure of adolescent connectedness: A manual for interpretation and scoring.* Unpublished manuscript, University of Texas, San Antonio.

Karcher, M. J. (2004). Connectedness and school violence: A framework for developmental interventions. In E. Gerler (Ed.), *Handbook of school violence* (pp. 7–42). Binghamton, NY: Haworth Press.

Karcher, M. J., & Finn, L. (2005). How connectedness contributes to experimental smoking among rural youth: Developmental and ecological analyses. *Journal of Primary Prevention, 26*, 25–36.

Karcher, M. J., & Lee, Y. (2002). Connectedness among Taiwanese middle school students: A validation study of the Hemingway Measure of Adolescent Connectedness. *Asia Pacific Education Review, 3*(1), 95–114.

Kohut, H. (1977). *Restoration of the self.* New York: International Universities Press.

Kohut, H., & Elson, M. (1987). *The Kohut seminars on self psychology and psychotherapy with adolescents and young adults.* New York: W. W. Norton.

Kuperminc, G. P., Blatt, S. J., & Leadbeater, B. J. (1997). Relatedness, self-definition, and early adolescent adjustment. *Cognitive Therapy and Research, 21*(3), 301–320.

Lang-Takac, E., & Osterweil, Z, (1992). Separateness and connectedness: Differences between genders. *Sex Roles, 27*, 277–289.

Lee, R. M., & Davis, C. (2000). Cultural orientation, past multicultural experience, and a sense of belonging on campus for Asian American college students. *Journal of College Student Development, 41*(1), 110–115.

Lee, R. M., Keough, K. A., & Seagal, J. D. (1999). *Belongingness, appraisal of campus climate, and perceived life stress in college women and men.* Unpublished manuscript, University of Minnesota–Twin Cities.

Lee, R. M., & Robbins, S. B. (1995). Measuring belongingness: The social connectedness and the social assurance scales. *Journal of Counseling Psychology, 42*(2), 232–241.

Lee, R. M., & Robbins, S. B. (1998). The relationship between social connectedness and anxiety, self-esteem, and social identity. *Journal of Counseling Psychology, 45*(3), 338–345.

Lerner, R. M., Fisher, C. B., & Weinberg, R. A. (2000). Toward a science for and of the people: Promoting the civil society through the application of developmental science. *Child Development, 71*, 11–20.

Lezin, N., Rolleri, L. A., Bean, S., & Taylor, J. (2004). Parent-child connectedness: Implications for research, interventions, and positive impacts on adolescent health. *ETR Associates, Parent-child connectedness BRIDGE project.* Retrieved July 17, 2006, from http://www.etr.org/recapp/forum/forumsummary200402.htm

Lynch, M., & Cicchetti, D. (1997). Children's relationships with adults and peers: An examination of elementary and junior high school students. *Journal of School Psychology, 35*(1), 81–89.

Mallinckrodt, B. (1991). Clients' representations of childhood emotional bonds with parents, social support, and formation of the working alliance. *Journal of Counseling Psychology, 38*, 401–409.

Maslow, A. H. (1968). *Toward a psychology of being.* Princeton, NJ: Van Nostrand.

Midgley, C., Feldlauffer, H., & Eccles, J. S. (1989). Student/teacher relations and attitudes towards mathematics before and after the transition to junior high. *Child Development, 60*, 981–992.

Nakkula, M., & Selman, R. (1991). How people "treat" each other: Pair therapy as a context for the development of interpersonal ethics. In J. L. Gewirtz & W. M. Kurtines (Ed.), *Handbook of moral behavior and development: Vol. 3: Application* (pp. 179–211). Hillsdale, NJ: Lawrence Erlbaum.

O'Donnell, J., Hawkins, J. D., & Abbott, R. D. (1995). Predicting serious delinquency and substance use among aggressive boys. *Journal of Consulting and Clinical Psychology, 63*, 529–537.

Olin, S. S. (2001). Youth violence: Report from the Surgeon General. *The Child, Youth, and Family Services Advocate, 24*(2), 1–7.

Patterson, G. R., Dishion, T. J., & Yoerger, K. (2000). Adolescent growth in new forms of problem behavior: Macro- and micro-peer dynamics. *Prevention Sciences, 1*, 3–13.

Prasad-Gaur, A., Hughes, J. H., & Cavell, T. (2001). Implications of aggressive children's positivity biased relatedness views for future relationships. *Child Psychiatry and Human Development, 31*(3), 215–230.

Resnick, M. D., Harris, L. J., & Blum, R. W. (1993). The impact of caring and connectedness on adolescent health and wellbeing. *Journal of Paediatrics & Child Health, 29,* S3–S9.

Richters, J. E., & Martinez, P. E. (1993). Violent communities, family choices, and children's chances: An algorithm for improving the odds. *Development and Psychopathology, 5,* 609–627.

Ripley, V. V., & Goodnough, G. E. (2001). Planning and implementing group counseling in a high school. *Professional School Counseling, 5,* 62–65.

Roth, J. L., & Brooks-Gunn, J. (2003). What is a youth development program? Identification of defining principles. In F. Jacobs, D. Wertlieb, & R. M. Lerner (Eds.), *Handbook of applied developmental science* (Vol. 2, pp. 197–223). Thousand Oaks, CA: Sage Publications.

Scales, P. C. (2005, December). Developmental assets and the middle school counselor. *Professional School Counseling,* 104–111.

Scales, P. C., & Leffert, N. (1999). *Developmental assets: A synthesis of the scientific research on adolescent development.* Minneapolis, MN: SEARCH Institute.

Schorr, L. B. (1988). *Within our reach: Breaking the cycle of disadvantage.* New York: Doubleday.

Soanes, C. (Ed.). (2003) *The Oxford compact English dictionary* (2nd ed.). Oxford, UK: Oxford University Press.

Stern, D. (1985). *The interpersonal world of the infant: A view from psychoanalysis and developmental psychology.* New York: Basic Books.

Sullivan, J. R., & Wright, N. (2002). The collaborative group counseling referral process: Description and teacher evaluation. *Professional School Counseling, 5,* 366–368.

van Aken, M. A. G., & Asendorpf, J. B. (1997). Support by parents, classmates, friends, and siblings in preadolescence: Covariation and compensation across relationships. *Journal of Social and Personal Relationships, 14*(1), 79–93.

XL
BULLYING AND PEER VICTIMIZATION

SUSAN M. SWEARER, ERIC S. BUHS, AND AMANDA B. SIEBECKER
University of Nebraska – Lincoln

KELLY BREY LOVE
Texas Children's Hospital/Baylor College of Medicine

COURTNEY K. MILLER
Catholic Social Services, Lincoln, Nebraska

Introduction

Bullying and peer victimization are ubiquitous phenomena that many students experience during their school years. While all students have the right to learn in a safe and nonthreatening environment, bullying usurps students of this basic right. This chapter will link theories and research about bullying behaviors, which will form the foundation for a review of effective school-based practice. Intervention programs that have been empirically evaluated will be presented, keeping in mind the developmental needs of students as they progress from preschool through high school.

Definitions

At the outset, we would like to provide working definitions for the constructs described in this chapter. We will define *bullying* according to the classic definition put forth by Dan Olweus: *Bullying* involves either physical or verbal negative actions inflicted by one or more persons upon another person. These actions are intentionally meant to cause harm and are repeated over time in a relationship characterized by an imbalance of strength and/or power (Olweus, 1993a). *Victimization* is defined in the following, "A student is being victimized when he or she is exposed, repeatedly and over time, to negative actions on the part of one of more other students" (Olweus, 1993a). Additionally, we have adopted the Institute of Medicine's (IOM) clinically accepted framework of "prevention," "treatment," and "maintenance" as a rubric for classifying empirically evaluated bullying prevention and intervention programs (IOM, 1994). The Institute of Medicine's framework is population-based, makes specific distinctions between prevention and treatment, and addresses multiple facets of risk and protective factors and their mutual effects. This framework is a useful rubric, as it emphasizes not only the importance of prevention and treatment, but also the importance of maintaining positive treatment gains over time.

Role of the School Counselor in Bullying Prevention and Intervention

The role of the school counselor in bullying prevention and intervention is vital. Often, school counselors are the first professionals in the schools to hear about bullying incidents. Additionally, school counselors are often trained in conflict resolution, individual counseling, and group counseling. These valuable skills lay the foundation for the school counselor to be the logical point person for bullying prevention and intervention efforts. As such, school counselors are key players in preventing, treating, and maintaining effective bullying programming.

Role of Type of School and Bullying

Researchers have examined whether school setting (i.e., geographic location) is related to bullying behaviors among youth. In the first, large-scale investigation ($N = 15,686$) of bullying among U.S. youth, there were no significant differences in frequency of being bullied among youth from urban, suburban, town, and rural areas (Nansel et al., 2001). This investigation, however, noted slight differences with regard to bullying others across geographic location. Approximately 2% to 3% fewer suburban youth endorsed participation in moderate bullying and 3% to 5% more youth in rural settings reported ever bullying.

Although the majority of research to date has been in urban and suburban school settings, several studies have specifically examined bullying in rural settings. The prevalence of bullying in seven rural elementary schools was examined by surveying students, parents, and teachers (Stockdale, Hangaduambo, Duys, Larson, & Sarvela, 2002). Surveys were completed by 739 fourth-, fifth-, and sixth-grade students, 367 parents, and 37 teachers. In this study, students reported higher prevalence of bullying than did parents or teachers, and their reports were associated with aggression, attitudes toward violence, and perceptions of school safety. Based on these results, these researchers concluded that bullying behavior is prevalent in rural elementary schools.

A more recent study conducted by Dulmus, Theriot, Sowers, and Blackburn (2004) examined the prevalence of bullying at three rural schools, sampling students in grades 3 through 8 with the Olweus Bully/Victim Questionnaire. Results indicated that of the 192 students included in this study, 158 children (82.3%) reported having experienced some form of bullying at least once in the past three months. While these results may suggest that school bullying is a larger problem in rural communities than in urban areas, additional research is warranted due to variations in the definition of bullying and methodological problems across studies.

The Explanatory Power of Theory

One weakness in the bullying literature is that much of the empirical work in this area is largely atheoretical; however, there are several cognitive and social theories that help clarify and provide explanation for the engagement in bullying behaviors. When school personnel understand the theoretical explanations that underlie bullying behaviors, logical, effective interventions can be developed. This next section will provide a brief overview of relevant cognitive and social theories that help explain social behaviors among students.

Social Information Processing Theory

Social information processing (SIP) is one of the most widely utilized theories to describe children's social and emotional functioning (Crick & Dodge, 1994; Dodge & Crick, 1990; Dodge et al., 2003; Shahinfar, Kupersmidt, & Matza, 2001). SIP suggests that individuals' unique biological composition, along with memories of previous experiences, impacts their interpretation of current experiences and is causally related to behavioral functioning (Crick & Dodge; Dodge & Crick). SIP consists of six components that include (1) encoding of external and internal stimuli, (2) mentally interpreting these stimuli, (3) selecting a specific goal, (4) constructing a certain response, (5) making a decision, and (6) engaging in a behavioral and/or emotional response (Crick & Dodge; Lemerise & Arsenio, 2000).

Theory of Mind

Theory of mind (ToM) has been defined as the ability of people to attribute mental states to themselves and others in order to explain and predict behavior (Premack & Woodruff, 1978; for a recent review, see Taylor, 1996). Operationally, ToM is divided into many developmental tasks, such as understanding of false beliefs, recognition of complex emotions, empathy, understanding of faux pas, and recognition of deception (Happé, 1994). ToM is essentially the ability to engage in higher order perspective-taking.

Theory of Homophily

The homophily hypothesis states that people who are similar to one another on the basis of certain attributes tend to associate with one another (Kandel, 1978). Homophily is divided into two components: (1) selection and (2) socialization (Kandel; Hogue & Steinberg, 1995). *Selection* refers to the tendency to choose friends on the basis of preexisting similarities. *Socialization*, on the other hand, refers to the tendency for similarity to increase as peers shape one another's behavior over time.

Dominance Theory

While homophily theory suggests that "birds of a feather flock together," dominance theory purports that the need to be "top dog" is related to social functioning. When attempting to understand children's social functioning, adults must understand their peer relationships in combination with their personality (Fleming, 1949). Dominance theory has guided empirical investigations of social relationships with regard to bullying and victimization, and it has helped explain why bullying behaviors peak in middle school (Pellegrini, 2002).

Attraction Theory

Another theory that has explanatory power for understanding bullying is attraction theory. Attraction theory explains perceived similarities between individuals and explains the general feeling of attraction between individuals

(Bukowski, Sippola, & Newcomb, 2000; Levy, O'Neal, Taylor, & Langley, 1990; McCormack & Smith, 1974; Moffitt, 1993; Shuntich, 1976). Byrne (1971) believed two individuals with similar attitudes and values are "attracted" to each other, as their perceived similarity decreases the likelihood for conflict. Shuntich found that students who were attitudinally similar to the each other liked the similar person significantly more and were significantly less aggressive toward that person compared with dissimilar students.

Social Learning Theory

Social learning theory posits that behavior is determined by the reciprocal interaction between cognitive, behavioral, and environmental influences (Bandura, 1977). This triadic reciprocity suggests that the person and the environment do not function independently, but instead, determine each other (Bandura, 2004). One of the most salient components of social learning theory is vicarious learning (i.e., modeling). Vicarious learning plays a large role in the future behavior of individuals (Bandura, 1977). In addition to observing behavior, individuals also encode the consequences of the behavior, thereby learning when and how to use the new behavior. Thus, individuals weigh the costs and benefits of engaging in a certain behavior (or not). Therefore, not all learned behaviors are used; rather it depends upon the factors that activate the behavior and the environmental conditions that sustain the behavior (Tedeschi & Felson, 1994).

Social Ecological Theory

Thus far, the theories reviewed relate to the individual (SIP, ToM), to peer group functioning (homophily, dominance, attraction), and to the interaction between the individual and other people (social learning theory). One unifying theory that encompasses the individual and the multiple contexts in which individuals function is social ecological theory. Social ecological theory is based on the assertion that the outcome of a given behavior or event is a result of the individual in relationship with the broader environment (i.e., family, peer group, classroom, school, community, culture, etc.; Bronfenbrenner, 1979). Social ecological theory is the only theory about bullying that specifically includes culture as a component of bullying.

Cultural Differences in Definitions, Prevalence, and Beliefs about Bullying

In a study of English and Swedish secondary students, a significantly larger percentage of English students believe that "calling someone names" is a form of bullying, whereas Swedish students did not. Conversely, a significantly higher percentage of Swedish students perceive that "leaving someone out of a group" can be categorized as a bullying behavior, while English students did not (Boulton, Bucci, & Hawker, 1999). Interestingly, both of these forms of bullying can be categorized as relational bullying; however, there was significant definitional discrepancy across cultures.

Similarly, Cerezo and Ato's (2005) study also found cross-cultural differences in a similar criterion for bullying, "Leave someone out of activities and games," posed in the above-mentioned study. This study looked at differences and similarities in bullying in middle school students in Spain and in England. This question was statistically significant for the students in Spain, but was not for the students in England, indicating a difference in definition across cultures. In a large study across 14 countries looking at definitional differences in the construct of bullying, researchers found that while differences across age were evident as to which activities constituted bullying, definitions of bullying remained relatively consistent across countries (P. K. Smith, Cowie, Olafsson, & Liefooghe, 2002).

Perhaps as a result of the differences in students' beliefs as to which behaviors compose bullying, prevalence rates also differ across countries. Recent studies conducted with English students illustrated a higher percentage of involvement in bullying than in other countries. On the whole, German students reported a relatively low frequency of bullying as compared with English students. In a study of 6- and 8-year-olds in England and Germany, 24% of English students reported being bullied weekly, whereas only 8% of German students reported this frequency. However, 2.5 to 4.5% of English students reported their role as being a bully, and 9.5% of German students reported this same role (Wolke, Woods, Stanford, & Schultz, 2001).

Menesini et al. (1997) conducted a study analyzing the prevalence rates of bullying among Italian and English primary and secondary school students. They found that 40% of Italian primary and 28% of Italian secondary school students reported being bullied "sometimes or more" in a school year, a percentage nearly twice as high as reported by the English students (Menesini et al.).

Recently, researchers have begun to look at reports of rates of bullying in relation to ethnicity and race. A study that examined seventh- and eighth-grade self-reported bullies and victims found no significant difference in involvement based on ethnicity (Seals & Young, 2003). Another study also found no significant difference between African American and Caucasian students regarding different types of bullying students were engaged in (verbal, physical, etc). Similarly, Kaufman et al. (1998) found that ethnicity was not as significant a factor in bullying as gender and grade level. Wolke et al. (2001) found similar results in their study of a younger population of 8-year-olds, finding ethnicity did not have a significant association with bullying interactions.

As evidenced by the definitional differences and varying prevalence rates of bullying across cultures and countries, some students appeared to hold culturally divergent beliefs about bullying as well. In Menesini et al.'s (1997) above-mentioned study, 48% of Italian students in primary grades and 60% in secondary grades reported that involvement in bullying "upset me a lot." Although English students reported higher prevalence rates of bullying, they also appeared to have reported less emotional impact, with 26% of English primary students and 12% of secondary students endorsing this same feeling (Menesini et al.).

In an Australian study, however, researchers found that both ethnicity and sex differentiated students attitudes toward bullying. Ethnic minorities placed greater importance on attributes proposed as consequences of bullying. No ethnic differences were found, however, for incidence of involvement in bullying, nor were there any differences found between ethnicities regarding attitudes toward bullying interventions (Nguy & Hunt, 2004).

Theory-Based Research

In the preceding section, we laid the theoretical framework for understanding social and cognitive theories that explain facets of human behavior. In this section, we will examine some of the empirical literature that has looked at bullying and victimization from these seven perspectives.

Social Information Processing Theory and Bullying

SIP researchers have found that aggressive children experience errors in social information processing, including (1) cue encoding, (2) cue interpretation, (3) response generation and selection, and (4) enactment (Dodge, 1986; Dodge, Pettit, McClaskey, & Brown, 1986; Feldman & Dodge, 1987; Milich & Dodge, 1984). In the case of engagement in bullying behaviors, at the cue encoding stage, bullies tend to seek fewer social cues before making hostile attributions regarding the intent of others (Dodge; Milich & Dodge). This often leads to a "misread" of both intent and environment. Research has identified that during cue interpretation, children who are aggressive utilize a hostile attribution bias regarding the behavior of others (Dodge; Dodge et al.). At the response generation phase of SIP, aggressive children have been found to identify more aggressive and fewer assertive responses than their nonaggressive peers (Dodge; Feldman & Dodge). In the enactment phase, Dodge et al. also identified that aggressive children lack the skills to enact competent responses to negative situations. Thus, the social information processing that occurs in students who bully others differs significantly from that in students who do not bully others. SIP theory provides a way of understanding how thinking processes are related to behaviors such as bullying.

Theory of Mind and Bullying

Theory of mind also explains how some bullies are so adept at bullying that adults may not notice these behaviors. The role ToM plays in bullying has been the subject of recent scholarly debate, generating two divergent views. On the one hand, Sutton, Smith, and Swettenham (1999b) discovered that children categorized as "ringleader" bullies appear to have superior ToM skills. On the other hand, Crick and Dodge (1999) indicated that the historical trend in research has identified an inverse relationship between perspective-taking abilities and aggressive behavior. What emerges from this debate is a heterogeneous view of bullies—one that accounts for both the bullies who have strong ToM skills and those who do not (Sutton, Smith, & Swettenham, 1999a; 1999c; 2001).

Sutton, Smith, and Swettenham (1999b) utilized ToM to define social cognition within the context of bullying. They had participants read 11 short stories designed to test understanding of mental states or emotions. Based on their results, they proposed that bullies may perceive and interpret social cues accurately, while displaying limitations with their abilities to select prosocial goals and generate positive response strategies and decisions. These observations could reflect past experiences and strategies that have been effective for gaining social status or social resources. This view represents bullying as a complex, functional behavior rather than a skill deficit, which is consistent with some evolutionary models of aggression (Hawley, 2003).

Happé and Frith (1996) evaluated the performance of 6- to 12-year-old children diagnosed with conduct disorder on false belief tasks. All of the children with conduct disorder passed the ToM tasks, though they demonstrated social deficits on an observational measure. Data have also indicated that relational methods of bullying increase with age (Rivers & Smith), that girls rely more on relational strategies when they bully (Bjorkqvist, Österman, & Kaukiainen, 1992; Rivers & Smith, 1994), and that girls perform better on ToM tasks than boys do (Baron-Cohen & Hammer, 1996). As a result, it is believed that ToM skills are more highly developed in individuals who utilize relational techniques to bully because they must understand and manipulate an entire social system. Bullying also represents a type of social interaction that can provide experiences that may develop social cognition in bullies, victims, and bystanders. Each individual involved in a bullying interaction might assume a specific and ongoing social role. Following each interaction, the bully's social status may advance while the victim's diminishes. These interactions could also reflect another predominant finding that aggressive children demonstrate a lack of empathy (Bjorkqvist, Österman, & Kaukiainen, 2000). While ToM is a useful theory to describe the manipulative qualities of some bullies, it does not explain the group phenomenon associated with some bullies. To understand these group dynamics, we turn to the theories of homophily, dominance, and attraction.

Theory of Homophily and Bullying

The homophily hypothesis has been used to explain within group similarity with respect to many types of externalizing behavior, such as antisocial behavior (Kiesner, Cadinu, Poulin, & Buccci, 2002; Kiesner, Poulin, & Nicotra, 2003), drug use (Kandel, 1978), and aggression (Espelage, Holt, & Henkel, 2003; Xie, Cairns, & Cairns, 1999). In general, adolescents tend to associate with friends who display the same behaviors and those behaviors tend to increase over time within the peer group.

Espelage et al. (2003) investigated peer influence on bullying behavior (e.g., teasing) and overt physical aggression (e.g., fighting). Significant within-group similarity was found in regard to both forms of self-reported aggression. This suggests that students who engage in bullying and/or fighting tend to associate with peers who also exhibit such behaviors. Finally, in conjunction with previous research on aggression, bullying tended to increase among peer groups who reported bullying others.

Salmivalli, Huttunen, and Lagerspetz (1997) also found a relationship between peer group affiliation and participation in bullying as either a bully, a reinforcer, an assistant, or a victim. Specifically, participants who endorsed bullying behaviors tended to affiliate with other participants who endorsed the same behaviors. Interestingly, the size of the peer group differed between the groups in that victims tended to have smaller peer groups, while bullies, reinforcers, and assistants tended to form larger peer groups. Furthermore, participants who were outside the peer group tended to be victims. Thus, bullying behavior may be influenced by group formation.

Homophily results in groupings of students based on many characteristics, one of which is social status. T. W. Farmer and E. Z. Farmer (1996) demonstrated that well-defined social structures exist in classrooms and that students tend to belong to clusters in which they share similar attributes. Although research is beginning to suggest that gender differences in bullying may not be as clear as was previously thought, research indicates that popular males tend to be more aggressive and popular females tend to exclude others who are unlike them (Adler, Kless, & Adler). Swearer and Cary (2003) found that both victims and bullies reported being "different" as the reason for either being bullied or bullying others. Therefore, dominant peer groups are formed that physically or relationally reject those who are different, which leads to less social support for victims of bullying. The homophily hypothesis suggests that if left alone, incidents of bullying would increase as groups of bullies become more similar through homophily and through the need to establish dominance.

Dominance Theory and Bullying

Peer affiliation has been shown to be a strong factor in mediating bullying and victimization (Mouttapa, Valente, Gallaher, Rohrbach, & Unger, 2004; Pellegrini & Bartini, 2000; Pellegrini, Bartini, & Brooks, 1999). It is during the transition from elementary school to middle school that bullying behavior may peak, ebbing and flowing as necessary to establish and maintain dominant peer relationships. In a longitudinal study conducted by Pellegrini and Long (2002), researchers found that bullying and aggression initially increased with the transition to middle school, and then declined as dominance was established. Further, Long and Pellegrini (2003) found that bullying covaried with dominance during the middle school years, showing that when bullying increased, dominance increased and when bullying decreased, dominance decreased. These findings are consistent with dominance theory in that individuals are ordered in a hierarchy (i.e., toughest to weakest) according to their access to resources and once the hierarchy is established, aggression deceases because individuals know who is most dominant (Pellegrini, 2002; Pellegrini & Bartini, 2001).

Attraction Theory and Bullying

Moffit (1993) stated that during that transition from childhood to adolescence, antisocial youth move from the fringes of the social group to a more powerful, visible status role. Moffitt further explained that adolescents often begin to engage in "social mimicry," in which adolescents adopt what are now seen as "successful behaviors." In this situation, adolescents who have not previously shown aggressive tendencies may begin to display aggressive behavior, as it is now being reinforced and valued by peers.

Similar to Moffitt's (1993) explanation of this increase in aggression from childhood to adolescence, Bukowski et al. (2000) defined attraction theory as youth desiring affiliation with peers demonstrating independent behaviors and avoidance of peers engaging in more prosocial behaviors. This desire for independence and more "adult" behaviors appears to be most prominent during the transition from childhood to adolescence.

In a study conducted with 217 students transitioning from elementary to middle school, Bukowski et al. (2000) confirmed this increase in attraction to aggressive classmates. They discovered boys nominated as attractive by their female classmates had aggression scores two-thirds of a standard deviation above the mean (Bukowski et al.). The authors discovered a significant difference between aggressive children attracted to peers displaying aggressive behaviors, and the attraction scores of children attracted to less aggressive peers.

In sum, attraction theory posits that aggressive children are viewed as "attractive," or well liked, by both aggressive and nonaggressive peers. Thus, students identified as bullies by their peers may appear more attractive as potential friends and more powerful than students who engage in low-aggression behaviors (e.g., pure victims or bystanders of bullying). These findings suggest that students categorized as "attractive" (e.g., physically attractive, attitudinally similar) are less likely to be bullied than "nonattractive" students (Garbarino & deLara, 2002).

Social Learning Theory and Bullying

In addition to the general theory of human behavior, Bandura (1978) applied social learning theory specifically to aggression. Bandura explained that vicarious or observational learning allows people to develop large behavioral repertoires of aggressive behavior, as opposed to learning through direct experience and trial and error. The actual response depends on the interpretation of the source, the learned responses, and the potential consequences. Maintenance of the behavioral response depends on anticipated positive consequences. In sum, vicarious learning leads to a large repertoire of behaviors, aversive stimulation leads to the activation of potential responses, and one particular response is chosen based on the perceived potential of positive consequences. Depending upon the learning history of the individual, aggressive or nonaggressive behaviors will be chosen.

While much of the research on social learning theory has focused on aggression, no current study has directly linked social learning theory and bullying. Many of the aggression studies, however, do investigate both relational and physical aggression. Tapper and Boulton (2005) used social learning theory to investigate the consequences of direct and indirect forms of aggression based on responses of the victim(s) and the bystander(s). Participants were observed using a micro video camera for a period ranging from 40 to 105 minutes. The observers then coded instances of aggression and the responses of the victim and the peers. The results indicated that the most common consequences of direct aggression were retaliation and victim withdrawal. On the other hand, peer support for the aggressor was most likely to occur when the aggression was either relational (indirect or direct) or indirect verbal aggression.

Hall, Herzberger, and Skowronski (1998) studied outcome expectances and the outcome values of aggressive behavior. Hall and colleagues suggested that aggressive children have certain expectations about the consequences of their behavior and attach value to those outcomes. Participants read stories in which a peer provoked them; one story asked them to imagine verbally retaliating and one asked them to imagine physically retaliating. They then measured the likelihood of physically and verbally retaliating and the outcome values attached to their choice. The results suggested that children high on self-reported aggression were less likely to expect being punished or to feel bad; rather, they expected to gain peer respect as a result of aggressive acts. Children who were more likely to expect being punished and/or who cared more about punishment scored lower on self-reported aggression. These studies provide some explanatory power for the engagement in bullying behaviors: Bullying is a learned behavior that is reinforced in many peer groups and settings (Garbarino & deLara, 2002).

Social Ecological Theory and Bullying

Given that bullying is not an isolated phenomenon, social ecological theory has been applied to the conceptualization of bullying behaviors in an effort to more fully understand its perpetuating cycle (Garbarino & deLara, 2002; Newman, Horne, & Bartolumucci, 2000; Olweus, 1993a; Swearer & Doll, 2001). Olweus (1997) pointed out research evidence which suggested that individual characteristics, as well as environmental factors (i.e., teacher attitudes, routines, etc.), play a major role in determining the extent to which bullying behaviors will manifest either in a classroom or in a school. This evidence also dispelled the myth that victimization is "caused" by external attributes of the individual, such as having red hair, wearing glasses, or being overweight.

The microsystem is defined as the *immediate setting* containing the individual and its influence on that individual. Examples of this may be the home or school and what influences each has on the child or student. The second level, the mesosystem, is seen as the *interrelations* among major settings or interactions between microsystems. Specific to bullying, an example would be the interrelations between home and school, as well as between peer groups, in terms of responses to and attitudes toward bullying behavior. The exosystem consists of *social structures* in which the individual may not specifically participate, but which have an influence on the individual (i.e., school policies, state legislation on bullying, etc.). The fourth system is the macrosystem. The macrosystem differs in that it does not refer to a specific context affecting the individual, but instead refers to general patterns for structures occurring at the other levels. Examples might be school or classroom structures (e.g., physical arrangement or layout) or societal and/or cultural attitudes toward bullying and victimization (Bronfenbrenner, 1977; Swearer & Espelage, 2004).

Bullying and victimization can be conceptualized as encompassing all contexts in which individual characteristics interact and are reciprocally affected by multiple contexts, factors, and interchanges. Of particular interest to the study of bullying behaviors within schools are the contexts of the family, school, community, and culture and their interchange with and influence on the individual student (Swearer & Doll, 2001). Given methodological and monetary constraints, few studies have attempted to examine bullying from a social ecological framework. One attempt to test a social ecological model found support for individual and school factors as salient in a social ecological framework (Swearer et al., 2006).

Theory-Based Practice

The IOM framework for prevention, treatment, and maintenance efforts to prevent bullying will be described, taking into account developmental differences across the school years. Areas of innovation will be discussed, including best practices in bullying prevention and intervention that emphasize home–school connections.

Best practices in bullying prevention involve schools first implementing Reynolds' (1986) three-stage multiple-gate screening procedure to identify youngsters who are at risk for bullying in school settings: (a) conducting large-group screening with self-report bullying measures; (b) 3 to 6 weeks later, retesting students who, on the basis of the large-group screening in Stage 1, meet cutoff score criteria for bullying and/or victimization; and (c) conducting individual, clinical interviews with students who manifest clinical levels of bullying and/or victimization at both Stage 1 and Stage 2 evaluations. Effective treatment of bullying typically includes schoolwide efforts augmented by individual therapy. Effective maintenance includes monitoring

Table 40.1 Bullying Prevention and Intervention Programs: Prevention, Treatment, and Maintenance

Intervention Name	Grades Intended	Targeted Behaviors/ Goals	Available Outcome Studies	IOM Spectrum
Bully Busters	K–8	Reduce & prevent bullying; increase teacher knowledge and skills	Newman-Carlson & Horne, 2004	Prevention, Treatment, & Maintenance
Second Step	Pre/K–9	Increase prosocial skills; decrease aggression	Frey et al., 2000; McMahon & Washburn, 2003; Sprague et al., 2001; Taub, 2002	Prevention & Treatment
Olweus' Bullying Prevention and Intervention Program	3–12	Reduce & prevent bullying; improve peer relationships	Carey, 2003; Endresen & Olweus, 2001; Eslea & Smith, 1998; Kallestad & Olweus, 2003; Kristensen & Smith, 2003; Olweus, 1991, 1992, 1993b, 1994, 1995a, 1995b, 1997a, 1997b, 1997c, 2003, 2004	Prevention & Treatment
Expect Respect	K–12	Prevent bullying and sexual harassment; create positive school climate	Meraviglia et al., 2003; Rosenbluth et al., 2004; Sanchez et al., 2001	Prevention & Treatment
Steps to Respect	3–6	Prevent bullying; improve peer relationships; increase bystander intervention	Frey et al. (2005); Hirschstein & Frey (2006)	Prevention

compliance with long-term goals, reducing bullying, and conducting ongoing evaluations to monitor progress.

This section reviews several available bullying/victimization intervention programs. While the included interventions and numerous other programs have been implemented in hundreds—perhaps even thousands—of settings, limiting the programs presented here to intervention with theoretical support and published evaluations of program effectiveness reduced the choices to a small handful (see Table 40.1). The following intervention programs were chosen because they are nationally or internationally recognized and have presented published, empirical evaluation data. This list is not intended to be exhaustive, but the published studies on which we relied here are readily available to the research and professional community. This information regarding the effectiveness of the interventions seems critical in that it allows both researchers and practitioners to enter into the bullying intervention realm with reasonable confidence that we can observe our critical professional commitment: to do no harm.

The Olweus Bullying Prevention Program

Dan Olweus, a Norwegian psychologist, developed and implemented the Olweus Bullying Prevention Program in Norway in the mid-1980s (Olweus, 1991). His program is among the most established and is probably the most widely applied intervention, both in Europe and in the United States. He developed this comprehensive intervention in response to the suicides of several Norwegian children associated with school bullying. These highly publicized deaths had a large impact in a small country such as Norway (population of ca. four million) and helped generate support for Olweus' large-scale, school-based efforts to intervene. The Olweus program has also spawned a number of notable intervention programs based on Olweus' work that will not be specifically discussed here due to space limitations (e.g., Pepler, Craig, O'Connell, Atlas, & Charach, 2003).

Theoretical/conceptual basis. Conceptually, Olweus has placed his intervention efforts within a larger philosophy that stresses the fundamental democratic right of students. Within a developmental perspective, Olweus has presented some degree of detail on his views of the causes of bullying, and he has maintained that bullying behavior is fostered by an interaction between parenting styles/behaviors (e.g., lack of warmth and involvement, permissiveness of aggressive behavior, and power-assertive discipline), the larger social environment (e.g., teacher attitudes and routines that tolerate or permit bullying), and children's temperament (e.g., highly active, easily emotionally aroused children are more likely to be aggressive). Victims, in Olweus' view, are characterized primarily by socially withdrawn behavior. Olweus' parent interviews have also indicated that victims tend to display higher levels of cautious and sensitive behaviors from early age, perhaps indicating temperament as a causal factor. He made no assertions as to parenting behaviors that may be related to victim status.

Contrary to the beliefs of many psychologists, Olweus dismissed anxiety and insecurity as causal factors in bullying behavior. He also maintained that the bullying risk factors above are unrelated to children's socioeconomic status. Additionally, he has attributed *increases* in bullying behavior to factors originating within children's social interactions such as social contagion, a weakening of inhibitions against aggressive behavior, diffusion of responsibility for bullying among the group, and changes in both bully and group perceptions of the victim. In a related focus on the larger social environment, Limber, Nation, Tracy, Melton, and Flerx (2004) cited the Olweus program as based on ecological theory and emphasizing related goals such as creation of a warm and caring school environment characterized by consistent involvement of adults in students' experiences, firm limits on student behavior related to bullying and victimization, and nonhostile/nonphysical consequences for violations of behavior standards.

Intervention components. Olweus' (1993a, 1993b, 1997) intervention efforts, following his conceptual tenets, focused on individual components (e.g., talks with bullies, victims, and parents; detailed individual intervention plans), as well as school-level components (e.g., adequate supervision of recess, staff discussion groups) and classroom level interventions (e.g., explicit antibullying rules, class meetings about bullying problems). The Olweus program has been implemented and evaluated relatively extensively in Norway and Europe, as well as in the United States. A thorough presentation of those findings is well beyond the scope of this chapter, and this section will focus on the American implementation as carried out by Limber and colleagues (e.g., Limber, Nation, Tracy, Melton, & Flerx, 2003; Olweus, Limber, & Mihalic, 1999).

Schoolwide components. This intervention program was implemented within 18 South Carolina middle schools (data below are from six schools completing two years of the study and six schools completing one year). The original Olweus program was modified to include schoolwide (as opposed to classroom-level) antibullying rules and broadened to involve the larger community. In the school year prior to the study, baseline data on bullying prevalence, student attitudes, and so forth was collected. The following August, one-day, schoolwide trainings occurred prior to the start of school, and staff discussed baseline data and subsequent implementation plans. Then, schools held a schoolwide special event (e.g., school assembly) to announce the program and its components to the students. The school staff also developed, announced, and enforced their own versions of schoolwide antibullying rules based on Olweus' (1993b) framework. The three basic guidelines were

1. We will not bully other students.
2. We will try to help students who are being bullied.
3. We will make a point to include students who are easily left out.

Staff also increased their monitoring of student behavior at empirically identified "hot spots" for bullying. Typical areas included recess/playgrounds, lunchrooms, hallways, bathrooms, and bus loading/unloading areas. School staff also developed school-specific programs for rewarding students who displayed prosocial behavior, for example, with tokens for redemption at the school store or entry into drawings for prizes.

Classrooms. The component was a class meeting held a minimum of every 2 weeks (20–30 minutes per session) to discuss bullying and peer relations. Many teachers led discussion of bullying prevalence and also used a video made available by program staff. Some meetings also included role playing, creative writing, and art projects to address the topic. Mental health support staff (either local, school-based personnel or graduate students provided by the program) were made available to assist teachers in conducting meetings and to help those uncomfortable leading such meetings.

Bullies and victims. Bullies and victims were also provided with individual-level support services and response protocols. Bullies were made immediately aware of their behavior by adult feedback, including disapproval and appropriate sanctions. Victims were protected from the aggressive behavior and given support in developing social skills and friendships. Adults were encouraged to directly intervene in all bullying episodes they witnessed and to engage support staff in resolution of the situations and subsequent monitoring.

The broader community. Parent and community involvement was also promoted. Parents were notified of the program via pamphlets and the program was also announced at PTA and parent–teacher meetings. Some schools presented more extensive information to parents via panel discussions and special events. Community organizations and media were encouraged to announce the program and raise community awareness of the issues.

Implementation fidelity. Limber and colleagues (2003) indicated that implementing some critical areas of the intervention components were a challenge for some schools and teachers. Challenging areas included maintaining the level of staff commitment to the program, maintaining high levels of involvement of staff over time (e.g., viewing the intervention as a 1-year effort rather than as systematic change), and teacher difficulty in holding classroom meetings.

Evidence Base. Research has indicated that the Olweus program has been successful in reducing levels of bullying and victimization in schools. The program evaluation data from Norwegian interventions (Olweus, 2003) indicated consistently lower levels of bullying and victimization and general antisocial behavior (including bullying) across early adolescent age groups. The American studies (Limber et al., 2003; Olweus et al., 1999) indicated consistently positive results, but with a somewhat lower magnitude of school-level effects relative to the Scandinavian studies. Significant reductions in bullying behaviors were generally strongest at year 1 follow-up (as opposed to year 2 follow-up) and indicated relatively large drops in bullying behavior for boys and girls. Findings from self-reports of victimization and of social isolation indicated a significant decrease for boys, but not for girls. Students also reported fewer incidences of bullying to parents. The authors maintain that the pattern of stronger and more consistently positive effects for boys over girls may be the result of the type of bullying/victimization addressed, with a relatively stronger or more effective emphasis on overt physical and verbal forms of aggression more typical in boys (as opposed to indirect forms of aggression that tend to occur more often with girls).

In sum, results indicate that the Olweus program is effective with early adolescent age groups, particularly for boys and/or direct forms of aggressive, bullying behaviors. The focus on school level variables precludes producing some data on the efficacy of the intervention relative to classroom and, especially, individual level effects. More fine-grained follow ups of the program effects are needed to contribute to a detailed understanding of the intervention efficacy in different types of classrooms and for the range of bullies and victims, especially with regard to gender differences.

Second Step

Second Step (Committee for Children, 2005) is a comprehensive violence prevention program developed by the Committee for Children and is one of the most extensively researched violence prevention programs available. To date, Second Step has been employed in the United States, Canada, Australia, Germany, New Zealand, Norway, and the United Kingdom. Second Step has also developed a

Spanish language version. Currently, Second Step is also the only program reviewed here that has curricula designed to serve pre-K through 4th grade (the other programs discussed here have been applied in ca. 5th to 8th grades).

While Second Step was not specifically designed as a bullying and victimization intervention, it does target direct and relational aggression. The primary focus of Second Step is to develop students' social-emotional skills in four areas: (1) empathy, (2) impulse control, (3) anger management, and (4) problem solving (Committee for Children, 2005). Frey, Hirchstein, and Guzzo (2000) suggested that competencies in these four areas serve as protective factors against problem behavior and peer relationship difficulties.

Theoretical basis. Second step is grounded in social learning theory (Frey et al., 2000). There is an emphasis on modeling, self-reflection, execution, and reinforcement. These constructs are considered necessary to the development and continued use of the specific skills taught through Second Step. The Committee for Children (2005) contends that aggressive children are at higher risk for more serious behavioral and emotional problems and that by providing direct instruction of specific skills and the opportunity to practice them, aggressive behaviors will decrease and positive social interactions will increase.

Though not explicitly framed as such by the authors, Second Step may also be conceptualized from an ecological systems perspective (Bronfenbrenner, 1979), similar to the Olweus program. Second Step is administered in a group format, typically within a classroom, and the authors also recommended that the program be implemented across all classrooms in a school. Frey et al. (2000) suggested that when this occurs, students are more likely to develop skills and maintain the program effects. Finally, at the family level, Second Step has developed a Family Guide for parents of students from preschool to fifth-grade ages.

Intervention Components. The Second Step program delivers content primarily through regularly scheduled, teacher-led lessons within small groups or at the classroom level.

Teachers. Teacher training is a universal component of the Second Step curriculum at all grade levels. Through a sequence of training sessions, teachers are instructed in how to model skills during student lessons. Throughout the program, positive reinforcement of skill use is also stressed. Students are then taught specific prosocial skills, which they then practice on a regular basis. Teachers generally conduct one to two 30-minute lessons per week with their students.

Elementary students. In the elementary curriculum, students practice prosocial behavior skills under the supervision of the teacher. Teachers follow the lesson plan, which includes lesson objectives, a script, discussion questions, role-plays, or other activities. With younger children, colorful puppets are sometimes are used to model problem solving and skill use. The plan also includes suggestions for modeling the skills throughout the week. (Committee for Children, 2005).

Middle school students. The middle school curriculum teaches students higher level skills and places more emphasis on changing attitudes and beliefs about aggression. The curriculum includes age-appropriate literature with relevant content. Lessons and discussions encourage students to try to understand characters' points of view and actively promote the development of perspective taking skills. Middle school students also engage in role plays and related discussion activities relevant to their daily experiences.

Evidence Base. As previously mentioned, Second Step provides a relatively strong degree of empirical evaluation, and a detailed review of all studies is beyond the scope of this chapter. The chapters in this review all included some form of teacher training prior to implementation of the program and were selected in order to be representative of the wide span of grade levels for which Second Step was designed. Studies summarized here include Sprague at al. (2001; grades K–8), Grossman et al. (1997; grades 2–3), Taub (2002; grades 3–5), and Van Shoiack-Edstrom, Frey, and Beland (2002; grades 6–8).

Sprague and colleagues (2001) conducted the most comprehensive analysis of the Second Step program by assessing its effects at all grade levels for which data were available at the time. This study did not, however, investigate the Second Step effects in isolation, but instead as part of a whole school program that involved the creation of new school rules as well as a schoolwide positive reinforcement and discipline program in addition to the Second Step curriculum. Sprague et al. measured their effectiveness with office referral data, perceptions of school safety, perceived behavioral support, and declarative knowledge of the Second Step curriculum. While an analysis of the unique effects attributable to the Second Step curriculum was not possible, findings indicated that students' declarative knowledge of the Second Step program components increased slightly (from 46% to 55%). Unfortunately, the authors did not administer the same tests to the control groups and could not rule out the role of maturation effects as a component of the increase. The analyses also indicated a decrease in office referrals for both middle school and elementary school participants (−82% and −51%, respectively), while the middle school control groups displayed a corresponding increase (82%) and elementary school controls presented only a slight increase (7.5%). The authors found no differences in changes in perceptions of school safety between the intervention and control school.

Grossman et al.'s (1997) analysis of the Second Step program included data from 12 schools serving similar socioeconomic and ethnic populations (6 intervention groups and 6 control groups). The Second Step curriculum was implemented with second- and third-grade students across the intervention groups. Observational data was collected on aggressive behaviors prior to intervention, directly following intervention, and 6 months after intervention. Grossman et al. found that physical aggression for the intervention group decreased, whereas these behaviors increased for the control students. This study is remarkable in the use of observational data and may provide some of the strongest evidence published indicating a decrease in aggression for intervention groups.

Taub (2002) evaluated the effectiveness of Second Step with third- to fifth-grade students in a primarily Caucasian, low SES, rural school context. Taub collected pre- and postintervention data and conducted a 1-year follow up. Teacher ratings of student behavior were gathered on three indices: "responds to directions from adults, engages appropriately with peers, and follows classroom rules" (p. 189) and two negative behaviors: "bothers/annoys/distracts other students and fights/argues with peers" (p. 190). Taub's findings indicated that intervention students displayed a decrease in antisocial behavior while the control school displayed an increase. Interestingly, the behavioral observations revealed a decline in observed prosocial behaviors for both schools; however, the decline was more severe for the comparison school than it was for the intervention school.

Van Shoiack-Edstrom et al. (2002) expanded the Second Step curriculum from one year duration to three years with groups of sixth- to eighth-grade students in the United States and Canada. The accompanying evaluation study used data gathered from the first 2 years of the program. The authors assessed intervention effectiveness by measuring student endorsement of aggression, verbal derogation, and social exclusion items. Additionally, they gathered data on students' perceived difficulties performing the adaptive social skills. This evaluation was also the only study in this review to include explicit measures of relational aggression. In year 1 of their study, the authors found no changes in the levels of social exclusion from pre- to postintervention, while the control group had a significant increase in social exclusion. Across the second year of the program, treatment groups showed a significant decrease in physical aggression, verbal derogation, and social exclusion, while control groups displayed either increased levels or displayed no change.

Second Step represents a broadly applied, highly visible intervention. While the targeted skills and behaviors extend well beyond bullying, per se, it is clear that the evidence supports contentions that the program should reduce bullying and victimization rates as well. Second Step is also the only program spanning early childhood and adolescent age groups and, as such, represents the only intervention program with an explicitly developmental framework.

The Expect Respect Program

While less visible than the Olweus program or Second Step, the Expect Respect program (Meraviglia, Becker, Rosenbluth, Sanchez, & Robertson, 2003) has also achieved recognition as a strategy with some empirical evaluation. The creators of Expect Respect based their intervention design on Olweus' program and research (Olweus et al., 1999); for their specific intervention components, they relied on Stein's Bullyproof program (Sjostrom & Stein, 1996). They developed their program to address traditional forms of bullying behavior, but also included a focus on bullying behaviors associated with sexual abuse and harassment. While these behaviors certainly fall under the standard definition of bullying, Expect Respect is notable for including the problems of sexual abuse and harassment as a central component of their program. The published intervention study was implemented once over the course of one school year in fifth-grade classrooms across six schools in the late 1990s in Austin, Texas.

Theoretical/conceptual basis. The program authors (Meraviglia et al., 2003; Rosenbluth, Whitaker, Sanchez, & Valle, 2003) do not explicitly cite or create a larger conceptual framework or causal model in their reports, aside from citing the work of Olweus et al. (1999) and the program developed by Stein (Sjostrom & Stein, 1996). They located their efforts within a larger context of violence prevention (the program, not coincidentally, was developed through a grant to a sexual and domestic violence prevention services provider). The authors stated that child contexts that tolerate bullying behavior foster increased aggressive behaviors and violence in adulthood and thus contribute to the incidence of sexual harassment and domestic violence, but do not explain specific processes via which this would occur. The intervention targets increasing bystander intervention as the behavioral means for decreasing bullying behaviors. The project "targeted the involvement of all members of the school community in recognizing and responding effectively to bullying and sexual harassment among students" (Rosenbluth et al., p. 212). The authors did not cite prior theoretical/causal models or present empirical support for the effectiveness of bystander intervention as a strategy for reducing harassing or aggressive behaviors in children.

Intervention Components. The program relied heavily on the *Bullyproof* model (Sjostrom & Stein, 1996) and presented classroom curriculum, staff training, policy development, parent education, and support services components. The program was implemented in fifth-grade classrooms (with matching control schools; see the following sections) in Texas. The students reflected the racially and socioeconomically diverse population of Austin, Texas (i.e., they included significant numbers of Hispanic and African American participants). No additional information has apparently been published on the precise number of classrooms engaged, but six program schools were involved (as well as six matched control schools), and the program involved 929 intervention students and 834 controls at the outset.

Classroom components. Twelve weekly *Bullyproof* sessions were administered in the intervention classrooms. These sessions targeted bystander intervention as the mechanism for reducing bullying and sought to increase the "ability and willingness," (Meraviglia et al., 2003) of bystanders to intervene. This increase might, in turn, decrease bullying. The curriculum also sought to aid students in distinguishing playful joking around versus hurtful teasing. Students were encouraged to "speak up or get help from an adult when they witnessed someone being mistreated" (Rosenbluth et al., 2003, p. 214) via writing assignments, role-playing, and class discussions.

Staff training. Two-tiered staff trainings were implemented by *Bullyproof* staff for project personnel. Counselors, teachers, and administrators received a single 6-hour training and other personnel (e.g., office staff, hall monitors) received 3 hours of training once per semester (i.e., twice) for the yearlong duration of the program. Staff were presented with prior research findings and were coached in intervention strategies targeting consistent staff responses across school contexts and the promotion of mutual respect among students (Rosenbluth et al., 2003). The training included discussions and activities.

Policy development. School administrators were trained to develop a policy supporting consistent staff responses to bullying and sexual harassment. Administrators were provided with a template or guideline for the development of the policies that were subsequently presented to school staff/parent advisory councils (Rosenbluth et al., 2003). Guidelines were then to be presented to staff, parents, and students with appropriate support for implementation (the authors report varied results in implementation of this component).

Parent education. Parents were provided with information through newsletters and presentations (attendance was voluntary and reported as "varying by site;" Rosenbluth et al., 2003, p. 215). The information presented related vocabulary, strategies for helping bullies/witnesses/victims, tips for responses and prevention, and described available community resources for coping support.

Support services. Counselors from the violence prevention center were made available to assist school counselors in providing support for children involved in bullying. Additional training was also provided to the school counselors themselves and included strategies for reducing victim vulnerability and alternatives to conflict resolution approaches. Counselors also received a manual on bullying, sexual abuse, dating violence, and domestic violence.

Program fidelity. The authors, throughout their publications, suggest that the fidelity of program implementation varied widely across schools and classrooms. This was especially true at the level of staff training and schoolwide policy dispersal and support. Some intervention school principals apparently did not provide significant discussion or dispersal of the policies. Two intervention schools (out of six) also declined to participate in a second year of the project.

Supporting Evidence. The project staff hypothesized that intervention students would "demonstrate greater increases in their levels of awareness of behaviors that constitute bullying . . . and sexual harassment" (Rosenbluth et al., 2003, p. 219). The authors maintained that, because of the increased awareness of bullying and so on, the intervention could logically be associated with either increases or decreases in reported bullying. It is not clear whether the authors would interpret either of these outcomes as evidence of reduced bullying problems for schools. Results supporting the program effects on bullying were extremely mixed. Control schools reported decreases in bullying behaviors, while intervention schools did not. Intervention students also reported no changes in the frequency at which they ignored bullying. Intervention students also reported an increase in witnessed bullying; it is unclear what this finding indicated (the authors attributed this to increased awareness). Both intervention and control students reported an increased intention to report bullying; however, students' reported likelihood of actually telling an adult about bullying did not change from pre- to postintervention. As the authors noted, several critical discontinuities between the stated program goals and focus and the pre- and postintervention survey items/variables that they used prevented more accurate or informative analyses from being carried out.

In sum, the evidence from the program is inconclusive as to the overall benefit to students, and the published empirical findings fall short of suggesting that Expect Respect is likely to produce reductions in bullying and associated problems for schools implementing the program. As the authors noted, the study did, however, appear to succeed in raising students' awareness of the problem—this would seem to be an important component of antibullying interventions. Perhaps future efforts at carrying out the program will provide improvements in the fidelity of implementation and will be able to more accurately assess targeted outcomes.

The Bully Busters Program

Bully Busters was developed by Dawn Newman-Carlson, Arthur Horne, and colleagues and the accompanying manuals were published in 2000 (Newman et al., 2000). Developed partially in response to Olweus' program (previously described), the authors created a program that was designed to be somewhat less comprehensive or extensive than the Olweus intervention, to be adapted to American schools, and that would still yield decreases in aggressive behavior. The results presented next were drawn from the single available journal article presenting Bully Busters and related empirical findings (Horner, Bartolomucci, & Newman-Carlson, 2003; Newman-Carlson & Horne, 2004). More detailed descriptions of the intervention, of course, can be obtained from the program manuals.

Theoretical/conceptual basis. The authors presented an unusually extensive and well-developed causal model based on Bronfenbrenner's (1979) ecological systems model and Albert Bandura's (1986) social learning model. The authors draw on the premise that environmental effects on children's behavior are transmitted through social learning/modeling and suggest that children raised in aggressive contexts (home and/or school, etc.) will be more aggressive themselves. A key component of their model is that this pattern will support children's beliefs that those who become victims deserve the treatment they receive by virtue of being weaker and, in a self-fulfilling process, because they are being victimized. Teachers, in the authors' view, play a critical role in this process in schools because they serve as models for student conduct regarding aggressive behavior in general and bullying in particular. Failure to intervene in bullying on the part of teachers is hypothesized to promote continued or increased bullying behavior.

Intervention Components. The Bully Busters intervention study was carried out by training teachers in a public U.S. middle school and was presented via collaboration with school counselors. Fifteen teachers completed the training and served as the treatment group. Fifteen of their colleagues not completing the training served as controls (they were not randomly assigned to groups). The program was implemented as a series of staff development workshops (three 2-hour workshops) with the components/modules as follows: increasing awareness, recognizing the bully, recognizing the victim, interventions for bullying behavior, interventions for victimization, prevention, relaxation, and coping skills.

Teachers were presented with training materials, participated in practice experiences, and were instructed to share the information and strategies they learned with their students. After the workshops, teachers participated in support teams that met every other week, where they problem-solved implementation of strategies and shared experiences related to their efforts to reduce bullying problems. Program fidelity was monitored through these meetings and by having teachers complete checklists on their intervention activities.

Evidence Base. Treatment and control teachers were given pre- and postintervention measures to evaluate their knowledge and use of the intervention skills, self-efficacy in dealing with problem students (e.g., disruptive, behavior disordered), and decreases in student aggression. Results indicated that the intervention group displayed significantly greater increases in skill knowledge and use and in self-efficacy in dealing with bullying related problems. The authors also reported that there was a decrease in bullying as measured by a decrease in reported referrals for aggressive behavior. An important caveat to the latter finding, however, is that the referrals measured a broad range of aggressive behaviors, including fighting, physical aggression (hitting, slapping), verbal aggression (verbal abuse), and so forth. While bullying involves these behaviors, many of them often occur outside the context of the bully/victim relationship/definition (as previously mentioned). Any reduction in students' aggressive behavior should certainly be regarded as a positive outcome, but this discrepancy reflects a common problem in the literature in that many outcome measures used tend to address aggressive behavior in general rather than identifying whether it occurs within bully/victim contexts (i.e., includes repeated interactions, involves a power differential between bully and victim, etc.).

Bully Busters, while lacking the larger implementation and empirical evaluation base of the Olweus or Second Step programs, represents a thoughtful and carefully created intervention program with thorough training and fidelity components. The level of detail the authors present regarding their conceptual/causal model and their evaluation strategy is also admirable. The commercial availability of the handbooks also contributes to the usefulness of the intervention and makes it perhaps (along with Second Step) the easiest program for prospective users to evaluate prior to implementation.

Steps to Respect

The *Steps to Respect* program (Committee for Children, 2001), is a schoolwide bullying prevention program for grades 3–6. This program is designed to foster students' socially responsible beliefs, develop social–emotional skills related to positive peer relations, and increase their ability to recognize, refute, and report bullying behavior. The program also seeks to raise staff and parent awareness and responsiveness to bullying problems.

Theoretical Basis. In a recent empirical article evaluating the effectiveness of the *Steps to Respect* program, Karin Frey and colleagues (Frey et al., 2005) explicitly cited a social information processing model (Crick & Dodge, 1994) as a basis for targeting children's beliefs and goals relative to bullying , as well as their cognitive–behavioral and affective skills. The program focused on changing children's cognitions regarding bullying (e.g., recognizing bullying) and learning more prosocial methods of responding to peers involved in bullying interactions. Hirchstein and Frey (2006) reported that grades 3–6 were chosen to include the age range within which evidence suggests children's attitudes and cognitions surrounding bullying and aggression become relatively stable. The curriculum also focused on fostering a general school and home climate in which aggressive behavior was not tolerated.

This broader program focused on addressing problems across home and school contexts also seemed to support an ecological perspective (e.g. Bronfenbrenner, 1979; Olweus, 1993a). This perspective supported the program's emphasis on a whole school approach that involved those staff directly involved in student learning, as well as counselors and administrators. Furthermore, the program advocated consistent parent involvement and supported transfer of skills learned at school to the home context.

Intervention Components

Schoolwide components. School personnel were provided with an overview of the Steps to Respect core program goals and content. Teachers, administrators, and counselors, in particular, received more in-depth training on how to intervene and work with students involved in bullying in addition to training on implementing the curriculum (Frey et al., 2005). The curriculum provided models of responses to bullying behavior and guidelines for coaching students involved in the different roles within bullying interactions.

Classrooms. Students participated in literature-based classroom lessons over 12–14 weeks. There were 11 skill lessons, which focused on social–emotional skills for peer relationships, how to be a responsible bystander, and how to recognize, respond to, and report bullying (Committee for Children, 2001). The skill lessons covered topics such as the role of respect in friendships, the role of bystanders in supporting/preventing bullying, promoting empathy for bullying victims, and improving students' group entry skills. The instructional methods included direct instruction, group discussions, and skills practice/role-playing.

Community. Parents were provided with information about the program and received letters throughout the program that described the skills their children were practicing and providing ideas on how to support these skills at home (Committee for Children, 2001). All school families also received annual letters updating parents on school-specific policies and activities related to bullying and aggression.

Implementation Fidelity. Frey et al. (2005) reported high levels of implementation fidelity for their study sample, not only in classroom lessons, but also in terms of schoolwide acceptance of the program components. Teachers in the group of participating schools ($N = 6$) reported having taught nearly all (99%) of the targeted skills. Classroom observers reported good overall lesson quality and a high (92%) learning objectives completion rate.

Evidence Base. Frey et al.'s (2005) published empirical study provided evidence indicating that the program was effective in reducing—relative to control groups—observed frequencies in bullying and in producing positive changes in student attitudes and beliefs regarding bullying and aggression. The positive effects were also strongest for children showing higher levels of negative behaviors at the study onset—this would presumably be the group most schools would hope their intervention efforts would be effective within. This is the only published study we know of that used actual observations of children's playground behavior—this additional source of data strengthens confidence in the evaluation findings.

As a caveat to these results, it is important to note that in a few cases, intervention groups actually displayed small increases in undesirable behaviors or attitudes, but because this increase was not as large as that displayed by control groups, the results thus indicated positive intervention effects. This finding may indicate that the problem of reducing raw rates of bullying behavior or attitudes supporting such behavior in schools is a daunting task, even for intensive intervention programs. Nonetheless, the random control trial evaluation completed here is exemplary among bullying intervention programs, and the authors' findings suggest that a program with a solid theoretical basis and good implementation practices can have positive effects on aggression and bullying in schools.

Future Directions

Synthesis

The interventions just discussed represent some of the better known efforts researchers and practitioners have made in decreasing bullying and victimization problems in schools. While evaluations of the results from their efforts are generally encouraging, it is also clear that the various program effects are not overwhelmingly or ubiquitously positive. Our review is consistent with research, which has found limited support for whole-school antibullying programs (J. D. Smith, Schneider, Smith, & Ananiadou, 2004). In accordance with the IOM (1994) framework, J. D. Smith and colleagues argued that the most important component of effective bullying prevention and intervention is systematic monitoring (i.e., maintenance). Therefore, programs are not necessarily the vital component for change; the people (i.e., school personnel, parents, students) who are committed to maintaining a culture of change are the vital component for change. The extensive effort and commitment that the published studies described on the part of participants is daunting and serves to stress the importance of careful evaluation of program elements and potential benefits/problems prior to engaging in the intervention. It is hoped the program summaries described in this chapter will provide an entry point for school practitioners considering similar efforts and provide a brief roadmap to the range of programs available.

Making sense of the conceptual support and causal models for some of the handful of available interventions with published empirical support is no easy task. In general, the published findings and reports do not explicitly cite clearly articulated and well-developed theoretical frameworks or create distinct causal models based on such frameworks (some of the programs reviewed here were notable exceptions in this regard)—the underlying causal models are critical for school personnel in creating evaluation components, diagnosing intervention problems, and revising less effective program elements as interventions progress. The bullying intervention field, in general, needs to improve this aspect of current and proposed intervention programs.

What is striking from this review is that many of the existing bullying prevention and intervention programs do not incorporate interventions based on theory. In fact, none of the published prevention and intervention programs address issues of homophily, dominance, and attractiveness theory in their programming. Thus, while theory guides us to specific interventions (e.g., have students in middle school stay in their same peer groups instead of changing groupings each year and thus setting up the need to establish dominance each year), existing programs are guided by broad social learning and social ecological theories. While these broad social theories are important for understanding the complexity of the bullying dynamic, they do not provide specific intervention strategies that can be easily implemented into myriad school settings.

While there is clearly some room for improvement, higher quality bullying interventions need to present a more developed and carefully crafted theoretical base. Such programs will also use carefully designed and selected pre/post measures to identify the specific problems present in a given context and to evaluate the effectiveness of the intervention in improving those problems. Using measures that accurately assess levels of the precise behaviors or attitudes targeted by the intervention, both before and after implementation, appears critical to understanding the program benefits, to program maintenance, and especially, to detecting any potential harmful effects.

Recommendations for Research and Practice

Effective bullying prevention and intervention must be data based. School personnel can follow the rubric for data-based decision making set forth in the book, *Bullying in American Schools: A Social-Ecological Perspective on Prevention and Intervention* (Espelage & Swearer, 2004). Individual schools can conduct whole-school surveys and/or questionnaires in order to assess the complexity of bullying that may occur in a particular school. These data can be used to guide prevention and intervention efforts. It is clear from this review and from the IOM framework, that maintenance of prevention and treatment efforts is vital. Bullying interventions are only helpful if they can be sustained. In fact, none of the programs reviewed in this chapter has a systematic plan for maintenance of a bully-free environment. There is a desperate need for rigorous testing of whole-school antibullying interventions (J. D. Smith et al., 2004), and there is a desperate need to identify inexpensive and realistic strategies for combating bullying that can be maintained over time. When school personnel partner with university researchers, we can collectively combat bullying in our nation's schools.

References

Adler, P. A., Kless, S. J., & Adler, P. (1992). Socialization to gender roles: Popularity among elementary school boys and girls. *Sociology of Education, 65,* 169–187.

Bandura, A. (1977). *Social learning theory.* Oxford, UK: Prentice-Hall.

Bandura, A. (1978). Social learning theory of aggression. *Journal of Communication, 28,* 12–29.

Bandura, A. (1986). *Social foundations of thought and action: A social cognitive theory.* Englewood Cliffs, NJ: Prentice-Hall.

Bandura, A. (2004). Model of causality in social learning theory. In A. Freeman, M. J. Mahoney, P. DeVito, & D. Martin (Eds.), *Cognition and psychotherapy* (2nd ed., pp. 25–44). New York: Springer Publishing.

Baron-Cohen, S., & Hammer, J. (1996). Is autism an extreme form of the male brain? *Advances in Infancy Research, 11,* 193–217.

Bjorkqvist, K., Österman, K. & Kaukiainen, A. (1992). The development of direct and indirect aggressive strategies in males and females. In K. Bjorkqvist & P. Niemela (Eds.), *Of mice and women: Aspects of female aggression* (pp. 51–64). San Diego, CA: Academic Press.

Bjorkqvist, K., Österman, K., & Kaukiainen, A. (2000). Social intelligence minus empathy = aggression? *Aggression and Violent Behaviour, 5,* 191–200.

Boulton, M. J., Bucci, E., & Hawker, D. D. (1999). Swedish and English secondary school pupils' attitudes towards, and conceptions of bullying: Concurrent links with bully/victim involvement. *Scandinavian Journal of Psychology, 40,* 277–284.

Bronfenbrenner, U. (1977). Toward an experimental ecology of human development. *American Psychologist, 32,* 513–531.

Bronfenbrenner, U. (1979). *The ecology of human development: Experiments by nature and design.* Cambridge, MA: Harvard University Press.

Bukowski, W. M., Sippola, L. K., & Newcomb, A. F. (2000). Variations in patterns of attraction of same- and other-sex peers during early adolescence. *Developmental Psychology, 36,* 147–154.

Byrne, D. (1971). The ubiquitous relationship: Attitude similarity and attraction: A cross-cultural study. *Human Relations, 24,* 201–207.

Cerezo, F., & Ato, M. (2005). Bullying in Spanish and English pupils: A sociometric perspective using the BULL-S questionnaire. *Educational Psychology, 25,* 353–367.

Committee for Children. (2001). *Steps to respect: A bullying prevention program.* Seattle, WA: Author

Committee for Children. (2005). *Second step violence prevention program.* Retrieved May 10, 2005, from http://www.cfchildren.org/ssf/ssf/ssindex

Crick, N. R., & Dodge, K. A. (1994). A review and reformulation of social information-processing mechanisms in children's social adjustment. *Psychological Bulletin, 115,* 74–101.

Crick, N. R., & Dodge, K. A. (1999). "Superiority" is in the eye of the beholder: A comment on Sutton, Smith, and Swettenham. *Social Development, 8*(1), 128–132.

Dodge, K. A. (1986). A social information processing model of social competence in children. In M. Perlmutter (Ed.), *The Minnesota symposium on child psychology* (pp. 77–125). Hillsdale, NJ: Erlbaum.

Dodge, K. A., & Crick, N. R. (1990). Social information-processing bases of aggressive behavior in children. *Personality and Social Psychology Bulletin, 16,* 8–22.

Dodge, K. A., Lansford, J. E., Burks, V. A., Bates, J. E., Petit, G. S., Fontaine, R., et al. (2003). Peer rejection of social information-processing factors in the development of aggressive behavior problems in children. *Child Development, 74,* 374–393.

Dodge, K. A., Pettit, G. S., McClaskey, C. L., & Brown, M. (1986). Social competence in children. *Monographs of the Society for Research in Child Development, 51*(2, Serial No. 213).

Doll, B., & Swearer, S. M. (2006). Cognitive-behavioral interventions for participants in bullying and coercion. In R. B. Mennuti, A. Freeman, & R. W. Christner (Eds.). *Cognitive-behavioral interventions in educational settings: A handbook for practice* (pp. 183-201). New York: Routledge.

Dulmus, C. N., Theriot, M. T., Sowers, K. M., & Blackburn, J. A. (2004). Student reports of peer bullying victimization in a rural school. *Stress, Trauma, and Crisis: An International Journal, 7*(1), 1–16.

Endresen, I. M. & Olweus, D. (2001). Self-reported empathy in Norwegian adolescents: Sex differences, age trends, and relationship to bullying. In A. Bohart & D. Stipek (Eds.) *Constructive and destructive behavior: Implications for family, school, and society* (pp. 147–165). Washington, DC: American Psychological Association.

Eslea, M. & Smith, P.K. (1998). The long-term effectiveness of anti-bullying work in primary schools. *Educational Research, 40*(2), 203-218.

Espelage, D. L., Holt, M. K., & Henkel, R. R. (2003). Examination of peer-group contextual effects on aggression during early adolescence. *Child Development, 74*(1), 205–220.

Espelage, D. L., & Swearer, S. M. (2003). Research on school bullying and victimization: What have we learned and where do we go from here? *School Psychology Review, 32,* 365–383.

Espelage, D. L., & Swearer, S. M. (Eds.). (2004). *Bullying in American schools: A social-ecological perspective on prevention and intervention.* Mahwah, NJ: Lawrence Erlbaum Associates, Inc.

Farmer, T. W., & Farmer, E. Z. (1996). Social relationships of students with exceptionalities in mainstream classrooms: Social networks and homophily. *Exceptional Children, 62*(5), 431–450.

Feldman, E., & Dodge, K. A. (1987). Social information processing and sociometric status: Sex, age and situational effects. *Journal or Abnormal Child Psychology, 15*, 211–227.

Fleming, C. (1949). *Adolescence: Its social psychology.* New York: International Universities Press, Inc.

Frey, K. S., Hirchstein, M. K., & Guzzo, B. A. (2000). Second step: Preventing aggression by promoting social competence. *Journal of Emotional & Behavioral Disorders, 8*, 102–112.

Frey, K. S., Hirschstein, M. K., Snell, J. L., Van Schoiack Edstrom, L., MacKenzie, E. P., et al. (2005). Reducing playground bullying and supporting beliefs: An experimental trial of the Steps to Respect program. *Developmental Psychology, 41*, 479–491.

Garbarino, J., & deLara, E. (2002). *And words can hurt forever: How to protect adolescents from bullying, harassment, and emotional violence.* New York: The Free Press.

Grossman, D. C., Neckerman, H. J., Koepsell, T. D., Liu, P. Y., Asher, K. N., Beland, K., et al. (1997). Effectiveness of a violence prevention curriculum among children in an elementary school: A randomized controlled trial. *Journal of the American Medical Association, 277*, 1605–1611.

Hall, J. A., Herzberger, S. D., & Skowronski, K. J. (1998). Outcome expectancies and outcome values as predictors of children's aggression. *Aggressive Behavior, 24*, 439–454.

Happé, F. (1994). An advanced test of theory of mind: Understanding of story characters' thoughts and feelings by able autistic, mentally handicapped, and normal children and adults. *Journal of Autism and Developmental Disorders, 24*(2), 129–154.

Happé, F., & Frith, U. (1996). Theory of mind and social impairment in children with conduct disorder. *British Journal of Developmental Psychology, 14*, 385–398.

Hawley, P. H. (2003). Prosocial and coercive configurations of resource control in early adolescence: A case for the well-developed Machiavellian. *Merrill-Palmer Quarterly, 49*, 279–309.

Hirschstein, M. K., & Frey, K. S. (2006). Promoting behaviors and beliefs that reduce bullying: The Steps to Respect program. In S. R. Jimerson & M. J. Furlong (Eds.), *The handbook of school violence and school safety: From research to practice* (pp. 309–323). Mahwah, NJ: Erlbaum.

Hogue, A., & Steinberg, L. (1995). Homophily of internalized distress in adolescent peer groups. *Developmental Psychology, 31*(6), 897–906.

Horne, A. M., Bartolomucci, C. L., & Newman-Carlson, D. (2003). *Bully busters: A teacher's manual for helping bullies, victims, and bystanders.* Champaign, IL: Research Press.

Institute of Medicine. (1994). *Reducing risks for mental disorders: Frontiers for preventive intervention research.* Washington, DC: National Academy Press.

Kallestad, J.H., & Olweus, D. Predicting teacher's and schools' implementation of the Olweus Bullying Prevention Program: A multilevel study. *Prevention & Treatment 6*, Article 21. Retrieved May 10, 2005 from http://journals.apa.org/prevention/volume6/pre0060021a.html.

Kandel, D. B. (1978). Homophily, selection, and socialization in adolescent friendships. *American Journal of Sociology, 84*(2), 427–436.

Kaufman, P., Chen, X., Choy, S. P., Chandler, K. A., Chapman, C. D., Rand, M. R., et al. (1998). *Indicators of school crime and safety.* Washington, DC: U.S. Department of Education and Justice.

Kiesner, J., Cadinu, M., Poulin, F., & Bucci, M. (2002). Group identification in early adolescence: Its relation with peer adjustment and it moderator effect on peer influence. *Child Development, 73*, 196–208.

Kiesner, J., Poulin, F., & Nicotra, E. (2003). Peer relations across context: Individual-network homophily and network inclusion in and after school. *Child Development, 74*(5), 1328–1343.

Kristensen, S. M., & Smith, P. K. (2003). The use of coping strategies by Danish children classed as bullies, victims, bully/victims, and not involved, in response to different (hypothetical) types of bullying. *Scandinavian Journal of Psychology, 44*(5), 479–488.

Lemerise, A., & Arsenio, W. F. (2000). An integrated model of emotion process and cognition in social information processing. *Child Development, 71*, 107–118.

Levy, R. S., O'Neal, E. C., Taylor, S. L., & Langley, T. (1990). Effect of attraction on interpersonal aggression. *The Journal of Social Psychology, 130*, 269–270.

Limber, S. P., Nation, M., Tracy, A. J., Melton, G. B., & Flerx, V. (2003). Implementation of the Olweus Bully Prevention programme in the southeastern United States. In P. K. Smith, D. Pepler, & K. Rigby (Eds.), *Bullying in schools: How successful can interventions be* (pp. 55–79). New York: Cambridge University Press.

Long, J. D., & Pellegrini, A. D. (2003). Studying change in dominance and bullying with linear mixed models. *School Psychology Review, 32*, 401–417.

McCormack, J., & Smith, D. (1974). The effects of attraction and attack on counteraggression. *Personality of Social Psychology Bulletin, 1*, 79–80.

McMahon, S. D., & Washburn, J. J. (2003). Violence prevention: An evaluation of program effects with urban African American students. *The Journal of Primary Prevention, 24*, 43–62.

Menesini, E., Eslea, M., Smith, P. K., Genta, M. L., Giannetti, E., Fonzi, A., et al. (1997). Cross-national comparison of children's attitudes towards bully/victim problems in school. *Aggressive Behavior, 23*, 245–257.

Meraviglia, M. G., Becker, H., Rosenbluth, B., Sanchez, E., & Robertson, T. (2003). The Expect Respect Project: Creating a positive elementary school climate. *Journal of Interpersonal Violence, 18*, 1347–1360.

Milich, R., & Dodge, K. A. (1984). Social information processing in child psychiatric populations. *Journal of Abnormal Child Psychology, 12,* 471–490.

Moffitt, T. E. (1993). Adolescence-limited and life-course persistent antisocial behavior: A developmental taxonomy. *Psychological Review, 100,* 674–701.

Mouttapa, M., Valente, T., Gallaher, P., Rohrbach, L. A., & Unger, J. B. (2004). Social network predictors of bullying and victimization. *Adolescence, 39*(154), 315–335.

Nansel, T. R., Overpeck, M., Pilla, R., Ruan, W. J., Simons-Morton, B., & Scheidt, P. (2001). Bullying behaviors among U.S. youth: Prevalence and association with psychosocial adjustment. *Journal of the American Medical Association, 285*(16), 2094–2100.

Newman, D. A., Horne, A. M., & Bartolumucci, C. L. (2000). *Bully busters: A teacher's manual for helping bullies, victims, and bystanders.* Champaign, IL: Research Press.

Newman-Carlson, D., & Horne, A. M. (2004). Bully busters: A psychoeducational intervention for reducing bullying behavior in middle school students. *Journal of Counseling & Development, 82,* 259–267.

Nguy, L., & Hunt, C. J. (2004). Ethnicity and bullying: A study of Australian high-school students. *Educational & Child Psychology, 21,* 78–94.

Olweus, D. (1990). Bullying among school children. In K. Hurrelmann & F. Losel (Eds.), *Health hazards in adolescence* (pp. 259–297). Oxford, UK: Walter De Gruyter.

Olweus, D. (1991). Bully/victim problems among school children: Basic facts and effects of a school based intervention program. In D. Pepler & K. Rubin (Eds.), *Development and treatment of childhood aggression* (pp. 411–448). Hillsdale, NJ: Lawrence Erlbaum Associates.

Olweus, D. (1992). Bullying among school children: Intervention and prevention. In R.D. Peters, R.J. McMahon, & V.L. Quinsey (Eds.) *Aggression and violence throughout the life span* (pp. 100–125). Thousand Oaks, CA: Sage Publications, Inc.

Olweus, D. (1993a). *Bullying at school: What we know and what we can do.* Malden, MA: Blackwell Publishers, Inc.

Olweus, D. (1993b). Bully/victim problems among schoolchildren: Long-term consequences and an effective intervention program. In S. Hodgins (Ed.), *Mental disorder and crime* (pp. 317–349). Thousand Oaks, CA: Sage Publications.

Olweus, D. (1994). Bullying at school: Long-term outcomes for the victims and an effective school-based intervention program. In L. R. Huesmann (Ed.), *Aggressive behavior: current perspectives* (pp. 97–130). New York: Plenum Press.

Olweus, D. (1995a). Bullying or peer abuse at school: Facts and interventions. *Current Directions in Psychological Science, 4*(6), 196–200.

Olweus, D. (1995b). Bullying or peer abuse in school: Intervention and prevention. In G. Davies, S. Lloyd-Bostock, M. McMurran, & C. Wilson (Eds.), *Psychology, law, and criminal justice: International developments in research and practice* (pp. 248–263). Oxford: Walter De Gruyter.

Olweus, D. (1997a). Bully/victim problems in school: Facts and intervention. *European Journal of Psychology of Education, 12*(4), 495–510.

Olweus, D. (1997b). Tackling peer victimization with a school-based intervention program. In D. P. Fry & K. Björkqvist (Eds.), *Cultural variation in conflict resolution: Alternatives to violence* (pp. 215–231). Hillsdale, NJ: Lawrence Erlbaum Associates, Inc.

Olweus, D. (1997c). Bully/victim problems in school: Knowledge base and an effective intervention program. *Irish Journal of Psychology, 18*(2), 170–190.

Olweus, D. (2003). Social problems in school. In A. Slater & G. Bremner (Eds.) *An introduction to developmental psychology,* (pp. 434–454). Malden, MA: Blackwell Publishing.

Olweus, D. (2004). The Olweus Bullying Prevention Programme: Design and implementation issues and a new national initiative in Norway. In P. K. Smith, D. Pepler, & K. Rigby (Eds.), *Bullying in schools: How successful can interventions be?* (pp. 13–36). New York, NY: Cambridge University Press.

Olweus, D., Limber, S., & Mihalic, S. (1999). Bullying prevention program. In D. S. Elliott (Series Ed.), *Blueprints for violence prevention: Book nine.* Boulder, CO: Center for the Study and Prevention of Violence.

Pellegrini, A. D. (2002). Bullying, victimization, and sexual harassment during the transition to middle school. *Educational Psychologist, 37*(3), 151–163.

Pellegrini, A. D., & Bartini, M. (2000). A longitudinal study of bullying, victimization, and peer affiliation during the transition from primary school to middle school. *American Educational Research Journal, 37*(3), 699–725.

Pellegrini, A. D., & Bartini, M. (2001). Dominance in early adolescent boys: Affiliative and aggressive dimensions and possible functions. *Merrill-Palmer Quarterly, 47,* 142–163.

Pellegrini, A. D., Bartini, M., & Brooks, F. (1999). School bullies, victims, and aggressive victims: Factors relating to group affiliation and victimization in early adolescence. *Journal of Educational Psychology, 91*(2), 216–224.

Pellegrini, A. D., & Long, J. D. (2002). A longitudinal study of bullying, dominance, and victimization during the transition from primary school through secondary school. *British Journal of Developmental Psychology, 20,* 259–280.

Pepler, D. J., Craig, W. M., O'Connell, P., Atlas, R., & Charach, A. (2003). Making a difference in bullying: Evaluation of a systematic school-based programme in Canada. In P. K. Smith, D. Pepler, & K. Rigby (Eds.), *Bullying in schools: How successful can interventions be* (pp. 125–129). New York: Cambridge University Press.

Premack, D., & Woodruff, G. (1978). Does the chimpanzee have a theory of mind? *Behavioural and Brain Sciences, 1*, 515–526.

Reynolds, W. M. (1986). A model for the screening and identification of depressed children and adolescents in school settings. *Professional School Psychology, 1*, 117–129.

Rivers, I., & Smith, P. K. (1994). Types of bullying behaviour and their correlates. *Aggressive Behaviour, 20*, 359–368.

Rosenbluth, B., Whitaker, D. J., Sanchez, E., & Valle, L. A. (2004). The expect respect project: Preventing bullying and sexual harassment in US elementary schools. In P. K. Smith, D. Pepler, & K. Rigby (Eds.), *Bullying in schools: How successful can interventions be* (pp. 211–233). New York: Cambridge University Press.

Salmivalli, C., Huttunen, A., & Lagerspetz, K. (1997). Peer networks and bullying in schools. *Scandinavian Journal of Psychology, 38*(4), 305–312.

Sanchez, E., Robertson, T.R., Lewis, C. M., Rosenbluth, B., Bohman, T., & Casey, D.M. (2001). Preventing bullying and sexual harassment in elementary schools: The Expect Respect Model. In R. Geffner & M. Loring (Eds.), *Bullying behavior: Current issues, research and intervention.* (pp. 157–180). Binghamton, NY: Haworth Press.

Seals, D., & Young, J., (2003). Bullying and victimization: Prevalence and relationship to gender, grade level, ethnicity, self-esteem, and depression. *Adolescence, 38*, 735–747.

Shahinfar, A., Kupersmidt, J. B., & Matza, L. S. (2001). The relation between exposure to violence and social information processing among incarcerated adolescents. *Journal of Abnormal Psychology, 110*, 136–141.

Shuntich, R. (1976). Some effects of attitudinal similarity and exposure on attraction and aggression. *Journal of Research in Personality, 10*, 155–156.

Sjostrom, L., & Stein, N. (1996). *Bullyproof: A teacher's guide on teasing and bullying for use with fourth and fifth grade students.* Wellesley, MA: Center for Research on Women.

Smith, J. D., Schnieder, B. H., Smith, P. K., & Ananiadou, K. (2004). The effectiveness of whole-school antibullying programs: A synthesis of evaluation research. *School Psychology Review, 33*, 547–560.

Smith, P. K., Cowie, H., Olafsson, R. F., & Liefooghe, A. P. D. (2002). Definitions of bullying: A comparison of terms used, age, and gender differences, in a fourteen-country international comparison. *Child Development, 73*, 1119–1133.

Sprague, J., Walker, H., Golly, A., White, K., Myers, D. R., & Shannon, T. (2001). Translating research into practice: The effects of a universal staff and student intervention on indicators of discipline and school safety. *Education & Treatment of Children, 24*, 495–511.

Stockdale, M. S., Hangaduambo, S., Duys, D., Larson, K., & Sarvela, P. (2002). Rural elementary students', parents', and teachers' perceptions of bullying. *American Journal of Health & Behavior, 26*(4), 266–277.

Sutton, J., Smith, P. K., & Swettenham, J. (1999a). Bullying and "theory of mind": A critique of the "social skills deficit" view of anti-social behaviour. *Social Development, 8*(1), 117–127.

Sutton, J., Smith, P. K., & Swettenham, J. (1999b). Social cognition and bullying: Social inadequacy or skilled manipulation? *British Journal of Developmental Psychology, 17*, 435–450.

Sutton, J., Smith, P. K., & Swettenham, J. (1999c). Socially undesirable need not be incompetent: A response to Crick and Dodge. *Social Development, 8*(1), 132–134.

Sutton, J., Smith, P. K., & Swettenham, J. (2001). "It's easy, it works, and it makes me feel good"—A response to Arsenio and Lemerise. *Social Development, 10*(1), 74–78.

Swearer, S. M., & Cary, P. T. (2003). Perceptions and attitudes toward bullying in middle school youth: A developmental examination across the bully/victim continuum. *Journal of Applied School Psychology, 19*, 63–79.

Swearer, S. M., & Doll, B. (2001). Bullying in schools: An ecological framework. *Journal of Emotional Abuse, 2*(2/3), 7–23.

Swearer, S. M., & Espelage, D. L. (2004). Introduction: A social-ecological framework of bullying among youth. In D. L. Espelage & S. M. Swearer (Eds.), *Bullying in American schools: A social-ecological perspective on prevention and intervention* (pp. 1–12). Mahwah, NJ: Lawrence Erlbaum.

Swearer, S. M., Peugh, J., Espelage, D. L., Siebecker, A. B., Kingsbury, W. L., & Bevins, K. S. (2006). A social-ecological model for bullying prevention and intervention in early adolescence: An exploratory examination. In S. R. Jimerson & M. J. Furlong (Eds.), *The handbook of school violence and school safety: From research to practice* (pp. 257–273). Mahwah, NJ: Lawrence Erlbaum Associates, Inc.

Tapper, K., & Boulton, M. J. (2005). Victim and peer group responses to different forms of aggression among primary school children. *Aggressive Behavior, 31*, 238–253.

Taub, J. (2002). Evaluation of the Second Step violence prevention program at a rural elementary school. *School Psychology Review, 31*, 186–200.

Taylor, M. (1996). A theory of mind perspective on social cognitive development. In R. Gelman & T. Kit-Fong Au (Eds.), *Perceptual and cognitive development* (pp. 283–329). London: Academic Press.

Tedeschi, J. T., & Felson, R. B. (1994). Learning theory and aggression. In J. T. Tedeschi & R. B. Felson (Eds.), *Violence, aggression, and coercive actions* (pp. 93–126). Washington, DC: American Psychological Association.

Van Shoiack-Edstrom, L., Frey, K. S., & Beland, K. (2002). Changing adolescents' attitudes about relational and physical aggression: An early evaluation of a school-based intervention. *School Psychology Review, 31,* 201–216.

Wolke, D., Woods, S., Stanford, K., & Schulz, H. (2001). Bullying and victimization of primary school children in England and Germany: Prevalence and school factors. *British Journal of Psychology, 92,* 673–697.

Xie, H., Cairns, R. B., & Cairns, B. D. (1999). Social networks and configurations in inner-city schools: Aggression, popularity, and implications for students with EBD. *Journal of Emotional and Behavioral Disorders, 7*(3), 147–155.

XLI
SCHOOL VIOLENCE

ANNE GREGORY
Curry School of Education, University of Virginia

ELISE CAPPELLA
New York University

Introduction

In the past 10 years, many communities were shaken by well-publicized shootings that resulted in multiple student deaths. Discussions about the problem of school violence increased. Fears of students as "super predators" were on the rise. While the events were certainly tragic, heightened concerns have not been grounded in the reality of declining violent crime in school settings over the past decade (National Center for Education Statistics [NCES], 2004). The chances of serious violent crime occurring in school are statistically quite low. During the school year 1999–2000, 16 of the 2,124 homicide victims who were school-aged children occurred in the school setting (NCES).

While violent crime may be rare, low-level aggression in schools is not uncommon. Thus, this chapter addresses prevalent behavior, to which many school staff are faced with on a daily basis. We define *aggression* as an intent or action to harm through verbal or physical force. A broad definition of aggression allows for a consideration of how delinquency in adolescents and young adults unfolds. For a group of serious offenders, aggressive actions begin early in life, gain momentum across the school years, and take on multiple and increasingly serious forms (Loeber, Burke, Lahey, Winters, & Zera, 2000). A preventive approach is called for in light of the escalation of aggressive behaviors across the school years.

Violence and Aggression in Schools

Rates of violence vary by the characteristics of the school. Violent crimes, including those against teachers, are more likely to happen in high schools than elementary or middle schools (NCES, 2004). Overall, urban schools have higher rates of violence than suburban and rural communities (NCES). Teachers in urban schools are more likely to be victims than those teaching in rural or suburban schools (NCES). Negative gang activities are particularly common in city schools, such that, in 1999, one third of city schools reported this as a problem (NCES, 1999). While urban schools have a particular confluence of poverty and violence, some evidence is suggestive that rural schools also have contextually specific patterns of violence. In 2003, students from rural areas, compared with urban and suburban areas, reported higher rates of bullying (NCES, 2004). A more in-depth study of three rural schools with students in grades three to eight also found high rates of bullying (Dulmus, Theriot, & Sowers, 2004). With greater residential stability and smaller populations in rural settings (Osgood & Chambers, 2003), perhaps rural students are more likely to attend years of schooling as a stable cohort leaving little room for reputations as victims or bullies to shift across the years.

Even with the variation in rates of violence across schools, there has been an overall downward trend in violence. A recent report issued by the U.S. Department of Education declared that school-based violent crimes against adolescents from 1992 to 2002 dropped by half (NCES, 2004). By 2003, 13% of high school students reported having been in a fight on school grounds—down from 16% in 2003. Similarly, students' reports of carrying weapons to school within the past month dropped from 12% to 6%.

Serious violent crime might be an infrequent occurrence, but low-level aggression appears to be more prevalent. The 1999 national school survey on crime and safety found that almost 30% of schools reported frequent bullying and almost 20% of schools reported frequent student acts of disrespect for teachers (NCES, 1999). In 2000, 3 million suspensions and 97,000 expulsions were reported. In some states, such as

Delaware and South Carolina, between 14% and 19% of the male students had been suspended (NCES, 2000). A study of 1992–1993 data from a random sample of disciplined 6th through 12th graders in 67 Florida school districts found that 47% of in- and out-of-school suspensions, corporal punishment, and expulsions were given for disruptive behavior in class, defiance of authority, or disrespectful behavior. The next largest offense, fighting, accounted for 9.5% of the disciplinary consequences (Florida Department of Education [DOE], 1995). The frequency of suspensions and expulsions and the reasons for such sanctions suggest that schools and counselors are faced with a serious problem of aggressive behavior.

Current Developments

"Get tough approach." Sociopolitical and historical developments affect how school violence and aggression is conceptualized and addressed. School counselors may have to navigate the tensions between a punishment orientation and a support orientation toward aggressive behavior. In response to increased public fear of school violence, many schools have taken an increasingly punitive, "get tough" approach. In the 1990s, zero tolerance policies were implemented across the states with a federal mandate passed in 1994, which called for a minimum 1-year expulsion for bringing a weapon to school (Gun-Free Schools Act). Critics of such policies argue that a mandate for expulsions does not take into account extenuating or contextual circumstances, which results in superfluous and overly punitive sanctions. The Harvard Civil Rights Project (2000) compiled case examples of children suspended or expelled for carrying sparklers, a Boy Scout pocketknife, a toenail clipper, and a toy ax for Halloween. They argued that punitive approaches to discipline may differentially affect African American and Latino students, who are overrepresented in suspensions and expulsions. In 1999, a survey showed that in grades 7 to 12, 20% of Hispanic students, 35% of African American students, and 15% of White students had ever been suspended or expelled (NCES, 2003). In light of the increasing numbers of students, particularly African American students, being suspended or expelled and with heightened fears of school violence, educational researchers (e.g., Devine, 1996) have documented the prison-like school environments that rely on video surveillance, metal detectors, and harsh sanctions.

Recognition of the complex needs of students provides a counterweight to the popularity of increased surveillance and harsh sanctions to reduce school violence. Some states and school districts are acknowledging the importance of addressing social and emotional development in school (Shriver & Weissberg, 2005), with states in every region across the United States mandating the teaching of social and emotional development alongside academic learning (National Association of State Boards of Education, 2005). In the mid-1990s, federal school safety funds spawned preventive interventions. Antibullying programs (e.g., Olweus, 1999), conflict mediation interventions (Johnson & Johnson, 1996), and on-campus suspension programs have become widespread. Concerns about the punitive approach of zero tolerance policies have generated new programs, such as a systematic school-based threat assessment to lower overreaction to a *perception* of student threat (Cornell et al., 2004). This may be helpful in addressing the problem of criminalizing youth, particularly youth of color.

Research-based interventions. Increasingly, school counselors may be asked to show the results of their interventions with evidence of decreased aggressive behavior and increased prosocial behavior. At the same time, counselors may be faced with the pressure to continue programs that are familiar to school staff, despite a lack of rigorous evidence that suggests they are helping. Currently, there is a federal push toward the use of evidence-based practice in schools, as seen in the establishment of the Institute for Education Sciences whose mission is to understand the effectiveness of education programs and improve academic achievement and access to educational opportunities for students. Efficacy and effectiveness research that utilizes experimental designs—randomly assigning schools, classrooms, or students to interventions—is prioritized in funding.

Faced with the pressure to show results, counselors may be called upon to ask critical questions of the research on interventions. This chapter aims to provide counselors with a knowledge base from which to raise such questions. It begins with an outline of the current research on the predictors of child and adolescent aggression. A theoretical understanding of how environmental factors interact with individual student characteristics to predict aggressive behavior will help counselors target risk factors specific to developmental stage and identify the reasons the intervention may help reduce aggressive behavior. With its focus on the prevention of serious school violence, the chapter then describes a range of research-based interventions. Several of the interventions focus on supporting students already identified as aggressive; others involve supporting individuals in the students' lives, namely teachers, parents, and peers. Also described are multilevel programs that intervene systematically across a range of settings and with different types of participants. Finally, the chapter provides counselors with concrete strategies to consider when selecting and developing interventions.

Aggressive Behavior in School

Individual Student Characteristics

Individual students differ in many ways—in their approach to social situations, in their struggles or successes with academic schoolwork, and in the ways their bodies are made up. These differences have been hypothesized to contribute to the behaviors students are likely to use in school. Researchers have isolated each of these individual characteristics to examine their relative contribution to the development and use of overt aggression in school settings. However, none of these factors operates separately from one another or outside the contexts of family, school, and community. We will outline the theory and evidence for the biological, cognitive, and academic differences associated with overt aggression, while keeping in mind the complex and interactive pathways through which aggression develops in students in school.

Biological factors. Possible biological contributors to overt aggression include genetic inheritance, temperament differences, neurotransmitter effects, and hormonal influences. This literature has been reviewed thoroughly elsewhere and will be summarized only briefly here (see Berman, Kavoussi, & Coccaro, 1997; Brain & Susman, 1997; Coie & Dodge, 1998).

Behavior-geneticists have postulated that a *tendency* toward aggressive behavior can be inherited, but aggressive behavior itself cannot (see Coie & Dodge, 1998). For example, biological genotypes passed down from parent to child may affect physiological processes, which influence a child's behavioral or cognitive style, which then interact with environmental factors to lead to behaviors. Twin and adoption studies from around the world support the theory. Genetic factors influence individual characteristics such as impulsivity and reactivity, and these may lead to a *disposition* toward externalizing behavior (e.g., Matheny, 1989), but there appears to be no relationship between genes and *actual* physical aggression or violence (Mednick, Gabrielli, & Hutchings, 1984; Raine, 1993).

Children's temperament has been hypothesized to relate to future behavior, in part through the stability of personality characteristics and in part through an interaction with environmental influences such as relationships with parents and peers. Early demonstrations of emotional regulation—for example, ability to inhibit inappropriate behaviors, cope with arousal, and organize for goal-oriented behavior when experiencing strong emotions—have been thought critical to children's later use of aggression (Dishion & Patterson, 1997). Research has demonstrated qualified support for these hypotheses: temperamental characteristics in preschool are stable over time (Bates, Bayles, Bennett, Ridge, & Brown, 1991), but a "difficult" temperament does not necessarily predict future delinquency (Caspi, Henry, McGee, Moffitt, & Silva, 1995; Earls & Jung, 1987). In addition, associations between early temperament and later aggression tend to be weak, confounded by use of maternal reports, and linked with parent–child attachment (Bates, Maslin, & Frankel, 1985) and the home environment (Earls & Jung). That said, *connections* between disposition and cognition (discussed next) may help to explain *some* children's aggressive responses to environmental stimuli (Dodge, 1991).

The framework for understanding the role of neurotransmitters in aggressive behavior is Gray's (1987) theory of brain function; in particular, his description of the behavioral facilitation and behavioral inhibition systems within the brain that launch or halt interactions with the environment. Although engagement or inhibition of activity is related to multiple neurotransmitters, concentration of *serotonin* metabolites in the cerebrospinal fluid is critical, such that low concentrations may lead to an increase in stress reactivity (Berman et al., 1997; Spoont, 1992). Studies of serotonin in children indicate that lower concentrations are, in fact, related to conduct disorder in adolescents (Pliszka, Rogeness, Renner, Sherman, & Broussard, 1988) and disruptive behavior disorders among children (Kruesi et al., 1992). However, investigators and theorists postulate a reciprocal transaction, such that the levels of neurotransmitters not only are genetically determined, but also respond to early environmental influences and socialization (see Rogeness, Javors, & Pliszka, 1992).

Finally, testosterone has been suggested to play an organizing or activating role in physically aggressive behavior, the former occurring during the perinatal period and the latter occurring during puberty (Brain & Susman, 1997). Study results have been conflicting (Inoff-Germain et al., 1988; Olweus, Mattsson, Schalling, & Low, 1988; Susman et al., 1987), and Archer (1994) attempted to explain the differences in theory and research in a dynamic model that posits early gender differences due to hormonally driven activity levels that lead boys and girls toward different play subcultures with a different need for physical aggression. These subcultures then interact with broader societal influences, individual temperaments, and baseline levels of testosterone. Later in adolescence, when testosterone levels are rising, a child's established patterns of aggression interact with hormones to produce more or less aggression, which fuels future testosterone if the aggression induces feelings of dominance and success. Although not empirically tested, this model is a compelling explanation of the role of testosterone as an *interacting* agent across time influencing children's aggression.

Social cognition. Beyond biological factors, individuals bring particular cognitive styles to social interactions (Dishion & Patterson, 1997). One of the most studied cognitive theories, social information processing, suggests that a social situation triggers a succession of cognitive and emotional operations that first represent, then interpret, the situation (Dodge & Schwartz, 1997). When these operations are effective and accurate, the social behavior is adaptive; when the operations are biased, the behavior is often maladaptive. A set of conscious and unconscious steps are hypothesized to occur repeatedly; however, children may develop patterns that simplify the steps and create relatively stable behavioral responses to situations over time (Huesmann, 1988; Schneider, 1991).

Researchers have used correlational studies with hypothetical social scenarios to examine the links between different aspects of the social cognitive processing model and children's aggressive behavior. For the most part, these studies have verified the connection between social information processing skills—for example, attending to and recalling social cues, requesting additional information, interpreting others' intentions, generating responses to the situation—and aggressive behavior (see Dodge & Frame, 1982; Dodge, Pettit, McClaskey, & Brown, 1986; Guerra & Slaby, 1989; Quiggle, Garber, Panak, & Dodge, 1992; Slaby & Guerra, 1988; Spivak & Shure, 1980). In addition, several studies indicate that aggressive children evaluate aggressive actions in a more positive light than do their nonaggressive peers (Guerra & Slaby), value the results of aggression more highly (Boldizar, Perry, & Perry, 1989), and have positive efficacy beliefs for the use of aggression (Crick & Dodge, 1989). However, the deficits in social information processing have been shown to differ based on the child's use of a particular subtype of aggression, in particular, reactive aggression (retaliation based in anger and frustration) and proactive aggression (unprovoked and goal-directed behavior; Dodge & Coie, 1987). Use of reactive aggression has been linked with hostile attributional biases, whereas use of proactive aggression is related to positive evaluations of aggressive behaviors and instrumental goals for social situations (Crick & Dodge, 1996).

Academic skills. An extensive body of research demonstrates a strong relationship between externalizing behavior problems and academic underachievement, with comorbidity up to 50% when including a broad set of externalizing syndromes and indications of school failure (Barkley, Fischer, Edelbrock, & Smallish, 1990; Hinshaw, 1992). A recent meta-analysis demonstrated that students with emotional behavior disorders (EBD) performed significantly worse across settings and subject areas than their nondiagnosed peers (R. Reid, Gonzalez, Nordness, Trout, & Epstein, 2004). A meta-analysis of the link between underachievement and delinquency revealed that academic difficulties were related to the onset, level, frequency, and persistence of delinquency in both males and females (Maguin & Loeber, 1996). Early in schooling, the link can be explained primarily by inattention and hyperactivity (Frick et al., 1991); in adolescence, the association grows increasingly robust (Hinshaw).

Paths between underachievement and delinquency have been hypothesized to be unidirectional (problems in one domain cause problems in the other; e.g., Hirschi, 1969; Rutter & Giller, 1983) or cyclical (bidirectional influences between domains). Deficits in academic skills may lead to aggressive behavior through task frustration, lack of motivation, low academic self-concept, and school disengagement (see Arnold et al., 1999). For example, continued academic problems may produce a negative association with schooling, thus increasing the likelihood of hostility, disobedience, and aggression in school (McEvoy & Welker, 2000). High levels of externalizing, on the other hand, have been thought to lead to academic problems through reduced time on task related to social skills deficits, inattention, or noncompliance (Arnold et al., 1999; McEvoy & Welker). Acting out in the classroom may help an underperforming student avoid academic tasks or may distract the teacher from the student's academic problems (Carr, Taylor, & Robinson, 1991).

Despite methodological problems, studies have provided some evidence of predictive, if not causal, pathways between academic skills and aggression. A subset of children with reading failure but no behavior problems in childhood has been shown to grow into adolescents with antisocial tendencies (Maughan, Gray, & Rutter, 1985). A delay in the onset of reading relates to later externalizing problems (e.g., McGee & Share, 1988), and aggression in middle childhood predicts low academic achievement in adulthood after controlling for early intelligence test scores (Huesmann & Eron, 1986). Finally, through such mechanisms as speech delay, familial adversity, and neurodevelopmental immaturity (e.g., Howlin & Rutter, 1987; Richman, Stevenson, & Graham, 1982; Tallal, Dukette, & Curtiss, 1989), aggression and learning are linked even before a child begins school (see Hinshaw, 1992). This provides additional support that the connection between aggression and achievement is complex and multifaceted, beginning early in development and interacting across contexts and domains to reinforce the relationship.

Final issues. The research summarized briefly provides theory and evidence of individual student factors within the biological, social–cognitive, and academic domains related to the use of aggression in schools. This extensive body of research has limitations. First, male students tend to be overrepresented and female students underrepresented in the study samples. This leads to a lack of complete knowledge about possible gender differences in the development of aggression, particularly as related to hormonal influences (e.g., Inoff-Germain et al., 1988; Susman et al., 1987) and links to achievement. A second and related limitation is that studies define aggression as overt or direct, rather than covert or indirect. An emerging area of interest among researchers and school personnel alike is the development and use of subtle forms of aggression in schools (see Crick, 1996; Underwood, 2003), but the pathways toward the use of social or relational aggression are less understood (see Kaukianinen et al., 1999; Xie, Swift, Cairns, & Cairns, 2002). Finally, although researchers have isolated these areas to study the development of aggression, most models are dynamic and comprehensive, linking biological, social–cognitive, and academic domains, as well as the multiple social contexts in which students live, work, and play.

Characteristics of the Social Context

Children traverse multiple social contexts as they develop across their years of schooling. The primacy of the home context shifts as they enter schooling and interact with peers. They encounter new adults in classrooms and are asked to abide by the structures of the daily school routines and rules. They draw on multiple communities outside of school and the home while being exposed to mass media and entertainment. In interaction with a child's attitudes and attributes, these social contexts provide key experiences that shape development, including acerbating or escalating aggressive or violent behavior. A review of the literature suggests that family, peers, neighborhoods, mass media, schools, and classrooms should be considered when examining the ecology of the developing child.

Family. Children can transfer negative behaviors learned with family members into the school setting (e.g., Earls, 1981). Family research has identified two areas of the home context that have been linked to children's and adolescents' aggressive and violent behavior: (a) parent–child interactions and (b) parenting practices. Focused on the patterned exchanges between parents and their children, Patterson and his colleagues have investigated a social interactional theory of the development of aggressive behavior (J. B. Reid, Patterson, & Snyder, 2002). Drawing on principles of operant conditioning, they have documented coercive cycles between parents and young children whereby a child's whining or tantrums are rewarded when a parent gives in to the child's request. These interlocking reinforcement patterns repeat themselves daily and children learn that aggressive behavior ushers in positive results. Investigators have also studied how children learn from adult modeling of aggression (Bandura, 1973), especially related to parents' discipline practices. From a social learning theory perspective, if an adult expresses anger by physically punishing the child, then the child may learn to do the same. Longitudinal studies have linked physical punishment to later aggression and delinquency (Eron, Huesmann, & Zelli, 1991; Farrington & Hawkins, 1991). Supervision during adolescence has also been studied as a parenting practice linked to aggression. Providing structure and adult guidance for adolescents has been posited as developmentally appropriate, even during a stage when needs for autonomy increase (Connell, 1990). Several longitudinal studies have shown that a lack of parent supervision is one of the strongest predictors of adolescent conduct disorder and delinquency (e.g., Hawkins, Herrenkohl, & Farrington, 1998).

Increasingly, scholars recognize that parenting practices should be considered within cultural context (Baumrind, 1991). Generalizations about the detrimental effects of particular parenting practices can be hard to make when for some families in certain neighborhood contexts such practices may be protective. For instance, Lansford, Deater-Deckard, Dodge, Bates, and Pettit (2004) showed that for African Americans, unlike for White adolescents, physical discipline such as spanking was linked to lower externalizing problems. A similar cultural specificity may be considered when examining the role of parental supervision and adolescent aggression. While some evidence shows that authoritative parenting may be linked to positive outcomes for adolescents from diverse groups (Gregory & Weinstein, 2004), culturally specific findings (Gonzales, Cauce, & Friedman, 1996; Steinberg, Lamborn, & Darling, 1994) present a more complex picture. Strict monitoring was adaptive for adolescents living in high-crime neighborhoods (Eamon, 2001; Gonzales et al., 1996), suggestive of the benefits of an authoritarian parenting style.

Peers. As early as 1939, Sutherland theorized that peers make up a crucial social context in which aggressive and violent norms are transmitted. Since then, empirical research has firmly established the reciprocal relationship between friendship networks and behavior (e.g., Dishion, French, & Patterson, 1995). Negative peer experiences (both peer rejection and "deviant" peer affiliation) have been cited as "on-ramps" to adolescent aggression (Laird, Jordan, Dodge, Pettit, & Bates, 2001). Aggressive children are more likely to be rejected by their classmates, which then increases the risk for later antisocial behavior (Asher & Coie, 1990). In fact, research has shown that the link between peer rejection and antisocial behavior is mediated by affiliation among aggressive peers (Dishion, Patterson, Stoolmiller, & Skinner, 1991). In the early years of schooling, a pattern of negative interactions with peers can become relatively stable across the school year for aggressive children (Snyder, 2002). These children are reinforced for their behavior, but often rejected by other peers. Seeking social niches that will hold them in high regard, they develop relationships with other aggressive children (Thornberry & Krohn, 1997). Longitudinal studies have shown that affiliation with an aggressive peer group is a powerful predictor of the persistence and progression of antisocial behavior (Moffit & Caspi, 2001; Patterson, Dishion, & Yoerger, 2000).

Within peer networks, friends may support and encourage each other's aggressive behavior through positive reinforcement and modeling. In observational studies of adolescents, researchers have shown that peers reinforce each other's aggressive talk and behavior through both verbal and nonverbal behavior (Buehler, Patterson, & Furniss, 1966; Dishion, Andrews, & Crosby, 1995; Dishion, Spracklen, Andrews, & Patterson, 1996). Moreover, displays of toughness and power can help an adolescent gain status and, for males, reinforce a type of masculine identity (Fagan & Wilkson, 1998). The processes of impression management, peer reinforced aggressive behavior, and expected gender roles need further examination. That said, research has firmly established that it is important to consider a teenager's friendship group to understand heightened aggression, especially during the adolescent years.

Neighborhood and media influences. A review of studies showed that differences in neighborhoods have a small to moderate effect on delinquency and violence (Leventhal & Brooks-Gunn, 2000). The mechanisms through which neighborhoods affect children's development include institutional resources, relationships, and the norms and collective efficacy in neighborhoods (Jencks & Mayer, 1990; Leventhal & Brooks-Gunn). For instance, access to high-quality childcare, with low adult-to-child ratios, is limited in poor neighborhoods (Fuller, Coonerty, Kipnis, & Choong, 1997); this resource is linked to positive behavioral outcomes (e.g., Benasich, Brooks-Gunn, & Clewell, 1992). Protective relationships may also be lacking or compromised in low-income communities. Economic hardship has been thought to increase parents' social isolation, stress, and depression, which then compromises their ability to provide monitoring (Conger et al., 2002). Lower monitoring predicts higher rates of delinquency (Hawkins, Herrenkohl, & Farrington, 1998). The benefits of watchful community members may also be compromised in low-income neighborhoods with high residential turnover. These neighborhoods have been shown to have weak norms to control aggressive behavior and low collective efficacy to change the neighborhood (Sampson, Morenoff, & Earls, 1999). Cut out from mainstream economic opportunities, key pathways out of poverty may be lost, which leaves generations trapped in poverty and exposed to violent neighborhoods (Hill, Fernando, Chen, & LaFrombois, 1994). Such exposure has been prospectively linked to greater aggressive behavior (Gorman-Smith & Tolan, 1998).

Increasing evidence has established a link between exposure to media violence and aggressive behavior (Anderson & Bushman, 2001). The link is robust and replicable, although not statistically large (Huesmann, Moise, & Podoloski, 1997). Experimental conditions in the lab have shown that exposure to violent media increases the likelihood of physical assault (see Anderson, Berkowitz, & Donnerstein, 2003, for a review). Longitudinal studies support the laboratory findings. For instance, in a study spanning over 25 years, Huesmann (1988) found that criminal convictions at age 30 were linked with preference for violent television in the third grade. Substantial evidence supports theories of observational learning of behaviors and cognitions to help explain why media exposure predicts aggression. Children replicate the behavior of admired television characters (Huesmann & Eron, 1986) who receive rewards for their acts of violence (Bandura, 1973). Via the media, children learn cognitive scripts for aggressive behavior and develop beliefs about the acceptability of aggression as a means to a goal (Huesmann et al., 1997).

Schools. Schools have been shown to differ in their rates of aggression and violence even when taking into account the characteristics of the enrolled students (Rutter, Maughan, Mortiore, & Ouston, 1979). Such differences have prompted inquiry into school policies, procedures, and structures that distinguish low from high aggressive schools. Three underlying theoretical approaches differentiate research in this area. The first approach implies that there is a developmental mismatch between students and the way schooling is organized such that the school either lacks appropriate monitoring or lacks appropriate autonomy. Said differently, schools are seen as under or overcontrolling. The second approach posits that students are not given the opportunity to bond with school whereby they do not become personally invested in the rules and in the community. The third approach suggests that schools' organization of students results in reinforcing maladaptive behavior. Research with these approaches has been conducted primarily at the elementary school level, yet evidence is suggestive that they may be helpful in understanding middle and high school effects on aggression.

Mismatched with young children's developmental needs, some schools may lack consistent, schoolwide expectations for behavior (Horner, Sugai, Lewis-Palmer, & Todd, 2001) or adequate supervision throughout the school grounds. Specific settings in the school may be particularly conducive to aggressive behavior. Using naturalistic observations of elementary students, Craig, Pepler, and Atlas (2000) found that, compared with behavior in classroom settings, children exhibited more aggression on the playground, where very little teacher intervention occurred. J. B. Reid and colleagues (1999) also showed that less supervision during recess was linked with higher levels of aggression. Additional settings such as hallways and lunchrooms may also need to be examined for their lack of appropriate supervision. Behavioral regulation, while underemployed in certain settings in the elementary school grades, may be implemented in a counterproductive manner in later grades without consideration for adolescents' increasing need for autonomy. Hyman and Perone (1998) argued that police presence, metal detectors, and locker searchers are displays of control and disrespect. Zero-tolerance and punitive suspension policies may also contribute to a culture of threat and control (Ayers, Dohrn, & Ayers, 2001). In repressive school environments, students may respond with moral indignation and active resistance (Giroux, 1983). Correlational research has shown that students' perceptions of feeling respected and perceiving clear and fair rules are linked to lower rates of discipline (Gottfredson, Gottfredson, & Hybl, 1993; Hollingsworth, Lufler, & Clune, 1984). Additional research on students' responses to school cultures of threat and surveillance is needed.

Schools may vary in the degree to which they offer the conditions that promote school bonding, which has been theorized as a factor that can lower aggression and violence. Combining social control theory (Hirschi, 1969) and developmental theory, Hawkins, Smith, and Catalano, (2004) have conceptualized school bonding as a commitment to doing well in school and an attachment to those at school, characterized by close emotional relationships. They posit that a strong social bond asserts an informal control on a student's behavior. Evidence to support their theory has accrued. Lowered school bonding has been linked to escalating aggression during the teen years (Hawkins, Guo, & Hill 2001). Relatedly, Battistich, Solomon, Watson, & Schaps (1997), in a longitudinal study across elementary grades, found that students' sense of community predicted lower delinquency.

School policies on tracking and ability grouping may also be linked to the problem of aggression. The drawbacks of homogenous grouping have been examined from the perspective of operant conditioning principles such that students who behave similarly reinforce each other's behavior and, by doing so, strengthen it. Some evidence is suggestive that classroom placement can have long-term effects on the escalation of aggression. Kellam, Ling, and Merisca (1998) found that first graders perceived as high in aggression had higher rates of aggression in sixth grade if they were placed in first-grade classrooms with high mean levels of aggression. They concluded that tracking aggressive children with similar children can have detrimental effects. Similarly, grouping lower achieving students together has been linked to increasing behavior difficulties over time (Werthamer-Larsson, Kellam, & Wheeler, 1991). In fact, some scholars have described the sorting of students as "structural violence." They argue that the monitoring of African American students as "behavior disordered" in special education serves to colonize and control this population of students, which leads to stigmatizing labels (Watts & Erevelles, 2004).

Classrooms. Classrooms in the early grades and the later grades have been shown to differ in levels of discipline problems (Baerveldt, 1992; Gregory, Nygreen, & Moran, 2006). Inquiry into what differentiates classrooms with higher levels of aggression and disruptive behavior can be grouped into three approaches. The first approach emphasizes the teachers' abilities to manage the classroom as a whole. Of importance are teachers' skills in engaging the students in academic tasks without being sidetracked by disruption. The second approach emphasizes the quality of teachers' relationships and interactions with individual students. The third approach focuses on teachers' attitudes and expectations that are brought into the classroom. While most of this research has been conducted at the elementary school level in single classrooms, some middle- and high-school-level research has sought to understand divergent behavior across classrooms (e.g., Gregory & Weinstein, in press).

The findings of Jacob Kounin (1970) are relevant today in understanding the importance of group management for well-run classrooms. Kounin found that more important than their specific discipline techniques, teachers with less aggression in their rooms were skilled at keeping the whole classroom on task and, thus, prevented escalating problems with aggression. Using systematic coding of videotaped elementary schools classrooms, Kounin found five skills that were linked with lower disruptions. "Withitness" is a teacher's preemptive actions and heightened awareness of behavior in the classroom. With quick and subtle interventions, a skilled teacher intervenes early to keep students engaged in the academic tasks. "Overlapping" is a teacher's ability to multitask with a focus on keeping the academic lesson going. He or she is able to address off-task behavior without derailing the lesson. "Momentum" helps transitions occur quickly with little time for losing students' motivation. "Smoothness" keeps the lessons focused with minimal deviations from the task at hand. "Group alerting" uses skills to keep each student engaged without letting some drift off. Overall, these teachers are able to anticipate problems with a focus on the antecedents of misbehavior (Emmer, Evertson, & Worsham, 2003; Evertson, Emmer, & Worhsam, 2003).

Indicators of well-run classrooms include how teachers interact with individual students. Reviews of research on classroom discipline have shown consistently that frequency of positive reinforcement is linked with orderly classrooms and low levels of misbehavior (see Doyle, 1985). The importance of positive feedback supports theories of operant conditioning, whereby behavior is strengthened when it is reinforced. The quality of interactions has also been examined from a relational standpoint. Close teacher relationships have been shown to serve as protective factors for young children at risk of negative discipline trajectories (Pianta, 1999). Evidence suggests that students' experience of teachers as nurturing with high academic expectations are linked to positive social and behavioral outcomes for middle school (Wentzel, 2002) and high school students (Gregory, 2004). Teachers, like parents, may help establish positive emotional climates with children (Davis, 2002). Within this climate, teachers may develop trust with students that enables them to effectively prevent or de-escalate aggressive behavior (Gregory). Or, teachers may develop effective regulatory processes with their students (via the relationship) to help students identify and control their emotions (Pianta & Weinstein, in press).

Teacher attitudes and expectations may exacerbate or prevent escalating aggression in the classroom. Research in this area asserts that teachers enter classrooms with preconceived notions of students, which affect their teaching practices. Though conducted mostly at the elementary school grade levels, research on teacher perceptions suggests that, on average, teachers are more likely to hold negative judgments of students of color than of White students (Weinstein, 2002). For instance, compared with teachers of color, White kindergarten teachers were more likely to report having conflict with their students of color (Saft & Pianta, 2001) and report overall higher rates of student difficulty in following directions (Rimm-Kaufman, Pianta, & Cox, 2000). From her ethnographic study of an elementary school, Ferguson (2000) argued that White teachers draw on stereotypes and their own fears of difference when they perceive "defiance" in African American students. In their large study of urban middle schools in the Midwest, Skiba and colleagues (2002) identified reasons for suspension given to African American students as more subjective compared with reasons for suspensions given to White students. In a path analysis explaining the disproportionate sanctioning of Black students, McCarthy and Hoge (1987) found that, despite Black and White students' similar self-reports of misconduct, teachers' evaluation of the students' demeanor explained a significant amount of the association between race and sanctions received. Additional research is needed to examine students' behavioral response to differential treatment.

Final issues. The social contextual effects on aggression often have small to moderate effect sizes, with meaningful implications for the escalation of aggressive behavior across schooling. That said, limitations of the empirical understanding of social contextual effects need to be highlighted. While it is helpful to pinpoint a given setting's particular effects on aggression, the reality of interacting settings is far more complex. Ecologically grounded research that accounts for the interacting influences encountered in a given day and across developmental stages is needed. The field is only beginning to address the generalizability and the cultural specificity of particular processes. Differences related to gender, social class, race and ethnicity, and region may influence how and why some social forces have more or less impact on some children's behavior.

Continuous and Reciprocal Interactions Between Individuals and Contexts

Individual attitudes and attributes interact with social contextual influences in a dynamic and reinforcing fashion (Rutter & Sroufe, 2000). Thus, across a child's life, genetic, neural, behavioral, and environmental systems likely interplay in a bidirectional manner (Gottlieb & Halpern, 2002). A life-course developmental model of aggressive behavior points to critical windows when particular risk factors play a greater or lesser role (J. B. Reid & Eddy, 1997). Longitudinal research has helped to identify when such risk factors set in motion negative developmental trajectories within particular subgroups of children. Confirmed by other studies, Patterson (1995) and Moffitt and Caspi (2001) delineated between early childhood onset of aggression, which is more likely to be life-course persistent, and adolescent onset of aggression, which is more likely to desist in early adulthood. These early-onset children often exhibit aggressive behavior outside the normative developmental levels before they start formal schooling. An interplay between individual factors (e.g., attentional problems, low verbal IQ, or irritable temperament) and family factors (e.g., disrupted inconsistent parenting, parents with a history of antisocial behavior, or coercive parenting) has been shown to be a strong predictor of such early onset. Thus, in these early years between infancy and 5 years of age, family and individual risks factors are particularly salient (J. B. Reid & Eddy).

When the "early-onset" children enter formal schooling, another set of risk factors exacerbate the aggressive behavior. School and peer factors such as a lack of positive teacher attention, academic underachievement, and rejection by peers, contribute to the "snowballing" of the problem. In high school, these children with histories of aggressive behavior are matched by another subgroup of later onset youth (Moffit and Caspi, 2001). For both groups of teens, a lack of adequate monitoring by parents accompanied by affiliation with high-risk peers exacerbates the aggressive behavior. Equipped with a developmental perspective that considers multiple pathways and risk factors that co-occur between individuals and their social contexts, school counselors can better understand how aggressive behaviors can become more wide-ranging in scope and seriousness across children's years in schooling.

Counseling Practice to Reduce School Violence

Current Practice in Schools

Recent efforts abound to study the effectiveness of school-based interventions to prevent violence and aggression (see Durlak & Wells, 1997; Henrich, Brown, & Aber, 1999; Johnson & Johnson, 1996; Leff, Power, Manz, Costigan, & Nabors, 2001; Wilson, Lipsey, & Derzon, 2003). Based in theory and research, most programs with evidence of effectiveness have been designed and evaluated by university researchers. These demonstration programs focus on building competence and/or addressing deficits within the individual student (e.g., cognitive processing skills, academic achievement), supporting and/or changing one or more social contexts (e.g., playground, classroom), or both. Prevention programs have been found to have the largest effects on the highest risk populations (Wilson, Gottfredson, & Najaka, 2001). Unlike demonstration programs, "routine practice programs"—those that currently exist in schools—generally have not been studied, have been shown to be minimally effective, or are evidence-based programs being inadequately implemented (see Wilson et al., 2003). In the following sections, we will outline some common routine practice programs and several effective demonstration programs to prevent and/or reduce aggression and violence in schools.

Routine practice programs. One common practice to reduce school violence involves the removal of disruptive students from the situation (e.g., detention or suspension) either alone or in combination with a parent–teacher conference (Gottfredson et al., 1993; Tolan & Guerra, 1994). Although research has demonstrated the importance of consistent consequences for violation of clear school rules (e.g., Colvin, Sugai, Good, & Lee, 1997), the long-term effectiveness of punitive disciplinary measures in reducing or preventing violence is not evident (see Skiba, Peterson, & Williams, 1997; Mayer, 1995). Similarly, when parent–teacher conferences are oriented toward problem solving and establishing consistent policies and communication across home and school, they may be helpful. However, when they occur only after negative events and emphasize punishment, their helpfulness in reducing the problem behavior is questionable.

A second widespread practice involves providing psychological testing and/or supportive counseling for individual students. Although an educational and psychological assessment may be a reasonable first step for the most disruptive students, it is not a realistic preventive or treatment solution given the tremendous resources needed to carry out this approach for all whose behavior and achievement may suggest it. In addition, supportive counseling (noncognitive behavioral therapy) has not been demonstrated to be effective in reducing aggression in the contexts in which disruptive children and youth act out (Wilson et al., 2001). Finally, even when school personnel try to implement evidence-based demonstration programs, for many reasons, the implementation of these interventions is often inadequate, thus reducing the likelihood of effectiveness. In a recent review, Gottfredson and colleagues (2004) found that only 57% of delinquency prevention activities in schools were implemented to a satisfactory level in terms of duration, intensity, and frequency of activities; content of programming; method of delivery; and participation among staff and students.

Demonstration programs. Many preventive and treatment programs designed and supported by a university-based research team have been the subject of rigorous examination documenting at least moderate effectiveness within particular school–community contexts when implemented with fidelity. The intervention programs are based in theory and research, and focus on the students (e.g., as individuals or groups), the social context (e.g., classroom, playground), or both (e.g., multilevel and whole school). A recent meta-analysis of school-based intervention effects on aggressive behavior indicates that well-implemented, intensive, teacher-administered, behavioral/academic/social competence programs can have a sizeable impact on student aggression (Wilson et al., 2003). We will discuss several of these programs next. In addition, we will describe some well-studied multimodal programs that may have smaller effects on aggressive behavior (see Wilson et al., 2003) but may have an impact *across* domains of student development such as social competence and academic learning. Given the differences in program effectiveness when programs are supported by a research team versus implemented without support, recommendations will be provided to counselors interested in utilizing an evidence-based approach in their schools to maximize the possibility of a positive impact on student aggression and violence.

Indicated or Treatment Programs

Typically, counselors intervene with individual students who already have demonstrated aggressive behavior with the aim of preventing the unfolding of a full-scale disorder. A recent meta-analysis showed that school-based programs that aim to prevent the escalation of aggression are most effective with students who already have exhibited aggressive behavior (Wilson et al., 2003). School interventions may be individual, parent, or group focused; however, the configuration of interventions with identified students is under strict scrutiny. With cost effectiveness a priority, schools often place aggressive children in group interventions, where students with similar difficulties interact in weekly meetings. Recent research on the negative peer influences in groups has raised questions about the unintended iatrogenic effects of group-format interventions at the elementary and middle schools (Boxer, Guerra, Huesmann, & Morales, 2005) and the high school level (Cho, Hallfors, & Sanchez, 2005). At this point, additional research is needed to understand whether mixed student groups are more or less beneficial than homogenous groups and whether high-aggressive or low-aggressive peers undermine or enhance intervention goals (Dishion & Dodge, 2005). With caution in mind, a well-studied group-based intervention follows. Then, we will describe a school-based parenting intervention, followed by a well-established individually focused intervention.

Anger Coping Program. The Anger Coping Program was designed as an 18-session, small–group format intervention with aggressive children (Lochman, Barry, & Pardini, 2003). The program draws on a social–cognitive approach, which emphasizes that children's perceptions of conflicts, encoding of relevant details, and interpretation of others' intentions are linked with their behavioral response (Crick & Dodge, 1996). Using a curriculum, group leaders address the following topics: anger management, perspective taking, socials skills training, goal setting, coping with peer pressure, emotional identification, problem solving, and relaxation training (Lochman et al., 2003). Sessions vary with a range of interactive tasks such as practicing calming self-talk while being teased, role-playing conflicts from different perspectives, and videotaping the negative consequences of an aggressive action.

The Anger Coping Program has been administered primarily in middle schools for boys identified as exhibiting aggressive behavior. It has been run as a single intervention (e.g., Lochman, 1992) and in combination with a parenting intervention (e.g., Lochman & Wells, 2004). Chorpita and his colleagues (2002) concluded in their review of three relevant studies that the intervention has a modest effect size in reducing aggressive behavior. In one study, only those who received a booster intervention the next school year showed significant reductions in classroom, off-task behavior (Lochman, 1992). The most recent published evaluation showed more promising results. The program was aimed at fifth- and sixth-grade boys who had relatively high aggressive ratings by parents and teachers (Lochman & Wells). Small groups of 4 to 6 boys participated in 32 sessions across 2 school years. The year after the intervention was completed, teachers rated the boys as improved in behavioral problems, anger management, and problem solving. No moderating effects of race were found such that the intervention effects held for the sample of White and African American boys. While the Anger Coping Program is a promising intervention, as mentioned previously, care should be taken when grouping aggressive children and adolescents in sustained "pull-out" programs (Dishion & Dodge, 2005).

Functional behavioral assessment and intervention. The 1997 and 2004 reauthorizations of the Individuals with Disabilities Education Act require schools to address discipline problems with students in special education using functional behavioral assessment and intervention. Grounded in behaviorist and social learning theory, functional analysis and intervention is frequently conducted with students exhibiting aggressive or disruptive behavior (Quinn et al., 2001). Crone and Horner (2003) described the procedures in detail. A teacher and counselor gather data about environmental factors that precede and follow the behavior. Hypotheses about the predictors and function of the behavior are developed. For instance, students may engage in problematic behaviors to obtain or escape something in the classroom (Ervin et al., 2001). Once hypotheses are formed about what drives the behavior, interventions are then designed to make the behavior irrelevant, inefficient, and ineffective (Crone & Horner, 2003). Interventions can include teaching a child an appropriate replacement behavior to obtain the desired goals or eliminating the reinforcers that strengthen the negative behavior (Ervin et al., 2001).

The functional approach to changing individual behavior in the classroom seems to be ahead of the research supporting its widespread use. While examination of 100 studies using functional behavioral assessment and intervention with 278 students showed positive short-term gains, most of the studies have been conducted with preschool and elementary students with disabilities (Ervin et al., 2001). Research with older students and those without disabilities is scarce. Moreover, long-term follow up to ascertain if the gains are sustained is rare. In addition, this approach can be quite time intensive and requires anywhere from 1 week to 30 days (Quinn et al., 2001). Thus, whether it is a cost-effective use of teacher and counselor time in comparison with classroom-wide interventions remains open to question. That said, a recent meta-analysis concluded that interventions based on learning principles and behavioral theory are most effective compared with other interventions such as mentoring or supportive counseling (Wilson et al., 2001). Thus, despite the fact the research on functional behavioral assessment and intervention is lagging, it is a promising approach that has become expected professional practice.

Parenting—The incredible years. For the past 20 years, Carolyn Webster-Stratton and her colleagues at the University of Washington Clinic have been developing interventions with young children to prevent the onset and escalation of conduct problems. After fine-tuning a parenting intervention, they developed child and teacher components (Webster-Stratton, 2005). Their program theory uses cognitive social learning principles with a focus on relationships. Using Patterson's interactional model (1982), they aimed to interrupt the coercive patterns that can become established between children and parents, which have been predictive of aggressive behavior. They also emphasized the importance of the emotional climate between parents and children with the goal of reducing harsh and inconsistent parenting and increasing warmth and positive interactions. Their programs relied heavily on videotaped parenting vignettes to model effective and ineffective parenting (see Webster-Stratton). The BASIC training program has 13 to 14 weekly 2-hour sessions and teaches parents of 2- to 7-year-olds how to positively engage, use praise and rewards effectively, set limits, and deal with noncompliance. The ADVANCE program aims to maintain treatment effects by lowering the detrimental effects of relationship distress and divorce, which were found to be predictors of treatment relapse. The program attempts to strengthen interpersonal skills in coping, communication, problem solving, social support, and self-care. They also offer four to six additional sessions that address how parents can promote their children's learning.

The BASIC parenting intervention has been studied extensively and summarized in more detail elsewhere (Webster-Stratton, 2005). The bulk of the research was with White middle-class families and children aged 2 to 6 years. However, they have extended their scope to include more diverse populations and children up to 10 years old. In brief, six randomized controlled trials have shown that the intervention improves parent–child interaction and reduces child conduct problems. The intervention has resulted in sustained gains for half to three quarters of the participants. A 3-year follow-up study showed that children with single parents or parents with relationship difficulties or negative life stress were less likely to sustain benefits. The intervention has also been successfully implemented with a low-income, Head Start population (M. J. Reid, Webster-Stratton, & Baydar, 2004). Children and their mothers with more difficulties benefited the most. The parent training has shown that behavioral improvements can generalize to the school setting. A recent study showed that the children of the parents in the intervention sustained improved classroom behavior across one school year, as rated by teachers (Webster-Stratton, Reid, & Hammond, 2004).

Universal or Single Context Programs

Beyond programs focused on students who already have demonstrated some aggressive behaviors, several setting-wide programs have evidence of effectiveness. Some of these are curricula with the primary goal of building skills and competencies within individual children, such as the Promoting Alternative THinking Strategies (PATHS) curriculum or classwide peer tutoring. These programs have the potential benefit of impacting both those students who may be at risk of developing aggressive tendencies, as well as those who already use aggression in school. Others are interventions whose primary goal is to alter the functioning of a setting, such as teacher consultation and playground restructuring. In this case, addressing environmental or structural characteristics related to the promotion of aggression may be especially critical, particularly for children in elementary school (e.g., J. B. Reid, Eddy, & Fetrow, 1999).

PATHS. The Promoting Alternative THinking Strategies program is a 60-lesson curriculum taught by the elementary school classroom teacher over one school year and integrated into the classroom curriculum with an emphasis on both changing the environment and educating the child (Greenberg, Kusche, & Mihalic, 1998). In particular, the program is designed to increase student self-control, emotion understanding, positive communication, prosocial behavior, and interpersonal problem solving. This theory-based program derives from the ABCD model of development (affective–behavioral–cognitive–dynamic) in which children's internal and external coping arises from their combined emotion awareness, cognitive understanding, and behavioral skills, with the affective component preceding the cognitive and behavioral functions (see Greenberg et al., 1998). Teaching methods for the 20- to 30-minute lessons include direct instruction, discussion, role plays, modeling, and reinforcement. Lessons focus on labeling and managing feelings, delaying gratification and controlling impulses, reading and interpreting social cues, using a procedure for problem solving and decision making, and developing nonverbal and verbal communication skills. Teachers are trained in a 3-day workshop at the beginning of the year, with ongoing support and consultation.

The PATHS curriculum is unusual in the rigor of the research base and its demonstrated effectiveness in both regular and special education classrooms (Greenberg & Kusche, 1993; Greenberg, Kusche, Cook, & Quamma, 1995). It has been tested in randomized, longitudinal studies with classroom observation components in Seattle-area first- to third-grade classrooms with approximately 60% White and 40% African American students and mainly low- to middle-income families. Positive outcomes include increased fluency and comfort in discussing basic feelings, as well as positive efficacy beliefs around managing and changing feelings. Among students at behavioral risk, teachers noted significant improvements in frustration, tolerance, social skills, task orientation, peer relations, and internalizing behaviors. Investigators mentioned significant variation regarding the level at which the teacher modeled cognitive and behavioral skills, shared emotions, and established an atmosphere of respect for varying beliefs and feelings (Greenberg et al., 1998). However, no outcomes were reported regarding differences by teacher ability or ways in which support staff attempted to bolster teacher skills. Finally, although the program includes generalization activities to be used outside the classroom and materials for families, outcomes generally have not been reported on the impact of nonclassroom and parent materials.

Peer tutoring. Peer tutoring, also called peer-assisted learning, has been used as a classroom-wide intervention aimed at raising achievement and increasing prosocial behaviors. Students are paired in fixed or reciprocal tutor–tutee roles. Primarily implemented in the elementary and middle schools, programs have addressed reading (Fuchs, Fuchs, & Burish, 2000) and mathematics (Fantuzzo, King, & Heller, 1992). Student tutors are trained to structure the tutoring time and use immediate corrective feedback with their tutee. Goals and rewards are built into the tutoring time to help the pair work efficiently and foster mutual motivation. The theoretical basis of peer tutoring is derived from research on the influence of classroom peers on behavior and motivation. It has been argued that in successful tutoring programs, students teach academic skills, model on-task behavior (Topping & Ehly, 2001), and foster academic and social motivation for learning (Rohrbeck, Ginsburg-Block, Fantuzzo, & Miller, 2003).

Given that academically targeted programs have been shown to reduce aggressive behavior (Wilson et al., 2003), the effectiveness of peer tutoring at raising academic outcomes shows promise for improving overall classroom behavior. A meta-analytic review that looked across effect sizes in 90 studies found that, on average, students in peer tutoring made moderate achievement gains (Rohrbeck et al., 2003). The programs were particularly beneficial for younger elementary students, low-income students, and urban students. While much of the research has focused on achievement gains, several studies have shown that peer tutoring is linked with improved behavior (Pigott, Fantuzzo, & Clement, 1986; Wolfe, Fantuzzo, & Wolfe, 1986). For instance, in a study with urban African American peer tutors, groups that were given rewards contingent on academic success were perceived by the teacher as showing lower negative classroom conduct (Fantuzzo et al., 1992).

Teacher consultation (Good behavior game). It has been argued that school counselors' roles should be expanded to include teacher consultation with the aim of increasing teacher capacity in classroom management (e.g., Adelman & Taylor, 2002). Drawing on behavioral consultation models, a counselor identifies the teacher's concern, gathers information about antecedents and consequences of the concern, develops a plan of intervention with the teacher, and determines the outcome of the intervention (Sladeczek, Kratochwill, Steinback, Kumke, & Hagermoser, 2003). A counselor may consult with a teacher to help implement specific programmatic interventions designed to improve classroom behavior. One such program is the Good Behavior Game (Barrish, Saunders, & Wolf, 1969), which draws on the premise that group-based rewards increase the likelihood that peers will be motivated to inhibit negative behavior. To implement the program, the teacher identifies a specific block of time when the game likely will have initial success. Then, the teacher, in consultation with the students, selects negative behaviors to decrease and chooses "activity rewards," such as extra time for free-choice reading. The teacher divides the students into teams, which receive points when they exhibit the predetermined negative behaviors. All the teams can win if they have fewer than the predetermined number of points (Embry & Straatemeier, 2001). The intervention has been found to be well liked by teachers (Tingstrom, 1994).

Embry (2002) offered a thorough review of the Good Behavior Game and its proven effectiveness in diverse classrooms. In short, implementation of the game lowered a range of negative behaviors across grades levels, in multiple settings in the school, and with at-risk populations. For instance, the program was associated with lowered disruptions with fourth graders (Barrish et al., 1969), elementary-age special education students (Darveaux, 1984; Grandy, Madsen, & De Mersseman, 1973), and adolescents (Salend, Reynolds, & Coyle, 1989). In a randomized trial in Baltimore with first graders, the game had the largest effect in reducing the aggressive behavior of students rated as high on aggression prior to the intervention (Dolan, Kellam, & Brown, 1993). Long-term effects of the classroom-centered intervention found that by sixth grade, the first graders who had played the game, relative to the control group, had fewer conduct problems and fewer suspensions (Ialongo, Poduska, Werthamer, & Kellam, 2001). A key ingredient appears to be peer pressure, such that positive peer norms are set and disruptive behavior is discouraged (see Hegerle, Kesecker, & Couch, 1979).

Playground interventions. Aggressive behavior in schools occurs most frequently in unstructured settings such as the lunchroom and playground (Craig & Pepler, 2000; Craig et al., 2000). Recent attention has been paid to the characteristics of safe and productive playgrounds, and programs targeting these characteristics have been shown to reduce aggression and violence among elementary school students. The characteristics include access to structured activities and an organized space (Bay-Hinitz, Peterson, & Quilitch, 1994), clear communication of rules and expectations (Colvin et al., 1997), sufficient and active supervision (Olweus, 1999), and incentives and consequences for positive and negative behavior (Eddy, Reid, & Fetrow, 2000). Although playground interventions may be imbedded in more comprehensive programs, research demonstrates that targeting these characteristics can reduce aggressive behavior. In one low-income, predominantly African American, urban elementary school, structured and organized games on the playground were associated with higher cooperative play and lower rough physical play over the school year, while active supervision by parent volunteers was associated with higher intercultural interaction (Leff, Costigan, & Power, 2004).

Another research team included a playground intervention in a multicomponent program (Linking the Interests of Families and Teachers; LIFT) in high juvenile crime neighborhoods within a small and majority Caucasian city. Researchers modified the Good Behavior Game (previously described) so students earned armbands from playground staff for clearly identified positive behaviors (toward a whole class reward) and negative behaviors were logged and subtracted from "good faith" points (adding to small group rewards; Eddy et al., 2000). The comprehensive program had a 3-year positive effect on elementary school children with high initial levels of aggression. Younger students had reduced playground aggression and hyperactive/inattentive behaviors, and older students had reduced arrests, delinquency, and drug use (J. B. Reid et al., 1999).

Finally, related to the peer tutoring program previously described, older peers have been trained to mediate conflicts on the playground as a supplement to the supervision by adults. In one well-implemented and evaluated program, older peers received 15 hours of training in recognizing and resolving conflicts, as well as ongoing support from a mediation team and playground supervisors. When eight trained and supported peer mediators were present on elementary school playgrounds in a middle-income, suburban community, there was an abrupt and sustained reduction in physical aggression that lasted for 2 years (Cunningham et al., 1998). Taken together, these intervention studies indicate the effectiveness of a strategy to target the *contexts* in which aggressive behaviors occur, not only the aggressive *individuals*.

Multilevel Programs

Programs designed to target multiple levels at which aggression develops and is impacted have been shown to be somewhat effective in preventing and reducing aggressive behavior in schools. These generally require more resources to implement, as well as more "buy-in" among school personnel, but the trade-off may be benefits across domains of development (e.g., reducing aggression *and* enhancing achievement).

Fast track. Based on research indicating that externalizing problems are multiply determined, the Conduct Problems Prevention Research Group (1999a, 1999b) designed, implemented, and studied a comprehensive school-based program to target risk and protective factors across universal and high-risk groups of first-grade students. The universal aspect of the program included the classroom-based PATHS curriculum addressing emotions, social behaviors, and social problem solving (described earlier), along with basic parent education and skills groups. The targeted program included student social skills groups, academic tutoring, parent–child pair work, peer pair work, and home visits for students identified as behaviorally disruptive (Conduct Problems Prevention Research Group). The universal program was delivered mainly by teachers after an intensive workshop and with regular consultation; the selective program was delivered by family/educational coordinators and paraprofessionals who received extensive and ongoing training and supervision.

This intervention study was unique in its scope and rigor. Researchers matched and randomly assigned 54 schools in diverse communities across the United States to intervention or control conditions, and studied the impact of the universal and high-risk components with classroom observations, as well as teacher, student, and parent reports, over a 3-year period. Initial positive effects were found for classroom climate, on-task behavior, and rule following among the universal population of students, and among parenting, aggressive behavior at school, coping skills, language arts grades, and peer acceptance for high-risk students across four sites (Conduct Problems Prevention Research Group, 1999a, 1999b). Differences were not found by site or student background (gender or race). Limitations to this intervention study include a lack of knowledge of program sustainability over time, the dosage necessary for a positive effect, the reasons why some students do not respond, and the role of school/classroom context in intervention impact. In addition, recent studies indicate that the long-term consequences for school behavior of this intensive and comprehensive program were less strong than anticipated (Conduct Problems Prevention Research Group, 2004).

Child Development Project. The Child Development Project aims to build "caring communities of learners" in elementary schools (Battistich, Schaps, Watson, & Solomon, 1996). Like the programs just described, the Child Development Project includes activities across multiple levels: (a) the school—principal leadership, schoolwide activities; (b) the classroom—developmental discipline; cooperative learning; values-rich, literature-based reading and language arts curricula, and a phonics-based reading program for struggling readers and, (c) the family—home activities to build home–school communication as well as understanding of family culture. Unlike these programs, however, the Child Development Project is designed not only to address the problem of aggressive behavior in school, but also to create a school *community* that more generally enhances student learning, cooperation, and respect.

Quasi-experimental studies with video observation of implementation quality and a range of student sociodemographic characteristics (ethnicity, income) showed short- and long-term positive results. In high implementation elementary schools, third- to sixth-grade students had lower rates of truancy, theft, substance use, and weapon carrying, and reported more sense of positive school community (Battistich et al., 1996). Follow-up studies indicated that when students in high-implementation elementary schools attend middle school, they had higher achievement and educational expectations, as well as lower misconduct and delinquent behavior than comparison students (Solomon, Battistich, Watson, Schaps, & Lewis, 2000). In addition, the phonics-based reading curriculum alone increased reading achievement for all students, but particularly for non-native English speakers (Battistich, 2000). A significant limitation of this program was that less than half of the schools that implemented the program did so to a high degree of fidelity. However, when implemented well, results indicated the potential importance of a universal emphasis on both academic learning and classroom/school culture as a means toward reducing behavioral problems among all students.

Positive Behavioral Interventions and Supports. Based on a public health model, Positive Behavioral Interventions and Supports (PBIS) emphasizes a three-tiered approach to preventing and addressing disruptive behaviors (Lewis & Sugai, 1999). The first tier (universal) targets all children and adults across the school setting with the idea that that every student needs clear instruction, support, and reinforcement regarding appropriate and inappropriate behaviors in and around the school building (Horner et al., 2001). The second tier (targeted) is geared toward children at risk for disruptive behavior, meaning they have engaged in problem behaviors in the past and have minimal access to protective supports. They are seen as unlikely to respond to universal interventions and in need of secondary-level interventions (e.g., daily report card, functional behavioral assessment) to move them in a more positive direction (Hawken & Horner, 2003; March & Horner, 2002). The third tier (intensive) is designed to provide team-based individualized and comprehensive services for those children with more severe behavioral problems who respond to neither universal nor targeted interventions (see Eber & Nelson, 1997). Across the three tiers, PBIS emphasizes the importance of measuring outcomes and using data for decision making, using practices with evidence of effectiveness, and attending to systems within the school to sustain the program.

The implementation and research data on PBIS is promising. Elementary and middle schools in primarily suburban, middle-income communities have been able to incorporate PBIS into their schools to high standards (e.g., Lewis, Sugai, & Colvin, 1998; Taylor-Greene & Kartub, 2000). Research studies with a pre/post design indicate a 20% to 60% reduction in discipline referrals and suspensions between the year before and the year after full implementation of PBIS (Lohrman-O'Rourke et al., 2000; Luiselli, Putnam, & Sunderland, 2002). These effects have been sustained over 6 years in schools that have continued to implement the program (Taylor-Greene & Kartub). Observational methods demonstrate that lower rates of discipline referrals are related to changes in disruptive behaviors in unstructured school settings such as the playground and hallway (Cushing, in press). What is not known is the ability of PBIS to be implemented to the same degree of fidelity and with the same effectiveness in urban low-income schools where the behavioral issues and school systems may be both qualitatively and quantitatively different from their suburban counterparts.

Final Issues

Although this section demonstrates the range of evidence-based interventions to prevent and reduce aggression in schools, there are several final issues to consider. First, intervention research tends to focus on overt forms of aggression and boys, rather than more subtle forms of aggression or girls. Recent efforts have been made to address the problem of relational or social aggression among girls (see Cappella & Weinstein, 2006; Leff, 2005), but these efforts are preliminary and must be linked with more comprehensive programs. Second, demonstration programs—in particular, those that operate at multiple levels—demand considerable resources. There is conflicting evidence regarding the importance of single- versus multiple-level approaches to addressing violence in schools, but research is clear regarding the importance of quality implementation. That said, few intervention studies describe implementation efforts, leaving gaps in understanding of methods for increasing implementation quality with school and community resources. Third, demonstration programs are developed and implemented most frequently in elementary schools, with middle and high schools receiving minimal attention. Although prevention with younger students is critical, given that aggression continues to develop through adolescence, older students deserve systematic efforts to create classroom and school environments in which prosocial behaviors are the norm. Fourth, with some exceptions, these interventions are largely a-contextual without consideration for peer and cultural norms—which may be critical to the effectiveness of a program. Finally, the evidence-based practice movement relies on a process that moves from highly controlled trials to wider dissemination within schools. A more ecologically valid approach to developing an understanding of what works may be an *iterative* process of research and development based not only in theory and research, but also within the school and community context in which the efforts exist.

Recommendations

The school counselor can play an integral role in assisting the school to prevent or address the problem of school violence by providing information and support around the use of evidence-based practices in their schools. However, given the multiple and complex realities of different school communities, there are several steps to consider prior to and during the process of implementing one of the previously discussed programs to maximize the potential benefit. From the research and theory on the development, prevention, and management of aggression in schools, we recommend the following guidelines when attempting to address school violence:

1. Collect and analyze data to understand where, when, and with whom aggression occurs.
   - Use existing datasets (e.g., discipline referrals) or gather new data (e.g., conversations or surveys with school staff).
   - Assess multiple forms of aggression, including physical, verbal, and relational aggression (Leff et al., 2001).

2. Coalesce key personnel and the school organization around the need for intervention within particular settings and/or groups of students.
   - Promote a supportive school climate around the prevention and reduction of aggression (Gottfredson et al., 2004).
   - Build school capacity to initiate and sustain an innovation (e.g., infrastructure and support, resources, and leadership; Sherman et al., 1997).
   - Prepare to integrate elements of the intervention into the structure of the school or setting (e.g., classroom, playground; Heller, 1990; Gottfredson et al., 2004).

3. Help school personnel select empirically supported activities with particular attention to the population with which and context within which the services have been tested.
   - Consider interventions designed to promote change within the individual child, as well as within the social context (e.g., universal, targeted, and indicated levels; Weissberg & Greenberg, 1998).
   - Multiple level programs accompanied by a clarification and communication of norms about behaviors are promising; however, it is more important to implement a less-resource heavy program well than a more-resource heavy program poorly (Durlak & Wells, 1997; Gottfredson et al., 2004; Sherman et al., 1997).
   - Intervene at the appropriate stage of development (e.g., early in the onset of problems for a student or setting) and during sensitive periods, such as transitions during the school day (Tolan, Guerra, & Kendall, 1995; Weissberg & Greenberg, 1998).

4. Monitor the implementation and/or adaptation of those programs or practices.
   - Adapt program content to ethnic and sociodemographic characteristics of students to maximize the potential that it has meaning in their lives, in particular if the program was tested in a demographically different school community than the one in which it will be implemented (Heller, 1990).
   - Provide extensive, quality training of personnel who deliver services, and provide supervision and support for ongoing delivery of services (Gottfredson et al., 2004).

5. Collect data to evaluate the progress of the intervention strategies and make adjustments as needed.
   - Think about the multiple outcomes that may be important to the school and collect data on those outcomes (e.g., different types of aggres-

sion, academic achievement, attendance) from multiple sources (e.g., teachers, students, school data).
- Allow sufficient time for the activities to work before making major adjustments to the intervention strategies; anticipate that the strongest results will be for the students and settings exhibiting the most problems at the start.

References

Adelman, H. S., & Taylor, L. (2002). School counselors and school reform: New directions. *Professional School Counseling, 5*(4), 235–248.

Anderson, C. A., & Bushman, B. J. (2001). Effects of violent video games on aggressive behavior, aggressive cognition, aggressive affect, physiological arousal, and prosocial behavior: A meta-analytic review of the scientific literature. *Psychological Science, 12*(5), 353–359.

Anderson, C. A., Berkowitz, L., & Donnerstein, E. (2003). The influence of media violence on youth. *Psychological Science in the Public Interest, 4*(3), 81–110.

Archer, J. (1994). Testosterone and aggression: A theoretical review. *Journal of Offender Rehabilitation, 21*, 3–39.

Arnold, D. H., Ortiz, C., Curry, J. C., Stowe, R. M., Goldstein, N. E., Fisher, P. H., et al. (1999). Promoting academic success and preventing disruptive behavior disorders through community partnership. *Journal of Community Psychology, 27*(5), 589–598.

Asher, S. R., & Coie, J. D. (1990). *Peer rejection in childhood.* New York: Cambridge University Press.

Ayers, W., Dohrn, B., & Ayers, R. (2001). *Zero tolerance: Resisting the drive for punishment in schools.* New York: The New Press.

Baerveldt, C. (1992). Schools and the prevention of petty crime: Search for a missing link. *Journal of Quantitative Criminology, 8*, 79–94.

Bandura, A. (1973). *Aggression: A social learning analysis.* Englewood Cliffs, NJ: Prentice Hall.

Barkley, R. A., Fischer, M., Edelbrock, C. S., & Smallish, L. (1990). The adolescent outcome of hyperactive children diagnosed by research criteria: An 8-year prospective follow-up study. *Journal of the American Academy of Child and Adolescent Psychiatry, 29*, 546–557.

Barrish, H. H., Saunders, M., & Wolf, M. M. (1969). Good behavior game: Effects of individual contingencies for group consequences on disruptive behavior in a classroom. *Journal of Applied Behavior Analysis, 2*, 119–124.

Bates, J. E., Bayles, K., Bennett, D. S., Ridge, B., & Brown, N. M. (1991). Origins of externalizing behavior problems at eight years of age. In D. J. Pepler & K. H. Rugin (Eds.), *The development and treatment of childhood aggression* (pp. 93–120). Hillsdale, NJ: Erlbaum.

Bates, J. E.; Maslin, C. A., & Frankel, K. A. (1985). Attachment security, mother–child interaction, and temperament as predictors of behavior-problem ratings at age three years. *Monographs of the Society for Research in Child Development, Vol. 50*, 167–193.

Battistich, V. (2000). *Summary of evaluation findings on the Child Development Project.* Oakland, CA: Developmental Studies Center.

Battistich, V., Schaps, E., Watson, M., & Solomon, D. (1996). Prevention effects of the Child Development Project: Early findings from an ongoing multisite demonstration trial. *Journal of Adolescent Research, 11*, 12–35.

Battistich, V., Solomon, V., Watson, M., & Schaps, E. (1997). Caring school communities. *Educational Psychologist, 32*(3), 137–151.

Baumrind, D. (1991). The influence of parenting style on adolescent competence and substance use. *Journal of Early Adolescence, 11*(1), 56–95.

Bay-Hinitz, A. K., Peterson, R. F., & Quilitch, H. R. (1994). Cooperative games: A way to modify aggressive and cooperative behaviors in young children. *Journal of Applied Behavior Analysis, 27*, 435–446.

Benasich, A. A., Brooks-Gunn, J., & Clewell, B. C. (1992). How do mothers benefit from early intervention programs? *Journal of Applied Developmental Psychology, 13*, 311–362.

Berman, M. E., Kavoussi, R. J., & Coccaro, E. F. (1997). Neurotransmitter correlates of human aggression. In D. M. Stoff, J. Breiling, & J. D. Maser (Eds.), *Handbook of antisocial behavior* (pp. 305–313). New York: John Wiley & Sons, Inc.

Boldizar, J. P., Perry, D. G., & Perry, L. C. (1989). Outcome values and aggression. *Child Development, 60*, 571–579.

Boxer, P., Guerra, N. G., Huesmann, L. R., & Morales, J. (2005). Proximal peer-level effects of a small-group selected prevention on aggression in elementary school children: An investigation of the peer contagion hypothesis. *Journal of Abnormal Child Psychology, 33*(3), 325–338.

Brain, P. F., & Susman, E. J. (1997). Hormonal aspects of aggression and violence. In D. M. Stoff, J. Breiling, & J. D. Maser (Eds.), *Handbook of antisocial behavior* (pp. 314–323). New York: John Wiley & Sons, Inc.

Buehler, R. E., Patterson, G. R., & Furniss, J. M. (1966). The reinforcement of behavior in institutional settings. *Behaviour Research and Therapy, 4*, 157–167.

Cappella, E., & Weinstein, R. S. (2006). The prevention of social aggression among girls. *Social Development.*

Carr, E. G., Taylor, J. G., & Robinson, S. (1991). The effects of severe behavior problems in children on the teaching behavior of adults. *Journal of Applied Behavior Analysis, 24*, 523–535.

Caspi, A., Henry, B., McGee, R. O., Moffitt, T. E., & Silva, P. A. (1995). Temperamental origins of child and adolescent behavior problems: From age 3 to age 15. *Child Development, 66,* 55–68.

Cho, H., Hallfors, D. D., & Sanchez, V. (2005). Evaluation of a high school peer group intervention for at-risk youth. *Journal of Abnormal Psychology, 33*(3), 363–374.

Chorpita, B. F., Yim, L. M., Donkervoet, J. C., Arensdorf, A., Amundsen, M. J., McGee, C., et al. (2002). Toward large-scale implementation of empirically supported treatments for children: A review and observations by the Hawaii Empirical Basis to Services Task Force. *Clinical Psychology: Science & Practice, 9*(2), 165–190.

Coie, J. D., & Dodge, K. A. (1998). Aggression and antisocial behavior. In W. Damon & N. Eisenberg (Eds.), *Handbook of child psychology: Vol. 3: Social, emotional, and personality development* (5th ed., pp. 779–862). New York: John Wiley & Sons, Inc.

Colvin, G., Sugai, G., Good, R. H., III., & Lee, Y. (1997). Using active supervision and precorrection to improve transition behaviors in an elementary school. *School Psychology Quarterly, 12,* 344–363.

Conduct Problems Prevention Research Group. (1999a). Initial impact of the Fast Track prevention trial for conduct problems: I. The high-risk sample. *Journal of Consulting and Clinical Psychology, 67,* 631–647.

Conduct Problems Prevention Research Group. (1999b). Initial impact of the Fast Track prevention trial for conduct problems: II. Classroom effects. *Journal of Consulting and Clinical Psychology, 67,* 648–657.

Conduct Problems Prevention Research Group (2004). The effects of the Fast Track Program on serious problem outcomes at the end of elementary school. *Journal of Clinical Child and Adolescent Psychology, 33,* 650–661.

Conger, R. D., Wallace, L. E., Sun, Y., Simons, R. L., McLoyd, V. C., & Brody, H. H. (2002). Economic pressure in African American families: A replication and extension of the family stress model. *Developmental Psychology, 38*(2), 179–193.

Connell, J. P. (1990). Context, self, and action: A motivational analysis of self-system processes across the life-span. In D. C. M. Beeghly (Ed.), *The self in transaction: Infancy to childhood* (pp. 61–97). Chicago: University of Chicago Press.

Cornell, D. G., Sheras, P. L., Kaplan, S., McConville, D., Douglass, J., Elkon, A., et al. (2004). Guidelines for student threat assessment: Field-test findings. *School Psychology Review, 33*(4), 527–546.

Craig, W. M., & Pepler, D. (2000). Observations of bullying and victimization in the school yard. In W. Craig (Ed.), *Childhood social development: The essential readings* (pp. 116–138). Malden, MA: Blackwell Publishers Inc.

Craig, W. M., Pepler, D., & Atlas, R. (2000). Observations of bullying in the playground and in the classroom. *School Psychology International, 21*(1), 22–36.

Crick, N. R. (1996). The role of overt aggression, relational aggression, and prosocial behavior in the prediction of children's future social adjustment. *Child Development, 67,* 2317–2327.

Crick, N. R., & Dodge, K. A. (1989). Children's evaluations of peer entry and conflict situations: Social strategies, goals, and outcome expectations. In B. Schneider, J. Nadel, G. Attili, & R. Weissberg (Eds.), *Social competence in developmental perspective* (pp. 396–399). Dordrecht, The Netherlands: Kluwer.

Crick, N. R., & Dodge, K. A. (1996). Social information processing mechanisms in reactive and proactive aggression. *Child Development, 67,* 993–1002.

Crone, D. A., & Horner, R. H. (2003). *Building positive behavior support systems in schools: Functional behavioral assessment.* New York: Guilford Press.

Cunningham, C. E., Cunningham, L. J., Martorelli, V., Tran, A., Young, J., & Zacharias, R. (1998). The effects of primary division, student-mediated conflict resolution programs on playground aggression. *Journal of Child Psychology & Psychiatry, 39*(5), 653–662.

Cushing, L. S. (in press). Validation and congruent validity of a direct observation tool to assess student social climate at school. *Journal of Positive Interventions.*

Darveaux, D. X. (1984). The Good Behavior Game plus merit: Controlling disruptive behavior and improving student motivation. *School Psychology Review, 13,* 510–514.

Davis, H. A. (2002). Conceptualizing the role and influence of student-teacher relationships on children's social and cognitive development. *Educational Psychologist, 38*(4), 207–234.

Devine, J. (1996). *Maximum security: The culture of violence in inner-city schools.* Chicago: University of Chicago Press.

Dishion, T. J., Andrews, D. W., & Crosby, L. (1995). Antisocial boys and their friends in early adolescence: Relationship characteristics, quality, and interactional process. *Child Development, 66,* 139–151.

Dishion, T. J., & Dodge, K. A. (2005). Peer contagion in interventions for children and adolescents: Moving towards an understanding of the ecology and dynamics of change. *Journal of Abnormal Child Psychology, 33*(3), 395–400.

Dishion, T. J., French, D. C., & Patterson, G. R. (1995). The development and ecology of antisocial behavior. In D. Cicchetti & D. Cohen (Eds.), *Manual of developmental psychopathology: Vol 2: Risk, disorder, and adaptation* (pp. 421–471). New York: Wiley.

Dishion, T. J., & Patterson, G. R. (1997). The timing and severity of antisocial behavior: Three hypotheses within an ecological framework. In D. M. Stoff, J. Breiling, & J. D. Maser (Eds.), *Handbook of antisocial behavior* (pp. 205–217). New York: John Wiley & Sons, Inc.

Dishion, T. J., Patterson, G. R., Stoolmiller, M., & Skinner,

M. S. (1991). Family, school, and behavioral antecedents to early adolescent involvement with antisocial peers. *Developmental psychology, 27,* 172–180.

Dishion, T. J., Spracklen, K. M., Andrews, D. W., & Patterson, G. R. (1996) Deviancy training in male adolescent friendships. *Behavior Therapy, 27,* 373–390.

Dodge, K. A. (1991). The structure and function of proactive and reactive aggression. In D. J. Pepler & K. H. Rubin (Eds.), *The development and treatment of childhood aggression* (pp. 201–218). Hillsdale, NJ: Erlbaum.

Dodge, K. A., & Coie, J. D. (1987). Social information-processing factors in reactive and proactive aggression in children's playgroups. *Journal of Personality and Social Psychology, 53,* 1146–1158.

Dodge, K. A., & Frame, C. L. (1982). Social-cognitive biases and deficits in aggressive boys. *Child Development, 53,* 620–635.

Dodge, K. A., Pettit, G. S., McClaskey, C. L., & Brown, M. M. (1986). Social competence in children. *Monographs of the Society for Research in Child Development, 51*(2, Serial No. 213), 1–85.

Dodge, K. A., & Schwartz, D. (1997). Social information processing mechanisms in aggressive behavior. In D. M. Stoff, J. Breiling, & J. D. Maser (Eds.), *Handbook of antisocial behavior* (pp. 171–180). New York: John Wiley & Sons.

Dolan, L. J., Kellam, S. G., & Brown, C. H. (1993). The short-term impact of two classroom-based preventive interventions on aggressive and shy behaviors and poor achievement. *Journal of Applied Developmental Psychology, 14*(3), 317–345.

Doyle, W. (1985). Classroom organization and management. In M. C. Wittrock (Ed.), *Handbook of research on teaching* (3rd ed., pp. 392–431). New York: MacMillan.

Dulmus, K., Theriot, M. T., & Sowers, K. M. (2004). Student report of peer bullying victimization in a rural school. *Stress, Trauma, and Crisis: An International Journal, 7*(1), 1–16.

Durlak, J. A., & Wells, A. M. (1997). Primary prevention mental health programs for children and adolescents: A meta-analytic review. *American Journal of Community Psychology, 25*(2), 115–152.

Eamon, M. K. (2001). Poverty, parenting, peer, and neighborhood influences on young adolescent antisocial behavior. *Journal of Social Service Research, 28*(1), 1–23.

Earls, F. (1981). Epidemiological child psychiatry: An American perspective. In. E. F. Purcell (Ed.), *Psychopathology of children and youth: A cross cultural perspective* (pp. 3–28). New York: Josial Macy Jr. Foundation.

Earls, F., & Jung, K. G. (1987). Temperament and home environment characteristics as causal factors in the early development of childhood psychopathology. *Journal of the American Academy of Child and Adolescent Psychiatry, 26,* 491–498.

Eber, L., & Nelson, C. M. (1997). School-based wraparound planning: Integrating services for students with emotional and behavioral needs. *American Journal of Orthopsychiatry, 67,* 385–395.

Eddy, M. J., Reid, J. B., & Fetrow, R. A. (2000). An elementary school-based prevention program targeting modifiable antecedents of youth delinquency and violence: Linking the interests of families and teachers (LIFT). *Journal of Emotional & Behavioral Disorders, 8*(3), 165–176.

Embry, D. D. (2002). The Good Behavior Game: A best practice candidate as a universal behavioral vaccine. *Clinical Child and Family Psychology Review, 5*(4), 273–297.

Embry, D. D., & Straatemeier, G. (2001). *The Pax acts game manual: How to apply the Good Behavior Game.* Tuscon, AZ: PAXIS Institute.

Emmer, E. T., Evertson, C. M., & Worsham, M. E. (2003). *Classroom management for secondary teachers* (6th ed.). Boston: Allyn and Bacon.

Eron, L. D., Huesmann, L. R., & Zelli, A. (1991). The role of parental variables in the learning of aggression. In D. J. Pepler & K. H Rubin (Eds.), *Development and treatment of childhood aggression* (pp. 169–188). Hillsdale, NJ, England: Lawrence Erlbaum Associates.

Ervin, R. A., Radford, P. M., Bertsch, K., Piper, A. L., Ehrhardt, K. E., & Poling, A. (2001). A descriptive analysis and critique of the empirical literature on school-based functional assessment. *School Psychology Review, 30*(2), 193–210.

Evertson, C. M., Emmer, E. T., & Worhsam, M. E. (2003). *Classroom management for elementary teachers* (6th ed.). Boston: Allyn and Bacon.

Fagan, J., & Wilkson, D. L. (1998). Social contexts and functions of adolescent violence. In D. S. Elliott, B. A. Hambrug, & K. R. Williams (Eds.), *Violence in American schools* (pp. 55–93). Cambridge, UK: Cambridge University Press.

Fantuzzo, J. W., King, J. A., & Heller, L. R. (1992). Effects of reciprocal tutoring on mathematics and school adjustment: A component analysis. *Journal of Educational Psychology, 84*(3), 331–339.

Farrington, D. P., & Hawkins, J. D. (1991). Predicting participation, early onset, and later persistence in officially recorded offending. *Criminal Behaviour & Mental Health, 1*(1), 1–33.

Ferguson, A. A. (2000). *Bad boys: Public school and the making of black masculinity.* Ann Arbor: University of Michigan Press.

Florida Department of Education. (1995). *Florida school discipline study.* Tallahassee, FL: Office of Policy Research. (ED384981)

Frick, P., Kamphaus, R. W., Lahey, B. B., Loeber, R., Christ, M. G., Hart, E., et al. (1991). Academic underachievement and the disruptive behavior disorders. *Journal of Consulting and Clinical Psychology, 59,* 289–294.

Fuchs, D., Fuchs, L. S., & Burish, P. (2000). Peer-assisted learning strategies: An evidence-based practice to promote reading achievement. *Learning Disabilities Research and Practice, 15*(2), 85–91.

Fuller, B., Coonerty, C., Kipnis, F. M., & Choong, Y. (1997). An unfair headstart: California families face gaps in preschool and child care availability. Berkeley, CA: Berkeley-Stanford PACE Center, Yale University, and the California Child Care Resource and Referral Network's Growing Up in Poverty Project.

Giroux, H. A. (1983). Theories of reproduction and resistance in the new sociology of education: A critical analysis. *Harvard Educational Review, 53*(3), 257–293.

Gonzales, N. A., Cauce, A. M., & Friedman, R. J. (1996). Family, peer, and neighborhood influences on academic achievement among African-American adolescents: One-year prospective effects. *American Journal of Community Psychology, 24*(3), 365–387.

Gorman-Smith, D., & Tolan, P. (1998). The role of exposure to community violence and developmental problems among inner-city youth. *Development & Psychopathology, 10*(1), 101–116.

Gottfredson, D. G., Gottfredson, D. C., Czeh, E. R., Cantor, D., Crosse, S. B., & Hantman, I. (2004) Toward safe and orderly schools: National study of delinquency prevention in schools. *U.S. Department of Justice.* September 15, 2005, from http://www.ncjrs.gov/pdffiles1/nij/205005.pdf

Gottfredson, D. C., Gottfredson, G. D., & Hybl, L. G. (1993). Managing adolescent behavior: A multiyear, multischool study. *American Educational Research Journal, 30*(1), 179–215.

Gottlieb, G., & Halpern, C. T. (2002). A relational view of causality in normal and abnormal development. *Development and Psychopathology, 14*, 421–435.

Grandy, G. S., Madsen, C. H., & De Mersseman, L. M. (1973). The effects of individual and interdependent contingencies on inappropriate classroom behavior. *Psychology in the Schools, 10*, 488–493.

Gray, J. A. (1987). *The psychology of fear and stress.* Cambridge, UK: Cambridge University Press.

Greenberg, M. T., & Kusche, C. A. (1993). *Promoting social and emotional development in deaf children: The PATHS project.* Seattle, WA: University of Washington Press.

Greenberg, M. T., Kusche, C. A., Cook, E. T., & Quamma, J. P. (1995). Promoting emotional competence in school-aged children: The effects of the PATHS curriculum. *Development and Psychopathology, 7*, 117–136.

Greenberg, M. T., Kusche, C., & Mihalic, S. F. (1998). *Blueprints for violence prevention, book ten: Promoting alternative thinking strategies (PATHS).* Boulder, CO: Center for the Study and Prevention of Violence.

Gregory, A. (2004). *A window on the discipline gap: Cooperation or defiance in the high school classroom.* Doctoral dissertation, University of California, Berkeley.

Gregory, A., & Weinstein, S. R. (in press). A window on the discipline gap: Defiance or cooperation in the high school classroom. *Journal of School Psychology.*

Gregory, A., & Weinstein, R. S. (2004). Connection and regulation at home and in school: Predicting growth in achievement for adolescents. *Journal of Adolescent Research, 19*(4), 405–427.

Gregory, A., Nygreen, K., & Moran, D. (2006). The Discipline gap and the normalization of failure. In P. Noguera and J. Wing, (Eds.). *Unfinished business; Closing the racial achievement gap in our schools.* (pp. 121–150) John Wiley & Sons: CA.

Guerra, N. G., & Slaby, R. C. (1989). Evaluative factors in social problem solving by aggressive boys. *Journal of Abnormal Child Psychology, 17*, 277–289.

Gun–Free Schools Act of 1990, Crime Control Act of 1990, Pub. L. 101–647, 18 U.S.C. ¶ 922.

Harvard Civil Rights Project. (2000). *Opportunity suspended: The devastating consequence of zero-tolerance and school discipline policy.* Retrieved September 10, 2005, from http://www.civilrightsproject.harvard.edu/convenings/zerotolerance/synopsis.php

Hawken, L. S., & Horner, R. H. (2003). Evaluation of a targeted intervention within a schoolwide system of behavior support. *Journal of Behavioral Education, 12*(3), 225–240.

Hawkins, J. D., Guo, J., & Hill, K. G. (2001). Long-term effects of the Seattle Social Development Intervention on school bonding trajectories. *Applied Developmental Science, 5*, 225–236.

Hawkins, J. D., Herrenkohl, T., & Farrington, D. P. (1998). A review of predictors of youth violence. In R. Loeber & D. P. Farrington (Eds.), *Serious & violent juvenile offenders: Risk factors and successful interventions* (pp. 106–146). Thousand Oaks, CA: Sage Publications, Inc.

Hawkins, J. D., Smith, B. H., & Catalano, R. F. (2004). Social development and social and emotional learning. In J. E. Zins, R. P. Weissberg, M. C. Wang, & H. J. Walberg (Eds.), *Building academic success on social and emotional learning: What does the research say?* (pp. 135–150). New York: Teachers College Press.

Hegerle, D. R., Kesecker, M. P., & Couch, J. V. (1979). A behavior game for the reduction of inappropriate classroom behaviors. *School Psychology Review, 8*, 339–343.

Heller, K. (1990). Social and community intervention. *Annual Review of Psychology, 41*, 141–168.

Henrich, C. C., Brown, J. L., & Aber, J. L. (1999). Evaluating the effectiveness of school-based violence prevention: Developmental approaches. *Social Policy Report, 13*, 1–16.

Hill, H. M., Fernando, I. S., Chen, S. A., & LaFrombois, T. D. (1994). Sociocultural factors in the etiology and prevention of violence among ethnic minority. In L. D. Eron, J. H. Gentry, P. Schlegel (Eds.), *Reason* to hope. *A psychosocial perspective on violence and youth* (pp. 59–98). Washington, DC: American Psychological Association.

Hinshaw, S. P. (1992). Academic underachievement, attention deficits, and aggression: Comorbidity and implications for intervention. *Journal of Consulting and Clinical Psychology, 60*(6), 893–903.

Hirschi, T. (1969). *Causes of delinquency.* Berkeley: University of California Press.

Hollingsworth, E. J., Lufler, H. S., & Clune, W. H. (1984). *School discipline: Order and autonomy.* New York: Praeger.

Horner, R. H., Sugai, G., Lewis-Palmer, T., & Todd, A. W. (2001). Teaching school-wide behavioral expectations. *Report on Emotional & Behavioral Disorders in Youth, 1*(4), 77–79.

Howlin, P., & Rutter, M. (1987). The consequences of language delay for other aspects of development. In W. Yule & M. Rutter (Eds.), *Language development and disorders* (pp. 271–294). Oxford, UK: MacKeith.

Huesmann, L. R. (1988). An information processing model for the development of aggression. *Aggressive Behavior, 14*, 13–24.

Huesmann, L. R. & Eron, L. D (1984). Cognitive processes and the persistence of aggressive behavior. *Aggressive Behavior, 10*, 243–251.

Huesmann, L. R., & Eron, L. D. (Eds.). (1986). *Television and the aggressive child: A cross-national comparison.* Hillsdale, NJ: Erlbaum.

Huesmann, L. R., Moise, J. F., & Podoloski, C. (1997). The effects of media violence on the development of antisocial behavior. In D. M. Stoff, J. Breiling, & J. D. Maser (Eds.), *Handbook of antisocial behavior* (pp. 181–193). New York: John Wiley & Sons, Inc.

Hyman, I. A., & Perone, D. C. (1998). The other side of school violence: Educator policies and practices that may contribute to student misbehavior. *Journal of School Psychology, 36*(1), 7–27.

Ialongo, N., Poduska, J., Werthamer, L., & Kellam, S. (2001). The distal impact of two first-grade preventive interventions on conduct problems and disorder in early adolescence. *Journal of Emotional & Behavioral Disorders, 9*(3), 146–160.

Inoff-Germain, G., Arnold, G. S., Nottelmann, E. D., Susman, E. J., Cutler, G. B., & Chrousos, G. P. (1988). Relations between hormone levels and observational measures of aggressive behavior of young adolescents in family interactions. *Developmental Psychology, 24*, 129–139.

Jencks, C., & Mayer, S. (1990). The social consequence of growing up in a poor neighborhood. In L. E. Lynn & M. F. H. McGeary (Eds.), *Inner-city poverty in the United States* (pp. 111–186). Washington, DC: National Academy Press.

Johnson, D. W., & Johnson, R. T. (1996). Conflict resolution and peer mediation programs in elementary and secondary schools: A review of the research. *Review of Educational Research, 66*(4), 459–506.

Kaukiainen, A., Bjorkqvist, K., Lagerspetz, K., Osterman, K., Salmivalli, C., Rothberg, S., et al. (1999). The relationships between social intelligence, empathy, and three types of aggression. *Aggressive Behavior, 25*, 81–89.

Kellam, S. G., Ling, X., & Merisca, R. (1998). The effect of the level of aggression in the first grade classroom on the course and malleability of aggressive behavior into middle school. *Development & Psychopathology, 10*(2), 165–185.

Kounin, J. S. (1970). *Discipline and group management in classrooms.* Oxford, UK: Holt, Rinehart, & Winston.

Kruesi, M. J. P., Hibbs, E. D., Zahn, T. P., Keysor, C. S., Hamburger, S. D., Bartko, F. F., et al. (1992). A 2-year prospective follow-up study of children and adolescents with disruptive behavior disorders. *Archives of General Psychiatry, 49*, 429–435.

Laird, R. D., Jordan, K. Y., Dodge, K. A., Pettit, G. S., & Bates, J. E. (2001) Peer rejection in childhood, involvement with antisocial peers in early adolescence, and the development of externalizing problems. *Development and Psychopathology, 13*, 337–354.

Lansford, J. E., Deater-Deckard, K., Dodge, K. A., Bates, J. E., & Pettit, G. S. (2004). Ethnic differences in the link between physical discipline and later adolescent externalizing behaviors. *Journal of Child Psychology and Psychiatry, 45*(4), 801–812.

Leff, S. S. (2005, July). *Joining with stakeholders to design a relational aggression program.* Poster presented at the Eighteenth NIMH Conference on Mental Health Services Research, Bethesda, MD.

Leff, S. S., Costigan, T., & Power, T. J. (2004). Using participatory research to develop a playground-based prevention program. *Journal of School Psychology, 42*(1), 3–21.

Leff, S. S., Power, T. J., Manz, P. H., Costigan, T. E., & Nabors, L. A. (2001). School-based aggression prevention programs for young children: Current status and implications for violence prevention. *School Psychology Review, 30*, 343–360.

Leventhal, T., & Brooks-Gunn, J. (2000). The neighborhood could live in: The effects of neighborhood residents on child and adolescent outcomes. *Psychological Bulletin, 126* (2), 309–337.

Lewis, T. J., & Sugai, G. (1999). Effective behavior support: A systems approach to proactive school-wide management. *Effective School Practices, 17*(4), 47–53.

Lewis, T. J., Sugai, G., & Colvin, G. (1998). Reducing problem behavior through a school-wide system of effective behavioral support: Investigation of a school-wide social skills training program and contextual interventions. *School Psychology Review, 27*, 446–459.

Lochman, J. E. (1992). Cognitive-behavioral intervention with aggressive boys: Three-year follow-up and preventive effects. *Journal of Consulting and Clinical Psychology, 60*(3), 426–432.

Lochman, J. E., Barry, T. D., & Pardini, D. A. (2003). Anger control training for aggressive youth. In A. E. Kazdin & J. R. Weisz (Eds.), *Evidence-based psychotherapies for children and adolescents* (pp. 263–281). New York: Guilford Press.

Lochman, J. E., & Wells, K. C. (2004). The Coping Power Program for preadolescent aggressive boys and their parents: Outcome effects at the 1-year follow-up. *Journal of Consulting & Clinical Psychology, 72*(4), 571–578.

Loeber, R., Burke, J. D., Lahey, B. B., Winters, A., & Zera, M. (2000). Oppositional defiant and conduct disorder: A review of the past 10 years, Part I. *Journal of the American Academy of Child & Adolescent Psychiatry, 39*(12), 1468–1484.

Lohrman-O'Rourke, S., Knoster, T., Sabatine, K., Smith, D., Horvath, B., & Llewellyn, G. (2000). School-wide application of positive behavior support in the Bangor Area School District. *Journal of Positive Behavior Interventions, 2,* 238–240.

Luiselli, J. K., Putnam, R. F., & Sunderland, M. (2002). Longitudinal evaluation of behavior support intervention in a public middle school. *Journal of Positive Behavioral Interventions, 4*(3), 182–188.

Maguin, E., & Loeber, R. (1996). Academic performance and delinquency. In M. Tonry (Ed.), *Crime and justice: A review of research* (Vol. 20, pp. 145–264). Chicago: University of Chicago Press.

March, R. E., & Horner, R. H. (2002). Feasibility and contributions of functional behavior assessment in schools. *Journal of Emotional and Behavioral Disorders, 10*(3), 158–170.

Matheny, A. P. (1989). Children's behavioral inhibition over age and across situations: Genetic similarity for a trait during change. *Journal of Personality, 57,* 215–226.

Maughan, B., Gray, G., & Rutter, M. (1985). Reading retardation and antisocial behavior: A follow-up into employment. *Journal of Child Psychology and Psychiatry, 26,* 741–758.

Mayer, G. R. (1995). Preventing antisocial behavior in the schools. *Journal of Applied Behavior Analysis, 28,* 467–478.

McCarthy, J. D., & Hoge, D. R. (1987). Social construction of school punishment. *Social Forces, 65*(4), 1101–1120.

McEvoy, A., & Welker, R. (2000). Antisocial behavior, academic failure, and school climate: A critical review. *Journal of Emotional and Behavioral Disorders, 8*(3), 130–140.

McGee, R., & Share, D. L. (1988). Attention deficit disorder hyperactivity and academic failure: Which comes first and which should be treated? *Journal of the American Academy of Child and Adolescent Psychiatry, 27,* 318–325.

Mednick, S. A., Gabrielli, W. F., Jr., & Hutchings, B. (1984). Genetic influences in criminal convictions: Evidence from an adoption cohort. *Science, 224,* 891–894.

Moffitt, T. E., & Caspi, A. (2001). Childhood predictors differentiate life-course persistent and adolescence-limited antisocial pathways among males and females. *Development & Psychopathology, 13*(2), 355–375.

National Association of State Boards of Education. (2005). *State-by-state emotional and social health education.* Retrieved October 1, 2005, from http://www.nasbe.org/

National Center for Education Statistics. (1999). *School survey on crime and safety.* Retrieved October 1, 2005, from http://www.nces.ed.gov/

National Center for Education Statistics. (2000). *OCR Elementary and Secondary Survey.* Retrieved October 1, 2005, from http://www.nces.ed.gov/

National Center for Education Statistics (2003). *Status and trends in the education of Hispanic students.* Retrieved October 1, 2005, from http"//www.nces.ed.gov/

National Center for Education Statistics. (2004) *Indicators of school crime and safety.* Retrieved October 1, 2005, from http://www.nces.ed.gov/

Olweus, D. (1999). Sweden. In P. K. Smith, Y. Morita, J. Junger-Tas, D. Olweus, R. Catalano, & P. Slee (Eds.), *The nature of school bullying: A cross-national perspective* (pp. 7–27). London: Routledge.

Olweus, D., Mattsson, A., Schalling, D., & Low, H. (1988). Circulating testosterone levels and aggression in adolescent males: A causal analysis. *Psychosomatic Medicine, 50,* 261–272.

Osgood, D. W., & Chambers, J. M. (2003). *Community correlates of rural youth violence.* Washington DC: U.S. Department of Justice, Juvenile Justice Bulletin.

Patterson, G. R. (1982). *Coercive family process.* Eugene, OR: Castalia.

Patterson, G. R. (1995). Coercion as a basis for early age of onset for arrest. (pp. 81¬105). In J. McCord (Ed.) *Coercion and punishment in long-term perspectives.* New York: Cambridge University Press.

Patterson, G. R., Dishion, T. J., & Yoerger, K. (2000). Adolescent growth in new forms of problem behavior: Macro- and micro-peer dynamics. *Prevention Science, 1*(1), 3–13.

Pianta, R. C. (1999). *Enhancing relationships between children and teachers.* Washington, DC: American Psychological Association.

Pigott, H. E., Fantuzzo, J. W., & Clement, P. (1986). The effects of reciprocal peer tutoring and group contingencies on the academic performance of elementary school children. *Journal of Applied Behavior Analysis, 19,* 93–98.

Pliszka, S. R., Rogeness, G. A., Renner, P., Sherman, J., & Broussard, T. (1988). Plasma neurochemistry in juvenile offenders. *Journal of the American Academy of Child and Adolescent Psychiatry, 27,* 588–594.

Quiggle, N., Garber, J., Panak, W. F., & Dodge, K. A. (1992). Social-information processing in aggressive and depressed children. *Child Development, 63,* 1305–1320.

Quinn, M. M., Gable, R. A., Fox, J., Rutherford, R. B., Jr., Van Acker, R., Conroy, M., et al. (2001). Putting quality functional assessment into practice in schools: A research agenda on behalf of E/BD students. *Education & Treatment of Children, 24*(3), 261–275.

Raine, A. (1993). *The psychopathology of crime: Criminal behavior as a clinical disorder.* New York: Academic Press.

Reid, J. B., & Eddy, J. M. (1997). The prevention of antisocial behavior; Some considerations in the search for effective interventions. In D. M. Stoff, J. Breiling, & J. D. Maser (Eds.), *Handbook of antisocial behavior* (pp. 343–355). New York: John Wiley & Sons.

Reid, J. B., Eddy, J. M. & Fetrow, R. A. (1999). Description and immediate impacts of a preventive intervention for conduct problems. *American Journal of Community Psychology, 27*(4), 483–517.

Reid, R., Gonzalez, J. E., Nordness, P. D., Trout, A., & Epstein, M. H. (2004). A meta-analysis of the academic status of students with emotional/behavioral disturbance. *The Journal of Special Education, 38*(3), 130–143.

Reid, J. B., Patterson, G. R., & Snyder, J. (2002). *Antisocial behavior in children and adolescents: A developmental analysis and model for intervention.* Washington, DC: American Psychological Association.

Reid, M. J., Webster-Stratton, C., & Baydar, N. (2004). Halting the development of conduct problems in Head Start children: The effects of parent training. *Journal of Clinical Child & Adolescent Psychology, 33*(2), 279–291.

Richman, N., Stevenson, J., & Graham, P. (1982). *Preschool to school: A behavioral study.* San Diego, CA: Academic Press.

Rimm-Kaufman, S. E., Pianta, R. C., & Cox, M. J. (2000). Teachers' judgments of problems in the transition to kindergarten. *Early Childhood Research Quarterly, 15*(2), 147–166.

Rogeness, G. A., Javors, M. A., & Pliszka, S. R. (1992). Neurochemistry and child and adolescent psychiatry. *Journal of the American Academic of Child and Adolescent Psychiatry, 31*, 765–781.

Rohrbeck, C. A., Ginsburg-Block, M. D., Fantuzzo, J. W., & Miller, T. R. (2003). Peer-assisted learning interventions with elementary school students: A meta-analytic review. *Journal of Educational Psychology, 95*(2), 240–257.

Rutter, M., & Giller, H. (1983). *Juvenile delinquency: Trends and perspectives.* Harmondsworth, U.K.: Penguin Books.

Rutter, M., Maughan, B., Mortiore, P., & Ouston, J. (1979). *Fifteen thousand hours.* Cambridge, MA: Harvard University Press.

Rutter, M., & Sroufe, L. A. (2000). Developmental psychopathology: Concepts and challenges. *Development and Psychopathology, 12*, 265–296.

Saft, E. W., & Pianta, R. C. (2001). Teachers' perceptions of their relationships with students: Effects of child age, gender, and ethnicity of teachers and students. *School Psychology Quarterly, 16*(7), 125–140.

Salend, S. J., Reynolds, C. J., & Coyle, E. M. (1989). Individualizing the good behavior game across type and frequency of behavior with emotionally disturbed adolescents. *Behavior Modification, 13*(1), 108–126.

Sampson, R. J., Morenoff, J. D., & Earls, F. (1999). Beyond social capital: Spatial dynamics of collective efficacy for children. *American Sociological Review, 64*(5), 633–660.

Schneider, D. J. (1991). Social cognition. *Annual Review of Psychology, 42*, 527–561.

Sherman, L. W., Gottfredson, D., MacKenzie, D., Eck, J., Reuter, P., & Bushway, S. (1997). *Preventing crime: What works, what doesn't, what's promising. A report to the United States Congress.* Washington, DC: National Institute of Justice.

Shriver, T. P., & Weissberg, R. P. (2005, August 16). No emotion left behind. *New York Times*, p. A15.

Slaby, R. C., & Guerra, N. G. (1988). Cognitive mediators of aggression in adolescent offenders: I. Assessment. *Developmental Psychology, 24*, 580–588.

Sladeczek, I., Kratochwill, T. R., Steinback, C. L., Kumke, P., & Hagermoser, L. (2003). Problem-solving consultation in the new millennium. In E. Cole, J. A. Ester, Siegel, & A. Jane (Eds.), *Effective consultation in school psychology* (pp. 60–86). Ashland, OH: Hogrefe & Huber Publishers.

Skiba, R., Michael, R. S., Nardo, A. C., & Peterson, R. (2002). The color of discipline: Sources of racial and gender disproportionality in school punishment. *The Urban Review, 34*(4), 317–342.

Skiba, R. J., Peterson, R. L., & Williams, T. (1997). Office referrals and suspension: Disciplinary intervention in middle schools. *Education & Treatment of Children, 20*(3), 295–313.

Snyder, J. (2002). Reinforcement and coercion mechanisms in the development of antisocial behavior: Peer relationships. In J. B Reid, G. R. Patterson, & J. Snyder (Eds.), *Antisocial behavior and children in adolescence: The developmental analysis on model for intervention* (pp. 101–122). Washington, DC: American Psychological Association.

Solomon, D., Battistich, V., Watson, M., Schaps, E., & Lewis, C. (2000). A six-district study of educational change: Direct and mediated effects of the Child Development Project. *Social Psychology of Education, 4*, 3–51.

Spivak, G., & Shure, M. B. (1980). Interpersonal problem-solving as a mediator of behavioral adjustment in preschool and kindergarten children. *Journal of Developmental Psychology, 1*, 29–44.

Spoont, M. R. (1992). Modulatory role of serotonin in neural information processing: Implications for human psychopathology. *Psychological Bulletin, 112*, 330–350.

Steinberg, L., Lamborn, S. D., & Darling, N. (1994). Over-time changes in adjustment and competence among adolescents from authoritative, authoritarian, indulgent, and neglectful families. *Child Development, 65*(3), 754–770.

Susman, E. J., Inoff-Germain, G., Nottelmann, E. D., Loriaux, L., Cutler, G. B., & Chrousos, G. P. (1987). Hormones, emotional dispositions, and aggressive attributes in young adolescents. *Child Development, 58,* 1114–1134.

Sutherland, E. H. (1939). *Principles of criminology* (3rd ed.). Philadelphis: Lippincott. Reid, Eddy, & Fetrow, 1999.

Tallal, P., Dukette, D., & Curtiss, S. (1989). Behavioral/emotional profiles of preschool language-impaired children. *Development and Psychopathology, 1,* 51–67.

Taylor-Greene, S. J., & Kartub, D. T. (2000). Durable implementation of school-wide behavior support: The high five program. *Journal of Positive Behavior Interventions, 2,* 233–245.

Thornberrry, T. P., & Krohn, M. D. (1997). Peers, drug use, and delinquency. In D. M. Stoff, J. Breiling, & J. D. Maser (Eds.), *Handbook of antisocial behavior* (pp. 218–233). New York: John Wiley & Sons.

Tingstrom, D. H. (1994) The good behavior game: An investigation of teachers' acceptance. *Psychology in the Schools, 31,* 57–65.

Tolan, P. H., & Guerra, N. G. (1994). Prevention of delinquency: Current status and issues. *Applied & Preventive Psychology, 3*(4), 251–273.

Tolan, P. H., Guerra, N. G., & Kendall, P. C. (1995). A developmental-ecological perspective on antisocial behavior in children and adolescents: Toward a unified risk and intervention framework. *Journal of Consulting and Clinical Psychology, 63*(4), 579–584.

Topping, K. J., & Ehly, S. W. (2001). Peer assisted learning: A framework for consultations. *Journal of Educational and Psychological Consultation, 12*(2), 113–132.

Underwood, M. K. (2003). *Social aggression among girls.* New York: Guilford Press.

Watts, I. E., & Erevelles, N. (2004). These deadly times: Reconceptualizing school violence. *American Educational Research Journal, 41*(2), 271–299.

Webster-Stratton, C. (2005). The incredible years: A training series for the prevention and treatment of conduct problems in young children. In E. D. Hibbs & P. S. Jensen (Eds.), *Psychosocial treatments for child and adolescent disorders: Empirically based strategies for clinical practice* (2nd ed., pp. 507–555). Washington, DC: American Psychological Association.

Webster-Stratton, C., Reid, M. J., & Hammond, M. (2004). Treating children with early onset conduct problems: Intervention outcomes for parent, child, teacher training. *Journal of Clinical Child and Adolescent Psychology, 33*(1), 105–124.

Weinstein, R. S. (2002). *Reaching higher: The power of expectations in schooling.* Cambridge, MA: Harvard University Press.

Weissberg, R. P., & Greenberg, M. T. (1998). School and community competence-enhancement and prevention programs. In W. Damon, I. E. Sigel, & K. A. Renninger (Eds.), *Handbook of child psychology: Vol. 4: Child psychology in practice* (5th ed., pp. 877–954). New York: John Wiley & Sons,.

Wentzel, K. R. (2002). Are effective teachers like good parents? Teaching styles and student adjustment in early adolescence. *Child Development, 73*(1), 287–301.

Werthamer-Larsson, L., Kellam, S. G., & Wheeler, L. (1991). Effect of first-grade classroom environment on shy behavior, aggressive behavior, and concentration problems. *American Journal of Community Psychology, 19*(4), 585–602.

Wilson, D. B., Gottfredson, D. C., & Najaka, S. S. (2001). School-based prevention of problem behaviors: A meta-analysis. *Journal of Quantitative Criminology, 17*(3), 247–272.

Wilson, S. J., Lipsey, M. W., & Derzon, J. H. (2003). The effects of school-based intervention programs on aggressive behavior: A meta-analysis. *Journal of Consulting & Clinical Psychology, 71*(1), 136–149.

Wolfe, J. A., Fantuzzo, J. W., & Wolfe, P. K. (1986). The effects of reciprocal peer management on the arithmetic proficiency of underachieving students. *Behavior Therapy, 17,* 253–265.

Xie, H., Swift, D. J., Cairns, B., & Cairns, R. B. (2002). Aggressive behaviors in social interaction and developmental adaptation: A narrative analysis of interpersonal conflicts during early adolescence. *Social Development, 11*(2), 205–224.

XLII
SUBSTANCE ABUSE

CHRIS WOOD AND LISA HINKELMAN
The Ohio State University

Introduction

Adolescent substance use and abuse is a significant concern in American society. Students in middle school and high school are using illicit substances, including marijuana, amphetamines, alcohol, and cigarettes at alarming rates. School counselors are likely to encounter students dealing with substance use and abuse issues on a regular basis. Doweiko (2002) discusses childhood and adolescence as a time when individuals are especially vulnerable to developing substance abuse disorders. This chapter is designed to provide the reader first with an overview of the prevalence, recent trends, and contributors to adolescent substance use and abuse. Next, information about how the school counselor can intervene in substance abuse situations is included, followed by an introduction and overview of the use of Motivational Interviewing (MI) in the school setting.

Using a case example, the reader will learn to identify a student's level of change within the stages of change model. Next, the principles of MI and the research that supports MI as an effective technique for working with substance use disorders are discussed. Finally, the reader will be provided with strategies for dealing with student resistance and with information on selecting effective treatment programs.

Prevalence

According to the Substance Abuse and Mental Health Services Administration (SAMHSA; 2004), nearly 19.5 million Americans, or 8.2% of the population, over the age of 12 currently use illicit drugs. The percentage of American youth who currently use illicit drugs is 11.2%. The National Institute on Drug Abuse (NIDA) reported in their 2004 Monitoring the Future Study that 51% of the population uses illicit drugs at some point throughout their lifetimes. Nearly 40% of 12th graders reported having used marijuana during the previous 12 months, 10% have used amphetamines, and 48% have used alcohol. SAMHSA also reported that approximately 10.9 million people between the ages of 12 and 20, or 29% of this age group, report drinking alcohol, with 19.2% of this age population engaging in binge drinking, and 6.1% identifying as heavy drinkers. Additionally, approximately 24% of adolescents ages 12 to 17 report smoking cigarettes, with 15% of the adolescent population classified as nicotine dependent (Johnston, O'Malley, Bachman, & Schulenberg, 2005). With this level of prevalence, it is likely that school counselors will encounter many students who are struggling with addictive behaviors.

Gender and Ethnicity

Much of the research that has been conducted on substance abuse has focused primarily on men and boys. Additionally, of the limited research that has specifically examined gender differences in substance use and abuse, ethnic minority girls have been underrepresented (Wallace et al., 2003). A recent national study on adolescent drug use found that use was lowest among African American and Asian American adolescents and highest among White students. Hispanic adolescents had rates of illicit drug use similar to, but slightly less than, their White counterparts had (Johnston et al., 2005).

Males reported higher rates of illicit drug use than females with specific differences in use of smokeless tobacco, steroids, and alcohol. Adolescent boys and girls have nearly identical rates of cigarette smoking (Johnston et al., 2005). Over the years, there has been a convergence in the drug usage rates of boys and girls with the prevalence of use becoming very similar among both genders. Researchers speculate that part of this is due to changes in gender role expectations and acculturation levels of young girls in present society (Wallace et al., 2003). Previously, it was considered "unladylike" for girls to smoke, drink, or engage in illicit drug use. More recently, the social taboos regarding expectations of femininity have changed, allowing girls increased opportunities to engage in activities and behaviors that were previously deemed inappropriate for their gender. While this change has resulted in increased opportunities for girls in a variety of arenas, it has also resulted in more girls choosing to engage in the use and abuse of licit and illicit substances.

Recent Trends

An understanding of the recent trends in adolescent substance use and the factors related to illicit drug use is imperative for a school counselor's effective intervention with substance abusing students. The usage reports of the adolescent substances use have remained relatively consistent over the past few years, maintaining a level lower than their peak in the early 1990s. However, there have been slight decreases reported by adolescents in the use of "any illicit drug" and similar decreases in the accessibility and use of drugs such as LSD, heroin, Rohypnol, and Ecstasy (Johnston et al., 2005). Slight increases were reported in the use of psychotherapeutic drugs taken nonmedically, including pain relievers, tranquilizers, stimulants and sedatives (SAMSHA, 2004) and significant increases were reported in the use of inhalants and OxyContin (Johnston et al., 2005). This trend indicates that adolescents are using substances that are readily available to them and that may be found in their home medicine cabinet or at their local grocery store. Accessing a family member's painkillers or purchasing items such as spray paint, cans of whipped cream, and other inhalants may not be readily apparent to parents and guardians, and as a result, substance use may not be identified for some time. School counselors can assist in training parents and families about these recent trends and help them to identifying the substances that might be in their homes that have the potential to be abused.

Contributors to Adolescent Substance Abuse

Children and adolescents experiment with alcohol and illicit substances for a variety of reasons. Adolescents report using substances as a way to experiment, to feel good, and to enhance social activities (Parks & Kennedy, 2004). Youth also attribute substance use to the influence of friends, the need for pleasure, and the personal curiosity associated with trying something new (De Micheli & Formigoni, 2002). While some adolescent substance experimentation appears somewhat innocuous and part of the typical adolescent experience, others report using substances as coping mechanisms for handling depression (Boys, Marsden, & Strang, 2001).

Researchers have attempted to understand the situational, familial, and environmental factors that contribute to adolescent substance use and abuse. Nunes and Parson (1995) reported that multiple factors impact adolescent substance abuse, including poor parent–child relationships; psychiatric disorders, especially depression; family and peer substance use; low academic motivation; behavioral problems; early cigarette use; low self-esteem; single-parent or stepparent families; and a high number of family stressors. The early use of tobacco and alcohol was also found to predict future substance use as well as accelerate the substance use by adolescents (Clark, Cornelius, Kirisci, & Tarter, 2005). Bailey and McCloskey (2005) found that adolescent girls with a history of sexual abuse were more likely to abuse illicit substances than girls who had not been previously sexually abused. Similarly, boys are also negatively impacted by abusive environments, and such environments can influence their future likelihood of substance use (Kirisci, Dunn, Mezzich, & Tarter, 2001). Specifically, researchers (Clark et al.; Kirisci et al.) have found that parents with a substance abuse diagnosis were more likely to abuse or neglect their children and that boys who were neglected as children and young adolescents were more likely to be substance abusers in late adolescence and early adulthood (Kirisci et al.).

Parents can be very influential in the lives of their adolescent children as it relates to substance use (Kelly, Comello, & Hunn, 2002; King, Vidourek, & Wagner, 2003; Nash, McQueen, & Bray, 2005), and children identify their parents as the people that have talked to them most about drug use (Kelly et al.). Adolescents who have a positive family environment have fewer friends that drink alcohol and have increased self-efficacy for refusing to drink alcohol (Nash et al.). Additionally, researchers have found that parents who spent a greater amount of time with their children were more likely to have children that did not use drugs. Conversely, parents who spent little time with their children and parents who use illicit substances are much more likely to have children who use drugs and alcohol (King et al.).

The school environment and school related factors are also related to adolescent substance use. D. J. Eitle and T. M. Eitle (2004) found that the school climate impacted the rates of illicit drug issues at the school. Specifically, schools that have students who are not committed to the mission of the school, that have predominately White students, that lack resources for students, and that have lower credentialed teachers and staff have a higher percentage of illicit drug offenses than other schools (Eitle & Eitle). Student truancy rates and grade point average are also predictors of drug use (Hallfors et al., 2002). Hallfors and colleagues discovered that the marijuana use of both 8th grade students and 12th grade students was correlated to their truancy rates and grade point averages. Students who were frequently truant and who had grade point averages below 2.5 were more likely to use illicit substances. Conversely, students who planned to attend college were less likely to use some illicit substances including cocaine, heroin, stimulants, and hallucinogens (Johnston, O'Malley, & Bachman, 2003).

Protective Factors

While there are numerous risk factors associated with adolescent substance abuse, there are several protective factors that help youth resist substance use and abuse. Risk factors, like those just mentioned, are antecedents that increase the probability that that substance abuse will exist, while protective factors serve as moderators and can reduce the effects of the exposure to risk (Hawkins, Van Horn, & Arthur, 2004). The goal is to build in enough protective factors in the lives of youth at risk to offset the exposure to the risk factors.

Clinton-Sherrod, Sobeck, Abbey, Agius, and Terry (2005) found that there are protective skills that adolescents can develop through their interactions with family, friends, community, and school that help youth abstain from using illicit substances. Specifically, their research found that African American sixth-grade students who had developed good decision-making skills, had higher self-efficacy, had lower peer pressure susceptibility, and had attitudes about school that were more positive were less likely to use substances. Other individual factors found serve as protective factors in youth substance abuse, including the ethnic and racial identity of urban African American young adults (Brook & Pahl, 2005). Brook and Pahl's research on African American youth found that adolescents with high levels of ethnic and racial identity, high identification with African American friends, and high valuation of their nuclear and extended families were able to resist the use of illicit substances.

As previously noted, individual characteristics can serve as protective factors; however, community and familial characteristics can also be protective factors in the lives of adolescents (Hays, Hays, & Mulhall, 2004). Communities that have appropriate and available child care, opportunities and rewards for prosocial involvement, and members with high social skills also enjoy a reduced rate of substance use (Hawkins et al., 2004; Hays et al.). Parenting style has also been found to relate to youth substance abuse, specifically, parenting that is authoritative and warm with higher levels of monitoring and lower levels of coerciveness is most effective in reducing adolescent substance use (Hays et al.).

School counselors are in a unique position to impact families and communities through collaboration with other school professionals including social workers, psychologists, nurses, and administrators to provide training and resources to parents and community members on the importance of protective factors in the lives of children. Through these strength-based collaborative efforts, school counselors can work to build resilient schools, families, neighborhoods, and communities with an emphasis on the strengths that an individual or family possesses rather than on the risk factors or deficits that are present. In this way, the school counselor can effectively serve as a resource and a liaison between the school, family, and community (McLaughlin & Vacha, 1993).

Prevention Efforts

In recognition of the prevalence, trends, and contributors to adolescent drug and alcohol use, the United States federal government allocated resources for the prevention of drug use among America's youth. In 1994, The Drug Free Schools Act was expanded into the Safe and Drug Free Schools and Communities Act. This Act was authorized under Title IV of the *Elementary and Secondary Education Act* (ESEA) of 1965 and was designed to provide local, state, and national funding for research-based drug and violence prevention programming in elementary and secondary schools and institutions of higher education. According to the White House Office of the Press Secretary (U.S. Department of Health & Human Services, 1998), the Safe and Drug-Free Schools Program provides support for prevention programming to 97% of America's school districts. Currently the Safe and Drug Free Schools and Communities Act is administered by the U.S. Department of Education under the No Child Left Behind Act of 2001 (P. L. 107-110). This effort is focused on comprehensive programming to promote safety, development, and positive outcomes for students while decreasing the use of alcohol, tobacco, and other drugs.

Through the administration of community service grants, governors' grants, and state formula grants, individual states can apply for funds to combat drugs and violence in their schools. Nationally, discretionary grants are available for through the Drug-Violence Prevention National Programs and include prevention programming for college campuses, school-based drug-testing programs, alcohol abuse programming, mentoring grants, and several additional drug and violence prevention programs (U.S. Office of Management and Budget and Federal Agencies [USOMB & FA], 2006).

In 2002, the U.S. Department of Education created a Safe and Drug-Free Schools office that is home to all federal safe schools, crisis response, alcohol and drug prevention, character education, and health and wellness programs, including Safe and Drug-Free Schools National Programs, Safe and Drug-Free Schools State Programs, Physical Education, School Counselors, School Emergency Response to Violence, Character Education, Civic Education, National Clearinghouse for Education Facilities, and Correctional Education ("Safe and Drug-Free Schools Office Created," 2002).

The Safe and Drug Free Schools Office provides state grants that are specifically designed to "help create and maintain drug-free, safe, and orderly environments for learning in and around schools" (USOMB & FA, 2006). These state grants are awarded to school districts with "research based approaches to drug and violence prevention to reduce youth crime and drug abuse" (USOMB & FA). Since 2002, this program has failed to demonstrate effectiveness in reducing youth drug use and violent crime, and has been deemed "ineffective" (USOMB & FA) by the U.S. government. The assessment of the program indicates that the funds are spread too thin to be effective, and that program is currently not performing. Thus, at the outset, there is little evidence that this government initiative has been effective in making an impact on the actual substance use of teens.

Role of the School Counselor in Intervention

In addition to the various governmental funding opportunities for substance abuse prevention programs, schools and communities also seek ways to reduce the substance abusing behavior of their students and the school counselor is often expected to support and implement substance abuse prevention and intervention programming. Lambie and Rokutani (2002) asserted that the school counselor has a unique opportunity to work closely with students, parents, teachers, and administrators and can use these relationships and access to intervene early in cases of suspected substance abuse. In order for the school counselor to effectively intervene in such situations, he or she must first understand the scope of the problem (Lambie & Rokutani). In addition to the contributors to and predictors of substance abuse mentioned previously, school counselors should be aware of additional warning signs and symptoms of substance abuse including changes in students' moods and behavior, drops in grades, truancies (Lambie & Rokutani), and increased sexual activity (Hallfors et al., 2002).

Lambie and Rokutani (2002) identified four tasks of school counselors in working with students with possible substance abuse issues, including identifying the warning signs of substance abuse, working with the student to develop an effective therapeutic alliance, supporting the family in order to promote change, and acting as a liaison between the student, family, school, and community agencies and/or treatment programs. The school counselor should be equipped with skills and confidence to intervene when he or she suspects that a student is abusing drugs or alcohol.

School counselors intervening with a student who is using drugs or alcohol need to be aware of the unique issues that exist in schools. The school setting does not provide the ideal environment for intensive substance abuse treatment. Moreover, school counselors do not have the time to provide such treatment given the many demands of their job. However, the school counselor can effectively support students, provide brief interventions that will assist students abusing substances, and provide linkages between the adolescent and the other systems in which he or she functions (Lambie & Rokutani, 2002). In doing this, the school counselor can increase the likelihood that students will enter and adhere to treatment.

There are times when students will disclose substance use or abuse to the school counselor and ask the school counselor to maintain the confidentiality of the student. The counselor's role in a situation where there are ethical or legal implications can be difficult to define and is often based upon state laws, school district policies, and interpretations of various ethical codes. While federal law protects the confidentiality of minors seeking drug or alcohol treatment (Fisher & Harrison, 2005), school counselors may not always be protected by this law. School counselors are not always considered "mental health professionals," and because they are not providing alcohol or drug diagnosis and treatment services, the federal regulations that govern confidentiality regarding substance abuse treatment might not apply uniformly to all school counselors (Fisher & Harrison).

While students are the school counselor's primary obligation, parents of minor students have legal rights to knowledge and information about their child. A school counselor has an ethical obligation to the student but a legal obligation to the parent (Remley & Herlihy, 2005). In order to work most effectively with students, the school counselor must develop an effective therapeutic relationship with the children. In adolescents, this rapport is generally fostered through a commitment of confidentiality on the part of the counselor (Remley & Herlihy), which has obvious limits. Remley and Herlihy and Stone (2005) suggested taking proactive steps regarding the handling of confidential information to minimize the negative impact on both students and parents.

Stone (2005) suggested informing students, parents, teachers, and school personnel about the limits of confidentially before it becomes an issue; informing teachers that the school counselor will consult with them when it is necessary and in the best interest of the child; and working with students to encourage them to share information with their parents, perhaps with the school counselor present as a support. It is also very important for school counselors to be knowledgeable about the school board policies; local, state, and federal regulations; and professional codes of ethics that govern their profession.

School counselors require an approach that takes into account the role of the school counselor and is consistent with the school counselor's unique position as a helping professional operating in the school setting. MI is an innovative approach school counselors can utilize in working to help students change problematic behaviors.

Motivational Interviewing

MI is a counseling approach developed by Miller and Rollnick (1991, 2002) that can assist students with the process of change. While originally conceptualized as an approach for working with individuals with addictive behaviors, the approach has been used successfully with a range of behavioral changes including physical exercise (Harland et al., 1999), weight reduction (Smith, Heckemeyer, Kratt, & Mason, 1997), bulimia (Treasure et al., 1999), marijuana use (Stephens, Roffman, & Curtin, 2000), and alcoholism (Project Match Research Group, 1997, 1998). Burke, Arkowitz, and Menchola (2003) conducted a meta-analysis of 30 controlled clinical research trials that investigated MI or Adaptations of Motivational Interviewing (AMI). Overall, they determined that the research supported the efficacy of AMIs for problems involving alcohol and drugs, as well as diet and exercise.

Using MI in Schools

MI is an ideal approach for school counselors to use in counseling students who exhibit addictive behaviors. The brief nature of MI poses a time/cost-effective strategy given the large student-to-school-counselor ratio that exists in many school settings. Moreover, since MI is designed to build in individuals the capacity for change rather than to be an actual treatment modality, the MI approach is consistent with the role of the school counselor in helping the student seek treatment rather than actually providing ongoing counseling for addictive behaviors. Lastly, the guiding principles of MI help to differentiate the school counselor from other educators/administrators who may have a more confrontational or disciplinarian orientation with the student.

The use of MI in schools requires a shift in theory and approach to working with students who use and abuse substances. The focus of MI is centered upon how motivated the people are to change as opposed to how resistant they are (Tevyaw & Monti, 2004). Adolescents are often challenging to work with in a therapeutic relationship due to their developmental level and their need for autonomy (Lambie & Rokutani, 2002); therefore, the use of a confrontational intervention can serve to completely disengage the student. Lambie (2004) posited, "A practical school counseling approach needs to provide strategies that in a brief amount of time would assist students who may be unmotivated to change" (p. 268).

MI utilizes a harm reduction approach, not an abstinence based approach, and the interventions are tailored specifically for each individual student and his or her present situation and level of motivation to change (Tevyaw & Monti, 2004). It is a brief intervention that is flexible and emphasizes the freedom of choice of the student (Lawendowski, 1998). Lawendowski asserted, "A brief, motivational intervention consisting of just one or two sessions holds promise as a treatment for adolescents with substance abuse problems" (p. 41). MI and motivational enhancement therapies are effective in decreasing substance use and increasing treatment engagement in adolescents (Tevyaw & Monti).

To counsel students with addictive behaviors, it is first necessary to have an understanding of both (a) how addictions develop and (b) how people change behaviors. The process of developing addictions and the process of changing addictive behaviors involve the same stages of change. With an understanding of the stages of change, school counselors can utilize MI techniques specific to the appropriate stage for the student. In this fashion, school counselors can facilitate a student's progression toward positive behavioral change.

Stages of Change

Prochaska and DiClemente (1982) developed a Transtheoretical Model (TTM) of behavioral change. This model posits 6 phases in the process of intentional behavior change that can be described as the Stages of Change (DiClemente, 2003). These stages are (a) precontemplation, (b) contemplation, (c) preparation, (d) action, (e) maintenance, and (f) termination. Movement through these stages of change is generally recursive and cyclical (see Figure 42.1). Each of these stages has unique characteristics. There is an identifiable "goal" to be achieved in each specific stage. Similarly, students engaged in the process of change must successfully complete the necessary tasks of each stage in order to successfully progress toward the subsequent stage. Figure 42.2 describes the student goals for each stage of change and the corresponding school counselor tasks for working with students in that stage. School counselors assisting individuals with the process of change can benefit from being aware of the stages of change, the goals for each stage, and the necessary tasks for each of the 6 stages.

Precontemplation

As Figure 42.1 illustrates, precontemplation is the stage prior to entering the cycle of change. Students in the precontemplation stage do not feel the need to change current patterns of behavior or do not see convincing reasons to consider behavioral change. Or they do not believe that the negative repercussions of the current behavior outweigh the costs of actively engaging in behavior change. "As long as the current pattern of behavior seems functional for the individual or no compelling reason arises to disrupt this pattern, an individual can remain in precontemplation for extended periods of time, even a lifetime" (DiClemente, 2003, p. 26).

Students in precontemplation may seem the most frequently encountered by school counselors. Generally, students in the precontemplation stage (precontemplators) are seen as highly "resistant" or unwilling to respond to counseling interventions. Conceptualizing students in the precontemplation stage as one of the four categories of precontemplators can assist school counselors in using more facilitative methods for helping students move toward change.

There are four types of precontemplators: (1) reluctant, (2) rebellious, (3) resigned, and (4) rationalizing (DiClemente, 1991; DiClemente & Velasquez, 2002). Each type of precontemplator is characterized by the primary way in which he or she avoids considering change.

Reluctant precontemplators are students who lack full awareness of their problematic addictive behavior and are therefore passively resistant. These students do not wish to risk change, as they do not see any potential benefits to changing their current status quo.

In contrast, rebellious precontemplators are actively resistant to change. Students who are rebellious precontemplators often have strong feelings against change and may have a heavy investment in their current addictive behavior. These students do not like being told what to do

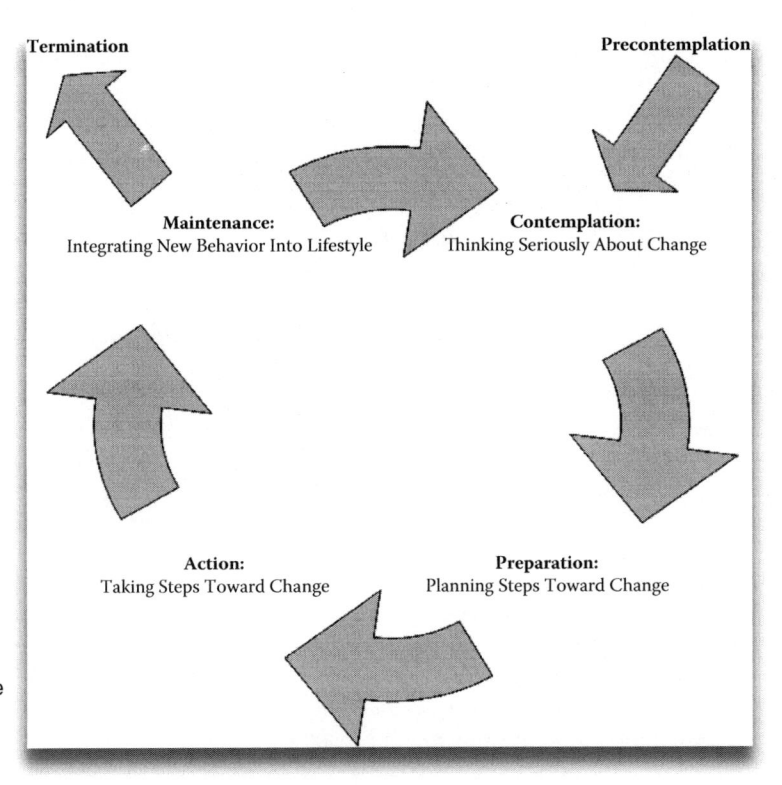

Figure 42.1 The Cycle of Change Adapted from DiClemente (2003).

Stage	Goal for Student	School Counselor Task
Precontemplation	Gaining awareness of the reasons for change; seriously considering possibility of change	• Increase student awareness of the reasons for considering change • Explore internal and environmental influences on maintaining the status quo
Contemplation	A reasoned evaluation that increases a student's commitment to change	• Help student weigh pros & cons of change • Help student tilt the decisional balance scale in favor of change
Preparation	A clearly articulated plan for change with sustaining student self-efficacy	• Assess the student's commitment to the change process • Help the student develop a plan for change that he/she believes has a strong likelihood for success
Action	Continued implementation of plan for change	• Support and affirm student's continued efforts toward change • Help student revise plan for change as necessary
Maintenance	Sustained new behavior that is mutually exclusive of previous behavior	• Reinforce student's commitment to new choices/lifestyle • Help student recover from setbacks and continue building on partial successes

Figure 42.2 The Stages of Change. Based on the work of DiClemente (2003) and Miller and Rollnick (2002).

and may even be hostile toward the proposal of a specific strategy for change.

Resigned precontemplators lack the energy to invest in change and are prepared to accept that their current behavior is inevitable. For these students, the problem seems overwhelming and the barriers to change are too great to warrant an investment of time or energy into the change process.

The fourth type of precontemplator is the rationalizing precontemplator. "These clients are not considering change because they have figured out the odds of personal risk, or they have plenty of reasons why the problem is not a problem or is a problem for others but not for them" (DiClemente, 1991, p. 193). Students who are rationalizing precontemplators sometimes like to "debate" their rationale for their current behavior—thus reinforcing their position against change.

The primary goal for the precontemplation stage is for the student to seriously consider the possibility of change. Since there has been little or no consideration of change of behavior in the foreseeable future, reaching this goal can be a formidable achievement. For the precontemplating student to envision change as a possibility requires successful completion of the major tasks in this stage.

The necessary tasks in the precontemplation stage include increasing student awareness of the need to change. Multiple internal and environmental influences impact the student reasoning for considering change: social pressure, human development, relationships, values, economic pressure, and so forth. Consideration of the current behavior within the context of these influences can compel a student to explore the possibility of changing current patterns of behavior.

Increasing concern about the current pattern of behavior is an important task for the precontemplation stage. This task involves gaining an awareness of potential reasons for change as well as those factors that may positively or negatively impact the student's ability to even begin to consider change.

Instilling hope is perhaps the most profound task for the precontemplation stage. This means exploring the barriers to change and generating productive strategies for overcoming such obstacles. Students in the precontemplation stage may lack hope due to previously unsuccessful change attempts in the current pattern or other patterns of behavior. It is important for the student in this stage to realize that a setback in the change process is expected and inherently different from a complete failure.

Contemplation

In the contemplation stage, the student is weighing the risks associated with change against the potential benefits. This analysis becomes a period of instability for the student. Students may struggle with ambivalent or confusing thoughts and feelings about a given behavior pattern as they consider the possibility of change. "The contemplation stage involves a process of evaluating risks and benefits, the pros and cons of both the current behavior pattern and the potential new behavior pattern" (DiClemente, 2003, p. 28).

Students in the contemplation stage are not yet ready to actively commit to the process of change. They are still gathering information and considering options. "Contemplation is the stage when clients are quite open to information and decisional balance considerations. Yet it is also the stage where many students are waiting for the one final piece of information that will compel them to change" (DiClemente, 1991, p. 195).

The goal for this stage, then, is a thoroughly reasoned evaluation that reinforces a student's decision to change. This evaluation should comprise the carefully considered risks and benefits of change. It is important for school counselors to remember that this goal involves an awareness of both sides of the change issue (costs and benefits) because failing to explore either side may hinder the accomplishment of the goal and tasks for the contemplation stage and create further ambiguity for the student.

The task for the contemplation stage is to conduct a thorough analysis of the advantages and disadvantages of the current behavior. This analysis needs to include both the affective and cognitive rewards of the current behavior and the stake involved in change. At the same time, the student needs to fully realize the costs of continuing the current behavior and the potential return on the investment in an endeavor to change. Again, it essential for the school counselor to help the student see the advantages as well as the disadvantages of the current behavior. Focusing only on the disadvantages of the current behavior (as traditional substance abuse models have done) may force students to oppositionally side with the advantages and hinder progression toward other stages.

Preparation

Students in the preparation stage are ready to make a change in the near future. "Preparation takes you from the decisions you make in the contemplation stage to the specific steps you take to solve the problem during the action stage" (Prochaska, Norcross, & DiClemente, 1994, p. 146). The decisional balance in the contemplation stage has been tipped in favor of change and students in this stage are determined to make an attempt at change.

The primary goal for the preparation stage is to formalize a plan of action. The plan of action needs to be a specific, detailed list of the steps necessary to engage in active progress toward change. The plan of action must include those crucial elements necessary to continue the student's initial energy toward action.

Inherent in a plan of action are several critical elements. Students must believe in the feasibility of the plan. They need to see the plan as possessing a strong likelihood for bringing about the desired outcome (the new behavior). Moreover, students need to believe in their own ability to successfully engage in the steps necessary to complete their plan of action. The tasks of the preparation stage involve reinforcing the students' commitments to change and helping them determine the best plans of action.

As part of the task of developing a plan of action there are several important considerations. The student's previous experiences with change should be considered to strategize a plan that has optimal potential for success. Similarly, considering the potential difficulties that could be encountered during the plan is also useful to prepare for action. Finally, as mentioned previously, the student's courage and competency to be successful in the plan are key components of the student's potential to implement any plan of action.

Action

The action stage is the implementation of the plan generated in the preparation stage. In the action stage, students make the move toward altering their behavior. This stage of change requires the greatest commitment of time and energy. For these reasons, this stage is also characterized by an attraction to the old patterns of behavior. It is often easier to return to the previous behavior than to follow through on the plan and begin to sustain a new behavior.

The goal for this stage is to establish a new pattern of behavior. In addition to the major task of implementing the plan of action, additional tasks include sustaining commitment in the face of obstacles to the plan and revising the plan as necessary in order to maintain the enterprise of change.

Maintenance

As Figure 42.1 represents, maintenance is the final stage before exiting the change process. In this stage, "the new behavior must become integrated into the lifestyle of the individual" (DiClemente, 2003, p. 29).

The maintenance stage is distinguished by the clear absence of the previous behavior and the sustained presence of the new behavior. There may still be, however, the urges and temptations to return to the previous behavior. "In the maintenance stage the person works to consolidate the gains made during the action stage and struggles to prevent relapse" (DiClemente & Velasquez, 2002, p. 212).

It is important to note that relapse is not a collapse of the change process. People often "recycle" through one or more stages before successfully negotiating the maintenance stage and exiting the change process into termination.

Success in the maintenance stage allows the new behavior to become "automatic" and the new "status quo" (DiClemente, 2003). Ultimately then, the student is able to exit the process of change (termination), with the new behavior as an integrated part of a new lifestyle.

Termination

Termination is the final exit from the process of change. This is not so much a stage as such but rather a new state of being where a new behavior has replaced the old behavior, and in fact, it would take a substantial amount of effort to go back to the old behavior. In reference to addictive behaviors, this state is sometimes referred to as "recovery." The goals and tasks of termination focus on the new way of being that does not include the previous behavior. "The entire gestalt of life now supports a new lifestyle committed to not engaging in the addictive behavior" (DiClemente, 2003, p. 201).

The preceding discussion of the stages of change addresses primarily the change process for addictive behaviors. As may already be apparent, however, the stages are indicative of any behavioral change. This process also applies to other behaviors that may be problematic for students, such as absenteeism, procrastination, bullying, and other achievement related behaviors. The remainder of this chapter explains in detail the tenets of MI. The following case example demonstrates how school counselors can identify the stages of change in the TTM and practically utilize MI with substance abusing students.

Case Example

Billy is a 16-year-old high school junior who was recently caught drinking at a school football game. When Billy returned from a one-week suspension, the principal asked the school counselor to speak to Billy and determine if Billy will seek counseling for his "problem." Before speaking with Billy, the school counselor gathers more information from Billy's school records. In the 9th grade, Billy was an honor student but his grades began to slip in the 10th grade, and he is currently failing two of his six classes according to his most recent progress report. Also noteworthy are the teacher comments on his progress reports and final grades. For 9th grade, teachers' comments included "Pleasure to have in class" and "Works conscientiously." In subsequent years, the teacher comments changed to "Work consistently lacks effort" and "Assignments not completed." School records also show an address change indicating that Billy moved to live with his mother at the start of 11th grade.

Case Example and the Stages of Change

This case example can be used to demonstrate how a school counselor can use the TTM stages of change to conceptualize work with a student. This conceptualization can help a school counselor understand Billy's situation and develop a strategy to help him. What stage(s) of change is Billy negotiating?

Billy has not come to see the school counselor voluntarily. Because he has not come to see the school counselor of his own accord, it seems unlikely that he will want to discuss treatment options for drug/alcohol. Most likely, Billy is in either the precontemplation or the contemplation stage. Perhaps the following exchange between Billy and his school counselor will help illuminate the stage of change regarding his behavior.

Billy: I don't see what the big deal is, everybody drinks at football games, I just happened to get caught.
School counselor: So one difference between you and your classmates is that your drinking has started to cause you some negative consequences.
Billy: Well, the suspension's not really that big a deal, it's my first one ever. It's just a matter of being in the wrong place at the wrong time.
School counselor: Getting caught was just a matter of bad luck and had nothing to do with your behavior.
Billy: Pretty much, I mean, most people don't actually bring their stuff to the game they drink before.
School counselor: So, another difference between you and some of your classmates is that you take alcohol with you to school events.
Billy: Yes, but I don't do it all the time.

Note that for every statement the school counselor makes, Billy takes an opposing perspective. This dialogue suggests that Billy is in the precontemplation stage. Although he does hint at some of the drawbacks of his behavior, he has convinced himself that change is unnecessary. For these reasons, Billy would most aptly be categorized as a rationalizing precontemplator.

Understanding the stage of change for Billy's problematic behavior allows the school counselor to select a strategy and specific techniques. The general principles of MI (Miller & Rollnick, 1991, 2002) provide a guiding character as well as specific strategies for school counselors to use in helping students with addictive behaviors in the different stages of change. Following these principles and the specific strategies for the stages of change will assist school counselors in helping students toward changing problematic behaviors.

MI posits four guiding principles to underscore the school counselor's orientation toward the student. These four principles underscore the character of the MI approach and the subsequent strategies for each stage of behavioral change. The principles are (a) express empathy, (b) develop discrepancy, (c) roll with resistance, and (d) support self-efficacy.

Express empathy. The first principle is to consistently express empathy immediately and throughout the change process. The emphasis should be on understanding the student's perspective and be free of blame or judgment. While a school counselor may not agree with the student behavior or approve of student choices, it is still possible to maintain a climate of acceptance.

An overall climate of acceptance facilitates change. Conversely, judgment and blame tend to immobilize the change process. A good way to think of this is to realize that a climate of acceptance frees people to change rather than forcing them to devote energy toward resisting judgment. School counselors need to realize that the school setting in general is not a climate of acceptance and that students (especially those with problematic behaviors) often feel judged by the adults in a school setting.

Related to the notion of acceptance is the understanding that ambivalence is normal and even a healthy part of the change process. "Ambivalence is accepted as a normal part of human experience and change, rather than seen as pathology or pernicious defensiveness" (Miller & Rollnick, 2002, p. 37). Often, ambivalent feelings and thoughts are seen as unhealthy manifestations of unwillingness to engage in positive change—"denial" or "resistance." An important concept of MI, however, is to view ambivalence as a normal part of the change process—to be respected with empathy as with all student experiences and perspectives. Understanding and accepting a student's ambivalence about change then becomes an essential component of being an empathic school counselor.

The principle of expressing empathy is demonstrated using counseling skills. Counseling skills are used to develop an awareness and understanding of student experiences. Through skillful reflective listening, the school counselor is able to step into the student's phenomenal space and thus empathically share his or her perspective. Moreover, counseling skills are also used to express the empathic understanding of student perspective through paraphrasing of messages and feelings.

Consider the opportunities for expressing empathy with Billy, the student described in the case example. Imagine that Billy is expressing ambivalence over his problematic behavior.

Billy: Well, I would like to do better in school, but I would hate to give up all the good times at parties with my friends.

School counselor: Part of you is worried that your excessive drinking and partying are creating difficulties for you at school and part of you can't seem to even imagine not going out drinking with your friends.

While other empathic statements are certainly possible, the school counselor's response provides an example of skillful reflective listening that expresses understanding of the student's perspective.

Develop discrepancy. The second principle that underlies MI is to develop discrepancy between a student's present behavior and his or her goals and values. It is important to note that the school counselor is to "develop" or "amplify" this discrepancy as initiated by the student and within the context of the student's perspective—and not to artificially "create" the discrepancy by imposing the school counselor's perspective or value system. In one sense, the school counselor is helping the student to identify and clarify the student's personal goals and values. Concurrently, the school counselor is helping to bring to the awareness of the student, the conflict between the student's current behavior and student's preferred state of being.

This discrepancy is of course the motivation for change. In order for change to occur, students must be aware of the discrepancy between their current behavior and their desired self. Moreover, it is the awareness of this discrepancy and the belief in their ability to successfully bring about change that fuels student energy to actively continue the process of change.

In utilizing the principal of developing discrepancy, the school counselor places the responsibility for change on the student. "When Motivational Interviewing is done well, it is not the counselor but the client who gives voice to concerns, reasons for change, self-efficacy, and intentions to change" (Miller & Rollnick, 2002, p. 39).

In the case example, the school counselor's last paraphrase to the student is an example of beginning to develop discrepancy.

School counselor: Part of you is worried that your excessive drinking and partying are creating difficulties for you at school and part of you can't seem to even imagine not going out drinking with your friends.

Here, the school counselor is using a paraphrase of message from the student and structuring the paraphrase so as to highlight the student concerns about his changing his present behavior. It is important to note the nonconfrontational style of the school counselor response.

Billy: I mean I know school is important and all that—but these are my last two years of high school and I don't want to miss out on anything.
School counselor: Tell me what is important to you about school.
Billy: Well I want to graduate on time. Also I'd like to go to college and eventually get a good job.
School counselor: So passing your classes and graduating with your classmates is something you value. You'd like to go to college and you see success in school as helping toward that. Tell me about the other values you mentioned, partying and friends.
Billy: I love to hang out with my friends. Most of us drink, but I guess it doesn't always have to be about that.

It is important to remember that ultimately the reasons for change come from the student, not the school counselor. The school counselor is helping the student see the discrepancies between the student's present behavior and the student goals or values. "When Motivational Interviewing is done well, it is not the school counselor but the client who gives voice to concerns, reasons for change, self-efficacy, and intentions to change" (Miller & Rollnick, 2002, p. 39).

Roll with resistance. The third foundational principle of MI is to "roll with resistance" (Miller & Rollnick, 2002). School counselors sometimes conceptualize resistance as a quality in the student—an unwillingness to move toward positive growth. In the MI approach, however, resistance is more appropriately conceptualized as a function of the school counselor–student dynamics. In one sense, resistance is created by confrontational encounter with another person or an interaction that engenders defensiveness on the part of the individual.

One way to deal with resistance or defensiveness is to try to overpower it with convincing arguments. This approach may just cause the student to become increasingly entrenched in his or her present position. Another approach, however is to avoid arguing or trying to convince the student of the need to change—but rather to roll with resistance and allow the student to drive the impetus for change.

Rolling with resistance calls for a school counselor to take several stances with a student. First, the school counselor should not argue for specified change or try to convince the student of the need to change. Similarly, the school counselor should not directly oppose defensiveness presented by the student. Rather, the school counselor should interpret the presence of resistance as a directive to change approaches. Consistently, the school counselor must maintain the attitude that the student is the primary resource for generating solutions to the current situation.

It is not the school counselor's responsibility to find all the answers—and attempting to do so may just cause a student to find fault in each proposed suggestion. Ultimately, the student will be living with the new lifestyle; it only makes sense that the changes are built on the strategies determined by the student.

School counselor: While part of you wants to reduce your partying, another part of you is worried about how your friends will react to such a change (*Develop discrepancy*).
Billy: I don't think I'm an alcoholic or anything. I mean, I've never hurt anybody else or myself, and I've never had any legal trouble or anything like that.
School counselor: I'm not here to "label" you as addict, diagnose any "problem," or convince you to do anything you don't want to do. I'm just here to help you take a look at your current situation and how you'd like things to be. One thing you feel proud about is that you've never hurt anyone else when you've been drinking (*Express empathy*). Tell me more about the things you feel good about in your social life (*Roll with resistance*).

Support self-efficacy. One of the most important guiding principles in the MI approach is the conviction to support self-efficacy. "Perceived self-efficacy refers to beliefs in one's capabilities to organize and execute the courses of action required to produce given attainments" (Bandura, 1997, p. 3). Obviously, the belief in one's ability to successfully bring about change is an important precursor to engaging in change. Students who do not believe they are able to go through the process of change successfully are less likely to even attempt change. Thus, a school counselor must consistently support the self-efficacy of students throughout the change process. The following dialogue highlights supporting self-efficacy in the process of change.

Billy: I don't know if I can really follow through with being part of a treatment group. I'm not very good at talking in front of others.
School counselor: You've been very good at sharing your perspective with me. You also mentioned that your friends really seem to trust and respect you. I believe those strengths could help you be very successful in a group.

Following the previously described guiding principles of MI, there are additional strategies that can assist a student with change. Facilitating "change-talk," responding appropriately to resistance, and strengthening the commitment to change are MI strategies that utilize specific counseling techniques to assist students.

Change-talk. Change-talk is dialogue between school counselor and student that is oriented toward the advantages of behavioral change. This dialogue tends to fall into four categories: (a) disadvantages of the status quo, (b) advantages of change, (c) optimism about change, and (d) intention to change (Miller & Rollnick, 2002). To facilitate change-talk a school counselor will want to ask specific, open-ended questions in the subsequent order of the four given categories. Consider how these open-ended questions can be used with the case example.

1. Disadvantages of status quo

School counselor: What worries you about your current situation?
Billy: I was already behind on assignments and now it's worse since I've been suspended. The week stresses me out so much I can only look forward to the weekend, and then I'm so exhausted from partying Friday night that I can't focus on doing any schoolwork Saturday.
School counselor: You're afraid that you are so far behind on assignments that catching up seems impossible. While you enjoy the release of partying Friday night, the consequences are you feel bad Saturday and can't get any homework done.
Billy: Yeah, it's kind of a bad trap I guess. I should cut back on my drinking—at least until I catch up.

The school counselor used an open-ended question to elicit the student's perspective on the disadvantages of the status quo. Then the school counselor carefully paraphrased the disadvantages expressed by the student.

School counselor: Why do you think you need to do something about your partying?
Billy: I guess I'm sick of feeling tired all the time—and it's not just the weekends anymore.
School counselor: In what ways does this concern you?
Billy: Well, I don't want to be like some loser drunk who can't hold down a job.
School counselor: What do you think will happen if you don't change anything?
Billy: I'll probably fail most of my classes and I won't be able to graduate with the rest of my class.

The preceding discussion between student and school counselor illustrates how the example open-ended questions can be used to evoke a discussion of the disadvantages of the status quo. The dialogue presented here is an accelerated example of a discussion that likely needs to be conducted in much greater depth with the student. It is important to note that in the example above, as with discussions in greater depth, the disadvantages of the status quo are those described by the student, not points argued by the school counselor.

2. Advantages of change

School counselor: How would you like things to be different?
Billy: I wish things were going better. I wish I weren't so far behind in school. I wish I wasn't so tired all the time.
School counselor: Describe how school could be better.
Billy: Well, I could be passing all my classes. I could be able to stay alert in class and understand what's going on.
School counselor: Describe how you'd like to be less "tired all the time."
Billy: I'd like it to be easier to get up in the morning and not feel like I'm dragging my body around for hours. I'd like to feel awake and alert, more able to focus and finish homework assignments.
School counselor: What would be the advantages of making some changes in your life?
Billy: I think I would feel much less stressed out if I were caught up in school. I'd feel better in the morning if I weren't out drinking the night before. My Mom would be less worried about me, my Dad might hassle me less. I could graduate high school next year.

3. Optimism about change

School counselor: What makes you think that if you decide to make a change you could do it?
Billy: Well, I'm that not sure I can really. But, I've got to do something. I can't afford to get busted again and I really want to make it through the year and not have to go to summer school to catch up.
School counselor: How confident are you—say on a scale from zero to ten where zero is not at all confident and 10 is extremely confident—regarding this change?
Billy: Probably a five for changing my partying and a four for passing all my classes . . . maybe a 4.5 overall.
School counselor: Why a 4.5 and not a zero?
Billy: Well, I know I need to do something. My mom came down on me pretty hard when I was suspended and I was able to cut back some. I know if I can cut back on drinking I will focus better and catch up in school.

Here, the school counselor has used an open-ended question to explore the student's optimism toward change. To further this understanding, the school counselor asks the student to rate his confidence on a scale of 1 to 10. This is another MI technique (sometimes called a "ruler") designed to assess the student's confidence and to further elicit change-talk. Notice that the school counselor asked why the student's assessment was not lower (and not the opposite). This encourages the student to express strengths toward change. Asking the student, "Why is it 4.5 and not 10?" would force the student to argue against change. The ruler technique can be used further as described in the following example.

4. Intention to change

School counselor: What would it take for you to go from 4.5 to a 5 or a 6?

Billy: If I had some sort of plan, I mean, if I knew what sort of steps I was going to take . . . and if, if I'd started the steps...then I'd feel more like an 8 or a 9, maybe even a 10 if I'd already started initiating the plan.

School counselor: What do you think you might do?

Billy: Well, I could just stay in weeknights or not drink on weekends, but then I wouldn't know what to do when I go out with friends. . . . I guess I can't really think of any other ways.

Here, the school counselor builds on the ruler technique by asking the student to describe how he might further progression toward change. Moreover, the school counselor is tapping into the student's current change strategies and the student's estimated probability of success for those strategies. In this respect, the school counselor has determined what the student believes is necessary to move toward change and has ascertained that the student lacks constructive strategies for moving toward change.

The case example illustrates some strategies for eliciting change-talk. Equally important is how a school counselor responds to change-talk. Miller and Rollnick (2002) encouraged the use of specific counseling skills as a means of furthering change-talk and enhancing intrinsic motivation. These skills include (a) elaborating change-talk, (b) summarizing change-talk, (c) affirming change-talk, (d) clarifying ambivalence, and (e) clarifying values.

Elaborating change-talk is accomplished when a school counselor encourages a student to expound on statements of change. The school counselor helps the student explore change-talk by using furthering responses such as, "Tell me more about . . . [student's change statement]," "What are some other reasons you might want to make a change?" or "Give me an example of . . ." (Miller & Rollnick, 2002, p. 87). The intent of these directive counseling responses is to help the student to further explore his or her intentions toward change.

Equally important in responding to student statements of change is stating a reflection of student change-talk. This skill can help student clarify ambivalence around change and continue exploration of intentions toward change. Recall the previous school counselor responses in the case example.

School counselor: You'd like to see yourself getting back on track in school and cutting back on your drinking. Right now you are discouraged about not passing your classes and partying keeps you exhausted most of the time.

The school counselor response reflects student change-talk. It is important for school counselors to be aware that reflecting student statements of change can sometimes engender psychological reactants in a student and elicit student statements against change.

School counselor: You'd like to end your pattern of partying and being exhausted the next day.

Billy: Well, going out with friends gives me relief from the stresses of school.

In such cases, it is necessary to use what Miller and Rollnick (2002) referred to as "double-sided reflection" (p. 101). Double-sided reflection can help a school counselor avoid being caught in the position of arguing for change while the student argues against it.

School counselor: You like the stress relief you feel from going out with friends and you hate feeling physically bad the next day after having been out partying with alcohol.

Summarizing change-talk is also another way for school counselors to assist students in exploring their feelings and thoughts about change. "In general, summaries are collections of change statements the person has made: disadvantages of the status quo, reasons for change, optimism about change, and desire to change" (Miller & Rollnick, 2002, p. 90). As with double-sided reflection, when reflecting change-talk, including both sides of ambivalence can be effective in facilitating student movement toward change.

Affirming change-talk is also an important school counselor response to student self-motivational change statements. Selective school counselor responses such as "That sounds like a good idea" and "That's a good point" (Miller & Rollnick, 2002, p. 91) can serve to reinforce a student's commitment to change and facilitate movement through the stages of change.

Clarifying ambivalence involves helping a student to examine each side of the conflict surrounding change. This might mean the school counselor and student evaluate separately the pros and cons for each of the change alternatives as well as the status quo. It is important that the school counselor and student complete this process for each alternative separately as well as the current behavior/status quo.

Clarifying values is equally important and intrinsically related to clarifying ambivalence. Students must be aware of their personal values in order to evaluate the advantages and disadvantages of change. Helping to discern what is truly important can help a student resolve ambivalence around change. Consider the following discussion.

School counselor: Let's talk about some of the options you have been considering for making changes in your life. We can evaluate the advantages and drawbacks of each. Let's start with your current lifestyle. What are some of the things you like about your current lifestyle?
Billy: Okay, I have a lot of friends. I always have someone to go do something with. And I like to go to parties and getting drunk.
School counselor: You like that you have many people who want to spend time with you. What else?
Billy: I like going to parties and getting drunk.
School counselor: You enjoy how you feel when you're drunk.
Billy: Yes, it feels good. I'm not worried about school or my Dad hassling me. And I'm funny when I'm drunk.
School counselor: So, drinking makes you forget about school and not be troubled by anyone's demands of you. Also, you enjoy being funny and you believe being drunk helps you be funny.
Billy: Well, I can be funny without being drunk, I mean maybe it just helps me feel loose enough to make jokes.
School counselors: Okay, so you value a sense of humor and you believe you can be very funny but you're not always so confident about displaying your sense of humor. What are some of the disadvantages of your current lifestyle?
Billy: Well, I'm tired all the time.
School counselor: Why do you think you're so tired?
Billy: Well, when I'm out late I feel tired and hungover the next day and it's hard for me to focus. Sometimes I get grumpy with my Mom for no reason. Also, I have a hard time understanding things from school and so I fall further behind.
School counselor: So feeling physically good is important to you. You also value your mother. Making progress in school is also important to you.
Billy: Yes, I do value my Mom, in fact that's part of why I want to stay on track toward graduation. Also, it would be nice to have both my Mom and Dad get off my back about school. I wish they could just trust me to take of things on my own.
School counselor: So you value handling things independently as well and you think your parents might give you more control over your life if you made some positive changes.

In the previous discussion, the student and school counselor are exploring some of the pros and cons of the student's current lifestyle. Moreover, they are discerning the student's values and how those values relate to the student's current lifestyle and the potential change(s) therein.

Values are imperative to the change process for students with addictive behaviors. As with other facets of counseling, it is important that school counselors explore with their students the relevancy of their personal values to lifestyle choices. These values need to be explored with an understanding of the student's cultural identity and in consideration of the student's worldview.

Cultural Considerations

It is essential for school counselors to realize that values are embedded in a social and cultural context. Therefore, school counselors need to understand the student's worldview and cultural identity in order to assist the student in exploring his or her values. Kluckhohn and Strodtbeck (1961) proposed a value-orientation model for the conceptualization of cultural values. While empirical evidence in support of this model is mixed (Carter, 1991), it can at least provide a framework for school counselors to use in exploring student values.

For example, some research indicates that African American students may have what Klockhohn and Strodtbeck (1961) defined as a collateral view of social relations (Carter & Helms, 1987). With this awareness and conceptual framework, a school counselor might wish to explore with an African American student his or her social support network, the value system of the student's family/social network, and determine how the student's current and future choices impact the student's social/family relations.

Dealing With Resistance

Some school counselors find the most challenging aspect of counseling students with addictive behaviors is encountering resistance. As mentioned previously, the MI approach takes a somewhat nontraditional view of resistance in the counseling relationship. Rather than interpreting resistance as a student trait that needs to be defeated, MI views resistance as a function of the counseling relationship. More specifically, resistance is in a sense, a reaction to what is happening in the counseling session and a signal to defer the current tactic in favor of another approach. While this view of resistance is in and of itself a strategy for working with resistance in the process of change, there are additional strategies that a school counselor might employ when encountering resistance: (a) simple reflection, (b) double-sided reflection, (c) amplified reflection, (d) reframing, and (e) agreeing with a twist. These are five techniques posited by MI to diminish resistance and foster progress through the stages of change (Miller & Rollnick, 2002).

Simple reflection. One response to resistance is a reflective listening statement (Miller & Rollnick, 2002). By acknowledging the student's disagreement, disbelief, doubts about change, or differing perception, a school counselor can avoid fostering increased defensiveness:

Billy: Who are you to tell me to stop partying? You've probably never had to put up with the kind of stress I'm dealing with. You've probably never even tried pot.
School counselor: It's hard for you to imagine that I could possibly understand what you're dealing with.

The principles of MI continue to apply when dealing with resistance and giving simple reflection. It is imperative that the school counselor continues to express empathy and to support self-efficacy in subsequent work with the student. Similarly, a school counselor may see an opportunity to deal with resistance and continue to develop discrepancy through double-sided reflection.

Double-sided reflection. Sometimes resistance may manifest itself in the counseling relationship through a student's continued exploration of only the one side of the change argument. In response to this type of resistance, it is helpful to use the previously discussed technique of double-sided reflection. Double-sided reflection is a technique that can assist school counselor and student in exploring both sides of ambivalence (Miller & Rollnick, 2002).

Billy: Yes, I'm going out drinking lot more than I used to, but it's not like I'm getting stoned or jacked up on coke all the time, I mean, I've only been drunk a few times at school activities and no one really sees me as an alcoholic.
School counselor: Part of you is concerned about your increased drinking and another part thinks it's also important to you that people don't view you as an "alcoholic."

When counseling students with addictive behaviors, double-sided reflection might also incorporate the facets of ambivalence that relate to decisions about change.

John: I know it makes sense to cut back on my partying if I'm going to start doing better in school, but I don't think you realize how much stress I'm under, it's like a hammer beating me down all the time!
School counselor: You'd really like to decrease your drinking and you are afraid of how you'll cope without drinking to help you deal with stress.

As with other strategies suggested throughout this chapter, double-sided reflection has potential application for many problematic student behaviors as well as for counseling students struggling with addictive behaviors. Just as student choices and behaviors in school are inherently connected with student addictive behaviors, counseling interventions in one area can be used to assist facilitating change in the other as well.

Amplified reflection. Another potentially effective method for responding to resistance is amplified reflection. "A related and quite useful response is to reflect back what the person has said in an amplified or exaggerated form—to state it in an even more extreme fashion" (Miller & Rollnick, 2002, p. 101). It is important to note that this should be done in a serious, straightforward tone that does not suggest sarcasm or criticism. A negative or sarcastic statement from the school counselor would likely only elicit greater resistance from the student.

Billy: I couldn't give up my partying with friends, I mean, what would they think—that I'm some kind of loser?
School counselor: You can't even imagine not drinking when out with your friends. You couldn't handle their reaction if you quit.

Or

Billy: You make it sound like I'm a raging alcoholic! I don't have a drinking problem!
School counselor: You don't see any negative consequences from your alcohol use—and you resent that I brought it up. In fact, you really see no connection at all between your partying and your problems in school.
Billy: Well, I know I need to take a look at how that stuff is impacting where I want to go . . . I mean, the partying isn't making it any easier to pass my classes.

In each of the two preceding examples, the school counselor used amplified reflection to respond to resistance in the counseling relationship. In the second example, the school counselor responded specifically to exploring the impact of the student's addictive behaviors on his lack of success in school. The school counselor's response utilizing amplified reflection elicited the student's arguments for exploring the relationship between addictive behaviors and problems in school.

Reframing. Sometimes students express resistance through a self-defeating, problematic, or counterproductive view of a situation. "A persistent use of a false or problematic perceptual frame indicates that the client is 'stuck' and likely to continue unless a change in perception can be engineered" (Gerber, 2003, p. 144). Reframing is the process of helping a student to alter the maladaptive frame into a new perceptual frame. More specifically, reframing in MI may mean helping to generate a more adaptive perception of the process of change.

Billy: I've tried to cut back on going out drinking before, but I always get back into it.
School counselor: You're very persistent. You're not afraid to try again when you aren't successful initially!

Or

Billy: I don't know why I should bother trying to do better in school, I've started out every semester swearing I'll do better and I end up putting off assignments until I'm flunking.
School counselor: You've done a great job noticing some of the mistakes you've made in getting to where you are—now you'll be able to avoid a lot of problems as we go through the process of changing.

Agreeing with a twist. Miller and Rollnick (2002) proposed another technique for rolling with resistance, which they have entitled "agreeing with a twist." This technique involves initially concurring with a student by reflecting their message coupled with a slight twist or modification of resistant momentum. "Agreement with a twist is basically a reflection followed by a reframe" (p. 105).

Billy: You're probably going to tell me I need to do some AA program or something. It wears me out just thinking about it.
School counselor: You're exactly right—if I were to make out a giant "to do" list for you it would probably just prevent you from starting to do anything. It's ironic isn't it—when you're told what you "have to do" it can actually prevent you from doing the very things you want to do.

These aforementioned strategies may provide some useful techniques for counseling students with addictive behaviors. When coupled with the philosophical perspective that resistance is an indicator for a school counselor to change approaches rather than a student's pure rejection of positive change, these techniques can assist school counselors in helping their students avoid the detrimental consequences of addictive behaviors.

Selecting a Treatment Program

Once a student has successfully negotiated the contemplation stage and determined that the negative consequences of the addictive behaviors warrant a behavioral change, a school counselor can be central in helping a student develop an action plan during the preparation stage. In assisting the student with developing an action plan, the process may benefit from the school counselor's developing a treatment plan that considers the unique characteristics of the student and then matching a treatment program with those attributes.

Some evidence suggests that matching student attributes to the specifically selected treatment when selecting treatment programs will increase the likelihood of treatment efficacy (Brown et al., 2002; Mattson, 1994; Project Match, 1997). In the broadest sense, this means considering factors such as student age, gender, severity of substance abuse, level of social support, and financial resources. On another level, school counselors might consider student preferences and cognitive, affective, or behavioral "style" in addition to cultural worldview in helping students to select a treatment approach. For example, a Mexican American student with a strong sense of family and joint decision making might benefit from bringing in his or her family to assist in selecting the treatment plan. Similarly, a school counselor might need to provide an alternate cognitive frame by labeling this step as a "plan for academic and career success" rather than a treatment plan, in order to avoid the stigma some cultures associate with seeking psychological help or therapy.

School counselors also need to consider indigenous treatment plans and/or traditional healers as potentially culturally responsive options for students. Fisher and Harrison (2005) described many such treatment options for groups such as African Americans, including programs such as the *Glide Memorial Methodist Church* in San Francisco, the *Free-N-One* recovery program, the *Nation of Islam* program, and the *African American Survivors Program*.

Using an assessment can also help a school counselor in developing a treatment plan with a student. There are no shortages of assessments to assist school counselors in determining the severity of student substance abuse (the Addiction Research Institute at the University of Texas provides a list of different assessments via their Web site, which is listed at the end of this chapter). School counselors can use assessments to assist students in determining suitable treatment.

Magura, Schildhaus, Rosenblum, and Gastfriend (2002) discussed using the American Society of Addiction Medicine (ASAM) Patient Placement Criteria in determining the appropriate level of treatment. The criteria outline four levels of care: (a) standard outpatient, (b) intensive outpatient, (c) residential, and (d) hospital. Moreover, these authors suggested using the following variables to determine the appropriate treatment level: acute detoxification and/or withdrawal, biomedical conditions, emotional/behavioral conditions, treatment acceptance/resistance, relapse potential, and recovery environment. Considering these variables can help school counselors in finding appropriate treatment programs and making referrals.

SAMHSA provides a Web site service that locates substance abuse treatment facilities nationally. School counselors can use this service as a starting point in an investigation of available referrals for their area.

Additional Considerations

Geographic location can have an influence on planning for treatment. Rural areas have the same rates of alcoholism and drug abuse yet often lack the same access to health care services (U.S. Department of Health and Human Services, 2007). For this reason, school counselors in rural areas may need to make special arrangements to help students get treatment. This may mean incorporating travel arrangements into the treatment planning process and/or connecting with rural primary care providers in order to secure substance abuse treatment. Consistent with culturally responsive counseling practice, school counselors in rural areas need to search for community sponsored programs and resources that may can be incorporated into the student's treatment plan.

A school counselor may also need to help a student negotiate a balance between treatment and school requirements. This may require a school counselor to advocate on behalf of a student with teachers/administration or assist a student by serving as a liaison between treatment facilities and the school.

It is important to note that in working with a student to determine treatment as part of the preparation stage, the process and outcome are contingent on the continued involvement and engagement of the student. The student is obviously the most important factor in any treatment formula.

Conclusion

What is the status of Billy in the case example? The school counselor has developed discrepancy between Billy's current addictive behaviors and the things Billy would like to accomplish. Billy has moved from precontemplation to contemplation. He is ready to explore further his ambivalence around his use of alcohol, his partying behaviors, and the behaviors he will need to change in order to become more successful in school. As he has already noted several disparaging aspects of his current behaviors, he is already beginning to tip the scale in favor of positive change. Soon he will be ready to explore options for beginning to alter his addictive behaviors and develop a plan of action, as the preparation stage necessitates.

It is imperative that the school counselor and Billy consider all potential implications of his plan of action. It may be useful for the school counselor and Billy to generate a menu of options for various potential plans and then evaluate each for the advantages/disadvantages and the probability of success. As always, the school counselor will continue to foster Billy's sense of self-efficacy by continuing to review the substantial progress he continues to make in improving his lifestyle by changing his addictive behaviors and improving his accomplishments in school.

Understanding the stages of change for behaviors can assist school counselors in working with students struggling with addiction. Knowledge of a student's current stage of change can help a school counselor conceptualize the necessary tasks for the student to continue on the path toward positive change. Moreover, the four guiding principles of MI—express empathy, develop discrepancy, roll with resistance, and support self-efficacy—can provide a solid foundation for counseling students with addictive behaviors. The specific MI counseling techniques introduced in this chapter provide school counselors with a repertoire of tools to help them further positive change in students and avoid the potential pitfalls posed by resistance.

Finally, while the case example demonstrates the stages of change and the use of specific counseling techniques, it is obviously a very simple example. The process of change is often difficult, impaired by frequent pitfalls and setbacks. It is important that school counselors not give up on the process of change, just as they ask students to continue to strive for positive change in their lives. Similarly, realizing the importance of addressing substance abuse by less confrontational means may require a substantial change in practice for individual school counselors and even the profession as a whole.

The following Web sites provide additional information relating to the chapter topics:

- Addiction Technology Transfer Center Network: http://www.nattc.org/
- Motivational Interviewing: http://www.motivationalinterview.org/

- National Clearinghouse for Drug and Alcohol Information (NCDAI): http://ncdi.samhsa.gov/
- National Institute on Drug Abuse: http://www.nida.nih.gov/ and http://www.drugabuse.gov
- National Institute on Alcohol Abuse and Alcoholism: http://www.niaaa.nih.gov/
- Practitioner resources on substance abuse: http://www.athealth.com/Practitioner/particles/FR_SubstanceAbuse.html
- National Institute of Mental Health: http://www.nimh.nih.gov/
- The United States Department of Labor—Substance Abuse Information Database (SAID): http://www.dol.gov/asp/programs/drugs/said/default.asp
- American Council for Drug Education: http://www.acde.org/
- Join Together Online—Boston University School of Health Project to reduce substance abuse and violence: http://www.jointogether.org/home/
- *Journal of Occupational Health Psychology*: http://www.apa.org/journals/ocp.html
- *Psychology of Addictive Behaviors*: http://www.apa.org/journals/adb/description.html
- Addictive Behaviors Research Center at University of Washington: http://depts.washington.edu/abrc/
- National Center on Addiction and Substance Abuse at Columbia University: http://www.casacolumbia.org
- Substance Abuse and Mental Health Services Administration (SAMHSA): http://www.samhsa.gov/
- SAMHSA Treatment Facility Locator: http://findtreatment.samhsa.gov/facilitylocatordoc.htm
- Addiction Research Institute, Center for Social Work Research, University of Texas: http://www.utexas.edu/research/cswr/nida/index.html
- American Society of Addiction Medicine (ASAM): http://www.asam.org/

References

Bailey, J.A., & McCloskey, L.A. (2005). Pathways to adolescent substance use among sexually abused girls. *Journal of Abnormal Child Psychology, 33,* 39–53.

Bandura, A. (1997). *Self-efficacy: The exercise of control.* New York: W. H. Freeman.

Boys, A., Marsden, J., & Strang, J. (2001). Understanding reasons for drug use amongst young people: A functional perspective. *Health education research, 16*(4), 457–469.

Brook, J. S., & Pahl, K. (2005). The protective role of ethnic and racial identity and aspects of an Africentric orientation against drug use among African American young adults. *The Journal of Genetic Psychology, 166*(3), 329–345.

Brown, T. G., Seraganian, P., Tremblay, J., & Annis, H. (2002). Matching substance abuse aftercare treatments to client characteristics. *Addictive Behaviors, 27,* 585–604.

Burke, B. L., Arkowitz, H., & Menchola, M. (2003). The efficacy of motivational interviewing: A meta-analysis of controlled clinical trials. *Journal of Consulting and Clinical Psychology, 71,* 843–861.

Carter, R. T. (1991). Cultural values: A review of empirical research and implications for counseling. *Journal of Counseling & Development, 70,* 164–173.

Carter, R. T. & Helms, J. E. (1987). The relationship of black value-orientations to racial identity attitudes. *Measurement and Evaluation in Counseling and Development, 19,* 185–195.

Clark, D. B., Cornelius, J. R., Kirisci, L., & Tarter, R. E. (2005). Childhood risk categories for adolescent substance involvement: A general liability typology. *Drug and Alcohol Dependence, 77*(1), 13–21.

Clinton-Sherrod, M., Sobeck, J., Abbey, A., Agius, E., & Terry, K. (2005). The role of psychosocial factors in the transition to substance abuse: Are they protective among urban minority adolescents? *Journal of Primary Prevention, 26*(6), 511–528.

De Micheli, D., & Formigoni, M. L. (2002). Are reasons for the first use of drugs and family circumstances predictors of future use patterns? *Addictive Behaviors, 27*(1), 87–100.

DiClemente, C. C. (1991). Motivational interviewing and the stages of change. In W. R. Miller & S. Rollnick (Eds.), *Motivational interviewing: Preparing people to change addictive behaviors* (pp. 191–202). New York: Guilford Press.

DiClemente, C. C. (2003). *Addiction and change: How addictions develop and addicted people recover.* New York: Guilford Press.

DiClemente, C. C., & Velasquez, M. M. (2002). Motivational interviewing and the stages of change. In W. R. Miller & S. Rollnick (Eds.), *Motivational interviewing: Preparing people for change* (pp. 201–216). New York: Guilford Press.

Doweiko, H. E. (2002). *Concepts of chemical dependency* (5th ed.). Pacific Grove, CA: Brooks/Cole.

Eitle, D. J., & Eitle, T. M. (2004). School and county characteristics as predictors of school rates of drug, alcohol, and tobacco offenses. *Journal of Health and Social Behavior, 45*(4), 408–421.

Fisher, G. L., & Harrison, T. C. (2005). *Substance abuse: Information for school counselors, social workers, therapists, and counselors* (3rd ed.). Boston: Allyn & Bacon.

Gerber, S. K. (2003). *Responsive therapy: A systematic approach to counseling skills* (2nd ed.). New York: Houghton Mifflin College/Lahaska Press.

Hallfors, D., Vevea, J. L., Iritani, B., Cho, H., Khatapoush, S., & Saxe, L. (2002). Truancy, grade point average, and sexual activity: A meta-analysis of risk indicators for youth substance use. *Journal of School Health, 72*(5), 205–212.

Harland, J., White, M., Drinkwater, C., Chin, D., Farr, L., & Howel, D. (1999) The Newcastle Exercise Project: A randomized controlled trial of methods to promote physical activity in primary care. *British Medical Journal, 319,* 828–831.

Hawkins, J. D., Van Horn, M. L., & Arthur, M. S. (2004). Community variation in risk and protective factors and substance use outcomes. *Prevention Science, 5*(4), 213–220.

Hays, S. P., Hays, C. E., & Mulhall, P. F. (2004). Community risk and protective factors and adolescent substance use. *The Journal of Primary Prevention, 24*(2), 125–141.

Johnston, L. D., O'Malley, P. M., & Bachman, J. G. (2003). *Monitoring the future. National survey results on drug use, 1975–2002: Vol. 2: College students and adults ages 19–40* (NIH Publication No. 03-5376). Bethesda, MD: National Institute on Drug Abuse.

Johnston, L. D., O'Malley, P. M., Bachman, J. G., & Schulenberg, J. E. (2005). *Monitoring the future: National results on adolescent drug use: Overview of key findings 2004.* Bethesda, MD: National Institute on Drug Abuse.

Kelly, K. J., Comello, M., & Hunn, L. (2002). Parent-child communication, perceived sanctions against drug use, and youth drug involvement. *Adolescence, 37*(148), 775–787.

King, K. A., Vidourek, R. A., & Wagner, D. I. (2003). Effect of parent drug use and parent-child time spent together on adolescent involvement in alcohol, tobacco, and other drugs. *Adolescent & Family Health, 3*(4), 171–176.

Kirisci, L., Dunn, M. G., Mezzich, A. C., & Tarter, R. E. (2001). Impact of parental substance use disorder and child neglect severity on substance use involvement in male offspring. *Prevention Science, 2*(4), 241–255.

Kluckhohn, F. R., & F. L. Strodtbeck. (1961). *Variations in value orientations.* Evanston, IL: Row, Peterson.

Lambie, G. W. (2004). Motivational enhancement therapy: A tool for professional school counselors working with adolescents. *Professional School Counseling, 7,* 268-276.

Lambie, G. W., & Rokutani, L. J. (2002). A systems approach to substance abuse identification and intervention for school counselors. *Professional School Counseling, 5*(5), 353–359.

Lawendowski, L. A. (1998). A motivational intervention for adolescent smokers. *Preventive Medicine, 27,* 39–46.

Magura, S., Schildhaus, S., Rosenblum, A., & Gastfriend, D. (2002). Substance user treatment program quality: Selected topics. *Substance Use & Misuse, 37,* 1185–1214.

Mattson, M. E. (1994). Patient-treatment matching: Rationale and results. *Alcohol Health & Research World, 18,* 287–285.

McLaughlin, T. F., & Vacha, E. F. (1993). Substance abuse prevention in the schools: Roles for the school counselor. *Elementary School Guidance & Counseling, 28*(2), 124–133.

Miller, W. R., & Rollnick, S. (1991). *Motivational interviewing: Preparing people to change addictive behavior.* New York: Guilford Press.

Miller, W. R., & Rollnick, S. (2002). *Motivational interviewing: Preparing people for change.* New York: Guilford Press.

Nash, S. G., McQueen, A., & Bray, J. H. (2005). Pathways to adolescent alcohol use: Family environment, peer influence, and parental expectations. *The Journal of Adolescent Health, 37*(1), 19–28.

Nunes, J. V., & Parson, E. B. (1995). Patterns of psychoactive substance use among adolescents. *American Family Physicians, 52,* 1693–1697.

Parks, K. A., & Kennedy, C. L. (2004). Club drugs: Reasons for and consequences of use. *Journal of Psychoactive Drugs, 36*(3), 295–302.

Prochaska, J. O., & DiClemente, C. C. (1982). Transtheoretical therapy: Towards a more integrative model of change. *Psychotherapy, 19,* 276–278.

Prochaska, J. O., Norcross, J. C., & DiClemente, C. C. (1994). *Changing for good: The revolutionary program that explains the six stages of change and teaches you how to free yourself from bad habits.* New York: W. Morrow.

Project MATCH Research Group. (1997). Matching alcoholism treatments to client heterogeneity: Project MATCH posttreatment drinking outcomes. *Journal of Studies on Alcohol, 58,* 7–29.

Project MATCH Research Group. (1998). Matching alcoholism treatments to client heterogeneity: Project MATCH three-year drinking outcomes. *Alcoholism: Clinical and Experimental Research, 23,* 1300–1311.

Remley, T. R., & Herlihy, B. (2005). *Ethical, legal, and professional issues in counseling* (2nd ed.). Upper Saddle River, NJ: Prentice Hall.

Safe and drug-free schools office created. (2002). *Inside School Safety, 7*(7), 7–8.

Smith, D. E., Heckemeyer, C. M., Kratt, P. P., & Mason, D. A. (1997). Motivational interviewing to improve adherence to a behavioral weight control program for older obese women with NIDDM: A pilot study. *Diabetes Care, 20,* 53–54.

Stephens, R. S., Roffman, R. A., & Curtin, L. (2000). Comparison of extended versus brief treatments for marijuana use. *Journal of Consulting and Clinical Psychology, 68,* 898–908.

Stone, C. (2005). *School counseling principles: Ethics and law.* Alexandria, VA: American School Counselor Association.

Substance Abuse and Mental Health Services Administration. (2004). *Results of the 2003 national survey on drug use and health.* Retrieved May 19, 2005, from http://www.oas.samhsa.gov/nhsda.htm

Tevyaw, T. O., & Monti, P. M. (2004). Motivational enhancement and other brief interventions for adolescent substance abuse: Foundations, applications, and evaluations. *Addiction, 99*(2), 63–75.

Treasure, J. L., Katzman, M., Schmidt, U., Troop, N., Todd, G., & de Silva, P. (1999). Engagement and outcome in the treatment of bulimia nervosa: First phase of a sequential design comparing motivation enhancement therapy and cognitive-behavioural therapy. *Behavioural Research and Therapy, 37,* 405–418.

U.S. Office of Management and Budget and Federal Agencies. (2006). *Safe and drug free schools state grants assessment.* Retrieved March 15, 2006, from http://www.whitehouse.gov/omb/expectmore/detail.10000200.2005.html

Wallace, J. M., Bachman, J. G., O'Malley, P. M., Schulenberg, J. E., Cooper, S. M., & Johnston, L. D. (2003). Gender and ethnic differences in smoking, drinking, and illicit drug use among American 8th, 10th, and 12th grade students, 1976–2000. *Addiction, 98,* 225–234.

7

Accountability and Professional Issues in School Counseling

XLIII
EVALUATING SCHOOL GUIDANCE AND COUNSELING PROGRAMS:
Past, Present, and Future

NORMAN C. GYSBERS
University of Missouri–Columbia

Education today is under intense pressure to be accountable for student academic achievement (No Child Left Behind Act, U.S. Department of Education, 2001). All educational programs, including guidance and counseling, are being asked to demonstrate their contributions to overall student success in general and student academic achievement in particular. As a result, it is not surprising to find that guidance and counseling program evaluation is in the forefront of professional discussion and action across the country (Dahir & Stone, 2003; Gysbers & Henderson, 2006; Isaacs, 2003; S. Johnson & Johnson, 2003; Myrick, 2003a).

School counselors, working within the framework of comprehensive guidance and counseling programs, are being asked to demonstrate that their work contributes to student success, particularly student academic achievement. Not only are school counselors being asked to tell what they do, but they are also being asked to demonstrate how what they do makes a difference in the lives of students. They are being asked to be accountable and to be answerable for their work.

Given the current emphasis on evaluation, is this a new phenomenon, or has our profession always been concerned about evaluating the impact of the work of school counselors? What is the profession doing today to respond to the current emphasis on evaluation? What does the future hold for evaluating school guidance and counseling programs? The three sections that follow provide answers to these questions.

The Past: The Evolution of Evaluation

As early as the 1920s, concerns about evaluation began to be raised. Payne (1924) pointed out that it was necessary to evaluate the work being done in guidance:

> What method do we have of checking the results of our guidance? For particular groups was it guidance, misguidance, or merely a contributing experience? We simply must work out some definite method of testing and checking the results of our work. If we do not, some other group will, with possibly disastrous results for our work. (p. 63)

Much of the work on evaluation in the early years focused on establishing standards for judging whether a guidance and counseling program was complete. The need to develop such standards to judge the completeness of a program arose because of the wide array of activities being conducted under the banner of guidance and counseling. Proctor (1930) stated the problem this way:

> One of the great needs in the field of guidance is some fairly objective means of comparing the guidance activities of one secondary school system with that of another. It is only in this manner that we shall ever arrive at an estimate of what constitutes a standard setup for the carrying out of a guidance program. (p. 58)

As work continued on identifying standards to measure what the standard setup for guidance and counseling should be, work was also underway in the 1930s to identify the possible outcomes of guidance and counseling programs. A number of writers, focusing on results, began to identify possible outcomes. For example, Christy, Stewart, and Rosecrance (1930), Hinderman (1930), and Rosecrance (1930) identified the following student outcomes that they thought would result from students' participating in guidance and counseling programs:

- fewer pupils dropping out of school,
- increase in the standard of scholarship,
- better morale in the student body,
- better all-around school life,
- fewer student failures and subject withdrawals,
- young people better informed about the future,
- satisfactory adjustment of graduates to community life and vocation and to a college or university,
- fewer disciplinary cases,
- fewer absences,
- more intelligent selection of subjects, and
- better study habits.

Not only did researchers focus on possible outcomes for guidance and counseling during these early years, but in addition, several of them undertook scientifically based studies to investigate the impact of guidance and counseling on the lives of students. Most notable were the studies conducted by Kefauver and Hand (1941) in the early 1930s and by Rothney and Roens (1950) in the latter part of the 1930s. In both longitudinal studies, these researchers found significant differences in favor of the experimental groups that had received guidance and counseling activities and services. Of particular interest to us today was the finding in the Kefauver and Hand study:

> [S]tudents in the experimental schools typically made slighter greater gains in mean scores on the Stanford Achievement Test than did the students (1) in the corresponding control situations, or (2) those who had been graduated by the two experimental schools prior to the 3-year period during which the study reported in this section of the volume was conducted. (p. 215)

Later, Rothney (1958) conducted the Wisconsin Counseling Study. In it, all 870 sophomores in the high schools in four communities in Wisconsin were placed in either an experimental group or a control group. The experimental groups received an intensive guidance program while the controls did not. On graduation day in June 1951, there were 690 graduates. Three follow-ups took place (a) 6 months after high school graduation, (b) 2.5 years after graduation, and (c) 5 years after graduation in 1956. Of the students who were living (685), 100% participated in the final follow-up. Here are the findings of this landmark study. Students who received counseling:

1. Achieved slightly higher academic records in high school and post–high school education.
2. Indicated more realism about their own strengths and weaknesses at the time they were graduated from high school.
3. Were less dissatisfied with their high school experiences.
4. Had different vocational aspirations.
5. Were more consistent in expression of, entering into, and remaining in their vocational choices, classified by areas.
6. Made more progress in employment during the 5-year period following high school graduation.
7. Were more likely to have gone on to higher education, to remain to graduate, and to plan for continuation of higher education.
8. Were more satisfied with their post–high school education.
9. Expressed greater satisfaction with their status 5 years after high school and were more satisfied in retrospect with their post–high school experiences.
10. Participated in more self-improvement activities after completing high school.
11. Looked back more favorably on the counseling they had obtained. (Rothney, 1958, pp. 479–480)

The 1960s, 1970s, and 1980s witnessed the rapid expansion of guidance and counseling in the schools. Increasing numbers of school counselors were employed, particularly at the elementary level. Interest in evaluation also increased. Numerous articles were written exhorting school counselors to evaluate their work and lamenting the fact that more was not being done (Pine, 1975; Rothney & Farwell, 1960; Wilson & Rotter, 1982). Tamminen and Miller (1968) expressed their concerns about the lack of attention to evaluating the impact of guidance and counseling programs very directly using the words *faith, hope,* and *charity*:

> Faith, hope, and charity have characterized the American attitude toward guidance programs—faith in their effectiveness, hope that they can meet important if not always clearly specified need, and charity in not demanding more evaluative evidence that the faith and hope are justified. (p. 3)

Some school districts, during this time, took on the task of being accountable. School counselors in Mesa, Arizona, for example, expressed a need to focus on results or outcomes.

Our main objective was, briefly stated, to reduce the size of our "universe" down to manageable size and then—within the parameters of this "new" definition of guidance—be responsible, i.e., *accountable*. We were committed to move toward a model of accountability—based not only upon what counselors did—but rather based on results or outcomes in terms of observable student behaviors. (McKinnon, n.d., p. iii)

Continued expressions of concern about the lack of evaluation of guidance and counseling programs were voiced during the 1990s. For example, Lee and Workman (1992) noted, "Compared to other areas of the profession, school counseling seems to have little empirical evidence to support claims that it has a significant impact on the development of children and adolescents" (p. 15). Gysbers, Hughey, Starr, and Lapan (1992) described the overall evaluation framework that guided Missouri's efforts to evaluate comprehensive school guidance programs. Two of the five questions that guided the evaluation process focused on the measurement of students' mastery of guidance competencies and the possible impact of the program on the climate and goals of the school.

Later in the 1990s, Whitson (1996) outlined a number of approaches to research that could be used in many settings, including school settings. She pointed out that school counselors were encountering increased pressure to be accountable and, hence, needed to be more active in outcome research. Then, Whitson and Sexton (1998) presented a review of school counseling outcome research published between 1988 and 1995. In their opening sentence, they stated, "In this era of accountability, school counselors increasingly are asked to provide information to parents, administrators, and legislators on the effectiveness of school counseling activities" (p. 412).

The Present: Personnel + Program = Results

The emphasis on evaluation that began in the 1920s has continued with renewed vigor in this the first decade of the 21st century. Trevisan and Hubert (2001) reiterated statements made over the past 20 years concerning the importance of program evaluation and of obtaining accountability data regarded student results. Foster, Watson, Meeks, and Young (2002) also reiterated the need for accountability for school counselors and offered the single-subject research design as a way to demonstrate effectiveness. Lapan (2001) stressed the importance of comprehensive programs of guidance and counseling "conceptualized as results-based systems" (p. 289). In his article, he described a framework for guidance program planning and evaluation. And, Hughes and James (2001) noted the importance of using accountability data with site-based management teams and other school personnel.

Given the intense pressure for school counselors, working within the framework of comprehensive guidance and counseling programs, to evaluate their work and to be accountable, what is the current thinking about evaluation? Gysbers and Henderson (2006) answered this question by describing three kinds of evaluation—namely, (1) personnel evaluation, (2) program evaluation, and (3) results evaluation. They used the formula Personnel + Program = Results to describe the relationships of these three types. The American School Counselor Association's (ASCA) *National Model* (2003) also answered this question by identifying three types of evaluation using similar titles: (1) school counselor performance standards (personnel evaluation), (2) program audit (program evaluation), and (3) results reports (results evaluation).

What is involved in these three types of evaluation? Personnel evaluation describes the standards and procedures used to evaluate the work of school counselors. Program evaluation describes the standards and procedures used to determine the degree to which a school district's (school building's) guidance and counseling program is being implemented. Results evaluation focuses on the impact that a school district's (building) guidance and counseling program and its activities and services are having on students, the district (building), and the community.

Each type of evaluation is important. Equally important, however, is how they relate to and interact with each other. School counselors must be doing the work of the comprehensive school guidance and counseling program full-time. At the same time, the program must be fully implemented. When school counselors are engaged full-time in the program, and the program is in place and functioning the way it should, it then becomes possible to conduct results evaluation to ascertain the contributions that the program maybe making to overall student success in general and student academic achievement specifically.

Personnel Evaluation

In the past, school counselors were evaluated using teacher evaluation procedures and forms. Teacher procedures and forms were used because the work of school counselors was not well defined and would often vary building by building across school districts. The traditional organizers for guidance and counseling in the schools, the position and services models, did not provide sufficient structure to clearly establish well-defined roles for school counselors.

When comprehensive school guidance and counseling program frameworks evolved in the 1970s and 1980s, however, the bases for clearly identifying and evaluating the work of school counselors emerged. It became possible to establish the duties of school counselors district wide within the framework of a comprehensive program using the language of the program. Once this happened, performance standards and criteria to evaluate the work of school counselors followed (ASCA, 2003; Henderson & Gysbers, 1998; Missouri Department of Elementary and Secondary Education, 2000).

Today, performance standards and criteria are being used with increasing frequency to supervise and evaluate school counselors. Performance standards are acknowledged measures of comparison used to make judgments about the scope of the work of school counselors within a comprehensive program. Once a sufficient number of performance standards have been identified, criteria are prepared that specify the important aspects of the standards. Enough criteria are needed to provide evaluators with confidence that each standard has been fulfilled.

Table 43.1 presents 6 standards and 15 criteria for performance-based professional school counselor evaluation developed by the Missouri Department of Elementary and Secondary Education (2000). Standards 1 through 4 were derived directly from the comprehensive guidance program framework used by the state of Missouri. Standards 5 and 6 focus on school counselors' communication and interaction within schools as well as school counselors' professional responsibilities. In Table 43.2, example descriptors are provided for the first 2 criteria. Each of the remaining 13 criteria also has descriptors that more fully explain the operational details of the criteria.

In Missouri, school counselor evaluation is both formative and summative. Ongoing professional development and supervision procedures using the standards and criteria constitute the formative part of the evaluation. Various forms used to conduct the formative part of the evaluation are available in the *Guidelines for Performance-Based Professional School Counselor Evaluation* document (Missouri Department of Elementary and Secondary Education, 2000; this document can be obtained at http://www.dese.mo.gov/divteachqual/profdev/Counselorscorrected2.pdf).

The summative part involves an evaluator's collecting and documenting the work of school counselors to be used in school counselor evaluation. Table 43.3 presents a data collection form using 2 example criteria from the standards and criteria found in Table 43.1. The information from the form in Table 43.3 is used to make judgments concerning school counselor performance for each of the 15 criteria based on a 3-point rating scale of "meets expectations," "progressing toward meeting expectation," and "does not meet expectations." See Table 43.4 for an example of this type of rating for the first 2 criteria.

Program Evaluation

What is program evaluation? How do we determine which activities and services and what organizational structure constitutes a program? What forms and procedures are used to conduct program evaluation?

Program evaluation is a procedure used to determine the degree to which a school district's comprehensive guidance and counseling program is in place and fully functioning. It can also be used as a self-study procedure to ascertain how a current program measures up before beginning a revision of the program. In other situations, such as in the state of Utah, program evaluation is conducted for purposes of funding (Utah State Office of Education, 2003).

"What constitutes a standard set-up for the carrying out of a guidance program" (Proctor, 1930, p. 58)? This question, asked many years ago, identifies a major issue in program evaluation today. Due to the work of Gysbers and Henderson (2006), Myrick (2003b), S. Johnson, C. Johnson, and Downs (2006), and the ASCA (2003), we know what activities, services, and organizational structure constitute a complete comprehensive guidance and counseling program.

Based on this knowledge it is possible to construct the forms and procedures used in program evaluation. This work begins with the development of standards and criteria. Just as was the case in personnel evaluation, enough standards are required to fully document that a complete comprehensive school guidance and counseling program is in place and functioning the way it should. Criteria are then needed for each standard to adequately specify the important aspects of each standard. It is important to understand that the standards and criteria must be derived directly from a comprehensive guidance and counseling program model to ensure that a complete program has been captured by the standards and criteria. The standards and criteria must match the desired program framework.

Once the standards and criteria have been chosen that fully represent a comprehensive guidance and counseling program, a scale is created for each of the criteria that can range from 1 to 5, 6, or 7 points. Sometimes a scoring guide that describes what an evaluator would look for at each point is provided. A scoring guide can also include examples of evidence evaluators would expect to find along with the documentation required to show the degree to which the standards and criteria have been met.

There are numerous examples of program evaluation forms available. States such as Missouri and Utah have developed forms based on their state models for comprehensive guidance and counseling programs. The ASCA (2003) included an example in their *National Model*. Care must be taken, however, in using state or national standards and criteria and the forms. Unless a local distinct has

Table 43.1 Standards and Criteria for Performance-Based Professional School Counselor Evaluation

Standard 1:	The professional school counselor implements the Guidance Curriculum Component through the use of effective instructional skills and the careful planning of structured group sessions for all students.
Criterion 1:	The professional school counselor teaches guidance units effectively.
Criterion 2:	The professional school counselor encourages staff involvement to ensure the effective implementation of the guidance curriculum.
Standard 2:	The professional school counselor implements the Individual Planning Component by guiding individuals and groups of students and their parents through the development of educational and career plans.
Criterion 3:	The professional school counselor, in collaboration with parents, helps students establish goals and develop and use planning skills.
Criterion 4:	The professional school counselor demonstrates accurate and appropriate interpretation of assessment data and the presentation of relevant, unbiased information.
Standard 3:	The professional school counselor implements the Responsive Services Component through the effective use of individual and small group counseling, consultation, and referral skills.
Criterion 5:	The professional school counselor counsels individual students and small groups of students with identified needs/concerns.
Criterion 6:	The professional school counselor consults effectively with parents, teachers, administrators and other relevant individuals.
Criterion 7:	The professional school counselor implements an effective referral process in collaboration with parents, administrators, teachers and other school personnel.
Standard 4:	The professional school counselor implements the System Support Component through effective guidance program management and support for other educational programs.
Criterion 8:	The professional school counselor provides a comprehensive and balanced guidance program in collaboration with school staff.
Criterion 9:	The professional school counselor provides support for other school programs.
Standard 5:	The professional school counselor uses professional communication and interaction with the school community.
Criterion 10:	The professional school counselor demonstrates positive interpersonal relations with students.
Criterion 11:	The professional school counselor demonstrates interpersonal relations with educational staff.
Criterion 12:	The professional school counselor demonstrates positive, interpersonal relations with parents/patrons.
Standard 6:	The professional school counselor fulfills professional responsibilities.
Criterion 13:	The professional school counselor demonstrates a commitment to ongoing professional growth.
Criterion 14:	The professional school counselor possesses professional and responsible work habits.
Criterion 15:	The professional school counselor follows the profession's ethical and legal standards and guidelines, as well as promotes cultural diversity and inclusivity in school policy and interpersonal relationships.

From: Missouri Department of Elementary and Secondary Education, 2000, "Guidelines for Performance-Based Professional School Counselor Evaluation," Jefferson City: Author, pp. 27–28. Reprinted with permission.

Table 43.2 Professional School Counselor Evaluation Criteria with Descriptors: An Example

Note: The descriptors provided are simply examples of student and counselor behaviors that may be used to document criteria. The descriptors provided are not intended to be an inclusive list. The observation and/or documentation of each criterion will vary based on the context.

Standard 1: The professional school counselor implements the Guidance Curriculum Component through the use of effective instructional skills and the careful planning of structured group sessions for all students.

Criterion 1: The professional school counselor teaches guidance units effectively.

The professional school counselor:

1. Organizes units for student mastery based on student needs.
2. Uses effective instructional strategies.
3. Establishes an environment conducive for student learning through the use of effective classroom management techniques.
4. Other. ...

Criterion 2: The professional school counselor encourages staff involvement to ensure the effective implementation of the guidance curriculum.

The professional school counselor:

1. Collaborates with or assists teachers in developing and/or teaching guidance units effectively.
2. Serves as a resource regarding guidance materials appropriate to the guidance units being taught.
3. Provides in-service training for teachers on guidance-related subject matter and guidance instruction methodology.
4. Other. ...

From: Missouri Department of Elementary and Secondary Education, 2000, "Guidelines for Performance-Based Professional School Counselor Evaluation," Jefferson City: Author, p. 29. Reprinted with permission.

---

adopted a state or national model completely, some modifications may be needed in the forms to reflect the nature and structure of the program the district has developed.

When and how often a district conducts program evaluation depends on the purposes to be achieved. For self-study purposes, the ASCA (2003) recommended that program evaluation be conducted when a program is being designed and yearly thereafter. The state of Utah uses program evaluation to determine whether a school district has met the standards for program organization and implementation in order to receive state funding (Utah State Office of Education, 2003). Whether program evaluation is done yearly or periodically, this type of evaluation provides the opportunity to determine if the written district program is the actual implemented district program. The results of program evaluation reveal where progress has been made or progress is lacking in overall comprehensive guidance and counseling program implementation.

Results Evaluation

Results evaluation is the process used to answer the question, What impact do comprehensive guidance and counseling programs (activities and services) have on students' success, particularly on students' academic achievement? Outcomes typically addressed in results evaluation include attendance, discipline referrals, grade point averages, achievement test scores, and classroom behaviors. Results evaluation focuses on how outcomes such as these may change due to students' participation in the district's comprehensive guidance and counseling program.

It is recommended that school counselors develop and carry out a results-based evaluation plan as a part of the

Table 43.3 Comprehensive Data Collection Form: Two Example Criteria

The Comprehensive Data Collection Form is used by both the administrator/supervisor and professional school counselor to summarize the documentation of each performance criterion over the course of the evaluation cycle. It should be maintained in the administrator's/supervisor's office with a copy in the PSC's portfolio. It should be reviewed periodically to determine the professional school counselor's progress. This document will provide an overview of the professional school counselor's performance to be used during the Evaluation Report. It serves as a composite of all the data collected. All data should be copied and discussed with the professional school counselor prior to entering it into the file.

Professional School Counselor _____   Beginning Date __/__/__
School _____   Ending Date __/__/__
Grade Level _____   Administrator/Supervisior _____

Data Collection:

CO-Classroom Observation	IC-Individual Conference	P-Porfolio
RS- Reflection Sheet	LR- Lesson Review	AR-Artifact
O-Other		

Standard 1: The professional school counselor implements the Guidance Curriculum Component through the use of effective instructional skills and the careful planning of structured group sessions for all students.

    Criterion 1: The professional school counselor teaches guidance units effectively.

    CO ____ IC ____ P ____ RS ____ LR ____ AR ____ Other _____

Data/Comments: Date __/__/__

PSC's initials _____   Administrator's/Supervisor's initials _____

    Criterion 2: The professional counselor encourages staff involvement to insure the effective implementation of the guidance curriculum.

    CO ____ IC ____ P ____ RS ____ LR ____ AR ____ Other _____

Data/Comments: Date __/__/__

PSC's initials _____   Administrator's/Supervisor's initials _____

From: Missouri Department of Elementary and Secondary Education, 2000, "Guidelines for Performance-Based Professional School Counselor Evaluation," Jefferson City: Author, p. 48. Reprinted with permission.

Table 43.4 Evaluation Report: Two Example Criteria

The Evaluation Report is used to summarize the administrator's/supervisor's rating of performance of each criterion at the end of the PSC evaluation process.

PSC _____ Administrator/Supervisor _____

Grade _____ School _____ Date __/__/__

Classification: Beginning PSC ___ Experienced PSC ___

The Proferssional School Counselor:	Meets Expectations	Progressing Toward Meeting Expectations	Does Not Meet Expectations
Criteria			
1. The professional school counselor teaches guidance units effectively.			
2. The professional school counselor encourages staff involvement to insure the effective implementation of the guidance curriculum.			

From: Missouri Department of Elementary and Secondary Education, 2000, "Guidelines for Performance-Based Professional School Counselor Evaluation," Jefferson City: Author, p. 61. Reprinted with persmission.

overall implementation of their district's comprehensive guidance and counseling programs. The outcomes to be addressed in the plan should come from the district's comprehensive school improvement plan, mission statement, and/or strategic plan. These documents contain outcomes chosen as important for a district to achieve. Since comprehensive guidance and counseling programs can make substantial contributions to the achievement of such outcomes, they can become the outcomes that are focused on in a results evaluation plan.

A results evaluation plan can focus on specific guidance and counseling activities or services chosen because they address specific outcomes identified in the district's comprehensive improvement plan. If this approach is chosen, then the plan needs to include the specific outcomes desired, the activities or services to be used that can address the desired outcomes, how the activities or services will be provided and by whom, the evaluation design to be used, how the data will be collected and analyzed, and what kind of report (e.g., PowerPoint presentation) will be prepared and to whom it will be presented.

As an illustration of a study that looked at the outcomes of a specific guidance and counseling activity, Brigman and Campbell (2003) tested a guidance curriculum titled "Student Success Skills" that focused on student cognitive, social, and self-management skills using a quasi-experimental, pre/post test design. School counselors conducted group sessions for students in grades 5, 6, 8, and 9. The treatment group scored significantly higher than control group on the reading and math scores of the Florida Comprehensive Assessment Test.

A results evaluation plan can also focus more broadly on the impact of an entire district guidance and counseling programs for K–12 or a specific grade grouping such as elementary, middle school, or high school districtwide or statewide. The same procedures identified previously would be used. To illustrate this approach, two statewide studies are presented—one conducted in Missouri and one in the state of Washington.

Lapan, Gysbers, and Petroski (2001) found that when 4,868 middle school classroom teachers in Missouri in 184 small, medium, and large sized middle schools rated guidance programs in their schools as more fully implemented, 22,601 seventh graders in these schools reported that they earned higher grades, school was more relevant for them, they had positive relationships with teachers, they were more satisfied with their education, and they felt safer in school. Sink and Stroh (2003), in a comparison of elementary students (grades 3 and 4) enrolled for several years in well-established comprehensive school counseling program schools with students enrolled in schools without such programs, found that students enrolled in schools with the well-established programs had significantly higher academic achievement test scores on the Iowa Tests of Basic Skills—Form M and the Washington Assessment of Student Learning.

In designing a results evaluation plan, several types of data can be used. Process data, the first type, describe what guidance and counseling activities and services were provided, when, and for whom. Process data provide evidence that guidance and counseling activities and services were actually provided. Perception data, the second type, tell us what students, parents, teachers, administrators, or others think about or feel about the activities and services and the work of school counselors. Outcome data (results data), the third type, are the actual behaviors of students as measured by attendance rates, discipline referral rates, grade point averages, and achievement test scores. All three types of data are useful in ascertaining the impact of comprehensive guidance and counseling programs on student behavior.

A major phase of developing and carrying out a results evaluation plan is the collection of the data. When will the results data be gathered and be whom? C. D. Johnson (1991) recommended that long-range, intermediate, and immediate data need to be considered. Long-range results data focus on how comprehensive guidance and counseling programs or the activities and services involved affect students after they leave school. Often collecting these kinds of data involves using a follow-up study design. Intermediate results focus on what impact the program has on students some period after they have participated in program activities and services while immediate results describe the impact of specific activities and services soon after they have been conducted.

The data collection schedule for results evaluation should be established prior to the initial date of the results evaluation period and should specify

- the guidance activity or service for which the data will be collected;
- the instrument(s) to be used;
- the group(s) or individuals from whom data will be collected;
- the time when data will be collected (pretest, posttest, end of year, and so forth) in relation to the process schedule; and
- the person(s) to be responsible for data collection.

The evaluation design chosen, including the types of comparisons to be made, will dictate most of the decisions relevant to the data collection schedule. Evaluation data collected for groups to make pretest/posttest comparisons or experimental group/control group comparisons need to conform closely to the time required to complete the chosen guidance and counseling activity. Pretest or baseline data need to be collected prior to the initiation of the guidance and counseling activities, and posttest data need to be collected at a specified time after completion of the guidance and counseling activities being evaluated (immediate results). Some designs also may require the collection of data at specified periods during the guidance and counseling activity period or as follow-up sometime after the completion of the guidance and counseling activity (intermediate or long-range results). All such data need to be collected on a predetermined schedule so that all persons involved in the results evaluation process can make plans and carry out the data collection in accordance with the design.

"School counselors do not have to be skilled statisticians to meaningfully analyze data" (ASCA, 2003, p. 51). This is true, but school counselors do need to master some basic statistical concepts to successfully analyze and interpret results data. In addition, school counselors need to know how to disaggregate data appropriately, enter data on spreadsheets such as Excel, do appropriate analyses, and develop graphs and charts displaying the data in understandable ways.

Disaggregating data is an important step in data analysis because it allows us to see if there are any students who are not doing as well as others. The ASCA (2003) suggested that the common fields for disaggregating data are as follows:

- gender,
- ethnicity,
- socioeconomic status (free and reduced lunch),
- vocational (multiperiod vocational program track),
- language spoken at home,
- special education,
- grade level, and
- teacher(s). (p. 50)

An important tool for results data analysis is a spreadsheet such as Excel. Spreadsheets allow us to enter results data and conduct various statistical procedures as appropriate. In addition, various charts and graphs can be created to show relationships of results data to possible outcomes such as state achievement test scores and external tests such as the SAT or ACT.

Some types of evaluation information are not easily adaptable to spreadsheet analyses, however, and may in fact be more meaningful when analyzed by counselors and their staff. For example, subjective counselor reports of guidance and counseling activities or certain types of student behaviors may lose meaning if quantified. These subjective analyses may be critical in the interpretation of other outcome data. In addition, small samples of activities or students may not warrant the use of computer analysis and thus will need to be handled manually. In such cases, precautions should be taken to reduce human error to a minimum by establishing checks and rechecks.

Finally, a results evaluation plan needs to emphasize how results data will be used. One use of such data is to demonstrate the contributions school counselors make to the goals of education as presented in the district's comprehensive school improvement plan. The second is how the data are used to enhance the district's current comprehensive guidance and counseling program. Results evaluation data serve to both prove and improve the program.

The Future: Bright and Full of Promise

It is well documented that evaluation has been part of professional discussion and action since the 1920s (Gysbers, 2004). Each decade of the 20th century saw repeated exhortations to conduct evaluation studies, particularly ones that focused on results. These decades also saw substantial efforts to actually conduct evaluation studies, including experimental control studies, to determine the impact of specific guidance and counseling activities and services as well as the overall impact of complete programs.

Given the past and present emphasis on evaluation, on being accountable, what about the future? I believe that the future is bright and full of promise because the profession is finally at a point of agreement that guidance and counseling is a program, not simply a set of services or a position. There is also general agreement about a common language that defines and describes the basic framework used to structure, organize, and sequence guidance and counseling activities and services K–12. In addition, there is general agreement that the content (student knowledge and skills) of guidance and counseling programs to be delivered to students can be organized around the three domains of academic, career, and personal/social.

Why is common language important for guidance and counseling programs? Common language enables school counselors, administrators, teachers, and parents or guardians to "coordinate their work and multiply the power of their intellects" (American College Testing Program, 1998, p. 9). Common language for guidance and counseling programs also allows these "individuals to communicate and replicate" (p. 9) guidance and counseling program activities. In addition, common language for guidance and counseling programs provides the basis for program, personnel, and results evaluation across a school district, grades K–12.

School counselors also have available at their fingertips technology that could not have been imagined years ago. Personal computers and software packages are available that can organize, analyze, and report results in various formats. This technology enables school counselors to take charge of results evaluation once they have mastered the basics of these software packages. The advances in hardware and software, that are sure to occur in the future, point to even more possibilities for evaluation.

Unfortunately, even with all of the knowledge and technology available today, some school counselors still see evaluation as a threat. What they need to do is rid their minds of the phobia of evaluation, of the persistent fear of evaluation that often leads to a compelling desire to avoid it. What will be required is a mindset that evaluation is simply a part of the guidance and counseling work that school counselors do in schools every day. It is a way that their work can be improved and its effectiveness demonstrated. It is important to begin each school year, semester, month, week, and day by being results oriented.

Finally, it is important to remember that evaluation talk is not enough. It is time for action. It is time for school counselors at all levels to accept the challenge of evaluation. The past has much to offer us concerning this challenge and how to address it. Let us use the wisdom of the past to address the challenge of evaluation today and into the future.

References

American College Testing Program. (1998, Spring). The power of a common language in workplace development. *Work Keys USA, 3,* 9.

American School Counselor Association. (2003). *The ASCA national model: A framework for school counseling programs.* Alexandra, VA: Author.

Brigman, G. & Campbell, C. (2003). Helping students improve academic achievement and school success behavior. *Professional School Counseling, 7,* 91–98.

Christy, E. B., Stewart, F. J., & Rosecrance, F. C. (1930). Guidance in the senior high school. *The Vocational Guidance Magazine, 9,* 51–57.

Dahir, C. A. & Stone, C. B. (2003). Accountability: A M.E.A.S.U.R.E. of the impact school counselors have on student achievement. *Professional School Counseling, 6,* 214–221.

Foster, L. H., Watson, T. S., Meeks, C., & Young, T. S. (2002). Single-subject research design for school counselors: Becoming an applied researcher. *Professional School Counseling, 6,* 146–154.

Gysbers, N. C. (2004). Comprehensive guidance and counseling programs: The evolution of accountability. *Professional School Counseling, 8,* 1–13.

Gysbers, N. C. & Henderson, P. (2006). *Developing and managing your school guidance and counseling program* (4th ed.). Alexandria, VA: American Counseling Association.

Gysbers, N. D., Hughey, K. F., Starr, M., & Lapan, R. T. (1992). Improving school guidance programs: A framework for program personnel and results evaluation. *Journal of Counseling and Development, 70,* 565–570.

Henderson, P. & Gysbers, N. C. (1998). *Leading and managing your school guidance program staff.* Alexandria, VA: American Counseling Association.

Hinderman, R. A. (1930). Evaluating and improving guidance services. *Nation's Schools, 5,* 47–52.

Hughes, D. K. & James, S. H. (2001). Using accountability data to protect a school counseling program: One counselor's experience. *Professional School Counseling, 4,* 306–309.

Issacs, M. L. (2003). Data-driven decision making: The engine of accountability. *Professional School Counseling, 6,* 228–295.

Johnson, C. D. (1991). Assessing results. In S. K. Johnson & E. A. Whitfield (Eds.), *Evaluating guidance programs: A practitioners guide* (pp. 43–55). Iowa City, IA: American College Testing Program.

Johnson, S. & Johnson, C. D. (2003). Results based guidance: A systems approach to student support programs. *Professional School Counseling, 6,* 180–184.

Johnson, S., Johnson, C., & Downs, L. L. (2006). *Building a results-based student support system.* Boston: Lahaska Press.

Kefauver, G. N. & Hand, H. C. (1941). *Appraising guidance in secondary schools.* New York: Macmillan.

Lapan, R. T. (2001). Results-based comprehensive guidance and counseling programs: A framework for planning and evaluation. *Professional School Counseling, 4,* 289–299.

Lapan, R. T., Gysbers, N. C., & Petroski, G. (2001). Helping 7th graders be safe and academically successful: A statewide study of the impact of comprehensive guidance programs. *Journal of Counseling and Development, 75,* 292–302.

Lee, C. C. & Workman, D. J. (1992). School counselors and research: Current status and future direction. *The School Counselor, 40,* 15–19.

McKinnon, B. E. (n.d.). *Toward accountability: A report on the Mesa approach to career guidance, counseling, and placement.* Mesa, AZ: Mesa Public Schools.

Missouri Department of Elementary and Secondary Education. (2000). *Guidelines for performance-based professional school counselor evaluation.* Jefferson City, MO: Author.

Myrick, R. D. (2003a). Accountability: Counselors count. *Professional School Counseling, 6,* 174–179.

Myrick, R. D. (2003b). *Developmental guidance and counseling: A practical approach* (4th ed.). Minneapolis, MN: Educational Media Corporation.

No Child Left Behind Act of 2001, Pub. L. No. 107-110, 115, Stat. 1434. (2001).

Payne, A. F. (1924). Problems in vocational guidance. *National Vocational Guidance Association Bulletin 2,* 61–63.

Pine, G. J. (1975). Evaluating school counseling programs: Retrospect and prospect. *Measurement and Evaluation in Guidance, 8,* 136–144.

Proctor, W. M. (1930). Evaluating guidance activities in high schools. *The Vocational Guidance Magazine, 9,* 58–66.

Rosecrance, F. C. (1930). Organizing guidance for the larger school system. *The Vocational Guidance Magazine, 9,* 243–249.

Rothney, J. W. M. (1958). *Guidance practices and results.* New York: Harper.

Rothney, J. W. M. & Farwell, G. F. (1960). The evaluation of guidance and personnel services. *Review of Educational Research, 30,* 168–175.

Rothney, J. W. M. & Roens, B. A. (1950). *Guidance of American youth: An experimental study.* Cambridge, MA: Harvard University Press.

Sink, C. A. & Stroh, H. R. (2003). Raising achievement test scores of early elementary school students through comprehensive school counseling programs. *Professional School Counseling, 6,* 350–364.

Tamminen, A. W. & Miller, G. D. (1968). *Guidance programs and their impact on students* (Research Project No. OE-5-85-035). St. Paul, MN: Department of Education.

Trevisan, M. S. & Hubert, M. (2001). Implementing comprehensive guidance program evaluation support: Lessons learned. *Professional School Counseling, 4,* 225–228.

Utah State Office of Education. (2003). *Comprehensive guidance performance review: Connecting program improvement and student learning.* Salt Lake City, UT: Author.

Whitson, S. C. (1996). Accountability through action research: Research methods for practitioners. *Journal of Counseling and Development, 74,* 616–623.

Whitson, S. C. & Sexton, T. L. (1998). A review of school counseling outcome research: Implications for practice. *Journal of Counseling and Development, 76,* 412–426.

Wilson, N. H. & Rotter, J. C. (1982). School counseling: A look into the future. *The Personnel and Guidance Journal, 60,* 353–357.

XLIV
RESEARCH IN AND ON SCHOOL COUNSELING

BRYAN S. K. KIM
University of Hawaii at Hilo

SAUL G. ALAMILLA
University of California, Santa Barbara

As is true for other areas in the field of education, there have been increasing pressures on the school counseling profession to be more accountable to the public concerning their relevance and effectiveness in helping students to be successful in the schools. The most recent example of this press of accountability has been the passing of the No Child Left Behind Act of 2001 (U.S. Department of Education, 2002) legislation. This law mandates school systems to be more accountable for the academic successes and failures of their students. An important consequence of this law, and the more general current trend on accountability, is that there now are even greater pressures on the school counseling profession to demonstrate its effectiveness in meeting students' emotional and social developmental needs and helping them to attain academic success.

Another source of this demand for accountability on the school counseling profession has been the increasing racial and ethnic diversification of our school systems. The past 4 decades in the United States have witnessed a dramatic increase in the number of individuals from diverse cultural backgrounds, mainly due to high immigration and birth rates among non-European American persons. Currently, African Americans and Latino Americans each represent 13% of the total U.S. population, with Asian Americans and American Indians representing 4% and 1%, respectively (U.S. Census Bureau, 2002). By the year 2050, it has been estimated that the number of racial and ethnic minority individuals will be nearly 50% of the U.S. population (U.S. Census Bureau). Already in California, Hawaii, and New Mexico, the number of "minority" persons represents over 50% of these states' populations, whereas Texas's minority population constitutes 48% (Hobbs & Stoops, 2002). An important implication of these data is that there will be a dramatic increase in the enrollment of students from diverse backgrounds in the school systems and that school personnel will be facing significant challenges posed by this increasing diversity. In particular, school counselors will be faced with meeting the unique needs of various cultural groups, while continuing to maintain their effectiveness with students from European American backgrounds. In addition, these demographic changes pose an important challenge for the school counseling profession to demonstrate and document their relevance and effectiveness in meeting the needs of the increasingly diverse student body.

One way in which the school counseling profession can demonstrate the important roles it plays in the lives of students is through research in and on school counseling. Research in and on school counseling can generate empirical evidence that can be used to demonstrate that school counselors are an integral part of the educational mission of the school systems. It can show that the practice of school counseling can have important and positive effects on the lives of students and the school community in general. It can show that the varied roles played by counselors in the schools help students cope with the many developmental challenges they face within the emotional, social, and academic arenas of their lives. Hence, research in and on counseling can be an important component of demonstrating accountability for the profession in meeting the needs of the student population.

Given this background, the purpose of this chapter is to describe and critique the current state of research in and on school counseling. First, we will present a conceptual framework that can be used to evaluate various facets of validity of research findings. This framework will be illustrated using a hypothetical counseling research study. Second, using this framework, we will critique the current state of school counseling research by examining two representative areas: (a) effectiveness of comprehensive school counseling programs and (b) efficacy of roles played by school counselors. We elected to choose these two areas of research because they seem most proximal to addressing the demand for accountability facing the school counseling profession. We should note that, although there may be some overlap between our review of comprehensive school counseling programs and that other chapters in this *Handbook* (e.g., Schmidt, Chapter 1, this volume), our focus will be on methodological strengths and limitations, in an attempt to help illustrate the general state of current research in and on school counseling. Third, we will examine the literature on the extent to which school counseling professionals are involved in research endeavors and the amount of attention devoted to empirical work in major school counseling publication outlets. Finally, we will offer directions for future research in and on school counseling.

A Conceptual Framework to Evaluate the Validity of Research Findings in School Counseling

The basic purpose of a research study is to isolate and assess the constructs of interest, to identify the relationship between the constructs, and simultaneously, to eliminate alternative hypotheses for the observed relationship (Heppner, Kivlighan, & Wampold, 1999). In this process, the concept of MAXMINCON is an important one to keep in mind (Kerlinger, 1986). MAXMINCON refers to *max*imizing the explained variance (i.e., controlled variation that is determined by the research design), *min*imizing the error variance (i.e., random error or noise), and *con*trolling irrelevant variables (e.g., using a covariate). When the explained variance between constructs of interest is at its greatest, the error variance is at its minimal, and the control variables have been fully and accurately identified, a study's results have the greatest chance of showing a true significant effect or relationship. However, a number of threats can jeopardize the validity of the study's findings. These threats are categorized into five types: (a) statistical conclusion validity, (b) internal validity, (c) construct validity of putative causes and effects, (d) external validity, and (e) hypothesis validity.

To illustrate these five threats, we would like to present a hypothetical research study that school counseling researchers might conduct. Imagine that you are a school counselor at a middle school who is interested in conducting an experimental study on the effects of a group intervention designed to enhance multicultural sensitivity among middle school students. Your idea for this research stemmed from your readings of the multicultural literature that suggested the importance of instilling awareness and knowledge about cultural diversity to adolescents. The literature suggested that this could lead individuals to function more effectively in our increasingly diverse society. After gaining approval to conduct research with human subjects from the school's administration, you randomly select 100 seventh graders from the entire seventh-grade class as participants in your study. Fortunately, you are able to gain informed consents from the parents of all 100 students and informed assents from all of these students to participate in your study.

To begin the study, you randomly assign 50 students to the experimental condition, and these students are again randomly divided into 5 groups of 10 students each. Each of these groups is given ten 50-minute group counseling sessions in which students learn about cultural diversity and to become more multiculturally aware, based on a manual you have developed. The groups meet 2 times each week and are facilitated by five different professional counselors whom you have trained. For the other 50 students, you also randomly divide them into 5 groups of 10 students each. Rather than receiving the treatment, they are shown a 50-minute *National Geographic* presentation about the animal kingdom across 10 meetings, held 2 times per week. Similar to the experimental condition, this control condition is facilitated by the five counselors who introduce and show the videotape presentation; however, no discussion is held after the showing to minimize contact between the counselors and students. After 5 weeks, you have the participants complete measures of multicultural self-efficacy to examine the differences between the two conditions on these scores.

Now, we turn our attention back to the five threats to validity and use this research example to illustrate these threats. Statistical conclusion validity refers to the extent to which researchers can be confident that the observed relationship between the variables of interest is accurate (Heppner et al., 1999). The threats that exist for this type of validity are related to making either Type I error (rejecting the null hypothesis when the null hypothesis is true) or Type II error (accepting the null hypothesis when the null hypothesis is not true). An example of a Type I error is finding a false significant relationship because of conducting numerous statistical tests. Conducting a large number of tests increases the likelihood of finding a significant relationship due to pure chance (this is also called fishing and error rate problem; Heppner et al.). In the preceding example, if you had administered several measures of multicultural competence and compared these scores separately to identify differences between the experimental and control condition without controlling for Type I error, you could be falsely concluding that the experimental condition had a positive effect because the significant differences could be due to chance. To avoid this situation, you might reduce the alpha level (e.g., Bonferroni correction) to conduct a more conservative statistical test. Alternatively, you might combine the scores of all of the measures into one score and simply conduct one comparison test (e.g., t-test).

In terms of Type II errors, a research study could lack adequate statistical sensitivity and not detect an effect or relationship when there is a true effect or relationship. One way this could occur is by having an insufficient sample size. Another way is to use instruments that have inadequate reliability (i.e., increased measurement error) that lead to a lack of statistical power. In the study just described, you could avoid a Type II error by conducting an a priori power analysis to determine the exact number of participants one might need given the alpha level for the statistical test(s), expected effect size (i.e., the size of the difference between the experimental and control groups), type of statistical test used (e.g., t-test, correlation, multivariate tests), and power of the statistical test (i.e., the degree to which you are willing to accept a Type II error—generally this is 20%, which leads to a power of .80). Often, researchers use a "rule of thumb"—for example, 20 participants per condition for a group counseling intervention. But this is a very rough and imprecise way of determining an optimal sample size, and it could lead to an inadequate number of participants. Regarding the issue of reliability, one could examine the internal consistency (e.g., Cronbach's alpha) of the scores from the measures used to ensure that the scores are relatively free of measurement error.

On a related note, an important consideration in avoiding Type I and Type II errors is to use the most appropriate statistical tests to analyze the data. In the previous example, five counselors each saw 10 students in both the experimental and control conditions. This situation creates dependence on each data point (i.e., outcome score) between the counselor and the student in each group. In other words, the participant scores are nested within the counselor to whom they were assigned. One way to address such a situation is to use tests such as hierarchical linear modeling that can account for the variance on the outcome score that is attributed to the counselor–student pairing. Without addressing this problem, the researcher would have made incorrect conclusions. In general, to avoid statistical analysis problems, we encourage school counseling researchers to consult with statistical books and/or consultants before engaging in data analyses.

Internal validity refers to the extent to which researchers can be confident that the causal relationship specified in the design of the study is indeed true. Essentially, internal validity of a study is increased when alternative and competing explanatory hypotheses are eliminated, thereby increasing the likelihood that the observed relationship with the dependent variables is indeed caused by the independent variables. Internal validity of a study is high when the independent variable(s) is manipulated, the participants are randomly assigned to comparison groups (typically treatment and control), and the research procedures (e.g., assessment, implementation of intervention) are given at the same time (Heppner et al., 1999). In studies involving experimental and control groups, there is a greater internal validity when both groups are equivalent on all characteristics except the independent variable that is being manipulated; this is usually accomplished via random assignment. When these conditions are not met, threats to internal validity are present.

Heppner et al. (1999) described a number of possible threats to internal validity. For example, when there is no manipulation of a variable in a study, the threat to internal validity is high, and a causal relationship cannot be made even when a statistically significant relationship is detected between the treatment experience and outcome variables of interest. An example of this type of a design is the one-group, pre/post test design in which there is no comparison group. Also, another design with high threat to internal validity is the correlational design in which there is no manipulation of the variables of interest. For these types of studies, only a relational conclusion can be made (e.g., a positive correlation exists between self-esteem and academic achievement). Even if a design employs a comparison group, when the participants are not randomly assigned into the two groups, threat to internal validity is present because a statistically significant difference between the two groups may be attributed to factors other than the intended treatment (i.e., pretreatment differences such as developmental level or achievement level). Also, when treatments are not given at the same time, threat to internal validity may be present because the treatment group at Time 1 may also receive unintended forms of treatment from external factors, which may not be present at Time 2 when the other group is offered the comparison condition. An internal validity problem also would exist if the group at Time 2 matured more quickly than the treatment group at Time 1; that is, it is not clear whether the observed difference between the two groups was due to the differential maturation rates or the treatments themselves.

Heppner et al. (1999) pointed out that the design that is least prone to threats to internal validity is the posttest only experimental control group design (see the following illustration).

$$R \quad X \quad O_1$$
$$R \quad \quad O_2$$

In this design, "R" refers to random assignment of participants to the two groups. "O_1" refers to posttest assessment in the first group, and "O_2" refers to the posttest assessment in the second group. "X" refers to the presence of treatment of interest; hence, treatment is given to the first group but not to the second group and the independent variable has two levels, treatment versus no treatment. This design meets the following conditions necessary for high internal validity: random assignment, manipulation of independent variable (i.e., treatment vs. no treatment), and the implementation of research procedures (e.g., assessment) at the same time.

In the preceding example, the study is designed to be free of threats to internal validity because you have randomly assigned participants into experimental and control groups. You also have a clear manipulation of your variable of interest (i.e., multicultural sensitivity training vs. no training), and the group counseling sessions are held at the same time. However, as you can imagine, this study is ideal in nature and such a design may not be possible in a typical school setting. In such a situation, a researcher might need to sacrifice some of the tenets of internal validity such as settling for nonrandom assignment and using existing classrooms to conduct the study. Here, the researcher would assign one classroom to the experimental condition and another to the control condition. In such a design, known as a quasi-experimental design, a major threat that is present, as previously mentioned, is that it is not clear whether the observed differences on the outcome scores are due to preexisting differences between the classes, for example, having a multicultural-focused curriculum in one class and another curriculum in the other class, or your intervention. To mitigate such a difference, it is important for researchers to ensure that if existing groups are going to be used over random assignment, the two groups are equal in as many aspects as possible (e.g., age, sex ratio, academic level, socioeconomic level, curriculum, and teachers' teaching and personality styles). For a study in which the experimental and control conditions cannot be given simultaneously, researchers should try to ensure that there is no major event, particularly related to multicultural sensitivity in our example, which is present for one group but not for another group. The presence of such an event is known as history, and this is one of the most serious threats to validity when the interventions are not administered simultaneously.

Construct validity of putative causes and effects refers to the extent to which the measured constructs accurately represent the constructs of interest (Heppner et al., 1999). A confound exists when there is ambiguity between the measured constructs and the constructs of interest. In essence, confound refers to having an alternative construct(s) embedded in the instruments that are designed to measure the construct of interest. Threats to construct validity usually occur when there is either an underrepresentation of the construct itself or an overrepresentation of construct irrelevancies. According to Heppner et al. (1999), specific threats to the construct validity of putative causes and effects might occur when (a) the construct is not fully explicated and the operationalization of the construct includes only a limited amount of construct representation, (b) the construct is assessed using only one measure and thus limiting the measurement of the full range of the construct, (c) the construct is measured using only one method such as self-reports, (d) subjects guess the experimental hypothesis and respond according to their guesses, (e) subjects feel anxious about the evaluation and do not respond accurately, and (f) the experimenter gives subtle messages that may affect the responses by the subjects.

In the example study presented previously, the group counselors used a manual that you developed based on extant literature on how multicultural sensitivity can be achieved. In designing this intervention, you have carefully included a comprehensive array of components that fully represents the constructs of multicultural sensitivity. In addition, you have carefully chosen instruments that assess self-reported, multicultural self-efficacy to determine the effects of your treatment program accurately. On the other hand, if such a measure was not taken and the group counseling intervention did not fully represent multicultural sensitivity, there may be a problem with construct validity. Also, if in administering the program, the five counselors in the treatment condition unknowingly deviated from the manual and perhaps were much nicer to their group members than to the students who watched *National Geographic* shows, the level of "niceness" of the counselors could become a confound, which is a serious threat to construct validity. Furthermore, another area of a potential construct validity problem is that the research study presented previously depended solely on self-reports of participants to assess their multicultural self-efficacy. In this regard, a stronger study would be to add a third-party observation (e.g., teacher or parent ratings) as a supplemental measure of students' multicultural self-efficacy. This method would strengthen the construct validity of the outcomes of group counseling.

External validity refers to the extent to which the results of a study are generalizable to other people, settings, and time (Heppner et al., 1999). A threat to external validity exists when there is an interaction between selection and treatment such that the treatment is effective on only the population on whom the treatment was tested. Given the increasing diversification of our school systems, as previously described, this threat is an important one to consider with respect to school counseling becoming more relevant and effective with non-European American clients. Another threat to external validity occurs when there is an interaction between setting and treatment such that the treatment is effective in only the setting in which the treatment was tested. Given the vastness of the United States, it is important to consider whether a treatment that was shown to be effective in one part of the country will be effective in another distant part. A final threat to external validity involves an interaction between history and treatment such that the treatment is effective only during the time that the treatment was tested. Hence, it is important to examine the current efficacy of a treatment method that was found to be effective during a previous time. To illustrate, in the preceding example study, you randomly selected the participants from all seventh graders in the school, which allowed the study to have a strong external validity in terms of its findings to the rest of the seventh-grade population in the school. However, one must be cautioned that the generalizability of the findings may not hold up in other schools, especially those schools with students whose characteristics are very different from the students in your school. In such a situation, it would be important for the study to be replicated in schools at other geographical locations and at other times to examine the extent to which the results are generalizable.

Finally, Wampold, Davis, and Good (1990) proposed hypothesis validity as an additional factor to consider when examining the rigor of a study. Wampold et al. described that threats to hypothesis validity can be present when there is an inconsequential hypothesis, such that the hypothesis of interest is not based on theory and does not result in convergence of theory (i.e., supporting the theory of interest while refuting alternative theories). Other threats to hypothesis validity involve having an ambiguous hypothesis such that the hypothesis is not stated in clear and falsifiable terms, having a lack of congruence between the experimental hypothesis and statistical hypothesis, and having a diffusion of statistical hypothesis (e.g., using an omnibus hypothesis when a more specific hypothesis should be used). In the study presented previously, the null hypothesis that was tested was that there would be no difference between the experimental and control conditions on the self-reported scores of multicultural self-efficacy, the alternative hypothesis being that there is a significant difference on multicultural self-efficacy. Because this hypothesis was based on extant theoretical literature on multicultural counseling, one can be confident that the study has hypothesis validity. However, if the hypothesis was not based on any theory—for example, that there would be a positive effect on students' career aspirations—there would be a concern about the validity of this hypothesis.

To summarize, a useful framework to critique the quality of research includes five domains: statistical conclusion validity, internal validity, construct validity of putative causes and effects, external validity, and hypothesis validity. These threats were illustrated using a hypothetical school counseling research study. Now, we turn our attention to existing research on school counseling. These studies will be described in the following section and evaluated based on this conceptual framework.

A Review and Critique of Current Research

Research on Comprehensive School Counseling Programs

In reviewing the research on comprehensive school counseling programs, it is helpful to begin with review articles; we found three of these types of articles. In one of the earlier reviews, Pine (1975) reviewed the extant research and found that studies on school counseling programs tended to examine a wide range of outcome variables including academic achievement, peer relations, personal adjustment, school attendance, school adjustment, self-concept, self-esteem, reduction of inappropriate behaviors, and setting realistic goals. In terms of the research methods that were employed, Pine listed the following: (a) experimental design (posttest only without control, pre/post test without control, and pre/post test with control), (b) descriptive method, (c) case study method, and (d) second person method. Pine concluded that there is evidence to support the effectiveness of school counseling programs but recommended that researchers use more formal methods for evaluating school counseling programs.

In the early 1990s, Borders and Drury (1992) conducted a review of articles on counseling programs that had been published between the 1960s and 1990 in peer-reviewed journals (e.g., *Journal of Counseling and Development, The School Counselor, Elementary School Guidance and Counseling,* and *Measurement and Evaluation in Counseling Development*). Based on their review, Borders and Drury identified the common characteristics, principles, scope, and nature of comprehensive school counseling programs. They found that there are four principles that characterize these programs: (1) they are substantive and systematic, with clearly delineated and measurable goals, objectives, and interventions; (2) they are fully integrated and integral to the general educational mission of the program (e.g., they work in tandem with and in service to other educational activities in the schools); (3) they possess a holistic and/or developmental theoretical focus (e.g., cognitive, social, and psychological factors that foster and advance the academic, personal, social, and career development of all students); (4) they are equally accessible to all students; and (5) they are guided by clearly written policies that uphold the confidentiality and protect the privacy of students and other participants (e.g., teachers and families).

In terms of effectiveness, Borders and Drury (1992) reported that (a) there was support for individual and small group counseling interventions (e.g., improved student self-esteem and academic achievement); (b) there was mixed support among and within students for classroom guidance interventions (e.g., one study reviewed revealed significant effects on kindergarten and first-grade but not on third-grade student attendance rates); and (c) there was support for consultation service interventions by showing a positive relationship between the intervention and student behavior, academic achievement, and self-concept.

However, Borders and Drury (1992) did not critique the research methodology of the articles under review, and hence, it is not known the extent to which these findings were based on rigorous and externally valid designs.

More recently, Gysbers (2004) reviewed the literature on school counseling programs that had been published between 1920 and 2003. Based on a sampling of empirical studies published during this time, Gysbers pointed out that these studies addressed two basic issues: "evaluating the impact of specific guidance and counseling activities and services and evaluating the impact of total programs of guidance and counseling" (p. 8). Gysbers also noted that the research designs used ranged from longitudinal to between or within group comparisons. Gysbers found that the results of these studies were generally supportive of vocational guidance and school counseling endeavors, with positive impacts on students' perceptions of the quality of their school and counseling experiences, grades, educational outlook, higher educational opportunities, and/or overall adjustment in and outside of the school environment.

While all three of these review articles are helpful in gaining a sense of the kinds of research work that currently exists on the effectiveness of comprehensive school counseling programs, they do not provide the full picture. In particular, each review article represented a different level of attention to the research rigor of the studies that were reviewed and none of them critiqued the studies in terms of the five types of validity threats. Hence, we would like to offer more detailed reviews of research studies examining the effectiveness of comprehensive school counseling programs with a particular focus on the design issues. This review is followed by a critique of the methodologies using the threats to the five validities as an evaluative framework.

In our search of the school counseling research literature, we identified only five published studies on comprehensive school counseling programs. Lavoritano and Segal (1992) evaluated the effectiveness of Remedial Education and Diagnostic Services (READS), a program that provides psychological and educational testing, counseling, and remedial education services by school counselors. The participants in the program were 152 elementary students from varied ethnic backgrounds and from 20 different schools who were referred to the program. In addition, 74 students were not referred to the program and, hence, did not receive the interventions; they were used as a comparison group. The dependent variables were participants' self-rated competency in six domains: (1) scholastic competence, (2) social acceptance, (3) athletic competence, (4) physical appearance, (5) behavioral conduct, and (6) general self-worth. The authors also investigated whether the participants' self-esteem as measured by the Self-Perception Profile for Children (SPCC; Harter, 1985) had higher scores after the intervention. In their preliminary analysis, the authors found that the students in the intervention group (i.e., students who were referred to the program) were significantly different in several characteristics: They were more likely to be males, they tended to come from single parent homes, they had a greater likelihood of having been retained a grade, they tended to be underachieving, and they tended to score low on the pretest measures on all six domains. In terms of the main research question with respect to the effects of the READS program, the authors conducted paired-samples t-tests on the pre/post test scores from the intervention group and found that their scores increased significantly on scholastic competence and decreased significantly on behavioral conduct. No differences were observed between the intervention and comparison group in several one-way analyses of covariance with the differing demographic characteristics as covariates.

Lapan, Gysbers, and Sun (1997) and Lapan, Gysbers, and Petroski (2001) examined the impact of the Missouri Comprehensive Guidance Programs (MCGP) programs among middle and high school students across the state of Missouri during a 7- to 10-year period. Lapan and colleagues (1997) noted that between 1985 and 1997 over 2,200 school counselors and administrators from more than 400 school districts in the state of Missouri had received training in the implementation and management of the MCGP and that over 97% of the state's school counselors were in the process of implementing MCGP. The MCGP is designed to help students with career planning and exploration, personal development (e.g., knowledge of self and of others), and educational and vocational development needs.

Lapan et al. (1997) examined the effects of MCGP on high school students' perceptions of academic achievement and campus climate. The data were obtained from the Missouri School Improvement Program (MSIP) database, which contained information from 22,964 high school students, 236 schools, and 434 school counselors from Missouri. The student outcome variables were assessed using the Secondary

Student Questionnaire (SSQ) that contained student-rated, single-item measures of their current grades, their perceptions of how well their educations were preparing them for the future, and how much they liked school. In addition, a 5-item measure was used to assess students' perception of school climate. Furthermore, counselors were assessed using a 32-item instrument on the degree to which the MCGP was being implemented in their schools. The data were analyzed using hierarchical linear modeling, which allows for the controlling of higher level variations such as differences between schools and school districts. The results indicated that schools with more fully implemented MCGP had students who reported having higher grades; better preparation for their futures, particularly in terms of their career goals; and positive school climate. In addition, positive effects of the program were maintained when differences between schools vis-à-vis enrollment size, student socioeconomic status, and percentage of minority students in the school were controlled.

Lapan et al. (2001) conducted a similar study but with a sample consisting of seventh-grade students and with a different set of outcome variables. Specifically, these researchers examined the impact of the MCGP on students' (a) perceptions of school safety, (b) satisfaction with their education, (c) perceptions of their grades, (d) perceptions of their relationships with their teachers, and (e) perceptions of the importance and relevance of their education to their futures. Again, using hierarchical linear modeling, the authors analyzed data from 22,601 seventh graders and 4,868 teachers from 184 schools and found that, while controlling for school variations on socioeconomic status and enrollment size, when counselors more fully implemented the MCGP (i.e., spent more time in classrooms; assisted students with personal, educational, and career issues; consulted with parents, teachers, and administrative staff when they engaged in individual and group counseling with students; and made appropriate referrals), students reported feeling safer in school, having better relationships with their teachers, having higher grades, being more satisfied with the educational experiences, perceiving their education experiences to be more relevant to their futures, and having a better quality of life. Interestingly, the authors also found that girls reported earning higher grades than boys did and European American students reported having higher grades than minority students did.

In another study examining a comprehensive school counseling program, Brigman and Campbell (2003) studied the effects of the Student Success Skills Program (SSS) on academic success and related behaviors among elementary, middle, and high school students. According to the authors, the SSS is designed to enhance the cognitive, social, and self-management skills that are related to academic success, and it is administered by counselors through classroom guidance and group counseling formats. In the study, the authors used a pre/post test experimental design in which participants in the SSS groups were compared with a control group from other schools with matching geographic location, race, and socioeconomic status. To participate in the SSS groups, 180 students were randomly selected from three elementary, one middle, and two high schools. These participants consisted of fifth, sixth, eighth, and ninth graders who scored between the 25th and 50th percentile on the Florida Comprehensive Assessment Test (FCAT) in reading. For the comparison group, data from the same number of students in the same grade levels with similar test scores were selected from nonparticipating schools. The results showed that participants in the SSS groups scored significantly higher on the FCAT reading and math scores than the students in the comparison groups.

Sink and Stroh (2003) examined whether elementary schools that have a well-established comprehensive school counseling program are enhancing student academic achievement more than schools without such a program. The authors randomly selected 150 public elementary schools in the state of Washington of various sizes and from various socioeconomic strata and collected data on 20,131 students in the third and fourth grades. Based on a multivariate analysis of covariance with a Bonferroni correction, Sink and Stroh found that, while controlling for length of enrollment and gender among students, students scored higher on measures of academic achievement (Iowa Tests of Basic Skills—Form M and the Washington Assessment of Student Learning) when a comprehensive school counseling program was implemented in their schools. Furthermore, increased academic achievement was observed especially among students from low socioeconomic status when their schools had a program in place.

As a whole, the results of these studies lend empirical support to the effectiveness of comprehensive school counseling programs. However, such findings are not without methodological limitations. Although many of these studies appear to have high levels of statistical conclusion and external validities given the large and representative sample sizes and the use of sophisticated data analytic strategies (HLM, MANCOVA with Bonferroni correction), one of the studies (Lavoritano & Segal, 1992) conducted numerous statistical tests without controlling for an inflated Type I error rate. In addition, some of the studies did not have comparison groups to examine the true effects of the school counseling programs. Hence, it is unclear whether the positive effects were indeed caused by the programs, which leads to internal validity concerns. Also, there are concerns about hypothesis and construct validity of the findings. In most of the studies, the authors noted that the observed effect sizes were relatively small. This raises questions about the extent to which the constructs used to assess the effectiveness of school counseling programs are adequate and if the most common choices of constructs meet the demands of accountability. It also raises the question of whether the effect sizes would have been larger if different outcome measures were used. In Lapan et al. (1997), for instance, student outcomes were assessed using single item measures, and hence, their psychometric adequacy cannot be known. Perhaps the use of more well-established measures of academic and social achievement might have led to larger effect sizes, thereby further strengthening the importance of the outcomes. Moreover, many of the measures used were self-reports, and as such, there was a general lack of objective achievement measures. For example, one of the outcome variables in Lapan et al. was student-reported grades. It could be speculated that the findings might have been strengthened if the actual grades of students were used instead. In addition to using well-established and objective outcome data, alternative methods of assessing student outcomes could have strengthened the studies. For example, Curcio, Mathai, and Roberts (2003) described the helpfulness of using the following types of evaluation tools in their evaluation work: (a) documents (e.g., minutes from counselor monthly meetings and counselor daily activity logs), (b) interviews with school counselors and principals, and (c) focus group discussions with parents, students, and teachers. However, despite all of these limitations in the current literature, it is also important to mention that the overall findings still provide valuable and important information vis-à-vis effectiveness.

We should note that the American School Counselor Association (ASCA; 2003) recently published *The ASCA National Model: A Framework for School Counseling Programs*, a document describing a model for developing and implementing comprehensive school counseling programs. This document offers a model of a comprehensive school guidance and counseling program based on four elements: (1) foundation, (2) delivery System, (3) management systems, and (4) accountability. The foundation element specifies that a guidance and counseling program should be based on a coherent philosophy and mission statement to guide the creation of the program that is related to the ASCA national standards and competencies. The delivery system component describes the mode in which the program is offered, including guidance workshops, individual services, responsive services, and support to systems. The management systems element details the relationship among the roles of school counselors, administrators, and an advisory council in developing, implementing, and evaluating the program. Finally, accountability, the fourth element, describes the importance of assessing whether and to what extent the program has made a positive difference in the lives of students. In proposing this model, the ASCA described the benefits to a variety of constituents including students, parents, teachers, administrators, education boards and departments, school counselors, counselor educators, and communities. While this model is promising, it should be noted that its validity with respect to applicability must also be examined. For example, future research is needed to examine the extent to which the model has been employed by school systems and the degree to which the model was useful in running effective programs.

Research on School Counselor Roles and Duties

In addition to examining the effectiveness of comprehensive school counseling programs in order to study the current state of research in and on school counseling, it is helpful to examine the research that has been done to investigate the efficacy of counselor roles and duties. In defining counselor roles and duties, Myrick (1993) proposed that the roles and duties could be categorized as either direct or indirect services. Myrick described direct services as including individual and group counseling and guidance activities. Indirect services include consultation, coordination (e.g., orchestrating guidance services through special events), and peer facilitation (e.g., "training" of peer counselors). On the other hand, Gysbers and Henderson (1994) proposed a four-category schema describing school counselor roles and duties. This schema include the following roles and duties: (a) guidance curriculum, (b) individual planning, (c) responsive services, and (d) system support. The implementation of a guidance curriculum refers to classroom or group activities designed for all students. Individual planning activities include assessing and advising students regarding their personal, educational, and career goals. Responsive services include preventive or remediation measures via individual, small group, and crisis counseling, and providing referrals and consultation services when and where appropriate. Finally, system support refers to conducting outcome research, professional and staff development, and supervision of school personnel.

Although there appears to be some clarity in terms of what counselor roles and duties ought to be, there has been tension between counselors and administrators about what roles and duties counselors must realistically assume in the school setting (Burnham & Jackson, 2000; Fitch, Newby, Ballestero, & Marshall, 2001). Some administrators believe that counselors should assist with administrative duties such as courses scheduling, coordinating or administering achievement tests, and disciplining students. In a survey of future school administrators, Fitch et al. found that 57% of the respondents rated record keeping, a role

ASCA deemed inappropriate for counselors, as a significant role for school counselors. Also, Burnham and Jackson, in a survey of counselors, found that no less than 65% of the participants reported having engaged in nonguidance or noncounselor related activities. According to ASCA (2003), activities that are appropriate for school counselors include counseling, consulting, academic and career guidance, interpretation of tests, and prevention programs. In light of this tension between some school administrators and counselors, it is imperative that the accountability efforts also focus on evaluating the efficacy of conventional school counselor roles and duties. Hence, in this section, we will examine the current research literature on school counselor roles and duties.

Unfortunately, however, our search of the research literature on counselor roles and duties led to only two articles. Fitch and Marshall (2004) examined the roles and duties of school counselors in terms of enhancing student academic success. The authors studied and compared the activities of school counselors at high- and low-achieving schools to determine if there was a relationship between school performance category and the perceived importance of different counseling duties and time spent on the duties. Participants were school counselors across 62 elementary, middle, and high schools in Kentucky. The participants completed a survey containing a list of 11 roles and duties that were based on the Kentucky School Counseling Standards (Education Professional Standards Board, 1996). The roles and duties were program management, curriculum implementation, counseling, consultation, coordination, assessment, maintenance of professional standards, leadership functions, professional development, advocacy work, and other related work (Fitch & Marshall); these activities are similar to those of ASCA standards. For each of these roles and duties, participants were asked to rate their perceptions of the importance and the amount of time spent on each role or duty. In addition, the participants also completed information on their schools' academic performance on the California Test of Basic Skills, which was used to classify each school as either high or low achieving.

The results indicated that for the ratings of importance of each role or duty, there were no significant differences between high- and low-achieving schools, except for the advocacy role; interestingly, participants in the low-achieving schools rated the advocacy role as more important than did counselors in the high-achieving schools (Fitch & Marshall, 2004). With respect to hours spent on each of the roles and duties, participants in high-achieving schools reported spending more time on program management, assessment, coordination activities, and adherence to professional standards (i.e., aligning their programs to prescribed models or standards) than counselors in low-achieving schools did. The authors also found that, similar to Burnham and Jackson's (2000) findings, counselors in both high- and low-achieving schools reported engaging in clerical activities more than in any other activity except for counseling activities (Fitch & Marshall, 2004). Despite these findings, however, Fitch and Marshall's findings also have some important limitations. The results may not be generalizable given that it was gathered from a convenience sample and in one state, namely, Kentucky. In addition, the study lacked any information about the students in each school. Information such as socioeconomic status and race/ethnicity could help to explain the findings and, at a minimum, should have been kept statistically constant between high- and low-achieving schools. This information also could have revealed the extent to which the findings are generalizable to other schools.

In a study that examined counselor roles and duties beyond those of the conventional direct service provider (e.g., individual and group counselor), Field and Baker (2004) explored nine high school counselors' views on the role of an advocate using a qualitative design. Field and Baker defined advocacy as the following:

> an approach to school counseling in which the counselor goes beyond the tradition verbal 'give and take,' based on theoretical premises and techniques. A school counselor advocates on behalf of an individual student, a student group, or about a student issue; incorporates multicultural competence; provides meaningful information and additional helping resources; and lends support, including appropriate interventions, beyond the four walls on an office. (p. 57)

The participants were divided into two groups and interviewed using a semistructured format. The analysis of the responses revealed the following themes: (a) advocacy required additional or extraordinary interventions, consisted of several interventions, and was focused exclusively on the student; (b) advocacy meant that counselors would support one another in their advocacy roles as well as support their profession; (c) advocacy constituted or was perceived as a belief system or structure, which predated professional training; (d) advocacy consisted of flexible and reflexive behaviors, which were guided by realistic expectations; (e) consistency in demonstrating advocacy beliefs and behaviors was viewed as essential by the counselors; (f) the counselors received positive feedback from students with respect to their advocacy work; (g) support from administrators was also expressed by the counselors; and (h) work overloads prevented counselors from implementing advocacy interventions or engaging in advocacy roles. While these findings are interesting, there are obvious limitations to these results. The limitations include the relatively small number of participants, data collection in groups that could be affected by social influence dynamics, and data analysis by two persons. Nonetheless, it should be pointed out that this is one of the few studies examining school counselors' implementation of the advocacy role.

While the findings from these two studies are useful, they do not offer a comprehensive view of the current research literature on the efficacy of counselor roles and duties. Hence, we further examined the school counseling literature in the area of counseling interventions. Although reviews of counseling intervention research are presented in the other chapters of this *Handbook*, particularly in Section VI, and they do not necessarily, directly bear on the efficacy of counselor roles and duties, we hoped that this examination would indirectly inform us on the type of counseling tasks that might be engaged in by counselors. We reasoned that counselor roles and duties could be shaped by the interventions they implement in the schools. This effort led us to a relatively recently published article that reviewed the intervention research literature in school counseling.

Whiston and Sexton (1998) reviewed research articles on school counseling interventions that were published between 1988 and 1995. They selected articles that (a) described activities or interventions performed by school counselors, (b) involved K–12 students or parents of school-aged children, and (c) assessed and described the outcome results of the intervention. These criteria led to the identification of 50 empirical studies. To organize these articles, the authors used the four-category schema of Gysbers and Henderson (1994) that was described previously. Based on this model, Whiston and Sexton classified 12 studies under the implementation of guidance curriculum category, 10 studies under the individual planning category, 25 studies under the responsive services category, and 3 studies under the system support category. The authors found that a majority of these studies were quantitative in nature ($n = 43$), while the remaining used qualitative, evaluative, or follow-up designs. Among the quantitative studies, 31 used descriptive field designs, 11 used experimental field designs, and 1 used an experimental laboratory design. The 12 studies with experimental designs had at least one control group, which suggests a high level of internal validity. However, the remaining 31 descriptive designs were not amenable to any causality conclusions. Also, Whiston and Sexton pointed out that treatment integrity was not documented in 42 of the 50 studies, which raises serious concerns about construct validity of the treatment variable. The authors also mentioned that only 2 of the 50 studies used random sampling, which suggests possible threats to external validity. Furthermore, the authors reported that the majority of quantitative studies did not use statistical tests to analyze the data, thereby raising concerns about the statistical conclusion validity. Based on these findings, Whiston and Sexton concluded, "a broad range of activities school counselors perform often result in positive changes for students . . . however, our conclusions are slightly more tentative due to our evaluations of the methodological limitations" (p. 422).

In summary, our review of the research literature on counselor roles and duties led to only two studies. Although the findings supported the efficacy of the various roles that school counselors play, they are not without methodological limitations. Also, although Whiston and Sexton's (1998) review article showed positive outcomes when counselors implemented the described counseling interventions within their varied roles as described by Gysbers and Henderson (1994), the findings are only indirectly related to the efficacy of counselor roles and duties, and they are limited by methodological concerns. Hence, the lack of available research on school counseling roles and duties poses a significant dilemma in terms of addressing the accountability press. Specifically, while the pressures have increased for the school counseling profession, there appears to be very limited research that can serve as evidence for the efficacy in the various counseling roles that school counselors play. To explore this issue further, we now turn our attention to the issue of the availability of researchers who are conducting school counseling research.

Availability of Researchers Who Are Conducting Research in and on School Counseling

Given the relative paucity of research on efficacy of counselor roles and duties and on comprehensive school counseling programs, it is helpful to examine the extent to which school counseling research is being conducted and to which the findings are published in school counseling journals. Bauman (2004) conducted a survey of 763 randomly selected ASCA school counselors from all 50 states and Puerto Rico. The survey contained 26 items that assessed counselors' views and activities concerning research and school counselors (Bauman). The results of the survey revealed the following: 78.1% of school counselors surveyed disagreed or strongly disagreed with the statement, "I am expected to conduct research as part of my job as a school counselor," whereas only 11.3% agreed or strongly agreed with this statement. Doctoral-degree-holding school counselors were more confident in their research abilities than were non-doctoral-degree-holding school counselors. The former group of school counselors also had more interests in collaborating with university researchers on research endeavors.

In terms of school counselors learning from research findings, Bauman's (2004) results showed that the publication most widely read by the respondents was the *ASCA School Counselor*, a magazine that publishes mainly practice-focused articles. Only 36% of the school counselors surveyed read the more research-focused *Professional School Counseling* or *Journal of Counseling and Development*. In short, the status quo of research in and on school counseling might be best illustrated by the following observations:

> a participant noted that many school counselors do not value what research can do for their program, and suggested that a lack of emphasis on research on [sic] graduate training programs might account for this . . . [whereas another] individual indicated that while her masters' degree program had prepared her well to conduct research, such endeavors [were] not valued by her workplace. (Bauman, 2004, p. 146)

In terms of journal space for articles on school counseling research, Bauman et al. (2002) examined the amount of pages devoted to reporting research findings in and on school counseling. The results indicated that only 25% of the first four volumes of the *Professional School Counseling* journal were devoted to empirical articles and only 19% and 28% of these studies primarily or marginally, respectively, were authored by school district affiliates. Furthermore, 22% of the school counselors surveyed were not keeping abreast of new research findings. Consistent with these results, Whiston and Sexton (1998) lamented about the relative lack of published research in their review of intervention articles. They noted, "[That] only 50 studies were published from 1988 through 1995 is somewhat disappointing" (p. 422).

In summary, it appears that master's level school counselors have little interest or confidence in conducting research. School counselors appear more interested in reading practice-oriented journals than research-oriented ones. Furthermore, research journals tend to devote relatively little space for empirical articles, which makes it more difficult for school counselors to share their research results with other professionals. Although these findings may seem disappointing, it is not surprising given that most school counselor training programs are geared toward practice (vs. research), and there is not a great deal of emphasis on research and publication (for suggestions concerning changes in the training sequence of school counselors to address this concern, see Steward, Neil, & Diemer, Chapter 2, this volume). Nonetheless, the findings raise serious concerns about whether the school counseling profession is well positioned to respond to the challenges of accountability needs. As Whiston and Sexton (1998) noted, "[If] school counseling activities are going to have a substantial empirical base then there needs to be increased interest in researching those activities" (pp. 422–423). They further noted, "We believe that school counselors, counselor educators or researchers, and leaders in professional organizations, such as the American Counseling Association (ACA) and the American School Counselor Association, should work together to increase the amount of outcome research in school counseling" (p. 425).

Implications for Future Research

Based on the findings from this review, several suggestions for future research can be offered. First, in future research studies, it is important to attend to the methodological issues cited previously. Given the many threats to validity present in the current school counseling literature, it is imperative that researchers make strong efforts to design studies that address the five types of validity threats. As previously described, the empirical literatures on the effectiveness of comprehensive school counseling programs and the efficacy of counselor roles and duties have several threats that limit the strength of their findings. Although there are no perfect studies (e.g., Bubble Hypothesis; Gelso, 1979), a concerted effort to enhance the rigor of research investigations in school counseling can go a long way toward strengthening the empirical knowledge base of the field and of the profession.

Second, given that most school counselors do not seem to be conducting research (and perhaps are not expected to), school counselor educators may need to engage in a greater level of research on school counseling. The productivity expectations for school counselor educators, as university faculty members, typically include some level of research publication. Given the current paucity of research in school counseling, particularly as it relates to efficacy of counselor roles and duties, it is imperative that faculty members engage in more research and publication. To this end, greater efforts should be made by ASCA and ACA to lobby departments of counselor education to increase the time and resources allotted for research activities and reduce other duties such as teaching and service. In addition, ASCA and ACA should lobby the Council for Accreditation of Counseling and Related Educational Programs (CACREP), the accreditation agency of many counselor education departments, to increase their standards regarding faculty research productivity.

Third, aside from the work of university faculty members, school counselors can be encouraged to engage in greater amount of research activities, at least in collaboration with counselor educators. Given that the pressures to be accountable to the public largely stems from school administrators, having school counselors conduct research and show evidence of program effectiveness and role efficacy to their school administrators may be one of the most effective means to meet the accountability press. In cases where significant outcomes are observed, the findings can be shared with other school counselors through various publication outlets. An added benefit of publishing such findings is that it can bring a positive light to the school in general (and even the school district) and to the school administrators in particular to further demonstrate their positive efforts to meet the academic and social needs of their students. To this end, we agree with the point made by Romano and Kachgal (2004) that having a greater level of research collaboration between school counselors and administrators and the university-based counseling researchers could lead to very fruitful results in addressing the accountability demands.

Several authors have proposed alternative methods in which school counselors can engage in more research endeavors. We strongly agree with this idea. Although the conceptual framework presented previously offers ways in which researchers can evaluate their work and strive to conduct more rigorous and valid studies, we realize that there are many limitations within the school setting that restrict the extent to which school counseling researchers have control over how research is conducted. For example, given the limited amount of material resources and time, it may be very difficult for school counselors to conduct true experimental studies in the schools. In recognition of this situation, we strongly believe that it may be just as fruitful if school counselors begin to engage in any and all types of research activities, regardless of how small the scope or limited the rigor of the activity might seem. We feel that doing so may lead to greater momentum for school counselors who then might eventually be able to establish a more rigorous and comprehensive research program in their schools. Collectively, such research activities also could lead to evidence-based practice that is based on methodological diversity, rather than just on experimental designs. To encourage this effort, what follows is a description of research designs representing methodological diversity.

One method is known as action research. Pine (1981) described action research as a descriptive investigation consisting of the following activities: (a) documentation (e.g., collecting, generating, organizing, and synthesizing information); (b) retrospection to accurately account for and reflect the actualities of school counseling effectiveness; and (c) case studies that may provide useful data for more in depth examination of the phenomena of interest.

Pine (1981) pointed out that these are activities that school counselors can carry out as part of their day-to-day professional duties, and that the findings can offer valuable information.

In another variation, Gillies (1993) described action research as "the application of the scientific method of fact-finding and experimentation to practical problems requiring action solutions" (p. 69). According to Gillies, counselors must ask, prior to the initiation of action research, the following queries: (a) what is the problem to be investigated, (b) what was the genesis of the problem, (c) what are the potential repercussions of overlooking the problem, (d) what is the desired outcome, and (e) how can this outcome or goal be attained/obtained?

Based on the consideration of these issues, one of four action research approaches could be chosen: (a) diagnostic action research, (b) participant action research, (c) empirical action research, or (d) experimental action research. According to Gillies (1993), diagnostic action research is appropriate for mundane issues and consists of identifying the problem, assessing causality, and considering and implementing solutions. In contrast, participant action research involves additional sources of information (e.g., teachers and parents) and consists of identifying concerns, defining the problem, inquiring about the need for additional information, collecting and analyzing data, brainstorming solutions, and collaboratively making and implementing suggestions to resolve the problem. The third approach is the empirical action research and this is a more formal research approach than the previously mentioned approaches. It is appropriate for examining the effects of counselor interventions using observational record keeping. Finally, experimental action research utilizes a control and experimental group as well as pre/post test measures. This method is most similar to the published research studies that have been previously described and is appropriate for contributing to theoretical advancement.

Another method is qualitative research. According to Heppner et al. (1999), "Qualitative research involves understanding the complexity of people's lives by examining individual perspectives in context" (p. 235). This method is based on the idea that there is no universal truth that is to be found, as in quantitative research, but that truth is subjective to each individual and that each person creates his or her ideas of the world that are shaped by the social, cultural, economic, and political forces in the environment. The most common method of data collection in qualitative research is through open-ended interviews where the researchers ask questions to participants regarding the issue at hand. The resultant responses are then analyzed for themes that may be similar to or different from the responses of other individuals. In school counseling research, a possible application of qualitative research is to ask the consumers of counseling about the specific benefits of counseling services. If school counselors could ask these questions to all of their clients and document their responses, they could begin to build a database of information about how people are benefiting from the counseling services.

A third method utilizes the single subject design. Citing the lack of outcome research on school counseling, Foster, Watson, Meeks, and Young (2002) discussed the benefits, as well as the limitations, of the single subject research design. Variations of the single subject design consisted of the following: (a) the A-B design, which is analogous to the pre/post test design but also includes a follow-up component; however, such a design does not rule out confounds, but is appropriate for assessing interventions aimed at acting out behavior; (b) the A-B-A-B design, which addresses the confound limitation of the former design; (c) the multiple baseline design, which is essentially a series of A-B designs; however, this design may be applied to the same individual when assessing varied behaviors, the same individual across different settings, and the same behavior with different individuals; and (d) the changing criterion design, which is another extension of the A-B design; however, in this case, as the criterion changes, the intervention also changes (i.e., design would be appropriate in behavioral interventions). Foster et al. argued that this type of design would address the challenges and critiques of the field as well as the concerns that many school counselors have regarding conducting research, namely, a lack of knowledge of research methodology or confidence in conducting research.

In general, these methods offer alternative ways for school counselors to conduct research activities. Although they are not without methodological limitations, we hope that these strategies will offer more attractive and doable options for school counselors interested in investigating scholarly problems in their school settings.

Finally, there is a need to increase the publication outlets for school counseling research. Currently, there is only one journal specifically devoted to school counseling, *Professional School Counseling* (*PSC*), and this outlet may not offer sufficient page space to meet the empirical accountability press. It should be added that *The School Counselor* and *Elementary School Guidance and Counseling* are no longer in existence, as they were combined to form the *PSC*. Although other journals have been mentioned in this chapter, such as the *Journal of Counseling and Development*, *PSC* is a counseling profession-wide journal that covers research work beyond school counseling. Perhaps efforts can be made to add an increased number of pages to *PSC* and consider other forms of publication such as an electronic journal. An electronic journal can have the same level of rigor in reviewing submitted manuscripts, but it is not bound by the high cost of printing that is associated with paper journals. In addition, the ASCA and the ACA might consider publishing the proceedings that focus on school counselor effectiveness from their annual meetings. This type of publication outlet might be less intimidating especially for beginning scholars and may lead to increased attendance at the conferences.

Conclusion

To conclude, we would like to quote Gysbers (2004), who stated,

> Today the issue of accountability is in the forefront of professional dialogue. . . . Not only are school counselors being asked to tell what they do, they also are being asked to demonstrate how what they do makes a difference in the lives of students. (p. 1)

We cannot agree more with his assessment. Hence, toward this end, we have reviewed the current research literature on school counseling and found several shortcomings, mainly related to methodological issues and the small quantity of research work. We hope that this chapter has offered useful information regarding the present status of research in and on school counseling, areas of strengths and shortcomings, and possible directions for future work.

References

American School Counselor Association. (2003). *The ASCA national model: A framework for school counseling programs*. Alexandria, VA: Author.

Bauman, S. (2004). School counselors and research revisited. *Professional School Counseling, 7*, 141–151.

Bauman, S., Siegel, J. T., Davis, A., Falco, L. D., Seabolt, K., & Szymanski, G. (2002). School counselors' interest in professional literature and research. *Professional School Counseling, 5*, 346–352.

Borders, L. D., & Drury, S. M. (1992). Comprehensive school counseling programs: A review for policymakers and practitioners. *Journal of Counseling and Development, 70*, 487–498.

Brigman, G., & Campbell, C. (2003). Helping students improve academic achievement and school success behavior. *Professional School Counseling, 7*, 91–98.

Burnham, J. J., & Jackson, C. M. (2000). School counselor roles: Discrepancies between actual practice and existing models. *Professional School Counseling, 4*, 41–49.

Curcio, C. C., Mathai, C., & Roberts, J. (2003). Evaluation of a school district's secondary counseling program. *Professional School Counseling, 6*, 296–303.

Education Professional Standards Board. (1996). *Guidance counselor standards.* Frankfort: Kentucky Department of Education.

Field, J. E., & Baker, S. (2004). Defining and examining school counselor advocacy. *Professional School Counseling, 8,* 56–63.

Fitch, T. J., & Marshall, J. L. (2004). What counselors do in high-achieving schools: A study on the role of the school counselor. *Professional School Counseling, 7,* 172–177.

Fitch, T., Newby, E., Ballestero, V., & Marshall, J. L. (2001). Future school administrators' perceptions of the school counselor's role. *Counselor Education and Supervision, 41,* 89–99.

Foster, L. H., Watson, T. S., Meeks, C., & Young, J. S. (2002). Single subject research design for school counselors: Becoming an applied researcher. *Professional School Counseling, 6,* 146–154.

Gelso, C. (1979). Research in counseling: Methodological and professional issues. *The Counseling Psychologist, 8,* 7–35.

Gillies, R. M. (1993). Action research in school counseling: Action research for school counselors. *The School Counselor, 41,* 69–72.

Gysbers, N. C. (2004). Comprehensive guidance and counseling programs: The evolution of accountability. *Professional School Counseling, 8,* 1–14.

Gysbers, N. C., & Henderson, P. (1994). *Developing and managing your school guidance program* (2nd ed.). Alexandria, VA: American Counseling Association.

Harter, S. (1985). *The self-perception profile for children.* Denver, CO: University of Denver.

Heppner, P. P., Kivlighan, D. M., & Wampold, B. E. (1999). *Research design in counseling* (2nd ed.). Belmont, CA: Brooks/Cole.

Hobbs, F., & Stoops, N. (2002). *Demographic trends in the 20th century: Census 2000 special reports.* Retrieved May 10, 2005, from http://www.census.gov/prod/2002pubs/censr-4.pdf

Kerlinger, F. N. (1986). *Foundations of behavioral research* (3rd ed.). New York: Holt, Rinehart & Winston.

Lapan, R. T., Gysbers, N. C., & Petroski, G. F. (2001). Helping seventh graders be safe and successful: A statewide study of the impact of comprehensive guidance and counseling programs. *Journal of Counseling and Development, 79,* 320–330.

Lapan, R. T., Gysbers, N. C., & Sun, Y. (1997). The impact of more fully implemented guidance programs on the school experiences of high school students: A statewide evaluation study. *Journal of Counseling and Development, 75,* 292–302.

Lavoritano, J., & Segal, P. B. (1992). Evaluating the efficacy of a school counseling program. *Psychology in the Schools, 29,* 61–70.

Myrick, R. D. (1993). *Developmental guidance and counseling: A practical approach* (2nd ed.). Minneapolis, MN: Educational Media.

Pine, G. J. (1975). Evaluating school counseling programs: Retrospect and prospect. *Measurement and Evaluation in Guidance, 8,* 136–144.

Pine, G. J. (1981). Collaborative action research in school counseling: The integration of research and practice. *Personnel and Guidance Journal, 59,* 495–501.

Romano, J. L., & Kachgal, M. M. (2004). Counseling psychology and school counseling: An underutilized partnership. *The Counseling Psychologist, 32,* 184–215.

Sink, C. A., & Stroh, H. R. (2003). Raising achievement test scores of early elementary school students through comprehensive school counseling programs. *Professional School Counseling, 6,* 350–364.

U.S. Census Bureau. (2002). *Projected migration by race and Hispanic origin, 1999 to 2100.* Retrieved May 10, 2005, from http://www.census.gov/population/projections/nation/summary/np-t7-c.txt

U.S. Department of Education. (2002). No child left behind act of 2001. Public law 107-110. Retrieved March 21, 2006, from http://www.ed.gov/policy/elsec/leg/esea02/107-110.pdf

Wampold, B. E., Davis, B., & Good, R. H. (1990). Hypothesis validity of clinical research. *Journal of Consulting and Clinical Psychology, 58,* 360–367.

Whiston, S. C., & Sexton, T. L. (1998). A review of school counseling outcome research: Implications for practice. *Journal of Counseling and Development, 76,* 412–426.

XLV

THE ESSENTIAL ROLE OF SCHOOL–COMMUNITY PARTNERSHIPS IN SCHOOL COUNSELING

MARY E. WALSH AND JILLIAN DePAUL
Boston College

One of the essential roles of school counselors is to "provide proactive leadership, which engages all stakeholders in the delivery of activities and services to help students achieve success in school" (American School Counselor Association [ASCA], 2003). Best practices call for school counselors, as school leaders who are often responsible for the coordination of resources and services that assist students, to be academically successful, to play a critical role in the development and implementation of school–community partnerships. Over the last decade, school–community partnerships have increased dramatically in the nation's school districts, reflecting an awareness of students' needs for support beyond classroom instruction.

However, throughout most of the 20th century, schools worked in relative isolation from the surrounding community. The high fences and walls that separated the school from the streets and roads of the neighborhood stood as a visible reminder of the inward focus of American schools. In the last quarter of the century, Parent Teacher Associations (PTAs), and health care providers (e.g., physicians and dentists) gradually assumed clearly defined, though narrow, roles in the community's schools. More recently, as schools began to reach out to their communities more broadly, they connected not only to families, but also to businesses, community social services and health agencies, libraries, universities, and more recently youth development organizations and family support centers. These connections between schools and local community institutions have resulted in many positive opportunities for students to participate in a range of supports for learning and healthy development.

Researchers have identified comprehensive school–community partnerships as one of the primary characteristics of effective schools. Partnerships with businesses, universities, and service learning centers are typically the direct responsibility of the school principals. The work of school counselors is most closely aligned with community agency partnerships that offer supports for student learning and healthy development. School counselors can and do play key roles in forming these collaborations (Fitch & Marshall, 2004; McWhirter, McWhirter, McWhirter, & McWhirter, 1998; Wohlstetter & Smyer, 1994). Leaders in the field of school counseling have recognized that school–community partnerships are critical to comprehensive student support. Recent practice guidelines have called on school counselors to build and maintain these linkages (ASCA, 1997, 2003; Campbell & Dahir, 1997).

Focus of This Chapter

This chapter will examine the role of school counselors in fostering and supporting school–community agency partnerships. After reviewing the evolution of school–community partnerships, with particular emphasis on their contribution to shaping the role of school counselors over decades, the chapter will discuss the fundamental developmental principles that simultaneously inform school–community partnerships and guide the practice of school counselors in this area. Following a discussion of the challenges inherent in school–community partnerships, the chapter will review "best practices" for the planning, implementation, and evaluation of school–community partnerships. Finally, this chapter will conclude with a discussion of the various models of school–community partnerships.

Brief History of School–Community Agency Partnerships

Historically, schools have long been aware of the need to respond to the nonacademic issues that can result in nonacademic barriers to learning (e.g., medical, social/environmental, emotional, familial concerns). Confronted by the pervasive effects of environmental stressors on learning and behavior, schools have traditionally sought to lessen the impact and address the consequences of those stressors on students. As early as 1890, reformers were advocating the provision of medical and dental examinations, lunches, summer programs, recreational activities, and child welfare officers in American schools (Tyack, 1992). In response, school systems gradually began to address a range of children's developmental, health, and nutritional needs. By 1940, annual medical and dental exams were provided, and school lunches became the norm by 1950 (Myrick, 1993; Tyack). While federal and local funding supported these efforts, the schools served as the primary locus and manager of the delivery of services.

As the decades progressed, federal and state governments began to increase funding to community-based agencies to address some of these needs (e.g., through entitlement programs for health care through Medicaid and for nutrition through the Food Stamp Program). In recent years, government-supported community health and mental health centers, hospitals, and social service agencies have provided an array of services to families and children. Neighborhood health centers, for example, now provide health care to a significant number of poor children. With the advent of these programs, the extent to which the school was held responsible for the delivery of comprehensive services decreased. This shift in responsibility is evident, for example, in the steady decrease in the number of school doctors over the past several decades.

While the government has supported the efforts of community agencies to increase care for the physical health needs of children, it has not been as responsive to their psychological needs. Recognizing that unmet psychological needs impact learning in significant ways, schools have made substantial efforts to respond to the mental health needs of children and families. Particularly in the last two decades, prevention and intervention programs in the domains of behavioral and emotional problems have expanded in local school systems. Schools are primary providers of mental health services to children. As a consequence, the profession of school guidance and counseling has evolved into a major provider of mental health services in schools (Gibson & Mitchell, 1990; Myrick, 1993; Short & Talley, 1997). What began as a profession devoted to preparing school children for the world of work broadened into one also dedicated to the adjustment of students to the demands of the school environment and then, gradually, assumed increasing responsibility for the emotional well-being of its students (Bauman, Davis, Falco, Seabolt, & Szymanski, 2003; Gibson & Mitchell; Myrick).

The growing demands for mental health services quickly exceeded the capacity of already overburdened school counselors, who were simultaneously responsible for group guidance, college advising, student scheduling, and many other tasks (Paisley & McMahon, 2001). As a result, counselors looked to community agencies, such as health care and mental health providers to form partnerships with the schools and assist with service delivery. Further, as school counselors recognized that fostering mental health requires a focus on prevention for all students, as well as intervention for the few, they sought out community partners who could provide supports and youth development opportunities (e.g., recreation, team-building, and sports). In recent years, the need for community partnerships with schools has intensified even more since the demands for increased academic achievement has led to cutbacks in a number of school-based student support services (e.g., counseling and health services, sports, art and music courses).

Why School–Community Partnerships Make Sense

Schools Cannot Do It Alone

The No Child Left Behind (NCLB) legislation (2001) has brought educational reform to every classroom in the country. The goals of this legislation—for every child to achieve his or her maximum potential—have been addressed through the development of curriculum standards and frameworks and new strategies for teaching and learning. The focus on improving academic achievement has been intense with every state and district aligning curricula to the national standards and frameworks and implementing intensive standardized testing to assess student outcomes. However, 6 years after the introduction of NCLB legislation, the country is still faced with a substantial academic "achievement gap." The achievement gap is a significant disparity in academic test scores between students of color, particularly Black and Hispanic students, and White students, as well as between students who experience poverty and those who do not (Barton, 2001, 2003; Campbell & Brigman, 2005; Isaacs, 2003; Newsom, 2003). The achievement gap has existed for decades and continues to persist despite the focus on improving teaching and learning strategies that resulted from the implementation of NCLB. This discrepancy in achievement has been described as one of the great civil rights issues of our era. It reflects social inequities that systemically deprive students of color and students in poverty of access to the resources and opportunities that are critical to breaking the cycle of poverty (Schorr & Schorr, 1988).

There is growing acknowledgement that NCLB's nearly exclusive focus on teaching and learning will not be sufficient to close the achievement gap. As has been demonstrated over many decades, academic achievement is not the result of a single factor (e.g., classroom teaching, neighborhood resources, family stability, genetic endowment, socioemotional development), but rather is the result of the complex interplay of all of these factors over the course of development. In her recent analysis, Linda Darling-Hammond (2000) estimated that improved teaching and learning practices account for about 40% to 60% of the achievement gap and that class size accounts for another 8%. The significant remainder of the achievement gap is thought to be accounted for by family and community issues (Darling-Hammond). Similarly, Rothstein (2004) argued that not only is there a range of factors (e.g., health risks, lack of educational enrichment opportunities, and home and neighborhood factors) contributing to the academic achievement gap, but that most of these factors are associated with poverty and constitute major obstacles to children's ability to learn.

Children living in poverty experience multiple nonacademic barriers to learning (Walsh & Murphy, 2003). For example, research demonstrates that children living in poverty are significantly limited in terms of their vocabulary and literacy levels (B. Hart & Risley, 2003). Children living in poverty are at high risk for obesity (Strauss & Pollack, 2001), which results in a number of health risks (e.g., asthma) and significant school absenteeism. In low-income children, vision problems are known to occur at twice the rate as in middle-income children (Rothstein, 2004). Further, children living in poverty are increasingly at risk for exposure to community violence, which has been shown to be negatively correlated with academic functioning (Walsh & Murphy). It is widely recognized that the emergence of the so-called "new morbidities" (e.g., sexual abuse, domestic and community violence, poverty, drug abuse, and homelessness; Bemak, 2000; Center for Mental Health in Schools, 2003; Dryfoos, 1990; Keys & Bemak, 1997) pose a a significant threat to children's well-being and ability to achieve in the classroom (Becker & Luthar, 2002; Greenberg et al., 2003; National Clearinghouse on Child Abuse and Neglect Information, 2004; Urban Institute, 2000).

While challenges to academic achievement are greatest for children living in poverty, the stakes are high for *all* of today's youth. The 2003 Youth Behavior Surveillance System update (Centers for Disease Control and Prevention [CDC], 2003) indicated that the a number of 14- to 17-year-olds in the United States are engaged in diverse problem behaviors. Results show that 45% of these students had drunk alcohol during the prior 30 days and 22% had smoked cigarettes and marijuana at least once during the prior 30 days. During the preceding 12 months, 33.2% had been involved in a physical fight; during the prior 30 days, 17% had carried a gun. Further, 46.7% had engaged in sexual intercourse; 37% of sexually active students had not used a condom at last sexual intercourse.

Reducing students' risks and enhancing their healthy development are challenges that need to be addressed. Schools rightfully acknowledge that they cannot do it alone and need the help of other institutions and resources (Lawson & Briar-Lawson, 1997; Payzant, 1992; Riley, 1998). Present-day educators, particularly school counselors, are quickly becoming aware of their need to join hands in an organized and deliberate manner with parents, community members, agency and clinic professionals, neighborhood organizations, institutions of higher education, and politicians in order to improve the life chances of children and youth (Alexander, Kruczek, Ramirez, & Zagelbaum, 2003; Carpenter-Aeby & Aeby, 2005; House & Hayes, 2002; Power, DuPaul, Shapiro, & Kazak, 2003; Williams, 2003).

Holistic Approach to Education

The critical role of school–community partnerships in supporting the learning and development of children is grounded in our current understanding of the human developmental process. Our best contemporary understandings of human development lead inevitably to the conclusion that no single societal institution or activity is sufficient to fully support the healthy development of our nation's children. Current understandings of human development serve not only as a conceptual basis for school–community partnerships, but also undergird the profession of school counseling (Akos, 2001; Galassi & Akos, 2004; Paisley, 2001).

For much of the 20th century, development was viewed as a universal process that unfolded in the same way for all children, regardless of the diversity of their experiences and environment. It is now recognized that development cannot be reduced to a series of stages that occur internally and universally, but rather is a product of a transaction between the child and his or her environments (Cicchetti & Sroufe, 2000). Further, emerging theoretical understandings view development as involving continuous interaction among the various domains of the child (i.e., biological, psychological, and social), occurring across the life span, and involving both risk and protective factors (Ford & Lerner, 1992; Walsh, Galassi, Murphy, & Park-Taylor, 2002; Walsh, Howard, & Buckley, 1999). We will now describe how these developmental principles assist educators and school counselors to understand not only that partnerships with the community are critical, but also how to implement them in practice.

Role of context. Contemporary best practices in education assume that knowledge is not simply "imparted to the child" in a one-way interaction, but rather is coconstructed by the child within the social contexts of school, family, and community (Airasian & Walsh, 1997). For example, children's understanding of and response to literary narratives or social studies lessons are grounded in their individual experiences in family, neighborhood, and cultural/ethnic identity. The greater the extent to which the new knowledge is embedded in the familial, social, political, and cultural dimensions of the child's world, the better the fit with the child's existing cognitive structures and the more effective the instruction.

In a similar vein, student support interventions typically coordinated or implemented by school counselors are effective insofar as they reflect the unique contexts that have already shaped the child. While the delivery of health and mental health care may seem, on the surface, to be an abstract and universal practice, it is now widely recognized that the effectiveness of health care practices is grounded in the cultural and social context in which they are delivered (Lubeck, Jessub, deVries, & Post, 2001; Segal, 1995). The recognition that children's unique contexts significantly shape their development has led school counselors to incorporate multicultural competencies into their practices. Best practices in student support recognize that connections with community resources better equip schools and school counselors to deliver contextually meaningful supports (Dryfoos, 1994b; Paavola et al., 1995; Schorr, 1997).

Bio-psycho-social levels of development. The role of school counselors positions them to recognize the mutually influential interaction between the biological, psychological, and social domains within the individual. For example, they regularly see students whose access to the curriculum is limited by chronic illness or family violence (Stallings, 1995). However, in many service settings, this recognition of the interdependence of the biological, psychological, and social levels of development has often been difficult to translate into practice. Traditional service providers have typically focused on a single aspect of development to the exclusion of others. For example, in schools, educators have focused primarily on cognitive development, while physical and socioemotional development was left to other professions. While these distinctions between various domains of development often define the boundaries of the various professions, they are, at best, artificial. Developmental theorists have pointed to the holistic or unitary nature of development and consider the various domains of development (e.g., cognitive vs. affective, biological vs. psychological) as the consequence of the particular perspective or angle from which development is viewed rather than as a reflection of "true cuts of nature" (Overton, 1998).

The complex issues facing today's children, however, can rarely be divided into the "discipline-shaped boxes" of the different professions. An effective response to student problems requires the services of a range of professionals, most of whom do not exist within the school and whose varied services must be integrated and coordinated with one another. School counselors play a critical role in implementing coordinated, comprehensive systems of care that involve both school and community agency staff representing a range of professions.

Development across the life span. An understanding that development occurs throughout the life span supports school counselors' recognition that education is a lifelong process. Development does not stop at the end of childhood or adolescence. Therefore, school counselors recognize the responsibility to prepare students for their entry into adulthood, the world of work, and responsible citizenship (Briztman, 2005). Fulfilling these responsibilities continues the legacy of school counseling, which originally focused on guiding students in their school-to-work transitions.

The life-span approach to development also acknowledges that adults who parent children continue to learn and develop both cognitively and emotionally. Supporting parents to enhance their skills and competencies, which has long been part of school counselors' work, ultimately leads parents to more effectively support their child's academic and social development. Parents can benefit from a range of supports and services that are typically available in the community. School counselors can work to increase parents' access to community services as well as formal learning opportunities that continue their education (e.g., high school equivalency, English language learning (ELL), computer training).

Risk and protective factors. For a number of years, school counselors have struggled with determining whether to focus primarily on enhancing strengths or remediating deficits. In today's schools, significant financial and human resources are focused on students who fail standardized tests. The focus on deficits in the academic arena is paralleled in the socioemotional realm as schools address a range of personal–social risks (e.g., drug taking, teen pregnancy, suicide). Unfortunately, within a deficit-focused system, schools with the highest achievement test failures have drastically cut art, sports, and other enrichment programs that support healthy development (Riley, 2002; Share, 2005).

The role of school counselors has been directly impacted by the strengths versus deficits debate. For decades, school counselors were viewed as the professionals who worked with students at risk. Fortunately, school counseling's close ties to the profession of counseling psychology helped school counselors in learning to maintain a strong recognition of the critical role of strengths in development. In recent years, as research on resilience and competence has demonstrated the powerful impact of strengths on development and learning, school counseling has become a clear voice for a simultaneous focus on both strengths and deficits at the educators' table (Benard, 1991; Education Trust, 2003; Garmezy, Masten, & Tellegen, 1984; Henderson & Milstein, 1996; Lerner, Walsh, & Howard, 1998).

Challenges in School–Community Partnerships

While early school–community partnerships were bold and important first steps in recognizing the potential of effective alliances between school and community, their shortcomings revealed chronic challenges inherent to this kind of collaborative endeavor. These challenges include (a) fragmentation and a limited range of services, (b) turf conflicts between school-based and community-based providers, and (c) insufficient funding.

Early partnerships often yielded a variety of discrete services, programs, and resources. For example, some community agencies provided programming in schools and classrooms that focused on a particular issue (e.g., bullying prevention). Some partnerships with local municipal agencies (e.g., police) addressed substance abuse prevention (e.g., the DARE project in the 1980s). Still others provided a service (e.g., mental health counseling) or youth development opportunity (e.g., YMCA recreation programs) for children and their families. As these partnerships began to multiply, many schools counted up to 20 or 30 community partners with whom they had one or another kind of collaborative arrangement.

While community partnerships significantly contribute to the school's capacity to support students, the proliferation of partnerships created significant challenges. The lack of coordination across partnerships often results in overlapping roles and functions. Community agencies can be unaware of the activities of other agencies in the school and unwittingly offer similar services or programs to the same populations of students. Services must be coordinated not only for the school as a whole, but also for individual students. It is not unheard of for individual students to be referred to duplicative services, which represents an inefficient use of resources and an ineffective way of addressing student problems. Oftentimes, aspects of student support that need a community partner (e.g., health education) may not be represented. The lack of integration and oversight typically results in fragmentation, duplication, and/or lack of services in key areas (Adelman & Taylor, 2002a; Lerner, 1995a).

The potential for community providers and their services to be marginalized within school operations presents an additional challenge to effective school–community partnerships. Over the years, school programs and services designed to address barriers to learning have often been viewed by school leaders as supplementary or auxiliary to the school's central mission of teaching and learning. Consequently, community providers often struggle to find their place in the day-to-day life of the school (Adelman & Taylor, 2002b; Osbourne & Collison, 1998). Further, external professionals may typically be pushed to the margins of school service provision as a result of turf conflicts with similar professionals in schools (e.g., community mental health professionals with school counselors and school psychologists). For example, school specialists might view agency professionals as discounting their own skills while external professionals may feel underappreciated and are sometimes not privy to knowledge about the unique culture of schools. These challenges require ongoing and honest conversations between in-school professionals (e.g., teachers, school counselors, and principals) and community agency professionals (e.g., mental health clinicians and social workers).

Finally, a significant challenge to the implementation of best practices in school–community partnerships is the lack of sufficient funding in both schools and community agencies. School-based funding for learning and healthy development is often eliminated or severely reduced when the school's budget tightens (Riley, 2002). At the same time, community agencies with similarly limited budgets struggle to make time spent in schools cost-effective by maximizing direct service hours to compile fee-for-service revenue. As a result, community agency representatives are often unable to devote time consistently to participating in school–agency staff meetings. This irregular participation is an obstacle for service coordination and efficiency.

School counselors are well situated to play a key role in addressing these challenges. Their training in the comprehensive needs of students, coupled with a systemic vision, places them in a unique position to facilitate the process of building and maintaining effective school–community partnerships and coordinating the services that result from these partnerships. If school counselors are effective at coordinating services, the tension between internal school professionals and external service providers will likely be significantly reduced. The systemic perspective of school counselors will also help them to support school administrators as they raise funds sufficient to sustain these partnerships. Finally, having been trained in the importance of empirically validated programs, school counselors know the essential role of evaluation in maintaining the effectiveness of their student support services and sustaining partnerships.

Best Practices in School–Community Partnerships

To respond to the challenges presented by school–community partnerships as well as to facilitate effective partnerships, school counselors can call on the significant literature that identifies "best practices" in this area. A review of the literature suggests that effective school–community partnerships (a) set goals for partnerships that are aligned with the goals of education reform, (b) promote student support services that are comprehensive, (c) provide coordinated services for students, (d) offer a continuum of prevention and intervention services to all students, (e) offer developmentally appropriate student support services, (f) increase family engagement in schools, (g) enhance schools' and agencies' ability to recognize and respond to a diverse community, (h) evaluate the effectiveness of the student and family support services they deliver, (i) be sustained over the long term, and (j) be supported by an identifiable infrastructure.

Alignment with the goals of education reform. Effective school–community partnerships align their goals with the goals of the education reform agenda as articulated in the NCLB. At the broadest level, school–community partnerships work to improve not only students' healthy development, but also their academic performance. Community agencies can no longer consider their goals opposed to, or even distinct from, the goals of teachers and school staff to promote the academic achievement of all students. At the same time, educators can no longer view the promotion of academic achievement as a goal that can be achieved apart from promoting students' well-being. Healthy development—physical, psychological, and social—must be the goal of school and community agency staff. Similarly, academic achievement must be viewed as a major responsibility of both the school and the community. Committing to the twin goals of academic success and healthy development will promote well-functioning school–community partnerships in which partners contribute in complementary ways to shared goals

NCLB has identified school–community partnerships as essential to achieving the goals of education reform. As a core element of education reform, these partnerships are expected to employ NCLB's major approaches; that is, they must be integrated within the whole school improvement plan for each school and district, they must yield outcome data that informs practice, they must collectively serve all students, and also they must continually engage families.

Comprehensive student support. Effective school–community partnerships promote what has come to be one of the gold standards in school counseling, comprehensive student support (Adelman & Taylor, 2002b). Comprehensive approaches to care ensure that the full range of a student's needs—educational, medical, psychological, social, recreational, and legal—is met. By engaging an array of community partnerships, a single school or school district can provide the full range of services and supports. While each provider may offer only one or two targeted services, together they make a number of important supports available for students and families. These supports not only address risks confronting students (e.g., acute health care) but also promote healthy development (e.g., opportunities for youth development).

School counselors are well positioned to ensure that comprehensive services are available to students. School counselors became familiar with the notion of comprehensive approaches as far back as the 1970s. At that time, guidance counselors were encouraged to shift the focus of their work to a broad range of guidance activities conducted on a regular, planned, and systemic basis to assist students in achieving a range of competencies (Gysbers & Henderson, 2000). Although the immediate and crisis needs of students continued to be addressed, a major focus of the new guidance programs was to provide all students with a range of opportunities to support their development. Guidance programs were consequently expanded to include a comprehensive range of services, such as assessment, information, consultation, counseling, referral, placement, follow up, and follow through (Gysbers & Henderson). School counselors were now expected not only to provide direct service, but also to work in consultative and collaborative relationships with other members of the guidance team as well as with school staff and parents. Gradually, as it became clear that school staff could not provide for all of the needs of students, school counselors were encouraged to integrate the services of community agencies and institutions in order to build comprehensive systems that could address the full range of student needs (Brabeck, Walsh, Kenny, & Comilang, 1997).

Coordination of services. Effective school–community partnerships require that services be coordinated, thus eliminating discrete and fragmented services. In delivering services, providers engage in a collaborative approach. Coordination is more efficient and cost-effective because it avoids the unnecessary duplication of services and can reduce the number of providers involved with a particular family or a program (Walsh, Brabeck, & Howard, 1999). In addition, the positive outcomes that are likely to result from a coordinated approach will reduce the need for additional services in the future. When services are coordinated, students and families can avoid falling through the proverbial cracks.

As an effective practice, coordination of services can occur at many levels. For example, various school- and community-based professionals may collaborate in developing an intervention for an individual student. Coordinated systems of care do not leave the child and family to determine their needs and seek various services on their own but, rather, help families to identify their needs, access the appropriate services, and integrate the recommendations and treatments suggested (Walsh & Park-Taylor, 2003). Similarly, prevention programs that focus on all students can be collaboratively designed to incorporate a number of service providers. For example, effective violence prevention often requires the expertise of educational, psychological, social, and health providers.

School counselors are well prepared to become school leaders in the provision of coordinated services that draw from both school-based and community agency providers. Counselors' understanding of the importance of embedding individual services within a holistic framework of student supports and their experience coordinating services at the individual level, classroom level, and schoolwide level enable them to integrate comprehensive, coordinated student support into the mission of the school.

Continuum of prevention and intervention. Effective community partnerships should assist schools in offering a continuum of prevention and intervention services for students and their families. Ideally, school counseling programs should provide a wide variety of services, ranging from broad-based prevention services that promote healthy development for all students to narrowly focused treatment for students who suffer from severe or chronic issues (Green & Keys, 2001).

In practice, the continuum of supports and services is generally described in terms of three levels (Adelman & Taylor, 2002a). The first level focuses on primary prevention and positive youth development for all students (Weissberg & O'Brien, 2004); it is generally delivered through systemic whole-school programs (e.g., social competence curricula) or through community-based opportunities for positive youth development (e.g., Boys and Girls Clubs). For example, implementing health education programs can enhance the healthy development of students and prevent nonacademic barriers to learning that are associated with poor physical health and emotional distress (Marx, Wooley, & Northup, 1998; McKenzie & Richmond, 1998). The second level is a prevention/early intervention program designed to identify and address student issues soon after they develop. School counselors can serve students on this level by coordinating the development of programs for students with specific issues (e.g., bullying prevention and friendship groups). Finally, the third level is a system of care that treats the severe and chronic problems that students face through a web of in-school and community-based services (e.g., mental health counseling, special education, and medical care). Implementing programs and interventions at all of these levels requires the integration of school and community resources to provide the most effective support.

While school counselors traditionally focused on the needs of at-risk or special needs students, more recently they have come to view all students as their clients (Education Trust, 2003; Gysbers, 2001). This indicates an overall shift away from exclusively addressing individual student problems or crises toward providing prevention services that help to protect all students from developing problems that interfere with learning and growth opportunities (P. J. Hart & Jacobi, 1992; Lee, 2005). Though prevention services are critical, some argue that they do not sufficiently enhance the positive competencies of the student (Galassi & Akos, 2004; House & Martin, 1998). Consistent with developmental research on risk and resilience, these researchers urge school counselors to function as "developmental advocates" by fostering prosocial skills and problem-solving competencies (P. J. Hart & Jacobi; Masten, Best, & Garmezy, 1990; Werner & Smith, 1992). Effective school–community partnerships can sharpen this focus by renewing school counselors' awareness of the powerful role of strengths in the lives of children.

In addition to offering services that meet a range of needs (health, social, psychological, etc.), communities also bring a wide range of youth and family support programs to school–community partnerships. The natural assets of communities—youth serving organizations, sports leagues, part-time job opportunities, neighbors with special skills—provide the means for children and youth to build upon their strengths and enhance their resilience in the face of substantial risks to their development (Benson, 1997; Benson, Galbraith, & Espeland, 1998). Community-based youth development programs can work in partnership with the schools to assist individuals and groups of children to avoid poor outcomes and increase the likelihood of good ones. Through their advocacy for school–community partnerships, school counselors can provide all students with opportunities to enhance their strengths and competencies and offer buffers to at-risk students that allow them to mature into healthy, well-functioning adults (Masten & Coatsworth, 1998; Rutter, 1985; Werner, 1989, 1990).

Expanding the capabilities of school counselors to treat all students as their clients should not detract from the services provided for at-risk students. Partnering with community agencies has positive results for students who struggle with emotional and behavioral needs. In the past, special education has been the default service for students with behavioral and emotional problems that interfered with learning. However, special education is not always the most effective way of addressing primary emotional and behavioral problems; the purpose of special education is to assist students with learning supports so that they can access the curriculum. Further, schools typically do not have the resources to address all of the complex emotional and behavioral needs of students and simultaneously provide support for and enhance the positive development of all students. By utilizing community services, the mental health needs of students are addressed more effectively and the school's resources are released to service the needs of all students (Kutash & Duchnowski, 2004).

Developmentally appropriate prevention and intervention. Effective school–community partnerships implement prevention and intervention programs that match the developmental tasks that students must negotiate. Schools are highly developmentally organized. They are aware of the developmental needs and abilities of children and tailor curriculum and instruction strategies accordingly. On the other hand, community agencies have less opportunity to shape interventions on the basis of sometimes subtle developmental distinctions among children. When school–community partnerships collaborate to design and implement prevention and intervention programs, the developmental expertise of schools is quite valuable. For example, many community agencies have faced challenges as they attempt to expand their after-school programs from elementary to middle school children. The after-school program model that was successful with elementary children is typically not efficacious with middle school children because of the developmental shift that occurs during the middle school transition. Through school–community partnerships, educational professionals can bring their extensive knowledge to bear on this issue and help agencies to design appropriate and successful programs for the middle school–aged group.

A developmental focus also informs prevention and intervention programs that support key transitions for students (Lerner & Kauffman, 1985). School counselors have long recognized that schools prepare students not simply for the next educational challenge, but for life. This recognition has led school counselors to support community partners that focus on the transition from school to work (Solberg, Howard, Blustein, & Close, 2004; Gysbers, 1997). While many high school graduates transition immediately into college, a large percentage move directly into jobs (Massachusetts Department of Education, 2004). Engaging the community to support critical developmental transitions is essential to providing the kind of education that will foster not only students' learning, but also their formation as responsible citizens (Betz, 1993; Chartrand, Strong, & Weitzman, 1995; Legum & Hoare, 2004).

Given that students' postsecondary transitions are largely influenced by the opportunities held by their particular environment, school counselors have engaged with community partners to provide systemic support for students' future planning (Lapan & Kosciulek, 2003; Lapan, Tucker, Kim, & Kosciulek, 2003). The School-to-Work Opportunities Act of 1994 advocated for the development of school-to-work community career systems, partnerships between the school and the community that create sustainable career opportunities for students (Hamilton & Hamilton, 1998). School counselors play a critical role in guiding students through the critical school-to-work transition. In fact, it has been shown that students who experience more adaptive transitions to work are more likely to have had school counselors play an active role in their career development process (Blustein, Phillips, Jobin-Davis, Finkelberg, & Roarke, 1997). School counselors can most effectively fill this important role in students' transitions by creating community career systems and reaching out to critical stakeholders in the community (e.g., parents, community leaders, businesses, and trade unions).

Family engagement. Effective school community partnerships extend supports not only to students but also to parents. The profession of school counseling is keenly aware of the significant role of programs that support parents (e.g., health promotion, ELL classes, continuing education, and parenting classes). These programs, often coordinated by school counselors in collaboration with community agencies, increase parental involvement in schools and educate parents about how to promote their children's academic achievement (Bryan & Holcomb-McCoy, 2004; Walsh et al., 1999).

The life-span orientation of school counselors has equipped them to direct the efforts of school–community partnerships toward supporting and enhancing the well-being of the adults in the community. The natural focus of schools on children and adolescents can often obscure the needs of their families. The linkage of school and community can create more opportunities for all professionals to work directly with parents and other community-based adults who play a significant role in the development of young people. Many school–community partnerships have documented significant increases in family participation in joint school–community programs (e.g., Coltoff, 1998). Adult-focused programs provide school counselors with opportunities to engage parents more directly in promoting the academic achievement of their children. Schools counselors can help the school to go beyond the typical parent–teacher meetings in order to provide parents with a sense of ownership regarding the school and their children's progress. In many well-developed school–community partnerships, schools have invited parents and caregivers to join the planning process and serve as classroom aides for new after-school programs for children. Development of parent resource centers, which are organized and staffed by parents, can be greatly facilitated by the leadership of the school counselor. Parents' presence at the school communicates that they value education. The degree to which parents value education is a major predictor of academic achievement (Ferguson, Jimerson, & Dalton, 2001).

School–community partnerships also present opportunities that focus directly on parent education and support (e.g., computer classes and ELL instruction). Positive developmental opportunities for parents enhance the quality of family life and thus contribute to the academic and healthy development of children. Through school–community partnerships, school counselors can become aware of the needs of the parents as well as the resources of the community to address those needs. School counselors can be instrumental in developing after-school and evening programs that directly serve parents. On the basis of assessments of parents' needs and a mapping of community resources, many schools have been able to develop parent education programs such as ELL, computer training, and parenting strategies for behavior management. School–community partnerships allow school counselors the unique opportunity to have a voice in designing services for parents that may indirectly foster the positive development of children.

Recognition of diversity. Best practices in student support call for services that are tailored to the unique strengths and needs of students and families from diverse backgrounds—that is, children and families who differ in terms of race, culture, class, sexual orientation, language, etc. Although students from marginalized groups are profoundly impacted by the dominant group, acculturation is a bilateral process. Families of diverse backgrounds are not only impacted by, but also substantially impact, their environment (Atkinson & Thompson, 1992). The mutual interaction between various cultural/ethnic groups and the dominant culture changes everyone to some degree. Recognizing the importance of context is essential to multicultural competence because it allows school counselors to create school climates and interventions that promote positive racial, cultural, gender, and socioeconomic identities among children (Coleman & Baskin, 2003; Helms, 1990; Vargas & Koss-Chioino, 1992). Sink (2002) suggested that "School counselors should facilitate student development and enhance the total school and community environment through the understanding and appreciation of cultural diversities."

Recently, as a result of the recognition that diverse students have diverse needs, the school counseling profession has worked to become multiculturally competent (Holcomb-McCoy, 2005). School counselors have realized that they must reach out and connect with various resources in the community that reflect the diversity of the students within the school in order to accentuate their strengths and respond to their needs (Constantine & Yeh, 2001; Holcomb-McCoy & Mitchell, 2005). Further, involvement with a community that reflects the diversity of the school enhances the general school climate and allows individual students to have a greater sense of school belonging, which often leads to the improvement of academic achievement (Roeser, Midgley, & Urdan, 1996).

The work of school counselors is also greatly informed by the socioeconomic diversity of students. This particular aspect of diversity poses particular challenges to urban schools because of the high concentration of poverty in America's cities. Though context is universally influential in child development, students living in urban contexts face particular challenges in their development and education—challenges that reinforce the need for partnerships with community agencies and resources (Barnett, Conley, & Green, 2005; Bryan, 2005). School counseling in urban contexts calls for particular competencies that enable school counselors to meet the specific needs of urban students. Chief among these urban school counselor competencies is a systemic perspective and the ability to collaborate with community stakeholders (Hernandez & Seem, 2004; Lee, 2005).

The recognition that unique nonacademic barriers to learning emanate from the conditions of poverty leads to the realization that these barriers cannot be addressed solely by focusing on the student. Community partners must be involved in school counselors' efforts to assist students in overcoming challenges presented by the community (e.g., community violence and lack of access to medical care). Just as community problems contribute to nonacademic barriers to learning and student needs, community strengths in resources and diversity can help address students' needs as well as promote resiliency. School counselors recognize that the urban systems in which young people develop should also be a center of attention for positive programming and intervention (Walz & Lee, 1998).

Evaluation of effectiveness. The growing mental health needs in schools have required school counseling to develop a broad repertoire of interventions to address both the issues facing at-risk children as well as prevention services aimed at a wider audience of students. As a consequence, the profession has built up a solid core of knowledge about the characteristics of effective interventions and prevention programs. Most school counselors recognize that interventions should be evidence based and should have defined and measurable outcomes.

In the face of a nearly limitless number of possible intervention and prevention strategies, school counselors can assist school–community partnerships to identify and implement research-based programs. In the selection of programs, school counselors facilitate community agencies' recognition that the most effective programs are based on an empirical assessment of the community's unique strengths and needs. Selection of evidence-based programming helps to focus the work of partnerships around specific, measurable outcomes. It helps partnerships to avoid global, nonfocused arrangements that operate on the assumption that programs of whatever type are good for children.

While evidence-based programs are effective in general, it is critical to determine effectiveness with specific populations and assess the fidelity of their implementation. Evaluation of program process and outcomes is an important dimension of the collaborative work of school–community partnerships. Accountability is particularly important to parents who want to be sure that their children and adolescents are receiving high-quality programs as well as to funders who are eager to ensure that their money is well spent.

Consistent with the approach of NCLB, evaluation data can inform the process of student support. Gathering and codifying this data can be a significant challenge to practitioners. School counselors often bring a range of skills to the evaluation process. Their training in research methods and statistics provides them with competencies and skills to make them effective collaborators in designing and implementing productive evaluations. They are also in a strong position to reach out to local university partners for support with research and evaluation. Evaluation of partnership programs can inform all providers of new and effective approaches to prevention and thus avoid wasting time and resources on less effective strategies.

Sustainability. In order to have maximum impact, effective school–community agency partnerships must be implemented over time. Abbreviated intervention and prevention programs have little lasting effect. The developmental research has made clear that change occurs over an extended period—not overnight. Only when partnerships exist over a significant period of time can the partners develop true reciprocity in that they learn to complement each other's strengths and limitations so that together they can maximize the potential for achieving positive outcomes for the school community.

In the past, partnerships between community agencies and schools were typically short lived, lasting as long as funding lasted. The older model in which either the school or the community agency was the sole source of funding often resulted in a lack of collaboration. Each partner would often feel that the other partner was not contributing its fair share. Recently, with funding shortages evident in education, health, and service sectors, new strategies for financial sustainability have evolved. Community agencies and schools have figured out creative ways to share positions that deliver services to children. In some school–community partnerships, third-party payers have provided funding for essential health services with schools and agencies collaborating in applying for these funds. For a number of partnerships, the federal government's after-school program—21st-Century Community Learning Centers federal program—has been a source of government funding to implement school-linked and school-based after-school programs. Corporations and foundations are increasingly stepping up to the table to support the development and at least short-term sustainability of these programs.

Sustainability is also enhanced by strategic utilization of specific resources in the community such as universities. In many communities, universities have brought considerable resources to school–community partnerships, particularly in terms of student interns (e.g., nurses, social workers, and counselors). It is recognized that financial resources are typically required for the operation of a school–community partnership; the synergies that arise from this partnership likely ensure that there is an overall financial saving. Operating the various units in the partnerships separately, without coordination, can be far more costly due to the lack of sharing resources.

Infrastructure. For many years successful school–community partnerships depended upon the time and effort of the principal as well as the time and effort of community agency administrators or staff in order for them to work smoothly and efficiently. However, the press of educational reform has all but consumed most principals in deepening the teaching and learning agenda of the school. Agency staff is similarly focused on delivering their primary service. For these reasons, attention to school–community partnerships is often marginalized in both school and agency. Consequently, there is little time on either the school's or the agency's part to sustain effective programs. Effective school–community partnerships require an infrastructure whose major task is to focus on sustaining and nurturing the partnership.

School–community collaborative programs not only require time to design and deliver, but in order to maintain the partnership, attention to both product and process are necessary. Each partner needs an opportunity to make adjustments along the way. Each partner needs feedback about what is working and what is not, and each partner must engage in the process of evaluating outcomes. Collaborative efforts are ultimately successful only when the partners labor together.

Effective school–community partnerships require a deliberate focus on nurturing and sustaining the relationship. A designated infrastructure, an individual or team whose major focus is the relationship itself, can often play this role. Such an infrastructure will typically transcend changes in staff in both school and community agencies and will be the vehicle through which communication occurs. The infrastructure can exist in the form of a person or a team at each site who takes responsibility for school partnerships. Such an infrastructure develops processes for the collaboration to function more smoothly (e.g., memoranda of agreements, periodic reviews, and strategies for identifying problems or challenges).

The best practices of school–community partnerships can best be understood through a description of a program that embodies them. The best practices of school–community partnerships will look different when implemented in the varied contexts of school systems and with different school cultures and community populations. One example of a school–community partnership that strives to adhere to these best practices in its own particular context is Boston Connects.

Boston Connects: Best Practices in Action

The Boston Connects program is a school–community-university partnership that brings comprehensive, coordinated student support to 3,300 students in two Boston neighborhoods—Allston/Brighton and Missions Hill/Roxbury—by linking nine Boston public elementary schools with community and university partners. Though there are many community agencies involved with each individual school, the lead community agency partner of Boston Connects is the YMCA of Greater Boston. As a lead agency, the YMCA represents all community agencies on the Boston Connects implementation team. The university partner of Boston Connects is Boston College, with involvement from multiple schools and departments including the Schools of Education, Social Work, and Nursing and Management. The School Counseling Program, housed in the Counseling Psychology program, has played the major role in program design and implementation.

Boston Connects began in 1995 as an effort to extend services and resources (e.g., health, mental health, and family services; after-school programs; and youth development opportunities) in one Boston public school. The program was taken to scale in 2001, extending to eight more Boston public elementary schools located in two Boston neighborhoods. Over the past 6 years, Boston Connects has worked to promote the learning and development of students, 85% of whom are children of color and 70% of whom live in conditions of poverty. As Boston Connects has grown, it has maintained its commitment to embodying the best practices of school–community partnerships. Thus, it serves as one effective illustration for the best practices outlined in this chapter.

In accordance with the goals of education reform, the mission of Boston Connects is to build a comprehensive, coordinated, and systemic web of services in active collaboration with community agencies and schools in order to provide school children with the supports, services, and resources they need to be academically successful. Though this mission establishes students' increasing academic success as a foremost goal for the partnership, it also explicitly acknowledges that this end cannot be met without the simultaneous goal of supporting students' development and well-being. Thus, in addition to working directly to improve students' academic achievement, through educational interventions such as tutoring and special education, Boston Connects also works to reduce nonacademic barriers to learning by providing supports for students' social, emotional, and physical well-being.

Boston Connects strives to support students comprehensively. Prior to the full implementation of school–community agency partnerships in Boston Connects schools, options for responding to at-risk students were more limited. The typical outcome for students who experienced learning challenges was a referral for a special education evaluation. Though the appropriate service for some students, this referral was an inappropriate response for many others. One of the main successes of Boston Connects has been the decrease of the percentage of referrals for special education evaluations, coupled with the increase of the range of alternative services and supports offered to meet the comprehensive needs of students. At one point in Boston, 24% of the student population was labeled special education, with significant overrepresentation of children of color. Coupled with the district's intense effort to reduce special education referrals, the Boston Connects schools have seen the percentage of children placed in special education drop to 14%.

Boston Connects has identified a wide array of prevention and early intervention programs for children who evidence some risk but are not appropriately classified as academically disabled. Among many others, these services include after-school programs, tutoring/academic support, mental health counseling, mentoring, health services, and summer school. Boston Connects has helped children to work through some of their challenges and receive supports from adults and peers in the community by dramatically increasing the number of students linked with a range of services. In just one academic year, from the fall of 2003 to the fall of 2004, the number of students receiving services and youth development resources increased by approximately 57%.

To ensure that the services and resources offered to students and families are coordinated, each Boston Connects school has a full-time school counselor, who is referred to within the program as a "school-site coordinator." A primary responsibility of this school counselor is the implementation of an effective student support process, through which each student, particularly those at risk, is assessed and referred for services and supports that enhance learning and development. The school counselor facilitates this process through the Student Support Team, an interdisciplinary group that consists of teachers, administrators, school counselors, and representatives from community partners, such as mental health agencies. This team assures not only that students are referred to appropriate prevention or intervention supports, but also that these services are not overlapping or redundant and routinely follow up with students, parents, and service providers. Further, the Student Support Information Database is a unique tool that enhances coordination of services by tracking referral information for each student.

In order to expand effective service and support connections for students, school counselors work with community agencies and other partners, always seeking to expand connections within the community. In this way, the school counselors create more opportunities for students to access various supports. By focusing efforts on coordinating services instead of the more traditional school counseling approach of delivering individual services (e.g., mental health counseling), school counselors can multiply the number of students served. Results from an analysis of the day-to-day activities of Boston Connects school counselors showed that activities supporting individual students (i.e., individual student appraisal and individual student services) composed 21% of all activities. Thus, school counselors were able to engage in a diverse array of other activities, such as family support and outreach (10%), school climate activities (14%), and service connections (29%; Walsh, Barrett, & DePaul, 2007).

The array of services and supports offered by Boston Connects falls along a continuum that ranges from whole-school prevention and youth development to small-group or classroom-level intervention for at-risk groups, and finally to early intervention for individual students exhibiting behavioral, emotional, or academic issues. A recent example of Boston Connects' whole-school prevention initiative is a health education and social competence curriculum that is currently being delivered to all students. This health program consists of two empirically validated curricula: (1) *Eat Well and Keep Moving*, the goal of which is to improve children's physical health knowledge, motivation, and efficacy and (2) *Skills for Growing*, which seeks to enhance students' social skills and emotional intelligence. Prevention specialists deliver the curriculum while raising awareness among the larger school community about the importance of physical and mental health. This initiative reflects Boston Connects' underlying philosophy that holds that children who are physically ill, fatigued, and undernourished cannot demonstrate their academic capacity, nor can students who are hampered by low self-esteem, poor emotional regulation, and inadequate social support. This curriculum seeks not only to educate, but also to empower students to care for themselves emotionally and physically.

In addition to whole-school supports, school counselors often organize and implement small-group services for classes or mixed-grade groups of students who demonstrate needs such as anger management or conflict resolution. Finally, individual students in need of services are identified through the prescribed Student Support Process and referred to services by the Student Support Team. These referrals are designed to meet the specific needs of the child and may include such recommendations as mental health counseling, a behavioral plan, or tutoring with university volunteers.

The continuum of prevention and intervention services constitutes the programmatic dimensions of what is referred to as "school climate." School climate reflects the physical and psychological aspects of the school that result in feelings and behaviors that can promote or impede learning. Social and emotional learning standards assist the school staff in identifying the developmentally appropriate behaviors that contribute to a positive school climate (Weissberg & O'Brien, 2004). One of the important roles of the school counselor is to facilitate the implementation of social and emotional learning standards and the development and maintenance of positive school climate.

The diversity of the perspectives represented on the interdisciplinary Student Support Team ensures that the supports offered to students are developmentally appropriate. The teams, which typically comprise teachers, principals, parents, and learning support staff, are facilitated by school counselors. Collaboration among these diverse professionals who collectively work across the age spectrum in the school assures that all aspects of the child's developmental level will be considered in the review. Further, the social competence curriculum implemented by Boston Connects' school counselors weekly in each classroom is designed around the developmentally organized social and emotional standards developed by the Collaborative for Social and Emotional Learning (CASEL; Weissberg & O'Brien, 2004). Finally, Boston Connects' commitment to serving the whole child ensures that supports and services will attend to those developmental challenges that often occur largely beyond school walls.

As one of Boston Connects' four major goals, increasing family engagement is seen as a critical pathway toward helping students achieve success in the classroom and beyond. Inherent to Boston Connects' mission for supporting students is the recognition of the importance of building a community that centers around school life. The investment of parents and caregivers is central to making this a meaningfully supportive community for students. Boston Connects counselors work directly with parents by facilitating their connection to community resources and services as well as supporting their engagement in the academic progress of their children. School counselors also collaborate with school and community professionals to offer opportunities for parents to enhance their personal and career development (e.g., ESL, job, and immigration counseling classes at the school).

Given that 85% of the students attending Boston Connects schools are children of color and nearly two thirds speak a second language at home, it is critical that the partnership acknowledge and appreciate the role of culture and ethnicity. The school counselors and prevention specialists employed by the program must be responsive to the critical impact of culture and ethnicity on the various prevention and intervention programs. For example, in accordance with findings that cultural adaptations to prevention curricula are often necessary for effectiveness (Resnicow, Soler, Braithwaite, Ahluwalia, & Butler, 2000), the prevention specialists have modified the social competence curriculum to reflect the specific cultural and ethnic identities of the student community. As another example, school counselors learn to appreciate the different meanings of mental health diagnoses and interventions across various ethnic groups and, therefore assist families in accessing services from multiculturally competent clinicians.

Recognizing the importance of evaluating effectiveness, researchers at Boston College are conducting an ongoing assessment of Boston Connects in an effort to identify the program's successes and the students' successes and to help the partnership evolve. Outcome evaluations of Boston Connects quantitatively assess the partnership's progress toward its stated goals of improving academic achievement, as well as increasing community agency involvement in schools and creating a more diverse array of student support referrals for students. Data have shown advancement toward several of these ends. For example, the program has demonstrated a positive impact on academic achievement. Students who receive services are making gains at the same rate and sometimes at a faster rate than students who are not in need of student support services. Without services, it can be reasonably assumed that students at risk would continue to fall further behind.

Equally important to assessing these quantitatively measured outcomes is the process evaluation, which takes a qualitative look at the manner in which these services are implemented. Several programmatic aspects of Boston Connects are designed as avenues for gaining feedback from a cross-section of involved parties, such as school counselors, teachers, principals, and parents. This valuable feedback from those involved on the ground level has often been used to make changes, both large and small, to all aspects of the program from service delivery at the individual schools to the level of program infrastructure.

Boston Connects has demonstrated its sustainability by not only maintaining its partnerships, but also expanding them and shaping its interventions based on the community's changing needs and strengths. Boston Connects began as a partnership with one Boston public school in 1995 and has grown into a far-reaching systemic intervention. Boston Connects in its current form began in 2001 and was scaled up from one public school to nine. The partnership's presence in these schools for a number of years has allowed relationships between community partners and school professionals to deepen, thereby improving and expanding the services offered to students. In addition, the continued presence of the partnership, coupled with the ongoing evaluation, allows Boston Connects to adapt its services and supports in response to the evolving needs and strengths of the ever-changing community.

Infrastructure

Boston Connects is based on a collaborative model, and thus, leadership is shared among the various stakeholders of the partnership. The complex program infrastructure includes school-based Student Support Teams and full-time school counselors, a cluster-wide Student and Family Instructional Support Center, and a Resource Advisory Council.

At the individual school level, the school counselor represents the program and enlists the support school and community professionals for the Student Support

Team. This team reviews individual students and whole classes, making referrals and recommendations for student support.

The Student and Family Instructional Support Center systematically links families, schools, and community agencies across the neighborhood. It serves as a central location where family and student support services and programmatic activities are delivered based on identified needs. For example, one of the services offered by this center is registration. The Student and Family Instructional Support Center is the only non-Boston Public Schools registration site in this "cluster" of schools. The BPS site location is far from the Boston Connects neighborhoods and a difficult commute, especially when using public transportation, as many Boston Connects families do. Offering this service is critical for Boston Connects families because of the center's proximity to their neighborhoods.

The Resource Advisory Council is a team of community, school, and university representatives that provides oversight, leadership, and advocacy in the coordination, integration, and strengthening of student support services and school–agency partnerships.

Models of School–Community Partnerships

The effort to link schools and community has resulted in the development of a number of models of school–community partnerships. These models range from tinkering at the margins of existing models of schooling (e.g., systems for referral to community agencies) to comprehensive efforts to partner with the community at more intensive levels.

The least intrusive model of school–community collaboration is a school-linked services approach in which a school articulates formal linkages and agreements for services with community agencies and resources. Somewhat more extensive is a school-based services model that delivers the services within the confines of the school building or in adjacent or nearby locations (Dryfoos, 1996). A number of school-based models incorporate one particular type of service (e.g., a school-based health clinic) while others offer a wide range of services (e.g., a Family Resource Center) to support the academic programs. Some of these services operate under the aegis and budget of the school system while others are funded by local city or town health or human service programs.

More ambitious than school-linked and school-based service approaches are models that attempt to transform the school and its personnel in the direction of more comprehensive approaches to addressing the needs of students. One salient example of this approach can be found in the development of what are referred to as community schools. Community schools have been variously defined, but generally, they integrate education with supports necessary for the healthy development of children, family and communities. In short, these schools weave together community development initiatives and school reform (Dryfoos, 1994). Community schools take many forms including full-service schools and extended-services schools. They incorporate a variety of innovative strategies and programs that lead to comprehensive delivery of education and related health and human services. Some well-known exemplars include the Children's Aid Society Community Schools Programs and the Texas School of the Future Project. Several of these models are being adapted in various cities around the country (Wang & Kovach, 1996), and many involve a partnership with a local university that provides various types of assistance for the implementation of these community schools.

Critical to all of these models is the design and development of a core infrastructure that enables and sustains the school–community partnership. One of the most effective kinds of infrastructure is embedded within the school and is focused on two elements of school functioning: the Student Support Team and process and the School Climate Team and process (Walsh & Brabeck, 2006). The Student Support Team and process matches individual students with appropriate supports, resources, and/or services, while the School Climate Team and process organizes all the school prevention activities and implements the social competence curriculum.

While a wide variety of school–community partnership models exist, each with unique features, all such partnerships are built on a common set of assumptions about the nature of child development. Advocates of these partnerships recognize that the development of children and youth is inextricably linked to their home, school, and sociocultural environments (Bronfenbrenner, 1979) and cannot be understood in isolation from these contexts. The development of the child in one context (e.g., the school) will be influenced by the conditions of the other contexts (e.g., the family and community). Instead of employing a narrow focus on the intellectual achievement of school children, school–community partnerships assume that cognitive development cannot be separated from either biological or sociocultural development (Bronfenbrenner; Lerner, 1986, 1995b). It is also understood that the adults who are critical to the child's life are themselves developing and benefit from support by the local school and community (Lerner, 1986, 1995b). Enhancing the development of adults will indirectly support the development of their children. Finally, school–community partnerships recognize the role of resilience in the development of children. Community resources that foster the development of children's strengths have been shown to contribute to improved academic outcomes (Masten et al., 1990; Werner, 1989, 1990).

These fundamental principles of development strongly suggest that not only the family but also the community must be part of the education of the whole child. A holistic view of human development makes clear that "it takes a village to raise a child" and it takes the partnership of family, school, and community to educate a child. School counselors, in their role as liaisons between teachers, parents, support personnel, and community resources, can be pivotal in forging strong school–community connections.

Vision of Schooling: The Whole Child

The most defining element of school–community partnerships that embody best practices and employ integrative models is their vision of schooling. School counselors' knowledge of students' biological, psychological, and social levels of development and their understanding of the impact of context, allows them to build school–community partnerships that champion a vision of schooling that sees, serves, and supports the whole child.

The division of the whole child into parts has framed the landscape in which school counselors have had to work over the years. Though unintentional, the assignment of teaching and learning (i.e., cognitive processes) to the schools and the personal–social needs of children (i.e., affective processes) to the community has become reified. On the one hand, there is little doubt that both educators and community providers are aware that cognitive and affective processes interact with and influence one another. On the other hand, as their roles have evolved, educators and community providers sometimes conducted their work as if these two processes were separate and unrelated aspects of the child (Eisner, 2005; Noddings, 2005). School–community partnerships redress this imbalance by deepening connections between school and community. Recognizing that children's development cannot be so simply divided, the school–community partnership movement has called on educators and human service professionals to recommit to a vision of the whole child.

In short, in helping to implement school–community partnerships, school counselors can restore to their role a balance between academic and personal–social emphases. The responsibility for enhancing academic as well as personal–social development renders the school counseling profession a critical part of the school's plan for educational reform (Gysbers, 2001; Gysbers & Henderson, 2000). In the context of school–community partnerships, school counselors can address the conditions that constitute barriers to learning and, at the same time, promote higher academic standards. This more balanced approach to education will lead school staff and community members to a renewed appreciation of both cognitive and affective needs of school children and to the necessity of linking the academic and personal–social domains (Marx et al., 1998; McKenzie & Richmond, 1998; Walsh et al., 1999).

The voice of the school counseling profession must be loud and unified in its call for the establishment and sustenance of interdependent community partnerships. In a culture that increasingly values individualism and autonomy, school counselors have recognized the undeniable truth that schools alone cannot provide optimal support for the healthy development of students. This recognition demonstrates not only their grounding in a unified professional philosophy but also, more importantly, their investment in the future of America's children and their unwavering commitment to enabling that future.

References

Adelman, H. S., & Taylor, L. (2002a). Building comprehensive, multifaceted, and integrated approaches to address barriers to student learning. *Childhood Education, 78,* 261–268.

Adelman, H. S., & Taylor, L. (2002b). School counselors and school reform: New directions. *Professional School Counseling, 5,* 235–248.

Airasian, P. W., & Walsh, M. E. (1997). Constructivist cautions. *Phi Delta Kappan, 78,* 444–449.

Akos, P. (2001). Creating developmental opportunity: Systemic and proactive interventions for elementary school counselors. In D. S. Sandhu (Ed.), *Elementary school counseling in the new millennium* (pp. 91–102). Alexandria, VA: American Counseling Association.

Alexander, C. M., Kruczek, T., Ramirez, M. C., & Zagelbaum, A. (2003). A review of the school counseling literature for themes evolving from the education trust initiative. *Professional School Counseling, 7,* 29–34.

American School Counselor Association. (2003). *The ASCA National Model: A framework for school counseling programs.* Alexandria, VA: Author.

Atkinson, D. R., & Thompson, C. E. (1992). Racial, ethnic, and cultural variables in counseling. In S. D. Brown & R. W. Lent (Eds.), *Handbook of counseling psychology* (2nd ed., pp. 349–382). New York: Wiley.

Barnett, K., Conley, J. A., & Green, A. G. (2005). Urban school counseling: Implications for practice and training (Special issue). *Professional School Counseling, 8,* 189–195.

Barton, P. E. (2001). *Facing the hard facts in education reform.* Princeton, NJ: Educational Testing Service.

Barton, P. E. (2003). *Parsing the achievement gap: Baselines for tracking progress.* Princeton, NJ: Educational Testing Service.

Bauman, S., Davis, A., Falco, L., Seabolt, K., & Szymanski, G. (2003). Trends in school counseling journals: The first fifty years. *Professional School Counseling, 7,* 79–90.

Becker, B. E., & Luthar, S. S. (2002). Social-emotional factors affecting achievement outcomes among disadvantaged students: Closing the achievement gap. *Educational Psychologist, 37,* 197–214.

Bemak, F. (2000). Transforming the role of the counselor to provide leadership in educational reform through collaboration. *Professional School Counseling, 3,* 323–331.

Benard, B. (1991). *Fostering resiliency in kids: Protective factors in the family, schools, and community.* San Francisco: Far West Laboratory for Educational Research and Development.

Benson, P. L. (1997). *All kids are our kids: What communities must do to raise caring and responsible children and adolescents.* San Francisco: Jossey-Bass.

Benson, P. L., Galbraith, J. & Espeland, P. (1998). *What kids need to succeed: Proven, practical ways to raise good kids* (Rev. ed.). Minneapolis, MN: Free Spirit Publishing.

Betz, N. E. (1993). Toward an integration of multicultural and career psychology. *Career Development Quarterly, 42,* 53–55.

Blustein, D. L., Phillips, S. D., Jobin-Davis, K., Finkelberg, S. L., & Roarke, A. E. (1997). A theory-building investigation of the school-to-work transition. *Counseling Psychologist, 25,* 364–402.

Brabeck, M., Walsh, M. E., Kenny, M., & Comilang, K. (1997). Interprofessional collaboration for children and families: Opportunities for counseling psychology in the 21st century. *Counseling Psychologist, 25,* 615–636.

Britzman, M. J. (2005). Improving our moral landscape through character education: An opportunity for school counselor leadership (Special issue). *Professional School Counseling, 8,* 293–295.

Bronfenbrenner, U. (1979). *The ecology of human development: Experiments by nature and design.* Cambridge, MA: Harvard University Press.

Bryan, J. (2005). Fostering education resilience and achievement in urban schools through school-family-community partnerships. *Professional School Counseling, 8,* 219–227.

Bryan, J., & Holcomb-McCoy, C. (2004). School counselor's perceptions of their involvement in school-family-community partnerships. *Professional School Counseling, 7,* 162–171.

Campbell, C. A., & Brigman, G. (2005) Closing the achievement gap: A structured approach to school counseling. *Journals for Specialists in Group Work, 30,* 67–82.

Campbell, C. A., & Dahir, C. A. (1997). *Sharing the vision: The national standards for school counseling programs.* Alexandria, VA: American School Counselor Association.

Carpenter-Aeby, T., & Aeby, V. G. (2005). Program evaluation and replications of school-based mental health services and family-community interventions with chronically disruptive students. *School Community Journal, 15,* 37–61.

Centers for Disease Control and Prevention. (2003). *Youth risk behavior surveillance system (YRBSS).* Atlanta, GA: U.S. Department of Health and Human Services.

Centers for Disease Control and Prevention. (2004). *U.S. obesity trends: 1985–2003.* Retrieved September 7, 2005, from http://www.cdc.gov/nccdphp/dnpa/obesity/trend/maps/index.htm

Center for Mental Health in Schools. (2003). *Youngsters mental health and psychosocial problems: What are the data?* Retrieved August 21, 2004, from http://smhp.psych.ucla.edu/pfdocs/prevalance/youthMH.pdf

Chartrand, J. M., Strong, S. R., & Weitzman, L. M. (1995). The interactional perspective in vocational psychology: Paradigms, theories, and research practices. In W. B. Walsh & S. H. Osipow (Eds.), *Handbook of vocational psychology: Theory, research, and practices* (2nd ed., pp. 35–65). Hillsdale, NJ: Lawrence Erlbaum Associates.

Cicchetti, D., & Sroufe, L. A. (2000). The past as prologue to the future: The times, they've been a-changin'. Development and psychopathology (Special issue). *Reflecting on the Past and Planning for the Future of Developmental Psychopathology, 12,* 255–264.

Coleman, H. L. K., & Baskin, T. (2003). Multiculturally competent school counseling. In D. B. Pope-Davis, H. L. K. Coleman, W. M. Ling, & R. L Torporek (Eds.), *Handbook of multicultural competencies in counseling and psychology* (pp. 103–113). Thousand Oaks, CA: Sage.

Coltoff, P. (1998). *Community schools: Education reform and partnership with our nation's social service agencies* (Report No. CWLA 0-87868-700-9). Washington, DC: Child Welfare League of America. (ERIC Document Reproduction Service No. ED421234)

Constantine, M. G., & Yeh, C. (2001). Multicultural training, self-construals, and multicultural competence of school counselors. *Professional School Counseling, 4,* 202–207.

Darling-Hammond, L. (2000, January 1). Teacher quality and student achievement: A review of state policy evidence. *Educational Policy Analysis Archives, 8*(1). Retrieved June 24, 2004, from http:// epaa.asu.edu/epaa/v8n1/

Dryfoos, J. G. (1990). *Adolescents at risk: Prevalence and prevention.* New York: Oxford University Press.

Dryfoos, J. G. (1994a). Full-service schools: A revolution in health and social services for children, youth and families. The Jossey-Bass Health Services, *The Jossey-Bass Social and Behavioral Science Series, and the Jossey-Bass Education Series.* San Francisco, CA: Jossey-Bass.

Dryfoos, J. G. (1994b). Medical clinics in junior high school: Changing the model to meet demands. *Journal of Adolescent Health, 15,* 549–557.

Dryfoos, J. G. (1996). Adolescents at risk: Shaping programs to fit the need. *Journal of Negro Education, 65,* 5–18.

Education Trust. (2003, October 28). *Challenging the myths: Re-thinking the role of school counselors.* Retrieved September 18, 2004, from http://www2.edtrust.org/NR/rdonlyres/0EF57A7F-B336-46A8-898D-981018AFBF11/0/counseling_train_broch.pdf

Eisner, E. W. (2005). Opening a shuttered window. *Phi Delta Kappan, 87,* 8–10.

Ferguson, P., Jimerson, S. R., & Dalton, M. J. (2001). Sorting out successful failures: Exploratory analyses of factors associated with academic and behavioral outcomes of retained students. *Psychology in the Schools, 38,* 327–341.

Fitch, T. J., & Marshall, J. L. (2004). What counselors do in high-achieving schools: A study on the role of the school counselor. *Professional School Counseling, 7,* 172–177.

Ford, D. H., & Lerner, R. M. (1992). *Developmental systems theory: An integrative approach.* Newbury Park, CA: Sage.

Galassi, J. P., & Akos, P. (2004). Developmental advocacy: Twenty-first century school counseling. *Journal of Counseling and Development, 82,* 146–157.

Garmezy, N., Masten, A. S., & Tellegen, A. (1984). The study of stress and competence in children: A building block for developmental psychopathology. *Child Development, 55,* 97–111.

Gibson, R. L., & Mitchell, M. H. (1990). *Introduction to counseling and guidance* (3rd ed.). New York: Macmillan.

Green, A., & Keys, S. (2001). Expanding the developmental school counseling paradigm: Meeting the needs of the 21st century student. *Professional School Counseling, 5,* 84–95.

Greenberg, M. T., Weissberg, R. P., O'Brien, M. U., Zins, J. E., Fredericks, L., Resnik, H., et al. (2003). Enhancing school-based prevention and youth development through coordinated social, emotional, and academic learning. *American Psychologist, 58,* 466–474.

Gysbers, N. C. (1997). Involving counseling psychology in the school-to-work movement: An idea whose time has come (Special issue). *CounselingPsychologist, 25,* 413–427.

Gysbers, N. C. (2001). School guidance and counseling in the 21st century: Remember the past into the future. *Professional School Counseling, 5,* 96–105.

Gysbers, N. C., & Henderson, P. (2000). *Developing and managing your school guidance program* (3rd ed.). Alexandria, VA: American Counseling Association.

Hamilton, M. A., & Hamilton, S. F. (1998). *Opening career paths for youth: What needs to be done? Who can do it?* Washington, DC: Youth Policy Forum.

Hart, B., & Risley, T. R. (2003). The early catastrophe: The 30 million word gap. *American Educator, 27,* 4–9.

Hart, P. J., & Jacobi, M. (1992). *From gatekeeper to advocate: Transforming the role of the school counselor.* New York: New York College Entrance Examination Board and the Achievement Council.

Helms, J. E. (Ed.). (1990). *Black and white racial identity: Theory, research, and practice.* Westport, CT: Greenwood Press.

Henderson, N., & Milstein, M. M. (1996). *Resiliency in schools: Making it happen for students and educators.* Thousand Oaks, CA: Corwin.

Hernandez, T. J., & Seem, S. R. (2004). A safe school climate: A systemic approach and the school counselor. *Professional School Counseling, 7,* 256–262.

Holcomb-McCoy, C. C. (2005). Investigating school counselors' perceived multicultural competence. *Professional School Counseling, 8,* 414–423.

Holcomb-McCoy, C. C., & Mitchell, N. (2005). A descriptive study of urban school counseling programs. *Professional School Counseling, 8,* 203–209.

House, R. M., & Hayes, R. L. (2002). School counselors: Becoming key players in school reform. *Professional School Counseling, 5,* 249–256.

House, R. M., & Martin, P. J. (1998). Advocating for better futures for all students: A new vision for school counselors. *Education, 119,* 284–291.

Isaacs, M. L. (2003). Data-driven decision making: The engine of accountability. *Professional School Counseling, 6,* 288–295.

Keys, S. G., & Bemak, F. (1997). Schools-family-community linked services: A school counseling role for the changing times. *School Counselor, 44,* 255–263.

Kutash, K., & Duchnowski, A. J. (2004). The mental health needs of youth with emotional and behavioral disabilities placed in special education in urban schools. *Journal of Child and Family Studies, 13,* 235–248.

Lapan, R. T., & Kosciulek, J. F. (2003). Toward a community career system program evaluation framework. *Professional School Counseling, 6,* 316–331.

Lapan, R. T., Tucker, B., Kim S., & Kosciulek, J. F. (2003). Preparing rural adolescents for post high-school transitions. *Journal of Counseling and Development, 81,* 329–342.

Lawson, H., & Briar-Lawson, K. (1997). *Connecting the dots: Progress toward the integration of school reform, school-linked services, parent involvement and community schools.* Oxford, OH: Miami University.

Lee, C. C. (2005). Urban school counseling: Contexts, characteristics and competencies. *Professional School Counseling, 8,* 184–188.

Legum, H. L., & Hoare, C. H. (2004). The impact of career intervention on at-risk middle school students' career maturity levels, academic achievement and self-esteem. *Professional School Counseling, 8,* 148–155.

Lerner, R., Walsh, M., & Howard, K. (1998). Developmental-contextual considerations: Person-context relations as the bases for risk and resiliency in child and adolescent development. In A. S. Bellack, & M. Hersen (Eds.), *Comprehensive clinical psychology* (Vol. 5, pp. 1–24). Oxford, UK: Persimmon.

Lerner, R. M. (1986). *Concepts and theories of human development* (2nd ed.). New York: Random House.

Lerner, R. M. (1995a). *America's youth in crisis: Challenges and options for programs and policies.* Thousand Oaks, CA: Sage.

Lerner, R. M. (1995b). Developing individuals within changing contexts: Implications of developmental contextualism for human development research, policy, and programs. In T. A. Kindermann & J. Valsiner (Eds.), *Development of person-context relations* (pp. 13–37). Hillsdale, NJ: Lawrence Erlbaum.

Lerner, R. M., & Kauffman, M. B. (1985). The concept of development in contextualism. *Developmental Review, 5,* 309–333.

Lubeck, S., Jessup P., deVries, M., & Post, J. (2001). The role of culture in program improvement. *Early Childhood Research Quarterly, 16,* 499–523.

Marx, E., Wooley, S. F., & Northup, D. (Eds.). (1998). *Health is academic: A guide to coordinated school health programs.* New York: Teachers College Press.

Massachusetts Department of Education. (2004). *Plans of high school graduates.* Retrieved May 18. 2006, from http://www.doe.mass.edu/news/news.asp?id=1946

Masten, A. S., Best, K. M., & Garmezy, N. (1990). Resilience and development: Contributions from the study of children who overcome adversity. *Development and Psychopathology, 2,* 425–444.

Masten, A. S., & Coatsworth, J. D. (1998). The development of competence in favorable and unfavorable environments: Lessons from research on successful children. *American Psychologist, 53,* 205–220.

McKenzie, F. D., & Richmond, J. B. (1998). Linking health and learning: An overview of coordinated school health programs. In E. Marx, S. Wolley, & D. Northrop (Eds.), *Health is academic: A guide to coordinated school health programs* (pp. 1–14). New York: Teachers College Press.

McWhirter, J. J., McWhirter, B. T., McWhirter, A. M., & McWhirter, E. H. (1998). *At-risk youth: A comprehensive response* (2nd ed.). Pacific Grove, CA: Brooks/Cole.

Myrick, R. D. (1993). *Developmental guidance and counseling: A practical approach* (2nd ed.). Minneapolis, MN: Educational Media Corporation.

National Clearinghouse on Child Abuse and Neglect Information. (2004). *Child Maltreatment 2002.* Retrieved June 24, 2004, from www.acf.hhs.gov/programs/cb/pubs/cm02/index.htm

Newsom, J. (2003). Education vital signs. Accountability: Struggling to comply. *American School Board Journal, 190,* 6–10.

No Child Left Behind Act. (2001). Retrieved September 3, 2004, from http://www.nochildleftbehind.gov/

Noddings, N. (2005). Identifying and responding to needs in education. *Cambridge Journal of Education, 35,* 147–159.

Osborne, J. L., & Collison, B. B. (1998). School counselors and external providers: Conflict of complement. *Professional School Counseling, 1,* 7–11.

Overton, W. F. (1998). Developmental psychology: Philosophy, concepts, methodology. In W. Damon & R. M. Lerner (Eds.), *Handbook of child psychology: Vol. 1: Theoretical models of human development* (5th ed., pp. 107–187). Hoboken, NJ: John Wiley & Sons.

Paavola, J. C., Cobb, C., Illback, R. J., Joseph, H. M., Torruellaa, A., & Talley, R. C. (1995). *Comprehensive and coordinated psychological services for children: A call for service integration.* Washington, DC: American Psychological Association.

Paisley, P. O. (2001). Maintaining and enhancing the developmental focus in school counseling programs. *Professional School Counseling, 4,* 271–277.

Paisley, P. O., & McMahon, H. G. (2001). School counseling for the 21st century: Challenges and opportunities. *Professional School Counseling, 5,* 106–115.

Payzant, T. W. (1992). New beginnings in San Diego: Developing a strategy for interagency collaboration. *Phi Delta Kappan, 74,* 139–146.

Power, T. J., DuPaul, G. J., Shapiro, E. S., & Kazak, A. E. (2003). *Promoting children's health: Integrating school, family, and community.* New York: Guilford Press.

Resnicow, K., Soler, R., Braithwaite, R. L. Ahluwalia, J. S., & Butler, J. (2000). Cultural sensitivity in substance use prevention. *Journal of Community Psychology, 28,* 271–290.

Riley, R. W. (1998). America goes back to school. *Our Children, 24,* 34 35.

Riley, R. W. (2002). What matters most. *American School Board Journal, 189,* 28–30.

Roeser, R. W., Midgley, C., & Urdan, T. C. (1996). Perceptions of school psychological environment and early adolescents' psychological and behavioral functioning in the school: The mediating role of goals and belonging. *Journal of Eductional Psychology, 88,* 408–422.

Rothstein, R. (2004). *Class and schools: Using social, economic, and educational reform to close the black-white achievement gap.* New York: Columbia University, Teacher's College.

Rutter, M. (1985). Resilience in the face of adversity: Protective factors and resistance to psychiatric disorder. *British Journal of Psychiatry, 147,* 598–611.

Schorr, L. B. (1997). *Common purpose: Strengthening families and neighborhoods to rebuild America.* New York: First Anchor Books.

Schorr, L. B., & Schorr, D. (1988). *Within our reach: Breaking the cycle of disadvantage.* Garden City, NY: Anchor Press.

Segal, B. (1995). Prevention and culture: A theoretical perspective. *Drugs and Society, 8,* 139–147.

Share, J. (2005). The cutting-edge challenge. *School Arts: The Art Education Magazine for Teachers, 104,* 23.

Short, R. J., & Talley, R. C. (1997). Rethinking psychology and schools: Implications of recent national policy. *American Psychologist, 52,* 234–240.

Sink, C. (2002). Comprehensive guidance and counseling programs and development. *Professional School Counseling, 6*, 130–137.

Solberg, V. S., Howard, K. A., Blustein, D. A., & Close, W. (2004). Connecting school-to-work: Career development in schools. *Counseling Psychologist, 30*, 705–725.

Stallings, J. A. (1995). Ensuring teaching and learning in the 21st century. *Educational Researcher, 24*, 4–8.

Strauss, R. M. & Pollack, H. A. (2001). Epidemic increase in childhood overweight, 1986–1998. *Journal of the American Medical Association, 286*, 2845–2848.

Tyack, D. (1992). Health and social services in public schools: Historical perspectives. *Future of Children, 2*, 19–37.

Urban Institute. (2000). *A new look at homelessness in America*. Retrieved June 24, 2004, from http://www.urban.org/url.cfm?ID=900302

Vargas, L. A., & Koss-Chioino, J. D. (Eds.). (1992). *Working with culture: Psychotherapeutic interventions with ethnic minority children and adolescents*. San Francisco: Jossey-Bass.

Walsh, M. E., Barrett, J. G., & DePaul, J. (2007). Day-to-day activities of school counselors: Alignment with new directions in the field and the ASCA National Model. *Professional School Counseling, 10*, 370–378.

Walsh, M. E., & Brabeck, M. M. (2006). Resilience and risk in learning: Complex interactions and comprehensive interventions. In R. J. Sternberg & R. F. Subotnik (Eds.), *Optimizing student success in school with the other three R's: Reasoning, resilience, and responsibility* (pp. 113–142). Greenwich, CT: Information Age Publishing.

Walsh, M. E., Brabeck, M. M., & Howard, K. A. (1999). Interprofessional collaboration in children's services: Toward a theoretical framework. *Children's Services: Social Policy, Research, and Practice, 2*, 183–208.

Walsh, M. E., Galassi, J. P., Murphy, J. A., & Park-Taylor, J. (2002). A conceptual framework for counseling psychologists in schools. *The Counseling Psychologist, 30*, 682–704.

Walsh, M. E., Howard, K. A., & Buckley, M. A. (1999). School counselors in school–community partnerships: Opportunities and challenges. *Professional School Counseling, 2*, 349–356.

Walsh, M. E., & Murphy, J. A. (2003). *Children, health and learning*. Westport, CT: Greenwood Publishing Group.

Walsh, M. E., & Park-Taylor, J. V. (2003). Comprehensive schooling and interprofessional collaboration: Theory, research, and practice. In M. M. Brabeck & M. E. Walsh (Eds.), *Meeting at the hyphen: Schools-universities-communities-professions in collaboration for student achievement and well being: 102nd Yearbook, Part 2* (pp. 8–44). Chicago: National Society for the Study of Education.

Walz, G. R., & Lee, C. C. (1998). *Social action: A mandate for counselors*. Alexandria, VA: American Counseling Association.

Wang, M., & Kovach, J. (1996). Bridging the achievement gap in urban schools: Reducing educational segregation and advancing resilience-promoting strategies. In B. Williams (Ed.), *Closing the achievement gap: A vision for changing beliefs and practices* (pp. 10–36). Alexandria, VA: Association for Supervision and Curriculum Development.

Weissberg, R. P., & O'Brien, M. U. (2004). What works in school-based social and emotional learning programs for positive youth development. *Annals of the American Academy of Political & Social Science, 59*, 86–97.

Werner, E. E. (1989). High-risk children in young adulthood: A longitudinal study from birth to 32 years. *American Journal of Orthopsychiatry, 59*, 72–81.

Werner, E. E. (1990). Protective factors and individual resilience. In S. J. Meisels & J. P. Shonkoff (Eds.), *Protective factors and individual resilience* (pp. 97–116). New York: Cambridge University Press.

Werner, E., & Smith, R. (1992). *Overcoming the odds: High risk children from birth to adulthood*. New York: Cornell University Press.

Williams, R. (2003). Reaching out in family therapy: Home-based, school, and community interventions. *Clinical Child Psychology and Psychiatry, 8*, 564–565.

Wohlstetter, P., & Smyer, R. (1994). Education by charter. In S. A. Mohrman, & P. Wohlstetter (Eds.), *School-based management: Organizing for high performance* (pp. 88–107). San Francisco: Jossey-Bass.

XLVI
LAW AND ETHICS IN SCHOOL COUNSELING

PATRICIA L. WOLLEAT
University of Wisconsin–Madison

The daily activities of school counselors take place within a complex of academic, social, cultural, political, legal, and professional influences (Remley, Hermann, & Huey, 2003), some of which are so basic to the functioning of schools as to be removed from the conscious awareness of students, staff, and the community; others are thrust into consciousness assuming a level of transparency that creates a palpable urgency to behave with deliberate consideration and reflection. The school counselor must have an appreciation both for the policies and practices that structure the foundational context and for the tools to deal ethically and effectively with the occasional dilemmas and crises.

The ethical challenges facing school counselors have been rendered immeasurably more complex as recognition of the diversity among their clients calls out for more sensitivity to the cultural context. Enrollment data illustrate the magnitude of this challenge. In 2002, 37.7% of enrolled elementary and secondary students were members of racial/ethnic minority groups, while among students in degree granting institutions of higher learning the percentage was 29.4%. These percentages have increased and continue to increase; for example, among fourth graders, 39.8% are racial/ethnic minorities, with 16.6% being African American and 17% being Hispanic. These data reflect the projected trends of increases, particularly in the Hispanic population. Whereas in 1999 the Hispanic population constituted 11%, by 2050 it is expected to be at 24%. The total racial/ethnic minority population is expected to top 50% by the middle of the 21st century.

The legal/ethical and cultural complexity of the context within which school counselors do their work distinguishes the role of professional school counselors from other counseling specialties and from other education professionals. Legally, the school is a unique institution, defined primarily by state law, with increasing influence of federal law. Layered in is also a tradition of local control of schools by elected school boards and other public officials and parental and citizen involvement in school affairs. Additionally, the primary clients are minors who lack the legal autonomy to make many types of decisions and instead are subject to the authority of their parents and the state. Thus, school counselors serve many interests, not the least of which is the professional belief (and cardinal ethical tenet) that a student/client's welfare is paramount as the anchoring principle of school counselor functioning, 1995; American School Counselor Association [ASCA], 2004).

School counselors vary considerably regarding both their awareness and their understanding of the contextual factors and in their perceptions of their competence to deal with a host of critical issues they may confront in their daily practice (Davis & Mickelson, 1994; Hermann, 2002). Among the highest frequency issues that school counselors reported confronting are deciding when to report child abuse, being pressured verbally to turn over confidential information, and determining whether a client poses a threat to self or others (Hermann). Davis and Mickelson noted that counselors were not always aware of the full array of issues in responding to specific scenarios relating to parental notification of alcohol and other drug abuse (AODA) issues, to release of student data to parents and third parties, to use of assessment tools outside of areas of competence, to participation in locker searches, and to work with clients who receive counseling elsewhere. These researchers also found, in part, that school counselors were more comfortable dealing with issues from an ethical perspective as compared with a legal perspective. This greater confidence in their ethical functioning may, in part, be a result of the tendency in professional training settings and the legal/ethical professional literature to focus on professional ethics (which are presumed universally applicable) as opposed to state law and local policies that vary from jurisdiction to jurisdiction. In addition, school counselors may experience a tension between the local aspects of their role (those rights and responsibilities that they share with other educators in their state and district that are regulated by state law and local policies) and the cosmopolitan dimensions that arise from their identification with the profession of school counseling across the country as embraced in professional codes of ethics (Davis & Mickelson; Pope & Bajt, 1988).

The goal of this chapter is to give school counselors a framework for understanding their professional responsibilities. While it cannot provide a treatise on every issue that may challenge school counselors, I hope that it will capture the necessary concepts and knowledge for analyzing at least the high frequency and emerging issues that may confront them. Optimally functioning school counselors are informed both by the best practice (Capuzzi, 2002) and by ethical traditions of the school counseling community, as well as by the laws and policies that regulate educational endeavors on federal, state, and local levels. Regional, cultural, political, and socioeconomic variability quickly dispels any hope, however, of a perfectly ordered world in which the interests of all parties seamlessly converge.

In order to shed light on this intricate mosaic of principles and policies, this chapter will be divided into four major sections: (1) a discussion of the major factors which compose the legal/ethical context of school counselor roles and functioning; (2) the sources of "regulation" affecting school counseling; (3) an explanation of some major ethical and legal concepts that are manifest in a variety of forms in the routine and not so routine transactions in which school counselors engage; and (4) a discussion of several situations fraught with complicated legal/ethical issues that are identified as high frequency in school counselors' work, are self-reported as issues in which school counselors lack confidence in their legal/ethical knowledge base, or are emergent issues that have been created by recent legal developments.

In addition to acquiring knowledge of ethical and legal principles, responsible school counselors understand how and when to apply them in a behavioral context. Toward this end, several authors have proposed protocols for ethical decision making (e.g., Cottone & Claus, 2000; Eberlein, 1987; Keith-Spiegel & Koocher, 1985; Kitchener, 1984). Typically, these protocols delineate a series of decision-making steps, including to (a) describe the situation, (b) define the issues, (c) consult legal and ethical guidelines, (d) evaluate the rights and responsibilities of all parties, (e) generate possible alternative courses of action, (f) analyze the consequences of each alternative, (g) present evidence that the projected consequences will occur, and (h) make the decision.

A more culturally responsive framework was proposed by Hansen and Goldberg (1999). They supplemented the conventional protocols with a matrix that includes an emphasis on cultural and clinical considerations in addition to the usual legal and ethical principles. Their seven considerations provide a framework for making culturally sensitive ethical decisions and include (1) moral principles and personal values; (2) clinical and cultural considerations; (3) ethics codes; (4) agency or employer policies; (5) federal, state, and local statutes; (6) rules and regulations; and (7) case law.

The addition of the *clinical and cultural* strand to the ethical decision-making protocol represents a first step in infusing multiculturalism into ethical decision making. Toporek and Williams (2006) proposed three additional measures: (a) clearer and more direct language in ethical codes for professionals to address social injustice, (b) guidelines for ethical decision making that reflect social justice, and (c) adjustments in training programs to broaden professionals' competencies by incorporating social justice interventions.

Although legal standards have yet to be established in the multicultural arena, there is no longer any question that ethical competence as a school counselor includes multicultural competence (Arrendondo & Toporek, 2004). Meeting multicultural competence standards (and their progeny) as proposed, for example, by Sue, Arrendondo, and McDavis (1992) and the American Psychological Association (APA; 2003) are excellent ways to ensure that a threshold of competence has been attained.

Because the professional responsibilities of school counselors are enacted against a matrix of interacting and sometimes competing regulatory policies and procedures promulgated within a complex, multicultural context, school counselors are often called upon to rationalize these discordant strands. This process of resolving potentially competing policies creates the opportunity for what Jacob-Timm and Hartshorne (1998) called "quality control" (p. 1). Some of these principles may appear to be constraints on professional behavior; viewed from another perspective, some may actually be considered to empower the counselors by freeing them from having to deliberate on and defend every action they take; others may be legitimately experienced as thwarting the goals and mission of school counseling.

Probably few professions are as subject to external constraints as school counseling is. One of the goals of this chapter is to identify these various sources of regulation and identify how they are implemented and enforced. How has school counseling become the subject of so much regulation and what are the sources of these constraints?

The Sociolegal Context of School Counseling

Three major social conditions account for the uniqueness of the school counselor role and school counselors' professional responsibilities: (a) the fact that most of the clients of school counselors are minors who legally lack autonomy (see Kaczmarek, 2000), being subject instead to the authority of their parents and the state; (b) the nature of the public school as a political institution, publicly funded and controlled by legislatures and elected boards; and (c) the long tradition of school counselors' professionally organizing at the local, state, and national levels. Each of these influences enters into the regulatory equation, resulting in a matrix of rights and responsibilities that together provide the foundation for the daily activities of the school counselor.

Minors' Autonomy

Children and adolescents possess remarkably few independent constitutional rights, their rights instead being derived from those of their parents and the state (Levesque, 2002). The historical view of children was that they were the property of their parents (usually the father), who could discipline, abuse, and even sell their children into slavery without interference by the state (Kramer, 1994). The interests of children were presumed to be coterminous with those of their parents; for example, if the parents had no rights, neither did the children. The trajectory of children's rights has been in the direction from the status of *property* to the status of *person*. However, even today, the rights of children remain limited and nebulous, being largely subservient to the authority of their parents and the state.

The evolution of the rights of children has taken place within the context of three limitations on children's autonomy (Levesque, 2002; Nurcombe & Partlett, 1994): (a) the parental presumption or the rights of parents, which are primary; (b) the *parens patriae* principle (i.e., the state is the parent) that empowers the state to act in the place of parents; and (c) the *police power* of the state, which allows the state to protect the community—adults and children alike—in the areas of public health, safety, welfare, and morals.

The earliest acknowledgement of children's rights separate from their parents came in the form of recognizing the *parens patriae* power of the state to step in to protect the child when the interests of the child diverged from those of their parents, the parents could not meet the needs of the child, or the child was being exploited by the newly industrialized society (Kramer, 1994). However, the rights of parents to control and raise their children as they saw fit remained paramount to the *parens patriae* power of the state. Children belonged to their parents and to the state but did not have rights as individual persons. When the state exercised its power, it was justified by protecting society's interests, not necessarily those of the child.

The year 1967 marked the beginning of a new era of children's rights. At this time, there was some legal acknowledgement of children's rights vis-à-vis the state, without being derived from the parents. The first court cases that acknowledged that children have some independent rights were in the area of due process protections in juvenile justice proceedings. These cases (*In re Gault*, 1967; *Kent v. United States*, 1966) mandated that juvenile court proceedings must contain the due process protections of the rights (a) to counsel, (b) against self-incrimination, (c) to notice of the charges against them, and (d) to cross-examine witnesses. In addition to these due process constitutional protections, children have been given some "rights" by statutes in specific areas, for example, requiring their consent to treatment in some instances. But rights of children remain rooted in the family or in some other form of custody—if not parents, a guardian or the state.

Since 1967, there has been an expansion of children's rights (Kramer, 1994). In 1969, Justice Fortas declared that children are *persons* under the Constitution (*Tinker v. Des Moines Independent Community School District*, 1969). There does, however, remain ambivalence as to how children are viewed, often related to whether they are viewed as in need of protection (e.g., in child abuse reporting statutes) or if the child is alleged to have committed a crime (e.g., in Wisconsin, a 17-year-old is considered an adult for criminal prosecution purposes, but a child for reporting victims of child abuse). Professional ethical codes encourage the school counselor to promote the autonomy of children and adolescents in developmentally appropriate ways within this evolving legal context.

The Role of Government in Education

Governmental policies at various levels have a profound effect on the professional responsibilities of school counselors. Governmental policies must be premised on the rights that Americans are afforded through the Constitution. Among the major constitutional concepts at the foundation of the ethical and legal challenges that face school counselors are privacy, due process, and equal protection of the law. Privacy, which many constitutional scholars deem to be at the very core of personal rights and responsibilities, will be discussed at length later in the chapter in relation to confidentiality. Due process is the constitutional protection that requires persons to be granted hearings before their rights may be taken away.

Equal protection requires that laws be applied equally across persons. For much of the history of the United States, unfortunately, equal protection has not always been honored—women, racial and ethnic minorities, GLBT individuals, and persons with disabilities have not always been treated equally under the law. Some of this discrimination has been dealt with by amending the Constitution (e.g., the 14th Amendment eliminating discrimination based on race); other bases of discrimination have been addressed by legislation. Among the important legislation applying equal protection principles in education are Title IX, which forbids discrimination in education on the basis of gender, and Individuals with Disabilities Education Act (IDEA), which grants a free and appropriate education to students with disabilities (see U.S. Department of Education Office of Civil Rights, 1991). The contemporary emphasis on multiculturalism in education and mental health interventions is a transformative outgrowth of the constitutional principles of equal protection.

Despite the growing role of the federal government in education, the most significant legal constraints on school counselors emanate from state and local laws and policies. "Public education is a creature of state law, usually mandated by state constitutions" (Kramer, 1994, Vol. 2, p. 434). This preeminence of state and local law is one of the reasons school counselors sometimes find their legal responsibilities confusing. Whereas federal laws and ethics codes of professional organizations have uniform nationwide application, state and local law is jurisdiction specific. Because of this variability across states and school districts, the literature on professional responsibilities tends to be heavily weighted toward ethical codes, federal legislation, and court decisions with nationwide application. Because it is a painstaking task to account for all the nuances in state law affecting the professional responsibilities of school counselors, some critical differences may be overlooked or minimized by authors, commentators, and counselor educators.

One of the foremost examples of jurisdictional variability of relevance to school counselors is state laws relating to child abuse. Although all states have some form of laws protecting children from abuse, they may differ in their specific contours in such areas as what behaviors or outcomes constitute child abuse and the circumstances under which mandatory reporting is required. It will not be possible in this chapter to delineate all of the specific differences in state laws. Instead, in this chapter, those areas of professional responsibilities that are the province of state law or local policy will be identified; school counselors are urged to get state- and local-specific advice on these issues.

Self-Regulation by Professional Communities

Although state and local laws vary across jurisdictions, all educators within a state's borders are subject to the same state laws and all educators in a given school district to the same board policies. However, members of different professions and disciplines within the same school may subscribe to different ethical codes. School counselors, for example, are represented by several professional organizations that have promulgated codes of ethics and developed mechanisms for adjudicating alleged ethical violations by their members (e.g., the American Counseling Association [ACA] and the ASCA). One Web site maintained by a prominent clinical psychologist (Pope, n.d.), to date, has identified over 100 ethical codes placed online by various psychological and mental health organizations. On the other hand, the professional organizations of some teaching disciplines promote no specific ethical codes, while special educators, administrators, and other student personnel professionals may be covered by ethical codes in various stages of development. The implication of this patchwork of ethical systems among different professions within a school means that the school counselor may at times be in ethical isolation, providing a lone voice advocating for a cherished ethical principle. This is not to say that other educators are behaving unethically or irresponsibly, only that the salience or relevance of particular ethical principles may be heightened for counselors as compared with other school professionals.

One of the most important functions that the national community of school counselors has performed is to advocate for all students. Consistent with the constitutional protection of equal protection, school counselors have also made a commitment to treat all students with respect and dignity. The preamble to the ASCA (2004) ethics code articulates this promise:

> Each person has the right to be respected, be treated with dignity and have access to a comprehensive school counseling program that advocates for and affirms all students from diverse populations regardless of ethnic/racial status, age, economic status, special needs, English as a second language or other language group, immigration status, sexual orientation, gender, gender identity/expression, family type, religious/spiritual identity and appearance. (Preamble)

ASCA's (2004) position is that counselors need to have the skills (e.g., see Constantine & Yeh, 2001) necessary to help members of all diverse populations to maximize their individual potential and to promote awareness and understanding of cultural and other sources of diversity in the school and community.

In summary, considering the minor status of school pupils, the preeminence of state and local law, and the heterogeneity of ethical systems across education professionals, it is not disputable that the school counselor exists within a very complex legal/ethical arena. In the rest of this chapter, we will deal with this complexity first, by identifying the sources of regulation or constraint and how the regulation is implemented and enforced, and second, by looking at some major ethical/legal concepts that cut across ethical decision making, and finally, by considering some specific situations that school counselors find to be highly prevalent or especially troubling

Sources of Regulation

It is eye opening and perhaps intimidating to consider the entire spectrum of entities that have something to say about how school counselors should go about their work. However, rather than being immobilized in the face of this multifaceted array of obligations and guidelines, counselors may be better served by attempting to understand the various interests that are advocated and how these interests may converge or diverge. It may be possible to reframe one's perceptions and see not just the constraints that are imposed, but also how the accumulated experience and wisdom of professional peers and elected officials may actually benefit and empower counselors to carry out their work more responsibly and efficiently. This efficiency may permit the counselors to serve more students more effectively. The sources of regulation of school counseling will be presented in order of those with the most narrow (but, perhaps, most powerful) scope of influence, for example, personal values, and proceed to those that are external and have more universal application, for example, federal legislation.

Values: Personal and Cultural

Professionally responsible behavior begins with the moral character of the school counselor (see Cohen & Cohen, 1999). Jordan and Meara (1999) asserted, "Principles, technical skills, and legal knowledge are necessary in evaluating a course of action but are not logically sufficient or necessarily primary. What is demanded of professionals is a dimension of character appropriately understood by way of virtues" (p. 144). Meara, Schmidt, and Day (1996) described the virtuous agent in the following words:

> One who (a) is motivated to do what is good, (b) possesses vision and discernment, (c) realizes the role of affect or emotion in assessing or judging proper conduct, (d) has a high degree of self-understanding and awareness, and, perhaps most importantly is connected with and understands the mores of community in moral decision making, policy setting and character development, and is alert to the legitimacy of client diversity in these respects. (pp. 28–29)

In distinguishing virtue ethics from principle ethics, the approach to ethical understanding embodied in most professional ethics codes, Jordan and Meara (1999) suggested that an appropriate question for examining virtue ethics is "Who am I?" as compared with "What should I do?"—the essential question related to principle ethics. Barnett (n.d.), following Kitchener's (1984) work on meta-ethics, proposed the following as the virtues that should underlie all ethics codes and ethical decisions:

> **Beneficence** is the virtue of helping others and providing services that are in the other individual's best interest; to do good. **Nonmalfeasance** is the virtue of not doing harm; ensuring that our actions do not result in harm to anyone. **Fidelity** is the virtue of faithfulness; being true to our commitments and obligations to others. A component of fidelity, **veracity**, implies we will be truthful and honest in all our endeavors. Promoting the **autonomy** of those we provide services to is one of our profession's overarching goals. **Justice** is the virtue of providing equal access to services and equal quality of services to all those with whom we come in contact. The virtue of **self-interest** stresses the importance of adequate and appropriate attention to our own self-care so our competence and judgment do not become impaired. (¶. 3)

Awareness of personal values and acting in congruence with universal virtues are necessary but not sufficient conditions for ethically responsible counselors. The culturally competent counselor must also have knowledge of the cultural value systems of their clients. Although the dimensions on which cultural values differ are manifold, many of them are captured in the dichotomy of *individualistic* (e.g., Eurocentric) versus *collectivistic* (e.g., Afrocentric) worldviews. Lu (1998) distinguished the individualistic worldview from the collective worldview on the basis of the weights cultures assign to individual versus group goals. The I/C dichotomy encompasses many specific cultural values such as the role of the family.

Clinical and Cultural Consideration

As noted earlier, Hansen and Goldberg (1999) added a major step in the ethical decision-making paradigm—considering the contextual cultural and clinical aspects of a situation. According to these authors, clinical judgment is involved in any "legal-ethical quandary," although most ethical decision-making protocols do not include it. Downing Hansen and Goldberg illustrated the interrelatedness of ethics and clinical judgment using the following example—the importance of a counselor's discerning, for example, whether a suicidal crisis is a genuine emergency or an attempt at manipulation. Another clinical consideration involves the developmental stage of the client. Ethically, competence requires that one adapt interventions and informed consent procedures to the age and cognitive competence of the client. Making treatment decisions informed by ethical principles is at the core of the ethical principle of competence.

According to Hansen and Goldberg (1999), "Cultural considerations are likewise often ignored or minimized when identifying salient variables, issues, and guidelines" (p. 496). They observed, "Issues such as the nature of multiple relationships, the use of barter, and boundaries of confidentiality take on different meaning when viewed from an informed multicultural perspective" (p. 497).

One of the most complete expositions of ethical quandaries viewed from a multicultural perspective was provided by Sadeghi, Fischer, and House (2003). Using a Delphi technique, they identified eight ethical dilemmas in multicultural counseling that are viewed as very important by counselors, most of whom work with a diverse set of clients. Most of these dilemmas arise from conflict between an individualistic worldview (which may be held by a majority counselor) and a collective worldview (which may represent the culture of a client). Although all of these dilemmas may not be directly relevant to the work of school counselors, they represent the extent to which ethics and multiculturalism are interrelated.

1. The counselor and client are faced with the client needing to choose between working on the symptoms of his or her emotional problems arising from a discrimination situation that has negative consequences, which conflicts with empowering the client to assert his or her civil rights although it would result in negative consequences for the individual.
2. The counselor and client are faced with the client's needing to choose between leaving his or her family to promote individual growth, which conflicts with assisting the client to stay and cope as a member of the cultural family.
3. The counselor and client are faced with the client needing to choose between ending an abusive relationship although it will result in him or her being a social outcast within the traditional culture, which conflicts with helping the client to stay in the marriage and cope with the situation.
4. The counselor and client are faced with the client needing to choose between seeking treatment based on Western medical practice to avoid negative health consequences, which conflicts with the client's cultural beliefs about health and illness.
5. Assisting a client with a problem while not having culturally specific competencies conflicts with not providing assistance although it could result in negative consequences for the individual.
6. Fostering independence of the client to solve his or her problems conflicts with the client's cultural expectation that the counselor offer solutions.
7. Achieving credibility with the client requires that the counselor compartmentalize his or her counseling values conflicts with the counselor maintaining his or her counseling values although the result would be a loss of credibility.
8. Using a standardized assessment is recognized by the funding agency to determine eligibility for treatment conflicts with using a culturally sensitive approach that is qualitative and more subjective and not recognized by the funding agency (Sadeghi et al., 2003, p. 185).

Among the dimensions of counselor functioning that potentially might be viewed through a cultural lens are assessment and diagnosis, goal setting, relationship parameters, intervention, and outcome evaluation. The ethically responsible school counselor has the competence to analyze each of these components from a multicultural perspective.

Local Policies

Whereas value, clinical, and cultural considerations focus on internal and case-specific dimensions, other relevant analyses involve external considerations. The most specific external level of influence is local policy and practice. Local control of public schools is an historic tradition in the United States. Although local school boards are increasingly subject to incentives and mandates from state and federal governments, much authority is vested in the local district to develop policies affecting both students and employees. Presumably local board policies are a reflection of community standards as school boards are elected entities. Given local control, policy differences might be expected across rural, urban, and suburban districts. Board policies may range from setting the calendar, to student discipline codes, to establishing the curriculum, and to developing personnel policies. Many of these board policies may directly affect the work of the school counselor, for example, their job descriptions and supervisory schemes—whether counselors are supervised by a central office guidance director or are evaluated by the school principal. Surprisingly, many school counselors are often more aware of state and federal laws than of their own districts' policies. Yet, there is considerable variability in local policy and even federal legislation may permit school districts to formulate local policies as long as they are made public. School counselors are advised to become thoroughly familiar with local policies regarding such issues as client confidentiality, reporting child abuse, and dual relationships with students (e.g., some districts forbid staff from giving rides to students or inviting them to their homes). In addition, school counselors must become familiar with the mores and folkways of their respective communities. Formal policies are often accessible through student and employee handbooks; some, but not all, districts place their policies online and make them accessible to the public as well. Some districts provide for individual building autonomy, possibly adding another layer of administrative policy. Folkways and mores will typically not be available through written media; counselors must, instead, use their observation skills and seek consultation with mentors to gain appreciation of informal networks and sentiments of the community.

School counselors are urged to get as much information as possible concerning board and building policies before accepting a position, thus, possibly avoiding some conflicts between the counselor's personal/professional ethical positions and local policies. Although local policies cannot contravene law and a counselor should not be asked to comply with practices that are patently illegal, some policies may nonetheless be in conflict with professional ethics codes, which boards may not be legally obligated to follow. The ACA ethical code urges counselors to work toward congruence of law, policy, and ethics. However, if congruence cannot be attained, the school counselor should keep in mind that the penalty for violating board policies that are not illegal may be an action against the job.

State Law

Typically the next level of regulation comes at the state level. Although some state professional associations have promulgated ethical codes, the most significant regulation at the state level comes through legal mechanisms. Each of the three branches of state government has a hand in creating law that affects school counselors. School counselors are affected not only by the general statutes that affect all citizens but also by a special set of statutes, often called the "school code," which refers to public schools specifically. For our purpose, school code will refer both to statutes and to the rules and regulations developed by state education agencies that have been empowered by the legislature to create such rules. School codes cover a plethora of matters including, for example, (a) requiring and setting criteria for approving, denying, and suspending educator licenses;

(b) approving counselor preparation programs that recommend counselors for the school counselor license; (c) setting standards for pupil/counselor ratios; (d) mandating the provision of certain counseling and guidance services; (e) nondiscrimination policies; (f) setting graduation and accountability standards; (g) providing privileged communication to clients of school counselors; and (h) implementing federal laws related to, for example, disclosure of pupil information (Family Educational Rights and Privacy Act [FERPA] of 1974), gender equity (Title IX), and services for students with disabilities (IDEA). In addition, school codes may set policies for funding of public education, including sources of funding and equalization formulas.

In addition to the school codes, other state laws affecting school counseling may include, for example, (a) mandating school counselors to be reporters of child abuse, (b) evidentiary rules that may recognize privileged communication for clients of school counselors, and (c) relationships among juvenile justice agencies and educational institutions. It cannot be stressed enough that state laws in these critical areas differ considerably, and it is a matter of ethical competence to become informed about the laws in the jurisdiction in which one practices.

State courts have also fashioned law that may affect school counselors through the imposition of liability for (a) failing to warn/protect third-party victims of client violence, (b) failing to prevent suicide (*Eisel v. Board of Education*, 1991), and (c) professional negligence or malpractice (*Sain v. Cedar Rapids Community School District*, 2001). Readers are cautioned that state law is highly variable and nowhere more so than in the areas just mentioned. Counselors are urged to get localized information regarding these potential venues for liability.

Depending on the nature of the state law or rule, various sanctions for a violation may be levied. For example, school counselors who violate the standards of their license may have their licenses suspended or revoked. Typically, the criteria for an action against a license fall into the categories of incompetence or immorality. The definitions of these criteria have been defined in Wisconsin law in PI 34.35(1)(c) and (d):

> (c) "Immoral conduct" means conduct or behavior which is contrary to commonly accepted moral or ethical standards and endangers the health, welfare, safety or education of any pupil.

> (d) "Incompetency" means a pattern of inadequate performance of duties or the lack of ability, legal qualifications or fitness to discharge required duties, and which endangers the health, welfare, safety or education of any pupil.

Other sanctions imposed by the state on individuals may include fines (e.g., for failing to report suspected child abuse or inappropriately disclosing confidential pupil information) or fines or withdrawal of financial support when a district violates a rule or law. School districts and, occasionally, individual counselors may be liable for claims for damages for harm to students as well.

The National Level

The final level of regulation is the national level. This level of regulation will be discussed in two parts—ethical codes as promulgated by professional organizations and federal law, both legislative and judicial.

Ethics Codes. A Web site maintained by Pope (n.d.), a noted authority on ethics in mental health, has identified nearly 100 codes of ethics promulgated by various mental health organizations. Such codes may be instructive to the public and to courts in the case of malpractice litigation and may be modeled by state licensing agencies as codes of conduct. Strictly speaking, however, professional ethical codes are enforceable only on and by their members. In their most fundamental sense, ethics codes are promises made to consumers that they will be treated with dignity and competence (see Hansen & Goldberg, 1999).

Jacob-Timm and Hartshorne (1998) asserted that ethical conduct is not synonymous with simple adherence to a set of ethical rules and standards. They pointed out, "Codes of ethics are imperfect guides to behavior" (p. 4). They cited the following reasons for their conclusion: (a) that ethics codes tend to be composed of broad abstract principles and are at times "vague and ambiguous" (p. 4); (b) that principles frequently compete with each other or with the law when applied to particular situations; and (c) that codes tend to be reactive, given the lengthy and thorough process by which codes are developed and amended. Within these limitations, Jacob-Timm and Hartshorne summarized the functions of ethical codes in ethical conduct as follows:

> Ethical codes thus provide guidance for the professional in his or her decision making. Ethical conduct, however, involves careful choices based on knowledge of codes and standards, ethical reasoning, and personal values. In many situations, more than one course of action is acceptable. In some situations, no course of action is completely satisfactory. In all situations, the responsibility for ethical conduct rests with the individual practitioner. (p. 4)

By tradition, school counselors have typically subscribed to the ACA (2005) *Code of Ethics and Standards of Practice* and the ASCA's (2004) *Ethical Standards for School Counselors.* These codes are compatible with each other, but the ASCA code is more specific in some areas that relate directly to working with minors in the schools, namely, responsibilities to parents, to colleagues, to associates, to the school, and to the community. In addition to the ethical code, ASCA has developed several formal positions statements covering the role of school counselors in such issues as HIV/AIDS, censorship, child abuse and neglect prevention, cross/multicultural counseling, parent consent for services, sexual orientation of youth, and students at risk.

Federal Law. Nationally, school counselors are impacted not only by their professional codes but also by federal law. The federal role in education is somewhat more complicated than that of the states because, under the common law, education was entrusted to parents and constitutionally it is a state function (Kramer, 1994). When Congress decides to enact legislation, it must find some constitutional authority to act. The concept of the "division of powers" between the federal and state governments as embodied in the 10th Amendment to the Constitution, reserves the function of education to the states. Thus, when Congress acts to regulate education it must do so indirectly through some other power. This is well exemplified in the National Defense Education Act (NDEA) of 1958, which is credited with providing funding to train the first significant cadre of school counselors in the 1960s (Herr, Cramer, & Niles, 2004). In this legislation, Congress used its *defense* powers to provide funding for education because the United States was behind the USSR in the race for space and it was believed that school counselors could help to identify and nurture scientifically and mathematically gifted students to aid in the national defense.

Since the early 1900s, the federal government has found ways to use its constitutional powers to regulate and provide financial assistance to schools, beginning with the Smith-Hughes Act in the early 1900s to provide for vocational education under the commerce power. Since NDEA, some of the most significant federal legislation that has affected the roles and functions of school counselors are the FERPA of 1974, which regulates disclosure of information from pupil records; Title IX, which provides for gender equity in all facets of education including career guidance and athletics; IDEA (formerly Public Law 94-142), which provides funds for educating students with disabilities; Sec. 504 of the Rehabilitation Act (USDE, 2007), which requires reasonable accommodations for persons with disabilities; and the Protection of Pupil Rights Amendment (PPRA, 2004), which requires parental consent for student participation in required surveys and evaluations that ask the student to reveal certain personal and family information. The most recent federal legislation related to education, the No Child Left Behind Act of 2001, requires, among other things, greater accountability for student outcomes in reading and mathematics. Some of these federal laws will be discussed in more detail in later sections of the chapter.

Legal and Ethical Concepts

Confidentiality

Perhaps no other principle promoting client welfare is as important as confidentiality. Confidentiality in the counseling relationship is so important that it is embodied in nearly every mental health ethics code (see, e.g., ACA *Code of Ethics* sec. B and ASCA *Ethical Standards for School Counselors* sec. A.1.), federal statutes, (e.g., *Confidentiality of Alcohol and Drug Abuse Patient Records* (2003) and U.S. Department of Health and Human Services), and even in opinions of the U.S. Supreme Court (e.g., *Jaffee v. Redmond,* 1996). Ethically and legally, school counselors are obligated to prevent disclosure of all communication (oral and written) pertaining to the counseling relationship. As will be explained later, confidentiality, however, is not absolute, and counselors have an obligation to share the limitations of confidentiality with their clients.

In attempting to understand this very complex notion of confidentiality, Figure 46.1 is intended to capture the essence of confidentiality.

The Confidentiality Presumption. The presumption of confidentiality supports a belief in the primacy of privacy within a counseling relationship; thus, any disclosure of otherwise confidential information must emanate from a value position that supersedes the value of privacy. The primacy of privacy within professional counseling relationships is supported by three principles. First, although the word *privacy* is not explicitly contained in the Constitution, interpreters of the Constitution have considered privacy to be a fundamental right of Americans. The mantle of privacy grants autonomy in making decisions about one's body and mind. Thus, clients are presumptively in control of the extent to which they choose to share their thoughts and feelings with others and what happens to the communication that is generated within the professional relationship.

Second, privacy, as implemented through confidentiality, is a necessary condition for clients to seek counseling. Without the promise of confidentiality, people might be reluctant to seek counseling and, thus, possibly leave some problems unaddressed. The possibility that some people might be reluctant to seek help absent a promise of confidentiality was a major grounds for a decision by the U.S. Supreme Court in the *Jaffee v. Redmond* (1996) case, which

---

THE CONFIDENTIALITY PARADIGM

The confidentiality presumption: All information generated within a counseling relationship is confidential

UNLESS

There is a valid reason to disclose the information

AND THEN

Disclose only the minimum amount of information necessary to accomplish the purpose of the disclosure

AND

Inform the client about the limits of confidentiality

Figure 46.1 The confidentiality paradigm.

prevented a social worker from testifying in federal court about her counseling relationship with a police officer who had killed a man in the line of duty. The Court reasoned that police officers and other public officials may experience a high level of stress and anxiety in the course of their duties and that officials and the public alike benefit from the availability of counseling within a confidential relationship. The benefit of access to a confidential counseling relationship was indeed considered by the court to be sufficiently valuable that it overcame a fundamental tenet of our system of jurisprudence—access to all of the evidence in a legal proceeding.

A third principle supporting the need for confidentiality in counseling relationships recognizes that the promise of confidentiality promotes efficacy in mental health treatment. Given the potential benefits of counseling and psychotherapy, it is crucial that the conditions to maximize effectiveness are provided—one of these conditions is the promise of confidentiality. The Supreme Court in *Jaffee v. Redmond* (1996) opined,

> Treatment by a physician for physical ailments can often proceed successfully on the basis of a physical examination, information supplied by the patient, and the results of diagnostic tests. Effective psychotherapy, by contrast, depends upon an atmosphere of confidence and trust in which the patient is willing to make a frank and complete disclosure of facts, emotions, memories, and fears. Because of the sensitive nature of the problems for which individuals consult psychotherapists, disclosure of confidential communications made during counseling sessions may cause embarrassment or disgrace. For this reason, the mere possibility of disclosure may impede development of the confidential relationship necessary for successful treatment. (sec. 3)

In addition to the constitutional protections of confidentiality as interpreted by the judicial branch, Congress and state legislatures have also passed statutes that protect confidentiality of educational and medical information. The general trend in these laws has been to provide access to records by those whom the records concern and to limit access to third parties. Among these statutes are the FERPA, initially passed in 1974, relating to educational records, and the Health Insurance Portability and Accountability Act of 1996 (HIPAA; USDHHS, 2007), relating to personal health information. In addition, many states have passed their own versions of laws, compatible with FERPA, relating to confidentiality of educational records (e.g., Wis. Stat. 118.125), and many have their own laws protecting confidentiality of medical records as well (e.g., Wis. Stat. 146.81-84). And, of course, both the ACA and ASCA ethical codes assert that confidentiality is among the most central of ethical principles.

In summary, the presumption of confidentiality occupies an almost sacred place in the professional responsibilities of counselors. It has attained this status through its association with a fundamental constitutional right, its importance in a client's decision to seek help, and its role in maximizing the effectiveness of counseling.

Valid Reasons to Disclose Otherwise Confidential Information. Given both the social and pragmatic value of confidentiality, the decision to disclose information must rest on a competing value that society or an official policy maker deems important enough to overcome the presumption of confidentiality (Isaacs & Stone, 1999; Taylor & Adelman, 1998). In certain respects, these situations may be thought of as limitations of or exceptions to the general rule of confidentiality. Among the valid reasons to disclose otherwise confidential information are (a) with the informed consent of the client or client representative—in schools, almost always the parents; (b) mandatory reporting, for example, of child abuse; (c) imminent harm to self or others; (d) when permitted by statute; and (e) pursuant to a court order.

Consent for disclosure. It is probably not completely accurate to describe *consent* as an exception to the presumption of confidentiality as *no disclosure without consent* is at the heart of the presumption. But considering it as an exception does provide the opportunity to call attention to the fact that disclosure of otherwise confidential information sometimes appears to be so frequent in schools that it may appear that disclosure is the norm. It must not be forgotten, however, that in each case of disclosure some kind of authorization for disclosure is required—*with appropriate consent* constitutes one of the major forms of authorization for disclosure.

Four important issues enter into a consideration of consent for disclosure: (a) the nature of the information protected from unauthorized disclosure; (b) what constitutes consent; (c) who has the power to consent to disclosure—the school, parents, or students; and (d) subjects' access to information. (*Informed consent* will also be discussed later in the chapter in relation to consent for participation in counseling activities. *Informed consent for disclosure of confidential information* is an analogous, but narrower, concept.)

What information is protected from unauthorized disclosure? School counselors must be concerned about two types of information—educational information as defined, for example, by FERPA, and confidential information (ACA, sec. B.1.C., 2005) or "information received in the counseling relationship" (ASCA, sec. A.2.f, 2004). Because FERPA authorizes disclosure of educational records without consent for certain purposes, for example, to school personnel who have a legitimate need to know, records that are personally kept by school counselors and that are not shared with others are not considered to be part of the educational record that falls under FERPA. Because these personal notes are likely to overlap with information that the ASCA and ACA codes consider confidential, school counselors can follow their professional ethics codes in deciding whether to disclose counseling information that is not covered by FERPA.

What constitutes consent? The professional ethics codes do not specifically define consent. However, there is a legal tradition in the medical and mental health fields as to what constitutes consent to disclose confidential information. Because giving consent to have otherwise confidential material disclosed involves surrendering the right to privacy, minimal standards for disclosure with consent must guarantee that the person is fully informed of the circumstances surrounding the disclosure and freely gives his or her consent. The FERPA requirements for consent for disclosure from a pupil's educational record are

(a) The parent or eligible student shall provide a signed and dated written consent before an educational agency or institution discloses personally identifiable information from the student's education records. . . .
(b) The written consent must:
   1. Specify the records that may be disclosed;
   2. State the purpose of the disclosure; and
   3. Identify the party or class of parties to whom the disclosure may be made
(c) When a disclosure is made under paragraph (a) of this section
   (1) If a parent or eligible student so requests, the educational agency or institution shall provide him or her with a copy of the records disclosed; and
   (2) If the parent of a student who is not an eligible student so requests, the agency or institution shall provide the student with a copy of the records disclosed. (34 C.F.R. 99.30)

Some state statutes and rules regarding informed consent might also include some specific date as to when the consent expires and a required notice to the recipient of the confidential information that the information must not be rereleased.

Who has the authority to consent to disclosure of counseling information? For the educational records of students under the age of 18, this authority is almost always going to be the parents. (Incidentally, FERPA gives this right to both parents unless there is a legal document that would limit access by one party; see U.S. Department of Education [USDE], 1999; Wilcoxon & Magnuson, 1999). FERPA expressly gives this right (and the right of access) to parents of pupils under 18 and, upon the student's reaching 18, to the student.

The issue of minors' rights to control information outside the scope of FERPA is less explicit, as state law and local policies may play a large role. State statutes may give minors over a certain age, often 14, the right to consent to disclosure of information from certain types of psychological treatment and to shield some information from parents or to require that both parents and minors consent to the release. It must be stressed, however, that these are very specific statutory rights and most do not pertain to the minor receiving services as a pupil in school (with perhaps the exception of AODA treatment). Nonetheless, school counselors should become familiar with the conditions under which minors may be able to give consent to the release of records independent from their parents in their own jurisdictions (Gustafson & McNamara, 1987). Counselors are also advised that it may be disrespectful to students to solicit their assent if refusal cannot be honored (Corrao & Melton, 1988).

For information generated within counseling that is not subject to FERPA, the school counselor may approach the issue of who has control of the disclosure of information with somewhat more flexibility in accordance with professional ethics codes (see Sullivan, Ramirez, Rae, Razo, & George, 2002). The ASCA (2004) ethics code presumes that disclosure of counseling information, when not required by law or imminent danger, will take place only with the consent of the student. The code also acknowledges, however, that the primacy of the duty to students must be balanced with the "inherent rights of parents to be the guiding voice in their children's lives" (sec. A.2.g; see also Mitchell, Disque, & Robertson, 2002).

A.2.f. [The professional school counselor] protects the confidentiality of information received in the counseling relationship as specified by federal and state laws, written policies and applicable ethical standards. Such information is only to be revealed to others with the informed consent of the student, consistent with the counselor's ethical obligation.

A.2.g [The professional school counselor] recognizes his/her primary obligation for confidentiality is to the student but balances that obligation with an understanding of the legal and inherent rights of parents/guardians to be the guiding voice in their children's lives.

B.2. Parents/Guardians and Confidentiality

The professional school counselor:

a. Informs parents/guardians of the counselor's role with emphasis on the confidential nature of the counseling relationship between the counselor and student.
b. Recognizes that working with minors in a school setting may require counselors to collaborate with students' parents/guardians.
c. Provides parents/guardians with accurate, comprehensive and relevant information in an objective and caring manner, as is appropriate and consistent with ethical responsibilities to the student.
d. Makes reasonable efforts to honor the wishes of parents/guardians concerning information regarding the student, and in cases of divorce or separation exercises a good-faith effort to keep both parents informed with regard to critical information with the exception of a court order.

Access to records. The concept of privacy and the right to control personal information includes not only the right to consent to disclosure, but the right of access to the information as well. The major privacy protections, for example, for educational records (FERPA), student participation in nonacademic testing and evaluation (PPRA), and personal health information (HIPAA), have served to strengthen access to records or materials either by parents, in the case of minors, or to the student/patient. In addition, FERPA permits parents and nonminor students to challenge and, if necessary, to correct information contained in the educational record. Although, ethically, students should be given the opportunity to examine information that is disclosed with their consent, there do not appear to be any universal legal provisions that specifically require access to or the opportunity to correct counseling information not covered by FERPA although some states may have statutes that afford that opportunity.

Mandatory Reporting. The most typical occasion for mandatory reporting is in the case of suspected child abuse, although some states also require reporting suspected abuse of other vulnerable populations such as the elderly and persons with disabilities. A few states may require the disclosure of information related to other crimes as well. In Wisconsin, for example, a therapist is required to report prior sexual exploitation by a therapist (a felony) if the client consents. Every state has some version of mandatory reporting for suspected child abuse. Mandatory reporting of child abuse is one of the circumstances in which a public policy entity, usually a state legislature, has balanced the need for protecting children from harm with the need for confidentiality within certain professional relationships and has weighed in on the side of reporting (Lambie, 2005). In other words, where school counselors have been named as mandatory reporters, most, if not all, of their discretion to report has been curtailed. Consistent with the mandatory reporting statutes, the ASCA (2004) ethical code permits disclosure without the consent of the victim or parents when the law requires that a report be made:

A.2.b. Keeps information confidential unless disclosure is required to prevent clear and imminent danger to the student or others or when legal requirements demand that confidential information be revealed. Counselors will consult with appropriate professionals when in doubt as to the validity of an exception.

There are both substantive and procedural differences across the states in these statutes, for example, how *abuse* is defined, whether "consensual" sexual contact between adolescents constitutes sexual abuse, whether the cultural background of the family is a mitigating factor, who the mandatory reporters are, the relationship of the reporter to the alleged victim, to whom reports are made, provisions for discretionary reporters, and sanctions for failing to report when required. School counselors are urged to become familiar with the contours of their own state's laws and local policies regarding reporting.

In order to encourage reporting, state statutes often provide immunity from all civil and criminal liability when a report is made in good faith. It is also the law in some states that employers may set up a reporting procedure that funnels reports through an intermediary, but it may be illegal to prevent an employee from reporting or to discipline an employee who does so in good faith.

Reporting suspected child abuse is a frequent legal/ethical issue confronted by school counselors (Hermann, 2002). Interestingly, it is also one in which counselors report a high level of confidence in their knowledge. Two possible hypotheses for the counselors' relative confidence in dealing with this issue are that confidence is gained by experience and/or that when a potential dilemma is codified into a law that requires a certain response, the ambiguity surrounding decision making is somewhat reduced.

Although some of the ambiguity regarding the decision to report has been reduced by legislation, the culturally sensitive counselor may also be confronted with conflicts between legal definitions of reportable abuse and differences across cultures and families regarding appropriate measures for disciplining a child. The extent to which cultural background should be considered in reporting is the subject of a significant ideological debate. Some states acknowledge cultural differences in their statutes (e.g., California)—most are silent. Fontes (2005) provided a compelling analysis of how parental disciplinary behavior may viewed as either abusive or culturally normative as a function of the counselor's own cultural background. The culturally sensitive school counselor may partially approach this dilemma by taking a proactive role in educating parents about the standards to which their state will hold them accountable. Because child protection is primarily a function of state law, it is incumbent upon the ethically responsible counselor to become familiar with the laws of their jurisdiction. Further, because child protection laws are often enforced at the county or parish level, it is also critical that counselors become familiar with the social service and law enforcement policies in their local jurisdiction.

Imminent harm to self or others. Because counselors may have a legal duty to protect potential victims of clients' violence (e.g., *Tarasoff v. The Regents of the University of California,* 1976), ethical codes typically permit disclosure without consent when a client threatens harm to others. Unlike in the case of child abuse, however, the duty to protect third parties in most states is not statutory, but based on court decisions (e.g., the seminal case, *Tarasoff,* in California; *Schuster v. Altenberg,* 1988, in Wisconsin), and therefore, not only may the duty to protect be different across the 50 states, but the actions that are required when a client threatens violence are less clear. What is clear, in most states, is that either a court or a legislature has weighed the value of confidentiality against harm to a third party and has decided that confidentiality must give way to protection from harm when a client is determined to harm a third party. However, in many states, there are no named mandatory reporters or explicit procedures for reporting, thus leaving room for more discretion by individual professionals and for school boards to develop local policies for preventing violence in the schools. The ASCA (2004) code requires that confidentiality be breached in the case of imminent danger to self or others.

A.7. Danger to Self or Others

The professional school counselor:

a. Informs parents/guardians or appropriate authorities when the student's condition indicates a clear and imminent danger to the student or others. This is to be done after careful deliberation and, where possible, after consultation with other counseling professionals.

Because the danger to self or others is an arena that is so saturated with state law and employer policies, school counselors are urged to get advice from experts on state law regarding the duty to protect in their own states. (Other issues related to dealing with high-risk individuals in schools will be discussed later in the chapter.)

The ACA and ASCA ethical codes, in addition to excepting imminent danger from confidentiality protection, have provided guidance on a specific type of potential harm—specifically, "to provide information to an identified third party who, by his/her relationship with the student, is at a high risk of contracting a disease that is commonly known to be communicable and fatal" (ASCA, sec. A.2.C). This provision also contains a caveat that some state laws may prevent this type of disclosure and, even if it is permitted, that warning be done with due regard for the client: The ASCA (2004) guidelines balance the need to disclose with the client's welfare:

A.2.c. [The professional school counselor] in absence of state legislation expressly forbidding disclosure, considers the ethical responsibility to provide information to an identified third party who, by his/her relationship with the student, is at a high risk of contracting a disease that is commonly known to be communicable and fatal. Disclosure requires satisfaction of all of the following conditions:

- Student identifies partner or the partner is highly identifiable
- Counselor recommends the student notify partner and refrain from further high-risk behavior
- Student refuses
- Counselor informs the student of the intent to notify the partner
- Counselor seeks legal consultation as to the legalities of informing the partner

Because of the stigma associated with certain infectious diseases (e.g., HIV/AIDS), many states have passed statutes that provide very high levels of confidentiality to medical information that concerns these diseases or have nondiscrimination policies that may protect those who are afflicted. Once again, it is the professional responsibility of the counselor to understand the laws of the state and local board policy regarding disclosure of this information and always to seek consultation before revealing this information.

Harm to self is another circumstance in which the principle of confidentiality is relaxed in the professional ethics codes. The need for confidentiality has been balanced against the potential loss of life by individuals who may not be prepared developmentally to act in their best interests. Although state courts have decided differently as to whether to impose legal liability on schools or school personnel (e.g., *Eisel*) for failing to prevent suicide, most commentators advise that when a school counselor becomes knowledgeable of a student's intent to commit suicide, confidentiality may be breached and the student's parents and school authorities must be notified (ASCA, 2004, sec. A.7.b; Remley & Sparkman, 1993). ASCA also recommended, if possible, student involvement in the disclosure process in the case of danger to both self and others.

The professional school counselor:

> b. Will attempt to minimize threat to a student and may choose to 1) inform the student of actions to be taken, 2) involve the student in a three-way communication with parents/guardians when breaching confidentiality or 3) allow the student to have input as to how and to whom the breach will be made. (ASCA, sec. A.7.b)

Other aspects of the school counselor's role in suicide prevention will be discussed later in the chapter.

Disclosure without consent as authorized by statute. The ASCA (2004) ethical code promotes confidentiality unless there is consent or imminent danger, or disclosure is required by law or school policies. One example of authorizing disclosure without consent is in FERPA. Under FERPA, educational records (educational records do not include counseling information that is maintained by the counselor for his or her eyes only) may be released without consent in circumstances as explained by the Family Policy Compliance Office (FPCO) of the U.S. Department of Education (2002) agency charged with enforcing FERPA.

> Generally, schools must have written permission from the parent or eligible student in order to release any information from a student's education record. However, FERPA allows schools to disclose those records, without consent, to the following parties or under the following conditions (34 CFR § 99.31):
>
> - School officials with legitimate educational interest;
> - Other schools to which a student is transferring;
> - Specified officials for audit or evaluation purposes;
> - Appropriate parties in connection with financial aid to a student;
> - Organizations conducting certain studies for or on behalf of the school;
> - Accrediting organizations;
> - To comply with a judicial order or lawfully issued subpoena;
> - Appropriate officials in cases of health and safety emergencies; and
> - State and local authorities, within a juvenile justice system, pursuant to specific State law. (USDE, 2002)

Schools may disclose, without consent, "directory" information such as a student's name, address, telephone number, date of birth, place of birth, honors, awards, and dates of attendance. However, schools must tell parents and eligible students about directory information and allow parents and eligible students a reasonable amount of time to request that the school not disclose directory information about them. Schools must notify parents and eligible students annually of their rights under FERPA. The actual means of notification (e.g., special letter, inclusion in a PTA bulletin, student handbook, or newspaper article) is left to the discretion of each school.

Recent changes to FERPA because of No Child Left Behind Act of 2001 require that parents be given an opportunity to opt their children out of "activities involving the collection, disclosure, or use of personal information collected from students for the purpose of marketing or for selling that information, or otherwise providing that information to others for that purpose" (¶ 14). Barring opt out, a local education authority (LEA) is permitted to disclose information without prior consent in the following circumstances:

> The requirements concerning activities involving the collection and disclosure of personal information from students for marketing purposes do not apply to the collection, disclosure, or use of personal information collected from students for the exclusive purpose of developing, evaluating, or providing educational products or services for, or to, students or educational institutions, such as the following:
>
> - College or other postsecondary education recruitment, or military recruitment.
> - Book clubs, magazines, and programs providing access to low-cost literacy products.

- Curriculum and instructional materials used by elementary schools and secondary schools.
- Tests and assessments used by elementary schools and secondary schools to provide cognitive, evaluative, diagnostic, clinical, aptitude, or achievement information about students.
- The sale by students of products or services to raise funds for school-related or education-related activities.
- Student recognition programs. (USDE, 2002, p. 5)

The exclusion of the need for parental consent to disclose information to military recruiters will be discussed later in the chapter.

Pursuant to a court order. Counseling information that is subject to confidentiality protections may be sought in several types of legal proceedings, some of which may not be related to educational matters (James & DeVaney, 1995). School counselors have reported dealing with requests and orders to testify to be infrequent but to be among those areas in which they lack confidence (Hermann, 2002). Some of these circumstances might include disputed child custody cases, juvenile court proceedings, and malpractice and other civil suits. In these situations, the confidential information may be considered as evidence that is necessary for a just outcome in the litigation. Our system of jurisprudence requires that judges and juries have access to all of the information relevant to a dispute and excludes evidence only when some other social value is deemed more important. This principle of jurisprudence may be in conflict with ethical protections for confidentiality. In some instances, the client or parent of a minor client may waive confidentiality and give consent to the disclosure. However, if a client does not wish to waive confidentiality, the presumption of confidentiality requires that a school counselor do everything possible to protect the privacy interests of the client. The ASCA (2004) ethical code, for example, advises the counselor to request "of the court that disclosure not be required when the release of confidential information may potentially harm a student or the counseling relationship" (A.2.d).

By 1996, 16 states had given weight to pupils' and families' privacy rights by including licensed school counselors in privileged communication statutes relating to procedures in state courts (Fischer & Sorenson, 1996). The U.S. Supreme Court decision in *Jaffee v. Redmond* (1996) provided the privilege to clients of licensed social workers in federal court proceedings. Privileged communication "is the right of a person in a 'special relationship' to prevent the disclosure in legal proceedings of information given in confidence in the special relationship" (Fischer & Sorenson, p. 18). Although privileged communication may be afforded through constitutional guarantees of privacy and at the discretion of judges, the protection is usually more certain under a privileged communication statute.

In those states that have passed privileged communication statutes, the relationship between school counselors and their clients is given the same status as those between clients and physicians, attorneys, psychologists, and priests and between spouses. Like the general presumption of confidentiality, the right of privileged communication legally must give way in several circumstances, for example, in homicide trials, in child abuse proceedings, and when the client has made his or her mental condition an issue in his or her claim or defense. Some commentators have remarked that the exceptions are so numerous that they swallow the rule. Even with the exceptions, however, the possibility of a privilege does force a party seeking information to provide specific authority for the privilege to be inoperable and does permit an arena for negotiations regarding narrowing the scope of the information that must be disclosed, if disclosure is required by a court.

How should a school counselor respond when confronted with a request for confidential information? The answer to this depends upon from whom the request is coming and the authority of the request. The school counselor should always seek consultation regarding the validity of a request to disclose confidential information. James and Devaney (1995) provided the following guidelines for a counselor who may become a witness in a legal proceeding: (a) record dates and times and details of conversations with lawyers, (b) consider retaining one's own attorney, (c) seek legal advice to determine if requested records are protected by a privilege, (d) discuss and ascertain client's wishes about disclosure, and (e) inform judge of ethical principles regarding confidentiality.

Some novice school counselors may be intimidated in the face of requests from attorneys or when presented with subpoenas, but they are not required to respond to requests for confidential information from attorneys. When served with a subpoena, a counselor should respond that the requested information is confidential and according to the counselor's ethical principles may not be disclosed because of the harm to the client or counseling relationship that may result from the disclosure. Even in cases where the client or parents of a minor client has provided consent for disclosure, the counselor should seek consultation concerning the validity of the waiver and to determine precisely what information should be disclosed. In cases where the counselor is not certain that the client is aware of the information that the counselor may need to disclose, the client or client's attorney should be informed. The best advice is that the client or parents should be informed whenever a disclosure is requested. In addition, FERPA very specifically requires that parents be notified when disclosure is requested pursuant to a valid subpoena or court order, as they may be entitled to a hearing on the issue. However, because the client is considered to be in control of counseling information, when a valid waiver of confidentiality does exist and/or clients/parents have been accorded their rights to notice and a hearing, such as is required under FERPA, the counselor is obliged to disclose the information.

The Minimum Necessary Rule

The minimum necessary rule requires that when there is a valid reason for a disclosure of information, the criterion for the nature and amount of information that should be disclosed is the minimum amount necessary to effectuate the purpose of the disclosure. The minimum necessary rule is expressed in the ACA and ASCA ethical codes and federal legislation such as HIPAA. There are several implications of this rule. First, it means that the framing of the consent document should be consistent with as limited a purpose as possible. Then, it means that the counselor, in consultation, should determine what information is essential for the purpose expressed in the waiver. Finally, it means that, just because a portion of a record may have been legally disclosed, other parts of the record are not automatically open to disclosure without authorization. Every disclosure requires specific authorization. A final corollary to the minimum necessary rule is that recipients of confidential information must be informed that they may not rerelease the information without consent from the client.

The Obligation to Discuss Limits of Confidentiality

As the protection of confidential information has become more formalized (e.g., through FERPA, PPRA) and more exceptions to confidentiality have been recognized, perhaps the most important obligation school counselors have regarding confidentiality is to ensure that clients understand the limits of confidentiality. The ASCA (2004) guidelines emphasize not only that limitations be discussed but also that "the meaning and limits of confidentiality are defined in developmentally appropriate terms to students" (A.2.a). This may be difficult when dealing with very young children; in these cases, the counselor may emphasize that any potential disclosure, however, will be in the context of helping the child (see Taylor & Adelman, 1989).

Consent for Treatment

Informed Consent Confidentiality of educational and counseling information may be thought of as one mechanism by which privacy is protected, informed consent for treatment/participation is another. Through informed consent, the client permits others to enter into his/her mental life and physical space. The legal history of informed consent to treatment stems from the common law notion that nonconsensual touching may give rise to a claim for assault and battery. Thus, in order to avoid a claim of battery, a physician, for example, would need to demonstrate that a patient had consented to the medical procedures performed. Today consent to treatment is also understood to be premised on the right to privacy, and in medicine, a failure to obtain informed consent can create malpractice liability. Counseling and psychotherapy are also considered treatments for which consent is required. The ASCA (2004) code requires that

A.2. The professional school counselor

a. Informs students of the purposes, goals, techniques and rules of procedure under which they may receive counseling at or before the time when the counseling relationship is entered. Disclosure notice includes the limits of confidentiality.

Neither the ACA or ASCA ethical guidelines explicitly state, however, that informed consent is *required* for participation in counseling. The ACA guidelines, in the section titled *Client Rights,* require two things that may, however, amount to informed consent—*Disclosure to Clients* and *Freedom of Choice.* The term *voluntary informed consent* is used in connection with minor clients.

Disclosure to clients. When counseling is initiated, and throughout the counseling process as necessary, counselors inform clients of the purposes, goals, techniques, procedures, limitations, potential risks, and benefits of services to be performed and other pertinent information. Counselors take steps to ensure that clients understand the implications of diagnosis, the intended use of tests and reports, fees, and billing arrangements. Clients have the right to expect confidentiality and to be provided with an explanation of its limitations, including supervision and/or treatment team professionals; to obtain clear information about their case records; to participate in the ongoing counseling plans; and to refuse any recommended services and be advised of the consequences of such refusal (see ACA, 2005, sec. A.2.b)

Freedom of choice. Counselors offer clients the freedom to choose whether to enter into a counseling relationship and to determine which professional(s) will provide counseling. Restrictions that limit choices of clients are fully explained (see ACA, 2005, A.2.a.)

Inability to give consent. When counseling minors or persons unable to give voluntary informed consent, counselors act in these clients' best interests (see ACA, 2005, B.3).

Next to the question of the need for consent, the most salient consent to treatment issue for school counselors is "Who is authorized to give consent?" The issue typically boils down to the following questions: "Under what conditions is the minor client able to give consent?" and "When is the consent of parents or guardians necessary?" As the reader may surmise, there is not a one-size-fits-all answer to these questions. Rather, the answer depends on the particular matrix of ethics, law, and policy that apply in specific jurisdictions in conjunction with the developmental stage of the minor and the nature of the proposed intervention (e.g., in some states minors may access AODA and medical treatment for sexually transmitted diseases without parental consent). The school counselor should begin the search to answer this question by addressing any local school policies that may be in place regarding assurances or notices that have been provided to students or parents regarding the consent process for entering into a counseling relationship or other guidance activities. As will be discussed in more detail in the following section, both FERPA and the PPRA require that school districts annually provide notice to parents regarding certain rights of parents and pupils, including the right of parents to give prior consent for their children to participate in certain required information gathering activities. In addition, LEAs may choose to provide greater assurances for parental consent for their children's participation. Thus, the appropriate starting place is LEA policies regarding parental and student rights.

Both the ACA and ASCA codes give nod to the rights of parents but stop short of requiring parental consent for children's participation in counseling and guidance activities. The ACA (2005) code frames the issue in terms of parental *inclusion* in the counseling process:

A.2.d. Inability to Give Consent

When counseling minors or persons unable to give voluntary consent, counselors seek the assent of clients to services, and include them in decision making as appropriate. Counselors recognize the need to balance the ethical rights of clients to make choices, their capacity to give consent or assent to receive services, and parental or familial legal rights and responsibilities to protect these clients and make decisions on their behalf. The primary responsibility of counselors is to respect the dignity and to promote the welfare of clients.

The ASCA (2004) code more explicitly recognizes their responsibilities to parents/guardians, but also stops short of requiring their consent for their children's participation in counseling activities:

B.1. The professional school counselor:

a. Respects the rights and responsibilities of parents/guardians for their children and endeavors to establish, as appropriate, a collaborative relationship with parents/guardians to facilitate the student's maximum development.
b. Adheres to laws, local guidelines and ethical standards of practice when assisting parents/guardians experiencing family difficulties that interfere with the student's effectiveness and welfare.
c. Respects the confidentiality of parents/guardians.
d. Is sensitive to diversity among families and recognizes that all parents/guardians, custodial and noncustodial, are vested with certain rights and responsibilities for the welfare of their children by virtue of their role and according to law.

The position of ASCA (1999) regarding the requirement for parental consent is perhaps more clearly stated in their position statement titled *The Professional School Counselor and Parent Consent for Services*. In this statement, ASCA took the position that parental consent is necessary only when required by law or local policy. At the same time, ASCA advocated that school counselors fully inform students and parents about the nature of their services, including the counselor's role, the nature of confidentiality, and the role of parents in a collaborative relationship.

In contrast to the ASCA position, the professional literature related to law and ethics for school psychologists assumes that parental consent is legally required in order to provide psychological services to minors (e. g., Jacobs-Timm & Hartshorne, 1998). They also proposed a secondary, but nonetheless important, developmentally appropriate role for minor clients to assent to the intervention as well. Jacobs-Timm and Hartshorne noted that there appears to be a legal trend toward greater levels of parental rights regarding their children's education.

One example of this trend toward a greater level of parental rights in the education of their children is the PPRA. This federal legislation began as the Hatch amendment to the Elementary and Secondary Education Act (ESEA) of 1974, was modified by the Grassley Amendment in 1994, and in its current form is known as the Tiahrt Amendment to the No Child Left Behind Act of 2001. The PPRA is codified at 20 U.S.C. sec. 1232h and its regulations are contained in 34 CFR Part 98.4. According to the FPCO of the U.S. Department of Education (2002) office charged with enforcing FERPA and the PPRA, the PPRA applies to the need for prior parental consent for *required* student participation in certain activities (e.g., the administration of surveys, analyses, and evaluations, and psychological treatment) that have the purpose of revealing

1. political affiliations or beliefs of the student or the student's parent;
2. mental and psychological problems of the student or the student's family;
3. sex behavior or attitudes;
4. illegal, antisocial, self-incriminating, or demeaning behavior;
5. critical appraisals of other individuals with whom respondents have close family relationships;
6. legally recognized privileged or analogous relationships, such as those of lawyers, physicians, and ministers;
7. religious practices, affiliations, or beliefs of the student or student's parent; or
8. income (other than that required by law to determine eligibility for participation in a program or for receiving financial assistance under such program). (USBE, 2002, pp. 3–4)

The PPRA requires that schools and contractors also make available for inspection by parents instructional materials that will be used in connection with Department of Education (ED)-funded surveys, analyses, or evaluations. In addition to the consent and inspection provisions relating to *required* ED-funded surveys, the PPRA requires any elementary or secondary school that receives funds for any programs funded by the ED to develop, in conjunction with parents, policies regarding the following:

1. The right of parents to inspect, upon request, a survey created by a third party before the survey is administered or distributed by a school to students.
2. Arrangements to protect student privacy in the event of the administration of a survey to students, including the right of parents to inspect, upon request, the survey, if the survey contains one or more of the same eight items of information noted above.
3. The right of parents to inspect, upon request, any instructional material used as part of the educational curriculum for students.
4. The administration of physical examinations or screenings that the school may administer to students.
5. The collection, disclosure, or use of personal information collected from students for the purpose of marketing or selling, or otherwise providing the information to others for that purpose.
6. The right of parents to inspect, upon request, any instrument used in the collection of information, as described in number 5. (USDE, 2002, p. 4)

These policies must be communicated to parents annually, preferably at the beginning of the school year, and, in a timely fashion, any substantive changes to the policies. As part of the required notification parents must also be informed of the opportunity to "opt out" of the following:

- Activities involving the collection, disclosure, or use of personal information collected from students for the purpose of marketing or for selling that information, or otherwise providing that information to others for that purpose.
- The administration of any third party (non-Department of Education funded) survey containing one or more of the above described eight items of information.
- Any non-emergency, invasive physical examination or screening that is: 1) required as a condition of attendance; 2) administered by the school and scheduled by the school in advance; and not necessary to protect the immediate health and safety of the student, or of other students. (USDE, 2002, p. 5)

The penalties for violating the PPRA include a withdrawal of federal funding from the school district. Recent court decisions have made it quite clear that individuals do not have a private right of action to collect damages for personal harm under the PPRA (FPCO, 2002). Many advocates of family and student privacy rights consider the lack of a private right to enforcement and the fact that consent is not defined as informed consent to weaken federal privacy protections for families. At the same time, more parents and students are becoming aware of their rights under the PPRA and are assisted by the FPCO and many other private organizations advocating for families to maximize the PPRA protections (e.g., by providing models of letters that parents can send to their school district to obtain the rights that they have been afforded).

School counselors should take note of several implications of the current PPRA: (a) the trend toward greater protection of parental rights in education; (b) the requirement that many materials and activities employed by school counselors (e.g., for classroom guidance activities or mental health screening) may be included in mandated policies for parental consent or inspection of instructional materials, curriculum, and surveys and situations in which opportunities for opting out may be required; (c) formal policies regarding requiring or exempting the need for parental consent for counseling and guidance activities will undoubtedly be more prevalent as LEA's are required to develop such policies if they already have not done so. The school counselor should be prepared to participate in the making of these policies from the perspective provided by their ethical codes, which place student welfare and developmentally appropriate levels of autonomy at the center. In addition, counselors might also advocate for the participation of parents and students in the formulation of these policies. The school counselor should also be reminded that their ethical principles may not be fully shared by other members of the educational community. Nonetheless, the professional counselor should continue to advocate those ethical principles and to continue to attempt to reconcile contrary policies with their ethical codes, keeping in mind, however, that despite their strong beliefs, violation of school board policy could result in personnel sanctions.

The Law of Negligence Negligence is a legal term that is applied to a situation in which a person who has a duty of care to another behaves in a way that falls below a standard of care and causes harm to the other. When a person commits negligence, he or she is considered to have committed a *tort*. When a professional commits negligence, the term *malpractice* is applied (Baerger, 2001). Most people are aware of the concept of professional negligence in the context of medical malpractice. Malpractice or professional negligence is also potentially applicable in the educational or counseling context. However, state courts have been hesitant to impose malpractice liability on schools for negligent teaching, for example, for failing to teach a student to read or not helping students to achieve certain achievement levels. Claims for educational malpractice have generally been foreclosed by the courts. On the other hand, claims about negligence that lead to physical injuries have a higher success rate.

Counselors may be somewhat more vulnerable than teachers to claims of negligence in their ongoing activities, but plaintiff victories remain few and far between. In a recent case (*Sain v. Cedar Rapids Community School District*, 2001) related to academic advising, the Iowa Supreme Court allowed a student to go to trial on claims that he had received inappropriate academic advising. On the other hand, plaintiffs (the individuals who have suffered the harm and are making the negligence claims) have had only a modicum of success in suits that attempt to place liability on the school or individual educators for failure to prevent violence or suicide (for a case where a school district was held liable, see *Eisel,* 1991). These issues will be discussed in more depth later in the chapter.

The potential for liability on the basis of negligence should not be disregarded by school counselors; at the same time, if they are in compliance with school policies, follow the principles and standards of practice of ACA and ASCA, and consult with supervisors and administrators when they have doubts, their risk of liability exposure will be lowered. It should also be noted that the legal principles relating to negligence and malpractice are matters of state law and cases decided in state courts are binding only in the state of origin. There is considerable variability across the states on many matters that relate to counselor's duties. It is, therefore, incumbent upon school counselors to get competent advice regarding their risk of liability for negligence in the areas that relate to their duties.

High Frequency Issues

Several studies surveying school counselors about the frequency of certain legal/ethical challenges and counselor confidence in dealing with those challenges have been conducted. A study by Hermann (2002) identified the following situations as ones that were either encountered by a high percentage of counselors or for which they do not feel well prepared: (a) identifying individuals who pose a danger to others, (b) identifying students who are at risk for suicide, (c) being asked to turn over verbal or written records, (d) determining whether to report suspected child abuse, (e) being subpoenaed to appear in a legal proceeding, and (f) expressing clients' dissatisfaction with counseling services. In this section, the first two of these issues will be considered, the others already having been discussed earlier in the chapter. The confidentiality and informed consent aspects of dealing with students at risk for suicide or posing a danger to others have been discussed earlier in the chapter but will be reviewed here and other dimensions of the issues will be identified. In addition, two emerging issues will be discussed in this section—the school counselor's obligation to present accurate information to students and the issues related to dealing with military recruiters in the school.

Because of the high stakes in many of these situations, the school counselor is urged to become thoroughly familiar with the professional literature on these issues. An excellent place to begin would be with the works cited in this chapter. Because of space limitations, only the very basic contours of these conflicts can be highlighted in this chapter.

Individuals Who Pose a Danger to Others

The school counselor must be concerned with at least two situations in which individuals may pose a danger to others—when the harm may come to victims within the school and when the danger is to individuals outside the school. The differences between these two situations may be negligible as far as counselors' actions are concerned, but the counselor's authority to act may come from different sources.

Preventing school violence is a very high priority following several high-profile, multiple-victim homicides in schools during the past decade (Dwyer, Osher, & Warger, 1998; Lamberg, 1998; Riley & McDaniel, 2000; Smaby, 1995; see also U.S. Department of Health and Social Services, 2001). According to Hermann and Finn (2003) and Bailey (2001), school officials, including school counselors, have a legal obligation to take action when students pose a risk of danger to others. At the same time, courts have been somewhat reluctant to hold schools liable for student-to-student violence, at least that violence that is not foreseeable (Hermann & Remley, 2000). Nonetheless, schools may be on notice to take several precautionary measures in order to fulfill their duties to student and staff safety. At a minimum, actions must pass a *reasonableness* test; that is, school counselors are expected to exercise that degree of care that would be exercised by other school counselors with similar education and experience. Although counselors do have a role in preventing imminent violence, they also have an ethical obligation to protect the rights of students.

School counselors have at least two major roles in violence prevention—educating students and staff about violence and assessing the risk of violence posed by a student (Reddy et al., 2003). Hermann and Finn (2002) described the role of the school counselor in threat assessment as follows:

> According to current school violence and student suicide jurisprudence, school counselors are justified in taking every threat of violence or suicide seriously. Yet, some courts have recognized that not all threats are serious threats to do harm. School counselors play a vital role in assessing these threats and working with administrators as they determine whether to remove a student from school because of a violent threat. According to legal dictates, threat assessment includes determining whether the language and context of the threat indicate a serious intent to do harm. A school counselor's previous interactions with the student are relevant in this determination, especially if the counselor has noted volatile behavior or the student has indicated suicidal ideation. Finally, school counselors need to consider other corroborating evidence such as the student's history of violent behavior. (p. 99)

The approach to assessing risk to violence recommended by Hermann and Finn (2003) emphasizes assessing risk on a case-by-case basis as opposed to employing the practice of profiling. *Profiling* is an a priori practice in which violence proneness is determined by identifying students who may share certain characteristics with previously violent individuals. Bailey (2001) and Vossekuil, Reddy, Fein, Borum, and Modzeleski (2000) urged caution in utilizing this method because research has shown that there is no valid profile of a school violence perpetrator. It may be stigmatizing or even a violation of a student's constitutional rights to have placement decisions (e.g., suspension) made on the basis of a profile alone.

On the other hand, Hermann and Finn (2003) believed that it is appropriate to consider the risk factors related to violent behavior when a student's behavior calls for attention (Kashani, Jones, Bumby, & Thomas, 1999). In Hermann and Finn's contrast of risk-factor analysis with profiling, they asserted that risk factors "encompass a broad range of indicators as opposed to one rigid, stereotypical profile" (p. 101). Risk factors for violence have been identified through research on individuals who have already engaged in violent behavior. Vossekuil et al. (2000), for example, analyzed 37 school shootings and discovered that the shootings were neither impulsive nor random. Most perpetrators had planned the shooting, engaged in behaviors of concern (e.g., looking for a weapon or expressing suicidal or homicidal thoughts in a school assignment), and told at least one other person of their plans. Many of the perpetrators were also found to have been alienated from the mainstream of the student body, had been bullied or teased, and had recently suffered a relationship loss.

When a counselor does determine that a "true threat" exists, he or she, after considering all of the indications of risk, must act to minimize the threat. If the threat is to the school setting, the counselor's findings can be reported to the administration or school security personnel. In a *Tarasoff*-type of situation, where the threat is to an individual outside of the school (e.g., to a parent), the counselor may have an obligation to warn or take some other action to protect the intended victim if it is determined that a threat exists. Ethical codes permit disclosure in this situation, and some urge that the student be involved, if possible, in the decision to warn or protect the intended victim. The need for confidentiality may enter into the school violence situation in another important way, protecting the anonymity of students or others who report to the counselor that another student is planning a violent act. As Vossekuil et al. (2000) found, 75% of perpetrators of school violence had told at least one other person of their plans. The receiver of this information may be more likely to tell someone who can help to avert a disaster if he or she does not fear retaliation or ostracism for "calling out" a peer.

Students at Risk for Suicide

Following a Maryland court case (*Eisel v. Board of Education,* 1991) in which school personnel were found liable for a student suicide, school counselors became more acutely aware of their responsibilities toward students at risk for suicide. In the *Eisel* case, school personnel failed to provide reasonable care to prevent the suicide. Other states have been reluctant to impose liability on schools for student suicides, and some commentators (e.g., Remley, Hermann, & Huey, 2003) suggest that courts may do so only when gross negligence is present. Nonetheless, the reasonableness standard of care and ethical principles place an obligation on school counselors to take action to prevent suicide (King, Price, Telljohann, & Wahl, 2000). Remley et al. identified the following as required under a reasonable care standard: "Taking every threat of suicide seriously, taking precautions to protect the child, and notifying the parents that the child is at risk for suicide" (p. 62).

Capuzzi (2002), in a very comprehensive article on preventing student suicide, after considering the legal and ethical mandates, advocated the "best practice" approach to suicide prevention. According to Capuzzi,

> Best practices are the aspirational standards an ethical and well-informed school counselor should seek to attain in the process of planning and implementing school-based prevention, crisis management, and postvention efforts. They can be distinguished from minimally acceptable practices which, though meeting most legal standards, may not provide maximum protection to students and their families. (p. 65)

The best practice approach, advocated by Capuzzi (2002), recommends that a comprehensive suicide prevention program be in place for all levels of schooling, including provisions for prevention, crisis responding, and postvention. At the prevention phase, Capuzzi recommended that (a) support for programs be obtained from all levels of administration; (b) all faculty and staff be educated about the characteristics of youth suicide, local and building policies and procedures for making referrals, and their roles in prevention; (c) crisis teams be developed and prepared; (d) access be provided to individual and group counseling for affected students; (e) parents be educated about the signs of suicide and any school protocols for dealing with students who are at risk; and (f) classroom presentations be offered to educate all students about suicide and how to access help for themselves and their friends. At the crisis management stage, Capuzzi acknowledged that the usual counseling skills that school counselors possess must be supplemented by crisis-oriented skills:

> The word *management* means that the professional involved must be prepared to apply skills that are different from those required for prevention or postvention counseling. An adolescent in crisis must be assessed, directed, monitored, and guided for the purpose of preventing an act of self-destruction. (p. 73)

Capuzzi (2002) suggested that the counselor be calm, supportive, and nonjudgmental and encourage self-disclosure. While the reality that suicide may be a choice may be acknowledged, it should not be *normalized* as a choice. He recommended that in-depth counseling not begin during the crisis stage and that assessment of the student and lethality be done with the collaboration of another professional. Among the management decisions that must be made at the crisis stage is taking measures to protect the student (e.g., not leaving the student alone or not sending the student home without being accompanied by a parent) if an assessment by at least two professionals determines the student to be at high risk. These measures include notifying parents, making a referral to an outside agency, and considering hospitalization. He further recommended that steps be taken that would not permit the student to return to school without clearance from a qualified professional.

Among a list of suggestions for the postvention phase, Capuzzi (2002) recommended a systemic response, including a meeting to provide consistent information to all faculty and staff. Although his best practice approach includes providing support for friends, classmates, and the deceased's family, he did not recommend that the victim be memorialized in school.

The school counselor should be reminded that confidentiality of counseling information is presumed to extend even into death. Therefore, the counselor should be vigilant about not disclosing information that may have been communicated within the confidential counseling relationship.

Military Recruitment of Students

Two acts of Congress in the early years of the 21st century, coupled with the war in Iraq, flamed historical controversy regarding the cooperation of schools in military recruitment. The current legal requirements for cooperation are contained in the Elementary and Secondary Education Act, as amended by the No Child Left Behind Act of 2001 (P.L. No. 107-110) and in the National Defense Act for Fiscal

Year 2002 (P.L. No. 107-107), the legislation that provided funding for the nation's armed forces in fiscal year 2002. Together these pieces of legislation require LEAs that receive any funds from ESEA to provide the same access to military recruiters as is extended to college recruiters and employers. This includes, for example, space at a career fair and disclosing directory information, including students' names, addresses, and telephone listings (USDE, 2002).

FERPA was also amended to exclude the requirement for parental consent to provide directory information to military recruiters. However, under FERPA, LEAs must notify parents that directory information will be disclosed to the military unless the parents take action to opt out (i.e., to notify the LEA that directory information must not be released to the military without their consent). LEAs may not make any policies that would prevent them from releasing the information to the military, other than in accordance with procedures for opting out.

Critics of the opt out policy are concerned that it places an affirmative duty on the parents to request to opt out as opposed to a policy respecting confidentiality that would require parental action if they wish to have directory information released. Although it is primarily an administrative responsibility to inform parents of the opportunity to opt out, the school counselor may want to be involved on the development of opt out procedures and provide oversight on the accuracy and accessibility of the documents that carry the required notices to parents and students.

Negligent Advising

School counselors were put on notice in 2001 that course advising is a function that may be scrutinized by courts. The occasion was a lawsuit brought by Bruce Sain, a senior at Jefferson High School in Cedar Rapids, Iowa, because he had been denied the opportunity to play basketball as a college freshman (*Sain v. Cedar Rapids Community School District*, 2001). The NCAA had found him ineligible to compete because he had not completed the required core English credits in high school. Coming into his senior year, he lacked three credits of English. He intended to take one course each trimester of his senior year to fulfill the requirement. He completed one course during the first trimester. After enrolling in an NCAA-approved course during the second trimester, Sain asked his counselor if he could transfer to a different English class. The counselor recommended a course entitled *Technical Communications*, which the counselor said would be consistent with his interest in computers and would count toward the NCAA core English requirement. He completed this course and another during the third trimester. However, shortly after graduation he was informed that he would be ineligible to play as a freshman and that he would lose his scholarship. The NCAA had determined that the Technical Communications course had not been approved because it had not appeared on a list of courses that the school had submitted for approval.

The trial court dismissed Sain's claim because it appeared to be a claim for educational malpractice, which, for a number of reasons, could not be brought in Iowa (or for that matter, in most other states). Sain appealed to the Iowa Supreme Court. There, the case took a very unexpected turn. The Iowa Supreme Court distinguished the claim of inappropriate advising from those usually falling under the educational malpractice rubric and, instead, advanced a novel theory under which Sain's claim would be able to go to trial. Instead of categorizing it as a claim alleging educational malpractice, the court found that it fit the requirements for the tort of *negligent representation*. Negligent representation is more commonly found in the business setting in cases against attorneys and accountants, in which a client relies to his or her detriment on information that proves to be inaccurate. Casting the case in this framework, the court ruled that the case should be allowed to go to trial.

The courts held,

> The tort of negligent misrepresentation is broad enough to include a duty for a high school guidance counselor to use reasonable care in providing specific information to a student when the guidance counselor has knowledge of the specific need for the information and provides the information to the student in the course of a counselor-student relationship, and a student reasonably relies upon the information under circumstances in which the counselor knows or should know that the student is relying upon the information. (*Sain v. Cedar Rapids Community School District*, 2001)

The decision has been both applauded (Willis, 2004) and derided (Abbott, 2002). What implications does it have for school counselors?

There are at least three provisions in the ASCA (2004) ethical code that have some bearing on the issue of providing accurate information to students:

A.1.d. Is knowledgeable of laws, regulations, and policies relating to students and strives to protect and inform students regarding their rights.

C.2.b. Provides professional personnel with accurate, objective, concise and meaningful data necessary to adequately evaluate, counsel and assist the student.

E.1.b. Monitors personal well-being and effectiveness and does not participate in any activity that may lead to inadequate professional services or harm to a student.

It can be inferred from these provisions that counselors have an ethical obligation to provide accurate information to students. Do counselors now have a legal duty as well (Stone, 2002)? State courts in prior similar situations have found that school counselors do have a duty to act reasonably in all aspects of their work, including academic advising. If they have not been found to be individually liable for negligent advising in the past, it may have been because it has been considered to be a variant of educational malpractice, which is a tort that has been foreclosed by most state courts (Henry, 2004); it may also be the case that many states have statutes which provide immunity to public employees for negligent acts. However, if other courts were to follow Iowa's lead and distinguish negligent advising from other instances of educational malpractice, statutory immunity may be all that stands between the counselor and liability. Under the negligent representation theory, the school district could still be found liable even if individual employees are given immunity.

The Iowa Supreme Court was quick to refute assertions that permitting the *Sain* case to go forward would discourage counselor/student interactions and limit the flow of important educational and career information. The court assured critics that their ruling would pertain to only individual, face-to-face interactions and concerning only the accuracy of information. The tort of negligent representation does not cover opinions or projections, only the accuracy of the information on which those opinions might be based. In addition, counselors should be reminded that *Sain* is precedent only in the state of Iowa. School counselors should seek consultation regarding their own state's laws on the applicability of the tort of negligent representation to information communicated during academic advising. They should also seek advice as to whether their state statutorily provides immunity to school counselors.

Following the *Sain* decision, Stone (2002) made several recommendations to school counselors that might lower their risk for liability in their roles as academic advisors:

> Continue to offer academic advising sessions to students. The *Sain* ruling should not deter the active pursuit of the role of career and academic advising, a role that has the greatest opportunity for implementing a social justice agenda to level the playing field for students. . . .
>
> Act as the reasonably competent professional would. If faced with a lawsuit, school counselors who practice with care and caution will pass the standard of care test. The courts are not asking for extraordinary care, only reasonable care. . . .
>
> Stay abreast of the information needed for competent academic advising. It is important to be able to demonstrate a working knowledge of procedures, policies, laws, ethical standards, and the school district's policies. . . .
>
> Empower others to take responsibility for having and giving the right information. For example, coaches could be in charge of advising students about NCAA regulations, and students could be encouraged to learn to become their own advocate in gathering information about college admissions, scholarships, and financial aid. . . .
>
> Require that students and parents sign off when they have been given critical information. For example, when seniors are given their personal credit check for their remaining graduation requirements, the school counselor can have them sign an acknowledgment that they have been told and understand what they need to do.
>
> Consult when appropriate. Best practice for school counselors is to always consult whenever they are unsure. School counselors never stand alone unless they fail to consult with others who are in a position to help.

Recommendations for School Counselors

We will take one more opportunity to remind the reader that this chapter makes no representation to be comprehensive in its coverage. It is best characterized as a primer on law and ethics in school counseling. Where might one go to increase ethical competence?

1. Among the major topical omissions in this chapter are dual/multiple relationships, testing and assessment, and responsibilities of the counselor as a practicum or internship supervisor. The reader is urged to obtain in-depth information on these topics. Most entry-level textbooks on ethics in counseling will cover these topics (e.g., see Corey, Corey, & Callahan, 2003; Welfel, 2002).
2. School counselors could also benefit immensely from graduate courses or in-depth continuing education on school law and the law of special education taught by experts in these fields.
3. Counselors are always urged to seek consultation from their peers and superiors when entering unfamiliar territory.

4. School counselors should become thoroughly familiar with the relevant policies of their local educational authority. In addition, they should avail themselves of relevant resources and services provided by their state departments of education.
5. In order to accommodate the cultural diversity of their clientele, school counselors should proactively include parents and community members in formulating counseling and guidance policies and encourage administrators to do the same.
6. Preservice school counselors are urged to expect substantial training in law and ethics in their graduate programs. This training should include not only an introduction to professional ethics codes, but also the relevant laws in the state in which the counselor will be licensed.
7. Preservice counselors should expect that their graduate preparation include attention to developing multicultural awareness and skills at a level that is congruent with the ethical principle of competence.
8. School counselors should demand access to competent legal advice by attorneys who are knowledgeable about the issues relevant to the roles and functions of school counselors.

Summary

We hope that the reader has acquired a broader and more complete understanding of the full array of entities whose laws, policies, and principles shape their daily work. It should be apparent, however, that legal and ethical issues are complicated and unique to each individual situation. Because of this complexity, this chapter should not serve as a substitute for school counselors' getting their own competent legal advice when faced with a conflictual situation. It is our expectation, however, that the school counselor will now be in a better position to know some of the critical questions to ask when consultation is sought.

References

Abbott, P. (2002). *Sain v. Cedar Rapids Community School District*: Providing special protection for student-athletes? [Electronic version]. *Brigham Young University Education and Law Journal, 2,* 291–309.

American Counseling Association. (2005). *American Counseling Association code of ethics and standards of practice.* Alexandria, VA: Author.

American Psychological Association. (2003). Guidelines on multicultural education, training, research, practice, and organizational change for psychologists [Electronic version]. *American Psychologist, 58,* 377–402.

American School Counselor Association. (1999, 2004). *Position statement: Parent consent for services.* Retrieved October 8, 2007, from http://www.schoolcounselor.org/content.asp?contentid=213

American School Counselor Association. (2004). *Ethical standards for school counselors.* Retrieved October 8, 2007, from http://www.schoolcounselor.org/content.asp?contentid=173

Arrendondo, P., & Toporek, R. (2004). Multicultural counseling competencies = ethical practice [Electronic version]. *Journal of Mental Health Counseling, 2,* 44–55.

Baerger, D. R. (2001). Risk management with suicidal patients: Lessons from case law [Electronic version]. *Professional Psychology: Research and Practice, 32,* 359–366.

Bailey, K. A. (2001). Legal implications of profiling students for violence [Electronic version]. *Psychology in the Schools, 38,* 141–155.

Barnett, J. E. (n.d.). *Yes, but is it ethical?* Retrieved May 7, 2005, from http://www.division42.org/MembersArea/Nws_Views/articles/is_it_ethical.html

Capuzzi, D. (2002). Legal and ethical challenges in counseling suicidal students. In T. P. Remley, Jr., M. A. Hermann, & W. C. Huey (Eds.), *Ethical and legal issues in school counseling* (2nd ed., pp. 64–81). Alexandria, VA: American School Counselor Association.

Cohen, E. D., & Cohen, G. S. (1999). *The virtuous therapist.* Belmont, CA: Wadsworth.

Confidentiality of alcohol and drug abuse patient records. (2003). *Code of Federal Regulations*, Chapter 42, Part 2.

Constantine, M. G., & Yeh, C. J. (2001). Multicultural training, self-construals, and multicultural competence of school counselors. *Professional School Counseling, 4,* 202–207.

Corey, G., Corey, M., & Callahan, P. (2003). *Issues and ethics in the helping professions* (6th ed.). Pacific Grove, CA: Brooks/Cole-Thompson Learning.

Corrao, J., & Melton, G. B. (1988). Legal issues in school-based behavior therapy. In J. C. Witt, S. N. Elliott, & F. M. Gresham (Eds.), *Handbook of behavior therapy in education* (pp. 377–399). New York: Plenum Press.

Cottone, R. R., & Claus, R. E. (2000). Ethical decision-making models: A review of the literature. *Journal of Counseling and Development, 78,* 275–283.

Davis, J. L., & Mickelson, D. J. (1994). School counselors: Are you aware of ethical and legal aspects of counseling? [Electronic version]. *The School Counselor, 42,* 5–13.

Dwyer, K., Osher, D., & Warger, C. (1998). *Early warning, timely response: A guide to safe schools.* Washington, DC: U.S. Department of Education.

Eberlein, L. (1987). Introducing ethics to beginning psychologists: A problem-solving approach. *Professional Psychology: Research and Practice, 18,* 353–359.

Eisel v. Board of Education of Montgomery, 597 A2d 447 (Md Ct. App. 1991).

Family Educational Rights and Privacy Act (FERPA). (1974). 20 U.S.C.A. § 1232g; 34 C.F.R. Part 99.

Fischer, L., & Sorenson, G. P. (1996). *School law for counselors, psychologists and social workers* (3rd ed.). New York: Longman.

Fontes, l. (2005). *Child abuse and culture: Working with diverse families*. New York: Guilford Press.

Grassley Amendment, S. 1017 of GOALS 2000: The Educate America Act under the heading "Protection of Pupils." 20 U.S.C. Section 1232h. (1994).

Gustafson, K. E., & McNamara, J. R. (1987). Confidentiality with minor clients: Issues and guidelines for therapists. *Professional Psychology: Research and Practice, 18*, 503–508.

Hansen, N. D., & Goldberg, S. G. (1999). Navigating the nuances: A matrix for consideration of ethical-legal dilemmas [Electronic version]. *Professional Psychology: Research and Practice, 30*, 495–503.

Henry, M. N. (2004). No child left behind? Educational malpractice litigation for the 21st century [Electronic version]. *California Law Review, 92*, 1117–1169.

Hermann, M. A. (2002). A study of legal issues encountered by school counselors and perceptions of their preparedness to respond to legal challenges. *Professional School Counseling, 6*, 12–19.

Hermann, M. A., & Finn, A. (2003) An ethical and legal perspective on the role of school counselors in preventing violence in schools. In T. P. Remley, Jr., M. A. Hermann, & W. C. Huey (Eds.). *Ethical and legal issues in school counseling* (2nd ed., pp. 94–110). Alexandria, VA: American School Counseling Association.

Hermann, M. A., & Remley, T. P., Jr. (2000). Guns, violence, and schools: The results of violence—Litigation against educators and students shedding more constitutional rights at the school house gate [Electronic version]. *Loyola Law Review, 46*, 389–439.

Herr, E. L., Cramer, S. H., & Niles, S. G. (2004). *Career guidance and counseling through the lifespan* (6th ed.). Boston, MA: Allyn & Bacon.

Individuals with Disabilities Education Act of 1997, P.L. No. 105-17, 34 CFR 300.574. (1997).

In re Gault. 387 U.S. 1. (1967).

Isaacs, M. L., & Stone, C. (1999). School counselors and confidentiality: Factors affecting professional choices. *Professional School Counseling, 2*, 258–266.

Isaacs, M. L., & Stone, C. (2001). Confidentiality with minors: Mental health counselors' attitudes toward breaching or preserving confidentiality. *Journal of Mental Health Counselors, 23*, 342–356.

Jacob-Timm, S., & Hartshorne, T. S. (1998). *Ethics and school law for psychologists* (3rd ed.). New York: John Wiley & Sons, Inc.

Jaffee v. Redmond. 18 U.S. 1; 116 S. Ct. 1923; 135 L. Ed. 2d 337; 1996 U.S. LEXIS 3879; 64 U.S.L.W. 4490. (1996).

James, S. H., & DeVaney, S. B. (1995). Preparing to testify: The school counselor as court witness [Electronic version]. *School Counselor, 43*, 97–102.

Jordan, A. E., & Meara, N. M. (1999). The role of virtues and principles. In D. N. Bersoff (Ed.), *Ethical conflicts in psychology* (pp. 141–145). Washington, DC: American Psychological Association.

Kaczmarek, P. (2000). Ethical and legal complexities inherent in professional roles with children and adolescent clients. *Counseling and Human Development, 33*, 1–21.

Kashani, J., Jones, M., Bumby, K., & Thomas, L. (1999). Youth violence: Psychosocial risk factors, treatment, prevention, and recommendations. *Journal of Emotional and Behavioral Disorders, 7*, 200–211.

Keith-Spiegel, P., & Koocher, G. P. (1985). *Ethics in psychology: Professional standards and cases*. New York: Random House.

Kent v. United States. 383 U.S. 541. (1966).

King, K. A., Price, J. H., Telljohann, S. K., & Wahl, J. (2000). Preventing adolescent suicide: Do high school counselors know the risk factors? *Professional School Counseling, 3*, 255–263.

Kitchener, K. S. (1984). Intuition, critical evaluation, and ethical principles: The foundation for ethical decisions in counseling psychology. *The Counseling Psychologist, 12*, 43–55.

Kramer, D. (1994). *Legal rights of children* (2nd ed., Vols. 1–3). Colorado Springs, CO: Shepard's/McGraw-Hill, Inc.

Lamberg, L. (1998). Preventing school violence: No easy answers. *Journal of the American Medical Association, 280*, 404–407.

Lambie, G. W. (2005). Child abuse and neglect: A practical guide for professional school counselors [Electronic version]. *Professional School Counseling, 8*(3).

Lawrence, G., & Kurpius, S. E. R. (2000). Legal and ethical issues involved when counseling minors in nonschool settings [Electronic version]. *Journal of Counseling and Development, 78*, 130–136.

Levesque, R. L. R. (2002). *Adolescents, sex, and the law: Preparing adolescents for responsible citizenship*. Washington, DC: American Psychological Association.

Lu, W. (1998). An interface between individualistic and collectivistic orientations in Chinese cultural values and social relations [Electronic version]. *The Howard Journal of Communications, 9*, 91–107.

Meara, N., Schmidt, L., & Day, J. (1996). Principles and virtues: A foundation for ethical decisions, policies, and character. *The Counseling Psychologist, 24*, 4–77.

Mitchell, C. W., Disque, J. G., & Robertson, P. (2002). When parents want to know: Responding to parental demands for confidential information [Electronic version]. *Professional School Counseling, 6*, 156–161.

Nurcombe, B., & Partlett, D. F. (1994). *Child mental health and the law*. New York: Free Press.

Pope, K. S. (n.d.). Ethics codes & practice guidelines for assessment, therapy, counseling, & forensic practice. Retrieved September 7, 2007, from http://www.kspope.com/ethcodes/index/php

Pope, K. S., & Bajt, T. R. (1988). When laws and values conflict: A dilemma for psychologists. In D. N. Bersoff (Ed.), *Ethical conflicts in psychology* (3rd ed., pp. 107–108). Washington, DC: American Psychological Association.

Protection of Pupil Rights Amendment (PPRA). (2004). *HB-rights.org*. Retrieved October 8, 2007, from http://www.hb-rights.org/5parents/ppra

Reddy, M., Borum, R., Berglund, J., Vossekuil, B., Fein, R., & Modzeleski, W. (2001). Evaluating risk for targeted violence in schools: Comparing risk assessment, threat assessment, and other approaches. *Psychology in the Schools, 38,* 157–173.

Remley, T. P., Jr., & Sparkman, L. B. (1993). Student suicide: The counselor's limited liability. *The School Counselor, 40,* 164–169.

Remley, T. P., Jr., Hermann, M. A., & Huey, W. C. (Eds.). (2003). *Ethical and legal issues in school counseling* (2nd ed.). Alexandria, VA: American School Counselor Association.

Riley, P. L., & McDaniel, J. (2000). School violence prevention, intervention, and crisis response. *Professional School Counseling, 4,* 120–125.

Sadeghi, M., Fischer, J. M., & House, S. G. (2003). Ethical dilemmas in multicultural counseling. *Multicultural Counseling and Development, 31,* 179–191.

Sain v. Cedar Rapids Community School District. 626. N.W.2d 115; Iowa Sup LEXIS 82 (Iowa Supreme Court, 2001).

Smaby, M. H. (1995). The school counselor as leader of efforts to have schools free of drugs and violence. *Education, 115*(4), 612–623.

Stone, C. (2002). Negligence in academic advising and abortion counseling: Courts rulings and implications. *Professional School Counseling, 6,* 28–35. (ERIC Document Reproduction Service No. EJ655208)

Sue, D. W., Arrendondo, P., & McDavis, R. J. (1992). Multicultural counseling competencies and standards: A call to the profession [Electronic version]. *Journal of Multicultural Counseling and Development, 20,* 64–88.

Sullivan, J. R., Ramirez, E., Rae, W. A., Razo, N. P., & George, C. A. (2002). Factors contributing to breaking confidentiality with adolescent clients: A survey of pediatric psychologists. *Professional Psychology: Research and Practice, 33.* Retrieved May 8, 2005, from http://www.apa.org/psycarticles.

Tarasoff v. The Regents of The University of California. 17 Cal. 3d 425, 551 P2d 332 (1976).

Taylor, L., & Adelman, H. S. (1989). Reframing the confidentiality dilemma to work in children's best interests. *Professional Psychology: Research and Practice, 20,* 79–83.

Taylor, L., & Adelman, H. S. (1998). Confidentiality: Competing principles, inevitable dilemmas. *Journal of Educational and Psychological Consultation, 9,* 267–275.

Tinker v. Des Moines Independent School District, 393 U.S. 503, 89 S. Ct. 733 (1969).

Toporek, R. L., & Williams, R. A. (2006). Ethics and professional issues related to the practice of social justice in counseling psychology. In R. L. Toporek, L. H. Gerstein, N. Fouad, G. Roysircar, & T. Israel (Eds.), *Handbook for social justice in counseling psychology: Leadership, vision, and action* (pp. 17–36). Thousand Oaks, CA: Sage.

U.S. Department of Education. (1999). *Rights of non-custodial parents in the Family Educational Rights and Privacy Act of 1974.* Washington, DC: Family Policy Compliance Office.

U.S. Department of Education. (2002, October 28). *Recent changes affecting FERPA & PPRA.* http://www.ed.gov/policy/gen/guid/fpco/pdf/ht102802.pdf

U.S. Department of Education. (2007). *The federal role in education.* Retrieved October 8, 2007, from http://www.ed.gov/about/overview/fed/role.html

U.S. Department of Education Office of Civil Rights. (1991). *The guidance counselor's role in ensuring equal educational opportunity.* Washington, DC: Author.

U.S. Department of Health and Human Services. (2001). *Youth violence: A report of the Surgeon General.* Rockville, MD: Author.

U.S. Department of Health & Human Services. (2007). *Medical privacy—National standards to protect the privacy of personal health information.* Retrieved October 8, 2007, from http://www.hhs.gov/ocr/hipaa/

Vossekuil, B., Reddy, M., Fein, R., Borum, R., & Modzeleski, W. (2000). *U.S.S.S. Safe School Initiative: An interim report on the prevention of targeted violence in schools.* Washington, DC: U.S. Secret Service, National Threat Assessment Center.

Welfel, E. R. (2002). *Ethics in counseling and psychotherapy.* Pacific Grove, CA: Brooks/Cole.

Wilcoxon, S. A., & Magnuson, S. (1999). Considerations for school counselors serving noncustodial parents: Premises and suggestions. *Professional School Counseling, 2,* 275–279.

Willis, S. P. (2004). Iowa school counselors had better get it right! *Iowa Law Review, 89,* 1093.

XLVII
PROFESSIONAL ACTIVITIES IN PROFESSIONAL SCHOOL COUNSELING

KEITH M. DAVIS, LAURIE L. WILLIAMSON, AND BARBARA A. SCARBORO

Appalachian State University

Introduction

This chapter discusses issues in professional school counseling regarding the professional activities and development of professional school counselors. Specifically discussed are (a) a brief history of the counseling profession; (b) credentialing, licensure, and accreditation in professional school counseling; (c) networking and collaboration; (d) partnering with local school systems; (e) technology; (f) differences in professional activities for school counselors based on geographical regions (rural, suburban, and urban) and grade levels (elementary, middle, and high school); (g) national, regional, and state school counseling organizations; and (h) the importance of advocacy as an underlying component for professional activities.

As professional school counselors move from their formal training to practice, it is important that they actively seek ways to maintain professional competence by keeping abreast of current changes in the school counseling profession. In doing so, they not only help promote the profession of school counseling, but also enhance their own senses of professional identity and advocacy for the constituents they serve (e.g., students, faculty, community, and society). To provide guidance for this professional development task we propose, in this chapter, a variety of ways in which professional school counselors can utilize professional activities and opportunities to maintain their professional identities, serve as advocates, and stay connected with each other as the school counseling profession continues to evolve.

Brief History of Professional School Counseling

Guidance and counseling as a profession was a latecomer to the field of education as the 1940s and 1950s witnessed a rapid expansion in the number of school counselors. School counseling was originally founded in the vocational movement that offered occupational assessment information and employment services. Thus, schools were encouraged to assist students in planning for their employment futures. Teaching and administration and their respective roles and responsibilities were already well established. Historically, teaching certification and experience has been a prerequisite for obtaining school counseling licensure in some states. Initially, school counselors were selected from within the ranks of the teaching staff. The standard expectation for school counselors was 1 to 2 years of teaching experience. The expectation that counselors were teachers first became established early in credentialing requirements. The struggle to define school counseling as a distinct profession continues today (Baker, 1994; Williamson, 1998).

It was the space race following the launch of Sputnik I, however, that really ignited the expansion of guidance and counseling services in the schools during the 1950s and 1960s. The National Defense Education *Act* (NDEA) of 1958 provided schools with financial support to hire counselors. The Congressional directive was to identify talented students and encourage them to pursue advanced study in math and science so that the United States would become more competitive with the then Soviet Union. The American Personnel and Guidance Association (APGA), which eventually became the American Counseling Association (ACA), and the American School Counselor Association (ASCA), which was established in 1952, worked together to increase interest in counselor training, preparation, and licensure (Lambie & Williamson, 2004).

In 1969, the vast majority of states required teaching experience for counseling licensure but the trend providing for substitute or comparable experience was becoming more evident. Robert Myrick (1993) reported that 21 states required teaching certification and/or one or more years of teaching experience. Changing professional identification from one role to another (teacher to counselor) requires a substantial paradigm shift that is often difficult to achieve (Baker, 1994; Baker & Herr, 1976; Cohen, 1961; Smith, 1994). This has led to an increasing number of states allowing certification as a school counselor for individuals who have completed master's level training but do not hold a teacher's certificate.

The need for schools to employ clinically capable school counselors is evidenced by the increase and severity of issues facing schools today. The National Education Commission on Time and Learning (1994) reported,

> Half of American children spend some portion of their childhood in a single-parent home; 20.8 million working mothers have children under the age of 17; family time has declined 40% since World War II; 40% of high school students care for themselves after school; and . . . students are bringing many more problems to school . . . receive less support outside school, and increasingly exhibit destructive behavior ranging from drug and alcohol abuse to gang membership and precocious sexual activity. (p. 3)

In addition, schools are experiencing varied enrollment trends. The number of school districts and schools has declined from 1937 to 1938, when the first numbers were documented, to the year 2000. Reportedly, 117,108 school districts encompassing 250,000 schools have decreased to 14,928 school districts and 92,012 schools. These statistics and contributing factors are chronicled on a dedicated Web site of the Rural School and Community Trust (n.d.; http://www.ruraledu.org) providing detailed information regarding the status of rural communities and education. After multiple incidences of consolidation, rural school closings created situations where students endure long round trip bus rides to schools, as well as getting up early to arrive at school on time. Rural information highlighted the advantages of smaller schools and districts promoting higher student achievement, even among economically challenged students. Other advantages included that these rural areas are more productive in social and economic domains. In contrast, urban schools districts are growing with additional pressure to ensure equity in education and resources across the districts. The focus of concern shifts to the resources that schools and students have, instead of what students learn. Small rural schools that are a part of an urban district tend to experience greater challenges in the areas of equitable resources and education. Despite the challenges, many rural areas are embracing their communities and are developing policies and procedures (i.e., additional funding, financial incentives) to support educational efforts. Recent immigration trends put additional pressure on schools in many areas, urban and rural, to address the unique needs of bilingual and bicultural children (Towner-Larsen, Granaello, & Sears, 2000).

The ASCA rose to the challenge of redefining the school counselor's role by developing the *ASCA National Standards for School Counseling Programs* (Campbell & Dahir, 1997). The *National Model* (ASCA, 2003) addresses the needs for a comprehensive and developmental approach to the delivery of services. The *National Model* values systemic activities that impact all students at all levels. School counselors are encouraged to consult and collaborate with a wide variety of educational and community resources. The ASCA model also provides school counselors with accountability strategies to demonstrate program effectiveness (Lambie & Williamson, 2004).

Professional organizations such as the ACA, the ASCA, and the Association for Counselor Education and Supervision (ACES) are calling for uniformity in counselor education and training and in licensure standards. National Board for Certified Counselors (NBCC) has developed criteria for a Nationally Certified School Counselor (NCSC). The National Board for Professional Teaching Standards (NBPTS) has developed criteria for National Board Certification. It is hoped that by achieving a level of national conformity, levels of consistency will be established and the availability of state reciprocity policies will be increased. As a result, school counseling will be empowered as a profession.

Credentialing, Licensure, and Accreditation in Professional School Counseling

What exactly do all of those confusing acronyms mean? There are accrediting boards to evaluate educational training programs as well as certification and licensure boards for individual professionals. School counseling training programs are monitored by two main organizations: the Council for Accreditation of Counseling and Related Educational Programs (CACREP) and the National Council for the Accreditation of Teacher Education (NCATE). These accreditation bodies develop and monitor the training standards of some professional school counseling programs (Figure 47.1).

Certification and Licensure

First, school counselors need to be licensed by the state Department of Education. But, they also have the opportunity to extend their professional development by meeting the criteria for national recognition. The NBCC was established in 1982 to support the standardization of the counseling profession by creating and monitoring a national certification system. The NBCC evaluates the professional training and competence of counselors from a wide variety of specialties by administering the National Counselor Examination (NCE) for licensure and certification. The NCE is designed to be general in nature and is intended to assess cognitive knowledge, regardless of individual areas of specialization. The NCE covers eight core areas: (a) human growth and development, (b) social and cultural foundations, (c) helping relationships (including counseling theories), (d) group work, (e) career and lifestyle development, (f) assessment and appraisal, (g) research and program evaluation, and (h) professional orientation. The examination is administered nationwide semiannually in April and October. Prerequisites for taking the examination include (a) a master's degree, (b) documented 2 years professional counseling experience, (c) 3,000 client contact hours, and (d) 100 hours of supervision (NBCC, n.d.).

Graduating from a CACREP program affords you the opportunity to waive the previously mentioned requirements and sit for the GSA-NCE (Graduate Student Administration-National Counselor Examination) at the end of your program. Satisfactory performance on the NCE is one of the criteria used by NBCC to identify professionals who may be eligible to become a National Certified Counselor (NCC). Being an NCC attests to your status as a professional counselor and advocate for the profession, and it is nationally recognized. You can also apply to receive specialty certification in the areas of (a) career, (b) gerontological, (c) school, (d) clinical mental health, and (e) addictions counseling. Certification is for a period of 5 years. At the conclusion of each 5-year cycle, you are required to document 100 contact clock hours of continuing education credit (NBCC, n.d.). Study guides for the NCE are available from the NBCC. (The contact information is National Board for Certified Counselors, Inc., 3 Terrace Way, Suite D, Greensboro, NC 27403-3660; phone 336-547-0607; fax 336-547-0017; e-mail nbcc@nbcc.org; and Web site http://www.nbcc.org)

After you have received initial certification as a counselor, many states offer licensure. Later in your career, you may choose to pursue your license and become a Licensed Professional Counselor (LPC). This designation affords you the opportunity to conduct private practice and receive third party payment from some insurance companies. LPCs are licensed by each individual state, and regulations vary from state to state. Generally, it is required that you (a) graduate with a master's degree from an accredited institution; (b) document 2 years of professional experience, 2,000 hours of supervised professional practice, 100 hours of clinical supervision (75 hours must be individual supervision and supervisors must be LPCs or equivalently credentialed mental health professionals with at least 5 years of counseling experience); (c) successfully pass the NCE; and (d) submit an acceptable Professional Disclosure Statement. Licensure is valid for 2 years, and you must earn 40 hours of continuing professional education credit during each 2-year renewal period.

School Counseling Licensure

In most states, a specialty area test is required by the state Department of Education in order to become a licensed school counselor. Many states use the Praxis (n.d.) series published by the Educational Testing Service (ETS) to evaluate mastery of basic counseling skills. School counselors frequently need to take the school counseling specialty portion of the Praxis to become licensed in that state as a school counselor. Qualifying scores vary from state to state (Praxis). Many states also require that all licensed school personnel pass a computer competency exam. Some states have included testing components that require the satisfactory demonstration of the use of word processing, database, spreadsheet, and Internet computer competencies. In 2005, the U.S. Department of Education, recognizing the increasing importance of technology, established action guidelines for the nation's school districts in preparing students for innovative approaches to learning through advances in educational technology. (The full text of the National Education Technology Plan is available at http://www.ed.gov/technology/plan.) It is a good idea to demonstrate the application of these competencies by developing a technology portfolio over the course of your career. A technology portfolio contains evidence of your technological skills, such as developing a parent brochure, an information Web page, or a PowerPoint presentation for staff development.

Every state has its own requirements; being licensed in one state does not necessarily translate into automatic licensure in another. A publication with information regarding state requirements for school counseling licensure and reciprocity with other states is available through the ASCA office. Professional organizations for school counselors include the ASCA (801 North Fairfax Street, Suite

Figure 47.1 Professional Organizations and Credentials for School Counselors.

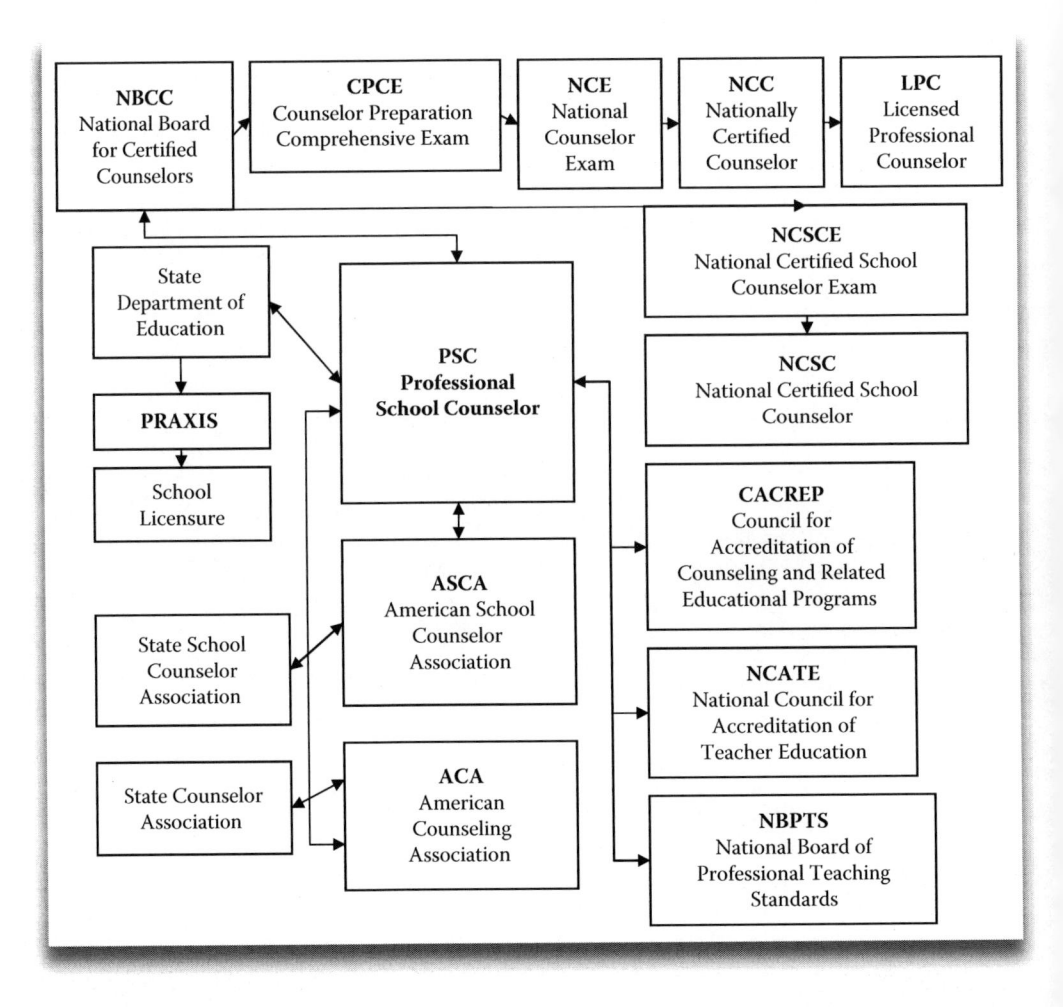

310, Alexandria, VA 22314; phone 703-683-2722 or 1-800-306-4722; fax 703-683-1619; e-mail asca@schoolcounselor.org; and Web site http://www.schoolcounselor.org) and the ACA (5999 Stevenson Avenue, Alexandria, VA 22304; phone 1-800-347-6647 ext. 222; fax 703-823-0252; and Web site www.counseling.org).

Advanced School Counseling Certification

The NCSC credential is a result of the joint efforts of the ACA, the ASCA, and the NBCC. Requirements include (a) a current NCC credential; (b) an advanced degree in a mental health field from an accredited institution; (c) coursework in appraisal of individuals, diversity in counseling, career development, and fundamentals of school counseling; (d) 3 years of postgraduate counseling experience and counseling supervision as a school counselor; and (e) a passing score on the National Certified School Counselor Exam (NCSCE). The NCSC is an attempt to standardize the school counseling certification process nationwide and provides criteria for school districts to provide school counselors with additional salary compensation (NBCC, n.d.). (The contact information is National Board for Certified Counselors, 3 Terrace Way, Suite D, Greensboro, NC 27403-3660; phone 336-547-0607; fax 336-547-0017; e-mail nbcc@nbcc.org; and Web site www.nbcc.org.)

Additionally, the NBPTS developed a board certification process for school counselors in 2002. The "Early Childhood Through Young Adulthood/School Counseling" certificate is appropriate for counselors who work with students ages pre-K–12th grade in educational settings. Requirements include a portfolio that demonstrates that your counseling practice meets the school counseling standards and that you monitor and refine your practice through continuous and in-depth reflection. Certification also requires an assessment process where counselors demonstrate content knowledge in the areas of (a) human growth and development, (b) school counseling program standards, (c) diverse populations, (d) theories, (e) data and change, and (f) collaboration (NBPTS, n.d.). Currently many states are providing additional salary compensation for school counselors who have successfully completed the board certification process. (The contact information is National Board for

Professional Teaching Standards National Office, 1525 Wilson Blvd., Suite 500, Arlington, VA 22209; phone 703-465-2700 or 1-800-228-3224; fax 703-465-2715; and Web site www.nbpts.org.)

Although all of the acronyms may be confusing, these organizations are important because they provide professional development opportunities, advocate for political and social support, and provide research-based resources. Membership in professional organizations is critical in promoting and advocating school counseling as a profession.

Networking and Collaborating

The DeWitt Wallace-Reader's Digest Fund contributed millions of dollars to jump-start an initiative to transform school counseling nationwide (Guerra, 1998). The multiyear initiative is called the *National Program for the Transformation of School Counseling* (NPTSC; Education Trust, 1999). The goal of the program is to improve the school counseling profession by transforming the preparation of counselors. Specifically, a large component of this preparation model includes training school counselors on how to meet the academic, career, and personal/social needs of underrepresented groups through social justice advocacy. This effort is aimed at closing the achievement gap of low-income students and students of color from other youth by promoting collaborative partnerships between local education (e.g., school counselors) and business, community activists, colleges, and whole communities so that all students will reach high levels of academic achievement.

Pedagogical trends encourage collaborative learning techniques (Gibson & Mitchell, 1992). Educators highlight the need for collaborative partnerships. Partnerships are forged between local schools, institutions of higher learning, and community leaders in business and industry in order to better prepare students for the modern work environment (Kurpius & Rozecki, 1992). One of the major problems identified by Guerra (1998) is that school counselors are trained in isolation from teachers, administrators, other school personnel, and the community, all of whom must collaborate to support and advocate success for all students.

Student counselors are trained in isolation from the other school professionals with whom they will be working on a daily basis. The NPTSC suggests that institutions of higher education must adapt their training programs in order to better integrate the training of school counselors with teachers. If collaborative teamwork in the schools is the ultimate goal, then it must be an integral part of the training process for teachers, counselors, and administrators.

There is minimal research available on promoting collaborative training programs. Only a few progressive programs provide opportunities for students to learn and collaborate across disciplines during their training. Shoffner and Williamson (2000) described an "innovative seminar" component of their training program in which counseling and administration students develop cooperative and collaborative strategies for working together in the school setting. Shoffner and Briggs (2001) created an interactive CD-ROM to challenge school counselors, teachers, and administrators to solve problems collaboratively.

Beesley (2004) suggested university training programs prepare students to facilitate "no-fault problem solving meetings" with teachers, students, and parents as active participants. This method was borrowed from the Ackerman Family Institute, which developed the model to stimulate cooperative planning and problem solving. Beesley also recommended that university programs develop advisory boards comprising school counselors, administrators, teachers, and members of the community to provide input and feedback on current issues, trends, and needs. Training programs need to develop curricula that focus on collaborative approaches to problem solving and provide students opportunities to practice collaborative or no-fault techniques. Finding ways to integrate the training of school counselors with that of other school professionals, particularly administrators and other pupil services personnel, is a vital need for the future.

The Counselor's Perspective

The No Child Left Behind Act (NCLB; U.S. Department of Education, 2001) is a federal mandate for public schools to effectively teach and ensure academic success for all students regardless of their race or socioeconomic status. In order for school counselors to better serve as advocates for all students, it becomes important for them to educate others within the school about their role and responsibilities. One of which is to promote social justice and to advocate for closing the achievement gap between minority and white students. Unfortunately, one of the most significant stressors identified by professional school counselors in the field is the lack of a clearly defined role (Kendrick, Chandler, & Hatcher, 1994; Studer & Allton, 1996). NCLB and the Education Trust (1999) initiative are among the developmental changes in the professions that have created changes in the roles and functions of school counselors within the schools. Thompson (2002) defined the changes as two dichotomous functions identified as administrative and therapeutic. Professional counselors indicate that the role of the school counselor is not well understood. Counselors' roles appear to have conflicting expectations from teachers, administration, and the counselors. Teachers perceive counselors as a part of the administration, administrators feel counselors are a part of the instructional staff, and counselors report a sense of "inbetween-ness" (Snyder & Daly, 1993; Welch & McCarroll, 1993). Both perceptions are complementary of the administrative role identified by Thompson. Part of the reason counselors may feel isolated or caught in the middle is due to a tradition established in many schools. The tradition fosters the belief that the teacher is ultimately responsible for the students' learning. Administrators, parents, or counselors are consulted with only when a problem arises. Job descriptions are most commonly carried out in isolation. Efforts to strengthen communication and relationships between all stakeholders need to become more vigorous.

One major study conducted by Amatea, Daniels, Bringman, and Vandiver (2004) implemented a 3-year, school-wide intervention strategy to promote a more collaborative work environment among counselors, teachers and parents in order to enhance student learning and achievement. Their success in creating organizational change is encouraging to those who want to promote a collaborative partnership model. Amatea et al. found that there must be authentic dialogue and cooperation between school and home for effective problem solving to occur. One key component to their program was a "no-fault" approach to problem solving. Another key factor appeared to be more actively involving students themselves by promoting student-led parent conferences and portfolio assessments. Their project is described clearly, and it could be feasibly duplicated as one way to advocate for student success and achievement. Of interest to those schools that want to implement such a program is a study conducted by Marlow, Bloss, and Bloss (2000). Recognizing that there are multiple learning modalities, they focused on social and Emotional Competency Education (ECE). ECE encourages collaboration between teachers and school counselors and promotes the premise that emotional, cognitive, and behavioral skills are the foundations for academic success. Essentially, you cannot teach a student who is unready to learn. Marlow et al. also identified attitudes and barriers to the collaboration movement such as time constraints, lack of clear guidelines, and confusion regarding role definitions, job descriptions, and evaluations. Similarly, Davis and Garrett (1998) described concrete ways that school counselors can educate and collaborate with teachers on their roles as student advocates. Specifically, they described the importance of the consulting and collaborative roles of school counselors as a way of enlisting teachers in a cofacilitation process for meeting the developmental needs of students. Ponec and Brock (2000) stressed the importance of teamwork among the professionals at school. Collaborating for student success is critical if we want to improve school counseling services and increase student advocacy and achievement.

Teachers-in-Training Questions

Unfortunately, most teachers and administrators do not seek and are not required to take course work in school counseling (Gibson & Mitchell, 1995). Prospective teachers and principals can graduate from their education training programs with no exposure to school counseling programs or to how school counselors serve in the role of advocate for students and student achievement. Many classroom teachers feel uncertain about the goals of the school counseling program in their schools and lack communication and involvement in the counseling program. The results of Gibson's (1990) study, in which teachers' opinions about school counseling programs were elicited, indicated that teachers generally felt uninformed about the school counselors' functions. The biggest concern highlighted in this study was the pervasive failure of school counselors to adequately communicate their roles and responsibilities, especially when it came to advocating for student achievement and success. Additional training in the areas of effective implementation of comprehensive school counseling programs and appropriate networking and integration of the school counseling program should be sought by new professionals. The success of the program and the effectiveness of the school counselor are directly impacted by the perceptions of administrators, teachers, and staff. Professional development is an ongoing, lifelong process for school counselors to stay of abreast of current trends and best practices for effective programming.

Teachers' Roles and School Counseling

Teacher support and participation are crucial to any program that involves students. The school counseling program is no exception. The teacher, more than any other professional in the school community, is in the best position to know the students. Teachers communicate with students on a daily basis and can establish relationships based on mutual trust and respect. Teacher support can be especially influential in determining how students view and use the services of a schools' counseling program. Teachers are a major source of student referrals, and counseling programs must therefore depend on alert faculty to ensure that students with counseling needs will not go unnoticed or unreferred. Teachers should orient and encourage students to seek and follow through with counselor assistance (Gibson & Mitchell, 1995). Professional school counselors are encouraged to meet with faculty and staff routinely to keep channels of communication open regarding the needs within the school and the counseling services available (Sink, 2005).

Areas of Potential Conflict

Teachers and counselors, however, do have different roles and job descriptions. That being the case, it is natural that conflict may develop between them. Researchers (Benshoff, Poidevant, & Cashwell, 1994; Cole, 1991; Idol & Baran, 1992; Kaplan, 1995; Studer & Allton, 1996; West & Cannon, 1988) have identified areas as having potential for conflict between teachers and counselors as (a) educational goals, (b) resources, (c) consultation efforts, (d) confidentiality, and (e) discipline.

Educational goals. Goals for educational and personal success are often perceived by teachers and counselors as being mutually exclusive. A teacher may not understand how personal counseling may benefit a student's academic learning. On the other hand, the counselor may view particular instructional practices in the classroom as detrimental to the student. An example might be that a student feels anxious about reading aloud in the classroom. The teacher is adamant that the student must complete the assignment and develop public speaking skills. The student feels trapped and comes to the counselor suffering from an anxiety attack. The student asks for the counselor's support. The counselor consults with the teacher and asks the teacher to consider some alternatives, such as allowing the student to tape record the readings or reducing the size of the audience. One hopes that the teacher, counselor, and student can agree to work together slowly and deliberately to build the student's confidence and ability to read aloud in class. Professional school counselors need to attend educational venues regularly to maintain professional skills and develop new areas of expertise. Conferences, in-services, and course work are all great ways to improve and expand one's repertoire of interventions and techniques (Remley & Herlihy, 2005).

Resources. Teachers and counselors often compete for the same limited resources, including time. Although time with students is the main conflict, competition may also come in the form of vying for money, equipment, supplies, physical space, and support services. An example might be competing with other faculty for budget money. How big is your piece of the pie? The resource teacher requests a budget based on the number of identified kids, which is often equivalent to a regular classroom teacher's budget. In other words, they are both providing for some 25 children. The school counselor, on the other hand, needs to advocate for the program and its mission to serve the entire school population. School counselors need materials for classroom guidance lessons (often used by 2 to 4 classes or 50 to 100 children at each grade level); small group activities; resource books for students, parents, and faculty; and so forth.

Consultation efforts. The roles of teacher and counselor are quite different from one another, and yet, when either professional takes on the role of consultant, there is considerable overlap. Unless teachers and counselors communicate and collaborate, there can be confusing or mixed messages provided to students, parents, and other educational and community supports. For example, a teacher has a student who is falling behind in math. The teacher requests that the parents make the student spend more time on homework, taking away privileges if necessary, until all assignments are complete. The counselor, meanwhile, learns that the student's grandfather recently died and encourages the parents to spend more unconditional time with their child and not to force homework battles. Both teacher and counselor need to share information and strategies on how best to support the student's academic as well as personal needs.

Confidentiality. Confidentiality is an ethical cornerstone in the counseling relationship. Confidentiality limits the information that counselors can share with teachers, parents, and administrators. A counselor promises not to reveal a client's information to anyone without the client's permission unless (a) the counselor's professional opinion is that the client intends harm to him or herself or another; (b) the client is the possible victim of abuse; or (c) the counselor is using the counseling information in clinical supervision. Teachers may not understand that counselors must abide by certain legal and ethical obligations. Unfortunately, from a teacher's perspective, confidentiality in the school setting limits the information available for sharing and problem solving. The counselor may appear self-important and uncooperative to the teacher who, on the other hand, is asked to share all information openly. School counselors need to be clear about their ethical and legal obligations. You will earn the respect and trust of others by handling situations as if they involved you personally. When and how would you want someone to share information about you? Advise others that you will divulge relevant information as needed, and ask them to trust your professional judgment. Your reputation will reflect your integrity.

Discipline. Counselors look for causes of behavior and identify poor self-esteem, dysfunctional families, and other interpersonal or intrapsychic issues that can lead to offending behavior. Counselors see discipline as student self-management. Counselors promote self-responsibility, behavior control, and personal accountability for actions. Teachers, on the other hand, are more whole-group student advocates who work to provide a safe, orderly, and productive learning environment for all. Teachers tend to look at the effects of the behavior and of how it may impede learning for others. Parents want the school to impart fair and equitable discipline that is consistent with community values. The best way to resolve tensions around discipline is to implement a schoolwide discipline program that is positive and proactive. Incentives and/or privileges range all the way from individual students, to teams, to grade levels, and to schoolwide achievements. A discipline committee consisting of students, parents, and faculty would monitor and refine the program as needed.

The best way to resolve discipline issues and many others is to conduct your school counseling program in a collaborative, consultation fashion. A collaborative relationship with teachers and administration is integral to implementing an effective school counseling program.

Collaborative Consultation

An effective school counseling program is based on mutual respect, trust, and communication between school professionals. Because the school counseling program is the responsibility of counselors, they must initiate communication and interaction with teachers and administrators; they must actively pursue teachers' and principals' involvement and assistance to prevent and avoid conflicts. One method used effectively in schools to promote communication among school personnel is called collaborative consultation. Collaborative consultation can occur among any group of teachers, counselors, and administrators. Each professional in the school setting can complement the role of the others to achieve effective interventions and maximum productivity. The intent of collaborative consultation is to generate creative solutions to problems that could not otherwise be generated independently. Collaborative consultation is a process characterized by shared decision making, mutuality, and reciprocity (Bryan, 2005; Davis, 2005; Erford, 2003; West & Cannon, 1988; West, Idol, & Cannon, 1989). Idol, Paolucci-Whitcom, and Nevin (1986) emphasized that diversity of expertise is a valuable resource. Joint approaches to problem solving produce better solutions. Examples of collaborative consultation include child study teams, student assistance programs, and advisory committees. The outcome of this team process will provide comprehensive and effective programs for all students.

School Counselor Education Programs and Local School Partnerships

In an effort to decrease the gap between professional school counselor training and professional school counselor practice, it becomes important for training programs to partner with local school systems in providing professional development opportunities for practicing school counselors. In our program, we accomplish this through providing in-service training to professional school counselors employed in local school systems, as well as making resources available to them through our school counseling library and resource center.

Once a year, our school counseling program faculty provides a 3-hour, in-service training at our university on a current topic germane to professional school counseling. School counselors from local school systems are invited to attend to learn about current issues and receive continuing education credits. School counseling students are required to attend, not only to learn about current information but, more important, to see the importance of how we promote and advocate the school counseling profession. Additionally, the school counseling program faculty is able to model how to organize and deliver a formal presentation to both students and professional school counselors alike. This modeling not only serves to encourage students and practicing school counselors to present themselves, either to their own school systems or at professional conferences, but also fulfills the ethical obligation within the ASCA (2004) for school counselors to contribute to "the development of the profession through sharing of skills, ideas, and expertise with colleagues" (F.2.b.).

Supervision for professional school counselors has been identified as a growing need. Unfortunately, many school counselors do not receive the type of counseling supervision they would like or need. In an effort to provide this growing service, we make available at our state conference a supervision session for those practicing school counselors who are interested in time-limited supervision. These supervision sessions are typically open forums for school counselors to discuss and share their own continued development as professional school counselors, as well as to discuss certain cases with which they are having difficulty. The wealth of school counselor experience in these sessions is the valuable opportunity to connect with one another and share ideas about what is or is not working in their comprehensive developmental guidance and counseling programs. It is also an opportunity to share with practicing school counselors the current trends in the school counseling profession as it relates to school counselor education and training, and is in keeping within the ethical standards of the ASCA (2004) "The professional school counselor . . . actively participates in local, state, and national associations fostering the development and improvement of school counseling" (F.2.a.).

Technology

The technological revolution has and will continue to have a tremendous impact on the school counseling profession and how the role can be performed from career and college counseling to parent involvement. Recognizing this, the ASCA has been diligent in incorporating aspects of technological use in their role and position statements, as well as ethical codes. As a result, more school counseling programs are requiring that their students demonstrate how they plan to incorporate technology within their comprehensive guidance and counseling programs, and state licensing and credentialing boards are requiring current professional school counselors to attend professional development training regarding use of technology.

The Web site for the ASCA contains excellent articles and links to articles regarding a variety of ways that currently practicing school counselors are incorporating technology within their comprehensive school counseling and guidance programs. For example, Stone (2004) described how a high school counselor advocates for closing the achievement gap through technology by using an online career choice module to help students decide which science and math courses to take to achieve their career goals. As a result, this high school counselor noted a 40% increase in African American students choosing higher level math and sciences courses over a 6-year period using the module. Other article links include the use of technology in career, assessment, appraisal, enrollment trends, data collection, and parental communication, as well as strategies for making access to technology an equitable process for all students.

Currently practicing school counselors are also finding that a link to their school counseling Web site from the school's primary Web site is an equally useful and efficient way to connect with parents and caregivers on a variety of topics (e.g., school counseling program mission, ongoing school counseling activities, potential groups for students, and testing information). Professional school counselors should not just know how to use (e.g., navigate) Web sites, but also how to build and maintain their own Web sites as a way to keep their constituents updated and informed on their comprehensive school counseling and guidance programs. Stone (2004) summed up other important aspects regarding the interface of technology and school counseling, stating,

> Technology plays a critical role in providing accurate, timely data from student information management systems. School counselors using this data increase their ability to be another set of eyes and ears for social justice and advocacy; monitoring patterns of course enrollment, student access and success in higher level academics; delivering career and academic advising; managing resources to extend the reach of the school counseling program. (2004, ¶ 2)

Professional Activities in Rural, Suburban, and Urban School Counseling

Professional school counselors work in rural, suburban, and urban school systems, but may not be familiar with the varying needs that each system may require. In changing economic times, school counselors working in rural areas face the erosion of the agricultural and manufacturing industry, while urban school counselors face a crumbling infrastructure, both resulting in poverty for their constituents and a lack of resources in their school systems. Suburban school counselors are no strangers to harder times and dwindling resources as well; however, it is evident through census information that these systems are not facing the same economic struggles as those of the more rural and urban systems (U.S. Census Bureau, 2000).

If the school counseling profession is to continue to advocate and meet the needs of its constituents, then it can do so only as a united profession, with unification coming through understanding the varying challenges and needs of professional school counselors representing all economic and geographical regions of the country. Within the context of how professional activities can help facilitate this understanding, it becomes more important for all school counselors to have mechanisms in place for communicating with one another in order to advocate for and promote the academic, vocational, and personal/social development of their students. Attending state school counseling conferences, sharing ideas and thoughts via school counseling listservs and professional interest networks (PINs), and gaining membership in professional school counseling organizations are all powerful ways to unite the school counseling profession as a voice for advocacy within political and social systems. One recent example of how such united advocacy has worked in the school counseling profession is the development of the Education Trust (2000) fund, an organization promoting and providing funding to school counseling training programs to help close the achievement gap for minority students. Another such example is the National Center for School Counseling Outcome Research (n.d.), which helps train school counselors in documenting how what they do works, so that school counselors can advocate and demonstrate data to school systems for the valuable work that professional school counselors do.

Reiterating once again that school counselors are part of the technological revolution, the ability to stay connected with the school counseling profession is more available now than at any other point in the profession's history. Using our collaborating and coordinating skills, professional school counselors are able to unite and advocate like never before through technology.

Professional Activities in Elementary, Middle, and High School Counseling

Professional school counseling roots are within secondary education, but are now found at all levels of a child's education providing essential services to promote the academic, vocational, and personal social needs. Although professional school counselors at all levels promote these services within their counseling, consulting, coordination, and collaborative roles, clearly children and adolescents have varying developmental needs and tasks. Thus, professional school counselors working within elementary, middle, and high schools may focus their professional activities to reflect advocating these varying developmental needs.

Elementary school counseling typically focuses on promoting and developing children's social skills, self-concept, and problem-solving skills. This is often carried out through group counseling and/or classroom guidance activities. Middle school counseling generally helps to assist in the transition from childhood to preadolescence. Much of the focus in middle school counseling is devoted to helping understand physical and social changes, including sexuality and peer acceptance. Middle school children have the ability to think more abstractly and begin developing rationales for their decision-making processes. In high school counseling, more emphases are placed on the career development of adolescents, preparing them for life after compulsory education, whether it is higher education or work. Although the argument can be rightfully made that all of these aspects are important at all levels of school counseling, differing developmental needs of children and adolescents may influence the degree to which certain services are employed by school counselors within elementary, middle, and high schools, which may in turn influence the degree to which school counselors seek professional activities that are more germane to their individual practice.

Within most professional school counseling organizations, there are distinctions and suborganizations that reflect the differing developmental levels and interests in school counseling. These distinctions provide a forum for professional school counselors to discuss and share issues and ideas specific to their developmental interests, through either newsletters or online listservs and PINs. Equally, school counseling state and national conferences typically have presentations and poster sessions specific to elementary, middle, and high school counseling. Colleges and universities are also increasingly providing advanced training to school counselors through evening, online, and summer school courses and institutes that target specific developmental levels. For example, at our university, we typically offer a summer institute course in creative and expressive arts techniques for use with children and adolescents, being sure that we address how each technique can be used at varying developmental levels. This type of integration helps to educate school counselors on how certain techniques can be used across a wide variety of developmental levels, and in the process, school counselors at all levels begin to see the connections and importance of transitional and developmental needs of all children and adolescents. Practicing school counselors are encouraged to continue their education after their formal training in order to keep up with the latest trends in working with a variety of age levels, and attending local colleges, universities, and workshops helps in promoting this professional identity and advocating for the profession by keeping abreast of current trends and research.

Another avenue for school counselors working at all levels of urban, suburban, and rural schools to continue their professional development, competence, and training is participation in their national, regional, and state counseling organizations.

National, Regional, and State School Counseling Organizations

School counseling programs throughout the country are placing a larger emphasis on school-counselors-in-training becoming more involved in their national, regional, and state school counseling organizations. Research has demonstrated that when students become involved in their professional organizations during their training, they are more likely to continue being involved and participating once they enter the school counseling profession (Erford, 2003).

Other than simply being a member of a professional school counseling organization, students and practicing professional school counselors have opportunities to not only attend conferences, but to present as well. By presenting at local, state, and national conferences, professional school counselors are adhering to the ASCA (2004) ethical standards by contributing "to the development of the profession through the sharing of skills, ideas and expertise with colleagues" (F.2.b.). Two typical methods of presenting at professional school counseling conferences are a formal short presentation and a poster presentation.

Professional and Poster Presentations

Several months before a conference, organizations will put out a call through either a Web site or mailing about upcoming professional conferences. There will be an option to submit a presentation proposal, for which potential presenters can choose between a formal lecture-style presentation and presenting information in poster session format. Either format requires a potential presenter to fill out a brief synopsis of the information to be presented, a title, and a shorter description of the informational session that will appear in the conference bulletin should it be accepted. Contact information is also required for all presenters. Potential presenters then submit their proposals to the organization for blind review, and they will be contacted by the organization on a decision. Typically, national conferences are larger and more competitive, while regional and state conferences stand a better chance of accepting a potential presentation proposal.

Formal lecture-style presentations are generally an hour, allowing time for questions. So, presenters should be prepared to deliver information in an organized and concise manner, realizing that not everything about a chosen topic can possibly be discussed in such a short time. Overhead projectors are generally provided by the conference location, while other technologies (e.g., PowerPoint, digital, video) for presenting are the presenter's responsibility. Presenters should always have handouts regarding the information they are presenting, and the number of handouts needed is hard to predict.

Presenting a poster session generally involves the presenters organizing information in bullet form on a three-winged poster board, with additional material available in handouts. Poster sessions at conferences are generally scheduled for 2 hours and all poster presenters organize their posters on tables so viewers can walk past and read the information. Poster presenters stand next to their posters, greet the viewers, and answer questions about their chosen topics. Usually, having a small supply of candy or trinkets on hand to pass out to viewers is gladly accepted.

Participation in professional organizations through attendance at national, regional, and state conferences not only keeps the school counselor abreast of current trends within the school counseling professional, but more important, brings counselors at all levels together from urban, suburban, and rural schools to share ideas, information, and resources. Through presentations and general mingling, school counselors can learn more about what may work in other schools, especially when it comes to advocating for the profession and how school counselors can be instrumental in advocating success for all students.

Activities in Advocacy

To conclude, we propose here the importance of advocacy in the school counseling role as an underlying component to promote the academic, career, and personal/social achievement of all students regarding the previously mentioned activities. In providing comprehensive and effective programs for all students, school counselors should continue their professional development in a way that incorporates advocacy activities as a focus. Advocacy, as identified by the *ASCA National Model* (ASCA, 2003) is a key leadership role for the school counselor. Generally defined and responsibilities not enumerated, the goal of advocacy is to promote academic, career, and personal/social success for all students. For example, current focus on academic achievement gaps among students based on ethnicity and socioeconomic status (Education Trust, 2000), school safety (Hernadez & Seem, 2004), and student empowerment for social justice are issues for school counselors to address. Social justice issues encompass, but are not limited to oppression, prejudice, racism, inequities in education policies, procedures, resources, and the socialization of students in schools and in communities. These issues illuminate the need for training and the importance of the school counselor's role as an advocate. Most counselor education programs have limited focus in advocacy and social justice issues and response training (Bemak & Chung, 2005; Trusty & Brown, 2005). Training school counselors in these areas would benefit the delivery of comprehensive programming. Additionally, the school counselor would assume a pervasive leadership role in identifying and addressing the unmet needs of students, parents, communities, and schools, thus, supporting and empowering students to learn, feel safe, and achieve with adequate resources and programs.

Advocacy competencies for school counselors have been operationalized and discussed in the context of school counselors' roles (Trusty & Brown, 2005). Advocacy for social justice and equity involves identifying unmet needs and taking action to alleviate the contributing factors that sustain injustices and inequities. The efforts to alleviate or minimize these factors bring about systemic change and place value on individual expression of those involved. To achieve this end, school counselors must be competent in three advocacy areas: (1) disposition, (2) knowledge, and (3) skills (Trusty & Brown). Disposition entails ethical practices and risk taking to join and empower students and parents to eliminate known situations that impede learning and equity. Knowledge of resolving conflict, mediation, resources, and models of advocacy and change are important in advocating for students and parents. Data supported problem identification and effective articulation to administration, boards, and community stakeholders with suggestions for resolution compose the knowledge component. The skill component includes the developmental counseling skills already incorporated in most counselor education training programs: problem identification, effective communication, collaboration, organization, and care of self to avoid burnout. School counselors must be aware of the perceptions of students, families, and systemic underpinnings to promote discussion and change. Presenting the information in an assertive, empathic, and professional manner to support systemic change while maintaining relationships and alliances is one of the challenges of advocacy. Stress management and reduction are important for self-care as advocacy activities can be challenging, demanding, and sometimes frustrating.

A key advocacy activity identified as a critical role for urban school counselors in particular is closing the achievement gaps between students of color and White students and between lower socioeconomic status and higher socioeconomic status students. Individual student needs, school resources, and access to needed services are sources of social injustices, inequities in schools, and the need for advocacy activities (Bemak & Chung, 2005). Some factors that perpetuate these issues include "negligence, low expectations, and job goals and outcomes adopted by school counselors and other school personnel" (p. 197) as important, but may not reflect the consensus of the students and parents. These issues include racism, sexism, violence, bullying, discrimination, and poverty. Confronting these issues as leaders for change, school counselors must assume the role of social advocate for systemic change. Lack of advocacy and social justice training was identified as the culprit for school counselors' perpetuating the injustices and inequities in schools.

Bemak and Chung (2005) proposed three ways to integrate advocacy training into counselor education existing curriculum. Social change, social reform, and school reform can be discussed in required courses and advocacy activity required during practicum and internship placements. This level of training is referred to as preservice training. After the school counselor is working in the field, in-service training reflective of social equity, leadership skills, and advocacy can be provided with emphasis on the academic success of all students including students with disabilities, students of color, and those from challenging socioeconomic situations. Furthermore, school counselor supervision can entail an advocacy focus. The supervisor being a professor or one with advocacy training and experience can support and provide productive feedback for school counselor advocacy activities.

It is essential for school counselors to focus on the academic, social, emotional, economic, political, and other environmental realities of students and families. A student's relationship to the school climate should be viewed from perspectives of personal and interpersonal (student to parent, school personnel, and community). These relationships set the climate of the school, establish acceptable behaviors, and establish policies and procedures for behavioral consequences and school safety.

As advocates, school counselors can design and implement a comprehensive school counseling program based on students', families', communities', and schools' assessed needs. Prevention and intervention programs for all students at each school level can be designed to address issues such as bullying, anger management/leadership skills, mediation, and violence prevention to reach all students. Groups and assemblies, instead of individual sessions, would maximize a school counselor's time and address the increasing number of students assigned to each school counselor (Hernandez & Seem, 2004). Counseling and guidance programs can be utilized in the classroom using evidence-based curriculum. Proactive and not reactive programs (e.g., character education and substance abuse prevention) can provide students with concrete information for good and productive decision making. The goals of these activities will establish or further promote feelings of safety, readiness to learn, and the opportunity of academic success for all students.

References

Amatea, E. S., Daniels, H., Bringman, N., & Vandiver, F. M. (2004). Strengthening counselor-teacher-family connections: The family-school collaborative consultation project. *Professional School Counseling, 8,* 47–56.

American School Counselor Association. (2003). *The ASCA national model: A framework for school counseling programs.* Alexandria, VA: Author.

American School Counselor Association. (2004). *Ethical standards for school counselors.* Alexandria, VA: Author.

Baker, S. B. (1994). Mandatory teaching experience for school counselors: An impediment to uniform certification standards for school counselors. *Counselor Education and Supervision, 33,* 314–326.

Baker, S. B., & Herr, E. L. (1976). Can we bury the myth? Teaching experience for the school counselor. *The Bulletin of the National Association of Secondary School Principals, 60,* 114–119.

Beesley, D. (2004). Teachers' perceptions of school counselor effectiveness: Collaborating for school success. *Education, 125*(2), 259–270.

Bemak, F., & Chung, R. C. (2005). Advocacy as a critical role for urban school counselors: Working toward equity and social justice. *Professional School Counseling, 8*(3), 196–202.

Benshoff, J. M., Poidevant, J. M., & Cashwell, C. S. (1994). School discipline programs: Issues and implications for school counselors. *Elementary School Guidance and Counseling, 28*, 163–169.

Bryan, J. (2005). Fostering educational resilience and achievement in urban schools through school-family-community partnerships. *Professional School Counseling, 8*(3), 219–227.

Campbell, C. A., & Dahir, C. A. (1997). *Sharing the vision: The national standards for school counseling programs.* Alexandria, VA: American School Counselor Association.

Cohen, N. K. (1961). Must teaching be a prerequisite for guidance? *Counselor Education and Supervision, 1*, 69–71.

Cole, C. G. (1991). Counselors and administrators: A comparison of roles. *NASSP Bulletin, 75*(534), 5–13.

Davis, K. M. (2005). School-based consultation. In C. A. Sink (Ed.), *Contemporary school counseling: Theory, research, and practice* (pp. 297–326). Boston: Lahaska Press.

Davis, K. M., & Garrett, M. T. (1998). Bridging the gap between school counselors and teachers: A proactive approach. *Professional School Counseling, 1*(5), 54–56.

Education Trust. (1999). *National initiative for transforming school counseling.* Washington, DC: Author.

Erford, B. T. (Ed.). (2003). *Transforming the school counseling profession.* Upper Saddle River, NJ: Merrill Prentice Hall.

Gibson, R. (1990). Teacher opinions of high school guidance programs: Then and now. *The School Counselor, 37*, 248–255.

Gibson, R. L., & Mitchell, M. H. (1995). *Introduction to counseling and guidance* (4th ed.). Englewood Cliffs, NJ: Prentice-Hall, Inc.

Guerra, P. (1998, February). Revamping school counselor education: The DeWitt Wallace-Reader's Digest fund. *Counseling Today, 19*, 36.

Hernadez, T. J., & Seem, S. R. (2004). A safe school climate: A systemic approach and the school counselor. *Professional School Counseling, 7*(4), 256–262.

Idol, L., & Baran, S. (1992). Elementary school counselor and special educators consulting together: Perilous pitfalls or opportunities to collaborate. *Elementary School Guidance and Counseling, 26*, 202–213.

Idol, L., Paolucci-Whitcom, P., & Nevin, A. (1986). *Collaborative consultation.* Austin, TX: Pro-Ed.

Kaplan, L. (1995). Principals versus counselors: Resolving tensions from different practice models. *The School Counselor, 42*, 261–267.

Kendrick, R., Chandler, J., & Hatcher, W. (1994). Job demands, stressors, and the school counselor. *The School Counselor, 41*, 365–369.

Kurpius, D. J., & Rozecki, T. (1992). Outreach, advocacy, and consultation: A framework for prevention and intervention. *Elementary School Guidance and Counseling, 26*, 176–189.

Lambie, G. W., & Williamson, L. L. (2004). The challenge to change from guidance counseling to professional school counseling: A historical proposition. *Professional School Counseling, 8*(2), 124–131.

Marlow, L., Bloss, K., & Bloss, D. (2000). Promoting social and emotional competency through teacher/counselor collaboration. *Education, 120*(4), 668–676.

Myrick, R. D. (1993). *Developmental guidance and counseling: A practical approach.* Minneapolis, MN: Educational Media Corporation.

National Board for Certified Counselors. (n.d.). *National counselor exam.* Retrieved May 1, 2005, from http://www.nbcc.org/exams/nce.htm

National Board for Professional Teaching Standards. (n.d.). *National board certification standards.* Retrieved May 1, 2005, from http://www.nbpts.org/standards/nbcert.cfm

National Center for School Counseling Outcome Research. (2000). Retrieved May 5, 2005, from http://www.umass.edu/schoolcounseling/2004ASCAppts.htm

National Education Commission on Time and Learning. (1994). *Prisoners of time.* Retrieved May 1, 2005, from http://www.ed.gov/pubs/PrisonersOfTime/index.html

Ponec, D. L., & Brock, B. L. (2000). Relationships among elementary school counselors and principals: A unique bond. *Professional School Counseling, 3*(3), 208–210.

Praxis. (n.d.). *Praxis II: Specialty exams.* Retrieved May 1, 2005, from http://www.ets.org/praxis/prxstate.html

Remley, T. P., Jr., & Herlihy, B. (2005). *Ethical, legal and professional issues in counseling* (2nd ed.). Upper Saddle River, NJ: Pearson.

The Rural School and Community Trust. (n.d.). General facts about rural education in the 50 states. Retrieved March 22, 2006, from http://www.ruraledu.org

Shoffner, M. F., & Briggs, M. K. (2001). An interactive approach for developing interprofessional collaboration: Preparing school counselors. *Counselor Education & Supervision, 40*(3), 193–201.

Shoffner, M. F., & Williamson, R. D. (2000). Engaging preservice school counselors and principals in dialogue and collaboration. *Counselor Education & Supervision, 40*(2), 128–141.

Sink, C. (2005). *Contemporary school counseling: Theory, research and practice.* Boston: Lahaska Press.

Smith, S. L. (1994). *Professional issues in counseling: Teaching experience as a requirement for the certification of school counselors* (Report No. CG026268). Greensboro: University of North Carolina. (ERIC Document Reproduction Service No. ED383974)

Snyder, B. A., & Daly, T. P. (1993). Restructuring guidance and counseling programs. *The School Counselor, 41*, 36–41.

Stone, C. B. (2004, March). Hands-on high-tech advocacy. *ASCA School Counselor*. Retrieved December 14, 2005, from http://www.schoolcounselor.org/article.asp?article=740&paper=91&cat=137

Studer, J. R., & Allton, J. A. (1996). The professional school counselor: Supporting and understanding the role of the guidance program. *NASSP Bulletin, 80*(581), 53–60.

Thompson, R. A. (2002). *School counseling: Best practices for working in the schools* (2nd ed.). New York: Brunner-Routledge.

Towner-Larsen, R., Granaello, D. H., & Sears, S. J. (2000). Supply and demand for school counselors: Perceptions of public school administrators. *Professional School Counseling, 3*(4), 270–276.

Trusty, J., & Brown, D. (2005). Advocacy competencies for professional school counselors. *Professional School Counseling, 8*(3), 259–265.

U.S. Census Bureau. (2000). *United States Census 2000*. Retrieved December 14, 2006, from http://www.census.gov/main/www/cen2000.html

U.S. Department of Education. (2001). *No Child Left Behind Act of 2001*. Retrieved March 23, 2006, from http://www.ed.gov/offices/OESE/esea/

Welch, I. D., & McCarroll, L. (1993). The future role of school counselors. *The School Counselor, 41*, 48–53.

West, J. F., & Cannon, G. (1988). Essential collaborative consultation competencies for regular and special educators. *Journal of Learning Disabilities, 21*, 45–53.

West, J. F., Idol, L., & Cannon, G. (1989). *Collaboration in the schools: An inservice and preservice curriculum for teachers, support staff, and administrators*. Austin, TX: Pro-Ed.

Williamson, L. L. (1998). School counseling—Is teaching experience really necessary? *Texas Counseling Journal, 26*, 28–33.

AUTHOR INDEX

A

Abbey, A., 719
Abbott, P., 806
Abbott, R. D., 654
Abeel, M., 235
Aber, J. L., 701
Aber, M. S., 146
Abercrombie, S., 347
Aboud, F. E., 588
Abrahamse, A., 95
Abrams, B. C., 488
Abrams, K., 636, 642, 644–645
Abreu, J. M., 68, 170, 185
Ackerman, B. P., 146
Ackerman, C., 546
Adair, M. K., 433
Adalbjarnardottir, S., 600
Adamowski, K., 464, 467, 470–473, 476
Adams, A. M., 185
Adams-Byars, J., 531
Adelman, H., 24, 83, 89, 296, 704, 769–771, 800
Adler, A., 404, 433
Adler, P., 501, 590–591, 677
Adler, P. A., 501, 590–591, 677
Aeby, V. G., 767
Ager, J., 56, 181, 564
Agius, E., 719
Agnew, T., 313, 315, 317
Agran, M., 162
Agras, W. S., 231
Ahia, C. E., 17
Ahluwalia, J. S., 777
Ahola-Sidaway, J., 505
Ainsworth, M. S., 655, 660
Airasian, P. W., 768
Aizcorbe, A. M., 270
Ajzen, I., 195
Akbar, N., 200

Akinbami, L. J., 223
Akin-Little, K. A., 388
Akman, J. S., 136, 140
Akos, P., 16, 19, 22–23, 28, 162–163, 171, 214, 413, 425, 499, 503–504, 604, 767, 771
Alagiri, P., 250
Alamilla, S., 751
Alan Guttmacher Institute, 243, 245
Albee, G. W., 382, 384, 389
Albers, A. B., 146, 149
Albert, B., 329
Albertini, V. I., 103
Aldarondo, F., 128–129, 131
Alder, N., 355
Alderman, G. L., 344
Alexander, C. M., 767
Alexander, D., 506
Alexander, J., 452
Alexander, K., 149, 639
Alexander, S. P., 600
Ali, S. R., 145–147, 151
Aligne, C. A., 223
Allan, J., 406
Allberg, W. R., 617–618
Allen, B. A., 640
Allen, J., 391, 398, 659
Allen, M., 459, 465, 467
Allen, S. J., 481
Allen-Meares, P., 322
Allington, R. L., 263, 267
Allton, J. A., 815, 817
Alson, A., 56
Alter, M. R., 614
Altmaier, E. M., 507
Alvarado, R., 388–389
Amaral, G., 235–236
Amatea, E. S., 89, 816
American Association of Suicidologists (ASS), 614
American Association of University Women (AAUW), 437, 595–596

American Counseling Association (ACA), 419, 442, 792
American Diabetic Association (ADA), 224–225, 229
American Psychiatric Association (APA), 382, 401
American Psychological Association (APA), 230–231, 272, 383, 432, 443, 786
American School Counselor Association (ASCA), xxix, 2, 9, 11–12, 15–18, 37–42, 45–46, 51, 163, 167–168, 272, 293, 295, 313–314, 413, 419, 431, 442, 452, 467–468, 471, 481, 533, 551, 556, 563, 597–598, 603–604, 628, 651, 668, 742, 744, 747, 758–759, 765, 785, 788, 792, 799–801, 806, 812, 818, 821
Amerikaner, M., 433
Ames, L., 432
Ananiadou, K., 687
Ancis, J. R., 189
Anctil, T. M., 157
Andersen, A., 229
Anderson, A., 604
Anderson, B. T., 505
Anderson, C. A., 698
Anderson, G. E., 640
Anderson, S., 213
Anderson, S. M., 20
Andrews, D. W., 698
Andrews, M. F., 481
Andrulis, D. P., 221
Angold, A., 149
Annunziata, J., 598
Ansbacher, H. L., 487–488
Anstrom, K., 271, 322
Antonak, R., 159, 161
Aponte, J. F., 555
Appleton, V. E., 412
Arata, C. M., 591
Arbona, C., 271
Archer, J., 695
Argo, T., 537
Arima, H., 413
Arkowitz, H., 721
Arman, J. F., 433
Armstrong, D., 463
Armstrong, S. A., 18, 406, 517
Arni, T. J., 282
Arnold, B., 68
Arnold, D. H., 696
Aro, H. M., 195–196
Aronson, J., 56, 183–184, 590
Arredondo, P., 18, 171, 324, 344, 435, 786
Arrington, E. G., 129
Arrow, H., 111
Arroyo, C. G., 56, 180, 195
Arsenio, W. F., 674
Arthur, M. S., 719
Ary, D. V., 249

Asay, P. A., 97
Aseltine, R. H., 619–620
Asendorpf, J. B., 656, 660
Asher, S. R., 116, 592–593, 697
Aspy, C. B., 20
Aspy, D., 357, 363
Association of American Universities, 21
Assouline, S. G., 535
Astin, A., 545
Astone, N. M., 147
Astramovich, R. L., 18
Atkinson, D. R., 97, 106, 182, 274, 323, 347, 507, 643, 773
Atlas, R., 680, 698
Ato, M., 675
Attneave, C., 450
Aubrey, R. F., 497
August, D., 186, 188
August, G. J., 383
Auinger, P., 223
Aumiller, K., 592
Avery, L., 542
Awender, M. A., 501
Axline, V., 521
Ayers, R., 699
Ayers, W., 699
Aylward, L. K., 467
Ayyash-Abdo, H., 463
Azcoitia, C. M., 353

B

Baca, L. M., 132
Bacchus, N., 86
Bachman, J. G., 717–719
Baer, E. C., 16
Baer-Barkley, K., 413
Baerger, D. R., 803
Baerveldt, C., 699
Baggerly, J., 22–23
Bagwell, C. L., 588, 592–593
Bailey, D. B., 166
Bailey, J. A., 718
Bailey, K. A., 804
Bajt, T. R., 786
Baker, J. A., 351, 353, 375
Baker, L., 259
Baker, M., 629
Baker, S., 197, 759
Baker, S. B., 11, 101–102, 127, 149–150, 163, 209, 276, 293–297, 397, 409, 431, 481, 497, 510, 642, 646–647, 811–812
Baldwin, B., 464
Baldwin, J. D., 247

Baldwin, J. I., 247
Balkin, R., 18, 406, 517
Ballast, D. L., 10
Ballestero, V., 467, 758
Ballif-Spanvill, B., 388
Baltes, P. B., 280
Balthazor, M., 589
Baltimore, M., 22–23
Balvanz, J., 517
Bamaca-Gomez, M. Y., 591
Bamossy, G., 148
Banaji, M., 170
Bandura, A., 161, 197, 211, 213, 278, 285, 391, 433, 487, 590, 675, 678, 685, 697–698, 727
Bank, L., 593
Banks, R. W., 322, 368
Baptiste, D. A., 100
Baptiste, L., 322
Baran, S., 817
Barbee, P. W., 19, 22
Bar-El, O., 410, 413–414
Barkhaus, R. S., 433
Barkley, R. A., 696
Barlow, S. H., 433
Barnes, P., 23
Barnett, K., 773
Barnett, W. S., 381, 390, 563
Baron-Cohen, S., 676
Barrera, M., Jr., 388–389
Barret, R. L., 312, 314
Barret, R. L, 314
Barrish, H. H., 704
Barry, C. M., 588
Barry, T. D., 702
Barth, R. P., 639
Bartini, M., 677
Bartolomucci, C. L., 678, 685
Barton, C., 29, 385
Barton, P., 199
Barton, P. E., 766
Basile, S. K., 7, 9
Baska, A., 531, 542
Baskhar, R., 170
Baskin, T., 271, 773
Bason, C. J., 433
Bass, C., 56–57, 127, 130, 565–566, 568–569
Bass, G. M., 542
Bates, J. E., 146, 695, 697
Bateson, G., 519
Battistich, V., 352, 354–357, 360–361, 368–369, 699, 706
Bauer, A. L., 20
Bauer, S. R., 411, 413
Bauman, K. E., 590–591
Bauman, L. J., 222
Bauman, S., 139, 178, 398, 613, 617, 760–761, 766

Baumeister, R., 352, 655–656, 659–660
Baumrind, D., 697
Baydar, N., 703
Bay-Hinitz, A. K., 705
Bayles, K., 695
Baytops, J. I., 146–147, 537
Beale, A., 352, 366
Beale, A. V., 501
Bean, S., 652
Beane, J. A., 26
Beardslee, W. R., 617
Bearman, P. S., 250
Beautrais, A. L., 462
Beauvais, F., 184, 548
Bebeau, M. J., 211
Beck, A., 625
Beck, A. T., 433
Beck, J., 625
Becker, B. E., 635, 641, 767
Becker, H., 683
Becker, H. J., 87–88
Beech, B. M., 130, 195
Beesley, D., 431, 443, 815
Behring, S. T., 492
Beidel, D. C., 599
Bekerman, Z., 80, 83, 91
Belaire, C., 17
Beland, K., 682–683
Belcastro, F., 540–541
Belgrave, F. Z., 181
Bell, E. L. J. E., 111
Bell, J. E., 450
Bell, L. A., 536–537
Bell, M., 260
Bell, S. K., 604
Bellamy, N., 388–389
Bell-Dolan, D. J., 592
Bellini, J., 310
Bemack, F., 91
Bemak, F., 18, 63, 69, 79, 102, 104–107, 146, 170, 185–186, 190, 197, 214, 301, 370–371, 433, 645–647, 767, 821–822
Benally, A., 535
Benally, N., 545
Benard, B., 411, 769
Ben Ari, R., 89
Benasich, A. A., 698
Benbow, C., 537–539, 552
Ben-David, M., 433
Benedetto, A. E., 130–132
Bennett, D. S., 695
Bennett, L., 437
Bennis, W., 470
Benshoff, J. M., 23, 315–316, 817
Benson, P. L., 384, 652, 667, 771
Benz, M. R., 165, 171

Berdahl, J. L., 111
Berenson, G. S., 229
Berg, B., 23
Bergan, J. R., 332, 487
Bergeron, L., 619
Bergin, J. J., 433
Berglund, M. L., 366, 381, 655
Berk, L., 401
Berkovitz, I. H., 413
Berkowitz, L., 698
Berla, N., 181
Berlin, B. M., 249
Berliner, D. C., 10
Berlyne, D. E., 519
Berman, M. E., 695
Bernal, M. E., 563, 565, 567
Bernard, C., 20
Bernard, J. M., 25, 303, 312, 316–317
Berndt, D. J., 549
Berndt, T. J., 588
Bernhardt, M., 406
Bernstein-Moore, R., 329
Berry, J. W., 58, 68–70, 96–97, 100–101, 184
Bertalanffy, L. von, 449, 489
Berthiaume, C., 619
Besett-Alesch, T. M., 18
Best, K. M., 771
Betancourt, H., 128
Bettinger, S., 525
Betz, N. E., 272, 278, 286, 505, 772
Beymer, L., 199
Bhana, A., 146
Bhandari, S., 220
Bhattacharya, G., 98–99
Bhopal, R. S., 249
Bickmore, K., 603
Biddle, B. J., 10, 112
Biederman, J., 405
Bierman, K. L., 592–593
Biever, J., 406
Biglan, A., 249
Bikos, L. H., 507
Bilides, D. G., 412, 426
Billops, A., 506
Billy, J. O. G., 249
Bina, C., 60
Bird, J., 624
Birman, D., 81, 84, 86–87
Birmingham, C. L., 231
Birmingham, S. M., 355
Bishop, J. B., 510
Bjorkqvist, K., 676–677
Black, B., 435
Black, K. A., 589
Black, M., 382
Blackbourn, J. M., 166

Blackburn, A. C., 546
Blackburn, J. A., 674
Blackman, L., 303, 316
Blackmon, S. M., 322–325
Blair, C., 640
Blalock, G., 161
Blanco, M., 383–384
Blatt, S. J., 490, 656
Bleuer, J. C., 52
Bliss, H. A., 222
Block, P., 343
Bloom, B. S., 432
Bloome, D., 259–260, 264
Bloomquist, M. L., 383
Bloss, D., 816
Bloss, K., 816
Blum, D. J., 433
Blum, R. W., 220, 231–232, 253, 652
Blumenson, R., 463
Blumenthal, S. J., 616
Blustein, D. L., 29, 150, 281, 498, 772
Bobby, C. L., 15
Bochner, S., 96, 100
Bodenhorn, N., 209, 212, 215
Boekeloo, B., 247
Boes, S., 21–22
Bogat, G. A., 412
Bogenschneider, K., 53, 55, 384
Bogliatto, C., 230
Bogo, R. J., 459, 619
Boivin, M., 588, 592
Bok, D., 56, 564
Boldizar, J. P., 696
Boldosser, S., 411
Bolton, B., 161
Bolton, I. M., 462–463, 474–475
Bolyard, C. W., 433
Bonde, L. O., 347
Bonica, C., 595
Bonny, A. E., 659
Bonstead-Bruns, M., 87
Bordeau, W. C., 127–131, 179
Borders, D., 310, 315–316
Borders, L. D., 19, 178, 203, 302, 312–313, 316, 385, 388, 755–756
Bordieu, P., 51
Bordonaro, A., 235
Borman, G. D., 53
Bornstein, M. H., 147
Borowsky, I. W., 618
Borquez, J., 146
Borum, R., 804
Boscardin, M. L., 170, 188
Bostain, D., 383
Bosworth, K., 370
Bouchey, H. A., 594

Boulton, M. J., 675, 678
Boutte, G., 385
Bouwsema, M., 653
Bowen, M. L., 163
Bowers, J., 18, 24, 38
Bowl, E., 17
Bowman, P., 186
Boxer, P., 127, 702
Boyce, W. T., 149
Boyd, J. D., 312
Boyd, W. L., 84
Boyer, E. L., 37, 453, 507
Boykin, 200
Boykin, A. W., 640
Boyle, M. H., 101
Boys, A., 718
Bozylinski, K., 229
Brabeck, M., 770–771, 778
Bradley, C., 299, 301, 433
Bradley, F. O., 179
Bradley, L. J., 23, 367–369, 371
Brain, P. F., 695
Braithwaite, R., 777
Brake, K. J., 433
Brammer, L. M., 340
Bramon-Bosch, E., 231
Brand, S., 653
Brandt, R., 353
Brannock, J. C., 136
Brantley, L. S., 413
Brantley, P. S., 413
Braswell, L., 601
Bray, J. H., 718
Brecheisen, B. K., 510–511
Brechman-Toussaint, M., 599
Brehm, K., 385
Breland, M. E., 472
Brendgen, M., 593–594
Brener, N. D., 249, 466
Brenner, B. R., 97
Brent, D. A., 475, 626
Breton, J., 619
Brewer, M., 616
Brewster, K. L., 249
Brey Love, K., xxix, 673
Briar-Lawson, K., 767
Bridger, R., 351
Bridges, S. K., 592
Briggs, M. K., 598, 815
Brigman, G., 18, 46, 333, 341–342, 406, 413, 451, 485, 746, 757, 766
Bringman, N., 89, 816
Brinton, B., 593
Brislin, R., 487
Britto, M. T., 659
Britton, T. P., 20

Britzman, M. J., 369, 768
Brock, S. E., 459, 464–465, 472–474
Brody, P., 472
Bronfenbrenner, U., xxviii, xxx, 52, 82, 84, 128, 145, 182, 279, 366, 383, 489, 564, 568, 597, 603, 653, 675, 679, 682, 686, 778
Brook, J. S., 719
Brookmeyer, K. A., 652
Brooks, A., 474–475
Brooks, D. K., 21
Brooks, F., 677
Brooks, V., 433
Brooks-Gunn, J., 146, 383, 652, 698
Brooks-McNamara, V., 645
Brotherton, W. D., 17
Brott, P. E., 309, 312
Broussard, T., 695
Brown, A., 10
Brown, B. B., 587–591, 594
Brown, C. H., 704
Brown, D., 150, 497, 508
Brown, D., 330, 340, 482–493
Brown, D., 4, 9–11, 215, 325, 821
Brown, E., 405
Brown, E. D., 146
Brown, J. L., 701
Brown, K., 406
Brown, M., 676
Brown, M. M., 696
Brown, M. T., 146–147, 511
Brown, N. M., 695
Brown, R. T., 226
Brown, S., 53, 329
Brown, S. D., 201, 278, 282–284, 286, 505, 510–511
Brown, T. G., 732
Brown-Chidsey, R., 170
Brownell, C. A., 587
Bruce, B., 231
Bruce, M. A., 18
Bruckner, H., 250
Bryan, J., 20, 152, 187, 214, 353, 370, 772–773, 818
Bryant, S., 481
Bubenzer, D. L., 21
Buboltz, W. C., Jr., 150
Bucci, E., 675
Bucci, M., 677
Buchanan, R., 81
Buck, M. R., 603
Buckley, K. W., 401
Buckley, T. R., xxviii, 111, 604, 768
Buckman, R., 599
Buckroyd, J., 412
Buehler, R. E., 698
Buescher, T. M., 542
Buhrmester, D., 588, 659
Buhs, E., xxix, 597–598, 673

Buka, S. L., 229
Bukowski, W. M., 587–588, 592, 594, 675, 678
Bull, F. C., 229
Bullis, M., 300, 302–303
Bumbarger, B., 389
Bumby, K., 804
Burdette, H. L., 229
Burgess, A. W., 464, 592–593
Buriel, R., 186
Burish, P., 704
Burke, B. L., 721
Burke, J. D., 693
Burlingame, G. M., 413, 433
Burnham, J. J., 294, 326, 413, 433, 758–759
Burnham, W., 9
Burns, L., 20
Burt, K., 467
Burwinkle, T., 229
Bushman, B. J., 698
Butchart, R. E., 178
Butler, J., 777
Butler, S. K., 17, 83, 96, 103, 105–108, 322–323, 325–326
Butts, H. F., 116
Byars-Winston, A. M., 511
Bybee, D., 181
Bynum, T. S., 638
Byrne, D., 675

C

Cabello, B., 492
Cadinu, M., 677
Cadwallader, T. W., 598
Cafaro, C. S., 615
Caffray, C. M., 412
Cairns, B. D., 644, 677, 697
Cairns, R. B., 644, 677, 697
Calderon, M., 186
Caldwell, 130
Caldwell, C. H., 116
Caldwell, K. A., 588
Caldwell, L. D., 195, 197, 200, 203
Caldwell, R. A., 412
Callahan, C. M., 535–537
Callahan, P., 808
Callan Stoiber, K., 483
Calvert, C., 506
Camacho-Gingerich, A., 527
Camburn, D., 249
Campanelli, M., 523
Campbell, C., 37–38, 46, 166, 197–198, 367, 398, 402, 406, 409, 411, 413, 421, 431, 501, 746, 757, 765–766, 812

Campbell, T., 335
Canetto, S. S., 384
Canino, G., 629
Cannon, G., 817–818
Capaldi, D., 593
Caplan, G., 333, 340, 345–346, 381–382, 450, 460, 464–465, 468, 482, 485–486
Caplan, M., 166
Caplan, R. B., 333, 340, 345–346, 382, 482, 485
Cappella, E., xxix, 693, 706
Capps, R., xxvii
Capps, S., 412
Capuzzi, D., 197, 463, 468, 470, 615, 625–626, 786, 805
Carey, J. C., 177, 188, 190, 271, 321, 324, 597–599, 602, 604
Carey, K., 330
Carkhuff, R. R., 20
Carlin, J. B., 230
Carlozzi, A. F., 19
Carlson, J., 23
Carlson, J., 385–386, 388
Carlson, J. D., 404
Carlson, J. M., 404
Carlson, N. S., 15, 18
Carlstrom, A. H., 286
Carney, J. V., 116, 462, 467, 469
Carpenter, S. L., 214, 353
Carpenter-Aeby, T., 767
Carr, E. G., 696
Carreon, A., 186
Carroll, J., 503, 518–520
Carroll, J. J., 20
Carroll, M. D., 228
Carter, B. F., 474–475
Carter, J. A., 20
Carter, P. L., 148, 153
Carter, R. T., xxviii, 28, 66–67, 71, 102, 111–112, 115–119, 121–122, 730
Carver, K., 594
Cary, P. T., 677
Casali, S. B., xxx, 129, 184
Casey, D., 462
Casey, J. A., 23
Casey-Cannon, S., 60, 70, 127–128
Cashwell, C., 17, 817
Caspi, A., 695, 698, 700
Cass, V. C., 136
Cassel, R., 403
Casson, J., 524
Casten, R., 563
Castro, F. G., 388–389
Catalano, R., 366, 381, 389–390, 564, 655, 659, 699
Catania, J. A., 596
Cates, D., 158
Cauce, A. M., 697

Cavell, T., 655
Ceballo, R., 146
Ceccarossi, K., 113
Center for Health and Health Care in Schools, 235
Center for Mental Health in the Schools, 622
Centers for Disease Control and Prevention (CDC), 219, 223–224, 227–228, 233, 236, 243, 245, 247, 249, 614, 622, 767
Cerezo, F., 675
Cernkovich, S. A., 591, 654
Chambers, J. M., 693
Chan, W., 234
Chandler, J., 413, 815
Chapman, B. E., 136
Charach, A., 680–681
Charkow Bordeau, W., 642
Charney, R. S., 353
Chartrand, J. M., 277, 772
Chatterji, P., 412, 605
Chaves, A. P., 150
Chavez, D., 186
Chavous, T. M., 56, 116–117, 127–128
Chea, P., 185
Cheek, N. H., 590
Chen, E., 149
Chen, L., 588
Chen, S. A., 698
Chen, X., 437, 592
Chen-Hayes, S., 79, 326
Chesswas, R. J. D., 355, 357–358, 363
Chiang, L., 66–67
Child, R. L., 189
Chiu, Y. W., 95–101
Chi-Ying Chung, R., 63, 69, 79, 102, 104–107, 170, 185–186, 190, 197, 433, 646–647, 821–822
Cho, H., 702
Chodorow, N., 655
Choi, Y., 564
Cho Kim, S., 563, 565–567
Choong, Y., 698
Chorpita, B. F., 702
Chrispeels, J. H., 87–88
Christenson, S. L., 490, 636, 641, 644–645
Christopher, J. S., 592
Christy, E. B., 740
Christy, M., 425
Chronister, K. M., 383
Chu, L., 617–618
Chun, K. M., 99
Chung, C. L. E., 101
Chung, I., 630
Chung, R. C.-Y., 63, 69, 79, 102, 104–107, 170, 185–186, 190, 197, 433, 646–647, 821–822
Ciarrochi, J., 211, 213

Cicchetti, D., 381, 389, 660, 767
Cicero, G., 199
Ciechalski, J. C., 12, 433
Clabby, J. F., 604
Claiborn, C. D., 19, 412
Clarini, J., 24
Clark, A., 404
Clark, A. J., 411
Clark, D. B., 718
Clark, J. N., 412
Clark, M. A., 23, 316
Clark, P., 23
Clark, R. D., 460
Clasen, R. D., 543
Clasen, R. E., 543
Claus, R. E., 786
Clauss-Ehlers, C. S., 517–518, 522, 525
Clay, D. L., 226
Clayton, C., 388
Clement, P., 704
Clemente, R., 84–85, 87–88, 329, 344, 347
Clewell, B. C., 698
Clinkenbeard, P. R., 548
Clinton-Sherrod, M., 719
Clore, G. L., 594
Close, W., 29, 281, 284–285, 498, 601, 772
Clune, W. H., 699
Coady, N. F., 20
Coatsworth, 772
Cobb, R., 594
Cobia, D., 21, 295, 517, 667
Cobitz, C., 23
Coccaro, E. F., 695
Cocco, K. M., 226
Cochran, J. L., 521–522
Cochran, L., 282
Cockrell, D. H., 112
Cockrell, K. S., 112, 116, 118
Coder, T. L., 467, 471
Coffey, C., 230
Cohen, D. A., 248
Cohen, E. D., 789
Cohen, G. S., 789
Cohen, J. J., 460, 472, 475
Cohen, M. A., 381
Cohen, N. K., 812
Cohn, S. J., 555
Coie, J. D., 382, 592–593, 695–697
Coker, A. L., 248
Colangelo, N., 531, 533–536, 538–542, 544–547
Colbert, R. D., xxx, 536
Cole, C. G., 817
Cole, K. L., 226
Cole, T. J., 232
Coleman, E., 136

Coleman, H. L. K., xxix, xxvii, xxx, 28–29, 49, 51, 53, 56–59, 70–72, 96, 99, 101, 127–130, 184–185, 219, 243, 253, 259, 271, 323, 351, 563–569, 635, 773
Coleman, J. K., 604
Coleman, J. M., 546
Coletti, S. D., 100
Coll, C. G., 147
Collignon, F., 87–88
Collins, C., 250
Collins, L., 353
Collins, W. A., 589, 594, 660
Collison, B. B., 84–85, 87–88, 769
Colten, M. E., 100
Coltoff, P., 773
Colvin, G., 403, 701, 705–706
Combs, D. C., 19
Comilang, K., 770
Comiskey, P. E., 411
Comly, E., 20
Committee for Children, 681–682, 686
Community Network for Youth Development, 366
Compton, S. N., 149
Conchas, G. Q., 86
Conduct Problems Prevention Research Group, 705–706
Conger, R. D., 146, 286, 698
Conger, R. E., 451
Conley, J. A., 773
Connell, J. P., 697
Connolly, J. A., 590, 594–595
Conoley, C. W., 486
Conoley, J. C., 486
Conrad, J., 592
Constantine, M. G., 101–102, 271–272, 321–325, 368, 773, 788
Constantine, N. A., 246
Conyers, L., 162
Conyne, R. K., 382–384
Cook, D. A., 67, 119
Cook, E. P., 132, 356, 383
Cook, E. T., 704
Cook, J. B., 433
Cook, L., 330, 482
Cooke, D. Y., 128–129
Cooksey, E. C., 249
Cookson, P. W., 352
Coonerty, C., 698
Cooper, C. R., 657
Corey, G., 406, 410, 413–414, 807
Corey, M., 410, 413–414, 807
Cormier, S., 482
Cornelius, J. R., 718
Cornell, D., 383, 469, 476, 694
Cornell, J. L., 247
Cornello, M., 718

Cornely, L., 91
Corrao, J., 795
Cort, K. A., xxix, 95, 635
Cortes, D. E., 97
Cortina, S., 226
Costa, F. M., 654
Costello, J. E., 149
Costigan, T., 701, 705
Cottone, R. R., 786
Couch, J. V., 705
Coupey, S. M., 222
Coutinho, M. J., 168
Cowan, E. W., 343
Cowen, E. L., 383, 389, 409
Cowen, R. L., 382
Cowie, H., 675
Cox, J. A., 21
Cox, M. J., 700
Coyle, E. M., 704
Craig, W., 590, 680, 698, 705
Cramer, S. H., 10, 398, 497, 501, 792
Crawford, I., 71
Crawford, P. B., 228
Creagh, M. G., 271
Crespi, T. D., 19, 312–313, 317
Crews, J., 20
Crick, N. R., 674, 676, 686, 696–697, 702
Crocitto, J. A., 625
Crockett, D., 597, 602
Crone, D. A., 702
Croninger, R. G., 437
Croom, G. L., 138
Crosby, A. E., 462
Crosby, E. G., 476
Crosby, L., 698
Crosnoe, R., 187, 635
Cross, W. E., 564
Crothers, M., 507
Crowe, M., 412
Crutchfield, L. B., 18, 23, 310, 312, 315–316, 421
Csikszentmihalyi, M., 565
Cudeck, R., 230
Cuellar, I., 68
Culbreth, J. R., 18
Cull, J. G., 625
Cunanan, E., 37
Cunningham, C. E., 705
Cunningham, C. M., 535
Cunningham, K., 547
Cunningham, P., 398
Cunningham, R. T., 200
Cunningham-Warburton, P., 66
Curcio, C. C., 758
Curtin, L., 721
Curtis, M. J., 483
Curtiss, S., 696

Cushing, L. S., 706
Cushway, D., 20
Cutler, D. L., 450
Cutler, J., 433

D

Dabrowski, K., 546, 549
Dadds, M., 405, 452
Daggett, W. R., 261–262
Dagley, J. C., 409, 433
Dahir, C. A., 16, 18, 37–38, 41, 43, 45–46, 112, 198, 234, 293, 301, 326, 330, 367, 398, 402, 409, 413, 421, 431, 468–469, 501, 739, 765, 812
Dalton, M. J., 773
Daly, T. P., 816
Damon, W., 366
Dana, R. H., 55, 64, 347
Dancer, D., 452
Dandeneau, C., 340, 351
D'Andrea, L. M., 20, 214
D'Andrea, M., 263, 267, 299, 413
Daniels, H., 89, 816
Dansby, V. S., 413
Dappen, L., 646
Darder, A., 188
Darley, J. M., 147
Darling, N., 697
Darling-Hammond, L., 112, 120, 767
Darlington, P., 180
Darou, W. G., 545
Darveaux, D. X., 704
Dauber, S., 639
D'Augelli, A. R., 138, 140, 604
Daunic, A. P., 603
Davenport, D. S., 17
David, C., 589
Davidman, L., 118
Davidman, P., 118
Davidson, B., 534
Davidson, J., 534
Davidson, M. M., 510
Davidson, W. S., II, 412
Davila, J., 594
Davis, A., 766
Davis, B., 755
Davis, C., 655
Davis, G. A., 235, 531, 533–535, 540, 546
Davis, J. B., 4–6, 276, 432, 497
Davis, J. L., 785–786
Davis, J. M., 462, 472, 475, 623
Davis, K. M., xxix, 811, 816, 818
Davis, L. E., 195, 198
Davis, L. J., 355, 357–358

Davis, T., 431–432, 438
Davis Sosenko, L. J., 358, 363
Dawkins, M. P., 96
Day, J., 789
Day-Vines, N. L., 146–147, 321, 326, 537
Deal, K. H., 22
Deane, F. P., 213
Deater-Deckard, K., 697
Deci, E. L., 160, 280, 286
Decker, R. H., 465, 468
Degirmencioglu, S. M., 589
Dela Cruz, K., 487
De la Luz, M, 566
DeLara, E., 678
De La Rosa, M. R., 383
Delgado-Gaitan, C., 87–88
Deligatti, N., 388
Delisle, J. R., 531, 534–536, 546–550
De Los Santos, J., 183
Delpit, L., 262, 267
Delquadri, J., 149
DeLuca, R. V., 433
Delucchi, K., 354
DeLucia-Waack, J. L., 412
Del Vecchio, A., 189
Delvenne, V., 230
Delworth, U., 22, 25, 310–312
DeMaris, A., 591
DeMartino, R., 620
DeMartino, R. A., 413
De Ment, T. L., 186
De Mersseman, L. M., 704
De Micheli, D., 718
Demmert, W. G., 185
Denbo, S. J., 564
DePaul, J., 776
DeRosier, M. E., 592–593
Derzon, J. H., 701–702
de Shazer, S., 405, 433
Devaney, S. B., 799
Developmental Studies Center, 361
Devine, J., 694
DeVoss, J. A., 481
DeVries, M., 768
Dewey, John, 6
Dexter-Mazza, E., 616
Diamond, J., 230
Diamond, L. M., 136, 594
DiCamillo, M. P., 603
DiClemente, C. C., 721–725
Diemer, M. A., 15, 761
Dietz, W. H., 229, 233
Dillard, J. M., 262
Dimmitt, C., 636–638, 644–645
Dinkmeyer, D. C., Jr., 404
Dinoff, B. L., 19

Dinsmore, J. A., 16
Dishion, T. J., 127, 660, 668, 695–698, 702
Disque, J. G., 795
Dixon, R. W., 433
Doan, J., 619
Dodge, K. A., 146, 381, 392, 593, 674, 676, 686, 695–697, 702
Dohn, H. H., 624
Dohrn, B., 699
Dolan, L. J., 704
Dolcini, M. M., 596
Doll, B., 160, 165, 197–198, 678–679
Dollarhide, C. T., 80, 91, 112, 114
Domanico, Y. B., 71
Domitrovich, C., 389
Donahue, P., 294
Donnenworth, E. E., 19
Donnerstein, E., 698
Donovan, C., 599
Donovan, J. E., 654
Dooley, C., 434, 440
Dorham, C. L., 127
Dornbusch, S., 86
Dorner, L., 82
Douzenis, C., 433
Dovidio, J. F., 117
Doweiko, H. E., 717
Downey, G., 595
Downs, L., 19–20, 45, 742
Downs, W. R., 591
Doyle, R. E., 488, 594
Doyle, W., 700
Drachman, D., 98
Draine, C., 98, 101
Dreikurs, R., 344, 487
Drew, N. S., 411
Drewnowski, A., 228
Drost, C., 128
Drotar, D., 226
Drury, A., 228
Drury, S. M., 203, 385, 388, 755–756
Dryfoos, J. G., 58, 381, 412, 767–768, 778
Dryler, H., 505
Duan, C., 213
Dubé, E. M., 594
DuBois, D. C., 162
DuBois, D. L., 152, 653, 659–660
Dubois, W. E. B., 177–178
Dubow, E. F., 127, 129
Duchnowski, A., 397, 772
Duffy, A., 405
Duffy, G., 260
Duffy, M., 214
Dukette, D., 696
Dukstein, R. D., 282
Dulmus, C. N., 622, 674, 693

Duncan, G. J., 146–147, 383
Dunn, M. G., 718
Dunphy, D., 590
DuPaul, G. J., 466, 767
Dupois, M., 139
Durlak, J., 382–383, 388–390, 425, 701, 707
Durodoye, B. A., 84
Duys, D., 674
Dwyer, K., 804
Dwyer, K. P., 459, 466
Dyck, R. J., 622
Dykeman, C., 412, 499, 506

E

Eagly, A. H., 170
Eamon, M. K., 697
Earls, F., 695, 697–698
Eastman, K. L., 99
Easton, A., 252
Eaton, W., 382
Eber, L., 706
Eberlein, L., 786
Eccles, J. S., 87, 149, 656
Eckermann, A. K., 98
Eckert, T. L., 466
Eddy, J. M., 700, 703
Eddy, M., 449, 705
Edelbrock, C. S., 696
Eder, D., 590–591
Education Trust, 37–39, 46, 49, 51, 481, 769, 771, 815, 821
Edwards, R. W., 548
Egan, G., 401
Eggert, L. L., 466, 619
Ehly, S., 185, 704
Ehrlich, G., 254
Eichenfield, G. A., 19
Eicher, S. A., 590
Eisner, E. W., 779
Eitle, D. J., 718–719
Eitle, T. M., 718–719
Ekstrom, R., 507
Elder, G. H., Jr., 146, 187
Eldridge, N., 405
Elias, M., 604
Elias, M. J., 209, 213, 389, 599
Eliason, G. T., 411
Eliassy, L., 89
Elizalde-Utnick, G., 483
Elkind, D., 425, 617
Ellen, J. M., 249, 596
Elliot, E. S., 510
Elliot, S. N., 483

Elliott, J., 104
Elliott, S. N., 112
Ellis, A., 296, 432–433
Ellsworth, B., 547
Elmore, P., 17
Elson, M., 655
Embry, D. D., 704
Embry, S. L., 17
Emmelkamp, P. M. G., 598
Emmer, E. T., 699
Emmett, J., 282
Emmons, C., 490
England, J. T., 16
English, K., 146
Ennett, S. T., 590–591
Enns, C. Z., 527
Entwisle, D., 147, 149, 639
Epp, L., 481
Epstein, J. L., 87–88, 355–356
Epstein, M. H., 696
Erb, C., 552
Erchul, W. P., 339, 482–483
Erevelles, N., 699
Erford, B., 43, 148, 196–197, 266, 295–297, 330, 435, 489, 533, 818, 820
Erickson, C. D., 322, 368
Erickson, D. B., 546
Erickson, E., 460, 464–465, 564, 566
Erickson, M., 405
Eriksen, K., 18, 26
Erikson, E. H., 432, 519, 588, 653
Eron, L. D., 696–698
Ertl, B., 462
Ervin, R. A., 702
Eschaback, L., 330
Eschenauer, R., 16, 79, 326
Espelage, D. L., 677, 679, 687
Espeland, P., 652, 771
Esquivel, G., 84, 88, 322
Estell, D. B., 644
Esters, I., 151
Etringer, B. D., 19
Evans, G. W., 146, 149
Evans, J., 232
Evans, K. M., 324, 551
Evans, M. A., 260
Evans, S. W., 198
Everly, G. S., Jr., 462
Evertson, C. M., 699

F

Fabian, S., 161–162
Facundo, A., 65

Fagan, J., 698
Fagot-Campagna, A., 224–225
Fairburn, C. G., 231
Fairchild, T. N., 314–315
Falbo, T., 182, 188
Falco, L., 766
Falicov, C. J., 450
Falk, R. F., 546
Fall, M., 213, 406
Fall, M., M., 517
Fantuzzo, J. W., 704
Faqua, D. R., 333
Farley, T. A., 248
Farmer, E. Z., 677
Farmer, T. W., 149, 598, 644, 677
Farrell, W., 405
Farrington, D., 654, 659, 697–698
Farrington, D. P., 697
Farris, A. M., 452, 506
Farwell, G. F., 740
Fassinger, R. E., 136
Faust, V., 9
Feagan, J. R., 112
Fedele, N. M., 434, 439–442
Feibig, D., 452
Fein, R., 460, 804
Feiring, C., 594–595
Feldhusen, J. F., 531
Feldlauffer, H., 656
Feldman, D., 406, 676
Feldman, S. S., 128
Feldstein, S. B., 312
Felfeli, M., 23
Felner, R. D., 653
Felson, R. B., 675
Fendrich, M., 196
Fenlon, M. J., 412
Fenton, R. E., 113
Ferguson, A. A., 700
Ferguson, M. P., 56, 564, 773
Fergusson, D. M., 249
Fernandes, A., 510
Fernando, I. S., 698
Ferreira, M. M., 370
Ferron, J., 146
Fetrow, R. A., 703, 705
Fiedler, E. D., 534
Field, J. E., 759
Field, S., 160, 165
Fielder, K. V., 548
Fillingame, L., 60, 128
Fincham, F., 594
Fine, M., 117–118, 120, 122, 166
Fineran, S., 437
Fink, C. M., 388
Finkelberg, S. L., 772

Finkelhor, D., 596
Finn, C. A., 412, 804
Finn, L., 659, 662
Finn-Stevenson, M., 385
Fiorini, J., 299, 301
First, J. M., 325
Fischer, J. M., 790
Fischer, L., 799
Fischer, M., 696
Fischer, T., 543
Fischetti, B. A., 19
Fish, M. C., 460, 472, 475
Fisher, B., 136, 140
Fisher, C., 235
Fisher, C. B., 113, 115–116, 652
Fisher, G. L., 720, 732
Fisher, M., 229–230
Fisher, P. H., 599
Fitch, T., 467, 476
Fitch, T. J., 758–759, 765
Fitzgerald, A., 593
Fitzgerald, P. W., 509
Fix, M. E., xxvii
Flament, M., 230
Flanigan, C. M., 329
Flanigan, G., 213
Flasher, A., 433
Flegal, K. M., 228
Fleming, C., 674
Flerx, V., 680–681
Fletcher, C. E. M., 600
Flickinger, S., 563
Flitton, B., 412
Flores, L. Y., 509–510
Florin, P., 391
Foley-Nicpon, M., 535, 548
Folsom, B., 509
Fong, M. L., 19
Fontaine, J. H., 138
Fontes, L., 321, 797
Ford, D. H., 280, 768
Ford, D. Y., 170, 180, 534–537, 542, 548
Fordham, S., 179–180, 183, 197
Forgas, J. P., 211
Formigoni, M. L., 718
Formoso, D., xxviii, 79
Forrest, G. C., 433
Forsyth, J. M., 115
Fortenberry, J. D., 249
Fortune, J., 22, 313
Fos, L., 433
Foster, C. M., 9
Foster, L. H., 604–605, 741, 763
Foster, S., 294
Foster, S. L., 592
Foster, V., 615

Fouad, N. A., 272, 278, 511
Fox, L. H., 544
Fox, N. A., 410
Frable, D. E. S., 146
Frame, C. L., 696
Frank, L. S., 357–359, 363, 368
Frankel, K. A., 695
Frankenberg, E., 111
Franklin, A. J., 68
Frantz, T. T., 398
Fraser, M. W., 600, 639–640
Frederickson, R. H., 544
Freedman, D., 229
Freeman, H. E., 605
Freeman, L., 412
Freeman, R., 230, 302
Freire, P., 25, 273
French, D. C., 592, 697
French, S. A., 231–232
Fretz, B. R., 482
Freud, S., 519
Freund, A. M., 280
Frevert, V., 404
Frey, C. P., 535
Frey, K. S., 452, 601, 605, 682–683, 686
Frey, L. L., 65, 68, 185, 431
Freytes, M., 22
Frick, P., 696
Fridman, A., 145
Fried, C., 184
Frieden, G., 25
Friedman, R. J., 697
Friend, M., 330, 482
Frith, U., 676
Fryxell, D., 463, 467
Fuchs, D., 704
Fuchs, L. S., 704
Fuertes, J. N., 435
Fuhriman, A., 433
Fujiki, M., 593
Fukunaga, C., 146
Fukuyama, M. A., 509
Fuligni, A. J., 105
Fulkerson, J. A., 230
Fuller, B., 698
Fuller, J. O., 164
Fuller, T., 195
Fulmore, C., 563
Fults, B. A., 546
Fundis, R., 537, 552
Furlong, M., 462
Furman, W., 588, 594–595
Furnham, A., 96, 100
Furniss, J. M., 698
Furr, S. R., 20
Fusick, L., 127–131, 179, 642

Fuson, S., 158
Futterman, D., 437

G

Gaa, J. P., 19
Gabrielli, W. F., Jr., 695
Gaertner, S. L., 117
Gahan, Father P., 669
Gainor, K. A., 322–323
Gaitan, C. D., 182, 188
Galassi, J. P., 23, 28–29, 214, 385, 604, 767–768, 771
Galasso, L., 412
Galbraith, J., 531, 534–536, 546–548, 550, 652, 771
Gallagher, J. J., 533, 549
Gallaher, P., 677
Gallegos, P. I., 185
Gallessich, J., 330, 346
Gandara, P., 186
Gant, L., 56, 181, 564
Gao, M., 231
Garbarino, J., 678
Garber, J., 592, 696
Garcia, E. E., 177, 185–186
Garcia Coll, C., 96, 99–100
Garcia-Vasquez, E., 185
Gardner, 166
Gardner, D. M., 229
Gardner, H., 26, 534, 536
Garland, A. F., 622
Garland, S., 466
Garlow, S. J., 629
Garmezy, N., 769, 771
Garner, P. W., 146, 411
Garrett, M. T., 816
Garrett, P., 146
Garry, E. M., 639
Gary, F., 629–630
Garza, R. T., 185
Gastfriend, D., 733
Gaubatz, M. D., 16–17
Gazda, G. M., 411, 419, 421
Ge, X., 146
Gee, G. C., 117
Gee, J. P., 261–262, 265
Geierstanger, S. P., 235–236
Gelso, C. J., 20, 482, 761
Gentemann, K. M., 602
Geoffroy, K. E., 314
George, C. A., 795
Gerber, P. J., 160
Gerber, S. K., 732
Gerhardstein, R., 410

Gerler, E. R., 11, 101–102, 127, 209, 276, 293–297, 397, 409, 411, 431, 433, 481, 669
Gerrity, D., 412
Gerton, J., 56, 71, 129, 184, 323, 563
Gesell, R., 432
Getz, H. G., 23, 313
Gianotti, T. J., 488
Gibbs, J., 97, 357, 367–369
Gibbs, R., 440
Gibson, M. A., 185
Gibson, R. L., 7, 9, 276, 397, 402, 766, 815–816
Gifford, E., 220
Gifford-Smith, M. E., 587
Gilat, I., 433
Gilbert, L. A., 598
Giles, H. C., 152
Gill, W. S., 625
Giller, H., 696
Gillette, M. D., 60
Gilliand, B. E., 405
Gillies, R. M., 503, 762
Gilligan, C., 432, 434, 653, 659
Gilliland, B. E., 461, 465–466, 470
Gilmore, M., 564
Gimenez, M., 27
Gimpel, G. A., 344
Ginsberg, R., 160
Ginsburg-Block, M. D., 704
Ginter, E. J., 411
Giordano, F. G., 17
Giordano, J., 100
Giordano, P. C., 591, 654
Giroux, H. A., 699
Gladding, S. T., 3–5, 11, 411, 414, 431, 482
Glaeser, B. C., 164
Glaize, D. L., 433
Glass, L., 537
Glasser, W., 296, 403, 411, 432–433
Glazer, N., 178
Glenn, E. E., 163
Gloria, A. M., 184–185
Glover, G., 519
Gold, R. S., 249
Goldberg, A., 590, 594–595
Goldberg, B., 412
Goldberg, M. E., 148
Goldberg, S. G., 786, 789–790, 792
Goldenberg, H., 182
Goldenberg, I., 182
Goldman, S., 617
Goldner, E. M., 231
Goldney, R., 621
Goldsmith, D., 536–537
Goldstein, S. B., 170
Goldston, D. B., 624–625
Goleman, D., 55, 211, 604

Goncalves, O. F., 23
Gonzales, N. A., 697
Gonzalez, J. E., 696
Gonzalez-Martinez, J. C., 170
Good, C., 184
Good, R. H., III, 701, 755
Goodman, E., 148
Goodman, R., 405
Goodman, R. W., 16, 18
Goodnough, G. E., 16, 148, 299, 413, 433, 660
Goodwin, A. L., 119
Goodwin, F., 4–6
Goodyear, R. K., 303, 312, 316–317
Gopaul-McNicol, S., 97
Gorczynski, J., 412
Gordon, E. W., 21, 326
Gordon, K. A., 187
Gordon, M., 83–84
Gordon, R. A., 18
Gore, S., 100
Gorkin, M., 621
Gorman-Smith, D., 467, 698
Gorn, G. J., 148
Gortmaker, S. L., 229
Goto, S. G., 117
Gottfredson, D. C., 388, 699
Gottfredson, D. G., 707
Gottfredson, G. D., 388, 699, 701
Gottfredson, L. S., 500, 503
Gottlieb, G., 700
Gould, M. S., 620
Gracie, J., 23
Graden, J. L., 481
Grady, W. R., 249
Graham, P., 696
Graham, P. A., 98
Graham, S., 122
Grall, M. B., 196
Gramzow, R. H., 115
Granaello, D. H., 812
Granato, L., 271, 322
Grandbois, 629
Grandy, G. S., 704
Granello, D. H., 18, 294, 310, 467
Granello, P. F., 18
Granley, M., 597
Grant, C. A., 60
Grant, S. K., 323
Grantham, T. C., 542, 548
Graun, K., 343
Gray, C. A., 164
Gray, G., 696
Gray, J. A., 695
Gray, K. C., 507
Gray, M. R., 594–595
Gray, N., 310

Green, A., 179, 182, 604–605, 771
Green, A. G., 773
Green, K. C., 545
Green, M. Y., 525
Green, S., 116
Greenberg, J. S., 548
Greenberg, K. R., 599–600
Greenberg, M., 80
Greenberg, M. T., 164, 216, 387, 389–390, 392, 703–704, 707, 767
Greene, K., 9, 17
Greenwald, A. G., 170
Greenwald, M., 24
Greenwood, A., 403
Greenwood, C. R., 149
Greer, B. B., 167
Greer, J. G., 167
Gregory, A., xxix, 58, 60, 693, 697, 699–700
Greif, G. L., 56
Greisler, P. C., 593
Gresham, F. M., 164
Gressard, C., 23
Greydanus, D. E., 231
Gridley, B. E., 20
Griffin, N. C., 412
Griffith, B. A., 25, 53
Grigg, W., 294
Grisdale, G. A., 316
Grissom, J., 640
Gross, A. M., 593
Gross, D. R., 463, 468, 470, 626
Gross, M. U. M., 535
Grossman, D., 212
Grossman, D. C., 682–683
Grossman, H., 403
Grossman, J. B., 152
Gruman, D., 309
Grunbaum, J. A., 248
Grunwald, B. B., 487
Guerra, N. G., 696, 702
Guerra, P., 19, 398, 701, 707, 815
Guest, M., 20
Guilkey, D. K., 249
Guo, J. J., 235, 699
Guo, S., 405
Gur, M., 249
Gurney, J. G., 224
Gushue, G. V., 102, 322
Gustafson, K. E., 795
Gustavson, C. B., 525–526
Gustke, C., 189
Gutierrez, H., 188
Gutkin, T. B., 330, 435, 483
Gutman, L. M., 149
Gutter, B. T., 56–57
Gutterman, J. T., 344

Guzman, B., 412
Guzzo, B. A., 601, 682
Gysbers, N., xxix, 3, 6, 8–11, 16, 39, 41, 46, 148, 166, 178, 196, 198, 203, 209, 215, 269, 276, 282, 285, 293, 295, 297, 314, 410, 498, 642, 666, 739, 741–742, 746, 748, 756–757, 763, 770–772, 779

H

Hache, G., 412
Hackett, G., 278, 286, 510
Hackney, H., 482
Hadar, E., 410
Hage, S. M., 381–383, 563
Hagermoser, L., 704
Hagerty, B. M., 653, 656, 659, 662
Haggerty, R., 382
Hahn, C. S., 147
Hakuta, K., 186, 188
Halberstadt, A., 98
Haley, M., 618
Halfon, N., 221–223
Hall, B., 98, 101
Hall, G. S., 518
Hall, J. A., 678
Hall, R. V., 149
Hall, S. P., xxviii, 111
Hall, T. M., 406
Hallfors, D. D., 702, 719–720
Halliday-Scher, K., 589
Halpalani, V., 129
Halpern, C. T., 700
Halpern-Felsher, B., 247, 249
Halterman, J. S., 223
Halverson, S. E., 313
Hamilton, M. A., 772
Hamilton, S. F., 772
Hamm, J. V., 185, 588
Hammer, J., 676
Hammond, M., 703
Han, B., 659
Hand, H. C., 740
Hand, J. Z., 437
Hangaduambo, S., 674
Hanjogiris, W. F., 136
Hanley-Maxwell, C., 157
Hannum, J. W., 490
Hansen, D. J., 599
Hansen, J. C., 340
Hansen, J. T., 17
Hansen, N. D., 786, 789–790, 792
Hanson, T., 355, 357–358
Hanson, W. E., 186–187

Hao, L., 87
Happé, F., 674, 676
Harachi, T., 564
Harber, K. D., 640
Hardesty, P. H., 262
Hardin, M. E., 598
Hardy, E., 312
Hargrove, B. K., 271–272
Harkins, K. F., 97
Harklau, L., 85
Harland, J., 721
Harmon, D., 535
Harold, R. D., 87
Harper, D. C., 226
Harper, G. W., 596
Harrington, T. F., 504
Harris, C. R., 537
Harris, J. J., 180, 535
Harris, K., 213
Harris, L. J., 652
Harris, T., 233
Harris-Bowlsbey, J., 498, 505
Harrison, H. M., 588–589, 594–595
Harrison, K., 181
Harrison, P. L., 600
Harrison, T. C., 487, 720, 732
Harry, B., 166–167
Hart, B., 767
Hart, C. H., 593
Hart, P., 37
Hart, P. J., 771
Harter, S., 588, 653, 662, 756
Hart-Johnson, T., 181
Hartley, M. T., 164
Hartman, J., 140, 412, 433
Hartshorne, T. S., 786, 792, 801
Hartung, P. L., 501, 504, 512
Hartup, W. W., 587–588
Harvey, A., 564
Harvey, W. B., 635, 640
Harvill, R. L., 419, 433
Harwood, R. L., 166
Hatch, T., 18, 24, 38
Hatcher, W., 815
Haub, A. L., 412–413
Haurin, R. J., 249
Hauser, R. M., 147
Haverkamp, B. E., 19
Havighurst, R. J., 432
Hawken, L. S., 706
Hawker, D. D., 675
Hawkins, J. D., 366, 381, 469, 654–655, 659, 697, 699, 719
Hawley, P. H., 676
Hay, P. J., 231
Hayden, D. C., 460, 466

Hayes, B. G., 23
Hayes, D. H., 339
Hayes, J. A., 20
Hayes, R. L., 40, 303, 316, 767
Hayes, S., 321
Hayes, T. J., 501
Haynes, O. M., 147
Hays, C. E., 719
Hays, D. G., 16
Hays, S. P., 719
Hayward, C., 599
Hazen, A., 433
Hazler, R. J., 116, 462, 467, 469
Hebert, T. P., 536
Heck, D. J., 588
Heckemeyer, C. M., 721
Heckman-Stone, C., 22
Hecter, J. M., 383
Hedley, A. A., 228
Heeren, T., 249
Hegerle, D. R., 705
Heller, K., 707
Heller, L. R., 704
Helms, J. E., xxvii, 66–67, 71, 118–119, 121–122, 128, 178, 180, 274, 564, 730, 773
Henderson, A., 181
Henderson, D., 517, 667
Henderson, D. A., 295, 416, 419
Henderson, N., 769
Henderson, P., 3, 6, 8–11, 16, 39, 41, 166, 203, 215, 293, 295, 297, 303, 312, 314, 410, 666, 739, 741–742, 758, 770, 779
Hendricks, J. E., 460–462, 464–465, 468, 473
Hendry, L. B., 659
Henggeler, S., 398
Heninger, M., 629
Henkel, R. R., 677
Henrich, C. C., 652, 701
Henry, B., 695
Henry, D. B., 467
Henry, M. N., 807
Hensley, F. A., 421
Hepler, N., 100
Heppner, M. J., 132, 356, 510
Heppner, P. P., 752–754, 762
Herek, G. M., 135
Herlihy, B., 310, 720–721, 817
Herman, J. L., 117
Hermann, M. A., 468, 785, 799, 803–805
Herman-Wenderoth, L., 229
Hernandez, T. J., 80, 91, 366, 370, 773, 821–822
Hernstein, R. J., 54
Herr, E. L., 10, 324, 398, 497–498, 501, 503, 506–507, 509, 521–522, 792, 812
Herre, K., 659

Herrell, A., 98
Herrenkohl, T., 697–698
Herring, R. D., 99–100, 179, 190, 412, 545
Herrling, S., 391
Hershberger, S. L., 140, 433
Herting, J. R., 466
Herting Wahl, K., 293
Hertz-Lazarowitz, R., 413
Hertzog, N. B., 535
Herzberger, S. D., 678
Hesketh, K., 229
Hess, A. M., 412
Hess, R. D., 87
Hett, G. G., 413–414
Hewes, G. M., 53
Heyward, S. M., 168
Hiatt-Michael, D. B., 602
Hill, C. L, 492
Hill, F. W., 470
Hill, H. M., 698
Hill, K. G., 699
Hill, M. S., 462
Hill, R., 564
Hillerbrand, E., 19
Hilliard, A. G., 197, 199
Hilton, T. L., 10
Himes, J. H., 228, 340
Hinderman, R. A., 740
Hines, P. L., 440, 636–637, 641, 643–644, 647
Hingson, R. W., 249
Hinkelman, L., 717
Hinkle, J. S., 300
Hinshaw, S. P., 696
Hirschi, T., 659–660, 696, 699
Hirschstein, M. K., 601, 682
Hirshfeld-Becker, D., 405
Hirt, J. B., 21–22
Hitchcock, R., 506
Hitlin, P., 596
Hlongwane, M. M., 433
Hlynsky, J. A., 231
Hoachlander, G., 26
Hoag, M. J., 413, 433
Hoagwood, K., 294, 326
Hoare, C. H., 597, 772
Hobson, S. M., 271
Hodges, E., 588
Hodges, E. V. E., 420
Hodges, S., 20
Hoek, H. W., 227, 230
Hoff, L. A., 464, 467–468, 470–473, 475–476
Hoffman, A., 160, 164–165
Hoffman, C. C., 459, 466
Hoffman, L., xxvii, 406
Hoffman, L. W., 146

Hoffman, M. A., 28
Hoffman, R. M., 16–17, 24–25
Hofsess, C. D., 506
Hoge, D. R., 700
Hoglund, W., 601
Hogue, A., 674
Hohenshil, T., 22
Holcomb, M. C., 122, 651
Holcomb-McCoy, C., 15–16, 128–130, 132, 146, 214, 271, 321–322, 326, 366, 369–370, 435, 772–773
Holder, D. W., 250
Holland, J., 276–277
Holland, J. L., 501
Hollingsworth, E. J., 699
Hollingworth, L. S., 544, 547, 549
Hollins, E. R., 120
Holloway, E. L., 310, 312
Holloway, S. D., 87
Holmbeck, G. N., 196
Holt, M. K., 677
Holzer, C. E., III, 197
Hom, A., 355–356
Homeyer, L. E., 519
Hong, E., 433
Honora, D., 654
Hoover, A. B., 433
Hoover-Dempsey, K. V., 87–88
Hopps, J., 145–146
Hord, R., 22
Hore, A. H., 433
Horne, A. M., 20, 409, 678, 685
Horner, R., 164, 698, 702, 706
Hornung, R. W., 659
Horowitz, F. D., 537
Horton-Parker, R., 316
House, R. M., 40, 196, 297, 384, 435, 767, 771, 790
Howard, D. E., 247
Howard, K. A. S., 29, 269, 272, 281, 284, 498, 768, 769, 771–772
Howard-Pitney, 620
Howlin, P., 696
Hoy, W. K., 490
Hoyt, K. B., 497, 509
Hoyt, W., 60
Hrabowski, F. A., 56
Huang, K., 70
Huang, L., 97
Hubbard, J., 594
Hubbard, L., 85, 211, 213, 215
Hubert, M., 741
Hudson, L., 506
Huesmann, L. R., 696–698, 702
Huey, W. C., 19, 785, 805

Huffine, C., 450
Hughes, C., 162
Hughes, D. C., 221
Hughes, D. K., 741
Hughes, J. H., 655
Hughey, K. F., 282, 741
Humes, C. W., 412
Hunn, L., 718
Hunsaker, M. D., 388, 534
Hunt, B., 20
Hunt, C. J., 676
Hunter, C., 117
Hunter, C. D., 66–67, 128, 130–131
Hunter, J., 137
Hunter, L., 209
Hunter-Ebeling, J., 472
Huss, S. N., 441
Hussey, D., 405
Hussong, A. M., 591
Husted, J., 548
Huston, A. C., 147
Hutchings, B., 695
Hutchinson, R., 567
Hutt, C., 519
Huttunen, A., 677
Hwang, M., 66–67, 70, 128, 131, 411
Hybl, L. G., 699
Hyman, C., 592, 699
Hymel, S., 425, 592

I

Ialongo, N., 195, 425, 704
Ibrahim, F. A., 64, 66
Idol, L., 482, 817–818
Igoa, C., 98, 101
Ilg, F., 432
Impara, J. C., 17
Ingersoll, E., 20
Inoff-Germain, G., 695, 697
Inose, M., 99–100, 103–104, 106, 129, 507
Institute Of Medicine (IOM), 673
Inzlicht, M., 184, 590
Ireland, M., 618–619
Ireys, H. T., 222
Isaacs, M., 413
Isaacs, M. L., 214, 739, 766, 794
Isaacson, L. E., 497, 508
Isernhagen, J. C., 646
Ito, A., 80, 91
Ivey, A. E., 20, 23, 60, 64, 189
Ivey, M. B., 60, 64, 189, 340
Izard, C. E., 146

J

Ja, D. Y., 321
Jackson, A., 235
Jackson, C. M., 294, 301–303, 413, 433, 758–759
Jackson, D. N., 339
Jackson, J. D., 27
Jackson, S. A., 21
Jackson, S. L., 282
Jacobi, M., 37, 771
Jacobs, D. G., 616, 618
Jacobs, E. E., 419, 433, 438, 463
Jacobs, L., 565
Jacobson, K. C., 662
Jacob-Timm, S., 786, 792, 801
James, D. C. S., 97–100
James, E. L., 343
James, I., 23
James, R. K., 405, 461, 465–466, 470
James, S. H., 741, 799
Jarchow, E., 367–369, 371
Jason, L. A., 482, 659
Javier, R. A., 527
Javors, M. A., 695
Jayaratne, E., 146
Jeffery, G., 412
Jencius, M., 23
Jencks, C., 698
Jensen, P., 412
Jepsen, D. A., 504, 507
Jerome, A., 459, 465
Jessell, J. C., 504
Jessor, R., 653–654, 659–660
Jessor, S. L., 653, 659–660
Jessup, P., 768
Jeynes, W. H., 53
Jimerson, S. R., 640, 773
Jobes, D. A., 463
Jobin-Davis, K., 772
Johnson, C., 742
Johnson, C. A., 383
Johnson, C. D., 24, 39, 45, 739, 747
Johnson, C. L., 228
Johnson, C. M., 326
Johnson, D., 411
Johnson, D. W., 600, 694, 701
Johnson, K., 460–462, 465
Johnson, L., 517
Johnson, L. S., 504, 510
Johnson, P., 64–65, 302–303
Johnson, R., 116–117
Johnson, R. T., 694, 701
Johnson, S., 97, 739, 742
Johnson, S. K., 24, 39, 45
Johnson, T., 548
Johnson, V., 406
Johnston, J. A., 510
Johnston, L. D., 717–719
Joiner, T. E., 195
Jolly, J. B., 625
Jones, C., 82
Jones, C. H., 413
Jones, D. S., 146
Jones, K. D., 23, 481
Jones, L. A., 433
Jones, L. K., 282
Jones, L. M., 296
Jones, M., 804
Jones, R. R., 451
Joo, E., 659
Jordan, A. E., 789
Jordan, J., 653, 662
Jordan, J. V., 431, 434, 442
Jordan, K., 17, 22
Jordan, K. Y., 697
Jouriles, E. N., 452
Joyce, P. R., 462
Joyner, B., 282
Joyner, K., 594
Juhnke, G. A., 16, 353, 624–625
Juliao, T. R., 587
Jung, K. G., 695
Juntunen, C. L., 97, 106, 182, 189, 296, 643
Jussim, L., 640
Juvonen, J., 122

K

Kachadourian, L., 594
Kachgal, M., xxx, 301, 384, 643, 647, 762
Kachgal, M. M., 28–29
Kaczmarek, P., 787
Kaduson, H. G., 406
Kaffenberger, C. J., 433
Kagan, H., 25
Kagan, J., 432
Kagan, N. I., 25
Kagan, S., 300
Kahn, B. B., 19, 519, 523
Kahn, H., 66
Kahn, K. B., 524
Kahn, W. J., 330–331, 339, 345–346, 348
Kailin, J., 112, 118
Kaiser, C. F., 549
Kaiser Commission on Medicaid and the Uninsured, 220–221
Kalafat, J., 462, 618, 620, 622
Kalish-Weiss, B., 521, 523
Kamatuka, N. A., 282

Kambon, K. K. K., 200
Kampwirth, T. J., 482, 487, 490
Kandel, D. B., 674, 677
Kandor, J. R., 15
Kang, H. W., 98
Kanitz, H. M., 271
Kantamneni, N., 269
Kantor, J. H., 599
Kao, G., 321–322
Kaplan, A. G., 431, 653
Kaplan, D. S., 636–637
Kaplan, D. W., 235
Kaplan, G., 98
Kaplan, H. B., 253, 636–637
Kaplan, L., 817
Kaplan, L. S., 314
Kapsch, L., 213
Karan, O. C., 636
Karcher, M. J., 355, 651–652, 654, 657, 659, 662, 664, 669
Karcher, S., 53, 60
Karenga, M., 566
Karno, M. P., 311
Karper, C., 23
Karshner, W. W., 544
Kartub, D. T., 706
Kasai, M., 527
Kashani, J., 804
Kaslow, N. J., 196
Kates, N., 101
Katz, L., 164
Katzman, D. K., 230
Kauffman, M. B., 772
Kaufman, C., 22
Kaufman, P., 675
Kaufmann, F., 542
Kaufmann, K., 113
Kaukiainen, A., 676–677, 697
Kavoussi, R. J., 695
Kay, L. F., 113
Kaye, W., 230
Kazak, A. E., 767
Kazdin, A. E., 452
Kearney, C. A., 638–639, 644
Keefe, K., 588
Keeler, G., 149
Kefauver, G. N., 740
Keisner, J., 195–197
Keitel, M. A., 84, 88
Keith-Spiegel, P., 786
Kelchner, K., 160, 162
Kellam, S., 425, 699, 704
Keller, T., 16, 18
Kelly, D. B., 271
Kelly, J. G., 81–82
Kelly, K. J., 718

Kelly, K. R., 18, 531
Kelly, K. T., 627
Kelsey, J. L., 145
Kendall, P. C., 707
Kendler, K. S., 230
Kendrick, R., 815
Kennedy, C. L., 718
Kennedy, N. J., 383
Kennickell, A. B., 270
Kenny, M. E., 29, 385, 770
Keough, K. A., 662
Keppel, K. G., 221
Kerewsky, S. D., 17, 383
Kerr, B. A., 412, 531, 534–536, 538–539, 542–546, 548–550, 552, 555
Kesecker, M. P., 705
Key, J. D., 226
Keys, S., 179, 182, 214, 301, 322, 329, 353, 366, 384, 604–605, 767, 771
Khan, L. K., 229
Kiesner, J., 195, 677
Kim, A. B., 68
Kim, B. S. K., 22, 68, 97, 185, 749
Kim, B. U., 96
Kim, C., 70
Kim, D., 355
Kim, K., 403
Kim, R., 411
Kim, S., 100, 196, 282
Kim, S. C., 57, 59, 563, 565–567
Kimmel, D. C., 139–140
Kindaichi, M. M., 324–325
King, G., 234
King, J. A., 704, 718
King, J. H., 20
King, K. A., 17, 460, 463, 465, 467, 470–471, 616, 620, 805
King, R., 503
King-Sears, M. E., 353
King-Sears, S. L., 214
Kinket, B., 118
Kinnison, L. R., 158
Kipnis, F. M., 698
Kirby, D., 245, 250–251
Kirisci, L., 718
Kirk, W. G., 618, 623, 625–626
Kiron, E., 565
Kirschenbaum, H., 604
Kiselica, M. S., 71, 325, 412
Kistner, J., 410, 589
Kitano, M. K., 535–537, 548
Kitayama, S., 64, 70, 72, 128
Kitchener, K. S., 419, 786, 789
Kite, M. E., 170
Kitzrow, M. A., 20
Kivlighan, D. M., 750–754

Kizner, L. R., 412
Kizner, S. R., 412, 433
Kjos, D., 23
Klebanov, P. K., 146
Klein, R. G., 599
Klein-Benham, M., 616
Kleine, P. A., 533
Kless, S. J., 501, 677
Klicker, R. L., 459, 467
Klonoff, E. A., 112
Klostermann, B. K., 659
Kluckhohn, F. R., 730
Kluckhon, C. K., 66
Kluckhon, F. R., 66, 72
Klute, C., 587, 589–591
Knell, S., 406
Knight, G. P., 563
Knudson, M. P., 627
Knudtson, L. F., 243, 253
Kobasa, S. C., 411
Kobayashi, R. B., 659
Koch, G. G., 591
Koch, J. M., 293
Kochenderfer, B. J., 588
Kofkin, J., 662
Kohatsu, E., 563, 565
Kohlberg, L., 25, 210–211, 432
Kohler, P. D., 160
Kohn, A., 357, 359, 363, 368–370
Kohn-Wood, L. P., 116
Kohut, H., 655, 659
Kokaly, M. L., 505
Kolko, D. J., 626
Koltyk, J., 567
Konold, T., 19, 503
Konstantinos, A., 51
Koocher, G. P., 786
Koonce, D., 180
Kopala, M., 322
Korn, W. E., 545
Kosciulek, J. F., 282, 772
Koss-Chioino, J. D., 132, 773
Kostoulas, K. K., 413
Kottman, T., 406
Kounin, Jacob, 699
Kovach, J., 778
Kowalchuk, R. K., 286
Kowalski, R. M., 592
Kozol, J., 112, 177, 489
Kraatz, R. A., 213
Kramer, D., 787–788, 792
Krappmann, L., 593
Kratochwill, T. R., 112, 332, 483, 487, 597, 704
Kratt, P. P., 721
Kraus, L. J., 282
Krauss, N. A., 221

Kreipe, R. E., 230
Kress, J. S., 209
Krieger, K., 23
Krishnakumar, A., 382
Krohn, M. D., 698
Kropp, R. Y., 247
Kruczek, T., 767
Kruesi, M. J. P., 695
Krug, E. G., 466
Kruger, A. C., 213
Kruger, E. A., 531, 535, 548
Krumboltz, J. D., 433
Kuehn, P. A., 98
Kuh, G. D., 335
Kulic, K. R., 409, 414, 418, 426, 433
Kulik, C. C., 538
Kulik, J. A., 538
Kumke, P., 704
Kumpfer, K. L., 384, 388–389, 391
Kundtson, L. F., 219
Kunjufu, K., 199
Kuo, J., 200
Kuo, Y., 22, 96
Kuperminc, G. P., 391, 490, 656, 659
Kupersmidt, J. B., 592–593, 674
Kupfer, D. J., 616
Kuranz, M., 352–353
Kurpius, D. J., 333, 815
Kurpius, S. E., 17–18
Kurpius, S. R., 542
Kusche, C., 164, 216, 703–704
Kush, F., 459, 619
Kushida, D., 492
Kuster, C. B., 381
Kutash, K., 397, 772
Kuttler, A. F., 594
Kuzniar, J., 488
Kwon, K.-L. K., 597
Kwong, A., 66–67

L

Ladany, N., 23, 189, 322, 324–325
Ladd, G., 116
Ladd, G. W., 116, 588, 592–593, 598
Ladson-Billings, G., 58, 60
LaFountain, R. M., 16, 411
LaFromboise, T., 56, 71, 129, 131, 184, 323, 545, 563, 565–566, 620, 698
Lagerspetz, K., 677
La Greca, A. M., 588–589, 594–595
Lahey, B. B., 693
Lai, E. W. M., 69
Lair, G., 403

Laird, R. D., 697
Laitinen, R., 162
Lake, J. K. J., 232
LaLonde, R. N., 97
Lamberg, L., 804
Lambert, M. J., 19
Lambert, S. F., 195
Lambie, G. W., 17, 720–721, 796, 812
Lamborn, N., 697
Lampe, R. E., 303, 312, 433
Lampert, C., 230
Landreth, G. L., 519, 521
Landrine, H., 112
Lang, W., 467
Langley, T., 675
Lang-Takac, E., 662
Lanning, W., 302
Lansford, J. E., 697
Lapan, R., 45, 148, 209, 269, 271, 282–283, 285, 741, 746, 756–758, 772
Lapan, T. T., 498, 504
LaPidus, J. B., 19
Lareau, A., 146
Larkin, R., 413
Larson, K., 674
Larson, L. M., 18
Larson, R. W., 594–595
Lashbrook, J. T., 591
Lasoff, D. L., 281, 510–511
Last, C. G., 401
Latendresse, S. J., 147
Lauer, P., 460, 466
Laursen, B., 589
Laursen, E. K., 355, 588
Laux, J. M., 616
LaVeist, T. A., 196
Lavoritano, J., 756–757
Lawrence, G., 17–18
Lawrence, M., 160
Lawson, D. M., 214
Lawson, H., 767
Lazarus, A. A., 411
Lazarus, M., 518
Lazear, K., 619
Lazos Vargas, S. L., 67
Leach, M. M., 19
Leadbeater, B. S., 490, 601, 656
Leary, M., 352, 592, 595
Leary, M. R., 655–656, 659–660
Lecuyer, C., 113
Lee, C., 111
Lee, C. C., 17, 37, 321, 324–326, 353, 369–370, 435, 597, 637, 639, 643–644, 741, 771, 773–774
Lee, J., 146, 152
Lee, J. L., 397
Lee, R. M., 352, 655, 659, 662

Lee, S., 104
Lee, S. J., 68, 95
Lee, S. M., 233
Lee, S. S., 383
Lee, V., 507
Lee, V. E., 437
Lee, Y., 657, 662, 701
Lee-Borden, N., 303
Leenaars, A. A., 475, 627
Leff, S. S., 701, 705–707
Leffert, N., 652
Legum, H. L., 772
Lehr, R., 412, 490
LeMare, L., 425, 592
Lemerise, A., 674
Lenhart, A., 596
Lenox, K., 592
Lent, R. W., 161–162, 201, 278, 286, 505
Lent, W. L., 510
Leon, G. R., 230
Leong, F. T. L., 501, 511–512
Lerner, A., 525
Lerner, R. M., 280, 384, 652, 768–769, 772, 778
Lester, J. N., 509
Leventhal, T., 698
Lever, N., 641
Levesque, R. L. R., 787
Levine, M. P., 230
Levy, D. M., 449
Levy, G. K., 412
Levy, R. S., 675
Lewin, K., 83, 383, 489
Lewis, A. C., 321
Lewis, C., 355
Lewis, C. C., 353, 355
Lewis, J., 537
Lewis, J. J., 64
Lewis, S., 464
Lewis, T. J., 706
Lewis-Palmer, T., 698
Lezin, N., 652
Li, L. C., 492
Liang, B., 433, 601
Liang, C. T. H., 97
Liaw, F. R., 640
Liberatos, P., 145, 147
Liberman, D. B., 19
Lickona, T., 210
Liddle, H. A., 452
Lieberman, M., 282
Liefooghe, A. P. D., 675
Liesener, J. J., 161–162
Lightfoot, J., 226
Likona, T., 469
Limber, S., 460, 680–681
Lin, M., 18

Lindemann, E., 460, 464
Lindsay, 113
Lindstrom, L., 165
Lindwall, J., xxix, 53, 59–60, 253, 351, 355
Lines, C. L., 19
Ling, X., 699
Link, B. G., 145
Linn, E., 437
Linskens, C. J., 259
Lintz, A., 85
Lipsey, M. W., 605, 701–702
Lissak, R. S., 449
Little, C., 542
Little, S. G., 388
Little, T. D., 593
Littrell, J. M., 303, 413, 420, 423, 433
Liu, W. M., 145–147, 151–152
Livneh, H., 159, 161
Lochman, J. E., 592–593, 702
Lock, J., 230
Locke, D. C., 65, 435–436, 643, 646
Lockhart, E. J., 158, 163, 167, 301, 322, 329, 366, 384
Loeber, R., 693, 696
Loesch, L. C., 3
Loganbill, C., 312
Logio, K. A., 230
Lohr, M. J., 589
Lohrman-O'Rourke, S., 706
Lomawaima, K. T., 178
Lonczak, H. S., 366, 381, 655
Long, J. D., 677
Long, K. L., 506
Lopez, E. C., 597
Lopez, E. J., 185
Lopez, S. R., 128
Lord, W., 433
Lorenz, F. O., 146, 286
Lorenz, J. A., 303
Lorion, R. P., 382, 389
Losch, N., 487
Losen, D., 177
Lotta, C. C., 531, 545
Louden-Gerber, G., 669
Love, R., 322
Lovecky, D. V., 531, 546
Low, H., 695
Lowry, R., 249
Lu, W., 789
Lubeck, S., 768
Lucas, M. S., 98–99
Lucas, T., 85, 88–91
Lufler, H. S., 699
Luhman, A., 537, 552
Luiselli, J. K., 706
Luke, M., 25

Lukin, L. E., 285
Lundberg, D. J., 23
Lundeen, C. A., 353
Luongo, P. F., 329
Lupkowski-Shoplik, A., 538–540
Lupton-Smith, H., 19
Lusterman, D.-D., 450
Luthar, S. S., 147, 389, 635, 641, 767
Luzzo, D. A., 17, 510
Lynch, E. W., 69, 98, 660
Lynch, R. H., 535
Lynch-Sauer, J., 653
Lynskey, M. T., 249
Lyons, H. Z., 22

M

Ma, P.-W., 63, 68–70, 104
Maccoby, E. E., 149
MacIntosh, R., 187–188
MacKenzie, D., 405
Mackey, L., 20
Mackler, B., 406
Mackler, L., 259
Madan-Bahel, A., 66–67
Madan-Swain, A., 226
Madden, M., 596
Maddi, S. R., 411
Maddux, C. D., 20
Maddy-Bernstein, C., 37
Madhok, R., 249
Madsen, C. H., 704
Maestas, M. V., 97
Maggs, J. L., 382
Magnuson, K., 96, 99–100
Magnuson, K. A., 147
Magnuson, S., 795
Magnussen, M., 425
Magourik Colbert, M., xxx
Magrab, P. R., 352
Maguin, E., 696
Magura, S., 733
Maher, E., 229
Mahler, J., 413
Mahoney, A. S., 555
Major, B., 115
Maker, C. J., 535–536
Maki, D. R., 23
Maldonado, R., 68
Maldonado-Colon, E., 65
Male, R. A., 544
Malgady, R. G., 97
Malley, P. B., 459, 619
Mallinckrodt, B., 655

Mallon, G. P., 137
Malone, S., 164
Mander, G., 20
Manley, R. S., 232
Mannarino, A. P., 425
Mannella, M., 405
Manning, M. L., 563
Manolis, C., 148
Manor, O., 228
Mansour, M., 235–236
Manz, P. H., 701
Manzi, A. J., 17, 504
Mar, Y., 89
March, R. E., 706
Margolis, R. L., 16
Marin, B. V., 347
Marin, G., 347
Marino, T., 19
Markiewitcz, D., 594
Marks, E. S., 342
Markus, H. R., 64, 70, 72, 123, 128, 181
Marland, S. Jr., 533
Marlow, L., 816
Marsden, J., 718
Marsh, L. D., 226
Marshall, B. C., 543
Marshall, J. L., 467, 758–759
Marshall, S., 196
Martens, B. K., 332, 482
Martin, D., 17
Martin, D. H., 248
Martin, P., 45, 518
Martin, P. J., 40, 196, 295, 297–298, 435, 771
Martin, S. S., 253
Martinez, C. R., Jr., 388–389
Martinez, P. E., 656
Martinez-Ponz, M., 285
Marx, E., 235, 771, 779
Masia-Warner, C., 599
Masiulis, B., 225
Maslin, C. A., 695
Maslovaty, N., 213
Maslow, A. H., 659
Mason, D. A., 721
Masson, R. L., 419, 433
Masten, A. S., 594, 769, 771–772, 779
Mathai, C. M., 613, 615–616, 758
Matheny, A. P., 695
Matlock-Hetzel, S., 214
Maton, K. I., 56
Matsumura, L. C., 338
Matthes, W. A., 309, 313
Matthews, C. O., 17
Matthews, K. A., 149
Matthews, S., 228
Mattson, M. E., 732

Mattsson, A., 695
Matza, L. S., 674
Mau, W., 87, 497, 505–507, 509–510
Maughan, B., 696, 698
Maumary-Gremaud, A., 592
Mayberry, R. M., 222
Mayer, J. D., 211
Mayer, S., 698
Mayne, T., 449
Mazzula, S., 115
McAdams, C. R., III, 615
McAdoo, H., 96
McAuliffe, G., 26
McBride, J. T., 223
McCall-Perez, Z., 85–86, 90
McCallum, A., 249
McCarn, S. R., 136
McCarroll, L., 816
McCarthy, M., 228
McCarty, T. L., 535
McCauley, A., 18
McCay, E., 352, 366
McClain, A. L., 214
McClaskey, C. L., 676, 696
McClellan, D. E., 164
McClelland, K., 117
McCloskey, L. A., 718
McClure, B. A., 18
McClure, G. T., 189
McCluskey, C. P., 638–639, 641, 644
McCoach, D. B., 537
McCollum, V., 310
McCord, J., 660
McCormack, J., 675
McCormick, J. S., 459–460, 465, 470, 475–476
McCoy, A. R., 639–640
McCreary, B. T., 195
McCubbin, L., 53, 60, 128, 563
McCurdy, B., 405
McDaniel, J., 804
McDaniel, S., 335
McDaniel, S. H., 450
McDaniels, C., 497
McDavis, R. J., 18, 171, 324, 344, 786
McDermott, P. A., 54
McDonald, G. J., 136
McDonald, J. L., 504
McDougall, P., 592–593
McDowell, E. E., 613, 616
McEachern, A. G., 300
McEvoy, A., 636–638, 644–645, 696
McEwan, R. T., 249
McFadden, J., 23
McFarland, W. P., 139
McGarty, D., 312
McGee, R. O., 695–696

McGhee, D. E., 170
McGlothlin, J. M., 16, 23
McGoldrick, M., 100
McGrath, J. E., 111
McHenry, S., 302
McIntosh, P., 67, 118
McKellar, R., 9
McKenna, N., 181, 233
McKenzie, F. D., 771, 779
McKenzie, J. A., 535
McKenzie, K., 406
McKeown, R. E., 618
McKinnon, B. E., 741
McKinnon, M., 505
McLaughlin, T. F., 719
McLemore, T. G., 592
McLeod, E. H., 213, 517
McLoyd, V. C., 146–147, 149, 153, 280
McMahon, G., 179
McMahon, H. G., 310, 766
McMahon, M., 313–314, 375, 501, 503
McMahon, S. D., 322
McMahon, T., 463
McMillan, B., 383–384
McMillian, M., 356
McNamara, J. R., 795
McNeal, R. E., 226
McNeil, B. W., 19, 22, 310–311
McQueen, A., 718
McWhirter, A., 382, 765
McWhirter, B., 382, 383, 765
McWhirter, E. H., 382, 507, 510, 765
McWhirter, J., 382, 635–636, 643, 645–646, 765
McWhirter, M. J., 641
Mead, G. H., 519
Meara, N. M., 789
Meath, J., 299–300
Meckstroth, E. A., 547
Mednick, S. A., 695
Medway, F. H., 486, 493
Meeks, C., 604, 741, 763
Mehan, H., 85, 89
Mehana, M., 53
Meichenbaum, R., 487
Meier, A. M., 249, 340
Meisels, S. J., 640
Melincoff, D. S., 322
Mellou, E., 518
Melton, G. B., 680–681, 795
Memis, J. P., 600
Men, M., 87
Menchola, M., 721
Mendaglio, S., 418, 536, 551
Mendelson, M. J., 588
Menesini, E., 675–676
Meraviglia, M. G., 683–684

Mercer, L., 592
Merisca, R., 699
Merrill, G., 4
Messinger, C. S., 147
Mester, R., 463
Metha, A., 463, 629–630
Metz, A. J., 284–285
Metzler, A. E., 509
Metzler, C. W., 249
Meyer, K. A., 599
Meyer, R. J., Jr., 310
Mezzich, A. C., 718
Michlin, M., 299–300
Mickelson, D. J., 785–786
Middleton, J. N., 112
Middleton, R. A., 171
Midgeley, E., 518
Midgley, C., 338, 656, 773
Mihalic, S. F., 164, 460, 680, 703
Mikulincer, M., 463
Milburn, N., 383
Mili, F., 222
Milich, R., 676
Milk, R., 118
Miller, C., xxix, 673
Miller, D. B., 56, 129, 187–188
Miller, D. L., 116
Miller, D. N., 466
Miller, D. W., 600, 603
Miller, F. W., 4–5, 7
Miller, G. A., 20
Miller, G. D., 740
Miller, G. E., 385
Miller, J. B., 431, 434, 653
Miller, J. Y., 659
Miller, L., 249
Miller, M., 150
Miller, T., 452
Miller, T. R., 704
Miller, W. R., 60, 721, 725–729, 731–732
Miller-Johnson, S., 592–593
Milligan, J., 537–538
Mills, R. S. L., 592
Millstein, S. G., 249
Milne, D. L., 23
Milner, V. S., 21, 198
Milos, M. E., 522
Milsom, A. S., 16, 162–163, 171, 413, 615
Milson, A., 164
Milstein, M. M., 769
Minde, T., 96
Minden, J., 467
Miner, J. L., 146
Minton, H. L., 136
Miranda, A., 404–405, 563
Miranda, G., 53, 60, 128

Mirowsky, J., 384
Mitchell, A. M., 10
Mitchell, C. W., 795
Mitchell, J., 462
Mitchell, J. T., 465–466, 471
Mitchell, K., 596
Mitchell, K. J., 596
Mitchell, K. M., 528
Mitchell, M. H., 7, 9, 276, 397, 402, 766, 815–816
Mitchell, N., 97, 99, 104–106, 326, 773
Mitchell, R. E., 383–384
Mitchum, N. T., 412
Miville, M. L., 177, 180, 183
Mobley, M., 636
Mock, M., 383
Modzeleski, W., 804
Moffitt, T. E., 675, 677–678, 695, 698, 700
Mohatt, G. V., 545
Mohr, P., 411
Moise, J. F., 698
Mok, D., 96
Moll, L. C., 88
Molnar, B. E., 229
Moloney, M., 160, 162
Monti, P. M., 721
Moon, M., 403
Moon, S. M., 531, 534, 537, 543
Moore, D., 406
Moore, E. J., 8, 39
Moore, K. A., 248
Moore, K. B., 270
Morales, A., 186–187
Morales, J., 702
Moran, D., 699
Moran, V. R., 186
Morenoff, J. D., 698
Morgan, O. J., 20
Morris, C. N., 398
Morris, J., 282
Morris, J. E., 535
Morris, T. L., 599
Morrison, D. M., 249
Morrison, G., 462
Morrow, L. M., 259–260
Morten, G., 274, 507
Mortiore, P., 698
Morton, G., 347
Mosak, H. H., 411
Mosconi, J., 282
Mott, R. L., 249
Motto, J. A., 626
Mouttapa, M., 677
Mrazek, P. J., 382, 392
Muffo, J. A., 21–22
Mufson, S. A., 412
Mukherjee, S., 226

Mulder, R. T., 462
Mulhall, P. F., 719
Muller, C., 635
Muller, L. E., 140, 412, 433
Mullis, F., 333, 341–342, 451, 485
Multon, K. D., 201, 278, 285
Munroe-Blum, H., 101
Murguia, A., 492
Murphy, J. A., 385, 767–768
Murphy, M. L., 459, 470
Murray, C., 54
Murray, G. C., 23
Murray, H., 83
Murray, I., 198
Muzina, D. J., 621
Myer, R. A., 472–473
Myers, J. E., 16, 18, 127, 129–130, 132, 309, 312, 598
Myers, L. J., 597
Myrick, R., 8, 11, 16, 39, 214, 293, 295–296, 412, 433, 438, 441, 742, 758, 766, 812

N

Nabors, L., 225, 701
Nachshol, R., 433
Nagin, D. S., 146, 149
Naglieri, J. A., 534
Najaka, S. S., 701
Nakkula, M., 653, 659–660, 669
Nangle, D. W., 599
Nansel, T. R., 673
Nanus, B., 470
Napolitano, S. A., 482
Narvaez, D., 211
Nash, S. G., 718
Nash, T., 225
Nastasi, B. K., 329
Nation, M., 382, 389–390, 680–681
National Association for Gifted Children (NAGC), 534–535, 555
National Association of State Boards of Education, 220
National Campaign to Prevent Teen Pregnancy, 244, 248–249, 251, 253–254
National Cancer Institute, 224
National Career Development Association (NCDA), 507
National Center for Children in Poverty, xxvii
National Center for Educational Statistics (NCES), 67, 112, 273, 535, 537, 635–636, 641, 646, 693–694
National Center for Health Statistics, 614
National Commission on Excellence in Education, 38
National Institute of Mental Health (NIMH), 230, 614

National Occupational Information Coordination
    Committee (NOICC), 498, 508
National Research Council, 269
National School Safety Center, 460
Naumberg, M., 519
Nauta, M. M., 505
Needham, B. L., 635
Neeman, J., 594
Neil, D. M., 15, 761
Neimeyer, G. J., 19
Neimeyer, R. A., 474
Nelson, C. M., 706
Nelson, K. W., 21
Nelson, L., 517
Nelson, L. J., 410
Nelson, M. D., 302–303
Nelson, M. L., 309, 311
Nelson, R. C., 18
Nelson, R. E., 467
Nemiroff, M. A., 598
Neufeldt, S. A., 310–312
Neumark-Sztainer, D., 227, 233
Nevill, D., 509
Neville, H. A., 67–68, 152, 636
Nevin, A., 482, 818
Newacheck, P. W., 221–223
Newby, E., 467, 758
Newcomb, A. F., 587–588, 592, 675
Newman, B. M., 211, 214
Newman, D. A., 678
Newman, J. L., 348
Newman, K. S., 151
Newman, P. R., 211, 214
Newman-Carlson, D., 20, 685
Newson, J., 766
New York State School Counselor Association, 45
Ng, K., 20
Ng'andu, N., 146
Nguy, L., 676
Nichols, S. L., 139
Nicotra, E., 677
Niles, S. G., 18–19, 498–499, 501, 503, 505, 792
Nin, A., 64
Nishina, A., 122
Nkomo, S. M., 111
Nobel, K. D., 549
Noddings, N., 352, 370, 779
Noel, C. J., 16, 299
Noll, E., 129, 322
Norcross, J. C., 724
Nordness, P. D., 696
Northam, E. A., 226
Northup, D., 771
Norton, R. A., 53, 60, 128, 563
Nosek, B., 170
Nugent, F. A., 6, 481

Nunes, J. V., 718
Nurcombe, B., 787
Nuttall, E. V., 65
Nwadiora, E., 96
Nye, C. H., 23
Nygreen, K., 699

O

Oakes, J. M., 145
Oates, G. L. S. C., 149
Ober, K., 443
Obiakor, F., 597
O'Brien, K. M., 132, 189, 281–282, 284–285, 356, 507
O'Brien, M., 537
O'Brien, M. U., 381, 771, 776–777
Ochs, L. A., 162
O'Connell, P., 680
O'Dea, J. A., 227, 233
Oden, M. H., 542, 546
O'Donnell, C., 619
O'Donnell, J., 654
O'Donnell, L., 619
Oetting, E. R., 184, 548
Offord, D. R., 101
Ofili, E., 222
Ogbu, J. U., 96, 179–180, 183, 197
Ogden, C. L., 228
O'Hanlon, W. H., 433
Ohnishi, H., 66
Okazaki, S., 101, 322
Olafsson, R. F., 675
Oldfield, R., 130, 195
Olin, S. S., 654, 659–660
Olisky, T., 130–132
Oliver, L. W., 282, 504, 510–511
Oliver, M. L., 111
Olmedo, E., 70
Olsen, L., 79, 83–85, 88, 90
Olson, L., 149
Olszewski-Kubilius, P. M., 536, 543, 545
Olweus, D., 460, 469, 673, 678, 680–681, 683, 686,
    694–695, 705
O'Malley, P. M., 717–719
Omizo, M. M., 214, 433, 488, 524
Omizo, S. A., 433, 524
O'Neal, E. C., 675
Orbach, I., 463
Orell, L. H., 340
Orellana, M. F., 82, 186
Orenstein, P., 535
Orfield, G., 177
Orme, S. F., 481
O'Rourke, K., 340, 351

Orr, D. P., 249
Orthner, D. K., 639–640
Ortiz, A. A., 65
Orton, G. L., 398
Osborn, C. J., 20
Osborne, J. L., 384
Osborne, S., 482
Osbourne, J. W., 180, 198, 769
Osgood, D. W., 693
Osguthorpe, R., 213
O'Shea, A. J., 504
O'Shea, J. A., 472
Osher, D., 459, 466, 804
Österman, K., 676–677
Osterman, K. F., 351, 354
Osterweil, Z., 662
Oswald, D. P., 168
Otis, A., 5
Ouston, J., 698
Overholser, J., 621
Overman, L. T., 53
Overton, W. F., 768
Owen, S. V., 66
Owens, D., 321
Oyserman, D., 56, 181, 564

P

Paavola, J. C., 768
Paganos, R. J., 162
Page, B. J., 309, 312–313, 316
Page, R. C., 413
Pahl, K., 719
Paikoff, R. L., 196
Paisley, P. O., 23, 178–179, 211, 213, 215, 303, 310, 315–316, 375, 766
Pajares, F., 182–183
Palma, T. V., 17, 504
Palmatier, L. L., 455, 461, 465, 469
Palmer, S., 165, 282
Palmo, A. J., 488
Panak, W. F., 592, 696
Paolucci-Whitcomb, P., 482, 818
Pappas, J. G., 316
Pardini, D. A., 702
Pare, P., 314
Pargament, K. I., 127
Parham, 180
Parham, T., 564
Park, S., 536
Parke, R. D., 55
Parker, J. G., 592–593
Parker, L. D., 65
Parker, W., 22

Parks, E. E., 66
Parks, K. A., 718
Park-Taylor, J., 385, 768, 771
Parra, G. R., 152
Parsad, B., 506
Parson, E. B., 718
Parsons, F., 4–5, 276, 432, 497
Parsons, R. D., 330–331, 339–340, 345–346, 348
Partin, R. L., 294
Partlett, D. F., 787
Passaro, P., 403
Passino, A. W., 412
Pastor, R., 411
Patchin, J. W., 638
Pate, R. H., 16, 615
Patel, D. R., 231
Pattee, L., 592
Patterson, C. J., 592
Patterson, C. P., 593
Patterson, G. A., 624
Patterson, G. J., 593
Patterson, G. R., 451, 660, 695–698, 700
Patterson, L. E., 187, 411
Patterson, T. E., 449, 453
Patterson, W. M., 624
Patton, G. C., 230
Patton, J. M., 146–147, 326, 535
Patton, J. R., 161, 166, 537
Patton, W., 313–314, 501
Patusky, K. L., 653
Paulus, L. E., 546
Pavelski, R., 462
Payne, A. F., 739
Payzant, T. W., 767
Peace, S. D., 303
Pearcy, J. N., 221
Pearlman, M., 405
Pearsall, J., 482
Pearson, B. Z., 186
Pearson, G., 316
Pearson, J. L., 476
Peck, B. M., 636–637
Pedersen, I. N., 347
Pedersen, P. B., 73, 177, 190, 597–599, 602, 604
Pederson, L., 645
Pederson, P., 128, 274
Pedro-Carroll, J., 412–413
Pellegrini, A. D., 674, 677
Peller, J. E., 433
Pelling, N., 23
Pennington, D., 312
Pentz, M. A., 391
Pepler, D., 590, 680, 698, 705
Pepper, F. C., 487
Peracchio, L. A., 148
Perez, W., 186

Perie, M., 294
Perls, F., 432
Perone, D. C., 699
Perrone, P. A., 544
Perry, C. L., 230
Perry, C. M., 355
Perry, D. G., 420, 696
Perry, M., 384
Perry, T., 197, 201
Perry, T. B., 588
Perusse, R., 16, 24, 148, 299
Petersen, S., 460
Peterson, G. W., 506
Peterson, J. S., 18, 409, 412, 414–416, 418, 420–421, 424, 536
Peterson, L. W., 598
Peterson, R. F., 705
Peterson, R. L., 701
Petras, H., 425
Petrie, S., 590
Petroski, G., 209, 269, 498, 746, 756–757
Petrowski, E. L., 18
Petterson, S. M., 146, 149
Pettit, G. S., 146, 676, 696–697
Pettit, N. W., 662
Pew, W. L., 404
Pew Hispanic Center, 178
Pfeffer, C. R., 617
Pfeiffer, A. M., 474, 536, 555
Phelps, L. A., 157, 316
Philips, S., 592
Philliber, S., 391, 659
Phillips, E. L., 231
Phillips, R. S. C., 653
Phillips, S. D., 772
Phillipson, L. C., 592
Philpot, C. L., 450
Phinney, J. S., 58, 127–130, 563–565
Piaget, J., 432, 519
Pianta, R. C., 700
Pickett, T., 145–146
Piechowski, M. M., 546–547
Pierson, M. R., 164
Pieterse, A. L., 66, 119
Pietrzak, D. R., 309
Pigott, H. E., 704
Piirto, J., 535, 546
Pike, K. C., 619
Pike, K. M., 229
Pilkington, J., 23
Pilkington, N. W., 604
Pinder, F. A., 509
Pine, G. J., 740, 755, 762
Piper, R. E., 118
Pitcher, G. D., 460, 464–466, 472
Pituc, S. T., xxvii, 63, 68, 104, 587, 589

Placier, P. L., 112
Plant, M. A., 249
Pliszka, S. R., 695
Plucker, J. M., 535
Podoloski, C., 698
Poduska, J., 425, 704
Pohan, C. A., 353
Poidevant, J. M., 817
Pokorny, A. D., 621
Poland, D. L., 542
Poland, S., 459–460, 464–467, 470, 472, 475–476, 614, 622–623, 626
Pollack, H. A., 767
Pollitt, E., 146
Ponterotto, J. G., 18, 128, 274, 435
Pope, K. S., 786, 788
Pope, M., 28
Pope-Davis, D. B., 152
Popenhagen, M. P., 460, 466–467
Popowicz, C. L., 510
Porfeli, E. J., 501
Porter, G., 481, 483
Porter, M., 195–196
Porter, R. Y., 518
Portes, A., 80–83, 86–87, 95
Portes, P. R., 107
Portman, T. A., 23
Post, J., 768
Poulin, F., 660, 677
Poureslami, M., 252
Powell, B., 669
Power, C., 228, 232
Power, T. J., 701, 705, 767
Powers, L., 160
Prasad-Gaur, A., 655
Prather, T., 162
Pratt, H. D., 231
Pratto, F., 111
Premack, D., 674
Presentacion, M., 405
Pressley, M., 260
Price, A. W., 196
Price, J. H., 17, 252, 460, 467, 616, 805
Price, J. M., 593
Price, R. H., 382, 389
Price, V., 195
Prieto, L. R., 22
Prilleltensky, I., 272, 383
Prilleltensky, O., 383
Prillman, D., 537
Prins, P. J. M., 598
Prinstein, M. J., 594
Probert, G. J., 509
Prochaska, J. O., 721, 724
Proctor, W. M., 739, 742
Project Match, 721, 732

Prout, H. T., 413, 598, 600
Prout, S. M., 214, 413, 598
Pryor, D. B., 403
Pryzwansky, W. B., 330, 340, 482–493
Pugh-Lilly, A. O., 152
Pulido, L., 82
Purdy, K. T., 588
Purkey, W. W., 16, 353, 357, 362–363
Purselle, D., 629
Putman, S. E., 397
Putnam, R. F., 706

Q

Qualley, R. M., 460, 466–467
Quamma, J. P., 704
Quierdo, A., 464–465
Quiggle, N., 696
Quilitch, H. R., 705
Quinn, A. C., 22
Quinn, M. M., 702
Quintana, S. M., 273, 564

R

Rachuba, L. T., 53
Rae, W. A., 795
Raine, A., 695
Rainey, L. M., 421
Rajani, N., 250–251
Rak, C. F., 187, 411
Ramirez, M. C., 767, 795
Ramos-McKay, J., 389
Ramsey, R., 467
Rand, K., 406
Randell, B. P., 619
Randolph, D. L., 343
Randolph, K. A., 639–640
Range, L. M., 626–627
Rapaport, R. J., 507
Rapee, R., 405
Rasheed, S., 150, 152, 507
Raskin, N. J., 411
Rasmussen, A., 146
Ray, D. C., 18, 406, 517, 519, 521, 528
Ray, K. E., 420
Ray, P. B., 313
Rayle, A. D., 127, 129–130, 132
Razo, N. P., 795
Realmuto, G. M., 383
Reardon, R., 509
Recio Adrados, J. L., 383

Recknor, J. C., 226
Reddy, M., 460, 804
Redivo, M., 599
Redwing, L., 548
Reed, A., 4–6, 276, 497
Reeder, G., 405
Reeder, J., 433
Reese, L. E., 388–389
Reeves, A., 17
Reeves, P. M., 303, 316
Reid, J., 449, 451
Reid, J. B., 697, 699–700, 703, 705
Reid, M., 659
Reid, M. J., 703
Reid, R., 696
Reiff, H. B., 160
Reinat, M., 271, 321
Reinhard, R., 525
Reinisch, J. M., 246
Reis, S. M., 535–536, 538, 540
Reiss, S., 522
Remez, L., 246–247
Remley, T. P., 19, 720–721, 804, 817
Remley, T. P., Jr., 19, 467–468, 720–721, 785, 798, 804, 805, 817
Renard, D., 23
Renner, P., 695
Rennie, D. L., 20
Renzulli, J. S., 535–536, 540
Resch, N. L., 152
Resnick, L. B., 276
Resnick, M. D., 231–232, 249, 618–619, 652, 659
Resnicow, K., 777
Rest, J., 211
Reyes, O., 482
Reynolds, A. J., 53, 639–640
Reynolds, A. L., 136, 321, 323
Reynolds, C. J., 704
Reynolds, W. M., 625, 679
Rhodes, J. E., 152
Rich, E., 232
Rich, Y., 89
Richards, P. S., 597
Richards, S., 160
Richardson, J., 312
Richert, S., 541
Richman, N., 696
Richmond, J. B., 771, 779
Richters, J. E., 656
Rickson, H., 232
Riddle, J., 433
Ridge, B., 695
Ridley, C. R., 492
Ries, L. A. G., 224
Ries, R. R., 542
Riester, A. E., 413

Riley, P. L., 804
Riley, R. W., 767, 769
Riley, S., 523
Rimm, S. B., 534–535, 540, 546
Rimm-Kaufman, S. E., 700
Rincon, C., 595
Rindfuss, R. R., 249
Ring, J. M., 95–101
Ringel, J., 381
Ripley, V., 43, 330, 433, 660
Risi, S., 410, 589
Risley, T. R., 767
Ritchie, M. H., 441
Riva, M. T., 412–413
Rivero, E., 87–88
Rivers, I., 676
Roarke, A. E., 772
Robbins, C., 253
Robbins, S., 509, 659, 662
Robbins, S. B., 352
Roberts, A. R., 460–461, 475
Roberts, C., 563, 565
Roberts, D., 563
Roberts, E. B., 302, 312–313
Roberts, J., 181, 758
Roberts, J. A., 148
Roberts, M. C., 226
Roberts, R., 127
Roberts, R. E., 116, 629
Robertson, J. A., 249
Robertson, P., 795
Robertson, T., 683
Robin, L., 249
Robins, S. B., 506
Robinson, M., 325
Robinson, N. M, 549
Robinson, S., 696
Robinson, T. L., 19
Robinson, T. R., 603
Robinson, V. P., 449
Robson, C., 520
Rodrigue, J. R., 196
Rodriguez, E. R., 184–185
Roedell, W. C., 538, 549
Roehlkepartain, E. C., 280
Roens, B. A., 740
Roeser, R. W., 773
Roessler, R. T., 161–162
Roffman, R. A., 721
Rogeness, G. A., 695
Rogers, C., 6, 8, 293, 295, 402–403, 432, 617
Rogers, C. R., 273, 411
Rogers, J. R., 616
Rogers, K. B., 538
Rogers, M. R., 597
Rogers, V., 405

Roggenbaum, S., 619
Rogler, L. H., 97, 383
Rohrbach, L. A., 677
Rohrbeck, C. A., 704
Rokutani, L., 23, 720–721
Rolle, A., 654
Rolleri, L. A., 652
Rollins, V. B., 324
Rollnick, S., 60, 721, 725–729, 731–732
Rollock, D., 96
Rolon-Dow, R., 181
Romano, J. L., xxx, 28–29, 293, 301, 381–384, 461,
    643, 647, 762
Romasz, T. E., 599–601, 605
Rome, E. S., 230–232
Romero, A. J., 116, 563, 565
Romo, H. D., 182, 188
Rones, M., 294, 326
Ronk, P., 472
Rønnestad, H., 309–312
Rose, C. D., 413–414
Rose, S. R., 591
Rose, T. B., 213
Rosecrance, F. C., 740
Rosenberg, M. S., 412
Rosenberger, E. W., 20
Rosenbloom, S. R., 113, 116
Rosenblum, A., 733
Rosenbluth, B., 683–684
Rosenthal, C. R., 433
Ross, C. E., 384
Ross, J. A., 224
Rossi, P. H., 145, 605
Rossi, R. J., 353–354, 356, 363
Roth, J. L., 652
Rotherham-Borus, M. J., 249, 391
Rothney, J. W. M., 544, 740
Rothstein, R., 767
Rotter, J. B., 65
Rotter, J. C., 740
Rouse, K., 113, 150
Rousso, H., 170
Rowden, L., 425, 592
Rowe, D. C., 662
Rowell, L. L., 433
Rowley, S. A., 127
Rowling, L., 226
Royal, G. P., 226
Roysircar, G., 96, 185, 435
Roysircar-Sodowsky, G., 65–66, 68, 97
Rozecki, T., 815
Ruben, H. L., 621
Rubin, K. H., 410, 592–593
Rubin, L., 425
Rudolph, L., 598
Rumbaut, R. G., 80–83, 86–87, 95, 127

Rumberger, R. W., 640–641
Rungta, S. A., 16
Rutter, M., 696, 698, 700, 772
Rutter, P. A., 619, 629
Ryan, C., 437
Ryan, J. A. M., 366, 655
Ryan, R. M., 160, 280, 286, 381
Ryan-Finn, K. D., 389
Ryan Krane, N., 282–284, 286, 511
Rye, D. R., 296
Ryerson, D. M., 620
Ryeson-Espino, S., 87

S

Saarni, C., 604
Sachs-Kapp, P., 139
Sadeghi, M., 790
Saenz, D. S., 563
Saginak, K. A., 112, 114
Sagrestano, L. M., 196
Salend, S., 538, 704
Salmivalli, C., 603, 677
Salovey, P., 211, 603
Salter, R., 316
Salzman, M., 413, 481, 487, 489, 491
Sameroff, A. J., 149
Sampson, J. P., Jr., 507
Sampson, R. J., 698
Sams, W., 19
Samuelson, P., 213
Sanborn, M. P., 534, 544
Sanchez, E., 683
Sanchez, L., 437
Sanchez, P., 271, 322
Sanchez, V., 702
Sanders, D. R., 413
Sanders, S. A., 246
Sanderson, C. A., 147
Sandfort, T. G. M., 135
Sandhu, D. S., 20, 404
Sandler, H. M., 87–88
Sandoval, J., 462, 464, 596–597, 600, 623
Sands, D. J., 160, 165
Sandstrom, M. J., 593
Sanger, M., 213
San Miguel, G., 178
San Miguel Bauman, S., 157
Santelli, J. S., 245–246, 249
Sanyika, 199
Saponaro, L. A., 592
Sapp, M., 405, 411
Sarason, S. B., 83
Sardi, V. A., 271, 322

Sarvela, P., 674
Satcher, J., 106
Satchere, D., 381
Satir, V., 449
Saunders, J., 195, 198
Saunders, M., 704
Sautner, B., 368, 375
Savickas, M. L., 277, 505, 509, 511
Savin-Williams, R. C., 140, 594
Scales, P. C., 280, 652
Scarboro, B., xxix, 811
Scarborough, J. L., 18
Schaefer, C., 406
Schaefer, C. E., 521
Schaeffer, C. M., 425
Schalling, D., 695
Schaps, E., 351–357, 360–361, 699, 706
Schatz, E., 552
Scheel, K. R., 22
Scher, D., 259
Scher, M., 598
Scherer, D., 19
Scherman, A., 433
Schetky, D. H., 547
Schiever, S. W., 547
Schildhaus, S., 733
Schimmel, C., 438
Schloss, P., 487
Schlossberg, S., 282
Schlundt, D. G., 229
Schmader, T., 115
Schmeelk-Cone, K. H., 116
Schmid, K., xxx, 81, 84
Schmidt, J. J., 3–5, 7–12, 15–16, 21, 276, 293, 296, 312, 314, 341, 357, 362, 382, 431–432, 438, 481, 483, 488, 493, 597–598, 600, 752
Schmidt, J. L., 314
Schmidt, L., 789
Schmidt, M. W., 433
Schmidt, N. B., 195
Schneider, B. H., 687
Schneider, D. J., 696
Schnurman-Crook, A., 23
Schoendorf, K. C., 223
Schön, D. A., 311–312
Schorr, D., 767
Schorr, L. B., 655, 767–768
Schuder, M. R., 640
Schuerger, J. M., 180
Schulenberg, J., 382, 717–718
Schulte, A., 330, 340, 482–493
Schultheiss, D. E. P., 17, 19, 504, 507, 511
Schultz, H., 675
Schunk, D. H., 537
Schuster, M. A., 248
Schwallie-Giddis, P., 38, 271, 322

Schwartz, A. E., 98–99
Schwartz, D., 696
Schwartz, I. M., 247
Schwartz, J. P., 381, 563
Schwartz, L. K., 170
Schwartz, M., 160, 168
Schwartz, W., 535
Schweinhart, L. J., 390–391
Schwiebert, V. L, 17
Schwimmer, J., 229
Sciarra, D., 4, 10, 322, 324, 401–403, 405–406, 438
Sciarra, P. T., 295, 431–432
Sclan, E. M., 112
Scott, J. M., 536, 543, 545
Scott, L., 351
Seabolt, K., 766
Seabrooks, J., 23
Seagal, J. D., 662
Seals, D., 675
Search Institute, 55, 359–360, 369, 371
Sears, S. J., 294, 467, 812
Seashore, K. R., 296, 300
Seeley, K., 536–537
Seem, S., 80, 91, 366, 370, 773, 821–822
Segal, P. B., 756–757
Segura-Herrera, T. A., 273
Seigle, P., 433, 601
Seligman, M. E. P., 384, 389, 565
Sellers, R. M., 117, 127–128
Selman, R., 653, 659–660, 669
Selzer, R., 230
Semino, S. J., 135
Seppanen, P., 296
Sergiovanni, T. J., 352, 354
Serpell, R., 259–260
Servaty-Seib, H. L., 409
Sesma, A., 280
Sexson, S. B., 226
Sexton, T. L., 148, 166, 214, 281, 433, 452, 510–511, 741, 760–761
Seymour, E., 504
Shaffer, D., 466
Shahar, G., 652
Shahinfar, A., 674
Shange, N., 526
Shapiro, E. S., 767
Shapiro, T. M., 111
Share, D. L., 696
Share, J., 769
Shaull, R., 25
Shaw, D., 260
Shea, M., 104
Shechtman, Z., 410, 411, 413–414, 433–434
Sheffield, D., 282
Sheldon, C. B., 38

Sheldon, K. M., 112
Sheldon, S. B., 355–356
Shelton, C. F., 343
Shelton, J. N., 117, 127
Shelton, N. J., 117
Shen, Y., 521–522
Shepard, J., 385–386, 388
Shepard, L., 640
Shepherd-Johnson, L., 83–84
Sheras, P., 383, 469, 476
Sheridan, S. M., 332, 481–482, 486, 597, 602
Sherman, J., 695
Sherman, L., 533–534
Sherman, L. W., 707
Sherry, A., 196
Shertzer, B., 7, 11
Shi, L., 220–221
Shneidman, E. S., 616, 631
Shoemaker, R. L., 10
Shoffner, M. F., 598, 815
Shon, S. P., 321
Shontz, F. C., 159, 161
Shorey, H., 406
Short, R. J., 766
Shostak, B., 522
Shouse, R. C., 84
Shriver, T. P., 694
Shrum, W., 590
Shuntich, R., 675
Shure, M., 216, 696
Shylo, K. R., 497
Sidanius, J., 111
Siebecker, A., xxix, 673
Siegle, D., 537
Siller, J., 159
Silva, P. A., 695
Silverman, L. K., 531, 533–535, 545–547, 549–550, 552–553
Silverthorn, N., 660
Simek-Morgan, L., 64
Simeonsson, R. J., 166
Simon, T. R., 462, 466
Simon, V. A., 594–595
Simonds, J. F., 463
Simons, H., 179
Simons, R. L., 146
Sink, C., 80, 91, 148, 269, 295, 406, 747, 757, 816
Sippola, L. K., 588, 675
Sire, J. W., 64
Siroskey-Sabdo, L. A., 433, 646–647
Sisson, C. F., 300, 302–303
Siwatu, K., 197
Sjostrom, L., 683–684
Skaggs, G., 212
Skiba, R., 700–701

Skinner, B. F., 405, 487
Skinner, M. J., 249
Skinner, M. S., 697
Skovholt, T., 309–312
Skowronski, K. J., 678
Skroban, S., 388
Slaby, R. C., 696
Sladeczek, I., 704
Slaikeu, K. A., 464, 473
Slap, G. B., 659
Slate, J. R., 413
Sleeter, C. E., 118
Sletta, O., 592
Sloper, P., 226
Sluzki, C. E., 100
Smaby, M. H., 20, 804
Smallish, L., 696
Smart, J., 166
Smith, A., 97, 100
Smith, B. H., 699
Smith, D., 675
Smith, D. C., 20, 463, 467
Smith, D. E., 721
Smith, E. A., 246–247
Smith, E. J., 383–384, 565
Smith, E. M., 548
Smith, E. P., 385, 387
Smith, J., 616, 620
Smith, J. D., 687
Smith, L., 509, 592
Smith, L. H., 540
Smith, M., 127, 487
Smith, M. A., 224
Smith, P., 388–389
Smith, P. K., 675–676, 687
Smith, P. L, 278
Smith, R., 771
Smith, S. E., 412
Smith, S. L., 18, 812
Smith, S. W., 603
Smith, T. B., 597
Smith-Davis, J., 98
Smolak, L., 230
Smoot, D. L., 592
Smothers, M. K., 269
Smyer, R., 765
Snyder, B. A., 816
Snyder, C., 406
Snyder, J., 697–698
Sobal, J., 228
Sobeck, J., 719
Sodowsky, G. R., 64–65, 69, 435
Solberg, S., 509
Solberg, V. A., 284–285

Solberg, V. S., 29, 269, 272, 278, 281, 284–286, 498, 772
Soleck, G., 145–146, 151
Soler, R., 777
Solomon, D., 352, 354–355, 361, 699, 706
Solorzano, L., 536
Sommerfeld, A., 60
Sophie, J., 136
Sorenson, G. P., 799
Sowa, C., 17
Sowers, J. A., 160
Sowers, K. M., 674, 693
Spagna, M. E., 162, 164, 166, 171
Spanierman, L. B., 67–68, 510
Sparkman, L. B., 467, 798
Sparks, R., 296
Specter, S. E., 228
Speight, S. L., 271–272, 283
Spence, S. H., 599
Spencer, H., 518
Spencer, M. B., 129, 196, 322
Spencer, S., 184
Spera, C., 53, 356
Spice, C. G., 315
Spice, W. H., 315
Spindler, G., 422
Spirito, A., 621
Spitzer, R. L., 231
Spivak, G., 696
Splete, H. H., 316
Spokane, A. R., 282, 504, 510–511
Spoont, M. R., 695
Spracklen, K. M., 698
Sprague, J., 466, 682
Spratt, E. G., 226
Sprinthall, N. A., 303
Srebalus, D. J., 22
Srinivasan, S., 229
Sroufe, L. A., 594, 700, 767
Stafford, A., 504
Stafford, J., 591
Stagnitti, K., 518–519
Stallings, J. A., 768
Standeven, B., 232
Stanford, K., 675
Stanley, J. C., 539
Stanley, P. H., 16, 353, 362, 367–370
Stanley, S. O., 149
Stanton-Salazar, R., 84, 86–87, 91
Starkman, N., 250–251
Starks, C., 113
Starr, M., 741
Steckler, A., 234
Steele, C. M., 56, 123, 129, 183–184, 197

Steele, D. M., 123
Stefanowski-Harding, S., 613, 617, 622–623
Stein, D., 463
Stein, D. M., 19
Stein, N., 683–684
Stein, R. E., 222
Steinback, C. L., 704
Steinberg, L., 594–595, 674, 697
Steinberg, S. J., 594
Steiner, H., 128, 230
Stephens, J., 510–511
Stephens, R. D., 459
Stephens, R. S., 721
Stephenson, M., 184
Stern, D., 655
Stern, S., 228
Stevens, G. D., 220–221
Stevens, H. B., 19
Stevens, J., 234
Stevens, N., 588
Stevens, P., 17
Stevenson, J., 696
Stevenson, J. F., 383–384
Steward, R. J., 15, 27, 761
Stewart, F. J., 740
Stickel, S. A., 299, 301–303, 411
Stief, T. M., 248
Stiefel, L., 98–99
Stillion, J. M., 613, 616
Stiver, I. P., 431, 434, 653
Stockdale, M. S., 674
Stockton, R., 23
Stoddard, J. J., 221
Stoiber, K. C., 597
Stolberg, A. L., 413
Stoltenberg, C. D., 19, 22, 25, 310–311
Stoltzfutz, J., 129, 322
Stone, C., 214, 721, 794, 807
Stone, C. B., 22–23, 37, 45–46, 112, 293, 301, 326, 437, 468–469, 739, 819
Stone, L. A., 179
Stone, S. C., 7, 11
Stoolmiller, M., 697
Storino, M., 604
Story, M., 228, 231–234
Stowischek, J., 162
St. Peter, R. F., 221–222
Straatemeier, G., 704
Strand, D., 526–527
Strang, J., 718
Straub, R. L., 460
Strauss, R. M., 767
Stringfield, S. C., 354, 356, 363
Strober, M., 230
Strodtbeck, F. L., 66, 72, 730

Stroh, H. R., 269, 747, 757
Strong, S. R., 277, 412, 772
Strunin, L., 249
Studer, J. R., 3, 9, 11, 19, 431, 438, 463, 815, 817
Stueve, A., 619
Stunkard, A. J., 228
Sturm, R., 381
Su, J., 231
Suárez-Orozco, C., 79, 81–88, 97
Suárez-Orozco, M., 79, 81–88, 97, 321
Substance Abuse and Mental Health Services Administration (SAMHSA), 717–718, 733
Sue, D., 64–67, 96–105, 107, 130, 189, 271–272, 275, 310, 436, 455, 471, 507, 511, 593–594, 597, 646
Sue, D. W., 18, 63–68, 95–105, 107, 130, 171, 177, 189, 271–272, 274–275, 310, 324, 344, 347, 436, 455, 471, 507, 511, 527, 593–594, 597, 646, 786
Sue, S., 99
Sue, W., 527
Sugai, G., 164, 698, 701, 706
Suh, S., 106
Sullivan, H. S., 518, 588, 594
Sullivan, J. R., 415, 660, 795
Sullivan, P. F., 229
Summerlin, M. L., 433
Summers, T., 250
Sun, Y., 148, 269, 756
Sundal-Hansen, L. S., 501
Sunderland, M., 706
Super, C. M., 277, 505
Super, D. E., 276–277, 432, 497–498, 500, 503, 505, 510–512
Surrey, J. L., 431, 440, 442, 653
Susman, E. J., 695
Sutton, J., 676
Sutton, J. M. J., 309, 312–313
Sutton, S. E., 413
Suwalsky, J. T. D., 147
Swanson, C. B., 177–178
Swanson, H. L., 164
Swanson, J. L., 272
Swearer, S. M., xxix, 482, 673, 677–679
Sweeney, D. S., 519
Sweeney, T. J., 18
Swettenham, J., 676
Swiatek, M. A., 538–540
Swick, K., 371
Swift, D. J., 697
Sylvester, M. S., 222
Synatschk, K. O., 315
Syverson, P. D., 21
Szalacha, L. A., 117
Szilagyi, P. G., 223

T

Szymanski, E. M., 162
Szymanski, G., 766

Tabish, K. R., 340
Taffe, R. C., 435
Tajfel, H., 567
Takeuchi, D. T., 117
Tallal, P., 696
Talley, R. C., 766
Talmadge, C. G., 96
Tamminen, A. W., 740
Tan, S., 87
Tan, V. L. M., 512
Tang, M., 19, 22
Tanner, J. F., Jr., 148
Tanney, B., 467
Tapper, K., 678
Tarakeshwar, 127
Tarter, R. E., 718
Tarver-Behring, S., 162, 164, 166, 171
Tatar, M., 80, 83, 91
Tatum, B. V., 535–537, 548
Taub, J., 682–683
Taylor, C., 601
Taylor, C. A., 433, 435
Taylor, J., 116, 652
Taylor, J. G., 497, 696
Taylor, L., 24, 83, 89, 296, 704, 769–771, 800
Taylor, M., 674
Taylor, R., 563, 565
Taylor, S. L., 675
Taylor, S. N., 248
Taylor, W. C., 196
Taylor-Greene, S. J., 706
Tedder, S. L., 433
Tedeschi, J. T., 675
Tellegen, A., 769
Telljohann, S. K., 252, 460, 467, 616, 805
Tencer Garrity, T. L., 185
Tennessen, J., 526–527
Terman, L., 542, 546
Terr, L. C., 461, 465
Terry, B., 149
Terry, K., 181, 719
Terry, R. A., 592–593
Terry, T., 351
Tevyaw, T. O., 721
Theberge, S. K., 636
Theriot, M. T., 674, 693
Thernstrom, A., 51, 127, 129–132, 564
Thernstrom, S., 51, 127, 129–132, 564

Thies, K. M., 222, 224–225
Thoma, S. J., 211
Thomas, C. R., 197
Thomas, D. E., 16, 181
Thomas, L., 804
Thomas, M. W., 460–462, 464–465, 468, 473
Thomas, N., 20
Thomas, S. R., 316
Thompson, C. E., 68, 118–119, 121, 323, 773
Thompson, C. L., 416, 419, 598
Thompson, E. A., 466, 619
Thompson, R. A., 294, 296, 298, 342, 599, 602, 815
Thoresen, C. E., 433
Thornberry, T. P., 698
Thornton, A., 249
Thousand, J. S., 597
Thull, B., 23
Thurlow, C., 589
Thurlow, M. L., 636, 641, 644–645
Thyer, B. A., 413
Tidwell, R., 412
Tienda, M., 321–322
Tierney, G., 106, 182
Tierney, R., 467, 643
Timberlake, T. L., 322, 368
Timmerman, G., 435
Tims, M. S., 591
Tingstrom, D. H., 704
Todd, A. W., 698
Todd, D. M., 81–82
Tolan, P. H., 381, 392, 467, 698, 701, 707
Tolan, S., 546–547
Tollerud, T. R., 404
Toloczko, A. M., 20
Tolson, J. M., 588–589
Tomlinson, M. J., 282
Tonemah, S. A., 536
Toporek, R. L., 435, 786
Topping, K. J., 704
Torres, L., 96
Torres, R. D., 188
Torres-Rivera, E., 20
Toth, S. L., 381
Toukmanian, S. G., 20
Tousignant, M., 619
Towner-Larsen, R., 812
Townsend, T. G., 181
Tracey, T. J. G., 506
Tracy, A. J., 433, 601, 680–681
Trainor, A., 166
Tranel Hall, T., 145
Travers, J. F., 112
Treasure, J. L., 231, 721
Tremblay, R. E., 146, 149
Trevisan, M. S., 741

Triandis, H. C., 274
Tribble, J. L., 17
Trice, A., 501, 503
Trickett, E. J., xxviii, xxx, 79, 81–82, 84, 86
Trimble, J., 70, 545
Troiden, R. R., 136
Troillett, A., 225
Troop, N. A., 231
Trotman, M. F., 535
Trout, A., 696
Truax, C. B., 528
Trueba, H. T., 87, 565
Trumble, B., 482
Trump, K. S., 461, 465, 467, 475
Trusty, J., 4, 9–11, 18, 20, 215, 325, 821
Tschann, J. M., 247
Tsolis, A., 312
Tucker, C. M., 182–183, 190, 282, 772
Tudor, J. F., 148
Turba, R., 22
Turner, J. C., 567
Turner, K., 113
Turner, R. J., 116
Turner, S. L., 282
Turner, S. M., 599
Tyack, D., 766
Tyson, C. A., 535

U

Udis, J., 597
Udry, J. R., 246–247, 594
Ullery, B., 21
Umana-Taylor, A. J., 591
Umemoto, D., 146
Underwood, M. K., 697
Ungar, R., 20, 644
Unger, J. B., 677
Updyke, J. F., 486, 493
Urbanovski, R., 214
Urberg, K. A., 588–589, 591
Urdan, T. C., 773
Urofsky, R., 17
Urtz, F. P., 524
U.S. Bureau of Labor Statistics, 270
U.S. Bureau of the Census, 95–96, 99, 127, 150, 269, 271, 347, 518, 751, 819
U.S. Department of Education (USDE), xxvii, 38, 45, 54, 58, 87, 95, 112–115, 123, 157, 160, 168, 321, 361, 437, 440, 443, 468–469, 531, 534–536, 547–548, 635–636, 641, 693, 739, 751, 788, 795, 799, 802, 806, 815

U.S. Department of Health and Human Services, 381, 392, 646, 719, 733, 804
U.S. Department of Labor, 498
Usher, C. H., 313, 316, 412, 646
U.S. Surgeon General, 381
Utay, J. M., 433
Utsey, S. O., 101, 322

V

Vacc, N. A., 3
Vacha, E. F., 719
Vacha-Haase, T., 17
Vaillancourt, T., 592
Valadez, J. R., 146
Valas, H., 592
Valdez, J., 405
Valente, T., 677
Valiga, M. J., 38
Valle, L. A., 683–684
Van Aken, M. A. G., 656, 660
Vanderkam, L., 534
Van Der Wielen, C., 118
Vandiver, F. M., 816
Vangstad, C., 420
Van Hoeken, D., 227, 230
Van Horn, M. L., 719
VanManen, T. M. A., 598
Van Shoiack-Edstrom, L., 682–683
VanTassel-Baska, J., 531, 537–538, 541–543, 550–552
Vantliver, F. M., 89
Vargas, L. A., 773
Varjas, K. M., 329
Varni, J., 229
Vaught, C. C., 313
Vega-Matos, C. A., 254
Velasquez, M. M., 722, 724
Vera, E. M., 16–17, 271–272, 283, 382–383, 388–389
Verdyn, C. M., 433
Verkuyten, M., 118
Vernez, G., 95
Vernon, A., 344, 414
Vespia, K. M., 22–23
Vidourek, R. A., 718
Villa, R. A., 597
Villanueva, I., 85
Vitaro, F., 588, 594
Vitousek, K. M., 229
von Bertalanffy, L., 449, 489
Von Cleve, E., 659
Vondracek, F. W., 501
Vossekuill, B., 460, 804

Vroon, P., 347
Vurembrand, N., 413

W

Wagener, D. K., 221
Wagner, A., 20
Wagner, D. I., 718
Wahl, J., 460, 467, 616, 805
Waidley, J. W., 316
Wake, M., 229
Walberg, H. J., 381, 388–390
Wald, J., 177
Waldo, M., 29, 385
Walker, H., 466
Walker, M., 434
Wallace, B. C., 117, 324–325
Wallace, J. M., 717–718
Wallace, S., 535
Wallace, S. A., 113
Walsh, M., 28-29, 385, 765, 767–772, 776, 778–779
Walter, J. D., 312
Walter, J. L., 433
Walters, E. E., 230
Walters, S. R., 235–236
Walton, J., 65
Walz, G. R., 37, 52, 164, 774
Wampold, B. E., xxx, 129, 184, 357, 752–755
Wandersman, A., 391
Wang, G. C. S., 99
Wang, M., 778
Wang, Y., 228
Wanko, M. A., 465
Wantz, R. A., 433
Ward, C. C., 40
Wardlaw, D., 619
Wardle, F., 131–132
Warger, C., 804
Warnes, E. D., 597
Warren, E. S., 18, 406, 517
Warter, E. H., 29, 385
Waters, E., 229
Waters, P. L., 662
Watkins, M. W., 476
Watley, D. J., 542
Watson, M., 352–355, 361, 699, 706
Watson, S. E., 596
Watson, T. S., 604, 741, 763
Watt, S. K., 19
Watts, I. E., 699
Watts, R., 404
Watts, R. E., 20
Watts, R. J., 322

Way, N., 113, 116, 588
Wayman, J. C., 187
Wearne, T. D., 501
Weaver, E., 4–6, 276
Webb, J., 533, 535, 547–550, 555
Webb, L., 333, 341–342, 405, 433, 451, 485
Webb, L. D., 412–413, 463, 629–630
Webb, N. B., 520, 598
Webber, M. P., 236
Weber, B., 463
Weber, T., 335
Webster-Stratton, C., 600, 703
Wechsler, H., 233
Wehmeyer, M. L., 160, 162, 165, 168, 170
Wei, X., 413
Weikart, D. P., 390, 391
Weinberg, R. A., 652
Weinberg, R. B., 465, 470, 472, 474
Weiner-Davis, M., 433
Weinick, R. M., 221
Weinrib, E., 526
Weinstein, R., 85
Weinstein, R. S., 706
Weinstein, S. R., 697, 699–700
Weiss, A., 626
Weiss, B., 519
Weissberg, R. P., 166, 381, 384, 388–390, 694, 707, 771, 776–777
Weist, M. D., 198, 517
Weisz, J. R., 519
Weitzman, L. M., 277, 772
Welch, I. D., 816
Welch, M., 481
Welch, S. L., 231
Welker, R., 636–638, 644–645, 696
Wellesley Centers for Women, 434–435, 444
Wells, A. M., 382–383, 390, 701, 707
Wells, K. C., 702
Welsh, M. P., 55
Wenckstern, S., 475, 627
Wengrower, H., 517–518
Wentzel, K., 116
Wentzel, K. R., 286, 588, 592, 700
Werner, E. E., 411, 771–772, 779
Werthamer, L., 704
Werthamer-Larrson, L., 699
Weslander, D. L., 313
West, C., 201
West, J. D., 21
West, J. F., 817–818
Westbrook, L. E., 222
Westefeld, J. S., 616
Wettersten, K. B., 278
Wheelan, S. A., 410

Wheeler, L., 699
Whelan, J. P., 604
Wheller, S., 17
Whipple, A. D., 640
Whiston, S. C., 18, 28–29, 148, 166, 214, 281–284, 326, 413, 433, 510–512, 760–761
Whitaker, D. J., 683–684
Whitaker, R. C., 229
White, G. P., 466, 485
White, J. F., 333, 341–342, 451
White, J. L., 198, 200
White, V. E., 18
Whitehead, T. L., 602
Whitehouse, S., 385
Whitlock, B., 180
Whitney-Thomas, J., 160, 162
Whiton, S., 347
Whitsell, S. S., 531
Whitson, S. C., 741
Whittle, B., 466
Wicker, L., 146
Wickrama, K. A. S., 286
Wiese, B. S., 280
Wiest, D., 403
Wiggins, J. D., 310, 313
Wiggins-Frame, M., 17
Wigram, T., 347
Wilcoxon, S. A., 795
Wilde, J., 189
Wilder, C., 604
Wiley, M. O., 313
Wilkerson, K, 310
Wilkinson, L., 483, 487
Wilkson, D. L., 698
Williams, C., 100
Williams, C. B., 115
Williams, C. L., 96, 101
Williams, D. J., 150
Williams, F. C., 83, 96, 103, 105–108, 323, 325
Williams, J., 229
Williams, J. H., 198
Williams, L. M., 433, 601
Williams, R., 767
Williams, R. A., 786
Williams, R. E., 488
Williams, T., 195, 198, 701
Williams, W., 403
Williamson, E. G., 5–6
Williamson, L. L., xxix, 811–812
Williamson, R. D., 815
Willis, S., 162
Willis, S. P., 806
Wilson, D. B., 701–704
Wilson, D. K., 196
Wilson, M. N., 129

Wilson, M. P., 462
Wilson, N., 355
Wilson, N. H., 740
Wilson, R., 541
Wilson, W. J., 49
Winebrenner, S., 531, 534, 536, 541, 549
Winsor, A., 351
Winters, A., 693
Wirt, J. B., 276
Wirt, R., 249
Wise, S. L., 435
Wittmer, J., 5–6, 459
Wladina, A., 51
Wodarski, J. S., 622
Wodarski, L. A., 622
Wohl, J., 555
Wohlstetter, P., 765
Wolak, J., 596
Wolf, L., 314
Wolf, M. M., 704
Wolf, W., 548
Wolfe, A. S., 71
Wolfe, D. A., 595
Wolfe, J. A., 704
Wolfe, P. K., 704
Wolfe, R., 230
Wolgien, C. S., 20
Wolin, S., 384
Wolin, S. J., 384
Wolke, D., 675
Wolleat, P. L., 785
Wong, E., 403
Wood, C., 717
Wood, C. N., 593
Wood, D. L., 222
Wood, G. A., 594
Wood, M., 148
Wood Dunn, N. A., 163
Woodfin, L., 181
Woodford, M. S., 23
Woodruff, G., 674
Woodruff, R., 22
Woods, S., 675
Woods, T., 601
Woodson, C. G., 198
Woody, D. E., 167
Wooley, S. F., 771
Workman, D. J., 741
Worsham, M. E., 699
Worth, S., 23
Worthington, R. L., 67–68, 296
Worzybt, J. C., 340, 351, 354
Wright, B. A., 159, 161
Wright, N., 415, 660
Wubbolding, R. E., 411

Wychoff, S., 196
Wyman, P. E., 413
Wynne, L., 335

X

Xie, H., 677, 697

Y

Yager, Z., 227, 233
Yalom, I. D., 286, 410–411, 599
Yamamoto, L. G., 222
Yang, A., 57, 59, 70, 129, 132, 563, 565–567
Yasui, M., 127, 129
Ybarra, M. L., 596
Yee, B., 537, 548, 552
Yeh, C. J., xxvii, xxx, 63, 66–70, 98–100, 103–104, 106, 127–131, 182–183, 271, 322, 507, 589, 643, 773, 788
Yemini, T., 614
Yih-Jiun, S., 406
Yoerger, K., 660, 698
Yoshikawa, H., 387
Yost, A. D., 98–99
Young, B. A., xxvii
Young, J., 675
Young, J. S., 17, 604, 763
Young, T. S., 741

Young-Hyman, D., 229
Young Rivers, R., 555
Yovanoff, P., 165
Yowell, C. M., 326

Z

Zagelbaum, A., 767
Zakriski, A. L., 593
Zambrano, E., 651
Zametkin, A. J., 614, 618
Zapata, A. L., 548
Zayas, L. H., 128–131
Zeichner, K., 60
Zelli, A., 697
Zephier, E., 228
Zera, M., 693
Zhang, Q., 228
Zheng, X., 101
Zhou, M., xxvii, 86, 99
Zigler, E., 56, 180, 195, 385, 622
Zimmerman, M. A., 116, 285
Zimmick, R., 20
Zimpfer, D. G., 21
Zinck, K., 413, 433
Zins, J. E., 314–315, 483
Zirkel, S., 590
Zisman, P., 590
Zuckerman, M., 178
Zuo, L., 542

SUBJECT INDEX

A

ABCD model of development, 703
Ability grouping, *See* Tracking and placement issues
Absenteeism and truancy, 272–273, 356, 638–639
Abstinence, 245, 247, 250–251
Academic achievement, 10, 51, *See also* Racial/ethnic minority students; Student performance outcomes
   accountability, *See* Accountability
   acculturation and, 184–185
   aggressive behavior and, 696
   caring environments and, 53, 59, 80, 356, *See also* Schools as caring communities
   college preparatory curriculum vs., 50, 51
   community involvement and, 58, *See also* School–community collaboration
   community or bridge programs, 189–190
   counselor advocacy roles, *See* Advocacy roles of counselors
   discrimination and, 52
   economic implications for non-graduates, 269–270
   emotional development vs., 563
   gender and, 51–52
   health and, 195–197
   intellective competence and, 54, 58
   locus of responsibility, 65
   parental involvement and, *See* Parental involvement
   poverty and, 51, 269–270, 537, 773
   racial identity and, 179–181, 322
   respect and, 58–59
   school failure, 635–647, *See also* Achievement gap; School failure
   school quality and, 53
   self-efficacy and, 183
   social class and, 51, 55, 99, 149, 294, *See also* Achievement gap; Socioeconomic status
   student accomplishment and, 50, 51
   student achievement data
      ASCA National Model and, 43, 45
      data-driven programs, 45, 51, 60
   students of color and, *See* Achievement gap
   teacher expectations and, 149, 638, 639, 640, 700
   teacher quality and, 53, 58
   "what works" interventions, 58–59
Academic failure, *See* Achievement gap; School failure
Academic press, 84–85
Academic records access, 794, 796
Academic self-efficacy, *See* Self-efficacy
Academic tracking, *See* Tracking and placement issues
Acceleration, 538–540
Access to records, 794, 796
Accountability, 112, 651, 758, *See also* Student performance outcomes
   ASCA National Model, 40, 44–45, 50–51, 217, 758
   evaluating school programs, *See* Program evaluation
   locus of responsibility, 65–66
   national standards for counseling programs, 38
   No Child Left Behind, *See* No Child Left Behind
   research, *See* Research
   school failure and, 636–637
Accreditation and certification, 298, 299, 402, 812–813, *See also* Counselor education and training
   advanced certification, 814–815
   CACREP minimal standards, 15–16, *See also* Council of Accredited Counseling and Related Educational Programs
   state licensure, 813
   supervision and, 19, *See also* Supervision
   teacher certification and, 28
Acculturation, 68–71, 96–97, 184–185, *See also* Assimilation
   academic achievement and, 184–185, 565
   acculturative stress, 69–70, 96
   "acting white," 179, 536, 548

Subject Index 865

cultural deprivation model, 101
culture shock, 69–70, 96, 98, 185
definition, 97
discussing issues of, 131
generation status, 97
group interventions, 443–444
intergenerational stresses, 82–83, 100, 323
psychological effects, 100–101
Acculturative environment of schools, 79–81, 83–89, 106, *See also* Acculturative press
effective schools and programs, 89–90
Acculturative press, *See also* Acculturation
academic press, 84–85
effective schools and programs, 89–90
immigrant parents and, 87–89
native language use in schools, 84
peer relationships and, 86
school adults and, 86–87
Achievement gap, 50, 51, 141, 177–190, 195, 197, 269, 294, 321–322, 564, 635, 766–767, *See also* Academic achievement; Racial/ethnic minority students; School failure
acculturation and, 184–185, *See also* Acculturation
anti-intellectualism and, 199
ASCA National Model and, 43
assessment issues, 189
caring communities and, 53, 59, 356
community or bridge programs, 189–190
computer technology and, 819
counselor advocacy roles and, 822, *See also* Advocacy roles of counselors
cultural identity and, 56–58, 564–565, *See also* Cultural identity; Racial identity
identity enhancement interventions, 563–583
discrimination effects, 52
effective school and personnel characteristics for improving, 188–190
future research directions, 190
gifted minority students, 536–537, 548
grade retention inequities, 640
graduation rates, 177
identity development theory, 179–181, *See also* Ethnic identity; Racial identity
interventions
African American Empowerment Curriculum, 195, 199–203
Afrocentric, 566
cognitive-behavioral, 182–183
Progressive School Counseling Advocacy Model, 195, 197–198
Transforming School Counseling Initiative, 296–297
"what works," 58–59
linguistic issues, 185–187, *See also* Language issues
literacy development, 262
No Child Left Behind and, 766–767

oppressive school conditions, 273
parental involvement and, 181–182
placement issues, 179, 189, 564
process model, 51–58
contextual factors, 52–53
cultural factors, 56–58
personal factors, 53–55
social stratification, 51–52
protective factors, 53–58, 187–188
public health concerns, 195–197
research, 183
resiliency, 53–58, 187–188
social class and poverty and, 51, 55, 99, 149, 269–270, 294, *See also* Poverty; Socioeconomic status
stereotype threat, 183–184
theory, 179
White teachers vs., 262
Achieving Success Identity Pathways, 284–286
Acting white, 179, 536, 548
Action plans, 43–44
Action research, 605, 762
Action stage, 724
Acute lymphoblastic leukemia (ALL), 224
Adaptive Success Identity Plan (ASIP), 509
Adlerian consultation, 344, 487–489
Adlerian therapy, 403–404
group work, 411, 432, 433, 488
play therapy, 406
Administrative supervision, 314
Administrator consultation, 345
Administrator training, 415
Adolescent connectedness, 651–669, *See also* Connectedness
Adolescent egocentrism, 617
Adolescent pregnancy, 243–244
academic performance outcomes, 253
alcohol and, 248–249
declining U.S. rates, 243, 245
preventive interventions, 391–392
Adolescent sexual health and development, *See* Adolescent pregnancy; Sexual health and development
Adolescent social class awareness, 147–148
Adolescent Suicide Awareness Program, 620
Adolescent thinking, 617
Advanced learning or gifted programs, 170, 198, *See also* Gifted and talented students
Advanced placement (AP), 539–540
Advanced school counseling certification, 814–815
Advisory council, 43
Advocacy roles of counselors, 18, 107, 112, 196, 297, 759, 788, 821–822, *See also* Social justice perspectives
ASCA National Model, 18, 821
competencies, 325

developmental advocates, 771
  facilitating systemic change, 37, 107, 197, 263, 297, 384
  immigrant students and, 106–107
  increasing community cultural sensitivity, 132
  training issues, 822
  tripartite model of multicultural counseling, 324
African American Empowerment Curriculum (AAEC), 195, 199–203
African American students, *See also* Diversity issues; Racial/ethnic minority students
  academic achievement issues, *See* Achievement gap
  academic aspiration patterns, 321, 507
  Afrocentric interventions, 566, 571–575
  contraceptive use, 246
  disciplinary effects, 697
  gifted and talented programs and, 170, 535
  harassment of Asian heritage students, 113, 116, 121
  health, 220–221
  internalized Eurocentric standards, 321–322
  perceived defiance by white teachers, 700
  public health issues, 195–197
  resiliency, 187
  school-based interventions, 198–199
  self-esteem and, 180
  sexual initiation, 248
  students with disabilities, 157
  suicide prevention/intervention issues, 629
African-centered educational psychology, 199–200
Afrocentric values, 181
  Kwanzaa intervention, 566, 571–575
Aggression, defined, 693, *See also* Violence and aggression
Aggressive-rejected students, 592
AIDS, 226–227, 245
Alcohol use, *See also* Substance abuse
  peer influence, 591
  suicide risk factor, 619
  teen pregnancy and, 248–249
  trends, 767
Alpha level, 753
America 2000, 38
American Counseling Association (ACA), 2, 812
  Code of Ethics and Standards of Practice, 792, 801
  training standards, 15
American Psychological Association (APA) ethical code, 313
American School Counselor Association (ASCA), 2, 11, 37, 167–168, 293, 812
  disability services standards, 163, 167
  Ethical Standards for School Counselors, 42, 139, 313–314, 468, 628, 788, 792, 800, 801
  gifted student program position statement, 533, 556
  group work and, 413
  multicultural competencies, 272, *See also* Multicultural competence
  national model, *See ASCA National Model*
  national standards, *See National Standards for School Counseling Programs*
  parental consent position statement, 801
  training standards, 295
Americans with Disabilities Act, 168
Anal sex, 246–248
Anger coping program, 702
Anger management, 201, 405, 492, 601
Annual calendar, 44
Anorexia nervosa, 227, 229–230
Anxiety disorders, 405
Appreciation, 274
Army Alpha Test, 276
Art expression, 520
Artistic-related careers, 277
Art Therapist Registered (ATR), 520
Art therapy, 520, 522–524, 598, *See also* Creative arts counseling
ASAP, 620
ASCA National Model, 9, 11, 12, 15–16, 39–46, 49–50, 102, 178–179, 261–262, 283, 294, 297, 398, 481, 812, *See also National Standards for School Counseling Programs*
  accountability for student outcomes, 40, 44–45, 50–51, 217, 758
  career development, 271
  counselor advocacy roles, 18, 325, 821
  delivery, 40, 41–43
  developmental-comprehensive perspective, 330
  equitable access to counseling, 127
  foundation, 40–41
  management, 40, 43–44
  outcome data disaggregation, 271
  prevention model, 384–385
  program evaluation and, 741, 744
  program supervision and, 314
  school counselor role definitions, 294, 366
  student achievement data and, 43
  vision of transformed school counselor, 40
ASCA School Counselor, 761
Asian Americans
  Adlerian lifestyle construct, 404
  career development, 104
  multidimensional identities, 70–71
  "1.5 generation," 97
  racial harassment issues, 113, 116, 121
  sandplay therapy, 527
  stereotypes, 72, 99, 103, 104, 321, 404
  suicide rates, 463
Assertiveness, 212
Assertiveness training intervention, 391

Assessment, *See also* Standardized testing; *specific tests or instruments*
 at-risk student identification, 471
 counselor training curriculum, 307
 counselor training standards, 17, 27
 crisis, 472–473
 evaluating school programs, *See* Program evaluation
 gifted and talented students, 550–551
 historical perspectives, 5, 7
 measuring connectedness, *See* Connectedness
 personality, 277
 racial/ethnic/sociocultural minority student and, 189
 school violence prevention and intervention, 702–703
 suicide risk, 623–625
 vocational guidance testing, 276, 277, 278–279, 282, 504
Assimilation, 68, 184, 522, *See also* Acculturation
 cultural deprivation model, 101
 Native American suicide and, 630
 racial identity vs., 179
Association for Counselor Education and Supervision (ACES), 9, 812
Association for Play Therapy (APT), 520
Association for Specialists in Group Work (ASGW), 432
Asthma, 223–224, 235–236
At-risk model of prevention, 382–383
At-risk students, *See also* Racial/ethnic minority students; Sexual health and development; Substance abuse; Suicide; Violence and aggression
 defining, 397–398
 grouping unconventional youth, 660, 668–669
 group work, *See* Group counseling interventions
 identifying and assessing, 471
 individual interventions, *See* Individual counseling interventions
 prevention programs, *See* Prevention
 school counselor liability issues, 468
 suicide risk assessment, 473
 unconventional connectedness, 653–654, 659–660
Attention deficit hyperactivity disorder (ADHD), 546
Attraction theory, 674–675, 677–678
Autism, 176
Autonomy, 119

B

BASIC parenting intervention, 703
Beauty self-image, 388
Beck Depression Inventory (BDI), 226, 625
Behavioral change models of prevention, 382–383, *See also* Group counseling interventions; Prevention
Behavioral consultation, 332, 484, 486–487
Behavioral play therapy, 521
Behavioral therapy, 404–405, 451
Behavior change intervention, motivational interviewing, 721–732
Belongingness, 352, 355, 655, 656, *See also* Connectedness
 gender differences, 662–663
 overall well-being and, 659
Biases, of counselors, *See* Counselor self-awareness of racial/ethnic/sociocultural orientations or biases
Bicultural competence, 56–57, 59, 71, 183, 185, 323, 565
Big Brothers/Big Sisters, 152
Bilingual counselors, 87
Bilingual or bicultural educational resources, 79, 85–86, *See also* Culturally appropriate interventions
 home-school liaisons, 88, 602
 native language retention and, 83
Bilingual students, *See also* English language learners
 academic achievement and, 186
 language brokering, 82, 100, 186–187
 native language use in schools, 84
 overrepresentation in special education, 65
Binge drinking, 591
Binge-eating disorder, 231
Biological factors in aggression, 695
Biracial friendships, 588
Biracial students
 identity issues, 129
 work with, 131–132
Body Mass Index (BMI), 227
Body weight, *See* Obesity and overweight
Bonferroni correlation, 753
Boston Connects, 775–778
Brain injury, 176
BRIDGES, 619
Bridge technique, 521
Brief family interventions, 166–167
Brown vs. Board of Education, 177
Bully Busters, 679, 685–686
Bullying, 329, 460, 673–687, *See also* Violence and aggression
 cultural differences, 675–676
 definition of terms, 673
 female students and, 153
 peer influence, 677
 prevention and intervention, 216, 385, 469, 601, *See also* Violence prevention
 best practices, 679–687
 Bully Busters, 679, 685–686

counselor roles, 673
culture of change, 687
effectiveness of programs, 687
Expect Respect, 679, 683–685
group work, 420
Olweus' program, 679, 680–681
recommendations, 687
Second Step programs, 679, 681–683
Steps to Respect, 679, 686
racial harassment issues, 116–117
reporting, 17
school setting and, 673–674, 693
social rejection and, 592
theory, 674–679
attraction theory, 674–675, 677–678
dominance theory, 674, 677
homophily, 674, 677
social ecological theory, 675, 678–679
social learning theory, 675, 678
theory of mind, 674, 676–677

C

Calm Heart: Ua Siab Tus Yees, 566–568, 576–579
Cancer, 224
Career centers, 509
Career development, 269, 277, 497–512, *See also* Vocational guidance
African American Empowerment Curriculum, 201
ASCA National Model, 271
assessment, 276, 277, 278–279, 282, 504
basic skills, 498
career interventions research, 281–282
classroom guidance activities, 501–503
collaborative intervention, 499
college level competencies, 507–510
computer-assisted systems, 507, 509
counselor training curriculum, 305
designing culturally responsive programs, 269–271, 283–286
developmental assets, 280, *See also* Developmental assets
developmental contextualism, 279–280
developmental theory, 277–278
diversity issues, 501, 504–508, 511–512
early emergence theory, 543–544
effectiveness, 510–511
elementary level competencies, 500–503
gender and, 501, 504–505, 542–543
gifted students and, 542–546, 552–553
group activities, 503
high school level competencies, 505–507
historical perspectives, 4–5, 276–277, 293, 497–498
immigrant students and, 104

internalized racism and, 322
intervention taxonomy, 499–500
locus of control and, 160
middle school level competencies, 503–505
multicultural competence issues, 283–284, 324, 325
multipotentiality, 544–546
person-environment fit models, 276, 277, 278
practice recommendations, 283–286
racial/ethnic role models, 325
research and future directions, 510–511
school counseling standards, 498–499
school dropouts and, 269–270, 641
school-to-work transition, 150, 152, 296, 507, 772
selection, optimization, and compensation model, 280
self-determination theory, 160, 161–162, 280–281
Social Cognitive Career Theory, 161, 162, 278
social justice and traditional approaches, 278–279
social justice perspective, 272–276, 283
student collaboration, 368
success identities, 285–286
Values-Based Career Counseling, 552–553
Career Development Assessment and Counseling (C-DAC) model, 512
Career Horizons, 284–285
Career portfolios, 504
Career self-efficacy, 278, 507
Caribbean immigrant parents, 105
The Caring Classroom, 357, 358–359, 364
Caring environments and student performance, 53, 59, 80
Caring school communities, 351–375, *See also* Schools as caring communities
Caring School Community (CSC), 361
CAST, 619
C-CARE, 619
CEDAR, 104
Center for Applied Research and Educational Improvement, 300
Center for Mental Health in the Schools, 622
Center for School Counseling Outcome Research, 300
Centers for Disease Control and Prevention (CDC), 233, 236, 466
Certification and accreditation, *See* Accreditation and certification
Character education, 210, 212, 469
Characterological distortion, 486
Chemotherapy, 224
Child abuse
parental discipline, 797
reporting, 311, 796
state laws regarding, 788
Child-centered play therapy, 521
Child Development Project (CDP), 355, 357, 360–362, 365, 706

Child Health Insurance Program (CHIP), 220
Child homicide, 460
Child mortality, 219
Children's Aid Society, 778
Children's legal rights, 787
Children's social class awareness, 147–148
Chinese culture, play therapy and, 522
Chinese immigrants, 96, 104
Chlamydia, 245, 246
Choice theory, 296, 403
Chowchilla bus incident, 465
Chronic illnesses, 222–227
    mental health and, 226
      services for students with, 225–227
    teacher training and, 226
Cigarette smoking, 717, 767
Civil Rights Act of 1964, 114–118
Civil Rights movement, 8
Class, *See* Social class and school counseling; Socioeconomic status
Classism, 145, 151
"The Classroom as Community," 357, 359, 364
Classroom discipline, 699–700, 704
Classroom guidance
    building caring school communities, 368
    career development, 501–503
    connectedness-promoting curriculum, 667–668
    diversity education, 368
    effectiveness, 756
    suicide prevention, 622
Classroom physical environment, 195
Classrooms, community building within, 355
Client-focused consultation, 332, 485
Climate, *See* School climate
Clinical judgment, 789–790
Clinical-services model, 6, 10
Clinical supervision, *See* Supervision
Cliques, 590–591
Code-switching, 201, 323
Cognitive-behavioral interventions, 213, 272, 405
    group work, 411, 433
    improving minority academic success, 182–183
    interpersonal interventions, 598
    play therapy, 406
Cognitive style and aggressive behavior, 696
Collaboration, 481, 816, *See also* Leadership roles for school counselors; Parental involvement
    building caring school communities, 368–369
    career development intervention, 499
    definition of terms, 481–483
    efficacy, 483
    Emotional Competency Education, 816
    scholarship of engagement, 451–452, 455
    school and community, *See* School–community collaboration
    school-based prevention model, 386
    school–family–community, 353, 355, 370–371, 450
    university, 300, 316, 555, 644, 762
Collaborative consultation services, 42, 333, 482, 818
Collaborative for Academic, Social, and Emotional Learning, 215
Collaborative training programs, 815
Collectivist cultural orientations, 72, 274–275, 322, 789
    connectedness and, 656–657
    gifted students and, 545
College preparatory curriculum, 50, 51
Color-blind orientations, 72, 119, 180, 188
Columbia TeenScreen Program, 620
Comic book conversations, 164
Communication skills, 212, 216, 385
Community collaboration, *See* School–community collaboration
Community counseling curriculum, 27
Community involvement and student achievement, 58, 189–190, *See also* School–community collaboration
Community mental health movement, 450, 464–465
Community of Caring program, 355
Community schools, 778, *See also* Schools as caring communities
Comprehensive Guidance Program Model (CGPM), 11, 293, 295
Comprehensive school counseling programs, 10–11, 269, 283–286, 295, 366, *See also specific components or programs*
    consultation and, 330
    culturally responsive career development programs, 269–271
    data-driven decision making, 45, 60
    essential services model, 10–11
    general systems theory, 449–450
    models, 9, 11, 39–46, *See also* ASCA National Model
    personal and social development and, 209, *See also* Personal and social development
    prescriptive vs. nonprescriptive, 10–11
    prevention strategies, 196
    research on, 755–758
    school–community partnership best practices, 770, *See also* School–community collaboration
    technological competence, 819
    terms, 11
Computer-assisted guidance systems, 507, 509
Computer competence, 819
Conferences of school counselors, 821
Confidentiality, x, 793–800
    access to records, 794, 796
    consultation and, 483
    counselor training standards, 17
    differing teacher and counselor perspectives, 817
    exceptions and consent, 794–800

group work and, 419
infectious diseases and, 797
minimum necessary rule, 800
presumption, 793
privileged communication, 799
protecting people from harm vs., 468, 803–805
reporting requirements, 311
revealing limits of, 800
substance abuse and, 720–721, 785
suicide risk vs., 623, 628, 798, 803, 805
violence risk and, 797
Conflict resolution skills, 60, 216, 602, *See also* Mediation
Adlerian approaches, 404
Conformity, 119
Conjoint family therapy, 449
Connectedness, 651–669
adolescent engagement and, 663
aggressive behavior and, 699
applied youth development, 652–653
attachment and social support, 655–656
balance, 659, 662
belongingness and schools as communities, 352, 355
building caring school communities, 369–370, *See also* Schools as caring communities
conventionality, 653–654
cultural orientations and, 656–657
defining, 654
developmental origins, 654
ecological perspectives, 653
family vs. non-familial, 657
gender differences, 662–663
graphical scale representation, 657–658
grouping unconventional youth, 660
measuring, 651
developmental assets framework, 652, 664–667
The Hemingway, 663–667, 669
overall well-being and, 659
research, 659–663
risk taking and, 659, 660
school guidance curriculum, 667–668
system support activities, 667
teacher education, 667
theory, 652–653, 658–659
Consent
ASCA position statement, 801
exception to confidentiality, 794–795
informed, 17, 18, 483, 800–803
parental, 801–803
Construct validity, 754
Consultation, 42, 329–348, 481
Adlerian, 344, 487–489
behavioral, 332, 484, 486–487
building caring school communities, 368–369
client-focused, 332

collaborative, 42, 333, 482, 818
communication strategies, 340–343
consultee-focused, 333
crisis-oriented, 332–333
cultural context, 331–332, 336, 491–493
definition of terms, 481–483
developmental-comprehensive perspective, 330
developmental-focused, 333
effectiveness, 339–340, 756
efficacy, 483
ethical and legal issues, 347–348, 483
Eurocentric perspectives, 491
evaluation of interventions, 485
exploring resistance, 343–344
gifted student's parents and teachers, 554
goals and objectives, 337–339
group-focused, 346
improving teacher classroom discipline, 704
levels, targets and contexts, 490–491
mental health issues, 333, 346, 464–465, 468
models, 483–490
modes, 331–332
monitoring and evaluating, 339
multicultural competence, 339–340, 344
objectivity in, 486
organizational, 489–490
practical definition, 330–331
problem-solving orientation, 331
process, 335–339, 490
research issues, 340, 493
system-focused, 335
transference and, 486
Transforming School Counseling Initiative, 330
working with students, 344–345
working with teachers or administrators, 345
Consultee-focused consultation, 333, 485–486
Contact, 119, 274
Contemplation stage, 723–724
Content pedagogy, 24
Contextual factors, *See specific factors*
Continuing education, 302, 309, 317
Contraception, 245–246, 248, 251
Contracts, "no suicide," 626–627
Contracts for caring classrooms, 358
Conventional and unconventional connectedness, 653–654
Coordinated school health programs (CSHPs), 234–237
Council of Accredited Counseling and Related Educational Programs (CACREP), 15–16, 162, 298–299, 301, 325, 402, 812–813
consultation and, 481
group work and, 413
Michigan State University school counseling training model, 24–29
Counseling, operational definition, 401

Counseling psychology training issues, 28–29
Counselor-assisted ethnic identity development, 128–133
Counselor education and training, 15–29, 293–307
   accreditation, *See* Accreditation and certification
   advocacy training, 822
   collaborative training programs, 815
   community counseling curriculum, 27
   Comprehensive Guidance Program Model (CGPM), 11, 293, 295
   continuing education, 302, 309, 317
   counseling psychology vs., 28–29
   creative arts school counseling, 520–521, 527
   critical school setting issues, 20–21
   curriculum integration, 26, 28
   developmental life-span emphasis, 23–24, 27
   developmental theory, 25, 293, 295–296, 310–311
   didactic and experiential instruction modes, 22, 25
   disability counseling competencies, 162–163, 171
   district, community and university collaboration, 300, 316
   facilitating self-awareness and personal development, 73
   fieldwork, 298–300, 302, 306, *See also* Supervision
   historical perspectives, 4
   "ideal" counselor-centered curriculum, 304–307
   immigrant students and, 107
   intervention for identity-impaired trainees, 22
   legal/ethical practice, 17–18
   literacy promotion, 268
   local school partnerships, 818
   mentoring, 22, 301–302
   Michigan State University school counseling training model, 24–29
   minimal standards and guidelines, 15–16
      assessment and diagnosis, 17, 27
      diversity issues, 16–17, 27
      extending training beyond, 21–24
      Research activities, 18–19, 28
   mock counseling sessions, 26–27
   multicultural competencies, 29, 302, 305, *See also* Multicultural competence
   National Model, 41–42, *See also* ASCA National Model
   National Program for the Transformation of School Counseling, 815
   online resources, 16
   outcome research, 303
   pedagogy and, 24–25
   phenomenological theory and, 25
   postgraduate training process, 21–22
   practicing school counselor involvement, 300
   presentation skills, 297–298
   prevention program development and, 392
   professional development schools, 316
   racial harassment issues, 123
   recommendations and future directions, 300–303
   reflective skills, 311–312
   regressive cognitive development, 310
   research, 300
   self-supervision skills, 302
   specific training needs, 301
   standardized curricula, 301
   student cohort composition effects, 28
   suicide prevention or intervention, 472, 615–616, 622, 631
   supervisor training, 303
   technology and, 22–23, 25
   theoretical bases and models, 294–298
   trainee personal development, 19–20
   Transforming School Counseling Initiative, 39, 49–51, 294, 296–297, 300
   university partnerships, 818, *See also* University-school collaboratives
Counselor interpersonal skills, 60
Counselor roles and responsibilities, *See* School counselor roles and responsibilities
Counselor self-awareness of racial/ethnic/sociocultural orientations or biases, 63–73, 95, 103, 130, 139, 188, 271–272, 310, 435, 642–643, *See also* Multicultural competence
   assessing worldview, 66
   class-associated biases, 152
   consultation and, 344
   critical case study, 71–73
   cultural value orientations, 66–67
   homophobic/heterosexist biases, 139
   implications for training, 73
   locus of control or responsibility, 64–66
   social class and, 152, 324
   white privilege, 67–68, 71–72
Counselor supervision, *See* Supervision
Countertransference (CT), 20
Creative arts counseling, 517–528
   art therapy, 522–524, 598
   counselor training, 520–521, 527
   drama therapy, 524–525
   implementation barriers, 517–518, 527
   interpersonal interventions, 598
   play therapy, 406, 517–522, 598
   poetry therapy, 525–526
   research, 519–520
   sandplay therapy, 526–527
   scheduling, 518
   theories of play, 518–519
   therapeutic vs. educational cultures, 517–518
Criminal background, 17–18
Criminalization of youth of color, 694
Crisis assessment, 472–473
Crisis Intervention Game, 474
Crisis management, 459–476, 625, 805
   barriers to crisis interventions, 466–467

common intervention errors, 474
crisis counseling, 42, 332–333
crisis intervention theory, 463–465
crisis preparation, 469–471
crisis prevention, 468–469
crisis typologies, 464–465
critical incident stress management, 465, 471–472
debriefing, 473, 475–476
definitions, 459
developmentally appropriate prevention and intervention, 474
diversity issues, 461
documentation, 468
evaluation of crisis interventions, 465–466
homeostasis, 465
legal and ethical considerations, 468
mental health consultation model, 468
mental health resources, 467
multicultural competence, 472
nature of crisis, 460–461
plans, 42
postvention, 474–476, 627, 805
prevention, 42
psychological first aid, 465, 473
risk factors, 463
school climate and, 460
school counselor involvement, 467, 470
school crises, 461–463
suicide prevention or response, *See* Suicide
training activities and content, 470–472
Crisis-oriented consultation, 42, 332–333
Crisis response teams, 470, 625
Critical consciousness, 273
Critical incident stress debriefing (CISD), 473, 475–476
Critical incident stress management (CISM), 465, 471–472
Cross-racial friendships, 588
Crowds, 589–590
Cubic model, 616–617
Cultural capital, 153
Cultural competence, *See* Multicultural competence
Cultural consciousness, 200–201, *See also* Counselor self-awareness of racial/ethnic/sociocultural orientations or biases; Cultural identity
Cultural deprivation model, 101
Cultural identity, 564, 565, *See also* Acculturation; Culturally appropriate interventions; Ethnic identity; Racial identity
achievement gap and, 56–58, 564–565
bicultural competence, 56–57, 59, 71, 183, 323, 565
career development model, 512
enhancement strategies, 563–583
Afrocentric *Kwanzaa* program, 566, 571–575
Hispanic program (*Fortaleciendo Nuestras Raíces*), 566, 580–595

Hmong program (*Calm Heart*), 566–568, 576–579
positive psychology, 564–565
research, 564
school counseling programs and, 568
student performance and, 56–58
Culturally appropriate interventions, 189, 471–472, *See also* Bilingual or bicultural educational resources; Multicultural competence
African American Empowerment Curriculum, 195, 199–203
Afrocentric *Kwanzaa* program, 566, 571–575
building caring school communities, 369
consultation and, 491–493
counselor-assisted ethnic identity development, 128–133
creative arts school counseling, 518
art therapy, 523–524
drama therapy, 525
play therapy, 521–522
poetry therapy, 526
sandplay therapy, 527
cultural identity enhancement strategies, 563–583
Hispanic program (*Fortaleciendo Nuestras Raíces*), 566, 580–595
Hmong program (*Calm Heart*), 566–568, 576–579
immigrant students and, 104
Progressive School Counseling Advocacy Model, 197–198
Strengthening Families Program, 391
substance abuse, 732
understanding home environments, 326
Culturally competent counselors, *See* Multicultural competence
Culturally competent teachers, 58, 60
Culturally diverse model, 101–102
Culturally responsive career development programs, 269–271, 283–286, *See also* Career development
Cultural pluralism, 84
Cultural translators, 106
Cultural values and biases self-awareness, *See* Counselor self-awareness of racial/ethnic/sociocultural orientations or biases
Culture, 64
affective presentation and, 322–323
family and, 72
worldview and, *See* Worldview
Culture brokering, 82, 100, 186–187, 602
Culture shock, 69–70, 96, 98

D

Data-driven programs, 45, 51, 60

Dating and romantic relationships, 594–595
Deaf-blindness, 176
Deafness, 175
Debriefing, 473, 475–476
DECIDE, 490
Decision making skills, 212, 214
Delinquency, *See also* Substance abuse; Violence and aggression
    caring school communities and, 355–356
    criminalization of youth of color, 694
    social rejection and, 592
Depression
    chronic illnesses and, 226
    gifted students and, 549–550
    racial harassment and, 116
    racial identity and, 180
    suicide risk factor, 463, 617, 619
Development, 220–221, 767–768
    ABCD model, 703
    bio-psycho-social levels, 768
    career development and theories of, 277–278
    class and, 146
    connectedness and, 654
    counselors as developmental advocates, 771
    counselor training curriculum, 306
    ecological frameworks, 279–280, 489, *See also* Ecological models
    emotional, *See* Emotional development
    exosystem contexts, 52
    group work goals, 420–421, 422, 432
    life-span approach, 768
    mental health and, 146
    microsystem/macrosystem/mesosystem framework, 52, 279–280, 489, 653, 679
    moral, 210–213, 313
    personal and social, *See* Personal and social development
    positive youth development approach, 252–253, 366–367
    prevention and intervention approaches, 469
    school–community partnership contexts, 767–769
    specific school counseling issues, 820
Developmental assets, 280, 359–360, 365
    connectedness assessment and, 652, 664–667
Developmental contextualism, 279–280
Developmental crisis, 462, 464–465
Developmental-focused consultation, 333
Developmental guidance and social class, 148–149
Developmental issues in counselor training, 19–20, 23–24, 25, 27
    consultation and, 330
    integrated developmental model, 310–311
Developmental Model for Counseling the Gifted, 553
Developmental model for counselor training, 25, 293, 295–296, 310–311
Developmental play therapy, 406

Developmental School Counseling and Guidance program, 314
Diabetes, 159, 224–225, 229
Diagnostic action research, 762
Diagnostic and Statistical Manual of Mental Disorders IV-TR (DSM-IV-TR), 230, 346, 382, 401
Diagnostic competence, 17
Diagnostic Testing and Prescriptive Instruction (DT-PI) model, 539
Directive approach to counseling, 5–6
DIRT, 623–624
Disability, *See also* Special education services; Students with disabilities; *specific disabilities*
    federal definitions, 175–176
    personal and familial adaptations, 159–160, 161
Disciplinary interventions, 693–694, 701
    as abusive, 797
    classroom control vs. aggressive behaviors, 699–700
    cultural differences in effects, 697
    differing teacher and counselor perspectives, 817–818
    racial/ethnic minorities and, 694, 700
Discipline, caring school communities and, 355–356
Discourses and literacy, 260–261
Discrimination and prejudice, 63, 86, *See also* Homophobia; Racial harassment; Racism; Stereotypes
    academic performance and, 52
    career choices and, 324, 325
    coping with, 64
    counselor awareness of, *See* Counselor self-awareness of racial/ethnic/sociocultural orientations or biases
    equal protection rights vs., 788
    ethnic identity development and, 128–129
    immigrant experiences, 86, 99–100, 103–104
    intervention programs, 214
    psychological effects, 115–116
    racial harassment vs., 115
    social class and, 147
Discrimination Model, 25
Disintegration, 119, 274
Disorder reduction model of prevention, 382–383
Dissonance, 119, 274
Diversity issues, xxvii, 450, *See also* Achievement gap; Culturally appropriate interventions; Multicultural competence; *specific minorities, problems*
    achievement gap, *See* Achievement gap
    bullying and, 675–676
    career development, 501, 504–508, 511–512
    caring school communities and, 353, 356
    classroom guidance, 368
    counselor training standards, 16–17, 27, 29

crisis management, 461
cultural diversity models, 101–102
cultural identity enhancement strategies, 563–583
demographic trends, 95, 271, 321, 435, 518, 751, 785
disability services issues, 157, 168, 170
discrimination, See Discrimination and prejudice
effective school–community partnerships and, 773
family–school relationship, 454–455
gifted students, 170, 534–537, 545, 548
group work, 412, 414–415, 434–438
identity, See Cultural identity; Ethnic identity; Racial identity
salad bowl metaphor, 353
school-based prevention model, 388–389
school communities and, 354
school counselor recruitment, 301–302, 326
student substance abuse and, 730, 732
suicide, 629–630
Documenting crises or incidents, 468
Document literacy, 261
Dominance theory, 674, 677
Double-sided reflection, 731
Down syndrome, 224
Drama therapy, 524–525
Dropouts, See School dropouts
Drug abuse, See Substance abuse
Due process, 787

E

Early emergence theory, 543–544
Early kindergarten admission, 538
Early preventive interventions, 390–391
Eating disorders, 147, 227, 229–233, 388
Ecological models, 128, 182, 189, 489, 642
  bullying theory and research, 675, 678–679, 685
  connectedness and, 653–654
  identity development theory, 279–280
  network therapy, 602–603
  prevention, 383
  social ecological theory, 675
  understanding school failure, 636
Ecology of school environments, 81–82
Ecosystemic therapy, 450
Educational records access, 794, 796
Education and training, See Counselor education and training
Education of All Handicapped Children Act, 10, 157
Education Trust, 37, 50, 51, 819
Efficacy, See Self-efficacy
Ego development of counselors, 19–20
Eisel v. Board of Education of Montgomery County, Maryland, 615, 805

Elementary and Secondary Education Act (ESEA), 8, 719
Elementary-level personal/social development interventions, 214
Elementary school counseling, 9–10, 820
Elementary School Counseling Demonstration Act, 10
Emancipatory Communitarian (EC) framework, 272
Emergency room health care, 221–222
Emotional Competency Education (ECE), 816
Emotional control, 201, 213
Emotional development, 220
  educational priorities vs., 563
  gifted students and, 546–547, 552–553
Emotional disturbance, 175, See also Depression
Emotional expression, 322–323, 461, 464, 492
Emotional first aid, 472
Emotional intelligence, 55, 59, 211
Emotional learning, 80
Emotional overexcitability, 547
Empathy, 20, 210, 213, 403
Empirical action research, 762
Employment, See Career development
Empowerment, tripartite model of multicultural counseling, 324
Empowerment groups for academic success (EGAS), 645–646
Enculturation, schools as agents of, 49
Engagement, 451–452
  adolescent connectedness and, 663
  caring school communities and, 355
English language learners (ELLs), xxvii, 98–99, 185–187, See also Bilingual students; Immigrant youth; Language issues
  drama therapy, 525
  effective schools and programs, 79–90
  placement issues, 85–86
Enrichment Triad/Revolving Door Identification Model, 540–541
Environmental press, 83
Equal protection rights, 787–788
Equity, See Social justice perspectives
Error variance, 752
Essential services model, 10–11
Ethical codes, 313–314, 788–789, 792, See also specific codes
  ACA *Code of Ethics and Standards of Practice*, 792, 801
  APA, 313
  ASCA *Ethical Standards for School Counselors*, 42, 139, 313–314, 468, 628, 788, 792, 800, 801
Ethical issues, 42, 785–786, See also Confidentiality; Legal issues
  clinical judgment, 789–790
  clinical supervision and, 313–314
  consultation, 347–348
  counselor training, 17–18, 305

crisis management and intervention, 468
   dealing with suicidal students, 628
   disability services, 167–168
   multicultural competence, 786
   professional codes, 788–789, See also Ethical codes
   recommendations for counselors, 807–808
Ethnic identity, 127–133, 564, 565, See also Racial identity
   acculturation and, See Acculturation
   biracial or multiethnic students, 129
   community building, 132
   counselor-assisted identity development, 128–133
   cultural consciousness and, 200–201
   cultural identity enhancement strategies, 563–587
   ecological models, 128
   interpersonal relationships and, 588
   multidimensionality and dynamics of, 70–71
   psychological well-being and, 129
   racism/discrimination vs., 128–129
   recommendations for counselors, 130–133
   student performance and, 56
   terminology, 128
Ethnicity
   defining, 178
   discussing issues of, 130–131
   social class and, 145, 154
Ethnic match, 130
Ethnocentrism, 177
Etiquette classes, 152
Evaluating school guidance and counseling programs, 413, 604–605, 739–748, See also Program evaluation
Evidence-based individual counseling, 398
Exceptional students, See Gifted and talented students; Students with disabilities
Existential values, 66, 72
Exosystem, 52, 279–280, 679
Expect Respect program, 679, 683–685
Experiential learning and counselor education, 22
Experimental action research, 762
Expulsion and suspension, 693–694
Extended-term mixed method (ETMM), 605
External validity, 754–755
Extracurricular activities, 58

F

Facilitation, 416–417
Failure identity, 403
False consciousness, 273
Familial connectedness, 657
Family contexts, 449, See also Parental involvement
   academic failure and, 637
   acculturation and intergenerational stresses, 82–83, 100, 323
   counselor liaison roles, 88, 451, 602, 643
   culture and, 72, 87
   designing culturally sensitive interventions, 326
   immigrant students and, 82, 87–89, 105
   marriage and heterosexism, 138
   multicultural counseling issues, 454–455
   National Education Goals, 181
   personal and social development and, 209
   psychological theory and research, 450–452
   scholarship of engagement, 451–452, 455
   school absenteeism and, 639
   school counseling role and objectives, 456
   school counselor interface, 451
   school–family–community partnership, 353, 355, 370–371, 450–453
   schools as communities, 353
   student aggressive behavior and, 697–700
   student performance and, 80
   substance abuse protective factors, 718
Family counseling, 386, 449, 601
   counseling students with disabilities, 166–167
   historical perspectives, 450
   sexual minorities and, 140–141
   terminology, 449, 450
Family genogram, 132
Family group therapy, 449, 450
Family network therapy, 449, 450
Family Service Association (FSA), 449
Female bullying, 153
FERPA, 794–796, 798–800, 806
Field theory, 489
Fieldwork requirements, 298–300, 302, 304, 306, See also Supervision
Fortaleciendo Nuestras Raíces: Strengthening Our Roots, 566, 580–583
Friendship, 587–589
Functional behavioral assessment and intervention, 702
Funding for school counseling, 7–8

G

Gang intervention programs, 340
Gateway behaviors, 382
Gay, Lesbian and Straight Education Network (GLSEN), 138
Gay, lesbian, bisexual and transgender issues, 507
   affirmative practices, 135, 139–142
   case example, 254–255
   dating and romantic relationships, 594–595
   Diversity Rooms, 139–140

eating disorders, 231
family counseling, 140
future research, 142
GLBTQ affirmative practices, 135, 139–142
group interventions, 437–438
group work, 140
key terms, 135
oral or anal intercourse risks, 247–248
positive role models, 140
proactive interpersonal interventions, 604
recommendations for counselors, 142
research, 137–139
school climate, 138
sex education and, 252
sexual identity development, 136–137, 249, 254
social support networks, 140–141
suicide risk, 463, 630
GEARUP, 189
Gender and career development, 501, 504–505
gifted students and, 542–543
Gender Aware Therapy, 598
Gender differences
academic achievement and, 51–52
aggressive behavior and, 697
bullying and, 677
connectedness and, 662–663
disability services issues, 168, 170
group composition issues, 418–419
relational aggression, 592
substance abuse, 717–718
Genderphobia, 138
General systems theory, 449–450
Genogram, 132
George-Barden Act, 7
Gestalt therapy, 432
Gifted and talented students, 198, 531–556
academic guidance, 537–538, 551–552
acceleration, 538–540
advanced placement, 539–540
ASCA position statement, 533, 556
career guidance, 542–546, 552–553
counseling and consulting interventions, 553–555
curricular modifications, 551
definition and identification, 534–536
developmental counseling model, 553
differentiation, 541–542
diversity issues, 170, 534–537, 545, 548
early emergence theory, 543–544
enrichment resources, 552, 555
Enrichment Triad/Revolving Door Identification
    Model, 540–541
group work, 420
high-stakes testing and, 541
identifying and assessing, 550–551
interpersonal relationships, 547–548
multiple intelligences, 536

multipotentiality, 544–546, 552
pullout programs, 540–541
social and emotional needs, 546–550
societal educational priorities and, 532
stress, 548
talent search, 539
underachievement and dropping out, 536–537
university-based guidance laboratories, 555
Goals 200, 38
Gonorrhea, 245, 246
Good Behavior Game, 704
Grade promotion and retention, 639–641
Grade skipping for gifted students, 538–539
Graffiti, 115
Grief expression, 20, 461, 464
Group counseling interventions, 409–426, 431–449,
    643
advantages, 431
aggregating at-risk youth, 660, 668–669
ASCA National Model, 42
barriers to, 413
building caring school communities, 367–368, 374
bullying prevention, 420
confidentiality, 419
counselor training curriculum, 305
definitions, 431
developmental goals, 420–421, 422, 432
diversity issues, 412, 414–415, 434–438
effectiveness, 756
elementary level, 439–440
empowerment groups, 645–646
evaluation and accountability, 443–444
facilitation and logistics, 416–418
"focused, but flexible" model, 421–425
gifted students and, 420, 554–555
high school level, 440
historical perspectives, 432
immigrant students and, 105
interpersonal interventions, 598–600
justified curriculum, 422
leadership skills, 439, 441–442
marketing, 415, 438
meeting topics, 423–424
middle school level, 440
needs assessment, 419
personal/social development interventions,
    214–215
planning, 412
practice guidelines and standards, 432
program evaluation, 413
promoting altruism, 443
purpose, 413–414, 431
racial/ethnic minority students and, 132
recommendations, 425–426
recruitment, 414–415, 441
relational-cultural model, 431, 434–435

remediation, 425
research, 411–413, 433–434, 443–444
rural and urban schools, 440
safe counseling environments, 442
scheduling, 441
sexual minorities and, 140, 437–438
size and composition, 418–419, 441
small vs. large groups, 409, 431
stages and dynamics, 410–411, 438–439
strengths focus, 411
subgrouping, 420
termination, 410–411
theoretical orientations, 411, 432–433
therapeutic factors, 410
Group crisis intervention, 473
Group-focused consultation, 346–347
Group racial identity, 121–122
Guidance laboratories, 555
Guidance movement, 4–5, *See also* Vocational guidance
Guided imagery, 132, 201

H

Haitian immigrants, 63, 64, 106
Hakoniwa, 527
Harborview Injury Prevention and Research Center (HIPRC), 619
Hawaiian culture, 492
Health care
    community agencies and, 766
    coordinated school health programs, 234–237
    emergency room use, 221–222
    poverty and, 767
    racial/ethnic minorities and, 219, 220–222
Health care worker cultural competencies, 222
Health crisis, 381
Health education, 220
Health impairment or disability definitions, 175–176
Health insurance, 220–221
Health Insurance Portability and Accountability Act (HIPAA), 794
Health Management Organizations (HMOs), 236
Health promotion and prevention issues, 195–197, 219–220, 383, *See also* Prevention
    Boston Connects program, 776
    integration across curriculum, 234
    Progressive School Counseling Advocacy Model, 195, 197–198
    school-based health centers, 234–237, 253
    schoolwide programs, 220, 223–224
    sexuality, 243–255, *See also* Sexual health and development
    weight-associated problems, 232–234
    well child health care, 220
Health records access, 794, 796
Health Status Indicators (HSIs), 221
Healthy People 2010, 220, 221
Hearing impairment, 175
Helping relationships, 1–2
Help-*Seek*ing behaviors, racial/ethnic and cultural differences, 322
The Hemingway: Measure of Adolescent Connectedness, 663–667, 669
Hepatitis B, 246
Herpes simplex virus, 246
Heterosexism, 135, 138, 139, *See also* Gay, lesbian, bisexual and transgender issues
High school dropouts, *See* School dropouts
High school graduation rates, 177
High school personal/social development interventions, 215
High/Scope Perry preschool project, 390–391
Hispanics, 95, 97, 339, *See also* Diversity issues; Racial/ethnic minority students
    academic aspirations, 507
    acculturation and, *See* Acculturation
    achievement gap, *See* Achievement gap
    Adlerian lifestyle construct, 404
    career counseling and, 510
    consultation and, 491
    contraceptive use, 246
    cultural identity enhancement strategies, 566, 580–583
    health, 220–221, 223, 232
    immigrant students, *See* Immigrant youth
    language concerns, *See* Language issues
    resiliency, 187
    self-esteem and, 180
    sexual initiation, 248
    students with disabilities, 157, 168
    suicide and, 461, 463, 629
History of school counseling, 1–12, 293, 811–812
    assessment, 5, 7
    elementary school, 9–10
    government funding, 7–8
    guidance movement, 4–5, 497–498, *See also* Career development; Vocational guidance
    personal and social development, 6–7
    prevention contexts, 382
    program models, 9
    psychological theories and approaches, 8
    race and ethnicity issues, 178–179
    school enrollment trends, 812
    special education services, 10
HIV/AIDS, 226–227, 245
    oral and anal sex and, 247
    sex education programs, 251
Hmong, 98, 566–568, 576–579

Holistic reading and writing experiences, 260
Homeostasis, 465
Homework and academic success, 637
Homicide, 460
Homophily, 674, 677
Homophobia, 135, 138
    counselor awareness of, 139
    group interventions, 140
Homosexuality, *See* Gay, lesbian, bisexual and transgender issues
Hope theory, 406
Hull House, 449
Humanistic group interventions, 411
Humanistic therapeutic approaches, 450–451
Human papillomavirus, 245, 246
Human Resource Training/Human Resource Development Model (HRT/HRD), 20
Human subjects consent, 18
Hypothesis validity, 755

I

I Can Problem Solve (ICPS), 216
Imaginary audience, 617
Imaginational overexcitability, 546
Immersion, 274
Immersion-Emersion, 119, 274
Immigrant youth, 63, 79, 95–108, 185–187, 323
    acculturation and, *See* Acculturation
    acculturative school environments, 79–80, 83–89, 106, *See also* Acculturative press
    career development, 104
    classroom climate for, 84
    collaborative support networks, 107
    counselor advocacy roles for, 89, 90
    counselor training, 107
    cultural deprivation model, 101
    culturally appropriate strategies, 104
    culturally diverse model, 101–102
    culture/language broker roles, 82
    ecology of family lives, 82
    effective schools and programs, 89–90
    intergenerational conflict, 82–83, 100
    linguistic issues, 80–81, 98–99, 185–187, *See also* Language issues
    migration patterns, 96–97
    native language use in schools, 84
    Newcomer Schools, 83, 90
    parent involvement, 87–89, 105
    peer relationships and, 86, 105
    placement issues, 85–86, 107
    practice issues and recommendations, 102–107
    psychological health, 100–101
    racism/discrimination experiences, 86, 99–100, 103–104
    resources for parents of, 81
    school adult relationships, 86
    school counselor involvement, 102
    social economic status, 99
    teacher-student relationships, 84
    voluntary and involuntary immigrants, 96
Immigration trends, 95
Immoral conduct, 791
Implicit Association Test, 170
Incompetency, 791
Indigenous healing methods, 189
Individual counseling interventions, 397–406, 643, *See also specific approaches, models or interventions*
    basic competencies, 401–402
    case law, 400
    definitions, 397–398, 401
    evidence-based treatments, 398
    facilitating school operations, 400
    federal mandates, 398–399
    gifted students and, 537–538, 553–554
    interpersonal interventions, 597–598
    model for, 398
    safe environments, 400–401
    scope of practice issues, 398–400
    sexual harassment, 598
    state mandate, 399–400
    theoretical orientations, 402–406
Individual-focused interventions, 272
Individualism, 65, 274–275, 565
    connectedness and, 656–657
    school environment, 72
    school failure and, 635–636
Individualistic cultural orientations, 789
Individualized education plan (IEP), 167
Individualized transition planning, 161, 167
Individual planning, 551–552
Individual student planning, 42, 397
    ASCA *National Model*, 297
    promoting connectedness, 668–669
Individuals with Disabilities Education Act (IDEA), 157–158, 163, 168, 222, 702, 788, 792
Individuation, 5, 434
Industrial Revolution, 4
Infectious diseases, 797
Informed consent, 17, 18, 483, 800–803
Institutionalized homophobia, 138
Insulin, 224–225
Integrated Curriculum Model, 542
Integrated developmental model, 310–311
Integration, 69, 96, 274

melting pot, 84, 102
salad bowl, 353
Intellective competence, 54, 58
Intellectual overexcitability, 547
Intelligence testing, 5, 54
Interest assessment, 277, 282, 504
Intergenerational conflict, 82–83, 100, 323
Internalization, 119
Internalized classism, 151
Internalized racism and career aspirations, 322
Internal locus of control, See Locus of control
Internal validity, 753–754
International Adult Literacy Survey (IALS), 261
International High School, 90
Internet resources, 16
Interpersonal intervention strategies, 596–605
    counselor roles, 602–603
    culture, 597
    developmental level and, 597
    group interventions, 598–600
    indirect interventions, 604
    individual interventions, 597–598
    network therapy, 602–603
    peer mediation, 600, 603–604
    professional staff training, 604
    program evaluation, 604–605
    schoolwide interventions, 600–602
    sexual minorities and, 604
    social phobia treatment, 599
    social power, 597
    TEAM intervention, 599–600
Interpersonal Process Recall, 25
Interpersonal relationships, 587–596
    adolescent connectedness and, 653–656, 659–660, See also Connectedness
    aggressive behavior and, 697–698
    dating and romantic relationships, 594–595
    friendship, 587–589
    gifted students and, 547–548
    identity formation and, 588
    immigrant students and, 86, 105
    relational aggression, 592
    research limitations, 596
    schools as communities, 353, 355
    sexuality, See Sexual health and development
    social networks, 589
        cliques, 590–591
        crowds, 589–590
        interventions, 601–602
        peer influence, 591
    social rejection, 592–594
Interpersonal skills for counselors, 60
Intervention and prevention, balanced approaches, 11
Introspection, 274
Invincibility, personal fable of, 617

Invitational Theory of Practice model, 16, 362–364, 365

J

Jaffee v. Redmond, 793–794, 799
Japanese Americans, 97
Japanese Noh Theater, 525
Journal of Counseling and Development, 761, 763
Juvenile diabetes, 224–225
Juvenile justice, 787

K

Kawaida, 572
Kelson v. City of Springfield, Oregon, 615
Kindergarten, early admission, 538
Korean immigrant youth, 106
Kujichagulia, 573
Kwanzaa intervention, 566, 571–575

L

Labeling and students with disabilities, 160, 166, 170
Language issues, 98–99, 185–187
    cultural brokers, 82, 100, 186–187, 602
    employment opportunities and, 99
    health care access and, 221–222
    immigrant academic achievement and, 80–81
    immigrant parental involvement and, 88
    intergenerational stresses, 82–83, 100
    interpersonal interventions, 597
    native language use in schools, 84
Leadership roles for school counselors, 297, 298, 370, 765, 821, See also Advocacy roles of counselors
    group work and, 439, 441–442
    implementing school–community partnerships, 765
    tripartite model of multicultural counseling, 324
Learning disabilities, See also Students with disabilities
    bilingual students and, 65
    labeling, 160
Learning how to learn, 81, 89
Least restrictive environments, 157
Legal issues, 785–786
    confidentiality, See Confidentiality
    consent, See Consent
    crisis management and intervention, 468
    equal protection rights, 787–788

federal law, 792–793, See also specific legislation
local policies, 790–791
military recruitment, 805–806
negligence, 803
negligent representation, 806–807
parens patriae and children's rights, 787
recommendations for counselors, 807–808
state laws and school codes, 791–792
suicide liability, 468, 615, 628, 791, 798
Lesbian, bisexual, and gay issues, See Gay, lesbian, bisexual and transgender issues
Leukemia, 224
Licensed Professional Counselor (LPC), 813
License suspension or revocation, 791
Licensure, 813
Life-course developmental model of aggressive behavior, 700–701
Life skills education for African-American males, 201
Life-span approach to development, 768, 772
Linking the Interests of Families and Children (LIFT), 451
Listening skills, 416
Literacy, 259–268
    acquisition processes and methods, 260–261
    contextual factors, 264, 266
    counselor training standards, 268
    definitions, 260, 261
    discourses, 260–261
    gaps in the literature, 263–264
    importance of in childhood, 259
    multicultural, 263, 267
    parental involvement and, 260
    phenomenological model for school counselor's role, 264–268
    promotion activities, 260
    school counselor and, 261–268
    skills instruction vs. whole-language approaches, 260
    students of color and, 262
    surveys, 261
Local school board policies, 790–791
Locus of control (LOC), 64–65, 72, 160
Locus of responsibility (LOR), 65–66, 72

M

Macrosystem, 52, 280, 489, 653, 679
Maintenance stage, 724–725
Malpractice, 803
    negligent representation, 806–807
Management agreements, 43
Mandatory reporting, 311, 796
Marginalization, 69
Marriage and heterosexism, 138

Master's level counselor education process, 21–22, See also Counselor education and training
Mastery learning, 58, 59, 183
Masturbation, 247
Maximizing Potential Model, 541
MAXMINICON, 752
MEASURE, 45
Mediation, 600, 602–604
Media violence, 697
Medicaid, 220–221
Medical Academy program, 89–90
Medical records access, 794, 796
MEETU, 473
Melting pot, 84, 102, 353
Mental health, See also Depression; Substance abuse; Suicide
    acculturation and, 100–101
    at-risk criteria for services, 196
    caring school communities and, 354
    chronic illnesses and, 226
    developmental challenges and, 195
    eating disorders and, 231
    ethnic identity and, 129
    immigrant youth and, 100–101
    need for community, 352
    obesity and overweight and, 229
    Progressive School Counseling Advocacy Model, 197–198
    psychoanalytic theory, 450
    racial/ethnic identity and, 180
    racial/ethnic minorities and, 146, 195, 196, 197
    racial harassment and, 115–116
    school counselor scope of practice, 399
    school counselor training models and, 295, 296
    school counselor understanding of, 401
    screening, 401
    social class and, 147, 153
    wellness model, 383
Mental health consultation, 333, 338, 340, 464–465, 468, 484, 485–486
Mental health services
    community mental health movement, 450
    consultation with, 346
    crisis intervention, See Crisis management
    gaps in, 381, 392
    preventive interventions, See Prevention
    school–community collaboration, 294, 766, 772
Mental retardation, 175
Mentoring in counselor training, 22, 301–302
Mentoring students, 105, 152, 184, 646
    peer mentoring, 368
Mesosystem, 52, 653, 679
Miami-Dade County Crisis Management Prevention Program, 620
Michigan State University school counseling training model, 24–29

Microcounseling Skills Training Model, 20
Microsystems, 52, 279, 489, 653, 679
Middle school counseling, 820
Middle school personal/social development interventions, 214–215
Midwestern Prevention Project, 388
Midwest Prevention Project, 391
Migration patterns, 96–97
Military recruitment, 805–806
Minority Identity Model, 274
Minority Student Achievement Network, 56
Minor's autonomy, 787
Mission statement, 40, 41
Mississippi Counseling Association, 314
Missouri Comprehensive Guidance Model (MCGM), 15, 16
Missouri Comprehensive Guidance Programs (MCGP), 756–757
Mock counseling sessions, 26–27
Model minority stereotype, 72, 99, 104, 321, 404
Montessori school system, 406
Moral action, 210
Moral character of counselors, 789
Moral development, 210–211, 212–213, 313
Moral feeling, 210
Moral knowing, 210
Motivation
   caring school communities and, 355
   self-determination theory, 160–162, 280–281
Motivational interviewing (MI), 60, 721–732
   case example, 725–732
   dealing with resistance, 730–731
   stages of change, 721–725
Multicultural competence, xxvii, 60, 102–103, 107–108, 146, 271–272, 283, 321, 324–326, 450, 642–643, *See also* Counselor self-awareness of racial/ethnic/sociocultural orientations or biases; Diversity issues
   advocacy competencies, 325
   bicultural competence, 56–57, 59, 71, 183, 185, 323
   career considerations, 324, 325
   career development interventions and, 511–512
   caring school communities and, 353
   consultation and, 339–340, 344, 491–493
   counseling psychology and counselor education, 29
   counselor racial identity attitudes, 120
   counselor training curricula, 29, 302, 305
   crisis intervention and, 472
   cultural identity enhancement strategies, 563–583
   disability-associated issues, 162–163, 171
   effective school–community partnerships and, 773–774
   ethical decision making, 786
   family involvement, 454–455
   gifted students and, 534
   group work and, 435–436
   health care workers and, 222
   identity issues, *See* Cultural identity; Ethnic identity; Racial identity
   improving minority academic success, 188–190
   interpersonal interventions, 597
   minimal standards for training, 16–17
   self-awareness of biases and values, *See* Counselor education and training
   student substance abuse and, 730
   training best practices, 324
   tripartite model of multicultural counseling, 324
   understanding student worldview and experiences, 103–104, 131
Multiculturalism, *See* Diversity issues; Multicultural competence
Multicultural literacy, 263, 267
Multicultural student identity issues, 129
Multidisciplinary team activities, 167
Multiple disabilities, 175
Multiple intelligences, 536
Multipotentiality, 544–546, 552
Multisetting approach to prevention, 386

N

National Adult Literacy Survey (NALS), 261
National Association for Gifted Children (NAGC), 555
National Board for Certified Counselors (NBCC), 812–813
National Board for Professional Teaching Standards (NBPTS), 24, 812
National Career Development Association, 5
National Career Development Guidelines, 498–499
National Certified Counselor, 813
National Certified School Counselor Exam (NCSCE), 814
National Council for Accreditation of Teacher Education, 162, 402, 812–813
National Counselor Examination (NCE), 813
National Defense Education Act (NDEA), 7–8, 276, 293, 295, 792–793, 811
National Education Goals, 181
National Institute on Drug Abuse, 215–217
Nationally Certified School Counselor (NCSC), 812, 813
National Model, See ASCA National Model
National Program for the Transformation of School Counseling, 815
National School Counselor Training Initiative, 398, 481
National Standards for School Counseling Programs, 38–39, 41, 51, 197–198, 297, 402, 431, 563, 812, *See also ASCA National Model*

National Study Group for the Affirmative Development of Academic Ability (NSGADAA), 54
National Vocational Guidance Association (NVGA), 5
A Nation at Risk, 10, 38
Native Americans
　culturally responsive consultation, 491–492
　health disparities, 225, 228, 234
　suicide prevention or intervention, 620
　suicide risk, 629–630
Navajo culture, 491–492, 527, 630
Negligent representation, 806–807
Network therapy, 602–603
Newcomer Schools, 83, 90
New student groups, 368
No Child Left Behind (NCLB), 18, 38, 45, 49–51, 112, 157–158, 198, 234, 443, 636–637, 751, 766, 793, 815
　achievement gap and, 766–767
　ASCA *National Standards and*, 297
　character education in, 469
　consultation issues, 340
　crisis management in, 468
　Protection of Pupil Rights Amendment, 802
　school–community partnership alignment, 770
No-fault problem solving, 815, 816
Noh Theater, 525
Nonverbal communication, 597, *See also* Creative arts counseling
Norming in groups, 410
North Carolina Master Plan for Guidance, 8
"No suicide" contracts, 626–627

O

Obesity and overweight, 225, 227–229, 767
Objectification, 522–524
Occupational self-efficacy, 278
Olweus Bullying Prevention Program, 679–681
Online harassment, 596
Open Circle Competency Program, 434–435
Oppression, 273
　false vs. critical consciousness, 273
　social justice model and, 384, *See also* Social justice perspectives
　wellness model vs., 383
Oral sex, 246–247
Oregon Social Learning Center (OSLC), 451
Organizational consultation, 489–490
Organizational racial identity, 121–122
Orthopedic impairment, 175
Other-esteem, 211, 214
Outcome-oriented school counseling program, 50
Overexcitability, 546–547

Overlap Model, 616
Overweight, *See* Obesity and overweight

P

Pain, 226
Pa ndau, 567, 576
Parens patriae, 787
Parental consent, 801–803
Parental expectations, as protective factor, 619
Parental involvement, *See also* Family contexts
　academic achievement/failure and, 53, 58, 149, 181–182, 637
　building caring school communities, 370, 374
　counselor facilitation of, 603
　effective school–community partnerships and, 772–773, *See also* School–family–community collaboration
　immigrant students and, 87–89, 105
　language issues, 88
　literacy development and, 260
　minority student performance improvement strategies, 58
　multicultural counseling issues, 454–455
　multisetting approaches for prevention, 386
　PATHS, 216
　social class and, 149, 151–152
　student-led parent conferences, 816
　students with disabilities and, 166–167
　supportive interventions for minority students, 190
Parental support for sexual minorities, 140
Parent education, 386
　effective school–community partnerships and, 773
　interpersonal interventions, 600, 603
　PET and STEP, 488
　school violence prevention and intervention, 703
　suicide awareness, 630
　violence prevention, 469, 684
Parent Effectiveness Training (PET), 488
Parenting practices, youth aggression and, 697
Parent-Management Training (PMT), 600
Parents, Families and Friends of Lesbians and Gays (PFLAG), 141
Participant action research, 762
PATHS, 216, 703–704, 705
Pathways curriculum, 234
Patriarchal power, 384
Pedagogy, 24–25
Peer counselors, 105, 388
Peer group supervision, 315–316
Peer mediation, 388, 600
Peer mentoring, 368
Peer pressure, 105, 151, 187, 535, 552, 591, 658, *See also* Interpersonal relationships

Peer tutoring, 704
People of color racial identity model, 119, 180
Perfectionism, 549, 553
Personal and social development, 209–217
    ASCA standards, 42, 209
    assertiveness, 212
    character, 209, 212, 469
    communication skills, 212
    comprehensive school guidance model, 209
    decision making, 212, 214
    emotional intelligence, 55, 59, 211
    family and, 209
    future research, 216–217
    historical perspectives, 6–7
    moral development, 210–211, 212–213
    outcome research, 212
    practice issues and recommendations, 214–215
    programs and resources, 215–216
    self-efficacy and, 211, 213, *See also* Self-efficacy
    self-esteem and, 211, 213–214, *See also* Self-esteem
Personal development of counselors, 19–20
Personalismo, 581
Personality measurement, 277, 278–279
Person-centered therapy, 213, 295, 402–403, 432–433
Person-environment fit model of career development, 276, 277, 278
Personnel evaluation, 741–742
Phenomenological models or approaches, 25, 145, 150–151, 153, 264–268
Physical activity, 229, 233, 234
Playground interventions and aggressive behavior, 705
Play therapy, 406, 517–522, *See also* Creative arts counseling
    counselor training, 520–521
    interpersonal interventions, 598
    theory, 518–519
Poetry therapy, 525–526
Popular cliques, 590
Positive Behavioral Interventions and Supports (PBIS), 706
Positive psychology, 387–388, 564–565
Positive youth development, 252–253, 366–367, 389
Possible selves, 181
Postgraduate counselor education process, 21–22, *See also* Counselor education and training
Post-traumatic stress disorder (PTSD), 116, 462
Postvention, 474–476, 615, 627, 805
Poverty, *See also* Socioeconomic status
    academic achievement and, 51, 269–270, 537, 773
    aggressive behavior and, 697, 767
    gifted students and, 537, 548
    health risks, 767
    immigrant households and, 99
    implications for schools and counseling, 146, 643
    protective factors and, 152

    psychological effects, 147, 153
Practicum and internship (fieldwork), 298–300, 302, 304, 306
Precontemplation stage, 722–723
Pregnancy, *See* Teen pregnancy
Prejudice, *See* Discrimination and prejudice; Homophobia
Preparation stage, 724
Preschool prevention program, 390–391
Prescriptive/nonprescriptive programs, 10–11
Presentation skills, 297–298, 821
Prevention, 42, 195–197, 381–392
    addressing school failure, 644
    Adlerian consultation, 489
    African American Empowerment Curriculum, 195, 199–203
    balanced approach, 11
    of bullying, *See* Bullying
    comprehensive school guidance model, 196
    consultation and collaboration targets, 490–491
    crisis prevention, 42, 468–469
    definition, 381–382
    developmental approaches, 469, 772
    effectiveness, 381, 389–390
    effective school–community partnerships and, 771–772
    group work, 409–426, *See also* Group counseling interventions
    health promotion model, 383, *See also* Health promotion and prevention issues
    historical context, 382
    models, 382–384
    outcome research, 201–202
    parental involvement and, 386
    positive youth development approach, 367
    postvention, 474, 627
    preschool project, 390–391
    public health issues, 195–197
    racial harassment issues, 123
    research, 389–390
    school-based model, 384–392
        assertiveness training intervention, 391
        classroom approaches, 385
        climate, 387–388
        cultural adaptation, 388–389
        curriculum, 388
        effective implementation, 386–389
        evaluation, 389
        High/Scope Perry preschool project, 390–391
        interpersonal interventions, 600–602
        Midwest Prevention Project, 391
        multisetting approaches, 386
        needs assessment, 387
        presentation, 388
        schoolwide approaches, 385–386
        Strengthening Families Program, 391

Teen Outreach Program, 391–392
school counselor training implications, 392
social justice model, 383–384
of substance abuse, *See* Substance abuse prevention and intervention
of suicide, *See* Suicide
of violence, *See* Violence prevention
Preventive health care, 219–220
obesity and eating disorders, 232–234
Primary prevention, 409, 424, *See also* Prevention
consultation and collaboration targets, 490
crisis prevention, 468–469
effective school–community partnerships and, 771
suicide, 614
Principals, individual counseling scope of practice and, 399–400
Principal training, 415
Privacy rights, 787, 793–794, *See also* Confidentiality
Privileged communication, 799
Problem-posing approach, 25
Problem-solving orientation, school counselor consultation model, 331
Problem-solving skills curriculum, 216
Process model of minority student achievement, 51–58, *See also* Achievement gap
Professional development, *See* Counselor education and training
Professional School Counseling, 761, 763
Professional school counseling conferences, 821
Professional self-regulation, 788–789, 792
Profiling, 804
Program-centered administrative consultation, 485
Program evaluation, 413, 604–605, 739–748, *See also* Research; Student performance outcomes
ASCA *National Model*, 741, 744
computer technology and, 748
data collection and analysis, 744–748
historical perspectives, 739–741
outcome variables, 740, 755, 758
personnel evaluation, 741–742
"personnel plus program equals results," 741
program evaluation, 742, 744
research on comprehensive school counseling programs, 755–758
school–community partnerships, 774
standards and criteria (table), 743
Program supervision, 314–315
Progressive education, 6
Progressive School Counseling Advocacy Model, 195, 197–198
Project Apogee, 541
Promoting Alternative Thinking Strategies (PATHS), 216, 703–704, 705
Prose literacy, 261
Protection of Pupil Rights Amendment (PPRA), 792, 801–802
Protective factors for minority academic achievement, 53–58, 187–188
Pseudo-Independence, 119, 274
Psychoanalytic theory, 450
Psychodrama, 524
Psychodynamic theories of play, 519
Psychoeducational drama, 524
Psychological first aid, 465, 473
Psychological or emotional disorders, *See* Mental health
Psychological triage, 472
Psychometric movement and vocational guidance, 276
Psychosocial adaptations to disability, 159–160, 161
Public health issues, 195–197, 219–227, *See also* Racial/ethnic minority health issues
Public school roles and functions, 111–112
acculturative environments, *See* Schools as acculturative environments
socialization, 80, 112
Puppets, 406

Q

Qualitative research, 762
Quantitative literacy, 261

R

Race, 128, 177–178, *See also* Ethnic identity; Racial identity
discussing issues of, 130–131
social class and, 145, 146–147
Race-based educational approach, 118
Racial climate, 121
Racial/cultural composition of school personnel, 112
Racial discrimination, *See* Discrimination and prejudice
Racial/ethnic minority health issues, 219–223
asthma, 223
contraceptive use, 245–246
diabetes, 225
eating disorders, 231–232
overweight and obesity, 228
Racial/ethnic minority students, *See also* Immigrant youth
academic achievement, *See* Achievement gap
academic aspirations, 321, 507
acculturation, *See* Acculturation
career decision-making issues, 324, 325

criminalization of, 694
demographic trends, 95, 271, 321, 435, 518, 751, 785
disability issues, 157, 168, 170
discrimination, *See* Discrimination and prejudice
disproportionate sanctioning, 694, 700
emotional expression and, 322–323
gifted and talented programs and, 170, 534–537, 548
harassment, *See* Racial harassment
help-*See*king behaviors, 322
historical school counseling issues, 178–179
identity development, *See* Ethnic identity; Racial identity
inappropriate placement or tracking, 179, 189
locus of control and responsibility, 64–66
mental health and, 146, 195, 196, 197
public health issues, 195–197
sexual minorities and, 142
suicide rates, 463
Racial/ethnic minority teachers, 112
Racial harassment, 111–123, *See also* Discrimination and prejudice
bullying and, 116–117
counselor training and, 123
discrimination vs., 115
identity orientations and responses to, 120–122
intervention strategies, 122–123
legal definitions, 114–118
microaggressions, 117
prevalence, 113–114, 116
prevention strategies, 123
psychological effects, 115–116
school officials' perceptions of, 116–118
teacher training and, 112
white teacher blindness to, 118
Racial identity, 118–119, 127, 564, *See also* Ethnic identity
academic achievement and, 179–181, 322
acculturation and, *See* Acculturation
"acting white," 179, 536, 548
Afrocentric values, 181
color-blind orientations, 72, 119, 180, 188
counselor-assisted identity development, 128–133
counselor attitudes and intervention approaches, 120
critique of whiteness, 122
cultural consciousness and, 200–201
discussing issues of, 131
false vs. critical consciousness, 273
groups and organizations, 121–122
interpersonal relationships and, 121, 588
mental health and, 180
Minority Identity Model, 274
models, 119, 180, 274
psychosocial adaptations, 323

resiliency and, 187
student performance and, 56
substance abuse protective factors, 719
white racial identity, 67, 71, 119, 274
Racially hostile environment, 114–115
Racial politics, schools hiding behind, 199
Racial socialization, 187, *See also* Racial identity
Racial stereotypes and career development, 501
Racism, 177, *See also* Achievement gap; Discrimination and prejudice; Racial harassment; White privilege
ethnic identity development and, 128–129
immigrant students and, 103–104
internalization, 69
interventions for combating, 189
social class and, 147
Rational emotive behavior therapy, 296, 432, 433
Reading skills development, *See* Literacy
Reality therapy, 403, 411, 432, 433
Recruiting counselors of color, 301–302, 326
Referral services, 42
Reflection, 348, 731
Reflective skills, 311–312
Reframing, 732
Refugees, 96–98, *See also* Immigrant youth
Rehabilitation Act, Section 504, 158, 167, 168
Reintegration, 119, 274
Relatedness, 655, 656
gender differences, 662–663
Relational aggression, 592, 682
Relational-cultural theory, 431, 434–435
Relationship issues, *See* Interpersonal relationships
Religion and spirituality
adolescent sexual behavior and, 249–250
immigrant students and, 106
Remedial Education and Diagnostic Services (READS), 756
Reporting requirements, 17, 311, 785, *See also* Confidentiality
Research, 751–763
action research, 605, 762
on comprehensive school counseling programs, 755–758
computer technology and, 819
on counselor roles and duties, 758–759
counselors as researchers-practitioners, 18–19, 28, 60, 760–761
counselor training curriculum, 306–307
human subjects informed consent, 18
outcome variables, 740, 755, 758
publication outlets, 761, 763
qualitative research, 762
recommendations for counselors, 761–763
single-subject design, 605, 763
training issues, 300
Transforming School Counseling Initiative, 300

university collaboration, 762
validity issues, 752–755, 761
Resilience
cultural identity and, 565
gifted students and, 537
group work, 411
health promotion model, 383
minority student performance and, 53–58, 187–188, 325
positive youth development approach, 366
Resistance, 274, 343–344, 730–731
Respect
effective school communities and, 354
respeto, 582
student performance and, 58–59
Responsibility Behavior Choice Program, 403
Responsive services interventions, 42
Results-based program evaluation, 744–748
Revolving Door Identification Model (RDIM), 540
Risk and protective factors, 57
Risk-taking and connectedness, 659, 660
Role models
moral development and, 212
sexual minorities and, 140
Role-playing, 26–27, 213, 470
Roles and responsibilities, *See* School counselor roles and responsibilities
Romantic and dating relationships, 594–595
Rural schools, 158
bullying and, 674, 693
gifted students and, 537
group work and, 440
substance abuse intervention issues, 733

S

SAD PERSONS scale, 624
Safe and Drug-Free Schools Program, 719–720
Safe counseling environments, 400–401, 442
Safe Zone, 252
Sain v. Cedar Rapids Community School District, 806–807
Salad bowl, 353
Sandplay therapy, 526–527
Scale to Assess Worldview, 66
Scholarship of engagement, 451–452
School and Family Intervention (SAFI) model, 90
School-based health centers (SBHCs), 234–237, 253
School-based prevention model, 384–392, *See also under* Prevention
School board policies, 790–791
School climate, 776, *See also* School environment; Schools as caring communities
academic failure and, 637

character education and, 212, 469
group work and, 420
immigrant youth and, 84
organizational consultation, 490
positive psychology, 387–388
school-based prevention model, 387–388
school crisis likelihood and, 460
substance abuse and, 718–719
truancy and, 639
School codes, 791–792
School–community collaboration, 294, 296, 353, 355, 398, 481, 765–779
best practices, 770–778
aligning with No Child Left Behind, 770
Boston Connects program, 775–778
comprehensive student support, 770
coordination of services, 771
developmentally appropriate prevention and intervention, 772
evaluating effectiveness, 774
evidence-based programs, 774
family engagement, 772–773, *See also* School–family–community collaboration
infrastructure and sustainability, 774–775
prevention and intervention continuum, 771–772
recognizing diversity, 773–774
collaborative training programs, 815
counselor training and supervision, 818
developmental contexts, 767–769
diversity issues, 773–774
historical perspectives, 766
implementation challenges, 769–770
mental health services and, 294, 766, 772
models, 778–779
university partnerships, 300, 316, 555, 644, 762
Whole Child vision of schooling, 779
School counseling curriculum, 41–42
School counseling department annual calendar, 44
School counseling profession
accreditation, *See* Accreditation and certification
conferences, 821
education, *See* Counselor education and training
history of, *See* History of school counseling
licensure, 813
recruiting counselors of color, 301–302, 326
supervision and job performance, 313, *See also* Supervision
terms and identity, 11
School counseling program organizational models, 49–50, *See also* ASCA National Model
School counseling program standards, *See* Standards-based school counseling programs
School counselor-centered training program, 304–307
School counselor criminal background, 17–18
School counselor moral character, 789

School counselor personal development, 19–20
School counselor personal identity, 11–12
School counselor racial identity attitudes, 120
School counselor roles and responsibilities, 49, 197–198, 375, 642–645, 815–816
   advocacy, *See* Advocacy roles of counselors
   ambiguities, 294
   ASCA *National Model*, 294, 366
   bullying prevention and intervention, 673, *See also* Bullying
   career development, *See* Career development
   collaboration, *See* Collaboration
   consultation, *See* Consultation
   crisis management and intervention, 467, 470
   cultural translators, 106
   educating school personnel about, 300
   facilitating systemic change, 37, 107, 197, 263, 297, 384
   family liaison, 88, 451, 601, 602, 643, *See also* Family contexts
   fostering caring school environments, 351–352
   helping immigrant students, 89, 90, 106–107
   job description, 400
   leadership, *See* Leadership roles for school counselors
   literacy development, 261–268
   multidisciplinary team activities, 167
   program evaluation, 605, 742
   researchers-practitioners, 18–19, 28, 60, 760–761
   research on, 758–759
   scope of practice issues, 398–400
   student health promotion, 146
   students with disabilities and, 167–168
   teacher conflict, 816–818
   teacher education, 84, 106–107, 604, 816
   training faculty knowledge, 301
   violence prevention, 196, 804
School counselor time management, 44
School counselor-to-student ratios, 19, 499, 507
School counselor values and biases, self-awareness of, *See* Counselor self-awareness of racial/ethnic/sociocultural orientations or biases
School crises, 461–463, *See also* Crisis management; Suicide; Violence and aggression
School dropouts, 635, 641–642
   economic life outcomes, 269–270
   gifted students and, 536
School environment, 72, *See also* Schools as caring communities
   aggressive behavior and, 693, 698–699
   bullying and, 673–674, 693
   climate, *See* School climate
   creating inviting environment, 347
   increasing cultural sensitivity, 132
   oppressive conditions and minority achievement discrepancies, 273
   organizational consultation, 489–490
   safe counseling environments, 400–401, 442
   supportive and caring environments, 351
School failure, 635–647, *See also* Achievement gap
   academic failure, 636–638
      aggressive behavior and, 696
      community/societal factors, 638
      family factors, 637
      risk factor identification, 644
      school factors, 637–638
   community/societal level, 646–647
   counselor roles and interventions, 642–645
   dropout, *See* School dropouts
   ecological systems theory, 636
   gifted students and, 536–537, *See also* Gifted and talented students
   grade promotion and retention, 639–641
   high-stakes testing and, 636–637, 646
   individualist perspectives and, 635–636
   intervention/prevention program examples, 645–646
   school counselor roles and interventions, 642–645
   school report card, 45
   schoolwide prevention/intervention program development, 644
   truancy and tardiness, 272–273, 356, 638–639
   White Eurocentric American culture and, 638
School–family–community collaboration, 152, 353, 355, 370–371, 450–453, *See also* Family contexts; Parental involvement; Schools as caring communities
   best practices, 772–773
   Boston Connects program, 777
   multicultural counseling, 454–455
   multisetting approaches for prevention, 386
School improvement data, 45
School nurse, 224
School quality and student performance, 53, *See also* School failure
School report card, 45
Schools as acculturative environments, 79–81, 83–89, 106, *See also* Acculturative press
   ecological perspective, 81–82
   effective schools and programs, 89–90
   resources for parents, 81
Schools as caring communities, 351–375, 778, *See also* Connectedness; School–community collaboration
   academic success, 356
   belongingness, 352, 355, *See also* Connectedness
   beneficial effects of, 354–356
   "The Caring Classroom," 357, 358–359, 364
   case example, 373–374
   challenges and future directions, 375
   Child Development Project, 357, 360–362, 365, 706
   "The Classroom as Community," 357, 359, 364

classroom guidance, 368
community building within classrooms, 355
community schools, 778
definition, 352
developmental assets, 357, 359–360, 365
diversity issues, 354, 356
engagement and participation, 355
implementation and evaluation, 371–373
individual and group level interventions, 367–368
Invitational Theory of Practice model, 362–364, 365
key elements, 353–354
multiculturally competent educational environments, 353
positive youth development approach, 366–367
school counselor involvement, 362, 363, 366–371
school–family–community collaboration, 353, 355
schoolwide initiatives, 369–370
sense of community, 353
theoretical frameworks, 357–365
Tribes TLC, 216, 357–358, 364, 368
School survival skills, 106
School-to-work transition, 150, 152, 296, 507, 772
School violence, See Violence and aggression
Schoolwide health programs, 220, 223
Search Institute, 357, 359–360
Secondary prevention, 424–425, 490–491, 614, See also Prevention
Second Step programs, 212, 216, 601, 679, 681–683
Secretary's Commission for Achieving Necessary Skills (SCANS), 276, 283
Section 504, 158, 167, 168
Selection, 674
Selection, optimization, and compensation model, 280
Self-awareness of biases, See Counselor self-awareness of racial/ethnic/sociocultural orientations or biases
Self-determination theory, 160, 161–162, 280–281, See also Locus of control
  interventions for students with disabilities, 164–165
Self-Directed Search (SDS), 277
Self-efficacy, 161, 183, 201, 211, 213, 278
  behavioral consultation, 487
  career, 278, 507
  caring school communities and, 354
  motivational interviewing intervention, 727
  Pathways intervention and, 234
  play therapy and, 406, 517
  Social Cognitive Career Theory, 161, 162, 278
Self-esteem, 211, 213–214
  connectedness and, 653
  counseling program effectiveness in changing, 756
  eating disorders and, 230
  interventions for students with disabilities, 166

media images and, 388
moral feeling, 210
racial harassment and, 116
racial identity and, 180
Self-Perception Profile for Children (SPCC), 756
Self-reflection, 311–312, 348
Self-supervision skills, 302
Sensual overexcitability, 546
Separation, 68, 184
Serotonin, 695
Services for Teens at Risk (STAR), 620
Settlement houses, 449
Sex differences, See Gender differences
Sex education, 243, 250, See also Sexual health and development
  abstinence-only curriculum, 250–251
  outcomes research, 250–251
  positive youth development approach, 252–253
  public preferences, 251–252
  sexual minorities and, 252
  social skills and, 254
Sexual abuse, counselor training issues, 20
Sexual harassment, 435–436
  definition, 436
  Expect Respect program, 683
  interpersonal interventions, 595–596, 598
Sexual health and development, 243–255, See also Sex education
  abstinence, 245, 250
  adolescent pregnancy rates, 243–245, See also Adolescent pregnancy
  age at sexual initiation, 248
  case examples, 254–255
  contraceptive use, 245–246, 248
  counselor and educator involvement, 253–254
  defining abstinence, 247
  diseases, See Sexually transmitted infections
  noncoital sexual behaviors, 246–248
  other health risk behaviors and, 248
  positive youth development approach, 252–253
  religion and, 249–250
Sexually transmitted infections (STIs), 245–247, 251
  HIV/AIDS, 226–227, 245, 247, 251
Sexual minority, defined, 135, See also Gay, lesbian, bisexual and transgender issues
Sexual orientation, See Gay, lesbian, bisexual and transgender issues
Shared vision and values of schools, 354, 369, 373, See also Schools as caring communities
Signs of Suicide (SOS), 620
Simpatia, 582
Single-subject research design, 605, 763
Skilled Counselor Training Model (SCTM), 20
Skills for Academic and Social Success (SASS) program, 599
SLAP, 623

Small groups, *See* Group counseling interventions
SOAR, 616, 620
Social class and school counseling, *See also* Socioeconomic status
   class indicators, 145
   counselors' class biases and, 152, 324
   developmental guidance, 148–149
   ethnicity and class, 154
   etiquette classes, 152
   indices and awareness issues, 147–148
   limitations in understanding class, 147–148
   multicultural competence, 146
   parental involvement and, 149, 151–152
   phenomenological/subjective approach, 145, 150–151, 153
   practice issues and recommendations, 150–153
   subjective phenomenological approach, 145
   vocational guidance, 149–150
   youth class awareness, 147–148
Social Class Worldview Model (SCWM), 147, 151
Social-cognitive approach to violence prevention, 702
Social Cognitive Career Theory (SCCT), 161, 162, 278
Social competency interventions, 601, *See also* Social skills
Social development, *See* Personal and social development
Social ecological theory, 675, 678–679, *See also* Ecological models
Social Effectiveness Therapy for Children (SET-C), 599
Social enrichment opportunities, 555
Social information processing theory (SIPT), 674, 676, 686, 696
Socialization, 80, 112, 674, *See also* Acculturation; Development; Personal and social development; *specific related models or theories*
Social justice perspectives, 272–276, 326, 821–822, *See also* Advocacy roles of counselors
   addressing school failure, 646
   culturally responsive career development programs, 283
   data-driven school counseling and, 51
   Emancipatory Communitarian (EC) framework, 272
   false vs. critical consciousness, 273
   National Program for the Transformation of School Counseling, 815
   prevention model, 383–384
   school counseling and, 275–276
   traditional career theory and, 278–279
Social learning theory, 451, 675
   behavioral consultation, 332, 484, 486–487
   bullying research, 678, 685
   school violence prevention and intervention, 702, 703

Social networks, *See under* Interpersonal relationships
Social phobia treatment, 599
Social power, 597
Social rejection, 592
Social skills
   Boston Connects program, 776
   interpersonal interventions, 599, 601
   intervention outcomes, 214, 434
   sex education and, 254
   social competency intervention, 601
   social rejection and, 593
   student performance and, 55, 80
   student socioeconomic status and, 49
   training for students with disabilities, 164
Social Skills Training (SST), 599
Social support systems, 49, *See also* Family contexts; Interpersonal relationships
   acculturative press and, 86–87
   connectedness and, 655–656, *See also* Connectedness
   immigrant students and, 107
   protective factors against poverty effects, 152
   schools as communities, 353
   sexual minority youth, 140–141
Socioeconomic status (SES), 145, *See also* Social class and school counseling
   academic achievement and, 51, 55, 99, 149, 269–270, 294, *See also* Achievement gap
   career choices and, 150
   class indicators, 146
   classism, 145, 151
   counseling and, 145–154, *See also* Social class and school counseling
   developmental outcomes and, 146
   eating disorders and, 232
   health status and, 220
   immigrant families, 99
   mental health and, 147, 153
   obesity and overweight and, 228–229
   racial/ethnic intersections, 145, 146–147
   supportive environments for students and, 49
Solution-focused therapy, 152, 405–406, 411, 433
Special education services, 157, *See also* Gifted and talented students; Students with disabilities
   bilingual students and, 65
   ethical, legal, and professional issues, 167–168
   historical perspectives, 10
   multidisciplinary team activities, 167
   qualifying disabilities, 175–176
   rural settings and, 158
Speech or language impairment, 175
Spirituality, *See* Religion and spirituality
Sputnik, 7
Standardized testing
   historical perspectives, 5

minority achievement gap and, 50, 184
    school failure and, 636–637, 646
Standards-based school counseling programs, 37–46
    advisory council, 43
    MEASURE, 45
    mission statement, 40, 41
    national model, *See ASCA National Model*
    National Standards for School Counseling Programs, 38–39, 41, 51, 197–198, 297, 402, 431, 563, 812
    planning, 43–44
    program audit/self-study, 44
    school counseling curriculum, 41–42
    student competencies, 38–39, 41
    using performance data, 43, 45
STAR, 620
State counseling programs, 820
State licensing, 813
Statistical conclusion validity, 752
Statistics and measurement curriculum, 306
Steps to Respect, 679, 686
Stereotypes
    Asian Americans and, 72, 99, 103, 104, 321, 404
    awareness of, 100, 104
    crowds and, 589
    gender and career development, 501
    labeling exercise intervention, 170
    secondary prevention interventions, 424–425
Stereotype threat, 187–188
Strategic Comprehensive Model (SCM), 11
Strengthening Families Program (SFP), 391
Strengths-based interventions, 104, 131, 190, 203, 565, 645, 719, 768–769, *See also* Resilience
    developmental assets, 280
    group work, 411
    school-based prevention model, 384
Structured play therapy, 521
Student accomplishment, 49, 50, 51, *See also* Academic achievement
    process model of minority student achievement, 51–58, *See also* Achievement gap
Student-centered classroom, 357
Student competencies, *National Standards for School Counseling Programs,* 38–39, 41
Student development, *See* Development
Student-directed learning strategies, 162
Student-led parent conferences, 816
Student performance outcomes, 50, 757–758, *See also* Academic achievement; Accountability
    African American Empowerment Curriculum and, 201–202
    ASCA National Model, 40, 44–45, 50–51
    developmental assets and, 360
    effective school and personnel characteristics for improving, 188–190

    family and, 80
    life outcomes and, 199
    linguistic issues, 80–81
    minority health outcomes and, 146
    organizational choices, 50–51
    process model of minority student achievement, 51–58
    program evaluation, 740, 755
    racial/ethnic minorities and, *See* Achievement gap
    school-based health centers and, 235–236
    school climate effects, 490
    school quality and, 53
    social skills and, 55, 80
    teen pregnancy and, 253
Student-school connectedness, *See* Connectedness
Students of color, academic performance of, *See* Achievement gap
Student Success Skills Program (SSS), 757
Student support services team, 42
Students with disabilities, 157–172, *See also* Special education services
    adult outcomes, 160, 162, 171
    brief family interventions, 166–167
    chronic illnesses, 222–227
    counselor training, 162–163, 171
    gender and, 168
    labeling, 160, 166, 170
    legislation, 157–158, 168
    psychosocial adaptations, 159–160, 161
    racial/ethnic minorities and, 157, 168, 170
    research directions, 171–172
    school counseling and, 159, 162–166
    self-determination interventions, 164–165
    self-determination theory, 160, 161–162
    Social Cognitive Career Theory, 161, 162
    social rejection and, 593
    social skills training, 164
    teacher or team consultations, 167
    transition planning, 161, 167
Student-to-counselor ratios, 19, 499, 507
Subgrouping, 420
Subjective/phenomenological approach, 145, 150–151, 153
Substance abuse, 717–734
    caring school communities and, 355–356
    confidentiality issues, 720–721, 785
    counselor training issues, 20
    cultural considerations, 730, 732
    gender differences, 717–718
    peer influence, 591
    prevalence, 717
    racial/ethnic minorities and, 719
    risk and protective factors, 718–719
    rural schools and, 733
    suicide risk factor, 463, 617, 619
    teen pregnancy and, 248–249

trends, 718, 767
Substance Abuse and Mental Health Services Administration, 215
Substance abuse prevention and intervention, 215, 719–720
    Child Development Project, 361
    developmental assets, 357, 360
    Midwest Prevention Project, 391
    motivational interviewing, 721–732
    online resources, 733–734
    school counselor and, 720–721
    treatment program selection, 732
Suburban school counseling issues, 819
Success identity, 403
Success Identity Pathways, 285–286
Suicidal Tendencies Scale, 625
Suicide
    confidentiality and liability issues, 468, 623, 628, 803, 805
    contagion, 475
    counselor training, 472, 615–616, 622, 631
    crisis situations and, 462–463
    danger signals, 623
    definition of terms, 613
    discussing issues of, 474
    diversity issues, 629–630
    effect on counselor, 621–622
    ethical issues, 628
    interventions, 615, 625–627
    legal issues, 468, 615, 791, 798
    "no suicide" contracts, 626–627
    parent education, 630
    posttraumatic stress responses, 462
    postvention, 474–476, 615, 627, 805
    prediction, 621
    prevention programs, 466, 614–615, 619–621, 622–625
        best practices, 805
        centers, 464
        curriculum, 622
        efficacy, 617, 619, 620
    protective factors, 618–619
    rates, 329, 460, 463, 613–614
    risk assessment and screening, 473, 623–625
    risk factors, 463, 617–619
    theory, 616–617
Suicide Ideation Questionnaire (SIQ), 625
Suicide Options, Awareness, and Relief (SOAR), 616, 620
Suicide Probability Scale (SPS), 625
Suicide Trajectory model, 616
Summer transition program, 285
Supervision, 299, 309–318
    administrative, 314
    barriers to, 312
    ethical issues, 313–314
    integrated developmental model, 310–311
    job performance and, 313
    local school partnerships, 818
    peer group, 315–316
    practice issues and recommendations, 316–317
    professional development schools, 316
    program, 314–315
    reflective skills, 311–312
    research, 312–314, 317
    self-supervision, 302
    training issues, 19, 23, 303
    videotaped sessions, 26
Support services, 42–43
Support system approach in counselor training, 296
Suspension and expulsion, 693–694
Syphilis, 246
Systematic Training for Effective Parenting (STEP), 488
System-focused consultation, 335
Systems-based prevention models, 383
Systems theory, 449–450, 489

T

Taiwan, 522
Talent search, 539
Tardiness interventions, 272–273, *See also* Truancy and tardiness
Teacher certification, 28
Teacher consultation, 345, *See also* Consultation
    building caring school communities, 368–369
    violence intervention (Good Behavior Game), 704
Teacher-counselor conflict, 816–818
Teacher criminal background, 18
Teacher cultural competence, 58, 60
Teacher education
    counselor roles, 84, 106–107, 604, 816
    pedagogy and, 24–25
    racial harassment issues, 112
    training about connectedness, 667
    working with chronically-ill students, 226
Teacher expectations and student performance, 149, 638, 639, 640, 700
Teacher homophobia, 138
Teacher quality and student performance, 53, 58
Teacher race/ethnicity demographics, 112
Teacher racial and sociocultural beliefs and attitudes, 112, 116
    blindness to racial oppression, 118
Teachers, individual counseling scope of practice and, 399
Teacher-student relationships, immigrant students and, 84, 86–87

Teach for America, 456
Teaching Empowerment through Active Means (TEAM), 599–600
TEAM intervention, 599–600
TeamMates, 646
Technological competence, 819
Technology and counselor education, 22–23, 25
Teen Outreach Program, 391–392
Teen pregnancy, *See* Adolescent pregnancy; Sexual health and development
Termination of groups, 410–411
Termination stage of change, 725
Tertiary prevention, 614–615
Testing, standardized, *See* Standardized testing
Testosterone, 695
Texas Association of School Boards, 111–123
Texas School of the Future Project, 778
Theme interference, 486
Theory of mind (ToM), 674, 676–677
Therapeutic relationship
    creative arts school counselor, 517
    substance abuse prevention and intervention, 720
Therapist-student ethnic match, 130
Time management, 44
Title IX, 788, 792
Tobacco-free environment policies, 224
Tort, 803
Tracking, *See* Tracking and placement issues
Tracking and placement issues
    academic failure and, 637–638
    at-risk assessment, 322
    gifted students and, *See* Gifted and talented students
    grouping aggressive youth, 699
    immigrant/ELL students, 85–86, 95, 107
    students of color and, 179, 189, 564
Traditional healing practices, 527, 630, 732
Training, *See* Counselor education and training
Trait-Factor Theory, 5–6
Transference, 486
Transformative Individual School Counseling model, 16
Transformed school counselor, 38
Transforming School Counseling Initiative, 39, 49, 50, 51, 294, 296–297, 300, 330
Transition planning, 161, *See also* School-to-work transition
    Career Horizons Summer transition program, 285
Traumatic brain injury, 176
Tribes TLC, 216, 357–358, 364, 368
Truancy and tardiness, 272–273, 356, 638–639
    substance abuse risk factor, 719
21st Century Program, 387
Type I diabetes, 224–225

Type I error, 492, 752
Type II diabetes, 224–225, 229
Type II error, 492, 752–753

U

Ujima, 574
Umoja, 571
Unconventional connectedness, 653–654
    grouping unconventional youth, 660, 668–669
    risk taking and, 659, 660
Undocumented immigrants, 82
Unemployment and school dropouts, 269, 641
University-school collaboratives, 300, 316, 555, 644, 762, 818
Upward Bound, 189
Urban schools, *See also* Poverty
    group work and, 440
    specific counselor issues, 819
    violence and aggression, 693
U.S. health care system, 220–221

V

Validity evaluation, 752–755, 761
Values-Based Career Counseling, 552–553
Vermont racial harassment prevention interventions, 123
Victimization, defined, 673, *See also* Bullying
Video supervision of counseling sessions, 26
Violence and aggression, 460, 693–708, *See also* Bullying; Crisis management
    academic underachievement and, 696
    attraction theory, 677–678
    biological factors, 695
    confidentiality and liability issues, 468, 797–798, 803–805
    counselor training issues, 20
    criminalization of youth of color, 694
    crisis situations and, 462–463
    dating violence, 595
    definition of terms, 693
    early childhood onset and progression, 700
    gender differences, 697
    individual characteristics, 695–697
    life-course developmental model, 700–701
    media exposure and, 697
    online harassment, 596
    poverty and, 767
    risk factors, 700, 804
    school bonding and, 699
    school or counselor liability, 615

school shootings, 329
social context, 697–700
    classroom discipline, 699–700
    culture, 697
    family, 697
    media, 698
    neighborhood, 698
    peers, 697–698
    school setting, 693, 698–699
social learning theory, 678
social rejection and, 592–593
trends, 693
Violence prevention, 196, 216, 451, 701–707, 804, *See also* Bullying; Crisis management; Prevention
    anger coping programs, 701
    character education, 469
    Child Development Project, 706
    demonstration programs, 701
    disciplinary interventions, 693–694, 699, 701
    Expect Respect program, 679, 683–685
    fast track, 705–706
    functional behavioral assessment and intervention, 701–702
    group work, 425
    parenting interventions, 469, 702
    PATHS, 216, 703–704, 705
    peer tutoring, 704
    playground interventions, 705
    Positive Behavioral Interventions and Supports, 706
    recommendations, 707–708
    research-based interventions, 694
    schoolwide social competency programs, 601
    Second Step programs, 212, 216, 601, 679, 681–683
    teacher consultation (Good Behavior Game), 704
    zero tolerance policies, 694
Visual impairment, 176
Vocational guidance, 497, *See also* Career development
    assessment, 276–279, 282, 504
    counselor training models and, 295
    historical perspectives, 4–5, 276–277, 293, 811–812
    person-environment fit models, 276, 277, 278
    social class and, 149–150
Vulnerability model, 473

W

Weight-related disorders, 225, 227–229
    preventive interventions, 232–234
Well child health care, 220
Wellness model, 383
White female school counselors, 435
White flight, 346
Whiteness, 67, 122
White privilege, 67–68, 71–72, 111, 130, 274
White racial identity, 67, 71, 119, 274
White teachers, racial/ethnic minority achievement vs., 262
Whole Child vision of schooling, 779
Whole-language approach to literacy development, 260
Wide Range Achievement Test-3, 323
Wisconsin Counseling Study, 740
Withdrawn-rejected students, 592
Worldview, 274, *See also* Culture; Diversity issues; Multicultural competence
    assessment of, 66
    collectivism vs. individualism, *See* Collectivist cultural orientations
    counselor awareness of, 64–66, 310, *See also* Counselor self-awareness of racial/ethnic/sociocultural orientations or biases
    cultural contradictions, 322
    discussing issues of, 130–131
    existential values, 66, 72
    social class and, 147

Y

Youth development programs, connectedness promotion in, 652–653
Youth Suicide Prevention Services, 474

Z

Zero tolerance policies, 694, 699
Zuni adolescents, 620